HOLT McDOUGAL

Literature

Grade 10

HOLT McDOUGAL

Typeset in *The Sans* from LucasFonts.

ART CREDITS

FRONT COVER, TITLE PAGE

top center Teacher's Discovery, Aubrun Hills, Michigan; *top right* © DEA/A. DAGLI ORTI/Getty Images; *bottom center* Getty Images; *center* Atlantide Phototravel/Corbis; *bottom left* Ken Kinzie/HMH Publishers.

BACK COVER

top left Marko Shark/Corbis; *center* Offering of the Heart (1400–1410). French tapestry from Arras. Wool and silk, 247 cm × 209 cm. Louvre, Paris. Photo © Réunion des Musées Nationaux/Art Resource, New York; *bottom left* McDougal Littell; *bottom right* Bettmann/Corbis.

ISBN 978-0-547-61847-0

4 5 6 7 8 9 10 0914 20 19 18 17 16 15 14 13 12

4500357623   B C D E F G

Creating *the future today*

HOLT MCDOUGAL LITERATURE creates the perfect environment for embracing the Common Core State Standards, making them accessible to every student. Each strand of the standards comes alive with scaffolded instruction, images, and unique technology tools to prepare students for the demands of the future.

Prepare for the future

The Common Core State Standards in Reading give equal attention to literary and informational texts. The focus on text analysis and critical thinking, including comparing and contrasting texts and mediums, prepares students to be analytical about resources and ideas.

HOLT MCDOUGAL LITERATURE is the only resource with **LINE NUMBERS** on every selection, making "citing textual evidence" a natural part of the reading process.

TEXT ANALYSIS WORKSHOPS in grades 6–10 begin each unit. Students apply newly learned skills in excerpts of quality text using Close Reading strategies. In grades 11 and 12, the workshops focus on the characteristics of genres in American and British texts.

ROLE OF SETTING	EXAMPLE SETTING
Setting can influence characters by • determining the living conditions and jobs available to them • shaping their personalities, their dreams, and their values	**A poor, drought-stricken Midwestern farm town in the 1930s** Despite months of grueling work, Joe's crops are failing again. Realizing that his life may never improve, he becomes bitter and angry.
Setting can create conflicts by • exposing the characters to dangerous weather, such as a storm or a drought • making characters endure a difficult time period, such as the Great Depression	The drought has lasted seven years, and most of the farms are failing. People have begun to sell their most prized possessions because they need money. Recently, Mrs. Wilkes sold her wedding band to buy shoes for her daughter.
Setting can serve as a symbol by • representing an important idea • representing a character's hopes, future, or predicament	Some people have planted a small flower garden in the town square. The garden is a symbol of their hope that their community can still thrive.

from Their Eyes Were Watching God

Novel by **Zora Neale Hurston**

It was a spring afternoon in West Florida. Janie had spent most of the day under a blossoming pear tree in the back-yard. She had been spending every minute that she could steal from her chores under that tree for the last three days. That was to say, ever since the first tiny bloom had opened. It had called her to come and gaze on a mystery. From barren brown stems to glistening leaf-buds; from the leaf-buds to snowy virginity of bloom. It stirred her tremendously.

EXEMPLARY TEXTS from Common Core State Standards and hundreds of other titles, including your favorite novels, are available to explore different worlds through reading.

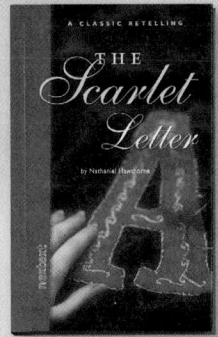  

NOVELWISE offers study guides and PowerPoint® presentations that support reading and discussion of your favorite novels.

WRITING WORKSHOPS show students how to craft and support an argument and to explain their ideas.

INFORMATIONAL TEXT requires students to apply academic vocabulary in texts with different purposes and structures. Seminal works of American history are important resources for Common Core State Standards.

CONNECTIONS: NONFICTION FOR COMMON CORE CD-ROM provides additional informational texts, including seminal or foundational American works, with specific connections to selections in *Holt McDougal Literature*.

Connections:
Nonfiction for Common Core

Features:
- A wealth of printable informational texts
- Connections to your grade-level literature anthology
- Suggestions for integrating nonfiction into your lessons

HOLT McDOUGAL
Literature
GRADES 6 – 12

COMMON CORE COMPANION

Students must think analytically and critically as they **COMPARE TEXTS** that differ in style, genre, medium, and purpose.

Before Reading
Sorry, Right Number
Teleplay by Stephen King

What sends a **CHILL** down your spine?

Reading for Information
MEMOIR Stephen King wrote a memoir of his life as a writer. Here are a few words of advice from the book.

from **On Writing**
Stephen King

By learning today

The Common Core State Standards are designed for every student. Tools to scaffold learning are seamlessly integrated in *Holt McDougal Literature*.

INTERACTIVE READERS contain selections from the Essential Course of Study with close reading support to scaffold and personalize learning.

ADAPTED INTERACTIVE READERS provide the same selections in an adapted format with additional vocabulary and comprehension support.

ENGLISH LANGUAGE LEARNER ADAPTED INTERACTIVE READERS use the same adapted selections with scaffolded instruction for English Language Learners, including academic vocabulary, language support, and a comprehensive Teacher's Guide.

AUDIO TUTOR CD provides an audio version of the adapted selections with the instructional material read in English or Spanish.

Holt McDougal Literature **is a comprehensive resource addressing all of the Common Core State Standards for English Language Arts with integrated instruction in Language and Speaking and Listening.**

The importance of acquiring academic vocabulary appropriate for college and career readiness is supported with every selection and reinforced with **WORDSHARP: AN INTERACTIVE VOCABULARY TUTOR CD,** which is also online to allow students to expand vocabulary independently.

GRAMMAR AND STYLE instruction at point of use within and following each selection reinforces students' command of conventions and supports their learning about language choices and style.

Language

◆ **GRAMMAR AND STYLE: Make Effective Word Choices**

In the following excerpts, notice how O. Henry uses verbs that help create vivid images for the reader:

> *With a whirl of skirts and with the brilliant sparkle still in her eyes, she fluttered out the door and down the stairs to the street.* (lines 55–57)
>
> *Instead of obeying, Jim tumbled down on the couch. . . .* (line 173)

Now study this model. Notice how the revisions in blue help you to better visualize Jim's trip to the shop. Use similar methods to revise your response to the prompt below.

STUDENT MODEL

Jim ~~walked~~ *scurried* to the shop; the store would close in just an hour. He reached into his right pocket, ~~took~~ *yanked* out the watch, and ~~held~~ *clasped* it in his hands.

COMMON CORE

L 3 Make effective choices for meaning or style. **W 3b** Use description to develop characters.

THE COMMON CORE STATE STANDARDS IN SPEAKING AND LISTENING prepare students for active participation in their future. **SPEAKING AND LISTENING WORKSHOPS** in many units teach the skills of successful group participation and the formal presentation of ideas in public settings.

With tools for *tomorrow*

Holt McDougal Literature's online platform provides easy access to teacher and student resources at point of use in the selection. HISTORY® film clips and full-length resources provide both motivation and context for texts.

ONLINE RESOURCES provide a wealth of instructional support material for Teacher and Student use.

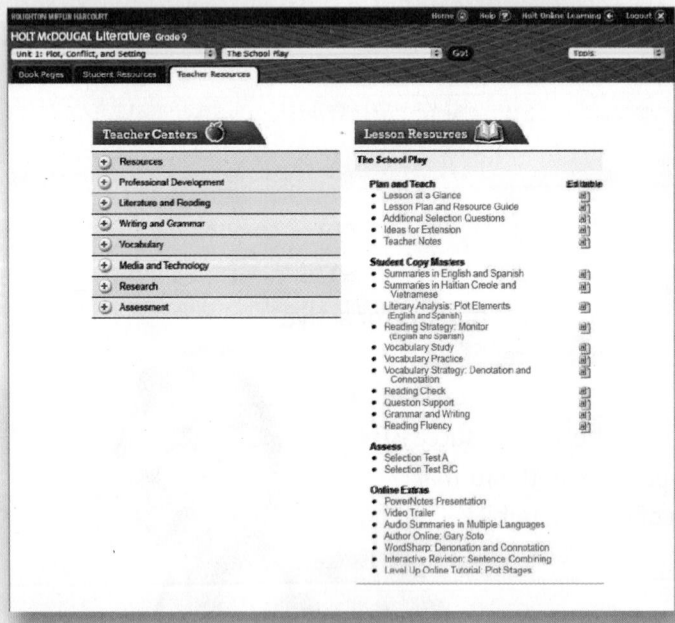

MEDIASMART DVD uses movie clips, commercials, political ads, documentaries, and news reports to bring media instruction to life with critical analysis and comparisons to other mediums.

Enhance learning of rigorous standards with **HISTORY®** video streaming and resources at point of use.

WRITESMART CD (also online) features interactive writing instruction, from prompts to the steps of the process, including editing and revision models. An editable **RUBRIC GENERATOR** allows teachers to customize assessment.

HOLT MCDOUGAL ONLINE ESSAY SCORING provides students with the practice and immediate constructive feedback that they need to improve as writers.

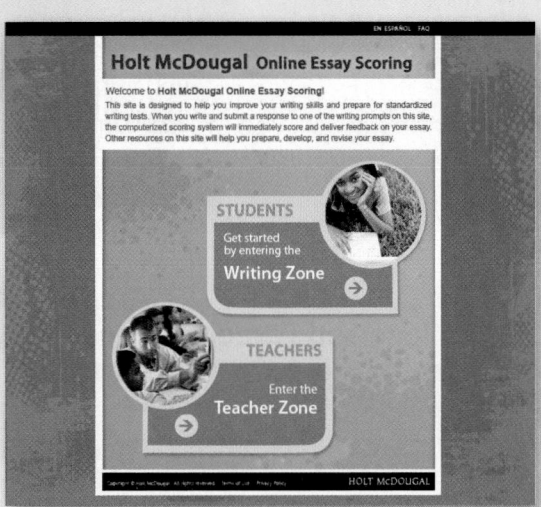

WHITEBOARD-READY LESSON DEMONSTRATIONS are available for the most challenging Common Core Standards.

POWERNOTES DVD (also online) provides point-of-use images, instructional information, and background knowledge with theater-quality video trailers.

COMMON CORE

English Language Arts
Common Core State Standards

The grades 9–10 standards on the following pages define what students should understand and be able to do by the end of grade 10. They correspond to the College and Career Readiness (CCR) anchor standards below by number. The CCR and grade-specific standards are necessary complements—the former providing broad standards, the latter providing additional specificity—that together define the skills and understandings that all students must demonstrate.

College and Career Readiness Anchor Standards for Reading

COMMON CORE STATE STANDARD

KEY IDEAS AND DETAILS

1. Read closely to determine what the text says explicitly and to make logical inferences from it; cite specific textual evidence when writing or speaking to support conclusions drawn from the text.

2. Determine central ideas or themes of a text and analyze their development; summarize the key supporting details and ideas.

3. Analyze how and why individuals, events, and ideas develop and interact over the course of a text.

CRAFT AND STRUCTURE

4. Interpret words and phrases as they are used in a text, including determining technical, connotative, and figurative meanings, and analyze how specific word choices shape meaning or tone.

5. Analyze the structure of texts, including how specific sentences, paragraphs, and larger portions of the text (e.g., a section, chapter, scene, or stanza) relate to each other and the whole.

6. Assess how point of view or purpose shapes the content and style of a text.

INTEGRATION OF KNOWLEDGE AND IDEAS

7. Integrate and evaluate content presented in diverse formats and media, including visually and quantitatively, as well as in words.

8. Delineate and evaluate the argument and specific claims in a text, including the validity of the reasoning as well as the relevance and sufficiency of the evidence.

9. Analyze how two or more texts address similar themes or topics in order to build knowledge or to compare the approaches the authors take.

RANGE OF READING AND LEVEL OF COMPLEXITY

10. Read and comprehend complex literary and informational texts independently and proficiently.

Reading Standards for Literature, Grades 9–10 Students

COMMON CORE STATE STANDARD	STUDENT EDITION
KEY IDEAS AND DETAILS	
1. Cite strong and thorough textual evidence to support analysis of what the text says explicitly as well as inferences drawn from the text.	FM46–FM47, 4, 36–37, 45, 48–49, 61, 78–79, 96, 148–157, 160, 182–182, 199, 202–203, 215, 218–219, 225, 252–253, 257, 292, 298, 308–309, 322, 324–325, 334, 342–343, 353, 354–355, 366, 371, 402, 438–439, 449, 452–453, 471, 510, 584–585, 596, 602–603, 609, 688–689, 693, 694–695, 707, 716–717, 735, 737, 754, 840, 856–857, 875, 886–887,892, 894–895, 899, 924, 984–985, 992, 998–999, 1042, 1017, 1020–1021,1025, 1066–1067, 1107, 1130–1131, 1141, 1273
2. Determine a theme or central idea of a text and analyze in detail its development over the course of the text, including how it emerges and is shaped and refined by specific details; provide an objective summary of the text.	4, 418, 426–427, 430, 435, 452–453, 471, 476–477, 481, 494, 688–689, 693, 694–695, 699, 707, 737, 754, 785, 786, 792, 810–811, 815, 893, 998–999, 1017, 1020–1021, 1022, 1025, 1042, 1058, 1066–1067, 1106,1107, 1109, 1206, 1266, R2
3. Analyze how complex characters (e.g., those with multiple or conflicting motivations) develop over the course of a text, interact with other characters, and advance the plot or develop the theme.	36–37, 45, 75, 176, 182–183, 199, 202–203, 214, 215, 218–219, 225, 258–259, 273, 308–309, 322, 342–343, 353, 402, 418, 452–453, 471, 584–585, 596, 984–985, 992, 1058, 1066–1067, 1074, 1083, 1107, 1110–1111, 1128, 1176, 1190, 1198–1199, 1219, 1237, 1248, 1257, 1273, 1288, 1310, R2
CRAFT AND STRUCTURE	
4. Determine the meaning of words and phrases as they are used in the text, including figurative and connotative meanings; analyze the cumulative impact of specific word choices on meaning and tone (e.g., how the language evokes a sense of time and place; how it sets a formal or informal tone).	4, 48, 53, 54, 64–65, 69, 75, 78–79, 90, 93, 94, 140–141, 147, 182, 196, 218, 223, 258–259, 264, 268, 308, 312, 314, 324, 331, 332, 342, 350, 354, 364, 367, 436, 593, 602–603, 607, 609, 688, 692, 698, 716, 721, 726, 732, 770, 778–779, 784, 786–787, 792, 794, 796, 801, 802–803, 809, 816–817, 820, 823, 840, 850, 856–857, 861, 865, 872, 875, 878–879, 882, 885, 886–887, 892, 894–895, 899, 908, 924, 934, 988, 998, 1005, 1010, 1042, 1070, 1078, 1085, 1100, 1105, 1110, 1116, 1130–1131, 1138, 1141, 1154, 1159, 1198, 1202, 1209, 1220, 1223, 1227, 1232, 1245, 1253, 1271, 1284, 1310, R2, R68
5. Analyze how an author's choices concerning how to structure a text, order events within it (e.g., parallel plots), and manipulate time (e.g., pacing, flashbacks) create such effects as mystery, tension, or surprise.	28, 48–49, 61, 78–79, 96, 160, 302, 308, 324–325, 334, 354–355, 371, 770, 778–779, 784, 786–787, 792, 794–795, 801, 802–803, 806, 809, 810–811, 815, 816–817, 823, 878–879, 885, 1110–1111, 1117, 1128, 1144–1145, 1158, 1190, 1219
6. Analyze a particular point of view or cultural experience reflected in a work of literature from outside the United States, drawing on a wide reading of world literature.	218, 223, 342–343, 352, 353, 354–355, 371, 418, 449, 438–439, 488–489, 496, 497, 694–695, 707, 934, 984–985, 992, 1058, 1064, 1094
INTEGRATION OF KNOWLEDGE AND IDEAS	
7. Analyze the representation of a subject or a key scene in two different artistic mediums, including what is emphasized or absent in each treatment (e.g., Auden's "Musée des Beaux Arts" and Breughel's *Landscape with the Fall of Icarus*).	716–717, 735, 1128, 1140, 1144–1145, 1161, 1294–1297
8. (Not applicable to literature)	

Reading Standards for Literature, Grades 9–10 Students, continued

COMMON CORE STATE STANDARD	STUDENT EDITION
9. Analyze how an author draws on and transforms source material in a specific work (e.g., how Shakespeare treats a theme or topic from Ovid or the Bible or how a later author draws on a play by Shakespeare).	452–453, 463, 584, 595, 596, 1064, 1130–1131, 1141, 1143, 1144–1145, 1161, 1190, 1198–1199, 1266
RANGE OF READING AND LEVEL OF TEXT COMPLEXITY **10.** By the end of grade 9, read and comprehend literature, including stories, dramas, and poems, in the grades 9–10 text complexity band proficiently, with scaffolding as needed at the high end of the range. By the end of grade 10, read and comprehend literature, including stories, dramas, and poems, at the high end of the grades 9–10 text complexity band independently and proficiently.	64–65, 75, 140–141, 147, 172, 252–253, 257, 258–259, 273, 298, 402, 414, 476–477, 481, 510, 628, 766, 770, 778–779, 784, 786–787, 794–795, 800, 802–803, 810–811, 816–817, 846, 930, 1054, 1058, 1066–1067, 1107, 1182, 1190, 1198–1199, 1237, 1273, 1288, 1316

Reading Standards for Informational Text, Grades 9–10 Students

COMMON CORE STATE STANDARD	STUDENT EDITION
KEY IDEAS AND DETAILS **1.** Cite strong and thorough textual evidence to support analysis of what the text says explicitly as well as inferences drawn from the text.	4, 98, 103, 118–119, 133, 160, 226–227, 235, 246, 251, 292, 336, 339, 379, 382–383, 389, 402, 510, 622, 646–647, 651, 652–653, 660, 754, 910, 913, 940–941, 949, 952–953, 965, 968–969, 978, 1042, 1290, 1293
2. Determine a central idea of a text and analyze its development over the course of the text, including how it emerges and is shaped and refined by specific details; provide an objective summary of the text.	4, 98, 103, 246, 251, 336, 337, 339, 374–375, 379, 382–383, 389, 402, 482–483, 487, 488–489, 496, 497, 510, 526, 572, 598, 601, 664–665, 675, 677, 678–679, 685, 687, 754, 824, 827, R2
3. Analyze how the author unfolds an analysis or series of ideas or events, including the order in which the points are made, how they are introduced and developed, and the connections that are drawn between them.	106–107, 115, 482–483, 487, 522–523, 526, 537, 556–557, 569, 572, 598, 601, 622, R2
CRAFT AND STRUCTURE **4.** Determine the meaning of words and phrases as they are used in a text, including figurative, connotative, and technical meanings; analyze the cumulative impact of specific word choices on meaning and tone (e.g., how the language of a court opinion differs from that of a newspaper).	98, 99, 106–107, 115, 118, 120, 128, 226–227, 231, 232, 235, 238–239, 245, 338, 374–375, 378, 379, 383, 386, 526, 532–533, 536, 537, 538–539, 540, 548, 549, 556–557, 558, 567, 598, 600, 622, 646, 649, 652–653, 658, 660, 668, 678, 682, 710, 713, 824, 825, 827, 900–901, 905, 908, 910, 911, 912, 934, 941, 946, 947, 952, 960, 963, 968, 975, 1292, R2, R68

Reading Standards for Informational Text, Grades 9–10 Students, continued

COMMON CORE STATE STANDARD	STUDENT EDITION
5. Analyze in detail how an author's ideas or claims are developed and refined by particular sentences, paragraphs, or larger portions of a text (e.g., a section or chapter).	118–119, 133, 160, 526, 532–533, 538–539, 545, 556–557, 569, 632, 638–639, 643, 646, 648, 652–653, 659, 660, 678–679, 682, 685, 754, 900–901, 905
6. Determine an author's point of view or purpose in a text and analyze how an author uses rhetoric to advance that point of view or purpose.	118, 129, 226–227, 235, 238–239, 245, 487, 526, 538–539, 545, 632, 652–653, 660, 710, 713, 754, 900–901, 908, 934, 940–941, 949, 952–953, 965, 968–969, 978, 980, 983
INTEGRATION OF KNOWLEDGE AND IDEAS	
7. Analyze various accounts of a subject told in different mediums (e.g., a person's life story in both print and multimedia), determining which details are emphasized in each account.	4, 104, 136–139, 340, 474, 548, 551, 552, 555, 575, 580, 582, 583, 601, 714, 996, 1026–1029, 1200, 1213, 1229, 1242, 1263, 1287, 1290, 1293
8. Delineate and evaluate the argument and specific claims in a text, assessing whether the reasoning is valid and the evidence is relevant and sufficient; identify false statements and fallacious reasoning.	482–483, 487, 632, 638–639, 643, 646–647, 651, 652–653, 660, 664–665, 674, 675, 678–679, 684, 685, 910, 913, 1290, 1293, R2
9. Analyze seminal U.S. documents of historical and literary significance (e.g., Washington's Farewell Address, the Gettysburg Address, Roosevelt's Four Freedoms speech, King's "Letter from Birmingham Jail"), including how they address related themes and concepts.	FM49–FM53, 632, 980, 983
RANGE OF READING AND LEVEL OF TEXT COMPLEXITY	
10. By the end of grade 9, read and comprehend literary nonfiction in the grades 9–10 text complexity band proficiently, with scaffolding as needed at the high end of the range. By the end of grade 10, read and comprehend literary nonfiction at the high end of the grades 9–10 text complexity band independently and proficiently.	172, 402, 414, 510, 628, 766, 846, 930, 1054, 1182, 1186, 1316

College and Career Readiness Anchor Standards for Writing

TEXT TYPES AND PURPOSES

1. Write arguments to support claims in an analysis of substantive topics or texts, using valid reasoning and relevant and sufficient evidence.

2. Write informative/explanatory texts to examine and convey complex ideas and information clearly and accurately through the effective selection, organization, and analysis of content.

3. Write narratives to develop real or imagined experiences or events using effective technique, well-chosen details, and well-structured event sequences.

PRODUCTION AND DISTRIBUTION OF WRITING

4. Produce clear and coherent writing in which the development, organization, and style are appropriate to task, purpose, and audience.

5. Develop and strengthen writing as needed by planning, revising, editing, rewriting, or trying a new approach.

6. Use technology, including the Internet, to produce and publish writing and to interact and collaborate with others.

RESEARCH TO BUILD AND PRESENT KNOWLEDGE

7. Conduct short as well as more sustained research projects based on focused questions, demonstrating understanding of the subject under investigation.

8. Gather relevant information from multiple print and digital sources, assess the credibility and accuracy of each source, and integrate the information while avoiding plagiarism.

9. Draw evidence from literary or informational texts to support analysis, reflection, and research.

RANGE OF WRITING

10. Write routinely over extended time frames (time for research, reflection, and revision) and shorter time frames (a single sitting or a day or two) for a range of tasks, purposes, and audiences.

COMMON CORE

Writing Standards, Grades 9–10 Students

COMMON CORE STATE STANDARD	STUDENT EDITION
TEXT TYPES AND PURPOSES	
1. Write arguments to support claims in an analysis of substantive topics or texts, using valid reasoning and relevant and sufficient evidence.	339, 610–619, 645, 742–751, 1298–1307, R28
a. Introduce precise claim(s), distinguish the claim(s) from alternate or opposing claims, and create an organization that establishes clear relationships among claim(s), counterclaims, reasons, and evidence.	610–619, 742–751, 1298–1307, R28
b. Develop claim(s) and counterclaims fairly, supplying evidence for each while pointing out the strengths and limitations of both in a manner that anticipates the audience's knowledge level and concerns.	610–619, 742–751, 1298–1307, R28
c. Use words, phrases, and clauses to link the major sections of the text, create cohesion, and clarify the relationships between claim(s) and reasons, between reasons and evidence, and between claim(s) and counterclaims.	610–619, 742–751, 1298–1307, R28
d. Establish and maintain a formal style and objective tone while attending to the norms and conventions of the discipline in which they are writing.	610–619, 742–751, 1298–1307, R28
e. Provide a concluding statement or section that follows from and supports the argument presented.	610–619, 742–751, 1298–1307, R28
2. Write informative/explanatory texts to examine and convey complex ideas, concepts, and information clearly and accurately through the effective selection, organization, and analysis of content.	103, 116, 148–157, 279, 390–399, 437, 473, 498–507, 571, 601, 713, 827, 828–837, 914–921, 983, 1030–1039, 1163, 1293, 1297, 1342–1363, R28
a. Introduce a topic; organize complex ideas, concepts, and information to make important connections and distinctions; include formatting (e.g., headings), graphics (e.g., figures, tables), and multimedia when useful to aiding comprehension.	148–157, 390–399, 498–507, 828–837, 838–839, 914–921, 983, 1030–1039, 1164–1173, 1342–1363, R28
b. Develop the topic with well-chosen, relevant, and sufficient facts, extended definitions, concrete details, quotations, or other information and examples appropriate to the audience's knowledge of the topic.	148–157, 251, 373, 390–399, 498–507, 809, 815, 828–837, 914–921, 983, 1030–1039, 1342–1363, R28

Writing Standards, Grades 9–10 Students, continued

COMMON CORE STATE STANDARD	STUDENT EDITION
c. Use appropriate and varied transitions to link the major sections of the text, create cohesion, and clarify the relationships among complex ideas and concepts.	148–157, 390–399, 498–507, 828–837, 914–921, 967, 983, 1030–1039, 1342–1363, R28
d. Use precise language and domain-specific vocabulary to manage the complexity of the topic.	148–157, 390–399, 498–507, 551, 555, 579, 828–837, 914–921, 983, 1030–1039, 1342–1363, R28
e. Establish and maintain a formal style and objective tone while attending to the norms and conventions of the discipline in which they are writing.	148–157, 390–399, 498–507, 677, 687, 828–837, 914–921, 983, 1030–1039, 1342–1363, R28
f. Provide a concluding statement or section that follows from and supports the information or explanation presented (e.g., articulating implications or the significance of the topic).	148–157, 390–399, 498–507, 823, 828–837, 914–921, 1030–1039, 1342–1363, R28
3. Write narratives to develop real or imagined experiences or events using effective technique, well-chosen details, and well-structured event sequences.	63, 280–289, 1164–1173, R28
a. Engage and orient the reader by setting out a problem, situation, or observation, establishing one or multiple point(s) of view, and introducing a narrator and/or characters; create a smooth progression of experiences or events.	280–289, 1164–1173, R28
b. Use narrative techniques, such as dialogue, pacing, description, reflection, and multiple plot lines, to develop experiences, events, and/or characters.	280–289, 1164–1173, R28
c. Use a variety of techniques to sequence events so that they build on one another to create a coherent whole.	280–289, 1164–1173, R28
d. Use precise words and phrases, telling details, and sensory language to convey a vivid picture of the experiences, events, setting, and/or characters.	237, 280–289, 1164–1173, R28
e. Provide a conclusion that follows from and reflects on what is experienced, observed, or resolved over the course of the narrative.	280–289, 1164–1173, R28
PRODUCTION AND DISTRIBUTION OF WRITING 4. Produce clear and coherent writing in which the development, organization, and style are appropriate to task, purpose, and audience. (Grade-specific expectations for writing types are defined in standards 1–3 above.)	FM57–FM59, 20, 151–152, 283–284, 393–394, 501–502, 613–614, 745–746, 831–832, 917–918, 967, 1033–1034, 1167–1168, 1301–1302, 1351–1352, R28

Writing Standards, Grades 9–10 Students, continued

COMMON CORE STATE STANDARD	STUDENT EDITION
5. Develop and strengthen writing as needed by planning, revising, editing, rewriting, or trying a new approach, focusing on addressing what is most significant for a specific purpose and audience. (Editing for conventions should demonstrate command of Language standards 1–3.)	20, 148–157, 160, 280–289, 292, 390–399, 402, 498–507, 520, 610–619, 742–751, 754, 828–837, 840, 914–921, 924, 1030–1039, 1042, 1163, 1164–1173, 1176, 1298–1307, 1310, 1342–1363, R28
6. Use technology, including the Internet, to produce, publish, and update individual or shared writing products, taking advantage of technology's capacity to link to other information and to display information flexibly and dynamically.	290–291, 838–839, 914–921, 922–923, 1164–1173, 1174–1175, 1364–1365, R28
RESEARCH TO BUILD AND PRESENT KNOWLEDGE	611–612, 914–921, 1030–1039, 1320, 1342–1363
7. Conduct short as well as more sustained research projects to answer a question (including a self-generated question) or solve a problem; narrow or broaden the inquiry when appropriate; synthesize multiple sources on the subject, demonstrating understanding of the subject under investigation.	
8. Gather relevant information from multiple authoritative print and digital sources, using advanced searches effectively; assess the usefulness of each source in answering the research question; integrate information into the text selectively to maintain the flow of ideas, avoiding plagiarism and following a standard format for citation.	551, 555, 917, 1030–1039, 1320, 1342–1363
9. Draw evidence from literary or informational texts to support analysis, reflection, and research.	139, 148–157, 390–399, 497, 498–507, 575, 713, 737, 785, 828–837, 877, 893, 913, 914–921, 1029, 1109, 1143, 1298–1307, 1320, 1342–1363
a. Apply *grades 9–10 Reading standards* to literature (e.g., "Analyze how an author draws on and transforms source material in a specific work [e.g., how Shakespeare treats a theme or topic from Ovid or the Bible or how a later author draws on a play by Shakespeare]").	148–157, 785, 831–832, 877, 893, 1143, 1298–1307
b. Apply *grades 9–10 Reading standards* to literary nonfiction (e.g., "Delineate and evaluate the argument and specific claims in a text, assessing whether the reasoning is valid and the evidence is relevant and sufficient; identify false statements and fallacious reasoning").	139, 393, 575, 713, 913, 914–921, 994, 1029, 1109, 1342–1363
RANGE OF WRITING	FM57–FM59, 148–157, 280–289, 390–399, 498–507, 610–619, 742–751, 828–837, 1030–1039, 1164–1173, 1298–1307
10. Write routinely over extended time frames (time for research, reflection, and revision) and shorter time frames (a single sitting or a day or two) for a range of tasks, purposes, and audiences.	

College and Career Readiness Anchor Standards for Speaking and Listening

COMPREHENSION AND COLLABORATION

1. Prepare for and participate effectively in a range of conversations and collaborations with diverse partners, building on others' ideas and expressing their own clearly and persuasively.

2. Integrate and evaluate information presented in diverse media and formats, including visually, quantitatively, and orally.

3. Evaluate a speaker's point of view, reasoning, and use of evidence and rhetoric.

PRESENTATION OF KNOWLEDGE AND IDEAS

4. Present information, findings, and supporting evidence such that listeners can follow the line of reasoning and the organization, development, and style are appropriate to task, purpose, and audience.

5. Make strategic use of digital media and visual displays of data to express information and enhance understanding of presentations.

6. Adapt speech to a variety of contexts and communicative tasks, demonstrating command of formal English when indicated or appropriate.

Speaking and Listening Standards, Grades 9–10 Students

COMMON CORE STATE STANDARD	STUDENT EDITION
COMPREHENSION AND COLLABORATION **1.** Initiate and participate effectively in a range of collaborative discussions (one-on-one, in groups, and teacher-led) with diverse partners on *grades 9–10 topics, texts, and issues*, building on others' ideas and expressing their own clearly and persuasively.	FM61–63, 276–279, 290–291, 508–509, 1040–1041, 1294–1297, 1308–1309
a. Come to discussions prepared, having read and researched material under study; explicitly draw on that preparation by referring to evidence from texts and other research on the topic or issue to stimulate a thoughtful, well-reasoned exchange of ideas.	FM61–63, 276–279, 508–509, 620–621, 1297, 1308–1309, R76
b. Work with peers to set rules for collegial discussions and decision-making (e.g., informal consensus, taking votes on key issues, presentation of alternate views), clear goals and deadlines, and individual roles as needed.	FM61–63, 508–509, 1308–1309, R76
c. Propel conversations by posing and responding to questions that relate the current discussion to broader themes or larger ideas; actively incorporate others into the discussion; and clarify, verify, or challenge ideas and conclusions.	FM61–63, 20, 290–291, 508–509, 620–621, 838–839, 922–923, 1308–1309, R76
d. Respond thoughtfully to diverse perspectives, summarize points of agreement and disagreement, and, when warranted, qualify or justify their own views and understanding and make new connections in light of the evidence and reasoning presented.	FM61–63, 20, 290–291, 400–401, 508–509, 1308–1309, R76
2. Integrate multiple sources of information presented in diverse media or formats (e.g., visually, quantitatively, orally) evaluating the credibility and accuracy of each source.	139, 290–291, 576–579, 583, 738–741, 1026–1029, 1174–1175, 1364–1365
3. Evaluate a speaker's point of view, reasoning, and use of evidence and rhetoric, identifying any fallacious reasoning or exaggerated or distorted evidence.	576–579, 738–741, 752–753, 1257, 1308–1309, R76, R84
PRESENTATION OF KNOWLEDGE AND IDEAS **4.** Present information, findings, and supporting evidence clearly, concisely, and logically such that listeners can follow the line of reasoning and the organization, development, substance, and style are appropriate to purpose, audience, and task.	158–159, 276–279, 400–401, 741, 752–753, 838–839, 1040–1041, 1308–1309, 1364–1365, R76

Speaking and Listening Standards, Grades 9–10 Students, continued

COMMON CORE STATE STANDARD	STUDENT EDITION
5. Make strategic use of digital media (e.g., textual, graphical, audio, visual, and interactive elements) in presentations to enhance understanding of findings, reasoning, and evidence and to add interest.	290–291, 838–839, 919, 922–923, 1174–1175, 1364–1365
6. Adapt speech to a variety of contexts and tasks, demonstrating command of formal English when indicated or appropriate. (See grades 9–10 Language standards 1 and 3 for specific expectations.)	752–753

College and Career Readiness Anchor Standards for Language

COMMON CORE STATE STANDARD

CONVENTIONS OF STANDARD ENGLISH

1. Demonstrate command of the conventions of standard English grammar and usage when writing or speaking.

2. Demonstrate command of the conventions of standard English capitalization, punctuation, and spelling when writing.

KNOWLEDGE OF LANGUAGE

3. Apply knowledge of language to understand how language functions in different contexts, to make effective choices for meaning or style, and to comprehend more fully when reading or listening.

VOCABULARY ACQUISITION AND USE

4. Determine or clarify the meaning of unknown and multiple-meaning words and phrases by using context clues, analyzing meaningful word parts, and consulting general and specialized reference materials, as appropriate.

5. Demonstrate understanding of figurative language, word relationships, and nuances in word meanings.

6. Acquire and use accurately a range of general academic and domain-specific words and phrases sufficient for reading, writing, speaking, and listening at the college and career readiness level; demonstrate independence in gathering vocabulary knowledge when considering a word or phrase important to comprehension or expression.

Language Standards, Grades 9–10 Students

COMMON CORE STATE STANDARD	STUDENT EDITION
CONVENTIONS OF STANDARD ENGLISH	
1. Demonstrate command of the conventions of standard English grammar and usage when writing or speaking.	20, 47, 155, 158–159, 283, 473, 505, 566, 613, 615, 620–621, 745, 749, 785, 835, 1030–1039, 1342–1363, R46
a. Use parallel structure.	505, 662, 752–753, 793, R46
b. Use various types of phrases (noun, verb, adjectival, adverbial, participial, prepositional, absolute) and clauses (independent, dependent; noun, relative, adverbial) to convey specific meanings and add variety and interest to writing or presentations.	63, 381, 393, 437, 547, 571, 677, 709, 893, 920, 967, 994, 1143, 1289, R46
2. Demonstrate command of the conventions of standard English capitalization, punctuation, and spelling when writing.	20, 151, 317, 317, 501, 617, 831, 920, 1298–1307, 1342–1363, R46
a. Use a semicolon (and perhaps a conjunctive adverb) to link two or more closely related independent clauses.	1037, 1305, R46
b. Use a colon to introduce a list or quotation.	151, 1342–1363, R46
c. Spell correctly.	617, 749, R68
KNOWLEDGE OF LANGUAGE	
3. Apply knowledge of language to understand how language functions in different contexts, to make effective choices for meaning or style, and to comprehend more fully when reading or listening.	16, 47, 116, 135, 155, 200, 217, 237, 275, 280–289, 323, 373, 451, 473, 615, 645, 662, 747, 785, 875, 981, 1109, R68
a. Write and edit work so that it conforms to the guidelines in a style manual (e.g., *MLA Handbook*, Turabian's *Manual for Writers*) appropriate for the discipline and writing type.	917, 1351–1352, 1362–1363

Language Standards, Grades 9–10 Students, continued

COMMON CORE STATE STANDARD	STUDENT EDITION
VOCABULARY ACQUISITION AND USE **4.** Determine or clarify the meaning of unknown and multiple-meaning words and phrases based on *grades 9–10 reading and content*, choosing flexibly from a range of strategies.	658, R68
a. Use context (e.g., the overall meaning of a sentence, paragraph, or text; a word's position or function in a sentence) as a clue to the meaning of a word or phrase.	16, 46, 106, 402, 597, 1176, R68
b. Identify and correctly use patterns of word changes that indicate different meanings or parts of speech (e.g., *analyze, analysis, analytical; advocate, advocacy*).	246, 248, 488, 493, 710, 711, 778, 783, 794, 798, 979, R68
c. Consult general and specialized reference materials (e.g., dictionaries, glossaries, thesauruses), both print and digital, to find the pronunciation of a word or determine or clarify its precise meaning, its part of speech, or its etymology.	16, 46, 62, 76, 84, 106, 114 140–141, 146, 182, 187, 236, 274, 335, 372, 380, 472, 644, 708, 909, 966, 993, 1018, 1108, 1124, R68
d. Verify the preliminary determination of the meaning of a word or phrase (e.g., by checking the inferred meaning in context or in a dictionary).	1124, R68
5. Demonstrate understanding of figurative language, word relationships, and nuances in word meanings	16, 36, 41, 202, 206, 450, 570, 676, 736, 1019, 1129, 1162
a. Interpret figures of speech (e.g., euphemism, oxymoron) in context and analyze their role in the text.	31, 1003
b. Analyze nuances in the meaning of words with similar denotations.	97, 216, 238, 244, 292, 436, 638, 641, 686, 950, 1142
6. Acquire and use accurately general academic and domain-specific words and phrases, sufficient for reading, writing, speaking, and listening at the college and career readiness level; demonstrate independence in gathering vocabulary knowledge when considering a word or phrase important to comprehension or expression.	FM66–FM67, 16, 134, 160, 292, 402, 510, 546, 661, 840, 876, 924, 1176, 1190, R68

Essential Course of Study

COMMON CORE

The **Essential Course of Study** designates an efficient and effective choice of selections for mastery of the Common Core State Standards.

ECOS

STRAND	Reading Literature	Reading Informational Text	Writing	Speaking and Listening	Language
UNIT 1					
Text Analysis Workshop: Plot, Setting, and Mood	Plot, Setting, and Mood RL 5				
Harrison Bergeron	Plot and Conflict RL 3 Draw Conclusions RL 1		Describe Plot and Conflict		Use Precise Language L 3, L 5 Greek Roots L 4c
Everyday Use	Conflict and Character RL 4, RL 5 Make Inferences RL 1		Write a Story Sequel W 3		Add Descriptive Details L 1b Prefixes L 4c
To Build a Fire	Setting and Conflict RL 4, RL 5 Predict RL 1				Connotation and Denotation L 5b
Writing Workshop: Literary Analysis: Short Story			Write Literary Analysis W 2a–f, W 4, W 5, W 9a (RL 1), W 10		Reciprocal Pronouns L 1, L 2, L 3
Speaking and Listening Workshop: Presenting a Response to a Short Story				Present a Response to a Short Story SL 4	Present a Response to a Short Story L 1
UNIT 2					
Text Analysis Workshop: Analyzing Characters	Character Development, Character Traits, Character Motivation RL 3				
The Possibility of Evil	Character Motivation RL 3 Make Inferences RL 1		Write a Scene		Use Modifiers L 3 Connotation and Denotation L 5, L 5b
The Teacher Who Changed My Life		Characterization in Nonfiction RI 4 Analyze Author's Purpose RI 1, RI 6	Write a Speech W 3d		Elaborate with Examples L 3 Latin Roots L 4c
A Marriage Proposal	Characters in a Farce RL 3, RL 4 Reading a Play RL 10		Write a Dialogue		Vary Sentence Types L 3 Latin Roots L 4c
Writing Workshop: Narrative: Short Story			Write a Short Story W 3a–e, W 4, W 5, W 10		Verb Tense L 1 Participles L 1b, L 2c, L 3
Technology Workshop: Producing a Video Narrative			Produce a Video Narrative W 6	Produce a Video Narrative SL 1c, SL 1d, SL 2, SL 5	

STRAND	Reading Literature	Reading Informational Text	Writing	Speaking and Listening	Language
UNIT 3					
Text Analysis Workshop: Narrative Devices	Choices About the Narrator; Choices About Time RL 5				
By the Waters of Babylon	First-Person Point of View RL 3, RL 4, RL 5 Make Inferences RL 1		Evaluate a Statement		Use Appropriate Language L 2, L 3
There Will Come Soft Rains	Chronological Order RL 4, RL 5 Draw Conclusions RL 1				Latin Roots L 4c, L 5b
Writing Workshop: Informative: Analysis of Literary Nonfiction			Write an Analysis of Literary Nonfiction W 2a–f, W 4, W 5, W 9b (RI 1, RI 4), W 10		Clauses L 1b Commas in Phrases and Clauses L 2
Speaking and Listening Workshop: Presenting a Literary Analysis				Present a Literary Analysis SL 1d, SL 4	
UNIT 4					
Text Analysis Workshop: Theme and Symbol	Theme and Symbol RL 2, RL 3, RL 6				
The Interlopers	Theme and Setting RL 2 Monitor Connotation		Analyze Theme W 2		Vary Sentence Structure L 1b, L 5b
When Mr. Pirzada Came to Dine	Theme and Character RL 2, RL 3 Draw Conclusions RL 1		Compare and Contrast Stories W 2		Add Descriptive Details L 3 Prefixes L 4c
Do not weep, maiden, for war is kind / the sonnet-ballad	Universal Theme RL 2, RL 10				
Writing Workshop: Informative: Comparison-Contrast Essay			Write a Comparison-Contrast Essay W 2a–f, W 4, W 5, W 9, W 10		Commas L 2 Parallelism L 1, L 1a
Speaking and Listening Workshop: Participating in a Group Discussion				Participate in a Group Discussion SL 1a–d	

STRAND	Reading Literature	Reading Informational Text	Writing	Speaking and Listening	Language
UNIT 5					
Text Analysis Workshop: Author's Purpose and Perspective		Author's Purpose and Perspective RI 3, RI 4, RI 5, RI 6			
The Plot Against People		Tone and Diction RI 3, RI 4 Recognize Classification			
Linked Selections					
Why Leaves Turn Color in the Fall		Author's Purpose RI 4, RI 6 Patterns of Organization RI 5	Reflect on Author's Message		Participial Phrases L 1b Specialized Vocabulary L 6
How a Leaf Works		Interpret Graphic Aids RI 4, RI 7	Use Information from Multiple Sources W 2d, W 8		
Media Study: News Reports			Redraft a New Story W 2d	View a TV Broadcast to Identify Purpose and Evaluate Credibility SL 2, SL 3	
And of Clay Are We Created	Author's Perspective RL 9 Characterization RL 3 Monitor RL 1				Latin Roots L 4a
Writing Workshop: Argument: Persuasive Letter			Write a Persuasive Letter W 1a–e, W 4, W 5, W 7, W 10		Passive Voice L 1 Dashes L 2 L 2c, L 3
Speaking and Listening Workshop: Conducting an Interview				Conduct an Interview SL 1a, SL 1c	Conduct an Interview L 1
UNIT 6					
Text Analysis Workshop: Argument and Persuasion		Analyze and Evaluate Arguments; Analyze Persuasive Techniques; Analyze Rhetorical Devices RI 5, RI 6, RI 8, RI 9			
Doing Nothing Is Something		Argument RI 5 Distinguish Fact from Opinion RI 8	Write an Editorial W 5		Add Rhetorical Questions L 3 Etymology L 4c, L 5b
I Acknowledge Mine		Persuasive Techniques RI 8 Summarize RI 2, RI 4	Write a Summary Set the Tone W 2e		Analogies L 5 Set the Tone L 1b
Use of Animals in Biomedical Research		Counterarguments RI 5, RI 8 Summarize and Critique RI 2, RI 4	Write a Summary W 2e		Formal Language L 3 Connotation L 5b

STRAND	Reading Literature	Reading Informational Text	Writing	Speaking and Listening	Language
UNIT 6 *continued*					
Media Study; Daisy / America's Back			Evaluate the Message	Persuasion in Political Ads SL 2, SL 3, SL 4	
Writing Workshop: Argument: Persuasive Essay			Write a Persuasive Essay W 1a–e, W 4, W 5, W 10		Subjunctive Mood L 1 Spelling L 2c, L 3
Speaking and Listening Workshop: Presenting an Argument				Present an Argument SL 3, SL 4, SL 6	Parallel Structure L 1a
UNIT 7					
Text Analysis Workshop: The Language of Poetry	Poetic Form RL 5 Poetic Elements RL 4, RL 10				
There Will Come Soft Rains / Meeting at Night / The Sound of Night	Sound Devices RL 4 Reading Poetry RL 5, RL 10		Interpret Theme W 9a (RL 2)		Use Precise Language L 3, L 4b
Sonnet 18 / Sonnet XXX of Fatal Interview	Sonnet RL 5 Reading Sonnets RL 2, RL 10		Interpret Theme W 2b		
Lord Randall / Ballad / Balada / Midwinter Blues	Ballad RL 5 Understand Dialect RL 4, RL 10		Support an Opinion W 2f		
Writing Workshop: Informative: Analysis of a Poem			Write a Response to Literature W 2a–f, W 4, W 5, W 9a (RL 1), W 10		Use Quotations Correctly L 2 Complex Sentences L 1
Technology Workshop: Creating a Class Blog			Create a Class Blog W 2a, W 6	Create a Class Blog SL 1c, SL 4, SL 5	
UNIT 8					
Text Analysis Workshop: Author's Style and Voice	Style and Voice RL 4				
The Pit and the Pendulum	Poe's Style RL 4 Paraphrase RL 1		Write Across Texts W 9a		Use Personification L 3 Foreign Words Used in English L 4b
Birches / Mending Wall	Frost's Style RL 4 Make Inferences RL 1		Analyze Dialogue W 9a (RL 2)		Use Verbals Effectively L 1b
Only Daughter / from Caramelo		Cisneros's Style and Voice RI 4, RI 5 Identify Author's Purpose RI 6			Etymology L 4c

STRAND	Reading Literature	Reading Informational Text	Writing	Speaking and Listening	Language
UNIT 8 *continued*					
Writing Workshop: Informative: Online Feature Article			Write an Online Feature Article W 2a–f, W 4, W 5, W 6, W 7, W 8, W 9b (RI 1)		Incorporating Quotations L 3a Absolute Phrases L 1b
Technology Workshop: Updating an Online Feature Article			Update an Online Feature Article W 6	Update an Online Feature Article SL 1c, SL 5	
UNIT 9					
Text Analysis Workshop: History, Culture, and the Author	Writer's Background; Historical and Cultural Context RL 4, RL 6	Writer's Background; Historical and Cultural Context RI 4, RI 6			
from *Farewell to Manzanar*		Cultural Characteristics RI 4, RI 6 Monitor RI 1	Write an Editorial W 4		Vary Sentence Structure L 1b Prefixes L 4c
A Eulogy for Dr. Martin Luther King, Jr.		Analyze Rhetorical Devices RI 6, RI 9	Cite Evidence W 2		
Marriage Is a Private Affair	Moral Dilemma RL 3, RL 6 Predict RL 1		Write Across Texts W 9b		Gerunds and Gerund Phrases L 1b Greek Roots L 4b
Writing Workshop: Informative: Cause- and-Effect Essay			Write a Cause-and-Effect Essay W 2 a–f, W 4, W 5, W 7, W 8, W 10		Transitions L 1 Sentence Variety L 2a
Speaking and Listening Workshop: Giving and Following Oral Instructions				Give and Follow Oral Instructions SL 1, SL 4	
UNIT 10					
Text Analysis Workshop: Greek Tragedy and Medieval Romance	Characteristics of Greek Tragedy; Characteristics of Medieval Romance RL 2, RL 3, RL 6, RL 10				
from *Don Quixote* / from *Man of La Mancha*	Parody Across Genres RL 5 Set a Purpose for Reading RL 1, RL 7, RL 9		Writing for Assessment W 2, W 5		Similes and Metaphors L 5
Writing Workshop: Narrative: Video Script			Write a Video Script W 2a, W 3a–e, W 4, W 5, W 6, W 10		Set Directions; Formatting a Script
Technology Workshop: Producing a Video			Produce a Video W 6	Produce a Video SL 2, SL 5	

STRAND	Reading Literature	Reading Informational Text	Writing	Speaking and Listening	Language
UNIT 11					
Text Analysis Workshop: Shakespearean Drama	Characteristics of Shakespearean Drama; The Language of Shakespeare RL 3, RL 5, RL 9, RL 10				The Language of Shakespeare L 6
The Tragedy of Julius Caesar	Shakespearean Tragedy RL 1, RL 3 Reading Shakespearean Drama RL 4, RL 9, RL 10	Behind the Curtain RI 7	Analyze Character Motives		Adjective Clauses L 1b
Media Study: from *Julius Caesar*	Evaluate the Film Clip RL 7		Evaluate the Film Clip W 2	Evaluate the Film Clip SL 1	
Writing Workshop: Argument: Critical Review			Write a Critical Review W 1a–e, W 4, W 5, W 9a (RL 7, 9) W 10		Spell Correctly L 2c Using Semicolons L 2a
Speaking and Listening Workshop: Evaluating a Presentation				Evaluate a Presentation SL 1a–d, SL 3, SL 4	
UNIT 12					
Research Strategies Workshop			Plan and Focus Research W 7, W 8, W 9		
Writing Workshop: Informative Text: Research Paper			Write a Research Paper W 2a–f, W 4, W 5, W 7, W 8, W 9b (RI 7)		Capitalizing Titles L 2 Integrating Quotations L 2b L 1, L 2b, L 3a
Technology Workshop: Creating a Web Site			Create a Web Site W 6	Create a Web Site SL 2	

HOLT McDOUGAL

Literature

Grade 10

COMMON CORE

EDITION

Typeset in *The Sans* from LucasFonts.

ART CREDITS

COVER, TITLE PAGE

top center Teacher's Discovery, Auburn Hills, Michigan; *top right* © DEA / A. DAGLI ORTI/Getty Images; *bottom center* Getty Images; *center* Atlantide Phototravel/Corbis; *bottom left* Ken Kinzie/HMH Publishers.

Art Credits are continued at the back of the book, following the Acknowledgments.

Printed in the U.S.A.

ISBN 978-0-547-61840-1

1 2 3 4 5 6 7 8 9 10   1426   20 19 18 17 16 15 14 13 12 11

4500000000   B C D E F G

HOLT McDOUGAL

Literature

Grade 10

Janet Allen

Arthur N. Applebee

Jim Burke

Douglas Carnine

Yvette Jackson

Carol Jago

Robert T. Jiménez

Judith A. Langer

Robert J. Marzano

Mary Lou McCloskey

Donna M. Ogle

Carol Booth Olson

Lydia Stack

Carol Ann Tomlinson

Special Contributor: Kylene Beers

HOLT McDOUGAL

HOUGHTON MIFFLIN HARCOURT

SENIOR PROGRAM CONSULTANTS

 **JANET ALLEN** Reading and Literacy Specialist; creator of the popular "It's Never Too Late"/"Reading for Life" Institutes. Dr. Allen is an internationally known consultant who specializes in literacy work with at-risk students. Her publications include *Tools for Content Literacy; It's Never Too Late: Leading Adolescents to Lifelong Learning; Yellow Brick Roads: Shared and Guided Paths to Independent Reading; Words, Words, Words: Teaching Vocabulary in Grades 4–12;* and *Testing 1, 2, 3 . . . Bridging Best Practice and High-Stakes Assessments.* Dr. Allen was a high school reading and English teacher for more than 20 years.

 **ARTHUR N. APPLEBEE** Leading Professor, School of Education at the University at Albany, State University of New York; Director of the Center on English Learning and Achievement. During his varied career, Dr. Applebee has been both a researcher and a teacher, working in institutional settings with children with severe learning problems, in public schools, as a staff member of the National Council of Teachers of English, and in professional education. He was elected to the International Reading Hall of Fame and has received, among other honors, the David H. Russell Award for Distinguished Research in the Teaching of English.

 **JIM BURKE** Lecturer and Author; Teacher of English at Burlingame High School, Burlingame, California. Mr. Burke is a popular presenter at educational conferences across the country and is the author of numerous books for teachers, including *School Smarts: The Four Cs of Academic Success; The English Teacher's Companion; Reading Reminders; Writing Reminders;* and *ACCESSing School: Teaching Struggling Readers to Achieve Academic and Personal Success.* He is the recipient of NCTE's Exemplary English Leadership Award and was inducted into the California Reading Association's Hall of Fame.

 **DOUGLAS CARNINE** Professor of Education at the University of Oregon; Director of the Western Region Reading First Technical Assistance Center. Dr. Carnine is nationally known for his focus on research-based practices in education, especially curriculum designs that prepare instructors of K–12 students. He has received the Lifetime Achievement Award from the Council for Exceptional Children and the Ersted Award for outstanding teaching at the University of Oregon. Dr. Carnine frequently consults on educational policy with government groups, businesses, communities, and teacher unions.

 **YVETTE JACKSON** Executive Director of the National Urban Alliance for Effective Education. Nationally recognized for her work in assessing the learning potential of underachieving urban students, Dr. Jackson is also a presenter for the Harvard Principal Center and is a member of the Differentiation Faculty of the Association for Supervision and Curriculum Development. Dr. Jackson's research focuses on literacy, gifted education, and cognitive mediation theory. She designed the Comprehensive Education Plan for the New York City Public Schools and has served as their Director of Gifted Programs.

 **CAROL JAGO** Teacher of English with thirty-two years of experience at Santa Monica High School in California; Author and nationally known Lecturer; and Past President of the National Council of Teachers of English. With varied experience in standards assessment and secondary education, Ms. Jago is the author of numerous books on education and is active with the California Association of Teachers of English, editing its scholarly journal *California English* since 1996. Ms. Jago also served on the planning committee for the 2009 NAEP Framework and the 2011 NAEP Writing Framework.

 **ROBERT T. JIMÉNEZ** Professor of Language, Literacy, and Culture at Vanderbilt University. Dr. Jiménez's research focuses on the language and literacy practices of Latino students. A former bilingual education teacher, he is now conducting research on how written language is thought about and used in contemporary Mexico. Dr. Jiménez has received several research and teaching honors, including two Fulbright awards from the Council for the International Exchange of Scholars and the Albert J. Harris Award from the International Reading Association.

 **JUDITH A. LANGER** Distinguished Professor at the University at Albany, State University of New York; Director of the Center on English Learning and Achievement; Director of the Albany Institute for Research in Education. An internationally known scholar in English language arts education, Dr. Langer specializes in developing teaching approaches that can enrich and improve what gets done on a daily basis in classrooms. Her publications include *Getting to Excellent: How to Create Better Schools* and *Effective Literacy Instruction: Building Successful Reading and Writing Programs.*

 **ROBERT J. MARZANO** Senior Scholar at Mid-Continent Research for Education and Learning (McREL); Associate Professor at Cardinal Stritch University in Milwaukee, Wisconsin; President of Marzano & Associates. An internationally known researcher, trainer, and speaker, Dr. Marzano has developed programs that translate research and theory into practical tools for K–12 teachers and administrators. He has written extensively on such topics as reading and writing instruction, thinking skills, school effectiveness, assessment, and standards implementation.

 **DONNA M. OGLE** Professor of Reading and Language at National-Louis University in Chicago, Illinois; Past President of the International Reading Association. Creator of the well-known KWL strategy, Dr. Ogle has directed many staff development projects translating theory and research into school practice in middle and secondary schools throughout the United States and has served as a consultant on literacy projects worldwide. Her extensive international experience includes coordinating the Reading and Writing for Critical Thinking Project in Eastern Europe, developing integrated curriculum for a USAID Afghan Education Project, and speaking and consulting on projects in several Latin American countries and in Asia.

 **CAROL BOOTH OLSON** Senior Lecturer in the Department of Education at the University of California, Irvine; Director of the UCI site of the National Writing Project. Dr. Olson writes and lectures extensively on the reading/writing connection, critical thinking through writing, interactive strategies for teaching writing, and the use of multicultural literature with students of culturally diverse backgrounds. She has received many awards, including the California Association of Teachers of English Award of Merit, the Outstanding California Education Research Award, and the UC Irvine Excellence in Teaching Award.

 **CAROL ANN TOMLINSON** Professor of Educational Research, Foundations, and Policy at the University of Virginia; Co-Director of the University's Institutes on Academic Diversity. An internationally known expert on differentiated instruction, Dr. Tomlinson helps teachers and administrators develop effective methods of teaching academically diverse learners. She was a teacher of middle and high school English for 22 years prior to teaching at the University of Virginia. Her books on differentiated instruction have been translated into eight languages.

 **SPECIAL CONTRIBUTOR:**
KYLENE BEERS Special Consultant; Former Middle School Teacher; nationally known Lecturer and Author on reading and literacy; and former President of the National Council of Teachers of English. Dr. Beers is the nationally known author of *When Kids Can't Read: What Teachers Can Do* and co-editor of *Adolescent Literacy: Turning Promise into Practice,* as well as articles in the *Journal of Adolescent and Adult Literacy.* Former editor of *Voices from the Middle,* she is the 2001 recipient of NCTE's Richard W. Halley Award, given for outstanding contributions to middle-school literacy.

ENGLISH LEARNER SPECIALISTS

MARY LOU McCLOSKEY Past President of Teachers of English to Speakers of Other Languages (TESOL); Director of Teacher Development and Curriculum Design for Educo in Atlanta, Georgia. Dr. McCloskey is a former teacher in multilingual and multicultural classrooms. She has worked with teachers, teacher educators, and departments of education around the world on teaching English as a second and foreign language. She is author of *On Our Way to English, Voices in Literature, Integrating English,* and *Visions: Language, Literature, Content.* Her awards include the Le Moyne College Ignatian Award for Professional Achievement and the TESOL D. Scott Enright Service Award.

LYDIA STACK International ESL consultant. Her areas of expertise are English language teaching strategies, ESL standards for students and teachers, and curriculum writing. Her teaching experience includes 25 years as an elementary and high school ESL teacher. She is a past president of TESOL. Her awards include the James E. Alatis Award for Service to TESOL (2003) and the San Francisco STAR Teacher Award (1989). Her publications include *On Our Way to English; Wordways: Games for Language Learning;* and *Visions: Language, Literature, Content.*

CURRICULUM SPECIALIST

WILLIAM L. McBRIDE Curriculum Specialist. Dr. McBride is a nationally known speaker, educator, and author who now trains teachers in instructional methodologies. A former reading specialist, English teacher, and social studies teacher, he holds a Masters in Reading and a Ph.D. in Curriculum and Instruction from the University of North Carolina at Chapel Hill. Dr. McBride has contributed to the development of textbook series in language arts, social studies, science, and vocabulary. He is also known for his novel *Entertaining an Elephant,* which tells the story of a burned-out teacher who becomes re-inspired with both his profession and his life.

MEDIA SPECIALISTS

DAVID M. CONSIDINE Professor of Instructional Technology and Media Studies at Appalachian State University in North Carolina. Dr. Considine has served as a media literacy consultant to the U.S. government and to the media industry, including Discovery Communications and Cable in the Classroom. He has also conducted media literacy workshops and training for county and state health departments across the United States. Among his many publications are *Visual Messages: Integrating Imagery into Instruction,* and *Imagine That: Developing Critical Viewing and Thinking Through Children's Literature.*

LARKIN PAULUZZI Teacher and Media Specialist; trainer for the New Jersey Writing Project. Ms. Pauluzzi puts her extensive classroom experience to use in developing teacher-friendly curriculum materials and workshops in many different areas, including media literacy. She has led media literacy training workshops, guiding teachers in the meaningful and practical uses of media in the classroom. Ms. Pauluzzi has taught students at all levels, from Title I Reading to AP English IV. She also spearheads a technology club at her school, working with students to produce media and technology to serve both the school and the community.

LISA K. SCHEFFLER Teacher and Media Specialist. Ms. Scheffler has designed and taught media literacy and video production curriculum, in addition to teaching language arts and speech. Using her knowledge of mass communication theory, coupled with real classroom experience, she has developed ready-to-use materials that help teachers incorporate media literacy into their curricula. She has taught film and television studies at the University of North Texas and has served as a contributing writer for the Texas Education Agency's statewide viewing and representing curriculum.

TEACHER ADVISORS

These are some of the many educators from across the country who played a crucial role in the development of the tables of contents, the lesson design, and other key components of this program:

Virginia L. Alford, MacArthur High School, San Antonio, Texas

Yvonne L. Allen, Shaker Heights High School, Shaker Heights, Ohio

Dave T. Anderson, Hinsdale South High School, Darien, Illinois

Kacy Colleen Anglim, Portland Public Schools District, Portland, Oregon

Jordana Benone, North High School, Torrance, California

Patricia Blood, Howell High School, Farmingdale, New Jersey

Marjorie Bloom, Eau Gallie High School, Melbourne, Florida

Edward J. Blotzer, Wilkinsburg Junior/Senior High School, Wilkinsburg, Pennsylvania

Stephen D. Bournes, Evanston Township High School, Evanston, Illinois

Barbara M. Bowling, Mt. Tabor High School, Winston-Salem, North Carolina

Kiala Boykin-Givehand, Duval County Public Schools, Jacksonville, Florida

Laura L. Brown, Adlai Stevenson High School, Lincolnshire, Illinois

Cynthia Burke, Yavneh Academy, Dallas, Texas

Hoppy Chandler, San Diego City Schools, San Diego, California

Gary Chmielewski, St. Benedict High School, Chicago, Illinois

Delorse Cole-Stewart, Milwaukee Public Schools, Milwaukee, Wisconsin

Kathy Dahlgren, Skokie, Illinois

Diana Dilger, Rosa Parks Middle School, Dixmoor, Illinois

L. Calvin Dillon, Gaither High School, Tampa, Florida

Dori Dolata, Rufus King High School, Milwaukee, Wisconsin

Jon Epstein, Marietta High School, Marietta, Georgia

Helen Ervin, Fort Bend Independent School District, Sugar Land, Texas

Sue Friedman, Buffalo Grove High School, Buffalo Grove, Illinois

Chris Gee, Bel Air High School, El Paso, Texas

Paula Grasel, The Horizon Center, Gainesville, Georgia

Rochelle L. Greene-Brady, Kenwood Academy, Chicago, Illinois

Christopher Guarraia, Centreville High School, Clifton, Virginia

Michele M. Hettinger, Niles West High School, Skokie, Illinois

Elizabeth Holcomb, Forest Hill High School, Jackson, Mississippi

Jim Horan, Hinsdale Central High School, Hinsdale, Illinois

James Paul Hunter, Oak Park-River Forest High School, Oak Park, Illinois

Susan P. Kelly, Director of Curriculum, Island Trees School District, Levittown, New York

Beverley A. Lanier, Varina High School, Richmond, Virginia

Pat Laws, Charlotte-Mecklenburg Schools, Charlotte, North Carolina

Diana R. Martinez, Treviño School of Communications & Fine Arts, Laredo, Texas

Natalie Martinez, Stephen F. Austin High School, Houston, Texas

Elizabeth Matarazzo, Ysleta High School, El Paso, Texas

Carol M. McDonald, J. Frank Dobie High School, Houston, Texas

Amy Millikan, Consultant, Chicago, Illinois

Eileen Murphy, Walter Payton Preparatory High School, Chicago, Illinois

Lisa Omark, New Haven Public Schools, New Haven, Connecticut

Kaine Osburn, Wheeling High School, Wheeling, Illinois

Andrea J. Phillips, Terry Sanford High School, Fayetteville, North Carolina

Cathy Reilly, Sayreville Public Schools, Sayreville, New Jersey

Mark D. Simon, Neuqua Valley High School, Naperville, Illinois

Scott Snow, Seguin High School, Arlington, Texas

Jane W. Speidel, Brevard County Schools, Viera, Florida

Cheryl E. Sullivan, Lisle Community School District, Lisle, Illinois

Anita Usmiani, Hamilton Township Public Schools, Hamilton Square, New Jersey

Linda Valdez, Oxnard Union High School District, Oxnard, California

Nancy Walker, Longview High School, Longview, Texas

Kurt Weiler, New Trier High School, Winnetka, Illinois

Elizabeth Whittaker, Larkin High School, Elgin, Illinois

Linda S. Williams, Woodlawn High School, Baltimore, Maryland

John R. Williamson, Fort Thomas Independent Schools, Fort Thomas, Kentucky

Anna N. Winters, Simeon High School, Chicago, Illinois

Tonora D. Wyckoff, North Shore Senior High School, Houston, Texas

Karen Zajac, Glenbard South High School, Glen Ellyn, Illinois

Cynthia Zimmerman, Mose Vines Preparatory High School, Chicago, Illinois

Lynda Zimmerman, El Camino High School, South San Francisco, California

Ruth E. Zurich, Brown Deer High School, Brown Deer, Wisconsin

COMMON CORE

OVERVIEW
Student Edition

LESSONS WITH EMBEDDED COMMON CORE INSTRUCTION

COMMON CORE
Look for the Common Core symbol throughout the book. It highlights targeted objectives to help you succeed in mastering the knowledge and skills you will need for college or for a career.

© Getty Images

COMMON CORE CONTENTS

COMMON CORE

CONTENTS IN BRIEF

Online at

Log in to learn more at thinkcentral.com, where you can access most program resources in one convenient location.

LITERATURE AND READING CENTER

- Author Biographies
- *PowerNotes* Presentations with Video Trailers
- Professional Audio Recordings of Selections
- Graphic Organizers
- Analysis Frames
- NovelWise

WRITING AND GRAMMAR CENTER

- Interactive Student Models*
- Interactive Graphic Organizers*
- Interactive Revision Lessons*
- *GrammarNotes* Presentations and Practice

*also available on WriteSmart CD-ROM

VOCABULARY CENTER

- *WordSharp* Interactive Vocabulary Tutor
- Vocabulary Practice Copy Masters

MEDIA AND TECHNOLOGY CENTER

- MediaScope: Media Literacy Instruction
- Digital Storytelling
- Speaking and Listening Support

RESEARCH CENTER

- Writing and Research in a Digital Age
- Citation Guide

Assessment Center

- Program Assessments
- Level Up Online Tutorials
- Online Essay Scoring

MORE TECHNOLOGY

Student One Stop

Access an electronic version of your textbook, complete with selection audio and worksheets.

Media Smart DVD-ROM

Sharpen your critical viewing and analysis skills with these in-depth interactive media studies.

FM11

The World of a Story
PLOT, SETTING, AND MOOD

● FICTION ● INFORMATIONAL TEXT ● MEDIA ● POETRY

> *Vocabulary Strategies*
>
> Greek roots: *syn, p. 46*   Connotation and denotation, *p. 97*
> Latin prefixes: *re-, p. 62*   Specialized vocabulary, *p.134*
> Latin prefixes: *dis-, p. 76*

COMMON CORE
UNIT 2

Word Portraits
CHARACTER DEVELOPMENT

• FICTION • INFORMATIONAL TEXT • POETRY • DRAMA • MEDIA

> ### Vocabulary Strategies
>
> Connotation and denotation, *p. 216*   Latin roots: *contra, p. 274*
> Latin roots: *sol, p. 236*

A Writer's Choice
NARRATIVE DEVICES

• FICTION • INFORMATIONAL TEXT

Vocabulary Strategies

Latin roots: *man, p. 335*   Latin roots: *plac, p.380*
Latin roots: *sen, p. 372*

COMMON CORE
UNIT 4

Message and Meaning
THEME

• FICTION • POETRY • INFORMATIONAL TEXT • ACROSS GENRES

Vocabulary Strategies

Connotation, *p. 436*   Prefixes: *im-, p. 472*
Analogies, *p. 450*

Why Write?
AUTHOR'S PURPOSE

• INFORMATIONAL TEXT • MEDIA • FICTION • POETRY

Making a Case
ARGUMENT AND PERSUASION

• INFORMATIONAL TEXT • FICTION • ACROSS GENRES • MEDIA

Vocabulary Strategies

Etymology, *p. 644*　　　　　Connotation, *p. 686*
Specialized vocabulary, *p. 661*　　Using a thesaurus, *p. 708*
Analogies, *p. 676*　　　　Similes and metaphors, *p.736*

FM23

COMMON CORE
UNIT 7

Sound and Sense
THE LANGUAGE OF POETRY

Signatures
AUTHOR'S STYLE AND VOICE

- **19TH-CENTURY WRITING** • **20TH-CENTURY WRITING**

STANDARDS FOCUS

*Style, Voice, Diction,
Tone, Imagery*

 HISTORY Video link at
thinkcentral.com

Poe's Style, Paraphrase

*Whitman's Style, Analyze
Sensory Details*

HISTORY Video link at
thinkcentral.com

Frost's Style, Make Inferences

Vocabulary Strategies

Foreign Words, *p. 876*   Etymology, *p. 909*

Product of the Times
HISTORY, CULTURE, AND THE AUTHOR

• INFORMATIONAL TEXT • FICTION • POETRY • MEDIA

STANDARDS FOCUS
Writer's Background, Historical and Cultural Influences

Video link at
thinkcentral.com

Memoir, Connect

INFORMATIONAL TEXT: LITERARY NONFICTION

Cultural Characteristics, Monitor

Video link at
thinkcentral.com

Historical Events in Memoirs, Distinguish Fact from Opinion

Analyze Rhetorical Devices

> ### Vocabulary Strategies
>
> Connotation and denotation, *p. 950*
> Prefixes: *in-, p. 966*
> Suffixes: *-ion, p. 979*
>
> Greek roots: *cosm, p. 993*
> Using a dictionary, glossary, or thesaurus, *p. 1018*

COMMON CORE
UNIT 10

Upholding Honor
GREEK TRAGEDY AND MEDIEVAL ROMANCE

• DRAMA • FICTION • ACROSS GENRES

Vocabulary Strategies

Etymology, *p. 1108*   Connotation, *p. 1142*
Analogies, *p. 1129*   Metaphors and similes, *p. 1162*

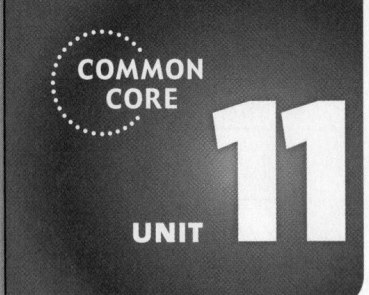

COMMON CORE

UNIT **11**

Shakespearean Drama
THE TRAGEDY OF JULIUS CAESAR

• DRAMA • MEDIA

STANDARDS FOCUS

Characteristics of Shakespearean Tragedy, The Language of Shakespeare

HISTORY Video link at **thinkcentral.com**

Tragedy, Tragic Hero, Soliloquy, Aside, Blank Verse, Dramatic Irony, Rhetorical Devices, Reading Shakespearean Drama

Analyze a Theater Review

Investigation and Discovery
THE POWER OF RESEARCH

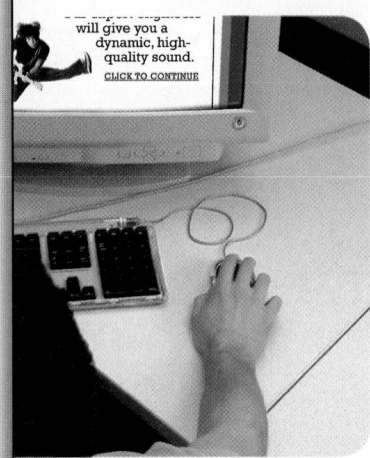

Student Resource Bank

Selections by Genre

Features

WriteSmart CD-ROM

Media Smart DVD-ROM

VOCABULARY STRATEGIES

pages 46, 62, 76, 97, 134, 216, 236, 274, 335, 372, 380, 436, 450, 472, 546, 570, 597, 644, 661, 676, 686, 708, 736, 876, 909, 950, 966, 979, 993, 1018, 1108, 1129, 1142, 1162

GRAMMAR AND STYLE

pages 47, 63, 77, 116, 135, 200, 217, 237, 275, 323, 373, 381, 437, 451, 473, 547, 571, 645, 662, 677, 687, 709, 785, 793, 877, 893, 951, 967, 994, 1019, 1109, 1143

STUDENT GUIDE TO ACADEMIC SUCCESS

STUDENT GUIDE

© Age Fotostock America, Inc.

FM39

The Common Core for Uncommon Achievement

Carol Jago

*"If you don't know where you are going,
any road will get you there." – Lewis Carroll*

The Common Core State Standards make clear where students are going. They describe what today's children need to know and be able to do to thrive in post-secondary education and the workplace. By focusing on results — the destination — rather than on the how — the means of transportation — the Common Core allows for a variety of teaching methods and many different classroom approaches. The challenge for teachers is to turn the daily journey towards this destination into an intellectual adventure.

One way to think about the Common Core is as a kind of GPS device to situate curriculum. While some students may choose the road less traveled, the objective is fixed. When students become lost through a wrong turn, teachers recalculate the route, providing a calm and confident voice that guides all students to academic achievement and deep literacy.

Shared Responsibility for Students' Literacy Development

The Common Core State Standards insist that the responsibility for helping students achieve literacy is not the sole responsibility of the English teacher. The introduction states clearly that, "instruction in reading, writing, speaking, listening, and language (should) be a shared responsibility within the school" (4). Citing NAEP Reading assessment test specification guidelines, the Common Core recommends that 55% of what students read in grade 8 and 70% in grade 12 should be informational text. These percentages are not meant to reflect the balance of reading materials in English class alone but rather the totality of what students should be reading across the curriculum in history/social studies, science, and technical subjects as well as in English. Given the type of reading that will be required of students in college and of graduates in the workplace, this distribution is both relevant and practical.

Understanding of Other Perspectives and Cultures

The Common Core also makes clear the importance of literature in the education of America's children. "Through reading great classic and contemporary works of literature representative of a variety of periods, cultures, and worldviews, students can vicariously inhabit worlds and have experiences much different from their own" (7). Reading literature demands that readers look inward, examine their beliefs in light of new information, consider the world through different eyes, take time for reflection. Such reading is a key to student learning.

The Purpose of Exemplar Texts

To describe the quality and complexity of the works students should read at each grade level, the Common Core offers lists of "exemplar texts." While some may choose to treat the texts on these lists as required reading, such usage would represent a misunderstanding of their purpose. "The choices should serve as useful guideposts in helping educators select texts of similar complexity, quality, and range for their own classrooms. They expressly do not represent a partial or complete reading list" (Appendix B, 2). The poems, stories, novels, and nonfiction that appear on the Common Core lists are intended as models for guiding — not dictating — text selection.

The Difference Between Persuasion and Argument

The Common Core writing standards describe the types and purposes for writing that students need to master. You will find extended definitions of argument, informative/ explanatory writing, and narrative writing in Appendix A. Of particular note is the distinction the Common Core draws between persuasion and argument. "When writing to persuade, writers employ a variety of persuasive strategies. One common strategy is an appeal to the credibility, character, or authority of the writer (or speaker). A logical argument, on the other hand, convinces the audience because of the perceived merit and reasonableness of the claims and proofs offered rather than either the emotions the writing evokes in the audience or the character or credentials of the writer" (24). Because of its importance for college and workplace readiness, argument holds a special place in the Common Core writing standards.

> *One way to think about the Common Core is as a kind of GPS device ...*

Complex Literary and Informational Texts

Throughout the Common Core document you will notice the anchor standard, "Read and comprehend complex literary and informational texts independently and proficiently." It isn't enough for students to read with a teacher by their side. They need to be able, often with a little help from their friends or from the habits of mind they learned from their teachers, to read for themselves. They need to be able, like Huck Finn, to head out for the territory on their own. Such a journey requires confidence in one's ability to navigate uncharted waters and to overcome challenges their teachers can't foresee or even imagine. As we guide students on the academic adventure that is high school, let us never forget that the path we tread is the path to intellectual freedom.

WORKS CITED

Common Core State Standards for English Language Arts and History/Social Studies, Science, & Technical Subjects. 2010.

Appendix B. Common Core State Standards for English Language Arts and History/Social Studies, Science, & Technical Subjects. 2010.

Carol Jago has taught middle and high school for over 30 years and was a member of the Common Core Initiative feedback team. She serves as Past President of the National Council of Teachers of English.

Understanding the Common Core State Standards

What are the English Language Arts Common Core State Standards?

The Common Core State Standards for English Language Arts indicate what you should know and be able to do by the end of your grade level. These understandings and skills will help you be better prepared for future classes, college courses, and a career. For this reason, the standards for each strand in English Language Arts (such as reading informational text or writing) directly relate to the College and Career Readiness Anchor Standards for each strand. The Anchor Standards broadly outline the understandings and skills you should learn by the end of high school so that you are well-prepared for college or for a career.

How do I learn the English Language Arts Common Core State Standards?

Your textbook is closely aligned to the English Language Arts Common Core State Standards. Every time you learn a concept or practice a skill, you are working on mastery of one of the standards. Each unit, each selection, and each workshop in your textbook connects to one or more of the standards for English Language Arts listed on the following pages.

The English Language Arts Common Core State Standards are divided into five strands: Reading Literature, Reading Informational Text, Writing, Speaking and Listening, and Language.

Reading Literature (RL)

This strand concerns the literary texts you will read at this grade level: stories, drama, and poetry. The Common Core State Standards stress that you should read a range of texts of increasing complexity as you progress through high school.

Reading Informational Text (RI)

Informational text includes a broad range of literary nonfiction, including exposition, argument, and functional text, such as personal essays, speeches, opinion pieces, memoirs, and historical and technical accounts. The Common Core State Standards stress that you will also read a range of informational texts of increasing complexity as you progress from grade to grade.

Writing (W)

The Writing strand focuses on your generating three types of texts: arguments, informative or explanatory texts, and narratives, as well as using the writing process and technology to develop and share your writing. The Common Core State Standards also emphasize research and specify that you should write routinely for both short and extended time frames.

Speaking and Listening (SL)

The Common Core State Standards focus on comprehending information presented in a variety of media and formats, on participating in collaborative discussions, and on presenting knowledge and ideas clearly.

Language (L)

The standards in the Language strand address the conventions of Standard English grammar, usage, and mechanics; knowledge of language; and vocabulary acquisition and use.

COMMON CORE DECODER

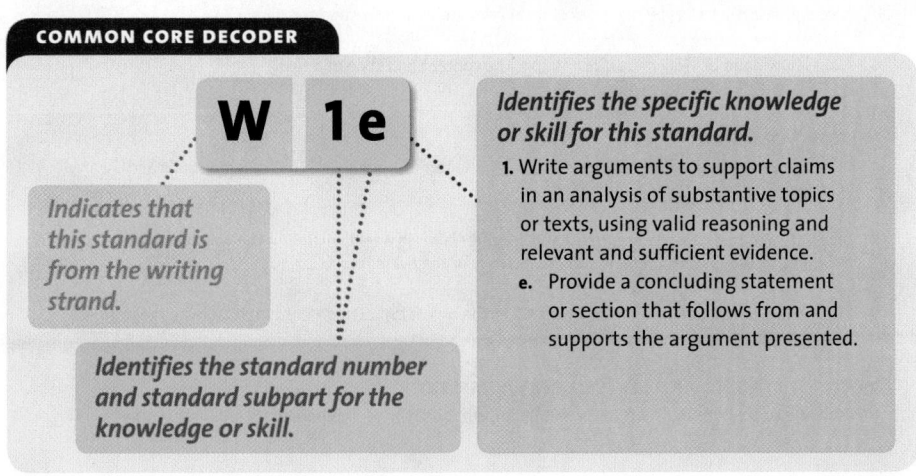

W 1 e

Indicates that this standard is from the writing strand.

Identifies the standard number and standard subpart for the knowledge or skill.

Identifies the specific knowledge or skill for this standard.

1. Write arguments to support claims in an analysis of substantive topics or texts, using valid reasoning and relevant and sufficient evidence.
   e. Provide a concluding statement or section that follows from and supports the argument presented.

English Language Arts
Common Core State Standards

COMMON CORE

Listed below are the English Language Arts Common Core State Standards that you are required to master by the end of grade 10. We have provided a summary of the concepts you will learn on your way to mastering each standard. The CCR anchor standards and high school grade-specific standards for each strand work together to define college and career readiness expectations—the former providing broad standards, the latter providing additional specificity.

College and Career Readiness Anchor Standards for Reading

COMMON CORE STATE STANDARDS

KEY IDEAS AND DETAILS

1. Read closely to determine what the text says explicitly and to make logical inferences from it; cite specific textual evidence when writing or speaking to support conclusions drawn from the text.

2. Determine central ideas or themes of a text and analyze their development; summarize the key supporting details and ideas.

3. Analyze how and why individuals, events, and ideas develop and interact over the course of a text.

CRAFT AND STRUCTURE

4. Interpret words and phrases as they are used in a text, including determining technical, connotative, and figurative meanings, and analyze how specific word choices shape meaning or tone.

5. Analyze the structure of texts, including how specific sentences, paragraphs, and larger portions of the text (e.g., a section, chapter, scene, or stanza) relate to each other and the whole.

6. Assess how point of view or purpose shapes the content and style of a text.

INTEGRATION OF KNOWLEDGE AND IDEAS

7. Integrate and evaluate content presented in diverse formats and media, including visually and quantitatively, as well as in words.

8. Delineate and evaluate the argument and specific claims in a text, including the validity of the reasoning as well as the relevance and sufficiency of the evidence.

9. Analyze how two or more texts address similar themes or topics in order to build knowledge or to compare the approaches the authors take.

RANGE OF READING AND LEVEL OF TEXT COMPLEXITY

10. Read and comprehend complex literary and informational texts independently and proficiently.

Reading Standards for Literature, Grades 9–10 Students

The College and Career Readiness Anchor Standards for Reading apply to both literature and informational text.

COMMON CORE STATE STANDARD	WHAT IT MEANS TO YOU
KEY IDEAS AND DETAILS	
1. Cite strong and thorough textual evidence to support analysis of what the text says explicitly as well as inferences drawn from the text.	You will use details and information from the text to support its main ideas—both those that are stated directly and those that are suggested.
2. Determine a theme or central idea of a text and analyze in detail its development over the course of the text, including how it emerges and is shaped and refined by specific details; provide an objective summary of the text.	You will analyze the development of a text's main ideas and themes by showing how they progress throughout the text. You will also summarize the main idea of the text as a whole without adding your own ideas or opinions.
3. Analyze how complex characters (e.g., those with multiple or conflicting motivations) develop over the course of a text, interact with other characters, and advance the plot or develop the theme.	You will analyze the development of a text's characters and how their actions, thoughts, and words contribute to the story's plot or themes.
CRAFT AND STRUCTURE	
4. Determine the meaning of words and phrases as they are used in the text, including figurative and connotative meanings; analyze the cumulative impact of specific word choices on meaning and tone (e.g., how the language evokes a sense of time and place; how it sets a formal or informal tone).	You will analyze specific words and phrases in the text to determine both what they mean individually as well as how they contribute to the text's tone and meaning as a whole.
5. Analyze how an author's choices concerning how to structure a text, order events within it (e.g., parallel plots), and manipulate time (e.g., pacing, flashbacks) create such effects as mystery, tension, or surprise.	You will analyze the ways in which the author has chosen to structure and order the text and determine how those choices affect the text's mood or tone.
6. Analyze a particular point of view or cultural experience reflected in a work of literature from outside the United States, drawing on a wide reading of world literature.	You will analyze the point of view or cultural experience of a work of literature from outside the United States.
INTEGRATION OF KNOWLEDGE AND IDEAS	
7. Analyze the representation of a subject or a key scene in two different artistic mediums, including what is emphasized or absent in each treatment (e.g., Auden's "Musée des Beaux Arts" and Breughel's Landscape with the Fall of Icarus).	You will compare and contrast how events and information are presented in visual and non-visual texts.
8. (Not applicable to literature)	

COMMON CORE FOCUS

RL 1 Cite strong and thorough textual evidence to support analysis of what the text says explicitly as well as inferences drawn from the text.

Literature: Citing Textual Evidence

Remind students of what it means to analyze and to draw inferences:

- To **analyze** something is to look at its different parts. For example, if you analyze a poem you might look at the different stanzas, the rhyme scheme, and the imagery.

- To **draw inferences,** or make inferences, is to figure out what a text means when it does not directly state something. You make inferences by combining what is stated with what you already know. For example, if a text says "José's hair and clothes were wet when he came inside," you might infer that it's raining outside.

Ask volunteers to read aloud each of the three stanzas in "The Tropics of New York." After each stanza, ask other volunteers to summarize it. Students may benefit from the review of unfamiliar types of fruit or vocabulary words such as *laden* ("loaded"), *rills* ("small streams"), *benediction* ("blessing"), *gaze* ("a steady look"), or *longing* ("desire").

Reading Standards for Literature, Grades 9–10 Students, continued

COMMON CORE STATE STANDARD	WHAT IT MEANS TO YOU
9. Analyze how an author draws on and transforms source material in a specific work (e.g., how Shakespeare treats a theme or topic from Ovid or the Bible or how a later author draws on a play by Shakespeare).	You will recognize and analyze how an author draws from and uses source material from other texts or other types of sources.
RANGE OF READING AND LEVEL OF TEXT COMPLEXITY 10. By the end of grade 10, read and comprehend literature, including stories, dramas, and poems, in the grades 9–10 text complexity band proficiently, with scaffolding as needed at the high end of the range.	You will demonstrate the ability to read and understand grade-level appropriate literary texts by the end of grade 10.

Spotlight on Common Core

COMMON CORE

RL 1 Cite strong and thorough textual evidence to support analysis of what the text says explicitly as well as inferences drawn from the text.

Literature: Citing Textual Evidence

The Common Core State Standards stress the importance of providing strong and thorough support for your analysis of any text that you read, from short stories, to poems, to opinion pieces. To support your analysis you need to provide **textual evidence**, which means using ideas and details from the text. You can do this in two ways:

1. identify the ideas and details that enable you to analyze what the text clearly states
2. identify the ideas and details that enable you to draw inferences, or make logical conclusions, about the text

Throughout this book, in questions about individual texts and in writing about texts, you will be asked to support your ideas with text evidence. Study the following example:

Read the following poem, "The Tropics in New York" by Claude McKay. Then answer the two questions that follow the poem.

> Bananas ripe and green, and ginger-root,
>   Cocoa in pods and alligator pears,
> And tangerines and mangoes and grape fruit,
>   Fit for the highest prize at parish fairs,
>
> 5 Set in the window, bringing memories
>   Of fruit-trees laden by low-singing rills,
> And dewy dawns, and mystical blue skies
>   In benediction over nun-like hills.
>
> My eyes grow dim, and I could no more gaze;
> 10   A wave of longing through my body swept,
> And, hungry for the old, familiar ways,
>   I turned aside and bowed my head and wept.

1. What imagery does the poet use to create the impression that New York is a tropical place? Support your response with text evidence.

2. What can you infer about the effect of the fruit, the dawn, the sky, and the hills on the speaker in the poem? Support your response with text evidence.

LEARN HOW Citing Textual Evidence The questions that follow "The Tropics in New York" both ask you to cite text evidence, but for different reasons. The first question directs you to probe what the poem says explicitly; the second question relates to the inferences you make in reading the poem.

To support your analysis, you need to identify specific ideas and details in the poem that will support your response to either type of question. These ideas and details can be specific words or **quotations** from the text, **paraphrases** of the text, or a **summary** of the text or of a relevant part of the text. Remember that to paraphrase, you use your own words instead of the exact words in the text. To summarize, you briefly retell what the text says, again in your own words.

Here are two examples of how to respond to the questions. Notice how the writer uses the types of text evidence to support each analysis.

1. What imagery does the poet use to create the impression that New York is a tropical place? Support your response with text evidence.

> In "The Tropics of New York," Claude McKay uses vivid visual imagery to create the initial impression that New York is a tropical place. The speaker begins by describing the bananas as "ripe and green" and then moves on to "dewy dawns," "mystical blue skies," and "nun-like hills." Each phrase creates a strong image for the reader, in sharp contrast to the more typical image of New York as a bustling urban area.

quotation marks correctly indicate that the poet's words are directly cited

2. What can you infer about the effect of the fruit, the dawn, the sky, and the hills on the speaker in the poem? Support your response with text evidence.

> In "The Tropics in New York," the speaker begins with descriptions that suggest that New York has the warmth, color, and lushness of a tropical climate. In the second stanza, however, the tone of the poem begins to shift, as the speaker states that the fruit sparks memories of another place, where trees are heavy with fruit and the water in small streams softly murmurs. In the final stanza, the speaker cannot bear his memories, saying "I could no more gaze; / A wave of longing through my body swept." He ends by crying, wishing for another time and place, all brought on by seeing the tropics in New York.

summary of the poem's first stanza

paraphrase of line 6 to discuss the speaker's memories

direct quotation to support the idea that the poem's speaker is sad

As you analyze texts throughout this book, be sure to use strong and thorough text evidence to support your ideas.

---

1. Some students may need help identifying any imagery at all before they can decide which images create the impression of a tropical place. Remind students that imagery is language that appeals to the reader's senses of sight, sound, smell, taste, and touch. Ask volunteers to identify the images they find in each stanza.

2. Point students to the third stanza and ask volunteers to identify every reference to the speaker's physical and emotional sensations.

LEARN HOW Citing Textual Evidence
Remind students that to state something *explicitly* is to say it directly or outright. It is the opposite of saying something *implicitly*, or implying something. When something is implied, it requires you to make an inference about its meaning.

To make sure students understand the difference between paraphrase and summary, write the following paraphrase and summary of the third stanza on the board without telling them which is which. Ask a volunteer to read each aloud and then ask the class to identify the paraphrase and the summary.

Paraphrase
My eyesight faded and I felt a wave of homesickness sweep through my body. Missing my old life, I bent down and cried.

Summary
The speaker missed his old home so much that he wept.

Explain that a summary will generally be shorter than a paraphrase, which should be about the same length or slightly shorter than the original text.

Reading Standards for Informational Text, Grades 9–10 Students

COMMON CORE STATE STANDARD	WHAT IT MEANS TO YOU
KEY IDEAS AND DETAILS	
1. Cite strong and thorough textual evidence to support analysis of what the text says explicitly as well as inferences drawn from the text.	You will use details and information from the text to support its main ideas—both those that are stated directly and those that are suggested.
2. Determine a central idea of a text and analyze its development over the course of the text, including how it emerges and is shaped and refined by specific details; provide an objective summary of the text.	You will analyze the development of a text's main ideas and themes by showing how they progress throughout the text. You will also summarize the main idea of the text as a whole without adding your own ideas or opinions.
3. Analyze how the author unfolds an analysis or series of ideas or events, including the order in which the points are made, how they are introduced and developed, and the connections that are drawn between them.	You will analyze the ways in which the author has chosen to structure and order the text and determine how those choices affect the text's central ideas.
CRAFT AND STRUCTURE	
4. Determine the meaning of words and phrases as they are used in a text, including figurative, connotative, and technical meanings; analyze the cumulative impact of specific word choices on meaning and tone (e.g., how the language of a court opinion differs from that of a newspaper).	You will analyze specific words and phrases in the text to determine both what they mean individually as well as how they contribute to the text's tone and meaning as a whole.
5. Analyze in detail how an author's ideas or claims are developed and refined by particular sentences, paragraphs, or larger portions of a text (e.g., a section or chapter).	You will examine specific portions of the text (sentences, paragraphs, or larger sections) to understand how they develop the author's ideas and claims.
6. Determine an author's point of view or purpose in a text and analyze how an author uses rhetoric to advance that point of view or purpose.	You will understand the author's purpose and analyze how the author uses language to effectively communicate that purpose.
INTEGRATION OF KNOWLEDGE AND IDEAS	
7. Analyze various accounts of a subject told in different mediums (e.g., a person's life story in both print and multimedia), determining which details are emphasized in each account.	You will compare and contrast the ways in which various media, such as newspapers, television, documentaries, blogs, and the Internet, portray the same events.
8. Delineate and evaluate the argument and specific claims in a text, assessing whether the reasoning is valid and the evidence is relevant and sufficient; identify false statements and fallacious reasoning.	You will evaluate the strength of the author's claims by examining the supporting details and reasoning and identifying any faults or weaknesses in them.

Reading Standards for Informational Text, Grades 9–10 Students, continued

COMMON CORE STATE STANDARD	WHAT IT MEANS TO YOU
9. Analyze seminal U.S. documents of historical and literary significance (e.g., Washington's Farewell Address, the Gettysburg Address, Roosevelt's Four Freedoms speech, King's "Letter from Birmingham Jail"), including how they address related themes and concepts.	▶ You will read and analyze influential documents and explain how they address important themes related to United States history and culture.
RANGE OF READING AND LEVEL OF TEXT COMPLEXITY	
10. By the end of grade 10, read and comprehend literary nonfiction in the grades 9–10 text complexity band proficiently, with scaffolding as needed at the high end of the range.	▶ You will demonstrate the ability to read and understand grade-level appropriate literary nonfiction texts by the end of grade 10.

Spotlight on Common Core

COMMON CORE · **RI 9** Analyze seminal U.S. documents of historical and literary significance (e.g., Washington's Farewell Address, the Gettysburg Address, Roosevelt's Four Freedoms speech, King's "Letter from Birmingham Jail"), including how they address related themes and concepts.

Informational Text: Analyzing Seminal U.S. Documents

The Common Core State Standards stress the importance of **analyzing** and **making connections** among seminal, or historic, U.S. documents. Reading and comparing themes and concepts among these important documents is one of the best ways to understand our history and our national experience.

Throughout your reading, you will be asked to analyze and make connections among historic documents. Many of these documents are also noted for their literary qualities. Use the techniques explained below to help you read these kinds of texts.

LEARN HOW Analyzing and Connecting Seminal U.S. Documents To understand a historic document's importance, you need to know something about its background or **historical context**. Asking questions like the ones below will help you understand its context better.

- Who is the document's author?
- Who was its audience?
- When was it written?
- Where was it written or presented?
- What is the document about?
- Why was it written?

Keep these questions in mind as you read the following excerpt from Patrick Henry's "Speech to the Second Virginia Convention." Also notice how one reader responded to her reading of this famous speech.

> *Background* In the years leading up to the American Revolutionary War, relations between the American colonists and England steadily worsened. England passed laws to restrict or punish the increasingly hostile colonies, which provoked more outrage among the colonists. Boston was specifically targeted for its bold defiance of English rule. One year before war was declared, the brilliant lawyer Patrick Henry addressed a convention of fellow Virginians who were undecided about whether to arm for war with England.

STUDENT GUIDE **FM49**

COMMON CORE FOCUS

RI 9 Analyze seminal U.S. documents of historical and literary significance (e.g., Washington's Farewell Address, the Gettysburg Address, Roosevelt's Four Freedoms speech, King's "Letter from Birmingham Jail"), including how they address related themes and concepts.

Informational Text: Analyzing Seminal U.S. Documents

Remind students that to **analyze** something is to look at its different parts. Explain that they will read excerpts from three historic documents and then **connect** the ideas they contain. Students should note that here the word *seminal* means of *historic importance*.

LEARN HOW Analyzing and Connecting Seminal U.S. Documents Tell students that each of the documents they will read is introduced by a "Background" note that provides **historical context**, or background information, about the document's author and the time in which he lived. Then, point out the bulleted questions that precede each document. These questions will help students analyze and interpret the document.

Have students read the questions, the "Background" note, and Patrick Henry's speech. Ask a student volunteer to identify the topic and Henry's opinion about it. How strongly does Henry feel about the topic? Ask students to cite evidence from the text to support their answers.

Tell students that "give me liberty or give me death!" is among the most famous quotations from the Revolutionary period. Ask students to speculate on why Henry's speech might have become so influential or why it might have helped inspire Virginia colonists to arm for war. If time allows, you might ask a student volunteer to give a dramatic reading of the speech's final paragraph.

---

from "Speech to the Second Virginia Convention,"
Richmond, March 23, 1775
Patrick Henry

> *speech by Patrick Henry, delivered to the Second Virginia Convention, 1775*

. . . They tell us, sir, that we are weak; unable to cope with so formidable an adversary. But when shall we be stronger? Will it be the next week, or the next year? Will it be when we are totally disarmed, and when a British guard shall be stationed in every
5 house? Shall we gather strength by irresolution and inaction? Shall we acquire the means of effectual resistance by lying supinely on our backs and hugging the delusive phantom of hope, until our enemies shall have bound us hand and foot? Sir, we are not weak if we make a proper use of those means which the God of

> *Henry addresses the audience with formal language. "Sir" likely refers to the leader of the convention.*

10 nature hath placed in our power. The millions of people, armed in the holy cause of liberty, and in such a country as that which we possess, are invincible by any force which our enemy can send against us. Besides, sir, we shall not fight our battles alone. There is a just God who presides over the destinies of nations, and who

> *His audience may believe that God is just and so will promote their cause.*

15 will raise up friends to fight our battles for us. The battle, sir, is not to the strong alone; it is to the vigilant, the active, the brave. Besides, sir, we have no election.[1] If we were base[2] enough to desire it, it is now too late to retire from the contest. There is no retreat but in submission and slavery! Our chains are forged!
20 Their clanking may be heard on the plains of Boston! The war is inevitable--and let it come! I repeat it, sir, let it come.

> *hostility with England could lead to war*

It is in vain, sir, to extenuate[3] the matter. Gentlemen may cry, Peace, Peace—but there is no peace. The war is actually begun! The next gale that sweeps from the north will bring to our ears
25 the clash of resounding arms! Our brethren are already in the field! Why stand we here idle? What is it that gentlemen wish? What would they have? Is life so dear, or peace so sweet, as to be purchased at the price of chains and slavery? Forbid it, Almighty God! I know not what course others may take; but as for me, give
30 me liberty or give me death!

> *Henry wants his audience to prepare for a war for independence and liberty.*

---

1. **election:** choice
2. **base:** dishonorable
3. **extentuate:** to underestimate or excuse

Questioning a text often leads to more questions, which can deepen your understanding of a document's context, meaning, and significance. Consider these examples:

- What do you know about the author's attitudes and beliefs?
- What events or situation probably influenced the author?
- Why do you think the author cared about the topic?

- What do you think the author was trying to achieve?
- Why might the author have chosen to make the points he or she made?

To answer some of these questions, you might have to research the author and the events and attitudes of the day. This helps you build the knowledge and insight necessary for a complete analysis.

As you read this excerpt from George Washington's "Farewell Address," keep these questions in mind. Notice how one reader responded.

Background As the nation's first president, George Washington helped bring the United States into being and saw it through its critical first years. He was revered then, as he still is, for his judgment, leadership, and wisdom. At the end of his presidency, he wrote a "Farewell Address," in which he expresses his faith in and concern for the new democratic government and liberty.

from "Farewell Address," Philadelphia, September 19, 1796
George Washington

. . . The basis of our political system is the right of the people to make and to alter their constitutions of government. But the Constitution which at any time exists, till changed by an explicit and authentic act of the whole people, is sacredly
5 obligatory[1] upon all. . . .
   . . . In all the changes to which you may be invited, remember that time and habit are at least as necessary to fix[2] the true character of governments as of other human institutions; that experience is the surest standard by which to test the real
10 tendency of the existing constitution of a country; . . . and remember, especially, that for the efficient management of your common interests, in a country so extensive as ours, a government of as much vigor[3] as is consistent with the perfect security of liberty is indispensable. Liberty itself will find in such
15 a government, with powers properly distributed and adjusted, its surest guardian. It is, indeed, little else than a name, where the government is too feeble to withstand the enterprises of faction,[4] to confine each member of the society within the limits prescribed by the laws, and to maintain all in the secure and
20 tranquil enjoyment of the rights of person and property.

1. **obligatory:** legally or morally binding
2. **fix:** establish
3. **vigor:** active strength
4. **faction:** conflict, dissension

Washington is leaving the presidency of the country he helped to establish. He believes in its democratic government.

Washington believes in the rights of the people, but says the Constitution must be preserved until changed by the "whole people."

It is important to give the new constitution time to work before making too many changes.

He supports a strong government, within limits.

Liberty is nothing but a name if the government cannot guard it by using laws that protect people's rights.

Many historic documents are also great works of literature. Patrick Henry's "Speech to the Second Virginia Convention" is as famous for its rhetorical excellence as it is for its historical significance. To analyze the literary value of a historic document, ask questions about the way the author expresses his or her ideas. Here are some questions to help you:

- What type of document is this: a letter? article? speech? journal?
- What type of language is used: formal? casual? technical? complex?

STUDENT GUIDE **FM51**

Direct students' attention to the bulleted questions that precede Washington's "Farewell Address." Ask students how these questions are different from the questions that preceded the Henry speech. Lead them to understand that these questions require greater understanding of the text and its historical context.

Have students read the questions, the "Background" note, and Washington's "Farewell Address." Students may have difficulty with Washington's prose style. Model how to paraphrase a challenging sentence by reading the document's second sentence aloud and then, on the board, paraphrasing each phrase. Help students see that rearranging the order of phrases may help clarify meaning:

"the current Constitution"

"is the law for everyone"

"until it is legally changed by an act (law) of the entire population."

Then read the phrases together as a coherent sentence. If time allows, have groups of two or three students paraphrase a difficult sentence. Remind them to refer to the footnotes or a dictionary for unfamiliar words. Have students choose a group member to read their paraphrases to the class.

Ask students to compare Washington's and Henry's attitudes about government and liberty. Lead them to understand that Henry values liberty above all things but doesn't address the idea of a democratic government. Washington stresses the delicate balance between a strong government and personal liberty.

As students read the questions that precede the Learned Hand speech, point out that they should recognize the emphasis on literary elements. Have students read the "Background" note. Then, ask volunteers to add anything they might know about life in America during the Great Depression and World War II. Tell students that the speech was given in New York City's Central Park. Ask them to imagine the mood of the audience, which was estimated to number almost one million people.

Then, have students read the Learned Hand speech. After students finish reading, ask them to compare Hand's concept of liberty with Henry's and Washington's. How do Hand's ideas about liberty differ from Henry's and Washington's?

Finally, ask students to comment on literary elements that are memorable and make the speech effective.

- Are there cultural references or references to other texts?
- How suitable is the author's style and tone for its purpose and audience?
- What, if anything, makes the language memorable: phrases? figurative language? symbols? imagery?
- What, if anything, makes the language persuasive: analogy? repetition? parallelism?

Try reading a document once to understand the author's ideas. Then read it again to examine *how* the author expresses these ideas. Multiple readings can help clarify why a document has literary value.

Consider these questions as you read the following excerpt from Learned Hand's "I Am an American Day Speech." Notice how he uses language to make the speech memorable and moving. Study how one reader responded to the document's literary and rhetorical qualities.

Background Learned Hand was a legal scholar and a federal judge from 1909 to 1961. Hand's judicial opinions are admired both for their well-argued clarity and literary craftsmanship. When Hand delivered his "I Am an American Day Speech," Americans were weary from ten years of economic depression and three years of a world war whose outcome was still uncertain. Against this backdrop, Hand addressed an enormous crowd that included many newly naturalized U.S. citizens. In the following excerpt he describes his idea of liberty.

from "I Am an American Day Speech" New York City, May 21, 1944
Learned Hand

> Speech, delivered to a crowd in New York City

. . . What then is the spirit of liberty? I cannot define it; I can only tell you my own faith. The spirit of liberty is the spirit which is not too sure that it is right; the spirit of liberty is the spirit which seeks to understand the mind of other men and women;
5 the spirit of liberty is the spirit which weighs their interests alongside its own without bias; the spirit of liberty remembers that not even a sparrow falls to earth unheeded; the spirit of liberty is the spirit of Him[1] who, near two thousand years ago, taught mankind that lesson it has never learned but never quite
10 forgotten; that there may be a kingdom where the least shall be heard and considered side by side with the greatest. And now in that spirit, that spirit of an America which has never been, and which may never be; nay, which never will be except as the conscience and courage of Americans who create it; yet in the
15 spirit of that America which lies hidden in some form in the aspirations of us all; in the spirit of that America for which our young men are at this moment fighting and dying; in that spirit of liberty and of America I ask you to rise and with me pledge our faith in the glorious destiny of our beloved country.

> Parallelism and repetition, "The spirit of liberty is," to persuade.

> Solemn but hopeful. His language is formal, but his words are appropriate for an event before citizens worried about World War II.

> Patriotic language: "pledge," "faith," "glorious destiny," "beloved." Unlike Henry or Washington, he defines liberty with several specific examples.

---

1. Traditionally, pronoun references to God or Jesus Christ are capitalized for clarification.

To deepen your analysis of significant historic documents, consider how they deal with related concepts and themes. You can ask these questions to help you to analyze:

- What topics or themes, if any, do these documents share?
- How does each author address them?
- How do the documents differ? Are the differences significant?

Study the following example to see how one student examined related ideas among the three historical documents that you read above.

> Three historic U.S. documents, spanning 170 years of American history, deal with the concepts of freedom and liberty. In 1775, in his "Speech to the Second Virginia Convention," Patrick Henry urges his fellow Virginians to arm for war with England. He compares English rule to slavery and claims that peace was not "so sweet" as to be "purchased at the price of chains and slavery," which leads to his statement "give me liberty or give me death." President George Washington discusses liberty in his "Farewell Address" from 1796. He fought for liberty, but as the head of the government, he is cautious. Washington believes that a strong democratic government is liberty's "surest guardian." Without this, liberty is an empty concept, since no one is safe from anyone else. Writing 150 years later in his "I Am an American Speech," Learned Hand describes his faith in liberty. His "spirit of liberty" is more complex and thoughtful than Henry's or Washington's. It also draws on religious beliefs as support for the ideal of human equality. With more American experience to look back on, both positive and negative, he says that liberty may never have truly existed in America, but he has faith that its spirit lives in its people. The three authors love liberty and are concerned about its well-being, but each author links liberty's survival with different things: rebellion, a strong democratic government, and the individual's "conscience and courage." However it is defined, liberty has been a central concept in American democracy, as these three historic documents demonstrate.

- topic and concept of related ideas
- relevant examples, summaries, and quotations develop a complex topic
- connects idea to earlier examples
- summarizes key differences among documents
- concluding section points to the documents' importance

As you study other significant historical documents, consider what they say about the past, what connections exist among them, and what insights they offer us today. Also consider how the language of the texts gives them literary significance as well.

Direct students to the questions that precede the sample student analysis of the three documents. Help students see that by responding to these questions, they are making connections among the three documents as the Common Core State Standards suggest.

Have students silently read the sample student analysis and the annotations. Then, ask them how well the analysis examines related ideas among the three historical documents. Would they add or change anything? Be sure that it is clear to them how the annotations help explain the analysis. You might review sections of the sample against related sections of the documents to verify that students understand which elements were analyzed and which aspects of the documents were compared.

College and Career Readiness Anchor Standards for Writing

TEXT TYPES AND PURPOSES

1. Write arguments to support claims in an analysis of substantive topics or texts, using valid reasoning and relevant and sufficient evidence.

2. Write informative/explanatory texts to examine and convey complex ideas and information clearly and accurately through the effective selection, organization, and analysis of content.

3. Write narratives to develop real or imagined experiences or events using effective technique, well-chosen details, and well-structured event sequences.

PRODUCTION AND DISTRIBUTION OF WRITING

4. Produce clear and coherent writing in which the development, organization, and style are appropriate to task, purpose, and audience.

5. Develop and strengthen writing as needed by planning, revising, editing, rewriting, or trying a new approach.

6. Use technology, including the Internet, to produce and publish writing and to interact and collaborate with others.

RESEARCH TO BUILD AND PRESENT KNOWLEDGE

7. Conduct short as well as more sustained research projects based on focused questions, demonstrating understanding of the subject under investigation.

8. Gather relevant information from multiple print and digital sources, assess the credibility and accuracy of each source, and integrate the information while avoiding plagiarism.

9. Draw evidence from literary or informational texts to support analysis, reflection, and research.

RANGE OF WRITING

10. Write routinely over extended time frames (time for research, reflection, and revision) and shorter time frames (a single sitting or a day or two) for a range of tasks, purposes, and audiences.

Writing Standards, Grades 9–10 Students

COMMON CORE STATE STANDARD	WHAT IT MEANS TO YOU
TEXT TYPES AND PURPOSES	
1. Write arguments to support claims in an analysis of substantive topics or texts, using valid reasoning and relevant and sufficient evidence.	You will write and develop arguments with strong evidence and valid reasoning that include
a. Introduce precise claim(s), distinguish the claim(s) from alternate or opposing claims, and create an organization that establishes clear relationships among claim(s), counterclaims, reasons, and evidence.	**a.** a clear organization of precise claims and counterclaims
b. Develop claim(s) and counterclaims fairly, supplying evidence for each while pointing out the strengths and limitations of both in a manner that anticipates the audience's knowledge level and concerns.	**b.** relevant and unbiased support for claims
c. Use words, phrases, and clauses to link the major sections of the text, create cohesion, and clarify the relationships between claim(s) and reasons, between reasons and evidence, and between claim(s) and counterclaims.	**c.** use of transitional words, phrases, and clauses to link information
d. Establish and maintain a formal style and objective tone while attending to the norms and conventions of the discipline in which they are writing.	**d.** a tone and style appropriate to the task
e. Provide a concluding statement or section that follows from and supports the argument presented.	**e.** a strong concluding statement or section that summarizes the evidence presented
2. Write informative/explanatory texts to examine and convey complex ideas, concepts, and information clearly and accurately through the effective selection, organization, and analysis of content.	You will write clear, well-organized, and thoughtful informative and explanatory texts with
a. Introduce a topic; organize complex ideas, concepts, and information to make important connections and distinctions; include formatting (e.g., headings), graphics (e.g., figures, tables), and multimedia when useful to aiding comprehension.	**a.** a clear introduction and organization, including headings and graphic organizers (when appropriate)
b. Develop the topic with well-chosen, relevant, and sufficient facts, extended definitions, concrete details, quotations, or other information and examples appropriate to the audience's knowledge of the topic.	**b.** sufficient supporting details and background information
c. Use appropriate and varied transitions to link the major sections of the text, create cohesion, and clarify the relationships among complex ideas and concepts.	**c.** appropriate transitions
d. Use precise language and domain-specific vocabulary to manage the complexity of the topic.	**d.** precise language and relevant vocabulary
e. Establish and maintain a formal style and objective tone while attending to the norms and conventions of the discipline in which they are writing.	**e.** a tone and style appropriate to the task
f. Provide a concluding statement or section that follows from and supports the information or explanation presented (e.g., articulating implications or the significance of the topic).	**f.** a strong concluding statement or section that restates the importance or relevance of the topic

STUDENT GUIDE **FM55**

Writing Standards, Grades 9–10 Students, continued

COMMON CORE STATE STANDARD	WHAT IT MEANS TO YOU
3. Write narratives to develop real or imagined experiences or events using effective technique, well-chosen details, and well-structured event sequences.	You will write clear, well-structured, detailed narrative texts that
a. Engage and orient the reader by setting out a problem, situation, or observation, establishing one or multiple point(s) of view, and introducing a narrator and/or characters; create a smooth progression of experiences or events.	**a.** draw your readers in with a clear topic and an interesting progression of events or ideas
b. Use narrative techniques, such as dialogue, pacing, description, reflection, and multiple plot lines, to develop experiences, events, and/or characters.	**b.** use literary techniques to develop and expand on events and/or characters
c. Use a variety of techniques to sequence events so that they build on one another to create a coherent whole.	**c.** have a coherent sequence and structure
d. Use precise words and phrases, telling details, and sensory language to convey a vivid picture of the experiences, events, setting, and/or characters.	**d.** use precise words and sensory details that keep readers interested
e. Provide a conclusion that follows from and reflects on what is experienced, observed, or resolved over the course of the narrative.	**e.** have a strong conclusion that reflects on the topic

PRODUCTION AND DISTRIBUTION OF WRITING

COMMON CORE STATE STANDARD	WHAT IT MEANS TO YOU
4. Produce clear and coherent writing in which the development, organization, and style are appropriate to task, purpose, and audience. (Grade-specific expectations for writing types are defined in standards 1–3 above.)	You will produce writing that is appropriate to the task, purpose, and audience for whom you are writing.
5. Develop and strengthen writing as needed by planning, revising, editing, rewriting, or trying a new approach, focusing on addressing what is most significant for a specific purpose and audience.	You will revise and refine your writing to address what is most important for your purpose and audience.
6. Use technology, including the Internet, to produce, publish, and update individual or shared writing products, taking advantage of technology's capacity to link to other information and to display information flexibly and dynamically.	You will use technology to share your writing and to provide links to other relevant information.

RESEARCH TO BUILD AND PRESENT KNOWLEDGE

COMMON CORE STATE STANDARD	WHAT IT MEANS TO YOU
7. Conduct short as well as more sustained research projects to answer a question (including a self-generated question) or solve a problem; narrow or broaden the inquiry when appropriate; synthesize multiple sources on the subject, demonstrating understanding of the subject under investigation.	You will engage in short and more complex research tasks that include answering a question or solving a problem by using multiple sources. The product of your research will demonstrate your understanding of the subject.

Writing Standards, Grades 9–10 Students, continued

COMMON CORE STATE STANDARD	WHAT IT MEANS TO YOU
8. Gather relevant information from multiple authoritative print and digital sources, using advanced searches effectively; assess the usefulness of each source in answering the research question; integrate information into the text selectively to maintain the flow of ideas, avoiding plagiarism and following a standard format for citation.	You will effectively conduct searches to gather information from different sources and assess the relevance of each source, following a standard format for citation.
9. Draw evidence from literary or informational texts to support analysis, reflection, and research. **a.** Apply grades 9–10 Reading standards to literature (e.g., "Analyze how an author draws on and transforms source material in a specific work [e.g., how Shakespeare treats a theme or topic from Ovid or the Bible or how a later author draws on a play by Shakespeare]"). **b.** Apply grades 9–10 Reading standards to literary nonfiction (e.g., "Delineate and evaluate the argument and specific claims in a text, assessing whether the reasoning is valid and the evidence is relevant and sufficient; identify false statements and fallacious reasoning").	You will paraphrase, summarize, quote, and cite primary and secondary sources, using both literary and informational texts, to support your analysis, reflection, and research.
RANGE OF WRITING **10.** Write routinely over extended time frames (time for research, reflection, and revision) and shorter time frames (a single sitting or a day or two) for a range of tasks, purposes, and audiences.	You will write for many different purposes and audiences both over short and extended periods of time.

Spotlight on Common Core

COMMON
CORE

W 4 Produce clear and coherent writing in which the development, organization, and style are appropriate to task, purpose, and audience.
W 10 Write routinely over extended time frames (time for research, reflection, and revision) and shorter time frames (a single sitting or a day or two) for a range of tasks, purposes, and audiences.

Writing: Maintaining Clarity and Coherence

The Common Core State Standards remind us that our ability to write clearly and coherently often determines our ability to share what we know with others. Whether writing directions to get to your house or summarizing several months of research, your writing should convey information in a way that readers can follow easily.

Before you begin writing, you should know the answers to a few important questions about your project. The answers to these questions will help you determine and plan your writing process. For example, what are you writing? A brief email to a friend normally doesn't require much time or forethought. On the other hand, a research report on a complex topic requires significant time for research and time to plan, draft, revise, edit, and publish the final report. Sometimes you may even need to start over and try a new approach. Thinking about the end product helps you decide how much time and what kind of attention to devote to it.

LEARN HOW Planning Your Writing Study the chart on page FM58. It provides some additional questions that you can ask yourself before you begin writing. Knowing the answers will help you plan your writing process and help you create superior work.

COMMON CORE FOCUS

W 4 Produce clear and coherent writing in which the development, organization, and style are appropriate to task, purpose, and audience.
W 10 Write routinely over extended time frames (time for research, reflection, and revision) and shorter time frames (a single sitting or a day or two) for a range of tasks, purposes, and audiences.

Writing: Maintaining Clarity and Coherence

LEARN HOW Planning Your Writing
Students might need to review some basic terminology related to these standards. Remind students that **coherent writing** is writing that readers can follow—the ideas follow one another logically and they all fit together. Then, review the terms *development, organization, style, task, purpose,* and *audience* as needed.

Enhance students' understanding of the material in the chart by asking them to provide their own sample answers to each question. Write their responses on the board, providing guidance as needed. Then ask:

- What other questions do you ask yourself before you begin a writing task?
- What other questions do you think might be helpful?

Personalizing this process will help students to use it.

LEARN HOW Using Writing Strategies
Go through the chart as a class, discussing the strategies in the left-hand column and the examples in the right-hand column. Challenge a student volunteer to restate each strategy in his or her own words. If necessary, provide definitions for the following terms in the left-hand column of the chart, and discuss examples.

- **Controlling idea or thesis statement:** the main proposition that a writer attempts to support in a piece of writing. (*Carter's efforts to find the tomb are the stuff of fiction—one of archaeology's most fascinating quests.*)

Planning Your Writing Process	
Question	Examples
What is my final product?	• *A research paper for a class website* • *A multimedia presentation* • *An analytic essay*
What is my topic?	• *The discovery of King Tut's tomb* • *Conditions and quality of the school's cafeteria* • *The differences between Shakespeare's Julius Caesar and the historical figure*
What is my purpose, or reason, for writing?	• *To give information about Howard Carter's discovery of King Tut's tomb in 1922* • *To argue that the school board should upgrade the school's cafeteria* • *To analyze Shakespeare's portrayal of Julius Caesar in light of the historical facts about Caesar*
Who is my audience?	• *My world history class* • *Our school board* • *My school's literary magazine*
How much time do I have? Am I writing over a short or extended period of time?	• *Two weeks* • *Four weeks* • *Two months*

Once you understand your task, purpose, audience, and time constraints, you can plan your writing process. For example, you can decide how much time you should spend researching your topic based on your purpose, audience, due date, and the end product. You might try drafting a schedule, using a calendar and what you know about how much time to allow for each step in the writing process.

LEARN HOW Using Writing Strategies Armed with a writing plan, you can now concentrate on producing clear and coherent writing. The **Writing Workshops** in this book give many strategies to help you write effectively. Study the chart below, which provides examples of some of these strategies. The highlighted text in the right column reflects the bold-faced points in the left column.

Writing Strategies	
DEVELOPMENT	WHAT DOES IT LOOK LIKE?
• Include a **memorable introduction** and concluding statement or section. • Utilize a **controlling idea or thesis statement**. • Introduce sufficient facts, definitions, **concrete details**, **quotations**, and other examples that are appropriate to the audience's knowledge of the topic.	*When discovered, King Tut's tomb yielded unimaginable riches and insights into the world of the ancient Egyptians. For the contemporary world, this discovery is a simple fact. Yet Englishman Howard Carter searched in Egypt's Valley of the Kings for over thirty years before he found the tomb in 1922. On entering the tomb, Carter wrote, "... as my eyes grew accustomed to the light, details of the room within emerged slowly from the mist, strange animals, statues, and gold—everywhere the glint of gold." Carter's efforts to find the tomb are the stuff of fiction—one of archaeology's most fascinating quests.*

Writing Strategies	
ORGANIZATION	**WHAT DOES IT LOOK LIKE?**
• Establish a **logical organization** that makes sense for the purpose and audience. • **Provide graphics, use formatting, or other text features to help aid comprehension,** if necessary. • **Use organizational patterns, such as cause-and-effect,** definitions, or compare-contrast **to help readers understand the relationship between ideas.** • Include words, phrases, and clauses that link sections of text and create cohesion, or flow. • **Introduce a topic, organize** complex ideas, **concepts, and information to make important connections** and distinctions.	*Narrative voice-over:* Every school day about 1200 Owens High School students stand in this line, waiting for poor-tasting, unhealthful food. As you can see, the line stretches out this door and down the hall. *Briefly interview waiting teens for their perspective.* *Voice-over:* Since Polk and Owens High Schools were merged, we have experienced tremendous overcrowding. The school cafeteria may be the worst example. In this presentation, we want to make the case for upgrading the cafeteria by adding another cashier and offering more healthful food choices.
LANGUAGE AND STYLE	**WHAT DOES IT LOOK LIKE?**
• Maintain a **formal style and objective tone** while adhering to **the conventions** of academic informative or explanatory writing. • Use **precise language and domain-specific vocabulary.** • Exhibit a strong command of grammar, usage, capitalization, punctuation.	Much of what most people know about Julius Caesar the historical figure comes from Shakespeare's play, The Tragedy of Julius Caesar. As the Caesar scholar Suz-anne Cross points out, "It is difficult, now, to separate the most famous Roman of them all from the most famous author of them all" ("Bestriding"). Still, modern readers wonder if Shakespeare's interpretation of Caesar is historically accurate. An analysis of the writings of Caesar's era suggests that Julius Caesar was a much more complex man than the arrogant and superstitious tyrant Shakespeare portrayed.

Authors use several strategies to maintain clarity and coherence in their writing. They apply these strategies to texts of varied lengths, purposes, and complexity. Be sure to notice these strategies as you analyze texts throughout this book, and be sure to use them to improve your own writing.

College and Career Readiness Anchor Standards for Speaking and Listening

COMMON CORE STATE STANDARDS

COMPREHENSION AND COLLABORATION

1. Prepare for and participate effectively in a range of conversations and collaborations with diverse partners, building on others' ideas and expressing their own clearly and persuasively.

2. Integrate and evaluate information presented in diverse media and formats, including visually, quantitatively, and orally.

3. Evaluate a speaker's point of view, reasoning, and use of evidence and rhetoric.

PRESENTATION OF KNOWLEDGE AND IDEAS

4. Present information, findings, and supporting evidence such that listeners can follow the line of reasoning and the organization, development, and style are appropriate to task, purpose, and audience.

• **Quotation:** textual evidence quoted from a source or someone's exact words enclosed in quotation marks. ("*. . . as my eyes grew accustomed to the light, details of the room within emerged slowly from the mist. . .*")

• **Organizational patterns:** particular arrangements of ideas and information; cause-effect organization expresses causal relationships between events, ideas, or trends. (*Since Polk and Owens High Schools were merged, we have experienced tremendous overcrowding.*)

• **Tone:** the writer's attitude toward the subject or readers, often expressed in the style of language—formal or informal—and the choice of words. (*An analysis of the writings of Caesar's era suggests that Julius Caesar was a much more complex man than the arrogant and superstitious tyrant Shakespeare portrayed.*)

College and Career Readiness Anchor Standards for Speaking and Listening, continued

COMMON CORE STATE STANDARDS

5. Make strategic use of digital media and visual displays of data to express information and enhance understanding of presentations.

6. Adapt speech to a variety of contexts and communicative tasks, demonstrating command of formal English when indicated or appropriate.

Speaking and Listening Standards, Grades 9–10 Students

COMMON CORE STATE STANDARD	WHAT IT MEANS TO YOU
COMPREHENSION AND COLLABORATION	
1. Initiate and participate effectively in a range of collaborative discussions (one-on-one, in groups, and teacher-led) with diverse partners on grades 9–10 topics, texts, and issues, building on others' ideas and expressing their own clearly and persuasively.	You will actively participate in a variety of discussions in which you
a. Come to discussions prepared, having read and researched material under study; explicitly draw on that preparation by referring to evidence from texts and other research on the topic or issue to stimulate a thoughtful, well-reasoned exchange of ideas.	**a.** have read any relevant material beforehand and have come to the discussion prepared
b. Work with peers to set rules for collegial discussions and decision-making (e.g., informal consensus, taking votes on key issues, presentation of alternate views), clear goals and deadlines, and individual roles as needed.	**b.** work with others to establish goals and processes within the group
c. Propel conversations by posing and responding to questions that relate the current discussion to broader themes or larger ideas; actively incorporate others into the discussion; and clarify, verify, or challenge ideas and conclusions.	**c.** initiate dialogue by asking and responding to questions and by relating the current topic to other relevant information
d. Respond thoughtfully to diverse perspectives, summarize points of agreement and disagreement, and, when warranted, qualify or justify their own views and understanding and make new connections in light of the evidence and reasoning presented.	**d.** respond to different perspectives and summarize points of agreement or disagreement when needed
2. Integrate multiple sources of information presented in diverse media or formats (e.g., visually, quantitatively, orally) evaluating the credibility and accuracy of each source.	You will integrate multiple sources of information, assessing the credibility and accuracy of each source.
3. Evaluate a speaker's point of view, reasoning, and use of evidence and rhetoric, identifying any fallacious reasoning or exaggerated or distorted evidence.	You will evaluate a speaker's argument and identify any false reasoning or evidence.

Speaking and Listening Standards, Grades 9–10 Students, continued

COMMON CORE STATE STANDARD	WHAT IT MEANS TO YOU
PRESENTATION OF KNOWLEDGE AND IDEAS	
4. Present information, findings, and supporting evidence clearly, concisely, and logically such that listeners can follow the line of reasoning and the organization, development, substance, and style are appropriate to purpose, audience, and task.	You will organize and present information to your listeners in a logical sequence and style that are appropriate to your task and audience.
5. Make strategic use of digital media (e.g., textual, graphical, audio, visual, and interactive elements) in presentations to enhance understanding of findings, reasoning, and evidence and to add interest.	You will use digital media to enhance and add interest to presentations.
6. Adapt speech to a variety of contexts and tasks, demonstrating command of formal English when indicated or appropriate.	You will adapt the formality of your speech appropriately, depending on its context and purpose.

Spotlight on Common Core

COMMON CORE

SL 1 Initiate and participate effectively in a range of collaborative discussions (one-on-one, in groups, and teacher-led) with diverse partners on grades 9–10 topics, texts, and issues, building on others' ideas and expressing their own clearly and persuasively.

Speaking and Listening: Participating in Group Discussions

The Common Core State Standards stress the importance of initiating and participating effectively in group discussions. Notice the knowledge and skills that **subparts a and c** of **SL 1** require of grade 10 students:

a. Come to discussions prepared, having read and researched material under study; explicitly draw on that preparation by referring to evidence from texts and other research on the topic or issue to stimulate a thoughtful, well-reasoned exchange of ideas.

c. Propel conversations by posing and responding to questions that relate the current discussion to broader themes or larger ideas; actively incorporate others into the discussion; and clarify, verify, or challenge ideas and conclusions.

Remember that effective group discussions are an important part of our democratic process. People may decide to discuss something with others because group discussions often help us to

- answer a question
- build understanding
- solve a problem

A group discussion can be about any topic and involve people of different ages, of different ethnic, cultural, and economic backgrounds—often with very different viewpoints. As diverse as they often are, productive group discussions provide a forum in which participants can respectfully and reasonably discuss a topic or issue—even when they disagree on how to resolve the issue. (See also the **Speaking and Listening Handbook** on page R81 for more information.)

COMMON CORE FOCUS

SL 1 Initiate and participate effectively in a range of collaborative discussions (one-on-one, in groups, and teacher-led) with diverse partners on *grades 9–10 topics, texts, and issues*, building on others' ideas and expressing their own clearly and persuasively.

Speaking and Listening: Participating in Group Discussions

Remind students that groups can be diverse and made up of people with very different backgrounds and opinions. Group discussions can range from an informal gathering of friends to plan a party to a school board meeting. A casual talk with friends, however, is a conversation, not a group discussion. Group discussions usually have a topic and a purpose or goal. Ask student volunteers to share examples of group discussions with the class.

Read Speaking and Listening Standard subpart **1a.** Remind students that *explicit* means *easily seen* or *clear*. To "explicitly draw on" preparation means to refer to it directly or clearly. Then, read subpart **1c.** Ask students to share examples of any of the behaviors given. Paraphrase the behaviors if necessary, for example:

Keep the discussion going by—

- *asking and answering questions that relate the discussion topic to a bigger idea or topic;*

- *involving others in the discussion;*

- *clarifying unclear information;*

- *verifying—or confirming—information, using evidence or other types of support;*

- *challenging ideas and conclusions.*

LEARN HOW Participating in Group Discussions As a class, review the questions and sample answers about basic information that group members—or participants—should know before participating in a discussion. Ask student volunteers to give sample answers from their own experiences.

Review the last question, "How should I prepare?" Ask students if they have ever come to a discussion unprepared or been part of a discussion in which someone was not prepared. What happened? How productive was the group as a result?

Review the section on preparation, especially the five points on preparing for a more formal group discussion. Expand on each point by giving examples or asking student volunteers to give examples.

LEARN HOW Participating in Group Discussions A discussion is likely to be successful when the participants know basic information about it. Study the following questions. The examples are from a journalism club meeting.

- What is the topic of the discussion?
  Example: how to make the school newspaper more useful, interesting, and widely read
- What is the goal of the discussion?
  Example: a list of recommendations for increasing the school newspaper's readership
- What kind of group is it?
  Example: 12 students and the faculty advisor
- What is my role or assignment?
  Example: to research digital formats of high-school newspapers
- How should I prepare?
  Example: research the topic online, through the library, and through interviews; bring notes and recommendations, including evidence; bring handouts of examples and other useful information

Preparation is an essential ingredient of productive group discussions. How much preparation you should do depends on the discussion. You may not need to prepare for an informal discussion about a topic you know well. A more formal discussion about an unfamiliar topic requires preparation. Here is how you can prepare:

- **read** any assigned materials
- **review** your role or assignment
- **research** the discussion topic by focusing on relevant, easily summarized information and by collecting and bringing supporting evidence
- **prepare** to express an informed opinion if asked
- **consider** other points of view

By preparing well, you can contribute by sharing relevant ideas and research, responding knowledgeably to questions, and making connections to related ideas. Knowing more about the topic also means you can listen more attentively, ask thoughtful questions, challenge ideas, and involve others in the discussion.

The chart below gives examples of these behaviors. Consider why these behaviors are effective. How well do you model them when you participate in group discussions?

Effective Behavior	What It Looks Like	
Sharing information that draws on your research	Maureen explains that some schools are getting school-district help in changing from print to digital. She comments, "Lincoln Public Schools created an online newspaper template for their high schools to use."	Maureen cites a fact from her research.
Connect the discussion topic to other related ideas	As Maureen answers another question, she says, "This relates to the larger issue of media convergence and the future of mainstream journalism."	She connects to a larger topic.
Listen attentively	Listening to Maureen's presentation, Ramón thinks, "I knew timeliness draws readers to online formats; I didn't know that strong visuals also mattered."	Due to his research, Ramón better understands the topic.
Ask thoughtful questions	After Maureen finishes speaking, Ramón asks her if she thinks the emphasis on visuals in digital versions of school newspapers is turning them into magazines.	Ramón connects visuals with magazine format.

continued

Effective Behavior	What It Looks Like
Respond knowledgeably to questions	Maureen considers Ramón's question before responding, "Madison High School's newspaper staff said that many students didn't distinguish between the two formats. Readership increased thirty-five percent when the paper went digital and added more visuals."
Challenge ideas and conclusions	As a follow-up question, Ramón asks, "Are there other reasons that could explain the increased readership?"
Involve others in the conversation	Maureen agrees that there could be other reasons; she then asks the group if they should consider the format issue separately from the readership issue.

Maureen responds with specific evidence.

Maureen's example may have other interpretations.

Maureen sees Ramón's point but invites the group to weigh in.

Reflect on the Discussion
- Think of a recent group discussion you participated in. How well prepared were the participants?
- How did you prepare for the discussion? What was the result of your preparation?
- What is one thing you might do differently in preparing for your next group discussion? Why will you make this change in your behavior?

In most of your classes and outside of school, you will have frequent opportunities to participate in group discussions. When you and the other participants are well prepared, discussions are more likely to be rational, stimulating, and productive.

College and Career Readiness Anchor Standards for Language

COMMON CORE STATE STANDARDS

CONVENTIONS OF STANDARD ENGLISH

1. Demonstrate command of the conventions of standard English grammar and usage when writing or speaking.

2. Demonstrate command of the conventions of standard English capitalization, punctuation, and spelling when writing.

KNOWLEDGE OF LANGUAGE

3. Apply knowledge of language to understand how language functions in different contexts, to make effective choices for meaning or style, and to comprehend more fully when reading or listening.

VOCABULARY ACQUISITION AND USE

4. Determine or clarify the meaning of unknown and multiple-meaning words and phrases by using context clues, analyzing meaningful word parts, and consulting general and specialized reference materials, as appropriate.

After the class has had a chance to read the rest of the lesson, ask students to form pairs. Each group should decide who will report their findings to the class. Tell students that they should read and discuss the "Reflect on the Discussion" questions and record their responses to the last bullet point. Then the "reporter" will share the group's findings with the class.

College and Career Readiness Anchor Standards for Language, continued

5. Demonstrate understanding of word relationships and nuances in word meanings.

6. Acquire and use accurately a range of general academic and domain-specific words and phrases sufficient for reading, writing, speaking, and listening at the college and career readiness level; demonstrate independence in gathering vocabulary knowledge when considering a word or phrase important to comprehension or expression.

Language Standards, Grades 9–10 Students

COMMON CORE STATE STANDARD	WHAT IT MEANS TO YOU

CONVENTIONS OF STANDARD ENGLISH
 1. Demonstrate command of the conventions of standard English grammar and usage when writing or speaking.
   a. Use parallel structure.
   b. Use various types of phrases (noun, verb, adjectival, adverbial, participial, prepositional, absolute) and clauses (independent, dependent; noun, relative, adverbial) to convey specific meanings and add variety and interest to writing or presentations.
	You will correctly use the conventions of English grammar and usage, including
	
	   a. parallel structure
	   b. phrases and clauses

2. Demonstrate command of the conventions of standard English capitalization, punctuation, and spelling when writing.
   a. Use a semicolon (and perhaps a conjunctive adverb) to link two or more closely related independent clauses.
   b. Use a colon to introduce a list or quotation.
   c. Spell correctly.
	You will correctly use the conventions of English capitalization, punctuation, and spelling, including
	
	   a. semicolons
	
	   b. colons
	   c. spelling

KNOWLEDGE OF LANGUAGE
 3. Apply knowledge of language to understand how language functions in different contexts, to make effective choices for meaning or style, and to comprehend more fully when reading or listening.
   a. Write and edit work so that it conforms to the guidelines in a style manual (e.g., MLA Handbook, Turabian's Manual for Writers) appropriate for the discipline and writing type.
	You will apply your knowledge of language in different contexts by
	
	   a. conforming to a style manual when writing and editing

COMMON CORE

Language Standards, Grades 9–10 Students, continued

COMMON CORE STATE STANDARD	WHAT IT MEANS TO YOU
VOCABULARY ACQUISITION AND USE	
4. Determine or clarify the meaning of unknown and multiple-meaning words and phrases based on grades 9–10 reading and content, choosing flexibly from a range of strategies.	You will understand the meaning of grade-level appropriate words and phrases by
a. Use context (e.g., the overall meaning of a sentence, paragraph, or text; a word's position or function in a sentence) as a clue to the meaning of a word or phrase.	a. using context clues
b. Identify and correctly use patterns of word changes that indicate different meanings or parts of speech (e.g., analyze, analysis, analytical; advocate, advocacy).	b. recognizing and adapting root words according to meaning or part of speech
c. Consult general and specialized reference materials (e.g., dictionaries, glossaries, thesauruses), both print and digital, to find the pronunciation of a word or determine or clarify its precise meaning, its part of speech, or its etymology.	c. using reference materials
d. Verify the preliminary determination of the meaning of a word or phrase (e.g., by checking the inferred meaning in context or in a dictionary).	d. inferring and verifying the meanings of words in context
5. Demonstrate understanding of figurative language, word relationships, and nuances in word meanings.	You will understand figurative language, word relationships, and slight differences in word meanings by
a. Interpret figures of speech (e.g., euphemism, oxymoron) in context and analyze their role in the text.	a. interpreting figures of speech in context
b. Analyze nuances in the meaning of words with similar denotations.	b. analyzing slight differences in the meanings of similar words
6. Acquire and use accurately general academic and domain-specific words and phrases, sufficient for reading, writing, speaking, and listening at the college and career readiness level; demonstrate independence in gathering vocabulary knowledge when considering a word or phrase important to comprehension or expression.	You will develop vocabulary knowledge at the college and career readiness level and demonstrate confidence in using it appropriately.

COMMON CORE FOCUS

L 6 Acquire and use accurately general academic and domain-specific words and phrases, sufficient for reading, writing, speaking, and listening at the college and career readiness level; demonstrate independence in gathering vocabulary knowledge when considering a word or phrase important to comprehension or expression.

Language: Building Useful Vocabularies

LEARN HOW Building Vocabulary Remind students that they use different vocabularies every day. They use an informal or conversational vocabulary when talking with friends or sending a text message. They probably use a more formal vocabulary when making a presentation, taking notes in class, or writing a research paper. The vocabulary we use depends on our audience and purpose.

Tell students they already use **specialized vocabularies** in each of their class subjects when they learn words that are specific to that subject or field. Write the names of several school subjects across the board, leaving room beneath the words for examples. Call on students to give examples of specialized vocabulary for each of these subjects.

Language Arts
hyperbole

irony

Math
divisor

equation

Refer students to the glossary in this textbook to remind them what kinds of words glossaries contain.

Spotlight on Common Core

 COMMON CORE

L 6 Acquire and use accurately general academic and domain-specific words and phrases, sufficient for reading, writing, speaking, and listening at the college and career readiness level; demonstrate independence in gathering vocabulary knowledge when considering a word or phrase important to comprehension or expression.

Language: Building Useful Vocabularies

The Common Core State Standards stress the importance of building a strong vocabulary made up of words from specific subject areas and academic vocabulary—words you use in all subject areas. The Standards also emphasize the need to take a skilled and flexible approach to word knowledge and usage.

LEARN HOW Building Vocabulary Most of the words we use every day are words we have heard before and know well. This vocabulary doesn't require much thought about its meaning or use. By contrast, the Common Core State Standards highlight two other kinds of vocabularies: specialized (or domain-specific) and academic. By understanding how and when to use each, you dramatically improve your chances for success in school.

Specialized vocabulary consists of words about a specific subject matter or area of study or work. They are usually introduced and studied in a class about a particular subject, such as the following examples from earth science:

> climate   electron   galaxy   ozone   precipitation   radioactive

In each of your classes, you need to understand subject-matter words in order to understand the subject. Typically, a subject-matter word's definition is usually provided when the word is introduced in a textbook. You can use the following tools to build these words into your vocabulary:

- flash cards to use on your own or with a partner
- your subject notebooks, in which you can write subject words, definitions, and examples
- word lists from your instructor or from your textbook

You can also look at the subject-matter words and terminology in your textbook. Those that appear in the glossary or have long entries in the index may be important to learn, study, and remember long after they are introduced. For example, the **Glossary of Literary & Nonfiction Terms** (page R102) in this textbook includes definitions of words that relate to the study of literature and nonfiction, such as *archetype, connotation,* and *memoir.*

Academic vocabulary consists of words about knowledge and learning—words you use in every subject area. Study these examples:

> cite   compound   coordinate   encounter   statistic   variable

You need to be able to understand and accurately use academic vocabulary because these words are often used to

- assess your understanding of key concepts
- communicate complex or abstract ideas

Many academic vocabulary words have different shades of meaning, depending on how they are used. You can use references, such as a dictionary or a thesaurus, to research a word if you are not sure of its meaning. You can also use the strategies mentioned above to help you review and use these words. (See also the **Academic Vocabulary Workshop** on page 16 of this book.)

Often academic vocabulary appears on quizzes and tests. If you come across an unfamiliar word on a test, you can use vocabulary strategies, such as using context clues or analyzing word structure, to infer the word's meaning. These techniques are discussed in the **Vocabulary and Spelling Handbook** on page R68 in this text.

You can also create an academic vocabulary notebook that you use for all your classes. To use this type of notebook, read several pages of text or class notes. Then, review the text and choose four or five words that you need to learn. Remember, academic vocabulary is not subject-matter specific. Finally, create an entry for the word in your notebook. Study the following example for the word *compound*:

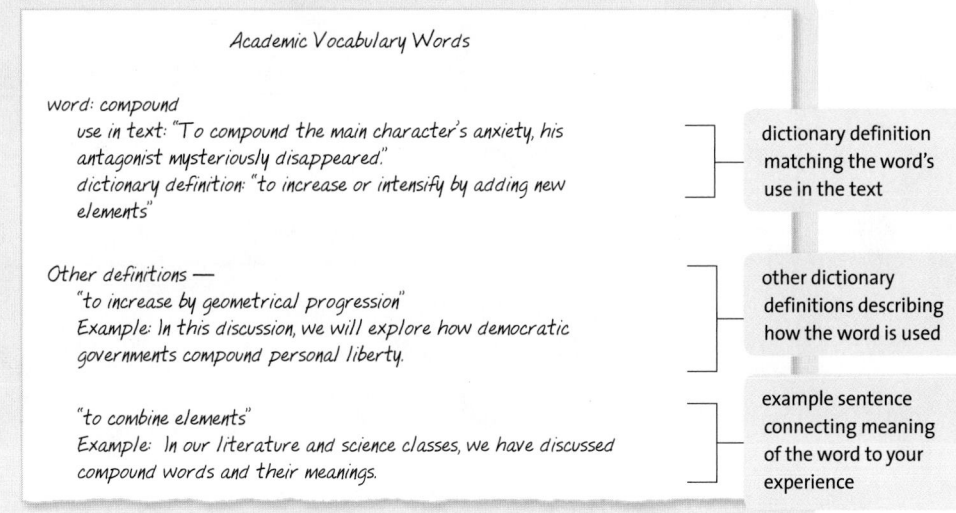

As you read or listen to people, notice when the academic vocabulary word is used. Try to use the word accurately yourself when you write or speak. Also, review your notebook regularly as you add more entries. In all of your classes and in your career you will be expected to use words with fluency, flexibility, and precision.

After students have read the lesson on **academic vocabulary,** divide them into groups of two or three. On the board, write eight or nine academic vocabulary words, such as the ones below. Write as many words as there are groups of two or three students:

factor   illustrate   implement   issue justify   objective   range   source structure   succeed   trace

Assign one word to each group. Then, tell students that each group should write a sentence that uses their word in as many different ways as the group can think of. Each sentence should be true and relate to the word's meaning. Emphasize that academic vocabulary words often have more than one meaning, and their meanings can vary depending on the way the word is used. If students' words have more than one definition, they should write sentences for each definition. Allow students to use dictionaries if available. Have groups present their sentences to the class.

To help students to demonstrate independence in acquiring vocabulary, make sure they have access to a dictionary and thesaurus in the classroom. Encourage students to consult these references when necessary.

The Power of Ideas

For help using this Introductory Unit, see

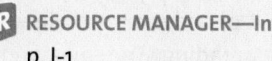 RESOURCE MANAGER—Introductory Unit
p. I-1

INTRODUCING THE ESSENTIALS

- Genres Workshop
- Reading Strategies Workshop
- Academic Vocabulary Workshop
- Writing Process Workshop

1

About the Art The artwork on this page illustrates literary selections in the anthology. *Under the Wave off Kanagawa* is the most famous woodblock print of Japanese artist Hokusai (1760–1849). For more information, see page 363.

Activity Ask students for their reactions to each piece of art on this page. Record brief notes about their impressions in a two-column chart. You may wish to revisit this chart after students view each image in a literary context. Compare their initial reactions with their later impressions of the artwork.

What Are Life's Big Questions?

The introductory unit provides an overview of the literary genres, reading strategies, and writing process that students will study in later units. It also introduces them to regularly appearing features, such as **Big Questions** and **Close Reads.** Encourage students to preview the unit by noting main headings, subheads, and graphic organizers, and by skimming through the first paragraph of each workshop. Discuss with students the unit title and section opener: "The Power of Ideas."

- What ideas have affected your life? *Students may offer a variety of answers ranging from science and philosophy to more personal experiences in which ideas brought about changes in actions or attitudes.*

- How can an idea have power? ***Possible answer:*** *An idea can have great power. It can influence people and change history.*

- What scientific or philosophical ideas have had profound, long-lasting effects? ***Possible answers:*** *Newton's theory of gravity; Einstein's theory of energy; ideas about freedom, democracy, and equality*

Pages 2 and 3 introduce students to the concept of **Big Questions.** Have them read and respond to the opening paragraph, which suggests that literature is a way to explore important ideas about life. As students read each **Big Question,** have them share their reactions. Ask whether these **Big Questions** apply to only one specific cultural period or historical era. ***Possible answer:*** *These ideas span many eras.*

The Power of Ideas

What Are Life's Big Questions?

Dignity, progress, justice—ideas like these resonate with all of us because they speak to the shared experiences that make us human. They also serve as the foundation for the big questions we all ask about the world. Consider the questions shown. How can your own experiences help you answer them? Through reading, discussing, and writing about literature, you can discover the answers that others have arrived at and gain new insights of your own.

Does love require SACRIFICE?

Our love for others—family, friends, significant others—can affect us in inexplicable, surprising ways. We might begin to put the needs of someone we love before our own, or we might make sacrifices that we never dreamed we'd make. Works such as W. D. Wetherell's "The Bass, the River, and Sheila Mant" and Chinua Achebe's "Marriage Is a Private Affair" will help you explore this question.

What is the price of FREEDOM?

In the 1960s, Martin Luther King Jr. led millions of African Americans in a fight for freedom. Along the way, his followers had to deal with violence, discrimination, and the assassination of Dr. King himself. From civil rights protesters to refugees fleeing their native countries, people of all times and cultures have faced oppression and injustice. Yet people often continue to fight for freedom in spite of the costs. What is the price of freedom? Is it ever too high?

Introductory Unit Resources

See resources on the **Teacher One Stop DVD-ROM** *and on* <u>**thinkcentral.com**</u>.

R **RESOURCE MANAGER INTRODUCTORY UNIT**
Lesson at a Glance and Note-Taking, pp. I-1– I-5

BEST PRACTICES TOOLKIT
Story Map, p. D14
Venn Diagram, p. A26
Character Traits Web, p. D7

TECHNOLOGY
- Teacher One Stop DVD-ROM
- Student One Stop DVD-ROM
- Write*Smart* CD-ROM
- GrammarNotes DVD-ROM
- Audio Anthology CD

How does heritage SHAPE US?

We are all the products of our experiences. In other words, who we are depends on such factors as when and where we grew up, the values that have been instilled in us, and the cultural and religious traditions that have been handed down from the previous generation. In this book, you will consider how your own heritage has shaped you as you read works by such authors as Rudolfo Anaya and Alice Walker.

When is ambition DANGEROUS?

Ambition is a powerful force that drives us to pursue personal goals and realize our dreams. But even the most well-intentioned person can be blinded by ambition. What happens when someone's pursuit of a goal becomes relentless or when he or she betrays those who offered support along the way? You will consider this question as you read William Shakespeare's *The Tragedy of Julius Caesar*.

COMMON CORE FOCUS

RL 1 Cite strong and thorough textual evidence to support analysis of what the text says explicitly as well as inferences drawn from the text. **RL 2** Determine a theme or central idea of a text and analyze in detail its development over the course of the text, including how it emerges and is shaped and refined by specific details; provide an objective summary of the text. **RL 4** Determine the meaning of words and phrases as they are used in the text, including figurative and connotative meanings; analyze the cumulative impact of specific word choices on meaning and tone (e.g., how the language evokes a sense of time and place; how it sets a formal or informal tone). **RI 1** Cite strong and thorough textual evidence to support analysis of what the text says explicitly as well as inferences drawn from the text. **RI 2** Determine a central idea of a text and analyze its development over the course of the text, including how it emerges and is shaped and refined by specific details; provide an objective summary of the text. **RI 7** Analyze various accounts of a subject told in different mediums (e.g., a person's life story in both print and multimedia), determining which details are emphasized in each account.

The Genres

Ask students to define each genre in their own words and share their definition with a partner. Discuss and compare their definitions with the information on the **Genres at a Glance** chart.

Discuss and Review Have students work in small groups to generate specific examples of each type of genre listed in the chart. Extend the discussion with these activities:

- Encourage students to explain differences among genres and forms using academic vocabulary.

- Remind students that some forms share characteristics of other genres. For example, magazine features may contain characters, dialogue, setting, and other literary techniques like those in fiction. Similarly, some novels and short stories are based on lives of real people and historical events. Encourage students to look for these qualities in selections from the anthology.

- Point out that each author, genre, and form offers a unique perspective on universal ideas and **Big Questions.** Invite student comments before moving on to the more detailed genre studies on pages 5–10.

Exploring Texts

If you've thought about questions like the ones on the preceding pages, you may have more in common with Shakespeare, Sophocles, and Gwendolyn Brooks than you realize. Throughout history, authors have searched for answers to thought-provoking questions and have shared their ideas through writing. By discussing and analyzing ideas in all forms of literature, you can learn how others see the world and arrive at your own deeply personal answers to the big questions in life.

COMMON CORE
Included in this workshop:
RL 1, RL 2, RL 4, RI 1, RI 2, RI 7

The Genres

By now you are familiar with the genres of literature—fiction, poetry, drama, and nonfiction—and many of their forms. In addition to traditional genres, this book contains other types of "texts," including movies, advertisements, and online news sites. These texts are worth reading and analyzing because they communicate many of the messages and ideas that you are exposed to daily.

Regardless of the genre, all texts can acquaint you with unfamiliar times and cultures and help you explore universal themes. Before you begin reading the selections in this book, review the characteristics of each genre.

GENRES AT A GLANCE

STORIES
Stories are narrative texts that spring from an author's imagination. It includes many subgenres, such as mystery and romance.
- novels   • short stories   • novellas

POETRY
Poetry is a type of literature in which words are chosen and arranged to create certain effects and to evoke emotional responses in readers.
- ballads   • sonnets   • narrative poems   • lyric poems

DRAMA
Drama is literature that is intended to be performed.
- comedies   • tragedies   • farces

NONFICTION
Nonfiction is writing about real people, events, and places.
- essays   • autobiographies   • news articles
- speeches   • biographies   • feature articles

TYPES OF MEDIA

Media are forms of communication that reach large numbers of people.
- TV shows   • news media   • advertising

DIFFERENTIATED INSTRUCTION

FOR STRUGGLING READERS

Note Taking For students who need help with note taking, hand out the note-taking copy master before discussing the genres. Have students read the introductory paragraphs silently. As you discuss the main points in the Literary Genres Workshop, have students record their ideas on the copy master.

R RESOURCE MANAGER—Copy Master
Note Taking p. I-2

FOR ENGLISH LANGUAGE LEARNERS

Vocabulary: Cognates Many of the genres and examples of genres have names that share linguistic roots with Spanish. Students whose first language is Spanish can use these examples to clarify their understanding:

English: *sonnet* / Spanish: *soneto*

English: *comedy* / Spanish: *comedia*

English: *farce* / Spanish: *farsa*

English: *biography* / Spanish: *biografía*

English: *Web site* / Spanish: *sitio web*

STORIES

Truth is stranger than fiction, as the old saying goes. Actually, the line between them is not always easy to define. At the heart of fiction is **narrative,** or the telling of a story. That story can be a work of pure imagination (science fiction, for example) or have roots in reality (such as historical fiction based on real people and events). Regardless of what inspired its creation, a work of fiction is usually one of three types.

- A **short story** is a brief work of fiction that can usually be read in one sitting. It often focuses on a single event or incident and develops only a few characters in depth.

- A **novel** is an extended work of fiction. Many novels have sweeping story lines that span long periods of time, involve intricate subplots, and develop a wide range of characters.

- A **novella** is longer than a short story but shorter than a novel. Most novellas take place over a short period of time and involve a limited number of characters.

Read the Model Set against the backdrop of the French Revolution, Charles Dickens's novel *A Tale of Two Cities* portrays characters who are swept along by the forces of history. Here, a French character named Lucie Manette receives some earthshattering personal news from the man who, years earlier, brought her to England. As you read, notice the elements of fiction that the author uses to communicate the idea of revelation.

LITERARY TERMS FOR FICTION
- plot
- conflict
- character
- setting
- theme
- narrator
- point of view
- flashback
- foreshadowing

from *A Tale* OF *Two Cities*
Novel by **Charles Dickens**

"Miss Manette, . . . when she [your mother] died—I believe broken-hearted—having never slackened her unavailing search for your father, she left you, at two years old, to grow to be blooming, beautiful, and happy, without the dark cloud upon you of living in uncertainty whether your father soon
5　wore his heart out in prison, or wasted there through many lingering years."

As he said the words he looked down, with admiring pity, on the flowing golden hair; as if he pictured to himself that it might have been already tinged with gray.

"You know that your parents had no great possession, and that what they
10　had was secured to your mother and to you. There has been no new discovery, of money, or of any other property; but—"

He felt his wrist held closer, and he stopped. The expression in the forehead, which had so particularly attracted his notice, and which was now immovable, had deepened into one of pain and horror.
15　"But he has been—been found. He is alive."

Close Read

1. Using terms from the list above, describe what is happening in this scene.

2. **Exploring a Big Question** The discovery of a long-lost family member is a heart-stopping revelation that deeply affects Miss Manette. What other kinds of revelations—both good and bad—can change people's lives?

STORIES

Have students read the introductory paragraph silently while you write the **Literary Terms for Fiction** on the board. Then invite them to name a memorable work of fiction. Encourage them to explain why the work impressed them, using **Literary Terms for Fiction** in their explanations.

Close Read

Introduce the model by pointing out that it is an excerpt from a famous novel by British author Charles Dickens (1812–1870). Call on a volunteer to read the model aloud. Then have students answer the Close Read questions.

Possible answers:

1. *In this scene, told from the third-person* point of view, *a man reveals some startling news to Miss Manette: her long-lost father has been found and is alive. He also discloses, in a* flashback, *that Miss Manette's mother had died of a broken heart while her daughter was very young. This excerpt may* foreshadow *future difficulties and conflicts that will evolve from the man's revelation.*

2. *Answers will vary but students may mention these revelations: discovering that (1) their families are moving far away; (2) a parent starts a new job; (3) a loved one falls ill or dies; (4) parents are getting divorced; (5) there will be a new addition to their family.*

CHECK UNDERSTANDING Ask for volunteers to explain the difference between a novel and a novella.

FOR STRUGGLING READERS

Concept Support Have students adapt a story map so that it includes these terms from the **Literary Terms for Fiction:** *plot, conflict, character, setting, theme, narrator.* Then have partners complete a story map by identifying these elements from a memorable work of fiction.

BEST PRACTICES TOOLKIT—Transparency
Story Map p. D14

FOR ENGLISH LANGUAGE LEARNERS

Language Support Remind students to use their knowledge of prefixes—word parts at the beginning of a word—to help them figure out the meanings of unfamiliar words. Point out that the prefixes *un-* and *im-* both mean "not" or "lack of." Define and discuss these words from the model:

- *unavailing* (line 2), "useless, unsuccessful"
- *uncertainty* (line 4), "doubt"
- *immovable* (line 13), "set, not moving"

POETRY

Have students read the first three paragraphs silently while you write the **Literary Terms for Poetry** and this poem on the board:

> A perfect picnic waited in the soft grass
> For a charming lad and a lovely lass,
> Spreading a blanket, about to recline,
> Hoping to chat and then to dine.
>
> Along came a pack of hungry hounds,
> Who lived and played on those very grounds,
> Who gave no thought to the darling pair,
> But saw only the picnic food sitting there.

Have students explain how the poem illustrates terms from the **Literary Terms for Poetry.**

Close Read

Read the model in a natural voice, following the poem's conversational flow. Then invite volunteers to read each stanza. You may also have students listen to the poem on the *Audio Anthology CD* before answering the **Close Read** questions.

Possible answers:

1. *Students may describe aspects of the poem's* form: *It is composed of three* stanzas; *the first and third stanzas each have six* lines; *the second has five lines. The lines are irregular in length. The poem has a conversational* rhythm *but no* rhyme. *Sound devices* include alliteration and assonance. *It also employs* imagery *and* figurative language, *such as metaphor (line 6).*

2. *Students may say that words can have the power to reassure people, especially young children.*

CHECK UNDERSTANDING Ask students to tell which stanza takes place in the present.

POETRY

Technically, poetry involves the artful selection and arrangement of words on a page. Poet Lucille Clifton, however, reminds readers that "poetry is a matter of life, not just a matter of language." A poem derives its power from the way its elements—language, form, and sounds—work together to communicate meaning and emotion.

You already know that poems are composed of short **lines** that are often grouped into **stanzas.** Some poets choose to craft traditional, highly structured poems, such as sonnets or haiku. Other poets, like Clifton, break with convention, often inventing unique forms that suit their subjects.

Poetry is meant to be heard, not just read. For that reason, a poem's sounds—for example, its jarring **rhythms** or singsong **rhymes**—are an essential part of its impact. Language also creates powerful effects. Through the use of **imagery** and **figurative language,** poets tap into our senses and prompt us to think about subjects in ways we might never have before.

Read the Model Here, a speaker reflects on a moment from her childhood that is still imprinted on her memory. As you read this poem, notice its form as well as its use of sound devices and imagery. How does the speaker's recollection of her feelings help you understand her idea of reassurance?

LITERARY TERMS FOR POETRY
- form
- line
- stanza
- speaker
- rhyme
- rhythm
- meter
- sound devices
- figurative language
- imagery

Making a Fist
Poem by **Naomi Shihab Nye**

For the first time, on the road north of Tampico,
I felt the life sliding out of me,
a drum in the desert, harder and harder to hear.
I was seven, I lay in the car
5 watching palm trees swirl a sickening pattern past the glass.
My stomach was a melon split wide inside my skin.

"How do you know if you are going to die?"
I begged my mother.
We had been traveling for days.
10 With strange confidence she answered,
"When you can no longer make a fist."

Years later I smile to think of that journey,
the borders we must cross separately,
stamped with our unanswerable woes.
15 I who did not die, who am still living,
still lying in the backseat behind all my questions,
clenching and opening one small hand.

6   THE POWER OF IDEAS

Close Read

1. Describe three poetic elements in "Making a Fist." Refer to the terms above for specific elements.

2. **Exploring a Big Question** Like the speaker, many of us turn to others for reassurance in moments of uncertainty. In your opinion, do words have the power to reassure us in such moments?

DIFFERENTIATED INSTRUCTION

FOR STRUGGLING READERS

Analysis Support: Poetry To help students apply the **Literary Terms for Poetry** to "Making a Fist" or another poem of your choice, have partners complete Core Analysis Frame: Poetry. Monitor their progress, offering assistance as requested or needed.

 BEST PRACTICES TOOLKIT—Transparency
Core Analysis Frame: Poetry pp. D21, D34

FOR ENGLISH LANGUAGE LEARNERS

Language: Skill Words Write these lines on the board, and have students identify one or more terms from the **Literary Terms for Poetry:**

> Little rockets zip and zoom,
> Hop, skip, bounce, and boom,
> Plop on the ground, plunk on me,
> A zillion acorns from the old oak tree.

Possible answers: sound devices, line, speaker, rhythm, meter, figurative language, imagery

DRAMA

Drama is broadly defined as any story that is performed by actors for an audience. A drama can be a live stage production, a movie, a television show, or a radio play. In a drama—whether it's a Shakespearean tragedy, a contemporary musical, or an experimental one-person show—the plot and the characters are developed primarily through **dialogue** and action.

While there's nothing quite as captivating as watching a performance unfold on stage or screen, a drama can also make good reading. By paying attention to the **stage directions**—the writer's instructions for the actors, the director, and the others working on the play—readers can visualize a performance in their minds. Stage directions often describe the characters' appearances, movements, and reactions, as well as the setting, scenery, and props. Such directions are usually set off from the dialogue in italics and parentheses.

Read the Model *Twelve Angry Men* is a television screenplay that was made into a movie in 1957 and again in 1997. In the drama, 12 jurors must decide the fate of a young man accused of murder. Here, the jurors have just heard the case and must now reach a verdict. Use the stage directions and dialogue to help you visualize the jurors' deliberations.

> **LITERARY TERMS FOR DRAMA**
> • plot
> • character
> • act/scene
> • stage directions
> • monologue
> • dialogue
> • aside
> • soliloquy

---

from

TWELVE Angry Men

Drama by **Reginald Rose**

from Act 1

Foreman. Anybody doesn't want to vote? (*He looks around the table. There is no answer.*) Okay, all those voting guilty raise your hands. (*Seven or eight hands go up immediately. Several others go up more slowly. Everyone looks around the table. There are two hands not raised, No. 9's and No. 8's. No. 9's hand goes up slowly*
5 *now as the foreman counts.*)

Foreman. . . . Nine . . . ten . . . eleven . . . That's eleven for guilty. Okay. Not guilty? (*No. 8's hand is raised*) One. Right. Okay. Eleven to one, guilty. Now we know where we are.

No. 3. Somebody's in left field. (*To No. 8*) You think he's not guilty?

10 **No. 8.** (*Quietly*). I don't know.

No. 3. I never saw a guiltier man in my life. You sat right in court and heard the same thing I did. The man's a dangerous killer. You could see it.

No. 8. He's nineteen years old.

No. 3. That's old enough. He knifed his own father. Four inches into the chest.
15 An innocent little nineteen-year-old kid. They proved it a dozen different ways.

> **Close Read**
>
> 1. Are all the jurors confident of their opinions? How can you tell?
>
> 2. **Exploring a Big Question** In our justice system, juries composed of 12 ordinary citizens must arrive at impartial and just verdicts. What qualities are essential for jurors to have in such high-stakes deliberations?

DRAMA

Have students read the first two paragraphs silently while you write the **Literary Terms for Drama** on the board. Ask them to use context clues to define the two boldfaced terms in the text. Then use these questions to compare drama and fiction:

• Which terms from the academic vocabulary are exclusive to drama? (*act, scene, stage directions*)

• Which elements from fiction are also used in drama? (*character, plot*)

• Which elements from drama may also be used in fiction? (*monologue, dialogue, aside*)

Close Read

Call on a volunteer to read the third paragraph. Then have students read the model silently. Next, assign roles and have a dramatic reading of the model. Afterward, have students answer the Close Read questions.

Possible answers:

1. *The stage directions show that seven or eight jurors are sure of the defendant's guilt, as they raise their hands immediately. Several others waver before raising their hands. Juror No. 8 is least certain of the defendant's guilt. Readers learn of this through the stage directions and ensuing dialogue.*

2. *Students may say that jurors should be open-minded and unbiased. They should examine the evidence without letting their emotions affect their judgment. Further, they should weigh all evidence before making a decision about guilt or innocence.*

CHECK UNDERSTANDING Have students identify information in the Foreman's first lines that is provided as stage directions.

FOR STRUGGLING READERS

Analysis Support: Dramatic Character Give students practice with the **Literary Terms for Drama** by asking these questions about the model:

• What information does the stage direction give in line 7? line 9? line 10? **Possible answers:** Line 7: Juror No. 8 votes not guilty. Line 9: Juror No. 3 addresses Juror No. 8. Line 10: Juror No. 8 replies in a quiet voice.

• Which act does the model come from? **Answer:** Act 1

• How many characters speak in the model? **Answer:** three characters

• What do you learn from the excerpt about the plot of the play? **Possible answer:** A nineteen-year-old man is on trial for murder and a jury is deciding his fate.

NONFICTION

Read the introductory paragraph and point out the terms *literary nonfiction* and *informational texts*. Offer additional examples of each, then ask students to provide examples as well. Discuss the characteristics of each type of nonfiction listed on the page. Point out that the **Literary Terms for Nonfiction** refer to terms that will be used in their study of nonfiction.

NONFICTION

You are probably used to seeing certain kinds of nonfiction in literature books. Works of **literary nonfiction,** including autobiographies and speeches, have long been studied for their historical significance and lyrical prose. Nonfiction also includes **informational texts,** such as news articles and instruction manuals that provide factual information. Since such texts are critical sources of information, you should learn how to read them with a careful and critical eye.

> **TERMS FOR NONFICTION**
> - purpose
> - text features
> - patterns of organization
> - argument
> - persuasion

TYPE OF NONFICTION	CHARACTERISTICS
AUTOBIOGRAPHY/BIOGRAPHY The true story of a person's life, told by that person (autobiography) or by another person (biography)	• Reveals details about significant events, people, and experiences in a person's life • Is told from the first-person point of view (autobiography) or from the third-person point of view (biography) • Presents the writer's own interpretations of his or her life (autobiography) or information gleaned from many sources (biography)
ESSAY A short work that focuses on a single subject. Common types include reflective, persuasive, and descriptive essays.	• May have the following purposes: to express feelings, to inform, to entertain, or to persuade • May be **formal,** with an organized structure and an impersonal style • May be **informal,** with a conversational style
SPEECH An oral presentation of the ideas, beliefs, or proposals of a speaker	• May be intended to express the speaker's feelings or to educate, entertain, persuade, or inspire an audience • Achieves its power through effective language, as well as through the vocal variations and gestures of the speaker
NEWS/FEATURE ARTICLES Informative writing in newspapers and magazines. News articles report on recent events. Feature articles focus on human-interest topics.	• Are primarily intended to inform or entertain • Convey information through headlines, photographs, quotations from sources, statistics, and examples • Aim to be objective and accurate
FUNCTIONAL TEXTS Writing that serves a practical purpose. Types include consumer documents, workplace documents, and procedural texts.	• Are written for a specific audience (for example, business clients or users of a product) • Often use charts, diagrams, and graphics to illustrate and clarify ideas • May include specialized jargon

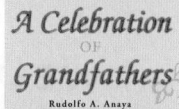

A Celebration of Grandfathers
Rudolfo A. Anaya

WORLD EVENTS

Girl, Trapped in Wat for 55 Hours, Die Despite Rescue Atter

Your e-mail account

❶ Creating a user name and password
Your user name should be at least seven characters You may use letters, numbers, and underscores.

Your password should be at least six characters and should include one number. Remember whether you used capital letters. Our system is case-sensitive!

❷ If you forget your password . . .
Select a security question from the menu below. You answer should be four or more characters. Make su it is something you will remember but will be diffic for others to guess.

DIFFERENTIATED INSTRUCTION

FOR STRUGGLING READERS

Nonfiction Word Webs Help students to create word webs illustrating key features of each type of nonfiction.

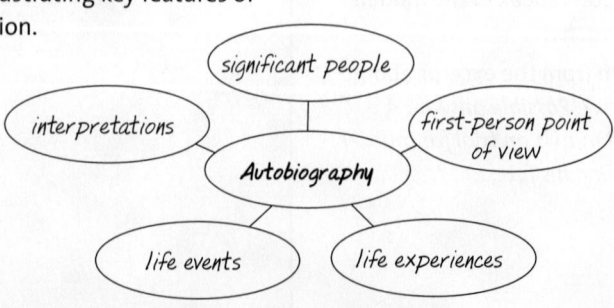

FOR ENGLISH LANGUAGE LEARNERS

Language: Skill Words Discuss the meanings of these terms from the chart:

- *style:* one's approach to writing
- *structure:* arrangement of materials; organization
- *impersonal:* straightforward, not reflecting personality

MODEL 1: AUTOBIOGRAPHY

Kaffir Boy is the autobiography of the black author Mark Mathabane, who grew up under the system of apartheid, or racial segregation, in South Africa. Here, he recalls a time in his childhood when the police raided the ghetto in which his family lived, intending to rid the neighborhood of people they considered "undesirable." Notice how Mathabane vividly illustrates fear.

from

Kaffir Boy   Autobiography by **Mark Mathabane**

. . . The darkness was impregnable, ominous; the more I stared into it, the blacker and blacker it became. I felt dizzy. I wanted to scream but my voice was paralyzed. Suddenly flashlights flared through the uncurtained window. Glass shattered somewhere nearby. I yearned to become invisible, to have the ground
5 beneath me open and swallow me until it was all over.
   "OPEN UP!" a voice bellowed by the window. "WE KNOW YOU'RE IN THERE!"
   I succeeded in reaching the bedroom door, fear all over me.

Close Read

1. How can you tell that this is an autobiographical—rather than a biographical—account?

2. **Exploring a Big Question**
Think about the intense fear that Mathabane experienced as a child. What are the physical and emotional effects of fear? Support your answer with details from the text.

MODEL 2: FEATURE ARTICLE

This article was published on September 6, 2004, ten years after apartheid was abolished in South Africa. As you read, consider the idea of progress.

SEPTEMBER 6, 2004

South Africa's Decade Of Freedom

by Michael Wines

JOHANNESBURG—"See this yard?" Tom Shiburi waves his hand toward a sprawling field of weeds in the township of Diepkloof (DEEP-kloof), close to
5 downtown Johannesburg. "We used to have some shacks here," he says. "Five thousand shacks—our last count came to something like 10,000 people. They've been relocated, all of them."
10 Shiburi is talking about the changes in the decade since South Africa abolished apartheid and embraced democracy. Under apartheid (the government-run system that forcibly
15 segregated blacks from whites and denied blacks basic rights), South Africa's white rulers herded millions of blacks into townships like Diepkloof, where they lived in tiny houses or in iron
20 shacks, many without electricity or water.
   But since South Africa's black majority came to power in 1994, the government has built and given 1.5 million homes to former shanty
25 dwellers—evidence of the transformation that has swept this nation in a blink of history's eye.

Close Read

1. How are the kinds of details in this article different from those in Mathabane's autobiography?

2. **Exploring a Big Question**
Consider what both excerpts reveal about life in South Africa before and after apartheid. What progress has been made in South Africa?

9

Explain that both models on this page cover the same topic, apartheid in South Africa. However, the genres, points of view, time frames, and information covered are different. Call on volunteers to read each one. Then have students answer the Close Read questions.

MODEL 1: AUTOBIOGRAPHY
Close Read

Possible answers:

1. *Kaffir Boy uses the first-person point of view. Mathabane shares his thoughts, feelings, and impressions of a childhood experience.*

2. *Fear can paralyze people; Mathabane, for example, could not speak because of his fear (lines 2–3). Fear can cause heightened anxiety, resulting in a racing heart, sweating, and shortness of breath or dizziness. Long-term effects include emotional trauma and anxiety disorders.*

MODEL 2: FEATURE ARTICLE
Close Read

Possible answers:

1. *The feature article includes more facts and background information than the autobiography, such as a definition of apartheid and statistics (lines 7–8, 17–18, 24).*

2. *A comparison of the excerpts reveals progress in South Africa: the country has "embraced" democracy and ended segregation; a black majority is in power; the government has built 1.5 million homes for former shanty dwellers, like Mathabane's family.*

CHECK UNDERSTANDING Have students explain how the purposes of the two models of nonfiction differ.

FOR STRUGGLING READERS

Analysis Support: Venn Diagram Use a Venn Diagram to show similarities and differences between the autobiography and the feature article. Possible characteristics to compare: point of view, time frame, information about apartheid.

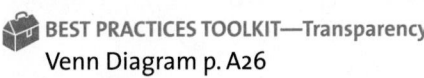
BEST PRACTICES TOOLKIT—Transparency
Venn Diagram p. A26

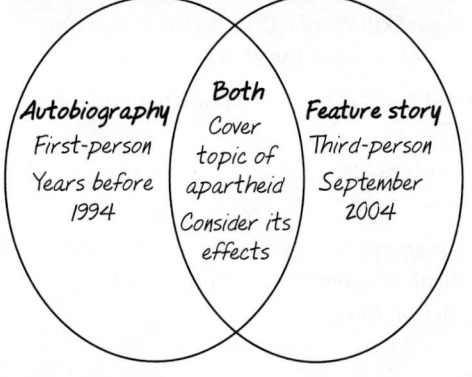

TYPES OF MEDIA

Have students read the introductory paragraph silently while you write the **Terms for Media** on the board. Then ask students to define *media literacy*. **Possible answer:** *the ability to critically analyze all kinds of media and to understand their purposes and effects* Use these activities to discuss the importance of media literacy:

- Ask students whether they believe everything they see or hear in the media, and why or why not. Encourage them to give examples.

- Have small groups brainstorm some effects of inaccurate or misleading information. Ask them to share their findings.

- Call on volunteers to identify the characteristics, purposes, and effects of each type of media in the chart.

CHECK UNDERSTANDING Ask students how an advertisement for a candidate differs from a news story about a candidate.

TYPES OF MEDIA

Subtle product placement in movies, exclusive stories on the nightly news, political campaign sites on the Web—media messages like these are pervasive today. For that reason, being literate now involves the ability to "read" media messages. To become **media literate,** you need to learn how to critically analyze such messages, as well as understand how they are shaping your perceptions of the world.

TERMS FOR MEDIA
• medium
• message
• purpose
• target audience

TYPES OF MEDIA	CHARACTERISTICS	
FEATURE FILMS Motion pictures that use narrative elements to tell a story	• Are intended to entertain and to generate profit • Create gripping narratives through cinematography, music, sets, and actors • Are at least one hour long	
NEWS MEDIA Accounts of current events as presented in newspapers and magazines and on TV, radio, and the Web	• Are meant to inform and to create viewer or reader loyalty • Medium (TV, Web, print) dictates the presentation and delivery of information • May be biased or inaccurate, so must be examined carefully	
TV SHOWS Programs broadcast on TV, including dramas, sitcoms, talk shows, and documentaries	• Are usually intended to entertain or inform • Are financed by sponsors who pay to air ads during the programs • Use visuals and sound effects to create compelling programming • Are typically 30–60 minutes in length	
ADVERTISING Paid promotion of products, services, candidates, or public service messages, using print and broadcast media	• Is designed to persuade a target audience to take action, buy a product or service, or support a candidate • Uses persuasive techniques, visuals, and sounds to sway an audience • Is strategically presented where and when it will have maximum exposure to the target audience	
WEB SITES Collections of "pages" on the Web. From a home page, users can navigate to other pages by clicking menus or hyperlinks.	• Can be accessed at any time by anyone with a computer and an Internet connection • Must be evaluated for reliability (because anyone can publish on the Web) • Convey information through text, graphics, audio, video, and animation	

DIFFERENTIATED INSTRUCTION

FOR STRUGGLING READERS

Comparison Matrix Use a Comparison Matrix chart to help students identify key features of each media and similarities and differences among them.

 BEST PRACTICES TOOLKIT—Transparency Comparison Matrix p. A24

FOR ENGLISH LANGUAGE LEARNERS

Language: Skill Words Discuss the meanings of these terms from the chart:

- *current events,* "events that are happening now"

- *sitcom,* "situation comedy; a short comedy on a limited topic"

- *documentary,* "a film on a factual, historical, political, or scientific topic, presented in a nonfiction format"

- *reliability,* "trustworthiness"

- *animation,* "a motion picture cartoon made from a series of filmed drawings"

Literature and Nonfiction Strategies

Jot your reactions and observations in your **Reader/Writer Notebook.**

❶ Ask the Right Questions

Analyzing literature is largely a matter of developing your ability to ask pointed, probing questions, such as the kinds described in the chart.

Kinds of Questions	Where to Look
Big questions about life and literature	▶ **Before Reading** pages (preceding every selection)
Questions that focus on text analysis and evaluation	▶ Side notes (alongside most selections) and **After Reading** pages (following every lesson)
Analysis Frames THINK central Go to thinkcentral.com. KEYWORD: HML10-11	▶ Guided questions for analyzing different genres

❷ Make Connections

To get meaning from literature and nonfiction, you have to make connections to your life, to other texts, and to the world at large. Try the following approaches:

• **Big Questions** The selections in this book are tied to big questions that affect all of our lives. Consider how the situations and experiences you read about relate to those in your own life.

• **Discussion/Writing** Share your insights with others or jot down your impressions in a journal. You might discuss or record

  • conflicts or events that you can personally relate to
  • characters who remind you of people you know
  • quotations that resonate with you
  • similar themes in other works

❸ Record Your Reactions

Keep track of your questions, observations, and reactions. Experiment with a variety of formats.

TWO-COLUMN NOTES

Jot down quotations and information from the selection in one column and your comments in the other.

Details in Kaffir Boy	My Impressions
"I yearned to become invisible, to have the ground beneath me open and swallow me." (lines 4–5)	Emphasizes the intense fear that paralyzed Mathabane; no wonder this experience has stayed with him after so many years.

GRAPHIC ORGANIZER

Use a variety of charts, diagrams, or other graphic organizers to help you interpret events, analyze characters, and draw conclusions.

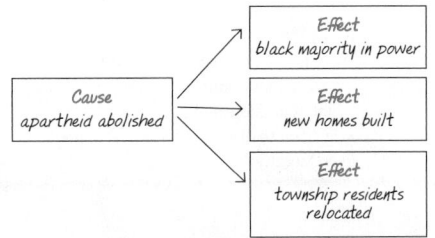

INTRODUCING THE ESSENTIALS   **11**

FOR STRUGGLING READERS

Concept Support Use these activities to reinforce the teaching in the text:

1. To develop questioning skills, write the Reporter's Questions on the board and have students use them as prompts to ask and answer questions about "South Africa's Decade of Freedom" on page 9.

2. For practice in **Big Questions,** have students look at the chart on page 8. Ask them to identify a **Big Questions** for "A Celebration of Grandfathers."

Possible answers: What is the value of experience? What is the importance of family?

3. Have students read the two-column notes and the cause-effect organizer against the text of each excerpt. Then ask them to use one of these organizers to record their reactions to the excerpt from *A Tale of Two Cities* on page 5.

Literature and Nonfiction Strategies

Ask students to describe how they have developed skills at a hobby, sport, or other activity. Point out that success in almost any activity requires learning skills or strategies along with lots of practice; the same is true with the study of literature. As you review the **Literature and Nonfiction Strategies,** point out that practicing these strategies will improve the quality of student work and enhance their enjoyment of literature.

1. **Ask the Right Questions**
   Tell students that asking and answering meaningful questions will help them to stay focused and to look for deeper meanings in literature. The chart shows what types of questions this anthology will teach them to ask and answer.

2. **Make Connections**
   Point out to students that readers connect with literature when the ideas, characters, experiences, or feelings engage them or touch them in some way. Ask them to quickly name

   • their favorite character
   • their least favorite character
   • the most exciting story
   • the most interesting real setting
   • the most exciting imaginary setting

   Point out that connections like these will help them to enjoy literature.

3. **Record Your Reactions**
   Suggest that students keep a **Reader/Writer Notebook** by their side when they read. They should try to use a format that makes sense with each genre they read. For example, two-column notes serve well when reading a memoir, whereas a cause-effect graphic works with an article that has a cause-effect organization.

Analysis Frames

The **Analysis Frames** on **thinkcentral.com** help students learn how to ask the right questions when reading, analyzing, and evaluating:

• fiction
• drama
• poetry
• literary nonfiction
• informational texts
• persuasive writing

COMMON CORE FOCUS

RL 1 Cite strong and thorough textual evidence to support analysis of what the text says explicitly as well as inferences drawn from the text. **RL 4** Determine the meaning of words and phrases as they are used in the text. **RI 1** Cite strong and thorough textual evidence to support analysis of what the text says explicitly as well as inferences drawn from the text. **RI 4** Determine the meaning of words and phrases as they are used in a text. **L 4** Determine or clarify the meaning of unknown and multiple-meaning words and phrases, choosing flexibly from a range of strategies.

Have students apply the **SKILLS AND STRATE-GIES FOR ACTIVE READING** to reading page 12.

- First, have them preview the page by reading the title, the introductory paragraph, and the red strategy subheads. Then ask them to identify the characteristics of an active reader. *Possible answer: engaged, alert, thoughtful*

- Have students set a purpose for reading page 12. *Possible answer: to learn how to read actively*

- Have students predict which strategy will be most useful for reading page 12, and to explain why.

- Ask which strategies they have used in the past and how they were helpful.

- Encourage students to visualize themselves practicing each skill on this page.

- Invite students to rate each skill on a useful-ness scale from 1 to 10. Ask them to explain their reasons.

Reading Strategies Workshop

Becoming an Active Reader

To explore life's big questions through reading, you need to be actively engaged. That means you should be picking up on essential details, questioning why events are unfolding as they are, and making connections between situations in the text and those in your life. When you are absorbed in a riveting television show or reading a review of a movie, you are using these skills and strategies—without consciously thinking about them. Throughout this book, you will apply the following skills and strategies to the texts you read.

SKILLS AND STRATEGIES FOR ACTIVE READING

Preview
Get a sense of a text before you start to read.
- Look for clues in the title, graphics, and subheadings.
- Skim opening paragraphs before you dive in.

Set a Purpose
Decide *why* you are reading a particular text.
- Ask: Am I reading for my own enjoyment, to learn about a topic, or for another reason?
- Think about how your purpose might affect the way you approach a text. Should you read slowly and analytically or simply settle back and enjoy?

Connect
Relate personally to what you are reading.
- Consider whether you've encountered people or situations like the ones described.
- Ask: If I were in this situation, how would I react?

Use Prior Knowledge
Call to mind what you already know about a topic.
- Before reading, jot down any relevant information or experiences that you bring to the text.
- As you are reading, use your notes to help you connect what you know to what you are learning.

Predict
Try to guess what will happen next.
- Note details about characters and events that hint at possible plot developments.
- Read on to discover whether your predictions were on target.

Visualize
Try to picture what is being described.
- Note descriptive details about characters, settings, and events that help you create sensory images.
- Use these details to help you "see" a scene unfolding as a movie in your mind.

Monitor
Check your own comprehension as you read.
- **Question** what is happening and why. For example, ask: What just happened? Why is the character acting this way?
- **Clarify** your understanding by rereading difficult parts or asking for help.
- **Evaluate** yourself as a reader. Ask: How well am I understanding the text?

Make Inferences
Use evidence in the text and what you know from experience to help you "read between the lines."
- Record details about characters, settings, and plot developments.
- Ask: How can common sense and my own experiences deepen my understanding of what's happening? (The chart below shows how one student made an inference about a character in the story on the next page.)

Details in "Where Is Here?"	What I Know	My Inference
The stranger remembers the room being "Dark by day, dark by night." (line 5)	During the day, houses are usually lit up.	There's something unusual or different about the stranger or his family.

12   THE POWER OF IDEAS

DIFFERENTIATED INSTRUCTION

FOR STRUGGLING READERS

Note Taking For those students who need help, hand out the note-taking copy master for the Reading Strategies Workshop. Read and discuss the introductory paragraph on this page. As students examine the **SKILLS AND STRATEGIES FOR ACTIVE READING,** assist them in completing the copy master as needed.

R RESOURCE MANAGER—Copy Master
Note Taking p. I-3

FOR ENGLISH LANGUAGE LEARNERS

Vocabulary Support Discuss the meanings of these terms from the **SKILLS AND STRATEGIES FOR ACTIVE READING** chart:

prior knowledge: information that you already know

visualize: picture in your mind

monitor: check or keep track of your progress

make inferences: use what you know along with what you read to figure out deeper meanings

In the story "Where Is Here?" by Joyce Carol Oates, a stranger revisits his childhood home. The current residents—a mother and a father—follow the stranger through their house as he recalls his memories of living there. As you read this excerpt from the story, use the **Close Read** questions to help you to make sense of the mysterious situation.

COMMON CORE

Included in this workshop:
RL 1, RL 4, RI 1, RI 4, L 4

from *Where Is Here?*

Short story by **Joyce Carol Oates**

Finally, as if remembering the presence of his hosts, and the necessity for some display of civility, the stranger expressed his admiration for the attractiveness of the room, and its coziness. He'd remembered it as cavernous, with a ceiling twice as high. "And dark most of the time," he said wonderingly.
5 "Dark by day, dark by night." The mother turned the lights of the little brass chandelier to their fullest: shadows were dispersed like ragged ghosts and the cut-glass fruit bowl at the center of the table glowed like an exquisite multifaceted jewel. The stranger exclaimed in surprise. He'd extracted a handkerchief from his pocket and was dabbing carefully at his face, where
10 beads of perspiration shone. He said, as if thinking aloud, still wonderingly, "My father was a unique man. Everyone who knew him admired him. He sat *here*," he said, gingerly touching the chair that was in fact the father's chair, at one end of the table. "And Mother sat *there*," he said, merely pointing. "I don't recall my own place or my sister's but I suppose it doesn't matter. . . . I see you
15 have four place settings, Mrs. . . . ? Two children, I suppose?" "A boy eleven, and a girl thirteen," the mother said. The stranger stared not at her but at the table, smiling. "And so too *we* were—I mean, there were two of us: my sister and me."

The mother said, as if not knowing what else to say, "Are you—close?"
20 The stranger shrugged, distractedly rather than rudely, and moved on to the living room.

This room, cozily lit as well, was the most carefully furnished room in the house. Deep-piled wall-to-wall carpeting in hunter green, cheerful chintz drapes, a sofa and matching chairs in nubby heather green, framed reproductions of
25 classic works of art, a gleaming gilt-framed mirror over the fireplace: wasn't the living room impressive as a display in a furniture store? But the stranger said nothing at first. Indeed, his eyes narrowed sharply as if he were confronted with a disagreeable spectacle. He whispered, "Here too! Here too!"

Close Read

1. **Connect** Think of a time when you returned to a place from your childhood, such as an old school or a previous home. In what ways was the place different from how you remembered it?

2. **Visualize** What impression do you have of the stranger so far? Cite details of his behavior that helped you to form a mental image.

Point out that each of the Close Read questions is keyed to one of the **SKILLS AND STRATEGIES FOR ACTIVE READING.** Encourage students to observe the kinds of information and insights generated by each skill and strategy.

MODEL: SHORT STORY
Close Read

Ask a volunteer to read aloud the introductory paragraph. Then have students preview the text by reading the title and skimming the first paragraph and Close Read questions. Before they read the story, have them set a purpose for reading it. ***Possible answer: Read to find out about the stranger's childhood.***

Possible answers:

1. *Students may say that the places from childhood seemed smaller or less impressive than they had remembered.*

2. *The stranger seems eccentric, excitable, and distracted, as evidenced by the following details: "The stranger exclaimed in surprise" (line 8); "The stranger shrugged, distractedly rather than rudely" (line 20); "Indeed, his eyes narrowed sharply as if he were confronted with a disagreeable spectacle" (lines 27–28).*

FOR ENGLISH LANGUAGE LEARNERS

Visualizing Point out that the stranger's childhood home is like a character in the story. Have students close their eyes and try to picture each room as you reread paragraphs 1 and 4. Then challenge partners to work together without the book to list every detail they can remember.

Possible answers:

3. *Readers can infer that the stranger did not have a good relationship with his father, as evidenced by his comment that the window seat was happy only "when Father wasn't home." He appears to have had a better relationship with his mother, who sounds imaginative and playful. She would join him on the window seat and imagine with him.*

4. *The father and mother appear to find him odd and imposing; they exchange a glance (line 45) that shows that both wish he would leave. The father makes a face conveying impatience, while the mother is more polite, not wishing to offend any guest in her home.*

5. *The riddles are not like the usual riddles that parents might tell children. They are eccentric, mysterious, esoteric, even unanswerable questions, not unlike the stranger himself, who is something of a riddle.*

6. *Students may predict that the stranger is a ghost. The evidence that supports this idea is his strange statement that "We've all been dead" (line 65) before he quickly corrects himself. Students may wish to listen to the entire story on the Audio Anthology CD to discover whether their predictions were correct.*

CHECK UNDERSTANDING Ask students how using various reading strategies increased their understanding and enjoyment of Oates's story.

He went to the fireplace, walking, now, with a decided limp; he drew his
30 fingers with excruciating slowness along the mantel as if testing its materiality. For some time he merely stood, and stared, and listened. He tapped a section of wall with his knuckles—"There used to be a large water stain here, like a shadow."

"Was there?" murmured the father out of politeness, and "Was there!"
35 murmured the mother. Of course, neither had ever seen a water stain there.

Then, noticing the window seat, the stranger uttered a soft surprised cry, and went to sit in it. He appeared delighted: hugging his knees like a child trying to make himself smaller. "This was one of my happy places! At least when Father wasn't home. I'd hide away here for hours, reading, daydreaming,
40 staring out the window! Sometimes Mother would join me, if she was in the mood, and we'd plot together—oh, all sorts of fantastical things!" The stranger remained sitting in the window seat for so long, tears shining in his eyes, that the father and mother almost feared he'd forgotten them. He was stroking the velvet fabric of the cushioned seat, gropingly touching the leaded
45 windowpanes. Wordlessly, the father and mother exchanged a glance: who was this man, and how could they tactfully get rid of him? The father made a face signaling impatience and the mother shook her head without seeming to move it. For they couldn't be rude to a guest in their house.

The stranger was saying in a slow, dazed voice, "It all comes back to me
50 now. How could I have forgotten! Mother used to read to me, and tell me stories, and ask me riddles I couldn't answer. 'What creature walks on four legs in the morning, two legs at midday, three legs in the evening?' 'What is round, and flat, measuring mere inches in one direction, and infinity in the other?' 'Out of what does our life arise? Out of what does our consciousness arise?
55 Why are we here? Where *is* here?'"

The father and mother were perplexed by these strange words and hardly knew how to respond. The mother said uncertainly, "Our daughter used to like to sit here too, when she was younger. It *is* a lovely place." The father said with surprising passion, "I hate riddles—they're moronic some of the time and
60 obscure the rest of the time." He spoke with such uncharacteristic rudeness, the mother looked at him in surprise.

Hurriedly she said, "Is your mother still living, Mr. . . . ?" "Oh no. Not at all," the stranger said, rising abruptly from the window seat, and looking at the mother as if she had said something mildly preposterous. "I'm sorry," the
65 mother said. "Please don't be," the stranger said, "We've all been dead—*they've* all been dead—a long time. " . . .

Close Read

3. Make Inferences Reread the boxed text. What can you infer about the stranger's relationship with his parents?

4. Monitor How do the father and the mother feel about the stranger? Cite details from lines 45–48 to support your answer.

5. Use Prior Knowledge Reread lines 49–55. How do these riddles compare with ones you know? Consider whether these riddles seem like ones that most parents would tell their children.

6. Predict What will the mother and the father find out about this stranger? Give reasons to support your prediction.

DIFFERENTIATED INSTRUCTION

FOR STRUGGLING READERS

Check Comprehension Adapt the Character Traits Web for support with questions 2, 3, and 6. Have students complete the web in pairs. Then discuss the questions with students, having them give evidence from the web to support their responses.

 **BEST PRACTICES TOOLKIT—Transparency**
Character Traits Web p. D7

Strategies That Work: Reading

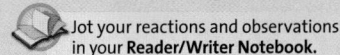 Jot your reactions and observations in your **Reader/Writer Notebook.**

❶ Read Independently

The best way to become a better reader is to make reading a daily habit. Try all kinds of texts, from news Web sites to classic novels.

What Should I Read?	How Will I Benefit?
Novels	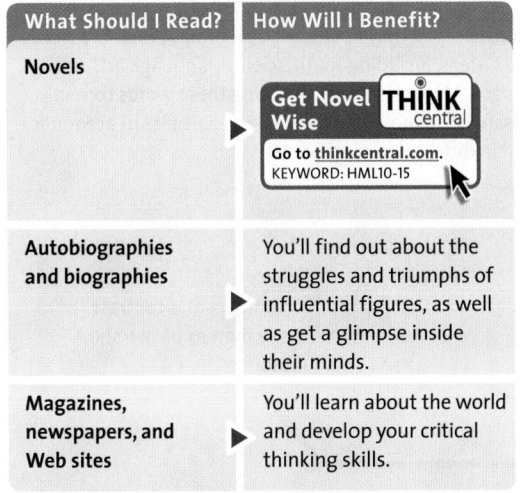 Get Novel Wise **THINK** central Go to **thinkcentral.com.** KEYWORD: HML10-15
Autobiographies and biographies	You'll find out about the struggles and triumphs of influential figures, as well as get a glimpse inside their minds.
Magazines, newspapers, and Web sites	You'll learn about the world and develop your critical thinking skills.

❷ Use Graphic Organizers

Graphic organizers, such as character webs, charts, and timelines, can help you understand characters and track twists and turns in a plot.

What the Stranger Sees	How the Stranger Reacts
Cozy, well-lit dining room	• Remembers the room being much darker • Starts perspiring • Recalls his family at the table
Well-furnished, nicely decorated living room	• Looks disturbed at first • Murmurs "Here too!" • Remembers a large water stain
A window seat	• Remembers this as a "happy place" • Starts acting like an overexcited child • Recalls crazy "riddles" his mother told him

❸ Build Your Vocabulary

Creating a personal word list can help you both build your vocabulary and become a better reader. Start a list in your **Reader/Writer Notebook,** adding words as you encounter them.

- **Choose your words.** Consider recording vocabulary words from the selections in this book. You might also include words that you encounter while reading newspapers and Web sites, such as unfamiliar terms connected to innovations or new technologies.
- **Go beyond the definitions.** Write synonyms, antonyms, and sentences to help you remember the words and their meanings.
- **Use the words often.** Studies have shown that you have to use a word multiple times to really learn it. Try to incorporate new words into your writing and discussions.

Word	Meaning
materiality (n) "Where Is Here?" line 30	**Definition:** being made of physical substance **Synonyms:** solidity, substantiality **Antonyms:** illusion, shadow **Sentence:** The knife sliced right through the vegetables, as if they had no materiality.

Strategies That Work: Reading

Review **Strategies That Work: Reading.** Point out that reading success is the result of using effective reading strategies. Emphasize that features in this text will help students develop effective reading skills.

1. **Read Independently**
   Have students do a quick personal survey of their independent reading. How many hours per day/week do they read? What types of reading do they do? Invite students to share titles and ideas from their readings, where appropriate, in class.

2. **Use Graphic Organizers**
   Explain that using graphic organizers increases understanding and recall of reading materials. Urge students to record graphic organizers in their **Reader/Writer Notebooks.**

3. **Build Your Vocabulary**
   Encourage students to internalize academic language by using new vocabulary words in original sentences that they share orally with a partner. Have the listening partner ask questions about the content of the sentences. The speaking partner then rewrites the sentences, clarifying the questions and presenting them orally. Have students repeat the partner process, reusing the words at least three times. Then, have partners shift roles and repeat the activity with different vocabulary words.

FOR STRUGGLING READERS

Concept Support Use these activities to reinforce the teaching in the text:

1. Keep a classroom list of "Best Sellers" with books highly recommended by students. You might also keep a longer list with students' ratings, four stars being the highest.

2. Hold a weekly "Vocabulary Jeopardy" game. Invite students to each submit 10 vocabulary cards with definitions to be used during a contest. Students may compete individually or on teams.

3. Invite students to share tips for learning and using new words. Also explain that each unit in the anthology opens with a feature that includes academic vocabulary—terms relating to the skills and strategies appearing in that unit's lessons. Encourage students to use those terms in writing and discussions, as well.

 THINK central

NovelWise

NovelWise is a Web site that helps students choose a novel or other book-length work to read. **NovelWise** also provides
- study guides
- reading strategies and literary elements instruction
- presentations to introduce classic novels
- project ideas

L 3 Apply knowledge of language to understand how language functions in different contexts, to make effective choices for meaning or style, and to comprehend more fully when reading or listening. **L 4a** Use context (e.g., the overall meaning of a sentence, paragraph, or text; a word's position or function in a sentence) as a clue to the meaning of a word or phrase. **L 4c** Consult general and specialized reference materials (e.g., dictionaries, glossaries, thesauruses), both print and digital, to find the pronunciation of a word or determine or clarify its precise meaning, its part of speech, or its etymology. **L 5** Demonstrate understanding of figurative language, word relationships, and nuances in word meanings. **L 6** Acquire and use accurately general academic and domain-specific words and phrases, sufficient for reading, writing, speaking, and listening at the college and career readiness level; demonstrate independence in gathering vocabulary knowledge when considering a word or phrase important to comprehension or expression.

Review the Academic Vocabulary word web with students. Starting with the box labeled Language Arts, in the upper right, read the questions aloud and ask for help with answers.

- **Language Arts:** Point out to students that a comparison highlights the similarities between things, and a contrast highlights the differences. Explain that a *theme* is the topic or subject of a discussion or piece of writing.

- **Science:** Explain that the word *alter* means "to change or modify some details." One process that might alter the salt content of ice is melting of the ice. As the ice melts, water could evaporate or mix with other liquids, affecting the salt content.

- **Other Languages:** Explain that the word *communicate* means "to share or exchange information or ideas." Point out to students that when learning a new language, written communication gives them the opportunity to plan and revise what they want to say and how they want to say it, so they can communicate clearly and effectively.

- **Geometry:** Tell students that to *identify* something means "to find or name the characteristics, nature, or qualities of someone or something." Explain that characteristics are "distinguishing attributes." Tell students that *polyhedra* is the plural form of *polyhedron*. To *identify* polyhedra, look for solids

Academic Vocabulary Workshop

What Is Academic Vocabulary?

The words you use during any given day change depending on the context, or setting, and on your purpose for using them. With family and friends you may be having a casual conversation or texting a quick message, and for those purposes you would use informal and conversational vocabulary. In school you must talk and write about the subjects you are studying, and to do so you often need to call upon another set of words. We call these words **academic vocabulary.**

COMMON CORE
Included in this workshop:
L 3, L 4a, L 4c, L 5, L 6

Cite, contemporary, statistic—you may encounter academic vocabulary words such as these in all subject areas, including math, science, language arts, social studies, and other languages. Understanding and using these words correctly will help you to be successful in school. This web shows examples of academic vocabulary words as used in different subject areas.

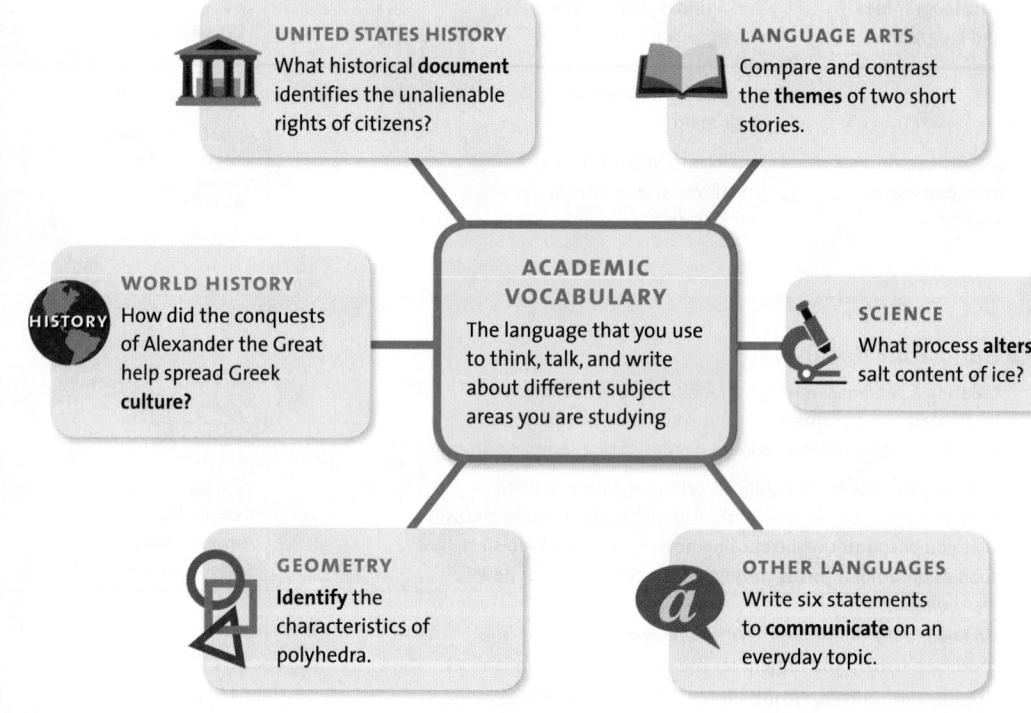

UNITED STATES HISTORY
What historical **document** identifies the unalienable rights of citizens?

LANGUAGE ARTS
Compare and contrast the **themes** of two short stories.

WORLD HISTORY
How did the conquests of Alexander the Great help spread Greek **culture?**

ACADEMIC VOCABULARY
The language that you use to think, talk, and write about different subject areas you are studying

SCIENCE
What process **alters** the salt content of ice?

GEOMETRY
Identify the characteristics of polyhedra.

OTHER LANGUAGES
Write six statements to **communicate** on an everyday topic.

DIFFERENTIATED INSTRUCTION

FOR ENGLISH LANGUAGE LEARNERS

Language Support Point out to students that the purpose of the web is to help them visualize the multiple content areas in which they use academic vocabulary words. Knowing the meaning of these academic vocabulary words will help English language learners to complete their assignments and do better on assessments. Provide students with alternate context for some of the terms listed on this page as follows:

- Learning another language can expose us to a different *culture*.

- What kind of *documents* might you read in a world history class?

- Writers *communicate* their ideas through a variety of genres and styles.

- What happens in geometry when you *alter* a square by attaching another square to one side?

- We used a guide to help us *identify* what kind of butterfly was in the garden.

The chart below identifies some of the academic vocabulary terms in this book. You will find these terms, as well as others, in activities labeled "Academic Vocabulary in Writing" and "Academic Vocabulary in Speaking." These activities will give you opportunities to practice using academic language.

Word	Definition	Example
author	a writer, the creator of something	What is the **author's** purpose in this essay?
cite	to quote from a source	**Cite** at least one online source and one print source in your essay.
contemporary	current; modern	Compare and contrast a **contemporary** poem with a poem written in the 19th century.
convince	to overcome doubts with argument or persuasion	Use evidence and reasoning to **convince** your audience.
crucial	extremely important; critical	Identify and explain one **crucial** event or issue that led to the Great Depression.
encounter	an unexpected meeting	What did Hitler's troops **encounter** when they invaded the Soviet Union?
emerge	to develop; to become something new	How does new growth **emerge** after a forest fire?
goal	aim or purpose	What **goal** are you trying to achieve by studying another language?
issue	concern or problem	Identify one **issue** the United Nations was formed to address.
statistic	numerical fact or quantity	Use facts and **statistics** to support your opinion.
survive	to live or remain in existence longer than expected	Why did some people **survive** the bubonic plague while others did not?
symbol	something that represents or suggests another thing	What **symbol** does the writer use to represent a lack of communication?
transmit	to communicate or hand off to others	How does one person **transmit** the flu to another?
vision	a mental or imaginative image	In one or two paragraphs, describe the **vision** of the framers of the Declaration of Independence.

whose faces are formed by closed plane figures bounded by three or more line segments.

- **World History:** Explain that *culture* is the "attitudes, behavior, or customs that characterize a group; the particular group having such attitudes, behavior, or customs." Tell students that as Alexander the Great, king of Macedonia, created his empire in the 300s BC, he also spread Greek culture.

- **United States History:** Explain to students that a *document* is a noun meaning "something printed or written that provides a record; something that provides evidence." Explain that the term *unalienable rights* refers to rights that cannot be changed or transferred. Tell students that the document that identifies unalienable rights in the United States is the Declaration of Independence. The Declaration states, "We hold these truths to be self-evident, that all men are created equal, that they are endowed by their Creator with certain unalienable Rights, that among these are Life, Liberty and the pursuit of Happiness."

FOR STRUGGLING READERS

Vocabulary Support Although this workshop focuses on academic vocabulary, students may need help with some of the other content-specific terms on this page. Use the following definitions for additional support.

- *persuasion:* the act of convincing someone
- *framers:* conceivers; The framers of the Declaration of Independence were the men who created, designed, and wrote the document.

FOR ADVANCED LEARNERS / PRE–AP

Challenge advanced learners to come up with other examples of questions using some of the academic vocabulary terms on this page. Compare and contrast the students' sentences with the examples on the page. Have students critique their sentences for clarity and proper use of the terms.

Academic Vocabulary in Action

Review the definition of *crucial* with students. Then have students complete the chart on their own or in pairs. See the chart below for possible responses.

Subject Area	Sentence
French	Learning to use the subjunctive tense is crucial to speaking French.
Drama	A crucial part of playing a role is the ability to follow directions.

Have students read the definition of *transmit*. Then ask them to fill out the chart, using a dictionary for help. Possible responses are provided in the chart below.

Word	Definition	Sentence
trans-atlantic	spanning or crossing the Atlantic	We took a trans-atlantic flight from Boston to Paris.
transfer	to convey, shift, or change from one place, person, or thing to another	She ordered a transfer of funds from her savings account to her checking account.
transport	to carry from one place to another	We called a taxi to transport us from the airport to the hotel.

Academic Vocabulary in Action

The terms below are taken academic vocabulary words that can be found in a variety of text types. Knowing the meanings of these terms is essential for completing the activities and lessons in this book as well as mastering test items.

crucial (adjective)

Defining the Word

The word *crucial* means "extremely important or critical." Something that is crucial is essential to something else. In a social studies class, you may learn that a free market is a crucial element in capitalism. As you read and study an author and her work, you may discover that her experience as an immigrant is a crucial element in her writing.

Using the Word

Now that you know the definition of *crucial*, practice using the word. Use a chart like the one shown to write sentences using the word *crucial* in various subject areas.

Subject Area	Sentence
Social Studies	A free market is a crucial element in capitalism.

transmit (verb)

Defining the Word

The word *transmit* means "to communicate or hand off to others." We may transmit a message via e-mail or a letter, and we may transmit a disease to someone else by sneezing. The Greek word root –trans– means "across" or "over" and is used as the base for many words in English.

Using the Word

Once you know the meaning of a root word, you are able to apply that meaning to other words built on the same root.

- In a chart like this one, make a list of other words you know that are formed from the root –trans–.
- Look up each word in the dictionary and write down its meaning.
- Write a sentence using each word.

Word	Definition	Sentence
transcend	to exceed or go over limits	That imaginative story transcends all belief.

DIFFERENTIATED INSTRUCTION

FOR ENGLISH LANGUAGE LEARNERS

Language Support Help students to understand the examples provided. Have pairs of students look up and share the meanings of some of the words used in the examples, including:

- *free market:* an economic market operating by free competition. The United States has a free-market economy.
- *capitalism:* an economic system in which the means of production and distribution are privately or corporately owned, and development is proportionate to the accumulation and reinvestment of profits gained in a free market. The United States has an economy based on capitalism, and the means of production and distribution are privately or corporately owned.

- *imaginative:* An imaginative story is creative and inventive and makes a reader believe in it.
- *belief:* a conviction or opinion. It is possible to have beliefs in ideas as well as more tangible things, such as people.

Strategies That Work: Vocabulary

 Record new vocabulary words in your **Reader/Writer Notebook.**

❶ Use Context Clues

The most important part of building your vocabulary is recognizing unfamiliar words as you read. When you encounter an unfamiliar word, look at the **context,** the words, phrases, or sentences that surround that word. Often the context can give you important clues to the word's meaning, as in the following example:

> The immigrants formed a new **community** when they arrived in the United States. They had common interests, and they began to form common traditions.

Even if you do not know what *community* means, you can figure out from the context that it means "a group of individuals with a common interest or characteristic."

❷ Clarify Word Definitions

If you cannot determine a word's meaning from its context, consult a dictionary. A dictionary entry will provide a word's pronunciation, parts of speech, origin, definitions, and sometimes even connotations—the different shades of meaning and associations taken on by words with similar definitions. When you are reading a textbook or manual, you may find definitions for unfamiliar words in a glossary at the back of the book.

> **circumnavigate** (sûr′kəm-năv′ĭ-gāt′) *v.*: to proceed completely around.

❸ Keep a Word List

Write down new academic terms in your **Reader/Writer Notebook.** Add to your list each time you take on a new reading assignment. In addition to listing the word and its definition, you might draw a symbol or picture to show you what the word represents or provide examples to remind you what the word means. Challenge yourself to use words from the list in your writing and discussions. The more frequently you use the words, the easier they will be to remember.

 Interactive Vocabulary THINKcentral
Go to **thinkcentral.com.**
KEYWORD: HML10-19

*For a complete list of terms in this book, see the **Academic Vocabulary Glossary** on pages R121–R122.*

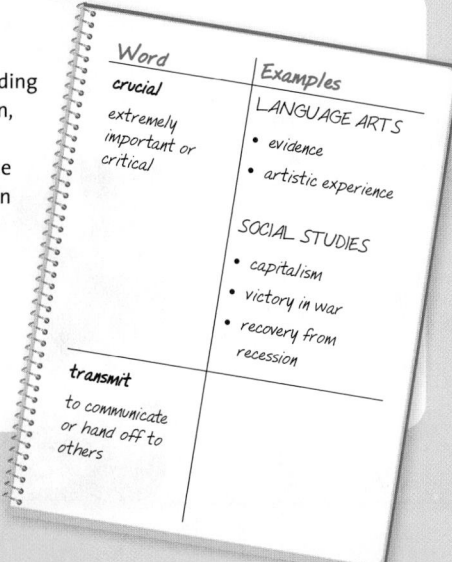

Word	Examples
crucial	LANGUAGE ARTS
extremely important or critical	• evidence
	• artistic experience
	SOCIAL STUDIES
	• capitalism
	• victory in war
	• recovery from recession
transmit	
to communicate or hand off to others	

Strategies That Work:
Vocabulary

Share with students that **Strategies That Work: Vocabulary** can be applied not only to Academic Vocabulary terms but also to unfamiliar words or phrases students will find in their reading. Encourage students to use these strategies in their reading both in and out of the classroom.

1. Use Context Clues

Ask students to identify the context clues in the example given. Explain that the context of an unfamiliar word may provide clues in definitions, restatements, or examples.

2. Clarify Word Definitions

Have students flip to the Glossary of Vocabulary in English and Spanish in the back of this book. Explain that this glossary provides pronunciations, parts of speech, and definitions for the vocabulary words in the selections in this book. Also included are the definitions of these vocabulary words in Spanish. Tell students that a glossary provides less information than a dictionary, but it may be easier to access and use because of its immediate availability. This textbook also includes a Glossary of Reading and Informational Terms and a Glossary of Literary Terms.

3. Keep a Word List

Encourage students to record new academic vocabulary in their **Reader/Writer Notebooks.** Explain that a strong vocabulary will help them to read and communicate more effectively. If you have a classroom computer, have students look at Interactive Vocabulary on **thinkcentral.com.**

FOR STRUGGLING READERS

Concept Support Use these activities to reinforce the teaching in the text:

1. For more help understanding context clues, have students go to the **Vocabulary and Spelling Handbook** in the back of this book. There they can find specific examples of context clues, including restatement, examples, comparison, contrast, and cause-and-effect relationships.

2. Invite students to share tips about using glossaries and dictionaries. Ask students if they use glossaries in textbooks in other subjects or if they have a particular online dictionary they like to use.

3. Suggest that students pair together and share their word lists. Have student pairs come up with other examples for some of the unfamiliar terms in their partners' notebooks. Alternatively, have students quiz each other on correct definitions.

 THINKcentral

WordSharp

WordSharp Vocabulary Tutor provides in-depth instruction in the use of vocabulary development strategies:

• identifying context clues
• applying knowledge of word parts and word origins
• using dictionaries and other resources
• recognizing specialized vocabulary
• studying word derivations

W 4 Produce clear and coherent writing in which the development, organization, and style are appropriate to task, purpose, and audience. **W 5** Develop and strengthen writing as needed by planning, revising, editing, rewriting, or trying a new approach, focusing on addressing what is most significant for a specific purpose and audience. **SL 1c** Propel conversations by posing and responding to questions that relate the current discussion to broader themes or larger ideas; actively incorporate others into the discussion; and clarify, verify, or challenge ideas and conclusions. **SL 1d** Respond thoughtfully to diverse perspectives, summarize points of agreement and disagreement, and, when warranted, qualify or justify their own views and understanding and make new connections in light of the evidence and reasoning presented. **L 1** Demonstrate command of the conventions of standard English grammar and usage when writing or speaking. **L 2** Demonstrate command of the conventions of standard English capitalization, punctuation, and spelling when writing.

Consider Your Options

Read the questions and answers under **Purpose, Audience,** and **Genre Format.** Discuss how these variables affect each other. For example, if the topic is chimpanzees and the audience is young adults, elicit how the genre format would change depending on the purpose.

- If the *purpose* is to persuade the audience to protect chimpanzees, the *genre format* might be an essay.

- If the *purpose* is to inform the audience, the *genre format* might be a research paper.

- If the *purpose* is to entertain the audience, the *genre format* might be a short story.

Repeat this process, changing the variables.

Writing Process Workshop

Expressing Ideas in Writing

The author E. L. Doctorow once said, "Writing is an exploration. You start from nothing and learn as you go." The journey from an unformed idea to a polished final draft proves that writing is indeed an exploration. Along the way, you can learn more about your own opinions and even enlighten, influence, or inspire others.

COMMON CORE
Included in this workshop:
W 4, W 5, SL 1c, SL 1d, L 1, L 2

Consider Your Options

You might want to describe a memorable experience in colorful detail, take a stand on a controversial issue, analyze the theme of a novel, or apply for a summer job. No matter what you decide to write about, you should start by considering three essential elements—your **purpose**, your **audience**, and the **format** of your writing.

PURPOSE	AUDIENCE	FORMAT
Why am I writing?	**Who are my readers?**	**Which format will best suit my purpose and audience?**
• to entertain	• other classmates	• essay • short story
• to inform or explain	• teacher	• letter • speech
• to argue or persuade	• friends	• poem • review
• to describe	• community members	• research paper • journal entry
• to express thoughts and feelings	• potential employer	• script • news article
• to inspire	• customer service department	• editorial • Web site
	• college admissions office	• summary
	• Web community	• multimedia presentation

DIFFERENTIATED INSTRUCTION

FOR STRUGGLING READERS

Note Taking An understanding of the writing process will help students communicate effectively—both in class and throughout their lives. If students need help, hand out the note-taking copy master for the Writing Process Workshop. As you discuss the main points on these four pages, have students record them on the copy master.

 RESOURCE MANAGER—Copy Master
Note Taking p. I-5

FOR ENGLISH LANGUAGE LEARNERS

Language: Skill Words Have students practice using the terms by identifying the *purpose, audience,* and *format* of each example.

- a funny short story for young children **Possible answer:** *purpose: to entertain; audience: children; format: short story*

- a research paper for doctors **Possible answer:** *purpose: to inform; audience: doctors; format: research paper*

- an advertisement for a new kind of backpack **Possible answer:** *purpose: to persuade; audience: students; format: advertisement*

Continue with the Process

Every writer follows a unique process for writing. Some writers, for example, dive right into drafting, letting their ideas develop as they go. Others revise their work countless times, generating one improved draft after another. As you tackle the **Writing Workshop** assignments in this book, you will start to adapt the following process to suit your own working style.

THE WRITING PROCESS

PLANNING/PREWRITING
Explore your ideas and decide what you want to write about. Once you've defined your purpose, audience, and format, develop and focus your ideas by using prewriting strategies, such as **freewriting** or **brainstorming** with others. Find additional strategies on page 23.

WHAT DOES IT LOOK LIKE?

Twelve Angry Men

Serving on a jury would be an exciting experience. Deciding someone's fate is a big responsibility, though. The eighth juror seemed to be the only one who took that responsibility to heart. Maybe I could write about the character of Juror No. 8.

DRAFTING
Transform your ideas into a rough draft, without worrying about errors. If you are writing an informal piece, such as a journal entry or a personal narrative, you might **draft to discover**—start writing with no set plan. If you are writing a formal essay, however, **draft from an outline.**

OUTLINE

I. Juror No. 8 has all the qualities that a responsible juror should have.

A. Is impartial (evidence is important, not feelings)
B. Stands up for his opinion even after other jurors ridicule him for being "in left field" (line 9)

REVISING
Critically evaluate your draft, looking for ways to improve development, organization, and style. Make sure your writing is clear and **coherent**, or easy to follow.

- Review the **rubric** on page 22.
- Enlist the help of a **peer reader.**
- Consider trying a new approach if something simply is not working.

PEER SUGGESTIONS

In Reginald Rose's Twelve Angry Men, Juror No. 8 is the only one to understand ~~what it means to be a good juror.~~ this weighty responsibility.

Suggestion: May want to grab readers with a creative statement. Try:"The jury has reached a verdict—one that will seal the fate of the defendant."

EDITING AND PUBLISHING
Proofread for errors in grammar, usage, **capitalization, punctuation, and spelling.** Use the **Proofreader's Checklist** to help you catch common mistakes. Get your writing out where others can read it. Where you publish, of course, depends on your **purpose, audience,** and **format.**

PUBLISHING OPTIONS

Jackie's Blog
My name is Jackie Zepeda, and I [...]
Music Academy. This site is whe[...]
with the world. For starters:

Continue with the Process

Determine Readiness Ask a volunteer to read the introductory paragraph. Then conduct a brief survey to determine students' familiarity with the writing process. Ask questions about their experiences at each stage.

- How do you generate ideas for a writing project?
- Do you write a draft from an outline or from a graphic organizer? Explain.
- What errors do you look for in your rough draft?
- Do you find a peer reader helpful? Explain.
- How do you decide that your writing is ready to turn in, send out, or publish?

FOR STRUGGLING READERS
Concept Support Draw a flow chart on the board to help students visualize the writing process. Explain that the arrows indicate the natural progression from one stage to the next. Encourage students to explain each stage; fill in details as needed.

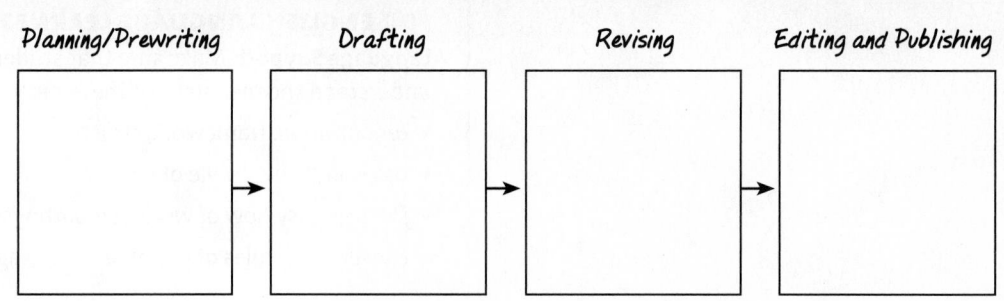

Planning/Prewriting → Drafting → Revising → Editing and Publishing

Scoring Rubric

Briefly discuss the Scoring Rubric, explaining that the rubric is a means by which students can evaluate their writing. (The word *rubric* refers to categorizing—here, categorizing a piece of writing according to its strengths.) Tell students that the best way to understand rubrics is to use them to score an actual piece of writing. Students will have the opportunity to work with a partner to evaluate what the wrote in the Writing Workshops. Students can score each other's writing using a rubric like the one on this page. They can then write a summary evaluation using the language of the rubric to explain the reasons for the score they gave their partner.

Scoring Rubric

Score	COMMON CORE TRAITS
6	• **Development** Includes a meaningful, engaging introduction; thoroughly develops the topic with well-chosen, relevant, and sufficient evidence; ends powerfully • **Organization** Logically organizes complex ideas, concepts, and information; uses appropriate and varied transitions to create cohesion and clarify relationships among ideas • **Language** Uses precise language in imaginative ways; maintains an appropriate style and tone for the audience and purpose; shows a strong command of conventions
5	• **Development** Has an engaging introduction; develops the topic with relevant, well-chosen evidence; has an effective concluding section • **Organization** Logically organizes ideas, concepts, and information; uses appropriate transitions to create cohesion and clarify relationships • **Language** Effectively uses precise language; maintains an appropriate style and tone for the audience and purpose; has a few errors in conventions
4	• **Development** Has an introduction, but it could be more engaging; lacks sufficient support for one or two ideas; has an adequate, though routine, concluding section • **Organization** Is logically organized, with one or two exceptions; could use a few more transitions to clarify the relationships among ideas • **Language** Includes some vague word choices; has one or two lapses in style and tone; includes a few distracting errors in conventions
3	• **Development** Has both an introduction and conclusion, but they are superficial or uninteresting; includes some unsupported ideas or irrelevant evidence • **Organization** Has some flaws in organization; needs more transitions • **Language** Uses words correctly, though language is unimaginative; has frequent lapses in style and tone; has some critical errors in conventions
2	• **Development** Has an unfocused, uninteresting introduction; does not develop most ideas; ends abruptly • **Organization** Has an illogical organization; lacks transitions throughout • **Language** Uses vague language and misuses some words; lapses into an inappropriate style and tone in many places; contains many distracting errors in conventions
1	• **Development** Lacks an introduction, development, and a concluding section • **Organization** Has no discernible organization; lacks transitions or uses inappropriate ones • **Language** Uses many words incorrectly; employs an inappropriate style and tone for the audience and purpose; has major problems with conventions

DIFFERENTIATED INSTRUCTION

FOR ENGLISH LANGUAGE LEARNERS

Language Support Make sure that students understand the meanings of these terms:

- *organization:* framework; structure
- *voice:* individual style of writing
- *fluency:* easy flow of words; smoothness
- *conventions:* rules of grammar and usage

Strategies That Work: Writing

Jot your writing ideas, plans, and notes in your **Reader/Writer Notebook.**

❶ Use Prewriting Strategies

The first step in any process is often the hardest—and that can be especially true of writing. Here are some strategies to help you get a strong start:

- **Freewrite.** Write continuously for 10 minutes, jotting down the ideas that pop into your head.
- **Chart your course.** Capture your ideas in a graphic organizer, such as a spider map or an observation chart.
- **Search for inspiration.** Look for quotations, photographs, headlines, and other sources of inspiration.
- **Brainstorm with others.** Hear what others have to say about your ideas.
- **Write from a prompt.** Consider the idea starters in the **Writing Workshops** for prompts and ideas for writing.

❷ Get Feedback from Peers

Often, peer readers can spot problems that you've overlooked. Consider the following guidelines.

When You're the Writer	When You're the Reader
• Make readers feel comfortable about responding honestly by listening respectfully to what they have to say.	• Be respectful and positive.
• Clarify what kind of feedback you want. Should your readers focus on content, structure, or both?	• Support your opinions with relevant observations, and give suggestions for improvement.
• Consider readers' comments and then make your own decisions about what to change.	• Ask questions to learn more about the writer's goals and ideas.
• Be willing to think about your writing in new ways.	• Don't rewrite the work yourself.

❸ Pay Attention to Details

Even minor mistakes, such as errors in grammar, punctuation, and spelling, can keep readers from taking your ideas seriously.

Use these spelling tips to make sure your writing is polished and correct.

- Review spelling rules on pages R72–R74.
- Avoid misusing commonly confused words, such as *accept* and *except*. (See page R75 for more examples.)
- Use the spell-check feature in your word-processing program or a dictionary.
- Read your draft backwards to catch mistakes your eye might miss while scanning over sentences you are very familiar with.

EXAMPLE

When Phillip wakes up, he is all alone on the island ~~accept~~ *except* for a member of the ship's crew and a cat. Soon, Phillip becomes blind. Overcoming that is a huge ~~obstical~~ *obstacle* for him.

Writing Online **THINK**central
Go to **thinkcentral.com.**
KEYWORD: HML10N-23

FOR STRUGGLING READERS

Concept Support Use these activities for reinforcement:

1. Review the first Writing Workshop (page 148) to show students an example of a prompt. Point out that they will be learning how to analyze a prompt for clues about format, purpose, and audience.

2. Ask students to brainstorm ideas about how peer readers might be useful at different stages in the writing process.

3. As students read the selections in this anthology, urge them to make notes about topics, style points, and other elements that they would like to attempt in their own writing. Invite students to use these selections as models to help them develop their individual writing style.

Strategies That Work:
Writing

Tell students that the suggestions in **Strategies That Work: Writing** can open up exciting possibilities for them as writers. Encourage them to apply these strategies whenever they write, regardless of the purpose or situation. They can help make their writing interesting, effective, and successful.

1. Use Prewriting Strategies
Review the five prewriting strategies for generating ideas. Discuss the benefits of each one. Ask students to share their experiences and recommendations.

2. Get Feedback from Peers
Explain that writers may get so caught up in their work that they lose perspective. Identifying the strengths and weaknesses of a piece of writing may become difficult after working on a paper for a while. A peer review brings a fresh eye to any project. Encourage peer writers to use the Scoring Rubric in order to give specific feedback about areas that need work. Emphasize the importance of being sensitive, respectful, and patient.

3. Pay Attention to Details
Suggest that students pay attention to the way that experienced writers write. Ask them to keep the Scoring Rubric in mind as they read literature and to ask, "What makes this writing work so well?" Encourage students to form writing groups. If you have a classroom computer, go to **thinkcentral.com** and show students examples of the writing resources.

Writing Online  **THINK**central

The **Writing Center** on **thinkcentral.com** includes Interactive Student Models, which show students how to read and critique others' writing. The **Writing Center** also includes
- Ideas for Writing
- Interactive Graphic Organizers
- Interactive Revision Lessons
- Writing Model Bank

The World of a Story

PLOT, SETTING, AND MOOD

- In Fiction
- In Nonfiction
- In Media
- In Poetry

25

About the Art French artist Bob Lescaux painted *Utopie* in 1999. For more information, see page 143.

INTRODUCE THE UNIT

The classroom, the soccer field, the kitchen, the mall—these are just some of the worlds in which tenth graders spend their time. Perhaps they also spend some time in the worlds that reading offers them. Have volunteers name some of the different "worlds" that they have visited by reading. What happened to them in those worlds? Did they laugh there? Did they tense up with worry or jump at an unexpected outcome? Did they meet unusual people in those worlds— or people just like themselves?

Have students think about the worlds that the images on this page suggest. Ask:

- What worlds do you travel to in these images? In other words, what kind of selection might each image illustrate? Why do you think so?
- Which image is more about the real world, and which is more about an inner world? Why do you think so?
- Which image seems to relate more to setting (time and place) and which more to mood (feeling or atmosphere)?

Tell students that the selections in Unit 1 will take them on many journeys, both real and imagined, where they will explore **plot, setting,** and **mood.** That is, they will explore the time, place, and atmosphere of these worlds. Students also will focus on events that lead them through rising action to a climax and resolution.

For help in planning this unit, see

 **RESOURCE MANAGER UNIT 1** pp. 1–10

UNIT 1

COMMON CORE

STRAND

Comparing Text Selections

STRAND	Text Analysis Workshop: Plot, Setting, and Mood pp. 28–35	Harrison Bergeron Short Story pp. 36–47	Everyday Use Short Story pp. 48–63	Searching for Summer Short Story pp. 64–77	To Build a Fire Short Story pp. 78–97	from *Deep Survival / How to Build a Fire Without Matches* Nonfiction / Diagram pp. 98–105
		Lexile: 840 Fry: 8 Dale-Chall: 6.6	Lexile: 810 Fry: 9 Dale-Chall: 5.7	Lexile: 810 Fry: 9 Dale-Chall: 5.7	Lexile: 970 Fry: 7 Dale-Chall: 6.1	Lexile: 920 Fry: 10 Dale-Chall: 7.5
Reading Literature	Setting and Mood pp. 28–29 RL 5 Plot and Story Analysis p. 30 RL 5 Analyze the Text pp. 31–35 RL 5	Plot and Conflict pp. 37, 40–45 RL 3 Draw Conclusions pp. 37–38, 40–41, 44–45 RL 1	Conflict and Character pp. 49, 53, 56, 59, 61 RL 1, RL 5 Figurative Language p. 54 RL 4 Make Inferences pp. 49, 50, 52, 54, 57, 61 Language Coach p. 53 RL 4	Setting and Mood pp. 65, 68, 71, 72 RL 4 Setting and Mood p. 75 RL 3 Monitor pp. 65, 66, 68, 72, 74, 75 RL 10 Language Coach pp. 69, 74 RL 4	Setting and Conflict pp. 79, 82, 84, 86, 88, 93, 96 RL 5 Predict pp. 79, 83, 85, 89, 92, 95–96 RL 1 Narrator p. 90 RL 4 Language Coach p. 93 RL 4 Word Relationships p. 94 RL 4	
Reading Informational Text			Interview p. 60			Use Text Features pp. 98–103 RI 1, RI 2 Language Coach p. 99 RI 4 Diagram p. 104 RI 7
Writing		Writing Prompt p. 47	Quickwrite p. 48 Writing Prompt p. 63 W 3	Writing Prompt p. 77		Writing Prompt p. 103 W 2
Speaking and Listening		Brainstorm p. 36 SL 1		Discuss p. 64 SL 1	What's the Connection? p. 78 SL 1	
Language		Precise Adjectives pp. 43, 47 L 3 Language Coach p. 41 L 5 Greek root *syn* p. 46 L 4c, L 5	Descriptive Details pp. 55, 63 L 1b Prefix *re-* p. 62 L 4c	Analyze Dialogue pp. 70, 77 L 3 Prefix *dis-* p. 76 L 4c	Language Coach p. 84 L 4c Language Coach p. 87 Connotation and Denotation p. 97 L 5b	

from **The Johnstown Flood** Historical Narrative pp. 106–117	**The Race to Save Apollo 13** Nonfiction pp. 118–135	**Media Study:** *from* **Apollo 13** Film Clip pp. 136–139	**Exile/Crossing the Border** Narrative Poems pp. 140–147	**Writing Workshop: Literary Analysis** pp. 148–157 *Speaking and Listening Workshop: Presenting a Response to a Short Story* pp. 158–159
Lexile: 1140 *Fry: 7* *Dale-Chall: 6.2*	*Lexile: 1080* *Fry: 10* *Dale-Chall: 8.1*			
			Narrative Poetry pp. 141–145, 147 RL 10 Reading Poetry pp. 141–142, 144–147 RL 4	
Mood pp. 107–108, 110, 112, 114, 115 RI 4 Chronological Order pp. 107–108, 110, 113, 115 RI 3 Language Coach p. 114 RI 4	Suspense in Nonfiction pp. 119, 121, 125, 127, 132–133 RI 6 Author's Purpose p. 129 RI 6 Take Notes pp. 119, 122, 126, 130, 133 RI 1, RI 4, RI 5 Language Coach p. 120, 128 RI 4	Suspense on Film pp. 136–139 RI 7		
Quickwrite p. 106 Writing Prompt p. 116 W 2	Writing Prompt p. 135	Analyze Accounts in Print and Film p. 139 W 9b (RI 7)	Quickwrite p. 140 Writing Prompt p. 147	Writing a Literary Analysis pp. 148–157 W 2a–f, W 4, W 5, W 9a, W 10
	Discuss p. 118 SL 1	Create a Storyboard p. 139 SL 2		Presenting a Response to a Short Story pp. 158–159 SL 4
Emphasize Action pp. 111, 116 L 3 Language Coach p. 114 L 4a	Sentence Flow pp. 130, 135 L 3 Specialized Vocabulary p. 134 L 6		Language Coach p. 146 L 4c	Drafting p. 151 L 2, L 2b Editing and Publishing p. 155 L 1, L 3 Delivering Your Presentation, p. 159 L 1

To see the complete Essential Course of Study, see pp. T23–T28.

 For additional lesson planning help, see **Teacher One Stop DVD.**

Instructional Support

Resource Manager Unit 1

UNIT SUPPORT
Academic Vocabulary, p. 3
Additional Academic Vocabulary, p. 4
Grammar Focus p. 5
Text Analysis Workshop pp. 9–10
Writing Workshop: Literary
Analysis p. 175

SELECTION SUPPORT*
Plan and Teach
Lesson planning pages
Additional leveled selection questions
Extension activities

Student Copy Masters
Selection summaries in four languages
Skills copy masters in English and Spanish
Vocabulary preteaching and support
Reading Check and Question Support
Reading Fluency

* Available for all selections

† Available on **thinkcentral.com**.

Language Handbook
Vocabulary Practice
Best Practices Toolkit†
PowerNotes DVD-ROM†
Connections: Nonfiction for Common Core CD-ROM†

Teacher One Stop DVD-ROM
Student One Stop DVD-ROM
Media*Smart* DVD-ROM *from* Apollo 13
Write*Smart* CD-ROM†
GrammarNotes DVD-ROM†
WordSharp CD-ROM†

Media**Smart**

Media Studies

Apollo 13

Finding Forrester

Tornado News Reports

"Daisy" / "America's Back"

The Aftermath of September 11

Differentiated Instruction

STRUGGLING READERS AND WRITERS	ENGLISH LANGUAGE LEARNERS	ADVANCED LEARNERS
Resource Manager Unit 1	**Resource Manager Unit 1**	**Resource Manager Unit 1**
Additional Selection Questions	Selection Summaries in English, Spanish, Vietnamese and Haitian Creole	Additional Selection Questions
Question Support	Skills Copymasters in Spanish	Ideas for Extension
Reading Fluency		**Diagnostic and Selection Tests**
Interactive Reader	**English Language Learner Adapted Interactive Reader Teacher's Guide**	Selection Tests B/C
Adapted Interactive Reader	**ELL Adapted Interactive Reader**	
Audio Tutor	**Audio Tutor**	
Level Up Online Tutorials	**Guide to English for Newcomers**	
Audio Anthology	**Audio Anthology**	
(with Audio summaries)	**Audio Summaries in Multiple**	
Diagnostic and Selection Tests	**Languages** (on **thinkcentral.com**)	
Selection Tests A/B		

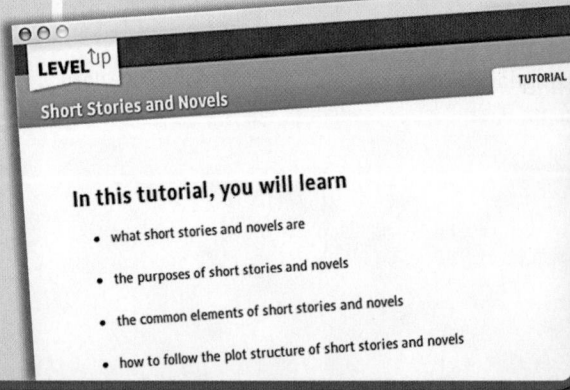

LEVEL up   TUTORIAL
Short Stories and Novels

In this tutorial, you will learn
- what short stories and novels are
- the purposes of short stories and novels
- the common elements of short stories and novels
- how to follow the plot structure of short stories and novels

Assessment and Reteaching

Diagnostic and Selection Tests

Unit and Benchmark Tests

ThinkCentral Online Assessment:

- All program assessments
- Level Up Online Tutorials

ExamView Test Generator on the Teacher One Stop DVD-ROM

Online Essay Scoring on **thinkcentral.com**

ThinkCentral Online Reteaching:

- Level Up Online Tutorials
- Reteaching Worksheets

Holt McDougal Online Essay Scoring

Welcome to Holt McDougal Online Essay Scoring!

This site is designed to help you improve your writing skills and prepare for standardized writing tests. When you write and submit a response to one of the writing prompts on this site, the computerized scoring system will immediately score and deliver feedback on your essay. Other resources on this site will help you prepare, develop, and revise your essay.

STUDENTS
Get started by entering the
Writing Zone

Professional Development

Video Center Based on interviews with program consultants and other educational experts, these videos feature classroom-ready teaching strategies.

Teacher Toolkit Includes a Teacher Handbook as well as a range of articles and handouts by program consultants and other educators.

Janet Allen

Jim Burke

Kylene Beers

Carol Jago

 **THINK central at a Glance**

One Location, Endless Resources

Find Resources Browse all *Holt McDougal Literature* components for the ones that meet your students' needs and match your teaching style.

Assess Progress and Reteach Assign electronic versions of program assessments to measure your students' mastery of the Common Core State Standards. On thinkcentral.com, some tests deliver online remediation tutorials to students who have not mastered skills.

 Interactive Whiteboard Lessons

Prepare your students for college and careers by teaching relevant, real-world skills through dynamic, interactive instruction. Go to **thinkcentral.com** to browse through all whiteboard lessons, including the following:

- Citing Textual Evidence
- Plot and Conflict
- Narrative Techniques
- Role of Setting

 Together Holt McDougal and HISTORY® are revolutionizing the study of English/language arts with video that helps students relive and re-imagine the people, places, and events they are discovering through reading. Look for selections with the HISTORY® icon.

Which stories are
WORTH reading?

Read the question and ask students for spontaneous responses. List their suggestions on the board. As students read the paragraph, relate its ideas to the list of responses.

ACTIVITY Have pairs of students compare their lists of criteria for a story worth reading. Have pairs merge their criteria with criteria from other pairs. Then ask student representatives to express the qualities that the group value most. Help students relate some of those qualities to the literary elements of plot, setting, and mood.

CHECK UNDERSTANDING Have students choose a selection that they have enjoyed and remembered but that has not yet been named during discussion of this page. Ask them to use the criteria from the *ACTIVITY* to explain why this story, too, is a "great read."

Which stories are
WORTH reading?

So many activities compete for your time and attention. You can spend your leisure time watching television, playing video games, or surfing the Internet. If you decide to invest your time reading a book, you want value for that investment. You want to be sure the story is worth reading, making you laugh, cry, or gasp in surprise.

ACTIVITY Which stories made you glad you had read them? What qualities made these stories so good? Create a list of your criteria for a "great read." Think about the following:

- Do you care more about the characters or the events that happen to them?
- Does suspense play a role in the stories you like?
- Are there certain places you like to read about?
- What emotions do you like to feel as you read?

Find It Online! THINK central
Go to **thinkcentral.com** for the interactive version of this unit.

26

Unit Resources

See resources on the **Teacher One Stop DVD-ROM** *and on* **thinkcentral.com**.

R RESOURCE MANAGER UNIT 1

UNIT AND BENCHMARK TESTS

BEST PRACTICES TOOLKIT

INTERACTIVE READER

ADAPTED INTERACTIVE READER

ELL ADAPTED INTERACTIVE READER

LANGUAGE HANDBOOK

VOCABULARY PRACTICE

TECHNOLOGY

⊚ Teacher One Stop DVD-ROM
⊚ Student One Stop DVD-ROM
⊚ PowerNotes DVD-ROM
⊚ Write*Smart* CD-ROM
⊚ Media*Smart* DVD-ROM
⊚ GrammarNotes DVD-ROM
⊚ Audio Anthology CD
⊚ Audio Tutor CD

Find It Online! THINK central

The interactive version of this unit on **thinkcentral.com** includes
- video and **PowerNotes** introductions to key selections
- audio support—listen or download
- **ThinkAloud** models
- **WordSharp** vocabulary tutorials
- interactive review and remediation

COMMON
CORE

Preview Unit Goals

TEXT ANALYSIS	• Analyze the author's choices on ordering events in a text
	• Analyze setting and its influence on mood and conflict
	• Analyze narrative techniques, including foreshadowing, irony, and suspense
	• Identify stages of plot and how characters advance the plot
READING	• Cite evidence to make inferences and draw conclusions
WRITING AND LANGUAGE	• Write an interpretive essay
	• Support key points with evidence from the text
	• Use descriptive details and improve sentence flow
VOCABULARY	• Determine figurative and connotative meanings of words
	• Understand and use specialized/technical vocabulary
	• Use word roots to help determine meaning
ACADEMIC VOCABULARY	• affect • establish
	• communicate • identify
	• definite
SPEAKING AND LISTENING	• Present a response to a short story
MEDIA AND VIEWING	• Analyze film techniques that create suspense

Media Smart DVD-ROM

Worthwhile Moments on Film
Discover how director Ron Howard re-creates the human drama and suspense of a real-life crisis in space. Page 136.

27

DIFFERENTIATED INSTRUCTION

FOR ENGLISH LANGUAGE LEARNERS

Academic Vocabulary Provide students with definitions of each Academic Vocabulary word.

affect (ə fekt') *v.* to influence; to create an effect upon

communicate (kə myōō'ni kāt') *v.* to share or exchange information or ideas

definite (def'ə nit) *adj.* certain; unquestionable

establish (ə stab' lish) *v.* to make stable or firm

identify (ī-děn'tə-fī') *v.* to find or name the characteristics, nature, or qualities of someone or something

Use the copy master to help students learn academic words they will use in this unit and on the Assessment Practice.

R **RESOURCE MANAGER—Copy Masters**
Academic Vocabulary p. 3
Additional Academic Vocabulary p. 4

Included in this unit: **RL 1, RL 3, RL 4, RL 5, RL 10, RI 1, RI 2, RI 3, RI 4, RI 5, RI 6, RI 7, RI 10, W 2, W 2a-f, W 3, W 4, W 5, W 9a, W 9b, W 10, SL 2, SL 4, L 1, L 1b, L 2, L 2b, L 3, L 4, L 4a, L 4c, L 5, L 5b, L 6**

Complete text of the Common Core State Standards is found in the correlation on p. T10. Standards covered in this unit are found in the standards overview (pp. 25A–25B) and on the lesson pages where they are taught.

Preview Unit Goals

This page outlines the skills and strategies covered in Unit 1. Explain to students how previewing material can help them become more effective readers.

To help students internalize new academic language in meaningful ways, have them work in small groups on the following speaking and writing activities. These activities will help students to acquire the unit literary concepts and the academic language needed to speak and write about these concepts.

Speaking For speaking practice with the academic vocabulary words in this unit, provide small groups of students with the following sentence frames for discussion:

- Suspenseful stories **affect** me in the following ways: _____.
- The setting of a story helps to **establish** a mood by _____.
- The **definite** purpose of a suspenseful story is to _____.
- A writer can **communicate** suspense by _____.
- I can **identify** my favorite suspenseful story: _____.

After students discuss each sentence frame, ask each group to share their responses to one of the sentence frames with the larger group.

Writing After students have discussed and shared their responses to the sentence frames, have students write a brief paragraph in which they respond to the following prompt: What is your favorite suspenseful story, movie, or television program? Write a brief paragraph in which you explain why it is suspenseful and why it is your favorite. In your paragraph, use at least three of the academic vocabulary words you have just discussed.

After students write their paragraphs, ask volunteers to read their response aloud to the group.

Focus and Motivate

RL 5 Analyze an author's choices concerning how to structure a text, order events, and create effects such as mystery, tension, or surprise.

Teach

Part 1: Setting and Mood

Setting Explain that the setting of some stories is crucial to the story's overall meaning. Use this activity to reinforce the importance of setting in certain stories:

1. Help students brainstorm a list of popular stories from literature or from films. List stories in which the setting is important.

2. Ask students to name the setting of each story and to describe clues that helped them identify it. If necessary, point out that a setting may be real or imaginary.

3. For each story, have students identify a story element, such as the conflict, mood, or character, that is affected by the setting. Record students' responses in a chart.

Setting		
Story Title	The Setting	Effect on Story Element

Mood Discuss how the mood of a story can change suddenly. Ask students to name a film in which an underdog triumphed against all odds. Prompt them with leading questions like these:

- Was there music? How did it change?
- Did images speed up or slow down?
- Did scenes become brighter or darker?
- How did characters' actions and words support the triumphant mood?

Explain that story writers also use details to create mood. Have students offer examples of details they might find in horror stories.

🧰 **BEST PRACTICES TOOLKIT— Transparency**
Analysis Frame: Setting pp. D21, D30

Plot, Setting, and Mood
Essential Course of Study ✓ **ECOS**

Every story transports you to a fictional world. You might be swept away by a love story set during the Civil War or mesmerized by a science fiction adventure that takes place on an uninhabited planet. No matter where and when they unfold, good stories allow you to experience times, places, and conflicts that are outside your everyday life. To understand why a story affects you as it does, you have to analyze the elements—plot, setting, and mood—that make up its world.

COMMON CORE
Included in this workshop:
RL 5 Analyze an author's choices concerning how to structure a text, order events, and create effects such as mystery, tension, or surprise.

Part 1: Setting and Mood

Almost every story happens in a particular time and place—for example, "long ago, in a galaxy far, far away," in a modern city, or during the Great Depression. The time and place of the story is its **setting.** Writers create setting through the following:

- details that suggest the time of day, year, season, or historical period
- descriptions of characters, clothing, buildings, weather, and landscapes

Another element that contributes to the world of a story is the **mood,** the feeling or atmosphere that a writer creates for readers. Whether it is mysterious or uplifting, a mood is developed through a writer's use of imagery and choice of words and details. Setting details, in particular, help to establish a mood.

In Jack London's "To Build a Fire" (page 80), the setting creates a mysterious, tense mood. The bleak story takes place on a wilderness trail in the Yukon Territory, a region in far northwestern Canada.

SETTING IN
TO BUILD A FIRE

Creates Tension
Can the man build a fire to warm his frozen limbs? He faces conflicts like this one as he struggles to survive.

Influences Character
Overconfident and inexperienced in the cold, the man learns a life-or-death lesson.

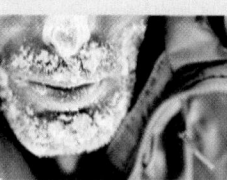

Helps Create Mood
The setting creates a mood of alienation and fear in the face of a natural world that is indifferent.

Serves as a Symbol
The man's frozen surroundings symbolize death and the indifference of nature to what people want.

DIFFERENTIATED INSTRUCTION

FOR STRUGGLING READERS

Note Taking For students who need help with note taking, hand out the note-taking copy master before discussing the page. Then have students read the first paragraph silently. Make sure they understand how to fill in their copy masters. As you discuss the main points of the paragraphs, have students record them on the copy master. Assist students as needed.

Sketch Setting Have students work in pairs or small groups to plan and sketch the setting of the model on page 29. Encourage students to label details in their sketches.

 RESOURCE MANAGER—Copy Master
Note Taking p. 9

MODEL: SETTING AND MOOD

At the beginning of the novel *Ethan Frome*, the narrator hears townspeople allude to a tragedy that ruined the life of the title character, Ethan. When a snowstorm hits the town, the narrator must spend the night at Ethan's, where he finally hears the entire tragic story. This excerpt begins as the storm is approaching.

from

Ethan Frome

Novel by **Edith Wharton**

. . . We set out for Starkfield with a good chance of getting there for supper. But at sunset the clouds gathered again, bringing an earlier night, and the snow began to fall straight and steadily from a sky without wind, in a soft universal diffusion more confusing than the gusts and eddies of the morning. It seemed
5 to be a part of the thickening darkness, to be the winter night itself descending on us layer by layer.

The small ray of Frome's lantern was soon lost in this smothering medium, in which even his sense of direction, and the bay's homing instinct, finally ceased to serve us. Two or three times some ghostly landmark sprang up to
10 warn us that we were astray, and then was sucked back into the mist; and when we finally regained our road the old horse began to show signs of exhaustion. I felt myself to blame for having accepted Frome's offer, and after a short discussion I persuaded him to let me get out of the sleigh and walk along through the snow at the bay's side. In this way we struggled on for another
15 mile or two, and at last reached a point where Frome, peering into what seemed to me formless night, said: "That's my gate down yonder." . . .

"Look here, Frome," I began, "there's no earthly use in your going any farther—" but he interrupted me: "Nor you neither. There's been about enough of this for anybody."
20 I understood that he was offering me a night's shelter at the farm, and without answering I turned into the gate at his side, and followed him to the barn, where I helped him to unharness and bed down the tired horse. When this was done he unhooked the lantern from the sleigh, stepped out again into the night, and called to me over his shoulder: "This way."
25 Far off above us a square of light trembled through the screen of snow. Staggering along in Frome's wake I floundered toward it, and in the darkness almost fell into one of the deep drifts against the front of the house. Frome scrambled up the slippery steps of the porch, digging a way through the snow with his heavily booted foot. Then he lifted his lantern, found the latch, and
30 led the way into the house. I went after him into a low unlit passage, at the back of which a ladder-like staircase rose into obscurity.

Close Read

1. Where and when does this story takes place? Describe the setting as completely as you can.

2. Reread lines 1–11. What mood do the setting details help to create? Support your answer.

3. What conflicts does the setting create for Ethan and the narrator?

4. Identify two setting details that may hint at the tragic story that the narrator will soon hear. Explain your choices. One detail has been boxed.

MODEL: SETTING AND MOOD
Close Read

1. ***Possible answer:*** *The story takes place in a town called Starkfield during a brutal winter. The time is early evening. Starkfield must be a rural town, because a farm and barn are mentioned (lines 20–22). The setting is not present-day, as suggested by the following clues: "Frome's lantern" (line 7), horse and sleigh transportation (lines 11 and 13), and expressions like "down yonder" (line 16).*

2. ***Possible answer:*** *The mood established in lines 1–11 is bleak and foreboding, as suggested by these details: "part of the thickening darkness," "smothering medium," "ghostly landmark," "sucked back into the mist," "old horse," and "signs of exhaustion."*

3. ***Possible answer:*** *Because of the winter storm, Ethan and the narrator cannot see anything. Even the lantern does not penetrate the heavy snowfall. As a result, they get lost and have to push the sleigh because the horse is too tired. Also, the narrator has to spend the night at Ethan's.*

4. ***Possible answer:*** *Details include "more confusing than the gusts and eddies of the morning" (line 4), "light trembled through the screen of snow" (line 25), and "ladder-like staircase rose into obscurity" (line 31).*

FOR ENGLISH LANGUAGE LEARNERS

Language: Skill Words List the following terms on the board: *character, detail, symbol, narrator.* Work with students to create Word Squares for each term, helping them identify the correct dictionary definitions. After students have completed their Word Squares, have them supply examples of each term.

BEST PRACTICES TOOLKIT—Transparency
Word Squares p. E10

FOR ADVANCED LEARNERS/PRE–AP*

Evaluate Setting Tell students to think of another story in which the setting was important. Have students write a brief essay that identifies the story, describes the setting, and evaluates the setting

* Pre–AP is a registered trademark of the College Entrance Examination Board. Use of the trademark does not constitute production, participation, sponsorship, or endorsement by the College Board.

Online Remediation

Are your students struggling with text analysis skills? Consider assigning them one or more **Level Up Online Tutorials** as remediation before beginning this unit. Log in to **thinkcentral.com** to view a list of the skills addressed by **Level Up**.

Teach

Part 2: Plot and Story Analysis

Conflicts in Plots Tell students that the basic framework for the development of a story hinges on a character's attempts to deal with the main conflict. Explain that a story may have more than one conflict, but it is the main conflict that is the point of greatest tension in the story. Review with students the types of conflict a character can face, asking for examples of each type.

Stages of a Typical Plot Point out that not every story fits neatly into the five stages shown in the chart. However, almost every story begins with an exposition followed by a rising action. Complications occur that make the main conflict more difficult to resolve. For example, a person trapped at home by a storm might suddenly lose electric power.

Draw a Plot Diagram on the board without labels. Starting at the beginning, the exposition, point to one section at a time and work with students to identify and label each section. Next, brainstorm one or two well-known stories from literature or film. Discuss the plot briefly. Then have students match plot details with the stages shown on the diagram. Try to include at least one story that does not include all five plot stages.

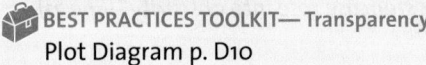 **BEST PRACTICES TOOLKIT— Transparency**
Plot Diagram p. D10

CHECK UNDERSTANDING

Give students the name of a well-known story that does not contain all five plot stages. Have students identify the missing stages.

Part 2: Plot and Story Analysis

A story is much more than the world in which the action unfolds. The real power of a story comes from *what happens* in that world. Most stories follow a **plot,** a series of scenes that traces a **conflict,** or struggle between opposing forces. The conflict can be **internal,** taking place within the mind of a character, or it can be an **external** conflict between a character and an outside force, such as another character, society, or nature.

Plot is usually talked about in terms of the following stages. In successful stories, each stage contains individual scenes that contribute to the plot as a whole. Keep in mind, however, that not every story follows this exact structure.

STAGES OF A TYPICAL PLOT	QUESTIONS FOR ANALYSIS
 **EXPOSITION** This part of a plot introduces the setting and characters and establishes a mood. It may also reveal the conflict or set the stage for it.	• What details help to establish the setting and create a mood? • What kind of person is the main character? • What, if anything, is revealed about the conflict?
 **RISING ACTION** Complications arise as the main character struggles to resolve the conflict. "The plot thickens" as suspense builds.	• What is the central conflict? • How do the characters respond to the conflict? • How does the conflict become more complicated?
 **CLIMAX** The climax is a turning point in the story and the moment of greatest suspense. Often the main character makes a decision or takes an action that makes the outcome of the conflict clear.	• What decision or action has the main character made or taken? • What impact might this decision or action have on the characters and the conflict? • How might the conflict be resolved?
 **FALLING ACTION** This stage shows the results of the decision or action that happened at the climax. Tension eases as the conflict is resolved.	• What is the outcome of the main character's decision or action? • What steps does the main character take to resolve the conflict?
RESOLUTION The resolution reveals the final outcome of the story and ties up any loose ends.	• How have the events and conflicts affected or changed the characters? • Through the resolution, what message might the writer be suggesting?

DIFFERENTIATED INSTRUCTION

FOR STRUGGLING READERS

Note Taking For students who need help, hand out the note-taking copy master for this page. After students read the top of the page, complete the first three items together. Tell students to fill in the rest of the copy master as they read the page. Remind them to take notes and not copy every detail from the chart.

R RESOURCE MANAGER—Copy Master
Note Taking p. 10

FOR ENGLISH LANGUAGE LEARNERS

Language: Skill Words On the board, list the literary terms shown in italics. Then give the examples in random order for students to match with the words.

• *complications:* The goal is in sight, but two more problems must be solved before it can be reached.

• *suspense:* Will the hero live or die?

• *outcome:* They lived happily ever after.

Part 3: Analyze the Text

In this story, a lovestruck teenager is faced with a difficult choice. As you read, use what you've learned about setting, mood, and plot to analyze the story.

THE BASS, THE RIVER, AND SHEILA MANT

Short story by **W. D. Wetherell**

There was a summer in my life when the only creature that seemed lovelier to me than a largemouth bass was Sheila Mant. I was fourteen. The Mants had rented the cottage next to ours on the river; with their parties, their frantic games of softball, their constant comings and goings, they appeared to me denizens of a
5 brilliant existence. "Too noisy by half," my mother quickly decided, but I would have given anything to be invited to one of their parties, and when my parents went to bed I would sneak through the woods to their hedge and stare enchanted at the candlelit swirl of white dresses and bright, paisley skirts.

Sheila was the middle daughter—at seventeen, all but out of reach. She
10 would spend her days sunbathing on a float my Uncle Sierbert had moored in their cove, and before July was over I had learned all her moods. If she lay flat on the diving board with her hand trailing idly in the water, she was pensive, not to be disturbed. On her side, her head propped up by her arm, she was observant, considering those around her with a look that seemed queenly
15 and severe. Sitting up, arms tucked around her long, suntanned legs, she was approachable, but barely, and it was only in those glorious moments when she stretched herself prior to entering the water that her various suitors found the courage to come near.

These were many. The Dartmouth heavyweight crew would scull by her
20 house on their way upriver, and I think all eight of them must have been in love with her at various times during the summer; the coxswain would curse at them through his megaphone but without effect—there was always a pause in their pace when they passed Sheila's float. I suppose to these jaded twenty-year-olds she seemed the incarnation of innocence and youth, while to me
25 she appeared unutterably suave, the epitome of sophistication. I was on the swim team at school, and to win her attention would do endless laps between my house and the Vermont shore, hoping she would notice the beauty of my flutter kick, the power of my crawl. Finishing, I would boost myself up onto our dock and glance casually over toward her, but she was never watching, and
30 the miraculous day she was, I immediately climbed the diving board and did my best tuck and a half for her, and continued diving until she had left and the sun went down and my longing was like a madness and I couldn't stop.

Close Read

1. The exposition transports you into the world of the story. What do you learn about the setting in lines 1–8? Describe the mood that the setting details help to create.

2. What does the boxed text reveal about the narrator's personality?

3. Consider the description of Sheila in lines 9–18 and the narrator's eagerness to impress her. What do you think the main conflict will be about?

Part 3: Analyze the Text
Close Read

1. *Possible answer: The setting is summer in a New England town near a river. It seems like a town with a lot of frequent vacationers who rent cottages (lines 1–3). The mood is easygoing, yet energetic and lighthearted.*

   IF STUDENTS NEED HELP . . . Draw attention to these and other details that suggest an easygoing, lighthearted mood: "the only creature that seemed lovelier to me than a largemouth bass" (lines 1–2), "denizens of a brilliant existence" (lines 4–5), "'Too noisy by half'" (line 5), and "stare enchanted at the candlelit swirl of white dresses and bright, paisley skirts" (lines 7–8).

2. *Possible answer: The boxed text shows that the narrator really cares what Sheila thinks of him. He seems both pathetically hopeful and insecure.*

3. *Possible answer: The main conflict will probably have something do to with the narrator trying to impress or date Sheila, who may ignore or rebuff him. The conflict will pit the narrator's eager interest in Sheila against her apparent disinterest in everything.*

FOR ENGLISH LANGUAGE LEARNERS

Vocabulary: Word Associations In a group, create a Cluster Diagram with *Water Activities* in the center circle. As students read the story, identify and briefly define terms associated with activities that take place on the water. Then cluster them according to whether they relate to boating, fishing, or swimming and diving:

boating: *crew, scull* (line 19); *coxswain* (line 21); *canoe* (line 52); *bow* (line 56); *paddling* (line 66); **fishing:** *bass* (line 2); *Mitchell reel* (line 59); *Pfleuger spinning rod* (line 60); *casts* (line 63); *line, drag* (line 64); *Rapala plug* (line 68); *worms* (line 107); *lure* (line 118); *spool* (line 121); **swimming and diving:** *laps* (line 26); *flutter kick, crawl* (line 28); *diving board* (line 30); *tuck and a half* (line 31)

BEST PRACTICES TOOLKIT—Transparency
Cluster Diagram p. B18

4. Possible answer: *The narrator finally gets enough nerve to ask Sheila out for the following evening. This makes the story more compelling because readers anticipate the date and wonder what will happen next.*

5. Possible answer: *Again, readers see the narrator's eagerness to impress Sheila. He seems like a considerate person, especially since he arranges the cushions in a way he thinks will be to Sheila's liking (line 56). Readers also learn that the narrator likes to fish and seems serious about his hobby (lines 59–65).*

6. Possible answer: *The mood becomes more peaceful and romantic than the bustling-with-energy summer afternoon scene in the first paragraph of the story.*

t was late August by the time I got up the nerve to ask her out. The tortured will-I's, won't-I's, the agonized indecision over what to say, the false starts toward her house and embarrassed retreats—the details of these have been seared from my memory, and the only part I remember clearly is emerging from the woods toward dusk while they were playing softball on their lawn, as bashful and frightened as a unicorn.

Sheila was stationed halfway between first and second, well outside the infield. She didn't seem surprised to see me—as a matter of fact, she didn't seem to see me at all.

"If you're playing second base, you should move closer," I said.

She turned—I took the full brunt of her long red hair and well-spaced freckles.

"I'm playing outfield," she said, "I don't like the responsibility of having a base."

"Yeah, I can understand that," I said, though I couldn't. "There's a band in Dixford tomorrow night at nine. Want to go?"

One of her brothers sent the ball sailing over the leftfielder's head; she stood and watched it disappear toward the river.

"You have a car?" she said, without looking up.

I played my master stroke. "We'll go by canoe."

I spent all of the following day polishing it. I turned it upside down on our lawn and rubbed every inch with Brillo, hosing off the dirt, wiping it with chamois until it gleamed as bright as aluminum ever gleamed. About five, I slid it into the water, arranging cushions near the bow so Sheila could lean on them if she was in one of her pensive moods, propping up my father's transistor radio by the middle thwart so we could have music when we came back. Automatically, without thinking about it, I mounted my Mitchell reel on my Pflueger spinning rod and stuck it in the stern.

I say automatically, because I never went anywhere that summer without a fishing rod. When I wasn't swimming laps to impress Sheila, I was back in our driveway practicing casts, and when I wasn't practicing casts, I was tying the line to Tosca, our springer spaniel, to test the reel's drag, and when I wasn't doing any of those things, I was fishing the river for bass.

Too nervous to sit at home, I got in the canoe early and started paddling in a huge circle that would get me to Sheila's dock around eight. As automatically as I brought along my rod, I tied on a big Rapala plug, let it down into the water, let out some line and immediately forgot all about it.

It was already dark by the time I glided up to the Mants' dock. Even by day the river was quiet, most of the summer people preferring Sunapee or one of the other nearby lakes, and at night it was a solitude difficult to believe, a corridor of hidden life that ran between banks like a tunnel. Even the stars were part of it. They weren't as sharp anywhere else; they seemed to have chosen the river as a guide on their slow wheel toward morning, and in the course of the summer's fishing, I had learned all their names.

I was there ten minutes before Sheila appeared. I heard the slam of their screen door first, then saw her in the spotlight as she came slowly down the path. As beautiful as she was on the float, she was even lovelier now—her

Close Read

4. In lines 33–48, the narrator makes a decision that sets the rising action in motion. Explain what his decision is. How does this scene make the story more compelling?

5. Reread lines 53–65. What more do you learn about the narrator and the kind of person he is?

6. Compare the description of the setting in the boxed text with that in the first paragraph of the story. How has the mood changed?

DIFFERENTIATED INSTRUCTION

FOR STRUGGLING READERS

Vocabulary Support Point out these words from the story. Have students read the context for each word and try to determine its approximate meaning.

- *indecision* (line 34), "uncertainty, not being sure"

- *chamois* (line 55), "cloth or towel"

- *dubious* (line 83), "doubtful, unconvinced"

- *antipathy* (line 106), "dislike"

- *surreptitiously* (line 113), "secretly"

- *concussion* (line 133), "blow or strike"

- *luminous* (line 181), "shining"

- *irretrievably* (line 190), "forever"

80 white dress went perfectly with her hair, and complimented her figure even
more than her swimsuit.

It was her face that bothered me. It had on its delightful fullness a very
dubious expression.

"Look," she said. "I can get Dad's car."

85 "It's faster this way," I lied. "Parking's tense up there. Hey, it's safe. I won't
tip it or anything."

She let herself down reluctantly into the bow. I was glad she wasn't facing me.
When her eyes were on me, I felt like diving in the river again from agony and joy.

I pried the canoe away from the dock and started paddling upstream. There

90 was an extra paddle in the bow, but Sheila made no move to pick it up. She
took her shoes off, and dangled her feet over the side.

Ten minutes went by.

"What kind of band?" she said.

"It's sort of like folk music. You'll like it."

95 "Eric Caswell's going to be there. He strokes number four."

"No kidding?" I said. I had no idea who she meant.

"What's that sound?" she said, pointing toward shore.

"Bass. That splashing sound?"

"Over there."

100 "Yeah, bass. They come into the shallows at night to chase frogs and moths
and things. Big largemouths. *Micropetrus salmonides*," I added, showing off.

"I think fishing's dumb," she said, making a face. "I mean, it's boring and
all. Definitely dumb."

Now I have spent a great deal of time in the years since wondering why
Sheila Mant should come down so hard on fishing. Was her father a
fisherman? Her antipathy toward fishing nothing more than normal
filial rebellion? Had she tried it once? A messy encounter with worms? It
doesn't matter. What does, is that at that fragile moment in time I would have
given anything not to appear dumb in Sheila's severe and unforgiving eyes.

110 She hadn't seen my equipment yet. What I *should* have done, of course,
was push the canoe in closer to shore and carefully slide the rod into some
branches where I could pick it up again in the morning. Failing that, I could
have surreptitiously dumped the whole outfit overboard, written off the forty
or so dollars as love's tribute. What I actually *did* do was gently lean forward,

115 and slowly, ever so slowly, push the rod back through my legs toward the stern
where it would be less conspicuous.

It must have been just exactly what the bass was waiting for. Fish will trail
a lure sometimes, trying to make up their mind whether or not to attack, and
the slight pause in the plug's speed caused by my adjustment was tantalizing

120 enough to overcome the bass's inhibitions. My rod, safely out of sight at last,
bent double. The line, tightly coiled, peeled off the spool with the shrill,
tearing zip of a high-speed drill.

Close Read

7. Describe Sheila's
personality. In what
ways does her attitude
create conflicts for the
narrator?

Close Read

7. *Possible answer:* *Sheila is inconsiderate and
rude. Her attitude creates conflicts for the
narrator because he has to try even harder
to impress someone who is not impressed
by anything and who is even revolted by the
narrator's other love: fishing (lines 102–103).*

IF STUDENTS NEED HELP . . . Remind students that Sheila's personality is revealed
by how she looks, what she says and does,
and by how other characters react to her.
Have students identify such details in lines
82–109. After a few have been found, ask
what type of person such an appearance or
action suggests.

FOR STRUGGLING READERS

Analysis Support: Plot Redraw the simple
Plot Diagram that you created on page 30.
Point out the rising action, explaining that
some people see this as a series of steps.
Have students think about what is happening in the story that creates a rising tension.
Ask them to identify at least three details
that are part of the rising action. ***Possible
answer:*** *Sheila says that fishing is dumb; the
narrator wonders what to do with the gear;
the fish bites; a loud noise results.*

FOR ENGLISH LANGUAGE LEARNERS

Language: Punctuation Direct students'
attention to the dialogue in lines 84–103.
Explain that the words inside quotation
marks are the words that a character says.
Each time a new speaker begins to talk, a
new paragraph begins. Ask students to find
examples of the speaker changing even
when the speaker is not identified (lines 94
and 95, lines 98 and 99).

8. Possible answer: *The narrator hooks a huge bass on his line, and he cannot let Sheila know about it.*

9. Possible answer: *The cutting back and forth between the narrator's struggle with the fish and Sheila's talking prolongs the suspense of the situation. Readers continue to wonder how the narrator will catch the bass and how he will manage to keep Sheila in the dark about his predicament. This is similar to the suspenseful situations featured in some action movies.*

10. Possible answer: *The river is slow and difficult to paddle, and the narrator realizes that he will encounter rocks, a shallow sandbar, and weeds—obstacles that could potentially sever the bass from his line.*

Four things occurred to me at once. One, that it was a bass. Two, that it was a big bass. Three, that it was the biggest bass I had ever hooked. Four, that
125 Sheila Mant must not know.

"What was that?" she said, half turning around.

"Uh, what was what?"

"That buzzing noise."

"Bats."

130 She shuddered, quickly drew her feet back into the canoe. Every instinct I had told me to pick up the rod and strike back at the bass, but there was no need to—it was already solidly hooked. Downstream, an awesome distance downstream, it jumped clear of the water, landing with a concussion heavy enough to ripple the entire river. For a moment, I thought it was gone, but then
135 the rod was bending again, the tip dancing into the water. Slowly, not making any motion that might alert Sheila, I reached down to tighten the drag.

While all this was going on, Sheila had begun talking and it was a few minutes before I was able to catch up with her train of thought.

"I went to a party there. These fraternity men. Katherine says I could get
140 in there if I wanted. I'm thinking more of UVM or Bennington. Somewhere I can ski."

The bass was slanting toward the rocks on the New Hampshire side by the ruins of Donaldson's boathouse. It had to be an old bass—a young one probably wouldn't have known the rocks were there. I brought the canoe back
145 out into the middle of the river, hoping to head it off.

"That's neat," I mumbled. "Skiing. Yeah, I can see that."

"Eric said I have the figure to model, but I thought I should get an education first. I mean, it might be a while before I get started and all. I was thinking of getting my hair styled, more swept back? I mean, Ann-Margret?
150 Like hers, only shorter."

She hesitated. "Are we going backwards?"

We were. I had managed to keep the bass in the middle of the river away from the rocks, but it had plenty of room there, and for the first time a chance to exert its full strength. I quickly computed the weight necessary to draw a
155 fully loaded canoe backwards—the thought of it made me feel faint.

"It's just the current," I said hoarsely. "No sweat or anything."

I dug in deeper with my paddle. Reassured, Sheila began talking about something else, but all my attention was taken up now with the fish. I could feel its desperation as the water grew shallower. I could sense the extra strain
160 on the line, the frantic way it cut back and forth in the water. I could visualize what it looked like—the gape of its mouth, the flared gills and thick, vertical tail. The bass couldn't have encountered many forces in its long life that it wasn't capable of handling, and the unrelenting tug at its mouth must have been a source of great puzzlement and mounting panic.

165 Me, I had problems of my own. To get to Dixford, I had to paddle up a sluggish stream that came into the river beneath a covered bridge. There was a shallow sandbar at the mouth of this stream—weeds on one side, rocks on the other. Without doubt, this is where I would lose the fish.

8. In lines 123–125, the main conflict comes into sharp focus. What is the narrator's conflict?

9. In the rising action, the story cuts back and forth between the narrator's struggle with the fish and Sheila's incessant talking. How does this heighten the **suspense**?

10. Reread lines 165–168. What conflicts are created by the setting?

DIFFERENTIATED INSTRUCTION

FOR STRUGGLING READERS

Comprehension To help students visualize the developing conflict, draw a large zigzag line across the board. For each peak, have students identify some detail of the narrator's interactions with Sheila. For each low point, have students identify some detail of the narrator's interaction with the fish.

FOR ENGLISH LANGUAGE LEARNERS

Vocabulary: Idioms Help students use context clues and tone to determine the meanings of these idioms: *got up the nerve* (line 33), "gained enough courage"; *showing off* (line 101), "trying to attract attention"; *No sweat* (line 156), "Do not worry"; *threw me off* (line 174), "confused me"; *There would be other Sheila Mants* (line 210), "I would meet other girls."

"I have to be careful with my complexion. I tan, but in segments. I can't
170 figure out if it's even worth it. I wouldn't even do it probably. I saw Jackie
Kennedy in Boston and she wasn't tan at all."

Taking a deep breath, I paddled as hard as I could for the middle, deepest
part of the bar. I could have threaded the eye of a needle with the canoe, but
the pull on the stern threw me off and I overcompensated—the canoe veered
175 left and scraped bottom. I pushed the paddle down and shoved. A moment of
hesitation . . . a moment more. . . . The canoe shot clear into the deeper water
of the stream. I immediately looked down at the rod. It was bent in the same,
tight arc—miraculously, the bass was still on.

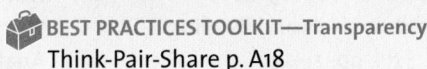

The moon was out now. It was low and full enough that its beam shone
180 directly on Sheila there ahead of me in the canoe, washing her in a
creamy, luminous glow. I could see the lithe, easy shape of her figure. I
could see the way her hair curled down off her shoulders, the proud, alert
tilt of her head, and all these things were as a tug on my heart. Not just Sheila,
but the aura she carried about her of parties and casual touchings and grace.
185 Behind me, I could feel the strain of the bass, steadier now, growing weaker,
and this was another tug on my heart, not just the bass but the beat of the river
and the slant of the stars and the smell of the night, until finally it seemed I
would be torn apart between longings, split in half. Twenty yards ahead of us
was the road, and once I pulled the canoe up on shore, the bass would be gone,
190 irretrievably gone. If instead I stood up, grabbed the rod and started pumping,
I would have it—as tired as the bass was, there was no chance it could get away.
I reached down for the rod, hesitated, looked up to where Sheila was stretching
herself lazily toward the sky, her small breasts rising beneath the soft fabric of
her dress, and the tug was too much for me, and quicker than it takes to write
195 down, I pulled a penknife from my pocket and cut the line in half.

With a sick, nauseous feeling in my stomach, I saw the rod unbend.

"My legs are sore," Sheila whined. "Are we there yet?"

Through a superhuman effort of self-control, I was able to beach the canoe and
help Sheila off. The rest of the night is much foggier. We walked to the fair—there
200 was the smell of popcorn, the sound of guitars. I may have danced once or twice
with her, but all I really remember is her coming over to me once the music was
done to explain that she would be going home in Eric Caswell's Corvette.

"Okay," I mumbled.

For the first time that night she looked at me, really looked at me.

205 "You're a funny kid, you know that?"

Funny. Different. Dreamy. Odd. How many times was I to hear that in the
years to come, all spoken with the same quizzical, half-accusatory tone Sheila
used then. Poor Sheila! Before the month was over, the spell she cast over me
was gone, but the memory of that lost bass haunted me all summer and haunts
210 me still. There would be other Sheila Mants in my life, other fish, and though
I came close once or twice, it was these secret, hidden tuggings in the night
that claimed me, and I never made the same mistake again.

Close Read

11. Lines 179–195 mark the
story's climax. Explain
what the narrator finally
chooses to do. Given his
thoughts and actions
in earlier scenes, is this
outcome believable?
Explain.

12. The falling action
(lines 196–205) shows
what happens after
the narrator makes his
choice. What are the
effects of his decision?

13. In the resolution (lines
206–212), the narrator,
now older, reflects on
his actions. What lesson
has he learned from his
experience?

FOR ENGLISH LANGUAGE LEARNERS

Vocabulary: Multiple-Meaning Words
Write these words from the story on the
board: *band* (line 47), *line* (line 195), and
funny (line 205). Have students find these
words in dictionaries and then work in pairs
to determine which meaning best fits the
context in the story. Ask volunteers to read
the meaning they chose. As a group, determine if the meaning is correct.

Close Read

11. *Possible answer:* The narrator chooses to
cut the bass loose; he chooses the girl over
the fish. Some students may be surprised,
because the narrator has put so much effort
into reeling in the bass. Others may say
that his decision was not surprising given
his strong feelings for Sheila.

12. *Possible answer:* The narrator and Sheila go
to the fair, where they dance once or twice.
Later, Sheila leaves the narrator to go home
with Eric Caswell. She tells the narrator that
he is a "funny kid."

13. *Possible answer:* Looking back, the narrator
realizes that he made a mistake by choosing
Sheila over the bass. He explains that his
interest in her faded quickly, but his regret
over the lost bass has haunted him over
the years.

Assess and Reteach

Assess

Have students summarize "The Bass, the River,
and Sheila Mant" by identifying exposition,
especially setting and mood, conflict, rising
action, climax, falling action, and resolution.

Reteach

*For students who are unable to apply the work-
shop skills to "The Bass, the River, and Sheila
Mant," select from these reteaching options:*

- Display a blank note-taking copy master
for this lesson.

  1. Ask students which parts were hard to
  complete. Focus instruction on only those
  parts.

  2. Have teams of students take turns
  identifying details for sections on the copy
  masters. Have one group suggest details.
  Then have another group either confirm
  the choice or offer an alternative.

- Have partners answer as many of the
questions from page 30 as possible, using
Think-Pair-Share to respond.

BEST PRACTICES TOOLKIT—Transparency
Think-Pair-Share p. A18

Focus and Motivate

COMMON CORE FOCUS

RL 1 Cite textual evidence to support analysis of what the text says explicitly as well as inferences drawn from the text. **RL 3** Analyze how complex characters develop over the course of a text, interact with other characters, and advance the plot. **L 3** Apply knowledge of language to make effective choices for meaning or style. **L 4c** Consult reference materials to determine or clarify a word's meaning or etymology. **L 5** Demonstrate understanding of word relationships.

SUMMARY

"Harrison Bergeron" is set in the United States in 2081, when laws require everyone to be average or handicapped into average sameness. One day, tall, brilliant 14-year-old Harrison Bergeron is arrested. He escapes and storms a TV studio. Removing his handicaps, he declares himself Emperor but is killed by authorities.

What if everyone were THE SAME?

Have students discuss the idea of an average society. After students complete the *BRAIN-STORM,* have them consider what sameness and diversity contribute to the world.

Essential Course of Study ECOS

Harrison Bergeron
Short Story by Kurt Vonnegut Jr.

What if everyone were THE SAME?

COMMON CORE

RL 1 Cite textual evidence to support analysis of what the text says explicitly as well as inferences drawn from the text. **RL 3** Analyze how complex characters develop over the course of a text, interact with other characters, and advance the plot. **L 5** Demonstrate understanding of word relationships.

What would the world be like if everyone were the same—average in intelligence, talents, appearance, and strength—and no one was better than anyone else? How do you think people would feel and act toward each other? Would they be happy and satisfied?

BRAINSTORM With your class, brainstorm possible advantages and disadvantages of a world where everyone is the same—exactly average. Try to generate as many ideas as possible.

Advantages	Disadvantages
no more jealousy	nothing to live up to

36

Selection Resources

See resources on the **Teacher One Stop DVD-ROM** *and on* **thinkcentral.com**.

 RESOURCE MANAGER UNIT 1
Plan and Teach, pp. 11–18
Summary, pp. 19–20†‡*
Text Analysis and Reading
 Skill, pp. 21–24†*
Vocabulary, pp. 25–27*
Grammar and Style, p. 30

DIAGNOSTIC AND SELECTION TESTS
Selection Tests, pp. 23–26

 BEST PRACTICES TOOLKIT
Definition Mapping, p. E6
New Word Analysis, p. E8
Story Map, p. D14
Analysis Frame, pp. D21, D32

INTERACTIVE READER

ADAPTED INTERACTIVE READER

ELL ADAPTED INTERACTIVE READER

TECHNOLOGY
⊘ **Teacher One Stop DVD-ROM**
⊘ **Student One Stop DVD-ROM**
⊘ **Audio Anthology CD**
⊘ **GrammarNotes DVD-ROM**
⊘ **Audio Tutor CD**
⊘ **ExamView Test Generator** on the Teacher One Stop

Find it Online!
Features on **thinkcentral.com** that support the selection include
• **PowerNotes** presentation
• **ThinkAloud** models to enhance comprehension
• **WordSharp** vocabulary tutorials
• interactive writing and grammar instruction

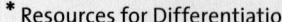

* Resources for Differentiation   † Also in Spanish   ‡ In Haitian Creole and Vietnamese

TEXT ANALYSIS: PLOT AND CONFLICT

The plot of a story is driven by a **conflict,** or struggle between opposing forces. In some stories, the conflict is between the main character and society. In "Harrison Bergeron," for example, the title character struggles with U.S. society in the year 2081. As you read, notice ways in which Harrison and the government oppose each other. Follow events to see who prevails.

READING SKILL: DRAW CONCLUSIONS

When you **draw conclusions,** you make judgments based on story details and your own prior knowledge. Use the following strategies to draw conclusions about the society depicted in "Harrison Bergeron":

- Note what results from the society's practices and laws.
- Apply your own knowledge to speculate about the motives of its officials.

As you read "Harrison Bergeron," use a chart like the one shown to make notes about the society. Also include your own thoughts or reactions about the information.

Details About Society	My Reactions
Constitutional amendments make everyone equal in every way.	It would be hard to enforce equality.
My Overall Conclusions	

▲ VOCABULARY IN CONTEXT

Vonnegut uses the following words in relating his futuristic tale. To see how many words you already know, substitute a different word or phrase for each boldfaced term. Write your answers in your *Reader/Writer Notebook.*

1. **vigilance** with the children crossing the street
2. **wince** in pain after the injection
3. filled with **consternation** at the thought
4. **cower** in the corner
5. **synchronize** our watches
6. **neutralizing** the impact

 Complete the activities in your **Reader/Writer Notebook.**

Meet the Author

Kurt Vonnegut Jr.
1922–2007

Serious Humor
Kurt Vonnegut Jr. was one of the most acclaimed satiric writers in America. After working briefly as a journalist, he began writing short stories in the late 1940s and continued writing stories, novels, dramas, and essays for more than 50 years. His fiction deals with sobering topics—war, brutality, and fear of technology. But Vonnegut writes with dark humor and elements of fantasy and even absurdity, which have given his writing lasting appeal.

Voice of Experience
During World War II, Vonnegut was held as a prisoner of war in Dresden, Germany. The city was leveled by a fierce firebombing, and the destruction and horror of that event became the focus of his most famous novel, *Slaughterhouse Five.* Vonnegut wrote in a preface to the novel that it was about "the inhumanity of many of man's inventions to man." Vonnegut's early work was not well received by critics, but since the 1970s he has been regarded as a major American writer.

BACKGROUND TO THE STORY
What's Your Handicap?
If you have ever run a footrace or played golf, you might know the sports term *handicap.* It refers to a way to even up a game so that good, average, and poor players can compete as equals. In a footrace, for example, faster runners might handicap themselves by giving slower runners a head start. In "Harrison Bergeron," people are given handicaps in daily life so that no one will be any stronger, smarter, or better looking than anyone else.

Author Online
THINK central
Go to **thinkcentral.com.**
KEYWORD: HML10-37

37

Teach

TEXT ANALYSIS COMMON CORE RL 3

● *Model the Skill:* **PLOT AND CONFLICT**

To model how to identify conflicts in a story, point out that a conflict can be either physical or psychological. It can be within a character, between characters, or between a character and an outside force. Ask what conflict might arise between a genius and a government that wants everyone to be average. Point out that the government might try to take away the genius's special gifts or hurt the genius.

GUIDED PRACTICE Have students identify conflicts in other stories.

READING SKILL COMMON CORE RL 1

■ *Model the Skill:* **DRAW CONCLUSIONS**

Have students read the text under **Serious Humor** and **Voice of Experience**. Then point out that Vonnegut experienced the war firsthand. Ask them to draw a conclusion as to why Vonnegut may have chosen to write a novel about World War II.

GUIDED PRACTICE Have students read the text under **What's Your Handicap?** Ask what they might conclude about a golfer with a huge handicap.

R RESOURCE MANAGER—Copy Master Draw Conclusions p. 23

VOCABULARY SKILL

COMMON CORE L 4

▲ VOCABULARY IN CONTEXT

DIAGNOSE WORD KNOWLEDGE Have all students complete Vocabulary in Context. Check their words and phrases against the following:

consternation (kŏn′stər-nā′shən) *n.* confused amazement or fear
cower (kou′ər) *v.* to crouch down in fear
synchronize (sĭng′krə-nīz′) *v.* to match the timing of
neutralize (nōō′trə-līz′) *v.* to counteract or cancel the effect of

vigilance (vĭj′ə-ləns) *n.* alert attention, watchfulness
wince (wĭns) *v.* to shrink or flinch involuntarily, especially in pain

PRETEACH VOCABULARY Use the following copy master to help students use context clues to determine the meaning of each boldfaced word.

R RESOURCE MANAGER—Copy Master Vocabulary Study p. 25

1. Read item 1 aloud, emphasizing *vigilance.*
2. Point out "so they seldom broke laws" and "the government was watching." Elicit possible meanings for *vigilance,* such as "watchfulness" or "alertness."
3. Repeat the procedure for items 2–6.

READ WITH A PURPOSE

Help students set a purpose for reading. Tell them to look for ways in which Harrison differs from his parents, especially his father, as they read the story.

READING SKILL   COMMON CORE
                                     RL 1

A *Model the Skill:* **DRAW CONCLUSIONS**

Model for students how to draw conclusions. Have students reread lines 1–17 and identify details that describe society in 2081. Have them record the details in their Details About Society charts. Then ask students how they think this society might treat someone who was not average.

Possible answer: *Specific details include: Laws require conformity (lines 4–6, 14–15), and this is maintained even in private homes (lines 15–17). The government requires that intelligent people wear government transmitters, which limit their ability to think (lines 15–17). This society is repressive and intrusive. It took away the Bergerons' young son (lines 9–10).*

VOCABULARY   COMMON CORE
                                  L 4

OWN THE WORD

vigilance: Tell students that *vigilance* is a noun and that the adjective form is *vigilant.* Then ask students to name times when they would be most *vigilant.* How might they show *vigilance*? Why is it necessary to be *vigilant*?

Possible answers: *in a crowd, away from home, when surrounded by strangers; watch people around them carefully, hold tight to their belongings; to prevent physical harm or theft.*

Harrison Bergeron

Kurt Vonnegut Jr.

The year was 2081, and everybody was finally equal. They weren't only equal before God and the law. They were equal every which way. Nobody was smarter than anybody else. Nobody was better looking than anybody else. Nobody was stronger or quicker than anybody else. All this equality was due to the 211th, 212th, and 213th Amendments to the Constitution, and to the unceasing **vigilance** of agents of the United States Handicapper General.

Some things about living still weren't quite right, though. April, for instance, still drove people crazy by not being springtime. And it was in that clammy month that the H-G men took George and Hazel Bergeron's fourteen-year-old 10 son, Harrison, away.

It was tragic, all right, but George and Hazel couldn't think about it very hard. Hazel had a perfectly average intelligence, which meant she couldn't think about anything except in short bursts. And George, while his intelligence was way above normal, had a little mental handicap radio in his ear. He was required by law to wear it at all times. It was tuned to a government transmitter.[1] Every twenty seconds or so, the transmitter would send out some sharp noise to keep people like George from taking unfair advantage of their brains. **A**

George and Hazel were watching television. There were tears on Hazel's cheeks, but she'd forgotten for the moment what they were about.

20 On the television screen were ballerinas.

A buzzer sounded in George's head. His thoughts fled in panic, like bandits from a burglar alarm.

"That was a real pretty dance, that dance they just did," said Hazel.

"Huh?" said George.

"That dance—it was nice," said Hazel.

"Yup," said George. He tried to think a little about the ballerinas. They weren't really very good—no better than anybody else would have been, anyway. They were burdened with sashweights[2] and bags of birdshot,[3] and

vigilance (vĭj′ə-ləns) *n.* alert attention, watchfulness

1 Targeted Passage

A DRAW CONCLUSIONS
Reread lines 1–17. Cite specific details that describe society in 2081. What is your opinion of the society so far?

Analyze Visuals ▶

Examine the image of the television announcer and the picture behind him. What does this painting suggest about television?

---

1. **transmitter:** an electronic device for broadcasting radio signals.
2. **sashweights:** lead weights used in some kinds of windows to keep them from falling shut when raised.
3. **birdshot:** tiny lead pellets made to be loaded in shotgun shells.

Detail of *TVTime-Announcer* (2002), Charles Foster-Hall. Acrylic on canvas, 16" × 20", 41cm x 51 cm. © Charles Foster-Hall.

DIFFERENTIATED INSTRUCTION

FOR ENGLISH LANGUAGE LEARNERS

Vocabulary Support Use Definition Mapping to teach these words: "amendments" (line 5), "intelligence" (line 12), "normal" (line 14), "mental" (line 14), "required" (line 14).

BEST PRACTICES TOOLKIT—Transparency Definition Mapping p. E6

FOR STRUGGLING READERS

In combination with the *Audio Anthology* CD, use one or more Targeted Passages (pp. 38, 41, 43, 44) to ensure that students focus on key story events, concepts, and skills. Targeted Passages are also good for English learners.

1 Targeted Passage [Lines 7–28]

This passage introduces the conflict of the story and the main characters.

• What happens to Harrison Bergeron, and how do his parents react? (lines 9–12)

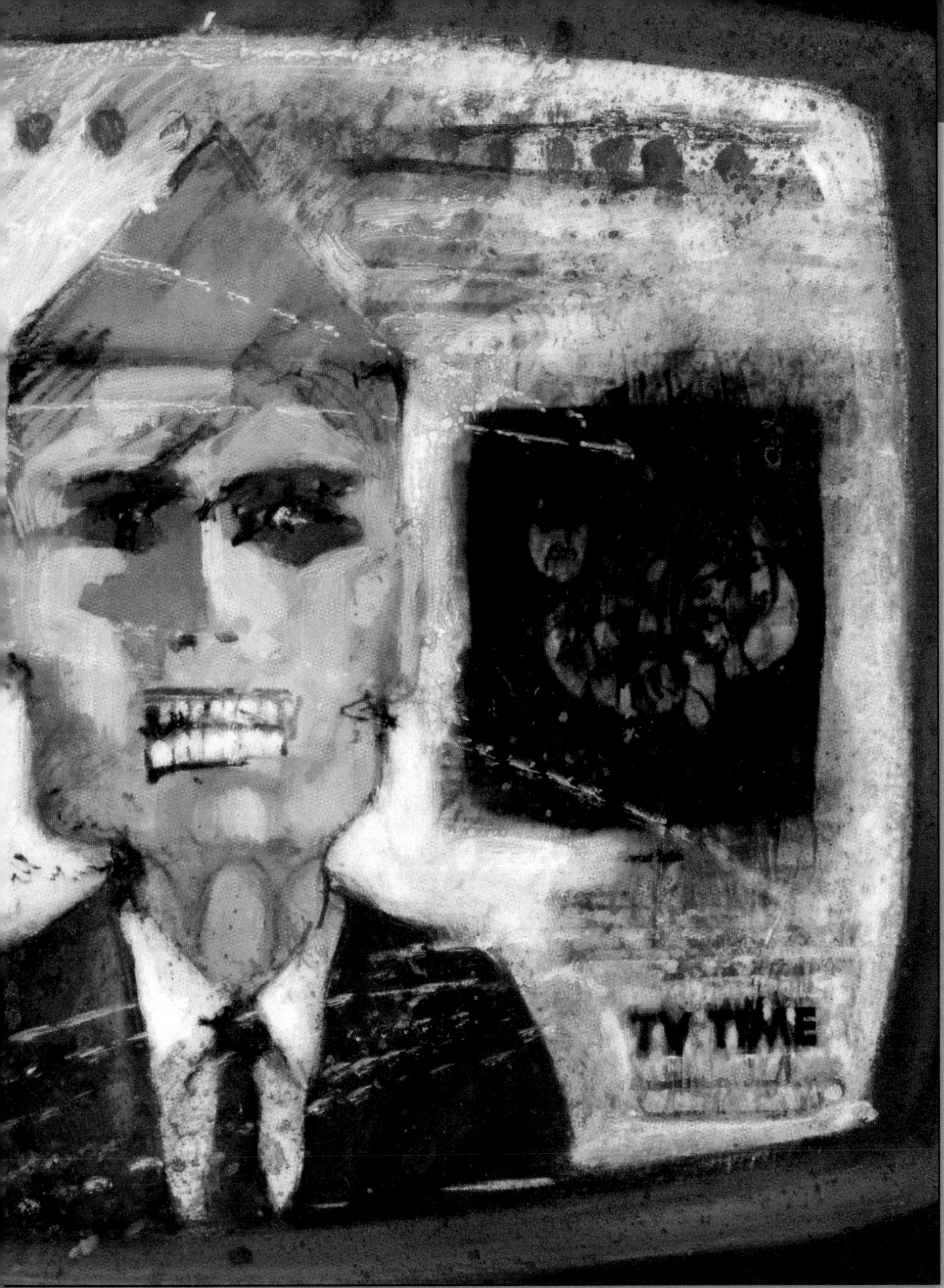

BACKGROUND

Utopian Society This story describes an attempt to create a Utopian, or perfect, society in the United States by abolishing all kinds of competition. For centuries, writers have described perfect societies: Plato wrote about one in *Republic*. The word *Utopian* comes from Sir Thomas More's book *Utopia*. George Orwell and Aldous Huxley both wrote famous satires on Utopian societies. This story is written in the same tradition.

Analyze Visuals

Possible answer: The announcer's strained face and gritted teeth suggest tension, and the triangular cap makes him appear to be either a puppet or a dunce. The graphics beside him are dark, murky, and confused, suggesting that the content of the television show is the same. The blurred lines create a barrier between the viewer and the announcer.

About the Art Contemporary artist Charles Foster-Hall was born in the United Kingdom, where he studied art, science, and engineering. He went on to Paris to study art, and he now lives in New York. He painted *TVTime-Announcer* in 2002. It is from a series of paintings called *TVTime*.

REVISIT THE BIG QUESTION

What if everyone were
THE SAME?

Discuss Based on lines 14–28, What does the government do to people who are above average in some way? *Possible answer: It handicaps them. George is considered to have above-average intelligence and is forced to wear a mental handicap radio (line 14). The ballerinas are "burdened with sashweights and bags of birdshot" (line 28) so that they are average.*

- What makes George and Hazel equal? (lines 4–6)
- Why does George have to try "to think a little about the ballerinas"? What do you think will happen to him as he is thinking? (lines 13–17)

FOR ADVANCED LEARNERS/PRE–AP

Make Judgments Begin a class discussion by asking students to think about how much control a government should have in the lives of its citizens. What controls are appropriate? When does the role of government go too far? Encourage students to use specific examples when expressing their opinions.

B DRAW CONCLUSIONS

Possible answer: *The society allows the government to disrupt people's thoughts by blasting them with noise (line 32). It does not allow people, like ballerinas, to be any better than anybody else. It makes them wear "sashweights and bags of birdshot" (line 28).*

C PLOT AND CONFLICT

Possible answer: *George thinks about his "abnormal son who was now in jail" (lines 51–52). Since above-average looks and abilities are considered abnormal and illegal by this government, Harrison was probably above average in some respects. Perhaps he was more attractive, more intelligent, or more talented than average.*

TIERED DISCUSSION PROMPTS

Direct students to lines 58–69. Use these prompts to help students think about George's plight:

Analyze What is ironic about Hazel's statement to George about not caring whether he is equal to her for a while? *Possible answer: Because Hazel is average, she cannot really ponder the meaning of that statement. She is not the one suffering like George is.*

Evaluate Do you think that George's situation is better or worse than Hazel's? *Students' responses should reflect whether it is better to have never known something or to have known and lost it.*

OWN THE WORD

wince: Tell students that the word *wince* refers to facial or body movements, such as grimacing or shuddering. Ask students to list situations that might cause them to *wince* as George did. *Possible answers: hearing bad news, having a cavity filled*

---

their faces were masked, so that no one, seeing a free and graceful gesture or a
30 pretty face, would feel like something the cat drug in. George was toying with
the vague notion that maybe dancers shouldn't be handicapped. But he didn't
get very far with it before another noise in his ear radio scattered his thoughts.

George winced. So did two out of the eight ballerinas.

Hazel saw him **wince.** Having no mental handicap herself, she had to ask
George what the latest sound had been.

"Sounded like somebody hitting a milk bottle with a ball peen hammer,"[4]
said George.

"I'd think it would be real interesting, hearing all the different sounds," said
Hazel, a little envious. "All the things they think up."

40 "Um," said George. B

"Only, if I was Handicapper General, you know what I would do?" said
Hazel. Hazel, as a matter of fact, bore a strong resemblance to the Handicapper
General, a woman named Diana Moon Glampers. "If I was Diana Moon
Glampers," said Hazel, "I'd have chimes on Sunday—just chimes. Kind of in
honor of religion."

"I could think, if it was just chimes," said George.

"Well—maybe make 'em real loud," said Hazel. "I think I'd make a good
Handicapper General."

"Good as anybody else," said George.

50 "Who knows better'n I do what normal is?" said Hazel.

"Right," said George. He began to think glimmeringly about his abnormal
son who was now in jail, about Harrison, but a twenty-one-gun salute in his
head stopped that. C

"Boy!" said Hazel, "that was a doozy, wasn't it?"

It was such a doozy that George was white and trembling, and tears stood
on the rims of his red eyes. Two of the eight ballerinas had collapsed to the
studio floor and were holding their temples.

"All of a sudden you look so tired," said Hazel. "Why don't you stretch out
on the sofa, so's you can rest your handicap bag on the pillows, honeybunch."
60 She was referring to the forty-seven pounds of birdshot in a canvas bag, which
was padlocked around George's neck. "Go on and rest the bag for a little
while," she said. "I don't care if you're not equal to me for a while."

George weighed the bag with his hands. "I don't mind it," he said. "I don't
notice it any more. It's just a part of me."

"You been so tired lately—kind of wore out," said Hazel. "If there was just
some way we could make a little hole in the bottom of the bag, and just take
out a few of them lead balls. Just a few."

"Two years in prison and two thousand dollars fine for every ball I took
out," said George. "I don't call that a bargain."

---

4. **ball peen hammer:** a hammer with a head having one flat side and one rounded side.

40 UNIT 1: PLOT, SETTING, AND MOOD

wince (wĭns) *v.* to shrink or flinch involuntarily, especially in pain

B DRAW CONCLUSIONS
How does the society affect the thoughts and reactions of the people? How does it influence their job performance?

C PLOT AND CONFLICT
George's thoughts reveal more about the conflict between Harrison and the society. On the basis of what you've read so far, what behavior do you think might be viewed as abnormal and illegal?

DIFFERENTIATED INSTRUCTION

FOR STRUGGLING READERS

Develop Reading Fluency Model for students an effective way to read the conversation between George and Hazel in lines 41–54. You might ask for a volunteer to read the dialog of one character while you read the other. Point out that the two characters often use nonstandard English when they talk. Then have pairs of students practice reading the dialogue aloud together.

 **RESOURCE MANAGER—Copy Masters**
Reading Fluency p. 31

FOR ADVANCED LEARNERS/PRE–AP

Evaluate Explain to students that this story is a satire and is designed to arouse mocking laughter. Point out that Hazel is described as someone with average intelligence. Ask students to find statements that Hazel makes and explain how the author mocks what is "average" through these statements. Ask students to consider what point the author is trying to make about the society depicted.

70 "If you could just take a few out when you came home from work," said Hazel. "I mean—you don't compete with anybody around here. You just set around."

"If I tried to get away with it," said George, "then other people'd get away with it—and pretty soon we'd be right back to the dark ages again, with everybody competing against everybody else. You wouldn't like that, would you?"

"I'd hate it," said Hazel.

"There you are," said George. "The minute people start cheating on laws, what do you think happens to society?"

80 If Hazel hadn't been able to come up with an answer to this question, George couldn't have supplied one. A siren was going off in his head.

"Reckon it'd fall all apart," said Hazel.

"What would?" said George blankly.

"Society," said Hazel uncertainly. "Wasn't that what you just said?"

"Who knows?" said George. **D**

The television program was suddenly interrupted for a news bulletin. It wasn't clear at first as to what the bulletin was about, since the announcer, like all announcers, had a serious speech impediment.[5] For about half a minute, and in a state of high excitement, the announcer tried to say, "Ladies and

90 gentlemen—"

He finally gave up, handed the bulletin to a ballerina to read.

"That's all right—" Hazel said of the announcer, "he tried. That's the big thing. He tried to do the best he could with what God gave him. He should get a nice raise for trying so hard."

"Ladies and gentlemen—" said the ballerina, reading the bulletin. She must have been extraordinarily beautiful, because the mask she wore was hideous. And it was easy to see that she was the strongest and most graceful of all the dancers, for her handicap bags were as big as those worn by two-hundred-pound men.

100 And she had to apologize at once for her voice, which was a very unfair voice for a woman to use. Her voice was a warm, luminous, timeless melody. "Excuse me—" she said, and she began again, making her voice absolutely uncompetitive.

"Harrison Bergeron, age fourteen," she said in a grackle[6] squawk, "has just escaped from jail, where he was held on suspicion of plotting to overthrow the government. He is a genius and an athlete, is under-handicapped, and should be regarded as extremely dangerous." **E**

A police photograph of Harrison Bergeron was flashed on the screen—upside down, then sideways, upside down again, then right side up. The

---

5. **speech impediment** (ĭm-pĕd′ə-mənt): a physical defect that prevents a person from speaking normally.
6. **grackle:** a blackbird with a harsh, unpleasant call.

D DRAW CONCLUSIONS
Reread lines 68–85. What do you think of George's reasons for not lightening his handicap bag?

Language Coach
Antonyms Reread lines 95–96. An **antonym** is a word that means the opposite of another word. Which word in this sentence is an antonym for *beautiful*?

Targeted Passage

E PLOT AND CONFLICT
Here the **rising action** begins. What more do you learn about the conflict between Harrison and the society?

READING SKILL COMMON CORE

D DRAW CONCLUSIONS RL 1

Possible answer: George's reasons seem rational in some ways. He does not want to go to prison and be fined (lines 68–69). He also seems to be concerned about how the actions of lightening his bag might affect others (lines 73–75). But his reasons also show that he has resigned himself to the government's ways. He feels that the laws hold society together and make it pleasant for everyone (lines 73–79).

TEXT ANALYSIS COMMON CORE

E *Model the Skill:* PLOT AND CONFLICT RL 3

Model how to identify and understand the plot's conflict.

- Break the question into two separate parts. Have students first focus on Harrison and what they know about him.

- Then ask what the government says and does with its news bulletin.

Possible answer: Harrison "was held on suspicion of plotting to overthrow the government"; he is a genius, an athlete, and "under-handicapped" (line 106). The society treats him like a dangerous criminal. They interrupt television shows, flash his picture, and warn the population about him.

Extend the Discussion Is Harrison's relationship to the government similar to his parents' relationship to the government?

FOR STRUGGLING READERS

2 Targeted Passage [Lines 95–103]

This passage shows the relationship between natural attributes and handicaps, and it also shows how someone who is compliant behaves.

- How can you tell that she is the strongest and most graceful dancer? (lines 97–99)

- Why does she apologize for her voice? (lines 100–104)

FOR ENGLISH LANGUAGE LEARNERS

Language Coach COMMON CORE L5

Antonyms *Answer:* *hideous;* Have students reread lines 97–103. Ask students to name antonyms, or opposites, for the following words: "easy," "strongest," and "graceful" (line 97); "unfair" (line 100); and "warm" (line 101).

Possible answer: *The figures are white, almost featureless blobs, who stare with blank eyes at what is before them. Their passivity and lack of color reflect George's and Hazel's resigned acceptance of their lives as well as their sameness.*

About the Art This painting, like the one on page 39, is also from Charles Foster-Hall's series *TVTime*.

REVISIT THE BIG QUESTION

What if everyone were
THE SAME?

Discuss In lines 111–125, how does Harrison remain above average, even with handicaps? What is ironic about how Harrison looks as compared to the other handicapped people?
Possible answer: *He "had outgrown hindrances faster than the H-G men could think them up" (lines 113–114). He challenges the government to keep thinking up ways to make him average. Harrison looks above average in his handicaps. He looks like a "walking junkyard" (line 120).*

TEXT ANALYSIS	COMMON CORE
	RL 3

⑤ PLOT AND CONFLICT

Possible answer: *He has been handicapped because he is so above average. For example, he is seven feet tall (line 111) and good-looking (line 122).*

IF STUDENTS NEED HELP . . . Have students work together to complete a Two-Column Chart. Label column 1 "Harrison's Handicaps," and label column 2 "Designed to make average . . . ."

🛠 BEST PRACTICES TOOLKIT—Transparency Two-Column Chart p. A25

VOCABULARY	COMMON CORE
	L 4

OWN THE WORD

consternation: Have students make a list of situations that might lead to feelings of *consternation.*

TVTime 2 (2002), Charles Foster-Hall. Acrylic on canvas, 16″ × 28″, 41 cm x 72 cm. © Charles Foster-Hall.

110 picture showed the full length of Harrison against a background calibrated in feet and inches. He was exactly seven feet tall.

The rest of Harrison's appearance was Halloween and hardware. Nobody had ever born heavier handicaps. He had outgrown hindrances faster than the H-G men could think them up. Instead of a little ear radio for a mental handicap, he wore a tremendous pair of earphones, and spectacles with thick wavy lenses. The spectacles were intended to make him not only half blind, but to give him whanging headaches besides.

Scrap metal was hung all over him. Ordinarily, there was a certain symmetry, a military neatness to the handicaps issued to strong people, but
120 Harrison looked like a walking junkyard. In the race of life, Harrison carried three hundred pounds.

And to offset his good looks, the H-G men required that he wear at all times a red rubber ball for a nose, keep his eyebrows shaved off, and cover his even white teeth with black caps at snaggle-tooth random. ⑤

"If you see this boy," said the ballerina, "do not—I repeat, do not—try to reason with him."

There was the shriek of a door being torn from its hinges.

Screams and barking cries of **consternation** came from the television set. The photograph of Harrison Bergeron on the screen jumped again and again,
130 as though dancing to the tune of an earthquake.

▲ Analyze Visuals

How would you describe the figures watching television? How well do they represent George and Hazel?

⑤ **PLOT AND CONFLICT**
Why has Harrison been so handicapped by the government?

consternation
(kŏn'stər-nā'shən)
n. confused amazement or fear

DIFFERENTIATED INSTRUCTION

FOR ENGLISH LANGUAGE LEARNERS
Language: Compound Nouns Explain that a compound word is two or more words that are put together to form one. Point out the compound noun "background" (line 110). Have students try to figure out its meaning in context and by defining *back* and *ground*. Ask pairs to find other compound nouns in the text and try to define them in the same way ("earphones" [line 115]; "headaches" [line 117]; "junkyard" [line 120]; "earthquake" [line 130]).

FOR ADVANCED LEARNERS/PRE–AP
Analyze Humor Have pairs analyze Vonnegut's style to determine how he injects humor into this story. For example, point out to students that he uses alliteration ("Halloween", "hardware", "heavier handicaps"—lines 112–113) when describing Harrison. Ask pairs to find examples of hyperbole, imagery, irony, and other literary devices from the story. Have pairs share their examples with the class and explain what the humor adds to the story.

George Bergeron correctly identified the earthquake, and well he might have—for many was the time his own home had danced to the same crashing tune. "My God—" said George, "that must be Harrison!"

The realization was blasted from his mind instantly by the sound of an automobile collision in his head.

When George could open his eyes again, the photograph of Harrison was gone. A living, breathing Harrison filled the screen.

Clanking, clownish, and huge, Harrison stood in the center of the studio. **G** The knob of the uprooted studio door was still in his hand. Ballerinas,
140 technicians, musicians, and announcers **cowered** on their knees before him, expecting to die.

"I am the Emperor!" cried Harrison. "Do you hear? I am the Emperor! Everybody must do what I say at once!" He stamped his foot and the studio shook.

"Even as I stand here—" he bellowed, "crippled, hobbled, sickened—I am a greater ruler than any man who ever lived! Now watch me become what I *can* become!"

Harrison tore the straps of his handicap harness like wet tissue paper, tore straps guaranteed to support five thousand pounds.
150 Harrison's scrap-iron handicaps crashed to the floor.

Harrison thrust his thumbs under the bar of the padlock that secured his head harness. The bar snapped like celery. Harrison smashed his headphones and spectacles against the wall.

He flung away his rubber-ball nose, revealed a man that would have awed Thor, the god of thunder.

"I shall now select my Empress!" he said, looking down on the cowering people. "Let the first woman who dares rise to her feet claim her mate and her throne!" **H**

A moment passed, and then a ballerina arose, swaying like a willow.
160 Harrison plucked the mental handicap from her ear, snapped off her physical handicaps with marvelous delicacy. Last of all, he removed her mask.

She was blindingly beautiful.

"Now—" said Harrison, taking her hand, "shall we show the people the meaning of the word dance? Music!" he commanded.

The musicians scrambled back into their chairs, and Harrison stripped them of their handicaps, too. "Play your best," he told them, "and I'll make you barons and dukes and earls."

The music began. It was normal at first—cheap, silly, false. But Harrison snatched two musicians from their chairs, waved them like batons as he sang
170 the music as he wanted it played. He slammed them back into their chairs.

The music began again and was much improved.

3 Targeted Passage

G GRAMMAR AND STYLE
Reread line 138. Notice how Vonnegut uses **the precise adjectives** *clanking, clownish, and huge* to create a vivid image of Harrison's appearance.

cower (kou'ər) *v.* to crouch down in fear

H PLOT AND CONFLICT
Reread lines 142–158. Notice how Harrison views himself in relation to other people. How do his views put him in conflict with the government?

HARRISON BERGERON **43**

G GRAMMAR AND STYLE COMMON CORE L 3

Identify Precise Adjectives Point out that the author uses precise adjectives that appeal to many senses, including sight and sound. Precise adjectives create images in readers' minds. Have students identify other precise adjectives in the story. *Possible answers:* "white and trembling" (line 55) appeal to sight; "warm" (line 101), "barking" (line 128), and "crashing" (line 132) appeal to sound; "wet" (line 148) and "rubber-ball" (line 154) appeal to touch

TEXT ANALYSIS COMMON CORE RL 3

H PLOT AND CONFLICT

Possible answer: Harrison declares himself Emperor (line 142), and says he is a "greater ruler than any man who ever lived"(line 146), directly challenging the government's authority. He also removes all his handicaps (lines 148–155), which is against the law.

TIERED DISCUSSION PROMPTS

Refer to lines 159–171, and use these prompts to help students understand the enormity of Harrison's "crimes":

Analyze How are Harrison's actions an attempt to overthrow the government? *Possible answer:* He not only breaks the laws but he tries to get others to do the same.

Synthesize Considering how the government punishes people for removing lead balls from their handicaps, how will Harrison most likely be punished? *Possible answer:* He would probably be locked up forever.

VOCABULARY COMMON CORE L 4

OWN THE WORD

cower: Have students create a semantic map for the word *cower*. Write the word in a center circle, and add the definition given. Draw spider legs from the center circle, and have students add synonyms to complete the map. *Possible answers: cringe, recoil, flinch, shrink*

FOR STRUGGLING READERS

3 Targeted Passage [Lines 159–171]

This passage explains why Harrison is such a threat to a government that insists everyone be equal in every way.

- What does Harrison do to the ballerina and the musicians? (lines 160–166)
- Why would the government disapprove of Harrison's actions? (line 166)
- Do you think his actions are fair to the ballerina and the musicians? (lines 162, 166–171)

FOR ENGLISH LANGUAGE LEARNERS

Comprehension: Transitions Point out these transition words that are used to create comparisons: "*like* bandits" (line 21); "'I am a greater ruler *than*'" (lines 145–146); "waved them *like* batons" (line 169); "*as though* synchronizing" (line 173); "leaped *like* deer" (line 181). Have pairs work together to write one sentence about the story that uses each of these transition words.

HARRISON BERGERON **43**

I DRAW CONCLUSIONS

Possible answer: Use of such playful verbs as "reeled, whirled, swiveled, flounced" (line 180), the comparison "They leaped like deer on the moon" (line 181), and the emphasis on kissing and love indicate that the narrator views it as joyful and exciting.

TEXT ANALYSIS

COMMON CORE

RL 3

J PLOT AND CONFLICT

Possible answer: when the Handicapper General shoots and kills Harrison

READING SKILL

COMMON CORE

RL 1

K DRAW CONCLUSIONS

Possible answer: George was shaken by a handicap signal (lines 197–198) and cannot remember what happened to his son. Hazel's mind is mixed up (line 203) and she forgets sad things (line 205).

VOCABULARY

COMMON CORE

L 4

OWN THE WORD

- **synchronize:** Have students complete this sentence: The coach said that the two divers were perfectly *synchronized* because.... *Possible answer:* they entered the water at exactly the same time.

- **neutralize:** Remind students that when a person's power is *neutralized*, his or her powers have been rendered ineffective. Have students refer to line 186 in which gravity was *neutralized*.

SELECTION WRAP–UP

READ WITH A PURPOSE Now that students have finished reading the selection, have them compare and contrast Harrison with his parents, especially his father. What choices does Harrison make that his father would not or could not make? *Possible answer: Harrison is willing to remove his handicaps; his father is not.*

Harrison and his Empress merely listened to the music for a while—listened gravely, as though **synchronizing** their heartbeats with it.

They shifted their weights to their toes.

Harrison placed his big hands on the girl's tiny waist, letting her sense the weightlessness that would soon be hers.

And then, in an explosion of joy and grace, into the air they sprang!

Not only were the laws of the land abandoned, but the law of gravity and the laws of motion as well.

180 They reeled, whirled, swiveled, flounced, capered, gamboled, and spun.

They leaped like deer on the moon.

The studio ceiling was thirty feet high, but each leap brought the dancers nearer to it.

It became their obvious intention to kiss the ceiling.

They kissed it.

And then, **neutralizing** gravity with love and pure will, they remained suspended in air inches below the ceiling, and they kissed each other for a long, long time. **I**

It was then that Diana Moon Glampers, the Handicapper General, came 190 into the studio with a double-barreled ten-gauge shotgun. She fired twice, and the Emperor and the Empress were dead before they hit the floor.

Diana Moon Glampers loaded the gun again. She aimed it at the musicians and told them they had ten seconds to get their handicaps back on.

It was then that the Bergerons' television tube burned out. **J**

Hazel turned to comment about the blackout to George. But George had gone out into the kitchen for a can of beer.

George came back in with the beer, paused while a handicap signal shook him up. And then he sat down again. "You been crying?" he said to Hazel.

"Yup," she said.

200 "What about?" he said.

"I forget," she said. "Something real sad on television."

"What was it?" he said.

"It's all kind of mixed up in my mind," said Hazel.

"Forget sad things," said George.

"I always do," said Hazel.

"That's my girl," said George. He winced. There was the sound of a riveting gun[7] in his head.

"Gee—I could tell that one was a doozy," said Hazel.

"You can say that again," said George.

210 "Gee—" said Hazel, "I could tell that one was a doozy." **K**

synchronize
(sĭng′krə-nīz′) *v.* to match the timing of

neutralize (nōō′trə-līz′) *v.* to counteract or cancel the effect of

I DRAW CONCLUSIONS
Reread lines 177–188. What words and phrases indicate how the **narrator** views this breaking of the laws?

J PLOT AND CONFLICT
How is the conflict resolved?

④ Targeted Passage

K DRAW CONCLUSIONS
Why do George and Hazel react this way to their son's death?

---

7. **riveting** (rĭv′ĭ-tĭng) **gun:** a power tool used to hammer bolts (called rivets) that are used in construction work and manufacturing to fasten metal beams or plates together.

DIFFERENTIATED INSTRUCTION

FOR STRUGGLING READERS

④ Targeted Passage [Lines 189–207]

This passage contains the climax and resolution of the story.

- What does Diana Moon Glampers do? (lines 189–191)

- How does George react to the events? Why does he hear the sound of "a riveting gun in his head" (lines 206–207)?

- What questions does he ask Hazel? (lines 198–202)

FOR ENGLISH LANGUAGE LEARNERS

Vocabulary: Idioms Use New Word Analysis to teach these story idioms: *drove people crazy* (line 8), "upset people"; *get away with* (line 73), "do something bad and not get caught"; *mixed up* (line 203), "confused"; *doozy* (lines 208, 210), "something special"; *You can say that again* (line 209), "I agree with you completely."

BEST PRACTICES TOOLKIT—Transparency New Word Analysis p. E8

Comprehension

1. **Recall** Why does the government handicap George but not Hazel?

2. **Recall** Why is the government looking for Harrison?

3. **Recall** What does the Handicapper General do to Harrison?

4. **Clarify** Why don't Harrison's parents respond with more feeling to what they have seen?

Text Analysis

● 5. **Analyze Plot and Conflict** Summarize the main conflict in "Harrison Bergeron." How is this conflict resolved? How does the resolution help to make the story successful?

6. **Recognize Climax** Recall that the climax, or turning point, is the high point of interest and tension in a story. What is the climax of this story?

■ 7. **Draw Conclusions** Look back at the chart you created as you read. What overall conclusions can you draw about the society depicted in the story? Consider how people must function and what has become "normal."

8. **Interpret Theme** What is Vonnegut saying about improving society by making everyone average? Support your opinion with evidence from the story.

9. **Evaluate** Would society have been better off with Harrison in charge? Using a chart like this one, predict the effects of Harrison's becoming emperor.

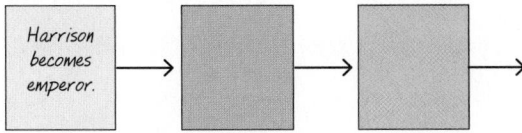

10. **Synthesize** Think about the criticisms of society made in "Harrison Bergeron." What aspects of today's society seem open to Vonnegut's criticisms?

Text Criticism

11. **Critical Interpretation** One critic has argued that Vonnegut portrays television as "a kind of desensitizing, numbing, and clearly thought-stifling, rather than thought-provoking, medium" that is partly responsible for the state of society. Do you agree or disagree? Support your opinion.

What if everyone were THE SAME?
Would you be happier if no one were better (or worse) than anyone else?

10. *rewarding effort rather than results; everybody having equal play time on sports teams regardless of whether they are good or not*

Text Criticism
Possible answers:
11. *Agree: The television shows mediocre or poor performances; it is a tool of the government. Disagree: The television is the least of people's problems. The Constitutional Amendments and the vigilant agents are the real cause of the society depicted.*

What if everyone were THE SAME?
Students might consider the positive and negative effects a lack of diversity would have on individuals and society as a whole. Students might also think about whether being equal means being the same.

RL 1 Cite textual evidence to support analysis of what the text says explicitly as well as inferences drawn from the text. **RL 3** Analyze how complex characters develop over the course of a text, interact with other characters, and advance the plot.

Practice and Apply

For preliminary support of post-reading questions, use these copy masters:

R RESOURCE MANAGER—Copy Masters
Reading Check p. 28
Analyze Plot and Conflict p. 21
Question Support p. 29

Additional selection questions are provided for teachers on page 15.

ANSWERS

Comprehension

1. *Hazel already has average intelligence.*

2. *He escaped from jail, where he was held on suspicion of plotting to overthrow the government.*

3. *She shoots and kills him.*

4. *Hazel's lack of intelligence and George's handicap keep them from remembering or focusing on it.*

Text Analysis
COMMON CORE RL 1, RL 3
Possible answers:

5. ● **COMMON CORE FOCUS** *Analyze Plot and Conflict Harrison Bergeron is in conflict with the government. He is an extraordinary person, and the government demands that he be equal to everybody else. He insists on being who he is and is killed by the government. The story's dramatic resolution warns readers what could happen in a society if freedom and diversity are not valued.*

6. *The climax is the scene in which Harrison and the ballerina are suspended in mid-air and are then shot and killed for their actions (lines 180–191).*

7. ■ **COMMON CORE FOCUS** *Draw Conclusions The society limits any potential for greatness. It is repressive, discriminatory, and dangerous (lines 1–6; 11–17; 55–62; 95–103; 112–117; 180–191).*

8. *Vonnegut is saying that making everyone average is no improvement; artists are compromised (lines 26–30, 100–101, 168); the handicaps harm people (lines 55–57); and humans are not allowed to reach their full potential (lines 145–147).*

9. *Yes. Harrison would remove peoples' handicaps and allow diversity to flourish.*

Vocabulary in Context
▲ VOCABULARY PRACTICE

1. *d*	4. *a*
2. *a*	5. *d*
3. *b*	6. *b*

 **RESOURCE MANAGER—Copy Master**
Vocabulary Practice p. 26

ACADEMIC VOCABULARY IN SPEAKING

Students should identify and discuss the social tendencies Vonnegut is warning against, for example, the desire for everyone to be equal, competing on a "level" playing field. Vonnegut seems to be recommending that people be wary of repressive governments that may try to limit potential for greatness.

VOCABULARY STRATEGY: THE GREEK ROOT *syn*

COMMON CORE L 4c

- Encourage students to begin by reading all the sentences and completing those that they can. For example, they will probably be familiar with *synonym* and *synchronizing*. Then have them look up any remaining definitions.

- Discuss other forms of the words. When *syndicate* is used as a verb, for instance, it might have various endings. A *synthesizer* is a musical instrument.

Possible answers:
1. *syndrome*
2. *synonym*
3. *syndicate*
4. *synchronize*
5. *synthesize*

 **RESOURCE MANAGER—Copy Master**
Vocabulary Strategy p. 27

Interactive Vocabulary THINK central

Keywords direct students to a **WordSharp** tutorial on **thinkcentral.com** or to other types of vocabulary practice and review.

Vocabulary in Context
▲ VOCABULARY PRACTICE

Write the letter of the word that is most different in meaning from the others.

1. (a) vigilance, (b) attention, (c) alertness, (d) laziness
2. (a) grin, (b) flinch, (c) wince, (d) shrink
3. (a) joy, (b) consternation, (c) happiness, (d) elation
4. (a) tower, (b) crouch, (c) cower, (d) cringe
5. (a) time, (b) synchronize, (c) set, (d) separate
6. (a) neutralize, (b) worsen, (c) lessen, (d) decrease

ACADEMIC VOCABULARY IN SPEAKING

- affect   • communicate   • definite   • establish   • identify

Identify the social tendencies Vonnegut is warning against in "Harrison Bergeron." Analyze the flaws of the society he depicts and discuss with a partner what Vonnegut seems to be recommending. Use at least one Academic Vocabulary word in your discussion.

VOCABULARY STRATEGY: THE GREEK ROOT *syn*

COMMON CORE

L 4c Consult reference materials to determine or clarify a word's meaning or etymology.

The vocabulary word *synchronize* contains the Greek word root *syn*, which means "together" or "similar." This root is found in a number of English words. To understand the meaning of words with *syn*, use context clues as well as your knowledge of the root.

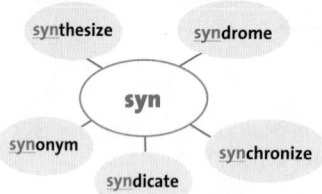

PRACTICE Write the word from the word web that best completes each sentence. Use context clues to help you or, if necessary, consult a dictionary or glossary.

1. A _____ is a group of symptoms that together indicate a disease.
2. A _____ is a word that has the same or a similar meaning to another word.
3. A _____ is a company that is made up of different parts, such as a newspaper, a magazine, and a TV network.
4. Swimmers often _____ their movements in an underwater ballet.
5. To _____ something is to combine separate elements to form a whole.

Interactive Vocabulary THINK central
Go to thinkcentral.com.
KEYWORD: HML10-46

DIFFERENTIATED INSTRUCTION

FOR ENGLISH LANGUAGE LEARNERS
Vocabulary: Cognates Ask students if any words in the word web have similar word parts and meanings in their languages. Encourage them to identify other words in their languages that begin with or contain *syn-*.

FOR ADVANCED LEARNERS/PRE–AP
The Greek Word Root *syn* Have students use the dictionary to find three additional words that begin with *syn-*. Have them write sentences for each word. The sentences should provide context clues to the words' meanings.

Language

◆ **GRAMMAR AND STYLE:** Use Precise Language

Review the **Grammar and Style** note on page 43. Vonnegut creates effective images, such as the image of Harrison in the TV studio, by using **precise adjectives.** When describing people, places, and events in your own writing, choose adjectives that allow readers to easily visualize them. Avoid using such adjectives as *good* and *nice,* which are too general to give readers a true sense of what is described.

COMMON CORE

L 3 Apply knowledge of language to make effective choices for meaning or style.

Here are two examples of Vonnegut's use of precise adjectives:

> *She must have been extraordinarily beautiful, because the mask she wore was hideous.* (lines 95–96)

> *Her voice was a warm, luminous, timeless melody.* (line 101)

Notice how the revisions in blue make this first draft more descriptive. Revise your own writing by using more precise adjectives.

STUDENT MODEL

Harrison Bergeron has a ~~big~~ *difficult* problem. He's ~~better~~ *smarter, stronger, and more attractive* than everyone else, and the government says that's ~~bad~~ *illegal.*

READING-WRITING CONNECTION

Increase your understanding of "Harrison Bergeron" by responding to this prompt. Then use the **revising tip** to improve your writing.

WRITING PROMPT

Short Constructed Response: Description
Imagine that a film version of "Harrison Bergeron" is being released and you have been assigned to write a blurb, or brief description, for a local newspaper. In **one or two paragraphs,** describe the plot and conflict in a way that makes people want to see the movie.

REVISING TIP

Review your response. How have you used precise adjectives to describe the people, places, and events in the film?

Interactive Revision THINK central

Go to **thinkcentral.com**.
KEYWORD: HML10-47

FOR STRUGGLING WRITERS

- Explain that a newspaper blurb must name the film and tell something about it. Discuss different details to include.
- Help students write a sentence that identifies the film and tells something about it.
- Help them write a sentence that states the main conflict.
- Discuss which parts of the story would be most likely to interest viewers.

Suggest that students use the first paragraph to name the film, its setting, main characters, and conflict. The second paragraph could describe one or more plot details.

Language

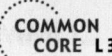
COMMON CORE L 3

◆ **GRAMMAR AND STYLE**

- Discuss why the revisions improve the draft. For example, *gigantic* is more accurate and descriptive than *big.* (To learn more about using language effectively, see **Writing Handbook**, page R29.)
- Write these sentences on the board and ask students to replace the adjectives with ones that are more precise:

> The noises that George heard were ~~loud~~. *thunderous and painful*

> Harrison wore *gigantic* ~~big~~ handicaps.

> One ballerina had a *soothing* ~~nice~~ voice.

 RESOURCE MANAGER—Copy Master
  Use Precise Language p. 30

READING-WRITING CONNECTION

- Encourage students to complete a story map, which will help them focus on the plot and conflict. Discuss what parts they will leave out so as not to give away the ending.

 **BEST PRACTICES TOOLKIT**—Transparencies
  Story Map p. D14
  Analysis Frame: Theme pp. D21, D32

THINK central

Writing Online

The following tools are available online at **thinkcentral.com** and on **Write*Smart* CD-ROM:**
- **Interactive Graphic Organizers**
- **Interactive Student Models**
- **Interactive Revision Lessons**
For additional grammar instruction, see **GrammarNotes** on **thinkcentral.com**.

Assess and Reteach

Assess

 DIAGNOSTIC AND SELECTION TESTS
  Selection Test A pp. 23–24
  Selection Test B/C pp. 25–26

Interactive Selection Test on **thinkcentral.com**

Reteach

Level Up Online Tutorials on **thinkcentral.com**

Reteaching Worksheets on **thinkcentral.com**
  Literature Lessons 5, 6, Reading Lesson 9, Vocabulary Lesson 6

Focus and Motivate

COMMON CORE FOCUS

RL 1 Cite textual evidence to support inferences drawn from the text. **RL 4** Determine the meaning of figurative language; analyze the cumulative impact of specific word choices on meaning and tone. **RL 5** Analyze an author's choices concerning how to structure a text. **W 3** Write narratives to develop events using well-structured event sequences. **L 1b** Use prepositional phrases to add variety and interest to writing. **L 4c** Consult reference materials to determine or clarify a word's meaning or etymology.

SUMMARY

In "Everyday Use," a mother and her younger daughter, Maggie, anxiously await a visit from Dee, the educated older daughter who left home. Dee wants to take household objects that reflect her African-American heritage, including two quilts promised to Maggie. Dee protests that Maggie does not appreciate their value. The mother sticks by her decision.

What makes something VALUABLE?

Discuss the question. After students complete the *QUICKWRITE*, elicit and discuss their criteria for calling something valuable.

Selection Resources

Before Reading

Essential Course of Study ECOS

Everyday Use
Short Story by Alice Walker

VIDEO TRAILER **THINK** central   KEYWORD: HML10-48

What makes something VALUABLE?

COMMON CORE

RL 1 Cite textual evidence to support inferences drawn from the text. **RL 4** Determine the meaning of figurative language; analyze the cumulative impact of specific word choices on meaning and tone. **RL 5** Analyze an author's choices concerning how to structure a text.

The word *value* means different things to different people. For example, an old vase might have high monetary value or high sentimental value. To some, it might have great historical, cultural, or artistic value. But others might think it's a useless piece of junk. Often people disagree over the value they assign to an object. Or they may agree that it is valuable, but not for the same reason.

QUICKWRITE If you could save only one precious possession of yours from being destroyed or left behind, what would you save? Write a short paragraph identifying the item and telling why it is valuable to you.

See resources on the **Teacher One Stop DVD-ROM** and on **thinkcentral.com**.

 RESOURCE MANAGER UNIT 1
Plan and Teach, pp. 33–40
Summary, pp. 41–42†‡*
Text Analysis and Reading
  Skill, pp. 43–46†*
Vocabulary, pp. 47–49*
Grammar and Style, p. 52

DIAGNOSTIC AND SELECTION TESTS
Selection Tests, pp. 27–30

 BEST PRACTICES TOOLKIT
Timeline, p. B23
Word Questioning, p. E9
Cluster Diagram, p. B18
Two-Column Chart, p. A25
Think-Pair-Share, p. A18
Venn Diagram, p. A26

INTERACTIVE READER
ADAPTED INTERACTIVE READER
ELL ADAPTED INTERACTIVE READER

TECHNOLOGY
- Teacher One Stop DVD-ROM
- Student One Stop DVD-ROM
- PowerNotes DVD-ROM
- Audio Anthology CD
- GrammarNotes DVD-ROM
- Audio Tutor CD
- ExamView Test Generator on the Teacher One Stop

Video Trailer  THINK central

Go to **thinkcentral.com** to preview the **Video Trailer** introducing this selection. Other features that support the selection include
- **PowerNotes** presentation
- **ThinkAloud** models to enhance comprehension
- **WordSharp** vocabulary tutorials
- interactive writing and grammar instruction

---

* Resources for Differentiation   † Also in Spanish   ‡ In Haitian Creole and Vietnamese

● TEXT ANALYSIS: CONFLICT AND CHARACTER

A story's plot progresses because of a **conflict,** or struggle between opposing forces. In "Everyday Use," the main conflict centers around two sisters, Dee and Maggie, and their mother, who narrates the story. Although the main conflict between these characters is worked out in the **resolution** of the story, some other conflicts linger unresolved.

As you read, pay attention to the conflicts and whether they are resolved. Also think about the differences in the characters' values and priorities.

Review: **Plot**

■ READING SKILL: MAKE INFERENCES

Because writers don't always tell you everything you need to know about a character, you must **make inferences,** or logical guesses, based on story details and your own experiences. For example, you might infer that the mother in this story prefers the outdoors from her comment "A yard like this is more comfortable than most people know. . . . It is like an extended living room." As you read, notice what the characters' words and actions tell you about their personalities and attitudes. Take notes on a chart like the one shown.

	Story Details	Inferences
Dee	thinks orchids are tacky flowers	is pretentious
Mama		
Maggie		

▲ VOCABULARY IN CONTEXT

Figure out the meaning of each boldfaced word from the context. In your *Reader/Writer Notebook,* write a sentence that shows your understanding of each word.

1. sneaky, **furtive** behavior
2. need time to **recompose** after your outburst
3. accept the club's **doctrine**
4. remember your **heritage** when you leave home

 Complete the activities in your **Reader/Writer Notebook.**

Meet the Author

Alice Walker
born 1944

A Humble Start
Alice Walker, one of America's most distinguished authors, comes from humble beginnings. She was the last of eight children born to sharecroppers Willie Lee and Minnie Tallulah Walker. Though money was scarce and life was hard, Walker loved the Georgia countryside where she grew up. Walker's childhood was shattered by a shooting accident when she was eight. She lost sight in one eye and had a disfiguring scar that left her intensely self-conscious. For years afterward, she felt like an outcast.

Travel, Activism, and Fame
Walker took comfort in reading and in writing poetry. With her mother's encouragement, she developed her talent for writing and did well in school. She graduated at the head of her high school class and received a college scholarship. During college, she became involved in the civil rights movement and traveled to Africa as an exchange student. After college, she devoted herself to writing and social activism. She has written more than 20 books, including *The Color Purple,* which won a Pulitzer Prize in 1983.

BACKGROUND TO THE STORY
Black Pride
"Everyday Use" takes place during the 1960s, when many African Americans were discovering their heritage. The "black pride" movement, which grew out of civil rights campaigns, called upon African Americans to celebrate their African roots and affirm their cultural identity. Many adopted African clothing, hairstyles, and names; some studied African languages.

Author Online
THINK central
Go to **thinkcentral.com.**
KEYWORD: HML10-49

49

Teach

TEXT ANALYSIS   COMMON CORE
                                       RL 1
                                       RL 5

● *Model the Skill:* CONFLICT AND CHARACTER

To model how to identify conflict, read aloud this example:

"You have no idea what that butter churn is worth," said Dan.

"Yes, I do. I used to use it every week," his mother replied.

The conflict is between Dan and his mother. Each feels the other does not understand the value of the butter churn.

GUIDED PRACTICE Have students name objects of value and tell how they can create conflict.

READING SKILL

■ *Model the Skill:* MAKE INFERENCES

Model how to make inferences by pointing out the phrases "humble beginnings," "the last of eight children," "money was scarce," and "loved the Georgia countryside" in **A Humble Start**. These details can lead to the following inferences about the Walker home: It was not fancy; it was crowded. Walker found things to love about it.

GUIDED PRACTICE Have students make an inference about the effect of Walker's accident on her vocation as a writer.

R RESOURCE MANAGER—Copy Master
Make Inferences p. 45

VOCABULARY SKILL   COMMON CORE
                                                             L 4

▲ VOCABULARY IN CONTEXT

DIAGNOSE WORD KNOWLEDGE Have all students complete Vocabulary in Context. Check their use of the words in sentences against the following:

doctrine (dŏk′trĭn) *n.* a set of rules, beliefs, or values held by a group
furtive (fûr′tĭv) *adj.* sneaky, secretive
heritage (hĕr′ĭ-tĭj) *n.* something passed down through generations, such as tradition, values, property

recompose (rē′kəm-pōz′) *v.* to restore to calm, to settle again

PRETEACH VOCABULARY Use the following copy master to help students create a word map for each boldfaced word in Part A.

R RESOURCE MANAGER—Copy Master
Vocabulary Study p. 47

1. Read the first phrase in Part A aloud.
2. Guide students in creating a word map like the one shown. Use the sidenotes in

the pupil edition as the source for definitions.

3. Repeat the procedure for the other phrases before assigning Part B.

READ WITH A PURPOSE

Help students set a purpose for reading. Tell them to read "Everyday Use" to understand how two ideas of a family's heritage can cause conflict.

READING SKILL

A *Model the Skill:* **MAKE INFERENCES**

To model how to make inferences, tell students that the story details and their own experiences will help them make inferences, or logical guesses, about the characters. Have students use their charts to record descriptive details about each sister. Then have students examine their details and make an inference.

	Story Details	Inferences
Maggie	"will be nervous ...will stand hopelessly" (line 7)	
Dee	"held life...in the palm of one hand" (lines 9–10)	

Possible answer: Maggie and her sister are opposites: Maggie is shy, "homely and ashamed" (line 8); her sister is a confident, successful person to whom the world has never said no (line 10).

Everyday Use

Alice Walker

I will wait for her in the yard that Maggie and I made so clean and wavy yesterday afternoon. A yard like this is more comfortable than most people know. It is not just a yard. It is like an extended living room. When the hard clay is swept clean as a floor and the fine sand around the edges lined with tiny, irregular grooves, anyone can come and sit and look up into the elm tree and wait for the breezes that never come inside the house.

Maggie will be nervous until after her sister goes: she will stand hopelessly in corners, homely and ashamed of the burn scars down her arms and legs, eying her sister with a mixture of envy and awe. She thinks her sister has held life always in
10 the palm of one hand, that "no" is a word the world never learned to say to her. **A**

You've no doubt seen those TV shows where the child who has "made it" is confronted, as a surprise, by her own mother and father, tottering in weakly from backstage. (A pleasant surprise, of course: What would they do if parent and child came on the show only to curse out and insult each other?) On TV mother and child embrace and smile into each other's faces. Sometimes the mother and father weep, the child wraps them in her arms and leans across the table to tell how she would not have made it without their help. I have seen these programs.

Sometimes I dream a dream in which Dee and I are suddenly brought
20 together on a TV program of this sort. Out of a dark and soft-seated limousine I am ushered into a bright room filled with many people. There I meet a smiling, gray, sporty man like Johnny Carson who shakes my hand and tells me what a fine girl I have. Then we are on the stage and Dee is embracing me with tears in her eyes. She pins on my dress a large orchid, even though she has told me once that she thinks orchids are tacky flowers.

In real life I am a large, big-boned woman with rough, man-working hands. In the winter I wear flannel nightgowns to bed and overalls during the day. I can kill and clean a hog as mercilessly as a man. My fat keeps me hot in zero weather. I can work outside all day, breaking ice to get water for washing; I can
30 eat pork liver cooked over the open fire minutes after it comes steaming from the hog. One winter I knocked a bull calf straight in the brain between the

Analyze Visuals ▶
What qualities do you associate with the woman in the painting? How closely does she match the story's **narrator**?

A **MAKE INFERENCES**
Reread lines 7–10. What can you infer about Maggie and her sister from this description? Which details led to your inference?

① **Targeted Passage**

Home Chores (1945), Jacob Lawrence. Gouache and graphite on paper, 29 1/2" × 21 1/16". Anonymous gift. The Nelson-Atkins Museum of Art, Kansas City, Missouri. F69-6. Photo by Jamison Miller © 2008 The Jacob and Gwendolyn Lawrence Foundation, Seattle/Artists Rights Society (ARS), New York.

DIFFERENTIATED INSTRUCTION

FOR ENGLISH LANGUAGE LEARNERS
Culture: Clarify Elicit from students prior knowledge about the terms *colored, Negro, black,* and *African American.* Put these terms on a timeline to show how *colored* was an early term used to describe people of African ancestry that gave way to *Negro* and was later followed by the terms *black* and *African American.*

🧰 **BEST PRACTICES TOOLKIT—Transparency**
Timeline p. B23

FOR STRUGGLING READERS
In combination with the *Audio Anthology CD,* use one or more Targeted Passages (pp. 50, 54, 59) to ensure that students focus on key story events, concepts, and skills. Targeted Passages are also good for English learners.

① **Targeted Passage [Lines 19–31]**
This passage helps readers begin to understand the relationship between Mama and Dee.

• What does Mama sometimes dream about? (lines 19–20)

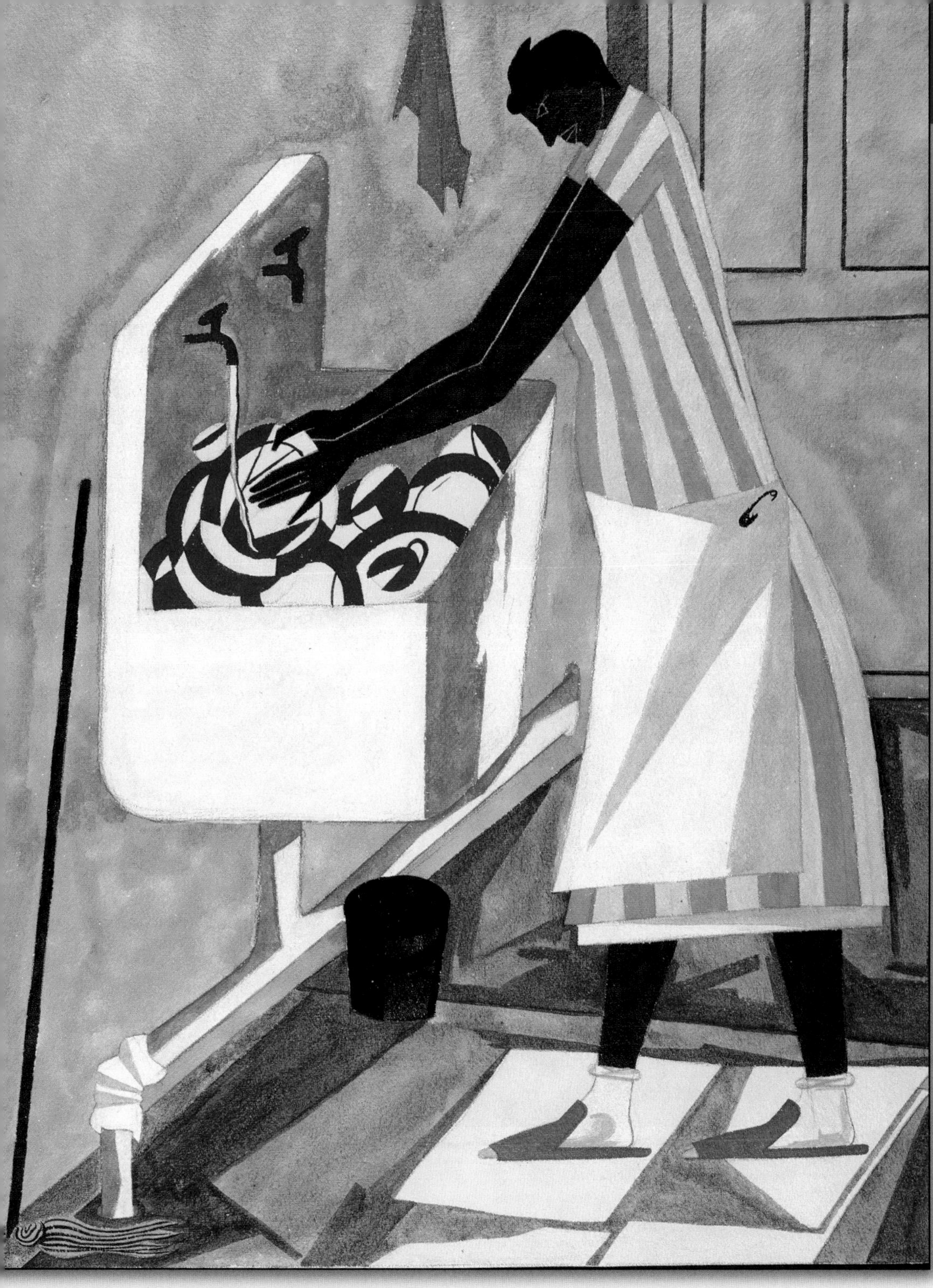

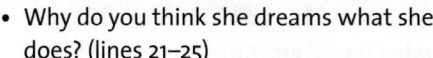

BACKGROUND

The Civil Rights Era: "A New Day for Us" This story is set in the 1960s—a time when two of the most significant pieces of Civil Rights legislation were passed. The Civil Rights Act of 1964 made segregation in public places illegal. The Voting Rights Act of 1965 made certain requirements for voting in the South, such as poll taxes and literacy tests, illegal. These civil rights created the "new day for us" to which the character Dee refers (lines 275–276).

CULTURAL CONNECTION

Civil Rights in the U.S. In the 1960s, the Mexican-American Civil Rights Movement, or Chicano Movement, also gained strength. In 1962, César Chávez began organizing farm workers in California. From 1966–1967, Reies Lopez Tijerina led the land grant movement in New Mexico. Students in East Los Angeles demanded more equitable education and a curriculum change. In 1968, the American Indian Movement (AIM) was formed. This group organized protests against racial discrimination of urban Native Americans.

Analyze Visuals

Possible answer: The woman in the painting appears to be strong, hardworking, and stoic. She may not care too much about appearances. Like the narrator, she seems to be a "large, big-boned woman with rough, man-working hands" (line 26).

About the Art Jacob Lawrence (1917–2000), an African-American artist of the Harlem Renaissance, painted *Home Chores* in 1945. Lawrence saw mother figures like the one in this painting as heroic because they often struggled to raise their children alone.

- Why do you think she dreams what she does? (lines 21–25)
- What does Mama look like in real life? How is her real-life image different from how she looks in her dream? (lines 26–31)

FOR ADVANCED LEARNERS/PRE–AP

Make Judgments Ask students to compare Mama and Dee. What character strengths do they share and what strengths make them different? Have students decide which they felt was the stronger character and support this decision from the story. ***Possible answer: Mama and Dee were both strong in their ability to face life, but Mama was ultimately stronger because she embraced both the good and the difficult in her heritage. Dee tried to separate her heritage from her childhood by leaving the house and her family behind.***

eyes with a sledge hammer and had the meat hung up to chill before nightfall. But of course all this does not show on television. I am the way my daughter would want me to be: a hundred pounds lighter, my skin like an uncooked barley pancake. My hair glistens in the hot bright lights. Johnny Carson has much to do to keep up with my quick and witty tongue.

But that is a mistake. I know even before I wake up. Who ever knew a Johnson with a quick tongue? Who can even imagine me looking a strange white man in the eye? It seems to me I have talked to them always with one
40 foot raised in flight, with my head turned in whichever way is farthest from them. Dee, though. She would always look anyone in the eye. Hesitation was no part of her nature. **B**

"How do I look, Mama?" Maggie says, showing just enough of her thin body enveloped in pink skirt and red blouse for me to know she's there, almost hidden by the door.

B MAKE INFERENCES
What do you infer about Mama from her description of herself? Cite specific details.

Analyze Visuals

Activity Ask students which character in the story most resembles the woman in this painting. *Possible answer: The woman resembles Maggie, as the figure is too thin and young to suggest the narrator and too conservatively dressed to suggest Dee. Also, she is seated quietly and passively, as Maggie might sit.*

About the Art William H. Johnson (1901–1970), another Harlem Renaissance artist, painted *Little Sweet* in 1944. Here the seated form of a woman is simplified by strong lines and angles, while the background and chair are painted in vibrant solid colors.

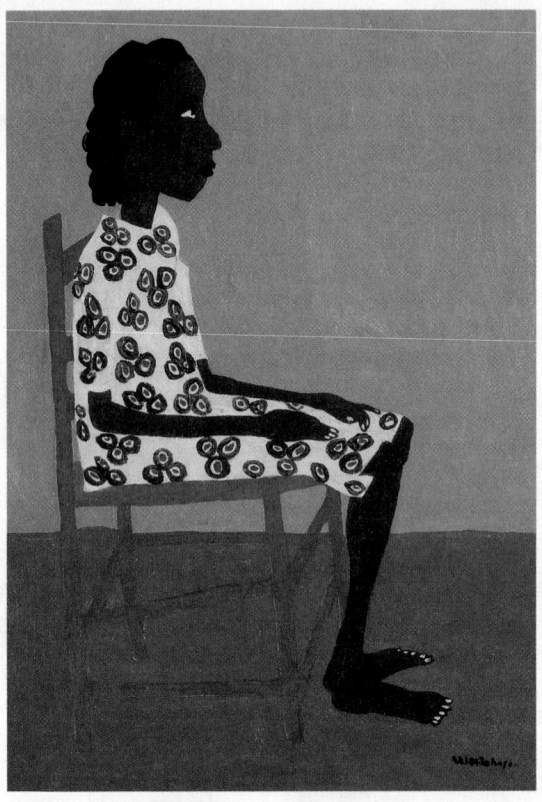

Little Sweet (1944), William H. Johnson. Oil on paperboard, 28″ × 22″. Smithsonian American Art Museum, Washington, D.C. Photo © Smithsonian American Art Museum, Washington, D.C./Art Resource, New York.

52   UNIT 1: PLOT, SETTING, AND MOOD

DIFFERENTIATED INSTRUCTION

FOR ENGLISH LANGUAGE LEARNERS
Vocabulary Support Use Word Questioning to teach these words: *concentration* (line 58), *style* (line 73), *trace* (line 151), *Civil* (line 152), *inspecting* (line 157), *portion* (line 262).

BEST PRACTICES TOOLKIT—Transparency
Word Questioning p. E9

FOR ADVANCED LEARNERS/PRE–AP
Evaluate Characters After students have finished reading the story, have them reread lines 33–36. In what ways is Mama's assessment of what Dee would want her to be like accurate or inaccurate? Then, ask students to discuss why a person would want somebody else to look a specific way. What does that say about Dee?

"Come out into the yard," I say.

Have you ever seen a lame animal, perhaps a dog run over by some careless person rich enough to own a car, sidle up to someone who is ignorant enough to be kind to him? That is the way my Maggie walks. She has been like this, 50 chin on chest, eyes on ground, feet in shuffle, ever since the fire that burned the other house to the ground.

Dee is lighter than Maggie, with nicer hair and a fuller figure. She's a woman now, though sometimes I forget. How long ago was it that the other house burned? Ten, twelve years? Sometimes I can still hear the flames and feel Maggie's arms sticking to me, her hair smoking and her dress falling off her in little black papery flakes. Her eyes seemed stretched open, blazed open by the flames reflected in them. And Dee. I see her standing off under the sweet gum tree she used to dig gum out of; a look of concentration on her face as she watched the last dingy gray board of the house fall in toward the red-hot brick 60 chimney. Why don't you do a dance around the ashes? I'd wanted to ask her. She had hated the house that much.

I used to think she hated Maggie, too. But that was before we raised the money, the church and me, to send her to Augusta[1] to school. She used to read to us without pity; forcing words, lies, other folks' habits, whole lives upon us two, sitting trapped and ignorant underneath her voice. She washed us in a river of make-believe, burned us with a lot of knowledge we didn't necessarily need to know. Pressed us to her with the serious way she read, to shove us away at just the moment, like dimwits, we seemed about to understand.

Dee wanted nice things. A yellow organdy dress to wear to her graduation 70 from high school; black pumps to match a green suit she'd made from an old suit somebody gave me. She was determined to stare down any disaster in her efforts. Her eyelids would not flicker for minutes at a time. Often I fought off the temptation to shake her. At sixteen she had a style of her own: and knew what style was. **C**

I never had an education myself. After second grade the school was closed down. Don't ask me why: in 1927 colored asked fewer questions than they do now. Sometimes Maggie reads to me. She stumbles along good-naturedly but can't see well. She knows she is not bright. Like good looks and money, quickness passed her by. She will marry John Thomas (who has mossy teeth 80 in an earnest face) and then I'll be free to sit here and I guess just sing church songs to myself. Although I never was a good singer. Never could carry a tune. I was always better at a man's job. I used to love to milk till I was hooked in the side in '49. Cows are soothing and slow and don't bother you, unless you try to milk them the wrong way.

I have deliberately turned my back on the house. It is three rooms, just like the one that burned, except the roof is tin; they don't make shingle roofs any more. There are no real windows, just some holes cut in the sides, like the portholes in a ship, but not round and not square, with rawhide holding the

---

1. **Augusta:** a city in Georgia.

COMMON CORE **RL 4**

Language Coach

Informal language
Reread the paragraph that begins with line 52. Walker uses sentence fragments such as "Ten, twelve years?" and "And Dee." to create an informal tone. What other fragments do you see on this page? [Hint: look for sentences that lack either a subject or a verb.]

C CONFLICT
Reread lines 52–74. What conflicts exist between Dee and her mother and sister?

TEXT ANALYSIS   COMMON CORE   RL 1 RL 5

C CONFLICT

Possible answer: *Dee is different from her mother and sister in appearance, ambition, and temperament. These differences create conflict. Dee is lighter-skinned than Maggie (line 52), with a strong sense of style (line 73) that clashes with her family's plainer appearance. She likes to read and forces her reading on her family (lines 63–65), who feel "trapped and ignorant underneath her voice" (line 65). She is more educated and ambitious than her mother and sister and wants nice things (line 69). Dee is also impatient with her family and their lack of ambition (lines 67–68).*

FOR ADVANCED LEARNERS/PRE–AP

Hypothesize The fire is a main event for these characters. Have students explore multiple purposes for its inclusion in the story. *Example: They should hypothesize not only about the cause of the fire, but also about the ways in which it continues to "burn" or "smoke" in the characters' lives.* Have students discuss the symbolic significance of the fire and the ways in which it represents unresolved conflict.

FOR ENGLISH LANGUAGE LEARNERS

Language Coach   COMMON CORE RL 4

Informal Language ***Answer:*** *Examples include the fragments that begin "A yellow organdy dress. . ." (lines 69–71), "After second grade. . ." (lines 75–76), and "Although I never. . ." (Line 81).* Have students rewrite the fragments they have identified to form complete sentences with subjects and verbs. Point out that these complete sentences are in formal English.

D MAKE INFERENCES

Possible answer: *Dee is difficult to get along with. Her "scalding humor" and tendency to erupt (line 96) suggest she can be mean and has a temper. She is a superior-acting faultfinder (lines 98–99). Only "furtive boys" (line 94) and "nervous girls" (line 95) hung around her. The boy she courted fled from her quickly (lines 98–100).*

COMMON CORE
RL 4

E FIGURATIVE LANGUAGE

Remind students that figurative language always involves imaginative comparisons between seemingly unlike things. Have students review the selection to find comparisons. To help students, ask them: To what does Mama compare Maggie's walk?

Possible answers: *Examples include comparing Maggie's walk to a lame dog (lines 47–51), comparing Asalamalakim's beard to a "a kinky mule tail" (line 109), Maggie's intake of breath sounding "like when you see the wriggling end of a snake" (lines 110–111), and "Maggie's hand is limp as a fish" (line 136).*

COMMON CORE
L 4

OWN THE WORD

- **furtive:** Explain that the Latin root of *furtive* is *fur*, meaning "thief." Have students explain how the Latin root of *furtive* relates to its definition. ***Possible answer:*** *Thieves are sneaky and do not want to get caught.*

- **recompose:** Tell students that the prefix *re-* means "again" and the Latin *com-* means "together" or "jointly." When you *compose* something, you put it together. Have students make a list of times when they felt they needed to *recompose* themselves.

---

shutters up on the outside. This house is in a pasture, too, like the other one.

90 No doubt when Dee sees it she will want to tear it down. She wrote me once that no matter where we "choose" to live, she will manage to come see us. But she will never bring her friends. Maggie and I thought about this and Maggie asked me, "Mama, when did Dee ever *have* any friends?"

She had a few. **Furtive** boys in pink shirts hanging about on washday after school. Nervous girls who never laughed. Impressed with her they worshiped the well-turned phrase, the cute shape, the scalding humor that erupted like bubbles in lye. She read to them.

When she was courting Jimmy T she didn't have much time to pay to us, but turned all her faultfinding power on him. He *flew* to marry a cheap city girl from 100 a family of ignorant flashy people. She hardly had time to **recompose** herself. D

furtive (fûr′tĭv) *adj.* sneaky, secretive

recompose (rē′kəm-pōz′) *v.* to restore to calm, to settle again

D MAKE INFERENCES
What do you learn about Dee from the way others respond to her?

When she comes I will meet—but there they are!

Maggie attempts to make a dash for the house, in her shuffling way, but I stay her with my hand. "Come back here," I say. And she stops and tries to dig a well in the sand with her toe.

It is hard to see them clearly through the strong sun. But even the first glimpse of leg out of the car tells me it is Dee. Her feet were always neat-looking, as if God himself had shaped them with a certain style. From the other side of the car comes a short, stocky man. Hair is all over his head a foot long and hanging from his chin like a kinky mule tail. I hear Maggie suck in
110 her breath. "Uhnnnh," is what it sounds like. Like when you see the wriggling end of a snake just in front of your foot on the road. "Uhnnnh."

Dee next. A dress down to the ground, in this hot weather. A dress so loud it hurts my eyes. There are yellows and oranges enough to throw back the light of the sun. I feel my whole face warming from the heat waves it throws out. Earrings gold, too, and hanging down to her shoulders. Bracelets dangling and making noises when she moves her arm up to shake the folds of the dress out of her armpits. The dress is loose and flows, and as she walks closer, I like it. I hear Maggie go "Uhnnnh" again. It is her sister's hair. It stands straight up like the wool on a sheep. It is black as night and around the edges are two long
120 pigtails that rope about like small lizards disappearing behind her ears. E

"Wa-su-zo-Tean-o!" she says, coming on in that gliding way the dress makes her move. The short stocky fellow with the hair to his navel is all grinning and he follows up with "Asalamalakim,[2] my mother and sister!" He moves to hug Maggie but she falls back, right up against the back of my chair. I feel her trembling there and when I look up I see the perspiration falling off her chin.

"Don't get up," says Dee. Since I am stout it takes something of a push. You can see me trying to move a second or two before I make it. She turns, showing white heels through her sandals, and goes back to the car. Out she peeks next with a Polaroid. She stoops down quickly and lines up picture after
130 picture of me sitting there in front of the house with Maggie cowering behind me. She never takes a shot without making sure the house is included. When

---

2. **Wa-su-zo-Tean-o!** (wä-sōō′zō-tē′nō) . . . **Asalamalakim!** (ə-săl′ə-mə-lăk′əm): African and Arabic greetings.

54 UNIT 1: PLOT, SETTING, AND MOOD

② Targeted Passage

COMMON CORE RL 4

E FIGURATIVE LANGUAGE
Figurative language is language that communicates meanings beyond the literal meanings of the words. Reread Mama's description of Dee's hair, which begins on line 118. Obviously, Dee's hair does not literally move like lizards. Here and in other places, Mama evokes images from her life spent on a farm. Her figurative language often reflects the historical and cultural setting of the story. What other examples of figurative language can you find?

DIFFERENTIATED INSTRUCTION

FOR STRUGGLING READERS

② Targeted Passage [Lines 101–125]

This passage contrasts Dee and her companion with the world they visit and helps prepare the reader for more conflict.

- How are Dee and her companion dressed? (lines 112–117)

- What do Dee and her companion say? (lines 121–123)

- Why do Dee's appearance and greeting surprise Mama and Maggie? (lines 91–92)

FOR ENGLISH LANGUAGE LEARNERS

Vocabulary: Multiple-Meaning Words Have students create Cluster Diagrams for each multiple-meaning word, writing each word in the center circle and the meanings for the word in the outer circles: "colored" (line 76), "bright" (line 78), "quickness" (line 79), "milk" (line 82), "stay" (line 103), "bear" (line 143), "sight" (line 175), "tops" (line 222), "backward" (line 238).

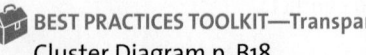

BEST PRACTICES TOOLKIT—Transparency
Cluster Diagram p. B18

◀ **Analyze Visuals**

Contrast the style and subject of this painting with those of the one on page 52. Does the contrast reflect the differences between the sisters in the story? Explain.

Portrait of a woman with golden headscarf (1900s), Attributed to Lo Babacar. Pikine, Senegal. Glass painting. Inv.:A.94.4.33 Musée des Arts d'Afrique et d'Oceanie, Paris. Photo © Arnaudet/ Réunion des Musées Nationaux/ Art Resource, New York.

a cow comes nibbling around the edge of the yard she snaps it and me and Maggie *and* the house. Then she puts the Polaroid in the back seat of the car, and comes up and kisses me on the forehead. **F**

Meanwhile Asalamalakim is going through motions with Maggie's hand. Maggie's hand is as limp as a fish, and probably as cold, despite the sweat, and she keeps trying to pull it back. It looks like Asalamalakim wants to shake hands but wants to do it fancy. Or maybe he don't know how people shake hands. Anyhow, he soon gives up on Maggie.

140   "Well," I say. "Dee."

"No, Mama," she says. "Not 'Dee,' Wangero Leewanika Kemanjo!"[3]

"What happened to 'Dee'?" I wanted to know.

"She's dead," Wangero said. "I couldn't bear it any longer, being named after the people who oppress me."

"You know as well as me you was named after your aunt Dicie," I said. Dicie is my sister. She named Dee. We called her "Big Dee" after Dee was born.

"But who was *she* named after?" asked Wangero.

"I guess after Grandma Dee," I said.

"And who was she named after?" asked Wangero.

---

3. **Wangero Leewanika Kemanjo** (wän-gâr′ō lē-wä-nē′kə kĕ-män′jō).

F GRAMMAR AND STYLE
Reread lines 131–134. Notice how Walker adds descriptive details through the use of **prepositional phrases** such as "around the edge of the yard," "in the back seat of the car," and "on the forehead."

Analyze Visuals

Possible answer: *The woman on page 52 seems humble and passive; her bare feet and simple dress also make her appear poor, like Maggie. In contrast, the woman on this page appears glamorous, well-dressed, and self-assured, like Dee. The contrast reflects the difference in attitude and circumstances between the two sisters.*

About the Art Babacar Lo is credited with painting *Portrait of a woman with golden headscarf* in the 1900s. This distinctive form of art, called glass painting, originated in Senegal and begins with an outline, traced in ink on the glass. Then successive layers of paint are added.

F GRAMMAR AND STYLE  COMMON CORE L 1b

Identify Descriptive Phrases Note that prepositional phrases function as adjectives and adverbs. They are modifiers that tell more about a person, place, thing, action, or other modifier. Have students find the words that the prepositional phrases in lines 131–134 modify. For example, "around the edge" is an adverb phrase that tells *where*; "of the yard" is an adjective phrase that modifies *edge*; and "on the forehead" is also an adverb phrase that tells *where*. Have students find other prepositional phrases and the words they modify in lines 112–120. Discuss how the phrases enrich the descriptive quality of the passage.

FOR STRUGGLING READERS

Comprehension: Conflict To help students understand the conflict over names, have them imagine themselves going home and telling the person who named them that they have changed their name. Invite students to speculate about the reaction to that news. Then ask how a person they were named for might feel in this situation.

FOR ENGLISH LANGUAGE LEARNERS

Comprehension: Comparisons Note the words that show comparison in these phrases: "hanging from his chin like a kinky mule tail" (line 109); "Maggie's hand is as limp as a fish, and probably as cold" (line 136); "sweet as a bird" (line 218). Pairs of students can then write one more original sentence using the comparison words *as* and *like*. Have them share their sentences with the group.

G CONFLICT

Possible answer: They are at odds because Dee has changed her name to Wangero. For Dee, this decision is a matter of black pride, because she does not want to be "named after the people who oppress" her (lines 143–144). Mama, however, seems to think that her attitude is ridiculous, because Dee is named after members of her own family.

REVISIT THE BIG QUESTION

What makes something

VALUABLE?

Discuss In lines 184–190, why does Dee regard the old benches, the butter dish, and the churn as valuable? *Possible answer: They are old; they are quaint; to her, they speak of a simpler life in the past that is now lost (for her). They represent her "true" heritage—something she is supposedly embracing.*

OWN THE WORD

doctrine Have students review the meaning of the word *doctrine.* Then have students give examples of groups or individuals that follow *doctrines.* **Possible answers:** *governments, religious and military organizations, scientists, philosophers*

---

150   "Her mother," I said, and saw Wangero was getting tired. "That's about as far back as I can trace it," I said. Though, in fact, I probably could have carried it back beyond the Civil War through the branches. **G**

"Well," said Asalamalakim, "there you are."

"Uhnnnh," I heard Maggie say.

"There I was not," I said, "before 'Dicie' cropped up in our family, so why should I try to trace it that far back?"

He just stood there grinning, looking down on me like somebody inspecting a Model A[4] car. Every once in a while he and Wangero sent eye signals over my head.

160   "How do you pronounce this name?" I asked.

"You don't have to call me by it if you don't want to," said Wangero.

"Why shouldn't I?" I asked. "If that's what you want us to call you, we'll call you."

"I know it might sound awkward at first," said Wangero.

"I'll get used to it," I said. "Ream it out again."

Well, soon we got the name out of the way. Asalamalakim had a name twice as long and three times as hard. After I tripped over it two or three times he told me to just call him Hakim-a-barber.[5] I wanted to ask him was he a barber, but I didn't really think he was, so I didn't ask.

170   "You must belong to those beef-cattle peoples down the road," I said. They said "Asalamalakim" when they met you, too, but they didn't shake hands. Always too busy: feeding the cattle, fixing the fences, putting up salt-lick shelters, throwing down hay. When the white folks poisoned some of the herd the men stayed up all night with rifles in their hands. I walked a mile and a half just to see the sight.

Hakim-a-barber said, "I accept some of their **doctrines,** but farming and raising cattle is not my style." (They didn't tell me, and I didn't ask, whether Wangero (Dee) had really gone and married him.)

We sat down to eat and right away he said he didn't eat collards and pork
180   was unclean. Wangero, though, went on through the chitlins and corn bread, the greens and everything else. She talked a blue streak over the sweet potatoes. Everything delighted her. Even the fact that we still used the benches her daddy made for the table when we couldn't afford to buy chairs.

"Oh, Mama!" she cried. Then turned to Hakim-a-barber. "I never knew how lovely these benches are. You can feel the rump prints," she said, running her hands underneath her and along the bench. Then she gave a sigh and her hand closed over Grandma Dee's butter dish. "That's it!" she said. "I knew there was something I wanted to ask you if I could have." She jumped up from the table and went over in the corner where the churn stood, the milk in it
190   clabber[6] by now. She looked at the churn and looked at it.

---

4. **Model A:** an automobile manufactured by Ford from 1927 to 1931.

5. **Hakim-a-barber** (hä-kē′mə-bär′bər).

6. **clabber:** curdled milk.

G CONFLICT
What is causing tension between Dee and Mama?

doctrine (dŏk′trĭn) *n.* a set of rules, beliefs, or values held by a group

---

DIFFERENTIATED INSTRUCTION

FOR STRUGGLING READERS

Comprehension Support Explain that Dee's comment about "being named after the people who oppress me" (lines 143–144) is a reference to the fact that African slaves lost their own names and were given the names of white people. That is why Dee no longer likes the name Mama gave her.

FOR ENGLISH LANGUAGE LEARNERS

Language: Conversational English Patterns Ask students to make a Two-Column Chart to restate these nonstandard usages in standard English: "he don't know how people shake hands" (lines 138–139), "those beef-cattle peoples down the road" (line 170), "These old things was just done by me and Big Dee" (lines 221–222), "I promised to give them quilts to Maggie, for when she marries John Thomas" (lines 235–236), "I reckon she would" (line 240).

 BEST PRACTICES TOOLKIT—Transparency Two-Column Chart p. A25

"This churn top is what I need," she said. "Didn't Uncle Buddy whittle it out of a tree you all used to have?"

"Yes," I said.

"Uh huh," she said happily. "And I want the dasher,[7] too."

"Uncle Buddy whittle that, too?" asked the barber.

Dee (Wangero) looked up at me.

"Aunt Dee's first husband whittled the dash," said Maggie so low you almost couldn't hear her. "His name was Henry, but they called him Stash."

"Maggie's brain is like an elephant's," Wangero said, laughing. "I can use the
200 churn top as a centerpiece for the alcove table," she said, sliding a plate over the churn, "and I'll think of something artistic to do with the dasher." **H**

When she finished wrapping the dasher the handle stuck out. I took it for a moment in my hands. You didn't even have to look close to see where hands pushing the dasher up and down to make butter had left a kind of sink in the wood. In fact, there were a lot of small sinks; you could see where thumbs and fingers had sunk into the wood. It was beautiful light yellow wood, from a tree that grew in the yard where Big Dee and Stash had lived.

After dinner Dee (Wangero) went to the trunk at the foot of my bed and started rifling through it. Maggie hung back in the kitchen over the dishpan.
210 Out came Wangero with two quilts. They had been pieced by Grandma Dee and then Big Dee and me had hung them on the quilt frames on the front porch and quilted them. One was in the Lone Star pattern. The other was Walk Around the Mountain. In both of them were scraps of dresses Grandma Dee had worn fifty and more years ago. Bits and pieces of Grandpa Jarrell's Paisley shirts. And one teeny faded blue piece, about the size of a penny matchbox, that was from Great Grandpa Ezra's uniform that he wore in the Civil War.

"Mama," Wangero said sweet as a bird. "Can I have these old quilts?"

I heard something fall in the kitchen, and a minute later the kitchen door
220 slammed. **I**

"Why don't you take one or two of the others?" I asked. "These old things was just done by me and Big Dee from some tops your grandma pieced before she died."

"No," said Wangero. "I don't want those. They are stitched around the borders by machine."

"That'll make them last better," I said.

"That's not the point," said Wangero. "These are all pieces of dresses Grandma used to wear. She did all this stitching by hand. Imagine!" She held the quilts securely in her arms, stroking them.
230 "Some of the pieces, like those lavender ones, come from old clothes her mother handed down to her," I said, moving up to touch the quilts. Dee (Wangero) moved back just enough so that I couldn't reach the quilts. They already belonged to her.

"Imagine!" she breathed again, clutching them closely to her bosom.

---

7. **dasher:** the plunger of a churn, a device formerly used to stir cream or milk to produce butter.

H MAKE INFERENCES
Reread lines 191–201. What do you learn about Dee and Maggie in these lines?

I MAKE INFERENCES
What might these noises mean?

H MAKE INFERENCES

Possible answer: *Maggie appears to know, or care, more about the family's past than Dee does; she knows her uncle whittled the dasher and what his nickname was (lines 197–198). Yet she tells her information in a low voice, as if she has no confidence, while Dee remains very certain of herself and her "artistic" (line 201) plans.*

I MAKE INFERENCES

Possible answer: *The fall could suggest that Maggie was so startled by Dee's request that she accidentally let something fall or even purposely knocked something down; the slamming of the kitchen door is a sign of behind-the-scenes anger on Maggie's part.*

FOR STRUGGLING READERS

Develop Reading Fluency Read aloud lines 191–201 to help students understand the conflict. Exaggerate Dee's confident, happy, laughing voice. Exaggerate Maggie's quiet, low voice. Now have students take turns reading the dialogue using tone and expression to bring the conflict to life.

R RESOURCE MANAGER—Copy Master
Reading Fluency p. 53

FOR ENGLISH LANGUAGE LEARNERS

Language: Conversational English Patterns
Point out these phrases and their meanings: *Well, there you are* (line 153), "there is the information"; *every once in a while* (line 158), "every few minutes or so"; *bits and pieces* (line 214), "small scraps"; *sweet as a bird* (line 218), "talking sweetly to get something." Have students share home-language equivalents for each phrase.

Analyze Visuals

Activity Have students reread the description of the family quilts in lines 210–217. In what ways are these quilts similar to Mitchell's *Crazy Quilt*? In what ways do they differ? *Possible answer: Both quilts are made of several different fabrics and pieces hand-sewn together. The family quilts were pieced with fabrics worn by beloved family members; Mitchell's contains hundreds of embroidered motifs of her own design.*

About the Art Like other "crazy quilts," Victoriene Mitchell's quilt is made up of irregularly shaped pieces of cloth sewn together. Mitchell (1829–1916) worked ten years to create her quilt, achieving a bold juxtaposition of embroidered motifs.

TIERED DISCUSSION PROMPTS

Direct students to lines 235–243. Use these prompts to help students understand the climax of the story:

Connect Does your family own any objects that reflect its heritage? Explain. *Students' answers will vary, but should connect to the quilts in the story.*

Analyze What does Dee mean when she calls Maggie "backward" (line 238)? *Possible answer: She means that Maggie is uneducated, unsophisticated, and old-fashioned. Maggie is unaware of the value of the quilts because she does not understand her own cultural heritage. Dee may even be suggesting that Maggie is stupid.*

Evaluate In what ways do these lines reflect greater conflict than any lines that have come before? *Possible answer: In these lines, Dee is name-calling instead of just implying her superiority, and Mama is openly disagreeing with Dee instead of just listening and taking things in.*

REVIST THE BIG QUESTION

What makes something
VALUABLE?

Discuss Based on lines 238–243, should a valuable object ever be put to everyday use? *Possible answers: Students may say that the quilts should be saved and cherished or that quilts are everyday objects.*

Crazy Quilt (1883-1893), Victoriene Parsons Mitchell. Textile. 195.6 cm x 163.2 cm. © Indianapolis Museum of Art/ Bridgeman Art Library.

"The truth is," I said, "I promised to give them quilts to Maggie, for when she marries John Thomas."

She gasped like a bee had stung her.

"Maggie can't appreciate these quilts!" she said. "She'd probably be backward enough to put them to everyday use."

240   "I reckon she would," I said. "God knows I been saving 'em for long enough with nobody using 'em. I hope she will!" I didn't want to bring up how I had offered Dee (Wangero) a quilt when she went away to college. Then she had told me they were old-fashioned, out of style.

DIFFERENTIATED INSTRUCTION

FOR STRUGGLING READERS

Concept Support Help students articulate what the quilts mean to Dee as compared with what they mean to Maggie by working with students to complete a Venn Diagram that compares and contrasts Dee's and Maggie's feelings.

 BEST PRACTICES TOOLKIT—Transparency
Venn Diagram p. A26

FOR ENGLISH LANGUAGE LEARNERS

Vocabulary: Phrasal Verbs Have students contrast the meanings of *stare down* (line 71) and *stare at*. Then have pairs participate in a Think-Pair-Share activity by looking up *sat down* (line 179), *hung back* (line 209), and *bring up* (line 241) in a dictionary and sharing the definitions with other students. Challenge students to come up with contrasting phrasal verbs.

BEST PRACTICES TOOLKIT—Transparency
Think-Pair-Share p. A18

"But they're *priceless*!" she was saying now, furiously; for she has a temper. "Maggie would put them on the bed and in five years they'd be in rags. Less than that!"

"She can always make some more," I said. "Maggie knows how to quilt."

Dee (Wangero) looked at me with hatred. "You just will not understand. The point is *these* quilts, these quilts!"

250 "Well," I said, stumped. "What would *you* do with them?"

"Hang them," she said. As if that was the only thing you *could* do with quilts. **J**

Maggie by now was standing in the door. I could almost hear the sound her feet made as they scraped over each other.

"She can have them, Mama," she said, like somebody used to never winning anything, or having anything reserved for her. "I can 'member Grandma Dee without the quilts."

I looked at her hard. She had filled her bottom lip with checkerberry snuff and it gave her face a kind of dopey, hangdog look. It was Grandma Dee and 260 Big Dee who taught her how to quilt herself. She stood there with her scarred hands hidden in the folds of her skirt. She looked at her sister with something like fear but she wasn't mad at her. This was Maggie's portion. This was the way she knew God to work.

When I looked at her like that something hit me in the top of my head and ran down to the soles of my feet. Just like when I'm in church and the spirit of God touches me and I get happy and shout. I did something I never had done before: hugged Maggie to me, then dragged her on into the room, snatched the quilts out of Miss Wangero's hands and dumped them into Maggie's lap. Maggie just sat there on my bed with her mouth open. **K**

270 "Take one or two of the others," I said to Dee.

But she turned without a word and went out to Hakim-a-barber.

"You just don't understand," she said, as Maggie and I came out to the car.

"What don't I understand?" I wanted to know.

"Your **heritage,**" she said. And then she turned to Maggie, kissed her, and said, "You ought to try to make something of yourself, too, Maggie. It's really a new day for us. But from the way you and Mama still live you'd never know it." **L**

She put on some sunglasses that hide everything above the tip of her nose and her chin.

280 Maggie smiled; maybe at the sunglasses. But a real smile, not scared. After we watched the car dust settle I asked Maggie to bring me a dip of snuff. And then the two of us sat there just enjoying, until it was time to go in the house and go to bed. ❧

J CONFLICT
Reread lines 238–252. Why doesn't Dee want Maggie to have the quilts?

③ Targeted Passage

K PLOT
This point is the **climax** of the story. How is the main conflict resolved?

heritage (hĕr′ĭ-tĭj) *n.* something passed down through generations, such as tradition, values, property

L CONFLICT
How does Dee view her mother and sister?

TEXT ANALYSIS   COMMON CORE
RL 1
RL 5

① Model the Skill: CONFLICT

To model how to understand the conflict over the quilts, use the board to write observations about why Maggie values the quilts and why Dee values the quilts.

Possible answer: *Dee feels the quilts are wasted on Maggie, who will put them to "everyday use" (line 239) and possibly wear them out (line 245). Dee thinks Maggie cannot appreciate the quilts as much as she can.*

TEXT ANALYSIS: *Review*

K PLOT

Possible answer: *Dee is put in her place when Mama gives the quilts to Maggie (line 268).*

TEXT ANALYSIS   COMMON CORE
RL 1
RL 5

L CONFLICT

Possible answer: *Dee views Maggie and her mother as African Americans who have not participated in the increased opportunities in the era of civil rights.*

VOCABULARY   COMMON CORE
L 4

OWN THE WORD

heritage: Tell students that the Latin root for *heritage* is *heres,* meaning "heir." Remind students that cities and towns, like people, have their own cultural *heritage.*

FOR STRUGGLING READERS

③ Targeted Passage [Lines 253–269]

This passage contains the story's climax and also reveals a great deal about Mama.

- What does Maggie say about the quilts? (lines 255–257)

- What do Maggie's words and appearance cause Mama to realize? (lines 262– 265)

- What does Maggie's response suggest about how Mama has acted toward Maggie in the past? (line 269)

FOR ADVANCED LEARNERS/PRE–AP

Evaluate Ask students whether they think Mama did the right thing by giving the quilts to Maggie. Break students into small groups, and have several groups list reasons to support Mama's decision. Have other groups find reasons not to support her decision. (For example, Mama finally supported Maggie and boosted her self-confidence. Or Mama may have alienated Dee for good instead of getting her back.) Have opposing small groups debate.

SELECTION WRAP–UP

READ WITH A PURPOSE Have students describe the story's conflicting ideas of what constitutes a family's heritage. Then ask students to compare Dee's idea of valuable to Maggie's idea of valuable. ***Possible answer:*** *For Dee, family heritage is embracing a culture that her family never experienced. She values things for their beauty. Maggie's idea of family heritage is learning skills from older generations and using things they have made.*

Reading for Information

INTERVIEW Excerpted is a 1992 interview Walker gave to Roland R. Freeman for his book *A Communion of the Spirits: African-American Quilters, Preservers, and Their Stories.*

Alice Walker} *on Quilting*

TIERED DISCUSSION PROMPTS

Use these prompts to help students understand the connection between "Everyday Use" and Alice Walker's own experience with quilting:

Connect What skills, hobbies, or passions have been passed down through the generations of your family? *Possible answer: Students may suggest anything from fishing or making a special recipe to collecting comic books.*

Analyze How is Walker's own identity wrapped up in her quilts? *Possible answer: The quilts consist of some of her own dresses and some of her own history. One quilt, the In Love and Trouble Quilt, expresses some of the values of a time period she lived through.*

Synthesize Walker's quilts are an expression of herself. How do quilts express identity for the characters in "Everyday Use"? *Possible answer: The quilts represent the characters' past, their heritage, their relatives, and their mentors. The quilts are also items that are precious and yet suitable for everyday use.*

Well, my mother was a quilter, and I remember many, many afternoons of my mother and the neighborhood women sitting on the porch around the quilting frame, quilting and talking, you know; getting up to stir something on the stove and coming back and sitting down. My mother also had a frame inside the house. Sometimes during the winter she would quilt and she often pieced quilts. Piecing . . . I'm really more of a piecer, actually, than I am a quilter, because I can get as far as piecing all of the little squares or sections together, and sometimes putting them together into big blocks, but then I always have to call in help—spreading it out on the frame, or spreading it out on the floor and putting the batting in and doing the actual quilting.

Alice Walker among her many quilts

[The first quilt] I worked on [was] the In Love and Trouble quilt. And I did that one when I was living in Mississippi. It was during a period when we were wearing African-inspired dresses. So all of the pieces are from dresses that I actually wore.

This yellow and black fabric I bought when I was in Uganda, and I had a beautiful dress made of it that I wore and wore and wore and eventually I couldn't wear it any more; partly I had worn it out and also I was pregnant, so it didn't fit, and I used that and I used the red and white and black, which was a long, floor-length dress that I had when I was pregnant with my daughter, Rebecca, who is now twenty-three. I took these things apart or I used scraps. I put them together in this quilt, because it just seemed perfect. Mississippi was full of political and social struggle, and regular quilts were all African American with emphasis on being here in the United States. But because of the African consciousness that was being raised and the way that we were all wearing our hair in naturals and wearing all of these African dresses, I felt the need to blend these two traditions. So it's a quilt of great memory and importance to me. I use it a lot and that's why it's so worn.

Comprehension

1. **Recall** How has Dee changed when she arrives to see her family?

2. **Recall** Why does Dee want the quilts?

3. **Recall** Who gets the quilts at the end of the story?

4. **Summarize** Why does Dee think Mama and Maggie don't understand their heritage?

COMMON CORE

RL 1 Cite textual evidence to support inferences drawn from the text. **RL 5** Analyze an author's choices concerning how to structure a text.

Text Analysis

5. **Make Inferences** Review the notes you took as you read. What positive and negative traits does each character have?

6. **Compare and Contrast** What makes the quilts valuable to Dee, and what makes them valuable to Maggie? Cite evidence.

7. **Analyze Plot** Reread lines 264–269. Explain why Mama makes the choice she does at the **climax** of the story. How does she feel about her choice?

8. **Analyze Conflict** Use the chart shown to explore the various ways that Dee is in conflict with her family. Which conflicts are resolved and which are not?

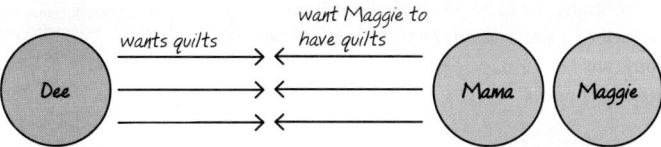

9. **Interpret Theme** What do you think Alice Walker is saying in "Everyday Use" about the nature of heritage? Support your answer.

10. **Synthesize** How do Walker's comments about quilting on page 60 affect your understanding of "Everyday Use"?

Text Criticism

11. **Historical Context** The story takes place in the late 1960s, a time of growing cultural awareness for African Americans. If the story were set in the present, would the conflicts within the family be different? Explain your answer.

What makes something VALUABLE?

Why might people disagree over why an object is valuable?

Practice and Apply

For preliminary support of post-reading questions, use these copy masters:

R RESOURCE MANAGER—Copy Masters

Reading Check p. 50
Conflict and Character p. 43
Question Support p. 51

Additional selection questions are provided for teachers on page 37.

ANSWERS

Comprehension

1. *Dee has changed her name and wears the hairstyle and clothing of someone who has embraced black pride.*
2. *She wants to hang the quilts to call attention to her African heritage.*
3. *Maggie gets the quilts.*
4. *Dee believes that using the quilts every day, as she assumes Maggie would do, is less practical than preserving them for the future.*

Text Analysis

COMMON CORE **RL 1, RL 5**

Possible answers:

5. ■ **COMMON CORE FOCUS** *Make Inferences*
   Positive: Mama accepts her own life; Maggie is humble; Dee is confident; Negative: Mama has a limited view of life; Dee can be overbearing; Maggie does not assert herself.
6. *Dee calls the quilts "priceless" (line 244). She recognizes them as part of her heritage (line 274) and wants to preserve them. For Maggie, the quilts are valuable for everyday use. She appreciates that they are the work of Grandma Dee and Big Dee, who taught her to quilt (259–260).*
7. *Mama realizes that Maggie needs the quilts for practical (lines 235–236), psychological (lines 258–263, 280), and emotional (lines 256–257) reasons. Mama is thrilled with her choice; it is like the "spirit of God" touching her (lines 265–266).*
8. ● **COMMON CORE FOCUS** *Analyze Conflict* *Dee changes her name; Mama and Maggie accept her change. Dee has moved away and adopted a "sophisticated lifestyle." Mama and Maggie still live at home and show no signs of changing their lifestyle.*
9. *Dee clearly values her past, just as Mama and Maggie do. The ways of the past (as*

---

represented by Maggie and Mama) are not necessarily worse than the new ways (represented by Dee and Hakim-a-barber).

10. *Walker explains that quilting is part of her own heritage, and is important to African-American heritage. She shows that quilts are valued in her culture, just as Dee, Maggie, and Mama all value quilts.*

Text Criticism

Possible answer:

11. *Dee might still feel embarrassed by her family and entitled to the quilts. Because embracing African heritage is not as new*

and fashionable, she might show her superiority in another way.

What makes something **VALUABLE?** Students might focus on the monetary value of something or its cultural or sentimental value. Suggest students consider what they would save first from their home in the event of a disaster.

ANSWERS

Vocabulary in Context

▲ VOCABULARY PRACTICE

1. *true*   3. *true*
2. *false*   4. *true*

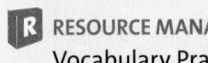 RESOURCE MANAGER—Copy Master
Vocabulary Practice p. 48

ACADEMIC VOCABULARY IN WRITING

Student answers should indicate that Dee communicates with broader gestures than Maggie does. Dee is much more straightforward and confrontational. Maggie tends to stand quietly, looking down, and scraping her feet together. She often lets her mother speak for her.

VOCABULARY STRATEGY:
THE PREFIX *re-*    COMMON CORE **L 4c**

Note that *re-* is often used as a prefix with action words. Ask which words in the web name actions. *(All do, although review and recall can also be nouns.)*

Possible answers:

1. *reaffirm*
2. *recompose*
3. *reboot*
4. *recall*
5. *review*

 RESOURCE MANAGER—Copy Master
Vocabulary Strategy p. 49

 **Interactive Vocabulary**

Keywords direct students to a **WordSharp** tutorial on **thinkcentral.com** or to other types of vocabulary practice and review.

Vocabulary in Context

▲ **VOCABULARY PRACTICE**

Write *True* or *False* for each statement.

1. Sneaking around is an example of **furtive** behavior.
2. When you **recompose** after a traffic accident, you become more agitated.
3. To believe in a certain group's **doctrine** is to follow their set rules.
4. If you deny your **heritage,** you refuse to acknowledge your cultural history.

ACADEMIC VOCABULARY IN WRITING

• affect   • communicate   • definite   • establish   • identify

Analyze how Dee and Maggie **communicate** their thoughts and feelings in this story. Notice both verbal communication (what they say, how they say it) and nonverbal communication (their facial expressions, gestures, and body language). Write one or two paragraphs to share your findings. Use at least one Academic Vocabulary word in your discussion.

VOCABULARY STRATEGY: THE PREFIX RE-

The vocabulary word *recompose* contains the Latin prefix *re-*, which means "again" or "back." This prefix is found in a number of English words. To understand the meaning of words with *re-*, use your knowledge of the base word as well as your knowledge of the prefix.

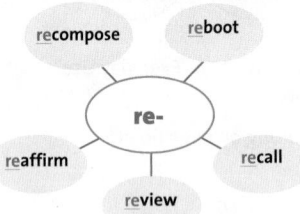

COMMON CORE

L 4c Consult reference materials to determine or clarify a word's meaning or etymology.

PRACTICE Write the word from the word web that best completes each sentence. Use context clues to help you or, if necessary, consult a dictionary.

1. To celebrate their anniversary, the couple decided to _____ their marriage vows.
2. She tried to _____ herself after her harsh scolding.
3. You need to _____ the computer after installing new software.
4. The toy company issued a _____ on a toy truck with dangerous parts.
5. Be sure to _____ your paper for spelling mistakes before submitting it.

Interactive Vocabulary
Go to **thinkcentral.com**.
KEYWORD: HML10-62

DIFFERENTIATED INSTRUCTION

FOR ENGLISH LANGUAGE LEARNERS

Vocabulary Activity Have students work in two or more teams to list more English words that begin with *re-*. Point out that most of the words will be verbs. Give each team one point for every verb, two for every noun.

Language

◆ **GRAMMAR AND STYLE: Add Descriptive Details**

Review the **Grammar and Style** note on page 55. By incorporating **prepositional phrases** into your writing, as Alice Walker does, you can add important details that show *what, when, where,* and *how* events are taking place. Here is an example from the story.

COMMON CORE

L 1b Use prepositional phrases to add variety and interest to writing. **W 3** Write narratives to develop events using well-structured event sequences.

> *After dinner Dee (Wangero) went to the trunk at the foot of my bed and started rifling through it. Maggie hung back in the kitchen over the dishpan. Out came Wangero with two quilts. They had been pieced by Grandma Dee and then Big Dee and me had hung them on the quilt frames on the front porch and quilted them.* (lines 208–212)

See how the revisions in blue add important descriptive details to this first draft. Revise your own writing by using these techniques.

STUDENT MODEL

Mama walks over to Dee and gives her a kiss. Dee frowns and wipes off the kiss. She crosses the room and sits down heavily.

on the cheek ^ *at Mama* ^
with a handkerchief ^ *on the bench* ^

READING-WRITING CONNECTION

YOUR TURN

Deepen your understanding of "Everyday Use" by responding to this prompt. Then use the **revising tip** to improve your writing.

WRITING PROMPT	REVISING TIP
Extended Constructed Response: Story Sequel Imagine that Dee visits the family again ten years after the events in "Everyday Use." Write **one page** showing what she, Mama, and Maggie are now like and how they interact. What conflicts between them are still unresolved?	Review your response. How have you used prepositional phrases that show *what, when, where,* and *how* events take place in your story sequel?

Interactive Revision

THINK central

Go to **thinkcentral.com**.
KEYWORD: HML10-63

FOR STRUGGLING WRITERS

- Have students discuss the character traits of Mama, Maggie, and Dee. Ask them to consider ways the characters may have changed.

- Before students begin drafting, suggest they work in pairs to discuss a possible conflict or other interaction that the characters might have, based on their history.

Language

COMMON CORE L 1b, W 3
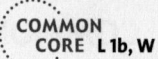

◆ **GRAMMAR AND STYLE**

Write this passage on the board, pointing out how the prepositional phrases (in blue) add descriptive details:

> *During Mama's recollection of the past, Hakim-a-barber and Dee arrive. Through the strong sun, Mama sees Dee get out of the car. She sees that Dee is dressed in a brightly colored African dress.*

Then ask students to add new prepositional phrases that tell *what, when, where,* and *how.* (For more on prepositional phrases, see **Grammar Handbook**, page R60.)

R RESOURCE MANAGER—Copy Master
Add Descriptive Details p. 52

READING-WRITING CONNECTION

Ask students to consider these questions: When Dee arrives, what is she wearing? Is she with anyone? How has she changed? Where is Maggie? Where is Mama? How have Maggie and Mama changed?

BEST PRACTICES TOOLKIT—Transparency
Comparison Matrix p. A24

Writing Online

THINK central

The following tools are available online at **thinkcentral.com** and on **Write*Smart* CD-ROM**:
- **Interactive Graphic Organizers**
- **Interactive Student Models**
- **Interactive Revision Lessons**

For additional grammar instruction, see **GrammarNotes** on **thinkcentral.com**.

Assess and Reteach

Assess

R DIAGNOSTIC AND SELECTION TESTS
Selection Test A, pp. 27–28
Selection Test B/C, pp. 29–30

Interactive Selection Test on **thinkcentral.com**

Reteach

Level Up Online Tutorials on **thinkcentral.com**

Reteaching Worksheets on **thinkcentral.com**
Literature Lesson 6, Reading Lesson 8, Vocabulary Lesson 2

Focus and Motivate

Searching for Summer
Short Story by Joan Aiken

COMMON CORE FOCUS

RL 3 Analyze how complex characters develop over the course of a text, interact with other characters, and advance the plot. RL 4 Determine the connotative meanings of words; analyze the cumulative impact of specific word choices on tone. RL 10 Read and comprehend literature, including stories. L 3 Make effective choices for meaning or style. L 4c Consult reference materials to determine a word's etymology.

SUMMARY

Set in a future after bombs have clouded the skies, "Searching for Summer" tells of Tom and Lily, who want to spend their honeymoon in sunshine. Instead, they get stuck in a dreary village before discovering a home bathed in sunshine. They spend three blissful days there, but then leave rather than reveal the cottage's location.

What do you take for
GRANTED?

Elicit that *to take for granted* means "not appreciate." Discuss the *BIG QUESTION* with students. After they complete the *DISCUSS* activity, have them explain their choices.

What do you take for
GRANTED?

COMMON CORE

RL 4 Determine the connotative meanings of words; analyze the cumulative impact of specific word choices on tone. RL 10 Read and comprehend literature, including stories.

There are many things in life that we assume will always be there. Air and water are two. But what if they disappeared? You've probably heard the saying "You never miss the water until the well runs dry." That means that we don't have appreciation for certain things until they're gone or scarce. "Searching for Summer" is set in a world that is missing something else we all take for granted.

DISCUSS Conduct an informal class survey, asking each person to name an everyday thing that is taken for granted. Choose the item mentioned most often, and as a class, discuss what you would do if this thing were suddenly gone or in short supply.

Things We Take for Granted
1. Air
2. Water

64

Selection Resources

See resources on the **Teacher One Stop DVD-ROM** *and on* **thinkcentral.com**.

RESOURCE MANAGER UNIT 1
Plan and Teach, pp. 55–62
Summary, pp. 63–64†‡*
Text Analysis and Reading
    Skill, pp. 65–68†*
Vocabulary, pp. 69–71*
Grammar and Style, p. 74

**DIAGNOSTIC AND SELECTION
    TESTS**
Selection Tests, pp. 31–34

BEST PRACTICES TOOLKIT
Word Squares, p. E10
Cluster Diagram, p. B18
Analysis Frame: Theme, p.
    D21, D32

TECHNOLOGY
🔘 **Teacher One Stop DVD-ROM**
🔘 **Student One Stop DVD-ROM**
🔘 **Audio Anthology CD**
🔘 **GrammarNotes DVD-ROM**
🔘 **ExamView Test Generator**
    on the Teacher One Stop

*** Resources for Differentiation   † Also in Spanish   ‡ In Haitian Creole and Vietnamese**

TEXT ANALYSIS: SETTING AND MOOD

A story may have more than one **setting**, and each setting may convey a different **mood**, or atmosphere. Imagine, for example, the emotional atmosphere in a gym packed with students watching their team winning an important game. Shouts, cheers, upbeat music, exciting plays—all these sights and sounds would create a mood of excitement and joyous anticipation. Now imagine how the mood would change if a character walked out of the gym into a long, dark, deserted hallway. To understand the relationship between the setting and the mood in a story, think about

• the sensory language that tells what a place is like
• the feelings conveyed by that language

In "Searching for Summer," you'll encounter two very different settings. As you read, notice the descriptions of each setting and think about the mood those details convey.

Review: **Conflict**

● READING STRATEGY: MONITOR

When you **monitor,** you check to make sure you understand what you are reading. If you don't understand a story, you may have to read more slowly, reread passages, or read aloud. Jot down any questions you have about the story's setting, characters, and events, and then answer them as you read further. Use a chart like the one shown. Additional monitoring questions are provided to help you clarify your understanding.

My Questions	My Answers
Why were the bombs banned?	probably because they caused too much destruction

▲ VOCABULARY IN CONTEXT

Classify the vocabulary words into three categories: "Words I Know Well," "Words I Think I Know," and "Words I Don't Know at All." Write a short definition in your *Reader/Writer Notebook* for words in the first two categories. After you read this short story, correct your definitions if necessary and define the new words you learn.

1. unavailing	2. disengage	3. rudimentary
4. wizened	5. voluble	6. commiserate
7. savoring	8. indomitable	

Complete the activities in your **Reader/Writer Notebook**.

Meet the Author

Joan Aiken
1924–2004

Literary Fathers
Joan Aiken (āˈkən) grew up in England in a literary household. Her father, Conrad Aiken, was an American poet, and her stepfather, Martin Armstrong, was a fiction writer. At an early age, she decided to follow in their footsteps.

A Writer's Life
In 1945 Aiken met and married journalist Ronald Brown. That same year, she began publishing poems and stories in magazines. Her first book for young adults, *All You've Ever Wanted and Other Stories,* appeared in 1953. About two years later, her husband died. To support herself and her two children, she worked as an editor for *Argosy,* a short story magazine, but continued to write at home. Her 1962 children's novel *The Wolves of Willoughby Chase* was a hit with critics and readers alike, enabling her to become a full-time writer. Aiken followed up with many other successful novels, including *Black Hearts in Battersea* and *The Whispering Mountain.* Though she is most often remembered as an author for young people, readers of all ages enjoy her stories.

BACKGROUND TO THE STORY

Nuclear Anxiety
Aiken wrote "Searching for Summer" in the 1950s, setting the story in a future "eighties"—perhaps the 1980s or 2080s. When the story was published, nuclear disaster was an ever-present threat. New nuclear weapons were being tested, and radioactive fallout rained down from the sky, polluting the environment.

Author Online
THINK central
Go to **thinkcentral.com.**
KEYWORD: HML10-65

65

Teach

● Model the Skill: SETTING AND MOOD

To model how to identify setting and mood, have students read the text under **Nuclear Anxiety.** Ask them to choose and describe a possible setting and mood for a story they might write, assuming the time period is one of nuclear anxiety. Point out that the setting could be a small town. The mood would be fearful and anxious.

GUIDED PRACTICE Ask students to develop their setting and mood by giving more descriptive details.

■ Model the Skill: MONITOR

Model for students how to monitor. Instruct students to read the text under **Literary Fathers** and **A Writer's Life.** Point out the following possible monitoring questions. *Who were Joan Aiken's fathers? Why did Joan work as an editor when she really loved writing?* Have students monitor their reading in a Reading Strategy chart.

GUIDED PRACTICE Ask students to try to answer their own questions.

R RESOURCE MANAGER—Copy Master
Monitor p. 67 (for student use while reading the selection)

VOCABULARY SKILL

▲ VOCABULARY IN CONTEXT

DIAGNOSE WORD KNOWLEDGE Have all students complete Vocabulary in Context. Check their definitions against the following:

commiserate (kə-mĭzˈə-rāt) *v.* to express sorrow or pity for another's troubles

disengage (dĭsˈĕn-gājˈ) *v.* to detach or remove oneself

indomitable (ĭn-dŏmˈĭ-tə-bəl) *adj.* not easily discouraged or defeated

rudimentary (rōōˈdə-mĕnˈtə-rē) *adj.* very basic, in the beginning stages

savoring (sāˈvər-ĭng) *n.* a full appreciation and enjoyment **savor** *v.*

unavailing (ŭnˈə-vāˈlĭng) *adj.* useless, ineffective

voluble (vŏlˈyə-bəl) *adj.* especially talkative, fluent with words

wizened (wĭzˈənd) *adj.* withered and dry

PRETEACH VOCABULARY Use the following copy master to help student predict the meaning of each boldfaced word in the copy master,

using context clues.

R RESOURCE MANAGER—Copy Master
Vocabulary Study p. 69

1. Read item 1 aloud, emphasizing *commiserate*.

2. Point out the word *kind* and the phrase *understand they had a difficult day.* Elicit possible meanings for commiserate, such as "sympathize."

3. Have students record their predictions.

4. Repeat the procedure for items 2–8.

SEARCHING FOR *Summer*

Joan Aiken

Lily wore yellow on her wedding day. In the eighties people put a lot of faith in omens and believed that if a bride's dress was yellow her married life would be blessed with a bit of sunshine.

It was years since the bombs had been banned, but still the cloud never lifted. Whitish gray, day after day, sometimes darkening to a weeping slate color or, at the end of an evening, turning to smoky copper, the sky endlessly, secretively brooded.

Old people began their stories with the classic, fairy-tale opening: "Long, long ago, when I was a liddle un, in the days when the sky was blue …" and
10 children, listening, chuckled among themselves at the absurd thought, because, *blue,* imagine it! How could the sky ever have been *blue?* You might as well say, "In the days when the grass was pink."

Stars, rainbows, and all other such heavenly sideshows had been permanently withdrawn, and if the radio announced that there was a blink of sunshine in such and such a place, where the cloud belt had thinned for half an hour, cars and buses would pour in that direction for days in an **unavailing** search for warmth and light. **A**

After the wedding, when all the relations were standing on the church porch, with Lily shivering prettily in her buttercup nylon, her father prodded
20 the dour and withered grass on a grave—although it was August, the leaves were hardly out yet—and said, "Well, Tom, what are you aiming to do now, eh?"

"Going to find a bit of sun and have our honeymoon in it," said Tom. There was a general laugh from the wedding party.

"Don't get sunburned," shrilled Aunt Nancy.

"Better start off Bournemouth[1] way. Paper said they had a half-hour of sun last Wednesday week," Uncle Arthur weighed in heavily.

Analyze Visuals ▶

How would you describe the **mood** of this painting? What qualities contribute to the mood?

unavailing (ŭn′ə-vā′lĭng) *adj.* useless, ineffective

A MONITOR
Reread lines 8–17. How have the sky and climate changed, and why?

① Targeted Passage

---

1. **Bournemouth** (bôrn′məth): a British seaside resort.

DIFFERENTIATED INSTRUCTION

FOR ENGLISH LANGUAGE LEARNERS

Vocabulary Support Use Word Squares to teach these words: *classic* (line 8), *insignificant* (line 61), *survey* (line 63), *individual* (line 92), *benefit* (line 168), *layer* (line 200).

BEST PRACTICES TOOLKIT—Transparency
Word Squares p. E10

FOR STRUGGLING READERS

In combination with the *Audio Anthology CD*, use one or more Targeted Passages (pp. 66, 68, 70, 72, 74) to ensure that students focus on key story events, concepts, and skills. Targeted Passages are also good for English learners.

① Targeted Passage [Lines 18–27]

This passage explains the goal of the newlyweds and shows that few others expect them to achieve it.

Nuclear Winter The setting described in "Searching for Summer" is not merely the result of one writer's imagination. The setting mirrors a situation that scientists now call Nuclear Winter. In the 1980s, scientists began predicting that Nuclear Winter would be a likely outcome of a nuclear war. Scientists estimated that nuclear bombs would generate huge quantities of dust and soot, which would be carried into Earth's atmosphere. There, the dust and soot would absorb sunlight. As a result, less sunlight would reach the ground, and days would become dark and overcast. Plants would not receive enough light for photosynthesis, and temperatures would plummet. These details are almost identical to those imagined by Aiken in this story which was written in the 1950s.

Analyze Visuals

Possible answer: The mood of the painting is gloomy and depressed. The lack of definition of the objects; the muted, gray, almost colorless scenes; and the general drabness of the painting contribute to the mood.

About the Art *Old Willow Lane 2* (1988) was painted by Mary Iverson (b. 1966). She is a Seattle artist who enjoys creating air paintings, a style that is created outside in natural light.

REVISIT THE BIG QUESTION

What do you take for

GRANTED?

Discuss In lines 13–27, what details show that the people in this story have an appreciation of sunlight? *Possible answer: Cars and buses head toward places that are reported to have sunshine (line 16). A half-hour of sun is considered a newsworthy event (lines 26–27).*

- Why is Lily shivering? (lines 4–7)
- What do Tom and Lily hope to do? (line 23)
- How do the others react? Why do you think they react this way? (lines 23–27)
- Why does Aunt Nancy say, "Don't get sunburned" (line 25)? (lines 4–7 and 13–14)

FOR ADVANCED LEARNERS/PRE–AP

Hypothesize After students read the first page of the story, engage the class in a discussion. How might world governments respond to Nuclear Winter if it occurred today? What might scientists try to do to fix the situation? Encourage students to consider how the food supply and drinking water would be affected. Would the same areas be inhabitable if the temperature dropped?

TEXT ANALYSIS   COMMON CORE
RL 4

B SETTING AND MOOD

Possible answer: The road is "gray and gritty" (line 32), and the countryside is gray and chilly (lines 36–37). These descriptions create a dreary, depressing mood.

READING STRATEGY   COMMON CORE
RL 10

C MONITOR

Possible answer: The sun is out so infrequently ("Last time I saw the sun was two years ago September" [lines 52–53]), that if it is out, people come in trucks and buses to see it.

TEXT ANALYSIS   COMMON CORE
RL 4

D *Model the Skill:* **SETTING AND MOOD**

Model for students how to identify setting and mood. Point out the phrase "people had given up bothering to take pride in their boroughs" in lines 59–60. Tell students they will need to use all their senses in order to understand the setting and mood. Ask students to think about what the town would smell like and sound like if no one took care of it. Have students use sensory details to describe how they perceive the town. Then have students describe the feelings those details convey to them.

Possible answer: The image makes me feel sad, discouraged, and hopeless.

Extend the Discussion How does the name "Molesworth" affect the feeling that you get from the description of the town?

"We'll come back brown as—as this grass," said Tom, and ignoring the good-natured teasing from their respective families, the two young people
30 mounted on their scooter, which stood ready at the churchyard wall, and chugged away in a shower of golden confetti. When they were out of sight, and the yellow paper had subsided on the gray and gritty road, the Whitemores and the Hoskinses strolled off, sighing, to eat wedding cake and drink currant[2] wine, and old Mrs. Hoskins spoiled everyone's pleasure by bursting into tears as she thought of her own wedding day when everything was so different.

Meanwhile Tom and Lily buzzed on hopefully across the gray countryside, with Lily's veil like a gilt banner floating behind. It was chilly going for her in her wedding things, but the sight of a bride was supposed to bring good luck, and so she stuck it out, although her fingers were blue to the knuckles.
40 Every now and then they switched on their portable radio and listened to the forecast. Inverness had seen the sun for ten minutes yesterday, and Southend[3] for five minutes this morning, but that was all. **B**

"Both those places are a long way from here," said Tom cheerfully. "All the more reason we'd find a nice bit of sunshine in these parts somewhere. We'll keep on going south. Keep your eyes peeled, Lil, and tell me if you see a blink of sun on those hills ahead."

But they came to the hills and passed them, and a new range shouldered up ahead and then slid away behind, and still there was no flicker or patch of sunshine to be seen anywhere in the gray, winter-ridden landscape. Lily began
50 to get discouraged, so they stopped for a cup of tea at a drive-in.

"Seen the sun lately, mate?" Tom asked the proprietor.

He laughed shortly. "Notice any buses or trucks around here? Last time I saw the sun was two years ago September; came out just in time for the wife's birthday." **C**

"It's stars I'd like to see," Lily said, looking wistfully at her dust-colored tea. "Ever so pretty they must be."

"Well, better be getting on I suppose," said Tom, but he had lost some of his bounce and confidence. Every place they passed through looked nastier than the last, partly on account of the dismal light, partly because people had given up
60 bothering to take a pride in their boroughs.[4] And then, just as they were entering a village called Molesworth, the dimmest, drabbest, most insignificant huddle of houses they had come to yet, the engine coughed and died on them. **D**

"Can't see what's wrong," said Tom, after a prolonged and gloomy survey.

"Oh, Tom!" Lily was almost crying. "What'll we do?"

"Have to stop here for the night, s'pose." Tom was short-tempered with frustration. "Look, there's a garage just up the road. We can push the bike there, and they'll tell us if there's a pub[5] where we can stay. It's nearly six anyway."

---

2. **currant:** a berry used to make jams, jellies, and wines.

3. **Inverness . . . Southend:** resort towns in the north and south of the British Isles.

4. **boroughs:** towns or districts.

5. **pub:** a British term for a tavern. Pubs in small towns sometimes serve meals and rent rooms to travelers.

B SETTING AND MOOD Reread lines 28–42. Note how the countryside looks and feels. What mood is created by this description?

C MONITOR Why are buses and trucks a sign that sunshine has been spotted in the area?

 **Targeted Passage**

D SETTING AND MOOD Reread lines 58–62. Picture what Molesworth looks like. What feeling do you get from that image?

DIFFERENTIATED INSTRUCTION

FOR STRUGGLING READERS

Targeted Passage [Lines 52–65]

This passage explains how the newlyweds are feeling about their trip and how they ended up in Molesworth, the setting for the major conflict.

- How have Tom's feelings changed since their journey began? (lines 56–57)

- What happened to the engine? (line 62)

- How does Lily react? Why do you think she reacts as she does? (line 64)

FOR ENGLISH LANGUAGE LEARNERS

Language: Modifiers Point out "dimmest, drabbest, most insignificant" (line 61) and explain that these words describe houses. Ask students to identify other pairs or clusters of adjectives in the story, such as "big, red-faced" (line 94); "bulging pale-gray bloodshot"; "stiff greasy black" (line 95); "yellow nylon" (line 170). Have students share their adjectives.

They had taken the bike to the garage, and the man there was just telling
them that the only pub in the village was the Rising Sun, where Mr. Noakes
70 might be able to give them a bed, when a bus pulled up in front of the
petrol[6] pumps.

"Look," the garage owner said, "there's Mr. Noakes just getting out of the
bus now. Sid!" he called.

But Mr. Noakes was not able to come to them at once. Two old people were
climbing slowly out of the bus ahead of him: a blind man with a white stick,
and a withered, frail old lady in a black satin dress and hat. "Careful now,
George," she was saying, "mind ee be careful with my son William."

"I'm being careful, Mrs. Hatching," the conductor said patiently, as
he almost lifted the unsteady old pair off the bus platform. The driver
80 had stopped his engine, and everyone on the bus was taking a mild and
sympathetic interest, except for Mr. Noakes just behind who was cursing
irritably at the delay. When the two old people were on the narrow pavement,
the conductor saw that they were going to have trouble with a bicycle that
was propped against the curb just ahead of them; he picked it up and stood
holding it until they had passed the line of petrol pumps and were going slowly
off along a path across the fields. Then, grinning, he put it back, jumped
hurriedly into the bus, and rang his bell.

"Old nuisances," Mr. Noakes said furiously. "Wasting public time.
Every week that palaver[7] goes on, taking the old man to Midwick Hospital
90 Outpatients and back again. I know what *I'd* do with 'em. Put to sleep, that
sort ought to be." **E**

Mr. Noakes was a repulsive-looking individual, but when he heard that Tom
and Lily wanted a room for the night, he changed completely and gave them a
leer that was full of false goodwill. He was a big, red-faced man with wet, full
lips, bulging pale-gray bloodshot eyes, and a crop of stiff greasy black hair. He
wore tennis shoes.

"Honeymooners, eh?" he said, looking sentimentally at Lily's pale prettiness.
"Want a bed for the night, eh?" and he laughed a disgusting laugh that
sounded like thick oil coming out of a bottle, heh-heh-heh-heh, and gave Lily
100 a tremendous pinch on her arm. **Disengaging** herself as politely as she could,
she stooped and picked up something from the pavement. They followed
Mr. Noakes glumly up the street to the Rising Sun.

While they were eating their baked beans, Mr. Noakes stood over their table
grimacing at them. Lily unwisely confided to him that they were looking for
a bit of sunshine. Mr. Noakes's laughter nearly shook down the ramshackle
building.

"Sunshine! Oh my gawd! That's a good 'un! Hear that, Mother?" he bawled
to his wife. "They're looking for a bit of sunshine. Heh-heh-heh-heh-heh-heh!

---

6. **petrol:** a British term for gasoline.

7. **palaver** (pə-lăv'ər): useless chatter.

COMMON CORE RL 4

Language Coach

Informal Language
Aiken's characters
speak informally, in a
regional **dialect**—the
vocabulary, grammar,
and pronunciation
of their setting. For
example, they use
"mind ee" (line 77)
and "good 'un!" (line
107). What other
examples of informal
language can you
find?

E CONFLICT
How does Mr. Noakes's
response to the Hatchings
differ from everyone
else's?

disengage (dĭs'ĕn-gāj')
v. to detach or remove
oneself

TEXT ANALYSIS: *Review*

E CONFLICT

Possible answer: *The other people respond
in a kind and considerate way, while
Mr. Noakes is totally unsympathetic toward
them. He curses "irritably at the delay"
(lines 81–82). He even goes so far as to suggest that they be put to sleep (lines 90–91).*

REVISIT THE BIG QUESTION

What do you take for
GRANTED?

Discuss In lines 90–102, how does Mr. Noakes
give you an appreciation for ordinary courtesy
and decency? *Possible answer: He shows how
unpleasant life can be when people lack these
qualities (lines 90–91, 98–100).*

VOCABULARY COMMON CORE L 4

OWN THE WORD

disengage: Have students complete this
sentence: Lily *disengaged* herself politely
from Mr. Noakes because. . . . ***Possible
answer:*** *He made her feel uncomfortable;
he had leered at her and pinched her.*

FOR ENGLISH LANGUAGE LEARNERS

Language Coach COMMON CORE RL 4
Informal Language Answer: *Examples
include: "Put to sleep, that sort ought to be"
(lines 90–91); "dja know what I'd do?" (lines
110–111); "I'd buy up the lot" (line 115).* Have
students work in pairs to rephrase the
informal language phrases into standard
English. For example, "dja know what I'd
do" could be rephrased as "Do you know I
would do?"

FOR ADVANCED LEARNERS/PRE–AP

Analyze Character Description Have pairs
find descriptive phrases that are used to
describe the physical appearance of Lily and
Mr. Noakes. How do these phrases help
accurately characterize each character? How
do the phrases show how different Lily and
Mr. Noakes are? For example, Lily's "pale
prettiness" (line 97) contrasts sharply with Mr.
Noakes's "bloodshot eyes, and a crop of stiff
greasy black hair" (line 95).

Analyze Visuals

Activity Ask students how the mood of this painting is different from the mood of *Old Willow Lane 2* on page 67. ***Possible answers:*** *This painting is bright, warm, and colorful, while the other is gray and colorless. This painting shows sunshine, and suggests a positive, uplifting mood, while the mood of* Old Willow Lane 2 *is depressing.*

About the Art Victoria Crowe (b. 1945) painted *Entrance to Erchless.* She is an appropriate artist for a story set in the British Isles. She studied art in London and teaches drawing and painting in Scotland.

Entrance to Erchless (1900s), Victoria Crowe. Oil on canvas, 96.5 cm × 111.7 cm. The Fleming-Wyfold Art Foundation. Photo © The Bridgeman Art Library.

 **GRAMMAR AND STYLE**

COMMON CORE L 3

Analyze Dialogue Spoken language differs from formal written language. For example, people include sentence fragments, contractions, and interjections in their spoken language. Authors use these elements in dialogue to make their characters sound real. Ask students to identify **fragments, contractions,** and **interjections** from lines 114–118. Have them identify other examples of fragments, contractions, and interjections as they read.

Why," he said, banging on the table till the baked beans leaped about,
110 "if I could find a bit of sunshine near here, permanent bit that is, dja know what I'd do?"

The young people looked at him inquiringly across the bread and margarine.

"Lido,[8] trailer site, country club, holiday camp—you wouldn't know the place. Land around here is dirt cheap; I'd buy up the lot. Nothing but woods. I'd advertise—I'd have people flocking to this little dump from all over the country. But what a hope, what a hope, eh? Well, feeling better? Enjoyed your tea? Ready for bed? Heh-heh-heh-heh, bed's ready for you." **F**

Avoiding one another's eyes, Tom and Lily stood up.

120 "I—I'd like to go for a bit of a walk first, Tom," Lily said in a small voice. "Look, I picked up that old lady's bag on the pavement; I didn't notice it till we'd done talking to Mr. Noakes, and by then she was out of sight. Should we take it back to her?"

"Good idea," said Tom, pouncing on the suggestion with relief. "Do you know where she lives, Mr. Noakes?"

"Who, old Ma Hatching? Sure I know. She lives in the wood. But you don't want to go taking her bag back, not this time o' the evening you don't. Let her worry. She'll come asking for it in the morning."

"She walked so slowly," said Lily, holding the bag gently in her hands. It
130 was very old, made of black velvet on two ring handles, and embroidered with beaded roses. "I think we ought to take it to her, don't you, Tom?"

---

8. **lido** (lī'dō): a British term for a public outdoor swimming pool.

70 UNIT 1: PLOT, SETTING, AND MOOD

3 Targeted Passage

F GRAMMAR AND STYLE
Reread lines 107–118. Notice how Aiken incorporates **sentence fragments, contractions,** and **interjections** into her dialogue to make it sound realistic.

DIFFERENTIATED INSTRUCTION

FOR STRUGGLING READERS

3 Targeted Passage [Lines 109–131]

This passage foreshadows the main problem and advances the plot.

- What would Mr. Noakes do if he found a bit of sunshine? (lines 114–117)

- How would Mr. Noakes's idea change the place? (lines 114–117)

- What does Lily find, and what does she want to do with it? (lines 121–123)

FOR ADVANCED LEARNERS/PRE–AP

Irony Irony refers to a contrast between appearance and actuality. Point out the irony of Noakes's plan: destroying natural beauty by bringing in masses of people to appreciate it. Have small groups research real places, such as national parks or seashores, in their community or elsewhere in the United States in which something similar has happened. Ask groups to present their findings to the class.

"Oh, very well, very well, have it your own way," Mr. Noakes said, winking at Tom. "Take that path by the garage; you can't go wrong. I've never been there meself, but they live somewhere in that wood back o' the village; you'll find it soon enough."

They found the path soon enough, but not the cottage. Under the lowering sky they walked forward endlessly among trees that carried only tiny and **rudimentary** leaves, **wizened** and poverty-stricken. Lily was still wearing her wedding sandals, which had begun to blister her. She held onto Tom's arm, 140 biting her lip with the pain, and he looked down miserably at her bent brown head; everything had turned out so differently from what he had planned. **G**

By the time they reached the cottage Lily could hardly bear to put her left foot to the ground, and Tom was gentling her along: "It can't be much farther now, and they'll be sure to have a bandage. I'll tie it up, and you can have a sit-down. Maybe they'll give us a cup of tea. We could borrow an old pair of socks or something. . . ." Hardly noticing the cottage garden, beyond a vague impression of rows of runner beans, they made for the clematis-grown[9] porch and knocked. There was a brass lion's head on the door, carefully polished.

"Eh, me dear!" It was the old lady, old Mrs. Hatching, who opened 150 the door, and her exclamation was a long-drawn gasp of pleasure and astonishment. "Eh, me dear! 'Tis the pretty bride. See'd ye s'arternoon when we was coming home from hospital."

"Who be?" shouted a voice from inside.

"Come in, come in, me dears. My son William'll be glad to hear company; he can't see, poor soul, nor has this thirty year, ah, and a pretty sight he's losing this minute—"

"We brought back your bag," Tom said, putting it in her hands, "and we wondered if you'd have a bit of plaster[10] you could kindly let us have. My wife's hurt her foot—"

160 My wife. Even in the midst of Mrs. Hatching's **voluble** welcome the strangeness of these words struck the two young people, and they fell quiet, each of them, pondering, while Mrs. Hatching thanked and **commiserated,** all in a breath, and asked them to take a seat on the sofa and fetched a basin of water from the scullery,[11] and William from his seat in the chimney corner demanded to know what it was all about.

"Wot be doing? Wot be doing, Mother?"

" 'Tis a bride, all in's finery," she shrilled back at him, "an's blistered her foot, poor heart." Keeping up a running commentary for William's benefit she bound up the foot, every now and then exclaiming to herself in wonder over 170 the fineness of Lily's wedding dress, which lay in yellow nylon swathes around the chair. "There, me dear. Now us'll have a cup of tea, eh? Proper thirsty you'm fare to be, walking all the way to here this hot day."

Hot day? Tom and Lily stared at each other and then around the room.

---

9. **clematis-grown:** covered with clematis, a flowering vine.

10. **plaster:** a British term for an adhesive bandage.

11. **scullery:** a small room in which dishwashing and other kitchen chores are done.

rudimentary
(rōō′də-mĕn′tə-rē)
adj. very basic, in the beginning stages

wizened (wĭz′ənd)
adj. withered and dry

G SETTING AND MOOD
Reread lines 136–141. What mood does the sensory language used to describe the woods convey to you?

voluble (vŏl′yə-bəl) *adj.* especially talkative, fluent with words

commiserate
(kə-mĭz′ə-rāt′) *v.* to express sorrow or pity for another's troubles

G SETTING AND MOOD

Possible answer: The "lowering sky" (lines 136–137) and the "rudimentary leaves, wizened and poverty-stricken" (line 138) suggest a gloomy, depressing mood.

IF STUDENTS NEED HELP . . . Have students visualize a darkened sky and trees with shriveled leaves. Then tell them to imagine themselves walking in those woods with blistered feet. What would their mood be?

TIERED DISCUSSION PROMPTS

Direct students to lines 154–172. Use these prompts to help students understand what the Hatchings are like:

Connect When you meet strangers, what kinds of behaviors help to make you comfortable? *Answers will vary, but students may suggest warmth, kindness, and an accepting or welcoming attitude.*

Analyze How are the Hatchings different from Mr. Noakes? *Possible answer: They are nice to Tom and Lily and to each other (lines 167–171), while Mr. Noakes made fun of Tom and Lily (lines 107–108) and spoke meanly about the Hatchings (lines 88–91).*

VOCABULARY COMMON CORE L 4

OWN THE WORD

• **rudimentary:** Have students provide synonyms for *rudimentary*. **Possible answers:** *fundamental, basic, elementary*

• **wizened:** The connotation of the word *wizened* is aged, or old, and wrinkled. Have students name things that could be described as *wizened*.

• **voluble:** Have students describe a circumstance in which they might be described as *voluble*. **Possible answer:** *when excited or nervous; at a party*

• **commiserate:** Ask students whether they have ever *commiserated* with someone. Have students explain with whom they *commiserated*, when, and why.

FOR ENGLISH LANGUAGE LEARNERS

Vocabulary: Phrasal Verbs Explain that *turned out* (line 141) means "proved to be." Help students come up with other phrasal verbs that use the main verb *turn*. Assign pairs one or two phrases to look up in a dictionary and have them share their definitions: *pulled up* (line 70), *picked up* (line 101), *made for* (line 147), *ran into* (line 249). Then, ask them to fill out a Cluster Diagram for each verb, putting the main verb in the center and the other

phrasal verbs in the outer circles.

BEST PRACTICES TOOLKIT—Transparency
Cluster Diagram p. B18

Then it was true, it was not their imagination, that a great dusty golden square of sunshine lay on the fireplace wall, where the brass pendulum of the clock at every swing blinked into sudden brilliance? That the blazing geraniums on the windowsill housed a drove of murmuring bees? That, through the window, the gleam of linen hung in the sun to whiten suddenly dazzled their eyes?

"The sun? Is it really the sun?" Tom said, almost doubtfully.

180 "And why not?" Mrs. Hatching demanded. "How else'll beans set, tell me that? Fine thing if sun were to stop shining." Chuckling to herself she set out a Crown Derby tea set, gorgeously colored in red and gold, and a baking of saffron[12] buns. Then she sat down and, drinking her own tea, began to question the two of them about where they had come from, where they were going. The tea was tawny and hot and sweet; the clock's tick was like a bird chirping; every now and then a log settled in the grate; Lily looked sleepily around the little room, so rich and peaceful, and thought, I wish we were staying here. I wish we needn't go back to that horrible pub. . . . She leaned against Tom's comforting arm.

190 "Look at the sky," she whispered to him. "Out there between the geraniums. Blue!" **H**

"And ee'll come up and see my spare bedroom, won't ee now?" Mrs. Hatching said, breaking off the thread of her questions—which indeed was not a thread, but merely a **savoring** of her pleasure and astonishment at this unlooked-for visit—"Bide here, why don't ee? Mid as well. The lil un's fair wore out. Us'll do for ee better 'n rangy old Noakes; proper old scoundrel 'e be. Won't us, William?" **I**

"Ah," William said appreciatively. "I'll sing ee some o' my songs."

A sight of the spare room settled any doubts. The great white bed, huge as 200 a prairie, built up with layer upon solid layer of mattress, blanket, and quilt, almost filled the little shadowy room in which it stood. Brass rails shone in the green dimness. "Isn't it quiet," Lily whispered. Mrs. Hatching, silent for the moment, stood looking at them proudly, her bright eyes slowly moving from face to face. Once her hand fondled, as if it might have been a baby's downy head, the yellow brass knob.

And so, almost without any words, the matter was decided.

Three days later they remembered that they must go to the village and collect the scooter which must, surely, be mended by now.

They had been helping old William pick a basketful of beans. Tom had 210 taken his shirt off, and the sun gleamed on his brown back; Lily was wearing an old cotton print which Mrs. Hatching, with much chuckling, had shortened to fit her.

It was amazing how deftly, in spite of his blindness, William moved among the beans, feeling through the rough, rustling leaves for the stiffness of concealed pods. He found twice as many as Tom and Lily, but then they, even on the third day, were still stopping every other minute to exclaim

---

12. **saffron:** a cooking spice that imparts an orange-yellow color to foods.

---

(4) **Targeted Passage**

H SETTING AND MOOD
Reread lines 174–191. Notice that the new setting conveys a different mood. How would you describe that mood?

savoring (sā′vər-ĭng) *n.* a full appreciation and enjoyment **savor** *v.*

I MONITOR
Reread lines 192–197. What is Mrs. Hatching saying? Try to clarify by reading her words aloud and then putting her statements in your own words.

TEXT ANALYSIS COMMON CORE RL 4

H SETTING AND MOOD

Possible answer: The mood is inviting—warm, bright, and colorful. The "great dusty golden square of sunshine" (lines 174–175), the "blazing geraniums" (line 176), the "murmuring bees" (line 177), and the blue sky (line 191) all suggest a mood of hope and happiness, a place filled with life.

READING STRATEGY COMMON CORE RL 10

I MONITOR

Possible answer: She's inviting them to see her spare bedroom and to stay with her (line 192). She says that she and her son can take care of them better than old Noakes can (line 196).

IF STUDENTS NEED HELP . . . Help students to work through the meaning of what Mrs. Hatching says by writing each question and statement that she makes.

VOCABULARY COMMON CORE L 4

OWN THE WORD

savoring: Have students list things or experiences that they might *savor*. **Possible answers:** *a favorite food, winning a race, a celebration*

DIFFERENTIATED INSTRUCTION

FOR STRUGGLING READERS

(4) **Targeted Passage** [Lines 179–212]
This passage shows why Tom and Lily decide to stay with the Hatchings, and what they do while they are there.

- What are the main reasons why Tom and Lily decide to stay with the Hatchings? (lines 186–191)

- What do Tom and Lily do while they are there? Do they seem happy? (lines 209–220)

FOR STRUGGLING READERS

Develop Reading Fluency Model for students how to read long, descriptive sentences with many commas. Read the line starting "Chuckling to herself . . ." (line 181) while students follow along. Point out how to pause at the commas and how to pace the reading to get the full effect of the description. Have pairs of students practice reading aloud the remainder of the paragraph through line 189.

R RESOURCE MANAGER—Copy Master
Reading Fluency p. 75

Yellow Dress (2003), Jeffrey T. Larson. Oil on linen, 12″ × 16″. © Daylight Fine Art.

◀ **Analyze Visuals**

How does the use of color affect the **mood** of this painting? Contrast the mood wih that of the painting on page 67.

over the blueness of the sky. At night they sat on the back doorstep while Mrs. Hatching clucked inside as she dished the supper, "Starstruck ee'll be! Come along in, do-ee, before soup's cold; stars niver run away yet as I do
220 know."

"Can we get anything for you in the village?" Lily asked, but Mrs. Hatching shook her head.

"Baker's bread and suchlike's no use but to cripple thee's innardses wi' colic.[13] I been living here these eighty year wi'out troubling doctors, and I'm not faring to begin now." She waved to them and stood watching as they walked into the wood, thin and frail beyond belief, but wiry, **indomitable**, her

indomitable
(ĭn-dŏm′ĭ-tə-bəl) *adj.*
not easily discouraged or defeated

---

13. **cripple . . . colic** (kŏl′ĭk): give yourself a bad case of indigestion.

Analyze Visuals

Possible answers: The vibrant colors, such as the woman's yellow dress, the purple, blue, and white flowers, and the green grass lend to the peaceful, bright, and hopeful mood of this painting. Old Willow Lane 2 suggests a depressing mood, shown by the gray color of the painting.

About the Art *Yellow Dress* (2003) was painted by the contemporary American artist Jeffrey T. Larson (born 1962). He has had many years of formal art training and is well versed in impressionism, as seen in this painting.

TIERED DISCUSSION PROMPTS

Direct students to lines 207–220. Use these prompts to help students understand how idyllic and wonderful this place is to Tom and Lily:

Connect What type of situation would be so pleasant for you that you might lose track of time? *Accept all reasonable answers.*

Analyze What details show the effects this place has on the couple? *Possible answer: Tom is tan (line 210). He and Lily stop to admire the blue sky (lines 216–217). They gaze at the stars at night (lines 217–218).*

Synthesize How does this place compare with everywhere else Tom and Lily have been? *Possible answer: It is much better. Lily is no longer cold. They are laughing and enjoying the sun and their view of the blue sky.*

VOCABULARY   COMMON CORE

L 4

OWN THE WORD

indomitable: Point out that *indomitable* is from the Latin prefix *in-*, meaning "not," and *domitare*, meaning " to tame." Someone who is *indomitable* cannot be subdued or conquered.

FOR ENGLISH LANGUAGE LEARNERS
Vocabulary: Multiple-Meaning Words
Remind students that many words in English have more than one meaning. A word's context can help students determine which meaning is correct. Have pairs use dictionaries to find the meanings of these selection words, using context clues to help them: *range* (line 47), *crop* (line 95), *sight* (line 155), *wood* (line 226), *dragged* (line 239), *grand* (line 252).

FOR ADVANCED LEARNERS/PRE–AP
Evaluate Point out to students that many cultures have described places that were a type of paradise on Earth, everywhere from Shangri-la to Atlantis to the Hindu city of Tripura. In legend, many such places are either hidden or else have been destroyed. Have students discuss if they think the Hatchings' home should remain hidden to avoid being destroyed. Have students support their opinions with evidence from the story.

black eyes full of zest. Then she turned to scream menacingly at a couple of pullets[14] who had strayed and were scratching among the potatoes.

Almost at once they noticed, as they followed the path, that the sky was
230 clouded over.

⑤ Targeted Passage

"It *is* only there on that one spot," Lily said in wonder. "All the time. And they've never even noticed that the sun doesn't shine in other places."

"That's how it must have been all over the world, once," Tom said.

At the garage they found their scooter ready and waiting. They were about to start back when they ran into Mr. Noakes.

"Well, well, well, well, *well!*" he shouted, glaring at them with ferocious good humor. "How many wells make a river, eh? And where did you slip off to? Here's me and the missus was just going to tell the police to have the rivers dragged. But hullo, hul*lo*, what's this? Brown, eh? Suntan? Scrumptious,"
240 he said, looking meltingly at Lily and giving her another tremendous pinch. "Where'd you get it, eh? That wasn't all got in half an hour, *I* know. Come on, this means money to you and me; tell us the big secret. Remember what I said; land around these parts is dirt cheap."

Tom and Lily looked at each other in horror. They thought of the cottage, the bees humming among the runner beans, the sunlight glinting in the red-and-gold teacups. At night, when they had lain in the huge sagging bed, stars had shone through the window, and the whole wood was as quiet as the inside of a shell. **ⓙ**

"Oh, we've been miles from here," Tom lied hurriedly. "We ran into a
250 friend, and he took us right away beyond Brinsley." And as Mr. Noakes still looked suspicious and unsatisfied, he did the only thing possible. "We're going back there now," he said. "The sunbathing's grand." And opening the throttle, he let the scooter go. They waved at Mr. Noakes and chugged off toward the gray hills that lay to the north. **ⓚ**

"My wedding dress," Lily said sadly. "It's on our bed."

They wondered how long Mrs. Hatching would keep tea hot for them, who would eat all the pasties.[15]

"Never mind, you won't need it again," Tom comforted her.

At least, he thought, they had left the golden place undisturbed. Mr. Noakes
260 never went into the wood. And they had done what they intended; they had found the sun. Now they, too, would be able to tell their grandchildren, when beginning a story, "Long, long ago, when we were young, in the days when the sky was blue . . ." ❧

---

14. **pullets:** young hens.
15. **pasties** (păs'tēz): a British term for meat pies.

TEXT ANALYSIS: *Review*

ⓙ CONFLICT

Possible answer: *Mr. Noakes sees that they are suntanned and asks where they got "it." He tells them "it" means "money to you and me" (line 242). They fear he will destroy this perfect spot.*

IF STUDENTS NEED HELP . . . Have students reread lines 114–117 to remind them what Mr. Noakes said he would do if he found a sunny spot.

READING STRATEGY

COMMON CORE RL 10

ⓚ MONITOR

Possible answer: *They lie about where they have been, "right away beyond Brinsley" (line 250), and they leave quickly in that direction. They decide to head toward the "gray hills" rather than let Mr. Noakes expose where the Hatchings live. They appreciate that the Hatchings' place exists and is untouched, and they do not want Mr. Noakes to know about it.*

SELECTION WRAP–UP

READ WITH A PURPOSE Now that students have finished reading the selection, have them compare and contrast their world to Tom and Lily's world. How do the different settings affect the attitudes of the people who live there? ***Possible answer:*** *In the real world, people take it for granted that they can see the sun and stars. In the story, people long for these things.*

⭐ **CRITIQUE** Have students think about the ending of the story and whether it was satisfying to them.

INDEPENDENT READING

If students are interested in reading other works by Joan Aiken, suggest *Jane Fairfax: The Secret Story of the Second Heroine in Jane Austen's Emma.*

COMMON CORE RL 4

Language Coach

Connotation Many words have positive or negative **connotations** (emotional associations). Reread lines 236-237. Do the words *glaring* and *ferocious* have positive or negative connotations?

ⓙ CONFLICT

Why do Mr. Noakes's statements fill Tom and Lily with horror?

ⓚ MONITOR

What do Tom and Lily decide to do?

DIFFERENTIATED INSTRUCTION

FOR STRUGGLING READERS

⑤ Targeted Passage [Lines 231–254]

This passage underscores the uniqueness of the Hatchings' place and why Tom and Lily want to protect it.

- What do Tom and Lily notice about the sky as they leave the Hatchings' place? (line 231)
- What do they realize about where the Hatchings live? (lines 231–233)

ENGLISH LANGUAGE LEARNERS

Language Coach

COMMON CORE RL 4

Connotation

Answer: *The words have negative connotations.* Have students reread lines 258–259. Have students point out words with positive connotations in those lines. ***Possible answers:*** *comforted (line 258) and golden (line 259).*

Comprehension

1. **Recall** Why are Tom and Lily riding around on their scooter at the beginning of the story?

2. **Recall** Why do Tom and Lily decide to visit the Hatchings?

3. **Clarify** Why don't Tom and Lily go back to the Hatchings' after picking up their scooter?

Text Analysis

4. **Monitor** Review the questions and answers you wrote while reading. What further insights did you gain into the setting, characters, and events?

5. **Interpret** Why does the sun shine only over the Hatchings' cottage?

6. **Contrast Setting and Mood** Contrast the Hatchings' cottage and yard with the rest of England "since the bombs." What differing moods are created by the sensory language used to describe these settings?

7. **Examine Conflicts** How would you describe the important conflicts in this story? Consider characters who are at odds and desires that are frustrated. Summarize the conflicts in a chart like the one shown.

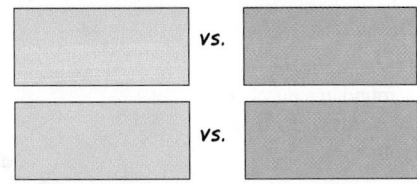

8. **Evaluate Actions** Do Tom and Lily do the right thing in not going back to the cottage? Explain your opinion.

9. **Draw Conclusions About Theme** What does the story suggest to you about the things people don't appreciate? Support your answer.

Text Criticism

10. **Author's Style** Many critics have commented on Aiken's ability to write stories that seem like folk tales. What elements of "Searching for Summer" remind you of "once upon a time" stories you read or heard as a child? Cite evidence from the story.

> **What do you take for GRANTED?**
>
> What would you do if blue skies disappeared?

COMMON CORE

RL 3 Analyze how complex characters develop over the course of a text, interact with other characters, and advance the plot. **RL 4** Analyze the cumulative impact of specific word choices on meaning and tone. **RL 10** Read and comprehend literature, including stories.

Text Criticism

Possible answer:

10. This story has characters who represent both good (Tom, Lily, the Hatchings) and evil (Mr. Noakes). It has a secret cottage deep in the woods (lines 136–138); a fantastical setting that is either totally gray (lines 4–7) or sunny and warm (lines 174–178); and an element of magic—the one sunny place in a gloomy world. Goodness is rewarded. The whole story almost seems like a legend. Characters begin their stories with "Long,

long ago . . ." (lines 8–9) or think of doing so (line 262).

> **What do you take for GRANTED?** Students might think about how gray skies affect them now and how permanently gray skies might affect them. Encourage students to consider the effects of gray skies on school, work, after school sports, socializing, and family outings.

Practice and Apply

For preliminary support of post-reading questions, use these copy masters:

R RESOURCE MANAGER—Copy Masters
Reading Check p. 72
Setting and Mood p. 65
Question Support p. 73

Additional selection questions are provided for teachers on page 59.

ANSWERS

Comprehension

1. *They are on their honeymoon in search of a place with sun.*

2. *They are returning Mrs. Hatching's purse.*

3. *They are afraid that Mr. Noakes will discover the sunlight there and ruin the place.*

Text Analysis
COMMON CORE RL 3, RL 4, RL 10

Possible answers:

4. ■ **COMMON CORE FOCUS** *Monitor*
   Possible insights: The clouds keep people from seeing stars as well as the sun (line 55). Mrs. Hatching does not realize the world has little sun (lines 180–181). Tom and Lily are good people (line 259).

5. *Perhaps because it always has and because the Hatchings believe that it always will.*

6. ● **COMMON CORE FOCUS** *Contrast Setting and Mood* *The Hatchings' home is described as "golden," "rich and peaceful," "quiet," and sunny (lines 174–210). These terms create a warm, comfortable mood. The rest of England is "Whitish gray," brooding, cold, with withered plants (lines 5–20). These terms create a gloomy mood.*

7. *everyone but the Hatchings vs. Nature; the Hatchings vs. Mr. Noakes; Tom and Lily vs. Mr. Noakes*

8. *Yes, because they preserved the spot forever. No, because they might have found a way to return to the cottage without giving away its location.*

9. *Many people live their lives not really appreciating something they have never lost or the fact that they have something others crave. The Hatchings take their sunny spot for granted; they do not fully appreciate it because they have not lost it.*

ANSWERS

Vocabulary in Context

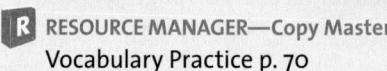
▲ VOCABULARY PRACTICE

1. *feeble*	5. *complex*
2. *connect*	6. *silent*
3. *blooming*	7. *distaste*
4. *accuse*	8. *effective*

R RESOURCE MANAGER—Copy Master
Vocabulary Practice p. 70

ACADEMIC VOCABULARY IN SPEAKING

Students should identify and discuss other themes that the story communicates, including the purity of young love, the appreciation of nature, the cruel nature of people toward the elderly and disabled, and human greed.

VOCABULARY STRATEGY:
THE PREFIX *dis-*

COMMON CORE **L 4c**

- Help students deconstruct the words that comprise more than a prefix and base word. For example, remove the suffix *-dis* from *disabled* and *discontinued*. Ask students for the meaning of each base word. Then have them suggest possible meanings for the complete words.

- Help them to use context clues by asking them questions and by pointing out key clues such as "crab" and "fisherman's net."

Possible answers:

1. *disengage*
2. *disinvite*
3. *disabled*
4. *disband*
5. *discontinued*

R RESOURCE MANAGER—Copy Master
Vocabulary Strategy p. 71

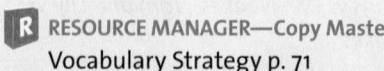
Interactive Vocabulary

Keywords direct students to a **WordSharp** tutorial on **thinkcentral.com** or to other types of vocabulary practice and review.

Vocabulary in Context

▲ VOCABULARY PRACTICE

Identify the word that is not related in meaning to the other words in the set.

1. indomitable, unconquerable, feeble, powerful
2. disengage, detach, remove, connect
3. withered, blooming, shrunken, wizened
4. sympathize, commiserate, pity, accuse
5. complex, rudimentary, basic, preliminary
6. voluble, talkative, fluent, silent
7. distaste, savoring, relishing, enjoyment
8. unavailing, useless, effective, futile

WORD LIST

commiserate
disengage
indomitable
rudimentary
savoring
unavailing
voluble
wizened

ACADEMIC VOCABULARY IN SPEAKING

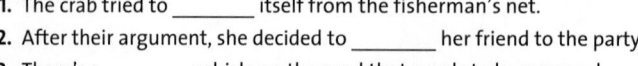
- affect   • communicate   • definite   • establish   • identify

COMMON CORE

L 4c Consult reference materials to determine or clarify a word's meaning or etymology.

One theme that Aiken's story conveys is the importance of sunlight. With a partner, **identify** and discuss other themes that the story **communicates.** Use at least one Academic Vocabulary word in your discussion.

VOCABULARY STRATEGY: THE PREFIX *dis-*

The vocabulary word *disengage* contains the Latin prefix *dis-*, which means "in different directions." This prefix is found in a number of English words. To understand the meaning of words with *dis-*, use your knowledge of the base word as well as your knowledge of the prefix.

PRACTICE Write the word from the word web that best completes each sentence. Use context clues to help you. If necessary, consult a dictionary or glossary.

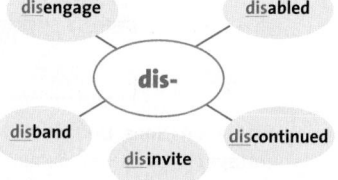

1. The crab tried to _____ itself from the fisherman's net.
2. After their argument, she decided to _____ her friend to the party.
3. There's a _____ vehicle on the road that needs to be removed.
4. The music group will _____ this month.
5. The store has _____ this brand of clothing.

Interactive Vocabulary

Go to **thinkcentral.com**.
KEYWORD: HML10-76

DIFFERENTIATED INSTRUCTION

FOR ENGLISH LANGUAGE LEARNERS

Vocabulary Practice Help students internalize the Academic Vocabulary words by pronouncing and defining the words aloud to them once. Ask students to repeat the words several times. Then create questions that include the words and have students answer the questions orally. Finally, have students form groups or teams and create their own questions and answers.

FOR ADVANCED LEARNERS/PRE–AP

Vocabulary in Writing Have students choose three vocabulary words and find other words that are based on the same root or base (*miserable, engaged, dominate, rudiments, savory, available, volume, wizen*). Encourage them to use dictionaries or other reference sources. Challenge them to use each word in a sentence that tells something about the story and then share their sentences.

Language

◆ **GRAMMAR AND STYLE:** Use Realistic Dialogue

COMMON CORE

L 3 Apply knowledge of language to make effective choices for meaning or style.

Review the **Grammar and Style** note on page 70. Aiken uses realistic dialogue to help shape her characters and bring them to life. When writing dialogue, follow her example by enlisting these techniques:

1. **Use contractions and interjections.** Contractions—such as *doesn't, we're,* and *they'll*—combine and shorten words, while interjections—such as *well, oh,* and *hey*—express emotion. You can incorporate both into your dialogue to make it sound more like everyday speech.

2. **Form sentence fragments.** Although sentence fragments should be avoided in formal writing, they are often used in dialogue. Here is an example from the story that highlights Aiken's use of these techniques.

> *"Can't see what's wrong," said Tom, after a prolonged and gloomy survey.*
>
> *"Oh, Tom!" Lily was almost crying. "What'll we do?"* (lines 63–64)

Notice how the revisions in blue make this first draft's dialogue sound more like real speech. Revise your own writing by making similar changes.

STUDENT MODEL

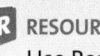

"Who wants to be the first to visit the new Rising Sun Resort? I̶ ̶a̶m̶ telling
 Not anywhere.
you, you̶ will never find a place like this. ̶T̶h̶e̶ ̶s̶u̶n̶ ̶i̶s̶ ̶b̶r̶i̶g̶h̶t̶,̶ ̶a̶n̶d̶ ̶t̶h̶e̶ ̶s̶k̶y̶ ̶i̶s̶ ̶b̶l̶u̶e̶
 Oh,
And did I mention the camp for the kids? What more could you want?"

READING-WRITING CONNECTION

Explore your understanding of "Searching for Summer" by responding to this prompt. Then use the **revising tip** to improve your writing.

WRITING PROMPT	REVISING TIP
Short Constructed Response: Description Imagine that Mr. Noakes has turned the woods into a resort. What would he say in a presentation to make people want to visit? What sensory language would he use? Write **one or two paragraphs** describing this resort, using the words, grammar, and pronunciation that Mr. Noakes would use.	Review your response. How have you used realistic dialogue to make the presentation sound like Mr. Noakes?

Interactive Revision THINK central

Go to **thinkcentral.com**. KEYWORD: HML10-77

FOR STRUGGLING WRITERS

- Explain that the presentation should make the place sound very appealing. Discuss different details students might include.

- Help students list features that might make people want to come to the resort.

- Discuss how Mr. Noakes speaks and the types of words he might use.

- Suggest that students begin by speaking the words and then writing them.

Language

COMMON CORE **L 3**

◆ **GRAMMAR AND STYLE**

- After students examine the student model, list additional contractions, as well as other interjections, such as *yes* and *wow*. (For more on dialogue, see the **Writing Handbook,** p. R36.)

- Write this dialogue on the board and revise to make it sound more realistic:

> *Yes, folks, this'll* ~~This will~~ *be the place of your dreams. Promise!*
>
> *Once you've* ~~you have~~ *been to Rising Sun Resort, you'll* ~~you will~~ *never want to go anywhere else.*

 RESOURCE MANAGER—Copy Master
Use Realistic Dialogue p. 74

READING-WRITING CONNECTION

- Suggest that students reread lines 114–117 to review Mr. Noakes's ideas about a holiday spot. Encourage them to visualize the scene that he describes and to add details that they imagine. Remind students that they should write from Mr. Noakes's point of view.

 **BEST PRACTICES TOOLKIT**—Transparency
Analysis Frame: Theme pp. D21, D32

Writing Online THINK central

The following tools are available online at **thinkcentral.com** and on **Write***Smart* CD-ROM:

- **Interactive Graphic Organizers**
- **Interactive Student Models**
- **Interactive Revision Lessons**

For additional grammar instruction, see **GrammarNotes** on **thinkcentral.com**.

Assess and Reteach

Assess

 DIAGNOSTIC AND SELECTION TESTS
Selection Test A, pp. 31–32
Selection Test B/C, pp. 33–34

Interactive Selection Test on **thinkcentral.com**

Reteach

Level Up Online Tutorials on **thinkcentral.com**

Reteaching Worksheets on **thinkcentral.com**
Literature Lesson 9, Reading Lesson 2

Focus and Motivate

Comparing Texts

To Build a Fire Video link at thinkcentral.com   **Essential Course of Study** ECOS

Short Story by Jack London

from **Deep Survival**

Nonfiction Book by Laurence Gonzales

How to Build a Fire Without Matches
Diagram

VIDEO TRAILER THINK central   KEYWORD: HML10-78

COMMON CORE FOCUS

RL 1 Cite evidence to support inferences drawn from the text. **RL 4** Determine the meaning of words as they are used in a text; analyze the cumulative impact of word choices on meaning and tone. **RL 5** Analyze how an author's choices concerning how to structure a text and order events within it create mystery and tension. **L 4c** Consult reference materials to determine a word's etymology. **L 5b** Analyze nuances in the meaning of words with similar denotations.

Should you trust your INSTINCTS?

COMMON CORE

RL 1 Cite evidence to support inferences drawn from the text. **RL 4** Determine the meaning of words as they are used in a text; analyze the cumulative impact of word choices on meaning and tone. **RL 5** Analyze how an author's choices concerning how to structure a text and order events within it create mystery and tension.

An instinct is unlearned, automatic behavior shown by all members of a species, such as birds building a nest. Do people, like animals, have instincts? If they do, when are they likely to use them? Are a person's instincts as good as, say, a dog's? The story "To Build a Fire" attempts to answer such questions.

SUMMARIES

"To Build a Fire" A man and a dog set out for a Yukon mining camp in dangerously cold weather. After he gets wet, the man builds a fire, but then extinguishes it. He cannot rebuild the fire and freezes to death.

from *Deep Survival* This selection identifies and analyzes patterns of thought and behavior shared by survivors of major disasters.

"How to Build a Fire Without Matches" The diagram shows the tools to build a fire.

What's the Connection?

Instinct, luck, fate, and the human ability to reason all play key roles in the main character's fight to stay alive in a harsh environment. After "To Build a Fire," you will read an excerpt from a nonfiction book and examine a visual that explore similar topics.

Should you trust your INSTINCTS?

Introduce the question, and clarify the term *instinct* by providing examples, such as fear, the will to survive, or the pursuit of pleasure.

What's the Connection?

Lead students in a discussion of what they think are the most important survival skills. Encourage students to cite specific examples from their own experiences and observations.

78

Selection Resources

 Video link at thinkcentral.com

Video Trailer THINK central

 RESOURCE MANAGER UNIT 1

Plan and Teach, pp. 77–82
Summary, pp. 83–84†‡*
Text Analysis and Reading
   Skill, pp. 85–88†*
Vocabulary, pp. 89–91*

DIAGNOSTIC AND SELECTION
   TESTS

Selection Tests, pp. 35–38

 BEST PRACTICES TOOLKIT

Two-Column Chart, p. A25
New Word Analysis, p. E8
Read Aloud/Think Aloud, p. A34

INTERACTIVE READER

ADAPTED INTERACTIVE READER

ELL ADAPTED INTERACTIVE READER

TECHNOLOGY

- Teacher One Stop DVD-ROM
- Student One Stop DVD-ROM
- PowerNotes DVD-ROM
- Audio Anthology CD
- GrammarNotes DVD-ROM
- Audio Tutor CD
- ExamView Test Generator on the Teacher One Stop

Go to **thinkcentral.com** to preview the **Video Trailer** introducing this selection. Other features that support the selection include
- **PowerNotes** presentation
- **ThinkAloud** models to enhance comprehension
- **WordSharp** vocabulary tutorials
- interactive writing and grammar instruction

* Resources for Differentiation   † Also in Spanish   ‡ In Haitian Creole and Vietnamese

TEXT ANALYSIS: SETTING AND CONFLICT

In some stories, the **setting** can create the conflict a character faces. It can even act as the **antagonist,** or opponent, of the main character. In "To Build a Fire," the setting is the Yukon wilderness, and the main character must battle the crippling cold to survive. The setting challenges him in other ways as well. As you read, notice details about this harsh setting and think about the choices the setting forces the character to make.

Review: Mood

READING STRATEGY: PREDICT

When you **predict,** you use text clues to guess what will happen next in a story. Predicting helps you become actively involved in what you are reading and gives you reasons to read on. To make sound predictions about what will happen in "To Build a Fire," use the following strategies:

• Think about the personality, actions, and thoughts of the main character when predicting how he will respond to his situation.

• Note passages of **foreshadowing,** or hints and clues about future plot events.

As you read, jot down at least three predictions and the clues you used to make them. Use a chart like the one shown.

Predictions	Text Clues
The man will ...	

Review: Draw Conclusions

▲ VOCABULARY IN CONTEXT

Jack London uses the following boldfaced vocabulary words in his suspenseful tale. To see how many vocabulary words you know, substitute a different word or phrase for each boldfaced term.

1. **intangible** fear
2. **conjectural** answer
3. baseless **apprehension**
4. **reiterate** the command
5. **smite** in anger
6. **imperative** action
7. forest **conflagration**
8. **peremptorily** dismiss

 Complete the activities in your **Reader/Writer Notebook.**

Meet the Author

Jack London
1876–1916

Teen Adventurer
Born to an indifferent mother and an absentee father, Jack London grew up in a poor neighborhood in Oakland, California. As a boy, his escape from poverty and loneliness was reading books. As a teenager, his escape was the sea. When he was 15, he borrowed money, bought a boat, and became an oyster pirate on the San Francisco Bay. At 17, he worked aboard a schooner that sailed the North Pacific. When he returned home, the only work he could find was low-paying manual labor. Fascinated by rags-to-riches stories he heard about people mining for gold in Canada's Yukon Territory, he sailed north at age 21.

Striking It Rich
London did not find gold in the Yukon, but he did find something valuable. Holed up during the fiercely cold Yukon winter, he read widely and listened to other gold prospectors tell stories about life in the frozen northland. Inspired by their tales and his own experiences, London returned to Oakland and began to write. In 1899, magazines began publishing his stories, and his writing career was on its way. His novels *The Call of the Wild, The Sea-Wolf,* and *White Fang* made him one of America's most popular, and financially successful, writers. Almost a century after his death, readers are still captivated by his stark, suspenseful stories.

Authors Online
Go to **thinkcentral.com**. KEYWORD: HML10-79

 THINK central

79

Teach

TEXT ANALYSIS

COMMON CORE
RL 5

● *Model the Skill:* SETTING AND CONFLICT

To model how to identify setting and conflict, remind students that *setting* refers to both the place and the time in which a story occurs. Point out that the Yukon is a cold, snowy, barren location with a small, scattered population. The weather is unpredictable. Explain that nature could act as an antagonist for someone traveling in this environment. For example, a blizzard or avalanche might occur, wild animals might attack, a person could get lost in the snow, or a person might develop frostbite.

GUIDED PRACTICE Have students explain why it might be difficult to get help if they ran into trouble in this setting.

READING STRATEGY

COMMON CORE
RL 1

■ *Model the Skill:* PREDICT

To model how to predict, have students reread the **Text Analysis.** Tell students to use text clues to make a prediction about the outcome of the story. Point out that one possibility is that the man will freeze to death because of a bad choice he makes.

GUIDED PRACTICE Ask students to identify the text clues they used to make a prediction.

R RESOURCE MANAGER—Copy Master
Predict p. 87 (for student use while reading the selection)

VOCABULARY SKILL

COMMON CORE
L 4

▲ VOCABULARY IN CONTEXT

DIAGNOSE WORD KNOWLEDGE Have all students complete Vocabulary in Context. Check their words and phrases against the following:

apprehension (ăp′rĭ-hĕn′shən) *n.* fear and worry for the future

conflagration (kŏn′flə-grā′shən) *n.* a large, destructive fire

conjectural (kən-jĕk′chər-əl) *adj.* involving guesswork

imperative (ĭm-pĕr′ə-tĭv) *adj.* urgently necessary

intangible (ĭn-tăn′jə-bəl) *adj.* unable to be perceived with the senses

peremptorily (pə-rĕmp′tə-rə-lē) *adv.* in a commanding way that does not allow for refusal or contradiction

reiterate (rē-ĭt′ə-rāt′) *v.* to repeat

smite (smīt) *v.* to inflict a heavy blow on; *past tense* **–smote** (smōt)

PRETEACH VOCABULARY Use the following copy master to help students evaluate their knowledge of each boldfaced word.

R RESOURCE MANAGER—Copy Master
Vocabulary Study p. 89

1. Read the first sentence in Part A aloud, emphasizing *apprehension.*

2. Point out the phrase *was not worried, but* and the word *nervously.* Elicit possible meanings for *apprehension.*

3. Repeat the procedure for items 2–8. Then have students complete Part B.

READ WITH A PURPOSE

Help students set a purpose for reading. Tell them to read to discover the danger of underestimating nature's power and of overestimating one's own.

TEXT ANALYSIS: *Review* COMMON CORE RL 4

A MOOD

Possible answer: *The author describes a setting that is "exceedingly cold and gray" (line 1), with "an intangible pall" (line 7), and "a subtle gloom" (lines 7–8). The mood conveyed is stark, cheerless, and lonely.*

IF STUDENTS NEED HELP ... Use a Two-Column Chart to draw students' attention to the details the author uses to describe the setting.

Image	How it makes me feel
"no sun nor hint of sun" (lines 5–6)	gloomy, unhappy

 BEST PRACTICES TOOLKIT—Transpareency
Two-Column Chart p. A25

Extend the Discussion How does the setting affect the man's mood?

VOCABULARY COMMON CORE L 4

OWN THE WORD

intangible: Point out to students that the word *intangible* comes from the Latin *in-*, meaning "not," and *tangere*, meaning "touch." Something *intangible* cannot be touched or perceived with the senses.

TO BUILD A FIRE

JACK LONDON

Day had broken cold and gray, exceedingly cold and gray, when the man turned aside from the main Yukon trail and climbed the high earth-bank, where a dim and little-travelled trail led eastward through the fat spruce timberland. It was a steep bank, and he paused for breath at the top, excusing the act to himself by looking at his watch. It was nine o'clock. There was no sun nor hint of sun, though there was not a cloud in the sky. It was a clear day, and yet there seemed an **intangible** pall over the face of things, a subtle gloom that made the day dark, and that was due to the absence of sun. This fact did not worry the man. He was used to the lack of sun. It had been days
10 since he had seen the sun, and he knew that a few more days must pass before that cheerful orb, due south, would just peep above the sky line and dip immediately from view.

The man flung a look back along the way he had come. The Yukon lay a mile wide and hidden under three feet of ice. On top of this ice were as many feet of snow. It was all pure white, rolling in gentle undulations where the ice jams of the freeze-up had formed. North and south, as far as his eye could see, it was unbroken white, save for a dark hairline that curved and twisted from around the spruce-covered island to the south, and that curved and twisted away into the north, where it disappeared behind another spruce-covered
20 island. This dark hairline was the trail—the main trail—that led south five hundred miles to the Chilcoot Pass, Dyea, and salt water; and that led north seventy miles to Dawson, and still on to the north a thousand miles to Nulato, and finally to St. Michael, on Bering Sea, a thousand miles and half a thousand more. **A**

Analyze Visuals ▶

How do you think it would feel to be in the **setting** of the photograph?

intangible (ĭn-tăn′jə-bəl) *adj.* unable to be perceived with the senses

① Targeted Passage

A MOOD
Reread lines 1–24. What mood is created by the description of the **setting**?

DIFFERENTIATED INSTRUCTION

FOR ENGLISH LANGUAGE LEARNERS

Language: Verb Tenses Remind students that many English verbs are irregular and do not follow the usual pattern for forming the past tense: adding *-ed*. Direct their attention to "spat" (line 41), explaining that it (and not *spitted*) is the past tense of *spit*. Follow the same procedure with these irregular verbs: "flung" (line 13), "thought" (line 55), "froze" (line 129), "broke" (line 133), and "clung" (line 152).

FOR STRUGGLING READERS

In combination with the *Audio Anthology CD*, use one or more Targeted Passages (pp. 80, 83, 88, 92, 95) to ensure that students focus on key story events, concepts, and skills. Targeted Passages are also good for English learners.

① Targeted Passage [Lines 1–17]

This passage identifies and describes the setting and the protagonist.

• Why was the day dark? (lines 5–6 and 10–12)

Reading Support

This selection on **thinkcentral.com** includes embedded **ThinkAloud** models—students "thinking aloud" about the story to model the kinds of questions a good reader would ask about a selection.

BACKGROUND

Klondike Gold Rush This story takes place during the Klondike Gold Rush, which began in 1897, almost half a century after the first major North American gold rush at Sutter's Mill in California. The Klondike River, a tributary of the Yukon River, runs through a corner of northwestern Canada called the Yukon Territory. By 1898, thousands of hopeful miners were pouring into the region. Most arrived in Skagway, Alaska, and traveled hundreds of miles by trail and then by boat to the gold fields around the town of Dawson Creek, Canada. Many of the miners were physically and emotionally unprepared for the severe conditions they encountered. Miners had to battle steep terrain, bitter cold, and frozen ground that was difficult to mine. Many lost their pack animals, their possessions, and even their lives. Only about a third of those who set off for the Klondike managed to complete the journey—and though some "Klondike Kings" became immensely rich, most of the miners were sorely disappointed.

Analyze Visuals

Possible answer: Such a setting would feel cold, lonely, and perhaps dangerous, but might also inspire a person with its beauty.

About the Art *Snow-Covered Trees* was photographed in Yellowstone National Park, Wyoming, by the award-winning nature photographer Jeff Vanuga.

- Where does the story take place? (line 2)
- What does this setting look and feel like? (lines 1–8, 11–20)
- What do you learn about the man? (lines 4–5, 9, 13)

FOR ADVANCED LEARNERS/PRE–AP

Make Judgments Point out to students that like the miners in the gold rush, the man in the story is risking his life for the possibility of becoming rich. Ask students if they think the risk is worth the cost. Ask students what kinds of risks they think are worth taking. Encourage students to be specific and explain their reasoning.

B DRAW CONCLUSIONS

Possible answer: *Because the man is literal-minded, alert to the surfaces of things (lines 29–30) but not to their deeper meanings (lines 32–36), he is probably not very deep or imaginative.*

IF STUDENTS NEED HELP . . . Encourage students to use the Read Aloud/Think Aloud strategy for this story. Model the strategy for them, showing how students might picture this character, make comparisons, and identify comprehension problems. Here is a possible dialogue you might use:

- This man does not seem to understand the severity of the cold.
- In that situation, I would be worried.
- Why is his lack of understanding a problem?

 BEST PRACTICES TOOLKIT—Transparency
Read Aloud/Think Aloud p. A34

C SETTING AND CONFLICT

Possible answer: *The cold is so extreme—causing his exposed skin to go numb (lines 62–63)—that the man will have to struggle to keep warm if he is to continue on his journey and even survive.*

Extend the Discussion Discuss the wisdom of traveling as "light" as this man does in weather this cold. Ask students what they would have worn and packed if they had been traveling in such a climate during that time period.

OWN THE WORD

conjectural: Have students review the meaning of the adjective *conjectural*. Then ask students to tell why they think the author describes the "field of immortality and man's place in the universe" as *conjectural*.

Possible answer: *One can only guess at the nature of immortality, as it is an unknown, not a fact.*

But all this—this mysterious, far-reaching hairline trail, the absence of sun from the sky, the tremendous cold, and the strangeness and weirdness of it all—made no impression on the man. It was not because he was long used to it. He was a newcomer in the land, a *chechaquo*, and this was his first winter. The trouble with him was that he was without imagination. He was quick and alert in the things of life, but only in the things, and not in the significances. Fifty degrees below zero meant eighty-odd degrees of frost. Such fact impressed him as being cold and uncomfortable, and that was all. It did not lead him to meditate upon his frailty as a creature of temperature, and upon man's frailty in general, able only to live within certain narrow limits of heat and cold; and from there on it did not lead him to the **conjectural** field of immortality and man's place in the universe. Fifty degrees below zero stood for a bite of frost that hurt and that must be guarded against by the use of mittens, ear flaps, warm moccasins, and thick socks. Fifty degrees below zero was to him just precisely fifty degrees below zero. That there should be anything more to it than that was a thought that never entered his head. **B**

As he turned to go, he spat speculatively. There was a sharp, explosive crackle that startled him. He spat again. And again, in the air, before it could fall to the snow, the spittle crackled. He knew that at fifty below spittle crackled on the snow, but this spittle had crackled in the air. Undoubtedly it was colder than fifty below—how much colder he did not know. But the temperature did not matter. He was bound for the old claim[1] on the left fork of Henderson Creek, where the boys were already. They had come over across the divide from the Indian Creek country, while he had come the roundabout way to take a look at the possibilities of getting out logs in the spring from the islands in the Yukon. He would be in to camp by six o'clock; a bit after dark, it was true, but the boys would be there, a fire would be going, and a hot supper would be ready. As for lunch, he pressed his hand against the protruding bundle under his jacket. It was also under his shirt, wrapped up in a handkerchief and lying against the naked skin. It was the only way to keep the biscuits from freezing. He smiled agreeably to himself as he thought of those biscuits, each cut open and sopped in bacon grease, and each enclosing a generous slice of fried bacon.

He plunged in among the big spruce trees. The trail was faint. A foot of snow had fallen since the last sled had passed over, and he was glad he was without a sled, travelling light. In fact, he carried nothing but the lunch wrapped in the handkerchief. He was surprised, however, at the cold. It certainly was cold, he concluded, as he rubbed his numb nose and cheekbones with his mittened hand. He was a warm-whiskered man, but the hair on his face did not protect the high cheek-bones and the eager nose that thrust itself aggressively into the frosty air. **C**

conjectural
(kən-jĕk′chər-əl) *adj.*
involving guesswork

B **DRAW CONCLUSIONS**
Based on the description in lines 25–40, what can you conclude about the man's personality?

C **SETTING AND CONFLICT**
What conflict does the setting create for the man?

---

1. **claim:** a tract of public land claimed by a homesteader or, as in this case, a miner.

DIFFERENTIATED INSTRUCTION

FOR STRUGGLING READERS

Develop Reading Fluency Have small groups read the story. The leader reads a paragraph aloud and asks questions about it. Another student summarizes the information and asks whether clarification is needed. Others work to clarify and predict what may happen.

Distribute the copy master and have students work in pairs or groups to practice fluency.

 **RESOURCE MANAGER—Copy Master**
Reading Fluency p. 94

FOR RELUCTANT READERS

Point out to students that, like the gold miners in the gold rush, the man in the story is risking his life for the possibility of becoming rich. On the board, write the following questions: What risk is important enough to justify ignoring your instincts? Should animals' instincts be important to people? Discuss with students how their ideas relate to the story.

Analyze Visuals

Activity What qualities does this photograph of the dog emphasize? *Possible answer: The photograph emphasizes the dog's watchfulness and determination.*

About the Art This photo, *Siberian Husky headshot*, is by Ted Wood, a photojournalist who has created several books about working dogs.

REVISIT THE BIG QUESTION

Should you trust your
INSTINCTS?

Discuss What do lines 68–72 suggest about the value of instinct? *Possible answer: Animal instinct can be more valuable and accurate than human judgment.*

At the man's heels trotted a dog, a big native husky, the proper wolf dog, gray-coated and without any visible or temperamental difference from its brother, the wild wolf. The animal was depressed by the tremendous cold. It knew that it was no time for travelling. Its instinct told it a truer tale than was told to the man by the man's judgment. In reality, it was not merely colder
70 than fifty below zero; it was colder than sixty below, than seventy below. It was seventy-five below zero. Since the freezing point is thirty-two above zero, it meant that one hundred and seven degrees of frost obtained.[2] The dog did not know anything about thermometers. Possibly in its brain there was no sharp consciousness of a condition of very cold such as was in the man's brain. But the brute had its instinct. It experienced a vague but menacing **apprehension** that subdued it and made it slink along at the man's heels, and that made it question eagerly every unwonted movement of the man as if expecting him to go into camp or to seek shelter somewhere and build a fire. The dog had
80 learned fire, and it wanted fire, or else to burrow under the snow and cuddle its warmth away from the air.

2 **Targeted Passage**

apprehension
(ăp′rĭ-hĕn′shən) *n.* fear and worry for the future

D PREDICT
What do you think the man and dog will do? Why?

---

2. **obtained:** existed.

READING STRATEGY — COMMON CORE — RL 1

D PREDICT

Possible answer: The man and dog will probably seek out the warmth of a fire at some point. The title of the story is "To Build a Fire," and fire is mentioned several times in the story (lines 51, 79–81). Also, the weather is bitterly cold (lines 71–72), so warmth may become necessary.

IF STUDENTS NEED HELP . . . Have students use their Predictions charts to help them identify details from the story's title and text (lines 50, 79–80) that can help them make this prediction.

FOR STRUGGLING READERS

2 **Targeted Passage** [Lines 66–81]

This passage introduces the dog and its instincts, which tell the dog that the cold is dangerous.

- What wild animal is related to the dog? (line 66)
- What do the dog's instincts tell it about traveling in the cold? (lines 68–72)
- What does the dog want? (lines 79–81)

FOR ADVANCED LEARNERS/PRE–AP

Analyze Absence of Names Draw students' attention to the fact that neither the man nor the dog is named in this story. How would the story be different if these characters were named? How might the omission of names enhance the impact of the story's theme? Have students answer these questions in a brief paragraph that explains the author's decision not to name the characters. Then invite them to share their responses with a small group or the whole class.

VOCABULARY — COMMON CORE — L 4

OWN THE WORD

apprehension: Remind students that *apprehension* is a noun. The verb form is *apprehend*, which means "to understand" or "to anticipate with anxiety." The adjective *apprehensive* means "fearful about the future."

Refer to lines 92–112 and use these prompts to help students recognize the man's lack of experience in such a setting:

Recall How does the man react to the progress he has made? *Possible answer: The man decides to celebrate his good progress by eating his lunch at the forks.*

Analyze How is the man's reaction different from the dog's? *Possible answer: The dog's tail is drooping with discouragement, whereas the man is delighted with their progress and feels like celebrating.*

Evaluate How effective is the technique of slowly revealing how little the man understands about survival in this kind of cold? *Possible answer: The narrator reveals the information gradually and almost casually so that the reader has to piece together the details to arrive at the conclusion. This technique is effective because it creates suspense and mirrors the man's gradual recognition of his own dangerous predicament.*

TEXT ANALYSIS COMMON CORE

Ⓔ SETTING AND CONFLICT RL 5

Possible answer: The man thinks that frostbite is a bit painful but not serious.

IF STUDENTS NEED HELP . . . Have them discuss the significance of lines 114–116 and 119–120. Point out that at first the man is just calmly aware of the cold, but that now he is physically affected.

Extend the Discussion Why do you think the man is unconcerned?

VOCABULARY COMMON CORE L 4

OWN THE WORD

reiterate: Have students list when or why they might *reiterate,* or repeat, something. *Possible answers: to keep from forgetting something; to be certain another person heard and understood information*

The frozen moisture of its breathing had settled on its fur in a fine powder of frost, and especially were its jowls, muzzle and eyelashes whitened by its crystalled breath. The man's red beard and mustache were likewise frosted, but more solidly, the deposit taking the form of ice and increasing with every warm, moist breath he exhaled. Also, the man was chewing tobacco, and the muzzle of ice held his lips so rigidly that he was unable to clear his chin when he expelled the juice. The result was that a crystal beard of the color and solidity of amber was increasing its length on his chin. If he fell down it

90 would shatter itself, like glass, into brittle fragments. But he did not mind the appendage. It was the penalty all tobacco chewers paid in that country, and he had been out before in two cold snaps. They had not been so cold as this, but by the spirit thermometer[3] at Sixty Mile he knew that they had been registered at fifty below and at fifty-five.

He held on through the level stretch of woods for several miles, crossed a wide flat . . . and dropped down a bank to the frozen bed of a small stream. This was Henderson Creek, and he knew he was ten miles from the forks. He looked at his watch. It was ten o'clock. He was making four miles an hour, and he calculated that he would arrive at the forks at half-past twelve. He decided

100 to celebrate that event by eating his lunch there.

The dog dropped in again at his heels, with a tail drooping discouragement, as the man swung along the creek bed. The furrow of the old sled trail was plainly visible, but a dozen inches of snow covered the marks of the last runners. In a month no man had come up or down that silent creek. The man held steadily on. He was not much given to thinking, and just then particularly he had nothing to think about save that he would eat lunch at the forks and that at six o'clock he would be in camp with the boys. There was nobody to talk to; and, had there been, speech would have been impossible because of the ice muzzle on his mouth. So he continued monotonously to chew tobacco and

110 to increase the length of his amber beard.

Once in a while the thought **reiterated** itself that it was very cold and that he had never experienced such cold. As he walked along he rubbed his cheekbones and nose with the back of his mittened hand. He did this automatically, now and again changing hands. But, rub as he would, the instant he stopped his cheekbones went numb, and the following instant the end of his nose went numb. He was sure to frost his cheeks; he knew that, and experienced a pang of regret that he had not devised a nose strap of the sort Bud wore in cold snaps. Such a strap passed across the cheeks, as well, and saved them. But it didn't matter much, after all. What were frosted cheeks? A

120 bit painful, that was all; they were never serious. Ⓔ

Empty as the man's mind was of thoughts, he was keenly observant, and he noticed the changes in the creek, the curves and bends and timber jams,[4] and

---

3. **spirit thermometer:** a thermometer in which temperature is indicated by the height of a column of colored alcohol.

4. **timber jams:** piled-up masses of floating logs and branches.

COMMON CORE L 4c

Language Coach

Homophones Words that sound the same but have different spellings and meanings are **homophones.** For example, in line 101, *creek* ("stream") is a homophone of *creak* ("a squeaking sound"). Use a dictionary to find the definitions of these other homophones that you will find in this story: *course/coarse, peace/piece, passed/past.*

reiterate (rē-ĭt′ə-rāt′) *v.* to repeat

Ⓔ SETTING AND CONFLICT

Notice the new problem created for the man. How does he view this problem?

DIFFERENTIATED INSTRUCTION

FOR ENGLISH LANGUAGE LEARNERS

Comprehension: Transitions Point out the transitional words and phrases in the story. Help students realize that these transitions often provide important information about time, sequence, and place. Discuss what students learn from each of these examples:

- "in that country" (line 91)
- "In a month" (line 104)
- "at six o'clock" (line 107)

FOR ENGLISH LANGUAGE LEARNERS

Language Coach COMMON CORE L 4c

Homophones *Answer:* course *means "a connected series of events";* coarse *means "rough";* peace *means "calm";* piece *means "a part of a whole";* passed *means "moved";* past *means "time that has elapsed."* Point out that two commonly confused homophones are *there* (line 100) and *their* (line 130).

---

always he sharply noted where he placed his feet. Once, coming around a bend
he shied abruptly, like a startled horse, curved away from the place where he
had been walking, and retreated several paces back along the trail. The creek
he knew was frozen clear to the bottom—no creek could contain water in that
arctic winter—but he knew also that there were springs that bubbled out from
the hillsides and ran along under the snow and on top the ice of the creek. He
knew that the coldest snaps never froze these springs, and he knew likewise
130 their danger. They were traps. They hid pools of water under the snow that
might be three inches deep, or three feet. Sometimes a skin of ice half an inch
thick covered them, and in turn was covered by the snow. Sometimes there
were alternate layers of water and ice skin, so that when one broke through he
kept on breaking through for a while, sometimes wetting himself to the waist.

That was why he had shied in such panic.

He had felt the give under his feet and heard the crackle of a snow-hidden
ice skin. And to get his feet wet in such a temperature meant trouble and
danger. At the very least it meant delay, for he would be forced to stop and
build a fire, and under its protection to bare his feet while he dried his socks
140 and moccasins. He stood and studied the creek bed and its banks, and decided
that the flow of water came from his right. He reflected awhile, rubbing his
nose and cheeks, then skirted to the left, stepping gingerly and testing the
footing for each step. Once clear of the danger, he took a fresh chew of tobacco
and swung along at his four-mile gait.[5] **F**

F PREDICT
What do you think will
happen? Why?

I n the course of the next two hours he came upon several similar traps.
Usually the snow above the hidden pools had a sunken, candied appearance
that advertised the danger. Once again, however, he had a close call; and
once, suspecting danger, he compelled the dog to go on in front. The dog did
not want to go. It hung back until the man shoved it forward, and then it
150 went quickly across the white, unbroken surface. Suddenly it broke through,
floundered to one side, and got away to firmer footing. It had wet its forefeet
and legs, and almost immediately the water that clung to it turned to ice. It
made quick efforts to lick the ice off its legs, then dropped down in the snow
and began to bite out the ice that had formed between the toes. This was a
matter of instinct. To permit the ice to remain would mean sore feet. It did
not know this. It merely obeyed the mysterious prompting that arose from the
deep crypts of its being. But the man knew, having achieved a judgment on the
subject, and he removed the mitten from his right hand and helped tear out
the ice particles. He did not expose his fingers more than a minute, and was
160 astonished at the swift numbness that **smote** them. It certainly was cold. He
pulled on the mitten hastily, and beat the hand savagely across his chest.

smite (smīt) *v.* to inflict
a heavy blow on; *past
tense*—**smote** (smōt)

---

5. **four-mile gait:** walking pace of four miles per hour.

Analyze Visuals

Activity What is suggested by putting the image of snowy trees next to the image of fire? *Possible answer: The wood from trees is used to fuel a fire. The snow suggests cold weather, which would make someone want a fire. The contrast between the trees and the fire highlights the human need for fire when confronted by snow and cold.*

TEXT ANALYSIS COMMON CORE RL 5

ⓖ SETTING AND CONFLICT

Remind students that the story's dangerous setting creates conflict for the character. Model for students how to determine the gravity of the man's situation by posing the following questions about the story's details:

- How long does it take for the man's fingers to become numb?
- What does he notice right after he smashes his fingers against his leg?
- What does he finally decide about his toes?

Possible answer: *The man's situation becomes more challenging because his fingers grow numb as soon as he exposes them to the cold. His toes are becoming numb as well.*

Extend the Discussion Do you think the man is beginning to worry? Why or why not?

At twelve o'clock the day was at its brightest. Yet the sun was too far south on its winter journey to clear the horizon. The bulge of the earth intervened between it and Henderson Creek, where the man walked under a clear sky at noon and cast no shadow. At half-past twelve, to the minute, he arrived at the forks of the creek. He was pleased at the speed he had made. If he kept it up, he would certainly be with the boys by six. He unbuttoned his jacket and shirt and drew forth his lunch. The action consumed no more than a quarter of a minute, yet in that brief moment the numbness laid hold of the exposed
170 fingers. He did not put the mitten on, but, instead, struck the fingers a dozen sharp smashes against his leg. Then he sat down on a snow-covered log to eat. The sting that followed upon the striking of his fingers against his leg ceased so quickly that he was startled. He had had no chance to take a bite of biscuit. He struck the fingers repeatedly and returned them to the mitten, baring the other hand for the purpose of eating. He tried to take a mouthful, but the ice muzzle prevented. He had forgotten to build a fire and thaw out. He chuckled at his foolishness, and as he chuckled he noted the numbness creeping into the exposed fingers. Also, he noted that the stinging which had first come to his toes when he sat down was already passing away. He wondered whether the
180 toes were warm or numb. He moved them inside the moccasins and decided that they were numb. ⓖ

> ⓖ **SETTING AND CONFLICT**
> Reread lines 162–181. How has the man's situation become more challenging? Cite details.

DIFFERENTIATED INSTRUCTION

FOR ENGLISH LANGUAGE LEARNERS

Comprehension: Analyisis Discuss how the man analyzes his situation, and point out the words and phrases that indicate that he is thinking: "noted" (line 177), "noted that" (line 178), "wondered whether" (line 179), "decided that" (lines 180–181).

He pulled the mitten on hurriedly and stood up. He was a bit frightened. He stamped up and down until the stinging returned into the feet. It certainly was cold, was his thought. That man from Sulphur Creek had spoken the truth when telling how cold it sometimes got in the country. And he had laughed at him at the time! That showed one must not be too sure of things. There was no mistake about it, it *was* cold. He strode up and down, stamping his feet and threshing his arms, until reassured by the returning warmth. Then he got out matches and proceeded to make a fire. From the under-growth, where high

190 water of the previous spring had lodged a supply of seasoned twigs, he got his firewood. Working carefully from a small beginning, he soon had a roaring fire, over which he thawed the ice from his face and in the protection of which he ate his biscuits. For the moment the cold of space was outwitted. The dog took satisfaction in the fire, stretching out close enough for warmth and far enough away to escape being singed.

When the man had finished, he filled his pipe and took his comfortable time over a smoke, then he pulled on his mittens, settled the ear flaps of his cap firmly about his ears, and took the creek trail up the left fork. The dog was disappointed and yearned back towards the fire. This man did not know cold.

200 Possibly all the generations of his ancestry had been ignorant of cold, of real cold, of cold one hundred and seven degrees below freezing point. But the dog knew; all its ancestry knew, and it had inherited the knowledge. And it knew that it was not good to walk abroad in such fearful cold. It was the time to lie snug in a hole in the snow and wait for a curtain of cloud to be drawn across the face of outer space whence this cold came. On the other hand, there was no keen intimacy between the dog and the man. The one was the toil slave[6] of the other, and the only caresses it had ever received were the caresses of the whip lash and of harsh and menacing throat sounds that threatened the whip lash. So the dog made no effort to communicate its apprehension to the man. It was not

210 concerned in the welfare of the man; it was for its own sake that it yearned back toward the fire. But the man whistled, and spoke to it with the sound of whip lashes, and the dog swung in at the man's heels and followed after. **H**

The man took a chew of tobacco and proceeded to start a new amber beard. Also, his moist breath quickly powdered with white his mustache, eyebrows, and lashes. There did not seem to be so many springs on the left fork of the Henderson, and for half an hour the man saw no signs of any. And then it happened. At a place where there were no signs, where the soft, unbroken snow seemed to advertise solidity beneath, the man broke through. It was not deep. He wet himself halfway to the knees before he floundered out to the firm

220 crust. He was angry, and cursed his luck aloud. He had hoped to get into camp with the boys at six o'clock, and this would delay him an hour, for he would have to build a fire and dry out his footgear. This was **imperative** at that low temperature—he knew that much; and he turned aside to the bank, which he climbed. On top, tangled in the underbrush about the trunks of several small

---

6. **toil slave:** a slave who performs hard labor.

TO BUILD A FIRE   **87**

H DRAW CONCLUSIONS
Who seems more knowledgeable about what to do—the man or the dog? Support your answer.

imperative (ĭm-pĕr′ə-tĭv)
adj. urgently necessary

---

spruce trees, was a high-water deposit[7] of dry firewood—sticks and twigs, principally, but also larger portions of seasoned branches and fine, dry, last year's grasses. He threw down several large pieces on top of the snow. This served for a foundation and prevented the young flame from drowning itself in the snow it otherwise would melt. The flame he got by touching a match to a
230 small shred of birch bark that he took from his pocket. This burned even more readily than paper. Placing it on the foundation, he fed the young flame with wisps of dry grass and with the tiniest dry twigs.

He worked slowly and carefully, keenly aware of his danger. Gradually, as the flame grew stronger, he increased the size of the twigs with which he fed it. He squatted in the snow, pulling the twigs out from their entanglement in the brush and feeding directly to the flame. He knew there must be no failure. When it is seventy-five below zero, a man must not fail in his first attempt to build a fire—that is, if his feet are wet. If his feet are dry, and he fails, he can run along the trail for half a mile and restore his circulation. But the
240 circulation of wet and freezing feet cannot be restored by running when it is seventy-five below. No matter how fast he runs, the wet feet will freeze the harder.

All this the man knew. The old-timer on Sulphur Creek had told him about it the previous fall, and now he was appreciating the advice. Already all sensation had gone out of his feet. To build the fire he had been forced to remove his mittens, and the fingers had quickly gone numb. His pace of four miles an hour had kept his heart pumping blood to the surface of his body and to all the extremities. But the instant he stopped, the action of the pump eased down. The cold of space smote the unprotected tip of the planet, and he,
250 being on that unprotected tip, received the full force of the blow. The blood of his body recoiled before it. The blood was alive, like the dog, and like the dog it wanted to hide away and cover itself up from the fearful cold. So long as he walked four miles an hour, he pumped the blood, willy-nilly, to the surface; but now it ebbed away and sank down into the recesses of his body. The extremities were the first to feel its absence. His wet feet froze the faster, and his exposed fingers numbed the faster, though they had not yet begun to freeze. Nose and cheeks were already freezing, while the skin of all his body chilled as it lost its blood. **⊙**

❸ Targeted Passage

⊙ SETTING AND CONFLICT
Reread lines 216–258. What new conflict with the setting is the man experiencing?

But he was safe. Toes and nose and cheeks would be only touched by the
260 frost, for the fire was beginning to burn with strength. He was feeding it with twigs the size of his finger. In another minute he would be able to feed it with branches the size of his wrist, and then he could remove his wet footgear, and, while it dried, he could keep his naked feet warm by the fire, rubbing them at first, of course, with snow. The fire was a success. He was safe. He

---

7. **high-water deposit:** debris left on the bank of a stream as the water recedes from its highest level.

Possible answer: The man's new conflict is that because he is wet, he is in more danger than he was before (lines 239–241). Also, because he has stopped walking, his heart is not pumping blood to his extremities, causing them to become numb quickly (lines 252–258).

IF STUDENTS NEED HELP . . .
- Have students read lines 236–242. Discuss why the man is in more danger now than he was before.
- Have students read lines 252–254. Point out that the man has stopped walking so that he can build the fire. Ask what the effect of stopping is.

DIFFERENTIATED INSTRUCTION

FOR STRUGGLING READERS

❸ Targeted Passage [Lines 236–258]
This passage explains why stopping to build a fire places the man in such danger.

- Why must the man build a fire? (lines 237–242)
- Why must a man with wet feet not fail in his first attempt to build a fire? (lines 239–242)
- Why does the man remove his mittens? What happens as a result? (line 246)
- How does walking affect the circulation of his blood? (lines 252–254)
- What happens to the blood when he stops walking? What effect does this have? (lines 254–258)

FOR ADVANCED LEARNERS/PRE–AP
Tone [small-group option] Have students discuss the tone of the narrative and whether it changes with the level of danger that the man faces. Ask students what the effect of the tone is, and have them speculate on the author's purpose in creating this tone.

remembered the advice of the old-timer on Sulphur Creek, and smiled. The old-timer had been very serious in laying down the law that no man must travel alone in the Klondike after fifty below. Well, here he was; he had had the accident; he was alone; and he had saved himself. Those old-timers were rather womanish, some of them, he thought. All a man had to do was to keep his
270 head, and he was all right. Any man who was a man could travel alone. But it was surprising, the rapidity with which his cheeks and nose were freezing. And he had not thought his fingers could go lifeless in so short a time. Lifeless they were, for he could scarcely make them move together to grip a twig, and they seemed remote from his body and from him. When he touched a twig, he had to look and see whether or not he had hold of it. The wires were pretty well down between him and his finger ends. **J**

All of which counted for little. There was the fire, snapping and crackling and promising life with every dancing flame. He started to untie his moccasins. They were coated with ice; the thick German socks were like sheaths of iron
280 halfway to the knees; and the moccasin strings were like rods of steel all twisted and knotted as by some **conflagration.** For a moment he tugged with his numb fingers, then, realizing the folly of it, he drew his sheath knife.

But before he could cut the strings, it happened. It was his own fault or, rather, his mistake. He should not have built the fire under the spruce tree. He should have built it in the open. But it had been easier to pull the twigs from the brush and drop them directly on the fire. Now the tree under which he had done this carried a weight of snow on its boughs. No wind had blown for weeks, and each bough was full freighted. Each time he had pulled a twig he had communicated a slight agitation to the tree—an imperceptible agitation,
290 so far as he was concerned, but an agitation sufficient to bring about the disaster. High up in the tree one bough capsized its load of snow. This fell on the boughs beneath, capsizing them. This process continued, spreading out and involving the whole tree. It grew like an avalanche, and it descended upon the man and the fire, and the fire was blotted out! Where it had burned was a mantle of fresh and disordered snow.

The man was shocked. It was as though he had just heard his own sentence of death. For a moment he sat and stared at the spot where the fire had been. Then he grew very calm. Perhaps the old-timer on Sulphur Creek was right. If he had only had a trail mate he would have been in no danger now. The trail
300 mate could have built the fire. Well, it was up to him to build the fire over again, and this second time there must be no failure. Even if he succeeded, he would most likely lose some toes. His feet must be badly frozen by now, and there would be some time before the second fire was ready. **K**

Such were his thoughts, but he did not sit and think them. He was busy all the time they were passing through his mind. He made a new foundation for a fire, this time in the open, where no treacherous tree could blot it out. Next he gathered dry grasses and tiny twigs from the high-water flotsam. He could not

J **DRAW CONCLUSIONS**
Reread lines 259–276. What pattern can you see in the man's attitude and behavior?

conflagration
(kŏn'flə-grā'shən) *n.* a large, destructive fire

K **PREDICT**
Do you think the man will be able to build a fire quickly enough to save his feet?

TO BUILD A FIRE **89**

FOR STRUGGLING READERS

Comprehension Support To make sure students understand exactly what is happening in lines 291–297, ask them what has happened to the fire the man built and what effect this key turn of events has on him.

READING SKILL: *Review* COMMON CORE

J **DRAW CONCLUSIONS** RL 1

Possible answer: *The pattern that is emerging in the man's attitude and behavior is that he repeatedly dismisses advice from "old-timers," arrogantly and naively believing that their advice is overly conservative and does not apply to someone who keeps his head (lines 268–270).*

READING STRATEGY COMMON CORE

K **PREDICT** RL 1

Some students will say yes, because he knows how to build a fire. Others will say no, *because now his fingers are numb and thus useless to him.*

IF STUDENTS NEED HELP . . . Before they answer the question, ask students to do a rapid inventory of the problems that the man is facing, including his "lifeless" fingers (lines 272, 274–276).

Extend the Discussion Ask students what is likely to happen if he fails to build a fire. ***Possible answer:*** *He will lose his feet to frostbite. He will die.*

VOCABULARY COMMON CORE

OWN THE WORD L 4

conflagration: Have students compare and contrast characteristics of a *conflagration* and a bonfire. ***Possible answer:*** *Both fires occur outdoors and are large. A* conflagration, *however, is destructive.*

REVISIT THE BIG QUESTION

Should you trust your

INSTINCTS?

Discuss Why does the man envy the dog? What details in lines 323–327 reinforce the idea that the dog is a creature of instinct? ***Possible answer:*** *The man envies the dog because it is "warm and secure in its natural covering" (line 327), meaning its fur. The emphasis on the dog's wolf-like qualities—"its wolf brush of a tail" (lines 323–324) and "its sharp wolf ears" (line 324)—emphasize that it is a wild animal that relies on instinct to survive.*

TEXT ANALYSIS	COMMON CORE
	RL 4

 **NARRATOR**

Ask for volunteers to read lines 315–327. Ask students to identify the phrases or sentences in the passage that describe the man's actions and then identify the phrases and sentences that describe the man's thoughts. Tell students that the narrator is omniscient because the narrator knows everything about what the man does and thinks.

Possible answer: *The change to first-person point of view makes the action seem more personal, intense, and suspenseful.*

---

bring his fingers together to pull them out, but he was able to gather them by the handful. In this way he got many rotten twigs and bits of green moss that
310 were undesirable, but it was the best he could do. He worked methodically, even collecting an armful of the larger branches to be used later when the fire gathered strength. And all the while the dog sat and watched him, a certain wistfulness in its eyes, for it looked upon him as the fire provider, and the fire was slow in coming.

When all was ready, the man reached in his pocket for a second piece of birch bark. He knew the bark was there, and though he could not feel it with his fingers, he could hear its crisp rustling as he fumbled for it. Try as he would, he could not clutch hold of it. And all the time, in his consciousness, was the knowledge that each instant his feet were freezing. This thought
320 tended to put him in a panic, but he fought against it and kept calm. **L**
He pulled on his mittens with his teeth, and threshed his arms back and forth, beating his hands with all his might against his sides. He did this sitting down, and he stood up to do it; and all the while the dog sat in the snow, its wolf brush of a tail curled around warmly over its forefeet, its sharp wolf ears pricked forward intently as it watched the man. And the man, as he beat and threshed with his arms and hands, felt a great surge of envy as he regarded the creature that was warm and secure in its natural covering.

After a time he was aware of the first faraway signals of sensations in his beaten fingers. The faint tingling grew stronger till it evolved into a stinging
330 ache that was excruciating, but which the man hailed with satisfaction. He stripped the mitten from his right hand and fetched forth the birch bark. The exposed fingers were quickly going numb again. Next he brought out his bunch of sulphur matches. But the tremendous cold had already driven the life out of his fingers. In his effort to separate one match from the others, the whole bunch fell into the snow. He tried to pick it out of the snow, but failed. The dead fingers could neither clutch nor touch. He was very careful. He drove the thought of his freezing feet, and nose, and cheeks, out of his mind, devoting his whole soul to the matches. He watched, using the sense of vision in place of that of touch, and when he saw his fingers on each side the bunch,
340 he closed them—that is, he willed to close them, for the wires were down, and the fingers did not obey. He pulled the mitten on the right hand, and beat it fiercely against his knee. Then, with both mittened hands, he scooped the bunch of matches, along with much snow, into his lap. Yet he was no better off.

After some manipulation he managed to get the bunch between the heels of his mittened hands. In this fashion he carried it to his mouth. The ice crackled and snapped when by a violent effort he opened his mouth. He drew the lower jaw in, curled the upper lip out of the way and scraped the bunch with his upper teeth in order to separate a match. He succeeded in getting one, which
350 he dropped on his lap. He was no better off. He could not pick it up. Then he

---

COMMON CORE RL 4

L NARRATOR
The **narrator** of a story is the character or voice that relates the story's events to the reader. In "To Build a Fire," the narrator is **omniscient,** or all-knowing and outside the action. London uses his omniscient narrator to create a detached, objective **tone.** This narrator is so detached that readers do not even know the man's name. Rewrite lines 315–320 from the point of view of the freezing man. How does the feel of the story change when the point of view changes from omniscient to **first-person**?

DIFFERENTIATED INSTRUCTION

FOR ENGLISH LANGUAGE LEARNERS
Vocabulary: Idioms and Sayings Help students understand the meanings of these idioms and sayings from the story: *had a close call* (line 147), "almost had an accident"; *keep his head* (lines 269–270), "remain calm"; *better off* (line 344), "in a better situation"; *at once* (line 363), "immediately."

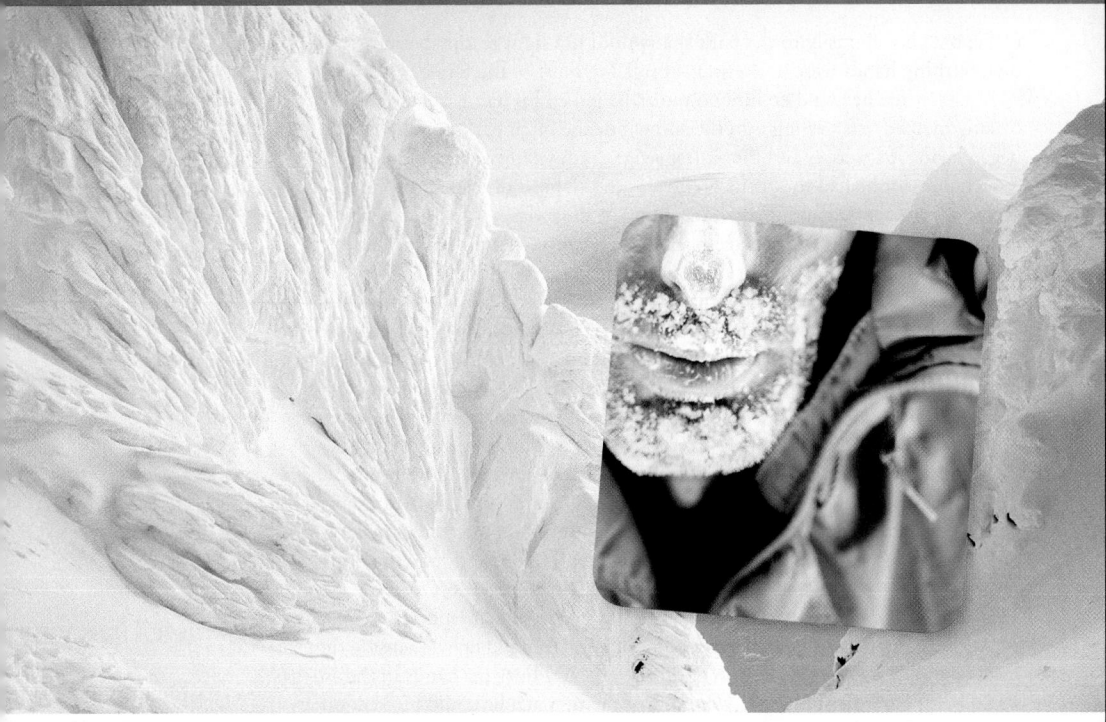

Analyze Visuals ▲

What effect is achieved by placing these two images together?

devised a way. He picked it up in his teeth and scratched it on his leg. Twenty times he scratched before he succeeded in lighting it. As it flamed he held it with his teeth to the birch bark. But the burning brimstone[8] went up his nostrils and into his lungs, causing him to cough spasmodically. The match fell into the snow and went out.

The old-timer on Sulphur Creek was right, he thought in the moment of controlled despair that ensued: after fifty below, a man should travel with a partner. He beat his hands, but failed in exciting any sensation. Suddenly he bared both hands, removing the mittens with his teeth. He caught the whole
360 bunch between the heels of his hands. His arm muscles not being frozen enabled him to press the hand heels tightly against the matches. Then he scratched the bunch along his leg. It flared into flame, seventy sulphur matches at once! There was no wind to blow them out. He kept his head to one side to escape the strangling fumes, and held the blazing bunch to the birch bark. As he so held it, he became aware of sensation in his hand. His flesh was burning. He could smell it. Deep down below the surface he could feel it. The sensation developed into pain that grew acute. And still he endured it, holding the flame

---

8. **brimstone:** sulfur, a chemical used in match heads.

TO BUILD A FIRE **91**

Analyze Visuals

Possible answer: The smaller photograph humanizes the larger image by showing the effects of that snowy setting on a man's face.

TIERED DISCUSSION PROMPTS

Refer to lines 356–367 and use these prompts to help students recognize what a dangerous situation the man is in:

Connect Think about a time when you realized that you had ignored good advice. How did you feel in that situation? *Students may say that they felt regret, frustration, or embarrassment.*

Analyze Why is it dangerous for all the matches to flare up at once? *Possible answer: If this fire does not light or goes out, there will be no matches left to build another.*

Evaluate Was it wise for the man to keep hold of the matches and ignore the pain of his burning flesh? *Answers will vary. Students may say that it was wise for the man to endure the pain because this was his last chance at making a fire. Others might argue that it was unwise because now his hands are even more injured and useless than before.*

FOR ENGLISH LANGUAGE LEARNERS

Comprehension: Description Work with students to identify all the body parts mentioned on these pages so that they can visualize what the man is doing. Most students will know *fingers* and *legs,* but discuss these words and phrases, pointing to your own body, if necessary: "nose and cheekbones" (line 62); "heels" (line 66); "beard and mustache" (line 84); "lips, chin" (line 87); "waist" (line 134); "sides" (line 322); "heels of his . . . hands" (lines 345–346); "lap" (line 350); "nostrils, lungs" (line 354); "flesh" (line 365); "hands and knees" (line 399).

of the matches clumsily to the bark that would not light readily because his own burning hands were in the way, absorbing most of the flame. ⓜ

370   At last, when he could endure no more, he jerked his hands apart. The blazing matches fell sizzling into the snow, but the birch bark was alight. He began laying dry grasses and the tiniest twigs on the flame. He could not pick and choose, for he had to lift the fuel between the heels of his hands. Small pieces of rotten wood and green moss clung to the twigs, and he bit them off as well as he could with his teeth. He cherished⁹ the flame carefully and awkwardly. It meant life, and it must not perish. The withdrawal of blood from the surface of his body now made him begin to shiver, and he grew more awkward. A large piece of green moss fell squarely on the little fire. He tried to poke it out with his fingers, but his shivering frame made him poke too far, and

380 he disrupted the nucleus of the little fire, the burning grasses and the tiny twigs separating and scattering. He tried to poke them together again, but in spite of the tenseness of the effort, his shivering got away with him, and the twigs were hopelessly scattered. Each twig gushed a puff of smoke and went out. The fire provider had failed. As he looked apathetically about him, his eyes chanced on the dog, sitting across the ruins of the fire from him, in the snow, making restless, hunching movements, slightly lifting one forefoot and then the other, shifting its weight back and forth on them with wistful eagerness.

    The sight of the dog put a wild idea into his head. He remembered the tale of the man, caught in a blizzard, who killed a steer and crawled inside the

390 carcass, and so was saved. He would kill the dog and bury his hands in the warm body until the numbness went out of them. Then he could build another fire. He spoke to the dog, calling it to him; but in his voice was a strange note of fear that frightened the animal, who had never known the man to speak in such a way before. Something was the matter, and its suspicious nature sensed danger—it knew not what danger, but somewhere, somehow, in its brain arose an apprehension of the man. It flattened its ears down at the sound of the man's voice, and its restless, hunching movements and the liftings and shiftings of its forefeet became more pronounced; but it would not come to the man. He got on his hands and knees and crawled toward the dog. This unusual posture again

400 excited suspicion, and the animal sidled mincingly away. ⓝ

    The man sat up in the snow for a moment and struggled for calmness. Then he pulled on his mittens, by means of his teeth, and got upon his feet. He glanced down at first in order to assure himself that he was really standing up, for the absence of sensation in his feet left him unrelated to the earth. His erect position in itself started to drive the webs of suspicion from the dog's mind; and when he spoke **peremptorily,** with the sound of whip lashes in his voice, the dog rendered its customary allegiance and came to him. As it came within reaching distance, the man lost his control. His arms flashed out to the dog, and he experienced genuine surprise when he discovered that his hands

410 could not clutch, that there was neither bend nor feeling in his fingers. He had

---

9. **cherished:** tended; guarded.

92   UNIT 1: PLOT, SETTING, AND MOOD

forgotten for the moment that they were frozen and that they were freezing more and more. All this happened quickly, and before the animal could get away, he encircled its body with his arms. He sat down in the snow, and in this fashion held the dog, while it snarled and whined and struggled.

But it was all he could do, hold its body encircled in his arms and sit there. He realized that he could not kill the dog. There was no way to do it. With his helpless hands he could neither draw nor hold his sheath knife nor throttle the animal. He released it, and it plunged wildly away, with tail between its legs, and still snarling. It halted forty feet away and surveyed him curiously, with 420 ears sharply pricked forward.

The man looked down at his hands in order to locate them, and found them hanging on the ends of his arms. It struck him as curious that one should have to use his eyes in order to find out where his hands were. He began threshing his arms back and forth, beating the mittened hands against his sides. He did this for five minutes, violently, and his heart pumped enough blood up to the surface to put a stop to his shivering. But no sensation was aroused in the hands. He had an impression that they hung like weights on the ends of his arms, but when he tried to run the impression down, he could not find it.

A certain fear of death, dull and oppressive, came to him. This fear quickly 430 became poignant as he realized that it was no longer a mere matter of freezing his fingers and toes, or of losing his hands and feet, but that it was a matter of life and death with the chances against him. This threw him into a panic, and he turned and ran along the old, dim trail. The dog joined in behind and kept up with him. He ran blindly, without intention, in fear such as he had never known in his life. Slowly, as he plowed and floundered through the snow, he began to see things again—the banks of the creek, the old timber jams, the leafless aspens, and the sky. The running made him feel better. He did not shiver. Maybe, if he ran on, his feet would thaw out; and, anyway, if he ran far enough, he would reach camp and the boys. Without doubt he would lose some 440 fingers and toes and some of his face; but the boys would take care of him, and save the rest of him when he got there. And at the same time there was another thought in his mind that said he would never get to the camp and the boys; that he would soon be stiff and dead. This thought he kept in the background and refused to consider. Sometimes it pushed itself forward and demanded to be heard, but he thrust it back and strove to think of other things. ◎

It struck him as curious that he could run at all on feet so frozen that he could not feel them when they struck the earth and took the weight of his body. He seemed to himself to skim along above the surface, and to have no

---

REVISIT THE BIG QUESTION
Should you trust your
INSTINCTS?

Discuss What detail in lines 432–437 suggests that instinct is pushing the man to run? What emotion fuels this instinct? *Possible answer: The author says that the man "ran blindly, without intention" (line 434). The emotion seems to be panic (lines 432–433).*

TEXT ANALYSIS   COMMON CORE   RL 5

◎ **SETTING AND CONFLICT**

Possible answer: The man's struggle has now become one of pure survival, of warding off death.

IF STUDENTS NEED HELP . . . Direct students to lines 429–445. Ask them what thoughts and fears now come into the man's head.

Extend the Discussion Why does the man refuse to think of his own death? *Possible answer: He has an instinct to survive, and such thoughts might make him stop trying.*

FOR ENGLISH LANGUAGE LEARNERS
Vocabulary: Multiple Meanings Many English words have more than one meaning. Direct students' attention to the uses of *struck* in lines 446–447. Point out the word's two meanings ("affected or caused him to feel" and "hit"), and discuss how students can use context clues to determine each meaning. Help students understand these other multiple-meaning words in the story: *snaps, springs* (line 129); *bed, banks* (line 140); *stamped* (line 183); *and frame* (line 379).

FOR ENGLISH LANGUAGE LEARNERS

Language Coach   COMMON CORE   RL 4
Etymologies *Possible answer: He's showing panic by "running blindly, without intention, in fear..." (line 434). Panikos* is different from the Greek root *pan* meaning "all." For example, *pandemic* (*pan + demos* for "people") means "all people," and *pantheon* (*pan + theos* for "gods") is "a temple dedicated to all the gods."

TIERED DISCUSSION PROMPTS

Refer to lines 451–462 and use these prompts to help students understand how the man's failure to build a fire has changed the outcome of the story:

Recall Why doesn't the man's new survival plan work? *Possible answer: His new plan to run all the way to camp fails because he is too tired.*

Analyze What has changed for the man since he tried to build a fire and failed? *Possible answer: He now fears death. He no longer feels cold. Running no longer brings sensation to his face, hands, or feet.*

Synthesize From what you know about surviving in cold and snowy environments and from what you learned from the story, why is the man feeling warm and comfortable? *Possible answer: The warmth may be a side effect of the frostbite and hypothermia that have set in, or it may be a hallucination caused by the decreased blood flow to the man's brain.*

VOCABULARY

COMMON CORE
RL 4

WORD RELATIONSHIPS

Point out to students that other word relationships can also help them infer word meanings. For example, if they are familiar with words that share a root with *conception*, such as *conceive* and *concept*, they may be able to guess the meaning of *conception* without finding a familiar synonym.

Possible answer: synonym: idea; *I think* conception *means "something that you think of."* Conception *seems to be related to* idea *because the man's conceptions are in his mind, according to line 475.*

---

connection with the earth. Somewhere he had once seen a winged Mercury,[10] 450 and he wondered if Mercury felt as he felt when skimming over the earth.

His theory of running until he reached camp and the boys had one flaw in it: he lacked the endurance. Several times he stumbled, and finally he tottered, crumpled up, and fell. When he tried to rise, he failed. He must sit and rest, he decided, and next time he would merely walk and keep on going. As he sat and regained his breath, he noted that he was feeling quite warm and comfortable. He was not shivering, and it even seemed that a warm glow had come to his chest and trunk. And yet, when he touched his nose or cheeks, there was no sensation. Running would not thaw them out. Nor would it thaw out his hands and feet. Then the thought came to him that the frozen portions of his 460 body must be extending. He tried to keep this thought down, to forget it, to think of something else; he was aware of the panicky feeling that it caused, and he was afraid of the panic. But the thought asserted itself, and persisted, until it produced a vision of his body totally frozen. This was too much, and he made another wild run along the trail. Once he slowed down to a walk, but the thought of the freezing extending itself made him run again.

And all the time the dog ran with him, at his heels. When he fell down a second time, it curled its tail over its forefeet and sat in front of him, facing him, curiously eager and intent. The warmth and security of the animal angered him, and he cursed it till it flattened down its ears appeasingly. This 470 time the shivering came more quickly upon the man. He was losing in his battle with the frost. It was creeping into his body from all sides. The thought of it drove him on, but he ran no more than a hundred feet, when he staggered and pitched headlong. It was his last panic. When he had recovered his breath and control, he sat up and entertained in his mind the conception of meeting death with dignity. However, the conception did not come to him in such terms. His idea of it was that he had been making a fool of himself, running around like a chicken with its head cut off—such was the simile that occurred to him. Well, he was bound to freeze anyway, and he might as well take it decently. With this newfound peace of mind came the first glimmerings of 480 drowsiness. A good idea, he thought, to sleep off to death. It was like taking an anesthetic. Freezing was not so bad as people thought. There were lots worse ways to die. ⚠

He pictured the boys finding his body the next day. Suddenly he found himself with them, coming along the trail and looking for himself. And, still with them, he came around a turn in the trail and found himself lying in the snow. He did not belong with himself any more, for even then he was out of himself, standing with the boys and looking at himself in the snow. It certainly was cold, was his thought. When he got back to the States he could tell the folks what real cold was. He drifted on from this to a vision of the old-timer

---

COMMON CORE RL 4

⚠ **WORD RELATIONSHIPS**
You can often **infer**, or guess, the meaning of an unfamiliar word by analyzing its relationship to other words. For example, the word *conception* (lines 474 and 475) may not be familiar to you. But if you can identify a nearby **synonym**, or word with nearly the same meaning, *conception*'s meaning may become clear. Which word in line 476 seems to be a synonym of *conception*? What do you think *conception* means? Explain your answers.

---

10. **Mercury:** the messenger of the gods in Roman mythology, who flew about by means of wings on his helmet and sandals.

DIFFERENTIATED INSTRUCTION

FOR ENGLISH LANGUAGE LEARNERS

Culture: Clarify Throughout the story, the man refers to grown men as "the boys" (line 483). Explain that at one time it was common to use the word *boys* to refer to "men" or "friends."

490 on Sulphur Creek. He could see him quite clearly, warm and comfortable, and smoking a pipe.

"You were right, old hoss;[11] you were right," the man mumbled to the old-timer of Sulphur Creek.

> Then the man drowsed off into what seemed to him the most comfortable and satisfying sleep he had ever known. The dog sat facing him and waiting. The brief day drew to a close in a long, slow twilight. There were no signs of a fire to be made, and, besides, never in the dog's experience had it known a man to sit like that in the snow and make no fire. As the twilight drew on, its eager yearning for the fire mastered it, and with a great lifting and shifting of
> 500 forefeet, it whined softly, then flattened its ears down in anticipation of being chidden by the man. But the man remained silent. Later the dog whined loudly. And still later it crept close to the man and caught the scent of death. This made the animal bristle and back away. A little longer it delayed, howling under the stars that leaped and danced and shone brightly in the cold sky. Then it turned and trotted up the trail in the direction of the camp it knew, where there were other food providers and fire providers. ◐ Q

⑤ Targeted Passage

Q PREDICT
Will the dog meet the same fate as the man? Why?

---

11. **old hoss:** old horse—here used as an affectionate term of address.

95

READING STRATEGY    **COMMON CORE**
RL 1

Q PREDICT

Possible answer: The dog will probably survive. First, it is not freezing; its fur has kept it warm. Also, it knows to return to camp, where there are "other food providers and fire providers" (line 506).

IF STUDENTS NEED HELP . . . Help students recognize that the dog's fur as well as its instincts are likely to keep it alive.

Extend the Discussion Does this dog seem different from your impression of a domesticated dog? Explain your response.

SELECTION WRAP-UP

READ WITH A PURPOSE Now that students have finished reading the selection, have them consider these questions: In what small yet critical ways did the man underestimate the danger of his trip? How did his body and mind fail him? *Possible answer: He ignores signals that indicate the weather is colder than he can withstand. When he becomes exhausted and numb, he loses his grip on his sanity.*

⭐ **CRITIQUE** Ask students whether they think the title "To Build a Fire" is a good choice for this story. Have them support their answers with evidence from the story.

INDEPENDENT READING

Students may also enjoy reading *Into the Wild* by Jon Krakauer, the true story of a young man's attempt to live in the Alaskan wilderness.

FOR STRUGGLING READERS

⑤ Targeted Passage [Lines 494–506]

This concluding passage describes the man's death and hints at the dog's survival.

- What has happened to the man? How do you know? (lines 494–495; line 502)

- What is the dog's first reaction? Do you think this reaction is caused by instinct or by something else? Explain. (lines 495–502)

- In which direction does the dog go after the man dies? Why? (lines 505–506)

FOR ADVANCED LEARNERS/PRE-AP

Tone Have students work in small groups to discuss why the author might have adopted and maintained the even, unemotional tone that he uses throughout the story. Have them consider alternative tones the author might have used and the effects that those different tones would have had on readers—and on the meaning of the story.

Practice and Apply

For preliminary support of post-reading questions, use these copy maseters:

R RESOURCE MANAGER—Copy Masters
Reading Check p. 92
Setting and Conflict p. 85
Question Support p. 93

Additional selection questions are provided for teachers on page 80.

ANSWERS

Comprehension

1. *He has to build a second fire because he gets wet after stepping into a hidden spring.*

2. *The man has built it below the branches of a snow-covered tree, which dumps its load of snow on the fire, extinguishing it.*

3. *He has difficulty because his hands are numb from the cold.*

4. *The man dies. The dog heads toward camp.*

Text Analysis

COMMON CORE RL 1, RL 5

Possible answers:

5. ● **COMMON CORE FOCUS** *Predict 1. The man will not seek shelter, but the dog will. 2. The man will be able to build a fire quickly.* **Text clues:** *1. The man lacks imagination (line 29), but the dog's instincts make it nervous (lines 76–77). 2. He knows how to build a fire, and he has plenty of matches.*

6. ● **COMMON CORE FOCUS** *Analyze Setting and Conflict Much of nature threatens the man's health and safety: The cold can kill him. The hidden springs are traps (line 130). The snow-laden tree puts out his fire. If he is unable to solve the challenges he faces he will die.*

7. *Qualities: overconfident, lacks imagination, a bit lazy* **Mistakes:** *travels alone, does not see the cold as a threat, builds a fire beneath a snowy tree.*

8. *The man does not fear dangerous cold, but the dog does. The man leaves the fire to push onward, whereas the dog stays by the fire. The message is that listening to one's instincts is important to survival.*

9. *The mood is unemotional, matter-of-fact, and reserved. The description of the frigid, icy setting reinforces that mood by echoing its emotional "coldness."*

10. *Some students will blame the man, because he was overconfident, ignored sound*

Comprehension

1. **Recall** Why must the man stop and build a second fire?

2. **Recall** What causes his second fire to go out?

3. **Recall** Why does the man have difficulty rebuilding the second fire?

4. **Clarify** What ultimately happens to the man and the dog?

Text Analysis

● 5. **Predict** Look at the chart you created as you read. What predictions did you make about events in the story? Tell what clues helped you guess correctly—or misled you. Cite evidence from the text in your response.

● 6. **Analyze Setting and Conflict** In what ways does the setting act as an **antagonist,** or opponent, of the man? How do the conflicts he face create **tension?** Cite evidence from the story.

7. **Evaluate Behavior** Identify at least three mistakes that the man makes. What traits or qualities within him cause him to make those mistakes? Record your ideas on a chart like the one shown.

Qualities		Mistakes
overconfident	→	travels alone
	→	
	→	

8. **Contrast Characters** Point out differences between the man and the dog. What message about instincts do you get from these contrasts?

9. **Analyze Mood** Describe the mood, or atmosphere, of the story. How does the description of setting contribute to the mood?

10. **Make Judgments** What do you blame most for the man's fate? Support your answer.

Text Criticism

11. **Philosophical Context** Two principles of the philosophy of **naturalism** are that (1) the universe is indifferent to humankind and (2) people are at the mercy of forces over which they have little control. How are these principles illustrated in "To Build a Fire"? Use examples from the story to support your answer.

> **Should you trust your INSTINCTS?**
>
> When is a person most likely to use his or her instincts?

COMMON CORE

RL 1 Cite evidence to support inferences drawn from the text. **RL 5** Analyze how an author's choices concerning how to structure a text, order events within it, and manipulate time create effects such as tension.

---

advice, was unable to see deeper patterns in the facts before him, and was unable to learn from the dog's instinctive behavior.

Text Criticism

Possible answer:

11. *The universe: the obstacles placed by nature in the man's path despite his suffering* **The forces:** *the dangerous setting and temperature are the result of natural laws that humans try to understand and tame—but that they can never entirely control.*

Should you trust your
INSTINCTS? Encourage students to use personal experience to consider the question. When have they, or someone they know, had an instinctive response to something? What was the result of listening to or ignoring those instincts?

Vocabulary in Context

▲ VOCABULARY PRACTICE

Decide whether each pair of words contains synonyms (words with the same meaning) or antonyms (words with opposite meanings).

1. intangible/touchable
2. conjectural/theorized
3. apprehension/anxiety
4. reiterate/restate
5. smite/caress
6. imperative/needless
7. conflagration/blaze
8. peremptorily/hesitantly

WORD LIST

apprehension
conflagration
conjectural
imperative
intangible
peremptorily
reiterate
smite

ACADEMIC VOCABULARY IN WRITING

• affect • communicate • definite • establish • identify

Working with a partner, **establish** a set of guidelines that you would give to someone about to set off into the Yukon. **Identify** and write down at least four important rules that he or she should follow. Try to use at least two Academic Vocabulary words in your guidelines.

VOCABULARY STRATEGY: CONNOTATION AND DENOTATION

A word's **denotation** is its basic dictionary meaning; its **connotation** is the overtones of meaning the word has taken on. For example, the vocabulary word *conflagration* means "a large fire," but it has negative connotations of total destruction, unlike the more neutral word *flame*. When you choose a word in writing, consider whether its connotation fits the context of the sentences and paragraphs surrounding it.

COMMON CORE

L 5b Analyze nuances in the meaning of words with similar denotations.

PRACTICE Choose the word that works best in each sentence.

1. The queen (assertively/peremptorily) ordered her attendants to stand.
2. The melody would (reiterate/echo) in his ears.
3. The excited children felt (anticipation/apprehension) as they entered the circus tent.
4. Examinations were (imperative/compulsory) for admission to the school.
5. There was an (intangible/unsubstantial) feeling of loss in the community.

Interactive Vocabulary THINK central

Go to **thinkcentral.com**.
KEYWORD: HML10-97

ANSWERS

Vocabulary in Context

▲ VOCABULARY PRACTICE

1. *antonyms*
2. *synonyms*
3. *synonyms*
4. *synonyms*
5. *antonyms*
6. *antonyms*
7. *synonyms*
8. *antonyms*

R RESOURCE MANAGER—Copy Master
Vocabulary Practice p. 90

ACADEMIC VOCABULARY IN WRITING

Student responses should identify rules such as "never travel alone" or "always bring warm clothes, food, and materials for starting a fire."

VOCABULARY STRATEGY: CONNOTATION AND DENOTATION

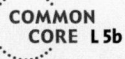

COMMON CORE L 5b

Introduce the topic of connotation by presenting pairs of words and asking students what each word suggests beyond its literal meaning, or denotation: *frosty, freezing; trot, lope; smooth, unbroken.*

Possible answers:

1. *peremptorily*
2. *echo*
3. *anticipation*
4. *compulsory*
5. *intangible*

R RESOURCE MANAGER—Copy Master
Vocabulary Strategy p. 91

Interactive Vocabulary THINK central

Keywords direct students to a **WordSharp** tutorial on **thinkcentral.com** or to other types of vocabulary practice and review.

Assess and Reteach

Assess

DIAGNOSTIC AND SELECTION TESTS
Selection Test A, pp. 35–36
Selection Test B/C, pp. 37–38

Interactive Selection Test on **thinkcentral.com**

Reteach

Level Up Online Tutorials on **thinkcentral.com**

Reteaching Worksheets on **thinkcentral.com**
Literature Lesson 6, Literature Lesson 9,
Reading Lesson 1, Vocabulary Lesson 17

DIFFERENTIATED INSTRUCTION

FOR ENGLISH LANGUAGE LEARNERS

Comprehension: Contrast Connotations of unfamiliar or difficult words may be hard for some students to grasp. To make the concept clearer, provide them with pairs of words in which one word has negative connotations and the other has neutral or positive connotations. Have students identify which word is negative in each pair: *slim, skinny* (negative); *sound, noise* (negative); *unusual, weird* (negative); *aroma, odor* (negative).

FOR ADVANCED LEARNERS/PRE–AP

Vocabulary Strategy Challenge students to look back through the story to find examples of words with strong connotations. Have them copy the sentences in which these words appear and circle the words that they selected. Then have them rewrite the sentences, replacing the circled words with other words having very different connotations. Invite students to share some of their sentence pairs with the class.

Focus and Motivate

COMMON CORE FOCUS

RI 1 Cite textual evidence to support analysis of what the text says explicitly. **RI 2** Provide an objective summary of the text. **RI 4** Determine the meaning of words as they are used in a text. **W 2** Write explanatory texts to examine and convey complex ideas, concepts, and information clearly and accurately.

SUMMARY

This selection identifies and analyzes 12 patterns of thought and behavior that survivors of major disasters have in common. These points add up to a reader's guide to surviving disaster, based on the attitudes and actions of actual survivors.

What's the Connection?

Introduce students to the PLAN strategy to help them preview the text and predict what it will be about. Then, as students read, they can use PLAN symbols in the summaries that they write. Explain how the symbols can help students recognize those sections of the text that require close reading.

📦 **BEST PRACTICES TOOLKIT—Transparency**
PLAN p. A22

Teach

Standards Focus: Use Text Features

Guide students in finding and using various text features to identify key ideas in a nonfiction text. Have students quickly preview the text. Then ask these questions to help them see the usefulness of text features:

- What word in the title relates to the story "To Build a Fire"?

- Based on your preview, do you think the numbers show time sequence or order of importance? Give your reasons.

- How do subheadings help you get a quick overview of the article's key ideas?

📘 **RESOURCE MANAGER—Copy Master**
Use Text Features p. 103

---

from Deep Survival
Nonfiction Book

COMMON CORE

RI 1 Cite textual evidence to support analysis of what the text says explicitly. **RI 2** Provide an objective summary of the text. **RI 4** Determine the meaning of words as they are used in a text.

What's the Connection?

In "To Build a Fire" you read about a man who is unable to save himself in a desperate situation. But what exactly does he do wrong? Could his fate have been different? In the following selection you'll learn what real people in desperate situations have done to save their lives.

Standards Focus: Use Text Features

Text features are design elements that highlight the organization of information and key ideas in a text. Like numbered steps in a recipe, they make a text easy to follow. For example, in the selection from *Deep Survival*, the following text features point out its key ideas:

- The **title** usually reveals the main topic of the piece.
- **Numbers** make the order of sequential information obvious or establish order of importance.
- **Subheadings**—boldfaced headings in the text—signal the start of new topics or sections and tell what they will be about.
- **Text in parentheses** explains whatever came just before it.

As you read the selection, use these features for help in finding and recording key ideas in the order the writer presents them. Record the writer's subheadings on a chart like the one shown, but then use the examples he gives as a basis for summarizing the key ideas—restating them in your own words.

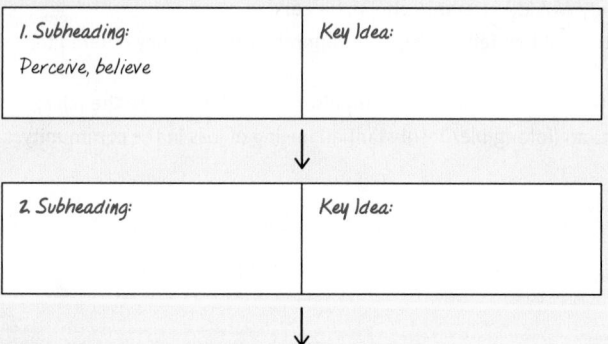

1. Subheading: Perceive, believe	Key Idea:

↓

2. Subheading:	Key Idea:

↓

Review: Summarize

Selection Resources

See resources on the **Teacher One Stop DVD-ROM** *and on* **thinkcentral.com**.

R **RESOURCE MANAGER UNIT 1**
Plan and Teach, pp. 95–99
Summary, pp. 101–102†‡*
Reading Skill, pp. 103–106

DIAGNOSTIC AND SELECTION TESTS
Selection Tests, pp. 39–42

TECHNOLOGY
💿 **Teacher One Stop DVD-ROM**
💿 **Student One Stop DVD-ROM**
💿 **Audio Anthology CD**
💿 **GrammarNotes DVD-ROM**
💿 **ExamView Test Generator** on the Teacher One Stop

* Resources for Differentiation   **† Also in Spanish**   **‡ Also in Haitian Creole and Vietnamese**

DEEP SURVIVAL
by LAURENCE GONZALES

Lauren Elder, sole survivor of a plane crash

I've been reading accident reports of various kinds for thirty or more years. Call me callous, but to me they're like silent comedy movies. People do the strangest things and get themselves into the most amazing predicaments. You want to go wake up Tolstoy and Dostoevsky and say: Hey, you think your characters are crazy. . . .

   In reading about cases in which people survived seemingly impossible circumstances, however, I found an eerie uniformity. Decades and sometimes even centuries apart, separated by culture, geography, race, language, and tradition, they all went through the
10 same patterns of thought and behavior. I eventually distilled those observations down to twelve points that seemed to stand out

Ⓐ USE TEXT FEATURES
Speculate about the meaning of the **title**. What topic do you predict the writer will discuss?

COMMON CORE RI 4
Language Coach
Root Words Look at this selection's title. The word *survival* includes the root *-viv-*, which means "to live." What are some other words that include this root? What do those words mean?

DEEP SURVIVAL **99**

Practice and Apply

INFORMATIONAL ANALYSIS   COMMON CORE
RI 1

Ⓐ USE TEXT FEATURES

Possible answer: *The title suggests that the writer will probably discuss survival in the most extreme circumstances.*

IF STUDENTS NEED HELP . . . Some students may be confused because they do not know the term *deep survival*. Tell them to make a prediction based on words that they do know; they can always change their predictions later.

DIFFERENTIATED INSTRUCTION

FOR STRUGGLING READERS

Options for Reading To complete the chart on page 98, have students work independently to identify the subheadings in the selection and then work with a partner to restate each subheading more fully as a key idea.

FOR ENGLISH LANGUAGE LEARNERS

Language Coach   COMMON CORE RI 4
Root Words
Answer: vibrant *means "full of life,"* revive *means "to restore life or consciousness,"* vivisect *means "to cut or dissect a living creature."* Have students practice using words with the root *-viv-* in sentences.

B *Model the Skill:* **USE TEXT FEATURES**

Model how to use text features. Explain that writers provide subheadings to alert readers to the key topics they are covering. Tell students to look for a pattern among subheadings. Ask how these subheadings are alike.

Possible answer: The points can be characterized as advice from the author about surviving a disaster. Some provide encouragement, others practical pointers. All include explanations within parentheses. There are 12 subheadings.

B USE TEXT FEATURES
Scan the boldfaced **subheadings** to get an overview of the points Gonzales makes. How would you characterize these points about survival? How many are there?

concerning how survivors think and behave in the clutch of mortal danger. Some are the same as the steps for staying out of trouble. Here's what survivors do:

1. Perceive, believe (look, see, believe). **B** Even in the initial crisis, survivors' perceptions and cognitive functions keep working. They notice the details and may even find some humorous or beautiful. If there is any denial, it is counterbalanced by a solid belief in the clear evidence of their senses. They immediately begin to recognize, acknowledge, and even accept the
20 reality of their situation. "I've broken my leg, that's it. I'm dead," as Joe Simpson [who survived a mountain-climbing accident in Peru] put it. They may initially blame forces outside themselves, too; but very quickly they dismiss that tactic and recognize that everything, good and bad, emanates from within. They see opportunity, even good, in their situation. They move through denial, anger, bargaining, depression, and acceptance very rapidly. They "go inside." Bear in mind, though, that many people, such as Debbie Kiley [who survived being lost at sea for five days without water], may have to struggle for a time before they get there.

2. Stay calm (use humor, use fear to focus). In the initial crisis,
30 survivors are making use of fear, not being ruled by it. Their fear often feels like and turns into anger, and that motivates them and makes them sharper. They understand at a deep level about being cool and are ever on guard against the mutiny of too much emotion. They keep their sense of humor and therefore keep calm.

3. Think/analyze/plan (get organized; set up small, manageable tasks). Survivors quickly organize, set up routines, and institute discipline. In successful group survival situations, a leader emerges often from the least likely candidate. They push away thoughts that their situation is hopeless. A rational voice emerges and is often actually heard,

Joe Simpson, survivor of a mountain-climbing accident

DIFFERENTIATED INSTRUCTION

FOR STRUGGLING READERS

Build Comprehension Explain that each subheading summarizes advice to readers and that the text fleshes out these pointers with examples of the thoughts and deeds of actual survivors. The text helps explain the subheadings. Show how words in the subheading often link to words in the text, sometimes in slightly altered forms. Ask students to find examples: "perceive", "perceptions" (lines 15, 16); "play", "entertain" (lines 62, 69).

FOR ENGLISH LANGUAGE LEARNERS

Vocabulary: Idioms Remind students that many words and phrases are idioms, expressions that do not mean exactly what they say. As an example, point out the idiom *bear in mind* (line 26). Discuss its meaning: "remember; take into consideration." Then follow a similar procedure with these idioms: *leave the rest behind* (line 50); *take great joy from* (line 52); *do their very best* (line 90); *pick themselves up* (lines 112–113); *keep their spirits up* (line 115).

40 which takes control of the situation. Survivors perceive that experience as being split into two people and they "obey" the rational one. It begins with the paradox of seeing reality—how hopeless it would seem to an outside observer—but acting with the expectation of success.

4. Take correct, decisive action (be bold and cautious while carrying out tasks). Survivors are able to transform thought into action. They are willing to take risks to save themselves and others. They are able to break down very large jobs into small, manageable tasks. They set attainable goals and develop short-term plans to reach them. They are meticulous about doing those tasks well. They deal with what is within their power from

50 moment to moment, hour to hour, day to day. They leave the rest behind.

5. Celebrate your successes (take joy in completing tasks). Survivors take great joy from even their smallest successes. That is an important step in creating an ongoing feeling of motivation and preventing the descent into hopelessness. It also provides relief from the unspeakable stress of a true survival situation.

6. Count your blessings (be grateful—you're alive). This is how survivors become rescuers instead of victims. There is always someone else they are helping more than themselves, even if that someone is not present. One survivor I spoke to, Yossi Ghinsberg, who was lost for weeks in the

60 Bolivian jungle, hallucinated about a beautiful companion. . . . Everything he did, he did for her.

7. Play (sing, play mind games, recite poetry, count anything, do mathematical problems in your head). C Since the brain and its wiring appear to be the determining factor in survival, this is an argument for expanding and refining it. The more you have learned and experienced of art, music, poetry, literature, philosophy, mathematics, and so on, the more resources you will have to fall back on. Just as survivors use patterns and rhythm to move forward in the survival voyage, they use the deeper activities of intellect to stimulate, calm, and entertain the mind. Counting becomes

70 important, too, and reciting poetry or even a mantra can calm the frantic mind. Movement becomes dance. One survivor who had to walk a long way counted his steps, one hundred at a time, and dedicated each hundred to another person he cared about. . . . Survivors often cling to talismans. They search for meaning and the more you know already, the deeper the meaning. They engage the crisis almost as a game. They discover the flow of the expert performer, in whom emotion and thought balance each other in producing action. "Careful, careful," they say. But they act joyfully and decisively. Playing also leads to invention, and invention may lead to a new technique, strategy, or a piece of equipment that could save you.

C USE TEXT FEATURES
Notice how the material in **parentheses** helps you understand point 7, **Play.** Read the rest of the section. Then explain in your own words how survivors "play."

FOR STRUGGLING READERS
Build Comprehension Help students sort out the pronouns on the page. Point out that the author occasionally uses *I* and *you*. However, more often the writer uses *they*. Ask students whom the pronoun *they* refers to (*survivors*).

FOR ADVANCED LEARNERS/PRE–AP
Style and Tone Have students analyze the author's style and tone, identifying its distinguishing features. Ask them to work independently to write a paragraph or two that states their conclusions and uses evidence from the text as support.

80

8. See the beauty (remember: it's a vision quest). Survivors are attuned to the wonder of the world. The appreciation of beauty, the feeling of awe, opens the senses. When you see something beautiful, your pupils actually dilate. This appreciation not only relieves stress and creates strong motivation, but it allows you to take in new information more effectively.

9. Believe that you will succeed (develop a deep conviction that you'll live). All of the practices just described lead to this point: Survivors consolidate their personalities and fix their determination. Survivors admonish themselves to make no more mistakes, to be very careful, and to 90 do their very best. They become convinced that they will prevail if they do those things.

10. Surrender (let go of your fear of dying; "put away the pain"). Survivors manage pain well. Lauren Elder, who walked out of the Sierra Nevada after surviving a plane crash, wrote that she "stored away the information: My arm is broken." That sort of thinking is what John Leach calls "resignation without giving up. It is survival by surrender." Joe Simpson recognized that he would probably die. But it had ceased to bother him, and so he went ahead and crawled off the mountain anyway. **D**

11. Do whatever is necessary (be determined; have the will 100 **and the skill).** Survivors have meta-knowledge: They know their abilities and do not over- or underestimate them. They believe that anything is possible and act accordingly. Play leads to invention, which leads to trying something that might have seemed impossible. When the plane in which Lauren Elder was flying hit the top of a ridge above 12,000 feet, it would have seemed impossible that she could get off alive. She did it anyway, including having to down-climb vertical rock faces with a broken arm. Survivors don't expect or even hope to be rescued. They are coldly rational about using the world, obtaining what they need, doing what they have to do.

12. Never give up (let nothing break your spirit). E There is 110 always one more thing that you can do. Survivors are not easily frustrated. They are not discouraged by setbacks. They accept that the environment (or the business climate or their health) is constantly changing. They pick themselves up and start the entire process over again, breaking it down into manageable bits. Survivors always have a clear reason for going on. They keep their spirits up by developing an alternate world made up of rich memories to which they can escape. They mine their memory for whatever will keep them occupied. They come to embrace the world in which they find themselves and see opportunity in adversity. In the aftermath, survivors learn from and are grateful for the experiences they've had.

D SUMMARIZE
A summary is a retelling of the main ideas and details of a text in your own words. In a sentence, summarize point 10, **Surrender.**

E USE TEXT FEATURES
Why do you think Gonzales placed this point last?

INFORMATIONAL ANALYSIS: Review   **COMMON CORE**   RI 2

D SUMMARIZE

Possible answer: Give in to the terrible reality of your plight, but don't give up.

IF STUDENTS NEED HELP . . .
Tell students that subheadings can help them summarize information because they usually identify the main ideas.

INFORMATIONAL ANALYSIS   **COMMON CORE**   RI 1

E USE TEXT FEATURES

Possible answer: Gonzales places this point last because it is the most important behavior or attitude, the one that enables a survivor to carry out all the other behaviors. By placing his key point last, Gonzales hopes it will stick in the reader's mind.

DIFFERENTIATED INSTRUCTION

FOR ENGLISH LANGUAGE LEARNERS
Language: Pronoun Referents Tell students that identifying whom or what a pronoun refers to can help them understand passages of text. Direct their attention to the pronouns "they" (line 111) and "it" (line 113). Work with students to identify the referents for these pronouns: "survivors" (line 110) and "entire process" (line 113).

Follow a similar procedure with these pronouns and referents from the selection:

- *them* (line 31), "survivors" (line 30)
- *which* (line 40), "rational voice" (line 39)
- *them* (line 48), "goals" (line 48)
- *that* (line 52), "[taking] great joy" (line 52)
- *who* (line 59), "Yossi Ghinsberg" (line 59)
- *it* (line 84), "appreciation" (line 83)

Comprehension

1. **Recall** What kinds of accidents happened to the people in *Deep Survival*?

2. **Paraphrase** What does it mean to "Perceive, believe"?

Text Analysis

● 3. **Analyze Text Features** Review the subheadings you jotted down as you read this selection. What is similar about the way in which they are stated? Why might Gonzales have chosen to phrase them this way?

4. **Make Generalizations** What general attitude do survivors seem to have?

5. **Apply** In what ways can you apply the 12 points to crises other than those involving physical survival in the outdoors?

COMMON CORE

RI 1 Cite textual evidence to support analysis of what the text says explicitly. RI 2 Provide an objective summary of the text. W 2 Write explanatory texts to examine and convey complex ideas, concepts, and information clearly and accurately.

Read for Information: Evaluate

WRITING PROMPT

Use Gonzales's principles for survival to evaluate the performance of the man in "To Build a Fire." How does he demonstrate effective survival behavior? What does he fail to do that survivors tend to do?

To answer this prompt you will need to do the following:

1. Create a checklist of effective survival behaviors based on the 12 principles in *Deep Survival*.

2. Reread "To Build a Fire," rating the man's survival skills based on your checklist.

3. Explain what you've discovered in a short paragraph. Then support your evaluation with evidence from the story and your checklist.

Evaluation on Specific Points

Yes No

1. ☐ ☐
2. ☐ ☐ → Summary → Evaluation with Evidence
3. ☐ ☐
4. ☐ ☐
5. ☐ ☐

FOR STRUGGLING WRITERS

Read for Information Help students evaluate the man's survival skills and then write a one-paragraph response to the prompt.

1. Suggest that students list the man's behaviors as they reread the story.

2. Help students evaluate the man's survival skills using their checklists and their notes.

3. Work with students to create a topic sentence for their paragraphs. This

sentence should be a general statement that rates the man's survival skills.

4. The other sentences in the paragraph should summarize the evidence that students recorded in their charts.

Practice and Apply

For preliminary support of post-reading questions, use these copy masters:

R RESOURCE MANAGER—Copy Masters
Reading Check p. 107
Question Support p. 108
Additional selection questions are provided for teachers on page 98.

ANSWERS

Comprehension

1. *mountain-climbing accidents, plane crashes, getting lost, breaking bones*

2. *It means "Recognize and accept the bad situation and look for opportunities."*

Text Analysis

COMMON CORE RI 1, RI 2

Possible answers:

3. ● **COMMON CORE FOCUS** *Analyze Text Features They are commands. Gonzales might have used them to urge readers to take action.*

4. **Make Generalizations** *optimistic, focused, resourceful, determined*

5. **Apply** *The points reflect an attitude that would help someone cope with an emotionally stressful or traumatic situation.*

Read for Information: Evaluate

 COMMON CORE W 2

Writing Prompt *Students may note that the man in "To Build a Fire" fails at point 1 because he does not recognize the severity of the crisis, fails at point 2 because he begins to panic, fails at point 4 because he is careless, fails at point 11 because he overestimates his skills, and fails at point 12 because he gives up.*

Assess and Reteach

Assess

DIAGNOSTIC AND SELECTION TESTS
Selection Test A, B/C pp. 39–40, 41–42

Interactive Selection Test on <u>thinkcentral.com</u>

Reteach

Level Up Online Tutorials on <u>thinkcentral.com</u>

Reteaching Worksheets on <u>thinkcentral.com</u>
Informational Text Lesson 1: Text Features

Practice and Apply

COMMON CORE FOCUS

RI 7 Analyze various accounts of a subject told in different mediums.

What's the Connection?

Have students look at the "How to Build a Fire" diagram. Ask students how this diagram relates to "To Build a Fire" and from *Deep Survival*. **Possible answers:** *The title of the short story "To Build a Fire" talks about building a fire. Whether or not the man in the story can successfully build a fire determines his survival. The text from* Deep Survival *talks about the importance of survival skills, such as building a fire.*

ANALYZE VISUALS · COMMON CORE · RI 7

1. EVALUATE

Possible answers: *Yes, this diagram is very clear. No, I think I would need more directions.*

ANALYZE VISUALS · COMMON CORE · RI 7

2. CONNECT

Possible answer: *The most likely survival situation I would face would be a flood, so starting a fire would not be my first priority. Instead, moving to higher ground would be my first priority.*

Diagram

Just as important as the ability to understand literary and expository selections is the ability to understand visual messages. The following diagram is from a survival manual. Consider how the image and the words work together to convey meaning. The questions to the right will help you.

COMMON CORE

RI 7 Analyze various accounts of a subject told in different mediums.

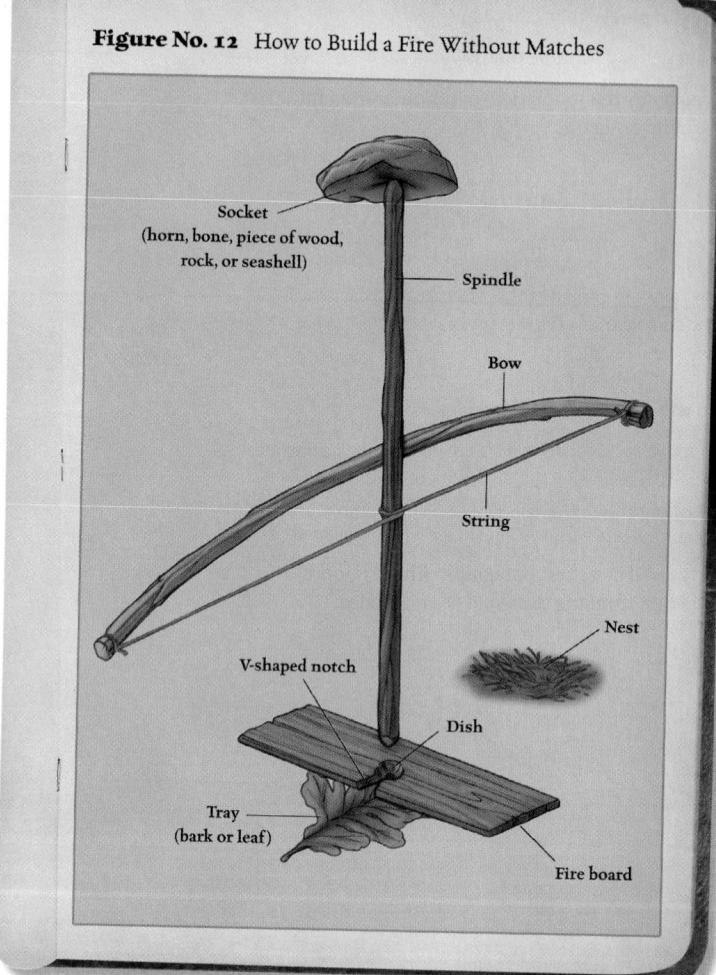

Figure No. 12 How to Build a Fire Without Matches

Socket
(horn, bone, piece of wood, rock, or seashell)

Spindle

Bow

String

Nest

V-shaped notch

Dish

Tray
(bark or leaf)

Fire board

1. **EVALUATE**
   If you were in a survival situation, do you think you could start a fire using only this diagram?

2. **CONNECT**
   In the survival situation you think you would personally be most likely to encounter, would building a fire be your first priority? If so, why? If not, what else would be?

Assessment Practice: Short Constructed Response

LITERARY TEXT: "TO BUILD A FIRE"

If you are able to analyze the literary elements in the stories you read, you will better appreciate literature. To strengthen your literary analysis skills, read the **short constructed response question** at left below and pay attention to the strategies suggested at right.

> In "To Build a Fire," how does the main character's opinion change regarding the advice given by the old-timer on Sulfur Creek? Support your answer with evidence from the story.

◀ STRATEGIES IN ACTION

1. Note that this question requires you to explain the man's opinion before the change as well as explain his opinion after the change.

2. Look for evidence that supports your answer. Evidence from the text can take the form of a **direct quotation**, a **paraphrase**, or a **synopsis with specific details**.

3. Make sure that any assertion you make is directly supported by evidence.

NONFICTION TEXT: "DEEP SURVIVAL"

Assessments often expect you to make thoughtful judgments about expository texts. Practice this important skill by answering the **short constructed response question** below.

> Having read "Deep Survival," do you believe you are now better prepared to survive a life-threatening disaster? Support your answer with evidence from the texts.

◀ STRATEGIES IN ACTION

1. Reread the text, noting places where the content confirms or contradicts your own knowledge and experience.

2. Make a judgment based on connections between the selection and your own life.

3. Include evidence for each connection you make.

COMPARING LITERARY AND NONFICTION TEXTS

You are likely to be tested on your ability to compare and contrast literary and nonfiction texts. Practice this valuable skill by applying the following **short constructed response question** to "To Build a Fire" and "Deep Survival."

> If the man in "To Build a Fire" had read "Deep Survival," might he have lived through his ordeal? Support your answer with evidence from both texts.

◀ STRATEGIES IN ACTION

1. Reread passages from both texts that you feel are key to answering the question.

2. The question asks you to make a prediction. Your answer should be based on evidence from both texts and your own experiences and knowledge of human behavior.

Assessment Practice: Short Constructed Response

LITERARY TEXT: "TO BUILD A FIRE"
Possible answer: *At first, the man refers to the old-timer as "rather womanish" and gloats that he was right and the old-timer was wrong. When his fire goes out, the man thinks "perhaps the old-timer was right." When he fails to rebuild his fire, the man finally admits that "the old-timer on Sulphur Creek was right" and he shouldn't be out alone after all.*

NONFICTION TEXT: "DEEP SURVIVAL" ***Possible answer:*** *After reading* Deep Survival, *I think that I'm better prepared to survive a life-threatening disaster. Suggestions such as "stay calm" and "get organized" seemed obvious, but I hadn't heard before that you should "celebrate your successes." Also, it never occurred to me before that it's important to "see the beauty" during a disaster.*

COMPARING LITERARY AND NONFICTION TEXTS ***Possible answer:*** *The man already possessed some of the survival skills on the* Deep Survival *list. He stayed calm, got organized, and took correct, decisive action. The man's downfall was his arrogance. Had he read* Deep Survival, *he would have scoffed at it, as he had scoffed at the old-timer from Sulphur Creek.*

DIFFERENTIATED INSTRUCTION

FOR STRUGGLING WRITERS

Make a Connection Tell students that in order to address the Comparing Literary and Nonfiction Texts prompt, they must first decide what information in "Deep Survival" would help the man in his situation. Have students reread the "Deep Survival" sub-headings and decide which of them would be useful to the man. Then have students address the next part of the prompt. Tell students to consider two things: Given what they know about the man's character, would he use the information? In what parts of his ordeal would the information prove most helpful? Have students look through "To Build a Fire" to find specific details to support their answers.

Focus and Motivate

COMMON CORE FOCUS

RI 3 Analyze how the author unfolds and develops a series of events, the order in which they occur, and the connections drawn between the events. **RI 4** Analyze the cumulative impact of specific word choices on meaning and tone. **W 2** Write explanatory texts to examine and convey complex ideas, concepts and information clearly and accurately. **L 3** Apply knowledge of language to make effective choices for meaning or style. **L 4a** Use context as a clue to the meaning of a word or phrase.

SUMMARY

This excerpt from *The Johnstown Flood* describes how a little girl named Gertrude Quinn survived the famous flood. When her house was destroyed, she climbed out of a hole in the house and grabbed onto a mattress. A man swam to her and threw her to people in a building on dry land. Gertrude was wrapped in blankets and taken to stay with the Metz family.

Is **SURVIVAL**
a matter of chance?

Explain that "a matter of chance" means that the cause is attributed to luck. Have students read the question and discuss the difference between luck, or chance, and quick thinking. After students discuss survival stories, have them complete the *QUICKWRITE*.

Selection Resources

---

from The Johnstown Flood
Historical Narrative by David McCullough

Is **SURVIVAL**
a matter of chance?

COMMON CORE

RI 3 Analyze how the author unfolds and develops a series of events, the order in which they occur, and the connections drawn between the events. **RI 4** Analyze the cumulative impact of specific word choices on meaning and tone. **L 4a** Use context as a clue to the meaning of a word or phrase.

If you listen to survivors' stories after a disaster, you are bound to hear phrases such as "If I hadn't turned back when I did . . ." or "It missed me by just inches. . . ." Is survival determined by pure luck? Or do some survivors make their own luck by thinking quickly and seeing opportunities for escape? Read this account of a little girl who survived one of the deadliest floods in U.S. history, and decide what accounts for her rescue.

QUICKWRITE With your class, discuss survival stories you have read or heard about. In each case, would you attribute survival to luck or other causes?

See resources on the **Teacher One Stop DVD-ROM** *and on* <u>thinkcentral.com</u>.

 RESOURCE MANAGER UNIT 1
Plan and Teach, pp. 111–118
Summary, pp. 119–120†‡*
Text Analysis and Reading
Skill, pp. 121–124*
Grammar and Style, p. 127

DIAGNOSTIC AND SELECTION TESTS
Selection Tests, pp. 43–46

 BEST PRACTICES TOOLKIT
Definition Mapping, p. E6
Think-Pair-Share, p. A18
Venn Diagram, p. A26
Draw It, p. A2
Two-Column Chart, p. A25

TECHNOLOGY
- Teacher One Stop DVD-ROM
- Student One Stop DVD-ROM
- Audio Anthology CD
- GrammarNotes DVD-ROM
- ExamView Test Generator on the **Teacher One Stop**

---

* Resources for Differentiation   † Also in Spanish   ‡ In Haitian Creole and Vietnamese

● TEXT ANALYSIS: MOOD

The Johnstown Flood is a **historical narrative,** a story about real events that occurred in the past. To tell the story of the horrifying events that occurred in Johnstown, Pennsylvania, in 1889, writer David McCullough creates a mood of tension and impending doom. **Mood** is the feeling or atmosphere that the writer creates for the reader. For example, think about the following description:

In the last few seconds, fighting the current around him that kept getting deeper and faster every second, he reached the hillside just as the wave pounded by below.

To understand how mood is created, notice the following as you read:

- the author's choice of words and phrases (**diction**) and their arrangement (**syntax**)
- details of setting
- imagery

As you read, look for descriptions of what Johnstown was like on the day of the flood and what Gertrude Quinn and her family saw, heard, and said.

Review: Conflict

■ READING SKILL: ANALYZE CHRONOLOGICAL ORDER

To help readers follow the chaotic events that took place during and after the Johnstown flood, McCullough presents them in **chronological** order, the structural pattern that presents events in the order in which they actually occurred in time. He also includes many **time-order signal words,** such as *before, after, then,* and *meanwhile* to show the connections between events.

As you read, look for such signal words and use them to record major events in the order that they occurred on a timeline like the one shown. Draw your timeline in your *Reader/Writer Notebook.*

| Mr. Quinn moves store goods to higher levels. | Mr. Quinn returns for dinner and shares his worries about the rising water. |

 Complete the activities in your **Reader/Writer Notebook.**

Meet the Author

David McCullough
born 1933

A Passion for the Past
To many Americans, David McCullough (mə-kŭl'ə) has a familiar face—and voice. He has hosted the PBS series *Smithsonian World* and *The American Experience* and has narrated many TV documentaries. First and foremost, however, McCullough is an award-winning writer of histories and biographies. His passion for writing about the past began in the 1960s when he saw old photographs of a tragic flood that had occurred about 70 years before in his native Pennsylvania. Unable to find well-written books about the tragedy, he decided to write one himself. The result was *The Johnstown Flood.* A master storyteller, McCullough has the gift of making the past come alive. "You scratch the surface of the supposedly dead past," he says, "and what you find is life."

BACKGROUND TO THE NARRATIVE
Dark Day in Johnstown
The facts about the Johnstown flood are well documented. A heavy downpour that began on May 30, 1889, caused a man-made lake high in the hills above Johnstown to overflow its banks. The surging water put tremendous pressure on the South Fork dam, and faulty repairs made to it in the past began to buckle. On the afternoon of May 31, the dam collapsed, releasing the entire contents of the lake. About 20 million tons of water rushed down the hills, smashing Johnstown with a wave of water three stories high. Minutes later, more than 2,000 people were dead, and the city lay in ruins.

Author Online **THINK** central
Go to **thinkcentral.com.**
KEYWORD: HML10-107

107

Teach

TEXT ANALYSIS COMMON CORE RI 4

● *Model the Skill:* **MOOD**

To model how to determine mood, point out the details and images in the example sentence that create a tense and frightening feeling: "fighting the current," "deeper and faster every second," "just as the wave pounded."

GUIDED PRACTICE Ask students to identify the mood created by this passage and state the details and images that create the mood:

> She limped from her tent, shivering, and frowned at the sky, the dark clouds moving over the ridge even faster now.

READING SKILL COMMON CORE RI 3

■ *Model the Skill:* **ANALYZE CHRONOLOGICAL ORDER**

To model how to analyze the structural pattern that presents events in chronological order, explain that writers use time-order signal words known as *transitions* to clarify the sequence of events. Then reread the **Background** and identify the time-order signal words and phrases, such as "in the past" and "later."

GUIDED PRACTICE Ask students to use signal words to create a timeline for the events described in the **Background**.

R RESOURCE MANAGER—Copy Master
Analyze Chronological Order p. 123 (for student use while reading the selection)

DIFFERENTIATED INSTRUCTION

FOR ENGLISH LANGUAGE LEARNERS
Comprehension: Transitions List the time-order signal words from the Background on the board, as well as the words listed in the **READING SKILL** in the pupil edition. Work with students to brainstorm a list of additional examples, such as *first, next,* and *finally.* Review the meaning of each signal word, and then invite students to use two or more examples in the same sentence.

FOR STRUGGLING READERS
Text Analysis Skill Support Write this sentence on the board: *With solemn faces and hunched backs, the survivors plodded through the mud in search of relics of their lost lives.* Model the skill by describing what you picture when you read about the "solemn faces and hunched backs" of the survivors. Invite students to describe their own mental pictures or sensory impressions. Then ask what kind of mood this image creates.

READING SKILL   COMMON CORE   RI 3

Ⓐ *Model the Skill:*
CHRONOLOGICAL ORDER

Model for students how to analyze chronological order. Identify the time-order signal words and phrases in lines 1–10. Then use them to arrange the events in chronological order on a timeline like the one on page 107.

Possible answer: *The signal words on (line 1), before (line 2), already (line 3), and at noon (line 7) tell you when the events took place.*

TEXT ANALYSIS   COMMON CORE   RI 4

Ⓑ MOOD

Possible answer: *The detail that tells about how Gertrude dangled her feet in the water, which covered the yard (lines 23–24), creates a mood of impending danger. The water, already rising, should not be high enough for Gertrude to dangle her feet in it from the porch. The detail of the "purple pansies floating face up . . . in the yellow water" (lines 27–28) also creates a mood of doom, because the flowers were no longer in the ground, and the water was yellow from contamination.*

The Johnstown Flood

David McCullough

On the morning of the 31st, James Quinn had gone to the store early to supervise the moving of goods to higher levels. Before leaving home he had told everyone to stay inside. One of his children, Marie, was already sick with measles, and he did not want the others out in the rain catching cold. He did, however, allow young Vincent to come along with him downtown to lend a hand.

At noon, when he had returned for dinner, the water had been up to his curbstone. He had been restless and worried through the meal, talking about the water rising in the streets and his lack of confidence in the South
10 Fork dam. Ⓐ

A few days before, he and his wife and the infant, Tom, and Lalia had gone to Scottdale for a christening, and Mrs. Quinn and the two children had stayed on to visit with her sister. Now Aunt Abbie and Libby Hipp were more or less running things, and he was doing his best to make sure they understood the seriousness of the situation.

"James, you are too anxious," his sister-in-law said. "This big house could never go."

In recalling the day years afterward, Gertrude felt sure that her father was so worried that he would have moved them all to the hill that morning, even
20 though he had no special place to take them, if it had not been for Marie. He was afraid of the effect the light might have on her eyes.

After dinner he had gone back to the store, and Gertrude slipped out onto the front porch where she began dangling her feet in the water, which, by now, covered the yard just deep enough for the ducks to sport about among the flowers. Everyone who survived the flood would carry some especially vivid mental picture of how things had looked just before the great wave struck; for this child it would be the sight of those ducks, and purple pansies floating face up, like lily pads, in the yellow water. Ⓑ

Analyze Visuals ▶
What does the photograph convey to you about the destructive force of the Johnstown flood?

Ⓐ CHRONOLOGICAL ORDER
What signal words in lines 1–10 tell you when the events took place?

① Targeted Passage

Ⓑ MOOD
Reread lines 22–28. What mood do these unusual details create?

DIFFERENTIATED INSTRUCTION

FOR ENGLISH LANGUAGE LEARNERS
Vocabulary Support Use Definition Mapping to teach these words: *survived* (line 25), *couple* (line 30), *lecture* (line 32), *visible* (line 153), *occupied* (line 180).

📁 BEST PRACTICES TOOLKIT—Transparency
Definition Mapping p. E6

FOR STRUGGLING READERS
In combination with the *Audio Anthology CD*, use one or more Targeted Passages (pp. 108, 111, 113, 114) to ensure that students focus on key story events, concepts, and skills. Targeted Passages are also good for English language learners.

BACKGROUND

The South Fork Dam The South Fork dam near the Quinns' home was originally designed to create a reservoir that could feed the Pennsylvania Canal. Retired from that purpose, the dam was taken over by a wealthy gentlemen's club. The club continued to raise the height of the dam without paying careful attention to proper construction techniques, such as allowing for water overflows. The dam became incapable of containing the water behind it. Last-minute efforts by townspeople and club members to provide for overflows proved insufficient, and the dam gave way early in the afternoon on May 31, 1889.

Analyze Visuals

Possible answer: *The photograph shows that the Johnstown Flood was incredibly destructive. The house is lying on its side, and its foundation is gone. The large uprooted tree broke through the toppled house.*

---

① Targeted Passage [Lines 8–21]

This passage describes the background and setting of the story and hints at its conflict.

- What is James Quinn worried about? (lines 8–10)

- How does his sister-in-law respond to his concerns? (lines 16–17)

- Why didn't Mr. Quinn move his family to the hill earlier in the morning? (lines 19–21)

FOR ADVANCED LEARNERS/PRE–AP

Analyze Effects Have students gather additional information about the Johnstown flood for cause-and-effect essays that focus on the short- and long-term effects of the flood on the Johnstown community. If students wish, they may adapt their essays for oral presentation to the class.

Is SURVIVAL
a matter of chance?

Discuss How do the words and actions of Gertrude's father in lines 29–39 show that he is worried about the family's survival? ***Possible answer:*** *He spanks her for not staying inside (lines 30–31), and he tells her of their "perilous position" (lines 32–33). He shouts, "'Run for your lives'" (line 38). He thinks this situation is life-threatening, not just inconvenient.*

TEXT ANALYSIS

Model the Skill: MOOD

Model for students how to identify details that create mood. As you read aloud lines 37–50, pause to list on the board details that suggest danger or fear. Next to each detail write the feeling it creates. After listing relevant evidence from the text, observe that the details help create a general feeling or atmosphere of terror.

Possible answer: *Some of the details that create a mood of terror include Gertrude's father's instructions to run for their lives (line 38), his face "white and terrified-looking" (line 42), his repeated command not to go back for anything (line 43), and the water being close to Rosemary's chin (lines 46–47).*

READING SKILL

D CHRONOLOGICAL ORDER

Possible answer: *Gertrude's father and some of his girls made it to dry land, while Libby, Gertrude, Aunt Abbie, and her baby turned back to the house.*

IF STUDENTS NEED HELP . . . Help students keep track of the correct order of events in the story by adding them to their timelines.

---

30 Shortly before four Gertrude's father suddenly appeared in front of her. He took her with one hand, with the other gave her a couple of quick spanks for disobeying his order to stay inside, and hurried her through the door.

"Then he gave me a lecture on obedience, wet feet, and our perilous position; he said he had come to take us to the hill and that we were delayed because my shoes and stockings had to be changed again. He was smoking a cigar while the nurse was changing my clothes. Then he went to the door to toss off the ashes."

It was then that he saw the dark mist and heard the sound of the wave coming. He rushed back inside, shouting, "Run for your lives. Follow me straight to the hill."

40 Someone screamed to him about the baby with the measles. He leaped up the stairs and in no more than a minute was back down with Marie wrapped in a blanket, his face white and terrified-looking.

"Follow me," he said. "Don't go back for anything. Don't go back for anything." Everyone started out the door except Vincent. Just where he was no one knew. Helen and Rosemary ran on either side of their father, holding on to his elbows as he carried the baby. When they got to the street the water was nearly to Rosemary's chin, but she kept going, and kept trying to balance the umbrella she had somehow managed to bring along. The hill was at most only a hundred yards away. All they had to do was get two short blocks to the end 50 of Main and they would be safe. **C**

James Quinn started running, confident that everyone was with him. But Aunt Abbie, who was carrying her baby, and Libby Hipp, who had Gertrude in her arms, had turned back.

When she reached the top of the steps that led from the yard down to the street, Aunt Abbie had had second thoughts.

"I don't like to put my feet in that dirty water," Gertrude would remember her saying. Libby said she would do whatever Aunt Abbie thought best, so they started back into the house.

"Well, I kicked and scratched and bit her, and gave her a terrible time, 60 because I wanted to be with my father," Gertrude said later. How the two women, each with a child, ever got to the third floor as fast as they did was something she was never quite able to figure out. Once there, they went to the front window, opened it, and looked down into the street. Gertrude described the scene as looking "like the Day of Judgment I had seen as a little girl in Bible histories," with crowds of people running, screaming, dragging children, struggling to keep their feet in the water.

Her father meanwhile had reached dry land on the hill, and turning around saw no signs of the rest of his family among the faces pushing past him. He grabbed hold of a big butcher boy named Kurtz, gave him Marie, told him to 70 watch out for the other two girls, and started back to the house. **D**

C MOOD
Reread lines 37–50. What details help create a mood of terror?

D CHRONOLOGICAL ORDER
Notice the signal word *meanwhile.* What two sets of actions occur at the same time?

DIFFERENTIATED INSTRUCTION

FOR ENGLISH LANGUAGE LEARNERS

Vocabulary: Idioms Explain that the idiomatic expression *[have] second thoughts* (line 55) means "change your mind" or "begin to doubt your opinion, decision, or plan." Then have student pairs use the Think-Pair-Share strategy to define these expressions: *saw no signs of* (line 68) and *with all his might* (lines 73–74).

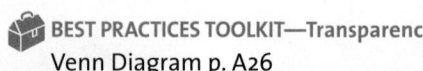 **BEST PRACTICES TOOLKIT—Transparency** Think-Pair-Share p. A18

FOR ADVANCED LEARNERS/PRE–AP

Compare and Contrast [small-group option] Have students research the account of Noah and the flood in the Hebrew Bible or another culture's account of a flood. Then ask students to complete a Venn Diagram that compares and contrasts this account with McCullough's description of the Johnstown Flood. Have students share their findings with the class.

BEST PRACTICES TOOLKIT—Transparency Venn Diagram p. A26

But he had gone only a short way when he saw the wave, almost on top of him, demolishing everything, and he knew he could never make it. There was a split second of indecision, then he turned back to the hill, running with all his might as the water surged along the street after him. In the last few seconds, fighting the current around him that kept getting deeper and faster every second, he reached the hillside just as the wave pounded by below. **E**

Looking behind he saw his house rock back and forth, then lunge sideways, topple over, and disappear.

80 Gertrude never saw the wave. The sight of the crowds jamming through the street had so terrified her aunt and Libby Hipp that they had pulled back from the window, horrified, dragging her with them into an open cupboard.

"Libby, this is the end of the world, we will all die together," Aunt Abbie sobbed, and dropped to her knees and began praying hysterically, "Jesus, Mary, and Joseph, Have mercy on us, oh, God . . ."

Gertrude started screaming and jumping up and down, calling "Papa, Papa, Papa," as fast as she could get it out.

The cupboard was in what was the dining room of an elaborate playhouse built across the entire front end of the third floor. There was nothing like it anywhere else in town, the whole place having been fitted out and furnished 90 by Quinn's store. There was a long center hall and a beautifully furnished parlor at one end and little bedrooms with doll beds, bureaus, washstands, and ingrain carpets on the floors. The dining room had a painted table, chairs, sideboard with tiny dishes, hand-hemmed tablecloths, napkins, and silverware.

From where she crouched in the back of the cupboard, Gertrude could see across the dining room into a miniature kitchen with its own table and chairs, handmade iron stove, and, on one wall, a whole set of iron cooking utensils hanging on little hooks. Libby Hipp was holding her close, crying and trembling.

Then the big house gave a violent shudder. Gertrude saw the tiny pots and 100 pans begin to sway and dance. Suddenly plaster dust came down. The walls began to break up. Then, at her aunt's feet, she saw the floor boards burst open and up gushed a fountain of yellow water.

"And these boards were jagged . . . and I looked at my aunt, and they didn't say a word then. All the praying stopped, and they gasped, and looked down like this, and were gone, immediately gone."

She felt herself falling and reaching out for something to grab on to and trying as best she could to stay afloat.

"I kept paddling and grabbing and spitting and spitting and trying to keep the sticks and dirt and this horrible water out of my mouth."

110 Somehow she managed to crawl out of a hole in the roof or wall, she never knew which. All she saw was a glimmer of light, and she scrambled with all her strength to get to it, up what must have been the lath[1] on part of the house

___

1. **lath:** a narrow strip of wood used to support plaster or tiles.

(2) Targeted Passage

● **GRAMMAR AND STYLE**
Reread lines 71–76. Notice how McCullough makes the scene's action come to life through the use of **strong verbs** and verb forms, such as *demolishing, surged,* and *pounded.*

● **GRAMMAR AND STYLE**   COMMON CORE L 3

Emphasize Action One reason authors use strong verbs is to emphasize the action in a story. Have students reread lines 71–76 and replace strong verbs with weaker verbs. For example, they can replace *surged* with *moved.* Ask students how the change affects readers' understanding of the action. Have students continue to identify strong verbs as they read the selection.

TIERED DISCUSSION PROMPTS

Direct students to lines 71–78. Use these prompts to help students understand the awful decision Gertrude's father had to make:

Connect Have you ever had to make a difficult decision? How did you make a choice? *Students' answers will vary.*

Analyze How would you describe the feelings of Gertrude's father at this point? *Possible answer: He probably felt scared, helpless, frustrated, and sad. He felt like he had no choice but to turn back (line 73).*

Evaluate Do you think Gertrude's father made the right choice? *Possible answer: Yes, he knew that he could not make it. If he died, he would be unable to help his family.*

REVISIT THE BIG QUESTION
Is SURVIVAL
a matter of chance?

In lines 106–112, how did Gertrude try to ensure her survival? *Possible answer: She fought to stay afloat (line 107). She crawled out of a hole in the roof or wall, moving toward a light that she saw (lines 110–113).*

FOR STRUGGLING READERS

(2) Targeted Passage [Lines 87–102]

This passage illustrates the flood's destructive power.

- What was the Quinns' house like? (lines 87–93)

- Why do you think the author describes the big house and playhouse in such detail? (lines 94–98)

- What happened to the playhouse, and to Gertrude's aunt and Libby? (lines 99–102)

FOR ADVANCED LEARNERS/PRE–AP

Analyze Personification Point out the phrase "the big house gave a violent shudder" (line 99) as an example of personification. Ask pairs to personify other inanimate objects in the selection, such as the flood, Gertrude's house, or Gertrude's mattress, in order to describe the actions of these objects during the events. Ask students how personification helps convey mood.

Analyze Visuals

Possible answer: *The drawing shows the flood in the middle of its wrath, doing the actual damage. It also shows a person's reaction to the flood. The photograph shows the aftermath of the flood and no people.*

TEXT ANALYSIS

COMMON CORE

RI 4

Ⓕ MOOD

Possible answer: *The incongruous image of the dead horse "bobbing up and down" like "a gigantic, gruesome rocking horse" (lines 122–123) intensifies the mood of hopelessness and panic. Because a rocking horse is a symbol of childhood fun, the contrast makes the situation seem even more surreal and ominous.*

IF STUDENTS NEED HELP . . . Review lines 118–123 and help students identify details that describe the dead horse and its movements.

REVISIT THE BIG QUESTION

Is **SURVIVAL**
a matter of chance?

What do the man's actions in lines 128–131 suggest about people's feelings about survival? *Possible answer:* *When people are in a desperate situation, they may be so concerned about their own survival that they are unaware of or indifferent to other people's problems. Self-preservation becomes paramount.*

A bridge washed away by the Johnstown Flood

◀ **Analyze Visuals**
What does the drawing communicate about the flood that the photo on page 109 does not?

underneath one of the gables.[2] She got through the opening, never knowing what had become of her aunt, Libby, or her baby cousin. Within seconds the whole house was gone and everyone in it.

The next thing she knew, Gertrude was whirling about on top of a muddy mattress that was being buoyed up by debris but that kept tilting back and forth as she struggled to get her balance. She screamed for help. Then a dead horse slammed against her raft, pitching one end of it up into the air and 120 nearly knocking her off. She hung on for dear life, until a tree swung by, snagging the horse in its branches before it plunged off with the current in another direction, the dead animal bobbing up and down, up and down, in and out of the water, like a gigantic, gruesome rocking horse. Ⓕ

Weak and shivering with cold, she lay down on the mattress, realizing for the first time that all her clothes had been torn off except for her underwear. Night was coming on and she was terribly frightened. She started praying in German, which was the only way she had been taught to pray.

A small white house went sailing by, almost running her down. She called out to the one man who was riding on top, straddling the peak of the roof and 130 hugging the chimney with both arms. But he ignored her, or perhaps never heard her, and passed right by.

"You terrible man," she shouted after him. "I'll never help you."

Then a long roof, which may have been what was left of the Arcade Building, came plowing toward her, looking as big as a steamboat and loaded down with perhaps twenty people. She called out to them, begging someone to

Ⓕ **MOOD**
What do the details about the dead horse contribute to the mood of the passage?

---

2. **gable:** a triangular portion of a roof.

DIFFERENTIATED INSTRUCTION

FOR ENGLISH LANGUAGE LEARNERS

Comprehension: Transitions Have students reread lines 116–123. Help them identify transition words that show sequence (*next, as, then,* and *until*). Have students use the Draw It strategy to create simple images of the selection events, using these transition words to determine the correct sequence of events.

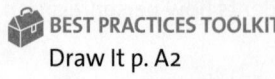 **BEST PRACTICES TOOLKIT**
Draw It p. A2

FOR STRUGGLING READERS

Develop Reading Fluency Have students read silently while read aloud the first three paragraphs on this page. Tell students to pay close attention to punctuation and how you use intonation and expression. Then have students echo reading, mimicking aspects of your delivery. Have students work in pairs or groups to practice fluency.

R RESOURCE MANAGER—Copy Master
Reading Fluency p. 128

save her. One man started up, but the others seemed determined to stop him. They held on to him and there was an endless moment of talk back and forth between them as he kept pulling to get free.

Then he pushed loose and jumped into the current. His head bobbed
140 up, then went under again. Several times more he came up and went under. Gertrude kept screaming for him to swim to her. Then he was heaving himself over the side of her raft, and the two of them headed off downstream, Gertrude nearly strangling him as she clung to his neck.

The big roof in the meantime had gone careening on until it hit what must have been a whirlpool in the current and began spinning round and round. Then, quite suddenly, it struck something and went down, carrying at least half its passengers with it. **G**

> Gertrude's new companion was a powerful, square-jawed millworker named Maxwell McAchren, who looked like John L. Sullivan.[3] How far she had
> 150 traveled by the time he climbed aboard the mattress, she was never able to figure out for certain. But later on she would describe seeing many flags at one point along the way, which suggests that she went as far up the Stony Creek as Sandy Vale Cemetery, where the Memorial Day flags could have been visible floating about in the water. Sandy Vale is roughly two miles from where the Quinn house had been, and when Maxwell McAchren joined her, she had come all the way back down again and was drifting with the tide near Bedford Street in the direction of the stone bridge.
>
> On a hillside, close by to the right, two men were leaning out of the window of a small white building, using long poles to carry on their own rescue
> 160 operation. They tried to reach out to the raft, but the distance was too great. Then one of them called out, "Throw that baby over here."
>
> McAchren shouted back, "Do you think you can catch her?"
>
> "We can try," they answered.
>
> The child came flying through the air across about ten to fifteen feet of water and landed in the arms of Mr. Henry Koch, proprietor of Koch House, a small hotel and saloon (mostly saloon) on Bedford Street. The other man in the room with him was George Skinner, a Negro porter, who had been holding Koch by the legs when he made the catch. The men stripped Gertrude of her wet underclothes, wrapped her in a blanket, and put her on a cot. Later she
> 170 was picked up and carried to the hill, so bundled up in the warm blanket that she could not see out, nor could anyone see in very well. **H**
>
> Every so often she could hear someone saying, "What have you got there?" And the answer came back, "A little girl we rescued." Then she could hear people gathering around and saying, "Let's have a look." Off would come part of the blanket in front of her face and she would look out at big, close-up faces looking in. Heads would shake. "Don't know her," they would say, and again the blanket would come over her face and on they would climb.

---

3. **John L. Sullivan:** a boxing champion in the late 1800s.

G CHRONOLOGICAL ORDER

Reread lines 128–147. Notice that several events take place in a short amount of time. Briefly summarize what happened, in order.

3 Targeted Passage

H CONFLICT

How is the conflict resolved? What builds suspense just before this resolution?

G CHRONOLOGICAL ORDER   RI 3

Possible answer: *First a small house went by carrying a man who did not answer Gertrude's cry for help (lines 128–131). Then a roof went by and one man jumped off and swam to her raft (lines 133–143). Finally, the roof sank, taking half of its passengers down with it (lines 144–147).*

Extend the Discussion Which of these events is most important to the story's plot?

TEXT ANALYSIS: *Review*

H CONFLICT

Possible answer: *The conflict is resolved when Mr. McAchren throws Gertrude to Mr. Koch, and he catches her (lines 164–165). The men's failed attempt to reach the raft (line 160) and unsure attempt to catch Gertrude (lines 162–163) build suspense.*

TIERED DISCUSSION PROMPTS

Use these prompts to help students understand the character of the remarkable man who saved Gertrude, as revealed in lines 136–147:

Recall How did the man help Gertrude? *Possible answer: He jumped from a roof and swam through the flood waters to join her on her raft.*

Analyze How would you characterize the man who helped Gertrude? *Possible answer: He is brave, caring, and selfless.*

Evaluate Which choice was more responsible for the man to make: being loyal to the group on the roof, or risking his life to help Gertrude? *Students' answers will vary but should be supported by details from the selection.*

FOR STRUGGLING READERS

3 Targeted Passage [Lines 148–177]

This passage shows that Gertrude had traveled a long way and that her survival was truly amazing.

- How did Gertrude guess at how far she had traveled on the raft? (lines 149–154)

- How did the men try to rescue Gertrude? (lines 158–160)

- How did Gertrude get from the raft to the saloon? (lines 161–166)

FOR ENGLISH LANGUAGE LEARNERS

Vocabulary: Phrasal Verbs Point out the phrasal verb *picked up* (line 170). Contrast its meaning with other phrasal verbs built on *pick*, such as *pick on* or *pick out*. Have student pairs repeat the process with other phrasal verbs, such as *slipped out* (line 22), *go back* (line 43), *called out* (line 135), and *carry on* (line 159). Then have students write a sentence using each phrasal verb.

Analyze Visuals

Activity Ask students what the cave entrance is constructed of and where the material probably came from. ***Possible answer:*** *It is constructed of wood planks, probably from houses destroyed in the flood.*

REVISIT THE BIG QUESTION
Is SURVIVAL
a matter of chance?

Based on lines 178–184, how do you think Gertrude's survival experience will affect her throughout her life? Do you think that it was simply a horrifying and traumatic event, or is it possible that she gained something positive from her experience? Explain. ***Possible answer:*** *Gertrude may become more fearful. She may question why she survived while others died and may relive her traumatic experiences through recurring memories or nightmares. On the other hand, Gertrude may become stronger and more self-confident, feeling that she can get through any crisis. She may feel lucky and grateful to those who helped her.*

SELECTION WRAP–UP

READ WITH A PURPOSE Have students sum up the events and actions that led to Gertrude's survival. Then ask them to come to a conclusion about how Gertrude survived. ***Possible answer:*** *Gertrude survived as a result of chance, her own courage and innate intelligence, and the ingenuity and quick thinking of others.*

★ **CRITIQUE** Ask students to evaluate whether the author includes enough details to help readers experience what being caught in a flood would be like.

Survivors of the Johnstown flood take shelter in a cave.

Gertrude never found out who it was that carried her up the hill, but he eventually deposited her with a family named Metz, who lived in a frame
180 tenement also occupied by five other families. The place looked like paradise to her, but she was still so terrified that she was unable to say a word as the Metz children, neighbors, and people in off the street jammed into the kitchen to look at her as she lay wrapped now in a pair of red-flannel underwear with Mason jars full of hot water packed all around her.

Later, she was put to bed upstairs, but exhausted as she was she was unable to sleep. In the room with her were three other refugees from the disaster, grown women by the name of Bowser, who kept getting up and going to the window, where she could hear them gasping and whispering among themselves. After a while Gertrude slipped quietly out of bed and across the
190 dark room. Outside the window, down below where the city had been, she could now see only firelight reflecting on the water. It looked, as she said later, for all the world like ships burning at sea. ✍ ❶

④ **Targeted Passage**

❶ MOOD
How has the mood changed at the end of the selection? What atmosphere does the last image create?

114   UNIT 1: PLOT, SETTING, AND MOOD

DIFFERENTIATED INSTRUCTION

FOR STRUGGLING READERS

④ **Targeted Passage** [Lines 185–192]

This passage invites students to think about Gertrude's survival and to consider how she might have felt at this point.

- Why do you think Gertrude could not sleep? (lines 185–186)

- Why did the Bowser women keep getting up and going to the window? (lines 186–189)

FOR ENGLISH LANGUAGE LEARNERS

Comprehension

1. **Recall** Where did Mr. Quinn order everyone to go when he heard the wave coming?

2. **Recall** Why didn't Gertrude go with Mr. Quinn?

3. **Recall** What happened to the Quinns' house?

4. **Clarify** How was Gertrude finally rescued?

Text Analysis

5. **Understand Chronological Order** Use the timeline you created as you read to summarize the story, noting how each event connects to the next.

6. **Identify Cause and Effect** What most accounts for Gertrude's miraculous survival—sheer luck, Gertrude's own actions, or others' actions? Give evidence from the narrative to support your answer.

7. **Analyze Mood** Describe the overall mood McCullough creates in his account of the Johnstown flood. How do the diction, syntax, and imagery used by the author help create this mood? Which passages are most effective?

8. **Compare and Contrast Settings** Both the excerpt from *The Johnstown Flood* and the story "To Build a Fire" are about people trying to survive in dangerous settings. Compare and contrast the settings and the roles they play in the selections. Record your ideas on a Venn diagram like the one shown.

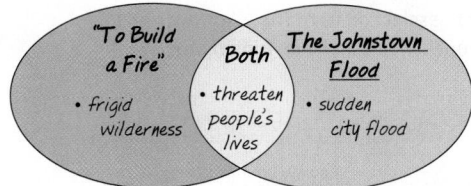

Text Criticism

9. **Critical Interpretations** David McCullough has said that in his writing he tries to make history "as interesting and human as it really was." Do you think he succeeds in doing so in the selection from *The Johnstown Flood?* Explain, giving examples from the narrative to support your opinion.

Is **SURVIVAL** a matter of chance?

What could increase your chances of surviving a disaster?

---

of Gertrude flying through the air (lines 164–165).

8. **"To Build a Fire":** *Yukon Territory, Alaska, 1890s; natural setting symbolizes death and nature's indifference; dangerous because of extreme cold; man tries to survive by building a fire; makes fatal mistake, does not survive;* **Both:** *setting is antagonist; strong mood; people need luck and skill to survive;* **The Johnstown Flood:** *Pennsylvania, 1889; unexpected event, not entirely natural; setting not symbolic, dangerous because of drowning risk; Gertrude floats on raft and is rescued*

Text Criticism

Possible answer:

9. *McCullough allows readers to feel what those living that history felt (lines 8, 42–44, 59–60, 82–86, 132, 185–186) and gives descriptive details about the flood.*

Is **SURVIVAL** a matter of chance?

Possible answer: *self-reliance, courage, practical skills*

For preliminary support of post-reading questions, use these copy maseters:

R RESOURCE MANAGER—Copy Masters
Reading Check p. 125
Mood p. 121
Question Support p. 126

Additional selection questions are provided for teachers on page 115.

ANSWERS

Comprehension

1. *Mr. Quinn ordered them to run to the hill.*

2. *Gertrude did not go with Mr. Quinn because Libby Hipp was carrying her, and Libby decided to turn back with Aunt Abbie.*

3. *The Quinns' house was struck by a huge wave and collapsed.*

4. *Maxwell McAchren swam to her raft and then threw her off the raft to Mr. Koch, who was standing in a building on dry ground.*

Text Analysis

COMMON CORE RI 3, RI 4

Possible answers:

5. ● **COMMON CORE FOCUS** *Understand Chronological Order* *Mr. Quinn moved goods at the store to avoid the rising water. As the water neared the Quinns' house, the family ran to the hill but Aunt Abbie, Libby, Gertrude, and the baby turned back. Mr. Quinn started back for them but changed his mind. When the house collapsed, only Gertrude survived. As Gertrude floated on the water, Mr. McAchren swam to her. McAchren threw Gertrude to Mr. Koch who gave her to a stranger. He carried her to the hill and left her with the Metz family.*

6. *Gertrude's survival was based on her own actions and the actions of others. She tried to survive by herself (lines 106–113), but she also relied on the help of strangers (lines 139–143, 164–165, 169–171). Luck played a role as well, in the arrival of the mattress as a raft (lines 116–118).*

7. ● **COMMON CORE FOCUS** *Analyze Mood* *The overall mood of this story is one of suspense and terror. Effective details that create this mood include Mr. Quinn's worries (line 8); his desperate actions (lines 38–70); the description of the Quinns' house collapsing and Gertrude's desperate survival attempt (lines 99–123); and the description*

COMMON CORE

RI 3 Analyze how the author unfolds and develops a series of events, the order in which they occur, and the connections drawn between the events. **RI 4** Analyze the cumulative impact of specific word choices on meaning and tone.

Language

COMMON CORE W 2, L 3

◆ **GRAMMAR AND STYLE**

- Have students read the student model and explain how the new verbs emphasize actions more effectively.

- Write these sentences on the board. Ask students to suggest stronger verbs to emphasize the action.

  McAchren g̶o̶t̶ jumped into the current and swam to Gertrude. When he got there, she h̶e̶l̶d̶ clung o̶n̶t̶o̶ his neck.

   RESOURCE MANAGER—Copy Master
  Emphasize Action p. 127

READING-WRITING CONNECTION

- Have students use a Two-Column Chart to list specific examples from the stories and the insights into human behavior that the examples show.

   BEST PRACTICES TOOLKIT—Transparency
  Two-Column Chart p. A25

Writing Online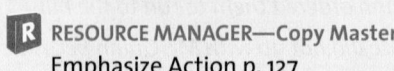

The following tools are available online at **thinkcentral.com** and on **WriteSmart CD-ROM:**
- **Interactive Graphic Organizers**
- **Interactive Student Models**
- **Interactive Revision Lessons**
For additional grammar instruction, see **GrammarNotes** on **thinkcentral.com**.

Assess and Reteach

Assess

 DIAGNOSTIC AND SELECTION TESTS
Selection Test A pp. 43–44
Selection Test B/C pp. 45–46

Interactive Selection Test on **thinkcentral.com**

Reteach

Level Up Online Tutorials on **thinkcentral.com**

Reteaching Worksheets on **thinkcentral.com**
Literature Lesson 42, Reading Lesson 6

Language

◆ **GRAMMAR AND STYLE: Emphasize Action**

COMMON CORE

L 3 Apply knowledge of language to make effective choices for meaning of style. **W 2** Write explanatory texts to examine and convey complex ideas, concepts and information clearly and accurately.

Review the **Grammar and Style** note on page 111. Like McCullough, you can create exciting action sequences by incorporating **strong verbs** into your writing. Choose verbs that create a vivid image for your reader. Avoid those that are too general or overused. Here are some examples of McCullough's use of strong verbs.

> *. . . the floor boards burst open and up gushed a fountain of yellow water.* (lines 101–102)

> *. . . a dead horse slammed against her raft . . .* (lines 118–119)

Notice how the revisions in blue use strong verbs to emphasize the action in this first draft. Revise your own writing by using similar techniques.

STUDENT MODEL

Gertrude and Amber were ~~taken~~ *washed* away by the floodwaters, and had to ~~hold~~ *cling* onto debris to stay afloat. However, both ~~met~~ *encountered* people who wanted to help them.

READING-WRITING CONNECTION

 **YOUR TURN** Increase your understanding of the selection from *The Johnstown Flood* by responding to this prompt. Then use the **revising tip** to improve your writing.

WRITING PROMPT

Extended Constructed Response
The story of Amber Colvin, on the next page, tells of a modern child who, like Gertrude Quinn, survived a deadly flood. What do the two stories suggest to you about survival in a disaster? What insights into human behavior do they give you? Write **three to five paragraphs** in response.

REVISING TIP

Review your response. How have you used strong verbs to create vivid images for your readers?

Interactive Revision
Go to **thinkcentral.com**.
KEYWORD: HML10-116

DIFFERENTIATED INSTRUCTION

FOR STRUGGLING WRITERS

- Have students work in small groups to identify selection examples and describe human insights for their charts.

- Adapt the assignment to three paragraphs: introduction, body paragraph with specific examples, and conclusion with insights.

MAGAZINE ARTICLE Though technology can help us predict natural disasters and often reduce the extent of their destructiveness, nature still has a mind of its own.

MICHAEL NEILL AND KEN MYERS

Nine-year-old Amber Colvin Rides Out a Killer Flood in Ohio

About 9:30 on the night of June 14, 1990, a flash flood hit the small town of Shadyside, Ohio, leaving death and destruction in its wake. Before the rain started, Dennis and Karen Colvin had driven to a nearby town to do errands and left their daughter, 9-year-old Amber, playing at home with her friend, 12-year-old Kerri Polivka. Suddenly the flood was in full force, and Amber and Kerri were on their own, fighting for their lives.

The Colvins' basement was inundated, and soon the girls were ankle-deep in water in the living room. At Kerri's suggestion, they got into the bathtub for protection, but within minutes the surging waters broke down the bathroom door and swept the tub from the floor. "It took me so far up I bumped my head on the ceiling," Amber recalls. . . .

When the two girls pressed their hands against the ceiling, it gave way, and they were flung out into the full fury of raging Wegee Creek. . . . As the tub splintered into pieces, Kerri was hit on the head—and was lost. "I tried to save her," says Amber, . . . "I saw her hair and tried to grab it. I pulled it up, then I had to let go." Amber then lunged out, grabbed a floating log—and clung to it all the way down the Wegee and into the Ohio River, 1¹/₂ miles away.

"I went under twice," she says, "once when the house went and the second time when I tried to save Kerri. . . . I was thinking there was no hope for me to live." Once she survived the millrace ride to the calmer Ohio, though, Amber realized she had a chance. She floated for seven miles more, at times dozing briefly as she gripped the log for eight hours, until it drifted ashore around 6:30 A.M. near Route 7. Amber managed to flag down Randy and Mitzie Ramsey of Bellaire. . . . "Amber was cold—but real alert and talkative," says Mitzie. . . .

When Dennis and Karen had tried to drive home the night before, they had been stopped at a police roadblock. The Colvins then walked down a hill untouched by the flood that stood behind their rented two-bedroom home, only to find the house had vanished, torn away by Wegee's waters. "Denny and I just held each other," says Karen. "Right there, I thought, there's no way. I thought she was dead," says Dennis. "Somebody was looking out for her, that's for sure."

Amber Colvin and her parents

DIFFERENTIATED INSTRUCTION

FOR ENGLISH LANGUAGE LEARNERS

Language: Punctuation Point out the ellipses in the text near the top of the second column. Explain that this punctuation indicates that some of the text has been left out. Have students work in pairs to find other examples of ellipses in the article. Discuss what might have been omitted, such as additional details or quotations about the event.

CONNECT

Use this selection either as support for the Writing Prompt on page 116 or as a mini-lesson on reading for information.

READING FOR INFORMATION

Point out that "Nine-year-old Amber Colvin Rides Out a Killer Flood in Ohio" is a magazine article. Have students preview the article, noting the headline and photo. Then ask these questions:

- What information does the headline provide? *Possible answer: It sums up the main idea of the article by telling the setting, main character, and main conflict.*

- How might the photo affect readers? *Possible answer: It might draw readers into the article by showing Amber and her parents as real, everyday people.*

- Why might the first paragraph be set off visually from the rest of the article? What kind of information do you find there? *Possible answer: The reader's attention is drawn to this section. This paragraph sets the scene and introduces key people in the account.*

TIERED DISCUSSION PROMPTS

Use the questions below to help students consider the true power of a flood:

Recall What happened after the girls went into the tub? *Possible answer: The water swept them into the Wegee Creek, where Kerri was lost.*

Analyze Do you think that Amber survived because of luck? *Possible answer: No. She survived by grabbing onto the log and holding on until she could get help.*

Synthesize Do you think that Gertrude's chances of survival would have been different had she experienced a flood in 1990 rather than in 1889? Explain. *Possible answer: No. Although the Ohio flood was more than 100 years later, people still cannot curb the power of a flood. Gertrude would still have had to try to survive as Amber did, and she would also have had to rely on others for help.*

Focus and Motivate

COMMON CORE FOCUS

RI 1 Cite evidence to support analysis of what the text says explicitly. **RI 4** Determine the meaning of words and phrases as they are used in a text. **RI 5** Analyze in detail how an author's ideas are developed and refined by particular sentences, paragraphs, or larger portions of text. **RI 6** Determine an author's point of view or purpose in a text. **L 3** Apply knowledge of language to make effective choices for meaning or style. **L 6** Acquire and use accurately domain-specific words and phrases.

SUMMARY

"The Race to Save *Apollo 13*" describes the efforts of flight director Eugene Kranz and his Houston staff in April 1970 to accomplish what appeared to be the impossible—the safe return of the astronauts after an explosion aboard the spacecraft.

How can we achieve the IMPOSSIBLE?

Have students read the question. Ask why people might initially think an emergency is an impossible situation. Have students complete the *DISCUSS* activity.

Selection Resources

The Race to Save *Apollo 13*
Nonfiction by Michael Useem

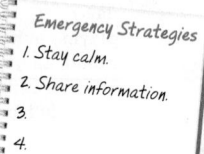
Video link at **thinkcentral.com**

How can we achieve the IMPOSSIBLE?

Some situations may seem hopeless at first. But when lives are at stake, people often find a way to achieve the impossible. In "The Race to Save *Apollo 13*," Michael Useem describes the extraordinary efforts of NASA employees to rescue astronauts aboard a damaged spacecraft.

DISCUSS With a small group, discuss strategies that can help people deal with an emergency. Share your list of strategies with the class.

Emergency Strategies
1. Stay calm.
2. Share information.
3.
4.
5.

118

See resources on the **Teacher One Stop DVD-ROM** and on **thinkcentral.com**.

Video link at
thinkcentral.com

 RESOURCE MANAGER UNIT 1
Plan and Teach, pp. 129–136
Summary, pp. 137–138†‡*
Text Analysis and Reading
   Skill, pp. 139–142†*
Vocabulary, pp. 143–145*
Grammar and Style, p. 148

**DIAGNOSTIC AND SELECTION
TESTS**
Selection Tests, pp. 47–50

 BEST PRACTICES TOOLKIT
Two-Column Chart, p. A25
New Word Analysis, p. E8
KWL, p. A21
Word Questioning, p. E9
Cluster Diagram, p. B18
Think-Pair-Share, p. A18

TECHNOLOGY
 Teacher One Stop DVD-ROM
 Student One Stop DVD-ROM
 Audio Anthology CD
 GrammarNotes DVD-ROM
 ExamView Test Generator
   on the Teacher One Stop

---

* Resources for Differentiation   † Also in Spanish   ‡ In Haitian Creole and Vietnamese

TEXT ANALYSIS: SUSPENSE IN NONFICTION

To draw the reader into a story, writers often create **suspense**—a feeling of excitement or tension about what will happen next. In nonfiction, a writer may create suspense by raising questions about the outcome of a situation or by emphasizing the risks involved. For example, in "The Race to Save *Apollo 13*," Michael Useem lets the reader know how much is at stake in the situation faced by the flight director.

He understood as well that his actions in the hours ahead might determine whether the U.S. space program experienced or avoided its biggest disaster.

As you read, notice the details that Useem included to increase the suspense of the narrative.

READING STRATEGY: TAKE NOTES

"The Race to Save *Apollo 13*" contains many details about equipment and procedures used in the space mission. When you read this type of information-rich text, take notes to help you understand and remember important information. Your notes may include

- key words and phrases from the text
- summaries (essential ideas rephrased in your own words)
- diagrams, charts, and other graphic organizers

As you read "The Race to Save *Apollo 13*," take notes about the problems people face and the solutions they find. Use a chart like the one shown.

Problem	Solution
The fuel cells that provided electricity to <u>Odyssey</u> were losing pressure.	The astronauts shut down all power in <u>Odyssey</u> and moved into the LEM.

▲ VOCABULARY IN CONTEXT

Michael Useem used the following boldfaced words to describe NASA procedures. To see how many you know, substitute a different word or phrase for each boldfaced term.

1. **replenish** our supplies
2. the ball's **trajectory** in the air
3. a **mandate** from my boss
4. her **innovative** approach
5. a **respite** from our labor
6. **collaborative** employees

Complete the activities in your **Reader/Writer Notebook.**

Meet the Author

Michael Useem
born 1942

Deciding Moments
Michael Useem (yōō-sēm') is a University of Pennsylvania professor who specializes in issues of leadership. "The Race to Save *Apollo 13*" is taken from his book *The Leadership Moment: Nine True Stories of Triumph and Disaster and Their Lessons for Us All*, which relates how leaders from various walks of life have made extremely difficult decisions during emergencies. Useem believes that their experiences illustrate what to do—and what not to do—in times of crisis.

BACKGROUND TO THE SELECTION

Space Race
In May 1961, President John F. Kennedy issued a challenge in a speech to Congress, stating that the United States should become the first nation to land astronauts on the moon and return them home safely. Kennedy believed this goal was necessary because the Soviet Union had recently sent a human into space.

The Apollo Program
Although Kennedy did not live to see it, NASA achieved his goal. In July 1969, the Apollo program successfully landed astronauts on the moon, and about 700 million television viewers around the world watched the historic moment. But after the mission ended, it was difficult to keep up this level of excitement. The launch of *Apollo 13* in April 1970 stirred little public interest. That changed when an oxygen tank exploded aboard the *Apollo 13* spacecraft *Odyssey*. In just moments, a seemingly routine mission became a full-blown crisis.

Author Online

THINK central

Go to **thinkcentral.com.**
KEYWORD: HML10-119.

119

Teach

TEXT ANALYSIS
COMMON CORE
RI 6

● *Model the Skill:* **SUSPENSE IN NONFICTION**

Model how to identify suspense in nonfiction. Explain that writers of speeches can create suspense for listeners. After students read **Space Race,** explain how President Kennedy's speech might have created suspense for his audience. Point out that the language or details of the speech may have stirred up excitement about the competition and anxiety about the uncertain outcome and what it might represent.

GUIDED PRACTICE Have students discuss examples of suspense in nonfiction they have read.

READING STRATEGY
COMMON CORE
RI 1
RI 4
RI 5

■ *Model the Skill:* **TAKE NOTES**

To model taking notes, have students read **The Apollo Program.** Point out the following key words and phrases and essential ideas as good examples of notes to take about story details: July 1969: the Apollo program, astronauts land on moon; 700 million TV viewers; then less interest until explosion on *Odyssey (Apollo 13)* in April 1970.

GUIDED PRACTICE Have students use their notes to summarize the passage.

R RESOURCE MANAGER—Copy Master
Take Notes p. 141 (for student use while reading the selection)

VOCABULARY SKILL
COMMON CORE
L 4

▲ VOCABULARY IN CONTEXT

DIAGNOSE WORD KNOWLEDGE Have all students complete Vocabulary in Context. Check their substitutions against the following:

collaborative (kə-lăb'ə-rə'tĭv) *adj.* done in cooperation with others
innovative (ĭn'ə-vā'tĭv) *adj.* able to create new, original ideas
mandate (măn'dāt') *n.* a command or instruction
replenish (rĭ-plĕn'ĭsh) *v.* to fill again
respite (rĕs'pĭt) *n.* a period of rest or relief

trajectory (trə-jĕk'tə-rē) *n.* the path of a moving body through space

PRETEACH VOCABULARY Use the following copy master to help students predict the meaning of each boldfaced word.

R RESOURCE MANAGER—Copy Master
Vocabulary Study p. 143

1. Read item 1 aloud, emphasizing *replenish*.
2. Point out the phrase "the supplies that they once had and needed again." Elicit

a possible meaning for *replenish*, such as "refill."

3. Repeat the process for items 2–6.

READ WITH A PURPOSE

Help students set a purpose for reading. Tell them to look for the ways that Eugene Kranz reacts to crisis.

BACKGROUND

Inside *Apollo 13* *Apollo 13* consisted of two main modules. The first one, code-named *Odyssey,* had two parts: a command module and a service module. The crew lived in and communicated with Mission Control from the *Odyssey* command module. The *Odyssey* service module, which was connected to the command module, contained all of the consumable supplies, such as water, oxygen, and fuel. The other main module of *Apollo 13* was the lunar landing module, code-named *Aquarius.* This module also had two parts. The first part was an operating base; the second, living quarters. Although none of the modules were spacious, the control module had couches for the three crew members' comfort. In the beginning of the selection, the astronauts are on *Odyssey* when they make contact with NASA.

> COMMON CORE RI 4
>
> **Language Coach**
>
> **Etymologies** Reread line 2. The word *astronaut* comes from the Greek words *astron,* meaning "star" and *nautēs,* meaning "sailor." Use a dictionary to find other words that use *astron* or *nautēs.*

Targeted Passage

The Race to Save APOLLO 13

Michael Useem

"What do you think we've got in the spacecraft that's good?"

"Hey, we've got a problem here."

The day was April 13, 1970. The voice was that of astronaut Jack Swigert, speaking from aboard the spacecraft Odyssey.

Almost immediately, NASA's Mission Control queried back: "This is Houston. Say again, please."

Astronaut and mission commander James Lovell responded this time: "Houston, we've had a problem."

For flight director Eugene Kranz, the message from *Apollo 13* presaged the test of a lifetime.

10   Only nine months earlier, on July 20, 1969, *Apollo 11* had landed Neil Armstrong and Buzz Aldrin in the Sea of Tranquillity,[1] fulfilling John F. Kennedy's promise to place a man on the moon before the end of the decade. Five months earlier, *Apollo 12* had placed Pete Conrad and Alan Bean in the Ocean of Storms. Just fifty-five hours earlier, at 1:13 P.M. on Saturday, April 11, 1970, *Apollo 13* had lifted up from the Kennedy Space Center on what to this moment had seemed a flawless trip to the moon's ridges of Fra Mauro.[2] Now, suddenly, the bottom was falling out.

---

1. **Sea of Tranquillity:** many areas of the moon are called seas or oceans, although the moon has no liquid water.

2. **Fra Mauro:** the area on the moon where *Apollo 13* was supposed to land.

DIFFERENTIATED INSTRUCTION

FOR ENGLISH LANGUAGE LEARNERS

> **Language Coach**   COMMON CORE RI 4
>
> **Etymologies** *Answers:*
> *astronomy, astronomer; astrophysics; nautical, nautilus, aeronaut, aquanaut.* Point out how etymology can help students decipher unusual words. While the *astro* in *astronaut* means "stars," the *aer* in *aeronaut* means "air" and the *aqua* in *aquanaut* means "water."

FOR STRUGGLING READERS

In combination with the *Audio Anthology* CD, use one or more Targeted Passages (pp. 120, 125, 127, 130, 132) to ensure that students focus on key story events, concepts, and skills. Targeted Passages are also good for English learners.

① Targeted Passage [Lines 6–17]

This passage establishes the setting of the selection and introduces both the main character and the major conflict.

NASA flight director Eugene Kranz at his console

NASA technician George Bliss was both transfixed and horrified by what he saw on his computer console[3] in a Houston back room. "We got more
20 than a problem," he warned colleague Sy Liebergot. The video screen told why: One of *Odyssey's* two oxygen tanks had broken down. The pressure in two of its three fuel cells, devices that use oxygen to generate electricity, was plummeting.

As Gene Kranz sifted through damage reports, the picture was distressing. The astronauts and their protective shell were unscathed, but it was evident that some kind of explosion had ripped through vital equipment. Two days into the flight, three quarters of the way to the moon, the astronauts were hurtling away from Earth at 2,000 miles per hour. The only practical way they could return was to round the moon and depend on its gravity to fire
30 them back like a slingshot. But this would require more than three days and demand more oxygen and electricity than Lovell and his crew had left. **A**

As flight director for *Apollo 13,* Kranz was the responsible official, and he was watching his mission spin out of control: his crew would consume their oxygen and power long before they neared Earth. Even if they survived to reenter the Earth's atmosphere, they would have no way to control their capsule's fiery plunge. Kranz could neither retrieve the astronauts nor **replenish** their supplies. He knew what options were out, yet he also knew he must somehow engineer a safe return. He understood as well that his

---

3. **computer console:** a computer's monitor and keyboard.

◀ **Analyze Visuals**

What can you **infer** from the expression on Eugene Kranz's face in the photograph?

A SUSPENSE

What facts in lines 24–31 help generate suspense?

replenish (rĭ-plĕn'ĭsh)
v. to fill again

Analyze Visuals

Possible answer: *Eugene Kranz looks serious and focused as he studies the computer monitor and console. He appears to be gathering and synthesizing information. His body language suggests that he is not panicked but confident and in control of the situation.*

TEXT ANALYSIS   COMMON CORE
                                      RI 6

A SUSPENSE

Possible answer: *The facts that generate suspense include "some kind of explosion had ripped through vital equipment" (line 26); "three quarters of the way to the moon" (line 27); "more than three days and . . . more oxygen and electricity [than the crew had]" (lines 30–31). All of these facts create suspense by making the reader question whether the astronauts' safe return is possible.*

IF STUDENTS NEED HELP . . . Begin a KWL chart. Help students to see that the information they know generates suspense that makes them want to find out what will happen to the astronauts. Encourage them to continue the chart, adding a *What I Have Learned* column, explaining their reactions to suspense and how their questions were resolved as they read on.

TOPIC: Apollo 13	What I Know	What I Want to Know
	Explosion ripped equipment	Will astronauts return safely?

 BEST PRACTICES TOOLKIT—Transparency KWL p. A21

VOCABULARY   COMMON CORE
                                      L 4

OWN THE WORD

replenish: Remind students that *replenish* is used in the context of "to fill again" and refers to items that need new stock or supplies. Have students list things their family *replenishes* at home. *Possible answers: groceries, gas in the family car, toothpaste, clothing*

- When does the selection take place? (line 2)
- Where are Jack Swigert and the other astronauts? (lines 2–3)
- Who is Eugene Kranz and where is he? (lines 4–8)
- What conflict is suggested here? (lines 19–23)

FOR ADVANCED LEARNERS/PRE–AP

Literary Features Have students discuss literary devices, such as character development, in this nonfiction selection. How do these devices help build suspense? How would the selection be different if Useem had used a textbook style?

Direct students to lines 46–67. Use these prompts to help students understand Kranz's predicament:

Connect Have you or someone you know ever been responsible for the safety of someone else? How does that experience help you understand Kranz's predicament? *Answers will vary.*

Analyze Why did Sy Liebergot allow himself to hope that the screen displays reflected only "sensor failure"? ***Possible answer:*** *During mock flights, he frequently saw "disastrous instrument readings that had later proved inaccurate" (lines 54–55), a much less frightening prospect than the astronauts being in real trouble.*

Evaluate Based on what you know about space flight and the information in the article, do you think that Kranz can save *Apollo?* *Students' answers will vary but should be supported by details from the article.*

READING STRATEGY

B TAKE NOTES

RI 1
RI 4
RI 5

Possible answer: *Kranz wanted to make sure that Mission Control didn't do anything to "blow [the] electrical power" or "lose fuel cell number two." He also wanted to prevent the officials from panicking by giving directions and encouraging discipline (lines 69–73).*

Extend the Discussion How would you evaluate Kranz as a leader? Why?

---

actions in the hours ahead might determine whether the U.S. space program
40 experienced or avoided its biggest disaster.

The Explosion's Wake

Hundreds of officials and engineers confronted the singular task of bringing the astronauts back alive. Four rotating flight teams—dubbed White, Black, Gold, and Maroon—were scheduled to spell one another during the mission's long days ahead. A backup crew for *Apollo 13* was on call to lend its expertise. Dozens of space program contractors were ready to assist.

Yet no one on the ground bore the burden that Eugene Kranz carried that evening and would continue to carry over the next four days. NASA's policy was unflinchingly clear: the flight director had the final call on all decisions. Moreover, "The flight director can do anything he feels is necessary for the
50 safety of the crew and the conduct of the flight regardless of the mission rules."

As Sy Liebergot, the frontline electrical official, gazed at his console in the minutes just after the explosion, he allowed himself to hope that the ominous screen displays might reflect sensor failure rather than a genuine problem. During NASA's countless simulations[4] of the flight, he had often seen disastrous instrument readings that had later proved inaccurate. The astronauts themselves were reporting that their oxygen tanks seemed fine, lending momentary support to Liebergot's hopeful search for instrumental error.

But Kranz was already learning from other flight officials that the problems were indeed real. The guidance officer reported that an onboard
60 computer was signaling a major glitch. The communications officer reported that the craft had mysteriously switched antennas. (As would be learned later, one had been hit by the explosion's debris.) And the astronauts themselves soon reported that one oxygen tank had emptied, two of the three fuel cells were generating no electricity, and two panels supplying power to the entire spacecraft were losing voltage. Lovell added even more distressing news: "We are venting[5] something into space." A glowing cloud was hovering outside *Odyssey,* suggesting rupture of its oxygen tanks.

"OK," called Kranz, sensing signs of panic in Mission Control. "Let's everybody keep cool. Let's make sure we don't do anything that's going to
70 blow our electrical power or cause us to lose fuel cell number two." Then he addressed what would have to be done. "Let's solve the problem." And finally he moved on to self-discipline: "Let's not make it any worse by guessing." **B**

By now, more bad news from *Odyssey.* Though a moon landing had been eliminated by the loss of the first oxygen tank and fuel cell, the

B TAKE NOTES
What problems did Kranz want to prevent at Mission Control?

---

4. **simulations:** here, mock space flights used to test procedures and train astronauts.

5. **venting:** discharging.

DIFFERENTIATED INSTRUCTION

FOR ENGLISH LANGUAGE LEARNERS

Vocabulary Support Use Word Questioning to teach these words: *teams* (line 42), *scheduled* (line 43), *final* (line 48), *communications* (line 60), *conclusions* (line 104), *protocols* (line 156), *virtually* (line 236).

📦 BEST PRACTICES TOOLKIT—Transparency
Word Questioning p. E9

FOR ENGLISH LANGUAGE LEARNERS

Vocabulary: Compound Nouns Explain to students that a compound word, such as *spacecraft* (line 3), is formed from two or more words. Have students determine its meaning by using context clues and their knowledge of the words *space* and *craft.* Have students define other compound nouns in the selection: *slingshot* (line 30), *frontline* (line 51), *shortcuts* (line 229), and *troubleshooting* (line 314). Then have students use dictionaries to check their definitions.

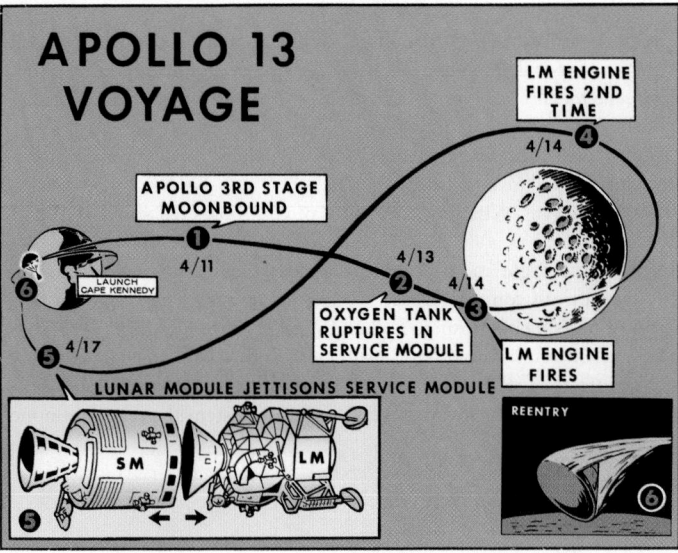

APOLLO 13
VOYAGE

LM ENGINE
FIRES 2ND
TIME
4/14 ④

APOLLO 3RD STAGE
MOONBOUND
① 4/11
4/13
② 4/14
③
OXYGEN TANK
RUPTURES IN
SERVICE MODULE
LM ENGINE
FIRES

⑥ LAUNCH
CAPE KENNEDY
⑤ 4/17

LUNAR MODULE JETTISONS SERVICE MODULE

REENTRY

SM   LM

⑤   ← →   ⑥

◄ **Analyze Visuals**

This diagram was created on April 15, 1970, to illustrate the plan for saving the *Apollo 13* voyage. What information does a graphic aid of this sort help clarify?

second system should still carry the astronauts safely home. Lovell noticed, however, that the pressure needle for the second tank was falling as well, and Liebergot was discovering the same thing. Normally the tank should register 860 pounds per square inch (psi); now it was approaching 300. The
80 explosion had come at 9:07 P.M., and the clock was now just past 10 P.M. At that rate of loss, the spaceship would exhaust all of its electricity and air sometime between midnight and 3 A.M.

Kranz telephoned the home of Chris Kraft—the former flight director and his onetime mentor, and now deputy director of the Manned Spacecraft Center. Kraft's wife pulled him out of the shower, and he heard Kranz urging, "Chris, you'd better get over here now. We've got a hell of a problem. We've lost oxygen pressure, we've lost a bus [an electrical power distribution system], we're losing fuel cells. It seems there's been an explosion." Kranz, age thirty-six, had worked with NASA for a decade, overseeing all Apollo
90 missions since taking over from Kraft when the prior Gemini series had come to an end. He was an experienced hand who sounded no undue alarm, solicited no unneeded counsel. Kraft raced to the space center, just ten miles away. When he arrived, Kranz brought his former mentor up to speed. . . .

With the oxygen for *Odyssey's* life support systems in rapid decline, Kranz barked rapid-fire demands for information and support to attack the problems.

Analyze Visuals

Possible answer: This diagram helps to clarify where and when each event in Apollo 13's journey occurred—or would have occured if all had gone according to plan. It also supports the text by simplifying complex information.

REVIST THE BIG QUESTION

How can we achieve the
IMPOSSIBLE?

Discuss In lines 83–92, how did Kranz's phone call show that he thought he was dealing with an impossible situation? *Possible answer: Kranz was "an experienced hand who sounded no undue alarm, solicited no unneeded counsel" (lines 91–92). However, he called his old mentor, Chris Kraft, at home and told him that he needed him to come in right away, an acknowledgment that he was facing a dire emergency.*

FOR ADVANCED LEARNERS/PRE–AP

Point of View Have students reread lines 83–92. Ask them to put themselves in Kranz's place and write an internal monologue from his point of view that explains why he decided to call Kraft. Remind students to cite specific evidence from the text and to consider what they know of Kranz's character and his responsibility to the mission. Invite students to present their monologues to the class.

How can we achieve the

IMPOSSIBLE?

Discuss In lines 94–102, how did Kranz react when faced with a situation that seemed impossible? ***Possible answer:*** *He didn't give up. He "barked rapid-fire demands for information and support to attack the problems" (line 95). He immediately thought of good questions to ask, and he was not deterred by a seemingly hopeless situation.*

Analyze Visuals

Activity Ask students to describe what they see in the control room, and how they think this picture might have changed during the emergency. ***Possible answer:*** *The control room is full of computers and notebooks. One screen appears to show an astronaut inside the spacecraft. There is a flag—a symbol of the United States. The control room is relatively empty, but during the emergency it probably filled up with computer engineers trying to help the astronauts.*

To the telemetry and electrical officer: "Will you take a look at the prelaunch data[6] and see if there's anything that may have started the venting?"
To the technicians running NASA's fast, on-site computers: "Bring up another computer . . . will you?"

100 *To the guidance and navigation officer:* "Give me a gross amount of the thruster propellants[7] consumed so far."
To Sy Liebergot: "What does the status of your buses tell you now?"

Off line, Liebergot and his backup engineer, George Bliss, were reaching even more forlorn conclusions: The single remaining oxygen tank was below 300 psi of pressure and losing another 1.7 psi each minute. If tank pressure fell below 100 psi, it would have insufficient force to move its precious contents into the fuel cells for power generation, and that point was just 116 minutes away. They made several attempts to stem the flow, but none succeeded.

110 *Liebergot:* "George, it looks grim."
Bliss: "Yes, it does."
Liebergot: "We're going down. We're losing it."
Bliss: "Yes, we are."

---

6. **prelaunch data:** information collected before launch of a spacecraft.
7. **thruster propellants:** fuel for rockets used to maneuver spacecraft.

Apollo 13 control room

DIFFERENTIATED INSTRUCTION

FOR STRUGGLING READERS

Develop Reading Fluency Point out that in lines 110–113, the names of people speaking are in italics and set off with a colon. The actual spoken words are in quotation marks. This punctuation sets off and highlights important conversations. Read the four lines of dialogue aloud to students, modeling proper intonation and pacing.

R RESOURCE MANAGER—Copy Master
Reading Fluency p. 149

FOR ADVANCED LEARNERS/PRE–AP

Research Have students research telemetry and create a Two-Column Chart that lists the main parts of a telemetry system in one column and what that part is used for in the second column. Then, have students diagram the telemetry system and label the parts.

BEST PRACTICES TOOLKIT—Transparency
Two-Column Chart p.A25

Now Liebergot was back on line with Kranz, arguing that the astronauts must move immediately into the attached lunar excursion module (LEM). Dubbed *Aquarius* on this mission, the LEM had been designed to set two astronauts on the moon and sustain life for several days. For three astronauts, *Aquarius* would be overcrowded, the power system would not work for long, and it would vaporize on reentry. But for the moment
120 it would have to do. The dying command module would support the astronauts for a matter of minutes; the LEM at least offered hours. Kranz again sought instant analysis. "I want you guys figuring our minimum power needed in the LEM to sustain life," he instructed a LEM technical group, which had anticipated no real action until the planned moon landing two days later. "And I want LEM manning around the clock."

The oxygen loss from *Odyssey* was accelerating to 3 psi per minute, and Bliss now estimated that they had eighteen minutes left before total power shutdown. A few moments later, he revised that down to seven minutes. And then, a moment later, to four. **C**
130 The Black Team had just taken over from White, and Glynn Lunney, who would spell Kranz at the director's console while the White Team stood down, sent up an urgent command: "Get 'em going in the LEM!" Lovell and Haise moved through the connecting hatch, and while Swigert stayed behind to wind down *Odyssey,* they powered up *Aquarius.* They worked frantically to transfer irreplaceable guidance data from the command module into the LEM computer in the seconds before everything was lost. Finally, Lovell radioed Houston, *"Aquarius* is up, and *Odyssey* is completely powered down."

There was a momentary relief, but with days to go, they had bought only
140 a little time. "OK, everybody," counseled Lunney, "we've got a lot of long-range problems to deal with."

Oxygen and Power
Among the mission's first long-range problems was that the return **trajectory** would miss the Earth by some forty thousand miles. The astronauts would need to fire the LEM's rocket in just five hours to close the gap. Producing the precision adjustment, however, would require immediate, massive recalibrations of instruments. By now the teams in Houston were humming, and they delivered the requisite data to Jim Lovell and his crew with an hour to spare.

While Glynn Lunney staffed the director's console, Kranz remained only
150 feet away, his mind turning over what to do next. He had already passed word that as soon as Houston had the fuel burn plan set, he would meet

C SUSPENSE
How do the references to time in lines 126–129 increase suspense?

trajectory
(trə-jĕk′tə-rē) *n.* the path of a moving body through space

TEXT ANALYSIS   COMMON CORE
RI 6

C *Model the Skill:* **SUSPENSE**

Model how to identify increasing suspense in a story. Explain that writers often use time to create suspense. When there is a limited amount of time to do something important, a sense of urgency is created. Have students identify the references to time in lines 126–129. Then point out to them that time gets shorter and shorter with each mention. ***Possible answers:*** *At first, Bliss estimated that the astronauts had 18 minutes before total power shutdown in Odyssey; quickly, he changed the estimate to 7 minutes, and then to 4 minutes. These time references create suspense by raising the question of whether the astronauts will be able to get out of Odyssey before total power shutdown.*

VOCABULARY   COMMON CORE
L 4

OWN THE WORD

trajectory: Remind students that *trajectory* is a noun that refers to "the path of a moving body through space" or "a chosen or taken course." Have students each write one sentence that demonstrates understanding of either definition.

FOR STRUGGLING READERS

2 Targeted Passage [Lines 114–121]

This passage helps students understand the importance of the astronauts' move from *Odyssey* to *Aquarius.*

• What was *Aquarius*? (line 115)

• How long could *Aquarius* support the astronauts? (line 117)

• How long could the command module support the astronauts? (lines 120–121)

FOR ENGLISH LANGUAGE LEARNERS

Vocabulary: Prefixes Remind students that a prefix is a letter or letters at the beginning of a word that change the meaning of the root word. The prefix *re-* means "back" or "again," so *recalibrations* (line 146) means "calibrations (or adjustments) that are done again." Have students find other words in the article with the prefix *re-.*

📁 **BEST PRACTICES TOOLKIT—Transparency** New Word Analysis p. E8

mandate
(măn′dāt′) n.
a command or
instruction

with his entire White Team in a nearby room. As it gathered, Kranz laid down his new **mandate:** "For the rest of this mission, I am pulling you men off console. The people out in that room will be running the flight from moment to moment, but it's the people in this room who will be coming up with the protocols they're going to be executing. From now on, what I want from every one of you is simple: options, and plenty of them." Their new name would be the Tiger Team, and for the remainder of the flight they would work and live in Room 210.

160 A mere twenty feet by twenty feet and windowless, Room 210 was bare except for several overhead TVs and tables along the walls, but its location was good: adjacent to the operations room and just a floor below the control room. Above all, it permitted the team to assemble all past and current data in one place. Now, Kranz believed, they could determine what had happened and was happening, essential for deciding what should happen next. **D**

D TAKE NOTES
Summarize the reasons Kranz created a new team that would work in a separate room.

Kranz pressed them to focus on solutions. He sought to build, he later reported, "a positive frame of mind that is necessary to work problems in a time-critical and true emergency environment." And he wanted quick answers to specific questions:

170 "How long can you keep the systems in the LEM running at full power?"

"Where do we stand on water? What about battery power? What about oxygen?"

"In three or four days we're going to have to use the command module again. I want to know how we can get that bird powered up and running from a cold stop . . . and do it all on just the power we've got left in the reentry batteries."

"I also want to know how we plan to align this ship if we can't use a star alignment. Can we use sun checks? Can we use moon checks? What about Earth checks?"

180 "I want options on . . . burns and midcourse corrections from now to entry."

"What ocean does it put us in?"

Once again, Kranz insisted on strategies and solutions without guesswork: "For the next few days we're going to be coming up with techniques and maneuvers we've never tried before," he concluded. "And I want to make sure we know what we're doing."

Kranz left his men to do their work and returned to the control room. Glynn Lunney of the Black Team had focused everybody on the forthcoming course correction, and minutes later Lovell and his colleagues

---

D Model the Skill:
TAKE NOTES

Model for students how to take notes. Remind students that taking notes will help them understand, summarize, and remember important information. Read lines 153–159, and point out the key phrase *Tiger Team*, and then discuss why the Tiger Team was created (line 156). Direct students to use their Problem and Solution note taking charts to record the information detailed in lines 156–169.

Possible answer: *Kranz created a new team, dubbed the Tiger Team, to create protocols that other teams would be carrying out (line 156). He put them in a separate room to avoid distractions, but he made sure that this room was close to both the operations and control rooms, giving the team access to all available mission data (lines 161–164).*

OWN THE WORD

mandate: Explain to students that *mandate* means "a command or instruction" that is given by one in an authoritative position, and the word connotes the need for people to obey. Ask students to provide synonyms for the word *mandate* that have similar connotations. **Possible answers:** *order, requirement*

DIFFERENTIATED INSTRUCTION

FOR ENGLISH LANGUAGE LEARNERS

Vocabulary: Idioms Use New Word Analysis to introduce and explain these idioms from the text: *the bottom was falling out* (line 17), "everything was going wrong"; *passed word* (lines 150–151), "told people"; *where do we stand on* (line 171), "explain our situation for"; *crunching the numbers* (line 201), "doing the math or calculations"; *gave . . . the green light* (lines 346–347), "gave permission."

BEST PRACTICES TOOLKIT—Transparency
New Word Analysis p. E8

FOR ADVANCED LEARNERS/PRE–AP

Evaluate Have students reread lines 170–182 and identify the main method that Kranz used to gather information. What other methods could he have used to pull together important information? Ask students whether they think Kranz's method was best. Why or why not?

190 executed a flawless blast of the LEM's engines. In one of the first bits of
good news since disaster struck, they had corrected their path perfectly.

Good news, though, was still in terribly short supply. The new course
required nearly four days for return, and *Aquarius* was provisioned for less
than two. The LEM's oxygen supply was not a problem since enough had
been placed on board for several moon walks, yet its supply of lithium
hydroxide was another story. This chemical was carried to remove carbon
dioxide accumulating in the cabin, but its LEM capacity was for two men
for two days, not for three men for twice that long. The available electricity
would last for even less time if *Aquarius* remained fully powered. Water, too,
200 was in desperately short supply. **E**

Kranz decided he wanted more seasoned talent crunching the numbers.
He sent the Tiger Team's electrical specialist back to the consoles on Tuesday
morning and in his place recruited Bill Peters from the Gold Team. Other
flight directors had sometimes found Peters slow to react and explain.
But Kranz had constructed a relationship with him, and he knew that he
brought exceptional experience: Peters had worked every space mission
since *Gemini 3* in 1965. "Peters was utterly brilliant," Kranz recalled, but he
could not explain himself well and one had to work with him to "bring out
the pieces."

210 After consulting with Kranz and the lead engineer for Grumman
Aerospace, the LEM maker, Peters was heartened by his preliminary
calculations: He could find ways to cut *Aquarius's* electrical flow from
55 amperes to 12, though this would require draconian[8] measures on
board: no computer, no guidance system, no heater, no panel display.
Communications would stay up, a fan would stir the air, and a little coolant
would circulate. Otherwise, all systems would be off.

Kranz also recruited another outsider, John Aaron, the Maroon Team's
twenty-seven-year-old electrical specialist. He understood power better than
anyone else, he was **innovative,** and he was unflappable—"Mr. Cool under
220 pressure" in Kranz's phrase. Kranz charged Aaron with a similar task for
conserving *Odyssey's* power, and together they took a first cut at the figures.
Their numbers were encouraging, and Aaron designed the plan. He believed
he could find the power to rev up the command module for reentry—but
only if almost all engineering corners were cut.

Aaron patiently presented his plan to a skeptical Tiger Team, reporting
that the powering up, normally a full day's affair, could take no more than
two hours. Bill Strahle, a guidance and navigation officer, interjected, "John,
you can't do it in that time." Aaron responded, "Well, now, that's what *I*

---

8. **draconian:** extremely harsh.

E SUSPENSE
What details in
lines 192–200 raise
questions about
the outcome of the
mission?

3 Targeted Passage

innovative
(ĭn′ə-vā′tĭv)
adj. able to create new,
original ideas

E SUSPENSE

Possible answer: *The new course planned
for the astronauts' return would take four
days, and* Aquarius *"was provisioned for
less than two" (lines 193–194). The supply
of lithium hydroxide, electricity, and water
(lines 195–200) were all inadequate. These
details raise questions about the outcome.*

REVIST THE BIG QUESTION

How can we achieve the
IMPOSSIBLE?

Discuss In lines 201–224, what decisions did
Kranz continue to make that show that he
thought "the impossible" was not truly impossible? ***Possible answer:*** *He recruited Bill Peters
and John Aaron as electrical specialists. Peters
identified ways to conserve electricity (lines
212–213), and Aaron thought he could "find
the power to rev up the command module for
reentry" (line 223). These recruiting decisions
show that Kranz believed that their impossible
situation was salvageable, if he put together a
team with the right combination of expertise
and talent.*

OWN THE WORD

innovative: Tell students that *innovative* is the adjectival form of the noun
innovation. The verb is *innovate.* Remind
students that a person who is *innovative* has original and creative ideas. Have
students list synonyms for each of the
three forms (adjective, noun, and verb)
of the word. ***Possible answers:*** *innovative
(adj.): inventive, fresh; innovation (noun):
creation, novelty; innovate (verb): alter,
change, create*

FOR STRUGGLING READERS

3 Targeted Passage [Lines 210–224]

This passage gives some hints that the
emergency might be resolved.

- How did Peters propose to cut
Aquarius's electrical flow? (lines 214–216)

- What was Aaron's task? (lines 222–224)

- How did their findings create some hope?
(lines 222–223)

FOR ADVANCED LEARNERS/PRE–AP

Characterization In three short paragraphs
(lines 201–224), Useem brings Bill Peters and
John Aaron to life. Have small groups work
together to discuss what the reader learns
about each man and the methods that
Useem uses to create characters in so few
lines.

TIERED DISCUSSION PROMPTS

Direct students to lines 231–242. Use these prompts to focus on decisions Kranz had to make:

Connect As a group leader, would you be better off handpicking your team in an emergency? Explain. *Answers will vary but should give details to support the response.*

Analyze Why did Kranz replace the Gold Team with the Tiger Team? ***Possible answer:*** *Kranz knew that any error of alignment or duration "would send the ship in a wrong direction with virtually no fuel remaining for any correction" (lines 235–237). He felt more comfortable with his own specially chosen team.*

Evaluate Did Kranz make the right decision? Explain. ***Possible answer:*** *Yes. The big burn worked. The Gold Team may have succeeded as well, but they did not have Kranz's absolute confidence. Leaders must make hard decisions that may offend others.*

COMMON CORE RI 4

Language Coach

Multiple-Meaning Words The word *fire* has more than one meaning. In line 232 it means "to ignite." What does it mean in the following sentences?
The fire burned many acres of forest.
The manager had to fire the lazy employee.

---

thought, Bill. But I think if we're willing to take a few shortcuts, we just 230 might be able to pull it off."

Late on the evening of Tuesday, April 14, nearly twenty-four hours after the accident, Lovell and crew rounded the moon and were scheduled to fire the LEM's rocket to accelerate their return to Earth. The engine burn, like virtually all other maneuvers of the past day, would be crucial, but this one would be especially so. The smallest error of alignment or duration would send the ship in a wrong direction with virtually no fuel remaining for any correction. Though the Gold Team was still on duty as the time of the scheduled firing approached, Kranz decided to install his own Tiger Team at the controls. His men quietly walked into Mission Control, muttered 240 apologies to their sitting counterparts, and took over the consoles. Under Kranz's direction, the "big burn" worked. Another essential milestone for the journey home had been reached, and the room erupted with cheers.

The moment's glow had barely passed when three men made their way from different directions to Kranz's workstation. Chris Kraft was one; Deke Slayton, astronaut and director of flight crew operations, the second. Max Faget, engineering director for the entire Manned Spacecraft Center, trailed slightly behind. "So what's our next step here, Gene?" opened Slayton, one of the original seven Mercury astronauts.

> *Kranz:* "Well, Deke, we're gonna work on that."
> 250 *Slayton:* "I'm not sure how much there is to work on. We're going to put the crew to bed, right?"
> *Kranz:* "Eventually, sure."
> *Slayton:* "Eventually may not do it, Gene. Their last scheduled sleep period was twenty-four hours ago. They're going to need some rest."

Now Kraft jumped in.

> *Kraft:* "How do we stand with that power-down problem, Gene?"
> *Kranz:* "It's coming along, Chris."
> *Kraft:* "We ready to execute it?"
> *Kranz:* "We're ready, but it's a long procedure and Deke thinks we ought 260 to get the crew ready to sleep first."
> *Kraft:* "Sleep? A sleep period's six hours! Take the crew off stream that long before powering down, and you're wasting six hours of juice you don't need to waste."

128 UNIT 1: PLOT, SETTING, AND MOOD

DIFFERENTIATED INSTRUCTION

FOR ENGLISH LANGUAGE LEARNERS

Language Coach COMMON CORE RI 4

Multiple-Meaning Words *Answers: "destructive burning" and "to dismiss from employment"* Tell students that context clues in a story will help students understand which meaning of a multiple-meaning word is being used. Have students identify other multiple-meaning words in lines 231–242 and use context clues to explain what they mean.

FOR RELUCTANT READERS

Connect to the Text Help students connect with the text by assigning students to read the parts of Kraft, Slayton, and Kranz aloud. Then engage the class in a discussion. Ask students which problem they would address first—letting the crew sleep or fixing the power down problem. Have students refer to the text to explain the reasons for their answers.

Slayton: "But if you keep them up and have them execute a complicated power-down when they're barely awake, someone's bound to screw something up. I'd rather spend a little extra power now than risk another disaster later."

Max Faget appeared, and Kranz drew him into the discussion.

Kranz: "Max, Deke and Chris were just telling me what they think our
270 next step ought to be."
Faget: "Passive thermal control,[9] right?"
Slayton, alarmed: "PTC?"
Faget: "Sure. That ship's had one side pointing to the sun and one pointing out to space for hours. If we don't get some kind of barbeque roll going on soon, we're going to freeze half our systems and cook the other half."
Slayton: "Do you have any idea what kind of pressure it's going to put on the crew to ask them to execute a PTC roll now?"
Kraft: "Or what kind of pressure it's going to put on the available power? I'm not sure we can afford to try something like that at the moment."
280 *Faget:* "I'm not sure we can afford not to."

The three-way argument escalated for several minutes, with each point and counterpoint more fiercely asserted than the last. Kranz said little throughout, mainly listening to what his three superiors had to say. Finally, he held up his hand, and they stopped speaking.

"Gentlemen," Kranz said, "I thank you
290 for your input." The discussion was over, his decision made: "The next job for this crew will be to execute a thermal roll. After that, they will power down their spacecraft. And finally, they will get some sleep. A tired crew can get over their fatigue, but if we damage this ship any further, we're not going to get over that." **F**

With the decision made, Kranz turned to his console, and Slayton and Faget turned to leave. Kraft lingered, considered objecting, but then quietly moved off as well. His protégé was in control, and he had ruled firmly. The

The Latin phrase on this insignia means "From the Moon, Knowledge."

---

9. **passive thermal control:** any method of controlling temperature on a spacecraft without using electricity.

COMMON CORE RI 6

F AUTHOR'S PURPOSE
An **author's purpose** is what the writer hopes to achieve in a particular work. The main purpose of this narrative is to show readers an example of leadership in a crisis. To achieve this purpose, Useem shares both important details and less important details with his readers. Reread lines 281–295, in which Useem shows how Kranz makes and expresses an important decision. If you were to summarize this passage for a friend, you would share only the most important details. Which details are most important to showing Kranz's leadership skills? The *less-important* details are not *unimportant* details, however. These details provide background and elaborate on the important details, help create suspense, and create a more complete picture of the event. What are some of the less important details in this passage?

Analyze Visuals

Activity Have students explain how the images on this insignia reflect the meaning of the Latin phrase. *Possible answer: The pioneering horses are leaving Earth, which looks diminutive in the background, and eagerly galloping toward the Moon while the Sun shines on them. They are heading toward the Moon for knowledge, fulfilling the Latin motto: Ex Luna, scientia (from the Moon, comes knowledge).*

READING STRATEGY COMMON CORE RI 6

F AUTHOR'S PURPOSE
Point out to students that the author's use of dialogue in lines 249–280 adds to the suspense about what Kranz's decision will be (lines 289–290). Explain to students that to make his decision, Kranz had to weigh the astronauts' requirement for sleep (lines 249–254) with the mission's need to have them execute a power-down procedure (line 256) and a thermal roll (lines 271–280). He also had to consider whether the exhausted astronauts could carry out the procedures without errors.

Answers: Important details: Kranz says little while the others argue. Kranz chooses a course of action—the crew will execute a thermal roll, power down the spacecraft, and get some sleep. Less important details: The argument takes several minutes. Kranz holds up his hand. Kranz calls his superiors "Gentlemen."

Extend the Discussion Would the selection have been as effective without dialogue?

FOR ENGLISH LANGUAGE LEARNERS
Comprehension: Transitions Reread lines 291–294 with students and identify the sequence signal words ("next," "after that," and "finally"). Point out how these words help the reader follow the order in which the actions take place. Direct students to lines 349–358, and have them identify transition words ("soon," "until," "then," "again and again," "another minute," "then," "moments later"). Ask pairs to write two sentences using each transition word or phrase.

FOR ADVANCED LEARNERS/PRE–AP
Evaluate Have partners research the Greek god Apollo. Ask them to consider whether "Apollo" was the best name for the United States Moon mission. What other names could they propose? Have them explain the logic of alternative name choices.

G GRAMMAR AND STYLE

COMMON CORE L 3

Analyze Sentence Flow Writers use coordinating conjunctions to link sentences. Have students reread lines 320–324 and identify the coordinating conjunctions (*and, but*) and the linked sentences. Ask them to read the sentences in sequence, without the coordinating conjunctions. What do the coordinating conjunctions contribute to the style and flow of the writing?

READING STRATEGY

COMMON CORE RI 1 RI 4 RI 5

H TAKE NOTES

Possible answer: Using the command module simulator, Ken Mattingly helped solve the repowering problem by testing and refining Aaron's scheme for a workable sequence (lines 317–327).

Extend the Discussion Ken Mattingly was supposed to be part of the crew of Apollo 13, until he was exposed to measles. In what ways might his involvement have been especially helpful?

VOCABULARY

COMMON CORE L 4

OWN THE WORD

- **respite:** Point out that *respite* comes from the Latin word *respectus*, meaning "refuge." Synonyms include *break, intermission,* and *pause.* Have students write sentences using *respite* correctly. Then have them rewrite their sentences using the synonym that best suits their original sentence.

- **collaborative:** Tell students that *collaborative* is the adjective form of the verb *collaborate* and the noun *collaboration.* All refer to working together toward a common end. Have students give examples of types of situations in which they might work *collaboratively* with other people. *Possible answers: house cleaning, debate team, community service project*

Targeted Passage ④

respite (rĕs′pĭt) *n.* a period of rest or relief

collaborative (kə-lăb′ə-rə′tĭv) *adj.* done in cooperation with others

G GRAMMAR AND STYLE

Reread lines 311–315. Rather than writing a series of short sentences, Useem uses the **coordinating conjunctions** *and* and *but* to join two sets of independent clauses.

H TAKE NOTES

How did Ken Mattingly help solve the problem of repowering the command module?

---

astronauts spent the next two hours performing their assigned tasks and
300 finally began a long-overdue slumber.

The Return

With the trajectory successfully fixed for the return to Earth, Kranz and his Tiger Team resumed their calculations and planning in Room 210. The biggest challenge: restarting the moribund command module. *Aquarius* had been life-sustaining, but the LEM would disintegrate on reentry. *Odyssey* would be life-returning: the command module came with a heat shield to endure reentry's 5,000 degrees Fahrenheit. For that, though, *Odyssey* would have to be coaxed back from dormancy—with a defunct regular electric supply and a mere two hours of power remaining in its auxiliary batteries.

It was now late Wednesday evening, and the Tiger Team had been
310 working relentlessly since Monday evening, struggling to surmount problem after problem if reentry were to succeed. Most of the team members had worked nonstop for more than forty-eight hours, and Kranz finally ordered a six-hour **respite.** Yes, they needed their sleep, but even more compelling was the fact that the most critical troubleshooting might finally be behind them. John Aaron, the electrical officer borrowed from the Maroon Team, had evidently found a way around *Odyssey*'s repowering problem. G

It was a **collaborative** solution. One of the command module's chief engineers, Arnie Aldrich, had worked with Aaron to ensure that the switches for the various systems would be thrown in a workable sequence so that
320 early systems would be ready for later ones as needed. Kranz himself had examined each step, and astronaut Ken Mattingly had tested everything in a nearby command module simulator. Mattingly had been scheduled to serve as the command module pilot for *Apollo 13,* but after he had been exposed to German measles, NASA had replaced him with Swigert. Severely disappointed at first, Mattingly now applied his insider's knowledge to testing and refining Aaron's scheme. Ultimately, it worked—at least on the simulator. H

To add to the tension, the fate of *Apollo 13* had become a global drama. The Soviet Union volunteered rescue vessels. Religious groups across
330 America and around the world prayed for the astronauts' safe deliverance. The Chicago Board of Trade added its own supplication, briefly suspending trading at 11 a.m. on Thursday "for a moment of tribute to the courage and gallantry of America's astronauts and a prayer for their safe return to Earth."

By Thursday evening, just eighteen hours before splashdown, the list of procedures to restart *Odyssey* was finalized and ready for transmission. Kranz, Aaron, and Aldrich pushed their way through the rows of consoles

---

DIFFERENTIATED INSTRUCTION

FOR STRUGGLING READERS

④ **Targeted Passage** [Lines 301–315]

This passage demonstrates the next major hurdle Kranz faced after the trajectory was fixed; it also hints at a hopeful resolution.

- Why couldn't the astronauts stay in *Aquarius* on their way back to Earth? (line 304)

- What would Kranz and his team have to do to *Odyssey*? Why? (lines 304–308)

FOR ENGLISH LANGUAGE LEARNERS

Vocabulary: Suffixes Explain that -*ly* is a suffix, or word ending, that means "in a certain way." For example: *successfully* (line 301) means "in a way that ends with success." Have partners create a Cluster Diagram with the -*ly* suffix in the middle and examples in the surrounding circles. Students can follow this procedure for the suffix -*less* in *flawless* (line 16).

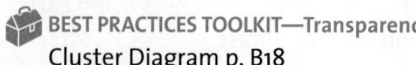
BEST PRACTICES TOOLKIT—Transparency
Cluster Diagram p. B18

The command module is recovered from the Pacific Ocean after splashdown.

in Mission Control to deliver the list. Mission Control would require nearly two hours to radio the start-up sequence, line by line, to Jack Swigert, who would have to copy each of the hundreds of technical instructions by hand.

340   Swigert and crew successfully followed the start-up protocol, moved back into *Odyssey,* and jettisoned *Aquarius.* By mid-Friday, the command module was approaching Earth's outer atmosphere at 25,000 miles per hour, and Kranz took the director's console for the final time. With four minutes to go before *Odyssey* hit the atmosphere's upper layers, Kranz stood and asked each of the system officers if they were ready. "Let's go around the horn once more before entry," he said. Each officer declared his readiness. Kranz gave the mission communicator, astronaut Joe Kerwin, the green light: "You can tell the crew they're go for reentry."

   Soon all radio contact with the crew was lost as intense heat enveloped

350 the plunging craft. Four minutes of anxious silence passed on the ground until the fiery spray around the capsule subsided; then Kranz instructed Kerwin to resume contact. *"Odyssey,"* Kerwin called. "Houston standing by,

Analyze Visuals

Activity Ask students to describe the command module. Does it look the way you expected it to look? *Possible answer: The command module is small and looks like it would be uncomfortable for three adults. It seems worn out and battered, not surprising, given its recent reentry.*

TIERED DISCUSSION PROMPTS

Direct students to lines 340–348. Use these prompts to help students focus on the last great hurdle for Mission Control:

Connect Think of a time when you worked hard at something and achieved all your interim goals, but the final outcome was still in doubt. How does that experience help you understand what Kranz and his team might have been feeling as the command module approached Earth's outer atmosphere? *Students' answers should reflect an understanding that Kranz and his team probably had mixed feelings. They had already accomplished amazing feats, giving them hope, but they must have also felt worry, fear, and anxiety.*

Analyze What was the point of Kranz asking each system officer if he was ready (lines 344–346)? *Possible answer: With only four minutes to go, there was no turning back, but Kranz showed, symbolically at least, that the entire operation had been collaborative.*

Evaluate How you would characterize Kranz as a leader at this point? *Possible answer: Kranz was determined and confident. As he gave Kerwin the green light (lines 346–348), he must have known that he had done everything he could have done.*

FOR ENGLISH LANGUAGE LEARNERS

Vocabulary: Phrasal Verbs Explain that some verbs pair up with a specific preposition to make a phrase with a different meaning from the verb. For example, *standing by* (line 352) means "waiting." Assign pairs phrasal verbs from the selection: *turning over* (line 150); *pulling . . . off* (lines 153–154); *coming up with* (line 184); *jumped in* (line 255); *drew . . . into* (line 268). Use Think-Pair-Share to help students use context to determine the meanings.

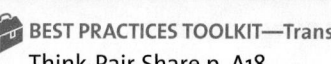 BEST PRACTICES TOOLKIT—Transparency
Think-Pair-Share p. A18

FOR ADVANCED LEARNERS/PRE-AP

Style Have students reread lines 340–341. Ask them why Useem might have compressed such a complex procedure into one sentence.

❶ SUSPENSE

Possible answer: *The writer built suspense by raising the question of whether the astronauts would survive reentry. His use of descriptive adjectives, such as "plunging craft" (line 350), "anxious silence" (line 350), and "fiery spray" (line 351), intensifies the suspense. So does the fact that the crew did not respond to Kerwin for "more blackout time than experienced on any other mission" (lines 354–355).*

Analyze Visuals

Activity Ask students how they think the astronauts were feeling at this point. *Possible answer: Smiling and waving at the crowd, the astronauts appear happy and relieved, though they must have been drained by their long ordeal. The fact that they are unshaven suggests that they had no time for personal care.*

SELECTION WRAP–UP

READ WITH A PURPOSE Now that students have finished reading the selection, have them compare and contrast Kranz's reactions to how they react under pressure. What are Kranz's strengths as a leader? *Possible answer: Kranz seeks help from experts, and he stays calm.*

⭐ **CRITIQUE** Have students evaluate Kranz's leadership style and skills. Would Kranz make a good mentor to another flight director?

---

❶ **SUSPENSE**
How did the writer build suspense in lines 349–355?

Targeted Passage

over." No response. Kranz: "Try again." Kerwin did, again and again, to no avail, and another minute passed, more blackout time than experienced on any other mission. ❶

Then, faintly, came the scratchy but unmistakable voice of astronaut Jack Swigert: "OK, Joe." Moments later Jim Lovell, Jack Swigert, and Fred Haise were floating down on three parachutes for a soft landing in the Pacific. Eugene Kranz punched the air.

360 Sy Liebergot faced weeks of recurrent nightmares about undervoltages. Jim Lovell declared the mission a failure, but, he added, "I like to think it was a successful failure." And Grumman Aerospace, maker of the LEM, sent a mock bill for more than $312,421 to North American Rockwell, producer of the command module, for a "battery charge, road call," and "towing fee" for returning *Odyssey* home.

Eugene Kranz, James Lovell, and their crews matched wits with a technology failure, and they won. They orchestrated thousands of actions—many minute, some momentous—to fix what seemed unfixable. In the end, they triumphed over one of NASA's worst nightmares.

❺

Astronauts Fred Haise, James Lovell, and John Swigert after their return to Earth

---

DIFFERENTIATED INSTRUCTION

FOR STRUGGLING READERS

❺ **Targeted Passage** [Lines 356–369]

This passage concludes the article by showing the final resolution of the *Apollo 13* emergency.

- How and where did the astronauts land? (lines 357–358)
- Why did Eugene Kranz punch the air? (line 359)
- Do you agree that the mission was a "successful failure"? (lines 366–369)

FOR ADVANCED LEARNERS/PRE–AP

Synthesize [small-group option] Have students think of a possible theme that is reflected in the statement "They orchestrated thousands of actions—many minute, some momentous—to fix what seemed unfixable" (lines 367–368). Then ask students to think of examples in history that would support this theme.

After Reading

Comprehension

1. **Recall** What was the original goal of *Apollo 13*?

2. **Recall** Why did NASA have to cancel the mission?

3. **Summarize** What were the main steps taken to save the astronauts?

Text Analysis

4. **Make Inferences** Why did astronaut James Lovell declare the *Apollo 13* mission "a successful failure"?

5. **Analyze Decisions** What skills, knowledge, and traits did Eugene Kranz look for when choosing members of the Tiger Team? Use a graphic organizer like the one shown to record your answer.

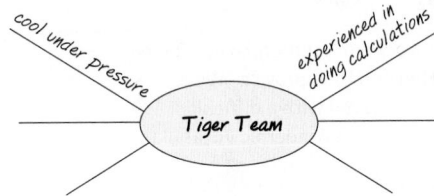

6. **Analyze Notes** Review the chart you created as you read. Which of the problems provided the biggest test of Kranz's leadership? Cite specific evidence to support your conclusion.

7. **Draw Conclusions** Why might the author have chosen to focus on the employees at Mission Control rather than on the astronauts in space? Support your answer.

8. **Interpret Main Idea** Reread lines 366–369. What idea does the writer express about the ways in which Kranz and his colleagues achieved the impossible?

9. **Make Judgments** Do you agree with NASA's policy of giving the flight director final authority on all decisions during the mission? Cite evidence to support your opinion.

10. **Predict** How might the space program have been affected if NASA had failed to rescue the astronauts aboard *Apollo 13*?

11. **Evaluate Suspense** Michael Useem included extensive technical information in his account of *Apollo 13*. How well did he balance the need to explain with the need to tell a suspenseful story? Find examples to support your answer.

> ### How can we achieve the IMPOSSIBLE?
> What qualities do you have that would help you deal with an emergency?

COMMON CORE

RI 1 Cite evidence to support analysis of what the text says explicitly. **RI 5** Analyze how an author's ideas are developed and refined.

Practice and Apply

For preliminary support of post-reading questions, use these copy masters:

> **R** **RESOURCE MANAGER**—Copy Masters
> Reading Check p. 146
> Suspense in Nonfiction p. 139
> Question Support p. 147
>
> Additional selection questions are provided for teachers on page 133.

ANSWERS

Comprehension

1. *Apollo 13's goal was to land on the Moon's Fra Mauro ridges (lines 16–17).*

2. *NASA canceled the mission because an explosion destroyed oxygen tanks and other vital equipment (lines 21–26) on the spacecraft.*

3. *First, Mission Control got the astronauts out of Odyssey (lines 130–138) and into the LEM Aquarius. Then, they figured out how to power up and return Odyssey and its crew to Earth.*

Text Analysis

COMMON CORE RI 1, RI 5

Possible answers:

4. *Lovell called it a failure because Apollo 13 never reached the Moon and a success because the astronauts returned home safely.*

5. *Kranz looked for intelligence, creativity, and determination. He wanted the Tiger Team to "[come] up with the protocols" (lines 155–156), "focus on solutions" (line 166), and remain positive.*

6. ● **COMMON CORE FOCUS** *Analyze Notes Kranz struggled most with the problem of the astronauts' requirement for sleep versus the need to complete a thermal roll and power-down; ultimately, he had to decide himself (lines 249–295).*

7. *Useem focused on Mission Control because that is where life-and-death decisions were made.*

8. *Kranz and his crew achieved the impossible by making successful decisions on small and large issues, step by step.*

9. *NASA's policy is well founded: When lives are at risk, somebody has to make final decisions to avoid second-guessing, procrastination, and wavering. For example, when the three-way argument about whether the astronauts should sleep or adjust the LEM's*

---

position continued for several precious minutes (lines 249–300), Kranz made a decision and executed it before it was too late to save the crew.

10. *Failing to rescue the astronauts might have undermined the entire Apollo program and jeopardized future missions. The failure would also have hurt the image of the space program in the eyes of the public and Congress, who fund the program.*

11. ● **COMMON CORE FOCUS** *Evaluate Suspense Useem succeeded by giving*

enough technical detail to explain the situation (lines 78–82, 126–129, 210–216, 301–308), without undermining his narrative. He balanced his technical explanations with more personal information, such as accounts of actual conversations.

> How can we achieve the
> **IMPOSSIBLE?** Students might consider qualities they admire in Kranz as well as in their peers and mentors, then compare those qualities to ones they possess.

ANSWERS

Vocabulary in Context

▲ VOCABULARY PRACTICE

1. *replenish*
2. *perimeter*
3. *question*
4. *innovative*
5. *action*
6. *collaborative*

 **RESOURCE MANAGER—Copy Master**
Vocabulary Practice p. 144

ACADEMIC VOCABULARY IN WRITING

Student responses will vary, but should identify a difficult problem from the student's life and the improvisation used to solve it. For example, a student might have left a textbook at school but had a friend scan and email pages home to her.

VOCABULARY STRATEGY: SPECIALIZED VOCABULARY

COMMON CORE L6

- As students review the words, remind them that they have multiple meanings. For example, *bus* usually refers to a vehicle. Point out that the first dictionary definition will not show the specialized meaning.

- Tell students to use context clues and the process of elimination. For example, Item 5 shows a definition for a verb, so they can eliminate four of the five words.

Possible answers:

1. *bus*
2. *satellite*
3. *protocols*
4. *transponder*
5. *vent*

 **RESOURCE MANAGER—Copy Master**
Vocabulary Strategy p. 145

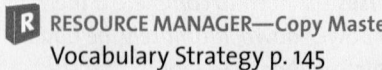

Interactive Vocabulary THINK central

Keywords direct students to a **WordSharp** tutorial on **thinkcentral.com** or to other types of vocabulary practice and review.

Vocabulary in Context

▲ VOCABULARY PRACTICE

Identify the word that is most different in meaning from the others.

1. remove, empty, replenish, discard
2. path, course, trajectory, perimeter
3. command, question, decree, mandate
4. standard, innovative, boring, unoriginal
5. rest, stillness, action, respite
6. oppositional, collaborative, solitary, dividing

WORD LIST
collaborative
innovative
mandate
replenish
respite
trajectory

ACADEMIC VOCABULARY IN WRITING

- affect   • communicate   • definite   • establish   • identify

The problems that *Apollo 13* encountered lacked a *definite* solution, which forced both the crew aboard the ship and the crew in Houston to improvise. Write a paragraph about a time in your life when you were faced with a difficult problem and had to improvise to solve it. Use at least one Academic Vocabulary word in your response.

VOCABULARY STRATEGY: SPECIALIZED VOCABULARY

The astronauts, scientists, and engineers who work at NASA have their own specialized vocabulary. This vocabulary includes terms such as *return trajectory*, which is the path of a spacecraft on its return to Earth. It is often possible to figure out the special meanings of words from the context. Otherwise, check a dictionary and look for labels—such as *space flight* and *computer science*—that may precede definitions and indicate special uses of a word.

PRACTICE Write the space flight term that matches each definition. If you need to, check a dictionary or glossary.

vent   protocols   bus   satellite   transponder

1. an electrical power distribution system
2. a small body that orbits a larger one
3. data transmissions between computers
4. an electronic device that combines a transmitter and a receiver
5. to release or discharge

COMMON CORE

L 6 Acquire and use accurately domain-specific words and phrases.

Interactive Vocabulary THINK central

Go to **thinkcentral.com**.
KEYWORD: HML10-134

DIFFERENTIATED INSTRUCTION

FOR ADVANCED LEARNERS/PRE–AP

Vocabulary in Writing Have students use at least four vocabulary words to write a paragraph that explains one of the problems Kranz faced and how he overcame it.

Language

◆ **GRAMMAR AND STYLE:** Improve Sentence Flow

COMMON CORE

L3 Apply knowledge of language to make effective choices for meaning or style.

Review the **Grammar and Style** note on page 130. Writing flows more smoothly when it doesn't merely consist of short, choppy sentences. Follow Michael Useem's example by inserting a **coordinating conjunction** (such as *and, but, for, or, so,* or *yet*) between two independent clauses to form a longer, **compound sentence** and to clarify the relationship between ideas. Remember to use a comma before a coordinating conjunction that joins two independent clauses. Here are two examples from the selection.

> *The astronauts and their protective shell were unscathed, but it was evident that some kind of explosion had ripped through vital equipment.* (lines 25–26)

> *He knew what options were out, yet he also knew he must somehow engineer a safe return.* (lines 37–38)

Notice how the revisions in blue use a coordinating conjunction to make smoother sentence structures. Revise your own writing by using similar techniques.

STUDENT MODEL

A small explosion has occurred aboard the <u>Odyssey.</u> Some vital equipment was damaged_{, but} The astronauts were not harmed.

READING-WRITING CONNECTION

YOUR TURN Increase your understanding of "The Race to Save *Apollo 13*" by responding to this prompt. Then use the **revising tip** to improve your writing.

WRITING PROMPT	**REVISING TIP**
Short Constructed Response: Press Release Imagine that you are working for NASA at the time of the *Apollo 13* crisis. Using information from the selection, write a **one- or two-paragraph press release** in which you describe events in the first hour after the explosion.	Review your response. How have you used coordinating conjunctions to make your writing flow more smoothly?

Interactive Revision THINK central

Go to **thinkcentral.com**.
KEYWORD: HML10-135.

FOR STRUGGLING WRITERS

- Remind students that a summary includes a main idea and supporting details.

- Review pages 120–123 with students and help them to note the important events that occurred after the explosion.

- Help students to write a topic sentence that identifies when the explosion happened and sets up the rest of the press release.

Language

COMMON CORE L3

◆ **GRAMMAR AND STYLE**

- After students examine the student model, have them describe their classroom by using sentences with coordinating conjunctions. (For more information on coordinating conjunctions, see **Grammar Handbook**, p. R63.)

- Write these sentences on the board. Have students suggest coordinating conjunctions to combine the two sentences.

> *The astronauts on* Odyssey *must have been afraid,. but ~~T~~they were also brave.*

> *Kranz could have let the astronauts sleep,. or ~~H~~he could have had them perform the thermal roll first.*

R RESOURCE MANAGER—Copy Master
Improve Sentence Flow p. 148

READING-WRITING CONNECTION

- Encourage students to review on pages 120–123 the first events that occurred after the explosion. Have them use a summarizing chart to record the most important information. Remind students that a press release should be succinct.

Writing Online  THINK central

The following tools are available online at **thinkcentral.com** and on **Write*Smart*** CD-ROM:
- Interactive Graphic Organizers
- Interactive Student Models
- Interactive Revision Lessons
For additional grammar instruction, see **GrammarNotes** on **thinkcentral.com**.

Assess and Reteach

Assess

DIAGNOSTIC AND SELECTION TESTS
Selection Test A pp. 47–48
Selection Test B/C pp. 49–50

Interactive Selection Test on **thinkcentral.com**

Reteach

Level Up Online Tutorials on **thinkcentral.com**

Reteaching Worksheets on **thinkcentral.com**
Literature Lesson 6, Study Skills Lesson 12

COMMON CORE FOCUS

RI 7 Analyze various accounts of a subject told in different mediums, determining which details are emphasized in each account. **W 9b (RI 7)** Draw evidence from informational texts; analyze various accounts of a subject told in different mediums, determining which details are emphasized in each account. **SL 2** Integrate multiple sources of information presented in diverse media or formats.

SUMMARY

This *Apollo 13* film clip takes place during a critical time window when three stranded astronauts attempt to return to Earth. On the ground, NASA engineers at Mission Control in Houston, Texas, try to solve technical problems, while the astronauts' friends and families tensely wait. In space, Jim Lovell, Jack Swigert, and Fred Haise face the possibility of death. After agonizing moments of silence, the astronauts finally make contact and parachute to safety.

What keeps you on the EDGE of your seat?

To help students explore the question, ask them to discuss a suspenseful movie—such as a mystery or a horror film—they have seen recently. How did the director increase the viewers' tension? What elements kept them on the edge of their seats?

BACKGROUND

Ron Howard was a child actor during the 1960s space race between the United States and the former Soviet Union. Always fascinated by space, Howard said, "I'm a storyteller. I'm not really an explorer. What I'm passionate about is telling stories in an effective way." To add realism to his film about the *Apollo 13* crisis, Howard used actual dialogue between NASA engineers and astronauts and incorporated the first scenes of real, unsimulated weightlessness, which were filmed aboard a NASA training aircraft.

What keeps you on the EDGE of your seat?

COMMON CORE

RI 7 Analyze various accounts of a subject told in different mediums, determining which details are emphasized in each account.

What type of movie do you prefer? Do you like the relentless tension created by nonstop action, or do you prefer the shock of a surprise ending? The scene you are about to view re-creates the tense moments that kept viewers glued to their television sets in 1970, waiting to see if the real *Apollo 13* crew would return home safely.

Background

Unlucky 13 Some people believe that the number 13 is unlucky, but those at the National Aeronautics and Space Administration (NASA) dismissed the superstitious belief. According to NASA, the flight of *Apollo 13* would be a routine mission. After all, *Apollo 11* and *Apollo 12* had already landed on the moon. What could possibly go wrong? The mission was to begin at 1:13 P.M. on April 11. In military time, that time is written as 13:13. *Apollo 13* was supposed to orbit the moon on April 13. Instead, an explosion weakened the ship's oxygen supply and battery life. The crew and the world were about to weather a major crisis.

The *Apollo 13* movie, based on the book *Lost Moon* by astronaut Jim Lovell with writer Jeffrey Kluger, recounts the nerve-racking events of the actual mission. Director Ron Howard captures every detail of NASA's race against time.

136

Media Study Resources

See resources on the **Teacher One Stop DVD-ROM** *and on* **thinkcentral.com**.

 RESOURCE MANAGER UNIT 1
Plan and Teach, pp. 151–154
Summary, pp. 155†*, 156‡*
Viewing Guide, p. 157
Close Viewing, p. 158
Media Activity, p. 159
Produce Your Own Media, p. 160

TECHNOLOGY
🔘 **Teacher One Stop DVD-ROM**
🔘 **Student One Stop DVD-ROM**
🔘 **MediaSmart DVD-ROM**
MediaScope on **thinkcentral.com**

* Resources for Differentiation † Also in Spanish ‡ In Haitian Creole and Vietnamese

Media Literacy: Creating Suspense on Film

In telling a suspenseful story, both writers and filmmakers aim to seize an audience's attention, making it anxious to learn the ultimate outcome. Writers ratchet up the tension primarily through the words that form the complications of the rising action or the vivid descriptions of characters' struggles. Filmmakers deliver suspense through a careful combination of visual and sound techniques.

How do directors keep viewers in suspense when the audience already knows the real-life ending? The secret, according to film director Ron Howard, is "simply storytelling." A director can use **camera shots, editing,** and **music** to tell a well-known story and still raise the level of suspense.

FILM TECHNIQUES	STRATEGIES FOR VIEWING	
Camera shots can build suspense by tracking the emotions of characters as they face certain struggles.	• Consider the effect of a **close-up shot** versus a **long shot.** The first conveys characters' emotions or thoughts, while the second shows characters in relation to their surroundings. Ask yourself: How do close-up shots help viewers sympathize with characters? • Watch for **point-of-view shots,** which show what a character sees. These shots give viewers an opportunity to experience what is happening from a character's point of view.	
Suspenseful scenes can be **edited** in a number of ways. Directors manipulate time, which can affect the flow of a scene.	• Notice how **parallel editing,** which is an editing technique that cuts from one shot to another, shows simultaneous action—often in different locations. Ask yourself: How do sudden shifts to different settings heighten the suspense? • Be aware that suspenseful scenes often rely on a **high-stakes deadline** or a race against time. Directors manipulate time to create suspense or increase viewers' anticipation. They can shorten time, turning minutes to seconds, or they can extend it, stretching a moment to a nail-biting extreme.	
Music can be a key element in a suspenseful scene. It can signal dramatic events, tense moments, or triumphant resolutions.	• Consider how **music** signals major events. You can often predict when something good or bad is about to happen through musical cues. • Notice how your emotions change when music is used. Ask yourself: What effect does the music have on me?	

MEDIA STUDY: TEACHING OPTIONS

Teaching Option 1: The Basics (1–2 Days)
1. Begin the Media Study using the material provided on pages 136–137.
2. Show the Introduction on MediaSmart. Then show the First Viewing. As they watch, have students use the Viewing Guide on page 138, along with the corresponding copy master on page 157 of the Resource Manager. Discuss their responses.
3. Return to the pupil book for the extension activities on page 139.

Teaching Option 2: In-Depth Study (2–3 Days)
1. Begin the Media Study using pages 136–137.
2. Show the Introduction and First Viewing from MediaSmart. Then continue on MediaSmart with the Media Lessons, using the teacher notes available in the Resources section.
3. Show the Guided Analysis presentation. Have students record their observations on the Student Viewing Guide available in the Resources section from MediaSmart.
4. Return to the book, page 139.

Media Literacy

To introduce the page, review with students the definition of *suspense.* Have them identify memorable suspenseful scenes from films they have seen and explain why these were so suspenseful. Ask students:

• How did you feel when you watched this scene?

• What film techniques increased the suspense?

On the board, record student responses to the second question. Make sure that *camera shots, editing,* and *music* are included on the list. Then discuss the chart on this page.

• **Camera Shots** Explore additional types of camera shots, such as eye-level shots or low-angle shots, and help students identify likely effects of these on mood. For example, how would a shot of a pool ball from the close-up, eye-level view of a player increase suspense about the game's outcome?

• **Editing** Remind students that films are edited to manipulate the viewers' sense of time and place. Point out that rapid cuts between shots telescope time and create fast-paced excitement, especially when the shots alternate between simultaneous events in different locations. Challenge students to make a timeline of parallel events as they watch the clip, indicating the three locations (*Odyssey* command module, Mission Control, and the living room) and what happens in each one, using different colors of ink.

• **Music** Have students think about different kinds of music that affect their emotions. Ask them to describe music that makes them happy, sad, or nervous. List features of each type of music for students to reference as they listen to the music in the clip. For example, screeching violins or pounding drums might create a tense, suspenseful mood. Challenge students to identify emotions the music evokes.

VIEWING GUIDE

1. Before students view the clip, tell them they will identify specific film techniques used to keep viewers on the edge of their seats. Encourage them to watch and listen for these elements:

   • the different types of **camera shots**, such as close-ups and point-of-view, and how these shots convey the way the astronauts, their families, and the Houston crew feel

   • the use of parallel **editing** to show the actions and reactions of people in each of the three locations and to heighten viewers' anticipation

   • the way **music** provides emotional cues to events that happen in the scene and creates suspense, increasing in tension as hope fades, then soaring into more uplifting music as relief explodes

2. Have students watch the film clip at least three times: once for camera shots, once for editing techniques, once for music. For the third viewing, have them view the clip with the volume turned off to help them understand how music contributes to the suspense in this scene.

R RESOURCE MANAGER—Copy Masters
   Viewing Guide p. 157
   Close Viewing p. 158
   Viewing Activity p. 159

Use this resource with the Viewing Guide:

🎬 **MediaSmart DVD-ROM**

MediaScope on **thinkcentral.com**

ANSWERS

FIRST VIEWING: Comprehension

1. *within three minutes of reentry into Earth's atmosphere*

2. *the South Pacific*

CLOSE VIEWING: Media Literacy

Possible answers:

3. *The close-ups reveal fear, anxiety, hope, dread, and, finally, elation and relief. They help viewers relate to the characters in the scene by putting viewers "in the scene."*

Media 💿 Smart DVD-ROM
• **Film Clip:** *Apollo 13*
• **Director:** Ron Howard
• **Rating:** PG
• **Genre:** Drama
• **Running Time:** 7.5 minutes

Viewing Guide for
Apollo 13

As you watch this scene, keep in mind that it occurs near the climax of *Apollo 13*. The astronauts are in the *Odyssey* command module. This is the only part of the spacecraft that has any chance to reenter Earth's atmosphere. At Mission Control, NASA workers stand by. Family members and others watch and wait.

Plan on viewing the scene several times. To help you analyze suspense, refer to the questions that follow.

NOW VIEW

FIRST VIEWING: Comprehension

1. **Recall** When does NASA expect to regain communication with Lovell, Haise, and Swigert?

2. **Clarify** Where does NASA expect the *Odyssey* command module will land?

CLOSE VIEWING: Media Literacy

3. **Make Inferences** What emotions are revealed through the **close-up shots** of family and friends? What effect do you think these shots have on viewers?

4. **Analyze Parallel Editing** The director uses parallel editing to show how people are waiting at different locations for the reentry of the command module. Describe two of the locations and explain why you think the director chose them.

5. **Analyze Sound** What kinds of sounds contribute to the realism of the event?

6. **Interpret Techniques** How would you describe the **music** soon after the command module goes into blackout?

7. **Evaluate Suspense** The director of *Apollo 13* uses several techniques to build suspense, including **close-up shots, long shots, music, absence of sound, voice-over,** and a **high-stakes deadline**. Which techniques kept you on the edge of your seat? Explain.

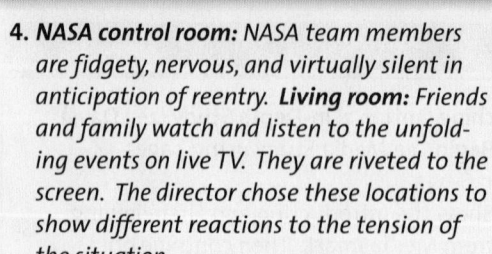

---

4. *NASA control room: NASA team members are fidgety, nervous, and virtually silent in anticipation of reentry. Living room: Friends and family watch and listen to the unfolding events on live TV. They are riveted to the screen. The director chose these locations to show different reactions to the tension of the situation.*

5. *Sounds include flames burning the capsule, the capsule shaking, helicopter blades spinning, control-room monitors beeping, and the TV anchor's worried voice.*

6. *The music is eerie and slightly ominous.*

7. *High-stakes deadline: The three-minute time window frames the scene with suspense. Absence of sound: The absence of sound reflects the silence of space and the paralyzing fear of those waiting. Close-up shots: The close-up shots convey emotional states and create tension.*

Write or Discuss

Analyze Accounts in Print and Film When making a film based on a real-life drama, most directors feel an obligation to be true to the original story. In the nonfiction account, "The Race to Save *Apollo 13*," the writer uses specific details to build suspense at critical moments. Does the filmmaker use the same details to create suspense in the film excerpt? Determine which details are emphasized in each account. To prepare, think about how the writer and the filmmaker used the techniques in each medium to incorporate

- facts
- references to time
- questions about outcome

In making the film, would you have emphasized different details? Why or why not?

COMMON CORE

W 9b (RI 7) Draw evidence from informational texts; analyze various accounts of a subject told in different mediums, determining which details are emphasized in each account. **SL 2** Integrate multiple sources of information presented in diverse media or formats.

Produce Your Own Media

Create a Storyboard A **storyboard** is a device that is used to plan the shooting of a film. It consists of a sequence of sketches showing what will appear in the film's shots. Storyboards help directors create a vision of the finished product. Using the student model as a guide, create a storyboard that depicts an event that is driven by a high-stakes deadline.

Media Tools
THINKcentral
Go to **thinkcentral.com**.
KEYWORD: HML10-139

HERE'S HOW Think of your storyboard as a rough sketch of a scene. Here are some tips to get you started:

- Be sure to include between eight and ten shots.
- Use close-up shots to show characters' emotions and to create tension.
- Vary shots to show different images or different actions taking place.
- Show how time is a critical factor.

Tech Tip

If a video camera is available, film the scene.

STUDENT MODEL

MEDIA STUDY **139**

Produce Your Own Media

Rubric: Create a Storyboard An effective story-board should

- depict an event with a high-stakes deadline
- incorporate both visuals and sounds
- include eight to ten shots, and indicate their sequence
- indicate and label a variety of shots, including close-ups, long shots, and point-of-view shots to capture the tension caused by the approaching deadline

- demonstrate the importance of time through the shortening or lengthening of the time frame in which events happen

R RESOURCE MANAGER—Copy Master
Produce Your Own Media p. 160

Assess and Reteach

Write or Discuss

COMMON CORE W 9b (RI 7), SL 2

Analyze Accounts in Print and Film Students should evaluate the ways in which the nonfiction account and the film select different details to create suspense. They should evaluate how the details add to the suspense of the print version and the film version of this event. Students should indicate what details they might have emphasized and explain how those selections would contribute to the film.

MEDIA STUDY WRAP—UP

Have students summarize what they have learned about film techniques directors use to create suspense. Ask students to use *close-up shot, long shot, point-of-view shot, parallel editing, high-stakes deadline,* and *music.*

RETEACH

For students who are unable to apply the Media Study Skills, select from these reteaching options:

- **Camera Shots** Have students put themselves in the places where the camera would go, so they can get a sense of how the shots will look. Experiment with a book. Place the book on a table, and have students bend down until the book is at eye level to experience an eye-level shot. Discuss how different camera angles change their perceptions of the book.
- **Editing** Ask students to name some of their favorite fast-paced movies and TV shows. Then have students name some slower-paced movies and shows. Discuss how the visuals are edited. How does the editing contribute to the pacing?
- **Music** Music in movies and on TV is designed to affect emotions. Draw a two-column chart on the board. Have students volunteer their favorite songs. List the titles in one column of the chart. Next have students explain what emotions they identify with the songs. Record those in the second column. Have students discuss the ways music is used in and TV programs.

Media Tools
THINKcentral

Media study keywords point to **MediaScope**, a Web site that helps students strengthen media analysis and production skills.

Exile
Poem by Julia Alvarez

Crossing the Border
Poem by Joy Harjo

SUMMARIES

"Exile" In this poem, the speaker addresses her father as she recalls the time when, as a ten-year-old, she and her family fled the Dominican Republic and arrived in New York City. Then she recalls walking with her father in New York City, trying to get used to her new home but feeling like an outsider.

"Crossing the Border" In this poem, the speaker describes what happens to her and others as they cross the border from the United States into Canada on their way to a meeting of indigenous people. A border guard eyes them suspiciously just because they are "Indians"; he even assumes that the "Moravian Town" they are heading for is a bar.

What makes you feel like an **OUTSIDER?**

Lead into the question by asking students to describe stories and movies in which a character has experienced alienation. Extend the discussion by having students complete the *QUICKWRITE.*

What makes you feel like an **OUTSIDER?**

Have you ever felt separate from others, like you did not belong? A sense of alienation can come from having a different ethnic background, being dressed differently, having different values, or other causes. Almost everyone has had such feelings at one time or another.

QUICKWRITE Write a brief journal entry about a time when you felt alienated. Where were you, and what made you feel different from others? Did the others intend to make you uncomfortable? What thoughts ran through your mind, and what did you end up doing? Exploring your own experience may help you understand the speakers in the two following poems.

I felt alienated when...

140

See resources on the **Teacher One Stop DVD-ROM** *and on* **thinkcentral.com**.

 RESOURCE MANAGER UNIT 1
Plan and Teach, pp. 161–168
Text Analysis and Reading
  Skill, pp. 169–172†*

DIAGNOSTIC AND SELECTION TESTS
Selection Tests, pp. 51–54

 BEST PRACTICES TOOLKIT
Cluster Diagram, p. B18

TECHNOLOGY
- Teacher One Stop DVD-ROM
- Student One Stop DVD-ROM
- Audio Anthology CD
- GrammarNotes DVD-ROM
- ExamView Test Generator
  on the **Teacher One Stop**

* Resources for Differentiation   † Also in Spanish   ‡ In Haitian Creole and Vietnamese

TEXT ANALYSIS: NARRATIVE POETRY

A **narrative poem** is a poem that tells a story. Like a short story, it contains characters, setting, and a plot driven by conflict. However, the narrative in a poem is much more condensed. The speaker begins to relate events immediately, without introducing himself or herself as a short story's narrator might. The story is developed through compact images instead of lengthy description or passages of dialogue. Time may shift abruptly, without clear transitions.

As you read "Exile" and "Crossing the Border," prepare to summarize the stories told in the poems. Ask these questions:

- Who are the characters?
- What are the settings?
- What conflicts do the characters face?
- How are the conflicts resolved?

READING STRATEGY: READING POETRY

The following strategies can help you unlock the meaning of the two poems in this lesson and other poetry you'll read.

- You must read a poem slowly, line by line. Notice how the poem is structured. Lines are grouped in **stanzas,** comparable to paragraphs in prose. Visualize the images in each stanza.

- It is especially important to interpret **figurative language** in poetry. Often, words in poems communicate ideas beyond their literal meaning. The speaker in "Exile," for example, refers to herself as swimming but is not physically doing so. The key to understanding the poem is seeing what she compares to swimming.

- Reading a poem aloud to yourself, to a partner, or in a small group will help you identify the speaker of a poem. As you read or listen to the poem, make inferences about gender, age, ethnicity, and attitudes. Using a graphic like the one shown, take notes about the speaker in each poem.

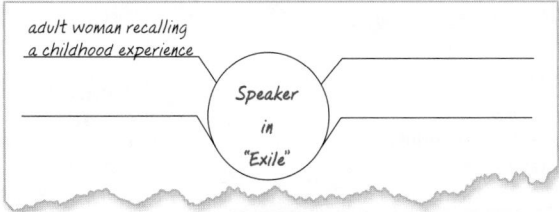

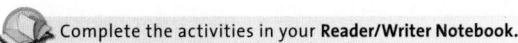

Complete the activities in your **Reader/Writer Notebook.**

Meet the Authors

Julia Alvarez
born 1950

American-Born Immigrant
Julia Alvarez was born in New York City. Shortly after her birth her family returned to their homeland, the Dominican Republic. At that time, it was ruled by Rafael Trujillo, a cruel dictator. The family was forced to flee in 1960 after Julia's father's participation in a failed plot to overthrow Trujillo. They returned to New York, where Alvarez had to adjust to a new language and way of life. "A lot of what I have worked through," she says, "has had to do with coming to this country and losing a homeland and a culture."

Joy Harjo
born 1951

Word Artist
Joy Harjo was born in Tulsa, Oklahoma. Her mother was part Cherokee, and her father was a full-blooded Muskogee, or Creek. Growing up, Harjo expected to become a visual artist but later decided to devote herself to poetry. Harjo often writes about the clash between Native American culture and the culture of mainstream America. She has noted that native women "constantly bump up against images of Indians that have nothing or nearly nothing to do with our lives."

Authors Online
Go to **thinkcentral.com.** KEYWORD: HML10-141

141

Teach

Model the Skill: NARRATIVE POETRY

To model how to make inferences and draw conclusions about elements of poetry, write these lines of poetry on the board and read them aloud:

> One balmy morn in early June,
> I cycled to my uncle's farm.
> The lettuces were in full bloom.
> The strawberries' ripe, honeyed charm
> Enticed me like a siren song—
> Likewise the chard, deep green and red.
> I didn't think I'd picked too long,
> But then the basket on my head
> Grew overfull . . . Its sides gave way . . .
> And so I lost my tasty haul that day!

Tell students what these lines convey about the main character, setting, and conflict in the story this poem is telling. The main character has bicycled to a farm to pick fruits and vegetables on a balmy morning in early June. The speaker's basket breaks and the produce spills.

GUIDED PRACTICE Ask students to think of poems and songs that tell a story.

Model the Skill: READING POETRY

Model how to draw conclusions about the structure and elements of poetry. Use the lines to reinforce students' understanding.

- Point out that the ten lines form a **stanza** unified by its rhyme scheme.

- Explain the meaning of the words *enticed* and *siren song* in line 5.

- Have students use the Graphic Organizer to list their inferences about the speaker.

GUIDED PRACTICE Ask students to describe what they visualize, taste, and hear when they read this stanza.

R RESOURCE MANAGER—Copy Master
Reading Poetry p. 171

DIFFERENTIATED INSTRUCTION

FOR STRUGGLING READERS

Rewrite the stanza written on the board for the **TEXT ANALYSIS** activity in the form of a paragraph, without line breaks:

> One balmy morn in early June, I cycled to my uncle's farm. The lettuces were in full bloom. The strawberries' ripe, honeyed charm enticed me like a siren song— likewise the chard, deep green and red. I didn't think I'd picked too long, but then the basket on my head grew overfull. . .

Its sides gave way. . . And so I lost my tasty haul that day!

Point out the sentences and punctuation, and then read the paragraph aloud. Explain to students that they can read poetry "in sentences," stopping or pausing slightly when they reach a punctuation mark rather than at the ends of lines—just as they would if they were reading prose. Then ask students to consider how the paragraph is different from the stanza of poetry.

READ WITH A PURPOSE

Help students set a purpose for reading by looking for expressions of alienation used in each poem. Have them look for similarities in the experiences of both writers.

TEXT ANALYSIS   COMMON CORE   RL 10

A NARRATIVE POETRY

Possible answer: The time is 1960, and the place is Ciudad Trujillo, the capital of the Dominican Republic. The people mentioned are the speaker, her parents (Papi and Mami), her sisters, and Papi's brothers. Their conflict is that they are fleeing their home-land. The adults are fearful of being dis-covered before they can get away. They are also worried about alarming the children, so they are pretending that they are simply going to the beach. The speaker senses that something is wrong because her uncles are "chuckling phony chuckles" (line 10), and her mother's "red eyes" (line 14) reveal that she has been crying.

Extend the Discussion Have students reread the biography of the poet and relate what they have read so far to events from her life.

READING STRATEGY   COMMON CORE   RL 4

B READING POETRY

Possible answer: The speaker is going with the flow and thus "swimming" in a figura-tive way. Instead of being frightened by what is happening, as she usually would be, she finds herself able to rise to the occa-sion rather than "sinking down" under the weight of her family's ordeal.

Exile

JULIA ALVAREZ

Ciudad Trujillo,[1] New York City, 1960

The night we fled the country, Papi,
you told me we were going to the beach,
hurried me to get dressed along with the others,
while posted at a window, you looked out

5 at a curfew-darkened Ciudad Trujillo,
speaking in worried whispers to your brothers,
which car to take, who'd be willing to drive it,
what explanation to give should we be discovered . . .

On the way to the beach, you added, eyeing me.
10 The uncles fell in, chuckling phony chuckles,
What a good time she'll have learning to swim!
Back in my sisters' room Mami was packing

a hurried bag, allowing one toy apiece,
her red eyes belying her explanation:
15 *a week at the beach so Papi can get some rest.*
She dressed us in our best dresses, party shoes. **A**

Something was off, I knew, but I was young
and didn't think adult things could go wrong.
So as we quietly filed out of the house
20 we wouldn't see again for another decade,

I let myself lie back in the deep waters,
my arms out like Jesus' on His cross,
and instead of sinking down as I'd always done,
magically, that night, I could stay up, **B**

---

1. **Ciudad Trujillo:** the name of the capital of the Dominican Republic from 1936–1961, which the dictator Trujillo renamed after himself.

Analyze Visuals ▶

How do you interpret this surrealistic painting, titled *Utopie* [Utopia]? What connections can you make between it and the poem "Exile"?

A NARRATIVE POETRY
Notice the place and time of events. Who are the people mentioned and what **conflicts** do they face?

B READING POETRY
The speaker is not literally floating in water. What is she actually doing?

DIFFERENTIATED INSTRUCTION

FOR ENGLISH LANGUAGE LEARNERS

The phrase "something was off" in line 17 is an idiom meaning that something seems suspi-cious. The speaker in the poem senses that something is off when her family lies to her about where they are going. Pair students and ask them to discuss whether they have ever been in a situation where they suspected that "something was off." What clues did they notice that made them suspicious? Ask students to start their discussion by completing the phrase "I noticed that something was off when …"

FOR STRUGGLING READERS

Options for Reading Read the poem aloud to students, emphasizing the drama and tension of the escape and then the wonder and bewilderment once the family reaches New York. You may want to have groups of students read sections of the poem together aloud. Appropriate sections are lines 1–16, 17–28, 29–36, 37–44, 45–56, 57–68.

Utopie (1999), Bob Lescaux. Oil on canvas, 81 cm × 65 cm. Private Collection. Photo © The Bridgeman Art Library.

25 floating out, past the driveway, past the gates,
    in the black Ford, Papi grim at the wheel,
    winding through back roads, stroke by difficult stroke,
    out on the highway, heading toward the coast.

    Past the checkpoint, we raced towards the airport,
30 my sisters crying when we turned before
    the family beach house, Mami consoling,
    there was a better surprise in store for us!

    She couldn't tell, though, until . . . until we were there.
    But I had already swum ahead and guessed
35 some loss much larger than I understood,
    more danger than the deep end of the pool. **C**

C NARRATIVE POETRY
What new **conflict** does the speaker recognize?

BACKGROUND

Trujillo's Rule in the Dominican Republic
Rafael Leonidas Trujillo Molina seized power in the Dominican Republic in 1930 and ruled for 30 brutal years. Citizens had little freedom and no opposition was permitted. His regime was noted for its corruption. That period was successful economically, but the benefits went mostly to a privileged few, especially members of the Trujillo family. Several attempts were made to overthrow Trujillo. The poet's father was involved in one attempt in 1960. Conspirators finally shot and killed Trujillo in 1961.

Analyze Visuals

Possible answer: Utopie *refers to a perfect place. The image of the boat sailing into the clouds symbolizes an escape to such a place. In a similar way, the family in "Exile" leave their homeland for New York City, a foreign place they hope will be a land of promise.*

About the Art Bob Lescaux (b. 1928) is a French artist who works in a style called surrealism, which began in Europe during the 1920s. This style attempts to evoke the strange, dreamlike images and feelings of the unconscious by portraying seemingly realistic images and objects in bizarre or incongruous juxtapositions.

TEXT ANALYSIS

COMMON CORE RL 10

C NARRATIVE POETRY

Possible answer: The speaker recognizes that once the family escapes from the Dominican Republic, they will face challenges and dangers in their new home.

TIERED DISCUSSION PROMPTS

Direct students to lines 29–32. Use these prompts to help students understand the speaker's parents motivation:

Analyze Why did Mami tell the sisters that there was a "better surprise" when they turned before the beach house? *Possible answer: Mami wanted to keep the girls calm.*

Evaluate In these circumstances, was Mami's lie to the girls justified? *Possible answer: Yes, Mami realized the family had to leave the country and needed to keep the girls as calm as possible.*

 **READING POETRY**

Possible answer: *The speaker and her father have been set adrift in the sense that they have been forced to leave their native country, which represents everything that has kept them secure and anchored to a sense of home and belonging.*

 *Model the Skill:* **NARRATIVE POETRY**

Model how to provide evidence that supports understanding by comparing line 45 with the setting at the beginning of the poem. Brainstorm with students the changes that the family has faced between the beginning of the poem and this time. *Possible answer:* *The new setting, New York City, sets up the conflict of adapting to a new place. Papi and the speaker both look and dress differently from the mannequins, which represent "ideal" Americans. The family will have to get used to a different way of life—different clothing, different values, different customs.*

 **READING POETRY**

Possible answer: *The comparison to swimmers brings to mind the idea of taking the risk of plunging into a new environment— one that might present new opportunities and joys or new dangers.*

REVISIT THE BIG QUESTION

What makes you feel like an OUTSIDER?

Discuss Based on lines 49–56, why does the mannequin family in the store window make the speaker and her father feel like outsiders? *Possible answer:* *The man and girl in the window look completely different from the speaker and her father. They represent an ideal American family, one that makes the speaker and her father feel like foreigners—outsiders— who don't belong in the United States.*

At the dark, deserted airport we waited.
All night in a fitful sleep, I swam.
At dawn the plane arrived, and as we boarded,
40   Papi, you turned, your eyes scanned the horizon

as if you were trying to sight a distant swimmer,
your hand frantically waving her back in,
for you knew as we stepped inside the cabin
that a part of both of us had been set adrift. **D**

45   Weeks later, wandering our new city, hand in hand,
you tried to explain the wonders: escalators
as moving belts; elevators: pulleys and ropes;
blond hair and blue eyes: a genetic code.

We stopped before a summery display window
50   at Macy's, *The World's Largest Department Store,*
to admire a family outfitted for the beach:
the handsome father, slim and sure of himself,

so unlike you, Papi, with your thick mustache,
your three-piece suit, your fedora hat, your accent.
55   And by his side a girl who looked like Heidi
in my storybook waded in colored plastic. **E**

We stood awhile, marveling at America,
both of us trying hard to feel luckier
than we felt, both of us pointing out
60   the beach pails, the shovels, the sandcastles

no wave would ever topple, the red and blue boats.
And when we backed away, we saw our reflections
superimposed, big-eyed, dressed too formally
with all due respect as visitors to this country.

65   Or like, Papi, two swimmers looking down
at the quiet surface of our island waters,
seeing their faces right before plunging in,
eager, afraid, not yet sure of the outcome. **F**

D **READING POETRY**
In what sense have the speaker and her father been "set adrift"?

E **NARRATIVE POETRY**
Notice that the **setting** has changed. What new **conflict** does it present?

F **READING POETRY**
What ideas does this comparison to swimmers bring to mind?

DIFFERENTIATED INSTRUCTION

FOR STRUGGLING READERS

Direct Address Make sure students recognize that throughout the poem, the speaker is speaking to her father, Papi, using the pronoun *you*. Point out that even though she is addressing her father, he is not necessarily physically present as she speaks her poem.

FOR ADVANCED LEARNERS/PRE–AP

Interpreting Poetry Ask students to explain the speaker's translations of the unfamiliar things her family encounters in New York City (lines 45–48). In particular, what does she mean by "genetic code"?

CROSSING THE BORDER

JOY HARJO

We looked the part. **G**
It was past midnight, well into
the weekend. Coming out of Detroit
into the Canada side, border guards
5 and checks. We are asked, "Who are you Indians
and which side are you from?"
Barney answers in a broken English.
He talks this way to white people
not to us. "Our kids."
10 My children are wrapped
and sleeping in the backseat.
He points with his lips to half-eyed
Richard in the front.
"That one, too."
15 But Richard looks like he belongs
to no one, just sits there wild-haired
like a Menominee would.
"And my wife. . . ." Not true.
But hidden under the windshield
20 at the edge of this country
we feel immediately suspicious.
These questions and we don't look
like we belong to either side.

"Any liquor or firearms?"
25 He should have asked that years ago
and we can't help but laugh.
Kids stir around in the backseat
but it is the border guard who is anxious.
He is looking for crimes, stray horses
30 for which he has no apparent evidence. **H**

G **READING POETRY**
Read the first stanza
aloud. What do you learn
about the speaker in the
poem?

H **NARRATIVE POETRY**
What is the **conflict**
between the border guard
and the Indians?

EXILE / CROSSING THE BORDER **145**

Prereading for this poem is found on page 140.

BACKGROUND

Native American Homelands Many Native Americans lived in Wisconsin and Michigan before Europeans settled there. Among them were the Menominee mentioned in the poem, of whom about 7,000 still live in Wisconsin. The speaker in the poem comes from Milwaukee, which has a sizable Native American population. Milwaukee has been the home to members of many indigenous people, including the Winnebago, Sauk, Fox, Ojibwa, Ottawa, and Potawatomi.

READING STRATEGY COMMON CORE RL 4

G Model the Skill: READING POETRY

To model how to make inferences and draw conclusions about the poem, have students reread lines 5–11. These lines contain clues about the speaker's ethnicity (line 5) and gender (lines 9–10). Have students read the remaining lines of the stanza to learn about the speaker's attitudes and record those clues in their graphic organizers. *Possible answer: The speaker is Native American, traveling with her children and a man named Barney. She recognizes that people often have prejudices against Native Americans.*

TEXT ANALYSIS COMMON CORE RL 10

H NARRATIVE POETRY

Possible answers: The conflict involves the guard's prejudicial assumption that the travelers must be guilty of some crime.

REVIST THE BIG QUESTION

What makes you feel like an OUTSIDER?

Discuss In lines 1–9, how does Barney's response to the guard reflect his alienation from mainstream society? *Possible answer: He talks differently to the guard as a white person than he would to the speaker and her children. His response suggests that he is intimidated by white people.*

FOR STRUGGLING READERS

Develop Reading Fluency Read the entire poem aloud to students, encouraging them to listen carefully for the story line. Then read a few lines at a time, and have students repeat what you have read with the same intonation and rhythm.

Distribute the copy master and have students work in pairs or groups to practice fluency.

R RESOURCE MANAGER—Copy Master
Reading Fluency p. 174

FOR ENGLISH LANGUAGE LEARNERS

Reading: Background On a map, point out the states of Michigan and Wisconsin. Show the journey the family would have made from Milwaukee to Detroit and then up to the Canadian border.

Analyze Visuals

Activity Ask students how the mood of the painting reflects the mood of the poem. *Possible answer: The stark contrast between the night sky and the red ground, together with the watchful "eyes" of the SUV, create a mood of wariness and isolation. Similarly, the speaker seems always to be on guard, wary of strangers and ready to confront the prejudice she has come to expect.*

READING STRATEGY COMMON CORE RL 4

① READING POETRY

Possible answer: Aspects of America that may follow the Indians into the north include the same kinds of prejudices.

TIERED DISCUSSION PROMPTS

Refer to lines 39–44 and use these prompts to help students understand why the border guard is so pleased:

Analyze Why does the border guard think that "Moravian Town" is a bar? *Possible answer: He thinks that all Native Americans like to drink.*

Synthesize Why is the border guard pleased in line 40? *Possible answer: He has been looking for "evidence" to confirm his prejudices about Indians and their bad habits; now he believes that he has found it.*

SELECTION WRAP–UP

READ WITH A PURPOSE Now that students have read both poems, reread lines 48 and 62–64 from "Exile" and lines 20–23 from "Crossing the Border." Point out that the speaker in each poem feels a sense of alienation from looking different. Ask students to think of other reasons why a person may feel alienated. *Possible answers: dressing or speaking differently, holding different political or moral views*

⭐ **CRITIQUE** Have students evaluate whether the speakers in the two poems are justified in feeling like outsiders.

"Where are you going?"
Indians in an Indian car, trying
to find a Delaware powwow
that was barely mentioned in Milwaukee.
35 Northern singing in the northern sky.
Moon in a colder air.
Not sure of the place but knowing the name
we ask, "Moravian Town?"

The border guard thinks he might have
40 the evidence. It pleases him.
Past midnight.
Stars out clear into Canada
and he knows only to ask,
"Is it a bar?"

45 Crossing the border into Canada,
we are silent. Lights and businesses
we drive toward could be America, too,
following us into the north. ①

Sport Utility Vehicle in Moonlight. Todd Davidson. © Todd Davidson/Getty Images.

COMMON CORE L 4c

Language Coach

Etymologies Reread line 34. Milwaukee is a city in Southeast Wisconsin. Its name means "good land" in the native Algonquian language. Look in a dictionary for word origins of other place names used in this poem: Detroit, Canada, Delaware, America.

---

① **READING POETRY**
What aspects of America might follow the Indians into the north?

DIFFERENTIATED INSTRUCTION

FOR STRUGGLING READERS

Comprehension: Clarify Meaning Make sure students understand that the Delaware (line 33) are another group of Native Americans, that a "powwow" is a meeting, and that "Moravian Town" is the name of a town.

FOR ENGLISH LANGUAGE LEARNERS

Language Coach COMMON CORE L 4c

Etymologies *Answer:*
Detroit: from French word détroit, meaning "strait"; Canada: from Iroquoian word kanata meaning "village" or "land"; Delaware: named after the first colonial governor of Virginia, French Baron De La Warr; America: Latin, derived from the name of Italian explorer Amerigo Vespucci

Comprehension

1. **Recall** In "Exile," where do the adults tell the speaker that the family is going?

2. **Clarify** Where does the family actually go?

3. **Recall** In "Crossing the Border," what border is the speaker trying to cross?

4. **Clarify** Why do the speaker and the others in the car want to cross the border?

Text Analysis

● 5. **Analyze Narrative Poetry** Using the following chart, analyze the narrative elements present in "Exile" and "Crossing the Border." Describe each element in the appropriate box.

Characters	Setting
Conflicts	Resolution (?)

6. **Interpret Figurative Language** Think about the experience Alvarez compares with swimming in "Exile." How fitting is the comparison?

7. **Make Inferences** In "Crossing the Border," how does the speaker feel after crossing into Canada? Explain how you know.

8. **Compare Speakers** Use the graphics you created as you read to describe the speaker in each poem. How do the speakers differ? How do they both express alienation?

■ 9. **Evaluate Poetry** Which poem more effectively tells a story? Which poem is more successful at creating a **mood**? Support your answers with evidence.

READING-WRITING CONNECTION

WRITING PROMPT	**REVISING TIP**
Extended Constructed Response: Story Passage How does a narrative poem differ from a short story? Write **three to five paragraphs** of a short story based on one of the poems. Then, in two or three sentences, comment on what is lost in the translation to prose.	If you wrote your response by hand, make sure your writing is legible. If you used a computer, be sure to use an easy-to-read font.

What makes you feel like an OUTSIDER?

How does alienation affect how people react to the world around them?

Practice and Apply

For preliminary support of post-reading questions, use these copy masters:

R RESOURCE MANAGER—Copy Masters
Narrative Poetry p. 169
Question Support p. 173

Additional selection questions are provided for teachers on page 165.

ANSWERS

Comprehension

1. *to the beach*

2. *to an airport to flee the country*

3. *the United States–Canadian border*

4. *to attend a powwow in Canada*

Text Analysis

COMMON CORE **RL 4, RL 10**

Possible answers:

5. ● **COMMON CORE FOCUS** *Analyze Narrative Poetry* **"Exile"**: *Characters: speaker and her family; Setting: Dominican Republic and New York City, 1960; Conflicts: family forced to flee and then feels alien in the U. S.; Resolution: speaker "plunges" into new culture but isn't sure of "outcome."* **"Crossing the Border"**: *Characters: speaker, her children, Barney, border guard; Setting: border between Michigan and Canada, past midnight; Conflict: Native Americans confronting white prejudice; Resolution: maybe none*

6. *The comparison works well, because "plunging" in to the water (lines 66–67) is a fitting metaphor for immersing oneself in a new culture, which requires taking risks.*

7. *The speaker feels disturbed by the exchange with the guard and worried that she will face similar prejudice in Canada.*

Assess and Reteach

8. *Students should note that the speaker in "Exile" feels like an outsider in a new country, while the speaker in "Crossing the Border" feels like an outsider in her own country. Both speakers express alienation through their silence.*

9. ■ **COMMON CORE FOCUS** *Evaluate Poetry Accept all well-supported answers.*

Language

READING-WRITING CONNECTION

After students have chosen a poem, ask them to write a plot summary organized by stanza. Encourage students to determine which ideas end and which continue into a new stanza.

What makes you feel like an OUTSIDER? *Possible answers:*
Alienation can make students feel they are not part of their community or school, and may prevent participation in activities.

Assess

DIAGNOSTIC AND SELECTION TESTS
Selection Test A, B/C pp. 51–54

Interactive Selection Test on **thinkcentral.com**

Reteach

Level Up Online Tutorials on **thinkcentral.com**

Reteaching Worksheets on **thinkcentral.com**
Literature Lesson 16: Narrative vs. Lyric Poetry

Focus and Motivate

COMMON CORE FOCUS

W 2a–f Write informative texts to examine complex ideas clearly through the effective selection and analysis of content. **W 4** Produce clear and coherent writing appropriate to task, purpose, and audience. **W 5** Develop and strengthen writing as needed by planning, revising, editing, rewriting, or trying a new approach, focusing on addressing what is most significant for a specific purpose and audience. **W 9a (RL 1)** Draw evidence from literary texts to support analysis. **W 10** Write routinely over shorter time frames for a range of tasks, purposes, and audiences. **L 1** Demonstrate command of the conventions of standard English grammar and usage. **L 2** Demonstrate command of the conventions of standard English punctuation. **L 2b** Use a colon to introduce a quotation. **L 3** Make effective choices for meaning or style.

WRITE WITH A PURPOSE

Explain to students that readers may not analyze a story in the same way. Remind them that their purpose is to make sense of the meaning of the work and convey their analyses clearly.

COMMON CORE TRAITS

Review the *COMMON CORE TRAITS* with students, focusing on development and organization of ideas. Compare the list of traits with the rubric on page 156.

ADDITIONAL TASKS

Write About a Play Write a review of a play or musical, explaining why you think your school drama department should put on a production of it.

Write About a Movie Write a movie review for your school newspaper. Explain why you think people should or should not go to see it.

Writing Online

The following tools are available online at **thinkcentral.com** and on **WriteSmart CD-ROM**:
- Interactive Graphic Organizers
- Interactive Student Models
- Interactive Revision Lessons

Writing Workshop
INFORMATIVE TEXT

Essential Course of Study ECOS

Literary Analysis

To analyze a work of literature—or determine meanings that are not obvious at first glance—you examine how the author uses language and literary elements to create meaning. In this workshop, you will learn how to write a literary analysis that looks closely at a short story and finds the meaning in it.

Complete the workshop activities in your **Reader/Writer Notebook**.

WRITE WITH A PURPOSE

WRITING TASK

Write a **literary analysis** of a short story you have read. Your analysis should use quotations and details from the story to develop your topic and help your audience find new meaning or significance in the work.

Idea Starters
- how conflict in "Harrison Bergeron" helps communicate the author's message
- how setting and mood in "Searching for Summer" affect the story's meaning
- how the author explores the role of heritage in "Everyday Use"

THE ESSENTIALS

Here are some common purposes, audiences, and formats for a literary analysis.

PURPOSES	AUDIENCES	FORMATS
• to examine complex ideas and concepts in literary texts • to convey the information clearly to others	• classmates and teacher • members of a reading club • readers of a literary magazine or Web site	• essay • literary journal article • oral presentation • blog • podcast

COMMON CORE TRAITS

1. DEVELOPMENT OF IDEAS
- presents an **engaging introduction**
- develops a **controlling idea** that offers an **analysis** of the short story's meaning
- supports key points of analysis with **relevant details** and **quotations from the text**
- concludes with a **summary of key points** and insights

2. ORGANIZATION OF IDEAS
- **organizes** ideas in a logical way
- uses varied **transitions** to create **cohesion** and **connect ideas**

3. LANGUAGE FACILITY AND CONVENTIONS
- establishes and maintains a **formal style** and **objective tone**
- includes **precise language**
- uses **reciprocal pronouns** correctly
- employs **correct grammar, mechanics**, and **spelling**

Writing Online

THINK central

Go to **thinkcentral.com**.
KEYWORD: HML10N-148

Writing Workshop Resources

R RESOURCE MANAGER UNIT 1

Plan and Teach, pp. 176–178
Prewriting–Editing, pp. 179–183
Writing Rubric, p. 184
Speaking and Listening, p. 185
Writing Support, p. 186*

 BEST PRACTICES TOOLKIT

Writing Template: Responding to Literature, p. C38

TECHNOLOGY

- **Teacher One Stop DVD-ROM**
- **Student One Stop DVD-ROM**
- **WriteSmart CD-ROM**
- **GrammarNotes DVD-ROM**

Writing Center on thinkcentral.com

*See resources on the **Teacher One Stop DVD-ROM** and on **thinkcentral.com**.*

* Resources for Differentiation

Planning/Prewriting

COMMON CORE **W 2a–f** Write informative texts to examine complex ideas clearly through the effective selection and analysis of content. **W 5** Develop writing as needed by planning. **W 9a (RL 1)** Draw evidence from literary texts to support analysis.

Getting Started

CHOOSE A STORY FOR ANALYSIS
Choose a short story to analyze for your essay. Reread short stories you have enjoyed, and think about what each story means.

▶ **ASK YOURSELF:**
- Which story do I keep thinking about long after having read it?
- What is the meaning or theme of this story?

THINK ABOUT AUDIENCE AND PURPOSE
As you begin to analyze the story you have selected, keep in mind that your **purpose** is to examine the author's use of language and story elements that shape the story's meaning. Your **audience** is likely to include people who have read the story and have their own ideas about its meaning.

▶ **ASK YOURSELF:**
- Who is my audience?
- Are they familiar with this short story?
- What ideas might my audience have about this story?
- What ideas and details do I have to share with my audience?
- What **domain-specific**, or specialized, vocabulary will my audience need to know in order to understand my analysis?

SELECT CONTENT DETAILS
Read the story a second or third time. In a reading log, list **stylistic elements** such as word choice, imagery, and tone. Write your thoughts about each item in the list.

▶ **WHAT DOES IT LOOK LIKE?**

Story Details	My Thoughts
"so clean and wavy"	It's a bare dirt yard, but she makes it sound wonderful.
"She never takes a shot without making sure the house is included."	This is Dee's own family, but she's acting like a tourist. That's insensitive.

WRITE A CONTROLLING IDEA
Review your reading log and identify the central idea behind the details you have listed and your own thoughts about it. Write a working **controlling idea**, or thesis statement, that explains this central idea. Then select key points from the story that prove your stance.

▶ **WHAT DOES IT LOOK LIKE?**

Controlling Idea
The author is saying that understanding and remembering your heritage is important.
Key Points
Key points covered in the body include the family home, Dee's name, and quilts.

DIFFERENTIATED INSTRUCTION

FOR ENGLISH LANGUAGE LEARNERS
Language: Reinforce Analytical Essay Terms Write these terms on the board, and review them with students:

- *organization:* how ideas are arranged and presented
- *introduction:* usually the first paragraph, which captures the reader's interest and states the controlling idea of the essay

- *body:* the main part of the essay, divided into paragraphs that present support for the controlling idea
- *evidence:* details that support the ideas in the body of the essay
- *concluding section:* the final section of the essay, which restates the controlling idea and summarizes the discussion with a final comment

---

Teach

Planning/ Prewriting
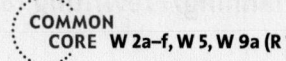**COMMON CORE** **W 2a–f, W 5, W 9a (R 1)**

▶ **CHOOSE A STORY FOR ANALYSIS** Explain to students that it is easier to write effectively if they are interested in what they are writing. Remind them that in order to convey the meaning of the story, they must understand it themselves.

▶ **THINK ABOUT AUDIENCE AND PURPOSE** Remind students that although they can expect their audience to have read the story, they should include some information for people who have not read it or who might have forgotten some of the story. Also, students should anticipate the audience's preconceived notions about the story's meaning and consider how to make use of them in their own writing.

▶ **SELECT CONTENT DETAILS** Model for students how to record stylistic elements in a reading log. Write or project on the board a copy of the reading log chart. Then, use a short story you have read in class to fill in story details and your thoughts about them. Remind students that their analyses should focus on stylistic elements, not just plot points.

▶ **WRITE A CONTROLLING IDEA** Remind students that a controlling idea must be specific, not general. The controlling idea will help the writer focus the essay and will guide readers' expectations, helping them to understand the author's ideas and arguments. Have students look at the controlling idea in the essay on page 153. Point out that the author has included the main supporting points in the controlling idea, which provides a basic outline for the reader.

R RESOURCE MANAGER—Copy Masters
Planning/Prewriting p. 179
Drafting p. 180
Revising pp. 181–182
Editing p. 183
Rubric p. 184
Writing Support p. 186

Planning/Prewriting *continued*

▶ **COLLECT EVIDENCE** Review the types of evidence students can use to support their key points: examples, quotations, and summaries. Remind students to use quotations in order to point out important words, highlight the author's use of stylistic elements, or make use of a particularly effective phrase or sentence. Explain that quotations must be written exactly as they appear in the short story and be enclosed in quotation marks.

YOUR TURN Give students time to find evidence in the stories they selected and to fill in their charts. If a student has trouble finding evidence to support his or her controlling idea, encourage that student to consider another approach for his or her analysis.

For interactive graphic organizers, see

💿 **Write***Smart* **CD-ROM**

Writing Center on thinkcentral.com

Planning/Prewriting *continued*

Getting Started

COLLECT EVIDENCE

Develop the **controlling idea** with well chosen, **relevant** (related) details as evidence that directly supports your points. Include a variety of each of the following:

Examples: specific instances from the story

Quotations: words, phrases, and sentences copied word-for-word from the story

Summaries: important information from the story summed up in your own words

Elaborate on, or explain, how each piece of evidence supports your controlling idea and affects the reader.

WHAT DOES IT LOOK LIKE?

Key Point	Evidence	Elaboration
Dee's name	summary: Dee takes African name; quotation: "You know as well as me you was named after your aunt Dicie." stylistic device: Dee (Wangero)	In rejecting her given name, which she shares with other family members, Dee shows she doesn't really understand the meaning of heritage.

PEER REVIEW Read your controlling idea to a peer who has read the short story. Then discuss the key points you intend to make and the evidence you've collected. Ask: Do you agree with my key points? Why or why not? Do I provide enough evidence to support them?

YOUR TURN In your *Reader/Writer Notebook,* develop your writing plan. Record a working version of your controlling idea. Then use a chart like the one on this page to organize your key points and evidence and make connections. Consider the following tips as you gather evidence:

- Collect a variety of relevant evidence, including concrete details, quotations, and summaries of story information, to develop your controlling idea.
- Double-check any quotations you plan to use to support your controlling idea. Record the exact words from the text and enclose them in quotation marks.
- Only cite stylistic elements that support your key points and help convey the meaning and message of your essay.
- If you have trouble finding supporting evidence for a key point, consider revising your controlling idea.

DIFFERENTIATED INSTRUCTION

FOR ENGLISH LANGUAGE LEARNERS

Writing: Controlling Idea Have students use sentence starters such as these to help them explore story elements and choose a focus:

- The main conflict happens when _____.
- The characters are changed by _____.
- The setting of the story is important because _____.
- The mood at the beginning of the story is _____.

- The author uses _____ (stylistic element) to _____.

FOR STRUGGLING WRITERS

Organize Supporting Evidence Remind students that the body of an essay contains several paragraphs, each paragraph clearly stating one idea that is supported by evidence. The details in each paragraph also support the controlling idea of the essay.

Drafting

The following chart shows how to organize your draft to create a coherent literary analysis.

COMMON CORE

W 4 Produce clear and coherent writing appropriate to task, purpose, and audience. **L 2** Demonstrate command of the conventions of standard English punctuation. **L 2b** Use a colon to introduce a quotation.

Organizing a Literary Analysis

INTRODUCTION
- Engage your **audience** by relating to their experiences. Identify the story's **title** and **author**.
- Include a clear **controlling idea** that presents your main idea, and note your **key points.**

▼

BODY
- Discuss one key point or **stylistic element** per paragraph, and cite **evidence** to back up your analysis.
- Maintain a **formal style** by using **precise language**, avoiding contractions and slang, and adopting an **objective**—neutral—**tone.**
- Use **varied transitions**, such as *at first, also*, and *another example*, to connect related ideas.

▼

CONCLUDING SECTION
- Summarize your key points and their **significance** to your topic.
- End with a question or statement for your audience to think about.

GRAMMAR IN CONTEXT: QUOTATIONS

Quotations from the short story can be used as evidence in your essay. Use quotation marks to enclose a direct quotation.

Type of Structure		Example
A directly quoted sentence begins with a capital letter. If the quotation is only a fragment of a sentence, it may begin with a lowercase letter.	▶	*The irony is obvious in Dee's statement that "She'd probably be backward enough to put them to everyday use!"*
Use a colon after an independent clause (complete sentence) that introduces a quotation.	▶	*The author reveals characters' emotions through key descriptions: "Dee (Wangero) looked at me with hatred."*
A direct quotation that includes character dialogue requires both single quotes and quotation marks. The character's words go inside the single quotes.	▶	*"'The quilts are priceless!' she exclaimed."*
A direct quotation can be set off from the rest of the sentence by a comma, a question mark, or an exclamation point, but not by a period.	▶	*"You know as well as me you was named after your aunt Dicie," Dee's mother replies.*

YOUR TURN

Develop a first draft. As you write, make sure to use correct punctuation and capitalization for any quotations you include in your analysis.

FOR ENGLISH LANGUAGE LEARNERS

Language: Punctuation Explain that periods and commas always appear inside quotation marks. Question marks and exclamation points appear inside quotation marks only when they are part of the quotations.

Write these examples on the board, and ask students whether the question marks or exclamation points should be placed inside or outside the quotation marks:

- My mother asked, "Where are you going*(?)*"
- Did you hear the officer shout, "Stop, or I'll shoot"*(?)*
- How strange it is to hear everyone tell me, "Have a nice day"*(!)*
- Rosa started laughing and said, "What a funny dog you have*(!)*"

Practice and Apply

Drafting

COMMON CORE W 4, L 2, L 2b

▶ *INTRODUCTION* Point out that the purpose of the introduction is to capture the reader's interest, as well as to introduce the controlling idea of the essay.

▶ *BODY* Remind students that quotations are only one type of evidence. Analytical essays should also include examples and summaries as evidence.

▶ *CONCLUDING SECTION* Remind students that the concluding section summarizes the key points in the essay and includes a final, thought-provoking question or statement. A focused and coherent concluding section will help the audience find new meaning or significance in the short story.

GRAMMAR IN CONTEXT: QUOTATIONS

For additional practice, write these two quotations on the board:

- "I believe," said the first lady, "that our souls are in our hands. For we do everything to the world with our hands. Sometimes I think we don't use our hands half enough; it's certain we don't use our heads."

- They all peered more intently at what their hands were doing. "Yes," said the third lady, "when you look back on a whole lifetime, it seems you don't remember faces so much as hands and what they did."

Have students select a fragment from either quotation and use correct punctuation when placing it in a sentence of their own. (***Example:** As one of the women remarks, "our souls are in our hands.")* Also, have students practice using a colon to quote one of the sentences in its entirety.

YOUR TURN

Have students complete the **Your Turn** exercise on their own. Remind them to use a quotation when the quotation would be more effective than a paraphrase.

For a template, see

BEST PRACTICES TOOLKIT—Transparency
Responding to Literature p. C38

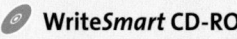

Write*Smart* CD-ROM
Writing Center on <u>thinkcentral.com</u>

Revising

COMMON CORE W5

Model the Skill Using a draft literary analysis on a transparency, model how to use the questions, tips, and strategies suggested in the chart to evaluate and revise. You might use an analytical essay by a student from another class or from last year. Be sure to remove the student's name from the analytical essay so that he or she is anonymous.

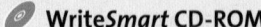

YOUR TURN Suggest that before exchanging analytical essays, students prepare questions about their own drafts. For instance, students might want to know how to improve the controlling idea, whether an example is relevant, or if they have expressed a particular idea clearly. After students have read each other's analytical essays, have them respond to the questions and make observations, including positive comments that will help their partners revise their drafts.

For interactive revision tools, see

WriteSmart CD-ROM

Writing Center on thinkcentral.com

Revising

When you revise, consider the content, organization, and style of your essay. The questions, tips, and strategies in the chart can help you improve your draft.

LITERARY ANALYSIS

Ask Yourself	Tips	Revision Strategies
1. Does the introduction grab the audience's interest? Does it include the name of the author and the title of the story?	▶ **Put a star** by sentences that get the audience interested. **Put a check mark** by the name of the author and the title of the story.	▶ **Add** an interesting opening sentence. **Add** the name of the author and the title of the story.
2. Does the introduction present a clear and engaging controlling idea? Does the introduction summarize key points?	▶ **Bracket** the controlling idea. **Label** each key point to be discussed in the body of the essay with *P1*, *P2*, and so on.	▶ If your controlling idea seems boring or obvious, **rewrite** it to make it more engaging. **Summarize** key points in the introduction.
3. Does the body include a paragraph for each key point? Is the order of key points effective?	▶ **Label** each paragraph with the key point it discusses. Then **number** your key points in order of importance.	▶ **Add** a paragraph for each key point. **Rearrange** the key points by putting the most important point last.
4. Is each key point supported by evidence, such as concrete examples and relevant quotations?	▶ **Circle** each piece of evidence for a key point. **Draw an arrow** from each item to the point it supports.	▶ **Add** evidence to support your key points. **Rearrange** evidence so that it is in the paragraph containing the point it supports.
5. Do I maintain a formal style and objective tone throughout?	▶ **Bracket** contractions, casual language, or vague word choices.	▶ **Reword** text to avoid contractions. **Replace** instances of informal language with precise, formal words.
6. Does the concluding section summarize key points and reflect on their overall meaning? Does it include a question or statement for the audience to think about?	▶ **Underline** the summary of key points and their meaning. **Highlight** the question or statement for your audience to think about.	▶ **Add** a summary of your key points and their meaning. **Add** a question or statement for your audience to ponder.

YOUR TURN **PEER REVIEW** Exchange your literary analysis with a classmate, or read your essay aloud to your partner. As you read and discuss the essays, focus on the controlling idea, evidence, and organization. Make sure to discuss the effect of the author's use of stylistic elements. If necessary, provide concrete suggestions for improvement.

DIFFERENTIATED INSTRUCTION

FOR STRUGGLING WRITERS
Stylistic Elements Remind students to include sentences about the author's use of stylistic elements, such as word choice and sensory language, in their essays. An important part of the essay is to analyze the effects of these techniques on the reader.

FOR STRUGGLING WRITERS
Writing: Concluding Section To help students develop concluding sections for their literary analyses, ask them: What does the short story mean to you? What are your key points? What do you want the audience to think about? Have students work in pairs to discuss and respond to these questions and help one another draft their concluding sections.

 **COMMON CORE** **W 5** Strengthen writing as needed by revising, editing, rewriting, or trying a new approach, focusing on addressing what is most significant for a specific purpose and audience.

ANALYZE A STUDENT DRAFT

Read this draft; note the comments on its strengths as well as the suggestions for improvement.

Heritage and "Everyday Use"

by Lydia Rodriguez, Eisenhower College Prep

1 At first, Alice Walker's story "Everyday Use" seems to be about minor conflicts. However, Walker uses mother-daughter conflicts to describe her beliefs about how people should honor their heritage. The conflicts Alice Walker discusses—over a family's home, a daughter's name, and some heirloom quilts—make the reader think about the larger question of heritage.

> In her introduction Lydia focuses on the **controlling idea** of her essay and the **key points** that will support her analysis.

2 The conflict over the family's home is clear from the beginning of the story. The mother loves the family home. When the family's previous home burned down years before, her daughter Dee showed no emotion. Now when Dee comes to visit, she poses her mother and sister in front of their house and snaps pictures like a tourist. The mother sees the family home as part of her heritage. But Dee sees it only as the backdrop for a photo.

> Lydia covers a key point in each body paragraph. She provides **concrete examples** as supporting **evidence** for this key point.

3 Dee and her mother also disagree about names. Dee tells her family that she has given herself an African name, Wangero Leewanika Kemanjo. She tells her mother that "Dee" is "dead," saying, "I couldn't bear it any longer, being named after the people who oppress me." Dee's mother replies, "You know as well as me you was named after your aunt Dicie." But her daughter rejects the name, preferring to forget all the Dees who came before her. The author highlights this conflict by referring to Dee by both names: Dee (Wangero).

> Lydia summarizes the story and offers **quotations** as evidence of this conflict. To strengthen her analysis, she could discuss a stylistic element.

LEARN HOW Explain the Effect of Stylistic Elements   Lydia presents her key point about the conflict over Dee's name but could make her analysis stronger by explaining how a **stylistic element** used by the author affects the reader.

LYDIA'S REVISION TO PARAGRAPH 3

But her daughter rejects the name, preferring to forget all the Dees who came before her. The author highlights this conflict by referring to Dee by both names: Dee (Wangero). ∧

Through the stylistic element of putting the African name in parentheses, the author expresses the idea that the African name Dee gave herself is not as important as the name Dee's mother gave her, the one that connects her to her family's heritage.

WRITING WORKSHOP **153**

ANALYZE A STUDENT DRAFT

Explain that the Student Draft on this page is the first half of a literary analysis. Model reading the draft and the annotations in blue, and explain that the yellow highlighting illustrates the student's language choices. Explain that the following *Learn How* mini-lessons provide helpful information about ways to improve this student draft as well as their own.

LEARN HOW **Explaining the Effect of Stylistic Elements**

- Tell students that, while a reader may recognize a stylistic element—a technique that imbues a text with meaning or feeling beyond what it says literally—the reader may not explicitly recognize its effect.

- Point out that when writing an essay, it is important to analyze and exemplify the effect of any stylistic element students reference.

- Have students look for stylistic elements in the story they are writing about. Ask them to find uses of stylistic elements that support the main ideas in their essays. Then have students analyze the effects of those examples on the story's reader.

Explain that the Student Draft is continued and completed on this page. Read the draft and annotations aloud and discuss. Ask students to comment on the student writer's use of supporting evidence from the story.

LEARN HOW Build an Effective Concluding Section

Explain how the revised concluding section differs from the one in the draft: While the draft states that the mother has a different understanding of their heritage, the revision actually explains what her understanding is. Point out that the final sentence of the revised student draft contains quoted fragments of Dee's statements in the short story. This creates a strong concluding section about the meaning of the story.

YOUR TURN Allow students to take time to revise their drafts. Remind them to include evidence from the stories—both quotations and summaries—to support their main points. Ask them to pay particular attention to their analyses of story elements, including stylistic elements. Have they explained the quotation, summary, or element and its effect on readers? Have they drawn explicit ties between it and the idea in their essay it is meant to support?

For interactive tools, see

 WriteSmart CD-ROM

Writing Center on thinkcentral.com

---

❹   The last and most important confrontation between Dee and her mother comes when Dee asks for two quilts. Dee wants to hang the quilts in her home. Her mother had offered her a quilt when she went away to school, but Dee had rejected it as "old-fashioned, out of style." Now, she tells her mother they are *"priceless!"* When the mother tells Dee that she promised the quilts to the younger daughter as a wedding gift, Dee reacts furiously: "Maggie can't appreciate these quilts. She'd probably be backward enough to put them to everyday use!" Dee can't see that "everyday use" is exactly why the quilts were made. She is more interested in owning a quilt that was intricately hand sewn than in remembering and appreciating the people who sewed it. This has the effect of making Dee seem more interested in material things, rather than in a true appreciation of her heritage.

> Lydia makes her most important **key point** in the final paragraph before the concluding section. She supports it with a summary of information from the story and quotations.

❺   As Dee storms out of the house, she tells her mother, "You just don't understand . . . your heritage." The fact is, the mother and Maggie understand their heritage in ways Dee never will.

> Although Lydia makes a general statement about the meaning of the story, her **concluding section** is weak.

LEARN HOW Build an Effective Concluding Section To make her conclusion as strong and effective as it can be, Lydia needs to restate her overall impression of the short story and add an interesting question or statement for her audience to think about.

LYDIA'S REVISION TO PARAGRAPH ❺

The fact is, the mother and Maggie understand their heritage in ways Dee never will. ∧

To the mother, heritage lies in the work of her ancestors; in the humble house that shelters her; in the memories of Grandma Dee, Stash, and Dicie; and in the lovingly pieced quilts that will keep Maggie and her husband warm. The author uses a series of conflicts between the mother and Dee to show that a family's heritage is not something "priceless" to be hung on a wall as a piece of art. Instead, it should be part of people's daily lives—for "everyday use."

YOUR TURN **PEER REVIEW** Use the feedback from your peers and teacher as well as the two "Learn How" lessons to revise your essay. Evaluate how well your work fits the purpose of a literary analysis, communicates the meaning you intended, and addresses your audience.

154   UNIT 1: PLOT, SETTING, AND MOOD

DIFFERENTIATED INSTRUCTION

FOR ENGLISH LANGUAGE LEARNERS

Writing: Concluding Section Remind students that the concluding section of an essay often begins with a summary of the main points and why the main points are significant. The last line of the concluding section should give the reader something to think about and might refer back to the opening lines of the essay or ask a relevant question. Have students review their concluding sections again to be certain they have incorporated these features.

FOR STRUGGLING WRITERS

Evidence Remind students to provide support for their ideas throughout the essay, including in the concluding section. Have students work in pairs to help each other pinpoint which ideas need further support and identify the evidence in the short story.

Editing and Publishing

W 5 Develop and strengthen writing by revising, editing, rewriting, or trying a new approach. **L 1** Demonstrate command of the conventions of standard English grammar and usage. **L 3** Make effective choices for meaning or style.

COMMON CORE

In the editing stage, proofread your essay to make sure that it is free of grammar, usage, spelling, and punctuation errors. Such errors can distract your audience from your ideas about the meaning of the short story.

GRAMMAR IN CONTEXT: RECIPROCAL PRONOUNS

Reciprocal pronouns are a type of indefinite pronoun that refers to something or someone that may or may not be specifically named. Writers use reciprocal pronouns *(each other, one another)* to convey a shared action or feeling among the members of a plural subject.

> *Dee and her mother also disagree about names.*
>
> [In the sentence, "with each other" could be added after "disagree." The **reciprocal pronoun** "each other" would show a shared feeling between the subjects of Dee and her mother.]

While editing her essay, Lydia noticed an opportunity to use a reciprocal pronoun.

> *Dee can't see that "everyday use" is exactly why the quilts were made.* ∧
> *This conflict with one another highlights the differences among Dee, her sister, and her mother.*
>
> [The conflict is shared by Dee, her sister, and her mother.]

PUBLISH YOUR WRITING

Finally, you will share your literary analysis with an audience. Here are some options:

- Submit your essay to the school literary magazine.
- Publish your essay on a Web site for the fans of the author's work.
- Adapt your essay into an oral presentation and deliver it to an audience that has read the story.

YOUR TURN Proofread your essay for errors. Make sure you have used reciprocal pronouns to note shared feelings or actions among the members of plural subjects. Then, publish your final essay where your intended audience is likely to see it.

Editing and Publishing

COMMON CORE W 5, L 1, L 3

GRAMMAR IN CONTEXT: RECIPROCAL PRONOUNS

Make sure that students understand the concept of a plural subject by having them identify them in the sentences in the student model essay *("Dee and her mother"; the mother and Dee")*.

Write this sentence on the board:

> Isabella was angry with her brother, and he was angry with her.

Have students rewrite the sentence using a reciprocal pronoun. *(Isabella and her brother were angry with each other.)*

PUBLISH YOUR WRITING

Brainstorm with students about additional places to publish their literary analyses.

YOUR TURN Allow students time to revise their essays. Remind them to check for plural subjects that would benefit from the use of reciprocal pronouns. Also remind them to make sure they have analyzed their evidence thoroughly and explained how it supports their main ideas.

FOR STRUGGLING WRITERS

Language: Reciprocal Pronouns Review the following information about pronouns and reciprocal pronouns with students:

- Pronouns are used in place of nouns or other pronouns. The words or word groups to which pronouns refer are called their antecedents.

- Pronouns should agree with their antecedents in number, gender, and person. For example: **The boy** took *his* lunch to the park.

- The reciprocal pronouns *each other* and *one another* are indefinite pronouns that convey a shared action or feeling among the members of a plural subject.

Scoring Rubric

Explain to students that the best way to understand rubrics is to use them to score actual writing. Have students use the rubric to evaluate the final copies of the literary analyses they wrote in the Writing Workshop. Ask students to score their essays and then write brief paragraphs using the language of the rubric to explain the reasons for their scores.

For Rubric Bank, see

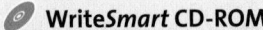 **WriteSmart CD-ROM**

Writing Center on **thinkcentral.com**

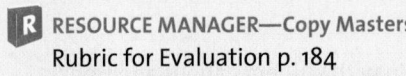

Assess

R **RESOURCE MANAGER**—Copy Masters
Rubric for Evaluation p. 184

Online Essay Scoring on **thinkcentral.com**

Reteach

Level Up Online Tutorials on **thinkcentral.com**
Reteaching Worksheets on **thinkcentral.com**

Writing Lesson 14: Writing a Controlling Idea

Writing Lesson 20: Integrating Quotations

Scoring Rubric

Use the rubric below to evaluate your literary analysis from the Writing Workshop or your response to the on-demand task on the next page.

LITERARY ANALYSIS

SCORE	COMMON CORE TRAITS
6	• **Development** Has an engaging introduction; includes a controlling idea with an insightful analysis of the short story; supports key points with relevant evidence; ends powerfully • **Organization** Arranges ideas in an effective, logical order; uses varied transitions to create cohesion and link ideas • **Language** Consistently maintains a formal style; uses precise language; shows a strong command of conventions
5	• **Development** Has an effective introduction; provides a controlling idea that offers an original analysis of the short story; supports key points with evidence; has a strong concluding section • **Organization** Arranges ideas logically; uses transitions to link ideas • **Language** Maintains a formal style; uses precise language; has a few errors in conventions
4	• **Development** Has an introduction that could be more engaging; includes a controlling idea that states an analysis of the short story; could use some more evidence; has an adequate concluding section • **Organization** Arranges ideas logically; could vary transitions more • **Language** Mostly maintains a formal style; needs more precise language at times; has a few distracting errors in conventions
3	• **Development** Has an adequate, though not memorable, introduction; has a controlling idea that makes an obvious statement about the short story; lacks sufficient support; has a routine concluding section • **Organization** Reflects some flaws in organization; needs more transitions to link related ideas • **Language** Frequently lapses into an informal style; uses some vague word choices; has some significant errors in conventions
2	• **Development** Has a weak introduction and a controlling idea that does not relate to the writing task; lacks specific evidence; has a weak concluding section • **Organization** Has organizational flaws; lacks transitions throughout • **Language** Uses an informal style and vague language; has many distracting errors in conventions
1	• **Development** Has no introduction or controlling idea; offers unrelated points as evidence; ends abruptly • **Organization** Includes a string of disconnected ideas with no overall organization • **Language** Uses an inappropriate style and vague, tired language; has major problems with grammar, mechanics, and spelling

Preparing for Timed Writing

COMMON CORE — **W 10** Write routinely over shorter time frames for a range of tasks, purposes, and audiences.

1. ANALYZE THE TASK — 5 MIN

Read the task carefully. Then, read it again, noting the words that tell the type of writing, the topic, the purpose, and the audience.

> **WRITING TASK** *Topic*  *Type of Writing*
>
> Choose a <u>short story that has personal meaning for you.</u> Write an <u>analysis</u> of the story
> *Audience*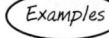
> to share with <u>a friend who has not read it.</u> In your essay, briefly summarize the story,
> identify a stylistic element the author uses to create the meaning you have gathered from
> it, and explain how the author uses that element to convey the story's meaning.
> ← *Purpose*

2. PLAN YOUR RESPONSE — 10 MIN

Consider these questions: What does the story mean to me? How does the author create that meaning? Respond to these questions with a controlling idea that provides the author and title of the story and briefly describes your ideas about the story's meaning. Then, list examples and details from the story as evidence to support your analysis.

> Controlling Idea
>
> Examples   Details

3. RESPOND TO THE TASK — 20 MIN

Begin drafting your essay. Follow these tips:

- Open your introduction by making a connection with your audience, for example, with a thought-provoking question. Add your controlling idea, then provide a brief summary (three to four sentences) of the story as it relates to your topic.
- Explain each key idea in its own body paragraph. Cite examples and details from the story as evidence to support each idea.
- Conclude with a summary of your key ideas and a statement or question about the broader meaning of the story as you understand it.

4. IMPROVE YOUR RESPONSE — 5–10 MIN

Revising Check your draft against the writing task. Does your draft clearly state your controlling idea about the meaning of the story? Have you included enough supporting evidence from the story? Do you end with a conclusion of the analysis?
Proofreading Find and correct errors in grammar, mechanics, and spelling. Make sure your edits are neatly written and legible.
Checking Your Final Copy Before you turn in your response, read it one more time to make sure that you have not missed any errors. Does your final essay represent your best work?

WRITING WORKSHOP **157**

COMMON CORE FOCUS

W 10 Write routinely over shorter time frames for a range of tasks, purposes, and audiences.

Preparing for Timed Writing

1. **Analyze the Task** Before students begin writing, encourage them to answer the following questions:
   - What is my time limit?
   - What are the core traits assessed in the scoring rubric?
   - Who is my audience?
   - What is my purpose?
2. **Plan Your Response** Point out to students that the scoring rubric emphasizes the need for relevant and specific evidence to support main ideas. Remind them to use specific examples, quotations, and summaries as evidence to back up each point.
3. **Respond to the Task** Remind students that their responses should be clearly focused. They should write an introduction with a clear controlling idea and a strong concluding section about the meaning of the work.
4. **Improve Your Response** Point out that the scoring rubric emphasizes showing a strong command of grammar, mechanics, and spelling. Remind students to proofread their essays and correct all errors.

Assess

Use the Scoring Rubric on page 156 to assess students' essays.

DIFFERENTIATED INSTRUCTION

FOR ENGLISH LANGUAGE LEARNERS

Writing: Proofreading Remind students that they can expect to make errors when responding to a writing task in a timed situation. While it may not be possible for them to correct all these errors, they should be aware of mistakes they commonly make in word choice, grammar, spelling, or mechanics. Encourage students to keep lists of their common errors and to look for and correct them before turning in timed writing assignments.

FOR STRUGGLING WRITERS

Analyzing Tasks Responding to a timed writing task can be difficult for struggling writers. Remind students to carefully read the task before starting to write. After writing but before handing in their work, students should review the task once again to be sure they have followed the instructions.

Focus and Motivate

COMMON CORE FOCUS

SL 4 Present information and supporting evidence clearly, concisely, and logically such that organization, development, and style are appropriate. **L1** Demonstrate command of the conventions of standard English grammar and usage when speaking.

SPEAK WITH A PURPOSE

Point out to students that their audience is likely to be composed of teachers and other students, although it might also include members of a reading club or readers of a literary magazine. Explain that practicing the presentation in advance will help students develop confidence and become more effective speakers.

COMMON CORE TRAITS

As students prepare to deliver their literary analyses remind them to keep in mind the *COMMON CORE TRAITS* of a strong oral presentation.

Practice and Apply

Adapting Your Essay

Model the Skill: **AUDIENCE**

Remind students that their listeners may not remember the short story or be able to reread it before the presentation. Explain to students the importance of beginning their presentations with a summary of the story they are analyzing. The summary should be brief, including all necessary information and no irrelevant details. For example, a speaker might summarize the beginning of "Embroidery" like this: "It's ten minutes to five, and three women are sitting together, doing embroidery and waiting for something to happen at five o'clock."

GUIDED PRACTICE Have students work in pairs to write three-sentence summaries of the short stories to which they are responding. Have them read the summaries aloud and give each other feedback.

R **RESOURCE MANAGER**—Copy Master
Speaking and Listening p. 185

Speaking & Listening Workshop

Presenting a Response to a Short Story

You have probably shared a response to a work before, such as telling your friend how much you liked a new song or movie, and why. When you talk about the meaning of a work, you are **presenting an analysis.**

Essential Course of Study **ECOS**

Complete the workshop activities in your **Reader/Writer Notebook.**

SPEAK WITH A PURPOSE	COMMON CORE TRAITS
TASK Adapt your literary analysis into an **oral presentation** that is appropriate for your audience. Practice delivering your presentation concisely so it is easy to follow.	**A STRONG ORAL PRESENTATION . . .** • presents the topic clearly and concisely • organizes information logically and coherently • offers compelling ideas and includes evidence to support them • uses effective verbal and nonverbal speaking techniques and shows a command of standard grammar and usage

COMMON CORE

SL 4 Present information and supporting evidence clearly, concisely, and logically such that organization, development, and style are appropriate. **L1** Demonstrate command of the conventions of standard English grammar and usage when speaking.

Adapting Your Essay

Because your audience will be listening to your literary analysis instead of reading it, you will need to adapt your essay to make it clear and easy to follow and use effective speaking techniques. Consider creating an outline of your main ideas and supporting details. In addition, follow these suggestions:

- **Audience** To help your audience follow your analysis, include a brief summary of the story to refresh their memories or to provide context for your ideas.
- **Introduction** Adapt the introduction of your essay to make it dramatic, but be sure to clearly and concisely state your controlling idea, or thesis.
- **Organization** Build interest and momentum. Present your ideas in a logical order, with strong supporting evidence from the story, so that listeners can follow your reasoning.
- **Conclusion** Sum up your key ideas and restate your analysis. End with a question or comment that gives your audience something to consider.
- **Scripting** Create a script. Neatly write a cue for your attention-getting introduction and controlling idea. Number key points and supporting evidence. Copy quotations just as they appear in the story. Underline words as a cue to emphasize them, and use long dashes to indicate dramatic pauses.

 **THINK** central
Speaking & Listening Online
Go to **thinkcentral.com.**
KEYWORD: HML10-158

> Dee tells her mother, "You just don't understand . . . your heritage," but it is *Dee* who does not understand it. The mother knows that her heritage is all around her—in her *house*, in her *family memories*, and in her beautiful *quilts*.

DIFFERENTIATED INSTRUCTION

FOR ENGLISH LANGUAGE LEARNERS

Language: Reinforce Literary Analysis Terms Explain to students that their oral presentations have the same goal as their literary analyses—to present an analysis of a short story and to provide evidence from the story to support their ideas.

Review key literary terms used in this and the writing workshop to discuss short stories:

- *character:* person in the story

- *conflict:* struggle between opposing forces that is a story's focus
- *mood:* feeling or atmosphere that a writer creates
- *plot:* the sequence of events in a story
- *setting:* time and place of the action of a story
- *theme:* underlying message about life or human nature that a writer wants the reader to understand

Delivering Your Presentation

The delivery of your literary analysis is as important as its content. Use both verbal and nonverbal techniques to clearly convey your information in a way that is appropriate for your audience and keeps everyone engaged.

Verbal Techniques

PACE	VOLUME	ENUNCIATION	STYLE
Vary your rate of speaking. Speak faster when you introduce your topic. Speak more slowly as you discuss your findings so that listeners can follow your line of reasoning.	Use an appropriate volume for the room in which you are speaking. Project your voice so that everyone in your audience can hear you.	Pronounce words clearly and read quotations carefully so that the audience understands the substance of your analysis.	Choose the style that is right for your audience and also for your topic. Use a conversational tone when speaking to classmates or friends. Avoid slang and colloquialisms in more formal settings or when discussing a serious topic.

Nonverbal Techniques

POSTURE	FACIAL EXPRESSIONS	GESTURES	EYE CONTACT
Stand up straight, but with a relaxed, comfortable stance. You will appear more authoritative, more engaging for audiences, and more confident. Turn to face different parts of the room. Walk toward or step back from the audience as your discussion requires.	Convey meaning with a variety of facial expressions, such as smiles, frowns, and raised eyebrows.	Use hand gestures to stress key points, to invite the audience to agree with your ideas, and to get or regain their attention.	Look directly at your audience. Make frequent eye contact with different individuals.

 YOUR TURN

As a Speaker Practice presenting your response to a friend, using appropriate verbal and nonverbal techniques described on this page. Afterward, ask for feedback on your delivery. Evaluate your audience's reaction and apply what you have learned to your actual presentation.

As a Listener Evaluate your friend's delivery of his or her presentation. Listen to make sure that the analysis is clear and effective and that evidence is organized in a way that makes ideas easy to follow. Provide feedback on the speaker's use of verbal and nonverbal techniques, such as pace, volume, and body language. Let the speaker know if his or her speech conventions and delivery style are appropriate for the audience and purpose. Determine whether information and ideas are presented logically and concisely, or if they instead detract from, or even undermine, the speaker's points.

FOR STRUGGLING STUDENTS

Scripting Tell students that one key to a good oral presentation is creating a script of the presentation in advance. Suggest that students put their scripts on small notecards, which are easy to hold and refer to during a presentation. A large piece of paper might distract both the presenter and the audience, and the presenter might be tempted to read from it rather than maintain eye contact with the audience.

Remind students that notes should contain important words and phrases, rather than full sentences or paragraphs. Quotations are the exception. Quotations should be carefully copied down in full, complete with any information necessary about which character said what to whom or where the quotation occurs in the plot.

Tell students to allow plenty of time to convert their essays into note form.

Delivering Your Presentation

Model the Skill: USE VERBAL AND NONVERBAL TECHNIQUES

Model the importance of good verbal and nonverbal techniques. Tell students in a low, monotonous voice, without facial expression or gesture and with your eyes on your notes, that verbal and nonverbal presentation affects how listeners absorb and react to what they hear. Then repeat the same information using variety in your pitch and tone, emphasizing important words, and maintaining eye contact.

GUIDED PRACTICE Have students work in pairs to adapt their literary analyses into oral presentations.

 YOUR TURN Have student pairs take turns delivering their presentations. Then have the listeners let their partners know which verbal and nonverbal techniques worked well. Then have students present their improved presentations to their partners.

Assess and Reteach

Assess

Use the *COMMON CORE TRAITS* to assess students' oral presentations.

A strong oral presentation
- focuses on a clear controlling idea
- has a logical structure
- offers compelling ideas and includes evidence to support them
- uses effective verbal and nonverbal speaking techniques

Reteach

Remind students to use visual cues, such as writing an outline on the board, and word cues, such as transitions, in their oral presentations. Have students work in pairs to identify key statements in their presentations that can be supported by visual and verbal cues.

Speaking and Listening Online THINK central
- Public speaking tips
- Strategies for effective listening

Assessment Practice

RL 1 Cite textual evidence to support analysis of what the text says explicitly as well as inferences drawn from the text. **RL 5** Analyze how an author's choices concerning how to structure a text create tension. **RI 1** Cite textual evidence to support analysis of what the text says explicitly as well as inferences drawn from the text. **RI 5** Analyze how an author's ideas are refined or developed by particular sentences. **W 5** Strengthen writing by revising and editing. **L 6** Acquire and use accurately general academic words sufficient for reading; demonstrate independence in gathering vocabulary knowledge.

CHECK READINESS

Read aloud the paragraph under **ASSESS,** and stress to students that this is not the full Unit Test but a way for the them to check their readiness for it. Then have students examine the skills standards listed under **REVIEW** and look back in the unit or in the **Student Resource Bank** for any skills they need to review.

READ THE TEXTS

Remind students to keep unit goals in mind as they read each passage, paying particular attention to these literary and reading skills:

- conflict
- mood
- make inferences
- draw conclusions

To help students focus on conflict, encourage them to ask questions such as

- Why do the women keep changing their minds about shelling the peas?
- Why didn't the Dundees leave Galveston?

ANSWER THE QUESTIONS

Direct students to pages R93–R101 of the **Handbook** to review test-taking strategies.

- Remind students to read through all the choices and eliminate any that are clearly wrong.

COMMON CORE

Assessment Practice

COMMON CORE

ASSESS
Taking this practice test will help you assess your knowledge of these skills and determine your readiness for the Unit Test.

REVIEW
After you take the practice test, your teacher can help you identify any standards you need to review.

COMMON CORE

RL 1 Cite textual evidence to support analysis of what the text says explicitly as well as inferences drawn from the text. **RL 5** Analyze how an author's choices concerning how to structure a text create tension. **RI 1** Cite textual evidence to support analysis of what the text says explicitly as well as inferences drawn from the text. **RI 5** Analyze how an author's ideas are refined or developed by particular sentences. **W 5** Strengthen writing by revising and editing. **L 6** Acquire and use accurately general academic words sufficient for reading; demonstrate independence in gathering vocabulary knowledge.

Practice Test THINK central
Take it at thinkcentral.com.
KEYWORD: HML10N-160

DIRECTIONS Read the two selections and the viewing and representing piece. Then, answer the questions that follow.

Embroidery   *by Ray Bradbury*

1   The dark porch air in the late afternoon was full of needle flashes, like a movement of gathered silver insects in the light. The three women's mouths twitched over their work. Their bodies lay back and then imperceptibly forward, so that the rocking chairs tilted and murmured. Each woman looked to her own hands, as if quite suddenly she had found her heart beating there.

2   "What time is it?"

3   "Ten minutes to five."

4   "Got to get up in a minute and shell those peas for dinner."

5   "But—" said one of them.

6   "Oh yes, I forgot. How foolish of me. . . ." The first woman paused, put down her embroidery and needle, and looked through the open porch door, through the warm interior of the quiet house, to the silent kitchen. There upon the table, seeming more like symbols of domesticity than anything she had ever seen in her life, lay the mound of fresh-washed peas in their neat, resilient jackets, waiting for her fingers to bring them into the world.

7   "Go hull them if it'll make you feel good," said the second woman.

8   "No," said the first. "I won't. I just won't."

9   The third woman sighed. She embroidered a rose, a leaf, a daisy on a green field. The embroidery needle rose and vanished.

10   The second woman was working on the finest, most delicate piece of embroidery of them all, deftly poking, finding, and returning the quick needle upon innumerable journeys. Her quick black glance was on each motion. A flower, a man, a road, a sun, a house; the scene grew under her hand, a miniature beauty, perfect in every threaded detail.

11   "It seems at times like this that it's always your hands you turn to," she said, and the others nodded enough to make the rockers rock again.

12   "I believe," said the first lady, "that our souls are in our hands. For we do *everything* to the world with our hands. Sometimes I think we don't use our hands half enough; it's certain we don't use our heads."

13   They all peered more intently at what their hands were doing. "Yes," said the third lady, "when you look back on a whole lifetime, it seems you don't remember faces so much as hands and what they did."

14   They recounted to themselves the lids they had lifted, the doors they had opened and shut, the flowers they had picked, the dinners they had made,

---

DIFFERENTIATED INSTRUCTION

FOR ENGLISH LANGUAGE LEARNERS

Assessment Practice: Work Backward
Prepare students by having them read the questions *before* reading the passages. Have pairs find unfamiliar words in test directions and questions and follow these steps:

1. Write each unfamiliar word on the board.
2. Have pairs offer definitions of words they think they know. Fill in correct definitions.
3. Help students find and understand the meanings of the remaining words.

Connect Point out that in both the short story and the newspaper article, people know disaster threatens. However, they do not know for certain how great the danger and the damage will be. Ask students to give examples of natural or human-made disasters that people must sometimes face.

all with slow or quick fingers, as was their manner or custom. Looking back, you saw a flurry of hands, like a magician's dream, doors popping wide, taps turned, brooms wielded, children spanked. The flutter of pink hands was the only sound; the rest was a dream without voices.

15   "No supper to fix tonight or tomorrow night or the next night after that," said the third lady.

16   "No windows to open or shut."

17   "No coal to shovel in the basement furnace next winter."

18   "No papers to clip cooking articles out of."

19   And suddenly they were crying. The tears rolled softly down their faces and fell into the material upon which their fingers twitched.

20   "This won't help things," said the first lady at last, putting the back of her thumb to each under-eyelid. She looked at her thumb and it was wet.

21   "Now look what I've done!" cried the second lady, exasperated. The others stopped and peered over. The second lady held out her embroidery. There was the scene, perfect except that while the embroidered yellow sun shone down upon the embroidered green field, and the embroidered brown road curved toward an embroidered pink house, the man standing on the road had something wrong with his face.

22   "I'll just have to rip out the whole pattern, practically, to fix it right," said the second lady.

23   "What a shame." They all stared intently at the beautiful scene with the flaw in it.

24   The second lady began to pick away at the thread with her little deft scissors flashing. The pattern came out thread by thread. She pulled and yanked, almost viciously. The man's face was gone. She continued to seize at the threads.

25   "What are you *doing*?" asked the other woman.

26   They leaned and saw what she had done.

27   The man was gone from the road. She had taken him out entirely.

28   They said nothing but returned to their own tasks.

29   "What time is it?" asked someone.

30   "Five minutes to five!"

31   "Is it supposed to happen at five o'clock?"

32   "Yes."

33   "And they're not sure what it'll do to anything, really, when it happens?"

34   "No, not sure."

35   "Why didn't we stop them before it got this far and this big?"

GO ON ➡

ITEM ANALYSIS

COMPREHENSION AND WRITTEN RESPONSE	ITEMS	UNIT PAGES
Conflict	8	28-35, 37, 49, 79
Setting	3	28-35, 65, 79
Mood	1, 23	28-35, 65, 107
Make Inferences	2, 8, 9, 15, 19, 20, 21, 22	49
Draw Conclusions	5, 10, 11, 14, 17, 18	37

VOCABULARY	ITEMS	UNIT PAGES
Connotation and Denotation	4, 6, 12, 13	97
Word Roots	7, 16	46

WRITING AND GRAMMAR	ITEMS	UNIT PAGES
Use Descriptive Details	2, 5	63, 116
Improve Sentence Flow	1, 3-4, 6	135

Practice Test

On **thinkcentral.com** students can complete an interactive version of this practice test *and* receive remediation for the skills they have not yet mastered.

FOR STRUGGLING READERS

Assessment Support Consider these options for completing the Assessment Practice:

- Have students "work backward" to review the test questions before reading the passages.

- Select random questions in the Assessment, and have students demonstrate how and where to look for the answers.

- Ask students to locate unfamiliar vocabulary words in the Assessment. Elicit the words' meanings from the class.

- Have students record useful testing words and definitions in their *Reader/Writer Notebooks* for later reference.

- Read the selections or parts of them aloud to aid in student comprehension.

36   "It's twice as big as ever before. No, ten times, maybe a thousand."

37   "This isn't like the first one or the dozen later ones. This is different. Nobody knows what it might do when it comes."

38   They waited on the porch in the smell of roses and cut grass. "What time is it now?"

39   "One minute to five."

40   The needles flashed silver fire. They swam like a tiny school of metal fish in the darkening summer air.

41   Far away a mosquito sound. Then something like a tremor of drums. The three women cocked their heads, listening.

42   "We won't hear anything, will we?"

43   "They say not."

44   "Perhaps we're foolish. Perhaps we'll go right on, after five o'clock, shelling peas, opening doors, stirring soups, washing dishes, making lunches, peeling oranges . . . "

45   "My, how we'll laugh to think we were frightened by an old experiment!" They smiled a moment at each other.

46   "It's five o'clock."

47   At these words, hushed, they all busied themselves. Their fingers darted. Their faces were turned down to the motions they made. They made frantic patterns. They made lilacs and grass and trees and houses and rivers in the embroidered cloth. They said nothing, but you could hear their breath in the silent porch air.

48   Thirty seconds passed.

49   The second woman sighed finally and began to relax.

50   "I think I just *will* go shell those peas for supper," she said. "I—"

51   But she hadn't time even to lift her head. Somewhere, at the side of her vision, she saw the world brighten and catch fire. She kept her head down, for she knew what it was. She didn't look up, nor did the others, and in the last instant their fingers were flying; they didn't glance about to see what was happening to the country, the town, this house, or even this porch. They were only staring down at the design in their flickering hands.

52   The second woman watched an embroidered flower go. She tried to embroider it back in, but it went, and then the road vanished, and the blades of grass. She watched a fire, in slow motion almost, catch upon the embroidered house and unshingle it, and pull each threaded leaf from the small green tree in the hoop, and she saw the sun itself pulled apart in the design. Then the fire caught upon the moving point of the needle while still it flashed; she watched the fire come along her fingers and arms and body, untwisting the yarn of her being so painstakingly that she could see it in all its

162

devilish beauty, yanking out the pattern from the material at hand. What it was doing to the other women or the furniture or the elm tree in the yard, she never knew. For now, yes now! it was plucking at the white embroidery of her flesh, the pink thread of her cheeks, and at last it found her heart, a soft red rose sewn with fire, and it burned the fresh, embroidered petals away, one by delicate one. . . .

Staying in Galveston, a Park Bench for Shelter

by Ian Urbina and John Schwartz
***from* The New York Times**

1 GALVESTON, Tex. –Those who make the barrier island here their home know this: Nature tries to wipe them out now and then. They live with that knowledge every day, though it does not come to the forefront of their thinking unless a storm is on the way.

2 The threat is anything but theoretical, as Daryl Thompson learned Saturday after making what he admitted was a bad decision.

3 Not only did he choose to ride out Hurricane Ike, but he did so outdoors. "I thought about going to the shelter," Mr. Thompson, who is homeless, said as he pushed his bike with two large water-logged bags balanced on top. "But I waited too long, then I was trapped."

4 Mr. Thompson said that at one point the wind was so strong that he kept getting blown off his feet. So he lay down underneath a park bench.

5 "I thought I might die," he said. "This thing tossed me like a salad."

6 The storm tossed much of the island the same way.

7 Along the seaway, wooden debris was stacked up like barricades, and things were askew in that way that only big storms can accomplish.

163

Make Inferences Point out that the women in "Embroidery" have known each other for a long time and that their conversation often centers around shared knowledge and experiences. Have students reread paragraphs 29–46 and take notes as they read. What shared experiences do the women talk about?

After students finish reading and taking notes, discuss the following examples, in addition to others students may have identified:

- They know something will happen at five o'clock.

- They have had some official communication about the event that did not give them accurate details.

- They have been through this before, but this time it will be bigger.

- There was a time when they could have prevented this from happening.

8   Dozens of palm trees were bent over. A boat sat in the middle of a road near 49th Street, even though no water flowed down the street. At the cemetery, statues of saints and the heads of white tombstones barely extended above muddy water.

9   Coast Guard helicopters buzzed overhead in an effort to check on rescue missions in response to more than 100 distress calls that came in during the night.

10   Late Saturday, city officials said there were no confirmed deaths, even though at least 17 buildings were destroyed. Property damage was "in the millions, if not hundreds of millions," said the city manager, Steve LeBlanc.

11   For residents of Galveston, which lost 6,000 people in 1900 in the nation's worst natural disaster, there is a grim calculation with each storm: Stay or go?

12   John Dundee, whose family has lived on the island for five generations, decided to stick out this storm after the misery of the 2005 evacuation for Hurricane Rita.

13   "My wife and I sat up in traffic for 27 hours, just trying to make it to my children's house in Waco," Mr. Dundee said. This time, they decided, "we felt we might be safer here than out on the highway," and they left their home on the unprotected west end of the island for his mother's home closer to town.

14   But then the surge predictions grew more and more ominous.

15   "We went back and forth and back and forth," Mr. Dundee said. By the time they decided to go, the water on the streets was waist deep—too much even for his Jeep.

16   Speaking from his home Saturday morning, a clearly relieved Mr. Dundee said, "We got beat up pretty bad, but everybody got through fine."

17   On Friday night, just hours before Hurricane Ike came ashore, Galveston's mayor, Lyda Ann Thomas, spoke by cellphone from the San Luis Hotel about why people stay in such a place, and why people go there.

18   Galveston has been on a building binge, with more than $6 billion in recent development—even after Hurricane Katrina underscored the risks of the Gulf Coast. The city's economy is on an upswing. And, as Ms. Thomas likes to say, "It only took 100 years."

19   Ms. Thomas's grandfather was I. H. Kempner, one of the men who helped revive the city after the storm in 1900. She said the risk was "just part of living here."

20   "The gulf sits here," Ms. Thomas said, "and at any moment—like today—it can rise up in wrath and overwhelm you."

21   "We've lost a lot today," she added. "But you know that's a part of our history."

164

22   Other residents, too, said they would ride the storm out again if given the option.

23   Ivy and Mike Gonzalez said they and their home had made it as they wandered out from the house, on Broadway. They added that it would have been much easier had the city not turned off the water and gas.

24   "We understand that they needed to take precautions, but I need a cup of coffee something vicious and the toilet needs flushing," said Ms. Gonzalez, adding that a couple of shingles had blown off their home but there was no other damage. . . .

25   Along Broadway and 29th, two teenagers kayaked on their way to check on a friend's house. Another boy walked up 21st Street with a fishing pole. "I'm not trying to catch anything," said the boy, Nick Parker, 11. "I'm just making sure there are no water moccasins."

26   Nick explained that he and his parents had waited too long to evacuate and had been trapped in their home. The water flooded their basement, he said, but no one was hurt. "Mostly, I'm here looking for someone else to play with," he said. "Hurricanes are boring. Maybe it's time to open the schools back up."

27   At Ball High School, which served as an evacuation shelter and where nearly 300 people rode out the storm, Michael W. Fox, who was staying at the shelter, said that all had gone smoothly, even though around midnight the first-floor auditorium was evacuated to the second floor as water flooded the building.

28   "It was civil and all, but by morning all anyone wanted to do was get out and check on their homes to see how bad things looked," Mr. Fox said as he waded through waist-deep water back to his home.

29   As she began pulling down the plywood from the front of her house on Avenue O, less than a half-mile from the water, Sara Rampton, 54, said her house was fine.

30   But tears began streaming down her face as she tried to explain what she did lose.

31   "My dog ran, and I lost my only photograph of my grandfather," said Ms. Rampton, explaining that as she tried to take her German shepherd, Gabriel, to a shelter when the storm started, he got spooked by the winds and bolted out the front door. She added that during the storm, water flooded part of her living room and the wind blew down her only photograph of her deceased grandfather.

GO ON →

165

FOR STRUGGLING READERS

Chronological Order Explain to students that "Staying in Galveston, a Park Bench for Shelter" consists of a number of interviews, so the information is not in chronological, or time, order. To help students understand the chronology of events, have them create timelines based on the information in the article.

Have students skim the article to identify dates and events. Tell students to list the dates and events as they read. After students have finished identifying dates and events, have them sketch a timeline that begins with points on the line for the 1800s and 1900. Ask students what other dates should be included on their timelines. Then have students fill in the events from their notes for each date.

🧰 BEST PRACTICES TOOLKIT—Transparency
Timeline p. B48

32   "You can replace everything else, and I'm sure they will rebuild," she said, wiping her face. "They can't rebuild all the personal things that get lost."

33   In 1900, the Great Storm, as it became known in the days before each hurricane was given a human name, changed one of the nation's most prosperous cities into a backwater.

34   That storm stopped what seemed to be an inexorable rise for Galveston, which considered itself a rival to New Orleans. It was the city with an opera house that had hosted Sarah Bernhardt, the city with the state's first telephone and its first electric light. And then, the storm.

35   "When I was growing up, people didn't like to talk about it," said Paul Burka, the senior executive editor of Texas Monthly magazine and a "B.O.I."—clubby old Galveston's abbreviation for "born on the island." The 1900 storm "was like a skeleton in the family closet," he said, because "that was the day that Galveston lost its destiny."

36   But the city did not stand still. Civic leaders like Kempner and John Sealy traveled to New York and Washington to persuade government and financial leaders that the island would soon be open for business again and to establish lines of credit.

37   Enormous undertakings followed. Galveston began building a seawall that is now 10 miles long and some 17 feet high, to break storm surges from the Gulf of Mexico. Workers raised the city's buildings on jacks—some by more than 10 feet—and filled in the space underneath with dredged soil.

38   The city survived, but it did not boom again. Its economic prominence was quickly grabbed by Houston, which dug a deepwater ship channel that allowed business to bypass the risky island port.

39   But life went on, and Galvestonians came to think of the threat of occasional hurricanes as something they could live with.

DIFFERENTIATED INSTRUCTION

FOR ENGLISH LANGUAGE LEARNERS

Assessment Vocabulary Explain to students that newspaper articles often use language specific to American culture. Lead students in identifying cultural terms in "Staying in Galveston, a Park Bench for Shelter," and discuss the meanings of the words or phrases.

Point out *kayaked* and *water moccasins* in paragraph 25 as two examples of cultural terms. Tell students that a *kayak* is a lightweight, watertight canoe that originated with the Inuit and Eskimo. The verb *kayaked* refers to someone using a *kayak* for transportation. Explain that a *water moccasin*, also known as a *cottonmouth*, is a venomous snake found in the southern United States.

Preparing Makes Sense. Get Ready Now.

Homeland Security

www.ready.gov

167

Reading Comprehension

Model a thinking process for answering multiple-choice questions.

1. **B is correct.** *The women speak very little except to speculate on what is about to happen at five o'clock. They are constantly checking the time. In paragraph 19, they find themselves crying. A lists positive feelings. C lists negative feelings, but the women are not ill or angry. D also lists positive feelings that are not in the story.*

2. **D is correct.** *In paragraph 35, one of the women asks the others why they didn't stop what was happening before it got to this point. A is incorrect because the story never says embroidery is a relaxing hobby. B is not relevant to the story, as none of the women is gossiping. C focuses on a pleasant activity, but the story focuses on fear of what is about to happen.*

3. **C is correct.** *The women keep checking the time as five o'clock nears, and they discuss past experiments, speculating on what will happen this time. A is incorrect because the story starts in the late afternoon. B and D are not mentioned in the story, so they are incorrect.*

4. **A is correct.** *The peas stand for all of the everyday chores the women do around the house. B addresses an emotional quality rather than a physical one. C and D are irrelevant because the story doesn't involve animals or a country's internal affairs.*

5. **D is correct.** *In paragraph 13, the third woman says that when you look back at your life, you remember "hands and what they did." Paragraph 14 lists many of the household activities their hands have done. A is incorrect because hands are more than just body parts in the story. Neither B nor C is true, because the women work with their hands all the time without mentioning manicures or pain.*

6. **A is correct.** *Twitching or jerking indicates tense emotions. The women are upset and crying and have stopped sewing. Because they are upset, their hands would not be calm, so B is wrong. C is incorrect because the women have stopped sewing. D is also incorrect because the women are no longer using their hands.*

Reading Comprehension

> **Use "Embroidery" (pp. 160–163) to answer questions 1–9.**

1. The mood of the women in this story is —
   A. cheerful and hopeful
   B. tense and fearful
   C. sick and angry
   D. peaceful and loving

2. One of the themes of this story is —
   A. embroidery is a relaxing hobby
   B. gossiping is not kind
   C. spending time with friends and family is enjoyable
   D. ignoring trouble does not stop it

3. At the beginning of the story, the three women are expecting —
   A. a day like any other day
   B. a dinner party later that night
   C. something unknown to happen at five o'clock
   D. an important visitor

4. Read the following dictionary entry.

   domestic\də měs'tǐk\ *adj.* **1.** of or relating to the family or household **2.** fond of homelife and household affairs **3.** tame (as in animals) **4.** of or relating to a country's internal affairs (as in taxes or highways).

   Which definition best explains why the unshelled peas in paragraph 6 are "symbols of domesticity?"
   A. Definition 1
   B. Definition 2
   C. Definition 3
   D. Definition 4

5. In paragraphs 11–14, hands symbolize —
   A. just another part of the body
   B. something that is pampered and manicured
   C. aches and pains
   D. the everyday activities of life

6. In paragraph 19, *twitched* means —
   A. jerked   C. sewed
   B. lay still   D. stroked

7. The word *exasperated* in paragraph 21 comes from the Latin root *asperare,* meaning "to make rough." *Exasperated* means —
   A. scrubbed clean
   B. helped
   C. breathed deeply
   D. irritated

8. In paragraphs 24–27, the second woman rips the embroidered man completely out of her embroidery because —
   A. she did not want the other women to be jealous of her fine stitching
   B. she was angry and afraid
   C. she knew she could do better
   D. she was not paying attention and tore too much of the man out

9. In paragraph 35, when one of the women says "Why didn't we stop them before it got this far and this big?" she means that —
   A. the three women should have prevented people from doing all experiments
   B. society should have made the women stop doing the experiments
   C. everything would have been all right if the experiment had stayed small
   D. people should have paid attention to what was happening and where it was leading

7. **D is correct.** *If your skin is irritated, it is also rough, and this would also be true of emotions. The woman was irritated because she made a mistake in her embroidery. It would not make sense to substitute A, B, or C for exasperated in the sentence.*

8. **B is correct.** *Since the woman cannot take out her feelings on the people carrying out the experiment, she takes them out on the embroidered man. She made a mistake in the embroidery, so A is wrong. C does not explain why she took out more than the face, where the mistake was. All the women are focusing intensely on their embroidery, so D is not correct.*

9. **D is correct.** *D also states an important theme in the story. It is not "all experiments" that threaten the women and their town, only a certain series of experiments, so A is wrong. The women are not doing the experiments, so B is also wrong. C is not a good answer, as the women are aware that the experiment is part of a series. They know that the danger was already there in the earlier stages.*

Use "Staying in Galveston" (pp. 163–166) to answer questions 10–16.

10. One of the main ideas of this article is —

A. Galveston is a great place to live

B. hurricanes are part of life in Galveston

C. that it is easy to ride out a hurricane

D. that Houston has a large port

11. Which sentence from the article best shows the power of the storm?

A. *"This thing tossed me like a salad."*

B. *Coast Guard helicopters buzzed overhead in an effort to check on rescue missions.*

C. *"I'm just making sure there are no water moccasins."*

D. *Along Broadway and 29th, two teenagers kayaked on their way to check on a friend's house.*

12. In paragraph 2, the phrase "anything but theoretical" means it is —

A. an idea

B. easy

C. expensive

D. real

13. A synonym for the word *binge* in paragraph 18 is —

A. bridge

B. design

C. overindulgence

D. slowdown

14. In paragraphs 29–32, Sara Rampton said that people cannot replace —

A. their homes

B. their telephones

C. their personal things

D. their coffee

15. People don't like to talk about the storm of 1900 because —

A. it is like a skeleton in the closet

B. nothing much happened

C. everyone is still grieving about their families' losses

D. it ended Galveston's economic power

16. The word *prominence* in paragraph 38 comes from the Latin root *prominere,* meaning "to jut out." *Prominence* means —

A. importance

B. flavor

C. politics

D. time

Use "Embroidery" and "Staying in Galveston" to answer questions 17–18.

17. All of the people in "Embroidery" and "Staying in Galveston" —

A. are women

B. faced a flood

C. survived the disaster

D. tried to stay in their homes

18. The message taught by "Embroidery" and "Staying in Galveston" is that —

A. people always manage to rebuild

B. disasters are usually avoidable

C. people should make every effort to get out of harm's way

D. there is nothing anyone can do to escape a disaster

GO ON

10. B is correct. *The article mentions several hurricanes that have affected Galveston. A is not mentioned in the article. C is incorrect because the article gives examples of how hard it is to ride out a storm. D is only mentioned briefly at the end of the article, so it is not the main idea.*

11. A is correct. *It shows how powerless the speaker was against the strength of the hurricane. Neither B nor C refers to the storm at all. D talks about the flooded street but does not mention the strength of the storm.*

12. D is correct. *A theory is an idea, and the phrase says "anything but," meaning that it is the opposite of an idea. It is real. A is the opposite of what it means, and B and C are both wrong.*

13. C is correct. *Often binge is used to refer to eating or drinking more than necessary. Here it means building more than necessary, which is clear because $6 billion was spent. A and B are wrong because they are not synonyms. D is the opposite of what is meant.*

14. C is correct. *Rampton talks about losing her dog and the only photograph of her grandfather. A, B, and D are incorrect because these items can be rebuilt or replaced.*

15. D is correct. *The city was booming before the storm and has not completely recovered its economic position since that time. A refers to the fact that people do not talk about the storm. B is clearly not correct because the storm caused a lot of damage. C is also wrong because the Great Storm occurred over 100 years ago, and the people alive today are no longer grieving.*

16. A is correct. *Something that is important stands out from the rest. B, C, and D are not definitions or synonyms of prominence.*

17. D is correct. *The women in "Embroidery" are at home even though they know the experiment will take place at five o'clock, and the people in Galveston didn't evacuate even though a hurricane was about to strike. A is incorrect because both men and women were interviewed in "Staying in Galveston." B and C are not correct because the women in "Embroidery" face an experiment not a flood, and they do not survive.*

18. C is correct. *If the people in either selection had evacuated before the events, they might have saved themselves, and possibly some of what they held dear. A is not true because Galveston never completely recovered from the 1900 hurricane. B is incorrect because people cannot control nature. D is also incorrect because in both selections the people knew in advance what was about to happen and had the chance to evacuate.*

19. B is correct.
Emergencies hit suddenly, so it is important to prepare for them. A is not the main idea of this poster. C is not correct because children should be involved, as shown in the poster. D is not the main message of the poster.

20. A is correct.
The people in the poster are calm. B is incorrect because the poster does not give instructions for writing a supply list. C is not correct because the poster does not target only single parents. D does not represent the main purpose of the photograph.

SHORT CONSTRUCTED RESPONSE

Possible responses:

21. *The women do not want to leave their familiar lives behind, as shown in their reminiscences in paragraphs 14 through 18. Moreover, they hope that, as with previous experiments, this one will not really harm them (paragraphs 33–34). They even think that their fear might be foolish: "how we'll laugh to think we were frightened by an old experiment!" (paragraph 45).*

22. *Many, like Daryl Thompson (paragraph 2), the Dundees (paragraph 12), and the Parkers (paragraph 26), waited too long and, by the time they decided to go, were unable to evacuate. Some stayed out of pride (paragraph 26) or to help out during the immediate aftermath of the storm.*

23. *The setting of "Embroidery" is the porch of a house in a small town just as it is about to be destroyed by an "experiment." The intimate setting allows the story to focus only on the effect of the situation on the three women. Readers see through the women's eyes and the mood of the story is mysterious and frightening.*

The setting of "Staying in Galveston" is the entire city of Galveston, and the mood is not as intense as that in "Embroidery." Instead, the mood here is somewhat more disinterested and factual. Nonetheless, the rubble-filled streets and destroyed homes underscore the effects of the hurricane.

Use the visual representation on page 167 to answer questions 19–20.

19. The main message of the poster is —
  - **A.** help others get ready for emergencies
  - **B.** don't wait to prepare for emergencies
  - **C.** only parents should prepare for emergencies
  - **D.** people should stay calm in emergencies

20. The designer of the poster most likely chose the photograph to —
  - **A.** emphasize calmly planning for emergencies
  - **B.** illustrate how to write a supply list
  - **C.** encourage single mothers to involve their children
  - **D.** encourage children to participate in planning

SHORT CONSTRUCTED RESPONSE
Write a short response to each question, using text evidence to support your response.

21. Why do the women in "Embroidery" continue to embroider instead of running to a shelter? Use evidence from the text to support your response.

22. What reasons do people give in "Staying in Galveston" for choosing not to evacuate? Use evidence from the text to support your response.

Write a short response to this question, using text evidence from both selections to support your response.

23. How do the settings in "Embroidery" and "Staying in Galveston" affect the mood of each selection? Use evidence from **both** selections to support your response.

170

DIFFERENTIATED INSTRUCTION

FOR ENGLISH LANGUAGE LEARNERS
Assessment Vocabulary To help students understand the Comprehension questions, teach or review the meanings of these vocabulary words:

mood: the feeling or atmosphere that a writer creates

symbol: a person, place, an object, or an activity that stands for something beyond itself

synonym: a word having the same or nearly the same meaning as another word

theme: underlying message about life or human nature

Revising and Editing

DIRECTIONS Read this passage, and answer the questions that follow.

> (1) With a weight of 13,632 tons and a length of 729 feet, the *Edmund Fitzgerald* was the largest carrier on the Great Lakes when it first sailed in 1958. (2) Seventeen years later, the ship would sink in Lake Superior. (3) At 2:20 p.m. on November 9th 1975 the *Fitzgerald* departed Superior, Wisconsin, destined for Detroit. (4) The National Weather Service issued gale warnings for the area. (5) Waves came onto the deck. (6) At approximately 7:15 that evening, the ship vanished from radar observation. (7) All 29 crew members were lost. (8) The next day, winds gusting up to 70 knots and waves cresting as high as 30 feet they shook the ship. (9) It was later discovered that the ship had dropped about 530 feet to the bottom of Lake Superior. (10) That day of November 10, 1975, will always be remembered.

1. What is the most effective way to improve the organization of the paragraph?
   A. Move sentence 1 to follow sentence 10
   B. Move sentence 2 to follow sentence 3
   C. Move sentence 3 to follow sentence 7
   D. Move sentence 8 to follow sentence 4

2. What is the most effective way to rewrite sentence 2 to convey a more somber tone?
   A. Seventeen years later, the doomed ship would sink in Lake Superior.
   B. Seventeen short years later, the ship would plunge below the surface of Lake Superior.
   C. Seventeen productive years later, the ship would finish its journey in Lake Superior.
   D. Seventeen years later, the hefty ship would dive into Lake Superior.

3. What is the best way to correct sentence 3?
   A. Change *departed* to *departing*
   B. Insert commas before and after *1975*
   C. Delete the comma after *Wisconsin*
   D. Make no change

4. Which transitional word or phrase could be added to the beginning of sentence 4?
   A. Consequently,
   B. Naturally,
   C. Shortly afterward,
   D. As a result,

5. What is the best example of a vivid verb to replace the phrase *came onto* in sentence 5?
   A. Battered
   B. Propelled
   C. Pushed
   D. Stirred

6. What change, if any, should be made to sentence 8?
   A. Insert a comma after **knots**
   B. Delete **they**
   C. Change **winds** to **wind's**
   D. Make no change

171

ANSWERS
Revising and Editing

1. **D** *is correct.* *Sentence 4 says that gales are forecast, and sentence 8 describes the gale the following day. A would take away the introduction to the paragraph. B is incorrect because sentence 2 refers directly to sentence 1. C is also wrong because sentence 3 tells about the ship leaving port, not about its disappearance.*

2. **A** *is correct.* *The adjective doomed adds a serious and gloomy feeling. B, C, and D do not convey gloominess.*

3. **B** *is correct.* *When writing a date consisting of the month, day, and year, commas should be placed around the year. A and C would add mistakes to the sentence. D is incorrect because the change in B is necessary.*

4. **D** *is correct.* *The transition helps clarify the relationship between the events in sentences 3 and 4. A indicates a causal relationship between the two sentences, which does not actually exist. B adds irony, which is inappropriate to the tone of the paragraph. C also indicates a causal relationship.*

5. **A** *is correct.* *The waves were hitting the deck, and* battered *means hit. B and C mean roughly the same thing, and are both wrong. D is erroneous because a deck cannot be stirred.*

6. **B** *is correct.* *Winds and waves are the subjects of the sentence. A and D would make the sentence ungrammatical. C is incorrect since a change is necessary.*

FOR STRUGGLING READERS

Assessment Support: Paragraph Organization and Word Choice Remind students that the ideas in paragraphs follow a certain order, such as chronology (time), importance, or cause and effect. Have students identify the order in the passage on page 171 (*chronological order*).

Explain that transitional phrases are used to help readers understand the organization of information within and between paragraphs.

Have students identify and explain the purpose of transitional expressions in the first four paragraphs of "Staying in Galveston."

Tell students that effective word choice makes writing more interesting and memorable. Ask them to identify the adjectives in paragraph 6 of "Embroidery" and explain how they affect the mood of the story.

COMMON CORE FOCUS

RL 10 Read and comprehend literature. **RI 10** Read and comprehend literary nonfiction.

INTRODUCE *GREAT READS*

In Unit 1, students have discussed a number of big questions. Invite students to tell which question they found most intriguing and why, and then focus attention on the three that appear on this page. Discuss the recommended books and their summaries, pointing out how each connects to the related question. Encourage students to choose one or more of these "great reads" to read independently.

COMMON CORE

RL 10 Read and comprehend literature. **RI 10** Read and comprehend literary nonfiction.

Ideas for Independent Reading

Which of the questions in Unit 1 intrigued you most? Continue exploring them with these additional works.

What if everyone were the same?

1984
by George Orwell

This novel is set in a bleak future world where citizens are constantly watched by the government, known as Big Brother. Individuality is forbidden, free thought is suppressed, and words never mean what they say.

Bless the Beasts and Children
by Glendon Swarthout

The heroes of this book are boys who are misfits at a summer camp. They're different from the popular, athletic boys, and working together they plot to free a pen of buffaloes that are to be slaughtered.

Colors of the Mountain
by Da Chen

The author of this memoir grew up in China during the Cultural Revolution, a time of great repression and conformity. Persecuted because of his family's form wealth, he endured and mad it to college.

What makes something valuable?

The Piano Lesson
by August Wilson

In this play, an African-American brother and sister clash over their family's legacy—a piano carved in designs by an enslaved ancestor. The brother wants to sell it to buy land; the sister wants to keep it.

Crazy in the Kitchen
by Louise DeSalvo

Several generations of Italian-American women battle in the kitchen over different ways of cooking. The author realizes that food represents a wealth of different values in the lives of her family members.

Brick Lane
by Monica Ali

Nazneen, born in Banglades is sent to England at age 18 to marry a Bengali immigran twice her age. Eventually she begins to ask what she want from life, what she finds of value.

Is survival a matter of chance?

The Perfect Storm
by Sebastian Junger

In October 1991, one of the worst storms in history occurred off the coast of New England. This true account describes the sinking of the fishing boat *Andrea Gail* and the dramatic attempts to rescue other vessels.

Left for Dead
by Beck Weathers

He was left for dead on the slopes of Mount Everest. His companions thought he had frozen. But his commitment to his wife and family woke Beck Weathers up in time to save his life, though not all of his fingers.

Isaac's Storm
by Erik Larson

In 1900, a hurricane destroyed much of Galveston, Texas. Over six thousand died. The book tells us why, and also ho those who survived did so.

Get Novel Wise **THINK** central

Go to **thinkcentral.com**.
KEYWORD: HML10-172

172

THINK central

NovelWise

The keyword on this page points to **NovelWise**, a Web site that helps students choose a novel or other book-length work to read. **NovelWise** also provides

• study guides
• reading strategies and literary elements instruction
• presentations to introduce classic novels
• project ideas

Word Portraits

CHARACTER DEVELOPMENT

- In Fiction
- In Nonfiction
- In Poetry
- In Drama
- In Media

173

INTRODUCE THE UNIT

How can you find out what someone is really like? When that "someone" is a character in literature, some clues come from the character's appearance, words, and actions. Other people's thoughts about and reactions to the character are indicators too. Even a character's name can be a telling detail. Ask students to imagine themselves writing a word portrait of someone they know. Where would they begin? Which details might they "brush on" thickly? Which might they present more subtly?

Invite students to apply their thoughts about word portraits to the pictures on this page. Ask the following type of questions.

- Who are these people?
- What are they doing, feeling, or thinking?
- If you were putting these characters into a story—separate stories or the same story— What names would you give them? Why?
- What are the first details that you would present about each of them?

If students suggest stereotypes, have them speculate about who these characters might be beneath their surface appearances. Explain that the selections in this unit will show both the expected and the unexpected sides of characters through various methods of **character development.** As students read and reflect, these word portraits will become more detailed and more interesting.

For help in planning this unit, see

R RESOURCE MANAGER UNIT 2
pp. 1–11

About the Art Michele Warner entitled this painting *Grandma*. For more information, see page 205.

UNIT 2

COMMON CORE STRAND

ECOS · ECOS · ECOS

	Text Analysis Workshop: Analyzing Characters pp. 176–181	Shoofly Pie Short Story pp. 182–201	The Possibility of Evil Short Story pp. 202–217	Like the Sun Short Story pp. 218–225	The Teacher Who Changed My Life Essay pp. 226–237	Linked Selections — A Celebration of Grandfathers Essay pp. 238–245
		Lexile: 860 / Fry: 5 / Dale-Chall: 6.0	Lexile: 110 / Fry: 8 / Dale-Chall: 6.0	Lexile: 740 / Fry: 7 / Dale-Chall: 6.2	Lexile: 1350 / Fry: 11 / Dale-Chall: 7.1	Lexile: 830 / Fry: 7 / Dale-Chall: 5.7
Reading Literature	Character Development p. 176 RL 3 Character Behavior pp. 178–179 RL 3 Analyze the Text pp. 180–181 RL 3	Character Traits pp. 183, 186, 189–193, 197, 199 RL 3 Connect pp. 183, 186, 195–196, 199 RL 1 Language Coach p. 196 RL 4	Character Motivation pp. 203, 206, 210–211, 215 RL 1, RL 3 Make Inferences pp. 203, 204, 207, 210, 212–213, 215 Symbolism p. 214 RL 3	Moral Dilemma pp. 219–220, 223, 225 RL 3 Predict pp. 219, 222, 225 RL 1 Allusion p. 223 RL 6 Character and Plot pp. 223, 225 RL 3 Language Coach p. 223 RL 4		
Reading Informational Text		Newspaper Article p. 201			Characterization in Nonfiction pp. 227–228, 230, 233, 235 RI 4 Author's Purpose pp. 227, 231, 234, 235 RI 6 Language Coach p. 231 RI 4 Reading p. 232 RI 4	Character Traits in Nonfiction pp. 239, 242–245 RI 4 Identify Author's Perspective pp. 239, 240, 243, 245 RI 6
Writing		Quickwrite p. 182 Writing Prompt p. 200	Writing Prompt p. 217	Quickwrite p. 218	Writing Prompt p. 237 W 3d	
Speaking and Listening			Discuss p. 202 SL 1		Discuss p. 226 SL 1	Debate p. 238 SL 1
Language		Sensory Details pp. 195, 200 L 3 Language Coach p. 187 L 4c	Modifiers pp. 209, 217 L 3 Connotation and Denotation p. 216 L 5b Language Coach pp. 206, 214 L 5		Analyze Examples pp. 232, 237 L 3 Latin Root sol p. 236 L 4c	Language Coach p. 244 L 5b

ECOS ✓   ECOS ✓

Linked Selections **Simply Grand: Generational Ties Matter** Magazine Article pp. 246–251 Lexile: 1110 Fry: 10 Dale-Chall: 7.5	**The Gift/Those Winter Sundays** Poems pp. 252–257	**A Marriage Proposal** Drama pp. 258–275	**Media Study:** from **Finding Forrester** Film Clip pp. 276–279	**Writing Workshop: Short Story** pp. 280–289 **Technology Workshop: Producing a Video Narrative** pp. 290–291
	Characters in Poetry pp. 253–254, 257 **RL 10** Make Inferences About the Speaker pp. 253–254, 256–257 **RL 1, RL 2**	Characters in a Farce pp. 259, 263, 265, 267, 269, 272–273 **RL 3** Reading a Play pp. 259–260, 262, 271, 273 **RL 10** Language Coach pp. 264, 268 **RL 4**		
Main Idea and Supporting Details pp. 246, 247, 249–250, 251 **RI 1, RI 2**				
Writing Prompt p. 251 **W 2b**	Quickwrite p. 252	Writing Prompt p. 275	Examine Stereotypes p. 279 **W 2**	Writing a Short Story pp. 280–289 **W 3 a–e, W 4, W 5, W 10** Producing a Video Narrative pp. 290–291 **W 6**
		Role-Play p. 258 **SL 1**	Characterization in Movies pp. 277–278 **SL 1, SL 4** Create a Cast List p. 279	Producing a Video Narrative **SL 1c–d, SL 2, SL 5**
Language Coach p. 248 **L 4b**		Vary Sentence Types pp. 263, 275 **L 3** Latin Root *contra* p. 274 **L 4c**		Drafting p. 283 **L 1** Editing and Publishing p. 287 **L 1b, L 2c, L 3**

ECOS ✓

To see the complete Essential Course of Study, see pp. T23–T28.

⊙ For additional lesson planning help, see **Teacher One Stop DVD.**

Instructional Support

Resource Manager Unit 2

UNIT SUPPORT
Academic Vocabulary p. 1

Additional Academic Vocabulary p. 2

Grammar Focus p. 3

Text Analysis Workshop pp. 7–8

Writing Workshop: Short Story p. 165

SELECTION SUPPORT*

Plan and Teach

Lesson planning pages

Additional leveled selection questions

Extension activities

Student Copy Masters

Selection summaries in four languages

Skills copy masters in English and Spanish

Vocabulary preteaching and support

Reading Check and Question Support

Reading Fluency

*Available for all selections

† Available on **thinkcentral.com**.

Language Handbook

Vocabulary Practice

Best Practices Toolkit†

PowerNotes DVD-ROM†

Connections: Nonfiction for Common Core CD-ROM†

Teacher One Stop DVD-ROM

Student One Stop DVD-ROM

Media*Smart* DVD-ROM *from* Finding Forrester

Write*Smart* CD-ROM†

GrammarNotes DVD-ROM†

WordSharp CD-ROM†

Differentiated Instruction

STRUGGLING READERS AND WRITERS	ENGLISH LANGUAGE LEARNERS	ADVANCED LEARNERS
Resource Manager Unit 2 Additional Selection Questions Question Support Reading Fluency **Interactive Reader** **Adapted Interactive Reader** Audio Tutor **Level Up Online Tutorials** **Audio Anthology** (with Audio summaries) **Diagnostic and Selection Tests** Selection Tests A/B	**Resource Manager Unit 2** Selection Summaries in English, Spanish, Vietnamese and Haitian Creole Skills Copymasters in Spanish **English Language Learner Adapted Interactive Reader Teacher's Guide** **ELL Adapted Interactive Reader** Audio Tutor **Guide to English for Newcomers** **Audio Anthology** **Audio Summaries in Multiple Languages** (on **thinkcentral.com**)	**Resource Manager Unit 2** Additional Selection Questions Ideas for Extension **Diagnostic and Selection Tests** Selection Tests B/C

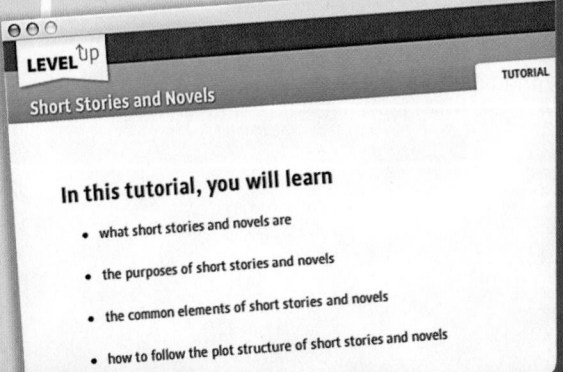

Assessment and Reteaching

Diagnostic and Selection Tests

Unit and Benchmark Tests

ThinkCentral Online Assessment:

- All program assessments
- Level Up Online Tutorials

ExamView Test Generator on the Teacher One Stop DVD-ROM

Online Essay Scoring on **thinkcentral.com**

ThinkCentral Online Reteaching:

- Level Up Online Tutorials
- Reteaching Worksheets

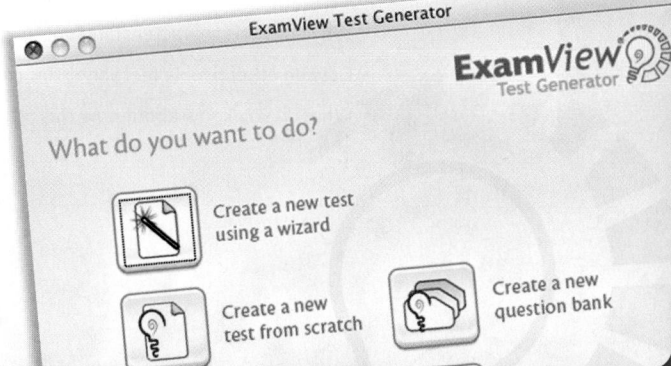

Professional Development

Video Center Based on interviews with program consultants and other educational experts, these videos feature classroom-ready teaching strategies.

Teacher Toolkit Includes a Teacher Handbook as well as a range of articles and handouts by program consultants and other educators.

Janet Allen

Kylene Beers

Jim Burke

Carol Jago

THINK central **at a Glance**

One Location, Endless Resources

Find Resources Browse all *Holt McDougal Literature* components for the ones that meet your students' needs and match your teaching style.

Assess Progress and Reteach Assign electronic versions of program assessments to measure your students' mastery of the Common Core State Standards. On thinkcentral.com, some tests deliver online remediation tutorials to students who have not mastered skills.

 Interactive Whiteboard Lessons

Prepare your students for college and careers by teaching relevant, real-world skills through dynamic, interactive instruction. Go to **thinkcentral.com** to browse through all whiteboard lessons, including the following:

- Character Development and Motivation
- Making Inferences
- Main/Central Idea and Details

 Together Holt McDougal and HISTORY® are revolutionizing the study of English/language arts with video that helps students relive and re-imagine the people, places, and events they are discovering through reading. Look for selections with the HISTORY® icon.

What makes a
CHARACTER live?

To introduce the page, read the question, restating it as "What makes a character seem like a real person to you?" Relate the paragraph to the image of characters that seem to "leap off the page" because the author has made them very lifelike and easy to visualize.

ACTIVITY Ask students to be specific in their responses to the questions. To extend the *ACTIVITY,* have pairs of students bring a memorable character to life for the class by acting out one of the character's distinctive qualities. Conclude by urging students to remember their responses as they meet and think about characters in upcoming selections.

CHECK UNDERSTANDING List the characters that students discussed. Then ask students to make a generalization about why these characters were memorable.

What makes a
CHARACTER live?

We can all remember reading about someone—real or fictitious—who seemed to come to life on the page. We can imagine what that character might say or do and can probably describe what he or she looks like. We can even imagine meeting that person and having a conversation.

ACTIVITY With a group of classmates, think of several memorable characters from books and movies. Describe each one, including details about appearance and personality. Then consider the following questions:

- Why does this character stand out in your memory?
- How do other people feel about this character?
- What do you know about how this person thinks and acts?

Find It Online! Go to **thinkcentral.com** for the interactive version of this unit.

174

Unit Resources

See resources on the **Teacher One Stop DVD-ROM** *and on* **thinkcentral.com**.

R RESOURCE MANAGER UNIT 2

UNIT AND BENCHMARK TESTS

BEST PRACTICES TOOLKIT

INTERACTIVE READER

ADAPTED INTERACTIVE READER

ELL ADAPTED INTERACTIVE READER

LANGUAGE HANDBOOK

VOCABULARY PRACTICE

TECHNOLOGY

- Teacher One Stop DVD-ROM
- Student One Stop DVD-ROM
- PowerNotes DVD-ROM
- Write*Smart* CD-ROM
- Media*Smart* DVD-ROM
- GrammarNotes DVD-ROM
- Audio Anthology CD
- Audio Tutor CD

THINK central

Find It Online!

The interactive version of this unit on **thinkcentral.com** includes
- video and **PowerNotes** introductions to key selections
- audio support—listen or download
- **ThinkAloud** models
- **WordSharp** vocabulary tutorials
- interactive review and remediation

Preview Unit Goals

TEXT ANALYSIS	• Analyze character traits and motivation • Analyze the methods writers use to develop complex characters • Analyze how characters advance the plot of a story • Analyze characters' moral dilemmas
READING	• Cite evidence to make inferences and generalizations • Identify central ideas and supporting details • Identify an author's perspective
WRITING AND LANGUAGE	• Write a narrative (short story) • Understand and use varied sentence types • Use precise verbs and modifiers
VOCABULARY	• Determine figurative and connotative meanings of words • Use reference materials to determine or clarify a word's etymology or meaning
ACADEMIC VOCABULARY	• dynamic • seek • individual • undergo • motive
MEDIA AND VIEWING	• Identify and analyze characterization and stereotypes in film • Produce a video narrative

Media Smart DVD-ROM

Creating Characters on Film

Explore the ways filmmakers portray characters in a riveting scene from *Finding Forrester*. Page 276.

175

COMMON CORE UNIT GOALS

RL 1, RL 2, RL 3, RL 4, RL 6, RL 10, RI 1, RI 2, RI 4, RI 6, RI 10, W 2, W 2b, W 3a-e, W 4, W 4b, W 5, W 6, W 10, SL 1, SL 1c, SL 1d, SL 2, SL 4, SL 5, L 1, L 1b, L 2c, L 3, L 4, L 4b, L 4c, L 5, L 5b, L 6

Complete text of the Common Core State Standards is found in the correlation on p. T10. Standards covered in this unit are found in the standards overview (pp. 173A–173B) are on the lesson pages where they are taught.

Preview Unit Goals

The listing on this page provides an overview of the skills and strategies covered in this unit. Point out that each skill strand is marked with a different color; explain that skills are color-coded in the same way throughout the text. As students read the page, encourage them to think about their ability to use each skill and strategy.

Ask students to write the Academic Vocabulary terms in their journal, leaving space to create their own definitions and to record examples as they work through the unit. Suggest that students use these terms frequently in class-room discussion as well as in their writing about the selections.

DIFFERENTIATED INSTRUCTION

FOR ENGLISH LANGUAGE LEARNERS

Academic Vocabulary Provide students with definitions of each Academic Vocabulary word.

dynamic (dī nam′ ik) *adj.* energetic; changing; in motion

individual (in′də vij′ōō əl) *adj*. existing as a single, separate thing or being

motive (mōt′iv) *n.* incentive; inner drive or desire that causes someone to act

seek (sēk) *v.* to look for or try to find

undergo (un′dər gō′) *v.* to endure, go through, or experience

Use the copy master to help students learn academic words they will use in this unit and on the Assessment Practice.

R RESOURCE MANAGER—Copy Masters
Academic Vocabulary p. 1
Additional Academic Vocabulary p. 2

Focus and Motivate

COMMON CORE FOCUS

RL 3 Analyze how complex characters develop over the course of a text, interact with other characters, and advance the plot or theme of a text.

Teach

Part 1: Character Development

Character Traits Point out that character traits can be physical traits, intellectual traits, or traits that reveal personality. For example, a character might be graceful and intelligent but reckless. To emphasize various ways that characters are developed, display several illustrations of stereotypical characters from either literature or film. These might include a bold pirate, a fairy princess, an evil villain, or a shy teenager. Ask students what aspects of the character's appearance show his or her personality. Then encourage them to develop these characters further by

- describing possible actions and words of each character
- describing how other characters might react to the character

Round and Flat Characters Explain that round characters seem real. Like real people, they have internal conflicts and a variety of traits, strengths, and weaknesses. A character traits web of a round character would have many notations. Flat characters, on the other hand, have few thoughts or traits. Ask students to give examples of flat characters from stories they have read. Encourage them to think of characters in folk tales as well as short stories.

BEST PRACTICES TOOLKIT Transparency
Analysis Frame: Character pp. D21, D26

Analyzing Characters *Essential Course of Study* ECOS

Slovenly manners, a magnetic personality, a competitive streak—these are the kinds of qualities that can shape your impressions of other people. For example, an egomaniac is probably not someone you would want as a friend. But finding out *why* that person behaves the way he or she does might change your opinion. Characters in literature can be just as complicated as real people. By closely analyzing characters, you can get more out of the stories you read and gain insights into human nature.

COMMON CORE

Included in this workshop:
RL 3 Analyze how complex characters develop over the course of a text, interact with other characters, and advance the plot or theme of a text.

Part 1: Character Development

Writers use many techniques to create their characters. Sometimes, the narrator of a story will tell you directly about a character, as in this example: "Enrique's active imagination often got him into trouble." More often, though, you will find out about characters indirectly. The writer may describe

- a character's physical appearance
- a character's actions, thoughts, and speech
- other characters' reactions to and comments about the character

By examining these characterization techniques, you can infer a character's **traits,** or qualities, such as insecurity or bravery. For example, what can you infer about this character from the following sentences? "Elena eyed her teammates critically. Am I the *only* one who knows how to play this game? she thought."

The extent to which a writer develops a character depends on the character's role in a story. Complex, highly developed characters, known as **round characters,** take center stage and seem the most lifelike. **Flat characters,** on the other hand, are one-sided.

ROUND CHARACTERS	FLAT CHARACTERS
Characteristics • are complex; exhibit a variety of traits • show a range of emotions • display strengths and weaknesses • often change over the course of a story	**Characteristics** • are defined by only one or two traits • show only a few emotions • may be stereotypes or stock characters • don't grow or change
Role in the Story • to serve as main characters who advance the plot • to help develop the theme	**Role in the Story** • to serve as minor characters who advance the plot or provide information • to reveal something about the main characters

---

DIFFERENTIATED INSTRUCTION

FOR STRUGGLING READERS

Note Taking For students who need help with note taking, hand out the note-taking copy master before discussing the page. Read the top paragraph aloud to students. Then ask volunteers to take turns reading aloud paragraphs or chart sections. Discuss each section after it is read, and have students record the definitions and main points on the copy master.

 RESOURCE MANAGER—Copy Master
Note Taking p. 7

How do Mrs. Wilson's thoughts about her daughter affect your impression not only of the daughter but also of Mrs. Wilson herself?

from The Opportunity

Short story by **John Cheever**

Mrs. Wilson sometimes thought that her daughter Elise was dumb. Elise was her only daughter, her only child, but Mrs. Wilson was not so blinded by love that the idea that Elise might be stupid did not occasionally cross her mind. The girl's father had died when she was eight, Mrs. Wilson had never
5 remarried, and the girl and her mother lived affectionately and closely. When Elise was a child, she had been responsive and lively, but as she grew into adolescence, as her body matured, her disposition changed, and some of the wonderful clarity of her spirit was lost. At sixteen she seemed indolent, and to have developed a stubborn indifference to the hazards and rewards of life.

Close Read

1. Based on Mrs. Wilson's thoughts about her daughter, how would you describe Elise?

2. What do Mrs. Wilson's thoughts reveal about the kind of mother she is? Cite details to support your answer.

MODEL 2: ROUND AND FLAT CHARACTERS

Here, a man named César reflects on the unfortunate turn his life has taken. As you read, pay attention to César's thoughts about his son.

from A Place Where the Sea Remembers

Novel by **Sandra Benítez**

When he was twenty-one, he had married Concha Ojeda. It was she who had allowed him to turn himself over to the sea. But now Concha was gone and in the months since the accident, the boy had gone mute and was clearly in decline. The boy needed a mother's love, he needed a father's strength, and
5 there was none of one and little left of the other. César thought of Concha's sister, who lived in Oaxaca. She had asked for the boy. She would raise him with her own, she had said at the wake. Since that time, César Burgos had agonized over his sister-in-law's offer and there were moments when he thought he would have to let the boy go.
10 He turned to his son, who sat at the table. . . .
"Why don't you speak?" Cesar cried, heat surging up his neck and into his cheeks.

Close Read

1. Is César a round or flat character? Cite details to support your answer.

2. Reread the boxed text. What do you learn about César from his thoughts about his sister-in-law's offer?

MODEL 1: CHARACTER TRAITS
Close Read

1. ***Possible answer:*** *Based on Mrs. Wilson's thoughts about her daughter, Elise seems aloof and unenthusiastic about life.*

2. ***Possible answer:*** *Mrs. Wilson seems like an overly concerned mother who loves her daughter very much and is confused about the recent change in her daughter's personality. Mrs. Wilson also seems to regret that she and Elise no longer live "affectionately and closely" (line 5).*

MODEL 2: ROUND AND FLAT CHARACTERS
Close Read

1. ***Possible answer:*** *César is a round character. He seems like a loving yet helpless father who has felt lost since his wife's death (lines 4–5). Despite his strong love for his son, César has moments when he feels he should let his son live with his sister-in-law (lines 7–9). César also exhibits some weaknesses when he loses his temper and yells at his son (lines 11–12).*

2. ***Possible answer:*** *Readers learn that César is emotionally torn about his sister-in-law's offer. It is clear that he loves his son very much, but at times, César feels like giving up and taking his sister-in-law up on her offer. César's thoughts reveal that he is not sure he is capable of giving his son what the boy needs.*

FOR STRUGGLING READERS

Concept Support Point out that character traits are different from moods or emotions. Moods and emotions often change quickly, while character traits are exhibited over time and in different circumstances. For example, a cheerful character might feel sadness upon losing a pet, but his cheer would eventually return. Read a paragraph or two from a familiar story and have students identify one of the character's traits and one of his or her emotions.

FOR ADVANCED LEARNERS/PRE–AP*

Analyze Alternatives Ask students to reread several folk tales and determine whether the characters are round or flat. Have students formulate theories about the characters and their roles in the stories.

* Pre-AP is a registered trademark of the College Entrance Examination Board. Use of the trademark does not constitute production, participation, sponsorship, or endorsement by the College Board.

THINKcentral

Online Remediation

Are your students struggling with text analysis skills? Consider assigning them one or more **Level Up Online Tutorials** as remediation before beginning this unit. Log in to **thinkcentral.com** to view a list of the skills addressed by **Level Up**.

Teach

Part 2: Character Behavior

Character Motivation Explain that a character's words and actions are often the result of his or her desire to attain a particular goal. To understand a character's motives, a reader needs to look at the actions of a character and ask why he or she does or says a particular thing. Read this story aloud:

> A star gymnast falls from the high bars at a state competition and sprains her ankle. It soon heals, but she avoids the bars for the rest of the season. The next season she refuses to try out for the team. She tells friends that she has simply lost interest in the sport.

Ask students what they think the girl's motivation is for dropping out of gymnastics. *Students might say that she has developed a fear of heights or that she is afraid she will get hurt or embarrass herself again.* Ask what her actions reveal about her character. *She may not be as fearless and competitive as she would want people to think.*

STATIC AND DYNAMIC CHARACTERS

After students read the chart, explain that of all the characters in a story, the main characters are most likely to be dynamic characters. In addition to the tips and questions in the chart, suggest that students ask themselves these questions:

- Does the character look or act differently at the end of the story? What might this difference indicate?
- Do other characters treat the character differently? If so, in what way?
- What might the character do in the future?

Help students develop mnemonics for remembering the difference between static and dynamic characters.

CHECK UNDERSTANDING

Have students write definitions of *character motivation, static characters,* and *dynamic characters.*

Part 2: Character Behavior

Once you understand *who* the characters are, the next questions concern *why* they act a certain way and *how* they change. Attempting to answer these questions not only takes you deeper into the story but also brings you closer to understanding the complexity of human behavior, including your own.

CHARACTER MOTIVATION

What prompted the man to steal a large sum of money? A character's **motivation**—the reasons behind his or her actions—can affect your perception of that character. For instance, the man might steal money to feed his family or to achieve a lifelong dream of wealth. How do these reasons affect your opinion of him?

Sometimes a character's motivation is stated directly in a story. Usually, though, you need to look for clues and details to try to figure out the motivation. As you read, pay attention to

- the narrator's direct comments about a character's motivation
- the character's actions, thoughts, and values
- the moral dilemmas, or questions, the character faces
- your own insights into human behavior

Possible Motives

Character

Resulting Action

STATIC AND DYNAMIC CHARACTERS

In addition to knowing why a character acts a certain way, it is important to analyze how a character changes as a result of the events in a story. A character might grow emotionally, learn a lesson, or alter his or her behavior. Characters who change and grow as the plot develops are **dynamic characters.** In contrast, characters who remain the same are **static characters.**

STRATEGIES FOR ANALYZING CHARACTER CHANGE

First examine the change:	Then analyze the meaning:
• Compare how a character was at the beginning of the story with how he or she is at the end.	• What lesson does the character learn, or what insight does he or she gain?
• Is the change **external,** such as in appearance or circumstance? Is it an **internal** change of attitude or belief?	• Does the change show personal growth, or does it lead to the character's downfall?
• What factors, events, or characters contributed to or caused the change?	• Would the character be motivated to change without the contributing factors?

178 UNIT 2: CHARACTER DEVELOPMENT

DIFFERENTIATED INSTRUCTION

FOR STRUGGLING READERS

Note Taking For those students who need help with note taking, hand out the note-taking copy master for this page. Read and discuss the top of the page. Then discuss one section at a time, allowing students time to complete one section before taking notes on the next.

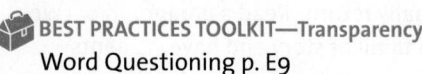

R RESOURCE MANAGER—Copy Master
Note Taking p. 8

FOR ENGLISH LANGUAGE LEARNERS

Concept Support: Character Terms On the board, write *motivation, dynamic character,* and *static character.* Have students work in pairs to make a Word Questioning diagram for each word or phrase. Identify dynamic objects, such as mobiles, and then contrast them with static objects, such as statues.

🧰 BEST PRACTICES TOOLKIT—Transparency
Word Questioning p. E9

MODEL 1: CHARACTER MOTIVATION

These two excerpts come from a story about a girl's initiation into a sorority. Why does Millicent want to join the exclusive club?

from **I N I T I A T I O N**

Short story by **Sylvia Plath**

What girl would not want to be one of the elect, no matter if it did mean five days of initiation before and after school, ending in the climax of Rat Court on Friday night when they made the new girls members? Even Tracy had been wistful when she heard that Millicent had been one of the five girls to
5   receive an invitation.

"It won't be any different with us, Tracy," Millicent had told her. "We'll still go around together like we always have, and next year you'll surely get in."

"I know, but even so," Tracy had said quietly, "you'll change, whether you think you will or not. Nothing ever stays the same."

10   And nothing does, Millicent had thought. How horrible it would be if one never changed . . . if she were condemned to be the plain, shy Millicent of a few years back for the rest of her life.

Close Read

1. The [boxed] text reveals how difficult it is to get into the sorority. Find another place that explains Millicent's more personal reason for wanting to belong.

2. What does Millicent's desire to join the sorority reveal about her?

MODEL 2: CHARACTER CHANGE

Now read to see how Millicent changes by the end of the story.

As part of her initiation, Millicent has had to ask strangers on a bus what they had for breakfast. One man answered cheerfully, "Heather birds' eyebrows on toast." His unusual response helped Millicent put the experience in perspective.

Outside, the sparrows were still chirping, and as she lay in bed Millicent visualized them, pale gray-brown birds in a flock, one like the other, all exactly alike.

And then, for some reason, Millicent thought of the heather birds. Swooping
5   carefree over the moors, they would go singing and crying out across the great spaces of air, dipping and darting, strong and proud in their freedom and their sometime loneliness. It was then that she made her decision.

Seated now on the woodpile in Betsy Johnson's cellar, Millicent knew that she had come triumphant through the trial of fire, the searing period of the ego
10   which could end in two kinds of victory for her. The easiest of which would be her coronation as a princess, labeling her conclusively as one of the select flock.

The other victory would be much harder, but she knew that it was what she wanted. It was not that she was being noble or anything. It was just that she had learned there were other ways of getting into the great hall, blazing with
15   lights, of people and of life.

Close Read

1. How has Millicent changed since the beginning of the story? Explain whether her change is external or internal.

2. What insight does Millicent gain? Cite details to support your answer.

FOR ENGLISH LANGUAGE LEARNERS

Culture: Clarify Explain to students that a sorority is an organized social club that allows only certain people (usually women) to join. In some schools, members of a sorority live together, eat together, and share in special activities. Many such clubs require that people who want to join must first go through an initiation, or ritual ceremony.

MODEL 1: CHARACTER MOTIVATION

Close Read

1. *Possible answer: "How horrible it would be if one never changed . . . if she were condemned to be the plain, shy Millicent of a few years back for the rest of her life"* (lines 10–12). Millicent hopes that belonging to the sorority will be her ticket to popularity, her ticket out of her ordinary life.

2. *Possible answers: Millicent cares about how others perceive her. She is not satisfied with her life right now and hopes that the sorority will improve her social situation. Millicent clearly cares about popularity, belonging, and having others look up to her.*

MODEL 2: CHARACTER CHANGE

Close Read

1. *Possible answer: Millicent has experienced an internal change by the end of the story. After hearing the man's unusual response about the heather birds, Millicent realizes that it is better to be independent and proud than dependent on a flock of others. She decides not to go through with joining the sorority.*

2. *Possible answer: Millicent realizes that joining a sorority is not her ticket to happiness, as evidenced by this text: "... she had learned there were other ways of getting into the great hall, blazing with lights, of people and of life" (lines 14–15). She realizes that happiness is not about being among a "select flock" (line 11) but about celebrating one's individuality.*

IF STUDENTS NEED HELP . . . Ask students to find words describing the sparrows and the heather birds. Discuss which kind of bird sounds more appealing. Then help students distinguish between the two kinds of victories described in lines 10–15.

Practice and Apply

Part 3: Analyze the Text

Close Read

1. **Possible answer:** *The wife seems like a nag who has hounded her husband about Brigid for years. Statements that reveal her personality include "You oughtn't to need to be told . . ." (line 7) and "Men don't like marrying into a family that has the like of her in it" (line 17).*

2. **Possible answer:** *The wife also wants to put Brigid in a home because Brigid will be able to receive proper care there.*

3. **Possible answer:** *The husband has a strong will because he stands up to his wife's unrelenting nagging (line 27). Also, he is a very caring brother who wants the best for his sister, Brigid.*

Part 3: Analyze the Text

The following excerpts are from a story set on a farm in Ireland. Two characters, husband and wife, are bickering over something that they have clearly argued about many times before. As you read, analyze the characters' traits, motivations, and changes.

---

from **Brigid**

Short story by **Mary Lavin**

"I see there's no use in talking about it," said the woman. "All I can say is God help the girls, with you, their own father, putting a drag on them so that no man will have anything to do with them after hearing about Brigid."

"What do you mean by that? This is something new. I thought it was
5 only the bit of bread and tea she got that you grudged the poor thing. This is something new. What is this?"

"You oughtn't to need to be told, a man like you that saw the world, a man that traveled like you did, a man that was in England and London."

"I don't know what you're talking about." He took up his hat and felt it to
10 see if the side he had placed near the fire was dry. He turned the other side toward the fire. "What are you trying to say?" he said. "Speak plain!"

"Is any man going to marry a girl when he hears her aunt is a poor half-witted creature, soft in the head, and living in a poke of a hut, doing nothing all day but sitting looking into the fire?"
15 "What has that got to do with anybody but the poor creature herself? Isn't it her own trouble?"

"Men don't like marrying into a family that has the like of her in it."

"Is that so? I didn't notice that you were put off marrying me, and you knew all about poor Brigid. You used to bring her bunches of primroses. And
20 one day I remember you pulling the flowers off your hat and giving them to her when she started crying over nothing. You used to say she was a harmless poor thing. You used to say you'd look after her."

"And didn't I? Nobody can say I didn't look after her. Didn't I do my best to have her taken into a home, where she'd get the proper care? You can't deny
25 that."

"I'm not denying it. You never gave me peace or ease since the day we were married. But I wouldn't give in. I wouldn't give in then, and I won't give in now, either. I won't let it be said that I had a hand or part in letting my own sister be put away."
30 "But it's for her own good."

Close Read

1. What do you learn about the wife's personality from the things she says to her husband? Cite specific statements to support your answer.

2. The boxed sentence gives one reason why the wife wants to put Brigid in a "home." What other motivation is revealed in this excerpt?

3. Reread lines 18–22 and 26–29. What do you learn about the husband's traits from the way he responds to his wife?

DIFFERENTIATED INSTRUCTION

FOR STRUGGLING READERS

Analysis Support: Character Traits To help students "hear" the conversation between the man and wife, have pairs of students read the excerpt aloud, using emphasis and tone of voice to emphasize character traits.

Later in the story, a sudden tragedy prompts the wife to reflect on her relationship with her husband and their argument over Brigid's care.

After their argument, the husband goes to visit Brigid at her tiny cottage within walking distance of the house. When he doesn't return by dark, his wife gets worried and goes to look for him. She finds his body at the cottage, his head badly burned by the hearth fire where he had fallen, while Brigid sits uncomprehending nearby.

It was dark at the pump, but she could hear people running the way she had pointed. Then when they had reached the cottage, there was no more running, but great talking and shouting. She sat down at the side of the pump, but there was a smell off her hands and desperately she bent forward and began to
5   wash them under the pump, but when she saw there was hair stuck to her fingers she wanted to scream again, but there was a great pain gathering in her heart, not yet the pain of loss, but the pain of having failed; failed in some terrible way.

    I failed him always, she thought, from the very start. I never loved him like he loved me; not even then, long ago, the time I took the flowers off my hat. It
10   wasn't for Brigid, like he thought. I was only making myself out to be what he imagined I was. I didn't know enough about loving to change myself for him. I didn't even know enough about it to keep him loving me. He had to give it all to Brigid in the end.

    He gave it all to Brigid; to a poor daft thing that didn't know enough to
15   pull him back from the fire or call someone when he fell down in a stroke. If it was anyone else was with him, he might have had a chance.

    Oh, how had it happened? How could love be wasted and go to loss like that? . . .

    Suddenly she thought of the heavy feet of the neighbors tramping the
20   boards of the cottage up in the fields behind her, and rising up, she ran back up the boreen.[1]

    "Here's the poor woman now," someone said, as she thrust past the crowd around the door.

    They began to make a way for her to where, on the settle bed, they had
25   laid her husband. But instead she parted a way through the people and went toward the door of the room off the kitchen.

    "It's Brigid I'm thinking about," she said. "Where is she?"

    "Something will have to be done about her now all right," someone said.

    "It will," she said, decisively, and her voice was as true as a bell.
30   She had reached the door of the room.

    "That's why I came back," she said, looking around her defiantly. "She'll need proper minding now. To think she hadn't the strength to run for help or pull him back a bit from the fire." She opened a door.

    Sitting on the side of the bed, all alone, she saw Brigid.
35   "Get your hat and coat, Brigid," she said. "You're coming with me."

---

1. **boreen:** a narrow country lane.

Close Read

1. Reread the boxed text. What motivated the wife to be kind to Brigid initially?

2. How does the wife change during the story? Explain the lesson she has learned by the end.

3. Do you think the wife would have changed had her husband not died? Support your opinion with evidence.

4. "Brigid" is the title of this story, yet Brigid herself never speaks. Is she a flat or round character? Support your answer.

FOR ENGLISH LANGUAGE LEARNERS

Pronoun Referents Explain the pronoun referents for *It* (line 1), *they* (line 2), and *him* (line 8). If necessary, explain how you determined this. Then have students work in mixed-language groups to find other pronouns and their referents in the italicized text at the top of page 181 and in the paragraph that begins on line 8 on the same page.

Close Read

1. *Possible answer: The wife was kind to Brigid because she wanted to look good in her husband's eyes.*

2. *Possible answer: The wife realizes that she failed her husband. She did not know enough about loving to change herself for him or to keep him loving her. She takes pity on Brigid, who was not able to help her brother out of the fire. The wife makes a decision that she should be the one to care for Brigid.*

3. *Answers will vary, but students may say that the wife probably would not have changed if her husband had not died. The wife had not changed her position in all the years she and her husband had argued about Brigid. It took a tragedy to change her.*

4. *Possible answer: Brigid is a flat, one-dimensional character, one who doesn't display emotion. Her role in the story is to advance the plot, which she does through her inaction and inability to save her brother, and to reveal the true nature of the husband and the wife.*

Assess and Reteach

Assess

Ask students to compare and contrast Brigid and the wife.

Reteach

For students who are unable to apply the workshop skills to "Brigid," select from these reteaching options:

1. Review with students the note-taking copy masters for this lesson.
   - Which methods helped to reveal the character of the wife in "Brigid"?
   - Which methods were not used?

2. Have students name characters from other stories and describe their traits or motivations. Have students support their responses with reasons.

COMMON CORE FOCUS

RL 1 Cite evidence to support inferences drawn from the text. **RL 3** Analyze how complex characters develop and interact with other characters. **RL 4** Determine the figurative meaning of words and phrases as they are used in a text. **L 3** Apply knowledge of language to make effective choices for style. **L 4c** Consult reference materials to determine or clarify a word's meaning or etymology.

SUMMARY

In "Shoofly Pie," Mattie distracts herself from the grief she feels after her mother's death by becoming a cook at the *Good for You Restaurant*. There, she comes into conflict with Johnny, the rude chef. After about six months, she leaves. She has made friends, resolved her conflict with Johnny, and coped, in some ways, with her grief.

Is there a cure for
GRIEF?

Write the term *grief* and elicit students' ideas about what the word means. Ask what causes grief and how it affects us. Read and discuss the Big Question. After students complete the *QUICKWRITE*, talk about the differences between coping with grief and curing it.

Shoofly Pie
Short Story by Naomi Shihab Nye

Is there a cure for
GRIEF?

COMMON CORE

RL 1 Cite evidence to support inferences drawn from the text. **RL 3** Analyze how complex characters develop and interact with other characters. **RL 4** Determine the figurative meaning of words and phrases as they are used in a text. **L 4c** Consult reference materials to determine or clarify a word's meaning or etymology.

The death of a loved one can be overwhelming. Yet people who experience such losses must eventually get on with their lives. In "Shoofly Pie," employees at a restaurant give new meaning to the term *comfort food* when they find a way to deal with grief.

QUICKWRITE With a small group, make a list of strategies that can help a person overcome grief. You may use the list that is shown to get started. Then write a short paragraph explaining which strategy or strategies might be most helpful to you or someone you know.

Ways of Dealing
with Grief
1. Talk to friends.
2. Keep busy.
3.
4.
5.

182

See resources on the **Teacher One Stop DVD-ROM** *and on* **thinkcentral.com**.

R RESOURCE MANAGER UNIT 2

Plan and Teach, pp. 9–16
Summary, pp. 17–18†‡*
Text Analysis and Reading
   Skill, pp. 19–22†*
Grammar and Style, p. 25

DIAGNOSTIC AND SELECTION TESTS
Selection Tests, pp. 55-58

BEST PRACTICES TOOLKIT

New Word Analysis, p. E8
Cluster Diagram, p. B18
Timeline, p. B23
Definition Mapping, p. E6
Word Questioning, p. E9
Plot Diagram, p. D10
Observation Chart, p. C7
Two Column Chart, p. A25

TECHNOLOGY
- Teacher One Stop DVD-ROM
- Student One Stop DVD-ROM
- Audio Anthology CD
- GrammarNotes DVD-ROM
- ExamView Test Generator
  on the **Teacher One Stop**

* Resources for Differentiation   † Also in Spanish   ‡ In Haitian Creole and Vietnamese

TEXT ANALYSIS: CHARACTER TRAITS

Characters often have consistent qualities, or **character traits**, that readers learn about over the course of a story. A trait may be a physical quality, such as clumsiness, or an aspect of the character's personality. In "Shoofly Pie," Nye sometimes directly describes a character trait. For example, we find out that the main character's boss is a good mentor in the following statement by the narrator:

That was the greatest thing about Riyad—he never made anyone feel stupid for not knowing something.

Instead of directly describing a character's traits, writers often let the reader draw conclusions about them. Your conclusions may be based on

- the character's words, thoughts, and actions
- what other characters say or think about the character

As you read "Shoofly Pie," note the traits of the main characters.

Review: Static and Dynamic Characters

READING SKILL: CONNECT

You can enhance your understanding and enjoyment of a story when you **connect** to it, or relate the content to your own experiences and knowledge. For example, you might connect your own experience of grief with the main character's grief in "Shoofly Pie." Ask the following questions to help make connections:

- Does a character remind me of myself or of someone I know?
- What do I know about the time, place, event, or situation described in the story?
- How is the story similar to other works I have read?

As you read "Shoofly Pie," record connections you make in a chart like the one shown.

Episode in the Story	My Connection
Mattie grieves over her mother's death.	When my uncle died, I stayed in my room all weekend.

Review: Compare and Contrast

 Complete the activities in your **Reader/Writer Notebook.**

Meet the Author

Naomi Shihab Nye
born 1952

Bicultural Upbringing
Like the character of Mattie, Naomi Shihab Nye (nī) is of Arab descent. She was raised in a bicultural household by her American mother and Palestinian father. As a teenager she spent a year in the Middle East and got to know her Palestinian grandmother, who became an important inspiration to her. Nye started writing poetry at age six, taking as subject matter her neighborhood's cats, squirrels, and trees.

In Praise of Diversity
Today, Nye is an award-winning poet and fiction writer. She still loves to write about familiar sights and sounds, but she also seeks to promote peace and cross-cultural understanding through her work. Nye believes that connections between people from different backgrounds enrich society as a whole: "I've never understood the impulse to be with people only like ourselves. How dull that would be."

BACKGROUND TO THE STORY

A Restaurant Remembered
Nye's inspiration for the Good for You Restaurant in "Shoofly Pie" came from her own memories. While attending college, she worked as a cook at a natural foods restaurant called the Greenwood Grocery. The experience left a lasting impression. Nye says that she has made several attempts in her writing to memorialize the "characters, flavors, and fragrances" of a place that has since passed out of existence.

Author Online **THINK** central
Go to **thinkcentral.com.**
KEYWORD: HML10-183

183

Teach

● *Model the Skill:* **CHARACTER TRAITS**

Tell students that Nye's character traits are described in in the short biography of the author in the textbook. Point out that some traits are directly described in the biography, such as Nye's bicultural heritage and her desire to promote cross-cultural understanding. Other traits are desribed indirectly through Nye's words. Tell students that they could conclude from what Nye says that she loves diversity.

GUIDED PRACTICE Have students describe the character traits of a favorite character from a book, movie, or TV show.

■ *Model the Skill:* **CONNECT**

To model how to connect, have students consider how their own memories might bring back interesting people, places, sights, sounds, or smells. Point out that Nye uses her memories to write "Shoofly Pie." Ask students what kinds of stories they could write based on their experiences.

GUIDED PRACTICE Have students name any other detail on this spread, including the details about grief and comfort food, with which they might connect, and jot down the connection.

R RESOURCE MANAGER—Copy Master
Connect p. 21 (for student use while reading the selection)

DIFFERENTIATED INSTRUCTION

FOR STRUGGLING READERS

Review Traits Explain that traits are the qualities shown by a character. List some of your traits, such as being left-handed, curious, easy-going, or social. Include a mix of physical and personality traits. Put them in a Cluster Diagram with your name in the middle. Ask students to make a similar cluster showing some of their own traits.

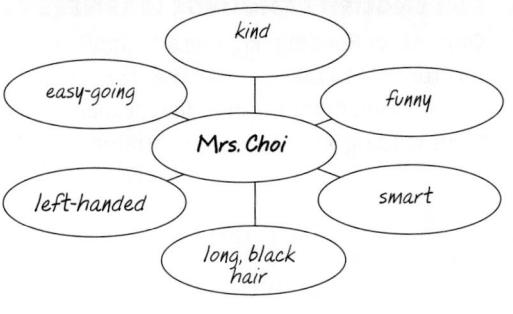

 BEST PRACTICES TOOLKIT—Transparency
Cluster Diagram p. B18

READ WITH A PURPOSE

Help students set a purpose for reading. Tell them to note the ways the different characters react to their grief.

SHOOFLY PIE

NAOMI SHIHAB NYE

*On our way somewhere we sat at this table—
wood clear-varnished, a design to hold the days:
two people talking toward the center;
candlelight on each face . . .*
　　　　　　　　　　—William Stafford [1]

Mattie couldn't believe she dropped the giant honey jar on the floor the moment the boss entered the kitchen after his overseas trip. Have you ever watched a gallon of honey ooze into a slow-motion golden dance around a mound of broken glass?

　　It might have looked glorious if she hadn't been the one who dropped it.

　　The boss stared at her with his deep eyes, his mouth wide open. "And you . . . must be . . . ?" he asked.

　　A secret voice in her head replied, *The idiot. The donkey.* But her real voice said, "The person they hired while you were out of town." Then she said, "I'm
10　so sorry—I'm also very sorry about your father," and knelt down.

　　You couldn't exactly use a *broom* on honey. A shovel maybe? She had a weird desire to stick both her hands into it.

　　Or, she might faint. Having never fainted before, she always imagined it as a way to escape a difficult scene. That, or going to the bathroom. "Excuse me," she'd said, many other times in her life. "I'll be right back." At her own mother's funeral recently, she'd spent a lot of time in the bathroom with her

Analyze Visuals ▶

Examine the photograph. What details help you form a mental image of the story's **setting**?

① **Targeted Passage**

---

1. **William Stafford (1914–1993):** an American poet who wrote about the daily concerns of people.

Middle-Eastern Cuisine The main character and the restaurant owner share a similar culinary heritage: the cuisines of Lebanon and Syria, as well as those of Jordan and Iraq, bear many similarities. These include a love of lamb; the use of garlic, cinnamon, and other spices; a reliance on the rich, salty, and sweet flavors of olives and dates; and the use of cultured (sour) milk in the form of leban, yogurt, and madzoon.

Cultural Connection In "Shoofly Pie," the characters use food as a means of communication and comfort. As in many families, food and the preparation of food is Mattie's link to her mother, who has died. Johnny, too, has fond memories of cooking with his grandfather. Have students tell about foods they might describe as "comfort foods" or foods that are a part of family traditions. For example, many cultures include pasta or noodle dishes at holiday times. Ask students what foods connote family or "comfort" in their cultures.

Analyze Visuals

Possible answer: The milk, the paper cups, and the bottles of flavored syrup all suggest a counter in a restaurant or café. The colorful menu board, decorated tiles, and yellow walls help form the image of a cheerful setting.

Activity Have students decide whether the details of the setting shown suggest a place that serves food that is "good for you."
Possible answers: Yes, the soup is veggie lentil. No, the bottles of syrup would be used in sweet sodas or coffee drinks.

- Who is the main character? (line 1)
- What is her first action in the story? (lines 1–2)
- Where is she? (line 2, lines 19–22)

FOR ADVANCED LEARNERS/PRE–AP

Analyze Have a volunteer read the quotation from William Stafford aloud. Discuss with students why they think the author chose to begin with this quotation. What information can they glean from it? Based on the quotation, what predictions can students make about what they will encounter in the short story?

A CONNECT
RL 1

Possible answer: *Mattie's reaction is believable because she feels embarrassed about dropping the jar of honey and thinks of ways to escape the situation.*

TEXT ANALYSIS   COMMON CORE

B CHARACTER TRAITS
RL 3

Possible answer: *Words might include* kind, patient, down-to-earth, accepting, *and* mild-mannered.

Extend the Discussion Does this portrayal of a boss seem realistic to you? Why or why not?

READING SKILL   COMMON CORE

C *Model the Skill:* CONNECT
RL 1

Tell students that their experiences enable them to connect with and better understand the story. Have students reread lines 53–58. Point out that in line 53, readers are told that the character "needed distraction." Explain that the next two lines tell why—the character's mother had died and her father was gone all day. Have students recall a time when they needed distraction from a difficult memory or event. Have students record their connections in their graphic organizers.

Possible answer: *A restaurant is a busy place. The work, as well as the customers and other workers, creates a constant distraction for Mattie.*

---

forehead pressed against the cool tiles. She felt safe, removed from the grief of what was waiting for her back in the world. **A**

In this case, a huge mess to clean up, and twelve sprouty salads to make, 20 *pronto.*[2] A bouquet of orders hung clipped to the silver line strung over the window between the kitchen and the dining room. She could peek out into the happier part of the restaurant, the eating domain, where regular people with purses and backpacks and boyfriends were waiting for their lunches.

How had she gotten into this?

Long ago, before her mother was diagnosed with cancer, when she still thought she just had migraine headaches, Mattie offered to make dinner by herself. She was twelve. During the whirl of washing lettuce, hulling fresh peas, stirring spaghetti sauce, and lighting the oven to heat the bread, she'd managed to pull down from the wall the giant shelf over the stove that held 30 matchbooks, tea, boxes, spice jars, recipes, birthday candles, half-empty sacks of Arabic coffee, yellowed grocery lists, vitamins, and her mother's favorite cabbage teapot with a china rabbit for a lid. One ear broke off the rabbit and chips of china fell into the spaghetti pot. Her mother came into the kitchen with a wet rag over her head to see what was happening.

Mattie should have known she was destined for disaster.

Today the boss squatted beside her. She felt comfortable to be in the presence of another American-of-Arab-descent, but it didn't seem the right moment to mention it. She'd seen his name on the mail that came in his absence. Despite her clumsiness, he was smiling and mild. "Thank you," he 40 said. "My father was a good man. As for the honey, I think I'll get one of those big scoops we use in the cooler and take care of it myself. Why don't you go back to what you were doing? Don't worry about it!" **B**

She stared after him. What a nice voice! Relieved, she turned back to the counter to sprinkle sunflower seeds and shaved cheese over the bowls of lettuce . . . and there was the empty honey bear sitting with its hat off, waiting for her to refill it for the waitress who had shoved it at her—Mattie would suggest the waitresses take care of such details themselves from now on.

Two weeks ago she'd never even thought about being a cook in a restaurant and now she was ready to help run the place.

50 The boss could have fired her. Some bosses were mean. She'd heard about them from her parents over the years. But suddenly she wanted this job very much. She needed it.

She needed the money, but even more, she needed distraction. It was too hard to be home by herself for the summer since her mother had died the first week of June. Her father was at work all day long until suppertime. Three days after the funeral, she'd gotten on a bus to ride downtown to the library and, in her distraction, had gotten off too early. She saw the *Good for You Restaurant* staring her in the face. **C**

That's what she needed. Something that was good for her.

60 So she stepped inside for a late lunch. After ordering an avocado sandwich

---

2. ***pronto*** (prŏn′tō): promptly.

A CONNECT
Reread lines 1–18. Based on your experiences, do you find Mattie's reaction to her accident believable? Why or why not?

B CHARACTER TRAITS
What words would you use to describe Mattie's boss?

C CONNECT
Recall a time when you did something to distract yourself from painful thoughts. Why might a restaurant job be a good distraction for Mattie?

DIFFERENTIATED INSTRUCTION

FOR STRUGGLING READERS

Start a Timeline Because not all of the story events are told in chronological order, and because some events in Mattie's earlier life also figure in the plot, encourage students to begin recording major events in pencil on a timeline. Note that students may need to shift some events as they learn more from the story.

 BEST PRACTICES TOOLKIT—Transparency
Timeline p. B23

FOR ENGLISH LANGUAGE LEARNERS

Vocabulary Support Use Definition Mapping to teach these words: *Despite* (line 39), *perspective* (line 111), *practitioners* (line 156), *innovative* (line 228), *coinciding* (line 284), *migrating* (line 343).

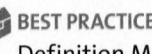 **BEST PRACTICES TOOLKIT—Transparency**
Definition Mapping p. E6

with cheese, she'd asked the waitress, "Do you like working here?" It was a cozy environment. Large, abstract paintings, mismatched chairs, real flowers in ceramic vases on each table. Ceiling fans, soft jazz playing.

The waitress sighed and shrugged.

Mattie asked, "Do you get to eat for free?"

"Sure. But who needs food? I'm not hungry. You get sick of food when you haul it around all day." She whispered, "Anyway, I'm too in love to think about food."

"With who?" (Mattie wondered why, when someone else whispered, you
70 whispered back.)

"The guy who washes dishes. Augie. If you go to the restroom, you can see him through the doorway. He has long blond hair and an earring."

Who didn't have an earring, these days? Even men who looked like Mattie's father had an earring.

So she walked back to the restroom just to see the love interest of a person she didn't even know, to distract herself from her own thoughts. The dishwasher looked bubbly and clean in his white apron. As if he washed himself between dishes. Slicked up and soapy. He grinned at Mattie when he caught her glance.

80 "He's cute," Mattie whispered to the waitress, upon her return. She ordered a bowl of fresh peach cobbler. She'd barely eaten in days.

"The problem with working here right now," the waitress said, "is—we're so shorthanded. Johnny's the main cook, but his grandpa died in Alabama, and he went over to help his grandma out two weeks ago. Plus, our boss Riyad was called to Beirut suddenly for his father's funeral—everyone is dying! Riyad's great, he helps out in the kitchen when he's here. But without them both, it's a nightmare! Riyad thought we needed an extra cook even before everybody left. Do you know anybody who'd like to be a cook?"

Fueled by her cobbler, Mattie was a danger to society. Plus, if everyone was
90 bereaved in this place, she'd fit right in. "I would."

"Do you have experience?"

"Of course!" Who didn't? She'd been inventing sandwiches and slicing elegant strips of celery for years. She made quick stir-frys for her parents and super-French-toast on the weekends. She'd often made her mother's sack lunches as well as her own—her mother had taught at a Montessori school where she had to heat up twenty little orange containers in the microwave at lunchtime every day. None of her students ate peanut butter anymore, she said—they ate curries, casseroles, and tortilla soup.

Mattie even read cookbooks for relaxation sometimes. While her mother
100 was dying, she couldn't concentrate very well on novels and found herself fixating on women's magazine recipes describing how to make cakes in the shapes of baby lambs and chicks.

"How do I apply?" The waitress dragged Sergio, temporary cook-in-command, to Mattie's table. He had a frantic glaze in his eyes, but asked a few questions and wrote her phone number down. Then he told her to show up

(2) Targeted Passage

TIERED DISCUSSION PROMPTS

Refer to lines 61–90 and use these prompts to help students understand how and why Mattie gets her job:

Connect Based on the story so far, would you want to work at the *Good for You Restaurant?* Students should cite evidence for their opinions.

Analyze Why do you think Mattie considers working at the *Good for You Restaurant? Possible answer: She needs money and distraction. It is a "cozy environment" (lines 61–62). She feels she would fit in (lines 89–90).*

Synthesize What is the *Good for You Restaurant* like? *Possible answer: It seems cozy, inviting, low-key, and friendly.*

REVISIT THE BIG QUESTION

Is there a cure for

GRIEF?

Discuss Based on lines 99–102, what does this passage suggest about the relationship between food and grief in Mattie's life? *Possible answer: Mattie read about food and recipes as a way to avoid grieving as her mother was dying. Food seems to provide a comforting distraction from grief.*

FOR STRUGGLING READERS

(2) **Targeted Passage** [Lines 82–98]

These lines help move the plot along and reveal character.

- What is the problem at the restaurant right now? (lines 82–87)
- Who suggests that Mattie could be the cook? (lines 89–90)
- What is Mattie's experience? (lines 92–96)

FOR ENGLISH LANGUAGE LEARNERS

Language Coach

Roots and Affixes

Answer: Referring to paintings, it might mean "to draw away from something"—maybe that means the painting does not resemble anything real. Point out the word *distraction* (line 53). Tell students that the prefix *dis-* means "apart." Have students use that information to tell what they think the word *distract* means.

Refer to lines 106–122 and use these prompts to help students understand how the story is beginning to establish the conflict in the plot:

Connect Have you ever been nervous about a first day at school or at a new job? How did you handle your nervousness? *Answers will vary.*

Analyze How do the other workers treat Mattie on her first day? *Possible answer: Augie is friendly, but Sergio treats her like his personal servant or "goon" (lines 118–122).*

Evaluate How well is the story leading up to the possibility of future conflict for Mattie? *Possible answer: Both Sergio and Johnny sound like trouble. Also, the reader knows that Mattie took the job impulsively and is not experienced. These details effectively establish the story's growing conflict.*

Analyze Visuals

Possible answer: The photograph suggests Mattie's experiences as a child cooking with her mother.

---

to work the next day. That was it. No application form, no interview. Mattie did not say, "I want to cook here because my mother just died." By the next day she'd applied for a health card, her backpack was stashed under the cash register, and her own white apron was tied around her neck.

110 Augie, the dishwasher, came out wiping his hands to welcome her.

Examining the menu closely from her new perspective, Mattie tried to memorize it on the spot, while Sergio juggled salad-making with the spreading of mayonnaise on homemade bread. His large hands looked awkward sprinkling wispy curls of carrot among lettuce and arugula leaves in the line-up of bowls.

Looking down onto the top of Mattie's head, he said, "Would you wash those flats of strawberries and mushrooms that just arrived—if we don't get this mushroom soup on for dinner soon . . . " which was how Mattie became his goon.

120 She wasn't sure "goon" was the right word, but that's what she felt like.

Do this, do that. He never said "please." He gave her the most tedious jobs and quoted Johnny as if Johnny were the god of cuisine.

◀ Analyze Visuals

Which of Mattie's childhood experiences does this photograph remind you of?

DIFFERENTIATED INSTRUCTION

FOR ENGLISH LANGUAGE LEARNERS
Language: Conversational English Patterns
Explain the meaning of some of the story's many informal phrases and locutions: *Do you get to eat for free?* (line 65); *Plus* (lines 84, 466); *Of course! Who didn't?* (line 92); *Do this, do that* (line 121); *not such a big deal* (line 137); *No way* (line 334); *That she did* (line 412); and *You wish* (line 460).

Culture: Clarify Students may help describe some of the foods in the story, or you may need to explain them: peach cobbler (line 81); curries, casseroles, and tortilla soup (line 98); vegeburger, Waldorf salad (line 149); buttermilk (line 255); peach smoothie (line 279); greens, corn bread, okra, coleslaw, pecan pie (lines 380–381).

Sergio didn't know the easiest way to peel raw tomatoes—dunk them into boiling water for three minutes, then pluck them out. That was one of the million little things she'd learned from her mother. Would she be remembering them forever? She could hear her mother's voice steering her among the giant spoons and chopping blocks—a hum of kindness, a *you-can-do-it* familiar tone.

130 Here in this place her mother had never been, it seemed easier to think about her. Easier than at home where every curtain, dusty corner, and wilting plant seemed lonesome right now. The shoes poking out from her mother's side of the bed. The calendar with its blank squares for the last two months. "You know," her mother had said, when there were just a few days left in her life, "this is the last thing in the world I ever wanted to do to you." It was easier right now to be in a madly swirling kitchen her mother had never seen.

"**W**ell, I don't *know* Johnny, okay?" Mattie said to Sergio on the fifth day of heavy labor, after she'd just chopped a line of cucumbers for the daily *gazpacho*.[3] "So he's not such a big deal to me, okay?"

"He will be when he gets back," Sergio said.

He was mixing fresh herb dressings. Mattie had snipped the basil up for 140 him with shiny shears. She peeled fifty cloves of garlic in a row. Even her bed at home would smell like garlic soon. She'd fallen immediately in love with the giant shiny pans, families of knives, containers of grated cheese and chopped scallions lined up to top the splendid House Vegetarian Chili. **D**

And she liked the view through the kitchen window into the dining room. She started guessing what a customer would order before the order had been turned in.

Every day the same young woman with short dark hair came in, sat alone under a cosmic painting (blue planets spinning in outer space), and ordered a vegeburger and a Healthy Waldorf Salad on the side. She wore dangling 150 earrings made of polished stones and glass. By the end of each meal she was patting her teary cheeks with a napkin.

Was it something she was reading?

Mattie had noticed her as she stood next to Sergio mixing up their Date/ Nut/Cream Cheese Delight in a huge bowl. It didn't take many brains to do that. So she could observe their crowd of eaters—bodybuilders, marathon-runners, practitioners of yoga, religion professors, and students.

"Do you know that girl?" She poked Sergio's side so he almost cut himself.

"Watch it! Who?"

"The crying one."

160 "Huh?"

Men didn't notice anything.

"The beautiful one who comes in here every day, orders exactly the same thing, and starts crying."

---

3. *gazpacho* (gə-spä'chō): a Spanish vegetable soup served cold.

D CHARACTER TRAITS
What impression do you get of Mattie's character from reading lines 135–143?

D CHARACTER TRAITS RL 3

Possible answer: Mattie thinks for herself; she is waiting to get to know Johnny before she takes Sergio's word about him (lines 135–137). She loves cooking (lines 140–143). She finds comfort in order and cleanliness.

TIERED DISCUSSION PROMPTS

Refer to lines 123–134 and use these prompts to help students understand the purpose Mattie's job serves for her:

Connect What situations in your life bring the encouraging voice of a parent, mentor, or friend to mind? *Answers should demonstrate an understanding of lines 123–127.*

Analyze How is her job at the restaurant helping Mattie cope with her grief? *Possible answer: It is easier for Mattie to think about her mother in a place like the restaurant than it is at home (lines 128–129); the "madly swirling kitchen" (line 134) seems to be enough to bring her mother to mind but not to make Mattie too sad.*

Compare In what ways is the restaurant like a filter, letting good memories in and keeping enormous grief out? *Possible answer: There's food, so it recalls good memories in the kitchen with her mother, but it is too busy to allow Mattie to dwell on her grief. It is also not the home of any specific memory of her mother.*

FOR ENGLISH LANGUAGE LEARNERS

Language: Modifiers Students may enjoy looking closely at, or need help with, these interesting choices of adjectives and adverbs: *a* you-can-do-it *familiar tone* (line 127); *madly swirling kitchen* (line 134); *sudsy head* (line 214); *Deep, dangerous tan* (line 218); *Explosive brown curls* (line 219); *he roared, lion-like* (line 231); *welcome-home kiss* (line 268); *bubbly embrace* (line 275); *nugget of pain* (line 358).

He stared disinterestedly through the window. "Actually she does look vaguely familiar."

Mattie speculated, "Maybe she hates our food, but she's obsessive-compulsive and can't go to any other restaurant. Maybe she's in love with Augie, too."

Mattie asked Riyad if she could ring the crying customer out.

170 "Sure. Do you know how to use the cash register?"

"No."

He showed her. That was the greatest thing about Riyad—he never made anyone feel stupid for not knowing something.

Mattie took the girl's bill and rang it up, whispering, "Is there anything we can do to make you feel better?"

The girl looked shocked. "Who *are* you?" she asked.

"I'm the person who puts dressing on your salad and makes your sandwich. I've noticed you through the window. Right there—see that little window we have? I started working here a few weeks ago. And you seem—upset. I
180 wondered if you could use—someone to talk to or anything."

The girl looked suspicious. "Do you know Johnny? The cook who runs this place?"

Him again. Mattie said, "He's on a trip. I've never seen his face."

"Just wait," the girl whispered. "It's the most amazing face you'll ever see." She shook her head "God! He drives me crazy."

"Me, too," Mattie said. She stepped away from the cash register so Riyad could ring up someone else.

The girl looked confused "But I thought you said . . . "

"I was just kidding, sorry. I don't know him. Is he your boyfriend?"

190 "Well, we were dating before he went to help his grandma. But right before he left, he said we were finished—well, he didn't say that *word* exactly, because I don't think he believes in beginnings and endings, but he said—we needed to follow different paths. God, I love him! I guess that's why I've been coming in so often. I'm hoping he'll be back and will have changed his mind." Her eyes filled up again.

Mattie handed her a Kleenex. "Has he called you since he's been gone? Has he written you at all?"

"Nothing. I've called him maybe four times. His grandma always answers and says Johnny's not there. She must be lying! But you see, Johnny hates to
200 talk on the phone. He doesn't believe in it. It makes him feel—disembodied. So I don't know if he's really not there or if he's simply—sticking to his principles."

"Sorry, but he sounds like a nutcase. How old is he, by the way?"

Her face sobered. "Twenty-one," she said. "But he says he's ageless."

Sergio suddenly stood behind Mattie with a ladle in one hand and a wire whisk in the other. "Are you taking a vacation? Or is this a coffee break I wasn't told about? If you're going to work here, you'll have to carry your weight."

It was his favorite dopey phrase.

Johnny returned the next day.

🅔 CHARACTER TRAITS
What do Mattie's interactions with the girl reveal about Mattie? Cite specific words or phrases to support your answer.

🅕 COMPARE AND CONTRAST
How does Mattie's impression of Johnny compare with the girl's description of him?

COMMON CORE
RL 3

🅔 CHARACTER TRAITS

Possible answer: Even though Mattie is compassionate—she "handed [the girl] a Kleenex" (line 196)—she is also straight-forward and observant. She seems eager to connect with people, even strangers.

READING SKILL: *Review*

COMMON CORE
RL 1

🅕 COMPARE AND CONTRAST

Possible answer: So far, Mattie probably thinks of Johnny as someone who is difficult to get along with rather than as a person whom someone else would adore. She refers to him as a "nutcase" (line 202), while the girl chalks up Johnny's behavior to "sticking to his principles" (line 201).

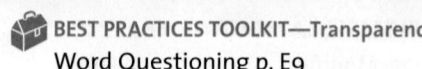

DIFFERENTIATED INSTRUCTION

FOR ENGLISH LANGUAGE LEARNERS
Vocabulary: Idioms Have students use Word Questioning to teach these idioms from the story: *love interest* (line 75), "person you are interested in romantically"; *shorthanded* (line 83), "in need of more workers"; *had a crush on* (line 278), "was infatuated with"; *lift a finger* (line 290), "make the slightest effort to help"; *went wild* (line 312), "got very excited"; *tag along* (line 476), "follow along after."

🧰 BEST PRACTICES TOOLKIT—Transparency
Word Questioning p. E9

Sergio was sick and didn't come in.

210 Riyad had to take his wife and babies to the doctor, too. Even with the *Good for You Restaurant*'s wholesome cuisine bolstering them, they'd all managed to get the flu.

So it was Johnny and Mattie on their own, with one lovesick waitress, another waitress with a sprained ankle, and Augie poking his sudsy head around the corner now and then to see if they needed plates.

Amazing face? Mattie couldn't see it. She thought he had an exaggerated square jaw, like Popeye[4] in a cartoon. Huge muscles under rolled-up white shirtsleeves. Deep, dangerous tan. Hadn't he heard about skin cancer? Explosive brown curls circled his head. He had great hair, yes. He also wore an 220 incredibly tight pair of faded jeans. Mattie couldn't imagine he felt very good inside them. **G**

"I'm sorry about your grandpa," she said.

Johnny stared at her hard. "I didn't realize you knew him."

That was mean. No way she would mention her mama when he was as mean as that. She hadn't even told Riyad or Sergio about her mother yet. Immediately Johnny started moving everything around. All the implements and condiments she'd rearranged to make them more available in a rush, all the innovative new placements of towels, tubs, cinnamon—*whoosh!*—he wanted to put things back exactly where they had been when he left.

230 And he was muttering. *Rub, rub, rub,* how dare anyone juggle the balance of his precious sphere? "Here!" he roared, lion-like, as he pulled a giant knife out from the lower shelf where Mattie had hidden it, finding it too large to be very useful. "Here is the sword of the goddess! My favorite sweet saber! And what is this pie on the Specials Board that I've never heard of in my life—*Shoofly?* Where did that come from?"

"Well, first from the Amish[5] communities in Pennsylvania. *Americana,*[6] you know? And now, from me." Mattie had suggested the recipe her second week, since it happened to be her personal favorite pie, and they'd sold out of it every day.

240 "*You?*"

He could make the simplest word sound like an insult. You didn't even want to be "you" anymore. "And who *are* you?"

She brandished her blender cap. "I'm the new—chef."

"Chef? I'm the chef around here. You're the cook, okay? Do you know the difference between the words?"

"I know the difference between lots of words. Between RUDE and NICE, for example." She stalked back to the dishwashing closet.

"Augie, break a plate over his head, will you?"

Augie looked shocked. "Johnny? Johnny's like—the mastermind! He 250 knows—everything! Did you know he even built the tables in this place?"

---

4. **Popeye:** a cartoon character with a prominent jaw.

5. **Amish:** a religious group valuing humility, family, and the simple life.

6. **Americana:** things distinctly American.

G CHARACTER TRAITS
What personality traits are suggested by this description of Johnny's appearance?

3 Targeted Passage

G CHARACTER TRAITS

Possible answer: The details suggest that Johnny cares a great deal about looking good and may risk skin cancer or discomfort to be sure that he does.

IF STUDENTS NEED HELP . . . Work with students to make a list of the details that describe Johnny. For example, "exaggerated square jaw," "huge muscles," "dangerously dark tan," "rolled-up shirtsleeves and skin-tight jeans." Discuss with students who they might cast to play Johnny in a movie version of the story and how that actor fits the character of Johnny.

REVISIT THE BIG QUESTION

Is there a cure for
GRIEF?

Discuss How does the brief exchange in lines 222–223 reflect different ways of approaching someone else's grief? *Possible answer: Mattie is polite—she offers a condolence but does not pry. Johnny is defensive, perhaps because he is still in mourning, and perhaps because he feels Mattie's comment oversteps a personal boundary about who is intimate enough to extend a condolence.*

FOR STRUGGLING READERS

3 Targeted Passage [Lines 222–247]

These lines help reveal the conflict between Mattie and Johnny.

- How does Johnny react when Mattie says she is sorry about his grandfather? (line 223)

- What does Johnny say when Mattie calls herself the new chef? (lines 244–245)

- How does Mattie feel about Johnny at this point? (lines 246–248)

FOR ENGLISH LANGUAGE LEARNERS

Vocabulary: Multiple-Meaning Words Have pairs of students work together to determine the meaning in context, as well as one other possible meaning (in another context) for each of the following words: *sphere* (line 231), *rising* (line 297), *raised* (line 365), *dashing* (line 394).

Analyze Visuals

Activity What activity is shown in the photograph, and how does it relate to the title? *Possible answer: Someone is rolling out a piecrust. This might be one of the steps in making shoofly pie.*

TEXT ANALYSIS

COMMON CORE

RL 3

⊕ CHARACTER TRAITS

Possible answer: Mattie shows that she thinks for herself. She shows that she values simple human decency, or being nice instead of rude (line 246), over being a "mastermind" (line 249).

TIERED DISCUSSION PROMPTS

Refer to lines 252–266 and use these prompts to help students understand the early relationship between Mattie and Johnny:

Connect Have you or someone you know ever been bossed around? How did you feel? *Answers will vary.*

Analyze How does Mattie respond to Johnny's authority? *Possible answer: She shows some independence by making shoofly pie that contains "Niceness" (line 259) and by talking back to him (lines 259, 265–266).*

Synthesize How does the shift in what the customers order foreshadow a shift in the relationship between Mattie and Johnny? *Possible answer: Johnny's authority can no longer be based on the feeling that he is the superior or more popular cook.*

"I don't care. He doesn't know *me.*" ⊕

She served nine pieces of Shoofly Pie that day. Arranging generous slices on yellow dessert plates, Mattie savored the sight of their crumbled toppings over the rich and creamy molasses interiors. Her mother used to love this pie.

That day no one ordered buttermilk pie, which apparently had been Johnny's specialty before he went away. His pie was still languishing in its full dish when Mattie wiped the counter at three P.M.

"What's *in* that pie of yours?" he asked her.

"Niceness."

260 During the lunch rush, Johnny had ordered Mattie around more rudely than Sergio ever did. But now she knew where Sergio learned it. Johnny snapped commands. *"Sauté! Stir!"* He kept insisting there were granules of raw sugar on the floor under his feet and making Mattie sweep when he had food all laid out.

"That's very unsanitary, Johnny, to sweep in the presence of food. Didn't your mama ever tell you?" Her words seemed to throw him into a funk.

When his weepy ex-girlfriend materialized, pressing her face up close to the kitchen window for what she hoped might be a welcome-home kiss, he tapped her forehead with his fingertips and busied himself. "Any chance we could 270 spend some time together?" she asked wistfully.

"Sharon, you know what I told you."

Tears welled up in her syrupy eyes.

She said, "Johnny, I think I can make you happy," as he slapped dill sauce around a grilled portabello mushroom on polenta. Ouch.

⊕ **CHARACTER TRAITS**
What traits does Mattie reveal in this incident?

DIFFERENTIATED INSTRUCTION

FOR STRUGGLING READERS

Plot Diagram Use the Plot Diagram to talk about how tension is building and action is rising. Plot the current point of the story about halfway to the climax. Have students identify the conflict and predict the climax.

🧰 BEST PRACTICES TOOLKIT—Transparency
Plot Diagram p. D10

FOR ADVANCED LEARNERS/PRE–AP

Indirect and Direct Characterization Have students choose one of the main characters and determine the main method of characterization. If the characterization is indirect, have students select and weigh textual evidence to show whether the characterization is achieved primarily through the character's words, thoughts, or actions; through the thoughts and words of other characters; or through a combination of methods.

The waitress and Augie had been found wrapped in a bubbly embrace in the broom closet that morning when Mattie whipped open the door looking for the mop.

Sergio now had a crush on a buff bodybuilder who came in every morning for a peach smoothie, dressed in a leopard-printed tank top. Even the Hell's
280 Angel who appeared only on Saturdays had slipped Mattie a note that said, "Good muffin, baby," drawn inside a heart.

Only Riyad, dear Riyad, seemed able to focus on food and the work right in front of him. One day after work Mattie had told him about her own Syrian heritage and her mom's death coinciding with his dad's. Did she only imagine it, or did tears well up in his eyes, too?

After that they both threw Arabic words into their talk. *"Yallah!"* Speed it up. *"Khallas!"* Enough already.

Some days Riyad refilled the bins of flour and apricots and sunflower seeds in the grocery section with careful attention. Some days he polished the front
290 window glass till it glittered. Lots of bosses might never lift a finger. One day Mattie found him down on his knees on a prayer rug in the cooler chanting in Arabic. She respected his devotion to service. He told her he had dreamed of owning a restaurant ever since he was a little boy who loved to eat, wandering the streets of Beirut. Only the ten-year war had made him leave his country. Mattie admitted she had trouble with Johnny's attitude. Riyad whispered, "Listen to this: When he first came to work here, he was our baker, not our chef. He asked me, 'Do I get paid while the bread's rising?'"

"**H**ave you been in the service or what?" Mattie asked Johnny, on her forty-fourth day at work. It was truly summer now, each day swelled full of ninety-
300 eight-degree heat. Midsummer in Texas, people forget what a cool breeze ever felt like.

"Why do you ask?"

"You act like a general. I think you'd like me to salute you."

"Well, you're full of it, too." ❶

He was furious that she had started revising the soup list. Today she was making a spicy peanut stew from Eritrea[7] with green beans and sweet potatoes.

"Where is Eritrea?" he asked her. "And what makes you think our customers will know of it if I don't?"

"East Africa. The whole world is tired of your black bean soup, Commander.
310 It's time to BRANCH OUT."

Johnny always stared at her as if he needed an interpreter.

Riyad went wild when he smelled that peanut stew cooking. "I want some! When will it be done?"

Mattie told Johnny the customers were also tired of his boring bouquet of alfalfa sprouts on top of his little salads, too. "Let's try lentil sprouts for a change.

---

7. **Eritrea** (ĕr'ĭ-trē'ə): a country in northeast Africa.

❶ CHARACTER TRAITS
What trait is Johnny suggesting that Mattie possesses?

REVISIT THE BIG QUESTION
Is there a cure for
GRIEF?

Discuss Grief can bring people together. How is that shown in lines 282–287? *Possible answer: When Riyad shows sympathy for Mattie, the reader infers that she feels closer to him as a result. Their ensuing switch to using Arabic words with each other shows sharing or increased intimacy.*

TEXT ANALYSIS   **COMMON CORE**   RL 3

❶ *Model the Skill:* CHARACTER TRAITS

Model your own thinking. Point out the word *too* in Johnny's comment, which suggests that he is accusing her of the same thing that she is accusing him of. Have students go back and tell how they interpret Mattie's comment in line 303.

Possible answer: *Johnny suggests that Mattie is also bossy or overbearing, or full of herself in her own way.*

FOR ENGLISH LANGUAGE LEARNERS
Language: Conversational English Patterns
There are many fragments in this selection. Have students restate each one as a complete sentence by adding a verb or both a subject and a verb, relying on context for information: *No application form, no interview* (line 106); *The crying one* (line 159); *Huge muscles under rolled-up white shirtsleeves. Deep-dangerous tan* (lines 217–218); *Enough already* (line 287); *East Africa* (line 309).

FOR ADVANCED LEARNERS/PRE–AP
Cultural Allusions Have students research and explain the bits of Arab culture that garnish the story. Students might investigate typical reasons for the emigration of Syrian and Lebanese citizens, the Ten-Year War, and the significance of the prayer rug.

Activity Does this photograph match your image of shoofly pie as it is described in the story? Why or why not? *Possible answer:* Yes. *In the story, shoofly pie is described as having a "rich and creamy molasses" filling and a crumbled topping (lines 253–254), and so does the pie in this photograph.*

Or nasturtiums.[8] Come on." Basically she was weary of watering them. She wanted to witness some different curls of life sprouting in the jars under the counters. Anyhow, an East Indian professor on the other side of town had just gotten E. coli[9] that was traced to alfalfa sprouts, and she felt nervous about them.

320   An anonymous food critic from the newspaper had eaten at the restaurant recently and written a glowing review. "Happy to say the *Good for You* menu offers new sparkle and a delectable, mysterious dessert called Shoofly Pie. Not to be missed." Mattie made three extras that day and they all sold out. A lady bought a whole one for her book club.

On the tenth of August, Johnny asked Mattie to sit down after work for a cup of mint tea with him.

"You think you're really clever, don't you?" he said, tapping his spoon on his cup.

"Not at all," she said, startled. "I certainly don't. In fact, I usually think I'm
330 pretty dumb. It's just that you were used to making all the decisions around here and it's been really hard for you to share them. I don't know why. I certainly wouldn't want to make all the decisions."

"You wouldn't?"

"No way. I think sharing them is better."

"You do, do you?"

He was staring at the top of her head as if she had two horns erupting.

---

8. **nasturtiums** (na-stûr′shəmz): a kind of edible flower.

9. **E. coli** (ē kō′lī): bacteria, certain strains of which can cause sickness.

DIFFERENTIATED INSTRUCTION

FOR STRUGGLING READERS

Develop Reading Fluency Read aloud the conversation between Mattie and Johnny that begins on line 327 and runs through line 384, using expression and pacing. Then have student pairs take parts and read the lines several times. As they increase fluency, suggest they add gestures and facial expressions, such as tapping a cup or giving a startled look.

Then he said, "Would you like to go to a movie with me?" and she almost fell over backwards out of her chair. Late afternoon sunlight had suspended in the air. She could smell the warm sweetness of molasses from the pies just out
340 of the oven.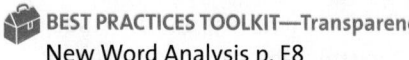

"Um—I'm sorry—I can't. It's not a good idea to mix business—and pleasure." She really wasn't much of a dater—now and then she went out with friends in groups, like migrating monarch butterflies, or ducks—but she simply could not imagine going around with this troublesome—chef.

He looked thunderstruck. "Are you serious?"

"Very."

He shrugged. "It was a good movie, too."

"Which one?"

"I'll never tell." Then he hissed, "What—do you just stick around home
350 with your mama after work and learn new recipes?"

Tears rose up in Mattie's eyes. He stared at her.

"My mother," she said, "died right before I started working here. For your information."

"Why didn't you tell me?"

"You weren't here. Plus, when you got back, you weren't very friendly."

One thing about loss—you decided whom to share it with. You could go around day after day and never give anyone a clue about what had been taken from you. You could hold it inside, a precious nugget of pain. Or you could say it out loud. When you trusted enough. When you felt like it. **K**
360 "I didn't feel like it."

You could place it on the table.

Johnny spoke softly now. "I'm sorry. But didn't you know I'd just been at my grandpa's funeral myself?"

"Yes."

"And he was like a daddy to me? He raised me when my own daddy took off? And my mama was already gone?"

Now tears shone in Johnny's eyes. It was a restaurant where every single person ended up crying at one time or another. "Well, I didn't know that," Mattie said. "That must have been really—hard."
370 She found herself with her hand on his arm.

"I'm sorry, too," she said. "I know you really loved your grandpa a lot."

He looked up sharply. "You do? How do you know that?"

"Trust me."

So many times during the days he'd mentioned little things his grandpa used to tell him. How to sharpen a knife. How to "swab the decks"—what Johnny called cleaning a counter.

Now he said, "Let me tell you about my grandpa's favorite corn bread," and he described it so deliciously, with raw pieces of fresh corn tucked into it, that Mattie had the idea they should concoct a meal based on beautiful things his
380 grandpa used to cook for him when he was growing up. Greens, corn bread, quick-fried okra, sweet potato casserole, vinegar coleslaw, pecan pie, and, since

GRAMMAR AND STYLE
Reread lines 337–340. Note how Nye chooses **adjectives** and **verbs** that appeal to the senses of sight, smell, and touch.

(4) Targeted Passage

K CONNECT
Think about the times when you shared grief with others. Why would Mattie only want to share grief with someone she trusts?

SHOOFLY PIE   **195**

**GRAMMAR
AND STYLE**
COMMON CORE
L 3

Analyze Sensory Details Ask students to identify the specific adjectives and verbs that appeal to the senses of sight, smell, and touch in this passage. *Possible answer:* **Sight:** *fell, suspended;* **Smell:** *smell;* **Touch:** *warm*

READING SKILL
COMMON CORE
RL 1

K CONNECT

Possible answer: Grief is personal. Often people can share it only with their closest friends and relatives—people who can be trusted.

FOR STRUGGLING READERS

(4) Targeted Passage [Lines 337–353]

These lines help to show how the relationship between Mattie and Johnny is changing.

• What does Johnny ask Mattie to do? (line 337)

• How does Mattie react? (lines 337–342)

• What information does Mattie tell Johnny about her personal life? (lines 352–353)

FOR ENGLISH LANGUAGE LEARNERS

Vocabulary: Phrasal Verbs Use New Word Analysis to teach these phrasal verbs from the story: *ring . . . out* (line 169); *sold out* (line 323); *came about* (line 400); *brought in* (line 415); *chose to* (line 429); and *move on* (line 467).

BEST PRACTICES TOOLKIT—Transparency New Word Analysis p. E8

their restaurant didn't serve meat, a special vegeburger seasoned with sage, his grandpa's favorite spice. They could do it In Memoriam (privately), but on the board they'd just call it "From Johnny's Grandpa's Special Recipes." **L**

They could even put white daisies on every table because they were his grandpa's favorite flowers.

The menu was so popular, they kept it up there three whole days. As customers were paying, they said, "Johnny, tell your grandpa we loved his food." No one told them he was dead.

390 Then Mattie said, "Okay, Riyad, what did YOUR daddy eat? Your turn."

For three days they served lentil soup, *baba-ghanouj*,[10] okra with rice, and falafel[11] sandwiches.

They played Arabic music in the restaurant.

Riyad seemed deeply emotional about it. He placed his father's dashing young photograph on the register. He gave Johnny and Mattie raises.

Sergio had left them by that time. He'd gone to sell boring used cars over on San Pedro, because he could make three times as much money over there. "But it won't taste as good," Mattie told him. They'd hired a grandmother, Lucy, to take his place. Lucy loved their new recipes as well as their old ones. She said,

400 "Did you know the name 'Shoofly' came about because the Amish people would shoo away the flies that came to land on their cooling pies when they took them out of the oven?"

Johnny said, "We don't have any flies in here. Mattie catches them in her fists the minute she sees them."

Then they did Mattie's mother's recipes. Mattie had a very hard time deciding which ones to do. Her mother had been a great cook, once upon a time, way back in the other world where things were still normal.

The menu board featured a special green salad with oranges and pecans, fragrant vegetable cous-cous with raisins, buttermilk biscuits, and of course,

410 Shoofly Pie for dessert. "I think your mother had a sweet tooth," Riyad said, staring dreamily at the full plates lined up on the counter.

"That she did," said Mattie, swallowing hard. Her mother had had everything: the best singing voice, the kindest heart, the kookiest wardrobe—she never felt shy about combining checks and stripes and wild colors.

Mattie brought in a tape of her mother's favorite blues singer, Lonnie Johnson, to play while they served her food. Mattie's father came over from his office to eat with them.

"This is kind of like that Anne Tyler book, *Dinner at the Homesick Restaurant*," he said. Mattie sat with him. He put his hand over her hand.

420 "What a rough summer, baby."

Mattie said, "It's also like our own private Days of the Dead." On November 2, people in South Texas made shrines to their beloved deceased family members or friends, arranging offerings of their favorite foods among the lit candles and incense.

---

10. **baba-ghanouj** (bä'bə gə-nōōsh'): Middle Eastern eggplant appetizer.

11. **falafel** (fə-lä'fəl): a Middle Eastern dish of fried, pureed chickpeas.

L CONNECT

Possible answer: *The thought of his grandfather's death brings back this personal memory. Because Johnny and Mattie share food, it may seem natural to him to share this memory now that some barriers between them are breaking down.*

TIERED DISCUSSION PROMPTS

Refer to lines 377–395 and use these prompts to help students understand how shared memories of loved ones become a kind of celebration that draws the characters together:

Connect What are some of your family's or friends' special recipes? *Answers will vary.*

Analyze How do the recipes serve as expressions of personal emotion? ***Possible answer:*** *Through the recipes, each person remembers and celebrates a loved one.*

Synthesize How does this menu change affect the *Good for You Restaurant*? ***Possible answer:*** *It makes it a more personal and emotional place. It helps draw those who work there closer. It also appears to be a hit with the customers, who like the variety and the food.*

REVISIT THE BIG QUESTION

Is there a cure for

GRIEF?

Discuss Based on lines 421–424, how can rituals surrounding food help diminish grief? ***Possible answer:*** *They bring people together. Family and friends join together and do something meaningful and satisfying in remembrance of the dead.*

L CONNECT

Think of a favorite dish that a relative or friend has prepared for you. Why might Johnny have chosen to describe his grandfather's corn bread to Mattie at this moment?

COMMON CORE RL 4

Language Coach

Meanings of Idioms Phrases that have a special meaning different from the literal meaning of each word are called **idioms**. Reread lines 410–411. What idiom does Riyad use to describe Mattie's mother? What do you think this idiom means?

DIFFERENTIATED INSTRUCTION

FOR ENGLISH LANGUAGE LEARNERS

Language Coach COMMON CORE RL 4

Meanings of Idioms *Answer: Riyad says that Mattie's mother had a sweet tooth. This idiom means that she likes sweet foods.* Point out the idiom *he drives me crazy* (line 185), and ask students what they think it means. Have students name examples of things that "drive them crazy."

FOR ADVANCED LEARNERS/PRE–AP

Identify the Literary Allusion Have students identify and research the allusion to Anne Tyler's novel *Dinner at the Homesick Restaurant*. Students should locate a synopsis of the book. Then have them explain what the connection is between the "In Memoriam" menus at the *Good for You Restaurant* and the title, characters, and plot of the novel.

"So who's homesick for Shoofly Pie?" asked a diner seated at the next table. "It's great!"

"Everybody," Mattie said. "Everybody who never lived a simple life." In some ways, you could choose what you remembered and what you did with it. Memories you chose to treasure would never fly away. They were like an adhesive stuck to the underside of your heart. Maybe they kept your heart in your body.

Riyad had an idea that they could offer their In Memoriam menus to the general public, too—letting people bring in groups of recipes belonging to someone they had loved who was gone now, and the *Good for You* staff would revise the recipes to become healthier, then serve special meals designated "Camille's Favorite Ratatouille Feast" or "Jim's Special Birthday Dinner" . . . what a thought.

"Is it creepy?" Johnny wondered out loud. "Will people feel like they eat here, then they die?"

"No," Mattie and Riyad said at once. "It's comforting. TRUST US."

"**H**ow do you think an omelette looks better, folded over or simply flipped? Should we slice the small strawberries in the fruit bowls or leave them whole?" Suddenly Johnny was so full of questions, Mattie could barely answer them all. He seemed to have softened somehow, like beans left to soak.

Sometimes when Mattie came in to work, she'd stop for a moment inside the door of the restaurant as if she were frozen. She'd stare all around the room—the tables, the chairs, the paintings, the vege-salt shakers—trying to remember how the place had looked to her before she'd known it from the inside out.

Now she had the recipes memorized, the arrangements of provisions on silver shelves inside the cooler, the little tubs the blueberries lived in. Even in the dreams she could hear the steady *clip-clip* of their best silver knife against the cutting board.

One day she told Johnny she admired his speed when he had ten things to do at once. He grinned at her so he *almost* looked handsome. He said, "Do you ever think how we'll all remember different things when we're old? When this restaurant feels like a far-away shadowy den we once inhabited together—I might remember the glint of the soup tureen in the afternoon light or the scent of comino, and you might remember—the gleam of my ravishing hair?"

"You wish." But she liked him now. She had to admit it. She really liked him.

One day Riyad said, "Everything is changing!" He gave Mattie a poem by Rumi[12] that read, "The mountains are trembling. Their map and compass are the lines in your palm." The first cold norther had swept down from the skies and everyone was wearing sweaters.

---

12. **Rumi** (rōō'mē): a 13th-century Persian mystic and poet.

CHARACTER TRAITS
How has Johnny's character softened? Cite details.

FOR ENGLISH LANGUAGE LEARNERS
Language: Possessive Nouns and Pronouns
This is a good opportunity to teach or review possessives, using *Johnny's Grandpa's Special Recipes* (line 384), *his grandpa's* (lines 385–386), and *his father's* (line 394). Have students work in groups to find additional possessives.

FOR ADVANCED LEARNERS/PRE-AP
Analyze Title and Symbol What significance does shoofly pie have in this story? What does it represent for Mattie? What do lines 425–427 suggest about Mattie's attitude toward the pie? Ask students to consider why Nye chose to title her story "Shoofly Pie." Then have them draw a conclusion about whether the pie is a symbol in the story.

That was the day she resigned. She had too much work to do at school now to keep on working here. Plus, she was feeling steadier. The restaurant had been Good for Her in all the ways it needed to be, and she could move on. She could cook better dinners for her father at home, with all her new experience. She could have dinner parties for his friends.

470   It shocked her how Johnny responded to the news of her departure. He shook his head and said, "No, no, no, baby," as if she were a little dog at his feet.

"What do you mean, no no no? Yes yes yes! I have homework piling up on me. I have a major paper to do that I haven't even started! My dad and I haven't even cleaned our house since my mom died. I'll miss this place terribly, but hey, I'll still come in and eat! And maybe you'll go to another movie someday and let me tag along, what do you say?"

Johnny stared at her. He'd been making Shoofly Pie on his own lately—good thing, because everyone still ordered it. Riyad and his wife presented Mattie with a mixed bunch of happy-looking flowers and a card: "This is your
480 home now, too!!! We love and appreciate you—free lunch any time!" Johnny kissed her, first time ever, on the top of her right ear. Her mother used to kiss her there. ❧

❺ Targeted Passage

TEXT ANALYSIS: *Review*   **COMMON CORE**

RL 3

ℕ STATIC AND DYNAMIC CHARACTERS

Possible answer: *Johnny has become more willing to ask questions (line 443); he grins and asks a personal, nostalgic question (lines 455–459); he shows sadness and humility when he asks Mattie to stay on (lines 470–471).*

SELECTION WRAP-UP

READ WITH A PURPOSE Now that students have finished reading the selection, have them compare and contrast ways the different characters handle their grief. Then have students decide which character they most relate or connect to and explain why. *Possible answer: Mattie, Riyad, and Johnny are all affected by their grief. Mattie is cautious who she trusts to tell about her loss. Riyad is sad in a quiet, contained way. Johnny seems to be acting out.*

⭐ **CRITIQUE** Have students decide whether this is a realistic story about grief. Why or why not?

INDEPENDENT READING

Students may want to read other selections by Naomi Shihab Nye. Suggest *Never in a Hurry: Essays on People and Places.*

DIFFERENTIATED INSTRUCTION

FOR STRUGGLING READERS

❺ **Targeted Passage** [Lines 470–482]

These lines are part of the story's falling action and resolution.

- How does Johnny react to the news that Mattie is leaving? (lines 470–471)

- What does Mattie suggest for the future? (lines 475–476)

- How do Johnny and Riyad say goodbye? (lines 478–481)

Comprehension

1. **Recall** Why is Mattie grieving?

2. **Recall** Why does Mattie decide to work at the restaurant?

3. **Recall** How does Johnny react when he first meets Mattie?

4. **Summarize** How do Mattie's and Johnny's feelings toward each other change over the course of the story?

◠ **COMMON CORE**

RL 1 Cite evidence to support inferences drawn from the text.
RL 3 Analyze how complex characters develop and interact with other characters.

Text Analysis

● 5. **Compare and Contrast Characters** What character traits do Mattie and Johnny have in common? In what ways are they different? Use a graphic organizer like the one shown to record your answers.

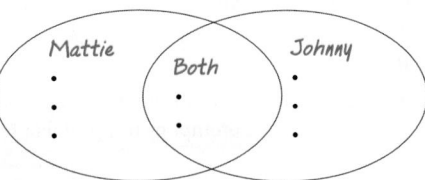

6. **Analyze Characters** A **foil** is a character who provides a striking contrast to another character. How does Riyad serve as a foil to Johnny's character?

◼ 7. **Connect** Review the chart you created as you read. How did the connections you made help you understand the effect of grief on one or more of the characters? Discuss specific examples in the story.

8. **Analyze Conflict** What incident in the story leads to a resolution of the **conflict,** or struggle, between Mattie and Johnny? Explain your answer.

9. **Draw Conclusions** Reread lines 465–482. Has Mattie gotten over her grief by the end of the story? Cite evidence to support your conclusion.

10. **Evaluate Characterization** Is Mattie a believable character? In your response, consider whether she acts and speaks the way a real person would and whether her relationships and interactions are believable.

Text Criticism

11. **Author's Style** Nye says she started writing things down in notebooks because she "wanted to remember everything. The quilt, the cherry tree, the creek. The neat whop of a baseball rammed perfectly with a bat." Using examples, explain how Nye's keen eye for detail brings the **setting** and **characters** to life in "Shoofly Pie."

> ### Is there a cure for **GRIEF?**
> How can people help each other deal with the loss of a loved one?

---

10. *Mattie is believable in many ways. She seems to withdraw into herself because of her grief. After a period of mourning, she seems to be coming out of it. She seems a bit unbelievable when she offers help to the crying woman in the restaurant.*

scallions lined up" (lines 142–143)—allow the reader to see the restaurant though Mattie's eyes. The description of Johnny—"He also wore an incredibly tight pair of faded jeans" (lines 219–220)—and the others offers clues to each character's traits.

Text Criticism

Possible answer:

11. *The description of the food and kitchen— "giant shiny pans, families of knives, containers of grated cheese and chopped*

> ### Is there a cure for **GRIEF?**
> Students might consider examples from their own experiences. How do people they know cope with grief? What, if anything seems to help?

Practice and Apply

For preliminary support of post-reading questions, use these copy masters:

R **RESOURCE MANAGER**—Copy Masters
  Reading Check p. 23
  Character Traits p. 19
  Question Support p. 24

Additional selection questions are provided for teachers on page 13.

ANSWERS

Comprehension

1. *Her mother died.*

2. *It is a distraction for her.*

3. *He is unkind to her. He may feel threatened by her.*

4. *Johnny comes to respect Mattie as a person and as a cook. As Johnny becomes kinder, Mattie begins to like him.*

Text Analysis

◠ **COMMON CORE RL 1, RL 3**

Possible answers:

5. ● **COMMON CORE FOCUS** *Character Traits* **Mattie:** *kind, quiet, resourceful, structured;* **Both:** *sure of themselves, grieving, good cooks;* **Johnny:** *a bit overbearing, wants to be in control, views the job as more than a distraction*

6. *Riyad is quiet and in control; Johnny is loud and, in many ways, out of control. Riyad can do lowly things like clean up honey and still be the boss; Johnny needs to be in control and have others obey him.*

7. ◼ **COMMON CORE FOCUS** *Connect* *Grief causes Mattie to get the job; grief may have helped Riyad share a bond with Mattie; grief may have caused Johnny to act out even more than usual; grief, celebration of memory, and a new friendship are the causes of some great menus.*

8. *When Johnny asks Mattie whether she stays home with her mama, Mattie tells him her mother died recently. This changes their relationship. Johnny realizes what he has in common with Mattie, and he stops being so overbearing. Having told her "secret," Mattie also begins to soften a little toward Johnny.*

9. *She may not be completely over it, but she has made progress: "she was feeling steadier" (line 466); "she could move on" (line 467). It may even be a good sign that she is willing to go to the movies with Johnny (lines 475–476).*

Language

COMMON CORE L3

◆ **GRAMMAR AND STYLE**

- Point out the two types of changes in the revision: verbs made more precise, and adjectives added to supply details about texture and appearance. (For more about adding sensory details, see the **Writing Handbook**, page R34.)

- Write this sentence on the board, and ask students to make it more vivid.

Mattie ~~wiped~~ scrubbed the stainless steel counter and ~~put the~~ heaved the heavy stacks of sturdy white dishes ~~away~~ into the cabinets overhead.

 RESOURCE MANAGER—Copy Master
Add Sensory Details p. 25

READING-WRITING CONNECTION

- Have students imagine themselves as observers in the restaurant where Johnny and Mattie cook side by side. For prewriting, suggest they use an Observation Chart to record the details they imagine.

 BEST PRACTICES TOOLKIT—Transparency
Observation Chart p. C7

Writing Online

The following tools are available online at **thinkcentral.com** and on **Write*Smart* CD-ROM**:
- **Interactive Graphic Organizers**
- **Interactive Student Models**
- **Interactive Revision Lessons**

For additional grammar instruction, see **GrammarNotes** on **thinkcentral.com**.

Assess and Reteach

Assess

DIAGNOSTIC AND SELECTION TESTS
Selection Test A, B/C pp. 55–58

Interactive Selection Test on **thinkcentral.com**

Reteach

Level Up Online Tutorials on **thinkcentral.com**

Reteaching Worksheets on **thinkcentral.com**
Literature Lesson 1

Language

◆ **GRAMMAR AND STYLE: Add Sensory Details**

COMMON CORE

L3 Apply knowledge of language to make effective choices for meaning or style.

Review the **Grammar and Style** note on page 195. You can appeal to your readers' senses, as Nye does, by carefully choosing **adjectives** and **verbs** that reflect what the characters see, hear, smell, touch, and taste. Here are two examples from the story.

> *Have you ever watched a gallon of honey ooze into a slow-motion golden dance around a mound of broken glass?* (lines 2–4)

> *Arranging generous slices on yellow dessert plates, Mattie savored the sight of their crumbled toppings over the rich and creamy molasses interiors.* (lines 252–254)

Notice how the revisions in blue create stronger sensory images in this first draft. Revise your response to the prompt by using similar techniques.

STUDENT MODEL

> Johnny ~~cut~~ ^{chopped} onions on the ^{wooden} board. Next to him, Mattie ~~put~~ ^{arranged} ^{sliced} vegetables on a ^{shiny} platter.

READING-WRITING CONNECTION

YOUR TURN Increase your understanding of "Shoofly Pie" by responding to this prompt. Then use the **revising tip** to improve your writing.

WRITING PROMPT	REVISING TIP
Short Constructed Response: Description Mattie and Johnny often have different approaches to cooking. Write a **one- or two-paragraph description** of them cooking a meal together.	Look back over your response. Did you use sensory details to appeal to your readers' senses? If not, revise your answer to include vivid adjectives and verbs that create strong sensory images.

Interactive Revision
Go to **thinkcentral.com**.
KEYWORD: HML10-200

DIFFERENTIATED INSTRUCTION

FOR STRUGGLING WRITERS

- Have students name tasks involved in making a meal, and then list them in the first column of a Two-Column Chart.

- In the second column, have students list some ingredients the cooks might use. Then have students complete sentences that begin with *Mattie* _____ or *Johnny* _____ by choosing one word from the first column and another from the second.

- Discuss ways to improve each sentence by adding describing words or more precise verbs.

- Have students decide on an order for their sentences and write their paragraphs.

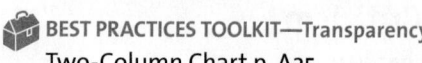 **BEST PRACTICES TOOLKIT—Transparency**
Two-Column Chart p. A25

NEWSPAPER ARTICLE In "Shoofly Pie," characters base menus on the favorite dishes of deceased loved ones. Connecting with the dead through food is an old Mexican tradition observed during the Day of the Dead holiday.

A Mexican Feast for Bodies and Souls

Dave Roos

Pan de muertos

Sometimes the smell of a steaming, freshly corn-husked tamale is enticing enough to wake the dead.

This time of year, in the mountainous Lake Pátzcuaro region of the Mexican state of Michoacán, villagers prepare a feast for their deceased as part of the annual Day of the Dead celebrations. From the end of October through early November, families dedicate ofrendas (home altars) to the recently departed, setting a lavishly adorned table with the loved one's favorite foods.

In this part of central Mexico, the table is crowded with indigenous classics like corundas, pyramidal tamales filled with salty cheese and poblano pepper; and churipo, a slow-simmered meat and vegetable stew in a ruddy broth of blended chilies, as well as more modern dishes like the regional staple sopa tarasca and the ubiquitous Day of the Dead treat, pan de muertos.

People here believe that the dead are guided by the alluring odors of their favorite foods during the long journey back from the world beyond. Once they arrive, they will share a meal with the living during an all-night vigil in the town cemetery.

The Day of the Dead is not Mexico's answer to Halloween, nor is it a Latin-American interpretation of All Saints' Day. Like Mexican food, itself a complex blend of indigenous and Spanish influences, the Day of the Dead is an inextricable mix of pre-Hispanic spiritualism and post-conquest Roman Catholicism. . . .

The ancient, soul-satisfying taste of slow-steamed corn tamale is the flavor of Pátzcuaro, and the best tamales are prepared by the Purhépecha peasants who commute daily from outlying villages to stock the town's bustling food market and sell handmade crafts in street-side stalls. . . .

If there is one food associated exclusively with the Day of the Dead—not only in Pátzcuaro, but all over Mexico—it is pan de muertos, a moist, eggy cake-bread generously coated with butter and sugar.

Alejandro Rivera Torres, the owner of RivePan bakery in Pátzcuaro, said he bakes and sells thousands of loaves of pan de muertos every season, in the traditional round shape with decorative "bones" or in the form of muertitos, little dead people flecked with pink sugar.

On a chilly November night in the pine mountains of Michoacán, a sweet slice of pan de muertos and a steaming cup of atole—a corn masa drink flavored with cinnamon, vanilla, or many types of fruit—do wonders to warm the souls of the living as they huddle all night in the cemetery sharing favorite traditional foods and fond memories with the spirits of their ancestors. . . .

READING FOR INFORMATION **201**

Focus and Motivate

Selection Resources

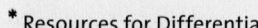

Essential Course of Study ECOS

The Possibility of Evil
Short Story by Shirley Jackson

VIDEO TRAILER THINK central   KEYWORD: HML10-202

How good are you at JUDGING people?

COMMON CORE

RL 1 Cite textual evidence to support inferences drawn from the text. **RL 3** Analyze how complex characters develop and interact with other characters. **L 5** Demonstrate understanding of word relationships.

The main character in "The Possibility of Evil" believes she can read into the hearts of those around her. Do you think it is so easy to judge people? Are you confident that you would recognize evil if you came face to face with it?

DISCUSS With a group, fill in a description wheel for the word *evil*. Then use the ideas you have brainstormed to create a definition of the word.

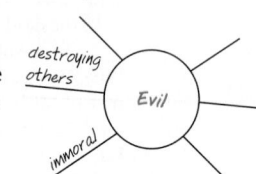

destroying others
immoral
Evil

10   10   10   10

202

TEXT ANALYSIS: CHARACTER MOTIVATION

One way of learning about a character is to consider his or her **motivation**—the reasons behind the character's actions. Writers usually do not directly state a character's motivation. Instead, readers often must figure out motivation by thinking about

- the character's words, thoughts, and actions
- how other characters react to him or her

In "The Possibility of Evil," Miss Strangeworth believes she acts in response to a *moral dilemma*: a choice between two options that violate one's moral principles. As you read, think about whether Miss Strangeworth is *really* motivated by moral principles, or if she has other reasons for her actions.

READING SKILL: MAKE INFERENCES

When you **make inferences** about a character, you apply your knowledge of human behavior to clues provided in the text. For example, if a character crosses to the other side of the street as another character approaches, you may infer that he or she doesn't like the other character.

As you read "The Possibility of Evil," note details that help you make inferences about the thoughts and feelings of characters. Use a diagram like the one shown here.

Details from Story	Inferences
After Tommy began working at the grocery, Miss Strangeworth called him Mr. Lewis.	She no longer thinks of Mr. Lewis as her friend or equal.

Review: **Evaluate, Predict**

▲ VOCABULARY IN CONTEXT

Figure out the meaning of each boldfaced word from the context provided. Write a sentence that shows your understanding of each word in your *Reader/Writer Notebook.*

1. **infatuated** with the hero of the novel
2. stared with **rapt** attention
3. a decision that isn't **negotiable**
4. **degraded** by trouble-seeking friends
5. could almost see through the **translucent** bowl
6. a **reprehensible** act that deserves punishment

Complete the activities in your **Reader/Writer Notebook.**

Meet the Author

Shirley Jackson
1919–1965

Horrifying Debut
Shirley Jackson established her reputation with her story "The Lottery," a chilling tale set in a quiet New England town. After the story was published in the *New Yorker* in 1948, outraged readers bombarded the magazine with letters and requests to cancel their subscriptions. Today, the story is considered a classic of gothic horror. The story's central premise, that ordinary humans are capable of great evil, became a recurring theme in Jackson's writing.

Sinister Small Towns
"The Possibility of Evil" and many of Jackson's other stories are set in small American towns that seem peaceful and friendly until their darker sides are revealed. Jackson herself experienced hostility in the small town where she lived, especially after she began publishing fiction. Her biographer, Judy Oppenheimer, wrote that "the idea of people talking about her, judging her, not just her work, made her extremely anxious. Shirley liked her privacy. She wanted to live anonymously in a small town, sending out her fearful disturbing messages to the rest of the world, without consequences."

Fear as a Tool
Jackson frequently suffered from panic attacks. Writing was one means of combating this condition. She once said, "I have always loved to use fear. To take it and make it work."

Author Online
THINK central
Go to **thinkcentral.com.**
KEYWORD: HML10-203

203

Teach

TEXT ANALYSIS COMMON CORE RL 1 RL 3

● *Model the Skill:* CHARACTER MOTIVATION

To model how to identify character motivation, have students read this passage:

> Mary ran to the kitchen, grabbing the fire extinguisher from the hall. Smoke poured from the doorway.

The passage gives clues about Mary's motives for getting the fire extinguisher: there is probably a fire in the kitchen.

GUIDED PRACTICE Ask students to explain what motivates the behavior of a character from a book, movie, or TV show.

READING SKILL

■ *Model the Skill:* MAKE INFERENCES

To model how to make inferences, have students read the text under **Horrifying Debut.** Tell students that they can make inferences about why some readers of the *New Yorker* canceled their subscriptions by noting the details in the text. They can infer that many readers of the *New Yorker* did not like to think of themselves as evil.

GUIDED PRACTICE Have students explain how their knowledge of human behavior helped them make the inference.

R RESOURCE MANAGER—Copy Master
Make Inferences p. 39

VOCABULARY SKILL

▲ VOCABULARY IN CONTEXT

DIAGNOSE WORD KNOWLEDGE Have all students complete Vocabulary in Context. Check their words and phrases against the following:

degraded (dĭ-grā′dĭd) *adj.* corrupted, depraved
infatuated (ĭn-făch′ōō-ā′tĭd) *adj.* intensely fond
negotiable (nĭ-gō′shə-bəl) *adj.* able to be bargained with
rapt (răpt) *adj.* fully absorbed; entranced
reprehensible (rĕp′rĭ-hĕn′sə-bəl) *adj.* deserving blame and criticism

translucent (trăns-lōō′sənt) *adj.* allowing light to shine through

PRETEACH VOCABULARY Use the following copy master to help students determine the meanings for each boldfaced vocabulary word needed to complete a CLOZE passage.

R RESOURCE MANAGER—Copy Master
Vocabulary Study p. 41

COMMON CORE
L 4

1. Read the first two sentences aloud.
2. Point out the phrases "accepted a bribe" and "steal from the elderly." Elicit a possible meaning for degraded, for example, "corrupted."
3. Repeat the process for sentences b–f.

READ WITH A PURPOSE
Help students to set a purpose for reading. Tell students to look for how Miss Strangeworth interacts with people in the town.

THE POSSIBILITY

of

Evil

Shirley Jackson

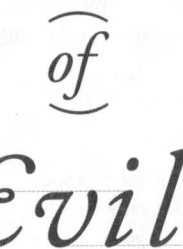

Miss Adela Strangeworth stepped daintily along Main Street on her way to the grocery. The sun was shining, the air was fresh and clear after the night's heavy rain, and everything in Miss Strangeworth's little town looked washed and bright. Miss Strangeworth took deep breaths, and thought that there was nothing in the world like a fragrant summer day.

She knew everyone in town, of course; she was fond of telling strangers—tourists who sometimes passed through the town and stopped to admire Miss Strangeworth's roses—that she had never spent more than a day outside this town in all her long life. She was seventy-one, Miss Strangeworth told the
10 tourists, with a pretty little dimple showing by her lip, and she sometimes found herself thinking that the town belonged to her. "My grandfather built the first house on Pleasant Street," she would say, opening her blue eyes wide with the wonder of it. "This house, right here. My family has lived here for better than a hundred years. My grandmother planted these roses, and my mother tended them, just as I do. I've watched my town grow; I can remember when Mr. Lewis, Senior, opened the grocery store, and the year the river flooded out the shanties[1] on the low road, and the excitement when some young folks wanted to move the park over to the space in front of where the new post office is today. They wanted to put up a statue of Ethan Allen"[2]—
20 Miss Strangeworth would frown a little and sound stern—"but it should have been a statue of my grandfather. There wouldn't have been a town here at all if it hadn't been for my grandfather and the lumber mill." **A**

---

1. **shanties** (shăn′tēz): roughly built cabins; shacks.
2. **Ethan Allen:** a Revolutionary War hero who led a group of soldiers, called the Green Mountain Boys, from what is now Vermont.

Analyze Visuals ▶
Examine the portrait. What impression do you have of the woman shown? Which **details** helped you form this impression?

① Targeted Passage

A MAKE INFERENCES
How does Miss Strangeworth feel about the contribution her family has made to the town?

Michele Warner/Illustration Works/ Getty Images.

READING SKILL

A *Model the Skill:* **MAKE INFERENCES**

Have students reread lines 9–22. Point out to students that lines 10–11 tell readers how Miss Strangeworth feels about the town. Explain that the lines that follow line 11 give details about why she feels this way. Have students make notes about these details in their Inferences charts to help them answer the question.

Possible answers: Miss Strangeworth is so proud of her family's contribution that she sometimes feels as if the town actually "[belongs] to her" (lines 10–11). She also believes that a statue of Ethan Allen, a Revolutionary War hero, was less fitting for a town park than a statue of her grand-father (lines 19–21), who built the first house on Pleasant Street. Although rightly proud of her family's contributions, Miss Strangeworth may hold them in higher esteem than they deserve (lines 11, 21–22).

DIFFERENTIATED INSTRUCTION

FOR ENGLISH LANGUAGE LEARNERS
Language: Verbs Remind students that adjectives modify nouns, and adverbs modify adjectives or other adverbs. Help students identify the verb and adverb in line 1 (*stepped*-verb; *daintily*-adverb). Then, give students these phrases and have them identify the verb and the modifiers: *everything . . . looked washed and bright* (lines 3–4); *you don't look well* (line 75); *she thought indulgently, looking at the delicately embroidered baby cap and the lace-edged carriage cover* (lines 83–84).

FOR STRUGGLING READERS
In combination with the *Audio Anthology CD*, use one or more Targeted Passages (pp. 204, 208, 210, 213, 214) to ensure that students focus on key story events, concepts, and skills. Targeted Passages are also good for English learners.

① Targeted Passage [Lines 1–14]
This passage introduces the story's setting and main character, Miss Strangeworth.

Reading Support

This selection on **thinkcentral.com** includes embedded **ThinkAloud** models—students "thinking aloud" about the story to model the kinds of questions a good reader would ask about a selection.

Analyze Visuals

Possible answer: *The subject appears to be a kind, gentle, respectable older woman. The details that suggest this interpretation are her almost-white hair, her smile, her pearls, her peaceful pose, and her pastime—knitting.*

About the Art Artist Michele Warner enjoys painting simple subjects like the older woman in this work, titled *Grandma*.

- How would you describe Miss Strangeworth physically? (lines 9–12)
- How would you characterize her? (lines 1, 3–11)
- What type of town does she live in? (lines 3–6)
- How does she feel about her town? (lines 8–22)

FOR ADVANCED LEARNERS/PRE–AP

Analyze Point out to students that Jackson was judged by her townspeople for the stories she wrote. Ask students whether they feel its appropriate to judge writers and other artists based on the work they produce. Encourage students to explain their reasoning using concrete examples.

B CHARACTER MOTIVATION   RL 1 RL 3

Possible answers: She may stop because she feels that she must be friendly to everybody. The phrase "had to stop" (lines 30–31) implies that she felt obligated to say hello; she wants everybody to think highly of her.

IF STUDENTS NEED HELP . . . Work with students to complete a Character Traits Web to help them understand Miss Strangeworth's motivations.

 BEST PRACTICES TOOLKIT—Transparency
Character Traits Web p. D7

TIERED DISCUSSION PROMPTS

Use these prompts to help students analyze new information about Miss Strangeworth in lines 50–61:

Connect Have you ever noticed a change in someone's appearance or behavior, but hesitated to ask whether he or she was okay? Explain why or why not. *Students may say they have, but hesitated, not wishing to pry.*

Analyze Why doesn't Miss Strangeworth say anything to Mr. Lewis about the changes she notices? *Possible answer: She thinks that "it was far too personal a subject to be introduced to Mr. Lewis, the grocer" (line 54). Her reference to him as "Mr. Lewis, the grocer" suggests that she feels above him and is not as sympathetic as she believes.*

Evaluate What does Miss Strangeworth's "gentle" reminder to Mr. Lewis suggest? *Possible answer: It suggests that she is not really concerned about Mr. Lewis. Otherwise, she would have overlooked his forgetting to remind her to buy tea (line 60).*

Miss Strangeworth never gave away any of her roses, although the tourists often asked her. The roses belonged on Pleasant Street, and it bothered Miss Strangeworth to think of people wanting to carry them away, to take them into strange towns and down strange streets. When the new minister came, and the ladies were gathering flowers to decorate the church, Miss Strangeworth sent over a great basket of gladioli; when she picked the roses at all, she set them in bowls and vases around the inside of the house her grandfather had built.

30   Walking down Main Street on a summer morning, Miss Strangeworth had to stop every minute or so to say good morning to someone or to ask after someone's health. When she came into the grocery, half a dozen people turned away from the shelves and the counters to wave at her or call out good morning. **B**

"And good morning to you, too, Mr. Lewis," Miss Strangeworth said at last. The Lewis family had been in the town almost as long as the Strangeworths; but the day young Lewis left high school and went to work in the grocery, Miss Strangeworth had stopped calling him Tommy and started calling him Mr. Lewis, and he had stopped calling her Addie and started calling her Miss

40   Strangeworth. They had been in high school together, and had gone to picnics together, and to high school dances and basketball games; but now Mr. Lewis was behind the counter in the grocery, and Miss Strangeworth was living alone in the Strangeworth house on Pleasant Street.

"Good morning," Mr. Lewis said, and added politely, "lovely day."

"It is a very nice day," Miss Strangeworth said as though she had only just decided that it would do after all. "I would like a chop, please, Mr. Lewis, a small, lean veal chop. Are those strawberries from Arthur Parker's garden? They're early this year."

"He brought them in this morning," Mr. Lewis said.

50   "I shall have a box," Miss Strangeworth said. Mr. Lewis looked worried, she thought, and for a minute she hesitated, but then she decided that he surely could not be worried over the strawberries. He looked very tired indeed. He was usually so chipper, Miss Strangeworth thought, and almost commented, but it was far too personal a subject to be introduced to Mr. Lewis, the grocer, so she only said, "And a can of cat food and, I think, a tomato."

Silently, Mr. Lewis assembled her order on the counter and waited. Miss Strangeworth looked at him curiously and then said, "It's Tuesday, Mr. Lewis. You forgot to remind me."

"Did I? Sorry."

60   "Imagine your forgetting that I always buy my tea on Tuesday," Miss Strangeworth said gently. "A quarter pound of tea, please, Mr. Lewis."

"Is that all, Miss Strangeworth?"

"Yes thank you, Mr. Lewis. Such a lovely day, isn't it?"

"Lovely," Mr. Lewis said.

Miss Strangeworth moved slightly to make room for Mrs. Harper at the counter. "Morning, Adela," Mrs. Harper said, and Miss Strangeworth said, "Good morning, Martha."

B CHARACTER MOTIVATION
Why does Miss Strangeworth take time to greet so many people?

(COMMON CORE L 5)

Language Coach

Antonyms Sometimes you can figure out an unfamiliar word's meaning by analyzing its relationship to other words. For example, a nearby word may clearly be an **antonym,** or a word opposite in meaning. Reread lines 52–53. What word in this passage seems to be an antonym of *chipper?* What do you think *chipper* means?

DIFFERENTIATED INSTRUCTION

FOR ENGLISH LANGUAGE LEARNERS

Language Coach   COMMON CORE L 5

Antonyms *Answer: tired;* Chipper *means energetic.* Point out that someone who is chipper is often lighthearted, too. What word in lines 52–53 is the antonym, or opposite of, *lighthearted? Answer: worried*

FOR ADVANCED LEARNERS/PRE–AP

Analyze Character Have students reread lines 23–29 and fill out the Character Traits and Textual Evidence chart to analyze what they learn about Miss Strangeworth's character from this paragraph. After students fill out the chart, have them discuss why she never gives away her roses. Is she stingy or overly proud? What do the roses represent to Miss Strangeworth?

 BEST PRACTICES TOOLKIT—Transparency
Character Traits and Textual Evidence p. D6

"Lovely day," Mrs. Harper said, and Miss Strangeworth said, "Yes, lovely," and Mr. Lewis, under Mrs. Harper's glance, nodded.

70 "Ran out of sugar for my cake frosting," Mrs. Harper explained. Her hand shook slightly as she opened her pocketbook. Miss Strangeworth wondered, glancing at her quickly, if she had been taking proper care of herself. Martha Harper was not as young as she used to be, Miss Strangeworth thought. She probably could use a good, strong tonic.[3]

"Martha," she said, "you don't look well."

"I'm perfectly all right," Mrs. Harper said shortly. She handed her money to Mr. Lewis, took her change and her sugar, and went out without speaking again. Looking after her, Miss Strangeworth shook her head slightly. Martha definitely did *not* look well. **C**

80 Carrying her little bag of groceries, Miss Strangeworth came out of the store into the bright sunlight and stopped to smile down on the Crane baby. Don and Helen Crane were really the two most **infatuated** young parents she had ever known, she thought indulgently, looking at the delicately embroidered baby cap and the lace-edged carriage cover.

"That little girl is going to grow up expecting luxury all her life," she said to Helen Crane.

---

3. **tonic:** a medicine for restoring and energizing the body.

C MAKE INFERENCES
What can you infer from the way Mrs. Harper reacts to Miss Strangeworth's comment?

infatuated
(ĭn-făch′ōō-ā′tĭd) *adj.* intensely fond

THE POSSIBILITY OF EVIL **207**

Analyze Visuals

Activity Ask students how the picture conveys a small-town feeling. *Possible answer: There are small buildings with large storefront windows. There is a flag flying from a building. Only a few people are walking along the sidewalk of a street like Main Street. There is no traffic. These details convey a small-town feeling.*

About the Art *Village Street Scene* was created by contemporary illustrator John Ward.

READING SKILL

C MAKE INFERENCES

Possible answer: Mrs. Harper responds abruptly when Miss Strangeworth says that she does not look well (lines 75–76). The fact that she does not speak to Miss Strangeworth again implies that she is upset, or perhaps offended by Miss Strangeworth's comment.

Extend the Discussion Miss Strangeworth didn't tell Mr. Lewis that he looked tired because it seemed too personal (lines 52–54), but she told Mrs. Harper that she didn't look well. Why?

FOR ENGLISH LANGUAGE LEARNERS

Develop Reading Fluency Have students listen to the entire story on the *Audio Anthology CD.* Then divide the story, and have students work in threes to look up unfamiliar words. Have each group share their words and definitions with the class.

Culture: Clarify Introduce the idea that certain words are indicative of American culture, such as *penny candy* (line 160), "individual pieces of candy that you can buy with small amounts of change"; and *soda shop* (line 271),

"an old-fashioned store where people buy ice cream sodas and candy."

FOR ADVANCED LEARNERS/PRE–AP

Analyze Setting Have students discuss the qualities that characterize a small town—for example, a small town's size and safety and the fact that everyone knows each other. Are these qualities advantages or disadvantages? Have students support their answers with examples from the story and from their own experiences.

VOCABULARY

COMMON CORE
L 4

OWN THE WORD

infatuated: Ask students how Don and Helen Crane might show that they are *infatuated* with their daughter. *Possible answer: They might dress their daughter in expensive clothes, push her in a beautiful carriage, and indulge her with gifts.*

THE POSSIBILITY OF EVIL **207**

Helen laughed. "That's the way we want her to feel," she said. "Like a princess."

"A princess can be a lot of trouble sometimes," Miss Strangeworth said
90 dryly. "How old is her highness now?"

"Six months next Tuesday," Helen Crane said, looking down with **rapt** wonder at her child. "I've been worrying, though, about her. Don't you think she ought to move around more? Try to sit up, for instance?"

"For plain and fancy[4] worrying," Miss Strangeworth said, amused, "give me a new mother every time."

"She just seems—slow," Helen Crane said.

"Nonsense. All babies are different. Some of them develop much more quickly than others."

"That's what my mother says." Helen Crane laughed, looking a little bit
100 ashamed.

"I suppose you've got young Don all upset about the fact that his daughter is already six months old and hasn't yet begun to learn to dance?"

"I haven't mentioned it to him. I suppose she's just so precious that I worry about her all the time."

"Well, apologize to her right now," Miss Strangeworth said. "*She* is probably worrying about why you keep jumping around all the time." Smiling to herself and shaking her old head, she went on down the sunny street, stopping once to ask little Billy Moore why he wasn't out riding in his daddy's shiny new car, and talking for a few minutes outside the library with Miss Chandler,
110 the librarian, about the new novels to be ordered, and paid for by the annual library appropriation. Miss Chandler seemed absentminded and very much as though she were thinking about something else. Miss Strangeworth noticed that Miss Chandler had not taken much trouble with her hair that morning, and sighed. Miss Strangeworth hated sloppiness. **D**

Many people seemed disturbed recently, Miss Strangeworth thought. Only yesterday the Stewarts' fifteen-year-old Linda had run crying down her own front walk and all the way to school, not caring who saw her. People around town thought she might have had a fight with the Harris boy, but they showed up together at the soda shop after school as usual, both of them looking grim
120 and bleak. Trouble at home, people concluded, and sighed over the problems of trying to raise kids right these days.

From halfway down the block Miss Strangeworth could catch the heavy scent of her roses, and she moved a little more quickly. The perfume of roses meant home, and home meant the Strangeworth House on Pleasant Street. Miss Strangeworth stopped at her own front gate, as she always did, and looked with deep pleasure at her house, with the red and pink and white roses massed along the narrow lawn, and the rambler[5] going up along the porch; and the neat, the unbelievably trim lines of the house itself, with its slimness and its washed white look. Every window sparkled, every curtain hung stiff

---

4. **plain and fancy:** every kind of.
5. **rambler:** a rose plant that grows upward like a vine, by clinging to a support.

rapt (răpt) *adj.* fully absorbed; entranced

2 Targeted Passage

D EVALUATE
Reread lines 90–114. Does Miss Strangeworth seem like a reasonable person? Explain your answer.

D EVALUATE

Possible answer: On the surface, Miss Strangeworth seems like a reasonable person, who is connected to and concerned with other townspeople. However, she also makes many personal, judgmental observations. She comments on Helen's baby, referring to her sarcastically (lines 89–90), and she says that Miss Chandler is "absentminded" and sloppy (lines 111–114). Her attitude seems superior and somewhat mean.

REVISIT THE BIG QUESTION

How good are you at

JUDGING people?

Discuss Direct students to lines 89–106. At this point in the story, there are hints that Miss Strangeworth may not be as benevolent as she seemed at first. Revisit the words that you used in your description wheel on page 202. Are Miss Strangeworth's comments about Helen's baby evil, or do they suggest only that something is slightly off balance? *Possible answer:* Ostensibly, Miss Strangeworth is telling Helen not to worry or be so fussy (lines 94 and 105–106), but at the same time she's planting seeds to undermine Helen's confidence (lines 85–86 and 89–90). Something seems to be off balance, at least.

VOCABULARY  COMMON CORE L 4

OWN THE WORD

rapt: Tell students that *rapt* means being fully absorbed; a synonym is *riveted*. Have students use both words in sentences.

DIFFERENTIATED INSTRUCTION

FOR STRUGGLING READERS

2 Targeted Passage [Lines 101–114]

This passage gives clues to Miss Strangeworth's character.

- Why does Miss Strangeworth tell Helen to apologize to her baby? (lines 103–104)
- What details does she notice about Billy Moore and Miss Chandler? (lines 108–113)
- Is Miss Strangeworth too concerned with things that are not her business? Explain. (lines 111–121)

FOR ENGLISH LANGUAGE LEARNERS

Vocabulary Support Use Word Squares to teach these words: *annual* (line 110), *debated* (line 138), *selected* (line 176), *convertible* (line 206), *potential* (line 308), *intense* (line 327).

 BEST PRACTICES TOOLKIT—Transparency Word Squares p. E10

130 and straight, and even the stones of the front walk were swept and clear.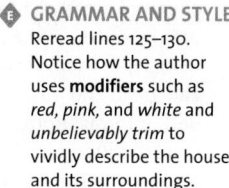
People around town wondered how old Miss Strangeworth managed to keep
the house looking the way it did, and there was a legend about a tourist once
mistaking it for the local museum and going all through the place without
finding out about his mistake. But the town was proud of Miss Strangeworth
and her roses and her house. They had all grown together.

Miss Strangeworth went up her front steps, unlocked her front door
with her key, and went into the kitchen to put away her groceries. She
debated having a cup of tea and then decided that it was too close to midday
dinnertime; she would not have the appetite for her little chop if she had tea
140 now. Instead she went into the light, lovely sitting room, which still glowed
from the hands of her mother and her grandmother, who had covered the
chairs with bright chintz[6] and hung the curtains. All the furniture was spare
and shining, and the round hooked rugs on the floor had been the work of
Miss Strangeworth's grandmother and her mother. Miss Strangeworth had put
a bowl of her red roses on the low table before the window, and the room was
full of their scent.

Miss Strangeworth went to the narrow desk in the corner, and unlocked
it with her key. She never knew when she might feel like writing letters, so
she kept her notepaper inside, and the desk locked. Miss Strangeworth's
150 usual stationery was heavy and cream-colored, with "Strangeworth House"

6. **chintz:** a colorful printed cotton fabric.

GRAMMAR AND STYLE
Reread lines 125–130.
Notice how the author
uses **modifiers** such as
red, pink, and *white* and
unbelievably trim to
vividly describe the house
and its surroundings.

▼ **Analyze Visuals**

Which details in this
painting fit Jackson's
description of the
story's **setting?**

The House with Roses (1936), Henri Le Sidaner. Oil on canvas. Private Collection. Photo © Visual Arts Library/Art Resource, New York.

THE POSSIBILITY OF EVIL **209**

**GRAMMAR
AND STYLE**

COMMON
CORE **L 3**

Analyze Modifiers Authors use modifiers
to help readers visualize a scene. Have
students identify the modifiers in lines
137–146 and then draw a picture of the
inside of Miss Strangeworth's house. How
does visualizing different parts of Miss
Strangeworth's house help them to understand her character?

Analyze Visuals

*Possible answer: The ramblers growing up and
over the doorway, the clean white paint, the
curtains in the window, and the trim lines of
the house fit the description of Miss Strangeworth's house. It appears pristine and beautiful, if a little old-fashioned—just like Miss
Strangeworth's house.*

About the Art The French postimpressionist
painter Henri Le Sidaner (1862–1939) is known
for his luminous landscapes and interiors. *The
House With Roses* is characteristic of his many
depictions of sun-drenched gardens and trel-
lises of roses set against stone houses.

FOR ENGLISH LANGUAGE LEARNERS
Vocabulary: Multiple-Meaning Words Call attention to the words *place* (line 133) and *spare*
(line 142). Remind students that some English
words have more than one meaning. Use the
Jigsaw strategy to discuss the meaning of
each word. Then have groups use context to
identify the meaning of *catch* (line 122), *lifting*
(line 182), and *trash* (line 213).

🧰 **BEST PRACTICES TOOLKIT**
Jigsaw Reading p. A1

FOR ADVANCED LEARNERS/PRE–AP
Analyze Have students discuss the point of
the anecdote about the tourist mistaking
Miss Strangeworth's house for a museum
(lines 131–135). What does this anecdote suggest about her character and her relationship
with the town?

engraved across the top, but, when she felt like writing her other letters, Miss Strangeworth used a pad of various-colored paper, bought from the local newspaper shop. It was almost a town joke, that colored paper, layered in pink and green and blue and yellow; everyone in town bought it and used it for odd, informal notes and shopping lists. It was usual to remark, upon receiving a note written on a blue page, that so-and-so would be needing a new pad soon—here she was, down to the blue already. Everyone used the matching envelopes for tucking away recipes, or keeping odd little things in, or even to hold cookies in the school lunch boxes. Mr. Lewis sometimes gave them to
160 the children for carrying home penny candy.

> Although Miss Strangeworth's desk held a trimmed quill pen, which had belonged to her grandfather, and a gold-frost fountain pen, which had belonged to her father, Miss Strangeworth always used a dull stub of pencil when she wrote her letters, and she printed them in a childish block print. After thinking for a minute, although she had been phrasing the letter in the back of her mind all the way home, she wrote on a pink sheet: DIDN'T YOU EVER SEE AN IDIOT CHILD BEFORE? SOME PEOPLE JUST SHOULDN'T HAVE CHILDREN, SHOULD THEY?
> She was pleased with the letter. She was fond of doing things exactly right.
> 170 When she made a mistake, as she sometimes did, or when the letters were not spaced nicely on the page, she had to take the discarded page to the kitchen stove and burn it at once. Miss Strangeworth never delayed when things had to be done.

③ Targeted Passage

After thinking for a minute, she decided that she would like to write another letter, perhaps to go to Mrs. Harper, to follow up the ones she had already mailed. She selected a green sheet this time and wrote quickly: HAVE YOU FOUND OUT YET WHAT THEY WERE ALL LAUGHING ABOUT AFTER YOU LEFT THE BRIDGE CLUB ON THURSDAY? OR IS THE WIFE REALLY ALWAYS THE LAST ONE TO KNOW? **F**
180   Miss Strangeworth never concerned herself with facts; her letters all dealt with the more **negotiable** stuff of suspicion. Mr. Lewis would never have imagined for a minute that his grandson might be lifting petty cash[7] from the store register if he had not had one of Miss Strangeworth's letters. Miss Chandler, the librarian, and Linda Stewart's parents would have gone unsuspectingly ahead with their lives, never aware of possible evil lurking nearby, if Miss Strangeworth had not sent letters to open their eyes. Miss Strangeworth would have been genuinely shocked if there *had* been anything between Linda Stewart and the Harris boy, but, as long as evil existed unchecked in the world, it was Miss Strangeworth's duty to keep her town
190 alert to it. It was far more sensible for Miss Chandler to wonder what Mr. Shelley's first wife had really died of than to take a chance on not knowing. There were so many wicked people in the world and only one Strangeworth left in town. Besides, Miss Strangeworth liked writing her letters. **G**

F MAKE INFERENCES
What is Miss Strangeworth suggesting in this letter to Mrs. Harper?

negotiable
(nĭ-gō'shə-bəl) *adj.* able to be bargained with

G CHARACTER MOTIVATION
What moral issue does Miss Strangeworth claim motivates her letters? What other reason for writing the letters is given in lines 180–193?

---

7. **petty cash:** a small fund of money kept handy for miscellaneous expenses.

DIFFERENTIATED INSTRUCTION

FOR STRUGGLING READERS

③ Targeted Passage [Lines 161–173]

This passage reveals Miss Strangeworth's true character.

- Why does Miss Strangeworth write her letters in childish block print? (lines 210–213)

- Think about Miss Strangeworth's encounters in the morning. To whom is she sending her letter now? (lines 166–168)

- How does Miss Strangeworth feel about the letter? (line 169)

FOR ENGLISH LANGUAGE LEARNERS

Vocabulary: Phrasal Verbs Point out that in English some verbs combine with prepositions to form verb phrases. Guide students to identify and define some of these phrases using Word Questioning: *sent over* (lines 27–28); *Ran out* (line 70); *went on* (line 107); *follow up* (line 175); *slipped out of* (line 241); *set off on* (line 256); *stood away* (line 281); *closed up* (line 283).

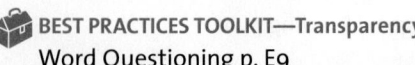 BEST PRACTICES TOOLKIT—Transparency
Word Questioning p. E9

She addressed an envelope to Don Crane after a moment's thought, wondering curiously if he would show the letter to his wife, and using a pink envelope to match the pink paper. Then she addressed a second envelope, green, to Mrs. Harper. Then an idea came to her and she selected a blue sheet and wrote: YOU NEVER KNOW ABOUT DOCTORS. REMEMBER
200 THEY'RE ONLY HUMAN AND NEED MONEY LIKE THE REST OF US. SUPPOSE THE KNIFE SLIPPED ACCIDENTALLY. WOULD DOCTOR BURNS GET HIS FEE AND A LITTLE EXTRA FROM THAT NEPHEW OF YOURS?

She addressed the blue envelope to old Mrs. Foster, who was having an operation next month. She had thought of writing one more letter, to the head of the school board, asking how a chemistry teacher like Billy Moore's father could afford a new convertible, but all at once she was tired of writing letters. The three she had done would do for one day. She could write more tomorrow; it was not as though they all had to be done at once.

She had been writing her letters—sometimes two or three every day for a
210 week, sometimes no more than one in a month—for the past year. She never got any answers, of course, because she never signed her name. If she had been asked, she would have said that her name, Adela Strangeworth, a name honored in the town for so many years, did not belong on such trash. The town where she lived had to be kept clean and sweet, but people everywhere were lustful and evil and **degraded,** and needed to be watched; the world was so large, and there was only one Strangeworth left in it. Miss Strangeworth sighed, locked her desk, and put the letters into her big, black leather pocketbook, to be mailed when she took her evening walk. ⓗ

degraded (dĭ-grā′dĭd) *adj.* corrupted, depraved

ⓗ **CHARACTER MOTIVATION**
Why do you think Miss Strangeworth calls the letters she sends "trash"? If she sees them as trash, why does she send them?

Mailboxes & Cosmos, Carl Schmalz, W.H.S. Watercolor. Courtesy of Pamela Dykstra.

THE POSSIBILITY OF EVIL **211**

Analyze Visuals

Activity Ask students how the table setting in the picture reminds them of the description of Miss Strangeworth's table setting. **Possible answer:** *The picture shows a table with nice silverware, a teacup and saucer, pretty napkins, fine china, and beautiful roses. It looks almost perfect, just like Miss Strangeworth's table.*

About the Art Sandra Speidel, who created *Coffee with Roses*, began illustrating, drawing, and painting as an adult. She has illustrated several books.

READING SKILL

❶ MAKE INFERENCES

Possible answer: She is interested in how Linda Stewart's father looks, because she sent a letter to his home earlier, suggesting that his daughter and the Harris boy were having an improper relationship. She thought Mr. Stewart looked "troubled" (line 258), which would suggest that he had received her letter.

Extend the Discussion How do you think Miss Strangeworth really feels about Mr. Stewart looking troubled?

VOCABULARY

COMMON CORE
L 4

OWN THE WORD

translucent: Give students these examples of things that are *translucent*: stained glass, ice, tracing paper. Point out that the word *transparent* is similar and means "clear."

She broiled her little chop nicely, and had a sliced tomato and good cup of
220 tea ready when she sat down to her midday dinner at the table in her dining room, which could be opened to seat twenty-two, with a second table, if necessary, in the hall. Sitting in the warm sunlight that came through the tall windows of the dining room, seeing her roses massed outside, handling the heavy, old silverware and the fine, **translucent** china, Miss Strangeworth was pleased; she would not have cared to be doing anything else. People must live graciously, after all, she thought, and sipped her tea. Afterward, when her plate and cup and saucer were washed and dried and put back onto the shelves where they belonged, and her silverware was back in the mahogany silver chest, Miss Strangeworth went up the graceful staircase and into her bedroom, which
230 was the front room overlooking the roses, and had been her mother's and her grandmother's. Their Crown Derby dresser set[8] and furs had been kept here, their fans and silver-backed brushes and their own bowls of roses; Miss Strangeworth kept a bowl of white roses on the bed table.

She drew the shades, took the
240 rose-satin spread from the bed, slipped out of her dress and her shoes, and lay down tiredly. She knew that no doorbell or phone would ring; no one in town would dare to disturb Miss Strangeworth during her afternoon nap. She slept, deep in the rich smell of roses.

translucent
(trăns-lōō′sənt) *adj.*
allowing light to shine through

After her nap she worked in her garden for a little while, sparing herself because of the heat; then she came in to her supper. She ate asparagus from
250 her own garden, with sweet-butter sauce, and a soft-boiled egg, and, while she had her supper, she listened to a late-evening news broadcast and then to a program of classical music on her small radio. After her dishes were done and her kitchen set in order, she took up her hat—Miss Strangeworth's hats were proverbial in the town; people believed that she had inherited them from her mother and her grandmother—and, locking the front door of her house behind her, set off on her evening walk, pocketbook under her arm. She nodded to Linda Stewart's father, who was washing his car in the pleasantly cool evening. She thought that he looked troubled. ❶

There was only one place in town where she could mail her letters, and
260 that was the new post office, shiny with red brick and silver letters. Although Miss Strangeworth had never given the matter any particular thought, she had

❶ MAKE INFERENCES
Why would Miss Strangeworth be interested in whether Linda Stewart's father looked troubled?

8. **Crown Derby dresser set:** a hairbrush, comb, and hand mirror made of fine china.

DIFFERENTIATED INSTRUCTION

FOR ADVANCED LEARNERS/PRE–AP

Analyzing Irony With Miss Strangeworth, everything seems perfect on the surface. Have students discuss how Shirley Jackson creates irony by juxtaposing what seems to be with what really is.

FOR ENGLISH LANGUAGE LEARNERS

Develop Reading Fluency Have students listen to the story on the *Audio Anthology CD*. Divide the story, and have students work in threes to practice reading portions of it aloud fluidly and smoothly. Before students begin, have them look up unfamiliar words in the dictionary to learn what they mean and how to pronounce them.

Distribute the copy master and have students work in pairs or groups to practice fluency.

Ⓡ RESOURCE MANAGER—Copy Master
Reading Fluency p. 47

always made a point of mailing her letters very secretly; it would, of course, not have been wise to let anyone see her mail them. Consequently, she timed her walk so she could reach the post office just as darkness was starting to dim the outlines of the trees and the shapes of people's faces, although no one could ever mistake Miss Strangeworth, with her dainty walk and her rustling skirts.

There was always a group of young people around the post office, the very youngest roller-skating upon its driveway, which went all the way around the building and was the only smooth road in town; and the slightly older
270 ones already knowing how to gather in small groups and chatter and laugh and make great, excited plans for going across the street to the soda shop in a minute or two. Miss Strangeworth had never had any self-consciousness before the children. She did not feel that any of them were staring at her unduly or longing to laugh at her; it would have been most **reprehensible** for their parents to permit their children to mock Miss Strangeworth of Pleasant Street. Most of the children stood back respectfully as Miss Strangeworth passed, silenced briefly in her presence, and some of the older children greeted her, saying soberly, "Hello, Miss Strangeworth."

Miss Strangeworth smiled at them and quickly went on. It had been a long
280 time since she had known the name of every child in town. The mail slot was in the door of the post office. The children stood away as Miss Strangeworth approached it, seemingly surprised that anyone should want to use the post office after it had been officially closed up for the night and turned over to the children. Miss Strangeworth stood by the door, opening her black pocketbook to take out the letters, and heard a voice which she knew at once to be Linda Stewart's. Poor little Linda was crying again, and Miss Strangeworth listened carefully. This was, after all, her town, and these were her people; if one of them was in trouble, she ought to know about it.

"I can't tell you, Dave," Linda was saying—so she *was* talking to the Harris
290 boy, as Miss Strangeworth had supposed—"I just *can't*. It's just *nasty*."

"But why won't your father let me come around anymore? What on earth did I do?"

"I can't tell you. I just wouldn't tell you for *any*thing. You've got to have a dirty dirty mind for things like that."

"But something's happened. You've been crying and crying, and your father is all upset. Why can't *I* know about it, too? Aren't *I* like one of the family?"

"Not anymore, Dave, not anymore. You're not to come near our house again; my father said so. He said he'd horsewhip you. That's all I can tell you: You're not to come near our house anymore."

300 "But I didn't *do* anything."

"Just the same, my father said . . ."

Miss Strangeworth sighed and turned away. There was so much evil in people. Even in a charming little town like this one, there was still so much evil in people. **J**

She slipped her letters into the slot, and two of them fell inside. The third caught on the edge and fell outside, onto the ground at Miss Strangeworth's

---

reprehensible
(rĕp'rĭ-hĕn'sə-bəl) *adj.*
deserving blame and criticism

④ **Targeted Passage**

J MAKE INFERENCES
How does Miss Strangeworth feel about the trouble she has caused Linda and Dave? Explain your answer.

THE POSSIBILITY OF EVIL **213**

FOR STRUGGLING READERS

④ **Targeted Passage** [Lines 267–288]

This passage demonstrates Miss Strangeworth's distorted view of herself and her secretive, duplicitous actions.

- Why does Miss Strangeworth mail her letters at night? (lines 261–265)
- What does the fact that Miss Strangeworth thinks of herself as "Miss Strangeworth of Pleasant Street" tell you about her? (line 275)
- Do the children seem to like her and think of her as a friendly old lady? (lines 273–278)

FOR ENGLISH LANGUAGE LEARNERS
Vocabulary: Pronoun Referents Have learners identify the referent of each underlined pronoun: *But the town was proud of Miss Strangeworth and her roses and her house. They had all grown together (lines 134–135); It was almost a town joke, that colored paper (line 153); She dropped a letter addressed to Don Crane .... Maybe it's good news for them (lines 315–316 and 323–324).*

REVIST THE BIG QUESTION
How good are you at
JUDGING people?

Discuss Direct students to lines 289–301 and ask if they think that Miss Strangeworth's reading of the relationship between Dave and Linda is accurate. *Possible answer: No, Linda is obviously disturbed by Miss Strangeworth's letter, describing it as "nasty" (line 290) and the author as having a "dirty dirty mind" (line 294). If she were doing what Miss Strangeworth implied, she would not react in this way.* Is what Miss Strangeworth did to them evil? *Possible answer: Yes, she suggested that something innocent was nasty and dirty, creating problems that were not deserved. Miss Strangeworth's thoughts and actions are evil; Dave's and Linda's are not.*

READING SKILL

J MAKE INFERENCES

Possible answer: Miss Strangeworth does not feel any remorse for hurting Linda and Dave; she simply "sighed and turned away," thinking there was "so much evil in people" (lines 302–303). She does not feel badly about bearing false witness or about causing trouble for two innocent teenagers.

Extend the Discussion How do you think Miss Strangeworth should feel about the trouble she has caused?

VOCABULARY   COMMON CORE   L 4

OWN THE WORD

reprehensible: Ask students what the adjective *reprehensible* describes in the text. *Possible answer: parents allowing their children to mock Miss Strangeworth* Have students give examples of behavior they consider *reprehensible*.

Main story text (center column)

feet. She did not notice it because she was wondering whether a letter to the Harris boy's father might not be of some service in wiping out this potential badness. Wearily Miss Strangeworth turned to go home to her quiet bed in her
310 lovely house, and never heard the Harris boy calling to her to say that she had dropped something. **K**

"Old lady Strangeworth's getting deaf," he said, looking after her and holding in his hand the letter he had picked up.

"Well, who cares?" Linda said. "Who cares anymore, anyway?"

"It's for Don Crane," the Harris boy said, "this letter. She dropped a letter addressed to Don Crane. Might as well take it on over. We pass his house anyway." He laughed. "Maybe it's got a check or something in it and he'd be just as glad to get it tonight instead of tomorrow."

"Catch old lady Strangeworth sending anybody a check," Linda said.
320 "Throw it in the post office. Why do anyone a favor?" She sniffed. "Doesn't seem to me anybody around here cares about us," she said. "Why should we care about them?"

"I'll take it over, anyway," the Harris boy said. "Maybe it's good news for them. Maybe they need something happy tonight, too. Like us."

Sadly, holding hands, they wandered off down the dark street, the Harris boy carrying Miss Strangeworth's pink envelope in his hand.

Miss Strangeworth awakened the next morning with a feeling of intense happiness and, for a minute, wondered why, and then remembered that this morning three people would open her letters. Harsh, perhaps, at first, but
330 wickedness was never easily banished, and a clean heart was a scoured heart. She washed her soft, old face and brushed her teeth, still sound in spite of her seventy-one years, and dressed herself carefully in her sweet, soft clothes and buttoned shoes. Then, going downstairs, reflecting that perhaps a little waffle would be agreeable for breakfast in the sunny dining room, she found the mail on the hall floor, and bent to pick it up. A bill, the morning paper, a letter in a green envelope that looked oddly familiar. Miss Strangeworth stood perfectly still for a minute, looking down at the green envelope with the penciled printing, and thought: It looks like one of my letters. Was one of my letters sent back? No, because no one would know where to send it. How did this
340 get here?

Miss Strangeworth was a Strangeworth of Pleasant Street. Her hand did not shake as she opened the envelope and unfolded the sheet of green paper inside. She began to cry silently for the wickedness of the world when she read the words: LOOK OUT AT WHAT USED TO BE YOUR ROSES. **L** 〜

Left column

K PREDICT

Possible answer: *She will be caught this time. Dave Harris saw that Miss Strangeworth was sending the letter, and he may bring it to the addressee, as it is a small town and everybody knows one another.*

TEXT ANALYSIS

COMMON CORE
RL 3

L SYMBOLISM

Have students reread the last two paragraphs of the story. Point out to students that the symbols of Miss Strangeworth's "sweet, soft clothes," "agreeable" breakfast, "sunny dinning room," and "Pleasant Street" serve to show her longing for a perfect, orderly life.

Possible Answer: *The roses might function as symbols for the idealized, perfect life that Miss Strangeworth feels she is losing as the town slips away from her. They might also symbolize her own attitude about her town, which appears to be beautiful and simple, but has (thorns) a cruel, hidden side.*

SELECTION WRAP–UP

READ WITH A PURPOSE Now that students have finished reading the selection, ask them how they think the destruction of the roses will affect Miss Strangeworth's life and future interactions with the people in the town. ***Possible answer:*** *Miss Strangeworth cries for the "wickedness of the world" (line 343) and will blame others, not recognizing that the destruction of her flowers was retribution for her own malice. She will not feel bad for her own evil actions.*

★ **CRITIQUE** Have students evaluate whether Miss Strangeworth was a believable character. Ask students to think about her life, her actions, and her motivation.

Right column

K PREDICT

What do you predict will happen because Miss Strangeworth failed to notice that she dropped the letter?

Language Coach

Commonly Confused Words Some words are easy to confuse. Reread lines 329–330. *Banished*, meaning "driven away," is easy to confuse with the word *vanished*. Should the following sentence be revised, and if so, how? *The clouds banished and the sun shone brightly.*

S Targeted Passage

COMMON CORE RL 3

L SYMBOLISM

Symbols are concrete elements in a story, such as a person, house, or object, that stand for something abstract, like freedom, safety, or evil. One function of symbols is to suggest additional information about a character, including information about his or her attitudes and beliefs. Reread the passages in "The Possibility of Evil" that focus on Miss Strangeworth's roses, particularly line 344. What might the symbol of the roses reveal about Miss Strangeworth's beliefs about her life and town?

Bottom section

DIFFERENTIATED INSTRUCTION

FOR STRUGGLING READERS

S Targeted Passage [Lines 327–344]

This passage concludes the story with Miss Strangeworth's evil deeds returning to haunt her.

- Why does Miss Strangeworth awake feeling happy? (lines 329–330)

- Why is Miss Strangeworth surprised to receive a green letter in the mail? (lines 338–339)

- What happened to Miss Strangeworth's roses? (lines 343–344)

Language Coach

Commonly Confused Words *Answer*: *The clouds* vanished . . . . Ask students for examples other words they commonly confuse. Write the words on the board, and work with students to clarify the meanings.

Comprehension

1. **Recall** What is Miss Strangeworth's reputation in town?

2. **Recall** How does she secretly warn people of "possible evil"?

3. **Recall** How is her secret activity discovered?

4. **Paraphrase** What is Miss Strangeworth's view of human nature?

Text Analysis

5. **Make Inferences** Review the chart you created as you read. Does Miss Strangeworth seem to understand the harm she is causing? Cite evidence to support your answer.

6. **Analyze Irony** Reread lines 219–238. Explain the irony, or the contrast between appearance and reality, in Miss Strangeworth's insistence upon living "graciously."

7. **Draw Conclusions About Motivation** The narrator offers more than one reason for Miss Strangeworth's secret activity. Do you think her main motivation is to address a moral dilemma—or is it something else? Use a graphic organizer like this one to answer.

Evidence from Text	My Own Knowledge and Experience	Conclusion

8. **Evaluate** Is the punishment that Miss Strangeworth receives at the end of the story appropriate? Explain why or why not.

9. **Predict** How will Miss Strangeworth's life in the town be different after her secret is discovered?

10. **Make Judgments About a Character** Review the definition you created for the word *evil* on page 202. Is Miss Strangeworth an evil person? Support your opinion with evidence from the text.

Text Criticism

11. **Social Context** Shirley Jackson's husband, the literary critic Stanley Edgar Hyman, said that her dark tales are not just expressions of her private fears but are "fitting symbols for our distressing world." What social or political issues are reflected in "The Possibility of Evil"? Use examples from the story in your response.

> ### How good are you at JUDGING people?
> What would you do if you encountered someone you thought evil?

COMMON CORE

RL 1 Cite textual evidence to support inferences drawn from the text. RL 3 Analyze how complex characters develop and interact with other characters.

Practice and Apply

For preliminary support of post-reading questions, use these copy masters:

R RESOURCE MANAGER—Copy Masters
Reading Check p. 44
Character Motivation p. 37
Question Support p. 45

Additional selection questions are provided for teachers on, see page 31.

ANSWERS

Comprehension

1. *She is the founder's granddaughter, a prim and proper elderly woman who grows beautiful roses and knows everyone.*

2. *She sends them unsigned letters that hint at evil actions done by people in their lives.*

3. *Dave Harris finds the letter she dropped and brings it to Don Crane.*

4. *She believes there are many wicked people in the world.*

Text Analysis

Possible answers:

5. ■ **COMMON CORE FOCUS** *Make Inferences* *She knows she upsets people. She turns away when she hears Linda crying (lines 289–304), telling herself that evil people are degrading her town and it's her duty to keep it clean.*

6. *Miss Strangeworth sips tea, uses lovely silverware, and has a neat house (lines 226–238). Yet, her intentions are hurtful, mean-spirited, and completely ungracious.*

7. ● **COMMON CORE FOCUS** *Character Motivation* *Have students answer whether or not Miss Strangeworth acts in response to a moral dilemma using specific examples from the text and their own experience. Answers will vary.*

8. *Evaluate* *Yes, the punishment fits the crime. She loved her roses and was quite proud of them. When they were destroyed, she cried "silently for the wickedness of the world" (line 343). She experienced the kind of hurt that she had inflicted on others.*

9. *Predict* *People will no longer treat her with the respect due to a kind older lady.*

10. *She is evil: she shows no remorse about destroying others. Writing malicious letters gives her pleasure (line 193).*

Text Criticism

Possible answer:

11. *Jackson may be commenting upon politicians and social commentators who use innuendo and false accusations to carry out their own agendas. Miss Strangeworth's destructive activities and subsequent downfall suggest that when people set themselves up as moral guardians, the results can only be destructive. Her story begs the question of whether society needs a moral guardian.*

How good are you at JUDGING people? Encourage students to consider what criteria they would use to decide that someone is evil. Have them also think about whether or not they have ever misjudged someone.

ANSWERS

Vocabulary in Context

▲ VOCABULARY PRACTICE

1. *a*	4. *d*
2. *b*	5. *c*
3. *a*	6. *a*

 RESOURCE MANAGER—Copy Master
Vocabulary Practice p. 42

ACADEMIC VOCABULARY IN WRITING

Sample response: Individuals *might* undergo *a variety of changes. They might become more suspicious of other people. They might become angry with loved ones. They might also take actions to* seek *the truth about the information in the note.*

VOCABULARY STRATEGY: CONNOTATION AND DENOTATION

COMMON CORE **L 5b**

- Suggest that students pay careful attention to context clues to determine the connotation of each word.
- If students experience difficulty, ask them to substitute a familiar synonym to determine which word makes sense in the sentence.

Possible answers:

1. *adoring*
2. *close*
3. *reprehensible*
4. *negotiable*
5. *corrupted*

 **RESOURCE MANAGER—Copy Master**
Vocabulary Strategy p. 43

Interactive Vocabulary

Keywords direct students to a **WordSharp** tutorial on **thinkcentral.com** or to other types of vocabulary practice and review.

Vocabulary in Context

▲ VOCABULARY PRACTICE

Choose the letter of the word that is most different in meaning from the others.

1. (a) disinterested, (b) infatuated, (c) lovesick, (d) smitten
2. (a) rapt, (b) inattentive, (c) absorbed, (d) immersed
3. (a) negotiable, (b) certain, (c) indisputable, (d) inarguable
4. (a) uplifted, (b) elevated, (c) honored, (d) degraded
5. (a) clear, (b) translucent, (c) dense, (d) transparent
6. (a) reprehensible, (b) admirable, (c) respectable, (d) praiseworthy

ACADEMIC VOCABULARY IN WRITING

> • dynamic • individual • motive • seek • undergo

How do you think Miss Strangeworth's neighbors react when they receive one of her letters? Write a paragraph describing several changes that characters might **undergo** after reading a note from Miss Strangeworth. Use at least one Academic Vocabulary word in your response.

VOCABULARY STRATEGY: CONNOTATION AND DENOTATION

A word's **denotation** is its basic dictionary meaning; its **connotation** is the overtones of meaning that it may take on. For example, the vocabulary word *infatuated* means "intensely fond," but it has connotations of an almost foolish obsession that *adoring* does not have. When you choose words in writing, be sure to consider whether their connotations fit the context of that particular sentence as well as that of your topic as a whole.

PRACTICE Choose the word that works best in each sentence. You can use a dictionary or thesaurus to help you.

1. The (infatuated/adoring) fans devoted their entire lives to their favorite movie star.
2. Pay (close/rapt) attention to what I am saying!
3. A (reprehensible/blameworthy) crime should be swiftly punished.
4. This issue is not a (negotiable/bargainable) one.
5. The politicians became (degraded/corrupted) by greed.

WORD LIST

degraded
infatuated
negotiable
rapt
reprehensible
translucent

COMMON CORE

L 5b Analyze nuances in the meaning of words with similar denotations.

Interactive Vocabulary THINK central

Go to **thinkcentral.com**.
KEYWORD: HML10-216

DIFFERENTIATED INSTRUCTION

FOR ENGLISH LANGUAGE LEARNERS

Language: Suffixes Point out that all the words in the word list are adjectives that modify nouns. The words *degraded* and *corrupted* can also be used as verbs. Explain that the suffix *-ed* changes a verb from a present tense (*degrade, corrupt*) to a past tense (*degraded, corrupted*). Ask students to write a sentence using each verb in the present tense and past tense.

Language

◆ **GRAMMAR AND STYLE:** Set the Scene

 **COMMON CORE**

L 3 Apply knowledge of language to make effective choices for meaning or style.

Review the **Grammar and Style** note on page 209. Shirley Jackson uses **modifiers,** words or groups of words that change or limit the meaning of other words, to precisely depict the details of a scene. Adjectives and adverbs, along with phrases and clauses, are examples of modifiers. Use modifiers to add descriptive details that draw the reader into a scene, as Jackson does in the following example:

> *Sitting in the warm sunlight that came through the tall windows of the dining room, seeing her roses massed outside, handling the heavy, old silverware and the fine, translucent china, Miss Strangeworth was pleased.* . . . (lines 222–225)

Notice how the revisions in blue help describe a scene more precisely. Revise your draft by adding modifiers.

STUDENT MODEL

Miss Strangeworth looks like an innocent ˄*, sweet* old lady. She ˄*deeply* loves her ˄*elegant* home and her ˄*beautiful* roses. However, her ˄*cruel* actions are far from innocent.

READING-WRITING CONNECTION

 YOUR TURN Enhance your understanding of "The Possibility of Evil" by responding to this prompt. Then use the **revising tip** to improve your writing.

WRITING PROMPT	REVISING TIP
Short Constructed Response: Analysis Has Miss Strangeworth lost her sanity? Is she truly **evil**? Using evidence from the text, write **one or two paragraphs** in response to these questions. Be sure to present a clear opinion in your answer, and use quotations from the story to support your argument.	Look back over your response. Did you use modifiers to add descriptive details? If not, revise your answer.

 **Interactive Revision** **THINK** central

Go to **thinkcentral.com**. KEYWORD: HML10-217

Language

COMMON CORE L 3

◆ **GRAMMAR AND STYLE**

Write on the board the paragraph that follows. (Revisions are shown in blue.) Then have students suggest modifiers to describe Miss Strangeworth's feelings about her roses and their destruction. (For more on using modifiers, see **Grammar Handbook,** page R57.)

Miss Strangeworth stepped into her garden, once lovely with her beloved red, pink, and white roses. She gazed sorrowfully upon the pitiful remains of her flower beds. Her magnificent roses were no longer standing. In their place was a horrid pile of dry, yellow leaves and faded, rotting flowers. She could not believe the cruel, evil world she lived in.

R RESOURCE MANAGER—Copy Master
  Set the Scene p. 46

READING-WRITING CONNECTION

• Ask students to review their definitions of *evil* and to reread pages 210–211. Have students use a character analysis frame to determine whether she is evil.

 BEST PRACTICES TOOLKIT—Transparency
  Analysis Frame: Character pp. D21, D26

Writing Online **THINK** central

The following tools are available online at **thinkcentral.com** and on **Write*Smart*** CD-ROM:
• Interactive Graphic Organizers
• Interactive Student Models
• Interactive Revision Lessons
For additional grammar instruction, see **GrammarNotes** on **thinkcentral.com**.

FOR STRUGGLING WRITERS

• Help students write a definition of evil.
• Direct students to the Targeted Passages on pages 204, 208, 210, 213, 214. Have them note what Miss Strangeworth does and how she feels. Have them record the information in a Two-Column Chart with the heads *Text* and *Evil or Not Evil.*

• Have students use their notes to write a one-sentence topic sentence that begins "Miss Strangeworth is (is not) evil because . . . ."

 BEST PRACTICES TOOLKIT—Transparency
  Two-Column Chart p. A25

Assess and Reteach

Assess

DIAGNOSTIC AND SELECTION TESTS
  Selection Tests A, B/C pp. 59–60, 61–62

Interactive Selection Test on **thinkcentral.com**

Reteach

Level Up Online Tutorials on **thinkcentral.com**

Reteaching Worksheets on **thinkcentral.com**
  Literature Lesson 2

Focus and Motivate

Like the Sun

Short Story by R. K. Narayan

SUMMARY

In "Like the Sun," Sekhar knows that the truth may be shocking. Nevertheless, he sets apart one day to be absolutely honest. His resolve is tested by his wife and then by a colleague. When his boss, the headmaster, asks Sekhar to comment on his musical talent, Sekhar tells the truth again. The price of his candor: he must grade 100 overdue papers that night.

How important is telling the TRUTH?

Ask students to identify some situations in which it is important to tell the truth and others in which it might be important not to be completely honest. Then ask the question. Have pairs formulate an answer and then complete the *QUICKWRITE*.

How important is telling the TRUTH?

We all know that honesty is the best policy. But sometimes the truth hurts people's feelings. In "Like the Sun," a schoolteacher is determined to be honest, even if it puts a strain on his relationships.

QUICKWRITE In a brief letter to an advice columnist, describe a situation in which telling the truth would have painful consequences. Then exchange letters with a partner and write a response to your partner's letter.

218

Selection Resources

● TEXT ANALYSIS: MORAL DILEMMA

The conflict in many short stories and longer works of fiction revolves around a character's **moral dilemma.** A character facing a moral dilemma must choose between two or more morally questionable options; for example, someone might have to choose between betraying a friend's trust or breaking a school rule. A character may also struggle to determine the right course of action or disagree with his or her society over what moral behavior is.

As you read a work of fiction that focuses on a moral dilemma, think about

- the moral choice the character faces
- what choice others expect the character to make
- the moral expectations of the character's culture or country

In "Like the Sun," the main character is concerned about the morality of telling the absolute truth. As you read, consider how this dilemma creates conflict for him, and think about the choices you would make if you were in his place.

■ READING STRATEGY: PREDICT

While reading a story, have you ever **predicted** that it would have a happy ending or that a character would get into trouble? When you make predictions, you guess what will happen in a story by using text clues and your own knowledge and experience. Even if your guesses turn out to be wrong, the process of making predictions can help you pay attention to important details.

As you read "Like the Sun," make predictions about the consequences of the main character's decision to tell the full truth. Use a chart like the one shown.

Event	Prediction	Outcome
Sekhar's wife serves him breakfast.	He will criticize her cooking and hurt her feelings.	She winces after he says the food isn't good.

 Complete the activities in your **Reader/Writer Notebook.**

Meet the Author

R. K. Narayan
1906–2001

Love of English
Born in southern India, R. K. Narayan (nä-rä′yän) is widely considered one of his country's greatest authors. As a young man, Narayan tried his hand at several professions, including teaching. When he decided to become a fiction writer in the 1930s, he chose to write in English, which was unusual for Indian writers at the time. In an interview Narayan noted, "I was never aware that I was using a different, a foreign, language when I wrote in English, because it came to me very easily. . . . And it's so transparent it can take on the tint of any country."

One Setting Fits All
Narayan set most of his novels and short stories in the fictional town of Malgudi, which was based in part on the place where he grew up. He created Malgudi for his first novel, *Swami and Friends* (1935). "As I sat in a room nibbling my pen and wondering what to write," he recalled, "Malgudi with its little railroad station swam into view."

BACKGROUND TO THE STORY
School Life in India
Sekhar, the main character in "Like the Sun," is a teacher in India, where schools are modeled on the British educational system. A headmaster, rather than a principal, is in charge of a school. Students progress through forms, which are the equivalent of grades in the United States. Sekhar teaches the third form, or ninth grade.

Author Online
THINK central
Go to **thinkcentral.com.**
KEYWORD: HML10-219

219

Teach

● *Model the Skill:* MORAL DILEMMA

Model how to identify a moral dilemma. Read aloud this example:

> Taisha decides to tell her best friend, Max, that he hasn't got what it takes to make the soccer team.

Point out that this decision represents a moral dilemma for Taisha. Explain that in choosing to tell Max the truth, Taisha risks causing conflict, hurting Max's feelings, and rupturing their friendship.

■ *Model the Skill:* PREDICT

Model for students how to make predictions. Read aloud this story event:

> A strict headmaster learns about two students cheating.

Remind students that they can use their own experiences and knowledge of human behavior to help them make predictions. They can also use details from the story to guide them.
Have students use a chart to predict what will happen next.

Event	Prediction	Outcome
Headmaster learns of cheating.	Students will be punished harshly.	Students never cheat again.

R RESOURCE MANAGER—Copy Master
Predict p. 61 (for student use while reading the selection)

DIFFERENTIATED INSTRUCTION

FOR STRUGGLING READERS

Story Map Have students use a Story Map to record key story elements. Begin by helping students name the time, place, and main character. Have students complete the rest of the map on their own as they read.

 BEST PRACTICES TOOLKIT—Transparency
Story Map p. D14

READ WITH A PURPOSE

Help students set a purpose for reading. Tell them to note how Sekhar's truth telling affects those around him.

A *Model the Skill:* **MORAL DILEMMA**

Point out that Sekhar's wife winces after he says that the food "isn't good" (line 13). Explain that her facial expression shows that Sekhar's honesty has hurt her feelings. Ask students whether they think Sekhar could have told his wife the truth in a different way.

Possible answer: Sekhar's wife would probably not agree, since she became angry at him for telling the truth about her cooking.

REVISIT THE BIG QUESTION

How important is telling the TRUTH?

Discuss Based on lines 1–4, what does Sekhar mean when he says that "truth . . . is like the sun" (line 1)? *Possible answer: He means that truth is powerful. It is too strong to look "straight in the face" (line 2). The truth needs softening or "tempering" (line 3); otherwise, it will cause pain.*

Like THE *Sun*

R. K. Narayan

Truth, Sekhar reflected, is like the sun. I suppose no human being can ever look it straight in the face without blinking or being dazed. He realized that, morning till night, the essence of human relationships consisted in tempering truth so that it might not shock. This day he set apart as a unique day—at least one day in the year we must give and take absolute Truth whatever may happen. Otherwise life is not worth living. The day ahead seemed to him full of possibilities. He told no one of his experiment. It was a quiet resolve, a secret pact between him and eternity.

The very first test came while his wife served him his morning meal. He 10 showed hesitation over a titbit, which she had thought was her culinary[1] masterpiece. She asked, "Why, isn't it good?" At other times he would have said, considering her feelings in the matter, "I feel full up, that's all." But today he said, "It isn't good. I'm unable to swallow it." He saw her wince and said to himself, Can't be helped. Truth is like the sun. **A**

His next trial was in the common room when one of his colleagues came up and said, "Did you hear of the death of so-and-so? Don't you think it a pity?"

"No," Sekhar answered. "He was such a fine man—" the other began. But Sekhar cut him short with: "Far from it. He always struck me as a mean and selfish brute."

20 During the last period when he was teaching geography for Third Form A, Sekhar received a note from the headmaster: "Please see me before you go home." Sekhar said to himself: It must be about these horrible test papers. A hundred papers in the boys' scrawls; he had shirked this work for weeks, feeling all the time as if a sword were hanging over his head.

The bell rang, and the boys burst out of the class.

Sekhar paused for a moment outside the headmaster's room to button up his coat; that was another subject the headmaster always sermonized about.

He stepped in with a very polite "Good evening, sir."

Analyze Visuals ▶

Examine the painting. What details suggest the **setting** of the story?

1 Targeted Passage

A **MORAL DILEMMA**
Sekhar believes that telling the truth is the moral choice. Do you think his wife would agree? Why or why not?

Detail of *The Dance of Krishna* (about 1650). Mewar, Rajasthan, India. From a manuscript of the Sur-Sagar. Opaque watercolor on paper, 11″ × 8¹⁄₈″. Collection Gopi Krishna, Patna, India.

---

1. **culinary** (kyōō′lə-nĕr′ē): having to do with cooking or the kitchen.

DIFFERENTIATED INSTRUCTION

FOR ENGLISH LANGUAGE LEARNERS

Vocabulary Support Use Word Questioning to teach these words: *unique* (line 4), *colleagues* (line 15), *inclinations* (line 44), *commenting* (line 68).

🧰 BEST PRACTICES TOOLKIT—Transparency
Word Questioning p. E9

FOR STRUGGLING READERS

In combination with the *Audio Anthology CD,* use one or more Targeted Passages (pp. 220, 223) to ensure that students focus on key story events, concepts, and skills. Targeted Passages are also good for English learners.

1 Targeted Passage [Lines 1–14]

These lines introduce the main character, the conflict, and the first event.

- What does Sekhar decide to do for one day? (lines 4–6)

- What trouble does he know this could cause? (lines 2–4)

- What is the "first test" of his resolution? (lines 9–14)

BACKGROUND

Indian Classical and Folk Music The central scene of this story features a performance of classical and folk music. In India instrumental and vocal music is often performed in small ensembles, like the group of three that performs in this story. Although classical music is played and appreciated only by an elite minority, folk music and classical music are often intertwined and are based on classical ragas: ancient melodic patterns. Vocalists and instrumentalists improvise on these patterns, often in performances that go on for long periods of time. These performances usually delight audiences, but when the vocalist or musicians are unskilled, as in this story, they can result in boredom or worse.

Analyze Visuals

Possible answer: The people in the painting and their musical instruments appear to be Indian. These details suggest that the story is set in India.

About the Art In this detail from the 17th-century painting *The Dance of Krishna, Krishna* is the blue-faced figure at the lower left who is playing a flute. In the full painting, he is leaping during a dance with five gopis, or female cowherds. In Indian legends, Krishna is a hero-god who destroyed wicked kings and demons across India. The bright reds, greens, oranges, blues, and yellows of this painting help to convey the ecstatic mood, for the dance is a cosmic one that expresses a fundamental truth about the power of love.

Direct students to lines 29–42. Use these prompts to help students understand Sekhar's dilemma:

Connect What is it like to be put on the spot to accept an invitation? *Possible answer: Being put on the spot is unpleasant; it can be hard to say no without offending.*

Analyze Why do you think Sekhar accepts the headmaster's invitation, even though he is clearly reluctant to go? *Possible answer: He probably feels that he cannot refuse an invitation from his headmaster without jeopardizing his job. He may also want to ingratiate himself with the headmaster because of his overdue test papers (line 22).*

READING STRATEGY   COMMON CORE   RL 1

B PREDICT

Possible answer: Sekhar will have a conflict between his vow to tell the truth and his opinion of the headmaster's music. Answers will vary as to how Sekhar will respond.

READING STRATEGY   COMMON CORE   RL 1

C *Model the Skill:* **PREDICT**

Model how to predict by reading lines 61–69 aloud. Point out to students line 65, "Sekhar pretended not to have heard the question." Tell students that in lines 67–69, Sekhar thinks to himself that the headmaster's singing is like croaking, "bellowing," and "loose window shutters in a storm." These text clues help students predict that what Sekhar will say might offend the headmaster. Have students enter the event, prediction, and outcome in their Predict charts.

Possible answer: The headmaster will be offended, embarrassed, or angry; Sekhar may have to face harmful consequences, such as the loss of salary and job security.

The headmaster looked up at him in a very friendly manner and asked,
30 "Are you free this evening?"

Sekhar replied, "Just some outing which I have promised the children at home—"

"Well, you can take them out another day. Come home with me now."

"Oh . . . yes, sir, certainly . . ." And then he added timidly, "Anything special, sir?"

"Yes," replied the headmaster, smiling to himself . . . "You didn't know my weakness for music?"

"Oh, yes, sir . . ."

"I've been learning and practicing secretly, and now I want you to hear me
40 this evening. I've engaged a drummer and a violinist to accompany me—this is the first time I'm doing it full-dress,[2] and I want your opinion. I know it will be valuable."

Sekhar's taste in music was well-known. He was one of the most dreaded music critics in the town. But he never anticipated his musical inclinations would lead him to this trial. . . . "Rather a surprise for you, isn't it?" asked the headmaster. "I've spent a fortune on it behind closed doors. . . ." They started for the headmaster's house. "God hasn't given me a child, but at least let him not deny me the consolation of music," the headmaster said, pathetically, as they walked. He incessantly chattered about music: how he began one day out
50 of sheer boredom; how his teacher at first laughed at him and then gave him hope; how his ambition in life was to forget himself in music.

At home the headmaster proved very ingratiating. He sat Sekhar on a red silk carpet, set before him several dishes of delicacies, and fussed over him as if he were a son-in-law of the house. He even said, "Well, you must listen with a free mind. Don't worry about these test papers." He added half humorously, "I will give you a week's time."

"Make it ten days, sir," Sekhar pleaded.

"All right, granted," the headmaster said generously. Sekhar felt really relieved now—he would attack them at the rate of ten a day and get rid of
60 the nuisance.

The headmaster lighted incense sticks. "Just to create the right atmosphere," he explained. A drummer and a violinist, already seated on a Rangoon mat, were waiting for him. The headmaster sat down between them like a professional at a concert, cleared his throat, and began an alapana,[3] and paused to ask, "Isn't it good Kalyani?"[4] Sekhar pretended not to have heard the question. The headmaster went on to sing a full song composed by Thyagaraja[5] and followed it with two more. All the time the headmaster was singing, Sekhar went on commenting within himself, He croaks like a dozen frogs. He is bellowing like a buffalo. Now he sounds like loose window shutters in a storm. **C**

---

2. **full-dress:** complete in every respect.

3. **alapana:** improvisational Indian music in the classical style.

4. **Kalyani:** traditional Indian folk songs.

5. **Thyagaraja:** a famous Indian composer (1767–1847).

B PREDICT
What **conflict** might arise between Sekhar and the headmaster? How do you think Sekhar will react to this conflict?

C PREDICT
What will happen if Sekhar expresses his opinion of the headmaster's singing?

DIFFERENTIATED INSTRUCTION

FOR STRUGGLING READERS

Develop Reading Fluency Remind students that India was an English colony for many years, and the characters in this story use proper British English. Point out some features of their speech: "Good evening, *sir*" (line 28 and throughout the selection); "*Rather* a surprise for you, isn't it?" (line 45); "I don't think I *shall* have a single friend left" (lines 96–97); "I must *positively* have them here tomorrow. . . ." (line 104).

With expression, read aloud the dialogue between Sekhar and the headmaster. Then have student pairs practice the dialogue themselves. Ask students to point out sections where they had trouble. Then reread those difficult or confusing sections aloud for students again.

Distribute the copy master and have students work in pairs or groups to practice fluency.

R RESOURCE MANAGER—Copy Master
Reading Fluency p. 65–66

70 The incense sticks burnt low. Sekhar's head throbbed with the medley of sounds that had assailed his eardrums for a couple of hours now. He felt half stupefied. The headmaster had gone nearly hoarse, when he paused to ask, "Shall I go on?" Sekhar replied, "Please don't, sir; I think this will do. . . ." The headmaster looked stunned. His face was beaded with perspiration. Sekhar felt the greatest pity for him. But he felt he could not help it. No judge delivering a sentence felt more pained and helpless. Sekhar noticed that the headmaster's wife peeped in from the kitchen, with eager curiosity. The drummer and the violinist put away their burdens with an air of relief. The headmaster removed his spectacles, mopped his brow, and asked, "Now, come out with your

80 opinion." **D**

"Can't I give it tomorrow, sir?" Sekhar asked tentatively.

"No. I want it immediately—your frank opinion. Was it good?"

"No, sir . . ." Sekhar replied.

"Oh! . . . Is there any use continuing my lessons?"

"Absolutely none, sir . . ." Sekhar said with his voice trembling. He felt very unhappy that he could not speak more soothingly. Truth, he reflected, required as much strength to give as to receive.

All the way home he felt worried. He felt that his official life was not going to be smooth sailing hereafter. There were questions of increment and

90 confirmation[6] and so on, all depending upon the headmaster's goodwill.

All kinds of worries seemed to be in store for him. . . . Did not Harischandra[7] lose his throne, wife, child, because he would speak nothing less than the absolute Truth whatever happened? **E**

At home his wife served him with a sullen face. He knew she was still angry with him for his remark of the morning. Two casualties for today, Sekhar said to himself. If I practice it for a week, I don't think I shall have a single friend left.

He received a call from the headmaster in his classroom next day. He went up apprehensively.

100 "Your suggestion was useful. I have paid off the music master. No one would tell me the truth about my music all these days. Why such antics at my age! Thank you. By the way, what about those test papers?"

"You gave me ten days, sir, for correcting them."

"Oh, I've reconsidered it. I must positively have them here tomorrow. . . ." A hundred papers in a day! That meant all night's sitting up! "Give me a couple of days, sir . . ."

"No. I must have them tomorrow morning. And remember, every paper must be thoroughly scrutinized." **F**

"Yes, sir," Sekhar said, feeling that sitting up all night with a hundred test

110 papers was a small price to pay for the luxury of practicing Truth. ❧

---

6. **increment and confirmation:** salary increases and job security.

7. **Harischandra:** a legendary Hindu king and the subject of many Indian stories. His name has come to symbolize truth and integrity.

COMMON CORE RL 4

Language Coach

Denotation/Connotation
Many words have positive or negative associations (connotations). Reread lines 70–71. Do the words *throbbed* and *assailed* have negative or positive connotations? Jot down a synonym with more neutral connotations for each word.

D **MORAL DILEMMA**
What dilemma does Sekhar face in this moment? What are the possible consequences of each choice he could make?

COMMON CORE RL 6

E **WORLD LITERATURE**
An **allusion** is a reference to a famous person, place, or event from history, literature, or mythology. In line 92, Narayan makes an allusion to Harischandra, a legendary Hindu king. Reread footnote 7, which describes Harischandra. How does this allusion help you understand the narrator's culture, view of himself, and his truth telling?

F **CHARACTER AND PLOT**
How has Sekhar's truthfulness affected his relationship with the headmaster?

TEXT ANALYSIS — COMMON CORE

D MORAL DILEMMA RL 3

Possible answer: Sekhar can either hold true to his vow of telling the truth and hurt his headmaster's feelings, or he can tell a lie and make his headmaster feel better. If he tells the truth, his headmaster will be upset and may take revenge on Sekhar. If he lies, he will betray his vow, and the headmaster will be happy, but will continue to look foolish.

TEXT ANALYSIS — COMMON CORE

E WORLD LITERATURE RL 6

Read lines 91–93 aloud to students, and then have a volunteer read the footnote. Tell students that the word *integrity* means "steadfast adherence to a strict moral or ethical code." Emphasize that Harischandra symbolizes, or stands for, these values.

Answer: The allusion to Harischandra helps the reader understand the importance of truth and integrity in Hindu stories and legends. Sekhar wants to live up to this legendary figure, but finds difficulty in living up to his ideals in the real world.

TEXT ANALYSIS — COMMON CORE

F CHARACTER AND PLOT RL 3

Possible answer: Sekhar has not lost his job, but he seems to be on the headmaster's bad side, as he has just been ordered to do the superhuman task of grading 100 papers in a single night.

FOR STRUGGLING READERS

2 Targeted Passage [Lines 82–110]

These lines contain the climax and resolution.

- What is the climax, or point of greatest tension? (lines 79–87)
- How did the headmaster treat Sekhar the next day? (lines 100–108)

FOR ENGLISH LANGUAGE LEARNERS

Language Coach — COMMON CORE RL 4

Denotation/Connotation
Answer: Negative; more neutral words for throbbed: *rang, vibrated;* for assailed: *hit, reached, entered.* Have students point out three neutral words in lines 70–71. *Possible answers: incense, medley, sounds*

SELECTION WRAP-UP

READ WITH A PURPOSE Have students consider how telling the truth affects Sekhar. By the end of the story, has Sekhar has changed his mind about the importance of telling the absolute truth? *Possible answer: Sekhar's truth is hard on him as well as on those around him (lines 74–75). Sekhar notes that Truth takes as much strength to give as to receive (lines 86–87), but he concludes that practicing Truth is a luxury worth the price (line 110).*

TIERED DISCUSSION PROMPTS

Use these prompts to help students see how Narayan and Dickinson present similar ideas about the truth:

Connect Think of a time when someone who cares about you told you something that wasn't completely true. What was that person's motive? How did you feel?

Analyze What does Dickinson mean by telling the truth "slant"? ***Possible answer:*** *She means that the truth may have to be worded carefully or adapted, as it sometimes is for children, when helping them come to terms with painful realities. If truth is not told slant, it may be too strong or "blinding" at first. Gradually, people can see the truth without being hurt by it.*

Evaluate Ask students to consider what the story and the poem say about telling the truth, and whether they agree with that message. ***Possible answer:*** *Both the story and the poem express the idea that the naked truth can offend and hurt people, and that smooth relations sometimes require people to temper, soften, or even "slant" the truth. Students will probably agree with this idea but may suggest that there are times when complete honesty is necessary, even if it causes pain.*

Tell all the Truth but tell it slant—
Emily Dickinson

Tell all the Truth but tell it slant—
Success in Circuit lies
Too bright for our infirm Delight
The Truth's superb surprise
5 As Lightning to the Children eased
With explanation kind
The Truth must dazzle gradually
Or every man be blind—

224

Comprehension

1. **Recall** What does Sekhar decide to do for one day?

2. **Recall** How is Sekhar tested during the day?

3. **Summarize** What negative consequences result from Sekhar's decision?

COMMON CORE

RL 1 Cite evidence to support inferences drawn from the text. RL 3 Analyze how characters with conflicting motivations develop and interact with others.

Text Analysis

4. **Analyze Character and Plot** Which of Sekhar's character traits most directly influence the story's plot? Explain your answer.

5. **Make Inferences** Reread lines 98–108. Do you think the headmaster is sincere when he thanks Sekhar for his honesty? Why or why not?

6. **Predict** Look back at the predictions you recorded as you read. How close were the predictions to what actually happened? Cite specific evidence that influenced your predictions.

7. **Moral Dilemma** In "The Possibility of Evil" and "Like the Sun," the main characters both hold a moral position that brings them into conflict with their communities. Compare and contrast the ways they respond to their **moral dilemmas**. Do you think they make the right decisions? Why or why not?

8. **Evaluate** How successful was Sekhar's experiment in telling the absolute truth? Use evidence from the story to support your opinion.

9. **Compare Literary Works** "The Possibility of Evil," "Like the Sun," and "Tell all the Truth but tell it slant—" all show different perspectives on telling the truth. What message about telling the truth does each work reveal? How are the messages similar? How are they different? Fill in a chart like this one to record your answer.

	"The Possibility of Evil"	"Like the Sun"	"Tell all the Truth ..."
Message about truth			
Similarities			
Differences			

Text Criticism

10. **Critical Interpretations** When asked why the problems of characters are often left unresolved at the end of his stories, Narayan responded, "Life is like that. We cannot manipulate life to suit fictional needs." Do you consider the ending of "Like the Sun" to be realistic? Cite evidence to support your opinion.

How important is telling the TRUTH?

Would you speak only the truth for an entire day? Why or why not?

---

seems to struggle with the problem of hurting people's feelings. Both characters remain firmly committed despite disapproval.

8. *Sekhar's experiment was a success. He stuck to his resolve and did not back down.*

9. *Mrs. Strangeworth fabricates hurtful stories and is malicious; Sekhar is trying to act with integrity. Sekhar thinks the truth is hard to look at directly. The speaker in the poem thinks the truth is "Too bright" and must be told "With explanation kind." Sekhar, however, doesn't seem to think that people should soften the truth.*

Text Criticism

Possible answer:

10. *It is realistic, because people often express gratitude for honest criticism and then retaliate against the truth-teller.*

How important is telling the TRUTH?

Have students consider the many kinds of half truths and white lies that people often tell. Then ask them whether they think they could avoid these even for a day.

Practice and Apply

For preliminary support of post-reading questions, use these copy masters:

R RESOURCE MANAGER—Copy Masters
Reading Check p. 63
Moral Dilemma p. 59
Question Support p. 64

Additional selection questions are provided for teachers on page 53.

ANSWERS

Comprehension

1. *He decides to tell the complete truth.*

2. *He is tested when his wife asks about her cooking, when he learns of someone's death, and when the headmaster asks for Sekhar's opinion of his musical talent.*

3. *He offends his wife and his colleague. He must correct 100 papers in one day.*

Text Analysis

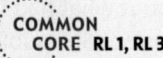

Possible answers:

4. *Sekhar's stubborn determination affects the plot. He knows that he will pay for his honesty (lines 91–97), but he persists.*

5. *Yes, because Sekhar has said what no one else dared (lines 100–101). The headmaster also is insulted and angry, so he makes Sekhar pay for not grading his test papers.*

6. ■ **COMMON CORE FOCUS** *Predict Students may have predicted that Sekhar would get fired or would be rewarded for his honesty.*

7. ● **COMMON CORE FOCUS** *Moral Dilemma Miss Strangeworth takes actions that harm other members of her society but—at least until the end—bring no harm upon her. She seems to enjoy them. Sekhar also hurts people's feelings, but he receives negative results from his actions. Sekhar*

Assess and Reteach

Assess

R RESOURCE MANAGER—Copy Masters
Selection Test A, B/C pp. 63–64, 65–66

Interactive Selection Test on **thinkcentral.com**

Reteach

Level Up Online Tutorials on **thinkcentral.com**

Focus and Motivate

COMMON CORE FOCUS

RI 1 Cite evidence to support inferences drawn from the text. **RI 4** Determine the meaning of figurative words and phrases in a text; analyze the impact of specific word choices on tone. **RI 6** Determine and analyze an author's purpose in a text. **W 3d** Use precise words and phrases to convey a vivid picture of the experiences, events, setting, and/or characters. **L 3** Apply knowledge of language to make effective choices for meaning or style. **L 4c** Consult reference materials to determine or clarify a word's meaning or etymology.

SUMMARY

In this personal essay, author Nicholas Gage pays tribute to the teacher who changed his life. When he was in the seventh grade, the demanding Marjorie Hurd asked him to write about what had happened to his family in Greece. She published his response, set him on a track toward a journalistic career, and has remained a lifelong friend.

Who has made you a **BETTER** person?

Introduce the Big Question. Then have students complete the *DISCUSS* activity. Have student groups take turns reporting their conclusions.

Selection Resources

Before Reading

Essential Course of Study **ECOS**

The Teacher Who Changed My Life
Essay by Nicholas Gage

VIDEO TRAILER THINK central KEYWORD: HML10-226

Who has made you a BETTER person?

COMMON CORE
RI 1 Cite evidence to support inferences drawn from the text. **RI 4** Determine the meaning of figurative words and phrases in a text; analyze the impact of specific word choices on tone. **RI 6** Determine and analyze an author's purpose in a text.

Sometimes one person can have a powerful effect on your life. When you look back, you realize how much you benefited from his or her influence. In "The Teacher Who Changed My Life," Nicholas Gage fondly recalls how he was challenged by his seventh-grade teacher, Miss Hurd.

DISCUSS In a small group, discuss well-known inspirational figures that you have heard about. What makes these people an inspiration to others? What qualities do they have in common? What have they inspired others to do?

226

See resources on the **Teacher One Stop DVD-ROM** *and on* **thinkcentral.com**.

 RESOURCE MANAGER UNIT 2
Plan and Teach, pp. 67–74
Summary, pp. 75–76†‡*
Text Analysis and Reading Skill, pp. 77–80†*
Vocabulary, pp. 81–83*
Grammar and Style, p. 86

DIAGNOSTIC AND SELECTION TESTS
Selection Tests, pp. 67–70

 BEST PRACTICES TOOLKIT
Definition Mapping, p. E6
New Word Analysis, p. E8
Cause-and-Effect Graphics, p. B16
Main Ideas and Details, p. B6

INTERACTIVE READER

ADAPTED INTERACTIVE READER

ELL ADAPTED INTERACTIVE READER

TECHNOLOGY
- Teacher One Stop DVD-ROM
- Student One Stop DVD-ROM
- PowerNotes DVD-ROM
- Audio Anthology CD
- GrammarNotes DVD-ROM
- Audio Tutor CD
- ExamView Test Generator on the **Teacher One Stop**

 **Video Trailer** THINK central

Go to **thinkcentral.com** to preview the **Video Trailer** introducing this selection. Other features that support the selection include
- **PowerNotes** presentation
- **ThinkAloud** models to enhance comprehension
- **WordSharp** vocabulary tutorials
- interactive writing and grammar instruction

* Resources for Differentiation   † Also in Spanish   ‡ In Haitian Creole and Vietnamese

● **TEXT ANALYSIS: CHARACTERIZATION IN NONFICTION**

Because writers of nonfiction portray real people rather than characters, they are limited in certain ways. A writer cannot make up facts about a real person. However, writers can shape the reader's attitude toward the person by using the same basic methods of **characterization** used in fiction. These are

- making direct comments about the person's nature
- describing the person's appearance
- quoting the person or describing his or her actions
- reporting what other people say or think about the person

As you read "The Teacher Who Changed My Life," notice how Gage shapes your attitude toward Miss Hurd.

● **READING SKILL: AUTHOR'S PURPOSE**

An **author's purpose** is what the writer hopes to achieve in a particular work. For example, the title of Gage's essay suggests that he wants to inform you about how a teacher influenced his life. In addition to providing information, writers may seek to persuade, to express ideas or emotions, or to entertain. A complex piece of writing often has more than one purpose.

As you read, notice how Gage's purposes affect the tone of his writing and his choice of details and words. Use a chart like the one shown in recording your analysis.

Purpose	How Purpose Affects Writing
To show influence of Miss Hurd	Narrates how she pushed him to write about his experiences

▲ **VOCABULARY IN CONTEXT**

To see how many vocabulary words you know, substitute a different word or phrase for each boldfaced term. Then write a brief definition of each boldfaced word you're familiar with in your *Reader/Writer Notebook.*

1. The defeat left him lonely and **isolated.**
2. I've learned a lot from my **mentor.**
3. He participated willingly and **avidly.**
4. She **emphatically** endorsed the candidate.
5. We need a **catalyst** to send us in a new direction.
6. They handled the awkward situation with great **tact.**

Complete the activities in your **Reader/Writer Notebook.**

Meet the Author

Nicholas Gage
born 1939

Narrow Escape
Nicholas Gage's original name was Nikos Gatzoyiannis (gät'zô-yän'ĭs). He was born in Lia, a village in northwestern Greece. Gage spent his early years with his mother, Eleni, and four older sisters. His father, Christos, had left to find work in the United States. After World War II, Eleni and her children found themselves caught in Greece's civil war between the Communists and the royalists. In 1947, Communist fighters gained control of Lia. When the Communists began to retreat in the spring of 1948, they took some children with them. Fearing that her children would be sent to Communist countries, Eleni made arrangements for the family to flee. Gage and three of his sisters escaped, but his mother and one sister were left behind. The Communists arrested Eleni, who was put on trial and executed. Eventually, Gage and his sisters joined their father in the United States.

BACKGROUND TO THE ESSAY

A Tireless Investigator
As an investigative reporter for the *New York Times* and the *Wall Street Journal,* Nicholas Gage reported on important issues such as organized crime and drug trafficking. But ever since childhood, he wanted to cover a more personal story. In 1980, Gage began researching a book about his mother's fate in the Greek civil war. His investigations led him to one of the judges who ordered Eleni's execution. Gage actually considered killing the judge, but he realized that if he took revenge he would "become like him, purging myself as he did of all humanity or compassion." Gage's award-winning book, *Eleni,* was published in 1983.

227

Teach

TEXT ANALYSIS
COMMON CORE
RI 4

● *Model the Skill:*
CHARACTERIZATION IN NONFICTION

To model how to identify characterization in nonfiction, read aloud this example:

> Coach Green always used to say, "That's not your best. You can do better."

Point out that the method of characterization used is quoting the person's words to show what he was like.

GUIDED PRACTICE Have students name a second detail that could add to the characterization of Coach Green.

READING SKILL
COMMON CORE
RI 6

■ *Model the Skill:* **AUTHOR'S PURPOSE**

To model how to identify the author's purpose, have students read **A Timeless Investigator** on page 227. Explain that the purpose of the paragraph is to provide students with biographical information about the author of the essay that follows. This purpose might affect the writing by keeping it concise and related to the topic of the essay.

GUIDED PRACTICE Have students explain the purpose of the background information about the essay.

R RESOURCE MANAGER—Copy Master
Author's Purpose p. 79

VOCABULARY SKILL

▲ **VOCABULARY IN CONTEXT**

DIAGNOSE WORD KNOWLEDGE Have all students complete Vocabulary in Context. Check the students' substitutions against the following:

avidly (ăv'ĭd-lē) *adv.* with great eagerness and enthusiasm
catalyst (kăt'l-ĭst) *n.* something or someone that brings about change
emphatically (ĕm-făt'ĭk-lē) *adv.* with strong emphasis

isolated (ī'sə-lā'tĭd) *adj.* separated from others
mentor (mĕn'tôr') *n.* a wise and trusted counselor or teacher
tact (tăkt) *n.* an understanding of the proper thing to do or say around others

PRETEACH VOCABULARY Use the following copy master to help students become familiar with word meanings and uses of each boldfaced word.

COMMON CORE
L 4

R RESOURCE MANAGER—Copy Master
Vocabulary Study p. 81

1. Read the first sentence in part A. Identify context clues such as *different* and *alone,* and discuss possible meanings for *isolated.*
2. Repeat the procedure for the remaining words in the chart.
3. Have students complete Part B independently.

READ WITH A PURPOSE

Help students set a purpose for reading. Tell students to look for the ways in which Hurd influences and inspires Gage.

REVISIT THE BIG QUESTION

Who has made you a
BETTER person?

Discuss Based on lines 1–6, how much influence did Miss Hurd have on Gage? ***Possible answer:*** *She had enormous influence: She "set the course of [his] life" (line 1) and "dragged [him] onto the path that would bring all the blessings [he has] received in America" (lines 2–3).*

TEXT ANALYSIS   COMMON CORE
                                      RI 4

Ⓐ *Model the Skill:*
CHARACTERIZATION IN NONFICTION

Have students reread lines 13–17. Then, draw this chart on the board and have students list the appropriate details under the correct branch.

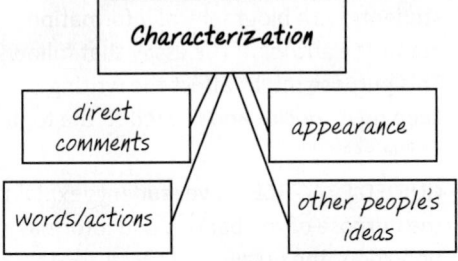

Possible answer: *He describes his appearance (line 13), describes his lack of action (lines 14–15), and reports his own secret thoughts about him (lines 14–15).*

Extend the Discussion How does Gage's description of his father prepare the reader to meet another highly influential adult in Gage's life?

The Teacher Who Changed *My Life*
Nicholas Gage

The person who set the course of my life in the new land I entered as a young war refugee—who, in fact, nearly dragged me onto the path that would bring all the blessings I've received in America—was a salty-tongued, no-nonsense schoolteacher named Marjorie Hurd. When I entered her classroom in 1953, I had been to six schools in five years, starting in the Greek village where I was born in 1939.

When I stepped off a ship in New York Harbor on a gray March day in 1949, I was an undersized 9-year-old in short pants who had lost his mother and was coming to live with the father he didn't know. My mother, Eleni
10 Gatzoyiannis,[1] had been imprisoned, tortured and shot by Communist guerrillas for sending me and three of my four sisters to freedom. She died so that her children could go to their father in the United States.

The portly, bald, well-dressed man who met me and my sisters seemed a foreign, authoritarian figure. I secretly resented him for not getting the whole family out of Greece early enough to save my mother. Ultimately, I would grow to love him and appreciate how he dealt with becoming a single parent at the age of 56, but at first our relationship was prickly, full of hostility. **Ⓐ**

As Father drove us to our new home—a tenement in Worcester, Mass.—and pointed out the huge brick building that would be our first school in America,
20 I clutched my Greek notebooks from the refugee camp, hoping that my few years of schooling would impress my teachers in this cold, crowded country. They didn't. When my father led me and my 11-year-old sister to Greendale Elementary School, the grim-faced Yankee principal put the two of us in a

Analyze Visuals ▶

What does this photograph suggest about the relationship between Nicholas Gage and Miss Hurd after he became an adult?

① **Targeted Passage**

Ⓐ **CHARACTERIZATION IN NONFICTION**
What methods of characterization does Gage use to explain his initial impression of his father?

---

1. **Eleni Gatzoyiannis** (ĕ-lĕ′nē gät′zō-yän′ĭs).

DIFFERENTIATED INSTRUCTION

FOR ENGLISH LANGUAGE LEARNERS

Vocabulary Support Use Definition Mapping to teach these words: *principal* (line 23), *facility* (line 24), *graded* (line 27), *immigrant* (line 34), *assigned* (line 49).

 BEST PRACTICES TOOLKIT—Transparency Definition Mapping p. E6

FOR STRUGGLING READERS

In combination with the *Audio Anthology CD*, use one or more Targeted Passages (pp. 228, 231, 234) to ensure that students focus on key story events, concepts, and skills. Targeted Passages are also good for English learners.

① **Targeted Passage [Lines 1–6]**

This introductory paragraph provides important details about both main characters: Miss Hurd and Gage.

Reading Support

This selection on **thinkcentral.com** includes embedded **ThinkAloud** models—students "thinking aloud" about the story to model the kinds of questions a good reader would ask about a selection.

BACKGROUND

Greek Immigration Between 1820 and 1992, about 700,000 Greeks legally immigrated to the United States. The largest number of Greeks immigrated between 1900 and 1920, when poor economic conditions drove them out of Greece. The Refugee Relief Act of 1953 admitted thousands of Greeks who were fleeing unstable political conditions and circumstances similar to those the Gage family experienced in the late 1940s. Many Greeks settled in urban areas, including large cities in Massachusetts and New York. Massachusetts, where the Gage family lived, has one of the largest Greek-American populations.

Cultural Connection Most cultures have core values that help people know how to live. For Greek Americans, *philotimo*, or "love of honor," is one of these values. It helps Greek Americans make moral choices and define right and wrong within the context of personal pride, honor, and duty to family and community. Invite students to name core values from their cultures that guide their lives.

Analyze Visuals

Possible answer: It suggests that they are good friends who enjoy each other's company.

- Who was Marjorie Hurd? (lines 3–4)
- When did Gage meet her? (line 4)
- What does Gage say that Marjorie Hurd did for him? (lines 1–3)

FOR ADVANCED LEARNERS/PRE–AP

Evaluate Engage students in a class discussion. Ask students how important they feel it is to have a mentor. What kind of help does a good mentor provide? What other sources could provide a similar kind of help? Encourage students to use specific examples from their own experience in explaining their points of view.

Analyze Visuals

Activity Ask students to guess the probable identity of each person in the photograph. *Possible answer: The youngest child is Gage. The three girls are his sisters. The man with the mustache could be a grandfather, and the other man an uncle.*

TIERED DISCUSSION PROMPTS

Direct students to lines 26–38. Use these discussion prompts to discuss Gage's characterization of himself as he faces a new school:

Connect Have you or someone you know ever had to enter a new school, group, or community? What was difficult about the experience? *Students should cite examples from their experiences to explain their answers.*

Synthesize Would you characterize Gage as someone with great ambition or drive before he met Miss Hurd? Explain. *Any answer is acceptable, but should be supported by details.*

 CHARACTERIZATION IN NONFICTION

Possible answer: These words show her no-nonsense attitude. They show that she will not put up with laziness.

IF STUDENTS NEED HELP ... Have them restate Hurd's words as statements Gage might make about her. Note how the exclamation points, emotion, and emphasis melt away.

OWN THE WORD

mentor: The author's *mentor* was Miss Hurd, an English teacher. Have students identify their own *mentors* and write a sentence or two describing how their "wise and trusted counselors or teachers" influenced them.

Nicholas Gage and his family at the harbor in Piraeus, Greece, ready to set out for the United States

class for the mentally retarded. There was no facility in those days for non-English-speaking children.

By the time I met Marjorie Hurd four years later, I had learned English, been placed in a normal, graded class and had even been chosen for the college preparatory track in the Worcester public school system. I was 13 years old when our father moved us yet again, and I entered Chandler Junior High 30 shortly after the beginning of seventh grade. I found myself surrounded by richer, smarter and better-dressed classmates, who looked askance at my strange clothes and heavy accent. Shortly after I arrived, we were told to select a hobby to pursue during "club hour" on Fridays. The idea of hobbies and clubs made no sense to my immigrant ears, but I decided to follow the prettiest girl in my class—the blue-eyed daughter of the local Lutheran minister. She led me through the door marked "Newspaper Club" and into the presence of Miss Hurd, the newspaper adviser and English teacher who would become my **mentor** and my muse.

A formidable, solidly built woman with salt-and-pepper hair, a steely eye 40 and a flat Boston accent, Miss Hurd had no patience with layabouts. "What are all you goof-offs doing here?" she bellowed at the would-be journalists. "This is the Newspaper Club! We're going to put out a *newspaper*. So if there's anybody in this room who doesn't like work, I suggest you go across to the Glee Club now, because you're going to work your tails off here!" **B**

mentor (mĕn'tôr') *n.* a wise and trusted counselor or teacher

B CHARACTERIZATION IN NONFICTION
Why might Gage have chosen to quote Miss Hurd's actual words in this paragraph?

230   UNIT 2: CHARACTER DEVELOPMENT

DIFFERENTIATED INSTRUCTION

FOR ENGLISH LANGUAGE LEARNERS

Vocabulary: Idioms Use New Word Analysis to introduce and teach these idioms from the essay: *layabouts* (line 40), "lazy people"; *goof-offs* (line 41), "people who avoid work."

 BEST PRACTICES TOOLKIT—Transparency New Word Analysis p. E8

FOR STRUGGLING READERS

Develop Reading Fluency Model for students the differences in intonation with a question mark, period, and exclamation point. Read aloud lines 39–44. Point out how a question mark means the tone goes up, a period has an even intonation, and an exclamation point places emphasis. Reread the question (lines 40–41, exclamation (line 42), and statement (line 42) and have students echo each reading.

I was soon under Miss Hurd's spell. She did indeed teach us to put out a newspaper, skills I honed during my next 25 years as a journalist. Soon I asked the principal to transfer me to her English class as well. There, she drilled us on grammar until I finally began to understand the logic and structure of the English language. She assigned stories for us to read and discuss; not
50 tales of heroes, like the Greek myths I knew, but stories of underdogs—poor people, even immigrants, who seemed ordinary until a crisis drove them to do something extraordinary. She also introduced us to the literary wealth of Greece—giving me a new perspective on my war-ravaged, impoverished homeland. I began to be proud of my origins. **C**

One day, after discussing how writers should write about what they know, she assigned us to compose an essay from our own experience. Fixing me with a stern look, she added, "Nick, I want you to write about what happened to your family in Greece." I had been trying to put those painful memories behind me and left the assignment until the last moment. Then, on a warm
60 spring afternoon, I sat in my room with a yellow pad and pencil and stared out the window at the buds on the trees. I wrote that the coming of spring always reminded me of the last time I said goodbye to my mother on a green and gold day in 1948.

Targeted Passage

2

COMMON CORE RI 4

Language Coach

Idioms The phrase "under Miss Hurd's spell," in line 45, is an **idiom,** or a figure of speech that isn't meant to be taken literally. How did the narrator feel about Miss Hurd? Why do you think he chose to describe his feelings with this idiom?

C AUTHOR'S PURPOSE Reread lines 45–54. Which **details** support Gage's purpose of explaining Miss Hurd's influence on him?

Nicholas Gage (top row, center) with his third-grade class

READING SKILL

COMMON CORE

RI 6

C *Model the Skill:* **AUTHOR'S PURPOSE**

Model how to identify the Author's Purpose. Remind students to look for the specific details and words Gage provides in lines 45–54. Have students record their analyses in their Author's Purpose charts introduced on page 227.

Possible answer: From Miss Hurd, he learned how to put out a newspaper (lines 45–46); the logic and structure of the English language (lines 48–49); stories of underdogs who triumphed (lines 50–52); and a new, proud perspective on his native land (lines 52–54).

Analyze Visuals

Activity Have students recall that Gage was nine years old when he came to America. Ask students why third grade was especially significant for Gage. *Possible answer: This was Gage's first year in an American school, one of the six schools he attended in five years before he met Miss Hurd.*

FOR STRUGGLING READERS

2 Targeted Passage [Lines 45–54]

This paragraph outlines some of the many important ways that Miss Hurd taught Gage.

• Why did Gage join Miss Hurd's English class? (lines 32–37)

• What did he learn from her? (lines 45–54)

• How did he change as a result of what he learned in her classroom? (lines 49, 53, 54)

FOR ENGLISH LANGUAGE LEARNERS

Language Coach

COMMON CORE
RI 4

Idioms *Answer: The narrator really liked Miss Hurd. He may have chosen this idiom to describe the effect she had on him.* Idioms can help in characterization. The author describes Miss Hurd as "salty-tongued" (line 3), and uses the idiom "work your tails off" (line 44) to give a concrete example of Miss Hurd's speech.

D READING

Look over lines 64–69 in which Gage uses a long, flowing sentence to describe the events in Greece. ***Possible answer***: *Gage had been trying not to think about what had happened to his family in Greece and how he had had to leave his mother behind. However, when he finally writes about it, he feels a sense of relief that is reflected in the long, flowing sentences as his experiences pour out of him onto paper.*

E GRAMMAR AND STYLE

COMMON CORE

L 3

Analyze Examples Review the terms *concrete noun* and *abstract noun*. Have students find concrete and abstract nouns in lines 75–79, and explain how these nouns work as examples to strengthen Gage's description. ***Possible answers:*** *mountain, minefields, lines, soldiers, refugee camp, execution, America, and* mother *are concrete.* Escape *and* spring *are abstract. The concrete nouns make the places and people specific; the abstract nouns sum up events and place the story in time.*

VOCABULARY

COMMON CORE

L 4

OWN THE WORD

tact: Have students provide synonyms for the noun *tact*. Then, have students give examples of situations in which someone was *tactful* or *tactless*.

I kept writing, one line after another, telling how the Communist guerrillas occupied our village, took our home and food, how my mother started planning our escape when she learned that the children were to be sent to re-education camps[2] behind the Iron Curtain[3] and how, at the last moment, she couldn't escape with us because the guerrillas sent her with a group of women to thresh wheat in a distant village. She promised she would try to
70 get away on her own, she told me to be brave and hung a silver cross around my neck, and then she kissed me. I watched the line of women being led down into the ravine and up the other side, until they disappeared around the bend—my mother a tiny brown figure at the end who stopped for an instant to raise her hand in one last farewell.

I wrote about our nighttime escape down the mountain, across the minefields and into the lines of the Nationalist soldiers, who sent us to a refugee camp. It was there that we learned of our mother's execution. I felt very lucky to have come to America, I concluded, but every year, the coming of spring made me feel sad because it reminded me of the last time I saw my mother.
80 I handed in the essay, hoping never to see it again, but Miss Hurd had it published in the school paper. This mortified me at first, until I saw that my classmates reacted with sympathy and **tact** to my family's story. Without telling me, Miss Hurd also submitted the essay to a contest sponsored by the Freedoms Foundation at Valley Forge, Pa., and it won a medal. The Worcester paper wrote about the award and quoted my essay at length. My father, by then a "five-and-dime-store chef," as the paper described him, was ecstatic with pride, and the Worcester Greek community celebrated the honor to one of its own.

For the first time I began to understand the power of the written word. A
90 secret ambition took root in me. One day, I vowed, I would go back to Greece, find out the details of my mother's death and write about her life, so her grandchildren would know of her courage. Perhaps I would even track down the men who killed her and write of their crimes. Fulfilling that ambition would take me 30 years.

Meanwhile, I followed the literary path that Miss Hurd had so forcefully set me on. After junior high, I became the editor of my school paper at Classical High School and got a part-time job at the Worcester *Telegram and Gazette*. Although my father could only give me $50 and encouragement toward a college education, I managed to finance four years at Boston University with
100 scholarships and part-time jobs in journalism. During my last year of college, an article I wrote about a friend who had died in the Philippines—the first person to lose his life working for the Peace Corps—led to my winning the Hearst Award for College Journalism. And the plaque was given to me in the White House by President John F. Kennedy.

---

2. **re-education camps:** camps where people were forced to go to be indoctrinated with Communist ideas and beliefs.

3. **behind the Iron Curtain:** on the Communist side of the imaginary divide between the democracies of Western Europe and the Communist dictatorships of Eastern Europe; in this case, the camps were in Albania.

COMMON CORE RI 4

D READING
A writer's **syntax and diction,** or sentence structure and word choice, help reveal his or her feelings about the subject. Look over lines 64–69, in which Gage uses a long, flowing sentence to describe the events in Greece. How does this syntax reflect what Gage was experiencing as he wrote?

tact (tăkt) *n.* an understanding of the proper thing to do or say around others

E GRAMMAR AND STYLE
Reread lines 82–88. Notice how Gage uses the **concrete noun** *medal* and **abstract nouns** such as *pride* and *honor* to describe responses to his essay.

DIFFERENTIATED INSTRUCTION

FOR STRUGGLING READERS
Review Cause and Effect Draw and label a Cause-and-Effect Graphic to review the relationship Gage establishes between Miss Hurd publishing Gage's essay and the events that followed in Gage's school, family, and community.

 BEST PRACTICES TOOLKIT—Transparency Cause-and-Effect Graphics p. B16

FOR ADVANCED LEARNERS/PRE–AP
Hypothesize About Historical Context [small-group option] Remind students that when young Gage's essay was published, anti-Communist fears were strong and rising in the United States. Have students speculate about the nature and concerns of the Freedoms Foundation and reasons, beyond literary merit, for the success of the essay.

For a refugee who had never seen a motorized vehicle or indoor plumbing until he was 9, this was an unimaginable honor. When the Worcester paper ran a picture of me standing next to President Kennedy, my father rushed out to buy a new suit in order to be properly dressed to receive the congratulations of the Worcester Greeks. He clipped out the photograph, had it laminated

110 in plastic and carried it in his breast pocket for the rest of his life to show everyone he met. I found the much-worn photo in his pocket on the day he died 20 years later. **ⓕ**

In our **isolated** Greek village, my mother had bribed a cousin to teach her to read, for girls were not supposed to attend school beyond a certain age. She had always dreamed of her children receiving an education. She couldn't be there when I graduated from Boston University, but the person who came with my father and shared our joy was my former teacher, Marjorie Hurd. We celebrated not only my bachelor's degree but also the scholarships that paid my way to Columbia's Graduate School of Journalism. There, I met the woman

120 who would eventually become my wife. At our wedding and at the baptisms of our three children, Marjorie Hurd was always there, dancing alongside the Greeks.

By then, she was Mrs. Rabidou, for she had married a widower when she was in her early 40s. That didn't distract her from her vocation of introducing young minds to English literature, however. She taught for a total of 41 years

ⓕ CHARACTERIZATION IN NONFICTION
What do the father's **actions** tell you about his feelings for his son?

isolated (ī′sə-lā′tĭd) *adj.* separated from others

Nicholas Gage (left) receiving the Hearst Award from President Kennedy in 1963

THE TEACHER WHO CHANGED MY LIFE   **233**

READING SKILL   COMMON CORE
RI 6

G AUTHOR'S PURPOSE

Possible answer: Words and details such as project, balky student, potential, bully and charm, tough love, and avidly all paint a picture of a teacher who is determined to make a difference in the lives of students from "troubled homes."

READING SKILL   COMMON CORE
RI 6

H Model the Skill: AUTHOR'S PURPOSE

Remind students that tone is an expression of the writer's attitude toward a subject, such as serious, bitter, or playful.

Possible answer: Gage's tone of sadness about his father's absence (line 145) is softened with joy by the presence of Miss Hurd (lines 148–149) which suggests that Gage's purpose is to highlight Miss Hurd's value in his life.

SELECTION WRAP-UP

READ WITH A PURPOSE Discuss with students whether they consider Miss Hurd a typical example of mentor. *Possible answer: On the one hand, Miss Hurd is a typical mentor because she inspires Gage. On the other, she's not typical because she uses "tough love," rather than a soft approach.*

VOCABULARY   COMMON CORE
L 4

OWN THE WORD

- **avidly:** Have students write sentences using the word *avidly*.
- **catalyst:** Ask students to explain what the author meant when he wrote, "[Miss Hurd] was the *catalyst* that sent me into journalism."
- **emphatically:** Ask students why they might say something *emphatically*.

and continually would make a "project" of some balky student in whom she spied a spark of potential. Often these were students from the most troubled homes, yet she would alternately bully and charm each one with her own special brand of tough love until the spark caught fire. She retired in 1981 at 130 the age of 62 but still **avidly** follows the lives and careers of former students while overseeing her adult stepchildren and driving her husband on camping trips to New Hampshire.

Miss Hurd was one of the first to call me on Dec. 10, 1987, when President Reagan, in his television address after the summit meeting with Gorbachev,[4] told the nation that Eleni Gatzoyiannis's dying cry, "My children!" had helped inspire him to seek an arms agreement "for all the children of the world."

"I can't imagine a better monument for your mother," Miss Hurd said with an uncharacteristic catch in her voice.

Although a bad hip makes it impossible for her to join in the Greek 140 dancing, Marjorie Hurd Rabidou is still an honored and enthusiastic guest at all our family celebrations, including my 50th birthday picnic last summer, where the shish kebab was cooked on spits, clarinets and *bouzoukis*[5] wailed, and costumed dancers led the guests in a serpentine line around our Colonial farmhouse, only 20 minutes from my first home in Worcester.

My sisters and I felt an aching void because my father was not there to lead the line, balancing a glass of wine on his head while he danced, the way he did at every celebration during his 92 years. But Miss Hurd was there, surveying the scene with quiet satisfaction. Although my parents are gone, her presence was a consolation, because I owe her so much.

150 This is truly the land of opportunity, and I would have enjoyed its bounty even if I hadn't walked into Miss Hurd's classroom in 1953. But she was the one who directed my grief and pain into writing, and if it weren't for her, I wouldn't have become an investigative reporter and foreign correspondent, recorded the story of my mother's life and death in *Eleni* and now my father's story in *A Place for Us*, which is also a testament to the country that took us in. She was the **catalyst** that sent me into journalism and indirectly caused all the good things that came after. But Miss Hurd would probably deny this **emphatically.**

A few years ago, I answered the telephone and heard my former teacher's 160 voice telling me, in that won't-take-no-for-an-answer tone of hers, that she had decided I was to write and deliver the eulogy at her funeral. I agreed (she didn't leave me any choice), but that's one assignment I never want to do. I hope, Miss Hurd, that you'll accept this remembrance instead. ❧

---

avidly (ăv′ĭd-lē) *adv.* with great eagerness and enthusiasm

G AUTHOR'S PURPOSE
Reread lines 123–132. What **words** and **details** in this paragraph help Gage pay tribute to Miss Hurd?

H AUTHOR'S PURPOSE
Reread lines 145–149. What purpose is suggested by Gage's **tone** in this paragraph?

catalyst (kăt′l-ĭst) *n.* something or someone that brings about change

emphatically (ĕm-făt′ĭk-lē) *adv.* with strong emphasis

③ Targeted Passage

---

4. **summit meeting with Gorbachev** (gôr′bə-chôf′): a high-level meeting between U.S. president Ronald Reagan and Mikhail Gorbachev, the last president of the Soviet Union.

5. **bouzoukis** (boŏ-zoō′kēz): traditional Greek stringed instruments resembling mandolins.

DIFFERENTIATED INSTRUCTION

FOR STRUGGLING READERS

③ Targeted Passage [Lines 159–163]

These lines help bring the essay to a close and explain the author's purpose.

- What did Miss Hurd request? (line 161)
- What does Gage mean by "this remembrance instead"? (line 163)
- What does this last paragraph tell you about the author's purpose in writing this piece? (lines 162–163)

FOR ENGLISH LANGUAGE LEARNERS

Vocabulary: Word Associations Note how some words, when grouped together, take on a particular meaning. Challenge students to name or find other examples in the essay: "last farewell" (line 74); "secret ambition" (line 90); "spark of potential" (line 127); "special brand of . . ." (line 129); "tough love" (line 129); "land of opportunity" (line 150).

Comprehension

1. **Recall** Why did Nicholas Gage come to the United States?

2. **Recall** What did Miss Hurd encourage him to write about?

3. **Recall** How did people react to Gage's essay?

4. **Paraphrase** According to Gage, what influence did Miss Hurd have on his career?

Text Analysis

● 5. **Analyze Characterization** For each method of characterization in the chart, give an example of how Gage uses it to convey Miss Hurd's personality. Which method gives you the most vivid impression of Miss Hurd? Explain your answer.

	Words and Actions	Physical Appearances	Gage's Comments
Example from text			
What it reveals about Miss Hurd			

6. **Make Inferences** What led Miss Hurd to take a special interest in Gage when he was her student?

7. **Draw Conclusions About Character** Does Gage offer a realistic or an idealized portrait of Miss Hurd in this essay? Support your conclusion with evidence from the text.

■ 8. **Examine Author's Purpose** Review the chart you created as you read. What is the main purpose of Gage's essay? Use evidence from the text to support your answer.

9. **Evaluate Actions** The essay that Gage wrote for Miss Hurd in the seventh grade was about a traumatic event in his life. Should a teacher publish such writing without the student's permission? Why or why not?

Text Criticism

10. **Author's Style** Some critics have complained that Nicholas Gage includes too many details in works such as *Eleni*, which is almost 500 pages long. Consider the kinds of details Gage included in "The Teacher Who Changed My Life." Would you say they are excessive, or do they serve an important function in conveying his message? Cite evidence in support of your opinion.

> ## Who has made you a **BETTER** person?
>
> How can a teacher inspire you to improve yourself?

COMMON CORE

RI 1 Cite evidence to support inferences drawn from the text. RI 6 Determine and analyze an author's purpose in a text.

THE TEACHER WHO CHANGED MY LIFE 235

Practice and Apply

For preliminary support of post-reading questions, use these copy masters:

R RESOURCE MANAGER—Copy Masters
Reading Check p. 84
Characterization in Nonfiction p. 77
Question Support p. 85

Additional selection questions are provided for teachers on see page 71.

ANSWERS

Comprehension

1. *His family was escaping the Communists.*

2. *Miss Hurd encouraged him to write about what happened to his family in Greece.*

3. *Gage's classmates reacted with sympathy and tact. Others reacted with great interest.*

4. *She set a "literary path" for him.*

Text Analysis
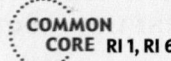
Possible answers:

5. ● **COMMON CORE FOCUS** *Analyze Characterization Words and Actions: Example: She has Gage write about what happened to his family in Greece (lines 56–59); Reveals: her insight into the most important event of Gage's life so far. Physical Appearance: Example: "solidly built woman with salt-and-pepper hair" (line 39); Reveals: She looks tough, she is not young, and she is beginning to gray. Gage's Comments: Example: "nearly dragged me onto the path" (lines 2–3); Reveals: what a strong, determined influence Miss Hurd was on Gage.*

6. *She knew he had recently immigrated from Greece (he still had an accent); she realized he had great potential.*

7. *It is a bit of both: Realistic: He shows her bellowing, almost threatening (lines 40–44); Idealized: Gage gives her credit for all his success, but, indeed, he had to have played a bit of a role himself.*

8. ■ **COMMON CORE FOCUS** *Examine Author's Purpose The main purpose is to pay tribute to Miss Hurd; to declare publicly how enormous her influence was upon him; and to thank her for it. Gage states his main purpose in the last two paragraphs of the essay (lines 150–163).*

---

9. *Students may call this act an invasion of privacy or an act of wisdom. They may note that ideas about students' privacy are different now than they were in 1953.*

> Who has made you a **BETTER** person? Ask students to think about teachers and coaches who inspired them to improve and why they responded to the encouragement.

Text Criticism

Possible answer:

10. *All the details either provide necessary background information about Gage and his family (lines 7–25, 61–79), or they help to create a single dominant impression of Miss Hurd as a remarkable teacher who changed Gage's life (lines 39–58, 95–104).*

THE TEACHER WHO CHANGED MY LIFE **235**

ANSWERS

Vocabulary in Context

 VOCABULARY PRACTICE

1. *synonyms*	**4.** *synonyms*
2. *antonyms*	**5.** *antonyms*
3. *antonyms*	**6.** *antonyms*

 RESOURCE MANAGER—Copy Master
Vocabulary Practice p. 82

ACADEMIC VOCABULARY IN WRITING

Students should describe a specific individual in their descriptions, explaining the changes that they underwent as a result of this person's influence. They should create dynamic portraits that explain how the mentor's influence led to change.

VOCABULARY STRATEGY:
THE LATIN ROOT *sol*

 **COMMON CORE** **L 4c**

- For each item, have students use their knowledge of the root and context clues to choose the correct word.
- The participial phrases in items 1 and 3 might make the task extra difficult for some students. You may restate these as follows:

1. *The young boy asked the police officer for help because he was accidentally _____ from his family.*

3. *She engages in _____ pursuits such as reading and drawing because she enjoys spending time alone.*

Possible answers:

1. *isolated*	**4.** *solitude*
2. *soliloquy*	**5.** *solo*
3. *solitary*	

 RESOURCE MANAGER—Copy Master
Vocabulary Strategy p. 83

Interactive Vocabulary

Keywords direct students to a **WordSharp** tutorial on **thinkcentral.com** or to other types of vocabulary practice and review.

Vocabulary in Context

 VOCABULARY PRACTICE

Decide whether the words in each pair are synonyms or antonyms.

1. mentor/advisor
2. tact/insensitivity
3. isolated/united
4. avidly/enthusiastically
5. catalyst/observer
6. emphatically/wearily

WORD LIST
avidly
catalyst
emphatically
isolated
mentor
tact

ACADEMIC VOCABULARY IN WRITING

- dynamic - individual - motive - seek - undergo

Write a description of an **individual** who had a strong positive influence on your life. Create a **dynamic** portrait that explains how this person changed you. Use at least one Academic Vocabulary word in your response. Here is an example of an opening:

> **SAMPLE OPENING**
>
> *Without a doubt, our neighbor Mr. Arisa is the **individual** who has changed my life the most, even though he only moved in six months ago.*

COMMON CORE

L 4c Consult reference materials to determine or clarify a word's meaning or etymology.

VOCABULARY STRATEGY: THE LATIN ROOT *sol*

The word *isolated* contains the root *sol*, from the Latin word *solus*, which means "alone." This root is found in a number of English words. To understand the meaning of words with *sol*, use context clues as well as your knowledge of the root.

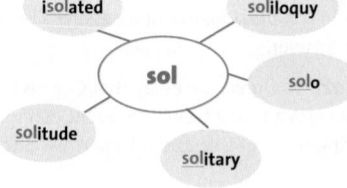

PRACTICE Write the word from the word web that best completes each sentence. Use context clues to help you, or consult a dictionary if necessary.

1. Accidentally _____ from his family, the young boy asked the police officer for help.
2. In the play, Hamlet performs a _____ in which he talks to himself.
3. Enjoying time alone, she engages in _____ pursuits such as reading and drawing.
4. They enjoyed the quiet _____ of a picnic on an empty stretch of beach.
5. The conductor quiets the rest of the orchestra so that the violinist can perform her _____ .

Interactive Vocabulary THINK central

Go to **thinkcentral.com**.
KEYWORD: HML10-236

DIFFERENTIATED INSTRUCTION

FOR ENGLISH LANGUAGE LEARNERS

Vocabulary: Roots Have students choose one of the words in the Vocabulary Strategy word web and create an additional web just for that word. The new word web can contain words related in meaning to the central word.

FOR ADVANCED LEARNERS/PRE–AP

Vocabulary in Writing Have students use at least three vocabulary words in a paragraph that retells some facts or experiences from Gage's life from an objective third-person point of view.

Language

◆ **GRAMMAR AND STYLE:** Elaborate With Examples

Review the **Grammar and Style** note on page 232. Illustrating your ideas with examples, as Gage does, can strengthen your message to readers. Note that Gage uses both concrete and abstract nouns in his examples to fully describe events and people's reactions to them. A **concrete noun** names an object that can be seen, heard, smelled, touched, or tasted (such as *sky, whistle, flower, book,* and *lemon*). An **abstract noun** names an idea, quality, or state (such as *democracy, independence, security, comfort,* and *sadness*).

> . . . *she told me to be brave and hung a silver cross around my neck.* . . .
> (lines 70–71)
>
> . . . *my classmates reacted with sympathy and tact* . . . . (line 82)

Notice how the revisions in blue use examples to strengthen the main points of this first draft. Use a similar method to revise your responses to the prompt.

COMMON CORE

L 3 Apply knowledge of language to make effective choices for meaning or style. **W 3d** Use precise words and phrases to convey a vivid picture of the experiences, events, setting, and/or characters.

> **STUDENT MODEL**
>
> Nick arrived in the United States when he was only nine years
> *His mother had just died, and he struggled to learn English.*
> old. It was a difficult time for him. But he eventually succeeded.
> *His courage and determination led him to write a prize-winning essay at age thirteen.*

READING-WRITING CONNECTION

Broaden your understanding of "The Teacher Who Changed My Life" by responding to this prompt. Then use the **revising tip** to improve your writing.

WRITING PROMPT	REVISING TIP
Extended Constructed Response: Speech Imagine that you are the author's father. Write a **three-to-five-paragraph speech** describing your son's life and your feelings for him.	Review your speech. Did you illustrate your ideas with examples? If not, revise your response with concrete and abstract nouns that fully describe events and people's reactions.

Interactive Revision THINK central

Go to **thinkcentral.com**.
KEYWORD: HML10-237

FOR STRUGGLING WRITERS

- Direct students to pertinent sections of the essay, such as lines 109–112.

- Have students list things Gage's father would most want to say about him.

- Create a rough outline: introduction, three body paragraphs, and a conclusion.

Language

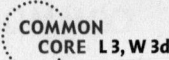
COMMON CORE L 3, W 3d

◆ **GRAMMAR AND STYLE**

- Have students identify the concrete and abstract nouns that are used in the revisions to the student model. For more on concrete and abstract nouns, see **Grammar Handbook**, page R46.

- Write this sentence on the board. Have students suggest revisions that would strengthen the point it makes.

  Hurd identified Gage as ~~someone~~ one of those "balky students" who needed ~~help~~ her oversight, her guidance, and her "tough love."

 RESOURCE MANAGER—Copy Master
Elaborate with Examples p. 86

READING-WRITING CONNECTION

- Suggest that students begin by locating details about Gage's father to get an impression of the man and his relationship with Gage.

BEST PRACTICES TOOLKIT—Transparency
Main Ideas and Details p. B6

> **Writing Online** THINK central
>
> The following tools are available online at **thinkcentral.com** and on **Write**Smart CD-ROM:
> - **Interactive Graphic Organizers**
> - **Interactive Student Models**
> - **Interactive Revision Lessons**
> For additional grammar instruction, see **GrammarNotes** on **thinkcentral.com**.

Assess and Reteach

Assess

DIAGNOSTIC AND SELECTION TESTS
Selection Test A pp. 67–68
Selection Test B/C pp. 69–70

Interactive Selection Test on **thinkcentral.com**

Reteach

Level Up Online Tutorials on **thinkcentral.com**

Reteaching Worksheets on **thinkcentral.com**
Literature Lesson 3, Reading Lesson 3, Vocabulary Lessons 7–8

Focus and Motivate

COMMON CORE FOCUS

RI 4 Analyze the impact of specific word choices on meaning and tone. **RI 6** Determine an author's point of view or purpose in a text. **L 5b** Analyze nuances in the meaning of words with similar denotations.

SUMMARY

In "A Celebration of Grandfathers," Rudolfo Anaya remembers his own grandfather, a farmer who taught him valuable lessons about living a fulfilling life. His grandfather and the life that he led are now gone, but Anaya recognizes that many lessons learned from the past still apply to the modern world.

Are OLD WAYS the best ways?

Ask students to describe some of the customs and traditions that they and their families enjoy. Then, ask the question. Before students *DEBATE*, remind them to keep in mind the traditions that they described earlier.

Selection Resources

See resources on the **Teacher One Stop DVD-ROM** and on **thinkcentral.com**.

R **RESOURCE MANAGER UNIT 2**
  Plan and Teach, pp. 87–94
  Summary, pp. 95–96†‡*
  Text Analysis and Reading
    Skill, pp. 97–100†*

DIAGNOSTIC AND SELECTION TESTS
  Selection Tests, pp. 71–74

BEST PRACTICES TOOLKIT
  Word Questioning, p. E9
  Character Traits and Textual
    Evidence, p. D6

TECHNOLOGY
  🖴 **Teacher One Stop DVD-ROM**
  🖴 **Student One Stop DVD-ROM**
  🖴 **Audio Anthology CD**
  🖴 **GrammarNotes DVD-ROM**
  🖴 **ExamView Test Generator**
    on the Teacher One Stop

* Resources for Differentiation   † Also in Spanish   ‡ In Haitian Creole and Vietnamese

---

A Celebration of Grandfathers
Essay by Rudolfo A. Anaya

Are OLD WAYS the best ways?

COMMON CORE

RI 4 Analyze the impact of specific word choices on meaning and tone. **RI 6** Determine an author's point of view or purpose in a text. **L 5b** Analyze nuances in the meaning of words with similar denotations.

In "A Celebration of Grandfathers," Rudolfo Anaya pays tribute to the customs and values of his elders. Today most people live in a society very different from the one he describes. Some still cherish tradition, but others embrace change.

DEBATE How much should tradition influence your life? With a group, stage a mini-debate about whether old ways are still the best ways.

238

TEXT ANALYSIS: CHARACTER TRAITS IN NONFICTION

Some types of nonfiction, such as memoirs and biographies, offer you a glimpse into people's lives. When you read such works, you get to know the **character traits,** or qualities, of individuals. Writers may focus on particular traits to help express ideas about life or provide insight into a time and place. For example, in "A Celebration of Grandfathers," Anaya describes what was special about his grandfather's generation in rural New Mexico.

They shared good times and hard times. They helped each other through the epidemics and the personal tragedies, and they shared what little they had. . . .

As you read, notice what Anaya reveals about his grandfather's traits.

READING SKILL: IDENTIFY AUTHOR'S PERSPECTIVE

People often look at a subject from different viewpoints. For example, a person who loves to ski will probably react to a snowstorm differently than someone who is concerned about getting to work on time would. The combination of beliefs, values, and feelings that influence how a writer looks at a subject is called the **author's perspective.** To determine the author's perspective in a personal essay, readers should examine clues such as the following:

- statements of opinion
- details the writer chooses to include
- the writer's tone, or attitude (such as a humorous or formal tone)

The writer's tone is an especially important clue to his or her perspective. The tone of an essay can reveal the writer's true feelings about the subject and can shape how you respond to the events described.

As you read "A Celebration of Grandfathers," use a chart like the one shown to identify how Anaya's perspective is revealed in his statements, details, and tone.

Statement, Detail, or Tone	What It Reveals About Perspective
For me [the farm] was a magical place.	Rural life has a special value.

 Complete the activities in your **Reader/Writer Notebook.**

Meet the Author

Rudolfo A. Anaya
born 1937

Storyteller's Gift
Rudolfo A. Anaya lives in New Mexico, where he was born and raised. He grew up listening to *cuentos* (stories and legends) that are part of the Hispanic oral tradition. Anaya has remarked that listening to his elders tell *cuentos* helped him hone his writing skills, noting that "the storyteller's gift is my inheritance."

A Breakthrough Novel
Anaya is best known for his first novel, *Bless Me, Ultima* (1972), the story of a boy in a small New Mexican village who struggles to find his identity. One of the first novels to represent the Mexican-American experience, it helped launch a vibrant Hispanic literary movement in the United States. Anaya's novels, plays, stories, and essays have earned him many literary awards, including the 2001 National Medal of Arts.

BACKGROUND TO THE ESSAY
Pride of Place
The landscape, culture, and history of New Mexico are important elements in Anaya's writing. During the first part of the 20th century, New Mexico still had a traditional agricultural economy. Its population consisted mainly of Native Americans and descendants of Spanish settlers, who first arrived there in the 1500s. Anaya's grandfather worked land along the Pecos River in the eastern part of the state, using methods that were probably not much different than those of his ancestors. By the late 1940s, however, this way of life was coming to an end. Many young people had moved into cities, depriving villages of the next generation of farmers.

Author Online
THINK central

Go to **thinkcentral.com.**
KEYWORD: HML10-239

239

Teach

● *Model the Skill:* **CHARACTER TRAITS IN NONFICTION**

To model how to identify character traits in nonfiction, read this example:

> Anaya writes about happy times spent with his grandfather. He describes the valley where he lived and the culture he was part of.

Tell students that Anaya's character traits are revealed by his choice of writing subject. Point out that the sentence portrays Anaya as a man who cares about history and is strongly attached to his cultural and physical surroundings.

GUIDED PRACTICE Ask students to read *Meet the Author* and then identify some of Anaya's other character traits.

■ *Model the Skill:* **IDENTIFY AUTHOR'S PERSPECTIVE**

To model how to identify author's perspective, write these statements on the board.

> Pat is an old factory worker.
> Pat is a veteran factory worker.

Point out that the second statement suggests that Pat is valued. The choice of the word *veteran* reveals the author's perspective.

GUIDED PRACTICE Ask students what perspective the selection title conveys.

R RESOURCE MANAGER—Copy Master
Identify Author's Perspective p. 99 (for student use while reading the selection)

DIFFERENTIATED INSTRUCTION

FOR STRUGGLING READERS

Author's Perspective Help students understand the term *author's perspective.* Draw two columns on the board, one labeled *Positive* and one labeled *Negative.* Write examples of positive and negative words and phrases that could be used to describe coyotes. Elicit other words from students. Explain how the words could be used to write about coyotes from two different perspectives, one positive and one negative.

FOR ENGLISH LANGUAGE LEARNERS

Language: Skill Words Write these words on the board and review them with students:

- *nonfiction:* prose writing that is based on real experience or factual knowledge
- *character traits:* qualities that a character has over a period of time

Contrast *nonfiction* with *fiction* and *character traits* with *feelings.* Have students give examples of each.

READ WITH A PURPOSE

Help students set a purpose for reading. Tell students to look for the ways in which Anaya's grandfather taught him lessons.

Ⓐ *Model the Skill:* IDENTIFY AUTHOR'S PERSPECTIVE

Model how to identify author's perspective by directing students' attention to these words and phrases: *respect* (lines 3 and 4); *wise* (line 6); *They had something important to share* (lines 6–7). Then discuss what this important knowledge was. Point out that the author's belief in the importance of their knowledge of how to live influences his writing. Have students make notes about the author's statements, details, and tone in their Perspective charts.

Possible answer: *Anaya values the old people, believing that they have wisdom, experience, and knowledge of how to live.*

Extend the Discussion What other types of lessons might the old people have shared?

A Celebration
OF
Grandfathers

Rudolfo A. Anaya

"Buenos días le de Dios, abuelo." God give you a good day, grandfather. This is how I was taught as a child to greet my grandfather, or any grown person. It was a greeting of respect, a cultural value to be passed on from generation to generation, this respect for the old ones.

The old people I remember from my childhood were strong in their beliefs, and as we lived daily with them, we learned a wise path of life to follow. They had something important to share with the young, and when they spoke, the young listened. These old *abuelos* and *abuelitas*[1] had worked the earth all their lives, and so they knew the value of nurturing, they knew the sensitivity of the
10 earth. . . . They knew the rhythms and cycles of time, from the preparation of the earth in the spring to the digging of the *acequias*[2] that brought the water to the dance of harvest in the fall. They shared good times and hard times. They helped each other through the epidemics and the personal tragedies, and they shared what little they had when the hot winds burned the land and no rain came. They learned that to survive one had to share in the process of life. . . . Ⓐ

Analyze Visuals ▶

What conclusions could you draw about the man in this photograph? What details led you to those conclusions?

❶ Targeted Passage

Ⓐ IDENTIFY AUTHOR'S PERSPECTIVE
What does Anaya's description of the old people reveal about his perspective?

---

1. *abuelos* (ä-bwĕʹlôs) . . . *abuelitas* (ä-bwĕ-lēʹtäs) *Spanish:* grandfathers . . . grannies.
2. *acequias* (ä-sĕʹkyäs) *Spanish:* irrigation ditches.

DIFFERENTIATED INSTRUCTION

FOR ENGLISH LANGUAGE LEARNERS

Vocabulary Support Use Word Questioning to teach these words: *generation* (line 3), *cycles* (line 10), *process* (line 15), *participant* (line 35), *transformation* (line 42).

 BEST PRACTICES TOOLKIT—Transparency Word Questioning p. E9

FOR STRUGGLING READERS

In combination with the *Audio Anthology CD*, use one or more Targeted Passages (pp. 240, 243, 244) to ensure that students focus on key story events, concepts, and skills. Targeted Passages are also good for English learners.

❶ Targeted Passage [Lines 1–8]

This passage identifies the feelings that Anaya had for his grandfather and for his grandfather's whole generation.

BACKGROUND

New Mexico Today Although the way of life is changing in New Mexico, Hispanics still make up a majority of the population in nine counties of the state, and Spanish is spoken at home by more than 30 percent of the people. The state's respect for its Hispanic heritage is also reflected in its two state songs, one of which is in Spanish.

Analyze Visuals

Possible answer: *The image reflects that the man lives a simple life, filled with hard work, long days in the sun, and a resigned acceptance of hardships and hard work.*

REVISIT THE BIG QUESTION
Are OLD WAYS
the best ways?

Discuss Based on lines 1–8, why was the tradition of respecting elders important to the author? *Possible answer: The old could teach him a wise way to live (line 6).*

- Why did Anaya greet grown people a certain way? (lines 2–4)

- What did Anaya learn from his daily contact with old people? (lines 5–6)

- Why did young people listen to the old? (lines 7–9)

FOR ADVANCED LEARNERS/PRE–AP

Aphorisms Explain that aphorisms are short sayings that express a wise thought. Have students identify one of the grandfather's aphorisms. *Examples: "Know where you stand" (lines 28–29); "Death is only this small transformation in life" (line 42).* Then have students write several original aphorisms. Invite them to illustrate and share their aphorisms in the form of a poster or multimedia presentation.

Analyze Visuals

Possible answer: *The man and the boy seem tethered to the land that seems as dry and harsh as the one Anaya describes.*

TEXT ANALYSIS   COMMON CORE   RI 4

B CHARACTER TRAITS

Possible answer: *The grandfather is a plain, quiet, calm man who doesn't waste words and offers practical advice (lines 28–29).*

TIERED DISCUSSION PROMPTS

Direct students to lines 16–25. Use these prompts to help students recognize the author's strong ties to the past:

Connect What place do you consider magical? Why? *Answers will vary.*

Analyze What details show the distance between the author's grandfather and the modern age? *Possible answer: The references to his ancestors (lines 17–18) and to the river and wind being the only things that marked time (lines 23–25) show the distance.*

Evaluate How does the author emphasize his regard for his grandfather? *Possible answer: The author points out that he saw his grandfather as a giant, even though he was really only five feet tall (lines 20–21).*

My grandfather was a plain man, a farmer from the valley called Puerto de Luna on the Pecos River. He was probably a descendant of those people who spilled over the mountain from Taos, following the Pecos River in search of farmland. There in that river valley he settled and raised a large family.

20   Bearded and walrus-mustached, he stood five feet tall, but to me as a child he was a giant. I remember him most for his silence. In the summers my parents sent me to live with him on his farm, for I was to learn the ways of a farmer. My uncles also lived in that valley, there where only the flow of the river and the whispering of the wind marked time. For me it was a magical place.

   I remember once, while out hoeing the fields, I came upon an anthill, and before I knew it I was badly bitten. After he had covered my welts with the cool mud from the irrigation ditch, my grandfather calmly said: "Know where you stand." That is the way he spoke, in short phrases, to the point. **B**

30   One very dry summer, the river dried to a trickle; there was no water for the fields. The young plants withered and died. In my sadness and with the impulse of youth I said, "I wish it would rain!" My grandfather touched me, looked up into the sky and whispered, "Pray for rain." In his language there was a difference. He felt connected to the cycles that brought the rain or kept

▲ Analyze Visuals

How does this photograph reflect the way of life that Anaya describes?

B CHARACTER TRAITS

Reread lines 16–29. What do you learn about the grandfather's traits in this passage?

242   UNIT 2: CHARACTER DEVELOPMENT

DIFFERENTIATED INSTRUCTION

FOR ENGLISH LANGUAGE LEARNERS

Reading Background Display a map of the Southwestern United States. Have students locate New Mexico and note its proximity to Mexico. Point out Taos, near the state's northern border, and the Pecos River.

FOR STRUGGLING READERS

Develop Reading Fluency Engage the class in echo reading. Read a sentence aloud, and then have the class echo it back. Guide students in pacing and intonation, and help them with the pronunciation of any difficult or unfamiliar vocabulary.

Distribute the copy master and have students work in pairs or groups to practice fluency.

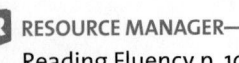 **RESOURCE MANAGER—Copy Master**
Reading Fluency p. 103

it from us. His prayer was a meaningful action, because he was a participant with the forces that filled our world; he was not a bystander.

A young man died at the village one summer. A very tragic death. He was dragged by his horse. When he was found, I cried, for the boy was my friend. I did not understand why death had come to one so young. My grandfather
40 took me aside and said: "Think of the death of the trees and the fields in the fall. The leaves fall, and everything rests, as if dead. But they bloom again in the spring. Death is only this small transformation in life." **C**

These are the things I remember, these fleeting images, few words.

I remember him driving his horse-drawn wagon into Santa Rosa in the fall when he brought his harvest produce to sell in the town. What a tower of strength seemed to come in that small man huddled on the seat of the giant wagon. One click of his tongue and the horses obeyed, stopped or turned as he wished. He never raised his whip. How unlike today, when so much teaching is done with loud words and threatening hands.
50 I would run to greet the wagon, and the wagon would stop. "*Buenos días le de Dios, abuelo,*" I would say. . . . "*Buenos días te de Dios, mi hijo,*"[3] he would answer and smile, and then I could jump up on the wagon and sit at his side. Then I, too, became a king as I rode next to the old man who smelled of earth and sweat and the other deep aromas from the orchards and fields of Puerto de Luna.

We were all sons and daughters to him. But today the sons and daughters are breaking with the past, putting aside *los abuelitos*. The old values are threatened, and threatened most where it comes to these relationships with the old people. If we don't take the time to watch and feel the years of their final
60 transformation, a part of our humanity will be lessened.

> I grew up speaking Spanish, and oh! how difficult it was to learn English. Sometimes I would give up and cry out that I couldn't learn. Then he would say, "*Ten paciencia.*" Have patience. *Paciencia,* a word with the strength of centuries, a word that said that someday we would overcome. . . . "You have to learn the language of the Americanos," he said. "Me, I will live my last days in my valley. You will live in a new time."
>
> A new time did come; a new time is here. How will we form it so it is fruitful? We need to know where we stand. We need to speak softly and respect others, and to share what we have. We need to pray not for material gain,
> 70 but for rain for the fields, for the sun to nurture growth, for nights in which we can sleep in peace, and for a harvest in which everyone can share. Simple lessons from a simple man. These lessons he learned from his past, which was as deep and strong as the currents of the river of life. **D**

He was a man; he died. Not in his valley but nevertheless cared for by his sons and daughters and flocks of grandchildren. At the end, I would enter his

---
3. *mi hijo* (mē ē'hō) *Spanish:* my son.

C CHARACTER TRAITS
What can you **infer** about Anaya's grandfather from this incident?

② **Targeted Passage**

D IDENTIFY AUTHOR'S PERSPECTIVE
How does the **tone** of lines 67–73 help reveal Anaya's perspective on life?

A CELEBRATION OF GRANDFATHERS **243**

C *Model the Skill:* **CHARACTER TRAITS**

Read and discuss line 42, in which the grandfather refers to "transformation." Explain to students that he feels that people also "bloom again." Lead students in recording the grandfather's character traits and supporting evidence in a Character Traits and Textual Evidence chart.

Quote	Explanation
"The leaves fall, and everything rests, as if dead. But they bloom again in the spring. Death is only this small transfor-mation in life."	Grandfather believes that death is a natural part of the life cycle, and that a rebirth follows it.

🧰 BEST PRACTICES TOOLKIT—Transparency
Character Traits and Textual Evidence
p. D6

Possible answer: The grandfather is religious and believes in life after death.

READING SKILL
COMMON CORE
RI 6

D **IDENTIFY AUTHOR'S PERSPECTIVE**

Possible answer: The tone of lines 67–73 is a descriptive and beautiful list of things people should do to make the world better. It helps show Anaya's respect for the past and for the simple aspects of life.

FOR STRUGGLING READERS

② **Targeted Passage [Lines 61–73]**

This passage shows the relationship Anaya sees among the past, present, and future generations.

- For Anaya, which Spanish word has a direct link to the past? (line 63)
- What suggestions does the author make for living well now? Who else voiced many of the same lessons? (lines 68–73)
- To whom does the author refer when he says *we*? (lines 67–71)

FOR ENGLISH LANGUAGE LEARNERS

Comprehension: Transitions Discuss the meaning of these contrast statements, explaining how the words *not for* and *but for* show ideas that are opposites or different: "We need to pray *not for* material gain, *but for* rain . . ."(lines 69–70). Ask students to work in pairs to find other words that signal opposite or different ideas.

REVISIT THE BIG QUESTION
Are **OLD WAYS** the best ways?

Discuss In lines 56–60, what does the author say will happen if young people abandon tradition entirely? **Possible answer:** *We will become less human (line 60).* Do you agree? *Answers will vary.*

room, which carried the smell of medications and Vicks. Gone were the aroma of the fields, the strength of his young manhood. Gone also was his patience in the face of crippling old age. Small things bothered him; he shouted or turned sour when his expectations were not met. It was because he could not care 80 for himself, because he was returning to that state of childhood, and all those wishes and desires were now wrapped in a crumbling, old body. **E**

"*Ten paciencia,*" I once said to him, and he smiled. "I didn't know I would grow this old," he said. . . .

I would sit and look at him and remember what was said of him when he was a young man. He could mount a wild horse and break it, and he could ride as far as any man. He could dance all night at a dance, then work the *acequia* the following day. He helped the neighbors; they helped him. He married, raised children. Small legends, the kind that make up every man's life.

He was ninety-four when he died. Family, neighbors, and friends gathered; 90 they all agreed he had led a rich life. I remembered the last years, the years he spent in bed. And as I remember now, I am reminded that it is too easy to romanticize[4] old age. Sometimes we forget the pain of the transformation into old age, we forget the natural breaking down of the body. . . . My grandfather pointed to the leaves falling from the tree. So time brings with its transformation the often painful wearing-down process. Vision blurs, health wanes; even the act of walking carries with it the painful reminder of the autumn of life. But this process is something to be faced, not something to be hidden away by false images. Yes, the old can be young at heart, but in their own way, with their own dignity. They do not have to copy the always-young 100 image of the Hollywood star. . . .

> I returned to Puerto de Luna last summer to join the community in a celebration of the founding of the church. I drove by my grandfather's home, my uncles' ranches, the neglected adobe washing down into the earth from whence it came. And I wondered, how might the values of my grandfather's generation live in our own? What can we retain to see us through these hard times? I was to become a farmer, and I became a writer. As I plow and plant my words, do I nurture as my grandfather did in his fields and orchards? The answers are not simple.
>
> "They don't make men like that anymore," is a phrase we hear when one 110 does honor to a man. I am glad I knew my grandfather. I am glad there are still times when I can see him in my dreams, hear him in my reverie. Sometimes I think I catch a whiff of that earthy aroma that was his smell. Then I smile. How strong these people were to leave such a lasting impression.

So, as I would greet my abuelo long ago, it would help us all to greet the old ones we know with this kind and respectful greeting: "*Buenos días le de Dios.*" ❧

---

4. **romanticize:** to view in an unrealistic or sentimental way.

E CHARACTER TRAITS
How did the grandfather change toward the end of his life?

③ Targeted Passage

COMMON CORE L 5b

Language Coach

Synonyms Words with the same or nearly the same meaning are **synonyms.** Reread the sentence in lines 110–111. What pair of synonyms appears in this sentence? How are these synonyms slightly different?

Comprehension

1. **Recall** What did Anaya's grandfather do for a living?

2. **Recall** Why did Anaya visit his grandfather each summer?

3. **Recall** What tradition from his past does Anaya want people to practice today?

4. **Summarize** What important lessons did Anaya learn from his grandfather?

Text Analysis

5. **Analyze Imagery** Anaya uses imagery—words and phrases that appeal to the reader's senses—to describe his grandfather. How do the images describing his childhood impressions of his grandfather contrast with the images describing the grandfather as he actually was?

6. **Character Traits** Anaya observed changes in his grandfather's **character traits** as he grew old. How did these changes affect his relationship with his grandfather? Cite evidence from the essay to support your inference.

7. **Analyze Author's Perspective** Review the chart that you created as you read. What beliefs, values, and feelings influence the way Anaya looks at "the pain of the transformation into old age"? Cite evidence.

8. **Interpret** Anaya poses the question "As I plow and plant my words, do I nurture as my grandfather did in his fields and orchards?" Why might Anaya consider his writing an attempt to "nurture"?

9. **Analyze Tone** What is the **tone** of this essay, and how do you know? Look back over the essay and identify words and details that reveal the tone. How does the tone help you share Anaya's perspective on events?

Text Criticism

10. **Biographical Context** "A Celebration of Grandfathers" was published in 1983. Fifteen years later, Anaya made the following statement in an interview: "The communal traditions of one generation are changed by the next, and we have to accept it and learn how the changes happen, and what is good or bad about that change. Sometimes you have to break free of family and community to find a new level of awareness for yourself." Compare this statement with the views that Anaya expresses in his essay.

> **Are OLD WAYS the best ways?**
>
> Which family traditions do you want to continue in your own life? Which do you want to leave behind?

COMMON CORE

RI 4 Analyze the impact of specific word choices on meaning and tone.
RI 6 Determine an author's point of view or purpose in a text.

Practice and Apply

For preliminary support of post-reading questions, use these copy masters:

R RESOURCE MANAGER—Copy Masters
Reading Check p. 101
Character Traits in Nonfiction p. 97
Question Support p. 102

Additional selection questions are provided for teachers on page 91.

ANSWERS

Comprehension

1. *The grandfather was a farmer.*

2. *to learn how to become a farmer*

3. *Anaya wishes everyone greeted old people with "Buenos dias le de Dios" and respect.*

4. *Anaya learned patience, prayer, love, respect for others, and the value of hard work.*

Text Analysis

COMMON CORE RI 4, RI 6

Possible answers:

5. *Though Anaya thought of his grandfather as a "giant" (line 21), the man was five feet tall and smelled "of earth and sweat" (lines 53–54). He was wise, a "participant with the forces that filled our world" (lines 35–36), who could direct horses with a click of his tongue (lines 47–48).*

6. *The characters exchanged roles, with Anaya reminding his grandfather to be patient (line 82).*

7. **COMMON CORE FOCUS Analyze Author's Perspective** *Anaya believes that the transformation to old age is part of nature (lines 93–94) and should be faced rather than hidden. He recalls when his grandfather pointed out the falling leaves (lines 93–94), and he states that old age should be faced (lines 97–98).*

8. *Anaya tries to help people grow.*

9. *The tone of the essay is one of respect and reverence. Anaya reveals the tone through his descriptions of his grandfather and the natural world, and through including Spanish words that reflect the language of his ancestors. The quiet respectful tone draws the reader in to share Anaya's perspective on the value of tradition and the simplicity of the past.*

Text Criticism

Possible answer:

10. *The essay questions how much of the past to keep; the quotation provides an answer.*

> **Are OLD WAYS the best ways?**
> Have students identify family traditions and think about which they want to continue as they become adults.

Assess and Reteach

Assess

DIAGNOSTIC AND SELECTION TESTS
Selection Test A, B/C pp. 71–72, 73–74

Interactive Selection Test on **thinkcentral.com**

Reteach

Level Up Online Tutorials on **thinkcentral.com**

Focus and Motivate

Simply Grand: Generational Ties Matter
Magazine Article

COMMON CORE FOCUS

RI 1 Cite textual evidence to support inferences drawn from the text. **RI 2** Determine a central idea and analyze how it is refined by specific details. **W 2b** Develop the topic with well-chosen and relevant facts, details, quotations, or other information and examples. **L 4b** Identify and correctly use patterns of word changes that indicate different meanings or parts of speech.

SUMMARY

This magazine article explores the importance of grandparents in children's lives and the ways that grandparents can use technology to stay in touch with grandchildren.

What's the Connection?

Divide the class into small groups and write *Grandparents* on the board. Have each group member in turn share something he or she knows about grandparents. Afterward, have one member of each group recite as many answers as the student remembers. List these on the board, asking the class to compare and contrast them.

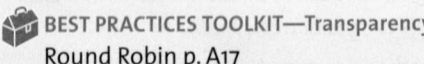
BEST PRACTICES TOOLKIT—Transparency
Round Robin p. A17

Teach

Standards Focus: Identify Main Idea and Supporting Details

Help students recognize the relationship between **main ideas** and **supporting details.** Explain how the main idea of the article is supported by the main ideas in each section and paragraph. Have students skim the article for the kinds of supporting details listed. Use questions to highlight the relationship.

- Why are grandparents so important?
- What problems do grandparents face today?
- How can technology help solve some of these problems?
- Which sentence tells the main idea about caregiving grandparents?

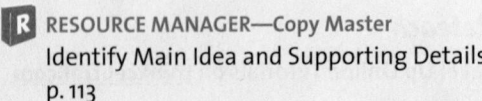
RESOURCE MANAGER—Copy Master
Identify Main Idea and Supporting Details
p. 113

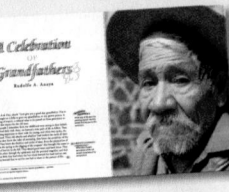

Use with
"A Celebration of Grandfathers,"
page 240.

COMMON CORE

RI 1 Cite textual evidence to support inferences drawn from the text. **RI 2** Determine a central idea and analyze how it is refined by specific details. **L 4b** Identify and correctly use patterns of word changes that indicate different meanings or parts of speech.

What's the Connection?

In "A Celebration of Grandfathers," Rudolfo Anaya recalls the deep bond he formed with his grandfather during the 1940s and expresses concern that children are no longer absorbing the traditions and values of their elders. In "Simply Grand: Generational Ties Matter," you will read about the efforts that grandparents make to maintain ties with their grandchildren in today's changing society.

Standards Focus: Identify Main Idea and Supporting Details

In nonfiction, the **main idea,** or **central idea,** is the most important idea, message, or opinion that the writer wants to communicate to the reader. A writer may state the main idea directly in the title or in a thesis statement or may only imply the idea, allowing the reader to infer it.

Writers develop a main idea through the use of **supporting details,** which appear throughout the body of an article or essay. References to supporting details may also appear in topic sentences or in subheadings. Supporting details can be

- facts or statistics
- statements from experts
- examples
- anecdotes

The chart below shows how the main idea was developed in "A Celebration of Grandfathers." Using a similar chart, record the main ideas and the most important supporting details in "Simply Grand."

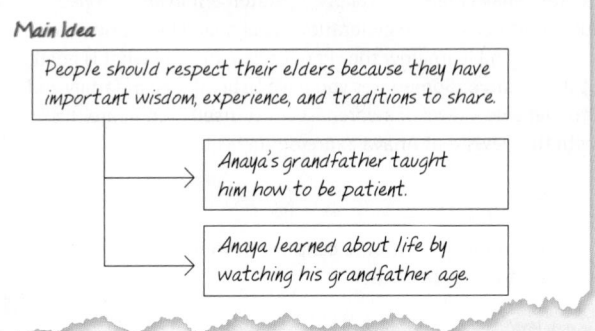

Main Idea

People should respect their elders because they have important wisdom, experience, and traditions to share.

→ Anaya's grandfather taught him how to be patient.

→ Anaya learned about life by watching his grandfather age.

Selection Resources

See resources on the **Teacher One Stop DVD-ROM** and on **thinkcentral.com**.

R RESOURCE MANAGER UNIT 2
Lesson Support,* pp. 105–109

DIAGNOSTIC AND SELECTION TESTS
Selection Tests, pp. 75–78

BEST PRACTICES TOOLKIT
pp. A17, B18

TECHNOLOGY

- Teacher One Stop DVD-ROM
- Student One Stop DVD-ROM
- Audio Anthology CD
- ExamView Test Generator on the Teacher One Stop

* Resources for Differentiation

FAMILY

SIMPLY GRAND:
Generational Ties Matter

by Megan Rutherford

There is a magical moment in the latter half of life when adults have a chance to reinvent themselves. They take on new names: Nana, Grandma, Bubbeh, Poppy, Grandpa, Zayde. They cast themselves in new roles: caregiver, mentor, pal, pamperer. They are filled with powerful new emotions that make them feel alive and vital. They become
10 grandparents.

"Every time a child is born, a grandparent is born too," says grandparenting guru and retired child psychologist Arthur Kornhaber. The bond between grandchild and grandparent is second only to the attachment between parent and child. Kornhaber calls it "clear love" because it has no strings attached. "There's always some
20 conditional element to parents' love. Grandparents are just glad to have you, and the child can feel that."

That love may be the emotional equivalent of superglue, but it needs

points of contact in order to stick. And today, like other family institutions, grandparenthood is being buffeted by sea changes. Working against the free exchange of
30 love are high divorce and remarriage rates, job stresses of dual-career parents (and grandparents), a global economy that puts vast distances between family members, and a pervasive bias against age spawned by the American obsession with youthfulness.

These impediments, however, are counterbalanced by innovations in travel, telecommunications, social
40 understanding, health, and life expectancy. Savvy parents and grandparents are harnessing these to strengthen intergenerational ties. "We have to reinvent ourselves as we go along, but we have more time to get it right," says Lillian Carson, a psychotherapist in Santa Barbara, California. . . . **A**

According to researchers, the better
50 the relationship between parent and grandparent, the greater the contact and closeness between grandparent and grandchild. "It's up to the parents to make the grandparents feel welcome and to send the message to their children that they're really integral," says Sally Newman, executive director of Generations Together at the

A MAIN IDEA AND
SUPPORTING DETAILS
What main, or controlling idea, can you **infer** from the first four paragraphs of this article?

READING FOR INFORMATION **247**

DIFFERENTIATED INSTRUCTION

FOR ENGLISH LANGUAGE LEARNERS
Vocabulary: Idioms Form two teams. Say an idiom aloud and have a student use it in a sentence. The other team can allow or question the usage. Examples of idioms:

- *no strings attached* (lines 18–19), "no limiting conditions"
- *sea changes* (line 28), "major changes"
- *stuff* (line 73), "many things"
- *state occasion* (lines 120–121), "major event"
- *set eyes on* (line 136), "saw"

INFORMATIONAL ANALYSIS   COMMON CORE

A MAIN IDEA AND   RI 1
SUPPORTING DETAILS   RI 2

Possible answer: *The important bond between grandparents and grandchildren is facing challenges, but many people are finding innovative ways to maintain this special relationship.*

IF STUDENTS NEED HELP . . . Tell students to begin by identifying the topic of the paragraphs as *grandparenthood.* Then, ask students what they learned about the topic. *Possible answers: Grandparents are important; new challenges exist; these are counterbalanced by several factors.* Help students combine these responses into one main, or controlling, idea.

Extend the Discussion What kinds of information do you think this article will contain?

TIERED DISCUSSION PROMPTS

Direct students to lines 70–109. Use these prompts to help students recognize the different ways that grandparents support grandchildren:

Connect What do you think grandparents and grandchildren can learn from each other? *Answers will vary.*

Analyze How do the supporting details in the text help you understand the relationship between grandparents and their grandchildren? *Possible answer: Examples help explain what grandchildren can learn from grandparents (lines 71–81). Statements explain why the relationship is precious to grandparents (lines 81–88). Examples help explain the topic sentence, which is stated at the beginning of each paragraph (lines 70–72, 90–91).*

Evaluate What facts would you choose to support the idea that small gestures by grandparents have a strong impact on grandchildren? *Possible answer: When Katie's grandmother sends her food and books, the girl knows that her grandmother loves her (lines 99–108).*

University of Pittsburgh. "The parents
60 should encourage frequent visits and not make the grandparents feel intrusive." And spending time together is essential, says Yaffa Schlesinger, who teaches sociology of the family at New York City's Hunter College. "If relationships are to be meaningful, they have to be deep in time. You cannot be friends with someone you met yesterday." . . .

70   No child can have too much love and attention. But that's not all grandparents have to offer. "Kids learn stuff from older people that they can't get from anybody else," says Newman. "Wisdom, patience, looking at things from many perspectives, tolerance, and hope. Older adults have lived through wars, losses, economic deprivations, and they give kids the security of
80 knowing that horrendous things can be survived." For the older generation, the relationship is equally precious. "Having grandchildren is the vindication of everything one has done as a parent. When we see our children passing on our values to another generation, we know we have been successful," says Margy-Ruth Davis, a new grandmother in New York City.

90   Keeping the gates open need not be expensive or arduous. Kathy Hersh, a Miami writer who is the mother of Katie, 11, and David, 7, sends a weekly packet of their photocopied poems, essays, teachers' notes, and report cards to their maternal grandparents in Indiana and their paternal grandmother, a widow, in Arizona. The grandparents respond in
100 kind. Kathy's mother sends homemade jam, cookies, fudge—and lots and lots of books. "It's not the value of the contents," says Kathy. "It's that the children have been thought of."

The value of that is beyond measure. "I know my grandmother is always going to love me and think everything I do is wonderful," Katie told her mother recently.

TECHNOLOGICAL AIDS

110 Other grandparents are discovering the miracles of the technological revolution. Margy-Ruth and Perry Davis are heartsick that they cannot be part of their granddaughter's daily life in Toronto. But she is already part of theirs, because the Davises have equipped their daughter with a digital camera, and every day she e-mails them a fresh picture of baby Tiferet.
120 "It's hard for every visit to be a state occasion, and it's hard not to be able to pop over and just look in for half an hour," says Margy-Ruth, "but at least this way I can watch the baby change day by day." . . .

The Davises are not alone in cultivating electronic intimacy. Indeed, anecdotal evidence suggests that keeping in touch with grandchildren
130 may be one of the main computer uses for seniors. Julia Sneden, a retired North Carolina kindergarten teacher, began e-mailing five-year-old Gina, her stepgranddaughter in California, several months before meeting her in person. When they finally set eyes on each other, they were already fast friends. . . .

Jacquie Golden of Salinas,
140 California, finds that e-mail has an unexpected advantage over the telephone when communicating with her teenage grandson Timothy Haines, a student at the University of Nebraska. "On the phone, he'll say everything is fine, his life is fine, his mother's fine, his friends are fine. With e-mail he opens up. He tells me how he's really doing,

---

⊙ COMMON CORE L 4b

Language Coach

Roots and Affixes
An affix added to the end of a word is called a **suffix**. *Vindication* (line 84) contains the suffix *-ion.* What other words in this paragraph contain the suffix *-ion?* How does this suffix change both of these words?

DIFFERENTIATED INSTRUCTION

FOR STRUGGLING READERS

Vocabulary Support Some students may become discouraged when they encounter difficult vocabulary, such as *economic deprivations* (line 78), *vindication* (line 84), *arduous* (line 91), and *onerous* (line 191). Draw attention to the context of the entire paragraph, and ask: What are some *horrendous things* that older people have survived? What suggests that *economic deprivations* are negative events?

FOR ENGLISH LANGUAGE LEARNERS

Language Coach   ⊙ COMMON CORE
L 4b
Roots and Affixes
Answer: attention, deprivation, generation: -ion changes the words from verbs to nouns. Have students work in pairs to look up the definitions of these words. Then have students practice using the words by including them in original sentences.

how rotten his last football game was,
150 and how school sucks. He gets down."

Many far-flung families have discovered a wonderful Web freebie: create-your-own family sites, where relatives equipped with passwords can post messages, share family anecdotes, keep track of birthdays, scan in snapshots—and see what the rest of their extended family has been up to. Valerie Juleson lives in Wilton,
160 Connecticut. Her 12 adult children—11 foster kids and one biological child—are spread out all over the United States and Europe, and her two grandchildren live in Florida. She keeps up with everyone through a website. **B**

MULTICULTURAL CHALLENGES

Meera Ananthaswamy has a double challenge in uniting her children and parents: distance and culture. After
170 emigrating with her parents from India to Canada in 1962, she moved with her husband and two daughters to Dallas three years ago. To maintain the closeness they felt when they all lived near one another in Hamilton, Ontario, the three generations try to get together at least twice a year. In addition, the two girls spend summers with their grandparents. Between visits, they
180 stay in touch through weekly phone calls. Perumal Rajaram tells his granddaughters stories from Hindu mythology, instructs them in Indian philosophy and takes them to the Hindu temple in Hamilton for additional prayers. "It gives them history and a sense of where they've come from," says Meera.

But sometimes Suma, 16, and
190 Usha, 13, find their grandparents' sense of tradition onerous. The girls like to wear jeans and shorts, which

Rajaram abhors. Then Meera steps in as interpreter. "I tell them, 'Your grandparents' definition of pretty is someone in a sari and not someone in short shorts. You've got to remember where your grandparents come from.'" . . .

200 Good communication and . . . [a] spirit of compromise have helped keep Meera's family close. That's not always the case in modern multicultural America, says sociology professor Schlesinger. The tragic irony is that many immigrants come to the U.S. in search of a better life for their children and grandchildren. But in order to achieve the goal set by their elders, the
210 younger generation must assimilate, and when they do, they become strangers who speak a different language and live by an alien code. "The grandparent has achieved his American Dream," says Schlesinger, "but at a terrible cost." . . .

FAMILY RITUALS

Even grandparents who have no physical or cultural divides separating them from their grandchildren may
220 yearn for ways to get closer. David Stearman and his wife Bernice are lucky enough to have all six grandkids living within a 25-minute drive of their home in Chevy Chase, Maryland. Nonetheless, the Stearmans are always looking for ways to enhance their togetherness. So Bernice has made a habit of taking the kids to "M&Ms"—movies and malls. David does
230 something a little more adventurous. For the past 10 summers, he has gone to camp with one—sometimes two—of his grandchildren. "The food is terrible, the beds are bad, there are no televisions or radios, but, man, you just feel good!" Stearman says. . . .

B MAIN IDEA AND SUPPORTING DETAILS
What supporting details appear in the discussion of technological aids? Which are the most important supporting details?

INFORMATIONAL ANALYSIS COMMON CORE

RI 1
RI 2

B Model the Skill: MAIN IDEA AND SUPPORTING DETAILS

Explain that the main, or controlling, idea of "Technological Aids" is that technology can help grandparents and grandchildren form close relationships. Remind students that supporting details include facts or statistics, statements from experts, examples, and anecdotes. Ask students to look through the article for an example of a family that uses technology to keep in touch. Then ask them to find statements and anecdotes about this family. Point out that these are all supporting details.

Possible answer: *The Davises use a digital camera to stay close to their distant family (lines 116–125); Jacquie Golden sees that e-mail has advantages over the telephone (lines 139–150); others, including the Julesons, use websites to keep in touch (lines 159–166).*

Extend the Discussion What other types of technology might someone use to keep in touch?

FOR ENGLISH LANGUAGE LEARNERS

Culture: Clarify Help students build meanings for the following terms: *superglue* (line 24), *American Dream* (line 215), *bungalow colony* (line 245), *single-parent and two-career households* (lines 277–278), *stay-at-home dad* (lines 283–284). Use a Cluster Diagram to elicit students' prior knowledge of these concepts. Then expand as needed.

🧰 **BEST PRACTICES TOOLKIT—Transparency**
Cluster Diagram p. B18

FOR ADVANCED LEARNERS/PRE–AP

Synthesize [small-group option] Have students reflect on what they have read about the wants and needs of grandparents and grandchildren. How would they change or adapt this article for the audience of a computer magazine? Have them discuss the question and then write proposals to describe their plan for an article.

Many families create and maintain their own rituals. That's what Beverly Zarin, a retired reading consultant, and
240 her husband Sol have done. For the past 20 years, the Zarins, who live in Connecticut, have vacationed together with their two sons and their sons' families for two weeks every summer in a bungalow colony in Maine. "That's been a tradition, a wonderful way to really get to know one another," she says. In November everyone heads for St. Louis, Missouri, for Thanksgiving
250 with the Zarins' son Larry and his family. At Passover the whole clan gathers at Beverly's house. "So we spend a good time together at least three times a year," says Beverly.

Other grandparents try to share the turning points of their own lives with their grandchildren. Forty years ago, Dorris Alcott of Timonium, Maryland took her first trip abroad, and her
260 exposure to new people and places forever changed the way she viewed the world. This summer she decided to give her granddaughter Sylviane, 16, the same experience. "I felt having this at her age would be far more memorable than any little bit of money I could leave her—plus I'd have her to myself for three weeks!" Sylviane was moved by the experience of traveling with her
270 grandmother. "I realized it was probably the last time I was ever going to spend that much time with her," she says, "and the first time too." As a result of the trip, Sylviane says, "I have more respect for my grandmother." . . .

CARING FOR CHILDREN

In a world with a shortage of good day care and an abundance of single-parent and two-career households, grandparents willing to care for their

280 grandchildren are highly prized. In the old days, such care was generally rendered by Grandma. Today the social forces that produced the stay-at-home dad have introduced the caregiver grandad. Peter Gross, a retired law professor, picks up grandsons Paul, 3, and Mark, 18 months, every weekday morning at 8:15 and cares for them in his San
290 Francisco home until 6 P.M. "It's a very close, intense relationship that's at the center of my life," says Gross. "What a relief to retire from the hurly-burly of the adult institutions of our world, where . . . politics and limitations tend to dominate, and move into this place of love and truth and nurturing and connection." **C**

Gross has a deep, everyday
300 relationship with his grandchildren that many grandparents would move halfway around the world to enjoy. In fact, that's just about what Judith Hendra did. This summer Hendra quit her job as a fund raiser for Beth Israel Medical Center in New York City, sold her loft, and moved with her husband, a free-lance photographer, and her German shepherd to Los Angeles to be
310 near her 18-month-old granddaughter Julia. "I reckon I have a window of opportunity of about 10 years before she turns into a California preteen, and then it'll be over," jokes Hendra. In the meantime Hendra, who plans to work part-time as a consultant, is looking forward to indulging a modest-sounding ambition: "I'd like to be a person who's taken for granted, who
320 picks Julia up from school and does ordinary things that are actually very important for kids. I don't want to be a special event." Now that's something special.

C MAIN IDEA AND SUPPORTING DETAILS
How does the information in lines 276–298 support the writer's main idea?

RI 1
RI 2

C MAIN IDEA AND SUPPORTING DETAILS

To help students identify the writer's main idea before they answer the question, call attention to the subtitle and first sentence in this part (lines 276–280). Guide students in using these details to state the main idea.

Possible answer: *The information provides one example of a way in which grandparents are finding creative ways to strengthen intergenerational relationships, while at the same time helping their adult children overcome childcare difficulties.*

DIFFERENTIATED INSTRUCTION

FOR ENGLISH LANGUAGE LEARNERS
Vocabulary: Multiple-Meaning Words
Identify these multiple-meaning words: *ties* (line 43), *closeness* (line 174), *clan* (line 251), *moved* (line 268). Have students work in pairs with English speakers. Have English speakers find the target words in a dictionary and English learners choose the meaning that best fits the context in the text. Ask volunteers to read the meaning aloud.

Language: Conversational English Patterns
Discuss the meaning of these phrases: *simply grand* (title), *second only to* (line 16), *need not be . . .* (line 90), *What a relief* (line 293), *I reckon* (line 311). Have student pairs create brief dialogues with one or two of the phrases and perform the dialogues for the class.

Comprehension

1. **Recall** Name two factors that can make it difficult for grandparents and grandchildren to develop a close relationship.

2. **Summarize** How do grandchildren benefit from having a close relationship with their grandparents?

Text Analysis

3. **Analyze Supporting Details** Review the supporting details in the chart you created and identify the kind of supporting detail (such as examples or anecdotes) that the writer used most often. What can you infer about the main idea from these supporting details?

4. **Compare and Contrast** In "A Celebration of Grandfathers" and "Simply Grand," Rudolfo A. Anaya and Megan Rutherford discuss how families are affected by changes in society. Compare and contrast their views on this topic.

COMMON CORE

RI 1 Cite textual evidence to support inferences drawn from text. RI 2 Determine a central idea and analyze how it is refined by specific details. W 2b Develop the topic with well-chosen and relevant facts, details, quotations, or other information and examples.

Read for Information: Make Generalizations

WRITING PROMPT

After reading "A Celebration of Grandfathers" and "Simply Grand," what general statements can you make about the grandparent-grandchild relationship? Write an essay in which you make three generalizations about this relationship. Use information from both selections and your own experience to support your response.

To answer this prompt, you will need to make generalizations. A **generalization** is an idea or statement that summarizes the general characteristics rather than the specific details of a subject. To make a generalization, follow these steps.

1. Gather evidence—facts, anecdotes, and observations—about the grandparent-grandchild relationship.

2. Look for patterns or connections among the pieces of evidence.

3. Make a general statement that characterizes the patterns or connections.

4. Review the evidence to make sure your generalizations are well supported and fair. Revise them if necessary.

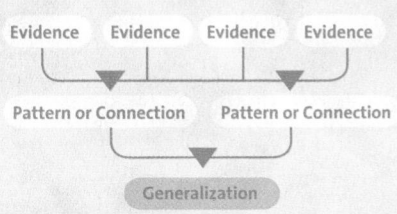

DIFFERENTIATED INSTRUCTION

FOR STRUGGLING WRITERS
Read for Information

- Tell students to record evidence on index cards, including one anecdote, fact, or observation on each card. This makes it easy to organize cards by key ideas.

- Remind students that an essay states a position on a topic. Have students begin with their generalization, state a position, and then support that position with key ideas supported by evidence.

- Remind students that when they look for patterns, they should be looking for similarities that will allow them to generalize. For example, point out that most of the grandparent-grandchild relationships in the article are long-distance ones.

FOR ADVANCED LEARNERS/PRE-AP
Read for Information Encourage students to research the topic in a library or on the Internet to find statistics and expert statements that they can incorporate into their essays.

Practice and Apply

For preliminary support of post-reading questions, use these copy masters:

R RESOURCE MANAGER—Copy Masters
Main Ideas and Supporting Details p. 113
Reading Check p. 117
Question Support p. 118

Additional selection questions are provided for teachers on page 108.

ANSWERS

Comprehension

1. **Possible answers:** *high divorce and remarriage rate, geographical distance*

2. **Possible answers:** *They receive unconditional love and they learn things.*

Text Analysis

COMMON CORE RI 1, RI 2, W 2b

Possible answers:

3. **Main Idea and Supporting Details** *The writer mainly used examples. Showing how the problems affect ordinary people helps readers understand the issues.*

4. *Anaya believes that many families are turning away from the wisdom of the elderly; Rutherford shows how many work to maintain bonds with the old.*

Read for Information: Make Generalizations

Writing Prompt *Possible answers: Grandparents have a great deal to offer grandchildren, including love, care, and wisdom; grandparents can provide cultural connections for grandchildren; grandparents make good caregivers for grandchildren with busy parents.*

Assess and Reteach

Assess

DIAGNOSTIC AND SELECTION TESTS
Selection Test A, B/C pp. 71–72, 73–74

Interactive Selection Test on **thinkcentral.com**

Reteach

Level Up Online Tutorials on **thinkcentral.com**

Reteaching Worksheets on **thinkcentral.com**
Reading Lesson 4: Recognizing Main Ideas and Details

Focus and Motivate

COMMON CORE FOCUS

RL 1 Cite strong and thorough textual evidence to support inferences drawn from the text.
RL 2 Determine two or more themes or central ideas of a text and analyze their development over the course of the text. **RL 10** Read and comprehend poems.

SUMMARIES

"The Gift" In this poem, the speaker, who is taking a splinter from his wife's hand, recalls how his father had removed a splinter from his hand when he was seven. Tenderly, he reflects on his father's gentleness.

"Those Winter Sundays" In this poem, the speaker remembers cold, winter Sundays when his father rose early to make a fire. He also recalls the anger within their household and his indifference toward his father's thoughtfulness.

How do you show you CARE?

Discuss the question with students. Ask them to recall occasions when someone showed them caring. Were the circumstances ordinary or unusual? Extend the discussion by having students complete the *QUICKWRITE*.

Selection Resources

See resources on the **Teacher One Stop DVD-ROM** and on **thinkcentral.com**.

 RESOURCE MANAGER UNIT 2
  Plan and Teach, pp. 119–126
  Text Analysis and Reading
    Skill, pp. 127–130†*

DIAGNOSTIC AND SELECTION TESTS
  Selection Tests, pp. 79–82

 BEST PRACTICES TOOLKIT
  Two-Column Chart, p. A25

TECHNOLOGY
  🔘 **Teacher One Stop DVD-ROM**
  🔘 **Student One Stop DVD-ROM**
  🔘 **Audio Anthology CD**
  🔘 **GrammarNotes DVD-ROM**
  🔘 **ExamView Test Generator**
    on the Teacher One Stop

* Resources for Differentiation   **†** Also in Spanish   **‡** In Haitian Creole and Vietnamese

---

The Gift
Poem by Li-Young Lee

Those Winter Sundays
Poem by Robert Hayden

How do you show you CARE?

COMMON CORE

RL 1 Cite evidence to support inferences drawn from the text.
RL 10 Read and comprehend poems.

Sometimes the most vivid memories are of ordinary events—for example, a relative tying your shoelaces when you were a child or cooking a favorite meal. What makes such moments special are the feelings you associate with them. In "The Gift" and "Those Winter Sundays," the speakers recall how their fathers showed love through simple acts of caring.

QUICKWRITE Make a list of ordinary events or routines that you remember from childhood. Then write a paragraph about one item on the list, explaining why the memory is meaningful to you.

Childhood Memories
1. *Visiting grandparents*
2. *Setting the dinner table*
3.
4.
5.

252

TEXT ANALYSIS: CHARACTERS IN POETRY

Characters in poetry are often created with **imagery**—words and phrases that appeal to the reader's senses. By using imagery, poets can create a vivid character in just a few words. For example, in "Those Winter Sundays," the speaker offers the following image of his father:

. . . cracked hands that ached
from labor in the weekday weather . . .

This phrase not only suggests the father's physical appearance but also hints at his personality and the hardship he endures.

As you read the two poems, notice the imagery each poet uses to create a character. Look for words that describe the character's

- appearance
- feelings or thoughts
- actions or behavior
- character traits

READING SKILL: MAKE INFERENCES ABOUT THE SPEAKER

To learn more about the speaker of a poem, readers can **make inferences,** or logical guesses based on clues in the text. For example, in "The Gift" the speaker describes how he reacted when his father began to remove a splinter from his palm.

To pull the metal splinter from my palm
my father recited a story in a low voice.
I watched his lovely face and not the blade.

You may infer from details in these lines that the speaker trusts his father and that they have a loving relationship.

As you read each poem, use a diagram like the one shown to help you organize inferences about the speaker.

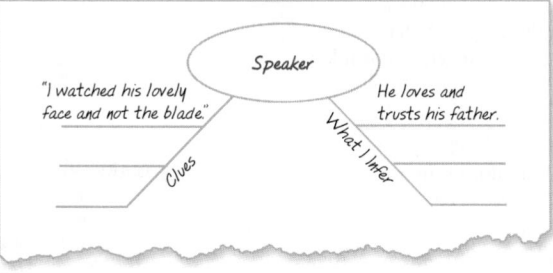
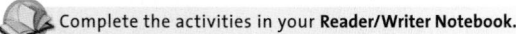

Complete the activities in your **Reader/Writer Notebook.**

Meet the Author

Li-Young Lee
born 1957

A Search for Identity
Li-Young Lee (lē-yŭng lē) was born in Indonesia, where his parents took refuge after fleeing from China. The Indonesian government imprisoned Lee's father in 1958 during a period of anti-Chinese persecution. After his release, the family lived in several Asian countries before settling in the United States when Lee was seven years old. Lee's childhood experiences have a strong influence on his poetry. He often writes about immigrants and examines the role that family and memory play in shaping identity.

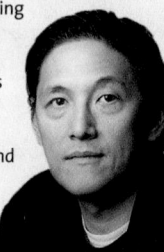

Robert Hayden
1913–1980

Poetry as Refuge
Robert Hayden grew up in a poor neighborhood in Detroit, Michigan. He was raised by neighbors from an early age after his biological parents separated. Although Hayden's foster parents made sacrifices for his education, their troubled marriage fueled spells of depression in him. Hayden sought escape from his "dark nights of the soul" by reading and writing poetry. His first collection came out in 1940 to little fanfare. However, by 1962, when "Those Winter Sundays" was published in the volume *A Ballad of Remembrance,* Hayden was on his way to becoming a prominent poet.

Authors Online
THiNK central
Go to **thinkcentral.com.** KEYWORD: HML10-253

253

DIFFERENTIATED INSTRUCTION

FOR STRUGGLING READERS

Concept Support Explain to students that the speaker in a poem is not necessarily the same as the poet, even if the poem seems to be autobiographical. To help students explore this concept, read aloud some lines of poetry in which the speaker is clearly different from the poet. Then work with students to find clues in the text that allow them to infer this difference.

Teach

TEXT ANALYSIS

● *Model the Skill:* **CHARACTERS IN POETRY**

To model how to identify characters in poetry, write these lines on the board and read them aloud:

> He sauntered up in his silk top hat,
> His cane danced before him, his hair all a-shine.
> With a tip and a bow and a one-two step,
> He offered his arm and asked, "Where shall we dine?"

Next, point out what these lines reveal about the character in the hat. Explain that the images of the character's clothing, gestures, and speech suggest an old-fashioned, elegant, and even eccentric person.

GUIDED PRACTICE Ask students to explain how images help create a vivid character in a favorite poem or song.

READING SKILL

COMMON CORE
RL 1
RL 10

■ *Model the Skill:* **MAKE INFERENCES ABOUT THE SPEAKER**

To model how to make inferences about the speaker, write these lines of poetry on the board under the lines from the **TEXT ANALYSIS** activity:

> I glared at this fool with his top hat and cane
> And replied in a voice tinged with mocking disdain,
> "Just who do you think you are to appear
> After leaving me waiting for more than a year?"

Point out that from these lines, students can infer that speaker was going out with the man in the top hat, and she is now angry with him because he went away but now expects to resume their relationship.

R RESOURCE MANAGER—Copy Master
Make Inferences About the Speaker
p. 129 (for student use while reading the selection)

READ WITH A PURPOSE

Help students set a purpose for reading. Tell students to look for the ways in which the speakers describe their fathers.

TEXT ANALYSIS

A Model the Skill: CHARACTERS IN POETRY

To model how to identify characters in poetry, read lines 6–13 aloud. On the board, create a two-column chart like the one below. Have students volunteer details for the image column. Then ask them what the images suggest and fill in the "What It Suggests" column.

Image	What It Suggests
voice: well of dark water, a prayer	deep voice, soft, tender, comforting

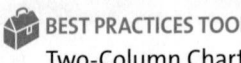 BEST PRACTICES TOOLKIT—Transparency
Two-Column Chart p. A25

Possible answer: *The father had a deep, tender, comforting voice; he had gentle hands; he used his hands to show love and to apply discipline.*

Extend the Discussion What impact might such a parent have on a child?

READING SKILL

COMMON CORE
RL 1
RL 10

B Model the Skill: MAKE INFERENCES

Have students fill out their Make Inferences diagrams. Tell them to fill in the "Clues" section of the diagram with details from lines 24–35 and then use those clues to fill in the "What I Infer" section.

Possible answer: *The speaker loved and trusted his father; he felt his father wouldn't let harm come to him.*

The Gift

LI-YOUNG LEE

To pull the metal splinter from my palm
my father recited a story in a low voice.
I watched his lovely face and not the blade.
Before the story ended, he'd removed
5 the iron sliver I thought I'd die from.

I can't remember the tale,
but hear his voice still, a well
of dark water, a prayer.
And I recall his hands,
10 two measures of tenderness
he laid against my face,
the flames of discipline
he raised above my head. **A**

Had you entered that afternoon
15 you would have thought you saw a man
planting something in a boy's palm,
a silver tear, a tiny flame.
Had you followed that boy
you would have arrived here,
20 where I bend over my wife's right hand.

Look how I shave her thumbnail down
so carefully she feels no pain.
Watch as I lift the splinter out.
I was seven when my father
25 took my hand like this,
and I did not hold that shard
between my fingers and think,
Metal that will bury me,
christen it Little Assassin,
30 Ore Going Deep for My Heart.
And I did not lift up my wound and cry,
Death visited here!
I did what a child does
when he's given something to keep.
35 I kissed my father. **B**

Analyze Visuals ▶
How does this painting reflect the **mood** of the poem?

A CHARACTERS IN POETRY
What do you learn about the father from **images** in this stanza?

B MAKE INFERENCES
Reread lines 24–35. What can you infer about the feelings of the **speaker** after his father removes the splinter?

Interwoven Hands. Todd Davidson. © Images.com/Corbis.

DIFFERENTIATED INSTRUCTION

FOR ENGLISH LANGUAGE LEARNERS

Options for Reading Read the first stanza aloud, and then select students to read the next two. Have students listen to the rest of the poem on the *Audio Anthology CD.*

FOR STRUGGLING READERS

Develop Reading Fluency Model how to read the poem for students. Point out that instead of stopping at the end of each line, students should look at the punctuation to tell them when to pause and when to stop. Explain to students that sometimes the punctuation will indicate a pause within a line, instead of at the end, as in in line 7. Read the poem aloud, one complete thought at a time, and have students echo the reading.

Distribute the copy master and have students work in teams or groups to practice fluency.

R RESOURCE MANAGER—Copy Master
Reading Fluency p. 132

BACKGROUND

Li-Young Lee and His Father Critics have noted that Li-Young Lee's poems create an atmosphere of silence reminiscent of classic Chinese poets. Lee himself was silent as a very young child. He did not speak in full sentences until he was three. At one time, Lee's father was personal physician to Mao Zedong, and people recognized in his father the combination of tenderness and austerity reflected in "The Gift."

Analyze Visuals

Possible answer: The crossed, interconnecting hands in the painting suggest strength and interdependence, a theme of the poem. The image of hands matches the speaker's memories of two experiences with hands—his own and his wife's. The painting's mood also matches the poem's mood of tenderness and caring.

TIERED DISCUSSION PROMPTS

Direct students to lines 1–5. Use these prompts to help students understand the relationship between the father and son:

Connect Describe a time when you or someone you know had an accident and an adult took care of you. *Answers will vary.*

Analyze Why did the speaker's father tell him a story while pulling the splinter from his palm? What effect did it have? ***Possible answer:*** *The speaker's father tells a story to calm and distract the speaker. The speaker listens to his father's voice rather than concentrate on the pain in his hand.*

Evaluate Was the father's storytelling appropriate to the situation? What else might be done to calm someone in this situation? ***Possible answers:*** *Yes. The boy was scared and needed reassurance. The story drew his attention away from his pain and worry. Singing a calming song might have had a similar effect.*

FOR STRUGGLING READERS

Sequence of Events Make sure students understand that the time sequence in the poem shifts twice—from the past to the present, then back to the past. Ask them how old the narrator is at the beginning of the poem. To what time does the poem shift forward in lines 18–23? To what time does it shift backward in lines 24–35?

FOR ADVANCED LEARNERS/PRE–AP

Storytelling Have students identify the biblical images and symbols that the poet uses for personal purposes in this poem. How do they reinforce the theme and meaning of the poem?

Prereading for this poem is found on page 252.

REVISIT THE BIG QUESTION

How do you show you CARE?

Discuss In lines 1–5, how did the father show his family caring? *Possible answer: He got up early to make the house warm, even on Sunday, his day off from hard work.*

Analyze Visuals

Activity Ask students how the painting supports the characterization of the father.

Possible answer: The hands, muscular, worn, and red, are those of a hard-working man who does physical labor outdoors.

About the Art *Vigour* is an oil painting created in 1932.

READING SKILL

COMMON CORE

RL 1
RL 10

C MAKE INFERENCES

Possible answer: The speaker's attitude toward his family was fearful, distant, and ungrateful as a child. Details: "No one ever thanked him" (line 5) and "fearing the chronic angers of that house" (line 9). The speaker's distance is suggested by his comment that he stayed in bed listening to his father make the fire, but did not thank him.

SELECTION WRAP–UP

READ WITH A PURPOSE Now that students have finished reading the selection, have them consider the images they have of the two fathers. How are the fathers alike? *Possible answer: Both fathers took the time to care for their children. One showed caring by removing a splinter, the other by splitting wood and shining shoes.*

⭐ **CRITIQUE** Which speaker do you think gives a better overall description of his father? Give your reasons for your choice.

INDEPENDENT READING

Suggest Lee's *Rose (New Poets of America)* and Hayden's *Collected Poems*, edited by Frederick Glaysher.

Those Winter Sundays

ROBERT HAYDEN

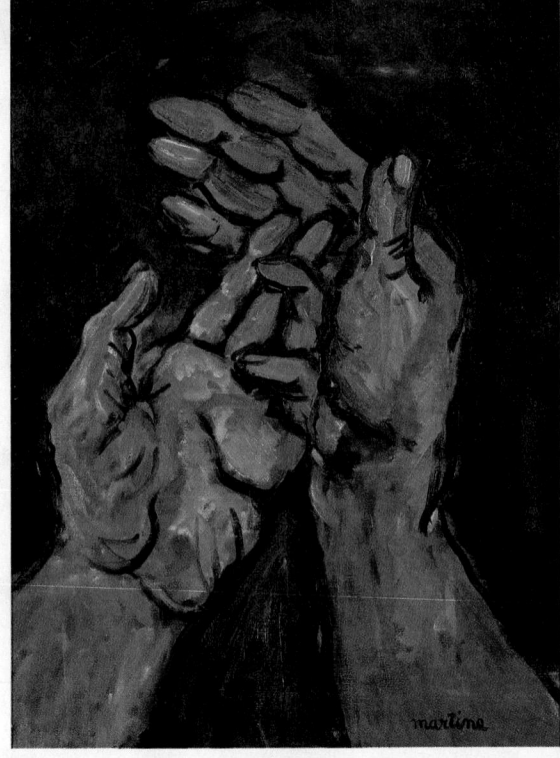

Vigour, Martine Levy. Musée d'Art Moderne, Troyes, France. Photo © Gerard Blot/ Réunion des Musées Nationaux/Art Resource, New York.

Sundays too my father got up early
and put his clothes on in the blueblack cold,
then with cracked hands that ached
from labor in the weekday weather made
5 banked fires blaze. No one ever thanked him.

I'd wake and hear the cold splintering, breaking.
When the rooms were warm, he'd call,
and slowly I would rise and dress,
fearing the chronic angers of that house, **C**

10 Speaking indifferently to him,
who had driven out the cold
and polished my good shoes as well.
What did I know, what did I know
of love's austere and lonely offices?

C MAKE INFERENCES
What can you infer about the **speaker's** attitude toward his family from clues in lines 1–9? Which details did you use to make this inference?

DIFFERENTIATED INSTRUCTION

FOR STRUGGLING READERS

Verb Tenses Focus on the verb tenses in the poem. Point out the use of the past tense in stanza 1 and the habitual past with *would* in stanza 2. Have students create sentences using the habitual past with *would*, asking and answering such questions as "What would you do on weekends when you were small?"

FOR ADVANCED LEARNERS/PRE–AP

Repetition Point out that Hayden repeats certain consonants throughout the poem. Ask students to identify these consonants and their frequency. How does this device contribute to the mood of the poem? What other repetition does the poet use? What effect does it have?

Comprehension

1. **Recall** What two incidents are described in "The Gift"?

2. **Recall** What does the speaker recall his father doing in "Those Winter Sundays"?

3. **Summarize** How does each speaker react to his father's act of caring?

COMMON CORE

RL 1 Cite strong and thorough textual evidence to support inferences drawn from the text. **RL 10** Read and comprehend poems.

Text Analysis

4. **Examine Characters in Poetry** Fill in a chart like the one shown with details that suggest the traits of the father in each poem. Then write a sentence describing each of these characters.

Father's Traits	"The Gift"	"Those Winter Sundays"
Physical traits		
Personality traits		

5. **Analyze Title** Why might Li-Young Lee have chosen to call his poem "The Gift"?

6. **Interpret** Reread the last two lines of "Those Winter Sundays." What does the speaker mean when he refers to "love's austere and lonely offices"?

7. **Make Inferences** Review the charts you created as you read. Based on your inferences, how would you characterize the father-son relationship in each poem?

8. **Compare and Contrast Speakers** Compare and contrast the attitudes of the speakers toward the experiences they describe in the poems.

9. **Analyze Author's Perspective** Both of the speakers are adults who look back on experiences from their childhood. How does this perspective influence the way each speaker views his experience?

Text Criticism

10. **Critical Interpretations** The poet Gerald Stern has spoken of "the large vision, the deep seriousness and the almost heroic ideal" in Li-Young Lee's poetry. How well does this phrase describe Lee's poem "The Gift"? Cite evidence from the text to support your opinion.

How do you show you CARE?

How could you show your feelings for someone who took care of you in childhood?

---

8. *The attitude of both speakers is grateful; but in "Those Winter Sundays" it is tinged with loss and regret.*

9. *As adults, both speakers have a deeper appreciation of their fathers. In "Those Winter Sundays," the speaker has come to understand the distance between him and his father.*

Text Criticism

10. *The father is described in heroic terms, as tender but strong. The act of removing a splinter is treated with the seriousness of a noble deed, supported by religious imagery.*

How do you show you CARE?

Students might first think about the caring their parents, teachers, or other special people showed them in childhood before they answer.

Practice and Apply

For preliminary support of post-reading questions, use these copy masters:

R RESOURCE MANAGER—Copy Masters
Characters in Poetry p. 127
Question Support p. 131

Additional selection questions are provided for teachers on page 123.

ANSWERS

Comprehension

1. *The speaker describes his father removing a splinter from his hand and himself taking a splinter out of his wife's hand.*

2. *He recalls his father getting up early on Sundays, dressing, making a fire, and polishing the speaker's shoes.*

3. *"The Gift": speaker kisses his father as child, expresses gratitude as adult; "Those Winter Sundays": speaker shows indifference as child, regret as adult*

Text Analysis

COMMON CORE RL 1, RL 10

Possible answers:

4. ● **COMMON CORE FOCUS** *Examine Characters in Poetry "The Gift":* Physical: lovely face, tender hand. Personality: caring, kind. The speaker's kind father provided a strong, supportive presence. *"Those Winter Sundays":* Physical: cracked hands; Personality: loving, undemonstrative. Though not affectionate, the speaker's father worked hard.

5. *His father gave him the gift of kindness, love, and reliability.*

6. *Love may involve thankless self-sacrifice.*

7. ● **COMMON CORE FOCUS** *Make Inferences "The Gift":* affectionate, appreciative, reciprocal; *"Those Winter Sundays":* restrained, regretful, distant

Assess and Reteach

Assess

DIAGNOSTIC AND SELECTION TESTS
Selection Test A pp. 79–80
Selection Test B/C pp. 81–82

Interactive Selection Test on **thinkcentral.com**

Reteach

Level Up Online Tutorials on **thinkcentral.com**

Reteaching Worksheets on **thinkcentral.com**
Literature Lesson 1, Reading Lesson 8

Focus and Motivate

COMMON CORE FOCUS

RL 3 Analyze how complex characters develop, interact with others, and advance the plot or develop the theme. **RL 4** Determine the connotative and figurative meaning of words and phrases. **RL 10** Read and comprehend dramas. **L 3** Apply knowledge of language to make effective choices for meaning or style. **L 4c** Consult reference materials to determine or clarify a word's etymology.

SUMMARY

In *A Marriage Proposal,* Lomov asks his neighbor Tschubukov for permission to marry Natalia, Tschubukov's daughter. Tschubukov agrees, but then the men quarrel. Exasperated, Tschubukov announces that Lomov and Natalia are engaged.

Why do people argue over SILLY THINGS?

Introduce the question. Invite volunteers to describe conflicts that resulted from pettiness. Allow students to use these scenarios for the *ROLE-PLAY* activity.

Selection Resources

Essential Course of Study **ECOS**

A Marriage Proposal
Drama by Anton Chekhov

Why do people argue over SILLY THINGS?

COMMON CORE

RL 3 Analyze how complex characters develop, interact with others, and advance the plot or develop the theme. **RL 4** Determine the connotative and figurative meaning of words and phrases. **RL 10** Read and comprehend dramas.

When two stubborn people have different opinions about something unimportant, a silly argument is likely to erupt. Such pettiness is displayed by the characters in *A Marriage Proposal,* who can't seem to agree on anything, even when they share the same goal.

ROLE-PLAY With a partner, brainstorm a scenario in which you have a difference of opinion about something of little importance. Then role-play an argument. Afterward, discuss any patterns that you noticed during the argument.

---

*See resources on the **Teacher One Stop DVD-ROM** and on **thinkcentral.com**.*

R **RESOURCE MANAGER UNIT 2**
Plan and Teach, pp. 133–140
Summary, pp. 141–142†‡*
Text Analysis and Reading
Skill, pp. 143–146†*
Vocabulary, pp. 147–149*
Grammar and Style, p. 152

DIAGNOSTIC AND SELECTION TESTS
Selection Tests, pp. 83–86

BEST PRACTICES TOOLKIT
New Word Analysis, p. E8
Core Analysis Frame: Drama,
pp. D21, D42
Character Traits Web, p. D7

INTERACTIVE READER

ADAPTED INTERACTIVE READER

ELL ADAPTED INTERACTIVE READER

TECHNOLOGY
- Teacher One Stop DVD-ROM
- Student One Stop DVD-ROM
- PowerNotes DVD-ROM
- Audio Anthology CD
- GrammarNotes DVD-ROM
- Audio Tutor CD
- ExamView Test Generator on the **Teacher One Stop**

THINK central

Find it Online!

Features on **thinkcentral.com** that support the selection include
- **PowerNotes** presentation
- **ThinkAloud** models to enhance comprehension
- **WordSharp** vocabulary tutorials
- interactive writing and grammar instruction

---

* Resources for Differentiation   † Also in Spanish   ‡ Also in Haitian Creole and Vietnamese

TEXT ANALYSIS: CHARACTERS IN A FARCE

A **farce** is a humorous play that includes ridiculous situations and dialogue. Characters in a farce are usually comical stereotypes who conform to a fixed pattern or are defined by a single trait. Notice in this speech from *A Marriage Proposal* how a character's trait is exaggerated for comic effect:

I have a weak heart, continual palpitation, and I am very sensitive and always getting excited.

As you read the play, create a chart for each character. Record details that help you identify the character's main trait or pattern of behavior.

weak heart — | Lomov's trait or pattern | — very sensitive

READING SKILL: READING A PLAY

To understand a play, you will need to read **stage directions** that describe the scenery and props, the actions of characters, or the tone in which dialogue should be delivered. Sometimes a stage direction will indicate one of the following:

- an **aside**—a short speech directed to the audience or a character but not heard by the other characters onstage
- a **monologue**—a long speech that is usually delivered by a character who is alone onstage

Asides and monologues can be used to reveal a character's private thoughts and feelings. As you read *A Marriage Proposal*, notice what each stage direction tells you about the characters.

▲ VOCABULARY IN CONTEXT

Complete each sentence with a word from the list. Then, in your *Reader/Writer Notebook*, write a brief definition of each word that is familiar to you.

WORD LIST	contrary	glutton	meditate	usurper

1. The scheming _____ tried to seize the king's throne.
2. I need to _____ on this issue awhile before deciding.
3. You insist on being _____ just to be different.
4. Please don't be a _____ at the dinner table.

 Complete the activities in your **Reader/Writer Notebook**.

Meet the Author

Anton Chekhov
1860–1904

Literary Detour
Anton Chekhov (chĕk'ôf) was a master of the short story as well as one of the most important modern playwrights. Born in southern Russia, he moved to Moscow as a young man and planned to become a doctor. While in medical school, he published many literary sketches to support his family. Although he received his medical degree in 1884, he never practiced medicine on a regular basis. Instead, he chose to pursue a writing career.

Early Success
Chekhov quickly won fame for his comical stories and farces, such as *A Marriage Proposal*. He considered humor to be an essential ingredient in all his work, but his writing grew more serious over time. Most of his full-length plays, including *Uncle Vanya*, *The Three Sisters*, and *The Cherry Orchard*, combine elements of tragedy and farce. Chekhov died from tuberculosis at age 44, when he was at the height of his career.

BACKGROUND TO THE PLAY

The Russian Gentry
A Marriage Proposal takes place on a country estate in late-19th-century Russia. The characters are members of the privileged class known as the gentry. These wealthy landowners employed peasants to work their fields, which allowed them to enjoy a life of leisure. Writers of farces often poked fun at the habits of the gentry, including their tendency to marry for economic gain rather than affection.

Author Online **THINK** central
Go to **thinkcentral.com**.
KEYWORD: HML10-259

259

Teach

TEXT ANALYSIS — COMMON CORE — RL 3

● *Model the Skill:*
CHARACTERS IN A FARCE

To model how to identify characters in a farce, read aloud this statement:

I am not argumentative. I only like to tell people when they are wrong, and most people usually are wrong.

Point out that the statement tells readers that the character is self-righteous, vain, and/or a perfectionist.

GUIDED PRACTICE Have students create a sentence that humorously characterizes an imaginary person.

R **RESOURCE MANAGER**—Copy Master
Characters in a Farce p. 143 (for student use while reading the selection)

READING SKILL — COMMON CORE — RL 10

■ *Model the Skill:* **READING A PLAY**

To model reading a play, read aloud this example, including the stage directions:

John *(rolling his eyes).* Yes, Pat, your idea is the best one I've heard yet.

Explain what the stage directions suggest about John's private thoughts. Tell students that rolling the eyes suggests that John doesn't want to talk to Pat or that he does not think that Pat's idea is good.

GUIDED PRACTICE Have students experiment with changing the stage directions to show that John likes Pat's idea.

VOCABULARY SKILL

▲ VOCABULARY IN CONTEXT

DIAGNOSE WORD KNOWLEDGE Have all students complete Vocabulary in Context. Check their answers against the following:

contrary (kŏn'trĕr'ē) *adj.* stubbornly uncooperative or contradictory
glutton (glŭt'n) *n.* a person who eats too much
meditate (mĕd'ĭ-tāt') *v.* to consider for a long time
usurper (yōō-sûrp'ər) *n.* someone who wrongfully takes possession of something

PRETEACH VOCABULARY Use the following copy master to help students predict the meaning of each boldfaced word.

R **RESOURCE MANAGER**—Copy Master
Vocabulary Study p. 147

1. Read item 1 aloud, emphasizing *contrary*.
2. Point out the word *disagreed*. Elicit possible meanings for *contrary*, such as "argumentative."

3. Have students fill in the chart.
4. Repeat the procedure for items 2–4.

READ WITH A PURPOSE

Help students set a purpose for reading. Tell them to look for places where the actors could use physical comedy to add to the humor.

A READING A PLAY

Possible answer: The details "reception room" and "country home in Russia" in the stage directions help readers visualize the setting of the play.

A Marriage
PROPOSAL

ANTON CHEKHOV

CHARACTERS

Stepan Stepanovitch Tschubukov (styĭ-pän' styĭ-pän'əv-yĭch chü-bü'kəf), a country farmer

Natalia Stepanovna (nə-täl'yə styĭ-pä-nôv'nə), his daughter (aged 25)

Ivan Vassiliyitch Lomov (ĭ-vän' vəs-yēl'yĭch lô'məf), Tschubukov's neighbor

SCENE

The reception room in Tschubukov's country home in Russia. Tschubukov discovered as the curtain rises. Enter Lomov, wearing a dress suit. **A**

TIME

The present [1890s]

A READING A PLAY
What information in the **stage directions** helps you visualize the **setting** of the play?

Tschubukov (*going toward him and greeting him*). Who is this I see? My dear fellow! Ivan Vassiliyitch! I'm so glad to see you! (*shakes hands*) But this is a surprise! How are you?

Lomov. Thank you! And how are you?

Tschubukov. Oh, so-so, my friend. Please sit down. It isn't right to forget one's neighbor. But tell me, why all this ceremony? Dress clothes, white gloves, and all? Are you on your way to some engagement, my good fellow?

Lomov. No, I have no engagement except with you, Stepan Stepanovitch.

Tschubukov. But why in evening clothes, my friend? This isn't New Year's!

1 Targeted Passage

Analyze Visuals ▶

What **mood** is suggested by this painting?

The Promenade (1917), Marc Chagall. Oil on canvas. Russian State Museum, St. Petersburg, Russia. Photo © Scala/Art Resource, New York. ©2008 Artists Rights Society (ARS), New York/ADAGP, Paris.

260 UNIT 2: CHARACTER DEVELOPMENT

DIFFERENTIATED INSTRUCTION

FOR ENGLISH LANGUAGE LEARNERS

Options for Reading Have students listen to *A Marriage Proposal* on the *Audio Anthology* CD. Then have small groups reread aloud different targeted sections of the play. Assign each student to a role.

FOR STRUGGLING READERS

In combination with the *Audio Anthology CD*, use one or more Targeted Passages (pp. 260, 265, 268, 272) to ensure that students focus on key events, concepts, and skills. Targeted Passages are also good for English learners.

1 Targeted Passage [Lines 1–9]

This passage introduces the play's two male characters. It hints at Lomov's reason for visiting Tschubukov but also begins to explore the characters' personalities.

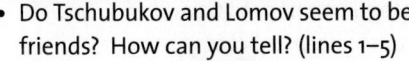

Reading Support

This selection on **thinkcentral.com** includes embedded **ThinkAloud** models—students "thinking aloud" about the story to model the kinds of questions a good reader would ask about a selection.

BACKGROUND

Russian Names Natalia's first and middle names are Natalia Stepanovna. Her middle name is a patronymic—a name that comes from the father's first name (Stepan Stepanovna). Her middle name takes the feminine form of her father's first name; his middle name takes the masculine form of his father's first name, which also was Stepan. Lomov's middle name indicates that his father's name is Vassily. The fact that the characters address each other by their patronymic as well as their first names indicates that they are speaking politely and formally, even though they are neighbors and have known each other for some time. (The English equivalent would be calling a neighbor "Mr.," "Mrs.," "Miss," or "Ms." and then his or her last name.) The formality points to that era's social expectations and thus helps call attention to Chekhov's farcical treatment of the gentry.

Analyze Visuals

Possible answer: *The mood suggested by this painting is a mix of dreamy surrealism, love, happiness, and humor.*

About the Art Created during the Russian Revolution of 1917, The *Promenade* is one of a series of paintings on the theme of love by Russian-born artist Marc Chagall (1887–1985). His innovative use of color and form in paintings, etchings, and even stained glass shows the artistic influence of both Russian expressionism and French cubism.

In *The Promenade*, Chagall clutches a bird in one hand while holding hands with his wife, Bella, who is flying over their town of Vitebsk. Chagall's simple color palette creates a hopeful mood. The elements in red frame the painting and draw the viewer's eye to Chagall. Bella's outstretched limbs and rippling dress may symbolize a flag, referring to Chagall's love of country.

- Do Tschubukov and Lomov seem to be friends? How can you tell? (lines 1–5)
- How is Lomov dressed? Why? (lines 6–7)
- Reread lines 7 and 8. What word, taken together with the play's title, suggests why Lomov is visiting Tschubukov?

FOR ADVANCED LEARNERS/PRE–AP

Hypothesize Have a student volunteer read the background to the play aloud. Engage the class in a discussion. Ask students: Given the background information and that the play is a farce, what do you expect from the play you are about to read? Point out that Chekhov wrote and set the play in the late 19th century. Ask students if they think humor from so long ago will still prove amusing to them and why or why not. Ask student what elements they think have helped this work to endure.

B Model the Skill:
READING A PLAY

Read aloud lines 10–16.

1. Tell students that the author gives a clue to Tschubukov's opinion of Lomov in Lomov's speech. Point out that in lines 11–12, Lomov says that he is again "turning to you [Tschubukov] for assistance."

2. Tell students that Tschubukov's assumption that Lomov wants money may mean that Lomov has borrowed money or other things from him in the past.

Possible answer: Tschubukov's aside shows that he is not quite as fond of Lomov as he appears to be. He says that he won't let Lomov borrow money from him, so he either does not trust Lomov or does not like him as much as he pretends.

Analyze Visuals

About the Art *The Window at the Country House* is another captivating painting by Marc Chagall. (See page 261.)

Activity How does the scene in this painting seem similar to the setting of the play? *Possible answer: The lush trees and grass suggest that this is a country house, and the play is set at a country house. The people at the table look serious and civilized, as Lomov and Tschubukov seem to be.*

---

10 **Lomov.** You see, it's simply this, that— (*composing himself*) I have come to you, Stepan Stepanovitch, to trouble you with a request. It is not the first time I have had the honor of turning to you for assistance, and you have always, that is—I beg your pardon, I am a bit excited! I'll take a drink of water first, dear Stepan Stepanovitch. (*He drinks.*)

Tschubukov (*aside*). He's come to borrow money! I won't give him any! (*to* Lomov) What is it, then, dear Lomov? **B**

Lomov. You see—dear—Stepanovitch, pardon me, Stepan—Stepan—dearvitch—I mean—I am terribly nervous, as you will be so good as to see—! What I mean to say—you are the only one who can help me, though I don't 20 deserve it, and—and I have no right whatever to make this request of you.

Tschubukov. Oh, don't beat about the bush, my dear fellow. Tell me!

Lomov. Immediately—in a moment. Here it is, then: I have come to ask for the hand of your daughter, Natalia Stepanovna.

B READING A PLAY
What does Tschubukov's **aside** reveal about him?

The Window at the Country House (1915), Marc Chagall. Tretyakov Gallery, Moscow, Russia. Photo © Scala/Art Resource, New York. © 2008 Artists Rights Society (ARS), New York/ADAGP, Paris.

262 UNIT 2: CHARACTER DEVELOPMENT

DIFFERENTIATED INSTRUCTION

FOR ENGLISH LANGUAGE LEARNERS
Language: Punctuation and Print Cues Point out the stage directions in lines 1, 2, and 10, explaining that the stage directions always will appear in italic type and within parentheses. Discuss the purpose for each stage direction thus far. For example, the stage direction "(*composing himself*)" (line 10) shows that Lomov is nervous but is trying to calm down so that Tschubukov will take him seriously. Also point out the appearance of dashes in the dialogue on pages 262 and 263. Explain that a dash often indicates that one character interrupts while another is speaking, as Tschubukov does to Lomov at the end of line 26. Dashes also can indicate that a character is struggling to speak, as Lomov does when he tries to find the words to explain his visit in lines 17–20.

Tschubukov (*joyfully*). Angel! Ivan Vassiliyitch! Say that once again! I didn't quite hear it!

Lomov. I have the honor to beg—

Tschubukov (*interrupting*). My dear, dear man. I am so happy that everything is so—everything! (*embraces and kisses him*) I have wanted this to happen for so

30 long. It has been my dearest wish! (*He represses a tear.*) And I have always loved you, my dear fellow, as my own son! May God give you his blessings and his grace and—I always wanted it to happen. But why am I standing here like a blockhead? I am completely dumbfounded with pleasure, completely dumbfounded. My whole being—! I'll call Natalia—

Lomov. Dear Stepan Stepanovitch, what do you think? May I hope for Natalia Stepanovna's acceptance?

Tschubukov. Really! A fine boy like you— and you think she won't accept on the minute? Lovesick as a cat and all that—! (*He goes out, right.*)

Lomov. I'm cold. My whole body is trembling as though I was going to take my examination! But the chief thing is to settle matters! If a person **meditates**

40 too much, or hesitates, or talks about it, waits for an ideal or for true love, he never gets it. Brrr! It's cold! Natalia is an excellent housekeeper, not at all bad looking, well educated—what more could I ask? I'm so excited my ears are roaring! (*He drinks water.*) And not to marry, that won't do! In the first place, I'm thirty-five—a critical age, you might say. In the second place, I must live a well-regulated life. I have a weak heart, continual palpitation, and I am very sensitive and always getting excited. My lips begin to tremble and the pulse in my right temple throbs terribly. But the worst of all is sleep! I hardly lie down and begin to doze before something in my left side begins to pull and tug, and something begins to hammer in my left shoulder—and in my head, too! I

50 jump up like a madman, walk about a little, lie down again, but the moment I fall asleep I have a terrible cramp in the side. And so it is all night long! (*Enter Natalia Stepanovna.*) **C**

Natalia. Ah! It's you. Papa said to go in: there was a dealer in there who'd come to buy something. Good afternoon, Ivan Vassiliyitch.

Lomov. Good day, my dear Natalia Stepanovna.

Natalia. You must pardon me for wearing my apron and this old dress: we are working today. Why haven't you come to see us oftener? You've not been here for so long! Sit down (*They sit down.*) Won't you have something to eat?

Lomov. Thank you, I have just had lunch.

60 **Natalia.** Smoke, do, there are the matches. Today it is beautiful, and only yesterday it rained so hard that the workmen couldn't do a stroke of work. How many bricks have you cut? Think of it! I was so anxious that I had the whole field mowed, and now I'm sorry I did it, because I'm afraid the hay will rot. It would have been better if I had waited. But what on earth is this? You are in evening clothes! The latest cut! Are you on your way to a ball? And you seem to be looking better, too—really. Why are you dressed up so gorgeously? **D**

meditate (mĕd'ĭ-tāt') *v.* to consider for a long time

C CHARACTERS IN A FARCE
What main trait does Lomov exhibit in his **monologue**?

D GRAMMAR AND STYLE
Reread lines 60–66. Chekhov uses **declarative, interrogative, imperative,** and **exclamatory** sentences to reflect Natalia's scattered thoughts.

A MARRIAGE PROPOSAL **263**

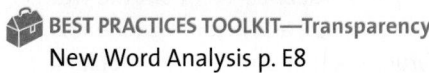
Vocabulary: Phrasal Verbs Explain that *dressed up* (line 66) means "wearing one's best clothes," whereas *dressed down* means "dressed casually" (or "scolded"). Have pairs of students use a dictionary to find the definitions of the phrasal verbs *give up* (line 169), *figure out* (lines 277–278), and *keep on* (line 285).

Direct students to lines 38–46. Use these prompts to help students explore Lomov's character:

Connect Have you or someone you know ever been nervous about asking for a favor? *Accept all reasonable responses.*

Analyze How does Lomov feel at this moment? *Possible answer: Lomov feels terrified. He is worried about rejection, but he feels driven to act (line 39).*

Evaluate What do you think of Lomov's decision to marry? Explain. *Possible answer: Lomov is making a poor decision because he is marrying not for love but because of social pressure (lines 43–44) and the wish to have someone take care of him (lines 41 and 44–45). Lomov never says that he loves Natalia; in fact, he rejects the idea of waiting for true love (lines 40–41).*

TEXT ANALYSIS | COMMON CORE RL 3

C CHARACTERS IN A FARCE

Possible answer: Lomov is nervous and is a bit of a hypochondriac. In this passage, he lists several real or imagined ailments.

D GRAMMAR AND STYLE | COMMON CORE L 3

Vary Sentence Types Have students identify the four sentence types in lines 60–66. Discuss the thoughts and emotions suggested in an example of each type.

VOCABULARY | COMMON CORE L 4

OWN THE WORD

meditate: Ask students: According to Lomov, on what might a person *meditate* too long? *Possible answer: on how they feel about Natalia*

A MARRIAGE PROPOSAL **263**

Why do people argue over
SILLY THINGS?

Discuss In lines 79–90, how does pettiness turn the beginning of a marriage proposal into an argument? Why would this moment strike the audience as ridiculous? ***Possible answer:*** *When Lomov mentions "my meadow" (line 77) at the beginning of his proposal, Natalia interrupts her suitor to challenge his ownership of the land. Lomov responds by defending his claim. The conversation quickly escalates into an argument because neither person can prove their position and neither will give in. This moment probably would strike the audience as ridiculous because the audience has just seen Lomov work up the courage to propose, only to allow himself to become sidetracked instead of saying what he has come to say.*

Lomov (*excited*). You see, my dear Natalia Stepanovna—it's simply this: I have decided to ask you to listen to me—of course it will be a surprise, and indeed you'll be angry, but!— (*aside*) How fearfully cold it is!

70 **Natalia.** What is it? (*a pause*) Well?

Lomov. I'll try to be brief. My dear Natalia Stepanovna, as you know, for many years, since my childhood, I have had the honor to know your family. My poor aunt and her husband, from whom, as you know, I inherited the estate, always had the greatest respect for your father and your poor mother. The Lomovs and the Tschubukovs have been for decades on the friendliest, indeed the closest, terms with each other, and furthermore my property, as you know, adjoins your own. If you will be so good as to remember, my meadows touch your birch woods.

Natalia. Pardon the interruption. You said "my meadows"—but are they yours?

80 **Lomov.** Yes, they belong to me.

Natalia. What nonsense! The meadows belong to us—not to you!

Lomov. No, to me! Now, my dear Natalia Stepanovna!

Natalia. Well, that is certainly news to me. How do they belong to you?

Lomov. How? I am speaking of the meadows lying between your birch woods and my brick earth.[1]

Natalia. Yes, exactly. They belong to us.

Lomov. No, you are mistaken, my dear Natalia Stepanovna, they belong to me.

Natalia. Try to remember exactly, Ivan Vassiliyitch. Is it so long ago that you inherited them?

90 **Lomov.** Long ago! As far back as I can remember they have always belonged to us.

Natalia. But that isn't true! You'll pardon my saying so.

Lomov. It is all a matter of record, my dear Natalia Stepanovna. It is true that at one time the title to the meadows was disputed, but now everyone knows they belong to me. There is no room for discussion. Be so good as to listen: my aunt's grandmother put these meadows, free from all costs, into the hands of your father's grandfather's peasants for a certain time while they were making bricks for my grandmother. These people used the meadows free of cost for about forty years, living there as they would on their own property. Later, however, when—

100 **Natalia.** There's not a word of truth in that! My grandfather, and my great grandfather, too, knew that their estate reached back to the swamp, so that the meadows belong to us. What further discussion can there be? I can't understand it. It is really most annoying.

Lomov. I'll show you the papers, Natalia Stepanovna.

Natalia. No, either you are joking or trying to lead me into a discussion. That's not at all nice! We have owned this property for nearly three hundred years, and

---

1. **brick earth:** clay suitable for making bricks.

Language Coach

Denotation/ Connotation Many words have positive or negative associations **(connotations)**. Reread lines 92–94. Does *dispute* or *discussion* have a more negative connotation? What denotation do they share?

DIFFERENTIATED INSTRUCTION

FOR STRUGGLING READERS

Comprehension Support As you reread lines 84–85, point out to students that "meadows," "birch woods," and "brick earth" are land. In other words, Natalia and Lomov are arguing about who owns certain nearby land. Have students discuss why they think the question of who owns the land would be so important to the characters.

FOR ENGLISH LANGUAGE LEARNERS

Language Coach   COMMON CORE
                                       RL 4
Denotation/Connotation
Answer: *Disputed is more negative. Both words involve debate.* Point out the words *swamp* (line 101) and *meadows* (line 102). Tell students that both are types of land. Ask students which word they think holds the more negative connotation.

now all at once we hear that it doesn't belong to us. Ivan Vassiliyitch, you will pardon me, but I really can't believe my ears. So far as I'm concerned, the meadows are worth very little. In all they don't contain more than five acres,
110 and they are worth only a few hundred rubles,[2] say three hundred, but the injustice of the thing is what affects me. Say what you will, I can't bear injustice.

Lomov. Only listen until I have finished, please! The peasants of your respected father's grandfather, as I have already had the honor to tell you, baked bricks for my grandmother. My aunt's grandmother wished to do them a favor—

Natalia. Grandfather! Grandmother! Aunt! I know nothing of them. All I know is that the meadows belong to us, and that ends the matter.

Lomov. No, they belong to me!

Natalia. And if you keep on explaining it for two days and put on five suits of evening clothes, the meadows are still ours, ours, ours! I don't want to take
120 your property, but I refuse to give up what belongs to us! **E**

Lomov. Natalia Stepanovna, I don't need the meadows, I am only concerned with the principle. If you are agreeable, I beg of you, accept them as a gift from me!

Natalia. But I can give them to you, because they belong to me! That is very peculiar, Ivan Vassiliyitch! Until now we have considered you as a good neighbor and a good friend; only last year we lent you our threshing machine so that we couldn't thresh until November, and you treat us like thieves! You offer to give me my own land. Excuse me, but neighbors don't treat each other that way. In my opinion, it's a very low trick—to speak frankly—

130 **Lomov.** According to you I'm a **usurper**, then, am I? My dear lady, I have never appropriated other people's property, and I shall permit no one to accuse me of such a thing! (*He goes quickly to the bottle and drinks water.*) The meadows are mine!

Natalia. That's not the truth! They are mine!

Lomov. Mine!

Natalia. Eh? I'll prove it to you! This afternoon I'll send my reapers into the meadows.

Lomov. W—h—a—t?

Natalia. My reapers will be there today!

140 **Lomov.** And I'll chase them off!

Natalia. If you dare!

Lomov. The meadows are mine, you understand? Mine!

Natalia. Really, you don't need to scream so! If you want to scream and snort and rage you may do it at home, but here please keep yourself within the limits of common decency.

Woman Reaping (before 1930), Marc Chagall. National Gallery, Prague, Czech Republic. Photo © Nimatallah/Art Resource, New York. © 2008 Artists Rights Society (ARS), New York/ADAGP, Paris.

---

2. **rubles** (rōō'bəlz): units of Russian money.

② Targeted Passage

E CHARACTERS IN A FARCE
Reread lines 104–120. What pattern of behavior appears evident in Natalia's responses to Lomov's claims?

usurper (yōō-sûrp'ər) *n.* someone who wrongfully takes possession of something

---

E *Model the Skill:*
CHARACTERS IN A FARCE

Model for students how to identify characters in a farce. After students reread lines 104–120, remind students that characters in a farce are usually comical stereotypes who conform to a fixed pattern or are defined by a single trait. Have students record details about Natalia's behavior in their Character Trait charts to help them answer the question.

Possible answer: *Natalia seems unbending. She is unwilling to admit to any claim of Lomov's, and she refuses to give up what she insists belongs to her family (lines 119–120).*

Analyze Visuals

About the Art *Woman Reaping* exhibits the use of strong color that is characteristic of many paintings by Marc Chagall. (See page 261.)

Activity How does this painting relate to the argument between Lomov and Natalia? ***Possible answer:*** *Natalia says that she will send her reapers into the meadows to prove that the meadows are hers (lines 136–137). The woman in this painting appears to be reaping a field or meadow.*

OWN THE WORD

usurper: Have students complete this sentence: Lomov says that Natalia accuses him of being a *usurper* because . . . ***Possible answer:*** . . . *Lomov claims the meadows for himself, while Natalia says they belong to her.*

FOR STRUGGLING READERS

② Targeted Passage [Lines 115–129]

This passage illustrates the content and silliness of Lomov and Natalia's argument.

• What is Lomov concerned about? What does he mean? (lines 121–122)

• What does Natalia call "peculiar"? What does she mean? (lines 124–125)

• Why does their talk about a "gift" sound foolish? (lines 122–128)

FOR ENGLISH LANGUAGE LEARNERS

Vocabulary: Multiple-Meaning Words Have students use a dictionary to find the meaning of each word that is correct for its context: *poor* (line 72), *terms* (line 76), *record* (line 92), *room* (line 94), *bear* (line 111), *low* (line 129), *common* (line 147). To check students' understanding, ask them to write a sentence that illustrates the correct meaning for the context and a sentence that illustrates another meaning of each word.

Analyze Visuals

Possible answer: *Natalia and Lomov are arguing over who owns some meadows. In this painting, people—perhaps peasants, such as those whom Lomov refers to in lines 158–160—are working on land that could be described as "meadows."*

About the Art Russian artist and theatrical designer Natalia Goncharova (1881–1962) painted *The Harvest*. She was one of the leaders of the Russian avant-garde. Although this scene of simple people working the land reveals her interest in neo-primitivism, Goncharova also is remembered for her paintings in the gritty, technological futurist style.

REVISIT THE BIG QUESTION

Why do people argue over SILLY THINGS?

Discuss In lines 153–165, does Tschubukov recognize that Lomov and Natalia are having a petty argument? Explain. *Possible answer: No; Tschubukov recognizes that an argument is going on, but he does not consider it petty. In fact, he enters into the argument himself, defending his daughter's claim that they own the meadows.*

The Harvest, Natalia Goncharova. Russian State Museum, St. Petersburg, Russia. Photo © Scala/Art Resource, New York. © 2008 Artists Rights Society (ARS), New York/ADAGP, Paris.

◀ **Analyze Visuals**
Which details in this painting suggest activities or locations that are discussed in the play?

Lomov. My dear lady, if it weren't that I were suffering from palpitation of the heart and hammering of the arteries in my temples, I would deal with you very
150 differently! (*in a loud voice*) The meadows belong to me!

Natalia. Us!

Lomov. Me! (*Enter* Tschubukov, *right.*)

Tschubukov. What's going on here? What is he yelling about?

Natalia. Papa, please tell this gentleman to whom the meadows belong, to us or to him?

Tschubukov (*to* Lomov). My dear fellow, the meadows are ours.

Lomov. But, merciful heavens, Stepan Stepanovitch, how do you make that out? You at least must be reasonable. My aunt's grandmother gave the use of the meadows free of cost to your grandfather's peasants; the peasants lived on
160 the land for forty years and used it as their own, but later when—

Tschubukov. Permit me, my dear friend. You forget that your grandfather's peasants never paid, because there had been a lawsuit over the meadows, and everyone knows that the meadows belong to us. You haven't looked at the map.

Lomov. I'll prove to you that they belong to me!

Tschubukov. Don't try to prove it, my dear fellow.

Lomov. I will!

DIFFERENTIATED INSTRUCTION

FOR ENGLISH LANGUAGE LEARNERS

Vocabulary: Idioms Write these idioms on the board and discuss their meanings: *beat about the bush* (line 21), "avoid giving a direct answer"; *deal with* (line 149), "respond to"; *darken my door* (line 209), "come to see me" (in an unwelcome way); *drop the subject* (line 336), "stop talking about it."

FOR ADVANCED LEARNERS/PRE–AP

Analyze Drama Have small groups of students discuss the questions on the Core Analysis Frame: Drama worksheet, using textual evidence to support their answers. Explain that students will have to wait to answer some of the plot, theme, writer's craft, and evaluate and critique questions until they have finished reading the play.

 BEST PRACTICES TOOLKIT—Transparency
Core Analysis Frame: Drama pp. D21, D42

Tschubukov. My good fellow, what are you shrieking about? You can't prove anything by yelling, you know. I don't ask for anything that belongs to you, nor do I intend to give up anything of my own. Why should I? If it has gone so far, my dear man, that you really intend to claim the meadows, I'd rather give them to the peasants than you, and I certainly shall!

Lomov. I can't believe it! By what right can you give away property that doesn't belong to you?

Tschubukov. Really, you must allow me to decide what I am to do with my own land! I'm not accustomed, young man, to have people address me in that tone of voice. I, young man, am twice your age, and I beg you to address me respectfully.

Lomov. No! No! You think I'm a fool! You're making fun of me! You call my property yours and then you expect me to stand quietly by and talk to you like a human being. That isn't the way a good neighbor behaves, Stepan Stepanovitch! You are no neighbor, you're no better than a land grabber. That's what you are!

Tschubukov. Wh—at? What did he say?

Natalia. Papa, send the reapers into the meadows this minute!

Tschubukov (*to* Lomov). What was that you said, sir?

Natalia. The meadows belong to us, and I won't give them up! I won't give them up! I won't give them up!

Lomov. We'll see about that! I'll prove in court that they belong to me.

Tschubukov. In court! You may sue in court, sir, if you like! Oh, I know you, you are only waiting to find an excuse to go to law! You're an intriguer,[3] that's what you are! Your whole family were always looking for quarrels. The whole lot!

Lomov. Kindly refrain from insulting my family. The entire race of Lomov has always been honorable! And never has one been brought to trial for embezzlement, as your dear uncle was!

Tschubukov. And the whole Lomov family were insane!

Natalia. Every one of them!

Tschubukov. Your grandmother was a dipsomaniac,[4] and the younger aunt, Nastasia Michailovna, ran off with an architect. 🄵

Lomov. And your mother limped. (*He puts his hand over his heart.*) Oh, my side pains! My temples are bursting! Lord in heaven! Water!!

Tschubukov. And your dear father was a gambler—and a **glutton**!

Natalia. And your aunt was a gossip like few others.

Lomov. And you are an intriguer. Oh, my heart! And it's an open secret that you cheated at the elections—my eyes are blurred! Where is my hat?

Natalia. Oh, how low! Liar! Disgusting thing!

---

3. **intriguer** (ĭn-trē′gər): a schemer.
4. **dipsomaniac** (dĭp′sə-mā′nē-ăk′): an alcoholic.

🄵 **CHARACTERS IN A FARCE**
Reread lines 189–198. How does Chekhov use exaggeration to create humor in this exchange of dialogue?

glutton (glŭt′n) *n.* a person who eats too much

Lomov. Where's my hat? My heart! Where shall I go? Where is the door? Oh—it seems—as though I were dying! I can't—my legs won't hold me— (*goes to the door*)

Tschubukov (*following him*). May you never darken my door again!

COMMON CORE RL 4

Language Coach

Meanings of Idioms
Groups of words that have a special meaning different from the meaning of each separate word are **idioms**. Reread line 209. If someone "darkens a door," what is that person doing, literally? What does Tschubukov really mean by this line?

210 **Natalia.** Bring your suit to court! We'll see! (*Lomov staggers out, center.*)

Tschubukov (*angrily*). The devil!

Natalia. Such a good-for-nothing! And then they talk about being good neighbors!

Tschubukov. Loafer! Scarecrow! Monster!

Natalia. A swindler like that takes over a piece of property that doesn't belong to him and then dares to argue about it!

Tschubukov. And to think that this fool dares to make a proposal of marriage!

Natalia. What? A proposal of marriage?

Tschubukov. Why, yes! He came here to make you a proposal of marriage.

220 **Natalia.** Why didn't you tell me that before?

Tschubukov. That's why he had on his evening clothes! The poor fool!

Natalia. Proposal for me? (*falls into an armchair and groans*) Bring him back! Bring him back!

Tschubukov. Bring whom back!

Natalia. Faster, faster, I'm sinking! Bring him back! (*She becomes hysterical.*)

Tschubukov. What is it? What's wrong with you? (*his hands to his head*) I'm cursed with bad luck! I'll shoot myself! I'll hang myself!

Natalia. I'm dying! Bring him back!

Tschubukov. Bah! In a minute! Don't bawl! (*He rushes out, center.*)

230 **Natalia** (*groaning*). What have they done to me? Bring him back! Bring him back!

Tschubukov (*comes running in*). He's coming at once! The devil take him! Ugh! Talk to him yourself, I can't!

Natalia (*groaning*). Bring him back!

Tschubukov. He's coming, I tell you! "Oh, Lord! What a task it is to be the father of a grown daughter!" I'll cut my throat! I really will cut my throat! We've argued with the fellow, insulted him, and now you've thrown him out!—and you did it all, you!

Natalia. No, you! You haven't any manners, you are brutal! If it weren't for you, he wouldn't have gone!

240 **Tschubukov.** Oh, yes, I'm to blame! If I shoot or hang myself, remember *you'll* be to blame. You forced me to do it! (*Lomov appears in the doorway.*) There, talk to him yourself! (*He goes out.*)

Lomov. Terrible palpitation! My leg is lamed! My side hurts me—

Natalia. Pardon us, we were angry, Ivan Vassiliyitch. I remember now—the meadows really belong to you.

③ Targeted Passage

DIFFERENTIATED INSTRUCTION

FOR STRUGGLING READERS

③ Targeted Passage [Lines 210–230]

This passage establishes a change (albeit a temporary one) in Natalia's attitude.

- What do Tschubukov and Natalia say about Lomov after Lomov leaves? (lines 212–216)

- What new piece of information does Natalia learn from her father? How does she react? (line 217; lines 220–230)

- Do you think that the issue about the meadows no longer matters? Explain. (lines 215–216)

FOR ENGLISH LANGUAGE LEARNERS

Language Coach COMMON CORE RL 4

Meanings of Idioms *Answer:* *standing in a doorway, thereby blocking the light; Tschubukov means to say, "Don't ever come to my home again."* Ask students for examples of modern idioms that express the sentiment "go away." Give students one or two examples to get them started, such as "take a hike" or "get lost."

Lomov. My heart is beating terribly! My meadows—my eyelids tremble—(*They sit down.*) We were wrong. It was only the principle of the thing—the property isn't worth much to me, but the principle is worth a great deal.

Natalia. Exactly, the principle! Let us talk about something else.

250 **Lomov.** Because I have proofs that my aunt's grandmother had, with the peasants of your good father—

Natalia. Enough, enough. (*aside*) I don't know how to begin. (*to* Lomov) Are you going hunting soon?

Lomov. Yes, heath cock shooting, respected Natalia Stepanovna. I expect to begin after the harvest. Oh, did you hear? My dog, Ugadi, you know him—limps!

Natalia. What a shame! How did that happen?

Lomov. I don't know. Perhaps it's a dislocation, or maybe he was bitten by some other dog. (*He sighs.*) The best dog I ever had—to say nothing of the price! I paid Mironov a hundred and twenty-five rubles for him.

260 **Natalia.** That was too much to pay, Ivan Vassiliyitch.

Lomov. In my opinion it was very cheap. A wonderful dog!

Natalia. Papa paid eighty-five rubles for his Otkatai, and Otkatai is much better than your Ugadi!

Lomov. Really? Otkatai is better than Ugadi? What an idea! (*He laughs.*) Otkatai better than Ugadi!

Natalia. Of course he is better. It is true Otkatai is still young; he isn't full grown yet, but in the pack or on the leash with two or three, there is no better than he, even—

Lomov. I really beg your pardon, Natalia Stepanovna, but you quite overlooked
270 the fact that he has a short lower jaw, and a dog with a short lower jaw can't snap.

Natalia. Short lower jaw? That's the first I ever heard that!

Lomov. I assure you, his lower jaw is shorter than the upper.

Natalia. Have you measured it?

Lomov. I have measured it. He is good at running though.

Natalia. In the first place, our Otkatai is pure-bred, a full-blooded son of Sapragavas and Stameskis, and as for your mongrel, nobody could ever figure out his pedigree; he's old and ugly and skinny as an old hag.

Lomov. Old, certainly! I wouldn't take five of your Otkatais for him! Ugadi is a
280 dog, and Otkatai is—it is laughable to argue about it! Dogs like your Otkatai can be found by the dozens at any dog dealer's, a whole pound full!

Natalia. Ivan Vassiliyitch, you are very **contrary** today. First our meadows belong to you, and then Ugadi is better than Otkatai. I don't like it when a person doesn't say what he really thinks. You know perfectly well that Otkatai is a hundred times better than your silly Ugadi. What makes you keep on saying he isn't?

G CHARACTERS IN A FARCE
How serious is Natalia's commitment to principle?

contrary (kŏn'trĕr'ē) *adj.* stubbornly uncooperative or contradictory

A MARRIAGE PROPOSAL **269**

Language: Possessives Using apostrophes in possessive nouns can be a challenge. Offer students some practice by writing these phrases and clauses on the board, omitting the apostrophes. Discuss where and why apostrophes should, or should not, be used in the underlined words.

• *your respected <u>father's</u> grandfather* (lines 112–113)

• *other <u>people's</u> property* (line 131)

• *I have <u>proofs</u> that my <u>aunt's</u> grandmother had* (line 250)

• *<u>his</u> lower jaw* (line 273)

• *a full-blooded son of <u>Sapragavas</u> and <u>Stameskis</u>* (lines 276–277)

• *by the <u>dozens</u> at any dog <u>dealer's</u>* (line 281)

• *the <u>hunters</u> who do the most talking* (line 297)

• *in <u>Maruskins's</u> meadows* (line 316)

TEXT ANALYSIS — COMMON CORE — RL 3

G CHARACTERS IN A FARCE

Possible answer: *Natalia does not have a strong commitment to principle. She has stopped arguing only because she has learned that Lomov wants to propose.*

IF STUDENTS NEED HELP . . . Elicit that these points are clues about Natalia's commitment:

• As soon as Lomov starts speaking, Natalia apologizes to him (line 244).

• She insists that he was right about the meadows (lines 244–245).

• When he continues to defend his claim, she tries to switch him to another subject (line 249).

Extend the Discussion What is on Natalia's mind when she urges Lomov to "talk about something else" (line 249)?

REVISIT THE BIG QUESTION

Why do people argue over
SILLY THINGS?

Discuss In lines 257–268, what pettiness again distracts Natalia and Lomov? Who do you think is responsible for starting the argument?
Possible answer: *Natalia and Lomov argue about whether her father's dog is better than Lomov's dog. Natalia starts the argument when she says that Lomov paid too much for his dog (line 260).*

VOCABULARY — COMMON CORE — L 4

OWN THE WORD

contrary: Tell students that when someone is being *contrary*, he or she is being stubbornly uncooperative; the opposite of cooperative. Ask students to use both *contrary* and *uncooperative* in a sentence.

Analyze Visuals

About the Art *Dog Lying in the Snow* shows one of the most frequently painted subjects by Franz Marc (1880–1916): an animal. The German-born Marc viewed animals as innocent creatures, in harmony with nature. This painting, which suggests a simple, pure beauty in the animal, may mirror the feelings that Lomov and Natalia have about their own dogs.

Activity How does this painting relate to the argument between Natalia and Lomov? *Possible answer: The painting shows a dog, and Natalia and Lomov are arguing about which dog is better: Tschubukov's Otkatai or Lomov's Ugadi.*

TIERED DISCUSSION PROMPTS

Direct students to lines 293–310. Use these prompts to examine this new argument between Natalia and Lomov:

Connect Have you ever continued to argue about something when you knew that you should have stopped? *Accept all reasonable responses.*

Evaluate At this point, do you think that Natalia and Lomov would make a good married couple? Why or why not? *Possible answer: Natalia and Lomov would not make a good married couple because they argue constantly, even about trivial things.*

Dog Lying in the Snow (1910–1911), Franz Marc. Oil on canvas, 62.5 cm × 105 cm. Stadelsches Kunstinstitut und Stadtische Galerie, Frankfurt am Main, Germany.

Lomov. I can see, Natalia Stepanovna, that you consider me either a blind man or a fool. But at least you may as well admit that Otkatai has a short lower jaw!

Natalia. It isn't so!

290 **Lomov.** Yes, a short lower jaw!

Natalia (*loudly*). It's not so!

Lomov. What makes you scream, my dear lady?

Natalia. What makes you talk such nonsense? It's disgusting! It is high time that Ugadi was shot, and you compare him with Otkatai!

Lomov. Pardon me, but I can't carry on this argument any longer. I have palpitation of the heart!

Natalia. I have always noticed that the hunters who do the most talking know the least about hunting.

Lomov. My dear lady, I beg of you to be still. My heart is bursting! (*He shouts.*)
300 Be still!

Natalia. I won't be still until you admit that Otkatai is better! (*Enter Tschubukov.*)

Tschubukov. Well, has it begun again?

Natalia. Papa, say frankly, on your honor, which dog is better: Otkatai or Ugadi?

Lomov. Stepan Stepanovitch, I beg of you, just answer this: has your dog a short lower jaw or not? Yes or no?

Tschubukov. And what if he has? Is it of such importance? There is no better dog in the whole country.

310 **Lomov.** My Ugadi is better. Tell the truth now!

DIFFERENTIATED INSTRUCTION

FOR STRUGGLING READERS

Comprehension Support Point out that in lines 297–298, Natalia is not really talking about hunting, even though she and Lomov have been discussing dogs used in hunting. What she means is that Lomov talks the most and therefore knows the least. Discuss what prompts her to insult Lomov in this way and how he responds to the insult.

FOR RELUCTANT READERS

Connect Help students to connect with the silliness of the play. Engage the class in a discussion of arguments they have engaged in or witnessed that, in retrospect, seem silly or humorous. Encourage students to use their experiences to draw parallels to the humor of the text.

Tschubukov. Don't get so excited, my dear fellow! Permit me. Your Ugadi certainly has his good points. He is from a good breed, has a good stride, strong haunches, and so forth. But the dog, if you really want to know, has two faults; he is old and he has a short lower jaw.

Lomov. Pardon me, I have a palpitation of the heart!—Let us keep to facts— just remember in Maruskins's meadows, my Ugadi kept ear to ear with Count Rasvachai and your dog was left behind.

Tschubukov. He was behind, because the count struck him with his whip.

Lomov. Quite right. All the other dogs were on the fox's scent, but Otkatai
320 found it necessary to bite a sheep.

Tschubukov. That isn't so!—I am sensitive about that and beg you to stop this argument. He struck him because everybody looks on a strange dog of good blood with envy. Even you, sir, aren't free from sin. No sooner do you find a dog better than Ugadi than you begin to—this, that—his, mine—and so forth! I remember distinctly.

Lomov. I remember something, too!

Tschubukov (*mimicking him*). I remember something, too! What do you remember? **H**

Lomov. Palpitation! My leg is lame—I can't—

330 **Natalia.** Palpitation! What kind of hunter are you? You ought to stay in the kitchen by the stove and wrestle with the potato peelings and not go fox hunting! Palpitation!

Tschubukov. And what kind of hunter are you? A man with your disease ought to stay at home and not jolt around in the saddle. If you were a hunter! But you only ride round in order to find out about other people's dogs and make trouble for everyone. I am sensitive! Let's drop the subject. Besides, you're no hunter.

Lomov. You only ride around to flatter the count! My heart! You intriguer! Swindler!

Tschubukov. And what of it? (*shouting*) Be still!

340 **Lomov.** Intriguer!

Tschubukov. Baby! Puppy! Walking drugstore!

Lomov. Old rat! Jesuit![5] Oh, I know you!

Tschubukov. Be still! Or I'll shoot you—with my worst gun, like a partridge! Fool! Loafer!

Lomov. Everyone knows that—oh, my heart!—that your poor late wife beat you. My leg—my temples—heavens—I'm dying—I—

Tschubukov. And your housekeeper wears the pants in your house!

---

5. **Jesuit** (jĕzh'ōō-ĭt): a member of a Roman Catholic religious order that was suppressed in Russia because of its resistance to the authority of the czar, the ruler of Russia. At the time, the term had the negative meaning of "one who schemes or plots."

H READING A PLAY
How does the **stage direction** clarify this speech?

READING SKILL   COMMON CORE
                                  RL 10

H READING A PLAY

Possible answer: The stage direction "mimicking him" (line 327) shows that Tschubukov is questioning Lomov's memory of the hunt in Maruskins's meadow. He is making fun of Lomov and is not respecting Lomov's points at all.

REVISIT THE BIG QUESTION

Why do people argue over

SILLY THINGS?

Discuss In lines 330–347, what do you learn about Tschubukov and Lomov from the pettiness of their insults? *Possible answer: Their remarks show that they are small-minded, insensitive, and self-centered.*

FOR STRUGGLING READERS

Comprehension Support Explain that Natalia's suggestion (lines 330–332) is sarcastic and insulting. She means that Lomov is weak and should do "women's work" (peeling potatoes) in the kitchen instead of pretending to be a hunter. Soon thereafter, Tschubukov insults Lomov by saying that his housekeeper is the one who makes the rules in his house (line 347); in other words, she is more masculine than he.

FOR ENGLISH LANGUAGE LEARNERS

Language: Verb Tenses Point out these irregular past-tense verbs and ask students to provide the base forms.

• *gave* (line 158) *Possible answer: give*

• *paid* (line 259) *Possible answer: pay*

• *heard* (line 272) *Possible answer: hear*

• *kept* (line 316) *Possible answer: keep*

• *struck* (line 318) *Possible answer: strike*

• *were* (line 319) *Possible answer: be*

• *found* (line 320) *Possible answer: find*

❶ CHARACTERS IN A FARCE

*Possible answer: Natalia's reaction is ridic-
ulous because she presumes that Lomov has
died and immediately turns from insults to
hysterical regret. Her sorrow seems all the
more ridiculous because when Lomov complained of feeling ill (lines 329, 348–350), she
belittled him (lines 330, 352).*

Extend the Discussion How could Natalia
have avoided this turn of events? Could
she do so without becoming inconsistent
in her character?

SELECTION WRAP–UP

READ WITH A PURPOSE Now that students
have finished reading the selection, engage
the class in a discussion about where physical
comedy could add to the humor. What actions
might the actors take to play up the silliness
in the dialogue? *Possible answers: Any time
Lomov talks about his physical ailments, the actor playing him could act out those ailments in
an exaggerated manner.*

⭐ **CRITIQUE** Ask students to state whether
they consider *A Marriage Proposal* to be a
funny play and to defend their responses.

INDEPENDENT READING

Students interested in farcical comedy may
want to read Oscar Wilde's *The Importance
of Being Earnest*, a play about mistaken identities, secret engagements, and romantic
entanglements.

Lomov. Here—here—there—there—my heart has burst! My shoulder is torn
apart. Where is my shoulder? I'm dying! (*He falls into a chair.*) The doctor!
350 (*faints*)

Tschubukov. Baby! Half-baked clam! Fool!

Natalia. Nice sort of hunter you are! You can't even sit on a horse. (*to* Tschubukov) Papa, what's the matter with him? (*She screams.*) Ivan Vassiliyitch! He
is dead!

Lomov. I'm ill! I can't breathe! Air!

Natalia. He is dead! (*She shakes* Lomov *in the chair.*) Ivan Vassiliyitch! What
have we done! He is dead! (*She sinks into a chair.*) The doctor—doctor! (*She
goes into hysterics.*) ❶

Tschubukov. Ahh! What is it? What's the matter with you?

360 **Natalia** (*groaning*). He's dead! Dead!

Tschubukov. Who is dead? Who? (*looking at* Lomov) Yes, he is dead! Good
God! Water! The doctor! (*holding the glass to* Lomov's *lips*) Drink! No, he won't
drink! He's dead! What a terrible situation! Why didn't I shoot myself? Why
have I never cut my throat? What am I waiting for now? Only give me a knife!
Give me a pistol! (Lomov *moves.*) He's coming to! Drink some water—there!

Lomov. Sparks! Mists! Where am I?

Tschubukov. Get married! Quick, and then go to the devil! She's willing! (*He
joins the hands of* Lomov *and* Natalia.) She's agreed! Only leave me in peace!

Lomov. Wh—what? (*getting up*) Whom?

370 **Tschubukov.** She's willing! Well? Kiss each other and—the devil take you both!

Natalia (*groans*). He lives! Yes, yes, I'm willing!

Tschubukov. Kiss each other!

Lomov. Eh? Whom? (Natalia *and* Lomov *kiss.*) Very nice! Pardon me, but what
is this for? Oh, yes, I understand! My heart—sparks—I am happy.
Natalia Stepanovna. (*He kisses her hand.*) My leg is lame!

Natalia. I'm happy too!

Tschubukov. Ahhh! A load off my shoulders! Ahh!

Natalia. And now at least you'll admit that Ugadi is worse that Otkatai!

Lomov. Better!

380 **Natalia.** Worse!

Tschubukov. Now the domestic joys have begun. Champagne!

Lomov. Better!

Natalia. Worse, worse, worse!

Tschubukov (*trying to drown them out*). Champagne, champagne!

*Translated from the Russian by
Hilmer Baukhage and Barrett H. Clark*

> ❶ **CHARACTERS
> IN A FARCE**
> What is ridiculous about
> Natalia's reaction?

④ **Targeted Passage**

DIFFERENTIATED INSTRUCTION

FOR STRUGGLING READERS

④ **Targeted Passage** [Lines 365–384]

In this concluding passage, Natalia finally
gets her proposal (in a way), and the audience
gets a hint at the characters' future.

- What does Tschubukov announce when
  he realizes that Lomov is alive? How does
  "Only leave me in peace!" (line 368) help
  explain his announcement? (lines 367–368)

- How do Lomov and Natalia say that they
  feel? Do you believe them? (lines 373–376)

- What does Natalia say that changes the
  mood? How does it change? (line 378;
  lines 379–384)

- When Tschubukov says, "Now the
  domestic joys have begun" (line 381), what
  is he predicting about the couple's married
  life? (lines 381–384)

- Why does Tschubukov keep calling for
  champagne? (line 384)

Comprehension

COMMON CORE

RL 3 Analyze how complex characters develop, interact with others, and advance the plot or develop the theme. RL 10 Read and comprehend dramas.

1. **Recall** Why does Lomov go to Tschubukov's home dressed in formal clothing?

2. **Recall** What two topics lead to petty arguments between Lomov and Natalia?

3. **Summarize** How does Tschubukov bring Lomov and Natalia together at the end of the play?

Text Analysis

● 4. **Reading a Play** Reread lines 38–52. Why might Chekhov have chosen to have Lomov express his thoughts alone onstage in a **monologue** instead of in dialogue with other characters?

● 5. **Examine Characters in a Farce** Review the chart you created as you read. How does Natalia cause Lomov's main trait or pattern of behavior to become even more exaggerated in the course of the play?

6. **Interpret Character Motivation** What seems to motivate Lomov's and Natalia's desire to marry each other? Cite evidence to support your answer.

7. **Analyze Irony** One important literary element that Chekhov uses in the play is irony, or the contrast between expectations and reality. Analyze the irony of the actions listed in this chart.

Action	Expectation	Reality
Tschubukov sends Natalia to talk with Lomov. (line 53)		
Lomov and Natalia agree to get married. (lines 367–375)		

8. **Identify Author's Perspective** The characters in *A Marriage Proposal* are members of the gentry. What does the play suggest about Chekhov's attitude toward this class of landowners? Cite evidence to support your answer.

9. **Evaluate Characters** Are Lomov and Natalia equally responsible for their arguments, or is one character more to blame? Explain your answer.

Text Criticism

10. **Critical Interpretations** The Russian writer Maxim Gorky said that there was always an element of sadness to Chekhov's humor: "One has only to read his 'humorous' stories with attention to see what a lot of cruel and disgusting things, behind the humorous words and situations, had been observed by the author with sorrow and were concealed by him." What sad realities underlie the humor in *A Marriage Proposal*?

> **Why do people argue over SILLY THINGS?**
> How would you help two people involved in a petty argument find common ground?

A MARRIAGE PROPOSAL **273**

---

8. The play suggests that Chekhov thinks that members of the gentry are greedy and petty, valuing land ownership and possessions over personal relationships.

9. Natalia is more responsible for their arguments, because she is the one who begins them (lines 79, 260, and 378). **OR** Lomov is to blame, because he is excitable and defensive (lines 112, 142–143, 264, 310). **OR** They are equally responsible, because neither is willing to let go of his or her position.

Text Criticism
Possible answer:
10. The sad realities are that the characters are greedy, self-righteous, very defensive when it comes to their possessions, and perhaps incapable of civil and loving relationships.

> Why do people argue over **SILLY THINGS?** Before answering, students might first think about how silly arguments sometimes camouflage deeper issues.

Practice and Apply

For preliminary support of post-reading questions, use these copy masters:

R RESOURCE MANAGER—Copy Masters
Reading Check p. 150
Reading a Play p. 145
Question Support p. 151

Additional selection questions are provided for teachers on page 137.

ANSWERS
Comprehension

1. *Lomov dresses formally because he intends to propose to Natalia.*

2. *Lomov and Natalia argue about who owns the meadows and who has the better dog.*

3. *Tschubukov joins the hands of Lomov and Natalia, announces that they are engaged, and calls for champagne to celebrate.*

Text Analysis
COMMON CORE RL 3, RL 10
Possible answers:

4. ■ **COMMON CORE FOCUS** *Reading a Play* Chekhov might have chosen a monologue because it lets the audience see, without interruption from other characters, Lomov's neurotic character (lines 45–51) and his reasons for wanting to marry Natalia (lines 39–45).

5. ● **COMMON CORE FOCUS** *Examine Characters in a Farce* The more that Natalia argues with Lomov, the more nervous and hypochondriacal he becomes (lines 148–149 and 206–207). These ailments continue until he faints (line 350).

6. *Lomov is motivated by society's expectations for someone of his age and by his wish to live a "well-regulated life" (lines 41–45). Natalia is motivated because she is a grown woman still living with her father, who seems eager to have her leave (lines 367–368).*

7. *Action: Tschubukov . . . ; Expectation: Natalia and Lomov will talk, and he will propose; Reality: They argue about the meadows.*
Action: Lomov and Natalia . . . ; Expectation: Natalia and Lomov will put aside their differences and be civil toward each other; Reality: Almost immediately, they start arguing again.

A MARRIAGE PROPOSAL **273**

Vocabulary in Context

▲ **VOCABULARY PRACTICE**

1. *true*
2. *false*
3. *true*
4. *true*

 RESOURCE MANAGER—Copy Master
Vocabulary Practice p. 148

ACADEMIC VOCABULARY IN WRITING

Possible answer: *My sister and I recently argued about what movie to go see. We did not* seek *the same goals. Her* motive *was to make her friends jealous by seeing a brand new movie. My* motive *was to see a movie I knew I would enjoy more. Finally we compromised by choosing my sister's movie, but we agreed that next week I get to pick.*

VOCABULARY STRATEGY:
THE LATIN ROOT *contra*

 COMMON CORE L 4c

- Have volunteers use a dictionary to look up each word in the word web. Invite comments about words in which other word parts help to shape meaning.

- For each **PRACTICE** sentence, help students use their knowledge of the root in combination with context clues (such as *inconsistent* in sentence 1 and *difference* in sentence 2) to determine the correct word choice.

Possible answers:

1. *contradict*
2. *contrast*
3. *Contraband*
4. *contravention*
5. *contrary*

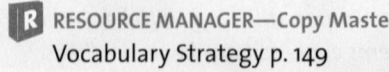 **RESOURCE MANAGER—Copy Master**
Vocabulary Strategy p. 149

Interactive Vocabulary

Keywords direct students to a **WordSharp** tutorial on **thinkcentral.com** or to other types of vocabulary practice and review.

Vocabulary in Context

▲ **VOCABULARY PRACTICE**

Decide if each statement is true or false.

WORD LIST
contrary
glutton
meditate
usurper

1. If you **meditate** on something, you give it a lot of thought.
2. A **usurper** respects other people's property.
3. You might be called a **glutton** if you eat a whole pie quickly.
4. A **contrary** friend seldom agrees with you.

ACADEMIC VOCABULARY IN WRITING

- dynamic   - individual   - motive   - seek   - undergo

Describe a silly or avoidable argument you had recently. As you tell what happened, explain each person's **motives**. Did each person in the argument **seek** the same goal? What was the outcome? Use at least two Academic Vocabulary words in your response.

VOCABULARY STRATEGY: THE LATIN ROOT *contra*

The word *contrary* contains the Latin root *contra*, which means "against." When *contra* is used as a prefix with English base words, as in *contrafactual*, you can easily figure out meanings. To understand other words containing *contra*, you may need to use context clues as well as your knowledge of the root.

COMMON CORE

L 4c Consult reference materials to determine or clarify a word's meaning or etymology.

PRACTICE Write the word from the word web that best completes each sentence. Use context clues to help you or, if necessary, consult a dictionary.

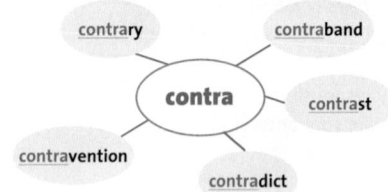

1. When you _____ yourself, you make inconsistent statements.
2. To _____ two things is to emphasize the difference between them.
3. _____ goods cannot be imported or exported abroad.
4. A _____ of international law is a serious violation.
5. He enjoys being _____ just to stir up debate.

Interactive Vocabulary **THINK** central

Go to **thinkcentral.com**.
KEYWORD: HML10-274

DIFFERENTIATED INSTRUCTION

FOR ENGLISH LANGUAGE LEARNERS

Vocabulary: Cognates Ask students to review the words in the Word List and the words in the word web. Then invite them to share any words from their home languages that are similar. Have them think of any words in their home languages that have the root *contra* and ask them if *contra* means "against" in those words too.

FOR ADVANCED LEARNERS/PRE-AP

Vocabulary in Writing Have students use the vocabulary words to write a paragraph about the arguments in *A Marriage Proposal* from the point of view of Lomov, Natalia, or Tschubukov. Have pairs of students who choose Lomov and Natalia or Lomov and Tschubukov compare their paragraphs to see which words are used for which character.

Language

◆ **GRAMMAR AND STYLE:** Vary Sentence Types

COMMON CORE

L 3 Apply knowledge of language to make effective choices for meaning or style.

Review the **Grammar and Style** note on page 263. When writing dialogue, use a mixture of sentence types to reflect characters' thoughts and emotions. A **declarative sentence** makes a statement. An **interrogative sentence** asks a question. An **exclamatory sentence** expresses strong emotion. An **imperative sentence** gives a command, request, or direction. Here is an example of how Chekhov uses a mixture of interrogative, declarative, and imperative sentences to convey his characters' emotions.

> **Lomov.** *Stepan Stepanovitch, I beg of you, just answer this: has your dog a short lower jaw or not? Yes or no?*
>
> **Tschubukov.** *And what if he has? Is it of such importance? There is no better dog in the whole country.*
>
> **Lomov.** *My Ugadi is better. Tell the truth now!* (lines 306–310)

Notice how the revisions in blue use a mixture of sentence types to better reflect the characters' emotions in this first draft. Revise your response to the prompt by using similar techniques.

STUDENT MODEL

Natalia. Your uncle gobbled up the whole wedding cake. *Who can eat so much?*

Lomov. ~~You're~~ *Stop* lying. He only took one piece.

READING-WRITING CONNECTION

Enhance your understanding of A *Marriage Proposal* by responding to this prompt. Then use the **revising tip** to improve your writing.

WRITING PROMPT	REVISING TIP
Short Constructed Response: Dialogue Suppose that Lomov and Natalia have just gotten married. Write a **half-page dialogue** in which they discuss the behavior of their relatives at the wedding. In your dialogue, include details that contribute to a definite **mood** or **tone**.	Review your dialogue. Did you vary the types of sentences the characters used? If not, revise to use a mixture of sentence types.

Interactive Revision

Go to **thinkcentral.com**.
KEYWORD: HML10-275

FOR STRUGGLING WRITERS

- Guide students to decide how they will portray the behavior of Lomov's and Natalia's relatives—for example, by vivid words or by examples.

- Help students brainstorm a list of sayings and comments that these characters might make about each other's relatives. Help students to write one line of dialogue for each character.

Language

COMMON CORE L3

◆ **GRAMMAR AND STYLE**

- After students examine the revisions in the student model, have them name the sentence types. ***Possible answer:*** *exclamatory, interrogative, imperative, and declarative*

- Write this dialogue on the board. Have students add variety by changing some of the declarative sentences to other sentence types. (For more on sentence types, see the **Grammar Handbook,** p. R59.)

  Natalia. Your aunt behaved so poorly~~.~~! Was s~~She~~ at least ~~must have been~~ ashamed of herself~~.~~?

  Lomov. You talk foolishly~~.~~! You are exaggerating. ~~Do you think y~~Your uncle was a complete gentleman~~.~~?

R RESOURCE MANAGER—Copy Master
   Vary Sentence Types p. 152

READING-WRITING CONNECTION

- Have students review lines such as 315–317 and 330–332 to help them reflect on the characters. Also have students review lines 189–202, in which the characters speak about some of their relatives.

 BEST PRACTICES TOOLKIT—Transparency
   Character Traits Web p. D7

Writing Online

The following tools are available online at **thinkcentral.com** and on **Write*Smart* CD-ROM:**
- **Interactive Graphic Organizers**
- **Interactive Student Models**
- **Interactive Revision Lessons**
For additional grammar instruction, see **GrammarNotes** on **thinkcentral.com**.

Assess and Reteach

Assess

DIAGNOSTIC AND SELECTION TESTS
   Selection Test A, B/C pp. 83–84, 85-86

Interactive Selection Test on **thinkcentral.com**

Reteach

Level Up Online Tutorials on **thinkcentral.com**

Focus and Motivate

⟨ COMMON CORE FOCUS

W 2 Write explanatory texts to convey complex ideas, concepts and information clearly through the effective selection, organization, and analysis of content. **SL 1** Come to discussions prepared, having read and researched material under study; explicitly draw on that preparation by referring to evidence from texts and other research. **SL 4** Present supporting evidence clearly such that listeners can follow the line of reasoning.

SUMMARY

In this film clip from *Finding Forrester*, Professor Crawford asks a prep school class to analyze some lines of poetry, but no one volunteers an answer. Annoyed, Crawford fires questions at one student, Coleridge. When Coleridge cannot even identify who wrote the poem, classmate Jamal Wallace tells him to say his own name. Jamal knows that British poet Samuel Taylor Coleridge wrote the poem. Crawford then makes a stereotypical remark about athletes such as Jamal. After a tense exchange, Crawford tells Jamal to leave.

What makes a character
BELIEVABLE?

Ask students to name actors whose performances were believable and to describe what made each of their characters seem real or memorable. Have students focus on the manner in which the actors spoke or moved and the way the actors responded to other characters.

BACKGROUND

Mike Rich, a radio news anchor, was inspired to write his first screenplay, *Finding Forrester*, by a radio interview he had conducted about famous American authors. Rich said, "I noticed that so many of them ... seemed to be eccentric, reclusive types. I thought a story that showed how someone helped a great writer break through that barrier of isolation and re-enter the world would make a terrific story, especially if that person were a teenager who is also in some way gifted."

Media Study

from Finding Forrester
Film Clip on **Media ● Smart DVD-ROM**

⟨ COMMON CORE

SL 1 Come to discussions prepared, having read and researched material under study; explicitly draw on that preparation by referring to evidence from texts and other research.

What makes a character
BELIEVABLE?

Think of a TV or movie character who captivated you. What was it about the actor's performance that convinced you of the character's believability? In this lesson, you'll view a movie scene that focuses on three characters. As you get a sense of each one, you'll see how film and performance techniques can influence your perceptions.

Background

Finding Friendship In the movie *Finding Forrester*, the main character is Jamal Wallace, who transfers from a high school in his tough urban neighborhood to a preparatory school with tough academic standards. Placed there on a basketball scholarship, Jamal is regarded as a star in the making. Few are aware that he is also an exceptional writer. The movie focuses on Jamal's unlikely friendship with a reclusive neighbor, William Forrester, a Pulitzer Prize-winning novelist who has begun helping Jamal tap his writing potential.

276

Media Study Resources

See resources on the **Teacher One Stop DVD-ROM** *and on* **thinkcentral.com**.

R **RESOURCE MANAGER UNIT 2**
Plan and Teach, pp. 155–158
Summary, pp. 159–160†‡*
Viewing Guide, p. 161
Close Viewing, p. 162
Media Activity, p. 163
Produce Your Own Media, p. 164

TECHNOLOGY
⊘ **Teacher One Stop DVD-ROM**
⊘ **Student One Stop DVD-ROM**
⊘ **Media*Smart* DVD-ROM**
MediaScope on **thinkcentral.com**

---

* Resources for Differentiation   † Also in Spanish   ‡ In Haitian Creole and Vietnamese

Media Literacy: Characterization in Movies

You're aware of the four basic methods in which characters are developed in fiction. In movies, characters are developed in similar ways but through camera techniques that show not only characters' physical appearance and actions but convey their emotions. In addition, actors use an array of performance techniques to add more dimension to characters.

WHAT DIRECTORS DO	WHAT ACTORS DO
Film Techniques Directors position characters within the "frame" of a screen or image, controlling the range of distance from the characters to viewers. This draws viewers' attention to characters' behavior and emotions.	**Performance Techniques** Actors rely on performance techniques to reveal characters' basic traits and to signal feelings or thoughts.
Strategies for Viewing • Put yourself at the scene through your awareness of **camera placement.** The camera often gets closer as the tension in a scene increases. Ask yourself: What character is drawing my attention? With whom do I sympathize? • Watch for **close-ups,** which reveal actors' facial expressions. Usually, the higher the emotional level of a scene, the more a director is likely to use close-ups. • Observe **camera movements.** Panning is when the camera scans a location from one side to the other.	**Strategies for Viewing** • Note an actor's use of **body language.** Viewers can make judgments based on a character's appearance and actions and make inferences about a character's thoughts and feelings. • Watch **facial expressions.** Look into characters' eyes, as **close-ups** permit, to read emotional signals. How do the eyes change to reveal suspicion? fear? wonder? • Listen to how an actor speaks the **dialogue,** which can reveal a character's personality or mood. The way an actor speaks and the words he or she says may change in formality and tone within the same movie. Note how different actors speak in different situations. Changes in their dialogue help reveal clues about their character.

MEDIA STUDY: TEACHING OPTIONS

Teaching Option 1: The Basics (1–2 Days)
1. Begin the Media Study using the material provided on pages 276–277.
2. Show the Introduction on Media*Smart*. Then show the First Viewing. As they watch, have students use the Viewing Guide on page 278, along with the corresponding copy master on page 161 of the Resource Manager. Discuss their responses.
3. Return to the pupil book for the extension activities on page 279.

Teaching Option 2: In-Depth Study (2–3 Days)
1. Begin the Media Study pp. 276–277.
2. Show the Introduction and First Viewing from Media*Smart*. Continue on Media*Smart* with the Media Lessons, using teacher notes in the Resources.
3. Show the Guided Analysis presentation. Have students record their observations on the Student Viewing Guide available in the Resources section from Media*Smart*.

Teach

Media Literacy

Ask what techniques help an actor make a character believable. On the board, list responses students might generate, such as realistic dialogue, gesture, costume, or tone of voice. Explain that film techniques such as shot composition, close-up, or camera movement also help create believable characters. Then discuss the chart on page 277.

• **Camera Placement** Explain that directors also frame actors in a certain way to reflect a character's state of mind. Ask how a character's position in the frame—foreground, center, or background—might suggest the importance of his or her state of mind.

• **Close-ups** Remind students that a close-up zooms in to reveal a detail. As students view the clip, have them watch for close-ups. Ask which characters or objects are featured in close-ups. What emotional signals do close-ups reveal?

• **Camera Movements** Remind students that a panning shot gives an overview, while a tracking shot often focuses on one character. Have students imagine viewing your classroom from a corner near the ceiling or from their own eyes as they move through the room. Ask how these images would differ. As they view the film clip, have students list panning or tracking shots that help lead viewers to certain characters.

• **Body Language and Facial Expressions** Have volunteers dramatize being bored, tired, annoyed, and so on, through gestures, posture, actions, and facial expressions. Challenge the rest of the class to guess the emotions in the dramatization.

• **Dialogue** Have students discuss how they speak in class, at home, or with friends, such as with formal language, jargon, or slang. After students view the clip, have them contrast how Crawford, Jamal, and Coleridge speak.

VIEWING GUIDE

1. Before students view the clip, tell them they will identify film and performance techniques used to create believable and engaging characters. Ask students to watch and listen for these elements:

   - the **composition** of shots that highlights the conflict between Professor Crawford and his students, Coleridge and Jamal

   - **close-ups** that reveal the facial expressions of Crawford, Coleridge, and Jamal and help viewers understand each character's emotions

   - uses of different types of **camera movements,** such as **panning** or **tracking shots,** that draw viewers' attention to one or more of the characters in a scene or make viewers feel they are there in the classroom

   - the way the three main actors in the scene use **body language, facial expressions,** and **dialogue** to convey characters' reactions and to reveal character traits, such as embarrassment

2. Encourage students to watch the film clip several times; for example, once for close-ups, once for shot composition, and so on. If possible, use the freeze-frame function to pause and illustrate the techniques discussed in the lesson.

R RESOURCE MANAGER—Copy Masters

   Viewing Guide p. 161
   Close Viewing p. 162
   Media Activity p. 163

Use this resource with the Viewing Guide:

MediaSmart DVD-ROM

MediaScope on **thinkcentral.com**

Media Smart DVD-ROM
- **Film Clip:** *Finding Forrester*
- **Director:** Gus Van Sant
- **Rating:** PG-13
- **Genre:** Drama
- **Running Time:** 4.5 minutes

278

Viewing Guide for
Finding Forrester

In an earlier scene, Professor Crawford has told Jamal that he doubts the student's ability to succeed academically. The clip you'll view occurs later in the movie, as the professor's English composition class is in session. View the clip once in its entirety and then several more times. Use these questions as you focus on the characters and their interactions.

NOW VIEW

FIRST VIEWING: Comprehension

1. **Recall** Why does Professor Crawford deliberately single out a certain student to identify the quotation on the chalkboard?

2. **Clarify** When Jamal identifies the quotation, how does Professor Crawford react?

CLOSE VIEWING: Media Literacy

3. **Draw Conclusions** Why do you think the director chose to shoot Coleridge almost entirely in close-ups?

4. **Analyze Techniques** As the confrontation between Jamal and Professor Crawford intensifies, what film techniques does the director use to convey the building tension?

5. **Analyze Characters** Choose Jamal, Coleridge, or Professor Crawford from the clip and write a brief profile based on what you've viewed. Describe what you think are that character's thoughts and feelings throughout the scene. Cite evidence from the film clip.

6. **Evaluate Acting** In your opinion, which one of the three main actors in the scene delivers the most convincing performance? Describe what appealed to you about the actor's basic appearance, dialogue delivery, and actions.

ANSWERS

FIRST VIEWING: Comprehension

1. *This student has the same last name as the author of the quotation (Coleridge).*

2. *Professor Crawford appears surprised.*

CLOSE VIEWING: Media Literacy

Possible answers:

3. *Close-up shots heighten the viewer's awareness of Coleridge's nervousness, embarrassment, and discomfort at being singled out and not knowing the answers. Close-ups allow the audience to recognize and empa-*

thize with Coleridge's emotional reaction.

4. *The director tightens the framing of close-ups on Jamal and Crawford as the scene progresses, and also quickens the pace of the editing.*

5. **Jamal:** *Jamal is a good student, very intelligent, and well-dressed. His calm facial expressions and low-key delivery of dialogue convey Jamal's controlled but strong emotions. Also, by responding confidently to Professor Crawford's challenges, Jamal proves that he is not only athletically gifted but also well-read and not easily intimidated.*

6. *The actor portraying Professor Crawford is extremely convincing as the arrogant and biased professor. His tone of voice conveys tremendous condescension toward Coleridge and suspicion, along with defensiveness, toward Jamal.*

Write or Discuss

Examine Stereotypes This pointed statement by Professor Crawford triggers the confrontation with Jamal: "Perhaps your skills *do* extend a bit beyond basketball." One of the most common shortcuts to characterization is the **stereotype,** an oversimplified representation of a person or group. This device has the virtue of saving time, but it can lead to dull predictability. To what degree do you think stereotyping is evident in this scene? What creative touches, if any, help the portrayals to rise above the usual predictability of stereotypes? Indicate specific shots, character actions, or dialogue to support your view. Keep these criteria in mind:

- your awareness of stereotypes
- the film techniques used by the director
- the nature of each actor's role and the performance techniques used

Produce Your Own Media

Create a Cast List Choose one of character-driven selections in this unit and imagine you're casting the roles for a movie version of the work. Create a cast list.

HERE'S HOW As you compose the cast list, consider these suggestions:

- For each character on the list, indicate the necessary traits to portray.
- Include the names of real-life actors whose appearance or well-known performances match the traits of the characters. Or present photos of classmates as the characters. As an "actor" poses for a shot, give directions about how to portray the character. List each character's basic traits.

STUDENT MODEL

Cast List for "Shoofly Pie"

Ashley Chin as Mattie
sensitive
observant
good-natured
spunky

Eric Russell as Johnny
gruff exterior
uncomfortable with change
sensitive

COMMON CORE

SL 4 Present supporting evidence clearly such that listeners can follow the line of reasoning. **W 2** Write explanatory texts to convey complex ideas, concepts and information clearly through the effective selection, organization, and analysis of content.

Media Tools **THINK** central

Go to **thinkcentral.com**.
KEYWORD: HML10-279

Tech Tip

Have classmates pose to resemble the characters, then photograph them.

MEDIA STUDY **279**

- **Camera Movements** Ask students how tracking and panning shots enable the viewer to pick up on character clues.
- **Body Language and Facial Expressions** Have students catalog the body language and facial expressions of their favorite TV characters as they watch their favorite TV shows.
- **Dialogue** Tell students that how a character speaks is as important as what he or she says.

Produce Your Own Media

Rubric: Create a Cast List A good cast

- lists all characters in a work of literature
- indicates important character traits that must be portrayed for each character on the list
- names actors or classmates whose physical appearance or character traits match those of characters they will portray
- provides sound reasons for casting choices

R RESOURCE MANAGER—Copy Master
Produce Your Own Media p. 164

Assess and Reteach

Write or Discuss

COMMON CORE SL 4, W 2

Examine Stereotypes In their written work or discussion, students should examine stereotypes in this scene, such as the stern scholar (Crawford), privileged underachiever (Coleridge), or African-American athlete (Jamal). Students should refer to specific film techniques, such as *framing, close-ups, panning, and tracking* shots that add dimension to characters. They should also explain how each actor brings his role to life through *body language, facial expressions,* and *dialogue*. For example, close-ups of Professor Crawford reveal his disbelief and anger, while close-ups of Jamal reveal his conviction and determination as the conflict in the scene escalates.

MEDIA STUDY WRAP–UP

Have students summarize what they have learned about film and performance techniques that actors or directors might use to create believable characters. Encourage them to use terms such as *close-up, pan, tracking shot, body language, facial expressions,* and *dialogue* in their explanations.

RETEACH

For students who are unable to apply the Media Study skills, select from these reteaching options:

- **Camera Placement** Define an area at the front of the class as the frame. Have a volunteer group step into the frame. Ask the class how they would position the volunteers within the frame to make one of them a main character and the rest minor characters.
- **Close-ups** Have student pairs stand on opposite sides of the classroom and say something to their partners. Then have students stand close together and repeat the statement. What new details do students notice?

Media Tools **THINK** central

Media study keywords point to **MediaScope**, a Web site that helps students strengthen media analysis and production skills.

Focus and Motivate

COMMON CORE FOCUS

W 3a–e Write narratives to develop real or imagined experiences or events using effective technique, well-chosen details, and well-structured event sequences. **W 4** Produce clear and coherent writing in which the development, organization, and style are appropriate to task, purpose, and audience. **W 5** Develop and strengthen writing as needed by planning, revising, editing, rewriting, or trying a new approach. **W 10** Write routinely over shorter time frames for a range of tasks, purposes, and audiences. **L 1** Demonstrate command of the conventions of standard English grammar and usage when writing. **L 1b** Use participial phrases to convey specific meanings and add variety. **L 2c** Spell correctly. **L 3** Apply knowledge of language to make effective choices for meaning or style.

WRITE WITH A PURPOSE

Remind students that when writing their short stories, they should choose a conflict they find interesting. Read aloud the two purposes of the workshop. Point out that most authors want to entertain and to convey a theme when they write.

COMMON CORE TRAITS

Review the *COMMON CORE TRAITS* with students, focusing primarily on the development of ideas. Compare the list of traits with the rubric on page 288.

ADDITIONAL TASKS

Write from an Advertisement Use photographs from advertisements to help you craft a short story. For example, photographs of a festival or vacation spot might give you ideas for the story's setting.
Possible subjects: working for a concert promoter, origins of a local business

Writing Workshop
NARRATIVE

Short Story
Essential Course of Study

When you write fiction, you can create a world just as you want it to be. The setting, characters, action, and dialogue are all of your own choosing. In this workshop, you will write a short story.

Complete the workshop activities in your **Reader/Writer Notebook**.

WRITE WITH A PURPOSE

WRITING TASK

Write a **short story** that is centered on an event or experience that you find interesting. Use sensory language, dialogue, and suspense to develop the story's setting, characters, plot, mood, and theme.

Idea Starters
• a character faces a challenge involving nature, such as a storm or natural disaster
• the main character becomes involved in a conflict with one or more other characters
• the main character struggles with conflicting feelings or ideas within himself or herself

THE ESSENTIALS

Here are some common purposes, audiences, and formats for short-story writing.

PURPOSES	AUDIENCES	FORMATS
• to entertain others	• classmates and teacher	• story for class
• to convey an idea about life or human nature	• family members	• children's book
	• readers of a literary magazine	• readers' theater
	• Web users	• video adaptation
		• podcast

COMMON CORE TRAITS

1. DEVELOPMENT OF IDEAS
• introduces, develops, and resolves a **central conflict**
• introduces and develops a **narrator** and **characters**
• uses techniques such as **dialogue** and **description** to develop the plot
• provides a **resolution** that follows from and reflects on the events in the story
• suggests a **theme**, or message, about life

2. ORGANIZATION OF IDEAS
• presents a smooth **sequence of events** to create a coherent story
• uses effective **pacing** to advance the plot

3. LANGUAGE FACILITY AND CONVENTIONS
• establishes and maintains a **point of view**
• includes **precise words and phrases, telling details**, and **sensory language**
• uses **participles** to vary sentence structure
• employs correct **grammar, mechanics**, and **spelling**

Writing Workshop Resources

R RESOURCE MANAGER UNIT 2
Plan and Teach, pp. 165–168
Prewriting–Editing, pp. 169–172
Writing Rubric, p. 174
Technology, p. 175
Writing Support, p. 176*

BEST PRACTICES TOOLKIT
Writing Template: Short Story
pp. C16, C39

TECHNOLOGY
⊘ **Teacher One Stop DVD-ROM**
⊘ **Student One Stop DVD-ROM**
⊘ **Write*Smart* CD-ROM**
⊘ **GrammarNotes DVD-ROM**

Writing Center on thinkcentral.com

*See resources on the **Teacher One Stop DVD-ROM** and on **thinkcentral.com**.*

* Resources for Differentiation

Planning/Prewriting

 COMMON CORE W 3a–e Write narratives to develop real or imagined experiences or events using effective technique, well-chosen details, and well-structured event sequences. W 5 Develop and strengthen writing as needed by planning.

Getting Started

FIND STORY IDEAS

Think about interesting **events** or **problems**, and then decide what **characters, settings,** and **plots** might bring that particular situation to life. Ask *what if* questions: "What if someone . . . ?" Write down whatever comes into your mind. Circle the ideas that interest you the most.

▶ **WHAT DOES IT LOOK LIKE?**

> Maybe something about (school) or sports
> (Girl/boy problems)
> What if a friend grows distant?
> The mall would be an interesting setting
> Being open to (new experiences)

THINK ABOUT AUDIENCE AND PURPOSE

Your **purpose** is to engage readers with a story that says something meaningful about life or human nature. Think about effective techniques that will help your audience relate to the story's **theme,** or message.

▶ **ASK YOURSELF:**

- Who is my target audience? Am I writing for more than one audience?
- What universal feelings and experiences do I want to share with my audience?
- How will I help my audience relate to this story?

IDENTIFY STORY ELEMENTS

Once you have ideas for your **short story,** you need to identify the **problem** that must be solved. Ask yourself: Who is the main **character**? What is the central **conflict**? From what **point of view,** or method of narration, will the story be told? For instance, use a first-person narrator to draw readers into one character's thoughts. Use a third-person narrator to reveal **multiple points of view.**

▶ **WHAT DOES IT LOOK LIKE?**

Main Character	Central Conflict	Point of View
Duane (football player)	Likes Tina but is too shy to ask her out	Third-person

PLOT YOUR STORY

Create a story graph to plot the sequence of events. Begin with the **exposition,** which sets up the conflict. Develop the complications in the **rising action,** where the **pace** quickens and suspense builds until the conflict reaches a **climax.** The **falling action** shows the events that lead to the **resolution** of the conflict.

TIP Adding **multiple plot lines** can create interest by introducing more layers of complexity to the story. For example, the story can follow the actions of more than one character.

▶ **WHAT DOES IT LOOK LIKE?**

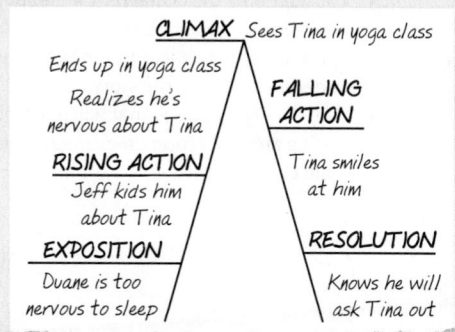

WRITING WORKSHOP **281**

DIFFERENTIATED INSTRUCTION

FOR ENGLISH LANGUAGE LEARNERS

Language: Reinforce Short Story Terms Write these terms on the board and review them with students:

- *characters:* the people or animals that are included in the events of the story
- *climax:* the point of maximum tension
- *conflict:* a struggle between opposing forces
- *dialogue:* a conversation between two or more characters in a story, set off by quotation marks

- *plot:* the sequence of events in a story
- *resolution:* the dénouement, or falling action, which ends the conflict
- *sensory language:* words and phrases that appeal to the five senses
- *suspense:* excitement or tension readers feel as they wait to find out how a story ends or a conflict is resolved
- *point of view:* the angle from which a story is told

Planning/ Prewriting

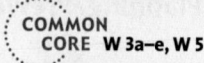 **COMMON CORE** W 3a–e, W 5

▶ **FIND STORY IDEAS** Remind students that conflicts happen every day and everywhere— at school, at home, in shops, on buses. Suggest that they think not only about conflicts they experience directly but also about ones they observe or hear about.

▶ **THINK ABOUT AUDIENCE AND PURPOSE** Explain to students that their classmates and family members—the bulk of their audience— may be familiar with the sorts of conflict students will write about. An audience that is familiar with the conflict will be able to understand the story's message and relate to the characters and setting.

▶ **IDENTIFY STORY ELEMENTS** Explore the concept of point of view with students. Discuss with students whether they would choose a first person or a third person narrator for the following plots: (1) how the team won the homecoming game, (2) choosing a birthday gift for a friend, (3) the first day at a new school. Have students support their ideas with reasons and examples.

▶ **PLOT YOUR STORY** Remind students that the events in the story should move the plot forward. Students should first chart all the action of the story and then reorder plot elements to build toward the climax. Tell students to delete plot elements that do not contribute to the progression toward the climax and resolution.

R RESOURCE MANAGER—Copy Masters
Planning/Prewriting, p. 169
Drafting, p. 170
Revising, pp. 171–172
Editing, p. 173
Rubric, p. 174
Writing Support, p. 176

Planning/Prewriting *continued*

▶ **DEVELOP MAIN CHARACTER** Remind students that sensory language is used to tell more about characters than what they look like. Remind students to describe how each character sounds, smells, or feels. For example, what kind of voice does a character have—raspy? high-pitched? Does he have an explosive laugh? Does she wear flowery perfume or smell like wet wool? Is her handshake firm or limp? These details bring characters alive for readers.

YOUR TURN Give students time to develop their writing plans and fill in their charts. If students have trouble coming up with story ideas, encourage them to think about problems they or their friends have encountered. Then have students develop ideas about their main characters and how they would react to conflict. Would their characters react differently than they or their friends would?

🧰 BEST PRACTICES TOOLKIT—Transparencies
   Plot Diagram p. D55
   Storyboard p. C51
   Story Frames p. C50

For interactive graphic organizers, see

💿 **Write*Smart* CD-ROM**

Writing Center on thinkcentral.com

Planning/Prewriting *continued*

Getting Started

DEVELOP MAIN CHARACTER
Write descriptions of the main character using **sensory language**, **telling details**, and **dialogue** that give a vivid picture of how that character thinks, acts, and feels; what motivates him or her; and what he or she looks and sounds like. As you choose details, keep in mind that they will also help define the story's **mood**, or atmosphere.

▶ **WHAT DOES IT LOOK LIKE?**

Duane
Details
Big, brawny guy
Extremely shy
Very anxious about asking Tina out—jumpy, stomach in knots, tight muscles, sort of defensive
Conflict causes insomnia—always tired, droopy eyes, falls asleep in class, no energy, groans, stumbles around
Dialogue
"I am sooooo tired. Do we have coffee?" Duane muttered.
"You asked Tina out yet?" Jeff said.
"Shut up, man! You're so loud," said Duane. "I'm just waiting for the right moment."

PEER REVIEW Describe the main character, conflict, and plot of your story to a peer. Ask for tips on making these elements more believable or interesting.

YOUR TURN In your *Reader/Writer Notebook,* develop your writing plan. Identify the main character of your story and its central conflict. Then, use a chart such as the one on this page to list precise details and dialogue that will bring the characters and actions in the story to life. Consider the following tips:

- Think of the visual images you have of the setting and your main character.
- Consider how the character's voice sounds and how he or she talks with the other characters.
- Think about the character's thoughts and feelings as he or she reacts to developments in the story.
- Use sensory language that will help your audience imagine the story's setting and the actions, movements, gestures, and feelings of your main character.

DIFFERENTIATED INSTRUCTION

FOR ENGLISH LANGUAGE LEARNERS
Culture: Connect Encourage students to use their own experiences about learning a new language in their stories. What conflicts and misunderstandings arose because of difficulties communicating? How were conflicts resolved? What positive experiences did students have that they could include in their stories? What messages about learning a new language would student writers like to convey to their audience?

FOR STRUGGLING WRITERS
Plan the Details Have students use these sen-tence starters to help them plan the details of their stories:

My main character is _____.

He/She has a conflict about _____.

My other characters are _____.

The setting of my story is _____.

Three important events in the story are

_____

In the conclusion, my main character

_____.

Drafting

Use this chart to organize a successful short story.

COMMON CORE

W 4 Produce clear and coherent writing in which the development, organization, and style are appropriate to task, purpose, and audience. **L 1** Demonstrate command of the conventions of standard English grammar and usage when writing.

Organizing Your Short Story

EXPOSITION

- Engage and orient readers by opening with a **detail** or a line of **dialogue** that introduces the conflict, the setting, and the characters.
- Establish the story's **point of view:** Who is telling the story, and what does he or she know?

RISING ACTION AND CLIMAX

- **Sequence events** in **chronological order.** Create a smooth progression by using **transitions,** such as *that morning, at school,* or *before the final bell,* to advance the plot and to clarify shifts in setting.
- Reveal the main character's personality and motivations through **dialogue.**
- Use **precise words, telling details,** and **sensory language** to develop the story's setting, characters, and mood.
- Build **suspense** by increasing the story's **pacing** and bringing its central **conflict** to a **climax.**

FALLING ACTION AND RESOLUTION

- End with a convincing **resolution** to the story's **conflict.**
- Give your readers a **theme to reflect on,** such as something interesting about life or human nature.

GRAMMAR IN CONTEXT: VERB TENSE

Verb tense tells the time of the action or idea that the verb expresses. Follow these tips:

When describing events that occur at the same time, use verbs in the same tense.

> Duane **groaned** tiredly as he **plopped** down at the kitchen table.
>
> [Both verbs are in the past tense because the two actions happened at the same time in the past.]

When describing events that occur at different times, use different tenses to show the sequence of events, or the order in which they happened.

> Duane's mother **had encouraged** him to try yoga before, but now she **pressed** him harder.
>
> [*Had encouraged* is in the past perfect tense, and *pressed* is in the past tense. The past perfect tense expresses an action that occurred before another action in the past.]

Although stories are usually told in the past tense, the present tense is used in dialogue.

> "You **know,** my yoga instructor **says** that new class **isn't** full yet."

YOUR TURN

Develop a first draft of your short story, following the structure outlined in the chart above. As you write, use consistent verb tenses to show a clear sequence of events.

FOR ENGLISH LANGUAGE LEARNERS

Verb Tense When students write about the past, they may have difficulty with the tenses of phrasal verbs. Write these phrasal verbs on the board:

- *add up*
- *do over*
- *dress up*
- *get through*
- *keep on*
- *look out*
- *make up*
- *point out*
- *show off*
- *take over*

Demonstrate how to form the past tense of *add up* by changing the form of the verb to *added* and keeping the preposition unchanged. Call on volunteers to change the other phrasal verbs to past tense. You may need to help students identify the past tense of common irregular verbs, such as *do* and *get.*

Drafting

COMMON CORE W 4, L 1

▶ **EXPOSITION** Offer students these examples of techniques they might use to open their stories, introduce their main characters, and establish point of view:

- a dialogue between the main character and someone else
- a question the narrator is asking himself or herself (first-person narrator) or the reader

▶ **RISING ACTION AND CLIMAX** Remind students that sensory language and realistic dialogue show characters' personalities and motivations. Write this sentence on the board: "Connor's little brother was sad because his dog had run away." Have students work in pairs to add sensory language to the sentence.

▶ **FALLING ACTION AND RESOLUTION** Explain that a satisfying conclusion answers the question "What happened in the end?"

GRAMMAR IN CONTEXT: VERB TENSE

Have students rewrite the following sentence pairs using consistent verb tense:

- Yesterday, the dog jumps on Isabella. Isabella fell down as the dog licks her face. *[Past tense: Yesterday, the dog jumped on Isabella. Isabella fell down as the dog licked her face. Present tense: The dog jumps on Isabella. Isabella falls down as the dog licks her face.]*

- I remembered to unplug my laptop before the server would come to the table. He trips anyway, and hot coffee spilled on me. *[Past tense: I remembered to unplug my laptop before the server came to the table. He tripped anyway, and hot coffee spilled on me. Present tense: I remember to unplug my laptop before the server comes to the table. He trips anyway, and hot coffee spills on me.]*

YOUR TURN

Have students complete the **Your Turn** exercise on their own. Then, have them exchange papers with another student and proofread the other person's paper.

For a short story writing template, see

 BEST PRACTICES TOOLKIT—Transparency
Writing Template: Short Story p. C39

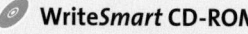 **WriteSmart CD-ROM**

Writing Center on thinkcentral.com

Revising

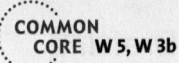

Model the Skill Using a draft story on a transparency, model how to use the questions, tips, and strategies suggested in the chart to evaluate and revise. You might use a story by a student from another class or from last year. Be sure to remove the student's name from the story so that he or she is anonymous.

Revising

As you revise your short story, consider the dialogue and sensory language that bring the setting, the main character, the conflict, and events in the plot to life. The goal is to determine whether you've effectively communicated these story elements to your intended audience. The following chart will help you revise and improve your draft.

SHORT STORY

Ask Yourself	Tips	Revision Strategies
1. Does the story begin in a way that engages the reader?	▶ **Underline** the dialogue, event, and details that engage readers.	▶ **Add** dialogue, action, or sensory language to engage your readers.
2. Does the sequence of events follow in chronological order?	▶ **Number** the events in order.	▶ **Rearrange** events so that each event builds logically on what happened before.
3. Is the conflict interesting and believable? Do the plot events build to a climax?	▶ **Double underline** the sentence(s) that reveal the conflict, then **draw stars** next to events or details that complicate the conflict and create suspense.	▶ **Add** details and events that develop the conflict and create suspense, yet keep the pace moving and the reader engaged.
4. Are believable characters, settings, and events developed through dialogue, description, and sensory language?	▶ **Bracket** examples of dialogue. **Place a check mark** next to each instance of descriptive or sensory language.	▶ **Add** dialogue to reveal characters' personalities and motivations. **Add** sensory language to give readers a vivid picture of the settings and events.
5. Is the point of view consistent both in the use of pronouns and in what the narrator does and does not know?	▶ **Circle** all the pronouns in the story that reveal the point of view. **Draw a wavy line** under text that reveals something the narrator would not know.	▶ **Correct** inconsistent pronouns. **Delete** or **reword** text that reveals something the narrator would not know. **Add** details that the narrator would know.
6. Is the conflict resolved in a logical and convincing way? Does the resolution convey a theme about life or human nature?	▶ **Highlight** the resolution of the conflict. **Place a star** next to any sentences that prompt readers to reflect on universal human experiences.	▶ **Elaborate** on the resolution to develop it more fully or to convey a theme about life or human nature.

YOUR
TURN

PEER REVIEW Exchange your short story with a classmate. Discuss whether you understand the personality of the main character, the conflict of the story, and the sequence of events that leads to its resolution. Suggest new approaches that might improve the story.

YOUR
TURN Suggest that, before exchanging papers, students make lists of questions they have about their own stories. For instance, students may want to know whether a character's emotions are clear from a certain action or if it is clear who is speaking in a particular dialogue. After students have read each other's stories, they should address these questions and add further comments based on their own observations. Remind students that criticism includes positive comments.

For interactive revision tools, see

💿 **Write*Smart* CD-ROM**

Writing Center on <u>thinkcentral.com</u>

DIFFERENTIATED INSTRUCTION

FOR STRUGGLING WRITERS

Add Descriptive Details To help students add descriptive details, present these examples:

1. Replace general words with more colorful, specific words.
   - tired: *droopy, exhausted, worn out*
   - went: *jogged, shuffled, dragged*
   - said: *giggled, boomed, whispered*

2. Use similes to compare with *like* or *as*.
   - happy: *as happy as a kid at his first birthday party*
   - ran: *I ran like a rabbit chased by a fox.*

3. Add language that appeals to the senses: sight, hearing, smell, touch, or taste.
   - The fire burned. It *sizzled* and *hissed*.
   - She smiled and then frowned. Her *wide grin* turned into a *sour pout*.

ANALYZE A STUDENT DRAFT

Read this draft; notice the comments on its strengths as well as suggestions for improvement.

COMMON CORE

W 5 Develop and strengthen writing as needed by revising, rewriting, or trying a new approach. **W 3b** Use narrative techniques such as dialogue to develop characters.

Sleepless
by Rose Kenwood, Central High School

The stairs groaned tiredly under Duane's bulk. Duane himself groaned tiredly as he plopped down at the kitchen table.

"Do we have coffee?" he muttered.

"Have you ever smelled coffee in this house?" his mother asked. "You know, my yoga instructor says that new class isn't full yet."

"I don't want to hear anything about yoga, Ma." Duane looked blearily for the chocolate puffs cereal.

"All right, but it can really help with insomnia," she said.

Duane grunted. He could just see himself in a leotard, stretching and taking deep breaths—and then his friends would walk by just as he was doing the Loser Lotus position.

At school, Duane ran into Jeff, one of the linebackers on the team.

"Hey man, you look wiped. Tackling people in your sleep now?" Jeff asked, laughing. "You should get some z's. You gonna practice today?"

"I'll be fine," Duane said, not sure if it was true. It had been nearly a week—more than six days!—since he'd managed to sleep more than a few hours. Maybe football was making him keyed up. Plus there was this girl. . . .

"You asked Tina out yet?" Jeff asked.

"Shut up, man! You're so loud," he said, trying to look cool. "I'm just waiting for the right moment."

"Well, don't wait too long—she's cool. Somebody else'll ask her."

Duane felt his heart rate increase and his shoulders tighten. "Lay off, Jeff," he said as the bell rang.

To capture readers' interest and introduce the main character, Rose uses **sensory language** and repetition.

Rose includes dialogue to bring her characters to life, but some of the dialogue should be revised to sound realistic.

Rose maintains a consistent **point of view,** using third-person pronouns in the narrative of her story. She focuses on a single character's thoughts through a third-person limited narrator.

In the dialogue between Duane and Jeff, Rose reveals the central **conflict** of the story—Duane's nervousness about asking Tina out.

LEARN HOW Use Sentence Fragments to Create Realistic Dialogue Rose includes dialogue to reveal Duane's personality and motivations. When people talk in a short story, however, they should sound the way they do in real life. Some of the dialogue in Rose's story seems unnatural. To make her dialogue more realistic, Rose should replace some complete sentences with sentence fragments.

ROSE'S REVISION TO DIALOGUE   *"Enough with the yoga,*

~~"I don't want to hear anything about yoga,~~ Ma."

FOR ENGLISH LANGUAGE LEARNERS

Language: Conversational English Patterns
Remind students that their short stories should incorporate realistic dialogue. Point out "Hey man" and "You should get some z's" in paragraph 8 of the Student Draft as examples of how teenagers really speak to one another. Have students identify other examples of realistic dialogue in the Student Draft. Explain the meaning of "You gonna" *(Are you going to)* and "else'll" *(else will)* if students do not understand these expressions.

FOR STRUGGLING WRITERS

Sensory Language Ask students to look through the Student Draft on this page to identify language that appeals to the five senses. For example, in paragraph 1, the writer uses "groaned tiredly" to describe the sound of the stairs and how Duane sounded as he "plopped down." Ask students to identify other words or phrases that appeal to sight, touch, sound, taste, or smell.

ANALYZE A STUDENT DRAFT

Explain that the Student Draft on this page is the first half of a short story. Model reading the draft and the annotations in blue, and explain that the yellow highlighting illustrates the student's language choices. Explain that the following *Learn How* mini-lessons provide helpful information about ways to improve this student draft as well as their own.

LEARN HOW   Use Sentence Fragments to Create Realistic Dialogue

- Read Duane's comment about yoga, "I don't want to hear anything about yoga, Ma," aloud. Then read: "Enough with the yoga, Ma." Point out that the second, revised line of dialogue reveals more about Duane's personality than the first, and the words sound like what a real person would say.

- Tell students that whether people speak in complete sentences or not depends on the situation they are in or how they are feeling. Ask students how Duane is feeling during the conversation with his mother. *(tired, discouraged)*

- Have students look for other lines of Duane's dialogue and suggest possible changes. *("Do we have coffee?" / "We got coffee?")*

ANALYZE A STUDENT DRAFT *continued*

Explain that the Student Draft is continued and completed on this page. Read the draft and annotations aloud and discuss. Ask students to comment on the student writer's resolution.

LEARN HOW Add Descriptive Detail

- Explain that in Rose's revision of her draft, she adds sensory language to describe the scene in the fifth paragraph on this page in more detail.

- Point out that "A deep, loud voice startled him" tells readers that Duane is tired and is paying no attention to the world around him.

- Have students place asterisks next to places in their drafts that might be strengthened by adding descriptive details.

 YOUR TURN Allow students to take time to revise their drafts. Remind them to include descriptive details to convey information about the plot, characters, and conflict. Ask students to pay particular attention to making their dialogue realistic.

For interactive revision tools, see

WriteSmart CD-ROM

Writing Center on thinkcentral.com

In homeroom, Duane's eyelids drooped during the daily announcements. "Yoga class meets during lunch period in the east gym. . . ." Before he knew it, the bell was ringing again.

"Duane, this is the second time this week you've fallen asleep during class. What's going on?" Mr. Clayton asked.

"Sorry, Mr. Clayton," Duane said, and stumbled out.

He floated in a half-wakeful state through his next four classes. At lunch, he found his stomach was too knotted to let him eat. He tried to joke with his buddies about the homecoming game but didn't have the energy.

He got up and started down the hall. A security guard stopped him.

"Do you have a pass?" the security guard asked.

"Uh, no, I, uh—"

"Are you on your way to yoga class?" the guard suggested.

"Yeah, yeah, it's in the east gym," he said with relief. The guard watched Duane closely as he walked down the hallway.

As soon as he opened the door to the east gym, a friendly voice said, "Hello! Grab a mat for yourself. We're just about to start."

The instructor was a big, muscular guy wearing shorts and a tank top. Duane kept his face down as he made his way to an empty spot on the floor.

"Let's start with a deep breath into your belly," the instructor said.

Duane breathed in. He dared to look around. Tina was right next to him. He choked a little and coughed. She glanced over and smiled warmly. Duane smiled back and took his first deep breath in days.

> Rose's **verb tenses** are **consistent.** She uses past tense for actions and present tense for dialogue.

> Rose uses transitional phrases to make the chronological **sequence of events** clear.

> In this paragraph Rose tells what Duane does, but she needs to add descriptive details to help her audience picture what happens.

> Rose's **resolution** follows from the conflict described over the course of the story. When Tina smiles at Duane, he knows he'll be able to overcome his shyness to ask her out.

LEARN HOW Add Descriptive Details Rose adds well-chosen details to explain why Duane leaves the lunchroom and what happens when he does. The sensory language she adds to describe the guard's voice helps readers imagine the scene.

ROSE'S REVISION

, the noise of the lunchroom fading as he walked.   *A deep, loud voice startled*
He got up and started down the hall, ~~A security guard stopped~~ him.

 YOUR TURN Use the feedback from your peers and teacher as well as the two "Learn How" lessons to revise your short story. Evaluate how well you have communicated your message about life by examining the characters, conflict, and plot.

DIFFERENTIATED INSTRUCTION

FOR STRUGGLING WRITERS

Transitions Explain that transitional words and phrases help readers understand the sequence of events in a story. Point out two examples of transitions in the student model: "At lunch" in the fourth paragraph on this page and "As soon as" in the tenth paragraph on this page.

1. Provide a series of model sentences that use transitions to show time order. Write the sentences on the board, and underline the transitional words and phrases.

- <u>When</u> Mindy got to school, she went right to the auditorium.

- She didn't see a soul. <u>After a while</u>, Amos wandered in.

- "Amos, you're so late!" Mindy screeched. <u>Before</u> Amos could answer, Mindy dragged out the props.

- "<u>As soon</u> as you're ready!" she yelled. "The play is tomorrow night."

- <u>Finally,</u> Amos seemed to wake up.

- <u>Then,</u> he jumped into action.

- <u>The next thing</u> Mindy knew, the props were finished.

- <u>The following evening,</u> Mindy went to the play.

2. Have students create sentences that show time order, using the transition words on the board.

R RESOURCE MANAGER—Copy Master
Writing Support, p. 176

Editing and Publishing

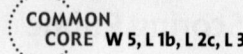 COMMON CORE

W 5 Strengthen writing by editing. **L 1b** Use participial phrases to convey specific meanings and add variety. **L 2c** Spell correctly. **L 3** Apply knowledge of language to make effective choices for meaning or style.

In the editing stage, you proofread your story to make sure that it is free of grammar, spelling, and punctuation errors. Read carefully to catch any spelling errors, even after doing a word-processing spell check. You don't want mechanical mistakes to distract your audience from what is happening in your narrative.

GRAMMAR IN CONTEXT: PARTICIPLES

A **participle** is a verb form that can be used as an adjective. Participles usually end in *-ing* or *-ed*. Writers use participles to provide information and vary sentence structure. Examine this sentence from Rose's draft:

> He could just see himself in a leotard, stretching and taking deep breaths.
> [The participles *stretching* and *taking* modify, or describe, the subject of the sentence—*He* (Duane). The participle *stretching* stands alone. *Taking* is part of a participial phrase: *taking deep breaths.* Instead of expressing the action of stretching and taking deep breaths in a separate sentence, Rose combines the information with the detail about Duane imagining himself in a leotard.]

As Rose edits her story, she sees an opportunity to vary sentence structure by using a participle in the last paragraph to break up a series of sentences that follow the subject-verb pattern.

> ~~Duane~~ breath̲e̲d̲ in, ~~He~~ dared to look around.
> *ing*

PUBLISH YOUR WRITING

You can share your short story with an audience. Here are some options:
- Send your story to a magazine or Web site that accepts stories from unpublished writers.
- Create a podcast of yourself reading your story aloud for others to enjoy.
- Adapt a key scene from your story into a script and produce a video adaptation. Enlist the help of some classmates to act out the parts of different characters.

 YOUR TURN Correct any spelling, capitalization, punctuation, or grammar errors in your story. Use participles and participial phrases to vary sentence structure and provide important information. Then, publish your story for your audience.

Editing and Publishing

 COMMON CORE **W 5, L 1b, L 2c, L 3**

GRAMMAR IN CONTEXT: PARTICIPLES

Remind students that a participle is a verb form that can be used as an adjective, and it usually ends in *-ing* or *-ed*. Participles provide information and add variety to sentence structure. For practice, have students identify the participles and participial phrases in the following sentences.

1. The smiling man ate another fried chicken wing. *(smiling)*
2. Ignored, she slipped out of the room. *(ignored)*
3. Visiting gardens, butterflies flit among the flowers. *(Visiting gardens)*

PUBLISH YOUR WRITING

Brainstorm with students additional ways to publish their stories.

YOUR TURN Allow students time to revise their stories. Remind them to check for sentences that could be combined using participial constructions. Ask them to check to see whether they can add more details to make their stories more effective.

FOR ENGLISH LANGUAGE LEARNERS

Participles Remind students that they can vary sentence structure in their short stories by using participles to break up a series of sentences that follow the subject-verb pattern. Write these sentence pairs on the board, and have students combine them using participles or participial phrases:

- Maria rode her bike. She got home fast. *(Riding her bike, Maria got home fast.)*
- The dog ran to the door. It barked and wagged its tail. *(The dog ran to the door, barking and wagging its tail.)*
- Damian looked around the room. He noticed Amy was at the party. *(Looking around the room, Damian noticed Amy was at the party.)*

FOR STRUGGLING WRITERS

Participial Phrases Write these verbs on the board: *arrive, lose, run away, take.* Have students create a sentence for each verb, using it in a participial phrase.

Scoring Rubric

Explain to students that the best way to understand rubrics is to use them to score actual writing. Have students use the rubric to evaluate the final drafts of their short stories. Ask students to score their own stories and then write a brief paragraph using the language of the rubric to explain the reasons for their scores.

For Rubric Bank, see

💿 **WriteSmart CD-ROM**

Writing Center on **thinkcentral.com**

Assess and Reteach

Assess

R **RESOURCE MANAGER**—Copy Masters
   Rubric for Evaluation, p. 174

Online Essay Scoring on **thinkcentral.com**

Reteach

Level Up Online Tutorial on **thinkcentral.com**

Reteaching Worksheets on **thinkcentral.com**

   Writing Lesson 21: Elaborate with Sensory
   Language

   Writing Lesson 32: Writing Dialogue

Scoring Rubric

Use the rubric below to evaluate your short story from the Writing Workshop or your response to the on-demand writing task on the next page.

SHORT STORY

SCORE	COMMON CORE TRAITS
6	• **Development** Skillfully introduces, develops, and resolves a conflict; develops compelling, believable characters; effectively uses dialogue and description • **Organization** Has a well-paced, smooth, coherent event sequence that builds to a strong climax and resolution • **Language** Consistently maintains a point of view; weaves in sensory language; shows a strong command of conventions
5	• **Development** Effectively introduces, develops, and resolves a conflict; develops interesting, believable characters; ably uses dialogue and description • **Organization** Has a coherent event sequence that builds to a climax and satisfactory resolution; uses effective pacing • **Language** Maintains a point of view; sentences have a variety of phrasing; includes sensory language; has a few errors in conventions
4	• **Development** Introduces, develops, and resolves a conflict; has interesting characters with some believable traits; could use more dialogue or description • **Organization** Includes some unnecessary events, resulting in uneven pacing • **Language** Mostly maintains a point of view; uses some sentence variety; needs more sensory language; has a few distracting errors in conventions
3	• **Development** Introduces and resolves a conflict, but needs more development; has some underdeveloped characters; needs more dialogue or description • **Organization** Has a confusing sequence caused by some extraneous events; has a lagging pace at times • **Language** Has a few lapses in point of view; sentence phrasing is repetitious; lacks enough sensory language; has some significant errors in conventions
2	• **Development** Introduces a conflict but does not develop or resolve it; inadequately develops characters; lacks sufficient dialogue and description • **Organization** Includes too many events that distract from the plot; has choppy pacing • **Language** Uses inconsistent point of view; sentences are simplistic; mostly lacks sensory language; has many distracting errors in conventions
1	• **Development** Has no identifiable conflict; includes underdeveloped characters; lacks any dialogue or description • **Organization** Has no apparent organization • **Language** Never establishes a clear point of view; sentences are simplistic; lacks sensory language; has major problems with conventions

Preparing for Timed Writing

COMMON CORE · **W 10** Write routinely over shorter time frames for a range of tasks, purposes, and audiences.

1. ANALYZE THE TASK — 5 MIN

Read the writing task carefully. Then, read it again, making note of the words that tell the type of writing, the topic, the audience, and the purpose.

WRITING TASK

Everyone feels shy or nervous sometimes. Write a <u>personal narrative or a short story</u> — *Type of Writing*
about a time you or a fictional character <u>overcame shyness or nervousness</u> to accomplish — *Topic*→
something. Use your narrative to <u>describe a meaningful experience or tell a meaningful</u>
<u>story</u> to (classmates). ← *Audience*   ←*Purpose*

2. PLAN YOUR RESPONSE — 10 MIN

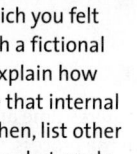

Identify a personal experience in which you felt shy or nervous or a situation in which a fictional character might feel that way, and explain how you or the character could overcome that internal conflict to accomplish something. Then, list other elements of your narrative, including what made the experience or situation meaningful.

Narrative Elements	Notes
People or Characters	
Setting	
Conflict	
Sequence of Events	
Resolution	
Meaning	

3. RESPOND TO THE TASK — 20 MIN

Begin drafting your narrative. Start with action or dialogue that introduces the conflict to your audience. As you write, keep the following points in mind:

- In the exposition, present the people or characters involved, the setting, the conflict, and any background information your audience might need.
- In the rising action, create a smooth sequence of events that builds to a climax, or high point of suspense.
- In the falling action and resolution, reflect on what was experienced over the course of the narrative.

4. IMPROVE YOUR RESPONSE — 5–10 MIN

Revising Compare your draft with the writing task. Does your draft tell a personal or fictional story about overcoming shyness or nervousness? Does your draft make the meaning of the experience or story clear to your classmates?

Proofreading Find and correct any errors in grammar, usage, or spelling. Make sure that your narrative is correctly punctuated and all edits are neatly written and legible.

Checking Your Final Copy Before you submit your narrative, examine it once more to make sure that you are presenting your best work.

WRITING WORKSHOP **289**

COMMON CORE FOCUS

W 10 Write routinely over shorter time frames for a range of tasks, purposes, and audiences.

Preparing for Timed Writing

1. **Analyze the Task** Before students begin writing, encourage them to answer the following questions:
   - What is my time limit?
   - What are the core traits assessed in the scoring rubric?
   - Who is my audience?
   - What is my purpose?

2. **Plan Your Response** Remind students that a story should place believable characters in a conflict situation that ends in a satisfying resolution. Tell students that when planning their responses, they should note important details about their characters and plot.

3. **Respond to the Task** Remind students that their responses should be focused and coherent. They should limit what they write to only one or two main characters and one conflict and resolution.

4. **Improve Your Response** Point out to students that the scoring rubric emphasizes using dialogue. Remind students to use realistic dialogue that is appropriate to the speaker and the situation. Also, have students check their verb tense sequences.

Assess

Use the Scoring Rubric on page 288 to assess students' stories.

FOR ENGLISH LANGUAGE LEARNERS

Writing: Proofreading Remind students that they can expect to make errors when responding to writing tasks in timed situations. Although it may not be possible for students to correct all their errors, they should be aware of ones they commonly make and proofread for them carefully. Students should check for errors in word choice, grammar, spelling, and usage.

FOR STRUGGLING WRITERS

Understanding the Task Responding to a timed writing task can be difficult for any writer. Remind students that it is important to read the task thoroughly before writing in order to comply with all aspects of the task. After students have written their answers, they should review the task one more time to be sure they have answered each part of the task as fully as possible and followed the instructions concerning audience, purpose, and tone.

Focus and Motivate

⬭ COMMON CORE FOCUS

W 6 Use technology to produce writing products. **SL 1c–d** Incorporate others in discussions; respond thoughtfully to diverse perspectives. **SL 2** Integrate multiple sources of information in diverse media. **SL 5** Use digital media.

PRODUCE WITH A PURPOSE

Tell students they will be presenting their videos for the class or other students at school. Remind students to select a key scene from their short stories for the video narrative.

COMMON CORE TRAITS

As students plan their videos, remind them to keep in mind the *COMMON CORE TRAITS* of a strong video presentation.

Practice and Apply

Planning The Video

Students may have trouble creating a script. Remind them that a video can be effective in creating mood and showing characters' emotions. Lighting, music, silence, lengths of shots, and other sound and camera effects will take the place of many of the words in the original story. Explain to students that when they want to explain background, they may need to write additional dialogue or narration.

R RESOURCE MANAGER—Copy Masters
Publishing with Technology, p. 175

Technology Workshop

Essential Course of Study **ECOS**

Producing a Video Narrative

Images can tell stories in ways that the written word cannot. Add sound to images, and you have a dynamic storytelling medium. A **video narrative** of one or more scenes from your short story can bring its characters, setting, and plot to life.

🖐 Complete the workshop activities in your **Reader/Writer Notebook.**

PRODUCE WITH A PURPOSE	*COMMON CORE TRAITS*
TASK Select a scene from your short story to feature in a **video narrative.** Once you have created your video, present it to a specific audience, such as your classmates or other students at your school.	**A STRONG VIDEO NARRATIVE . . .** • focuses on one or more scenes • includes images and sound • is based on an engaging script • uses action and dialogue to grab viewers' interest

⬭ COMMON CORE

W 6 Use technology to produce writing products.
SL 1c–d Incorporate others in discussions; respond thoughtfully to diverse perspectives.
SL 2 Integrate multiple sources of information in diverse media.
SL 5 Use digital media.

Planning the Video

Creating a video narrative requires time and preparation. The following guidelines can help you with the process.

- **Focus on a Scene** Think about the action you want to portray. Choose a scene that makes sense without extra explanation or that could be expanded for your narrative.
- **Cast the Characters and Choose a Setting** Ask classmates to portray your characters. Adjust the scene's setting to a location you can shoot. If a scene is set on the moon, for example, move the action inside the moon base.
- **Create a Script** Map out dialogue and action, and consider using a voice-over—an off-screen narrator who provides background information or the thoughts and feelings of the main character. Also, include notes on visual effects and sound effects in your script if applicable.
- **Storyboard Your Scene** Use sketches to show what shots you will need. Include a variety of perspectives, such as establishing shots, medium shots, and close-ups. Consider including shots from a key character's point of view.

Media Tools **THINK central**
Go to **thinkcentral.com.**
KEYWORD: HML10-290

Video	Audio
Image Description: MEDIUM SHOT of the class, with HIGH CAMERA ANGLE on DUANE and TINA	[soothing music plays in background] [voice-over] Duane couldn't believe it. He was going to have to do yoga after all. [Duane, in low mumble to himself as he puts mat down] If only Ma could see me now . . . [voice-over] Then, he spotted Tina.

DIFFERENTIATED INSTRUCTION

FOR ENGLISH LANGUAGE LEARNERS
Language: Reinforce Technology Terms
Review key technology terms used in this workshop:

- *scene:* episode in the plot
- *script:* text of a play, film, or broadcast
- *storyboard:* set of drawings or pictures that tell a story
- *video:* visual elements

- *audio:* sound elements
- *rehearse:* practice by repetition
- *props:* items in a production that are not scenery, lighting/sound, or wardrobe
- *costumes:* clothing worn by the characters

Producing the Video

You will need a video camera and some expertise to produce your video. Find out what kind of equipment and technical help are available at your school, in your community, or among your friends. If equipment is not available, act out the scene in a theatrical production.

- **Rehearse** Prepare your actors. Give them the script and show them the storyboards. Make sure they are familiar with their lines and actions. Rehearse the sequence of actions and any dialogue between characters, providing clear and specific instructions, until you and the cast feel confident about how the scene plays out.

- **Assemble Props and Equipment** Gather everything you need before recording. Make sure that cast members have any costumes or props they need. To avoid shaky results, place the camera on a tripod or a steady surface such as a table while recording.

- **Roll Camera!** Follow the script and storyboards in shooting your video. You may want to ask one or more classmates to help you direct the scene or do the recording. If so, tell anyone helping exactly what they should do to help shooting go smoothly.

- **Edit Your Masterpiece** Use an editing software program, if available, to assemble the best footage. (Otherwise, shoot scenes in sequence.) Then, record voice-overs if needed, add music if you wish, and create a title screen and credits.

Presenting the Video

TALK BACK

Sharing your video with an audience is half the fun. After your classmates or intended audience have viewed your video, hold a discussion in which viewers can share reactions to your work. Follow these suggestions to make sure you get helpful feedback.

- Be prepared to discuss all aspects of the video, from the acting and the plot to the choice of music and camera shots.

- Encourage your classmates to ask questions about your narrative or technical choices. When appropriate, clarify the effects you were trying to achieve. Ask: Did I succeed in achieving my intended effects? What parts of my video could I improve?

- Consider all constructive criticism. Respond thoughtfully and respectfully to suggestions—even when you disagree.

 YOUR TURN Use the guidelines on these pages to plan, produce, and present a video of one or more scenes from your short story. Use feedback from your viewers to help you evaluate your own work. Edit or re-record portions of your video to incorporate others' suggestions for improvement.

291

Producing the Video

Have students work in groups to choose and storyboard a scene from one of the short stories students wrote. After groups choose their scenes, suggest that students decide who will operate the camera, who will be responsible for scenery, props, and sound effects, and who the actors will be.

If the school cannot provide equipment and/or technology help, elicit from students which of them are familiar with the process of making videos and have access to equipment.

Presenting the Video

Arrange a screening of students' videos. Assemble an audience and provide comment cards for them to complete. Have students use the feedback to make their final edits.

YOUR TURN Allow students plenty of time and space to produce their videos. Students may wish to invite friends and family members to preview the video and then use that audience's responses to help them create the final version.

Assess

Use the *COMMON CORE TRAITS* to assess students' videos.

A strong video narrative
- focuses on one or more scenes
- includes images and sound
- is based on an engaging script
- uses action and dialogue to grab viewers' interest

Reteach

Remind students that a printed story requires readers to create the world of the story in their imaginations. Visual presentations show that world.

THINK central

Media Tools

Keywords for using technology direct students to **MediaScope,** a Web site that helps them strengthen media analysis and production skills.

Assessment Practice

RL 1 Cite textual evidence to support analysis of what the text says explicitly as well as inferences drawn from the text. **RL 3** Analyze how complex characters develop over the course of a text, interact with other characters, and advance the plot or theme of a text. **RI 1** Cite textual evidence to support analysis of what the text says explicitly as well as inferences drawn from the text. **RI 6** Determine an author's point of view or purpose in a text. **W 5** Strengthen writing by revising and editing. **L 5b** Analyze nuances in the meaning of words with similar denotations. **L 6** Acquire and use accurately general academic words sufficient for reading; demonstrate independence in gathering vocabulary knowledge.

CHECK READINESS

Read aloud the paragraph under **ASSESS** and stress to students that this is not the full Unit Test, but a way for them to check their readiness for it. Then have students examine the skills standards listed under **REVIEW** and look back in the unit or in the **Student Resource Bank** for any skills they need to review.

READ THE TEXTS

Remind students to keep unit goals in mind as they read each passage, paying particular attention to these literary and reading skills:

- character traits
- character motivation
- make generalizations
- make inferences

To help students focus on characters while reading, encourage them to ask questions such as

- How are the uncles in "Uncles" different from the uncle in "Tío Nano"?
- Who gets upset in each passage? What do they do and why?

ANSWER THE QUESTIONS

Direct students to pages R93–R101 of the **Handbook** to review test-taking strategies.

- Tell students not to change an answer unless they can articulate why another answer is correct. Tell them that, often, a strong hunch is right.

Assessment Practice

ASSESS
Taking this practice test will help you assess your knowledge of these skills and determine your readiness for the Unit Test.

REVIEW
After you take the practice test, your teacher can help you identify any standards you need to review.

COMMON CORE

RL 1 Cite textual evidence to support analysis of what the text says explicitly as well as inferences drawn from the text. **RL 3** Analyze how complex characters develop over the course of a text, interact with other characters, and advance the plot or theme of a text. **RI 1** Cite textual evidence to support analysis of what the text says explicitly as well as inferences drawn from the text. **RI 6** Determine an author's point of view or purpose in a text. **W 5** Strengthen writing by revising and editing. **L 5b** Analyze nuances in the meaning of words with similar denotations. **L 6** Acquire and use accurately general academic words sufficient for reading; demonstrate independence in gathering vocabulary knowledge.

Practice Test
THINK central
Take it at **thinkcentral.com**.
KEYWORD: HML10N-292

DIRECTIONS Read the following selections, and then answer the questions.

from Tío Nano   *by Lionel G. García*

1   Hernando Carrejo, *Tío* Nano we called him, was a master at timing his visits at mealtime. We could see him coming from the highway by the courthouse two blocks away, stooped from the weight of two suitcases full of clothes to be sold to the people living in the south Texas ranches. From his home in Laredo, he would take the bus or hitch a ride that would get him past Freer and around the ranching community of La Rosita. From there he would work his way through the ranches showing off his wares. In a few days, hungry and tired, he would find his way back to the main road and hitch a ride to San Diego to see his favorite cousin, my grandmother.

2   Then came the depression, and my grandmother grew tired of feeding and housing so many people, especially *Tío* Nano, who ate enough for two men, and we were told to be on the lookout for him. Anyone seeing *Tío* Nano coming down the road was to alert my grandmother, giving her time to hide not only the food she was cooking, but herself. We were supposed to tell him she was not home, that she had left town.

3   We were playing out in the street close to the courthouse one late morning when an old black car coming from the direction of Freer stopped at the corner. We heard *Tío* Nano's distinctive slurred voice thanking the driver for the ride and we saw him climb out of the car, shiny rear-end first, having a difficult time getting his suitcases out from the back seat. We dropped everything and ran home before he could turn around to see us.

4   My grandmother was in the kitchen when we arrived.

5   "What in Heaven's name happened to you?" she asked.

6   "*Tío* Nano," Cota managed to spit out before going to the faucet to get a drink of water.

7   "He's here?" my grandmother inquired, her face ashen, looking at all of us one at a time.

8   "Yes," we said.

9   "God in Heaven," she cried out. "I have to hide the food."

10   She grabbed for two dirty hand towels to grasp the pot of boiling beans and rushed with it into the bathroom. She came running out of the bathroom and snatched the plate of tortillas and raced it to the bathroom where she had just hidden the beans. As she was running back out, she said, "Tell him I'm gone. Tell him I left. Went to Alice to buy groceries, and I won't return until . . . Well, not today. That won't work. Tell him I got sick and had to go see Dr. Dunlap."

DIFFERENTIATED INSTRUCTION

FOR ENGLISH LANGUAGE LEARNERS
Assessment Practice: Work Backward Tell students to read the questions *before* they read the passages. Have pairs find unfamiliar words in test directions and questions and follow these steps:

1. Write each word on an index card.
2. Look up the meaning in a dictionary and write it on the back of the card.
3. Use the cards to practice the words with your partner and to teach them to others.

Culture: Clarify Explain that lines 10–11 of "Tío Nano" refer to the Great Depression, which began in 1929 and lasted through the 1930s. People all over the world lost their jobs, and in many areas, food was scarce. Because so many people were out of work during this period, salespeople had a hard time finding customers with the money to make purchases.

from **Uncles**   *by Margaret Atwood*

1   Once in a while Susanna's mother would make an appearance on the porch. "Susanna, don't show off," she would say, or, "Susanna, don't pester your uncles." Then an uncle would say, "She's no trouble, Mae." Mostly Susanna's mother stayed in the kitchen, doing the dishes along with the aunts, which in Susanna's opinion was where they belonged.

2   It was the aunts who brought most of the food for the Sunday dinners. They would arrive with roasts, lemon meringue pies, cookies, jars of their own pickles. Her mother might cook some potatoes, or make a jellied salad. Not a great deal was expected of her, because she was a war widow; she was still getting over the loss, and she had a child to bring up single-handed. On the outside it didn't seem to bother her. She was cheerful and rounded, and slow-moving by nature. The uncles had clubbed together to buy her the house, because she was their little sister, they had all grown up on a farm together, they were close.

3   The aunts had a hard time forgiving this. It would come up at the dinner table, in oblique references to how you had to scrimp to meet two sets of mortgage payments. The uncles would look at their wives with baffled reproach, and pass their plates down to Susanna's mother for another helping of mashed potatoes. You could not turn your own flesh and blood out on the streets to starve. Susanna knew this because she heard an uncle saying it as he lumbered down the front walk to his car.

4   "You didn't have to get such a big house," the aunt said. "It's almost as big as ours." Her high heels clipped on the cement as she hurried to keep up. All of the aunts were small, brisk women, with short legs.

5   Susanna was rocking in the giant white wicker rocker on the porch. She stopped rocking and scrunched down so her head was out of sight, to listen in.

6   "Come on, Adele," said the uncle. "You wouldn't want them living in a hut."

7   "She could get a job." This was an insult and the aunt knew it. It would mean that the uncle could not provide.

8   "Who would look after Susanna?" said the uncle, coming to a stop while he hunted for his keys. "Not you, that's for sure."

9   There was a note of bitterness in the uncle's voice that was new to Susanna. She felt sorry for him. For the aunt she felt no pity.

ASSESSMENT PRACTICE   **293**

ITEM ANALYSIS

COMPREHENSION AND WRITTEN RESPONSE	ITEMS	UNIT PAGES
Character Traits	5, 8, 10, 14, 15, 16	176–181, 183, 239
Character Motivation	2, 4, 6, 9, 16	176–181, 203
Make Generalizations	11, 12, 13	251
Make Inferences	1, 3, 7, 8, 10	203, 253

VOCABULARY	ITEMS	UNIT PAGES
Connotation and Denotation	4, 5, 6, 7	216
Word Roots	1, 2, 3	236, 274

WRITING AND GRAMMAR	ITEMS	UNIT PAGES
Modifiers and Verbs	1, 2, 4	200, 217
Sentence Types	3, 5	275

Practice Test

On **thinkcentral.com** students can complete an interactive version of this practice test *and* receive remediation for the skills they have not yet mastered.

Reading Comprehension

Model a thinking process for answering multiple-choice questions.

1. **B is correct.** *Paragraph 1 explains that the uncle is visiting his favorite cousin, "my grandmother." The word* my *indicates the narrator's relation to the other family members.* A, C, *and* D *are incorrect.*

2. **D is correct.** *The uncle's motive is hunger, and J illustrates it. A shows the effect of the motive, so it is incorrect. B concerns the narrator's sighting of the uncle, not motivation. C illustrates the effect of the uncle's work, so it is incorrect.*

3. **A is correct.** *The clues are "clothes to be sold" and "showing off his wares" (paragraph 1). B and C identify the occupations of other characters, so they are incorrect. D is a loose association with the word* courthouse *but is unrelated to the uncle.*

4. **B is correct.** *Paragraph 2 states this choice as a motive. A is not stated or implied. Nothing in the text suggests a lack of space, so C is incorrect. D might erroneously be inferred from the clause "my grandmother grew tired of feeding . . . so many people"; however, the next phrase, "especially Tío Nano," suggests that she is not tired of cooking for the children.*

5. **B is correct.** *"Hungry and tired" (paragraph 1) shows the uncle's fatigue, while paragraph 2 shows the grandmother's. Furthermore, B is correct by process of elimination: A and C might apply to one character but not both; D is totally untrue.*

6. **D is correct.** *Her reactions are shown in paragraphs 9–10. A is completely incorrect. B is what she wants the children to tell the uncle, not what she does. C may have happened, but it did not happen in reaction to the uncle's sudden arrival, so H is incorrect.*

7. **B is correct.** *This response can be inferred from the remark "'She's no trouble, Mae'" (paragraph 1) and the fact that they shared Sunday dinners. The evidence suggests the opposite of A and C. No evidence supports or disproves D, so it is not a good response.*

8. **D is correct.** *From paragraph 7, readers can infer that the aunt is attacking the uncle's self-respect. No evidence at all supports A*

Reading Comprehension

> **Use the excerpt from "Tío Nano" (p. 292) to answer questions 1–6.**

1. The story of *Tío* Nano is told through the eyes of —
   - **A.** the grandmother
   - **B.** a grandchild
   - **C.** a doctor
   - **D.** an uncle

2. In paragraph 1, which of the following phrases illustrates *Tío* Nano's motives?
   - **A.** *his favorite cousin, my grandmother*
   - **B.** *We could see him coming from the highway*
   - **C.** *stooped from the weight of two suitcases*
   - **D.** *was a master at timing his visits at mealtime*

3. From paragraph 1, you can infer that *Tío* Nano's occupation is most likely that of a —
   - **A.** salesman
   - **B.** bus driver
   - **C.** rancher
   - **D.** lawyer

4. What motivates the grandmother in the story to change her feelings about feeding *Tío* Nano?
   - **A.** *Tío* Nano's appetite seems to increase every time he visits.
   - **B.** The depression has made it harder for her to feed and house her relatives.
   - **C.** There is no room for *Tío* Nano and his two heavy suitcases.
   - **D.** She is tired of cooking all day long for the children.

5. How are *Tío* Nano and the grandmother in the story alike?
   - **A.** They both enjoy riding around in the south Texas countryside.
   - **B.** They both become tired from working so hard.
   - **C.** They both use the children to give other people false information.
   - **D.** They both are ill often and cannot get their work done.

6. The grandmother reacts to news of *Tío* Nano's arrival by —
   - **A.** preparing a big meal to welcome him to the house
   - **B.** getting sick and runs out to the doctor's office
   - **C.** sending the children out to play for the afternoon
   - **D.** hiding the food and asking the children to say she is gone

> **Use the excerpt from "Uncles" (p. 293) to answer questions 7–12.**

7. From paragraph 1, what can you infer about the relationship between Susanna and her uncles?
   - **A.** She annoys them.
   - **B.** They get along well.
   - **C.** The uncles ignore her.
   - **D.** They don't talk much.

8. In paragraph 7, Adele knowingly insults her husband's —
   - **A.** determination
   - **B.** honesty
   - **C.** loyalty to family
   - **D.** ability to provide

9. The uncles' main motivation for buying their sister a house is that —
   - **A.** they want to keep their sister and Susanna from living with them
   - **B.** they want to cause their wives extra work
   - **C.** they think their sister needs a house big enough for the Sunday dinners
   - **D.** they care about their sister and Susanna as family members

or B. *Although the aunt criticizes the uncle for how he shows his loyalty, loyalty per se cannot be inferred as the issue.*

9. **D is correct.** *The text states the uncles bought the house "because she was their little sister" and "they were close" (paragraph 2). No evidence supports A, B, or C.*

10. **C is correct.** *The text states that she "scrunched down . . . to listen in" (paragraph 5). "To listen in" suggests curiosity. A, B, and D are incorrect; none of them are implied in the passage.*

11. **C is correct.** *The text states that the "aunts had a hard time forgiving" their husbands' buying Mae a house (paragraph 3). Also, the discussion between the aunt and uncle supports this answer. No evidence supports A or D, and B is definitely untrue, as shown by the ungracious "oblique references" to two mortgage payments.*

10. Susanna hides on the porch and listens to her aunt and uncle's conversation out of —

    A. alarm

    B. boredom

    C. curiosity

    D. indifference

11. Which generalization is true of the aunts?

    A. They enjoy cooking and doing the dishes after dinner.

    B. They behave graciously toward Susanna and her mother.

    C. They resent their husbands' support of Susanna's mother.

    D. They are nice to Susanna because they wish they had daughters.

12. Which generalization is true about the uncles?

    A. They expect family members to help one another.

    B. They have no disappointments in their lives.

    C. The Sunday dinners are their favorite weekly event.

    D. They sympathize with their wives' disapproval.

Use both selections to answer question 13.

13. Which of the following generalizations is true about the main characters in both selections?

    A. They want to acquire better cars and better houses.

    B. Family relationships are important to them.

    C. They believe that children should be seen but not heard.

    D. The uncles are unpopular with everyone else in the family.

SHORT CONSTRUCTED RESPONSE
Write three or four sentences to answer each question.

14. How does the author reveal the grandmother's character in the excerpt from "Tío Nano"? Give one example each of two methods of characterization.

15. Identify three character traits of Susanna in the excerpt from "Uncles." Support your answer with examples from the selection.

Write two to three paragraphs to answer this question.

16. How do *Tío* Nano and Susanna's uncles compare or contrast in terms of their behavior, their positions in life, or any other characteristics they exhibit? Support your answer with details from the selections.

GO ON ➡

---

12. **A is correct.** *Paragraph 3 suggests that the uncles expect to look out for one another. The bitterness (paragraph 9) suggests that B and D are untrue. No evidence supports C.*

13. **B is correct.** *Tío Nano has a favorite cousin; the uncles look after their sister. No evidence supports A, C, or D.*

SHORT CONSTRUCTED RESPONSE
Possible responses:

14. *The author reveals character through the character's words and details that other characters observe about her. Examples of the former include "I have to hide the food" (paragraph 9) and "Tell him I got sick and had to go see Dr. Dunlap" (paragraph 10). Examples of the latter include "my grandmother grew tired of feeding ... so many people, especially Tio Nano" (paragraph 2).*

15. *Susanna is judgmental, as shown by her opinion that her aunts belong in the kitchen (paragraph 1). She is observant and curious, as shown by her eavesdropping (paragraph 5). She is loyal to her uncle, as shown by her feeling sorry for him (paragraph 9).*

16. *The uncle in "Tío Nano"*

    a. *likes to eat: is a master at visiting at mealtimes; eats enough for two men*

    b. *likes his family, or at least claims to: "his favorite cousin, my grandmother" (paragraph 1)*

    c. *is probably not successful at his work during the depression: His suitcases are heavy on his return trip from the ranches.*

    d. *is selfish: doesn't appear to give or do anything in return for meals at the grandmother's house*

    The uncles in "Uncles"

    a. *like to eat: Sunday dinners are large, and the uncles ask for more potatoes.*

    b. *have a sense of family obligation: provide for wives and sister; have weekly dinner; seem to enjoy Susanna*

    c. *are somewhat successful: bought their sister a house; one owns a car; wives bring most of the dinner*

    d. *are generous: bought the house for the sister; pay for most of the Sunday meal; spend time with Susanna*

DIFFERENTIATED INSTRUCTION

FOR ENGLISH LANGUAGE LEARNERS

Vocabulary Support On the board, write the italicized vocabulary terms from the following bulleted list. Then read the examples in random order, and have students match each example to the appropriate term. Elicit additional examples.

- *character traits:* kind, cranky, loving
- *character motivation:* fear, greed, love
- *generalization:* Family dinners are always interesting.

Vocabulary

1. **C is correct.** A cannot be correct because the narrator says that the voice is slurred, which is the opposite of clear. The roots suggest something that is separated from other things and therefore different. B makes no sense, since the narrator recognizes the voice. D makes no sense in the context.

2. **C is correct.** A cannot be correct because difficult means "hard," and not challenging would mean "easy." B is incorrect. D, fake, sounds like facilis, but is unrelated to difficult, so D is incorrect.

3. **C is correct.** A fits the context, but the root suggests a message arriving by an indirect rather than a dishonest path. B makes no sense in the context. D is incorrect because the uncles feel reproachful, so they clearly have understood the message.

4. **C is correct.** We learn that Tío Nano is hungry and tired, so weary fits. Although stooped suggests being bent over and looking down, it has no connotations of considering others inferior, so A is incorrect. A man who arrives at mealtimes probably is not submissive, so B is wrong. Although Tío Nano is unsuccessful, nothing suggests that he is weak, so D is incorrect.

5. **D is correct.** Urgency is suggested by Cota's needing water. Cota is not described as angry or sloppy, so A and C are incorrect. Although real spitting is disrespectful, spit is used figuratively, so B is incorrect.

6. **D is correct.** Clubbed suggests a group united by choice. Although the uncles are friendly to their sister, friendliness has little to do with buying her a house, so A is incorrect. Since clubbed refers to the uncles, B (snobbery), which describes an aunt, is incorrect. C is incorrect because the text has nothing to do with violence.

7. **B is correct.** Trudged conveys a lack of gaiety that matches the uncles' bafflement. Marched suggests anger or determination, which does not match the bafflement, so A is incorrect. No evidence suggests walking unsteadily, so C is also incorrect. Walked has almost no connotations, so D is incorrect.

Vocabulary

Use your knowledge of context clues and Latin word roots to answer the following questions.

1. The prefix *dis-* means "apart," and the Latin root *-stinct-* means "to separate." In paragraph 3 of "Tío Nano," *distinctive* means —
   A. clear
   B. common
   C. different
   D. likely

2. The word *difficult* in paragraph 3 of "Tío Nano" contains the root of the Latin word *-facilis-* and the prefix *dif-*. If *dif-* means "not" in the word *difficult*, what does *facilis* mean?
   A. Challenging
   B. Dizzy
   C. Easy
   D. Fake

3. The Latin word *ob* means "toward," and the root *-liqu-* means "slanting." In paragraph 3 of "Uncles," the word *oblique* means —
   A. dishonest
   B. exact
   C. indirect
   D. misunderstood

Use your knowledge of connotation and denotation to answer the following questions.

4. The connotation of the word *stooped* in paragraph 1 in "Tio Nano" suggests that Tío Nano —
   A. looked down on other people
   B. had a submissive personality
   C. was weary from his work
   D. was a weak person

5. The word *spit* in paragraph 6 in "Tio Nano" has the connotation of —
   A. anger
   B. disrespect
   C. sloppiness
   D. urgency

6. The word *clubbed* in paragraph 2 of "Uncles" has the connotation of —
   A. friendliness
   B. snobbery
   C. violence
   D. unity

7. Which word has nearly the same connotation as the word *lumbered* in paragraph 3 of "Uncles"?
   A. Marched
   B. Trudged
   C. Staggered
   D. Walked

296

DIFFERENTIATED INSTRUCTION

FOR ENGLISH LANGUAGE LEARNERS

Test-Taking Strategies: Understanding Instructions Read aloud instructions that identify multistep tasks. After each set of instructions, ask students how they might proceed. For example, for item 14 on page 295, students must

- name two methods of characterization in the passage
- for each method, give one example from the passage

Use a similar procedure with the **Revising and Editing** questions. Although students need to do only one thing, they must go through multiple steps, as follows:

1. For item 5, reread sentence 11 in the passage.
2. Recall what *an exclamatory sentence* is.
3. Read all the answer choices.
4. Decide which revision, if any, would create an exclamatory sentence.

Revising and Editing

DIRECTIONS Read this passage, and answer the questions that follow.

(1) Many people aren't aware of challenge faced by designers who customize rooms. (2) Sometimes, designers put on jumpsuits, gloves, and glasses to test a room. (3) There's a reason why they do this. (4) They want people with physical limitations to have functional homes. (5) One designer tests a kitchen by making a cup of tea. (6) She tries to open a drawer and finally has to take off her glove. (7) She puts a cup of water in the microwave. (8) Unable to see the settings, she decides to switch on a light. (9) The switch is across the room and is a struggle to reach for someone in a bulky jumpsuit—or for an elderly person. (10) Instead, she guesses which buttons to push. (11) Suddenly she hears a crackle and realizes the tea bag has caught fire.

1. What change, if any, should be made in sentence 1?
   A. Insert *an* before challenge
   B. Change *challenge* to **challenges**
   C. Insert a comma after *designers*
   D. Make no change

2. What change, if any, should be made to sentence 2?
   A. Change *Sometimes* to **Furthermore**
   B. Add descriptive adjectives to *jumpsuits, gloves,* and *glasses*
   C. Use a simile to compare *designers* to something more familiar
   D. Make no change

3. What is the most effective way to rewrite sentence 3 as an interrogative sentence?
   A. Why do they do this?
   B. There's a reason why they do this!
   C. They do this for a reason.
   D. Do this for a reason.

4. What is the most effective way to rewrite sentence 6?
   A. She tries to open a blue drawer and finally has to take off her black glove.
   B. She desperately tries to open a large drawer and finally has to take off her glove.
   C. She tries to pull on a drawer and finally has to take off her large glove.
   D. She struggles to open a drawer and finally has to yank off her cumbersome glove.

5. What is the most effective way to rewrite sentence 11 as an exclamatory sentence?
   A. Insert a comma before *and*
   B. Change the final punctuation
   C. Change *realizes* to **screams**
   D. Make no change

297

FOR ENGLISH LANGUAGE LEARNERS

Assessment Support: Sentence Types Write these sentences on the board, and have students identify each as declarative, interrogative, exclamatory, or imperative:

- Do you think family is important?
- Name your closest relative.
- I have eight cousins.
- Your parents are so nice!
- My mother designs rooms.
- Did her tea bag really catch fire?

RL 10 Read and comprehend literature. **RI 10** Read and comprehend literary nonfiction.

INTRODUCE *GREAT READS*

In Unit 2, students have discussed a number of big questions. Invite students to tell which question they found most intriguing and why, and then focus attention on the three that appear on this page. Discuss the recommended books and their summaries, pointing out how each connects to the related question. Encourage students to choose one or more of these "great reads" to read independently.

UNIT 2
Great Reads

Ideas for Independent Reading

What helps someone overcome grief? How does one person improve another's life? Find out by reading these additional works.

COMMON CORE

RL 10 Read and comprehend literature. **RI 10** Read and comprehend literary nonfiction.

Is there a cure for grief?

Let Their Spirits Dance
by Stella Pope Duarte

Teresa Ramirez's brother Jesse died in Vietnam 30 years ago. When her mother, 80, decides to travel to Washington to find his name on the Vietnam Memorial wall, Teresa hopes this journey will help free her mother from her long grief.

A Death in the Family
by James Agee

This novel by one of America's most respected writers chronicles a family's grief after the father's death in an auto accident. Readers see how quickly happiness can turn to devastation.

In the Midst of Winter
edited by Mary Jane Moffat

The writers in this anthology express their grief over the loss of a family member or an animal companion. Can writing about grief help one get past it?

How good are you at judging people?

A Separate Peace
by John Knowles

The narrator of this novel remembers his high school friend Phineas, a talented athlete whom he accidentally crippled in a moment of misperception and envy.

Twelve Angry Men
by Reginald Rose

A jury must decide whether a teenager is guilty of murder. When the jurors take their first poll, all but one vote to convict the boy. Will the majority convince the holdout to change his mind?

The Heart Is a Lonely Hunter
by Carson McCullers

This classic novel portrays five outcasts in a Depression-era Southern town. McCullers reveals the complexities of humans in search of love.

Who has made you a better person?

The Color of Water: A Black Man's Tribute to His White Mother
by James McBride

McBride honors his mother, who experienced rejection, isolation, and poverty but ensured that each one of her 12 children went to college.

Death Be Not Proud
by John Gunther

The writer's son Johnny was stricken with a brain tumor when he was 17. As Johnny struggled with his illness, he never lost hope and inspired everyone around him. His father honored his memory with this book.

A Lesson Before Dying
by Ernest J. Gaines

Grant Wiggins is asked to help a young death-row inmate prepare to die. The prisoner is a victim of racism, as is Grant, who chafes at the limits it places on his life. The two men help each other resist the crippling efffects of hatred.

Get Novel Wise

THINK central

Go to **thinkcentral.com**.
KEYWORD: HML10-298

298

NovelWise   **THINK** central

The keyword on this page points to **NovelWise**, a Web site that helps students choose a novel or other book-length work to read. **NovelWise** also provides

- study guides
- reading strategies and literary elements instruction
- presentations to introduce classic novels
- project ideas

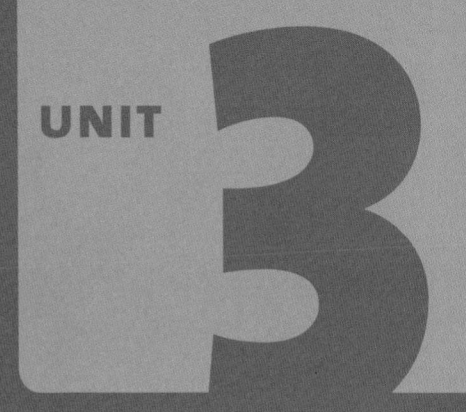

UNIT 3

A Writer's Choice

NARRATIVE DEVICES

- **In Fiction**
- **In Nonfiction**

About the Art Ando Hiroshige created this woodblock print, called *Sudden Shower over Shin-Ohashi Bridge and Atake*, in the 1800s. For more information, see page 359.

INTRODUCE THE UNIT

Call attention to the scenes of rain showers and talk briefly about the story each one tells. Point out that just as an artist makes choices about how to share an idea visually, a writer must consider a variety of **narrative devices** when telling a story. Ask what types of choices a writer makes. Elicit that among those choices are (1) who will tell the story and from what point of view and (2) how best to order the events or ideas that the writer wants to share.

Invite students to use *Sudden Shower over Shin-Ohashi Bridge and Atake* and the photograph to consider how a writer's choices influence the resulting story. Ask:

- If you were to write a story based on one of these works, who would you choose to narrate the story?
- What might happen in the story?
- How might the story begin?
- How might the story change if another person told the story?

Finally, explain that in discussing the selections in this unit, students will focus on the decision writers make in choosing narrative devices. These devices, including the choice of narrator and point of view and the order in which events are presented, are key to making a story interesting.

For help in planning this unit, see

R **RESOURCE MANAGER UNIT 3**
pp. 1–10

UNIT 3

<table>
<tr><th>COMMON CORE STRAND</th><th>ECOS
Text Analysis Workshop: Narrative Devices
pp. 302–307</th><th>ECOS
By the Waters of Babylon
Short Story
pp. 308–323

Lexile: 800
Fry: 5
Dale-Chall: 5.1</th><th>ECOS / Comparing Text Selections
There Will Come Soft Rains
Short Story
pp. 324–335

Lexile: 910
Fry: 9
Dale-Chall: 6.1</th><th>Comparing Text Selections
Inside the Home of the Future/Car of the Future
Newspaper Article/Ad
pp. 336–341

Lexile: 1300
Fry: 12
Dale-Chall: 6.1</th><th>The Doll's House
Short Story
pp. 342–353

Lexile: 760
Fry: 6
Dale-Chall: 5.9</th></tr>
<tr><td>Reading Literature</td><td>Choices About Narrator pp. 302–303
Choices About Time pp. 304–305 RL 5
Analyze the Text pp. 306–307</td><td>First-Person Point of View pp. 309, 312, 315, 322 RL 3, RL 4
Make Inferences pp. 309–310, 313, 316, 318, 322 RL 1
Language Coach pp. 312, 314 RL 4</td><td>Chronological Order pp. 325–326, 331, 334 RL 4, RL 5
Draw Conclusions pp. 325–326, 328, 330–331, 333–334 RL 1
Language Coach p. 332 RL 4</td><td></td><td>Omniscient Point of View pp. 343–344, 346, 348, 352, 353 RL 3, RL 6
Connect pp. 343, 346, 348, 351, 353 RL 1
Language Coach p. 350 RL 4
World Literature p. 352 RL 6</td></tr>
<tr><td>Reading Informational Text</td><td></td><td></td><td></td><td>Central Idea pp. 337, 339 RI 2
Synthesize pp. 336–339 RI 1, RI 4
Language Coach p. 338 RI 4
Advertisement p. 340 RI 7</td><td></td></tr>
<tr><td>Writing</td><td></td><td>Writing Prompt p. 323</td><td></td><td>Writing Prompt p. 339 W 1</td><td></td></tr>
<tr><td>Speaking and Listening</td><td></td><td>Discuss p. 308 SL 1</td><td>What's the Connection? p. 324 SL 1</td><td></td><td>Survey p. 342 SL 1</td></tr>
<tr><td>Language</td><td></td><td>Punctuation p. 317 L 2
Use Appropriate Language pp. 317, 323 L 3</td><td>Latin Root man p. 335 L 4c
Figurative Language p. 331 L 5b</td><td></td><td></td></tr>
</table>

The Seventh Man Short Story pp. 354–373	The Man in the Water Short Story pp. 374–381	Dyaspora Essay pp. 382–389	Writing Workshop: Analysis of Literary Nonfiction pp. 390–399 Speaking & Listening Workshop: Presenting a Literary Analysis pp. 400–401
Lexile: 910 Fry: 4 Dale-Chall: 5.6	Lexile: 950 Fry: College Dale-Chall: 6.7	Lexile: 1140 Fry: 9 Dale-Chall: 6.6	
Foreshadowing and Flashback pp. 355–356, 358, 360, 362, 369, 371 RL 5, RL 6 Monitor pp. 355-356, 358, 360, 362, 364-365, 367, 371 RL 1 Language Coach pp. 364, 367 RL 4 Symbol p. 366 RL 1			
Interview p. 370	Reflective Essay pp. 375, 377, 379 RI 1 Identify Main Idea and Supporting Details pp. 375–376, 379 RI 1, RI 4 Syntax and Diction p. 378 RI 4	Second-Person Point of View pp. 383–384, 389 RI 2 Analyze Sensory Details pp. 383, 386, 388, 389 RI 4 Language Coach p. 386 RI 4	Analysis of Literary Nonfiction pp. 390–400 RI 1, RI 4
Quickwrite p. 354 Writing Prompt p. 373 W 2b	Quickwrite p. 374 Writing Prompt p. 381		Writing an Analysis of Literary Nonfiction pp. 390–399 W 2a–f, W 4, W 5, W 9b, W 10
		Discuss p. 382 SL 1	Presenting a Literary Analysis pp. 400-401 SL 1d, SL 4
Add Descriptive Details pp. 361, 373 L 3 Latin Root sen p. 372 L 4c	Write Concisely pp. 377, 381 L 1b Language Coach p. 378 Latin Root plac p. 380 L 4c		Drafting p. 393 L 1b Editing and Publishing p. 397 L 2

To see the complete Essential Course of Study, see pp. T23–T28.

For additional lesson planning help, see **Teacher One Stop DVD.**

ECOS

Instructional Support

Resource Manager Unit 3

UNIT SUPPORT

Academic Vocabulary p. 3

Additional Academic Vocabulary p. 4

Grammar Focus p. 5

Text Analysis Workshop pp. 9–10

Writing Workshop: Analysis of
Literary Nonfiction p. 141

SELECTION SUPPORT*

Plan and Teach

Lesson planning pages

Additional leveled selection questions

Extension activities

Student Copy Masters

Selection summaries in four languages

Skills copy masters in English and Spanish

Vocabulary preteaching and support

Reading Check and Question Support

Reading Fluency

*Available for all selections

† Available on **thinkcentral.com.**

Language Handbook

Vocabulary Practice

Best Practices Toolkit†

PowerNotes DVD-ROM†

**Connections: Nonfiction for
Common Core** CD-ROM†

Teacher One Stop DVD-ROM

Student One Stop DVD-ROM

Write*Smart* CD-ROM†

GrammarNotes DVD-ROM†

WordSharp CD-ROM†

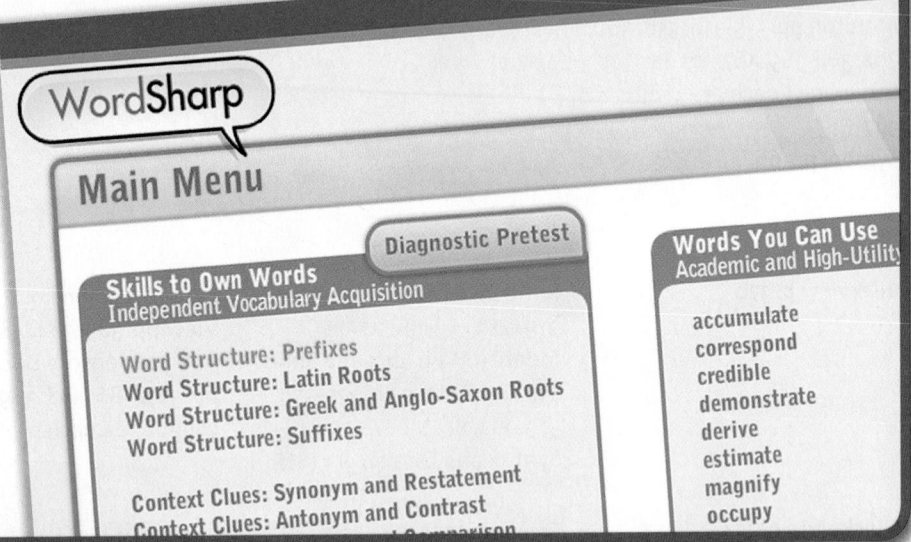

Differentiated Instruction

STRUGGLING READERS AND WRITERS	ENGLISH LANGUAGE LEARNERS	ADVANCED LEARNERS
Resource Manager Unit 3	**Resource Manager Unit 3**	**Resource Manager Unit 3**
Additional Selection Questions	Selection Summaries in English, Spanish, Vietnamese and Haitian Creole	Additional Selection Questions
Question Support		Ideas for Extension
Reading Fluency	Skills Copymasters in Spanish	**Diagnostic and Selection Tests**
Interactive Reader	**English Language Learner Adapted Interactive Reader Teacher's Guide**	Selection Tests B/C
Adapted Interactive Reader	**ELL Adapted Interactive Reader**	
Level Up Online Tutorials	**Audio Tutor**	
Audio Tutor	**Guide to English for Newcomers**	
Audio Anthology	**Audio Anthology**	
(with Audio summaries)	**Audio Summaries in Multiple Languages** (on **thinkcentral.com**)	
Diagnostic and Selection Tests		
Selection Tests A/B		

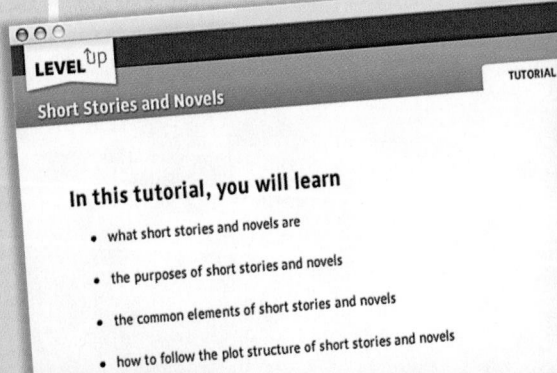

Assessment and Reteaching

Diagnostic and Selection Tests

Unit and Benchmark Tests

ThinkCentral Online Assessment:

- All program assessments
- Level Up Online Tutorials

ExamView Test Generator on the Teacher One Stop DVD-ROM

Online Essay Scoring on **thinkcentral.com**

ThinkCentral Online Reteaching:

- Level Up Online Tutorials
- Reteaching Worksheets

Holt McDougal Online Essay Scoring

Welcome to Holt McDougal Online Essay Scoring!

This site is designed to help you improve your writing skills and prepare for standardized writing tests. When you write and submit a response to one of the writing prompts on this site, the computerized scoring system will immediately score and deliver feedback on your essay. Other resources on this site will help you prepare, develop, and revise your essay.

STUDENTS
Get started by entering the
Writing Zone →

Professional Development

Video Center Based on interviews with program consultants and other educational experts, these videos feature classroom-ready teaching strategies.

Teacher Toolkit Includes a Teacher Handbook as well as a range of articles and handouts by program consultants and other educators.

Janet Allen

Jim Burke

Kylene Beers

Carol Jago

 **at a Glance**

One Location, Endless Resources

Find Resources Browse all *Holt McDougal Literature* components for the ones that meet your students' needs and match your teaching style.

Assess Progress and Reteach Assign electronic versions of program assessments to measure your students' mastery of the Common Core State Standards. On thinkcentral.com, some tests deliver online remediation tutorials to students who have not mastered skills.

 Interactive Whiteboard Lessons

Prepare your students for college and careers by teaching relevant, real-world skills through dynamic, interactive instruction. Go to **thinkcentral.com** to browse through all whiteboard lessons, including the following:

- Point of View
- Narrative Techniques
- Word Choice and Tone
- Figurative Language and Imagery

 Together Holt McDougal and HISTORY® are revolutionizing the study of English/language arts with video that helps students relive and re-imagine the people, places, and events they are discovering through reading. Look for selections with the HISTORY® icon.

HISTORY

How do you
TELL a tale?

Introduce the page by reading the question. Have students recall a story that they have enjoyed and share what they remember about its narrator. Talk about what the narrator knew and how close he or she was to the story's action and characters. Also discuss how the story might have been different if the narrator had been a different type of person.

ACTIVITY Have pairs of students preview the questions to get a sense of how a story might be told in an unusual way. Then have students discuss memorable events from the story they chose. Ask them how the writer's choices affected the story—perhaps by making it exciting, surprising, or interesting in terms of character development.

CHECK UNDERSTANDING Have students answer the question at the top of the page in their own words. Help them identify aspects of their answers as examples of narrative devices and a writer's choices.

Find It Online! **THINK** central

Go to **thinkcentral.com** for the interactive version of this unit.

How do you
TELL a tale?

Writers of stories do not follow a formula. Instead, they make deliberate choices about how to tell stories that will engage readers. Some writers choose narrators who observe events from an unusual vantage point. Other writers choose to tell their stories backwards. Writers might even decide to mislead readers on purpose simply for the element of surprise.

ACTIVITY With a partner, think of a book, movie, or television program that told a story in an unusual way. Discuss the techniques or devices the writer used to capture your interest and make the story memorable. Consider the following:

• Is there anything unusual about the narrator?

• Are the events arranged in any special order?

• Are there any unexpected plot twists?

300

Unit Resources

See resources on the **Teacher One Stop DVD-ROM** and on **thinkcentral.com**.

R RESOURCE MANAGER UNIT 3

UNIT AND BENCHMARK TESTS

BEST PRACTICES TOOLKIT

INTERACTIVE READER

ADAPTED INTERACTIVE READER

ELL ADAPTED INTERACTIVE READER

LANGUAGE HANDBOOK

VOCABULARY PRACTICE

TECHNOLOGY

🖭 **Teacher One Stop DVD-ROM**

🖭 **Student One Stop DVD-ROM**

🖭 **PowerNotes DVD-ROM**

🖭 **Write*Smart* CD-ROM**

🖭 **Media*Smart* DVD-ROM**

🖭 **GrammarNotes DVD-ROM**

🖭 **Audio Anthology CD**

🖭 **Audio Tutor CD**

Find It Online! **THINK** central

The interactive version of this unit on **thinkcentral.com** includes

• video and **PowerNotes** introductions to key selections

• audio support—listen or download

• **ThinkAloud** models

• **WordSharp** vocabulary tutorials

• interactive review and remediation

Preview Unit Goals

TEXT ANALYSIS	• Identify and analyze point of view: first person, second person, third-person limited, and third-person omniscient
	• Analyze an author's choices concerning how to structure a text and manipulate time, including flashback and foreshadowing
	• Analyze various accounts of a subject told in different mediums
	• Read and analyze a reflective essay
READING	• Use strategies for reading, including connecting and monitoring
	• Synthesize ideas and information; support an opinion
	• Cite textual evidence to support inferences and conclusions
	• Analyze sensory details
WRITING AND LANGUAGE	• Write an analysis of literary nonfiction
	• Use a consistent point of view
	• Add descriptive details; use similes to compare ideas
	• Use phrases to write concisely
	• Use vocabulary and sentence structures appropriate to formal language
SPEAKING AND LISTENING	• Present a literary analysis
VOCABULARY	• Use word roots to help determine meaning
ACADEMIC VOCABULARY	• consequent • shift
	• crucial • survive
	• initial

Complete text of the Common Core State Standards is found in the correlation on p. T10. Standards covered in this unit are found in the standards overview (pp. 299A–299B) and on the lesson pages where they are taught.

Preview Unit Goals

The main skills and strategies taught in Unit 3 are presented on this page. Challenge students to articulate something that they already know about each skill and term. Also urge them to note some personal goals in their journals. As you review the color-coding of the skill strands, invite students to page through the unit to see how the color-coding reappears.

Have students record the Academic Vocabulary terms in their journals, with a preliminary definition for each term. Urge students to confirm and perhaps refine the definitions as they read, discuss, and write about the selections in the unit.

301

DIFFERENTIATED INSTRUCTION

FOR ENGLISH LANGUAGE LEARNERS

Academic Vocabulary Provide students with definitions of each Academic Vocabulary word.

consequent (kän'si kwent') *adj.* following as an effect or result

crucial (krōō' shəl) *adj.* extremely important; critical

initial (i nish'əl) *adj.* occurring at the beginning

shift (shift) *v.* to change course; to move or transfer

survive (sər vīv') *v.* to live longer than expected; to remain in existence

Use the copy master to help students learn academic vocabulary they will use in this unit and on the Assessment Practice.

R RESOURCE MANAGER—Copy Masters
Academic Vocabulary p. 3
Additional Academic Vocabulary p. 4

Focus and Motivate

COMMON CORE FOCUS

RL 5 Analyze an author's choices concerning how to manipulate time (pacing, flashbacks) and create mystery, tension, or surprise.

Teach

Part 1: Choices About the Narrator

Point of View Explain that the **narrator** of a story is not the author but an invented voice that tells the story. Tell students that the choice of narrator can affect how involved readers become with the story and its characters.

Advantages and Disadvantages of Each Point of View After reading, use questions like those that follow to help students appreciate advantages and disadvantages of each point of view. Record their responses in a chart like the one shown.

Point of View	Advantages	Disadvantages
First-Person		
Third-Person Limited		
Third-Person Omniscient		

- The first-person point of view describes events exactly as one character first experiences them. How can this point of view help make a story vivid and real and create a subjective tone? How does this limit what readers learn?

- Why would the third-person limited point of view help readers feel connected to a particular character? How might it limit readers' understanding of story background?

- Why might the third-person omniscient point of view be useful for telling a story about an impending disaster that involved many people? How might it create a detached tone?

 **BEST PRACTICES TOOLKIT—Transparency**
   Analysis Frame: Author's Craft
      pp. D21, D24

UNIT 3
Text Analysis Workshop

Narrative Devices *Essential Course of Study* ECOS

What conflicts will drive the plot? Who will the characters be? Against what backdrop will the story develop? Beyond these considerations, a writer must make two other critical choices when crafting a story: *who* tells the story and *how* the events will unfold in time. As a reader, you should be aware of how these choices affect your perceptions of the characters and your understanding of events.

COMMON CORE
Included in this workshop:
RL 5 Analyze an author's choices concerning how to manipulate time (pacing, flashbacks) and create mystery, tension, or surprise.

Part 1: Choices About the Narrator

Point of view refers to the vantage point from which a story is told. Point of view is created by a writer's choice of **narrator,** the voice that tells the story. This choice affects whether the narrator is a character in the story or an outside observer. It also influences the story's tone plus what you know and how you feel about its characters.

POINT OF VIEW	STRATEGIES FOR ANALYSIS
FIRST PERSON *The narrator* • is a main or minor character in the story • refers to him- or herself as *I* or *me* • presents his or her own thoughts, feelings, and interpretations • lacks direct access to the thoughts of other characters • creates a subjective tone	**Consider the source.** You may feel connected to a first-person narrator because he or she seems to be talking directly to you. However, don't trust everything the narrator tells you. Ask: • Is the narrator trustworthy or unreliable? • How might the narrator's opinions of other characters affect what he or she says about them?
THIRD-PERSON LIMITED *The narrator* • is not a character in the story but an outside observer • zooms in on the thoughts and feelings of one character—usually the protagonist • creates an objective tone	**Understand the limitations.** Because you learn only one character's thoughts, you don't get the big picture. Ask: • How might the character's thoughts affect readers' impressions of characters and events? • What more would an omniscient narrator be able to convey?
THIRD-PERSON OMNISCIENT *The narrator* • is not a character in the story but an outside observer • is "all knowing"; has access to the thoughts and feelings of all characters • may create a very detached tone	**Take advantage of the insights.** When an omniscient narrator tells the story, you become "all knowing" too. Ask: • How do different characters react to the same event? • How do the characters perceive each other?

302 UNIT 3: NARRATIVE DEVICES

DIFFERENTIATED INSTRUCTION

FOR STRUGGLING READERS

Note Taking For students who need help with note taking, hand out the note-taking copy master before discussing the page. Read the top paragraph aloud to students. As you discuss the main points in the paragraph and chart sections, have students record them on the copy master.

Illustrate Points of View Have students create drawings or images to help them remember various points of view. For example, they might draw a person writing in a diary for first-person narrator or show a fly on the wall to remember third-person omniscient narrator.

R RESOURCE MANAGER—Copy Master
   Note Taking p. 9

MODEL 1: FIRST-PERSON POINT OF VIEW

In this excerpt, the narrator learns that her sister, Lalla, has broken off her wedding engagement. How does the narrator react to this news?

---

from Lalla
Short story by **Rosamunde Pilcher**

. . . it was a call from London and it was Allan Sutton.
"I have to speak to Lalla."
His voice sounded frantic. I said cautiously, "Is anything wrong?"
"She's broken off our engagement. I got back from the office and found a
5 letter from her and my ring. She said she was coming home. She doesn't want
to get married.". . .

I found myself caught up in a tangle of conflicting emotions. Enormous
sympathy for Allan; a reluctant admiration for Lalla, who had the courage to
take this shattering decision; but, as well, a sort of rising excitement.

Close Read

1. Review the boxed text. What do you learn about the narrator's feelings?

2. How would this scene be different if Allan were the narrator?

MODEL 2: THIRD-PERSON POINT OF VIEW

Here, a visitor prompts Luis and his father, Mr. Cintrón, to reflect on the past. Notice how the omniscient narrator lets you in on the characters' thoughts.

---

from Catch the Moon
Short story by **Judith Ortiz Cofer**

"Please call me Naomi, Señor Cintrón. You know my mother. She is the
director of the funeral home. . . ." Mr. Cintrón seemed surprised at first; he
prided himself on having a great memory. Then his friendly expression changed
to one of sadness as he recalled the day of his wife's burial. Naomi did not finish
5 her sentence. She reached over and placed her hand on Mr. Cintrón's arm for a
moment. Then she said "Adiós" softly, and got in her shiny white car. She waved
to them as she left, and her gold bracelets flashing in the sun nearly blinded Luis.
    Mr. Cintrón shook his head. "How about that," he said as if to himself.
"They are the Dominican owners of Ramirez Funeral Home." And, with a sigh,
10 "She seems like such a nice young woman. Reminds me of your mother when
she was her age."
    Hearing the funeral parlor's name, Luis remembered too. The day his mother
died, he had been in her room at the hospital while his father had gone for
coffee. The alarm had gone off on her monitor and nurses had come running in,
15 pushing him outside. After that, all he recalled was the anger that had made him
punch a hole in his bedroom wall.

Close Read

1. Find one example in which the narrator reveals Mr. Cintrón's thoughts. Then find one example in which Luis's thoughts are described.

2. Describe Luis's and Mr. Cintrón's feelings about their loss. What emotions is each character dealing with?

TEXT ANALYSIS WORKSHOP **303**

MODEL 1: FIRST-PERSON POINT OF VIEW

Close Read

1. *Possible answer: The narrator has conflicting emotions about Lalla's broken engagement in that she admires her sister's bravery, sympathizes with Allan, and also feels a rising excitement.*

2. *Possible answer: If Allan were the narrator, the focus would be on his feelings rather than on the sister's. Readers would be able to know just what he thought when he found the letter and ring instead of learning from someone else only that "his voice sounded frantic."*

MODEL 2: THIRD-PERSON POINT OF VIEW

Close Read

1. *Possible answer: The narrator reveals Mr. Cintrón's thoughts at the beginning, pointing out that Mr. Cintrón prided himself on having a great memory and also recalled the day of his wife's burial. The narrator reveals Luis's thoughts in the last paragraph, noting that he remembers the day of his mother's death and his angry reaction to that death.*

2. *Possible answer: Mr. Cintrón is saddened by the memories of his wife's funeral. He clearly misses his wife, as is evidenced by his comment to Luis, "Reminds me of your mother when she was her age." Luis had originally felt anger at his mother's death, but he seems to have moved beyond it, since he remembered it only after hearing the funeral parlor's name.*

FOR ENGLISH LANGUAGE LEARNERS

Language: Pronoun Referents Identify for students the different referents for *I* in "Lalla" (lines 2, 3, 4, and 7). Help them distinguish between the ones that refer to the narrator and the ones used in dialogue. Have pairs of students find other pronouns in the second model and ask each other to which noun each pronoun refers.

FOR ADVANCED LEARNERS/PRE–AP

Hypothesize Points of View Ask students to hypothesize and write a paragraph describing how their lives might be different if they could experience the world from a point of view other than the first-person point of view. Then, have them write a paragraph describing their day from this alternate point of view. Invite volunteers to share their ideas with the class.

Online Remediation

Are your students struggling with text analysis skills? Consider assigning them one or more **Level Up Online Tutorials** as remediation before beginning this unit. Log in to **thinkcentral.com** to view a list of the skills addressed by **Level Up**.

Teach

Part 2: Choices About Time

Foreshadowing After students read the page, explain that suspense is the excitement or tension that readers or viewers feel as they wonder what might happen next. Writers create suspense to hold readers' interest. Ask students to recall stories they have read or films they have seen that contained **fore-shadowing.** Have volunteers identify hints about events that happened later in the story.

Flashback Explain that **flashback** allows a writer to provide background information about a character, setting, or event. For example, if two characters dislike each other, a flashback might explain the reasons why.

To illustrate how flashbacks change the sequence of events, draw a simple timeline on the board.

```
2      3      1              4
├──────┼──────┼──────────────┤
```

Explain that the numerals on the timeline show the order in which the events shown in the second set of pictures on page 304 actually occurred. To clarify the actual chronology of the events, read this story as you point to the corresponding picture and numeral:

> Once a man and his family spent happy times together. Years later, the man was in a plane crash. After the crash, he thought back to the time he spent with his family. Then he shifted his thoughts back to the present, where he was stranded on an island.

Emphasize that the third picture depicts an event that actually happened at an earlier time. Point out that writers sometimes introduce a flashback without offering clues to the shift in time, so it is important that readers make a mental note of the chronological order of events in a story as they read.

Part 2: Choices About Time

In addition to making choices about point of view, writers make choices about how time is going to unfold in a story. Most writers choose to tell a story in chronological order. Sometimes, though, a writer will use techniques such as flashback or foreshadowing to create specific effects.

If you've ever watched a horror movie, you know about **foreshadowing,** or the use of hints to build suspense about what will happen next. Those hints might be shots of foreboding settings or statements like "I'll be right back"—sure signs of lurking danger. Writers also use foreshadowing to create edge-of-your-seat effects. As you read any story, look for similar hints—repeated details or characters who make important statements or behave in unusual ways.

What clues in this familiar movie scenario hint at a disastrous plane crash?

| Flashes of lightning signal an approaching storm. | A passenger reassures others: "There's nothing to worry about." | The pilot loses control of the aircraft. | The aircraft crashes on a remote island. |

A flashback is another device frequently used in movies. In literature, a **flashback** is an account of an event or a conversation that happened before the beginning of the story. It interrupts the chronological order of events to reveal information that can help readers understand the characters or the current situation. To spot a flashback, look for phrases that signal a shift in time, such as "he remembered that day" or "as a young child."

How does this flashback help you to understand the character's emotions?

  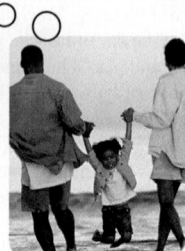 

| Remnants of the crash remain on the beach. | One survivor's thoughts turn toward home. | He remembers time spent with his family years earlier. | Jolted to the present, he realizes he may never see his family again. |

DIFFERENTIATED INSTRUCTION

FOR STRUGGLING READERS

Note Taking For those students who need help, hand out the note-taking copy master for this page. Read and discuss the top of the page, reviewing the term *chronological order.* Then discuss each paragraph separately, allowing students time to complete one section of the copy master before taking notes on the next.

 RESOURCE MANAGER—Copy Master
Note Taking p. 10

FOR ENGLISH LANGUAGE LEARNERS

Vocabulary: Prefixes Draw a word web on the board with the prefix *fore-* in the center. Around it, write the words *foreshadow, fore-head, foresee, foresight, forethought, fore-ground.* Explain that *fore-* means either "in front" or "before." Have teams of students first predict what each word in the web means. Help students check their definitions in a dictionary.

MODEL: FLASHBACK

"Sophistication" is a story about a young man and woman who want to look sophisticated in each other's eyes. Here, the characters reflect on an awkward encounter from their past. As you read, consider how the flashback helps you understand the characters and their current situation.

from SOPHISTICATION

Short story by **Sherwood Anderson**

When the moment of sophistication came to George Willard his mind turned to Helen White, the Winesburg banker's daughter. . . . Once on a summer night when he was eighteen, he had walked with her on a country road and in her presence had given way to an impulse to boast, to make
5 himself appear big and significant in her eyes. Now he wanted to see her for another purpose. He wanted to . . . try to make her feel the change he believed had taken place in his nature. . . .

Helen White was thinking of George Willard even as he wandered gloomily through the crowds thinking of her. She remembered the summer evening when
10 they had walked together and wanted to walk with him again. She thought that the months she had spent in the city, the going to theaters and the seeing of great crowds wandering in lighted thoroughfares, had changed her profoundly. She wanted him to feel and be conscious of the change in her nature.

The summer evening together that had left its mark on the memory of both
15 the young man and woman had, when looked at quite sensibly, been rather stupidly spent. They had walked out of town along a country road. Then they had stopped by a fence near a field of young corn and George had taken off his coat and let it hang on his arm. "Well, I've stayed here in Winesburg—yes— I've not yet gone away but I'm growing up," he had said. "I've been reading
20 books and I've been thinking. I'm going to try to amount to something in life.

"Well," he explained, "that isn't the point. Perhaps I'd better quit talking."

The confused boy put his hand on the girl's arm. His voice trembled. The two started to walk back along the road toward town. In his desperation George boasted, "I'm going to be a big man, the biggest that ever lived here in
25 Winesburg," he declared. . . .

The boy's voice failed and in silence the two came back into town and went along the street to Helen White's house. At the gate he tried to say something impressive. Speeches he had thought out came into his head, but they seemed utterly pointless. . . .
30 On the warm fall evening as he stood in the stairway and looked at the crowd drifting through Main Street, George thought of the talk beside the field of young corn and was ashamed of the figure he had made of himself.

Close Read

1. What do you learn about George's thoughts in lines 1–7?

2. What do you learn about Helen's thoughts in lines 8–13?

3. Later, a flashback takes you to the summer evening that has loomed in George's and Helen's memories. Where does this flashback begin? Explain.

4. Review the boxed details. What do they reveal about George's behavior? Explain whether you think he impressed Helen.

5. How does the flashback help you understand George? Consider how he thinks he has changed since that evening.

MODEL: FLASHBACK

Close Read

1. *Possible answer:* *In lines 1–7, readers learn that George wants to see Helen White so that he can explain how he has changed. He realizes that the last time they saw each other, he behaved immaturely.*

2. *Possible answer:* *In lines 8–13, readers learn that Helen also feels that she has changed and matured, and wants to share these changes with George.*

3. *Possible answer:* *The flashback begins in line 14, with the sentence "The summer evening together that had left its mark . . ." Readers are then carried back to that summer evening to learn what transpired between the young man and woman.*

4. *Possible answer:* *The boxed details reveal that George boasted because he was desperate to impress Helen. Students will likely think that he did not impress Helen.*

5. *Possible answer:* *The flashback helps readers understand that George himself was embarrassed by his behavior, even at the time. Readers see how ridiculously George behaved and why he wants so badly to redeem himself in Helen's eyes. When he first met Helen, he wanted her to think he was a significant, important person. Now he wants to show that he has matured since then.*

IF STUDENTS NEED HELP . . . Direct their attention to this phrase in line 6: "He wanted to . . . try to make her feel the change." Contrast this motive with "he tried to say something impressive" (lines 27–28).

CHECK UNDERSTANDING

Have students identify the point of view used in "Sophistication." Then ask how a flashback differs from foreshadowing.

FOR ENGLISH LANGUAGE LEARNERS

Language: Verb Tenses Remind students that some verbs change form to show when the action occurred. Write on the board these verbs from the model: "came" (line 1) and "wanted" (line 5). Point out that both are in the past tense. They show actions that began and ended at a certain time in the past. Then write these verbs on the board: "had walked" (line 3) and "had given" (line 4). Draw attention to the helping verb

had, explaining that these verbs show a past action or situation that ended before another one began.

Have pairs of students look through the model and try to find at least two additional examples of both tenses. Invite students to compare the verbs that they chose.

Practice and Apply

Part 3: Analyze the Text

Close Read

1. **Possible answer:** *You can see inside Ashoke's and Ashima's minds in lines 20–21, when the narrator says, "It has never occurred to either of them to question Ashima's grandmother's selection," and then again in line 26, when they think, "But this isn't possible." You can see inside Mr. Wilcox's mind when you learn that he is "unamused," in line 6.*

2. **Possible answer:** *The omniscient narrator helps readers understand that to Ashoke and Ashima, the thought of naming their baby themselves or naming the child after a relative is unthinkable. Mr. Wilcox does not understand their feelings because he has grown up with different traditions.*

3. **Possible answer:** *If readers could not see Ashoke's and Ashima's thoughts, then they might be less likely to sympathize with the characters or to understand their viewpoint.*

Part 3: Analyze the Text

Use what you've learned about point of view and sequence to analyze the two excerpts that follow.

The first excerpt is from a novel about a family from Bengal, India, that is making a new life in the United States. In keeping with Bengali tradition, the husband and wife are waiting for word from a family elder about what the name of their baby will be. How does the third-person omniscient point of view influence your understanding of the characters?

from THE NAMESAKE
Novel by **Jhumpa Lahiri**

. . . they are told by Mr. Wilcox, compiler of hospital birth certificates, that they must choose a name for their son. For they learn that in America, a baby cannot be released from the hospital without a birth certificate. And that a birth certificate needs a name.

5   "But, sir," Ashima protests, "we can't possibly name him ourselves."

Mr. Wilcox, slight, bald, unamused, glances at the couple, both visibly distressed, then glances at the nameless child. "I see," he says. "The reason being?"

"We are waiting for a letter," Ashoke says, explaining the situation in detail.

"I see," Mr. Wilcox says again. "That is unfortunate. I'm afraid your only 10 alternative is to have the certificate read 'Baby Boy Ganguli.' You will, of course, be required to amend the permanent record when a name is decided upon."

Ashima looks at Ashoke expectantly. "Is that what we should do?"

"I don't recommend it," Mr. Wilcox says. "You will have to appear before a judge, pay a fee. The red tape is endless."

15   "Oh dear," Ashoke says.

Mr. Wilcox nods, and silence ensues. "Don't you have any backups?" he asks. Ashima frowns. "What does it mean, 'backup'?"

"Well, something in reserve, in case you didn't like what your grandmother has chosen."

20   Ashima and Ashoke shake their heads. It has never occurred to either of them to question Ashima's grandmother's selection, to disregard an elder's wishes in such a way.

"You can always name him after yourself, or one of your ancestors," Mr. Wilcox suggests, admitting that he is actually Howard Wilcox III. "It's a fine 25 tradition. The kings of France and England did it," he adds.

But this isn't possible, Ashima and Ashoke think to themselves. This tradition doesn't exist for Bengalis, naming a son after father or grandfather, a daughter after mother or grandmother. This sign of respect in America and Europe, this symbol of heritage and lineage, would be ridiculed in India. 30 Within Bengali families, individual names are sacred, inviolable. They are not meant to be inherited or shared.

Close Read

1. For each character—Ashoke, Ashima, and Mr. Wilcox—find one example where you can "see" inside that character's mind.

2. This excerpt is about a clash between Bengali and American traditions. Through the omniscient narrator, what do you learn about how Ashoke's and Ashima's thoughts differ from those of Mr. Wilcox?

3. How would your impression of the characters be different if you did not know Ashoke's and Ashima's thoughts?

DIFFERENTIATED INSTRUCTION

FOR STRUGGLING READERS

Vocabulary Support Introduce these words from *The Namesake.* Have students read the context for each word and suggest a possible meaning for it. After students have finished the excerpt, have them find definitions for any words that are still unclear to them.

- *compiler* (line 1), "one who collects and puts together"

- *alternative* (line 10), "other choice"

- *ensues* (line 16), "follows"

- *disregard* (line 21), "purposely ignore"

- *ridiculed* (line 29), "mocked, laughed at"

- *inviolable* (line 30), "not able to be violated or dishonored"

Now read this excerpt from a novel about friendship and growing up. In this scene, the main character visits the private school he attended as a teenager. His destination is a tree on the property, where, years earlier, something terrible happened. As you read, notice how the flashback and the point of view affect your impression of the main character.

from A Separate Peace
Novel by **John Knowles**

There were several trees bleakly reaching into the fog. Any one of them might have been the one I was looking for. Unbelievable that there were other trees which looked like it here. It had loomed in my memory as a huge lone spike dominating the riverbank, forbidding as an artillery piece, high
5 as the beanstalk. Yet here was a scattered grove of trees, none of them of any particular grandeur.

Moving through the soaked, coarse grass I began to examine each one closely, and finally identified the tree I was looking for by means of certain small scars rising along its trunk, and by a limb extending over the river, and
10 another thinner limb growing near it. This was the tree, and it seemed to me standing there to resemble those men, the giants of your childhood, whom you encounter years later and find that they are not merely smaller in relation to your growth, but that they are absolutely smaller, shrunken by age. In this double demotion the old giants have become pigmies[1] while you were looking
15 the other way.

The tree was not only stripped by the cold season, it seemed weary from age, enfeebled, dry. I was thankful, very thankful that I had seen it. So the more things remain the same, the more they change after all—*plus c'est la même chose, plu ça change.* Nothing endures, not a tree, not love, not even a death by violence.
20 Changed, I headed back through the mud. I was drenched; anybody could see it was time to come in out of the rain.

The tree was tremendous, an irate, steely black steeple beside the river. I was [not going to] climb it. . . . No one but Phineas could think up such a crazy idea. He of course saw nothing the slightest bit intimidating about it. He
25 wouldn't, or wouldn't admit it if he did. Not Phineas.

"What I like best about this tree," he said in that voice of his, the equivalent in sound of a hypnotist's eyes, "what I like is that it's such a cinch!" He opened his green eyes wider and gave us his maniac look, and only the smirk on his wide mouth with its droll, slightly protruding upper lip reassured us that he
30 wasn't completely goofy.

"Is that what you like best?" I said sarcastically. I said a lot of things sarcastically that summer; that was my sarcastic summer, 1942.

---

1. **pigmies:** people of unusually small size.

Close Read

1. From what point of view is this story told? Explain how you can tell. How does the point of view contribute to the tone of the story?

2. At what point does the story switch from the present to the past? Cite the clues that signaled this flashback.

3. Reread lines 3–21. What do you learn about the narrator from his own thoughts about the tree and his past?

4. Review the boxed text. What do the descriptions of the tree—in the present and in the flashback— help to emphasize?

TEXT ANALYSIS WORKSHOP **307**

Close Read

1. *Possible answer: The story is told from the first-person point of view, because the narrator uses* I *and* me. *This helps create a personal, intimate tone.*

2. *Possible answer: The story switches from the present to a flashback in line 22. A line space and a contrasting image of the tree signal the flashback. Another clue occurs in lines 31–32, when the narrator says, "I said a lot of things sarcastically that summer; that was my sarcastic summer, 1942."*

3. *Possible answer: Readers learn that the tree has haunted the narrator for years. He remembers it as ominous and looming, but later finds it to be small and shriveled.*

4. *Possible answer: The descriptions show how the tree that now seems small and shrunken was once tremendous and strong. This emphasizes the powerful effect of time.*

Assess and Reteach

Assess

Ask students to find examples of these terms in the workshop models: *point of view, first-person point of view, narrator, third-person limited point of view, foreshadowing, third-person omniscient point of view, flashback.*

Reteach

For students who are unable to apply the workshop skills to the excerpts from *The Namesake* and *A Separate Peace*, select from these reteaching options:

1. Review with them the note-taking copy masters for this lesson. Have students identify each literary element exemplified.
   - "Nothing endures, not a tree, not love, not even a death by violence." (*foreshadowing*)
   - "Hearing the funeral parlor's name, Luis remembered too. The day his mother died . . . ." (*flashback*)
   - "Now he wanted to see her for another purpose . . . ." "Helen White was thinking of George Willard . . . ." (*third-person omniscient point of view*)

2. Read the previous passages aloud to the class and have them respond in a Whip Around.

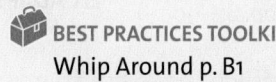 **BEST PRACTICES TOOLKIT**
Whip Around p. B1

FOR ENGLISH LANGUAGE LEARNERS
Vocabulary: Idioms Read aloud these idioms and share their meanings. Then have students work in pairs to create sentences with each idiom.

- *broken off* (line 4, "Lalla"), "ended suddenly"
- *growing up* (line 19, "Sophistication"), "becoming older and more mature"

- *red tape* (line 14, *The Namesake*), "time wasted on governmental paperwork"
- *it's such a cinch* (line 27, *A Separate Peace*), "it's so easy"

Focus and Motivate

COMMON CORE FOCUS

RL 1 Cite textual evidence to support inferences drawn from the text. **RL 3** Analyze how complex characters advance the plot. **RL 4** Analyze the impact of word choices on meaning and tone. **RL 5** Analyze an author's choices concerning how to manipulate time. **L 2** Demonstrate command of the conventions of standard English punctuation. **L 3** Apply knowledge of language to make effective choices for meaning or style.

SUMMARY

In "By the Waters of Babylon," the narrator, the son of a priest in an apparently traditional culture, sets off on a quest for knowledge to the mysterious and forbidden "Place of the Gods." The narrator discovers that this "great Dead Place" was not home to the gods but a thriving city destroyed in a cataclysmic war—a city once known as "newyork."

Does **KNOWLEDGE**
come at a price?

Introduce the question, then discuss whether gaining knowledge can have negative consequences. Continue the exploration by having students complete the *DISCUSS* activity.

Selection Resources

Essential Course of Study **ECOS**

By the Waters of Babylon
Short Story by Stephen Vincent Benét

VIDEO TRAILER THINK central KEYWORD: HML10-308

Does **KNOWLEDGE**
come at a price?

○ **COMMON CORE**

RL 1 Cite textual evidence to support inferences drawn from the text. **RL 3** Analyze how complex characters advance the plot. **RL 4** Analyze the impact of word choices on meaning and tone. **RL 5** Analyze an author's choices concerning how to manipulate time.

How much knowledge should a person or society have? When, if ever, should our pursuit of knowledge be limited? In "By the Waters of Babylon," you will meet John, a character who learns through a difficult journey that knowledge can come at a price.

DISCUSS Think about a time when your desire for knowledge got you into a tough situation. Then create a cause-effect chart like the one shown to represent this experience. Share your chart with your classmates, and then discuss if pursuing knowledge is ever worth risking trouble.

What I Wanted to Know (Cause)	What I Did	What Happened (Effect)
Who my older sister liked	Read her electronic journal	I found out we both liked the same guy.

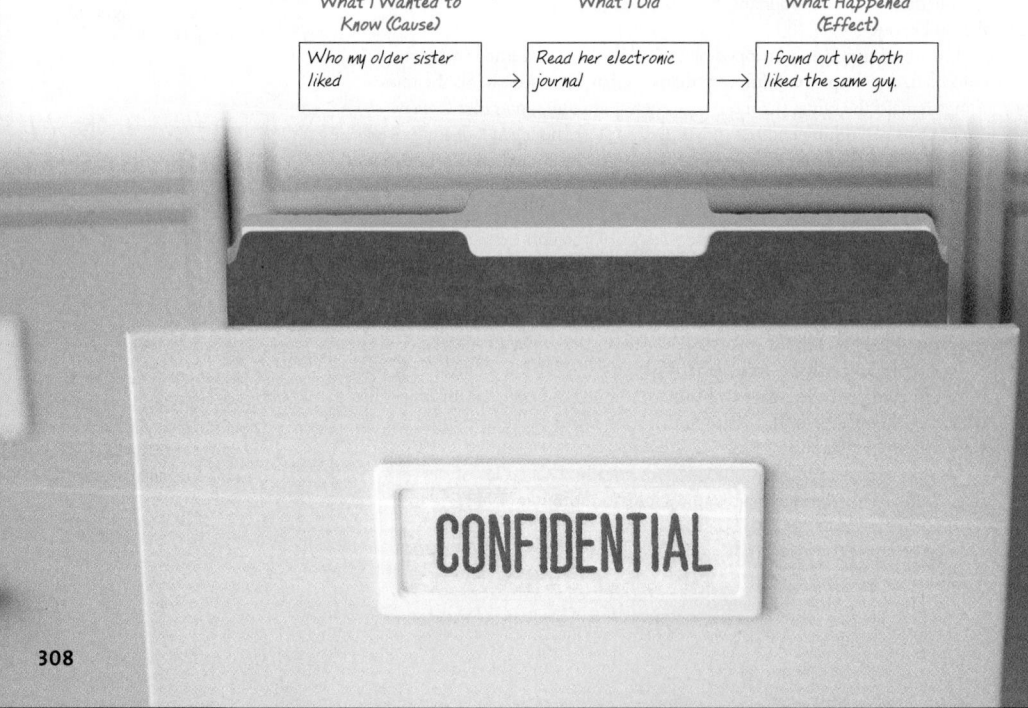

CONFIDENTIAL

See resources on the **Teacher One Stop DVD-ROM** *and on* **thinkcentral.com**.

 RESOURCE MANAGER UNIT 3
Plan and Teach, pp. 11–18
Summary, pp. 19–20 † ‡*
Text Analysis and Reading
   Skill, pp. 21–24*
Grammar and Style, p. 27

DIAGNOSTIC AND SELECTION TESTS
Selection Tests, pp. 87–90

 BEST PRACTICES TOOLKIT
Word Squares, p. E10
Making Inferences, p. A13
Three-Column Journal, p. B10
Main Ideas and Details, p. B6

INTERACTIVE READER

ADAPTED INTERACTIVE READER

ELL ADAPTED INTERACTIVE READER

TECHNOLOGY
- **Teacher One Stop DVD-ROM**
- **Student One Stop DVD-ROM**
- **PowerNotes DVD-ROM**
- **Audio Anthology CD**
- **GrammarNotes DVD-ROM**
- **Audio Tutor CD**
- **ExamView Test Generator** on the Teacher One Stop

Video Trailer

Go to **thinkcentral.com** to preview the **Video Trailer** introducing this selection. Other features that support the selection include
- **PowerNotes** presentation
- **ThinkAloud** models to enhance comprehension
- **WordSharp** vocabulary tutorials
- interactive writing and grammar instruction

---

* Resources for Differentiation   † In Spanish   ‡ In Haitian Creole and Vietnamese

TEXT ANALYSIS: FIRST-PERSON POINT OF VIEW

"By the Waters of Babylon" is a short story told from the **first-person point of view.** The narrator is John, a character who speaks directly to the reader, using the pronoun *I*. He introduces himself in the following way:

My father is a priest; I am the son of a priest. I have been in the Dead Places near us, with my father—at first, I was afraid.

Everything in the story is presented through John's eyes. At times, he does not fully understand what he sees or experiences. Such a narrator is called a **naive narrator.** However, remember that the author and the narrator are not the same person. The author uses John's naive perspective to help reveal the **tone,** his attitude toward the story's subject.

As you read "By the Waters of Babylon," notice how the author's choice of point of view and narrator affects what you learn about the story's characters, events, and tone.

Review: Foreshadowing

READING SKILL: MAKE INFERENCES

When a character narrates a story, you know only as much as the character knows. By making **inferences,** or educated guesses, you can figure out information that the narrator does not tell you. Use the following strategies to make inferences about the setting of "By the Waters of Babylon":

• Notice the names of places.
• Notice how these places may resemble places that you know.

As you read the story, jot down important details that help you understand the different sites John visits on his journey. Use a chart like the one shown.

Places	Important Details	My Inferences
1. Dead Places	Only priests and sons of priests can visit.	
2. the great river		
3. the Place of the Gods		

Review: Draw Conclusions

 Complete the activities in your **Reader/Writer Notebook.**

Meet the Author

Stephen Vincent Benét
1898–1943

A Literary Family
Stephen Vincent Benét (bĭ-nā′) grew up in a home where literature was valued and enjoyed. When he was young, Benét and his two siblings, William and Laura, spent many evenings listening to their father, a colonel in the U.S. Army, read poetry and historical stories. Their mother was also an avid reader and occasionally wrote verse to entertain family and friends. With their upbringing, the Benét children seemed likely to lead artistic lives. In fact, each became a successful writer, making *Benét* a well-known name in American literature.

A Proud American
Much of Stephen Vincent Benét's writing is based on American history and folklore. Among his most famous works is the epic Civil War poem *John Brown's Body,* for which he won a Pulitzer Prize in 1929. A second Pulitzer came in 1944, following Benét's death, for *Western Star,* a long narrative poem about the history of America. Benét also received acclaim for his fiction. His best-known story, "The Devil and Daniel Webster," won the 1937 O. Henry Award and became the basis of a play, an opera, and a film.

BACKGROUND TO THE STORY

About the Title
The title of this selection is an **allusion,** or reference, to Psalm 137 in the Bible. The psalm expresses the sorrow of the Jews over their enslavement in Babylon and the destruction of Zion, their homeland. The psalm begins: "By the waters of Babylon, there we sat down and wept, when we remembered thee, O Zion."

Author Online

THINK central

Go to thinkcentral.com.
KEYWORD: HML10-309

309

Teach

TEXT ANALYSIS   COMMON CORE   RL 3 / RL 4

● *Model the Skill:* **FIRST-PERSON POINT OF VIEW**

To model how to see the connection between the form of narration and the tone, read aloud this example:

> As I walked through the house, I was amazed by the oil paintings and marble sculptures. I felt as though I were inside a museum rather than a home. Could this shabbily dressed man be a millionaire?

Explain how the first-person point of view affects readers' perceptions of the house and its owner. Because readers see the house and its owner through the narrator's eyes, they are likely to share his or her amazement as well as his or her appraisal of the "shabbily dressed man."

GUIDED PRACTICE Elicit other examples of stories written from a first-person point of view, and ask how the point of view affected readers' knowledge and perceptions.

READING SKILL   COMMON CORE   RL 1

■ *Model the Skill:* **MAKE INFERENCES**

Use the preceding example to model the skill of making inferences by recording information on a Make Inferences chart that you draw on the board. Write one Important Detail on the chart, such as "Narrator is amazed by art." Then write an inference that students could make from this detail, such as "The man must not look refined." Tell students that another Important Detail could be "wonders if man is millionaire." Ask students what they would infer from that detail.

GUIDED PRACTICE After students read **A Proud American,** ask them to infer what kinds of books Benét probably most enjoyed reading.

R RESOURCE MANAGER—Copy Master
Make Inferences p. 23 (for student use while reading the selection)

DIFFERENTIATED INSTRUCTION

FOR STRUGGLING READERS

Vocabulary Support Explain that the term "naive narrator" is an extension of the meaning of the adjective *naive.* The word *naive* usually means "unsophisticated, innocent, or lacking in worldly wisdom," as in *Many voters are politically naive* or *Until they have had some experience in the world, most young adults are naive.*

Concept Connect Explain that an **allusion** is a reference that assumes that readers share a common knowledge base with the writer. The title of the selection is an allusion to psalms that appear in the Hebrew Bible, also known as the Old Testament portion of the Christian Bible. The psalms are poems and hymns addressed to God.

READ WITH A PURPOSE

Help students set a purpose for reading. Ask them to look for the reasons that drove John to seek knowledge.

A Model the Skill: MAKE INFERENCES

Model the process of making inferences by drawing on the board the Make Inferences graphic organizer. Refer students to lines 11–17. Point out that there are nearby Dead Places, that they contain houses, and the houses contain old bones and metal. The Dead Places are forbidden to all but priests or sons of priests.

Possible answer: The story appears to take place after some cataclysmic event (lines 8–9, 14) in some traditional or fictional culture. The Dead Places are thought to be haunted (lines 6–9, 14–15) and unclean (line 4). They are restricted to priests and sons of priests, who may go there only to search for metal (lines 2–4).

By the Waters of Babylon

Stephen Vincent Benét

The north and the west and the south are good hunting ground, but it is forbidden to go east. It is forbidden to go to any of the Dead Places except to search for metal, and then he who touches the metal must be a priest or the son of a priest. Afterwards, both the man and the metal must be purified. These are the rules and the laws; they are well made. It is forbidden to cross the great river and look upon the place that was the Place of the Gods—this is most strictly forbidden. We do not even say its name, though we know its name. It is there that spirits live, and demons—it is there that there are the ashes of the Great Burning. These things are forbidden—they have been

10 forbidden since the beginning of time.

My father is a priest; I am the son of a priest. I have been in the Dead Places near us, with my father—at first, I was afraid. When my father went into the house to search for the metal, I stood by the door, and my heart felt small and weak. It was a dead man's house, a spirit house. It did not have the smell of man, though there were old bones in a corner. But it is not fitting that a priest's son should show fear. I looked at the bones in the shadow and kept my voice still. **A**

Then my father came out with the metal—a good, strong piece. He looked at me with both eyes, but I had not run away. He gave me the metal to hold—I

20 took it and did not die. So he knew that I was truly his son and would be a priest in my time. That was when I was very young—nevertheless, my brothers would not have done it, though they are good hunters. After that, they gave me the good piece of meat and the warm corner by the fire. My father watched over me—he was glad that I should be a priest. But when I boasted or wept without a reason, he punished me more strictly than my brothers. That was right.

After a time, I myself was allowed to go into the dead houses and search for metal. So I learned the ways of those houses—and if I saw bones, I was no longer afraid. The bones are light and old—sometimes they will fall into dust if you touch them. But that is a great sin.

Analyze Visuals ▶

Examine the painting shown. How do the primitive images and style of this work relate to the story's **characters** and **setting**?

❶ Targeted Passage

A MAKE INFERENCES
What can you infer so far about the **setting** of the story? Write details about the Dead Places in your chart.

Birsay Ceremony (1996), Gloria Wallington. Monotype. Private Collection. Photo © Bridgeman Art Library.

DIFFERENTIATED INSTRUCTION

FOR ENGLISH LANGUAGE LEARNERS

Options for Reading Have students listen to parts of the story several times on the *Audio Anthology CD*. Ask them to summarize the key events in each part. Then have students independently read the whole story.

FOR STRUGGLING READERS

In combination with the *Audio Anthology CD*, use one or more Targeted Passages (pp. 310, 314, 316, 321) to ensure that students focus on key events, concepts, and skills. Targeted Passages are also good for English learners.

❶ Targeted Passage [Lines 2–21]

This passage introduces the priest and his son, who is the narrator, and the concept of the Dead Places and the Place of the Gods.

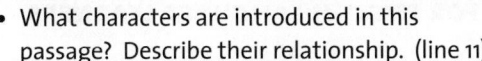

Reading Support

This selection on **thinkcentral.com** includes embedded **ThinkAloud** models—students "thinking aloud" about the story to model the kinds of questions a good reader would ask about a selection.

Analyze Visuals

Possible answer: *The primitive and mystical nature of the painting matches the story's setting. Like the story, the painting appears to depict a traditional culture or a place where civilization as we know it does not exist. The tallest of the three figures in the painting might be a priest or spiritual leader, a notion supported by the mysterious symbols in the picture. Similarly, the story focuses on a priest and his son.*

About the Art English artist Gloria Wallington paints landscapes and creates monotypes. Like many of her pictures, *Birsay Ceremony* reflects her interest in Celtic myth and Pictish life and times. Birsay, ancient capital of Scotland's Orkney Islands, was once a center of Viking power.

TIERED DISCUSSION PROMPTS

Direct students to lines 2–25. Use these prompts to help students understand the relationship between father and son:

Connect The narrator says that "it is not fitting that a priest's son should show fear" (lines 15–16). Have you ever been in a situation where you were afraid but did not want to show your fear? How did you conceal your feelings? *Answers will vary.*

Analyze What can you tell about the relationship between the narrator and his father? *Possible answer: The narrator has great respect for his father; both father and son take very seriously the narrator's destiny to "be a priest in [his] time" (lines 20–21).*

Evaluate Do you think the narrator's father is doing a good job of preparing his son to be a priest? Give reasons for your answer. *Possible answer: The father does seem to be doing a good job. He helps his son overcome his fears of the Dead Places. He also watches over his son (lines 23–24) and appropriately punishes him (lines 24–25).*

- What characters are introduced in this passage? Describe their relationship. (line 11)

- Who is permitted to go to the Dead Places? for what reason? (lines 3–4)

- Where are people strictly forbidden to go? Why? (lines 2, 5–7, 9–10; 8–9)

- What is the narrator destined to become? (lines 20–21)

FOR ADVANCED LEARNERS/PRE–AP

Analyze Figurative Language Benét uses figurative language to convey the narrator's thoughts and feelings, as in "it was like a fire in my heart" (lines 35–36) and "my spirit was a cool stone" (line 48). Have students identify other such similes and metaphors in the story. Then have them write original similes and metaphors that similarly convey the narrator's thoughts and feelings.

B POINT OF VIEW

Possible answer: The narrator reveals his perseverance (lines 34–35: "that was hard and took a long time"); his love of knowledge (lines 35–36); his curiosity (lines 37–38: "I asked myself many questions that I could not answer, but it was good to ask them"); and his imagination (lines 38–39: "it seemed to me that it was the voice of the gods as they flew through the air").

REVISIT THE BIG QUESTION

Does KNOWLEDGE
come at a price?

Discuss Based on lines 35–36 and 43, what does the narrator mean when he says, "my knowledge and my lack of knowledge burned in me"? How does this statement relate to his earlier statement that knowledge "was like a fire in my heart" (lines 35–36)? *Possible answer: The narrator has a passion for knowledge. He is excited by what he already knows, but the desire to learn more "burns" inside him.*

Cultural Connection The narrator must go on a journey in order to become an adult in the eyes of his tribe. Many cultures around the world practice similar coming-of-age rituals. In the Jewish tradition, a bar mitzvah (or bat mitzvah for girls) marks the passage into adulthood. A ceremony and feast at the age of 13 indicates the child's passage into adulthood. Many Native American groups mark this passage through vision quests. When a boy reaches his early teens, he is sent on a quest outside the village. The boy prays and fasts until he receives a sign from his guardian spirit, usually in the form of an animal. Only then can he return to his village as a man.

30   I was taught the chants and the spells—I was taught how to stop the running of blood from a wound and many secrets. A priest must know many secrets—that was what my father said. If the hunters think we do all things by chants and spells, they may believe so—it does not hurt them. I was taught how to read in the old books and how to make the old writings—that was hard and took a long time. My knowledge made me happy—it was like a fire in my heart. Most of all, I liked to hear of the Old Days and the stories of the gods. I asked myself many questions that I could not answer, but it was good to ask them. At night, I would lie awake and listen to the wind—it seemed to me that it was the voice of the gods as they flew through the air. **B**

40   We are not ignorant like the Forest People—our women spin wool on the wheel; our priests wear a white robe. We do not eat grubs from the tree; we have not forgotten the old writings, although they are hard to understand. Nevertheless, my knowledge and my lack of knowledge burned in me—I wished to know more. When I was a man at last, I came to my father and said, "It is time for me to go on my journey. Give me your leave."

    He looked at me for a long time, stroking his beard; then he said at last, "Yes. It is time." That night, in the house of the priesthood, I asked for and received purification. My body hurt, but my spirit was a cool stone. It was my father himself who questioned me about my dreams.

50   He bade me look into the smoke of the fire and see—I saw and told what I saw. It was what I have always seen—a river, and, beyond it, a great Dead Place and in it the gods walking. I have always thought about that. His eyes were stern when I told him—he was no longer my father but a priest. He said, "This is a strong dream."

    "It is mine," I said, while the smoke waved and my head felt light. They were singing the star song in the outer chamber, and it was like the buzzing of bees in my head.

    He asked me how the gods were dressed, and I told him how they were dressed. We know how they were dressed from the book, but I saw them as if 60 they were before me. When I had finished, he threw the sticks three times and studied them as they fell.

    "This is a very strong dream," he said. "It may eat you up."

    "I am not afraid," I said and looked at him with both eyes. My voice sounded thin in my ears, but that was because of the smoke.

    He touched me on the breast and the forehead. He gave me the bow and the three arrows.

    "Take them," he said. "It is forbidden to travel east. It is forbidden to cross the river. It is forbidden to go to the Place of the Gods. All these things are forbidden."

70   "All these things are forbidden," I said, but it was my voice that spoke and not my spirit. He looked at me again.

B POINT OF VIEW
Reread lines 30–39. Think about how the **first-person point of view** affects your impression of the narrator. What important inner qualities does he reveal?

Language Coach

Formal Language Narrators sometimes use formal language to create a mood or fit a situation. In line 50, John uses the word *bade*, which is a more formal version of *asked*. Why do you think the writer chose to have John use formal language in this situation?

DIFFERENTIATED INSTRUCTION

FOR ENGLISH LANGUAGE LEARNERS

Vocabulary Support Use Word Squares to teach these words: *ignorant* (line 40), *image* (line 193), *labored* (line 322), *approach* (line 353).

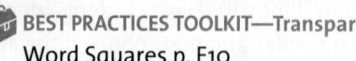 **BEST PRACTICES TOOLKIT—Transparency**
Word Squares p. E10

FOR ENGLISH LANGUAGE LEARNERS

Language Coach   COMMON CORE RL 4

Formal Language *Possible answer: John is participating in a religious ceremony and speaks formally in this role. Have students read lines 67–69, noting the formal language. Ask each student to adapt the language to informal language to express the same ideas. Then, ask for volunteers to share their adaptation orally.*

"My son," he said. "Once I had young dreams. If your dreams do not eat you up, you may be a great priest. If they eat you, you are still my son. Now go on your journey." **C**

I went fasting, as is the law. My body hurt but not my heart. When the dawn came, I was out of sight of the village. I prayed and purified myself, waiting for a sign. The sign was an eagle. It flew east.

Sometimes signs are sent by bad spirits. I waited again on the flat rock, fasting, taking no food. I was very still—I could feel the sky above me and
80 the earth beneath. I waited till the sun was beginning to sink. Then three deer passed in the valley, going east—they did not wind me or see me. There was a white fawn with them—a very great sign.

I followed them, at a distance, waiting for what would happen. My heart was troubled about going east, yet I knew that I must go. My head hummed with my fasting—I did not even see the panther spring upon the white fawn. But, before I knew it, the bow was in my hand. I shouted, and the panther lifted his head from the fawn. It is not easy to kill a panther with one arrow, but the arrow went through his eye and into his brain. He died as he tried to spring—he rolled over, tearing at the ground. Then I knew I was meant to go
90 east—I knew that was my journey. When the night came, I made my fire and roasted meat.

It is eight suns' journey to the east, and a man passes by many Dead Places. The Forest People are afraid of them, but I am not. Once I made my fire on the edge of a Dead Place at night, and next morning, in the dead house, I found a good knife, little rusted. That was small to what came afterward, but it made my heart feel big. Always when I looked for game, it was in front of my arrow, and twice I passed hunting parties of the Forest People without their knowing. So I knew my magic was strong and my journey clean, in spite of the law.

100 Toward the setting of the eighth sun, I came to the banks of the great river. It was half a day's journey after I had left the god road—we do not use the god roads now, for they are falling apart into great blocks of stone, and the forest is safer going. A long way off, I had seen the water through trees, but the trees were thick. At last, I came out upon an open place at the top of a cliff. There was the great river below, like a giant in the sun. It is very long, very wide. It could eat all the streams we know and still be thirsty. Its name is Ou-dis-sun, the Sacred, the Long. No man of my tribe had seen it, not even my father, the priest. It was magic, and I prayed.

Then I raised my eyes and looked south. It was there, the Place of the Gods.
110 How can I tell what it was like—you do not know. It was there, in the red light, and they were too big to be houses. It was there with the red light upon it, mighty and ruined. I knew that in another moment the gods would see me. I covered my eyes with my hands and crept back into the forest. **D**

C MAKE INFERENCES
Why do you think the narrator's father allows the narrator to travel to the Place of the Gods, even though it is forbidden?

D MAKE INFERENCES
Reread lines 100–113. In what ways do the great river and the Place of the Gods resemble places you know?

C MAKE INFERENCES RL 1

Possible answer: The narrator's father realizes that his son has a burning need to know more and, like his son, the father recognizes the son's "very strong dream" (line 62) as a compelling force. The father may also feel that since his son is destined to become a priest, it is appropriate for him to pursue his dream. What he learns on his quest will make him a better priest.

IF STUDENTS NEED HELP... Have them discuss how the narrator's words in line 63 probably affect his father's decision.

D MAKE INFERENCES RL 1

Students may see a resemblance between the great river and a major waterway in their own part of the country. The Place of the Gods may remind students of ancient ruins they have seen in pictures or perhaps in person—"too big to be houses ... mighty and ruined" (lines 111–112). Remind students to record their answers on the copy masters.

FOR ENGLISH LANGUAGE LEARNERS
Vocabulary: Multiple-Meaning Words Guide students to identify multiple-meaning words, such as *wound* (line 31), *spells* (line 33), *hurt* (line 33), *sink* (line 80), and *parties* (line 97). Have students refer to a dictionary to write sentence pairs using two meanings of each word. Clarify that multiple-meaning words may have different pronunciations, such as *wound*, or they may be different parts of speech, such as *hurt*.

FOR ADVANCED LEARNERS/PRE–AP
Hypothesize Direct students' attention to lines 101–103. Have students work in small groups to conjecture what the "god roads" are and why "they are falling apart into great blocks of stone" (line 102).

Activity Ask students which of Wallington's paintings, this one or the one on page 311, better captures the mood of the story. Have them give reasons for their choices. *Students may choose either painting, but they should provide thoughtful reasons to support their opinions.*

About the Art Like her work on page 311, Gloria Wallington's *Midsummer Night, 1994* has a primitive, mystical air. Crudely defined shapes evoke, rather than actually depict, a scene that appears to be one of worship.

Midsummer Night, 1994 (1994), Gloria Wallington. Monotype, 24 × 31 cm.
Private Collection. Photo © Bridgeman Art Library.

Surely, that was enough to do, and live. Surely it was enough to spend the night upon the cliff. The Forest People themselves do not come near. Yet, all through the night, I knew that I should have to cross the river and walk in the places of the gods, although the gods ate me up. My magic did not help me at all, and yet there was a fire in my bowels, a fire in my mind. When the sun rose, I thought, "My journey has been clean. Now I will go home from my 120 journey." But, even as I thought so, I knew I could not. If I went to the Place of the Gods, I would surely die, but, if I did not go, I could never be at peace with my spirit again. It is better to lose one's life than one's spirit, if one is a priest and the son of a priest.

Nevertheless, as I made the raft, the tears ran out of my eyes. The Forest People could have killed me without fight, if they had come upon me then, but they did not come. When the raft was made, I said the sayings for the dead and painted myself for death. My heart was cold as a frog and my knees like water, but the burning in my mind would not let me have peace. As I pushed the raft from the shore, I began my death song—I had the right. It was a fine song.

② Targeted Passage

> **COMMON CORE RL 4**
>
> **Language Coach**
>
> **Meanings of Idioms** Idioms are groups of words that have a special meaning different from the meaning of each separate word. Reread lines 120–122. The idiom *at peace* means "tranquil about" or even "dead." What does *at peace* mean in these lines?

DIFFERENTIATED INSTRUCTION

FOR STRUGGLING READERS

② Targeted Passage [Lines 114–127]

This passage shows the narrator's courage, commitment, and sense of responsibility. He decides to go on, despite his belief that he will die.

• What conflict is the narrator experiencing? (lines 120–123)

• What does the narrator decide to do? Why? (lines 120–123)

• What does the narrator's decision reveal about his character? (lines 122, 124, 126–127)

FOR ENGLISH LANGUAGE LEARNERS

> **Language Coach**   **COMMON CORE RL 4**
>
> **Meanings of Idioms** *Answer: tranquil about* Have students identify other idioms in the story or in common usage. Point out line 43, in which the narrator says "My lack of knowledge burned in me," as an example.

130 *"I am John, son of John," I sang. "My people are the Hill People.*
They are the men.
I go into the Dead Places, but I am not slain. I take the metal from the Dead
Places, but I am not blasted.
I travel upon the god roads and am not afraid. E-yah! I have killed the
panther; I have killed the fawn!
E-yah! I have come to the great river. No man has come there before.
It is forbidden to go east, but I have gone, forbidden to go on the great river,
but I am there.
Open your hearts, you spirits, and hear my song.
140 *Now I go to the Place of the Gods; I shall not return.*
My body is painted for death and my limbs weak, but my heart is big as I go
to the Place of the Gods!" **Ⓔ**

All the same, when I came to the Place of the Gods, I was afraid, afraid.
The current of the great river is very strong—it gripped my raft with its hands.
That was magic, for the river itself is wide and calm. I could feel evil spirits
about me, in the bright morning; I could feel their breath on my neck as I
was swept down the stream. Never have I been so much alone—I tried to
think of my knowledge, but it was a squirrel's heap of winter nuts. There was
no strength in my knowledge anymore, and I felt small and naked as a new-
150 hatched bird—alone upon the great river, the servant of the gods.

Yet, after a while, my eyes were opened, and I saw. I saw both banks of the
river—I saw that once there had been god roads across it, though now they
were broken and fallen like broken vines. Very great they were, and wonderful
and broken—broken in the time of the Great Burning when the fire fell out of
the sky. And always the current took me nearer to the Place of the Gods, and
the huge ruins rose before my eyes.

I do not know the customs of rivers—we are the People of the Hills. I tried
to guide my raft with the pole, but it spun around. I thought the river meant
to take me past the Place of the Gods and out into the Bitter Water of the
160 legends. I grew angry then—my heart felt strong. I said aloud, "I am a priest
and the son of a priest!" The gods heard me—they showed me how to paddle
with the pole on one side of the raft. The current changed itself—I drew near
to the Place of the Gods. **Ⓕ**

When I was very near, my raft struck and turned over. I can swim in our
lakes—I swam to the shore. There was a great spike of rusted metal sticking
out into the river—I hauled myself up upon it and sat there, panting. I had
saved my bow and two arrows and the knife I found in the Dead Place, but
that was all. My raft went whirling downstream toward the Bitter Water. I
looked after it, and thought if it had trod me under, at least I would be safely

Ⓔ POINT OF VIEW
Think about how the
first-person point of view
helps create suspense.
How might your interest
be affected if a different
narrator told of John's
journey?

Ⓕ POINT OF VIEW
Reread lines 157–163.
What details suggest that
John is a **naive narrator**?

TEXT ANALYSIS   COMMON CORE   RL 3
                                        RL 4

Ⓔ POINT OF VIEW

Possible answer: If the story were told in
the third person, it would not be as exciting
or suspenseful, because we would not be experiencing events through John's eyes. The
first-person point of view helps us identify
with John and feel what he is feeling.

Extend the Discussion Why do you suppose the author waits until line 130 to reveal the narrator's name? What does that
name tell you about the narrator?

REVISIT THE BIG QUESTION
Does **KNOWLEDGE**
come at a price?

Discuss Based on lines 147–150, why does John
say, "There was no strength in my knowledge
anymore" (lines 148–149)? *Possible answer:*
John has ventured into a place where no one
else has gone before. He does not know what
to expect, feels he is surrounded by evil spirits
and magic, and is alone and afraid.

TEXT ANALYSIS   COMMON CORE   RL 3
                                        RL 4

**Ⓕ Model the Skill: POINT OF
VIEW**

To model for students how to discover
details about the narrator, reread the
explanation of **naive narrator** on page 309.
Talk about why John knows so little about
his surroundings.

Possible answer: John says, "I do not know
the customs of rivers—we are the People
of the Hills" (line 157). He speaks of "the
Bitter Water of the legends" (lines 159–160),
which perhaps refers to the ocean. He says
that the gods "showed me how to paddle"
(line 161).

FOR ENGLISH LANGUAGE LEARNERS

Language: Verb Tenses Direct students' attention to lines 157–171. Have students focus on
the many irregular past-tense verb forms in
these paragraphs, such as *tried* (line 157), *spun*
(line 158), *thought* (line 158), *heard* (line 161),
drew (line 162), *struck* (line 164), and *swam*
(line 165). Review with students that English
has many irregular past and past-perfect verb
forms. Help students list the present-tense
forms of each verb. To extend the activity,
have students work in teams to identify

irregular past tenses on previous pages of the
story. Have teams exchange their lists and
check the validity of one another's entries.
The team with the most correct entries wins.

READING SKILL

G MAKE INFERENCES

Possible answer: A conflagration of enormous proportions must have occurred at the Place of the Gods some time ago, resulting in the loss of many lives and destroying buildings and roads.

IF STUDENTS NEED HELP . . . Work together to complete their Make Inferences graphic organizers.

🧰 BEST PRACTICES TOOLKIT—Transparency Making Inferences p. A13

READING SKILL

H MAKE INFERENCES

Possible answer: The shattered stone image was probably a statue of George Washington.

---

170 dead. Nevertheless, when I had dried my bowstring and restrung it, I walked forward to the Place of the Gods.

It felt like ground underfoot; it did not burn me. It is not true what some of the tales say, that the ground there burns forever, for I have been there. Here and there were the marks and stains of the Great Burning, on the ruins, that is true. But they were old marks and old stains. It is not true either, what some of our priests say, that it is an island covered with fogs and enchantments. It is not. It is a great Dead Place—greater than any Dead Place we know. Everywhere in it there are god roads, though most are cracked and broken. Everywhere there are the ruins of the high towers of the gods. **G**

180 How shall I tell what I saw? I went carefully, my strung bow in my hand, my skin ready for danger. There should have been the wailings of spirits and the shrieks of demons, but there were not. It was very silent and sunny where I had landed—the wind and the rain and the birds that drop seeds had done their work—the grass grew in the cracks of the broken stone. It is a fair island—no wonder the gods built there. If I had come there, a god, I also would have built.

How shall I tell what I saw? The towers are not all broken—here and there one still stands, like a great tree in a forest, and the birds nest high. But the towers themselves look blind, for the gods are gone. I saw a fish hawk, catching
190 fish in the river. I saw a little dance of white butterflies over a great heap of broken stones and columns. I went there and looked about me—there was a carved stone with cut letters, broken in half. I can read letters, but I could not understand these. They said UBTREAS. There was also the shattered image of a man or a god. It had been made of white stone, and he wore his hair tied back like a woman's. His name was ASHING, as I read on the cracked half of a stone. I thought it wise to pray to ASHING, though I do not know that god. **H**

How shall I tell what I saw? There was no smell of man left, on stone or metal. Nor were there many trees in that wilderness of stone. There are many pigeons, nesting and dropping in the towers—the gods must have loved them,
200 or, perhaps, they used them for sacrifices. There are wild cats that roam the god roads, green-eyed, unafraid of man. At night they wail like demons, but they are not demons. The wild dogs are more dangerous, for they hunt in a pack, but them I did not meet till later. Everywhere there are the carved stones, carved with magical numbers or words.

I went north—I did not try to hide myself. When a god or a demon saw me, then I would die, but meanwhile I was no longer afraid. My hunger for knowledge burned in me—there was so much that I could not understand. After a while, I knew that my belly was hungry. I could have hunted for my meat, but I did not hunt. It is known that the gods did not hunt as we
210 do—they got their food from enchanted boxes and jars. Sometimes these are still found in the Dead Places—once, when I was a child and foolish, I opened

G MAKE INFERENCES
Reread lines 172–179. What can you infer about the events that occurred at the Place of the Gods?

🔢 Targeted Passage

H MAKE INFERENCES
Reread lines 187–196. What famous person do you think the "shattered image" depicts?

316 UNIT 3: NARRATIVE DEVICES

DIFFERENTIATED INSTRUCTION

FOR STRUGGLING READERS

🔢 **Targeted Passage** [Lines 172–204]

In this passage, John enters the Place of the Gods and tries to put into words all that he sees. He discovers that it differs in some ways from what he had expected.

- How does the Place of the Gods prove to be different from what John had expected? (lines 172–173, 181–182)

- Summarize what John sees as he walks through the Place of the Gods. (lines 184–185, 189–191, 193–195, 203–204)

Develop Reading Fluency Read aloud the paragraph beginning on line 180 in a manner that conveys John's fear and wonder as he walks into the City of the Dead. Have the students practice reading portions of the passage using intonation to convey different levels of fear or wonder.

Distribute the copy masters and have students practice fluency.

🇷 RESOURCE MANAGER—Copy Master Reading Fluency p. 28

such a jar and tasted it and found the food sweet. But my father found out and punished me for it strictly, for, often, that food is death. Now, though, I had long gone past what was forbidden, and I entered the likeliest towers, looking for the food of the gods.

I found it at last in the ruins of a great temple in the mid-city. A mighty temple it must have been, for the roof was painted like the sky at night with its stars—that much I could see, though the colors were faint and dim. It went down into great caves and tunnels—perhaps they kept their slaves there.
220 But when I started to climb down, I heard the squeaking of rats, so I did not go—rats are unclean, and there must have been many tribes of them, from the squeaking. But near there, I found food, in the heart of a ruin, behind a door that still opened. I ate only the fruits from the jars—they had a very sweet taste. There was drink, too, in bottles of glass—the drink of the gods was strong and made my head swim. After I had eaten and drunk, I slept on the top of a stone, my bow at my side.

When I woke, the sun was low. Looking down from where I lay, I saw a dog sitting on his haunches. His tongue was hanging out of his mouth; he looked as if he were laughing. He was a big dog, with a gray-brown coat, as
230 big as a wolf. I sprang up and shouted at him, but he did not move—he just sat there as if he were laughing. I did not like that. When I reached for a stone to throw, he moved swiftly out of the way of the stone. He was not afraid of me; he looked at me as if I were meat. No doubt I could have killed him with an arrow, but I did not know if there were others. Moreover, night was falling.

I looked about me—not far away there was a great, broken god road, leading north. The towers were high enough, but not so high, and while many of the dead houses were wrecked, there were some that stood. I went toward this god road, keeping to the heights of the ruins, while the dog followed. When I had reached the god road, I saw that there were others behind him. If I
240 had slept later, they would have come upon me asleep and torn out my throat. As it was, they were sure enough of me; they did not hurry. When I went into the dead house, they kept watch at the entrance—doubtless they thought they would have a fine hunt. But a dog cannot open a door, and I knew, from the books, that the gods did not like to live on the ground but on high.

I had just found a door I could open when the dogs decided to rush. Ha! They were surprised when I shut the door in their faces—it was a good door, of strong metal. I could hear their foolish baying beyond it, but I did not stop to answer them. I was in darkness—I found stairs and climbed. There were many stairs, turning around till my head was dizzy. At the top was another
250 door—I found the knob and opened it. I was in a long small chamber—on one side of it was a bronze door that could not be opened, for it had no handle. Perhaps there was a magic word to open it, but I did not have the word. I turned to the door in the opposite side of the wall. The lock of it was broken, and I opened it and went in.

COMMON CORE L2

◆ **PUNCTUATION**

Dashes are used to indicate parenthetical information, or information that is not part of the main story. (Don't confuse a dash with a hyphen, which is used to join words together.) Look back over lines 216–226. What kind of information is introduced after each dash?

◆ **GRAMMAR AND STYLE**
Reread lines 235–244. Notice how Benét uses **formal language** that lacks contractions and contains complex sentence structure.

◆ **PUNCTUATION** COMMON CORE L2

Punctuation Remind students that dashes are similar to parentheses. Both types of punctuation indicate additional information. Have students skim all of page 317 to find more examples of the use of the dash in the story.

Possible answer: The main thread of the story here describes what John sees in the Place of the Gods. After each dash, John tells us his thoughts about and his reactions to what he sees.

◆ **GRAMMAR AND STYLE** COMMON CORE L3

Analyze Language Benét's use of formal language is consistent with the mood of the story and the nature of the narrator's quest. Formal language helps establish a serious and somber tone, which is appropriate for a quasi-religious journey such as this one to a forbidden place. Ask students to identify other places in the story where Benét uses carefully chosen formal language to support the mood of the story and the state of mind of the narrator. (*lines 110–113, 124–129, 205–215*) To extend the activity, challenge students to rewrite these sections of text in a more casual, conversational style. Discuss how the paraphrased sections alter the feel of the story.

FOR STRUGGLING READERS

Comprehension Support After students read lines 209–213, ask them to explain the meaning of "enchanted boxes and jars" (line 210). Then elicit or explain that, as the narrator says, "often, that food is death" (line 213) either because it is old or because it is foreign to the palate and stomach of the People of the Hills.

FOR ADVANCED LEARNERS/PRE–AP

Predict [small-group option] Have students speculate about the identity of the Dead Place and predict how the story might end, citing evidence to support their predictions.

READING SKILL COMMON CORE RL 1

K MAKE INFERENCES

Possible answer: *The "place of great riches" may bring to mind a posh apartment in a high-rise building.*

IF STUDENTS NEED HELP . . .

- Direct students' attention to key descriptive details: "a small anteroom" (line 256); windows overlooking the city (line 260); floor coverings and soft, deep chairs (lines 261–262); paintings, sculptures, and books (lines 263–268).
- Remind students that in the preceding paragraph, John describes how he entered the building and walked up numerous flights of stairs (lines 245–254).

TIERED DISCUSSION PROMPTS

Direct students to lines 271–280. Use these prompts to help students understand John's bewilderment:

Connect Have you ever encountered a machine or device that left you wondering about its purpose and use? How did you learn more about it? *Answers should reflect understanding of the situation described.*

Analyze What discoveries puzzle John in the "place of great riches"? Explain the mystery of these discoveries. ***Possible answer:*** *John sees the "washing place" but does not understand the concept of hot and cold running water (lines 271, 277–278). Similarly, he sees the "cooking place" but does not understand the concept of a gas or electric stove (lines 272–273). Nor does he understand that electricity provides light with "neither oil nor wick" (lines 274–275).*

Within, there was a place of great riches. The god who lived there must have been a powerful god. The first room was a small anteroom—I waited there for some time, telling the spirits of the place that I came in peace and not as a robber. When it seemed to me that they had had time to hear me, I went on. Ah, what riches! Few, even, of the windows had been broken—it was all as it had been. The great windows that looked over the city had not been broken at all, though they were dusty and streaked with many years. There were coverings on the floors, the colors not greatly faded, and the chairs were soft and deep. There were pictures upon the walls, very strange, very wonderful—I remember one of a bunch of flowers in a jar—if you came close to it, you could see nothing but bits of color, but if you stood away from it, the flowers might have been picked yesterday. It made my heart feel strange to look at this picture—and to look at the figure of a bird, in some hard clay, on a table and see it so like our birds. Everywhere there were books and writings, many in tongues that I could not read. The god who lived there must have been a wise god and full of knowledge. I felt I had a right there, as I sought knowledge also. K

Nevertheless, it was strange. There was a washing place but no water—perhaps the gods washed in air. There was a cooking place but no wood, and though there was a machine to cook food, there was no place to put fire in it. Nor were there candles or lamps—there were things that looked like lamps, but they had neither oil nor wick. All these things were magic, but I touched them and lived—the magic had gone out of them. Let me tell one thing to show. In the washing place, a thing said "Hot," but it was not hot to the touch—another thing said "Cold," but it was not cold. This must have been a strong magic, but the magic was gone. I do not understand—they had ways—I wish that I knew.

It was close and dry and dusty in the house of the gods. I have said the magic was gone, but that is not true—it had gone from the magic things, but it had not gone from the place. I felt the spirits about me, weighing upon me. Nor had I ever slept in a Dead Place before—and yet, tonight, I must sleep there. When I thought of it, my tongue felt dry in my throat, in spite of my wish for knowledge. Almost I would have gone down again and faced the dogs, but I did not.

I had not gone through all the rooms when the darkness fell. When it fell, I went back to the big room looking over the city and made fire. There was a place to make fire and a box with wood in it, though I do not think they cooked there. I wrapped myself in a floor covering and slept in front of the fire—I was very tired.

Now I tell what is very strong magic. I woke in the midst of the night. When I woke, the fire had gone out, and I was cold. It seemed to me that all around me there were whisperings and voices. I closed my eyes to shut them

K MAKE INFERENCES
Reread lines 255–270. What does this "place of great riches" remind you of?

DIFFERENTIATED INSTRUCTION

FOR ENGLISH LANGUAGE LEARNERS

Language: Verb Tenses Direct students' attention to lines 255–270. Have pairs of students identify *all* of the verbs in this paragraph and list their forms in a Three-Column Journal with these headings: *Infinitives, Past Tense,* and *Past Perfect.* Tell students to underline the form of each verb that appears in the passage. Focus attention on the irregular past and past-perfect forms, such as *must have been* (lines 255–256), *came* (line 257), *had had* (line 258), *had been broken* (line 259), *had been* (line 260), *were* (lines 261, 262, 263, 268), *came* (line 264), stood (line 265), *made* (line 266), *felt* (line 270), and *sought* (line 270).

BEST PRACTICES TOOLKIT—Transparency
Three-Column Journal p. B10

318 UNIT 3: NARRATIVE DEVICES

Selassie Monoliths, 1998 (1998), Charlie Millar. Oil on canvas, 111.7 × 96.5 cm.
Private Collection. Photo © Bridgeman Art Library.

out. Some will say that I slept again, but I do not think that I slept. I could feel
the spirits drawing my spirit out of my body as a fish is drawn on a line.

Why should I lie about it? I am a priest and the son of a priest. If there are
spirits, as they say, in the small Dead Places near us, what spirits must there
300 not be in that great Place of the Gods? And would not they wish to speak?
After such long years? I know that I felt myself drawn as a fish is drawn on a
line. I had stepped out of my body—I could see my body asleep in front of the
cold fire, but it was not I. I was drawn to look out upon the city of the gods.

It should have been dark, for it was night, but it was not dark. Everywhere
there were lights—lines of light—circles and blurs of light—ten thousand

Direct students to lines 309–340. Use these prompts to help students understand John's vision and his reaction to it:

Connect In your experience, how can a vivid dream or daydream affect a person's point of view? *Answers will vary, but students should recognize the power of dreams to change a person's perspective.*

Analyze How does John's vision explain what happened to the gods? ***Possible answer:*** *John sees a thriving city that is destroyed by the weapons of the gods at war: "fire falling out of the sky and a mist that poisoned" (lines 334–335), turning the city into a "Dead Place" (lines 338–339).*

Evaluate John comments that "not all they did was well done—even I could see that" (lines 329–330). How is this observation likely to affect John's view of the gods? ***Possible answer:*** *John may begin to question the extent of their wisdom and power—and their "magic"—because clearly they are less than perfect.*

TEXT ANALYSIS: *Review*

COMMON CORE

RL 5

🄛 **FORESHADOWING**

Possible answer: *The dream is foreshadowed early in the story, lines 50–60, in John's conversation with his father about his dreams of the "great Dead Place and in it the gods walking."*

---

torches would not have been the same. The sky itself was alight—you could barely see the stars for the glow in the sky. I thought to myself "This is strong magic" and trembled. There was a roaring in my ears like the rushing of rivers. Then my eyes grew used to the light and my ears to the sound. I knew that I
310 was seeing the city as it had been when the gods were alive.

That was a sight indeed—yes, that was a sight: I could not have seen it in the body—my body would have died. Everywhere went the gods, on foot and in chariots—there were gods beyond number and counting, and their chariots blocked the streets. They had turned night to day for their pleasure—they did not sleep with the sun. The noise of their coming and going was the noise of many waters. It was magic what they could do—it was magic what they did.

I looked out of another window—the great vines of their bridges were mended, and the god roads went east and west. Restless, restless, were the gods and always in motion! They burrowed tunnels under rivers—they flew in the
320 air. With unbelievable tools they did giant works—no part of the earth was safe from them, for, if they wished for a thing, they summoned it from the other side of the world. And always, as they labored and rested, as they feasted and made love, there was a drum in their ears—the pulse of the giant city, beating and beating like a man's heart.

Were they happy? What is happiness to the gods? They were great; they were mighty; they were wonderful and terrible. As I looked upon them and their magic, I felt like a child—but a little more, it seemed to me, and they would pull down the moon from the sky. I saw them with wisdom beyond wisdom and knowledge beyond knowledge. And yet not all they did was well done—even I
330 could see that—and yet their wisdom could not but grow until all was peace.

Then I saw their fate come upon them, and that was terrible past speech. It came upon them as they walked the streets of their city. I have been in the fights with the Forest People—I have seen men die. But this was not like that. When gods war with gods, they use weapons we do not know. It was fire falling out of the sky and a mist that poisoned. It was the time of the Great Burning and the Destruction. They ran about like ants in the streets of their city—poor gods, poor gods! Then the towers began to fall. A few escaped— yes, a few. The legends tell it. But, even after the city had become a Dead Place, for many years the poison was still in the ground. I saw it happen; I saw
340 the last of them die. It was darkness over the broken city, and I wept. 🄛

All this, I saw. I saw it as I have told it, though not in the body. When I woke in the morning, I was hungry, but I did not think first of my hunger, for my heart was perplexed and confused. I knew the reason for the Dead Places, but I did not see why it had happened. It seemed to me it should not have happened, with all the magic they had. I went through the house looking for an answer. There was so much in the house I could not understand—and yet I am a priest and the son of a priest. It was like being on one side of the great river, at night, with no light to show the way.

🄛 **FORESHADOWING**
John's "dream" is foreshadowed earlier in the story. Where in the story does Benét prepare the reader for this dream?

DIFFERENTIATED INSTRUCTION

FOR STRUGGLING READERS

Comprehension Support To check understanding, ask students to explain the meaning of these words and phrases in the context of the story: *chariots* (line 313); *They had turned night to day* (line 314); *they did not sleep with the sun* (lines 314–315); *fire falling out of the sky and a mist that poisoned* (lines 334–335); *It was like being on one side of the great river, at night, with no light to show the way* (lines 347–348).

FOR ADVANCED LEARNERS/PRE–AP

Synthesize: First-Person Narrative Have students reread the narrator's description of "the city of the gods," lines 304–340. Then have them read lines 349–360. Ask students to write a first-person narrative from the point of view of the "god" sitting in the chair, using details from the narrator's account, their inferential skills, and their imaginations. Have volunteers read their narratives aloud.

Then I saw the dead god. He was sitting in his chair, by the window, in a
350 room I had not entered before, and for the first moment, I thought that he was
alive. Then I saw the skin on the back of his hand—it was like dry leather. The
room was shut, hot and dry—no doubt that had kept him as he was. At first I
was afraid to approach him—then the fear left me. He was sitting looking out
over the city—he was dressed in the clothes of the gods. His age was neither
young nor old—I could not tell his age. But there was wisdom in his face and
great sadness. You could see that he would have not run away. He had sat at
his window, watching his city die—then he himself had died. But it is better to
lose one's life than one's spirit—and you could see from the face that his spirit
had not been lost. I knew that, if I touched him, he would fall into dust—and
360 yet, there was something unconquered in the face.

That is all of my story, for then I knew he was a man—I knew then that
they had been men, neither gods nor demons. It is a great knowledge, hard to
tell and believe. They were men—they went a dark road, but they were men.
I had no fear after that—I had no fear going home, though twice I fought off
the dogs and once I was hunted for two days by the Forest People. When I saw
my father again, I prayed and was purified. He touched my lips and my breast;
he said, "You went away a boy. You come back a man and a priest." I said,
"Father, they were men! I have been in the Place of the Gods and seen it! Now
slay me, if it is the law—but still I know they were men."

370 He looked at me out of both eyes. He said, "The law is not always the same
shape—you have done what you have done. I could not have done it my time,
but you come after me. Tell!"

I told, and he listened. After that, I wished to tell all the people, but he
showed me otherwise. He said, "Truth is a hard deer to hunt. If you eat too
much truth at once, you may die of the truth. It was not idly that our fathers
forbade the Dead Places." He was right—it is better the truth should come
little by little. I have learned that, being a priest. Perhaps, in the old days, they
ate knowledge too fast. **M**

Nevertheless, we make a beginning. It is not for the metal alone we go to
380 the Dead Places now—there are the books and the writings. They are hard
to learn. And the magic tools are broken—but we can look at them and
wonder. At least, we make a beginning. And, when I am chief priest, we
shall go beyond the great river. We shall go to the Place of the Gods—the
place newyork—not one man but a company. We shall look for the images
of the gods and find the god ASHING and the others—the gods Lincoln
and Biltmore[1] and Moses.[2] But they were men who built the city, not gods or
demons. They were men. I remember the dead man's face. They were men who
were here before us. We must build again. ◠

(4) Targeted Passage

M DRAW CONCLUSIONS
Reread lines 376–378.
What idea about
knowledge do you
think Benét is trying
to communicate?

---

1. **Biltmore:** the name of a once-famous hotel in New York City.
2. **Moses:** Robert Moses (1888–1981), a New York City public official whose name appears
   on many bridges and other structures built during his administration.

REVISIT THE BIG QUESTION
Does KNOWLEDGE
come at a price?

Discuss Based on lines 373–378, what is the
price of keeping truth and knowledge from
coming out too quickly? *Possible answer:
Progress advances more slowly. The people are
treated like children, while the priests are all-
powerful.*

READING SKILL: Review   COMMON CORE   RL 1

M DRAW CONCLUSIONS

*Possible answer: Benét is suggesting that
humans slow down to better understand
and weigh new knowledge, because
knowledge alone is not wisdom. "Eating"
knowledge too fast can have disastrous
consequences.*

Extend the Discussion In what ways is
truth "a hard deer to hunt" (line 374)?

SELECTION WRAP–UP

READ WITH A PURPOSE Now that students
have finished reading the selection, have them
summarize the changes that John's desire for
knowledge brought to him and to his people.
*Possible answer: John discovered courage
within himself and learned the truth about the
gods. He is seeking wider knowledge for his
people and wants to build again what was lost.*

⭐ **CRITIQUE** Have students evaluate
the twist at the end of the story and explain
why they were or were not surprised. Ask
students if the ending effectively supports
Benét's message.

INDEPENDENT READING

Students may be interested in other titles
by Stephen Vincent Benét, such as *America*,
published in 1944, and *The Devil and Daniel
Webster and Other Stories*, published in 1975.

FOR STRUGGLING READERS

(4) Targeted Passage [Lines 349–377]

In this passage, John realizes the truth about
the "gods." He shares that truth with his
father, who cautions him to guard it wisely.

• What startling truth does John learn? What
effect does his new knowledge have on
him? (lines 361–363, 369; 364)

• What does John want to do with his newly
acquired knowledge? Why doesn't he do
what he wants to do? (lines 373; 373–377)

FOR ADVANCED LEARNERS/PRE–AP

Synthesize Invite students to reread lines
379–388. Have students write a brief essay
explaining whether this paragraph—and the
story as a whole—conveys a hopeful or pes-
simistic message. Have volunteers share their
essays with the class.

Practice and Apply

For preliminary support of post-reading questions, use these copy masters:

R RESOURCE MANAGER—Copy Masters
Reading Check p. 25
First-Person Point of View p. 21
Question Support p. 26

Additional selection questions are provided for teachers on page 15.

ANSWERS

Comprehension

1. *John plans to be a priest, like his father.*

2. *John is eager to gain more knowledge.*

3. *There are no gods living in the "Place of the Gods." It is a city built by humans.*

4. *The story takes place in and near New York City, in the future after a cataclysmic war.*

Text Analysis

COMMON CORE **RL 1, RL 3**

Possible answers:

5. *Possible answer: The tone of the story is a sense of both wonder and terror of what human beings can accomplish through knowledge, especially technological knowledge. John's point of view helps the reader participate in the wonder and terror he feels.*

6. ● COMMON CORE FOCUS **Make Inferences** *The Place of the Gods is New York City. Long ago, there was a cataclysmic war, during which bombs dropped on the city and caused near-total death and destruction.*

7. *The theme is that knowledge is gained at a price. John learns the truth about the Place of the Gods, knowledge that alters his world view (lines 361–363). The people from New York had great knowledge, but the weapons they made with this knowledge destroyed them (lines 334–336).*

8. *The words of the psalm describe the Jews' sorrow over the destruction of their homeland. These words echo in the story, because John, too, weeps with sorrow (lines 339–340) when he grasps the fate of his homeland during "the time of the Great Burning and the Destruction" (lines 335–336).*

9. ● COMMON CORE FOCUS **Compare Points of View** *A third-person omniscient narrator would have presented a less compel-*

Comprehension

1. **Recall** What profession does John plan to have?

2. **Recall** Why does John set out on his journey?

3. **Recall** What does John discover to be untrue about the Place of the Gods?

4. **Clarify** When and where does this story take place?

Text Analysis

5. **Analyze** What is the **tone** of this story? How does the use of John as a narrator affect the tone?

● 6. **Make Inferences About Setting** Review the chart you completed as you read. What can you infer about the Place of the Gods and the events that took place there long ago?

7. **Draw Conclusions** What is the **theme,** or message, of this story? Cite evidence to support your conclusion.

8. **Understand Allusion** The **Background** on page 309 explains the biblical allusion, or reference, in the story's title. How do the words of the psalm relate to the discoveries John makes about the Great Burning and the gods?

● 9. **Compare Points of View** With a **first-person narrator,** you see the story unfold through the eyes of one character. Think about how John reacts to other characters and the way he describes the story's events. Would a **third-person omniscient narrator**—a narrator who sees into the minds of all characters in a story—have presented a more compelling picture of the events in "By the Waters of Babylon"? Cite evidence from the story to support your opinion.

10. **Evaluate Narrative Devices** John is an example of a **naive narrator**—a narrator with limited knowledge, who does not fully understand what he experiences. Why did Benét choose this kind of narrator for "By the Waters of Babylon"?

Text Criticism

11. **Historical Context** This story was published in 1937, when the threat of a second world war loomed large over the face of Europe. In what ways is this historical context reflected in the story? Explain your answer.

> ### Does **KNOWLEDGE** come at a price?
> What are some of the consequences of obtaining knowledge?

COMMON CORE

RL 1 Cite textual evidence to support inferences drawn from the text. **RL 3** Analyze how complex characters advance the plot.

ling picture than a first-person narrator. A first-person narrator allows readers to share John's thoughts, feelings, and interpretations directly. For example, we share John's fears in approaching the Place of the Gods (lines 109–150) and his wonder as he describes it (lines 172–204).

10. *Benét chose a naïve narrator because this enables readers to share the story's gradual revelations with John as they occur, making the tale suspenseful and surprising.*

Text Criticism

11. *Possible answer: People of the time feared that a second world war could destroy the world. The story appears to have its roots in such fear, because the advanced weaponry of the "gods" at war did indeed destroy their world.*

> Does **KNOWLEDGE** come at a price? *Possible answer: Knowledge carries with it responsibility for wise use and for poor choices.*

Language

◆ **GRAMMAR AND STYLE: Use Appropriate Language**

Review the **Grammar and Style** note on page 317. Benét uses **formal language** to convey the dark mood of the story. You, too, can use formal language when the audience and purpose require a quality of seriousness in your writing. Here are some guidelines to follow:

1. **Avoid using contractions.** Contractions tend to make writing sound more like everyday speech than formal writing.

2. **Use more complex sentence structure and vocabulary.** Short, simple sentences and informal language, such as slang, are more appropriate for casual communication.

Here is an example of Benét's use of formal language:

> *How shall I tell what I saw? The towers are not all broken—here and there one still stands, like a great tree in a forest, and the birds nest high. But the towers themselves look blind, for the gods are gone.* (lines 187–189)

Notice how the revisions in blue in the student model make the language of this first draft more appropriate for the audience and purpose. Use similar techniques to revise your response to the prompt.

> **STUDENT MODEL**
>
>   *may appear to be*
> Knowledge ~~seems like it can be~~ dangerous. But ~~it's~~ *it is* people using the
>
> knowledge who are the real danger.

READING-WRITING CONNECTION

YOUR TURN Enrich your understanding of "By the Waters of Babylon" by responding to this prompt. Then use the **revising tip** to improve your writing.

WRITING PROMPT	REVISING TIP
Short Constructed Response: Evaluation Do you agree with John that too much **knowledge** can harm people and that "truth should come little by little"? Write a **one-to-two-paragraph response**, drawing on the story and real-life events.	Review your response. Did you use formal language, including avoiding contractions and using complex sentence structure and vocabulary? If not, revise to increase the formality of your answer.

Interactive Revision
Go to **thinkcentral.com**.
KEYWORD: HML10-323

◆ **GRAMMAR AND STYLE**

- After students examine the student model, ask how the revisions changed the tone.

- Write this passage on the board, and ask students to suggest revisions to give it a more serious, formal tone. (Sample revisions appear in blue.)

 *~~There's no question that~~ John is unquestionably qualified to become ~~has what it takes to be a priest. He's smart. He's got a curious mind. He's got guts.~~ is intelligent, inquisitive, and courageous.*

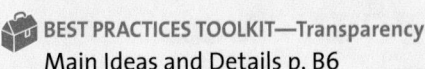 **RESOURCE MANAGER—Copy Master**
Use Appropriate Language p. 27

READING-WRITING CONNECTION

- Encourage students to think in specific terms rather than generalities. The knowledge that harmed people was, in part, knowledge of weapon-making. How might scientific knowledge help—or harm—society?

 BEST PRACTICES TOOLKIT—Transparency
Main Ideas and Details p. B6

> **THINK** central
> **Writing Online**
>
> The following tools are available online at **thinkcentral.com** and on **WriteSmart CD-ROM**:
> - **Interactive Graphic Organizers**
> - **Interactive Student Models**
> - **Interactive Revision Lessons**
>
> For additional grammar instruction, see **GrammarNotes** on **thinkcentral.com**.

DIFFERENTIATED INSTRUCTION

FOR STRUGGLING WRITERS

- Limit the scope of the assignment to one well-developed paragraph.

- Help students state their agreement or disagreement in a topic sentence.

- Guide students to generate specific reasons, examples, and details to support their topic sentences.

Assess and Reteach

Assess

DIAGNOSTIC AND SELECTION TESTS
Selection Test A, B/C pp. 87–88, 89–90

Interactive Selection Test on **thinkcentral.com**

Reteach

Level Up Online Tutorials on **thinkcentral.com**
Literature Lessons 8, 10

COMMON CORE

L 3 Apply knowledge of language to make effective choices for meaning or style.

Focus and Motivate

COMMON CORE FOCUS

RL 1 Cite textual evidence to support analysis of what the text says explicitly as well as inferences drawn from the text. **RL 4** Determine the figurative meaning of words in a text. **RL 5** Analyze an author's choices concerning how to structure a text and order the events within it. **L 4c** Consult reference materials to determine or clarify a word's etymology.

SUMMARIES

"There Will Come Soft Rains" An advanced home completes automated tasks while outside, a charred wall contains silhouettes of the family members. When a falling tree branch causes a fire, the house tries to save itself.

"Inside the Home of the Future" This newspaper article focus on efforts to create automated homes.

The Car of the Future This 1950 advertisement is a look at the future.

Is **TECHNOLOGY** taking over?

Introduce the question, and have students complete the *QUICKWRITE.*

What's the Connection?

Discuss technological advances and ask students to describe technological advances they may see in the future.

Selection Resources

There Will Come Soft Rains
Short Story by Ray Bradbury

Inside the Home of the Future
Newspaper Article by Kelly Greene

The Car of the Future
Advertisement

Essential Course of Study **ECOS**

VIDEO TRAILER **THINK** central KEYWORD: HML10-324

Is **TECHNOLOGY** taking over?

COMMON CORE

RL 1 Cite textual evidence to support analysis of what the text says explicitly as well as inferences drawn from the text. **RL 5** Analyze an author's choices concerning how to structure a text and order the events within it. **RL 4** Determine the figurative meaning of words in a text.

Which technological innovations have improved the quality of everyday life? Which ones have had a negative impact? In "There Will Come Soft Rains," you will read about the far-reaching consequences of technology on one particular home.

What's the Connection?

The following short story depicts a futuristic society in which human misuse of technology has had cataclysmic results. After reading "There Will Come Soft Rains," you will read an expository text and view a visual that share a more positive view of technological innovation.

Section 3

THE CELL PHONE IS HERE TO STAY

WOULD YOU PASS ME THE SALT, HONEY?

COMING RIGHT UP, DEAR!

CAN I BE EXCUSED?

OLSEN

1823

© www.CartoonStock.com

324

 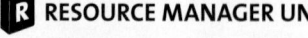
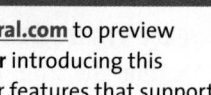

TEXT ANALYSIS: CHRONOLOGICAL ORDER

Writers make choices about how to organize events in a story. The most straightforward way of structuring a story is to describe events in **chronological order**—the sequence in which events occur. To determine chronological order in a story, look for the following:

- words that identify time, such as *six o'clock* and *today*
- words that signal order, such as *before, next,* and *last*
- breaks in the chronological flow of events

As you read "There Will Come Soft Rains," think about the reasons Ray Bradbury might have chosen to present this science fiction story in chronological order.

READING SKILL: DRAW CONCLUSIONS

A **conclusion** is a judgment based on evidence in the story and your own prior knowledge. Use the following strategies to analyze information about the house in the story:

- Analyze details about the family and their routine.
- Analyze details about the areas near the house.
- Identify changes in the performance of the house.

As you read the story, record and analyze important details. Later you will draw conclusions about what happened.

Important Details	My Thoughts
It's morning and the house is empty.	The people are gone. The house still acts as though they're there.

Review: Compare and Contrast

▲ VOCABULARY IN CONTEXT

Substitute a different word or phrase for each boldfaced vocabulary word. Write a brief definition of each boldfaced word in your *Reader/Writer Notebook*.

1. The **silhouette** of the great oak is visible for miles.
2. Your increasing **paranoia** is making you a nervous wreck.
3. To **manipulate** a puppet properly requires practice.
4. The sight of the rattlesnake made Don **tremulous.**
5. She is **oblivious** to the mess all around her.
6. This is a **sublime** piece of cheesecake!

 Complete the activities in your **Reader/Writer Notebook.**

Ray Bradbury
born 1920

Prophet of the Future
Ray Bradbury is one of America's best-known science fiction and fantasy writers. His most chilling stories comment on the human consequences of progress. "Science ran too far ahead of us too quickly," Bradbury once remarked, "and the people got lost in a mechanical wilderness." Sadly, Bradbury has lived to see some of his frightening concerns become fact.

A Magical Childhood
Bradbury's interest in science fiction and fantasy emerged when he was growing up in Waukegan, Illinois. He devoured the popular culture of his day, including movies, radio shows, comics, and science fiction magazines. He was also a fan of the local library, where he enjoyed books by such early science fiction writers as H. G. Wells and Jules Verne. While various writers have influenced his style, his themes are drawn primarily from his own childhood.

BACKGROUND TO THE STORY
Technology: No Guarantee
Before 1900, electric machines were used primarily in workplaces. With the spread of electricity, however, families enjoyed modern appliances in their homes. In the early 20th century, many household machines, such as the vacuum cleaner and the toaster, became available for the first time.

Science fiction writers of this period often created works featuring utopias—or ideal worlds—in which machines freed people of difficult tasks. In "There Will Come Soft Rains," Bradbury challenges this idea by presenting a society harmed by modern technology.

Author Online THINK central

Go to thinkcentral.com.
KEYWORD: HML10-325

325

TEXT ANALYSIS COMMON CORE RL 4 RL 5

● Model the Skill: CHRONOLOGICAL ORDER

To model how to place events in chronological order, read aloud this example:

Jen's alarm rang at 6:40 A.M., 20 minutes earlier than usual. Her mother had already left for work. First, Jen took a shower and got dressed. Before breakfast, she reviewed her science notes. She left for school a few minutes after 8:00.

Tell students that the following words indicate time or signal order: 6:40 A.M., First, Before, after, 8:00.

GUIDED PRACTICE Elicit other examples of words that indicate time or signal order.

READING SKILL COMMON CORE RL 1

■ Model the Skill: DRAW CONCLUSIONS

Use the preceding example to model drawing conclusions.

- **Details:** Jen set her alarm "20 minutes earlier than usual." Before leaving for school, she reviewed her science notes.
- **Conclusion:** Jen probably has a science test.

GUIDED PRACTICE What can students conclude about Bradbury's attitude toward technology?

R RESOURCE MANAGER—Copy Master
Draw Conclusions p. 41

VOCABULARY SKILL COMMON CORE L 4

▲ VOCABULARY IN CONTEXT

DIAGNOSE WORD KNOWLEDGE Have all students complete Vocabulary in Context. Check their words or phrases against the following:

manipulate (mə-nĭp′yə-lāt′) *v.* to move, operate, or handle

oblivious (ə-blĭv′ē-əs) *adj.* paying no attention, completely unaware

paranoia (păr′ə-noi′ə) *n.* an irrational fear of danger or misfortune

silhouette (sĭl′ōō-ĕt′) *n.* an outline that appears dark against a light background

sublime (sə-blīm′) *adj.* supreme, splendid

tremulous (trĕm′yə-ləs) *adj.* trembling, unsteady

PRETEACH VOCABULARY Use the following copy master to help students predict the meaning of each boldfaced word.

R RESOURCE MANAGER—Copy Master
Vocabulary Study p. 43

1. Read the first item aloud, emphasizing *silhouette*.
2. Call attention to the phrases "window shade was drawn" and "someone inside the well-lit room." Elicit possible meanings for *silhouette,* such as "outline."
3. Repeat the procedure for the other items.

READ WITH A PURPOSE

Help students set a purpose for reading. Tell them to look for the house's personality.

TEXT ANALYSIS | COMMON CORE
RL 4
RL 5

Ⓐ CHRONOLOGICAL ORDER

Possible answer: "seven o'clock" *(line 1),* "The morning house" *(lines 2–3),* "The clock ticked on" *(line 3),* "Seven-nine, breakfast time" *(line 4),* "breakfast stove" *(line 5),* "Today is" *(line 8)*

READING SKILL | COMMON CORE
RL 1

Ⓑ *Model the Skill:* DRAW CONCLUSIONS

To model how to draw conclusions, read aloud lines 14–20. Use the board to fill out a Draw Conclusions graphic organizer. Discuss various reasons that the house is quiet, and help students draw the conclusion that the days is unusual because no one is home.

Possible answer: *There is no one in the house slamming doors or walking on the carpets, heading to school or work, as the house is apparently accustomed to (lines 14–15). The garage door opens, waiting for someone to get into the car, but no one does (lines 19–20).*

THERE WILL COME
Soft Rains

Ray Bradbury

In the living room the voice-clock sang, *Tick-tock, seven o'clock, time to get up, time to get up, seven o'clock!* as if it were afraid that nobody would. The morning house lay empty. The clock ticked on, repeating and repeating its sounds into the emptiness. *Seven-nine, breakfast time, seven-nine!*

In the kitchen the breakfast stove gave a hissing sigh and ejected from its warm interior eight pieces of perfectly browned toast, eight eggs sunnyside up, sixteen slices of bacon, two coffees, and two cool glasses of milk.

"Today is August 4, 2026," said a second voice from the kitchen ceiling, "in the city of Allendale, California." It repeated the date three times for memory's
10 sake. "Today is Mr. Featherstone's birthday. Today is the anniversary of Tilita's marriage. Insurance is payable, as are the water, gas, and light bills." Ⓐ

Somewhere in the walls, relays[1] clicked, memory tapes glided under electric eyes.

Eight-one, tick-tock, eight-one o'clock, off to school, off to work, run, run, eight-one! But no doors slammed, no carpets took the soft tread of rubber heels. It was raining outside. The weather box on the front door sang quietly: "Rain, rain, go away; rubbers, raincoats for today . . ." And the rain tapped on the empty house, echoing.

Outside, the garage chimed and lifted its door to reveal the waiting car.
20 After a long wait the door swung down again. Ⓑ

At eight-thirty the eggs were shriveled and the toast was like stone. An aluminum wedge scraped them into the sink, where hot water whirled them down a metal throat which digested and flushed them away to the distant sea. The dirty dishes were dropped into a hot washer and emerged twinkling dry.

---

1. **relays:** devices that automatically turn switches in electric circuits on and off.

326   UNIT 3: NARRATIVE DEVICES

Analyze Visuals ▶
Examine this image. What details convey the orderliness of the family that lives in the house?

 **Targeted Passage**

Ⓐ **CHRONOLOGICAL ORDER**
Reread lines 1–11. Which words and phrases tell you that the story is organized in chronological order?

Ⓑ **DRAW CONCLUSIONS**
Reread lines 14–20. Which story details suggest that this is an unusual day for the family?

DIFFERENTIATED INSTRUCTION

FOR ENGLISH LANGUAGE LEARNERS

Vocabulary Support Use Definition Mapping to teach these words: *reveal* (line 19), *emerged* (line 24), *panels* (line 63), *ceased* (line 148), *reinforcements* (line 154).

📦 BEST PRACTICES TOOLKIT—Transparency
Definition Mapping p. E6

FOR STRUGGLING READERS

In combination with the *Audio Anthology CD,* use one or more Targeted Passages (pp. 326, 328, 331, 333) to ensure that students focus on key events, concepts, and skills. Targeted Passages are also good for English learners.

① **Targeted Passage [Lines 5–21]**

This passage establishes time and place, introduces the technologically remarkable house, and suggests the absence of occupants.

Reading Support

This selection on **thinkcentral.com** includes embedded **ThinkAloud** models—students "thinking aloud" about the story to model the kinds of questions a good reader would ask about a selection.

Analyze Visuals

Possible answer: *The orderliness of the family is conveyed by the neatness of the property and the obvious care that the owners have taken. For example, the grass is neatly trimmed, the path appears to have been recently swept, and the house is an unblemished white. Nothing appears to be out of place.*

REVISIT THE BIG QUESTION

Is TECHNOLOGY
taking over?

Based on lines 1–18, what features of the house in the story suggest that it is a wonder of technology? *Possible answer: A "voice-clock" announces the time and hurries the house's inhabitants along (lines 1–2). The breakfast stove automatically prepares a perfect breakfast (lines 5–7). A voice from the kitchen ceiling provides reminders of special occasions and bills due (lines 10–11). A "weather box on the front door" announces the weather conditions (lines 16–17).*

- What is the setting of the story? (lines 17–18)
- How would you describe the house?
- What happens to the eggs and toast? What does this suggest about the house's occupants? (line 21)

FOR ADVANCED LEARNERS/PRE–AP

Make Comparisons Compare this house with the house in the City of the Gods from "By the Waters of Babylon." How were the two houses similar in setting, contents, and history? How are they different?

Center column (story text)

Nine-fifteen, sang the clock, *time to clean.*

Out of warrens in the wall, tiny robot mice darted. The rooms were acrawl with the small cleaning animals, all rubber and metal. They thudded against chairs, whirling their mustached runners, kneading the rug nap, sucking gently at hidden dust. Then, like mysterious invaders, they popped into their
30 burrows. Their pink electric eyes faded. The house was clean.

Ten o'clock. The sun came out from behind the rain. The house stood alone in a city of rubble and ashes. This was the one house left standing. At night the ruined city gave off a radioactive glow which could be seen for miles.

Ten-fifteen. The garden sprinklers whirled up in golden founts, filling the soft morning air with scatterings of brightness. The water pelted windowpanes, running down the charred west side where the house had been burned evenly free of its white paint. The entire west face of the house was black, save for five places. Here the **silhouette** in paint of a man mowing a lawn. Here, as in a photograph, a woman bent to pick flowers. Still farther over, their images
40 burned on wood in one titanic instant, a small boy, hands flung into the air; higher up, the image of a thrown ball, and opposite him a girl, hands raised to catch a ball which never came down.

The five spots of paint—the man, the woman, the children, the ball—remained. The rest was a thin charcoaled layer.

The gentle sprinkler rain filled the garden with falling light.

Until this day, how well the house had kept its peace. How carefully it had inquired, "Who goes there? What's the password?" and, getting no answer from lonely foxes and whining cats, it had shut up its windows and drawn shades in an old-maidenly preoccupation with self-protection which bordered
50 on a mechanical **paranoia.**

It quivered at each sound, the house did. If a sparrow brushed a window, the shade snapped up. The bird, startled, flew off! No, not even a bird must touch the house!

The house was an altar with ten thousand attendants, big, small, servicing, attending, in choirs. But the gods had gone away, and the ritual of the religion continued senselessly, uselessly.

Twelve noon.

A dog whined, shivering, on the front porch.

The front door recognized the dog voice and opened. The dog, once huge
60 and fleshy, but now gone to bone and covered with sores, moved in and through the house, tracking mud. Behind it whirred angry mice, angry at having to pick up mud, angry at inconvenience.

For not a leaf fragment blew under the door but what the wall panels flipped open and the copper scrap rats flashed swiftly out. The offending dust, hair, or paper, seized in miniature steel jaws, was raced back to the burrows. There, down tubes which fed into the cellar, it was dropped into the sighing vent of an incinerator which sat like evil Baal[2] in a dark corner.

---

2. **Baal** (bā'əl): an idol worshiped by certain ancient peoples of the Middle East.

Left column

READING SKILL — COMMON CORE   RL 1

C DRAW CONCLUSIONS

Possible answer: This futuristic society prizes technology as a means of eliminating chores and making day-to-day life easier and more convenient. The nature of the devices—such as the automatic, self-cleaning sink (lines 21–24) and the robotic cleaning mice (lines 26–29)—also suggests that the society values cleanliness and order. With so many labor-saving devices, people in this society—at least, those people who can afford the devices—should have ample time to pursue leisure activities.

READING SKILL — COMMON CORE   RL 1

D DRAW CONCLUSIONS

Possible answer: The house and the surrounding city have suffered an atomic blast. Silhouettes are all that remain of the family members who lived in the house.

IF STUDENTS NEED HELP . . .

- Have students reread lines 31–33. Discuss possible reasons why "[t]he house stood alone in a city of rubble and ashes." Then ask what could cause "the ruined city" to give off "a radioactive glow."

- Have students reread lines 35–44. Call attention to the words *charred, burned,* and *charcoaled.* Then discuss why the "west face of the house was black" except for the silhouettes.

VOCABULARY — COMMON CORE   L 4

OWN THE WORD

- **silhouette:** Ask students when or why they might see someone in *silhouette.*

- **paranoia:** Point out that *paranoia* is from the Latin prefix *para-*, meaning "mind," and *paranoos,* meaning "madness." A person suffering from *paranoia* is said to be *paranoid.* Have students explain when or why a person might feel *paranoid.*

Right column

C DRAW CONCLUSIONS
Think about the **setting** of this story. What do you learn about the society from the house's many automated features?

2 Targeted Passage

silhouette (sĭl'ōō-ĕt') *n.* an outline that appears dark against a light background

D DRAW CONCLUSIONS
Reread lines 31–44. Based on the story details about the city, what do you think has happened?

paranoia (păr'ə-noi'ə) *n.* an irrational fear of danger or misfortune

---

DIFFERENTIATED INSTRUCTION

FOR STRUGGLING READERS

2 Targeted Passage [Lines 31–44]

This key passage suggests that an atomic blast destroyed the city and vaporized the house's family members.

- Why was the west face of the house black? How did the silhouettes get there? (lines 39–40)

- What event occurred during the "one titanic instant"? What makes you think so? (lines 32–33)

FOR ENGLISH LANGUAGE LEARNERS

Vocabulary: Conversational English Patterns
Note the slightly antiquated language and sentence structure in these examples: "The rooms were acrawl with . . ." (lines 26–27); "'Who goes there?'" (line 47); "It quivered at each sound, the house did" (line 51); "For not a leaf fragment blew under the door but what the wall panels flipped open . . ." (lines 63–64). Stress that this kind of language is more suited to literary use than everyday speech.

10:00

The dog ran upstairs, hysterically yelping to each door, at last realizing, as the house realized, that only silence was here.

70 It sniffed the air and scratched the kitchen door. Behind the door, the stove was making pancakes which filled the house with a rich baked odor and the scent of maple syrup.

The dog frothed at the mouth, lying at the door, sniffing, its eyes turned to fire. It ran wildly in circles, biting at its tail, spun in a frenzy, and died. It lay in the parlor for an hour.

Two o'clock, sang a voice.

Delicately sensing decay at last, the regiments of mice hummed out as softly as blown gray leaves in an electrical wind.

Two-fifteen.

80 The dog was gone.

In the cellar, the incinerator glowed suddenly and a whirl of sparks leaped up the chimney. **E**

Two thirty-five.

Bridge tables sprouted from patio walls. Playing cards fluttered onto pads in a shower of pips. Martinis manifested on an oaken bench with egg-salad sandwiches. Music played.

> **E COMPARE AND CONTRAST**
> Compare the actions of the dog with those of the house. What does the dog's death suggest about the house?

THERE WILL COME SOFT RAINS **329**

Analyze Visuals

Activity How does the illustration relate to the setting and atmosphere of the story?

Possible answer: *The sleek, modern kitchen depicted in the illustration is suggestive of the futuristic kitchen in the story, especially since there is no evidence of human life.*

E COMPARE AND CONTRAST

Possible answer: *The dog is in a frenzy, dying and alone. It searches in vain for the family, lured toward the kitchen by the smell of pancakes, only to perish at the door (lines 68–75). Meanwhile, the house continues mindlessly on its automated and mechanized course, cleaning up mud (lines 61–62) and making pancakes for no one (lines 70–72), oblivious to the dog's pathetic plight. The dog's death, followed by the house's efficient disposal of its body (lines 77–82), suggests that the house is trying to go on, but it is only a matter of time until it, too, succumbs.*

FOR STRUGGLING READERS

Comprehension Support Direct students' attention to lines 73–82. Help students use textual clues to infer how the house dealt with the body of the dog. Explain that in this context, *regiments* are many robot mice that work in an orderly way. Point out that the regiments of mice come out and then the dog is gone. Next, the incinerator glows suddenly, as if something has been put in it. Ask what happened to the dog and explain, if necessary.

FOR ENGLISH LANGUAGE LEARNERS

Vocabulary: Multiple-Meaning Words Help students identify words with more than one meaning, such as *spun* (line 74), *wind* (line 78), *Bridge* (line 84), and *cards* (line 84). Have pairs complete a Cluster Diagram, placing the multiple-meaning word in the center and the definitions in the outer cells.

🗂 **BEST PRACTICES TOOLKIT—Transparency**
Cluster Diagram p. B18

F DRAW CONCLUSIONS

Possible answer: *The nursery's furnishings suggest that there are young children in the family. The imaginative re-creation of nature suggests that the family appreciates nature but may be more accustomed to experiencing it through technological media than through firsthand experience.*

TIERED DISCUSSION PROMPTS

Direct students to lines 83–110. Use these prompts to help students understand the role that technology plays in the house:

Analyze How is the family's daily schedule of activities reflected in the house's technological programming? ***Possible answer:*** *In the early afternoon, the house provides playing cards, martinis, sandwiches, and music (lines 83–86). In the late afternoon, the nursery creates "the children's hour" and then draws a hot bath (lines 90–105). Subsequently, the house provides dinner, lights a fire in the hearth, offers a cigar, and later warms the beds (lines 106–110).*

Synthesize Without humans living in the house, how long do you think the house's technology will continue to function? Why? *Students should defend their responses.*

OWN THE WORD

- **manipulate:** Ask students how they might *manipulate* a computer's keyboard. ***Possible answers:*** *typing documents, sending e-mails*

- **tremulous:** Have students complete this sentence to show they understand the meaning of *tremulous*: The mouse was *tremulous* because. . . .

But the tables were silent and the cards untouched.

At four o'clock the tables folded like great butterflies back through the paneled walls.

90 *Four-thirty.*

The nursery walls glowed.

Animals took shape: yellow giraffes, blue lions, pink antelopes, lilac panthers cavorting in crystal substance. The walls were glass. They looked out upon color and fantasy. Hidden films clocked through well-oiled sprockets, and the walls lived. The nursery floor was woven to resemble a crisp, cereal meadow. Over this ran aluminum roaches and iron crickets, and in the hot still air butterflies of delicate red tissue wavered among the sharp aroma of animal spoors! There was the sound like a great matted yellow hive of bees within a dark bellows, the lazy bumble of a purring lion. And there was the patter of 100 okapi[3] feet and the murmur of a fresh jungle rain, like other hoofs, falling upon the summer-starched grass. Now the walls dissolved into distances of parched weed, mile on mile, and warm endless sky. The animals drew away into thorn brakes and water holes.

It was the children's hour. F

Five o'clock. The bath filled with clear hot water.

Six, seven, eight o'clock. The dinner dishes **manipulated** like magic tricks, and in the study a *click.* In the metal stand opposite the hearth where a fire now blazed up warmly, a cigar popped out, half an inch of soft gray ash on it, smoking, waiting.

110 *Nine o'clock.* The beds warmed their hidden circuits, for nights were cool here.

Nine-five. A voice spoke from the study ceiling:

"Mrs. McClellan, which poem would you like this evening?"

The house was silent.

The voice said at last, "Since you express no preference, I shall select a poem at random." Quiet music rose to back the voice. "Sara Teasdale. As I recall, your favorite. . . ."

> *"There will come soft rains and the*
> *   smell of the ground,*
> *And swallows circling with their*
> 120 *   shimmering sound;*
>
> *And frogs in the pools singing at night,*
> *And wild plum trees in* ***tremulous*** *white;*
>
> *Robins will wear their feathery fire,*
> *Whistling their whims on a low fence-wire;*

F DRAW CONCLUSIONS
What do the nursery's furnishings tell you about the family and their relationship to the natural world?

manipulate
(mə-nĭp′yə-lāt′) *v.* to move, operate, or handle

tremulous (trĕm′yə-ləs)
adj. trembling, unsteady

---

3. **okapi** (ō-kä′pē): an antelope-like hoofed mammal of the African jungle.

DIFFERENTIATED INSTRUCTION

FOR STRUGGLING READERS

Concept Support: Sensory Details Direct students' attention to lines 92–103. Elicit or explain that Bradbury uses sensory details to bring the narrative to life. Help students complete a Two-Column Chart to identify sensory details. Then ask what effect the description of the nursery had on them.

BEST PRACTICES TOOLKIT—Transparency
Two-Column Chart p. A25

Develop Reading Fluency Read aloud lines 92–103 twice, first using a monotone voice,

and then an animated voice, emphasizing sensory details. Discuss the change in listening interest that accompanies a change in voice emphasis. Have student pairs practice reading as they vary the type of emphasis used.

Distribute the copy masters and have students work in pairs or groups to practice fluency.

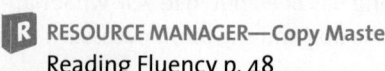
RESOURCE MANAGER—Copy Master
Reading Fluency p. 48

And not one will know of the war, not one
Will care at last when it is done.

Not one would mind, neither bird nor tree,
If mankind perished utterly;

And Spring herself, when she woke at dawn
130   Would scarcely know that we were gone." **G**

The fire burned on the stone hearth and the cigar fell away into a mound of quiet ash on its tray. The empty chairs faced each other between the silent walls, and the music played.

At ten o'clock the house began to die. **H**
The wind blew. A falling tree bough crashed through the kitchen window. Cleaning solvent, bottled, shattered over the stove. The room was ablaze in an instant!

"Fire!" screamed a voice. The house lights flashed, water pumps shot water from the ceilings. But the solvent spread on the linoleum, licking, eating,
140   under the kitchen door, while the voices took it up in chorus: "Fire, fire, fire!"

The house tried to save itself. Doors sprang tightly shut, but the windows were broken by the heat and the wind blew and sucked upon the fire. **A**

The house gave ground as the fire in ten billion angry sparks moved with flaming ease from room to room and then up the stairs. While scurrying water rats squeaked from the walls, pistoled their water, and ran for more. And the wall sprays let down showers of mechanical rain.

G DRAW CONCLUSIONS
What do you think is the **theme,** or main message, of the poem?

H CHRONOLOGICAL ORDER
How has the marking of time changed in the story? Explain.

③ Targeted Passage

COMMON CORE L 5b

A FIGURATIVE LANGUAGE
Personification is the giving of human qualities to an inanimate object. Reread line 141. How does the personification of the house in this line reflect the rise of artificial intelligence technologies?

THERE WILL COME SOFT RAINS   **331**

FOR STRUGGLING READERS

③ Targeted Passage [Lines 134–146]

This passage signals the beginning of the end for the house, as a falling tree branch causes a fire to start in the kitchen.

- What causes the fire? (lines 135–136)
- How does the house respond to the fire? (line 138)
- Reread line 134. What does this sentence suggest about what will happen?

FOR ADVANCED LEARNERS/PRE–AP

Analyze Author's Technique From the moment the fire starts (line 136) through the end of the story, Bradbury depicts the events as a life-or-death battle between opposing forces. Have students write a brief essay analyzing how the author turns the action into an almost-human conflict.

Is TECHNOLOGY
taking over?

Discuss Based on lines 147–162, how does Bradbury's description of the spreading fire suggest the limits of technology? ***Possible answer:*** *As sophisticated as the house's protective mechanisms are, technology cannot overcome the primitive natural force of fire.*

Analyze Visuals

Possible answer: Moderately effective. The story's illustrations are more effective at conveying the chronological order of events for the end of the story than for preceding parts. The first illustration (p. 327) shows the outside of the house at 7:00 A.M. The next illustration (p. 329) shows the kitchen at 10:00 A.M. but offers no strong sense of chronology. Then there is a huge gap in time: the next illustration (p. 331) shows the fire beginning in the kitchen 12 hours later. The subsequent effects of the fire are then depicted in the illustration on page 332.

But too late. Somewhere, sighing, a pump shrugged to a stop. The quenching rain ceased. The reserve water supply which had filled baths and washed dishes for many quiet days was gone.

150　　The fire crackled up the stairs. It fed upon Picassos and Matisses[4] in the upper halls, like delicacies, baking off the oily flesh, tenderly crisping the canvases into black shavings.

Now the fire lay in beds, stood in windows, changed the colors of drapes! And then, reinforcements.

From attic trapdoors, blind robot faces peered down with faucet mouths gushing green chemical.

The fire backed off, as even an elephant must at the sight of a dead snake. Now there were twenty snakes whipping over the floor, killing the fire with a clear cold venom of green froth.

160　　But the fire was clever. It had sent flame outside the house, up through the attic to the pumps there. An explosion! The attic brain which directed the pumps was shattered into bronze shrapnel on the beams.

The fire rushed back into every closet and felt of the clothes hung there.

The house shuddered, oak bone on bone, its bared skeleton cringing from the heat, its wire, its nerves revealed as if a surgeon had torn the skin off to let the red veins and capillaries quiver in the scalded air. Help, help! Fire! Run, run! Heat snapped mirrors like the first brittle winter ice. And the voices wailed Fire,

---

4. **Picassos and Matisses:** paintings by the famous 20th-century artists Pablo Picasso (pǐ-kä′sō) and Henri Matisse (mə-tēs′).

COMMON CORE RL 4

Language Coach

Word Meanings The suffix *-s* usually means "more than one," but sometimes it gives a new meaning to the base word from which it derives, or comes. In line 154, *reinforcements* refers to additional troops. How does that meaning apply in the story? What does the singular form, *reinforcement,* mean?

▼ **Analyze Visuals**

Review all of the illustrations in the story. Together, how effective are they at conveying the story's **chronological order** of events? Explain.

DIFFERENTIATED INSTRUCTION

FOR ENGLISH LANGUAGE LEARNERS

Language Coach
COMMON CORE RL 4

Word Meanings *Possible answer: The house's automatic fire protection systems are activated like additional army troops joining a battle;* reinforcement *means "something that strengthens."* Ask students to think about the way different endings can change the meaning of the base word. For instance, *troop* as a verb means "to gather or go in a group." *Troops* are soldiers, and a *trooper* can be a police officer.

FOR ADVANCED LEARNERS/PRE–AP

Evaluate Language The power of the story comes in large part from imaginative imagery and strong verbs. For example, Bradbury writes that the fire "crackled up the stairs" (line 150) and that the robots attacked the fire "with a clear cold venom of green froth" (lines 158–159). Have students identify other such examples of imagery and vivid verbs that they consider especially effective.

fire, run, run, like a tragic nursery rhyme, a dozen voices, high, low, like children dying in a forest, alone, alone. And the voices fading as the wires popped their
170 sheathings like hot chestnuts. One, two, three, four, five voices died.

In the nursery the jungle burned. Blue lions roared, purple giraffes bounded off. The panthers ran in circles, changing color, and ten million animals, running before the fire, vanished off toward a distant steaming river. . . .

Ten more voices died. In the last instant under the fire avalanche, other choruses, **oblivious,** could be heard announcing the time, playing music, cutting the lawn by remote-control mower, or setting an umbrella frantically out and in the slamming and opening front door, a thousand things happening, like a clock shop when each clock strikes the hour insanely before or after the other, a scene of maniac confusion, yet unity; singing, screaming, a
180 few last cleaning mice darting bravely out to carry the horrid ashes away! And one voice, with **sublime** disregard for the situation, read poetry aloud in the fiery study, until all the film spools burned, until all the wires withered and the circuits cracked.

> The fire burst the house and let it slam flat down, puffing out skirts of spark and smoke.
>
> In the kitchen, an instant before the rain of fire and timber, the stove could be seen making breakfasts at a psychopathic rate, ten dozen eggs, six loaves of toast, twenty dozen bacon strips, which, eaten by fire, started the stove working again, hysterically hissing!
> 190 The crash. The attic smashing into kitchen and parlor. The parlor into cellar, cellar into sub-cellar. Deep freeze, armchair, film tapes, circuits, beds, and all like skeletons thrown in a cluttered mound deep under.
>
> Smoke and silence. A great quantity of smoke. **J**
>
> Dawn showed faintly in the east. Among the ruins, one wall stood alone. Within the wall, a last voice said, over and over again and again, even as the sun rose to shine upon the heaped rubble and steam:
>
> "Today is August 5, 2026, today is August 5, 2026, today is . . ." ❧

oblivious (ə-blĭv′ē-əs) *adj.* paying no attention, completely unaware

sublime (sə-blīm′) *adj.* supreme, splendid

④ **Targeted Passage**

J DRAW CONCLUSIONS
What idea about technology does Bradbury convey in the burning of the house?

FOR STRUGGLING READERS

④ **Targeted Passage** [Lines 184–197]

This passage concludes the story with a frenzy of activity as the house collapses. Only a single wall remains—ironically, with a voice announcing the start of a new day.

- What finally happens to the house? (lines 190–192)

- Compare lines 186–189 with lines 5–7. How does Bradbury's description of events in the kitchen reflect the altered mood of the story?

- Why do you think Bradbury did not end the story after "Smoke and silence" (line 193)? What do lines 194–197 add to the story?

READING SKILL COMMON CORE

J DRAW CONCLUSIONS RL 1

Possible answer: *Technology in itself is powerful but mindless. It must be controlled through human effort and used wisely, not blindly depended upon. Technology alone could neither save the house from the fire nor protect the people from the atomic blast that destroyed the city. In fact, technology was responsible for the atomic blast. The story warns that technology must be developed very carefully, or it may destroy those who created it.*

VOCABULARY COMMON CORE

OWN THE WORD L 4

- **oblivious:** Ask students if they have ever been *oblivious* to a situation or of people around them. Have them explain the situation.

- **sublime:** Have students provide two or three synonyms for *sublime*. ***Possible answers:*** *splendid, magnificent, grand*

SELECTION WRAP-UP

READ WITH A PURPOSE Now that students have finished reading the selection, have them give a one or two sentence description of the house's personality. ***Possible answer: With the "gods" the house exists to serve gone (lines 54–56, the house is on the brink of insanity. It continues going through the motions in a desperate attempt to retain some sense of normality.***

⭐ **CRITIQUE** Point out that the story is unusual because it lacks characters and dialogue. Ask students if they liked this technique and how well they thought it suited the theme.

INDEPENDENT READING

If students are interested in reading about a lifestyle that Ray Bradbury favors, suggest *Dandelion Wine,* a novel about summertime in a small town.

Practice and Apply

For preliminary support of post-reading questions, use these copy masters:

R **RESOURCE MANAGER**—Copy Masters
Reading Check p. 46
Chronological Order p. 39
Question Support p. 47

Additional selection questions are provided for teachers on page 33.

ANSWERS

Comprehension

1. *The story takes place in Allendale, California, in early August 2026.*

2. *The house announces the time and the weather, prepares breakfast, and cleans itself.*

3. *At the story's beginning, the empty house carries out its programmed daily tasks. A falling tree branch causes a fire. The house tries to save itself but is finally destroyed.*

Text Analysis

COMMON CORE **RL 1, RL 5**

Possible answers:

4. ● **COMMON CORE FOCUS** *Draw Conclusions The family and the city have been destroyed by an atomic blast. The house stands alone amid the rubble (lines 31–32), while the "ruined city gave off a radioactive glow" (line 33). Only silhouettes of the McClellans (lines 38–42) remain.*

5. *Technology is powerful but must be handled wisely lest it become destructive. In the story, technology is used to create a wonder home, but human misuse of technology leads to self-destruction.*

6. *The third-person narrator's flat, objective tone and matter-of-fact reporting of events underplays the horror of the family's demise. Readers learn early that something cataclysmic has occurred, leaving them to wonder what will happen next. The house becomes a character, engaged in a life-or-death fight with the fire.*

7. ● **COMMON CORE FOCUS** *Chronological Order Bradbury chose chronological order to build suspense. Readers see the house go through a daily routine despite the absence of its human occupants.*

After Reading

Comprehension

1. **Recall** When and where does the story take place?

2. **Recall** List three functions the house performs.

3. **Summarize** Describe the changes the house undergoes during the story.

Text Analysis

● 4. **Draw Conclusions** Review the chart you filled in as you read. What has happened to the McClellan family and the town? Use details to support your conclusion.

5. **Interpret Theme** What do you think is the theme, or main message, of the story? Cite evidence from the story to support your answer.

6. **Examine Point of View** In the third-person point of view, a narrator outside the action describes events and characters. How does the third-person narrator of "There Will Come Soft Rains" maintain the reader's interest in a story where there are no human characters? Explain.

● 7. **Analyze Chronological Order** Consider how the story would have been different if it had included numerous **flashbacks,** or scenes that recall earlier experiences. Why might Bradbury have chosen to follow chronological order? Cite evidence from the story to support your opinion.

8. **Compare Literary Works** Review Stephen Vincent Benét's "By the Waters of Babylon," pages 310–321. Use a chart to compare the characters, events, and setting of the Benét story with those in Bradbury's "There Will Come Soft Rains." Which author presents the most disturbing view of society and its technology?

	"By the Waters of Babylon"	"There Will Come Soft Rains"
Characters		
Events		
Setting		

Text Criticism

9. **Author's Style** Many critics admire Bradbury for his use of **imagery,** or words and phrases that appeal to the five senses. Find three examples of imagery in "There Will Come Soft Rains," and discuss how they contribute to your experience of the story.

Is **TECHNOLOGY** taking over?
Are people becoming too dependent on technology?

COMMON CORE

RL 1 Cite textual evidence to support analysis of what the text says explicitly. **RL 5** Analyze an author's choices concerning how to structure a text and order the events within it.

---

8. *Charts will vary. Students should note that both stories suggest a future where a cataclysm destroys a city. Bradbury's story is more disturbing, because it lacks the hopeful note that ends Benét's story.*

Text Criticism

Possible answer:

9. *Bradbury's description of the nursery (lines 92–103) is filled with sensory imagery; "ten billion angry sparks moved with flaming ease from room to room" (lines 143–144);* the fire "fed upon" the paintings, "baking off the oily flesh, tenderly crisping the canvases into black shavings" (lines 150–152). *Such imagery brings the story to life, helping readers to imagine its look, sound, smell, and feel.*

Is **TECHNOLOGY** taking over? *Possible answer: If people are no longer capable of performing work, then perhaps they are too dependent on technology.*

Vocabulary in Context

▲ **VOCABULARY PRACTICE**

Choose the word that best completes the sentence.

1. Leon has overcome his_____and now enjoys friendships and social activities.

2. The cellist knows how to skillfully_____his instrument to make beautiful music.

3. In her old age, my great aunt walks in a_____manner.

4. Jenna enjoys all kinds of winter activities and is_____to the cold.

5. Critics agree that the artist's recent painting is her most_____work yet.

6. The young girl left a chalky_____of her hand on the sidewalk.

WORD LIST

manipulate
oblivious
paranoia
silhouette
sublime
tremulous

ACADEMIC VOCABULARY IN WRITING

• consequent • crucial • initial • shift • survive

COMMON CORE

L 4c Consult reference materials to determine or clarify a word's etymology.

Imagine a future time when technology fails and causes widespread trouble. Write a paragraph describing the **initial** crisis and the **consequent** problems. Use at least one Academic Vocabulary word in your response.

VOCABULARY STRATEGY: THE LATIN ROOT *man*

The vocabulary word *manipulate* stems from the Latin root *man*, which means "hand." To understand the meaning of words with *man*, use context clues as well as your knowledge of the root.

PRACTICE Write the word from the word web that best completes each sentence. Use context clues to help you, or, if necessary, consult a dictionary.

1. They_____these clothes in another country.

2. Before typewriters and printers, a book_____was written only by hand.

3. I am not sure how to_____this complicated-looking tool.

4. Many factories still depend on_____labor, rather than machines.

manipulate

manual — **man** — **man**ufacture

manuscript

Interactive Vocabulary THINK central

Go to **thinkcentral.com**.
KEYWORD: HML10-335

ANSWERS

Vocabulary in Context

▲ **VOCABULARY PRACTICE**

1. *paranoia*   4. *oblivious*

2. *manipulate*   5. *sublime*

3. *tremulous*   6. *silhouette*

 RESOURCE MANAGER—Copy Master
Vocabulary Practice p. 44

ACADEMIC VOCABULARY IN WRITING

Possible answer: *In the* initial *crisis, all forms of electrical and battery power suddenly became useless. One* consequent *problem was a breakdown in global communication.*

VOCABULARY STRATEGY: THE LATIN WORD ROOT *man*

COMMON CORE **L 4c**

• The word part *script* comes from the Latin *scriptus* ("to write") and *facture* comes from the Latin *facere* ("to make").

• For each item, help students use context clues and their knowledge of the root to determine word meaning and choose words.

Possible answers:

1. *manufacture*   3. *manipulate*

2. *manuscript*   4. *manual*

 RESOURCE MANAGER—Copy Master
Vocabulary Strategy p. 45

Interactive Vocabulary THINK central

Keywords direct students to a **WordSharp** tutorial on **thinkcentral.com** or to other types of vocabulary practice and review.

Assess and Reteach

Assess

DIAGNOSTIC AND SELECTION TESTS
Selection Test A pp. 91–92
Selection Test B/C pp. 93–94

Interactive Selection Test on **thinkcentral.com**

Reteach

Level Up Online Tutorials on **thinkcentral.com**

Reteaching Worksheets on **thinkcentral.com**
Reading Lessons 6, 9, 12

DIFFERENTIATED INSTRUCTION

FOR ENGLISH LANGUAGE LEARNERS

Vocabulary: Word Game Divide students into teams for a pantomime game using the vocabulary words.

1. List words on the board and review the meanings.

2. Assign a player on each team a word to pantomime. The rest of that student's team should guess the word.

3. Have the students continue the game, with a different player from each team

pantomiming each of the remaining vocabulary words.

FOR ADVANCED LEARNERS/PRE–AP

Vocabulary in Writing Challenge students to use at least four vocabulary words in a paragraph written from the point of view of a future archaeologist piecing together the events that occurred in Allendale in 2026.

Focus and Motivate

COMMON CORE FOCUS

RI 1 Cite textual evidence to support analysis of what the text says explicitly as well as inferences drawn from the text. **RI 2** Determine a central idea of a text and analyze its development, how it emerges and is shaped and refined by specific details; provide an objective summary. **RI 4** Determine the meaning of words as they are used in a text. **W 1** Write arguments to support claims in an analysis of substantive topics or texts, using valid reasoning and relevant and sufficient evidence.

SUMMARY

This article focuses on the efforts of researchers and labs to create automated homes that would facilitate everyday tasks. The article describes many of the advances being developed.

What's the Connection?

Use an SQ3R organizer to help students read the selection. Direct students to

1. Scan the article for information in the title, headings, and pictures, then predict what they expect to learn from it.

2. Write questions based on a skim of the text, such as *What kinds of tasks can an "intelligent house" perform? Who will benefit from automation in the home?*

3. Answer the questions as they read.

4. Summarize important points of the article.

 **BEST PRACTICES TOOLKIT—Transparency** SQ3R p. A23

Teach

Standards Focus: Synthesize

- Discuss with students how synthesizing ideas and information from different materials is like assembling a jigsaw puzzle. Each source provides additional pieces that gradually form a more detailed picture.

- Elicit why it is important to consider the genre of each source and weigh its content accordingly. For example, a newspaper article is likely to provide objective factual information, while a short story will not.

R RESOURCE MANAGER—Copy Master
Skills Focus pp. 57, 59

Inside the Home of the Future

Newspaper Article

COMMON CORE

RI 1 Cite textual evidence to support analysis of what the text says explicitly as well as inferences drawn from the text. **RI 2** Determine a central idea of a text and analyze its development, how it emerges and is shaped and refined by specific details; provide an objective summary. **RI 4** Determine the meaning of words as they are used in a text.

What's the Connection?

In "There Will Come Soft Rains," you read about a fictional house of the future that featured a variety of "smart" mechanical devices. The article you are about to read will tell you about actual "intelligent" houses that may be in your future.

Standards Focus: Synthesize

When you read different materials on a related topic, you **synthesize**—or put together—facts, ideas, and details from each source. As a result, you gain a fuller understanding of the topic than you would if you had simply relied on one text. Here's how you can synthesize information from two or more selections.

- Determine the central idea and details of each selection.
- Record questions that come to you as you learn new information.
- Note any conflicts in the information presented.
- Reread each selection to answer your questions and fill in gaps in your understanding.

To help you synthesize information from the Bradbury story and the following article, complete a chart like the one started here.

Source	Central Ideas and Details	Questions and New or Conflicting Information
"There Will Come Soft Rains"	Technology can improve living conditions, but it can also worsen them.	
"Inside the Home of the Future"		

Selection Resources

See resources on the **Teacher One Stop DVD-ROM** and on **thinkcentral.com**.

R RESOURCE MANAGER UNIT 3
Lesson Support, pp. 49–53

DIAGNOSTIC AND SELECTION TESTS
Selection Tests, pp. 95–98

BEST PRACTICES TOOLKIT
p. A23

TECHNOLOGY
- **Teacher One Stop DVD-ROM**
- **Student One Stop DVD-ROM**
- **GrammarNotes DVD-ROM**
- **ExamView Generator** on the **Teacher One Stop**

* Resources for Differentiation

Inside the Home of the Future

BY KELLY GREENE

As you pour the detergent into your last load of laundry, you realize the bottle is almost empty. But instead of making a mental note to add it to your grocery list, or running to the kitchen to scribble it down, you simply say out loud, "Remember: Buy laundry detergent." The word "remember" is picked up by a microphone in the wall and triggers a 10 computer to transcribe your words to your to-do list.

It might sound like a sci-fi vision of the future. But it's actually a project called Audio Notes, currently in the works at the Georgia Institute of Technology's 5,000-square-foot Aware Home, a combination house and laboratory in Atlanta where scientists are dreaming up futuristic housing technology.

20 "I love that shopping list," says Eileen Lange, a 68-year-old retiree from Lithonia, Ga., who toured the house and tried out some of its projects last year.

Researchers and commercial labs around the country are building experimental homes to test technology that could make domestic life easier and extend the independence of older homeowners. Such efforts go beyond so-30 called universal design, a trend toward building houses with wider doorways,

grab bars and adjustable kitchen cabinets that took off in the early 1990s.

"These are lifestyle services empowered by a new generation of technology," says Joseph Coughlin, director of the Massachusetts Institute of Technology's AgeLab in Cambridge. Ⓐ

In many cases, the mechanics for the 40 gizmos already exist—mainly wireless sensors, cellphones, broadband access and home computers. What's been missing, and what researchers now are trying to develop, are ways to harness the hardware to run your entire house with little effort or technological savvy— letting you turn up the heat remotely, anticipating when you want the lights on, or deciding automatically how long 50 your food should cook. . . .

Here's a look at what's in store for your home of the future. Ⓑ

The Intelligent House

Would you like your home to "know" you better? Computer scientists at the University of Texas-Arlington are building a home with this scenario as the goal:

At 6:15 A.M., the house turns up the heat, without programming, because it 60 has learned on its own that it needs 15

Practice and Apply

TIERED DISCUSSION PROMPTS

Direct students to lines 1–78. Use these prompts to help students understand who can benefit from high-tech homes, and how:

Connect What types of technology do you rely on in your home? *Answers will vary.*

Analyze How will technology help older homeowners and others keep their independence? *Possible answer: The technology can let people dictate lists (lines 6–11), can turn heat on and off automatically (lines 58–62), and can supervise health maintenance (lines 62–71). It can also make daily living easier in a number of other ways (lines 72–78).*

INFORMATIONAL ANALYSIS   COMMON CORE   RI 2

Ⓐ CENTRAL IDEA

Remind students that as they read, they should look for phrases and opinions that show the author's perspective and then evaluate the writing to determine bias. *Possible answers: Comparison of current method (remembering and writing list) with voice-activated shopping list; Moves beyond 1990s designs to lifestyle services*

INFORMATIONAL ANALYSIS   COMMON CORE   RI 1   RI 4

Ⓑ SYNTHESIZE

Possible answer: Researchers are developing an automated to-do list that can record spoken reminders; much of the technology needed for automated homes already exists.

DIFFERENTIATED INSTRUCTION

FOR ENGLISH LANGUAGE LEARNERS
Options for Reading After discussing the purpose of reading a newspaper article, have students read one section at a time. Discuss the sections and elicit, then answer, any specific questions students have. Use questions 1 and 2 on page 339 to assess comprehension.

FOR STRUGGLING READERS
Vocabulary Support Have students work in small groups to define challenging words and phrases in the article, such as *futuristic* (line 19), *domestic* (line 27), *broadband access* (line 41), *technological savvy* (line 46), and *simulated* (line 90). Have students use the words and phrases in sentences.

Vocabulary: Multiple-Meaning Words Help students identify words that have more than one meaning, such as *load* (line 2), *note* (line 4), *vision* (line 12), *commercial* (line 24), and *harness* (line 44). With the aid of a dictionary, have students write sentence pairs using two meanings of each word. Explain or elicit that multiple-meaning words, such as *commercial*, may be different parts of speech.

COMMON CORE

RI 1
RI 4

C SYNTHESIZE

Possible answer: Technology can help control the climate of a house (lines 58–62); it can provide various conveniences, such as starting the kitchen coffee maker, turning on the morning news, and running the shower (lines 62–67); it can monitor food supplies and place grocery orders (lines 73–76); it can help monitor visitors to the house (lines 92–102).

INFORMATIONAL ANALYSIS

COMMON CORE

RI 1
RI 4

D *Model the Skill:* SYNTHESIZE

To model how to synthesize information from the two selections, draw the graphic organizer from page 336 on the board. Then begin to fill in the main ideas and details, plus the students' questions about the material, as you discuss the information with the class.

Possible answer: The view of technology presented in the article is very positive, focusing exclusively on its benefits without mentioning any drawbacks. "There Will Come Soft Rains" presents a more balanced view, highlighting benefits but also showing in stark terms the possible negative consequences of misused technology.

---

minutes to warm up before your alarm goes off. At 7 A.M., when your alarm sounds, it signals the bedroom light and kitchen coffee maker to turn on. When you step into the bathroom, the morning news pops up on a video screen, and the shower turns on automatically. While you shave, the house senses (through the floor) that you are two pounds over your 70 ideal weight; it adjusts your suggested menu and displays it in the kitchen.

When you leave home after breakfast, the house locks itself. Later that morning, it notes that the refrigerator is low on milk and cheese, and it places a grocery order to be delivered just before you get home. When you arrive, the food is there and the house has cranked up the hot tub for you.

What's powering all the automation 80 is something called machine learning, which would enable the computer monitoring the house to observe a resident's habits for a while, and then anticipate individual needs and make decisions about what to turn on and off, says Diane Cook, the project's manager.

At the University of Florida in Gainesville, researchers are using a cellphone to run a home. (So far, the "home" 90 is a simulated apartment inside a lab, but there's a real house under construction that should be finished in June.) When someone rings the doorbell, you either hear it or feel your cellphone vibrating. Then you can open your phone and see a picture of the person at the door. (A video camera relays the picture.) If you recognize the visitor, you can push a 100 button on your cellphone to unlatch the door. If it's dark and you can't see the visitor, you can push another button to turn on an outside light. **C**

The project, started three years ago, has "evolved from focusing just on smart phones to the smart house," says William Mann, who heads Florida's Rehabilitation Engineering Research Center on Technology for Successful Aging. . . .

Language Coach

Roots and Affixes A **prefix** is an affix (word part) added before a root or base. Reread lines 79–86. The prefix *anti-* in *anticipate* means "before." How does understanding the prefix help you figure out what *anticipate* means?

C SYNTHESIZE
Summarize the various tasks that technology can assist in completing.

D SYNTHESIZE
How positive is the view of technology presented in the article? Does "There Will Come Soft Rains" present a similar or different view?

Kicked-Up Kitchen

Scientists are devoting considerable 110 attention to this room, where busy families can be distracted by caring for children, parents or both.

One tool on the drawing board, Georgia Tech's Cook's College, would use four cameras mounted under the kitchen cabinets to film your hands as you mix ingredients on the countertop below. The pictures, formatted like a filmstrip, would show what you've done most recently. 120 That way, if you're interrupted by a phone call, or children needing help with homework, you can review what you've done to see whether you already had added the salt, for example, or to recall how many cups of flour you had sifted.

Since the cameras are focused on the counter, not on your face, study participants who have seen the tool haven't felt self-conscious about being filmed. 130 "It avoids the bad-hair-day issue," says Dr. Mynatt.

At the University of Florida, researchers are working on microwave ovens that can read a new kind of label, known as radio-frequency identification tag. Such labels can store more information than bar codes and are expected to replace them eventually, says Dr. Mann, who heads the project. . . . 140 A range at the LifeWise Home in Bowie, Md., built by the National Center for Senior Housing Research, first acts as a refrigerator, so you can pop in a casserole in the morning, then set it to bake later in the afternoon. If two hours pass after the cooking time has finished and you haven't removed the dish from the oven, it turns back into a refrigerator.

"It's great for someone who's working, 150 or [busy] during the day with volunteer work," says Charlotte Wade, the program director for the center. . . . It could also prevent people with memory loss from eating spoiled food. **D**

DIFFERENTIATED INSTRUCTION

FOR ENGLISH LANGUAGE LEARNERS

Language Coach

Roots and Affixes *Possible answer: Because the computer observes and then* anticipates *before deciding what to do, it sounds like* anticipate *has to do with planning in advance.* Have students use a dictionary to compare the words *antecedent* and *antibiotic*. What do the prefixes *ante* and *anti* mean in these words? (*Ante* means "before"; *anti* means "against.")

FOR RELUCTANT READERS

Connect with the Stories After students read lines 79–86, call attention that the computer learns to "anticipate" people's needs and "make decisions" (lines 84–85). Like the house in "There Will Come Soft Rains," the computer is, in effect, taking charge. Ask students to debate whether, based on what they know from this article, technology can really take over our lives.

Comprehension

1. **Recall** Describe three capabilities of the houses mentioned in the article.

2. **Recall** Who is intended to benefit from living in such homes? How?

Text Analysis

3. **Synthesize** Review the ideas and information you noted on your chart. How is Bradbury's fictional home of the future similar to actual homes being developed by researchers? Support your answer with details from both texts.

4. **Evaluate** What is the most useful innovation described in the article? Explain your answer.

⬤ **COMMON CORE**

RI 1 Cite textual evidence to support analysis of what the text says explicitly as well as inferences drawn from the text. **RI 2** Determine a central idea of a text and analyze its development, how it emerges and is shaped and refined by specific details; provide an objective summary. **W 1** Write arguments to support claims in an analysis of substantive topics or texts, using valid reasoning and relevant and sufficient evidence.

Read for Information: Support an Opinion

WRITING PROMPT

Is technology more harmful or helpful to us? Consider both the advantages and disadvantages of living in a heavily mechanized society. Use your objective summaries of both the short story and the newspaper article to help you form an opinion.

To answer this prompt, you will have to support an opinion. An **opinion** is a statement that expresses an individual's beliefs, feelings, or thoughts. To support your opinion, you will need to follow these steps:

1. State your opinion on whether technology is more harmful or helpful to us.

2. Use your summary statements to find evidence from each selection that supports your opinion.

3. Recall personal knowledge or experiences that support your opinion.

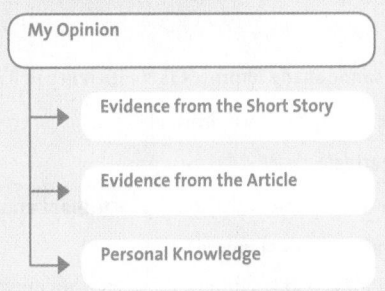

My Opinion

Evidence from the Short Story

Evidence from the Article

Personal Knowledge

Review the evidence to make sure that your opinion is adequately supported; revise your opinion if necessary.

INSIDE THE HOME OF THE FUTURE **339**

For preliminary support of post-reading questions, use these copy masters:

R RESOURCE MANAGER—Copy Masters
Reading Check p. 61
Question Support p. 62
Support an Opinion p. 57

Additional selection questions are provided for teachers on page 52.

ANSWERS

Comprehension

1. *Capabilities include an automated to-do list that records spoken reminders (lines 3–11), weight sensors (lines 67–71), food supply monitors that place grocery orders (lines 73–76).*

2. *All homeowners benefit from an easier domestic life. Older homeowners benefit from extended independence (lines 27–29).*

Text Analysis

⬤ **COMMON CORE** RI 1, RI 2, W 1

Possible answers:

3. ***Synthesize*** *Bradbury's home responds to occupants' desires and needs by preparing meals, giving reminders, cleaning, and performing daily tasks. Real homes do the same by automatically turning on appliances, monitoring food supplies, and placing grocery orders.*

4. *Students should provide thoughtful responses.*

Read for Information: Support an Opinion

Writing Prompt *Responses will vary, but students should support their opinions with evidence from the two selections and personal knowledge or experiences.*

Assess and Reteach

Assess

DIAGNOSTIC AND SELECTION TESTS
Selection Tests A, B/C pp. 95–96, 97–98

Interactive Selection Test on thinkcentral.com

Reteach

Level Up Online Tutorials on thinkcentral.com

Researching Worksheets on thinkcentral.com
Reading Lesson 14

FOR STRUGGLING WRITERS

Read for Information Encourage students to carefully consider both sides of the question and establish a clear opinion before starting to write. Remind them that many technological advancements have both positive *and* negative aspects. For example, the Internet makes a world of knowledge widely available, but it also opens the door to identity theft and other crimes.

FOR ADVANCED LEARNERS/PRE–AP

Hypothesize Ask students to imagine how technology will advance over the next century. What will the home of the future look like? What features will it have? Have students share with the class their conceptions of the home of the future by either drawing a picture or writing a brief essay.

Practice and Apply

COMMON CORE FOCUS

RI 7 Analyze various accounts of a subject told in different mediums.

Advertisement

To help students connect "The Car of the Future" with "There Will Come Soft Rains" and "Inside the Home of the Future," ask students to look at the poster and list technological innovations in this futuristic, 1950 automobile. (**Answer:** *automatic drive, power steering, hydraulic power windows, air-conditioning, cruise control, shoulder belts*) What does this feature infer about current technological innovations? (**Answer:** *Advances that seem commonplace now were exciting and innovative to a previous generation, and what is cutting-edge now will be commonplace to future generations.*)

ANALYZE VISUALS   COMMON CORE   RI 7

1. INTERPRET

Possible answer: *The aerodynamic shape is the only feature described in the text that can be seen in the image. Answers may vary as to whether this supports or takes away from the effectiveness.*

ANALYZE VISUALS   COMMON CORE   RI 7

2. ANALYZE

Possible answer: *The car seems quite low to the ground (only the bottom half of the wheels can be seen) and overall is low and smooth. The only projecting features are tailfins, which add to the sense of motion and aerodynamicness.*

ANALYZE VISUALS   COMMON CORE   RI 7

3. MAKE JUDGMENTS

The features described make the car seem very exciting and modern; students may point out that they have not seen this car in pictures or movies of the 1950s, which would indicate it did not sell well.

Advertisement

You have just read a short story and a newspaper article that express differing views of technology. The selections' writers used words to present their ideas. Now you will analyze a print advertisement that uses both words and an image to inform and persuade readers. To help you, answer the questions at right.

COMMON CORE

RI 7 Analyze various accounts of a subject told in different mediums.

1950

THE GREAT AMERICAN AUTOSHOW *PRESENTS*

The Car of the FUTURE

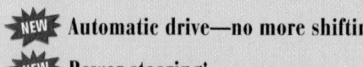

- Low, aerodynamic shape improves fuel efficiency to 35 mpg!
- **NEW** Automatic drive—no more shifting!
- **NEW** Power steering!
- Hydraulic power windows raise and lower without cranking!
- Air-conditioning comes standard!
- Windshield wipers that reach the entire windshield!
- "Cruise Control" lets you take your foot off the accelerator—and keep on going!
- Shoulder seatbelts provide the most advanced safety technology ever!

1. **INTERPRET**
   Which feature or features described in the text of the advertisement can be seen in the image of the car? Does having more features than can be seen in the image support or take away from the effectiveness of the advertisement?

2. **ANALYZE**
   What features in the image support the claim that the car has an aerodynamic shape?

3. **MAKE JUDGMENTS**
   Do you think this car sold well? Why or why not?

340   UNIT 3: NARRATIVE DEVICES

Assessment Practice: Short Constructed Response

LITERARY TEXT: "THERE WILL COME SOFT RAINS"

Assessments expect you to draw conclusions as you read literary texts. Practice this skill by answering the **short constructed response question** below.

> After reading "There Will Come Soft Rains," what can the reader conclude about the author's view of technology? Support your answer with evidence from the story.

◄ **STRATEGIES IN ACTION**

1. *Skim the story, looking for specific passages dealing with technology.*
2. *Form an opinion based on these passages.*
3. *Make sure that your opinion is directly supported by evidence.*

NONFICTION TEXT: "INSIDE THE HOME OF THE FUTURE"

Being able to recognize details that support a text's main idea will help you better understand what you read. Practice the skill of recognizing supporting details by answering the **short constructed response question** below.

> How does the author of "Inside the Home of the Future" support the idea that technology can be beneficial? Include evidence from the text in your answer.

◄ **STRATEGIES IN ACTION**

1. *Reread the article, noting details that support the idea that technology is beneficial.*
2. *Remember that the evidence from the text can be in the form of a **direct quotation**, a **paraphrase**, or a **specific synopsis**.*
3. *Include the evidence you find in your answer.*

COMPARING LITERARY AND NONFICTION TEXTS

Some assessment questions ask you to compare and contrast literary and nonfiction texts. Practice this valuable skill by answering the following **short constructed response question** about "There Will Come Soft Rains" and "Inside the Home of the Future."

> How are the views of technology expressed in "There Will Come Soft Rains" and "Inside the Home of the Future" similar and different? Support your answer with evidence from both texts.

◄ **STRATEGIES IN ACTION**

1. *Note that the question asks you to explain how the views in each text are alike <u>and</u> different.*
2. *Make a general statement of how the views are alike and different, and then look for specific evidence from both texts that support your general statement.*

THERE WILL COME SOFT RAINS / INSIDE THE HOME OF THE FUTURE / CAR OF THE FUTURE **341**

Assessment Practice: Short Constructed Response

LITERARY TEXT: "THERE WILL COME SOFT RAINS" Students should draw the conclusion that the author believes technology can be useless and even dangerous. Possible examples to cite from the story include the hungry dog that cannot get food from an automated kitchen making breakfast and the atomic bomb that destroyed the city and killed the family.

NONFICTION TEXT: "INSIDE THE HOME OF THE FUTURE" Students may respond that the author uses specific examples to show how technology can be beneficial. Examples students may include in their responses as evidence are Audio Notes, a house run by a cell phone, and a range that serves as both a refrigerator and an oven.

COMPARING LITERARY AND NONFICTION TEXTS Students may discuss how both illustrate technology as helpful, giving specific details from each selection to support this idea. To discuss the selections' differences, students may note that "There Will Come Soft Rains" also shows technology as impractical, citing specific details from that story as evidence.

DIFFERENTIATED INSTRUCTION

FOR STRUGGLING WRITERS

Tell students to identify six key features of the "Home of the Future." Have them use this information to write an advertisement similar to the one for the car of the future pictured on page 340.

- Use one or two concise sentences to highlight each feature.
- Work in teams to practice the skill of editing and refining the sentences.

- Point out the population groups that would benefit from various features.

Focus and Motivate

COMMON CORE FOCUS

RL 1 Cite textual evidence to support inferences drawn from the text. **RL 3** Analyze how complex characters develop over the course of a text. **RL 4** Determine the connotative meaning of words and phrases as they are used in a text. **RL 6** Analyze a particular point of view reflected in world literature.

SUMMARY

In 1880s New Zealand, the Burnell sisters are given a doll's house. At school, Isabel, the oldest, enjoys the popularity that results from inviting classmates to see it. She ignores Lil and Else Kelvey, whose mother is a washer-woman. But Kezia, the youngest Burnell, invites them. When her aunt sees them, she shoos them off. Despite this treatment, odd little Else Kelvey speaks and smiles for the first time in the story.

What makes someone POPULAR?

Introduce the question, and together discuss some of the things people do in order to be popular. Ask students if popularity stems from the quality of a person's character or from something else. Continue this inquiry by having students complete the *SURVEY* activity and share their results with the class.

The Doll's House
Short Story by Katherine Mansfield

What makes someone POPULAR?

COMMON CORE

RL 1 Cite textual evidence to support inferences drawn from the text. **RL 3** Analyze how complex characters develop over the course of a text. **RL 4** Determine the connotative meaning of words and phrases as they are used in a text. **RL 6** Analyze a particular point of view reflected in word literature.

How do people act when they are trying to join the "in" crowd? Sometimes they behave badly by bragging about new possessions or by making fun of others. In "The Doll's House," you will read about a group of girls whose pursuit of popularity brings out the worst in their nature.

SURVEY What makes someone popular at your school? With a partner, brainstorm the qualities that well-liked students seem to possess. You may choose to add to or delete from the list shown. Afterward, ask a small group of students to rank the qualities in order of importance. Tally their responses and discuss the results.

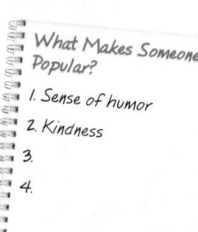

What Makes Someone Popular?
1. Sense of humor
2. Kindness
3.
4.

Selection Resources

See resources on the **Teacher One Stop DVD-ROM** *and on* **thinkcentral.com**.

 RESOURCE MANAGER UNIT 3
    Plan and Teach, pp. 65–72
    Summary, pp. 73–74†‡*
    Text Analysis and Reading
      Skill, pp. 75–78†*

DIAGNOSTIC AND SELECTION TESTS
    Selection Tests, pp. 99–102

 BEST PRACTICES TOOLKIT
    Three-Column Journal, p. B10
    New Word Analysis, p. E8

TECHNOLOGY
    🖋 **Teacher One Stop DVD-ROM**
    🖋 **Student One Stop DVD-ROM**
    🖋 **GrammarNotes DVD-ROM**
    🖋 **ExamView Test Generator**
      on the **Teacher One Stop**

*Resources for Differentiation   † Also in Spanish   ‡ In Haitian Creole and Vietnamese

TEXT ANALYSIS: OMNISCIENT POINT OF VIEW

A story written from the **third-person point of view** has a narrator who is not a character but an outside observer. Sometimes this type of narrator is **omniscient,** or all knowing, and has the power to reveal the thoughts and feelings of more than one character. In "The Doll's House," for example, the omniscient narrator describes the private wishes of several characters, including those of the Burnell children.

The Burnell children could hardly walk to school fast enough the next morning. They burned to tell everybody, to describe, to—well—to boast about their doll's house before the school bell rang.

Unlike stories written from the first-person point of view, stories with an omniscient point of view offer a wider, and perhaps more reliable, perspective. Writers often use such a point of view when they wish to examine broad social issues. As you read the story, think about how its point of view affects the **tone** of the story. Consider how the writer's ability to show the thoughts and perspective of *all* of the characters in the story allows her to reveal her attitude toward the events she describes.

Review: **Symbol**

READING STRATEGY: CONNECT

When you **connect** to a story, you relate its content to your own knowledge and experiences. This strategy can deepen your understanding of the characters, their actions, and the story's overall message. As you read "The Doll's House," make connections between the characters' world and your own. Record your observations in a chart like the one shown.

Characters' Experiences	My Experiences
The Burnell girls are thrilled by the doll's house.	I felt excited when my parents gave me my first bike.

Review: **Make Inferences**

 Complete the activities in your **Reader/Writer Notebook.**

Meet the Author

Katherine Mansfield
1888–1923

A Bold Spirit
Born Kathleen Beauchamp in Wellington, New Zealand, Katherine Mansfield was the third child of a wealthy merchant father and a class-conscious mother. When she was five, her family moved to the rural settlement of Karori, where she excelled in the artistic pursuits of writing and playing the cello. Although Mansfield enjoyed country life, she felt constrained by her family's traditional values. A fiercely independent teen, Mansfield, at 19, settled in London, England. There she enjoyed great creative freedom.

Breaking New Ground
Although she lived only to the age of 34, Mansfield was a master of the short story and developed a distinctive prose style. Her best works reflect her use of experimental narrative techniques to offer vivid insights into characters' thoughts. Mansfield never returned to New Zealand, though she remained close to her homeland in spirit. Many of her stories, including "The Doll's House," recall her childhood experiences.

BACKGROUND TO THE STORY
The Better Sort
This story is set in the late 1800s in New Zealand, which was then a colony of Great Britain. When the British emigrated there, they took with them not only their possessions but the social prejudices of their native land. At the time, British society was divided along rigid class lines. Birth usually determined a person's class, and climbing the social scale was difficult. In her fiction, Mansfield criticized this elitist system.

Author Online
THINK central
Go to **thinkcentral.com.**
KEYWORD: HML10-343

343

Teach

● *Model the Skill:* **OMNISCIENT POINT OF VIEW**

To model how to identify the omniscient point of view, read this example:

> The boys laughed at Juan's joke, which made him feel good. But Paul didn't think it was very funny. He didn't like being picked on. Juan never gave a second thought to Paul's feelings. He just wanted to be liked by the other boys.

Tell students that the example is written in the **omniscient point of view.** Point out that the narrator reveals the thoughts and feelings of more than one character. Readers know what both Juan and Paul think.

GUIDED PRACTICE Ask if this sentence is in the omniscient point of view:

> I got tired of wishing Antoine would like me.

■ *Model the Skill:* **CONNECT**

To model how to connect to a story, read aloud the three-line excerpt from the Text Analysis section on this page.

Ask students if they have ever boasted about a new possession or honor. Tell students that if they have, they can relate, or understand, the excitement of the Burnell children. Explain that relating to any story in a personal way will help them understand the characters and their actions better.

GUIDED PRACTICE Ask students how they might relate to a story about two teenagers who find themselves in charge of a group of young children during an emergency.

 RESOURCE MANAGER—Copy Master
Connect p. 77 (for student use while reading the selection)

DIFFERENTIATED INSTRUCTION

FOR STRUGGLING READERS

Connect Ask students if they have ever read a story or seen a movie that featured a character for whom they felt sorry. Point out that such a reaction is a way of connecting to a story. Then read aloud the two bulleted examples, and ask students how they themselves relate to each character's problem.

- Bonita's palms sweated as she read her report to the class.
- When Zahir gave the wrong answer, he wondered if they thought he was dumb.

FOR ENGLISH LANGUAGE LEARNERS

Language: Skill Words Give students these examples of the use of the terms *third-person* and *omniscient:*

- *He, she,* and *it* are <u>third-person</u> pronouns.
- Not even a genius can be <u>omniscient</u>.

Ask students if they have seen the term *third-person* when learning to conjugate verbs. Then point out that *omniscient* comes from the Latin *omnis* ("all") and *sciens* ("knowing").

Practice and Apply

READ WITH A PURPOSE

Help students set a purpose for reading. Tell them to look for the reasons Isabel was popular.

TEXT ANALYSIS

COMMON CORE
RL 3
RL 6

Ⓐ Model the Skill: POINT OF VIEW

Point out that readers get information in three ways: the narrator directly commenting (lines 1–5), the narrator relating a character's opinion (lines 7–8), or a character speaking (lines 6–7). Have students use a Three-Column Journal to track facts about the doll's house in the story.

Narrator's Direct Comments	Narrator Relates Character's Opinions	Character's Speech, Actions
doll's house from Mrs. Hay	very sweet of her	
doll's house is very big		
smells of paint		

Possible answer: *Through direct comments of the narrator, we learn that the doll's house was sent by Mrs. Hay, required two men to carry it, and that it smelled of fresh paint.*

 BEST PRACTICES TOOLKIT—Transparency Three-Column Journal p. B10

❧ THE ❧
Doll's House

Katherine Mansfield

When dear old Mrs. Hay went back to town after staying with the Burnells she sent the children a doll's house. It was so big that the carter[1] and Pat carried it into the courtyard, and there it stayed, propped up on two wooden boxes beside the feed-room door. No harm could come to it; it was summer. And perhaps the smell of paint would have gone off by the time it had to be taken in. For, really, the smell of paint coming from that doll's house ("Sweet of old Mrs. Hay, of course; most sweet and generous!")—but the smell of paint was quite enough to make any one seriously ill, in Aunt Beryl's opinion. Even before the sacking was taken off. And when it was. . . . Ⓐ

10   There stood the doll's house, a dark, oily, spinach green, picked out with bright yellow. Its two solid little chimneys, glued on to the roof, were painted red and white, and the door, gleaming with yellow varnish, was like a little slab of toffee. Four windows, real windows, were divided into panes by a broad streak of green. There was actually a tiny porch, too, painted yellow, with big lumps of congealed paint hanging along the edge.

But perfect, perfect little house! Who could possibly mind the smell? It was part of the joy, part of the newness.
"Open it quickly, some one!"
The hook at the side was stuck fast. Pat pried it open with his penknife, and
20   the whole house front swung back, and—there you were, gazing at one and the same moment into the drawing room and dining room, the kitchen and two bedrooms. That is the way for a house to open! Why don't all houses open like that? How much more exciting than peering through the slit of a door into a mean little hall with a hat stand and two umbrellas! That is—isn't it?—what you long to know about a house when you put your hand on the knocker. Perhaps it is the way God opens houses at dead of night when He is taking a quiet turn with an angel. . . .

"O-oh!" The Burnell children sounded as though they were in despair. It was too marvelous; it was too much for them. They had never seen anything

Analyze Visuals ▶

Think about the purpose of a doll's house like the one shown. Would it be regularly played with or displayed for company? Explain.

Ⓐ POINT OF VIEW Reread lines 1–9. What do you learn about the doll's house from the direct comments of the narrator?

❶ Targeted Passage

---

1. **carter:** delivery person.

DIFFERENTIATED INSTRUCTION

FOR ENGLISH LANGUAGE LEARNERS

Options for Reading Have students listen to the *Audio Anthology CD* and read the dialogue in parts to prepare for an oral presentation. Assign difficult roles to proficient readers. Have students practice in pairs or in groups before they read in front of the class.

FOR STRUGGLING READERS

In combination with the *Audio Anthology CD*, use one or more Targeted Passages (pp. 344, 346, 347, 348, 349, 352) to ensure that students focus on key story events, concepts, and skills. Targeted Passages are also good for English learners.

❶ Targeted Passage [Lines 16–27]

In this passage, the narrator expresses an excitement about the doll's house that reflects the joy of the children in the story.

- How is the tone of the sentences in lines 16–17 reflected in the dialogue in line 18?
- How does the narrator describe the children's reaction to the doll's house? (lines 16–17)
- Why does the narrator think all houses should be like the doll's house? (lines 22–24)

FOR ADVANCED LEARNERS/PRE–AP

Compare Point of View In this story, the omniscient narrator tells what different people are thinking. Ask students to read lines 1–43 and record the reactions to the doll's house from the adult's perspective and from the children's perspective. Have them summarize the adult's perspective in one sentence and the children's perspective in a second sentence. How do the perspectives differ?

B CONNECT

Students who find the Burnells' reactions to the doll's house believable should be able to relate specific experiences when they or someone they know received a wonderful gift. Students who find the Burnells' reactions unbelievable should state what specifically seems unrealistic in the girls' reactions.

Extend the Discussion Think about the doll's house as you read lines 28–30 (beginning on page 344) and the full sentence in lines 34–35. Does the description of the interior make the children's reactions seem credible, even though they may differ from your experiences?

C POINT OF VIEW

Possible answer: Information provided by the omniscient narrator causes readers to see the Burnells as conceited and competitive. Readers learn that the girls want to boast and anticipate being looked up to by their classmates.

IF STUDENTS NEED HELP . . . Lines 52–57, in particular, are dense with information about the Burnells' plan for visitors to the doll's house. Focus students on that paragraph by having students list character traits for the Burnells and the text lines in which those traits are revealed.

---

30 like it in their lives. All the rooms were papered. There were pictures on the walls, painted on the paper, with gold frames complete. Red carpet covered all the floors except the kitchen; red plush chairs in the drawing room, green in the dining room; tables, beds with real bedclothes, a cradle, a stove, a dresser with tiny plates and one big jug. But what Kezia liked more than anything, what she liked frightfully, was the lamp. It stood in the middle of the dining room table, an exquisite little amber lamp with a white globe. It was even filled all ready for lighting, though, of course, you couldn't light it. But there was something inside that looked like oil, and that moved when you shook it. **B**

The father and mother dolls, who sprawled very stiff as though they had 40 fainted in the drawing room, and their two little children asleep upstairs, were really too big for the doll's house. They didn't look as though they belonged. But the lamp was perfect. It seemed to smile at Kezia, to say, "I live here." The lamp was real.

The Burnell children could hardly walk to school fast enough the next morning. They burned to tell everybody, to describe, to—well—to boast about their doll's house before the school bell rang.

"I'm to tell," said Isabel, "because I'm the eldest. And you two can join in after. But I'm to tell first."

There was nothing to answer. Isabel was bossy, but she was always right, and 50 Lottie and Kezia knew too well the powers that went with being eldest. They brushed through the thick buttercups at the road edge and said nothing.

"And I'm to choose who's to come and see it first. Mother said I might."

For it had been arranged that while the doll's house stood in the courtyard they might ask the girls at school, two at a time, to come and look. Not to stay to tea, of course, or to come traipsing through the house. But just to stand quietly in the courtyard while Isabel pointed out the beauties, and Lottie and Kezia looked pleased. . . . **C**

But hurry as they might, by the time they had reached the tarred palings[2] of the boys' playground the bell had begun to jangle. They only just had time 60 to whip off their hats and fall into line before the roll was called. Never mind. Isabel tried to make up for it by looking very important and mysterious and by whispering behind her hand to the girls near her, "Got something to tell you at playtime."

Playtime came and Isabel was surrounded. The girls of her class nearly fought to put their arms around her, to walk away with her, to beam flatteringly, to be her special friend. She held quite a court under the huge pine trees at the side of the playground. Nudging, giggling together, the little girls pressed up close. And the only two who stayed outside the ring were the two who were always outside, the little Kelveys. They knew better than to come 70 anywhere near the Burnells.

---

2. **palings:** fence stakes.

B CONNECT
Think back to the excitement you felt when you received a favorite gift. On the basis of your experience, do you find the Burnells' reactions to the doll's house believable? Why, or why not?

C POINT OF VIEW
Reread lines 44–57. Notice what the **omniscient narrator** reveals about the Burnells. How does this information shape your opinion of the girls?

 **Targeted Passage**

DIFFERENTIATED INSTRUCTION

FOR STRUGGLING READERS

 **Targeted Passage** [Lines 64–70]

In this paragraph, the author introduces the Kelveys and, with them, the story's theme or message begins to take shape.

- How is Isabel treated by her classmates? (lines 64–66)

- Why do the Kelvey girls avoid coming "anywhere near" the Burnells? (lines 69–70)

- What does this say about the Kelveys' status among their classmates? (lines 68–69)

Develop Reading Fluency Direct students to lines 44–70. Help them locate the dialogue in lines 47–48, 52, and 62–63 and identify the speaker. Ask students how Isabel would sound when speaking to her sisters and to her friends. What narrator's lines could be read with Isabel's voice? Read the lines aloud, distinguishing the sounds of dialogue from the narration. Then have pairs of students practice together, taking turns reading the narrator's lines and Isabel's dialogue.

The Daughters of Edward Darley Boit (1882), John Singer Sargent. Oil on canvas, 221.93 × 222.57 cm. Gift of Mary Louisa Boit, Julia Overing Boit, Jane Hubbard Boit and Florence D. Boit in memory of Edward Darley Boit. Museum of Fine Arts, Boston. Photo © Museum of Fine Arts, Boston.

For the fact was, the school the Burnell children went to was not at all the kind of place their parents would have chosen if there had been any choice. But there was none. It was the only school for miles. And the consequence was all the children in the neighborhood, the Judge's little girls, the doctor's daughters, the storekeeper's children, the milkman's, were forced to mix together. Not to speak of there being an equal number of rude, rough little boys as well. But the line had to be drawn somewhere. It was drawn at the Kelveys. Many of the children, including the Burnells, were not allowed even to speak to them. They walked past the Kelveys with their heads in the air, and

▲ **Analyze Visuals**

Examine the figures and the setting in the painting. How well do they match your impression of the people and furnishings of the Burnell household? Explain.

❸ Targeted Passage

THE DOLL'S HOUSE 347

Analyze Visuals

Possible answer: *The figures and setting of the painting match the description of the Burnells. The painting depicts a family with daughters much like the Burnells. The children's clothes, their somewhat serious demeanor, and the fine rug suggest a home and lifestyle similar to the Burnells', where the adults do not want their children's friends in the house.*

About the Art *The Daughters of Edward Darley Boit* typifies the work of John Singer Sargent (1856–1925) in its portrayal of people in a plush interior bathed in strong, pure light. As the work suggests, Singer often painted portraits of upper-class friends and patrons.

FOR STRUGGLING READERS

❸ Targeted Passage [Lines 71–79]

The narrator's comments in this passage show how rigid divisions in social class affect the Burnells and the Kelveys.

- Why is the school "not at all the kind of place" the Burnells would choose? (lines 71–76)

- What is meant by "the line had to be drawn somewhere"? (line 77)

- Why were so many students not allowed to associate with the Kelveys? (lines 77–79)

FOR ENGLISH LANGUAGE LEARNERS

Vocabulary: Idioms Use New Word Analysis to teach the idioms used on these pages: *burned to tell* (line 45), "anxious to say"; *whip off (their hats)* (line 60), "remove quickly"; *fall into line* (line 60), "take place in a line or queue"; *the line had to be drawn* (line 77), "a boundary had to be created"

 BEST PRACTICES TOOLKIT—Transparency New Word Analysis p. E8

as they set the fashion in all matters of behavior, the Kelveys were shunned by everybody. Even the teacher had a special voice for them, and a special smile for the other children when Lil Kelvey came up to her desk with a bunch of dreadfully common-looking flowers. **D**

They were the daughters of a spry, hardworking little washerwoman, who went about from house to house by the day. This was awful enough. But where was Mr. Kelvey? Nobody knew for certain. But everybody said he was in prison. So they were the daughters of a washerwoman and a jailbird. Very nice company for other people's children! And they looked it. Why Mrs. Kelvey made them so conspicuous was hard to understand. The truth was they

90 were dressed in "bits" given to her by the people for whom she worked. Lil, for instance, who was a stout, plain child, with big freckles, came to school in a dress made from a green art-serge[3] tablecloth of the Burnells', with red plush sleeves from the Logans' curtains. Her hat, perched on top of her high forehead, was a grown-up woman's hat, once the property of Miss Lecky, the postmistress. It was turned up at the back and trimmed with a large scarlet quill. What a little guy[4] she looked! It was impossible not to laugh. And her little sister, our Else, wore a long white dress, rather like a nightgown, and a pair of little boy's boots. But whatever our Else wore she would have looked strange. She was a tiny wishbone of a child, with cropped hair and enormous

100 solemn eyes—a little white owl. Nobody had ever seen her smile; she scarcely ever spoke. She went through life holding on to Lil, with a piece of Lil's skirt screwed up in her hand. Where Lil went our Else followed. In the playground, on the road going to and from school, there was Lil marching in front and our Else holding on behind. Only when she wanted anything, or when she was out of breath, our Else gave Lil a tug, a twitch, and Lil stopped and turned around. The Kelveys never failed to understand each other. **E**

Now they hovered at the edge; you couldn't stop them listening. When the little girls turned round and sneered, Lil, as usual, gave her silly, shamefaced smile, but our Else only looked.

110 And Isabel's voice, so very proud, went on telling. The carpet made a great sensation, but so did the beds with real bedclothes, and the stove with an oven door.

When she finished Kezia broke in. "You've forgotten the lamp, Isabel."

"Oh, yes," said Isabel, "and there's a teeny little lamp, all made of yellow glass, with a white globe that stands on the dining room table. You couldn't tell it from a real one."

"The lamp's best of all," cried Kezia. She thought Isabel wasn't making half enough of the little lamp. But nobody paid attention. Isabel was choosing the two who were to come back with them that afternoon and see it. She chose

120 Emmie Cole and Lena Logan. But when the others knew they were all to have

 Targeted Passage

---

3. **art-serge** (ärt-sûrj): a type of woven wool.

4. **guy**: British term for an odd-looking person.

TEXT ANALYSIS | COMMON CORE | RL 3 RL 6

D POINT OF VIEW

Possible answer: *The townspeople all shun the Kelveys. The omniscient point of view allows the reader to see that status is very important in this community. The writer seems to note the cruelty in the ways in which the townspeople treat the Kelveys. She seems to view the Kelveys with a more sympathetic eye.*

Extend the Discussion Why might the author have the narrator call Lil's flowers "dreadfully common-looking" in line 83? Is the storyteller an unreliable narrator?

READING STRATEGY | COMMON CORE | RL 1

E CONNECT

Possible answer: *Story details show that the Kelveys are disliked because they are different in a number of ways: Their mother is a washerwoman, and their father is said to be in prison. The girls have strange appearances and wear used clothes (lines 88–99). Else never smiles and rarely speaks (lines 99–104). Students may admit that Lil and Else would be treated in their school just as they are treated in the story, or students may claim that their school is more democratic in spirit.*

D POINT OF VIEW
What do you learn about the townspeople? Explain how the omniscient point of view allows you to see problems that may affect an entire community. What do you think is the writer's attitude toward the townspeople? toward the Kelveys?

E CONNECT
Reread lines 84–106. Find details that explain why the Kelveys are disliked. How might Lil and Else be treated at your school?

DIFFERENTIATED INSTRUCTION

FOR STRUGGLING READERS

④ Targeted Passage [Lines 98–120]

In this passage, Mansfield tells and shows readers more about her characters.

- What character traits of Else's do we learn from the narrator? (lines 100–105)

- Describe Else's relationship with Lil. (lines 101–106)

- What do you learn about Isabel from her words and actions and from the narrator? (lines 110, 118–119)

FOR ADVANCED LEARNERS/PRE-AP

Analyze Tone Have students read lines 84–125, analyzing Mansfield's tone, or her attitude toward her subject—in this case, the Kelveys. Encourage students to focus on diction by examining word connotations. How are readers swayed to sympathize with the Kelveys, especially Else? What might the tone indicate about the author's social views? Invite students to share their conclusions with the class.

a chance, they couldn't be nice enough to Isabel. One by one they put their arms round Isabel's waist and walked her off. They had something to whisper to her, a secret. "Isabel's my friend."

Only the little Kelveys moved away forgotten; there was nothing more for them to hear.

Days passed, and as more children saw the doll's house, the fame of it spread. It became the one subject, the rage. The one question was, "Have you seen Burnells' doll's house? Oh, ain't it lovely!" "Haven't you seen it? Oh, I say!"

Even the dinner hour was given up to talking about it. The little girls sat
130 under the pines eating their thick mutton sandwiches and big slabs of johnny cake spread with butter. While always, as near as they could get, sat the Kelveys, our Else holding on to Lil, listening too, while they chewed their jam sandwiches out of a newspaper soaked with large red blobs. . . .

"Mother," said Kezia, "can't I ask the Kelveys just once?"

"Certainly not, Kezia."

"But why not?"

"Run away, Kezia; you know quite well why not." **F**

F MAKE INFERENCES
Think about how Kezia's family acts toward her. Why might she want to share the doll's house with the Kelveys?

> *A*t last everybody had seen it except them. On that day the subject rather flagged. It was the dinner hour. The children stood together under the pine trees, and suddenly, as they looked at the Kelveys eating out of their paper, always by themselves, always listening, they wanted to be horrid to them. Emmie Cole started the whisper.
>
> "Lil Kelvey's going to be a servant when she grows up."
>
> "O-oh, how awful!" said Isabel Burnell, and she made eyes at Emmie.
>
> Emmie swallowed in a very meaning way and nodded to Isabel as she'd seen her mother do on those occasions.
>
> "It's true—it's true—it's true," she said.
>
> Then Lena Logan's little eyes snapped. "Shall I ask her?" she whispered.
>
> "Bet you don't," said Jessie May.
>
> 150 "I'm not frightened," said Lena. Suddenly she gave a little squeal and danced in front of the other girls. "Watch! Watch me! Watch me now!" said Lena. And sliding, gliding, dragging one foot, giggling behind her hand, Lena went over to the Kelveys.
>
> Lil looked up from her dinner. She wrapped the rest quickly away. Our Else stopped chewing. What was coming now?

5 Targeted Passage

"Is it true you're going to be a servant when you grow up, Lil Kelvey?" shrilled Lena.

What makes someone POPULAR?

Discuss Based on lines 126–137, how has the doll's house become a symbol of popularity among the children? *Possible answer: The Burnells, the most popular girls at school, get to choose who may or may not see their doll's house. By choosing certain girls, the Burnells are showing their approval of those girls.*

READING SKILL: *Review*

F MAKE INFERENCES RL 1

Possible answer: Kezia's family seems to ignore her or order her around. She may want to share the doll's house with the Kelveys for attention. Or she might sense common ground since they, too, are ignored.

IF STUDENTS NEED HELP . . . Have them reread lines 39–51 (p. 346) and lines 113–137 (pp. 348–349) and list details about Kezia.

FOR STRUGGLING READERS

5 Targeted Passage [Lines 138–155]

In this passage, conflict builds.

- Where are the Kelveys sitting in relation to the other girls? (lines 141, 152–153)

- What do the girls whisper about Lil Kelvey? (line 143)

- What is Lena going to ask Lil? (lines 143, 148)

FOR ENGLISH LANGUAGE LEARNERS

Language: Conversational English Patterns
Tell students that this story has dated British usages, such as the *dinner hour* (line 129), "lunchtime"; *rather flagged* (line 139), "died down"; and *sell* (line 159), "setback." Have small groups list five more unfamiliar terms. They can trade lists and write a definition and sentence for each usage.

Activity Have students compare or contrast Homer's portrayal of little girls in this painting with Mansfield's portrayal of them in her story. *Possible answer: Mansfield is concentrating in this story on the mean streak some little girls have, whereas Homer is showing little girls as purer, more innocent beings.*

About the Art Winslow Homer (1836–1910) painted *Apple Picking* a few years before the time when Mansfield set her story. *Apple Picking* is one of many watercolors done in the summer of 1878 at Houghton Farm in New York. Like its counterparts, it depicts farm children as figures tied to idyllic landscapes through deft strokes of paint and the interplay of light and form.

Dead silence. But instead of answering, Lil only gave her silly, shamefaced smile. She didn't seem to mind the question at all. What a sell for Lena! The girls began to titter.

Lena couldn't stand that. She put her hands on her hips; she shot forward. "Yah, yer father's in prison!" she hissed, spitefully.

This was such a marvelous thing to have said that the little girls rushed away in a body, deeply, deeply excited, wild with joy. Someone found a long rope, and they began skipping. And never did they skip so high, run in and out so fast, or do such daring things as on that morning.

In the afternoon Pat called for the Burnell children with the buggy and they drove home. There were visitors. Isabel and Lottie, who liked visitors, went upstairs to change their pinafores. But Kezia thieved out at the back. Nobody was about; she began to swing on the big white gates of the courtyard.

COMMON CORE RL 4

Language Coach

Denotation/Connotation
The images or feelings connected to a word are its **connotations**. Reread lines 159–160. How do you think the girls are feeling as they *titter*? Why do you think the author chose this word instead of *laugh*?

Apple Picking (1878), Winslow Homer. Watercolor and gouache on paper, laid down on board, 7″ × 8³/₆″. Daniel J. Terra Collection 1992.7. Photo © Terra Foundation for American Art, Chicago, Illinois/Art Resource, New York.

DIFFERENTIATED INSTRUCTION

FOR ADVANCED LEARNERS/PRE–AP

Identifying Conflict Have students identify the conflicts at this point in the story. Then have them discuss how they think these conflicts will be resolved. Suggest that students use a Three-Column Journal to track the conflicts. Label the first column "Conflicts," the second "Resolution Prediction," and the third "Story Resolution."

 BEST PRACTICES TOOLKIT—Transparency
Three-Column Journal p. B10

FOR ENGLISH LANGUAGE LEARNERS

Language Coach   **COMMON CORE RL 4**

Denotation/Connotation
Possible answer: To titter *is "to laugh nervously." The girls might be feeling that a line has been crossed.* Laughed *wouldn't convey this feeling.* Have students look for other words in the story that have images or feelings connected to them. For example, point out *hissed* in line 162. What feeling is conveyed by this word?

Presently, looking along the road, she saw two little dots. They grew bigger, they were coming towards her. Now she could see that one was in front and one close behind. Now she could see that they were the Kelveys. Kezia stopped swinging. She slipped off the gate as if she was going to run away. Then she hesitated. The Kelveys came nearer, and beside them walked their shadows, very long, stretching right across the road with their heads in the buttercups. Kezia clambered back on the gate; she had made up her mind; she swung out.

"Hullo," she said to the passing Kelveys.

They were so astounded that they stopped. Lil gave her silly smile. Our
180 Else stared.

"You can come and see our doll's house if you want to," said Kezia, and she dragged one toe on the ground. But at that Lil turned red and shook her head quickly.

"Why not?" asked Kezia.

Lil gasped, then she said, "Your ma told our ma you wasn't to speak to us."

"Oh well," said Kezia. She didn't know what to reply. "It doesn't matter. You can come and see our doll's house all the same. Come on. Nobody's looking."

But Lil shook her head still harder.

"Don't you want to?" asked Kezia.

190 Suddenly there was a twitch, a tug at Lil's skirt. She turned round. Our Else was looking at her with big, imploring eyes; she was frowning; she wanted to go. For a moment Lil looked at our Else very doubtfully. But then our Else twitched her skirt again. She started forward. Kezia led the way. Like two little stray cats they followed across the courtyard to where the doll's house stood. **G**

"There it is," said Kezia.

There was a pause. Lil breathed loudly, almost snorted; our Else was still as a stone.

"I'll open it for you," said Kezia kindly. She undid the hook and they looked inside.

200 "There's the drawing room and the dining room, and that's the—"

"Kezia!"

Oh, what a start they gave!

"Kezia!"

It was Aunt Beryl's voice. They turned round. At the back door stood Aunt Beryl, staring as if she couldn't believe what she saw.

"How dare you ask the little Kelveys into the courtyard?" said her cold, furious voice. "You know as well as I do, you're not allowed to talk to them. Run away, children, run away at once. And don't come back again," said Aunt Beryl. And she stepped into the yard and shooed them out as if they were chickens.

210 "Off you go immediately!" she called, cold and proud. **H**

> **G** MAKE INFERENCES
> Reread lines 190–194. Notice how Lil responds to Else. What does this tell you about their relationship?

> **H** CONNECT
> Aunt Beryl forbids Kezia to play with the Kelveys. How would you respond if you were in Kezia's position?

Activity How does the illustration on this page relate to the illustration on page 345? **Possible answer:** This illustration shows what someone would see by opening the doll's house (as it is shown on page 345) and looking into the dining room. The lamp is referred to in line 36, lines 113–118, and in line 230.

TEXT ANALYSIS   COMMON CORE

RL 3
RL 6

❶ POINT OF VIEW

Possible answer: The omniscient narrator reveals that Aunt Beryl has other motives for mistreating the Kelveys in addition to her need to feel superior; she is upset over a "threatening" letter she received from a man named Willie Brent. The omniscient narration allows us to see Aunt Beryl's actual reasons for scolding Kezia, and makes her seem crueler and more hypocritical than if we didn't know her real reasons.

TEXT ANALYSIS   COMMON CORE

RL 6

❶ WORLD LITERATURE

Encourage students to think beyond the time frame of this story and consider the factors which divide children in schools today. Although rigid social structures may have disappeared, brainstorm comparable social differences in today's society.

Possible answer: Accept all reasonable, thoughtful responses.

SELECTION WRAP-UP

READ WITH A PURPOSE Now that students have finished reading the selection, have them decide why Isabel was more popular than her sisters. **Possible answer:** Isabel was the oldest daughter in an upper class family, and because of this she expected to be popular.

⭐ **CRITIQUE** Ask students if they find the story's characters one-dimensional—in this case, simply virtuous or simply shallow—or complex.

They did not need telling twice. Burning with shame, shrinking together, Lil huddling along like her mother, our Else dazed, somehow they crossed the big courtyard and squeezed through the white gate.

"Wicked, disobedient little girl!" said Aunt Beryl bitterly to Kezia, and she slammed the doll's house to.

The afternoon had been awful. A letter had come from Willie Brent, a terrifying, threatening letter, saying if she did not meet him that evening in Pulman's Bush, he'd come to the front door and ask the reason why. But now that she had frightened those little rats of Kelvey's and given Kezia a good
220 scolding, her heart felt lighter. That ghastly pressure was gone. She went back to the house humming. ❶

When the Kelveys were well out of sight of the Burnells', they sat down to rest on a big red drainpipe by the side of the road. Lil's cheeks were still burning; she took off the hat with the quill and held it on her knee. Dreamily they looked over the hay paddocks,[5] past the creek, to the group of wattles[6] where Logan's cows stood waiting to be milked. What were their thoughts?

Presently our Else nudged up close to her sister. But now she had forgotten the cross lady. She put out a finger and stroked her sister's quill; she smiled her rare smile.
230 "I seen the little lamp," she said, softly. ❶
Then both were silent once more. ☙

⑥ **Targeted Passage**

---

5. **paddocks** (pădʹəks): areas of fenced-in land.

6. **wattles** (wŏtʹlz): acacia trees.

352   UNIT 3: NARRATIVE DEVICES

❶ **POINT OF VIEW**
Reread lines 204–221. What does the omniscient narrator reveal about Aunt Beryl and her motives for treating the Kelveys so poorly? How does this contribute to the **tone** of the story?

COMMON CORE RL 6

❶ **WORLD LITERATURE**
Mansfield grew up in New Zealand and many of her stories recall her childhood experiences. Reread the Background to the Story on page 343. Do you think the situation in this story could still happen today, with children anywhere in the world?

DIFFERENTIATED INSTRUCTION

FOR STRUGGLING READERS

⑥ **Targeted Passage** [Lines 218–231]
Mansfield resolves conflict and expresses theme at the close of the story through the narrator's comments and the actions and speech of her characters.

- How has the episode at the doll's house affected Lil and Else differently? (lines 223–224, 227–230)

- What happens at the end of the story to show that seeing the doll's house has had a profound effect on Else? (line 228)

FOR RELUCTANT READERS

Connect with the story The important characters of this story are all girls, and doll's houses are considered toys for girls. To help students connect with the meaning of the story, refer them to the Big Question: What makes someone POPULAR? Ask students to retell the story using characters and an item to which they can relate. They might want to place themselves in the action as one of the characters.

Comprehension

1. **Recall** Describe the doll's house that the Burnells receive.

2. **Recall** Under what conditions are the girls' friends allowed to see the doll's house?

3. **Recall** Why are the Burnells not allowed to speak to the Kelveys?

4. **Clarify** Why does Else smile at the end of the story?

Text Analysis

5. **Compare and Contrast Characters**
What are the similarities and differences between Isabel Burnell and Lil Kelvey? Use a Venn diagram like the one shown to explore your answer.

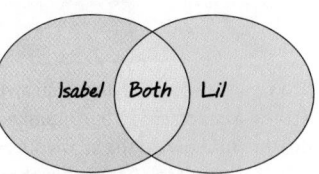

6. **Identify Symbol** A person, a place, or an object that represents something beyond itself is a **symbol.** Two objects that might be considered symbols in this story are the doll's house and the little lamp. What values do these objects symbolize?

7. **Draw Conclusions About Theme** Think about the story's theme, or main message. What does the story reveal about popularity? Use evidence to support your conclusion.

● 8. **Connect** **Writing** "The Doll's House," Mansfield painted a picture of traditional New Zealand society. Despite the different location and time period, how are the characters, events, and ideas presented in the story relevant to your own experiences? Review the chart you completed as you read. Support your answer with information from the chart and the story.

● 9. **Analyze Point of View** In the story, the **omniscient narrator** sees into the minds of several of the story's characters. How might your sense of the town and its residents be different if the story were told through the eyes of just one character—Aunt Beryl, for example? How would this affect the story's **tone**?

Text Criticism

10. **Critical Interpretations** "The notion that human beings adopt masks and present themselves to their fellows under assumed personalities," wrote one biographer, "was one of [Mansfield's] literary obsessions." How does this comment apply to the story? Cite specific examples to support your answer.

> **What makes someone POPULAR?**
> What are some positive ways to achieve popularity?

COMMON CORE

RL 1 Cite textual evidence to support inferences drawn from the text. **RL 3** Analyze how complex characters develop over the course of a text. **RL 6** Analyze a particular point of view reflected in world literature.

Practice and Apply

For preliminary support of post-reading questions, use these copy masters:

R **RESOURCE MANAGER**—Copy Masters
Reading Check p. 79
Omniscient Point of View p. 75
Question Support p. 80

Additional selection questions are provided for teachers on page 69.

ANSWERS

Comprehension

1. *dark green with yellow trim, smells of paint, two chimneys and a porch*

2. *Their friends can see the doll's house only if they come in pairs, are quiet, and stay out of the Burnells' house.*

3. *The Burnells are not allowed to speak to the Kelveys because the Kelveys are from too low a social class.*

4. *She has seen the lamp in the doll's house.*

Text Analysis   COMMON CORE RL 1, RL 3, RL 6

Possible answers:

5. *Similarities: Isabel and Lil are about the same age and both have younger sisters. Differences: Isabel is bossy, talkative, popular, and upper-class; Lil is quiet, shy, unpopular, and lower-class.*

6. *The house may symbolize the socially stratified world that Kezia and Else live in. The lamp symbolizes the ability to see beyond these limits to a world of openness.*

7. *Popularity is not always based on good traits, but on surface things, like appearance and social status.*

Assess and Reteach

Assess

DIAGNOSTIC AND SELECTION TESTS
Selection Test A, B/C pp. 99–100, 101–102

Interactive Selection Test on **thinkcentral.com**

Reteach

Level Up Online Tutorials on **thinkcentral.com**

Reteaching Worksheets on **thinkcentral.com**
Literature Lesson 10

---

8. ● **COMMON CORE FOCUS** *Connect Incorporating details from their charts, student responses should connect or contrast details from the story with aspects of their own experiences.*

9. ● **COMMON CORE FOCUS** *Omniscient Point of View If the story were told from Aunt Beryl's point of view, readers might see the Kelveys as awful and see the Burnells or Lena Logan as gracious and respectable.*

Text Criticism

Possible answer:

10. *Mansfield's obsession with "the notion that human beings adopt masks" is reflected in the snobbery and hypocrisy of the story's characters.*

> What makes someone **POPULAR?** Students might consider positive ways to achieve popularity and use popularity for the greater good.

Focus and Motivate

⊙ COMMON CORE FOCUS

RL 1 Cite evidence to support inferences drawn from the text. **RL 4** Determine the meaning of words as they are used in the text. **RL 5** Analyze an author's choices concerning how to manipulate time and create tension or surprise. **RL 6** Analyze a particular point of view reflected in world literature. **W 2b** Develop the topic with well-chosen, relevant details and examples. **L 3** Apply knowledge of language to make effective choices for meaning and style. **L 4c** Consult general reference materials to determine or clarify a word's etymology.

SUMMARY

In "The Seventh Man," the central narrator tells about the most tragic event of his life. When he was ten, he watched as his best friend, K., drowned during a typhoon. As the survivor, he was haunted by K.'s death. He finally returned to the scene of the tragedy and shed his guilt.

Can you RECOVER from tragedy?

Ask the question, then have students complete the *QUICKWRITE*. Encourage them to explore both physical and mental methods of recovery.

Selection Resources

The Seventh Man
Short Story by Haruki Murakami

Can you RECOVER from tragedy?

⊙ COMMON CORE

RL 1 Cite evidence to support inferences drawn from the text. **RL 4** Determine the meaning of words as they are used in the text. **RL 5** Analyze an author's choices concerning how to manipulate time and create tension or surprise. **RL 6** Analyze a particular point of view reflected in world literature.

We've all read stories in which a violent turn of events—a heart attack, a car crash, an earthquake—results in an individual's sudden death. But how do the survivors who are left behind recover? In "The Seventh Man," the main character describes the troubles and triumphs he experienced following a devastating childhood tragedy.

QUICKWRITE With a group, list several tragic events that you know about from the news. Think about the lasting effects of the events on the survivors. Select one event and write a paragraph about specific resources or methods that you think might help the survivors recover from their difficult experiences.

354

See resources on the **Teacher One Stop DVD-ROM** and on **thinkcentral.com**.

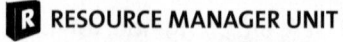

R RESOURCE MANAGER UNIT 3
Plan and Teach, pp. 81–88
Summary, pp. 89–90†‡*
Text Analysis and Reading
  Skill, pp. 91–94†*
Vocabulary, pp. 95–97*
Grammar and Style, p. 100

DIAGNOSTIC AND SELECTION
  TESTS
Selection Tests, pp. 103–106

📦 BEST PRACTICES TOOLKIT
Word Squares, p. E10
Cluster Diagram, p. B18
T Chart, p. A25
Character Traits Web, p. D7

TECHNOLOGY
💿 **Teacher One Stop DVD-ROM**
💿 **Student One Stop DVD-ROM**
💿 **Audio Anthology CD**
💿 **GrammarNotes DVD-ROM**
💿 **ExamView Test Generator**
  on the **Teacher One Stop**

---

* Resources for Differentiation   † Also in Spanish   ‡ In Haitian Creole and Vietnamese

TEXT ANALYSIS: FORESHADOWING AND FLASHBACK

When crafting stories, writers often rely on two narrative techniques to engage readers: foreshadowing and flashback.

- **Foreshadowing** is a writer's use of hints or clues to indicate situations that will occur later in a story. Writers often build suspense through foreshadowing.
- A **flashback** is an episode that interrupts the action of the story's plot to show an experience that happened at an earlier time. Writers usually provide important background information in flashbacks.

As you read "The Seventh Man," notice how the author uses both foreshadowing and flashback to build your interest in the story.

READING STRATEGY: MONITOR

When you read, you should pause occasionally to check, or **monitor,** your understanding of a story. As you read "The Seventh Man," use the following techniques to help you monitor your own comprehension:

- **Predicting:** Predict what might happen next based on details in the story.
- **Questioning:** Ask yourself questions about ideas, events, and characters in the story.

Use a chart like the one shown to jot down places in the story where you paused to make a prediction or ask a question.

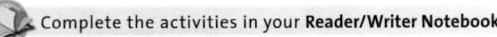

Passages Where I Paused to Check My Understanding	
Predictions	Questions

Review: Visualize

▲ VOCABULARY IN CONTEXT

Restate each phrase below by substituting a different word or words for the boldfaced term. Then, write a brief definition of each boldfaced word in your *Reader/Writer Notebook.*

1. a vengeful act of **savagery**
2. **ominous** dark shadows
3. a **delirium** caused by fever
4. a **premonition** of the future
5. a farewell full of **sentiment**
6. a **reconciliation** between enemies

Complete the activities in your **Reader/Writer Notebook.**

Meet the Author

Haruki Murakami
born 1949

Affinity with the West
Born to parents who were teachers of literature, Haruki Murakami (hä-rōō'kē mŏŏr'ä-kä'mē) grew up in Kyoto (kē-ō'tō) and Kobe (kō'bē), Japanese cities known for rich educational and cultural resources. An only child, Murakami often escaped loneliness and his parents' strictness by reading. As a teen, Murakami developed a taste for Western literature, favoring fiction by Leo Tolstoy, F. Scott Fitzgerald, and Truman Capote over traditional Japanese works. Today, he is a best-selling author whose novels and stories are valued for the way they elegantly combine Eastern and Western influences.

Consumer Culture
Murakami often writes about the spiritual emptiness experienced by the Japanese of his generation. In his youth, the Japanese were poor but idealistic. That idealism disappeared in the late 1960s, when Japan became a prosperous nation. In its place arose a society that looked for fulfillment in consumption and found boredom and disappointment instead.

BACKGROUND TO THE STORY
Tsunamis and Typhoons
Japan consists of four main islands and numerous smaller ones. Because the rock underlying these islands are constantly shifting, Japan is subject to frequent earthquakes. When the earthquakes occur out at sea, they whip up tsunamis, or tidal waves, which wreak havoc along the coast. The country also experiences typhoons, tropical storms that produce high winds and ocean surges.

Author Online
THINK central
Go to thinkcentral.com.
KEYWORD: HML10-355

355

Teach

TEXT ANALYSIS — COMMON CORE — RL 5, RL 6

● *Model the Skill:*
FORESHADOWING AND FLASHBACK

To model how to make inferences regarding plot development, read aloud the following lines:

> "This is my sad story," began Max. "I was only six when it happened."

Point out that Max shifts from the present to the past when he says, "I was only six." The word "sad" suggests the tragedy to come.

GUIDED PRACTICE Ask students to describe a memorable event in their lives, using a word or phrase that foreshadows something about what happened.

READING STRATEGY — COMMON CORE — RL 1

■ *Model the Skill:* **MONITOR**

Direct students' attention to the **Consumer Culture** paragraph. Help them speculate about the contents of the paragraph by listing questions they hope will be answered by reading. For example, *What does consumerism have to do with Murakami?* Tell them to pause to ask additional questions as they read.

GUIDED PRACTICE Ask students how monitoring techniques aided comprehension.

R RESOURCE MANAGER—Copy Master
Monitor p. 93 (for student use while reading the selection)

VOCABULARY SKILL — COMMON CORE — L 4

▲ VOCABULARY IN CONTEXT

DIAGNOSE WORD KNOWLEDGE Have all students complete Vocabulary in Context. Check their rephrasing of the words against the following:

delirium (dĭ-lîr'ē-əm) *n.* a temporary state of mental confusion usually resulting from high fever or shock

ominous (ŏm'ə-nəs) *adj.* menacing; threatening

premonition (prē'mə-nĭsh'ən) *n.* a hunch or feeling about the future; a foreboding

reconciliation (rĕk'ən-sĭl'ē-ā'shən) *n.* the act of settling or resolving

savagery (săv'ĭj-rē) *n.* extreme violence or cruelty

sentiment (sĕn'tə-mənt) *n.* feeling or emotion

PRETEACH VOCABULARY Use the following copy master to help students predict meanings for each boldfaced word in Part A.

R RESOURCE MANAGER—Copy Master
Vocabulary Study p. 95

1. Read the first pair of sentences in Part A aloud, emphasizing *savagery.*
2. Point out the word "brutal" in the first sentence and the phrase "no caring or kindhearted" in the second. Elicit possible meanings for *savagery*, such as "severe brutality."
3. Repeat the procedure for items b–f.

READ WITH A PURPOSE

Help students set a purpose for reading. Ask them to determine what the wave symbolized to the seventh man.

ADDITIONAL TEACHING OPPORTUNITY

Frame Story: Direct students to lines 1–29. Tell them that "The Seventh Man" is a **frame story,** or a story within a story. Explain that in a frame story there are two narrators. The frame story narrator (outer narrator) introduces the frame—the setting and situation in which the inner story is told. The central narrator (inner narrator) tells the story that is the heart of the selection.

READING STRATEGY   COMMON CORE   RL 1

Ⓐ MONITOR

Possible answer: A small group is "huddled in a circle" (line 4); the man may be the seventh member to tell his story.

TEXT ANALYSIS   COMMON CORE   RL 5   RL 6

Ⓑ *Model the Skill:* FORESHADOWING

To model how to make inferences about plot development, read aloud lines 1–13.

- Point out that in the lines in quotation marks, the man tells about the past. The lines without quotation marks describe what is happening in the present.

- Make sure students understand that *foreshadowing* normally refers to clues about what will happen next. In this story, however, the foreshadowing is about what already happened in the past and will be told next, in a flashback.

Possible answer: The man begins his story "'It happened . . . when I was ten years old'" (line 2), suggesting that he will tell more about his past. In lines 12–13, the man says that the event took away "'precious years that can never be replaced,'" hinting that he will tell more about the event. The man says, "'In my case, it was a wave'" (line 25), again suggesting that he will explain more about what happened in his past.

The Seventh Man

Haruki Murakami

"A huge wave nearly swept me away," said the seventh man, almost whispering. "It happened one September afternoon when I was ten years old."

The man was the last one to tell his story that night. The hands of the clock had moved past ten. The small group that huddled in a circle could hear the wind tearing through the darkness outside, heading west. It shook the trees, set the windows to rattling, and moved past the house with one final whistle. Ⓐ

"It was the biggest wave I had ever seen in my life," he said. "A strange wave. An absolute giant."

He paused.

10   "It just barely missed me, but in my place it swallowed everything that mattered most to me and swept it off to another world. I took years to find it again to recover from the experience—precious years that can never be replaced."

The seventh man appeared to be in his mid-fifties. He was a thin man, tall, with a moustache, and next to his right eye he had a short but deep-looking scar that could have been made by the stab of a small blade. Stiff, bristly patches of white marked his short hair. His face had the look you see on people when they can't quite find the words they need. In his case, though, the expression seemed to have been there from long before, as though it were part

20   of him. The man wore a simple blue shirt under a grey tweed coat, and every now and then he would bring his hand to his collar. None of those assembled there knew his name or what he did for a living.

He cleared his throat, and for a moment or two his words were lost in silence. The others waited for him to go on.

"In my case, it was a wave," he said. "There's no way for me to tell, of course, what it will be for each of you. But in my case it just happened to take the form of a gigantic wave. It presented itself to me all of a sudden one day, without warning. And it was devastating." Ⓑ

Ⓐ **MONITOR**
Why do you think the man is called "the seventh man"?

 **Targeted Passage**

Ⓑ **FORESHADOWING**
Reread lines 1–28. Which details suggest that you will learn more about the man's past?

Katsura Moonlight (1982), Clifton Karhu. 30/100. Woodblock, 40 × 30 cm. The Tolman Collection, Tokyo.

DIFFERENTIATED INSTRUCTION

FOR ENGLISH LANGUAGE LEARNERS

Vocabulary Support Use Word Squares to teach these words: *recover* (line 12), *adulthood* (line 50), *precise* (line 52), *area* (line 56), *impact* (line 187), *clarity* (line 214).

🧰 BEST PRACTICES TOOLKIT—Transparency
Word Squares p. E10

FOR STRUGGLING READERS

In combination with the *Audio Anthology CD,* use one or more Targeted Passages (pp. 356, 358, 364, 369) to ensure that students focus on key story events, concepts, and skills. Targeted Passages are also good for English learners.

 **Targeted Passage** [Lines 1–13]

This passage introduces the central narrator, the key event in his life, and the idea of going back into his past.

☉ FLASHBACK

RL 5
RL 6

Possible answer: *The seventh man begins to talk about the town where he grew up, his family, and his best friend, K. This information "sets up" the story, allowing the listeners and readers to enter the seventh man's world.*

READING STRATEGY

☉ MONITOR

Possible answer: *The narrator befriends K. because he is "such a sweet, pure-hearted boy" (lines 44–45). He also knows that because other kids look up to him, he can protect the frail K. (lines 42–43).*

---

grew up in a seaside town in the Province of S. It was such a small town, I doubt that any of you would recognize the name if I were to mention it. My father was the local doctor, and so I led a rather comfortable childhood. Ever since I could remember, my best friend was a boy I'll call K. His house was close to ours, and he was a grade behind me in school. We were like brothers, walking to and from school together, and always playing together when we got home. We never once fought during our long friendship. I did have a brother, six years older, but what with the age difference and differences in our personalities, we were never very close. My real brotherly affection went to my friend K. **☉**

K. was a frail, skinny little thing, with a pale complexion and a face almost pretty enough to be a girl's. He had some kind of speech impediment,[1] though, which might have made him seem retarded to anyone who didn't know him. And because he was so frail, I always played his protector, whether at school or at home. I was kind of big and athletic, and the other kids all looked up to me. But the main reason I enjoyed spending time with K. was that he was such a sweet, pure-hearted boy. He was not the least bit retarded, but because of his impediment, he didn't do too well at school. In most subjects, he could barely keep up. In art class, though, he was great. Just give him a pencil or paints and he would make pictures that were so full of life that even the teacher was amazed. He won prizes in one contest after another, and I'm sure he would have become a famous painter if he had continued with his art into adulthood. He liked to do seascapes. He'd go out to the shore for hours, painting. I would often sit beside him, watching the swift, precise movements of his brush, wondering how, in a few seconds, he could possibly create such lively shapes and colors where, until then, there had been only blank white paper. I realize now that it was a matter of pure talent. **☉**

One year, in September, a huge typhoon hit our area. The radio said it was going to be the worst in ten years. The schools were closed, and all the shops in town lowered their shutters in preparation for the storm. Starting early in the morning, my father and brother went around the house nailing shut all the storm doors, while my mother spent the day in the kitchen cooking emergency provisions. We filled bottles and canteens with water, and packed our most important possessions in rucksacks[2] for possible evacuation. To the adults, typhoons were an annoyance and a threat they had to face almost annually, but to the kids, removed as we were from such practical concerns, it was just a great big circus, a wonderful source of excitement.

Just after noon the color of the sky began to change all of a sudden. There was something strange and unreal about it. I stayed outside on the porch, watching the sky, until the wind began to howl and the rain began to beat against the house with a weird dry sound, like handfuls of sand. Then we closed the last storm door and gathered together in one room of the darkened house, listening to the radio. This particular storm did not have a great deal

☉ FLASHBACK
In lines 29–38, what information interrupts the present action of the story? Explain.

☉ MONITOR
Why do you think the narrator chooses to befriend K.?

② Targeted Passage

---

1. **speech impediment:** an obstacle to speaking clearly, such as a lisp or stammer.
2. **rucksacks:** knapsacks.

DIFFERENTIATED INSTRUCTION

FOR STRUGGLING READERS

② Targeted Passage [Lines 56–71]

This passage introduces the typhoon, shows how the narrator's family prepares for the storm, and hints at future destruction.

- What details suggest this typhoon will be extremely dangerous? (lines 57–58)
- How does the narrator's family prepare for the storm? (lines 59–62)
- Why would kids find typhoons "a wonderful source of excitement"? (line 65)

FOR ENGLISH LANGUAGE LEARNERS

Culture: Connect Invite volunteers to share their knowledge of typhoons, tsunamis, earthquakes, or other natural disasters that might have occurred in their home countries or regions. Ask students to describe how they think the narrator and his family might have felt as they prepared for the storm.

Sudden Shower over Shin-Ohashi Bridge and Atake (1800's), Ando Hiroshige or Utagawa. Plate 58 from *One Hundred Famous Views of Edo*. Woodblock color print. © Brooklyn Museum of Art, Brooklyn, New York. Photo © Bridgeman Art Library.

of rain, it said, but the winds were doing a lot of damage, blowing roofs off houses and capsizing ships. Many people had been killed or injured by flying debris. Over and over again, they warned people against leaving their homes. Every once in a while, the house would creak and shudder as if a huge hand were shaking it, and sometimes there would be a great crash of some heavy-sounding object against a storm door. My father guessed that these were tiles blowing off the neighbors' houses. For lunch we ate the rice and omelettes my mother had cooked, waiting for the typhoon to blow past.

Analyze Visuals

Activity Ask students to compare and contrast the scene in this print with the story's description of the early stages of the typhoon (lines 66–79). *Possible answer: Similarities: The print shows driving rain, and the hunched pedestrians suggest the desire to take refuge from the storm. The sky has changed color, as in the story, and it looks "strange and unreal" (line 67). **Differences:** The weather in the print is not as severe as in the story. People are still out walking and boating, whereas in the story, people are warned to stay home.*

About the Art Ando Hiroshige (1797–1858) is one of the masters of the Japanese school of art known as *ukiyo-e*—"pictures of the floating world." Hiroshige, who often rendered buildings and bridges in snow, rain, and mist, was known for his close observation of detail, though *ukiyo-e* always contain at least a hint of the unreal.

REVISIT THE BIG QUESTION
Can you RECOVER
from tragedy?

Discuss Based on lines 72–74, do you know that this typhoon will be something that will take a great deal of **recovery**? *Possible answer: The winds are destroying houses (lines 72–73), and people have already been killed or hurt. Families will have to fix their homes again, heal, and possibly mourn the loss of loved ones.*

FOR ENGLISH LANGUAGE LEARNERS
Vocabulary: Word Associations Write these common word associations on the board and read them aloud in context: "all of a sudden" (line 66), "Every once in a while" (line 75), "every which way" (line 132), "I had never seen anything like it in my life" (lines 179–180), "frozen in place" (line 194), "in twos and threes" (line 200), "stood rooted" (line 205), "What good would it do" (line 206), "All at once" (line 215), "take a long, hard look" (lines 329–330). Have pairs of students create an original sentence with each example. Collect the sentences, and ask an accelerated reader to read aloud all the sentences for each example. Tell students to signal when they think a sentence is not a valid example of the word association, and to explain why.

80 But the typhoon gave no sign of blowing past. The radio said it had lost momentum almost as soon as it came ashore at S. Province, and now it was moving north-east at the pace of a slow runner. The wind kept up its savage howling as it tried to uproot everything that stood on land.

Perhaps an hour had gone by with the wind at its worst like this when a hush fell over everything. All of a sudden it was so quiet, we could hear a bird crying in the distance. My father opened the storm door a crack and looked outside. The wind had stopped, and the rain had ceased to fall. Thick, grey clouds edged across the sky, and patches of blue showed here and there. The trees in the yard were still dripping their heavy burden of rainwater.

90 "We're in the eye of the storm," my father told me. "It'll stay quiet like this for a while, maybe fifteen, twenty minutes, kind of like an intermission. Then the wind'll come back the way it was before."

I asked him if I could go outside. He said I could walk around a little if I didn't go far. "But I want you to come right back here at the first sign of wind."

I went out and started to explore. It was hard to believe that a wild storm had been blowing there until a few minutes before. I looked up at the sky. The storm's great "eye" seemed to be up there, fixing its cold stare on all of us below. No such "eye" existed, of course: we were just in that momentary quiet spot at the center of the pool of whirling air.

100 While the grown-ups checked for damage to the house, I went down to the beach. The road was littered with broken tree branches, some of them thick pine boughs that would have been too heavy for an adult to lift alone. There were shattered roof tiles everywhere, cars with cracked windshields, and even a doghouse that had tumbled into the middle of the street. A big hand might have swung down from the sky and flattened everything in its path.

K. saw me walking down the road and came outside.

"Where are you going?" he asked.

"Just down to look at the beach," I said.

Without a word, he came along with me. He had a little white dog that
110 followed after us.

"The minute we get any wind, though, we're going straight back home," I said, and K. gave me a silent nod. **F**

The shore was a 200-yard walk from my house. It was lined with a concrete breakwater—a big dyke[3] that stood as high as I was tall in those days. We had to climb a short flight of steps to reach the water's edge. This was where we came to play almost every day, so there was no part of it we didn't know well. In the eye of the typhoon, though, it all looked different: the color of the sky and of the sea, the sound of the waves, the smell of the tide, the whole expanse of the shore. We sat atop the breakwater for a time, taking in the view without
120 a word to each other. We were supposedly in the middle of a great typhoon, and yet the waves were strangely hushed. And the point where they washed against the beach was much farther away than usual, even at low tide. The

---

3. **dyke:** a barrier built along the edge of a body of water to prevent flooding.

Sidebar (left margin)

E FORESHADOWING

Possible answer: *The father's warning builds suspense because he tells the son to come back "'at the first sign of wind'" (line 94). His statement alerts the reader that he suspects dangerous wind will return and that the typhoon will continue its destruction. His warning also sets up the possibility that the boy will not come back when he should, and the reader suspects that something bad will happen as a result.*

Extend the Discussion Do you think that the father should have let his son go out?

F *Model the Skill:* **MONITOR**

Read lines 80–92 aloud. Discuss what happened when the wind was blowing in the earlier part of the storm. Then point out the father's factual information about being in the eye of the storm. Have students use their Reading Strategy charts from page 355 to write predictions based on this information.

Possible answer: *The narrator and K. will get stuck on the beach when the wind starts blowing again.*

Sidebar (right margin)

E FORESHADOWING
Reread lines 93–94. How does the father's warning build **suspense**, or excitement?

F MONITOR
Predict what might happen next to the narrator and K.

DIFFERENTIATED INSTRUCTION

FOR ENGLISH LANGUAGE LEARNERS
Language: Contractions Explain to students that "wind'll" (line 92) is a nonstandard contraction. However, it is formed as many other contractions are—by combining a noun or pronoun and a verb part, and omitting some letters. Create a three-column chart with the headings "Noun + Verb," "Pronoun + Verb," and "Verb + Negative Word." Point out "We're" and "It'll" (line 90). Have students categorize the contractions, using the chart.

Break students into groups of three, and assign each group several pages of the story to search for other contractions to categorize.

white sand stretched out before us as far as we could see. The whole, huge space felt like a room without furniture, except for the band of flotsam[4] that lined the beach.

We stepped down to the other side of the breakwater and walked along the broad beach, examining the things that had come to rest there. Plastic toys, sandals, chunks of wood that had probably once been parts of furniture, pieces of clothing, unusual bottles, broken crates with foreign writing on them, and 130 other, less recognizable items: it was like a big candy store. The storm must have carried these things from very far away. Whenever something unusual caught our attention, we would pick it up and look at it every which way, and when we were done, K.'s dog would come over and give it a good sniff. ⑥

We couldn't have been doing this more than five minutes when I realized that the waves had come up right next to me. Without any sound or other warning, the sea had suddenly stretched its long, smooth tongue out to where I stood on the beach. I had never seen anything like it before. Child though I was, I had grown up on the shore and knew how frightening the ocean could be—the **savagery** with which it could strike unannounced.

140 nd so I had taken care to keep well back from the waterline. In spite of that, the waves had slid up to within inches of where I stood. And then, just as soundlessly, the water drew back—and stayed back. The waves that had approached me were as unthreatening as waves can be—a gentle washing of the sandy beach. But something **ominous** about them—something like the touch of a reptile's skin—had sent a chill down my spine. My fear was totally groundless—and totally real. I knew instinctively that they were alive. They knew I was here and they were planning to grab me. I felt as if some huge, man-eating beast were lying somewhere on a grassy plain, dreaming of the moment it would pounce and tear me to pieces with its sharp 150 teeth. I had to run away.

"I'm getting out of here!" I yelled to K. He was maybe ten yards down the beach, squatting with his back to me, and looking at something. I was sure I had yelled loud enough, but my voice did not seem to have reached him. He might have been so absorbed in whatever it was he had found that my call made no impression on him. K. was like that. He would get involved with things to the point of forgetting everything else. Or possibly I had not yelled as loudly as I had thought. I do recall that my voice sounded strange to me, as though it belonged to someone else.

Then I heard a deep rumbling sound. It seemed to shake the earth. Actually, 160 before I heard the rumble I heard another sound, a weird gurgling as though a lot of water was surging up through a hole in the ground. It continued for a while, then stopped, after which I heard the strange rumbling. Even that was not enough to make K. look up. He was still squatting, looking down at

---

4. **flotsam:** refuse or debris from a ship.

---

⑥ GRAMMAR AND STYLE
Reread lines 126–133. To highlight the boys' intense curiosity, Murakami uses a **simile** to compare the littered beach to a candy store.

savagery (săv′ĭj-rē) *n.* extreme violence or cruelty

ominous (ŏm′ə-nəs) *adj.* menacing; threatening

---

⑥ **GRAMMAR AND STYLE**   COMMON CORE L 3

Analyze Similes Remind students that a simile compares two unlike things using *like*, *as*, or *than*. The comparison helps readers picture or understand an image—in this case, what the beach looks like. Ask students how the comparison of the beach to a candy store helps them understand what the beach looks like and how the narrator and K. feel about everything they see on the beach. Ask students to find other similes in the story (for example, in lines 178 and 205) and explain how they add expressive details to the story.

TIERED DISCUSSION PROMPTS

Direct students to lines 140–163. Use these prompts to help students understand the rising action of the tragedy and the basis of the narrator's guilt:

Analyze What causes the narrator to decide to suddenly leave the beach? *Possible answer: the narrator's knowledge of typhoons, the appearance of the waves (lines 146–150), the way they receded from the beach (line 142), the sound of the water (lines 159–162), and instinct (lines 144–147).*

Evaluate Does the narrator do enough to warn K.? Explain. *Possible answer: No, he knew that there was impending danger. In his mind he yelled, and yet his "voice sounded strange . . . as though it belonged to someone else" (lines 157–158).*

VOCABULARY   COMMON CORE L 4

OWN THE WORD

• **savagery:** Point out that *savagery* is a noun form that indicates a condition of being *savage*. As a noun, *savage* refers to an uncivilized or brutal person. As an adjective, the word can be used to describe a wild, brutal, or cruel person.

• **ominous:** Expand on the meaning of *ominous* by providing students with analogies. For example, you might say, "Dark clouds suggest *ominous* weather. In a movie, an evil character's theme song is often *ominous* music."

FOR STRUGGLING READERS

Develop Reading Fluency Reread lines 144–150 with the students, pointing out that words and phrases like "ominous" (line 144), "planning to grab me" (line 147), and "man-eating beast . . . pounce and tear me to pieces" (lines 148–149) foreshadow danger. Read these words aloud in a manner that sounds foreboding. Then have students locate other examples of phrases that foreshadow danger and have volunteers read their examples aloud with appropriate intonation and emphasis.

Ⓡ **RESOURCE MANAGER—Copy Master**
Reading Fluency p. 101

FOR ADVANCED LEARNERS/PRE–AP

Analyze Imagery Point out line 136, "the sea had suddenly stretched its long, smooth tongue." Explain that the narrator personifies the sea, speaking about it as if it is a living thing. Have pairs of students work together to write five sentences in which they personify the sea, the wind, and the typhoon.

Possible answer: *The wave is huge, like the narrator's description of the wave in the story: as "tall as a three-story building" (line 180). The wave looks like the snake that the narrator describes, and it also appears "poised to strike" (line 179). The end of the wave appears to have teeth or talons, making it look as fierce as the wave the narrator describes.*

About the Art *Under the Wave off Kanagawa* is the most famous work by Hokusai (1760–1849), a premier artist of the Japanese woodblock print. In this print, a giant wave eclipses everything: boats, people, and, quite nearly, the majestic and sacred Mt. Fuji in the lower right-hand corner of the detail.

READING STRATEGY   **COMMON CORE**
                                RL 1

H MONITOR

Possible answer: *The wave has engulfed or "swallowed" (line 184) K. and pulled him out to sea. He may have drowned.*

TEXT ANALYSIS   **COMMON CORE**
                           RL 5
                           RL 6

O FORESHADOWING

Possible answer: *The amount of water that the wave pulls from the shore (line 193) suggests that another wave will appear. The return of the silence that had preceded the first wave (line 195) and the man's own statement that such "waves often came in twos and threes" (line 200) both foreshadow the appearance of another wave.*

---

something at his feet, in deep concentration. He probably did not hear the rumbling. How he could have missed such an earth-shaking sound, I don't know. This may seem odd, but it might have been a sound that only I could hear—some special kind of sound. Not even K.'s dog seemed to notice it, and you know how sensitive dogs are to sound.

170   I told myself to run over to K., grab hold of him, and get out of there. It was the only thing to do. I *knew* that the wave was coming, and K. didn't know. As clearly as I knew what I ought to be doing, I found myself running the other way—running full speed toward the dyke, alone. What made me do this, I'm sure, was fear, a fear so overpowering it took my voice away and set my legs to running on their own. I ran stumbling along the soft sand beach to the breakwater, where I turned and shouted to K.

"Hurry, K.! Get out of there! The wave is coming!" This time my voice worked fine. The rumbling had stopped, I realized, and now, finally, K. heard my shouting and looked up. But it was too late. A wave like a huge snake with its head held high, poised to strike, was racing towards the shore. I had

180   never seen anything like it in my life. It had to be as tall as a three-story building. Soundlessly (in my memory, at least, the image is soundless), it rose up behind K. to block out the sky. K. looked at me for a few seconds, uncomprehending. Then, as if sensing something, he turned towards the wave. He tried to run, but now there was no time to run. In the next instant, the wave had swallowed him. **H**

The wave crashed on to the beach, shattering into a million leaping waves that flew through the air and plunged over the dyke where I stood. I was able to dodge its impact by ducking behind the breakwater. The spray wet my clothes, nothing more. I scrambled back up on to the wall and scanned the shore. By then the wave had turned and, with a wild cry, it was rushing

190   back out to sea. It looked like part of a gigantic rug that had been yanked by someone at the other end of the earth. Nowhere on the shore could I find any trace of K., or of his dog. There was only the empty beach. The receding wave had now pulled so much water out from the shore that it seemed to expose the entire ocean bottom. I stood along on the breakwater, frozen in place.

The silence came over everything again—a desperate silence, as though sound itself had been ripped from the earth. The wave had swallowed K. and disappeared into the far distance. I stood there, wondering what to do. Should I go down to the beach? K. might be down there somewhere, buried in the sand . . . But I decided not to leave the dyke. I knew from experience that big

200   waves often came in twos and threes. **O**

I'm not sure how much time went by—maybe ten or twenty seconds of eerie emptiness—when, just as I had guessed, the next wave came. Another gigantic roar shook the beach, and again, after the sound had faded, another huge wave raised its head to strike. It towered before me, blocking out the sky, like a deadly cliff. This time, though, I didn't run. I stood rooted to the sea wall, entranced, waiting for it to attack. What good would it do to run, I

Examine the illustration. How does this image of a great wave compare with your mental picture of the wave in the story?

H MONITOR
What has happened to K.? Explain.

O FORESHADOWING
Reread lines 185–200. Which details foreshadow the appearance of another wave?

Detail of *Under the Wave off Kanagawa*, Hokusai.
© Historical Picture Archive/Corbis.

DIFFERENTIATED INSTRUCTION

FOR STRUGGLING READERS
Concept Support Help students follow the events by asking them to sketch or diagram and label the scene that the narrator describes. Have them draw the dyke/breakwater, the beach where K. is sitting, and the movements of the narrator, which they can represent by a dotted line. Help students begin this diagram by telling them where to sketch the narrator's home, reminding them that it is 200 yards from the shore (line 113).

FOR ENGLISH LANGUAGE LEARNERS
Vocabulary: Multiple-Meaning Words Have students study the following words in context and then look them up in the dictionary. Ask them to write the meaning of each word, followed by an example sentence. Have students share their sentences with the class: *trace* (line 192), *wrestling* (line 239), *executed* (line 334), *leafed* (line 335).

TIERED DISCUSSION PROMPTS

Direct students to lines 157–184. Use these prompts to help students understand the actions that will haunt the narrator for more than 40 years:

Recall What happens the first time the narrator shouts to K.? *Possible answer: The narrator's voice "sounded strange" (line 157)—probably because of fear—and K. doesn't seem to hear him.*

Analyze K. realizes the danger he faces when it is too late. How does this fact intensify the tragedy? *Possible answer: K. must have felt horror; he surely had time to know he would die because he "tried to run" (line 183). Also, the narrator saw his best friend, K., experience this awful knowledge.*

Synthesize Given the narrator's summary of his actions versus his thoughts, what might a reader think about instinct versus logic? *Possible answer: A reader might wonder why the narrator's survival instinct dominates his instinct to help. A reader might conclude that the survival instinct overrules other instincts.*

FOR ADVANCED LEARNERS/PRE–AP

Researching an Artist Have students do library and Internet research into the life and work of the Japanese artist Hokusai, whose woodblock print appears on this page. Encourage students to explore Hokusai's influence on Western artists, particularly the French impressionists. Invite students to share their research findings with the class. Interested students may want to create a multimedia presentation that includes reproductions of Hokusai's artwork.

thought, now that K. had been taken? Or perhaps I simply froze, overcome with fear. I can't be sure what it was that kept me standing there.

The second wave was just as big as the first—maybe even bigger. From
210 far above my head it began to fall, losing its shape, like a brick wall slowly crumbling. It was so huge that it no longer looked like a real wave. It was like something from another, far-off world, that just happened to assume the shape of a wave. I readied myself for the moment the darkness would take me. I didn't even close my eyes. I remember hearing my heart pound with incredible clarity.

The moment the wave came before me, however, it stopped. All at once it seemed to run out of energy, to lose its forward motion and simply hover there, in space, crumbling in stillness. And in its crest,[5] inside its cruel, transparent tongue, what I saw was K.

Some of you may find this impossible to believe, and if so, I don't blame
220 you. I myself have trouble accepting it even now. I can't explain what I saw any better than you can, but I know it was no illusion, no hallucination. I am telling you as honestly as I can what happened at that moment—what really happened. In the tip of the wave, as if enclosed in some kind of transparent capsule, floated K.'s body, reclining on its side. But that is not all. K. was looking straight at me, smiling. There, right in front of me, so close that I could have reached out and touched him, was my friend, my friend K. who, only moments before, had been swallowed by the wave. And he was smiling at me. Not with an ordinary smile—it was a big, wide-open grin that literally stretched from ear to ear. His cold, frozen eyes were locked on mine. He was
230 no longer the K. I knew. And his right arm was stretched out in my direction, as if he were trying to grab my hand and pull me into that other world where he was now. A little closer, and his hand would have caught mine. But, having missed, K. then smiled at me one more time, his grin wider than ever. **J**

 seem to have lost consciousness at that point. The next thing I knew, I was in bed in my father's clinic. As soon as I awoke the nurse went to call my father, who came running. He took my pulse, studied my pupils, and put his hand on my forehead. I tried to move my arm, but couldn't lift it. I was burning with fever, and my mind was clouded. I had been wrestling with a high fever for some time, apparently. "You've been asleep
240 for three days," my father said to me. A neighbor who had seen the whole thing had picked me up and carried me home. They had not been able to find K. I wanted to say something to my father. I *had* to say something to him. But my numb and swollen tongue could not form words. I felt as if some kind of creature had taken up residence in my mouth. My father asked me to tell him my name, but before I could remember what it was, I lost consciousness again, sinking into darkness.

---

5. **crest:** the top of a wave.

③ Targeted Passage

COMMON CORE RL 4

Language Coach

Multiple Meanings
Many words have more than one meaning. Reread the sentence in lines 211–213. *Assume* can mean "suppose," "put on," or "take control of." Which meaning best fits its use in this passage? Use *assume* this way in a new sentence.

J MONITOR
What might explain the strange image that the narrator sees in the wave?

READING STRATEGY
COMMON CORE

RL 1

J MONITOR

Possible answer: The narrator was distraught; he was in a heightened emotional state. Because of his traumatized state, the narrator may have seen strange images that were not really there. Some students may say that as a boy, the seventh man saw K.'s body but that the smile was really a mouth frozen in anguish or a last gasp for air. Others might interpret the event as a "white light" experience in which the boy's fear of his own death subliminally triggers an image of either a happy "other world," as evidenced by his friend's welcoming smile, or a scary world, as evidenced by K.'s "cold, frozen eyes" and outstretched hand.

REVISIT THE BIG QUESTION
Can you **RECOVER**
from tragedy?

Discuss Based on lines 234–246, what problems does the seventh man face as he tries to recover? *Possible answer: He was unconscious and briefly regains consciousness (line 234). He cannot lift his arm (line 238), has a high fever (line 238), a "clouded" mind (line 238), and he cannot talk (line 243). Then, he loses consciousness again (line 245).*

DIFFERENTIATED INSTRUCTION

FOR STRUGGLING READERS

③ Targeted Passage [Lines 207–217]
This passage helps students understand the fear the man felt as a boy.

- Why do you think the narrator did not run from the second wave? (lines 207–208)
- How do you picture the second wave, based on the man's description? (lines 209–213)
- What does "I readied myself for the moment the darkness would take me" (line 213) mean?

FOR ENGLISH LANGUAGE LEARNERS

Language Coach COMMON CORE RL 4

Multiple Meanings *Answer:*
"put on": *The spy* assumed *the identity of a mail carrier.* Have students locate two other multiple meaning words in the selection, and have them identify the best meaning for each word in its context.
Possible answers: wash up *(line 253), come ashore;* blow *(line 261), shock*

Altogether, I stayed in bed for a week on a liquid diet. I vomited several times, and had bouts of **delirium.** My father told me afterwards that I was so bad that he had been afraid that I might suffer permanent neurological[6] damage from the shock and high fever. One way or another, though, I managed to recover—physically, at least. But my life would never be the same again.

They never found K.'s body. They never found his dog, either. Usually when someone drowned in that area, the body would wash up a few days later on the shore of a small inlet to the east. K.'s body never did. The big waves probably carried it far out to sea—too far for it to reach the shore. It must have sunk to the ocean bottom to be eaten by the fish. The search went on for a very long time, thanks to the cooperation of the local fishermen, but eventually it petered out.[7] Without a body, there was never any funeral. Half crazed, K.'s parents would wander up and down the beach every day, or they would shut themselves up at home, chanting sutras.[8]

As great a blow as this had been for them, though, K.'s parents never chided me for having taken their son down to the shore in the midst of a typhoon. They knew how I had always loved and protected K. as if he had been my own little brother. My parents, too, made a point of never mentioning the incident in my presence. But I knew the truth. I knew that I could have saved K. if I had tried. I probably could have run over and dragged him out of the reach of the wave. It would have been close, but as I went over the timing of the events in my memory, it always seemed to me that I could have made it. As I said before, though, overcome with fear, I abandoned him there and saved only myself. It pained me all the more that K.'s parents failed to blame me and that everyone else was so careful never to say anything to me about what had happened. It took me a long time to recover from the emotional shock. I stayed away from school for weeks. I hardly ate a thing, and spent each day in bed, staring at the ceiling. **K**

K. was always there, lying in the wave tip, grinning at me, his hand outstretched, beckoning. I couldn't get that picture out of my mind. And when I managed to sleep, it was there in my dreams—except that, in my dreams, K. would hop out of his capsule in the wave and grab my wrist to drag me back inside with him.

And then there was another dream I had. I'm swimming in the ocean. It's a beautiful summer afternoon, and I'm doing an easy breaststroke far from shore. The sun is beating down on my back, and the water feels good. Then, all of a sudden, someone grabs my right leg. I feel an ice-cold grip on my ankle. It's strong, too strong to shake off. I'm being dragged down under the surface. I see K.'s face there. He has the same huge grin, split from ear to ear, his eyes locked on mine. I try to scream, but my voice will not come. I swallow water, and my lungs start to fill.

I wake up in the darkness, screaming, breathless, drenched in sweat.

---

6. **neurological:** relating to the nervous system.

7. **petered out:** came to an end.

8. **sutras:** short religious texts meant to be chanted.

delirium (dǐ-lîr′ē-əm) *n.* a temporary state of mental confusion usually resulting from high fever or shock

K MONITOR
As you reread lines 234–274, question the narrator's reaction to the tragedy. Do you think it is believable? Explain.

Direct students to lines 289–317. Use these prompts to help students understand how the tragedy affected the seventh man throughout his life:

Connect Do you think that you would have wanted to live somewhere else if you were the seventh man? Why or why not? *Students' answers should explain why they do or do not feel that the man's feelings are valid.*

Analyze What is the impact of K.'s death on the seventh man's life up to this point? *Possible answer: K.'s death has a totally negative impact on the seventh man's life. The seventh man continues to have nightmares (lines 302–305), never marries because of the nightmares (line 306), still fears the water and is unable to go to the beach or to swim (lines 312–315).*

TEXT ANALYSIS   COMMON CORE   RL 1

L SYMBOL

Have students reread lines 318–330. Point out words and phrases that are clues about what the watercolors symbolize, such as "reawaken the old terror" and "K.'s spirit" in lines 325–326.

Possible answer: The watercolors symbolize the spirit of K.—a "sweet, pure-hearted boy" (line 45) who was "so full of life" (line 48) and "liked to do seascapes" (line 51)—and remind the narrator of the tragedy and his own guilt and loss.

VOCABULARY   COMMON CORE   L 4

OWN THE WORD

premonition: Point out that *premonition* comes from the Latin word *praemonitus*, meaning "to forewarn." Ask students to describe a time when they had a *premonition*. When did this happen? What was the forewarning?

At the end of the year I pleaded with my parents to let me move to another 290 town. I couldn't go on living in sight of the beach where K. had been swept away, and my nightmares wouldn't stop. If I didn't get out of there, I'd go crazy. My parents understood and made arrangements for me to live elsewhere. I moved to Nagano Province in January to live with my father's family in a mountain village near Komoro.[9] I finished elementary school in Nagano and stayed on through junior and senior high school there. I never went home, even for holidays. My parents came to visit me now and then.

I live in Nagano to this day. I graduated from a college of engineering in the City of Nagano and went to work for a precision toolmaker in the area. I still work for them. I live like anybody else. As you can see, there's nothing unusual 300 about me. I'm not very sociable, but I have a few friends I go mountain climbing with. Once I got away from my hometown, I stopped having nightmares all the time. They remained a part of my life, though. They would come to me now and then, like debt collectors at the door. It happened when I was on the verge of forgetting. And it was always the same dream, down to the smallest detail. I would wake up screaming, my sheets soaked with sweat.

That is probably why I never married. I didn't want to wake someone sleeping next to me with my screams in the middle of the night. I've been in love with several women over the years, but I never spent a night with any of them. The terror was in my bones. It was something I could never share with 310 another person.

I stayed away from my hometown for over forty years. I never went near that seashore—or any other. I was afraid that if I did, my dream might happen in reality. I had always enjoyed swimming, but after that day I never even went to swim in a pool. I wouldn't go near deep rivers or lakes. I avoided boats and wouldn't take a plane to go abroad. Despite all these precautions, I couldn't get rid of the image of myself drowning. Like K.'s cold hand, this dark **premonition** caught hold of my mind and refused to let go.

premonition
(prē′mə-nĭsh′ən) *n.*
a hunch or feeling about the future; a foreboding

 hen, last spring, I finally revisited the beach where K. had been taken by the wave.

320   My father had died of cancer the year before, and my brother had sold the old house. In going through the storage shed, he had found a cardboard carton crammed with childhood things of mine, which he sent to me in Nagano. Most of it was useless junk, but there was one bundle of pictures that K. had painted and given to me. My parents had probably put them away for me as a keepsake of K., but the pictures did nothing but reawaken the old terror. They made me feel as if K.'s spirit would spring back to life from them, and so I quickly returned them to their paper wrapping, intending to throw them away. I couldn't make myself do it, though. After several days of indecision, I opened the bundle again and forced myself to take a long, hard 330 look at K.'s watercolors. **L**

COMMON CORE RL 1

L SYMBOL
A **symbol** is a person, a place, an object, or an activity that stands for something beyond itself. What do K.'s watercolors symbolize to the narrator? What evidence from the text helps you infer the meaning of the watercolors?

---

9. **Nagano Province . . . village near Komoro:** a northwestern area of Japan and a town in that area.

DIFFERENTIATED INSTRUCTION

FOR ENGLISH LANGUAGE LEARNERS

Vocabulary: Compound Nouns Remind students that in English, compound words, such as *windshields* (line 103), *doghouse* (line 104), and *breakwater* (lines 114 and 126), are formed by combining two smaller words. You might also point out that some compounds use a hyphen to combine words—for example, *earth-shaking* (line 165) and *far-off* (line 212). Assign groups to search two or three story pages for compound words. Have groups record on separate index cards each of the smaller words in the compound words. Then have each group scramble its cards and pass them to another group in order to reconstruct the original compound words or create other new ones with those word parts.

Most of them were landscapes, pictures of the familiar stretch of ocean and sand beach and pine woods and the town, and all done with that special clarity and coloration I knew so well from K.'s hand. They were still amazingly vivid despite the years, and had been executed with even greater skill than I recalled. As I leafed through the bundle, I found myself steeped in warm memories. The deep feelings of the boy K. were there in his pictures—the way his eyes were opened on the world. The things we did together, the places we went together began to come back to me with great intensity. And I realized that his eyes were my eyes, that I myself had looked upon the world back then with the

340 same lively, unclouded vision as the boy who had walked by my side.

I made a habit after that of studying one of K.'s pictures at my desk each day when I got home from work. I could sit there for hours with one painting. In each I found another of those soft landscapes of childhood that I had shut out of my memory for so long. I had a sense, whenever I looked at one of K.'s works, that something was permeating my very flesh.

Perhaps a week had gone by like this when the thought suddenly struck me one evening: I might have been making a terrible mistake all those years. As he lay there in the tip of the wave, surely K. had not been looking at me with hatred or resentment; he had not been trying to take me away with him. And

350 that terrible grin he had fixed me with: that, too, could have been an accident of angle or light and shadow, not a conscious act on K.'s part. He had probably already lost consciousness, or perhaps he had been giving me a gentle smile of eternal parting. The intense look of hatred I thought I saw on his face had been nothing but a reflection of the profound terror that had taken control of me for the moment.

The more I studied K.'s watercolor that evening, the greater the conviction with which I began to believe these new thoughts of mine. For no matter how long I continued to look at the picture, I could find nothing in it but a boy's gentle, innocent spirit.

360 I went on sitting at my desk for a very long time. There was nothing else I could do. The sun went down, and the pale darkness of evening began to envelop the room. Then came the deep silence of night, which seemed to go on forever. At last, the scales tipped, and dark gave way to dawn. The new day's sun tinged the sky with pink.

It was then I knew I must go back.

I threw a few things in a bag, called the company to say I would not be in, and boarded a train for my old hometown.

I did not find the same quiet, little seaside town that I remembered. An industrial city had sprung up nearby during the rapid development of the

370 Sixties, bringing great changes to the landscape. The one little gift shop by the station had grown into a mall, and the town's only movie theater had been turned into a supermarket. My house was no longer there. It had been demolished some months before, leaving only a scrape on the earth. The trees in the yard had all been cut down, and patches of weeds dotted the black

---

Language Coach

Synonyms Words with the same or nearly the same meaning are **synonyms.** Reread line 335. Which word is a synonym for "immersed"?

M MONITOR
How do you know the narrator is recovering from the tragedy?

TIERED DISCUSSION PROMPTS

Direct students to lines 341–365. Use these prompts to help students understand the reason behind the seventh man's recovery:

Connect Has looking back at old photographs or pictures ever changed your feelings about the past? Explain. *Answers will vary.*

Analyze What is soothing to the man about K.'s pictures? *Possible answer: They are "soft landscapes of childhood" (line 343) that help the man recall the young, innocent K., and realize that that person could not hate him.*

Evaluate Is it believable that looking at K.'s art again could change the man's thinking so profoundly? Why or why not? *Possible answer: Yes, because when the man sees K.'s innocence and gentleness revealed through his art, he realizes that K. could not have been looking at him in hatred. This insight frees the man from his guilt and allows him to interpret the tragedy differently.*

READING STRATEGY   COMMON CORE

M MONITOR   RL 1

Possible answer: The narrator is recovering because he is able to look at K.'s paintings again (line 342). He actually thinks he made "a terrible mistake all those years" (line 347). He thinks that K. was not looking at him with hatred; instead, he thinks that was just a reflection of the terror he himself felt (lines 348–355). He is able to shed some of the blame and is therefore recovering.

FOR ENGLISH LANGUAGE LEARNERS

Vocabulary: Phrasal Verbs Have pairs use a dictionary to create Cluster Diagrams with the infinitive form of the main verb (underlined verb) and all phrasal verbs they know of or find in the outer circles. Share the first example with learners and create the Cluster Digram for them to use as models: *"taking in"* (line 119), *grab hold of* (line 169), *locked on* (line 229), *gave way to* (line 363), *sprung up* (line 369), *cut down* (line 374), *sat down* (line

384), *dreamed up* (line 389), *fell silent* (line 415).

BEST PRACTICES TOOLKIT—Transparency
Cluster Diagram p. B18

Language Coach   COMMON CORE
                              RL 4
Synonyms *Answers: permeating; personal* Have students think of synonyms for the words *recover* and *tragedy*. **Possible answers:** *regain, reclaim; disaster, fatal event*

Analyze Visuals

Activity How do the waves in this print differ from the wave in the print on page 363? How do the different prints connect to the narrator at different points in the story?

Possible answer: The waves in this print are less awesome and frightening than the wave on page 363. They do not have the monster-like characteristics. The wave on page 363 reflects the time when the narrator thought of a wave as deadly. Now the narrator is willing to come to terms with the sea and no longer perceives it solely as a source of disaster and tragedy.

About the Art In *The Wave*, Ando Hiroshige (1797–1858), known for his lyricism, shows gently cresting waves that do not obliterate the shore, swallow boats and people, or eclipse Mt. Fuji. Rather, they mirror the shape of other natural elements in the scene.

The Wave (1800's), Ando Hiroshige or Utagawa. From the series *One Hundred Views of the Provinces.* Woodblock print, 37.3 × 25.5 cm. Galerie Janette Oster, Paris. Photo © Bridgeman Art Library.

stretch of ground. K.'s old house had disappeared as well, having been replaced by a concrete parking lot full of commuters' cars and vans. Not that I was overcome by **sentiment.** The town had ceased to be mine long before.

I walked down to the shore and climbed the steps of the breakwater. On the other side, as always, the ocean stretched off into the distance, unobstructed,
380 huge, the horizon a single straight line. The shoreline, too, looked the same as it had before: the long beach, the lapping waves, people strolling at the water's edge. The time was after four o'clock, and the soft sun of late afternoon embraced everything below as it began its long, almost meditative descent

sentiment (sĕn′tə-mənt)
n. feeling or emotion

 **VISUALIZE**
As you read lines 378–408, visualize the sea and the seventh man. What is the impact of this scene?

368 UNIT 3: NARRATIVE DEVICES

 **VISUALIZE**

Possible answer: The impact of this scene is great. The details about the "gentle seascape" (line 385), and of the man walking into the sea (lines 391–393) and collapsing facedown in the water (lines 405–407), help the reader see and feel the extent to which sadness and guilt had taken over the man's life. These details also help the reader almost physically feel the guilt and fear being lifted from the seventh man's shoulders.

OWN THE WORD

sentiment: Ask students to give examples of experiences that could cause someone to feel emotion, or *sentiment.*

DIFFERENTIATED INSTRUCTION

FOR ADVANCED LEARNERS/PRE–AP

Analyze Have small groups compare how the man characterizes the wave that took K. at the beginning of the story and how he characterizes the waves at the end of the story. Do the waves or the sea really change, or does the man's view of them change? What do the man's actions in lines 391–397 symbolize?

to the west. I lowered my bag to the sand and sat down next to it in silent appreciation of the gentle seascape. Looking at this scene, it was impossible to imagine that a great typhoon had once raged here, that a massive wave had swallowed my best friend in all the world. There was almost no one left now, surely, who remembered those terrible events. It began to seem as if the whole thing were an illusion that I had dreamed up in vivid detail.

390 And then I realized that the deep darkness inside me had vanished. Suddenly. As suddenly as it had come. I raised myself from the sand, and, without bothering to take off my shoes or roll up my cuffs, walked into the surf and let the waves lap at my ankles.

Almost in **reconciliation**, it seemed, the same waves that had washed up on the beach when I was a boy were now fondly washing my feet, soaking black my shoes and pant cuffs. There would be one slow-moving wave, then a long pause, and then another wave would come and go. The people passing by gave me odd looks, but I didn't care.

I looked up at the sky. A few grey cotton chunks of cloud hung there,
400 motionless. They seemed to be there for me, though I'm not sure why I felt that way. I remembered having looked up at the sky like this in search of the "eye" of the typhoon. And then, inside me, the axis of time gave one great heave. Forty long years collapsed like a dilapidated house, mixing old time and new time together in a single swirling mass. All sounds faded, and the light around me shuddered. I lost my balance and fell into the waves. My heart throbbed at the back of my throat, and my arms and legs lost all sensation. I lay that way for a long time, face in the water, unable to stand. But I was not afraid. No, not at all. There was no longer anything for me to fear. Those days were gone.

I stopped having my terrible nightmares. I no longer wake up screaming
410 in the middle of the night. And I am trying now to start life over again. No, I know it's probably too late to start again. I may not have much time left to live. But even if it comes too late, I am grateful that, in the end, I was able to attain a kind of salvation, to effect some sort of recovery. Yes, grateful: I could have come to the end of my life unsaved, still screaming in the dark, afraid.

The seventh man fell silent and turned his gaze upon each of the others. No one spoke or moved or even seemed to breathe. All were waiting for the rest of his story. Outside, the wind had fallen, and nothing stirred. The seventh man brought his hand to his collar once again, as if in search for words. ◉

"They tell us that the only thing we have to fear is fear itself; but I don't
420 believe that," he said. Then, a moment later, he added: "Oh, the fear is there, all right. It comes to us in many different forms, at different times, and overwhelms us. But the most frightening thing we can do at such times is to turn our backs on it, to close our eyes. For then we take the most precious thing inside us and surrender it to something else. In my case, that something was the wave." ❧

Translated by Jay Rubin

4 Targeted Passage

reconciliation
(rĕk′ən-sĭl′ē-ā′shən) *n.* the act of settling or resolving

◉ **FLASHBACK**
Reread lines 415–418. Which details tell you that you have just completed reading a flashback?

THE SEVENTH MAN **369**

FOR STRUGGLING READERS

4 Targeted Passage [Lines 399–414]

This passage shows the resolution of the central narrator's internal conflict.

- What does "Forty long years collapsed like a dilapidated house" (line 403) mean?
- Why did the man collapse in the water? (line 405)
- Has the man really recovered from K.'s death? Cite evidence. (lines 409–410)

TEXT ANALYSIS — COMMON CORE

◉ **FLASHBACK** — RL 5 / RL 6

Possible answer: The seventh man lets his gaze fall "upon each of the others. . . . All were waiting for the rest of his story" (lines 415–417). The others are the people who have been listening to his story. The seventh man "brought his hand to his collar once again" (line 418) now that the flashback has ended, just as he did at the beginning of the story (line 21) before he began his tale.

VOCABULARY — COMMON CORE

OWN THE WORD — L 4

reconciliation: Have students list experiences that required *reconciliation.* **Possible answer:** *amicably resolving a dispute with someone*

SELECTION WRAP–UP

READ WITH A PURPOSE Now that students have finished reading the selection, have them explain what the wave symbolizes to the seventh man (lines 25–26, 420–425). **Possible answer:** *The wave symbolizes the way fear follows someone who does not meet it head on.*

⭐ **CRITIQUE** Ask students whether they think the seventh man's transformation and recovery are believable. Why or why not?

INDEPENDENT READING

If students enjoy reading fiction about the ocean, recommend Yann Martel's *Life of Pi.* In it, students will read about Pi's treacherous journey on a lifeboat.

THE SEVENTH MAN **369**

TIERED DISCUSSION PROMPTS

Use these prompts to help students understand Haruki Murakami's ideas about writing and how those ideas might have affected "The Seventh Man":

Connect If you could interview Murakami about his writing, what questions would you ask? *Accept all reasonable answers.*

Analyze Murakami says that he prefers to write his stories in the first person. In "The Seventh Man," the flashback story is told in the first person, but lines 1–28 of the story are told from a third-person point of view. What is the effect of using two points of view? *Possible answer: When the seventh man tells his flashback inner story, we experience his thoughts and feelings. We see him more objectively from the perspective of the outer narrator and the other members of the group when third person is used. The use of both perspectives allows us to view the seventh man both as an individual and as one of many people who are attempting to recover from a tragedy or trauma.*

Evaluate Do you think Murakami's style is more Japanese or Western? Why? *Answers will vary, but students should support their answers with evidence from the selection and from the interview.*

Reading for Information

INTERVIEW In this interview, the acclaimed Japanese author Haruki Murakami offers fascinating insights into his own writing process. He also demonstrates a rich understanding of contemporary world literature.

An Interview with HARUKI MURAKAMI

Larry McCaffrey and Sinda Gregory

Larry McCaffrey: I think just about all of your [stories] are in first person. Have you ever thought about not writing in first person?

Haruki Murakami: Yes, for a short time I tried to write in the third person, but it didn't work out.

LM: What's the problem? Is it not as interesting? Is it the voice?

HM: When I tried to use third person, I just felt like I became a god. But I don't want to be a god. I don't know everything. I can't write everything. I'm just myself. I would write something just as myself. I don't mean that I really am the protagonist but that I can envision what my protagonist sees and experiences. . . . I'm forty-six and married, but when I'm writing I can become twenty-five and unmarried. I can walk around in somebody else's shoes—and feel those shoes. Writing becomes your second life. That's good.

LM: Some critics, both in the U.S. and Japan, have said that your work is not really Japanese. Do you yourself think of yourself as having a distinctly Japanese sensibility?

HM: The opinion that my books are not really Japanese seems to me to be very shallow. I certainly think of myself as being a Japanese writer. . . . At first I wanted to be an international writer, but eventually saw that I was nothing but a Japanese writer. But even in the beginning I wasn't only borrowing Western styles and rules. I wanted to change Japanese literature from the inside, not the outside. So I basically made up my own rules.

Sinda Gregory: Could you give us some examples of what you mean?

HM: Most literary purists in Japan love beautiful language and appreciate sensitivity rather than energy or power. This beauty is admired for its own sake, and so their styles use a lot of very stiff, formal metaphors that don't sound natural or spontaneous at all. These writing styles get more and more refined, to the point where they resemble a kind of bonsai. I don't like such traditional forms of writing; it may sound beautiful, but it may not communicate. Besides, who knows what beauty is? So in my writing, I've tried to change that. I like to write more freely, so I use a lot of long and peculiar metaphors that seem fresh to me. . . .

SG: What's been the reaction of American readers to your work? I'm wondering especially about your younger readers.

HM: I found it very interesting when I visited universities in the U.S. that many students are interested in Japanese literature and culture. What I noticed was that they seemed to be reading contemporary Japanese books simply as novels rather than as "Japanese novels." They're reading my books or ones by Amy Yamada or Banana Yoshimoto the same way they had begun to read García Márquez and Vargas Llosa and other Latin American novelists a few years ago. It takes a while for this kind of change to take place. Writers from different countries are changing each other and finding global audiences more easily nowadays; it's a small world and a world which is getting smaller. I think that's a great thing.

Comprehension

1. **Recall** At what location does the story begin and end?

2. **Clarify** Why have the people in the group come together?

3. **Summarize** Describe the tragedy that changed the seventh man's life.

COMMON CORE

RL 1 Cite evidence to support inferences drawn from the text.
RL 5 Analyze an author's choices concerning how to manipulate time and create tension or surprise.
RL 6 Analyze a particular point of view reflected in world literature.

Text Analysis

4. **Understand Cause and Effect** In what ways has the tragedy affected the seventh man? Review the story for specific examples. Use a chart like the one shown to help you organize your thoughts. An example has been filled in for you.

Cause	Effects on the Seventh Man
K.'s death ⟶	1. He loses consciousness.

5. **Interpret Foreshadowing** What point in the story held the most **suspense**, or tension, for you? In what way was this event foreshadowed earlier in the story? Give specific examples from the story to support your answer.

6. **Analyze Flashback** "The Seventh Man" is told almost exclusively in flashback. The narrator recounts events that took place before the beginning of the story. How does this technique help you understand the seventh man and his struggle to recover from tragedy?

7. **Evaluate an Opinion** The seventh man concludes that the worst thing we can do when we are frightened is "to turn our backs on [fear], to close our eyes." Do you agree or disagree with this opinion? Explain your answer.

8. **Monitor** Review the notes you took as you read. What aspect of the story was the most challenging for you? How did **predicting** or **questioning** help you understand this difficult part?

9. **Compare Literary Works** In what ways does Murakami's writing seem fresh and imaginative? Use information from both "The Seventh Man" and "An Interview with Haruki Murakami" to support your answer.

Text Criticism

10. **Critical Interpretations** In Murakami's later fiction, notes one literary critic, "we see the theme of isolation and Murakami's assertion of the need for communication and greater understanding between people." Would you say that "The Seventh Man" deals with these issues? Explain.

Can you RECOVER from tragedy?

Do you think talking about the tragedy helps? Why or why not?

THE SEVENTH MAN **371**

9. *He uses "peculiar" metaphors about the wave, he "double narrates" the story, and he writes the seventh man's story in the first person.*

Text Criticism

Possible answer:

10. *Yes, the seventh man lived alone and suffered by himself for a long time. Once he tells his story, it is apparent that he needed to communicate and have others understand.*

Can you RECOVER from tragedy? Some students may feel that talking helps work through grief, but others may think it prolongs the pain.

Practice and Apply

For preliminary support of post-reading questions, use these copy masters:

R RESOURCE MANAGER—Copy Masters
Reading Check p. 98
Foreshadowing and Flashback p. 91
Question Support p. 99
Additional selection questions are provided for teachers on page 85.

ANSWERS

Comprehension

1. *The story begins and ends in a house with a small group of people.*

2. *The group members may have come together to hear one another's stories or perhaps to wait out the storm.*

3. *When the seventh man was ten years old, he and his best friend, K., were on a beach. A typhoon caused an enormous wave to engulf K. and carry him out to sea. The seventh man felt he could have rescued K. had he tried harder.*

Text Analysis
COMMON CORE RL 1, RL 5, RL 6
Possible answers:

4. *The effects of K.'s death on the narrator include his nightmares, his decision to leave home and never return, the fact that he never marries, and his refusal to swim or go near water again (lines 289–317).*

5. ● **COMMON CORE FOCUS** *Foreshadowing* The most suspenseful event was wondering if K. would escape the wave. This was foreshadowed by the boy's premonition of the wave's danger (lines 140–163) and the father's warning (line 94).

6. ● **COMMON CORE FOCUS** *Flashback* The extended flashback helps you understand why K.'s death so strongly impacted the narrator's life. The flashback also helps you appreciate how difficult it was for the man to recover from the tragedy.

7. *Agree:* If you do not address your fear, then you will never overcome it. *Disagree:* If you ignore your fear, it will go away.

8. ● **COMMON CORE FOCUS** *Monitor* The most difficult part of the story was realizing what was real and unreal about what the narrator saw and felt. When I questioned the details and reread the text, the real and unreal became clearer.

THE SEVENTH MAN **371**

ANSWERS

Vocabulary in Context

▲ **VOCABULARY PRACTICE**

1. *true*   4. *false*
2. *false*   5. *true*
3. *false*   6. *true*

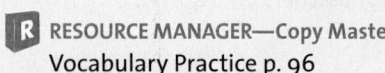 **RESOURCE MANAGER—Copy Master**
Vocabulary Practice p. 96

ACADEMIC VOCABULARY IN WRITING

Possible answer: *If you're going to* survive *an avalanche, quick and clear thinking are* crucial. *When the snow or ice starts to* shift, *crouch low. Keep your mouth shut—now is not the time to call out for help. After the movements stop, try to kick your way to the surface.*

VOCABULARY STRATEGY:  **COMMON CORE L 4c**
THE LATIN ROOT *sen*

- For each item, tell students to use their knowledge of context clues and the root *sen* to help them figure out which word best completes the sentence.

- Model the strategy by pointing out that in item 1, *over* and *reason* are the context clues: *over* signals that *reason* is superior to the missing word (*sentiment*), which has something to do with "to feel."

Answers:

1. *sentiment*
2. *sensitive*
3. *sensation*
4. *sensual*
5. *sensory*

 **RESOURCE MANAGER—Copy Master**
Vocabulary Strategy p. 97

Interactive Vocabulary    **THINK central**

Keywords direct students to a **WordSharp** tutorial on **thinkcentral.com** or to other types of vocabulary practice and review.

Vocabulary in Context

▲ **VOCABULARY PRACTICE**

Decide if each statement is true or false.

1. Individuals who commit acts of **savagery** are cruel or violent.
2. An **ominous** cloud is one that pleases or delights.
3. If you are experiencing **delirium,** your thoughts are clear.
4. A **premonition** is a recollection of the past.
5. Personal letters are often filled with **sentiment.**
6. People settle their differences in a **reconciliation.**

WORD LIST
delirium
ominous
premonition
reconciliation
savagery
sentiment

ACADEMIC VOCABULARY IN WRITING

- consequent   - crucial   - initial   - shift   - survive

Using at least two Academic Vocabulary words, write a paragraph describing what it would be like to **survive** another type of natural disaster. Here is an example of an opening:

> **SAMPLE OPENING**
>
> If you're going to survive an avalanche, quick and clear thinking are **crucial.**

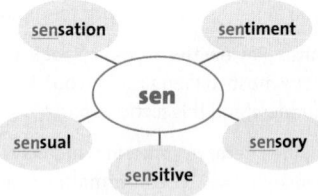 **COMMON CORE**

L 4c Consult general reference materials to determine or clarify a word's etymology.

VOCABULARY STRATEGY: THE LATIN ROOT *sen*

The vocabulary word *sentiment* stems from the Latin root *sen,* which means "to feel." To understand the meaning of words with *sen,* use context clues as well as your knowledge of the root.

PRACTICE Write the word from the word web that best completes each sentence. Use context clues to help you, or, if necessary, consult a dictionary.

1. I choose reason over _____ when making an important decision.
2. He is very _____ to what others say about him.
3. A feather on your skin is a ticklish _____.
4. She enjoys the _____ delight of a gourmet meal.
5. A three-dimensional movie is a unique _____ experience.

Interactive Vocabulary **THINK central**

Go to **thinkcentral.com.**
KEYWORD: HML10-372

DIFFERENTIATED INSTRUCTION

FOR ENGLISH LANGUAGE LEARNERS

Vocabulary: Cognates Have students create a T Chart with *sen* words that are cognates (words that are similar in their home languages and in English). If students' home languages do not have these relationships with English, have them copy the word web from the book and add more English words to it, creating a sentence with each word. Allow students to use a dictionary for this activity.

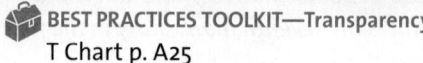 **BEST PRACTICES TOOLKIT—Transparency**
T Chart p. A25

Language

◆ **GRAMMAR AND STYLE:** Add Descriptive Details

Review the **Grammar and Style** note on page 361. Throughout the story, Murakami uses similes to clarify events and give energy to his writing. A **simile** is a direct comparison of two different things, actions, or feelings, using the words *like* or *as*. In your own writing, use similes to help readers understand unusual experiences by comparing them to more familiar things, as Murakami does. Here is an example from the story.

> *Forty long years collapsed like a dilapidated house, mixing old time and new time together in a single swirling mass.* (lines 403–404)

Notice how the revisions in blue add clarity and interest to this first draft. Revise your response to the prompt below by using a similar technique.

STUDENT MODEL

The giant wave swept away the seventh man's world. The wave symbolized *, like an explosion in his peaceful life*

a terrible experience and a fear he couldn't forget that seemed to follow him everywhere. *like an evil shadow*

READING-WRITING CONNECTION

YOUR TURN Increase your understanding of "The Seventh Man" by responding to this prompt. Then use the **revising tip** to improve your writing.

WRITING PROMPT	**REVISING TIP**
Extended Constructed Response: Analysis A **symbol** is a person, a place, or an object that represents something beyond itself. In what ways does water symbolize both the painful and peaceful experiences of the seventh man? Write **three or four paragraphs** in response, using information from the story to support your answer.	Review your response. Did you use similes to clarify events and give energy to your writing? If not, revise your answer.

Interactive Revision THINK central
Go to **thinkcentral.com**.
KEYWORD: HML10-373

FOR STRUGGLING WRITERS

- Limit the length of the assignment to two paragraphs—a "painful experience" paragraph and a "peaceful experience" paragraph.

- Have students work in small groups to generate a list of peaceful experiences and a list of painful experiences.

Language

COMMON CORE L 3, W 2b

◆ **GRAMMAR AND STYLE**

- After students examine the student model, discuss how the revisions added clarity and interest.

- Write this sentence on the board, and ask students to add a simile that adds interest, depth, or clarity to the sentence. (A sample simile is shown in blue.)

Suddenly, the wave rose up like water blowing from the head of a whale and washed over K.

 RESOURCE MANAGER—Copy Master
Add Descriptive Details p. 100

READING-WRITING CONNECTION

- Have students reread the beginning of the story, where the central narrator recounts K.'s tragic death, and the end of the story, where the narrator returns home to the beach.

 **BEST PRACTICES TOOLKIT**—Transparency
Character Traits Web p. D7

Writing Online THINK central

The following tools are available online at **thinkcentral.com** and on **WriteSmart CD-ROM:**
- **Interactive Graphic Organizers**
- **Interactive Student Models**
- **Interactive Revision Lessons**
For additional grammar instruction, see **GrammarNotes** on **thinkcentral.com**.

Assess and Reteach

Assess

DIAGNOSTIC AND SELECTION TESTS
Selection Test A pp. 103–104
Selection Test B/C pp. 105–106

Interactive Selection Test on **thinkcentral.com**

Reteach

Level Up Online Tutorials on **thinkcentral.com**

Reteaching Worksheets on **thinkcentral.com**
Literature Lesson 8, Reading Lesson 2, Vocabulary Lesson 7

Focus and Motivate

COMMON CORE FOCUS

RI 1 Cite strong and thorough textual evidence to support inferences drawn from the text.
RI 2 Determine a central idea of a text and analyze its development over the course of the text, including how it is shaped by specific details.
RI 4 Analyze the cumulative impact of specific word choices on meaning and tone. **L 1b** Use various types of phrases to convey specific meanings and add variety and interest to writing. **L 4c** Consult reference materials to determine or clarify a word's meaning and etymology.

SUMMARY

Roger Rosenblatt reflects on the emotional impact of the crash of Air Florida Flight 90, in which 78 people were killed. He examines the heroism of rescuers who risked and gave their lives so that others could live.

Can ordinary people be HEROES?

Introduce the question. In preparation for the *QUICKWRITE*, have students discuss examples of heroes who risk their lives for strangers.

The Man in the Water
Essay by Roger Rosenblatt

Can ordinary people be HEROES?

COMMON CORE

RI 2 Determine a central idea of a text and analyze its development over the course of the text, including how it is shaped by specific details.
RI 4 Analyze the cumulative impact of specific word choices on meaning and tone.

When disaster strikes, people react in different ways. Some struggle to save themselves, others crumble in fear, and a few rare individuals risk their own lives to save the lives of strangers. In "The Man in the Water," you will read about an ordinary man whose selfless acts made him a hero.

QUICKWRITE With a group, use a description wheel like the one shown to list qualities that define a hero. Then write a short paragraph about a particular person who possesses these traits. Make sure to indicate whether the hero is a public figure or an ordinary person.

374

Selection Resources

See resources on the **Teacher One Stop DVD-ROM** and on **thinkcentral.com**.

R RESOURCE MANAGER UNIT 3
Plan and Teach, pp. 103–110
Summary, pp. 111–112†‡*
Text Analysis and Reading
  Skill, pp. 113–116†*
Vocabulary, pp. 117–119*
Grammar and Style, p. 122

DIAGNOSTIC AND SELECTION TESTS
Selection Tests, pp. 107–110

BEST PRACTICES TOOLKIT
New Word Analysis, p. E8
Venn Diagram, p. A26

TECHNOLOGY
 Teacher One Stop DVD-ROM
Student One Stop DVD-ROM
Audio Anthology CD
GrammarNotes DVD-ROM
ExamView Test Generator
  on the **Teacher One Stop**

---

* Resources for Differentiation   † Also in Spanish   ‡ In Haitian Creole and Vietnamese

TEXT ANALYSIS: REFLECTIVE ESSAY

A **reflective essay** is an essay in which the writer makes a connection between a personal observation and a universal idea—such as love, courage, or freedom. Roger Rosenblatt's essay contains narration as well as reflection. As he tells the story of a disaster, he makes choices, as a fiction writer would, about the order in which to present events and the perspective from which to present them. He also makes stylistic choices about **diction** (the words he uses) and **syntax** (the arrangement of words) to create effects, such as the **voice** and tone of the selection, rhythm of language, and emphasis of ideas. Notice how the choices Rosenblatt makes involve you in the story.

READING SKILL: IDENTIFY MAIN IDEA AND SUPPORTING DETAILS

A reflective essay, like most essays, has a thesis, or **main idea.** If you are unsure of the main idea, you can usually figure it out from the **supporting details**—that is, the facts and other evidence included in the essay to reinforce the central idea.

In "The Man in the Water," Rosenblatt explores why a 1982 airplane crash is memorable. He develops his main idea over the course of several paragraphs. Jot down each part of his main idea as you find it. Then, beneath each statement, write a few details that support it.

Statement	Statement

Supporting Details	Supporting Details

▲ VOCABULARY IN CONTEXT

The following words are key to understanding Rosenblatt's essay about a real-life hero. Restate each phrase, using a different word or words for the boldfaced term. Write your answers in your *Reader/Writer Notebook*.

1. to straighten a **chaotic** bedroom
2. freedom **emblemized** by the American flag
3. the **flailing** goose drying its wings
4. an **implacable** child who cannot be quieted

*Complete the activities in your **Reader/Writer Notebook**.*

Meet the Author

Roger Rosenblatt
born 1940

Star Journalist
Roger Rosenblatt is a native of New York City and holds a Ph.D. in literature and writing from Harvard University. In 1975, after teaching at his alma mater, he became a professional journalist. During his lengthy writing career, he has regularly contributed to news publications, such as the *Washington Post* and *Time*, and has won several prestigious awards. Today, he is viewed as one of the finest American essayists, approaching his work with, as one critic noted, "uncommon clarity, conciseness, eloquence and humor."

Man of the World
Known for his sensitivity and literary flair, Rosenblatt has won praise for several nonfiction books on controversial topics, including *Witness: The World Since Hiroshima*, which examines the impact of the atomic bomb on different aspects of modern life. His best-known book is perhaps *Children of War*, an investigation into the lives of children in various war-torn nations.

BACKGROUND TO THE ESSAY

The Crash of Flight 90
One of the most publicized air disasters occurred on January 13, 1982, when Air Florida Flight 90 departed from Washington National Airport. Failing to gain enough altitude on takeoff, the passenger jet crashed into the nearby 14th Street Bridge and slid into the icy Potomac River. Seventy-eight people died in the disaster—some of them in the plane, some in their cars on the bridge, and some in the frigid waters of the Potomac. Ice on the jet's wings was the probable cause of the accident.

Author Online
THINK central
Go to thinkcentral.com.
KEYWORD: HML10-375

375

Teach

TEXT ANALYSIS   COMMON CORE   RI 2

● *Model the Skill:* **REFLECTIVE ESSAY**

Explain that in writing this essay, Rosenblatt included the perspectives, or viewpoints, of several people involved with the disaster. Point out that "seeing" an event through the eyes of more than one person can broaden understanding of the event.

GUIDED PRACTICE Have students compare accounts of an event that many of them have witnessed.

READING SKILL   COMMON CORE   RI 1   RI 4

■ *Model the Skill:* **IDENTIFY MAIN IDEA AND SUPPORTING DETAILS**

To model how to identify the main idea and supporting details, read aloud the paragraph under **Star Journalist.** Point out that Rosenblatt has worked hard to become a "star journalist." This is the main idea. Tell students that one detail that supports this idea is that he has "won several prestigious awards."

GUIDED PRACTICE Have students find the main idea and two supporting details in **Man of the World.**

R RESOURCE MANAGER—Copy Master
Identify Main Idea and Supporting Details p. 115 (for student use while reading the selection)

VOCABULARY SKILL   COMMON CORE   L 4

▲ VOCABULARY IN CONTEXT

DIAGNOSE WORD KNOWLEDGE Have all students complete Vocabulary in Context. Check their definitions against the following:

chaotic (kā-ŏt'ĭk) *adj.* extremely confused or disordered

emblemized (ĕm'blə-mīzd') *adj.* represented; symbolized **emblemize** *v.*

flailing (flā'lĭng) *adj.* waving vigorously **flail** *v.*

implacable (ĭm-plăk'ə-bəl) *adj.* impossible to calm or satisfy; relentless

PRETEACH VOCABULARY Use the following copy master to help students predict meanings for each boldfaced word.

R RESOURCE MANAGER—Copy Master
Vocabulary Study p. 117

1. Read item 1 aloud, emphasizing *chaotic*.

2. Point out the phrase "running in all directions." Elicit possible meanings for *chaotic*, such as "in a state of confusion."

3. Have students record their predictions.

4. Repeat the procedure for items 2–4.

Practice and Apply

READ WITH A PURPOSE

Help students set a purpose for reading. Tell them to look for reasons that people risk their lives for others.

READING SKILL	COMMON CORE
	RI 1
	RI 4

A Model the Skill: CENTRAL IDEA

To model how to find the main idea, read aloud lines 15–21 and point out the phrases that Rosenblatt uses to describe nature ("indifferent," line 19) and human nature ("rose to the occasion," line 21).

Possible answer: *Rosenblatt's main point is that although nature is indifferent to human beings and may cause a disaster, human nature may rise to the occasion.*

VOCABULARY	COMMON CORE
	L 4

OWN THE WORD

- **chaotic:** Tell students that *chaotic* is the adjective form of *chaos*. Synonyms for *chaos* include *clutter, disarray,* and *jumble.* Have students write a sentence using *chaos* and one of these synonyms as a context clue.

- **emblemized:** Remind students that *emblemized* is related to the noun *emblem,* a "symbol" or "badge" used to represent something. Have students list several *emblems* that they recognize in their community. ***Possible answers:*** *logos, signs*

- **flailing:** Ask students to explain why they think the author chose to use the word *flailing* in line 20. ***Possible answer:*** *Although people struggled with terror and panic, they had the courage to help one another to survive the disaster.*

376 UNIT 3: NARRATIVE DEVICES

The Man in the Water

Roger Rosenblatt

Targeted Passage ①

chaotic (kā-ŏt′ĭk) *adj.* extremely confused or disordered

emblemized (ĕm′blə-mīzd′) *adj.* represented; symbolized **emblemize** *v.*

flailing (flā′lĭng) *adj.* waving vigorously **flail** *v.*

A CENTRAL IDEA

Reread lines 15–21. What point is Rosenblatt making about nature and human nature?

As disasters go, this one was terrible, but not unique, certainly not among the worst on the roster of U.S. air crashes. There was the unusual element of the bridge, of course, and the fact that the plane clipped it at a moment of high traffic, one routine thus intersecting another and disrupting both. Then, too, there was the location of the event. Washington, the city of form and regulations, turned **chaotic,** deregulated, by a blast of real winter and a single slap of metal on metal. The jets from Washington National Airport that normally swoop around the presidential monuments like famished gulls are, for the moment, **emblemized** by the one that fell; so there is that detail.

10 And there was the aesthetic clash as well—blue-and-green Air Florida, the name a flying garden, sunk down among gray chunks in a black river. All that was worth noticing, to be sure. Still, there was nothing very special in any of it, except death, which, while always special, does not necessarily bring millions to tears or to attention. Why, then, the shock here?

Perhaps because the nation saw in this disaster something more than a mechanical failure. Perhaps because people saw in it no failure at all, but rather something successful about their makeup. Here, after all, were two forms of nature in collision: the elements and human character. Last Wednesday, the elements, indifferent as ever, brought down Flight 90. And

20 on that same afternoon, human nature—groping and **flailing** in mysteries of its own—rose to the occasion. A

Of the four acknowledged heroes of the event, three are able to account for their behavior. Donald Usher and Eugene Windsor, a park police helicopter team, risked their lives every time they dipped the skids into the water to pick up survivors. On television, side by side in bright blue jumpsuits, they described their courage as all in the line of duty. Lenny Skutnik, a twenty-eight-year-old employee of the Congressional Budget Office, said: "It's something I never thought I would do"—referring to his jumping into the water to drag an injured woman to shore. Skutnik added

30 that "somebody had to go in the water," delivering every hero's line that

376 UNIT 3: NARRATIVE DEVICES

DIFFERENTIATED INSTRUCTION

FOR ENGLISH LANGUAGE LEARNERS

Vocabulary Support Use New Word Analysis to teach these words: *element* (line 2), *section* (line 37), *invested* (line 44), *capacity* (line 47), *relaxed* (line 51), *commenced* (line 66).

 **BEST PRACTICES TOOLKIT**—Transparency New Word Analysis p. E8

FOR STRUGGLING READERS

In combination with the *Audio Anthology CD,* use one or more Targeted Passages (pp. 376, 378) to help students focus on key events,

concepts, and skills. Targeted Passages are also good for English learners.

① Targeted Passage [Lines 2–9]

This passage sets the scene by focusing on unusual details about the airplane crash.

- What is the first "unusual element" that Rosenblatt describes? (line 3)

- For Rosenblatt, what is notable about the crash location in Washington, D.C.? (lines 5–7)

- What mood or atmosphere do these details help create? (lines 6–9)

A park police helicopter pulls two survivors from the Potomac River following the crash of Air Florida Flight 90.

is no less admirable for its repetitions. In fact, nobody had to go into the water. That somebody actually did so is part of the reason this particular tragedy sticks in the mind.

But the person most responsible for the emotional impact of the disaster is the one known at first simply as "the man in the water." (Balding, probably in his fifties, an extravagant mustache.) He was seen clinging with five other survivors to the tail section of the airplane. This man was described by Usher and Windsor as appearing alert and in control. Every time they lowered a lifeline and flotation ring to him, he passed it on to
40 another of the passengers. "In a mass casualty, you'll find people like him," said Windsor. "But I've never seen one with that commitment." When the helicopter came back for him, the man had gone under. His selflessness was one reason the story held national attention; his anonymity another. The fact that he went unidentified invested him with a universal character. For a while he was Everyman, and thus proof (as if one needed it) that no man is ordinary. **C**

Still, he could never have imagined such a capacity in himself. Only minutes before his character was tested, he was sitting in the ordinary plane among the ordinary passengers, dutifully listening to the stewardess telling
50 him to fasten his seat belt and saying something about the "no smoking sign." So our man relaxed with the others, some of whom would owe their lives to him. Perhaps he started to read, or to doze, or to regret some harsh remark made in the office that morning. Then suddenly he knew that the trip would not be ordinary. Like every other person on that flight, he was desperate to live, which makes his final act so stunning. **D**

B GRAMMAR AND STYLE
Reread lines 23–25. Notice how Rosenblatt includes the **appositive phrase**, or **noun phrase,** "a park police helicopter team" to describe concisely who the two men are.

C REFLECTIVE ESSAY
In Rosenblatt's view, why did "the man in the water" give the story greater significance?

D REFLECTIVE ESSAY
Notice how Rosenblatt shifts back in time and assumes the perspective of the man, even though he cannot really know what the man was thinking. What does this perspective add to your impression of the man?

THE MAN IN THE WATER   **377**

THE MAN IN THE WATER   **377**

 **SYNTAX AND DICTION**

Read aloud lines 62–64, with appropriate pacing and emphasis. Then have volunteers read the same lines to demonstrate their understanding of the ideas and drama in the words.

Possible answer: *"that kept our thoughts on him, and which keeps our thoughts on him still" (lines 62–63); "the one making no distinctions", "the other acting wholly on distinctions", "the other acting wholly on distinctions" (lines 68–69)*

REVISIT THE BIG QUESTION

Can ordinary people be **HEROES?**

Discuss In lines 75–80, how is the anonymous man a hero "to those who observed him"? **Possible answer:** *He "gave a lifeline to the people gasping for survival" (lines 78–79). His selfless act assured observers that the possibility of heroism exists in all human beings.*

VOCABULARY   COMMON CORE   L 4

OWN THE WORD

implacable: Point out that the word *implacable* comes from the Latin *im-* or *in-*, meaning "not," and *placable* meaning "easily calmed." Tell students that one synonym for *implacable* is *unyielding.*

SELECTION WRAP-UP

READ WITH A PURPOSE Now that students have finished reading the selection, have them identify reasons why a person might risk his or her life for others. **Possible answers:** *work, seeing others in danger, being in the right place at the right time*

⭐ **CRITIQUE** Have students identify which event or statement in the essay they found most meaningful. They should support their choices with evidence from the selection.

Language Coach

Frequently Misused Words Reread lines 57–58. *Affect* is a verb meaning "to influence": *The weather affected her commute. Effect* is a noun meaning "a result": *Jimmy's scolding had no effect on his noisy sister.* How is *effect* used in lines 57–58?

COMMON CORE   RI 4

 **SYNTAX AND DICTION**

Diction refers to the writer's word choice, and **syntax** refers to the arrangement of those words. Writers use diction and syntax—important components of **voice**—to create effects. For example, Rosenblatt uses sentence fragments in line 64 to create drama and emphasis. These fragments slow the reader down and call attention to the ideas they express. The fragments are also **parallel,** with a repeated grammatical structure that adds to the rhythm of the language and shows that the two subjects—man in nature and man in the water—are equal ideas. Where else in this paragraph do you see repeated diction or syntax? What effect does it create?

implacable (ĭm-plăk'ə-bəl) *adj.* impossible to calm or satisfy; relentless

---

For at some moment in the water he must have realized that he would not live if he continued to hand over the rope and ring to others. He *had* to know it, no matter how gradual the effect of the cold. In his judgment he had no choice. When the helicopter took off with what was to be the last survivor, he 60 watched everything in the world move away from him, and he deliberately let it happen.

Yet there was something else about the man that kept our thoughts on him, and which keeps our thoughts on him still. He was *there*, in the essential, classic circumstance. Man in nature. The man in the water. ⑤ For its part, nature cared nothing about the five passengers. Our man, on the other hand, cared totally. So the timeless battle commenced in the Potomac. For as long as that man could last, they went at each other, nature and man: the one making no distinctions of good and evil, acting on no principles, offering no lifelines; the other acting wholly on distinctions, 70 principles, and, one supposes, on faith.

Since it was he who lost the fight, we ought to come again to the conclusion that people are powerless in the world. In reality, we believe the reverse, and it takes the act of the man in the water to remind us of our true feelings in this matter. It is not to say that everyone would have acted as he did, or as Usher, Windsor, and Skutnik. Yet whatever moved these men to challenge death on behalf of their fellows is not peculiar to them. Everyone feels the possibility in himself. That is the abiding wonder of the story. That is why we would not let go of it. If the man in the water gave a lifeline to the people gasping for survival, he was likewise giving a lifeline to those 80 who observed him.

The odd thing is that we do not even really believe that the man in the water lost his fight. "Everything in Nature contains all the powers of Nature," said Emerson. Exactly. So the man in the water had his own natural powers. He could not make ice storms, or freeze the water until it froze the blood. But he could hand life over to a stranger, and that is a power of nature too. The man in the water pitted himself against an **implacable,** impersonal enemy; he fought it with charity; and he held it to a standoff. He was the best we can do.

 **Targeted Passage**

January 25, 1982

DIFFERENTIATED INSTRUCTION

FOR STRUGGLING READERS

 **Targeted Passage** [Lines 81–88]

This passage presents a paradox, or apparent contradiction. Even though the anonymous man died, Rosenblatt says that he didn't lose his fight.

• How does the Emerson quotation apply to the man in the water? (line 83)

• How did the man use his powers? (line 85)

• Why does Rosenblatt say that the man in the water didn't lose his fight? (lines 86–88)

FOR ENGLISH LANGUAGE LEARNERS

Language Coach

Frequently Misused Words *Answer: Rosenblatt means "He had to know it, no matter how gradual the result of the cold."* Have students write sentences using both *effect* and *affect.* **Possible answer:** *The lighting effect was artistic, but the diners complained that it affected their ability to eat.*

Comprehension

1. **Recall** What disaster is described in this essay?

2. **Recall** How did the anonymous man respond to the disaster?

3. **Summarize** What eventually happened to the man in the water?

Text Analysis

4. **Clarify** Rosenblatt defines the struggle between the man and the water in broad terms. What does the struggle represent?

5. **Make Inferences** Why do you think Rosenblatt chose to focus on the anonymous man in the water rather than on one of the other three acknowledged **heroes** of the disaster?

● 6. **Examine Reflective Essay** Reflective essays relate a writer's personal observations to universal ideas. Such essays are loosely structured and may use some of the same narrative techniques that fictional stories do. What would this essay lose without paragraphs 5 and 6 (lines 47–61)? What would it lose without paragraph 7 (lines 62–70) or the final paragraph?

● 7. **Draw Conclusions About the Central Idea** Review the chart you completed as you read. What is the central idea of the essay? Cite evidence to support your answer.

8. **Analyze Tone** A writer's tone is the attitude that he or she takes toward a subject. It can be described in many different ways, including serious, bitter, playful, or sympathetic. In your own words, describe Rosenblatt's tone toward the man in the water. Cite specific words and phrases to explain your thinking.

9. **Evaluate Opinion** Rosenblatt concludes that "we do not even really believe that the man in the water lost his fight [with nature]." Do you agree or disagree with this opinion? Cite evidence to support your answer.

10. **Make Generalizations** Do you think that most people are capable of acting as heroically as the man in the water? Give examples from the essay and real life to support your opinion.

Text Criticism

11. **Critical Interpretations** "For me," Rosenblatt once stated, "the essay is a continuous search for an answer to a question." In your opinion, what question did Rosenblatt set out to answer in "The Man in the Water"? Cite evidence to support your interpretation.

> **Can ordinary people be HEROES?**
>
> What heroic qualities do you have?

COMMON CORE

RI 1 Cite strong and thorough textual evidence to support inferences drawn from the text. **RI 2** Determine a central idea of a text and analyze its development over the course of the text, including how it is shaped by specific details. **RI 4** Analyze the cumulative impact of specific word choices on meaning and tone.

65–66); "he was likewise giving a lifeline to those who observed him" (lines 79–80); and "He was the best we can do" (lines 87–88).

9. *Agree, because he saved other people; disagree, because he drowned in the end.*

10. *Many people are capable of acting heroically, as the examples of Donald Usher, Eugene Windsor, and Lenny Skutnik show. Examples from real life might include heroic actions by the military, police, and firefighters.*

Text Criticism
Possible answer:

11. *He set out to answer the question "Why did the Air Florida disaster have such a profound impact on people?" The body of the essay, focusing on the anonymous man, is an attempt to answer this question.*

> Can ordinary people be
> **HEROES?** Encourage students to not only identify heroic qualities they have but also to discuss *why* they consider these qualities heroic.

Practice and Apply

For preliminary support of post-reading questions, use these copy masters:

R RESOURCE MANAGER—Copy Masters
Reading Check p. 120
Reflective Essay p. 113
Question Support p. 121

Additional selection questions are provided for teachers on page 107.

ANSWERS

Comprehension

1. *Air Florida Flight 90 crashed into the Potomac River in Washington, D.C.*

2. *He gave up his chance to be rescued so that he could save other passengers.*

3. *He slipped under the water and drowned.*

Text Analysis
COMMON CORE RI 1, RI 2, RI 4

Possible answers:

4. *The man represents the best elements of human nature, while the water represents the neutral, indifferent attitude of nature.*

5. *He probably focused on the anonymous man because the man's anonymity made him seem universal (line 44).*

6. ● **COMMON CORE FOCUS** *Reflective Essay* Without paragraphs 5 and 6, the reader might find it hard to connect with the man on a personal or emotional level. Without the last paragraph, the theme of the essay would not be as clear. This paragraph helps the reader appreciate the heroic nature of the man's actions. If the essay didn't have paragraph 7, it would lose some of the drama and rhythm created by Rosenblatt's use of diction and syntax.

7. ● **COMMON CORE FOCUS** *Identify Main Idea and Supporting Details* The main idea is that the selfless heroism of the anonymous man represents all that is best in human nature. Although he died, he did not really lose his battle against the elements. His goal was to save his fellow travelers and in this he triumphed (lines 81–88).

8. *The writer's tone might be described as admiring. Descriptions that support this analysis include "invested him with a universal character" (line 44); "which makes his final act so stunning" (line 55); "Our man, on the other hand, cared totally" (lines*

Vocabulary in Context

▲ VOCABULARY PRACTICE

1. *antonyms*
2. *synonyms*
3. *synonyms*
4. *antonyms*

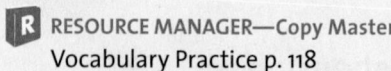 **RESOURCE MANAGER—Copy Master**
Vocabulary Practice p. 118

ACADEMIC VOCABULARY IN SPEAKING

Ask each pair of students to share orally a brief summary of their discussion, including use of one or more Academic Vocabulary words. Challenge students to use one of the words in another context during the day.

VOCABULARY STRATEGY: THE LATIN ROOT *plac*

 **COMMON CORE L 4c**

- Students may profit from working in groups for this activity.
- Before students complete the activity, have them take turns suggesting definitions for the words in the spokes of the web.

Possible answers:

1. *placebo*
2. *placate*
3. *implacable*
4. *placid*

 **RESOURCE MANAGER—Copy Master**
Vocabulary Strategy p. 119

Interactive Vocabulary THINK central

Keywords direct students to a **WordSharp** tutorial on **thinkcentral.com** or to other types of vocabulary practice and review.

Vocabulary in Context

WORD LIST
chaotic
emblemized
flailing
implacable

▲ VOCABULARY PRACTICE

Decide whether the words in each pair are synonyms or antonyms.

1. chaotic/ordered
2. emblemized/symbolized
3. flailing/waving
4. implacable/consolable

ACADEMIC VOCABULARY IN SPEAKING

- consequent • crucial • initial • shift • survive

Part of the significance of the man in the water is that he gave his life to save others. Discuss with a partner how the perspective of this essay would **shift** if the man had **survived** the ordeal. Refer to evidence from the text and use at least one Academic Vocabulary word in your discussion.

VOCABULARY STRATEGY: THE LATIN ROOT *plac*

COMMON CORE

L 4c Consult reference materials to determine or clarify a word's meaning or etymology.

The word *implacable* stems from the Latin root *plac,* which means "to please or soothe." To understand the meaning of words with *plac,* use context clues as well as your knowledge of the root.

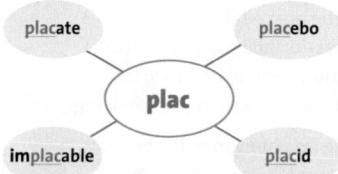

PRACTICE Choose the word from the word web that best completes each sentence. Use context clues to help you, or, if necessary, consult a dictionary.

1. The doctor prescribed a medicine-free _____ pill to satisfy the patient.
2. She gave the crying baby a pacifier to _____ her.
3. His _____ boss was so difficult to please.
4. They lived a _____ , unhurried existence in the mountains.

Interactive Vocabulary THINK central

Go to **thinkcentral.com**.
KEYWORD: HML10-380

DIFFERENTIATED INSTRUCTION

FOR ADVANCED LEARNERS/PRE–AP

Vocabulary in Writing Have students use at least two vocabulary words in a paragraph about a hero, written in Rosenblatt's style.

Language

COMMON CORE

L 1b Use various types of phrases to convey specific meanings and add variety and interest to writing.

◆ **GRAMMAR AND STYLE: Write Concisely**

Review the **Grammar and Style** note on page 377. One way Rosenblatt is able to keep his writing concise is by using appositive phrases. An **appositive** is a noun or pronoun that identifies or renames another noun or pronoun. An **appositive phrase**, or **noun phrase,** is made up of an appositive plus its modifiers. By incorporating appositive phrases into your writing, you can convey information about a person or thing in one sentence. Here are two examples from the essay:

Washington, the city of form and regulations, turned chaotic . . . (lines 5–6)

Lenny Skutnik, a twenty-eight-year-old employee of the Congressional Budget Office, said . . . (lines 26–28)

Notice how the revisions in blue in the student model use appositive phrases to make the writing of this first draft more concise. Use a similar technique to revise your own writing.

> **STUDENT MODEL**
>
> In "The Man in the Water," Roger Rosenblatt writes about the disaster ^, an award winning author and essayist,
>
> that befell Air Florida Flight 90. ^, a passenger jet ~~Roger Rosenblatt is an award winning~~
>
> ~~author and essayist. The plane was a passenger jet.~~ Unlike an objective
>
> news reporter, Rosenblatt assumes the perspective of the man in the
>
> water. ~~That man was~~ an ordinary American hero.

READING-WRITING CONNECTION

YOUR TURN

Increase your understanding of "The Man in the Water" by responding to this prompt. Then use the **revising tip** to improve your writing.

WRITING PROMPT	REVISING TIP
Short Constructed Response: Analysis What do you learn in "The Man in the Water" that you would probably not learn in a news report of the same tragedy? Use what you know about reflective essays and narrative techniques to write a **one- or two-paragraph response.**	Review your response. Have you used **appositive phrases** to make your writing more concise? If not, revise.

Interactive Revision **THINK**central

Go to **thinkcentral.com.**
KEYWORD: HML10-381

FOR STRUGGLING WRITERS

- Help students fill out their diagrams by listing factual details they might expect to find in a news report, such as *who, what, when, where, why,* and *how.*

- Guide students in citing specific details Rosenblatt includes in his essay.

- Help students compare and contrast Rosenblatt's details in the reflective essay with details that might be found in a news report.

Language

◆ **GRAMMAR AND STYLE**

- After students examine the examples and the student model, elicit that appositives and appositive phrases allow a writer to compress two or more sentences into a single sentence. (For more about appositives and appositive phrases, see page R60 in the **GRAMMAR HANDBOOK.**)

- Write this passage on the board. Have students suggest appositives and appositive phrases that would make the passage more concise. (Sample revisions are shown in blue.)

An anonymous man, known simply as "the man in the water," saved five other passengers' lives. ~~He was known simply as "the man in the water."~~

R RESOURCE MANAGER—Copy Master
Write Concisely p. 122

READING-WRITING CONNECTION

- Have students reread the essay to identify specific examples of the elements of a reflective essay. Then have students use a Venn Diagram to compare elements of a news report and a reflective essay.

R BEST PRACTICES TOOLKIT—Transparency
Venn Diagram p. A26

> **THINK** central
>
> **Writing Online**
>
> The following tools are available online at **thinkcentral.com** and on **Write*Smart* CD-ROM:**
> - **Interactive Graphic Organizers**
> - **Interactive Student Models**
> - **Interactive Revision Lessons**
>
> For additional grammar instruction, see **GrammarNotes** on **thinkcentral.com.**

Assess and Reteach

Assess

DIAGNOSTIC AND SELECTION TESTS
Selection Test A, B/C pp. 107–108, 109–110

Interactive Selection Test on **thinkcentral.com**

Reteach

Level Up Online Tutorials on **thinkcentral.com**

Focus and Motivate

COMMON CORE FOCUS

RI 1 Cite textual evidence to support inferences drawn from the text. **RI 2** Determine the central idea of a text and analyze how it emerges and is shaped and refined by specific details. **RI 4** Determine the connotative meaning of words and phrases as they are used in a text.

SUMMARY

In this emotionally charged essay, Joanne Hyppolite describes her childhood after moving with her family from Haiti to Boston. She includes details about the customs and values she experiences in her home, then contrasts them to her life outside as someone growing up as an American. She shows how this combination makes her a "dyaspora child"—disconnected from one place, but not truly connected to another.

Can you be from two CULTURES at once?

Ask the question. Explain that cultural identity is the feeling of identifying with a particular group or culture. After students complete the *DISCUSS* activity, point out that their lists show some of the difficulties they might have leaving their culture to live in a different culture.

Selection Resources

See resources on the **Teacher One Stop DVD-ROM** and on **thinkcentral.com**.

R RESOURCE MANAGER UNIT 3
Plan and Teach, pp. 125–132
Summary, pp. 133–134†‡*
Text Analysis and Reading
  Skill, pp. 135–138†*

DIAGNOSTIC AND SELECTION TESTS
Selection Tests, pp. 111–114

BEST PRACTICES TOOLKIT
Word Squares, p. E10

TECHNOLOGY
- Teacher One Stop DVD-ROM
- Student One Stop DVD-ROM
- Audio Anthology CD
- GrammarNotes DVD-ROM
- ExamView Test Generator on the **Teacher One Stop**

* Resources for Differentiation   † Also in Spanish   ‡ In Haitian Creole and Vietnamese

---

Before Reading

Dyaspora
Essay by Joanne Hyppolite

Can you be from two CULTURES at once?

COMMON CORE

RI 1 Cite textual evidence to support inferences drawn from the text. **RI 2** Determine the central idea of a text and analyze how it emerges and is shaped and refined by specific details. **RI 4** Determine the connotative meaning of words and phrases as they are used in a text.

When asked about cultural identity, many of us simply respond, "I'm an American." For others, however, the matter is not as clear. People who have left their native countries to settle in the United States often feel torn between two cultures. In "Dyaspora," you will read about one woman's struggles to be both Haitian and American.

DISCUSS List the aspects of home that you would miss most if you had to move abroad. Then, share your list with a partner, and discuss how you might adjust to living in a new country.

What I Would Miss Most About Home
1. Family and friends
2. Favorite TV shows
3.
4.
5.

382

TEXT ANALYSIS: SECOND-PERSON POINT OF VIEW

Although writers of nonfiction usually choose to use the first-person or third-person points of view, they sometimes create works that use another, more unusual point of view: **second person.** In this point of view, the writer directly addresses an audience by using the pronouns *you* and *yours.* For example, in "Dyaspora," Joanne Hyppolite remarks:

In your neighborhood when you tell people you are from Haiti, they ask politely, "Where's that?" You explain and because you seem okay to them, Haiti is okay to them.

For readers, the second-person point of view often generates a sense of instant recognition. They may feel as though they know the author and share in the author's experiences. As you read "Dyaspora," think about its point of view and how that view affects you as a reader.

READING SKILL: ANALYZE SENSORY DETAILS

Authors use **imagery**, or **sensory details,** to appeal to one or more of the five senses—sight, hearing, smell, taste, and touch. In the selection, Hyppolite offers an abundance of sensory details to help readers connect to her particular way of life. For example, she allows readers to "hear" the sounds of her home by describing her parents' accents and their favorite Haitian music. To analyze sensory details in the selection, think about

- the sense or senses to which each detail appeals
- the idea or emotion each detail is meant to evoke

As you read "Dyaspora," record sensory details that help you understand Hyppolite's experiences. Use a chart like the one shown here.

Sensory Detail	Sense(s) Appealed to	Idea or Emotion
On Sundays in your house, "Dominika-anik-anik" floats from the speakers of the record player....	Sound	

Review: Make Inferences, Compare and Contrast

 Complete the activities in your **Reader/Writer Notebook.**

Meet the Author

Joanne Hyppolite
born 1969

An Avid Reader
Joanne Hyppolite (ē-pō'lĕt') was born in Haiti but grew up primarily in Boston, Massachusetts. When she was young, she began visiting her local library. Reading ignited her imagination. "I loved disappearing into the world that the writer created," she once stated.

A Bridge Builder
At age 12, Hyppolite was inspired to write a story of her own. Soon hundreds of stories filled her notebooks. She continued to hone her craft while pursuing a bachelor's degree at the University of Pennsylvania. In 1995, Hyppolite published her first book, *Seth and Samona*, a children's story about friendship between a Haitian-American boy and an African-American girl. Today, she continues to write fiction for both children and adults. Through her books, she hopes to "debunk stereotypes" about Haitians and to build bridges between Haitian and American cultures.

BACKGROUND TO THE ESSAY

The Haitian Diaspora
In 1915, American troops invaded Haiti to restore order to a country ravaged by revolutions. When they left in 1934, conditions deteriorated and grew even worse during the dictatorship of François Duvalier (1957–1971). As a result, thousands of Haitians, like Hyppolite's parents, emigrated to other countries, particularly Cuba, the Dominican Republic, and the United States. In recent years, Haitians have fled in even greater numbers because of economic hardship and civil unrest.

Author Online
THINK central
Go to **thinkcentral.com.**
KEYWORD: HML10-383

383

Teach

TEXT ANALYSIS
COMMON CORE
RI 2

● *Model the Skill:* **SECOND-PERSON POINT OF VIEW**

To model how to determine the point of view, read aloud this passage:

> When you are ten and move from America to Japan, you are confused about your identity. You remember enough of your home to feel American. But you are comfortable in Japan too. You wonder which culture is yours.

Point out to students the pronouns that identify the second-person point of view of the passage: "you," "your," "yours".

GUIDED PRACTICE Have students discuss how the effect of the passage might be different if told from a first- or third-person point of view.

READING SKILL
COMMON CORE
RI 4

■ *Model the Skill:* **ANALYZE SENSORY DETAILS**

To model how to analyze sensory details, read aloud this sentence:

> In a crowded American city, the beeping horns; the aroma of food; and the bright, beaming nighttime lights signal that you are home.

Identify a sensory detail, such as "the beeping horns," and discuss with students the sense it appeals to (hearing) and the idea it invokes (noise).

GUIDED PRACTICE Ask students to identify other sensory details in the sentence and the feelings they evoke.

R RESOURCE MANAGER—Copy Master
Analyze Sensory Details p. 137
(for student use while reading the selection)

DIFFERENTIATED INSTRUCTION

FOR STRUGGLING READERS
Reading Skill Support: Sensory Details To help students understand and recognize sensory details, have them work in pairs to write five sentences about their surroundings. Each sentence should include at least one sensory detail. Have pairs exchange their sentences and identify the sensory details, the senses they appeal to, and the ideas the sentences convey.

FOR ADVANCED LEARNERS/PRE–AP
Point of View Challenge students to write a short autobiographical essay about their lives that involves at least one other person. Have them first write the passage using the second-person point of view and then using the third-person omniscient point of view. Break students into small groups to share their essays. Have them discuss how their two versions differed.

READ WITH A PURPOSE

Help students set a purpose for reading. Tell them to look for examples of cultural differences the author experiences daily.

TEXT ANALYSIS   COMMON CORE

Ⓐ Model the Skill: POINT OF VIEW

RI 2

To model how to determine the point of view, reread the first paragraph with students using first-person pronouns. Point out to students how the use of *I* and *me* allows the reader to focus on the narrator's experience. Reread the paragraph again and discuss how the use of *you* draws the reader into the experience.

Possible answer: *The intended audience of this essay is the reader. The author uses the pronoun you so that readers can place themselves in the story and identify with the author's experiences.*

DYASPORA

Joanne Hyppolite

When you are in Haiti they call you *Dyaspora.*[1] This word, which connotes both connection and disconnection, accurately describes your condition as a Haitian American. Disconnected from the physical landscape of the homeland, you don't grow up with a mango tree in your yard, you don't suck *kenèps* in the summer, or sit in the dark listening to stories of *Konpè* Bouki and Malis.[2] The bleat of *vaksins* or the beating of a *Yanvalou* on *Rada* drums are neither in the background or the foreground of your life.[3] Your French is nonexistent. Haiti is not where you live. Ⓐ

Your house in Boston is your island. As the only Haitian family on the
10 hillside street you grow up on, it represents Haiti to you. It was where your *granmè* refused to learn English, where goods like ripe mangoes, plantains, *djondjon,* and hard white blobs of mints come to you in boxes through the mail.[4] At your communion and birthday parties, all of Boston Haiti seems to gather in your house to eat *griyo* and sip *kremas.*[5] It takes forever for you to kiss every cheek, some of them heavy with face powder, some of them damp with perspiration, some of them with scratchy face hair, and some of them giving

Analyze Visuals ▶

What **mood** is suggested by this painting?

Ⓐ POINT OF VIEW
Reread lines 1–8. Who do you think is the intended audience, or the "you," of this essay?

① Targeted Passage

---

1. ***Dyaspora,*** or **diaspora** (dī-ăs'pər-ə): scattered people originally located in one place.
2. **Disconnected . . . and Malis:** Away from Haiti, you don't have a mango tree in your yard, eat Haitian fruits in the summer, or listen to Haitian stories at night.
3. **The bleat . . . your life:** The musical sounds of Haitian horns or drums playing island dances are not part of your life's experiences.
4. **It was . . . the mail:** It was where your grandmother refused to learn English and where you received packages of tropical fruits, vegetables, and mint candies sent from Haiti.
5. ***griyo*** (grē'yō) . . . ***kremas*** (krä'mäs): fried spiced pork and alcoholic drinks made with coconut.

Detail of *Dance* (1996), Francks Deceus. Mixed media on canvas, 76.2 cm x 101.6 cm. © Francks Deceus/Bridgeman Art Library.

DIFFERENTIATED INSTRUCTION

FOR ENGLISH LANGUAGE LEARNERS

Vocabulary Support Use Word Squares to teach these words: *physical* (line 3), *encounter* (line 18), *inevitably* (line 42), *perceptions* (line 113), *status* (line 114).

📦 BEST PRACTICES TOOLKIT—Transparency
Word Squares p. E10

FOR STRUGGLING READERS

In combination with the *Audio Anthology CD,* use one or more Targeted Passages (pp. 384, 388) to ensure that students focus on key events, concepts, and skills. Targeted Passages are also good for English learners.

① Targeted Passage [Lines 1–14]

This passage introduces life as a Haitian American living in Boston.

- How does the author feel about being a Haitian American? (lines 1–3)

- What aspects of her Haitian culture does she
  no longer experience? What aspects does
  she still experience? (lines 4–7; lines 11–14)

- What does she mean by "Your house in Boston is your island"? (line 9)

READING SKILL

B Model the Skill: SENSORY DETAILS

To model how to understand sensory details, draw the Reading Skill chart from page 383 on the board. Point out sensory details in lines 13–18, such as "heavy with face powder" and "perfume" in lines 15 and 17, and enter these details in the chart. Then ask students to identify other details, as well as the senses the details appeal to and the emotions or ideas the details evoke.

Possible answer: *The sensory details that convey Hyppolite's discomfort include "heavy with face powder" (line 15), "damp with perspiration" (lines 15–16), "scratchy face hair" (line 16), and "perfume head-rush" (line 17).*

READING SKILL

C SENSORY DETAILS

Possible answer: *The unfamiliarity of the Haitian terms helps readers share the differences between the world most of them know and the world Hyppolite is describing. Words such as "Bien-être" (line 46) and "Kreyòl" (line 47) help readers recognize the French roots of Haiti and hear the dialect that Hyppolite hears in her home.*

REVISIT THE BIG QUESTION

Can you be from two
CULTURES at once?

Discuss In lines 22–44, how do the author's house and family life reflect her cultural identity? **Possible answer:** *Her family listens to Haitian music (line 23) and eats Haitian food (lines 32–35). Family members have two names (line 28), and the house is decorated as it would be in Haiti (line 36). The family discusses and follows Haitian culture and politics (lines 40–44).*

---

you a perfume head-rush as you swoop in. You are grateful for every smooth, dry cheek you encounter. In your house, the dreaded *matinèt*[6] which your parents imported from Haiti just to keep you, your brother, and your sister
20 in line sits threateningly on top of the wardrobe. It is where your mother's *andeyò Kreyòl*[7] accent and your father's *lavil*[8] French accent make sometimes beautiful, sometimes terrible music together. On Sundays in your house, "Dominika-anik-anik" floats from the speakers of the record player early in the morning and you are made to put on one of your frilly dresses, your matching lace-edged socks, and black shoes. Your mother ties long ribbons into a bow at the root of each braid. She warns you, your brother and your sister to "respect your heads" as you drive to St. Angela's, never missing a Sunday service in fourteen years. In your island house, everyone has two names. The name they were given and the nickname they have been granted so that your mother is
30 Gisou, your father is Popo, your brother is Claudy, your sister is Tinou, you are Jojo, and your grandmother is Manchoun. Every day your mother serves rice and beans and you methodically pick out all the beans because you don't like *pwa*.[9] You think they are ugly and why does all the rice have to have beans anyway? Even with the white rice or the *mayi moulen*,[10] your mother makes *sòs pwa*—bean sauce. You develop the idea that Haitians are obsessed with beans. In your house there is a mortar and a pestle as well as five pictures of Jesus, your parents drink Café Bustelo[11] every morning, your father wears *gwayabèl* shirts . . . , and you are punished when you don't get good grades at school. You learn about the behavior of husbands from conversations your aunts have.
40 You are dragged to Haitian plays, Haitian *bals,* and Haitian concerts where in spite of yourself *konpa* rhythms make you sway. You know the names of Haitian presidents and military leaders because political discussions inevitably erupt whenever there are more than three Haitian men together in the same place. Every time you are sick, your mother rubs you down with a foul-smelling liquid that she keeps in an old Barbancourt rum bottle under her bed. You splash yourself with Bien-être[12] after every bath. Your parents speak to you in *Kreyòl,* you respond in English, and somehow this works and feels natural. But when your mother speaks English, things seem to go wrong. She makes no distinction between he and she, and you become the pronoun police. Every
50 day you get a visit from some *matant* or *monnonk* or *kouzen* who is also a *marenn* or *parenn* of someone in the house.[13] In your house, your grandmother

COMMON CORE RI 4

Language Coach

Denotation/Connotation
The images or feelings connected to a word are the word's **connotations**. Reread line 35. The word *obsessed* means "to think about excessively, be haunted by." What effect does the use of this word have on the tone of the selection?

---

6. **matinèt** (mä′tē-nĕt′): a small whip.

7. **andeyò Kreyòl** (än′dā-yō′ krā-yōl′): country Creole, a language spoken by Haitians, based on French and various African languages.

8. **lavil** (lä-vēl′): city.

9. **pwa** (pwä): beans.

10. **mayi moulen** (mä′yē mōō′lĕn): milled or ground corn.

11. **Café Bustelo** (kä-fā′ bōō-stā′lō): a brand of Cuban coffee.

12. **Bien-être** (byŏn-ĕt′rə): a French brand of perfumed bath products.

13. **Every day . . . the house:** Every day, you have aunts, uncles, or cousins visit.

DIFFERENTIATED INSTRUCTION

FOR STRUGGLING READERS

Comprehension Support Explain to students that "respect your heads" (lines 26–27) means to respect your teachers. When the author refers to being the "pronoun police" (line 49), she is saying that she feels that she must correct her mother's grammar.

Develop Reading Fluency Use the notes at the bottom of the page to model correct pronunciations for students.

FOR ENGLISH LANGUAGE LEARNERS

Language Coach COMMON CORE RI 4
Denotation/Connotation
Possible answer: *It gives the selection a bemused, humorous tone.* Explain to students that the meaning or feeling of the sentences would change if *happen* replaced *erupt* in line 43 and *tied* replaced *lassoed* in line 57.

has a porcelain *kivèt* she keeps under her bed to relieve herself at night. You pore over photograph albums where there are pictures of you going to school in Haiti, in the yard in Haiti, under the white Christmas tree in Haiti, and you marvel because you do not remember anything that you see. You do not remember Haiti because you left there too young but it does not matter because it is as if Haiti has lassoed your house with an invisible rope. **D**

60 Outside of your house, you are forced to sink or swim in American waters. For you this means an Irish-Catholic school and a Black-American neighborhood. The school is a choice made by your parents who strongly believe in a private Catholic education anyway, not paying any mind to the busing crisis that is raging in the city. The choice of neighborhood is a condition of the reality of living here in this city with its racially segregated neighborhoods. Before you lived here, white people owned this hillside street. After you and others who looked like you came, they gradually disappeared to other places, leaving you this place and calling it bad because you and others like you live there now. As any *dyaspora* child knows, Haitian parents are not familiar with these waters. They say things to you like, "In Haiti we

70 never treated white people badly." They don't know about racism. They don't know about the latest styles and fashions and give your brother grief every time he sneaks out to a friend's house and gets his hair cut into a shag, a high-top, a fade. They don't know that the ribbons in your hair, the gold loops in your ears, and the lace that edges your socks alert other children to your difference. So you wait until you get to school before taking them all off and out and you put them back on at the end of your street where the bus drops you off. Outside your house, things are black and white. You are black and white. Especially in your school where neither you nor any of the few other Haitian girls in your class are invited to the birthday parties of the white kids in your

80 class. You cleave to these other Haitian girls out of something that begins as solidarity but becomes a lifetime of friendship. You make green hats in art class every St. Patrick's day and watch Irish step-dancing shows year after year after year. You discover books and reading and this is what you do when you take the bus home, just you and your white schoolmates. You lose your accent. You study about the Indians in social studies but you do not study about Black Americans except in music class where you are forced to sing Negro spirituals as a concession to your presence. They don't know anything about Toussaint Louverture[14] or Jean-Jacques Dessalines.[15] **E**

In your neighborhood when you tell people you are from Haiti, they ask

90 politely, "Where's that?" You explain and because you seem okay to them, Haiti is okay to them. They shout "Hi, Grunny!" whenever they see your

---

D MAKE INFERENCES
What can you infer so far about Hyppolite and how she feels about being a Haitian American?

E COMPARE AND CONTRAST
Reread lines 59–88. Compare Hyppolite's Haitian values and her American experiences. How do you know that she is struggling to belong to both cultures?

---

14. **Toussaint Louverture (1743—1803)** (tōō-sā' lōō-vĕr-tōōr'): a black general who struggled for Haitian independence.
15. **Jean-Jacques Dessalines (1758—1806)** (zhô-zhôk dĕ'sä-lēṅ): African-born emperor of Haiti who defeated the French in 1803 to win independence for the island.

DYASPORA **387**

TIERED DISCUSSION PROMPTS

Direct students to lines 59–103. Use these prompts to help students understand Hyppolite's difficult situation:

Connect Have you ever felt that you did not really belong to a group that you had to spend time with? How would you describe this experience? *Students should identify relevant personal experiences.*

Analyze What does the author mean when she says, "You are black and white" (line 77)? *Possible answer:* Hyppolite is trying to live as both a white person and a black person. Her school is predominantly white, her neighborhood is African American, and her family experiences are predominantly Haitian.

Evaluate Do you think the transition from inside her home to outside—from family to school, for example—was more difficult than Hyppolite makes it sound? Explain. *Possible answers:* Yes, Hyppolite says she is "forced to sink or swim in American waters" (lines 59–60). Though she says that "You get so you can jump between worlds with the same ease that you slide on your nightgown" (lines 101–103), it probably wasn't very easy.

FOR ENGLISH LANGUAGE LEARNERS

Vocabulary: Idioms Discuss the meanings of these idioms with students: *You are dragged* (line 40), "you are forced"; *forced to sink or swim* (line 59), "you are forced to fail or succeed"; *paying any mind to* (line 62), "paying attention to"; *familiar with these waters* (line 69), "knowledgeable of these situations"; *give [your brother] grief* (line 71), "give a difficult time." Have pairs create sentences with each idiom.

FOR ADVANCED LEARNERS/PRE–AP

Research [small-group option] Have students reread lines 85–88 and discuss how Hyppolite feels about her studies. Ask students what changes could be made to her curriculum to make it more relevant. Have small groups research this idea and make suggestions for new studies. For example, students may suggest studying particular Haitian-American writers or leaders, and they may suggest learning about important African-American history as well.

DYASPORA **387**

READING SKILL

F SENSORY DETAILS

Possible answer: Hyppolite translates
sentences between her grandmother and
a neighbor (lines 92–93). She tastes and is
familiar with "sweet potato pie" (line 93),
and she learns to "jump double-dutch" and
"dance the puppet and the white boy" (lines
95–96). She can "jump between worlds
with . . . ease" (line 102) now.

READING SKILL: *Review*

G MAKE INFERENCES

Possible answer: The high school students
now think that they know about Haiti.
However, their image of Haiti is stereotypical—it's where people "have tuberculosis" (line 108) and "eat cats" (line 109).
Her schoolmates think she is an "aberration" (line 110) because she looks and talks
like them. They essentially ignore the
Haitian part of her and do not change their
opinions of her homeland.

SELECTION WRAP–UP

READ WITH A PURPOSE Now that students
have finished reading the selection, have them
compare Hyppolite's cultural experiences with
those of her mother. Why were their experiences different? *Possible answer: Hyppolite
functioned in English during the school day,
where she mixed with girls of other races and
backgrounds. Her mother was more isolated
and did not speak English well.*

★ CRITIQUE Ask students whether they think
Hyppolite effectively shows how difficult it
is for many children to adapt to two cultures
while holding onto both.

INDEPENDENT READING

Students interested in reading more about
acculturation might enjoy *Red Hot Salsa:
Bilingual Poems on Being Young and Latino in
the United States* by Lori Marie Carlson. Featured writers include Gary Soto, Gina Valdés,
and Martín Espada.

---

grandmother on the stoop and sometimes you translate a sentence or two
between them. In their houses, you eat sweet potato pie and nod because you
have that too, it's made a little different and you call it *pen patat* but it's the
same taste after all. From the girls on the street you learn to jump double-
dutch,[16] you learn to dance the puppet and the white boy. You see a woman
preacher for the first time in your life at their church. You wonder where down
South is because that is where most of the boys and girls on your block go for
vacations. You learn about boys . . . through these girls because this subject is
100 not allowed in your island/house. You keep your street friends separate from
your school friends and this is how it works and you are used to it. You get
so you can jump between worlds with the same ease that you slide on your
nightgown every evening. F

Then when you get to high school, things change. People in your high
school and your neighborhood look at you and say, "You are Haitian?" and
from the surprise in their voice you realize that they know where Haiti is
now. They think they know what Haiti is now. Haiti is the boat people on
the news every night. Haiti is where people have tuberculosis. Haiti is where
people eat cats. You do not represent Haiti at all to them anymore. You are
110 an aberration because you look like them and you talk like them. They do
not see you. They do not see the worlds that have made you. You want to say
to them that you are Haiti, too. Your house is Haiti, too, and what does that
do to their perceptions? You have the choice of passing but you don't. You
claim your *dyaspora* status hoping it will force them to expand their image
of what Haiti is but it doesn't. Your sister who is younger and very sensitive
begins to deny that she is Haitian. She is American, she says. American. G

You turn to books to lose yourself. You read stories about people from other
places. You read stories about people from here. You read stories about people
from other places who now live here. You decide you will become a writer.
120 Through your writing they will see you, *dyaspora* child, the connections and
disconnections that have made you the mosaic that you are. They will see
where you are from and the worlds that have made you. They will see you. ∾

F SENSORY DETAILS

Which sensory details
tell you that Hyppolite is
feeling more comfortable
as a Haitian American?

 Targeted Passage

G MAKE INFERENCES

Why do people begin
to treat Hyppolite
differently?

---

16. **double-dutch:** a jump-rope game involving two ropes.

DIFFERENTIATED INSTRUCTION

FOR STRUGGLING READERS

 Targeted Passage [Lines 104–122]

This passage shows how difficult it is for Hyppolite to be a Haitian American and how she
intends to deal with that difficulty.

- Why does Hyppolite not represent Haiti to
her schoolmates? (lines 107–109)

- Why does Hyppolite choose to tell others
she is Haitian American? Why does her sister deny her ethnicity? (line 114–115; 115–116)

- What makes Hyppolite decide to
become a writer? (lines 120–122)

FOR ENGLISH LANGUAGE LEARNERS

Vocabulary: Multiple-Meaning Words
Direct students to the words *serves* (line 31),
natural (line 47), *slide* (line 102), and *mosaic*
(line 121). Have pairs use diction-aries to
determine the meaning of each word that
best fits the context of the sentence. Have
volunteers read the meanings they chose.
Discuss the meanings as a group.

Comprehension

1. **Recall** What does *dyaspora* mean?

2. **Summarize** Describe the ways in which Hyppolite's home reflects the values and customs of her native country.

3. **Clarify** What decision does Hyppolite make at the end of the essay?

Text Analysis

● 4. **Examine Point of View** Consider how the second-person point of view of this essay affects you as a reader. Does Hyppolite's use of *you* and *yours* help you to relate to her unusual experiences? Cite evidence from the essay to support your answer.

● 5. **Analyze Sensory Details** Review the chart you created as you read. Of the images and sensory details you recorded, which ones were most effective in conveying Hyppolite's Haitian heritage? Explain your response.

6. **Compare and Contrast** In Hyppolite's experience, what are the similarities and differences between Haitian and American cultures? Use a graphic organizer like the one shown to record details from the essay.

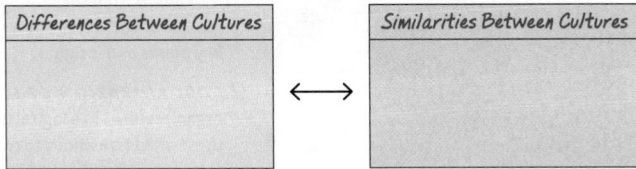

Differences Between Cultures		Similarities Between Cultures
	⟷	

7. **Make Inferences** How does Hyppolite's attitude toward her own cultural identity change during the course of the essay? Support your answer with specific details.

8. **Evaluate** Hyppolite concludes, "Through your writing they will see you, *dyaspora* child, the connections and disconnections that have made you the mosaic that you are." Evaluate Hyppolite's essay. Does it succeed in conveying the "mosaic" quality of immigrant life in America? Cite evidence from the essay to support your response.

Text Criticism

9. **Social Context** What does Hyppolite say about the way Americans perceive Haiti and Haitian Americans? Cite evidence to support your claim.

Can you be from two CULTURES at once?
How do you define your cultural identity?

COMMON CORE

RI 1 Cite textual evidence to support inferences drawn from the text. **RI 2** Determine the central idea of a text and analyze how it emerges and is shaped and refined by specific details.

DYASPORA **389**

Practice and Apply

For preliminary support of post-reading questions, use these copy masters:

R RESOURCE MANAGER—Copy Masters
Reading Check p. 139
Second-Person Point of View p. 135
Question Support p. 140

Additional selection questions are provided for teachers on page 129.

ANSWERS

Comprehension

1. Dyaspora *means "scattered people who initially lived in one place."*

2. *eats Haitian food, listens to Haitian music, hears Kreyòl; values family*

3. *Hyppolite decides to become a writer.*

Text Analysis
COMMON CORE RI 1, RI 2
Possible answers:

4. ● COMMON CORE FOCUS *Examine Point of View* Use of "your" house (lines 9–39) and "your" school (lines 75–88) places readers into situations Hyppolite describes.

5. ■ COMMON CORE FOCUS *Analyze Sensory Details* These details convey the sounds of Hyppolite's heritage: "andeyò Kreyòl" (line 21), "Dominika-anik-anik" (line 23), and "konpa rhythms" (line 41).

6. *Differences: language; school curriculum; fashion Similarities: value education; eat some similar foods (line 93)*

7. *She tries to be more American by removing her ribbons, gold earrings, and lace-edged socks before school and by losing her accent (lines 59–88). In high school, she claims her Haitian identity and tries to represent Haiti to her classmates (lines 112–122).*

Assess and Reteach

Assess
DIAGNOSTIC AND SELECTION TESTS
Selection Test A, B/C pp. 111–112, 113–114

Interactive Selection Test on **thinkcentral.com**

Reteach
Level Up Online Tutorials on **thinkcentral.com**

Reteaching Worksheets on **thinkcentral.com**
Literature Lesson 10, Reading Lesson 12

---

8. *Hyppolite's essay conveys the "mosaic" quality of immigrant life in America. She provides readers with a glimpse inside her home—the food, the sounds, the "foul-smelling liquid" in the "old Barbancourt rum bottle" (lines 44–45). They have also been able to see her at school, "study[ing] about the Indians" (lines 81–85) and in her neighborhood, translating her grandmother's words and learning to jump rope (lines 91–96).*

Text Criticism
Possible answer:

9. *Hyppolite says that Americans view Haitians in a stereotypical manner (lines 104–116).*

Can you be from two CULTURES at once?
Encourage students to discuss not only their cultural identities but also the factors they use to define these identities.

Focus and Motivate

COMMON CORE FOCUS

W 2a–f Write informative/explanatory texts to examine complex ideas clearly and accurately through the effective selection, organization, and analysis of content. **W 4** Produce clear and coherent writing. **W 5** Develop and strengthen writing as needed by planning, revising, editing, rewriting, or trying a new approach. **W 9b (RI 1, 4)** Draw evidence from literary nonfiction to support analysis. **W 10** Write routinely over shorter time frames for a range of tasks, purposes, and audiences. **L 1b** Use various types of clauses to convey specific meanings and add variety and interest. **L 2** Demonstrate command of the conventions of standard English capitalization, punctuation, and spelling.

WRITE WITH A PURPOSE

Remind students that their purpose is to share a well-reasoned analysis of literary nonfiction with an audience.

COMMON CORE TRAITS

Review the *COMMON CORE TRAITS* with students, concentrating on development of ideas and organization of ideas. Compare the list of traits with the rubric on page 398.

ADDITIONAL TASKS

Write About a Television Ad Write an analysis of a television ad, describing the ad's images and sound and explaining how these elements affect its message.
Possible subjects: health, new technology

Write About Fine Art Choose an abstract work of art and write an analysis of it.

Writing Online

The following tools are available online at **thinkcentral.com** and on **WriteSmart** CD-ROM:
• Interactive Graphic Organizers
• Interactive Student Models
• Interactive Revision Lessons

Writing Workshop
INFORMATIVE TEXT

Essential Course of Study **ECOS**

Analysis of Literary Nonfiction

The nonfiction texts in this unit are personal essays, reflecting each author's thoughts or feelings about an experience. To analyze an essay, or determine its deeper meaning, you examine how the author uses stylistic elements to help you connect with an experience. In this workshop, you will learn how to write an analysis of literary nonfiction that examines the effects of an author's choices.

Complete the workshop activities in your **Reader/Writer Notebook**.

WRITE WITH A PURPOSE

WRITING TASK

Write a **literary analysis** of an essay. In your response, analyze the author's use of stylistic elements and their effects, using quotations and other evidence from the essay to support your ideas and convey your understanding of the essay's meaning to your audience.

Idea Starters
• the effect of a particular point of view used in an essay
• the use of complex sentences in the essay "The Man in the Water" by Roger Rosenblatt
• the effect of sensory language in the essay "Dyaspora" by Joanne Hyppolite

THE ESSENTIALS

Here are some common purposes, audiences, and formats for literary analysis.

PURPOSES	AUDIENCES	FORMATS
• to examine complex ideas and concepts in an essay • to effectively convey your analysis of an essay to others	• classmates and teacher • readers of a literary magazine • Web users	• essay for class • literary journal • oral presentation • blog • podcast script

COMMON CORE TRAITS

1. DEVELOPMENT OF IDEAS
• presents an **engaging introduction**
• develops a **controlling idea** that offers an **analysis** of the author's style
• supports key points of analysis with **relevant details** and **quotations from the text**
• concludes with a **summary of key points** and **insights**

2. ORGANIZATION OF IDEAS
• **organizes** ideas in a logical way
• uses varied **transitions** to create **cohesion** and **connect ideas**

3. LANGUAGE FACILITY AND CONVENTIONS
• establishes and maintains a **formal style** and **objective tone**
• includes **precise language** and **domain-specific vocabulary**
• uses **commas** correctly
• employs correct **grammar, mechanics,** and **spelling**

Writing Online THINK central
Go to **thinkcentral.com**.
KEYWORD: HML10N-390

Writing Workshop Resources

 RESOURCE MANAGER UNIT 3
Plan and Teach, pp. 141–144
Prewriting–Editing, pp. 145–149
Writing Rubric, p. 150
Speaking and Listening p. 151
Writing Support, p. 152*

 BEST PRACTICES TOOLKIT
Writing Template: Literary Analysis pp. C16, C30

TECHNOLOGY
⊘ **Teacher One Stop DVD-ROM**
⊘ **Student One Stop DVD-ROM**
⊘ **WriteSmart CD-ROM**
⊘ **GrammarNotes DVD-ROM**
Writing Center on thinkcentral.com

See resources on the **Teacher One Stop DVD-ROM** *and on* **thinkcentral.com**.

* Resources for Differentiation

Planning/Prewriting

 COMMON CORE **W 2a–f** Write informative/explanatory texts to examine complex ideas clearly and accurately through the effective selection, organization, and analysis of content. **W 5** Develop and strengthen writing as needed by planning.

Getting Started

CHOOSE AN ESSAY

Reread essays that have interested you. Consider what each essay means to you. Think about the **stylistic elements**—techniques such as word choice, point of view, and sensory language—that are used in each essay and their **effect**.

▶ **ASK YOURSELF:**
- What is the meaning of the experience described in this essay?
- What stylistic elements does the author use, and what is their effect on my understanding of the meaning of the essay?

THINK ABOUT AUDIENCE AND PURPOSE

As you begin to analyze the essay you have selected, keep in mind that your **purpose** is to consider the author's use of stylistic elements and to convey your understanding of the author's meaning to your **audience.** Your audience is likely to include people who have read the essay and have their own ideas about its meaning.

▶ **ASK YOURSELF:**
- Who is my audience? Are they familiar with this essay? Why might they be interested in an analysis of this essay?
- What ideas might my audience have about the meaning of this essay?
- What insights do I have to share with my audience?
- What **domain-specific,** or specialized, **vocabulary** might I need to explain to my audience?

GATHER DETAILS

Read the essay a second or third time. Look for **stylistic elements** that the author uses. List the elements you identify and record your ideas about their **effects** in a chart.

▶ **WHAT DOES IT LOOK LIKE?**

"Dyaspora"

Stylistic Element	Effect
second-person point of view	readers "become" the author
juxtaposition of you and they	highlights cultural differences, how it feels to be outsider
sensory language	help readers connect with author's experience and her thoughts and feelings

WRITE A CONTROLLING IDEA

Review your chart and examine how the author's use of stylistic elements creates meaning. Write a **controlling idea** that explains the effect of these elements.

▶ **WHAT DOES IT LOOK LIKE?**

Controlling Idea: Joanne Hyppolite uses various stylistic elements in "Dyaspora" to help readers understand her experience as a Haitian American.

DIFFERENTIATED INSTRUCTION

FOR ENGLISH LANGUAGE LEARNERS

Language: Reinforce Literary Analysis Terms Write these terms on the board and review them with students:

- *organization:* how ideas are arranged and presented in an essay. Writers can organize ideas in different ways.

- *tone:* an expression of the writer's attitude toward a subject. The tone of a work might be playful or serious. Writers communicate tone through their choices of words and details.

- *point of view:* refers to the method of narration used in a short story, novel, narrative poem, or work of nonfiction. In a work told from a first-person point of view, the narrator is a character in the story or essay. In a work told from a third-person point of view, the narrator is outside the action, not one of the characters.

- *sensory language:* words and phrases that appeal to one or more of the five senses. Sensory language tells how things look, sound, smell, taste, and feel.

Teach

Planning/ Prewriting

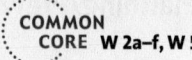 **COMMON CORE** **W 2a–f, W 5**

▶ **CHOOSE AN ESSAY** Remind students that in order to write an effective literary analysis of an essay, they need to choose an essay that interests or fascinates them. Advise students to reread their chosen essays, highlighting or marking examples of stylistic elements that they might use in their analyses.

▶ **THINK ABOUT AUDIENCE AND PURPOSE** Explain to students the importance of focusing on their audience. Point out that all members of their audience may not have read their chosen essay, and those who have read it may have analyzed it differently. Encourage students to provide background information to help the audience understand their analyses.

▶ **GATHER DETAILS** Explain that rereading the essay will help students identify the author's use of stylistic elements. Review with students the examples listed in the chart, and discuss the effect of each element.

▶ **WRITE A CONTROLLING IDEA** Explain that the controlling idea sums up the overall point of the analysis—how the author uses stylistic elements to create meaning—and helps the audience understand the rest of the analysis. The controlling idea may be a single sentence or longer, but it should identify the element or elements that the writer will focus upon and suggest why readers might care about them. Read the sample controlling idea on page 391 aloud to students, and discuss how it effectively tells readers what the rest of the analysis will be about.

R **RESOURCE MANAGER—Copy Masters**
Planning/Prewriting p. 145
Drafting p. 146
Revising pp. 147–148
Editing p. 149
Rubric p. 150
Writing Support p. 152

Planning/Prewriting *continued*

▶ **COLLECT EVIDENCE** Explain to students that they will need to include details from the essay in their literary analyses. At times, students may summarize information in order to help the audience understand a particular stylistic element. At other times, students may use direct quotations and examples. Remind students that the various kinds of support also include paraphrased lines or short passages and details such as images, actions, and dialogue. Remind students to choose evidence that best supports their controlling ideas.

▶ **ORGANIZE YOUR IDEAS** Explain that key points are the main ideas or insights that students want to include in their literary analyses. Point out the structure in the sample outline on page 392. Explain to students that in the sample, *A, B,* and *C* are the key points—examples of stylistic elements—and the numbers are the supporting evidence for each point. Suggest that students use an outline such as this to organize key points and supporting evidence for their literary analyses.

 YOUR TURN Give students time to choose an essay, gather details, form a controlling idea, gather evidence, and organize their selected ideas into outlines. Have students reread the essays they have chosen for analysis and find additional evidence independently.

For interactive graphic organizers, see

🖸 **Write*Smart* CD-ROM**

Writing Center on thinkcentral.com

Planning/Prewriting *continued*

Getting Started

COLLECT EVIDENCE

Next, gather relevant evidence to sufficiently develop your controlling idea. Make sure each piece of evidence you choose supports your explanation of the author's use of stylistic elements.

- **quotations:** words, phrases, and sentences taken directly from the essay
- **concrete details:** specific examples from the essay
- **summaries:** important ideas from the essay summed up in your own words

Elaborate on, or explain, how the evidence supports your controlling idea.

▶ **WHAT DOES IT LOOK LIKE?**

Stylistic Element: Juxtaposition

Evidence		
Quotation	Detail	Summary
"When you are in Haiti they call you Dyaspora"	In the neighborhood in Boston, "they" are people who are not from Haiti.	You and they draw attention to differences the author experiences at home, in her neighborhood, and at school.

Elaboration/Explanation The author combines and contrasts the pronouns you and they to highlight her experience as an outsider.

ORGANIZE YOUR IDEAS

Use an outline to organize your **key points** and supporting **evidence** in a **logical structure.** To determine the order in which you will present your key points, think about which stylistic element is most important. Then, emphasize that point by placing it last in your discussion.

▶ **WHAT DOES IT LOOK LIKE?**

Introduction and controlling idea
A. Second-person point of view
  1. "When you are in Haiti they call you Dyaspora."
  2. Ends essay with word you
B. Juxtaposition
  1. You/they at home, in neighborhood, at school
  2. "They" = people in neighborhood not from Haiti
C. Sensory language
  1. "heavy with face powder," "damp with perspiration," "scratchy face hair," "a perfume head-rush"
  2. smell nasty liquid for rubdowns when ill

PEER REVIEW Share with a peer who has read the essay the evidence you have collected to support your key points. Ask your peer to identify which key points need more support.

 YOUR TURN In your *Reader/Writer Notebook*, develop your writing plan. Record a working version of your controlling idea. Then, use a chart like the one at the top of this page to organize your key points and evidence. Consider the following tips as you gather evidence:

- Collect supporting evidence about stylistic elements.
- Double-check any quotations you plan to use to support your controlling idea. Record the exact words from the text and enclose them in quotation marks.
- If you have trouble finding supporting evidence for a stylistic element, consider reworking or trying a new approach to your controlling idea.

392 UNIT 3: NARRATIVE DEVICES

DIFFERENTIATED INSTRUCTION

FOR STRUGGLING WRITERS

Organization Have students use this outline to help them organize their evidence:

Controlling idea and key points

  A. My first piece of evidence is _____.
    1. A key point is _____.
    2. A key point is _____.
  B. My second piece of evidence is _____.
    1. A key point is _____.
    2. A key point is _____.

Drafting

Use this chart to organize your literary analysis.

COMMON CORE

W 4 Produce clear and coherent writing. **W 9b (RI 1, 4)** Cite textual evidence; determine the meaning of words and phrases as they are used in the text. **L 1b** Use various types of clauses to convey specific meanings and add variety and interest.

Organizing Your Literary Analysis

INTRODUCTION

- Engage your **audience** by relating the meaning of the essay to experiences people share.
- Give the **author's name** and the **title** of the essay.
- Explain your **controlling idea** clearly, identifying the overarching effect of a stylistic element.

▼

BODY

- Discuss one **key point** per paragraph. Use clear, coherent, and **precise language** to convey the complexity of the essay. Use appropriate and varied **transitions** between paragraphs to keep the essay flowing.
- Use a variety of **evidence—quotations, concrete details,** and **facts**. If necessary, define any **domain-specific vocabulary.**
- Maintain a **formal style** and **objective tone** by avoiding contractions and using unbiased, clear language.

▼

CONCLUDING SECTION

- Summarize your **key points** and reflect on their overall **meaning.**
- End with a **concluding statement** that follows from and supports your controlling idea.

GRAMMAR IN CONTEXT: RESTRICTIVE AND NONRESTRICTIVE CLAUSES

You can use restrictive and nonrestrictive relative clauses to add details. A **restrictive clause** contains information necessary to the meaning of a sentence. A **nonrestrictive clause** contains information that adds to but does not change the sentence's basic meaning. For example, you need more information to understand who the writer of this sentence means by *people*:

> The author says people call her <u>Dyaspora</u>.

The writer could provide that information by adding the restrictive clause *who live in Haiti.*

> The author says people **who live in Haiti** call her <u>Dyaspora</u>.

The clause *who live in Haiti* is restrictive because without it the sentence means *all* people call the author *Dyaspora*. The clause restricts, or limits, the meaning of *people* to *people who live in Haiti.*

To provide information that adds variety or interest, but that is not essential to the meaning of the sentence, the writer might add a nonrestrictive clause to the sentence:

> The author says people who live in Haiti call her <u>Dyaspora</u>, **which is a term for scattered people originally located in one place.**

YOUR TURN

Develop a first draft of your analysis. Use restrictive and nonrestrictive clauses correctly to add details or background information to your sentences.

FOR ENGLISH LANGUAGE LEARNERS

Restrictive and Nonrestrictive Clauses Remind students that a restrictive clause contains information necessary to the meaning of a sentence. A nonrestrictive clause contains information that adds to but does not change the sentence's basic meaning. Have students identify whether the underlined clauses in the following sentences are restrictive or nonrestrictive.

My neighbor, <u>whom I have known for ten years</u>, is going to help me plant a garden. *(nonrestrictive)*

My neighbor and I are going to plant a vegetable garden <u>for his elderly father</u>. *(restrictive)*

Have students practice composing sentences with restrictive and nonrestrictive clauses.

Practice and Apply

Drafting

COMMON CORE W 4, W 9b (RI 1, 4), L 1b

▶ **INTRODUCTION** Tell students to look at the Student Draft on page 395 for an example of an engaging introduction that states a clear controlling idea. Remind students that their introductions should identify the effect of the evidence they will discuss in their analyses.

▶ **BODY** Help students consider these additional organizational methods for their literary analyses:

- **Order of Importance** Key points are arranged in order either from least important to most important, or from most to least

- **Order of Impression** Key points are arranged in order from most obvious to least obvious, or from least obvious to most obvious.

Remind students to support key points with strong evidence from the literary text.

▶ **CONCLUDING SECTION** Stress that students should close with more than a summary. Suggest that they ask themselves, "Why does this matter to my readers?"

GRAMMAR IN CONTEXT: RESTRICTIVE AND NONRESTRICTIVE CLAUSES

For additional practice, have students rewrite the following sentences using restrictive clauses.

- The author says people in Boston eat *griyo* and sip *kremas*. *[People from Haiti who live in Boston eat* griyo *and sip* kremas.*]*

- The author says parents do not think white people were treated badly. *[The author says Haitian parents do not think white people were treated badly in Haiti.]*

YOUR TURN

Ask students to complete the **Your Turn** activity independently. Remind students to add details by including restrictive and nonrestrictive clauses in their analyses. Suggest that students write their drafts double-spaced so that they can make revisions more easily later.

For a literary analysis writing template, see

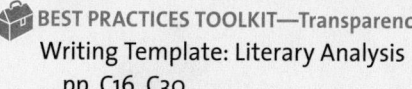 **BEST PRACTICES TOOLKIT—Transparency** Writing Template: Literary Analysis pp. C16, C30

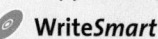 **WriteSmart CD-ROM**

Writing Center on thinkcentral.com

Revising

COMMON CORE W 5

Model the Skill Using a draft literary analysis on a transparency, model how to use the questions, tips, and strategies suggested in the chart to evaluate and revise. You might use the literary analysis of a student from another class or from last year. Be sure to remove the student's name from the literary analysis so that he or she is anonymous.

YOUR TURN Suggest that students, after reading their partners' drafts, take one minute to freewrite a response that explains why they feel the draft does or does not include a clear controlling idea and supporting key points. Then allow students a few minutes to share their responses with one another. Remind students to begin by making a positive comment about the draft, followed by a clear suggestion on how their partners can strengthen the controlling idea with additional evidence.

For interactive revision tools, see

💿 **Write*Smart* CD-ROM**

Writing Center on thinkcentral.com

Revising

When you revise, determine whether you've achieved your purpose and effectively communicated your ideas to your intended audience. The questions, tips, and strategies in the chart below can help you revise, rewrite, and improve your draft.

LITERARY ANALYSIS

Ask Yourself	Tips	Revision Strategies
1. Does the introduction grab the audience's interest?	**Put a star** by sentences that get the audience interested.	**Add** an interesting opening sentence.
2. Does the introduction present a clear and coherent controlling idea about the author's use of stylistic elements?	**Bracket** the controlling idea. **Put a check mark** next to each stylistic element.	**Rewrite** your controlling idea to include consideration of the author's use of stylistic elements.
3. Does the body include a paragraph for each key point? Do transitions clarify relationships among ideas? Is the order of key points logical?	**Draw a wavy line** below key points. **Highlight** transitional words. **Number** your key points in order of importance.	**Create** a separate paragraph for each key point. **Add** transitions to connect ideas. **Rearrange** the key points so that the most important point is discussed last.
4. Is each key point supported by well-chosen and sufficient evidence, such as quotations and concrete details?	**Circle** each piece of evidence. **Draw an arrow** from each item to the point it supports.	**Add** quotations and other evidence to support your key points. **Rearrange** evidence so that it is in the paragraph containing the point it supports.
5. Does the essay discuss the effects of stylistic elements?	**Write an E** next to discussion of the effect of each stylistic element.	**Add** a sentence or two to explain the effect of each element.
6. Does the concluding section summarize key points and follow from and support the ideas in the essay?	**Underline** the summary of key points and their meaning.	**Add** a summary of your key points and a sentence or two about their meaning.

YOUR TURN ***PEER REVIEW*** Exchange your essay with a partner, or read it aloud to your partner. As you read, focus on the controlling idea, supporting evidence, and organization. Discuss whether the key points are clear, and provide concrete suggestions for improvement.

DIFFERENTIATED INSTRUCTION

FOR ENGLISH LANGUAGE LEARNERS

Writing: Concluding Section Provide students with sentence frames such as these to help them develop their concluding section:

- My controlling idea is _____.
- My key points are _____, _____, and _____.
- I want the audience to question/think about _____.

FOR STRUGGLING WRITERS

Writing: Quotations Have students practice punctuating words, phrases, and sentences that are direct quotations. Remind students that periods go inside closing quotation marks. Have students complete the punctuation in these sentences from the student model:

- Sensory language include relatives' cheeks "heavy with face powder" and "damp with perspiration(.")
- We can say that we "see where you are from and the worlds that have made you(.")

ANALYZE A STUDENT DRAFT

Read this draft; note comments on its strengths and suggestions for improvement.

COMMON CORE — W 5 Develop and strengthen writing as needed by revising, editing, rewriting, or trying a new approach.

Be Me, See Me
by David Wong, Connally High School

1 Does anyone know what it's like to be me? It's a question that comes to mind when you're struggling in a difficult situation. It's a question Joanne Hyppolite asks in her essay "Dyaspora" about her own experience as a Haitian American. Hyppolite became a writer to share that experience. In "Dyaspora," she uses stylistic elements to help others understand what it's like to be her.

2 First, where readers might expect a first-person or third-person point of view, Hyppolite makes an unusual choice. Her choice of the second-person point of view draws readers directly into her experience. "When you are in Haiti they call you *Dyaspora*," she says in the first sentence. Through the pronoun *you,* we identify with Hyppolite right away. You could say we "become" her. We experience what she has experienced. "Your house in Boston is your island," she says. "Outside of your house, you are forced to sink or swim in American waters," she explains later. Hyppolite uses the second-person point of view for the entire essay ending it with the word *you.*

3 The author also uses juxtaposition effectively to help readers understand her experience. By combining the contrasting pronouns *you* and *they* she highlights her experience as an outsider. She uses the element in the essay's first sentence to describe herself as an outsider in Haiti. Later, the juxtaposition of *you* and *they* draws attention to differences the author experiences at home, in her neighborhood, and at school.

> The **introduction** opens with a question to grab the audience's interest and helps readers connect with the topic of the essay. The **controlling idea** of the essay is explained in clear and coherent language.

> David devotes a paragraph to each **key point** and provides evidence to support it.

> David needs to cite a greater *variety of evidence* to support his point about juxtaposition.

LEARN HOW Use a Variety of Evidence The writer presents his key point about juxtaposition and **summarizes** information from the text as supporting evidence. He could strengthen his point by including **quotations** and **concrete details.**

DAVID'S REVISION TO PARAGRAPH 3

Later, the juxtaposition of *you* and *they* draws attention to differences the author experiences at home, in her neighborhood, and at school. *"They" are Haitian immigrant parents, like Hyppolite's own. "They" are parents who "don't know that the ribbons in your hair, the gold loops in your ears, and the lace that edges your socks alert other children to your difference." "They" are people in the neighborhood who are not from Haiti.*

ANALYZE A STUDENT DRAFT

Explain that the Student Draft on this page is the first half of a literary analysis. Model reading the draft and the annotations in blue, and explain that the yellow highlighting illustrates evidence the student cites to support his analysis. Explain that the following *Learn How* mini-lessons hold helpful information about ways to improve this student draft as well as their own.

LEARN HOW Use a Variety of Evidence

- Tell students that quotations are evidence that is taken directly from the literary text. Quotations support the student's analysis.
- Ask students to think about whether the student writer's addition of quotations and examples is effective and to explain their responses.
- Have students identify places in their drafts where they can add direct quotations to support a point.

FOR ADVANCED LEARNERS/PRE–AP

Synthesize Ideas Have students look for a quotation that unifies the core ideas in the literary work. The quotation might exemplify the theme, demonstrate something about a character, provide a lesson for real life, or be crucial in some other way. The introduction should make a statement about the quotation, and the body of the essay should provide evidence to support the statement.

Explain that the Student Draft is continued and completed on this page. Read the draft and annotations aloud and discuss. Ask students to comment on the student writer's use of transitions and sensory language.

LEARN HOW Summarize Key Points

- Explain that a common mistake students make when writing literary analyses is not summarizing their key points.
- Point out that the sentences the student writer added clearly summarize his key points and controlling idea.
- Have students check to make sure their concluding sections include statements for further thought and summarize their key points.

YOUR TURN Ask students to complete the **Your Turn** activity independently. Remind students to find places in their literary analyses where they should include additional evidence or summaries of key points to support their controlling ideas.

For interactive revision tools, see

📀 **Write***Smart* **CD-ROM**

Writing Center on thinkcentral.com

ANALYZE A STUDENT DRAFT *continued*

❹ Finally, the author includes sensory language to help readers connect with her. These details convey smells, sounds, and sights familiar to the author. They take us to family celebrations where we kiss relatives' cheeks "heavy with face powder," "damp with perspiration," covered "with scratchy face hair," and offering "a perfume head-rush." We hear the melody "Dominika-anik-anik" floating through the house on Sunday mornings. We listen in on the private conversations of aunts and the men's explosive political discussions. We smell the nasty liquid the author's mother keeps in an old rum bottle under the bed for rubdowns when the author is sick. These details not only help us share in the author's experiences. They also help us think and feel what the author thinks and feels about her experiences.

❺ In the end, we can tell the author that we understand her experience as a *Dyaspora* better after reading her essay. We can say that we "see where you are from and the worlds that have made you."

> The writer uses **transitions** effectively to move from one paragraph to the next. The transitional word *finally* signals the last point in his discussion.

> After providing evidence of the use of sensory language, the writer explains the **effect** of this **stylistic element** on the reader.

> The **concluding section** discusses the meaning of the information in the essay, but the writer forgets to summarize key points for his audience.

LEARN HOW Summarize Key Points To bring his essay to a close, the writer needs to summarize its key points and controlling idea.

DAVID'S REVISION TO PARAGRAPH ❺

In the end, we can tell the author that we understand her experience as a *Dyaspora* better after reading her essay.

In "Dyaspora," Joanne Hyppolite combines the stylistic elements of point of view, juxtaposition, and sensory language to create a vivid picture of her experiences. These elements help us "be" her, and so "see" her.

 YOUR TURN

PEER REVIEW Use the feedback from your peers and teacher as well as the two "Learn How" lessons to revise, edit, rewrite, or try a new approach to your essay as needed.

DIFFERENTIATED INSTRUCTION

FOR ENGLISH LANGUAGE LEARNERS

Comprehension: Transitions Point out that the transitions that appear in the student model are only a few of many possibilities. Discuss transitions that link ideas within sentences, such as *and*, and within paragraphs, such as *later*. Next, identify the transitions that link paragraphs to each other, such as *First* and *Finally*. Have students suggest other transitions that could be used in the student model.

To provide English learners with additional writing support, see

R RESOURCE MANAGER—Copy Master
Writing Support p. 152

Editing and Publishing

 COMMON CORE **W 5** Develop and strengthen writing as needed by editing. **L 2** Demonstrate command of the conventions of standard English capitalization, punctuation, and spelling.

In the editing stage, proofread your essay to make sure it is free of grammar, usage, spelling, and punctuation errors. Careless mistakes in the mechanics of writing can distract your audience from your ideas about the meaning of the essay.

GRAMMAR IN CONTEXT: COMMAS IN NONRESTRICTIVE PHRASES AND CLAUSES

To provide details and background information, writers use a variety of phrases and clauses. The presence or absence of commas tells the reader how the phrase or clause relates to the main ideas of the sentence. Commas are not used to set off restrictive phrases or clauses because the information they contain is needed to complete the main idea of the sentence. Examine these examples from the draft:

> We hear the melody "Dominika-anik-anik" floating through the house on Sunday mornings.
>
> [restrictive phrase: *floating through the house on Sunday mornings*]

> We smell the nasty liquid the author's mother keeps in an old rum bottle under the bed for rubdowns when the author is sick.
>
> [restrictive clause: *when the author is sick*]

Nonrestrictive phrases and clauses, on the other hand, need commas. The commas signal that the information contained in nonrestrictive phrases and clauses can be left out without affecting the meaning of the sentence.

When the writer proofread his draft, he identified and corrected these examples of a nonrestrictive phrase and clause by adding commas:

> Hyppolite uses the second-person point of view for the entire essay, ending it with the word you.

> They take us to family celebrations, where we kiss relatives' cheeks "heavy with face powder," "damp with perspiration," covered "with scratchy face hair," and offering "a perfume head-rush."

PUBLISH YOUR WRITING

Finally, you will share your literary analysis with an audience. Here are some options:

- Submit your essay to the school literary magazine.
- Publish your essay on a Web site for fans of the author's work.
- Adapt your essay into an oral presentation and deliver it to an audience that has read the essay.

 YOUR TURN Proofread your essay for errors. Make sure that commas are used to set off nonrestrictive phrases and clauses. Then, publish your final essay.

FOR STRUGGLING WRITERS

Commas in Nonrestrictive Phrases and Clauses Help students determine whether they have inserted commas correctly in the nonrestrictive phrases and clauses in their literary analyses. Have them review the examples in the Grammar in Context box on page 397. Then tell students to review their own work and ask themselves whether information in a sentence is necessary to the meaning of the sentence (restrictive clause) or whether the information could be left out without changing the meaning (nonrestrictive clause). Remind students that nonrestrictive phrases and clauses need commas.

Editing and Publishing

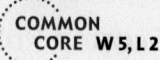 **COMMON CORE W 5, L 2**

GRAMMAR IN CONTEXT: COMMAS IN NONRESTRICTIVE PHRASES AND CLAUSES

Remind students that a *restrictive clause* contains information necessary to the meaning of a sentence. A *nonrestrictive clause* contains information that adds to but does not change the sentence's basic meaning. Nonrestrictive clauses use commas. Remind students that restrictive clauses do not use commas because the information they contain is needed to complete the main idea of the sentence. For practice, have students identify if commas are needed in the following sentences.

1. They call you *Dyaspora* when you are in Haiti. *(no)*
2. They show us the *matinèt* which is used to keep children in line. *(yes, to set off the nonrestrictive clause beginning with* which)
3. We hear the Haitian music which makes us sway with its *konpa* rhythms. *(yes, to set off the nonrestrictive clause beginning with* which)

PUBLISH YOUR WRITING

Brainstorm with students about additional ways to publish their literary analyses.

YOUR TURN Allow students time to proofread their drafts. Remind them to pay close attention to the use of restrictive and nonrestrictive clauses. Also remind students to offer evidence to support key points, use transition words, and craft effective concluding sections.

Scoring Rubric

Tell students that the best way to understand a scoring rubric is to use it to score actual writing. Provide the class with copies of a student's literary analysis with the student's name removed. Work as a class to evaluate the literary analysis by using the scoring rubric. Have students score the analysis and write a brief paragraph using the language of the scoring guide to explain the reasons for their score.

For Rubric Bank, see

📀 **WriteSmart CD-ROM**

Writing Center on thinkcentral.com

Assess and Reteach

Assess

R RESOURCE MANAGER—Copy Master
Rubric for Evaluation p. 150

Online Essay Scoring on thinkcentral.com

Reteach

Level Up Online Tutorials on thinkcentral.com

Reteaching Worksheets on thinkcentral.com

Writing Lesson 12: Patterns of Paragraph Organization

Writing Lesson 23: Elaborate with Incidents, Examples, and Quotations

Scoring Rubric

Use the rubric below to evaluate your literary analysis from the Writing Workshop or your response to the on-demand task on the next page.

LITERARY ANALYSIS

SCORE	COMMON CORE TRAITS
6	• **Development** Has an engaging introduction; includes a controlling idea with an insightful analysis of the author's style; supports key points with relevant evidence; ends powerfully • **Organization** Arranges ideas in an effective, logical order; uses varied transitions to create cohesion and link ideas • **Language** Consistently maintains a formal style; uses precise language; shows a strong command of conventions
5	• **Development** Has an effective introduction; provides a controlling idea that offers an original analysis of the author's style; supports key points with evidence; has a strong concluding section • **Organization** Arranges ideas logically; uses transitions to link ideas • **Language** Maintains a formal style; uses precise language; has a few errors in conventions
4	• **Development** Has an introduction that could be more engaging; includes a controlling idea that states an analysis of the author's style; could use some more evidence; has an adequate concluding section • **Organization** Arranges ideas logically; could vary transitions more • **Language** Mostly maintains a formal style; needs more precise language at times; has a few distracting errors in conventions
3	• **Development** Has an adequate, though not memorable, introduction; has a controlling idea that makes an obvious statement about the author's style; lacks sufficient support; has a routine concluding section • **Organization** Reflects some flaws in organization; needs more transitions to link related ideas • **Language** Frequently lapses into an informal style; uses some vague word choices; has some significant errors in conventions
2	• **Development** Has a weak introduction and a controlling idea that does not relate to the writing task; lacks specific evidence; has a weak concluding section • **Organization** Has organizational flaws; lacks transitions throughout • **Language** Uses an informal style and vague language; has many distracting errors in conventions
1	• **Development** Has no introduction or controlling idea; offers unrelated points as evidence; ends abruptly • **Organization** Includes a string of disconnected ideas with no overall organization • **Language** Uses an inappropriate style and vague, tired language; has major problems with grammar, mechanics, and spelling

Preparing for Timed Writing

COMMON CORE · **W 10** Write routinely over shorter time frames for a range of tasks, purposes, and audiences.

1. ANALYZE THE TASK · 5 MIN

Read the task carefully. Then, read it again, noting the words that tell the type of writing, the topic, the purpose, and the audience.

> **WRITING TASK**
>
> "Whatever you do will be insignificant, but it is very important that you do it."
>
> *Type of writing* ↘   ↙ *Topic*   ↙ *Audience* —Mahatma Gandhi
>
> Write a <u>literary analysis</u> of <u>this quotation</u> for <u>your peers</u> by <u>explaining what it means to you and offering specific examples or experiences from your life that illustrate the idea it expresses.</u>
>
>   ↑ *Purpose*

2. PLAN YOUR RESPONSE · 10 MIN

First, paraphrase the quotation by stating it in your own words. Next, list stylistic elements that make the quotation powerful, and make a few notes about their effect on the meaning of the quotation. Then, list examples or experiences from your life that support or explain your analysis of the quotation.

> Paraphrase:
> _____
> Stylistic Elements:
> Effect on Meaning:
> _____
> Example #1:
> Example #2:

3. RESPOND TO THE TASK · 20 MIN

Begin drafting your analysis. Follow these tips:

- Open with an observation or anecdote that will grab the attention of your audience. State your controlling idea about the meaning of the quotation.
- In the body, discuss how stylistic elements make the quotation powerful. Present examples from your own life that support the controlling idea.
- In the concluding section, reflect on the meaning of the quotation and close with an insightful comment.

4. IMPROVE YOUR RESPONSE · 5–10 MIN

Revising Check your draft against the task. Does your draft analyze the quotation? Do you discuss how stylistic elements make the quotation powerful? Do you provide examples or experiences from your own life to support your analysis? Do you conclude with an insight based on the quotation?

Proofreading Find and correct errors in grammar, usage, and spelling. Make sure your edits are neatly written and legible.

Checking Your Final Copy Examine your response again to make sure that you have not missed any errors.

DIFFERENTIATED INSTRUCTION

FOR STRUGGLING WRITERS

Organization To help students organize their ideas in order of importance, provide the following framework.

Beginning Paragraph

- Identify the questions.
- State your controlling idea.

Middle Paragraphs

- Give the least important key idea.
  - —Provide evidence from the text.
  - —Connect the evidence and key idea.
- Give the next most important key idea.
  - —Provide evidence from the text.
  - —Connect the evidence and key idea.
- Give the most important key idea.
  - —Provide evidence from the text.
  - —Connect the evidence and key idea.

End Paragraph

- Summarize the key points.
- Explain why they matter.

COMMON CORE FOCUS

W 10 Write routinely over shorter time frames for a range of tasks, purposes, and audiences.

Preparing for Timed Writing

1. **Analyze the Task** Before students begin writing, encourage them to answer the following questions:
   - What is my time limit?
   - What are the core traits assessed in the scoring rubric?
   - Who is my audience?
   - What is my purpose?

2. **Plan Your Response** Point out to students that the scoring rubric emphasizes the importance of using quotations, examples, and summaries to elaborate on key points. Remind students to use proper punctuation when citing direct quotations.

3. **Respond to the Task** Remind students to focus consistently on a clear controlling idea. Encourage them to use specific examples, summaries, and quotations that support their controlling ideas.

4. **Improve Your Response** Point out that the scoring rubric emphasizes using effective organizational strategies. Remind students to use transitions to ensure a smooth and clear writing style.

Assess

Use the Scoring Rubric on page 398 to assess each student's analysis.

Focus and Motivate

SL 1d Respond thoughtfully to diverse perspectives and summarize points of agreement and disagreement. **SL 4** Present information, findings, and supporting evidence clearly, concisely, and logically.

SPEAK WITH A PURPOSE

Tell students that even though they may not speak in public on a regular basis, public speaking skills will give them confidence to share their analyses with others. Point out that the qualities of a good speaker, such as confidence and poise, can be achieved through practice and hard work.

COMMON CORE TRAITS

As students prepare to deliver their speeches, remind them to keep in mind the *COMMON CORE TRAITS* of a strong oral presentation.

Practice and Apply

Adapting Your Essay

Model the Skill: ORGANIZATION

Students may need additional help developing an introduction for their oral presentations that helps the audience focus on the controlling idea. Provide students with this sample opening introductory question for a presentation about immigration: "What challenges do immigrants face when they move to a new country?" Then model how to begin adapting this question for use in an oral presentation. You might suggest answering the opening question with evidence from the selection, such as quotations from the author.

GUIDED PRACTICE Have students work in pairs to adapt their literary analyses into oral presentations. Suggest that students find quotations from quotation collections or online resources to include in their introductions.

R RESOURCE MANAGER—Copy Master
Speaking and Listening p. 151

Speaking & Listening Workshop

Presenting a Literary Analysis
Essential Course of Study **ECOS**

When you watch a TV program that profiles someone, the techniques used to tell the story—interviews, video clips, still photos, narration, and soundtrack—can help you connect with the person's experiences. When you tell a friend about it, you explain how the storytelling elements helped make the person's life meaningful to you. Your personal response to the program is similar in many ways to an **oral presentation of your analysis** of an essay.

*Complete the workshop activities in your **Reader/Writer Notebook.***

SPEAK WITH A PURPOSE	*COMMON CORE TRAITS*
TASK Adapt your literary analysis into an **oral presentation.** Practice your presentation, and then deliver it to an appropriate audience who has read the essay.	**A STRONG ORAL PRESENTATION . . .** • focuses on a clear controlling idea • has a logical structure • offers compelling ideas and includes supporting evidence • includes language that is appropriate to the audience and task

COMMON CORE

SL 1d Respond thoughtfully to diverse perspectives and summarize points of agreement and disagreement. **SL 4** Present information, findings, and supporting evidence clearly, concisely, and logically.

Speaking & Listening Online

Go to **thinkcentral.com**.
KEYWORD: HML10-400

Adapting Your Essay

Your audience will be listening to your analysis rather than reading it, so you will have to present your reasoning and evidence in a way that listeners can follow. Here are some suggestions:

• **Organization** On note cards, make notes for each part of your presentation: your introduction; each key idea and its supporting evidence; and your concluding section. Arrange the note cards for key ideas in order of importance. Consider opening with a question, personal observation, or a quotation from the essay. Elaborate on your key ideas to make them easier for your listeners to understand. Copy quotations you plan to use word-for-word as they appear in the essay. Explain the context of any quotations, examples, or summaries that you share from the text. Use transitions to connect ideas. Close with a comment that shows your appreciation of the effects the author created in the essay and its meaning.

Key Idea 1
Second-person point of view
Quote: "When you are in Haiti they call you Dyaspora"
We "become" her.

• **Cueing** Add delivery cues to your note cards. Underline words in your controlling idea and quotations that you want to emphasize. Include dashes for pauses.

DIFFERENTIATED INSTRUCTION

FOR ENGLISH LANGUAGE LEARNERS
Language: Reinforce Oral Presentation Terms Explain to students that an oral presentation has the same goal as writing a literary analysis—to present an analysis of an essay and support it with evidence from the text. Review key terms used in the Writing Workshop and in this workshop:

• *audience:* the people who will hear the oral presentation, such as classmates and the teacher

• *evidence:* summaries, quotations, and examples used to support key ideas

• *organization:* how ideas are arranged and presented. An oral presentation has an introduction, key ideas supported by evidence, and a concluding section.

Delivering Your Presentation

MAKE THE CONNECTION

Both the structure and the delivery of your oral presentation should support your controlling idea and help you achieve your purpose. When you deliver your presentation, use verbal and nonverbal techniques to help your listeners connect with you and what you are saying. Practice the techniques below as you rehearse your presentation. Then, use them to deliver your response.

Verbal	Nonverbal
Speaking Rate Vary the pace, or speed, of your delivery. Use a faster pace in your introduction. Speak more slowly for effect as you elaborate on key ideas.	**Eye Contact** Make frequent eye contact with your audience. Look at different individuals as you make different points.
Enunciation Speak clearly so that everyone can understand exactly what you say. Take care to begin and end each word distinctly.	**Gestures** Use natural hand and arm gestures to emphasize key ideas, to invite your audience to agree with you, or to get or regain their attention.
Language Conventions Adopt a tone that is appropriate for your audience. Use a conversational tone when speaking to classmates or other people your age. Avoid slang and colloquialisms in more formal settings.	**Facial Expressions** Vary your facial expressions to hold the interest of your listeners and to convey meaning. Smile, frown, or raise your eyebrows as appropriate.

As a Speaker Practice presenting your response to a group of friends or family members, using appropriate verbal and nonverbal techniques. Ask for feedback, and apply it to your presentation.

As a Listener Evaluate a classmate's presentation using these points:
- Clearly states and keeps focus on a controlling idea
- Follows a logical structure that helps achieve the purpose of the presentation and makes the speaker's meaning clear
- Makes convincing points and includes supporting evidence
- Uses pace, volume, enunciation, eye contact, facial expressions, gestures, and language conventions effectively
- Demonstrates a speaking style that is appropriate to the purpose of the presentation and aids the audience in understanding its meaning

Provide feedback to your classmates by responding thoughtfully to the different perspectives they have to offer. As you discuss the presentation with your classmates, sum up points of agreement and disagreement. When there is disagreement, justify your own view, but also be willing to consider the views of others.

401

FOR STRUGGLING STUDENTS

Deliver Your Oral Presentation Some students may prepare good presentations but have trouble with delivery. Pair these students with students who have strong speaking skills. Have the partners deliver the presentations to the writers. This approach will help writers see how they might include more verbal and nonverbal techniques and strategies to improve their delivery.

Delivering Your Presentation

Model the Skill: MAKE THE CONNECTION

Point out to students that they automatically modify their speech and gestures in everyday conversation. Have a conversation with a volunteer, and model for students how the pace and tone of speech changes with the subject matter and emotions of the conversation.

GUIDED PRACTICE Have students work in pairs to adapt their literary analyses into oral presentations.

 YOUR TURN Have students exchange drafts of their presentations. Instruct partners or groups to use sticky notes to mark places where the audience could have a greater connection with the speaker if the speaker were to use more verbal or nonverbal techniques. Then have pairs deliver their presentations, incorporating the feedback they received.

Assess and Reteach

Assess

Use the *COMMON CORE TRAITS* to assess students' presentation. A strong oral presentation:
- focuses on a clear controlling idea
- has a logical structure
- offers compelling ideas and includes supporting evidence
- includes language that is appropriate to the audience and task

Reteach

Some students may have trouble making convincing points that are supported by evidence from the essay. Have students work with a partner to first identify the key points they want to share with the audience. Then have partners revisit the literary analysis and identify and mark places where evidence can be used to support each key point.

Speaking and Listening Online
- Public speaking tips
- Strategies for effective listening

Assessment Practice

COMMON CORE FOCUS

RL1 Cite textual evidence to support inferences drawn from the text. **RL3** Analyze how complex characters develop, interact with others, and advance the plot. **RI1** Cite textual evidence to support analysis of what the text says explicitly as well as inferences drawn from the text. **RI2** Determine a central idea of a text; provide an objective summary. **W5** Strengthen writing by revising and editing. **L4** Use context as a clue to the meaning of a word. **L6** Acquire and use accurately general and academic words sufficient for reading; demonstrate independence in gathering vocabulary knowledge.

CHECK READINESS

Read aloud the paragraph under **ASSESS** and stress to students that this is not the full Unit Test, but a way for them to check their readiness for it. Then have students examine the skills standards listed under **REVIEW** and look back in the unit or in the **Student Resource Bank** for any skills they need to review.

READ THE TEXTS

Remind students to keep unit goals in mind as they read each passage, paying particular attention to these literary and reading skills:

- point of view
- draw conclusions
- support an opinion

To help students focus on point of view while reading, encourage them to ask questions such as

- Who is telling the story "Babysitting Helen"?
- What relationship does the narrator have with Audra Thomas?

ANSWER THE QUESTIONS

Direct students to pages R93–R101 of the **Handbook** to review test-taking strategies.

Remind students to read through all the choices, eliminate any that are clearly wrong, and then choose the *best* answer.

ASSESS
Taking this practice test will help you assess your knowledge of these skills and determine your readiness for the Unit Test.

REVIEW
After you take the practice test, your teacher can help you identify any standards you need to review.

COMMON CORE

RL1 Cite textual evidence to support inferences drawn from the text. **RL3** Analyze how complex characters develop, interact with others, and advance the plot. **RI1** Cite textual evidence to support analysis of what the text says explicitly as well as inferences drawn from the text. **RI2** Determine a central idea of a text; provide an objective summary. **W5** Strengthen writing by revising and editing. **L4** Use context as a clue to the meaning of a word. **L6** Acquire and use accurately general academic words sufficient for reading; demonstrate independence in gathering vocabulary knowledge.

Practice Test
THINK central
Take it at **thinkcentral.com**.
KEYWORD: HML10N-402

Assessment Practice

DIRECTIONS Read the two selections and the flier. Then, answer the questions that follow.

Babysitting Helen   *by Kathy Stinson*

1   It wasn't till Trish was talking on the phone to Gavin about their plan for Saturday that her mother told her she would be baby-sitting that night. Trish covered the mouthpiece. "I can't, Mom. I'm going out with Gavin."

2   "I already said you'd do it."

3   "Without even asking me?"

4   "Barb Stanley needs someone to stay with Helen for a few hours."

5   "Gavin, can I call you back? Yeah, love you too, bye." Trish picked her books up from the counter and hugged them to her chest. "You said I would babysit Barb's *mother*? That weird old lady who came for lunch and kept going 'Isn't that marvelous?' every time she made the wooden gull flap its wings?"

6   "It's just for a few hours. Barb said Helen will probably sleep the whole time. And Trish," her mother argued, "you do see Gavin every day."

7   Trish stomped upstairs to her room. Didn't mothers know anything about *love*?

....

8   Trish shoved her homework and a couple of tapes into her knapsack, just in case Gavin wasn't home when she called him from Helen's. She threw on her coat and flung her knapsack over her shoulder.

9   Helen was awake when Trish arrived. She was watching TV. Four brightly colored barrettes—pink and red rabbits—were stuck haphazardly into her wispy white hair. Her brown sweater was on inside out.

10   Barb ushered Trish into the kitchen. "Mom had a longer nap than usual this afternoon," she said. "She wanted to make a cake this morning. I guess it tired her out. I'm sorry," Barb explained, "but with the long nap . . ."

11   "Does she know who I am?" Trish interrupted. "Won't she think it's kind of weird having a babysitter?"

12   "I'm afraid Mom doesn't know who many people are any more," Barb said. "And you can just tell her you came over to watch TV."

13   Trish shook her head. "What's with the barrettes?"

14   "My granddaughter left them here last weekend." Barb scribbled a phone number on a pad by the phone. "And for some reason, Mom has decided there's going to be a party tonight. So, just play along, okay? She'll get tired soon without anything actually happening." As she slipped out the back door Barb added, "Don't let her out of your sight for more than a few minutes, eh? She gets into things."

402   UNIT 3: NARRATIVE DEVICES

DIFFERENTIATED INSTRUCTION

FOR ENGLISH LANGUAGE LEARNERS
Assessment Practice: Work Backward
Prepare students by having them read the questions *before* reading the passages. Have pairs find unfamiliar words in test directions and questions and follow these steps:

1. Write each word on an index card.

2. Look up the meaning in a dictionary and write it on the back of the card.

3. Use the cards to practice the words with your partner and to teach them to others.

Culture: Clarify Explain to students that in many cultures, it is an honor to care for elderly relatives. In countries throughout the world, family units live together in one house or in several houses clustered together. Families that practice this way of living are able to care for one another throughout each stage of life.

15   Right.

16   "Thank you for coming, Trish."

17   In the living room Helen was fixed on the TV. Trish sat down where she'd be able to watch them both. Crayons and old-fashioned stickers were scattered over the coffee table. Barb must have dug them out of some old box for the granddaughter's visit last weekend, Trish figured. And that must be her, the granddaughter—the little girl in the photo on the piano.

18   "Are you here for the party?" Helen said.

19   "Um, yeah."

20   "Your outfit is lovely."

21   Trish glanced down at her jeans and the old sweatshirt she only wore when she knew she wouldn't run into anybody that mattered. "Thanks. Um. You look lovely too."

22   Helen laughed. She was a tiny woman but her laugh came from deep inside and went on and on. Trish wondered what she'd said that was so funny.

23   "Would you just look at that!" Trish followed Helen's gaze to the TV, where a mechanical pink rabbit was marching across the screen beating a drum. "Isn't that the darndest thing?"

24   For the next fifteen minutes Trish and Helen watched "Golden Girls". Helen sat quietly through the funniest bits and laughed when nothing funny was happening at all. She seemed to like the commercials better than the show, and when the battery bunny started across the screen with his drum again, Helen laughed and exclaimed, "Would you just look at that! Isn't that the darndest thing?"

25   Trish pretended to laugh along at the boring rabbit with its ability to keep on going and going and going.

26   When the rabbit stopped, Helen got up and looked out the window. "Where is everyone?"

27   "Barb just went out for a little while," Trish said. "She'll be back soon. Why don't you come watch the rest of your show?" Or better yet, she thought, why don't you go to bed so I can call Gavin?

28   "Where do you live?" Helen demanded to know. Before Trish could answer, Helen said, "You live in the bottom of our garden, don't you?"

29   "Well actually," Trish said, "I live up the street. You know the Carters? They're my parents."

30   "At the bottom of our garden," Helen said. "That's just what I thought." Then she wandered away in the direction of the kitchen.

31   Trish could hear canisters being moved around on the counter and the scraping of a chair across the tiled floor. Don't leave her alone, Barb had said.

 GO ON

ITEM ANALYSIS

COMPREHENSION AND WRITTEN RESPONSE	ITEMS	UNIT PAGES
Point of View	2, 16	302–307, 309, 343, 383
Chronological Order	12, 14	302–307, 325, 355
Symbol	6	373
Draw Conclusions	1, 3, 5, 7, 8, 9, 10, 11, 17, 18, 19	325
Synthesize Ideas and Support an Opinion	20–22	336, 339

VOCABULARY	ITEMS	UNIT PAGES
Word Meanings	4, 13, 15	335

WRITING AND GRAMMAR	ITEMS	UNIT PAGES
Simile	1	373
Appositive Phrases	2	381
Sentence Structure	3–6	323

Practice Test

On **thinkcentral.com** students can complete an interactive version of this practice test *and* receive remediation for the skills they have not yet mastered.

FOR STRUGGLING READERS

Assessment Support Consider these options for completing the Assessment Practice:

- Have students "work backward" to review the test questions *before* reading the passages.

- Select random questions in the Assessment, and have students demonstrate *how* and *where* to look for the answers.

- Ask students to locate unfamiliar vocabulary words in the Assessment. Elicit the words' meanings from the class.

- Have students record useful testing words and definitions in their journals for later reference.

- Read the selection or parts of them aloud to aid in student comprehension.

But she couldn't check up on a grown woman like she was some two year old. As a peach-skinned model on the TV smoothed moisturizer onto her cheeks, Trish concentrated on the sounds in the kitchen. When something heavy banged against the counter onto the floor, Trish leapt from her chair, thinking 911.

32   She found Helen standing on the counter. "Dear, would you just pass me that tin of beans that fell?" Helen said.

33   Trish held up a hand, as if it might keep Helen from falling, and retrieved the tin from under the edge of the cupboards.

34   "Helen, it's time to come down now," Trish's heart had stopped beating, but from her mouth came her calm trying-to-reason-with-a-three-year-old voice. "Take my hands, I'll help you."

35   Helen turned back to the open cupboard. "But I haven't found what I'm looking for."

36   If Helen fell, she'd break something for sure. And if she broke a hip—well, didn't old people get pneumonia and die if they had to stay in bed for too long?

37   "What are you looking for?" Trish asked, fighting not to cry. "Maybe I can find it for you."

38   Helen stared into the cupboard for a long moment. "I've forgotten." Her knees shaking, she reached her hands down to Trish. "My mind—" She leaned against Trish as she lowered herself to the chair pushed up against the counter. "It's not what it used to be, you know."

39   Surprised at how little Helen weighed, Trish lifted her the rest of the way down. Relief when Helen's feet touched the floor made Trish want to hug Helen. She wished, unexpectedly and momentarily, that her own mother was there to hug her.

40   Trish picked the canisters up off the floor, where Helen had set them out of her way, and returned them to the counter. "Would you like a piece of chocolate cake?"

41   "Would that help my mind, do you think?"

42   "It can't hurt," Trish said. "You get some plates and I'll cut the cake."

43   Trish was pushing the knife through the layers of chocolate when Helen said, "I don't think we can do that yet." She touched her hands to the pink and red rabbits in her hair. "Everyone isn't here."

44   "Right." Trish followed Helen back to the living room.

45   Helen picked up the photo of Barb's little granddaughter on the piano. "We used to have such lovely parties. She adored getting all fancied up." Helen held the photo closer to her face. "I don't remember that dress though."

46   "Who do you think—?" Trish swallowed, "Who is that in the picture, Helen?"

47   "Why, it's Barbara. Do you know Barbara?" She set the photo back on the piano. "Of course, you live in the bottom of the garden don't you. You can go home now if you'd like."

404

DIFFERENTIATED INSTRUCTION

FOR ENGLISH LANGUAGE LEARNERS
Vocabulary Support Use Word Questioning to teach these words from "Babysitting Helen":

gull (paragraph 5), *stomped* (paragraph 7), *knapsack* (paragraph 8), *ushered* (paragraph 10), *tin* (paragraph 32), *trembling* (paragraph 53), *continents* (paragraph 75), *rumpled* (paragraph 79).

BEST PRACTICES TOOLKIT—Transparency
Word Questioning p. E9

Language: Third-Person Point of View
Point out to students that "Babysitting Helen" is told in third-person point of view. The narrator is outside the action, not one of the characters in the story.

48   "No, I think . . . I think I'd like to stay—" Trish took a deep breath, "for the party."

49   Helen smoothed her skirt and sat down in front of the TV. "I love parties, don't you?" There was effort in her words. When the battery bunny came on she said, "Would you just look at that. Isn't that the darndest thing?" But her eyes were without laughter. Trish knew how upset and out of control little kids got when they were up much past bedtime. Would Helen get like that if she got overtired trying to stay up, waiting for something that wasn't going to happen?

50   "Maybe you'd like to go to bed now," Trish suggested.

51   "You know I can't miss the party." The look in Helen's eyes reminded Trish of a TV movie she'd seen in which a girl, all dolled up, was starting to realize no one was going to show up for her party. "Not," Helen said, composing herself, "after you've gone to so much trouble."

52   Trish looked at her watch. Barb wouldn't be home for another two hours. Should she—could she—try to give Helen her party?

53   Trish slid onto the piano bench and slowly, softly, started to pick out the notes of the first party song that came to her. *Hap-py birth-day to you, Hap-py birth-day to you . . .* Standing beside Trish, Helen began to move her head back and forth to the rhythm. *Hap-py birth-day, Hap-py birth-day . . .* Helen swayed, her eyes closed and a trembling smile on her lips, as Trish played.

54   It's working, Trish thought. If this will keep Helen happy, I'll play all night. But in the middle of the next time through, Helen stopped moving and opened her eyes. Her expression was cross.

55   "What is it? Do you want me to stop playing?"

56   "Your playing is lovely." Helen placed her hands on her hips. "But it's not much of a party without hats now, is it."

57   Party hats? She'd never find any in this house. Trish picked up the TV guide. "I wonder if there are any good movies on tonight."

58   "Every good party," Helen insisted, "has hats."

59   What was it with this party thing? Helen couldn't concentrate on anything for more than two minutes, but she was determined there was going to be a party—with hats. Trish sighed. Party hats. Party hats.

60   In the kitchen cupboard, she had seen paper plates. She'd brought pencil crayons for her map homework—Helen was supposed to be asleep—and of course, there were the stickers and crayons too.

61   "Look," said Trish. "We'll make hats." She knelt beside the coffee table. "With these stickers, we'll make beautiful hats."

62   "I can make a hat!" Helen grabbed a plate and a sticker. "You live in the bottom of the garden, don't you?"

63   "Yes," Trish said. "Will you come and visit me there some day?"

64   "That would be lovely, dear." Helen rubbed the sticker over her tongue.

GO ON ➡

405

FOR STRUGGLING READERS

Comprehension: Transitions To aid student comprehension of the selections, remind students that writers use transitions to link ideas. Tell students that transitions link ideas within sentences and within paragraphs and link one paragraph to another.

Point out the following examples of transitions in the selection:

- "<u>And</u> for some reason, Mom has decided there's going to be a party tonight. So, just play along, okay?"

- <u>When</u> the rabbit stopped, Helen got up and looked out the window.

- <u>When</u> something heavy banged against the counter onto the floor, Trish leapt from her chair, thinking 911.

- <u>The second time</u> Trish played it, Helen's feet were lifting off the ground. <u>The third time</u>. . . .

65 "Not too much," Trish said. "You'll lick off all the glue."

66 "I know that!" Helen laughed from deep inside.

67 Trish watched as Helen stuck stickers on her paper plate, licking and sticking, licking and sticking, one after another till two paper plates were covered. Please, energetic bunny, you've got to wear down soon.

68 Trish tied Helen's hat around her head.

69 "You, too," Helen insisted.

70 "There," Trish said, her hat in place. "Now, ready for bed?"

71 "Don't be so silly." Helen planted herself firmly beside the piano. "The party is just beginning!"

72 Helen swayed through the first round of "Happy Birthday." The second time Trish played it, Helen's feet were lifting off the ground. The third time, she was swaying in circles, a spring in every step.

73 Trish played on as Helen danced. And then Helen began to sing.

74 *Happy birthday to you, Happy birthday to you.* Her voice was strong, her face radiant. *Happy birthday, dear Ed-ward*, she belted out, *Happy Birthday to yoo-oouu!*

. . . .

75 When Barb came home, Trish was watching "Saturday Night Live" and coloring in the continents on her geography map. Beside her on the sofa, Helen was asleep, chocolate cake crumbs on her chest, home-made party hat perched crookedly on her head.

76 Barb eyed the three plates on the coffee table. Each held a fork, a few crumbs, and a birthday candle. "Did you have company?"

77 "I'm—not exactly."

78 Barb rummaged in her purse. "I'm sorry if Mom gave you a hard time."

79 Trish rumpled the money Barb handed her into the pocket of her jeans. "She's a neat lady." Careful not to disturb any of the stickers, Trish slid the hat Helen had made for her into her knapsack. "I'll come back and party with her any time." Trish opened the door to leave. "Barb?" she asked, "Who is Edward?"

80 "Edward? My father's name was Edward." Barb looked at Trish, puzzled. "Why?"

81 "That's who the party was for tonight," Trish said.

82 "Dad died two years ago."

83 "But when was his birthday?"

84 "November 24th. That's—"

85 Trish nodded. "Tonight."

86 From the sofa came a contented sigh. Barb and Trish turned. Helen was smiling in her sleep.

406

DIFFERENTIATED INSTRUCTION

FOR ENGLISH LANGUAGE LEARNERS

Assessment Support: Punctuation and Print Cues Help students understand the dialogue in the story and who is speaking. Point out that quotation marks set off the dialogue between Trish and Helen on page 406. Helen's singing of "Happy Birthday" (paragraph 74) is indicated by italic type, without quotation marks. Have students find other examples of dialogue in the story and identify who is speaking.

Assessment Support: Point of View Remind students that the term *point of view* in Reading Comprehension item 2 refers to the method of narration. "Babysitting Helen" is told in third-person, and "About A Girl" is told from first-person point of view—the narrator is a character in the story.

About a Girl

by Karen Olsson
from **Texas Monthly**

1   BLESSED AS I AM WITH AN ordinary memory, I am able to reconstruct my first meeting with Audra Thomas, which took place last February at her family's house, as a series of discrete moments.

2   One: On the way there, I crept along in heavy Dallas traffic, increasingly discouraged as the hour of the interview drew near, then pulled over at a gas station to call the Thomases and tell them I would be late. The day was cool and windy and thickly gray; I remember shouting into the pay phone.

3   Two: I drove, some forty minutes later, just past the blinking light that announces the town of Celina and turned into the subdivision where the Thomases live, Morgan Lake Estates. There had been a harsh storm earlier in the week, a pelting of icy rain and snow, and while most of the residue had melted, patches of snow still dotted the winter lawns.

4   Three: I waited outside the front door of the Thomases' house until it opened, and there was Audra: a big girl, slightly knock-kneed, with strikingly pale skin and thick brown eyebrows. Her eyes wandered shyly in my direction without making contact directly. Audra can't really see, and I'd known that before I arrived, yet I felt suddenly shy myself, unsure of what to do instead of shaking hands. We sat down on the living room couch and began to talk.

5   There are certain things I remember because I happened to jot them down in my notebook: that the couch was covered in a dark plaid fabric, and resting on it was a throw patterned with a golf motif; that on the wall was a tapestry of a forest scene illustrating a Bible passage. There are other things I didn't write down and don't remember: For instance, I recall that Audra wore gray pants, but her shirt—a white blouse, maybe?—is lost to me, and though I suspect she had on a silver necklace, I might have merely inferred that because she wore a silver necklace the other times I saw her.

6   She was soft-spoken at first, but she quickly grew more animated, looking upward and gesturing rapidly as she spoke, a knowing half-smile on her face. She told me that she'd lived in Texas since she was two, that she'd attended elementary school in Plano, that for the eighth grade she'd gone to the Texas School for the Blind and Visually Impaired, in Austin. While she knew all this, she didn't remember any of it, for she does not have an ordinary memory. In 1996, when Audra was in the fifth grade, she fell off a playground swing and hit her head, and afterward her mind seemed to turn against her. She lost most of her vision and was able to make things out only if they were an inch or two in front of her eyes. She no longer saw colors, only shades of gray. She lost the ability to tolerate touches and smells and other sensations. She also began to forget past experiences. Worse, her amnesia was ongoing, and at her lowest

GO ON ➡

407

FOR ENGLISH LANGUAGE LEARNERS

Assessment Vocabulary To improve student reading comprehension, have student pairs identify unfamiliar words in "About A Girl" before they answer the Reading Comprehension questions. Then have them determine the meanings of the words using context clues or a dictionary, thesaurus, or glossary.

FOR STRUGGLING READERS

Reading Comprehension: Transitions To help students answer Reading Comprehension items 12 and 14, discuss the use of transitions to show time sequence. Help students locate these examples in "About A Girl": "last February" (paragraph 1), "on the way there" (paragraph 2), "some forty minutes later" (paragraph 3). Have students find other examples of time-sequence transitions in the selection.

point the days just fell away. At a time when she should have been starting the sixth grade, she was reduced to playing with infant toys, and her mother was caring for her around the clock.

7   Since then, Audra has not regained what she lost, but she has grown into her own person; in May she graduated from Celina High School, and this fall she'll start college. Though she doesn't remember things that happened to her more than four or five months ago, she can learn and retain information—about places she's lived or school subjects or what's been in the news. "I'm a big geek," she volunteered early in our conversation. In particular, she is a big current-events geek: In the tenth grade she won a statewide Current Issues and Events academic contest by scoring higher than any other student in her division on a test of state, national, and world affairs. . . . She has tended over the past year to get into arguments with other kids about U.S. foreign policy; in the spring, she was voted the most opinionated girl in the senior class. "I scare people," she said. "They see me coming with my cane and they are like, 'Oh, my gosh, get out of the way!'"

8   As I recall our first interview, what stands out is not any one of the immediate details—the jewelry Audra might have been wearing or the living room decor or even anything she said—but rather my initial sense of her person, which emerged gradually and is much harder to put into words, and has no doubt been influenced by my subsequent visits. I remember how it felt to sit there with her, this bright, half-smiling, wry seventeen-year-old . . . , who explained that she sometimes walks straight into trees—who charmed me, really. Most of the other moments I remember from that day are also bound up with how I felt: my anxiety about arriving late, my nervousness at the door.

9   By the time you read this, or not long after, Audra will have forgotten how that day felt to her. And this is what I find most arresting: not that she can't remember what happened, but that she can't remember the way things *felt*, and that lacking such memories, she is nevertheless such a strong presence, such a lively person. She talks about herself with self-deprecating humor, and more than once she said to me, "I have no life." It's the sort of thing a teenager says when she's bored and stuck at home much of the time, yet coming from Audra, it resonates in other ways. After her accident, she was deprived of her regular middle-class girlhood; she really did have no life. In the years since, with the help of her family, she's built a life for herself—and more to the point, she's constructed a self for herself, after having been cut off from the girl she was. But what is it to have a life with no lasting memories? A self with so little internal evidence of its own past? . . .

10   ONE SUNDAY IN APRIL, AUDRA and I went to the Modern Art Museum in Fort Worth because she is interested in art and art history. None of the other visitors seemed the least bit surprised to see a blind girl with a cane

408

DIFFERENTIATED INSTRUCTION

FOR ENGLISH LANGUAGE LEARNERS

Assessment Vocabulary To help students understand the Reading Comprehension questions, teach or review these vocabulary terms:

- *theme:* an underlying message about life or human nature that a writer wants the reader to understand

- *symbol:* a person, a place, an object, or an activity that stands for something beyond itself

- *evidence:* specific pieces of information that support a thesis, such as facts, quotations, examples, or summaries

making her way through the galleries, but I was still trying to figure it out: How is it that a person who can't see colors except as varying shades of gray, who can make out forms only from very close up or through a magnifying viewer, likes to look at paintings?

11   A new exhibit had just opened, a retrospective of the work of Philip Guston, and we proceeded through it as follows: Audra would walk right up to a canvas and eyeball it, sometimes tracing a contour in the air with her finger, because tracing helps her to see things better. "Oh, hello," she'd say when she came across a new figure or a change of color. She asked questions: "Okay, there's a big splotch here where it's lighter?"

12   "Yeah, it's pink there, and the paint's applied really thickly," I said, trying to help her and feeling inadequate to the task. Every so often a museum guard would tell us we were too close to the canvas. "Hey, cut us some slack, will you?" I'd think. "The girl can barely see!" Audra would back off and look at the painting through a little black telescope she'd brought, which helped her see the picture in its entirety.

13   After a while I thought I was beginning to understand Audra's way of looking. She didn't care for busy or complex paintings, in which it was hard to connect all the pieces, or paintings without much color contrast, in which she couldn't tell different sections apart. "I like stuff more on the abstract side, stuff that's simpler," she said. "I like to look until it clicks with me." She seemed to be actively assembling the images in her head, laboring to perceive each painting in a manner superficially different from how a sighted person would look at anything, but perhaps not entirely different. To some degree, we all create what we're looking at and what we remember.

GO ON ➡

FOR ENGLISH LANGUAGE LEARNERS

Assessment Support: Contractions Point out that the writer of "About A Girl" uses informal language in her article. Have students identify contractions in the selection, which tend to make the writing sound more like everyday speech than formal language does.

FOR STRUGGLING READERS

Assessment Support Have students review the selections again and read the Assessment directions carefully before beginning the Assessment Practice.

Reading Comprehension

Model a thinking process for answering multiple-choice questions.

1. **B is correct.** *When something is ironic, the actual result is different from the expected result. The title is ironic because Helen is not a baby, but a grown woman. A is incorrect because this answer does not make the title ironic. C is incorrect because Helen's poor memory is a given, not ironic. D is incorrect because the story is not entirely about a birthday party.*

2. **D is correct.** *The author's use of the third-person limited point of view allows the reader to know only Trish's thoughts and changing feelings throughout the story. A is incorrect because this point of view does not explain why Helen acts the way she does. B is also incorrect because, in the beginning, Trish complains about having to babysit Helen. C is incorrect because the reader does not know the feelings of everyone else in the story.*

3. **C is correct.** *Helen wants to have a birthday party for her husband, who died two years before, because she still loves him. A is incorrect because the story doesn't mention tactics. B is incorrect because the story focuses on Helen, not Trish. D is not the theme of the story.*

4. **B is correct.** *The word* haphazardly *means "disorganized." Thus, "scattered with no pattern" is the correct answer. A, C, and D are all incorrect because they are not the correct meanings of the word* haphazardly.

5. **A is correct.** *At the beginning of the story, Helen's daughter tells Trish that Helen has baked a cake. When people bake cakes, it is usually for a special occasion. B, C, and D are incorrect because these items aren't the first clues the reader is given.*

6. **A is correct.** *The rabbit that keeps going is symbolic of how Helen continues to talk about the party. B is incorrect because the bunny is not connected to Trish. C is mentioned at the beginning of the story, but it is not a symbol of anything. D is incorrect because the bunny represents something else.*

Reading Comprehension

> **Use "Babysitting Helen" (pp. 402–406) to answer questions 1–9.**

1. The title "Babysitting Helen" is ironic because —
   A. Trish doesn't want to babysit
   B. Helen is an old woman, not a baby
   C. Helen doesn't remember things
   D. the story is about a birthday party

2. The author tells this story from the third-person limited point of view to —
   A. explain why Helen acts the way she does
   B. show how enjoyable babysitting is
   C. let the reader know how everyone in the story thinks and feels
   D. let the reader know only Trish's thoughts and changing feelings

410

7. **D is correct.** *In paragraph 31, Trish thinks that "she couldn't check up on a grown woman like she was some two year old." A is incorrect because Helen does not promise not to get into trouble. B and C are incorrect because Trish worries about what would happen if Helen did get hurt.*

8. **C is correct.** *Trish wants to give Helen a party, and it is the first song she can think of to play. A is incorrect because it is not mentioned in the story. B is also incorrect because it, too, is not mentioned in the story. D is incorrect because Helen does not ask Trish to play the piano.*

3. One of the themes of this story is —
   A. babysitting tactics
   B. that you have to do chores
   C. the power of love
   D. the power of a quest

4. In paragraph 9, *haphazardly* means —
   A. in neat rows
   B. scattered with no pattern
   C. vertically
   D. down her back

5. The first clue that tonight is special for Helen is the —
   A. cake she baked
   B. photo on the piano
   C. birthday hats
   D. birthday song

6. The rabbit that keeps going is a symbol of —
   A. Helen
   B. Trish
   C. Trish's homework
   D. nothing, it's just a bunny

7. In paragraphs 30–31, Trish does not follow Helen into the kitchen because —
   A. Helen promises not to get into trouble
   B. Trish wants Helen to get hurt
   C. Trish knows everything will be okay
   D. Trish does not want to treat Helen like a baby

8. Trish plays the birthday song because —
   A. she knows it is Helen's birthday
   B. it is time for her piano practice
   C. she wants to give Helen a party
   D. Helen asks her to play

9. Helen forgets many things but remembers —
   A. why she went into the kitchen
   B. her husband's birthday
   C. where Trish lives
   D. who the little girl in the picture is

   > **Use "About a Girl" (pp. 407–409) to answer questions 10–15.**

10. One of the themes of "About a Girl" is —
    A. human memory is mysterious
    B. we are nothing without memories
    C. computers are helpful
    D. family memories are important

11. The author begins the article with "Blessed as I am with an ordinary memory…" because —
    A. she appreciates being able to remember absolutely everything
    B. she wants readers to count their blessings
    C. she wants to show that she is ordinary
    D. she wants readers to value something they take for granted

12. Audra lost vision and memory when —
    A. she fell off a bike
    B. she was born
    C. she fell off a swing
    D. she was in a car accident

13. The word *amnesia* in paragraph 6 means —
    A. pain
    B. forgetfulness
    C. happiness
    D. amiableness

GO ON

9. **B is correct.** *Helen sings "Happy Birthday" to Edward, her husband. A is incorrect because Helen admits that she has forgotten why she came into the kitchen. C is incorrect because Helen thinks that Trish lives at the bottom of the garden. D is incorrect because Helen states that the girl in the picture is her daughter, Barbara, instead of her granddaughter.*

10. **A is correct.** *The narrator states that Audra will not remember something that happened to her and wonders what life would be like if she couldn't remember her own past. B is incorrect because Audra's life is full, even if she doesn't have many memories. C is incorrect because computers are not mentioned in the story. D is incorrect because the article is about memories in general, not specific ones.*

11. **D is correct.** *Something that is "ordinary" is something that most people take for granted. A is incorrect because the author doesn't remember everything, such as the color of the shirt Audra was wearing when they first met. B is incorrect because she wants readers to understand Audra's situation. C is incorrect because "ordinary" describes memory, not the author.*

12. **C is correct.** *The author tells the reader that the reason Audra lost her sight is because "she fell off a playground swing and hit her head." A, B, and D are incorrect because these instances are not the reason why Audra lost her sight.*

13. **B is correct.** *The word* amnesia *means "a partial or total loss of memory." A, C, and D are incorrect because they do not match the meaning of* amnesia.

14. **D is correct.** *The author talks about how people create memories from the bit of information they can remember. A is incorrect because the article is not written in chronological order. B is incorrect because the article has a specific structure. C is incorrect because although the author did not remember a few details, they were insignificant to the story.*

15. A *is correct.* *What gets the author's attention is that Audra can't remember the way things felt. B is incorrect because this is not the meaning of the word as it is used in paragraph 9. C is incorrect because deactivating means "making something inactive." D is incorrect because the two ideas are not incompatible, or contradictory.*

16. C *is correct.* *Trish lives down the street from Helen, and Karen is a journalist. A and B are incorrect because although the selections mention Helen, Audra, and relatives, the selections themselves are not told through their eyes. D is incorrect because teachers are not mentioned in either selection.*

17. B *is correct.* *Audra has lost the ability to remember how things felt. However, Helen shows emotion at times when talking. A is incorrect because both Helen and Audra can remember things that happened in the past. C is incorrect because Helen does not remember most people. D is incorrect because the reader is not given clues that Helen remembers places.*

18. B *is correct.* *The photo indicates that club members will cut and paste their memories into a scrapbook. Although club members might share their photos and mementos, A and C are incorrect because neither is the purpose of the meetings. D is incorrect because club members are not making quilts.*

19. D *is correct.* *The advertisement does not indicate that any certain population is invited to the club meetings. Therefore, A, B, and C are incorrect.*

SHORT CONSTRUCTED RESPONSE

Possible responses:

20. *Trish realizes that watching Helen is not that painful. In paragraph 79, she states that Helen is a "neat lady" and that she will "come back and party with her any time."*

21. *Although Audra is not the "typical teenager," in paragraph 9, she states that she "has no life." The author follows this statement with "It's the sort of thing a teenager says when she's bored." The author is implying that teenagers say this when they have nothing to do, but that Audra makes this statement because her lack of memories makes her feel as if she doesn't have a life.*

---

14. Why doesn't the author present events in the order in which they happened?

   A. The author wrote the article in the order in which she took her notes.

   B. The article's structure is not important because the story is so compelling.

   C. The author did not remember key details.

   D. The structure suggests the scattered way people often recall memories.

15. In paragraph 9, the word *arresting* means —

   A. attracting attention

   B. being under arrest

   C. deactivating

   D. contradictory

> Use "Babysitting Helen" and "About a Girl" to answer questions 16–17.

16. "Babysitting Helen" and "About a Girl" are told through the eyes of —

   A. Helen and Audra

   B. relatives

   C. people outside of the family

   D. their teachers

17. What does Helen remember that Audra cannot?

   A. Events

   B. Feelings

   C. People

   D. Places

> Use the flier on page 410 to answer questions 18–19.

18. During club meetings, members will —

   A. share their photos and mementos

   B. cut and paste to make memory books

   C. discuss their most vivid memories

   D. collect scraps of fabric to make quilts

19. The Scrapbook Club is for —

   A. Springville's senior citizens

   B. only young adults

   C. experienced scrappers only

   D. anyone who wants to scrapbook

SHORT CONSTRUCTED RESPONSE
Write a short response to each question, using text evidence to support your response.

20. In "Babysitting Helen," how do Trish's feelings about "babysitting" change? Support your response with evidence from the story.

21. What does Audra mean when she says that she has "no life"? Support your response with evidence from the selection.

Write a short response to the following question, using text evidence from both selections to support your response.

22. How does the idea of memories apply to both selections? Support your response with evidence from **both** selections.

412

---

22. *Helen remembers long-ago memories. In paragraph 45, she remembers that her daughter, now grown, used to like getting "fancied up." Although her husband died two years ago, she still remembers and celebrates his birthday. However, she doesn't remember a commercial she saw just a few moments before, nor does she remember why she went into the kitchen.* *Audra, on the other hand, remembers nothing about her life for longer than a few months or so. In paragraph 9, the narrator states that "Audra will have forgotten..." This indicates to the reader that Audra only retains her memories for a short time. The memories of Helen and Audra are quite different in that Helen's memory loss is a result of getting older, while Audra's memory loss is a result of an accident.*

Revising and Editing

DIRECTIONS Read this passage, and answer the questions that follow.

> (1) Video games have changed a lot in the last 20 years. (2) The arcade was once the only place kids could play games with advanced graphics. (3) An arcade is a building containing video-game machines. (4) Later, Atari makes it possible for kids to play some arcade games at home. (5) Because Atari was one of the original home gaming systems. (6) The Internet allows kid's to play against opponents all over the world.

1. What is the most effective way to revise sentence 1 using a simile?
   A. Video games, along with other electronic devices, have changed a lot in the last 20 years.
   B. As any kid will tell you, video games have changed a lot in the last 20 years.
   C. The difference between video games today and those from 20 years ago is like night and day.
   D. As the times have changed, so have video games and the people who play them.

2. What is the most effective way to combine sentences 2 and 3 using an appositive phrase?
   A. An arcade, which is a building that contains video-game machines, was once the only place where kids could play games, with advanced graphics.
   B. Kids, interested in games with advanced graphics, had to go to the arcade, which housed video-game machines.
   C. An arcade is a building containing video-game machines and is where kids went to play games with advanced graphics.
   D. An arcade, a building containing video-game machines, was once the only place kids could play games with advanced graphics.

3. What change, if any, should be made in sentence 4?
   A. Change *makes* to **made**
   B. Change *possible* to **impossible**
   C. Change *to play* to **playing**
   D. Make no change

4. What change, if any, should be made in sentence 5?
   A. Insert a comma after *Because*
   B. Delete *Because*
   C. Change *was* to **were**
   D. Make no change

5. What change, if any, should be made in sentence 6?
   A. Delete the apostrophe in *kid's*
   B. Insert a comma after *opponents*
   C. Change *opponents* to **opponent's**
   D. Make no change

6. What transition could be added to the beginning of sentence 6?
   A. As a result,
   B. Meanwhile,
   C. Now,
   D. However,

413

Revising and Editing

1. **C is correct.** *The phrase "like night and day" is the only simile among the answer choices.* A *contains a prepositional phrase.* B *and* D *contain subordinate clauses.*

2. **D is correct.** *The appositive phrase "a building containing video-game machines" explains the meaning of* arcade. A *uses an adjective clause to define* arcade. B *uses a participial phrase to define* arcade, *and* C *uses a compound predicate.*

3. **A is correct.** A *is correct because the sentence is referencing events that happened in the past.* B *and* C *are incorrect because they do not make sense in the sentence.* D *is incorrect because the sentence needs to be changed to past tense.*

4. **B is correct.** *Deleting the word* Because *makes the fragment a complete sentence.* A *is incorrect because inserting a comma after "Because" does not change the fragment into a complete sentence.* C *is incorrect because the subject is singular.* D *is incorrect because the sentence does need a change.*

5. **A is correct.** *"Kid's" is incorrect because it should be the plural "kids."* B *is incorrect because there is no need to add a comma.* C *is incorrect because "opponents" does not need to be changed.* D *is wrong because the sentence is incorrect and needs to be changed.*

6. **C is correct.** *The sentence needs a transition that shows the contrast of video game systems in the past and using the Internet today.* A, B, *and* D *are not the correct transitions that could be added to the beginning of the sentence.*

DIFFERENTIATED INSTRUCTION

FOR STRUGGLING READERS
Assessment Support: Similes Review with students that similes are figures of speech that make comparisons between two unlike things using the words *like* or *as*.

COMMON CORE FOCUS

RL 10 Read and comprehend literature. **RI 10** Read and comprehend literary nonfiction.

INTRODUCE *GREAT READS*

In Unit 3, students have discussed a number of big questions. Invite students to tell which question they found most intriguing and why, and then focus attention on the three that appear on this page. Discuss the recommended books and their summaries, pointing out how each connects to the related question. Encourage students to choose one or more of these "great reads" to read independently.

COMMON CORE

RL 10 Read and comprehend literature. **RI 10** Read and comprehend literary nonfiction.

Ideas for Independent Reading

Can learning ever harm you? Is there anything wrong with being liked? Consider these questions when you read these works.

Does knowledge come at a price?

Fahrenheit 451
by Ray Bradbury

Montag is a fireman. His job is to burn books, which are forbidden in a future society. One day he smuggles home a book and begins to read. What will happen if he is found out?

Nervous Conditions
by Tsitsi Dangarembga

Tambudzai is delighted at the chance to leave her tiny Rhodesian village and be educated at the home of her wealthy uncle. The more she learns, however, the more critical she becomes of both her parents' and her uncle's worlds.

The Curious Incident of the Dog in the Night-Time
by Mark Haddon

When a 15-year-old autistic boy discovers his neighbor's poodle stabbed to death, he vows to solve the crime. Ultimately, he learns who killed the dog but also uncovers other secrets that turn his life upside down.

What makes someone popular?

Shattering Glass
by Gail Giles

Simon Glass is an overweight, clumsy geek until a popular clique decides to turn him into the high school Class Favorite. As they transform Simon, they begin to hate him, and the final result is chilling.

Death of a Salesman
by Arthur Miller

This classic American play tells us that salesmen don't only sell their wares; they must also sell themselves. And unpopular salesmen don't do well. The salesman Willy Loman is liked, but he's not well liked, and that is his tragedy.

Pygmalion
by George Bernard Shaw

By giving the Cockney flower-seller Eliza Doolittle lessons in speech and manners, Professor Henry Higgins transforms her into the toast of London society. But Eliza has much to teach Professor Higgins in return.

Can ordinary people be heroes?

The White Rose: Munich 1942–1943
by Inge Scholl

The German brother and sister Hans and Sophie Scholl, who hated everything Adolf Hitler stood for, worked with friends to resist the Third Reich. They were arrested, tried, and executed for distributing anti-Hitler leaflets. Their story is told by their sister.

In the Time of the Butterflies
by Julia Alvarez

Alvarez combines history and fiction in this account of the three heroic Mirabal sisters, who worked against the Trujillo dictatorship in the Dominican Republic and were assassinated. They used the code name *mariposas*, or "butterflies."

Stone Soup for the World
by Marianne Larned

This book collects 100 inspiring accounts of "everyday heroes" who improved their communities and nations. The volume also lists many volunteer organizations that interested readers can join.

Get Novel Wise

Go to **thinkcentral.com**.
KEYWORD: HML10-414

414

NovelWise

The keyword on this page points to **NovelWise**, a Web site that helps students choose a novel or other book-length work to read. **NovelWise** also provides
- study guides
- reading strategies and literary elements instruction
- presentations to introduce classic novels
- project ideas

Message and Meaning

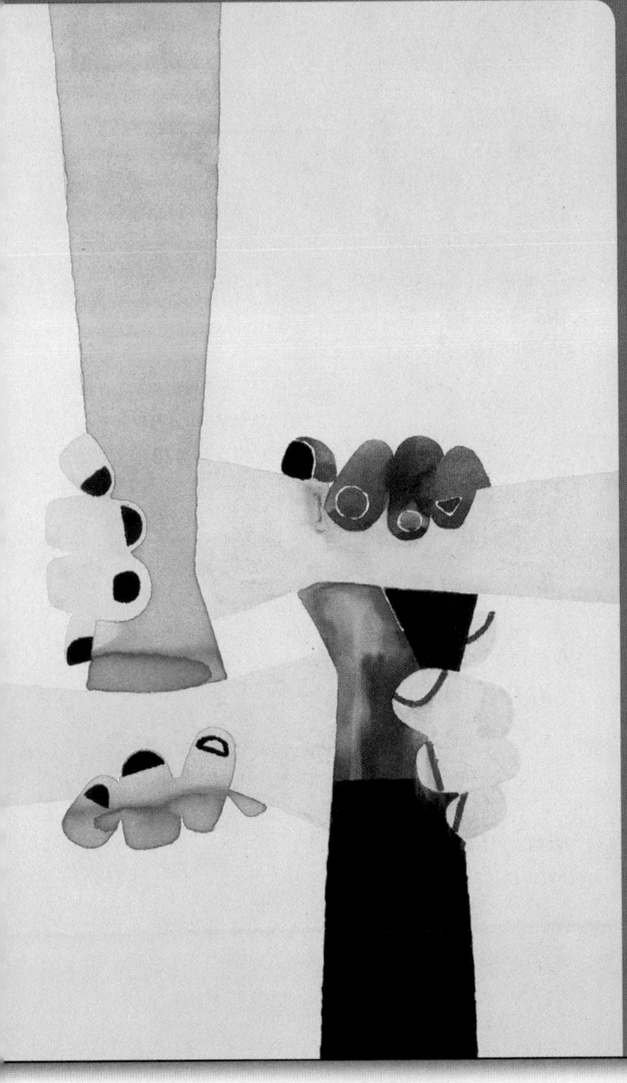

THEME

- In Fiction
- In Poetry
- In Nonfiction
- Across Genres

415

About the Art George Giusti (1908–1991) created this painting for a 1955 series called *Great Ideas of Western Man*. The image as it appears in the series is coupled with this thematic quotation from reformer Jane Addams: "Civilization is a method of living, an attitude of equal respect for all men." For more information, see page 485.

INTRODUCE THE UNIT

"Slow and steady wins the race," "In union there is strength," "Never trust a flatterer"— these lessons, or morals, are stated at the end of three of Aesop's ancient fables. Each moral is the theme of its story. Unlike fables, most modern stories do not end with a succinct thematic statement. However, almost every story has a theme, or some kind of message or life lesson.

Other kinds of artistic expression present themes as well. To illustrate, invite students to consider the theme of the painting and the photograph on this page. To elicit ideas, ask:

- What do you think the different colors in the painting mean?
- What messages might the clasping hands represent?
- How can you tell that the people in the photograph are suffering?
- What lessons might people learn by thinking about the photograph?
- What theme or themes might connect these two images?

Point out that learning to explore themes is one mark of a critical reader or viewer. Then explain that as students read the selections in the unit, they will develop this skill by considering the **message and meaning** in fiction, poetry, and nonfiction. They will also think about the ways in which authors convey themes to their readers.

For help in planning this unit, see

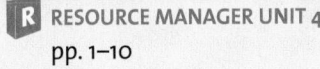 RESOURCE MANAGER UNIT 4
   pp. 1–10

	Text Analysis Workshop: Theme and Symbol pp. 418–425	**The Interlopers** Short Story pp. 426–437	**Two Friends** Short Story pp. 438–451	*Comparing Texts Selections*	
STRAND				**When Mr. Pirzada Came to Dine** Short Story pp. 452–475	**Interview with Jhumpa Lahiri/ Refugee Aid Society** pp. 470–474
		Lexile: 1230 Fry: 10 Dale-Chall: 6.8	Lexile: 960 Fry: 6 Dale-Chall: 6.5	Lexile: 1170 Fry: 9 Dale-Chall: 6.6	
Reading Literature	Themes in Literature pp. 418–425 Identify Theme p. 420 Analyze the Text pp. 421–425 RL 2, RL 3, RL 6	Theme and Setting pp. 427–428, 431, 433–435 RL 2 Archetype p. 430 RL 2 Monitor pp. 427 430, 432, 435	Symbol pp. 439, 442, 444, 447, 449 RL 6 Make Inferences pp. 439, 440, 442–443, 445–447, 449 RL 1 World Literature p. 448	Theme and Character pp. 453, 457–458, 460–462, 467, 469, 471 RL 2, RL 3 Draw Conclusions pp. 453–454, 456, 459, 463–465, 468, 471 RL 1 Allusion p. 463	
Reading Informational Text					Interview p. 470 Web Site p. 474 RI 7
Writing		Writing Prompt p. 437 W 2	Quickwrite p. 438 Writing Prompt p. 451	Writing Prompt p. 473 W 2	
Speaking and Listening		Role-Play p. 426 SL 1		What's the Connection? p. 452 SL 1	
Language		Vary Sentence Structure pp. 432, 437 L 1b Connotation p. 436 L 5b Language Coach p. 430	Write Concisely pp. 446, 451 L 3 Analogies p. 450 L 5 Language Coach p. 446	Add Descriptive Details pp. 458, 473 L 3 The prefix im- p. 472 L 4c Language Coach p. 464	

Do not weep, maiden, for war is kind/the sonnet-ballad Poem/Sonnet pp. 476–481	*from Tolerance* Persuasive Essay pp. 482–487	*Letter to a Young Refugee from Another/ Song of P'eng-ya* Essay/Poem pp. 488–497	*Writing Workshop: Comparison-Contrast Essay* pp. 498–507 *Speaking and Listening Workshop: Participating in a Group Discussion* pp. 508–509
	Lexile: 850 *Fry: 9* *Dale-Chall: N/A*	*Lexile: 1040* *Fry: College* *Dale-Chall: 6.0/N/A*	
Universal Theme pp. 477–478, 480–481 RL 2 Understand Verbal Irony pp. 477–478, 481 RL 10		Author's Message Across Genres pp. 489–490, 492–496 RL 2, RL 6 Comparing Themes Across Genres pp. 494, 496 RL 2 Writing for Assessment p. 497 RL 2, RL 6	
	Persuasive Essay pp. 483–484, 486, 487 RI 2, RI 6 Analyze Reasons and Evidence pp. 483, 486–487 RI 8	Set a Purpose for Reading p. 489 RI 2 Comparing Themes Across Genres pp. 494, 496 RI 2 Writing for Assessment p. 497 RI 7	
		Quickwrite p. 488 Writing for Assessment p. 497 W 9 (RI 7)	Writing a Comparison-Contrast Essay pp. 498–507 W 2a–f, W 4, W 5, W 9, W 10
Discuss p. 476 SL 1	Role-Play p. 482 SL 1		Participating in a Group Discussion pp. 508–509 SL 1a–d
	Language Coach p. 484	Language Coach p. 493 L 4b	Drafting p. 501 L 2 Editing and Publishing p. 505 L 1, L 1a

To see the complete Essential Course of Study, see pp. T23–T28.

For additional lesson planning help, see **Teacher One Stop DVD.**

Instructional Support

Resource Manager Unit 4

UNIT SUPPORT

Academic Vocabulary p. 3

Additional Academic Vocabulary p. 4

Grammar Focus p. 5

Text Analysis Workshop pp. 9–10

Writing Workshop: Comparison-Contrast Essay p. 125

SELECTION SUPPORT*

Plan and Teach

Lesson planning pages

Additional leveled selection questions

Extension activities

Student Copy Masters

Selection summaries in four languages

Skills copy masters in English and Spanish

Vocabulary preteaching and support

Reading Check and Question Support

Reading Fluency

* Available for all selections

† Available on **thinkcentral.com**.

Language Handbook

Vocabulary Practice

Best Practices Toolkit†

PowerNotes DVD-ROM†

Connections: Nonfiction for Common Core CD-ROM†

Teacher One Stop DVD-ROM

Student One Stop DVD-ROM

Write*Smart* CD-ROM†

GrammarNotes DVD-ROM†

WordSharp CD-ROM†

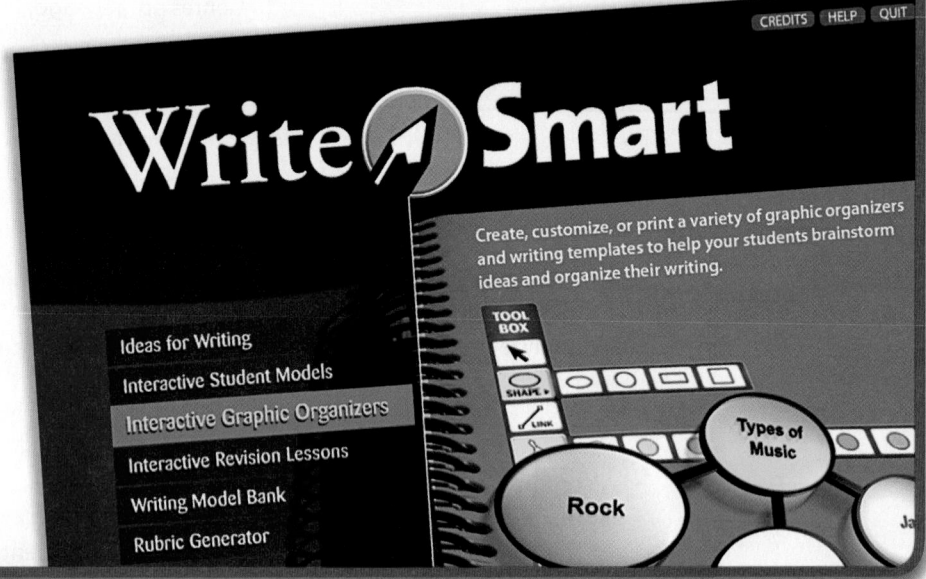

Differentiated Instruction

STRUGGLING READERS AND WRITERS	ENGLISH LANGUAGE LEARNERS	ADVANCED LEARNERS
Resource Manager Unit 4	**Resource Manager Unit 4**	**Resource Manager Unit 4**
Additional Selection Questions	Selection Summaries in English, Spanish, Vietnamese and Haitian Creole	Additional Selection Questions
Question Support	Skills Copymasters in Spanish	Ideas for Extension
Reading Fluency	**English Language Learner Adapted**	**Diagnostic and Selection Tests**
Interactive Reader	**Interactive Reader Teacher's Guide**	Selection Tests B/C
Adapted Interactive Reader	**ELL Adapted Interactive Reader**	
Audio Tutor	Audio Tutor	
Level Up Online Tutorials	**Guide to English for Newcomers**	
Audio Anthology	**Audio Anthology**	
(with Audio summaries)	**Audio Summaries in Multiple**	
Diagnostic and Selection Tests	**Languages** (on **thinkcentral.com**)	
Selection Tests A/B		

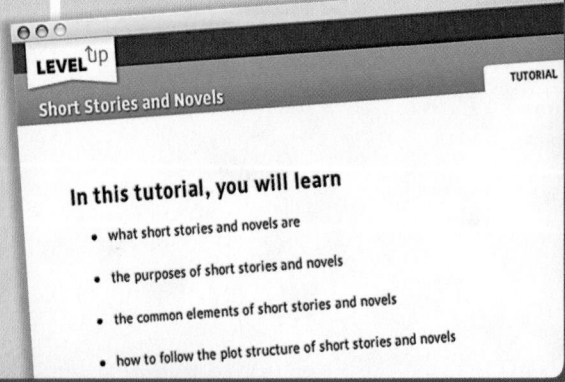

Assessment and Reteaching

Diagnostic and Selection Tests

Unit and Benchmark Tests

ThinkCentral Online Assessment:

- All program assessments
- Level Up Online Tutorials

ExamView Test Generator on the Teacher One Stop DVD-ROM

Online Essay Scoring on **thinkcentral.com**

ThinkCentral Online Reteaching:

- Level Up Online Tutorials
- Reteaching Worksheets

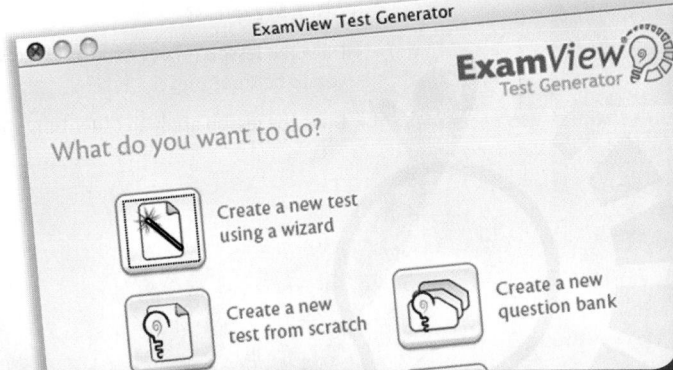

ExamView Test Generator

ExamView Test Generator

What do you want to do?

Create a new test using a wizard

Create a new test from scratch

Create a new question bank

Professional Development

Video Center Based on interviews with program consultants and other educational experts, these videos feature classroom-ready teaching strategies.

Teacher Toolkit Includes a Teacher Handbook as well as a range of articles and handouts by program consultants and other educators.

Janet Allen

Jim Burke

Kylene Beers

Carol Jago

THINK central **at a Glance**

One Location, Endless Resources

Find Resources Browse all *Holt McDougal Literature* components for the ones that meet your students' needs and match your teaching style.

Assess Progress and Reteach Assign electronic versions of program assessments to measure your students' mastery of the Common Core State Standards. On thinkcentral.com, some tests deliver online remediation tutorials to students who have not mastered skills.

 Interactive Whiteboard Lessons

Prepare your students for college and careers by teaching relevant, real-world skills through dynamic, interactive instruction. Go to **thinkcentral.com** to browse through all whiteboard lessons, including the following:

- Theme/Central Idea
- Role of Setting
- Comparing Texts
- Evaluating Arguments

 Together Holt McDougal and HISTORY® are revolutionizing the study of English/language arts with video that helps students relive and re-imagine the people, places, and events they are discovering through reading. Look for selections with the HISTORY® icon.

415D

What are life's big LESSONS?

To introduce the page, read the question. Then write several examples of life's big **lessons** on the board:

> Cheaters never win.
>
> Don't rely on others to make you happy.
>
> The truth will always be uncovered, no matter how you try to hide it.

Discuss how these or other lessons might be learned (1) through personal experience and (2) through the experiences of other people.

ACTIVITY Suggest some movies or books that have simple themes. Then propose more complex works. For example, begin with *Star Wars* and its major theme: Evil is strong, but good can overcome it. Then propose a classic story, such as *Romeo and Juliet*. Discuss how Shakespeare uses this play to express **lessons** about love, hatred, maturity, and family relationships. Point out that such universal themes endure, often making classics of the stories in which they appear.

CHECK UNDERSTANDING Have students explain why readers might enjoy or appreciate a book or movie more if they are aware of its theme, or lesson.

What are life's big LESSONS?

You can't find them in a textbook. You can't discover them in a class. The way you will learn life's most important lessons will be through your own experiences and through encounters with the words, accomplishments, and ideas of others. Sometimes these lessons, or themes, will show up in the fiction you read and the movies you watch.

ACTIVITY Think of a book or a movie that taught you something about life or human nature. Then answer the following:

- What lesson or theme was the author or director trying to express?

- Does the lesson reflect what your experience has shown you to be true?

- Does the lesson apply to other times and other places?

Find It Online!
Go to **thinkcentral.com** for the interactive version of this unit.

416

Unit Resources

See resources on the **Teacher One Stop DVD-ROM** *and on* **thinkcentral.com**.

R RESOURCE MANAGER UNIT 4

UNIT AND BENCHMARK TESTS

⊞ BEST PRACTICES TOOLKIT

INTERACTIVE READER

ADAPTED INTERACTIVE READER

ELL ADAPTED INTERACTIVE READER

LANGUAGE HANDBOOK

VOCABULARY PRACTICE

TECHNOLOGY

- ⊘ **Teacher One Stop DVD-ROM**
- ⊘ **Student One Stop DVD-ROM**
- ⊘ **PowerNotes DVD-ROM**
- ⊘ **Write*Smart* CD-ROM**
- ⊘ **Media*Smart* DVD-ROM**
- ⊘ **GrammarNotes DVD-ROM**
- ⊘ **Audio Anthology CD**
- ⊘ **Audio Tutor CD**

THINK central

Find It Online!

The interactive version of this unit on **thinkcentral.com** includes

- video and **PowerNotes** introductions to key selections
- **audio support**—listen or download
- **ThinkAloud** models
- **WordSharp** vocabulary tutorials
- interactive review and remediation

Preview Unit Goals

TEXT ANALYSIS	• Determine a theme or central idea and analyze its development • Identify and interpret symbol • Identify and interpret verbal irony • Analyze and compare authors' messages across genres • Determine an author's point of view or purpose and analyze an author's use of rhetoric
READING	• Make inferences and draw conclusions; cite evidence • Monitor comprehension • Analyze and evaluate reasons and evidence
WRITING AND LANGUAGE	• Write a comparison-contrast essay • Use transitions to clarify the relationships between ideas • Use adverbs to add descriptive detail • Use subordinate clauses to improve sentence flow
SPEAKING AND LISTENING	• Participate in a group discussion
VOCABULARY	• Determine the connotative meanings of words as they are used in a text • Use prefixes to determine the meanings of words
ACADEMIC VOCABULARY	• alter • theme • layer • unify • symbol

ON BOSTON | MARATHO

417

UNIT GOALS

Included in this unit: **RL 1, RL 2, RL 3, RL 4, RL 6, RL 10, RI 1, RI 2, RI 6, RI 7, RI 8, RI 10, W 1, W 2, W 2a–f, W 4, W 5, W 9, W 10, SL 1a–d, L 1a, L 1b, L 2, L 3, L 4b, L 4c, L 5, L 6**

Complete text of the Common Core State Standards is found in the correlation on p. T10. Standards covered in this unit are found in the standards overview (pp. 415A–415B) and on the lesson pages where they are taught.

Preview Unit Goals

The goals on this page are an overview of the main skills and strategies presented in Unit 4. As you read the goals aloud, point out the color-coding of each skill category, and answer any initial questions that students may have. Urge students to use the list to set some personal goals for themselves, as well.

Discuss what students know about the Academic Vocabulary. As a class, develop initial definitions that students can copy into their **Reader/Writer Notebooks** and later refine. Throughout the unit, remind students to reinforce their understanding by using these terms in speaking and writing about the selections.

DIFFERENTIATED INSTRUCTION

FOR ENGLISH LANGUAGE LEARNERS

Academic Vocabulary Provide students with definitions of each Academic Vocabulary word.

alter (ôl′tər) *v.* to change or modify some details

layer (lā′ər) *n.* a single thickness, fold, or level

symbol (sĭm′bəl) *n.* something that represents something else; an object, mark, or sign

theme (thēm) *n.* a topic or subject of a discussion or piece of writing

unify (yōō′ nə fī′) *v.* to make into one; to bring together into a unit

Use the copy master to help students learn academic words they will use in this unit and on the Assessment Practice.

🔲 RESOURCE MANAGER—Copy Masters
Academic Vocabulary p. 3
Additional Academic Vocabulary p. 4

Focus and Motivate

COMMON CORE FOCUS

RL 2 Determine a theme or central idea of a text and analyze in detail its development, including how it emerges and is shaped and refined by specific details; provide an objective summary of the text. **RL 3** Analyze how complex characters develop the theme. **RL 6** Analyze a particular point of view in a work of world literature.

Teach

Part 1: Universal Themes in Literature

Theme Clarify for students that a theme is a general message that emerges from the specific subject of a literary work. It is an observation or insight about human nature that the author chooses to communicate. Have students verbalize the theme of their favorite fairy tale or fable. A student who chooses "The Tortoise and the Hare," for example, may state the theme as the importance of working steadily toward long-term goals.

Universality Point out that as human beings we share many of the same problems and have similar reactions to archetypal experiences. Universal themes deal primarily with our continuing concerns about birth, death, life, love, good, evil, anger, hatred, ambition, fear, and relationships.

Symbols Explain to students that literary symbols are specific representations of more abstract ideas. To help students understand that symbols can have more than one meaning and use, have them brainstorm for ideas connected with, for example, the moon, a handkerchief, fire, and water. Then have them connect symbols with ideas such as love of country, love of fellow humans, desire for peace, and social status. Finally, have them list possible purposes for using each of the symbols they have listed.

BEST PRACTICES TOOLKIT—Transparency
Analysis Frame: Theme pp. D21, D32

Text Analysis Workshop

Theme and Symbol

Essential Course of Study ECOS

When a friend inquires about a movie you saw recently, you might describe it by saying something like "It's about a Guatemalan girl who moves to New York and adjusts to life in an unfamiliar world." While it is true you've described the *topic* of the movie, you're not communicating its *big idea*. If you continue by saying "It's really about finding a way to fit in without losing your uniqueness," you are talking about theme. A **theme** is an underlying message about life that a writer wants to convey. Whether that message is about fitting in, love, or another timeless topic, it can often prompt you to think about human nature in a new way.

COMMON CORE

Included in this workshop:
RL 2 Determine a theme or central idea of a text and analyze in detail its development, including how it emerges and is shaped and refined by specific details; provide an objective summary of the text. **RL 3** Analyze how complex characters develop the theme. **RL 6** Analyze a particular point of view in a work of world literature.

Part 1: Themes in Literature

Despite the diversity in the world, many themes show up again and again in literature, no matter what the culture, time period, or country. These **universal themes** deal with archetypal experiences—that is, experiences common to all cultures. For example, the theme "With great power comes great responsibility" has been explored in stories as varied as ancient epics, myths, and today's comics.

"WITH GREAT POWER COMES GREAT RESPONSIBILITY"

Valmiki's *Ramayana* India C. 250 B.C.	Virgil's *Aeneid* Rome C. 20 B.C.	*Spider-Man* United States 1962–present

Theme and Symbol A writer has many tools he or she can use to develop a theme. Symbols, for example, can serve to powerfully reinforce a theme. A **symbol** is something concrete—a person, place, object, or activity—that represents an abstract idea. Among their many functions, symbols can help establish thematically appropriate moods, provide information about characters, reveal an author's perspective, and even show readers something about a work's historical context. Here are some examples of symbols and the ideas they might communicate:

- a bleak winter setting (isolation or death)
- a small child (innocence)
- a physical challenge, such as climbing a mountain (a character's emotional growth)

418 UNIT 4: THEME

DIFFERENTIATED INSTRUCTION

FOR STRUGGLING READERS

Note Taking For students who need help, hand out the note-taking copy master. As you identify main points, have students list these on the copy master. Later, students can complete the copy master with text details.

Charting Clues Have students chart theme clues in the model on page 419, focusing on Sylvia's interaction with the tree.

Type of Clue	Example from Story
Thoughts	climb is harder
Actions	keeps climbing
Setting	tree lengthens

 RESOURCE MANAGER—Copy Master
Note Taking p. 9

In this story, a farm girl named Sylvia meets a hunter in search of a rare bird. Wanting to impress the hunter, Sylvia decides to help look for the heron. In the end, however, she makes a difficult choice—to protect the bird. As part of her initial effort to help, Sylvia climbs a tree to look for the heron. As you read, consider what the tree and Sylvia's climb might symbolize.

from A White Heron

Short story by **Sarah Orne Jewett**

Half a mile from home, at the farther edge of the woods, where the land was highest, a great pine tree stood, the last of its generation. Whether it was left for a boundary mark, or for what reason, no one could say; the woodchoppers who had felled its mates were dead and gone long ago, and a whole forest
5 of sturdy trees, pines and oaks and maples, had grown again. But the stately head of this old pine towered above them all and made a landmark for sea and shore miles and miles away. Sylvia knew it well. She had always believed that whoever climbed to the top of it could see the ocean; and the little girl had often laid her hand on the great rough trunk and looked up wistfully at those
10 dark boughs that the wind always stirred, no matter how hot and still the air might be below. Now she thought of the tree with a new excitement, for why, if one climbed it at break of day, could not one see all the world, and easily discover whence the white heron flew? . . .

There was the huge tree asleep yet in the paling moonlight, and small and
15 silly Sylvia began with utmost bravery to mount to the top of it. . . .

The way was harder than she thought; she must reach far and hold fast, the sharp dry twigs caught and held her and scratched her like angry talons, the pitch made her thin little fingers clumsy and stiff as she went round and round the tree's great stem. . . .
20 The tree seemed to lengthen itself out as she went up, and to reach farther and farther upward. It was like a great mainmast to the voyaging earth; it must truly have been amazed that morning through all its ponderous frame as it felt this determined spark of human spirit wending its way from higher branch to branch. Who knows how steadily the least twigs held themselves to advantage
25 this light, weak creature on her way! The old pine must have loved his new dependent. More than all the hawks, and bats, and moths, and even the sweet-voiced thrushes, was the brave, beating heart of the solitary gray-eyed child. And the tree stood still and frowned away the winds that June morning while the dawn grew bright in the east.
30 Sylvia's face was like a pale star, if one had seen it from the ground, when the last thorny bough was past, and she stood trembling and tired but wholly triumphant, high in the tree-top. Yes, there was the sea with the dawning sun making a golden dazzle over it, and toward that glorious east flew two hawks. . . . Truly it was a vast and awesome world!

Close Read

1. What is special about the pine tree? Cite details in the first paragraph to support your answer. One detail has been boxed.

2. Find three details in lines 14–32 that suggest just how challenging Sylvia's climb is. What archetypal experience might her climb symbolize?

3. Consider Sylvia's decision to protect the bird, as well as the symbolic meanings of the tree and the climb. What might the writer be using Sylvia's decision and symbolism to say about how people should treat their natural surroundings?

TEXT ANALYSIS WORKSHOP **419**

MODEL: THEME AND SYMBOL
Close Read

1. *Possible answer: The pine tree is special as an old and stately landmark, visible from far away. It is a part of nature that has endured, having been spared by wood-choppers. Supporting text details include: "the stately head of this old pine towered above them all and made a landmark" (lines 5–6) and "great rough trunk" (line 9).*

2. *Possible answer: Details from the text that support the challenge of Sylvia's climb: "Sylvia began with utmost bravery" (line 15), "The way was harder than she thought" (line 16), "twigs caught and held her and scratched her like angry talons" (line 17), "The tree seemed to lengthen itself out as she went up" (line 20), "determined spark of human spirit" (line 23), and "trembling and tired but wholly triumphant" (lines 31–32). The physical challenge of Sylvia's climb may represent the archetypal experience of maturing from a small, silly child to someone who can make an important decision, such as protecting the heron.*

3. *Possible answer: The writer uses the symbolic nature of the tree, the heron, and Sylvia's decision to protect the bird to say that people should both respect and actively protect the natural world. Nature is beautiful and important; it should be cherished, not destroyed. Sylvia's final decision to protect the heron emphasizes this theme, as she comes to realize that she should play her part in protecting nature.*

FOR ENGLISH LANGUAGE LEARNERS

Vocabulary: Multiple Meanings Have students find two meanings for these words from the model: *break* (line 12), *fast* (line 16), *pitch* (line 18), and *awesome* (line 34). Ask students to write sentences to illustrate each meaning and then identify which meaning is used in the story.

FOR ADVANCED LEARNERS/PRE–AP

Analyze Theme Have students read the workshop independently. Have them form reading groups and choose a short story to analyze together. Direct them to use the questions on page 420 to make their interpretations of its theme.

Online Remediation

Are your students struggling with text analysis skills? Consider assigning them one or more **Level Up Online Tutorials** as remediation before beginning this unit. Log in to **thinkcentral.com** to view a list of the skills addressed by **Level Up**.

Teach

Part 2: Identify Theme

Plot and Conflict Tell students that plot, conflict, and theme are inseparable in fiction. The plot is the series of events in which the characters attempt to work out the main conflict. The way in which they do this and the changes they undergo (or don't) as a result will provide clues about the author's vision of the world and life created in the work.

Expressing Theme Tell students that after studying all the questions in the chart, readers can also ask themselves: What message does the author want me to take away from this selection? The answer will yield an instinctive statement of theme. Clarify that there is no right or wrong way to state theme. Every reader has his or her own way of putting a story's central insight into words. To be valid, however, the theme statement has to be defensible. Students need to cite evidence from the plot, setting, conflict, characters, symbols, and title that prove the statement to be true. Have students answer the question given above, then return to the questions in the chart to find supporting evidence for their answers. Also remind students that theme never completely explains a piece of literature; theme is one of the many elements that make up the whole.

CHECK UNDERSTANDING

Have students define *plot*, *conflict*, and *theme* in their own words.

Part 2: Identify Theme

Sometimes the theme of a story is stated directly by a character or the narrator. Most of the time, however, the theme is implied, and readers must analyze elements in the text—the setting, the characters, and the symbols, for example—to uncover the story's deeper meaning. Use the questions below to summarize each story element. This will help you identify the theme of any story you read.

CLUES TO THEME

TITLE
The title may refer to a significant idea explored in the story. Ask
- To what in the story does the title refer?
- What ideas or symbols does the title highlight?
- Does the title have more than one meaning?

 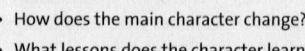 

CHARACTERS
Characters' actions and motivations may reflect the message of the story. Ask
- What are the main character's key traits and motivations? Consider how the writer might want readers to feel about the character.
- How does the main character change?
- What lessons does the character learn?

PLOT AND CONFLICT
A story revolves around conflicts that are central to the theme. Ask
- What is the main conflict in the story?
- How is the conflict resolved?
- Is the resolution portrayed as a positive or a negative outcome?

SETTING
The setting's significance to the characters and the conflict can suggest the theme. Ask
- How does the setting influence the characters?
- How does the setting affect the plot?
- What larger idea or issue might the setting represent?

IMPORTANT STATEMENTS
The narrator or the characters may make statements that hint at the theme. Ask
- What key comments do the characters or the narrator make? Take note of statements about values and ideas.
- What message or attitude about life do these statements reveal?

SYMBOLS
Symbols can powerfully reinforce the theme. Ask
- What characters, objects, places, or events have symbolic significance in the story?
- What ideas do these symbols communicate?

Remember, some works of literature have more than one theme, but typically only one is dominant. When you describe a theme of a work, be sure to use one or two complete sentences, not single words or phrases. For example, "love" expresses a topic, not a theme. "People often find love where they least expect it," however, is a valid way to state a theme.

DIFFERENTIATED INSTRUCTION

FOR STRUGGLING READERS
Note Taking Hand out the note-taking copy master for this page before discussing the Clues to Theme chart. As you cover each element, help students summarize the use of each clue type.

 RESOURCE MANAGER—Copy Master
Note Taking p. 10

FOR ENGLISH LANGUAGE LEARNERS
Language: Skill Words On the board, list the literary terms shown in italics:
- *plot:* the series of events in a story
- *conflict:* struggle between characters or forces
- *characters:* people or animals in a story
- *setting:* the time and place of the story
- *symbols:* the people, places, object, or events that stand for abstract ideas

Have students give an example for each term.

Practice and Apply

Part 3: Analyze the Text

As you read the following story, use the questions provided to help you identify the theme and understand the symbolism of the cranes.

CRANES

Short story by **Hwang Sunwŏn**

BACKGROUND This story takes place at the end of the Korean War (1950–1953), a civil war that pitted the Communist government of North Korea against the more democratic government of South Korea. At the end of World War II, the Korean peninsula had been divided along the line of 38° north latitude, commonly called the 38th parallel. During the Korean War, intense fighting along this border shifted control of nearby villages back and forth between the North Koreans and South Koreans. One of these villages is the setting of "Cranes."

The northern village lay snug beneath the high, bright autumn sky, near the border at the Thirty-eighth Parallel.

White gourds lay one against the other on the dirt floor of an empty farmhouse. Any village elders who passed by extinguished their bamboo pipes
5 first, and the children, too, turned back some distance off. Their faces were marked with fear.

As a whole, the village showed little damage from the war, but it still did not seem like the same village Sŏngsam[1] had known as a boy.

At the foot of a chestnut grove on the hill behind the village he stopped and
10 climbed a chestnut tree. Somewhere far back in his mind he heard the old man with a wen[2] shout, "You bad boy, climbing up my chestnut tree again!"

The old man must have passed away, for he was not among the few village elders Sŏngsam had met. Holding on to the trunk of the tree, Sŏngsam gazed

---

1. **Sŏngsam** (səng'säm').
2. **wen:** a harmless skin tumor.

Close Read

1. The title of this story is one clue to the theme. As you read, look for details that explain the significance of birds known as cranes.

2. The boxed details describe a peaceful setting—not one you might expect in a story about war. Which details in lines 1–8 suggest that the residents are unsettled by their seemingly calm surroundings?

TEXT ANALYSIS WORKSHOP **421**

Part 3: Analyze the Text

Close Read

1. Tell students that the significance of the title does not become clear until the end of the story. Question 10 on page 425 will help them explore the symbolism of the cranes and thus understand the title's significance.

2. *Possible answer: Details that suggest an unsettled atmosphere include "empty farmhouse" (lines 3–4); "extinguished their bamboo pipes" (line 4); "children, too, turned back some distance off" (line 5); "faces were marked with fear" (lines 5–6); and "did not seem like the same village Sŏngsam had known as a boy" (lines 7–8).*

FOR STRUGGLING READERS

Vocabulary Support Introduce these words from "Cranes." Have students locate the words in the story and then think aloud to figure out the meanings from context.

- *extinguished* (line 4), "put out the fire"
- *converted* (line 17), "changed into"
- *stunned* (line 18), "very surprised"
- *glared* (line 52), "stared angrily"
- *averted* (line 61), "turned away"

- *contracted* (line 71), "caught"
- *espied* (line 105), "saw"
- *specimens* (line 114), "special examples"

Analysis Support: Symbols Have students start a three-column chart like the one shown. Under *Symbols & Clues*, have them list possible symbols, such as the gourds, the chestnut tree, and the 38th Parallel. As they find symbols, students can list the line numbers. After reading, have students fill in the *Significance* column.

Symbols & Clues	Lines	Significance
climbing chestnut tree	10	childhood; guilt

3. Possible answers: *Sŏngsam may be motivated by his curiosity about what happened to his childhood friend since they last saw each other. Students may also say that perhaps Sŏngsam views Tŏkchae as an enemy and thus wants to interrogate him himself.*

4. Possible answer: *The flashback to Sŏngsam and Tŏkchae's childhood shows readers that Tŏkchae was a caring, generous friend. Not only did he pluck the painful burrs off of Sŏngsam, but he also shared his chestnuts, perhaps to make his friend feel better.*

IF STUDENTS NEED HELP . . . Help students fill in two Sequence Chains, one for the present events in the story and one for the past events. Doing so should enable students to follow the flashbacks that are essential to understanding the theme.

BEST PRACTICES TOOLKIT—Transparency
Sequence Chain p. B21

---

15 up at the blue sky for a time. Some chestnuts fell to the ground as the dry clusters opened of their own accord.

A young man stood, his hands bound, before a farmhouse that had been converted into a Public Peace Police office. He seemed to be a stranger, so Sŏngsam went up for a closer look. He was stunned: this young man was none other than his boyhood playmate, Tŏkchae.[3]

20 Sŏngsam asked the police officer who had come with him from Ch'ŏnt'ae[4] for an explanation. The prisoner was the vice-chairman of the Farmers' Communist League and had just been flushed[5] out of hiding in his own house, Sŏngsam learned.

Sŏngsam sat down on the dirt floor and lit a cigaret.

25 Tŏkchae was to be escorted to Ch'ŏngdan[6] by one of the peace police. After a time, Sŏngsam lit a new cigaret from the first and stood up. "I'll take him with me."

Tŏkchae averted his face and refused to look at Sŏngsam. The two left the village.

30 Sŏngsam went on smoking, but the tobacco had no flavor. He just kept drawing the smoke in and blowing it out. Then suddenly he thought that Tŏkchae, too, must want a puff. He thought of the days when they had shared dried gourd leaves behind sheltering walls, hidden from the adults' view. But today, how could he offer a cigaret to a fellow like this?

35 *O*nce, when they were small, he went with Tŏkchae to steal some chestnuts from the old man with the wen. It was Sŏngsam's turn to climb the tree. Suddenly the old man began shouting. Sŏngsam slipped and fell to the ground. He got chestnut burrs all over his bottom, but he kept on running. Only when the two had reached a safe place where the old man could not overtake them

40 did Sŏngsam turn his bottom to Tŏkchae. The burrs hurt so much as they were plucked out that Sŏngsam could not keep tears from welling up in his eyes. Tŏkchae produced a fistful of chestnuts from his pocket and thrust them into Sŏngsam's . . . Sŏngsam threw away the cigaret he had just lit, and then made up his mind not to light another while he was escorting Tŏkchae.

---

3. **Tŏkchae** (tŏk'jă').
4. **Ch'ŏnt'ae** (chən'tă').
5. **flushed:** driven from hiding.
6. **Ch'ŏngdan** (chəng'dän').

3. What do you think motivates Sŏngsam to take Tŏkchae with him? Explain your answer.

4. What does Sŏngsam's flashback to his childhood in lines 35–43 tell you about Tŏkchae's character and their friendship?

DIFFERENTIATED INSTRUCTION

FOR STRUGGLING READERS

Comprehension: Symbols Help students draw some conclusions about the chestnuts and what they may represent in the story. Use the chart begun on page 421.

Symbols & Clues	Lines	Significance
climbing **chestnut** tree	10	childhood; guilt
stealing **chestnuts** with Tŏkchae.	35–43	forbidden item that bonds boys

45 They reached the pass at the hill where he and Tŏkchae had cut fodder[7] for cows until Sŏngsam had to move to a spot near Ch'ŏnt'ae, south of the Thirty-eighth Parallel, two years before the liberation.

Sŏngsam felt a sudden surge of anger in spite of himself and shouted, "So how many have you killed?"

50 For the first time, Tŏkchae cast a quick glance at him and then looked away.

"You! How many have you killed?" he asked again.

Tŏkchae looked at him again and glared. The glare grew intense, and his mouth twitched.

"So you managed to kill quite a few, eh?" Sŏngsam felt his mind becoming
55 clear of itself, as if some obstruction had been removed. "If you were vice-chairman of the Communist League, why didn't you run? You must have been lying low with a secret mission."

Tŏkchae did not reply.

"Speak up. What was your mission?"

60 Tŏkchae kept walking. Tŏkchae was hiding something, Sŏngsam thought. He wanted to take a good look at him, but Tŏkchae kept his face averted.

Fingering the revolver at his side, Sŏngsam went on: "There's no need to make excuses. You're going to be shot anyway. Why don't you tell the truth here and now?"

65 "I'm not going to make any excuses. They made me vice-chairman of the League because I was a hardworking farmer and one of the poorest. If that's a capital offense,[8] so be it. I'm still what I used to be—the only thing I'm good at is tilling the soil." After a short pause, he added, "My old man is bedridden at home. He's been ill almost half a year." Tŏkchae's father was a widower, a poor,
70 hardworking farmer who lived only for his son. Seven years before his back had given out, and he had contracted a skin disease.

"Are you married?"

"Yes," Tŏkchae replied after a time.

"To whom?"

75 "Shorty."

"To Shorty?" How interesting! A woman so small and plump that she knew the earth's vastness, but not the sky's height. Such a cold fish! He and Tŏkchae had teased her and made her cry. And Tŏkchae had married her!

"How many kids?"

80 "The first is arriving this fall, she says."

Sŏngsam had difficulty swallowing a laugh that he was about to let burst forth in spite of himself. Although he had asked how many children Tŏkchae

7. **fodder:** coarsely chopped hay or straw used as food for farm animals.

8. **capital offense:** a crime calling for the death penalty.

Close Read

5. Reread lines 45–64. How has the war affected Sŏngsam's opinion of his former friend? Cite details that helped you to understand Sŏngsam's view of Tŏkchae.

6. What details in lines 65–80 remind Sŏngsam that Tŏkchae has a human side? One detail has been boxed.

Close Read

5. *Possible answer:* Sŏngsam's feelings toward Tŏkchae have changed. He seems to be disgusted by him and distrustful. He feels "a sudden surge of anger" (line 48) because he thinks Tŏkchae may have murdered many people. He suspects that his former friend must be "lying low with a secret mission" (line 57) or "hiding something" (line 60).

6. *Possible answer:* Sŏngsam is reminded of Tŏkchae's human side when Tŏkchae talks about his father as being hardworking, poor, and ill (lines 68–69). Then, when he finds out that Tŏkchae is married to someone they teased together as boys, the two begin to talk (lines 72–80).

FOR STRUGGLING READERS
Analysis Support: Theme Help students explain Tŏkchae's reaction to Sŏngsam's accusations. Have students support their analysis with specific details from the story. *Possible answer: Tŏkchae finds it difficult to look his friend in the eye, perhaps because of fear or disappointment at who Sŏngsam has become. Tŏkchae also seems angry, because he glares at Sŏngsam. He also refuses to make excuses and says that he is no differ-* ent than he used to be. Then discuss how Tŏkchae's reaction may provide a clue to the theme. *Possible answer: The theme may have something to do with friendship and how it must be changed or maintained, depending on the circumstances.*

7. Possible answer: *Sŏngsam begins to change when he realizes that he and Tŏkchae are similar. Both were faced with the difficult decision of whether to leave their farmland and familiar lives for safety reasons. Tŏkchae decided to stay with his sick father. In contrast, Sŏngsam left his family behind and has been haunted by his decision ever since. In line 101, Songsam walks "with his face averted," as if the company of his friend and the memory of his friend's decision are painful to him.*

---

had, he could not help wanting to break out laughing at the thought of the wife sitting there with her huge stomach, one span around. But he realized

85 that this was no time for joking.

"Anyway, it's strange you didn't run away."

"I tried to escape. They said that once the South invaded, not a man would be spared. So all of us between seventeen and forty were taken to the North. I thought of evacuating, even if I had to carry my father on my back. But Father

90 said no. How could we farmers leave the land behind when the crops were ready for harvesting? He grew old on that farm depending on me as the prop and the mainstay of the family. I wanted to be with him in his last moments so I could close his eyes with my own hand. Besides, where can farmers like us go, when all we know how to do is live on the land?"

95 Sŏngsam had had to flee the previous June. At night he had broken the news privately to his father. But his father had said the same thing: Where could a farmer go, leaving all the chores behind? So Sŏngsam had left alone. Roaming about the strange streets and villages in the South, Sŏngsam had been haunted by thoughts of his old parents and the young children, who had been left with

100 all the chores. Fortunately, his family had been safe then, as it was now.

*T*hey had crossed over a hill. This time Sŏngsam walked with his face averted. The autumn sun was hot on his forehead. This was an ideal day for the harvest, he thought.

When they reached the foot of the hill, Sŏngsam gradually came to a halt. In

105 the middle of a field he espied a group of cranes that resembled men in white, all bent over. This had been the demilitarized zone[9] along the Thirty-eighth Parallel. The cranes were still living here, as before, though the people were all gone.

Once, when Sŏngsam and Tŏkchae were about twelve, they had set a trap

110 here, unbeknownst to the adults, and caught a crane, a Tanjŏng crane.[10] They had tied the crane up, even binding its wings, and paid it daily visits, patting its neck and riding on its back. Then one day they overheard the neighbors whispering: someone had come from Seoul[11] with a permit from the governor-general's office to catch cranes as some kind of specimens. Then and there

---

9. **demilitarized zone:** an area—generally one separating two hostile nations or armies—from which military forces are prohibited.

10. **Tanjŏng** (tän'jəng') **crane:** a type of crane found in Asia.

11. **Seoul** (sōl): the capital and largest city of South Korea.

7. Line 101 marks a change in Sŏngsam's behavior. What does this change reveal about what's going on inside him? Reread lines 95–100 and summarize what motivates the change.

DIFFERENTIATED INSTRUCTION

FOR STRUGGLING READERS

Comprehension: Symbol Help students draw some conclusions about the Tanjŏng cranes and what they may represent. Use the chart begun on page 421.

Symbols & Clues	Lines	Significance
cranes still here	105–106	cranes unchanged
caught a **crane** with Tŏkchae	109–126	cranes were a bond
boys can free **crane**	117–119	people have power

Lead students to see that the cranes may stand for the two men's friendship, which has endured despite their current status as enemies. Point out that Sŏngsam has the power to free Tŏkchae, just as the boys once had the power to free their captured crane. Stress the fact that Tŏkchae is innocent of wrongdoing and guilty only of being a devoted son, facts that Sŏngsam has come to understand.

the two boys had dashed off to the field. That they would be found out and
punished had no longer mattered; all they cared about was the fate of their
crane. Without a moment's delay, still out of breath from running, they untied
the crane's feet and wings, but the bird could hardly walk. It must have been
weak from having been bound.

The two helped the crane up. Then, suddenly, they heard a gunshot. The
crane fluttered its wings once or twice and then sank back to the ground.

The boys thought their crane had been shot. But the next moment, as
another crane from a nearby bush fluttered its wings, the boys' crane stretched
its long neck, gave out a whoop, and disappeared into the sky. For a long while
the two boys could not tear their eyes away from the blue sky up into which
their crane had soared.

"Hey, why don't we stop here for a crane hunt?" Sŏngsam said suddenly.
Tŏkchae was dumbfounded.

"I'll make a trap with this rope; you flush a crane over here."

Sŏngsam had untied Tŏkchae's hands and was already crawling through the
weeds.

Tŏkchae's face whitened. "You're sure to be shot anyway"—these words
flashed through his mind. Any instant a bullet would come flying from
Sŏngsam's direction, Tŏkchae thought.

Some paces away, Sŏngsam quickly turned toward him.

"Hey, how come you're standing there like a dummy? Go flush a crane!"
Only then did Tŏkchae understand. He began crawling through the weeds.

A pair of Tanjŏng cranes soared high into the clear blue autumn sky,
flapping their huge wings.

Translated by Peter H. Lee

Close Read

8. In what ways is Tŏkchae like the crane? Cite specific descriptions of the crane that could also apply to Tŏkchae.

9. Why does Sŏngsam push Tŏkchae to flush a crane?

10. What might the two cranes symbolize? Use details from the text to summarize your answer.

11. Considering the clues in the story, what do you think the writer is saying about friendship? State the story's theme and summarize the details that helped you arrive at your conclusion.

Close Read

8. *Possible answer: Tŏkchae is like the crane because he, too, is imprisoned. He is being treated by government officials as a "specimen" whose activities and wrongdoings must be studied closely.*

9. *Possible answer: Sŏngsam pushes Tŏkchae to flush a crane because he wants to set Tŏkchae free.*

10. *Possible answer: The pair of cranes symbolizes the friendship of the two men that transcends the conflict dividing their country. The cranes still live in the demilitarized zone (lines 106–108), and so should these two friends, in Sŏngsam's view. The cranes once showed the two the value of freedom (lines 115–126), and now have done so again.*

11. *Possible answer: The theme can be stated in these ways: friendship should be valued more than other things, such as political beliefs or laws; being faithful to higher values of love, friendship, and truth brings freedom, whereas struggles for power and control bring only imprisonment and death.*

Assess and Reteach

Assess

Have students use their Clues to Theme notes to summarize how the title, plot, conflict, characters, setting, and symbols contribute to the theme.

Reteach

For students who are unable to apply the workshop skills to "Cranes," review with them the note-taking copy masters for this lesson. Have students read aloud the information they recorded about theme and symbol. Then write a blank copy of the chart from page 421 on the board. Help students complete it with information from "A White Heron." Students should supply examples of words, thoughts, characters' actions, and setting that provide clues about the theme.

FOR STRATEGIC READERS

Comprehension: Characters' Actions

Discuss with students similarities and differences between Sŏngsam and Tŏkchae as characters. If necessary, point out that both are prisoners—Tŏkchae because he was a Communist and Sŏngsam because he is trapped in his role as a policeman. They have similar values about the land, but Tŏkchae refused to leave his family while Sŏngsam did leave. Then ask students what clues the characters' similarities and differences provide to the theme. *Possible answer: The difference between the two men highlights the theme of valuing friendship, for it helps Sŏngsam remember Tŏkchae as a friend and an individual much like himself, rather than than as a political enemy. This leads Sŏngsam to choose friendship and freedom above political allegiance.*

Essential Course of Study ECOS

The Interlopers
Short Story by Saki

VIDEO TRAILER THINK central KEYWORD: HML10-426

COMMON CORE FOCUS

RL 2 Determine a theme of a text and analyze in detail how it emerges and is shaped and refined by specific details. **W 2** Write explanatory texts to examine and convey complex ideas, concepts, and information clearly and accurately through the effective analysis of content. **L 1b** Use various types of clauses to convey specific meanings and add variety and interest to writing. **L 5b** Analyze nuances in the meanings of words with similar denotations.

SUMMARY

Ulrich and Georg despise one another because of a family feud over land. One night they meet and are pinned by fallen tree branches during a storm. As a result, they agree to be friends. Sadly, they are "rescued" by wolves, not men.

What's wrong with holding a GRUDGE?

Discuss the question. After students *ROLE-PLAY*, work with them to brainstorm a list of reasons why they might hold grudges. Have them perform their scenes.

What's wrong with holding a GRUDGE?

COMMON CORE

RL 2 Determine a theme of a text and analyze in detail how it emerges and is shaped and refined by specific details.

Both history and literature are full of individuals who bear grudges, or feelings of great resentment, against others. This situation occurs so often in literature that it can be classified as an **archetype**—a pattern that appears in works all over the world and in different time periods. Recall, for example, the Montagues and Capulets—Romeo and Juliet's warring relatives. In "The Interlopers," you will read about two neighboring families whose ongoing feud has dire consequences.

ROLE-PLAY With a partner, imagine a scenario in which a long-standing grudge exists between the two of you. Think about what your relationship once involved. For example, maybe you were teammates or best friends. Also consider what event led to your disagreement. Then role-play a chance meeting. How do you behave toward each other? Do you remain angry or make up? Afterward, discuss what the hazards of holding the grudge have been.

426

See resources on the **Teacher One Stop DVD-ROM** *and on* **thinkcentral.com**.

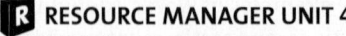 **RESOURCE MANAGER UNIT 4**
Plan and Teach, pp. 11–18
Summary, pp. 19–20†‡*
Text Analysis and Reading
   Skill, pp. 21–24†*
Vocabulary, pp. 25–27*
Grammar and Style, p. 30

DIAGNOSTIC AND SELECTION TESTS
Selection Tests, pp. 115–118

 **BEST PRACTICES TOOLKIT**
Definition Mapping, p. E6
Story Map, p. D14
Two-Column Chart, p. A25
Analysis Frame: Setting, p.
   D21, D30

INTERACTIVE READER

ADAPTED INTERACTIVE READER

ELL ADAPTED INTERACTIVE READER

TECHNOLOGY
- **Teacher One Stop DVD-ROM**
- **Student One Stop DVD-ROM**
- **PowerNotes DVD-ROM**
- **Audio Anthology CD**
- **GrammarNotes DVD-ROM**
- **Audio Tutor CD**
- **ExamView Test Generator**
   on the **Teacher One Stop**

Video Trailer

Go to **thinkcentral.com** to preview the **Video Trailer** introducing this selection. Other features that support the selection include
- **PowerNotes** presentation
- **ThinkAloud** models to enhance comprehension
- **WordSharp** vocabulary tutorials
- interactive writing and grammar instruction

* Resources for Differentiation   † Also in Spanish   ‡ In Haitian Creole and Vietnamese

TEXT ANALYSIS: THEME AND SETTING

In a short story, a **theme** is a message about life or human nature that the writer wants to communicate to readers. Often, the **setting** of a story, or where and when it takes place, helps convey this message. To understand how setting might contribute to theme, ask yourself the following questions:

- What aspects of the setting are emphasized?
- How does the setting affect the characters?
- How does the setting relate to the story's main conflict?

"The Interlopers" takes place in a forest whose ownership has been disputed by two families for generations. As you read, think about what Saki is saying about human nature and how the story's setting helps make this message clear.

READING STRATEGY: MONITOR

Good readers automatically check, or **monitor,** their comprehension of what they read. One way they accomplish this is by **clarifying** difficult passages. Strategies such as rereading, reading aloud, and summarizing can make tough parts easier to understand.

As you read "The Interlopers," stop and clarify the points in the story that are confusing to you. Use a chart like this one.

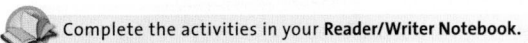

Confusing Passage	→	How I Clarified My Understanding	→	My New Understanding

▲ VOCABULARY IN CONTEXT

Saki uses the following words to tell his tale of resentments and greed. Categorize each word as "Know Well," "Think I Know," or "Don't Know." Then, in your *Reader/Writer Notebook*, write a brief definition of each word that is familiar to you.

WORD LIST		
acquiesce	languor	pinioned
condolence	marauder	precipitous
draft	pestilential	succor
interloper		

Know Well	Think I Know	Don't Know

Complete the activities in your **Reader/Writer Notebook.**

Meet the Author

Saki
1870–1916

Full of Surprises
"Saki" (sä'kē) was the pen name of Hector Hugh Munro, a British fiction writer of the early 20th century. He was considered one of the finest wits and storytellers of his generation. Written in the years leading up to World War I, his works convey the mixed sentiments of the time. Many of his short stories are **satires**, darkly humorous pieces that reveal flaws in social customs and institutions. Like the fiction of American icon O. Henry, Saki's narratives often feature surprise endings.

A World Traveler
At the age of 32, Saki began a long career as a newspaper correspondent. While on assignment, he lived in various places, including the Balkans, Russia, and France. In 1908, after his father died, Saki settled in London. There, at the age of 38, he began to write fiction, incorporating many of the exotic places he had visited into his works. For example, "The Interlopers" is set in the Carpathians, a mountain range in eastern Europe that Saki knew through his many journeys.

A Tragic End
Unfortunately, Saki's career as a fiction writer was short-lived. Following the outbreak of World War I, he enlisted in the British army. "I have always looked forward to the romance of a European war," he once remarked. In November 1916, he was killed by a German sniper during an attack at Beaumont-Hamel, France. He was 46 years old.

Author Online
THINK central
Go to **thinkcentral.com.**
KEYWORD: HML10-427

427

Teach

● *Model the Skill:* THEME AND SETTING

To model how setting can help convey a theme, read aloud this example:

> The sea was calm at the moment, but a wind had come up from the west and the sky was turning dark. Tom, the more experienced sailor, wanted to return to shore, but Joe refused, saying, "Trust me."

Guide students in applying the three questions on the pupil page to this passage.

GUIDED PRACTICE Have students name stories they have read or movies they have seen in which the setting contributed to the theme, such as the Arctic setting in "To Build a Fire."

READING STRATEGY

■ *Model the Skill:* MONITOR

To model how to monitor reading, have students read **Full of Surprises.** Point out that many of Saki's works are characterized as satires. Tell students the works are called satires because they ridicule customs and institutions.

GUIDED PRACTICE Have students read **A Tragic End** and clarify why Saki fought in World War I.

R RESOURCE MANAGER—Copy Master
Monitor p. 23 (for student use while reading the selection)

▲ VOCABULARY IN CONTEXT

DIAGNOSE WORD KNOWLEDGE Have all students complete Vocabulary in Context. Check their definitions against the following:

acquiesce (ăk'wē-ĕs') *v.* to agree or give in to
condolence (kən-dō'ləns) *n.* an expression of sympathy
draft (drăft) *n.* a gulp or swallow
interloper (ĭn'tər-lō'pər) *n.* one that intrudes in a place, situation, or activity
languor (lăng'gər) *n.* a lack of feeling or energy
marauder (mə-rôd'ər) *n.* one who raids and loots
pestilential (pĕs'tə-lĕn'shəl) *adj.* likely to spread and cause disease
pinioned (pĭn'yənd) *adj.* restrained or immobilized **pinion** *v.*
precipitous (prĭ-sĭp'ĭ-təs) *adj.* extremely steep
succor (sŭk'ər) *n.* help in a difficult situation

PRETEACH VOCABULARY Use the following copy master to help students predict meanings for each boldfaced word.

R RESOURCE MANAGER—Copy Master
Vocabulary Study p. 25

READ WITH A PURPOSE

Help students set a purpose for reading. Tell them to look for clues about what kind of men Ulrich and Georg are.

A THEME AND SETTING

Possible answer: *The aspects of the natural setting that are emphasized include "forest of mixed growth" (line 1), "eastern spurs of the Carpathians" (line 1), "winter night" (line 2), wild game (lines 3, 4) and "dark forest" (line 6).*

OWN THE WORD

- **interloper:** Tell students that another way to describe an *interloper* is someone who is a meddler, a person who iterferes.

- **precipitous:** Remind students that *precipitous* is the adjective form of the noun *precipice*, "an extremely steep mass of rock" or "the brink of a dangerous situation." Have students write a sentence for both meanings of the word *precipice*.

- **acquiesce:** Ask students to name synonyms for the verb *acquiesce*. **Possible answers:** *accede, accept, agree, assent, consent*

THE Interlopers

SAKI

In a forest of mixed growth somewhere on the eastern spurs of the Carpathians,[1] a man stood one winter night watching and listening, as though he waited for some beast of the woods to come within the range of his vision, and, later, of his rifle. But the game[2] for whose presence he kept so keen an outlook was none that figured in the sportman's calendar as lawful and proper for the chase; Ulrich von Gradwitz[3] patrolled the dark forest in quest of a human enemy. **A**

The forest lands of Gradwitz were of wide extent and well stocked with game; the narrow strip of **precipitous** woodland that lay on its outskirt was not remarkable for the game it harbored or the shooting it afforded, but it was the most jealously guarded of all its owner's territorial possessions. A famous lawsuit, in the days of his grandfather, had wrested it from the illegal possession of a neighboring family of petty landowners; the dispossessed party had never **acquiesced** in the judgment of the Courts, and a long series of poaching affrays[4] and similar scandals had embittered the relationships between the families for three generations. The neighbor feud had grown into a personal one since Ulrich had come to be head of his family; if there was a

---

1. **eastern spurs of the Carpathians** (kär-pā′thē-ənz): the edges of a mountain range in central Europe.
2. **game:** animals hunted for food or sport.
3. **Ulrich von Gradwitz** (ōōl′rĭкн fôn gräd′vĭts).
4. **poaching affrays** (ə-frāz′): noisy quarrels about hunting on someone else's property.

428   UNIT 4: THEME

interloper (ĭn′tər-lō′pər) *n.* one that intrudes in a place, situation, or activity

1 Targeted Passage

A THEME AND SETTING What aspects of the story's natural setting are emphasized in this introductory paragraph?

precipitous (prĭ-sĭp′ĭ-təs) *adj.* extremely steep

acquiesce (ăk′wē-ĕs′) *v.* to agree or give in to

FOR ENGLISH LANGUAGE LEARNERS

Vocabulary Support Use Definition Mapping to teach these words: *illegal* (line 11), *series* (line 13), *code* (line 43), *release* (line 55), *region* (line 123), *dramatic* (line 137).

 BEST PRACTICES TOOLKIT—Transparency Definition Mapping p. E6

FOR STRUGGLING READERS

In combination with the *Audio Anthology CD*, use one or more Targeted Passages (pp. 428, 432, 434) to ensure that students focus on key events, concepts, and skills. Targeted Passages are also good for English learners.

1 Targeted Passage [Lines 4–15]

This passage introduces one of the two main characters and explains the conflict between Ulrich and his neighbor.

Reading Support

This selection on **thinkcentral.com** includes embedded **ThinkAloud** models—students "thinking aloud" about the story to model the kinds of questions a good reader would ask about a selection.

BACKGROUND

The Carpathian Mountains consist of a long stretch of low to medium peaks that run through Romania in southeastern Europe. The winters in that area are relatively mild, with low temperatures not usually exceeding –10 degrees Celsius. The region is covered with fir and spruce trees and is home to many large carnivorous animals, such as bears, wolves, and lynx.

Analyze Visuals

Activity Ask students to compare this photograph to the setting of the story. ***Possible answer:*** *The photograph shows a "dark forest" (line 6) of "mixed growth" (line 1). The forest in the photograph looks like a quiet place where wild animals might roam.*

- Who or what is the "game" that Ulrich waits for? (line 6, lines 17–19)
- Why does Ulrich guard the land? (lines 10–15)
- How did the land come into Ulrich's possession? (lines 10–13)

FOR ADVANCED LEARNERS/PRE–AP

Make Judgements Point out that Saki's experience traveling as a journalist informed his writing. Ask: Must a writer visit a place in order to create an accurate setting? Is using imagination alone sufficient? Encourage students to use specific examples of other authors and stories they have read in order to explain their points.

THE INTERLOPERS **429**

B MONITOR

Possible answer: The two men's families have been fighting for three generations over who owns a forest (lines 10–16). Ulrich and Georg have continued the feud and made it personal. Instead of trying to end their feud, they continually wish ill to one another (lines 19–22).

TEXT ANALYSIS COMMON CORE RL 2

C ARCHETYPE

Help students to clarify the meaning of *archetype.* Ask students to name some examples of "good" archetypes versus "evil" archetypes that they have encountered in movies. Create a master list on the board and discuss with the class how the same archetype is repeated in the different films.

Possible answer: Students may suggest that the initial conflict becomes meaningless to later generations yet can still lead to negative results for both sides. Students may cite examples such as Romeo and Juliet, where the conflict between the families caused the deaths of their children.

VOCABULARY COMMON CORE L 4

OWN THE WORD

marauder: Tell students that *maraud* is a verb meaning "to raid in search of plunder." By adding the suffix *-er,* the verb becomes a noun used to describe who is raiding and looting. From the story, ask students to identify who Ulrich von Gradwitz considered *marauders.* **Possible answer:** *a neighboring family headed by Georg Znaeym*

---

man in the world whom he detested and wished ill to it was Georg Znaeym,[5] the inheritor of the quarrel and the tireless game-snatcher and raider of the disputed border-forest. The feud might, perhaps, have died down or been
20 compromised if the personal ill-will of the two men had not stood in the way; as boys they had thirsted for one another's blood, as men each prayed that misfortune might fall on the other, and this wind-scourged winter night Ulrich had banded together his foresters to watch the dark forest, not in quest of four-footed quarry, but to keep a lookout for the prowling thieves whom he suspected of being afoot from across the land boundary. The roebuck,[6] which usually kept in the sheltered hollows during a storm wind, were running like driven things tonight, and there was movement and unrest among the creatures that were wont to sleep through the dark hours. Assuredly there was a disturbing element in the forest, and Ulrich could guess the quarter from
30 whence it came. **B**

He strayed away by himself from the watchers whom he had placed in ambush on the crest of the hill, and wandered far down the steep slopes amid the wild tangle of undergrowth, peering through the tree trunks and listening through the whistling and skirling[7] of the wind and the restless beating of the branches for sight or sound of the **marauders.** If only on this wild night, in this dark, lone spot, he might come across Georg Znaeym, man to man, with none to witness—that was the wish that was uppermost in his thoughts. And as he stepped around the trunk of a huge beech, he came face to face with the man he sought.

40 The two enemies stood glaring at one another for a long silent moment. **C**

Each had a rifle in his hand, each had hate in his heart and murder uppermost in his mind. The chance had come to give full play to the passions of a lifetime. But a man who has been brought up under the code of a restraining civilization cannot easily nerve himself to shoot down his neighbor in cold blood and without a word spoken, except for an offense against his hearth and honor. And before the moment of hesitation had given way to action a deed of Nature's own violence overwhelmed them both. A fierce shriek of the storm had been answered by a splitting crash over their heads, and ere they could leap aside a mass of falling beech tree had thundered down on
50 them. Ulrich von Gradwitz found himself stretched on the ground, one arm numb beneath him and the other held almost as helplessly in a tight tangle of forked branches, while both legs were pinned beneath the fallen mass. His heavy shooting boots had saved his feet from being crushed to pieces, but if his fractures were not as serious as they might have been, at least it was evident that he could not move from his present position till someone came to release him. The descending twigs had slashed the skin of his face, and he had to wink away some drops of blood from his eyelashes before he could take in a general

---

5. **Georg Znaeym** (gā-ôrg′ tsnä′ĕm).
6. **roebuck:** a male roe deer.
7. **skirling:** a shrill cry or sound.

B MONITOR
Clarify your understanding of why Ulrich and Georg are enemies by rereading or reading aloud lines 7–30.

marauder (mə-rôd′ər) *n.* one who raids and loots

COMMON CORE RL 2

C ARCHETYPE
An **archetype** is a pattern that appears repeatedly in literature, such as star-crossed lovers, a search for treasure, or a battle against evil. The plot of "The Interlopers" centers around the archetypal plot of enemies who have inherited a feud. Consider what other literary works you have read that contain feuds. What theme, or central idea, usually develops from a plot involving an inherited feud?

Language Coach

Homophones Many words sound alike but have different spellings. Reread lines 47–50. The word *ere* is an old-fashioned word with several homophones, including *err.* Which word means "to make a mistake"? Which word means "before"? How can you tell?

DIFFERENTIATED INSTRUCTION

FOR STRUGGLING READERS

Comprehension Support Point out to students that "Nature's own violence" is the storm (lines 46–55). This storm forces the men to face their conflict. Have students use a Story Map to outline the important information they already know and to record information they learn as they continue reading.

 BEST PRACTICES TOOLKIT—Transparency Story Map p. D14

FOR ENGLISH LANGUAGE LEARNERS

Language Coach

Homophones Answer: *Ere means "before"; you can tell by substituting the definition into the sentence. You can tell* err *means "to make a mistake" because it is related to the word* error *("mistake"). Point out the old-fashioned adjective* wont *(line 28), and tell students that a homophone for it is the verb* want. *Ask students to decide which word means "accustomed or used" and which means "desire."*

view of the disaster. At his side, so near that under ordinary circumstances he could almost have touched him, lay Georg Znaeym, alive and struggling, but obviously as helplessly __pinioned__ down as himself. All around them lay a thick-strewn wreckage of splintered branches and broken twigs. **D**

Relief at being alive and exasperation at his captive plight brought a strange medley of pious thank offerings and sharp curses to Ulrich's lips. Georg, who was nearly blinded with the blood which trickled across his eyes, stopped his struggling for a moment to listen, and then gave a short, snarling laugh.

"So you're not killed, as you ought to be, but you're caught, anyway," he cried; "caught fast. Ho, what a jest, Ulrich von Gradwitz snared in his stolen forest. There's real justice for you!"

And he laughed again, mockingly and savagely.

60

pinioned (pĭn′yənd) *adj.* restrained or immobilized **pinion** *v.*

D THEME AND SETTING
How does the natural setting, particularly the fallen tree, affect Ulrich and Georg?

THE INTERLOPERS **431**

FOR ENGLISH LANGUAGE LEARNERS

Vocabulary: Roots Explain to students that many pairs of nouns and verbs have the same root, such as *wreckage* (line 61) and *wreck*, and *relief* (line 62) and *relieve*. Have small groups find on pages 431–434 other nouns that share a root with a verb. Have students use a Two-Column Chart to record the nouns in the left column and the verb form in the right column.

Noun Form	Verb Form
• wreckage	• wreck
• relief	• relieve

🧰 **BEST PRACTICES TOOLKIT—Transparency**
Two-Column Chart p. A25

D *Model the Skill:* **THEME AND SETTING**

Possible answer: *Both men are trapped under the fallen tree, blown down by the wind (lines 47–49). They are injured and unable to move (lines 49–61). They are forced to recognize their own helplessness.*

REVISIT THE BIG QUESTION

What's wrong with holding a **GRUDGE?**

Discuss Based on lines 63–69, what is surprising about Georg's comment to Ulrich?
Possible answer: Despite the fact that Georg is seriously hurt, he is pleased that Ulrich is at least caught, if not killed. Instead of focusing on his own desperate situation, Georg thinks first of their **grudge** *and his hatred for Ulrich.*

VOCABULARY   COMMON CORE   L 4

OWN THE WORD

pinioned: Point out that when a person is *pinioned*, he or she is restrained or immobilized by binding the arms. Have students write a sentence using the word *pinioned*.

GRAMMAR AND STYLE

COMMON CORE L 1b

Improve Sentence Flow Point out that a subordinate clause can be used as an adjective, an adverb, or a noun to allow writers to express ideas that are difficult to express in one word. Ask students what part of speech this subordinate clause is (adverb) and what idea it expresses. Point out other subordinate clauses in the story (such as, "Even when he had accomplished that operation," line 95). Have students find other subordinate clauses in the story and identify the idea each expresses.

READING STRATEGY

Model the Skill: MONITOR

Model for students how to monitor their reading. Point out lines 76–79, and explain that Georg is threatening Ulrich and sarcastically saying that his men could pretend to be clumsy and roll the tree over Ulrich. Have students record this discussion clarifying these lines in their Clarifying charts.

Possible answer: Both men threaten to enlist their foresters to kill the other.

VOCABULARY

COMMON CORE L 4

OWN THE WORD

• **condolence:** Remind students that a *condolence* is an expression of sympathy. Have students suggest situations in which they would offer someone their *condolences*.

• **draft:** Remind students that *draft* is used as a noun in this story and means "a gulp or swallow." Point out that *draft* has multiple meanings. Have students use dictionaries to look up other meanings of *draft* and then write sentences using other forms and meanings of the word.

---

70 "I'm caught in my own forest land," retorted Ulrich. "When my men come to release us, you will wish, perhaps, that you were in a better plight than caught poaching on a neighbor's land, shame on you."

Georg was silent for a moment; then he answered quietly.

"Are you sure that your men will find much to release? I have men, too, in the forest tonight, close behind me, and they will be here first and do the releasing. When they drag me out from under these branches, it won't need much clumsiness on their part to roll this mass of trunk right over on the top of you. Your men will find you dead under a fallen beech tree. For form's sake I shall send my **condolences** to your family."

80 "It is a useful hint," said Ulrich fiercely. "My men had orders to follow in ten minutes' time, seven of which must have gone by already, and when they get me out—I will remember the hint. Only as you will have met your death poaching on my lands, I don't think I can decently send any message of condolence to your family."

"Good," snarled Georg, "good. We fight this quarrel out to the death, you and I and our foresters, with no cursed interlopers to come between us. Death . . . to you, Ulrich von Gradwitz."

"The same to you, Georg Znaeym, forest thief, game-snatcher."

Both men spoke with the bitterness of possible defeat before them, for each 90 knew that it might be long before his men would seek him out or find him; it was a bare matter of chance which party would arrive first on the scene.

Both had now given up the useless struggle to free themselves from the mass of wood that held them down; Ulrich limited his endeavors to an effort to bring his one partially free arm near enough to his outer coat pocket to draw out his wine flask. Even when he had accomplished that operation, it was long before he could manage the unscrewing of the stopper or get any of the liquid down his throat. But what a heaven-sent **draft** it seemed! It was an open winter,[8] and little snow had fallen as yet, hence the captives suffered less from the cold than might have been the case at that season of the year; nevertheless, 100 the wine was warming and reviving to the wounded man, and he looked across with something like a throb of pity to where his enemy lay, just keeping the groans of pain and weariness from crossing his lips.

"Could you reach this flask if I threw it over to you?" asked Ulrich suddenly; "there is good wine in it, and one may as well be as comfortable as one can. Let us drink, even if tonight one of us dies."

"No, I can scarcely see anything; there is so much blood caked around my eyes," said Georg, "and in any case I don't drink wine with an enemy."

Ulrich was silent for a few minutes and lay listening to the weary screeching of the wind. An idea was slowly forming and growing in his brain, an idea that 110 gained strength every time that he looked across at the man who was fighting

---

8. **open winter:** a mild winter.

GRAMMAR AND STYLE
Reread lines 70–72. Saki uses the **subordinate clause** "When my men come to release us" to tell how Ulrich thinks he will be rescued.

condolence (kən-dō'ləns) *n.* an expression of sympathy

MONITOR
Summarize in one or two sentences what each man threatens to do if rescued.

Targeted Passage

draft (drăft) *n.* a gulp or swallow

DIFFERENTIATED INSTRUCTION

FOR STRUGGLING READERS

Targeted Passage [Lines 89–107]
This passage shows the seriousness of the men's situation and the story's turning point.

• Are Ulrich and Georg confident that they will be rescued? (lines 89–91)

• What does Ulrich find in his pocket? (lines 94–95)

• What question does Ulrich ask Georg? (line 103)

FOR ENGLISH LANGUAGE LEARNERS

Vocabulary: Multiple-Meaning Words Have students identify the words on page 432 that have multiple meanings: *poaching* (line 72); *mass, trunk, top* (line 77); *form* (line 78); *matter, chance* (line 91); *crossing* (line 102). List each word on the board. Have students form two teams. Have one member of the first team choose a word and use it in two sentences, one sentence for each meaning of the word. If the word is used incorrectly, the other team gets a turn. Repeat for each word.

so grimly against pain and exhaustion. In the pain and **languor** that Ulrich himself was feeling the old fierce hatred seemed to be dying down. **G**

"Neighbor," he said presently, "do as you please if your men come first. It was a fair compact. But as for me, I've changed my mind. If my men are the first to come, you shall be the first to be helped, as though you were my guest. We have quarreled like devils all our lives over this stupid strip of forest, where the trees can't even stand upright in a breath of wind. Lying here tonight, thinking, I've come to think we've been rather fools; there are better things in life than getting the better of a boundary dispute. Neighbor, if you will help
120 me to bury the old quarrel I—I will ask you to be my friend."

Georg Znaeym was silent for so long that Ulrich thought, perhaps, he had fainted with the pain of his injuries. Then he spoke slowly and in jerks.

"How the whole region would stare and gabble if we rode into the market square together. No one living can remember seeing a Znaeym and a von Gradwitz talking to one another in friendship. And what peace there would be among the forester folk if we ended our feud tonight. And if we choose to make peace among our people, there is none other to interfere, no interlopers from outside. . . . You would come and keep the Sylvester night[9] beneath my roof, and I would come and feast on some high day at your castle. . . . I would
130 never fire a shot on your land, save when you invited me as a guest; and you should come and shoot with me down in the marshes where the wildfowl are. In all the countryside there are none that could hinder if we willed to make peace. I never thought to have wanted to do other than hate you all my life, but I think I have changed my mind about things too, this last half-hour. And you offered me your wine flask. . . . Ulrich von Gradwitz, I will be your friend."

For a space both men were silent, turning over in their minds the wonderful changes that this dramatic reconciliation would bring about. In the cold, gloomy forest, with the wind tearing in fitful gusts through the naked branches and whistling around the tree trunks, they lay and waited for the help that
140 would now bring release and **succor** to both parties. And each prayed a private prayer that his men might be the first to arrive, so that he might be the first to show honorable attention to the enemy that had become a friend. **H**

Presently, as the wind dropped for a moment, Ulrich broke silence.

"Let's shout for help," he said; "in this lull our voices may carry a little way."

"They won't carry far through the trees and undergrowth," said Georg, "but we can try. Together, then."

The two raised their voices in a prolonged hunting call.

"Together again," said Ulrich a few minutes later, after listening in vain for an answer halloo.

150 "I heard something that time, I think," said Ulrich.

"I heard nothing but the **pestilential** wind," said Georg hoarsely.

---

9. **Sylvester night:** New Year's Eve, the feast day of Saint Sylvester (Pope Sylvester I).

---

languor (lăng'gər) *n.* a lack of feeling or energy

G THEME AND SETTING
In what ways are Ulrich's actions influenced by the natural setting and its conditions? Cite specifics from lines 92–112.

succor (sŭk'ər) *n.* help in a difficult situation

H THEME AND SETTING
Reread lines 113–142. How has the setting brought about changes in the **conflict** between Ulrich and Georg?

pestilential (pĕs'tə-lĕn'shəl) *adj.* likely to spread and cause disease

---

G THEME AND SETTING

Model how to understand the how setting affects a character's actions. Read lines 92–112 aloud to students. Point out that the setting is a cold winter night, which causes Ulrich to drink from his wine flask to warm himself. Ask students how the fallen tree, another detail of the setting, affects Ulrich.

Possible answer: Ulrich is trapped outside on a cold winter night. To keep warm, he drinks from his wine flask. He looks across to Georg with "a throb of pity" (line 101) and offers him a drink. He realizes that one of them might die (line 105), and as he listens to the "weary screeching of the wind" (lines 108–109) an idea forms in his mind; their desperate situation seems to make his "old fierce hatred" (line 112) subside.

**TEXT ANALYSIS   COMMON CORE
RL 2**

H THEME AND SETTING

Possible answer: The fallen tree traps Ulrich and Georg into a situation where they are forced to face each other. Ulrich warms himself with wine in the chilly night and offers some to Georg. This friendly gesture thaws the hatred that each one feels for the other.

**VOCABULARY   COMMON CORE
L 4**

OWN THE WORD

- **languor:** Have students create a semantic map for *languor*. Write the word in the center circle along with the definition. Draw spider legs from the center circle and have students add antonyms to complete the map.

- **succor:** Point out that *succor* comes from the Latin word *succurrere*, which means "to run to the aid of." Have students write a sentence using *succor* correctly.

- **pestilential:** Ask students why they think Saki used the word *pestilential* in line 151.

FOR STRUGGLING READERS

Comprehension Point out to students that Ulrich wants to become friends with Georg (lines 113–120). But, more important, he also begins to recognize that people and relationships are more important than things. He says, "there are better things in life than getting the better of a boundary dispute" (lines 118–119). Discuss with students the importance of this statement and how they can infer a larger message from it to apply to their own lives.

FOR ADVANCED LEARNERS/PRE–AP

Analyze Setting [small-group option] Tell students to work in small groups to answer questions in the Analysis Frame: Setting questions for "The Interlopers." Then have students discuss ways the setting contributes to one or more themes in the story. Have students summarize their ideas for the class.

BEST PRACTICES TOOLKIT—Transparency
Analysis Frame: Setting pp. D21, D30

What's wrong with holding a GRUDGE?

Discuss Based on lines 163–167, what does the surprise ending suggest about holding grudges? *Possible answer: Holding grudges is a waste of time. People never know what will happen in their lives, and they should not waste years being angry over things that ultimately do not matter.*

TEXT ANALYSIS
COMMON CORE
RL 2

❶ THEME AND SETTING

Possible answer: The conclusion of the story suggests that the wolves are going to kill Ulrich and Georg (lines 163–167).

Analyze Visuals

Possible answer: The shadowy photographs suggest a mysterious, suspenseful, and ominous mood; the photograph of the wolf creates a frightening mood.

SELECTION WRAP-UP

READ WITH A PURPOSE Now that students have finished reading the selection, discuss with students what they learned about Ulrich and Georg. Are these two men similar or different? *Possible answer: Although they are feuding, Ulrich and Georg are similar. They are both determined and filled with hate.*

⭐ **CRITIQUE** Have students evaluate the effectiveness of the surprise ending.

INDEPENDENT READING

If students are interested in reading other works by Saki, suggest "The Open Window," a short story about a girl whose tale terrifies a visitor.

434 UNIT 4: THEME

There was silence again for some minutes, and then Ulrich gave a joyful cry.

"I can see figures coming through the wood. They are following in the way I came down the hillside."

Both men raised their voices in as loud a shout as they could muster.

"They hear us! They've stopped. Now they see us. They're running down the hill towards us," cried Ulrich.

"How many of them are there?" asked Georg.

"I can't see distinctly," said Ulrich; "nine or ten."

160 "Then they are yours," said Georg; "I had only seven out with me."

"They are making all the speed they can, brave lads," said Ulrich gladly.

"Are they your men?" asked Georg. "Are they your men?"

"No," said Ulrich with a laugh, the idiotic chattering laugh of a man unstrung with hideous fear.

"Who are they?" asked Georg quickly, straining his eyes to see what the other would gladly not have seen.

"*Wolves*." 〰 ❶

❸ Targeted Passage

❶ THEME AND SETTING
How does nature get the better of Ulrich and Georg at the story's conclusion?

◀ Analyze Visuals
Review the photographs in this lesson. What **mood** do they help create?

434 UNIT 4: THEME

DIFFERENTIATED INSTRUCTION

FOR STRUGGLING READERS

❸ Targeted Passage [Lines 155–167]

This passage shows the men's hopeful excitement and the tragic ending that dashes it.

• Who does Ulrich think he sees running down the hill? (lines 154, 161)

• Why do you think that Ulrich has "the idiotic chattering laugh of a man unstrung with hideous fear" (lines 163–164)?

FOR STRUGGLING READERS

Develop Reading Fluency Model for students the correct pronunciation of the names *Ulrich* and *Georg*. Then have students work in pairs and practice reading the dialogue between Ulrich and Georg in lines 153–167. Have students practice the lines several times to develop fluency. Invite volunteers to read the dialogue aloud to the class.

Distribute the copy masters and have students work in pairs or groups to practice fluency.

R RESOURCE MANAGER—Copy Master
Reading Fluency p. 31

Comprehension

1. **Recall** Why is Ulrich in the forest?

2. **Recall** Why are the von Gradwitz and Znaeym families fighting?

3. **Summarize** What happens to Ulrich and Georg when they are in the forest?

COMMON CORE

RL 2 Determine a theme of a text and analyze in detail how it emerges and is refined by specific details; provide an objective summary.

Text Analysis

4. **Identify Conflict** Use a chart like the one shown to record an example of each kind of conflict found in the story. Then explain the nature of the conflict.

Kind of Conflict	Example from the Story	Explanation
Character vs. character		
Character vs. nature		
Character vs. self		

5. **Analyze Climax** Identify the climax of the story. How do Ulrich and Georg begin to change at this **turning point?** Cite evidence to support your claim.

6. **Understand Irony** A contrast between what is expected and what really occurs is called irony. Think about what you thought would happen at the conclusion of "The Interlopers" and what actually does happen. How is the ending of the story ironic?

7. **Interpret Title** Who or what are the interlopers? Give two interpretations of the story's title.

● 8. **Examine Theme and Setting** Think about the story's setting and the way it affects Ulrich and Georg. What theme related to setting do you think Saki communicates in the story? Cite evidence to support your claim.

● 9. **Monitor** Review the chart you created as you read. How has clarifying your reading helped you to better understand the story? Offer two personal examples to support your answer.

Text Criticism

10. **Critical Interpretations** "Saki came to the short story as a satirist," argues one literary critic, "and never averted his eye from the darker side of human nature, a place where not only social ineptness, pomposity, and foolishness are rooted but criminality as well." What human vices or follies does Saki ridicule in the story?

> ### What's wrong with holding a GRUDGE?
>
> Why do you think grudges appear so often in literature?

---

9. ● **COMMON CORE FOCUS** *Monitor* Students' answers should reflect an understanding of the story and strategy.

Text Criticism
Possible answer:

10. *Saki depicts human beings as pompous and foolish. Ulrich and Georg each think he is controller of the forest lands. Instead, the men are dominated by nature.*

What's wrong with holding a
GRUDGE? *Possible answer:*
Grudges introduce conflict into literature and involve readers in the interplay between characters and in the resolution of the conflict. Grudges are archetypal experiences.

For preliminary support of post-reading questions, use these copy masters:

R RESOURCE MANAGER—Copy Masters
Reading Check p. 28
Theme and Setting p. 21
Question Support p. 29

Additional selection questions are provided for teachers on page 15.

ANSWERS

Comprehension

1. *Ulrich is looking for poachers, specifically Georg and his foresters.*

2. *The families are fighting over the ownership of the forest lands.*

3. *The two men are pinned down by a fallen tree, agree to be friends, and are forced to wait for rescuers who never come.*

Text Analysis

Possible answers:

4. *Character vs. Character: Ulrich vs. Georg; life-long enemies who fight over land Character vs. Nature: The men vs. the storm and forest; both men are trapped after the storm. Character vs. Self: Ulrich vs. himself; he gives up hating Georg.*

5. *Throughout the story the conflict revolved around the feud, the hatred the men had for each other. The story's climax is when Ulrich and Georg agree to become friends.*

6. *I expected the men would be rescued and become friends. Ironically, wolves arrive and threaten the men.*

7. *The title could refer to both the men and to the wolves. The men intrude on the wolves and vice versa. Each man also thinks of the other as an intruder on his land.*

8. ● **COMMON CORE FOCUS** *Theme and Setting* One theme is that nature has control over humankind (lines 47–65, 165–167); the "fierce shriek of the storm" interrupts the men just as they plan to act (lines 47–48).*

ANSWERS

Vocabulary in Context

▲ VOCABULARY PRACTICE

1. *similar*	6. *similar*
2. *different*	7. *similar*
3. *similar*	8. *different*
4. *different*	9. *different*
5. *different*	10. *similar*

 **RESOURCE MANAGER—Copy Master**
Vocabulary Practice p. 26

ACADEMIC VOCABULARY IN WRITING

Possible answer: *The wolves in this story are a* symbol *of unpredictable fate. They could also be viewed as a* symbol *of nature's power. Changing the wolves to another animal that preys on humans, such as a bear, might not* alter *the* theme *greatly. However, changing the wolves to a vulture might* alter *the* symbol *to emphasize cruelty.*

VOCABULARY STRATEGY: CONNOTATION

COMMON CORE L 5b

• Have students create a simple sentence using one of the words and then replace that word with other words that mean the same.

• Have them consider how the meaning of the sentence is changed.

Possible answers:

1. *pale: neutral; pasty: negative; fair: positive*

2. *exotic: positive; strange: negative; unusual: neutral*

3. *flimsy: negative; light: neutral; feathery: positive*

4. *brilliance: positive; brightness: neutral; glare: negative*

5. *discriminating: positive; picky: negative; selective: neutral*

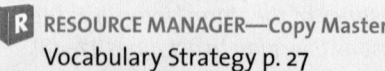 **RESOURCE MANAGER—Copy Master**
Vocabulary Strategy p. 27

Interactive Vocabulary THINK central

Keywords direct students to a **WordSharp** tutorial on **thinkcentral.com** or to other types of vocabulary practice and review.

Vocabulary in Context

▲ VOCABULARY PRACTICE

Decide whether each pair of terms are similar or different.

1. precipitous/steep	6. draft/sip
2. acquiesce/dispute	7. succor/assistance
3. marauder/raider	8. pestilential/healthful
4. condolence/indifference	9. interloper/guest
5. languor/energy	10. pinioned/pinned down

WORD LIST

acquiesce
condolence
draft
interloper
languor
marauder
pestilential
pinioned
precipitous
succor

ACADEMIC VOCABULARY IN WRITING

• alter • layer • theme • unify • symbol

How might the wolves be a **symbol** in this story? Consider how changing the wolves to another animal might **alter** the symbolic meaning. Explain your interpretation in a paragraph. Use at least one Academic Vocabulary word in your response.

VOCABULARY STRATEGY: CONNOTATION

COMMON CORE

L 5b Analyze nuances in the meanings of words with similar denotations.

The term *connotation* refers to an attitude or feeling connected to a word. For example, *languor* and *sluggishness* could both be defined as "a lack of physical or mental energy," but Saki's use of *languor* to describe Ulrich's condition connotes a dreaminess not associated with *sluggishness*. Writers are aware of the connotations of words and often use them to evoke specific feelings or moods. If you are unable to determine a word's connotation by looking at the word alone, consider it in the context of the sentence, sentences, or paragraphs that surround it.

PRACTICE Place the words in each numbered item below on a continuum to show the positive, negative, or neutral connotations associated with each word. Then compare your answers with those of a classmate.

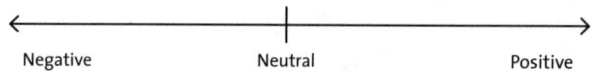

Negative	Neutral	Positive

1. pale, pasty, fair
2. exotic, strange, unusual
3. flimsy, light, feathery
4. brilliance, brightness, glare
5. discriminating, picky, selective

Interactive Vocabulary THINK central

Go to **thinkcentral.com**.
KEYWORD: HML10-436

DIFFERENTIATED INSTRUCTION

FOR ENGLISH LANGUAGE LEARNERS

Vocabulary: Cognates Have students look up each vocabulary word from the ***Word List*** in a bilingual dictionary and write a synonym for the word in their home language. Then, ask them to identify which words are cognates and how they identified them.

FOR ADVANCED LEARNERS/PRE–AP

Vocabulary in Writing Have students use at least three of the vocabulary words to write a first-person account (as either Ulrich or Georg) that explains why the man feels as he does about his neighbor.

Language

COMMON CORE

L 1b Use various types of clauses to convey specific meanings and add variety and interest to writing. W 2 Write explanatory texts to examine and convey complex ideas, concepts, and information clearly and accurately through the effective analysis of content.

◆ **GRAMMAR AND STYLE: Vary Sentence Structures**

Review the **Grammar and Style** note on page 432. Saki uses subordinate clauses to vary his sentence structures and add important details. A **subordinate** (or **dependent**) **clause** contains a subject and a verb but does not express a complete thought as a sentence does. Subordinate clauses answer the questions *how, how many, how much, to what degree, what kind, which one, why, when,* and *where.* They may be introduced by words like *because, if, since, when, where, who,* and *whom.* Here are three examples of subordinate clauses from the story:

> *The neighbor feud had grown into a personal one since Ulrich had come to be head of his family; if there was a man in the world whom he detested and wished ill to it was Georg Znaeym....* (lines 15–17)

Notice how the revisions in blue use subordinate clauses to join sentences. Doing so creates sentence variety and adds detail to this first draft. Use similar methods to revise your responses to the prompt.

> **STUDENT MODEL**
>
> Ulrich and Georg are enemies. ~~They~~ who have held a grudge against each other for a long time. ^When They meet in the forest. ^The old war picks up where it left off. ^If A tree ~~falls~~ hadn't first fallen on top of them. ~~Otherwise,~~ they might have killed each other immediately.

READING-WRITING CONNECTION

YOUR TURN Explore the topics of context and theme in "The Interlopers" by responding to this prompt. Then use the **revising tip** to improve your writing.

WRITING PROMPT	REVISING TIP
Extended Constructed Response: Analysis In the story, Saki cleverly explores the theme of hunting. In **three to five paragraphs,** analyze the message Saki conveys about hunters and their prey.	Review your response. Have you varied the structure of your sentences? If not, revise to include subordinate clauses that add important details.

Interactive Revision THINK central
Go to **thinkcentral.com**.
KEYWORD: HML10-437

FOR STRUGGLING WRITERS

- Limit the length of the assignment to three paragraphs.
- Help students review the parts of the story that specifically relate to hunting, and discuss with them what Saki might be saying about human beings and prey.
- Have pairs help one another write a thesis statement that reflects a theme and find details to include in the body paragraph.

Language

◆ **GRAMMAR AND STYLE**

- Have students read the Student Model aloud, first without the edits and then with the edits to emphasize the improvement. (For more on subordinate clauses, see page R62 in the **GRAMMAR HANDBOOK**.)

- Write this passage on the board. Have students revise it by using subordinate clauses to join sentences.

> When Ulrich and Georg are faced with possible death~~.~~, ~~t~~They begin to feel differently about each other. Because w~~W~~ar and near-death experiences are life-altering~~.~~, ~~t~~They cause people to think about what is really important.

R RESOURCE MANAGER—Copy Master
Improve Sentence Flow p. 30

READING-WRITING CONNECTION

- Have students review lines 19–39 and the end of the story when both men are confronted by the wolves.

Writing Online THINK central

The following tools are available online at **thinkcentral.com** and on **Write*Smart* CD-ROM:**
- **Interactive Graphic Organizers**
- **Interactive Student Models**
- **Interactive Revision Lessons**
For additional grammar instruction, see **GrammarNotes** on **thinkcentral.com**.

Assess and Reteach

Assess

DIAGNOSTIC AND SELECTION TESTS
Selection Test A, B/C pp. 115-116, 117-118

Interactive Selection Test on **thinkcentral.com**

Reteach

Level Up Online Tutorials on **thinkcentral.com**

Reteaching Worksheets on **thinkcentral.com**:
Literature Lessons 9, 11, Reading Lesson 2, Vocabulary Lesson 17

Focus and Motivate

COMMON CORE FOCUS

RL 1 Cite strong textual evidence to support analysis of what the text says explicitly as well as inferences drawn from the text. **RL 6** Analyze a particular point of view reflected in a work of world literature. **L 3** Apply knowledge of language to make effective choices for meaning or style. **L 5** Demonstrate understanding of word relationships.

SUMMARY

"Two Friends" tells of the last meeting of Messieurs Morissot and Sauvage, good friends who go on a fishing trip. As they enjoy a day of fishing, they are captured by Prussian soldiers. When both Frenchmen refuse to give the officer a password, they are shot.

What would you do for a **FRIEND?**

Ask the question. After students have read the paragraph and completed the *QUICKWRITE,* call on volunteers to share their paragraphs about friendship.

Selection Resources

See resources on the **Teacher One Stop DVD-ROM** *and on* <u>thinkcentral.com</u>.

R RESOURCE MANAGER UNIT 4
Plan and Teach, pp. 33–40
Summary, pp. 41–42†‡*
Text Analysis and Reading
   Skill, pp. 43–46†*
Vocabulary, pp. 47–49*
Grammar and Style, p. 52

DIAGNOSTIC AND SELECTION TESTS
Selection Tests, pp. 119–122

BEST PRACTICES TOOLKIT
Word Questioning, p. E9
Three-Column Journal, p. B10
Venn Diagram, p. A26
Analysis Frame: Theme,
   pp. D21, D32

TECHNOLOGY
⊘ **Teacher One Stop DVD-ROM**
⊘ **Student One Stop DVD-ROM**
⊘ **Audio Anthology CD**
⊘ **GrammarNotes DVD-ROM**
⊘ **ExamView Test Generator**
   on the **Teacher One Stop**

 *** Resources for Differentiation**   † Also in Spanish   ‡ In Haitian Creole and Vietnamese

---

Two Friends
Short Story by Guy de Maupassant

What would you do for a FRIEND?

COMMON CORE
RL 1 Cite textual evidence to support analysis of what the text says explicitly as well as inferences drawn from the text. **RL 6** Analyze a particular point of view reflected in a work of world literature.

Faced with a life-or-death situation, do people who have a close friendship come to each other's aid? Or do they only worry about saving their own skins? In this short story, you will meet two men who remain true to each other in the face of great peril.

QUICKWRITE With a group, list meaningful acts of friendship you've witnessed or experienced. Add to or delete from the list that is shown. Then write a paragraph describing how far you would go for your closest friends.

> *Acts of Friendship*
> 1. Rescued friend from a dangerous situation
> 2. Consoled friend when his grandparent died
> 3. Enjoyed many summers together at camp
> 4.
> 5.

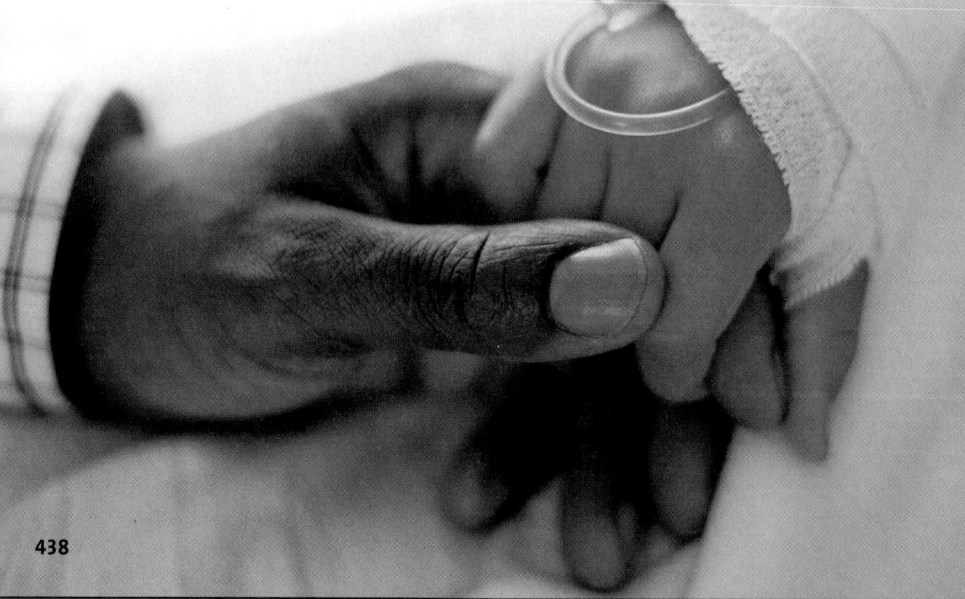

438

TEXT ANALYSIS: SYMBOL

A **symbol** is a person, place, object, or activity that represents something beyond itself. Flags, for example, often serve as symbols of national heritage and patriotism. In literature, a symbol takes its meaning from its context. In "Two Friends," for example, the bleak landscape might be said to symbolize the loss of vitality in France. To identify other symbols in the selection, use these strategies as you read:

- Note what is described at length or repeated.
- Note words that suggest broad ideas about humanity.

Review: Setting

READING SKILL: MAKE INFERENCES ABOUT CHARACTER

Skilled readers **make inferences,** or logical guesses, about characters on the basis of story details and their own knowledge. Sometimes called "reading between the lines," making inferences allows readers to build a more complete understanding of the characters and the entire story.

As you read the selection, pay attention to the details that Maupassant uses to describe the two friends and the Prussian soldiers. Record your inferences about these characters in an organizer like the one shown.

Character Details	+	My Experiences	=	My Inferences
Morrisot fishes every Sunday from early morning until dark.	+	Fishing requires calm, patience, and an enjoyment of the outdoors.	=	Morrisot probably demonstrates all these qualities.

▲ VOCABULARY IN CONTEXT

To see how many vocabulary words you already know, substitute a different word or phrase for each boldfaced term.

1. She sat in her room **dejectedly** after she lost the race.
2. **Fanatical** followers of the band waited hours for tickets.
3. This relaxing vacation has **rejuvenated** my spirits!
4. Why the **pensive** look on your face?
5. The clown's **eccentric** costume made the children laugh.
6. This **atrocity** should not go unpunished.
7. This large tree will **afford** some nice shade for our picnic.
8. The child remained **unperturbed** during the storm.

 Complete the activities in your **Reader/Writer Notebook.**

Meet the Author

Guy de Maupassant
1850–1893

Learning from a Master
In 1867, at the age of 17, Guy de Maupassant (gē' də mō-pă-säɴ') met Gustave Flaubert, a family friend and one of France's most respected novelists. Flaubert served as Maupassant's mentor, offering him advice, including the following message: "Whatever you want to say, there is only one word to express it, only one verb to give it movement, only one adjective to qualify it." Maupassant went on to become a celebrated author in his own right.

On Fire!
Although Maupassant wrote several novels, his specialty was the short story, a form he helped popularize. From 1880 to 1890, Maupassant enjoyed his most prolific years as an author, remarkably producing 300 stories. His best works are often characterized by precise language and realistic portrayals of everyday life.

BACKGROUND TO THE STORY

The Franco-Prussian War
For most of the 1800s, Germany was a collection of separate German-speaking states. Among these, the northern state of Prussia emerged as the most powerful. Under the leadership of the Prussian chancellor Otto von Bismarck, the German states began to unite. In July 1870, fearing a unified Germany, Emperor Napoleon III of France began what was later called the Franco-Prussian War. "Two Friends" takes place in 1871, while Paris is under siege, or attack, by the Prussian army. The story reflects Maupassant's firsthand experiences of the war, in which he fought briefly as a young French soldier.

Author Online
THINK central
Go to thinkcentral.com.
KEYWORD: HML10-439

439

Teach

TEXT ANALYSIS   COMMON CORE   RL 6

● Model the Skill: SYMBOL

Explain that symbols act as a type of shorthand to communicate complicated, emotionally rich ideas. Discuss symbols in stories students have read. Emphasize the symbolic role setting or activities can play.

GUIDED PRACTICE Have students explain the symbolism of the game in this example:

Every Thanksgiving my cousins and I played basketball, no matter what the weather. The grownups cheered us on. Some even joined in the traditional game.

READING SKILL   COMMON CORE   RL 1

■ Model the Skill: MAKE INFERENCES ABOUT CHARACTER

To model how to make inferences about character, have students reread **On Fire!** and Background. Tell students that this information will help them make an inference about how Maupassant's background influenced the details in this story.

GUIDED PRACTICE Have students infer why Maupassant accepted advice from Gustave Flaubert.

R RESOURCE MANAGER—Copy Master
Make Inferences About Character p. 45 (for student use while reading the selection)

VOCABULARY SKILL   COMMON CORE   L 4

▲ VOCABULARY IN CONTEXT

DIAGNOSE WORD KNOWLEDGE Have all students complete Vocabulary in Context. Check their words and phrases against the following:

afford (ə-fôrd') *v.* to provide or offer
atrocity (ə-trŏs'ĭ-tē) *n.* a very cruel or brutal act
dejectedly (dĭ-jĕk'tĭd-lē) *adv.* in a disheartened, depressed way
eccentric (ĭk-sĕn'trĭk) *adj.* strange; peculiar
fanatical (fə-năt'ĭ-kəl) *adj.* extremely enthusiastic

pensive (pĕn'sĭv) *adj.* thoughtful in a wistful, sad way
rejuvenated (rĭ-jōō'və-nā'tĭd) *adj.* made new or young again **rejuvenate** *v.*
unperturbed (ŭn'pər-tûrbd') *adj.* calm and serene; untroubled

PRETEACH VOCABULARY Use the following copy master to help students predict the meaning of each boldfaced word.

R RESOURCE MANAGER—Copy Master
Vocabulary Study p. 47

1. Read the first two sentences in the passage aloud, emphasizing *dejectedly*.
2. Point to *miserable*. Elicit meanings for *dejectedly*, such as "sadly."
3. Help students find a similar definition in Part B (item 4). Repeat the procedure.

Help students set a purpose for reading. Tell students to look for details about how Morissot and Sauvage feel about the Prussians and the war.

READING SKILL **COMMON CORE** RL 1

A *Model the Skill:* **MAKE INFERENCES**

Explain to students that to make an inference about the relationship between individuals in the story, they must understand to whom the reciprocal pronouns refer. Tell students that "each other" in line 21 refers to Morissot and Sauvage.

Possible answer: *There is a reciprocal, friendly relationship between the two men.*

VOCABULARY **COMMON CORE** L 4

OWN THE WORD

- **dejectedly:** Remind students that the word *dejectedly* is the adverbial form of *dejected*, which refers to being low in spirits or depressed. Antonyms for the adverb include *blissfully, cheerfully, happily,* and *joyfully.* Have students write two sentences: one with *dejected* or *dejectedly* and one that uses an antonym.

- **fanatical:** Tell students that *fanatical* is the adjective form of the noun *fanatic,* which refers to a person who is extremely enthusiastic or has excessive zeal about a situation. *Fanatical* often has a negative connotation of someone being rabid, extremist, or revolutionary. Have students find synonyms that have a more positive connotation for *fanatical.*
Possible answers: *devotee, enthusiast, fan*

TWO FRIENDS

GUY DE MAUPASSANT

Targeted Passage ①

Paris was under siege, in the grip of famine, at its last gasp. There were few sparrows on the rooftops now, and even the sewers were losing some of their inhabitants. The fact is that people were eating anything they could get their hands on.

One bright January morning Monsieur Morissot[1] was strolling **dejectedly** along one of the outer boulevards, with an empty stomach and his hands in the pockets of his old army trousers. He was a watchmaker by trade and a man who liked to make the most of his leisure. Suddenly, he came upon one of his close friends, and he stopped short. It was Monsieur Sauvage,[2] whom he had
10 got to know on fishing expeditions.

Every Sunday before the war it was Morissot's custom to set off at the crack of dawn with his bamboo rod in his hand and a tin box slung over his back. He would catch the Argenteuil train and get off at Colombes, from where he would walk to the island of Marante. The minute he reached this land of his dreams he would start to fish—and he would go on fishing till it got dark.

And it was here, every Sunday, that he met a tubby, jolly little man by the name of Sauvage. He was a haberdasher[3] from the Rue Notre-Dame-de-Lorette, and as **fanatical** an angler[4] as Morissot himself. They often spent half the day sitting side by side, rod in hand, with their feet dangling over
20 the water. And they had become firm friends.

There were some days when they hardly spoke to each other. On other occasions they would chat all the time. But they understood each other perfectly without needing to exchange any words, because their tastes were so alike and their feelings identical.

---

1. **Monsieur Morissot** (mə-syœ' mô-rē-sō').
2. **Sauvage** (sō-väzh').
3. **haberdasher:** one who sells men's clothing, such as shirts, hats, and gloves.
4. **angler:** a fisherman.

A **MAKE INFERENCES**
Reread lines 16–24. What can you infer about Morisott and Sauvage from the details of their friendship?

DIFFERENTIATED INSTRUCTION

FOR ENGLISH LANGUAGE LEARNERS

Vocabulary Support Use Word Questioning to teach these words: *identical* (line 24), *confirm* (line 33), *mutual* (line 33), *detect* (line 115), *abandoned* (line 120), *collapsed* (line 229).

 BEST PRACTICES TOOLKIT—Transparency Word Questioning p. E9

FOR STRUGGLING READERS

In combination with the *Audio Anthology CD,* use one or more Targeted Passages (pp. 440, 443, 445, 446, 448) to ensure that students focus on key story events, concepts, and skills. Targeted Passages are also good for English learners.

① **Targeted Passage [Lines 1–20]**

This introductory passage describes the wartime setting of the story and sets up the

"Two Friends" is set in January 1871, when the German occupation of France was nearly complete. France declared war on Prussia on July 19, 1870, but on August 4 the Prussians, who were extremely well prepared, crossed the border into Alsace, defeating the French and beginning their march on Paris. On September 1, Prussian forces captured French emperor Napoleon III and 100,000 of his troops. The emperor was deposed and a provisional government for national defense (which eventually became the Third French Republic) was created. Parisians continued to resist the Prussian offensive, enduring many hardships. Food was so scarce that many Parisians ate rats (mentioned in lines 2–3) to survive. The city finally surrendered on January 28, 1871. After a brief occupation, Prussian forces withdrew from the city.

Analyze Visuals

Possible answer: *The two men are sitting close together at a table, facing each other. They seem to be involved in an enjoyable conversation.*

About the Art Pierre Auguste Renoir (1841–1919) was a founder of impressionism and was one of its most popular representatives. *At the Inn of Mother Anthony* reflects the impressionists' idea of giving viewers the general impression of a scene or object, rather than rendering every detail with clear precision. The painting also shows that Renoir, like other impressionists, enjoyed creating lighting effects that make a scene appear to glow.

friendship between Morissot and Sauvage, its two main characters.

- What is Paris like at this time? (lines 1–4)
- Why does Morissot have an empty stomach and wear old army trousers (lines 6–7)? (line 1)
- How did Morissot and Sauvage originally become friends? (lines 11–20)
- What does the expression "before the war" (line 11) suggest about them? (lines 1–4)

FOR ADVANCED LEARNERS/PRE-AP

Compare and Contrast Have a student volunteer read aloud Flaubert's message to Maupassant. Challenge students to experiment with writing using Flaubert's standards. Have students spend no more than five minutes rewriting the first line of the story. Then, in a classroom discussion, have students compare and contrast their sentences with Maupassant's. How are the sentences similar and different? Were students able to write to Flaubert's standards? How does their word choice reflect their voices as writers?

B SYMBOL

Possible answer: *The fishing trips might symbolize the characters' friendship and the peaceful beauty that marked their lives before the outbreak of the war.*

REVISIT THE BIG QUESTION

What would you do for a FRIEND?

Discuss How does the moment in lines 44–51 show that there is a deep friendship between Morissot and Sauvage? *Possible answer: Their deep friendship is suggested by their emotional response when they meet unexpectedly.*

C Model the Skill: MAKE INFERENCES

Have students reread lines 48–65. Tell students that based on the details in these lines, they can infer that the war has brought the men sadness and a longing for the past. Remind students to record their answers on their Make Inferences About Character charts.

Possible answer: The war has brought the men sadness and a longing for the past. They wonder when they will be able to fish again (lines 53–57); and twice they drink, probably to dull their sadness (lines 58–65).

OWN THE WORD

- **rejuvenated:** Have students explain why the author chose the word *rejuvenated* in the phrase "... when the *rejuvenated* sun sent floating over the river..."

- **pensive:** Have students create a semantic map for the word *pensive*.

On spring mornings at about ten o'clock, when the <u>rejuvenated</u> sun sent floating over the river that light mist which moves along with the current, warming the backs of the two enthusiastic fishermen with the welcome glow of a new season, Morissot would say to his neighbor:

"Ah! It's grand here, isn't it?"

30   And Monsieur Sauvage would reply:

"There's nothing I like better."

This simple exchange of words was all that was needed for them to understand each other and confirm their mutual appreciation.

In the autumn towards the close of day, when the sky was blood-red and the water reflected strange shapes of scarlet clouds which reddened the whole river, and the glowing sun set the distant horizon ablaze, making the two friends look as though they were on fire, and touching with gold the russet leaves which were already trembling with a wintry shudder, Monsieur Sauvage would turn to Morissot with a smile and say:

40   "What a marvelous sight!"

And Morissot, equally taken up with the wonder of it all, but not taking his eyes off his float, would answer:

"It's better than walking down the boulevards, eh?" **B**

As soon as the two friends had recognized each other, they shook hands warmly, feeling quite emotional over the fact that they had come across each other in such different circumstances. Monsieur Sauvage gave a sigh and remarked:

"What a lot has happened since we last met!"

Morissot, in mournful tones, lamented:

50   "And what awful weather we've been having! This is the first fine day of the year."

And, indeed, the sky was a cloudless blue, brilliant with light.

They started to walk on together side by side, **pensive** and melancholy. Then Morissot said:

"And what about those fishing trips, eh? *There's* something worth remembering!"

"When shall we be able to get back to it?" mused Monsieur Sauvage.

They went into a little café and drank a glass of absinthe.[5] Then they resumed their stroll along the boulevards.

60   Morissot suddenly stopped and said:

"What about another glass of the green stuff, eh?"

"Just as you wish," consented Monsieur Sauvage, and they went into a second bar.

When they came out they both felt very fuzzy, as people do when they drink alcohol on an empty stomach. The weather was very mild. A gentle breeze caressed their faces. **C**

---

5. **absinthe:** a syrupy green alcoholic beverage that has a licorice flavor.

rejuvenated (rĭ-jōō'və-nā'tĭd) *adj.* made new or young again **rejuvenate** *v.*

B SYMBOL
Reread lines 25–43. Notice that the men's fishing trips are described at length and in vivid detail. What might these experiences symbolize?

pensive (pĕn'sĭv) *adj.* thoughtful in a wistful, sad way

C MAKE INFERENCES
What inferences can you make so far about how the war has affected the two men?

DIFFERENTIATED INSTRUCTION

FOR ENGLISH LANGUAGE LEARNERS

Language: Modifiers Use a Three-Column Journal to help students explore the use of modifiers in this story. In the left-hand column, have them write nouns with strong modifiers. In the middle column, have them write the modifiers. In the right-hand column, have them write other modifiers that they might use to describe the same nouns. Start with these examples:

noun	modifier	other modifiers
sun (line 25)	rejuvenated	newborn, glorious
leaves (line 37)	russet	red, dying,

 **BEST PRACTICES TOOLKIT—Transparency**
Three-Column Journal p. B10

Monsieur Sauvage, who felt even more fuddled[6] in this warm air, stopped and said:

"What about it, then? Shall we go?"

70 "Go where?"

"Fishing!"

"But where can we go?"

"To our island, of course. The French frontline is near Colombes. I know the colonel in command—fellow called Dumoulin. I'm sure we'd have no trouble in getting through."

Morissot began to quiver with excitement.

"Right!" he said. "I'm your man!"

And the two friends separated and went off to get their fishing tackle.

An hour later they were striding down the main road together. They reached
80 the villa in which the colonel had set up his headquarters. When he heard their request, he smiled at their **eccentric** enthusiasm but gave them permission. They set off once again, armed with an official pass.

eccentric (ĭk-sĕn′trĭk) *adj.* strange; peculiar

They soon crossed the frontline, then went through Colombes, which had been evacuated, and now found themselves on the fringe of the area of vineyards which rise in terraces above the Seine. It was about eleven o'clock.

On the opposite bank they could see the village of Argenteuil, which looked deserted and dead. The hills of Orgemont and Sannois dominated the horizon, and the great plain which stretches as far as Nanterre was empty, completely empty, with nothing to be seen but its leafless cherry trees and gray earth.

90 Pointing towards the high ground Monsieur Sauvage muttered:

"The Prussians are up there."

And as the two friends gazed at the deserted countryside, they felt almost paralyzed by the sense of uneasiness which was creeping through them.

② **Targeted Passage**

The Prussians! They had never so much as set eyes on them, but for four months now they had been aware of their presence on the outskirts of Paris, occupying part of France, looting, committing **atrocities,** reducing people to starvation . . . the invisible yet all-powerful Prussians. As they thought of them, a kind of superstitious dread was added to their natural hatred for this unknown, victorious race.

atrocity (ə-trŏs′ĭ-tē) *n.* a very cruel or brutal act

100 "What if we should happen to run into some of them?" said Morissot nervously.

Monsieur Sauvage gave the sort of reply which showed that cheerful Parisian banter survived in spite of everything.

"Oh, we'll just offer them some nice fish to fry!"

Even so, they were so worried by the silence of the surrounding countryside that they hesitated about going any further.

It was Monsieur Sauvage who finally made up his mind.

"Come on!" he said. "We'll go on—but we must keep a sharp lookout!" **D**

D MAKE INFERENCES
What does the men's decision to continue their fishing trip reveal about their personalities and view of the world?

---

6. **fuddled:** drunk and confused.

Refer to lines 64–78 and use these prompts to explore the two characters' decision:

Summarize What happens in this passage? *Possible answer: The friends decide to go to their favorite fishing spot, despite the fact that fighting is taking place nearby.*

Analyze What factors seem to figure into the characters' thinking? *Possible answer: They are a little drunk (lines 64–67), and they are not completely realistic about the possible danger.*

Evaluate Do you think that these characters are making the right decision? Why or why not? *Possible answer: No. They are risking their lives for a mere hobby. They should wait until the war is over and they can fish safely.*

READING SKILL   COMMON CORE
                                     RL 1

D MAKE INFERENCES

Possible answer: The decision shows that Morissot and Sauvage have a childlike optimism. They do not adequately fear enemy soldiers or combat zones. Naively, they figure that if approached by the Prussians, they will offer the soldiers some of their fish (lines 100–104).

Extend the Discussion What is so important about fishing that the men are willing to risk their lives to continue their trip?

VOCABULARY   COMMON CORE
                                     L 4

OWN THE WORD

- **eccentric:** Tell students that *eccentric* comes from the Greek word *ekkentros,* meaning "out of center," and refers to something strange or peculiar. Have students complete the following sentence: The neighbors found the man *eccentric* because. . . .

- **atrocity:** Remind students that *atrocious* is the adjective form meaning "very evil or cruel" or "exceptionally bad." Have students use *atrocious* in sentences.

FOR STRUGGLING READERS

② **Targeted Passage [Lines 90–99]**

This passage sets up the story's main conflict: the two friends versus the Prussians.

- How can you tell that the friends are entering dangerous territory? How do they feel about this environment? (lines 86–89, 92–93)

- What do they know about the Prussians? How does that knowledge make them feel? (lines 94–99)

- How much personal contact have they had with the Prussians? Explain. (line 94)

FOR ENGLISH LANGUAGE LEARNERS

Vocabulary: Phrasal Verbs Point out the phrasal verbs *set up* (line 80) and *set off* (line 82) on this page. Challenge students to write a sentence for each phrasal verb. After volunteers share their sentences, ask them to use a dictionary to find and share other phrasal verbs with *set* (such as *set down, set forth,* and *set out*).

ⓔ SYMBOL

Possible answer: *The gudgeon might symbolize Morissot and Sauvage. The friends have tricked themselves into believing that there is nothing to worry about and that they run little risk by fishing in this area. Perhaps they will draw the attention of the Prussians, just as live bait attracts the attention of bigger fish.*

Analyze Visuals

Activity How does this painting capture the friends' feeling about fishing? *Possible answer: The painting shows two fishermen who appear at peace with each other, with the gold-washed setting, and with fishing itself. The image could illustrate the narrator's comment that Morissot and Sauvage "were overcome by a delightful sense of joy" (lines 126–127).*

About the Art At first a student of impressionism, Paris-born Georges Seurat (1859–1891) went on to develop his own theories about the way that the mind creates images and about the use of color. The painting on this page reflects the artistic movement that he led, called neoimpressionism. Seurat's best-known technique was pointillism, the creation of images using dots or small brush strokes of color. His best-known painting using this technique is *Sunday Afternoon on the Island of La Grand Jatte* (1884–1886), for which the painting on this page was a study.

OWN THE WORD

afford: Point out that *afford* has several definitions and students can use context clues to determine the intended meaning of the word. In line 110, *afford* means "to provide or offer." *Afford* can also mean "to have financial means," "to spare or give up," or "to bear without disadvantage to oneself."

And they scrambled down the slope of one of the vineyards, bent double,
110 crawling on their hands and knees, taking advantage of the cover **afforded** by the vines, keeping their eyes wide open and their ears on the alert.

All that now separated them from the riverbank was a strip of open ground. They ran across it, and as soon as they reached the river, they crouched amongst the dry rushes.

Morissot pressed his ear to the ground to see if he could detect the sound of marching feet. He could hear nothing. They were alone, completely alone.

They told each other there was nothing to worry about, and started to fish.

Opposite them the deserted island of Marante concealed them from the other bank. The little building which once housed the restaurant was closed
120 and shuttered, and looked as though it had been abandoned for years.

It was Monsieur Sauvage who caught the first fish—a gudgeon. Morissot caught the second, and then, almost without a pause, they jerked up their rods time after time to find a little silvery creature wriggling away on the hook. This really was a miraculous draft of fishes. ⓔ

They carefully placed each fish into a fine-meshed net which was suspended in the water at their feet. And as they did so they were overcome by a delightful sense of joy, the kind of joy you only experience when you resume something you really love after being deprived of it for a long time.

afford (ə-fôrd') *v.*
to provide or offer

ⓔ SYMBOL
A gudgeon is both a small fish used as bait and a person who is easily tricked. On the basis of this information, whom or what might the gudgeon symbolize?

Line fishermen, study for *La Grand Jatte* (1883), Georges Seurat. Oil on canvas, 16 cm × 25 cm. Musée d'Art Moderne, Troyes, France. Photo © Réunion des Musées Nationaux/Art Resource, New York.

DIFFERENTIATED INSTRUCTION

FOR STRUGGLING READERS

Comprehension Support Explain that when the author says, "This really was a miraculous draft of fishes" (lines 123–124), he is making an allusion to the Bible. Luke 5:1–11 records a story of how Jesus produced "a miraculous draft of fishes" for some fishermen. By using this allusion, Maupassant suggests that the friends' fishing is more than a mere enjoyable hobby and becomes something spiritual.

A kindly sun was shedding its warmth across their backs. They were so
130 absorbed that they no longer heard, or thought, or paid the least attention to
the outside world. What did anything matter now? They were fishing!

But suddenly, the bank beneath them shook with a dull rumble which
seemed to come from underground.

The distant cannon were starting to fire again.

Morissot turned his head, and above the bank, over to the left, he saw the
great bulk of Mont Valérien. On the mountainside was a white plume of
smoke, showing where the gunpowder had just bellowed out.

Almost immediately another jet of smoke spurted from the fort on the
summit, and a few seconds later the rumble of another detonation reached
140 their ears.

Other cannon shots followed, and every now and then the mountain spat
out its deadly breath, exhaled its clouds of milky vapor, which rose slowly into
the calm sky above. **F**

"There they go again!" said Monsieur Sauvage with a shrug of his shoulders.
Morissot, who was anxiously watching the feather on his float as it bobbed
up and down, was suddenly filled with the anger of a peace-loving man for
these maniacs who indulge in fighting.

"They've got to be really stupid," he growled, "to go on killing each other
like that!"

150 "They're worse than animals," said Monsieur Sauvage.
Morissot, who had just caught another fish, called out:

"And it'll never be any different so long as we have governments!"

"Oh, no," disagreed Monsieur Sauvage. "The Republic[7] would never have
declared war . . ."

"Look!" interrupted Morissot. "Under kings you have war against other
countries. Under republican governments you have civil war."

And they began to argue, in a calm and friendly way, sorting out all the world's
great political problems with the commonsense approach of mild and reasonable
men. On one point they were in absolute agreement: mankind would never be
160 free. And as they talked, Mont Valérien went thundering on without respite,
demolishing French homes with its cannonades,[8] pounding lives to dust, crushing
human beings to pulp, putting an end to so many dreams, to so many long-awaited
joys, so much long-expected happiness, tearing into the hearts of all those wives
and daughters and mothers with pain and suffering that would never be eased.

"Such is life," said Monsieur Sauvage.

"Better to call it death," laughed Morissot. **G**

But at that moment they both gave a start, scared by the feeling that
somebody had been walking just behind them. They looked round and saw
standing above them four men, four tall, bearded men, armed to the teeth,

F SETTING
Compare and contrast this fishing trip with earlier ones described in the story. How has the setting changed?

③ Targeted Passage

G MAKE INFERENCES
Reread lines 157–166. Why is the argument between Morissot and Sauvage **ironic**?

---

7. **the Republic:** the Second Republic of France (1848–1852), which was France's first truly representative government.

8. **cannonades:** numerous firings of cannons.

TWO FRIENDS **445**

FOR STRUGGLING READERS

③ Targeted Passage [Lines 144–166]

The discussion in this passage sheds light on one of the story's main theme: that warfare is part of the human condition.

- How does Morissot feel about war? How does Sauvage feel about it? (lines 144–166)
- What idea do they agree with completely? (lines 159–160)
- As the friends talk, what is happening nearby? How does that activity help prove their point? (lines 160–164)

FOR ADVANCED LEARNERS/PRE–AP

Research Historical Connections Refer students to Morissot's statement about war in lines 155–156. Ask students to think of some societies they have studied that are or were ruled by monarchs, and other societies that have or have had representative governments. Instruct students to find and share with the class a few historical examples that support or refute Morissot's statement.

F SETTING

Possible answer: *The setting of this fishing trip is not calm and peaceful, as was the setting of earlier fishing trips. The sun is shining (line 129), as it did then (lines 25–26 and 36), but now the friends hear cannon shots and see the smoke of cannons (lines 132–140).*

IF STUDENTS NEED HELP . . . Have them re-read lines 25–33 and 34–43, which describe two earlier fishing trips. Help students compare those passages to lines 129–143 by discussing questions like these:

- How is the sun described in each passage? How does it affect the fishermen?
- During which fishing trip are the fishermen interrupted? How does the interruption change the scene?

Have students fill in a Venn Diagram with details from each scene, paying close attention to the type and amount of detail.

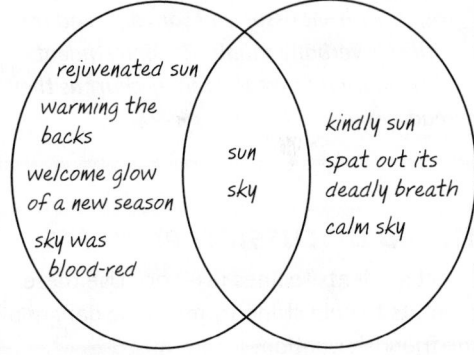

- rejuvenated sun warming the backs
- welcome glow of a new season
- sky was blood-red

sun
sky

- kindly sun spat out its deadly breath
- calm sky

💼 **BEST PRACTICES TOOLKIT—Transparency**
Venn Diagram p. A26

G MAKE INFERENCES

Possible answer: *The argument is ironic because Morissot and Sauvage are calmly arguing about political problems while a battle is going on around them (lines 160–166).*

Extend the Discussion There are three types of irony: dramatic, situational, and verbal. How are any or all of these types of irony at work in the passage?

TWO FRIENDS **445**

◆ GRAMMAR AND STYLE

COMMON CORE L 3

Write Concisely Break the sentence into five short sentences, adding *they were* to every sentence after the first one. Elicit that the result is a series of dull, choppy sentences. Discuss the fact that a compound predicate (which in this case is in the passive voice) uses fewer words and flows more smoothly than would a sequence of sentences with a single predicate in each sentence. Also point out the sense of speed that is created by joining the predicate in a series. Have volunteers identify other sentences with compound predicates in the story.

READING SKILL

COMMON CORE RL 1

❶ MAKE INFERENCES

Possible answer: *The reader can infer that the Prussians are uncaring and perhaps unprincipled. The soldiers are physically rough with Morissot and Sauvage, and their officer is verbally rough. Remind students to fill in their Make Inferences chart as they read.*

TIERED DISCUSSION PROMPTS

Direct students to lines 183–200. Use these prompts to help students grasp the danger of the friends' situation:

Connect How do you feel about the friends at this point in the story? Why? *Accept all reasonable responses.*

Analyze How does the officer try to get the password from the men? ***Possible answer:*** *He uses fear by threatening to kill them. He also preys on their emotions by asking about their families.*

Evaluate Maupassant does not have his characters speak in self-defense. He does not make them explain themselves. What might Maupassant be suggesting by this omission? ***Possible answer:*** *He might be suggesting that the friends realize that the Prussian officer will not believe them. The two Frenchmen are so attuned to each other that each comes to this conclusion on his own without talking to or signaling the other.*

---

170 dressed like liveried[9] footmen, with flat military caps on their heads—and rifles which they were pointing straight at the two friends.

The fishing rods dropped from their hands and went floating down the river.

In a matter of seconds they were seized, tied up, hustled along, thrown into a boat and carried across to the island. ◆

Behind the building which they had thought deserted they saw a group of about twenty German soldiers.

A sort of hairy giant who was sitting astride a chair and smoking a large clay pipe asked them in excellent French:

180   "Well, messieurs, did the fishing go well?"

One of the soldiers placed at the officer's feet the net full of fish which he had been careful to bring along. The Prussian smiled and said:

"Well, well! I can see you didn't do badly at all! . . . But I have to deal with a very different matter. Now, listen to me carefully, and don't get alarmed . . . As far as I am concerned you are a couple of spies sent out here to keep an eye on me. I've caught you and I've every right to shoot you. You were obviously pretending to fish as a cover for your real purposes. It's too bad for you that you've fallen into my hands. But war is war . . . Now, since you've come out here past your own lines, you're bound to have a password so you can get back.
190 Just give me that password and I'll spare your lives." ❶

The two friends, ghastly pale, stood there side by side with their hands trembling. They said nothing.

"Nobody will ever get to know about it," continued the officer. "You will go back without any trouble, and the secret will go with you . . . If you refuse to cooperate, you'll die—straight away. So take your choice!"

They stood there motionless, keeping their mouths firmly shut.

The Prussian, who was still quite calm, pointed in the direction of the river and said:

"Just think! In five minutes you'll be at the bottom of that river. In five
200 minutes! You must have families. Think of them!"

The rumbling of the cannon was still coming from Mont Valérien.

The two fishermen simply stood there, refusing to speak. The German now gave some orders in his own language. Then he moved his chair some distance away from the prisoners. Twelve men marched up and formed a line twenty yards from them with their rifles at their sides.

"I'll give you one minute to make up your minds," called the officer. "And not two seconds more."

Then he jumped to his feet, went up to the two Frenchmen, took Morissot by the arm, and led him to one side. Then he said to him in a very low voice:

210   "Quick! Just let me have that password! Your friend won't know you've told me. I'll make it look as though I've taken pity on you both."

---

9. **liveried:** uniformed.

◆ GRAMMAR AND STYLE
Reread lines 174–175. By using a **compound predicate**, Maupassant is able to describe a series of actions in one concise sentence.

❹ Targeted Passage

❶ MAKE INFERENCES
What can you infer about the Prussian soldiers from their actions toward the fishermen?

Language Coach

Fixed Expressions Some concepts have a standard, or fixed, way of being expressed. Reread line 211. Which fixed expression in this sentence means "shown mercy to"?

DIFFERENTIATED INSTRUCTION

FOR STRUGGLING READERS

❹ Targeted Passage [Lines 183–205]

This passage focuses on the conflict that leads to the climax of the story.

- What accusation does the officer make against Morissot and Sauvage? What does he want from them? (lines 185–186; lines 188–190)

- How do Morissot and Sauvage respond? (lines 191–192)

- How does the arrival of the 12 soldiers signal the climax of the story? (lines 194–195)

FOR ENGLISH LANGUAGE LEARNERS

Language Coach

Fixed Expressions *Answer: taken pity on* Have students read line 94. Point out that the fixed expression *set eyes on them* means "seen them." Ask students what they think the fixed expression *to run into* in line 100 means.

Morissot said nothing.

The Prussian then dragged Monsieur Sauvage to one side and made the same proposition to him.

Monsieur Sauvage said nothing.

So they were pushed together again, side by side.

It was then that Morissot happened to glance down at the net full of gudgeon which was lying in the grass a few yards away.

220 A ray of sunlight fell on the heap of glittering fish, which were still quivering with life. As he looked at them he felt a momentary weakness. In spite of his efforts to hold them back, tears filled his eyes. **K**

"Farewell, Monsieur Sauvage," he mumbled.

And Monsieur Sauvage replied:

"Farewell, Monsieur Morissot."

They shook hands, trembling uncontrollably from head to foot.

"Fire!" shouted the officer.

Twelve shots rang out simultaneously.

J MAKE INFERENCES
Why do Morissot and Sauvage refuse to offer the Prussian officer a password?

K SYMBOL
Reread lines 216–221. How does this description contribute to your understanding of the fish as a symbol in the story?

Detail of *Execution of the Emperor Maximilian* (1867), Édouard Manet. Oil on canvas, 77¹⁄₈″ × 102¹⁄₄″. Museum of Fine Arts, Boston. Gift of Mr. and Mrs. Frank Gair Macomber (30.444).

TWO FRIENDS   **447**

FOR ADVANCED LEARNERS/PRE–AP

Evaluate Characterization Have students reread the description of Morissot and Sauvage's final moments in lines 216–225. Instruct them to consider what Maupassant reveals about the characters through their words and actions. Then ask students to write a paragraph in which they evaluate the realism and the importance of his final characterization of the two friends. Invite students to exchange and compare evaluations.

FOR STRUGGLING READERS

Develop Reading Fluency Model for students how to read the exchange between the Prussian, Morissot, and Sauvage. Read aloud, starting with line 80. Pause and use proper intonation for the ellipses in lines 183 and 188 and for the dashes in lines 195 and 254. Have students echo the reading.

Have students work in pairs to practice fluency.

R RESOURCE MANAGER—Copy Master
Reading Fluency p. 53

READING SKILL   COMMON CORE   RL 1

J MAKE INFERENCES

Possible answer: *Morissot and Sauvage may not have a password. If they do, they probably consider revealing it a traitorous act.*

TEXT ANALYSIS   COMMON CORE   RL 6

K *Model the Skill:* **SYMBOL**

Model for students how to identify symbols. Remind students that to interpret a symbol, they want to think about what the fish might represent in a broad sense. Point out to students that the author says the fish are "quivering with life" (lines 219–220). Ask students to consider who or what else is quivering with life.

Possible answer: The fish symbolize the happier times that Morissot and Sauvage once knew. They also symbolize the friends: both the fish and the friends are near death, and both were caught because they did not realize the danger around them.

Analyze Visuals

Activity How does this painting reflect the plot and mood of this scene in the story?
Possible answer: In both cases, soldiers are firing rifles to execute someone. The painting's dark colors and black figures create a grim mood. The executioners and the executed are faceless, suggesting the dehumanizing nature of war.

About the Art Edouard Manet (1832–1883) tried to distance himself from the impressionists, but his work shows their influence. Art historians consider him an early modernist.

What would you do
for a FRIEND?

Discuss Direct students to lines 228–244. In what sense is the way that Morissot and Sauvage died fitting in terms of their friendship? *Possible answer: Morissot and Sauvage protected each other, and each refused to claim an advantage that the other did not have. Now they have died together, and their bodies have been disposed of together in the river they loved.*

VOCABULARY

COMMON CORE
L 4

OWN THE WORD

unperturbed: Tell students that *unperturbed* is related to the verb *perturb*, which comes from Latin meaning "to throw into disorder." The prefix *un-* means "not" or "opposite from." Have students write a sentence using *unperturbed* correctly.

● WORLD LITERATURE

Possible answer: *Maupassant may have witnessed such brutality while a soldier. He also clearly hated the Prussians. The same story could take place in other parts of the world during wartime.*

SELECTION WRAP–UP

READ WITH A PURPOSE Now that students have finished reading the selection, ask them if they think that Morissot and Sauvage's feelings about the war are reflected in how they interact with the Prussian. *Possible answer: The men feel fear and hatred toward the Prussian army. These feelings are reflected in their refusal to help the Prussian.*

★ **CRITIQUE** Ask students whether they think that Maupassant developed two believable main characters or whether they think that the two main characters were simply too naive for the situation in which they were living.

INDEPENDENT READING

Recommend *The Chosen* by Chaim Potok to students who would like to read another story about devoted friendship.

Monsieur Sauvage fell like a log onto his face. Morissot, who was taller, swayed, spun round, then collapsed on top of his friend, with his face staring
230 up at the sky and the blood welling from where his coat had been burst open across his chest.

The German shouted out more orders. His men went off and came back with some lengths of rope and a few heavy stones which they fastened to the feet of the two bodies. Then they carried them to the riverbank.

All the time Mont Valérien continued to rumble, and now it was capped by a great mountain of smoke.

Two soldiers got hold of Morissot by the head and feet. Two others lifted up Monsieur Sauvage in the same way. The two bodies were swung violently backwards and forwards, then thrown with great force. They curved through
240 the air, then plunged upright into the river, with the stones dragging them down, feet first.

The water spurted up, bubbled, swirled round, then grew calm again, with little waves rippling across to break against the bank. There was just a small amount of blood discoloring the surface.

The officer, still quite **unperturbed,** said, half aloud:

"Well, now it's the fishes' turn."

As he was going back towards the building, he noticed the net full of gudgeon lying in the grass. He picked it up, looked at the fish, then smiled, and called out:
250 "Wilhelm!"

A soldier came running up. He was wearing a white apron. The Prussian officer threw across to him the catch made by the two executed fishermen, and gave another order:

"Fry me these little creatures—straight away, while they're still alive. They'll be delicious!"

Then he lit his pipe again. 🐚 ●

Translated by Arnold Kellett

⑤ Targeted Passage

unperturbed
(ŭn'pər-tûrbd') *adj.* calm and serene; untroubled

● WORLD LITERATURE
Maupassant was a soldier during the Franco-Prussian war, at which time this story is set. How do you think this experience may have influenced his particular point of view in this story? Could this same story take place at another time and in another part of the world?

DIFFERENTIATED INSTRUCTION

FOR STRUGGLING READERS

⑤ Targeted Passage [Lines 237–256]

This passage brings the story to a close and sheds light upon the officer's character.

- What happens to the bodies of Morissot and Sauvage? (lines 237–244)

- What does the officer mean by "Well, now it's the fishes' turn"? (line 246) What does the comment show about his attitude toward the Frenchmen? (lines 239–244)

- What is the officer's final action? What does it reveal about him? (lines 254–255; 245–256)

FOR ADVANCED LEARNERS/PRE–AP

Analyze Theme Have students work in small groups to answer the questions in the Analysis Frame: Theme. Have students consider symbols in the story and the wartime setting as they answer the questions.

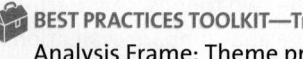 **BEST PRACTICES TOOLKIT—Transparency** Analysis Frame: Theme pp. D21, D32

Comprehension

1. **Recall** Who are Morissot and Sauvage?

2. **Recall** How do the wartime conditions affect their habits?

3. **Recall** What prompts the two Frenchmen to cross the frontline of the war?

4. **Summarize** What happens to Morissot and Sauvage as a result of their venturing into enemy territory?

Text Analysis

● 5. **Make Inferences** Review the chart you made as you read. Do Morissot and Sauvage seem to understand the dangers of war? Cite evidence to support your answer.

● 6. **Interpret Symbol** References to fish and fishing are repeated throughout the story. What do they symbolize? To help you interpret their meaning, create a chart like the one shown. Record descriptions of fish and fishing as well as the ideas you associate with them.

Descriptions of Fish/Fishing	Associations

7. **Examine Setting and Theme** Reread lines 25–40 and 118–143. Compare the conditions on the island of Marante before and during the Prussian occupation. What theme about war do these changes communicate?

8. **Analyze Irony** Explain the contrast between what you expected and what actually happens at the end of the story. Support your answer with details.

9. **Draw Conclusions** Describe how Morissot and Sauvage behave while in the enemy camp. What conclusions can you draw about their friendship from their final actions?

Text Criticism

10. **Biographical Context** "War! When I think of this word," declared Maupassant, "I feel bewildered, as though they were speaking to me of sorcery, of the Inquisition, of a distant, finished, abominable, monstrous, unnatural thing." How are Maupassant's feelings about war reflected in the story? Support your response with details.

What would you do for a FRIEND?

Would you truly be willing to give your life for a friend?

Text Criticism

Possible answer:

10. *Maupassant shows the Prussians acting in an "abominable" and "monstrous" way— namely, the cruel and senseless execution of two innocent Frenchmen.*

What would you do for a FRIEND?
Students will consider the extent of help they are willing to give to different kinds of friends.

COMMON CORE

RL 1 Cite textual evidence to support analysis of what the text says explicitly as well as inferences drawn from the text.
RL 6 Analyze a particular point of view reflected in a work of world literature.

Practice and Apply

For preliminary support of post-reading questions, use these copy masters:

R RESOURCE MANAGER—Copy Masters
Reading Check p. 50
Symbol p. 43
Question Support p. 51

Additional selection questions are provided for teachers on page 37.

ANSWERS

Comprehension

1. *Morissot and Sauvage are two Frenchmen who became friends through fishing.*

2. *The war has made fishing unsafe.*

3. *their great desire to fish together again*

4. *Morissot and Sauvage are captured, accused of being spies, and executed.*

Text Analysis

COMMON CORE RL 1, RL 6

Possible answers:

5. ■ **COMMON CORE FOCUS** *Make Inferences Morissot and Sauvage know of events in Paris (lines 94–99) and of the dangers of war (lines 148–164), but only in a general sense. They seem not to apply the threat of danger to themselves personally.*

6. ● **COMMON CORE FOCUS** *Symbol Charts will vary. Students may conclude that fishing may symbolize what France was like before the war. The fish may symbolize victims of war.*

7. *The island's change from idyllic fishing spot to cruel military encampment reflects the theme that war is destructive.*

8. *The reader expects that the two friends will be released because they are harmless fishermen, not enemy spies. Instead, the Prussians execute them.*

9. *When interrogated separately, each man refuses to speak in an attempt to save his life (lines 208–215). Also, neither man offers up his friend to save his own life. These men apparently value their friendship more than their lives.*

Vocabulary in Context

▲ VOCABULARY PRACTICE

1. *true*	5. *false*
2. *false*	6. *true*
3. *false*	7. *false*
4. *true*	8. *true*

 **RESOURCE MANAGER—Copy Master**
Vocabulary Practice p. 48

ACADEMIC VOCABULARY IN WRITING

Possible answer: *The story of Morissot and Sauvage emphasizes the* theme *that the Prussians are cruel and indifferent to the French people they rule. The Prussian officer kills two men who were guilty of nothing more than fishing. Exposing the Prussians' brutality should help to* unify *people to oppose them.*

VOCABULARY STRATEGY: ANALOGIES

COMMON CORE **L5**

- For each practice item, suggest that students identify the relationship in the first pair of words before they look for a vocabulary word that establishes the same relationship in the second pair of words.

- Help students read each analogy—for example, "*Intelligent* is to *clever* as *strange* is to _____."

- Follow up by inviting volunteers to create original analogies and submit them for class discussion.

Possible answers:

1. *eccentric (synonym)*
2. *fanatical (degree of intensity)*
3. *dejected (cause and effect)*
4. *rejuvenated (antonym)*
5. *atrocity (cause and effect)*

 **RESOURCE MANAGER—Copy Master**
Vocabulary Strategy p. 49

Interactive Vocabulary THINK central

Keywords direct students to a **WordSharp** tutorial on **thinkcentral.com** or to other types of vocabulary practice and review.

Vocabulary in Context

▲ VOCABULARY PRACTICE

Decide if each statement is true or false.

1. To **afford** privacy to someone is to offer it to him or her.
2. To be **unperturbed** is to be disturbed and agitated.
3. To be **rejuvenated** is to be worn down and tired.
4. If you are **fanatical** about something, you are obsessed with it.
5. An **eccentric** person has a normal, traditional way of doing things.
6. An **atrocity** is offensive and outrageous.
7. To speak **dejectedly** is to speak with excitement and energy.
8. If you are **pensive,** you are thoughtful.

WORD LIST

afford
atrocity
dejectedly
eccentric
fanatical
pensive
rejuvenated
unperturbed

ACADEMIC VOCABULARY IN WRITING

- alter - layer - symbol - theme - unify

Imagine that you are a reporter writing at the time of the story. How could your writing help to **unify** opposition to the Prussians? Write a paragraph article about what happened to Morissot and Sauvage. Consider the **theme** that you want to highlight. Use at least one Academic Vocabulary word in your response.

VOCABULARY STRATEGY: ANALOGIES

Analogies express relationships between pairs of words. Some common relationships are described in the chart below.

 **COMMON CORE**

L5 Demonstrate understanding of word relationships.

Type	Relationship
Synonym	means the same as
Antonym	means the opposite of
Cause and effect	results in or leads to
Degree of intensity	is less (or more) than

Complete each analogy by choosing the appropriate vocabulary word. Identify the kind of relationship on which the analogy is based.

1. intelligent : clever :: strange : _____
2. annoyed : furious :: interested : _____
3. gift : delighted :: problem : _____
4. bored : excited :: fatigued : _____
5. goodwill : charity :: cruelty : _____

Interactive Vocabulary THINK central
Go to **thinkcentral.com**.
KEYWORD: HML10-450

DIFFERENTIATED INSTRUCTION

FOR STRUGGLING READERS

Comprehension: Vocabulary As students work through the **Vocabulary Practice**, help them find context clues. For example, for item 2, *disturbed* and *agitated* are antonyms for *unperturbed*, so that statement is false. In item 6, *offensive* and *outrageous* appropriately describe an *atrocity* or other strongly negative action, so the statement is true.

FOR ADVANCED LEARNERS/PRE–AP

Vocabulary in Writing Have students complete the activity by using at least five of the vocabulary words to write a newspaper feature article about someone—themselves or a fictional other person—who enjoys the activity. The article would include information about the person and activity and some quotations from him or her. Work with students to plan a format for sharing the finished articles.

Language

◆ **GRAMMAR AND STYLE: Write Concisely**

Review the **Grammar and Style** note on page 446. A **predicate** indicates what a subject is or does or what happens to a subject. By combining predicates, you can avoid writing a series of short, choppy sentences that begin with the same noun or pronoun. Here are two additional examples of how Maupassant uses **compound predicates** to make his writing more concise:

Then he jumped to his feet, went up to the two Frenchmen, took Morissot by the arm, and led him to one side. (lines 208–209)

The water spurted up, bubbled, swirled round, then grew calm again . . . (line 242)

Notice how the revisions in blue use compound predicates to concisely describe a series of events. Use similar methods to revise your own writing.

STUDENT MODEL

The fishing scene is especially effective. On their last day, Morrisot and
Sauvage receive a pass. ~~They also~~ [*and*] cross enemy lines. ~~Morrisot and Sauvage~~ [*They*]
then scramble down a hill ~~and~~ crawl on their hands and knees [*and*] ~~Finally~~ ~~they~~
reach their beloved fishing ground.

READING-WRITING CONNECTION

YOUR TURN

Deepen your understanding of "Two Friends" by responding to this prompt. Then use the **revising tip** to improve your writing.

WRITING PROMPT	REVISING TIP
Short Constructed Response: Analysis What scenes in "Two Friends" stick out in your mind as particularly memorable? Choose one that you find especially effective. Then, write a **one- to two-paragraph analysis** of the scene, describing how it contributes to the plot as a whole.	Review your response. Have you used compound predicates to make your writing more concise? If not, revise.

Interactive Revision
THINK central
Go to **thinkcentral.com**.
KEYWORD: HML10-451

COMMON CORE

L3 Apply knowledge of language to make effective choices for meaning or style.

FOR STRUGGLING WRITERS

- Limit the length of the assignment to two paragraphs.
- If students struggle to identify memorable scenes that advance the plot, meet with them in a group to brainstorm a list of moments in the story that shocked, surprised, intrigued, or touched them. Have students write about the scenes that contain these moments.

Language

COMMON CORE **L3**

◆ **GRAMMAR AND STYLE**

- Make sure that students can identify the verbs in the examples from the story and the model. Ask students to explain how the edits in the model make the writing smoother.

- Write the passage that follows on the board. Have students make revisions by combining predicates. (For more information about compound predicates, see p. R59 in the **GRAMMAR HANDBOOK.**)

*Morissot and Sauvage were captured~~.~~ and
~~They were~~ brought before a Prussian officer.
He ordered them to divulge the password.
When they refused, the officer threatened
them, ~~and he~~ promised them their freedom~~.~~,
and ~~f~~Finally~~,~~ ~~he~~ had them shot.*

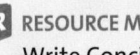
RESOURCE MANAGER—Copy Master
Write Concisely p. 52

READING-WRITING CONNECTION
Have students note lines in the memorable scenes they select. Remind students that symbolism is important to understanding this selection.

Writing Online
THINK central

The following tools are available online at **thinkcentral.com** and on **Write*Smart* CD-ROM:**
- **Interactive Graphic Organizers**
- **Interactive Student Models**
- **Interactive Revision Lessons**
For additional grammar instruction, see **GrammarNotes** on **thinkcentral.com**.

Assess and Reteach

Assess

DIAGNOSTIC AND SELECTION TESTS
Selection Test A pp. 119–120
Selection Test B/C pp. 121–122

Interactive Selection Test on **thinkcentral.com**

Reteach

Level Up Online Tutorials on **thinkcentral.com**

Reteaching Worksheets on **thinkcentral.com:**
Literature Lesson 30, Reading Lesson 8

Focus and Motivate

COMMON CORE FOCUS

RL 1 Cite textual evidence to support analysis of what the text says explicitly as well as inferences drawn from the text. **RL 2** Determine a theme of a text and analyze how it emerges and is refined by specific details. **RL 3** Analyze how complex characters develop the theme. **W 2** Write explanatory texts to examine and convey complex ideas, concepts, and information clearly and accurately through the effective analysis of content. **L 3** Apply knowledge of language to make effective choices for meaning or style. **L 4c** Consult general reference materials to determine or clarify a word's meaning or etymology.

SUMMARIES

"When Mr. Pirzada Came to Dine" Lilia, the narrator, remembers how her Indian family befriended a Pakistani scholar.

"Interview with Jhumpa Lahiri" Lahiri talks about *The Interpreter of Maladies* story collection.

"Refugee Aid Society" photo of Russian refugees waiting at a refugee camp

When do world
CONFLICTS affect us?

Have students complete the *QUICKWRITE*.

What's the Connection?

Ask: What difficulties do young immigrants encounter?

Selection Resources

When Mr. Pirzada Came to Dine
Short Story by Jhumpa Lahiri

Interview with Jhumpa Lahiri
Transcript of NewsHour with Jim Lehrer

Refugee Aid Society Web Site

VIDEO TRAILER **THINK** central KEYWORD: HML10-452

When do world
CONFLICTS affect us?

COMMON CORE

RL 1 Cite textual evidence to support analysis of what the text says explicitly as well as inferences drawn from the text.
RL 2 Determine a theme of a text and analyze how it emerges and is refined by specific details.
RL 3 Analyze how complex characters develop the theme.

How do you respond when you learn about a conflict in a distant part of the world? For some, the matter is quickly forgotten in the rush to take care of everyday concerns. For others, however, a faraway conflict can become intensely personal. In the following selection, you will read about how a young girl tries to ease the worries of a man whose loved ones live in a war-torn country.

What's the Connection?

Conflicts can affect people both near the conflict and on the other side of the world. In the short story you're about to read, you'll see how a conflict in Pakistan affects a young girl in the United States. Then you'll read an expository selection and examine a visual that both address the same issue.

SECTION 2 LOCAL NE

Conflict in Middle East drives up oil prices

452

WASHINGTON–Sources confirmed

See resources on the **Teacher One Stop DVD-ROM** and on **thinkcentral.com**.

 RESOURCE MANAGER UNIT 4
Plan and Teach, pp. 55–62
Summary, pp. 63–64†‡*
Text Analysis and Reading Skill, pp. 65–68†*
Vocabulary, pp. 69–71*
Grammar and Style, p. 74

DIAGNOSTIC AND SELECTION TESTS
Selection Tests, pp. 123–126

 BEST PRACTICES TOOLKIT
Word Squares, p. E10
New Word Analysis, p. E8
Think-Pair-Share, p. A18
Word Questioning, p. E9
Three-Column Journal, p. B10

INTERACTIVE READER

ADAPTED INTERACTIVE READER

ELL ADAPTED INTERACTIVE READER

TECHNOLOGY
- **Teacher One Stop DVD-ROM**
- **Student One Stop DVD-ROM**
- **PowerNotes DVD-ROM**
- **Audio Anthology CD**
- **GrammarNotes DVD-ROM**
- **Audio Tutor CD**
- **ExamView Test Generator** on the **Teacher One Stop**

THINK central
Video Trailer
Go to **thinkcentral.com** to preview the **Video Trailer** introducing this selection. Other features that support the selection include
- **PowerNotes** presentation
- **ThinkAloud** models to enhance comprehension
- **WordSharp** vocabulary tutorials
- interactive writing and grammar instruction

---

* Resources for Differentiation   † Also in Spanish   ‡ In Haitian Creole and Vietnamese

TEXT ANALYSIS: THEME AND CHARACTER

Sometimes, a story's **theme**, or central idea, is stated directly or is obvious after a first reading. More often, a theme must be pieced together after careful study. One way to discover a theme is to analyze the thoughts, words, and actions of a story's **main character**. As you read the selection, ask yourself the following questions about Lilia, the main character:

- How does she react to other characters?
- What conflicts does she experience?
- How does she change over time?

READING SKILL: DRAW CONCLUSIONS

Remember that when you **draw conclusions,** you gather pieces of information—from your reading and from what you already know—to make judgments. Use the following strategies to help you draw conclusions about how the political events in Pakistan affect the story's characters:

- Note how the characters behave before and after the outbreak of violence in Pakistan.
- Identify any changes in the characters' habits.

As you read, use a chart like this one to take notes.

Details About Characters	My Thoughts
At first, Lilia and her family share relaxed meals with Mr. Pirzada.	Lilia and her family are thoughtful to include Mr. Pirzada in their meals.

▲ VOCABULARY IN CONTEXT

Jhumpa Lahiri uses the boldfaced words in her story of internal and external conflicts. Try to figure out the meaning of each boldfaced word from the context. Then in your *Reader/Writer Notebook*, write down the meaning of each word.

1. measure to **ascertain** clothing size
2. restrict an individual's **autonomy**
3. meet a **compatriot** overseas
4. celebrate a nation's **sovereignty**
5. dress **impeccably** for the occasion
6. the **imperceptible** actions of a magician
7. **assail** an enemy in battle
8. **concede** victory to an opponent

Complete the activities in your **Reader/Writer Notebook.**

Meet the Author

Jhumpa Lahiri
born 1967

Fighting to Fit In
Born in London, Jhumpa Lahiri (jōōm′pə lə-hē′rē) grew up in Rhode Island, the daughter of Indian educators. As a student she often felt displaced. She recalls, "I didn't belong. I looked different and felt like an outsider." Lahiri's self-confidence improved when she began to write fiction. "I started writing ten page 'novels' during recess," she explains. "[It] allowed me to observe and make sense of things without having to participate."

Pulitzer Prize Sensation
As an adult, Lahiri continued to write stories based on her own struggles as an immigrant child. In 2000, she received the prestigious Pulitzer Prize for *The Interpreter of Maladies,* her debut work of fiction. The short story collection, which includes "When Mr. Pirzada Came to Dine," depicts individuals trying hard to succeed in their adopted homeland—the United States.

BACKGROUND TO THE STORY

A Nation Divided
The story takes place in 1971, the year in which civil war erupted in Pakistan. At the time, Pakistan had two distinct parts, West Pakistan and East Pakistan, which were divided by more than a thousand miles of Indian soil. Major linguistic, cultural, and economic differences also separated the two sections. West Pakistan was home to many different ethnic groups. East Pakistan, on the other hand, had a more homogeneous population. East Pakistanis were resentful of the political power wielded by West Pakistanis. From this civil war came a new nation, Bangladesh.

Author Online
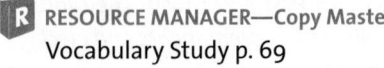
Go to **thinkcentral.com.**
KEYWORD: HML10-453

453

Teach

TEXT ANALYSIS — **COMMON CORE** RL 2 RL 3

● *Model the Skill:* **THEME AND CHARACTER**

To model how to identify theme and character, read this passage:

> Kayla waved to her parents and then slowly drove off. Moving into her own place was not an easy step, but Kayla knew it was an essential one.

Tell students that the theme of a story with this passage might be that growing up means taking on adult responsibilities.

GUIDED PRACTICE Discuss other actions that would support the same theme.

READING SKILL — **COMMON CORE** RL 1

■ *Model the Skill:* **DRAW CONCLUSIONS**

Use *Meet the Author* to model the concept of drawing conclusions. Example:

- Lahiri's parents were Indian.
- When she was young, Lahiri often "felt like an outsider."
- I can conclude that this story probably draws from Lahiri's personal experience.

GUIDED PRACTICE Ask students how their prior knowledge can help them draw conclusions.

R RESOURCE MANAGER—Copy Master
Draw Conclusions p. 67

VOCABULARY SKILL

▲ VOCABULARY IN CONTEXT

DIAGNOSE WORD KNOWLEDGE Have all students complete Vocabulary in Context. Check their definitions against the following:

ascertain (ăs′ər-tān′) *v.* to discover with certainty

assail (ə-sāl′) *v.* to attack or deliver a blow

autonomy (ô-tŏn′ə-mē) *n.* freedom; independence

compatriot (kəm-pā′trē-ət) *n.* a person from one's own country

concede (kən-sēd′) *v.* to admit or acknowledge, often reluctantly

impeccably (ĭm-pĕk′ə-blē) *adv.* perfectly, flawlessly

imperceptible (ĭm′pər-sĕp′tə-bel) *adj.* impossible or difficult to notice

sovereignty (sŏv′ər-ĭn-tē) *n.* complete independence and self-governance

PRETEACH VOCABULARY Use the following copy master to help students use context clues to predict the meaning of each boldfaced word.

R RESOURCE MANAGER—Copy Master
Vocabulary Study p. 69

1. Read the first sentence in Part A aloud, emphasizing *autonomy.*
2. Point out the phrase "free and independent nation." Elicit possible meanings for *autonomy,* such as "independence."
3. Have students record their ideas.

COMMON CORE L 4

READ WITH A PURPOSE

Help students set a purpose for reading. Tell students to look for details about the relationship between Lilia and her friend Dora.

READING SKILL

COMMON CORE
RL 1

A DRAW CONCLUSIONS

Possible answer: Taken as a whole, the details suggest that Mr. Pirzada leads a less refined and less comfortable life, and a far more solitary and lonely life, in New England than he did in Dacca.

VOCABULARY

COMMON CORE
L 4

OWN THE WORD

- **ascertain:** Tell students that synonyms for *ascertain* include *determine, discover, find, learn.* Have students write two sentences, one with *ascertain* and one with a synonym.

- **autonomy:** Tell students that *autonomy* is taken from the Greek word *autonomos,* which means "self-ruling." Ask students to list ways in which U.S. citizens are *autonomous.* **Possible answer:** *They vote on constitutional amendments and elect representatives.*

WHEN *Mr. Pirzada Came to Dine*

Jhumpa Lahiri

In the autumn of 1971 a man used to come to our house, bearing confections in his pocket and hopes of **ascertaining** the life or death of his family. His name was Mr. Pirzada,[1] and he came from Dacca,[2] now the capital of Bangladesh, but then a part of Pakistan. That year Pakistan was engaged in civil war. The eastern frontier, where Dacca was located, was fighting for **autonomy** from the ruling regime in the west. In March, Dacca had been invaded, torched, and shelled by the Pakistani army. . . . By the end of the summer, three hundred thousand people were said to have died. In Dacca Mr. Pirzada had a three-story home, a lectureship in botany[3] at the university, a wife
10 of twenty years, and seven daughters between the ages of six and sixteen whose names all began with the letter A. "Their mother's idea," he explained one day, producing from his wallet a black-and-white picture of seven girls at a picnic, their braids tied with ribbons, sitting cross-legged in a row, eating chicken curry off of banana leaves. "How am I to distinguish? Ayesha, Amira, Amina, Aziza, you see the difficulty."

Each week Mr. Pirzada wrote letters to his wife, and sent comic books to each of his seven daughters, but the postal system, along with most everything else in Dacca, had collapsed, and he had not heard a word of them in over six months. Mr. Pirzada, meanwhile, was in America for the year, for he had
20 been awarded a grant from the government of Pakistan to study the foliage of New England. In spring and summer he had gathered data in Vermont and Maine, and in autumn he moved to a university north of Boston, where we lived, to write a short book about his discoveries. The grant was a great honor, but when converted into dollars it was not generous. As a result, Mr. Pirzada lived in a room in a graduate dormitory, and did not own a proper stove or a television set. And so he came to our house to eat dinner and watch the evening news. **A**

---

1. **Pirzada:** (pēr-zä'də).
2. **Dacca:** (dăk'ə).
3. **botany** (bŏt'n-ē): the science or study of plants.

454 UNIT 4: THEME

---

ascertain (ăs'ər-tān') *v.* to discover with certainty

autonomy (ô-tŏn'ə-mē) *n.* freedom; independence

① Targeted Passage

Analyze Visuals ▶

In what way does the photograph help establish the **setting?**

A DRAW CONCLUSIONS
What details in lines 8–27 tell how Mr. Pirzada's life in New England is different from his life in Dacca?

DIFFERENTIATED INSTRUCTION

FOR ENGLISH LANGUAGE LEARNERS

Vocabulary Support Use Word Squares to teach these words: *located* (line 5), *successive* (line 65), *estimation* (line 91), *label* (line 135), *anticipating* (line 198), *removed* (line 280).

BEST PRACTICES TOOLKIT—Transparency
Word Squares p. E10

FOR STRUGGLING READERS

In combination with the *Audio Anthology CD*, use one or more Targeted Passages (pp. 454, 459, 462, 463, 469) to ensure that students focus on key events, concepts, and skills. Targeted Passages are also good for English learners.

① Targeted Passage [Lines 2–23]

This introductory passage describes the conflict in Pakistan and explains why Mr. Pirzada

---

Reading Support

This selection on **thinkcentral.com** includes embedded **ThinkAloud** models—students "thinking aloud" about the story to model the kinds of questions a good reader would ask about a selection.

BACKGROUND

East Pakistan Becomes Bangladesh The civil war in Pakistan broke out in March 1971, and it did not end until December of that year. Thousands of people died in the fighting, and millions of refugees fled to neighboring India. With the end of the war, the former province of East Pakistan became the independent nation of Bangladesh. Today, that country's capital and largest city is Dhaka, also spelled Dacca, as it is in Lahiri's story.

Analyze Visuals

Possible answer: *The photograph helps establish the setting by suggesting a warm, inviting home, such as the home of the narrator's family for Mr. Pirzada. In addition, the yellow leaves on the tree outside suggest autumn, the time of year that the narrator mentions in the first sentence.*

REVISIT THE BIG QUESTION
When do world
CONFLICTS affect us?

Discuss Based on lines 1–27, how is the title of this story connected to a conflict that is going on in the world? *Possible answer: Mr. Pirzada comes to the narrator's home to eat dinner and to watch the evening news on TV (lines 26–27) so that he can find out about a conflict in his homeland of Pakistan. A civil war is occurring there, and Mr. Pirzada is concerned for the survival of his wife and children in the city of Dacca (lines 2–3). Over the course of these dinners, Lilia expands her knowledge of the world.*

is alone in the United States instead of with his family in Dacca.

- What conflict does this passage describe? (lines 4–5)
- Where is Dacca, and why is it important to Mr. Pirzada? (lines 3–4, 8–10)
- Why is Mr. Pirzada alone in New England? (lines 19–23)
- How might ongoing events in Pakistan make Mr. Pirzada feel? Why? (lines 16–19)

FOR ADVANCED LEARNERS/PRE-AP

Analyze Have students read the first paragraph of the story and then ask students what point of view the story is written in (*first person*). Point out that students are studying theme and character in this selection. Ask students whether or not they feel writing in first person is a good way to express character. What are the advantages and drawbacks of this point of view? Have students reference examples from other works they have read to support their opinions.

B *Model the Skill:* DRAW CONCLUSIONS

Model how to draw conclusions for students.

1. Direct their attention to lines 40–41. Have them discuss the significance of Lilia's comment "by the end of September I had grown so accustomed to Mr. Pirzada's presence."

2. Direct their attention to line 43. Elicit that Lilia assumes that there will be four people at dinner—an assumption that suggests that Mr. Pirzada usually dines with her family.

3. Have students use their Draw Conclusions charts to record details about the characters and their thoughts.

Possible answer: Details that suggest that Mr. Pirzada is a welcome guest include the fact that he has been a guest many times, the comment that Lilia has become accustomed to his being there, and Lilia's asking her mother for a fourth glass because she expects him to come.

REVISIT THE BIG QUESTION

When do world
CONFLICTS affect us?

Discuss Based on what he says in lines 50–59, how does Lilia's father feel about Partition as a solution to the **conflict** between Hindus and Muslims? *Possible answer: His tone, especially his use of the phrase "sliced up . . . like a pie," suggests disapproval.*

OWN THE WORD

compatriot: Tell students that *patriot* means "one who loves and defends one's country." Addition of the prefix *com-*, which means "with" or "together" changes the word to mean "a person from one's own country."

At first I knew nothing of the reason for his visits. I was ten years old, and was not surprised that my parents, who were from India, and had a number
30 of Indian acquaintances at the university, should ask Mr. Pirzada to share our meals. It was a small campus, with narrow brick walkways and white pillared buildings, located on the fringes of what seemed to be an even smaller town. The supermarket did not carry mustard oil, doctors did not make house calls, neighbors never dropped by without an invitation, and of these things, every so often, my parents complained. In search of **compatriots**, they used to trail their fingers, at the start of each new semester, through the columns of the university directory, circling surnames familiar to their part of the world. It was in this manner that they discovered Mr. Pirzada, and phoned him, and invited him to our home.

40   I have no memory of his first visit, or of his second or his third, but by the end of September I had grown so accustomed to Mr. Pirzada's presence in our living room that one evening as I was dropping ice cubes into the water pitcher, I asked my mother to hand me a fourth glass from a cupboard still out of my reach. She was busy at the stove, presiding over a skillet of fried spinach with radishes, and could not hear me because of the drone of the exhaust fan and the fierce scrapes of her spatula. I turned to my father, who was leaning against the refrigerator, eating spiced cashews from a cupped fist. **B**
     "What is it, Lilia?"
     "A glass for the Indian man."
50   "Mr. Pirzada won't be coming today. More importantly, Mr. Pirzada is no longer considered Indian," my father announced, brushing salt from the cashews out of his trim black beard. "Not since Partition.[4] Our country was divided. 1947."
     When I said I thought that was the date of India's independence from Britain, my father said, "That too. One moment we were free and then we were sliced up," he explained, drawing an X with his finger on the countertop, "like a pie. Hindus here, Muslims there. Dacca no longer belongs to us." He told me that during Partition Hindus and Muslims had set fire to each other's homes. For many, the idea of eating in the other's company was still unthinkable.
60   It made no sense to me. Mr. Pirzada and my parents spoke the same language, laughed at the same jokes, looked more or less the same. They ate pickled mangoes with their meals, ate rice every night for supper with their hands. Like my parents, Mr. Pirzada took off his shoes before entering a room, chewed fennel seeds after meals as a digestive, drank no alcohol, for dessert dipped austere biscuits[5] into successive cups of tea. Nevertheless my father insisted that I understand the difference, and he led me to a map of the world taped to the wall over his desk. He seemed concerned that Mr. Pirzada might take offense if I accidentally referred to him as an Indian, though I could not really imagine Mr. Pirzada being offended by much of anything. "Mr. Pirzada

compatriot
(kəm-pā′trē-ət) *n.*
a person from one's own country

B DRAW CONCLUSIONS
Which details in lines 40–47 suggest that Mr. Pirzada is a welcome guest in Lilia's home?

---

4. **Partition:** the division in 1947 of the Indian subcontinent into two independent countries, India and Pakistan, after British withdrawal.

5. **biscuits:** a British term for cookies or crackers.

DIFFERENTIATED INSTRUCTION

FOR ENGLISH LANGUAGE LEARNERS

Vocabulary: Word Associations Explain that Lahiri's story contains many common, useful phrases and expressions that are well worth learning. Have students study these phrases in context and then quiz one another on their meanings: "on the fringes of" (line 32), "dropped by" (line 34), "every so often" (line 35), "My stomach tightened" (line 230), "the more . . . the more" (line 236), "safe and sound" (line 241), "drawing closer and closer" (line 446), "nothing short of" (line 447).

FOR ADVANCED LEARNERS/PRE–AP

Research Hindus and Muslims [small-group option] Have students research cultural, political, and religious similarities and differences between Hindus and Muslims. Ask students to summarize their findings either in a detailed chart or in a short report. Have volunteers share their work with the class, relating their findings to the conflict referred to in Lahiri's story.

70 is Bengali, but he is a Muslim," my father informed me. "Therefore he lives in East Pakistan, not India." His finger trailed across the Atlantic, through Europe, the Mediterranean, the Middle East, and finally to the sprawling orange diamond that my mother once told me resembled a woman wearing a sari[6] with her left arm extended. Various cities had been circled with lines drawn between them to indicate my parents' travels, and the place of their birth, Calcutta, was signified by a small silver star. I had been there only once and had no memory of the trip. "As you see, Lilia, it is a different country, a different color," my father said. Pakistan was yellow, not orange. I noticed that there were two distinct parts to it, one much larger than the other, separated

80 by an expanse of Indian territory; it was as if California and Connecticut constituted a nation apart from the U.S.

My father rapped his knuckles on top of my head. "You are, of course, aware of the current situation? Aware of East Pakistan's fight for **sovereignty?**"

I nodded, unaware of the situation. **C**

We returned to the kitchen, where my mother was draining a pot of boiled rice into a colander. My father opened up the can on the counter and eyed me sharply over the frames of his glasses as he ate some more cashews. "What exactly do they teach you at school? Do you study history? Geography?"

"Lilia has plenty to learn at school," my mother said. "We live here now,

90 she was born here." She seemed genuinely proud of the fact, as if it were a reflection of my character. In her estimation, I knew, I was assured a safe life, an easy life, a fine education, every opportunity. I would never have to eat rationed food, or obey curfews, or watch riots from my rooftop, or hide neighbors in water tanks to prevent them from being shot, as she and my father had. "Imagine having to place her in a decent school. Imagine her having to read during power failures by the light of kerosene lamps. Imagine the pressures, the tutors, the constant exams." She ran a hand through her hair, bobbed to a suitable length for her part-time job as a bank teller. "How can you possibly expect her to know about Partition? Put those nuts away."

100 "But what does she learn about the world?" My father rattled the cashew can in his hand. "What is she learning?"

We learned American history, of course, and American geography. That year, and every year, it seemed, we began by studying the Revolutionary War. We were taken in school buses on field trips to visit Plymouth Rock,[7] and to walk the Freedom Trail, and to climb to the top of the Bunker Hill Monument.[8] We made dioramas out of colored construction paper depicting George Washington crossing the choppy waters of the Delaware River, and

---

6. **sari** (sä'rē): a garment worn mostly by women of Pakistan and India, consisting of a length of fabric with one end wrapped around the waist to form a skirt and the other draped over the shoulder or covering the head.

7. **Plymouth Rock:** a boulder in Plymouth, Massachusetts, said to be the site where the Pilgrims disembarked from the *Mayflower*.

8. **Freedom Trail . . . Bunker Hill Monument:** historic sites in Boston, which commemorate critical events in the American struggle for independence from Great Britain.

WHEN MR. PIRZADA CAME TO DINE **457**

---

sovereignty
(sŏv'ər-ĭn-tē) *n.*
complete independence and self-governance

C THEME AND CHARACTER
Reread lines 50–84. In this passage, Lilia's father shares information about India and Pakistan. Does she understand the conflict between these two nations? Explain.

TEXT ANALYSIS

COMMON CORE
RL 2
RL 3

C THEME AND CHARACTER

Possible answer: Lilia does not understand the conflict; she says, "It made no sense to me" (line 60). She sees only the similarities between Indians and Pakistanis in language, appearance, and customs (lines 60–65).

Extend the Discussion Do you think that Lilia's father expects too much from her, considering her age? Why or why not?

TIERED DISCUSSION PROMPTS

Direct students to lines 50–99. Use these prompts to help students understand the characters:

Analyze Why does Lilia's mother tell her husband, "We live here now, she was born here" (lines 89–90)? *Possible answer: Lilia's father has been focusing on their past in India, especially the matter of Partition. Her mother is trying to make him see that Lilia's more immediate concern in school is learning the history of the United States, where she was born and lives today.*

Synthesize How would you describe the parents' feelings about their heritage and their adopted homeland? *Possible answer: Lilia's mother appreciates their Indian heritage but seems willing to embrace life in the United States. Her father seems more inclined to dwell on their ties to India.*

FOR STRUGGLING READERS

Concept Support Point out that in lines 92–97, Lilia's thoughts and the quoted comment from her mother refer to hardships that Lilia's parents left behind when they came to the United States. From that evidence, the reader can conclude that a large part of the reason that Lilia's parents left India was to escape difficulty and even the threat of violence.

FOR ENGLISH LANGUAGE LEARNERS

Culture: Clarify Display a map of India, Pakistan, and Bangladesh. Have students locate each of the three nations and then find Dacca (Dhaka), where Mr. Pirzada's family lives. Review the geopolitical information in lines 3–8 and lines 50–83. Make clear that at the time in which the story is set, Bangladesh was known as East Pakistan, and East Pakistan and West Pakistan were separated.

VOCABULARY

COMMON CORE
L 4

OWN THE WORD

sovereignty: Ask students explain whether or not *sovereignty* and *autonomy* could be synonymous. Students may consult a dictionary or thesaurus if necessary. *Possible answer: synonymous, as both words refer to self-government and independence*

we made puppets of King George wearing white tights and a black bow in his hair. During tests we were given blank maps of the thirteen colonies, and asked to fill in names, dates, capitals. I could do it with my eyes closed.

T̲he next evening Mr. Pirzada arrived, as usual, at six o'clock. Though they were no longer strangers, upon first greeting each other, he and my father maintained the habit of shaking hands.

"Come in, sir. Lilia, Mr. Pirzada's coat, please."

He stepped into the foyer, **impeccably** suited and scarved, with a silk tie knotted at his collar. Each evening he appeared in ensembles of plums, olives, and chocolate browns. He was a compact man, and though his feet were perpetually splayed, and his belly slightly wide, he nevertheless maintained an efficient posture, as if balancing in either hand two suitcases of equal weight. His ears were insulated by tufts of graying hair that seemed to block out the unpleasant traffic of life. He had thickly lashed eyes shaded with a trace of camphor,[9] a generous mustache that turned up playfully at the ends, and a mole shaped like a flattened raisin in the very center of his left cheek. 🅔 On his head he wore a black fez[10] made from the wool of Persian lambs, secured by bobby pins, without which I was never to see him. Though my father always offered to fetch him in our car, Mr. Pirzada preferred to walk from his dormitory to our neighborhood, a distance of about twenty minutes on foot, studying trees and shrubs on his way, and when he entered our house his knuckles were pink with the effects of the crisp autumn air.

"Another refugee, I am afraid, on Indian territory."

"They are estimating nine million at the last count," my father said.

Mr. Pirzada handed me his coat, for it was my job to hang it on the rack at the bottom of the stairs. It was made of finely checkered gray-and-blue wool, with a striped lining and horn buttons, and carried in its weave the faint smell of limes. There were no recognizable tags inside, only a hand-stitched label with the phrase "Z. Sayeed, Suitors" embroidered on it in cursive with glossy black thread. On certain days a birch or maple leaf was tucked into a pocket. He unlaced his shoes and lined them against the baseboard; a golden paste clung to the toes and heels, the result of walking through our damp, unraked lawn. Relieved of his trappings, he grazed my throat with his short, restless fingers, the way a person feels for solidity behind a wall before driving in a nail. Then he followed my father to the living room, where the television was tuned to the local news. As soon as they were seated my mother appeared from the kitchen with a plate of mincemeat kebabs with coriander chutney.[11] Mr. Pirzada popped one into his mouth.

---

9. **camphor** (kăm′fər): a fragrant compound from an Asian evergreen tree, used in skin-care products.

10. **fez** (fĕz): a man's felt hat in the shape of a flat-topped cone, worn mainly in the eastern Mediterranean region.

11. **mincemeat kebabs** (kə-bŏbz′) . . . **chutney** (chŭt′nē): an Indian or Pakistani dish consisting of pieces of spiced meat that have been placed on skewers and roasted, with an accompanying relish made of fruits, spices, and herbs.

impeccably (ĭm-pĕk′ə-blē) *adv.* perfectly, flawlessly

🅔 **GRAMMAR AND STYLE**
Reread lines 117–123. Lahiri's use of the adverbs *perpetually, slightly, thickly,* and *playfully* helps to create a vivid image of Mr. Pirzada.

TEXT ANALYSIS

🅓 **THEME AND CHARACTER** — RL 2, RL 3 · COMMON CORE

Possible answer: Several details suggest that Lilia is dissatisfied with her history class. Her statement that every year began with a study of the Revolutionary War (line 103) implies boredom and annoyance, as does her subsequent listing of activities. This feeling is further supported by her statement that she could fill in a map of the colonies with her eyes closed (line 110).

🅔 GRAMMAR AND STYLE — COMMON CORE · L 3

Add Descriptive Details Writers use adverbs to add many kinds of descriptive details. For example, adverbs may tell where, when, how, and to what extent. Adverbs can also define the degree of an adjective or another adverb. To illustrate how adverbs can enrich description, have students read lines 117–123 twice, first without the four adverbs listed and then with them in place. Then ask students to find other examples of Lahiri's use of adverbs. Examples might include *heartily* (line 147), *calmly* (line 217), *safely* (line 361), and *suddenly* (line 392). Challenge students to use some of the adverbs they identify in original sentences.

VOCABULARY — COMMON CORE · L 4

OWN THE WORD

impeccably: Explain to students that the word *impeccably* is an adverb; the adjective is *impeccable*. Have students name situations when they would want to be "impeccably suited." *Possible answer: dressing for an interview or a wedding*

DIFFERENTIATED INSTRUCTION

FOR ENGLISH LANGUAGE LEARNERS
Language: Modifiers Direct students' attention to lines 115–129. Explain that this paragraph contains many adjective-noun combinations that help give readers a clear, detailed image of Mr. Pirzada. Ask pairs of students to list as many of these combinations as they can. Remind them that the adjectives do not have to appear directly beside the nouns. Elicit or provide adjective-noun combinations such as these:

- *silk tie* (line 115)
- *compact man* (line 117)
- *belly slightly wide* (line 118)
- *efficient posture* (line 119)
- *graying hair* (line 120)
- *unpleasant traffic* (line 121)
- *generous mustache* (line 122)
- *flattened raisin* (line 123)
- *black fez* (line 124)
- *knuckles were pink* (line 129)
- *crisp autumn air* (line 129)

"One can only hope," he said, reaching for another, "that Dacca's refugees are as heartily fed. Which reminds me." He reached into his suit pocket and gave me a small plastic egg filled with cinnamon hearts. "For the lady of the house," he said with an almost **imperceptible** splay-footed bow.

150 "Really, Mr. Pirzada," my mother protested. "Night after night. You spoil her."

"I only spoil children who are incapable of spoiling." **F**

It was an awkward moment for me, one which I awaited in part with dread, in part with delight. I was charmed by the presence of Mr. Pirzada's rotund elegance, and flattered by the faint theatricality of his attentions, yet unsettled by the superb ease of his gestures, which made me feel, for an instant, like a stranger in my own home. It had become our ritual, and for several weeks, before we grew more comfortable with one another, it was the only time he spoke to me directly. I had no response, offered no comment, betrayed no

160 visible reaction to the steady stream of honey-filled lozenges, the raspberry truffles, the slender rolls of sour pastilles. I could not even thank him, for once, when I did, for an especially spectacular peppermint lollipop wrapped in a spray of purple cellophane, he had demanded, "What is this thank-you? The lady at the bank thanks me, the cashier at the shop thanks me, the librarian thanks me when I return an overdue book, the overseas operator thanks me as she tries to connect me to Dacca and fails. If I am buried in this country I will be thanked, no doubt, at my funeral."

It was inappropriate, in my opinion, to consume the candy Mr. Pirzada gave me in a casual manner. I coveted each evening's treasure as I would a jewel, or

170 a coin from a buried kingdom, and I would place it in a small keepsake box

imperceptible
(ĭm′pər-sĕp′tə-bel) *adj.* impossible or difficult to notice

F DRAW CONCLUSIONS
What do Mr. Pirzada's words and actions reveal about his feelings for the people of Dacca?

② Targeted Passage

WHEN MR. PIRZADA CAME TO DINE **459**

Analyze Visuals

Activity Have students locate words in the story that Lilia uses to describe what this photograph shows. *Possible answer: Lilia refers to the "honey-filled lozenges, the raspberry truffles," and the "sour pastilles" (lines 160–161), and she says that she places Mr. Pirzada's gifts of candy in "a small keepsake box" (line 170).*

F DRAW CONCLUSIONS

Possible answer: Mr. Pirzada is concerned about and feels sympathy for the refugees in Dacca. He shows up nightly at Lilia's family's house to watch the TV news (line 111), and he comments that he hopes the refugees from Dacca "are as heartily fed" as he is in Lilia's home (lines 146–147).

TIERED DISCUSSION PROMPTS

Direct students to lines 150–167. Use these prompts to help students explore the early relationship between Mr. Pirzada and Lilia:

Analyze Why does Lilia have conflicting feelings about Mr. Pirzada? *Possible answer: Lilia finds Mr. Pirzada's manner charming and flattering (lines 154–155) but also somewhat disconcerting, sometimes making her feel like a stranger in her own home (lines 156–157).*

Evaluate Do you think that Mr. Pirzada likes Lilia, or is he merely being polite? Explain. *Possible answer: Mr. Pirzada appears to like Lilia, always bringing her candy and suggesting that she is a child who cannot be spoiled (line 152). While politeness and gratitude may play a part, he probably would not bring gifts if he did not feel positively toward Lilia, who may remind him of his daughters in Dacca (lines 10–11).*

OWN THE WORD

imperceptible: Point out that the prefix *im-* means "not." Remind students that *imperceptible* means "impossible or difficult to notice." Ask students what they think the word *perceptible* means. *Possible answer: capable of being noticed; able to be perceived*

FOR STRUGGLING READERS

② Targeted Passage [Lines 148–167]

This passage introduces the relationship between Mr. Pirzada and Lilia by focusing on the gifts that he brings her.

- What do the gifts that Mr. Pirzada brings to Lilia have in common? (lines 159–161)
- What delights her about his visits? (lines 154–155)
- How does Mr. Pirzada respond when Lilia thanks him? (lines 161–167)

FOR ENGLISH LANGUAGE LEARNERS

Culture: Connect Ask students if they have eaten Indian or Pakistani food. Point out the various text references to foods, such as in line 144 and lines 180–185. Ask students if they know other foods from these countries, such as basmati rice, mango lassis, tandoori chicken, various types of curries, lentils, naan (bread), and cucumber-yogurt sauce. If possible, provide samples of a few of these foods by enlisting the aid of students and family members from these countries.

COMMON CORE

RL 2
RL 3

Ⓖ Model the Skill: THEME AND CHARACTER

Model for students how to identify theme and character. Have students reread lines 150–170. Point out that Lilia and Mr. Pirzada have a routine built around the exchange of the candy. This is their first means of communication on which they build their friendship.

Possible answer: *The gifts are special to Lilia because they come from the elegant and charming Mr. Pirzada, who presents them to her as an expression of affection. For this reason, she places the candies in a special keepsake box, the only memento of a grandmother she never knew.*

Extend the Discussion Have students discuss why they think Mr. Pirzada is important to Lilia.

Analyze Visuals

Activity Discuss how this photograph reflects the activity at Lilia's home. **Possible answer:** *The photograph shows plates of food in front of a television set. In the story, Mr. Pirzada and the others eat dinner while gathered in front of the TV to watch the news.*

---

made of carved sandalwood beside my bed, in which, long ago in India, my father's mother used to store the ground areca nuts[12] she ate after her morning bath. It was my only memento of a grandmother I had never known, and until Mr. Pirzada came to our lives I could find nothing to put inside it. Every so often before brushing my teeth and laying out my clothes for school the next day, I opened the lid of the box and ate one of his treats. Ⓖ

That night, like every night, we did not eat at the dining table, because it did not provide an unobstructed view of the television set. Instead we huddled around the coffee table, without conversing, our plates perched on the edges of

180 our knees. From the kitchen my mother brought forth the succession of dishes: lentils[13] with fried onions, green beans with coconut, fish cooked with raisins in a yogurt sauce. I followed with the water glasses, and the plate of lemon wedges, and the chili peppers, purchased on monthly trips to Chinatown and stored by the pound in the freezer, which they liked to snap open and crush into their food.

Before eating Mr. Pirzada always did a curious thing. He took out a plain silver watch without a band, which he kept in his breast pocket, held it briefly to one of his tufted ears, and wound it with three swift flicks of his thumb and

Ⓖ THEME AND CHARACTER

Consider the way Lilia cares for the gifts she receives from Mr. Pirzada. Why are they special to her?

---

12. **areca** (ə-rē′kə) **nuts:** seeds of the betel palm, chewed as a stimulant.

13. **lentils:** cooked seeds of a beanlike plant native to southwest Asia, a staple in Indian and Pakistani cuisine.

DIFFERENTIATED INSTRUCTION

FOR STRUGGLING READERS

Vocabulary Support Use New Word Analysis to teach these words from the story:

- *memento* (line 173), "something that serves as a reminder"
- *unobstructed* (line 178), "not blocked"
- *succession* (line 180), "series of items"
- *duration* (line 190), "the time during which something lasts"

 BEST PRACTICES TOOLKIT—Transparency New Word Analysis p. E8

FOR ADVANCED LEARNERS/PRE–AP

Analyze Character Have students reflect upon what Lilia calls the "curious thing" (line 186) that Mr. Pirzada does with his watch before eating. Have them consider what might prompt his action, especially since he never seems to consult the watch while it is out of his pocket (lines 190–192). Ask students to compare their ideas with partners. Then have them read on to verify their responses.

forefinger. Unlike the watch on his wrist, the pocket watch, he had explained
190 to me, was set to the local time in Dacca, eleven hours ahead. For the duration
of the meal the watch rested on his folded napkin on the coffee table. He never
seemed to consult it.

Now that I had learned Mr. Pirzada was not an Indian, I began to study him
with extra care, to try to figure out what made him different. I decided that the
pocket watch was one of those things. When I saw it that night, as he wound it
and arranged it on the coffee table, an uneasiness possessed me; life, I realized,
was being lived in Dacca first. I imagined Mr. Pirzada's daughters rising from
sleep, tying ribbons in their hair, anticipating breakfast, preparing for school.
Our meals, our actions, were only a shadow of what had already happened
200 there, a lagging ghost of where Mr. Pirzada really belonged. ⓗ

At six-thirty, which was when the national news began, my father raised the
volume and adjusted the antennas. Usually I occupied myself with a book, but
that night my father insisted that I pay attention. On the screen I saw tanks
rolling through dusty streets, and fallen buildings, and forests of unfamiliar
trees into which East Pakistani refugees had fled, seeking safety over the Indian
border. I saw boats with fan-shaped sails floating on wide coffee-colored rivers,
a barricaded university, newspaper offices burnt to the ground. I turned to
look at Mr. Pirzada; the images flashed in miniature across his eyes. As he
watched he had an immovable expression on his face, composed but alert, as
210 if someone were giving him directions to an unknown destination.

During the commercial my mother went to the kitchen to get more rice,
and my father and Mr. Pirzada deplored the policies of a general named
Yahyah Khan. They discussed intrigues I did not know, a catastrophe I could
not comprehend. "See, children your age, what they do to survive," my father
said as he served me another piece of fish. But I could no longer eat. I could
only steal glances at Mr. Pirzada, sitting beside me in his olive green jacket,
calmly creating a well in his rice to make room for a second helping of lentils.
He was not my notion of a man burdened by such grave concerns. I wondered
if the reason he was always so smartly dressed was in preparation to endure
220 with dignity whatever news **assailed** him, perhaps even to attend a funeral at
a moment's notice. I wondered, too, what would happen if suddenly his seven
daughters were to appear on television, smiling and waving and blowing kisses
to Mr. Pirzada from a balcony. I imagined how relieved he would be. But this
never happened.

That night when I placed the plastic egg filled with cinnamon hearts in the
box beside my bed, I did not feel the ceremonious satisfaction I normally did.
I tried not to think about Mr. Pirzada, in his lime-scented overcoat, connected
to the unruly, sweltering world we had viewed a few hours ago in our bright,
carpeted living room. And yet for several moments that was all I could
230 think about. My stomach tightened as I worried whether his wife and seven
daughters were now members of the drifting, clamoring crowd that had flashed
at intervals on the screen. In an effort to banish the image I looked around my

ⓗ **THEME AND CHARACTER**
Reread lines 186–200. What insight about Mr. Pirzada does Lilia gain from seeing him tend to his pocket watch?

assail (ə-sāl') *v.* to attack or deliver a blow

WHEN MR. PIRZADA CAME TO DINE   **461**

TEXT ANALYSIS
COMMON CORE RL 2 RL 3

ⓗ THEME AND CHARACTER

Possible answer: *Seeing Mr. Pirzada tend to his pocket watch makes Lilia realize just how closely connected he remains to his family, even though they are far away.*

Extend the Discussion Lilia says that seeing Mr. Pirzada with his pocket watch makes her feel possessed by uneasiness (line 196). What does she mean, and why do you think she feels that way?

REVISIT THE BIG QUESTION
When do world **CONFLICTS** affect us?

Discuss In lines 201–232, how does Lilia's father try to educate his daughter about the ongoing conflict in Pakistan? What effect does his effort have on Lilia? Cite evidence from the story to support your answer. ***Possible answer:*** *Lilia's father insists that she watch the TV news report (line 203). He also draws her attention to the plight of the children (line 214). The effect of his effort is to make Lilia acutely aware of the events in Pakistan and to open her eyes to how these events are affecting Mr. Pirzada and his family. The proof that Lilia is getting the message is that she loses her appetite (line 215) and that later, her stomach tightens as she worries about Mr. Pirzada's wife and daughters (lines 230–232).*

VOCABULARY
COMMON CORE L 4

OWN THE WORD

assail: Remind students that *assail* means "to attack or deliver a blow" and comes from the Latin word for "to jump on or onto." Ask students why they think the author chose to use the word *assailed* in line 220. What meaning does the word convey? ***Possible answer:*** *Mr. Pirzada searched for news about his family's welfare. Hearing that they were imprisoned or dead might make him feel as though he had been attacked or given a vicious blow or beating.*

FOR ENGLISH LANGUAGE LEARNERS
Vocabulary: Multiple-Meaning Words Have students use a dictionary to find the meaning of each word that is correct for its context: *ground* (line 172), *dishes* (line 180), *occupied* (line 202), *composed* (line 209), *helping* (line 217), *smartly* (line 219), *passages* (line 250), *initial* (line 323), *posed* (line 332), *watch* (line 362), *place* (line 374), *faint* (line 402), *smear* (line 402), *missing* (line 410). To check students' understanding, ask them to write a sentence that illustrates the correct meaning for the context and a sentence that illustrates another meaning of each word. For additional reinforcement, help students look for other examples of multiple-meaning words in the story, and help them use the words correctly in original sentences.

WHEN MR. PIRZADA CAME TO DINE   **461**

Activity Ask students what details in lines 232–241 they can see in this photograph.
Possible answer: The photograph shows Lilia's keepsake box (line 238) against a wall that appears to be covered by white and violet paper (line 234). The piece of candy, though round, in the photograph suggests the square of white chocolate that Lilia eats (lines 238–241).

room, at the yellow canopied bed with matching flounced curtains, at framed class pictures mounted on white and violet papered walls, at the penciled inscriptions by the closet door where my father had recorded my height on each of my birthdays. But the more I tried to distract myself, the more I began to convince myself that Mr. Pirzada's family was in all likelihood dead. Eventually I took a square of white chocolate out of the box, and unwrapped it, and then I did something I had never done before. I put the chocolate
240 in my mouth, letting it soften until the last possible moment, and then as I chewed it slowly, I prayed that Mr. Pirzada's family was safe and sound. I had never prayed for anything before, had never been taught or told to, but I decided, given the circumstances, that it was something I should do. That night when I went to the bathroom I only pretended to brush my teeth, for I feared that I would somehow rinse the prayer out as well. I wet the brush and rearranged the tube of paste to prevent my parents from asking any questions, and fell asleep with sugar on my tongue. ❶

No one at school talked about the war followed so faithfully in my living room. We continued to study the American Revolution, and learned
250 about the injustices of taxation without representation, and memorized passages from the Declaration of Independence. During recess the boys would divide in two groups, chasing each other wildly around the swings and seesaws, Redcoats against the colonies. In the classroom our teacher, Mrs. Kenyon, pointed frequently to a map that emerged like a movie screen from the top

---

❸ Targeted Passage

❶ THEME AND CHARACTER
Reread lines 201–247. Think about the **internal conflict** Lilia experiences. How has her interest in Pakistan changed since the beginning of the story? Explain who or what has prompted this change.

COMMON CORE
RL 2
RL 3

❶ THEME AND CHARACTER

Possible answer: Lilia's interest in Pakistan has increased as she has learned more about the situation there and has watched events unfold on television. Also, her interest has become personalized: she now connects events with Mr. Pirzada, whom she has gotten to know and like, and she worries about his family.

IF STUDENTS NEED HELP . . . Use an Open Mind diagram to help students identify Lilia's mixed feelings:

bored by/now disturbed by TV images

once unsure of/now concerned for Mr. Pirzada

interested in/now worried about his family

BEST PRACTICES TOOLKIT—Transparency
Open Mind p. D9

DIFFERENTIATED INSTRUCTION

FOR STRUGGLING READERS

❸ Targeted Passage [Lines 236–245]
This passage explores Lilia's deepening concern for Mr. Pirzada and his family.

- What happens when Lilia tries to distract herself? How do you think she feels toward Mr. Pirzada's family? (lines 236–237), (line 241)

- What does Lilia do that she has never done before? (lines 239–243)

- What do the candies seem to represent for Lilia? Why? (lines 239–245)

FOR STRUGGLING READERS

Develop Reading Fluency Model how to read long, descriptive sentences. Read lines 232–236 aloud to the class. Point out that although this is one long sentence, the commas break up the sentence into smaller thoughts. Remind students that commas act as a pause in the sentence. Lead the class in a unison reading of the sentence, paying particular attention to pacing at the commas.

of the chalkboard, charting the route of the *Mayflower,* or showing us the location of the Liberty Bell. Each week two members of the class gave a report on a particular aspect of the Revolution, and so one day I was sent to the school library with my friend Dora to learn about the surrender at Yorktown. Mrs. Kenyon handed us a slip of paper with the names of three books to look
260 up in the card catalogue. We found them right away, and sat down at a low round table to read and take notes. But I could not concentrate. I returned to the blond-wood shelves, to a section I had noticed labeled "Asia." I saw books about China, India, Indonesia, Korea. Eventually I found a book titled *Pakistan: A Land and Its People.* I sat on a footstool and opened the book. The laminated jacket crackled in my grip. I began turning the pages, filled with photos of rivers and rice fields and men in military uniforms. There was a chapter about Dacca, and I began to read about its rainfall, and its jute[14] production. I was studying a population chart when Dora appeared in the aisle. **J**

"What are you doing back here? Mrs. Kenyon's in the library. She came to
270 check up on us."

I slammed the book shut, too loudly. Mrs. Kenyon emerged, the aroma of her perfume filling up the tiny aisle, and lifted the book by the tip of its spine as if it were a hair clinging to my sweater. She glanced at the cover, then at me.

"Is this book a part of your report, Lilia?"

"No, Mrs. Kenyon."

"Then I see no reason to consult it," she said, replacing it in the slim gap on the shelf. "Do you?" **K**

A s weeks passed it grew more and more rare to see any footage from Dacca on the news. The report came after the first set of commercials,
280 sometimes the second. The press had been censored, removed, restricted, rerouted. Some days, many days, only a death toll was announced, prefaced by a reiteration of the general situation. . . . More villages set ablaze. In spite of it all, night after night, my parents and Mr. Pirzada enjoyed long, leisurely meals. After the television was shut off, and the dishes washed and dried, they joked, and told stories, and dipped biscuits in their tea. When they tired of discussing political matters they discussed, instead, the progress of Mr. Pirzada's book about the deciduous trees[15] of New England, and my father's nomination for tenure, and the peculiar eating habits of my mother's American coworkers at the bank. Eventually I was sent upstairs to do my homework,
290 but through the carpet I heard them as they drank more tea, and listened to cassettes of Kishore Kumar, and played Scrabble on the coffee table, laughing and arguing long into the night about the spellings of English words. I wanted to join them, wanted, above all, to console Mr. Pirzada somehow. But apart from eating a piece of candy for the sake of his family and praying for their safety, there was nothing I could do. They played Scrabble until the eleven

14. **jute:** the fiber from an Asian plant, used for sacking and cording.

15. **deciduous** (də-sĭj′ōō-əs) **trees:** trees that shed or lose leaves at the end of the growing season.

WHEN MR. PIRZADA CAME TO DINE **463**

J ALLUSION
An **allusion** is a reference to a well-known character, event, or place from literature or history. Reread lines 248–258. What allusions appear in these lines? How do they help illustrate the situation facing Mr. Pirzada's family?

④ Targeted Passage

K DRAW CONCLUSIONS
How has the conflict in Pakistan affected the lives of Lilia's classmates and her history teacher, Mrs. Kenyon? Explain.

TEXT ANALYSIS

J ALLUSION
Tell students that the author gives them a key to decoding the allusions in this section by providing one broad topic under which all the other allusions fall, the American Revolution.

Possible answer: Allusions to various events in American history appear in these lines. These events show the American struggle for independence, a struggle that Mr. Pirzada's country is engaged in at the time of the story. However, Lilia's school is focused only on American history and is uninterested in Pakistani/Indian current events.

READING SKILL · COMMON CORE · RL 1

K DRAW CONCLUSIONS
Possible answer: It has not affected the lives of Lilia's classmates or of Mrs. Kenyon. They seem indifferent to the war.

IF STUDENTS NEED HELP . . .
- Compare lines 248–251 with lines 102–110. Discuss how studying the American Revolution is a tradition at Lilia's school.
- Have students reread the conversation in lines 274–277. Discuss why Mrs. Kenyon disregards the book that Lilia is reading and then takes it from her.

Extend the Discussion What conclusions can you draw about Mrs. Kenyon?

TIERED DISCUSSION PROMPTS
Direct students to lines 278–295. Use these prompts to help students recognize Lilia's changing attitude:

Analyze What does Lilia notice that is different about the news reports that she, her parents, and Mr. Pirzada listen to? *Possible answer: Footage from East Pakistan has grown more rare because the press has been censored. The news contains only death tolls and brief reports of violence.*

Synthesize How has Lilia's growing awareness of world events affected her relationship with Mr. Pirzada? *Possible answer: Lilia is more sensitive to the worry and pain that Mr. Pirzada must be feeling.*

FOR STRUGGLING READERS

④ Targeted Passage [Lines 260–277]
In this passage, Lilia's increasing interest in Pakistan and its political conflict clashes with the lack of concern that others have for the conflict.
- Why do you think Lilia is having trouble concentrating (line 261)? (lines 248–249)
- What book does Lilia choose to read? (lines 263–264)
- What does Mrs. Kenyon say to Lilia about the book? Why? (lines 276–277)

FOR ENGLISH LANGUAGE LEARNERS
Language: Possessives Call attention to the title *Pakistan: A Land and Its People* (line 264). Point out that there is no apostrophe in "Its." Explain that possessive nouns have apostrophes but that possessive pronouns do not, even when they end in -s. Discuss these additional examples of possessive nouns: "Mr. Pirzada's family" (line 241), "At the McIntyres'" (line 418), "Dora's house" (line 431).

WHEN MR. PIRZADA CAME TO DINE **463**

READING SKILL COMMON CORE RL 1

L DRAW CONCLUSIONS

Possible answer: *The scarcity of news from Dacca creates a kind of lull in the lives of Lilia's parents and Mr. Pirzada. During this lull, they pass the time with long, leisurely meals (lines 283–284), conversation, and games of Scrabble (line 291).*

REVISIT THE BIG QUESTION

When do world CONFLICTS affect us?

Discuss Direct students to lines 308–315. When Mr. Pirzada says, "Hang the news tonight" (lines 312–313), has he forgotten about the conflict in Pakistan? Explain. ***Possible answer:*** *Mr. Pirzada has not forgotten about the conflict in Pakistan; it still weighs heavily on his mind. At this moment, however, he gives priority to the carving of Lilia's Halloween pumpkin. Perhaps he uses this activity as an escape from the pain and anxiety he feels for his family and his people. Perhaps he feels that this activity connects him to his children in Dacca.*

o'clock news, and then, sometime around midnight, Mr. Pirzada walked back to his dormitory. For this reason I never saw him leave, but each night as I drifted off to sleep I would hear them, anticipating the birth of a nation on the other side of the world. L

L DRAW CONCLUSIONS How does the scarcity of news from Dacca affect Lilia's parents and Mr. Pirzada?

One day in October Mr. Pirzada asked upon arrival, "What are these large orange vegetables on people's doorsteps? A type of squash?"

"Pumpkins," my mother replied. "Lilia, remind me to pick one up at the supermarket."

"And the purpose? It indicates what?"

"You make a jack-o'-lantern," I said, grinning ferociously. "Like this. To scare people away."

"I see," Mr. Pirzada said, grinning back. "Very useful."

The next day my mother bought a ten-pound pumpkin, fat and round, and placed it on the dining table. Before supper, while my father and Mr. Pirzada were watching the local news, she told me to decorate it with markers, but I wanted to carve it properly like others I had noticed in the neighborhood.

"Yes, let's carve it," Mr. Pirzada agreed, and rose from the sofa. "Hang the news tonight." Asking no questions, he walked into the kitchen, opened a drawer, and returned, bearing a long serrated knife. He glanced at me for approval. "Shall I?"

I nodded. For the first time we all gathered around the dining table, my mother, my father, Mr. Pirzada, and I. While the television aired unattended we covered the tabletop with newspapers. Mr. Pirzada draped his jacket over the chair behind him, removed a pair of opal cuff links, and rolled up the starched sleeves of his shirt.

Language Coach

Homophones Many words sound alike but have different spellings. The word *aired* (line 317) is a homophone of *erred* ("made a mistake"). *Aired* can mean "put out in fresh air" or "broadcasted (over radio or television)." Which meaning fits here? How can you tell?

"First go around the top, like this," I instructed, demonstrating with my index finger.

He made an initial incision and drew the knife around. When he had come full circle he lifted the cap by the stem; it loosened effortlessly, and Mr. Pirzada leaned over the pumpkin for a moment to inspect and inhale its contents. My mother gave him a long metal spoon with which he gutted the interior until the last bits of string and seeds were gone. My father, meanwhile, separated the seeds from the pulp and set them out to dry on a cookie sheet, so that we could roast them later on. I drew two triangles against the ridged surface for the eyes, which Mr. Pirzada dutifully carved, and crescents for eyebrows, and another triangle for the nose. The mouth was all that remained, and the teeth posed a challenge. I hesitated.

"Smile or frown?" I asked.

"You choose," Mr Pirzada said.

As a compromise I drew a kind of grimace, straight across, neither mournful nor friendly. Mr. Pirzada began carving, without the least bit of intimidation, as if he had been carving jack-o'-lanterns his whole life. He had nearly finished

DIFFERENTIATED INSTRUCTION

FOR STRUGGLING READERS

Vocabulary Support Have students use a Think-Pair-Share activity to explore the meanings of words connected with the carving of Lilia's pumpkin: *serrated* (line 314), *incision* (line 323), *dutifully* (line 330), *grimace* (line 335). In pairs, have students create a brief original scene using the vocabulary words in context. Have each pair share their scene with the class. Urge students to use context clues and, as needed, a dictionary.

FOR ENGLISH LANGUAGE LEARNERS

Language Coach

Homophones ***Answer:*** *Broadcasted* fits the context of a family watching TV. Point out the words *night* (line 297), *see* (line 307), and *time* (line 316). Pronounce each word as a model for students. Then ask students to pronounce each word individually, emphasizing the long vowel sounds in each word. Have students work in pairs to create a list of homophones for each of the words.

when the national news began. The reporter mentioned Dacca, and we all
turned to listen: An Indian official announced that unless the world helped
340 to relieve the burden of East Pakistani refugees, India would have to go to
war against Pakistan. The reporter's face dripped with sweat as he relayed the
information. He did not wear a tie or jacket, dressed instead as if he himself
were about to take part in the battle. He shielded his scorched face as he
hollered things to the cameraman. The knife slipped from Mr. Pirzada's hand
and made a gash dipping toward the base of the pumpkin.

"Please forgive me." He raised a hand to one side of his face, as if someone had
slapped him there. "I am—it is terrible. I will buy another. We will try again."

"Not at all, not at all," my father said. He took the knife from Mr. Pirzada,
and carved around the gash, evening it out, dispensing altogether with the
350 teeth I had drawn. What resulted was a disproportionately large hole the size of
a lemon, so that our jack-o'-lantern wore an expression of placid astonishment,
the eyebrows no longer fierce, floating in frozen surprise above a vacant,
geometric gaze.

For Halloween I was a witch. Dora, my trick-or-treating partner, was a
witch too. We wore black capes fashioned from dyed pillowcases and
conical hats with wide cardboard brims. We shaded our faces green with a
broken eye shadow that belonged to Dora's mother, and my mother gave us two
burlap sacks that had once contained basmati rice, for collecting candy. That
year our parents decided that we were old enough to roam the neighborhood
360 unattended. Our plan was to walk from my house to Dora's, from where I

DRAW CONCLUSIONS
How does Mr. Pirzada react to the latest news report from Dacca?

READING SKILL — COMMON CORE — RL 1

DRAW CONCLUSIONS

Possible answer: Mr. Pirzada reacts to the news report—the threat of war between India and Pakistan—with shock and concern. His shock is suggested by the fact that the knife abruptly slips from his hand, making a gash in the pumpkin.

IF STUDENTS NEED HELP . . . Compare lines 344–345 with lines 323–324. Discuss why Mr. Pirzada, who had handled the knife so skillfully at first, might drop the knife now.

Extend the Discussion Why does Lilia's father immediately take the knife from Mr. Pirzada and carve around the gash (lines 348–350)?

Analyze Visuals

Activity Discuss whether the pumpkin in the photograph matches the one that Lilia describes. Have students cite textual evidence to support their answers. *Possible answer: The pumpkin in the photograph is a close match. Like Lilia's pumpkin, this one is round (line 308); it has triangle-shaped eyes and nose, along with crescent-shaped eyebrows (lines 329–331). The mouth of the pumpkin in the photograph seems a good representation of the hole that results when Lilia's father carves around the gash that Mr. Pirzada accidentally made (lines 348–353).*

FOR STRUGGLING READERS
Comprehension Support Discuss the TV news report that so startles Mr. Pirzada that he drops his knife (lines 344–345). To make sure that students understand the intensity of the news, direct their attention to these details in lines 341–344: the reporter's sweaty face, his battle-ready clothing, his act of shielding his scorched face, and his yelling at the cameraman.

FOR ADVANCED LEARNERS/PRE–AP
Research a Crisis Direct students to research the crisis caused by refugees fleeing from East Pakistan into India and the reasons behind India's threat to go to war against Pakistan because of it (lines 339–341). Ask students to write a paragraph or two about this crisis and its eventual resolution. Have students compare their findings with partners or in small groups. Ask volunteers to share their findings with the class.

TIERED DISCUSSION PROMPTS

Direct students to lines 367–400. Use these prompts to help students understand Mr. Pirzada's concern for Lilia:

Connect How do you feel about Mr. Pirzada at this point in the story? Why? *Accept all reasonable responses.*

Analyze What questions does Mr. Pirzada ask to indicate that he is somewhat worried about Lilia? How else does he indicate concern? *Possible answer: Mr. Pirzada asks if Lilia will be warm enough (line 370) and if there is any danger in going trick-or-treating (line 388). He also asks what would happen if it rained or if the girls lost their way (line 397). He indicates concern by offering to accompany the girls (line 391).*

Evaluate Do you feel that Mr. Pirzada's concern is appropriate? Why or why not? *Possible answer: Mr. Pirzada's concern seems overblown, but there may be two justifications for it. For one thing, Halloween customs are new to him, so it may be natural for him to have questions. In addition, his expressions of concern for Lilia and Dora probably reflect the fear that he feels for his family in Pakistan.*

VOCABULARY

COMMON CORE

L 4

OWN THE WORD

concede: Remind students that *concede* means "to admit something, often reluctantly." Have students complete the following sentence to illustrate that they understand the meaning of the word. José *conceded* that . . . . *Possible answer: he had lost the election.*

---

was to call to say I had arrived safely, and then Dora's mother would drive me home. My father equipped us with flashlights, and I had to wear my watch and synchronize it with his. We were to return no later than nine o'clock.

When Mr. Pirzada arrived that evening he presented me with a box of chocolate-covered mints.

"In here," I told him, and opened up the burlap sack. "Trick or treat!"

"I understand that you don't really need my contribution this evening," he said, depositing the box. He gazed at my green face, and the hat secured by a string under my chin. Gingerly he lifted the hem of the cape, under which I

370 was wearing a sweater and zipped fleece jacket. "Will you be warm enough?"

I nodded, causing the hat to tip to one side.

He set it right. "Perhaps it is best to stand still."

The bottom of our staircase was lined with baskets of miniature candy, and when Mr. Pirzada removed his shoes he did not place them there as he normally did, but inside the closet instead. He began to unbutton his coat, and I waited to take it from him, but Dora called me from the bathroom to say that she needed my help drawing a mole on her chin. When we were finally ready my mother took a picture of us in front of the fireplace, and then I opened the front door to leave. Mr. Pirzada and my father, who had not gone

380 into the living room yet, hovered in the foyer. Outside it was already dark. The air smelled of wet leaves, and our carved jack-o'-lantern flickered impressively against the shrubbery by the door. In the distance came the sounds of scampering feet, and the howls of the older boys who wore no costume at all other than a rubber mask, and the rustling apparel of the youngest children, some so young that they were carried from door to door in the arms of their parents.

"Don't go into any of the houses you don't know," my father warned.

Mr. Pirzada knit his brows together. "Is there any danger?"

"No, no," my mother assured him. "All the children will be out. It's a

390 tradition."

"Perhaps I should accompany them?" Mr. Pirzada suggested. He looked suddenly tired and small, standing there in his splayed, stockinged feet, and his eyes contained a panic I had never seen before. In spite of the cold I began to sweat inside my pillowcase.

"Really, Mr. Pirzada," my mother said, "Lilia will be perfectly safe with her friend."

"But if it rains? If they lose their way?"

"Don't worry," I said. It was the first time I had uttered those words to Mr. Pirzada, two simple words I had tried but failed to tell him for weeks, had said

400 only in my prayers. It shamed me now that I had said them for my own sake.

He placed one of his stocky fingers on my cheek, then pressed it to the back of his own hand, leaving a faint green smear. "If the lady insists," he **conceded**, and offered a small bow.

concede (kən-sēd') *v.* to admit or acknowledge, often reluctantly

---

DIFFERENTIATED INSTRUCTION

FOR STRUGGLING READERS

Explore Sensory Details Direct students' attention to the description in lines 380–386. Elicit or explain that Lahiri uses details that appeal to the senses to bring this scene in the narrative to life. Help students identify the vivid sensory words (for example, *flickered, scampering, howls,* and *rustling*) and the senses to which they appeal.

Comprehension Support Help students understand the importance of lines 398–400 by discussing these points:

- Lilia has worried about Mr. Pirzada and his family but has not known how to say so.
- When she speaks, her "Don't worry" applies to his concern for her, not for his family.
- Lilia feels that she has spoken selfishly. At this moment, there seems to be no way to tell Mr. Pirzada what she really means.

We left, stumbling slightly in our black pointy thrift-store shoes, and when we turned at the end of the driveway to wave good-bye, Mr. Pirzada was standing in the frame of the doorway, a short figure between my parents, waving back.

"Why did that man want to come with us?" Dora asked.

"His daughters are missing." As soon as I said it, I wished I had not. I felt 410 that my saying it made it true, that Mr. Pirzada's daughters really were missing, and that he would never see them again.

"You mean they were kidnapped?" Dora continued. "From a park or something?"

"I didn't mean they were missing. I meant, he misses them. They live in a different country, and he hasn't seen them in a while, that's all."

We went from house to house, walking along pathways and pressing doorbells. Some people had switched off all their lights for effect, or strung rubber bats in their windows. At the McIntyres' a coffin was placed in front of the door, and Mr. McIntyre rose from it in silence, his face covered with 420 chalk, and deposited a fistful of candy corns into our sacks. Several people told me that they had never seen an Indian witch before. Others performed the transaction without comment. As we paved our way with the parallel beams of our flashlights we saw eggs cracked in the middle of the road, and cars covered with shaving cream, and toilet paper garlanding the branches of trees. By the time we reached Dora's house our hands were chapped from carrying our bulging burlap bags, and our feet were sore and swollen. Her mother gave us bandages for our blisters and served us warm cider and caramel popcorn. She reminded me to call my parents to tell them I had arrived safely and when I did I could hear the television in the background. My mother did not seem 430 particularly relieved to hear from me. When I replaced the phone on the receiver it occurred to me that the television wasn't on at Dora's house at all. Her father was lying on the couch, reading a magazine, with a glass of wine on the coffee table, and there was saxophone music playing on the stereo.

After Dora and I had sorted through our plunder, and counted and sampled and traded until we were satisfied, her mother drove me back to my house. I thanked her for the ride, and she waited in the driveway until I made it to the door. In the glare of her headlights I saw that our pumpkin had been shattered, its thick shell strewn in chunks across the grass. I felt the sting of tears in my eyes, and a sudden pain in my throat, as if it had been stuffed with the sharp 440 tiny pebbles that crunched with each step under my aching feet. I opened the door, expecting the three of them to be standing in the foyer, waiting to receive me, and to grieve for our ruined pumpkin, but there was no one. In the living room Mr. Pirzada, my father, and mother were sitting side by side on the sofa. The television was turned off, and Mr. Pirzada had his head in his hands.

What they heard that evening, and for many evenings after that, was that India and Pakistan were drawing closer and closer to war. Troops from

THEME AND CHARACTER
Reread lines 388–415. According to Lilia, why is Mr. Pirzada protective of her? Explain how she, in turn, is protective of Mr. Pirzada.

Analyze Visuals

Activity Have students compare and contrast this photograph with the photograph on page 460. *Possible answer: The photographs are similar in that both show food placed in front of a televised news report. The differences are that now the food is only boiled eggs (as described in line 458), and the picture on the screen now is clearly an image of war.*

READING SKILL

COMMON CORE

RL 1

◉ DRAW CONCLUSIONS

Possible answer: Pakistan's civil war greatly upsets Lilia's family and Mr. Pirzada during its 12-day duration. Their customary routines are abandoned. Mr. Pirzada is too worried and distracted to bring candy, and Lilia's mother serves only the simplest of meals. Sometimes Mr. Pirzada stays so late, watching the news, that he sleeps on the couch. The family and Mr. Pirzada are preoccupied with what Lilia calls "a single fear" (line 464).

both sides lined the border, and Dacca was insisting on nothing short of independence. The war was soon to be waged on East Pakistani soil. The United States was siding with West Pakistan, the Soviet Union with India and
450 what was soon to be Bangladesh. War was declared officially on December 4, and twelve days later, the Pakistani army, weakened by having to fight three thousand miles from their source of supplies, surrendered in Dacca. All of these facts I know only now, for they are available to me in any history book, in any library. But then it remained, for the most part, a remote mystery with haphazard clues. What I remember during those twelve days of the war was that my father no longer asked me to watch the news with them, and that Mr. Pirzada stopped bringing me candy, and that my mother refused to serve anything other than boiled eggs with rice for dinner. I remember some nights helping my mother spread a sheet and blankets on the couch so that Mr.
460 Pirzada could sleep there, and high-pitched voices hollering in the middle of the night when my parents called our relatives in Calcutta to learn more details about the situation. Most of all I remember the three of them operating during that time as if they were a single person, sharing a single meal, a single body, a single silence, and a single fear. ◉

 *I*n January, Mr. Pirzada flew back to his three-story home in Dacca, to discover what was left of it. We did not see much of him in those final weeks of the year; he was busy finishing his manuscript, and we went to Philadelphia to spend Christmas with friends of my parents. Just as I have

◉ DRAW CONCLUSIONS
Note the way Lilia's family and Mr. Pirzada behave during the 12 days of war compared with their earlier shared experiences. How has Pakistan's civil war affected them?

DIFFERENTIATED INSTRUCTION

FOR ENGLISH LANGUAGE LEARNERS
Vocabulary: Word Associations Have students study these common phrases and expressions and then record them in a notebook, along with context sentences that show their meaning: *did not see much of* (line 466), *For a long time* (line 470), *did not hear from* (lines 470–471), *Every now and then* (line 478), *thanked us for our hospitality* (line 488), *express his gratitude* (line 490), *there was no need to* (line 500).

FOR STRUGGLING READERS
Comprehension Support Call attention to the repetition of the word *single* in lines 463–464. Elicit or explain that Lahiri repeats the word to convey a sense of unity in the face of adversity. Invite pairs of students to paraphrase the sentence; then call on volunteers to share and compare their paraphrases.

no memory of his first visit, I have no memory of his last. My father drove him
470 to the airport one afternoon while I was at school. For a long time we did not
hear from him. Our evenings went on as usual, with dinners in front of the
news. The only difference was that Mr. Pirzada and his extra watch were not
there to accompany us. According to reports Dacca was repairing itself slowly,
with a newly formed parliamentary government. The new leader, Sheikh
Mujib Rahman, recently released from prison, asked countries for building
materials to replace more than one million houses that had been destroyed
in the war. Countless refugees returned from India, greeted, we learned, by
unemployment and the threat of famine. Every now and then I studied the
map above my father's desk and pictured Mr. Pirzada on that small patch of
480 yellow, perspiring heavily, I imagined, in one of his suits, searching for his
family. Of course, the map was outdated by then.

Finally, several months later, we received a card from Mr. Pirzada
commemorating the Muslim New Year,[16] along with a short letter. He was
reunited, he wrote, with his wife and children. All were well, having survived
the events of the past year at an estate belonging to his wife's grandparents
in the mountains of Shillong. His seven daughters were a bit taller, he wrote,
but otherwise they were the same, and he still could not keep their names in
order. At the end of the letter he thanked us for our hospitality, adding that
although he now understood the meaning of the words "thank you" they
490 still were not adequate to express his gratitude. To celebrate the good news
my mother prepared a special dinner that evening, and when we sat down
to eat at the coffee table we toasted our water glasses, but I did not feel like
celebrating. Though I had not seen him for months, it was only then that I felt
Mr. Pirzada's absence. It was only then, raising my water glass in his name, that
I knew what it meant to miss someone who was so many miles and hours away,
just as he had missed his wife and daughters for so many months. He had no
reason to return to us, and my parents predicted, correctly, that we would never
see him again. Since January, each night before bed, I had continued to eat, for
the sake of Mr. Pirzada's family, a piece of candy I had saved from Halloween.
500 That night there was no need to. Eventually, I threw them away. 🕮 Ⓟ

⑤ Targeted Passage

Ⓟ THEME AND CHARACTER
Why does Lilia throw away her remaining candies?

---

16. **Muslim New Year:** an important Islamic holiday and observance that marks the Prophet Muhammad's emigration from Mecca to Medina, a turning point in Islamic history.

WHEN MR. PIRZADA CAME TO DINE **469**

FOR STRUGGLING READERS

⑤ Targeted Passage [Lines 482–500]

This concluding paragraph reveals the fate of Mr. Pirzada's family and the insight that Lilia gains while thinking about them.

- What happened to Mr. Pirzada and his family? (lines 483–488)
- What does Lilia's mother do to celebrate? Why doesn't Lilia feel like celebrating? (lines 490–496)

- What thought occurs to Lilia as she raises her water glass in a toast? (lines 494–496)

Comprehension Support In line 481, Lilia comments that by the time the refugees returned from India, her father's map had become outdated. Clarify the comment by explaining that East Pakistan had become the independent nation of Bangladesh. You may want to review lines 65–81 with students, and point out the description of the use of yellow and orange on the map.

REVISIT THE BIG QUESTION
When do world
CONFLICTS affect us?

Discuss Based on lines 493–498, how does Lilia finally come to understand the effects of the conflict in Pakistan on Mr. Pirzada? ***Possible answer:*** *Lilia's understanding comes when she realizes how she misses Mr. Pirzada and how similar his feelings must have been as he thought about his distant family while in the United States.*

TEXT ANALYSIS

Ⓟ THEME AND CHARACTER RL 2 RL 3

Possible answer: *Lilia has associated the candies with her prayers for Mr. Pirzada's family (lines 239–247). Now that she knows that he and his family are safe, she no longer needs to pray for them and therefore no longer needs the candy.*

SELECTION WRAP–UP

READ WITH A PURPOSE Now that students have finished reading the selection, have them compare Lilia's friendship with Dora to her friendship with Mr. Pirzada. What do these relationships show about the nature of friendship? ***Possible answer:*** *There are different kinds of friendships. Lilia and Dora have one type of friendship, because they are peers. Lilia and Mr. Pirzada have a different type, because he is an adult. Each friendship is important in its own way.*

⭐ **CRITIQUE** Ask students why they do or do not think that Lahiri has created a believable ten-year-old girl in Lilia. Remind students to keep in mind the cultural influences affecting Lilia.

INDEPENDENT READING
If students would like to read about another immigrant family coping with world conflicts as they strive to make a life in the United States, suggest *Esperanza Rising* by Pam Muñoz Ryan.

WHEN MR. PIRZADA CAME TO DINE **469**

TIERED DISCUSSION PROMPTS

Use these prompts to help students understand the connection between Lahiri's personal life and the characters and events in stories such as "When Mr. Pirzada Came to Dine":

Restate In your own words, tell what Elizabeth Farnsworth means when she calls Lahiri an "interpreter of maladies." ***Possible answer:*** *When Farnsworth calls Lahiri an "interpreter of maladies," she means that through her writing, Lahiri can help other people better understand feelings of longing and facing loss in life.*

Analyze How has Lahiri's family background influenced her writing? ***Possible answer:*** *Lahiri's writing reflects her observation of her parents' experience as Indian immigrants and her understanding of their feelings—especially their feelings of loss about what they had given up to come to the United States.*

Synthesize Think about Saki and about Guy de Maupassant, the other two authors you have already met in Unit 4. Which author do you think would identify more closely with what Lahiri says in this interview about personal connections to stories? Why? ***Students should make a logical defense of their choices. For example, they may suggest that Maupassant's experiences in the Franco-Prussian War gave him a closer personal connection to the subject of "Two Friends" than Saki had to the subject of "The Interlopers."***

Interview

You have just read a short story by Jhumpa Lahiri about conflicts faced by immigrants. Now, you'll read an interview that examines the sources of her inspiration.

NewsHour
FROM A NEWSHOUR WITH JIM LEHRER TRANSCRIPT

JHUMPA LAHIRI, PULITZER PRIZE WINNER

Elizabeth Farnsworth: Tell us about the title of [your] book. It's an unusual title, "Interpreter of Maladies." Where does it come from?

Jhumpa Lahiri: The title is . . . Well, it's the title of one of the stories in the book. And the phrase itself was something I thought of before I even wrote that story. I thought of it one day after I ran into someone I knew. I asked him what he was doing with himself, and he told me he was working as an interpreter in a doctor's office in Brookline, Massachusetts, where I was living at the time, and he was translating for a doctor who had a number of Russian patients. And he was fluent in English and Russian. And on my way home, after running into him, I thought of this . . . I just heard this phrase in my head. And I liked the way it sounded, but I wasn't quite sure what it meant, but I wrote it down. I just wrote down the phrase itself. And for years, I sort of would try to write a story that somehow fit the title. And I don't think it happened for maybe another four years that I actually thought of a story, the plot of a story that corresponded to that phrase.

EF: It occurred to me that you're kind of an interpreter of maladies yourself in these stories.

JL: I guess that's what has . . . That's the way it's turned out, yeah. But I didn't know . . . At the time, I wasn't aware of it.

EF: There's longing and loss in these stories, the longing and loss that often comes with the life of an immigrant. Is this your longing and loss, do you think, as the child of immigrants, or is this more the longing and loss of your parents' generation coming through?

JL: Both. I think that, in part, it's a reflection of what I observed my parents experiencing and their friends, their circle of fellow Indian immigrant friends. It's also, in part, drawn from my own experiences and a sense of . . . I always say that I feel that I've inherited a sense of that loss from my parents because it was so palpable all the time while I was growing up, the sense of what my parents had sacrificed in moving to the United States, and in so many ways, and yet at the same time, remaining here and building a life here and all that that entailed.

EF: One of the stories that raises these issues is called "When Mr. Pirzada Came to Dine." It begins like this: "In the autumn of 1971 a man used to come to our house bearing confections in his pocket and hopes of ascertaining the life or death of his family." I love that beginning. Tell us a little bit about the story. . . .

JL: Sure. This story is based on a gentleman who . . . used to come to my parents' house in 1971 from Bangladesh. He was at the University of Rhode Island. And I was four, four years old, at the time, and so I actually don't have any memories of this gentleman. But I've heard . . . I heard through my parents what his predicament was. And when I learned about his situation, which was that he was in the United States during the Pakistani civil war and his family was back in Dacca, I just sort of . . . I was so overwhelmed by this information that I wrote this story based on that . . . Based on that experience in my parents' life.

Comprehension

1. **Recall** Why does Mr. Pirzada begin coming to Lilia's house?

2. **Recall** How does Lilia react to the gifts Mr. Pirzada brings?

3. **Clarify** Why does Lilia's father want her to learn about Indian and Pakistani history?

Text Analysis

4. **Analyze Character** Lilia becomes more concerned about Pakistan and its civil unrest as she becomes better acquainted with Mr. Pirzada. Show Lilia's growing cultural awareness by completing a timeline like the one shown. Fill in each blank with an appropriate story detail.

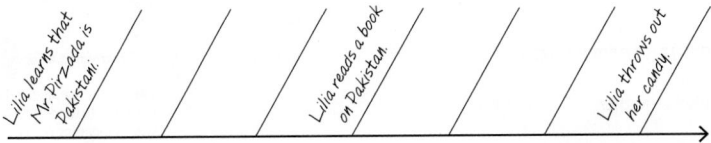

5. **Examine Character Relationship** Lilia states that Mr. Pirzada is protective of her because he misses his own daughters. How is the relationship between Lilia and Mr. Pirzada like that of a father and a daughter?

6. **Interpret Theme and Character** What theme do you think Lahiri is trying to communicate through the experiences of Lilia? Cite evidence in your answer.

7. **Draw Conclusions** Review the chart you created. Explain which characters are most affected by the conflict in Pakistan. Why do you think the conflict becomes a personal matter for some, but not for all, of the characters?

8. **Evaluate** Reread lines 482–500. Does the outcome of the story seem believable? Why or why not? In your response, explain how well the story resolves Lilia's inner conflict.

9. **Compare Literary Works** Reread the interview with Lahiri on page 470. What details in the interview enhance your understanding of the characters and events depicted in "When Mr. Pirzada Came to Dine"? Explain your response.

Text Criticism

10. **Author's Style** Lahiri is admired for her penetrating insights into human behavior. Find examples of such insights in the story and discuss how they add to the story's impact.

When do world **CONFLICTS** affect us?

What can make a far-away conflict become personal to you?

COMMON CORE

RL 1 Cite textual evidence to support analysis of what the text says explicitly as well as inferences drawn from the text.
RL 2 Determine a theme of a text and analyze how it emerges and is refined by specific details.
RL 3 Analyze how complex characters develop the theme.

Practice and Apply

For preliminary support of post-reading questions, use these copy masters:

R RESOURCE MANAGER—Copy Masters
Reading Check p. 72
Theme and Character p. 65
Question Support p. 73

Additional selection questions are provided for teachers on page 59.

ANSWERS

Comprehension

1. *Lilia's parents invite him to eat dinner and watch the TV news with them.*

2. *Lilia is not quite sure how to react at first, but she comes to treasure the gifts.*

3. *He wants her to learn of her heritage and the world outside the United States.*

Text Analysis

COMMON CORE RL 1, RL 2, RL 3

Possible answers:

4. *Lilia learns that Mr. Pirzada's family lives in Dacca and may be in danger; Lilia sees that people in her community are not affected by events in Dacca; Lilia grows in her wish to console Mr. Pirzada; Lilia shares Mr. Pirzada's fear and concern as she and her family continue to follow events in Pakistan.*

5. *Mr. Pirzada seems fatherly when he brings Lilia candies and is affectionate toward her (lines 147–148, 159–163) and when he worries about her on Halloween (lines 370–397). Lilia is daughterly when she looks forward to seeing him and worries about his family (lines 230–247).*

6. ● **COMMON CORE FOCUS** *Theme and Character* *One theme may be that part of maturing is learning about other people and caring about their welfare. Lilia becomes more mature as she does so.*

7. ■ **COMMON CORE FOCUS** *Draw Conclusions Mr. Pirzada is most affected by the conflict, because his family lives in the disputed area. Lilia's parents are less affected, because they were born in that part of the world but have lived in the United States for years. Lilia never has lived in that part of the world, but she is affected because of her empathy for Mr. Pirzada. For Dora and Mrs. Kenyon, the conflict is merely an impersonal news story.*

8. *The outcome seems believable; Lilia's increased awareness, genuine concern, and*

---

growing maturity reflect the resolution of her inner conflict.

9. *Details include Lahiri's observation of the experiences of her parents and their immigrant friends, the sense of loss that she inherited from her parents, and her memory of the gentleman who used to come to her parents' house in 1971.*

Text Criticism

10. *Examples will vary. For instance, Lilia is moved by events to pray, for the first time,*

for Mr. Pirzada's family (lines 238–247). Later, she realizes that she now knows what it means to miss someone (lines 494–496). Such insights help readers connect with the story, because they can understand Lilia's feelings.

When do world **CONFLICTS** affect us?

A far-away conflict becomes personal when someone you know is affected by it.

Vocabulary in Context

▲ VOCABULARY PRACTICE

1. *doubt*
2. *restriction*
3. *compatriot*
4. *sovereignty*

5. *impeccably*
6. *imperceptible*
7. *assail*
8. *correct*

 RESOURCE MANAGER—Copy Master
Vocabulary Practice p. 70

ACADEMIC VOCABULARY IN SPEAKING

Possible answer: *The carving of the pumpkin adds an interesting* layer *to the meaning of the story. The event shows how Lilia's family has adopted American holiday customs, which Mr. Pirzada is eager to share with them. When Mr. Pirzada hears bad news about East Pakistan while carving the pumpkin, he slips. This suggests a* theme *about how people may cover up their feelings and only let them slip during times of sudden stress.*

VOCABULARY STRATEGY: THE PREFIX *im-*

COMMON
CORE **L 4c**

- Model for students how to use the parts of a word to understand its meaning.

- Elicit or provide additional examples of words beginning with the prefix *im-*, such as *impossible*, *immortal*, and *immature*. Have students define the words and use them in sentences.

Answers:

1. *immoderate*
2. *imperfect*
3. *impenetrable*

4. *improbable*
5. *imperceptible*

 RESOURCE MANAGER—Copy Master
Vocabulary Strategy p. 71

Vocabulary in Context

▲ VOCABULARY PRACTICE

Identify the word that is not related in meaning to the other words in the set. If necessary, use a dictionary to check the definitions of words.

1. doubt, ascertain, discover, realize
2. freedom, autonomy, independence, restriction
3. stranger, foreigner, compatriot, outsider
4. sovereignty, dependence, neediness, reliance
5. messily, sloppily, carelessly, impeccably
6. obvious, imperceptible, tangible, distinct
7. greet, assail, welcome, embrace
8. admit, allow, concede, correct

WORD LIST
ascertain
assail
autonomy
compatriot
concede
impeccably
imperceptible
sovereignty

ACADEMIC VOCABULARY IN SPEAKING

- alter   • layer   • symbol   • theme   • unify

COMMON CORE
L 4c Consult general reference materials to determine or clarify a word's meaning or etymology.

Each of the events in the story adds another **layer** of meaning. Choose one event and tell how it connects to one of the key story **themes**. Use at least one Academic Vocabulary word in your response.

VOCABULARY STRATEGY: THE PREFIX *im-*

The vocabulary word *imperceptible* contains the Latin prefix *im-*. This prefix often means "not" and is used in many English words. To understand the meanings of words that begin with *im-*, use context clues and your knowledge of the prefix.

PRACTICE Write the word from the word web that best completes each sentence. Use context clues to help you or, if necessary, consult a dictionary.

1. You seem to spend an _____ amount of time with your friend Janey.
2. An _____ shirt may have one sleeve that is longer than the other.
3. The _____ fortress resisted attackers for decades.
4. Your explanation seems highly _____. What really happened?
5. The wings of a hummingbird flutter so fast as to be almost _____.

imperceptible   imperfect   improbable   **im-**   immoderate   impenetrable

Interactive Vocabulary **THINK** central

Go to thinkcentral.com.
KEYWORD: HML10-472

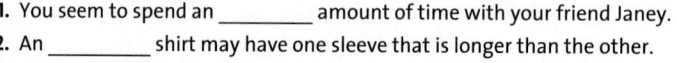 **DIFFERENTIATED INSTRUCTION**

FOR ENGLISH LANGUAGE LEARNERS

Vocabulary: Word Maps Have students use Word Questioning for each of the words. Then have them use each vocabulary word correctly in a sentence.

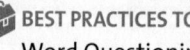 **BEST PRACTICES TOOLKIT— Transparency**
Word Questioning p. E9

FOR ADVANCED LEARNERS/PRE–AP

Vocabulary in Writing Challenge students to use as many vocabulary words as they can in a letter written by Mr. Pirzada's wife to her husband during the conflict in Pakistan. Invite students to compare letters in small groups to see the various ways in which they used the words.

Language

◆ **GRAMMAR AND STYLE: Add Descriptive Details**

Review the **Grammar and Style** note on page 458. There, Lahiri uses **adverbs** to effectively convey details about her character's physical appearance. Here are two other examples of how Lahiri uses adverbs to reveal personal qualities of Lilia and Mr. Pirzada:

> "You make a jack-o'-lantern," I said, grinning *ferociously*. "Like this. To scare people away." (lines 305–306)

> I could only steal glances at Mr. Pirzada, sitting beside me in his olive green jacket, *calmly* creating a well in his rice to make room for a second helping of lentils. (lines 215–217)

Notice how the revisions in blue improve the descriptive power of this first draft through the addition of adverbs. Use similar methods to revise your responses to the prompt below.

> **STUDENT MODEL**
>
> "The Interlopers" seems to take place in the early twentieth century,
> *violently*
> in central Europe. The two main characters hate each other. However,
> *dramatically*
> everything changes when the two are caught in the same fate.

COMMON CORE

L 3 Apply knowledge of language to make effective choices for meaning or style. **W 2** Write explanatory texts to examine and convey complex ideas, concepts, and information clearly and accurately through the effective analysis of content.

READING-WRITING CONNECTION

 YOUR TURN Broaden your understanding of "When Mr. Pirzada Came to Dine" by responding to this prompt. Then use the **revising tip** to improve your writing.

WRITING PROMPT	**REVISING TIP**
Extended Constructed Response: Comparison and Contrast The stories in this unit are from different time periods, but they share a similar theme about conflict: "After a time, hatred becomes pointless." Compare and contrast the ways each story expresses these theme. Using examples from the stories, write a **three-to-five-paragraph response.**	Review your response. Did you use adverbs to convey details? If not, revise your answer to include adverbs in your descriptions.

Interactive Revision **THINK** central
Go to **thinkcentral.com**.
KEYWORD: HML10-473

Language

COMMON CORE L 3, W 2

◆ **GRAMMAR AND STYLE**

- As you examine the examples from the story and the student model, discuss how the highlighted words enrich the text. (For more on adverbs, see page R57 in the **GRAMMAR HANDBOOK**.)

- Write this passage on the board. Ask students to suggest adverb insertions that add detail to the description. (Sample revisions are shown in blue.)

> We *anxiously* watched the images on the television screen, hoping for some good news. Mr. Pirzada shifted *uneasily* in his seat. "Try to remain calm," I told him *softly*.

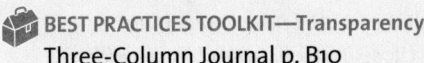 RESOURCE MANAGER—Copy Master
Add Descriptive Details p. 74

READING-WRITING CONNECTION

- Have students use a Three-Column Journal or other graphic organizer to record details about each of the stories.

 BEST PRACTICES TOOLKIT—Transparency
Three-Column Journal p. B10

> **Writing Online** **THINK** central
>
> The following tools are available online at **thinkcentral.com** and on **WriteSmart** CD-ROM:
> - **Interactive Graphic Organizers**
> - **Interactive Student Models**
> - **Interactive Revision Lessons**
> For additional grammar instruction, see **GrammarNotes** on **thinkcentral.com**.

FOR STRUGGLING WRITERS

- For review, have students summarize each of the stories read thus far in Unit 4.

- Have students work in small groups to discuss how each story reveals the theme about conflict. Then have groups share and compare their conclusions.

- Suggest that students organize their writing by focusing first on similarities among the stories and then on differences.

Practice and Apply

COMMON CORE FOCUS

RI 7 Analyze various accounts of a subject told in different mediums, determining which details are emphasized in each account.

Web Site

Have students look at the "Refugee Assistance" photo. Ask students how the photo relates to the short story "Mr. Pirzada Came to Dine" and the interview with Jhumpa Lahiri. *Possible answers: In both the interview and the story, Lahiri addresses how it feels to be an immigrant and a refugee. The photo is a graphic representation of the emotional toll on refugees that Lahiri talks about in both the story and the interview.*

ANALYZE VISUALS   COMMON CORE   RI 7

1. INTERPRET

Possible answer: The Refugee Aid Society consists of many people reaching out to help those in need around the world.

ANALYZE VISUALS   COMMON CORE   RI 7

2. ANALYZE

Possible answer: The purpose of the photograph of the refugees is to help people make a personal connection with refugees and be moved to assist them. The photograph shows that refugees are real people with families and children. They have no homes and have few material possessions—perhaps only the clothes they are wearing. The people in the photograph look tired, worried, and unsure of what to do next.

Web Site

Images can help you understand the effects of conflicts. The image below is from an aid society's Web site. Consider how the words, images, and graphics work together, and answer the questions below.

COMMON CORE

RI 7 Analyze various accounts of a subject told in different mediums, determining which details are emphasized in each account.

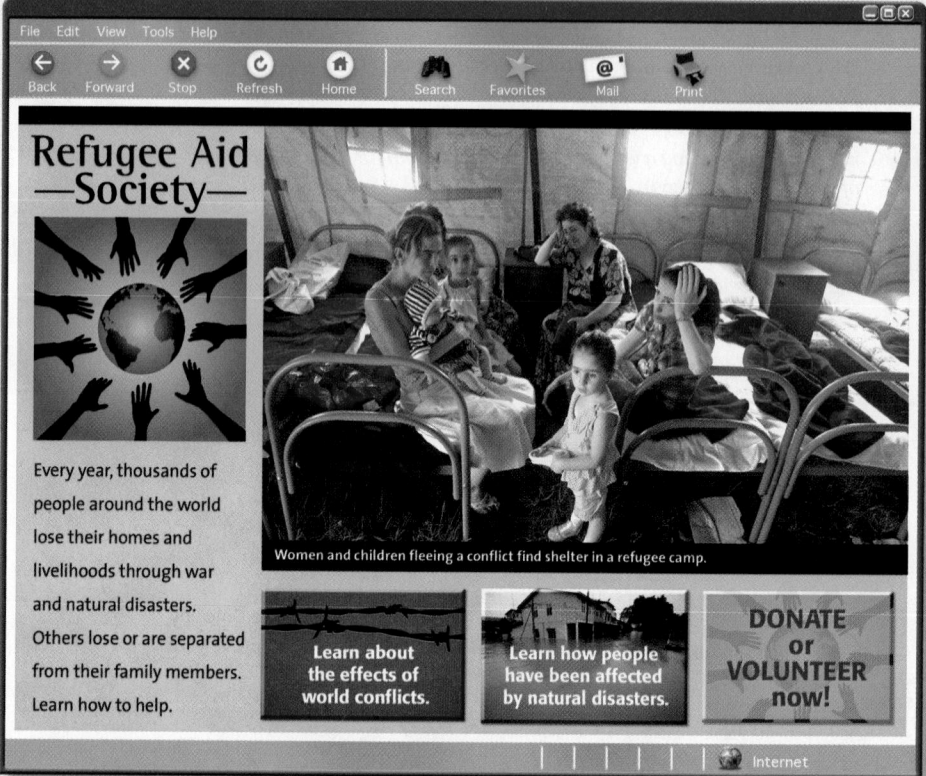

Women and children fleeing a conflict find shelter in a refugee camp.

1. INTERPRET
Examine the Refugee Aid Society's graphic in the upper left corner of the Web page. What impression does this graphic give you about this society and its goals?

2. ANALYZE
What is the purpose of including the photograph of the refugees? What does the photograph reveal about the refugees' situation?

474   UNIT 4: THEME

Assessment Practice: Short Constructed Response

LITERARY TEXT: "WHEN MR. PIRZADA CAME TO DINE"

Assessments often expect you to analyze the literary elements authors include in their written works. Practice analyzing a symbol by answering the **short constructed response question** below.

> In "When Mr. Pirzada Came to Dine," what does the candy that Lilia eats each night and eventually throws away represent? Support your answer with evidence from the story.

◀ **STRATEGIES IN ACTION**

1. Reread the text closely before deciding on your answer.
2. Note the significance of the candy to Lilia and to the events of the story.
3. Make sure your answer can be supported by evidence in the story.

NONFICTION TEXT: "JHUMPA LAHIRI, PULITZER PRIZE WINNER"

When responding to assessment questions, you are expected to go beyond the text to form thoughtful judgments. Practice this skill by answering the **short constructed response question** below.

> After reading the interview, what insight might a reader gain about Jhumpa Lahiri's writings? Support your answer with evidence from the selection.

◀ **STRATEGIES IN ACTION**

1. Reread the interview, paying attention to how the details relate to Lahiri's works.
2. Remember the evidence from the text can be in the form of a **direct quotation**, a **paraphrase**, or a **specific synopsis**.
3. Include the evidence you find in your answer.

COMPARING LITERARY AND NONFICTION TEXTS

You are likely to answer assessment questions that ask you to compare literary and nonfiction works. Practice this valuable skill by applying the following **short constructed response question** to "When Mr. Pirzada Came to Dine" and "Jhumpa Lahiri, Pulitzer Prize Winner."

> How do the details portrayed in Jhumpa Lahiri's interview mirror the events in her short story "When Mr. Pirzada Came to Dine"? Support your answer with evidence from both selections.

◀ **STRATEGIES IN ACTION**

1. State generally how the two works share similarities.
2. Review the details that appear in the interview. Then skim the short story, looking for similar details. Use these examples as evidence to support your general statement.

WHEN MR. PIRZADA ... / JHUMPA LAHIRI ... / REFUGEE AID SOCIETY WEB SITE   **475**

Assessment Practice: Short Constructed Response

LITERARY TEXT: "WHEN MR. PIRZADA CAME TO DINE" **Possible answer:** *At first, the candy represents tokens of friendship from Mr. Pirzada. As Lilia's friendship with Mr. Pirzada grows, Lilia comes to empathize with Mr. Pirzada and worries about his family so much that she prays for the first time. The candies become part of her prayer ritual. She says, "As I chewed it slowly, I prayed Mr. Pirzada's family was safe and sound." When she finds out that Mr. Pirzada's family is safe and he has been reunited with them, she throws the candy away because she no longer needs to pray.*

NONFICTION TEXT: "JHUMPA LAHIRI, PULITZER PRIZE WINNER" **Possible answer:** *Lahiri says that her writing in Interpreter of Maladies is partly what she observed from her Indian immigrant parents. She conveys the sense of loss she felt from her parents. Her writing also comes from personal experience. The character of Mr. Pirzada is based on a man who visited her parents' home.*

COMPARING LITERARY AND NONFICTION TEXTS **Possible answer:** *In "Mr. Pirzada," Lahiri communicates a sense of loss through the character of Mr. Pirzada, as he worries about his family in war torn Pakistan. In the interview, Lahiri says growing up she had a "sense of what my parents sacrificed in moving to the United States." She illustrates that sense of sacrifice and adjustment immigrants experience through Lilia's parents. In one scene, Lilia's mother states, "We live here now, she was born here," explaining why Lilia learns about the United States instead of India.*

DIFFERENTIATED INSTRUCTION

FOR STRUGGLING WRITERS

Short Constructed Response Help students to organize their thoughts with a graphic organizer. Ask students to point out what important information the prompt gives them as guidelines for their response. Have students create a two-column chart and label the first column "Details from the Interview" and the second column "Events from the Story." Tell students to record some of the main points about the interview in the first column. Then have students look in "Mr. Pirzada" for corresponding details for the second column. Finally, have students use the information in their graphic organizers to write their answers.

Focus and Motivate

COMMON CORE FOCUS

RL 2 Determine a theme of a text and analyze in detail how it emerges and is refined by specific details. **RL 10** Read and comprehend poems.

SUMMARIES

"Do not weep, maiden, for war is kind"
The speaker of this poem addresses people whose loved ones have died in war: a woman who has lost a lover, a baby who has lost a father, and a mother who has lost a son. The speaker seems to praise the glory of war, but the bitterly ironic tone reveals the message.

"the sonnet-ballad" In this poem, the speaker addresses her mother, describing her beloved's departure for war and asking, "where is happiness?" Lamenting his certain death, the speaker likens death to a temptress who will steal her love from her.

Who are the VICTIMS of war?

Ask the question, and relate it to the photograph. As students complete the *DISCUSS* activity, encourage partners to list possible victims of war. Have groups compile and share a master list of victims and of reasons that wars are fought.

Selection Resources

Before Reading

Essential Course of Study **ECOS**

Do not weep, maiden, for war is kind
Poem by Stephen Crane

the sonnet-ballad
Poem by Gwendolyn Brooks

Who are the VICTIMS of war?

COMMON CORE

RL 2 Determine a theme of a text and analyze in detail how it emerges and is refined by specific details. **RL 10** Read and comprehend poems.

What effect does war have on the soldiers who engage in battle and on loved ones who are left behind? These poems show how ordinary citizens can become victims when countries wage war.

DISCUSS Do you know anyone who has been involved in war, either as a participant or as a bystander? With a partner, discuss the effects of war as you have heard them described or as you imagine them. Then with a larger group, discuss why people have fought wars throughout history.

476

See resources on the **Teacher One Stop DVD-ROM** and on **thinkcentral.com**.

R RESOURCE MANAGER UNIT 4
Plan and Teach, pp. 77–82
Text Analysis and Reading
Skill, pp. 83–86†*

DIAGNOSTIC AND SELECTION TESTS
Selection Tests, pp. 127–130

BEST PRACTICES TOOLKIT
Reflection Chart, p. B8
Read Aloud, p. A34

INTERACTIVE READER

ADAPTED INTERACTIVE READER

ELL ADAPTED INTERACTIVE READER

TECHNOLOGY
- Teacher One Stop DVD-ROM
- Student One Stop DVD-ROM
- PowerNotes DVD-ROM
- Audio Anthology CD
- GrammarNotes DVD-ROM
- Audio Tutor CD
- ExamView Test Generator on the **Teacher One Stop**

THINK central

Find it Online!
Features on **thinkcentral.com** that support the selection include
- **PowerNotes** presentation
- **ThinkAloud** models to enhance comprehension
- **WordSharp** vocabulary tutorials
- interactive writing and grammar instruction

---

* Resources for Differentiation   † Also in Spanish   ‡ In Haitian Creole and Vietnamese

TEXT ANALYSIS: UNIVERSAL THEME

Although literary works may belong to different time periods and cultures, they often express the same message about human nature or life. In these cases, the message is called a **universal theme.** Universal themes reflect experiences that are common to most people, such as growing older or falling in love. The poems you are about to read were written 50 years apart and are the works of two distinguished authors, Stephen Crane and Gwendolyn Brooks. As you read each poem, use these strategies to discover the poems' shared message:

- Identify the **speaker,** or the voice that "talks" to the reader.
- Notice key **images** and think about their meaning.
- Identify examples of **repetition,** or words and phrases that are repeated in the poem. Think about their meaning.
- Consider the **mood,** or the overall feeling, created by the poem.

READING SKILL: UNDERSTAND VERBAL IRONY

Unlike fiction writers, poets typically communicate their messages in little space and few words. They often rely on different techniques to help them craft compact works of great power. One important literary technique is **verbal irony**—saying one thing but meaning the opposite. The first line of Crane's poem provides an example of such irony:

Do not weep, maiden, for war is kind.

War, by definition, cannot be considered kind. Clearly, Crane intends the reader to think something entirely different about war. Many poems, particularly those involving social criticism or protest, feature this technique. As you read the two poems, record examples of verbal irony and explain what you think they mean. In your *Reader/Writer Notebook,* create a graphic organizer like the one shown to help you.

Poem	Examples of Verbal Irony	Explanations
Crane's poem	Do not weep, maiden, for war is kind. (line 1)	War is cruel.

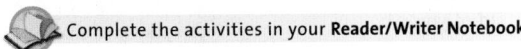 Complete the activities in your **Reader/Writer Notebook.**

Meet the Authors

Stephen Crane
1871–1900

Chronicler of War
When his Civil War novella *The Red Badge of Courage,* published in 1895, achieved enormous success, Stephen Crane felt embarrassed, since he had no firsthand experience of war. However, he soon took a job as a foreign correspondent, covering wars in Cuba and Greece. His experience of spending 30 hours in a lifeboat, after being shipwrecked near Cuba, inspired his famous story "The Open Boat." Although he died at 29, Crane left behind a prodigious number of literary works, many of which are considered classics.

Gwendolyn Brooks
1917–2000

Poet and Activist
Raised on Chicago's South Side, Gwendolyn Brooks remained devoted to this neighborhood and its black community throughout her life. In her early poetry, Brooks was strongly influenced by traditional literary forms. Empowered by black activism, she turned to free verse in the 1960s, striving to write poems that the people she wrote about would read. In 1950, Brooks won the Pulitzer Prize for poetry, the first African American so honored.

Authors Online
Go to thinkcentral.com. KEYWORD: HML10-477

THINK central

Teach

● *Model the Skill:* **UNIVERSAL THEME**

To model how to identify universal theme, write this poem on the board:

> A more unpleasant date she'd had
> She could not remember when.
> Closing the door quite tightly,
> She said, "Can't wait to see *him* again."

Help students state, in a sentence, the universal theme that the poem expresses. Point out that one possible theme is that establishing a romantic relationship can be difficult to do.

GUIDED PRACTICE Discuss how details in these lines help students understand the theme.

■ *Model the Skill:* **UNDERSTAND VERBAL IRONY**

To model how to understand verbal irony, discuss the verbal irony in the poem on the board. Point out that since the date was "unpleasant," and she "clos[ed] the door quite tightly," the speaker probably doesn't want to see the man again. Explain that the verbal irony lies in the line "Can't wait to see *him* again." The speaker says the opposite of what she means.

GUIDED PRACTICE Invite students to suggest examples of verbal irony that might appear in everyday conversation.

R RESOURCE MANAGER—Copy Master Understand Verbal Irony p. 85 (for student use while reading the selections)

DIFFERENTIATED INSTRUCTION

FOR STRUGGLING LEARNERS

Skill Support Discuss these examples of verbal irony from common speech:

- "I love seeing the dentist! It's such fun to have a tooth drilled!"
- A person with a terrible cold: "How am I? I've never felt better."
- A beach vacationer on the fourth day of rain: "Isn't this weather just perfect?"
- A person who lost his or her job: "Well, now I have that free time I wanted."

FOR ADVANCED LEARNERS/PRE–AP

Analyze Theme Types Remind students that not all themes are universal. Some themes are more limited, closely reflecting the time period and/or culture in which they were written. Ask students to list several literary works that they have read, including historical fiction, and identify the theme or themes in each work. Then have students classify the themes, deciding if each is limited or universal.

READ WITH A PURPOSE

Help students set a purpose for reading. Tell students to note the different writing styles Crane and Brooks use in their poems.

READING SKILL · COMMON CORE RL 10

A *Model the Skill:* **VERBAL IRONY**

Remind students that verbal irony is saying one thing but meaning the opposite. Point out the phrase "for war is kind" in line 1. Ask students if they think that war is kind. Tell students that most people would agree that war is the opposite of "kind," so this phrase is an example of verbal irony. Have students reread lines 1–11 and record examples of irony in their Reading Skills charts to help them answer the question.

Possible answer: *These lines demonstrate verbal irony in that the speaker expresses the horror of war by speaking of its opposite—the valor of war. He twice says that "War is kind" (lines 1 and 5), but he contrasts that statement with images such as a soldier presumably shot from his steed (lines 2–3), hoarse regimental drums (line 6), and a corpse-covered field (line 11).*

 BEST PRACTICES TOOLKIT—Transparency
Reflection Chart p. B8

TEXT ANALYSIS · COMMON CORE RL 2

B *Model the Skill:* **UNIVERSAL THEME**

Remind students that identifying images is a key to understanding theme. Tell students that as they discover images they should keep in mind what message the author is trying to communicate to readers.

Possible answer: *In stanza 1, the main image is of the maiden's lover throwing his hands in the air and falling dead from the horse, which continues running in fright. In stanza 3, the main image is of the baby's father collapsing and dying in a battlefield trench. In stanza 5, the main image is of the mother's son being buried in a brightly colored shroud. The common element is that the images illustrate the death of a soldier.*

Do not weep, maiden, for war is kind

Stephen Crane

Do not weep, maiden, for war is kind.
Because your lover threw wild hands toward the sky
And the affrighted steed ran on alone,
Do not weep.
5 War is kind.

　Hoarse, booming drums of the regiment,
　Little souls who thirst for fight,
　These men were born to drill and die.
　The unexplained glory flies above them,
10　Great is the Battle-God, great, and his Kingdom—
　A field where a thousand corpses lie. **A**

Do not weep, babe, for war is kind.
Because your father tumbled in the yellow trenches,
Raged at his breast, gulped and died,
15 Do not weep.
War is kind.

　Swift blazing flag of the regiment,
　Eagle with crest of red and gold,
　These men were born to drill and die.
20　Point for them the virtue of slaughter,
　Make plain to them the excellence of killing
　And a field where a thousand corpses lie.

　Mother whose heart hung humble as a button
　On the bright splendid shroud of your son,
25　Do not weep.
　War is kind. **B**

A **VERBAL IRONY**
Reread lines 1–11. In what way do these lines demonstrate verbal irony? Explain.

B **UNIVERSAL THEME**
Reread stanzas 1, 3, and 5. Identify the **images** of war presented in each stanza. What do these images have in common?

478　UNIT 4: THEME

Gloria Triptych (detail of despairing woman), Giuseppe Mentessi. Right panel. Galleria d'Arte Moderna, Rome. Photo © Dagli Orti/The Art Archive.

DIFFERENTIATED INSTRUCTION

FOR ENGLISH LANGUAGE LEARNERS

Options for Reading Read the poem aloud, stopping at the end of each stanza to clarify words or concepts and to discuss Crane's meaning. Then ask students to read the poem aloud with a partner. To call attention to the poem's structure, ask one student to read aloud stanzas 1, 3, and 5 and the other student to alternate with stanzas 2 and 4.

 BEST PRACTICES TOOLKIT—Transparency
Read Aloud p. A34

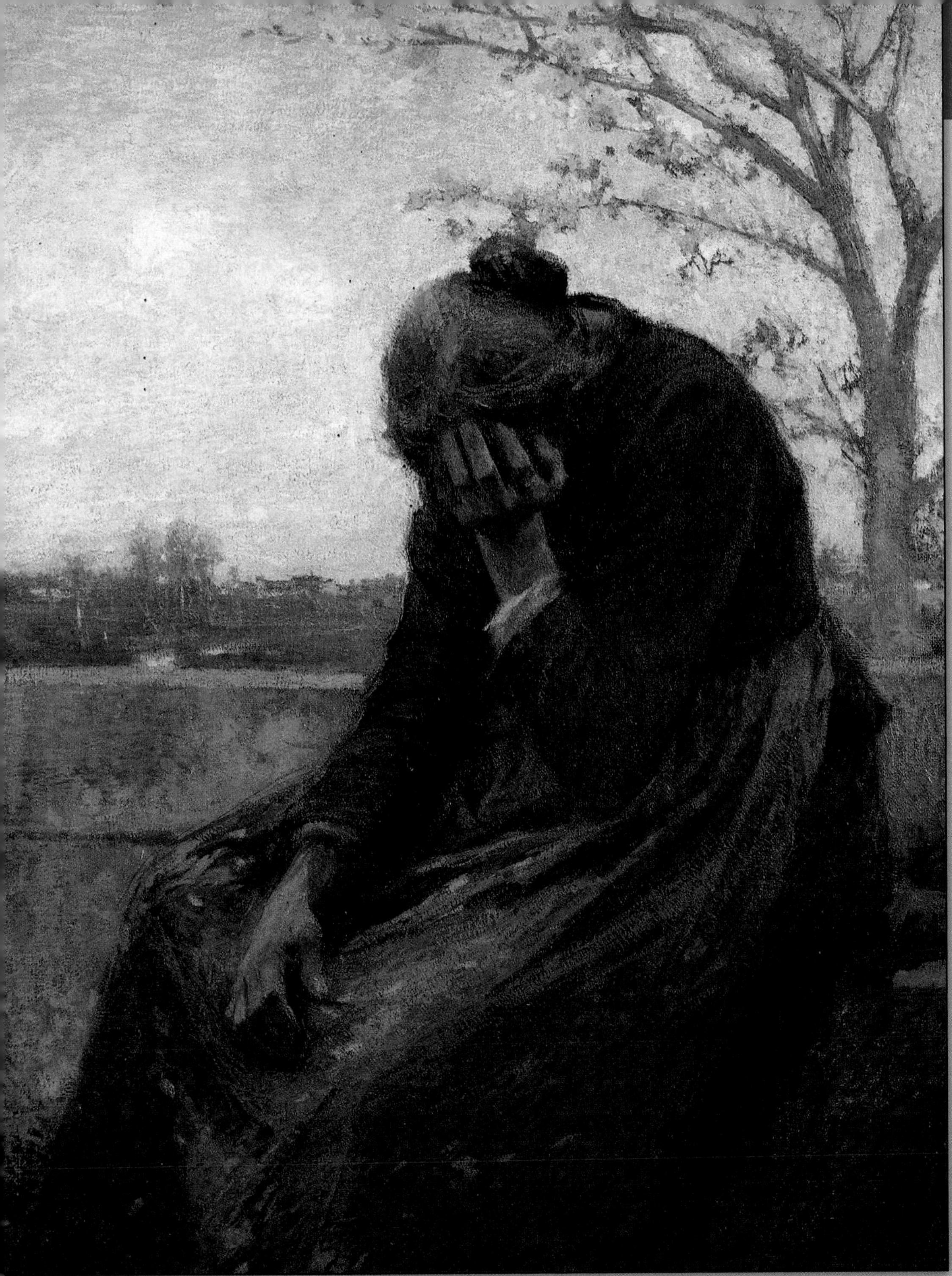

Reading Support

THINK central

This selection on **thinkcentral.com** includes embedded **ThinkAloud** models—students “thinking aloud” about the story to model the kinds of questions a good reader would ask about a selection.

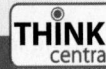

Analyze Visuals

Activity Ask students to identify the stanza of Crane’s poem that has the strongest connection to the painting. ***Possible answer:*** *The poem’s final stanza, which describes a grieving mother, has the strongest connection to the painting.*

About the Art Giuseppe Mentessi (1857–1931) demonstrated a social consciousness in many of his works. In particular, the Italian artist used his art to raise awareness of the poverty and desperation that marked the lives of many people living in the Italian countryside. With *Gloria*, Mentessi ventured into the arena of war protest, a passion that grew during World War I. *Gloria* is a triptych, or a painting done on three panels. The right panel is represented here.

REVISIT THE BIG QUESTION

Who are the **VICTIMS** of war?

Discuss Who are the victims of war in Crane’s poem? ***Possible answer:*** *A maiden and her lover, a baby and its father, and a mother and her son, all could be considered the victims in this poem.*

FOR STRUGGLING READERS

Vocabulary Support

- *affrighted* (line 3), “scared”
- *steed* (line 3), “horse”
- *regiment* (line 6), “group of soldiers”
- *trenches* (line 13), “ditches dug into a battlefield to hide and protect soldiers”
- *shroud* (line 24), “cloth used to wrap a body for burial”

FOR ADVANCED LEARNERS/PRE–AP

Evaluate Techniques Ask students to consider the literary techniques that Crane uses to convey the theme of this poem. Suggest that they pay particular attention to Crane’s use of imagery and verbal irony. Then have students gather in a group to discuss this question: Does Crane effectively use literary techniques to express his theme, or does the theme get lost because these techniques are so obvious?

Prereading for this poem is found on page 476.

COMMON CORE
RL 2

C UNIVERSAL THEME

Possible answer: *Death is presented as a temptress who lures the speaker's lover away from her. This image hints that the theme will relate to the seductive nature of war and the pain of those left behind.*

Analyze Visuals

Possible answer: *Both the sculpture and the painting convey a sorrowful mood.*

About the Art Kathe Kollwitz (1867–1945) lived in Germany during the tumultuous years of the Nazi regime.

ADDITIONAL TEACHING OPPORTUNITY

Dramatic Monologue Point out to students that this poem is an example of a dramatic monologue—a poem in which a speaker addresses a silent or absent listener in a moment of intense emotion. The speaker's words often reveal details about his or her personality, feelings, and circumstances. Ask students what they learn about the speaker in this poem.

SELECTION WRAP–UP

READ WITH A PURPOSE Now that students have finished reading the selection, ask students which poet's style they prefer. What is it about that poet's writing that appeals to them? *Possible answer: Answers will vary. Some students may prefer the third-person narrative and multiple stanzas in Crane's poem. Others may prefer the first-person, one stanza poem by Brooks.*

⭐ **CRITIQUE** Ask students which poem they found more moving and why.

INDEPENDENT READING

If students would like to read another work by Stephen Crane, suggest *The Red Badge of Courage,* the story of a soldier's experiences during the American Civil War.

the sonnet-ballad
Gwendolyn Brooks

Oh mother, mother, where is happiness?
They took my lover's tallness off to war,
Left me lamenting. Now I cannot guess
What I can use an empty heart-cup for.
5 He won't be coming back here any more.
Some day the war will end, but, oh, I knew
When he went walking grandly out that door
That my sweet love would have to be untrue.
Would have to be untrue. Would have to court
10 Coquettish death, whose impudent and strange
Possessive arms and beauty (of a sort)
Can make a hard man hesitate—and change.
And he will be the one to stammer, "Yes."
Oh mother, mother, where is happiness? **C**

C UNIVERSAL THEME
Explain how death is presented in the poem. What clues does this **image** give you about theme?

◀ Analyze Visuals
How would you compare the **mood** of this sculpture with that of the painting on page 479?

Lamentation: Memorial for Ernst Barlach (1940), Käthe Kollwitz. Bronze. © 2008 Artists Rights Society (ARS), New York/VG Bild-Kunst, Bonn.

DIFFERENTIATED INSTRUCTION

FOR STRUGGLING READERS

Develop Reading Fluency Have students participate in an echo reading of this poem. Ask students to listen to "the sonnet-ballad" on the *Audio Anthology CD.* Then read aloud a few lines at a time, pausing to allow students time to repeat the lines with the same intonation and rhythm. Finally, have partners practice reading the poem aloud with expression and appropriate pacing.

Distribute the copy masters and have students work in pairs or groups to practice fluency.

R RESOURCE MANAGER—Copy Masters
Reading Fluency p. 88

Vocabulary Support

- *lamenting* (line 3), "grieving," "mourning"
- *court* (line 9), "try to gain the love of"
- *Coquettish* (line 10), "characterized by pretended interest in romance"
- *impudent* (line 10), "rudely disrespectful"
- *stammer* (line 13), "speak hesitantly"

Increase students' familiarity with these words by asking them to use each in a sentence.

Comprehension

1. **Recall** Whom does the speaker address in Crane's poem?

2. **Recall** In "the sonnet-ballad," where has the speaker's lover gone?

Text Analysis

3. **Analyze Imagery** Think about the various images in each poem. Select one lasting image from each poem and explain its impact.

4. **Make Inferences** According to the speaker of each poem, why do people fight wars? Cite evidence to support your answer.

5. **Interpret Verbal Irony** Look back over the chart you created as you read. What does the use of verbal irony in the poems tell you about the writers' attitudes toward war? Support your answer with examples from the poems.

6. **Draw Conclusions About Universal Theme** Create a chart like the one shown, identifying the literary elements in each poem. Then use this information to state the universal theme expressed by both poems.

	Crane's Poem	Brooks's Poem
Speaker		
Key images		
Repetition		
Mood		

Universal Theme

7. **Evaluate** Which poem makes the strongest statement about war and its victims? Give evidence from the poems to support your opinion.

Text Criticism

8. **Historical Context** Both poems reflect the wartime experiences of earlier generations. Crane's poem was published in 1899, following Cuba's war for independence. Brooks wrote and published "the sonnet-ballad" following World War II. What aspects of these poems might be different if the authors were alive today and writing about current world events?

Who are the VICTIMS of war?

How does war affect ordinary people?

COMMON CORE

RL 2 Determine a theme of a text and analyze in detail how it emerges and is refined by specific details. RL 10 Read and comprehend poems.

Practice and Apply

For preliminary support of post-reading questions, use these copy masters:

R RESOURCE MANAGER—Copy Masters
Universal Theme p. 83
Question Support p. 87

Additional selection questions are provided for teachers on page 80.

ANSWERS

Comprehension

1. *The speaker addresses a maiden, a baby, and a mother, all of whom have lost a loved one as a soldier in battle.*

2. *The lover has gone off to war.*

Text Analysis

COMMON CORE RL 2, RL 10

Possible answers:

3. **Crane:** *The horse that runs alone suggests that when a soldier dies, war and life goes on.* **Brooks:** *Death's coquettishness shows why some people are drawn to battle.*

4. **Crane:** *People fight wars for the enjoyment of fighting (line 7), for personal glory (line 9), for religious reasons (line 10), and for national pride (lines 17–18).* **Brooks:** *People fight wars because they see war as beautiful, grand, and alluring (lines 7 and 10–12).*

5. **COMMON CORE FOCUS** *Verbal Irony Crane's verbal irony suggests that he finds war cruel and brutal. Brooks suggests that she sees war as tragically attractive.*

6. **COMMON CORE FOCUS** *Universal Theme Crane's Poem: Speaker: third person; Key images: loved ones crying, soldiers*

dying; Repetition: "Do not weep," "War is kind"; Mood: bitter, hopeless Brooks's Poem: Speaker: first person; Key images: girl lamenting, soldier leaving, death seducing; Repetition: "Oh mother, mother, where is happiness?" and "would have to be untrue"; Mood: melancholy Universal Theme: War harms soldiers and their loved ones.

7. *Crane's poem makes the stronger statement, because it depicts the death of three soldiers and the sadness of their loved ones.*

Text Criticism

Possible answer:

8. *The poems might include references to modern aspects of war, such as computer technology, equipment and tactics, and female soldiers, which did not exist when either poem was written.*

Who are the VICTIMS of war? Possible answer: *Ordinary people experience separation from loved ones during war, as well as death, food shortages, and loss of their homes.*

Assess and Reteach

Assess

DIAGNOSTIC AND SELECTION TESTS
Selection Test A pp. 127–128
Selection Test B/C pp. 129–130

Interactive Selection Test on **thinkcentral.com**

Reteach

Level Up Online Tutorials on **thinkcentral.com**

Reteaching Worksheets on **thinkcentral.com**
Literature Lesson 11: Theme, Motif, and Epiphany
Literature Lesson 36: Irony

Focus and Motivate

COMMON CORE FOCUS

RI 2 Determine a central idea of a text to analyze its development over the course of a text.
RI 6 Determine an author's point of view in a text and analyze how an author uses rhetoric to advance that point of view. **RI 8** Delineate and evaluate the argument and specific claims in a text, assessing whether the reasoning is valid and the evidence is relevant and sufficient.

SUMMARY

In this World War II–era essay, novelist E. M. Forster reacts to the deadly ideological divisions of the time by preaching tolerance. Forster maintains that the goal of brotherly love in worldly affairs is unrealistic. While allowing that tolerance may be a "dull virtue," the author argues that it is the "proper spirit" for avoiding brutality and rebuilding the war-torn world of the 1940s.

How ACCEPTING are you?

Introduce the question. Ask students to identify problems resulting from intolerance, and then discuss together ways of bridging these gaps and practicing tolerance. Continue this inquiry by having students complete the *SURVEY* activity and share their results with the class.

Selection Resources

Before Reading

from Tolerance
Essay by E. M. Forster

How ACCEPTING are you?

COMMON CORE

RI 2 Determine a central idea of a text and analyze its development over the course of a text. **RI 6** Determine an author's point of view in a text and analyze how an author uses rhetoric to advance that point of view. **RI 8** Delineate and evaluate the argument and specific claims in a text, assessing whether the reasoning is valid and the evidence is relevant and sufficient.

Our global community consists of billions of people belonging to various religions, races, and ethnic groups. What is the best way to build strong alliances between different individuals, groups, and nations? According to the following selection, the answer can be found in practicing tolerance—or respect for the beliefs and customs of others.

SURVEY With a partner, create a brief survey about the importance of tolerance. Add to or subtract from the example shown. Ask a small group of classmates to complete the survey. Share the results with your whole class.

Survey About Tolerance
1. How is tolerance practiced in your school? Give an example.
2. How is tolerance practiced in the world? Give an example.
3. In what ways do you practice tolerance? Give an example.

482

See resources on the **Teacher One Stop DVD-ROM** and on **thinkcentral.com**.

 RESOURCE MANAGER UNIT 4
Plan and Teach, pp. 89–96
Summary, pp. 97–98†‡*
Text Analysis and Reading
    Skill, pp. 99–102†*

DIAGNOSTIC AND SELECTION TESTS
Selection Tests, pp. 131–134

🧰 **BEST PRACTICES TOOLKIT**
Two-Column Chart, p. A25

TECHNOLOGY
💿 **Teacher One Stop DVD-ROM**
💿 **Student One Stop DVD-ROM**
💿 **Audio Anthology CD**
💿 **GrammarNotes DVD-ROM**
💿 **ExamView Test Generator**
on the **Teacher One Stop**

---

* Resources for Differentiation   † Also in Spanish   ‡ In Haitian Creole and Vietnamese

TEXT ANALYSIS: PERSUASIVE ESSAY

A **persuasive essay** is a short work of nonfiction written primarily to persuade readers to adopt the writer's message, or **central idea.** The central idea of a persuasive essay is typically a position on an issue or a topic. For example, Forster states his thesis as follows:

In public affairs, in the rebuilding of civilisation, something much less dramatic and emotional [than love] is needed, namely, tolerance.

A strong persuasive essay also uses **rhetoric**—powerful language, **persuasive techniques,** and a clear and logical **argument** to be convincing. As you read Forster's persuasive essay, be on the lookout for these elements.

READING SKILL: ANALYZE REASONS AND EVIDENCE

To check whether Forster's essay contains a clear and logical argument, analyze the **reasons** and **evidence** he provides to support his thesis. Specifically, make sure that he backs up each reason with at least one piece of evidence. Also check to see whether each reason logically supports his thesis. Recording the reasons and evidence in a graphic organizer such as the one shown here can help you do this. Add or subtract boxes as needed.

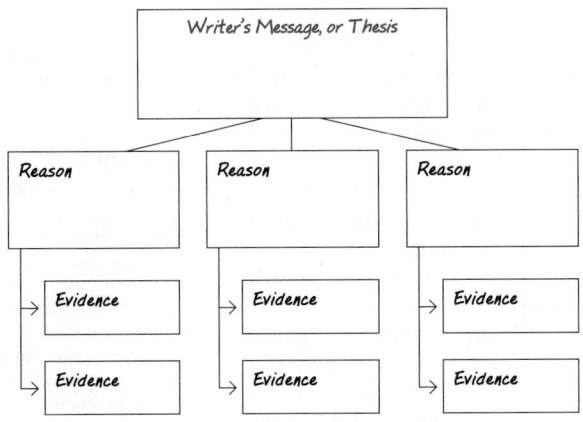

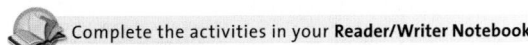
Complete the activities in your **Reader/Writer Notebook.**

Meet the Author

E. M. Forster
1879–1970

The Worst Years
Edward Morgan Forster spent the early part of his life frustrated with the private boys' school that he attended in England, where he suffered the taunts of classmates and the severity of teachers. His subsequent years at Cambridge University were much happier. There, he expanded his intellectual horizons, made close friends, and dedicated himself to literature.

Literary Triumph
Forster began publishing stories soon after graduation and published his first novel in 1905. A number of acclaimed novels followed. The best known of these—*A Room with a View* (1908), *Howards End* (1910), and *A Passage to India* (1924)—have enjoyed a resurgence of popularity sparked by successful film adaptations. During the 1930s and 1940s, Forster turned increasingly to social criticism and virtually gave up writing fiction.

BACKGROUND TO THE ESSAY

On the Air
This essay is one of several that Forster broadcast over the radio during and just after World War II (1939–1945) and later collected in his volume *Two Cheers for Democracy* (1951). In these essays, Forster often explores the means by which citizens of democracies can counter the spread of the kind of thinking that leads to brutal dictatorships—like that of Nazi Germany, Britain's foe during the war. With their claims of racial superiority and their mass murder of ethnic groups that they branded undesirable, the Nazis were the supreme example of intolerance.

Author Online
THINK central
Go to **thinkcentral.com.**
KEYWORD: HML10-483

DIFFERENTIATED INSTRUCTION

FOR STRUGGLING READERS
Concept Support: Analyze Reasons and Evidence Ask students if they've ever read a newspaper editorial, a letter to an editor, or a political speech. Explain that all are examples of persuasive essays. Then ask students to give reasons that support these arguments:

• Teachers should talk to each other so they don't all assign homework the same day.

• School should begin later in the day.

FOR ENGLISH LANGUAGE LEARNERS
Culture: Connect Explain that in World War II, England suffered bombings and food shortages. People took shelter in the tube, or subway station, and had to wait in long queues, or lines. Invite volunteers to give other examples of hardships that nations face during times of war or political disruption.

Teach

TEXT ANALYSIS COMMON CORE
RI 2
RI 6

● *Model the Skill:* PERSUASIVE ESSAY

To model how to understand a persuasive essay, write this excerpt from a persuasive essay on the board:

> Starting school in early August is a bad idea. It gives schools more time to prepare for standardized tests, but it robs students of their summer breaks. We want our summers back!

Point out that a persuasive essay tries to get readers to think or act in a certain way—to accept the writer's position and perhaps take action. Explain that the writer wants readers to think that school should not begin in early August. Point out the powerful language that appeals to the emotions. For example, the word "robs" is dramatic, and the last sentence creates a sense of urgency.

GUIDED PRACTICE Ask students to rewrite the excerpt to include other examples of powerful language. For more on persuasion, see **Reading Handbook,** pages R21–R26.

READING SKILL COMMON CORE
RI 8

■ *Model the Skill:* ANALYZE REASONS AND EVIDENCE

To model how to analyze reasons and evidence, return to the excerpt on the board. Point out that the writer provides this reason to support his or her thesis: Starting school in early August interferes with students' summer breaks. Point out that the writer must now go on to support this reason with evidence, such as facts, expert opinions, or personal experience.

GUIDED PRACTICE Ask students to think of a specific piece of evidence that could support this reason.

R RESOURCE MANAGER—Copy Master
Analyze Reasons and Evidence p. 101 (for student use while reading the selection)

READ WITH A PURPOSE

Help students set a purpose for reading. Tell students to look for supporting ideas that they find particularly persuasive.

TEXT ANALYSIS

COMMON CORE

RI 2
RI 6

Ⓐ *Model the Skill:*
PERSUASIVE ESSAY

Remind students that in a persuasive essay, the author puts forth a thesis that he then supports. Point out that in lines 1–3, Forster cites a problem: rebuilding civilization. He points to a thesis idea: "A sound state of mind" is needed to rebuild civilization. Note that the rhetorical questions (lines 6–8) are persuasive devices. Invite students to use a chart like the one below to track the techniques he uses in support of his thesis.

Thesis: Sound state of mind and proper spirit are needed for rebuilding civilization.	
Powerful Language	Persuasive Techniques
"only sound foundation"	unanswered questions
"inspired"	use of "must"
"cataclysms . . . threatening to destroy us"	confidence

 BEST PRACTICES TOOLKIT—Transparency
Two-Column Chart p. A25

Possible answer: *Forster says that a sound state of mind, inspired by the proper spirit, is needed to create a sound foundation for civilization.*

Extend the Discussion Why might Forster wait to answer the questions in lines 6–8?

TOLERANCE

E. M. Forster

Analyze Visuals ▶

In what way does the painting illustrate **tolerance** among different people?

Surely the only sound foundation for a civilisation is a sound state of mind. Architects, contractors, international commissioners, marketing boards, broadcasting corporations will never, by themselves, build a new world. They must be inspired by the proper spirit, and there must be the proper spirit in the people for whom they are working. . . .

What though is the proper spirit? . . . There must be a sound state of mind before diplomacy or economics or trade conferences can function. But what state of mind is sound? Here we may differ. Most people, when asked what spiritual quality is needed to rebuild civilisation, will reply "Love." Men must
10 love one another, they say; nations must do likewise, and then the series of cataclysms which is threatening to destroy us will be checked. **Ⓐ**

Respectfully but firmly, I disagree. Love is a great force in private life; it is indeed the greatest of all things: but love in public affairs does not work. It has been tried again and again: by the Christian civilisations of the Middle Ages, and also by the French Revolution, a secular movement which reasserted the brotherhood of man.[1] And it has always failed. The idea that nations should love one another, or that business concerns or marketing boards should love one another, or that a man in Portugal should love a man in Peru of whom he has never heard—it is absurd, unreal, dangerous. It leads us into perilous and
20 vague sentimentalism.[2] "Love is what is needed," we chant and then sit back, and the world goes on as before. The fact is we can only love what we know personally. And we cannot know much. In public affairs, in the rebuilding of civilisation, something much less dramatic and emotional is needed, namely, tolerance. Tolerance is a very dull virtue. It is boring. Unlike love, it has always had a bad press. It is negative. It merely means putting up with people, being able to stand things. No one has ever written an ode[3] to tolerance or raised a

---

1. **French Revolution . . . brotherhood of man:** The French Revolution, which lasted from 1789 to 1799, had the motto "Liberty! Equality! Brotherhood!"
2. **sentimentalism** (sĕn'tə-mĕn'tl-ĭz'əm): a tendency toward too much tender, often shallow emotion.
3. **ode** (ōd): a usually formal poem on a serious subject.

Ⓐ **PERSUASIVE ESSAY**
Reread lines 1–11. According to Forster, what is needed to create a sound foundation for civilization?

Language Coach

Oral Fluency Part of reading aloud fluently is correct pronunciation. In words ending with *-gue*, the *g* is pronounced /g/, and the *-ue* is silent. Read aloud the full sentence in lines 19–20, paying attention to pronunciation.

"Civilization is a method of living, an attitude of equal respect for all men." From the series *Great Ideas of Western Men* (1955), George Giusti. India ink and gouache on paper, 24⁷/₈" × 18⁵/₁₆". Gift of the Container Corporation of America. Smithsonian American Art Museum, Washington, D.C. Photo © Smithsonian American Art Museum, Washington, D.C./Art Resource, New York.

DIFFERENTIATED INSTRUCTION

FOR ENGLISH LANGUAGE LEARNERS

Language Coach

Oral Fluency *Answer:* *Be sure students pronounce* vague *correctly —*/vāg/. Give students practice saying *vague*. First have students each write an original sentence using *vague*. Then have students work in pairs. Tell students to swap sentences and read the sentences aloud. Encourage partners to monitor each other's pronunciation.

FOR STRUGGLING READERS

In combination with the *Audio Anthology CD*, use one or more Targeted Passages (pp. 484, 486) to ensure that students focus on key ideas, concepts, and skills. Targeted Passages are also good for English learners.

❶ Targeted Passage [Lines 12–24]

Point out that the author uses this passage to persuade readers that love is not the answer to world problems. Ask these questions:

- What logic does Forster use in lines 12–16 to argue his point?

- In lines 16–21, how does Forster make the goal of global love sound ridiculous?

- How do lines 21–24 sum up the point and lead into a new idea?

FOR ADVANCED LEARNERS/PRE–AP

Analyze Tone Have students work in pairs to analyze the tone of the essay. They should study Forster's diction, focusing on specific word connotations. They can also examine sentence length and usage to see what tone of formality Forster tries to strike. Finally, pairs can examine how the author uses repetition and word choice to bring readers to his point of view.

BACKGROUND

World War II In lines 8–9, Forster talks of how to "rebuild civilisation." Is he exaggerating? Consider the damage of World War II. Cities lay in ruin, Nazi death camps were exposed, and the United States had used atom bombs against Japan.

Analyze Visuals

Possible answer: The painting illustrates tolerance among people by showing hands of different colors clasped together.

About the Art Italian-born George Giusti (1908–1991) worked as an illustrator and designer, and this work shows his knack for using simple images to capture ideas. Each of the four hands holds and is held by another hand. The resulting square seems to convey the power in unity.

TIERED DISCUSSION PROMPTS

Direct students to lines 7–26. Use these prompts to help students see how Forster strikes a pragmatic tone:

Connect What are your thoughts about Forster's ideas at this point in the essay? Explain. *Accept all reasonable answers.*

Analyze How does Forster contrast the call for love with his own idea? *Possible answer: He says a call for love is absurd and tolerance is "less . . . emotional," which makes his own argument sound logical.*

REVISIT THE BIG QUESTION
How ACCEPTING
are you?

Discuss Based on lines 24–30, why does Forster believe people will need tolerance after the war? *Possible answer: Forster believes that people will need tolerance to rebuild together, despite different backgrounds and overcrowding.*

B PERSUASIVE ESSAY

RI 2
RI 6

Possible answer: *Forster's repetition emphatically drives home his point that tolerance is a necessary state of mind for rebuilding after the war.*

READING SKILL

COMMON CORE

RI 8

C *Model the Skill:* ANALYZE REASONS AND EVIDENCE

Draw the Reading Skill graphic organizer on the board. Read lines 31–44 aloud, and have students volunteer reasons and evidence they identify in the paragraph.

Possible answer: *Forster has said that the "world is very full of people" (line 31), that most people will not know or like each other (lines 32–35), and that the alternative to tolerance is the actions of the Nazis (lines 37–39).*

TEXT ANALYSIS

COMMON CORE

RI 2
RI 6

D PERSUASIVE ESSAY

Possible answer: *Forster may have included common complaints to help readers identify with his position: Our inevitable irritation in everyday life requires that we remember to be tolerant.*

SELECTION WRAP–UP

READ WITH A PURPOSE What was more persuasive: referencing everyday irritations or the actions of the Nazis? **Possible answer:** *Everyday irritations were more persuasive because they are more easy to relate to.*

⭐ **CRITIQUE** Have students rate the strength of Forster's argument for tolerance, using a scale of 1 to 10, with 1 as weakest and 10 as strongest.

INDEPENDENT READING

For students who want to read another work about tolerance, suggest *Witness* by Karen Hesse.

---

statue to her. Yet this is the quality which will be most needed after the war. This is the sound state of mind which we are looking for. This is the only force which will enable different races and classes and interests to settle down
30 together to the work of reconstruction. **B**

The world is very full of people—appallingly full; it has never been so full before, and they are all tumbling over each other. Most of these people one doesn't know, and some of them one doesn't like; doesn't like the colour of their skins, say, or the shapes of their noses, or the way they blow them or don't blow them, or the way they talk, or their smell, or their clothes, or their fondness for jazz or their dislike of jazz, and so on. Well, what is one to do? There are two solutions. One of them is the Nazi solution. If you don't like people, kill them, banish them, segregate them, and then strut up and down proclaiming that you are the salt of the earth.[4] The other way is much less
40 thrilling, but it is on the whole the way of the democracies, and I prefer it. If you don't like people, put up with them as well as you can. Don't try to love them: you can't; you'll only strain yourself. But try to tolerate them. On the basis of that tolerance a civilised future may be built. Certainly I can see no other foundation for the postwar world. **C**

For what it will most need is the negative virtues: not being huffy, touchy, irritable, revengeful. I have lost all faith in positive militant ideals; they can so seldom be carried out without thousands of human beings getting maimed or imprisoned. Phrases like "I will purge this nation," "I will clean up this city," terrify and disgust me. They might not have mattered when the world was
50 emptier: they are horrifying now, when one nation is mixed up with another, when one city cannot be organically separated from its neighbours. . . .

I don't then regard tolerance as a great eternally established divine principle, though I might perhaps quote "In my Father's house are many mansions"[5] in support of such a view. It is just a makeshift,[6] suitable for an overcrowded and overheated planet. It carries on when love gives out, and love generally gives out as soon as we move away from our home and our friends and stand among strangers in a queue[7] for potatoes. Tolerance is wanted in the queue; otherwise we think, "Why will people be so slow?"; it is wanted in the tube,[8] or "Why will people be so fat?"; it is wanted at the telephone, or "Why are they so deaf?"
60 or conversely, "Why do they mumble?" It is wanted in the street, in the office, at the factory, and it is wanted above all between classes, races, and nations. It's dull. And yet it entails imagination. For you have all the time to be putting yourself in someone else's place. Which is a desirable spiritual exercise.  **D**

---

4. **salt of the earth:** the finest or noblest people. The expression derives from a statement in the New Testament of the Bible (Matthew 5:13).

5. **"In my Father's house are many mansions":** Heaven is a place of diversity. The quotation is from the New Testament of the Bible (John 14:2).

6. **makeshift:** a temporary substitute for something else.

7. **queue** (kyōō): a chiefly British expression for a line of people.

8. **tube:** a British term for the Underground, or London subway.

B PERSUASIVE ESSAY
Why might Forster's repetition of "this is" be considered a persuasive technique? Explain.

C ANALYZE REASONS AND EVIDENCE
What reasons and evidence has Forster given so far to support his message about tolerance?

2 Targeted Passage

D PERSUASIVE ESSAY
Reread lines 52–63. Think about why Forster might have chosen to include commonplace complaints. How effective are they at persuading you to agree with his position?

DIFFERENTIATED INSTRUCTION

FOR STRUGGLING READERS

2 Targeted Passage [Lines 55–63]

The author sums up his case, using logic and language devices to persuade.

- According to Forster, when is it that love "gives out," or stops working? (lines 55–57)

- What situation does Forster imagine in order to show when tolerance is needed? (lines 57–61)

- Does Forster truly see tolerance as "dull"? (lines 62–63)

FOR STRUGGLING READERS

Develop Reading Fluency Have students work in pairs. Instruct students to take turns reading the text aloud, one paragraph at a time. After a reader has finished reading a paragraph, have students pause so that the listener can paraphrase what they just heard.

Distribute the copy masters and have students work in pairs or groups to practice fluency.

R RESOURCE MANAGER—Copy Master
Reading Fluency p. 105

Comprehension

1. **Recall** According to Forster, what quality do most people believe will improve the world?

2. **Clarify** Why does Forster disagree with this popular opinion?

3. **Recall** Why is tolerance, in Forster's eyes, a "very dull virtue"?

4. **Summarize** In your own words, restate the message, or **thesis,** of the essay.

Text Analysis

● 5. **Analyze Reasons and Evidence** Review the essay and the notes you made as you read. Which reasons and evidence best support Forster's thesis? Do you think any of his evidence is inaccurate? Explain your response.

6. **Understand Rhetorical Questions** When crafting persuasive essays, writers often include rhetorical questions, or questions that do not require responses. Find three different rhetorical questions in the essay. Then describe the effect the questions have on you as a reader. Use a graphic organizer like the one shown to help you.

Rhetorical Question	Effect
→	
→	
→	

7. **Draw Conclusions** Reread lines 52–61. Why do you suppose Forster uses examples drawn from everyday life to illustrate the need for tolerance?

8. **Interpret Text** Reread lines 62–63. What does Forster mean by his final point that tolerance requires imagination? Explain your response.

● 9. **Evaluate Persuasive Essay** Think about the effectiveness of the essay. After reading it, do you share Forster's position about tolerance? Why or why not?

10. **Make Judgments** Forster's essay was broadcast on British radio around the time of World War II. Who might benefit most from hearing or reading the essay today? Explain your opinion.

How **ACCEPTING** are you?

How can you increase tolerance in your school or community?

COMMON CORE

RI 2 Determine a central idea of a text and analyze its development over the course of a text. RI 6 Analyze how an author uses rhetoric to advance point of view or purpose in a text. RI 8 Delineate and evaluate the argument and specific claims in a text, assessing whether the reasoning is valid and the evidence is relevant and sufficient.

Practice and Apply

For preliminary support of post-reading questions, use these copy masters:

R RESOURCE MANAGER—Copy Masters
Reading Check p. 103
Persuasive Essay p. 99
Question Support p. 104

Additional selection questions are provided for teachers on page 93.

ANSWERS

Comprehension

1. *Most believe love will improve the world.*

2. *Forster doesn't think we can love people outside our immediate circle.*

3. *In Forster's eyes, tolerance is a "very dull virtue" (line 24) because "it merely means putting up with people" (line 25).*

4. *Possible answer: After the destruction caused by the war, tolerance of people and their differences is more important than love.*

Text Analysis

COMMON CORE RI 2, RI 6, RI 8

Possible answers:

5. ● COMMON CORE FOCUS *Analyze Reasons and Evidence* **Best supporting reasons:** *crowded and diverse world; we can annoy one another (lines 31– 36);* **Best evidence:** *the Nazis and common intolerance (lines 37–40).*

6. *"What though is the proper spirit?" (line 6)* **Effect:** *I want the answer; "But what state of mind is sound?" (lines 7–8)* **Effect:** *makes me read on; "Well, what is*

Assess and Reteach

Assess

DIAGNOSTIC AND SELECTION TESTS
Selection Test A pp. 131–132
Selection Test B/C pp. 133–134

Interactive Selection Test on **thinkcentral.com**

Reteach

Level Up Online Tutorials on **thinkcentral.com**

Reteaching Worksheets on **thinkcentral.com:**
Informational Text Lesson 14: Elements of an Argument

Informational Text Lesson 15: Persuasive Techniques

---

one to do?" (line 36) **Effect:** *I think Forster knows what to do.*

7. *to persuade by having readers identify with these common reactions and by showing that the author's view of tolerance is practical*

8. *Tolerance requires a person to imagine being in another's shoes, and Forster seems to suggest that compassion doesn't come without mental effort.*

9. ● COMMON CORE FOCUS *Persuasive Essay* *Students should apply thoughtfulness and logic in evaluating Forster's position.*

10. *Politicians, corporate heads, and community leaders, and people bent on mutual destruction might also benefit.*

How **ACCEPTING** are you?
Students might first identify occasions when intolerance caused conflict in their school or community, and then propose ways to increase understanding.

Focus and Motivate

SUMMARY

"Letter to a Young Refugee from Another"
In this essay, Andrew Lam describes how he survived as a refugee by being fierce, alert, and hopeful. He also explains the importance of not giving in to hate or allowing oneself to forget.

"Song of P'eng-ya" The speaker in this poem is a man who describes his family's dangerous escape from soldiers to the warm sanctuary provided by an old friend.

What if you had to FLEE your country?

Discuss the question with students. Ask them what they would miss most and what they would expect to find ahead of them as refugees. Extend the discussion by having students form small groups to complete the *QUICKWRITE*. Have groups share their word webs with the class.

Selection Resources

Comparing Across Genres

Letter to a Young Refugee from Another
Essay by Andrew Lam

Song of P'eng-ya
Poem by Tu Fu

What if you had to FLEE your country?

How would you feel if political events forced you to leave your home, your belongings, and your entire community? In these two selections, you will learn about the powerful emotions and numerous hardships displaced people, or refugees, experience.

QUICKWRITE With a small group, create a word web that details some of the challenges a refugee might face. Then write a short paragraph in which you imagine what it would be like to live in an entirely new culture.

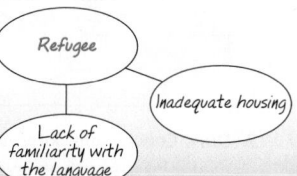

Refugee — Inadequate housing — Lack of familiarity with the language

488

See resources on the **Teacher One Stop DVD-ROM** and on **thinkcentral.com**.

R RESOURCE MANAGER UNIT 4
Plan and Teach, pp. 107–114
Summary, pp. 115–116†‡*
Text Analysis and Reading
Skill, pp. 117–121†*

**DIAGNOSTIC AND SELECTION
TESTS**
Selection Tests, pp. 135–138

BEST PRACTICES TOOLKIT
Word Questioning, p. E9
Main Ideas and Details, p. B6

TECHNOLOGY
- Teacher One Stop DVD-ROM
- Student One Stop DVD-ROM
- Audio Anthology CD
- GrammarNotes DVD-ROM
- ExamView Test Generator
  on the **Teacher One Stop**

---

* Resources for Differentiation   † Also in Spanish   ‡ In Haitian Creole and Vietnamese

● TEXT ANALYSIS: AUTHOR'S MESSAGE ACROSS GENRES

When you read, it is important to keep in mind the **genre** of a work—whether the work you are reading is nonfiction, fiction, drama, poetry, or myth. A writer's choice of genre can greatly affect how the central message of a piece is communicated.

For example, writers of nonfiction usually rely on direct statements and evidence to convey their **messages**. Poets, on the other hand, rely more heavily on imagery, figurative language, and mood to express their **themes**. You can see this for yourself in the essay and poem that follow. Both focus on a similar topic—the experiences of a refugee—but in each the writer conveys his unique message with the elements and techniques of his particular genre. As you read, try to determine each writer's message by paying attention to the following.

In the Essay	In the Poem
• direct statements	• words and phrases describing the speaker's thoughts and feelings
• facts, examples, and other details drawn from the writer's experiences	• vivid imagery
• the list of directions for how to feel and behave	• figurative language
• tone	• mood
• the writer's final piece of advice	• the lesson or message you take away

■ READING STRATEGY: SET A PURPOSE FOR READING

Sometimes people enjoy reading as a leisure activity, without a particular goal in mind. More often, and especially for school, you **set a purpose** for your reading—that is, you establish a particular reason to read a text. In this lesson, your purpose for reading is to identify the central themes, or messages, of the selections. As you read, think about your impressions of the refugees and their experiences. After you read, you will use the **Points of Comparison** chart on page 496 to help you compare and contrast the messages of the two selections.

 Complete the activities in your **Reader/Writer Notebook.**

Meet the Authors

Andrew Lam
born 1964

Word Painter
At the age of 11, Andrew Lam found himself thrown into an unfamiliar culture. After fleeing Saigon, South Vietnam, one day before the city fell to the North Vietnamese, Lam's family settled in northern California. In time, Lam fell in love with his new language and way of life. Today, his passion for words is conveyed not only in his fiction but also in articles for the Pacific News Service and in commentaries for National Public Radio.

Tu Fu
712–770

Unlucky in Life
Though considered one of China's greatest poets, Tu Fu (dōō' fōō') was unlucky in both his personal and his professional lives. His poetic genius went unrecognized during his lifetime, and he didn't advance far in his chosen political career. In addition, Tu Fu endured poverty and uncertainty, owing in part to the revolts and unrest that afflicted the region of China where he lived.

Authors Online
Go to thinkcentral.com. KEYWORD: HML10-489
THINK central

489

DIFFERENTIATED INSTRUCTION

FOR STRUGGLING READERS
Understanding Author's Message Ask students to describe the setting of the photograph on page 488. Does the man on the suitcases look comfortable? Why or why not? What would it be like to have to fit everything you owned into a few suitcases?

Teach

TEXT ANALYSIS   COMMON CORE
RL 2
RL 6

● *Model the Skill:* AUTHOR'S MESSAGE ACROSS GENRES

To model how to identify an author's message across genres, clarify the characteristics of an essay for students. Tell them that an essay is a short work of nonfiction prose that focuses on a single subject. Some essays are formal in tone, developing a structured, logical argument, while others are informal and even conversational in tone, using a looser structure.

Also clarify that an essay may include many of the characteristics of poetry that are listed in the right column of the chart on this page. Point out that, for example, an essay may express the writer's personal thoughts and feelings, and it may use vivid imagery and figurative language. Tell students that one key difference between the genres, however, is that a poem is more likely to suggest rather than directly state its theme. Poetry also tends to evoke strong emotion through word choice and sound devices.

GUIDED PRACTICE Ask students to identify a story and a poem that express the same theme.

R RESOURCE MANAGER—Copy Master Author's Message Across Genres p. 117 (for student use while reading the selections)

READING STRATEGY   COMMON CORE
RI 2

■ *Model the Skill:* SET A PURPOSE FOR READING

Ask students to reread **Tu Fu: Unlucky in Life** in *Meet the Authors.* Point out that one possible purpose for reading is to find out who Tu Fu was and how he was unlucky in life.

GUIDED PRACTICE Ask students to suggest a purpose for reading "Letter to a Young Refugee from Another."

489

READ WITH A PURPOSE

Help students set a purpose for reading. Tell students to look for details about what life is like for the refugees.

Letter to a Young Refugee from Another

Andrew Lam

Targeted Passage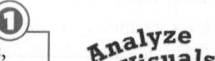

> On the news last night I saw you amidst a sea of desperate Albanian refugees, and afterward I couldn't get the image out of my mind. You with your wide eyes and shy smile, your hand gripping your mother's as if it were a life saver, you are repeating my story of 24 years ago.

Listen, even if I know so little about your country's tumultuous history, even if I don't know your name, I think I know what you are going through. When I was eleven, about your age, I too fled from my homeland with my mother and sister and grandmother when the communist tanks came rolling into Saigon, Vietnam. We ended up in a refugee camp[1] in Guam[2] while our father
10 was left behind. **A**

Back then I couldn't make any sense out of what had happened to me or my family. History, after all, is always baffling to the young. One day I was reading my favorite book in my mother's rose garden, my dogs sleeping lazily at my feet, and the next day I was running for my life with a small backpack in which I only managed to save my stamp collection. Everything else was burnt: photographs, mementos, books, toys, letters, and clothes.

For the first few days in the refugee camp, I walked about as if in a kind of somnambulist[3] trance. Something had slipped loose within me, a familiar tapestry quickly unraveling. Only years later, only after many revisitations
20 to the scene in my mind, did it slowly dawn on me what I had experienced: terror—a natural reaction to the fact that I was dispossessed, an exile.

---

1. **refugee camp:** a shelter for people displaced by war, political oppression, religious persecution, or famine.

2. **Guam** (gwäm): a Pacific island that is an unincorporated territory of the United States.

3. **somnambulist** (sŏm-năm′byə-lĭst): a person who sleepwalks.

490   UNIT 4: THEME

Analyze Visuals ▶

Which **details** in the photograph suggest that the woman and child are experiencing hardships?

A AUTHOR'S MESSAGE
Whom is the author addressing in the essay? Why?

DIFFERENTIATED INSTRUCTION

FOR ENGLISH LANGUAGE LEARNERS

Vocabulary Support Use Word Questioning to teach these words: *reaction* (line 21), *crucial* (line 25), *flexibility* (line 40), *displaced* (line 59), *consumes* (line 81), *commit* (line 88).

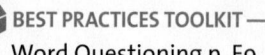 BEST PRACTICES TOOLKIT —Transparency
Word Questioning p. E9

FOR STRUGGLING READERS

In combination with the *Audio Anthology CD*, use one or more Targeted Passages (pp. 490, 493) to ensure that students focus on key concepts and skills. Targeted Passages are also good for English learners.

1 Targeted Passage [Lines 1–4]

This passage explains how one image on television evoked a flood of feeling that

BACKGROUND

The Fall of Saigon On April 29, 1975, the United States evacuated its few remaining troops, advisers, and diplomats from Vietnam's capital city, Saigon. The next day, North Vietnamese tanks rolled into the city. The South Vietnamese put up little resistance. North Vietnamese troops took over the presidential palace. The next year, North and South Vietnam became the Socialist Republic of Vietnam. The new capital was Hanoi, in the north. Saigon was renamed Ho Chi Minh City, and a military government ran the united country.

Analyze Visuals

Possible answer: The chained fence, the drab clothing, the child's intent gaze, the woman's sorrowful expression, and her hand held protectively over the child's face all suggest hardships.

Activity Ask students what message the photographer is trying to convey. *Possible answer: Life is difficult as an exile or in a refugee camp.*

REVISIT THE BIG QUESTION

What if you had to

FLEE your country?

Dicuss Have students reread lines 17–21. Ask them to explain the effects of the author's traumatic experience as a refugee. *Possible answer: The author experienced terror for the first time, a feeling he will never forget. He walked around in a daze (lines 17–18) and felt like he was falling apart (lines 18–19).*

prompted the author to write the essay.

- What image did the author see on television? (lines 2–3)
- How did the image affect him? (line 2)
- What did the image remind him of? (line 4)

FOR ADVANCED LEARNERS/PRE–AP

Compare and Contrast Engage students in a class discussion about the merits of the two genres they are reading. Ask students if they feel an essay or a poem is a more effective way to communicate the plight of refugees. What makes that particular format effective? Encourage students to explain their reasoning using other essays and poems they have read as supporting examples.

B AUTHOR'S MESSAGE

RL 2
RL 6

Possible answer: Refugee life is difficult; surviving it requires courage, strength, and cunning.

IF STUDENTS NEED HELP . . . Ask them to find the words the author uses to describe "the road ahead" (line 24)—that is, life as a refugee.

C *Model the Skill:* AUTHOR'S MESSAGE

RL 2
RL 6

Remind students that focusing on the writer's list of directions for how to feel and behave is one way to find the message in the essay. Work with them to state the main idea of each paragraph. Have students fill out a Main Idea and Details chart to help them.

Rise early.

↓

1. *Food lines are long, no matter how early you are there.* 2. *Protect yourself from rising sun.* 3. *It can take half a day for food.*

Pretend to be helpless.

↓

1. *Tell server that grandmother is bedridden.* 2. *Cry.* 3. *Don't be ashamed to beg.* 4. *Swallow your pride.*

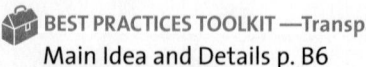 **BEST PRACTICES TOOLKIT** —Transparency
Main Idea and Details p. B6

Possible answer: Rise early, pretend to be helpless, be aggressive, stay alert, and remain hopeful.

My young friend, there are so many things I want to tell you, so many experiences I want to share with you, but, most of all, I want to warn you that the road ahead is a very difficult and treacherous one, and you must be brave and strong and cunning. There are crucial things you should learn and learn quickly, and then there are things you must mull over for the rest of your life. **B**

    The immediate thing is to learn to rise as early as possible. The food line is always long and no matter how early you are there, there will always be a line. You must have a hat or a scarf to protect your head from the cold and then
30 from the rising sun, since it can take half a day for food.

    When you get to the end of the line, try to act as helpless and as sad as possible. Tell the server that your frail grandmother is bedridden and cannot wait in line, that you are, in fact, feeding her. Cry if you can. Try not to feel ashamed. That you never begged before in your life means nothing. Swallow your pride. Another plate will save you or your mother or sister many hours of waiting for the next meal and will give them time to stand in line for medicine or clothes, depending on your immediate needs.

    Listen carefully, a new reality is upon you, and you must rise to it as best you can. It entails a drastic change in your nature and in your thinking. It
40 requires new flexibility and cunning. Be aggressive even when you are naturally shy. Be brave even when only days earlier you still hugged your teddy bear going to sleep.

    Be fierce. Do not let others take advantage of you. Do not show that you are weak. In the worst circumstances, the weak get left out or beaten and robbed. Arm yourself, if you can, with a knife or a stone, and guard your family and possessions like a mad dog its bone. People can sense that you are willing to fight for what you have left, and most will back away.

    Be alert. Listen to gossips and news. Find out what is coming down the line: food, donated clothes, blankets, tents, and medicines. Always get more than
50 you need, if you can manage it, because extra can be traded with others for something you don't have or can be given away to the elderly and feeble who are not as quick as you. An extra blanket is so helpful on a cold spring night, as you, I'm sure, have already found out.

    Be hopeful. No, more than that. Don't give up hope. Maybe your father has made it somewhere else, to another camp possibly. The same can be said of your aunts and cousins, friends, and neighbors. Never give up hope. Soon enough the camp will organize, and there'll be a newsletter with information regarding lost relatives looking for each other, or a bulletin board with names and agencies that will track displaced loved ones. Go every day to check and
60 see whether your father has sent word. Console your inconsolable mother and sister. Hug them as often as you can. **C**

    I close my eyes now and cast my mind back to that time spent in the refugee camp, and all I hear are the sounds of weeping. I imagine it is not

B AUTHOR'S MESSAGE
Reread lines 22–26. On the basis of this passage, what appears to be the message of the essay?

C AUTHOR'S MESSAGE
In lines 27–61 the author offers a **list,** or catalog, of do's and don'ts for the young Albanian refugee. **Summarize** the main points of the list.

DIFFERENTIATED INSTRUCTION

FOR ENGLISH LANGUAGE LEARNERS

Vocabulary Support Encourage students to practice using these expressions in sentences: *for the rest of your life* (line 26), "as long as you live"; *as best you can* (lines 38–39), "trying your hardest"; *By the same token* (line 75), "similarly; likewise"; *Commit . . . to memory* (lines 88–89), "remember"; *from the top of your lungs* (line 91), "as loudly as you can".

FOR ADVANCED LEARNERS/PRE–AP

Literary Techniques in Nonfiction Remind students that nonfiction writers often employ literary techniques to bring their stories to life. Have students discuss Andrew Lam's use of characterization, setting, theme, and figurative language. Ask, Are these techniques effective in his essay?

that different than what you are hearing now each morning, each afternoon, and each night. Throughout the green tent city that flapped incessantly in the wind was the music of sorrow and grief. A woman who saw her husband shot in front of her wailed until she was hoarse and breathless. A man who left his feeble father behind cried quietly into his blanket. A woman whose teenage son was kept behind stared out into the dark as if she had lost her mind. For 70 a while, the sound of weeping was my refugee camp lullaby.

Indeed, life in limbo[4] is difficult and humiliating, but you must remember that being robbed of what you loved does not speak to your weakness or frailty. It only speaks of the inhumanity and fear and hatred of those who caused you to flee and endure in this new dispossessed reality.

By the same token, I implore you, do not give in to their hatred. I know it is very hard, if not impossible, for someone who has just been forced out of his homeland, but you must try. Those who killed and robbed and caused so much pain and suffering to you, your family, and your people are, in fact, trying to make you into their own image, even if they don't realize it yet. They 80 want you to hate just like them, and they want you to be consumed with the fire of their hatred. Don't hate. Hatred consumes oppressed and oppressors alike and its terrible expressions—revenge is chief among them—always result in blood and tears and injustice and unspeakable suffering, especially for the innocent.

Don't hate. Love instead. Love what you lost, love what you still have, and love those who suffered along with you, for their suffering and yours are part of your inheritance.

And don't forget. Commit everything—each blade of grass, each teary-eyed child, each unmarked grave—to memory. Then when you are older, tell your 90 story. Tell it on your bruised knees, if you must. Tell it at the risk of madness. Scream it from the top of your lungs, the way a wounded bird would sing its last song. For though the story of how you suffered, how you lost your home, your loved ones, and how you triumphed is not new, it must always be told. And it must be heard. It is the only light we ever have against the overwhelming darkness. ✍ **D**

---

4. **limbo:** a state of being disregarded or forgotten.

COMMON CORE L 4b

Language Coach

Affixes Many words are created by adding a prefix or a suffix to a common base or root. The word *possess* means "to have or own." By adding the suffix *-ion*, the word changes from a verb to a noun. A *possession* is something owned, property. What other word based on *possess* occurs in line 74? What does it mean? Use a dictionary if you need help finding the definition of affixes.

②

D **AUTHOR'S MESSAGE**
What important piece of advice does the author end with?

TIERED DISCUSSION PROMPTS

Direct students to lines 75–87. Use these prompts to help students understand Lam's insights about the vicious circle created by hate and revenge:

Connect What do you think is the most natural reaction toward someone who causes pain and suffering? How would you react? *Responses should reflect an understanding that a natural reaction is to feel anger, hatred, or a desire to seek revenge.*

Analyze According to Lam, what is the inevitable result of seeking revenge? *Possible answer: Innocent people suffer (lines 82–84).*

Synthesize How would you sum up Andrew Lam's conclusions about hate and revenge? How do you think Lam came to his conclusions? *Possible answer: Hate and revenge turn victims into victimizers and establish a vicious circle that causes more innocent people to suffer. Lam learned from observation and experience about the terrible price of hatred.*

TEXT ANALYSIS   **COMMON CORE**

D **AUTHOR'S MESSAGE**   RL 2 RL 6

Possible answer: *The author advises the boy to commit his refugee experiences to memory and share his stories.*

FOR ENGLISH LANGUAGE LEARNERS

Language Coach   **COMMON CORE** L 4b

Affixes *Answer:* Dispossessed *means "deprived of one's belongings." The refugees no longer possess the things they love.* Point out the word *displaced* (line 59), which is a derivation of the verb *place*. Tell students that the meaning of *place* is "put in a particular physical environment." Ask students how they think adding the prefix *dis-* changes the meaning of the word. What does *displace* mean?

② Targeted Passage [Lines 88–95]

This passage brings the essay full circle—back to the subject of memory. Remind students that an image on television brought back to the author a flood of feeling and memory, which caused him to write the letter.

- What does the author tell the refugee to remember? (lines 88–89)
- Why does the author say that the refugee must tell the story? (lines 92–95)

Prereading for this poem is found on page 488.

READING STRATEGY

E COMPARING THEMES ACROSS GENRES

Remind students of the various types of genres that exist: poems, short stories, novels, play. Then have them name various types of nonfiction genres. *Possible answer: The speaker in the essay recounts his experience and gives advice; the tone is matter of fact. The speaker of the poem has had a similar experience but recounts it using strong visual imagery. Rebel soldiers have forced the speaker and his family to flee over dangerous trails at night, by moonlight. They left with nothing and were forced to beg.*

IF STUDENTS NEED HELP . . . Reread the first line of the poem. After pausing, reread the fifth line.

TEXT ANALYSIS

COMMON CORE
RL 2
RL 6

F AUTHOR'S MESSAGE

Possible answer: Images that convey the hardships of refugee life are "baby girl in her hunger bit me" (line 9), "squirmed and wailed" (line 12), "Ten days, half in rain and thunder" (line 15), "mud and slime" (line 16), "trails slick, clothes wet and clammy" (line 18), "Mountain fruits served for rations" (line 21), "low-hung branches" as shelter (line 22).

Song
of P'eng-ya
Tu Fu

I remember when we first fled the rebels,[1]
hurrying north over dangerous trails;
night deepened on P'eng-ya Road,[2]
the moon shone over White-water Hills.
5 A whole family endlessly trudging,
begging without shame from the people we met:
valley birds sang, a jangle of soft voices;
we didn't see a single traveler returning. **E**
The baby girl in her hunger bit me;
10 fearful that tigers or wolves would hear her cries,
I hugged her to my chest, muffling her mouth,
but she squirmed and wailed louder than before.
The little boy pretended he knew what was happening;
importantly he searched for sour plums to eat.
15 Ten days, half in rain and thunder,
through mud and slime we pulled each other on.
There was no escaping from the rain,
trails slick, clothes wet and clammy;
getting past the hardest places,
20 a whole day advanced us no more than three or four li.[3]
Mountain fruits served for rations,
low-hung branches were our rafter and roof. **F**
Mornings we traveled by rock-bedded streams,
evenings camped in mists that closed in the sky.
25 We stopped a little while at the marsh of T'ung-chia,[4]
thinking to go out by Lu-tzu[5] Pass;

E COMPARING THEMES ACROSS GENRES

When you compare and contrast themes across genres, you look for ways in which the messages of the selections are the same and are different. Recall the essay you just read. How does the speaker of the essay differ from the speaker of this poem? In this poem, what has happened to the speaker and his family?

F AUTHOR'S MESSAGE

Reread lines 9–22. Which **images** strongly convey the physical hardships of refugee life?

---

1. **rebels:** troops led by the traitorous general An Lu-shan, who attacked and captured the Chinese capital of Ch'ang-an in A.D. 756.

2. **P'eng-ya** (pŭng'yä') **Road:** a road to the town of P'eng-ya, about 130 miles north of Ch'ang-an. Tu Fu and his family passed through P'eng-ya as they sought safety from the rebel forces.

3. **three or four li** (lē): less than a mile and a half.

4. **T'ung-chia** (tŏŏng'jyä').

5. **Lu-tzu** (lōō'dzŭ').

DIFFERENTIATED INSTRUCTION

FOR STRUGGLING READERS

Questions and Answers Ask students to find and read the lines in the poem that answer these questions: In what direction did the speaker's family flee? *(line 2)* Why did the speaker hug the baby girl to his chest? *(line 10)* How long did they travel? *(line 15)* Why was the traveling so slow? *(lines 17–20)* What did they eat? *(line 21)*

FOR STRUGGLING READERS

Develop Reading Fluency Read the first six lines aloud, and discuss the setting and the characters. Then have students listen to the *Audio Anthology CD* as they read along.

Distribute the copy masters and have students work in pairs or groups to practice fluency.

R RESOURCE MANAGER—Copy Master
Reading Fluency p. 124

an old friend there, Sun Tsai,[6]
ideals higher than the piled-up clouds;
he came out to meet us as dusk turned to darkness,
30 called for torches, opening gate after gate,
heated water to wash our feet,
cut strips of paper to call back our souls.[7]
Then his wife and children came;
seeing us, their tears fell in streams. **G**
35 My little chicks had gone sound to sleep;
he called them to wake up and eat from his plate,
said he would make a vow with me,
the two of us to be brothers forever.
At last he cleared the room where we sat,
40 wished us goodnight, all he had at our command.
Who is willing, in the hard, bleak times,
to break open, lay bare his innermost heart?
Parting from you, a year of months has rounded,
Tartar tribes[8] still plotting evil,
45 and I think how it would be to have strong wings
that would carry me away, set me down before you. **H**

Translated by Burton Watson

---

6. **Sun Tsai** (soōn' dzǐ').

7. **cut strips of paper to call back our souls:** It was believed that the soul could leave the body when a person was frightened. The ritual referred to here was intended to restore the souls of the frightened travelers.

8. **Tartar tribes:** the forces of An Lu-shan.

SONG OF P'ENG-YA   **495**

G AUTHOR'S MESSAGE
Reread lines 27–34.
The phrase "ideals higher than the piled-up clouds" and "tears fell in streams" are examples of **figurative language.**
What ideas or emotions do they suggest?

H AUTHOR'S MESSAGE
Describe the **mood,** or feeling, conveyed by the poem. In the end, does the poet send a message of hope or one of hopelessness?

Analyze Visuals

Activity: How does the photograph support the mood of the second half of the poem?
Possible answer: The photograph supports the feelings of civility, comfort, and hope—feelings similar to those generated in the speaker by his old friend, Sun Tsai, after the speaker's harrowing escape.

REVISIT THE BIG QUESTION
What if you had to
FLEE your country?
Based on lines 27–42, what comforts the speaker, now that he and his family are refugees? *Possible answer: His friend's kindness, hospitality, tears, and vows of brotherhood comfort the speaker.*

TEXT ANALYSIS   COMMON CORE
G AUTHOR'S MESSAGE   RL 2 RL 6
Possible answer: These examples of figurative language suggest both hope and sorrow.

TEXT ANALYSIS   COMMON CORE
H AUTHOR'S MESSAGE   RL 2 RL 6
Possible answer: The ending conveys a sorrowful mood because the friends have been separated (line 43), but the speaker sends the hopeful message that they will meet again (lines 45–46).

SELECTION WRAP-UP

READ WITH A PURPOSE Ask students how the life of refugees was described in the two works. What did the refugees lose? *Possible answer: Life was frightening and uncertain. The refugees in both selections lost their homes and their possessions.*

⭐ **CRITIQUE** Whose message—Andrew Lam's or Tu Fu's—is most hopeful? Give your reasons.

FOR RELUCTANT READERS

Connect To help students connect with the text, have them work in small groups to answer the following questions: If you had to flee your home with only a backpack, what would you take? What possessions would you miss the most if you had to leave them behind? What would you be unable to replace if it were lost?

Invite the groups to report their answers to the class at large. Hold a class discussion comparing and contrasting what items students thought would be important enough to take with them and the reasons for their choices.

Practice and Apply

For preliminary support of post-reading questions, use these copy masters:

R RESOURCE MANAGER—Copy Masters
Reading Check p. 122
Comparing Across Genres p. 117
Question Support p. 123
Additional selection questions are provided for teachers on page 111.

ANSWERS

Comprehension

1. *They have both experienced the dislocation and trauma of a refugee life.*

2. *The author cautions the young refugee against hating the oppressors because hatred only leads to more pain and degradation (lines 75–84). The author advises the young refugee to love instead, as a way of maintaining personal integrity and humanity (lines 85–87).*

3. *The speaker and his family suffer displacement, hunger, humiliation, and bad weather on the P'eng-ya Road.*

4. *Sun Tsai welcomes the speaker and his family into his home, heats water to wash their feet, performs a ritual to protect them, gives them a place to sleep, lets the speaker's children eat off his plate, and makes a vow of eternal brotherhood (lines 29–38).*

Text Analysis
COMMON CORE RL 2, RL 6

Possible answers:

5. *The first-person point of view allows closer identification with the refugees' feelings and trials. A third-person point of view might offer more objectivity and a broader perspective of society.*

6. *The images of the children hungry and wailing, of the family battling rain and mud, and of branches as shelter convey a mood of sorrow and desperation.*

Comparing Across Genres

Possible answers:

Time Period: Essay—1970s   Poem—700s
Situation: Essay—The author recalls his own refugee experience. Poem—The speaker describes fleeing his homeland with his young family.

Qualities: Essay—attentiveness, aggressiveness, cunning, determination, protectiveness, hope

Poem—attentiveness, resourcefulness, determination, hope

Author's message: Essay—Be strong and you will persevere. Poem—Friendship comforts us in the worst of times.

Techniques: Essay—examples, repetition, characterization Poem—sensory images, figurative language, characterization

---

Comprehension

1. **Recall** What do the author of the essay and the Albanian refugee have in common?

2. **Clarify** According to the essay, why should refugees love, instead of hate, those who have caused them pain?

3. **Recall** What hardships does the speaker of Tu Fu's poem face on P'eng-ya Road?

4. **Summarize** In the poem, how does Sun Tsai help the speaker's family?

Text Analysis

5. **Analyze Point of View** Both the essay and the poem are written from first-person points of view. Think about the effect each point of view has on you as the reader. How might your understanding of refugees and their hardships be different if third-person observers narrated the accounts?

6. **Examine Imagery and Mood** The feeling or atmosphere a writer creates for readers is called a mood. The mood of a piece might be described, for example, as somber, mysterious, cheerful, or joyful. Mood is often established by imagery—vivid words and phrases that appeal to the senses. Cite three examples of imagery in "Song of P'eng-ya" and tell how they help establish the poem's mood and its message.

Comparing Across Genres

Now that you have read both selections about refugee life, you are ready to identify each author's message. The following **Points of Comparison** chart will help you get started.

Points of Comparison	In the Essay	In the Poem
In what time period does this take place?		
What situation does the person face?		
What qualities help the person survive?		
Write a sentence stating the **author's message** as you interpret it.		
What techniques does the author rely on most?		

> **What if you had to FLEE your country?**
> What difficulties would you face in adapting to a new culture?

> What if you had to **FLEE** your country? Students might mention the challenges of finding new homes, making new friends, and adjusting to new laws and customs.

Writing for Assessment

COMMON CORE
RI 2, RL 6, W 9 (RI 7)

1. READ THE PROMPT

In writing assessments, you will often be asked to **compare and contrast** works of literature that are from different time periods and that explore a similar theme. You are now going to practice writing an essay that requires this type of focus.

> Although living more than a thousand years apart, both Andrew Lam and Tu Fu experienced displacement from their homelands. In their works, both authors attempt to give readers an impression of their lives as political exiles. In a four- or five-paragraph essay, compare and contrast how the two authors explore this theme. Do the selections offer a similar message about refugee life? In what ways do the messages differ? Cite evidence to support your response.

◀ **STRATEGIES IN ACTION**

1. *I need to write an essay that will show similarities and differences in two selections.*
2. *I have to consider each author's message about refugee life.*
3. *I need to include examples or quotations from the two works.*

2. PLAN YOUR WRITING

- Review the answers you provided for the **Points of Comparison** chart on page 496.
- Using your chart, find examples to use as evidence for the points you will develop in your essay. If necessary, review the selections again to identify more examples.
- Create an outline to organize your main points.

> I. Lams' essay
>   A. Theme
>   B. Author's attitude
> II. Tu Fu's poem
> III. Similarities
> IV. Differences

3. DRAFT YOUR RESPONSE

Introduction Introduce the topic—refugee life—and then explain that you will be comparing and contrasting the messages of the selections.

Body State and explain Andrew Lam's main idea in one paragraph and Tu Fu's theme in another. In a third paragraph, compare the two messages. In a fourth paragraph, contrast the messages. Make sure to support your statements with examples and quotations from the selections.

Conclusion Wrap up your essay with a final thought about refugee life and a brief summary of your main points.

Revision Check your use of transitional words and phrases to connect your ideas within and between paragraphs. Words and phrases such as *likewise*, *both*, and *in the same way* signal similarities. *Nevertheless* and *however* signal differences.

Writing for Assessment

COMMON CORE RL 2, RL 6, W 9 (RI 7)

1. READ THE PROMPT

Suggest that students review **Author's Message Across Genres** on page 489. Remind them that narrators and speakers sometimes state their messages directly. Then ask a volunteer to reread the first question in the prompt. ("Do the selections offer a similar message about refugee life?") Suggest that it might be helpful to begin with this question: *What do you learn about refugee life in each selection?*

2. PLAN YOUR WRITING

After students review the **Points of Comparison** chart on page 496, begin an outline on the board. Encourage students to suggest heads and subheads as well as details from each work.

I. Refugee Life
  A. turmoil, anguish, fear
  B. physical and emotional danger
  C. strategies for survival
  D. sources of comfort
II. Letter to a Young Refugee from Another
  A. political situation
  B. refugee camp

Assess and Reteach

Assess

DIAGNOSTIC AND SELECTION TESTS
  Selection Test A pp. 135–136
  Selection Test B/C pp. 137–138

Interactive Selection Test on **thinkcentral.com**

Reteach

Level Up Online Tutorials on **thinkcentral.com**

Reteaching Worksheets on **thinkcentral.com**:
  Literature Lesson 11: Theme, Motif, and Epiphany
  Reading Lesson 3: Determining Author's Purpose

---

3. DRAFT YOUR RESPONSE

Encourage students to identify in their outlines where they plan to add quotes and other supporting evidence. Suggest that they reference specific lines from the essay or poem.

- Remind students to make sure that they allow for an introduction, body, and conclusion in their outlines. Have them highlight this information.
- Limit the length of the assignment to four paragraphs: one paragraph for the intro-

duction, two paragraphs for the body (one for each selection), and one paragraph for the conclusion.

- Help students find one quotation from each selection to support their ideas about the message. Remind them to reference this information in their outlines.

Focus and Motivate

⋯ COMMON CORE FOCUS

W 2a–f Write informative/explanatory texts to examine complex ideas clearly and accurately through the effective selection, organization, and analysis of content. **W 4** Produce clear and coherent writing. **W 5** Develop and strengthen writing as needed by revising, editing, rewriting, or trying a new approach. **W 9** Draw evidence from texts to support analysis. **W 10** Write routinely over shorter time frames for a range of tasks, purposes, and audiences. **L 1** Demonstrate command of the conventions of standard English grammar and usage. **L 1a** Use parallel structure. **L 2** Demonstrate command of the conventions of standard English capitalization, punctuation, and spelling.

WRITE WITH A PURPOSE

Tell students to choose two subjects that they are familiar with or are interested in. Remind them that their purpose is to describe the similarities and differences between their two chosen subjects.

COMMON CORE TRAITS

Review the *COMMON CORE TRAITS* with students, concentrating on development of ideas and organization of ideas. Compare the list of traits with the rubric on page 506.

ADDITIONAL TASK

Write About Travel Write an essay for a travel magazine that compares and contrasts two similar travel destinations. Begin your research online.
Possible Subjects: two vacation spots, two national parks

Writing Online · THINK central

The following tools are available online at **thinkcentral.com** and on Write*Smart* CD-ROM:
• Interactive Graphic Organizers
• Interactive Student Models
• Interactive Revision Lessons

Writing Workshop
INFORMATIVE TEXT

Essential Course of Study ECOS

Comparison-Contrast Essay

Which novel is more exciting? Which political candidate will be a stronger leader? To answer such questions, you must compare and contrast; doing so can give you a deeper understanding of each subject and help you make a more informed choice between them. In this workshop, you will write a comparison-contrast essay—an essay that identifies the similarities and differences between two subjects.

 Complete the workshop activities in your **Reader/Writer Notebook**.

WRITE WITH A PURPOSE

WRITING TASK

Write a **comparison-contrast essay** in which you identify the similarities and differences between two subjects. Make sure to include a controlling idea that is supported by details, quotations, and other evidence.

Idea Starters
• two literary works
• two sports or extracurricular activities
• two brands of a product

THE ESSENTIALS

Here are some common purposes, audiences, and formats for comparison-contrast writing.

PURPOSES	AUDIENCES	FORMATS
• to gain a deeper understanding of two subjects • to aid decision making	• classmates and teacher • newspaper or magazine readers • consumers	• essay for class • newspaper or magazine review • consumer Web site

⋯ COMMON CORE TRAITS

1. DEVELOPMENT OF IDEAS
• presents an **engaging introduction** that identifies the subjects
• includes a **controlling idea** that states the overarching comparison and contrast
• supports key points with **relevant evidence,** such as facts, concrete details, and quotations
• concludes with a **summary of key points** and an **insight** about the subjects

2. ORGANIZATION OF IDEAS
• **organizes** ideas using a logical structure
• uses varied **transitions** to clarify relationships among ideas

3. LANGUAGE FACILITY AND CONVENTIONS
• establishes and maintains a **formal style** and **objective tone**
• includes **precise language** and **domain-specific vocabulary**
• uses **parallel structure** to clarify and emphasize ideas
• employs correct **grammar, usage, and spelling**

Writing Online THINK central

Go to **thinkcentral.com**.
KEYWORD: HML10N-498

Writing Workshop Resources

 **RESOURCE MANAGER UNIT 4**
Plan and Teach, pp. 125–128
Prewriting–Editing, pp. 129–133
Writing Rubric, p. 134
Speaking and Listening, p. 135
Writing Support, p. 136*

 BEST PRACTICES TOOLKIT
Writing Template: Compare-Contrast pp. C23, C24

TECHNOLOGY
 Teacher One Stop DVD-ROM
⊘ **Student One Stop DVD-ROM**
⊘ **Write*Smart* CD-ROM**
⊘ **GrammarNotes DVD-ROM**
Writing Center on thinkcentral.com

*See resources on the **Teacher One Stop DVD-ROM** and on **thinkcentral.com**.*

* Resources for Differentiation

Planning/Prewriting

 COMMON CORE W 2a–f Write informative/explanatory texts to examine complex ideas clearly and accurately through the effective selection, organization, and analysis of content. **W 5** Develop and strengthen writing as needed by planning.

Getting Started

CHOOSE YOUR SUBJECTS

Select two subjects to compare and contrast. Make sure there is a good reason to compare and contrast the two subjects. Avoid choosing subjects that are too similar.

▶ **ASK YOURSELF:**
- How are the two subjects similar?
- How are the two subjects different?
- Why are their similarities and differences important?

BRAINSTORM SIMILARITIES AND DIFFERENCES

Use a Venn diagram to make important connections and distinctions between the two subjects. List every similarity and difference that occurs to you. Consider various aspects or features of your subjects. For example, if you are comparing two literary works, consider characters, theme, setting, conflict, resolution, and author's techniques. Then, identify the strength of each similarity and difference, keeping only the strongest points and deleting the weaker ones.

▶ **WHAT DOES IT LOOK LIKE?**

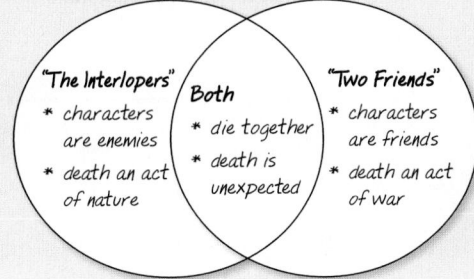

"The Interlopers"
* characters are enemies
* death an act of nature

Both
* die together
* death is unexpected

"Two Friends"
* characters are friends
* death an act of war

THINK ABOUT AUDIENCE AND PURPOSE

As you begin to brainstorm your subjects, keep in mind your **purpose**—to compare and contrast two subjects for your **audience**. Focus on what is most significant for your specific purpose and your audience.

▶ **ASK YOURSELF:**
- Who is my target audience? Who would be most interested in the subjects of my comparison?
- What message do I want to communicate to my audience?
- What aspects of my subjects might my audience want to know more about?
- What **domain-specific,** or specialized, **vocabulary** will my audience already be familiar with?

WRITE A CONTROLLING IDEA

Explain the **controlling idea,** or focus, of your essay in precise language. Make important connections and distinctions between the two subjects. Be prepared to refine your controlling idea as you draft your essay.

▶ **WHAT DOES IT LOOK LIKE?**

> *Controlling Idea:* "The Interlopers" and "Two Friends" have similar messages about life and death, but their characters differ in important respects.

Planning/ Prewriting

 COMMON CORE W 2a–f, W 5

▶ **CHOOSE YOUR SUBJECTS** Remind students that to make a clear distinction between similarities and differences, there must be a good reason to compare and contrast the two subjects. Have students list possible similarities and differences. If there are more similarities than differences, suggest students choose different subjects.

▶ **BRAINSTORM SIMILARITIES AND DIFFERENCES** Suggest that students use a Venn Diagram like the one on page 499 or a different organizer that fits the data and suggests a format for their essays. Make sure students understand that in order to write effective comparison-contrast essays, they should include only the strongest similarities and differences.

▶ **THINK ABOUT AUDIENCE AND PURPOSE** Make sure students understand who their audience is and what its interests are. Remind students to include background information for people who are unfamiliar with the two subjects of their essays.

▶ **WRITE A CONTROLLING IDEA** Tell students that their controlling ideas should name both the subjects and the points of comparison they will address in their essays. Suggest that students use the information from their graphic organizers to identify the strongest points of comparison between the two subjects. Encourage students to revise or rework their controlling ideas as they draft their essays.

📋 **BEST PRACTICES TOOLKIT—Transparencies**
Venn Diagram p. A26
Y Chart p. A27

R **RESOURCE MANAGER—Copy Masters**
Planning / Prewriting p. 129
Drafting p. 130
Revising pp. 131–132
Editing p. 133
Rubric p. 134
Writing Support p. 136

DIFFERENTIATED INSTRUCTION

FOR ENGLISH LANGUAGE LEARNERS
Language: Reinforce Compare and Contrast Terms: Write these terms on the board and review them with students:

- *to compare:* to look for things or qualities that are similar or alike
- *to contrast:* to look for things or qualities that are different
- *connections:* ways in which things and people are related or linked to each other
- *distinctions:* ways in which things or people differ from each other

- *controlling idea:* one or two sentences summarizing the main idea of an essay. In a comparison-contrast essay, the controlling idea names the literary works or the subjects and the points of comparison. For example:

The pairs of characters in both "Two Friends" and "The Interlopers" face their deaths together. Although the men in "The Interlopers" have long been enemies, they, too, discover the value of friendship.

Planning/Prewriting *continued*

▶ **COLLECT SUPPORTING EVIDENCE** If students are comparing non-literary subjects, they may need to conduct research in order to support their ideas with evidence. Remind students to use a variety of evidence. When using direct quotations, students should record the source title and page numbers and then copy the words precisely, using ellipses to show omitted material and brackets to add words or phrases for clarification.

 Give students time to choose their two subjects, develop a controlling idea, and begin filling out their charts. Have students research and find additional evidence independently.

For interactive graphic organizers, see

 Write*Smart* CD-ROM

Writing Center on thinkcentral.com

R RESOURCE MANAGER—Copy Master
Writing Support p. 136

Planning/Prewriting *continued*

COLLECT SUPPORTING EVIDENCE

Choose **relevant quotations** and **concrete details** that support your controlling idea. Be sure to select and record sufficient supporting details for each key similarity or difference you plan to include in your essay. If you are comparing and contrasting texts, make sure to note the page number where you find each detail or quotation.

▶ **WHAT DOES IT LOOK LIKE?**

Story Element	"The Interlopers"	"Two Friends"
characters' relationship with each other	"each prayed that misfortune might fall on the other" (p. 430)	"they understood each other perfectly" (p. 440)
characters' experiences	meet in forest; both characters are hunting, one is hunting for the other (p. 430)	meet by accident in the street (p. 440)
characters' deaths	die by accident (tree falls on them, wolves attack) (pp. 430–434)	killed on purpose (soldiers shoot them) (p. 447)

PEER REVIEW Read your controlling idea to a classmate and share the evidence you have gathered to support it. Then, ask: Is my controlling idea clear? Is my supporting evidence convincing? Do I need to revise or try a new approach to my controlling idea?

 In your *Reader/Writer Notebook,* develop your writing plan. Record your controlling idea. Then, use a chart such as the one on this page to collect supporting evidence. Consider the following tips as you gather relevant evidence:

- As part of your supporting evidence, collect quotations from a text or review, a commercial or ad, or from someone you know who has used the product, participated in the activity, or has experience with the subjects.
- Copy quotations word-for-word exactly as they appear. Use ellipses (. . .) to show omitted material and brackets ([ ]) to add words or phrases for clarification.
- Choose concrete details to illustrate your key points. If you cite details from a text, use your own words to paraphrase them.

DIFFERENTIATED INSTRUCTION

FOR ENGLISH LANGUAGE LEARNERS

Writing: Controlling Idea Have students use these sentence starters to help them develop their controlling ideas:

- The subjects or works I will compare are _____ and _____.
- Their messages are _____.
- The main similarity or difference is _____.
- The key element I will discuss is _____.

FOR STRUGGLING WRITERS

Collect Evidence Have students brainstorm a list of key words they might use in an Internet search on their chosen subjects and a list of categories for possible experts, such as teachers, scientists, and so on. Emphasize that an individual's expertise is usually limited to a specific field. Thus, a scientist is most likely an expert only in his or her specialty, not in other scientific areas.

Drafting

COMMON CORE **W 4** Produce clear and coherent writing. **W 9** Draw evidence from texts to support analysis. **L 2** Demonstrate command of the conventions of standard English capitalization, punctuation, and spelling.

The following chart shows a structure for organizing an effective comparison-contrast essay.

Organizing Your Comparison-Contrast Essay

INTRODUCTION
- State the **subjects** you will compare and contrast.
- Explain your **controlling idea**—the overarching comparison and contrast—in precise language.

▼

BODY
- Use one of the following **structures** to present your points of comparison in a clearly organized way:
  Block Structure—discusses all the points relating to the first subject before moving on to the second subject
  Point-by-Point Structure—compares or contrasts both subjects, one point at a time
- Cite **relevant facts, concrete details,** and other **evidence** from your chart to support your key points.
- Use appropriate and varied **transitions,** such as *also, however,* and *unlike,* to link ideas, create cohesion, and signal similarities and differences.
- Establish and maintain a **formal style** and **objective tone** by avoiding contractions and slang and by adopting a neutral attitude.

▼

CONCLUDING SECTION
- Summarize the **key points** and restate the controlling idea.
- Close with an insight that follows from and supports your controlling idea.

GRAMMAR IN CONTEXT: COMMA PLACEMENT IN CONTRASTING EXPRESSIONS

A variety of words and phrases can be used to contrast ideas. The expressions below are used to signal **contrasts,** or differences. Use commas to set off these expressions from the rest of the sentence.

Expressions	Example
but, however, instead, on the other hand, in contrast, unlike, yet	*The two stories convey a similar message about death and fate. Their portrayals of this theme are very different, however.*

YOUR TURN
Develop a first draft of your comparison-contrast essay, following the structure outlined in the chart above. Include a variety of contrasting expressions to signal important distinctions, using commas to set off such expressions from the rest of the sentence.

WRITING WORKSHOP **501**

FOR ENGLISH LANGUAGE LEARNERS
Comma Placement in Contrasting Expressions Remind students that they can identify a contrasting expression by the commas that set it off from the rest of the sentence. Ask students to identify the contrasting expressions in the following sentences from the Student Model. Then have students find other examples in the Student Model.

- "In 'Two Friends,' <u>on the other hand</u>, Morissot and Sauvage share a deep friendship."
- "The pairs of characters undergo very different experiences, <u>however</u>."

FOR ADVANCED LEARNERS/PRE–AP
Analyze Stylistic Elements [paired activity option] Have students write several paragraphs that analyze and compare the stylistic elements two literary texts. Urge them to include some of this analytical evidence in their essays. Refer students to the Analysis Frame: Author's Craft for help.

 BEST PRACTICE TOOLKIT—Copy Master
Analysis Frame: Author's Craft pp. D21, D24

Drafting
COMMON CORE **W 4, W 9, L 2**

▶ **INTRODUCTION** Tell students to look at the Student Draft on page 503 for an example of an attention-grabbing introduction. Remind students that their introductions should state the subjects that will be compared and contrasted.

▶ **BODY** Remind students to include details that clearly support their points. Students will also need to include transitions to connect ideas between sentences and paragraphs and to signal similarities or differences. Have students identify the transitional words and phrases in the Student Draft on page 503.

▶ **CONCLUDING SECTION** Stress that after reading a comparison-contrast essay, the audience should be able to understand how the two subjects are similar and different. Explain that an additional insight leaves readers with ideas to ponder.

GRAMMAR IN CONTEXT: COMMA PLACEMENT IN CONTRASTING EXPRESSIONS

For additional practice, have students insert commas after the contrasting expressions in the following sentences.

- In contrast the two stories portray the idea of death and fate in two different ways. *[In contrast,]*
- Morissot and Sauvage in "Two Friends" share a deep friendship. However Ulrich von Gradwitz and Georg Znaeym in 'The Interlopers" share a deep, lifelong hatred. *[However,]*

YOUR TURN
Ask students to complete the **Your Turn** activity independently. Remind students to include commas in contrasting expressions. Suggest that students write their drafts double-spaced so that they can make revisions more easily later.

For compare-contrast writing templates, see

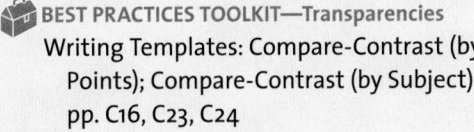 BEST PRACTICES TOOLKIT—Transparencies
Writing Templates: Compare-Contrast (by Points); Compare-Contrast (by Subject) pp. C16, C23, C24

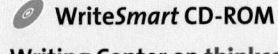 **Write*Smart* CD-ROM**
Writing Center on <u>thinkcentral.com</u>

WRITING WORKSHOP **501**

Revising

Model the Skill Using a draft essay on a transparency, model how to use the questions, tips, and strategies suggested in the chart to evaluate and revise. You might use the essay of a student from another class or from last year. Be sure to remove the student's name from the essay so that he or she is anonymous.

Revising

As you revise, consider the controlling idea, supporting evidence, and organization of your comparison-contrast essay. The goal is to determine whether you've achieved your specific purpose and effectively communicated your ideas to your intended audience. The questions, tips, and strategies in the following chart will help you revise and improve your draft.

COMPARISON-CONTRAST ESSAY

Ask Yourself	Tips	Revision Strategies
1. Does the introduction grab the audience's attention?	▶ **Underline** sentences in the introduction that engage readers.	▶ **Add** an interesting question, fact, or observation to get readers' attention.
2. Does the introduction identify the subjects and state a clear and coherent controlling idea?	▶ **Circle** the subjects. **Bracket** the controlling idea.	▶ If necessary, **add** the subjects or an overarching statement that explains the controlling idea.
3. Does the writing establish and maintain a formal style and objective tone?	▶ **Bracket** contractions, casual slang, or informal language.	▶ **Reword** text to avoid contractions. **Replace** instances of informal language with precise, formal words.
4. Is each point of comparison supported by well-chosen and sufficient evidence, such as facts and concrete details?	▶ **Circle** each piece of evidence. **Draw an arrow** to connect it to the point it supports.	▶ **Add** evidence for any point that does not have a corresponding circle.
5. Are appropriate and varied transitions used to connect and contrast ideas?	▶ **Place a check mark** next to each transitional word or phrase.	▶ **Add** transitional words or phrases where needed to clarify the relationships between ideas.
6. Does the concluding section follow and sum up ideas? Does it give the audience something to think about?	▶ **Double underline** the summary of key points in the concluding section. **Underline** the insight offered to readers.	▶ **Add** an overarching view of key points or a final observation about the significance of the comparison and contrast.

YOUR TURN
Suggest that students, after reading their partners' drafts, take one minute to freewrite a response explaining whether or not the points of comparison were clear. Then allow students a few minutes to share their responses with one another. Students should begin by making a positive comment about the draft, followed by clear suggestions on how their partners can make their points clear.

For interactive revision tools, see

 Write*Smart* CD-ROM

Writing Center on thinkcentral.com

YOUR TURN **PEER REVIEW** Exchange your comparison-contrast essay with a classmate, or read it aloud to your partner. As you read and comment on your classmate's essay, focus on the controlling idea, supporting evidence, and organization. Discuss whether the points of comparison and contrast are clear. If necessary, provide concrete suggestions for improvement, using the revision strategies in the chart.

DIFFERENTIATED INSTRUCTION

FOR STRUGGLING WRITERS

Organization To help students organize their ideas, provide the following framework for them:

Introduction

- Clearly identify the subjects or the two literary works.
- State your controlling idea (see page 499).

Body (number of points will vary)

- Name the first subject or literary work.

    —Present the first point of comparison, and give examples from the first subject.

    —Present the second point of comparison, and give examples from the first subject.

- Name the second subject or literary work.

    —Present the first point of comparison, and give examples from the second subject.

    —Present the second point of comparison, and give examples from the second subject.

Concluding Section

- Restate the subjects and points of comparison.
- Summarize the points.

Practice and Apply

ANALYZE A STUDENT DRAFT

Read this draft; notice its strengths as well as suggestions for improvement.

COMMON CORE

W 5 Develop and strengthen writing as needed by revising, editing, rewriting, or trying a new approach.

Defying Death: "The Interlopers" and "Two Friends"
by Jason Wilkes, Leyden High School

❶ How can people find meaning in life when death could come at any time? The experiences of characters in the short stories "The Interlopers" by Saki and "Two Friends" by Guy de Maupassant offer insights into this question. The two stories convey a similar message about death and fate. Their portrayals of this theme are very different, however.

❷ The relationships between the characters in the two stories are totally dissimilar, at least at the beginning of each story. Ulrich von Gradwitz and Georg Znaeym in "The Interlopers" are inheritors of a family land dispute and share a deep, lifelong hatred: "as boys they had thirsted for one another's blood, as men each prayed that misfortune might fall on the other." Von Gradwitz jealously guards the land, hoping to find his enemy illegally hunting there and thus be justified in killing him.

❸ In "Two Friends," on the other hand, Morissot and Sauvage share a deep friendship. They met while fishing and "understood each other perfectly . . . because their tastes were so alike and their feelings identical." Their relationship endures, even though they know little of each other's lives and have no contact beyond their shared hobby.

❹ In both stories the bond between characters grows. The pairs of characters undergo very different experiences, however. In "The Interlopers" the two enemies tramp through the forest, Znaeym hunting for game and von Gradwitz hunting for Znaeym. The characters in "Two Friends," in contrast, meet accidentally in the street. Overjoyed to see each other after a long separation they decide to go fishing, ignoring the fact that their country is at war.

> The **introduction** hooks the audience with a question and identifies the **subjects** that will be compared and contrasted. The compelling idea, or general focus of the essay, is spelled out in the **controlling idea.**

> To support his point about the characters' hatred, Jason provides a **quotation** and concrete **details** from the text.

> Jason uses a clear **point-by-point structure** to organize his discussion.

> Jason needs to check his use of introductory phrases to determine whether commas would help make his sentences clearer.

LEARN HOW Use Commas after Introductory Phrases Jason begins several sentences in paragraph 4 with introductory phrases. The short prepositional phrases he uses do not need punctuation because the meaning is clear without it. However, Jason needs to insert a comma after the participial phrase that begins the final sentence to avoid confusing readers.

JASON'S REVISION TO PARAGRAPH ❹

Overjoyed to see each other after a long separation, they decide to go fishing, . . .

ANALYZE A STUDENT DRAFT

Explain that the Student Draft on this page is the first half of a comparison-contrast essay. Model reading the draft and the annotations in blue, and explain that the yellow highlighting illustrates the student's language choices. Explain that the following *Learn How* mini-lessons include helpful information about ways to improve this student draft as well as their own.

LEARN HOW Use Commas after Introductory Phrases

- Explain that introductory phrases provide sentence variety and help make essays more interesting to read. Point out that introductory phrases can be prepositional phrases or participial phrases.

- Tell students that an example of a prepositional phrase from the Student Model is "In both stories" (paragraph 4). This short prepositional phrase does not need a comma, as the meaning is clear without it. Then have students review the student writer's revisions of paragraph 4.

- Have students think about whether the student writer's use of introductory phrases is effective. Then ask them to think of another type of phrase that the writer might have used in the sentence.

- Have students identify places in their drafts where they can add an introductory phrase and revise sentences in which introductory phrases need commas.

ANALYZE A STUDENT DRAFT *continued*

Explain that the Student Draft is continued and completed on this page. Read the draft and annotations aloud, and discuss them. Ask students to comment on the student writer's use of a variety of sentence structures.

 LEARN HOW Use Transitional Phrases

- Explain that a common mistake students make when writing comparison-contrast essays is forgetting to use transitions to connect ideas.

- Point out that the transitional phrase added by the student writer—"in sharp contrast"—clarifies the contrast in ideas between paragraphs 5 and 6.

- Have students place asterisks next to places in their drafts that can be strengthened by adding transitional phrases.

YOUR TURN Ask students to complete the **Your Turn** activity independently. Remind students to find places in their essays where they can effectively use commas after introductory and transitional phrases.

For interactive revision tools, see

 WriteSmart CD-ROM

Writing Center on **thinkcentral.com**

ANALYZE A STUDENT DRAFT *continued*

5 These dissimilar experiences nevertheless lead to all four characters' deaths—deaths that are shocking and unexpected. In "The Interlopers" von Gradwitz and Znaeym meet just as a violent storm erupts. Before they can kill each other, a tree falls on them both. Realizing that they are both doomed unless someone comes to find them, von Gradwitz offers Znaeym an end to their feud and a pledge of friendship. Znaeym accepts and together they shout for help. As they await their death from approaching wolves, the bonds of their hatred have turned to friendship.

> Jason uses a **variety of sentence structures.** Two sentences begin with prepositional phrases (one short and one long), and one with a participial phrase. The third sentence opens with a dependent clause.

6 The relationship between Morissot and Sauvage in "Two Friends" is consistent throughout the story. While the two are fishing, Prussian soldiers capture them. In the end neither speaks because neither wants to betray the other. The soldiers shoot them both. The two men die together, victims of the same fate as von Gradwitz and Znaeym in "The Interlopers."

> Jason turns from a discussion of the characters in "The Interlopers" to an examination of the characters in "Two Friends." A transitional phrase would help mark this shift and make the contrast between the stories clearer.

7 In these short stories Saki and Maupassant present different pairs of characters with different lives who unexpectedly meet the end that comes to us all eventually—death. Both authors seem to be saying that in a world full of natural or political enemies all people have is each other. Through friendship we can defy death. Friends help us find meaning in life.

> The **concluding section** summarizes key points and offers an insightful observation about life, death, and friendship.

LEARN HOW Use Transitional Phrases To show how the ideas in paragraph 6 contrast with those in paragraph 5, Jason adds a transitional phrase.

JASON'S REVISION TO PARAGRAPH 6

 In sharp contrast,
The relationship between Morissot and Sauvage in "Two Friends" is consistent throughout the story.

YOUR TURN Use the feedback from your peers and teacher as well as the two "Learn How" lessons to revise, rewrite, or try a new approach to your essay as needed. Evaluate how well you conveyed your controlling idea and addressed what is most significant for your specific purpose and audience.

DIFFERENTIATED INSTRUCTION

FOR ENGLISH LANGUAGE LEARNERS

Comprehension: Transitional Words and Phrases Be sure students understand the concept of compare and contrast. Use this activity to illustrate how transitions can be used within and between paragraphs to point out **similarities** and **differences**:

1. Hold up pictures of two different men.

2. Use words and phrases such as *both, in addition to, instead,* and *but* to model a series of sentences that compare and contrast the men.

Both men are happy to be neighbors. *(similarity)*

In addition to being neighbors, they are friends. *(similarity)*

They **also** play in a tournament together. *(similarity)*

On the other hand, the men's daily lives are different. *(difference)*

Bob has one child, **but** Michael has three. *(difference)*

Michael works on his home computer **instead** of driving to work. *(difference)*

Editing and Publishing

COMMON CORE
W 2c Use transitions to clarify the relationships among ideas.
W 5 Strengthen writing by editing.
L 1 Demonstrate command of the conventions of standard English grammar and usage. L 1a Use parallel structure.

In the editing stage, you proofread your essay to make sure that it is free of grammar, spelling, usage, and punctuation errors. Mistakes can distract and confuse your audience about the points you want to make.

GRAMMAR IN CONTEXT: PARALLELISM

Using stylistic elements such as parallel structure can help you clarify and emphasize ideas in your essay. **Parallel structure** refers to words, phrases, and sentences with the same grammatical form. Expressing related ideas in a similar way makes your writing more balanced and effective.

Examine these examples of parallel structure in Jason's draft:

> "... *as boys* they had thirsted ... *as men* each prayed ..."
>
> [parallel words]

> In "The Interlopers" the two enemies tramp through the forest, Znaeym **hunting for game** and von Gradwitz **hunting for Znaeym.**
>
> [parallel phrases]

As Jason edits his essay, he sees an opportunity to use parallel structure to strengthen his concluding section.

> *Through friendship we can*
> Through friendship we can defy death. ~~Friends help us find meaning in life.~~
> ˄

PUBLISH YOUR WRITING

Think about how you might share your comparison-contrast essay with an audience. Here are some options:

- Organize a group discussion in which you and several classmates talk about your interpretations of the essay.
- Use your essay to prepare a computer slide presentation for an interested local organization or group.
- Submit your essay to an online literary magazine or your school newspaper.

YOUR TURN Correct any errors in your essay. Develop and strengthen the writing as needed. Use commas where needed in contrasting expressions and after introductory phrases. Apply stylistic elements such as parallel structure, where appropriate, to bring balance to your writing. Then, publish your essay for your audience.

Editing and Publishing

COMMON CORE   W 2c, W 5, L 1, L 1a

GRAMMAR IN CONTEXT: PARALLELISM

Remind students that parallel structure refers to the words, phrases, and sentences with the same grammatical form. For practice, have students rewrite the following sentences using parallel structure.

- Death can be shocking. Death can be unexpected. Death can be unwelcome. *[Death can be shocking, unexpected, and unwelcome.]*
- Morissot and Sauvage were concerned with saving their friendship. Protecting each other was also important to them. *[Morissot and Sauvage were concerned with saving their friendship. Morissot and Sauvage were concerned with protecting each other.]*

PUBLISH YOUR WRITING

Brainstorm with students about additional ways to publish their comparison-contrast essays.

YOUR TURN Allow students time to proofread their drafts. Remind them to check for correct comma usage with contrasting expressions and introductory phrases. Also remind students to use parallel structure in their essays to strengthen the balance of their writing.

FOR ENGLISH LANGUAGE LEARNERS

Parallelism: Provide students with several examples and non-examples of parallel structure. Discuss why each one is or is not parallel.

Parallel: Seeing is believing.

Not: Seeing something will make you believe it.

Parallel: Waste not, want not.

Not: Do not waste, so you have what you want.

Parallel: To live is to love.

Not: All living people love.

FOR STRUGGLING WRITERS

Writing: Concluding Section Provide students with sentence frames such as these to help them revise their concluding sections.

- The two subjects I compare are _____ and _____.
- I sum up my ideas by _____.
- I want the audience to think about _____.

Scoring Rubric

Tell students that the best way to understand a scoring rubric is to use it to score actual writing. Provide the class with copies of a student's essay with the student's name removed. Work as a class to evaluate the essay by using the scoring rubric. Have students score the essay and write a brief paragraph using the language of the scoring guide to explain the reasons for their score.

For Rubric Bank, see

WriteSmart CD-ROM

Writing Center on **thinkcentral.com**

Assess and Reteach

Assess

R **RESOURCE MANAGER**—Copy Master
Rubric for Evaluation p. 134

Online Essay Scoring on **thinkcentral.com**

Reteach

Level Up Online Tutorials on **thinkcentral.com**
Reteaching Worksheets on **thinkcentral.com**

Writing Lesson 9: Revising for Parallelism

Writing Lesson 14: Writing a Controlling Idea

Scoring Rubric

Use the rubric below to evaluate your comparison-contrast essay from the Writing Workshop or your response to the on-demand task on the next page.

COMPARISON-CONTRAST ESSAY

SCORE	COMMON CORE TRAITS
6	• **Development** Has an engaging introduction; includes a controlling idea with an insightful analysis of similarities and differences between subjects; supports key points with relevant evidence; ends powerfully • **Organization** Arranges ideas in an effective, logical order; uses varied transitions to create cohesion and link ideas • **Language** Consistently maintains a formal style and objective tone; uses precise language; shows strong command of conventions
5	• **Development** Has an effective introduction; provides a controlling idea with an original analysis of similarities and differences between subjects; supports key points with evidence; has a strong concluding section • **Organization** Arranges ideas logically; uses transitions to link ideas • **Language** Maintains a formal style and objective tone; uses precise language; has a few errors in conventions
4	• **Development** Has an introduction that could be more engaging; includes a controlling idea that clearly states similarities and differences; could use more evidence; ends adequately • **Organization** Arranges ideas logically; could vary transitions more • **Language** Mostly maintains a formal style and objective tone; needs more precise language at times; has a few errors in conventions
3	• **Development** Has an adequate, though not memorable, introduction; has a controlling idea with an obvious statement about similarities and differences between subjects; lacks sufficient support; has a routine concluding section • **Organization** Reflects some flaws in organization; needs more transitions • **Language** Frequently lapses into an informal style or biased tone; uses some vague word choices; has some significant errors in conventions
2	• **Development** Has a weak introduction and a controlling idea that does not relate to the writing task; lacks specific evidence; has a weak concluding section • **Organization** Has organizational flaws; lacks transitions throughout • **Language** Uses an informal style and vague language; has many errors in conventions
1	• **Development** Has no introduction or controlling idea; offers unrelated points as evidence; ends abruptly • **Organization** Includes disconnected ideas with no overall organization • **Language** Uses an inappropriate style and vague, tired language; has major problems with grammar, usage, and spelling

Preparing for Timed Writing

COMMON CORE

W 10 Write routinely over shorter time frames for a range of tasks, purposes, and audiences.

1. ANALYZE THE TASK — 5 MIN

Read the task carefully. Then, read it again, noting the words in the task that tell the type of writing, the topic, the audience, and the purpose.

WRITING TASK ↙ *Type of writing*   *Purpose* ↘

Write a short <u>article</u> for your school newspaper that <u>compares and contrasts</u>
<u>two examples of a form of entertainment, such as movies, video games, or</u> ← *Possible topics*
<u>musical performers</u> that <u>other students</u> might enjoy.
        ↖ *Audience*

2. PLAN YOUR RESPONSE — 10 MIN

Identify two movies, two video games, or two musical performers with which you are familiar. Then, use a Venn diagram to list similarities and differences between the two. Remember to consider specific aspects of the two subjects, such as characters, story line, and special effects for movies.

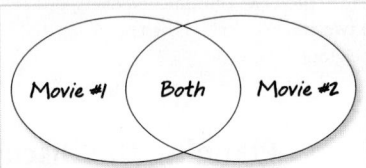

Movie #1   Both   Movie #2

3. RESPOND TO THE TASK — 20 MIN

Begin drafting your essay. Remember to use the point-by-point or block organizational structure. As you write, keep the following tips in mind:

- In the introduction, identify the subjects and include a controlling idea that gives an overall impression of the similarities and differences between the subjects.
- In the body, state several points of comparison and contrast. Support each point with relevant, well-chosen concrete details and examples.
- Your concluding section should summarize your controlling idea and close with an insight about your subjects.

4. IMPROVE YOUR RESPONSE — 5–10 MIN

Revising Compare your draft with the task. Does your draft compare and contrast two examples of a form of entertainment? Will the information help your peers determine which of the two they might enjoy more?

Proofreading Find and correct any errors in grammar, usage, punctuation, or spelling. Make sure that your article and any edits are neatly written and legible.

Checking Your Final Copy Before you submit your article, examine it once more to make sure that you are presenting your best work.

WRITING WORKSHOP   **507**

DIFFERENTIATED INSTRUCTION

FOR STRUGGLING WRITERS

Use Transitions Remind students to use transitions to help them move from one key point to the next and to point out similarities and differences in the two subjects they compare in their responses. Provide the following list of transition words and phrases for students to use in their writing: *in addition, for example, finally, in both cases, in contrast, however.* Have students think of other transitional words and phrases they might use.

COMMON CORE FOCUS

W 10 Write routinely over shorter time frames for a range of tasks, purposes, and audiences.

Preparing for Timed Writing

1. **Analyze the Task** Before students begin writing, encourage them to answer the following questions:
   - What is my time limit?
   - What are the core traits assessed in the scoring rubric?
   - Who is my audience?
   - What is my purpose?

2. **Plan Your Response** Point out to students that the scoring rubric emphasizes the importance of clearly stating the similarities and differences between subjects. Remind students to consider different aspects of the two subjects as they plan their responses.

3. **Respond to the Task** Remind students to use a clear organizational structure in the opening paragraphs of their responses. They should include examples that support their controlling ideas and an observation in their concluding sections.

4. **Improve Your Response** Point out that the scoring rubric emphasizes using effective organizational strategies. Remind students to use transitions to ensure a smooth and clear writing style.

Assess

Use the Scoring Rubric on page 506 to assess students' responses.

Focus and Motivate

COMMON CORE FOCUS

SL 1a–d Initiate and participate effectively in a range of collaborative discussions with diverse partners.

SPEAK WITH A PURPOSE

Tell students that with practice they will gain confidence in sharing their ideas in group discussions. Point out that joining a discussion group with others who are interested in comparing and contrasting the same two subjects will also help students gain confidence.

COMMON CORE TRAITS

As students prepare to participate in a group discussion, remind them to keep in mind the *COMMON CORE TRAITS* of an effective group discussion.

Practice and Apply

Planning the Discussion

Model the Skill: ASSIGN ROLES

Students may need help understanding the role of group leader. Remind students that the leader keeps the discussion going, listens to others, and encourages participation. Ask for two or three volunteers to act as participants in a model group. Model the role of the group leader by suggesting a topic or two that the group might discuss. Write those ideas on the board, and then ask the volunteers what ideas they have for topics. Write their ideas on the board, and then hold a vote to decide which topic interests the group the most.

GUIDED PRACTICE Have groups of three practice taking turns in the role of group leader. Suggest that students offer each other feedback on ways they can improve their performance as a leader. Monitor their practice and offer guidance as needed.

R RESOURCE MANAGER—Copy Master
Speaking and Listening p. 135

Speaking & Listening Workshop

Essential Course of Study **ECOS**

Participating in a Group Discussion

Participating cooperatively in a **group discussion** is a way to share information and your own ideas to get feedback. It is also an opportunity to listen to others, learn from them interactively, and build on their ideas. A group discussion about the similarities and differences of two subjects can help you and other group members understand the subjects better.

Complete the workshop activities in your **Reader/Writer Notebook**.

SPEAK WITH A PURPOSE	COMMON CORE TRAITS
TASK Participate in a **group discussion** in which you and others compare and contrast two literary works you have read in class, two consumer products, or two other subjects chosen by the group.	**PARTICIPANTS IN A GROUP DISCUSSION . . .** • come to the discussion prepared • work with peers to set rules for the discussion • pose and respond to questions that relate to the discussion • respond thoughtfully to diverse perspectives • build on each others' ideas

COMMON CORE

SL 1a–d Initiate and participate effectively in a range of collaborative discussions with diverse partners.

Planning the Discussion

Follow these suggestions to share information and plan your group discussion:

• **Form a Discussion Group** Form a group with three or more classmates who are interested in comparing and contrasting the same two subjects.

• **Assign Roles** Review the responsibilities of each group member and assign roles:

Leader:	leads group in choosing a discussion topic, keeps discussion moving, keeps track of time, and guides interaction of group members
Participant:	creates a list of main points before discussion, contributes relevant information, listens attentively, asks pertinent questions, and clarifies or elaborates on ideas
Recorder:	using the list of main points from each participant, checks off points that are discussed and takes notes, adding information or insights as needed

Speaking & Listening Online
Go to **thinkcentral.com**.
KEYWORD: HML10-508

• **Agree on Rules for the Discussion** As a group, come to a consensus regarding the discussion rules. Consider how participants will take turns speaking, and how and when alternate or opposing views will be expressed. Set clear goals for the discussion and consider whether you want to set time limits on each person's contributions.

• **Prepare to Participate** Read and research the material to be discussed. Make notes citing evidence you can use during the discussion to support your ideas or stimulate an exchange of ideas.

508 UNIT 4: THEME

DIFFERENTIATED INSTRUCTION

FOR ENGLISH LANGUAGE LEARNERS
Language: Reinforce Group Discussion Terms
Explain to students that the group discussion has the same goal as writing a comparison-contrast essay—to compare and contrast two things. Review key terms used in the Writing Workshop and in this workshop:

• *compare:* identify similarities

• *contrast:* identify differences

• *controlling idea:* the focus of an essay or discussion

• *transitions:* words or phrases that connect one idea to another

Holding the Group Discussion

PARTICIPATE ACTIVELY

Remember that to participate in a group discussion fully, you not only share your own ideas and respond to questions about them; you also listen carefully to other members of the group and ask questions when the information and ideas they present need clarification or elaboration. This two-way line of communication allows group members to interact and to build on each other's ideas. Follow these guidelines for a group discussion:

- **Get Started** The group leader should identify the topic of discussion the group has chosen and ask a general lead-in question, such as, "What are the main similarities and differences of the subjects?" The recorder should note each question and check off or add to the observations members jotted down during planning.
- **Share Information and Ideas** Respond to the question posed by the leader, referring to your notes as needed. Make any related points that support your answer.
- **Listen to Others** Take notes that summarize points of agreement and disagreement. Make new connections in light of the reasoning presented.
- **Respond and Comment Further** Respond thoughtfully and respectfully to other points of view. Pose questions that relate the discussion to larger ideas and that challenge ideas and conclusions. Incorporate others' ideas into the discussion and build on them.
- **Sum It Up** When everyone has had a chance to share their information and ideas, the group leader should ask the recorder to summarize the content of the discussion.

YOUR TURN
As a Speaker Speak clearly at an appropriate volume and speed. Maintain a respectful, cooperative tone—whether you agree or disagree with a group member.

As a Listener Listen closely to make sure you can follow each group member's ideas and supporting evidence. When you need more information, ask questions for clarification and elaboration.

509

FOR STRUGGLING STUDENTS

Conduct the Group Discussion Some students may have trouble sharing their ideas in a group. Pair these students with students who have strong discussion skills. Have the partners discuss their essays with one another. This approach will help participants better understand how to express their ideas and participate actively in a group discussion.

Holding the Group Discussion

Model the Skill: PARTICIPATE ACTIVELY

Point out that an effective group discussion is one in which all students are actively involved. Explain that if only a few students in a group participate, not all ideas are heard or shared. Tell students that participation by all members is important in order to build on one another's ideas. Have a conversation with a volunteer, and model for studentas how to actively participate.

GUIDED PRACTICE Have students work in pairs to practice listening to their partner's ideas and asking questions.

YOUR TURN Remind students that when participating in a group discussion, they should be respectful when they speak and be good listeners while others are talking. Explain the importance of being prepared before the discussion begins. Have groups of three practice taking turns listening and speaking.

Assess and Reteach

Assess

Use the *COMMON CORE TRAITS* to assess students' discussions.

Participants in a group discussion
- come to the discussion prepared
- work with peers to set rules for the discussion
- pose and respond to questions that relate to the discussion
- respond thoughtfully to diverse perspectives
- build on each others' ideas

Reteach

Some students may have trouble asking others to clarify or elaborate on their ideas. Suggest this sentence starter for students who need help: "I don't quite understand what you mean. Can you explain further?"

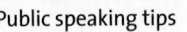

Speaking and Listening Online THINK central
- Public speaking tips
- Strategies for effective listening

Assessment Practice

RL 1 Cite textual evidence to support analysis of what the text says explicitly as well as inferences drawn from the text. **RL 2** Determine a theme of a text. **RI 1** Cite textual evidence to support analysis of what the text says explicitly as well as inferences drawn from the text. **RI 2** Determine a central idea of a text. **W 5** Strengthen writing by revising and editing. **L 6** Acquire and use accurately general academic words sufficient for reading; demonstrate independence in gathering vocabulary knowledge.

CHECK READINESS

Read aloud the paragraph under **ASSESS** and stress to students that this is not the full Unit Test, but a way for them to check their readiness for it. Then have students examine the skills standards listed under **REVIEW** and look back in the unit or in the **Student Resource Bank** for any skills they need to review.

READ THE TEXTS

Remind students to keep unit goals in mind as they read each passage, paying particular attention to these literary and reading skills:

- theme
- draw conclusions
- analyze authors' messages

To help students focus on drawing conclusions while reading, encourage them to ask questions such as

- In what way did PD's music touch people's lives?
- How are people affected by Nadja's music?

ANSWER THE QUESTIONS

Direct students to pages R93–R101 of the **Handbook** to review test-taking strategies.

Remind students to read each set of directions carefully, looking for key words. After they complete the first item, students may want to reread the directions to ensure that they understand what is being asked.

Assessment Practice

ASSESS
Taking this practice test will help you assess your knowledge of these skills and determine your readiness for the Unit Test.

REVIEW
After you take the practice test, your teacher can help you identify any standards you need to review.

COMMON CORE

RL 1 Cite textual evidence to support analysis of what the text says explicitly as well as inferences drawn from the text. **RL 2** Determine a theme of a text. **RI 1** Cite textual evidence to support analysis of what the text says explicitly as well as inferences drawn from the text. **RI 2** Determine a central idea of a text. **W 5** Strengthen writing by revising and editing. **L 6** Acquire and use accurately general academic words sufficient for reading; demonstrate independence in gathering vocabulary knowledge.

Practice Test THINK central
Take it at thinkcentral.com.
KEYWORD: HMLN10-510

DIRECTIONS Read the two selections and the viewing and representing piece. Then, answer the questions that follow.

The Heartbeat of the Soul of the World
by René Saldaña Jr.

1   On the day of PD's funeral, the sun beat down on the crowd gathered at the cemetery. A good many of us from the barrio were there. A few from the high school marching band were also in attendance. The heat made us all slouch, sweaty and heavy.

2   PD's family took up the two rows of chairs directly in front of the coffin, the lid closed for the sake of PD's mother. She had cried and cried when she heard her boy was dead. Just another night out with friends, on his way home, the officer told her. He'd got in a wreck. The other driver'd been drinking. Somehow PD's right arm had been cut off cleanly just below the elbow. His face and head misshapen but without a bruise or scratch. This last part the cop didn't tell her. She saw for herself at the morgue.

3   That night, a few hours after news of the wreck, one of the boys in Peñitas, hiding from his parents on the roof of his house, nearly fell from his perch when he heard PD's mom screaming out her dead son's name: "Ay, mi Pedro, mi Pedrito. Ay, Diosito Santo. Porqué, Diosito?" The boy thought it was La Llorona crying out for her drowned babies, and that's when he almost fell.

4   Today at the funeral, PD's mom was all cried out. All she did was grab at her chest and moan, wrinkle her face, moan some more. Times like these—the heat oppressive, your son dead—what can you do?

5   Mr. Stevens, the band director, had found a place in the very last row of chairs, not covered by the canopy. He was wearing dark sunglasses, his green tweed jacket, and he'd trimmed his scraggly red-blond beard. He was older, maybe forty-five, maybe fifty, and scrawny. He looked like he was carrying the load of the world on his skinny shoulders. He looked beaten.

6   Mr. Stevens had been hired on as an assistant director at the high school six years back, and when the old band director retired, he took over. He loved jazz and the blues, couldn't get enough of the South Texas *conjunto* music since first he'd heard it one Saturday morning on a public radio station, and had all kinds of music playing in his office and over the speakers in the band hall when class wasn't in session.

7   One day three years ago, frustrated by his students' lack of enthusiasm for the piece they were taking to competition, he stopped a rehearsal midway, pulled out a couple of LPs and a record player from his office, and said to the

---

DIFFERENTIATED INSTRUCTION

FOR ENGLISH LANGUAGE LEARNERS
Assessment Practice: Work Backward
Prepare students by having them read the questions *before* reading the passages. Have pairs find unfamiliar words in test directions and questions and follow these steps:

1. Write each word on an index card.
2. Look up the meaning in a dictionary and write it on the back of the card.
3. Use the cards to practice the words with your partner and to teach them to others.

Culture: Connect Invite Spanish-speaking students to translate the sentence spoken by PD's mom in "The Heartbeat of the Soul of the World," paragraph 3, into English. Ask students how the translation helps them to understand PD and the theme of the story. Then ask volunteers to share their knowledge of the meanings of other Spanish words in the story, such as *conjunto* and *bajo sexto*.

students, "This is Miles Davis. Listen. It's his heart and soul. He's showing you the world's core through his music. The clay and fire. He's letting you in on its secrets, every one of them. That's how you need to be playing. . . . Now listen to this. It's Coltrane. . . ." He propped up the LP covers on the chalkboard railing behind him for his students to see.

8   One kid said, "This is Black music, man. You're a gringo, we're Hispanic. What's it have to do with you? Or us?"

9   "This isn't Black music. It's not even music. It's beyond music." They all stared at their teacher blankly. "It's hard to explain," he said, "but, wait—wait right here, okay?" He left the hall, and in a few moments returned with a CD. He didn't cut Coltrane off, just turned him down. It was still there, a buzz in the corner by the trumpet section. Then Stevens played Narciso Martinez. "See?" he said after a few moments. "Now do you hear it? The secrets are here, too. Like a heaviness. Can you hear the weight in the music? It's in the *bajo sexto* and the accordion." He closed his eyes and tapped the beat on his chest.

10   Some of the band members giggled, nervous that their director had lost his mind. The same kid from before said, "You think we're Mexicans, Stevens?" Some more students laughed.

11   But not PD.

12   He was still lost on Miles and Coltrane, especially Coltrane, shutting out all the noise: the kid complaining, Melissa next to PD blowing the spit out of her trumpet, Stevens talking, the others laughing. Just Coltrane now, buzzing somewhere in the corner, a raspy river of sound. Then Narciso and his accordion joined in. PD closed his eyes and imagined Coltrane and Narciso on a stage—the one a Black guy and the other a Mexican. Just two guys on a dark stage playing a sax and an accordion; then no Coltrane and no Narciso, just their music on the stage. Their sounds swirling together, and an explosion next, then the notes showering down on PD, who was standing in the middle of the stage now, crying and laughing. How can that happen? he wondered. The music, its heaviness, in his chest, a slush of tears in there, and laughter.

13   PD got what Mr. Stevens was saying. Stevens looked at the record player like he could see these same guys on stage too.

14   "It's about the music," he said, biting at his fingernails. "It's about their souls, our souls." He let Narciso play through to the end of the song.

15   Everyone stayed quiet until the song was over, then Stevens turned it all off. But PD got it stuck in his mind. It played in his ears the rest of the day, all through English II, Algebra I, history, on up to marching practice in the afternoon heat, where he was unable to concentrate on the steps he had already

GO ON ➡️

ITEM ANALYSIS

COMPREHENSION AND WRITTEN RESPONSE	ITEMS	UNIT PAGES
Theme	2, 10, 12, 13, 15	418–425, 427, 453, 477
Symbol	1	418–425, 439
Draw Conclusions	3, 5, 6, 7, 8, 9, 19, 20, 21, 23	453
Analyze and Compare Authors' Messages	17, 18, 22	489

VOCABULARY	ITEMS	UNIT PAGES
Connotation and Denotation	4, 11, 14, 16	436

WRITING AND GRAMMAR	ITEMS	UNIT PAGES
Vary Sentence Structure	1, 2, 3, 4, 6	437, 451
Adverbs	5	473

Practice Test

On **thinkcentral.com** students can complete an interactive version of this practice test *and* receive remediation for the skills they have not yet mastered.

FOR STRUGGLING READERS

Assessment Support Consider these options for completing the Assessment Practice:

• Have students "work backward" to review the test questions *before* reading the passages.

• Select random questions in the Assessment, and have students demonstrate *how* and *where* to look for the answers.

• Ask students to locate unfamiliar vocabulary words in the Assessment. Elicit the words' meanings from the class.

• Have students record useful testing words and definitions in their journals for later reference.

• Read the selection or parts of them aloud to aid in student comprehension.

memorized, mucking it up for all of the marching band, forcing them to have to start over.

16 But Coltrane, man, he got to PD something fierce. And Narciso, too. He began to mix up the sax and the accordion. It was supposed to be Coltrane, his sound; instead, PD kept hearing the same music, Coltrane's, but coming out of Narciso's accordion. PD shook his head, and was somehow able to get through that afternoon's band practice.

17 Next day, Mr. Stevens heard music down the hall from his office, a trumpet, and for a second he thought it was somebody playing his record from yesterday. He sat on his clunky chair, heavy with the music, almost like he was drowning in a river rushing past. He got up finally, his eyes half closed as he walked, listening to the music. It was Coltrane he heard, but on a trumpet from one of the practice rooms. Stuff he'd heard before but never heard before, not quite like this, if you get what I mean. Harder, maybe like early Coltrane playing his older stuff, but on a trumpet. He walked through the empty hall. Beyond the hall. That's where it was coming from.

18 He walked to the practice rooms and saw through the glass it was PD, playing his trumpet, his back to the door, the door slightly ajar.

19 PD sitting there, his back to the world beyond the door, his head dipping to a beat.

20 Stevens imagined PD had his eyes closed, the boy's right knee rising and falling to that same beat. Then it was that Stevens noticed the boy playing the same song over and over, what he'd played to the students yesterday, and with it something else mixed in, that harder primal sound—those're the only words he could use to try to explain to himself the boy's playing: hard, base, basic, primal, crude, original, the world's soul exposed. He heard the accordion coming out of this boy's trumpet, and a sax. This boy, third-chair trumpet, a sophomore, good enough at playing and marching, not exceptional, but just good enough. Stevens couldn't understand this boy's playing right now.

21 Then PD turned, his trumpet on his lap, and looked at Stevens. "Sorry. I should go." PD had decided to skip English II. He began to put away his horn. "What's that you were playing? I mean, I know what it is, but . . ." He looked over PD's shoulder. "Where's your sheet music?"

22 "No sheet music. Playing from memory."

23 "From yesterday?"

24 The boy nodded.

25 "But it was such a short moment. You couldn't have—"

26 "It was long enough. That John Coltrane is good. And Narciso Martinez, also. You wouldn't think that they're so much alike, that they can say the same thing to you, being different like they are. But . . ."

27 "Yeah, you wouldn't know it at all. I mean to say, *most* people wouldn't know it. But you got it."

512

FOR ENGLISH LANGUAGE LEARNERS

Assessment Vocabulary Write these literary terms from the Assessment items on the board, and review them with students:

- *theme:* an underlying message about life or human nature that a writer wants a reader to understand

- *flashback:* an account of a conversation, an episode, or an event that happened before the beginning of a story. Often a flashback interrupts the chronological flow of a story to give the reader information needed to understand a character's present situation.

- *symbol:* a person, a place, an object, or an activity that stands for something beyond itself. For example, doves symbolize peace, and acorns symbolize growth.

28   "I think so."

29   PD clasped shut his instrument case and left the band hall. Mr. Stevens walked back to his office, all the while shaking his head.

30   Two or three days later, Stevens loaned several CDs to PD. Some more jazz, some blues, a bit of classical, something that sounded foreign to PD, maybe Jewish. Lots more stuff. But PD didn't have a CD player, so he took one from a teacher's room, and he listened to all the music at home. For a week he kept the player and the music, and he couldn't sleep hardly. Then, before hopping on the bus to go to an away football game with the band that Friday afternoon, he handed back the music to Mr. Stevens. "Thanks," he said. Earlier, he'd snuck back to that teacher's room and replaced the CD player, right where he'd found it.

31   The following Monday, Mr. Stevens asked PD, "So? What did you think?"

32   "It's so clear. They're all telling me the same thing."

33   "What's that?"

34   "It's about suffering. More than that—the struggle. But the overcoming it too. I could hear the heaviness. It weighs a ton, man."

35   The two became fast friends. Dig it—an old white dude and a young Chicano kid. Who would've thought? I'm not saying they hung out at lunchtime or dared each other to go steal a soda from the corner store, or talked in secret about their girlfriends. Seeing them in class, you wouldn't even guess they knew each other except for in the band hall, as teacher and student. Stevens didn't promote PD to first chair, and PD didn't call Mr. Stevens by his first name, not in private, and definitely not in public. But they were good friends, the best.

36   PD's senior year, Stevens got PD a gig. That's what he called it, a gig. At some cafe downtown in McAllen. PD had been working on some of his own stuff this last year—Indio Blues, he called it. That night at the cafe, Stevens played a bit of the bass guitar—*toam-tum-tum*—a heartbeat that vibrated just underneath the tiled floor all the way to PD's feet, then up his legs and spine; and soon his own heart matched the tempo of the bass.

37   He was nervous—the lights all on him, his stomach vibrating from Stevens's bass—so he closed his eyes, put his trumpet to his lips, and played. Man, the first set he dragged out for close to a half hour, nonstop. But it wasn't the same song for that long. He'd take a deep breath and change directions, and Stevens had to play catch-up. When PD finished, Stevens stopped—dead cold, in the middle of some riff he was on; but it worked. You know how it is—you come to the end when the end comes. That's that.

38   PD was exhausted after two more sets just like the first one—sweaty, drooping at the shoulders, but blowing his Indio Blues solid, all the way through to the end.

FOR STRUGGLING READERS

Assessment Practice: Remind students of these test-taking tips:

- Read the directions carefully. Look at the passages and questions to get an overview of what is expected.

- Tackle the questions one at a time rather than thinking about the whole test.

- Refer back to the reading selections as needed.

39   Then he played every weekend at different places. Stevens backing him up, but most times he'd just quit playing the bass and listen. That's how good this kid was. Nobody cried because of his playing. He didn't bring people to their knees. Nobody fainted. But they heard it was their song he was playing, some people looking around to see if the others knew their secrets were being exposed in the notes. Embarrassed. But every one of them, their hearts in their throats. Happy and sad all at once.

40   This week, we lost—the bunch of us—we lost something of his music in PD's passing. Each of us some different note of his, but each just as heavy.

41   This afternoon, Stevens, under his sunglasses, cried. So did PD's family and friends. They cried because he was gone—no more of his early morning practicing on his horn, waking everybody in the whole house, in the entire neighborhood. Stevens cried because he'd heard PD play that first time in the band hall. He'd played behind him at the coffeehouses in town. Now, Stevens heard only the memory of the sound, reverberating, a buzz, the heartbeat of the soul of the world. His shoulders shaking under the load of it all. He cried, wondering if the memory was enough.

42   This afternoon, at the cemetery, the sun pounded down something fierce. A trying heat—and there was no tent big enough to keep it off us all.

514

The Power of Music

by Nadja Salerno-Sonnenberg
from **Nadja on My Way**

1   This is something I know for a fact: You have to work hardest for the thing you love the most. And when it's music that you love, you're in for the fight of your life.

2   It starts when your blood fills with music and you know you can't live without it. Every day brings a challenge to learn as much possible and to play even better than you did the day before.

3   You may want to achieve fame and glory, or you may want to play for fun. But whenever you fall in love with music, you'll never sit still again.

4   Music is more important than we will ever know. Great music can pull you right out of your chair. It can make you cry, or laugh, or feel a way you've never felt before. It can make you remember the first person you loved . . . Music has that power.

5   Just imagine a world without music. What would you whistle when you walked down the street? How could you make a movie? How could you have a ball game without an organist leading the crowd when you're down by a run in the ninth?

6   You could be the most successful doctor in the world, but if you never turn on the radio, never go to a concert, never sing in the shower, never see *The King and I*[1]—then you can't be a total, fulfilled human being. It's impossible.

7   When you realize how vital music is, you realize a musician's fight is quite a noble, heroic endeavor. It didn't always seem that way to me. There was a time, years ago, when I felt discouraged and it seemed selfish to put so much time into music. Being a musician didn't seem as useful to others as being a surgeon, or even a good politician.

8   But I came to understand that it's a great, great gift to help people forget their everyday life and be uplifted. And better than uplifted, to be inspired; that's what music can do. It's important to us all, and I'm proud to put mind and muscle into recording, concerts, teaching, and studying: into being a musician.

---

1. **The King and I:** well-known American musical and one of the most widely performed shows in the musical theater. A movie version was made in the 1950s.

515

9   Emotionally, music has brought me an enormous amount of joy and an enormous amount of despair and frustration. Because of music, I have learned what a battle is. I've won most, but not all—not by a long shot.

10   It's a reward to see people affected at my concerts and, after concerts, hearing from them. Mothers have come backstage and said, "My son saw you on TV and he decided to play the violin."

11   During a master class in Aspen, a young girl played the Bruch G minor Concerto for me. I had played the Bruch there, and she played it exactly the way I did. I was thrilled and embarassedly happy to have affected a young violinist in that way.

12   Yet I will never feel satisfied because there are always many goals ahead. Some days I can't believe I've come as far as I have—and how much farther I want to go.

13   I wrote this book about my life work, and this book may also be about yours. Being a musician is never easy. It takes guts or stupidity to walk onstage and play the violin. You may have a bad day in front of thousands.

14   No matter what happens through your life, though, the music is always there. Friends can run away, but Brahms never will.

15   And he's listening.

The World Comes to you

Music Festival

July 13–15
Stanton Park
12–9 pm

Admission
Adults $12
Children $5

Get your groove on to the music of cultures from around the world
How does music affect culture? How does culture affect music?

Hear The Music ◆ Feel The Beat

LATIN SAMBA   *Indie Rock*

Celtic   *Bunggul*   Polka
    Reggae   & much more

✳ World Music ✳
World Food ✳ World Fun
in a World Class Festival

Brought to you
by the World Travelers Society

517

DIFFERENTIATED INSTRUCTION

FOR ENGLISH LANGUAGE LEARNERS

Have students study the Visual before answering Reading Comprehension items 19 and 20. Suggest they ask themselves: Who made and who sponsored the flyer? What is the flyer's purpose? Who is the target audience? What messages are communicated?

ANSWERS

Reading Comprehension

Model a thinking process for answering multiple-choice questions.

1. **A is correct.** *Throughout the selection, the author discusses and shares the different ways that music touches and affects people. B, C, and D are incorrect because the words do not make sense when substituted for* heartbeat *in the title.*

2. **C is correct.** *The text gives examples of ways music crosses cultural barriers. A is incorrect. Although driving and drinking are mentioned at the beginning of the text, that is not one of the themes. B is incorrect because the message is not about the school band. D is incorrect because the story is about the effects of music on people, not the friendships.*

3. **D is correct.** *The author's use of a flashback allows the reader to understand the importance of PD's music to the people around him. A is incorrect because the reader knows what more than one character is thinking. B is incorrect because the reader is already aware of PD's death, which is told at the beginning of the text. C is incorrect because although the author seems to enjoy jazz music, this is not the reason for the flashback.*

4. **B is correct.** *The word* barrio *in Spanish means "neighborhood." A, C and D are incorrect because these are not the meanings of* barrio.

5. **B is correct.** *Mr. Stevens energizes his students by playing music CDs for them. A is incorrect because although Mr. Stevens does tell the students stories about great players, this is not how he excites them. C and D are incorrect because he does not do either of these things.*

6. **D is correct.** *In paragraph 9, Mr. Stevens tells the students, "The secrets are here, too. Like a heaviness. Can you hear the weight in the music?" A is incorrect because although Mr. Stevens might feel that jazz is the greatest form of music, this is not the reason for his explanation. B is incorrect because it is only a detail shared by Mr. Stevens. C is incorrect because although this is stated in paragraph 9, Mr. Stevens says this only to explain that music carries weight, or depth.*

Reading Comprehension

Use "The Heartbeat of the Soul of the World" (pp. 510–514) to answer questions 1–11.

1. The word "heartbeat" in the title refers to —
   A. music
   B. soul
   C. friends
   D. the world

2. One of the themes of this story is —
   A. driving and drinking don't mix well
   B. being in the school band is fun
   C. music crosses cultural barriers
   D. friends matter

3. The author's use of a flashback to tell the story —
   A. lets readers know what one character is thinking
   B. hints at what is about to happen
   C. persuades readers to enjoy jazz music
   D. lends greater significance to the events from the past

4. In paragraph 1, the word *barrio* means —
   A. church
   B. neighborhood
   C. school
   D. town

5. In paragraph 7, Mr. Stevens excites his band students about music by —
   A. telling them stories about great players
   B. playing jazz by Miles Davis and John Coltrane for them
   C. dismissing class early
   D. making them practice longer

6. In paragraphs 7–9, Mr. Stevens tries to explain to his students that —
   A. jazz is the greatest form of music
   B. music is made of clay and fire
   C. playing certain instruments adds weight to music
   D. music can help people feel the world's secrets

7. When PD hears the music in paragraph 12, he imagines —
   A. John Coltrane and Narciso Martinez playing together
   B. himself on stage being cheered by an audience
   C. himself writing music
   D. the band performing this music in competition

8. When Mr. Stevens finds PD playing the trumpet in paragraphs 17–25, he —
   A. is angry that PD is not in class
   B. is surprised that PD can play the song after hearing it only once
   C. thinks about getting PD a gig
   D. scolds PD for making mistakes in band practice the day before

9. A few days after Mr. Stevens first plays John Coltrane for the class he gives PD —
   A. sheet music for the songs he had played
   B. a CD player
   C. a trumpet and an accordion
   D. a variety of CDs, including jazz and classical

518

7. **A is correct.** *In paragraph 12, PD imagines John Coltrane and Narciso Martinez on the same stage, playing together. B is incorrect because PD can see himself on the stage crying and laughing but no audience cheering him. C and D are incorrect because they were not stated in the text.*

8. **B is correct.** *Mr. Stevens states, "But it was such a short moment. You couldn't have—." This statement indicates that he is surprised that PD can play the song after hearing it only once. A is incorrect because*

Mr. Stevens is not angry. C is incorrect. Although this does end up happening later in the text, Mr. Stevens does not immediately get PD a gig after he finds him playing. D is incorrect because Mr. Stevens does not scold PD.

9. **D is correct.** *In paragraph 30, Mr. Stevens loans PD some CDs. A is incorrect because this is not stated in the text. B is incorrect because PD borrows a CD player from a teacher, not from Mr. Stevens. C is incorrect because this does not happen in the text.*

10. In paragraphs 32–34, PD tells Mr. Stevens that the music tells him —
  A. about suffering and overcoming it
  B. about joy and happiness
  C. about love
  D. about why music matters

11. In paragraph 36 the word *gig* means —
  A. computer memory
  B. a dance
  C. a chance to play
  D. part of a band uniform

Use "The Power of Music" (pp. 515–516) to answer questions 12–16.

12. One of the main ideas of this article is that —
  A. music enriches life
  B. the author is a great musician
  C. people don't practice music enough
  D. you have to practice if you want to be good

13. One assumption the author of the article makes is that —
  A. great music is emotional
  B. *The King and I* is the worst musical ever
  C. only musicians work hard for the thing they love most
  D. there is music in everyone's life

14. In paragraph 6, the word *fulfilled* means —
  A. carried out
  B. complete
  C. mature
  D. successful

15. The author believes that music can —
  A. inspire people
  B. tell a story
  C. teach new things
  D. improve math skills

16. In paragraph 9, the word *frustration* means the opposite of —
  A. difficulty
  B. hardship
  C. perfection
  D. satisfaction

Use "The Heartbeat of the Soul of the World" and "The Power of Music" to answer questions 17–18.

17. PD and the author of "The Power of Music" would agree that music is —
  A. always fun
  B. a hobby
  C. life itself
  D. a chore

18. Why might music sometimes frustrate PD and the author of "The Power of Music"?
  A. Their families do not always appreciate their playing.
  B. People do not always pay them enough.
  C. Practice and performing interfere with other things they want to do.
  D. They can't always make music that says what they want it to say.

GO ON

519

10. A is correct. In paragraph 34, PD states, "It's about suffering. More than that—the struggle. But the overcoming it too." B, C, and D are incorrect because these emotions are not mentioned in paragraphs 32–34.

11. C is correct. The word gig means "a musical performance." A is incorrect because although gig is a term that also has a technical meaning, it is not the meaning used in paragraph 36. B and D are incorrect because they are not meanings for gig.

12. A is correct. The emotions and feelings the author shares, such as "you know you can't live without it," allude to the point that music enriches, or enhances, life. B and D are incorrect because they are details, not the main idea. C is incorrect because this is not stated in the text.

13. D is correct. In paragraphs 5–6, the author provides scenarios in which people need music in their lives. A is incorrect because although the author may feel that great music is emotional, this is not an assumption that is stated in the text. B is incorrect because the author feels that The King and I is a musical that everyone must see. C is incorrect because the author mentions other careers that require hard work.

14. B is correct. The definition of fulfilled as it is used in paragraph 6 is "complete." A, C, and D are incorrect because these are not the meanings of fulfilled as it is used in paragraph 6.

15. A is correct. In paragraph 8, the author states "I came to understand that it's a great, great gift to help people forget their everyday life and be uplifted. And better than uplifted, to be inspired." B is incorrect because although the author might feel that music tells a story, this is not supported by the details in the text. C and D are incorrect because they are not supported by details in the text.

16. D is correct. The meaning of frustration is "dissatisfaction." So, the opposite meaning of frustration is "satisfaction." A and B are incorrect because they are synonyms for the word frustration. C is incorrect because perfection is not an antonym of frustration.

17. C is correct. Details provided in both selections support the statement that music is "life itself." A is incorrect because in "The Power of Music," the author talks about working hard and being "in for the fight of your life." B is incorrect because both people feel that music is not simply "a hobby." D is incorrect because both people enjoy music, thus, they do not see it as "a chore."

18. D is correct. Both talk about how people respond to their music and how it affects them. The musicians try to get it right, but in "The Power of Music," the author mentions that sometimes that doesn't happen. A is incorrect because in both selections people supported both PD and the author of "The Power of Music." B is incorrect because pay is not mentioned in either selection. C is incorrect because playing music was the most important thing in both of their lives.

19. D is correct. *The visual shows that people all over the world listen to music. This is supported by the various kinds of music listed on the bottom of the flyer. A is incorrect because the visual does not support "the smallness of the world." B is incorrect because the illustration does not indicate that world music is changing. C is incorrect because although many people might say that the world is a small place, this is not the reason the designer chose the illustration.*

20. A is correct. *The flyer asks how music and culture interact and affect each other. B, C, and D are incorrect because they are not supported by the illustration or by the text on the flyer.*

SHORT CONSTRUCTED RESPONSE

Possible responses:

21. *Everyone lost PD's talent and his music. In paragraph 40, the writer states, "This week, we lost—the bunch of us—we lost something of his music in PD's passing." People who had heard him play in the coffeehouses around town realized that he was playing about them. Now that is gone, and his family and friends, especially Mr. Stevens, have to rely on their memories of PD's playing and wonder if that will be enough.*

22. *The mixture of facts and opinions in the selection strengthens the author's case that music is the most important thing in life. The author wants readers to see how deeply music affects people by giving examples of how people react to it. Also, she specifically talks about how some people responded to her music.*

23. *The third-person point of view in "The Heartbeat of the Soul of the World" is effective because it allows the reader to experience the emotions the characters felt when they lost their friend. Further, PD's music influenced those around him and the people who heard him play in the coffeehouses. The first-person point of view in "The Power of Music" is effective in its own way. The message the author is trying to convey is one of personal feelings and thus, telling the story in first-person achieves this goal best.*

> **Use the visual representation on page 517 to answer questions 19–20.**

19. The designer of this flyer most likely chose the illustration —
   A. to illustrate the smallness of the world
   B. to emphasize the changing nature of world music
   C. to show that the world is a small place
   D. to show that people all over the world listen to music

20. One purpose of the festival is to explore —
   A. how music and culture interact
   B. how music affects politics
   C. how music is created
   D. how to use music in movies

SHORT CONSTRUCTED RESPONSE
Write a short response to each question, using text evidence to support your response.

21. What has been lost with PD's death? Support your response with evidence from the text.

22. What is the effect of the author's use of both opinions and facts in "The Power of Music"? Use text evidence to support your response.

Write a short response to the following question, using text evidence from both selections to support your response.

23. What impact does the point of view have in "The Heartbeat of the Soul of the World" and "The Power of Music"? Support your response with evidence from **both** texts.

DIFFERENTIATED INSTRUCTION

FOR ENGLISH LANGUAGE LEARNERS

Assessment Vocabulary To help students better understand Reading Comprehension items 13 and 19, teach or review these key vocabulary words:

- *assumption:* a statement accepted as true without proof

- *designer:* someone who invents, conceives, or arranges

- *flyer:* a circular for mass distribution

Revising and Editing

DIRECTIONS Read this passage, and answer the questions that follow.

> (1) The landscape around us tell a story. (2) The rocks they examine are hundreds of millions of years old. (3) Geologists study the origin, its history, and the earth's structure. (4) Some hills and valleys have been around for a shorter period of time. (5) Just 10,000 years ago, mile-thick glaciers scraped away everything in their path, creating large basins. (6) Glaciers are enormous, slow-moving sheets of ice. (7) The glaciers melted and filled the basins with water. (8) The most recent glacier's formed the Great Lakes.

1. What change, if any, should be made to sentence 1?
   A. Change *landscape* to **landscapes**
   B. Change *story* to **stories**
   C. Change *tell* to **tells**
   D. Make no change

2. What is the most effective way to improve the organization of the paragraph?
   A. Move sentence 1 to follow sentence 2
   B. Move sentence 2 to follow sentence 3
   C. Move sentence 3 to follow sentence 4
   D. Move sentence 8 to the beginning of the paragraph

3. How should sentence 3 be revised to create parallel structure?
   A. Geologists study the original, history, and the earth's structure.
   B. Geologists' earth study includes the origin, historical, and structures.
   C. Geologists study origins, history, and the structure of the earth.
   D. Geologists study the earth's origin, its history, and its structure.

4. Which transition should be added to the beginning of sentence 4?
   A. For example,   C. However,
   B. Obviously,   D. And,

5. What is the most effective way to revise sentence 5 to include an adverb?
   A. Just 10,000 years ago, wide, mile-thick glaciers scraped away everything in their path, creating large basins.
   B. Just 10,000 years ago, mile-thick glaciers scraped away everything in their broad path, creating large basins.
   C. Just 10,000 years ago, mile-thick glaciers relentlessly scraped away everything in their path, creating large basins.
   D. Just 10,000 years ago, mile-thick glaciers scraped away almost everything in their path, creating large basins.

6. What change, if any, should be made to sentence 8?
   A. Insert a comma after **recent**
   B. Change *glacier's* to **glaciers**
   C. Change *Great* to **great**
   D. Change *Lakes* to **lakes**

 STOP

521

Revising and Editing

1. **C is correct.** The verb tell needs to change to tells for the sentence to have proper subject-verb agreement. A is incorrect because there is only one landscape around us at a given time. B is incorrect because it would not be grammatically correct to have the singular article a before a plural noun. D is incorrect because there is a change needed to the sentence.

2. **B is correct.** By moving sentence 2 to follow sentence 3, the organization of the paragraph is smoother, and the reader knows who "they" refers to in sentence 2. A, C, and D are incorrect because moving them to different places would not improve the paragraph's organization.

3. **D is correct.** Each singular noun is preceded by a possessive. A is incorrect because the word original does not make sense in the context. B is incorrect because "earth study" is awkward and "origin, historical, and structures" are not parallel. C is incorrect because "origins" is plural while history and structure are singular.

4. **C is correct.** The transition shows connection and contrast to the idea about the age of the rocks. A is incorrect because "shorter periods of time" is not an example of "millions of years." B is incorrect because it does not make sense in the sentence. D is incorrect because sentence 4 is not a continuation of the thought in sentence 3.

5. **C is correct.** The adverb relentlessly modifies the verb scraped. A, B, and D are incorrect because they have additional adjectives—wide, broad, and almost—not adverbs.

6. **B is correct.** Glacier's is a possessive noun and needs to be changed to glaciers, a plural noun. A is incorrect because a comma is not needed after recent. C and D are incorrect because Great Lakes is a proper noun.

RL 10 Read and comprehend literature. **RI 10** Read and comprehend literary nonfiction.

INTRODUCE *GREAT READS*

In Unit 4, students have discussed a number of big questions. Invite students to tell which question they found most intriguing and why, and then focus attention on the three that appear on this page. Discuss the recommended books and their summaries, pointing out how each connects to the related question. Encourage students to choose one or more of these "great reads" to read independently.

UNIT 4
Great Reads

Ideas for Independent Reading

Which questions in Unit 4 did you wish you could examine further? These books can help you extend your explorations.

COMMON CORE

RL 10 Read and comprehend literature. **RI 10** Read and comprehend literary nonfiction.

What would you do for a friend?

Of Mice and Men
by John Steinbeck

Farm workers George and Lennie are best friends in Depression-era California. George protects Lennie, who is bigger and stronger but mentally slow. They drift from job to job, dreaming of buying their own farm, but circumstances shatter their dreams.

Gilgamesh
trans. by Stephen Mitchell

This is a new English translation of the world's oldest book. Gilgamesh, the powerful, arrogant king of Uruk, is humanized through his close friendship with Enkidu. When Enkidu is killed, Gilgamesh sets out on a quest to find immortality.

Four Spirits
by Sena Jeter Naslund

This novel looks at a 1963 Birmingham, Alabama, church bombing through the eyes of several characters, including a black woman and a white woman who become good friends as they work in the civil rights movement.

Who are the victims of war?

The Underdogs
by Mariano Azuela

This novel of the Mexican Revolution follows a band of guerrillas over years spent fighting government forces. At first, the guerrillas are high-minded and idealistic; later, they become just as oppressive as their opponents.

Fallen Angels
by Walter Dean Myers

The Vietnam War is shown from the perspective of Richie Perry, a young black soldier from Harlem. His experiences confuse and terrify him and bring him to an unexpected maturity.

Catch-22
by Joseph Heller

The soldier Yossarian wants no part of war because—no surprise—people are trying to kill him. He spends his time thinking of ways to get out but is thwarted by a powerful and absurd military system.

How accepting are you?

Dreams from My Father
by Barack Obama

President Obama was born to a white mother from Kansas and a black father from Kenya. His memoir tells how he worked to accept his racial heritage and gained success as an attorney and community organizer.

Twilight: Los Angeles, 1992
by Anna Deavere Smith

Presented are the actual words of about 45 people interviewed by Smith after the 1992 Los Angeles riots. The voices—black, white, Asian, and Latino—reveal how differently people view the world and offer insight into the causes of the riots.

Us and Them: A History of Intolerance in America
by Jim Carnes

This book explores 14 examples of intolerance in America, from the case of Mary Dyer, who was executed for her Quaker faith in 1660, to the Crown Heights riot in 1991, in which African Americans and Hasidic Jews clashed.

Get Novel Wise **THINK** central

Go to **thinkcentral.com**.
KEYWORD: HML10-522

522

THINK central

NovelWise

The keyword on this page points to **NovelWise**, a Web site that helps students choose a novel or other book-length work to read. **NovelWise** also provides

- study guides
- reading strategies and literary elements instruction
- presentations to introduce classic novels
- project ideas

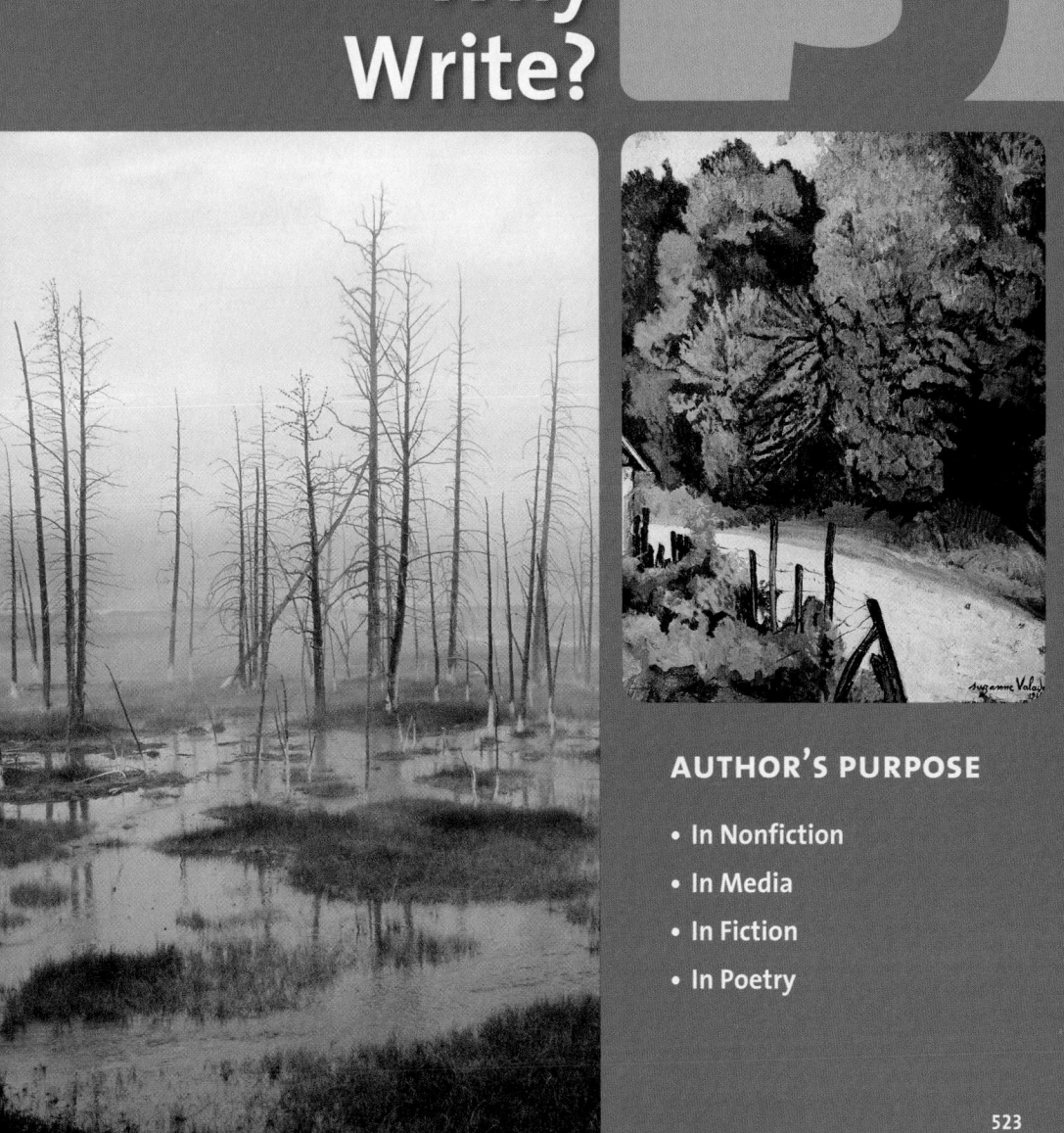

UNIT 5

Why Write?

AUTHOR'S PURPOSE

- In Nonfiction
- In Media
- In Fiction
- In Poetry

523

Some people write because they enjoy recording events. Other people write only when they are required to do so, such as when they must prepare a book report or explain a scientific experiment. Still other people write to present a persuasive argument or to share entertaining or inspiring thoughts.

A writer's creativity comes from his or her life experiences, including daily activities, books or other reading material, or pictures. Invite students to consider how the pictures on this page might inspire a writer. Use these discussion prompts:

- What kind of nonfiction might one of these images illustrate?
- How might either image help convey the ideas in a magazine article? in a news report?
- What ideas for a story or poem come to mind as you think about these images?

Discuss the fact that the same source can inspire various kinds of writing and reasons for writing. Then tell students that as they read the selections in this unit, they will consider the **author's purpose** for writing works of nonfiction, fiction, and poetry and for creating various types of media.

For help in planning this unit, see

R RESOURCE MANAGER UNIT 5
pp. 1–10

About the Art (Left) Photograph of trees burned in a forest fire at Yellowstone National Park. (Right) Suzanne Valadon (1865–1938) painted *Path through the Forest*.

UNIT 5

COMMON CORE

STRAND	Text Analysis Workshop: Author's Purpose and Perspective pp. 526–531	The Plot Against People Humorous Essay pp. 532–537	Linked Selections — Why Leaves Turn Color in the Fall Essay pp. 538–547	Linked Selections — How a Leaf Works / Tree Planting Guide Textbook Diagrams / Procedural Document pp. 548–555	Blowup: What Went Wrong at Storm King Mountain / How to Survive a Wildfire Narrative Nonfiction / Procedural Document pp. 556–575
		Lexile: 1250 Fry: 11 Dale-Chall: 7.6	Lexile: 1150 Fry: 8 Dale-Chall: 7.1	Lexile: 940 Fry: 5 Dale-Chall: 4	Lexile: 1170, 960 Fry: 7, 7 Dale-Chall: 7.4, 7-8
Reading Literature					
Reading Informational Text	Purpose and Perspective pp. 526–527 RI 6 Organization and Format pp. 528–529 RI 3, RI 5 Analyze the Text pp. 430–431	Tone and Diction pp. 533–534, 536, 537 RI 4 Recognize Classification pp. 533–534, 536–537 RI 3 Language Coach p. 536 RI 4	Author's Purpose pp. 539–540, 543–545 RI 4, RI 6 Organization pp. 539, 542, 545 RI 5 Language Coach p. 540 RI 4	Interpret Graphic Aids pp. 549–551 RI 7 Evaluate Graphics pp. 552–555 RI 7 Technical Meanings p. 549 RI 4	Narrative Nonfiction pp. 557, 560–562, 566, 569 RI 3 Take Notes pp. 557, 560, 562–563, 565, 569 Evaluate Grapics pp. 573–575 RI 2 Synthesize Information pp. 573–575 RI 7 Language Coach pp. 558, 567 RI 4
Writing		Quickwrite p. 532	Writing Prompt p. 547	Writing Prompt p. 551 W 2d, W 8 Writing Prompt p. 555 W 2d, W 8	Writing Prompt p. 571 W 2 Writing Prompt, p. 575 W 9b (RI 7)
Speaking and Listening			Discuss p. 538 SL 1		Discuss p. 556 SL 1
Language			Add Descriptive Details pp. 544, 547 L 1b Specialized Vocabulary p. 546 L 6		Add Descriptive Details pp. 565, 571 L 1b Gerunds p. 566 L 1 Analogies p. 570 L 5

Media Study: News Reports TV Newscast Clip/Web Page pp. 576–579	*Getting From Here to There* Procedural Documents pp. 580–583	*And of Clay Are We Created / Girl, Trapped in Water for 55 Hours, Dies Despite Rescue Attempts* Short Story / News Article pp. 584–601	*Peruvian Child / Lady Freedom Among Us* Poems pp. 602–609	*Writing Workshop: Persuasive Letter* pp. 610–619 *Speaking and Listening Workshop: Conducting an Interview* pp. 620–621
		Lexile: 1330 *Fry: 12* *Dale-Chall: 8.0*		
		Author's Perspective pp. 585–586, 588, 591–592, 594, 596 **RL 9** Allusion p. 595 **RL 9** Monitor pp. 585, 588–589, 591, 594, 596 **RL 1** Language Coach pp. 593, 595 **RL 4**	Author's Purpose and Imagery pp. 603–604, 606, 609 **RL 4** Make Inferences pp. 603–604, 606–607, 609 **RL 1** Language Coach, p. 607 **RL 4**	
	Interpret Graphic Aids pp. 580–583 **RI 7** Synthesize Sources pp. 581–582 **RI 7**	Analyze a News Article pp. 598–600 **RI 2, RI 3** Language Coach p. 600 **RI 4** Writing Prompt p. 601 **RI 7**	Interview p. 608	
	Writing Prompt p. 583 **W 2**	Quickwrite p. 584 Writing Prompt p. 601 **W 2**		Writing a Persuasive Letter pp. 610–619 **W 1a–e, W 4, W 5, W 7, W 10**
Credibility in News Reports pp. 577–579 **SL 2, SL 3**	Read for Information p. 583 **SL 2**		Discuss p. 602 **SL 1**	Conducting an Interview pp. 620–621 **SL 1a, SL 1c**
		Latin Root *fort* p. 597 **L 4a**		Drafting p. 613 **L 1** Revising pp. 614-616 **L 1, L 3** Editing and Publishing p. 617 **L 2, L 2c** Conducting an Interview pp. 620–621 **L 1**

ECOS

To see the complete Essential Course of Study, see pp. T23–T28.

For additional lesson planning help, see **Teacher One Stop DVD.**

Instructional Support

Resource Manager Unit 5

UNIT SUPPORT

Academic Vocabulary, p. 3

Additional Academic Vocabulary, p. 4

Grammar Focus p. 5

Text Analysis Workshop pp. 9–10

Writing Workshop: Persuasive
Letter p. 185

SELECTION SUPPORT*

Plan and Teach

Lesson planning pages

Additional leveled selection questions

Extension activities

Student Copy Masters

Selection summaries in four languages

Skills copy masters in English and Spanish

Vocabulary preteaching and support

Reading Check and Question Support

Reading Fluency

*Available for all selections

† Available on **thinkcentral.com**.

Language Handbook

Vocabulary Practice

Best Practices Toolkit†

PowerNotes DVD-ROM†

Connections: Nonfiction for
Common Core CD-ROM†

Teacher One Stop DVD-ROM

Student One Stop DVD-ROM

Media*Smart* DVD-ROM

Early Warnings / Kye the Storm
Chaser

Write*Smart* CD-ROM†

GrammarNotes DVD-ROM†

WordSharp CD-ROM†

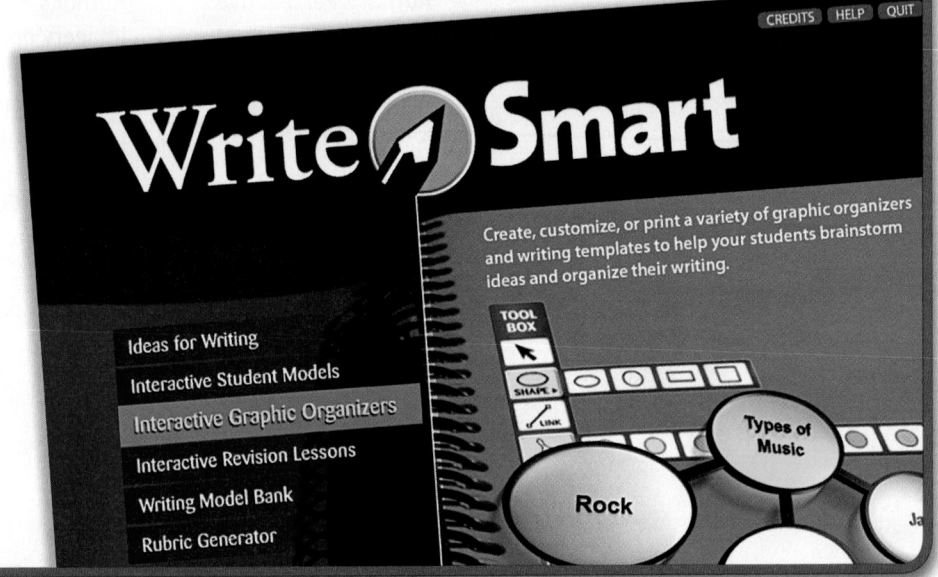

Differentiated Instruction

STRUGGLING READERS AND WRITERS	ENGLISH LANGUAGE LEARNERS	ADVANCED LEARNERS
Resource Manager Unit 5 Additional Selection Questions Question Support Reading Fluency **Interactive Reader** **Adapted Interactive Reader** **Level Up Online Tutorials** **Audio Anthology** (with Audio summaries) **Diagnostic and Selection Tests** Selection Tests A/B	**Resource Manager Unit 5** Selection Summaries in English, Spanish, Vietnamese and Haitian Creole Skills Copymasters in Spanish **English Language Learner Adapted Interactive Reader Teacher's Guide** **ELL Adapted Interactive Reader** **Audio Tutor** **Guide to English for Newcomers** **Audio Anthology** **Audio Summaries in Multiple Languages** (on **thinkcentral.com**)	**Resource Manager Unit 5** Additional Selection Questions Ideas for Extension **Diagnostic and Selection Tests** Selection Tests B/C

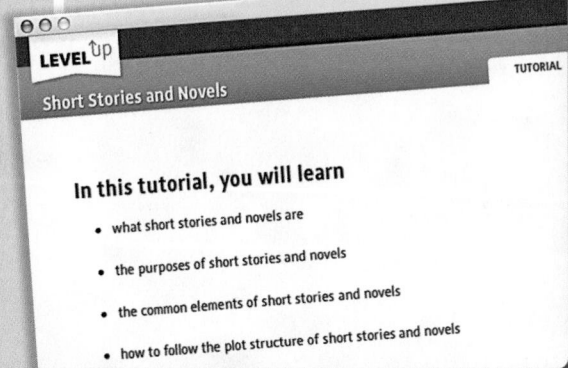

Assessment and Reteaching

Diagnostic and Selection Tests

Unit and Benchmark Tests

ThinkCentral Online Assessment:

- All program assessments
- Level Up Online Tutorials

ExamView Test Generator on the Teacher One Stop DVD-ROM

Online Essay Scoring on **thinkcentral.com**

ThinkCentral Online Reteaching:

- Level Up Online Tutorials
- Reteaching Worksheets

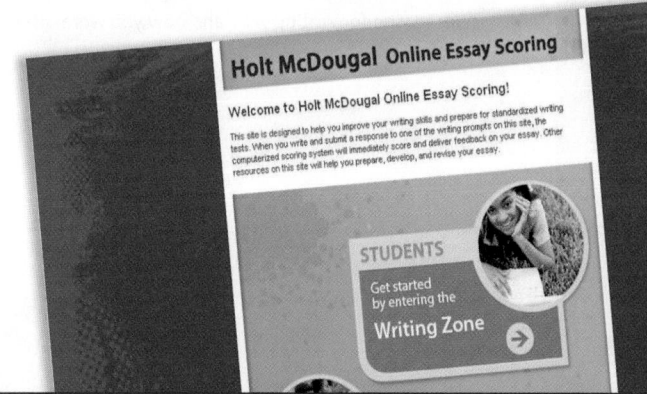

Holt McDougal **Online Essay Scoring**

Welcome to Holt McDougal Online Essay Scoring!

This site is designed to help you improve your writing skills and prepare for standardized writing tests. When you write and submit a response to one of the writing prompts on this site, the computerized scoring system will immediately score and deliver feedback on your essay. Other resources on this site will help you prepare, develop, and revise your essay.

STUDENTS

Get started by entering the **Writing Zone** ➔

Professional Development

Video Center Based on interviews with program consultants and other educational experts, these videos feature classroom-ready teaching strategies.

Teacher Toolkit Includes a Teacher Handbook as well as a range of articles and handouts by program consultants and other educators.

Janet Allen

Jim Burke

Kylene Beers

Carol Jago

THINK central at a Glance

One Location, Endless Resources

Find Resources Browse all *Holt McDougal Literature* components for the ones that meet your students' needs and match your teaching style.

Assess Progress and Reteach Assign electronic versions of program assessments to measure your students' mastery of the Common Core State Standards. On thinkcentral.com, some tests deliver online remediation tutorials to students who have not mastered skills.

 Interactive Whiteboard Lessons

Prepare your students for college and careers by teaching relevant, real-world skills through dynamic, interactive instruction. Go to **thinkcentral.com** to browse through all whiteboard lessons, including the following:

- Author's Purpose and Perspective
- Text Structure and Meaning
- Analyzing Informational Text
- Word Choice and Tone

 **HISTORY**

Together Holt McDougal and HISTORY® are revolutionizing the study of English/language arts with video that helps students relive and re-imagine the people, places, and events they are discovering through reading. Look for selections with the HISTORY® icon.

Why **WRITE?**

Ask the question, then read and discuss the opening paragraph. Have students consider what materials they might **write** to achieve these goals:

- recording the details of a current event
- entertaining a lonely friend
- persuading an adult neighbor to vote
- giving directions to a cultural event

Draw students' attention to the image of the man writing. Discuss the possible purpose or purposes for his writing.

ACTIVITY Model the *ACTIVITY* by naming an influential piece of writing and describing the author's original intention for the piece, as well as your own response to it. For example, the "I Have a Dream" speech given in 1963 by Martin Luther King, Jr., was meant to encourage his audience to work tirelessly but peacefully toward social equality. You might then describe how King's words helped you imagine what a world without prejudice might be like.

CHECK UNDERSTANDING Have students complete this sentence in as many ways as they can, based on the text and on their own insights:
One reason that people write is to _____.

Why **WRITE?**

What if you had the ability to inspire others, or make them laugh, or change the way they think? What if you could teach people something new or share the solution to an important problem?

You can. Through writing, anyone—including you—can achieve goals like these. That's why the world is so dependent on words. People need them to accomplish a wide variety of purposes, from communicating weekend plans to protesting an unfair law.

ACTIVITY Think of individuals who have affected you with their words. These individuals might be songwriters, politicians, advertisers, or novelists. Write down what each person wrote, what you think his or her reason for writing was, and how you were affected.

Find It Online!  THINK central

Go to **thinkcentral.com** for the interactive version of this unit.

524

Unit Resources

See resources on the **Teacher One Stop DVD-ROM** *and on* **thinkcentral.com**.

R RESOURCE MANAGER UNIT 5

UNIT AND BENCHMARK TESTS

BEST PRACTICES TOOLKIT

INTERACTIVE READER

ADAPTED INTERACTIVE READER

ELL ADAPTED INTERACTIVE READER

LANGUAGE HANDBOOK

VOCABULARY PRACTICE

TECHNOLOGY

- **Teacher One Stop DVD-ROM**
- **Student One Stop DVD-ROM**
- **PowerNotes DVD-ROM**
- **Write*Smart* CD-ROM**
- **Media*Smart* DVD-ROM**
- **GrammarNotes DVD-ROM**
- **Audio Anthology CD**
- **Audio Tutor CD**

Find It Online! THINK central

The interactive version of this unit on **thinkcentral.com** includes

- video and **PowerNotes** introductions to key selections
- **audio support**—listen or download
- **ThinkAloud** models
- **WordSharp** vocabulary tutorials
- interactive review and remediation

Preview Unit Goals

TEXT ANALYSIS	• Identify and analyze author's perspective • Analyze the cumulative effect of specific word choices on tone and meaning • Analyze imagery and author's purpose • Analyze functional texts
READING	• Recognize and analyze patterns of organization • Interpret and evaluate graphic aids; use graphic aids to record information • Synthesize information from multiple sources
WRITING AND LANGUAGE	• Write an argument (persuasive letter) • Use participles and participial phrases; use adverb clauses
SPEAKING AND LISTENING	• Conduct an interview
VOCABULARY	• Acquire and use domain-specific vocabulary
ACADEMIC VOCABULARY	• author • issue • document • vision • goal
MEDIA AND VIEWING	• Analyze how events and information are presented in different mediums • Evaluate the ways information is presented in nonprint sources

News with a Purpose
Determine the credibility of news sources in coverage of tornadoes. Page 576.

UNIT GOALS

Included in this unit: **RL 1, RL 3, RL 4, RL 9, RL 10, RI 1, RI 2, RI 3, RI 4, RI 5, RI 6, RI 7, RI 10, W 1a–e, W 2, W 2d, W 4, W 5, W 7, W 8, W 9b, W 10, SL 1a, SL 1c, SL 2, SL 3, L 1, L 1b, L 2, L 2c, L 3, L 4a, L 5, L 6**

Complete text of the Common Core State Standards is found in the correlation on p. T10. Standards covered in this unit are found in the standards overview (pp. 523A–524B) and on the lesson pages where they are taught.

Preview Unit Goals

The goals on this page identify the main skills and strategies that students will meet in this unit's reading selections. Have students scan the list and consider what they already know about each goal. Note the color-coding of each strand, then urge students to watch for the colors to be repeated throughout the unit.

Point out the Academic Vocabulary at the bottom of the page. Invite students to write the list in their **Reader/Writer Notebooks,** along with a definition for each term. Encourage students to return to and refine the definitions as they read, discuss, and write about the selections in Unit 5.

DIFFERENTIATED INSTRUCTION

FOR ENGLISH LANGUAGE LEARNERS

Academic Vocabulary Provide students with definitions of each Academic Vocabulary word.

author (ô'thər) *n.* a writer; a creator of something

document (däk'yōō mənt) *n.* something printed or written that provides a record; something that provides evidence

goal (gōl) *n.* an aim, purpose, or specific result one tries to achieve

issue (ish'ōō) *n.* a concern or problem

vision (vizh' ən) *n.* a mental or imaginative image; something seen in a dream or trance

Use the copy master to help students learn academic words they will use in this unit and on the Assessment Practice.

 RESOURCE MANAGER—Copy Masters
Academic Vocabulary p. 3
Additional Academic Vocabulary p. 4

RI 3 Analyze how the author unfolds and develops a series of events, including the order in which the points are made, how they are introduced and developed, and the connections that are drawn between them. **RI 4** Analyze the cumulative impact of specific word choices on meaning and tone. **RI 5** Analyze in detail how an author's ideas or claims are developed by sentences, paragraphs, or larger sections of the text. **RI 6** Determine an author's point of view or purpose in a text.

Teach

Part 1: Purpose and Perspective

Author's Purpose Identifying an author's purpose for writing can aid comprehension. Every author has a specific reason for writing, but may have less important reasons as well. In order to identify the author's main purpose for writing, readers should consider

• the subject and tone of the work
• the intended audience
• the choice of details and words
• the effect of the work on readers

Author's Perspective Choose a high-interest topic, such as locker searches. Discuss how personal factors, such as age, gender, ethnicity, economic status, religion, or politics, might influence a writer's perspective. Even if a reader knows nothing about a writer's background, clues to perspective can be found by:

• **Direct Statements** What details reveal the writer's values or beliefs?

• **Word Choice/Tone** What does the writer's choice of words and phrases tell you about his or her attitude toward the subject?

• **Selection of Facts** Are the facts important and relevant? Does the writer choose only facts that support his or her perspective?

• **Focus or Emphasis** What aspect of the subject is emphasized? What is left out?

BEST PRACTICES TOOLKIT—Transparency
Analysis Frame: Author's Craft pp. D21, D24

Author's Purpose and Perspective

An article crammed with statistics, an essay filled with emotional appeals, a business letter, an e-mail from a friend—no matter what you are reading, usually you can scan just the first few lines to find out whether the writing is informative or persuasive, impersonal or revealing. Without realizing it, you are picking up on clues to an author's purpose and perspective, both of which affect what you read and how you read it.

Part 1: Purpose and Perspective

You already know that an **author's purpose**—a writer's reason for crafting a particular work—can be one or more of the following:

• to inform
• to entertain
• to persuade
• to express thoughts or feelings

The purpose of a text is usually obvious. Perspective, though, can be more difficult to detect. An **author's perspective** is the unique combination of ideas, values, and beliefs that influences the way a writer looks at a topic. Most writers do not intentionally broadcast their values, especially journalists, who strive to report "just the facts." In some essays and speeches, however, writers' beliefs are revealed in subtle ways.

As you read any text, look for direct statements in which the writer explicitly expresses his or her beliefs. Also pay attention to the writer's choice of words and **details** and his or her **tone,** or attitude toward a subject. All these elements can serve as clues to an author's perspective, as you'll notice in this example.

Essential Course of Study ECOS

COMMON CORE

Included in this workshop:
RI 3 Analyze how the author unfolds and develops a series of events, including the order in which the points are made, how they are introduced and developed, and the connections that are drawn between them. **RI 4** Analyze the cumulative impact of specific word choices on meaning and tone. **RI 5** Analyze in detail how an author's ideas or claims are developed by sentences, paragraphs, or larger sections of the text. **RI 6** Determine an author's point of view or purpose in a text.

Can you imagine being on a waiting list that is 87,000 people long?

Last year, nearly 87,000 people were on the list for an organ transplant. My sister was one of them. A heart transplant saved her life, but not everyone on the list is as fortunate. Every day, an average of 17 people die while waiting for a compatible organ.

The thought of organ donation used to make me squeamish. But watching my sister get a second chance at life made me realize how vital this act of giving is. Learn about organ donation, and find out if you can save a life.

by Ginny García

Become an Organ Donor

PURPOSE To persuade

• **Phrases** such as *how vital this act of giving is* and the author's direct **call to action** provide clues to the purpose.

• The author makes her case by including alarming statistics.

PERSPECTIVE That of someone whose opinion of organ donation has been shaped by a personal experience

• **Words and phrases** like *second chance at life* convey an impassioned, hopeful **tone.**

• **Direct statements** reveal what the author used to think about organ donation and how she feels about it now.

DIFFERENTIATED INSTRUCTION

FOR STRUGGLING READERS

Note Taking For students who need help with note taking, hand out the note-taking copy master before discussing this page. As volunteers read aloud each section, discuss the main points, and have students record them on the copy master.

R RESOURCE MANAGER—Copy Master
Critical Reading Workshop, p. 9

FOR ENGLISH LANGUAGE LEARNERS

Language: Skill Words Briefly define each purpose for writing. Help students match examples to a likely main purpose: funny story (*to entertain*), a news report (*to inform*), a nature poem (*to express feelings*), a campaign speech (*to persuade*)

MODEL 1: PURPOSE

To figure out the purpose of a particular work, you often have to examine the writer's choice of details. You should also consider the intended audience. Use these clues to determine the author's purpose in this excerpt.

from Go Fast, Turn Easier

Feature article by **Chris Anthony**

Skiing slowly in powder[1] is like jogging through oatmeal: Not only does it feel weird and look silly, but it's downright difficult. Effortless powder skiing is fast powder skiing. You need speed to power through and rise above the snowpack. If you drive your boards under the snow without enough momentum, they'll
5 nosedive until you slow to a stop.

Most people think powder skiing means hard work. They drop in and get low in an effort to manhandle their skis around. Forget muscling the turn: The key is to be on top of the snow *before* you start turning. . . .

---

1. **powder:** deep, dry, light snow that has not yet been packed down by skiers or machines.

Close Read

1. Is this article intended for expert skiers, people with some experience in skiing, or novices? Support your answer.

2. Consider the boxed details and the intended audience. What is the author's primary purpose?

MODEL 2: PURPOSE AND PERSPECTIVE

The author of "Go Fast, Turn Easier" is a knowledgeable skier. Beyond that information, readers don't learn much about his beliefs and values. In the excerpt from "Snow Immobile," the author's perspective on a different winter sport— snowboarding—comes across clearly. As you read, look for clues that reveal both the author's purpose and his perspective.

from SNOW IMMOBILE

Essay by **Dave Barry**

For those of you who, for whatever reason, such as a will to live, do not participate in downhill winter sports, I should explain that snowboarding is an activity that is very popular with people who do not feel that regular skiing is lethal enough. These are of course young people, fearless people, people with
5 100 percent synthetic bodies who can hurtle down a mountainside at 50 mph and knock down mature trees with their faces and then spring to their feet and go, "Cool."

Close Read

1. The author includes exaggerated details like the one in the box. Find two more examples. What do they suggest about his purpose?

2. Does this author appear to be a fan of snowboarding? Cite details that help you to detect his perspective on snowboarding.

TEXT ANALYSIS WORKSHOP **527**

MODEL 1: PURPOSE
Close Read

1. *Possible answer:* This article is intended for skiers with some experience. The writer assumes an audience of skiers who can already ski well enough to control their skis at high speeds ("Effortless powder skiing is fast powder skiing," lines 2–3), but who are also likely to make certain common mistakes ("If you drive your boards under the snow . . . slow to a stop," lines 4–5).

2. *Possible answer:* The boxed details indicate that the writer's primary purpose is to inform. The statements are addressed to "you" and give specific instructions on how to ski better.

MODEL 2: PURPOSE AND PERSPECTIVE
Close Read

1. *Possible answer:* Exaggerated details include "popular with people who do not feel that regular skiing is lethal enough" (lines 3–4), "people with 100 percent synthetic bodies" (lines 4–5), and "knock down mature trees with their faces" (line 6). These humorous details make it clear that the writer's purpose is to entertain.

2. *Possible answer:* The writer is apparently not a fan of snowboarding, as revealed by the boxed detail and the details cited in question 1. The perspective he reveals by exaggerating the dangers of snowboarding is that of a person who is no longer young and who does not enjoy taking risks.

FOR STRUGGLING READERS
Analysis Support: Purpose

- Discuss how Model 1 would be different if the writer's purpose were to express his feelings about powder skiing. (*The details would describe the writer's experiences rather than giving instructions on skiing.*)

- Discuss how Model 2 would be different if the writer's purpose were to inform people of the dangers of snowboarding. (*The*

details would be factual rather than exaggerated.)

Analysis Support: Perspective After students read and discuss Model 2, ask them to choose another sport. Write *Positive Perspective* and *Negative Perspective* on the board. Help students generate details about the sport that writers with a positive and negative perspective on the sport would emphasize in a description.

Online Remediation

THINK central

If your students are struggling with critical reading skills, consider assigning them one or more **Level Up Online Tutorials** as remediation before beginning this unit. Log in to **thinkcentral.com** to view a list of the skills addressed by **Level Up**.

Part 2: Organization and Format

Organization Before students read page 528, briefly review the meanings of these terms, and ask students to give examples of the kinds of information likely to be presented in each organizational pattern:

- **Chronological order:** events presented in order of time sequence (*historical account, memoir, news report, instructions*)

- **Classification organization:** things or ideas grouped with others that share common characteristics (*geographic description grouped by landforms, climate conditions, or vegetation; survey grouped by types, such as dogs or musical instruments*)

- **Cause-and-effect organization:** an event presented with its causes, effects, or both (*analysis of the significance of a historical event, explanation of why a natural phenomenon occurs*)

- **Compare-and-contrast order:** things or ideas discussed in terms of how they are similar to and different from each other (*a consumer report on different brands of a product, a review of two books by the same author or on the same topic*)

Tell students that it is not unusual to find a variety of patterns of organization within one piece of writing.

Format After students have read page 528, ask them to scan a textbook to identify examples of subheadings. Ask them to observe and point out how headings, titles, boldface, italics, color, or graphics are used to help clarify the content and organization of the material.

CHECK UNDERSTANDING

Have students explain what kinds of organization they might find in an article about how to build a birdhouse.

Part 2: Organization and Format

To achieve their purpose and present ideas logically, writers use thoughtfully chosen **patterns of organization,** such as **chronological order** and **classification organization.** By noticing the organizational pattern that is used in a work, you can more easily see relationships among ideas. Here are two other patterns:

- **Cause-and-effect organization** establishes relationships between events, ideas, or trends. A writer might use this pattern to help readers understand a scientific phenomenon or to explain how one historical event brought about another. **Signal Words:** *because, as a result, consequently, since*

- **Compare-and-contrast organization** highlights similarities and differences between two or more subjects. This pattern is used to show the benefits of one subject over another or to compare an unfamiliar subject with a familiar one. **Signal Words:** *similarly, also, like, in contrast, while, but, unlike*

Sometimes readers need more than a few signal words to help them follow information. For example, think about the last time you read an in-depth feature article like the one shown here. In such complex texts, writers use **text features,** such as **titles, subheadings,** and **graphic aids,** to help readers locate information quickly.

The **title** reveals the subject of the article—the flu season.

The Flu Strikes Again

Feature article by **Faye Danahan**

Downtown resident Samantha Shaw says she always knows when winter is approaching. "The coughing and sneezing on the train, in restaurants, at the gym—I'm surrounded by germs. Let the flu season begin!"

This Year More Severe Than Last
Shaw isn't the only one who's apprehensive. Experts state that flu cases are already up 5 percent from last year at this time. If this month is any indication, Chicago could see a severe 30 percent overall increase in cases this year as compared to last.

How to Stay Healthy
Even if you can't get a flu vaccination, there are some precautions you can take. *Continued on page 26A*

Subheadings reflect the controlling, or main, ideas of the sections.

Words and phrases signal differences between this year's flu season and last year's.

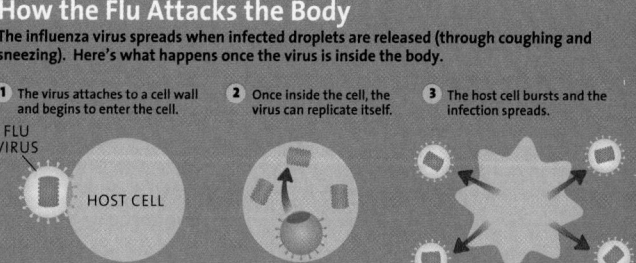

How the Flu Attacks the Body
The influenza virus spreads when infected droplets are released (through coughing and sneezing). Here's what happens once the virus is inside the body.

1. The virus attaches to a cell wall and begins to enter the cell.
2. Once inside the cell, the virus can replicate itself.
3. The host cell bursts and the infection spreads.

FLU VIRUS

HOST CELL

A **graphic aid** helps readers understand how the flu virus spreads.

Continued on page 26A

528

DIFFERENTIATED INSTRUCTION

FOR STRUGGLING READERS
Note Taking For students who need help, hand out the note-taking copy master for this page. As they read and discuss the main points on the page, have students record them on the copy master. Assist as needed.

R RESOURCE MANAGER—Copy Master
Critical Reading Workshop, p. 10

Concept Support Provide students with sentences or pairs of sentences that use signal words for cause-and-effect and compare-and-contrast. Then ask them to use the signal words in their own sentences.

- *cause-and-effect:* As a result of her efforts, Jenny was made captain of the team.
- *compare-and-contrast:* Unlike Noah, Henry was extremely tall.

MODEL: ORGANIZATION AND FORMAT

This author explains how fear and anxiety can affect athletes at pivotal moments. Notice how the author uses specific patterns of organization and text features to help you understand difficult scientific concepts.

10	20	30	40	50	60	70

from
At Home in the Discomfort Zone

Feature article by **Kevin Foley**

Fear and Anxiety Fear is sudden and arresting, a blind-side Holyfield punch. It can start with a sloppy foothold, a hooked ski edge, or an ill-timed paddle stroke. As your body veers toward trouble—cliff, tree, Class V hole the size of a Winnebago—neurons relay electrical impulses from your eyes to your

5 brain's gumball-size amygdala, which sounds the alarm to the hypothalamus. The two structures begin gushing hormones, urging the adrenal glands to start pumping epinephrine, norepinephrine, and cortisol, three stress hormones that ramp up glucose production, increase heart rate, speed up your breathing, and often leave you sweating like a goose at a down-jacket factory. On the upside,

10 though, fear is turbocharging muscles and the brain for confrontation or evasive action—the classic fight-or-flight response—and that can help performance.

Anxiety is a more plodding matter, says

15 Mary Meagher, a psychologist in the behavioral neuroscience group at Texas A&M University, and it's a reaction that's more troublesome to athletes. "Fear and anxiety have different underlying brain circuitry," she says. "Anxiety

20 is future-oriented; it's about potential threats. You're uncertain, aroused at a low level, with clenched muscles and increased pain sensitivity." . . . Anxiety stimulates the amygdala, triggering the production of

25 cortisol but generating less heart-whumping adrenaline than fear does. Fear inspires alarm and action, often suddenly and acutely, outstripping thought; anxiety unfolds more slowly, disrupting thought and evaluation.

30 Thus anxiety is more insidious, magnifying injuries, hindering movements, and knocking athletes out of the blessed neural harmony of competitive flow. But it's more easily controlled than fear.

TIPS
- **Think positive.** You've heard it before, but studies by Meagher and others have shown just how well positive thinking can reduce anxiety's physical effects. . . .
- **Mentally practice overcoming adversity.** Focus on controlling your breathing (slow and deep, not rapid and shallow), on staying in the present moment (you're on the rock, not plummeting from it), and on visualizing success (you're pulling fluidly through the move).

Close Read

1. Reread lines 3–9. What pattern of organization does the author use to explain what happens when "your body veers toward trouble"?

2. In lines 14–33, the author uses compare-and-contrast organization to explain the differences between fear and anxiety. One difference is boxed. Find two other differences.

3. Identify two text features in the article, and explain how they help you as a reader.

MODEL: ORGANIZATION AND FORMAT

Close Read

1. *Possible answer: The pattern of organization used in lines 3–9 is cause-and-effect. The writer describes the chain reaction of chemical effects that begin with a fearful situation. Each effect is the cause of another effect.*

2. *Possible answer: Besides the boxed text, the writer also explains these differences between fear and anxiety: Fear is about an immediate threat, whereas anxiety is about potential threats (lines 1–3 and 19–21); fear causes sudden alarm, whereas anxiety unfolds more slowly (lines 26–29); fear can help athletes, whereas anxiety tends to be distracting (lines 9–13 and 30–33); anxiety is easier to control than fear (line 33).*

3. *Possible answer: One helpful text feature is the subheading "Fear and Anxiety." Because the title of the article does not make the topic entirely clear, this subheading provides important information. Another helpful text feature is the "TIPS" sidebar. Its bulleted subheadings let the reader determine the main points at a glance.*

DIFFERENTIATED INSTRUCTION

FOR STRUGGLING READERS

Analysis Support: Organization Tell students that noticing the organizational patterns in writing makes it easier for readers to take quick, efficient notes. For example, the cause-and-effect information in lines 3–9 can be recorded using arrows to show the chain reaction, while the compare-and-contrast information throughout the article can be recorded in two lists, one for the characteristics of fear and the other for the contrasting characteristics of anxiety. Work with students to demonstrate these note-taking methods on the board.

Practice and Apply

Part 3: Analyze the Text

Close Read

1. **Possible answer:** *You would expect to find information on how the Supreme Court arrived at its decision under the subheading "Legal Reasoning." The word* reasoning *is the clue.*

2. **Possible answer:** *The subheadings and the boxed details suggest that the author's primary purpose is to inform readers about the historical background of the case and the legal reasoning that led to the court's decision. The boxed clue "Textbook feature" indicates that the audience is students.*

3. **Possible answers:** *Text features that aid in understanding the article are the title, which tells the subject of the article; the subheadings, which divide the article into sections and tell what each section is about; the use of boldface (lines 6–7) and italic (lines 27–29) to highlight the landmark decision; and the "Legal Sources" sidebar, which highlights laws relevant to the case.*

4. **Possible answer:** *The writer's perspective on the ruling is that he or she agrees with it but also understands why some saw it as legally debatable at the time: "While the correctness of the* Brown *ruling . . . seems obvious today, some justices had difficulty agreeing to it. One reason was the force of legal precedent" (lines 8–11). Nothing else about the writer's perspective is revealed; the facts on both sides of the case are presented objectively.*

Part 3: Analyze the Text

In 1954, in *Brown* v. *Board of Education of Topeka*, the Supreme Court ruled that racial segregation in public schools was unconstitutional. This landmark decision overturned an earlier ruling that endorsed "separate but equal" facilities for blacks and whites. Use what you've learned in this workshop to compare two texts on this historic case.

Brown v. Board of Education of Topeka

Textbook feature

ORIGINS OF THE CASE In the early 1950s, the school system of Topeka, Kansas, operated separate schools for "the two races"—blacks and whites. Reverend Oliver Brown protested that this was unfair to his eight-year-old daughter Linda. Although the Browns lived near a "white" school,
5   Linda was forced to take a long bus ride to her "black" school across town.

THE RULING **The Court ruled that segregated public schools were "inherently" unequal and therefore unconstitutional.**

LEGAL REASONING While the correctness of the *Brown* ruling—which actually involved five segregation cases from across the nation—seems
10 obvious today, some justices had difficulty agreeing to it. One reason was the force of legal precedent. The *Plessy* v. *Ferguson* decision endorsing segregation had stood for over 50 years. It clearly stated that "separate but equal" facilities did not violate the Fourteenth Amendment.
     Thurgood Marshall, the NAACP lawyer who argued *Brown*, spent
15 years laying the groundwork to chip away at Jim Crow—the local laws that required segregated facilities. Marshall had recently won two Supreme Court decisions in 1950 that challenged segregation at graduate schools. Then in 1952, the Supreme Court agreed to hear the Browns' case.
20 The Court deliberated for two years before deciding how to interpret the Fourteenth Amendment.
     In the end, Chief Justice Earl Warren carefully sidestepped *Plessy,* claiming that segregated schools were not and never could be equal. On Monday,
25 May 17, 1954, Warren read the unanimous decision:

> *"Does segregation of children in public schools . . . deprive children of . . . equal educational opportunities? We believe that it does."*

30   —*Brown* v. *Board of Education of Topeka*

LEGAL SOURCES

U.S. Constitution
Fourteenth Amendment, Equal Protection Clause (1868):

"No state shall . . . deny to any person within its jurisdiction the equal protection of the laws."

Related Case
Plessy v. *Ferguson* (1896): Established doctrine of "separate but equal"

Close Read

1. Under which subheading would you expect to find information on how the Supreme Court arrived at its decision?

2. Examine the subheadings and the boxed details. What is the author's primary purpose?

3. Identify two text features that add to your understanding of the text. Explain your choices.

4. How much can you tell about the author's perspective on *Brown* v. *Board of Education?* Explain your answer.

DIFFERENTIATED INSTRUCTION

FOR STRUGGLING READERS

Analysis Support: Perspective Remind students that an author's perspective may be conveyed through tone. These texts contain similar content but use different tones. Ask students to contrast the tones and to point out words that create the difference in these examples:

Textbook: "protested that this was unfair to his eight-year-old daughter" (lines 3–4)

Speech: "saw the viciousness of segregation and could no longer tolerate it" (line 9)

Textbook: "the correctness of the *Brown* ruling . . . seems obvious" (lines 8–10)

Speech: "The decision struck down an American apartheid founded on ignorance, hatred, and violence." (lines 2–3)

Textbook: "[Chief Justice] Warren read the unanimous decision" (lines 25–26)

Speech: "a unanimous Supreme Court ignited a torch for tomorrow, a torch of freedom and hope" (lines 29–30)

In 2004, U.S. Secretary of Education Rod Paige gave the following speech at the dedication ceremony for the *Brown* v. *Board of Education* National Historic Site. As you read Paige's remarks, try to determine his purpose and his perspective. How do they influence what you learn about the momentous case?

from Grand Opening Dedication Speech   by **Rod Paige**

. . . *Brown* v. *Board of Education* was a triumph of the human spirit, a reaffirmation of constitutional and human rights. The decision struck down an American apartheid[1] founded on ignorance, hatred, and violence. It was, and remains today, a statement of hope and expectation, a belief that the American
5 people will rise above prejudice, ignorance, and classification to find our common humanity.

Today it is right that we remember Oliver Brown, Linda Brown, and all of the plaintiffs involved in the case. They were parents, students, and neighbors who saw the viciousness of segregation and could no longer tolerate it. These
10 parents rose above the terrible turbulence of history and conflict to fight for freedom—freedom for their children, for themselves, and for all Americans. . . .

For me, the decision was more than a legal ruling; it was a ruling on a way of life. I grew up in rural, segregated Mississippi. We lived with segregation and the racism that inspired it every single day. African Americans understood
15 the moral imperative guiding Oliver Brown and everyone involved in the case. We felt the tenacious hold of segregation on our country and our culture. And we knew its terrible consequences—centuries of prejudice, waste, division, and even death.

For us, it came as no surprise that the battleground was the educational
20 system. Our schools reflected segregationist thinking; they institutionalized separation. By example, many of our schools taught inequality, incivility, callousness, disregard, exclusion, and disrespect. It was a vicious circle. Racism was the cause, and the result, of such teaching, generation after generation, for over 250 years. It still has a hold on our schools today as we confront re-
25 segregation and the exclusion of millions of children from a quality education.

There are some who say the decision remains unfulfilled. They are right! *Brown* opened the doors of our schools. Now we must build on that decision to make education fully inclusive and fair. . . .

On May 17, 1954, thanks to a handful of Americans, a unanimous
30 Supreme Court ignited a torch for tomorrow, a torch of freedom and hope. That torch still burns brightly today. . . .

---

1. **apartheid:** "apartness"—a separation of people according to their race.

Close Read

1. How do the boxed details in the speech differ from those in the textbook feature? Explain what the details suggest about Paige's purpose.

2. Consider Paige's choice of words and phrases in lines 1–11. Would you describe his tone as inspirational or angry? Support your answer.

3. Think about Paige's tone and his description of his early years in lines 12–24. What can you infer about his perspective on the *Brown* v. *Board of Education* decision?

4. In lines 21–24, Paige uses cause-and-effect organization to talk about racism. Summarize what he says about the "vicious circle."

Close Read

1. ***Possible answer:*** *Paige uses lofty, impassioned language in the boxed text rather than the neutral language of the textbook article. His details suggest a purpose to express his thoughts and feelings.*

2. ***Possible answer:*** *Paige's tone in lines 1–11 is inspirational. He calls the* Brown *ruling "a triumph of the human spirit" (line 1) and describes it as a "statement of hope and expectation" that people can find their "common humanity" (lines 4–6).*

3. ***Possible answer:*** *Paige's tone and the description of his early years in segregated Mississippi (lines 12–24) suggest that his perspective on the* Brown *ruling has been shaped by his own experiences of racism.*

4. ***Possible answer:*** *Paige shows that racism is a "vicious circle" that causes policies that, in turn, cause racism. For example, racism led to school segregation, which instilled racism in the minds of the students and passed bigotry to the next generation.*

Assess and Reteach

Assess

Have students briefly contrast the purpose and perspective of the textbook article and the speech.

Reteach

For students who are unable to apply the workshop skills to the texts, choose from these reteaching activities:

Have students review their worksheet masters for pages 526 and 528.

- Ask them to review the article on page 530 and explain how they identify its purpose to inform. Have students also explain how they excluded other purposes.

- Write on the board these clues to a writer's perspective: word choice, tone, choice of facts and details, information about the writer's life, direct statements. Have students find examples in the speech and link each to Paige's perspective.

FOR ENGLISH LANGUAGE LEARNERS

Vocabulary: Prefixes Call attention to these words in lines 21–22: *inequality, incivility, disregard, disrespect*. Explain that the prefixes *in-* and *dis-* often mean "not." Help students define each base word and combine its meaning with that of the prefix to define the whole word. Point out that *in-* can also mean "in," as in *involved* (lines 8, 15). Help students link the word to the meaning "in."

FOR ADVANCED LEARNERS/PRE–AP*

Analyze Purpose and Perspective Have students use the library or Internet to find two pieces of writing on the same topic written for different purposes or from two perspectives. Ask students to analyze the two works and to point out specific details that reveal the differences.

Focus and Motivate

COMMON CORE FOCUS

RI 3 Analyze how the author unfolds a series of ideas, including the order in which the points are made. **RI 4** Determine the meaning of words and phrases as they are used in a text; analyze the cumulative impact of specific word choices on meaning and tone.

SUMMARY

In "The Plot Against People," a humorous essay, Russell Baker reveals that inanimate objects are sentient and that they have a goal: "to resist man and ultimately defeat him." He uses the format of a scientific report to describe inanimate objects—tools, appliances, and other modern conveniences—that attempt to achieve this goal by breaking down, getting lost, or not working after their first use.

When are little things a **BIG DEAL?**

Introduce the question. Elicit that an annoyance is not a life-changing trauma, but it may seem so at the time. After students have completed the *QUICKWRITE* activity, come to a class consensus on the meaning of annoyance.

Selection Resources

Essential Course of Study  **ECOS**

The Plot Against People
Humorous Essay by Russell Baker

When are little things a **BIG DEAL?**

(When are little things a BIG DEAL?)

COMMON CORE

RI 3 Analyze how the author unfolds a series of ideas, including the order in which the points are made. **RI 4** Determine the meaning of words and phrases as they are used in a text; analyze the cumulative impact of specific word choices on meaning and tone.

Keys get lost. Computers crash. Every day, people encounter problems, inconveniences, and other annoyances that make life stressful. In the following essay, Russell Baker proposes an interesting theory about why such things happen.

QUICKWRITE What are some of the things that annoy you when they break down, don't work, or get lost? Make a short list of about five items. Then choose the one that annoys you the most and explain why to a classmate.

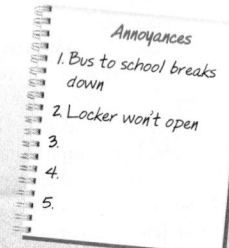

Annoyances
1. Bus to school breaks down
2. Locker won't open
3.
4.
5.

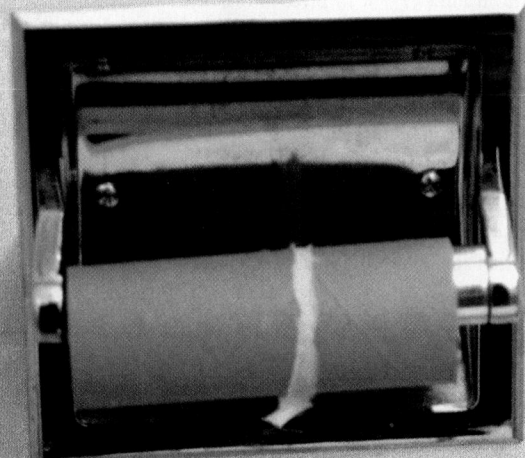

See resources on the **Teacher One Stop DVD-ROM** *and on* **thinkcentral.com**.

 RESOURCE MANAGER UNIT 5
Plan and Teach, pp. 11–18
Summary, pp. 19–20†‡*
Text Analysis and Reading Skill, pp. 21–24†*

DIAGNOSTIC AND SELECTION TESTS
Selection Tests, pp. 139–142

 BEST PRACTICES TOOLKIT
New Word Analysis, p. E8

INTERACTIVE READER

ADAPTED INTERACTIVE READER

ELL ADAPTED INTERACTIVE READER

TECHNOLOGY
- Teacher One Stop DVD-ROM
- Student One Stop DVD-ROM
- PowerNotes DVD-ROM
- Audio Anthology CD
- GrammarNotes DVD-ROM
- Audio Tutor CD
- ExamView Test Generator on the **Teacher One Stop**

 **THINK** central

Find it Online!
Features on **thinkcentral.com** that support the selection include
- **PowerNotes** presentation
- **ThinkAloud** models to enhance comprehension
- **WordSharp** vocabulary tutorials
- interactive writing and grammar instruction

---

* Resources for Differentiation   † Also in Spanish   ‡ In Haitian Creole and Vietnamese

TEXT ANALYSIS: TONE AND DICTION

While reading an essay, you might notice that the writer seems serious, mocking, or sentimental. That quality of the writing is known as the **tone**, or the writer's attitude toward a subject. One way the writer creates tone is through **diction**, the word choice and the arrangement of the words, or **syntax.** Notice how Russell Baker uses formal, scientific language in this sentence.

The goal of all inanimate objects is to resist man and ultimately to defeat him, and the three major classifications are based on the method each object uses to achieve its purpose.

Instead of the word "things," Baker writes "inanimate objects." Also, Baker's sentence structure is complicated, or suitable for a scientific paper. The contrast between his elevated style and the everyday topic creates a humorous tone. As you read his essay, notice the diction and details Baker uses to create tone.

READING SKILL: RECOGNIZE CLASSIFICATION

Pattern of organization refers to how a writer arranges ideas and information. Common patterns of organization include

- cause and effect
- chronological order
- comparison and contrast

A fourth pattern of organization is **classification.** To classify is to sort ideas or objects into groups that share common characteristics. This type of organization is revealed in Baker's thesis statement: "Inanimate objects are classified scientifically into three major categories—those that don't work, those that break down, and those that get lost."

As you read, use a chart like the one shown to identify examples of each category identified in the thesis statement. In the third column, note important characteristics of each group.

Category	Examples	Characteristics
Things that don't work		
Things that break down	car, washing machine	create maximum frustration for people
Things that get lost		

 Complete the activities in your **Reader/Writer Notebook.**

Meet the Author

Russell Baker
born 1925

Early Hardships
Russell Baker suffered grief and hardship early in life. He lost his father at the age of five and witnessed his suddenly widowed mother make the painful decision to leave his sister with relatives who were in a better financial position to provide for her. This sad beginning, however, did not dampen Baker's attitude or his desire to succeed in life. He credits his mother with encouraging him to set high goals: "She would make me make something of myself."

"Casual" Columnist
Baker's sharp eye for detail and ability to provide insightful commentary on little things made journalism the ideal career for him. He had always loved news and the appealing stories newspapers contained. Baker knew that he eventually wanted to write for one. "I marveled at the places newspapers could take me," he once noted.

His Observer column, which ran from 1962 to 1998 in the *New York Times*, showcased Baker's talent for capturing details. He described it as "a casual column without anything urgent to tell humanity." Baker wrote about everyday occurrences, such as shopping for groceries and watching television, with wit and humor. His talent for relating personal stories to a universal audience has made him popular with critics and readers alike.

Authors Online
Go to **thinkcentral.com.** KEYWORD: HML10-533

THINK central

533

Teach

● *Model the Skill:* TONE AND DICTION

To model how to identify tone, read aloud this passage:

> I searched everywhere for my glasses: under the couch, on the kitchen counter, even in my sock drawer. They were nowhere to be found. How was I going to study without my glasses? In a panicked gesture, I placed my hand on my head. But instead of hair, I felt the steel frame of my glasses.

Point out that the choice and arrangement of words suggest the narrator's frantic search and worry about studying and create a tone of panic.

GUIDED PRACTICE Ask students for a title that reflects the tone of the example.

■ *Model the Skill:* RECOGNIZE CLASSIFICATION

To model how to recognize classification, give two examples for each of these categories of food: food you might eat in a fast-food restaurant, food you might eat in an upscale restaurant, food you might make at home. Give students the following examples: hamburgers, grilled chicken sandwiches; chicken marsala, lobster; spaghetti, vegetable soup.

GUIDED PRACTICE Have students define *classification* in their own words.

R RESOURCE MANAGER—Copy Master Recognize Classification p. 23 (for student use while reading the selection)

DIFFERENTIATED INSTRUCTION

FOR STRUGGLING READERS
Develop Reading Fluency Read aloud terms related to the Reading Skill, such as *classification, classify, category, characteristics,* enunciating syllables and emphasizing stressed syllables. Have students repeat each term. Then have student pairs practice reading the Targeted Passage on page 534 aloud. Distribute the copy masters and have students work in pairs or groups to practice fluency.

R RESOURCE MANAGER—Copy Master Reading Fluency p. 27

FOR ADVANCED LEARNERS/PRE-AP
Analyze Across Media [paired-activity option] Explain that TV shows have a tone in that each show expresses the attitude that its creative team takes toward its subject. Ask students to list five TV shows and describe the tone of each show.

Help students set a purpose for reading. Tell them to read to discover how different categories of objects plot against people.

A TONE AND DICTION

Possible answer: *The word choice creates an image of a machine that is alive, very intelligent, and hostile toward people.*

IF STUDENTS NEED HELP . . . Have students look up the meaning of the word *cunning*. Discuss its negative connotation.

B *Model the Skill:* CLASSIFICATION

Read lines 20–27 aloud. Point out the "objects that get lost" category in line 24 and the examples in line 21. Have students record these in the first two columns of their Reading Skill charts. Then, with students, identify details that show how the objects operate, and have students list them in the third column of their charts.

Possible answer: *Objects in the second category get lost (line 24). Details that show how these objects operate include the idea that getting lost is an intentional act (line 25), the reference to a secret method of locomotion (line 26), and the idea that these objects can hide their movement (line 27).*

ADDITIONAL TEACHING OPPORTUNITY

Author's Purpose Recall that **author's purpose** is what the writer hopes to achieve in a particular work. Refer students to lines 1–8 and ask: What might Baker's purpose be for writing this essay?

The Plot Against People
Russell Baker

Analyze Visuals ▶

How would you describe the **tone** of this painting? What qualities has the artist given to the toasters?

WASHINGTON, June 17 — Inanimate objects are classified scientifically into three major categories—those that don't work, those that break down, and those that get lost.

The goal of all inanimate objects is to resist man and ultimately to defeat him, and the three major classifications are based on the method each object uses to achieve its purpose. As a general rule, any object capable of breaking down at the moment when it is most needed will do so. The automobile is typical of the category.

1 Targeted Passage

10   With the cunning typical of its breed, the automobile never breaks down while entering a filling station with a large staff of idle mechanics. It waits until it reaches a downtown intersection in the middle of the rush hour, or until it is fully loaded with family and luggage on the Ohio Turnpike. **A**

Thus it creates maximum misery, inconvenience, frustration, and irritability among its human cargo, thereby reducing its owner's life span.

Washing machines, garbage disposals, lawn mowers, light bulbs, automatic laundry dryers, water pipes, furnaces, electrical fuses, television tubes, hose nozzles, tape recorders, slide projectors—all are in league with the automobile to take their turn at breaking down whenever life threatens to flow smoothly for their human enemies.

20   Many inanimate objects, of course, find it extremely difficult to break down. Pliers, for example, and gloves and keys are almost totally incapable of breaking down. Therefore, they have had to evolve a different technique for resisting man.

A Plausible Theory

They get lost. Science has still not solved the mystery of how they do it, and no man has ever caught one of them in the act of getting lost. The most plausible theory is that they have developed a secret method of locomotion which they are able to conceal the instant a human eye falls upon them. **B**

A TONE AND DICTION
Notice Baker's choice of the words "cunning" and "breed" in line 9. What image does this choice of words create for the reader?

B CLASSIFICATION
In lines 20–27, Baker moves from discussing the first category to describing the second. What details show how objects in this category operate?

Toasters on Hills (1998), Charles Kaufman. Acrylic on canvas, 60 cm × 80 cm. © 2002 Charles Kaufman.

DIFFERENTIATED INSTRUCTION

FOR ENGLISH LANGUAGE LEARNERS
Vocabulary Support Use New Word Analysis to teach these words: *method* (line 5), *capable* (line 6), *maximum* (line 13), *evolve* (line 22), *inherent* (line 37), *constitutes* (line 39).

 **BEST PRACTICES TOOLKIT—Transparency** New Word Analysis p. E8

FOR STRUGGLING READERS
In combination with the *Audio Anthology CD*, use one or more Targeted Passages (pp. 534, 536) to ensure that students focus on key events, concepts, and skills. Targeted Passages are also good for English learners.

1 Targeted Passage [Lines 1–8]
This passage introduces the essay's subject and main idea. It also establishes the humorous tone and pattern of organization (classification) that Baker uses in the essay.

Reading Support

THINK central

This selection on **thinkcentral.com** includes embedded **ThinkAloud** models–students "thinking aloud" about the story to model the kinds of questions a good reader would ask about a selection.

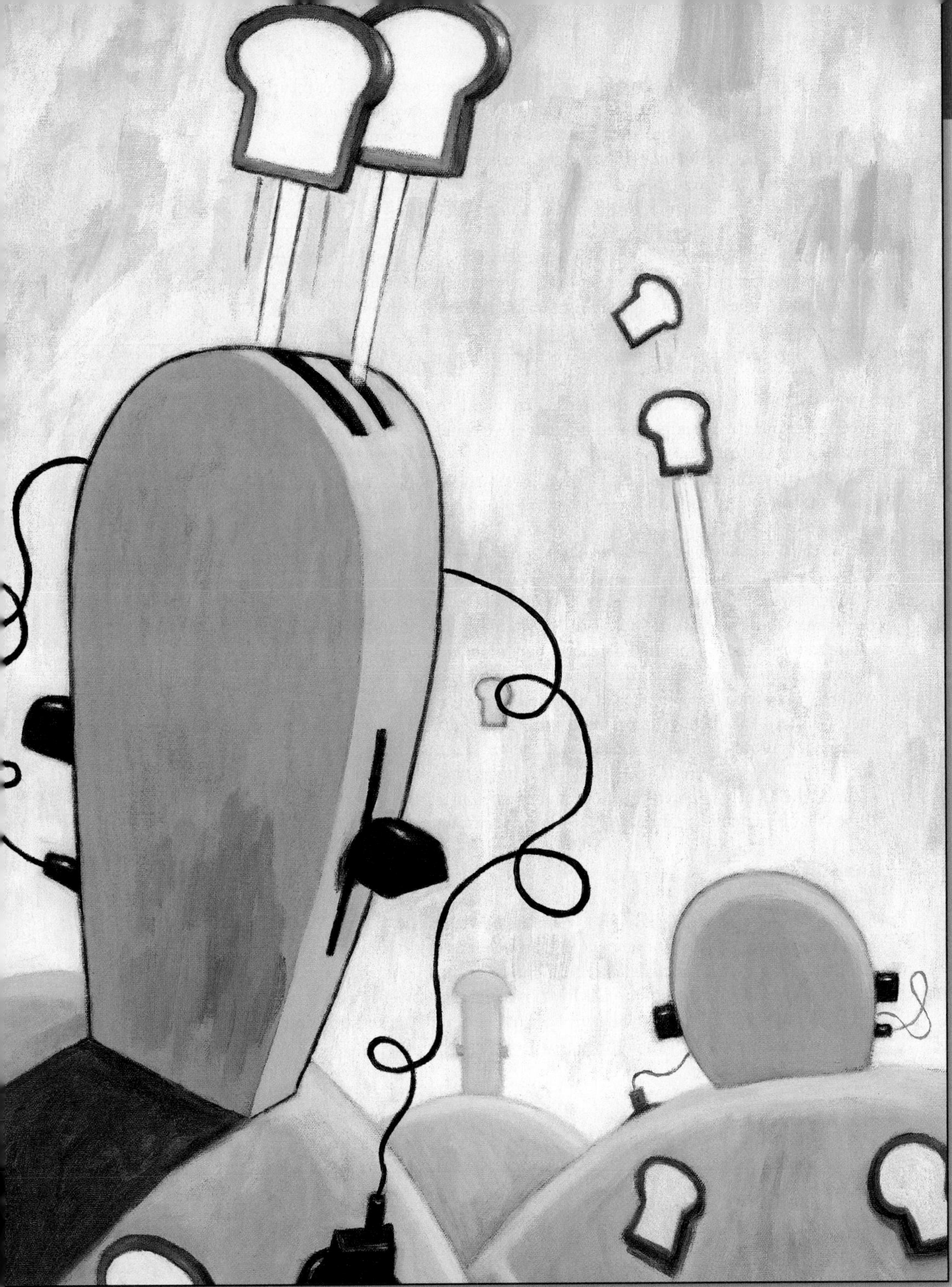

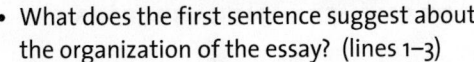

TIERED DISCUSSION PROMPTS

Direct students to lines 15–19. Use these prompts to help students grasp Baker's use of irony in this essay:

Analyze In this paragraph, Baker offers a theory about why things break down. What is that theory? ***Possible answer:*** *Baker's theory is that the objects that he names break down on purpose to frustrate their human enemies.* Why is Baker's statement ironic? ***Possible answer:*** *Baker's theory differs dramatically from reality—namely, the fact that things break down because parts wear out or construction was shoddy. It is ironic because both he and we know the truth.*

Evaluate Not all irony is humorous. Is this example humorous? Defend your view. ***Possible answer:*** *This example of irony is humorous. The reader laughs at the absurd idea that inanimate objects are plotting against people. The reader may also laugh at himself or herself for relying on these conveniences and for taking it so hard when they break down.*

Analyze Visuals

Possible answer: The tone is playful. The toasters seem alive and willful, popping out toast energetically, perhaps to communicate or to compete.

About the Art Charles Kaufman's Toasters on Hills is part of a series of "Toaster Paintings." He began painting seriously after studying modern masters such as Picasso, Matisse, and van Gogh in Budapest in 1990. Still, his paintings reflect the style and sense of humor of his earlier work as a cartoonist.

- What does the first sentence suggest about the organization of the essay? (lines 1–3)
- In which sentence does Baker present the main idea of the essay? In your own words, what is that main idea? (lines 4–6)
- What general rule does Baker name (lines 6–7)? What does the statement suggest about the tone of the essay? (lines 6–7)

FOR ADVANCED LEARNERS/PRE–AP

Analyze Personification Ask students to write a paragraph or two about the ways in which Baker makes inanimate objects appear human. For example, how does he suggest that they have the power to think? What motives does he ascribe to them? Urge students to cite examples from the essay to support their ideas. Have students share and compare their analyses in small groups.

It is not uncommon for a pair of pliers to climb all the way from the cellar to the attic in its single-minded determination to raise its owner's blood
30 pressure. Keys have been known to burrow three feet under mattresses. Women's purses, despite their great weight, frequently travel through six or seven rooms to find hiding space under a couch.

Scientists have been struck by the fact that things that break down virtually never get lost, while things that get lost hardly ever break down.

A furnace, for example, will invariably break down at the depth of the first winter cold wave, but it will never get lost. A woman's purse, which after all does have some inherent capacity for breaking down, hardly ever does; it almost invariably chooses to get lost. **C**

Some persons believe this constitutes evidence that inanimate objects are
40 not entirely hostile to man, and that a negotiated peace is possible. After all, they point out, a furnace could infuriate a man even more thoroughly by getting lost than by breaking down, just as a glove could upset him far more by breaking down than by getting lost.

Not everyone agrees, however, that this indicates a conciliatory attitude among inanimate objects. Many say it merely proves that furnaces, gloves, and pliers are incredibly stupid.

The third class of objects—those that don't work—is the most curious of all. These include such objects as barometers, car clocks, cigarette lighters, flashlights, and toy-train locomotives. It is inaccurate, of course, to say that
50 they never work. They work once, usually for the first few hours after being brought home, and then quit. Thereafter, they never work again.

In fact, it is widely assumed that they are built for the purpose of not working. Some people have reached advanced ages without ever seeing some of these objects—barometers, for example—in working order.

Science is utterly baffled by the entire category. There are many theories about it. The most interesting holds that the things that don't work have attained the highest state possible for an inanimate object, the state to which things that break down and things that get lost can still only aspire. **D**

They Give Peace

They have truly defeated man by conditioning him never to expect anything
60 of them, and in return they have given man the only peace he receives from inanimate society. He does not expect his barometer to work, his electric locomotive to run, his cigarette lighter to light, or his flashlight to illuminate, and when they don't, it does not raise his blood pressure.

He cannot attain that peace with furnaces and keys and cars and women's purses as long as he demands that they work for their keep. ❧ **E**

② Targeted Passage

TEXT ANALYSIS   COMMON CORE   RI 4

C Model the Skill: TONE AND DICTION

Read aloud lines 35–38, and point out that formal language usually creates a serious tone. Discuss whether Baker's attitude in these lines is serious. Have students identify other words in lines 28–38 that describe his attitude.

Possible answer: *Baker uses multisyllabic, "formal" terms, such as "invariably" (line 35) and "inherent capacity" (line 37). His attitude isn't serious: The idea of a furnace's getting lost or a purse's breaking down is humorous, as is the suggestion that a purse would choose to get lost.*

READING SKILL   COMMON CORE   RI 3

D CLASSIFICATION

Possible answer: *The third class is the most curious because these objects quit after one use and seem built for that very purpose.*

TEXT ANALYSIS   COMMON CORE   RI 4

E TONE AND DICTION

Possible answer: *Baker uses long sentences and formal language, such as "inanimate society," "illuminate," and "attain" to discuss simple, ordinary objects in a fanciful way, thereby creating irony and humor.*

C TONE AND DICTION
Reread lines 35–38. In what ways does Baker imitate formal writing in this passage? How serious is his attitude?

COMMON CORE RI 4

Language Coach

Roots and Affixes In nouns, the suffix *-ory* often means "the place where an action is performed" (as in *observatory*). In adjectives, it means "performing the action of." Which part of speech results when *-ory* is added to *conciliate* ("win over")? What does *conciliatory* (line 44) mean?

D CLASSIFICATION
Why is the third class of objects "the most curious of all"?

E TONE AND DICTION
Reread lines 59–65. How do Baker's **diction** and **syntax** contribute to the humor in this passage?

SELECTION WRAP–UP

READ WITH A PURPOSE Ask students: Do you agree or disagree with Baker's classification of objects? *Answers will vary.*

⭐ **CRITIQUE** Would this essay have been as effective if Baker had not imitated the style of a scientific paper? Why or why not?

DIFFERENTIATED INSTRUCTION

FOR STRUGGLING READERS

② Targeted Passage [Lines 47–65]
This passage describes the third class of objects and brings the essay to a close.

• What characteristic do the items in this class have in common? (lines 50–51)

• What theory explains their behavior? (lines 56–57)

• How are the first two groups similar? How are both different from the third group? (lines 64–65)

FOR ENGLISH LANGUAGE LEARNERS

Language Coach   COMMON CORE RI 4

Roots and Affixes *Answer: The suffix* -ory *forms an adjective here.* Conciliatory *means "winning over" or "soothing."* Name other words with the suffix *-ory,* such as *laboratory, inventory, exploratory,* and *investigatory.* Then ask students to identify the part of speech and offer a definition of each word.

Comprehension

1. **Recall** According to Baker, how does the breakdown of inanimate objects affect humans?

2. **Recall** What reason does Baker give for calling furnaces, gloves, and pliers "incredibly stupid"?

3. **Clarify** How have things that don't work "attained the highest possible state"?

Text Analysis

● 4. **Recognize Classification** Review the classification chart you created. Explain what distinguishes the three classes of objects from each other and what links them. Why do you think Baker chose to discuss them in the order he did?

5. **Connect** What objects in your own life fit into the classes Baker describes?

6. **Interpret Title** What is "the plot against people"? Would "Life's Little Nuisances" be as effective a title for an essay about annoyances? Explain why or why not.

● 7. **Analyze Tone and Diction** How would you describe the overall tone of Baker's essay? What aspects of the essay created the tone—elevated diction and syntax, unexpected images, or other factors? Use a chart like the one shown to provide examples that support your answer.

Key Element	Evidence from Text	Description of Tone
Diction		
Syntax		
Images		
Other		

8. **Identify Author's Purpose** Considering Baker's tone and diction in this selection, what do you think his purpose is for writing about this subject? Use strong evidence from the text to support your answer.

9. **Evaluate** *New York Times* critic Christopher Buckley said this about humorous writing: "We should always treat light things humorously and serious things lightly." Evaluate Baker's essay with respect to Buckley's comment.

When are little things a BIG DEAL?

How do you respond to life's annoyances? What are the advantages of responding with humor?

COMMON CORE

RI 3 Analyze how the author unfolds a series of ideas, including the order in which the points are made. RI 4 Determine the meaning of words and phrases as they are used in a text; analyze the cumulative impact of specific word choices on meaning and tone.

Practice and Apply

For preliminary support of post-reading questions, use these copy masters:

R RESOURCE MANAGER—Copy Masters
Reading Check p. 25
Tone and Diction p. 21
Question Support p. 26

Additional selection questions are provided for teachers on page 15.

ANSWERS

Comprehension

1. *The breakdown creates maximum misery and frustration and thereby shortens human lives (lines 13–14).*

2. *These objects are "stupid" for not choosing the most excruciating way to frustrate humans: getting lost.*

3. *Things that don't work have "attained the highest possible state" by conditioning humans to expect nothing from them.*

Text Analysis

COMMON CORE RI 3, RI 4

Possible answers:

4. ■ COMMON CORE FOCUS *Recognize Classification Things that break down do so at inconvenient times; things that get lost can't break down, so they hide; things that don't work have conditioned people to expect little of them. All three categories resist human desires, causing frustration and suffering. Baker ordered the categories according to their level of evolution, and his outlandish theory adds to the irony and humor.*

Assess and Reteach

Assess

DIAGNOSTIC AND SELECTION TESTS
Selection Test A pp. 139–140
Selection Test B/C pp. 141–142

Interactive Selection Test on **thinkcentral.com**

Reteach

Level Up Online Tutorials on **thinkcentral.com**

Reteaching Worksheets on **thinkcentral.com**
Literature Lessons 40, 43

---

5. *Answers will vary but may include computers and cell phones; eyeglasses and keys; and cheap ballpoint pens.*

6. *"The plot against people" is inanimate objects' deliberate efforts to resist and frustrate people. "Life's Little Nuisances" would not be as effective a title, because more humor arises from the idea that objects have intentions and motives.*

7. ● COMMON CORE FOCUS *Tone and Diction The overall tone is light and humorous. The contrast between the elevated diction and the common, everyday subject creates humor, as does the complicated*

syntax. Incongruous images, such as the cunning automobile and stealthily climbing pliers.

8. *Baker's purpose is to entertain and amuse through word choices and details.*

9. *As Buckley suggests, Baker's essay treats light things humorously.*

When are little things a BIG DEAL?
Have students think about how humor helps them cope with life's difficulties.

Focus and Motivate

COMMON CORE FOCUS

RI 4 Determine the meaning of words and phrases as they are used in a text. **RI 5** Analyze in detail how an author's ideas or claims are developed by sentences, paragraphs, or larger portions of text. **RI 6** Determine an author's point of view or purpose in a text. **L 1b** Use various types of phrases to convey meanings and add variety and interest to writing. **L 6** Acquire and use accurately domain-specific words and phrases.

SUMMARY

In this poetic essay, Diane Ackerman explains why autumn leaves turn color and fall from their trees. She reflects on things that autumn leaves remind us of, including our own mortality.

Can **BEAUTY** be captured in words?

Read the question aloud, and have volunteers propose brief answers. Then have students complete the *DISCUSS* activity, and invite them to share the challenges of capturing beauty in words.

Selection Resources

Before Reading

Essential Course of Study **ECOS**

Why Leaves Turn Color in the Fall

Essay by Diane Ackerman

VIDEO TRAILER | **THINK** central | KEYWORD: HML10-538

Can **BEAUTY** be captured in words?

COMMON CORE

RI 4 Determine the meaning of words and phrases as they are used in a text. **RI 5** Analyze in detail how an author's ideas or claims are developed by sentences, paragraphs, or larger portions of text. **RI 6** Determine an author's point of view or purpose in a text.

How would you describe a beautiful sunset to someone who had not seen it? How would you explain this same sunset to a child who wondered why it occurred? Would explaining the sunset make it seem more beautiful, or less? In the following essay, Diane Ackerman captures the beauty of autumn leaves while explaining the scientific concepts behind their occurrence.

DISCUSS Describe to a partner, in as much detail as you can, a beautiful scene from nature. This might be a sunset (as mentioned before), a flock of birds taking wing, or any other natural phenomenon. Afterward, discuss how easy—or hard—it was for you to convert the scene to words and for your partner to visualize the scene.

538

See resources on the **Teacher One Stop DVD-ROM** and on **thinkcentral.com**.

 RESOURCE MANAGER UNIT 5
Plan and Teach, pp. 29–36
Summary, pp. 37–38†‡*
Text Analysis and Reading
  Skill, pp. 39–42†*
Vocabulary, pp. 43–45*
Grammar and Style, p. 48

**DIAGNOSTIC AND SELECTION
  TESTS**
Selection Tests, pp. 143–146

 BEST PRACTICES TOOLKIT
Word Questioning, p. E9
Whip Around, p. B1
T Chart, p. A25

INTERACTIVE READER

ADAPTED INTERACTIVE READER

ELL ADAPTED INTERACTIVE READER

TECHNOLOGY
- **Teacher One Stop DVD-ROM**
- **Student One Stop DVD-ROM**
- **PowerNotes DVD-ROM**
- **Audio Anthology CD**
- **GrammarNotes DVD-ROM**
- **Audio Tutor CD**
- **ExamView Test Generator**
  on the Teacher One Stop

THINK central

Video Trailer

Go to **thinkcentral.com** to preview the **Video Trailer** introducing this selection. Other features that support the selection include
- **PowerNotes** presentation
- **ThinkAloud** models to enhance comprehension
- **WordSharp** vocabulary tutorials
- interactive writing and grammar instruction

---

* Resources for Differentiation   † Also in Spanish   ‡ In Haitian Creole and Vietnamese

TEXT ANALYSIS: AUTHOR'S PURPOSE

Author's purpose is the reason why a writer writes. An author may write to explain a process, to describe a scene, to reflect on an idea, or, in the case of Diane Ackerman, to do all three. Her overall purpose in this essay is to explain why leaves turn color and fall from trees. To that end, she uses scientific terms.

A corky layer of cells forms at the leaves' slender petioles, then scars over. Undernourished, the leaves stop producing the pigment chlorophyll, and photosynthesis ceases.

Ackerman also wants to describe the beauty of autumn leaves, and to that end she uses poetic diction and **imagery,** words and phrases that re-create sensory experiences.

They glide and swoop, rocking in invisible cradles. They are all wing and may flutter from yard to yard on small whirlwinds or updrafts, swiveling as they go.

As you read, determine the main purpose of each paragraph— to explain, to describe, or to reflect.

● READING SKILL: PATTERNS OF ORGANIZATION

Ackerman uses at least three **patterns of organization:**

- **cause and effect,** to explain a process
- **comparison and contrast,** to show likeness and difference
- **main idea and supporting details,** to present insights

As you read, look for cause-and-effect organization. Fill out two cause-and-effect chains—one to show why leaves turn color and another to show why they fall.

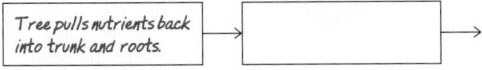

Tree pulls nutrients back into trunk and roots. → →

▲ VOCABULARY IN CONTEXT

Diane Ackerman conveys the richness of her subject by using the following boldfaced words. Define each word.

1. **stealth** in her smooth, silent movement
2. a judge issuing an **edict** in the courtroom
3. an athlete, tall and **robustly** built
4. a painter's son, **predisposed** to the arts
5. **adaptation** of an animal to its environment
6. the monkey's **capricious,** unpredictable nature

 Complete the activities in your **Reader/Writer Notebook.**

Meet the Author

Diane Ackerman
born 1948

Done It All
Diane Ackerman considers herself a nature writer "if what we mean by Nature is . . . the full sum of Creation." She has worked as a sports journalist and a crisis counselor as well as a writer-in-residence. She has dared to fly planes, scuba dive, swim with a whale, and sit on an alligator with its mouth taped shut. Naturally, she has written about all of these experiences. She often finds herself "in a state of complete rapture about a discipline or field," which helps explain why science and natural history are so often incorporated into her work.

Science and Poetry
Ackerman's interest in science began in childhood when she raised turtles and observed that plums hanging from a tree looked like bats. She lives in upstate New York on two acres of wooded land that includes a portion set aside for deer. She is an accomplished poet as well as a nature writer. One of her works is a verse play about Sor Juana Inés de la Cruz, a 17th-century Mexican nun who was a poet and a scientist.

Authors Online
Go to **thinkcentral.com.** KEYWORD: HML10-539

THINK central

539

Teach

TEXT ANALYSIS   COMMON CORE
RI 4
RI 6

● *Model the Skill:* AUTHOR'S PURPOSE

To model how to determine the author's purpose, read this passage aloud:

> The natural beauty of Lighthouse Beach is spectacular. The blue-green ocean slowly laps against the sand, awakening the tiny creatures asleep in their shells.

Point out that the author uses poetic language and imagery. Tell students that the author's purpose is to describe.

GUIDED PRACTICE Have students identify the author's purpose in a different passage.

READING SKILL   COMMON CORE
RI 5

■ *Model the Skill:* PATTERNS OF ORGANIZATION

Write this passage on the board:

> When a meteoroid falls into the earth's atmosphere, it burns up, and a trail of light appears as a shooting star.

On the board, draw a cause-and-effect chain to show the pattern: meteoroid falls, burns up, trail of light appears.

GUIDED PRACTICE Have students fill out a cause-and-effect chain to explain a natural event.

[R] RESOURCE MANAGER—Copy Master
Analyze Cause and Effect p. 41

VOCABULARY SKILL

COMMON CORE
L 4

▲ VOCABULARY IN CONTEXT

DIAGNOSE WORD KNOWLEDGE Have all students complete Vocabulary in Context. Check their definitions against the following:

adaptation (ăd′ăp-tā′shən) *n.* the process of adjusting to suit one's surroundings
capricious (kə-prĭsh′əs) *adj.* impulsive, unpredictable
edict (ē′dĭkt′) *n.* a command issued by an authority
predisposed (prē′dĭ-spōzd′) *v.* inclined to something in advance

robustly (rō-bŭst′lē) *adv.* in a strong, powerful way
stealth (stĕlth) *n.* a concealed manner of acting

PRETEACH VOCABULARY Use the following copy master to help students predict meanings for each boldfaced word.

[R] RESOURCE MANAGER—Copy Master
Vocabulary Study p. 43

1. Read item 1 aloud, emphasizing *stealth.*

2. Point out the phrase "oftentimes arrives undetected." Elicit possible meanings for *stealth,* such as "sneakiness."

3. Have students record their predictions.

4. Repeat the procedure for items 2–6.

Practice and Apply

READ WITH A PURPOSE

Have students read to discover why leaves turn color and fall off trees in the autumn.

Ⓐ AUTHOR'S PURPOSE

Remind students that explanatory writing often uses scientific terms, descriptive writing often uses imagery and poetic language, and reflective writing often talks about ideas. Guide students to conclude that since all the details in the paragraph fall under the category of either imagery or poetic language, the purpose of the paragraph must be to describe.

Possible answer: Ackerman's purpose is to describe the arrival of autumn (line 1). She uses vivid sensory details, such as "Early-morning frost sits heavily on the grass" (lines 4–5) and "baggage of chilly nights" (line 8).

OWN THE WORD

- **stealth:** *Stealth* refers to a "concealed manner of acting," and successfully describes how time, as marked by seasons, tends to sneak up on us. Have students link this noun to other nouns to paint a similar picture. *Possible answer: stealth of a burglar*

- **edict:** *Edict* is a strong word that refers to a "command issued by an authority." Ask students why they think it is effective in lines 14–15. *Possible answer: Used with the word* rules, *it reminds the reader that without the sun, all living things would die*

Why Leaves Turn Color in the Fall

DIANE ACKERMAN

The **stealth** of autumn catches one unaware. Was that a goldfinch perching in the early September woods, or just the first turning leaf? A red-winged blackbird or a sugar maple closing up shop for the winter? Keen-eyed as leopards, we stand still and squint hard, looking for signs of movement. Early-morning frost sits heavily on the grass, and turns barbed wire into a string of stars. On a distant hill, a small square of yellow appears to be a lighted stage. At last the truth dawns on us: Fall is staggering in, right on schedule, with its baggage of chilly nights, macabre holidays, and spectacular, heart-stoppingly beautiful leaves. Soon the leaves will start cringing on the trees, and roll up

10 in clenched fists before they actually fall off. Dry seedpods will rattle like tiny gourds. But first there will be weeks of gushing color so bright, so pastel, so confettilike, that people will travel up and down the East Coast just to stare at it—a whole season of leaves. Ⓐ

Where do the colors come from? Sunlight rules most living things with its golden **edicts.** When the days begin to shorten, soon after the summer solstice on June 21, a tree reconsiders its leaves. All summer it feeds them so they can process sunlight, but in the dog days of summer the tree begins pulling nutrients back into its trunk and roots, pares down, and gradually chokes off its leaves. A corky layer of cells forms at the leaves' slender petioles,[1] then scars

20 over. Undernourished, the leaves stop producing the pigment chlorophyll, and photosynthesis[2] ceases. Animals can migrate, hibernate, or store food to prepare for winter. But where can a tree go? It survives by dropping its leaves,

---

1. **petioles:** the stalks of leaves.

2. **chlorophyll . . . photosynthesis:** Chlorophyll is the green pigment in plants that is necessary for photosynthesis, the process by which plants use sunlight, water, and carbon dioxide to produce food.

COMMON CORE   RI 4

Language Coach

Denotations/Connotations The feelings and ideas associated with a word are its **connotations.** *Staggering* and *toddling* both mean "moving unsteadily." *Toddling* suggests youth; what does *staggering* (line 7) suggest?

①

Ⓐ AUTHOR'S PURPOSE
What seems to be Ackerman's purpose in the first paragraph? Support your answer with specific details.

edict (ē′dĭkt′) *n.* a command issued by an authority

stealth (stĕlth) *n.* a concealed manner of acting

DIFFERENTIATED INSTRUCTION

FOR ENGLISH LANGUAGE LEARNERS

Language Coach   COMMON CORE RI 4

Denotations/Connotations
Answer: old age, drunkenness, or exhaustion Lead students to explore the connotations of other words in the first paragraph. Point out that the word *baggage* (line 8) often connotes something that is unwanted, *cringing* (line 9) connotes fear, and *gushing* (line 11) suggests something overwhelming.

FOR STRUGGLING READERS

In combination with the *Audio Anthology CD,* use one or more Targeted Passages (pp. 540, 544) to ensure that students focus on key events, concepts, and skills. Targeted Passages are also good for English learners.

① **Targeted Passage** [Lines 7–21]

This passage introduces students to the signs of fall in the Northeast and explains how trees change their leaves.

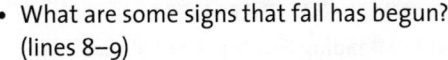

Reading Support

This selection on **thinkcentral.com** includes embedded **ThinkAloud** models—students "thinking aloud" about the story to model the kinds of questions a good reader would ask about a selection.

BACKGROUND

Autumn In the Northern Hemisphere, autumn officially begins on the autumnal equinox (September 22 or 23), when day and night are the same length. The season officially ends on the winter solstice (December 21 or 22), the shortest day of the year. As autumn progresses, the sun rises and sets more and more to the south, causing the days to shorten and the nights to lengthen. Depending on the previous summer's weather, leaf color may start to change before the official start of autumn, also known as fall. In the northeastern United States, the leaves are usually entirely off the trees well before the official end of the season.

Analyze Visuals

Activity Ask students to compare this photograph of leaves with Ackerman's description of leaves in lines 7–13 and 48–57. Which does a better job of capturing the beauty of the leaves, the visual image or the words? Ask students to explain their responses. *Students should support their answers with reasons.*

TIERED DISCUSSION PROMPTS

Direct students to lines 1–13. Use these prompts to help students understand the imaginative imagery that Ackerman uses to describe the arrival of fall:

Analyze What visual image does Ackerman conjure up in lines 7–9? *Possible answer: She presents an image of fall as a traveler staggering under the weight of heavy bags.*

Evaluate How effective is Ackerman's imagery in describing the arrival of fall? Explain. *Accept all thoughtful responses.*

- What are some signs that fall has begun? (lines 8–9)
- What does Ackerman mean when she says, "Sunlight rules most living things with its golden edicts"? (lines 14–15)
- What happens to a tree's leaves during the summer? (lines 16–19)
- What happens to the leaves when the tree starts to hold onto its nutrients? (lines 19–21)

FOR ENGLISH LANGUAGE LEARNERS

Vocabulary Support Use Word Questioning strategies to teach these words: *schedule* (line 7), *defining* (line 27), *occurs* (line 34), *achieve* (line 36), *varies* (line 42), *respond* (line 59).

 BEST PRACTICES TOOLKIT—Transparency Word Questioning p. E9

B *Model the Skill:* PATTERNS OF ORGANIZATION

Read lines 14–24 aloud. Point out transitions such as *when* and *soon after* (line 15) that signal causes and effects.

Possible answer:

Days begin to shorten. (line 15)

↓

Tree pulls nutrients back into its trunk and roots. (lines 17–19)

↓

Corky layer of cells forms at petioles and scars over. (lines 19–20)

↓

Leaves become undernourished. (line 20)

↓

Leaves stop producing chlorophyll. (line 20)

↓

Photosynthesis stops. (line 21)

↓

Leaves die and fall off. (lines 22–24)

C PATTERNS OF ORGANIZATION

Possible answer:

Leaves stop producing chlorophyll.

↓

Chlorophyll no longer hides the yellow and red pigments (lines 25–26)

↓

The leaves turn color.

OWN THE WORD

robustly: The adverb *robustly* comes from the Latin *robus* meaning "oak, strength."

---

and by the end of autumn only a few fragile threads of fluid-carrying xylem[3] hold leaves to their stems. B

A turning leaf stays partly green at first, then reveals splotches of yellow and red as the chlorophyll gradually breaks down. Dark green seems to stay longest in the veins, outlining and defining them. During the summer, chlorophyll dissolves in the heat and light, but it is also being steadily replaced. In the fall, on the other hand, no new pigment is produced, and so we notice the other
30 colors that were always there, right in the leaf, although chlorophyll's shocking green hid them from view. With their camouflage gone, we see these colors for the first time all year, and marvel, but they were always there, hidden like a vivid secret beneath the hot glowing greens of summer. C

The most spectacular range of fall foliage occurs in the northeastern United States and in eastern China, where the leaves are **robustly** colored, thanks in part to a rich climate. European maples don't achieve the same flaming reds as their American relatives, which thrive on cold nights and sunny days. In Europe, the warm, humid weather turns the leaves brown or mildly yellow. Anthocyanin, the pigment that gives apples their red and turns leaves red or
40 red-violet, is produced by sugars that remain in the leaf after the supply of nutrients dwindles. Unlike the carotenoids, which color carrots, squash, and corn, and turn leaves orange and yellow, anthocyanin varies from year to year, depending on the temperature and amount of sunlight. The fiercest colors occur in years when the fall sunlight is strongest and the nights are cool and dry (a state of grace scientists find vexing to forecast). This is also why leaves

---

3. **xylem:** plant tissue through which water and nutrients are conducted.

B PATTERNS OF ORGANIZATION
In lines 14–24, the pattern of organization switches from main idea and supporting details to cause and effect. Fill out a cause-and-effect chain to show why leaves fall.

C PATTERNS OF ORGANIZATION
Use lines 25–33 to fill out a cause-and-effect chain showing the process of leaves changing color.

robustly (rō-bŭst'lē) *adv.* in a strong, powerful way

DIFFERENTIATED INSTRUCTION

FOR ENGLISH LANGUAGE LEARNERS

Comprehension: Transitions Point out the contrast statement in line 32 and the signal word *but*. Organize students into three groups. Have Group 1 find three contrast statements with *but* on page 540 (lines 9–13, 16–19, 21–22). Have Group 2 find three contrast statements with the signal words *but* or *though* on page 543 (lines 53, 61–64, 69–71). Have Group 3 find three contrast statements with *but* or *although* on page 544 (lines 99–100, 101–103, 104–105).

FOR STRUGGLING READERS

Develop Reading Fluency Read aloud lines 25–33 pausing at commas and stopping at periods. Have students repeat each sentence aloud, mimicking your pacing. Then have student pairs practice reading the entire passage aloud, using punctuation to pace themselves. Distribute the copy masters and have students work in teams or pairs to practice fluency.

R RESOURCE MANAGER—Copy Master
Reading Fluency p. 49

appear dizzyingly bright and clear on a sunny fall day: The anthocyanin flashes like a marquee.[4]

Not all leaves turn the same colors. Elms, weeping willows, and the ancient gingko all grow radiant yellow, along with hickories, aspens, bottlebrush
50 buckeyes, cottonweeds, and tall, keening poplars. Basswood turns bronze, birches bright gold. Water-loving maples put on a symphonic display of scarlets. Sumacs turn red, too, as do flowering dogwoods, black gums, and sweet gums. Though some oaks yellow, most turn a pinkish brown. The farmlands also change color, as tepees of cornstalks and bales of shredded-wheat-textured hay stand drying in the fields. In some spots, one slope of a hill may be green and the other already in bright color, because the hillside facing south gets more sun and heat than the northern one.

An odd feature of the colors is that they don't seem to have any special purpose. We are **predisposed** to respond to their beauty, of course. They
60 shimmer with the colors of sunset, spring flowers, the tawny buff of a colt's pretty rump, the shuddering pink of a blush. Animals and flowers color for a reason—**adaptation** to their environment—but there is no adaptive reason for leaves to color so beautifully in the fall any more than there is for the sky or ocean to be blue. It's just one of the haphazard marvels the planet bestows every year. We find the sizzling colors thrilling, and in a sense they dupe us. Colored like living things, they signal death and disintegration. In time, they will become fragile and, like the body, return to dust. They are as we hope our own fate will be when we die: Not to vanish, just to sublime[5] from one beautiful state into another. Though leaves lose their green life, they bloom
70 with urgent colors, as the woods grow mummified day by day, and Nature becomes more carnal, mute, and radiant.

We call the season "fall," from the Old English *feallan,* to fall, which leads back through time to the Indo-European *phol,* which also means to fall. So the word and the idea are both extremely ancient, and haven't really changed since the first of our kind needed a name for fall's leafy abundance. As we say the word, we're reminded of that other Fall, in the garden of Eden, when fig leaves never withered and scales fell from our eyes. Fall is the time when leaves fall from the trees, just as spring is when flowers spring up, summer is when we simmer, and winter is when we whine from the cold.

80 Children love to play in piles of leaves, hurling them into the air like confetti, leaping into soft unruly mattresses of them. For children, leaf fall is just one of the odder figments of Nature, like hailstones or snowflakes. Walk down a lane overhung with trees in the never-never land of autumn, and you will forget about time and death, lost in the sheer delicious spill of color. Adam and Eve concealed their nakedness with leaves, remember? Leaves have always hidden our awkward secrets.

But how do the colored leaves fall? As a leaf ages, the growth hormone, auxin, fades, and cells at the base of the petiole divide. Two or three rows of

---

4. **marquee:** a lighted billboard, such as those used at movie theaters.

5. **sublime:** to transform directly into another state.

D AUTHOR'S PURPOSE
Using scientific **diction**—the terms *anthocyanin* and *carotenoids*—helps Ackerman explain the difference between the pigments found in leaves. How do they differ?

predisposed
(prē'dĭ-spōzd') *v.*
inclined to something in advance

adaptation
(ăd'ăp-tā'shən) *n.*
the process of adjusting to suit one's surroundings

E AUTHOR'S PURPOSE
Reread lines 65–71. Here Ackerman reflects on the deaths of living things, including human beings. What does she say we hope for ourselves?

F AUTHOR'S PURPOSE
Reread lines 72–86. What seems to be Ackerman's purpose in each paragraph? Cite specific words and phrases to support your answers.

TEXT ANALYSIS — COMMON CORE

D AUTHOR'S PURPOSE — RI 4 RI 6

Possible answer: Anthocyanin is a red pigment that varies based on temperature and the amount of sunlight (lines 39–43). Carotenoids are orange and yellow pigments that do not vary (lines 41–42).

TEXT ANALYSIS — COMMON CORE

E AUTHOR'S PURPOSE — RI 4 RI 6

Possible answer: Ackerman says that people hope they won't vanish when they die. Instead, they hope to go from one beautiful state into another (lines 68–69).

TEXT ANALYSIS — COMMON CORE

F AUTHOR'S PURPOSE — RI 4 RI 6

Possible answer: The author informs readers about the origin of the word "fall" (lines 72–73) and refers to Adam and Eve's fall in the biblical garden of Eden (lines 76–77, 84–86). She also reflects on what falling leaves mean to children (lines 80–82).

REVISIT THE BIG QUESTION
Can **BEAUTY** be captured in words?

Discuss In lines 58–65, Ackerman says we are "predisposed" to respond to the beauty of autumn leaves because they "shimmer with the colors of sunset, spring flowers . . . the shuddering pink of a blush." What do you think of this idea?

VOCABULARY — COMMON CORE

OWN THE WORD — L 4

• **predisposed:** Explain that *predisposed* is related to the verb *dispose,* which can mean "to put into a receptive frame of mind." The prefix *pre-* means "before."

• **adaptation:** Have students use a thesaurus to create semantic maps for *adaptation.*

FOR ENGLISH LANGUAGE LEARNERS

Comprehension: Transitions Remind students that this selection has many cause-and-effect statements. Have pairs find the cause-and-effect statements on pages 543 and 544 (lines 55–57, 61–62, 109–110). Invite students to submit a cause to the class and ask for the effect. Record causes and effects on the board.

FOR ADVANCED LEARNERS/PRE–AP

Synthesize Point out Ackerman's references to Adam and Eve and the garden of Eden (lines 76–77, 84–86). Have small groups read this biblical story in the book of Genesis and then consider Ackerman's statement that "Leaves have always hidden our awkward secrets" (lines 85–86). Ask students to link this statement to the Adam and Eve story. How is the essay's description of fall reflected in this account?

Possible answer: *The photos on pages 541 and 542 emphasize the beautiful colors of fall leaves. The photo on page 544 shows how falling leaves "glide and swoop" (line 91).*

◀ **Analyze Visuals**

Study the photographs on this page and on pages 541 and 542. What qualities of autumn leaves are brought out in each photo? How do the photos add to the visual appeal of the selection?

GRAMMAR AND STYLE

COMMON CORE
L 1b

Analyze Descriptive Details Point out to students that these phrases help readers visualize falling leaves. Have students find other participial phrases in the essay and explain how they add descriptive details.

small cells, lying at right angles to the axis of the petiole, react with water, then
90 come apart, leaving the petioles hanging on by only a few threads of xylem. A light breeze, and the leaves are airborne. They glide and swoop, rocking in invisible cradles. They are all wing and may flutter from yard to yard on small whirlwinds or updrafts, swiveling as they go. Firmly tethered[6] to earth, we love to see things rise up and fly—soap bubbles, balloons, birds, fall leaves. They remind us that the end of a season is **capricious,** as is the end of life. We especially like the way leaves rock, careen, and swoop as they fall. Everyone knows the motion. Pilots sometimes do a maneuver called a "falling leaf," in which the plane loses altitude quickly and on purpose, by slipping first to the right, then to the left. The machine weighs a ton or more, but in one pilot's
100 mind it is a weightless thing, a falling leaf. She has seen the motion before, in the Vermont woods where she played as a child. Below her the trees radiate gold, copper, and red. Leaves are falling, although she can't see them fall, as she falls, swooping down for a closer view.

At last the leaves leave. But first they turn color and thrill us for weeks on end. Then they crunch and crackle under foot. They *shush,* as children drag their small feet through the leaves heaped along the curb. Dark, slimy mats of leaves cling to one's heels after a rain. A damp, stuccolike mortar[7] of semidecayed leaves protects the tender shoots with a roof until spring, and makes a rich humus.[8] An occasional bulge or ripple in the leafy mounds signals
110 a shrew or a field mouse tunneling out of sight. Sometimes one finds in fossil stones the imprint of a leaf, long since disintegrated, whose outlines remind us how detailed, vibrant, and alive are the things of this earth that perish. ❧ **H**

G GRAMMAR AND STYLE
Reread lines 91–93. Ackerman effectively uses the **participial phrases** "rocking in invisible cradles" and "swiveling as they go" to vividly describe the falling leaves.

capricious
(kə-prĭsh'əs)
adj. impulsive, unpredictable

② Targeted Passage

H AUTHOR'S PURPOSE
Think about Ackerman's purpose in the last paragraph. How is her purpose supported by her **diction** and use of **imagery**?

---

6. **tethered:** fastened, as if with a rope.
7. **stuccolike mortar:** a bonding material that is like a soft, sticky plaster.
8. **humus:** decomposed organic matter that provides nutrients for plants.

TEXT ANALYSIS

COMMON CORE
RI 4
RI 6

H AUTHOR'S PURPOSE

Possible answer: *Her purpose is to describe the look, sound, and feel of fall leaves. She uses onomatopoetic words such as crunch, crackle, and shush (line 105). Images such as "Dark, slimy mats" (lines 106–107) and "damp, stuccolike mortar" (line 107) describe the texture of wet fallen leaves. The image of the fossilized leaf (lines 110–112) gives a sense of permanence to something impermanent.*

VOCABULARY

COMMON CORE
L 4

OWN THE WORD

capricious: Have students list actions that might make them appear *capricious*.

SELECTION WRAP-UP

READ WITH A PURPOSE Ask students: How do you respond to the change of seasons and the colors of fall? Have students use details and sensory language in their responses. *Student answers will vary.*

⭐ **CRITIQUE** Have students evaluate whether this essay is primarily informative, descriptive, or reflective and support their opinions.

DIFFERENTIATED INSTRUCTION

FOR STRUGGLING READERS

② Targeted Passage [Lines 93–103]

This passage allows students to reflect on what falling leaves look like and how people respond to them.

- According to Ackerman, why do people love to see falling leaves? (lines 93–94)
- How do falling leaves remind us of the end of life? (line 95)
- How do falling leaves resemble the pilot's "falling leaf" maneuver? (lines 97–100)

FOR ENGLISH LANGUAGE LEARNERS

Language: Modifiers Point out Ackerman's frequent use of adjectives to describe nature. Lead a Whip Around activity, asking students to call out a noun-adjective pair that they found particularly striking. Record the pairs in a T Chart on the board. Review that verbs such as *become* and *grow* may join nouns to adjectives.

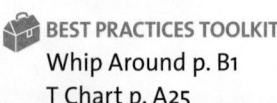
BEST PRACTICES TOOLKIT
Whip Around p. B1
T Chart p. A25

Comprehension

1. **Recall** How does dropping its leaves in autumn help a tree to survive?

2. **Paraphrase** What does Ackerman mean by autumn's "stealth"?

3. **Paraphrase** In what ways do the bright colors of autumn "dupe" us?

Text Analysis

4. **Identify Author's Purpose** In which parts of her essay is Ackerman's purpose to explain? to describe? to reflect? Are these purposes compatible? Explain your answer.

5. **Analyze Patterns of Organization** Use the cause-and-effect chains you created to explain why leaves turn color and why they fall. Be specific.

6. **Recognize Contrasts** What contrasts are pointed out in the essay? Cite examples.

7. **Analyze Language** Ackerman's language can be very poetic, filled with sensory **imagery.** Skim the essay and record notable examples. Which examples best describe the beauty of fall? Explain your answer.

> **Sensory Imagery**
> • "Early-morning frost sits heavily ..." (lines 4–5)
> •
> •

8. **Interpret Author's Message** Explain the connection Ackerman sees between fall leaves and human beings. How close does the connection seem to you?

9. **Evaluate Interpretations** One critic has said that Ackerman's nonfiction is "a creative blend of journalism, science, and poetry; it is her poetic vision that makes her nonfiction so successful." Would you say that this is true of her essay? Cite strong text evidence to support your answer.

Can **BEAUTY** be captured in words?

How do you define beauty?

COMMON CORE

RI 5 Analyze in detail how an author's ideas or claims are developed by sentences, paragraphs, or larger portions of text. **RI 6** Determine an author's point of view or purpose in a text.

Practice and Apply

For preliminary support of post-reading questions, use these copy masters:

R RESOURCE MANAGER—Copy Masters
Reading Check p. 46
Author's Purpose p. 39
Question Support p. 47

Additional selection questions are provided for teachers on page 33.

ANSWERS

Comprehension

1. *Dropping its leaves allows a tree to use less energy in the winter.*

2. *Ackerman means that autumn arrives quickly, without clear, unmistakable signs.*

3. *Because the colors are bright, they seem to signal life, but they actually signal death.*

Text Analysis
COMMON CORE RI 5, RI 6

Possible answers:

4. **● COMMON CORE FOCUS** *Author's Purpose Ackerman's purpose is to* **explain** *in the passages that tell why leaves turn color and fall (lines 16–33, 39–47, 87–90). Her purpose is to* **describe** *in the opening paragraph describing the arrival of fall (lines 1–13), in the passage discussing the different colors of leaves (lines 48–61), and in the last two paragraphs describing leaves as they fall and lie on the ground (lines 91–110). Her purpose is to* **reflect** *in the passages about the word fall (lines 72–79), about the garden of Eden (lines 75–77, 84–86), and about death (lines 65–71, 110–112). Accept all reasonable answers about compatibility.*

5. **■ COMMON CORE FOCUS** *Patterns of Organization Leaves turn color when they stop producing the green pigment chlorophyll, and their red and yellow pigments show through (lines 25–26). As the days get shorter (line 15), a tree pulls back its nutrients into its trunk and roots (lines 17–19). A corky layer of cells forms at the petioles and scars over (lines 19–20), causing the leaves to become undernourished and to stop producing chlorophyll (lines 20–21). As a result, photosyn-thesis stops (line 21), and the leaves die and fall off the tree (lines 22–24).*

6. *The vivid fall colors in the northeastern United States and eastern China are contrasted with the duller colors in Europe (lines 34–38). The red pigment anthocyanin*

---

is contrasted with the orange and yellow carotenoids (lines 39–47). The lively color of fall leaves is contrasted with the death it signals (lines 66–67). Earthbound people are contrasted with weightless, falling leaves (lines 93–94).

7. *Examples include "a small square of yellow appears to be a lighted stage" (line 6), "a symphonic display of scarlets" (lines 51–52), and "lost in the sheer delicious spill of color" (line 84).*

8. *Ackerman sees both fall leaves and human beings as impermanent and*

doomed to die. Some students may see a close connection; others may think that it's a stretch.

9. *Agree: Ackerman's poetic style engages readers and broadens their understanding of science. Disagree: Ackerman's poetic style detracts from the essay's clarity.*

Can **BEAUTY** be captured in words?
Before students answer, have them consider whether they agree that "Beauty is in the eye of the beholder."

Vocabulary in Context

▲ VOCABULARY PRACTICE

1. *stealth*
2. *capricious*
3. *edict*
4. *Adaptation*
5. *robustly*
6. *predisposed*

 **RESOURCE MANAGER—Copy Master**
Vocabulary Practice p. 44

ACADEMIC VOCABULARY IN WRITING

*Possible answer: In my **vision**, spring is the most beautiful season. The bright green of new leaves overcomes the gray, brown, and white of winter. Daily changes **document** the rapid growth and rejuvenation of spring.*

VOCABULARY STRATEGY: SPECIALIZED VOCABULARY

COMMON CORE **L 6**

1. organic
2. compost
3. hydrocarbon
4. solstice
5. deciduous

 **RESOURCE MANAGER—Copy Master**
Vocabulary Strategy p. 45

Interactive Vocabulary

THINK central

Keywords direct students to a **WordSharp** tutorial on **thinkcentral.com** or to other types of vocabulary practice and review.

Vocabulary in Context

▲ VOCABULARY PRACTICE

Choose the word that best completes each sentence.

1. With great _____, the lioness tracked her prey.
2. Try not to be _____; think before you act!
3. Our teacher's _____ was that tardy students would be locked out.
4. _____ to a new environment ensures the survival of a species.
5. He shook my hand _____, showing great enthusiasm.
6. As an animal lover, I am _____ to veterinary school.

WORD LIST
adaptation
capricious
edict
predisposed
robustly
stealth

ACADEMIC VOCABULARY IN WRITING

• author   • document   • goal   • issue   • vision

What is your favorite season of the year? **Document** your response by writing a paragraph describing that season. Share your **vision** by creating strong images of the season. Use at least one Academic Vocabulary word in your response.

VOCABULARY STRATEGY: SPECIALIZED VOCABULARY

Biologists and other scientists have their own **specialized vocabulary**— terms specifically suited to their particular fields of study. This vocabulary includes words such as *chlorophyll*, which names the pigment necessary for *photosynthesis*, the name of the process by which plants use sunlight to convert water and carbon dioxide into food. It is often possible to figure out the meaning of a specialized vocabulary term from context. Other times, you will need to look up the terms.

PRACTICE Match each definition below with the appropriate term from the selection. If you need to, check a dictionary or glossary.

compost   deciduous   organic   solstice   hydrocarbon

1. having properties characteristic of living organisms
2. a mixture of decaying matter
3. a compound consisting of hydrogen and carbon
4. the time of year when the sun is farthest from the equator
5. losing foliage at the end of the growing season

COMMON CORE

L 6 Acquire and use accurately domain-specific words and phrases.

Interactive Vocabulary   THINK central
Go to **thinkcentral.com**.
KEYWORD: HML10-546

DIFFERENTIATED INSTRUCTION

FOR STRUGGLING READERS

Vocabulary Practice Have students use context clues to help them choose the correct word for each sentence. For example, for item 1, a lioness would track her prey with sneakiness (stealth). For item 5, a person who shook hands with great enthusiasm would shake hands strongly (robustly).

FOR ENGLISH LANGUAGE LEARNERS

Vocabulary: Cognates Have students identify the words from the Word List that have Romance language cognates. Then ask students which two suffixes almost always indicate that there will be a similar word in Spanish (*-tion* becomes *-ción*; *-ly* becomes *-mente*). Have students find other *-tion* and *-ly* words in the essay and write them, their meanings, and their equivalents in a Three-Column Journal.

 BEST PRACTICES TOOLKIT—Transparency
Three-Column Journal p. B10

Language

◆ GRAMMAR AND STYLE: Add Descriptive Details

 COMMON CORE

L 1b Use various types of phrases to convey meanings and add variety and interest to writing.

Review the **Grammar and Style** note on page 544. Note how Ackerman uses participial phrases to create images of falling leaves.

A **participle** is a verb form (verbal) that acts as an adjective. It modifies a noun or a pronoun. A **participial phrase** consists of a participle plus its modifiers and complements. Here are some examples of how Ackerman uses participles and participial phrases to enrich her writing with imaginative details.

> . . . they were always there, hidden like a vivid secret beneath the hot *glowing greens of summer.* (lines 32–33)

> *Children love to play in piles of leaves, hurling them into the air like confetti, leaping into soft unruly mattresses of them.* (lines 80–81)

Notice how the revisions in blue enliven this first draft by incorporating participles and participial phrases. Try making similar changes when revising your own writing.

STUDENT MODEL

> *growing*   *Moving from junior high to high school,*
> Like leaves during a season, people change as they age. We do not
>   *Losing their leaves*
> always like the same clothes, music, or activities that we used to. ~~When~~
> ~~they lose their leaves,~~ trees do not die, they just become something
>   *exciting and challenging*
> different. Our old selves do not die as we go through changes, either.

READING-WRITING CONNECTION

 YOUR TURN
Expand your understanding of "Why Leaves Turn Color in the Fall" by responding to this prompt. Then use the **revising tip** to improve your writing.

WRITING PROMPT	REVISING TIP
Extended Constructed Response: Reflection What do autumn leaves tell humans about themselves? What does their **beauty** mean? Respond in **three to five paragraphs,** drawing on Ackerman's ideas or your own original ideas.	Review your response. Have you used participial phrases to add descriptive details?

 **Interactive Revision** THINK central
Go to **thinkcentral.com**.
KEYWORD: HML10-547

FOR STRUGGLING WRITERS

- Limit the assignment to three paragraphs.
- Help students review the pertinent parts of the story. Discuss the ideas with students, and help them write a thesis statement.
- Have pairs help each other find supporting details in the story.

Language

◆ GRAMMAR AND STYLE

- After students read the Student Model, have them identify the noun or pronoun that the participial phrase and participles are modifying ("they," "piles of leaves").

- Write this passage on the board. Have students revise it by adding either participial phrases or participles:

> *Falling from trees and disintegrating,* l~~Leaves~~ remind us of our own death. *Encouraged,* w~~We~~ hope to move to another beautiful state, as leaves do.

R RESOURCE MANAGER—Copy Master
Add Descriptive Details p. 48

READING-WRITING CONNECTION

- Have students review lines 65–69, 80–86, 93–95, and 110–112. Ask students to form an opinion statement about the meaning of autumn leaves. Point out that their statement is not factual.

Writing Online THINK central

The following tools are available online at **thinkcentral.com** and on **Write*Smart*** CD-ROM:
- **Interactive Graphic Organizers**
- **Interactive Student Models**
- **Interactive Revision Lessons**
For additional grammar instruction, see **GrammarNotes** on **thinkcentral.com**.

Assess and Reteach

Assess

DIAGNOSTIC AND SELECTION TESTS
> Selection Test A pp. 143–144
> Selection Test B/C pp. 145–146

Interactive Selection Test on **thinkcentral.com**

Reteach

Level Up Online Tutorials on **thinkcentral.com**

Reteaching Worksheets on **thinkcentral.com**
> Literature Lesson 27: Simile and Metaphor
> Reading Lesson 3: Determining Author's Purpose

Focus and Motivate

COMMON CORE FOCUS

RI 4 Determine the technical meaning of words and phrases used in a text. **RI 7** Analyze various accounts of a subject told in different mediums, determining which details are emphasized in each account. **W 2d** Use domain-specific vocabulary to manage the complexity of the topic. **W 8** Gather relevant information from multiple print sources.

SUMMARY

The two graphic aids in "How a Leaf Works" explain and depict the process of photosynthesis and what the inside of a leaf looks like, including descriptions of its cells and tissues.

What's the Connection?

Use PLAN to help students preview the graphic aids.

- Direct students to the Photosynthesis graphic. Write the title (*Photosynthesis*) in the center circle of the web.

- Have students write the subheads (the phrases in boldface beside each number) in the outer circles.

- Have students add related words to the phrases in the outer circles

- Have students add details as they read and reflect on what they have learned.

🗂 **BEST PRACTICES TOOLKIT—Transparency**
PLAN p. A22

Teach

Standards Focus: Interpret Graphic Aids

Guide students through the process of examining and interpreting a graphic aid. Help students identify each element in the diagrams; point out the blue tab that holds the title for each graphic and links between parts. Have students scan the text, and write a sentence describing what is being represented.

R **RESOURCE MANAGER—Copy Master**
Interpret Graphic Aids p. 59

How a Leaf Works  Essential Course of Study ECOS
Textbook Diagrams

Use with "Why Leaves Turn Color in the Fall," page 540.

⊙ **COMMON CORE**

RI 4 Determine the technical meaning of words and phrases used in a text. **RI 7** Analyze various accounts of a subject told in different mediums, determining which details are emphasized in each account.

What's the Connection?

You just read a rather poetic yet scientific description of why leaves turn color in the fall. Now you will learn from a few well-designed graphic aids why leaves are green in the first place.

Standards Focus: Interpret Graphic Aids

A **graphic aid** is a visual illustration of a verbal statement. Graphic aids include photographs, diagrams, maps, and equations. Well-made graphics clarify the text they accompany, making complex information easier to understand. Graphics may also emphasize details that the text does not. Determining which information comes from graphics, which from text, and which from both, can help you more fully comprehend the process. You can use these guidelines to interpret and evaluate most graphic aids:

- Read the title, headings, and captions first to get the main idea.
- On maps and complex graphic aids, look for a key or legend to see how colors and symbols are used.
- Use the obvious meanings of symbols such as arrows to help you read the visual information.
- Pay attention to labels that identify specific details.
- Study the information in the graphic, looking for patterns or basic concepts.
- Ask yourself, "Is this graphic clear? Does it help explain the text or add visual appeal?"

As you read the pages that follow, complete a chart like the one shown. State in your own words what each graphic aid shows.

Type of Graphic Aid	What It Shows
Magnified photograph of a leaf cell	
Cutaway diagram of a chloroplast	
Schematic diagram of photosynthesis	
Chemical equation for photosynthesis	
Cutaway diagram of a leaf	

Selection Resources

*See resources on the **Teacher One Stop DVD-ROM** and on **thinkcentral.com**.*

R **RESOURCE MANAGER UNIT 5**
Lesson Support,* pp. 51–64

DIAGNOSTIC AND SELECTION TESTS
Selection Tests, pp. 147–150

INTERACTIVE READER

ADAPTED INTERACTIVE READER

ELL ADAPTED INTERACTIVE READER

TECHNOLOGY

🔘 **Teacher One Stop DVD-ROM**
🔘 **Student One Stop DVD-ROM**
🔘 **PowerNotes DVD-ROM**
🔘 **Audio Tutor CD**
🔘 **ExamView Test Generator on the Teacher One Stop**

* Resources for Differentiation

Practice and Apply

Photosynthesis

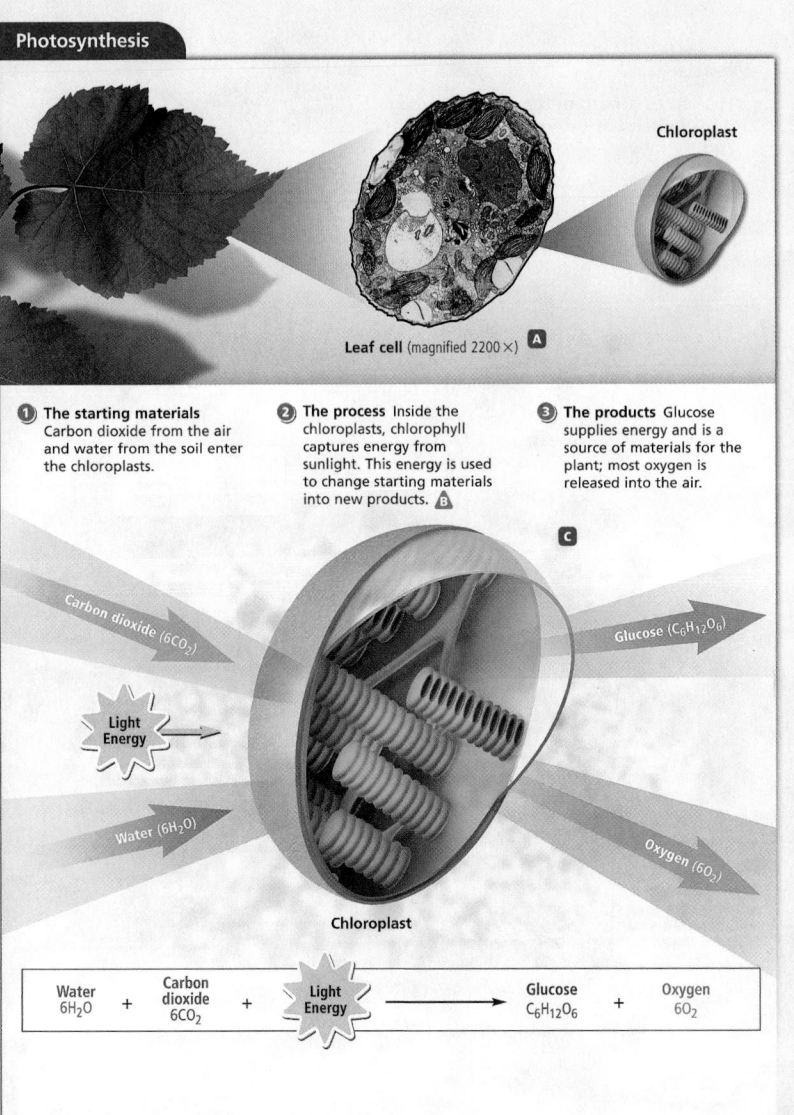

Leaf cell (magnified 2200×) **A**

Chloroplast

1 **The starting materials** Carbon dioxide from the air and water from the soil enter the chloroplasts.

2 **The process** Inside the chloroplasts, chlorophyll captures energy from sunlight. This energy is used to change starting materials into new products. **B**

3 **The products** Glucose supplies energy and is a source of materials for the plant; most oxygen is released into the air.

C

Carbon dioxide (6CO₂)

Glucose (C₆H₁₂O₆)

Light Energy

Water (6H₂O)

Oxygen (6O₂)

Chloroplast

| Water $6H_2O$ | + | Carbon dioxide $6CO_2$ | + | Light Energy | → | Glucose $C_6H_{12}O_6$ | + | Oxygen $6O_2$ |

A **INTERPRET GRAPHIC AIDS**
Science textbooks often include **photographs** of structures magnified to many times their actual size. What does this photo of a leaf cell show you about chloroplasts?

COMMON CORE RI 4

B **TECHNICAL MEANINGS**
Many English words are derived from Greek root words. The root *chloro-* comes from the Greek *chlóros,* meaning "pale green." English words containing the root *chloro-* are used in many biological terms. Reread the text under step 2. What words contain *chloro-?* What do you think these words mean? (Hint: *-plast* means "to form" and *-phyll* means "leaf.")

C **INTERPRET GRAPHIC AIDS**
A **schematic diagram** uses lines, symbols, and words to help readers picture processes or objects not normally seen. What do the arrows in this schematic diagram communicate?

Reading Online!  THINK central

Features on **thinkcentral.com** that support the selection include
• **PowerNotes** presentation
• **ThinkAloud** models to enhance comprehension

DIFFERENTIATED INSTRUCTION

FOR ENGLISH LANGUAGE LEARNERS

Options for Reading Have students help one another to fill out the chart on page 548. Ask pairs to first identify which of the two graphic aids they should look at for each graphic aid example. Then have them work together to tell what each of the identified parts of the graphic aids shows.

INFORMATIONAL ANALYSIS  COMMON CORE RI 7

A INTERPRET GRAPHIC AIDS

Possible answer: *The photograph of a leaf cell shows that chloroplasts are green and that there are many of them inside a leaf cell.*

VOCABULARY COMMON CORE RI 4

B TECHNICAL MEANINGS

Point out the words *energy* and *sunlight* in step 2 on the graphic aid. Tell students that *energy* comes from the Greek root *energos,* meaning "active." The Greek word for *sun* is *helios.*

Possible answer: Chloroplast *and chlorophyll contain* chloro-. *From the roots,* chloroplast *means "forming green." It is the microorganelle that performs photosynthesis.* Chlorophyll *means "the green pigment in leaves."*

INFORMATIONAL ANALYSIS COMMON CORE RI 7

C *Model the Skill:* INTERPRET GRAPHIC AIDS

Point out the numbered captions that describe the steps in the process of photosynthesis, and read the text aloud. Note the correlation between the captions and the schematic diagram and the illustrated chart below it. Then have students use the captions and the diagram to answer the question about the arrows.

Possible answer: *The arrows in this schematic diagram indicate that some materials are coming into the chloroplast (carbon dioxide, light energy, and water), and other materials are leaving the chloroplast (glucose and oxygen).*

INFORMATIONAL ANALYSIS

D INTERPRET GRAPHIC AIDS

Possible answer: The chloroplasts are located in the upper layer of leaf cells. They look like tiny green peas.

Extend the Discussion How are the cells in which the chloroplasts are located different from the cells on the surface of the leaf?

Inside a Leaf

The leaf is an organ that produces sugars. It is made up of different types of cells and tissues.

D INTERPRET GRAPHIC AIDS
A **cutaway diagram** shows an object with the outer part removed to reveal the interior. Notice the different layers of cells in this cutaway diagram of a leaf. Where are the chloroplasts located? What do they look like?

Cells at the surface produce a waxy cuticle that keeps the leaf from losing water.

Most chloroplasts are located in cells of the upper layer of the leaf.

Xylem transports water and nutrients up from the roots.

Carbon dioxide, oxygen, and water vapor move into and out of the leaf through stomata.

Phloem transports energy-rich compounds made in the leaf down to other parts of the plant.

Reading Support

THINK central

This selection on **thinkcentral.com** includes embedded **ThinkAloud** models—students "thinking aloud" about the story to model the kinds of questions a good reader would ask about a selection.

DIFFERENTIATED INSTRUCTION

FOR STRUGGLING READERS
Develop Reading Fluency Read aloud the scientific terms used in the graphic aids. Have students repeat the terms in unison, copying your pronunciations. Then have student pairs practice pronouncing and using the terms to describe what each graphic aid illustrates.

FOR ENGLISH LANGUAGE LEARNERS
Comprehension: Task Support Have groups of students use Cause-and-Effect Graphics to record the process by which a leaf works. Refer them back to page 548 to use the guidelines for interpreting graphic aids. Invite groups to compare their results, resolve any differences, and create a collective chart on the board.

 BEST PRACTICES TOOLKIT—Transparencies Cause-and-Effect Graphics pp. B16, B37–B39

Comprehension

1. **Recall** Where does photosynthesis take place?

2. **Recall** What does a plant do with the products of photosynthesis?

3. **Paraphrase** Review the equation at the bottom of page 549. Paraphrase this equation.

Text Analysis

4. **Interpret Graphic Aids** What parts of a leaf are shown in the cutaway diagram on page 550, titled "Inside a Leaf"? What are their different functions?

5. **Compare Texts** How would you compare the experience of reading the graphic aids with the experience of reading "Why Leaves Turn Color in the Fall"? Which source did you find more informative? Explain your answer.

Read for Information: Use Information from Multiple Sources

WRITING PROMPT

On the basis of the information in the textbook diagrams and Diane Ackerman's essay, explain (1) the process of photosynthesis, (2) the reason leaves are green in summer, and (3) the reason leaves turn color in the fall. Define scientific terms in your explanation.

To respond to this prompt, you will need to synthesize information from multiple sources having to do with photosynthesis and the color of leaves. Then you will need to paraphrase this information. Following these steps can help:

1. Review the chart you created as you read, noting what the schematic diagram of photosynthesis showed you.

2. Review the diagram labeled "Inside a Leaf," looking for more details you could add to your explanation. Jot them down.

3. Review Diane Ackerman's essay, identifying and taking notes on passages that discuss photosynthesis, the green color of leaves, and the process of color change.

4. Using your notes from all three sources, describe the three topics in the order listed in the prompt.

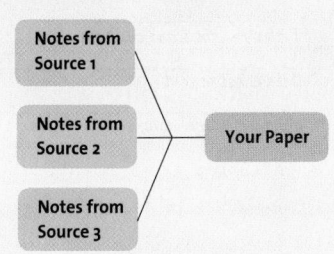

Notes from Source 1

Notes from Source 2 → Your Paper

Notes from Source 3

COMMON CORE

RI 7 Analyze various accounts of a subject told in different mediums, determining which details are emphasized in each account. **W 2d** Use domain-specific vocabulary to manage the complexity of the topic. **W 8** Gather relevant information from multiple print sources.

Practice and Apply

For preliminary support of post-reading questions, use these copy masters:

R RESOURCE MANAGER—Copy Masters

Reading Check p. 63

Question Support p. 64

Use Information from Multiple Sources p. 60

Additional selection questions are provided for teachers on page 54.

ANSWERS

Comprehension

1. *inside chloroplasts*

2. *A plant uses glucose for food and energy and releases oxygen.*

3. *Carbon dioxide, water, and light energy react to form glucose and oxygen.*

Text Analysis   COMMON CORE RI 7

Possible answers:

4. **Interpret Graphic Aids** *waxy cuticle—keeps leaf from losing water; chloroplasts—produce food; xylem—transports nutrients from roots; phloem—transports compounds from leaf; stomata—allow gases and water vapor to move in and out of the leaf*

5. *Accept reasonable responses.*

Read for Information: Use Information from Multiple Sources   COMMON CORE W 2d, W 8

Writing Prompt *Possible answers: In photosynthesis, plants combine water, carbon dioxide, and light energy to create glucose and oxygen; summer's leaves are green because of chlorophyll; fall's leaves turn color because the plant stops feeding and can't make chlorophyll.*

Assess and Reteach

Assess

DIAGNOSTIC AND SELECTION TESTS

Selection Test A, B/C pp. 147–148, 149-150

Interactive Selection Test on thinkcentral.com

Reteach

Level Up Online Tutorials on thinkcentral.com

FOR STRUGGLING WRITERS

Read for Information

- Have students create a three-column chart using the three topics in the writing prompt. Have students write their notes as they review Ackerman's essay, the graphic aids, and the chart they completed while reading.

- Help students use their notes to create a thesis statement for each topic. Students can use these statements when writing their paragraphs.

FOR ADVANCED LEARNERS/PRE–AP

Read for Information Encourage students to include more detailed information about one of these topics from at least one additional source, such as a science textbook.

Focus and Motivate

COMMON CORE FOCUS

RI 7 Analyze various accounts of a subject told in different mediums, determining which details are emphasized in each account. **W 2d** Use domain-specific vocabulary to manage the complexity of the topic. **W 8** Gather relevant information from multiple print sources.

SUMMARY

"How to Plant a Tree" is a procedural document that outlines the steps in tree selection and planting. The text of this how-to document is supported by several graphic aids: a plant zone map of the United States, a chart of five popular trees and their hardiness zones, and a tree-planting diagram.

What's the Connection?

Use a KWL chart to help students connect the tree-planting how-to essay with previous selections on related topics. Direct students to write what they already know about trees in the first column of the chart. Ask them what they would like to know, and tell them to list questions in the second column. After reading, students may record additional information they have learned in the third column of the chart.

 BEST PRACTICES TOOLKIT—Transparency
KWL p. A21

Teach

Standards Focus: Evaluate Graphics

- Evaluating graphics involves determining the relevance, significance, and reliability of the information, as well as judging their general effectiveness, practical use, and visual appeal.

- Encourage students to think about what each graphic aid adds to their understanding of the procedural document.

RESOURCE MANAGER—Copy Master
Evaluate Graphics p. 73

How to Plant a Tree
Functional Document

Use with "Why Leaves Turn Color in the Fall," page 540, and "How a Leaf Works," page 548.

COMMON CORE

RI 7 Analyze various accounts of a subject told in different mediums, determining which details are emphasized in each account.

What's the Connection?

In the previous two selections you read a scientific essay about why leaves change color in the fall and examined graphic aids to learn more biological facts about leaves. Now you will read a how-to essay on the topic of planting trees.

Standards Focus: Evaluate Graphics

Most functional documents use graphics—visual representations such as diagrams or illustrations—to make the processes they describe more complete and easier to understand. When you evaluate a graphic in a functional document or any other type of text, you consider how well the graphic helps the text achieve its purpose. The following questions can help you evaluate most graphics.

- How do the graphics relate to the purpose of the document?
- Are the graphics clear and easy to understand?
- Are titles, headings, and captions clear? Do they help you understand the main idea of each graphic?
- Do the graphics include details that are not provided in the text?
- Is the information up-to-date, reliable, and verifiable?
- Are the graphics visually appealing? Are the text and graphics arranged well on the page?

As you read the functional document on the next two pages, complete a chart like the one shown for each graphic aid.

Graphic: Zone Map	
Graphic element	**Details**
Purpose	
Clarity	
Titles, headings, and captions	
Details not in text	
Up-to-date, reliable, and verifiable	
Visual appeal	

Selection Resources

See resources on the **Teacher One Stop DVD-ROM** *and on* **thinkcentral.com**.

R RESOURCE MANAGER UNIT 5
Lesson Support,* pp. 65–78

DIAGNOSTIC AND SELECTION TESTS
Selection Tests, pp. 151–154

 BEST PRACTICES TOOLKIT
KWL, p. A21

TECHNOLOGY

- **Teacher One Stop DVD-ROM**
- **Student One Stop DVD-ROM**
- **ExamView Test Generator** on the Teacher One Stop

* Resources for Differentiation

Tree Planting Guide

Brought to you by **Great Trees** and **greattrees4U.net,** your local and online tree experts.

Selecting Your Tree

When selecting a tree, you need to determine which is the best kind of tree for you and the region where you live.

Step 1. Decide what kind of tree you want. Go to greattrees4U.net or browse our nursery for trees that interest you.

Step 2. Check your planting area. Consider whether a fully-grown tree will fit in the area you are considering. Choose an evergreen for year-round shade and protection from wind and noise. Choose a deciduous tree for summer shade and winter sunshine.

Step 3. Know Your Zone. The United States and Canada are divided into 11 Plant Hardiness Zones. The map below shows the 10 zones in the United States (excluding Alaska and Hawaii). Find your region on the map.

Step 4. Determine whether the type of tree you want to plant will survive in your hardiness zone.

Step 5. Check greattrees4U.net or talk with our nursery specialists to learn about special local conditions, such as soil quality, that may affect how well your tree will grow in your neighborhood.

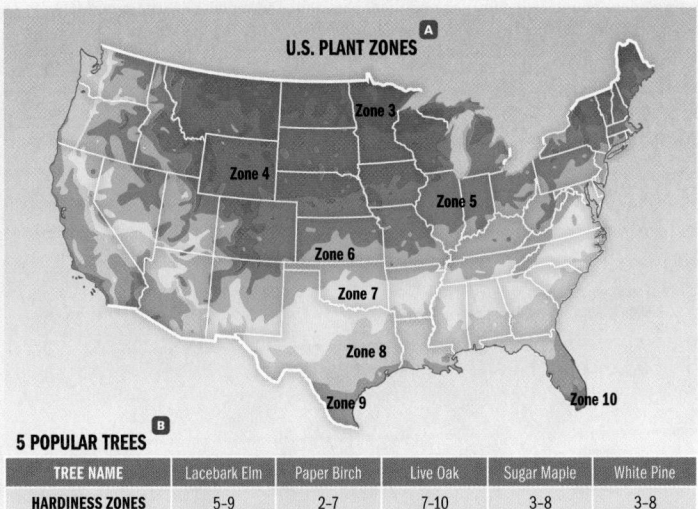

U.S. PLANT ZONES Ⓐ

Zone 3
Zone 4
Zone 5
Zone 6
Zone 7
Zone 8
Zone 9
Zone 10

5 POPULAR TREES Ⓑ

TREE NAME	Lacebark Elm	Paper Birch	Live Oak	Sugar Maple	White Pine
HARDINESS ZONES	5–9	2–7	7–10	3–8	3–8

Ⓐ **EVALUATE GRAPHICS**
What part of the text does this graphic support? What purpose does it serve?

Ⓑ **EVALUATE GRAPHICS**
Is the chart easy to understand? Which tree can survive in the least number of zones?

Practice and Apply

Ⓐ *Model the Skill:* EVALUATE GRAPHICS

To model how to evaluate graphics, ask the Skills Focus questions on page 552 about the zone map. Then draw a two-column chart on the board to help students evaluate the map.

Graphic: Zone Map

Graphic element	Details
Purpose	The purpose of the map is to show the hardiness zones.
Clarity	The color coding is clear and easy to understand.
Titles, headings, and captions	The title describes the content of the map. The zone labels are clear.

Possible answer: *The graphic supports Step 3. Its purpose is to show where the hardiness zones are.*

Ⓑ EVALUATE GRAPHICS

Possible answer: *Yes. The live oak can survive in only four zones.*

Extend the Discussion What trees would not survive in the southernmost part of Texas?

DIFFERENTIATED INSTRUCTION

FOR ENGLISH LANGUAGE LEARNERS

Options for Reading Have students work in pairs to read and summarize the steps in selecting a tree and the information in the graphics. Have one partner read the five steps aloud and the other partner summarize them. Then have students reverse roles. To check comprehension of the graphics, have student pairs examine the map and the chart and then summarize what each shows in one or two sentences.

FOR STRUGGLING READERS

Develop Reading Fluency Read the introduction and steps for selecting a tree aloud to the class, pausing at commas and stopping briefly at periods and at the end of steps. Ask students to identify the Web site. Then have student pairs practice reading the steps to each other. Circulate around the room to assist students with pronunciations of unfamiliar words.

Use these prompts to help students understand the steps in planting a tree.

Connect Is planting a tree harder or easier
than you imagined? Explain. ***Possible answer:*** *Accept all reasonable answers.*

Apply What besides the tree itself would
you need to plant a tree? ***Possible answer:***
You would need a shovel, mulch, and water.

Speculate Why might a newly planted
tree not survive? ***Possible answer:*** *A newly
planted tree might not survive if its roots did
not penetrate the soil, if it were not watered
enough, or if it did not have enough mulch
to keep water from evaporating or to provide
nutrients.*

INFORMATIONAL ANALYSIS COMMON CORE RI 7

C EVALUATE GRAPHICS

Possible answer: *The diagram shows stakes,
which the text doesn't mention. Yes, you
need stakes to support the tree.*

Extend the Discussion How does the ridge
of soil aid water penetration?

Tree Planting Guide, continued

Planting Your Tree

Once you have selected and purchased your tree, it's time to do some work.
Remember: The tree you are planting may live for decades to come. Give it a good
start by working carefully to plant the tree properly.

Step 1. Call before you dig. Your local utility companies can tell you the locations of
any underground lines and cables.

Step 2. Dig a hole twice as wide as the tree's root ball and slightly less deep. Roughen
the sides and bottom of the hole with your shovel so that root tips can
penetrate the native soil.

Step 3. Remove the tree's container or burlap, and then place the root ball in the hole.
The top of the root ball should be 1/2 to 1 inch above the surrounding soil.
Look at your tree from several directions to make sure it is standing straight.

Step 4. Refill the hole with soil a few inches at a time, using the same native soil that
you dug up to make your hole. As you fill the hole, press down firmly on the
soil or add water to collapse air pockets.

Step 5. Form a temporary dam by making a ridge of soil around the tree's base to
encourage water penetration.

Step 6. Pile mulch (bark, wood chips, or leaves) 3–4 inches deep around the tree, leaving a 6-inch circle around the base of the trunk. Mulch keeps surface water
from evaporating and provides nutrients to the soil.

Step 7. Give your tree a good soaking after planting. Add more soil if the ground
settles too much.

C EVALUATE GRAPHICS
What piece of
information does this
diagram give that the
text does not? Is this
information important
to completing the
task? Explain.

C

Top of root ball
slightly above ground

Stakes for support, if needed

Mulch 3–4 inches deep

Hole refilled
with native soil;
water to settle

Soil ridge to aid
water penetration

Root ball, removed from container

Hole 2 times as wide
as root ball

DIFFERENTIATED INSTRUCTION

FOR STRUGGLING READERS
Comprehension Support Point out that the
actions taken in steps 4–7 ensure that the
newly planted tree has the best chance for
survival. Identify the purpose of each step: the
method of adding soil after placing the root
ball in the ground anchors the young tree; the
soil ridge keeps water from running off and
away from the planting site; the mulch helps
hold water and keeps it from drowning the
newly planted tree; added soil keeps the tree
anchored.

FOR ADVANCED LEARNERS/PRE–AP
Plan Plantings How do trees enhance the
environment? Challenge students to work in
small groups or with a partner to design a plan
for planting trees on the school grounds or at
another location in their community. Have
students identify native deciduous and conifer-
ous trees appropriate for the chosen location.
Have groups share their plans with the class
and explain the purpose of the trees and the
designs they have chosen.

Comprehension

1. **Recall** What does the zone map tell you?

2. **Recall** Why should you call utility companies before you dig?

3. **Paraphrase** Why should you put mulch around the tree?

Text Analysis

4. **Synthesize Information from Multiple Graphics** If Clara lives in Houston, Texas, would a live oak survive in her yard? Would one survive in her cousin Jerry's yard in North Dakota? Explain.

5. **Evaluate Graphics** Review the notes you recorded in your chart. On the basis of your answers to the evaluation questions, are the graphics in this document clear and visually appealing?

COMMON CORE

RI 7 Analyze various accounts of a subject told in different mediums, determining which details are emphasized in each account. **W 2d** Use domain-specific vocabulary to manage the complexity of the topic. **W 8** Gather relevant information from multiple print sources.

Read for Information: Synthesizing Information from Graphics

WRITING PROMPT

Larry has just returned to South Carolina from a vacation in Northern Maine. He would like to plant some trees in his yard to bring beautiful fall foliage to his neighborhood. He knows nothing about selecting and planting trees or why leaves change colors, so you must advise him. Which trees should he plant? How will the fall foliage compare to the foliage he saw in Maine? Write 2–3 paragraphs advising Larry on his project. Use information from "Why Leaves Turn Color in the Fall," the textbook diagrams, and the functional document for planting a tree to support your response.

To respond to this prompt, you will need to synthesize information from multiple graphical and textual sources to draw conclusions about the ideas presented. Follow these steps:

1. Review the graphic organizers you created as you read the three selections. Note any information that relates to your topic.

2. Review the steps for selecting and planting a tree, including the graphics. Keep in mind the region in which Larry lives.

3. Review the textbook diagrams. Will any information there affect Larry's tree choice?

4. Review Ackerman's essay, identifying and taking notes on passages that discuss regional differences.

5. State your conclusion in a topic sentence. Then, support your conclusion with information from the selections.

FOR STRUGGLING WRITERS

Read for Information

- Have students work with partners to review the graphical and textual sources for information relevant to the writing topic. Suggest that each pair create a two-column chart to collect information, listing sources in the first column and making notes on relevant information from each source in the second column.

- Direct students to use the information in their charts to draw conclusions. Then have them state their conclusions in topic

sentences. Remind students that they can revise their topic sentences as needed later.

FOR ADVANCED LEARNERS/PRE–AP

Respond Orally Have student pairs adapt their responses to the writing prompt as a script for a skit in which Larry meets with a landscape architect to discuss a detailed planting plan for his yard. Have student pairs perform their skits twice so that both students have an opportunity to play the role of the landscape architect and provide specific, accurate answers to Larry's questions orally.

Practice and Apply

For preliminary support of post-reading questions, use these copy masters:

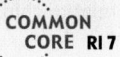 **RESOURCE MANAGER—Copy Masters**

Reading Check p. 77
Question Support p. 78
Synthesize p. 74

Additional selection questions are provided for teachers on page 68.

ANSWERS

Comprehension

1. *where in the US certain plants will grow*

2. *to avoid utility lines and cables*

3. *When mulch decomposes, it releases nutrients.*

Text Analysis

COMMON CORE RI 7

4. *Clara can plant a live oak, which grows in zone 9; it would not thrive in North Dakota, zones 3 and 4.*

5. *Answers will vary. The USDA zone map clearly shows where the zones are. Colors are visually appealing, with cooler colors for cooler zones and warmer colors for the warmer zones. Some labels of states or cities might be helpful. Both maps are clear and visually appealing. The tree diagram is fairly clear. All the necessary parts are well labeled. The art is simple, and not as visually appealing as a photo might be.*

Read for Information: Synthesizing Information from Graphics

COMMON CORE W 2d W 8

Writing Prompt *Paragraphs should indicate that Larry can plant any of the trees listed in the chart on page 553 except the paper birch. According to the Ackerman article, though, Larry will not get as vibrant colors from his trees as those in Maine because "the most spectacular range of fall foliage occurs in the northeastern United States . . . thanks in part to the a rich climate."*

Assess and Reteach

Assess

DIAGNOSTIC AND SELECTION TESTS

Selection Test A, B/c pp. 151–152, 153–154

Interactive Selection Test on **thinkcentral.com**

Reteach

Level Up Online Tutorials on **thinkcentral.com**

Focus and Motivate

COMMON CORE FOCUS

RI 3 Analyze how the author unfolds and develops a series of events, the order in which they occur, and the connections drawn between events. **RI 4** Determine the meaning of words and phrases used in a text. **RI 5** Analyze in detail how an author's ideas or claims are developed by sentences. **W 2** Write explanatory texts to examine and convey complex ideas, concepts, and information clearly and accurately through the effective analysis of content. **L 1** Demonstrate command of the conventions of standard English grammar and usage. **L 1b** Use various types of clauses to convey specific meanings and add variety and interest to writing. **L 5** Demonstrate understanding of word relationships.

SUMMARY

In "Blowup: What Went Wrong at Storm King Mountain," Sebastian Junger recounts a 1994 disaster in which 14 firefighters died while battling a Colorado wildfire. Junger explains why he thinks it turned deadly.

What can we learn from **DISASTER?**

Ask the question and have students share how they react to news of a disaster. Before students begin the *DISCUSS* activity, have them list a few disasters, past or present. Then, invite groups to share their lists.

Selection Resources

 RESOURCE MANAGER UNIT 5
Plan and Teach, pp. 79–86
Summary, pp. 87–88†‡*
Text Analysis and Reading
   Skill, pp. 89–92†*
Vocabulary, pp. 93–95*
Grammar and Style, p. 98

DIAGNOSTIC AND SELECTION TESTS
Selection Tests, pp. 155–158

BEST PRACTICES TOOLKIT
Reciprocal Teaching, p. A35
New Word Analysis, p. E8
Cluster Diagram, p. B18
Venn Diagram, p. A26

TECHNOLOGY
🔵 **Teacher One Stop DVD-ROM**
🔵 **Student One Stop DVD-ROM**
🔵 **Audio Anthology CD**
🔵 **GrammarNotes DVD-ROM**
🔵 **ExamView Test Generator**
   on the Teacher One Stop

See resources on the **Teacher One Stop DVD-ROM** *and on* **thinkcentral.com**.

Video link at **thinkcentral.com**

*** Resources for Differentiation   † Also in Spanish   ‡ In Haitian Creole and Vietnamese**

Blowup: What Went Wrong at Storm King Mountain

Video link at **thinkcentral.com**

Narrative Nonfiction by Sebastian Junger

What can we learn from **DISASTER?**

COMMON CORE

RI 3 Analyze how the author unfolds and develops a series of events, the order in which they occur, and the connections drawn between events. **RI 4** Determine the meaning of words and phrases used in a text. **RI 5** Analyze in detail how an author's ideas or claims are developed.

When you hear about a disaster, what's your reaction? Do you pay attention to the details so you can prevent the same thing from happening to you? You wouldn't be alone in trying to learn a lesson from tragedy. People do it all the time—especially those who are paid to risk their lives when disaster strikes. The selection you are about to read is both a description and an analysis of what caused a small wildfire to flare into a deadly blaze, seemingly without warning.

DISCUSS In a small group, discuss a disaster that took lives or caused great damage to property. Note what went wrong and whether the catastrophe might have been avoided. Then write down your group's top two or three recommendations for averting a similar disaster or reducing its damage.

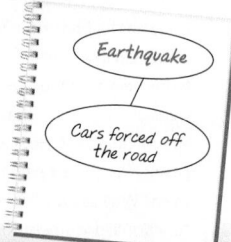

Earthquake

Cars forced off the road

556

● TEXT ANALYSIS: NARRATIVE NONFICTION

Narrative nonfiction is writing that tells a true story. Just as in a fictional story, the details in narrative nonfiction help bring the characters, settings, and events to life. For example, notice how the details in this passage from "Blowup: What Went Wrong at Storm King Mountain" convey the experiences of one firefighter who was caught in that blaze.

I was roughly one hundred and fifty feet from the top of the hill, and the fire got there in ten or twelve seconds. I made it over the top and just tumbled and rolled down the other side. . . .

As you read, notice other elements of good storytelling.

● READING STRATEGY: TAKE NOTES

When reading a text that has an obvious method of organiza-tion, it's a good idea to record the key ideas and information in that text on a graphic organizer. Here are some ideal pairings:

- a **timeline** for chronological order
- a **diagram** for spatial order, or position in space
- a **cause-and-effect chain** for cause-and-effect order

Sebastian Junger uses several patterns of organization, with chronological order being particularly important. As you read, record the main events of the disaster on a timeline.

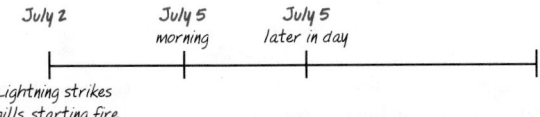

Review: **Patterns of Organization, Graphic Aids**

▲ VOCABULARY IN CONTEXT

The following boldfaced words help the author deliver his dramatic account of a fire. To see how many you already know, substitute a different word or phrase for each one. Then, in your *Reader/Writer Notebook*, write a definition for each word.

1. **deflect** blame from himself by accusing another
2. a rowdy **contingent** of football players at the hotel
3. forces **conspire** to create tragedy
4. a **conceivably** simple plan that went wrong
5. a **rigorous** course load at school

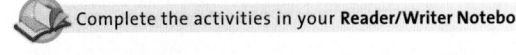

Complete the activities in your **Reader/Writer Notebook.**

Meet the Author

Sebastian Junger
born 1962

Describing Danger
Sebastian Junger is most famous for his first book, *The Perfect Storm*—a nonfiction account of the *Andrea Gail*, a commercial fishing boat wrecked in an Atlantic storm. Originally, he had intended to write a book about people with dangerous jobs—an idea he got while recovering from a leg injury suffered while climbing trees for a tree-removal company. But a chapter on the *Andrea Gail* turned into a whole volume—and a bestseller.

World-Traveling Journalist
Despite his success as a book author, Junger considers himself a magazine journalist. He has traveled to Kosovo, Sierra Leone, and Afghanistan on assignments for such publications as *National Geographic*. *Fire*, published in 2001, is a collection of his magazine articles. It includes "Blowup: What Went Wrong at Storm King Mountain." Junger says he felt compelled to write about "situations where people are in one form or another being confronted with forces that are way beyond their control."

BACKGROUND TO THE SELECTION
One of the biggest firefighting disasters in the United States occurred July 6, 1994, on Storm King Mountain in Colorado. Fourteen firefighters died in a blowup, or sudden explosion of flames, on the windy, dried-out slopes. Today the dead are memorialized with crosses at the spots where they fell and plaques along the route of the fire.

Author Online **THINK** central
Go to **thinkcentral.com.**
KEYWORD: HML10-557

557

Teach

● *Model the Skill:* NARRATIVE NONFICTION

To model how to identify narrative nonfiction, explain that a narrative is any type of writing that tells a story: fiction, nonfiction, or poetry. Narrative nonfiction includes biographies, autobiographies, and magazine articles about real events. Emphasize that while narrative nonfiction tell stories, the story details are factual and describe real people, places, and events.

GUIDED PRACTICE Ask students for other examples of narrative nonfiction.

READING STRATEGY

■ *Model the Skill:* TAKE NOTES

To model how to take notes, write this pas-sage on the board:

> Hurricane Rita struck the Gulf Coast on Saturday, September 24, 2005. On Thursday, September 22, three million people had already started to evacuate. They had learned the deadly lessons of Hurricane Katrina, which had slammed into the Gulf Coast on August 29.

Point out that either a timeline or a cause-and-effect chain would be a helpful way to take notes on this passage.

GUIDED PRACTICE Ask: Which graphic organizer might help you take notes on an article about Katrina's aftermath.

VOCABULARY SKILL COMMON CORE
L 4

▲ VOCABULARY IN CONTEXT

DIAGNOSE WORD KNOWLEDGE Have all stu-dents complete Vocabulary in Context. Check their words, phrases, and definitions against the following:

conceivably (kən-sēv′ə-blē) *adv.* possibly
conspire (kən-spīr′) *v.* to plan or plot secretly
contingent (kən-tĭn′jənt) *n.* a gathering of people representative of a larger group
deflect (dĭ-flĕkt′) *v.* to fend off or avert the direction of something

rigorous (rĭg′ər-əs) *adj.* strict, uncompromising

PRETEACH VOCABULARY Use the copy master to help students predict the meaning of each boldfaced word.

R RESOURCE MANAGER—Copy Master
Vocabulary Study p. 93

1. Read item 1 aloud, emphasizing *deflect*.
2. Point out the phrase *batting it away*. Elicit possible meanings for *deflect*, such as "turn away."

3. Have students record their predictions.
4. Repeat the procedure for items 2–5.

READ WITH A PURPOSE

Help students set a purpose for reading. Have them preview the selection title and subtitle and then read to identify the factors that created a disaster on Storm King Mountain.

TIERED DISCUSSION PROMPTS

Use these prompts to help students explore the dramatic opening to this selection (lines 1–21):

Connect Have you ever heard the "thunderous sound" of your own heart or felt it racing? Describe the physical sensations and emotions you were feeling. *Accept all thoughtful answers.*

Analyze What details indicate that Junger is about to tell a tragic story? *Possible answer: Tragic details include the facts that despite the radio warnings, 14 people died in a fire that initially had not seemed serious, and that they died within sight of onlookers.*

Evaluate This selection begins in the middle of the action. Do you find the opening effective or confusing? Why? *Possible answer: The opening may be a little confusing, but it is effective because it is so dramatic. It makes the reader want to read on to learn how such a terrible event could have happened.*

BLOWUP:

WHAT WENT WRONG AT STORM KING MOUNTAIN

Sebastian Junger

> The main thing Brad Haugh remembers about his escape was the thunderous sound of his own heart. It was beating two hundred times a minute, and by the time he and the two smoke jumpers[1] running with him had crested a steep ridge in Colorado, everyone behind them was dead.
>
> Their coworkers on the slope at their backs had been overrun by flames that Haugh guessed were three hundred feet high. The fire raced a quarter mile up the mountain in about two minutes, hitting speeds of eighteen miles an hour. Tools dropped in its path were completely incinerated. Temperatures reached two thousand degrees—hot enough to melt gold or fire clay.

10 "The fire blew up behind a little ridge below me," Haugh said later. "People were yelling into their radios, 'Run! Run! Run!' I was roughly one hundred and fifty feet from the top of the hill, and the fire got there in ten or twelve seconds. I made it over the top and just tumbled and rolled down the other side, and when I turned around, there was just this incredible wall of flame."

Haugh was one of forty-nine fire fighters caught in a wildfire that stunned the nation with its swiftness and its fury. Fourteen elite fire fighters perished on a spine of Storm King Mountain, seven miles west of Glenwood Springs, Colorado. They died on a steep, rocky slope in a fire initially so small that the crews had not taken it seriously. They died while cars passed within sight on
20 the interstate below and people in the valley aimed their camcorders at the fire from garage roofs.

There were many other fire fighters on Storm King when Brad Haugh crested the ridge, yet he feared that he and the two men with him were the only ones on the mountain left alive. That thought—not the flames—caused him to panic. He ran blindly and nearly knocked himself unconscious against a tree. Fires were spotting all around him as the front of the flames chased him. The roar was deafening; "a tornado on fire" was how he later described it. The light, he remembered, was a weird blood-red that fascinated him even as he ran.

Analyze Visuals ▶

How would you feel if you were photographing this scene?

❶ Targeted Passage

COMMON CORE RI 4

Language Coach

Etymology A word's history is called its **etymology.** The word *elite*, pronounced /ā lēt´/, comes from a Latin word *eligere*, meaning "to pick out or choose." Reread lines 16–18. Use the etymology of *elite* to figure out its meaning in this sentence.

---

1. **smoke jumpers:** people who fight forest fires by parachuting to remote locations. Once on the ground, they carry heavy supplies on their backs and hike over rough terrain.

The 1994 South Canyon fire on Storm King Mountain

DIFFERENTIATED INSTRUCTION

FOR ENGLISH LANGUAGE LEARNERS

Language Coach   **COMMON CORE RI 4**

Etymology *Answer:*
Since elite *comes from a word meaning "to choose," it must mean something like "chosen." I think here it means that these firefighters were chosen, or recognized, as the best.* Have students use a dictionary to identify a word related to *elite* that can be used as a noun, adjective, or verb and also comes from the Latin word *eligere.*
Answer: elect

FOR STRUGGLING READERS

In combination with the *Audio Anthology CD,* use one or more Targeted Passages (pp. 558, 562, 566, 568) to ensure that students focus on key story events, concepts, and skills. Targeted Passages are also good for English learners.

❶ Targeted Passage [Lines 1–9]

This passage introduces someone who survived the fire and who will be a key character in the narrative. It also establishes the severity and swiftness of the blaze.

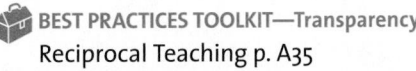

The two smoke jumpers with him were Eric Hipke and Kevin Erickson.
30 Hipke had been so badly burned the flesh was hanging off his hands in strips.
Haugh paused briefly to collect himself, then led the two men about a hundred
yards down the mountain, stopping only long enough to wrap Hipke's hands
in wet T-shirts. As they started down again, the fire was spreading behind
them at a thousand acres an hour, oak, pinyon, and juniper spontaneously
combusting[2] in the heat.

"I didn't have any nightmares about it later," said Haugh. "But I did keep
waking up in the night very disoriented. . . ."

T he South Canyon fire, as it was called, ignited on Saturday, July 2, as
a lightning strike in the steep hills outside Glenwood Springs. At first
40 people paid it little mind because dry lightning had already triggered
thirty or forty fires across the drought-plagued state that day; another wisp
of smoke was no big deal. But this blaze continued to grow, prompting the
Bureau of Land Management[3] (BLM) district office in Grand Junction to
dispatch a seven-member crew on the morning of July 5 to prepare a helicopter
landing site, designated H-1, and start cutting a fire line along a ridge of Storm
King. At this point the blaze was cooking slowly through the sparse pinyon
and juniper covering the steep drainage below. Glenwood Springs was visible
to the east, and a pricey development called Canyon Creek Estates was a mile
to the west. Interstate 70 followed the Colorado River one thousand feet
50 below, and occasionally the fire fighters could see rafters in brightly colored life
jackets bumping through the rapids. **B**

The BLM crew worked all day, until chain-saw problems forced them to
hike down to make repairs. Replacing them were eight smoke jumpers from
Idaho and Montana (eight more would be added the next morning) who
parachuted onto the ridgetop to continue cutting fire line. They worked until
midnight and then claimed a few hours' sleep on the rocky ground.

Just before dawn, on the morning of July 6, Incident Commander Butch
Blanco led the BLM crew back up the steep slope. Arriving at the top, Blanco
discussed strategy with the smoke jumper in charge, Don Mackey. At about the
60 same time, the BLM office in Grand Junction dispatched one additional crew
to the fire, the twenty-member Prineville Hotshots, a crack interagency unit
from Oregon whose helmet emblem is a coyote dancing over orange flame.

The smoke jumpers had cleared another landing spot, H-2, on the main
ridge, and around twelve-thirty in the afternoon, a transport helicopter settled
onto it. The first **contingent** of the Prineville crew ran through the rotor wash
and crouched behind rocks as the chopper lifted off to pick up the rest of the
unit from below. They'd been chosen alphabetically for the first flight in: Beck,
Bickett, Blecha, Brinkley, Dunbar, Hagen, Holtby, Johnson, and Kelso. Rather

---

2. **spontaneously combusting:** self-igniting through an internal chemical action.

3. **Bureau of Land Management:** an agency within the U.S. Department of the Interior, in charge of sustaining the health, diversity, and productivity of public lands.

560 UNIT 5: AUTHOR'S PURPOSE

A NARRATIVE
NONFICTION
What does Junger focus
on in this seven-paragraph
introduction? Why might
he have chosen to begin his
nonfiction narrative
this way?

B TAKE NOTES
Reread lines 38–51. What
is Junger able to convey
through a shift back in
time? Note events on
your timeline.

contingent (kən-tĭn′jənt)
n. a gathering of people
representative of a larger
group

DIFFERENTIATED INSTRUCTION

FOR STRUGGLING READERS

Develop Reading Fluency Select a paragraph from the selection, and read it aloud smoothly and at a moderate pace. Model correct pronunciation and how to pause at punctuation, including commas, colons, and parentheses. Have students practice reading the same paragraph aloud in small groups until they can read it fluently.

FOR ENGLISH LANGUAGE LEARNERS

Vocabulary: Idioms Use New Word Analysis to teach these idioms from the selection: *collect himself* (line 31), "become calm"; *paid it little mind* (line 40), "did not pay much attention to it"; *no big deal* (line 42), "not important"; *pushed it* (line 94), "moved as quickly as he could"; *wait it out* (line 108), "wait until the danger had passed."

 BEST PRACTICES TOOLKIT—Transparency
New Word Analysis p. E8

than wait for their crew mates, these nine hotshots started downslope into the
70 burning valley. **C**

The layout of Storm King Mountain is roughly north-south, with a central spine running from the 8,793-foot summit to H-2. Another half mile south along this ridge was the larger site, H-1. The fire had started on a steep slope below these cleared safe areas and was spreading slowly.

The strategy was to cut a wide firebreak[4] along the ridgetop and a smaller line down the slope to contain the blaze on the southwestern flank of the ridge. Flare-ups would be attacked with retardant drops[5] from choppers. If there were problems, crews could easily reach H-1 in five or ten minutes and crawl under their fire shelters—light foil sheets that resemble space blankets
80 and **deflect** heat of up to six hundred degrees.

---

4. **firebreak:** a natural or constructed barrier used to stop fires that may occur.
5. **retardant drops:** the air-dropping of chemicals to help retard or delay the spread of fire.

C NARRATIVE NONFICTION
What do you learn from Junger's **characterization** of the smoke jumpers?

deflect (dĭ-flĕkt') v. to fend off or avert the direction of something

D GRAPHIC AIDS
Study the graphic shown. What does it tell you about the progress of the fire? What other spatial relationships does it show?

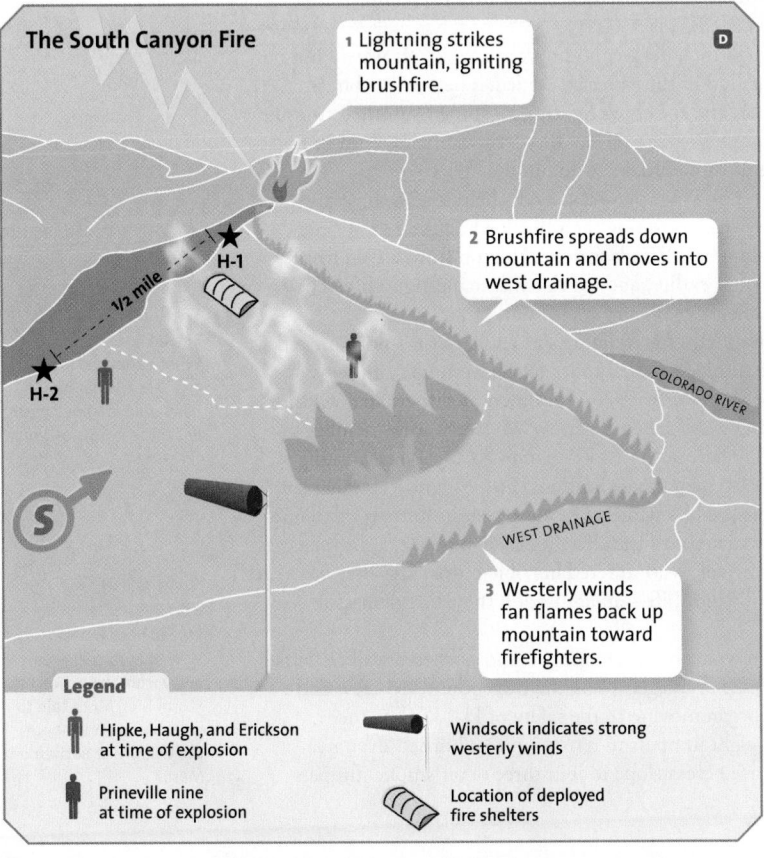

The South Canyon Fire

1 Lightning strikes mountain, igniting brushfire.

2 Brushfire spreads down mountain and moves into west drainage.

H-1

½ mile

H-2

COLORADO RIVER

WEST DRAINAGE

3 Westerly winds fan flames back up mountain toward firefighters.

S

Legend

Hipke, Haugh, and Erickson at time of explosion

Prineville nine at time of explosion

Windsock indicates strong westerly winds

Location of deployed fire shelters

BLOWUP: WHAT WENT WRONG AT STORM KING MOUNTAIN **561**

Model how to take notes. Read aloud lines 104–108, and then list the following events on the board:

3:00 P.M. Crew begins widening fire line

3:20 P.M. Cold front moves in

3:50 P.M. Haugh and swamper ordered to ridgetop to wait out fire

Point out that the events are listed on the board in chronological, or time, order. Have students enter these events on their Reading Strategy timelines.

Possible answer: *Around 3:50 p.m., Haugh and his swamper were ordered to climb to the ridgetop, considered a safe place. A cold front had moved in at about 3:20, and its winds were bringing the fire back to life.*

TEXT ANALYSIS

COMMON CORE

RI 3

F NARRATIVE NONFICTION

Possible answer: *Junger breaks away because the Battlement Mesa fire blew up under conditions similar to those developing on Storm King Mountain. The information helps explain what is happening on Storm King Mountain. It also supports the idea that the Bureau of Land Management could have learned from past tragedies.*

If students need help . . . Discuss the similarities between the two fires by completing a Venn Diagram like this one:

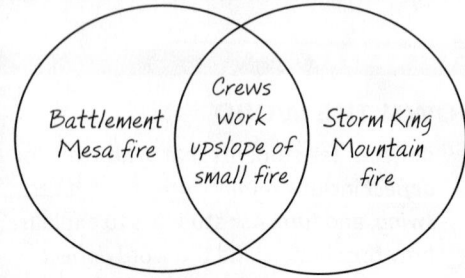

BEST PRACTICES TOOLKIT—Transparency
Venn Diagram p. A26

"It was just an ugly little creeper," the BLM's Brad Haugh said of the early stages of the fire. Every summer, fire fighters like Haugh put out thousands of blazes like this one all over Colorado; at this point there was no reason to think South Canyon would be any different.

The second half of the Prineville crew dropped onto H-2 around 3:00 P.M. and began widening the primary fire line. Two hundred feet below, Haugh was clearing brush with his chain saw on a 33 percent slope. That meant the ground rose one foot for every yard climbed, roughly the steepness of a sand dune. The grade near the top was closer to 50 percent. He wore bulky Kevlar
90   sawyer's chaps and a rucksack loaded with two gallons of water weighing fifteen pounds, a folding knife, freeze-dried rations, and some toilet articles. He also carried a folding fire shelter and a Stihl 056 chain saw that weighed ten or twelve pounds. Even loaded down as he was, Haugh could probably have reached the ridgetop in less than one minute if he had pushed it, and H-1 in five or ten minutes. Wildfires rarely spread faster than one or two miles an hour, and the vast majority of fire fighters are never compelled to outrun them—much less fight to survive them. By conventional fire evaluation standards, Haugh was considered safe.

② Targeted Passage

About three-thirty Haugh took his second break of the day. It was so hot he
100 had already consumed a gallon of the water he carried. The fire was burning slowly in the drainage floor, and the crews fighting it—nine from the Prineville unit and twelve smoke jumpers—were several hundred feet below him in thick Gambel oak, some of the most flammable wood in the West.

Around 3:50 Haugh and his swamper—a sawyer's helper who flings the cut brush off the fire line—were finishing their break when their crew boss announced they were pulling out. Winds were picking up from a cold front that had moved in a half hour earlier, and the fire was snapping to life. They were ordered to climb to the ridgetop and wait it out. **E**

It's rare for an entire mountainside to ignite suddenly, but it's not unheard
110 of. If you stand near H-2 and look several miles to the west, you can see a mountain called Battlement Mesa. In 1976, three men died there in a wildfire later re-created in a training video called *Situation #8.* Every crew member on Storm King would certainly have seen it. In *Situation #8,* a crew is working upslope of a small fire in extremely dry conditions. Flames ignite Gambel oak and race up the hill, encouraged by winds. The steep terrain funnels the flames upward, and fire intensity careens off the chart, a classic blowup. Four men are overrun, three die. The survivor, who suffered horrible burns, says they were never alerted to the critical wind shift—an accusation the BLM denied at the time. . . . **F**

120   At about 4:00 P.M. high winds hit the mountain and pushed a wall of flames north, up the west side of the drainage. Along the ridge, the BLM crew and the upper Prineville unit began moving to the safety of H-1. Below them, Don Mackey ordered his eight jumpers to retreat up to a burned-over area beneath H-1. He then started cross-slope to join three other smoke jumpers

E TAKE NOTES
Reread lines 104–108. What happened around 3:50 P.M.? What had happened at about 3:20? Put these events on your timeline.

F NARRATIVE NONFICTION
Reread lines 109–119. Why does Junger break away from the action on Storm King Mountain to give information about the wildfire at Battlement Mesa?

DIFFERENTIATED INSTRUCTION

FOR STRUGGLING READERS

② Targeted Passage [Lines 85–98]

Filled with technical details, this passage focuses on firefighter Brad Haugh and describes the challenging working conditions for the crews on Storm King Mountain.

- How steep is the ground on which the crews are working? Why is the steepness an important detail? (lines 87–89)

- What kind of work is Haugh doing? How hard does that work seem to you? (line 87)

- What clothing is Haugh wearing? What equipment is he carrying? How do both things make his job more challenging or more dangerous? (lines 89–93)

- Junger claims that "Haugh was considered safe" (line 98) as he battled the fire. Do you think Haugh was safe? Explain. (lines 93–97)

deployed with the Prineville nine. Apparently, no one had advised them that the situation was becoming desperate. In the few minutes it took Mackey to join the twelve fire fighters, the fire jumped east across the drainage. "I radioed that in," said Haugh. "And then another order came to evacuate." That order came from Butch Blanco on the ridgeline, who was hurriedly conducting
130 the evacuation. "This was a much stronger warning than the previous one," recalled Haugh. "I sent my swamper to the ridgetop with a saw and radioed that as soon as the lower Prineville contingent came into sight below me, I would bump up to the safety zone."

Suddenly, fierce westerly winds drove the fire dangerously close—though still hidden behind the thick brush—to the unsuspecting fire fighters. "The crew was unaware of what was behind them," said Haugh. "They were walking at a slow pace, tools still in hand and packs in place." As Haugh watched them, a smoke jumper appeared at his side. "He said that his brother-in-law was down in the drainage, and he wanted to take his picture."

140 That fellow was Kevin Erickson, and Don Mackey was his brother-in-law, now in serious trouble below. As Erickson aimed his camera, everything below him seemed to explode. "Through the viewfinder, I saw them beginning to run, with fire everywhere behind them," Erickson said. "As I took the picture, Brad grabbed me and turned me around. I took one more look back and saw a wall of fire coming uphill." Closing in on Haugh and Erickson were smoke jumper James Thrash and the twelve other fire fighters in a ragged line behind him. Though Blanco and others were now screaming, "Run! Run! Run!" on the radio, Thrash chose to stop and deploy the fire shelter he would die in. Eric Hipke ran around him and followed Haugh and Erickson up the hill. The
150 three-hundred-foot-high flames chasing them sounded like a river thundering over a waterfall. **G**

I n his book *Young Men and Fire,* Norman Maclean writes that dying in a forest fire is actually like experiencing three deaths: first the failure of your legs as you run, then the scorching of your lungs, finally the burning of your body. That, roughly, is what happens to wood when it burns. Water is driven out by the heat; then gases are superheated inside the wood and ignited; finally, the cellulose is consumed. In the end nothing is left but carbon.

This process is usually a slow one, and fires that burn more than a few acres per hour are rare. The South Canyon fire, for example, only burned fifty acres
160 in the first three days. So why did it suddenly rip through two thousand acres in a couple of hours? Why did one hillside explode in a chain reaction that was fast enough to catch birds in midair?

Fire typically spreads by slowly heating the fuel in front of it—first drying it, then igniting it. Usually, a walking pace will easily keep fire fighters ahead of this process. But sometimes a combination of wind, fuel, and terrain **conspires** to produce a blowup in which the fire explodes out of control. One explanation for why South Canyon blew up—and the one most popular in

G TAKE NOTES
Summarize what happened at about 4:00 P.M. Then add your summary to your timeline—in proper order.

conspire (kən-spīr′) *v.* to plan or plot secretly

FOR STRATEGIC READERS

Comprehension Support Make these points as you discuss Junger's use of Norman Maclean's book (lines 152–157):

- The reference to dying reminds readers how this story will end.
- Comparing a body to a piece of wood helps show the impersonality of the fire.
- The passage at first seems to go off on a tangent, but Junger smoothly returns to his subject in the next paragraph.

FOR ADVANCED LEARNERS/PRE–AP

Evaluate an Analogy Have students discuss the analogy that Junger makes between the death of a person in a forest fire and the destruction of wood when it burns (lines 152–157). Ask them whether this unexpected comparison is effective. Challenge students to explain the impact that each part of the analogy makes on the reader.

G TAKE NOTES

Possible answer: At about 4:00 p.m., high winds pushed the fire north. The firefighters were ordered to evacuate, but the fire suddenly exploded. They literally ran for their lives in advance of the fire.

TIERED DISCUSSION PROMPTS

Direct students to lines 134–151. Use these prompts to help students grasp the fire's deadly turn:

Analyze In what ways does Kevin Erickson's firsthand account of the scene convey a sense of urgency to the reader? *Possible answer: Through his camera, Erickson sees the fire explode. His firsthand account allows the reader to share his experience on the mountain.*

Synthesize You already know that this fire will end in tragedy. How does Junger still manage to create tension and suspense in this passage? *Possible answer: Junger creates tension and suspense by showing how unaware the firefighters were of the danger. He keeps the reader waiting for the moment when the crews realize that the fire is near.*

VOCABULARY   COMMON CORE
                                        L 4
OWN THE WORD

conspire: Ask students why they think the author chooses *conspires* in the sentence "But sometimes a combination of wind, fuel, and terrain *conspires* to produce a blowup." *Possible answer: The author is stressing that conditions can change unexpectedly for the worst during a fire.*

Analyze Visuals

Activity On the basis of the information in this photograph, *discuss* which senses would be affected when facing a wildfire. ***Possible answer:*** *The sense of touch would be affected because of the fire's heat. Sight would be affected because the fire obscures the onlookers' view. Onlookers also would smell the burning vegetation and hear the roar of the flames.*

TIERED DISCUSSION PROMPTS

Refer students to lines 163–187. Use these prompts to help students understand how a mountainside can explode:

Connect Junger explains that a mountain can sometimes have a creepy feeling before it explodes into flame (lines 179–181). Have you or someone you know ever had a creepy feeling or premonition that something was wrong? How did the situation turn out? *Accept all reasonable responses.*

Analyze In this passage, Junger provides two possible explanations for why the mountain blew up. Which one does he seem to think is more plausible? How do you know? ***Possible answer:*** *Junger thinks that the superheating explanation is more plausible. He discusses it in more detail (lines 171–187), and he notes that some survivors felt that something was wrong (lines 182–183).*

Synthesize On the basis of what you have learned about wildfires, do you think that these crews should have been prepared for superheating? Defend your answer. ***Possible answer:*** *The crews should have been prepared for superheating. Even though it is a "rare phenomenon" (line 171), experienced firefighters should have known about superheating and about other cases in which it had created explosions.*

A fire fighter observing the South Canyon fire

Glenwood Springs—was that it was just so . . . steep and dry up there and the wind blew so hard that the mountain was swept with flame. That's plausible; similar conditions in other fires have certainly produced extreme fire behavior. The other explanation turns on a rare phenomenon called superheating.

Normally, radiant heat[6] drives volatile[7] gases—called turpines—out of the pinyon and juniper just minutes before they are consumed. But sometimes hot air rises up a steep slope from a blaze and drives turpines out of a whole hillside full of timber. The gases lie heavily along the contours of the slopes, and when the right combination of wind and flame reaches them, they explode. It's like leaving your gas stove burners on for a few hours and then setting a match to your kitchen.

A mountainside on the verge of combustion is a subtle but not necessarily undetectable thing; there are stories of crews pulling out of a creepy-feeling canyon and then watching it blow up behind them. Turpines have an odor, and that's possibly why some of the Prineville survivors said that something had "seemed wrong." The westward-facing hillside had been drying all afternoon in the summer sun. Hot air was sucked up the drainage as if it were

---

6. **radiant heat:** heat that passes through the air, heating solid objects that in turn heat the surrounding area.
7. **volatile:** explosive.

564 UNIT 5: AUTHOR'S PURPOSE

DIFFERENTIATED INSTRUCTION

FOR ENGLISH LANGUAGE LEARNERS

Comprehension: Transitions Explain that contrasts are often indicated by signal words and phrases such as *however* and *on the other hand* but that other, less common phrases also can be used. Discuss the contrast signaled by "That's plausible . . . The other explanation" (lines 169–171) and "Normally . . . But sometimes" (lines 172–175).

an open flue. The powerful winds that hit around 4:00 P.M. blew the fire up the drainage at the hottest time of day. And turpines, having baked for hours, could **conceivably** have lit the whole hillside practically at once. **H**

When Storm King blew, Haugh had to run 150 feet straight up a fire
190 line with poor footing. Despite **rigorous** conditioning—he is a runner and a bodybuilder—his heart rate shot through the roof and his adrenal glands dumped enough epinephrine[8] into his system to kill a house cat. Behind him, sheets of flame were laid flat against the hillside by 50 mph winds. The inferno roared through inherently combustible vegetation that had been desiccated,[9] first by drought, then by hot-air convection, finally by a small grass fire that flashed through a few days earlier. The moisture content of the fine dead fuels was later estimated to be as low as 2 or 3 percent—absolutely explosive. As Haugh ran, panicked shouts came over the tiny radio clipped to his vest for people to drop their equipment and flee. One brief thought flashed through his mind—"So this is what it's like to run for your life"—and he didn't think
200 again until he reached the ridgetop.

Above him, the BLM and upper Prineville crews had abandoned hope of reaching H-1 and scrambled toward H-2. When that route too was blocked, they turned and plunged over the ridge. Due south, one hundred feet below **I** H-1, the eight smoke jumpers who had been ordered out by Don Mackey fifteen minutes earlier were crawling under their foil shelters to wait out the approaching fire storm. At Canyon Creek far below, a crew of fresh smoke jumpers who were preparing to hike in watched in horror as eight little silver squares appeared on the mountainside. Meanwhile, hidden from view by smoke, Mackey, the Prineville nine, and the three smoke jumpers were running
210 a race only one of them, Hipke, would win.

In the end twelve of the dead were found along the lower fire line. Prineville hotshot Scott Blecha had also run past Thrash but lost his race a hundred feet from the ridgeline. The rest were in two main groups below a tree—*the* tree, as it came to be known, where Haugh had started his run—a few clumped so close together that their bodies were actually touching. Only smoke jumpers Thrash and Roger Roth had deployed their shelters, but the blistering heat disintegrated the foil. Kathi Beck died alongside Thrash, partly under his shelter. It seemed that in his last agony, Thrash may have tried to pull her in. In addition, Richard Tyler and Robert Browning, two fire fighters deployed
220 earlier to direct helicopter operations, perished just north of H-2, only a few hundred feet from a rocky area that might have saved them. **J**

The Prineville nine's dash for safety ended after three hundred feet. They were caught just three or four seconds before Haugh himself cleared the ridgetop, and he could hear their screams over his radio. Reconstructing the details of the victims' agonized last seconds would occupy many hours of professional counseling for the survivors.

---

8. **epinephrine:** another name for adrenaline, a natural chemical released by the body that speeds up heartbeats, improves breathing, and increases blood flow to muscles during exercise.

9. **desiccated:** thoroughly dried out.

H TAKE NOTES
Based on Junger's explanation of super-heating, what might have been happening for several hours before 4:00 P.M.? Indicate this possible occurrence on your timeline.

conceivably
(kən-sēv'ə-blē) *adv.*
possibly

rigorous (rĭg'ər-əs) *adj.*
strict, uncompromising

I GRAMMAR AND STYLE
Reread lines 201–203. Notice how Junger uses the **adverb clause** "When that route too was blocked" to describe at what point the Prineville crew plunged over the ridge. Adverb clauses help to add important details to writing, telling when or where something happened, for example.

J PATTERNS OF ORGANIZATION
Why do you think Junger chose to present these details in spatial order?

READING STRATEGY

H TAKE NOTES

Possible answer: Before 4:00 P.M., volatile gases called turpines might have been seeping out of the pinyon and juniper for hours and pooling along the ground. Once the wind carried the flames forward, these gases could have exploded when the fire reached them.

I GRAMMAR AND STYLE   COMMON CORE **L 1b**

Add Descriptive Details Elicit that the information in the adverb clause "When that route too was blocked" is important because it reveals the growing desperation of the situation. To reinforce the concept, have students identify and explain the usefulness of the clause "When Storm King blew" (line 188).

READING STRATEGY: *Review*   COMMON CORE **RI 5**

J PATTERNS OF ORGANIZATION

Possible answer: Putting these details in spatial order helps readers visualize how the fire reached the firefighters. It also allows Junger to speculate about what the firefighters were doing in their last moments, based on the locations and positions of their bodies. Finally, showing that some of the firefighters were very close to safety when they died adds poignancy and irony to the account.

VOCABULARY   COMMON CORE **L 4**

OWN THE WORD

- **conceivably:** Point out that *conceivably* is related to the verb *conceive,* meaning "to form or develop." The adjective *conceivable,* which is the base of the adverb, describes a situation as being possible or in development.

- **rigorous:** Tell students that *rigorous* has the connotation of hard work. Ask students to list situations where they might need to be *rigorous.* ***Possible answers:*** *playing a sport; cleaning the house; studying*

FOR RELUCTANT READERS
Connect to the Text To help students connect with the firefighters' experience, use a Cluster Diagram to explore Haugh's dramatic thought in line 199: "So this is what it's like to run for your life." Write the quotation in the center of a Cluster Diagram, and add students' ideas about "what it's like to run for your life" around it. To generate ideas, ask: What would you feel as you were running for your life? What would you think about?

 BEST PRACTICES TOOLKIT—Transparency
Cluster Diagram p. B18

FOR ADVANCED LEARNERS/PRE–AP
Analyze Figurative Language Point out that Junger uses the language of competition to describe the firefighters' struggle—for example, saying that some of the smoke jumpers were "running a race only one . . . would win" (lines 209–210). Ask students to make some notes about this figurative language and why Junger might have decided to use it. Then have students gather for a group discussion of their analyses.

Dying in a fire is often less a process of burning than of asphyxiation.[10] Their suffering was probably intense but short-lived. Pathologists looked for carbon in their lungs and upper airways and found none, which meant the victims weren't breathing when the fire passed over them. Their lungs were filled with fluid, their throats were closed in laryngeal spasms—responses to superheated air—and their blood contained toxic levels of carbon monoxide. This gas, given off during incomplete combustion, displaces oxygen in the blood and kills very quickly.

"They died after a few breaths at most," said Rob Kurtzman, a pathologist at the Grand Junction Community Hospital, "probably in less than thirty seconds. All the body changes—the charring, the muscle contractions, the bone fractures—happened after they were dead." **L**

About four-thirty Haugh, Erickson, and Hipke staggered onto Interstate 70. Just an hour before, they had enjoyed a well-earned break on the mountain; now fourteen people were dead. But all they knew at that point was that Blanco, the incident commander, was calling out names on the radio and a lot of people weren't answering.

Haugh and Erickson laid Hipke in the shade of a police cruiser and doused him with water to lower his body temperature and prevent him from going into shock. Blanco climbed back up toward the fire to look for more survivors but found none. The eight smoke jumpers who'd deployed their shelters below H-1 emerged, shaken but unhurt. They were saved not by their shelters but by having deployed them on previously burned ground. The fire was still pumping at this point, and Glenwood Springs was now in danger. Flames were racing eastward along the upper ridges, and the BLM command post at nearby Canyon Creek had begun ordering residents to evacuate.

Haugh's BLM crew had survived. The other Prineville Hotshots—the upper placements—made it out as well. They had snaked their way down the east side of the ridge through a hellish maze of spot fires and exploding trees. Two of them had tried to deploy their shelters but were dragged onward by friends.

Word quickly filtered back to BLM officials in Grand Junction that something terrible had happened on Storm King. Mike Mottice, the agency's area manager, had driven past the blowup and arrived at his Glenwood Springs office around 5:00 P.M. Minutes later crews began arriving from the mountain, and Mottice realized for the first time that there were people unaccounted for. "I hoped that the fire shelters would save them," he said. "But that evening some smoke jumpers confirmed that there were deaths." . . .

The next morning investigators began to measure things, ponder the dynamics of the mountain, and coax secrets from the dead.

The first question was how fast the fire had moved, and Haugh's estimate—that the last three hundred feet were covered in about twelve seconds—turned out to be close. In the end, the investigators confirmed that the fire had

---

10. **asphyxiation:** the medical term for suffocation.

A plane releasing fire retardant on the blaze

covered the quarter-mile slope in about two minutes, hitting its top speed of
270   18 mph in the dried-out Gambel oak.

The next question was why it had done that. Fire behavior is determined by
an incredibly complicated interaction of fuel, terrain, and wind, and there are
mathematical models describing the interaction. (The models are programmed
into hand-held calculators carried by most incident commanders these days.)
The deadly hillside faced west at a 33 to 50 percent slope, and the vegetation
on it possessed burning characteristics described in a formula called Fuel
Model Number Four. The moisture content of the small dead fuels on Storm
King Mountain was around 3 percent. And the live Gambel oak (which had
only been partly burned earlier) was several times drier than normal. In a light
280   wind, according to this model, those conditions would produce twenty-three-
foot flames spreading at a maximum of seven hundred feet an hour.

That's a manageable fire, or at least one that can be outrun, but an increase
in wind speed can change the situation dramatically. At 7:20 P.M. on Tuesday
(less than twenty-four hours before the blowup), the National Weather Service
issued a "Red Flag" fire warning for the area around Glenwood Springs. Dry
thunderstorms were expected the following morning, followed by southwest
winds gusting up to 30 mph. A cold front would come through sometime that
afternoon, swinging the winds to the northwest.

COMMON CORE RI 4

Language Coach

Multiple Meanings
Some words have
specialized meanings.
A *model* is usually a
small version of a larger
object. What does it
mean in line 273? (Line
276 gives a clue.) In
line 287, *front* means
"boundary between
different air masses."
What does *front* usually
mean?

Analyze Visuals

Activity Ask students to study both the caption and the photograph and then to make at least one inference based on this written and visual information. *Possible answer: Because the photograph shows that the house is extremely close to the fire—close enough for the people who live there to see the smoke and the plane releasing fire retardant—we can infer that the residents of the house are worried that they are in danger. The photograph also shows a vehicle with its side and back doors open, suggesting that people are packing up in preparation for evacuating to safety.*

TIERED DISCUSSION PROMPTS

Direct students to lines 271–295. Use these prompts to help students understand why the fire intensified:

Summarize What is Junger's theory about why the Storm King Mountain fire escalated out of control? *Possible answer: Junger's theory is that gusting winds caused the fire to intensify from a "manageable fire, or least one that can be outrun" (line 282) to one with huge flames that were racing up the mountain much faster than a "human can run" (line 292). The moisture content of the vegetation and the slope of the hillside had not been a threat as long as the wind had remained light.*

Analyze What does Junger mean when he says that the fire "exploded in a mathematically predictable way" (lines 294–295)? *Possible answer: He means that the mathematical models that are used to describe the behavior of fires would have predicted the intensification of this particular fire—if someone had thought to factor in the National Weather Service's warning about gusting winds (lines 283–288).*

Evaluate How well does Junger support his theory about the Storm King Mountain fire? Explain. *Students will probably think that Junger presents ample evidence to support his theory. Some students may suggest that his argument would have been stronger if he had quoted experts to support his theory.*

FOR ENGLISH LANGUAGE LEARNERS

Language Coach   COMMON CORE
                                 RI 4
Multiple Meanings *Answer: A* front *usually means "the part of something that faces forward." In line 276,* model *seems to refer to a formula that predicts future behavior.* Provide pairs of sentences that illustrate the multiple meanings of each word. For example, *"Temperatures dropped when the cold front moved in. They painted the front of their house first."* Then have students work with partners to create their own sentence pairs.

FOR ADVANCED LEARNERS/PRE–AP

Analyze Tone [small-group option] Ask students to analyze Junger's tone—his attitude toward his subject or readers—as he tries to explain why the fire exploded (lines 271–295). For example, is Junger's tone objective? friendly? angry? Have students prepare and share an oral or written analysis about the effect of factual passages like this one upon the reader. Have them also discuss why Junger might be committed to including such passages in his narrative.

Analyze Visuals

Activity This photograph shows Storm King Mountain 10 years after the fire. Ask students what the photograph reveals about the changes that have taken place on the mountain since the tragedy. *Possible answer: The photograph shows that while there is new vegetation, the trees have not regained their leaves and may be dead. The photograph also shows that the mountain is now the site of a memorial honoring the firefighters who died.*

REVISIT THE BIG QUESTION

What can we learn from
DISASTER?

Discuss How does the reference in lines 289–295 to the Battlement Mesa fire remind the reader of the human tragedy in this disaster? *Possible answer: The reference underscores the idea that perhaps some or all of the deaths at Storm King Mountain could have been avoided if people had learned from what happened at Battlement Mesa.*

READING STRATEGY: *Review*   **COMMON CORE**   **RI 5**

 **PATTERNS OF ORGANIZATION**

Possible answer: Junger uses spatial order and time order in his explanation. A chart might be useful for recording specific measurements. A diagram might be good for taking notes on spatial details.

SELECTION WRAP–UP

READ WITH A PURPOSE Have students summarize "what went wrong" during the Storm King Mountain fire. Then ask them: Could the fire and the loss of life have been prevented? Have students explain their answers. *Possible answer: High winds that accompanied a cold front caused the fire to spread and created fast-moving flames that firefighters could not control or outrun. Accept all thoughtful answers.*

⭐ **CRITIQUE** How easy was it to follow Junger's narrative? Explain.

INDEPENDENT READING

Students may enjoy reading Sebastian Junger's other essays about dangerous jobs in his collection *Fire.*

Fire fighter Eric Hipke revisits Storm King Mountain in 2004.

Gusts of 35 mph, plugged into Fuel Model Number Four, produce sixty-
290 four-foot flames racing up the mountain at up to fifteen feet per second. In the superdry Gambel oak, the rate of spread would have been almost twice that— much faster than any human can run. The lessons of the Battlement Mesa fire (detailed in the *Situation #8* video) had not been learned: A small fire on steep ground covered with extremely dry vegetation had once more exploded in a mathematically predictable way—again, with tragic results. . . . **N**

"I know in my heart," said Haugh, "that the twelve persons who died in that part of the fire were unaware of what was happening." By the time the Prineville nine and the three smoke jumpers with them saw the horror coming—by the time great sheets of flame hit the dry Gambel oak and frantic
300 voices over the radio screamed at them to run—they had only twenty seconds to live. They must have died in a state of bewilderment almost as great as their fear. ॰ஓ

④ **Targeted Passage**

N PATTERNS OF ORGANIZATION
Reread lines 271–295. What pattern of organization does Junger use to explain fire behavior? What type of graphic organizer would you use to record details from this passage?

DIFFERENTIATED INSTRUCTION

FOR STRUGGLING READERS

④ **Targeted Passage** [Lines 296–302]

This concluding passage offers Haugh's reflections about what happened to his fallen coworkers.

- How does Haugh characterize the last seconds of his coworkers' battle? (lines 296–297)

- Why did the firefighters have "only twenty seconds to live" (lines 300–301) when they "saw the horror coming"? (lines 298–299)

- According to Junger, what must the firefighters have been feeling when they died? Why? (lines 301–302)

Comprehension

1. **Recall** How were Brad Haugh and the other two men with him able to escape the fire?

2. **Recall** How did the fire originally begin on July 2?

3. **Recall** What effect did the cold front have on the fire?

4. **Clarify** Why did so many fire fighters die?

COMMON CORE

RI 3 Analyze how the author unfolds and develops a series of events, the order in which they occur, and the connections drawn between events. **RI 5** Analyze in detail how an author's ideas or claims are developed.

Text Analysis

5. **Examine Notes** Using the timeline you created, explain what happened on Storm King Mountain. How long had the fire burned before the first crew arrived? When did the situation on the mountain become a disaster?

6. **Interpret Information** Junger has been praised for delivering a lot of technical information while telling a good story. What did you learn from the selection about wildfires and how to fight them?

7. **Analyze Cause and Effect** Junger proposes that a phenomenon called superheating could have caused the blowup. Reread the passage about superheating (lines 171–187). Then use a cause-and-effect chart to show how it occurs.

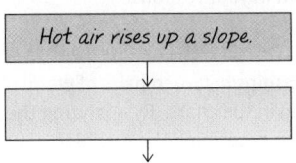

Hot air rises up a slope.

8. **Evaluate Narrative Nonfiction** Where is Junger strongest as a storyteller? Cite passages employing **suspense, foreshadowing,** vivid **characterization,** or other elements you found particularly effective.

9. **Apply Ideas** Junger believes that people with dangerous jobs are more heroic than people who participate in extreme sports. Do you think the fire fighters portrayed in "Blowup" are heroic? Explain why or why not.

What can we learn from DISASTER?

What lesson have you learned from witnessing or reading about a disaster?

---

8. ● **COMMON CORE FOCUS** *Narrative Nonfiction Junger is a strong storyteller in the opening paragraphs, which involve the reader in Brad Haugh's sensations as he runs for his life. Junger vividly describes the victims' final moments (lines 211–234). He also creates suspense as he describes how the fire intensified (lines 120–151). Junger's reference to a similar fire foreshadows the tragic blowup to come (lines 109–119).*

9. *Students who believe that the firefighters are heroic may note how dangerous and strenuous their jobs are, how diligently they worked, and how tragically they died. Students who do not think that the firefighters are heroic may view them as victims, noting that they were unaware of the seriousness of their situation and unprepared for what happened.*

What can we learn from **DISASTER?** Students may describe survival techniques for specific types of disasters or reflect on what a specific disaster taught them about what is most important in life.

Practice and Apply

For preliminary support of post-reading questions, use these copy masters:

R RESOURCE MANAGER—Copy Masters
Reading Check p. 96
Narrative Nonfiction p. 89
Question Support p. 97

Additional selection questions are provided for teachers on page 83.

ANSWERS

Comprehension

1. *The three men outran the fire to the top of a ridge, where the fire stopped.*

2. *The fire began with a lightning strike.*

3. *The cold front created high winds, which spread the fire.*

4. *Firefighters died because the fire exploded around them before they knew what was happening, and they could not outrun the fast-moving flames.*

Text Analysis

COMMON CORE RI 3, RI 5

Possible answers:

5. ● **COMMON CORE FOCUS** *Take Notes The fire had burned for three days. On July 2, the fire was ignited by a lightning strike. On the morning of July 5, a crew was sent to prepare a helicopter landing site and cut a fire line. At dawn on July 6, the Prineville Hotshots arrived. At 4:00 P.M. the situation became a disaster when high winds hit the mountain and spread the fire, which then exploded. The firefighters ran for their lives, but 14 did not make it.*

6. *Among the many things that the reader learns is that wildfires are fought by cutting fire breaks and dropping flame retardant from planes, that most wildfires travel relatively slowly unless wind gusts increase the rate of speed, and that blowups can occur when volatile gases are driven out of the trees by hot air and then ignite.*

7. *Hot air rises up a slope. The hot air drives turpines (volatile gases) out of the timber. The turpines lie along the hillside. Wind and flame reach the turpines. The turpines explode. A blowup occurs.*

ANSWERS

Vocabulary in Context

▲ VOCABULARY PRACTICE

1. *false*	4. *false*
2. *true*	5. *false*
3. *true*	

 **RESOURCE MANAGER—Copy Master**
Vocabulary Practice p. 94

ACADEMIC VOCABULARY IN WRITING

Possible answers: *What was your primary* goal *in writing this article? What* issues *would you like to write about in the future? What* authors *have inspired you through their choice of topics or writing style?*

VOCABULARY STRATEGY: ANALOGIES

COMMON CORE L5

- For each item, help students identify the relationship between the words in the first pair. Have them state this relationship in a sentence. Model the thought process of determining the relationship in item 1 by saying, "If you create an <u>interruption</u>, you cause someone to become <u>distracted</u>. So the relationship between the words is that the first word is the cause and the second word is the effect."

- As students work to complete the analogies, suggest that they test different words from the Word List until they find the one that creates a relationship that matches the relationship of the first pair.

Possible answers:

1. *deflect*; results in or leads to
2. *rigorous*; is grammatically related to
3. *conceivably*; means the opposite of
4. *contingent*; is a part of

 **RESOURCE MANAGER—Copy Master**
Vocabulary Strategy p. 95

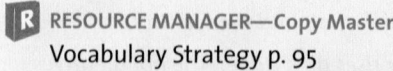

Interactive Vocabulary   THINK central

Keywords direct students to a **WordSharp** tutorial on **thinkcentral.com** or to other types of vocabulary practice and review.

Vocabulary in Context

▲ VOCABULARY PRACTICE

Decide if each statement is true or false.

1. To **deflect** criticism means to attract it all the time.
2. A **contingent** is often a smaller group of people.
3. To **conspire** with people is to act together with them.
4. If it can **conceivably** rain today, this means there is no chance of it happening.
5. A **rigorous** course of study is easy and will teach very little.

WORD LIST

conceivably
conspire
contingent
deflect
rigorous

ACADEMIC VOCABULARY IN WRITING

- author • document • goal • issue • vision

Write three questions you might ask the **author** in an interview. Consider **issues** that relate to the Storm King disaster or to writing nonfiction. Use at least one Academic Vocabulary word in your response.

VOCABULARY STRATEGY: ANALOGIES

Analogies express relationships between pairs of words. Some common relationships are described in the chart. By analyzing the relationship between words in analogies, you can determine the meaning of words you're unfamiliar with.

COMMON CORE
L5 Demonstrate understanding of word relationships.

Type	Relationship
Part to a whole	is a part of
Antonym	means the opposite of
Cause and effect	results in or leads to
Grammar	is grammatically related to

PRACTICE Complete each analogy by choosing the appropriate word from the Word List. Identify the kind of relationship on which the analogy is based.

1. interruption : distract :: obstacle : _____
2. indignation : indignant :: rigor : _____
3. slightly : greatly :: impossibly : _____
4. school : class :: military : _____

Interactive Vocabulary   THINK central

Go to **thinkcentral.com**.
KEYWORD: HML10-570

DIFFERENTIATED INSTRUCTION

FOR ENGLISH LANGUAGE LEARNERS

Comprehension: Task Support Assign pairs of students to write a statement that is true for every false statement in the **Vocabulary Practice**. Have students identify the word or words in the original sentence that make it not true. Then have them think of words or phrases that accurately reflect the meaning of the vocabulary word. Call on volunteers to share their new sentences for class discussion.

FOR ADVANCED LEARNERS/PRE-AP

Vocabulary in Writing Have students use the five vocabulary words in a brief newspaper story that reports the disaster on Storm King Mountain. Display the results and invite students to see how their classmates used the words.

Language

◆ **GRAMMAR AND STYLE:** Add Descriptive Details

Review the **Grammar and Style** note on page 565. An **adverb clause** tells *where, why, how, when,* or *to what degree* something was done. It is typically introduced by a subordinating conjunction such as *after, as, because, since, until, when,* and *where.* In the following excerpts, notice how Junger uses adverb clauses to explain when certain events occurred. Also pay attention to the structure of these sentences; notice where the adverb clauses are placed.

> *As they started down again, the fire was spreading behind them at a thousand acres an hour, oak, pinyon, and juniper spontaneously combusting in the heat. (lines 33–35)*
>
> *All the body changes—the charring, the muscle contractions, the bone fractures—happened after they were dead.* (lines 237–238)

Notice how the revisions in blue enhance the description in this first draft. Revise your responses to the prompt by including adverb clauses, making sure to set them off with a comma when they come <u>before</u> independent clauses.

> **STUDENT MODEL**
>
> *As they walk up and down steep slopes,*
> People who fight wildfires need to be very strong. They must haul their
> *Since chain saws can weigh 10 to 12 pounds and two gallons of water can weigh 17 pounds,*
> food, water, and equipment, such as chain saws and fire shelters. This is a
> difficult task.

COMMON CORE

L 1b Use various types of clauses to convey specific meanings and add variety and interest to writing. **W 2** Write explanatory texts to examine and convey complex ideas, concepts, and information clearly and accurately through the effective analysis of content.

READING-WRITING CONNECTION

 YOUR TURN Deepen your understanding of "Blowup: What Went Wrong at Storm King Mountain" by responding to this prompt. Then use the **revising tip** to improve your writing.

WRITING PROMPT	REVISING TIP
Extended Constructed Response: Identification What is the most important lesson to be learned from the **disaster** on Storm King Mountain? Write **three to five paragraphs** discussing mistakes made and offering one or more proposals for the future.	Review your response. Did you use adverb clauses to add descriptive details? If not, revise your draft. Pay attention to the structure of the sentences you create.

Interactive Revision THINK central
Go to **thinkcentral.com**.
KEYWORD: HML10-571

FOR STRUGGLING WRITERS

- Have students work in small groups to list mistakes that they think were made on Storm King Mountain.

- Suggest that students focus on one mistake from their list.

- Help students brainstorm to come up with a possible solution to this mistake.

- Help students generate a proposal that might prevent another disaster.

Language

 **COMMON CORE L 1b, W 2**

◆ **GRAMMAR AND STYLE**

- Have students review the **Grammar and Style** note on page 565 and read the student model.

- Write this passage on the board. Have students add adverb clauses based on the bracketed prompts. (Sample revisions are shown in blue.)

> *Haugh realized the fire was growing [why?] because the winds had picked up. He started to run [how?] as fast as he could [where?] up the mountain.*

R RESOURCE MANAGER—Copy Master
Add Descriptive Details p. 98

READING-WRITING CONNECTION

- Have students reread lines 289–302 as they think about lessons to be learned from the fire. Ask students to decide which mistake was most important and to offer a proposal that addresses this problem.

Writing Online THINK central

The following tools are available online at **thinkcentral.com** and on **WriteSmart** CD-ROM:
- Interactive Graphic Organizers
- Interactive Student Models
- Interactive Revision Lessons
For additional grammar instruction, see **GrammarNotes** on **thinkcentral.com**.

Assess and Reteach

Assess

DIAGNOSTIC AND SELECTION TESTS
Selection Test A pp. 155–156
Selection Test B/C pp. 157–158

Interactive Selection Test on **thinkcentral.com**

Reteach

Level Up Online Tutorials on **thinkcentral.com**

Reteaching Worksheets on **thinkcentral.com**
Informational Text Lesson 2, Vocabulary Lesson 23

Focus and Motivate

⊙ COMMON CORE FOCUS

RI 2 Determine a central idea of a text. **RI 3** Analyze how the author unfolds and develops a series of events, the order in which they occur, and the connections drawn between the events. **RI 7** Analyze various accounts of a subject told in different mediums determining which details are emphasized in each account. **W 9b (RI 7)** Draw evidence from literary nonfiction; analyze various accounts of a subject told in different mediums.

SUMMARY

"How to Survive a Wildfire" is a procedural document that explains how to escape a wildfire. The text of this how-to document is supported by two kinds of graphic aids: illustrations of what to do in the event of a wildfire and a bar graph of causes of wildfires.

What's the Connection?

Use a KWL chart to prepare students for reading the procedural document on surviving a wildfire. For the first column, have students recall what they already know about wildfires. In the second column, have them write questions about what they want to know. After reading, have students write what they have learned.

🧰 **BEST PRACTICES TOOLKIT—Transparency**
KWL p. A21

Teach

Standards Focus: Synthesizing Information from Graphics

- Have students identify titles, headings, captions, and labels in the graphics included in this how-to essay document. Point out that titles and headings often directly state main ideas.

- As students view and interpret graphics, encourage them to tap their own knowledge and experience by asking, "What do I know about what this graphic shows?"

- Before synthesizing information from multiple graphics, suggest that students ask these questions: Why is this graphic included with the others? What information does it provide that the others do not?

R **RESOURCE MANAGER—Copy Master**
Synthesize p. 107

Reading for Information

How to Survive a Wildfire
Functional Document

What's the Connection?

Use with "Blowup: What Went Wrong at Storm King Mountain," page 558.

⊙ **COMMON CORE**

RI 2 Determine a central idea of a text. **RI 3** Analyze how the author unfolds and develops a series of events, the order in which they occur, and the connections drawn between the events.

In "Blowup: What Went Wrong at Storm King Mountain," you read an account of three firefighters who escaped a horrific wildfire explosion. You also viewed photos and a diagram that illustrated the extent of the fire. Now you will read a how-to essay that provides both written and visual information about surviving a wildfire.

Standards Focus: Synthesizing Information from Graphics

Not only can you **synthesize,** or combine, information from several written sources on a topic, you can also synthesize information from several visual sources. Synthesizing information from multiple graphics, such as photographs, diagrams, maps, and charts, helps you develop your understanding of that topic. To help synthesize information from multiple graphics, use these guidelines:

- Interpret the main idea presented in each graphic by reading the titles, headings, captions, labels, and legends.
- Develop your thoughts about each idea presented in the graphics by connecting the ideas to your knowledge and personal experience.
- Note the relationships between the ideas presented in the graphics. Are there similarities? Are there contradictions?
- Combine the information you gathered—main ideas, thoughts, and relationships—into a summary statement.

Complete a chart like the one below to synthesize information from some of the graphics that appear in "Blowup: What Went Wrong at Storm King Mountain" and "How to Survive a Wildfire.

Graphic	Main Idea	My Thoughts
photo on page 559	The South Canyon fire was large and intense.	I've seen wildfires, but none as big as this one.
diagram on page 561	Wind caused the fire to nearly surround the firefighters.	
"Know Your Surroundings" graphic		
"What to Do if the Fire Approaches" graphic		
Summary Statement:		

Selection Resources

See resources on the **Teacher One Stop DVD-ROM** *and on* <u>thinkcentral.com</u>.

R **RESOURCE MANAGER UNIT 5**
Lesson Support,* pp. 99–112

DIAGNOSTIC AND SELECTION TESTS
Selection Tests, pp. 159–162

🧰 **BEST PRACTICES TOOLKIT**
KWL, p. A21

TECHNOLOGY
- 💿 **Teacher One Stop DVD-ROM**
- 💿 **Student One Stop DVD-ROM**
- 💿 **Audio Anthology CD**
- 💿 **ExamView Test Generator** on the **Teacher One Stop**

* Resources for Differentiation

How to Survive a Wildfire

Wildfires destroy millions of acres of property every year in the United States—and they also sometimes take lives. However, there are ways to survive if a wildfire threatens your campsite or home.

If a wildfire approaches, don't panic. Keeping a calm awareness of your surroundings and your situation can give you the best chance of survival.

Know Your Surroundings

First, quickly think over what you know of the surrounding terrain. Where are roads, lakes, rivers, or areas of rocky ground located in relation to you and the fire? Your best chance of escaping a fire is by traveling in an area where there is little vegetation, such as a road or stream.

Know Your Surroundings

Rocky ground · Hill · Fire · Road · Stream **A**

Remember, vegetation is what burns, so head for any bare areas. Avoid areas of dry or dead plants that will burn quickly. Knowing your trees can also help. Evergreen trees burn more quickly than deciduous trees (trees that shed their leaves), so avoid pine trees if possible.

Additionally, wildfires travel uphill more quickly than they travel downhill, so if you are on a hillside, travel downward. **B**

A EVALUATE GRAPHICS
What should this person do to avoid the fire?

B SYNTHESIZE INFORMATION
Look at the graphic on page 561, which illustrates the Storm King Mountain fire. According to this graphic and the information in this article, why were the Prineville nine in a vulnerable position?

INFORMATIONAL ANALYSIS · COMMON CORE · RI 2

A EVALUATE GRAPHICS

Possible answer: The person should move away from the fire to an area free of vegetation, such as the road, stream, or rocky ground.

Extend the Discussion What advantages does the person shown have?

INFORMATIONAL ANALYSIS · COMMON CORE · RI 7

B SYNTHESIZE INFORMATION

Possible answer: They were uphill from the fire, and fires move uphill quickly.

DIFFERENTIATED INSTRUCTION

FOR ENGLISH LANGUAGE LEARNERS
Transitions To aid comprehension, identify transitional words and phrases in the document. Explain that transitions connect ideas within and between sentences. Read aloud the first section of the document, pausing at words or phrases that signal relationships between ideas (*First, Additionally*). Discuss what these transitions indicate (sequence, addition). Continue reading, pausing to identify and discuss other examples.

C EVALUATE GRAPHICS

Possible answer: *Answers will vary. The graphic shows the correct way to protect oneself from a wildfire. The person is crouching in a ditch and covering himself with a wet coat.*

IF STUDENTS NEED HELP . . .

Have students read aloud the labels and use them as prompts to describe what a person should do to when trapped by an approaching fire.

D *Model the Skill:* SYNTHESIZE INFORMATION FROM GRAPHICS

To model how to synthesize information from multiple graphics, infer the main idea of the graphic on this page from its labels and the accompanying text, connect those ideas to what you know or have experienced, and identify similarities or differences between the graphics. Record this information in a chart like the one on page 572. Then review the information and write a summary statement in the chart.

Graphic	Main Idea	My Thoughts
Graphic on page 555; chart on this page	Lightning was the cause of the Storm King Mountain fire; burning debris is the most common cause of fire.	I've never heard of a fire caused by lightning. I have heard of fires caused by arson and burning debris.

Possible answer: *The Storm King Mountain fire was caused by lightning, which is not the most common cause of wildfires. The most common cause is burning debris.*

If the Fire Approaches

If you become trapped by an approaching fire, try to find or dig a ditch and crouch down as low as possible. If you can, cover yourself with a blanket or coat (preferably wet). Staying low will help you avoid inhaling smoke.

C EVALUATE GRAPHICS
How does this graphic help you understand the procedure it illustrates?

Alternatively, crouch low in the middle of a stream or lake. Try to keep as much of your body below the surface of the water as possible.

Once the fire has passed, move upwind to where the fire has already burned the vegetation.

Preventing Wildfires

To help ensure that you never have to try to survive a wildfire, do what you can to prevent wildfires. Observe burn bans. Monitor any fires or campfires and extinguish them thoroughly. Be careful when using equipment around dry vegetation. D

D SYNTHESIZE INFORMATION FROM GRAPHICS
What is the most common cause of wildfires? Use this chart and the graphic illustrating the Storm King Mountain fire on page 561 to determine whether the Storm King Mountain fire was started by the most common cause of wildfires.

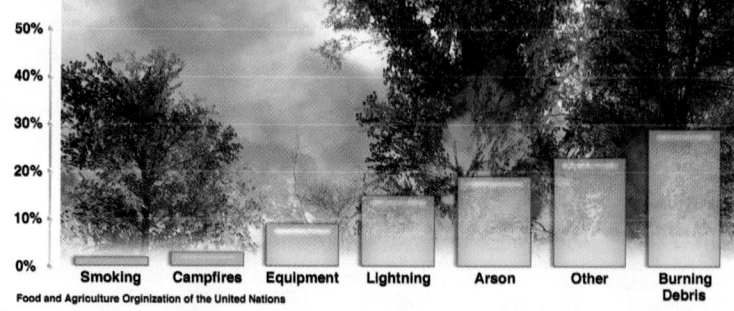

DIFFERENTIATED INSTRUCTION

FOR STRUGGLING READERS

Comprehension Support Help students interpret the bar graph. Identify the parts of the graph: vertical axis, horizontal axis, scale, bars, and bar labels. Discuss what the scale, or numbers, on the vertical axis represent and what the bars on the horizontal axis represent (*percentage of fires, causes of fires*). Explain how to read across from the top of a bar to the vertical axis to determine the percentage of fires with a particular cause. Then, give students practice reading the

graph by asking them to determine the percentage of fires with each cause.

FOR ADVANCED LEARNERS/PRE–AP

Hypothesize What would you do if you were caught by a wildfire? Have students synthesize what they learned both from the account of the fire on Storm King Mountain and from the how-to essay to write a brief short story from a first-person point of view about escaping from a wildfire. Invite students to share their stories with the class.

Comprehension

1. **Recall** What areas should you move to if a wildfire threatens you?

2. **Recall** Does a wildfire move faster uphill or downhill?

Text Analysis

3. **Evaluate Graphics** Does the graphic "Know Your Surroundings" present information effectively? Explain.

4. **Evaluate Graphics** What activities do you think might fall under the "Other Human Activity" category of the "Causes of Wildfires" graph?

● 5. **Synthesize Information from Graphics** How do the graphics in this article help you understand the steps necessary to escape, survive, or prevent a wildfire?

COMMON CORE

RI 7 Analyze various accounts of a subject told in different mediums determining which details are emphasized in each account. **W 9b (RI 7)** Draw evidence from literary nonfiction; analyze various accounts of a subject told in different mediums.

Read for Information: Use Information from Multiple Sources

WRITING PROMPT

Given the information presented in the photographs and graphic in "Blow-up: What Went Wrong at Storm King Mountain" and in the three graphics in "How to Escape a Wildfire," what conclusions can you draw about wildfire prevention and safety? Respond in 2–3 paragraphs.

To respond to this prompt,

1. Consider how each graphic and photograph adds to your knowledge of wildfire safety and how it affects you as a reader.

2. Review the chart you created as you read. The thoughts you noted and your summary statement are good sources of information for your response.

Graphic	Main Idea	My Thoughts
photo on page 559	The South Canyon fire was large and intense.	I've seen wildfires, but none as big as this one.
diagram on page 561	Wind caused the fire to nearly surround the firefighters.	
"Know Your Surroundings" graphic		
"What to Do if the Fire Approaches" graphic		
"Causes of Wildfires" graph		
Summary Statement:		

Practice and Apply

For preliminary support of post-reading questions, use these copy masters:

R RESOURCE MANAGER—Copy Masters
Reading Check p. 111
Question Support p. 112
Synthesize p. 107
Additional selection questions are provided for teachers on page 102.

ANSWERS

Comprehension

1. *You should move to an area that is free of dry vegetation and conifers.*

2. *uphill*

Text Analysis

COMMON CORE **RI 7**

3. *Answers will vary. The graphic illustrates how a person should think about his or her position and that of the fire and the surrounding terrain.*

4. *Answers may include fireworks, downed power lines, and controlled burns that go out of control.*

5. ● **COMMON CORE FOCUS** *Synthesize*
Answers will vary. The first two graphics illustrate steps one should take if threatened with, or trapped by, a wildfire. The graph lists causes of wildfires, which people should know in order to avoid accidentally causing a fire.

Read for Information: Use Information from Multiple Sources

COMMON CORE **W 9b**

Writing Prompt *Answers will vary. Students should mention that wildfires can be exacerbated by natural forces, and that people should be careful to avoid causing wildfires. Students should also observe that if one knows what to do, one can increase one's likelihood of surviving a wildfire.*

Assess and Reteach

Assess

DIAGNOSTIC AND SELECTION TEST
Selection Test A, B/C pp. 159–160, 161–162

Interactive Selection Test on thinkcentral.com

Reteach

Level Up Online Tutorials on thinkcentral.com

FOR STRUGGLING WRITERS

Read for Information

- Remind students to combine what they already know about the topic with information from textual and graphical sources.

- Tell students to begin with a brief introductory paragraph that states their main idea about wildfire prevention and safety, present their conclusions with reasons and supporting evidence in a longer body paragraph, and then conclude with a brief paragraph in which they summarize their key points.

FOR ADVANCED LEARNERS/PRE–AP

Explain a Process Have students work in small groups to create a procedural document about how to prevent wildfires. Tell students to include both text and graphics in their document. Have each group present its document to the rest of the class, and have the class select the document that combines text and graphics most effectively to explain how to prevent wildfires.

COMMON CORE FOCUS

SL 2 Integrate multiple sources of information presented in diverse media or formats, evaluating the credibility and accuracy of each source.
SL 3 Evaluate a speaker's point of view, reasoning, and use of evidence and rhetoric, identifying any fallacious reasoning or exaggerated or distorted evidence.

SUMMARY

Robert Hager narrates an in-depth report about tornadoes from *NBC Nightly News with Tom Brokaw*. This newscast tells how tornadoes form and how scientists try to predict tornadoes in order to save lives. It cites experts from the Universities of Colorado and Illinois, and the National Weather Service, and includes video footage. The Web report offers an individual storm chaser's experiences with tornadoes, including home videos.

Is the news always RELIABLE?

To help students explore the Big Question, ask them to identify many different news sources, including newspaper reports, TV and radio broadcasts, public service announcements, posters, magazine articles, the Internet, and school gossip. Which news sources are most reliable? What different elements make a news source seem credible?

BACKGROUND

Tornado chasers travel around areas prone to tornadoes, such as Tornado Alley in the Great Plains, looking for twisters. They collect data for government agencies, conduct storm-chasing tours, or work for private companies that provide weather-related information to airports, farmers, and the public. To find and study tornadoes, tornado chasers need different kinds of equipment, including maps; laptop computers; weather radios; two-way radios; satellite images; global positioning systems; and video, still, and digital cameras.

Media Study

News Reports

Essential Course of Study ECOS

TV Newscast Clip/ Web Page on Media Smart DVD-ROM

Is the news always RELIABLE?

COMMON CORE

SL 2 Integrate multiple sources of information presented in diverse media or formats, evaluating the credibility and accuracy of each source. **SL 3** Evaluate a speaker's point of view, reasoning, and use of evidence and rhetoric, identifying any fallacious reasoning or exaggerated or distorted evidence.

Where might you find a headline like this one: "Celebrity Secrets Exposed"? If you guessed the news source to be a supermarket tabloid, you'd probably be right. There's an endless variety of news sources out there. By critically examining two sources in this lesson, you'll explore how to make judgments about their reliability and usefulness.

Background

Twister Tendencies Every spring brings news of tornadoes, the most violent of all storms. Although these spiral-shaped windstorms can occur in most parts of the world, they happen most often in the United States, especially in a region known as Tornado Alley. This region includes part of Texas, Oklahoma, Kansas, Nebraska, and Iowa. The newscast and Web page you'll explore cover a series of tornadoes in Alabama that arose at the start of the 1998 tornado season.

576

Media Study Resources

See resources on the **Teacher One Stop DVD-ROM** *and on* **thinkcentral.com**.

R RESOURCE MANAGER UNIT 5
- Plan and Teach, pp. 113–116
- Summary, pp. 117†*, 118‡*
- Viewing Guide, p. 119
- Close Viewing, p. 120
- Viewing Activity, p. 121
- Produce Your Own Media, p. 122

TECHNOLOGY
- ⊘ **Teacher One Stop DVD-ROM**
- ⊘ **Student One Stop DVD-ROM**
- ⊘ **Media*Smart* DVD-ROM**
- **MediaScope on thinkcentral.com**

* Resources for Differentiation   † Also in Spanish   ‡ In Haitian Creole and Vietnamese

Media Literacy: Credibility in News Reports

The ideal news report is objective, accurate, and thorough. When writing a news story, a journalist relies upon **sources**—people or published materials that provide information on the report's topic. These sources may not always be as reliable or credible as they seem. **Credibility** refers to the believability and trustworthiness of both the sources and the report itself. Since the journalist chooses the sources, the reader or viewer needs to be prepared to question the credibility of both the journalist and the publisher. How an individual source or journalist sees the facts and details of the news story and his or her conscious or unconscious biases can influence how the report is communicated and affect the report's credibility.

QUESTIONS TO ASK ABOUT A TV NEWSCAST

- From what **news outlet**, or station, is the story broadcast? What sense do you have of the outlet's reputation and that of the **news anchor** or **field reporters**?
- Is the person delivering the report an experienced anchor with a reputation for excellence, and is he or she affiliated with a reputable news agency? If not, what background qualifies this person to deliver the news?
- Is the primary **purpose** of the report to inform, persuade, or entertain? Are there clues in the title? What other purpose is evident? How might the report's **formality** or **tone** be different if the purpose were different?
- Who is the report's intended **audience**? How might this audience affect the report's **formality** or **tone**?
- Are the **facts** and **statistics** that appear in the report relevant and reliable? Are documented sources provided?
- What interviews are included? Are the interview **sources** witnesses to an event? Are the sources **experts** on the topic of the story? What biases might sources have?

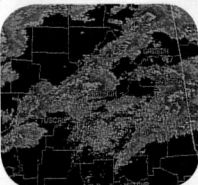

QUESTIONS TO ASK ABOUT A WEB REPORT

- Where is the Web site published? Who is its creator or **webmaster**?
- What is the report's **purpose**? Does the purpose influence the report's **formality** or **tone**?
- Does the page offer complete details about a report?
- What **sources** are cited? Can **facts** be confirmed in other sources? Are **links** provided to credible news sources or other viewpoints?
- Does the Web news report show the **date** and **time** the report was originally published?
- How does the Web site's intended audience influence its **formality** and **tone**?

Kye The Storm Chaser

My Latest Tornado News

- My Tornado Videos
- Tornado Watch (My Region Only)
- Tornado Alley Facts
- The Fujita Scale
- Kye's Tornado Photos
- About Kye
- National Weather Service
- More Links

MEDIA STUDY **577**

Teach

Media Literacy

COMMON CORE SL 2, SL 3

Review with students the definition of *credibility*. Have them identify elements that generally point to the credibility of a print or electronic news report. Ask where the information for the report comes from. Why is this source believable? Which facts and statistics seem most accurate? On the board, list responses students may generate, such as scientific experts, data, government officials, video footage, or reliable eyewitnesses. Make sure that *facts, statistics, sources,* and *experts* are included on the list. Then discuss the two charts on page 577.

- **Questioning Strategies for a TV Newscast** Explain to students that different factors may affect the trustworthiness of a news report. Discuss how a person who has experienced a frightening tornado may remember the events through the lens of fear or relief at being alive. Point out that a scientist from a particular research project may analyze tornado data hoping mostly to confirm his or her scientific theory. As students view the film clip, have them jot down information about the sources used to put the report together, and consider how, if at all, each source might be biased.

- **Questioning Strategies for a Web Report** Emphasize that news reports on the Internet have to be carefully evaluated, because anyone can post anything on the Web. Have students view your school's or town's home page. Point out that these pages are posted by institutions, which already gives them credibility beyond individual sites. Work with students to identify additional elements that show the page's reliability, such as contact information, frequent updates, and informative purpose. Challenge students to look for similar elements as they view the Web page.

MEDIA STUDY: TEACHING OPTIONS

Teaching Option 1: The Basics (1–2 Days)
1. Begin the Media Study using the material provided on pages 576–577.
2. Show the Introduction on Media*Smart*. Then show the First Viewing. As they watch, have students use the Viewing Guide on page 578, along with the corresponding copy master on page 119 of the Resource Manager. Discuss their responses.
3. Return to the pupil book for the extension activities on page 579.

Teaching Option 2: In-Depth Study (2–3 Days)
1. Begin the Media Study pages 576–577.
2. Show the Introduction and First Viewing from Media*Smart*. Continue with the Media Lessons, using the teacher notes available in the Resources section.
3. Show the Guided Analysis presentation. Have students record their observations on the Student Viewing Guide available in the Resources section from Media*Smart*.
4. Return to the pupil book, page 579.

Practice and Apply

VIEWING GUIDE

1. Before students view the clip and study the Web page, tell them they will be asked to think critically about the purpose and credibility of these news reports. Encourage them to watch and listen for these elements:

   - the TV station that broadcasts the tornado report and the **news anchor** and **reporter** who delivered it
   - the stated and implied **purpose** of the two reports
   - the believability of Robert Hager's information **sources** and **experts**, and of Kye's Web links
   - the reliability of tornado **facts** and **statistics** on Kye's Web page and in the newscast

2. Have students watch the film clip several times, focusing each time on a different aspect, such as source credibility or fact documentation. Have them explore each part of Kye's Web page and follow the links included. To help them evaluate the Web page's credibility, urge them to compare the facts posted to those in the newscast.

R RESOURCE MANAGER—Copy Masters

Viewing Guide p. 119
Close Viewing p. 120
Viewing Activity p. 121

Use this resource with the Viewing Guide:

MediaSmart **DVD-ROM**

MediaScope on **thinkcentral.com**

ANSWERS

FIRST VIEWING: Comprehension

1. *Scientists are trying to learn how to better predict tornadoes so that they can warn people about them.*

2. *The National Weather Service Web site would have the latest information about tornadoes.*

CLOSE VIEWING: Media Literacy

Possible answers:

3. *Visual and sound techniques used in newscasts and on Web sites add an emotional and sometimes sensational dimension to news coverage. They can also make the audience feel as though they are eyewitnesses to the events being reported.*

Media⬛Smart DVD-ROM

- **News Format 1:** "NBC News: Early Warnings: Predicting Tornadoes"
  NBC Anchor: Tom Brokaw
  NBC Correspondent: Robert Hager
  Running Time: 3 minutes
  Genre: TV newscast
- **News Format 2:** "Kye the Storm Chaser"
  Genre: Web site

HOME

About Kye

When I can steal a moment from chasing storms across Tornado Alley, I'm posting news on this site to convey the excitement of being in the path of a tornado.

578

Viewing Guide for
News Reports

View the TV newscast clip a few times. Examine the Web page closely. As you do so, think critically about the basic purpose or purposes and judge the credibility of each news form.

NOW VIEW

FIRST VIEWING: Comprehension

1. **Summarize** In general, what does the TV newscast report that scientists are trying to learn about tornadoes?

2. **Clarify** In using Kye's Web page, which one of the links would you choose if you wanted to find out the latest information about tornadoes nationwide?

CLOSE VIEWING: Media Literacy

3. **Analyze Media Techniques** How do the different visual and sound techniques available to newscasts and Web sites affect how they cover the news?

4. **Analyze Credibility** Explain what specific features you think give the TV newscast credibility.

5. **Make Judgments** In general, the purpose of the TV news report and the Web site is to inform. Read more details about Kye in the second small image on this page. What other purpose might there be for Kye's delivery of news? Does this other purpose affect how the news is presented?

6. **Compare Types of Sources** How do two of the sources in the newscast clip differ from Kye, the source of the Web site?

7. **Compare Credibility** Draw a credibility scale like the one shown. Number it from 1—"not at all credible"—to 5—"extremely credible." Then rate each of the two news forms according to the scale. Give at least one reason for each rating.

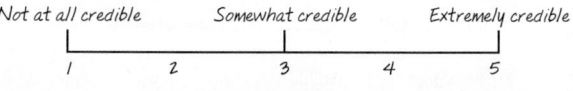

Not at all credible   Somewhat credible   Extremely credible

1   2   3   4   5

---

4. *It is from a reputable news source (NBC) and is presented by a well-known, reliable news anchor (Brokaw). An experienced reporter (Hager) interviews three experts in the field, provides facts and statistics, and intends primarily to inform viewers about the subject matter.*

5. *Kye's Web site could entertain readers with her excitement about tornadoes. Yes; when an additional purpose in news coverage is to entertain, particular details may be emphasized or even exaggerated to make a good story and to keep the audience engaged.*

6. *The newscast sources are researchers or scientists studying the science of tornadoes. Kye is an amateur tornado chaser who studies or observes the effects of tornadoes.*

7. **NBC News rating: 5** *NBC's news report is extremely credible. It intends solely to inform, and the sources used are all experts in their fields.*

   Kye the Storm Chaser rating: 2 *Kye's site is somewhat credible because it gives eyewitness views of tornadoes, but Kye is an enthusiastic amateur, not a scientist.*

Write or Discuss

Evaluate a News Source Review the questioning strategies on page 577 for newscasts and Web news. Based on the knowledge you gained from using these strategies, evaluate the type of information you can get from each of these sources. Cite evidence in your response.

Produce Your Own Media

Highlight Credible Characteristics Find an example of a credible news story in print or electronic form. Examine the story and the news format closely, pinpointing whatever specific features make the report credible. Then redraft the report to make it seem unreliable. Present your report to the class.

HERE'S HOW Use the following suggestions when writing your new version:
- Refer to the questions on page 577 to form your criteria for credibility.
- As a class, compare news stories. Single out choices that meet all of your criteria. Because your classmates will be your report's audience, they will be familiar with the media literacy concepts discussed in this media story.

PROFESSIONAL MODEL

Note the characteristics that make this news story credible.

COMMON CORE

SL 2 Integrate multiple sources of information, evaluating the credibility and accuracy of each source. SL 3 Evaluate a speaker's point of view, reasoning, and use of evidence and rhetoric.

Media Tools
Go to **thinkcentral.com**.
KEYWORD: HML10-579

Tech Tip

If equipment is available, record a TV newscast. Pause at points to present its credible features.

MEDIA STUDY **579**

Produce Your Own Media

R RESOURCE MANAGER—Copy Master
Produce Your Own Media p. 122

Rubric A redrafted news story that is unreliable should
- be based on a credible print or electronic news story
- contain few, if any, reliable facts or statistics
- include few, if any, documented sources
- include few, if any, comments by interview sources or experts
- include altered photographs or captions, if appropriate

Write or Discuss
COMMON CORE SL 2, SL 3

Evaluate a News Source In their written work or discussions, students should summarize the type of information available on newscasts and Web news. They should tell when they might use this information and provide clear, logical reasons for their choices. In their evaluations, students should refer to specific questioning strategies they used to evaluate a news source. For example, they might ask themselves whether a TV news report includes reliable *facts* and *statistics* or which credible *sources* are cited in a Web site.

MEDIA STUDY WRAP-UP

Have students summarize what they have learned about questioning strategies to evaluate the credibility of newscasts and Web news sites. Encourage them to use terms such as *source, news outlet, news anchor, field reporter, URL, domain, Web master,* and *links* in their explanations.

RETEACH

Discuss these additional questions with students having difficulty evaluating the credibility of the TV newscast and Web site.

- What words, images, or sounds are used in the newscast? On the Web page? What words, images, or sounds have been left out of each?
- What is the point of view of each source in the newscast? What is Kye's point of view?
- How does the newscast affect how I think about the topic? How does the Web page affect how I think? How does each make me feel?

Media Tools

Media study keywords point to **MediaScope**, a Web site that helps students strengthen media analysis and production skills.

Focus and Motivate

RI 7 Analyze various accounts of a subject told in different mediums determining which details are emphasized in each account. **W 2** Write explanatory texts to examine and convey complex ideas, concepts, and information clearly and accurately through the effective analysis of content. **SL 2** Integrate multiple sources of information presented in diverse media or formats, evaluating the credibility and accuracy of each source.

SUMMARY

"Getting from Here to There" presents two maps of the transit system in Houston, Texas. One is a map of Houston's entire METRORail system, and the other is a detail map that focuses on the Texas Medical Center area.

Teach

Standards Focus: Interpret Graphic Aids

- Examine the elements of the two transit maps with students. Point out each map's title, legend, scale, and the colors and symbols used.

- Ask students under what circumstances they might use the first, larger map, and when they might need the second, more detailed map.

R RESOURCE MANAGER—Copy Master
Interpret Graphic Aids p. 131

Reading for Information

Getting From Here to There
Functional Documents

Standards Focus: Interpret Graphic Aids

COMMON CORE

RI 7 Analyze various accounts of a subject told in different mediums determining which details are emphasized in each account.

Transit maps provide details of routes and stations for a city's public transportation system. Transit maps are useful tools for finding your way around, but they can be very confusing if you don't know how to read them. Good navigators break down the information the map provides and combine it with personal knowledge and common sense to find their way.

- Read the title of the map to learn what information the map presents.
- Check for a key, or **legend,** that provides information about the symbols the map uses, as well as a **scale,** which provides information about how distance on the map translates to distance in the real world.
- Look for landmarks, street names, and neighborhoods marked on the map.
- Consider the map's use of different colors. What does each color represent?
- Examine the lines that represent bus routes and train lines. Do they intersect with any other lines? If so, can you transfer to another route at those intersections? How can you tell?
- Use your knowledge of how transportation systems work to help you figure out the best choices for your travel.

As you view the transit maps that follow, use a chart like the one below to interpret the information on each map.

According to the title, what does this map show?	
How many modes of transportation are identified on the map?	
How much area does the map cover?	
What elements does the map use to make the information clear?	
What other useful information does the map provide?	

Selection Resources

See resources on the **Teacher One Stop DVD-ROM** and on **thinkcentral.com**.

R **RESOURCE MANAGER UNIT 5**
Lesson Support,* pp. 123–136

DIAGNOSTIC AND SELECTION TESTS
Selection Tests, pp. 163–166

TECHNOLOGY
- Teacher One Stop DVD-ROM
- Student One Stop DVD-ROM
- ExamView Test Generator on the Teacher One Stop

* Resources for Differentiation

Practice and Apply

These two maps illustrate part of the transit system in Houston, Texas. One is a map of the entire METRORail system; the other is a **detail map**—a small, zoomed-in section of a map. Use the maps to answer the questions below and on the After Reading page.

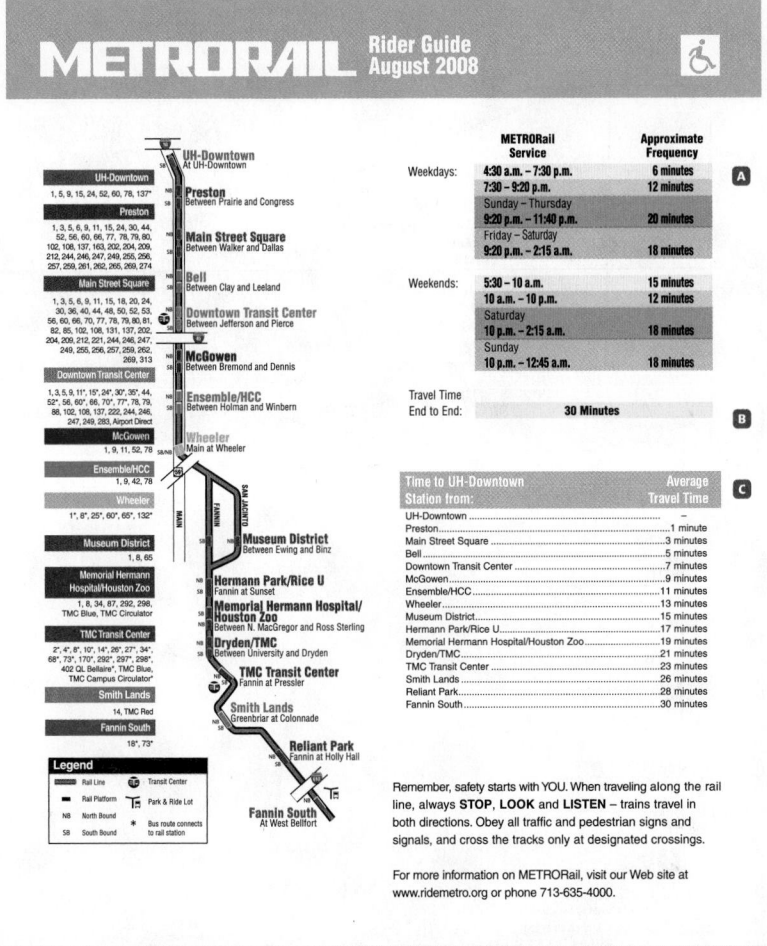

METRORAIL Rider Guide August 2008

Weekdays:	METRORail Service	Approximate Frequency
	4:30 a.m. – 7:30 p.m.	6 minutes
	7:30 – 9:20 p.m.	12 minutes
	Sunday – Thursday	
	9:20 p.m. – 11:40 p.m.	20 minutes
	Friday – Saturday	
	9:20 p.m. – 2:15 a.m.	18 minutes
Weekends:	5:30 – 10 a.m.	15 minutes
	10 a.m. – 10 p.m.	12 minutes
	Saturday	
	10 p.m. – 2:15 a.m.	18 minutes
	Sunday	
	10 p.m. – 12:45 a.m.	18 minutes

Travel Time End to End:	**30 Minutes**

Time to UH-Downtown Station from:	Average Travel Time
UH-Downtown	–
Preston	1 minute
Main Street Square	3 minutes
Bell	5 minutes
Downtown Transit Center	7 minutes
McGowen	9 minutes
Ensemble/HCC	11 minutes
Wheeler	13 minutes
Museum District	15 minutes
Hermann Park/Rice U.	17 minutes
Memorial Hermann Hospital/Houston Zoo	19 minutes
Dryden/TMC	21 minutes
TMC Transit Center	23 minutes
Smith Lands	26 minutes
Reliant Park	28 minutes
Fannin South	30 minutes

Remember, safety starts with YOU. When traveling along the rail line, always **STOP**, **LOOK** and **LISTEN** – trains travel in both directions. Obey all traffic and pedestrian signs and signals, and cross the tracks only at designated crossings.

For more information on METRORail, visit our Web site at www.ridemetro.org or phone 713-635-4000.

A INTERPRET GRAPHIC AIDS
Identify the map's **legend.** What information does the legend provide?

B INTERPRET GRAPHIC AIDS
What other information, besides a map of the METRORail, does this page provide? When might you use this information?

C SYNTHESIZE SOURCES
If you were a visitor to Houston, what information might you need in addition to this METRORail map to understand where the METRORail can take you?

INFORMATIONAL ANALYSIS — COMMON CORE — RI 7

A *Model the Skill:* INTERPRET GRAPHIC AIDS

To model how to interpret graphic aids, point out the colors and symbols on the map and think aloud as you use the legend to interpret them, or understand their meaning. Say, for example: "According to the legend, the colors on the map represent different rail lines."

Possible answer: *The legend provides information about symbols on the map for rail platforms, northbound and southbound routes, transit centers, park and rides, and places where a bus route connects to the light rail.*

INFORMATIONAL ANALYSIS — COMMON CORE — RI 7

B INTERPRET GRAPHIC AIDS

Possible answer: *It provides information about frequency of METRORail service and estimated travel time between various stops. Someone might use this information when planning how long a trip might take.*

INFORMATIONAL ANALYSIS — COMMON CORE — RI 7

C SYNTHESIZE SOURCES

Possible answer: *Visitors to Houston might need more information about areas surrounding the METRORail line and what visitor destinations are within walking distance of various stops.*

DIFFERENTIATED INSTRUCTION

FOR ENGLISH LANGUAGE LEARNERS

Preview Have students preview the two maps. Tell them to read the titles, skim the legends, and scan the maps themselves to identify unfamiliar terms or symbols. Define specialized vocabulary and clarify symbols that may be confusing. Then have students use what they have learned from their preview to set a purpose for reading the maps, or examining them more closely. Have students use this sentence frame to set a purpose: *I'm going to use this map to figure out _____.*

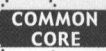
D Model the Skill: INTERPRET GRAPHIC AIDS

Model for students how to interpret graphic aids using a chart like the one on page 580. Read each question in the chart, examine the map, and answer the question, recording the answer in the chart.

According to the title, what does this map show?	The title indicates that the map shows the Texas Medical Center Area of the transit system.
How many modes of transportation are identified on the map?	

Possible answer: *The different colored lines and circles represent different bus routes and their numbers.*

E SYNTHESIZE SOURCES

Possible answer: *You can use the two maps to figure out how to get to the Texas Medical Center area by train from other places in the system, and once at the Texas Medical Center how to travel by bus to places in that area.*

IF STUDENTS NEED HELP . . .
Point out the Texas Medical Center (TMC) stop on the METRORail map.

F Model the Skill: INTERPRET GRAPHIC AIDS

Model for students how to evaluate the design of a document by choosing one specific feature, such as the legends, and pointing out the differences between them. Then tell them which one you find more visually appealing, based on those differences. Say, for example: "The legend on the second map is much larger and therefore easier to read."

Possible answer: *I think the first map is more visually appealing. Its main colors, such as bright orange, are much bolder than those of the other map, and they stand out more on the white background.*

D INTERPRET GRAPHIC AIDS
What do the different colored lines and circles represent?

E SYNTHESIZE SOURCES
How would you use this map and the METRORail map together to navigate Houston's transit system?

COMMON CORE RI 7

F INTERPRET GRAPHIC AIDS
Documents of the same type, such as these two transit maps, often have many of the same graphic features. Even so, these two maps have significant design differences that affect how clearly and attractively they present their information. From each map's particular use of color to the **font,** or text style, of its title and labels, the two maps are visually distinct. Which map do you think is more visually appealing? Support your answer with specific examples from the maps.

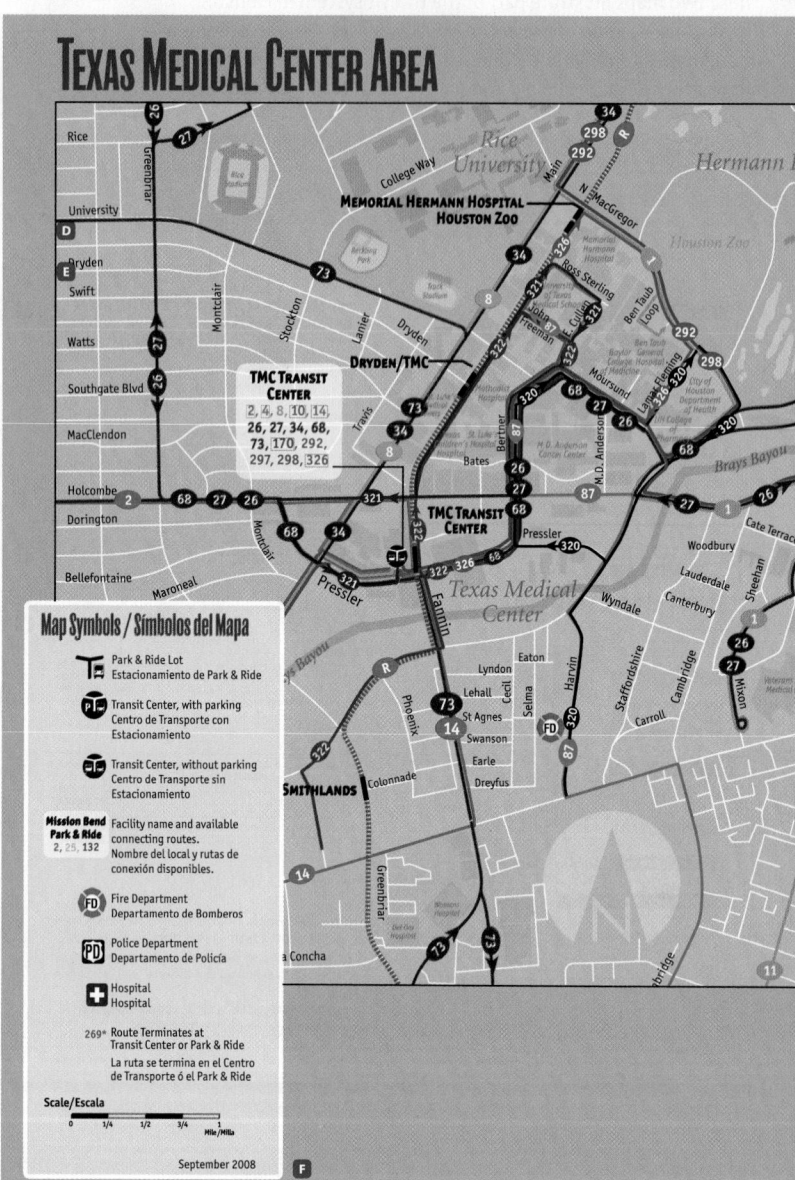

DIFFERENTIATED INSTRUCTION

FOR STRUGGLING READERS

Comprehension Support To help students interpret the Texas Medical Center map, start a round robin in which each student uses information in the map to describe a trip he or she might take. Model the process, saying, for example: "I am at [place on bus route]. To get to [another place on bus route], I would take bus # X" or "I would take bus #X to [another place] and then transfer to bus #Y." Then have students describe their own itineraries.

FOR ADVANCED LEARNERS/PRE-AP

Analyze Routes and Schedules How can you get from here to there? How fast can you get from here to there? Challenge individual students or student pairs to use the maps to figure out the shortest routes from places in the greater transit system to locations in the Texas Medical Center Area or to calculate the shortest times between two places on the METRORail.

Comprehension

1. **Recall** What section of Houston does the detail map portray?

2. **Recall** List three Houston sites that the METRORail visits.

Text Analysis

● 3. **Interpret Graphic Aids** How long would it take to travel by METRORail from Main Street Square to the Houston Zoo?

● 4. **Interpret Graphic Aids** Could you transfer from bus 26 to bus 297 at the TMC Transit Center?

5. **Synthesize Sources** Describe how you could use Houston public transit to travel from Rice University Stadium to Reliant Park.

COMMON CORE

RI 7 Analyze various accounts of a subject told in different mediums determining which details are emphasized in each account. **W 2** Write explanatory texts to examine and convey complex ideas, concepts, and information clearly and accurately. **SL 2** Integrate multiple sources of information presented in diverse media or formats.

Read for Information: Use Information from Multiple Sources

WRITING PROMPT

Create a transit map for your neighborhood, including information on available transit options and routes, as well as map elements, such as a legend, color-coding, and neighborhood landmarks.

To respond to this prompt, analyze the graphical elements of both transit maps you have just seen. Synthesize the information from these sources with your knowledge of your own neighborhood. Follow these steps:

1. Review both transit maps, and think about how they are structured and what elements they include. Which elements did you find most useful? How could you use similar elements in your own map?

2. Consider the transportation needs of your neighborhood. What kinds of transportation will you include on your map (for example: bus routes, rail, bike paths)?

3. Review the chart you created as you examined each map. How would you want each question answered about your own map?

4. If necessary, create practice sketches of your transit map to help you think through your plan.

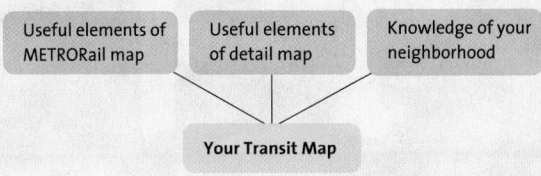

Useful elements of METRORail map → Useful elements of detail map → Knowledge of your neighborhood → **Your Transit Map**

FOR STRUGGLING WRITERS

Read for Information

- Tell students to model elements of their maps after the transit maps for Houston.
- Suggest that students use color-coding and a variety of symbols for neighborhood landmarks, such as parks, museums, and other sights.

FOR ADVANCED LEARNERS/PRE-AP

Plan an Itinerary Have students choose a major city in the United States that they would like to visit. Direct them to do research on the Internet to identify the public transportation options in the city they have selected, and then use transit maps and other information they gather to plan a one-day itinerary for touring the city to share with the class.

Practice and Apply

For preliminary support of post-reading questions, use these copy masters:

R RESOURCE MANAGER—Copy Masters
  Reading Check p. 135
  Question Support p. 136
  Synthesize p. 132

  Additional selection questions are provided for teachers on page 126.

ANSWERS

Comprehension

1. *the Texas Medical Center area*

2. *Answers may include Downtown, Main Street Square, Downtown Transit Center, Museum District, Hermann Park, Rice University, Memorial Hermann Hospital, Houston Zoo, TMC Travel Center, Reliant Park.*

Text Analysis   COMMON CORE RI 7

3. ● **COMMON CORE FOCUS** *Interpret Graphic Aids approximately 16 minutes*

4. ● **COMMON CORE FOCUS** *Interpret Graphic Aids Yes, you could transfer from bus 26 to bus 297 at the TMS Transit Center.*

5. *bus 26 or 27 to the TMC Transit Center, then METRORail to Reliant Park*

Read for Information   COMMON CORE W 2 SL 2

Writing Prompt *Maps will vary but should include a legend, color-coding, and neighborhood landmarks and should indicate the routes of at least one form of transportation.*

Assess and Reteach

Assess

DIAGNOSTIC AND SELECTION TESTS
  Selection Test A pp. 163–164
  Selection Tests B/C pp. 165–166

Interactive Selection Test on thinkcentral.com

Reteach

Level Up Online Tutorials on thinkcentral.com

Reteaching Worksheets on thinkcentral.com
  Reading Lessons 4, 21

Focus and Motivate

COMMON CORE FOCUS

RL 1 Cite textual evidence to support analysis of what the text says explicitly. **RL 3** Analyze how complex characters develop and interact with other characters. **RL 4** Determine the meaning of words and phrases as they are used in a text. **RL 9** Analyze how an author draws on and transforms source material in a specific work. **L 4a** Use context as a clue to the meaning of a word or phrase.

SUMMARY

In the short story "And of Clay Are We Created," Isabel Allende tells about a 13-year-old victim of a volcanic eruption. For three days, the girl is buried up to her neck in water and clay, while a reporter works to get help for her and to keep her spirits up. Her prolonged death forces the reporter to confront buried memories in his own life.

Can reporters always stay OBJECTIVE?

Introduce the question, and be sure students understand the term *objective*—"without bias, detached." Ask how being objective can help or hinder a reporter's task. Extend the discussion by having students complete the *QUICKWRITE.*

Essential Course of Study ECOS

And of Clay Are We Created
Short Story by Isabel Allende

Can reporters always stay OBJECTIVE?

COMMON CORE

RL 1 Cite textual evidence to support analysis of what the text says explicitly. **RL 3** Analyze how complex characters develop and interact with other characters. **RL 9** Analyze how an author draws on and transforms source material in a specific work.

Should journalists remain detached and objective when reporting a tragedy? Or should they express their personal feelings and become involved with helping victims? What is the proper role of the news media?

QUICKWRITE Imagine that a reporter is interviewing a victim of a tragedy, such as a deadly accident or hurricane. What is usually said in such interviews? Write a brief dialogue between the reporter and the person involved. Discuss the true feelings reporters and victims might have about each other.

584

Selection Resources

See resources on the **Teacher One Stop DVD-ROM** *and on* **thinkcentral.com**.

 RESOURCE MANAGER UNIT 5
Plan and Teach, pp. 137–144
Summary, pp. 145–146†‡*
Text Analysis and Reading
   Skill, pp. 147–150†*
Vocabulary, pp. 151–153*

DIAGNOSTIC AND SELECTION TESTS
Selection Tests, pp. 167–170

 BEST PRACTICES TOOLKIT
Jigsaw Reading, p. A1
Cluster Diagram, p. B18
Character Traits Web, p. D7
Character Traits and Textual
   Evidence, p. D6

INTERACTIVE READER

ADAPTED INTERACTIVE READER

ELL ADAPTED INTERACTIVE READER

TECHNOLOGY
⬤ **Teacher One Stop DVD-ROM**
⬤ **Student One Stop DVD-ROM**
⬤ **PowerNotes DVD-ROM**
⬤ **Audio Anthology CD**
⬤ **GrammarNotes DVD-ROM**
⬤ **Audio Tutor CD**
⬤ **ExamView Test Generator**
   on the **Teacher One Stop**

 THINK central

Find it Online!

Features on **thinkcentral.com** that support the selection include
• **PowerNotes** presentation
• **ThinkAloud** models to enhance comprehension
• **WordSharp** vocabulary tutorials
• interactive writing and grammar instruction

---

* Resources for Differentiation   † Also in Spanish   ‡ In Haitian Creole and Vietnamese

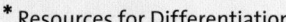

TEXT ANALYSIS: AUTHOR'S PERSPECTIVE

An **author's perspective** is a unique blend of feelings, values, and beliefs that a writer brings to a subject. "And of Clay Are We Created" contains echoes of Isabel Allende's own life experiences as a former journalist and an exile from her native country. Her journalistic experience, for example, is reflected in her descriptions of a disaster scene and her exploration of a reporter's thoughts and feelings.

Carefully read the information about Allende on this page. Then, as you read her short story, draw on what you know of her life to help you understand her perspective.

Review: Characterization

READING STRATEGY: MONITOR

Monitoring is checking your understanding as you read and adjusting your reading strategies to improve comprehension. The following strategies may be useful:

- **adjust your reading rate**—that is, read more slowly
- **reread**—go back over the text for clarification
- **visualize**—picture characters, events, or settings
- **question**—ask about events or characters

As you read, use a chart like this one to note the passages that you are having trouble understanding, and decide which of the strategies will best improve your comprehension.

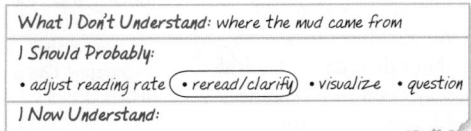

> *What I Don't Understand:* where the mud came from
> *I Should Probably:*
> • adjust reading rate • reread/clarify • visualize • question
> *I Now Understand:*

▲ VOCABULARY IN CONTEXT

Allende uses the following words to tell her story. Categorize these words as "Words I Know Well," "Words I Think I Know," and "Words I Don't Know." In your *Reader/Writer Notebook*, write a definition for the words in the first two categories.

WORD LIST		
embody	resignation	tenacity
fortitude	stratagem	tribulation
pandemonium	stupor	

Complete the activities in your **Reader/Writer Notebook.**

Meet the Author

Isabel Allende
born 1942

Creative Storyteller
Allende remembers having "acquired the vice of storytelling at a rather early age." She became a respected magazine and television journalist in her native Chile, but once admitted, "I could never be objective. I exaggerated and twisted reality...."

Political Exile
In 1973, Allende's uncle Salvador Allende, the president of Chile, was assassinated. A military government seized control, and a period of terror and violence began. Allende's family went into exile, moving to Venezuela; later Allende moved to the United States. She found it hard to get work as a journalist and turned to creative writing in 1981. Her first novel, *The House of the Spirits,* became an international bestseller.

A Mother's Loss
In 1991, Allende's daughter Paula was stricken with an incurable disease. During the months of hospitalization that followed, Allende began a memoir for Paula, who eventually died. In *Paula,* considered her finest and most revealing work, Allende explores sickness, loss, and tragedy. She says that the book may have been "written with tears, but [they were] very healing tears."

BACKGROUND TO THE SHORT STORY

Volcanic Disaster
Allende's story is based on a real event. On November 13, 1985, the Nevado del Ruiz volcano in Colombia erupted. The intense heat from the eruption melted the mountain's icecap and sent a torrent of water, ash, mud, and rocks into the valley below and onto the town of Armero. More than 20,000 people died. (See **Reading for Information** on page 598.)

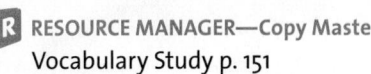
Author Online
Go to **thinkcentral.com.**
KEYWORD: HML10-585

585

Teach

TEXT ANALYSIS COMMON CORE RL 9

● *Model the Skill:* **AUTHOR'S PERSPECTIVE**

Explain how these experiences might alter an author's perspective:

- growing up in another country
- experiencing the death of a child
- living in poverty
- being a scientific researcher

Observe that such experiences would influence awareness of foreign cultures, sensitivity to loss and poverty, and respect for scientific study.

GUIDED PRACTICE Ask students to think of another life experience that could influence an author's perspective.

READING STRATEGY COMMON CORE RL 1

■ *Model the Skill:* **MONITOR**

To model monitoring, write the following passage on the board. Point out the descriptive details and explain that the visualize strategy would help to picture the scene and understand it better.

> Scarlet ibis, sipping daintily, stream bubbling, fish gurgling, sun washing

GUIDED PRACTICE Ask what kind of material might require monitoring by adjusting reading rate and questioning.

 **RESOURCE MANAGER**—Copy Master
Monitor p. 149 (for student use while reading the selection)

VOCABULARY SKILL COMMON CORE L 4

▲ VOCABULARY IN CONTEXT

DIAGNOSE WORD KNOWLEDGE Have all students complete Vocabulary in Context. Check their definitions against the following:

embody (ĕm-bŏd′ē) *v.* to give shape to or visibly represent

fortitude (fôr′tĭ-tōōd′) *n.* strength of mind; courage

pandemonium (păn′də-mō′nē-əm) *n.* a wild uproar or noise

resignation (rĕz′ĭg-nā′shən) *n.* passive acceptance of something; submission

stratagem (străt′ə-jəm) *n.* a clever trick or device for obtaining an advantage

stupor (stōō′pər) *n.* a state of mental numbness, as from shock

tenacity (tə-năs′ĭ-tē) *n.* the quality of holding persistently to something; firm determination

tribulation (trĭb′yə-lā′shən) *n.* great distress or suffering

PRETEACH VOCABULARY Use the following copy master to help student predict meanings for each boldfaced word.

RESOURCE MANAGER—Copy Master
Vocabulary Study p. 151

1. Read the first pair of sentences in Part A aloud, emphasizing *embody*.

2. Point out the words "a symbol of." Elicit possible meanings for *embody*.

3. Repeat the procedure for items b–h.

READ WITH A PURPOSE

Help students set a purpose for reading. Have students read to find out how a reporter tries to save a young girl trapped in rubble from a volcanic eruption and in a way saves himself.

TEXT ANALYSIS

COMMON CORE

RL 9

A *Model the Skill:*
AUTHOR'S PERSPECTIVE

Explain that a journalist is trained to report the facts of an event, answering the questions *who, what, when, where, why,* and *how,* while also trying to generate strong reader interest. Have students re-read the paragraph and list the descriptive details the author uses.

Possible answer: *The author reveals her journalistic background when she accurately describes the volcano's effect on the cotton fields—"curling them like waves of foam" (lines 11–12). She also creates suspense by mentioning the predictions of the geologists that went unheeded by the townspeople.*

Extend the Discussion How might the author's report of the volcano change if she had experienced it firsthand?

AND OF *Clay* ARE WE *Created*

Isabel Allende

They discovered the girl's head protruding from the mud pit, eyes wide open, calling soundlessly. She had a First Communion name,[1] Azucena.[2] Lily. In that vast cemetery where the odor of death was already attracting vultures from far away, and where the weeping of orphans and wails of the injured filled the air, the little girl obstinately clinging to life became the symbol of the tragedy. The television cameras transmitted so often the unbearable image of the head budding like a black squash from the clay that there was no one who did not recognize her and know her name. And every time we saw her on the screen, right behind her was Rolf Carlé,[3] who had gone there on assignment, never
10 suspecting that he would find a fragment of his past, lost thirty years before.
First a subterranean[4] sob rocked the cotton fields, curling them like waves **A** of foam. Geologists had set up their seismographs[5] weeks before and knew that the mountain had awakened again. For some time they had predicted that the heat of the eruption could detach the eternal ice from the slopes of the volcano, but no one heeded their warnings; they sounded like the tales of frightened old women. The towns in the valley went about their daily life, deaf to the moaning of the earth, until that fateful Wednesday night in November when a prolonged roar announced the end of the world, and walls of snow broke loose, rolling in an avalanche of clay, stones, and water that descended
20 on the villages and buried them beneath unfathomable meters of telluric[6] vomit. As soon as the survivors emerged from the paralysis of that first awful terror, they could see that houses, plazas, churches, white cotton plantations, dark coffee forests, cattle pastures—all had disappeared. Much later, after soldiers and volunteers had arrived to rescue the living and try to assess the

Analyze Visuals ▶

Study the painting. How do you **interpret** the girl's expression?

① Targeted Passage

A AUTHOR'S PERSPECTIVE
Think about Allende's former job as a journalist. How is her background reflected in the following paragraph? Cite specific details to support your answers.

---

1. **First Communion name:** a name traditionally given to a Roman Catholic child at the time of the child's first participation in the rite of Holy Communion.
2. **Azucena** (ä-sōō-sĕ'nə).
3. **Rolf Carlé** (rälf kär'lā).
4. **subterranean** (sŭb'tə-rā'nē-ən): underground.
5. **seismographs** (sīz'mə-grăfs'): instruments that record the intensity and duration of earthquakes.
6. **telluric** (tĕ-lŏŏr'ĭk): relating to the earth.

Niña (1943), Julia Diaz. Oil on canvas, 30 cm × 35 cm. Courtesy of the Julia Diaz Foundation.

586 UNIT 5: AUTHOR'S PURPOSE

DIFFERENTIATED INSTRUCTION

FOR ENGLISH LANGUAGE LEARNERS

Options for Reading: Jigsaw Reading Have student groups use Jigsaw Reading to read short portions of the story. Regroup students to include experts on each section. Have group members share what they have learned.

BEST PRACTICES TOOLKIT
Jigsaw Reading p. A1

FOR STRUGGLING READERS

Use one or more Targeted Passages (pp. 586, 592, 595) to ensure that students focus on key story events, concepts, and skills. Targeted Passages are also good for English learners.

① Targeted Passage [Lines 1–10]

This passage introduces the setting and the central conflict.

• Who is the child? What had happened to her? (lines 1–2)

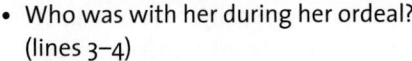

Reading Support

This selection on **thinkcentral.com** includes embedded **ThinkAloud** models—students "thinking aloud" about the story to model the kinds of questions a good reader would ask about a selection.

BACKGROUND

Blocked Roadways After the eruption of Nevado del Ruiz, rescue workers began immediately to assess the damage and plan for medical attention for the victims. However, roads and bridges had been damaged, making helicopters the only viable transportation option. Since few helicopters were available during the first 48 hours after the blast, most victims could not be transported to hospital care. In addition, the main hospital of Armero had been destroyed, and alternate facilities quickly became overwhelmed. Rolf Carlé's attempts to get a pump would have been hampered by damaged communication systems and blocked roadways.

Analyze Visuals

Possible answer: The girl's expression is thoughtful, interested, and sad.

About the Art Julia Diaz was born in San Salvador, El Salvador, in 1917. A renowned portrait painter, Diaz is admired for her sensitive portrayals of mothers and children.

- Who was with her during her ordeal? (lines 3–4)
- How did the world come to know the child? (lines 6–8)

FOR ENGLISH LANGUAGE LEARNERS

Reading: Background Explain that the selection is fiction though based on a real event. A short nonfiction article about the event follows.

FOR ADVANCED LEARNERS/PRE–AP

Research Allow students to become experts by researching and choosing a way to share additional information about one of these topics:

- volcanic eruptions
- the 1985 eruption of the Nevado del Ruiz volcano in Colombia
- organizations that aid disaster victims

READING STRATEGY

B Model the Skill: MONITOR

Use a questioning technique to monitor reading of lines 29–34. Ask these questions to model the technique:

- Where was the narrator when the station called?
- What emotions does the narrator feel when Rolf is called away?

Have students record answers to the questions in the third row of a chart.

Possible answer: *The narrator of the story is Rolf Carlé's girlfriend.*

TEXT ANALYSIS

C AUTHOR'S PERSPECTIVE

Possible answer: *Allende's perspective is that the camera lens can distance reporters and protect them emotionally from the events they are describing.*

Extend the Discussion Is distance from the event useful or harmful to reporters?

VOCABULARY

OWN THE WORD

- **tenacity:** Have students create a semantic map for *tenacity*. Write the word in the center circle along with its definition. Have students use a thesaurus to find synonyms to complete the web. **Possible answers:** *bullheadedness, doggedness, obstinacy, pigheadedness, willfulness*

- **fortitude:** Remind students that *fortitude* refers to "strength of mind; courage." Ask students to complete the following sentence to show an understanding of this noun: *Jason needs great fortitude . . .*

---

magnitude of the cataclysm,[7] it was calculated that beneath the mud lay more than twenty thousand human beings and an indefinite number of animals putrefying in a viscous soup.[8] Forests and rivers had also been swept away, and there was nothing to be seen but an immense desert of mire.

30 When the station called before dawn, Rolf Carlé and I were together. I crawled out of bed, dazed with sleep, and went to prepare coffee while he hurriedly dressed. He stuffed his gear in the green canvas backpack he always carried, and we said goodbye, as we had so many times before. I had no presentiments. I sat in the kitchen, sipping my coffee and planning the long hours without him, sure that he would be back the next day. **B**

He was one of the first to reach the scene, because while other reporters were fighting their way to the edges of that morass in jeeps, bicycles, or on foot, each getting there however he could, Rolf Carlé had the advantage of the television helicopter, which flew him over the avalanche. We watched on our screens the footage captured by his assistant's camera, in which he was up to
40 his knees in muck, a microphone in his hand, in the midst of a bedlam of lost children, wounded survivors, corpses, and devastation. The story came to us in his calm voice. For years he had been a familiar figure in newscasts, reporting live at the scene of battles and catastrophes with awesome **tenacity**. Nothing could stop him, and I was always amazed at his equanimity in the face of danger and suffering; it seemed as if nothing could shake his **fortitude** or deter his curiosity. Fear seemed never to touch him, although he had confessed to me that he was not a courageous man, far from it. I believe that the lens of a camera had a strange effect on him; it was as if it transported him to a different time from which he could watch events without actually participating in them.
50 When I knew him better, I came to realize that this fictive distance seemed to protect him from his own emotions. **C**

Rolf Carlé was in on the story of Azucena from the beginning. He filmed the volunteers who discovered her, and the first persons who tried to reach her; his camera zoomed in on the girl, her dark face, her large desolate eyes, the plastered-down tangle of her hair. The mud was like quicksand around her, and anyone attempting to reach her was in danger of sinking. They threw a rope to her that she made no effort to grasp until they shouted to her to catch it; then she pulled a hand from the mire and tried to move but immediately sank a little deeper. Rolf threw down his knapsack and the rest of
60 his equipment and waded into the quagmire, commenting for his assistant's microphone that it was cold and that one could begin to smell the stench of corpses.

"What's your name?" he asked the girl, and she told him her flower name. "Don't move, Azucena," Rolf Carlé directed, and kept talking to her, without a thought for what he was saying, just to distract her, while slowly he worked his way forward in mud up to his waist. The air around him seemed as murky as the mud.

---

7. **cataclysm** (kăt'ə-klĭz'əm): a violent and sudden change in the earth's crust.
8. **putrefying** (pyōō'trə-fī'ĭng) **in a viscous soup:** rotting in a thick soup.

B MONITOR
Reread lines 29–34. Who is the **narrator** of the story?

tenacity (tə-năs'ĭ-tē) *n.* the quality of holding persistently to something; firm determination

fortitude (fôr'tĭ-tōōd') *n.* strength of mind; courage

C AUTHOR'S PERSPECTIVE
Based on the narrator's comments about the effect of a lens on Rolf Carlé, what would you say is Allende's perspective on news reporting?

DIFFERENTIATED INSTRUCTION

FOR ENGLISH LANGUAGE LEARNERS

Vocabulary: Prefixes Write these words on the board, underlining their prefixes: *presentiments* (line 33), *microphone* (lines 40 and 61), *transported* (line 48), *discovered* (line 53), *distract* (line 65), *transmission* (line 80), *transport* (line 96). Have students create Cluster Diagrams with one prefix in the center of each diagram. Discuss the meaning of each prefix and challenge students to find other words with these prefixes in the story

or in the dictionary. Finally, have a volunteer locate another story word with a common prefix—for example, *decomposing* (line 160). Work as a group to complete a Cluster Diagram for that prefix.

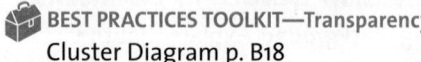
BEST PRACTICES TOOLKIT—Transparency
Cluster Diagram p. B18

It was impossible to reach her from the approach he was attempting, so he retreated and circled around where there seemed to be firmer footing. When finally he was close enough, he took the rope and tied it beneath her arms, so they could pull her out. He smiled at her with that smile that crinkles his eyes and makes him look like a little boy; he told her that everything was fine, that he was here with her now, that soon they would have her out. He signaled the others to pull, but as soon as the cord tensed, the girl screamed. They tried again, and her shoulders and arms appeared, but they could move her no farther; she was trapped. Someone suggested that her legs might be caught in the collapsed walls of her house, but she said it was not just rubble, that she was also held by the bodies of her brothers and sisters clinging to her legs. **D**

"Don't worry, we'll get you out of here," Rolf promised. Despite the quality of the transmission, I could hear his voice break, and I loved him more than ever. Azucena looked at him but said nothing.

During those first hours Rolf Carlé exhausted all the resources of his ingenuity to rescue her. He struggled with poles and ropes, but every tug was an intolerable torture for the imprisoned girl. It occurred to him to use one of the poles as a lever but got no result and had to abandon the idea. He talked a couple of soldiers into working with him for a while, but they had to leave because so many other victims were calling for help. The girl could not move, she barely could breathe, but she did not seem desperate, as if an ancestral **resignation** allowed her to accept her fate. The reporter, on the other hand, was determined to snatch her from death. Someone brought him a tire, which he placed beneath her arms like a life buoy, and then laid a plank near the hole to hold his weight and allow him to stay closer to her. As it was impossible to remove the rubble blindly, he tried once or twice to dive toward her feet but emerged frustrated, covered with mud, and spitting gravel. He concluded that he would have to have a pump to drain the water, and radioed a request for one but received in return a message that there was no available transport and it could not be sent until the next morning.

"We can't wait that long!" Rolf Carlé shouted, but in the **pandemonium** no one stopped to commiserate. Many more hours would go by before he accepted that time had stagnated and reality had been irreparably distorted. **E**

A military doctor came to examine the girl and observed that her heart was functioning well and that if she did not get too cold she could survive the night.

"Hang on, Azucena, we'll have the pump tomorrow," Rolf Carlé tried to console her.

"Don't leave me alone," she begged.

"No, of course I won't leave you."

D MONITOR
Visualize Azucena, Rolf, and the others. Why can't the rescuers pull Azucena out?

resignation
(rĕz′ĭg-nā′shən) *n.* passive acceptance of something; submission

pandemonium
(păn′də-mō′nē-əm) *n.* a wild uproar or noise

E CHARACTERIZATION
Consider Rolf's efforts to save Azucena. What do they suggest about him?

AND OF CLAY ARE WE CREATED **589**

COMMON
CORE

RL 3

F CHARACTERIZATION

Possible answer: *In lines 108–124, readers learn that Rolf is caring, optimistic, and uninformed about women and girls. We learn that Azucena is 13 and has not traveled outside her town. The last two sentences suggest that Rolf is protective and strong, with great emotional, mental, and physical endurance.*

Analyze Visuals

Activity What element of the story is evoked by the art? **Possible answer:** *The hand- and footprints evoke the idea of leaving a mark in a soft surface, like the mud in which Azucena has impressed her mark.*

About the Art *Sosteniendo el Tiempo* (Sustaining Time) was created by Satenik Tekyan in 1998. The artist was born in 1962 in Argentina to Armenian parents. Her art reflects her feeling of cultural displacement from her homeland. She studied art in Buenos Aires and works as a drawing professor.

Someone brought him coffee, and he helped the girl drink it, sip by sip. The warm liquid revived her, and she began telling him about her small life, about
110 her family and her school, about how things were in that little bit of world before the volcano erupted. She was thirteen, and she had never been outside her village. Rolf Carlé, buoyed by a premature optimism, was convinced that everything would end well: the pump would arrive, they would drain the water, move the rubble, and Azucena would be transported by helicopter to a hospital where she would recover rapidly and where he could visit her and bring her gifts. He thought, She's already too old for dolls, and I don't know what would please her; maybe a dress. I don't know much about women, he concluded, amused, reflecting that although he had known many women in his lifetime, none had taught him these details. To pass the hours he began
120 to tell Azucena about his travels and adventures as a news hound, and when he exhausted his memory, he called upon imagination, inventing things he thought might entertain her. From time to time she dozed, but he kept talking in the darkness, to assure her that he was still there and to overcome the menace of uncertainty. **F**

That was a long night.

Many miles away, I watched Rolf Carlé and the girl on a television screen. I could not bear the wait at home, so I went to National Television, where I

F CHARACTERIZATION
What do you learn about Rolf and Azucena in lines 108–124? What do the last two sentences suggest about Rolf's character?

Sosteniendo el Tiempo (1998), Satenik Tekyan. Mixed media, 95 cm × 80 cm. www.artesur.com/satenik.

DIFFERENTIATED INSTRUCTION

FOR ADVANCED LEARNERS/PRE–AP

Analyze Foreshadowing Point out that the author prepares readers for the story's ending with small clues. Ask students to reread the story, looking for these clues. For example, the word *premature* (line 112) helps prepare the reader for a coming disappointment. Have students make lists of words and lines that foreshadow the ending, then share these with the class.

FOR RELUCTANT READERS

Connect to the Text Discuss how Rolf and Azucena pass the time. Ask students to put themselves in Rolf's place. How would they encourage the trapped girl? What experiences of their own would they share with her? Then have students consider what it would be like to be trapped in the mud and rubble. What kind of support would they want from others? What would help them forget about their situation, if only for a short while? Have pairs of students role-play Rolf and Azucena in this scene.

often spent entire nights with Rolf editing programs. There, I was near his
world, and I could at least get a feeling of what he lived through during those
130 three decisive days. I called all the important people in the city, senators,
commanders of the armed forces, the North American ambassador, and the
president of National Petroleum, begging them for a pump to remove the silt,
but obtained only vague promises. I began to ask for urgent help on radio
and television, to see if there wasn't *someone* who could help us. Between
calls I would run to the newsroom to monitor the satellite transmissions that
periodically brought new details of the catastrophe. While reporters selected
scenes with most impact for the news report, I searched for footage that
featured Azucena's mud pit. The screen reduced the disaster to a single plane
and accentuated the tremendous distance that separated me from Rolf Carlé;
140 nonetheless, I was there with him. The child's every suffering hurt me as it
did him; I felt his frustration, his impotence. Faced with the impossibility
of communicating with him, the fantastic idea came to me that if I tried, I
could reach him by force of mind and in that way give him encouragement. I
concentrated until I was dizzy—a frenzied and futile activity. At times I would
be overcome with compassion and burst out crying; at other times, I was so
drained I felt as if I were staring through a telescope at the light of a star dead
for a million years. **G**

I watched that hell on the first morning broadcast, cadavers[9] of people and
animals awash in the current of new rivers formed overnight from the melted
150 snow. Above the mud rose the tops of trees and the bell towers of a church
where several people had taken refuge and were patiently awaiting rescue
teams. Hundreds of soldiers and volunteers from the civil defense were clawing
through rubble searching for survivors, while long rows of ragged specters
awaited their turn for a cup of hot broth. Radio networks announced that
their phones were jammed with calls from families offering shelter to orphaned
children. Drinking water was in scarce supply, along with gasoline and food.
Doctors, resigned to amputating arms and legs without anesthesia, pled that
at least they be sent serum and painkillers and antibiotics; most of the roads,
however, were impassable, and worse were the bureaucratic obstacles that
160 stood in the way. To top it all, the clay contaminated by decomposing bodies
threatened the living with an outbreak of epidemics. **H**

Azucena was shivering inside the tire that held her above the surface.
Immobility and tension had greatly weakened her, but she was conscious
and could still be heard when a microphone was held out to her. Her tone
was humble, as if apologizing for all the fuss. Rolf Carlé had a growth of
beard, and dark circles beneath his eyes; he looked near exhaustion. Even
from that enormous distance I could sense the quality of his weariness, so
different from the fatigue of other adventures. He had completely forgotten
the camera; he could not look at the girl through a lens any longer. The
170 pictures we were receiving were not his assistant's but those of other reporters

---

9. **cadavers** (kə-dăv′ərz): dead bodies.

G MONITOR
Reread lines 141–147 and
clarify what the narrator
attempts to do. How does
the effort make her feel?

H AUTHOR'S
PERSPECTIVE
Reread lines 130–161. What
would you say is Allende's
perspective on politicians
and other officials?

TIERED DISCUSSION PROMPTS
Direct students to lines 126–147. Use these
prompts to help students understand how
Azucena's struggle affects the narrator:

Connect Have you ever felt unable to help
a friend or loved one solve or endure a
problem? Explain. *Accept all reasonable
responses.*

Analyze What can you tell about the narrator from her response to problems? *Possible
answer: The narrator's actions show that she
is an active problem-solver who is willing to
use influence to get help.*

Evaluate Do you think the narrator did ev-
erything she could to help Rolf and Azucena?
Do you think she could have done more?
Accept all reasonable responses.

FOR STRUGGLING READERS
Comprehension Support Have students fill
out a Character Traits Web with information
about the narrator. Encourage students to
reread the story looking for clues to the narrator's personality. After students have filled
in their webs, have volunteers share their
information and create a master
Character Traits Web.

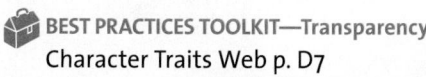
BEST PRACTICES TOOLKIT—Transparency
Character Traits Web p. D7

FOR ENGLISH LANGUAGE LEARNERS
Vocabulary: Idioms List these idioms on the
board and explain their meanings: *in the face
of* (line 44), "despite"; *From time to time* (line
122), "occasionally"; *To top it all* (line 160), "in
addition to everything else." Have students
find the sentences in the selection that
contain the idioms, and then paraphrase the
sentences using the definitions.

Left column

TEXT ANALYSIS: *Review*

COMMON CORE
RL 3

❶ CHARACTERIZATION

Possible answer: *The observations in lines 165–180 suggest that Rolf has lost his objectivity and is no longer acting as a reporter.*

TEXT ANALYSIS

COMMON CORE
RL 9

❷ AUTHOR'S PERSPECTIVE

Possible answer: *Allende criticizes the way the media manages to get the technical resources it needs, while the victims of the disaster cannot. She is critical of the media exploiting the victims of tragedy, distributing images of them without helping them at all (lines 184–190).*

IF STUDENTS NEED HELP . . . Have students find evidence from the story that identifies negative character traits of the reporters. Use the Character Traits and Textual Evidence graphic organizer to record the text and the traits each example reflects.

Character Trait	
Quote: "reporters who had appropriated Azucena" (line 170)	Trait: greedy for a news story

BEST PRACTICES TOOLKIT—Transparency
Character Traits and Textual Evidence
p. D6

VOCABULARY

COMMON CORE
L 4

OWN THE WORD

- **embody:** Point out that the verb *embody* can also mean "personify." Have students give examples of objects or people who *embody* something.

- **stupor:** Tell students that *stupor* comes from the Latin *stupere*, which means "be stunned." Have students write sentences that demonstrate their understanding of the word.

Right column (story text)

who had appropriated Azucena, bestowing on her the pathetic responsibility of **embodying** the horror of what had happened in that place. With the first light Rolf tried again to dislodge the obstacles that held the girl in her tomb, but he had only his hands to work with; he did not dare use a tool for fear of injuring her. He fed Azucena a cup of the cornmeal mush and bananas the army was distributing, but she immediately vomited it up. A doctor stated that she had a fever but added that there was little he could do: antibiotics were being reserved for cases of gangrene.[10] A priest also passed by and blessed her, hanging a medal of the Virgin around her neck. By evening a gentle, persistent
180 drizzle began to fall. ❶

"The sky is weeping," Azucena murmured, and she, too, began to cry.
"Don't be afraid," Rolf begged. "You have to keep your strength up and be calm. Everything will be fine. I'm with you, and I'll get you out somehow."

Reporters returned to photograph Azucena and ask her the same questions, which she no longer tried to answer. In the meanwhile, more television and movie teams arrived with spools of cable, tapes, film, videos, precision lenses, recorders, sound consoles, lights, reflecting screens, auxiliary motors, cartons of supplies, electricians, sound technicians, and cameramen: Azucena's face was beamed to millions of screens around the world. And all the while Rolf
190 Carlé kept pleading for a pump. The improved technical facilities bore results, and National Television began receiving sharper pictures and clearer sound, the distance seemed suddenly compressed, and I had the horrible sensation that Azucena and Rolf were by my side, separated from me by impenetrable glass. I was able to follow events hour by hour; I knew everything my love did to wrest the girl from her prison and help her endure her suffering; I overheard fragments of what they said to one another and could guess the rest; I was present when she taught Rolf to pray and when he distracted her with the stories I had told him in a thousand and one nights beneath the white mosquito netting of our bed. ❷

200 When darkness came on the second day, Rolf tried to sing Azucena to sleep with old Austrian folk songs he had learned from his mother, but she was far beyond sleep. They spent most of the night talking, each in a **stupor** of exhaustion and hunger and shaking with cold. That night, imperceptibly, the unyielding floodgates that had contained Rolf Carlé's past for so many years began to open, and the torrent of all that had lain hidden in the deepest and most secret layers of memory poured out, leveling before it the obstacles that had blocked his consciousness for so long. He could not tell it all to Azucena; she perhaps did not know there was a world beyond the sea or time previous to her own; she was not capable of imagining Europe in the years of the war. So
210 he could not tell her of defeat, nor of the afternoon the Russians had led them to the concentration camp to bury prisoners dead from starvation. Why should he describe to her how the naked bodies piled like a mountain of firewood resembled fragile china? How could he tell this dying child about ovens and gallows? Nor did he mention the night that he had seen his mother naked,

---

10. **gangrene:** death and decay of body tissue, usually resulting from injury or disease.

Right margin annotations

embody (ĕm-bŏd′ē) *v.* to give shape to or visibly represent

❶ **CHARACTERIZATION**
Reread lines 165–180. What do these observations suggest has happened to Rolf? Explain your answer.

② **Targeted Passage**

❷ **AUTHOR'S PERSPECTIVE**
Allende gives a behind-the-scenes view of broadcasting a news story. What criticisms of the media does she seem to be suggesting?

stupor (stōō′pər) *n.* a state of mental numbness, as from shock

DIFFERENTIATED INSTRUCTION

FOR STRUGGLING READERS

② **Targeted Passage** [Lines 184–203]

This passage shows how Rolf and Azucena are managing after one day trapped in the mud.

- What does Azucena do when reporters ask her questions? (lines 184–185)

- What does Rolf ask for when reporters bring their cameras? (lines 189–190)

- How do Rolf and Azucena feel after spending a night together? (lines 202–203)

FOR ENGLISH LANGUAGE LEARNERS

Culture: Clarify Draw attention to the priest mentioned in lines 178–179 who blesses Azucena. Explain that in the Catholic religion, priests are often asked to say a blessing over a person who is about to die. The blessing offers hope for delivery to heaven after death.

Resurrection (2000), Stevie Taylor. Pastel on paper. Private Collection. Photo © Bridgeman Art Library.

Analyze Visuals

Activity How does the pose of the figure in the art recall the characters of both Rolf and Azucena? *Possible answer: The crouched position of the figure recalls Rolf locked inside the armoire and Azucena curled up in the mud.*

About the Art *Resurrection* was painted in 2000 by the English artist Stevie Taylor (b. 1949). It is typical of Taylor's work, which is influenced by psychology and science fiction.

shod in stiletto-heeled red boots, sobbing with humiliation. There was much he did not tell, but in those hours he relived for the first time all the things his mind had tried to erase. Azucena had surrendered her fear to him and so, without wishing it, had obliged Rolf to confront his own. There, beside that hellhole of mud, it was impossible for Rolf to flee from himself any longer, and the
220 visceral terror he had lived as a boy suddenly invaded him. He reverted to the years when he was the age of Azucena and younger, and, like her, found himself trapped in a pit without escape, buried in life, his head barely above ground; he saw before his eyes the boots and legs of his father, who had removed his belt and was whipping it in the air with the never-forgotten hiss of a viper coiled to strike. Sorrow flooded through him, intact and precise, as if it had lain always in his mind, waiting. He was once again in the armoire[11] where his father locked him to punish him for imagined misbehavior, there where for eternal hours he had crouched with his eyes closed, not to see the darkness, with his hands over his ears to shut out the beating of his heart, trembling,
230 huddled like a cornered animal. Wandering in the mist of his memories he

---

11. **armoire** (ärm-wär´): a large wardrobe or cabinet.

> **COMMON CORE RL 4**
>
> **Language Coach**
>
> **Roots and Affixes** A word's **root** may contain its core meaning. The Latin root *vert* means "to turn." Reread lines 220–225. Which word contains this root? What do you think the word means? (Hint: The prefix *re-* means "back.")

FOR ENGLISH LANGUAGE LEARNERS

Culture: Clarify Students from countries that did not participate in World War II may not understand the references in lines 200–214. Explain that Rolf is Austrian. His country and its ally, Germany, lost the war against Russia and its allies. The conquering Russians made Austrians help bury those murdered in German concentration camps. After the defeat, many Austrians and Germans relocated to South America.

FOR ENGLISH LANGUAGE LEARNERS

> **Language Coach**   **COMMON CORE RL 4**
>
> **Roots and Affixes** *Answer:* Reverted means *"turned back or returned to a former state."* Work with students to identify and define other verbs that contain the root *vert* combined with different prefixes, such as *avert* ("turn away"), *convert* ("turn around"), *divert* ("turn aside"), *invert* ("turn upside down or inside out"), *subvert* ("overturn").

found his sister, Katharina, a sweet, retarded child who spent her life hiding, with the hope that her father would forget the disgrace of her having been born. With Katharina, Rolf crawled beneath the dining room table, and with her hid there under the long white tablecloth, two children forever embraced, alert to footsteps and voices. Katharina's scent melded with his own sweat, with aromas of cooking, garlic, soup, freshly baked bread, and the unexpected odor of putrescent[12] clay. His sister's hand in his, her frightened breathing, her silk hair against his cheek, the candid gaze of her eyes. Katharina . . . Katharina materialized before him, floating on the air like a flag, clothed in the white

240 tablecloth, now a winding sheet, and at last he could weep for her death and for the guilt of having abandoned her. He understood then that all his exploits as a reporter, the feats that had won him such recognition and fame, were merely an attempt to keep his most ancient fears at bay, a **stratagem** for taking refuge behind a lens to test whether reality was more tolerable from that perspective. He took excessive risks as an exercise of courage, training by day to conquer the monsters that tormented him by night. But he had to come face to face with the moment of truth; he could not continue to escape his past. He was Azucena; he was buried in the clayey mud; his terror was not the distant emotion of an almost forgotten childhood, it was a claw sunk in his throat.

250 In the flush of his tears he saw his mother, dressed in black and clutching her imitation-crocodile pocketbook to her bosom, just as he had last seen her on the dock when she had come to put him on the boat to South America. She had not come to dry his tears, but to tell him to pick up a shovel: the war was over and now they must bury the dead.

"Don't cry. I don't hurt anymore. I'm fine," Azucena said when dawn came.

"I'm not crying for you," Rolf Carlé smiled. "I'm crying for myself. I hurt all over." **L**

The third day in the valley of the cataclysm began with a pale light filtering through storm clouds. The president of the republic visited the area in his

260 tailored safari jacket to confirm that this was the worst catastrophe of the century; the country was in mourning; sister nations had offered aid; he had ordered a state of siege; the armed forces would be merciless; anyone caught stealing or committing other offenses would be shot on sight. He added that it was impossible to remove all the corpses or count the thousands who had disappeared; the entire valley would be declared holy ground, and bishops would come to celebrate a solemn mass for the souls of the victims. He went to the army field tents to offer relief in the form of vague promises to crowds of the rescued, then to the improvised hospital to offer a word of encouragement to doctors and nurses worn down from so many hours of **tribulations.** Then

270 he asked to be taken to see Azucena, the little girl the whole world had seen. He waved to her with a limp statesman's hand, and microphones recorded his emotional voice and paternal tone as he told her that her courage had served as an example to the nation. Rolf Carlé interrupted to ask for a pump, and the

---

12. **putrescent** (pyoō-trĕs′ənt): rotting and foul-smelling.

Side margin annotations

stratagem (strătʹə-jəm) *n.* a clever trick or device for obtaining an advantage

K MONITOR
In line 220 a **flashback** begins in which Rolf recalls his childhood in a defeated Austria after World War II. **Reread** this description, through line 254. What terrible memories does he have?

L AUTHOR'S PERSPECTIVE
Rolf was exiled from his homeland, as Allende was exiled from her native Chile. Given Rolf's experiences, what might Allende be saying about the consequences of burying one's past and leaving one's family?

tribulation
(trĭbʹyə-lāʹshən) *n.* great distress or suffering

Left column annotations

READING STRATEGY — COMMON CORE RL 1

K MONITOR

Possible answer: Rolf remembers whippings from his father, his fear of the dark when he was locked inside an armoire as a punishment, and his love for his retarded sister Katharina.

Extend the Discussion How does the narrator link Rolf's memories to Azucena's experience?

TEXT ANALYSIS — COMMON CORE RL 9

L AUTHOR'S PERSPECTIVE

Possible answer: Allende is saying that past memories cannot be repressed forever. People must mourn for the home and family they have lost if they are to become emotionally healthy (lines 246–249).

VOCABULARY — COMMON CORE L 4

OWN THE WORD

- **stratagem:** Share with students that *stratagem* is related to the word *strategy,* which means "a plan of action." Both words come from the Greek words *stratos,* meaning "army," and *agein,* meaning "lead."

- **tribulation:** Have students give examples of situations that can cause *tribulation* or "great distress or suffering."

DIFFERENTIATED INSTRUCTION

FOR ADVANCED LEARNERS/PRE–AP

Research Have students research the impact of the disaster on Armero, the town that inspired Allende's story. Have them explore how, if at all, the town honors those who died, and if the area has become the holy ground that the story suggests. Invite students to share the information from their research with the class.

FOR ENGLISH LANGUAGE LEARNERS

Vocabulary: Idioms Use New Word Analysis to help students learn the idioms *come face to face* (lines 246–247), "confront," and *glued to the screen* (line 276), "unable to stop watching the screen."

 BEST PRACTICES TOOLKIT—Transparency
New Word Analysis p. E8

president assured him that he personally would attend to the matter. I caught a glimpse of Rolf for a few seconds kneeling beside the mud pit. On the evening news broadcast, he was still in the same position; and I, glued to the screen like a fortune teller to her crystal ball, could tell that something fundamental had changed in him. I knew somehow that during the night his defenses had crumbled and he had given in to grief; finally he was vulnerable. The girl had
280 touched a part of him that he himself had no access to, a part he had never shared with me. Rolf had wanted to console her, but it was Azucena who had given him consolation.

I recognized the precise moment at which Rolf gave up the fight and surrendered to the torture of watching the girl die. I was with them, three days and two nights, spying on them from the other side of life. I was there when she told him that in all her thirteen years no boy had ever loved her and that it was a pity to leave this world without knowing love. Rolf assured her that he loved her more than he could ever love anyone, more than he loved his mother, more than his sister, more than all the women who had slept in his arms,
290 more than he loved me, his life companion, who would have given anything to be trapped in that well in her place, who would have exchanged her life for Azucena's, and I watched as he leaned down to kiss her poor forehead, consumed by a sweet, sad emotion he could not name. I felt how in that instant both were saved from despair, how they were freed from the clay, how they rose above the vultures and helicopters, how together they flew above the vast swamp of corruption and laments. How, finally, they were able to accept death. Rolf Carlé prayed in silence that she would die quickly, because such pain cannot be borne. ⓜ

By then I had obtained a pump and was in touch with a general who had
300 agreed to ship it the next morning on a military cargo plane. But on the night of that third day, beneath the unblinking focus of quartz lamps and the lens of a hundred cameras, Azucena gave up, her eyes locked with those of the friend who had sustained her to the end. Rolf Carlé removed the life buoy, closed her eyelids, held her to his chest for a few moments, and then let her go. She sank slowly, a flower in the mud.

⓷ Targeted Passage

You are back with me, but you are not the same man. I often accompany you to the station, and we watch the videos of Azucena again; you study them intently, looking for something you could have done to save her, something you did not think of in time. Or maybe you study them to see yourself as if
310 in a mirror, naked. Your cameras lie forgotten in a closet; you do not write or sing; you sit long hours before the window, staring at the mountains. Beside you, I wait for you to complete the voyage into yourself, for the old wounds to heal. I know that when you return from your nightmares, we shall again walk hand in hand, as before. ❧

Translated by Margaret Sayers Peden

COMMON CORE RL 4

Language Coach

Derivations Words that are formed from another word or base are **derivations**. What word in line 282 is derived from the word *console*? What does it mean? Use the derivation *inconsolable* to describe a character in this story.

COMMON CORE RL 9

ⓜ ALLUSION

An **allusion** is a reference to another literary work, a famous person or event, or a religious concept. "And of Clay Are We Created" makes numerous references to Christianity and the Bible, especially in the references to "clay," which in the Bible represents human mortality. Reread lines 293–296. What do you think Allende means when she says that Rolf and Azucena were "freed from the clay"?

REVISIT THE BIG QUESTION

Can reporters always stay OBJECTIVE?

Discuss Based on lines 306–314, was Rolf Carlé able to remain objective? What happened to make him lose his objectivity? *Possible answer: Rolf became emotionally involved with the fate of a disaster victim and tried everything to save her. In the process, he stopped being an objective reporter.*

TEXT ANALYSIS   COMMON CORE RL 9

ⓜ ALLUSION

Point out lines 297–298 in which Allende writes "how together they flew above the vast swamp of corruption and laments." Ask students to describe the picture this brings to their minds and explain how this idea supports being "freed from the clay."

Answer: *Allende means that they were freed from fear of death, and were joined in spiritual connection.*

SELECTION WRAP-UP

READ WITH A PURPOSE Have students think about the irony and the tragedy of the requested pump arriving the day after Azucena's death. Why didn't the author write the story so that the pump arrived in time to save her? *Possible answer: Azucena's death is essential to the message the author wishes to convey. It helps free not only Azucena but also Rolf from pain and suffering.*

★ **CRITIQUE** Do you think the connection between Rolf's past and Azucena's suffering is a believable one? Explain.

INDEPENDENT READING

Another account of heroism during tragedy is *The Real Guardians: Five True Stories of Coast Guard Heroes and Their Rescues in New Orleans Following Hurricane Katrina* by Darrel Creacy and Carlito Vicencio.

FOR STRUGGLING READERS

⓷ Targeted Passage [Lines 299–305]

This passage concludes the story and tells how Azucena died and how Rolf shared her last moments.

- What happened to Azucena? Who watched her death? (lines 302–303)

- What did Rolf Carlé do after her death? (lines 303–304)

FOR ENGLISH LANGUAGE LEARNERS

Language Coach

COMMON CORE RL 4

Derivations *Answer:* consolation, *meaning "comfort"; Rolf Carlé was* inconsolable *as he finally gave in to his grief.* Have student pairs create additional sentences that contain the words *console*, *consolation*, and *inconsolable* and read them aloud to the whole group.

Practice and Apply

For preliminary support of post-reading questions, use these copy masters:

R RESOURCE MANAGER—Copy Masters
Reading Check p. 154
Author's Perspective p. 147
Question Support p. 155

Additional selection questions are provided for teachers on page 141.

ANSWERS

Comprehension

1. *A volcano eruption created a mudslide that buried the town.*

2. *Rolf Carlé is a reporter covering the disaster.*

3. *She is buried up to her neck in the mud and trapped by the bodies of her brothers and sisters clinging to her legs.*

4. *He remembers burying bodies in concentration camps, witnessing his mother's humiliation, experiencing abuse by his father, comforting his sister, and seeing the sister he abandoned in his dreams.*

Text Analysis

COMMON CORE RL 1, RL 3, RL 9

Possible answers:

5. ◼ **COMMON CORE FOCUS** *Monitor Students may have reread, questioned, read more slowly, or visualized, depending on the passages.*

6. *Rolf comforts and reassures Azucena as she dies. Azucena enables Rolf to face his emotions. Their relationship becomes almost like that of a brother and sister sharing a fundamental love.*

7. *Azucena is more accepting of her fate than Rolf is. This may be because she knows what she can endure or because Rolf is used to overcoming obstacles.*

8. ● **COMMON CORE FOCUS** *Author's Perspective It seems that Allende does not value objectivity in reporting. She seems to value caring, compassion, involvement, and real assistance more. Rolf becomes a more noble character as he abandons his role as a reporter to comfort Azucena.*

9. *Allende's choice of narrator helps readers see Rolf as a television viewer would but also gives them insight into his personality and his history. The narrator also shares an insider's knowledge of the news media and describes Rolf with loving eyes. If Rolf*

Comprehension

1. **Recall** What disaster has happened in the town?

2. **Recall** Who is Rolf Carlé?

3. **Recall** What prevents Azucena from being rescued?

4. **Clarify** What memories disturb Rolf as he waits in the night with Azucena?

Text Analysis

5. **Monitor Understanding** Look back at the notes you made as you read. What strategies did you use to increase your understanding?

6. **Analyze Characterization** What do Rolf and Azucena do for each other? How would you describe the relationship that develops between them? Use a chart to plan your answer.

> What Rolf Does for Azucena:
>
> What Azucena Does for Rolf:
>
> Relationship:

7. **Contrast Attitudes** Contrast Azucena's attitude toward her fate with Rolf's feelings about it. What might account for the difference?

8. **Identify Author's Perspective** Do you think Allende values objectivity in reporting? Support your opinion with strong textual evidence.

9. **Analyze Point of View** How does Allende's choice of narrator contribute to the story? Consider what this narrator was able to present that Rolf Carlé as narrator would not have been able to provide.

10. **Interpret Theme** State what the story suggests to you about the role of the media in a tragedy. What other messages do you draw from the story?

Text Criticism

11. **Biographical Context** Allende, in reflecting on a photograph of Omaira Sanchez, the trapped girl who inspired her story, commented: "We've never met her and are living at the other end of the world, yet we've been brought together because of her. She never dies, this girl. . . . She's born every instant." What does this statement reveal about Allende's values?

> **Can reporters always stay OBJECTIVE?**
>
> Should a reporter's duty to remain objective always take priority over other ethical considerations? Explain.

COMMON CORE

RL 1 Cite textual evidence to support analysis of what the text says explicitly. **RL 3** Analyze how complex characters develop and interact with other characters. **RL 9** Analyze how an author draws on and transforms source material in a specific work.

---

had been the narrator, he might not have seemed so sympathetic. He also could not have presented a broader picture of the tragedy, because he never leaves Azucena's side.

10. *The story suggests that media "objectivity" is cruel. The media offers no real assistance to suffering people. Other possible messages are that people should help each other endure pain, and that some tragedies are too big to repair.*

Text Criticism
Possible answer:

11. *The statement reveals that Allende values human solidarity and compassion.*

> Can reporters always stay **OBJECTIVE?** Students might describe life-and-death situations or specific instances in which other ethical considerations might appeal to a reporter's humanity and override his or her duty to remain objective.

Vocabulary in Context

▲ VOCABULARY PRACTICE

Decide whether the words in each pair are **synonyms** (words that have similar meanings) or **antonyms** (words that have opposite meanings). You can use a dictionary or thesaurus to help you.

1. tenacity/laziness
2. fortitude/weakness
3. resignation/acceptance
4. pandemonium/chaos
5. stupor/enthusiasm
6. embody/represent
7. stratagem/scheme
8. tribulation/hardship

WORD LIST

embody
fortitude
pandemonium
resignation
stratagem
stupor
tenacity
tribulation

ACADEMIC VOCABULARY IN WRITING

> • author   • document   • vision   • goal   • issue

Briefly retell part of the story from the trapped girl's point of view. Your **goal** for writing is to capture Azucena's experiences. Use at least one Academic Vocabulary word in your response.

COMMON CORE

L 4a Use context as a clue to the meaning of a word or phrase.

VOCABULARY STRATEGY: THE LATIN WORD ROOT *fort*

The vocabulary word *fortitude* stems from the Latin root *fort,* which means "strong." To understand the meaning of words with *fort,* use context clues as well as your knowledge of the root.

PRACTICE Choose the word from the word web that best completes each sentence. Use context clues to help you or, if necessary, consult a dictionary.

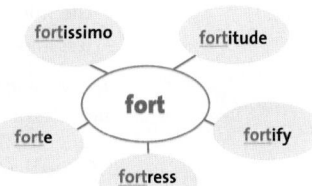

1. In music, to play a piece _____ is to play in a very loud manner.
2. She showed great _____ during her mother's funeral.
3. This exercise will _____ the muscles in your upper body.
4. Painting is her _____; she is a very talented artist.
5. Building a solid _____ will keep enemies at bay.

Interactive Vocabulary THINK central

Go to **thinkcentral.com**.
KEYWORD: HML10-597

DIFFERENTIATED INSTRUCTION

FOR ENGLISH LANGUAGE LEARNERS

Vocabulary: Cognates Have students work with a partner with the same home language. Have them write the vocabulary words that have cognates in their home language, such as *tenacidad,* Spanish for *tenacity.* Have students work with a dictionary to find translations to English for each cognate.

FOR ADVANCED LEARNERS/PRE–AP

Vocabulary in Writing Have students write a newspaper article about the events of the story using four or more vocabulary words. Have students exchange their articles with a partner for review and revision.

ANSWERS

Vocabulary in Context

▲ VOCABULARY PRACTICE

1. *antonyms*   5. *antonyms*
2. *antonyms*   6. *synonyms*
3. *synonyms*   7. *synonyms*
4. *synonyms*   8. *synonyms*

R RESOURCE MANAGER—Copy Master
Vocabulary Practice p. 152

ACADEMIC VOCABULARY IN WRITING

Possible answer: *I've been trapped here for several days now and doubt that I will ever escape. The reporter said the goal is simple, but I do not believe it. The issue is not simply draining the water that surrounds me.*

VOCABULARY STRATEGY: THE LATIN WORD ROOT *fort*

COMMON CORE L 4a

For each item, help students use their understanding of the word root and context clues to select the correct answer.

Possible answers:

1. *fortissimo*   4. *forte*
2. *fortitude*   5. *fortress*
3. *fortify*

R RESOURCE MANAGER—Copy Master
Vocabulary Strategy p. 153

Interactive Vocabulary THINK central

Keywords direct students to a **WordSharp** tutorial on **thinkcentral.com** or to other types of vocabulary practice and review.

Assess and Reteach

Assess

DIAGNOSTIC AND SELECTION TESTS
Selection Test A, B/C pp. 167–168, 169-170

Interactive Selection Test on **thinkcentral.com**

Reteach

Level Up Online Tutorials on **thinkcentral.com**

Reteaching Worksheets on **thinkcentral.com**
Literature Lesson 45, Reading Lesson 2, Vocabulary Lesson 7

Focus and Motivate

 COMMON CORE FOCUS

RI 2 Determine the central idea of a text and analyze its development over the course of the text. **RI 3** Analyze how the author unfolds and develops a series of events, the order in which they occur, and the connections drawn between the events. **RI 4** Determine the meaning of words and phrases as they are used in a text. **RI 7** Analyze various accounts of a subject told in different mediums. **W 2** Write explanatory texts to examine and convey complex ideas.

SUMMARY

In this news article, Julia Preston relates the causes of the death of Omaira Sanchez, a girl buried up to her neck by volcanic debris in Armero, Colombia.

What's the Connection?

Use a KWL chart to help prepare students for the selection.

 BEST PRACTICES TOOLKIT—Transparency
KWL p. A21

What I Know	What I Want to Know	What I Learned
A volcano erupted.	How many were hurt?	
A girl is trapped in floodwater.	How old is the girl?	
	Will she be rescued?	

Teach

Standards Focus: Analyze a News Article

Have students scan the article and identify each of these elements: headline, captions, and lead. Explain that reporters often present the most important details first because they assume that many readers will not complete the entire article before moving on to the next article.

R RESOURCE MANAGER—Copy Master
Analyze a News Article p. 165

Girl, Trapped in Water for 55 Hours, Dies Despite Rescue Attempts
News Article

Use with "And of Clay Are We Created," page 586.

 COMMON CORE

RI 2 Determine the central idea of a text and analyze its development over the course of the text. **RI 3** Analyze how the author unfolds and develops a series of events, the order in which they occur, and the connections drawn between the events. **RI 4** Determine the meaning of words and phrases as they are used in a text.

What's the Connection?

Often, fiction writers discover ideas for stories in real events. Isabel Allende based her short story "And of Clay Are We Created" on actual news accounts about a girl trapped in floodwater after a volcano eruption in Colombia. The news article you are about to read reports what happened to the girl, Omaira Sanchez, who was the inspiration for Allende's fictional Azucena.

Standards Focus: Analyze a News Article

A **news article** is a factual account of a real-life event. The author's purpose for writing a news article is to inform or explain. News articles typically provide the following elements:

- a **headline** summarizing the article
- photographs with **captions,** or lines of explanation
- a **lead**—the first few sentences of an article, which are meant to grab the reader's attention. The lead often contains the story's **central idea,** or main idea, as well.
- answers to the questions *who, what, when, where, why, and how,* the story's **most important** details.
- less important details arranged in order of decreasing importance

As you read the following news article, note the information it provides, and record the information on a chart like the one shown.

Elements of News Article	Information Provided
Headline	
Photos and Captions	
Lead	
Answers to who, what, when, where, why, and how questions	
Additional details	

Selection Resources

See resources on the **Teacher One Stop DVD-ROM** *and on* **thinkcentral.com**.

R RESOURCE MANAGER UNIT 5
Lesson Support,* pp. 157–170

DIAGNOSTIC AND SELECTION TESTS
Selection Tests, pp. 171–174

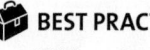 **BEST PRACTICES TOOLKIT**
KWL, p. A21

TECHNOLOGY
- 💿 **Teacher One Stop DVD-ROM**
- 💿 **Student One Stop DVD-ROM**
- 💿 **Audio Anthology CD**
- 💿 **ExamView Test Generator** on the **Teacher One Stop**

* Resources for Differentiation

Practice and Apply

Girl, Trapped in Water for 55 Hours, Dies Despite Rescue Attempts

Rescue efforts to save Omaira Sanchez

by Julia Preston

Armero, Colombia—Omaira Sanchez, a 13-year-old girl trapped up to her neck for more than 55 hours in floodwaters, died yesterday morning despite rescuers' frantic efforts to free her. **B**

Omaira's legs were pinned in the ruins of what was once her home by a cement slab and by the body of an
10 aunt who drowned in the avalanche

of mud that rolled over Armero Wednesday night.

Trapped in the chilly water the little girl shivered violently and her hands turned a deathly white. Finally her blood pressure dropped so low she suffered a heart attack, according to Alejandro Jimenez, 23, a medical student volunteer at the
20 disaster site who attended the child.

A **ANALYZE A NEWS ARTICLE**
What do you learn from this photograph and its caption?

B **ANALYZE A NEWS ARTICLE**
Which of the six journalistic questions are answered in the first paragraph of the article?

INFORMATIONAL ANALYSIS COMMON CORE

A ANALYZE A NEWS ARTICLE RI 2 RI 3

Possible answer: *From the photograph and its caption, you learn the girl's name, Omaira Sanchez, and you see that she is trapped up to her neck in muddy water while rescuers work to free her.*

INFORMATIONAL ANALYSIS COMMON CORE

B ANALYZE A NEWS ARTICLE RI 2 RI 3

Possible answer: *The first paragraph answers these journalistic questions: Who—Omaira Sanchez, a 13-year-old girl; What—died despite rescue efforts; Where— Armero, Colombia; When— yesterday.*

IF STUDENTS NEED HELP . . . Remind students that the journalistic questions are *who, what, when, where, why,* and *how.*

TIERED DISCUSSION PROMPTS

Refer students to lines 7–20. Use these prompts to discuss the reporter's initial statements about the disaster:

Connect Have you ever been in or heard about other seemingly impossible situations? How does that help you understand Sanchez's dilemma? *Students should connect previous experiences with Sanchez's situation.*

Analyze What details does the reporter include to help readers connect to Omaira's situation? *Vivid details—being trapped by the aunt's body, the cement slab, and Omaira's white hands—help readers connect to her terrible situation (lines 7–15).*

Evaluate Does the reporter do a good job of presenting the most important information first? *Possible answer: Yes, most of the reporter's questions (who, what, where, when, why, and how) are answered within the first few paragraphs.*

DIFFERENTIATED INSTRUCTION

FOR STRUGGLING READERS

Comprehension Support To check students' understanding—and to complete the chart on page 598—have students read the article independently. Then have them work in pairs to identify the elements of the article that convey information. Elicit from students that some information is repeated in several places; for example, the details of the photograph are written in the article even though they are obvious from the photograph and caption.

FOR ENGLISH LANGUAGE LEARNERS

Options for Reading Have students work in pairs to read the article. Direct partners to take turns reading aloud. After each paragraph, have partners stop to discuss the information in the paragraph. If either partner is unclear about the text's meaning, have the listening partner reread the paragraph.

INFORMATIONAL ANALYSIS · COMMON CORE

**RI 2
RI 3**

⊙ ANALYZE A NEWS ARTICLE

Possible answer: *The photograph shows how a mudflow has covered the fields over a wide area and caused great destruction. It helps the reader understand the difficulties involved in the rescue.*

IF STUDENTS NEED HELP . . . Point out that the caption to the photograph helps the viewer interpret the image. Ask a volunteer to read it aloud.

INFORMATIONAL ANALYSIS · COMMON CORE

**RI 2
RI 3**

⊙ *Model the Skill:* ANALYZE A NEWS ARTICLE

To model how to analyze a news article, draw a chart on the board like the one on page 598. Write the question about Jimenez in the first column in the row about the six journalistic questions, and underline the word *How*. Reread aloud to find an answer to the question, and record it in the second column of the chart.

Possible answer: *Jimenez is one of the rescuers who works to save Omaira Sanchez (lines 18–20).*

⊙ ANALYZE A NEWS ARTICLE
What information does this photograph convey to you?

Mudflow covering the fields after the Nevado del Ruiz eruption

"You can imagine how I feel," said Jimenez, looking drawn and exhausted yesterday morning. "We stayed up all night trying to save her." ⊙

About a dozen ₃₀ rescuers from the Colombian Air Force, the Red Cross, and fire departments of towns near Armero radioed increasingly desperate pleas since Thursday for an electric pump to keep the fetid waters from rising above the girl's chin. They called for ₄₀ picks, shovels, and winches to clear away rubble trapping her.

At 2 P.M. yesterday, four hours after Omaira died, a Colombian radio station announced that 18 water pumps ₅₀ had just arrived in a town 45 miles from Armero. To the end, rescue workers dug with their bare hands at the cement slab leaning on Omaira's numb legs, and bailed the water with tin cans.

₆₀ Someone stretched a dirty blue-and-white checkered tablecloth over the scene of tragedy, a scene that, displayed in newspapers around the world yesterday, came to represent the horror of the disaster.

⊙ ANALYZE A NEWS ARTICLE
How is Alejandro Jimenez involved in the events?

COMMON CORE RI 4

Language Coach

Etymology A word's **etymology** is its history. The Latin word *foetere* means "to stink." Use this Latin root to figure out the meaning of a word in line 38.

600 UNIT 5: AUTHOR'S PURPOSE

DIFFERENTIATED INSTRUCTION

FOR STRUGGLING READERS

Develop Reading Fluency Draw attention to the map on the page. Say the name of a place and have students find it on the map. Pronounce the place-name again, and have students say it. Repeat for other place-names. Then ask students to name the country and the continent where the story takes place and to identify nearby oceans and countries. Correct students' pronunciations, and have them practice further as needed.

FOR ENGLISH LANGUAGE LEARNERS

Language Coach · COMMON CORE RI 4

Etymology *Answer: The word* fetid *means "stinking."* Have students name other things that might be described as *fetid*. **Possible answers:** *garbage, compost, a swamp, a sewer, standing water*

Comprehension

1. **Recall** What caused Omaira Sanchez to be trapped?

2. **Summarize** What efforts did rescue workers make to try to save Omaira?

Text Analysis

3. **Read a News Article** What details are provided by Alejandro Jimenez? What would have been the effect if he had not been mentioned or quoted?

4. **Analyze Details** What do the details about the pumps' arrival and the checkered tablecloth contribute to the article?

5. **Evaluate Graphic Aids** Explain what each photograph adds to your understanding of the events. Which of the two photographs has greater emotional impact? Give reasons for your answer.

○ **COMMON CORE**

RI 2 Determine the central idea of a text and analyze its development over the course of the text. **RI 3** Analyze how the author unfolds and develops a series of events, the order in which they occur, and the connections drawn between the events. **RI 7** Analyze various accounts of a subject told in different mediums. **W 2** Write explanatory texts to examine and convey complex ideas.

Read for Information: Compare Accounts

WRITING PROMPT

A news article and a short story are very different forms of writing, with different purposes and different strengths. Compare and contrast the article about Omaira Sanchez with Allende's story about Azucena. What elements do the pieces have in common? What elements are specific to each form, and what is their effect on you as a reader? Ultimately, which piece affected you more strongly? Why?

To respond to this prompt, you will need to compare and contrast, following these steps:

1. Create a large Venn diagram like the one shown.

2. On one side, note elements found only in the short story, such as the inner thoughts of the characters.

3. On the other side, note elements found only in the news article, such as photographs of the scene.

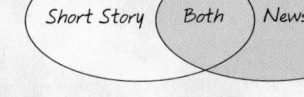
Short Story   Both   News Article

4. In the middle, note elements the two pieces have in common.

5. Weigh the elements on each side, and decide which piece affected you more strongly.

Practice and Apply

For preliminary support of post-reading questions, use these copy masters:

R RESOURCE MANAGER—Copy Masters
Reading Check p. 169
Question Support p. 170
Compare Forms p. 166

Additional selection questions are provided for teachers on page 160.

ANSWERS

Comprehension

1. *debris from a mudslide*

2. *Rescue workers radioed for a pump, requested tools to clear rubble, dug with bare hands, and bailed water with a cup.*

Text Analysis

○ **COMMON CORE RI 2, RI 3, RI 7, W 2**

Possible answers:

3. ● **COMMON CORE FOCUS** *Analyze a News Article* Jimenez offers first-hand information about the rescue attempt that helps the reader better appreciate the heroic efforts.

4. ● **COMMON CORE FOCUS** *Analyze Details* make the story more tragic; pumps could have saved Sanchez; tablecloth shows how rescue workers treated her with dignity

5. *first shows Omaira and how hard rescuers worked to save her; second shows the extent of the mudflow; the first photograph gains greater impact, shows the tragedy's human faces*

Read for Information: Compare Accounts

Writing Prompt *Possible answer: Though both the story and the article share a tragic plot, the story is more gripping because it reveals more human emotion.*

Assess and Reteach

Assess

DIAGNOSTIC AND SELECTION TESTS
Selection Tests A, B/C pp. 171–172, 173-174

Interactive Selection Test on thinkcentral.com

Reteach

Level Up Online Tutorials on thinkcentral.com

Reteaching Worksheets on thinkcentral.com
Informational Text Lesson 1: Text Features

FOR STRUGGLING WRITERS

Read for Information

- Explain that the graphic organizer is a good way to get ideas flowing before answering the writing prompt in an essay.

- Invite students to organize their essays by explaining the details of first one form and then the other.

- Limit the essay to three to five paragraphs.

FOR ADVANCED LEARNERS/PRE–AP

Read for Information Have students extend their essays to discuss elements of newspaper articles that are common but do not appear in the article in this passage. For example, some articles may include police reports or a timeline of the disaster. Have students comment in their essays on how these elements might have impacted the effectiveness of this article.

Focus and Motivate

RL 1 Cite textual evidence to support inferences drawn from the text. **RL 4** Analyze the cumulative impact of specific word choices on meaning.

SUMMARIES

"Peruvian Child" While in Peru visiting an Incan site with a tour group, the speaker encounters a poor, bedraggled child holding a faceless doll. According to the speaker, most people would rather have a photograph of such a child as a souvenir than actually hold her in their arms or confront her poverty.

"Lady Freedom Among Us" The speaker presents Lady Freedom, a famous statue that sits atop the Capitol Building in Washington, D.C., as if she were a homeless person from whom we might recoil if we encountered her on the streets. Yet though she is gritty and weathered, this symbol of freedom is one of us.

What do we **OWE** others?

Read the question aloud, and ask students how they respond to people in need. Then complete the *DISCUSS* activity as a class, inviting volunteers to share their self-ratings about how much responsibility they take for others.

Selection Resources

Peruvian Child
Poem by Pat Mora

Lady Freedom Among Us
Poem by Rita Dove

What do we **OWE** others?

COMMON CORE

RL 1 Cite textual evidence to support inferences drawn from the text. **RL 4** Analyze the cumulative impact of specific word choices on meaning.

How do you react when you encounter a homeless person or see a child in great need? Do you ignore the person, or do you help? In the poems that follow, two poets express their views on the extent of our responsibility toward the less fortunate.

DISCUSS Think about the following aphorisms, or sayings: "You are your brother's keeper," "Mind your own business," "Charity begins at home." Plot them on a continuum ranging from no responsibility for others to great responsibility. Then rate yourself on the continuum. As a class, discuss how much responsibility you take for the welfare of others.

602

See resources on the **Teacher One Stop DVD-ROM** and on **thinkcentral.com**.

 RESOURCE MANAGER UNIT 5
Plan and Teach, pp. 171–178
Text Analysis and Reading
  Skill, pp. 179–182†*

**DIAGNOSTIC AND SELECTION
  TESTS**
Selection Tests, pp. 175–178

BEST PRACTICES TOOLKIT
Read Aloud/Think Aloud, p.
A34

TECHNOLOGY
- Teacher One Stop DVD-ROM
- Student One Stop DVD-ROM
- Audio Anthology CD
- GrammarNotes DVD-ROM
- ExamView Test Generator
  on the Teacher One Stop

---

* Resources for Differentiation   † Also in Spanish   ‡ In Haitian Creole and Vietnamese

● TEXT ANALYSIS: AUTHOR'S PURPOSE AND IMAGERY

Poets do not always write poems to simply express a personal feeling. Sometimes poets write to inform or persuade readers. Even a poem that simply describes a person or a scene, such as the two poems that follow, can have a strong **purpose.**

An important clue to a poet's **purpose** is the way he or she uses **imagery,** or words and phrases that re-create sensory experiences. Consider this imagery from "Peruvian Child."

Still in the middle of my path is the child
with no smile who stared at us.

What picture of the child is created in your mind? How do you think the poet wants you to feel about the child?

As you read the poems, think about the images they convey and what purpose they support.

● READING SKILL: MAKE INFERENCES

Poetry is a very compressed form of writing. Because not everything is stated explicitly, you must **make inferences,** or read between the lines, in order to enrich your understanding. For example, in "Peruvian Child," you must infer that the speaker is a person on a guided tour, though this is never stated.

Record your inferences in your *Reader/Writer Notebook* as you read the poems, using a chart like the one shown. Include clues from the text to support your inferences.

Inferences	Clues from Text
Speaker is someone on a guided tour.	"our guide said" "We wanted ... to hold a picture"

 Complete the activities in your **Reader/Writer Notebook.**

Meet the Authors

Pat Mora
born 1942

Upholding Heritage
Pat Mora considers herself lucky to be bilingual. She grew up speaking both English and Spanish in El Paso, Texas, a city on the U.S.-Mexican border. She remembers as a child wishing that she had learned about her Mexican heritage in school. Today she uses her writing and other activities to help kindle an interest in Latino culture. In 1997, she founded Día de los Niños/Día de los Libros (Children's Day/Book Day), which celebrates children's literacy on April 30 of each year.

Rita Dove
born 1952

Poet Laureate
At 41, Rita Dove was the youngest person ever to be appointed U.S. Poet Laureate (1993–1995). In response to a request to speak at a ceremony in Washington, D.C., commemorating the 200th anniversary of the Capitol, she wrote "Lady Freedom Among Us." "Lady Freedom" refers to the 19-foot Statue of Freedom that rests on top of the white dome of the Capitol. The statue depicts a woman in eagle-feathered headdress who carries a sword and shield.

Authors Online
Go to thinkcentral.com. KEYWORD: HML10-603

THINK central

603

Teach

TEXT ANALYSIS

COMMON CORE
RL 4

● *Model the Skill:* AUTHOR'S PURPOSE AND IMAGERY

To model how to use imagery to determine an author's purpose, write these lines on the board and read them aloud:

Jostling for the best position,
cameras held aloft like torches,
they flashed their glistening eyes
at the Masterpiece, never looking.

Describe the picture these lines of poetry create in your mind. Explain that the lines create a picture of tourists taking flash photographs of a famous work of art without even looking at it. The poet wants us to disapprove of them for not even examining the art they are supposedly admiring.

GUIDED PRACTICE Ask students what images a poet might use to describe tourists more sympathetically.

READING SKILL

COMMON CORE
RL 1

■ *Model the Skill:* MAKE INFERENCES

To model how to make inferences, point out the clues in the lines of poetry on the board that helped you infer that the speaker is describing tourists. Explain that the people described are holding cameras. They are taking pictures ("flashed their glistening eyes") of a "Masterpiece" and they must jostle one another to get near it.

GUIDED PRACTICE Ask students to identify clues that help them infer that the poet wants readers to disapprove of the tourists.

R RESOURCE MANAGER—Copy Master
Make Inferences p. 181 (for student use while reading the selection)

DIFFERENTIATED INSTRUCTION

FOR STRUGGLING READERS

Make Inferences Guide students in making inferences based on everyday scenarios:

- You wake up, look out your window, and see people wearing gloves, scarves, and hats. *(It's cold outside.)*

- You sneeze ten times in one hour and your throat hurts. *(You're getting a cold.)*

- Your friend throws his books in his locker, slams the door, and stomps away. *(He is in a bad mood or angry.)*

FOR ADVANCED LEARNERS/PRE–AP

Use Imagery Challenge students to write a brief poem with a specific purpose in mind. Tell them that they should not explicitly state their purpose but that they should write in such a way that the reader must infer it. Remind students that using imagery is one way to accomplish this goal, because imagery can suggest meaning without directly stating it. Have students trade poems with a partner and work to identify each other's purpose.

READ WITH A PURPOSE

Help students set a purpose for reading. Suggest that they read to discover connections between the two poems.

TEXT ANALYSIS — COMMON CORE RL 4

A *Model the Skill:*
AUTHOR'S PURPOSE AND IMAGERY

Read lines 1–5 aloud, and point out the comparison between the child and women in outdoor markets. Explain that the image suggests that the child's life has been hard and that she is old beyond her years. Observe that the poet's purpose is to elicit readers' sympathy for the child.

Possible answer: The child's eyes look like those of the women who work in outdoor markets and who view the tourists as if they are prison "guards." Readers can infer that the child's eyes look old and wary, suggesting that she has already had a difficult life. The poet may want readers to feel sorry for the child because she does not have the cheerful, innocent look of a "typical" child.

READING SKILL — COMMON CORE RL 1

B *Model the Skill:*
MAKE INFERENCES

To model how to make inferences, list clues from the text in column 2 of a Make Inferences chart like the one shown on page 603. Then lead students to use the clues to make an inference about the tourists' values in column 1.

Possible answer: The tourists want to photograph the child as though she were a tourist attraction (like the spring mentioned in lines 14–15), rather than a real child. They are too self-involved, detached, or uncaring to concern themselves with her poverty-stricken life; she is just a bit of local color. The tourists seem to value having a souvenir of their trip over making any real human connection with the people they encounter—or doing anything to help them.

Peruvian Child

Pat Mora

Still in the middle of my path is the child
with no smile who stared at us. Her eyes
even then the eyes of women who sell chickens
and onions in outdoor markets. The women
5   who stare at us as if we are guards. **A**

She whispered to the doll with no face,
smoothed the red and blue scraps
of cloth on the path, ironed them with her hand,
wrapped and re-wrapped the doll, hair
10   mud-tangled as the child's, and the dog's,
and the llama's that followed the child's
small bare feet after she bundled the doll
in the striped *manta* on her back.

The matted group stood by the edge of the spring
15   watching us drink clear, holy water of the Inca,
a fountain of youth, our guide said.
We wanted, as usual, to hold a picture
of the child in a white border, not to hold her
mud-crusted hands or feet or face,
20   not to hold her, the child in our arms. **B**

A AUTHOR'S PURPOSE AND IMAGERY
Reread lines 1–5. How do the child's eyes look, and what do they suggest about her life? Speculate about the poet's purpose in describing such eyes.

B MAKE INFERENCES
Reread lines 17–20. What do the tourists want? What does this say about their values?

604   UNIT 5: AUTHOR'S PURPOSE

DIFFERENTIATED INSTRUCTION

FOR ENGLISH LANGUAGE LEARNERS

Options for Reading Read aloud "Peruvian Child" once. Then do so again, pausing at the end of each stanza for questions, explanations, or discussion.

 **BEST PRACTICES TOOLKIT—Transparency**
Read Aloud/Think Aloud p. A34

Vocabulary Support Draw students' attention to the word *manta* in line 13 of the poem. Explain to students that *manta* is in italic type because it is a Spanish word, and foreign words usually appear in italics. The word means "blanket" or "rug." Ask students to decide which translation better fits how the word is used in this poem.

BACKGROUND

The Ancient Inca The reference to the "holy water of the Inca" (line 15) reveals that the tourists in this poem are visiting an ancient Inca spring thought to be the legendary "fountain of youth" (lines 16) that could bestow eternal life. At the time of the Spanish conquest in 1532, the Inca empire dominated the Pacific coast and Andean mountain region of South America, extending almost 2,000 miles from Ecuador to central Chile. Native Americans, most of whom are descendants of the Inca, make up about 45 percent of the present-day population of Peru.

Poverty in Contemporary Peru According to the World Bank, in 2001 about 55 percent of Peru's population lived in poverty, while almost 25 percent lived in extreme poverty (defined as living on less than $1 a day). Poverty is concentrated in rural areas and among native peoples, who have a poverty rate of about 70 percent. Children are also among the poorest. According to UNICEF, of the 3.8 million Peruvians living in extreme poverty, 2.1 million are children.

Analyze Visuals

Possible answer: Framing the child's face in a snapshot makes her seem like a souvenir of a vacation rather than a real child (just as the poem describes in lines 17–20).

TIERED DISCUSSION PROMPTS

Use these prompts to help students understand the poet's attitude toward the child and toward the tourists:

Analyze In describing the child, why do you think the speaker focuses on the girl's doll? *Possible answer: The faceless doll presents a heartbreaking image that epitomizes both the child's poverty and her nurturing attitude. The doll's facelessness symbolizes the girl herself. She is faceless to the tourists, who don't really see her. Her nurturing behavior toward her doll contrasts with the tourists' insensitivity toward her as a human being.*

Synthesize Based on your reading of the poem and your own experience, do you think that taking photographs prevents you from seeing your subject—or does it actually help you see things more clearly? Explain. *Accept all thoughtful responses.*

FOR STRUGGLING READERS

Comprehension Support Students may need help understanding lines 4–5: "The women who stare at us as if we are guards." Ask students what kind of guards the speaker is referring to (prison guards). Discuss what the girl's attitude toward the tourists might be if she is staring at them as if they are guards. Elicit that she may see them as powerful and threatening and thus may feel afraid of them. Like the women, she may feel imprisoned by her life and view the tourists as free.

FOR ADVANCED LEARNERS/PRE–AP

Analyze Irony Ask students to consider why it is ironic that the tourists are drinking water that is supposedly from "a fountain of youth" (line 16), while the child stares at them with "the eyes of women who sell chickens and onions in outdoor markets" (lines 3–4). *Possible answer: It is ironic that the tourists are drinking from a fountain of youth, while poverty has robbed the child of her youth.*

Prereading for this poem is found on page 602.

Lady Freedom Among Us

Rita Dove

don't lower your eyes
or stare straight ahead to where
you think you ought to be going

don't mutter *oh no*
5 *not another one*
get a job   *fly a kite*
go bury a bone **C**

with her oldfashioned sandals
with her leaden skirts
10 with her stained cheeks and whiskers and heaped up trinkets
she has risen among us in blunt reproach

she has fitted her hair under a hand-me-down cap
and spruced it up with feathers and stars
slung over one shoulder she bears
15 the rainbowed layers of charity and murmurs
all of you   even the least of you **D**

don't cross to the other side of the square
don't think *another item to fit on a tourist's agenda*

consider her drenched gaze   her shining brow
20 she who has brought mercy back into the streets
and will not retire politely to the potter's field

C **MAKE INFERENCES**
Think about the title of the poem. Though "Lady Freedom" refers to a famous statue, what situation is described in the poem?

D **AUTHOR'S PURPOSE AND IMAGERY**
Notice the similarities between the description of the homeless woman's appearance in lines 8–16 and the images of the statue on page 607. What purpose might this comparison serve?

606   UNIT 5: AUTHOR'S PURPOSE

READING SKILL
C MAKE INFERENCES

COMMON CORE
RL 1

Possible answer: *A pedestrian's encounter with a homeless person is the situation being described in this section of the poem.*

IF STUDENTS NEED HELP . . . Have them divide their inference chart (see page 603) into two subcategories, as shown.

Inferences	Clues from Text
Speaker is talking to someone who ...	
is going somewhere, probably on foot	"don't lower your eyes / or stare straight ahead to where / you think you ought to be going"
Speaker is talking about someone who ...	
is poor or homeless	"not another one / get a job"

TEXT ANALYSIS
D AUTHOR'S PURPOSE AND IMAGERY

COMMON CORE
RL 4

Possible answer: *The purpose of the comparison is to point out that the ideals embodied by the statue, such as freedom and dignity, should be applied to real people who live among us and deserve our respect—even the homeless.*

IF STUDENTS NEED HELP . . . Ask students to imagine that the statue pictured on page 607 stepped down from her pedestal and began walking through the streets. How might people react to such a woman?

REVISIT THE BIG QUESTION
What do we **OWE** others?

Discuss Reread the stanzas that begin with the word *don't*. Based on lines 1–18, what is our simplest level of responsibility toward the subject of the poem? **Possible answer:** *Our simplest level of responsibility is to at least notice her; we should not ignore her or pretend she is not there.*

606 UNIT 5: AUTHOR'S PURPOSE

DIFFERENTIATED INSTRUCTION

FOR STRUGGLING READERS

Develop Reading Fluency Have students listen to the audio recording of the poem several times. Then have them work in pairs to practice reading the poem aloud. Finally, assess comprehension with basic questions and discuss text ideas. Distribute the copy masters and have students work in pairs or groups to practice fluency.

R **RESOURCE MANAGER—Copy Master**
Reading Fluency p. 184

Comprehension Support Make sure that students understand the reference to "the potter's field" in line 21. Explain that a potter's field is a burial place for poor or unknown people. The term was first used in the New Testament (Matthew 27:27). Discuss what the speaker means when she says that Lady Freedom "will not retire politely to the potter's field." Elicit that like Lady Freedom, the homeless won't simply go away because they look forlorn and are outside the mainstream.

having assumed the thick skin of this town
its gritted exhaust its sunscorch and blear
she rests in her weathered plumage
25 bigboned   resolute

    don't think you can ever forget her
    don't even try
    she's not going to budge

    no choice but to grant her space
30 crown her with sky
    for she is one of the many
    and she is each of us **E**

COMMON CORE RL 4

Language Coach

Etymology The word *plumage* (line 24) comes from the Old French word *plume*, meaning "feather." Look at the photos on this page—to what do you think "weathered plumage" refers?

E **MAKE INFERENCES**
Reread lines 31–32. Who do "she" and "many" and "us" represent?

607

READING SKILL   **COMMON CORE** RL 1

E **MAKE INFERENCES**

Possible answer: "She" represents both a homeless woman and the statue of Lady Freedom. The "many" are the homeless, and "us" are all the people in society.

Analyze Visuals

Activity Ask students to explain how viewing this photograph of the statue helps them understand the poem. *Possible answer: The photograph helps readers better visualize the description in lines 8–25.*

About the Art The statue *Lady Freedom* (also known as the *Statue of Freedom*) stands on top of the dome of the Capitol in Washington, D.C. Designed by Thomas Crawford (1814–1859), the nearly 20-foot bronze statue was commissioned in 1855 and completed after Crawford's death. He had intended the statue to wear a liberty cap, a symbol of freed slaves. However, Jefferson Davis, then secretary of war and later president of the Confederacy, objected to the design, and Crawford changed the cap to a plumed helmet. Originally named *Armed Liberty*, *Lady Freedom* holds a laurel wreath and shield in her left hand and a sword in her right. The statue was installed in 1863, during the Civil War.

SELECTION WRAP—UP

READ WITH A PURPOSE Now that students have read the poems, ask them to place the tourists from "Peruvian Child" in the situation described in "Lady Freedom Among Us." How might the tourists react to the homeless woman described in Dove's poem? *Possible answer: The tourists would probably react to the woman in the same way they reacted to the child: they would not want to get involved or bother themselves with her. However, they probably would not want to photograph her.*

⭐ **CRITIQUE** Have students identify the element of each poem that had the greatest impact on them and explain why.

INDEPENDENT READING

Students may enjoy reading other works by Pat Mora. Suggest *My Own True Name: New and Selected Poems for Young Adults, 1984–1999.*

FOR ENGLISH LANGUAGE LEARNERS

Language Coach   COMMON CORE RL 4

Etymology *Answer:*
The statue has a feathered headdress. The plumage has been subjected to harsh weather conditions; it is neither bright nor flashy. Have students use the word *plumage* in sentences that do not refer to the statue.

FOR ADVANCED LEARNERS/PRE–AP

Analyze Style Ask students to copy the poem in their notebooks, inserting conventional capitalization and punctuation marks where the original seems grammatically incorrect. Then have students work in small groups to compare their "conventional" versions of the poem with Dove's original. Encourage students to discuss the effects of Dove's stylistic choices on the meaning and tone of the poem.

TIERED DISCUSSION PROMPTS

Use these prompts to help students understand how Rita Dove's ideas about freedom, as expressed in this interview, connect to her poem "Lady Freedom Among Us":

Connect What does the word *freedom* mean to you? Write a brief definition to explain your interpretation. *Accept all reasonable answers.*

Analyze In this interview, what does Dove imply about how freedom affects the way human beings relate to one another? ***Possible answer:*** *Dove implies that people cannot really be free if they do not allow themselves to connect to other people. Freedom does not mean that we are free simply to retreat to the privacy of our own lives ("I've got my life . . . ") and ignore the less fortunate (such as the homeless). Dove implies that freedom requires us to connect to other people, perhaps even take responsibility for them, not retreat from them.*

Evaluate Do you think that Dove's poem accomplishes her purpose, as expressed in this interview? In other words, does the poem make us "think more deeply about freedom and how it affects the way human being relates to human being"? Why or why not? *Encourage students to provide reasons and textual evidence to support their evaluations.*

Reading for Information

INTERVIEW Journalist Bill Moyers interviewed Rita Dove for his PBS television series *The Language of Life: A Festival of Poets.*

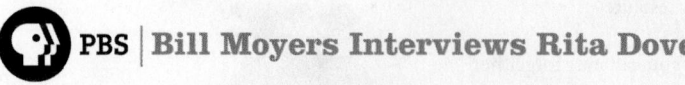

PBS | **Bill Moyers Interviews Rita Dove**

MOYERS: How is life as our poet laureate?

DOVE: Very hectic but extremely gratifying. Even more people than I had hoped are interested in poetry—I've got letters backed up to the ceiling from all kinds of people and from students of all ages. People often simply want to know where they can find poetry.

MOYERS: I can imagine Thomas Jefferson doing a double take upon finding you the poet laureate sitting here in the Jefferson Building at the Library of Congress, which houses his original library. You must know that he felt blacks were innately incapable of writing poetry. . . .

DOVE: Yes. It's troublesome to read those words and then to read other words of Jefferson's which really make a wonderful case for the equality of all men. It's a paradox I've been wrestling with. . . .

MOYERS: If Jefferson were here today, which poem would you read to him?

DOVE: I would read him "Lady Freedom Among Us," which is about his city, Washington, D.C., and which also has something to do with the body politic and with the political person. That poem would be closer than most to what he was comfortable with and knew in his life.

MOYERS: You wrote that one day after the statue of Lady Freedom was removed for cleaning and then brought back by helicopter to her place atop the Capitol Building right across from where we're sitting. That was in—

DOVE: In September 1993—about a month before the statue was brought back. Lady Freedom had been haunting me—sitting in the parking lot looking forlorn—so when the historian of Congress asked me if I would like to say a few words at the ceremony for her reinstallation I thought, "I have more than a few words to say."

MOYERS: What do you hope we'll take away from that poem?

DOVE: I would like us to think more deeply about freedom and how it affects the way human being relates to human being. That's why I wanted us to experience Lady Freedom as a human being—if we saw someone like her on the street, would we shy away from her obvious idealism and sense of herself? Hence the poem's comparisons to homeless people, who remind us that we are in this together. We really can't just imagine these people and think, "I've got my life and I'm going to keep going." They remind us that we're all connected.

608

608 UNIT 5: AUTHOR'S PURPOSE

Comprehension

1. **Recall** According to the speaker in Pat Mora's poem, what does the Peruvian child look like?

2. **Recall** How does the tour group respond to the child?

3. **Clarify** What typical responses to the homeless are presented in "Lady Freedom Among Us"? What clues in the poem tell you this?

Text Analysis

4. **Make Inferences** Review the inference chart you created. Which poem required you to infer more in order to understand its meaning? Explain.

5. **Analyze Author's Purpose and Imagery** What is Mora's purpose in "Peruvian Child"? Explain how her purpose is supported by the imagery she uses to describe the child and the tour group.

6. **Interpret Imagery and Author's Purpose** In Rita Dove's poem, what ideas are brought to mind by the imagery used to describe Lady Freedom? What might be the purpose of the poem?

7. **Synthesize** What did the interview with Rita Dove on page 608 contribute to your understanding of "Lady Freedom Among Us"?

8. **Compare and Contrast Texts** Compare and contrast the poets' views about the level of responsibility we have to the less fortunate. Use a Venn diagram to note the similarities and differences between Mora's and Dove's messages. Cite examples, or textual evidence, from the poems.

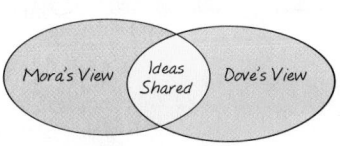
Mora's View | Ideas Shared | Dove's View

9. **Apply Ideas** Apply the ideas in these poems to your own experience. Do you accept the poets' views about how people should act toward the less fortunate? Explain.

Text Criticism

10. **Social Context** In her interview with Bill Moyers, Dove said that she wanted people to consider freedom and how it affects the way people relate to each other. Does the freedom we value as a society make people more inclined or less inclined to take responsibility for poverty and homelessness?

What do we OWE others?
What are the best ways to help the less fortunate?

COMMON CORE

RL 1 Cite textual evidence to support inferences drawn from the text. RL 4 Analyze the cumulative impact of specific word choices on meaning.

Practice and Apply

For preliminary support of post-reading questions, use these copy masters:

R RESOURCE MANAGER—Copy Masters
Author's Purpose and Imagery p. 179
Question Support p. 183

Additional selection questions are provided for teachers on page 175.

ANSWERS

Comprehension

1. *The child has no smile and old eyes. She is dirty, with tangled hair and muddy feet.*

2. *The tour group wants to take a photo of the child but does not want to hold her.*

3. *Responses include avoiding eye contact, thinking criticisms, moving away, and trying to forget. Clues are in lines that begin with "don't" and describe these actions.*

Text Analysis

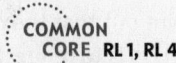
COMMON CORE RL 1, RL 4

Possible answers:

4. ■ **COMMON CORE FOCUS** *Make Inferences* "Lady Freedom Among Us" requires more inferences because the speaker does not directly describe what she sees.

5. ● **COMMON CORE FOCUS** *Author's Purpose and Imagery* Mora's purpose is to make readers take more responsibility for helping poor children. She describes a desperately needy child and uncaring tourists who want to possess an image of her as a souvenir.

6. ● **COMMON CORE FOCUS** *Author's Purpose and Imagery* Dove's imagery describes Lady Freedom as a homeless woman who is dressed bizarrely yet still possesses great dignity. Dove's purpose

Assess and Reteach

Assess

DIAGNOSTIC AND SELECTION TESTS
Selection Test A, B/C pp. 175–176, 177-178

Interactive Selection Test on **thinkcentral.com**

Reteach

Level Up Online Tutorials on **thinkcentral.com**

Reteaching Worksheets on **thinkcentral.com**
Reading Lesson 3, Reading Lesson 8

---

may be to make people view the homeless with respect.

7. *The interview clarifies Dove's purpose—to make people think about how they relate to and are connected to others.*

8. *Both poets think that we have a responsibility to help the less fortunate. Mora criticizes people who treat the poor as tourist attractions, while Dove criticizes those who disrespect the homeless.*

9. *Some students may think that hugging a child is condescending or that it is wise to avoid the homeless, who may be unstable.*

Text Criticism

Possible answer:

10. *Less: Valuing freedom may make us view people as responsible for their own bad choices. More: Valuing freedom may make us think that everyone should be free to enjoy a good life.*

What do we OWE others? *Possible answer: The best ways show respect for the recipient's dignity and humanity.*

Focus and Motivate

COMMON CORE FOCUS

W 1a–e Write arguments to support claims, using valid reasoning and relevant and sufficient evidence. **W 4** Produce clear and coherent writing in which the development, organization, and style are appropriate to task, purpose, and audience. **W 5** Develop and strengthen writing as needed by planning, revising, and editing, focusing on a specific purpose. **W 7** Conduct research to answer a question. **W 10** Write routinely over shorter time frames for a range of tasks, purposes, and audiences. **L 1** Demonstrate command of the conventions of standard English grammar and usage. **L 2** Demonstrate command of the conventions of standard English capitalization, punctuation, and spelling. **L 2c** Spell correctly. **L 3** Use knowledge of language to make effective choices for meaning or style.

WRITE WITH A PURPOSE

Point out that the purpose of most persuasive letters is to request action. Explain that how students present their proposals depends, in part, on their audience. Tell students to determine whether their audience is an individual, company, group, or organization.

COMMON CORE TRAITS

Review the *COMMON CORE TRAITS*, focusing on development and organization of ideas. Compare the list of traits with the rubric on page 618.

ADDITIONAL TASK

Write about Yourself Write a persuasive letter to an organization or business to convince them of your qualifications for a position or an award. **Possible subjects:** summer job, internship, volunteer opportunity, scholarship

Writing Online

The following tools are available online at **thinkcentral.com** and on **WriteSmart CD-ROM:**
- Interactive Graphic Organizers
- Interactive Student Models
- Interactive Revision Lessons

Writing Workshop

ARGUMENT

Persuasive Letter

Have you ever read or heard a persuasive argument that inspired you to act on an issue or cause? Strong persuasive writing can often sway people to adopt a different point of view. In this workshop, you will write a letter that convinces others to accept and take action on a proposal.

 Complete the workshop activities in your **Reader/Writer Notebook.**

WRITE WITH A PURPOSE

WRITING TASK

Write a **persuasive letter** in the form of a proposal to an organization or group. You will need to conduct some research to find evidence that supports your proposal. Use a standard business-letter format.

Idea Starters
- propose a community project
- propose a student advisory board for the school cafeteria
- propose a new city law

THE ESSENTIALS

Here are some common purposes, audiences, and formats for persuasive proposals.

PURPOSES	AUDIENCES	FORMATS
• to persuade people to agree with your claim • to motivate others to take action	• company or organization • school board • community members • local officials	• business letters • proposals • project plans • speeches • blogs • documentaries

COMMON CORE TRAITS

1. DEVELOPMENT OF IDEAS
- includes an **introduction** that identifies an issue and states a **precise claim**
- fairly develops the claim with **valid reasons** and **relevant evidence,** using **research**
- anticipates and addresses **questions, concerns,** and **opposing claims**
- offers a **concluding section** that follows from and supports the claim

2. ORGANIZATION OF IDEAS
- establishes **clear, logical relationships** among claims, reasons, and evidence
- uses **transitions** to create cohesion and link ideas

3. LANGUAGE FACILITY AND CONVENTIONS
- maintains a **formal style** and **objective tone**
- uses the **active voice** for strong and **clear writing**
- employs correct **grammar, punctuation,** and **spelling**

Writing Online

Go to **thinkcentral.com.**
KEYWORD: HML10N-610

Writing Workshop Resources

R **RESOURCE MANAGER UNIT 5**
Plan and Teach, pp. 185–188
Prewriting–Editing, pp. 189–193
Writing Rubric, p. 194
Speaking and Listening, p. 195
Writing Support, p. 196*

BEST PRACTICES TOOLKIT
Mapping Main Ideas and Details, pp. C6, C46
Business Writing: Letter, p. C41

TECHNOLOGY
- **Teacher One Stop DVD-ROM**
- **Student One Stop DVD-ROM**
- **WriteSmart CD-ROM**
- **GrammarNotes DVD-ROM**

Writing Center on thinkcentral.com

*See resources on the **Teacher One Stop DVD-ROM** and on **thinkcentral.com.***

* Resources for Differentiation

Planning/Prewriting

 **COMMON CORE** **W 1a–e** Write arguments to support claims, using valid reasoning and relevant and sufficient evidence. **W 5** Develop and strengthen writing as needed by planning. **W 7** Conduct research to answer a question.

Getting Started

CHOOSE AN ISSUE

For your persuasive letter, consider a **substantive issue**—one that matters to a substantial number of people. List a few issues that matter to you. Consider issues that inspire strong differences in opinion; a persuasive piece of writing addresses opposing viewpoints, not issues on which most people already agree.

▶ **ASK YOURSELF:**

- Which issue do I care about the most?
- What possible proposal can I think of to address this issue?
- What reasons can I think of to support my proposal?
- What are some opposing opinions that other people might have?

THINK ABOUT AUDIENCE AND PURPOSE

As you think about your topic more deeply, keep in mind your **purpose**—to convince your **audience** to accept your proposal. To be successful, you need to consider your audience's **knowledge about the topic** and anticipate their potential **concerns**.

▶ **ASK YOURSELF:**

- Who is my audience? What do I want my audience to believe or do?
- What concerns might my audience have? How will my proposal look from their point of view?
- What background information might my audience need?
- What aspects of the issue might my audience want to know more about?

RESEARCH YOUR AUDIENCE

Once you have determined the issue and your proposal, you need to **identify** the specific person, department, and office location to which you will address your letter. The more **specific** you can get, the more precisely you can target your proposal to that audience.

▶ **WHAT DOES IT LOOK LIKE?**

What department in this organization handles proposals?	City Council Members/ City of Cary
What is the office for this department located?	212 Academy Street Cary, NC 27511
Who could address my proposal?	City Council Members

STATE YOUR CLAIM

Confidently and precisely state your proposal in a **claim**. Make sure your claim can be supported by valid **reasons**. If you discover that there are no substantial arguments to back up your claim, then you should rework it or try a new approach.

▶ **WHAT DOES IT LOOK LIKE?**

| **Claim:** The city needs a skate park. |
| **Reason #1:** Teenagers need a place to skate that's safe and fun. |
| **Reason #2:** A good location is available. |
| **Reason #3:** Skate parks have many positive effects. |

DIFFERENTIATED INSTRUCTION

FOR ENGLISH LANGUAGE LEARNERS

Language: Reinforce Persuasive Terms Review terms students need to know to write a persuasive letter. Make sure that students understand the words' meanings, especially words that have multiple meanings, such as *argument* and *claim*.

argument: a statement for or against an issue or idea

claim: a statement that proposes a particular action or idea

logical: reasonable and valid

opinion: a belief

opposing: different or opposite

persuasive: convincing

viewpoint: the way a person sees or interprets an issue

Teach

Planning/ Prewriting

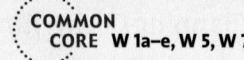 **COMMON CORE W 1a–e, W 5, W 7**

▶ **CHOOSE AN ISSUE** Review the task, and emphasize that students' persuasive letters will propose, or suggest, a project of some kind. Tell students to list interests they have that might lead to a proposal. Then have students brainstorm creative ideas they could propose in each area of interest.

▶ **THINK ABOUT AUDIENCE AND PURPOSE** Point out that although the audience of a persuasive letter is usually a specific person or group, the writer usually does not know the recipient personally. Explain that the information students gather about their audience will be factual, not personal, and related to the proposal itself. Remind students that they may need to provide their audience some background information about the issue addressed in their letters.

▶ **RESEARCH YOUR AUDIENCE** Identify print and online sources students can consult to find the information they need to address and send their letters.

▶ **STATE YOUR CLAIM** To help students identify their claims, have them respond to these questions in one sentence:

- Why am I writing this letter?
- What do I hope to accomplish?

Remind students that their claims should appear in the first paragraph of their persuasive letters.

R RESOURCE MANAGER—Copy Masters
  Planning / Prewriting p. 189
  Drafting p. 190
  Revising pp. 191–192
  Editing p. 193
  Rubric p. 194
  Writing Support p. 196

Planning/Prewriting *continued*

▶ **GATHER SUPPORT FOR YOUR CLAIM** Tell students that an effective persuasive letter is brief—often only one page in length—which means it must include only the most important information about a topic, without repetition. As students identify main ideas and important details to include in their letters, encourage them to think about information that their audiences need to know about their topics.

▶ **ANTICIPATE READER CONCERNS** Emphasize that by anticipating recipients' questions and concerns, students can strengthen their claims and the chances that the claims will be adopted. To identify questions their audiences might have, suggest that students consider general concerns about the topics they have chosen and formulate them as questions. Then have students jot down notes about how they would answer each question.

YOUR TURN Give students time to choose their topics, gather relevant information about their audiences, state their claims, and identify reasons and evidence that support those claims. Then, to help students better address audience concerns, have them write down anticipated questions along with possible responses.

For interactive graphic organizers, see

Write*Smart* CD-ROM

Writing Center on thinkcentral.com

Planning/Prewriting *continued*

Getting Started

GATHER SUPPORT FOR YOUR CLAIM

To be convincing, you need to provide **evidence** that supports your claim and anticipates the audience's **concerns**. Research the issue to find evidence that clearly supports your claim and strengthens the argument you are presenting.

▶ **WHAT DOES IT LOOK LIKE?**

> I. Evidence that a good location is available
>   A. Vacant lot owned by Calvin Davis, Cary businessman
>   B. Owner wants to deed land to city
>   C. Lot is large and is on city bus line

ANTICIPATE READER CONCERNS

Consider any **questions**, **concerns**, or **opposing** (alternate) **claims** that your audience might raise. Your letter must anticipate your readers' questions and address their concerns with informed responses. Clearly distinguish your claim from opposing ones and explain the limitations of other viewpoints.

▶ **WHAT DOES IT LOOK LIKE?**

Questions/Opposing Claims	My Response
Where will the city get money to build a skate park?	Contributions from local businesses, park passes sold to users
Skate parks aren't safe.	Post rules ("Wear a helmet," "Park closes at dusk")

PEER REVIEW Share with a classmate the claims, reasons, and evidence you have outlined. Explain the anticipated concerns your readers might have and how you plan to address them. Discuss the limitations and strengths of your arguments.

YOUR TURN In your *Reader/Writer Notebook*, develop your writing plan. Write a sentence that explains the purpose of your persuasive letter. Then, use an outline to organize your claim and its supporting reasons and evidence. Consider the following tips:

- Make sure your claim is precise enough to clearly distinguish it from alternate or opposing claims.
- Research the issue and make sure that any evidence and information you use is accurate. Consider all valid arguments for and against your claim. Write down all reasons and evidence that strengthen your claim, and respond to opposing ones.
- Clearly show the relationships between your claim and the reasons and evidence you use in your argument.

DIFFERENTIATED INSTRUCTION

FOR ENGLISH LANGUAGE LEARNERS

Writing: Types of Details List the different types of supporting evidence on the board and discuss each. Remind students that background information includes the basic facts a recipient needs to know about a topic, that examples include specific instances or illustrations, and that explanations include reasons and their supporting details. Point out that A and B in the outline provide background information about the lot's location and the owner's intention, while C offers an explanation as to why that location would be good for a public skate park. Together, the three points support the claim that a good location is available. Encourage students to support their claims with a variety of evidence.

FOR STRUGGLING WRITERS

Map Main Ideas and Details Instead of an outline, have students use Mapping Main Ideas and Details to organize the main ideas they will present and the details they will cite to support each idea. Model how to use a graphic organizer to map main ideas and supporting ideas using the main idea and details about the location on Mockingbird Lane shown in outline form.

 BEST PRACTICES TOOLKIT— Transparency Mapping Main Ideas and Details, pp. C6, C46

Drafting

COMMON CORE

W 4 Produce clear and coherent writing in which the development, organization, and style are appropriate to task, purpose, and audience.
L 1 Demonstrate command of the conventions of standard English grammar and usage.

This chart shows how to organize a persuasive letter. For proper formatting of a business letter, see pages 615–616.

Organizing Your Persuasive Letter

INTRODUCTION

- Introduce yourself and then provide relevant **background information** as necessary.
- State your **claim** precisely, and explain why you are writing the letter.

▼

BODY

- Support your claim with **valid reasoning** and **relevant** and **sufficient evidence** from your research.
- Present ideas in a **logical order** that clearly establishes relationships between claims, reasons, and evidence.
- Address reader questions and concerns by providing a well-informed response. Acknowledge any anticipated **opposing claims** and explain their limitations.
- Use **transitions**—words, phrases, and clauses such as *furthermore* or *for example*—to create **cohesion**, or flow.
- Maintain a **formal style** with a confident voice. Use an **objective**, or unbiased, **tone** that isn't defensive.

▼

CONCLUDING SECTION

- **Restate** your claim, and remind members of your audience why their support matters.
- End with a **call to action** telling readers what to do to support your claim.

GRAMMAR IN CONTEXT: ACTIVE AND PASSIVE VOICE

Voice is the form certain verbs take to indicate whether the subject of the verb performs or receives the action. When the subject of the verb performs the action, the verb is in the **active** voice. When the subject of a verb receives the action, the verb is in the **passive** voice. Using verbs in the active voice will help make the writing in your persuasive letter clear, concise, and direct. Notice the differences between the following sentences.

Active Voice	Passive Voice
To keep people safe, most cities and towns **post** rules that skate-park users must follow.	To keep people safe, rules that skate-park users must follow **are posted** by most cities and towns.

The sentence in the active voice emphasizes the subject, "most cities and towns." The active voice makes the sentence stronger and more concise than the sentence in the passive voice.

 YOUR TURN Develop a first draft of your letter, following the structure outlined in the *Organizing Your Persuasive Letter* chart above. As you write, use the active voice wherever possible and appropriate.

FOR ENGLISH LANGUAGE LEARNERS

Active and Passive Voice Help students differentiate between the active and passive voice:

- A verb in the active voice has a direct object, which tells who or what receives the action.

Example: The city built a <u>skate park</u>.

- A verb in the passive voice does not have a direct object but is often followed by prepositional phrase that begins with *by*, which tells who or what performs the action.

Example: A skate park was built <u>by the city</u>.

Discuss the subject and verb and direct object or object of a preposition in the examples.

FOR STRUGGLING WRITERS

Discuss Content Have students meet with partners to discuss the organization and content of their persuasive letters. Students should take turns sharing the introductions, bodies, and concluding sections of their letters. Listening partners should provide feedback and offer suggestions on how to improve the way information is presented.

Practice and Apply

Drafting

COMMON CORE W 4, L 1

▶ **INTRODUCTION** Tell students that the first paragraph is the most important part of a persuasive letter; the first paragraph explains the letter's purpose to its audience. Remind students to express the purpose and claim in clear, concise language. Have students locate the writer's statement of purpose and claim in the Student Draft on page 615.

▶ **BODY** With students, skim the body paragraphs in the Student Draft on pages 615–616, pointing out that each paragraph focuses on a main idea (i.e., location of a skate park, questions about a skate park, benefits of a skate park). Observe that in some cases all the information in the body of a persuasive letter can be conveyed in a single paragraph.

▶ **CONCLUDING SECTION** Emphasize the importance of expressing thanks to the letter's recipient, as well as of explaining why his or her support matters. Have students locate the writer's expression of appreciation on page 616 of the Student Draft. Point out that it closes the letter on a courteous and respectful note.

GRAMMAR IN CONTEXT: ACTIVE AND PASSIVE VOICE

For additional practice, have students write the following sentences in the active voice.

- Many young people in our city are attracted to skateboarding. [*Skateboarding attracts many young people in our city.*]
- Money to build a skate park has been contributed by local businesses. [*Local businesses have contributed money to build a skate park.*]

 YOUR TURN Ask students to complete the **Your Turn** activity independently. Remind students to use the active voice wherever possible and appropriate. Suggest that students double-space their drafts so that they can make revisions more easily later.

For a business letter writing template, see

 BEST PRACTICES TOOLKIT— Transparency
Business Writing: Letter, p. C41

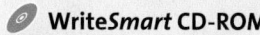 **Write*Smart* CD-ROM**
Writing Center on <u>thinkcentral.com</u>

Revising

Model the Skill Using a draft on a transparency or electronic whiteboard, model how to use the questions, tips, and strategies suggested in the chart to evaluate and revise. You might use a student's persuasive letter or a persuasive letter of your own. If you use the former, be sure to remove the student's name so that he or she is anonymous.

YOUR TURN Before exchanging drafts, have students write a short note to their partners about the parts of their persuasive letter they consider weak and would like help with. After reading, tell students to begin their feedback to their partners with a positive comment. Remind students not to tell their partners what to do but to ask questions and make suggestions, instead. Emphasize that students do not need to make revisions based on every suggestion their partners offer.

For interactive revision tools, see

WriteSmart CD-ROM

Writing Center on thinkcentral.com

Revising

As you revise, consider the stated claim, main reasons, supporting evidence, and organization of your persuasive letter. The goal is to determine whether you've achieved your purpose and effectively communicated your ideas to your intended audience. The questions, tips, and strategies in the following chart will help you revise your draft and rewrite where necessary.

PERSUASIVE LETTER

Ask Yourself	Tips	Revision Strategies
1. Are my purpose and claim clearly and precisely stated in the first paragraph?	▶ **Put a wavy line** under the sentence that states the claim.	▶ **Add or revise** the first paragraph to state your purpose and claim clearly and precisely.
2. Are there at least two valid reasons that support the claim? Is each reason sufficiently supported by relevant evidence?	▶ **Underline** each reason. **Circle** each piece of evidence and **draw an arrow** to the reason it supports.	▶ **Add** valid reasons or **revise** existing ones to make your position clear. **Add** relevant evidence to ensure you have sufficient support for your claim.
3. Does the organization of my letter establish clear relationships among ideas?	▶ **Label** claims, reasons, and evidence by sequence or in order of importance.	▶ **Rearrange** your text to follow an order of importance or a logical sequence.
4. Are audience concerns and opposing claims anticipated and addressed with persuasive responses?	▶ **Put a bracket** around any question, concern, or opposing claim. **Put a check mark** next to your response.	▶ **Add** sentences that identify audience concerns and address the opposing claims with a well-informed response.
5. Do I use appropriate transitions to clearly establish relationships among related parts of the argument?	▶ **Put a star** next to each transition.	▶ **Add** transitional words or phrases that smoothly link and clarify relationships among major sections of the text.
6. Does the concluding section restate the claim and include a call to action?	▶ **Put a box** around the restatement of the claim. **Highlight** the call to action.	▶ **Add** a sentence that restates your claim. **Add** a call to action if one is missing.

YOUR TURN **PEER REVIEW** Exchange your persuasive letter with a classmate, or read it aloud to your partner. As you read and comment on each other's letters, focus on the stated claim, the reasoning and supporting evidence, and the argument's organization. Decide if the letter follows the formal style and format of a business letter. Give each other concrete suggestions for improvement, using the revision strategies in the chart.

DIFFERENTIATED INSTRUCTION

FOR ENGLISH LANGUAGE LEARNERS

Writing: Concluding Section Remind students that *gratitude* means "thanks." Discuss ways students can express their thanks to the recipients of their persuasive letters. Write these statements on the board:

- Thank you for your time/attention/consideration.
- Thank you for considering the ideas I have proposed/suggested.

FOR STRUGGLING WRITERS

Use Color Have students use colored pens or pencils when commenting on their partners' drafts. Colored comments will help make suggestions stand out. (Students may wish to avoid using red so that their partners do not feel their drafts are being corrected.) Students may also wish to use Color Coding when revising their own drafts.

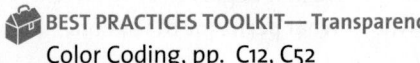

BEST PRACTICES TOOLKIT— Transparency
Color Coding, pp. C12, C52

ANALYZE A STUDENT DRAFT

Read this draft; notice the comments on its strengths as well as suggestions for improvement.

COMMON CORE

W 1d Maintain a formal style. **W 5** Strengthen writing by revising or editing. **L 1** Demonstrate command of the conventions of standard grammar and usage. **L 3** Use knowledge of language to make effective choices for meaning or style.

623 Harmony Drive
Cary, NC 27519

April 14, 2011

City Council Members
City of Cary
212 Academy St.
Cary, NC 27511

Dear City Council Members:

❶ As a teenaged skateboarder, I have often searched online to find the nearest skate park. There are very few skate parks in our area, so many avid skateboarders get totally bored. The solution to this problem is to create a skate park in our city. To you, this may sound a bit crazy, but please share this letter at the next council meeting and consider building a skate park in our city.

❷ There is an excellent location for a skate park on Mockingbird Lane. A Cary businessman, Calvin Davis, owns a vacant lot there. In a recent newspaper interview, Mr. Davis said he will not build on the lot himself. Instead, he wants to deed the land to the city of Cary. The lot would be great place for a skate park. Not only is it big, but it is also on the bus line, so young people could get there.

The heading, inside address, and salutation follow correct business letter **formatting**.

The author clearly states her **purpose** and her **claim** in the opening paragraph, but she needs to replace some words and phrases with more *formal diction*.

In this body paragraph, the author concisely presents a **reason** and **supporting evidence** for her proposal about building a skate park.

LEARN HOW Use Formal Diction Diction is a writer's choice of words, phrases, and sentence structures. When writing a persuasive letter, use formal diction and eliminate any slang. To correct errors in diction, read your draft aloud. If a word or phrase sounds like you would say it to a friend in casual conversation, replace it.

MARTI'S REVISION TO PARAGRAPH ❶

. . . There are very few skate parks in our area, so many avid skateboarders ~~get totally bored~~. *do not have* The solution to this problem is to create a skate park in *an exciting* Cary. ~~To you, this may sound a bit crazy, but~~ please share this letter at the *and safe* next council meeting and consider building a skate park in our city. *place to skate.*

ANALYZE A STUDENT DRAFT

Explain that the Student Draft on this page is the first half of a persuasive letter. Model reading the draft and the annotations in blue, and explain that the yellow highlighting illustrates the student's language choices. Explain that the following *Learn How* mini-lessons provide helpful information about ways to improve this student draft as well as their own.

LEARN HOW Use Formal Diction

- Tell students that proper diction helps ensure that the recipient takes the persuasive letter seriously.

- Explain to students that using formal language and sentence structures will also improve the tone of their writing. Ask students why the revisions to the student's draft sound better.

- Point out that in revising, the student writer deleted informal words and phrases that echoed the sound of casual conversation and replaced them with more formal language.

FOR ENGLISH LANGUAGE LEARNERS

Use Formal Diction Pair English language learners with students who are fluent in English. Have English language learners read aloud their drafts to their partners. As they read, their partners should listen for words and phrases and sentence structures that sound too casual for a business letter. Have listening partners offer specific suggestions about deleting or replacing words or phrases or revising sentences to create a more formal, serious tone.

FOR ADVANCED LEARNERS/PRE–AP

Write a Procedural Document Have students work in pairs or small groups to draft a set of instructions or a procedural guide for use by community members. Remind students to use a logical order and reader-friendly formatting to present information. Then, have students write a persuasive letter to frame and present the document to community leaders or local officials.

Explain that the Student Draft is continued and completed on this page. Read the draft and annotations aloud and discuss. Ask students to comment on the student writer's anticipation of readers' questions.

LEARN HOW Write an Effective Concluding Section

- Explain that although the writer restates the purpose of the letter and expresses appreciation to her audience, her concluding section is weak because she does not tell the letter's recipients where they can go for more information.

- Point out that the details the student writer added to the letter provide specific contact information. The writer gives the name and address of the owner of the empty lot on Mockingbird Lane.

- Have students review the concluding section in their own drafts to make sure that in addition to including a summary of their purpose and claim in writing and an expression of thanks to the recipients, it tells them where they can get more information on the topic.

YOUR TURN Ask students to complete the **Your Turn** activity independently. Tell them to find two places in their drafts where conversational or informal diction is used and rewrite these sentences using formal English. Also direct students to evaluate the effectiveness of their concluding section by asking these questions: Have I wrapped up my key points? Did I express gratitude to the recipients? Did I tell the recipients where they can find additional information?

For interactive revision tools, see

Write*Smart* **CD-ROM**

Writing Center on thinkcentral.com

---

3 Finding a location for a skate park is not enough, however. A lot of other questions have to be answered. For example, where will the city find money to build a skate park? How can the city protect the safety of users of the park? We can get some answers from cities and towns that already have skate parks. In some places, local businesses have contributed money to build a skate park. Other cities and towns continue to pay for skate parks after they are built by requiring people to buy passes to use them. To keep people safe, most cities and towns post rules (such as "Wear a helmet," or "Park closes at dusk") that skate-park users must follow.

> Marti anticipates city council members' concerns and **opposing opinions** and provides a response.

4 Finally, studies show that sports have a positive effect on young people. A skate park would have the following benefits for our city's youth:
- It would give teens a chance to be outdoors and get exercise.
- It would give teens something to do after school and on weekends.
- It would keep teens out of trouble.

> The bulleted list is reader-friendly **formatting** that clearly presents more **reasons** that strengthen the claim.

5 We need to build a skate park in our community.

6 I hope that with the information I have provided, you will consider building a skate park in Cary. Thank you for your attention.

> In the concluding section, Marti restates her claim, but fails to include a call to action.

Sincerely,
Marti Borland
Marti Borland

LEARN HOW Write an Effective Concluding Section A persuasive letter should convince readers that an issue is important enough to merit action. Marti revises this section to show where readers can get more information.

MARTI'S REVISION TO PARAGRAPH 5

We need to build a skate park in our community. *As the owner of the empty lot, Calvin Davis would be interested in this plan. He can be reached at 900 Mockingbird Lane, Cary.*

YOUR TURN Use the feedback from your peers and teacher as well as the two "Learn How" lessons to revise your persuasive letter. Evaluate how clearly, concisely, and accurately you have presented and organized information.

DIFFERENTIATED INSTRUCTION

FOR STRUGGLING WRITERS

Anticipate Questions If students have difficulty anticipating recipients' questions about the topics of their persuasive letters, have them read their drafts aloud in small groups. Then have group members brainstorm unanswered questions about the topic of each letter. As students revise their drafts, tell them to respond to at least two of the questions suggested by members of the group.

Editing and Publishing

COMMON CORE

W 5 Strengthen writing as needed by editing. L 2 Demonstrate command of the conventions of standard English capitalization, punctuation, and spelling. L 2c Spell correctly.

In the editing stage, check your persuasive letter to make sure you use correct spelling, punctuation, and grammar. Careless spelling mistakes can detract from the credibility of the information you provide and may prevent you from achieving your purpose in writing.

GRAMMAR IN CONTEXT: USING DASHES TO EMPHASIZE PARENTHETICAL INFORMATION

Parentheses are often used in a sentence to include examples or other explanatory information. When you want to emphasize or draw attention to examples and explanations, however, use dashes to set off the information.

As Marti edits her letter, she notices a sentence where she could use dashes to include and emphasize parenthetical information.

> To keep people safe, most cities and towns post rules (such as "Wear a helmet," or "Park closes at dusk") that skate-park users must follow.

PUBLISH YOUR WRITING

Here are some options for sharing your persuasive letter with an audience:
- Send the letter to the addressee.
- Display your letter in school, or post it to a school-sponsored Web page.
- Turn your letter into an informative demonstration or presentation.
- Produce a documentary by videotaping interviews with people who provide evidence that supports your claim.

 YOUR TURN Proofread your persuasive letter, correcting misspellings and any other errors in conventions. Use dashes where appropriate to emphasize examples or explanatory information. Then, send, display, or post your letter.

Editing and Publishing

COMMON CORE W 5, L 2, L 2c

GRAMMAR IN CONTEXT: USING DASHES TO EMPHASIZE PARENTHETICAL INFORMATION

Stress that dashes are used to draw attention to information. For practice, in the following sentences, have students replace the parentheses with dashes to emphasize parenthetical information:

- Responsible skateboarders use equipment (such as a helmet, elbow pads, and knee pads) to stay safe.
- Skate park locations suggested in the past (Morgan Street and Bristol Drive) are less convenient because they are not near a bus stop.
- These ideas for raising money for a skate park (contributions from local businesses and park passes) have been successful in other cities and towns.

PUBLISH YOUR WRITING

Brainstorm with students additional ways to publish their persuasive letters.

 YOUR TURN Allow students time to proofread their drafts. Remind them to use dashes where appropriate to include and emphasize parenthetical information. Also remind students to use the active voice wherever possible and appropriate, to make their writing concise and clear.

FOR ENGLISH LANGUAGE LEARNERS

Using Dashes to Emphasize Parenthetical Information Point out that commas, parentheses, and dashes all can be used to mark a break in the thought expressed in a sentence and to set off additional information. Offer students these explanations:

- Commas frequently set off appositives and appositive phrases that identify or explain a noun or pronoun but do not affect the meaning of a sentence.

Example: Mr. Davis, a local businessman, owns an empty lot that would be perfect for a skate park.

- Parentheses usually signal information that is not of major importance in a sentence.

Example: Mockingbird Lane (a quiet suburban street) is located on the city bus line.

- Dashes often draw attention to examples, explanations, and other information of interest.

Example: I urge you to look into this great location—Mockingbird Lane—as soon as possible.

Scoring Rubric

Tell students that the best way to understand a scoring rubric is to use it to score actual writing. Have students use the rubric to evaluate the final copy of the persuasive letter they wrote in the Writing Workshop. Ask them to score their writing and then write a brief paragraph using the language of the rubric to explain the reasons for their score.

For Rubric Bank, see

WriteSmart CD-ROM

Writing Center on **thinkcentral.com**

Assess and Reteach

Assess

R RESOURCE MANAGER—Copy Master
Rubric for Evaluation p. 194

Online Essay Scoring on **thinkcentral.com**

Reteach

Level Up Online Tutorials on **thinkcentral.com**

Reteaching Worksheets on **thinkcentral.com**

    Writing Lesson 3: Thinking About Purpose, Audience, and Form (RAFT)

    Informational Texts Lessons 18–19

Scoring Rubric

Use the rubric below to evaluate your persuasive letter from the Writing Workshop or your response to the on-demand task on the next page.

PERSUASIVE LETTER

SCORE	COMMON CORE TRAITS
	• **Development** States a precise claim on a substantive topic; supports the claim with valid reasons and relevant evidence; ably addresses reader concerns and opposing claims; ends with a call to action • **Organization** Is logically organized to persuasive effect; uses transitions to create cohesion and show relationships among the claim, reasons, and evidence • **Language** Consistently maintains a formal style and objective tone; shows a strong command of conventions
	• **Development** States a precise claim on an interesting topic; offers valid reasons and evidence; responds to reader concerns and opposing claims; ends with a call to action • **Organization** Is logically organized; uses transitions to show the relationships among the claim, reasons, and evidence • **Language** Uses a formal style and objective tone; has a few errors in conventions
	• **Development** States a clear claim; offers mostly valid support; needs to more thoroughly address reader concerns; has an adequate concluding section • **Organization** Presents a logical organization, with one or two exceptions; could use a few more transitions • **Language** Mostly uses a formal style, but sounds defensive at times; includes a few distracting errors in conventions
	• **Development** Makes a broad claim; provides some relevant support but not enough; dismisses other viewpoints without response; includes a vague call to action • **Organization** Has some flaws in organization; needs more transitions to show how parts of the text relate • **Language** Often lapses into an informal style or defensive tone; has several errors in conventions
	• **Development** Has a weak claim; offers irrelevant reasons and insufficient evidence; fails to acknowledge other viewpoints; has no call to action • **Organization** Has major organizational flaws; lacks transitions throughout • **Language** Uses an informal style and defensive tone; has many errors in conventions
	• **Development** Lacks a claim; provides no support; ignores potential reader concerns and opposing claims; ends abruptly • **Organization** Has no organization and transitions • **Language** Uses an inappropriate style and tone; has major problems with grammar, mechanics, and spelling

Preparing for Timed Writing

COMMON CORE **W 10** Write routinely over shorter time frames for a range of tasks, purposes, and audiences.

1. ANALYZE THE TASK · 5 MIN

Read the task carefully. Then, read it again, noting the words in the task that tell the type of writing, the topic, the audience, and the purpose.

WRITING TASK *Type of writing* *Audience* *Purpose*

Write a <u>persuasive letter</u> to a <u>company</u> to <u>convince them to invest in a product or service that you are sure will be very profitable for the company.</u> Use your imagination to make up a product and/or company name if necessary. *Possible topics*

2. PLAN YOUR RESPONSE · 10 MIN

The task asks you to persuade a company about the value of your product or service. Ask yourself: What is the product or service? What reasons do I have for writing to this company? What evidence do I have to show that the product or service will be profitable? Record your ideas in a chart.

Product/Service:	
Reasons:	Evidence:

3. RESPOND TO THE TASK · 20 MIN

Begin drafting your letter. As you write, also follow these tips:

- Precisely state your claim in the first paragraph of the letter.
- In the body paragraphs, describe your product or service and the reasons you think it is appropriate for the company. Include accurate evidence to support your claim. Anticipate the company's concerns and offer a response.
- In the last paragraph, ask the company's representative to respond.

4. IMPROVE YOUR RESPONSE · 5–10 MIN

Revising Compare your draft with the task. Does your draft include introductory, body, and concluding paragraphs? Is your claim logically developed with valid reasons and sufficient evidence? Do you address opposing claims? Is your tone formal and objective? Do you end with a call to action?

Proofreading Take the remaining time to find and correct any errors in grammar, punctuation, or spelling.

Checking Your Final Copy Read your letter a final time to make sure that all your edits are neat and that your letter is legible.

COMMON CORE FOCUS

W 10 Write routinely over shorter time frames for a range of tasks, purposes, and audiences.

Preparing for Timed Writing

1. **Analyze the Task** Before students begin writing, encourage them to answer the following questions:
   - What is my time limit?
   - What are the core traits assessed in the scoring rubric?
   - Who is my audience?
   - What is my purpose?

2. **Plan Your Response** Point out that the scoring rubric emphasizes the importance of showing a clear purpose for writing. Tell students to identify a topic, reasons, and support by using a chart like the one shown. Remind students to state the purpose in the first paragraph of their letters.

3. **Respond to the Task** Remind students to provide accurate and logical evidence that supports the claim, to anticipate any opposing arguments, and to include a call to action.

4. **Improve Your Response** Observe that the scoring rubric emphasizes using appropriate diction. Tell students to set aside a few minutes of their writing time to review word choice and sentence structure in their letters to ensure that their diction sets and maintains an appropriate tone for their audiences and purposes.

Assess

Use the Scoring Rubric on page 618 to assess students' letters.

DIFFERENTIATED INSTRUCTION

FOR ENGLISH LANGUAGE LEARNERS

Writing: Analyzing Tasks Read the task aloud to students and make sure they understand the type of writing, purpose, audience, and topic. If necessary, restate the task so that students fully understand what they are being asked to do. Discuss any words or phrases in the task that students may not fully understand, such as *company, product, service,* and *value*.

FOR STRUGGLING WRITERS

List and Discuss Reasons Explain to students that their letters must identify and thoroughly explain how their product or service will benefit the company. Remind students to use a chart like the one shown to identify the reasons and evidence they need to back up their claims. Tell students that they may discuss all the reasons in a single body paragraph and then discuss the evidence, or they can devote a body paragraph to a discussion of each reason supported by evidence.

Focus and Motivate

COMMON CORE FOCUS

SL 1a, c Come to discussions prepared; propel conversations by posing and responding to questions and incorporating others in the discussion. **L1** Demonstrate command of standard English grammar and usage when speaking.

SPEAK WITH A PURPOSE

Tell students that interviewing an expert, the person who is the subject of one's research, or an eyewitness is an excellent way to gather information on a topic. Explain that an interview often yields information that is not available from other sources. Emphasize that the success of an interview depends on carefully prepared questions that are relevant to the topic and follow-up questions that ask for clarification or elaboration.

COMMON CORE TRAITS

As students prepare to conduct their interviews, remind them to keep in mind the *COMMON CORE TRAITS* of a strong interview.

Practice and Apply

Planning the Interview

Model the Skill: PREPARE QUESTIONS

Point out that a good interviewer asks questions that elicit, or draw out, the most information. Tell students that they can prepare for an interview by thinking about what they want to know and then phrasing questions that will elicit informative responses. Model how to phrase interview questions. Explain that instead of asking a yes or no question such as "Did you enjoy the experience?" or "Did you learn from the experience?" you might ask, "What was the best part of the experience?" or "What did you learn from the experience?"

GUIDED PRACTICE Have students prepare a list of five questions for their interviews. Remind students to prepare questions that cannot be answered with single-word responses such as *yes* or *no*.

R RESOURCE MANAGER—Copy Master
Speaking and Listening, p. 195

Speaking & Listening Workshop

Conducting an Interview

Essential Course of Study ECOS

Where do you go to get evidence that you can use to support an argument? You can choose from many print and online resources. Sometimes, however, your best source for interesting or accurate information is an **interview** with an expert on a subject, a person who is the topic of your research, or someone who was an eyewitness to an event or has firsthand knowledge of your topic.

 Complete the workshop activities in your **Reader/Writer Notebook**.

SPEAK WITH A PURPOSE	*COMMON CORE TRAITS*
TASK Conduct an **interview** with someone who has expert knowledge or firsthand experience to obtain support for your claim. Ask prepared questions, listen carefully to your interviewee's responses, and follow up by asking for clarification or elaboration.	**TO CONDUCT A STRONG INTERVIEW, YOU . . .** • demonstrate knowledge of the topic • pose questions that relate to the topic • listen carefully and respond appropriately • ask for clarification or elaboration of responses • take accurate notes • use appropriate language and grammar

COMMON CORE

SL 1a, c Come to discussions prepared; propel conversations by posing and responding to questions and incorporating others in the discussion. **L1** Demonstrate command of standard English grammar and usage when speaking.

Planning the Interview

Use these tips to plan your interview:

• **Identify an Interviewee** Think about what you want or need to know about your topic. Then, brainstorm people to interview. Narrow your list to two or three people you would be interested in interviewing. Work through your short list of possible interviewees until one agrees to be interviewed.

• **Make Arrangements** Use a checklist to make arrangements. Bring along a friend or family member if you do not personally know the interviewee.

  ❑ Set up a mutually convenient time and place to meet. Choose a quiet place where there will be no distractions or interruptions.

  ❑ Set up a time to speak by phone if it is not convenient to conduct the interview in person.

  ❑ Ask for permission ahead of time if you plan to record or videotape the interview.

  ❑ Remember to be courteous and thank the person for agreeing to be interviewed.

• **Prepare Questions** Think about what you hope to learn from the person you will interview. Before the interview, review your research and reread any material that might be relevant. If applicable, do research to learn more about your interviewee's experience. Avoid creating a script, but write a few open-ended questions to start the conversation. Phrase questions so that they will elicit, or draw out, the most information. Be sure to ask questions that relate to your topic, and avoid questions with answers that could easily be looked up or found elsewhere.

THINK central
Speaking & Listening Online
Go to **thinkcentral.com**.
KEYWORD: HML10-620

DIFFERENTIATED INSTRUCTION

FOR ENGLISH LANGUAGE LEARNERS
Language: Reinforce Interview Terms Clarify key terms used in this workshop:

• *interview:* a conversational situation in which one person gathers information from another person

• *interviewer:* the person asking questions in an interview

• *interviewee:* the person responding to questions in an interview

• *expert:* a person with special knowledge of a subject

• *eyewitness:* a person who sees or is present at an event

• *elaboration:* adding information in the form of facts, statistics, examples, explanations

• *clarification:* making information clear through definitions or explanations

• *script:* a written text for an interview or other oral presentation

• *technique:* a way of doing something

Conducting the Interview

Follow these suggestions to ask questions and listen responsively:

- **Use Proper Language** Maintain a formal and objective style that uses proper conventions of English grammar, even if the interviewee uses slang or informal language.

- **Vary Your Approach** Use a variety of techniques, questions, and responses to keep the conversation with your interviewee going.

Interview Techniques	Question and Sentence Frames
Invite the interviewee to describe, narrate, explain, evaluate, compare, and reveal.	• What was the sequence of events that led you to _____? • What can you tell me about _____? • What are/were your reasons for _____?
Avoid questions that can be answered with "yes" or "no."	• What do you like best (or least) about _____? [*instead of* Do you like _____?] • What is most challenging about _____? [*instead of* Is that challenging?]
Ask for more detail about a point by using *who, what, where, when, why,* and *how* questions.	• What was the outcome of _____? • Why did you decide to _____? • How do you feel about _____?
Respectfully clarify or challenge ideas if you are having difficulty understanding, need more information, or found research that contradicts the information given.	• What do you mean by _____? • I'm confused by _____. Please clarify. • Please elaborate on your comment about _____.
To prevent possible misunderstandings, pause periodically to summarize, synthesize, or highlight the speaker's ideas.	• Let me summarize what you said about _____. • May I quote you as saying _____? • What I think you said about _____ is _____.

- **Be a Good Listener** Listen attentively, using eye contact and facial expressions to communicate interest. Show respect by not interrupting.

- **Take Notes** Even when recording an interview, take notes, including what you notice about the interviewee's attitude. List key words and phrases that highlight the speaker's ideas. Synthesize the person's main points and examples he or she uses. Accurately quote important information and statements that might be controversial or misunderstood.

- **Wrap Up** Ask your interviewee if there is anything else he or she wants to share. Explain how the conversation has been helpful to you, and thank the interviewee. Then, send the interviewee a thank-you note.

 YOUR TURN Come prepared to pose questions that draw on your research about the topic. Throughout the interview, pay close attention to what your interviewee is saying. Stay on topic and resist the temptation to interrupt.

621

Assessment Practice

CHECK READINESS

Read aloud the paragraph under **ASSESS** and stress to students that this is not the full Unit Test, but a way for them to check their readiness for it. Then have students examine the skills standards listed under **REVIEW** and look back in the unit or in the **Student Resource Bank** for any skills they need to review.

READ THE TEXTS

Remind students to keep unit goals in mind as they read each passage, paying particular attention to these literary and reading skills:

- author's purpose
- author's perspective
- tone

To help students focus on tone while reading, encourage them to ask questions such as

- How would the author read it?
- How does the purpose of each selection provide a clue to its tone?

ANSWER THE QUESTIONS

Direct students to pages R93–R101 of the **Handbook** to review test-taking strategies.

- As students prepare to answer multiple-choice questions, remind them to read through all the choices, eliminate any that are clearly wrong, and then choose the answer that is the most accurate.

- Also remind students not to look for patterns in the answer choices. Writers of assessment questions are careful to avoid such patterns.

COMMON CORE

Assessment Practice

ASSESS
Taking this practice test will help you assess your knowledge of these skills and determine your readiness for the Unit Test.

REVIEW
After you take the practice test, your teacher can help you identify any standards you need to review.

Practice Test **THINK** central

Take it at **thinkcentral.com**.
KEYWORD: HML10N-622

DIRECTIONS Read the following selections, and then answer the questions.

from Spiders Up Close

1   Of the more than 34,000 species of spiders named so far (with another estimated 136,000 yet to be named), all are predators, their bodies designed to catch and consume their prey: insects.

Top-notch Predators

2   Hanging head-down from the hub of her web, the silver argiope (*Argiope argentata*) feels her trap begin to quiver, indicating the presence of prey. Determining direction by the vibration of the radial web spokes, she scrambles toward a grasshopper that is frantically struggling in a sticky thread. Working quickly, she wraps her victim in silk. Then she gives it a paralyzing bite with her jaws, or chelicerae, and regurgitates digestive enzymes that begin to liquefy the insect. Leaving her mummified meal suspended from the web, the spider returns to her control post to wait for more victims.

3   **Ingenious Hunters**   Few creatures have developed more varied techniques to capture their prey than the spider. Although 60 percent of spiders, including the orb-weaving *A. argentata,* fashion some sort of aerial trap with silk, the rest do not spin webs at all but pursue their prey in other deadly ways.

4   A jumping spider (family Salticidae) can leap on its prey from a distance, impaling it with venom-delivering fangs. Its leaping prowess is astonishing, especially considering that it has no enlarged muscular hindlegs to propel it. Researchers suggest that hydrostatic pressure builds up in the legs, suddenly releasing and popping the spider forward—as much as forty times its own body length.

5   Jumping spiders are stalkers like cats, but some spiders simply run down their prey. Wolf spiders (family Lycosidae) have earned their name for their speedy pursuit of prey. The much larger tarantulas are also generally runners, often lurking in underground burrows until they detect vibrations of prey on the soil outside their lair.

6   Bolas spiders (family Araneidae) do their hunting with a short silk thread tipped with a drop of glue; they hold one end of the thread and fling the sticky end at passing prey. To improve their chances, these spiders emit a pheromone that mimics that of female moths; approaching male moths looking for a mate are likely to become lunch instead. . . .

DIFFERENTIATED INSTRUCTION

FOR ENGLISH LANGUAGE LEARNERS
Assessment Practice: Work Backward Prepare students by having them read the questions *before* reading the passages. Have pairs find unfamiliar words in test directions and questions and follow these steps:

1. Write each word on an index card.
2. Look up the meaning in a dictionary and write it on the back of the card.

3. Use the cards to practice words with your partner and to teach them to others.

7   *Dolomedes*, the fishing spiders (family Pisauridae), venture right onto the water surface to hunt, sometimes diving to capture insects and small fish. The surface of the water acts as their web. By touching the water with their legs, these spiders detect vibrations of passing insects. Supported by surface tension, they dash out to subdue prey. The king of the fishers is the water spider (*Argyroneta aquatica*); it weaves an air-filled diving bell out of silk and can remain submerged in the water inside it for weeks.

from How to Write a Letter
by Garrison Keillor

1   A blank white eight-by-eleven sheet can look as big as Montana if the pen's not so hot—try a smaller page and write boldly. Or use a note card with a piece of fine art on the front; if your letter ain't good, at least they get the Matisse. Get a pen that makes a sensuous line, get a comfortable typewriter, a friendly word processor—whichever feels easy to the hand.

2   Sit for a few minutes with the blank sheet in front of you, and meditate on the person you will write to, let your friend come to mind until you can almost see her or him in the room with you. Remember the last time you saw each other and how your friend looked and what you said and what perhaps was unsaid between you, and when your friend becomes real to you, start to write.

3   Write a salutation—*Dear* You—and take a deep breath and plunge in. A simple declarative sentence will do, followed by another and another and another. Tell us what you're doing and tell it like you were talking to us. Don't think about grammar, don't think about lit'ry style, don't try to write dramatically, just give us your news. Where did you go, who did you see, what did they say, what do you think?

4   If you don't know where to begin, start with the present moment: *I'm sitting at the kitchen table on a rainy Saturday morning. Everyone is gone and the house is quiet.* Let your simple description of the present moment lead to something else, let the letter drift gently along.

5   The toughest letter to crank out is one that is meant to impress, as we all know from writing job applications; if it's hard work to slip off a letter to a friend, maybe you're trying too hard to be terrific. A letter is only a report to someone who already likes you for reasons other than your brilliance. Take it easy.

 GO ON

ITEM ANALYSIS

COMPREHENSION AND WRITTEN RESPONSE	ITEMS	UNIT PAGES
Author's Purpose	5, 9, 10, 12	526–531, 539, 603
Author's Perspective	6, 7, 11, 14	526–531, 585
Tone	4, 8, 9, 13	526–531, 533
Patterns of Organization	1, 2, 3	526–531, 539

VOCABULARY	ITEMS	UNIT PAGES
Metaphors and Similes	1, 2, 3, 4, 5	

WRITING AND GRAMMAR	ITEMS	UNIT PAGES
Participles and Participial Phrases	2, 3, 5	547
Adverb Clauses	1, 4	571

 THINK central

Practice Test

On **thinkcentral.com** students can complete an interactive version of this practice test *and* receive remediation for the skills they have not yet mastered.

FOR STRUGGLING READERS

Assessment Support Consider these options for completing the Assessment Practice:

- Have students "work backward" to review the test questions before reading the passages.

- Select random questions in the Assessment and have students demonstrate how and where to look for answers.

- Ask students to locate unfamiliar vocabulary words in the Assessment. Elicit the words' meanings from the class.

- Have students record useful testing words and definitions in their journal for later reference.

- Read the selections or parts of them aloud to aid in student comprehension.

Reading Comprehension

Model a thinking process for answering multiple-choice questions.

1. **C is correct.** *The title and subheadings reflect key ideas. A, B, and D are incorrect because the article contains no captions, footnotes, or boldfaced words.*

2. **D is correct.** *The article examines types of spiders. A is incorrect because the article does not trace causes. B is a weak choice because although several types of spiders are discussed, finding similarities and differences is not the point of the article. C is incorrect because time order is irrelevant to this non-narrative article.*

3. **A is correct.** *The paragraph contrasts spiders that stalk with spiders that run down their prey. B is a weaker choice because the point is to show similarities and differences between the two methods of hunting, not to describe groups. C is a weak choice, for it refers to a paragraph structure that is used in all patterns of organization. D is incorrect because the paragraph does not mention causes and effects of the hunting methods.*

4. **A is correct.** *Expressions such as "Its leaping prowess is astonishing" (paragraph 4) and "have earned their name" (paragraph 5) convey admiration. B is incorrect because the author does not express fear or alarm. C is incorrect because although the subject could be treated in a gloomy way, the author seems happy to discuss spider predation. D is incorrect because the author gives no sign that the essay is other than serious.*

5. **D is correct.** *The author provides unusual information in nearly every sentence, making the article enjoyable reading. A is a weaker choice because although the author probably has positive feelings about spiders, he or she does not express them outright. B is a weak choice because the author does not try to change readers' minds or make them take action. C is incorrect because the author conveys facts about spiders without revealing his feelings.*

6. **D is correct.** *Keillor emphasizes that a letter to a friend should flow naturally, without excessive care about formalities (paragraphs 3 and 6). A is incorrect because*

---

6   Don't worry about form. It's not a term paper. When you come to the end of one episode, just start a new paragraph. You can go from a few lines about the sad state of pro football to the fight with your mother to your fond memories of Mexico to your cat's urinary-tract infection to a few thoughts on personal indebtedness and on to the kitchen sink and what's in it. The more you write, the easier it gets, and when you have a True True Friend to write to, a *compadre,* a soul sibling, then it's like driving a car down a country road, you just get behind the keyboard and press on the gas.

Reading Comprehension

Use "Spiders Up Close" (pp. 622–623) to answer questions 1–5.

1. Which text features help you recognize the article's pattern of organization?
   - **A.** Captions
   - **B.** Footnotes
   - **C.** Title and subheadings
   - **D.** Boldfaced words in text

2. Which overall pattern of organization does the author use?
   - **A.** Cause and effect
   - **B.** Comparison and contrast
   - **C.** Chronological order
   - **D.** Classification

3. In paragraph 5 the author describes how different spiders catch their prey using —
   - **A.** comparison and contrast
   - **B.** classification
   - **C.** main idea and supporting details
   - **D.** cause and effect

4. The author's tone can best be described as —
   - **A.** admiring
   - **B.** alarmed
   - **C.** gloomy
   - **D.** ironic

5. The author's two purposes for writing the article are to —
   - **A.** reflect and express feelings
   - **B.** inform and persuade
   - **C.** express feelings and entertain
   - **D.** inform and entertain

Use "How to Write a Letter" (pp. 623–624) to answer questions 6–10.

6. Which statement best describes the author's perspective?
   - **A.** He is tired of receiving poorly written letters.
   - **B.** He thinks writing a good letter is hard work.
   - **C.** He believes letter writing is a way to impress your friends.
   - **D.** He thinks letter writing should be like having a conversation.

7. The author's perspective is most clearly revealed in his —
   - **A.** references to job applications and term papers
   - **B.** list of letter-writing do's and don'ts
   - **C.** suggestion for an appropriate salutation
   - **D.** use of slang and sincere expressions

Keillor does not complain about letters that he has received. B is incorrect because Keillor emphasizes that writing a letter should seem natural. C is contradicted in paragraph 5.

7. **D is correct.** *Nonstandard expressions in the article include* ain't *and* lit'ry; *sincere expressions include* compadre *and* soul sibling. *A is incorrect because the article is about personal letters. B is incorrect because the article contains no such list. C is incorrect because the suggestion for a salutation (paragraph 3) is only a minor detail.*

8. **B is correct.** *The author's emphasis on being natural reassures the reader that writing a letter is not as hard as it may seem. A is incorrect because Keillor varies his sentences and includes interesting details. C is incorrect because the author appears to mean what he says. D is incorrect because the author presents letter-writing as something with which he, too, has struggled.*

9. **B is correct.** *The rapid movement from one homey detail to another creates humor based on real life. A is incorrect because the*

8. The tone of "How to Write a Letter" can best be described as —

   A. monotonous

   B. reassuring

   C. sarcastic

   D. superior

9. Which tone does the author adopt in paragraph 6 to help convey his purpose?

   A. Agitated

   B. Humorous

   C. Regretful

   D. Showy

10. The author's purpose for writing this essay is to —

    A. clarify

    B. complain

    C. give advice

    D. persuade

SHORT CONSTRUCTED RESPONSE
Write three or four sentences to answer each question.

11. Find two words in paragraphs 3 and 4 of "Spiders Up Close" that express the author's attitude toward spiders. Explain how those words reflect that attitude.

12. The author achieves two purposes in paragraph 6 in "Spiders Up Close." What are those purposes? Cite words and images that the author uses to convey each purpose.

13. How do these sentences from paragraph 5 of "How to Write a Letter" illustrate the tone of the essay?

    "A letter is only a report to someone who already likes you for reasons other than your brilliance. Take it easy."

Write a paragraph to answer this question.

14. What is the author's perspective on writing in general, according to "How to Write a Letter"? Give at least three examples of images or word choices in this essay that reveal his perspective, and explain how they do so.

GO ON ➡

---

overall feeling of the passage is relaxed. C is incorrect because the author does not describe a situation or issue about which he has regrets. D is incorrect because although the author shows cleverness, showing off knowledge or skill is not the point of the passage.

10. **C is correct.** Keillor gives advice on how to write a letter. A is a weaker choice because the article does more than clarify; it gives how-to advice. B is incorrect because the comments about the troubles of letter-writing are too mild to be called complaints. D is a weaker answer because Keillor is not trying to get the reader to share his views.

SHORT CONSTRUCTED RESPONSE

Possible responses:

11. Words that express the author's attitude toward spiders include *ingenious* (paragraph 3), *varied* (paragraph 3), and *astonishing* (paragraph 4). These words have a positive connotation, and the author would not have used them unless he or she felt that spiders were admirable.

12. One purpose of these lines is to inform. Expressions and images that help achieve that purpose include "hold one end of the thread" (paragraph 6), "fling the sticky end" (paragraph 6), and "emit a pheromone" (paragraph 6), which name steps in the Bolas spider's hunting method. The other purpose is to entertain. To achieve that purpose, the author makes a humorous word choice—"to become lunch" (paragraph 6)—to describe what happens to prey. In addition, the author's precise, detailed imagery for the Bolas spider's hunting behavior is entertaining as well as informative.

13. In these sentences, Keillor addresses the reader directly as "you," uses a colloquial idiom ("Take it easy"), and reassures the reader about the task of letter-writing. These details help create an informal, relaxed tone.

14. In general, Keillor seems to enjoy writing. He admits that writing can be daunting (paragraph 1) but affirms, "The more you write, the easier it gets" (paragraph 6). In addition, the invitation "Take a deep breath and plunge in" (paragraph 3) presents writing as an enjoyable adventure. Keillor even seems to enjoy the physical details of writing: "Try a smaller page and write boldly" (paragraph 1); "Get a pen that makes a sensuous line" (paragraph 1). The overall effect is of a person who enjoys what he does—and who knows that he does it well.

Vocabulary

1. **B** *is correct. The name* wolf spider *compares a spider to a wolf, but the spider is not literally a wolf.* A *and* D *address literal descriptions.* C *is incorrect because the name* tarantula *does not compare the spider to something else.*

2. **D** *is correct. The spider is not literally a king, only figuratively so.* A *and* C *are literal statements.* B *is incorrect because "stalkers like cats" is a simile, not a metaphor.*

3. **A** *is correct. "As big as Montana" is a figurative comparison, and the use of* as *makes it a simile.* B *is incorrect because "come to mind until you can almost see her or him" is arguably not figurative and does not use* like *or* as. C *is incorrect because although "to crank out" is figurative, it does not use* like *or* as. D *is incorrect because although calling a letter a report is figurative, the comparison does not use* like *or* as.

4. **C** *is correct.* C *is the only choice that offers a comparison using* like *or* as *(in this case,* like*). The language in* A *is metaphorical; the language in* B *and* D *is literal.*

5. **D** *is correct. The idea of a letter drifting implies a figurative comparison, and the absence of* like *or* as *makes the expression a metaphor.* A, B, *and* C *are all literal descriptions.*

Vocabulary

> **Use context clues and your knowledge of similes and metaphors to answer the following questions.**

1. In the article "Spiders Up Close," which spider name is an example of a metaphor?
   A. *jumping spider*
   B. *wolf spider*
   C. *tarantula*
   D. *silver argiope spider*

2. Which expression from "Spiders Up Close" is an example of a metaphor?
   A. *Hanging head-down from the hub of her web*
   B. *Jumping spiders are stalkers like cats*
   C. *The much larger tarantulas are also generally runners*
   D. *The king of the fishers is the water spider*

3. Which expression from "How to Write a Letter" is an example of a simile?
   A. *A blank white eight-by-eleven sheet can look as big as Montana*
   B. *let your friend come to mind until you can almost see her or him*
   C. *The toughest letter to crank out is one that is meant to impress*
   D. *A letter is only a report to someone who already likes you*

4. Which expression from "How to Write a Letter" is an example of a simile?
   A. *take a deep breath and plunge in*
   B. *When you come to the end of one episode*
   C. *it's like driving a car down a country road*
   D. *you can almost see her or him in the room*

5. Which expression from "How to Write a Letter" is an example of a metaphor?
   A. *get a comfortable typewriter*
   B. *Sit for a few minutes*
   C. *don't try to write dramatically*
   D. *let the letter drift gently along*

DIFFERENTIATED INSTRUCTION

FOR ENGLISH LANGUAGE LEARNERS
Review Assessment Terms On the board write the terms shown in italics. Then, give the examples in random order and have students classify them. Elicit additional examples from students.

- *author's perspective:* Garrison Keillor thinks that a friendly letter shouldn't try to impress the reader.

- *tone and diction:* In "How to Write a Letter," Keillor's use of colloquial words and phrases makes him sound friendly.

- *author's purpose:* Keillor writes to help his readers become better letter-writers.

- *pattern of organization:* The author of "Spiders Up Close" discusses spiders according to their hunting methods.

- *metaphor and simile:* In "Spiders Up Close," the author compares the water spider's silk vehicle to a diving bell.

Revising and Editing

DIRECTIONS Read this passage, and answer the questions that follow.

> (1) American history has many famous heroes, but Sybil Ludington is one who is less well known. (2) In 1777, Sybil was just sixteen years old. (3) Her father was an officer in the New York militia. (4) One night, the British attacked a nearby town. (5) Someone had to alert the militiamen in the area. (6) Sybil volunteered to call the soldiers to arms. (7) She rode forty miles that night.

1. Which is the most effective way to add an adverb clause to sentence 2?

   A. In 1777, Sybil was just sixteen years old, and the Revolutionary War was raging.

   B. In 1777, during the Revolutionary War, Sybil was just sixteen years old.

   C. Sybil was just sixteen years old in 1777, when the Revolutionary War was raging.

   D. Sybil was a sixteen-year-old girl in 1777.

2. Which is the most effective way to add a participial phrase to sentence 3?

   A. Her father was an officer in the New York militia, leading a force of local soldiers.

   B. Her father led a force of local soldiers as an officer in the New York militia.

   C. An officer in the New York militia, her father led a force of local soldiers.

   D. Her father was an officer in the New York militia who led a force of local soldiers.

3. Which is the most effective way to add a participial phrase to sentence 4?

   A. One night, the British attacked a nearby town; colonists stored supplies there.

   B. One night, the British attacked a nearby town and stole supplies.

   C. One night, the British attacked a nearby town, stealing colonists' supplies.

   D. One night, the British attacked a nearby town where colonists stored supplies.

4. Which is the most effective way to add an adverb clause to sentence 6?

   A. Because the messenger and his horse were too weary to travel, Sybil volunteered to call the soldiers to arms.

   B. The messenger and his horse were too weary to travel, so Sybil volunteered to call the soldiers to arms.

   C. The messenger and his horse were too weary to call the soldiers to arms, but Sybil felt fine.

   D. The messenger and his horse were too weary to travel; Sybil volunteered to call the soldiers to arms.

5. Which is the most effective way to add a participial phrase to sentence 7?

   A. She rode forty miles that night and roused the militia to action.

   B. She rode forty miles that night, rousing the militia to action.

   C. She rode forty miles that night to rouse the militia to action.

   D. She rode forty miles that night; she roused the militia to action.

STOP

627

ANSWERS
Revising and Editing

1. C *is correct.* *The clause is "when the Revolutionary War was raging." A is incorrect because the added "and the Revolutionary War was raging" is an independent clause, not a subordinate clause. B is incorrect because the added "during the Revolutionary War" is a prepositional phrase, not a clause. D is incorrect because it merely rearranges the words of the original sentence.*

2. A *is correct.* *The participial phrase "leading a force of local soldiers" modifies the noun* soldier. *B is incorrect because it contains no participle. C is incorrect because the revision adds an appositive phrase, not a participial phrase. D is incorrect because the revision adds an adjective clause, not a participial phrase.*

3. C *is correct.* *"Stealing colonists' supplies" is the participial phrase. A is incorrect because the revision adds an independent clause, not a participial phrase. B is incorrect because "and stole supplies" is part of a compound predicate with "attacked a nearby town," not a separate phrase. D is incorrect because the revision adds an adjective clause, not a participial phrase.*

4. A *is correct.* *The clause "Because the messenger and his horse were too weary to travel" modifies the verb* volunteered. *B, C, and D are incorrect because all three are compound sentences consisting of two independent clauses, rather than complex sentences; in addition, H is incorrect because the revision changes the meaning of the sentence.*

5. B *is correct.* *The participial phrase "rousing the militia to action" modifies the pronoun* she. *A is incorrect because the revision creates a compound predicate rather than a separate phrase. C is incorrect because "to rouse the militia to action" is an infinitive phrase, not a participial phrase. D is incorrect because the revision adds an independent clause, not a participial phrase.*

FOR STRUGGLING READERS

Assessment Support: Participial Phrases Tell students that participial phrases can serve as adjectives or adverbs in a sentence. Help them to recognize and correct dangling participial phrases. Write this sentence on the board: *Finally getting the water it needed, the rain fell on the village.* Work with students to explain why this sentence contains a dangling participial phrase. ***Answer:** The participial phrase should modify* village, *not* rain. *The correct sentence might read: "The village finally got the water it needed when the rain fell."*

COMMON CORE FOCUS

RL 10 Read and comprehend literature. **RI 10** Read and comprehend literary nonfiction.

INTRODUCE *GREAT READS*

In Unit 5, students have discussed a number of big questions. Invite students to tell which question they found most intriguing and why, and then focus attention on the three that appear on this page. Discuss the recommended books and their summaries, pointing out how each connects to the related question. Encourage students to choose one or more of these "great reads" to read independently.

Ideas for Independent Reading

Which of the questions in Unit 5 intrigued you the most? Continue exploring them with these additional works.

COMMON CORE

RL 10 Read and comprehend literature. **RI 10** Read and comprehend literary nonfiction.

Can beauty be captured in words?

Cultivating Delight: A Natural History of My Garden
by Diane Ackerman

A naturalist and writer, Ackerman celebrates the color, the animals, and the changing seasons in her garden. She also digresses into such topics as the origins of the word *tulip.*

Pilgrim at Tinker Creek
by Annie Dillard

This is a highly spiritual and poetic meditation on nature, modeled on Thoreau's *Walden.* Dillard records and reflects on the beauty and cruelty she sees around her home near Tinker Creek in Virginia.

West with the Night
by Beryl Markham

Much of this memoir describes the stunning beauty of East Africa, where Markham grew up. She recalls the varied landscapes, wildlife, and people of the region.

What can we learn from disaster?

Triangle: The Fire That Changed America
by David Von Drehle

In 1911, a fire at the Triangle Shirtwaist Company factory killed 146 people—most of them Jewish and Italian immigrant women. The tragedy led to massive labor organizing and widespread factory reforms.

Fitzgerald's Storm: The Wreck of the Edmund Fitzgerald
by Dr. Joseph MacInnis

Part natural history, part investigative history, this book describes the sinking of the *Edmund Fitzgerald,* an ore carrier that went down in a storm on Lake Superior in 1975. Twenty-nine men died.

The Greatest Disaster Stories Ever Told
edited by Lamar Underwood

This book offers accounts of 17 disasters, including the deadly chemical spill in Bhopal, India; the space shuttle *Challenger* explosion; and the September 11 terrorist attack on the World Trade Center.

What do we owe others?

There Are No Children Here
by Alex Kotlowitz

Kotlowitz, a *Wall Street Journal* reporter, follows the lives of two young boys growing up in a Chicago housing project. They live in constant terror of gang violence and worry that they will not reach adulthood.

Alabanza
by Martín Espada

Alabanza means "praise" in Spanish, and the title poem of this collection remembers the immigrant restaurant workers killed in the World Trade Center attack. The remaining poems also praise the poor and forgotten.

Family Matters
by Rohinton Mistry

A grandfather in Bombay is increasingly unable to care for himself. His daughter and her family, living in straitened circumstances, take him in, and each family member learns something about responsibility for others.

Get Novel Wise

THINK central

Go to **thinkcentral.com.**
KEYWORD: HML10-628

THINK central

NovelWise

The keyword on this page points to **NovelWise,** a Web site that helps students choose a novel or other book-length work to read. **NovelWise** also provides

- study guides
- reading strategies and literary elements instruction
- presentations to introduce classic novels
- project ideas

Making a Case

6

ARGUMENT AND PERSUASION

- In Nonfiction
- In Fiction
- Across Genres
- In Media

629

INTRODUCE THE UNIT

There are many ways to make a case—that is, to present an argument—in support of an idea, including delivering a speech, graphing data, or creating an advertisement. The success of a case depends greatly upon the persuasive strategies used to argue it. For example, both images on this page make a case for respecting animal rights. However, the persuasive strategies differ. The painting depicts a group of primates living in an unblemished natural world. The photograph presents the pleading expression of a caged chimpanzee.

Invite students to consider the persuasive power of the images. Offer these questions to start the discussion:

- How does each image make a case for animal rights? How are the cases similar or different?
- What caption would you write for the painting? for the photograph? What details guided your decision?

Explain to students that the selections in this unit will show how several writers have used **argument and persuasion** to make their cases in nonfiction, fiction, across genres, and in the media.

For help in planning this unit, see

R RESOURCE MANAGER UNIT 6
pp. 1–10

About the Art French primitive painter Henri Rousseau (1844–1910) created *The Merry Jesters* around 1906. The painting is typical of his jungle scenes: It offers the viewer a fresh, innocent view of a setting that is more a product of Rousseau's imagination than of his personal experience—but a setting that is precise and compelling just the same.

UNIT 6

STRAND	Text Analysis Workshop: Argument and Persuasion pp. 632–637	Doing Nothing Is Doing Something — Persuasive Essay pp. 638–645 — Lexile: 1170, Fry: 7, Dale-Chall: 7.3	Abolishing the Penny Makes Good Sense — Editorial pp. 646–651 — Lexile: 1040, Fry: 11, Dale-Chall: 7.2	On Nuclear Disarmament — Speech pp. 652–663 — Lexile: 970, Fry: 12, Dale-Chall: 7.4	I Acknowledge Mine — Essay pp. 664–677 — Lexile: 1110, Fry: 12, Dale-Chall: 7.0	Use of Animals in Biomedical Research — Position Paper pp. 678–687 — Lexile: 1380, Fry: College, Dale-Chall: 8.9
Reading Literature						
Reading Informational Text	The Analysis of an Argument pp. 632–633 RI 5, RI 6, RI 8 The Craft of Persuasion pp. 634–636 RI 5, RI 6, RI 8 Analyze the Text p. 637	Argument pp. 639, 641, 643 RI 5 Fact/Opinion pp. 639, 641–643 RI 8	Evidence pp. 647, 649–651 RI 8 Deductive Reasoning pp. 647–648, 651 RI 1, RI 5 Author's Claim, p. 648 RI 5 Language Coach, p. 649 RI 4	Rhetorical Devices pp. 653, 656, 660 RI 6 Inductive Reasoning pp. 653–654, 656–658, 660 RI 5, RI 8 Author's Claim p. 659 RI 5 Language Coach p. 658 RI 4	Persuasive Techniques pp. 665, 668, 671, 674, 675 RI 8 Summarize pp. 665–666, 671–672, 675, 677 RI 2 Language Coach p. 668 RL 4	Counterarguments pp. 679–685 RI 5, RI 8 Summarize and Critique pp. 679, 680–683, 685, 687 RI 2, RI 5 Author's Claim p. 682 RI 5 Language Coach, p. 682 RI 4 Synthesize p. 684 RI 8
Writing		Writing Prompt p. 645 W 5	Quickwrite p. 646	Writing Prompt p. 662	Writing Prompt p. 677 W 2e	Writing Prompt p. 687 W 2e
Speaking and Listening		Discuss p. 638 SL 1		Survey p. 652 SL 1	Debate p. 664 SL 1	Discuss p. 678 SL 1
Language	Academic Vocabulary pp. 632, 634, 636	Rhetorical Questions pp. 642, 645 L 3 Etymology p. 644 L 4c Language Coach p. 641 L 5b		Repetition, pp. 657, 662 L 1a, L 3 Specialized Vocabulary, p. 661 L 6	Set the Tone pp. 668, 677 L 1b Analogies p. 676 L 5	Formal Language, pp. 684, 687 L 3 Connotation p. 686 L 5b

The Blue Stones Allegory pp. 688–693	Comparing Texts Selections		How Much Land Does a Man Need? / from The New Testament Short Story / Scriptural Writing pp. 716–737	 Media Study: Daisy / America's Back Political Ads pp. 738–741	 Writing Workshop: Persuasive Essay pp. 742–751 Speaking and Listening Workshop: Presenting an Argument pp. 752–753
	A Chip of Glass Ruby Short Story pp. 694–709	The Question of South Africa / Stop Apartheid Now! Speech / Poster pp. 710–715			
Lexile: 980 Fry: 6 Dale-Chall: 5-6	Lexile: 990 Fry: 7 Dale-Chall: 6.3	Lexile: 1240 Fry: 10 Dale-Chall: 9-10	Lexile: 1110/1150 Fry: 7/8 Dale-Chall: 5.8/6.8		
Allegory pp. 689, 692–693 RL 2 Paraphrase pp. 689, 690, 693 RL 1 Symbolism p. 690 RL 2 Language Coach, p. 692 RL 4	Theme and Persuasion pp. 695, 699, 704, 707 RL 2, RL 6 Draw Conclusions pp. 695, 696, 698, 702–703, 706–707 RL 1 Language Coach p. 698 RL 4		Didactic Literature pp. 717–718, 723, 727, 733–735 RL 7 Set a Purpose for Reading p. 717 RL 1 AFFIXES P. 732 RL 4 Language Coach pp. 721, 726, 732 RL 4		
		Analyze a Speech pp. 711–713 RI 4, RI 6 Poster p. 714 RI 7			
Quickwrite p. 688	Writing Prompt p. 709	Writing Prompt p. 713 W 9b (RI 6)	Writing for Assessment p. 737 W 9 (RI 7)	Persuasion in Political Ads p. 739 SL 2, SL 3 Evaluate the Message p. 741 SL 2, SL 4	Writing a Persuasive Essay pp. 742–751 W 1a–e, W 4, W 5, W 6, W 10
	What's the Connection? p. 694 SL 1		Discuss p. 716 SL 1		Presenting an Argument pp. 752–753 SL 3, SL 4, SL 6
	Vary Sentence Types pp. 703, 709 L 1b Thesaurus p. 708 L 4c	Language Coach p. 711 L 4b	Similes/Metaphors p. 736 L 5		Drafting p. 745 L 1 Revising pp. 746–748 L 3 Editing and Publishing p. 749 L 1, L 2c Use Parallel Structure p. 752 L 1a

ECOS ✓

To see the complete Essential Course of Study, see pp. T23–T28.

 For additional lesson planning help, see **Teacher One Stop DVD.**

Instructional Support

Resource Manager Unit 6

UNIT SUPPORT

Academic Vocabulary p. 3

Additional Academic Vocabulary p. 4

Grammar Focus p. 5

Text Analysis Workshop pp. 9–10

Writing Workshop: Persuasive Essay p. 197

SELECTION SUPPORT*

Plan and Teach

  Lesson planning pages

  Additional leveled selection questions

  Extension activities

Student Copy Masters

  Selection summaries in four languages

  Skills copy masters in English and Spanish

  Vocabulary preteaching and support

  Reading Check and Question Support

  Reading Fluency

* Available for all selections

† Available on **thinkcentral.com**.

Language Handbook

Vocabulary Practice

Best Practices Toolkit†

PowerNotes DVD-ROM†

Connections: Nonfiction for Common Core CD-ROM†

Teacher One Stop DVD-ROM

Student One Stop DVD-ROM

Media*Smart* DVD-ROM

Daisy / America's Back

Write*Smart* CD-ROM†

GrammarNotes DVD-ROM†

WordSharp CD-ROM†

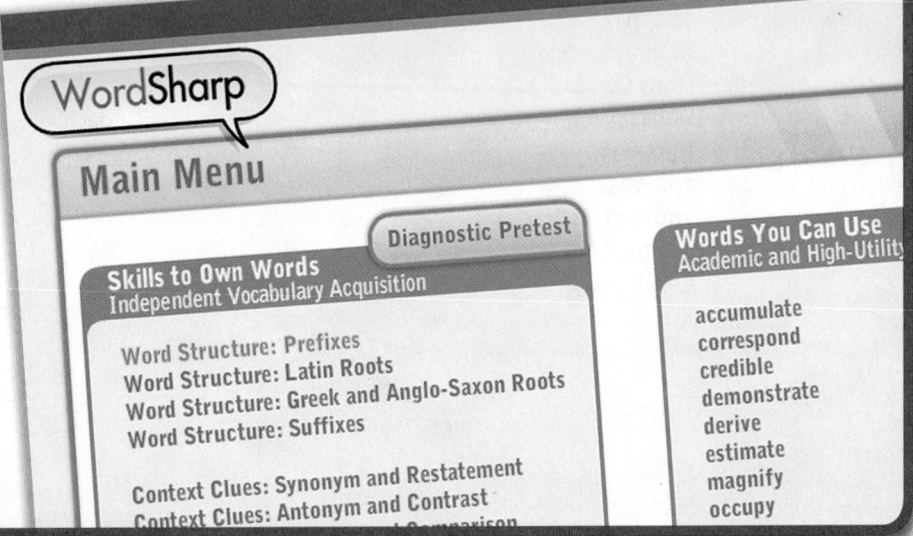

Differentiated Instruction

STRUGGLING READERS AND WRITERS

Resource Manager Unit 6

Additional Selection Questions

Question Support

Reading Fluency

Interactive Reader

Adapted Interactive Reader

Audio Tutor

Level Up Online Tutorials

Audio Anthology

(with Audio summaries)

Diagnostic and Selection Tests

Selection Tests A/B

ENGLISH LANGUAGE LEARNERS

Resource Manager Unit 6

Selection Summaries in English, Spanish, Vietnamese and Haitian Creole

Skills Copymasters in Spanish

English Language Learner Adapted Interactive Reader Teacher's Guide

ELL Adapted Interactive Reader

Audio Tutor

Guide to English for Newcomers

Audio Anthology

Audio Summaries in Multiple Languages (on **thinkcentral.com**)

ADVANCED LEARNERS

Resource Manager Unit 6

Additional Selection Questions

Ideas for Extension

Diagnostic and Selection Tests

Selection Tests B/C

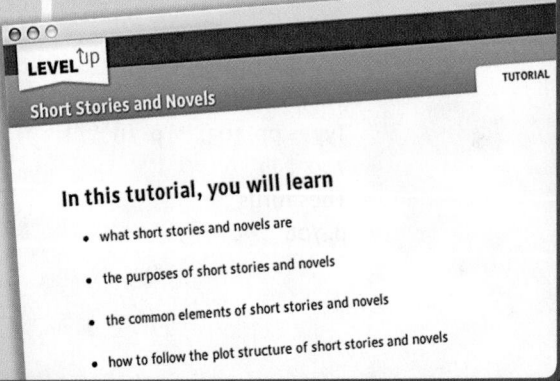

Assessment and Reteaching

Diagnostic and Selection Tests

Unit and Benchmark Tests

ThinkCentral Online Assessment:

- All program assessments
- Level Up Online Tutorials

ExamView Test Generator on the Teacher One Stop DVD-ROM

Online Essay Scoring on **thinkcentral.com**

ThinkCentral Online Reteaching:

- Level Up Online Tutorials
- Reteaching Worksheets

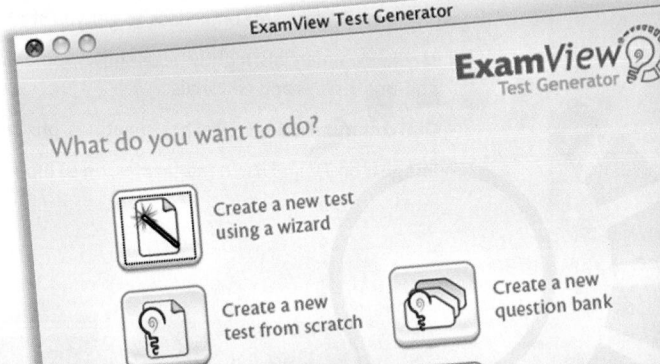

ExamView Test Generator

ExamView Test Generator

What do you want to do?

Create a new test using a wizard

Create a new test from scratch

Create a new question bank

Professional Development

Video Center Based on interviews with program consultants and other educational experts, these videos feature classroom-ready teaching strategies.

Teacher Toolkit Includes a Teacher Handbook as well as a range of articles and handouts by program consultants and other educators.

Janet Allen

Jim Burke

Kylene Beers

Carol Jago

THINK central **at a Glance**

One Location, Endless Resources

Find Resources Browse all *Holt McDougal Literature* components for the ones that meet your students' needs and match your teaching style.

Assess Progress and Reteach Assign electronic versions of program assessments to measure your students' mastery of the Common Core State Standards. On thinkcentral.com, some tests deliver online remediation tutorials to students who have not mastered skills.

 Interactive Whiteboard Lessons

Prepare your students for college and careers by teaching relevant, real-world skills through dynamic, interactive instruction. Go to **thinkcentral.com** to browse through all whiteboard lessons, including the following:

- Evaluating Arguments
- Writing Effective Arguments
- Using Parallel Structure

HISTORY

Together Holt McDougal and HISTORY® are revolutionizing the study of English/language arts with video that helps students relive and re-imagine the people, places, and events they are discovering through reading. Look for selections with the HISTORY® icon.

Can you be
PERSUADED?

Present the question, then call on volunteers to read the opening paragraphs aloud. As students consider the questions ask them what the writer of each of the following messages might be trying to **persuade** them to do:

• a TV ad for a new shampoo

• a political campaign poster

• a speech about saving the environment

Using these examples, have students suggest several criteria that make a persuasive message successful.

DISCUSS To get students started, have them think of advertisements they have seen around the school. Point out that a brand or company name is an advertisement, as are posters that promote attendance at school events, support of sports teams, and academic excellence. Encourage group representatives to note key discussion points and then share them with the class.

CHECK UNDERSTANDING Have students complete this sentence in as many reasonable ways as they can: *You know that a message is trying to persuade you when _____.*

Can you be
PERSUADED?

We all like to think that we're strong-minded, that we know what we believe and want. We also like to imagine that we're not easily swayed by what others might say or do. But is this really the case?

Every day we are bombarded with persuasive messages. How many of these messages are you aware of? How actively do you analyze the ideas being presented?

DISCUSS With a group of classmates, record the different kinds of persuasive messages you encounter in a day. Rank them according to how effective you think they are, and discuss why the good ones work so well. Here are some ideas to get you started.

• **Media:** commercials, nightly news shows, radio talk shows, Internet pop-ups, essays and editorials

• **Oral communication:** speeches, meetings, phone solicitors

• **Images:** on TV shows, in magazines, on billboards

Find It Online!  Go to **thinkcentral.com** for the interactive version of this unit.

630

Unit Resources

See resources on the **Teacher One Stop DVD-ROM** *and on* **thinkcentral.com**.

R RESOURCE MANAGER UNIT 6

UNIT AND BENCHMARK TESTS

BEST PRACTICES TOOLKIT

INTERACTIVE READER

ADAPTED INTERACTIVE READER

ELL ADAPTED INTERACTIVE READER

LANGUAGE HANDBOOK

VOCABULARY PRACTICE

TECHNOLOGY

- Teacher One Stop DVD-ROM
- Student One Stop DVD-ROM
- PowerNotes DVD-ROM
- Write*Smart* CD-ROM
- Media*Smart* DVD-ROM
- GrammarNotes DVD-ROM
- Audio Anthology CD
- Audio Tutor CD

Find it Online!

The interactive version of this unit on **thinkcentral.com** includes

• video and **PowerNotes** introductions to key selections

• audio support—listen or download

• **ThinkAloud** models

• **WordSharp** vocabulary tutorials

• interactive review and remediation

Preview Unit Goals

TEXT ANALYSIS	• Analyze theme; understand allegory and symbolism • Interpret didactic literature • Analyze and evaluate an argument, including claim, support, reasons, evidence, and counterargument • Identify and analyze persuasive and rhetorical devices
READING	• Draw conclusions; summarize; critique; paraphrase • Distinguish fact from opinion
WRITING AND LANGUAGE	• Write an argument (persuasive essay) • Use repetition and rhetorical questions to add impact • Use compound-complex sentences to vary sentence structure
SPEAKING AND LISTENING	• Present an argument
VOCABULARY	• Understand words derived from Germanic and Greek affixes • Use reference materials to determine or clarify a word's etymology or meaning
ACADEMIC VOCABULARY	• cite • objective • controversy • statistic • convince
MEDIA AND VIEWING	• Recognize and analyze persuasive techniques in advertising • Integrate information presented in diverse media

Media Smart DVD-ROM

Creating Characters on Film

Persuasion in Political Ads

Examine two iconic ads that are blueprints for today's most powerful and persuasive political ads. Page 738

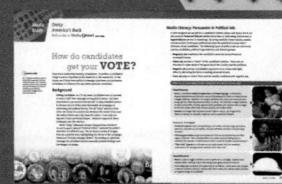

631

COMMON CORE **UNIT GOALS**

Included in this unit: **RL 1, RL 2, RL 4, RL 6, RL 7, RL 10, RI 1, RI 2, RI 4, RI 5, RI 6, RI 7, RI 8, RI 9, RI 10, W 1a-e, W 2, W 2e, W 4, W 5, W 9, W 9b, W 10, SL 2, SL 3, SL 4, SL 6, L 1, L 1a, L 1b, L 2c, L 3, L 4b, L 4c, L 5, L 5b, L 6**

Complete text of the Common Core State Standards is found in the correlation on pp. T10. Standards covered in this unit are found in the standards overview (pp. 629A–629B) and on the lesson pages where they are taught.

Preview Unit Goals

Explain to students that the Unit Goals summarize the main skills and strategies taught in Unit 6. As students read through the list, encourage them to make some informal predictions about the kinds of selections that they will be reading. Point out the color-coding of the strands and remind students that they will see this coding used within the lessons as well as on this page.

Invite students to read the Academic Vocabulary silently. Call on volunteers to define familiar terms and to use a dictionary for help with unfamiliar terms. Ask students to record all of the terms in their **Reader/Writer Notebooks,** along with a definition for each one. Throughout the unit, they can return to the list to refine or clarify the original definitions.

DIFFERENTIATED INSTRUCTION

FOR ENGLISH LANGUAGE LEARNERS

Academic Vocabulary Provide students with definitions of each Academic Vocabulary word.

cite (sīt) *v.* to quote from some source such as a book, Internet article, or speech

controversy (kän′trə vər′se) *n.* a debate or quarrel over opposing opinions

convince (kən vins′) *v.* to overcome any doubts with argument or persuasion

objective (əb-jĕk′tĭv) *n.* something worked toward or striven for

statistic (stə tis′tik) *n.* numerical fact or quantity

Use the copy master to help students learn academic words they will use in this unit and on the Assessment Practice.

 RESOURCE MANAGER—Copy Masters
Academic Vocabulary p. 3
Additional Academic Vocabulary p. 4

Focus and Motivate

COMMON CORE FOCUS

RI 5 Analyze how an author's claims are developed and refined by sentences, paragraphs, or larger portions of text. **RI 6** Determine an author's purpose in a text and analyze how an author uses rhetoric. **RI 8** Evaluate the argument and specific claims, assessing whether the reasoning is valid and the evidence is relevant and sufficient. **RI 9** Analyze seminal U.S. documents of historical and literary significance.

Teach

Part 1: The Analysis of an Argument

Parts of an Argument Draw on the board a large outline of the diagram on page 632.

- Ask students to suggest a claim that a reader might encounter in an editorial. Write it in the top of the diagram.
- For each column, have students suggest a possible supporting reason and an example of evidence proving that reason.
- Ask students why a persuasive writer often

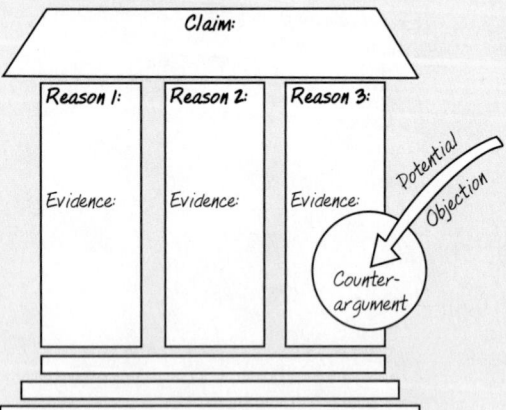

brings up objections that an opponent might make. Have students suggest an objection to their claim and a counterargument.

 BEST PRACTICES TOOLKIT—Transparency
Analysis Frame: Persuasion pp. D21, D44

Text Analysis Workshop

Argument and Persuasion

Essential Course of Study ECOS

In today's world, you are faced with choices every day, from which brand of gym shoes you should buy to which presidential candidate deserves your support. Along with every choice comes a barrage of persuasive messages. TV ads, speeches, editorials, petitions—all are aimed at influencing your beliefs and actions. How do you understand the shifts in perspective among messages on the same topic and separate the logical arguments from powerful appeals that aren't based on sound reasoning? By learning how to analyze arguments, you will be better able to make informed choices about decisions that matter.

Part 1: The Analysis of an Argument

COMMON CORE

Included in this workshop:
RI 5 Analyze how an author's claims are developed and refined. **RI 6** Determine an author's purpose in a text and analyze how an author uses rhetoric. **RI 8** Evaluate the argument and specific claims, assessing whether the reasoning is valid and the evidence is relevant and sufficient. **RI 9** Analyze seminal U.S. documents of historical and literary significance.

Like a pair of gym shoes, an argument may be constructed of high-quality parts, or it might be poorly made. To analyze an argument, you first need to understand its parts. A strong argument typically includes

- a **claim**, or the writer's position on a problem or an issue. The perspective revealed in the claim may change from argument to argument.

- **support**, which includes reasons and evidence that help to justify the claim

- a **counterargument**, or a brief argument that negates objections to the claim that "the other side" is likely to raise

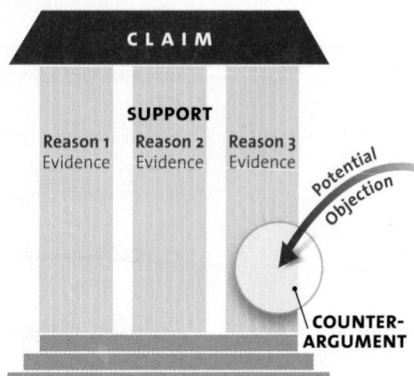

STRATEGIES FOR EVALUATING AN ARGUMENT

- **Check the claim.** What is the writer trying to convince you to do or believe? Consider whether the reasons given actually support the claim.

- **Examine the evidence.** Does the information come from a trustworthy source? Is there enough of it to make the case?

- **Look for logic.** Watch for errors in logic, such as **hasty generalizations**, or conclusions drawn from too little evidence. (Example: "Our student president is a football player, and he's doing a terrible job. Athletes shouldn't be elected to the student council.")

- **Consider the counterargument.** Has the writer adequately dealt with likely objections?

DIFFERENTIATED INSTRUCTION

FOR STRUGGLING READERS
Note Taking For students who need help with note taking, hand out the note-taking copy master before discussing this page. As volunteers read aloud each section, discuss the main points, and have students record them on the copy master.

R RESOURCE MANAGER—Copy Master
Note Taking p. 9

FOR ENGLISH LANGUAGE LEARNERS
Language: Skill Words Provide concrete context for *support, evidence, argument,* and *claim.* (Legs *support* a table; police use hair as *evidence*; they had an *argument* over what to eat; he *claims* to be a good hitter.) Link the everyday and literary meanings.

MODEL 1: CLAIM AND SUPPORT

As you read this excerpt from a feature article, look for the claim that the author is making. Is it effectively supported?

from Youth ✔oter Participation

Feature article from **Ad Council**

The right to vote for the leaders of our state and nation is a freedom that separates our country from so many others in the world. In order for democracy to work in America, people must exercise this privilege.

Voting is a way to have a voice in our government—whether you want to ensure that your children receive the best education; or that you will collect your social security benefits upon retirement; or that your taxes will support research for life-threatening diseases. Our leaders, whether it be your local mayor or the President, make decisions that affect your life.

Close Read

1. Identify the author's claim, or position.

2. What reason is given to support the claim? In your opinion, is the reason strong? Support your answer.

MODEL 2: COUNTERARGUMENT

The same article continues with a counterargument, or a different perspective on the issue. As you read, notice the potential objection that the author anticipates. How does the author counter the opposing viewpoint?

Why don't people vote? Many people say that it's because they don't think it will matter. Imagine if everyone felt that way—we could never elect a president or a congressman. There have been many, many elections, locally and nationally, that have been decided by less than 100 votes.

5   **1776**—One vote gave America the English language instead of German.
1845—One vote brought Texas into the Union.
1868—One vote allowed Andrew Johnson to escape impeachment.
1920—The 19th Amendment to the U.S. Constitution gave women the right to vote.

Close Read

1. Reread the boxed text. In your own words, explain the opposing argument that the author anticipates. What is the author's response?

2. Reread the evidence that the author gives to counter the opposing viewpoint. Is this evidence effective? Support your viewpoint.

MODEL 1: CLAIM AND SUPPORT
Close Read

1. *Possible answer: The writer's claim is that democracy only works if people exercise their right to vote (lines 2–3).*

2. *Possible answer: The supporting reason given is that voting gives people a voice in their government (line 4). Some students may say the reason is strong because the writer gives examples of important government decisions that affect people's lives (lines 4–8). Others may say the writer fails to give examples that would relate to the intended audience of young people, and thus does not support the claim effectively.*

MODEL 2: COUNTERARGUMENT
Close Read

1. *Possible answer: The opposing argument anticipated in the boxed text is that one person's vote doesn't matter. The writer refutes this by saying no official would ever be elected if everyone felt this way (lines 2–3). The writer then gives examples of historic decisions in which every vote indeed counted because the results were very close.*

2. *Possible answer: Students may say that the evidence to counter the opposing viewpoint is effective because it shows that history was influenced by one or a small number of voters. Others may feel that the evidence could have been more effective if it had included more recent examples.*

FOR STRUGGLING READERS

Analysis Support: Claim Remind students that the purpose of persuasive writing is to convince readers to do or believe something. As students begin reading Model 1, tell them to determine the writer's claim by asking themselves: What does the writer want me to do or believe?

Analysis Support: Counterargument After students read Model 2, reinforce the concept of counterargument by presenting students with a claim and a supporting reason—for example, we should stop mountaintop mining because it has devastating effects on fish and wildlife—and asking them to raise an objection. Provide a counterargument to their objections. Then reverse roles: students present a claim and a reason, you raise an objection, and they give a counterargument.

Online Remediation   THINK central

If your students are struggling with critical reading skills, consider assigning them one or more **Level Up Online Tutorials** as remediation before beginning this unit. Log in to **thinkcentral.com** to view a list of the skills addressed by **Level Up**.

Teach

Part 2: The Craft of Persuasion

Persuasive Techniques After students read the first two paragraphs, brainstorm with them to come up with types of persuasive writing, such as consumer ads, editorials, campaign fliers, speeches recruiting volunteers to a cause, fundraising letters, and reviews. List ideas on the board.

Have a volunteer read each row of the chart. After the example is read, ask students to match it to a genre from the list on the board. Then work together to create similar examples for other genres. For example, a bandwagon appeal on a campaign flier might be: Stand with your neighbors. Vote for Joe Lynch.

For each type of appeal, ask students to name examples of products, causes, or issues that writers might promote by using that appeal. For instance, an emotional appeal to fear might be used by a writer promoting the use of bike helmets.

CHECK UNDERSTANDING

Have students describe at least two ways to evaluate an argument.

Part 2: The Craft of Persuasion

Even when you know how to evaluate an argument, it's easy to be swayed by appeals that bypass your brain and go straight to your heart. Allowing feelings to influence your decisions is not always a mistake. However, you should be aware of how powerful language and emotion can be used to affect you.

PERSUASIVE TECHNIQUES

Many of the following techniques that appear in contemporary political debates are probably familiar to you. What additional examples have you encountered?

TECHNIQUE	EXAMPLE
Appeals by Association	
Bandwagon Appeal Taps into people's desire to belong or be a part of a group	Everyone supports safer streets. Don't YOU?
"Plain Folks" Appeal Implies that ordinary people are on "our side" or that a candidate is like a regular person	At last, a tax plan created with real families and real budgets in mind.
Testimonial Relies on endorsements from celebrities or satisfied customers	As a well-known television personality, I've played a senator on TV. But candidate Amelia Lopez is the real thing!
Transfer Connects a product, a candidate, or a cause with a positive image or idea	Take pride in being an American. Re-elect Governor Frank.
Emotional Appeals	
Appeal to Pity, Fear, or Vanity Uses strong feelings, rather than facts and evidence, to persuade. These appeals may include **fallacies** such as appeals to commonly held opinions, false dilemmas, and personal attacks.	**Appeal to Vanity** Some people think the traffic situation is just fine. But those who really understand how the world works know we need a new bridge.
Appeal to Values	
Ethical Appeal Taps into people's values or moral standards	If you believe in education, vote against cutting after-school programs. With your help, we can keep these programs going strong.
Word Choice	
Loaded Language Uses words with positive or negative connotations to stir people's emotions	The proven candidate who has the trust and voice of the American people.

634 UNIT 6: ARGUMENT AND PERSUASION

DIFFERENTIATED INSTRUCTION

FOR STRUGGLING READERS

Note Taking For students who need help, hand out the note-taking copy master for Part 2. As they read and discuss the main points about Persuasive Techniques, have students record these in Part A of the copy master. Have students record information from page 637 in Part B of the copy master.

R RESOURCE MANAGER—Copy Master
Note Taking p. 10

FOR ENGLISH LANGUAGE LEARNERS

Language: Skill Words Explain the term *bandwagon* by telling students that at one time politicians campaigned by traveling through the streets on a bandwagon, a decorated wagon that carried a brass band and was pulled by a team of horses. People would show their support for the candidate by "hopping on the bandwagon," and thus bandwagon became an expression meaning "attracts many enthusiastic supporters."

MODEL 1: PERSUASION IN SPEECHES

Here, a senator tries to persuade his audience—the U.S. Congress—to work harder to combat the country's hunger crisis. What techniques does he use to enhance his argument?

from # HUNGER AWARENESS

Speech by **Senator Edward Kennedy**

Today is National Hunger Awareness Day, and it is an opportunity for all of us in Congress to pledge a greater effort to deal effectively with this festering problem that shames our nation and has grown even more serious in recent years.

5 The number of Americans living in hunger, or on the brink of hunger, . . . now includes 13 million children. . . .

These Americans deserve higher priority by all of us in Congress. Day in and day out, the needs of millions of Americans living in poverty have been overlooked, and too often their voices have been silenced.

10 These are real people, struggling every day to get by. They are single mothers serving coffee at the local diner at 5 A.M. and cleaning houses in the afternoon, yet are still unable to afford both shelter and food. They are low-wage workers holding down two jobs, yet still forced to make impossible choices between feeding their family, paying the rent, and obtaining decent

15 medical care. They are children who go to bed hungry every night whose parents can't afford to give them more than a single slim meal a day.

Close Read

1. One example of loaded language is boxed. Find two more examples.

2. Identify another persuasive technique, used in lines 10–16. Is it effective? Explain your opinion.

MODEL 2: PERSUASION IN THE MEDIA

On this billboard, language and visuals work together to send a persuasive message.

YOU'LL NEVER MISS ONE CAN,   BUT SHE WILL.

Feed the hungry. One can...   and one should.

Close Read

1. Reread the text on this billboard. What techniques are being used to persuade you? Cite specific words or phrases to support your answer.

2. Consider the photographs and the layout. Do these visual elements contribute to the power of the message? Explain your opinion.

MODEL 1: PERSUASION IN SPEECHES

Close Read

1. *Possible answer: Besides the boxed text, other examples of loaded language are "shames our nation" (line 3), "voices have been silenced" (line 9), "real people, struggling every day to get by" (line 10), "impossible choices" (lines 13–14), "children who go to bed hungry" (line 15), and "a single slim meal a day" (line 16).*

2. *Possible answer: Another persuasive technique used in lines 10–16 is the "plain folks" appeal, signaled by the words "real people" (line 10) and elaborated with details about people's everyday struggles. Most students will say it is effective because it shows readers that the poor are decent, hardworking people just like them.*

MODEL 2: PERSUASION IN THE MEDIA

Close Read

1. *Possible answer: The persuasive technique used in the billboard text is an emotional appeal to pity ("but she will") and an ethical appeal ("One can . . . and one should").*

2. *Possible answer: The visual elements contribute strongly to the power of the message. The first photo shows in bright, cheerful colors a shopping cart full of groceries, reminding viewers that they "can" help because they have plenty for themselves. The second, more somber-colored photo shows a child's sad face, arousing sympathy, guilt, and a desire to protect. Some students may say, however, that the ad is manipulative because it seeks to arouse guilt in viewers.*

DIFFERENTIATED INSTRUCTION

FOR STRUGGLING READERS

Analysis Support: Loaded Words Reinforce the concept of loaded words. Ask students to restate each phrase from the speech in less emotionally-charged language.

- "festering problem" (*serious problem*)

- "shames our nation" (*troubles our nation*)

- "their voices have been silenced" (*their voices haven't been heard*)

- "struggling" (*trying*)

- "impossible choices" (*difficult choices*)

FOR ENGLISH LANGUAGE LEARNERS

Vocabulary: Puns in Advertising Tell students that ad writers often use puns to create clever, memorable slogans. Explain that a pun is a play on words, usually involving two different meanings of the same word or words. Ask students what two different meanings for "one can" are used on the billboard. ("*a single metal container*" and "*someone is able*")

RHETORICAL DEVICES

After students have read the instructions and chart, ask two volunteers to read the example of repetition aloud. Have one student read it as written, and the other student replace the second *Freedom* with *It* and the third *Freedom* with *Liberty*. Ask students to compare the effects of the two versions.

Explain that parallelism may include repeated words, but its main feature is repeated grammatical elements or structure. For example, King begins each sentence with a verb phrase followed by a prepositional phrase. Read aloud a version without the parallelism: *Let us rise up tonight and be ready. We must stand together with great determination, because now is the time to move on. These are powerful, challenging days, and we can make America what it ought to be.* Invite a volunteer to read the original version. Ask students to comment on the difference.

Close Read

1. **Possible answer:** *One example of repetition is "for me, for me" (line 5), which stresses Quindlen's conviction that people must act for themselves, not for what others want. The first sentence contains parallelism (lines 1–3), which emphasizes that both the old and new "notions" create rigid and simplistic distinctions between men and women. Other examples of parallelism are the paired infinitive phrases "to make ... to acknowledge" (lines 7–8) and the string of infinitive phrases beginning with "to go to professional school" (lines 11–12).*

2. **Possible answer:** *The boxed text draws an analogy between kinds of music and kinds of personal choices. Jingles and the music of pied pipers are compared with what the "'theys'" do. The "symphony" or "melodies spun out by your own heart" are compared with a person's individual, unique choices and decisions. This analogy might appeal to students because they identify strongly with certain kinds of music and have a strong desire to express themselves, yet also feel pressure to conform.*

RHETORICAL DEVICES

Without powerful language—or **rhetoric**—even skillfully crafted arguments can seem uninspired. To make their messages more memorable, writers use rhetorical devices, such as repetition, parallelism, analogies, and rhetorical questions. Notice how the use of language strengthens the arguments shown.

RHETORICAL DEVICE	EXAMPLE
repetition Uses the same word or words more than once for emphasis	Freedom leads to prosperity. Freedom replaces the ancient hatreds among the nations with comity and peace. Freedom is the victor. —Ronald Reagan, speech at Brandenburg Gate
parallelism Uses similar grammatical constructions to express ideas that are related or equal in importance. Often creates a rhythm.	Let us rise up tonight with a greater readiness. Let us stand with a greater determination. And let us move on in these powerful days, these days of challenge to make America what it ought to be. —Martin Luther King Jr., "I've been to the mountaintop" speech

Here, the journalist Anna Quindlen gives advice to graduating students. How does she enhance her message with rhetorical devices?

from COMMENCEMENT ADDRESS
Speech by **Anna Quindlen**

Set aside the old traditional notion of female as nurturer and male as leader; set aside, too, the new traditional notions of female as superwoman and male as oppressor. Begin with that most terrifying of all things, a clean slate. Then look, every day, at the choices you are making, and when you ask yourself why
5 you are making them, find this answer: for me, for me. Because they are who and what I am, and mean to be.

This is the hard work of your life in the world, to make it all up as you go along, to acknowledge the introvert, the clown, the artist, the reserved, the distraught, the goofball, the thinker. You will have to bend all your will not
10 to march to the music that all of those great "theys" out there pipe on their flutes. They want you to go to professional school, to wear khakis, to pierce your navel, to bare your soul. These are the fashionable ways. The music is tinny, if you listen close enough. Look inside. That way lies dancing to the melodies spun out by your own heart. This is a symphony. All the rest are jingles.

Close Read

1. Find one example each of repetition and parallelism. For each example, explain what the wording helps to emphasize.

2. Another device that Quindlen uses is an **analogy,** or a comparison between two things. Explain the analogy in the boxed text. Why might it appeal to students?

DIFFERENTIATED INSTRUCTION

FOR ENGLISH LANGUAGE LEARNERS

Language: Skill Words Draw parallel lines on the board and note that the lines run in the same direction but do not cross. Sentences, clauses, or phrases are likewise parallel if their parts line up when they are written one above the other. Write on the board, one above the other, these sentences from Model 1, page 635: "They are single mothers" and "They are low-wage workers" (lines 12–13). Help students identify the parallel parts of the sentences.

FOR STRUGGLING READERS

Analysis Support: Repetition and Parallelism Help students identify repetition and parallelism in these quotations:

- "Injustice anywhere is a threat to justice everywhere."

- "Ask not what your country can do for you. Ask what you can do for your country."

- "Men, their rights and nothing more. Women, their rights and nothing less."

- "... give me liberty, or give me death."

Part 3: Analyze the Text

Through the AmeriCorps network, young volunteers do service work while earning money toward their college education. As you read this article from the AmeriCorps Web site, use what you have learned to evaluate the argument being presented. What techniques are used to persuade you to join the organization?

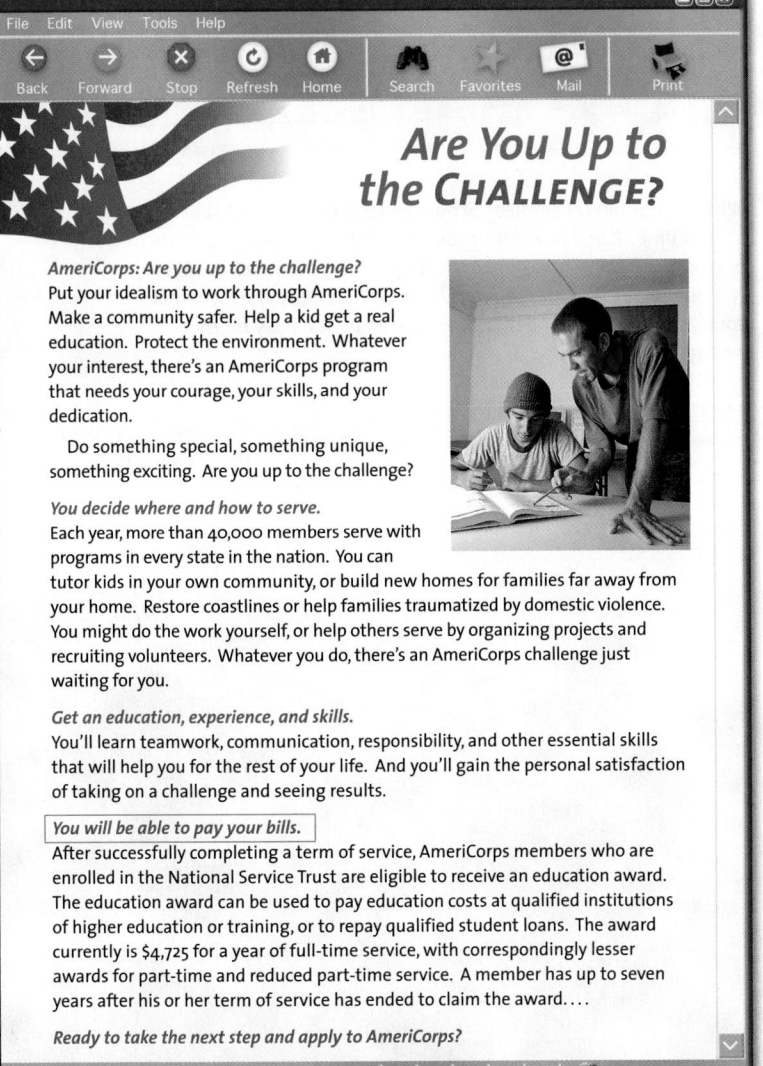

Are You Up to the CHALLENGE?

AmeriCorps: Are you up to the challenge?
Put your idealism to work through AmeriCorps. Make a community safer. Help a kid get a real education. Protect the environment. Whatever your interest, there's an AmeriCorps program that needs your courage, your skills, and your dedication.

Do something special, something unique, something exciting. Are you up to the challenge?

You decide where and how to serve.
Each year, more than 40,000 members serve with programs in every state in the nation. You can tutor kids in your own community, or build new homes for families far away from your home. Restore coastlines or help families traumatized by domestic violence. You might do the work yourself, or help others serve by organizing projects and recruiting volunteers. Whatever you do, there's an AmeriCorps challenge just waiting for you.

Get an education, experience, and skills.
You'll learn teamwork, communication, responsibility, and other essential skills that will help you for the rest of your life. And you'll gain the personal satisfaction of taking on a challenge and seeing results.

> You will be able to pay your bills.

After successfully completing a term of service, AmeriCorps members who are enrolled in the National Service Trust are eligible to receive an education award. The education award can be used to pay education costs at qualified institutions of higher education or training, or to repay qualified student loans. The award currently is $4,725 for a year of full-time service, with correspondingly lesser awards for part-time and reduced part-time service. A member has up to seven years after his or her term of service has ended to claim the award....

Ready to take the next step and apply to AmeriCorps?

Close Read

1. One reason that the author uses to persuade readers to join AmeriCorps is boxed. Identify two other reasons. In your opinion, are they convincing?

2. What persuasive techniques are being used in this article? Give specific examples to support your answer.

3. Find one example of parallelism and explain its effect.

4. Reread the boxed reason. Does the evidence that follows support the reason? (Consider: How much does four years of college cost?)

5. How do the images and the use of color add to the article's message?

FOR ADVANCED LEARNERS/PRE–AP

Analyze Arguments and Persuasive Techniques Have students look up famous quotations on the Internet to find examples of various persuasive techniques and rhetorical devices. Ask them to prepare a short oral analysis of the arguments, techniques, and devices. Invite students to share their examples with the class.

Practice and Apply

Part 3: Analyze the Text

Close Read

1. *Possible answers: Besides the boxed reason, other reasons given for joining AmeriCorps are that it's exciting (line 9), flexible (line 10), and educational (line 18). Students' evaluations will vary, but they should support their opinions.*

2. *Possible answers: The main persuasive technique used is an appeal to values: helping people or the environment (lines 3–4, 12–14) and getting an education (lines 18–20, 23–26). Other techniques used are the bandwagon appeal: "40,000 members serve" (line 11); an emotional appeal to pity: "families traumatized" (line 14); and loaded language: "idealism" (line 2), "courage" (line 6), "special . . . unique . . . exciting" (lines 8–9), "challenge" (line 9), "satisfaction" (line 20).*

3. *Possible answer: One example of parallelism is "Make a community safer. . . . the environment" (lines 3–4). The parallel structure of the sentences emphasizes the verbs and thus the many ways to help. Another example is "something special . . . exciting" (lines 8–9), which creates a rhythm emphasizing the three adjectives.*

4. *Possible answer: Students may say that the evidence following the boxed reason does not strongly support it. The education award is "$4,725" (line 27), not nearly enough to cover tuition at most colleges.*

5. *Possible answer: Red type highlights key ideas. The American flag adds to the message by connecting AmeriCorps membership with patriotism. The photo enhances the appeal to helping values.*

Assess and Reteach

Assess

Ask students what persuasive arguments and techniques would work in a speech on a topic such as the need for daily exercise.

Reteach

If students are unable to apply the workshop skills, review the note-taking copy masters. Ask volunteers to explain each term. Urge other students to offer refinements. List ways each technique or device could be applied and have students do the same.

Focus and Motivate

COMMON CORE FOCUS

RI 5 Analyze how an author's ideas or claims are developed and refined. **RI 8** Delineate and evaluate the argument and specific claims in a text, assessing whether the reasoning is valid. **W 5** Develop and strengthen writing as needed by revising, focusing on what is most significant for a specific purpose. **L 3** Apply knowledge of language to make effective choices for meaning or style. **L 4c** Consult reference materials to determine or clarify the etymology of a word. **L 5b** Analyze nuances in the meaning of words with similar denotations.

SUMMARY

In "Doing Nothing Is Something," Anna Quindlen champions the idea of creating downtime for children as a means of fueling their creativity. Quindlen argues that parents should give their children what she calls "the gift of enforced boredom," at least during the summer.

How should you spend your
FREE TIME?

Introduce the question and ask students how important it is to have leisure time, and why. Continue the exploration by having students complete the *DISCUSS* activity.

Essential Course of Study ECOS

Doing Nothing Is Something
Persuasive Essay by Anna Quindlen

VIDEO TRAILER **THINK** central KEYWORD: HML10-638

How should you spend your FREE TIME?

COMMON CORE

RI 5 Analyze how an author's ideas or claims are developed and refined. **RI 8** Delineate and evaluate the argument and specific claims in a text, assessing whether the reasoning is valid. **L 5b** Analyze nuances in the meaning of words with similar denotations.

What is your typical day like? School and homework must take up a lot of time. If you have other commitments, such as a job, sports practice, or family chores, then there's probably not much room in your life for leisure. In this essay, Anna Quindlen explores whether young people have enough leisure time or are too busy for their own good.

DISCUSS If you had more free time, how would you spend it? Make a list of things you would do—or not do. Then discuss with a partner how you would benefit from the extra free time.

Free Time
1. Draw cartoons.
2. Take long walks.
3.
4.
5.

638

Selection Resources

See resources on the **Teacher One Stop** DVD-ROM and on **thinkcentral.com**.

R RESOURCE MANAGER UNIT 6
Plan and Teach, pp. 11–18
Summary, pp. 19–20†‡*
Text Analysis and Reading
  Skill, pp. 21–24†*
Vocabulary, pp. 25–27*
Grammar and Style, p. 30

DIAGNOSTIC AND SELECTION TESTS
Selection Tests, pp. 179–182

BEST PRACTICES TOOLKIT
Word Squares, p. E10
Outline, p. B19

INTERACTIVE READER

ADAPTED INTERACTIVE READER

ELL ADAPTED INTERACTIVE READER

TECHNOLOGY
- Teacher One Stop DVD-ROM
- Student One Stop DVD-ROM
- PowerNotes DVD-ROM
- Audio Anthology CD
- GrammarNotes DVD-ROM
- Audio Tutor CD
- ExamView Test Generator on the **Teacher One Stop**

THINK central

Video Trailer

Go to **thinkcentral.com** to preview the **Video Trailer** introducing this selection. Other features that support the selection include
- **PowerNotes** presentation
- **ThinkAloud** models to enhance comprehension
- **WordSharp** vocabulary tutorials
- interactive writing and grammar instruction

*** Resources for Differentiation   † Also in Spanish   ‡ In Haitian Creole and Vietnamese**

● TEXT ANALYSIS: ARGUMENT

At the heart of every argument is a **claim,** the writer's position on an issue. To convince readers that a claim is valid, a writer must offer **support,** which may consist of

- reasons that explain or justify an action, a belief, or a decision
- evidence in the form of facts, statistics, examples, or the views of experts

In "Doing Nothing Is Something," Anna Quindlen discusses a topic particular to contemporary U.S. society. Over the years, United States' culture has undergone a cultural shift in the use of leisure time. Quindlen claims that this shift in perspective is detrimental to children and the adults they will become.

As you read, use a chart like the one shown to help you identify Anna Quindlen's claim and the support she provides.

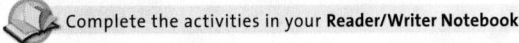

Claim: We need to allow children to have downtime in the summer.	
Reason	Evidence
Children are overscheduled.	A suburb set aside one night free of homework, athletic practices, and after-school events.

■ READING SKILL: DISTINGUISH FACT FROM OPINION

A **fact** is a statement that can be proved, such as, "Most U.S. households have Internet access." An **opinion** is a statement of belief, such as, "I think people rely too much on the Internet."
People often use words and phrases such as *I think, I believe, perhaps,* and *maybe* to state their opinions—but not always. To identify opinions that lack such telltale words and phrases, remember that an opinion cannot be proved; at best, an opinion can only be supported.

▲ VOCABULARY IN CONTEXT

The following vocabulary words help Quindlen make her point about free time. To see how many words you know, match each word from the list with its synonym.

WORD LIST	contemptuous	hiatus	prestigious
	deficit	laudable	

1. prominent   2. shortfall   3. break
4. disdainful   5. praiseworthy

 Complete the activities in your **Reader/Writer Notebook.**

Meet the Author

Anna Quindlen
born 1952

A Fresh Voice
Anna Quindlen was hired as a reporter by the *New York Times* in 1977, just three years after graduating from college. She gave up her full-time job in 1985 to stay home with her children and work on a novel. However, an editor convinced her to write a column about marriage and parenthood. Quindlen's voice stood out among the *Times* columnists, most of whom were men who focused on politics. She has earned widespread acclaim for her ability to address important social issues through her personal experiences. In 1992, she won a Pulitzer Prize for the columns she had initially viewed as "a way to make a little bit of money while writing my novel."

Family Portraits
While Quindlen achieved success as a columnist, she continued to pursue her dream of writing fiction. Her first novel, *Object Lessons,* became a best-seller when it was published in 1991, and other successful novels have followed. Although she tackles controversial subjects, such as domestic violence, Quindlen's fiction, like her columns, is rooted in observations of family life. She said that anyone who reads her books would realize that "family is central to my existence."

Author Online
THINK central
Go to **thinkcentral.com.**
KEYWORD: HML10-639

639

Teach

● *Model the Skill:* ARGUMENT

To model how to identify an author's argument, share this passage:

> Electronic entertainment harms children. Kids stay indoors, passively watching TV instead of playing outside with friends.

Point out that the author begins with the statement that electronic entertainment harms children. Explain that the writer supports the claim by saying that kids give up exercise and interaction with friends in favor of electronic entertainment.

GUIDED PRACTICE Elicit additional support for the writer's claim.

R RESOURCE MANAGER—Copy Master
Argument p. 21

■ *Model the Skill:* DISTINGUISH FACT FROM OPINION

To model how to distinguish fact from opinion, read **Meet the Author**. Discuss which statements are facts and which are opinions. Dates and events mentioned are facts. Quindlen's comment about "anyone who reads her books" is an opinion; it can't be proved.

GUIDED PRACTICE Elicit other examples of facts and opinions.

▲ VOCABULARY IN CONTEXT

DIAGNOSE WORD KNOWLEDGE Have all students complete Vocabulary in Context. Check their words and phrases against the following:

contemptuous (kən-tĕmp′chōō-əs) *adj.* scornful or disrespectful
deficit (dĕf′ĭ-sĭt) *n.* a shortfall or deficiency
hiatus (hī-ā′təs) *n.* a gap or break in continuity
laudable (lô′də-bəl) *adj.* worthy of high praise
prestigious (prĕ-stē′jəs) *adj.* having a great reputation; highly respected

PRETEACH VOCABULARY Use the following copy master to help students predict the meaning of each boldfaced word.

R RESOURCE MANAGER—Copy Master
Vocabulary Study p. 25

1. Read item 1, emphasizing *contemptuous.*
2. Point out the word *scorn.* Elicit possible meanings for *contemptuous,* such as "lacking in respect."

3. Have students record their predictions.
4. Repeat the procedure for items 2–5.

BACKGROUND

Textbooks of Old Describing the textbooks on her children's desks, Quindlen writes: "The number of uncut pages at the back grows smaller and smaller" (lines 3–6). She is referring to the way in which books used to be published, with folded pages that the reader had to cut apart to separate. Quindlen's metaphor is a colorful way of describing the approaching end of the school year.

REVISIT THE BIG QUESTION

How should you spend your
FREE TIME?

Discuss In lines 8–14, did Quindlen enjoy her summer leisure time as a child? How can you tell? *Possible answer: Quindlen seems to have enjoyed her leisure, as evidenced by her saying that she feels "glee" at remembering those summers (lines 8–9) and in her catalog of memories (lines 10–14).*

Analyze Visuals

Possible answer: The photograph suggests a relaxed, contemplative, dreamy mood.

Doing Nothing Is Something

by Anna Quindlen

Analyze Visuals ▶
What **mood** does this photograph suggest to you?

Summer is coming soon.
I can feel it in the softening of the air, but I can see it, too, in the textbooks on my children's desks. The number of uncut pages at the back grows smaller and smaller. The looseleaf is ragged at the edges, the binder plastic ripped at the corners. An old remembered glee rises inside me.
10 Summer is coming. Uniform skirts in mothballs. Pencils with their points left broken. Open windows. Day trips to the beach. Pickup games. Hanging out.

DIFFERENTIATED INSTRUCTION

FOR ENGLISH LANGUAGE LEARNERS
Vocabulary Support Use Word Squares to teach these words: *psychological* (line 65), *research* (line 66), *unstructured* (lines 79–80), *culture* (line 90), *evidence* (line 114), *computer* (line 165).

🧰 BEST PRACTICES TOOLKIT—Transparency
Word Squares p. E10

FOR STRUGGLING READERS
In combination with the *Audio Anthology CD,* use one or more Targeted Passages (pp. 641, 642) to ensure that students focus on key events, concepts, and skills. Targeted Passages are also good for English learners.

①Targeted Passage [Lines 16–37]
This passage introduces the author's positive view of leisure as Quindlen associates the approaching summer with recollections of her own childhood summers.

Targeted Passage

How boring it was. **①**

Of course, it was the making of me, as a human being and a writer. Downtime is where we become ourselves, looking into the middle
20 distance, kicking at the curb, lying on the grass or sitting on the stoop and staring at the tedious blue of the summer sky. I don't believe you can write poetry, or compose music, or become an actor without downtime, and plenty of it, a **hiatus** that passes for boredom but is really the quiet moving of the wheels inside that fuel creativity.
30 And that, to me, is one of the saddest things about the lives of American children today. Soccer leagues, acting classes, tutors—the calendar of the average middle-class kid is so over the top that soon Palm handhelds will be sold in Toys "R" Us. Our children are as overscheduled as we are, and that is saying something. **Ⓐ**
40 This has become so bad that parents have arranged to schedule times for unscheduled time. Earlier this year the privileged suburb of Ridgewood, N.J., announced a Family Night, when there would be no homework, no athletic practices and no after-school events. This was terribly exciting until I realized that this was not one night a week,
50 but one single night. There is even a free-time movement, and Web site: familylife1st.org. Among the frequently asked questions provided online: "What would families do with family time if they took it back?"

Let me make a suggestion for the kids involved: how about nothing? It is not simply that it is pathetic to consider the lives of children who
60 don't have a moment between piano and dance and homework to talk about their day or just search for split ends, an enormously satisfying leisure-time activity of my youth. There is also ample psychological research suggesting that what we might call "doing nothing" is when human beings actually do their best thinking, and when creativity comes
70 to call. Perhaps we are creating an entire generation of people whose ability to think outside the box, as the current parlance[1] of business has it, is being systematically stunted by scheduling.

A study by the University of Michigan quantified[2] the downtime **deficit**; in the last 20 years American kids have lost about four unstruc-
80 tured hours a week. There has even arisen a global Right to Play movement: in the Third World it is often about child labor, but in the United States it is about the sheer labor of being a perpetually busy child. In Omaha, Neb., a group of parents recently lobbied for additional recess. Hooray, and yikes. **Ⓑ**

How did this happen? Adults did
90 it. There is a culture of adult distrust that suggests that a kid who is not playing softball or attending science-enrichment programs—or both— is huffing or boosting cars: if kids are left alone, they will not stare into the middle distance and consider

---

1. **parlance** (pär'ləns): a particular manner of speaking.
2. **quantified:** expressed as a number or quantity.

COMMON CORE L 5b

Language Coach

Word Definitions
Downtime (in line 18) originally meant the time when a machine in a factory was shut down for repairs; today, it can refer to any time not working. Use the word *downtime* in a sentence of your own.

hiatus (hī-ā'təs) *n.* a gap or break in continuity

deficit (děf'ĭ-sĭt) *n.* a shortfall or deficiency

Ⓐ DISTINGUISH FACT FROM OPINION
Is the last statement in this paragraph a fact or an opinion? Explain your answer.

Ⓑ ARGUMENT
What evidence does Quindlen supply in lines 76–88 to support her claim? Add this evidence to your chart.

- What details and images does Quindlen recall from her own childhood? What do these memories have in common? (lines 19–23; line 27)
- What does Quindlen think of children's lives today? (lines 34–35)
- What examples does she give to prove her point? (lines 32–33)

FOR ENGLISH LANGUAGE LEARNERS

Language Coach   **COMMON CORE** L 5b

Word Definitions
Answer: Students' answers may vary as long as they use the word correctly. Ask students to compare the words *downtime* and *hiatus.* Can the words be used interchangeably? How do the meanings differ? *Possible answer: Since* downtime *originally referred to time out for repair, it still carries the connotation or rest for renewal, while* hiatus *is simply a time away from something.*

Reading Support

This selection on **thinkcentral.com** includes embedded **ThinkAloud** models—students "thinking aloud" about the story to model the kinds of questions a good reader would ask about a selection.

READING SKILL   **COMMON CORE** RI 8

Ⓐ DISTINGUISH FACT FROM OPINION

Answer: It is an opinion. It expresses a belief that cannot be proved.

TEXT ANALYSIS   **COMMON CORE** RI 5

Ⓑ *Model the Skill:* ARGUMENT

Possible answer: To support her claim, Quindlen cites a scientific study indicating that "kids have lost about four unstructured hours a week" (lines 79–80), the Right to Play movement to conditions in the United States (lines 80–85), and a local parent campaign for more recess (lines 85–87).

VOCABULARY   **COMMON CORE** L 4

OWN THE WORD

- **hiatus:** Have students complete the following sentence to demonstrate their understanding of the word. During my *hiatus* from school.... *Possible answer: I plan to visit my grandparents.*
- **deficit:** Tell students that *deficit* comes from the Latin word meaning "it is lacking." Have students use dictionaries to find synonyms for *deficit. Possible answers: inadequacy, insufficiency*

READING SKILL

 *Model the Skill:* DISTINGUISH FACT FROM OPINION

Remind students that a fact is a statement that can be proved. An opinion is a statement of belief.

Possible answer: *Quindlen cites the fact that although presidential aide Karen Hughes had only one weekday dinner with her son, she was praised for her "dedication to family time" (lines 120–123).*

 GRAMMAR AND STYLE

COMMON CORE

L 3

Add Rhetorical Questions Explain that a rhetorical question is a question that doesn't require an answer. Such a question is a device that persuasive writers and speakers often use to suggest that their arguments are so strong that the answer is obvious.

VOCABULARY

COMMON CORE

L 4

OWN THE WORD

- **prestigious:** Have students list people or things that they consider *prestigious*. ***Possible answers:*** *colleges, awards*

- **contemptuous:** Point out that the adjective *contemptuous* comes from *contempt*, meaning "despised or disrespected," and the suffix *ous*, which means "full of."

- **laudable:** Remind students that *laudable* means "worthy of high praise." Tell them that the verb *laud* means "to praise highly." Have students use both words in sentences.

SELECTION WRAP–UP

READ WITH A PURPOSE Now that students have finished reading the selection, ask : What is the author's main idea? ***Possible answer:*** *Children need unstructured time.*

---

prestigious
(prĕ-stē′jəs) *adj.* having a great reputation; highly respected

contemptuous
(kən-tĕmp′chōō-əs) *adj.* scornful or disrespectful

laudable (lô′də-bəl) *adj.* worthy of high praise

 DISTINGUISH FACT FROM OPINION

Reread lines 109–126. What fact does Quindlen include to support her opinion that parents have too little leisure time?

GRAMMAR AND STYLE

Reread lines 150–163. Quindlen uses **rhetorical questions** to make the idea of doing nothing sound more appealing than the usual summertime activities.

---

the meaning of life and how come your nose in pictures never looks the way you think it should, but 100 instead will get into trouble. There is also the culture of cutthroat and unquestioning competition that leads even the parents of preschoolers to gab about **prestigious** colleges without a trace of irony: this suggests that any class in which you do not enroll your first grader will put him at a disadvantage in, say, law school.

Finally, there is a culture of 110 workplace presence (as opposed to productivity). Try as we might to suggest that all these enrichment activities are for the good of the kid, there is ample evidence that they are really for the convenience of parents with way too little leisure time of their own. Stories about the resignation of presidential aide Karen Hughes unfailingly reported her 120 dedication to family time by noting that she arranged to get home at 5:30 one night a week to have dinner with her son. If one weekday dinner out of five is considered **laudable,** what does that say about what's become commonplace?

Summer is coming. It used to be a time apart for kids, a respite from the clock and the copybook, the 130 organized day. Every once in a while, either guilty or overwhelmed or tired of listening to me keen[3] about my monumental boredom, my mother would send me to some rinky-dink park program that consisted almost entirely of three-legged races and making things out of Popsicle sticks.

---

3. **keen:** cry out in grief.

Now, instead, there are music camps, sports camps, fat camps, probably 140 thin camps. I mourn hanging out in the backyard. I mourn playing Wiffle ball in the street without a sponsor and matching shirts. I mourn drawing in the dirt with a stick.

Maybe that kind of summer is gone for good. Maybe this is the leading edge of a new way of living that not only has no room for contemplation but is **contemptuous** 150 of it. But if downtime cannot be squeezed during the school year into the life of frantic and often joyless activity with which our children are saddled while their parents pursue frantic and often joyless activity of their own, what about summer? Do most adults really want to stand in line for Space Mountain or sit in traffic to get to a shore house that 160 doesn't have enough saucepans? Might it be even more enriching for their children to stay at home and do nothing? For those who say they will only watch TV or play on the computer, a piece of technical advice: the cable box can be unhooked, the modem removed. Perhaps it is not too late for American kids to be given the 170 gift of enforced boredom for at least a week or two, staring into space, bored out of their gourds, exploring the inside of their own heads. "To contemplate is to toil, to think is to do," said Victor Hugo. "Go outside and play," said Prudence Quindlen. Both of them were right.

Targeted Passage

---

642 UNIT 6: ARGUMENT AND PERSUASION

DIFFERENTIATED INSTRUCTION

FOR STRUGGLING READERS

Targeted Passage [Lines 150–177]

This concluding passage stresses the need to give kids at least some time to do nothing.

- According to Quindlen, how should parents enforce boredom? (lines 160–162, 166–168)

- What does Quindlen believe would be the result of enforced boredom? (lines 172–175)

FOR ENGLISH LANGUAGE LEARNERS

Vocabulary: Idioms and Sayings Help students understand these idioms and sayings from the story: *Hanging out* (line 14), "relaxing"; *looking into the middle distance* (lines 19–20), "staring into space"; *over the top* (line 35), "excessive"; *think outside the box* (line 72), "think creatively"; *huffing or boosting cars* (line 94), "inhaling fumes or stealing cars"; *rinky-dink* (line 134), "shoddy"; *bored out of their gourds* (line 172), "completely bored."

Comprehension

1. **Recall** What were Quindlen's summers like when she was a child?

2. **Recall** What change does Quindlen propose in her essay?

3. **Clarify** What does the word *nothing* mean in the essay's title?

Text Analysis

● 4. **Analyze an Argument** Review the chart you created as you read. What evidence does Quindlen provide to support her claim?

■ 5. **Distinguish Fact from Opinion** Identify whether each statement listed in the chart is a fact or an opinion. Use a chart like the one shown to record your answers.

Statement	Fact or Opinion?
"I don't believe you can write poetry, or compose music, or become an actor without downtime...." (lines 23–26)	
"... in the last 20 years American kids have lost about four unstructured hours a week." (lines 78–80)	
"I mourn hanging out in the backyard." (lines 140–141)	

6. **Examine Support** How does the Victor Hugo quotation in lines 173–175 support Quindlen's claim?

7. **Make Judgments** Quindlen notes that children today are enrolled in soccer leagues, music camps, and sports camps—pursuits that may be quite enjoyable. Explain whether you agree with her that such activities are not leisure. What perspective does Quindlen offer about "downtime".

8. **Synthesize Concepts** What does the essay suggest about our society's values? Cite evidence in your response.

9. **Evaluate an Argument** How effective is Quindlen's argument in this essay? Support your opinion with evidence from the text.

How should you spend your FREE TIME?
Would you like to spend time doing nothing? Why or why not?

---

8. The essay suggests that society values goal-directed activity over contemplative, purely creative activity. Evidence includes Quindlen's discussions of "the culture of adult distrust" (lines 90–100) and "the culture of cutthroat ... competition" (lines 100–108).

9. Students should support their opinions by citing specific lines or passages and by evaluating Quindlen's use of evidence to support her claim.

How should you spend your FREE TIME? Students might cite examples from the selection to support their arguments about the value of spending time doing nothing.

For preliminary support of post-reading questions, use these copy masters:

R RESOURCE MANAGER—Copy Masters
Reading Check p. 28
Distinguish Fact from Opinion p. 23
Question Support p. 29

Additional selection questions are provided for teachers on page 15.

ANSWERS

Comprehension

1. *Quindlen's childhood summers were leisurely, sometimes boring.*

2. *Quindlen proposes that children be allowed to have more free time without structured activities—especially in summer.*

3. *Nothing means not participating in organized sports, music lessons, and similarly structured activities.*

Text Analysis COMMON CORE RI 5, RI 8

Possible answers:

4. ● **COMMON CORE FOCUS** *Argument Quindlen's reasons are that (1) downtime provides an opportunity for children to develop their creativity and that (2) children are overscheduled during the school year.*

5. ■ **COMMON CORE FOCUS** *Distinguish Fact from Opinion The first statement is an opinion; the second and third statements are fact.*

6. *Hugo says that contemplation is work. The quotation relates to Quindlen's claim, because Quindlen argues that "doing nothing" helps children put their minds to work creatively by giving them time to think.*

7. *Some students may argue that such activities are too structured to qualify as leisure. Others may believe that if kids find such activities relaxing and fun, then the activities would qualify as leisure.*

RI 5 Analyze how an author's ideas or claims are developed and refined. **RI 8** Delineate and evaluate the argument and specific claims in a text, assessing whether the reasoning is valid.

ANSWERS

Vocabulary in Context

▲ VOCABULARY PRACTICE

1. *c*   4. *a*
2. *d*   5. *b*
3. *d*

R RESOURCE MANAGER—Copy Master
Vocabulary Practice p. 26

ACADEMIC VOCABULARY IN WRITING

Possible answer: Statistics *show that students have less free time today than ever before. Homework assignments require a great deal of time. Many students also play important roles in daily family life. In order to* ***convince*** *their parents to grant them new freedoms, they accept time-consuming new responsibilities.*

VOCABULARY STRATEGY: ETYMOLOGY

 COMMON CORE L 4c

- Explain that an etymology traces the history and development of a word back to its earliest known form and shows changes in spelling and meaning that have occurred in the word over time.
- Point out that that foreign words—such as the Latin words *hiātus* and *hiāre* in the example—appear in italics. Also explain that some dictionaries use the symbol < to mean "derived from."

Answers:
1. *Latin*
2. *Latin, Middle English*
3. *contemnere, "to scorn"*

R RESOURCE MANAGER—Copy Master
Vocabulary Strategy p. 27

Interactive Vocabulary

 THINK central

Keywords direct students to a **WordSharp** tutorial on **thinkcentral.com** or to other types of vocabulary practice and review.

Vocabulary in Context

▲ VOCABULARY PRACTICE

Choose the letter of the word that is most different in meaning from the others. If necessary, use a dictionary to check the precise meanings of words you are unsure of.

1. (a) prestigious, (b) reputable, (c) infamous, (d) eminent
2. (a) hiatus, (b) gap, (c) respite, (d) renewal
3. (a) surplus, (b) excess, (c) sufficiency, (d) deficit
4. (a) despicable, (b) admirable, (c) laudable, (d) commendable
5. (a) disdainful, (b) deferential, (c) scornful, (d) contemptuous

WORD LIST
contemptuous
deficit
hiatus
laudable
prestigious

ACADEMIC VOCABULARY IN WRITING

- cite • controversy • convince • objective • statistic

Why do you think young people often lack free time? **Cite** at least three specific reasons. Use at least one Academic Vocabulary word in your response. Here is an example of one reason.

> **SAMPLE REASON**
>
> *In addition to spending plenty of time studying, students whose* ***objective*** *is college must be involved in extracurricular activities, too.*

VOCABULARY STRATEGY: ETYMOLOGY

The **etymology** of a word, or its origin and history, can provide insight into the word's meaning. You can learn about a word's etymology by looking up the word or its root in a dictionary. Information about the etymology will appear near the beginning or end of the dictionary entry.

hi•a•tus (hī-ā′təs) *n., pl.* **–tus•es** or **hiatus 1.** A gap or interruption in space, time, or continuity; a break: *"We are likely to be disconcerted by . . . hiatuses of thought"* (Edmund Wilson). **2.** *Linguistics* A slight pause that occurs when two immediately adjacent vowels in consecutive syllables are pronounced, as in *reality* and *naive*. **3.** *Anatomy* A separation, aperture, fissure, or short passage in an organ or body part. [Latin *hiatus,* from past participle of *hiare,* to gape.] —**hi•a′tal** (-āt′l) *adj.*

PRACTICE Look up the following italicized words in a dictionary, noting each word's derivation and meaning. Also look for clues to explain its spelling. Then answer the questions.

1. What language is the original source of the word *deficit*?
2. Through which languages can the history of *laudable* be traced?
3. From which Latin word does *contemptuous* derive, and what does the Latin word mean?

COMMON CORE

L 4c Consult reference materials to determine or clarify the etymology of a word.

Interactive Vocabulary • THINK central

Go to **thinkcentral.com**.
KEYWORD: HML10-644

DIFFERENTIATED INSTRUCTION

FOR STRUGGLING WRITERS

Develop Reading Fluency Pronounce all the vocabulary words for this selection aloud. Then have students repeat the pronunciations as you modeled them. Have students work in pairs to practice pronouncing the words until they can say them fluently. Then have students use the words in sentences to demonstrate comprehension.

FOR ADVANCED LEARNERS/PRE–AP

Vocabulary in Writing Challenge students to use as many vocabulary words as they can in a brief composition that explores ways in which they could tap into their creativity by doing nothing. For example, students might suggest putting aside time during the week just to think.

Language

◆ **GRAMMAR AND STYLE:** Add Rhetorical Questions

Review the **Grammar and Style** note on page 642. Quindlen uses **interrogative sentences** to pose a series of **rhetorical questions,** or questions that do not require answers, encouraging readers to think about issues. Revise your response to the prompt by employing these techniques:

1. **Include one or more rhetorical questions in your editorial.** Rhetorical questions can help you focus your audience's thoughts on an issue.

2. **Use rhetorical questions sparingly so that they retain their impact.** Add rhetorical questions only when you really need to underscore a point. Here is one student's example.

> **STUDENT MODEL**
>
> Are we supposed to feel sorry for kids who are lucky enough to participate in a variety of activities? Do we really think kids are too overscheduled just because they spend their days at soccer practice and music lessons instead of looking up at the sky?

Notice how the revision in blue helps to highlight the message in this first draft.

> **STUDENT MODEL**
>
> I know plenty of kids who do volunteer work in the summer or take courses in subjects not taught at school. ∧ *Would they really be better off hanging out at the pool?*

◆ COMMON CORE

L 3 Apply knowledge of language to make effective choices for meaning or style. **W 5** Develop and strengthen writing as needed by revising, focusing on what is most significant for a specific purpose.

READING-WRITING CONNECTION

YOUR TURN Explore the ideas presented in "Doing Nothing Is Something" by responding to this prompt. Then use the **revising tip** to improve your writing.

WRITING PROMPT	REVISING TIP
Extended Constructed Response: Editorial Write a **three-to-five-paragraph editorial** in which you argue that children reap greater benefits from participating in structured activities.	Review your response. Did you include rhetorical questions, though sparingly? If not, revise your response to include either more or fewer rhetorical questions.

Interactive Revision THINK central
Go to **thinkcentral.com.**
KEYWORD: HML10-645

FOR STRUGGLING WRITERS

- Limit the length of the assignment to two or three paragraphs.
- Have small groups of students discuss the possible benefits of structured activities.
- Offer advice as students draft the statement of their claim. Then help them use an outline to organize their argument.

 **BEST PRACTICES TOOLKIT—Transparency**
Outline p. B19

Language

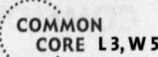 COMMON CORE L 3, W 5

◆ **GRAMMAR AND STYLE**

- After students examine the second model, discuss how the inserted rhetorical question improves the draft.

- Write this passage on the board. Ask students to suggest a rhetorical question to enhance the text. (Sample revisions are shown in blue.)

> *I think that Quindlen should consider why she could have the kind of unstructured, "go outside and play" summer that she enjoyed as a child. Was it because her mom didn't work?*

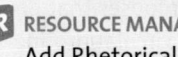 **RESOURCE MANAGER—Copy Master**
Add Rhetorical Questions p. 30

READING-WRITING CONNECTION

Point out that students are countering Quindlen's claim, so they should recall how she supported her view. In addition, explain that because of the editorial's length, students should probably explore two or three benefits.

> **Writing Online** THINK central
>
> The following tools are available online at **thinkcentral.com** and on Write*Smart* CD-ROM:
> - **Interactive Graphic Organizers**
> - **Interactive Student Models**
> - **Interactive Revision Lessons**
> For additional grammar instruction, see **GrammarNotes** on **thinkcentral.com.**

Assess and Reteach

Assess

DIAGNOSTIC AND SELECTION TESTS
Selection Test A pp. 179–180
Selection Test B/C pp. 181–182

Interactive Selection Test on **thinkcentral.com**

Reteach

Level Up Online Tutorials on **thinkcentral.com**

Reteaching Worksheets on **thinkcentral.com**
Reading Lesson 5: Distinguishing Fact from Opinion
Informational Text Lesson 14: Elements of an Argument
Vocabulary Lesson 25: Etymologies

Focus and Motivate

COMMON CORE FOCUS

RI 1 Cite strong textual evidence to support analysis of what the text says explicitly as well as inferences drawn from the text. **RI 4** Determine the meaning of words as they are used in a text. **RI 5** Analyze in detail how an author's claims are developed by a particular paragraph. **RI 8** Delineate and evaluate the argument and specific claims in a text, assessing whether the reasoning is valid and the evidence is relevant and sufficient.

SUMMARY

In "Abolishing the Penny Makes Good Sense," economist Alan S. Blinder proposes that pennies be withdrawn from circulation. In his editorial he explains why he thinks the penny is a problem. He predicts how retailers would cope without the penny and outlines a plan for determining sales tax in a penny-free economy. Blinder concludes by offering a suggestion for ending Americans' sentimental attachment to the penny.

Why keep what is no longer **USEFUL?**

Ask the question, and then use the photograph of the typewriter to introduce the idea that sometimes people keep things that are no longer useful. After students have read the paragraph, ask them to list examples of tools and appliances that have outlived their useful-ness. Then suggest that they focus on one of these items for the *QUICKWRITE.* Encourage volunteers to share their responses.

Selection Resources

Before Reading

Abolishing the Penny Makes Good Sense
Editorial by Alan S. Blinder

Why keep what is no longer USEFUL?

COMMON CORE

RI 1 Cite textual evidence to support analysis of what the text says explicitly as well as inferences drawn from the text. **RI 4** Determine the meaning of words as they are used in a text. **RI 5** Analyze in detail how an author's claims are developed by a particular paragraph. **RI 8** Delineate and evaluate the argument and specific claims in a text, assessing whether the reasoning is valid and the evidence is relevant and sufficient.

Are there old tools or appliances in your home that nobody ever uses? What keeps your family from throwing them away? In "Abolishing the Penny Makes Good Sense," economist Alan Blinder denies the usefulness of one of the most common objects in our society.

QUICKWRITE Write a paragraph about a device or an object that has outlived its usefulness. Explain what caused it to lose value, and discuss why some people might be reluctant to get rid of it.

646

See resources on the **Teacher One Stop DVD-ROM** and on **thinkcentral.com**.

R RESOURCE MANAGER UNIT 6
Plan and Teach, pp. 31–38
Summary, pp. 39–40†‡*
Text Analysis and Reading
  Skill, pp. 41–44†*

**DIAGNOSTIC AND SELECTION
  TESTS**
Selection Tests, pp. 183–186

BEST PRACTICES TOOLKIT
Word Questioning, p. E9

TECHNOLOGY
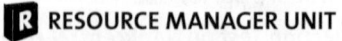 Teacher One Stop DVD-ROM
Student One Stop DVD-ROM
Audio Anthology CD
GrammarNotes DVD-ROM
ExamView Test Generator
  on the **Teacher One Stop**

---

* Resources for Differentiation   † Also in Spanish   ‡ In Haitian Creole and Vietnamese

TEXT ANALYSIS: EVIDENCE

Writers use **evidence** to show that their arguments and conclusions are valid. Alan Blinder presents a variety of evidence in "Abolishing the Penny Makes Good Sense," including family anecdotes and observations like this one:

Few people nowadays even bend down to pick a penny off the sidewalk.

Anecdotal evidence is based on personal experience. Other types of evidence include:

- **empirical** evidence (based on scientific research)
- **logical** evidence (based on sound reason or facts)

As you read, evaluate the evidence Blinder presents.

READING SKILL: ANALYZE DEDUCTIVE REASONING

When you arrive at a conclusion by applying a general principle to a specific situation, you are organizing your ideas by using **deductive reasoning.** Here is an example:

General Principle: Any student caught cheating will be suspended.
Specific Situation: Jeremiah was caught cheating.
Conclusion: Jeremiah will be suspended.

Writers often use deductive reasoning in arguments without stating the general principle. They just assume that readers will recognize and agree with the principle.

Careful readers don't always assume the general principle is sound, however. They identify it, as well as the other parts of the argument, and then ask whether each part is really true.

To analyze Alan Blinder's deductive reasoning, complete the following chart as you read his editorial.

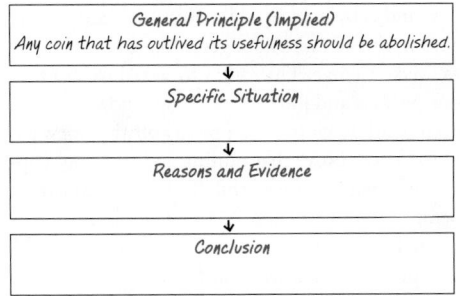

General Principle (Implied)
Any coin that has outlived its usefulness should be abolished.

↓

Specific Situation

↓

Reasons and Evidence

↓

Conclusion

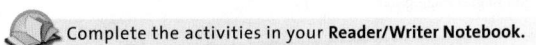

Complete the activities in your **Reader/Writer Notebook.**

Meet the Author

Alan S. Blinder
born 1945

Money Matters

Alan S. Blinder is a professor of economics at Princeton University. The author of numerous articles and essays, Blinder has also influenced economic policy from within government. He served on the Council of Economic Advisors, which advises the president on economic issues, and from 1994 to 1996 he helped oversee the nation's banking system as vice chairman of the Federal Reserve Board. An economist who collaborated on a textbook with Blinder noted that "when Alan offered a criticism of something I had done, it was almost invariably right. I never could think of a good counterargument."

BACKGROUND TO THE EDITORIAL

The Ever-Changing Penny
The first U.S. penny was minted in 1793. Made of solid copper, it was about the size of a quarter. Since that time, the penny has been redesigned 11 times, with the Lincoln penny making its debut in 1909 to mark the 100th anniversary of Lincoln's birth. The composition of the penny has changed over the years as well. In 1982 the government switched from a mostly copper penny to one that is 97% zinc with a copper coating. Had the mint continued to make pennies out of copper, the cost to produce each one would have been greater than one cent.

Diminishing Value
A penny doesn't go as far as it once did. In the 1930s a penny could buy a lollipop, a pencil, or a handful of peanuts. Today, you would be hard-pressed to find anything that costs only one cent.

Author Online

THINK central

Go to **thinkcentral.com.**
KEYWORD: HML10-647

647

Teach

TEXT ANALYSIS · COMMON CORE · RI 8

● Model the Skill: EVIDENCE

To model how to evaluate evidence, read aloud the editorial's title, "Abolishing the Penny Makes Good Sense." Then discuss which of the following items might provide valid evidence for Blinder's claim:

1. an anecdote about the problems created by using pennies
2. a count of the number of pennies in the author's pocket

Point out that both items are relevant to the writer's argument and support his claim.

GUIDED PRACTICE Elicit valid evidence for a claim that people should walk a mile a day for their health.

READING SKILL · COMMON CORE · RI 1 · RI 5

■ Model the Skill: ANALYZE DEDUCTIVE REASONING

Help students identify and explain the flaw in this example of deductive reasoning:

General Principle: All flowers bloom in the spring.

Specific Situation: Mums are flowers.

Conclusion: Mums bloom in the spring.

Point out that many flowers, including mums, do not bloom in the spring. Therefore, the general principle is not sound.

GUIDED PRACTICE Have students invent a general principle, specific situation, and conclusion of their own.

R RESOURCE MANAGER—Copy Master
Analyze Deductive Reasoning p. 43 (for student use while reading the selection)

DIFFERENTIATED INSTRUCTION

FOR STRUGGLING READERS
Develop Reading Fluency Students may consider fiction, with dialogue and vivid descriptions, easier to read than an editorial. Read aloud lines 7–17, modeling the tone of the author's subtle humor and sarcasm. Then have student pairs practice reading these lines and the final paragraph, mimicking your tone, pacing, and pronunciation.

R RESOURCE MANAGER—Copy Master
Reading Fluency p. 47.

FOR ADVANCED LEARNERS/PRE–AP
Evaluate Deductive Reasoning Ask students to sketch out an original argument (general principle → specific situation → conclusion). Then have them exchange their argument with a partner and consider specific situations that might contradict the general principle in their partner's argument. Have partners collaborate on improving the general principle so that it will be true in all situations. Call on volunteers to share their final arguments with the class.

READ WITH A PURPOSE

Help students set a purpose for reading. Tell them to look for three arguments the author gives in favor of abolishing the penny.

TEXT ANALYSIS · COMMON CORE · RI 5

A AUTHOR'S CLAIM

Possible answer: The author claims that abolishing the penny would have great benefits to individuals and government with virtually no costs. If the writer stated the claim in the final paragraph, the reader would have to speculate about the writer's claim while reading the piece.

READING SKILL · COMMON CORE · RI 1 · RI 5

B *Model the Skill:* DEDUCTIVE REASONING

Point out the evidence and reasons that Blinder provides in this passage to support his statement of the specific situation. Help students add this information to the third box of their Deductive Reasoning charts.

Possible answer: The specific situation is that (in Blinder's opinion) the penny has outlived its usefulness (lines 7–8).

Extend the Discussion Reread the title of Blinder's editorial. How can you tell that the title expresses his conclusion rather than his general principle?

REVISIT THE BIG QUESTION

Why keep what is no longer USEFUL?

Discuss Based on lines 7–17, do pennies have any usefulness to you? What do you use pennies for? *Possible answer: Yes, pennies are often useful for paying the exact amount of cash. Also, cashiers usually cannot make change for you without using pennies.*

Targeted Passage ①

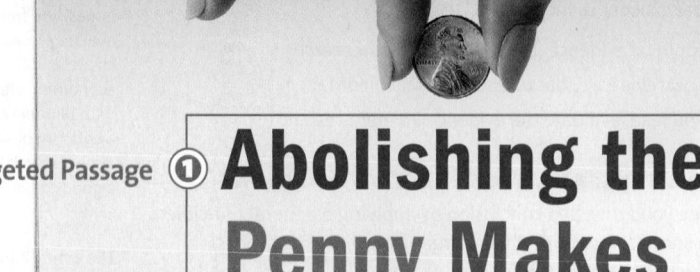

Abolishing the Penny Makes Good Sense

by Alan S. Blinder

COMMON CORE RI 5

A AUTHOR'S CLAIM
Editorial writers usually want their readers to understand the **claim,** or point, of their piece right away. What claim is the author is making in the first paragraph? How would this editorial be different if the writer stated the claim in the final paragraph of the piece instead of the first?

B DEDUCTIVE REASONING
Reread lines 7–17. What is the specific situation Blinder intends to prove exists? Restate this situation in your own words on your chart.

An economist rarely has the opportunity to recommend a policy change that benefits 200 million people, imposes costs on virtually no one, and saves the government money to boot. But I have such a suggestion to offer the nation as a holiday gift: Let's abolish the penny. **A**

Yes, the old copperhead has outlived its usefulness and is by now a public nuisance—something akin to the gnat. Pennies get in the way when

10 we make change. They add unwanted weight to our pockets and purses. Few people nowadays even bend down to pick a penny off the sidewalk. Doesn't that prove that mining and minting[1] copper into pennies is wasteful? Today, if it rained pennies from heaven, only a fool would turn his umbrella upside down: The money caught would be worth less than the ruined umbrella. **B**

---

1. **minting:** stamping coins from metal.

DIFFERENTIATED INSTRUCTION

FOR ENGLISH LANGUAGE LEARNERS

Vocabulary Support Use Word Questioning to teach these words: *economist* (line 1), *accumulated* (line 21), *tradition* (line 96), *currency* (line 99), *income* (line 101), *motivates* (line 122).

 BEST PRACTICES TOOLKIT—Transparency Word Questioning p. E9

FOR STRUGGLING READERS

In combination with the *Audio Anthology CD*, use one or more Targeted Passages (pp. 648, 650) to ensure that students focus on key ideas, concepts, and skills. Targeted Passages are also good for English learners.

① **Targeted Passage [Lines 1–6]**

This passage contains the hook that makes the reader want to read further.

- What is the profession of Blinder, the author? What evidence supports that idea? (lines 1, 5)

I have been antipenny for years, but final proof came about two years ago. I used to dump my pennies into a shoe box. Eventually, I accumulated several hundred. Dismayed by the ever-growing collection of useless copper, I offered the box to my son William, then 8, warning him that the bank would take the pennies only if he neatly wrapped them in rolls of 50. William, obviously a keen, intuitive economist, thought the matter over carefully for about two seconds before responding: "Thanks, Dad, but it's not worth it." If it's not worth the time of an 8-year-old to wrap pennies, why does the U.S. government keep producing the things? **G**

91 Billion in Circulation

More than the time of 8-year-olds is involved. Think how often you have waited in line while the customers ahead of you fumbled through their pockets or purses for a few—expletive deleted—pennies. A trivial problem? Yes, until you multiply your wasted seconds by the billions of cash transactions that take place in our economy each year. I estimate that all this penny-pinching wastes several hundred million hours annually. Valuating[2] that at, say, $10 an hour adds up to several billion dollars per year, which is more than enough to justify this column.

We also must consider the cost of minting and maintaining the penny supply. There are roughly 91 billion pennies circulating, and every year

the U.S. Treasury produces 12 billion to 14 billion more, at a cost of about $90 million. Since this expenditure just produces a nuisance for society, it should be at the top of everyone's list of budget cuts.

There are no coherent objections to abolishing the penny. It has been claimed, apparently with a straight face, that eliminating pennies would be inflationary,[3] because all those $39.99 prices would rise to $40. Apart from the fact that such increases would be penny-ante,[4] the claim itself is ludicrous. A price such as $39.99 is designed to keep a four from appearing as the first digit—something the retailer deems psychologically important. In a penny-less society merchants probably would change the number to $39.95, not raise it to $40. Even if only one-fifth of all merchants reacted this way, abolishing the penny would be disinflationary.

Sales tax poses a problem. How would a penny-free economy cope with, for instance, a 7% sales tax on a $31 purchase, which comes to $2.17? The answer leads to the second part of my suggestion. Let all states and localities amend their sales taxes to round all tax bills to the next-highest nickel. In the example, the state would collect $2.20 instead of $2.17. The customer would lose 3¢ but—if my previous arguments are correct—would actually be better off without the pennies. What other tax leaves the taxpayer happier for having paid it?

---

2. **valuating:** placing a value on.

3. **inflationary:** causing an increase in the price of goods.

4. **penny-ante** (ăn'tē): a business deal on a trivial scale.

COMMON CORE RI 4

Language Coach

Prefixes The prefix *anti-* comes from the Greek word for "against." English speakers often create new words, such as *antipenny* (line 18), by adding a prefix to an existing word. What does *antipenny* mean?

G EVIDENCE
In your opinion, is the anecdote Blinder offers in lines 18–35 truly "final proof" that the penny has no value? Why or why not?

TEXT ANALYSIS

COMMON CORE
RI 8

G EVIDENCE

Possible answer: *The anecdote is not "final proof" because Blinder's son might not be a typical 8-year-old. Also, the value of the penny cannot be judged by a child.*

IF STUDENTS NEED HELP . . . Ask them what Blinder implies when he says his son "thought the matter over carefully for about two seconds" (lines 29–30). Does he mean that his son gave too quick an answer or that the answer was so obvious that he didn't need more time?

TIERED DISCUSSION PROMPTS

Direct students to lines 62–79. Use these prompts to help students explore the author's argument:

Connect Would you be more likely to buy something that is priced at $39.99 than at $40.00? Why or why not? *Answers will vary, but students should recognize that $39.99 seems less expensive than $40.00.*

Analyze What does Blinder mean when he says that abolishing the penny would be disinflationary (lines 78–79)? *Possible answer: He means that prices will go down, lowering inflation, because merchants would round prices down by five cents rather than merely one cent.*

Synthesize Can you think of arguments for keeping the penny in circulation? *Accept all reasonable answers.*

- What is Blinder's proposal? Why do you think that he waits until the end of the paragraph to state it? (line 6)

- What benefits does Blinder think his proposal will have? (lines 2–4)

- What play on words can you find in the title of the editorial?

FOR ENGLISH LANGUAGE LEARNERS

Language Coach

COMMON CORE
RI 4

Prefixes *Answer: against pennies* Ask students to think of other words with the prefix *anti-* and give their meanings.

Why keep what is no longer **USEFUL?**

Discuss Based on lines 121–136, do you believe that something that has only sentimental value can be useful—or is the idea of useful-ness tied to practical value? Explain. *Accept all thoughtful answers.*

 *Model the Skill:* EVIDENCE

Remind students that evidence includes anecdotes, observations, examples, sta-tistics, and the views of experts. Sound evidence is relevant to the argument and sufficient to support a claim or reason.

Possible answer: The evidence is somewhat relevant. It shows that other countries have abolished useless units of currency. On the other hand, the fact that abolishing coins has been done in other countries is not definitive proof that the United States also should do so.

SELECTION WRAP-UP

READ WITH A PURPOSE Ask students: Which of the author's arguments for abolishing the penny do you consider most compelling? *Accept all thoughtful answers.*

⭐ **CRITIQUE** Ask students if they agree with Blinder that his idea is "obviously correct" (line 139). Why or why not?

After pennies are struck at the U.S. Mint, they must be inspected for imperfections before they can be released.

Sentimental Value

Only tradition explains our stub-born attachment to the penny. But sometimes traditions get ridiculous. Surely the smallest currency unit
100 a country uses should be related to its average income. Yet countries with lower standards of living than the United States have minimum currency units worth more than 1¢—while we have been minting the penny for two centuries.

Even England, as tradition-bound a nation as they come, is more progressive in this matter than the
110 United States. Years ago the smallest unit of British currency was the far-thing, equal to one-quarter of what was then called a penny. As England grew richer, the farthing gave way to the half-penny, then to the old penny, and finally to the new penny, which is the equivalent of 9.6 far-things. During this same time, all the stodgy United States did was
120 abolish the half-penny. ⓓ

ⓓ **EVIDENCE**
Reread lines 107–120. What type of **evidence** does the author provide here? Is it relevant to his argument? Explain.

② Targeted Passage

Sure, the penny has sentimental value. That motivates the last part of my suggestion. Rather than call in all the pennies and melt them, which would be too expensive and perhaps heartrending, the govern-ment should simply announce that it is demonetizing[5] the penny as of next January—and let collectors
130 take many of the pesky coppers out of circulation. After hobbyists and investors accumulated what-ever stockpiles they desired, the rest could be redeemed by the govern-ment—wrapped neatly in rolls of 50, of course.

Let's get penny-wise and abolish the 1¢ piece. The idea is so logical, so obviously correct, that I am sure
140 the new Congress will enact it dur-ing its first days in office.

---

5. **demonetizing** (dē-mŏn′ĭ-tī′zĭng): depriving of value.

DIFFERENTIATED INSTRUCTION

FOR STRUGGLING READERS

② Targeted Passage [Lines 121–136]

This passage tells how the abolition of the penny might be accomplished.

- According to Blinder, why should the government not collect and melt pennies? (lines 121–122)

- What does he think the government should do instead? (lines 126–129)

- What would hobbyists and investors do with pennies? What would the rest of the population do? (lines 121–131; lines 131–136)

- What would you do with your pennies if they were taken out of circulation?

Task Support Work with students to add reasons and evidence to the third box of their deductive-reasoning charts. *Example: The U.S. Treasury spends $90 million a year to produce pennies (lines 56–58).* Then make sure students understand that Blinder's conclusion is the same thing as his proposal, which he uses as the title of his editorial.

Comprehension

1. **Recall** What is the author's opinion of the penny?

2. **Recall** In what ways does the penny inconvenience people?

3. **Summarize** According to the author, how will customers be affected at checkout lines if the penny is abolished?

COMMON CORE

RI 1 Cite textual evidence to support analysis of what the text says explicitly as well as inferences drawn from the text. **RI 8** Delineate and evaluate the argument and specific claims in a text, assessing whether the reasoning is valid and the evidence is relevant and sufficient.

Text Analysis

4. **Examine an Argument** For each objection to abolishing the penny listed in the chart shown, summarize the **counterargument** that the author makes to refute the objection.

Objection	Counterargument
Inflation would result.	
People would pay more in sales taxes.	
The penny is part of our tradition.	

5. **Analyze Deductive Reasoning** Review the chart you created as you read. What is the strongest reason that the author presents to support his conclusion that the penny has lost its usefulness? Explain your answer.

6. **Analyze Tone** What tone does the author use when discussing arguments in favor of keeping the penny? Cite examples from the text.

7. **Interpret a Statement** What does the author intend to suggest in the last paragraph when he says that his "idea is so logical, so obviously correct, that I am sure the new Congress will enact it during its first days in office"?

8. **Predict an Outcome** The author speculates about how merchants and consumers would respond if the penny is abolished. What do you predict will happen if the penny is removed from circulation? Give reasons for your prediction.

9. **Make Judgments** The author states in the opening paragraph that abolishing the penny would impose "costs on virtually no one." Do you agree with his characterization of how the change would affect people? Cite evidence to support your opinion.

10. **Evaluate Evidence** Does the author provide sufficient evidence to support his conclusion that the penny should be abolished? Explain why or why not.

11. **Evaluate an Unstated Assumption** Look at the chart on page 647 and note Blinder's unstated general principle. Do you agree with this basis for Blinder's argument? Explain why or why not.

> **Why keep what is no longer USEFUL?**
> Do only useful things have value?

Practice and Apply

For preliminary support of post-reading questions, use these copy masters:

R RESOURCE MANAGER—Copy Masters
Reading Check p. 45
Evidence p. 41
Question Support p. 46

Additional selection questions are provided for teachers on page 35.

ANSWERS

Comprehension

1. *Blinder believes that the penny is useless and a nuisance.*

2. *The penny inconveniences people by weighing down their pockets and wasting their time.*

3. *Customers will save time because they won't have to fumble for pennies or wait while someone ahead of them does.*

Text Analysis

COMMON CORE RI 1, RI 8

Possible answers:

4. *Inflation would not result, for merchants would probably round prices down instead of rounding up; people would not mind paying more in sales taxes if the change saved them time; the penny can remain part of our tradition, for people would be able to collect them.*

5. ● **COMMON CORE FOCUS** *Analyze Deductive Reasoning* The strongest reason is that few people bend down to pick up pennies— a sign that pennies have little or no value.

6. *The author tends to use a sarcastic or dismissive tone. In lines 69–70, he uses "ludicrous" to describe the claim that abolishing the penny is inflationary.*

7. *that Congress won't abolish the penny because lawmakers aren't swayed by logic and common sense*

8. *Most people will not mind. Some people might be upset because they are collectors or because they will end up losing money.*

9. *No, because Blinder underestimates the effect of abolishing the penny on poor people. Also, it is difficult to predict what effect this change could have on the economy.*

10. ● **COMMON CORE FOCUS** *Evidence No, because too much of his evidence consists of anecdotes and observations rather than hard facts.*

11. *Yes, because coins should be evaluated for their usefulness in the economy, not for their sentimental or value as collectibles.*

> **Why keep what is no longer USEFUL?** *Possible answer: Value has nothing to do with usefulness. Value is a measure of the importance a person attaches to something.*

Assess and Reteach

Assess

DIAGNOSTIC AND SELECTION TESTS
Selection Test A pp. 183–184
Selection Test B/C pp. 185–186

Interactive Selection Test on <u>thinkcentral.com</u>

Reteach

Level Up Online Tutorials on <u>thinkcentral.com</u>

Reteaching Worksheets on <u>thinkcentral.com</u>
Informational Text Lesson 12: Inductive vs. Deductive Reasoning

Informational Text Lesson 16: Evaluating Evidence

Focus and Motivate

COMMON CORE FOCUS

RI 4 Determine the meaning of words as they are used in a text. **RI 5** Analyze how an author's claims are developed and refined by a particular paragraph. **RI 6** Analyze how an author uses rhetoric to advance point of view or purpose in a text. **RI 8** Delineate and evaluate the argument and specific claims in a text, assessing whether the reasoning is valid and the evidence is relevant and sufficient. **L1a** Use parallel structure. **L 3** Apply knowledge of language to make effective choices for meaning or style. **L 6** Acquire and use accurately domain-specific words and phrases.

SUMMARY

In his speech "On Nuclear Disarmament," Carl Sagan argues against the production of nuclear weapons. We must act now, he says, to avoid a nuclear war.

What would make the world SAFER?

Discuss the question with students. Ask them to think about the concept of security. Extend the activity by having the students complete the *SURVEY*.

On Nuclear Disarmament

 HISTORY Video link at **thinkcentral.com**

Speech by Carl Sagan

What would make the world SAFER?

COMMON CORE

RI 4 Determine the meaning of words as they are used in a text. **RI 5** Analyze how an author's claims are developed and refined by a particular paragraph. **RI 6** Analyze how an author uses rhetoric to advance a point of view or purpose. **RI 8** Delineate and evaluate the argument and specific claims in a text, assessing whether the reasoning is valid and the evidence is relevant and sufficient.

The newspapers are full of reports about war, epidemics, terrorism, and environmental crises. Some problems are so serious that they may threaten civilization. In his speech on nuclear disarmament, delivered in 1988, scientist Carl Sagan argues for rethinking ideas about how to maintain security.

SURVEY Ask six people to identify something that can be done to make the world a safer place. Present the results of your survey to the class.

652

Selection Resources

See resources on the **Teacher One Stop DVD-ROM** and on **thinkcentral.com**.

 HISTORY Video link at **thinkcentral.com**

 **RESOURCE MANAGER UNIT 6**
Plan and Teach, pp. 49–56
Summary, pp. 57–58†‡*
Text Analysis and Reading
   Skill, pp. 59–62†*
Vocabulary, pp. 63–65*
Grammar and Style, p. 68

**DIAGNOSTIC AND SELECTION
   TESTS**
Selection Tests, pp. 187–190

BEST PRACTICES TOOLKIT
New Word Analysis, p. E8
T Chart, p. A25

TECHNOLOGY
- **Teacher One Stop DVD-ROM**
- **Student One Stop DVD-ROM**
- **Audio Anthology CD**
- **GrammarNotes DVD-ROM**
- **ExamView Test Generator
   on the Teacher One Stop**

* Resources for Differentiation   † Also in Spanish   ‡ In Haitian Creole and Vietnamese

TEXT ANALYSIS: RHETORICAL DEVICES

In persuasive writing, rhetorical devices can make the writer's ideas more compelling and memorable. Carl Sagan uses the following devices in his speech "On Nuclear Disarmament":

- **Repetition**—the use of the same word, phrase, or sentence more than once for emphasis
- **Parallelism**—the use of similar grammatical constructions to express related ideas. Sagan opens his speech with a sentence that includes the parallel phrases "ancestors of some of us, brothers of us all."

As you read, notice how Sagan uses these rhetorical devices.

READING SKILL: ANALYZE INDUCTIVE REASONING

When you are led by specific evidence to form a general principle, or generalization, you are following **inductive reasoning.** Carl Sagan uses inductive reasoning when he presents **evidence**—examples and facts from past wars and then, from these, makes a generalization about warfare. When you encounter inductive reasoning, examine the evidence and the concluding generalization to see whether

- the evidence is valid and provides sufficient support for the conclusion
- the writer overgeneralizes, or draws a conclusion that is too broad

As you read, use a graphic organizer like the one shown to help you analyze Sagan's inductive reasoning.

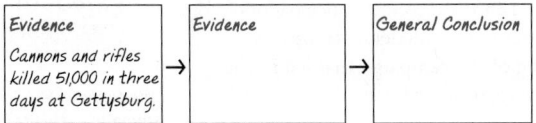

Evidence		Evidence		General Conclusion
Cannons and rifles killed 51,000 in three days at Gettysburg.	→		→	

▲ VOCABULARY IN CONTEXT

In the speech you are about to read, Sagan uses the following words. In your *Reader/Writer Notebook,* write a sentence for the words you already know. After you have read the selection, check to see if you used those words correctly.

WORD LIST		
annihilate	contending	precursor
carnage	malice	reconcile

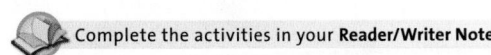

Complete the activities in your **Reader/Writer Notebook.**

Meet the Author

Carl Sagan
1934–1996

Popular Scientist
Carl Sagan's gift for explaining science to the general public helped make him one of the most famous scientists of his time. The astronomer is best known for writing and narrating a television series about astronomy and related topics. The series, *Cosmos,* was watched by 400 million viewers, or, as Sagan put it, 3 percent of the world's population.

No Nukes!
A staunch opponent of nuclear weapons, Sagan promoted the idea that even a limited nuclear war would devastate life on Earth by causing global temperatures to plunge. Although some scientists disputed this "nuclear winter" theory, it probably helped spur efforts in the 1980s to reduce the number of nuclear weapons held by the United States and the Soviet Union.

BACKGROUND TO THE SPEECH
The Cold War
In 1988, Carl Sagan delivered "On Nuclear Disarmament" in Gettysburg, Pennsylvania, to mark the 125th anniversary of a famous Civil War battle. At the time of the speech, the United States and the Soviet Union were still locked in a decades-long rivalry known as the cold war. Both nations had tens of thousands of nuclear warheads in their arsenals. According to some military strategists, these weapons prevented direct conflict because each side knew that it could be destroyed in a counterattack. This state of affairs was known as a balance of terror. However, many people feared that a crisis could spark a nuclear war between the superpowers.

Author Online
THINK central
Go to **thinkcentral.com.**
KEYWORD: HML10-653

653

Teach

TEXT ANALYSIS
COMMON CORE
RI 6

● *Model the Skill:* **RHETORICAL DEVICES**

To model how to identify rhetorical devices, share this passage:

> Our leaders should work to preserve our families, to preserve our schools, and to preserve our future.

Point out that the word *work,* used once, is part of all three parallel phrases. Explain that the phrases beginning "to preserve our" are parallel.

GUIDED PRACTICE Have students use repetition and parallelism in a sentence.

READING SKILL
COMMON CORE
RI 5
RI 8

■ *Model the Skill:* **ANALYZE INDUCTIVE REASONING**

Read aloud the following facts: "Hitler's rise to power was considered 'impossible,' and so was the explosion of the *Challenger.* Yet both occurred." Explain that one generalization that can be made, based upon these facts, is that supposedly impossible things can happen.

GUIDED PRACTICE Have students make an overgeneralization about these facts.

R RESOURCE MANAGER—Copy Master
Analyze Inductive Reasoning p. 61

VOCABULARY SKILL
COMMON CORE
L 4

▲ VOCABULARY IN CONTEXT

DIAGNOSE WORD KNOWLEDGE Have all students complete Vocabulary in Context. Check their words and phrases against the following:

annihilate (ə-nī′ə-lāt′) *v.* to destroy completely
carnage (kär′nĭj) *n.* massive slaughter
contending (kən-tĕn′dĭng) *adj.* struggling in rivalry **contend** *v.*
malice (măl′ĭs) *n.* a desire to harm others
precursor (prĭ-kûr′sər) *n.* something that comes before and signals or prepares the way for

what will follow
reconcile (rĕk′ən-sīl′) *v.* to restore friendly relations

PRETEACH VOCABULARY Use the following copy master to help students determine meanings for each boldfaced word.

R RESOURCE MANAGER—Copy Master
Vocabulary Study p. 63

1. Read item 1 aloud, emphasizing *annihilate* in both sentences.

2. Point out the phrases "wipe out" and "kill." Elicit possible meanings for *annihilate,* such as "kill."

3. Repeat the procedure for items b–f.

4. Have students complete the paragraph.

Practice and Apply

READ WITH A PURPOSE

Help students set a purpose for reading. Tell them to look for the author's arguments for why war is now a global rather than a national issue.

READING SKILL · COMMON CORE · RI 5 RI 8

A Model the Skill: INDUCTIVE REASONING

Make sure students understand that Sagan is presenting statistics about the Battle of Gettysburg, which took place in 1863. Also suggest that Sagan is presenting evidence that may lead to a general conclusion later in the speech. At this point, however, he is citing these statistics to show "the first hint ... of what technology bent to the purposes of war might be capable" (lines 4–5). We can predict that his generalization will have something to do with this basic idea.

Possible answer: Sagan states that 51,000 people were killed (line 1), a few hundred artillery pieces with a range of a few miles were used (lines 11–14), and the most powerful artillery held 20 pounds, or about one-hundredth of a ton, of TNT (lines 14–16).

VOCABULARY · COMMON CORE · L 4

OWN THE WORD

precursor: Have students explain how the balloon in line 9 functioned as a *precursor*. *Possible answer:* The balloon, used for reconnaissance in 1863, came before modern-day reconnaissance technology, such as satellites.

On Nuclear Disarmament

Carl Sagan

Analyze Visuals ▶

In what other contexts have you seen images like this one used?

Fifty-one thousand human beings were killed or wounded here, ancestors of some of us, brothers of us all. This was the first full-fledged example of an industrialized war, with machine-made arms and railroad transport of men and materiel. This was the first hint of an age yet to come, our age; an intimation of what technology bent to the purposes of war might be capable. The new Spencer repeating rifle was used here. In May 1863, a reconnaissance balloon of the Army of the Potomac[1] detected movement of Confederate troops across the Rappahannock River, the beginning of the campaign that led to the Battle of Gettysburg. That balloon was a **precursor** of air forces and strategic
10 bombing and reconnaissance satellites.

① Targeted Passage

precursor (prĭ-kûr′sər) *n.* something that comes before and signals or prepares the way for what will follow

A few hundred artillery pieces were deployed in the three-day battle of Gettysburg. What could they do? What was the war like then? . . . Ballistic projectiles, launched from the cannons that you can see all over this Gettysburg Memorial, had a range, at best, of a few miles. The amount of explosive in the most formidable of them was some twenty pounds, roughly one-hundredth of a ton of TNT.[2] It was enough to kill a few people. **A**

But the most powerful chemical explosives used eighty years later, in World War II, were the blockbusters, so-called because they could destroy a city block. Dropped from aircraft, after a journey of hundreds of miles, each

A INDUCTIVE REASONING
What statistics does Sagan provide as **evidence** in lines 1–16?

1. **Army of the Potomac:** the Union army that defeated Confederate forces near the town of Gettysburg, Pennsylvania. The battle was a turning point in the Civil War.
2. **TNT:** a chemical compound used as an explosive.

654 UNIT 6: ARGUMENT AND PERSUASION

DIFFERENTIATED INSTRUCTION

FOR ENGLISH LANGUAGE LEARNERS

Vocabulary Support Use New Word Analysis to teach these words: *technology* (line 5), *strategic* (line 9), *nuclear* (line 42), *identification* (line 97), *expanded* (line 98), *challenge* (line 137).

 BEST PRACTICES TOOLKIT—Transparency New Word Analysis p. E8

FOR STRUGGLING READERS

In combination with the *Audio Anthology CD,* use one or more Targeted Passages (pp. 654, 657, 659) to ensure that students focus on key story events, concepts, and skills. Targeted Passages are also good for English learners.

① Targeted Passage [Lines 1–10]

This passage introduces the idea that the Civil War was a forerunner of modern warfare and the nuclear age.

BACKGROUND

History of Nuclear Weapons "Technology bent to the purposes of war" (line 5) created the nuclear age when scientists learned to split atoms in a process called *fission* in 1939. The first atomic bomb, tested in New Mexico in 1945, was the result of this scientific breakthrough. When scientists learned to combine the nuclei of atoms, the more powerful hydrogen bomb was invented in the 1950s.

Nuclear Weapons Today Although the technology that underpins nuclear weapons was developed in the United States, many countries throughout the world now either have nuclear weapons or are working to produce them. The Nuclear Non-Proliferation Treaty, or NPT, tries to control the spread of nuclear weapons by preventing new nuclear weapon states from emerging and by having the established nuclear states pledge to disarm. There are five "declared nuclear states," according to the provisions of the NPT: the United States, Russia, France, Britain, and China. In addition, India, Pakistan, and Israel are known to possess nuclear weapons. Other countries suspected of having nuclear capabilities or nuclear weapons programs include Iran and North Korea. Nations that have given up their nuclear arsenals, dismantled their weapons programs, or are in the process of doing so include Ukraine, Kazakhstan, South Africa, and Libya.

Analyze Visuals

Possible answer: An image like this might be found in history books discussing World War II and the atomic bombs dropped on Japan. Other contexts might include antiwar or antinuclear posters.

- How many soldiers died at Gettysburg? (line 1)
- How was the Civil War an example of industrialized war? (lines 3–4)
- What were some of the new weapons used at Gettysburg? (lines 6–7)
- Which Civil War weapons were the predecessors to some of our modern weapons? (lines 9–10)

FOR ADVANCED LEARNERS/PRE–AP

Evaluate Have students work in small groups to analyze Sagan's statement "We make mistakes. We kill our own" (lines 63, 74). Ask students to list the evidence he provides to support this claim. Have them evaluate whether this phrase strengthens Sagan's argument or just serves a rhetorical purpose. Encourage groups to share their conclusions with the class.

Analyze Visuals

Activity Ask students how the composition of the photograph on this page emphasizes the relationship between its two main images. *Possible answer: The cannon in the foreground and the gravestones in the background emphasize that this type of weapon caused the deaths of the soldiers.*

Possible answer: The evidence helps the reader contrast the enormous destructive power of thermonuclear weapons (hydrogen bombs) with that of the less-destructive weapons used at Gettysburg (lines 1–16) and during World War II (lines 17–25).

Remind students that parallelism is the use of similar grammatical constructions to express related ideas. Ask students if they also see the use of repetition in these lines.

Possible answer: Sagan uses parallelism to emphasize that each technological advance increased the explosive power of weapons 1,000 times: "a thousand times more . . . a thousand times more . . . a thousand times more still. A thousand times a thousand, times a thousand is a billion" (lines 32–35).

annihilate: The word *annihilate* comes from the Latin word *annihilare,* meaning "to reduce to nothing." Ask students to explain why *annihilate* was used in line 23. *Possible answer: The two Japanese cities were reduced to nothing.*

The Soldiers' National Cemetery in Gettysburg National Military Park

20 carried about ten tons of TNT, a thousand times more than the most powerful weapon at the Battle of Gettysburg. A blockbuster could kill a few dozen people.

At the very end of World War II, the United States used the first atomic bombs to **annihilate** two Japanese cities. Each of those weapons had the equivalent power of about ten thousand tons of TNT, enough to kill a few hundred thousand people. One bomb.

A few years later the United States and the Soviet Union developed the first thermonuclear[3] weapons, the first hydrogen bombs. Some of them had an explosive yield equivalent to ten million tons of TNT; enough to kill a few million people. One bomb. Strategic nuclear weapons can now be launched to 30 any place on the planet. Everywhere on earth is a potential battlefield now. **B**

Each of these technological triumphs advanced the art of mass murder by a factor of a thousand. From Gettysburg to the blockbuster, a thousand times more explosive energy; from the blockbuster to the atomic bomb, a thousand times more; and from the atomic bomb to the hydrogen bomb, a thousand times still more. A thousand times a thousand, times a thousand is a billion; in less than one century, our most fearful weapon has become a billion times more deadly. But we have not become a billion times wiser in the generations that stretch from Gettysburg to us. **C**

> 3. **thermonuclear** (thûr′mō-nōō′klē-ər): based on the process of nuclear fusion, in which atomic nuclei combine at high temperatures, releasing energy.

annihilate (ə-nī′ə-lāt′) *v.* to destroy completely

B INDUCTIVE REASONING How is the **evidence** in this paragraph related to evidence provided earlier in the speech?

C RHETORICAL DEVICES Reread lines 32–38. What idea does Sagan stress through the use of **parallelism**?

DIFFERENTIATED INSTRUCTION

FOR STRUGGLING READERS

Comprehension Support Read aloud the sentence that begins, "Each of these technological triumphs" (line 31). Point out that the phrase "technological triumphs" is used ironically. Sagan does not really mean that it is a triumph to kill millions of people. Then point out that he uses the phrase "mass murder" to refer to war. Explain that Sagan uses strong language and techniques to convey his dislike of warfare.

FOR ENGLISH LANGUAGE LEARNERS

Comprehension: Task Support To help students understand the English words for multiples of 100, work with them to complete a T Chart with the columns labeled *English* and *Home Language.* Under *English,* write the words *hundred, thousand, million,* and *billion.* Then have students write these numbers in their home languages.

 **BEST PRACTICES TOOLKIT—Transparency** T Chart p. A25

The souls that perished here would find the **carnage** of which we are now
40 capable unspeakable. Today, the United States and the Soviet Union have
booby-trapped our planet with almost sixty thousand nuclear weapons. Sixty
thousand nuclear weapons! Even a small fraction of the strategic arsenals
could without question annihilate the two **contending** superpowers, probably
destroy the global civilization, and possibly render the human species extinct.
No nation, no man should have such power. We distribute these instruments
of apocalypse[4] all over our fragile world, and justify it on the grounds that it
has made us safe. We have made a fool's bargain.

The 51,000 casualties here at Gettysburg represented one-third of the
Confederate army and one-quarter of the Union army. All those who died,
50 with one or two exceptions, were soldiers. The best-known exception was a
civilian in her own house who thought to bake a loaf of bread and, through
two closed doors, was shot to death; her name was Jennie Wade. But in the
global thermonuclear war, almost all the casualties will be civilians, men,
women, and children, including vast numbers of citizens of nations that
had no part in the quarrel that led to the war, nations far removed from the
northern mid-latitude "target zone." There will be billions of Jennie Wades.
Everyone on earth is now at risk. . . . **D**

Two months before Gettysburg, on May 3, 1863, there was a Confederate
triumph, the Battle of Chancellorsville. On the moonlit evening following the
60 victory, General Stonewall Jackson and his staff, returning to the Confederate
lines, were mistaken for Union cavalry. Jackson was shot twice in error by his
own men. He died of his wounds.

We make mistakes. We kill our own.

> There are some who claim that since we have not yet had an accidental
> nuclear war, the precautions being taken to prevent one must be adequate.
> But not three years ago we witnessed the disasters of the *Challenger*[5] space
> shuttle and the Chernobyl[6] nuclear power plant, high-technology systems, one
> American, one Soviet, into which enormous quantities of national prestige had
> been invested. There were compelling reasons to prevent these disasters. In
> 70 the preceding year, confident assertions were made by officials of both nations
> that no accidents of that sort could happen. We were not to worry. The experts
> would not permit an accident to happen. We have since learned that such
> assurances do not amount to much.

We make mistakes. We kill our own. **E**

This is the century of Hitler and Stalin, evidence—if any were needed—that
madmen can seize the reins of power of modern industrial states. If we are
content in a world with nearly sixty thousand nuclear weapons, we are betting
our lives on the proposition that no present or future leaders, military or
civilian—of the United States, the Soviet Union, Britain, France, China, Israel,

---

4. **apocalypse** (ə-pŏk′ə-lĭps′): total devastation.
5. *Challenger:* an American space shuttle that exploded in 1986, killing all seven crew members.
6. **Chernobyl** (chər-nō′bəl): a town in the Ukraine (then part of the Soviet Union) that was the
site of a major nuclear power plant accident in 1986.

carnage (kär′nĭj) *n.*
massive slaughter

contending
(kən-tĕn′dĭng) *adj.*
struggling in rivalry
contend *v.*

D INDUCTIVE REASONING
What new point does
Sagan make with the
historical **evidence** he
discusses in lines 48–57?

② Targeted Passage

E GRAMMAR AND STYLE
The two simple sentences
in line 74 also appear
earlier and later in the
speech. Consider how
this **repetition** serves
to link and emphasize
essential points.

REVISIT THE BIG QUESTION

What would make the world SAFER?

Discuss Based on lines 39–74, why does Sagan
believe that we have made "a fool's bargain"
by accepting the theory that nuclear weapons
will ensure our security? *Possible answer: He
thinks there is ample historical evidence that an
accidental nuclear war could happen—a war
that would destroy the whole planet.*

READING SKILL   COMMON CORE

D INDUCTIVE REASONING   RI 5 / RI 8

*Possible answer: Nuclear war will not
only kill millions of people, but most of
the victims will be civilians, not soldiers—
"billions of Jennie Wades" (line 56) will
be killed.*

E GRAMMAR AND STYLE   COMMON CORE L 1a / L 3

*Possible answer: The repetition
of the phrase "a few" in lines 21, 24, and
28 emphasizes how the force of weapons
has grown and unifies these statistics. The
repetition of the words "a thousand" and
"a billion" in lines 31–38 creates a rhythm
that further reinforces how the growth of
destructive weapons is out of control.*

VOCABULARY    COMMON CORE L 4

OWN THE WORD

- **carnage:** Have students create a semantic map for *carnage.* Write the word and
  its definition in the center circle. Draw
  spider legs out from the center circle,
  and have students offer synonyms to
  complete the map. *Possible answers:
  massacre, slaughter*

- **contending:** Ask students if they have
  ever had to *contend* with someone or
  something. Have them explain who,
  when, and why they *contended* or are
  contending with that situation.

FOR STRUGGLING READERS

 Targeted Passage [Lines 64–73]

This passage reinforces Sagan's thesis that we
should be very concerned about an accidental
nuclear war.

- Why do some people claim that we are doing enough to prevent nuclear war? (lines
  64–65)

- What events does Sagan cite as examples
  of disasters that were deemed impossible?
  (lines 66–67)

Develop Reading Fluency Tell students that
repetition is also used to unify a speech and
to create appealing or memorable rhythms.
Read aloud lines 63–74. Point out how these
lines create a powerful rhythm that further
emphasizes Sagan's message. Have students
read the lines after you, and encourage students to emphasize the rhythm of the lines.

R RESOURCE MANAGER—Copy Master
Reading Fluency p. 69

TIERED DISCUSSION PROMPTS

Direct students to lines 85–89. Use these prompts to help students understand why Sagan criticizes the relationship between the United States and the Soviet Union:

Connect Does Sagan's description of the nuclear competition worry you? Why or why not? *Accept all reasonable responses.*

Analyze What does Sagan suggest "propelled" (line 86) the United States and the Soviet Union toward hostile relations with each other? *Possible answer: He suggests that each side became more obsessed with "malefactions" (line 87), or acts of wrongdoing, committed by the other. Each side threatened to launch deadly attacks against the other in response to these acts.*

Synthesize Is the United States today "locked in a deadly embrace" (line 85) with any other nation or power, "never seeing the big picture" (line 89)? Explain your opinion. *Accept all well-reasoned answers.*

READING SKILL · COMMON CORE RI 5 RI 8

F *Model the Skill:* INDUCTIVE REASONING

On the board, draw a graphic organizer like the one on page 653. Have students suggest evidence from lines 108–121 for you to record in the organizer. Then ask students what conclusion Sagan draws.

Possible answer: Sagan draws the conclusion that nations can no longer gain from competition and conflict. We must all learn to cooperate or we will "perish together" (line 114).

VOCABULARY · COMMON CORE L 4

OWN THE WORD

malice: Have students use the noun *malice* in sentences. Then ask students to identify the adjective form of the word (*maliciously*) and use it in sentences.

---

80 India, Pakistan, South Africa, and whatever other nuclear powers there will be—will ever stray from the strictest standards of prudence. We are gambling on their sanity and sobriety even in times of great personal and national crisis, all of them, for all times to come. I say this is asking too much of us. Because we make mistakes. We kill our own. . . .

We have made a fool's bargain. We have been locked in a deadly embrace with the Soviet Union, each side always propelled by the abundant malefactions of the other; almost always looking to the short term—to the next congressional or presidential election, to the next party congress—and almost never seeing the big picture.

90 Dwight Eisenhower, who was closely associated with this Gettysburg community, said, "The problem in defense spending is to figure out how far you should go without destroying from within what you are trying to defend from without." I say we have gone too far. . . .

The Civil War was mainly about union; union in the face of differences. A million years ago, there were no nations on the planet. There were no tribes. The humans who were here were divided into small family groups of a few dozen people each. They wandered. That was the horizon of our identification, an itinerant family group. Since them, the horizons have expanded. From a handful of hunter-gatherers, to a tribe, to a horde, to a small city-state, to

100 a nation, and today to immense nation-states. The average person on the earth today owes his or her primary allegiance to a group of something like a hundred million people. It seems very clear that if we do not destroy ourselves first, the unit of primary identification of most human beings will before long be the planet Earth and the human species. To my mind, this raises the key question: whether the fundamental unit of identification will expand to embrace the planet and the species, or whether we will destroy ourselves first. I'm afraid it's going to be very close.

The identification horizons were broadened in this place 125 years ago, and at great cost to North and South, to blacks and whites. But we recognize that

110 expansion of identification horizons as just. Today there is an urgent, practical necessity to work together on arms control, on the world economy, on the global environment. It is clear that the nations of the world now can only rise and fall together. It is not a question of one nation winning at the expense of another. We must all help one another or all perish together. **F**

On occasions like this it is customary to quote homilies; phrases by great men and women that we've all heard before. We hear, but we tend not to focus. Let me mention one, a phrase that was uttered not far from this spot by Abraham Lincoln: "With **malice** toward none, with charity for all. . . ." *Think* of what that means. This is what is expected of us, not merely because

120 our ethics command it, or because our religions preach it, but because it is necessary for human survival.

COMMON CORE RI 4

Language Coach

Roots and Affixes A root contains a word's core meaning. An affix at the beginning of a root or base is a **prefix**. The root *fac* means "to do." The prefix *mal-* means "evil." Reread line 87. What do you think *malefactions* are?

F INDUCTIVE REASONING
What **conclusion** does Sagan draw in lines 108–114?

malice (măl'ĭs) *n.* a desire to harm others

DIFFERENTIATED INSTRUCTION

FOR ENGLISH LANGUAGE LEARNERS

Language Coach · COMMON CORE RI 4

Roots and Affixes *Possible answer: wrongdoing* Ask students to use their knowledge of the prefix *mal-* to define *malice*, which is a vocabulary word on page 658, and *malefactor*.

FOR ADVANCED LEARNERS/PRE–AP

Research the Cold War Explain that Sagan delivered this speech in 1988, three years before the collapse of the Soviet Union and the end of the Cold War. Have students work in small groups to research an aspect of the Cold War or its aftermath. Then have groups present their findings to the class.

Here's another: "A house divided against itself cannot stand." Let me vary it a little: A species divided against itself cannot stand. A planet divided against itself cannot stand. And [to be] inscribed on this Eternal Light Peace Memorial, which is about to be rekindled and rededicated, is a stirring phrase: "A World United in the Search for Peace."

The real triumph of Gettysburg was not, I think, in 1863 but in 1913, when the surviving veterans, the remnants of the adversary forces, the Blue and the Gray, met in celebration and solemn memorial. It had been the war that set
130 brother against brother, and when the time came to remember, on the fiftieth anniversary of the battle, the survivors fell, sobbing, into one another's arms. They could not help themselves. **G**

It is time now for us to emulate them, NATO and the Warsaw Pact,[7] Israelis and Palestinians, whites and blacks, Americans and Iranians, the developed and the underdeveloped worlds.

We need more than anniversary sentimentalism and holiday piety and patriotism. Where necessary, we must confront and challenge the conventional wisdom. It is time to learn from those who fell here. Our challenge is to **reconcile**, not *after* the carnage and the mass murder, but *instead* of the
140 carnage and the mass murder.

It is time to act. ❧

---

7. **Warsaw Pact:** an alliance of the Soviet Union and other Communist nations.

⊙ COMMON CORE RI 5

G AUTHOR'S CLAIM
Writers often take time to develop claims over course of an entire text, or in this case, speech. Reread lines 127–132. How is Sagan's claim against the development of nuclear weapons highlighted in this paragraph?

reconcile (rĕk′ən-sīl′) v. to restore friendly relations

③ **Targeted Passage**

FOR STRUGGLING READERS

③ **Targeted Passage [Lines 136–140]**

This passage sums up Sagan's message and makes a persuasive appeal to the audience.

- What does Sagan mean by "anniversary sentimentalism" and "holiday piety and patriotism"? (lines 136–137)

- What is the "conventional wisdom" that must be challenged? (lines 104–107)

- What lessons are to be learned from the soldiers who fought at Gettysburg? (lines 127–132)

FOR ADVANCED LEARNERS/PRE-AP

Counterargument Have students work in small groups to craft a counterargument to Sagan's main argument. Suggest that they first outline Sagan's claims and evidence opposing nuclear weapons. Then have students argue against his view, offering evidence to support their own points. Invite volunteers to present their arguments to the class.

TEXT ANALYSIS   COMMON CORE   RI 5

G AUTHOR'S CLAIM

Possible answer: Sagan uses the example of the reconciliation of Civil War veterans to show how adversaries should unite based on their common humanity.

Analyze Visuals

Activity Ask students what kind of event is depicted in this photograph. *Possible answer: The photograph depicts a march or rally of people who oppose the spread of nuclear weapons.*

VOCABULARY   COMMON CORE   L 4

OWN THE WORD

reconcile: *Reconciliation* is the noun form of the verb *reconcile.* Both mean "to restore friendly relations." Have students write sentences using both words.

SELECTION WRAP–UP

READ WITH A PURPOSE Now that students have finished reading the selection, ask them: Why would a war in the 21st century be so much more deadly than a war in the 19th century? *Possible answer: Technology has increased the killing capacity of weapons by billions; people make mistakes; casualties would spread far beyond combatants.*

★ **CRITIQUE** Ask students to rate Sagan's speech on a scale of 1 to 5, with 5 the highest. Suggest that they come up with one rating for the effectiveness of the speech's argument and another for its use of language. Then have them average these numbers into an overall score.

INDEPENDENT READING
Suggest *Thirteen Days: A Memoir of the Cuban Missile Crisis* by Robert F. Kennedy to students interested in a behind-the-scenes account of the days leading to the brink of nuclear war.

Practice and Apply

For preliminary support of post-reading questions, use these copy masters:

R RESOURCE MANAGER—Copy Masters
Reading Check p. 66
Rhetorical Devices p. 59
Question Support p. 67

Additional selection questions are provided for teachers on page 53.

ANSWERS

Comprehension

1. *Rifles, reconnaissance balloons, and artillery pieces were used at Gettysburg.*

2. *Blockbuster bombs, atomic bombs, and thermonuclear weapons were developed.*

3. *A war could still occur by accident or because of the actions of a world leader who is insane or foolhardy.*

Text Analysis
COMMON CORE RI 4, RI 5, RI 6, RI 8

Possible answers:

4. ● COMMON CORE FOCUS
   Rhetorical Devices *Sagan emphasizes the irony that weapons developed to keep us safe have actually put us and "our fragile world" (line 46) in much greater danger.*

5. *Sagan argues that society's ever-expanding horizon of identification suggests that we will evolve to the point where humans identify with the whole "planet and the species" (line 106)—unless we "destroy ourselves first" (line 106). Once we have expanded our "unit of identification" (line 105) to include the whole species, we will begin to realize that one nation cannot win "at the expense of another" (lines 113–114), and that we "now can only rise and fall together" (lines 112–113).*

6. *The "real triumph" was that the veterans realized that they were really brothers who should not have fought against each other.*

7. ● COMMON CORE FOCUS **Analyze Inductive Reasoning** *Conclusions should be supported by sound reasoning and examples from the article.*

8. *Individual Actions: write letters to politicians and newspapers, sign petitions, support peace candidates; Group Activities: join peace organizations, participate in protest marches, join discussion or study groups*

Comprehension

1. **Recall** What weapons were used in the Battle of Gettysburg?

2. **Recall** What developments in warfare occurred during and shortly after World War II?

3. **Summarize** According to Sagan, why should we reject assurances that a nuclear war will not occur?

Text Analysis

● 4. **Examine a Rhetorical Device** What idea does Sagan emphasize with his **repetition** of the statement, "We have made a fool's bargain"?

5. **Examine an Argument** Sagan states that as society has evolved, humans have gone from identifying with small groups to identifying with enormous nation-states. How does this idea relate to the main **claim** of his argument?

6. **Make Inferences** What does Sagan mean when he says that "the real triumph of Gettysburg" was the behavior of surviving veterans who attended the 50th anniversary of the battle, in 1913?

■ 7. **Analyze Inductive Reasoning** Review the graphic organizer you created as you read. Does Sagan provide sufficient **support** for his conclusion about nuclear weapons and **security**? Explain why or why not.

8. **Analyze a Conclusion** At the end of his speech, Sagan says it is "time to act" to prevent nuclear war. In a chart like the one shown, identify specific actions that individuals and groups can take in response to Sagan's call for action.

Preventing Nuclear War	
Individual Actions	**Group Activities**
•	•
•	•
•	•

9. **Compare Texts** Compare and contrast the techniques of argument used in Sagan's speech and Alan Blinder's editorial "Abolishing the Penny Makes Good Sense."

10. **Make Conclusions** Sagan became famous for helping the general public understand scientific concepts. How well does he explain the complex issues involved with nuclear weapons? Cite evidence to support your opinion.

What would make the world SAFER?

Is nuclear disarmament still an important issue? Why or why not?

COMMON CORE

RI 4 Determine the meaning of words as they are used in a text. **RI 5** Analyze how an author's claims are developed and refined by a particular paragraph. **RI 6** Analyze how an author uses rhetoric to advance a point of view or purpose. **RI 8** Delineate and evaluate the argument and specific claims in a text, assessing whether the reasoning is valid and the evidence is relevant and sufficient.

9. *Blinder uses deductive reasoning, reaching a conclusion by applying a general principle to a specific situation. Sagan uses inductive reasoning, presenting evidence to build toward a general conclusion.*

What would make the world SAFER? *Students may argue that, with the end of the Cold War, nuclear war is less likely. Other students may counter that there is increased danger of nuclear weapons falling into the hands of terrorists.*

10. *Sagan provides clear general reasons for disarmament, saying that "even a small fraction" of our nuclear arsenals could "destroy the global civilization" (lines 42–44) and that "the nations of the world now can only rise and fall together" (lines 112–113). However, he does not discuss the difficulty of getting all nations with nuclear weapons to give them up.*

Vocabulary in Context

▲ VOCABULARY PRACTICE

Decide whether the words in each pair are synonyms or antonyms.

1. annihilate/preserve
2. carnage/bloodshed
3. contending/cooperating
4. malice/hatred
5. precursor/aftermath
6. reconcile/antagonize

WORD LIST

annihilate
carnage
contending
malice
precursor
reconcile

ACADEMIC VOCABULARY IN SPEAKING

- cite - controversy - convince - objective - statistic

Is Carl Sagan's speech "On Nuclear Disarmament" as relevant today as it was in 1988? Share your opinion in a discussion. Support your ideas with facts and reasons to **convince** others that your opinion is logical. Use the Academic Vocabulary words in your discussion.

VOCABULARY STRATEGY: SPECIALIZED VOCABULARY

Specialized vocabulary is vocabulary specifically suited to a particular occupation or field of study. Politicians and military personnel often use specialized vocabulary when talking about war. This vocabulary includes terms such as *ballistic*, which refers to the movements of missiles and other weapons propelled through the air. It is often possible to figure out the meaning of a specialized vocabulary term from context. Otherwise, look up the term in a dictionary.

COMMON CORE

L 6 Acquire and use accurately domain-specific words and phrases.

PRACTICE Write the term that matches each definition. If you need to, check a dictionary.

| arsenal | casualties | deploy | disarmament | reconnaissance |

1. military people lost through death, injury, sickness, or capture
2. a stock of weapons
3. the reduction of a nation's military forces and equipment
4. an inspection of an area to gather military information
5. to position troops or equipment in readiness for combat

Interactive Vocabulary

THINK central

Go to **thinkcentral.com**.
KEYWORD: HML10-661

DIFFERENTIATED INSTRUCTION

FOR ENGLISH LANGUAGE LEARNERS

Vocabulary Activity Have students work in groups without dictionaries to create a word web for each word in the word list. When they have finished, have them compare their webs with those of other groups. Encourage them to add more descriptors. Finally, have them check the meaning of the vocabulary words in a dictionary. They may choose to add more items to their webs.

FOR ADVANCED LEARNERS/PRE–AP

Vocabulary in Writing Ask students to use at least four vocabulary words in a brief editorial expressing their opinions on the issue of nuclear disarmament.

ANSWERS

Vocabulary in Context

▲ VOCABULARY PRACTICE

1. *antonyms*	4. *synonyms*
2. *synonyms*	5. *antonyms*
3. *antonyms*	6. *antonyms*

 **RESOURCE MANAGER**—Copy Master
Vocabulary Practice p. 64

ACADEMIC VOCABULARY IN SPEAKING

Possible answer: *The public's fear of nuclear attack may have lessoned somewhat since 1988, but the issue of nuclear weaponry remains crucial today. The controversy that Sagan discussed is still vital because nuclear disarmament has not take place. Statistics show that in 2002, the United States had more than 10,000 nuclear weapons, and Russia had more than 8,000.*

VOCABULARY STRATEGY: SPECIALIZED VOCABULARY

COMMON CORE L 6

- Help students practice using context clues to determine the meaning of specialized words. Read this sentence:

  *Soldiers waited for the **bombardment** to begin, hoping that the artillery attack would be brief.*

- Ask students if there is a context clue that suggests the meaning of *bombardment* ("artillery attack"). Have them offer definitions for *bombardment*.

Answers:

1. *casualties*	4. *reconnaissance*
2. *arsenal*	5. *deploy*
3. *disarmament*	

 **RESOURCE MANAGER**—Copy Master
Vocabulary Strategy p. 65

Interactive Vocabulary **THINK** central

Keywords direct students to a **WordSharp** tutorial on **thinkcentral.com** or to other types of vocabulary practice and review.

Language

COMMON CORE L 1a, L 3

◆ **GRAMMAR AND STYLE**

- After they review the note on page 657 and the student model, have students add sentences using repetition and parallel structure to make their writing more memorable.

- Write these sentences on the board. Have students suggest revisions that include repetition and parallel structure.

It is time to come together. ~~We can~~ *It is time to make the world a safer place.* ~~We must~~ *It is time to think seriously.* ~~Now we must~~ *It is time to act.*

R RESOURCE MANAGER—Copy Master
Use Rhetorical Devices p. 68

READING-WRITING CONNECTION

Suggest that students review the Statistical Illustration on page 663. Have students add up the numbers of nuclear weapons recorded on the chart and then compare this number to the number of weapons cited by Sagan in his speech. Encourage students to use that comparison as evidence in their arguments.

Writing Online

THINK central

The following tools are available online at **thinkcentral.com** and on **Write*Smart* CD-ROM**:

- Interactive Graphic Organizers
- Interactive Student Models
- Interactive Revision Lessons

For additional grammar instruction, see **GrammarNotes** on **thinkcentral.com**.

Assess and Reteach

Assess

DIAGNOSTIC AND SELECTION TESTS
Selection Test A pp. 187–188
Selection Test B/C pp. 189–190

Interactive Selection Test on **thinkcentral.com**

Reteach

Level Up Online Tutorials on **thinkcentral.com**

Reteaching Worksheets on **thinkcentral.com**
Literature Lesson 35: Rhetorical Devices

Informational Text Lesson 12: Inductive vs. Deductive Reasoning

---

Language

◆ **GRAMMAR AND STYLE:** Use Rhetorical Devices

COMMON CORE

L 1a Use parallel structure.
L 3 Apply knowledge of language to make effective choices for meaning or style.

Review the **Grammar and Style** note on page 657. Using **repetition** and **parallel structure**, as Sagan does in his speech, can reinforce important messages and ideas. Use these techniques to revise your responses to the prompt:

1. **Repeat powerful words or phrases that will draw attention to a key point.** In this example, Sagan repeats the participial phrase "divided against itself" to stress the necessity of nations working together:

   . . . *"A house divided against itself cannot stand." Let me vary it a little: A species divided against itself cannot stand. A planet divided against itself cannot stand.* (lines 122–124)

2. **Use repetition** and **parallel structure to link related ideas.** Repeating important words or phrases in a parallel grammatical structure can indicate to readers that ideas appearing at different points in the piece are related.

Notice how the revisions in blue strengthen the message in this first draft.

> **STUDENT MODEL**
>
> Sagan believes it is ~~a mistake~~ *foolish* to seek safety in terrible weapons, *foolish to* trust politicians to make the right decisions, and *foolish to* set nation against nation.

READING-WRITING CONNECTION

YOUR TURN

Explore the message in "On Nuclear Disarmament" by responding to this prompt. Then use the **revising tip** to improve your writing.

WRITING PROMPT	REVISING TIP
Short Constructed Response: Write Across Texts Is the world a safer place today than it was when Sagan gave his speech? Use Sagan's speech and the nuclear weapons chart on page 663 to write a **one- or two-paragraph response.**	Review your response. Did you use repetition to draw attention to key points and to link related ideas? If not, revise your response.

Interactive Revision

THINK central
Go to **thinkcentral.com**.
KEYWORD: HML10-662

DIFFERENTIATED INSTRUCTION

FOR STRUGGLING WRITERS

- Explain how the security of the world was at risk when Sagan gave his speech.

- Help students write a sentence that describes the nuclear threat today.

- Help students organize their responses:

  Beginning: Briefly state Sagan's argument about nuclear weapons.

  Middle: Summarize the information in the chart.

Close: State and develop an opinion about whether the world is safer now.

Reading for Information

STATISTICAL ILLUSTRATION When Carl Sagan delivered his speech "On Nuclear Disarmament" in 1988, the United States and the Soviet Union had about 60,000 nuclear weapons pointed at each other. This chart shows estimated amounts of nuclear weapons 20 years later. Note that the end of the cold war led to reductions in some nuclear stockpiles.

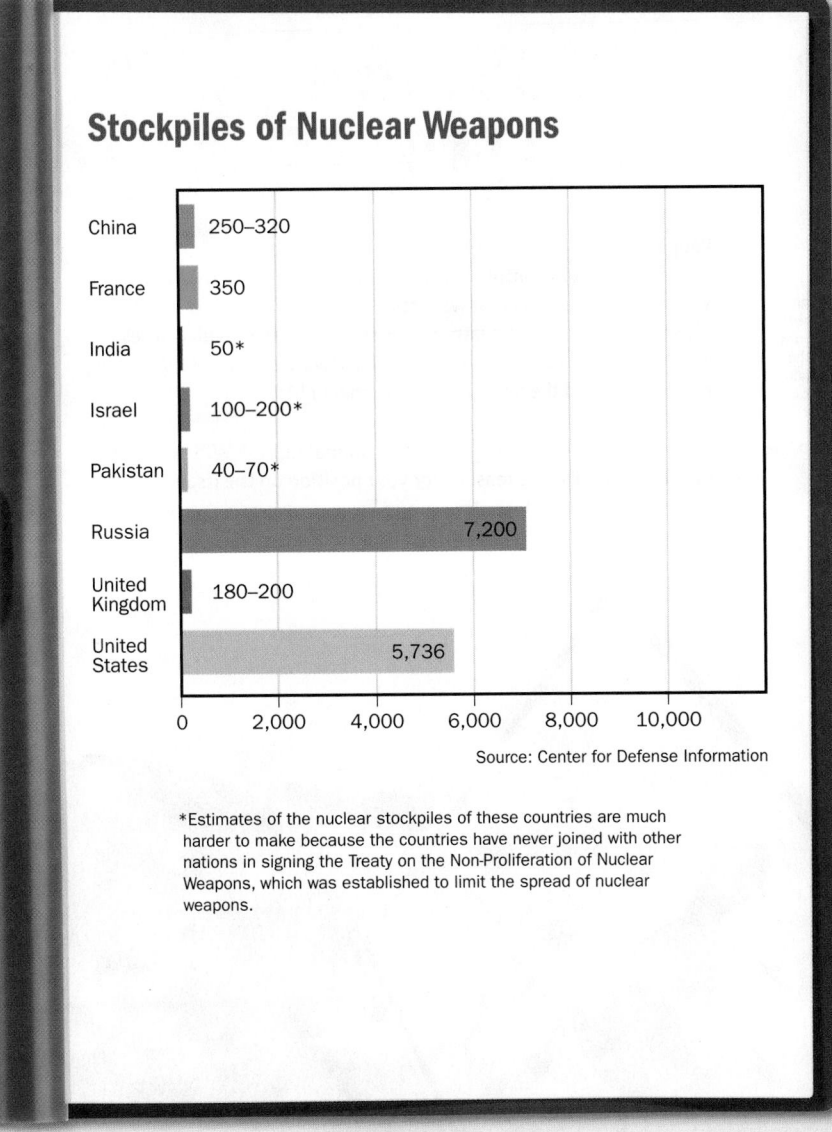

Stockpiles of Nuclear Weapons

Country	
China	250–320
France	350
India	50*
Israel	100–200*
Pakistan	40–70*
Russia	7,200
United Kingdom	180–200
United States	5,736

Source: Center for Defense Information

*Estimates of the nuclear stockpiles of these countries are much harder to make because the countries have never joined with other nations in signing the Treaty on the Non-Proliferation of Nuclear Weapons, which was established to limit the spread of nuclear weapons.

READING FOR INFORMATION **663**

CONNECT

Use this selection either as support for the READING-WRITING CONNECTION prompt on page 662 or as a mini-lesson on reading for information.

READING FOR INFORMATION

Point out that "Stockpiles of Nuclear Weapons" is a statistical illustration. Then ask these questions:

- What information is given along the vertical (left) axis and the horizontal (bottom) axis? *Possible answers: The vertical axis displays the names of the countries that have nuclear weapons. The horizontal axis shows numbers of weapons in increments of two thousand.*

- How is the number of weapons in each country represented on the chart? *Possible answer: A colored bar keyed to the horizontal axis is displayed. A precise or estimated number is given at the end of the bar.*

TIERED DISCUSSION PROMPTS

Use these prompts to help students understand that statistical information can change over time:

Connect The chart reflects information that differs from information found in Sagan's speech. Have you ever changed your opinion about something because the facts changed? *Accept all reasonable responses.*

Analyze What can you infer about the number of weapons given in the chart considering the numbers supposedly held by India, Israel, and Pakistan? *Possible answer: We can infer that the totals are not exact. They may be higher, since India, Israel, and Pakistan have not reported their weapons.*

Synthesize On the basis of what you have learned, do you think the changing number of nuclear stockpiles would have influenced Sagan's beliefs about the threat of nuclear destruction? Explain. *Possible answers: Some students may say that Sagan would feel less threatened because there are fewer nuclear weapons. Others may argue that although there are fewer weapons, more countries have them—and that situation could be even more dangerous.*

Focus and Motivate

COMMON CORE FOCUS

RI 2 Determine a central idea of a text and analyze its development, how it emerges and is shaped and refined by specific details; provide an objective summary of the text. **RI 4** Determine the meaning of words and phrases as they are used in a text. **RI 8** Delineate and evaluate the argument and specific claims in a text, assessing whether the reasoning is valid and the evidence is relevant and sufficient. **W 2e** Establish and maintain a formal style and objective tone. **L 1b** Use various types of phrases. **L 5** Demonstrate an understanding of word relationships.

SUMMARY

In "I Acknowledge Mine," Jane Goodall—a naturalist, animal-rights activist, and conservationist—describes the pitiful conditions at labs that use chimpanzees for medical research. Goodall argues passionately for more humane and ethical treatment of these animals.

Do animals have RIGHTS?

Ask students to tell what animal rights means to them. Continue this exploration by having students complete the *DEBATE* activity.

Selection Resources

See resources on the **Teacher One Stop DVD-ROM** and on **thinkcentral.com**.

R RESOURCE MANAGER UNIT 6
Plan and Teach, pp. 71–78
Summary, pp. 79–80†‡*
Text Analysis and Reading
  Skill, pp. 81–84†*
Vocabulary, pp. 85–87*
Grammar and Style, p. 90

DIAGNOSTIC AND SELECTION TESTS
Selection Tests, pp. 191–194

BEST PRACTICES TOOLKIT
Word Squares, p. E10
Cluster Diagram, p. B18

INTERACTIVE READER

ADAPTED INTERACTIVE READER

ELL ADAPTED INTERACTIVE READER

TECHNOLOGY
- Teacher One Stop DVD-ROM
- Student One Stop DVD-ROM
- PowerNotes DVD-ROM
- Audio Anthology CD
- GrammarNotes DVD-ROM
- Audio Tutor CD
- ExamView Test Generator on the **Teacher One Stop**

Video Trailer THINK central

Go to **thinkcentral.com** to preview the **Video Trailer** introducing this selection. Other features that support the selection include
- **PowerNotes** presentation
- **ThinkAloud** models to enhance comprehension
- **WordSharp** vocabulary tutorials
- interactive writing and grammar instruction

* Resources for Differentiation   † Also in Spanish   ‡ In Haitian Creole and Vietnamese

---

Before Reading

Essential Course of Study **ECOS**

I Acknowledge Mine
Essay by Jane Goodall

VIDEO TRAILER **THINK** central | KEYWORD: HML10-664

Do animals have RIGHTS?

COMMON CORE

RI 2 Determine a central idea of a text and analyze its development, how it emerges and is shaped and refined by specific details; provide and objective summary of the text. **RI 8** Delineate and evaluate the argument and specific claims in a text, assessing whether the reasoning is valid and the evidence is relevant and sufficient.

People express their love for animals in a variety of ways, such as pampering pets or contributing money to protect natural habitats. But we often buy products that were tested on animals, and such tests can cause suffering or even death. In this selection, Jane Goodall raises questions about our moral responsibility toward chimpanzees used in medical labs and the importance of animal rights.

DEBATE Should our society recognize animal rights? With a group of classmates, list the reasons for your position on the issue. Then debate the topic with another group.

664

TEXT ANALYSIS: PERSUASIVE TECHNIQUES

Writers use **persuasive techniques** to help convince readers about an issue. Such techniques include **emotional appeals**—statements intended to stir up strong feelings. In the following example, Jane Goodall includes disturbing details and emotionally charged words to arouse pity in readers:

. . . young chimpanzees, in similar tiny prisons, rocked back and forth or from side to side, far gone in misery and despair.

Emotional appeals can be an important element of an effective argument. However, writers sometimes exaggerate problems or use appeals to pity to cover up logical fallacies, or flawed reasoning. As you read "I Acknowledge Mine," pay attention to Goodall's use of emotional appeals.

READING STRATEGY: SUMMARIZE

When you **summarize** an argument, you briefly restate the text's main ideas and important information. A summary is a brief retelling of the main facts, it is not a critique. When you summarize, you should

- present ideas and information in the same order in which they appear in the text
- leave out examples and details that are not essential for understanding the writer's key points
- refrain from critiquing, or evaluating, the writer's ideas

As you read, use a chart like the one shown to help you summarize important ideas and information.

Main Idea	Details
Chimpanzees in the lab suffered from overcrowding and isolation.	The youngest were kept in pairs in small, dark cages.
	Older ones lived alone, without any companionship or stimulation.

VOCABULARY IN CONTEXT

To see how many vocabulary words you know, substitute a different word or phrase for each boldfaced word.

1. Poverty is a **stark** reality.
2. The crowd was loud and **boisterous.**
3. This pill can **alleviate** pain.
4. Must you disagree so **stridently?**
5. I admit my **complicity** in the error.

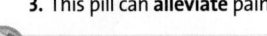 Complete the activities in your **Reader/Writer Notebook.**

Meet the Author

Jane Goodall
born 1934

Call of the Wild
Beginning in 1960, British naturalist and author Jane Goodall devoted herself to observing the behavior of wild chimpanzees in the Gombe Stream Chimpanzee Reserve in Tanzania. There, Goodall made some startling discoveries. For example, she saw chimpanzees make and use tools, disproving the theory that only humans use them. She also observed a chimpanzee "adopt" a younger, orphaned chimpanzee.

Championing Chimps
Goodall's observations over several decades support her belief that chimpanzees are highly intelligent creatures capable of feeling emotions and forming long-term relationships. As a leading authority on chimpanzee behavior, Goodall has written dozens of books, ranging from scholarly works to illustrated children's books. Today, she dedicates her time to lecturing about wildlife conservation and animal welfare.

BACKGROUND TO THE ESSAY
Chimpanzees and Research
Because about 98 percent of chimpanzees' genetic material is identical to ours, they have long been used by researchers for studying the progression and treatment of human diseases. In recent years, they have been used in the study of hepatitis C and HIV. The use of chimpanzees in research has grown increasingly controversial, however, and has been banned in some nations, including Great Britain, Sweden, and New Zealand.

Author Online
THINK central
Go to **thinkcentral.com.**
KEYWORD: HML10-665

665

Teach

TEXT ANALYSIS   COMMON CORE   RI 8

Model the Skill: PERSUASIVE TECHNIQUES

To model how to analyze persuasive techniques, read aloud this example:

Millions of pounds of recyclable materials get dumped in landfills each year, thanks to lazy people or careless municipalities that don't bother recycling.

Emotional appeals are one technique used by persuasive writers. Point out that the following words appeal to the emotions: *dumped, lazy, careless, bother.*

GUIDED PRACTICE Ask students to find examples of emotionally charged words in ads or letters to the editor.

READING STRATEGY   COMMON CORE   RI 2

Model the Skill: SUMMARIZE

Summaries should include the main points of a text. A summary of **Call of the Wild** might include: British naturalist Jane Goodall noted surprising behaviors when she studied wild chimpanzees in Tanzania. She observed them making tools and saw one chimp adopt an orphan.

GUIDED PRACTICE Have students summarize **Championing Chimps.**

 RESOURCE MANAGER—Copy Master
Summarize p. 83

VOCABULARY SKILL   COMMON CORE   L 4

VOCABULARY IN CONTEXT

DIAGNOSE WORD KNOWLEDGE Have all students complete Vocabulary in Context. Compare their words or phrases against the following definitions:

alleviate (ə-lē'vē-āt') *v.* to make easier or provide relief

boisterous (boi'stər-əs) *adj.* noisy and lacking in restraint or discipline

complicity (kəm-plĭs'ĭ-tē) *n.* association or partnership in a crime or offense

stark (stärk) *adj.* harsh or grim
stridently (strīd'nt-lē) *adv.* harshly; conspicuously

PRETEACH VOCABULARY Use the following copy master to help students predict meanings for each boldfaced word.

R RESOURCE MANAGER—Copy Master
Vocabulary Study p. 85

1. Read item 1 aloud, emphasizing *stark.*
2. Point out the phrase "should live in open, bright spaces." Elicit possible meanings for

stark, such as "terrible."

3. Have students record their predictions.
4. Repeat the procedure for items 2–10.

Practice and Apply

READ WITH A PURPOSE

Help students set a purpose for reading. Tell them to identify the reasons that Goodall believes chimpanzees in particular deserve more compassionate treatment from researchers.

READING STRATEGY   COMMON CORE   RI 2

 SUMMARIZE

Possible answer: *Goodall decided to help chimpanzees in medical research labs after viewing a videotape that showed monkeys and chimpanzees suffering in a laboratory.*

IF STUDENTS NEED HELP... Remind them to restate the main idea and most important information, leaving out nonessential details.

VOCABULARY   COMMON CORE   L 4

OWN THE WORD

stark: Remind students that *stark* means "harsh or grim." Have students use the adjective in sentences to describe colors, seasons, places, songs, or other nouns of their choice.

I
—Acknowledge—
Mine

Jane Goodall

Analyze Visuals ▶

What aspects of this photograph give it an **emotional appeal?**

It was on December 27, 1986, that I watched the videotape that would change the pattern of my life. I had spent a traditional Christmas with my family in Bournemouth, England. We all sat watching the tape, and we were all shattered. Afterward, we couldn't speak for a while. The tape showed scenes from inside a biomedical research laboratory, in which monkeys paced round and round, back and forth, within incredibly small cages stacked one on top of the other, and young chimpanzees, in similar tiny prisons, rocked back and forth or from side to side, far gone in misery and despair. I had, of course, known about the chimpanzees who were locked away in medical research laboratories.
10 But I had deliberately kept away, knowing that to see them would be utterly depressing, thinking that there would be nothing I could do to help them. After seeing the video I knew I had to try. . . .

① Targeted Passage

Ⓐ SUMMARIZE
How would you summarize the information in lines 1–12?

The videotape had revealed conditions inside Sema, a federally funded laboratory in Maryland. Goodall took action, criticizing Sema for violating government standards and causing psychological harm to chimpanzees. The president of Sema denied these charges. Several months after Goodall first viewed the videotape, she received permission to visit the laboratory.

Even repeated viewing of the videotape had not prepared me for the **stark** reality of that laboratory. I was ushered, by white-coated men who smiled
20 nervously or glowered, into a nightmare world. The door closed behind us. Outside, everyday life went on as usual, with the sun and the trees and the birds. Inside, where no daylight had ever penetrated, it was dim and colorless. I was led along one corridor after another, and I looked into room after room

stark (stärk) *adj.* harsh or grim

666   UNIT 6: ARGUMENT AND PERSUASION

DIFFERENTIATED INSTRUCTION

FOR ENGLISH LANGUAGE LEARNERS

Vocabulary Support Use Word Squares to teach these words: *medical* (line 9), *depressing* (line 11), *violating* (line 14), *contact* (line 55), *confined* (line 83), *ethical* (line 207).

 BEST PRACTICES TOOLKIT—Transparency
Word Squares p. E10

FOR STRUGGLING READERS

In combination with the *Audio Anthology CD*, use one or more Targeted Passages (pp. 666, 672, 674) to ensure that students focus on key story events, concepts, and skills. Targeted passages are also good for English learners.

① Targeted Passage [Lines 1–12]

This passage introduces the subject of the essay, sets its tone, and establishes the author's persuasive purpose.

• What is the subject of the essay? (lines 8–12)

Reading Support

This selection on **thinkcentral.com** includes embedded **ThinkAloud** models–students "thinking aloud" about the story to model the kinds of questions a good reader would ask about a selection.

BACKGROUND

Chimpanzee Populations Today the world's chimpanzee population is an estimated 150,000 to 200,000. This number represents a decline from more than one million chimps that once lived in the central part of Africa. Large numbers of chimpanzees are now found in only about ten countries. There are several reasons for their decline: illegal capture and hunting, logging, road building, and clearing of land for farms, which destroys their habitat. Efforts are underway to conserve habitat and to create corridors that connect the forests where these primates live.

Analyze Visuals

Possible answer: *The photograph's emotional appeal comes from the sad eyes of the chimpanzee, the framing of its face in the iron door, and the suggestion that it is imprisoned in a dark cage or room behind the door.*

- What effect does the videotape have on Jane Goodall? (lines 4, 11–12)

- How does the description of the videotape set the tone of the essay? (lines 7–8)

- What do you think Goodall will try to persuade readers to do or think in this essay? (lines 11–12)

FOR ADVANCED LEARNERS/PRE–AP

Analyze Passive Voice Point out that teachers generally encourage students to limit the use of the passive voice. Ask students to discuss why Goodall may have chosen to use the passive voice to describe the plight of the lab chimpanzees. Is the construction effective here? Why or why not?

Do animals have
RIGHTS?

Discuss Direct students to lines 26–33, and ask what words and images Goodall uses to describe the lives of laboratory chimpanzees. What idea about animal rights does she imply?
Possible answer: The words "crammed," "tiny," "cramped," "objects," "economical" and the image of faces peering "out from the semidarkness" suggest that people are ignoring the chimps' rights.

TEXT ANALYSIS   COMMON CORE RI 8

B Model the Skill: PERSUASIVE TECHNIQUES

To model how to analyze persuasive techniques, read the paragraph aloud, emphasizing the sentence fragment that answers each question. Point out that rhetorical questions can sometimes have obvious answers, such as these sentence fragments.
Possible answer: to emphasize her point, focus attention on plight of chimpanzees

---

C GRAMMAR AND STYLE   COMMON CORE W 2e L 1b

Set the Tone Ask students to explain why this comparison creates a sad tone.
Possible answer: Readers can easily sympathize with orphaned refugee children and can transfer their emotional reaction to animals in a similar plight.

---

lined with small, bare cages, stacked one above the other. I watched as monkeys paced around their tiny prisons, making bizarre, abnormal movements.

   Then came a room where very young chimpanzees, one or two years old, were crammed, two together, into tiny cages that measured (as I found out later) some twenty-two inches by twenty-two inches at the base. They were two feet high. These chimp babies peered out from the semidarkness of their

30 tiny cells as the doors were opened. Not yet part of any experiment, they had been waiting in their cramped quarters for four months. They were simply objects, stored in the most economical way, in the smallest space that would permit the continuation of life. At least they had each other, but not for long. Once their quarantine was over they would be separated, I was told, and placed singly in other cages, to be infected with hepatitis or AIDS or some other viral disease. And all the cages would then be placed in isolettes.

   What could they see, these infants, when they peered out through the tiny panel of glass in the door of their isolette? The blank wall opposite their prison. What was in the cage to provide occupation, stimulation, comfort? For those

40 who had been separated from their companions—nothing. I watched one isolated prisoner, a juvenile female, as she rocked from side to side, sealed off from the outside world in her metal box. A flashlight was necessary if one wanted to see properly inside the cage. All she could hear was the constant loud sound of the machinery that regulated the flow of air through vents in her isolette. **B**

   A "technician" (for so the animal-care staff are named, after training) was told to lift her out. She sat in his arms like a rag doll, listless, apathetic. He did not speak to her. She did not look at him or try to interact with him in any way. Then he returned her to her cage, latched the inner door, and closed her isolette, shutting her away again from the rest of the world.

50 I am still haunted by the memory of her eyes, and the eyes of the other chimpanzees I saw that day. They were dull and blank, like the eyes of people who have lost all hope, like the eyes of children you see in Africa, refugees, who have lost their parents and their homes. Chimpanzee children are so like human children, in so many ways. They use similar movements to express their feelings. And their emotional needs are the same—both need friendly contact and reassurance and fun and opportunity to engage in wild bouts of play. And they need love. **C**

   Dr. James Mahoney, veterinarian at the Laboratory for Experimental Medicine and Surgery in Primates (LEMSIP), recognized this need when he began

60 working for Jan Moor-Jankowski.[1] Several years ago he started a "nursery" in that lab for the infant chimpanzees when they are first taken from their mothers. It was not long after my visit to Sema that I went for the first of a number of visits to LEMSIP.

   Once I was suitably gowned and masked and capped, with paper booties over my shoes, Jim took me to see his nursery. Five young chimps were there at the time, ranging in age from about nine months to two years. Each one was

---

1. **Jan Moor-Jankowski:** director of LEMSIP.

COMMON CORE RI 4

Language Coach

Connotations A **connotation** is the positive or negative attitude or feeling associated with a word. The words *object* and *stored* (line 32) normally do not evoke many feelings. Why do the words have negative connotations here?

B PERSUASIVE TECHNIQUES

Reread lines 37–44. Why might Goodall have chosen to include **rhetorical questions**—questions that do not require answers—in her appeal to the reader's sympathy?

C GRAMMAR AND STYLE

Reread lines 50–53. Notice how Goodall uses **imagery** and **figurative language**—comparing the chimpanzees to orphaned refugee children—to convey a sad **tone**.

DIFFERENTIATED INSTRUCTION

FOR ENGLISH LANGUAGE LEARNERS

Language: Verb Tenses Remind students that in the passive voice, the subject of a sentence is often not stated. In addition, the subject does not "do" the action of the verb. Ask students to change these phrases from the passive voice to the active voice (with the subject doing the action):

- "A 'technician' . . . was told to lift her out." (lines 45–46) *Possible answer: A supervisor told the "technician" to lift her out.*

- "they are subjected to far harsher treatment." (line 152) *Possible answer: Scientists subject them to far harsher treatment.*

- "Animals in labs are used in different ways." (line 169) *Possible answer: Scientists use lab animals in different ways.*

- "animals are injected with . . . different amounts." (line 171) *Possible answer: Scientists inject animals with different amounts.*

FOR ENGLISH LANGUAGE LEARNERS

Language Coach   COMMON CORE RI 4

Connotations *Possible answer: The words* stored *and* economical *have a negative connotation here because they describe how living animals are being treated like senseless objects.* Point out to students that *boisterous* as it is used in line 79 has a positive connotation—it contrasts these infants with the chimpanzee in line 46.

dressed in children's clothes—"to keep their diapers on, really," said the staff member who was with them. (Someone is always with them throughout the day.) The infants played vigorously around me as I sat on the soft red carpet, surrounded by toys. I was for the moment more interesting than any toy, and almost immediately they had whisked off my cap and mask. Through a window these infants could look into a kitchen and work area where, most of the time, some human activity was going on. They had been taken from their mothers when they were between nine and eighteen months old, Jim said. He brings them into the nursery in groups, so that they can all go through the initial trauma together, which is why some were older than others. And, he explained, he tries to do this during summer vacation so that there will be no shortage of volunteer students to help them over their nightmares. Certainly these **boisterous** youngsters were not depressed.

I stayed for about forty minutes, then Jim came to fetch me. He took me to a room just across the corridor where there were eight young chimpanzees who had recently graduated from the nursery. This new room was known as "Junior Africa," I learned. Confined in small, bare cages, some alone, some paired, the youngsters could see into the nursery through the window. They could look back into their lost childhood. For the second time in their short lives, security and joy had been abruptly brought to an end through no fault of their own. Junior Africa: the name seems utterly appropriate until one remembers all the infants in Africa who are seized from their mothers by hunters, rescued and cared for in human families, and then, as they get older, banished into small cages or tied to the ends of chains. Only the reasons, of course, are different. Even these very young chimpanzees at LEMSIP may have to go through grueling experimental procedures, such as repeated liver biopsies[2] and the drawing of blood. Jim is always pleading for a four-year childhood before research procedures commence, but the bodies of these youngsters, like those of other experimental chimps, are rented out to researchers and pharmaceutical companies. The chimpanzees, it seems, must earn their keep from as early an age as possible.

During a subsequent visit to LEMSIP, I asked after one of the youngsters I had met at the nursery, little Josh. A real character he had been there, a born group leader. I was led to one of the cages in Junior Africa, where that once-assertive infant, who had been so full of energy and zest for life, now sat huddled in the corner of his barred prison. There was no longer any fun in his eyes. "How can you bear it?" I asked the young woman who was caring for him. Her eyes, above the mask, filled with tears. "I can't," she said. "But if I leave, he'll have even less."

This same fear of depriving the chimpanzees of what little they have is what keeps Jim at LEMSIP. After I had passed through Junior Africa that first day, Jim took me to the windowless rooms to meet ten adult chimps. No carpets or toys for them, no entertainment. This was the hard, cold world of the adult research

boisterous (boi'stər-əs) *adj.* noisy and lacking in restraint or discipline

2. **biopsies:** removals of tissue samples from a living body for examination.

TIERED DISCUSSION PROMPTS

Direct students to lines 64–97. Use these prompts to help students understand how Goodall uses comparison and contrast to underscore the horror of the chimpanzees' situation:

Recall In your own words, describe how the chimpanzees are treated in the nursery and then after they are transferred to "Junior Africa." *Possible answer: The infants in the nursery have a chance to play in an open area surrounded by toys. In "Junior Africa," the young chimps are confined in small cages, alone or with a partner, and subjected to experimental procedures.*

Analyze Why does Jane Goodall present this contrast between the nursery and "Junior Africa"? *Possible answer: The contrast emphasizes what the chimpanzees have lost. It also shows readers that the chimpanzees behave like human children, suggesting that their experience of being caged is as devastating as it would be for human children. Both points appeal to readers' emotions.*

Synthesize What is the effect of this emotional appeal? *Possible answer: It makes us feel sad, horrified, and angry; in other words, the reader feels the same way Goodall does.*

Analyze Visuals

Activity What aspect of the text is illustrated by the image of the tiny chimp squatting at the edge of the page? How does the chimp appeal to our emotions? *Possible answer: The photograph probably represents little Josh, whose zest for life was cut short by his confinement in a "barred prison" (lines 99–103). The chimp looks sad and isolated at the bottom of the blank margin. The image elicits pity, sadness, and perhaps a desire to help.*

VOCABULARY COMMON CORE
L 4

OWN THE WORD

boisterous: Tell students that the word *boisterous* can connote rude behavior. Have students list situations when people's actions might be considered *boisterous*.

FOR RELUCTANT READERS

Have students review the discussion of persuasive techniques on page 665. Then have students work in groups to identify the most emotionally charged passages in the selection. Point out lines 20–25, 26–36, 37–44, and 50–57 as examples. Tell each team to separate the emotional appeals from the facts and compare them. Ask students: What facts retain their emotional appeal even when the persuasive words are removed? Why? Have student groups draw conclusions and then take turns reporting their conclusions to the class.

Do animals have
RIGHTS?

Based on lines 116–126, why does Goodall focus on Jojo? How does she humanize him? How does this treatment affect your understanding of animal rights? *Possible answer: She describes one chimp's plight to illustrate the suffering of all chimpanzees in research laboratories. She humanizes Jojo by mentioning his name, suggesting that he dreams of his lost life, and showing his heartbreaking gestures. This humanizing treatment makes the reader feel that Jojo should enjoy the same rights as people.*

Analyze Visuals

Activity Why is Goodall in a mask in the photograph? How does the picture appeal to our emotions? *Possible answer: She wears a mask so that she won't contaminate the chimps or perhaps be contaminated by them. The picture appeals to our emotions by showing a chimpanzee seeking contact with Goodall. The cage and Goodall's lab clothing contrast with this very human gesture.*

110 chimps at LEMSIP. Five on each side of the central corridor, each in his own small prison, surrounded by bars—bars on all sides, bars above, bars below. Each cage measured five feet by five feet and was seven feet high, which was the legal minimum cage size at that time for storing adult chimpanzees. Each cage was suspended above the ground, so that feces and food remains would fall to the floor below. Each cage contained an old car tire and a chimpanzee. That was all.

JoJo's cage was the first on the right as we went in. I knelt down, new cap and mask in place, along with overalls and plastic shoe covers and rubber gloves. I looked into his eyes and talked to him. He had been in his cage at least ten years. He had been born in the African forest. . . . Could he remember, I
120 wondered? Did he sometimes dream of the great trees with the breeze rustling through the canopy, the birds singing, the comfort of his mother's arms? Very gently JoJo reached one great finger through the steel bars and touched one of the tears that slipped out above my mask, then went on grooming the back of my wrist. So gently. Ignoring the rattling of cages, the clank of steel on steel, the violent sway of imprisoned bodies beating against the bars, as the other male chimps greeted the veterinarian.

His round over, Jim returned to where I still crouched before JoJo. The tears were falling faster now. "Jane, please don't," Jim said, squatting beside

A chimpanzee greets Jane Goodall at the Laboratory for Experimental Medicine and Surgery in Primates.

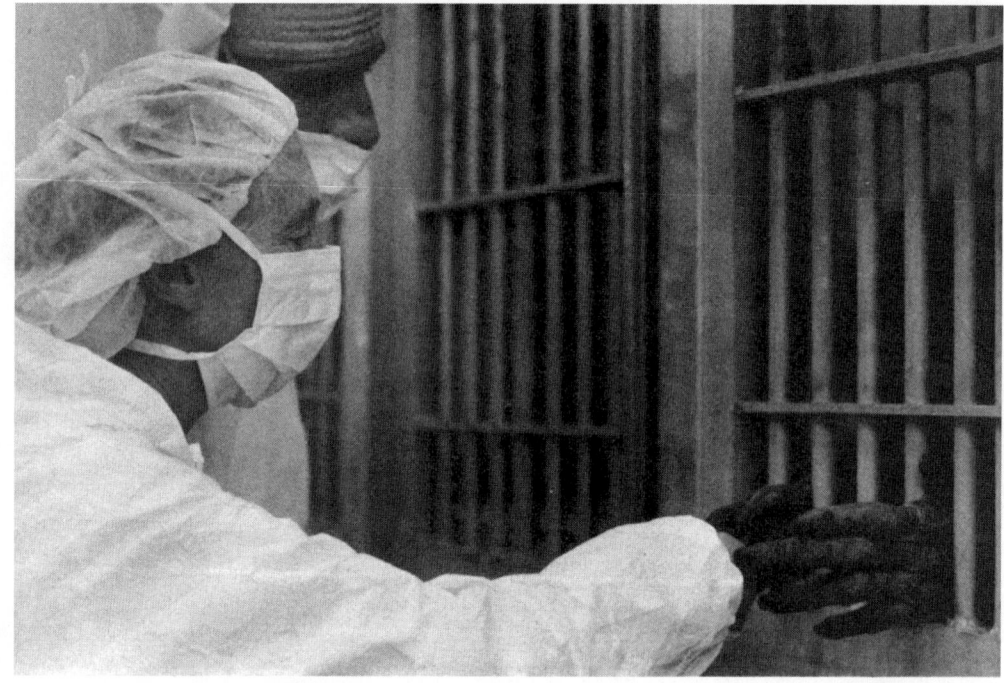

DIFFERENTIATED INSTRUCTION

FOR STRUGGLING READERS
Develop Reading Fluency Model for each group how to read in a way that reflects the emotions the author wishes to evoke. Read aloud lines 37–40, 116–124, and 209–218, using expression and pacing. Instruct students to pause at commas, periods, and elipses and to use a questioning tone when they see a question mark. Then have student groups practice reading the lines until they can do so fluently. Have volunteers take turns reading the passages aloud to the class.

FOR ADVANCED LEARNERS/PRE–AP
Analyze Author's Style Remind students that nonfiction writers use literary elements to make their work richer, livelier, and more compelling. Ask students to discuss Goodall's use of setting, character, and theme in this essay. What conflicts does she establish? Is there a resolution?

me and putting his arm around me. "Please don't. I have to face this every
130 morning of my life." **D**

I also visited [the pharmaceutical company] Immuno's two labs in
Austria. The first of these, where hepatitis research is conducted and where
chimpanzees are used to test batches of vaccine, was built some time ago.
There I got no farther than the administration building. I was not allowed
into the chimpanzee rooms because I had not had a hepatitis shot. And—how
unfortunate!—the closed-circuit TV monitors could not, for some reason, be
made to work that day. In the lobby, though, there were two demonstration
cages, set there so the public could see for itself the magnificent and spacious
housing that Immuno was planning for its chimpanzee colony. (This they
140 felt was necessary because of all the criticisms that were being made about
the small size of the existing cages, dangerous criticisms leading to expensive
lawsuits.) The present cages, I knew, were not very large. The new ones looked
identical to those at LEMSIP. . . .

To my mind, it should be required that all scientists working with laboratory
animals, whatever the species, not only know something about the animals
and their natural behavior, but see for themselves how their protocols[3] affect
individual animals. Researchers should observe firsthand any suffering they
cause, so that they can better balance the benefit (or hoped-for benefit) to
humanity against the cost in suffering to the animal. Laboratory chimpanzees
150 are prisoners, but they are guilty of no crimes. Rather, they are helping—
perhaps—to **alleviate** human suffering. Yet in some of the labs I have described,
and in others around the world, they are subjected to far harsher treatment than
we give to hardened criminals. Surely we owe them more than that. **E**

Even if all research labs could be redesigned to provide the best possible
environment for the chimpanzee subjects, there would still be one nagging
question—should chimpanzees be used at all? . . . Of course I wish I could
wave a wand and see the lab cages standing empty. Of course I hate the
suffering that goes on behind the closed doors of animal labs. I hate even more
the callous attitude that lab personnel so often show toward the animals in
160 their power—deliberately cultivated, no doubt, to try to protect themselves
from any twinge of guilt. . . . Our children are gradually desensitized to
animal suffering. ("It's all right, darling; it's only an animal.") The process
goes on throughout school, culminating in the frightful things that zoology,
psychology, veterinary, and medical students are forced to do to animals in
the process of acquiring knowledge. They have to quell empathy if they are to
survive in their chosen fields, for scientists do things to animals that, from the
animals' point of view, are torture and would be regarded as such by almost
everyone if done by nonscientists.

Animals in labs are used in different ways. In the quest for knowledge,
170 things are done to them to see what happens. To test the safety of various
products, animals are injected with or forced to swallow different amounts

---

3. **protocols** (prō'tə-kôlz'): plans for scientific experiments.

D PERSUASIVE TECHNIQUES
Reread lines 116–130.
What details help make
this passage a powerful
emotional appeal?

alleviate (ə-lē'vē-āt') v.
to make easier or
provide relief

E SUMMARIZE
Briefly restate the key
point that Goodall makes
in lines 144–153.

TEXT ANALYSIS   COMMON CORE

RI 8

D PERSUASIVE TECHNIQUES

*Possible answer: This passage gets its pow-
erful emotional appeal from these details:
the description of Jojo's lost life in Africa,
Jojo gently touching a finger to Goodall's
wrist, the rattling of cages, the violent sway
of bodies beating against bars, Goodall's
tears, and Jim Mahoney's words.*

READING STRATEGY   COMMON CORE

RI 2

E SUMMARIZE

*Possible answer: Researchers have an
obligation to the animals they use. First,
researchers should learn about the animals
and their natural behaviors to truly understand how their experiments affect these
animals. Researchers should also observe
the suffering they cause so that they can
weigh the benefits against that suffering.
Finally, researchers should stop treating lab
animals more harshly than they do criminals, since these animals are supposedly
helping humans and not being punished for
crimes.*

TIERED DISCUSSION PROMPTS

Direct students to lines 154–168. Use
these prompts to help students understand
Goodall's basic message:

Recall What nagging question does Goodall
pose in this passage? *Possible answer:
Should we use chimpanzees in medical
research at all?*

Evaluate Do you agree with Goodall's comparison between research on chimpanzees
and torture? *Accept all reasonable and
well-supported responses.*

VOCABULARY   COMMON CORE

L 4

OWN THE WORD

alleviate: *Alleviate* means "to make
easier or provide relief." Have students
write sentences that demonstrate their
understanding of the word.

FOR ENGLISH LANGUAGE LEARNERS

Language: Modifiers Placement of modifiers
is a key issue for English language learners. Remind students that adjectives modify
nouns and pronouns, while adverbs modify
verbs, adjectives, and other adverbs. Ask
students to identify these modifiers and their
parts of speech:

• "There is an <u>angry</u> debate, <u>ongoing</u> and
<u>abrasive</u>, about the role of . . ." (lines
178–179)—*adjectives*

• "A <u>fully</u> <u>adult</u> <u>male</u> chimpanzee" (line
225)—*adverb, adjective, adjective.*

• "one <u>especially</u> <u>memorable</u> event" (line
227)—*adverb, adjective*

• "We had communicated most <u>truly</u>" (lines
235–236)—*adverb*

Then have small groups find additional examples of modifiers and identify their parts
of speech.

to see how sick they get, or if they survive. The effectiveness of medical procedures and drugs are tried out on animals. Surgical skills are practiced on animals. Theories of all sorts, ranging from the effects of various substances to psychological trauma, are tested on animals. What is so shocking is the lack of respect for the victims, the almost total disregard for their living, feeling, sometimes agonizing bodies. And often the tortures are inflicted for nothing. There is an angry debate, ongoing and abrasive, about the role of animals in medicine. Even though I am not qualified to judge a dispute of this
180 magnitude, which has become so polarized, it seems obvious that extremists on both sides are wrong. The scientists who claim that medical research could never have progressed at all without the use of animals are as incorrect as the animal-rights activists who declare **stridently** that no advances in medicine have been made due to animal research.

stridently (strīd'nt-lē) *adv.* harshly; conspicuously

Let me return to chimpanzees and to the question of whether we are justified in using them in our search for medical knowledge. Approximately three thousand of them languish in medical research laboratories around the world, somewhat more than half this number (about one thousand eight hundred) in the United States. Today, as we have seen, they are primarily
190 used in infectious-disease research and vaccine testing; even though they have seldom shown even minor symptoms of either AIDS or hepatitis, the experimental procedures are often stressful, the conditions in which they are maintained typically bleak. . . .

Humans are a species capable of compassion, and we should develop a heightened moral responsibility for beings who are so like ourselves. Chimpanzees form close, affectionate bonds that may persist throughout life. Like us, they feel joy and sorrow and despair. They show many of the intellectual skills that until recently we believed were unique to ourselves. They may look into mirrors and see themselves as individuals—beings who have consciousness
200 of "self." Do they not, then, deserve to be treated with the same kind of consideration that we accord to other highly sensitive, conscious beings—ourselves? Granted, we do not always show much consideration to one another. That is why there is so much anguish over human rights. That is why it makes little sense to talk about the "rights" of chimpanzees. But at least where we desist from doing certain things to human beings for ethical reasons, we should desist also from doing them to chimpanzee beings. We no longer perform certain experiments on humans, for ethical reasons. I suggest that it would be logical to refrain also from doing these experiments on chimpanzees.

 **Targeted Passage**

F SUMMARIZE
Summarize Goodall's proposal for determining whether experiments on chimpanzees are justified.

Why do I care so much? Why, in order to try to change attitudes and
210 actions in the labs, do I subject myself repeatedly to the personal nightmare of visiting these places, knowing that I shall be haunted endlessly by memories of my encounters with the prisoners there? Especially in their eyes, those bewildered or sad or angry eyes. The answer is simple. I have spent so many years in the forests of Gombe, being with and learning from the chimpanzees. I consider myself one of the luckiest people on earth. It is time to repay something of the debt I owe the chimpanzees, for what they have taught me

READING STRATEGY  COMMON CORE

RI 2

F Model the Skill: SUMMARIZE

Help students complete their Reading Strategy charts to identify the main idea. Point out the supporting details in the passage, including the statements that chimpanzees are very "like ourselves" (line 195), they "form close, affectionate bonds" (line 196), "they feel joy and sorrow and despair" (line 197), and "they show many intellectual skills" we thought were unique to humans (lines 196–198).

Possible answer: *We should stop performing experiments on chimpanzees, creatures that are like humans in many ways, because we refrain from performing those experiments on humans for ethical reasons. The standard of what is ethical for human beings should be applied to chimpanzees.*

VOCABULARY COMMON CORE

L 4

OWN THE WORD

stridently: Tell students that *stridently* is the adverbial form of the adjective *strident*. Point out that *strident* can be a synonym for *boisterous*. Have students consult a dictionary to compare and contrast the meanings and usages of the two words.

DIFFERENTIATED INSTRUCTION

FOR STRUGGLING READERS

 **Targeted Passage** [Lines 194–208]

In this passage, Goodall shifts from an emotional appeal to make a reasoned argument about chimpanzee research.

- How are chimpanzees and people alike? (lines 196–200)

- What rhetorical question does Goodall ask in this passage? Why does she ask it? (lines 200–202)

- What ethical argument does Goodall make against any experiments on chimpanzees? (lines 206–208)

Vocabulary: Multiple Meanings Have partners write these multiple-meaning words in the center of Cluster Diagrams: *bear* (line 103), *hard* (line 109), *cold* (line 109), *round* (line 127), *bonds* (line 196), *groom* (line 225). Have students use context clues or a dictionary to determine possible meanings, then write those meanings in the outer circles.

 BEST PRACTICES TOOLKIT—Transparency Cluster Diagram p. B18

about themselves, about myself, about the place of humans and chimpanzees in the natural world.

When I visit JoJo in his tiny steel prison I often think of David Greybeard, 220 that very special chimpanzee who, by his calm acceptance of my presence, first helped me to open the door into the magic world of the chimpanzees of Gombe. I learned so much from him. It was he who introduced me to his companions, Goliath and Mike and the Flo family and all the other unique, fascinating personalities who made up his community at that time. David even allowed me to groom him. A fully adult male chimpanzee who had lived all his life in the wild actually tolerated the touch of a human hand.

There was one especially memorable event. I had been following David one day, struggling through dense undergrowth near a stream. I was thankful when he stopped to rest, and I sat near him. Close by I noticed the fallen red fruit of 230 an oil nut palm, a favorite food of chimpanzees. I picked it up and held it out to David on the palm of my hand. For a moment I thought he would ignore

Do animals have
RIGHTS?

Direct students to lines 215–226. Ask them why Goodall feels that she owes a debt to chimpanzees. Why has her experience caused her to speak out on behalf of these animals' rights? ***Possible answer:*** *She learned so much about herself from chimpanzees and about the relationship of people to the natural world. Goodall understands their intrinsic value, not only to themselves but also to people.*

Analyze Visuals

Activity Why might the photograph affect us emotionally? Which of Goodall's points does it illustrate? ***Possible answer:*** *It shows the close bonds that chimpanzees form with their family members. It illustrates Goodall's point that people and chimpanzees are not so different, after all.*

FOR ADVANCED LEARNERS/PRE–AP

Evaluate Points of View Have students identify Goodall's arguments about research on chimpanzees. Then challenge students to raise an objection that "the other side" might express. Encourage students to set aside their personal opinions about animal research. Invite students to share their ideas in a roundtable discussion.

my gesture. But then he took the nut, let it fall to the ground and, with the same movement, very gently closed his fingers around my hand. He glanced at my face, let go of my hand, and turned away. I understood his message: "I don't want the nut, but it was nice of you to offer it." We had communicated most truly, relying on shared primate signals that are deeper and more ancient than words. It was a moment of revelation. I did not follow David when he wandered off into the forest. I wanted to be alone, to ponder the significance of what had happened, to enshrine those moments permanently in my mind.

240   And so, when I am with JoJo, I remember David Greybeard and the lessons he taught me. I feel deep shame—shame that we, with our more sophisticated intellect, with our greater capacity for understanding and compassion, have deprived JoJo of almost everything. Not for him the soft colors of the forest, the dim greens and browns entwined, or the peace of the afternoon when the sun flecks the canopy and small creatures rustle and flit and creep among the leaves. Not for him the freedom to choose, each day, how he will spend his time and where and with whom. Nature's sounds are gone, the sounds of running water, of wind in the branches, of chimpanzee calls that ring out so clear and rise up through the treetops to drift away in the hills. The comforts

250   are gone, the soft leafy floor of the forest, the springy branches from which sleeping nests can be made. All are gone. Here, in the lab, the world is concrete and steel; it is loud, horrible sounds, clanging bars, banging doors, and the deafening volume of chimpanzee calls confined in underground rooms. It is a world where there are no windows, nothing to look at, nothing to play with. A world where family and friends are torn apart and where sociable beings are locked away, innocent of crime, into solitary confinement. **G**

It is we who are guilty. I look again into JoJo's clear eyes. I acknowledge my own **complicity** in this world we have made, and I feel the need for forgiveness. He reaches out a large, gentle finger and once again touches the

260   tear trickling down into my mask.   **③ Targeted Passage**

Some of the laboratories discussed in this selection have changed their practices, partly in response to Jane Goodall's criticism and recommendations. For example, Sema, which is now called Diagnon, no longer keeps chimpanzees in isolettes. The chimpanzees now live in more spacious, well-lit cubicles, and they are sometimes allowed to have contact with other chimpanzees. **H**

Comprehension

1. **Recall** What made Goodall decide to investigate research laboratories?

2. **Recall** What conditions did she find in the laboratories that she visited?

3. **Recall** How did the chimpanzee named David Greybeard behave when he came in contact with Goodall in the forests of Gombe?

4. **Clarify** Why does Goodall believe it is important for scientists who work with laboratory animals to know about their natural behavior?

Text Analysis

5. **Examine an Argument** Review the chart you created as you read. How would you **summarize** Goodall's proposals to improve the treatment of chimpanzees in laboratories?

6. **Interpret a Statement** Reread lines 194–208. How do you interpret Goodall's remarks about human rights and the rights of chimpanzees?

7. **Analyze Support** How does the example of Goodall's experiences with David Greybeard support her argument?

8. **Make Inferences** How does Goodall seem to feel about James Mahoney, the veterinarian who guided her visit to LEMSIP?

9. **Identify an Author's Perspective** What beliefs, values, and feelings influence the way Goodall views experimentation on chimpanzees? Support your answer with evidence.

10. **Draw Conclusions** Does Goodall think that chimpanzees should be treated differently from other animals used in laboratory experiments? Cite evidence to support your conclusion.

11. **Evaluate Persuasive Techniques** Does Goodall use **emotional appeals** appropriately in her argument, or are do these appeals contain **rhetorical or logical fallacies**—that is, appeals to false situations, appeals to pity, or personal attacks? Provide examples to support your opinion.

Do animals have RIGHTS?

Should it be against the law to perform medical research on animals?

COMMON CORE

RI 2 Determine a central idea of a text and analyze its development, how it emerges and is shaped and refined by specific details; provide and objective summary of the text. RI 8 Delineate and evaluate the argument and specific claims in a text, assessing whether the reasoning is valid and the evidence is relevant and sufficient.

Practice and Apply

For preliminary support of post-reading questions, use these copy masters:

R RESOURCE MANAGER—Copy Masters
Reading Check p. 88
Persuasive Techniques p. 81
Question Support p. 89

Additional selection questions are provided for teachers on page 75.

ANSWERS

Comprehension

1. *She watched a video showing the poor treatment of chimpanzees and monkeys.*

2. *She found chimpanzees kept in tiny, bare cages, isolated from stimulation.*

3. *David Greybeard accepted Jane Goodall and introduced her to other wild chimps.*

4. *Researchers need this knowledge to understand how laboratory procedures affect the chimps, so that they can eliminate unnecessary suffering.*

Text Analysis

COMMON CORE RI 2, RI 8

Possible answers:

5. ● **COMMON CORE FOCUS** *Summarize Researchers should learn about the natural behavior of chimps and provide them with better housing and more opportunities to interact and exercise; researchers should refrain from experiments that are unethical to perform on humans.*

6. *Granting chimpanzees legal rights makes little sense in a world where human rights are often ignored, but chimps should share humans' right to humane treatment.*

7. *Goodall's experience with David Greybeard shows that chimps are highly intelligent with advanced social skills. He gently refused the nut she offered (lines 232–234), introduced her to his companions (lines 222–224), and allowed her to groom him (lines 224–225).*

8. *She admires James Mahoney for his efforts to improve the lives of lab chimps.*

---

9. *Goodall's views on experimentation are influenced by love and respect for animals. She believes that chimps are much like humans (lines 196–200) and that it is thus wrong to make them suffer.*

10. *Goodall's recognition of their intelligence, social bonds, and similarity to humans suggests that she believes chimps should be treated with the same respect as people. She does not argue against all animal research, however.*

11. ● **COMMON CORE FOCUS** *Persuasive Techniques Answers will vary. Students who think her emotional appeals are excessive may point to examples such as the description of her crying during her interaction with Jojo (lines 122–123).*

Do animals have RIGHTS?

Students may agree or disagree, but should base their answers on arguments presented by Goodall.

ANSWERS

Vocabulary in Context

▲ **VOCABULARY PRACTICE**

1. *false*   4. *false*

2. *true*   5. *false*

3. *true*

R **RESOURCE MANAGER—Copy Master**
Vocabulary Practice p. 86

ACADEMIC VOCABULARY IN SPEAKING

Sample response: *Many controversies relate to our economy. People have often disagreed about ways to limit our country's dependence on imported fuel. The impact of immigration, both legal and illegal, is often debated, with both sides offering statistics to back-up their conclusions. The role of the government in the market economy is also frequently disputed.*

VOCABULARY STRATEGY:
ANALOGIES

COMMON CORE L5

Help students to identify simple examples for each relationship in the chart:

- racket : tennis :: (club) : golf
- big : huge :: (small) : tiny
- cold : hot :: bland : (spicy)
- joke : laughter :: insult : (tears)
- cry : crying :: (talk) : talking

Answers:

1. *complicity (cause to effect)*

2. *stridently (grammar)*

3. *boisterous (antonyms)*

4. *alleviate (object to purpose)*

5. *stark (synonyms)*

R **RESOURCE MANAGER—Copy Master**
Vocabulary Strategy p. 87

Keywords direct students to a **WordSharp** tutorial on **thinkcentral.com** or to other types of vocabulary practice and review.

Vocabulary in Context

▲ **VOCABULARY PRACTICE**

Decide whether each statement is true or false.

1. To **alleviate** a problem is to make it worse.

2. A **boisterous** child may disrupt a quiet restaurant.

3. If you have **complicity** in a crime, you had involvement in it.

4. An elegantly decorated room can be described as **stark**.

5. To speak **stridently** is to ask in a sweet, quiet manner.

WORD LIST
alleviate
boisterous
complicity
stark
stridently

ACADEMIC VOCABULARY IN SPEAKING

- cite   • controversy   • convince   • objective   • statistic

Identify and discuss three issues that have inspired heated public **controversy.** Try to describe each of the issues **objectively.** Use at least one Academic Vocabulary word in your response.

VOCABULARY STRATEGY: ANALOGIES

Analogies express relationships between pairs of words. Some common analogy relationships are described in the chart.

COMMON CORE

L5 Demonstrate understanding of word relationships.

Type	Relationship
Object to purpose	is used for
Synonyms	means the same as
Antonyms	means the opposite of
Cause to effect	results in or leads to
Grammar	is grammatically related to

PRACTICE Complete each analogy by choosing the appropriate vocabulary word. Then, identify the kind of relationship on which the analogy is based.

1. generosity : gratitude :: _____ : guilt

2. grateful : gratefully :: strident : _____

3. selfish : generous :: calm : _____

4. alarm : protect :: aspirin : _____

5. practical : useful :: bleak : _____

Interactive Vocabulary
Go to **thinkcentral.com.**
KEYWORD: HML10-676

DIFFERENTIATED INSTRUCTION

FOR ENGLISH LANGUAGE LEARNERS

Vocabulary: Synonyms/Connotations Before students complete the Vocabulary Practice with analogies, have mixed-language pairs create a word web for each item in the Word List, for either synonyms or connotations. Remind them that they should not list other words in a given family (stridently/strident) for this activity.

FOR ADVANCED LEARNERS/PRE–AP

Vocabulary in Writing Have students write a letter to the editor about their debate topic or another issue of concern in the current news. Ask them to use as many of the words from the Word List as possible. Invite students to mail their letters to a local newspaper or post them in the class as part of a class newsletter.

Language

◆ **GRAMMAR AND STYLE:** Set the Tone

Review the **Grammar and Style** note on page 668. **Tone** is a writer's attitude toward a subject—humorous, angry, or sarcastic, for example—as expressed through **word choice, imagery,** and **formal** or **informal language.** In her writing, Goodall uses imagery and figurative language to express sadness and outrage over the treatment of chimpanzees. Note how she effectively uses nouns, adjectives, and participles to create disturbing images in the following example:

> *Here, in the lab, the world is* concrete and steel; *it is loud,* horrible sounds, clanging bars, banging doors, *and the* deafening *volume of chimpanzee calls confined in underground rooms.* (lines 251–253)

Notice how the revisions in blue help to establish a neutral, objective tone in this first draft. When you revise your own writing, be sure your choice of language and use of imagery match the tone you want to convey.

STUDENT MODEL

Goodall points out that these ~~poor~~ chimpanzees spend all day and night in confinement ~~, like prisoners~~. When they ~~gaze sadly~~ *look out* from their ~~small, dark~~ cages, ~~they can see only a stark wall.~~ *there is nothing to provide them with stimulation.*

READING-WRITING CONNECTION

YOUR TURN

Deepen your understanding of "I Acknowledge Mine" by responding to this prompt. Then use the **revising tip** to improve your writing.

WRITING PROMPT	REVISING TIP
Extended Constructed Response: Summary Write a **three-to-five-paragraph objective summary** of Goodall's essay. Keep in mind that your summary should impartially restate Goodall's main ideas and important details, not critique her argument.	Review your response. Have you used participial phrases to add descriptive details?

Interactive Revision **THINK** central

Go to **thinkcentral.com**.
KEYWORD: HML10-677

I ACKNOWLEDGE MINE **677**

COMMON CORE

RI 2 Provide an objective summary of the text. **W 2e** Establish and maintain a formal style and objective tone. **L 1b** Use various types of phrases.

Language

COMMON CORE RI 2, W 2e, L 1b

◆ **GRAMMAR AND STYLE**

- Point out the importance of thinking about the tone before writing. Help students to list words that might describe the tone of an acceptance speech, then have them think about the tone of a personal response. Ask students whether the tone of each would be formal or informal.

- Write this opening of an acceptance speech on the board. Have students suggest revisions for a more suitable tone.

Dear friends, I thank you ~~for your cool award. It means a lot to me that you understand why we have to stop all medical research on chimps.~~ for making a difference in this world. I thank you for understanding that our cruel and unusual treatment of chimpanzees must end—and end immediately. I thank you from the bottom of my heart.

R RESOURCE MANAGER—Copy Master
Set the Tone p. 90

READING-WRITING CONNECTION

Refer students to READING STRATEGY: SUMMARIZE on page 665. Remind them that a summary is a brief restatement of all of the text's main ideas and important information.

THINK central

Writing Online

The following tools are available online at **thinkcentral.com** and on Write*Smart* **CD-ROM:**
- **Interactive Graphic Organizers**
- **Interactive Student Models**
- **Interactive Revision Lessons**

For additional grammar instruction, see **GrammarNotes** on **thinkcentral.com**.

FOR STRUGGLING WRITERS

- Limit the length of the assignment to three paragraphs.

- Remind students to present ideas and information in the same order in which they appear in the text.

- Encourage students to leave out examples and details that are not essential for understanding the writer's key points.

- Remind students to refrain from critiquing, or evaluating, the writer's ideas.

Assess and Reteach

Assess

DIAGNOSTIC AND SELECTION TESTS
Selection Test A pp. 191–192
Selection Test B/C pp. 193–194

Interactive Selection Test on **thinkcentral.com**

Reteach

Level Up Online Tutorials on **thinkcentral.com**

Focus and Motivate

SUMMARY

In this position paper, the AMA responds to objections to using animals in biomedical research. The AMA maintains that people would suffer if laws ended or further regulated experiments on animals.

Do the **ENDS** justify the means?

Introduce the question, and have students restate Goodall's objections to animal research. You may wish to start students on their balance-scale diagrams for the *DISCUSS* activity by suggesting the topic of agricultural biotechnology.

Selection Resources

Essential Course of Study ECOS

Use of Animals in Biomedical Research
Position Paper by the American Medical Association

Do the **ENDS** justify the means?

You have read about Jane Goodall's objections to some aspects of animal research. In "Use of Animals in Biomedical Research," the American Medical Association addresses the issue of whether improving human health outweighs the suffering of animals in medical laboratories.

DISCUSS Think of a situation in which an unpleasant or disturbing action may lead to a worthy outcome. Create a balance scale like the one shown. Jot down the possible benefits of the action in one box and the harm caused by the action in the other. Share your balance scale with your classmates, and discuss whether the possible benefits outweigh the harm.

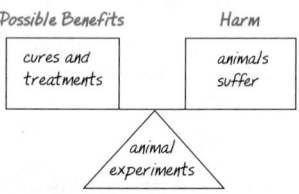

Possible Benefits — cures and treatments

Harm — animals suffer

animal experiments

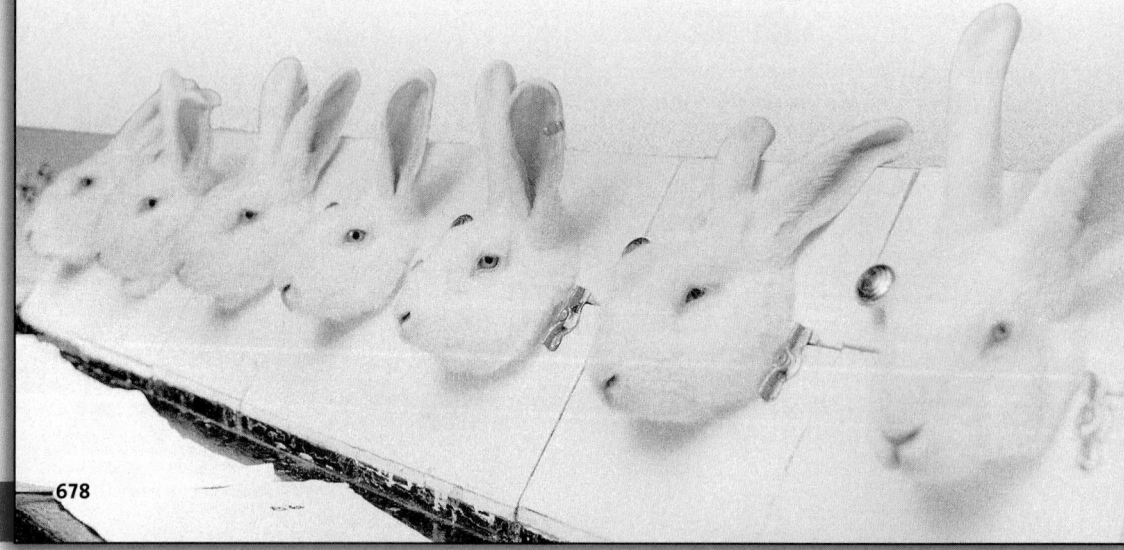

See resources on the **Teacher One Stop DVD-ROM** *and on* **thinkcentral.com**.

 **RESOURCE MANAGER UNIT 6**
Plan and Teach, pp. 91–98
Summary, pp. 99–100†‡*
Text Analysis and Reading Skill, pp. 101–104†*
Vocabulary, pp. 105–107*
Grammar and Style, p. 110

DIAGNOSTIC AND SELECTION TESTS
Selection Tests, pp. 195–198

 BEST PRACTICES TOOLKIT
Word Squares, p. E10
Think-Pair-Share, p. A18

INTERACTIVE READER

ADAPTED INTERACTIVE READER

ELL ADAPTED INTERACTIVE READER

TECHNOLOGY
- Teacher One Stop DVD-ROM
- Student One Stop DVD-ROM
- PowerNotes DVD-ROM
- Audio Anthology CD
- GrammarNotes DVD-ROM
- Audio Tutor CD
- ExamView Test Generator on the **Teacher One Stop**

THINK central

Find it Online!
Features on **thinkcentral.com** that support the selection include
- **PowerNotes** presentation
- **ThinkAloud** models to enhance comprehension
- **WordSharp** vocabulary tutorials
- interactive writing and grammar instruction

---

* Resources for Differentiation   † Also in Spanish   ‡ In Haitian Creole and Vietnamese

TEXT ANALYSIS: COUNTERARGUMENTS

Although the American Medical Association is firmly in favor of using animals in research, it does not ignore the views of opponents. Instead, it states the opponents' views and then disputes them with **counterarguments.** As you read "Use of Animals in Biomedical Research," use a chart like the one shown to keep track of counterarguments in the selection.

Opposing Viewpoint	Counterargument	Support for Counterargument
Animal experimentation isn't needed.	Most modern medical advances have required such experiments.	Many Nobel Prizes have been awarded for medical research involving animals.

READING STRATEGY: SUMMARIZE AND CRITIQUE

To **summarize** an argument, you restate the argument's main points. A summary should include only information that appears in the original text. When you want to discuss your opinions about or criticisms of an argument, you write a **critique.** A critique allows you to share more of your own ideas than you would in a summary, but these ideas must be backed up by examples and evidence.

In the article you are about to read, "Use of Animals in Biomedical Research," the authors summarize animal rights' arguments and then critique them. As you read, practice this strategy yourself by summarizing the American Medical Association's arguments and developing your own critique.

▲ VOCABULARY IN CONTEXT

Figure out the meaning of each word from the context provided, and, in your *Reader/Writer Notebook*, write a sentence that shows your understanding.

1. support from a **proponent** of this plan
2. a **speculative** and unreliable conclusion
3. a speech full of insincere **rhetoric**
4. obstacles that **impede** our progress

 Complete the activities in your **Reader/Writer Notebook.**

American Medical Association
Founded in Philadelphia in 1847, the American Medical Association (AMA) is the largest professional organization for physicians in the United States. The AMA identifies its core purpose as the promotion of "the science and art of medicine and the betterment of public health." The AMA formulates policies on a wide range of health care and ethical issues, such as tobacco use and discrimination against AIDS patients. Many important studies have been published in the prestigious *Journal of the American Medical Association.*

Animal Rights Versus Animal Welfare
Discussions of animal protection often distinguish between the animal rights and animal welfare movements. Animal rights advocates believe that all experimentation on animals is wrong, even if it relieves human suffering. According to People for the Ethical Treatment of Animals (PETA), the world's largest animal rights organization, "animals, like humans, have interests that cannot be sacrificed or traded away just because it might benefit others.... Animals are not ours to use for food, clothing, entertainment, or experimentation." Animal welfare advocates, on the other hand, do not entirely rule out the use of animals in research, but they believe that the animals should be treated as humanely as possible. The animal welfare movement also calls for a reduction in the numbers of animals used in research and for the development of experimental procedures that do not require animals.

Teach

● *Model the Skill:* COUNTERARGUMENTS

To model how to identify counterarguments, read aloud this example:

> Some have criticized jaywalking tickets as "order for order's sake." But cities with strong jaywalking enforcement have fewer accidents involving pedestrians.

Point out the viewpoint that jaywalking tickets are needless enforcement. The counterargument is that they increase safety.

GUIDED PRACTICE Ask students to think of another pairing of an argument and a counterargument.

 RESOURCE MANAGER—Copy Master
Counterarguments p. 101

■ *Model the Skill:* SUMMARIZE AND CRITIQUE

Read aloud the following summary of "I Acknowledge Mine":

> In "I Acknowledge Mine," the author describes the pitiful conditions at labs that use chimpanzees for medical research and argues passionately for ethical treatment of these animals.

Suggest that a critique might state: "Ms. Goodall argues passionately for the ethical treatment of laboratory chimpanzees, but little of her argument is based on scientific fact." Point out that the second phrase contains an opinion.

GUIDED PRACTICE Ask students to write critiques of the Goodall essay.

VOCABULARY SKILL

▲ VOCABULARY IN CONTEXT

DIAGNOSE WORD KNOWLEDGE Have all students complete Vocabulary in Context. Check their sentences against the following:

impede (ĭm-pēd') *v.* to obstruct or hinder
proponent (prə-pō'nənt) *n.* a person who pleads for or supports a cause
rhetoric (rĕt'ər-ĭk) *n.* grand but empty talk
speculative (spĕk'yə-lə-tĭv) *adj.* based on guesses and theories rather than fact

PRETEACH VOCABULARY Use the following copy master.

R RESOURCE MANAGER—Copy Master
Vocabulary Study p. 105

1. Read the first sentence in Part A aloud, emphasizing *impede.* Point out the words "progress" and "difficult." Elicit possible meanings for *impede,* such as "get in the way of."
2. Repeat the procedure for items 2–4.

READ WITH A PURPOSE

Help students set a purpose for reading. Tell them to look for facts that support the use of animals in biomedical research.

TIERED DISCUSSION PROMPTS

Direct students to lines 1–19. Use these prompts to help students see how the AMA uses the history of animal research to support its arguments:

Connect How do you feel about the way in which animals have been used for research in the past? *Accept all reasonable responses.*

Analyze Why do you think the AMA begins its position paper by citing medical discoveries that were made throughout history as a result of animal research by famous historical figures? *Possible answer: Citing key discoveries by famous historical figures suggests that animal research has been crucial to medical advances.*

Evaluate How effective is the paper's introduction? *Possible answer: The introduction is effective in tying animal research to medical advances. Plus, by appealing to historical precedent and the authority of famous people, the AMA adds legitimacy to its argument.*

READING STRATEGY

COMMON CORE
RI 2
RI 5

A *Model the Skill:* **SUMMARIZE AND CRITIQUE**

To model how to summarize, read the the first four lines of the paragraph aloud. Point out that lines 20–24 identify the three general purposes, and the rest of the paragraph provides a more detailed explanation of each.

Possible answers: The three general purposes for which animals are used in experiments today are biomedical and behavioral research, education, and testing of drugs and other products. This paragraph outlines the information that will be discussed in more detail later in the article.

Use of Animals in Biomedical Research

American Medical Association

Targeted Passage

Animals have been used in experiments for at least 2,000 years, with the first reference made in the third century B.C. in Alexandria, Egypt, when the philosopher and scientist Erisistratus used animals to study body functions.

Five centuries later, the Roman physician Galen used apes and pigs to prove his theory that veins carry blood rather
10 than air. In succeeding centuries, animals were employed to discover how the body functions or to confirm or disprove theories developed through observation. Advances in knowledge made through these experiments included Harvey's demonstration of the circulation of blood in 1622, the effect of anesthesia on the body in 1846, and the relationship between bacteria and disease in 1878.
20 Today, animals are used in experiments for three general purposes: (1) biomedical and behavioral research, (2) education, (3) drug and product

A SUMMARIZE AND CRITIQUE
Summarize the information presented in lines 20–39. Why do you think the authors include this information?

testing. . . . Biomedical research increases understanding of how biological systems function and advances medical knowledge. . . . Educational experiments are conducted to educate and train students in medicine, veteri-
30 nary medicine, physiology,[1] and general science. In many instances, these experiments are conducted with dead animals. . . . Animals also are employed to determine the safety and efficacy[2] of new drugs or the toxicity[3] of chemicals to which humans or animals may be exposed. Most of these experiments are conducted by commercial firms to fulfill government requirements. . . . **A**

Use of Animals Rather than Humans

40 A basic assumption of all types of research is that man should relieve human and animal suffering. One objection to the use of animals in

---

1. **physiology** (fĭz′ē-ŏl′ə-jē): a branch of biology that deals with the functioning of organisms.
2. **efficacy** (ĕf′ĭ-kə-sē): the capacity to produce a desired effect.
3. **toxicity** (tŏk-sĭs′ĭ-tē): the quality of being poisonous or harmful.

DIFFERENTIATED INSTRUCTION

FOR ENGLISH LANGUAGE LEARNERS

Vocabulary Support Use Word Squares to teach these words: *philosopher* (lines 4–5), *conducted* (line 32), *environments* (line 63), *alternative* (line 146), *fundamental* (line 240), *legislatures* (lines 267–268).

 BEST PRACTICES TOOLKIT—Transparency
Word Squares p. E10

FOR STRUGGLING READERS

In combination with the *Audio Anthology CD*, use one or more Targeted Passages (pp. 680, 682, 684) to ensure that students focus on key information, concepts, and skills. Targeted Passages are also good for English learners.

1 Targeted Passage [Lines 24–39]

This passage explains some of the general purposes for which animals are currently used in experiments.

biomedical research is that the animals are used as surrogates for human beings. This objection presumes the equality of all forms of life; animal rights advocates argue that if the tests are for the benefit of man, then man should serve
50 as the subject of the experiments. There are limitations, however, to the use of human subjects both ethically, such as in the testing of a potentially toxic drug or chemical, and in terms of what can be learned. The process of aging, for instance, can best be observed through experiments with rats, which live an average of two to three years, or with some types of monkeys, which live 15
60 to 20 years. Some experiments require numerous subjects of the same weight or genetic makeup or require special diets or physical environments; these conditions make the use of human subjects difficult or impossible. By using animals in such tests, researchers can observe subjects of uniform age and background in sufficient numbers to determine if findings are consistent and
70 applicable to a large population. **B**

Animals are important in research precisely because they have complex body systems that react and interact with stimuli much as humans do. The more true this is with a particular animal, the more valuable that animal is for a particular type of research. One important property to a researcher is discrimination—the extent to which an
80 animal exhibits the particular quality to be investigated. The greater the degree of discrimination, the greater the reliability and predictability of the information gathered from the experiment. **C**

For example, dogs have been invaluable in biomedical research because of the relative size of their organs com-

pared to humans. The first successful kidney transplant was performed in a
90 dog, and the techniques used to save the lives of "blue babies," babies with structural defects in their hearts, were developed with dogs. Open-heart surgical techniques, coronary bypass surgery,[4] and heart transplantation all were developed using dogs.

Another important factor is the amount of information available about a particular animal. Mice and rats play
100 an extensive role in research and testing, in part because repeated experiments and controlled breeding have created a pool of data to which the findings from a new experiment can be related and given meaning. Their rapid rate of reproduction also has made them important in studies of genetics and other experiments that require observation over a number of generations.
110 Moreover, humans cannot be bred to produce "inbred strains"[5] as can be done with animals; therefore, humans cannot be substituted for animals in studies where an inbred strain is essential.

Scientists argue repeatedly that research is necessary to reduce human and animal suffering and disease. Biomedical advances depend on research with animals, and not using
120 them would be unethical because it would deprive humans and animals of the benefits of research. . . .

Benefits of Animal Experimentation

The arguments advanced by animal rights activists in opposing the use of animals in biomedical research . . . are scientific, emotional, and philosophic. . . . The scientific challenge raised by animal rights activists goes to the heart

---

4. **coronary bypass surgery:** open-heart surgery to improve the blood supply to the heart.

5. **inbred strains:** groups of animals produced by the mating of siblings over at least 20 generations, resulting in individuals as genetically similar as possible.

B COUNTERARGUMENTS
What counterargument is given to dispute the view that humans should be the subjects of experiments that benefit humans?

C SUMMARIZE AND CRITIQUE
Summarize the information presented in this paragraph. What critique do you think an animal rights activist might present in response to this information?

Reading Support

This selection on **thinkcentral.com** includes embedded **ThinkAloud** models–students "thinking aloud" about the story to model the kinds of questions a good reader would ask about a selection.

Analyze Visuals

Activity Ask students what the presentation of this photograph on the page implies about the animal. *Possible answer: The paper clip and slightly askew photograph suggest that the rat is a lab animal whose photograph is attached to a research file. The rat seems trapped on the page, staring straight at the viewer as if looking out from a cage.*

TEXT ANALYSIS COMMON CORE

B Model the Skill: COUNTERARGUMENTS RI 5 RI 8

Help students fill out their Counterarguments charts. Direct students to the opposing view introduced in lines 47–50. Point out that the rest of the paragraph details several specific counterarguments to the opposing view.

Possible answer: Some experiments cannot be performed on humans because the length of the human lifespan makes the tests impractical or because the tests require many genetically similar subjects, special diets, or environments. There are also ethical limitations on the use of humans for certain tests.

READING STRATEGY COMMON CORE

C SUMMARIZE AND CRITIQUE RI 2 RI 5

Possible answer: Summary: Animals are valuable in research because their body systems function much like humans. The more closely an animal exhibits the quality being studied, the more reliable the information gathered. Critique: By this reasoning, humans are the most ideal subjects because there are no variables to consider.

- What are the three general purposes for animal experiments today? (lines 24, 27–28, 34–35)
- According to the AMA, how does biomedical research benefit people? (lines 24–27)
- Why would the government require commercial firms to perform animal tests? (lines 37–39)

FOR STRUGGLING READERS
Develop Reading Fluency Point out to students that with scholarly, scientific writing it is

easy to get lost in the complex sentence structure. Model for students the reading of the sentence beginning on line 224, emphasizing the pause at the comma. Divide the class into two groups. The first group reads together to the comma, then the second reads to the period. Lines 99–105 can be read the same way. Distribute the copy masters and have students work in teams or pairs to practice fluency.

R RESOURCE MANAGER—Copy Master
Reading Fluency p. 111

BACKGROUND

Animal Experiments The Humane Society of the United States estimates that scientists in the United States perform experiments on more than a million animals annually. Some animal-rights advocates, however, estimate that as many as 100 million animals are used worldwide each year. Mice and rats account for about 90 percent of these subjects.

READING STRATEGY   COMMON CORE
                                     RI 2
                                     RI 5

 SUMMARIZE AND CRITIQUE

Possible answer: The animal rights argument is: If animals are so important to research, why hasn't more been accomplished? The authors critique it by providing examples of the many advances in medical science made possible by using animals in experiments.

TEXT ANALYSIS   COMMON CORE
                                     RI 5

 AUTHOR'S CLAIM

Possible answer: The writer relates emotional, exaggerated statements made by the opposition and then counters with an unemotional statement with facts about the positive results of animal testing.

REVISIT THE BIG QUESTION

Do the **ENDS** justify the means?

Discuss Based on lines 149–154, why isn't Ingrid Newkirk's statement about the failure of animal research a convincing argument? How does the weakness of this statement reinforce the AMA's argument?

Possible answer: Newkirk's statement assumes an all-or-nothing stance—if animal research were effective, it would solve all problems. The possibility that it does solve some problems is not considered. By citing this transparently weak argument, the authors raise doubts about all arguments against animal research.

---

of the issue by asking whether animal 130 experiments are necessary for scientific and medical progress and whether all the experiments being performed and all the animals being used are justified and required. Scientists insist that they are; animal rights activists insist that they are not.

Scientists justify use of animals in biomedical research on two grounds: the contribution that the information makes 140 to human and animal health and welfare, and the lack of any alternative way to gain the information and knowledge. Animal rights activists contest experiments that utilize animals on both these grounds and assert that this practice no longer is necessary because alternative methods of experimentation exist for obtaining the same information.

In an appearance on the *Today* show 150 in 1985, Ingrid Newkirk, representing People for the Ethical Treatment of Animals (PETA), stated: "If it were such a valuable way to gain knowledge, we should have eternal life by now." This statement is similar in spirit to one made in 1900 by an antivivisectionist[6] who stated that, given the number of experiments on the brain done up to then, the insane asylums of Washington, D.C. 160 should be empty.

Scientists believe that such assertions miss the point. The issue is not what *has not* been accomplished by animal use in biomedical research, but what *has* been accomplished. A longer life span has been achieved, decreased infant mortality[7] has occurred, effective treatments have been developed for many diseases, and the quality of life has been 170 enhanced for mankind in general.

One demonstration of the critical role that animals play in medical and scientific advances is that 54 of 76 Nobel Prizes awarded in physiology or medicine since 1901 have been for discoveries and advances made through the use of experimental animals. Among these have been the Prize awarded in 1985 for the studies (using 180 dogs) that documented the relationship between cholesterol and heart disease; the 1966 Prize for the studies (using chickens) that linked viruses and cancer; and the 1960 Prize for studies (using cattle, mice, and chicken embryos) that established that a body can be taught to accept tissue from different donors if it is inoculated[8] with different types of tissue prior to birth 190 or during the first year of life, a finding expected to help simplify and advance organ transplants in the future. Studies using animals also resulted in successful culture of the poliomyelitis[9] virus; a Nobel Prize was awarded for this work in 1954. The discovery of insulin and treatment of diabetes, achieved through experiments using dogs, also earned the Prize in 1923.

200 In fact, virtually every advance in medical science in the 20th century, from antibiotics and vaccines to antidepressant drugs and organ transplants, has been achieved either directly or indirectly through the use of animals in laboratory experiments. The result of these experiments has been the elimination or control of many infectious diseases—smallpox, poliomyelitis, measles—and 210 the development of numerous life-saving techniques—blood transfusions, burn therapy, open-heart and brain surgery.

---

6. **antivivisectionist** (ăn′tē-vĭv′ĭ-sĕk′shən-ĭst): someone opposed to the act of operating on live animals for science experiments.

7. **infant mortality:** the death rate during the first year of life.

8. **inoculated** (ĭ-nŏk′yə-lā′tĭd): injected.

9. **poliomyelitis** (pō′lē-ō-mī′ə-lī′tĭs): a highly infectious viral disease that generally affects children and may lead to paralysis and deformity. Also called *polio*.

Targeted Passage

 SUMMARIZE AND CRITIQUE

Identify the argument that the article summarizes in lines 137–148. What critique do the authors offer in response?

COMMON CORE RI 5

 AUTHOR'S CLAIM

Writers often develop their claims by offering opposing arguments, and then restating their own position. Explain how the writer does this in lines 149–170.

COMMON CORE RI 4

Language Coach

Commonly Confused Words *Infectious* (line 208) means "caused by microscopic agents such as bacteria and viruses." *Contagious* means "spreading from person to person." All contagious diseases are infectious, but not all infections are contagious. Can you think of an example of a disease that is infectious but not contagious?

DIFFERENTIATED INSTRUCTION

FOR STRUGGLING READERS

② Targeted Passage [Lines 200–212]

In this passage, the AMA argues that animal research has helped scientists make great medical advances.

- What medical advances have resulted from animal research? (lines 202–203)

- How have people benefited from these advances? (lines 207–212)

- What might animal subjects in burn-therapy experiments have gone through? (line 211)

FOR ENGLISH LANGUAGE LEARNERS

Language Coach   COMMON CORE
                                   RI 4

Commonly Confused Words *Possible answer: Malaria is an infectious disease spread by mosquitoes—therefore, it is not contagious.* Ask students why people with contagious diseases are often quarantined.

Possible answer: to prevent widespread outbreak of the disease

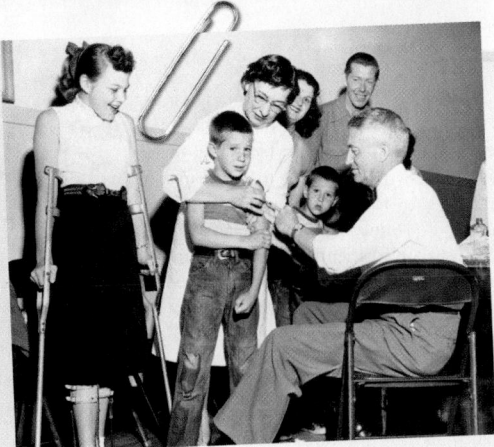

A boy is vaccinated for polio in 1955 under the gaze of his sister, who became paralyzed from a polio infection. The first polio vaccine was developed through experiments on animals.

This has meant a longer, healthier, better life with much less pain and suffering. For many, it has meant life itself. Often forgotten in the **rhetoric** is the fact that humans *do* participate in biomedical research in the form of clinical trials. They experience pain and are injured, 220 and in fact, some of them die from this participation. Hence, scientists are not asking animals to be "guinea pigs" alone for the glory of science. . . . **F**

Scientists feel that it is essential for the public to understand that had scientific research been restrained in the first decade of the 20th century as antivivisectionists and activists were then and are today urging, many millions of 230 Americans alive and healthy today would never have been born or would have suffered a premature death. Their parents or grandparents would have died from diphtheria, scarlet fever, tuberculosis, diabetes, appendicitis, and countless other diseases and disorders. . . .

The Danger of Restricting Research

The activities and arguments of animal rights and animal welfare activists and organizations present the American 240 people with some fundamental decisions that must be made regarding the use of animals in biomedical research.

The fundamental issue raised by the philosophy of the animal rights movement is whether man has the right to use animals in a way that causes them to suffer and die. To accept the philosophical and moral viewpoint of the animal rights movement would require a total ban 250 on the use of animals in any scientific research and testing. The consequences of such a step were set forth by the Office of Technology Assessment (OTA) in its report to Congress: "Implementation of this option would effectively arrest most basic biomedical and behavioral research and toxicological testing in the United States." The economic and public health consequences of that, the OTA warned 260 Congress, "are so unpredictable and **speculative** that this course of action should be considered dangerous." **G**

No nation and no jurisdiction within the United States has yet adopted such a ban. Although . . . laws to ban the use of animals in biomedical research have been introduced into a number of state legislatures, neither a majority of the American people nor their elected representatives 270 have ever supported these bills.

Another aspect of the use of animals in biomedical research that has received little consideration is the economic consequences of regulatory change. Clearly, other nations are not curtailing the use of animals to any significant degree. Some of these, like Japan, are major competi-

rhetoric (rĕt′ər-ĭk) *n.* grand but empty talk

F COUNTERARGUMENTS
What opposing viewpoints are disputed in lines 200–223?

speculative
(spĕk′yə-lə-tĭv) *adj.* based on guesses and theories rather than fact

G SUMMARIZE AND CRITIQUE
What critique do the authors offer in lines 251–262? Is this critique effective? Why or why not?

FOR ENGLISH LANGUAGE LEARNERS
Comprehension: Transitions Have students work in a Think-Pair-Share activity to identify signal words and phrases like "In fact" (line 200), "Hence" (line 221), "Although" (line 265), "therefore" (line 301), and "However" (line 306). Discuss how these words explain the connections among the ideas in the passage.

 **BEST PRACTICES TOOLKIT—Transparency**
Think-Pair-Share p. A18

FOR ADVANCED LEARNERS/PRE–AP
Analyze an Argument Have students evaluate the reasoning in this selection by looking for errors in logic, such as circular reasoning, either/or fallacy, oversimplification, overgeneralization, false cause, and hasty generalization. For more on faulty reasoning, see **Reading Handbook,** page R23.

TEXT ANALYSIS   COMMON CORE

F COUNTERARGUMENTS   RI 5 RI 8

Possible answer: The opposing viewpoints are (1) animal research has not achieved much (lines 152–154); and (2) if the testing benefits people, people should serve as the subjects of the experiments (lines 47–50).

IF STUDENTS NEED HELP . . . Suggest that they first identify the AMA's counterarguments and then look back through the selection to find the opposing viewpoints the AMA is refuting.

READING STRATEGY   COMMON CORE

G SUMMARIZE AND CRITIQUE   RI 2 RI 5

Possible answer: A ban on the use of animals in ways that would cause them to suffer and die would stop basic research and testing. That dangerous economic and public health consequences might result is a strong and effective critique.

Analyze Visuals

Activity Ask students how this photograph helps support the AMA's argument. *Possible answer: The photograph shows the effects of polio: the girl with crutches and leg braces. It also shows the solution to polio: an injection of vaccine that is being given to her brother.* Then ask students if the illustrations on pages 618 and 620 support the AMA's thesis. Have students explain their answers. *Student responses will vary.*

VOCABULARY   COMMON CORE

OWN THE WORD   L 4

- **rhetoric:** Tell students that another meaning of *rhetoric* is "using language effectively and persuasively."
- **speculative:** Tell students that the word *speculative* has a connotation of something risky or dangerous. Have students offer examples of things that might be or are *speculative*.

GRAMMAR AND STYLE   COMMON CORE   L 3

Identify Formal Language

Formal language is used in most informational texts, including articles and research reports. Ask students to identify examples of complex vocabulary and sentence structure, standard punctuation, and lack of contractions in this position paper.

TEXT ANALYSIS   COMMON CORE   RI 5   RI 8

❶ COUNTERARGUMENTS

Possible answer: The counterargument is that while everyone wants to limit animal suffering, restrictions on animal research may lead to greater human suffering.

TEXT ANALYSIS   COMMON CORE   RI 8

❷ SYNTHESIZE INFORMATION

Before students construct their answers, have them summarize the two viewpoints and the evidence the authors offer to support their opinions.

Possible answer: Goodall expresses concern for the welfare of animals used in research but also acknowledges the benefit of using animals. Students should choose the article they think uses the most convincing evidence and back up their opinions with details from the text.

VOCABULARY   COMMON CORE   L 4

OWN THE WORD

- **proponent:** Have students write sentences using the word *proponent*.
- **impede:** Have students identify synonyms for *impede*.

SELECTION WRAP-UP

READ WITH A PURPOSE Ask students: Which parts of the AMA's argument are most and least persuasive? Why? *Possible answer:* most persuasive: animal research has led to medical advances; least persuasive: economic consequences of regulatory change

---

❶ GRAMMAR AND STYLE

Reread lines 313–325. Because this paper is written for a professional audience, it contains **formal language,** including complex vocabulary and sentence structure, standard punctuation, and a lack of contractions.

proponent (prə-pō′nənt) *n.* a person who pleads for or supports a cause

impede (ĭm-pēd′) *v.* to obstruct or hinder

❶ COUNTERARGUMENTS

What counterargument is made in response to the animal welfare movement in lines 326–336?

Targeted Passage ③

COMMON CORE RI 8

❷ SYNTHESIZE INFORMATION

Now you have read two different articles on the use of animals for scientific research. Think about the ideas and details in each text. What is the central idea of each article? Synthesize the information in both articles and decide which one presents the best evidence. Explain your choice using evidence from the texts.

tors of the United States in biomedical research. Given the economic climate in the United States, our massive trade

280 imbalance, and our loss of leadership in many areas, can the United States afford not to keep a leading industry, i.e., biomedical science, developing as rapidly as possible? Many nations are in positions to assume leadership roles, and the long-term economic impact on our citizens could be profound. This economic impact would be expressed in

290 many ways, not the least of which would certainly be a reduction in the quality and number of health services available for people who need them.

Through polls and by other means, the American people have indicated that they support the use of animals in research and testing. At the same time they have expressed a strong wish that the animals be protected against

300 any unnecessary pain and suffering. The true question, therefore, is how to achieve this without interfering with the performance of necessary research. Scientists already comply with a host of federal, state, municipal, and institutional guidelines and laws. However, in this era of cost containment, they fear that overregulation will become so costly that research progress will suffer.

310 Scientists emphasize that a reasonable balance must be achieved between increased restrictions and increased cost.

What must be recognized, say scientists, is that it is not possible to protect all animals against pain and still conduct meaningful research. No legislation and no standard of humane care can eliminate this necessity. The only alternative is either to eliminate

320 the research, as animal rights adherents urge, and forego the knowledge and the benefits of health-related research that would result, or to inflict the pain

and suffering on human beings by using them as research subjects. ❶

The desire by animal welfare **proponents** to ensure maximum comfort and minimal pain to research animals is understandable and appeals

330 to scientists, the public, and to legislators. But what also must be recognized and weighed in the balance is the price paid in terms of human pain and suffering if overly protective measures are adopted that **impede** or prevent the use of animals in biomedical research. ❶

In short, the American people should not be misled by emotional appeals and philosophic rhetoric on this issue.

340 Biomedical research using animals is essential to continued progress in clinical medicine. Animal research holds the key for solutions to AIDS, cancer, heart disease, aging, and congenital defects.[10] In discussing legislation concerning animal experimentation, the prominent physician and physiologist Dr. Walter B. Cannon stated in 1896 that "... the antivivisectionists are the second of the

350 two types Theodore Roosevelt described when he said, 'Common sense without conscience may lead to crime, but conscience without common sense may lead to folly, which is the handmaiden of crime.'"

The American Medical Association has been an outspoken proponent of biomedical research for over 100 years, and that tradition continues today. The

360 Association believes that research involving animals is absolutely essential to maintaining and improving the health of the American people. The Association is opposed to any legislation or regulation that would inappropriately limit such research, and actively supports all legislative efforts to ensure the continued use of animals in research, while providing for their humane treatment. ❷

---

10. **congenital defects:** defects present at birth.

DIFFERENTIATED INSTRUCTION

FOR STRATEGIC READERS

③ Targeted Passage [Lines 337–355]

Here the AMA warns against emotional appeals and urges common sense.

- Why does the AMA think that Roosevelt's statement is relevant to its argument? (lines 351–355)

- What did Theodore Roosevelt mean when he said that "conscience without common sense may lead to folly"? (lines 351–355)

FOR ADVANCED LEARNERS/PRE-AP

Evaluating Evidence Have students evaluate the evidence the AMA provides in its position paper. Ask them if they think the AMA's arguments lack important facts or if they leave any questions or arguments unanswered.

Comprehension

1. **Recall** What is the AMA's position on the use of animals in medical research?

2. **Recall** How important has animal research been to medical science?

3. **Clarify** How do the animal rights and animal welfare movements differ from each other?

4. **Summarize** According to the AMA, what consequences will result from banning or restricting the use of animals in medical experiments?

Text Analysis

● 5. **Summarize and Critique** Why do you think the authors chose to summarize animal rights activists' arguments and then critique them? How does this strategy help their argument?

6. **Interpret Statements** Reread lines 301–336. Does the AMA favor any changes in current practice to minimize the pain and suffering of research animals? Give reasons for your interpretation.

7. **Draw Conclusions** What values have influenced the AMA's position on animal research? Cite evidence to support your conclusion.

8. **Make Judgments** Does the AMA fairly represent the opposing viewpoints of the animal rights movement in this paper? Explain why or why not.

9. **Evaluate Support** Consider the **reasons** and **evidence** that the AMA gives to support the view that animal research is necessary for medical science. Does the AMA provide sufficient support for its claim? Explain your opinion.

● 10. **Evaluate Counterargument** Supporters of animal rights argue that it is morally wrong for humans to use animals in a way that causes them to suffer or die. Review the chart you created as you read. Does the AMA offer a satisfactory counterargument to this viewpoint? Cite evidence to support your opinion.

11. **Compare Texts** The AMA's position on animal research differs greatly from the views expressed by Jane Goodall in "I Acknowledge Mine." Compare and contrast the techniques that the AMA and Goodall use to persuade readers.

> ## Do the ENDS justify the means?
> Are humans justified in using animals in medical research? Why or why not?

COMMON CORE

RI 2 Determine a central idea of a text; provide an objective summary of the text. RI 5 Analyze how an author's ideas or claims are developed and refined. RI 8 Delineate and evaluate the argument and specific claims in a text.

Practice and Apply

For preliminary support of post-reading questions, use these copy masters:

R RESOURCE MANAGER—Copy Masters
Reading Check p. 108
Counterarguments p. 101
Question Support p. 109

Additional selection questions are provided for teachers on page 95.

ANSWERS

Comprehension

1. *The AMA holds that using animals in medical research is necessary and should not be limited by more regulations.*

2. *Animal research has been crucial in almost every medical advance in the last century.*

3. *The animal-rights movement wants to ban all research in which animals suffer (lines 243–251), while the animal-welfare movement wants to minimize the suffering of research animals (lines 326–329).*

4. *According to the AMA, humans and animals will suffer and die because new medicines won't be developed (lines 224–236), and the United States will lose the economic benefits of research that will be conducted in other nations (lines 271–293).*

Text Analysis

COMMON CORE RI 2, RI 5, RI 8

Possible answers:

5. ● **COMMON CORE FOCUS**
Summarize and Critique Summarizing and critiquing the opposing arguments allows the authors to show the merit of their own viewpoint, point by point.

6. *No: The AMA says that scientists already comply with many rules (lines 304–306) and that overly protective measures would impede or prevent animal research (lines 306–309).*

7. *AMA values are that scientific progress is crucial (lines 360–363) and human life is more important than animal life (lines 42–55).*

8. *No: the AMA represents opposing views as "emotional appeals and philosophic rhetoric" (lines 338–339). Little space is provided for animal-rights arguments; there are few quotes or facts about experiments. Yes: the AMA presents some of the animal-rights opposing arguments (lines 47–50, 127–134) and quotes the head of PETA (lines 152–154).*

---

9. *Yes: the AMA cites Nobel Prizes awarded for breakthroughs resulting from animal experiments (lines 173–199) and medical advances that improve people's health and extend their lives (lines 200–214). No: the AMA does not justify animal suffering, even for the sake of medical advances.*

10. ● **COMMON CORE FOCUS** *Counterarguments Yes: medical advances offset the suffering and death of animals. No: the AMA has not addressed the issue of whether animals have inherent rights.*

11. *Goodall uses emotional appeals and bases her argument on experience. The AMA tries to persuade through logic, using counterarguments to refute opposing views.*

> Do the **ENDS** justify the means?
> Students may agree or disagree but should support either opinion with evidence from this selection or the selection by Jane Goodall.

ANSWERS

Vocabulary in Context

▲ **VOCABULARY PRACTICE**

1. *speculative*   3. *proponent*
2. *rhetoric*   4. *impede*

 RESOURCE MANAGER—Copy Master
Vocabulary Practice p. 106

ACADEMIC VOCABULARY IN SPEAKING

Possible answer: *Statistics help to convince an audience that an argument is supported by facts. The AMA cites a statistic that "54 of the 76 Nobel Prizes awarded in physiology or medicine since 1901 have been for discoveries and advances made through the use of animal experimentation." The AMA's objective is to show that animal experimentation has led to considerable scientific progress.*

VOCABULARY STRATEGY: CONNOTATION

 COMMON CORE L 5b

- Have students cite reasons explaining their choices of where words go on the scale.
- Point out that in items 1 and 3, the context includes *study* as "a field of knowledge."

Possible answers:

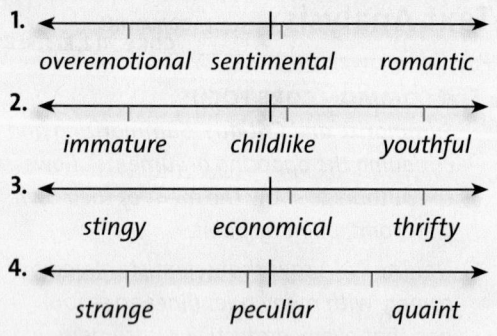

1. overemotional sentimental romantic
2. immature childlike youthful
3. stingy economical thrifty
4. strange peculiar quaint

 **RESOURCE MANAGER—Copy Master**
Vocabulary Strategy p. 107

Interactive Vocabulary THINK central

Keywords direct students to a **WordSharp** tutorial on **thinkcentral.com** or to other types of vocabulary practice and review.

Vocabulary in Context

▲ **VOCABULARY PRACTICE**

Choose the word from the list that best completes each sentence.

1. Until we get the facts from the proper sources, everything is _____.
2. Concrete actions speak louder than empty _____.
3. As a _____ of conservation, she signed a petition for the preservation of wetlands.
4. I do not want to _____ your work, so please let me know if I'm a distraction.

WORD LIST
impede
proponent
rhetoric
speculative

ACADEMIC VOCABULARY IN SPEAKING

- cite   • controversy   • convince   • objective   • statistic

How do **statistics** affect an argument? Use the AMA's article as the basis for a discussion. Analyze three statistics **cited** in the article. Why was each statistic included, and how does it affect the overall argument? Use at least one Academic Vocabulary word in your response.

VOCABULARY STRATEGY: CONNOTATION

A word's **connotation** is the overtone of meaning that it has beyond its **denotation,** or basic meaning. Some connotations may be positive or negative. For example, although the nouns *rhetoric* and *discourse* can both be used to refer to written or oral expression in language, *rhetoric* can have a negative connotation because it can suggest language that is empty or insincere. When you choose words in writing, be sure to consider whether their connotations fit the context of the sentence and of the larger piece you are writing.

PRACTICE Place the words in each group on a continuum like the one shown, to identify whether they have positive, negative, or neutral connotations. You can use a dictionary or thesaurus to help you. Then compare your answers with those of a classmate.

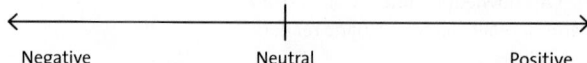

Negative   Neutral   Positive

1. sentimental, overemotional, romantic
2. childlike, youthful, immature
3. thrifty, economical, stingy
4. strange, quaint, peculiar

COMMON CORE

L 5b Analyze nuances in the meaning of words with similar denotations.

 **Interactive Vocabulary** THINK central

Go to **thinkcentral.com**.
KEYWORD: HML10-686

DIFFERENTIATED INSTRUCTION

FOR ENGLISH LANGUAGE LEARNERS

Vocabulary: Connotations Have students work in small groups to identify words to complete connotation triads (negative-neutral-positive) like those in the Vocabulary Strategy. Have them use these words from the text: "guinea pigs" (negative), "folly" (negative), and "justify" (positive). Have groups read a triad to another group, who can then try to plot the words in the correct order.

FOR ADVANCED LEARNERS/PRE–AP

Vocabulary: Applying Connotations Challenge students to form triads using the four vocabulary words for this selection. Then have them write a two- or three-paragraph essay agreeing with or arguing against the AMA's position on animals in biomedical research. Have students use at least one of the new synonyms from each triad.

Language

◆ **GRAMMAR AND STYLE: Consider Audience**

Review the **Grammar and Style** note on page 684. When deciding how to craft a particular piece of writing, it is important to consider your audience. For example, your writing style in an e-mail to a friend will probably differ from the style you use in a research paper. For most school and business communication, you should use **formal language.** Typically, this style of language does not contain contractions and consists of standard punctuation and more complex vocabulary and sentence structure. Here is an example of how the American Medical Association uses formal language in its position paper.

> *Animal rights activists contest experiments that utilize animals on both these grounds and assert that this practice no longer is necessary because alternative methods of experimentation exist for obtaining the same information.* (lines 143–148)

Notice how the revisions in blue create a more formal writing style. Use similar methods to revise your responses to the prompt.

◠ **COMMON CORE**

RI 2 Provide an objective summary of a text. **W 2e** Establish and maintain a formal style. **L 3** Make effective choices for meaning or style.

STUDENT MODEL

Medical research on animals is part of a tradition that goes back
hundreds of years. Many
~~a long ways. Lots of~~ scientific advances have come from it. ~~This~~ *which* shows the

importance of this research.

READING-WRITING CONNECTION

 Explore the ideas presented in "Use of Animals in Biomedical Research" by responding to this prompt. Then use the **revising tip** to improve your writing.

YOUR TURN

WRITING PROMPT	REVISING TIP
Extended Constructed Response: Summarize In two to three paragraphs, write a **summary** of the American Medical Association's arguments for using animals in biomedical research. Remember, this is a summary, so only include information from the article. Do not include a critique—your criticisms of or perspective on the arguments.	Review your response. Did you use formal language like that the American Medical Association uses in its paper? If not, revise for a more formal style.

Interactive Revision THINK central

Go to thinkcentral.com.
KEYWORD: HML10-687

FOR STRUGGLING WRITERS

- Remind students that a summary restates the argument's main points.

- Point out that a summary should only include information that appears in the original text.

- Remind students to cite details and direct quotes from the AMA's position paper.

- Review the elements of formal language.

- Encourage students to avoid short, choppy sentences.

Language

 **COMMON CORE RI 2, W 2e, L 3**

◆ **GRAMMAR AND STYLE**

- Write these sentences on the board and ask students to supply formal alternatives:

  I ~~didn't buy~~ did not accept your claims. You ~~hit it on the head~~ are entirely correct. The ~~paper's a bit thin~~ paper is somewhat short on facts.

- Remind students to use a thesaurus when they are writing for an audience that will respond best to formal language.

R RESOURCE MANAGER—Copy Master
Consider Audience p. 110

READING-WRITING CONNECTION

- Remind students to identify what they believe are the two or three most important arguments presented by the American Medical Association.

- Encourage students to create outlines to plan the topic sentence and supporting details of each paragraph.

- Ask them to cite details and direct quotes from the AMA's position paper.

Writing Online  THINK central

The following tools are available online at **thinkcentral.com** and on **WriteSmart CD-ROM:**
- **Interactive Graphic Organizers**
- **Interactive Student Models**
- **Interactive Revision Lessons**
For additional grammar instruction, see **GrammarNotes** on **thinkcentral.com**.

Assess and Reteach

Assess

DIAGNOSTIC AND SELECTION TESTS
Selection Test A pp. 195–196
Selection Test B/C pp. 197–198

Interactive Selection Test on **thinkcentral.com**

Reteach

Level Up Online Tutorials on **thinkcentral.com**

Reteaching Worksheets on **thinkcentral.com**
Informational Text Lesson 14: Elements of an Argument

Focus and Motivate

COMMON CORE FOCUS

RL 1 Cite textual evidence to support analysis of what the text says explicitly. **RL 2** Determine a theme or central idea of a text. **RL 4** Determine the meaning of words and phrases as they are used in a text.

SUMMARY

"The Blue Stones" is a story about the cost of greed and jealousy. A sea captain's wife, jealous of his ship and the figurehead mounted on it, removes the gemstones that served as the figurehead's eyes. As a result of the wife's actions, both she and the ship become blind, and the ship and her husband are lost.

What problems are caused by **JEALOUSY** and **GREED?**

Ask students whether there is a relationship between jealousy and greed. Introduce the question, and lead into the *QUICKWRITE* activity.

The Blue Stones

Allegory by Isak Dinesen

What problems are caused by **JEALOUSY** and **GREED?**

COMMON CORE

RL 1 Cite textual evidence to support analysis of what the text says explicitly. **RL 2** Determine a theme or central idea of a text. **RL 4** Determine the meaning of words and phrases as they are used in a text.

Jealousy and a desire for wealth are part of the human experience. But what happens when these feelings go too far? The selection you are about to read is about a woman whose jealousy and greed lead her to make an unwise decision.

QUICKWRITE Have you ever experienced or witnessed a time when jealousy or greed caused conflict? How did the conflict arise? What resulted from the conflict? Write two or three paragraphs describing the conflict and its outcome.

688

Selection Resources

See resources on the **Teacher One Stop DVD-ROM** and on **thinkcentral.com**.

R RESOURCE MANAGER UNIT 6
Plan and Teach, pp. 113–120
Text Analysis and Reading Skill, pp. 121–124†*

DIAGNOSTIC AND SELECTION TESTS
Selection Tests, pp. 199–202

TECHNOLOGY
- Teacher One Stop DVD-ROM
- Student One Stop DVD-ROM
- GrammarNotes DVD-ROM
- ExamView Test Generator on the **Teacher One Stop**

* Resources for Differentiation   † Also in Spanish   ‡ In Haitian Creole and Vietnamese

TEXT ANALYSIS: ALLEGORY

An **allegory** is a story that functions on two levels: a literal level and a symbolic level. The literal story may tell a tale that seems ordinary, of people and events. However, on the symbolic level, the allegory is likely to teach a moral lesson, relying on characters and events to represent abstract ideas or concepts, such as freedom, evil, or goodness.

To be effective, the allegory must succeed on both levels. It must tell an interesting story, and it must convey an important symbolic theme or lesson.

As you read "The Blue Stones," think about the literal and symbolic levels of this allegory. Consider what the characters, objects, and events might stand for besides their literal meaning. Then think about how specific symbols work together to form the allegory's moral lesson.

READING SKILL: PARAPHRASE

When you **paraphrase**, you restate ideas from a text in your own words. Paraphrasing helps you better understand difficult or complex texts. A paraphrase should be shorter than or about the same length as the original source, and should contain all of the source's significant information.

As you read "The Blue Stones," paraphrase the allegory to help you understand the symbolic meaning of characters and events. Use a chart like the one below.

What the story describes	My paraphrase
There was once a skipper who named his ship after his wife. He had the figurehead of it beautifully carved, just like her, and the hair of it gilt.	There once was a sea captain who named his ship after his wife and had a figurehead on it carved and painted to look just like her.

 Complete the activities in your **Reader/Writer Notebook**.

Meet the Author

Isak Dinesen
1885–1962

Out of Africa
The story you are about to read is an allegory by Isak Dinesen that tells a traditional-sounding tale. However, Dinesen is best known for *Out of Africa*, an autobiographical account of her years in British East Africa, now Kenya.

Born Karen Blixen in Denmark, Dinesen's spirit of adventure was often at odds with her sheltered upbringing. After her father died and the cousin she loved refused to marry her, she defiantly set sail for Africa to marry the cousin's twin brother, Bror Blixen-Finecke. In 1914, the couple established a coffee plantation in what is now Kenya. Blixen-Finecke was a wayward, faithless husband who often left Dinesen on her own. After the couple divorced in 1921, Dinesen ran the six-thousand-acre farm by herself for ten years.

Although Dinesen is often regarded as the European author who best captured the beauty of the African landscape, she wrote equally accomplished works about northern Europe and the Danish upper class. Many of her stories celebrate the power of women. After she returned to Denmark in 1931, she published *Seven Gothic Tales*, stories set in Europe hundreds of years ago and featuring mysterious events and persecuted heroines. She published *Out of Africa* in 1937.

Author Online
THINK central
Go to **thinkcentral.com**.
KEYWORD: HML10-689

689

Teach

● *Model the Skill:* **ALLEGORY**

To illustrate the function of allegory, as well as model how to interpret one, read students this story:

> A dog lay down to sleep in the cows' feeding trough. When the cows wanted to eat their straw, the dog would not let them.

Explain to students that there are two stories in these lines. The literal story tells of a dog that slept in the straw and kept the cows from eating their food. Point out that, although the dog could not eat the straw, he did not want anyone else to have it. On the allegorical level, the dog symbolizes a person who doesn't want others (the cows in the story) to have something even though the person has no use for it himself.

GUIDED PRACTICE Ask students to suggest moral lessons that might be drawn from the story about the dog. Then ask them to list other allegories. They may have ideas from movies, books, or even fables.

READING SKILL   COMMON CORE
RL 1

■ *Model the Skill:* **PARAPHRASE**

To model how to paraphrase, read aloud the first paragraph of **Meet the Author.** Draw a Paraphrase chart on the board and fill in the first column with help from student volunteers. Record that the story is an allegory, the author is Isak Dinesen, Dinesen lived in British East Africa, and she is best known for *Out of Africa*, an autobiographical work. Then lead students to write paraphrases, or restatements, of this information.

GUIDED PRACTICE Have students paraphrase the other two paragraphs about Isak Dinesen.

R RESOURCE MANAGER—Copy Master
Paraphrase p. 123 (for student use while reading this selection)

DIFFERENTIATED INSTRUCTION

FOR ADVANCED LEARNERS/PRE–AP

Write an Allegory Remind students that the fables, proverbs and maxims they have learned since childhood are the seeds from which allegories grow. Ask students to suggest fables and then look for the maxims within. For instance, "The Tortoise and the Hare" could be summed up with "It doesn't matter how you start the race; the important thing is how you finish it." After discussing a number of these, have each student choose a proverb or maxim and create a one- or two- paragraph allegory to express it on both the literal and the symbolic levels.

Connect with the Author Ask students to research the life and writings of Isak Dinesen/ Karen Blixen-Finecke. Have them read other examples of her writing. What life experiences do they believe impacted the subject of her writing? What connections are there between her life and her stories that "celebrate the power of women?"

READ WITH A PURPOSE

Help students set a purpose for reading. Ask them to read "The Blue Stones" to find out why the skipper would not give the blue stones to his wife.

TEXT ANALYSIS — COMMON CORE RL 2

Ⓐ Model the Skill: SYMBOLISM

To model how to understand symbolism, read lines 1–9 aloud. Point out that the skipper and his wife view the figurehead differently. Have students identify what the wife says about the figurehead (line 3) and what the skipper says (lines 4–9).

Possible answer: The figurehead symbolizes the man's wife or his love for his wife. Clues include the description of her as "you yourself" (spoken by the skipper in line 5), and the descriptions of her as very similar to the wife.

READING SKILL — COMMON CORE RL 1

Ⓑ Model the Skill: PARAPHRASE

Remind students that paraphrasing means restating text in their own words. Lead students in adding information from this part of the story to their Paraphrase charts.

Possible answer: A skipper has carved a figurehead to look like his wife. After he helped a king, he received two precious blue stones that he had placed in the figurehead like eyes. The wife wanted the stones for earrings, but he refused.

REVISIT THE BIG QUESTION

What problems are caused by JEALOUSY and GREED?

Discuss In lines 12–16, why does the wife want the blue stones? Ask students to decide whether she is driven by jealousy or greed and to explain their answers. *Possible answers: Since the wife was already jealous of the figurehead, she probably wants them because her husband gave them to the figurehead. She was driven by a mixture of jealousy and greed, but jealousy was likely the strongest.*

The Blue Stones

ISAK DINESEN

There was once a skipper who named his ship after his wife. He had the figurehead of it beautifully carved, just like her, and the hair of it gilt. But his wife was jealous of the ship. "You think more of the figurehead than of me," she said to him. "No," he answered, "I think so highly of her because she is like you, yes, because she is you yourself. Is she not gallant, full-bosomed; does she not dance in the waves, like you at our wedding? In a way she is really even kinder to me than you are. She gallops along where I tell her to go, and she lets her long hair hang down freely, while you put yours up under a cap. But she turns her back to me, so that when I want a kiss I come home to Elsinore." Ⓐ

10 Now once, when this skipper was trading at Trankebar, he chanced to help an old native king flee traitors in his own country. As they parted, the king gave him two big blue, precious stones, and these he had set into the face of his figurehead, like a pair of eyes to it. When he came home he told his wife of his adventure, and said: "Now she has your blue eyes too." "You had better give me the stones for a pair of earrings," said she. "No," he said again. "I cannot do that, and you would not ask me if you understood." Ⓑ

Analyze Visuals ▶

How does the photograph of this figurehead help evoke the **mood** of this allegory?

❶ Targeted Passage

Ⓐ SYMBOLISM
What do you think the figurehead symbolizes? What clues in the story help you understand its symbolic meaning?

Ⓑ PARAPHRASE
Paraphrase what has happened in this allegory so far.

DIFFERENTIATED INSTRUCTION

FOR ENGLISH LANGUAGE LEARNERS

Compound Words Explain that the word *figurehead* is a compound word composed of *figure* and *head*. The word has two meanings: "a figure on the prow of a ship" and "a person with nominal leadership but no actual authority." Have students work in groups to suggest meanings for the following compound words: *centerpiece, switchboard, swordfish,* and *sweatshop*. After the groups have determined meanings based on the individual words, have them look up each compound word in a dictionary to see how the combined meaning differs from that of the individual words.

FOR STRUGGLING READERS

Use one or more Targeted Passages (pp. 690, 692) to ensure that students focus on key story events, concepts, and skills. Targeted Passages are also good for English learners.

❶ Targeted Passage [Lines 1–9]

This passage introduces the characters and the conflict.

• Who are the main characters? (lines 1–3)

Possible answer: *The figurehead is a mysterious figure that seems to belong to another time and place. The photograph helps create the mood of "Blue Stones," which is a folktale.*

About the Art Carved around 1860, this figurehead once graced the prow of the English boat *Kathelina*. A diadem, which is a crown or headband, adorns the woman's head, and she clutches a rose in her hand.

- Why is the wife jealous of the figurehead? (line 3)
- How does the skipper feel about the figurehead? (lines 4–7)
- How does the skipper feel about his wife? (lines 5–6, 9)

FOR STRUGGLING READERS

Develop Reading Fluency Point out that this selection is written in the style of a fable or a fairy tale, with phrases such as "There was once a skipper" (line 1) and "he chanced to help" (line 10). Students may find the language stilted and difficult to read. Read aloud the first four lines, demonstrating the shift in voice between narrator, wife, and skipper. Then have student groups practice reading the selection aloud. Ask groups to identify the lines or sentences they consider most difficult to read. Have a representative of each group read the difficult lines aloud to the class and explain what aspects make the passage particularly challenging.

Language Coach

Prefixes The **prefix** *in-* or *im-* often means "not." When this prefix appears at the beginning of a word, it often negates the meaning of the rest of the word, such as *inactive*, meaning "not active," or *inaudible*, meaning "not audible." Reread line 24. What do you think is the meaning of *incurable*?

Still the wife could not stop fretting about the blue stones, and one day, when her husband was with the skippers' corporation, she had a glazier of the town take them out, and put two bits of blue glass into the figurehead instead,
20 and the skipper did not find out, but sailed off to Portugal. But after some time the skipper's wife found that her eyesight was growing bad, and she could not see to thread a needle. She went to a wise-woman, who gave her ointments and waters, but they did not help her and in the end the old woman shook her head, and told her that this was a rare and incurable disease, and that she was going blind. "Oh, God," the wife then cried, "that the ship was back in the harbor of Elsinore. Then I should have the glass taken out, and the jewels put back. For did he not say that they were my eyes?" But the ship did not come back. Instead the skipper's wife had a letter from the Consul of Portugal, who informed her that she had been wrecked, and gone to the bottom with
30 all hands. And it was a very strange thing, the Consul wrote, that in broad daylight she had run straight into a tall rock, rising out of the sea.

© ALLEGORY
What is the literal meaning of the blue stones in this story? What is their symbolic meaning?

② Targeted Passage

© ALLEGORY

Possible answer: The literal meaning of the blue stones is expensive stones are valued by the man and his wife for different purposes. The stones symbolize sight or understanding.

SELECTION WRAP–UP

READ WITH A PURPOSE Now that students have finished reading the selection, ask them: What is the message of the story? *Possible answer: The story says that the effects of jealousy can be destructive and permanent.*

INDEPENDENT READING

If students are interested in reading more short fiction by Isak Dinesen, they might enjoy the other short stories in *Winter's Tales*.

DIFFERENTIATED INSTRUCTION

FOR STRUGGLING READERS

② Targeted Passage [lines 22–31]

This passage contains the climax and resolution of the story.

- What has happened to the wife's eyes? (lines 24–25)

- What did the skipper say about the blue stones? (line 27)

- What happened to the ship? (lines 29–31)

- What has happened to the figurehead's eyes? (line 31)

FOR ENGLISH LANGUAGE LEARNERS

Language Coach · COMMON CORE RL 4

Prefixes *Answer:*

not curable Ask students to think of another word in which the prefix *in-* means "not" and use this word in a sentence.

Possible answers: inaccurate, incorrect, ineffective, insoluble; Although the gift was inexpensive, he had insufficient funds to make the purchase.

Comprehension

1. **Recall** Whom does the ship's figurehead resemble?

2. **Recall** What does the wife want the skipper do to with the blue stones?

3. **Clarify** When does the wife's eyesight begin to fail?

COMMON CORE

RL 1 Cite textual evidence to support analysis of what the text says explicitly. **RL 2** Determine a theme or central idea of a text.

Text Analysis

● 4. **Analyze Symbolism and Allegory** What are the literal and symbolic meanings of each character or object from the allegory? Use a chart like this one to record your answers.

Character or Object	Literal meaning	Symbolic Meaning
the ship's figurehead		
the blue stones		
the skipper		
the wife		

● 5. **Explain the Function of Allegory** The function of allegories is often to teach a lesson or illustrate an important theme to the reader. How does this allegory function thematically?

● 6. **Analyze Characterization** Are the characters in this allegory **round,** fully-developed **characters,** or are they **flat characters,** who have one outstanding trait or role? Why do you think the author chose this form of characterization?

● 7. **Paraphrase** Paraphrase the events in this allegory. You can use your answer to question B on page 690 to help you get started.

8. **Make Judgments** Does this allegory effectively teach its lesson or convey its theme? Explain.

> **What problems are caused by JEALOUSY and GREED?**
>
> How can we avoid these problems? Explain.

Practice and Apply

ANSWERS

Comprehension

1. *The figurehead resembles the skipper's wife.*

2. *The wife wants the skipper to give the stones to her for earrings.*

3. *The wife's eyesight begins to fail when she removes the stones from the figurehead.*

Text Analysis

COMMON CORE RL 1, RL 2

Possible answers:

4. ● **COMMON CORE FOCUS** *Allegory* The literal meaning of the ship's figurehead is a ship figurehead, and the symbolic meaning is the skipper's wife or his love for her. The literal meaning of the blues stones is precious stones, and the symbolic meaning is vision or understanding. The literal meaning of the skipper is a ship skipper, and the symbolic meaning is trust or loyalty. The literal meaning of the wife is a wife consumed by jealousy and greed, and the symbolic meaning is jealousy and greed.

5. *The allegory functions thematically by showing that people should trust their loved ones and not become overwhelmed by jealousy or greed.*

6. *The characters are flat, which helps them function as symbols in an allegory rather than as real people.*

Assess and Reteach

Assess

DIAGNOSTIC AND SELECTION TESTS

Selection Test A pp. 199–200

Selection Test B/C pp. 201–202

Interactive Selection Test on **thinkcentral.com**

Reteach

Level Up Online Tutorials on **thinkcentral.com**

Reteaching Worksheets on **thinkcentral.com**

Language and Literary Devices Lesson 32: Allegory

Study Skill Lesson 12: Paraphrasing

---

7. ● **COMMON CORE FOCUS** *Paraphrase*
Answers will vary. Students should paraphrase the allegory—retell it in their own words, including all of the events in the allegory.

8. *Answers will vary. Students should support their answers with reasons.*

> **What problems are caused by JEALOUSY and GREED?**
> *Students may suggest that jealousy and greed can be avoided by trusting those you love and by being content with what you have.*

COMMON CORE FOCUS

RL 1 Cite textual evidence to support analysis of what the text says explicitly as well as inferences from the text. **RL 2** Determine a theme of a text and analyze in detail its development, including how it is refined by specific details. **RL 4** Determine the meaning of words and phrases as they are used in a text. **RL 6** Analyze a particular point of view reflected in a work of world literature. **L 1b** Use various types of clauses to convey specific meanings and add variety and interest to writing. **L 4c** Consult specialized reference materials to determine or clarify a word's precise meaning or etymology.

SUMMARIES

"A Chip of Glass Ruby" Mrs. Bamjee, an Indian who lives in South Africa, is imprisoned for her politics, and her husband realizes that her compassionate nature is what attracted him to her.

"from The Question of South Africa" Desmond Tutu argues that until apartheid is removed, South Africa will remain a land of division and unrest.

"Stop Apartheid Now!" This poster portrays the message of standing up against oppression.

What would you
SACRIFICE for justice?

Ask the question. Then discuss the meaning of sacrifice.

What's the Connection?

Discuss standing up for what is right. What are the consequences of being involved?

A Chip of Glass Ruby
Short Story by Nadine Gordimer

The Question of South Africa
Speech by Desmond Tutu

Stop Apartheid Now!
Poster by Trocaire

What would you SACRIFICE for justice?

COMMON CORE

RL 1 Cite textual evidence to support analysis of what the text says explicitly as well as inferences drawn from the text. **RL 2** Determine a theme of a text and analyze in detail its development, including how it is refined by specific details. **RL 6** Analyze a particular point of view reflected in a work of world literature.

During times of injustice, change often comes from ordinary people who are willing to sacrifice their comfort or security to stand up for an ideal. "A Chip of Glass Ruby" portrays one such person, a housewife who struggles against South Africa's system of racial segregation.

What's the Connection?

In the following literary selection, you will consider the theme of sacrifice and how it affects not only the individual but also families. After you read "A Chip of Glass Ruby" you'll read an expository selection and a visual that explore similar themes.

694

---

*See resources on the **Teacher One Stop DVD-ROM** and on **thinkcentral.com**.*

R RESOURCE MANAGER UNIT 6
Plan and Teach, pp. 149–154
Summary, pp. 155–156
Text Analysis and
    Reading Skill, pp. 157–160
DIAGNOSTIC AND SELECTION TESTS
Selection Tests, pp. 203–206

BEST PRACTICES TOOLKIT
Think-Pair-Share, p. A18
Three-Column Journal,
    p. B10
Cluster Diagram, p. B18

TECHNOLOGY
- Teacher One Stop DVD-ROM
- Student One Stop DVD-ROM
- Audio Anthology CD
- GrammarNotes DVD-ROM
- ExamView Generator on the Teacher One Stop

* Resources for Differentiation

TEXT ANALYSIS: THEME AND PERSUASION

Just as essayists and speech writers can **persuade** readers to take action or adopt a certain position, fiction writers can persuade readers to feel differently about important issues. By creating stories in which characters must grapple with injustice, for example, a fiction writer can develop important **themes** about society and its values.

As you read "A Chip of Glass Ruby," notice how Nadine Gordimer makes use of narrative techniques to tell a story that is both interesting and persuasive.

READING SKILL: DRAW CONCLUSIONS

When you **draw conclusions** about elements in a story, you use information from the story and your own prior knowledge to make judgments. For example, if a character often exaggerates his own problems and does not show sympathy for other characters, you would probably conclude that the character is self-centered.

As you read "A Chip of Glass Ruby," note the behavior of the main characters and their attitudes toward events. Use a chart like the one shown to organize your observations.

Event	Behavior/Attitude	
	Bamjee	Mrs. Bamjee
Arrival of duplicating machine		

▲ VOCABULARY IN CONTEXT

Gordimer uses the following boldfaced words to help illuminate the faults of racial segregation in South Africa. Use context clues to determine the meaning of these words. Write your answers in your *Reader/Writer Notebook*.

1. I was **disarmed** by his friendly smile.
2. She looked **morose** after hearing the bad news.
3. Don't **patronize** people just because they lack experience.
4. The stranger's **presumption** caused great offense.
5. His fine **repute** was ruined by scandal.

 Complete the activities in your **Reader/Writer Notebook**.

Meet the Author

Nadine Gordimer
born 1923

A Voice Against Racism
One of South Africa's leading authors, Nadine Gordimer often explores the destructive influence of racism on people's daily lives. Gordimer's highly acclaimed novels and short stories deliver a powerful political message; several of her books were banned in her homeland for many years. Although Gordimer has stated that she does not consider herself to be a political writer, she recognizes that her work has been strongly affected by the extreme politics she experienced in South Africa when it was racially segregated. Gordimer won the Nobel Prize in literature in 1991.

BACKGROUND TO THE STORY

Life Under Apartheid
"A Chip of Glass Ruby" is set in South Africa during the period of apartheid, a system of racial segregation and discrimination that was formally established in the 1950s. Every citizen was classified as either white, colored (mixed race), Asian (of East Indian ancestry), or Bantu (native black). Strictly enforced laws set limits on the lives of the nonwhite majority. The Group Areas Act forced nonwhites to live in certain areas, and "pass laws" required black South Africans to carry passes identifying where they could and could not go. Although Asians did not have to carry passes, their movements were restricted. For decades, activists struggled to overturn apartheid. Many blacks died during strikes and protests; others were imprisoned. Apartheid was officially abolished in 1991.

Author Online

THINK central

Go to thinkcentral.com.
KEYWORD: HML10-695

695

Teach

TEXT ANALYSIS

COMMON CORE
RL 2
RL 6

● *Model the Skill:* **THEME AND PERSUASION**

Point out that persuasive messages come in all different forms—not just essays, editorials, position papers, and speeches. Explain that a speech would probably present evidence and reasons to support its argument and might use rhetorical devices such as parallelism. A story might portray characters working for a peace organization.

GUIDED PRACTICE Have students suggest stories, poems, movies, or songs with a persuasive message.

READING SKILL

COMMON CORE
RL 1

■ *Model the Skill:* **DRAW CONCLUSIONS**

To model how to draw conclusions, describe a character who works two jobs to pay her way through college and who also volunteers at a homeless shelter. Discuss conclusions that could be drawn about the character based on this information. For example, this character is hardworking, serious about her education, and generous toward the less fortunate.

GUIDED PRACTICE Have students explain a conclusion they have drawn about a character from a story, novel, or movie.

R **RESOURCE MANAGER**—Copy Master
Draw Conclusions p. 139

VOCABULARY SKILL

▲ VOCABULARY IN CONTEXT

DIAGNOSE WORD KNOWLEDGE Have all students complete Vocabulary in Context. Check their words and phrases against the following:

disarm (dĭs-ärm') *v.* to win over; to make less hostile
morose (mə-rōs') *adj.* gloomy; sullen
patronize (pā'trə-nīz') *v.* to behave in a manner that shows feelings of superiority
presumption (prĭ-zŭmp'shən) *n.* behavior or language that is boldly arrogant or offensive

repute (rĭ-pyoot') *n.* reputation; fame

PRETEACH VOCABULARY Use the following copy master to help students predict the meaning of each boldfaced word.

R **RESOURCE MANAGER**—Copy Master
Vocabulary Study p. 141

1. Read the first sentence in Part A aloud, emphasizing *disarmed*.
2. Point out "calm" and "eased his mind."

Elicit possible meanings for *disarmed*, such as "won over."

COMMON CORE
L 4

3. Repeat the procedure for items 2–5.

READ WITH A PURPOSE

Help students set a purpose for reading. Tell them to look for what motivates Mrs. Bamjee's behavior.

A Model the Skill: DRAW CONCLUSIONS

To help students answer this question, have them add this event to their Reading Skill charts.

Possible answer: Bamjee and Mrs. Bamjee have sharply different attitudes toward black South Africans. Bamjee feels that the blacks' problems are theirs alone and that Indians shouldn't become involved. Mrs. Bamjee, by contrast, thinks that injustice should concern everyone and that she has a responsibility to be involved.

IF STUDENTS NEED HELP . . .

- Call students' attention to Bamjee's statement in lines 5–7: "We don't have to carry passes; let the natives protest against passes on their own . . . Let them go ahead with it." Discuss how he distinguishes himself from the black South Africans and why, therefore, he doesn't want to protest on their behalf.

- Direct students' attention to line 4. Discuss what Mrs. Bamjee means when she says, "We've all got the same troubles" and why her comment sparks such a negative reaction from her husband.

A Chip
of
Glass Ruby

Nadine Gordimer

When the duplicating machine was brought into the house, Bamjee said, "Isn't it enough that you've got the Indians' troubles on your back?" Mrs. Bamjee said, with a smile that showed the gap of a missing tooth but was confident all the same, "What's the difference, Yusuf? We've all got the same troubles."

"Don't tell me that. We don't have to carry passes; let the natives protest against passes on their own; there are millions of them. Let them go ahead with it." A

The nine Bamjee and Pahad children were present at this exchange as they were always; in the small house that held them all there was no room for
10 privacy for the discussion of matters they were too young to hear, and so they had never been too young to hear anything. Only their sister and half-sister, Girlie, was missing; she was the eldest, and married. The children looked expectantly, unalarmed and interested, at Bamjee, who had neither left the room nor settled down again to the task of rolling his own cigarettes, which had been interrupted by the arrival of the duplicator. He had looked at the thing that had come hidden in a washbasket and conveyed in a black man's taxi, and the children turned on it too, their black eyes surrounded by thick lashes like those still, open flowers with hairy tentacles that close on whatever touches them.

 Targeted Passage

A DRAW CONCLUSIONS
How do Bamjee and Mrs. Bamjee differ in their attitudes toward native black people?

Untitled, Chandragupta Thenuwara. Oil on canvas.

DIFFERENTIATED INSTRUCTION

FOR ENGLISH LANGUAGE LEARNERS

Options for Reading Assign individual students to read dialogue for specific characters. Have the remaining students take turns reading the part of the narrator.

FOR STRUGGLING READERS

In combination with the *Audio Anthology CD,* use one or more Targeted Passages (pp. 696, 698, 700, 706) to ensure that students focus on key story events, concepts, and skills. Targeted Passages are also good for English learners.

1 Targeted Passage [Lines 1–12]

This passage introduces Bamjee and Mrs. Bamjee and their family and establishes their attitudes about the black population of South Africa.

Analyze Visuals

Activity Ask students what aspects of the story they see reflected in the painting. Have students turn back to the painting after they have finished reading the story to analyze it again. *Possible answer: The woman in the painting is dressed in traditional Indian clothing, as Mrs. Bamjee dresses.*

About the Art Arun Mishra (b. 1963) is a well known Indian artist who frequently paints images of women. Mishra feels especially drawn to the raw beauty of working female laborers. These women convey an aura of sensibility, confidence, and innocence to him.

BACKGROUND

The Anti-Apartheid Movement "A Chip of Glass Ruby" is set during the early days of the anti-apartheid (a-PAR-tied) movement. Beginning in 1952, the African National Congress (ANC), in cooperation with the South African Indian Congress, began to organize nonviolent boycotts, strikes, and marches to protest the government's apartheid policies, particularly its pass laws. In 1960 a protest campaign was organized in which thousands of blacks invited arrest by presenting themselves at police stations without their passes, as in Gordimer's story. On March 21, 1960, the police opened fire on a crowd of such protesters in Sharpeville, near Johannesburg. They killed 69 people in what became known as the Sharpeville Massacre.

- What triggers the disagreement between Bamjee and Mrs. Bamjee? (line 1)
- How are blacks being treated differently from Indians? (line 5)
- Are the Indians being well treated? How do you know? (lines 1–2)
- Who are the other members of this family? How much do they know about the disagreement that opens the story? (lines 8–12)

FOR ADVANCED LEARNERS/PRE–AP

Make Comparisons Ask students to identify the various descriptions of Mrs. Bamjee and note who is describing her. With this information, have students compare the way that Mrs. Bamjee is seen by Mr. Bamjee, the children, Dr. Khan, the policemen, and the neighbors. Which people describe her appearance? Which ones see her personality? Have students write descriptions of Mrs. Bamjee that bring together all these elements.

Connect Do you know anyone who is wrapped up in a political or charitable cause? If so, describe this person. *Answers will vary.*

Analyze How would you characterize Mrs. Bamjee based on what you learn about her in this passage? *Possible answer: Mrs. Bamjee is a high-energy, down-to-earth, nurturing woman who leads a busy life. She takes care of a house full of children yet stays up late to copy leaflets (line 41). She seems more concerned about her political activities than her appearance, as the unflattering physical description of her in lines 35–37 suggests.*

Synthesize In what ways is Mrs. Bamjee a traditional person? In what ways is she untraditional? *Possible answer: Mrs. Bamjee is traditional in her clothing and in the way she takes care of her children. She is untraditional in her political involvement and in her decision to stop wearing the chip of glass ruby that her mother gave her (lines 38–40).*

READING SKILL   COMMON CORE
                                             RL 1

B DRAW CONCLUSIONS

Possible answer: Bamjee's reaction suggests that he either does not care about the plight of the Africans or that he does not want to get involved on their behalf.

VOCABULARY   COMMON CORE
                                             L 4

OWN THE WORD

repute: Have students create a semantic map for *repute*. Write the word and its definition in the center circle. Draw spider legs from the center circle, and have students use a thesaurus to add synonyms to complete the web.

---

20 "A fine thing to have on the table where we eat," was all he said at last. They smelled the machine among them; a smell of cold black grease. He went out, heavily on tiptoe, in his troubled way.

"It's going to go nicely on the sideboard!" Mrs. Bamjee was busy making a place by removing the two pink glass vases filled with plastic carnations and the hand-painted velvet runner with the picture of the Taj Mahal.[1]

After supper she began to run off leaflets on the machine. The family lived in that room—the three other rooms in the house were full of beds—and they were all there. The older children shared a bottle of ink while they did their homework, and the two little ones pushed a couple of empty milk bottles in 30 and out the chair legs. The three-year-old fell asleep and was carted away by one of the girls. They all drifted off to bed eventually; Bamjee himself went before the older children—he was a fruit-and-vegetable hawker[2] and was up at half past four every morning to get to the market by five. "Not long now," said Mrs. Bamjee. The older children looked up and smiled at him. He turned his back on her. She still wore the traditional clothing of a Moslem woman, and her body, which was scraggy and unimportant as a dress on a peg when it was not host to a child, was wrapped in the trailing rags of a cheap sari,[3] and her thin black plait was greased. When she was a girl, in the Transvaal[4] town where they lived still, her mother fixed a chip of glass ruby in her nostril; but she had 40 abandoned that adornment as too old-style, even for her, long ago.

She was up until long after midnight, turning out leaflets. She did it as if she might have been pounding chilies.

Bamjee did not have to ask what the leaflets were. He had read the papers. All the past week Africans had been destroying their passes and then presenting themselves for arrest. Their leaders were jailed on charges of incitement,[5] campaign offices were raided—someone must be helping the few minor leaders who were left to keep the campaign going without offices or equipment. What was it the leaflets would say—"Don't go to work tomorrow," "Day of Protest," "Burn Your Pass for Freedom"? He didn't want to see. **B**

50 He was used to coming home and finding his wife sitting at the table deep in discussion with strangers or people whose names were familiar by **repute.** Some were prominent Indians, like the lawyer, Dr. Abdul Mohammed Khan, or the big businessman, Mr. Moonsamy Patel, and he was flattered, in a suspicious way, to meet them in his house. As he came home from work next day, he met Dr. Khan coming out of the house, and Dr. Khan—a highly educated man—said to him, "A wonderful woman." But Bamjee had never

② Targeted Passage

COMMON CORE RL 4

Language Coach

Multiple-Meaning Words Some words, such as *fixed* and *chip* (line 39), have multiple meanings. In this sentence *fixed* means "attached" and *chip* means "a small piece." Write a sentence for each word using one of its other meanings. Use a dictionary if necessary.

B DRAW CONCLUSIONS
What does Bamjee's reaction to the leaflets suggest about him?

repute (rĭ-pyōōt') *n.* reputation; fame

---

1. **Taj Majal** (täzh mä-häl'): a beautiful white marble building in India.

2. **hawker:** a peddler who sells goods by calling out.

3. **sari** (sä'rē): a garment worn by East Indian women and girls, consisting of a long cloth wrapped around the body, with one end draped over the shoulder.

4. **Transvaal** (trăns-väl'): a province in northeast South Africa.

5. **charges of incitement:** accusations that the defendants have tried to persuade others to commit illegal actions.

DIFFERENTIATED INSTRUCTION

FOR STRUGGLING READERS

② Targeted Passage [Lines 33–49]

This passage clarifies Mrs. Bamjee's political activity—and the risk that she takes in doing it.

- How does Mrs. Bamjee's clothing reflect her values? How does the chip of glass ruby emphasize the duality of her personality? (lines 35–40)

- How has the South African government been dealing with protesters? (lines 45–46)

- How does Bamjee feel about what his wife is doing? (lines 34–35, 49)

FOR ENGLISH LANGUAGE LEARNERS

Language Coach   COMMON CORE
                                             RL 4

Multiple-meaning words *Possible answers:* I fixed *the flat tire on my sister's bike. My favorite cookies are chocolate* chip. Ask students to find two more multiple-meaning words on this page (*runner, run off*).

caught his wife out in any **presumption;** she behaved properly, as any Moslem woman should, and once her business with such gentlemen was over would never, for instance, have sat down to eat with them. He found her now back
60 in the kitchen, setting about the preparation of dinner and carrying on a conversation on several different wavelengths with the children. "It's really a shame if you're tired of lentils, Jimmy, because that's what you're getting— Amina, hurry up, get a pot of water going—don't worry, I'll mend that in a minute; just bring the yellow cotton, and there's a needle in the cigarette box on the sideboard."

"Was that Dr. Khan leaving?" said Bamjee.

"Yes, there's going to be a stay-at-home on Monday. Desai's ill, and he's got to get the word around by himself. Bob Jali was up all last night printing leaflets, but he's gone to have a tooth out." She had always treated Bamjee as
70 if it were only a mannerism that made him appear uninterested in politics, the way some woman will persist in interpreting her husband's bad temper as an endearing gruffness hiding boundless goodwill, and she talked to him of these things just as she passed on to him neighbors' or family gossip. **G**

"What for do you want to get mixed up with these killings and stonings and I don't know what? Congress[6] should keep out of it. Isn't it enough with the Group Areas?"

She laughed. "Now, Yusuf, you know you don't believe that. Look how you said the same thing when the Group Areas started in Natal. You said we should begin to worry when we get moved out of our own houses here in the
80 Transvaal. And then your own mother lost her house in Noorddorp,[7] and there you are; you saw that nobody's safe. Oh, Girlie was here this afternoon; she says Ismail's brother's engaged—that's nice, isn't it? His mother will be pleased; she was worried." **D**

"Why was she worried?" asked Jimmy, who was fifteen, and old enough to **patronize** his mother.

"Well, she wanted to see him settled. There's a party on Sunday week at Ismail's place—you'd better give me your suit to give to the cleaners tomorrow, Yusuf."

One of the girls presented herself at once. "I'll have nothing to wear, Ma."
90 Mrs. Bamjee scratched her sallow face. "Perhaps Girlie will lend you her pink, eh? Run over to Girlie's place now and say I say will she lend it to you."

The sound of commonplaces often does service as security, and Bamjee, going to sit in the armchair with the shiny armrests that was wedged between the table and the sideboard, lapsed into an unthinking doze that, like all times of dreamlike ordinariness during those weeks, was filled with uneasy jerks and starts back into reality. The next morning, as soon as he got to market, he heard that Dr. Khan had been arrested. But that night Mrs. Bamjee sat up making a new dress for her daughter; the sight **disarmed** Bamjee, reassured him again, against his will, so that the resentment he had been making ready

---

6. **Congress:** the African National Congress (ANC), one of the main groups that opposed apartheid.
7. **Natal** (nə-tăl') ... **Noorddorp** (nôrt'dôrp): provinces in South Africa.

A CHIP OF GLASS RUBY **699**

presumption
(prĭ-zŭmp'shən) *n.* behavior or language that is boldly arrogant or offensive

COMMON CORE RL 2
G THEME AND PERSUASION
Reread lines 69–73. Mrs. Bamjee compares her husband's attitude toward her political activities to a husband's "endearing" bad temper. Why would Mrs. Bamjee be so casual when talking about important matters? This comment about Mrs. Bamjee might be a clue to the story's theme.

D THEME AND PERSUASION
Reread lines 66–83. What does this dialogue suggest about the responsibilities of individuals?

patronize (pā'trə-nīz') *v.* to behave in a manner that shows feelings of superiority

disarm (dĭs-ärm') *v.* to win over; to make less hostile

TEXT ANALYSIS COMMON CORE RL 2
G THEME AND PERSUASION
Point out the phrases "only a mannerism" and "appear uninterested" in line 70. Explain that Mrs. Bamjee downplays her husband's indifference with these words.

Possible answer: She speaks casually so as not to indicate that her husband's indifference bothers her; she would like her husband to embrace activism and fight injustice too.

TEXT ANALYSIS COMMON CORE RL 2 RL 6
D THEME AND PERSUASION
Possible answer: The dialogue suggests that because injustice puts everyone at risk, individuals have a responsibility to fight injustice wherever they find it.

TIERED DISCUSSION PROMPTS
Use lines 69-99 to help students understand the relationship between Mr. and Mrs. Bamjee:

Recall In what way do Bamjee and Mrs. Bamjee disagree? *Possible answer: Mrs. Bamjee wants to take an active role in protesting government policies; Bamjee does not want to get involved.*

Evaluate Are both characters fooling themselves? Explain. *Possible answer: Yes. Mrs. Bamjee is fooling herself when she insists that her husband doesn't believe what he says (lines 77–81). Bamjee is fooling himself when he is falsely comforted by his wife's domestic routines and ignores the dangerous reality of her political activities.*

VOCABULARY COMMON CORE L 4
OWN THE WORD
- **presumption:** Remind students that *presumption* refers to arrogant or offensive language or behavior.
- **patronize:** Tell students that *patronize* can also mean "to go to as a regular customer."
- **disarm:** Have students demonstrate their understanding of *disarm* by completing the following sentence: "The playful puppy *disarmed . . . .*"

FOR STRUGGLING READERS
Vocabulary Support Introduce these words from "A Chip of Glass Ruby." Have students read the context for each word and then suggest a synonym to replace it.
- *wavelengths* (line 61), "particular lines of thought"
- *mannerism* (line 70), "characteristic way of acting; trait"
- *sallow* (line 89), "of a sickly yellowish color"

FOR RELUCTANT READERS
Help students see the connection between dialect and reading interest. Read line 74 aloud: "What for do you want to get mixed up with these killings and stonings . . .?" Ask students to think about what Mr. Bamjee is saying, and then have them repeat the line with the word *Why* replacing *What for.* Have them look for other examples of dialect in the selection and suggest standard English equivalents for the nonstandard English patterns. Examples may include lines 86, 90, and 169.

all day faded into a **morose** and accusing silence. Heaven knew, of course, who
100 came and went in the house during the day. Twice in that week of riots, raids,
and arrests, he found black women in the house when he came home; plain
ordinary native women in doeks,[8] drinking tea. This was not a thing other
Indian women would have in their homes, he thought bitterly; but then his
wife was not like other people, in a way he could not put his finger on, except
to say what it was not: not scandalous, not punishable, not rebellious. It was,
like the attraction that had led him to marry her, Pahad's widow with five
children, something he could not see clearly.

morose (mə-rōs′) *adj.*
gloomy; sullen

When the Special Branch[9] knocked steadily on the door in the small
hours of Thursday morning, he did not wake up, for his return to
110 consciousness was always set in his mind to half past four, and that was more
than an hour away. Mrs. Bamjee got up herself, struggled into Jimmy's raincoat
which was hanging over a chair, and went to the front door. The clock on
the wall—a wedding present when she married Pahad—showed three o'clock
when she snapped on the light, and she knew at once who it was on the other
side of the door. Although she was not surprised, her hands shook like a very
old person's as she undid the locks and the complicated catch on the wire
burglar-proofing. And then she opened the door and they were there—two
colored policemen in plain clothes. "Zanip Bamjee?"
   "Yes."
120   As they talked, Bamjee woke up in the sudden terror of having overslept.
Then he became conscious of men's voices. He heaved himself out of bed in
the dark and went to the window, which, like the front door, was covered
with a heavy mesh of thick wire against intruders from the dingy lane it
looked upon. Bewildered, he appeared in the room, where the policemen were
searching through a soapbox of papers beside the duplicating machine. "Yusuf,
it's for me," Mrs. Bamjee said.
   At once, the snap of a trap, realization came. He stood there in an old shirt
before the two policemen, and the woman was going off to prison because of
the natives. "There you are!" he shouted, standing away from her. "That's what
130 you've got for it. Didn't I tell you? Didn't I? That's the end of it now. That's the
finish. That's what it's come to." She listened with her head at the slightest tilt
to one side, as if to ward off a blow, or in compassion.
   Jimmy, Pahad's son, appeared at the door with a suitcase; two or three of the
girls were behind him. "Here, Ma, you take my green jersey." "I've found your
clean blouse." Bamjee had to keep moving out of their way as they helped their
mother to make ready. It was like the preparation for one of the family festivals
his wife made such a fuss over; wherever he put himself, they bumped into
him. Even the two policemen mumbled, "Excuse me," and pushed past into
the rest of the house to continue their search. They took with them a tome

③ Targeted Passage

Analyze
Visuals ▶

How does the painting
reflect what is happening
in the story?

---

8. **doeks** (dŭks): cloth head coverings.

9. **Special Branch:** the South African secret police.

700   UNIT 6: ARGUMENT AND PERSUASION

Untitled, Jagath Weerasinghe.

What would you SACRIFICE for justice?

Discuss Based on lines 108–126, what sacrifice
has Mrs. Bamjee made? Why has she done so?
*Possible answer: Mrs. Bamjee has sacrificed both
her personal safety and her freedom (which is
taken away by her arrest) because she wants to
stand in opposition to injustice.*

Analyze Visuals

*Possible answer: The painting shows a woman
standing in her doorway, looking out, and
bracing herself against the jamb. Mrs. Bamjee
might have looked this way as she opened the
door for the police.*

About the Art The artist uses color, light,
and shadow to emphasize the figure of the
woman. Muted tones keep the less important
objects—the furnishings and interior of the
house—in the background.

VOCABULARY

COMMON
CORE
L 4

OWN THE WORD

morose: Ask students if they have ever
felt *morose*, or "gloomy or sullen." Have
them write a short explanation about
when and why they felt *morose*.

DIFFERENTIATED INSTRUCTION

FOR STRUGGLING READERS

③ Targeted Passage [Lines 117–138]

In this passage, Mrs. Bamjee is arrested, and
family members react.

- Who has come to Mrs. Bamjee's home at
  this early hour? Why? (lines 117–118, 128)

- Explain this sentence: "At once, the snap of
  a trap, realization came." (line 127)

- What do the children do before Mrs. Bamjee
  leaves? How is their reaction to the arrest different from Bamjee's? (lines 133–138)

FOR ADVANCED LEARNERS/PRE–AP

Hypothesis [paired-activity option] Direct
students to this statement, which reflects
Bamjee's thoughts: "Heaven knew, of course,
who came and went in the house during the
day" (lines 99–100). Instruct students to look
for evidence throughout the story that helps
them draw conclusions about why Bamjee
did not try to stop his wife from her activism.
Ask students to share their conclusions and
evidence with the class.

TIERED DISCUSSION PROMPTS

Direct students to lines 120–132. Use these prompts to help students focus on Bamjee's reaction to his wife's arrest:

Connect Have you ever been startled awake in the middle of the night? How did you feel? How might that experience help you understand Bamjee's initial response to the arrival of the police? *Answers will vary, but students should recognize the disorientation that marks such moments.*

Analyze How does Bamjee react once he realizes what is happening? *Possible answer: He erupts in anger at his wife and takes an I-told-you-so attitude.*

Evaluate Do you think that Bamjee's reaction is fair? Why or why not? *Possible answer: Fair: Bamjee was opposed to his wife's activities, so his reaction was understandable. Unfair: He did not stop her from her activism. Whether fair or unfair, as her husband, he should be supportive of her and concerned about her welfare instead of shouting and stepping away (line 129).*

FOR ENGLISH LANGUAGE LEARNERS

Vocabulary: Idioms Have pairs of students determine the meaning of these idioms, either from context or from a dictionary:

- *It's going to go nicely* (line 23), "It will look good with"
- *setting about* (line 60), "beginning"
- *put his finger on* (line 104), "figure out"
- *That's what it's come to* (line 131), "This is the result"
- *made such a fuss over* (line 137), "became so excited about"
- *had set her heart on* (line 149), "wanted very much, was determined to get"

140 that Nehru[10] had written in prison; it had been bought from a persevering traveling salesman and kept, for years, on the mantelpiece. "Oh, don't take that, please," Mrs. Bamjee said suddenly, clinging to the arm of the man who had picked it up.

The man held it away from her.

"What does it matter, Ma?"

It was true that no one in the house had ever read it; but she said, "It's for my children."

"Ma, leave it." Jimmy, who was squat and plump, looked like a merchant advising a client against a roll of silk she had set her heart on. She went into
150 the bedroom and got dressed. When she came out in her old yellow sari with a brown coat over it, the faces of the children were behind her like faces on the platform at a railway station. They kissed her goodbye. The policemen did not hurry her, but she seemed to be in a hurry just the same.

"What am I going to do?" Bamjee accused them all.

The policemen looked away patiently.

"It'll be all right. Girlie will help. The big children can manage. And Yusuf—" The children crowded in around her; two of the younger ones had awakened and appeared, asking shrill questions.

"Come on," said the policemen.

160 "I want to speak to my husband." She broke away and came back to him, and the movement of her sari hid them from the rest of the room for a moment. His face hardened in suspicious anticipation against the request to give some message to the next fool who would take up her pamphleteering until he, too, was arrested. "On Sunday," she said. "Take them on Sunday." He did not know what she was talking about. "The engagement party," she whispered, low and urgent. "They shouldn't miss it. Ismail will be offended." **E**

They listened to the car drive away. Jimmy bolted and barred the front door and then at once opened it again; he put on the raincoat that his mother had taken off. "Going to tell Girlie," he said. The children went back to bed. Their
170 father did not say a word to any of them; their talk, the crying of the younger ones and the argumentative voices of the older, went on in the bedrooms. He found himself alone; he felt the night all around him. And then he happened to meet the clock face and saw with a terrible sense of unfamiliarity that this was not the secret night but an hour he should have recognized: the time he always got up. He pulled on his trousers and his dirty white hawker's coat and wound his grey muffler up to the stubble on his chin and went to work.

$\mathbf{T}$he duplicating machine was gone from the sideboard. The policemen had taken it with them, along with the pamphlets and the conference reports and the stack of old newspapers that had collected on top of the
180 wardrobe in the bedroom—not the thick dailies of the white men but the

E DRAW CONCLUSIONS
What conclusions can you draw about Mrs. Bamjee based on her behavior in lines 160–166?

---

10. **Nehru** (nā′rōō): Jawaharlal (jə-wä′hər-läl′) Nehru, nationalist leader in India's movement for self-governance and the first prime minister of independent India.

E *Model the Skill:* **DRAW CONCLUSIONS**

To model how to draw conclusions, read lines 160–166 with students. Have them list Mrs. Bamjee's last actions and words before she is taken away.

Possible answer: Mrs. Bamjee's behavior shows that even in the midst of a personal crisis, she still is thinking about others— even more so than about herself.

IF STUDENTS NEED HELP . . . Have them review what is said about the engagement party in lines 81–90.

Extend the Discussion If Bamjee were the one being arrested, how do you think his thoughts would differ from Mrs. Bamjee's?

DIFFERENTIATED INSTRUCTION

FOR STRUGGLING READERS
Build Understanding: Similes Direct students' attention to lines 148–149 and 151–152. Elicit or explain that Gordimer uses similes (comparisons with *like* or *as*) to create vivid descriptions. Help students identify what is being compared in the two similes. Then examine other similes in the story, such as those in lines 17–19 and 263–264. To extend the activity, invite students to write and share a few similes of their own.

FOR ENGLISH LANGUAGE LEARNERS
Language: Conversational English Patterns Have students identify the words that are missing but implied in each of these items:

- "Perhaps Girlie will lend you her pink, eh?" (lines 89–90), *dress*

- "Going to tell Girlie" (line 169), *I'm*

- "Such a kind lady" (line 214), *She's*

thin, impermanent-looking papers that spoke up, sometimes interrupted by suppression or lack of money, for the rest. It was all gone. When he had married her and moved in with her and her five children, into what had been the Pahad and became the Bamjee house, he had not recognized the humble, harmless, and apparently useless routine tasks—the minutes of meetings being written up on the dining-room table at night, the government blue books that were read while the latest baby was suckled, the employment of the fingers of the older children in the fashioning of crinkle-paper Congress rosettes—as activity intended to move mountains. For years and years he had not noticed
190 it, and now it was gone.

The house was quiet. The children kept to their lairs, crowded on the beds with the doors shut. He sat and looked at the sideboard, where the plastic carnations and the mat with the picture of the Taj Mahal were in place. For the first few weeks he never spoke of her. There was the feeling, in the house, that he had wept and raged at her, that boulders of reproach had thundered down upon her absence, and yet he had said not one word. He had not been to inquire where she was; Jimmy and Girlie had gone to Mohammed Ebrahim, the lawyer, and when he found out that their mother had been taken—when she was arrested, at least—to a prison in the next town, they had stood about
200 outside the big prison door for hours while they waited to be told where she had been moved from there. At last they had discovered that she was fifty **F** miles away, in Pretoria.[11] Jimmy asked Bamjee for five shillings to help Girlie pay the train fare to Pretoria, once she had been interviewed by the police and had been given a permit to visit her mother; he put three two-shilling pieces on the table for Jimmy to pick up, and the boy, looking at him keenly, did not know whether the extra shilling meant anything, or whether it was merely that Bamjee had no change.

It was only when relations and neighbors came to the house that Bamjee would suddenly begin to talk. He had never been so expansive in his life as he
210 was in the company of these visitors, many of them come on a polite call rather in the nature of a visit of condolence. "Ah, yes, yes, you can see how I am— you see what has been done to me. Nine children, and I am on the cart all day. I get home at seven or eight. What are you to do? What can people like us do?"

"Poor Mrs. Bamjee. Such a kind lady."

"Well, you see for yourself. They walk in here in the middle of the night and leave a houseful of children. I'm out on the cart all day; I've got a living to earn." Standing about in his shirtsleeves, he became quite animated; he would call for the girls to bring fruit drinks for the visitors. When they were gone, it was as if he, who was orthodox if not devout and never drank liquor,
220 had been drunk and abruptly sobered up; he looked dazed and could not have gone over in his mind what he had been saying. And as he cooled, the lump of resentment and wrongedness stopped his throat again. **G**

---

11. **Pretoria** (prĭ-tôr′ē-ə): the administrative capital of South Africa.

F GRAMMAR AND STYLE
Reread lines 196–201. Notice how Gordimer forms a **compound-complex sentence** by connecting a series of independent and subordinate clauses.

G DRAW CONCLUSIONS
Reread lines 208–222. Why does Bamjee feel so resentful about his wife's imprisonment?

A CHIP OF GLASS RUBY   703

F GRAMMAR AND STYLE

Vary Sentence Structure By using compound-complex sentences, Gordimer adds a distinctive flow to her writing style. Ask students to rewrite the sentence in lines 196–201 as a series of simple sentences. After you or a volunteer reads the sentences aloud, discuss how the change to simple sentences alters the feel of the text. Urge students to find other examples of compound-complex sentences in the story, as in lines 69–73 and 167–169.

READING SKILL   COMMON CORE   RL 1

G DRAW CONCLUSIONS

Possible answer: *Bamjee feels resentful because he sees himself as a victim. In his view, he is paying the price for his wife's activism, for her imprisonment leaves him having to care for the children in addition to working all day.*

IF STUDENTS NEED HELP . . . Ask:
- Where is Bamjee during the day?
- Who cared for the children and the household before Mrs. Bamjee went to prison? Who cares for them now?
- What does Bamjee mean when he says, "you see what has been done to me" (line 212)?

FOR ENGLISH LANGUAGE LEARNERS
Language: Word Associations Have students study these phrases and expressions: "you'd better" (line 87); "Heaven knew [knows]" (line 99); "He had never been so . . . as he was" (lines 209–210); "see for yourself" (line 215); "that's how she is" (line 290). Elicit additional examples that demonstrate correct use of these expressions in context. Reinforce learning by having students quiz each other.

FOR ADVANCED LEARNERS/PRE–AP
Analyze Tone Have students work in small groups to discuss Gordimer's tone in the story. Ask them to find evidence that suggests whether Gordimer seems to express approval or disapproval of any of the characters, or whether she remains neutral throughout. Have the groups take notes on their discussions and then compare their conclusions.

⊕ Model the Skill: THEME AND PERSUASION

To model how to analyze theme and persuasion, have students refer to lines 231–243. Read aloud Jimmy's dialogue, and point out that the author is using Jimmy's dialogue to provide background on the racial struggle.

Possible answer: *Jimmy appears to view his mother's political activity with pride. He feels that his mother is in jail for a good cause, and he thinks that the teacher is angry because he feels that his rights are threatened by the efforts to empower the natives. His comments to Bamjee in lines 235–240 suggest that he understands and supports his mother.*

Extend the Discussion When Bamjee asks, "Did she ever think of this?" (line 234)—referring to the situation that her family now finds itself in—Jimmy replies, "That's why Ma's *there*" (line 235). What does this exchange suggest about how differently Bamjee and Jimmy view the situation?

REVISIT THE BIG QUESTION

What would you
SACRIFICE for justice?

Discuss Based on lines 250–257, how has Mrs. Bamjee's sacrifice affected Bamjee emotionally? *Possible answer: Mrs. Bamjee's sacrifice has left Bamjee angry, confused, and frustrated. He cannot understand why the "good plain Moslem woman" (lines 252–253) whom he had married would do something so unconventional—and so problematic for him.*

Bamjee found one of the little boys the center of a self-important group of championing brothers and sisters in the room one evening. "They've been cruel to Ahmed."

"What has he done?" said the father.

"Nothing! Nothing!" The little girl stood twisting her handkerchief excitedly.

An older one, thin as her mother, took over, silencing the others with a gesture of her skinny hand. "They did it at school today. They made an example of him."

230 "What is an example?" said Bamjee impatiently.

"The teacher made him come up and stand in front of the whole class, and he told them, 'You see this boy? His mother's in jail because she likes the natives so much. She wants the Indians to be the same as natives.' "

"It's terrible," he said. His hands fell to his sides. "Did she ever think of this?"

"That's why Ma's *there*," said Jimmy, putting aside his comic and emptying out his schoolbooks upon the table. "That's all the kids need to know. Ma's there because things like this happen. Petersen's a colored teacher, and it's his black blood that's brought him trouble all his life, I suppose. He hates anyone who says everybody's the same because that takes away from him his bit of whiteness that's

240 all he's got. What d'you expect? It's nothing to make too much fuss about." ⊕

"Of course, you are fifteen and you know everything," Bamjee mumbled at him.

"I don't say that. But I know Ma, anyway." The boy laughed.

There was a hunger strike among the political prisoners, and Bamjee could not bring himself to ask Girlie if her mother was starving herself too. He would not ask; and yet he saw in the young woman's face the gradual weakening of her mother. When the strike had gone on for nearly a week, one of the elder children burst into tears at the table and could not eat. Bamjee pushed his own plate away in rage.

250 Sometimes he spoke out loud to himself while he was driving the vegetable lorry.[12] "What for?" Again and again: "What for?" She was not a modern woman who cut her hair and wore short skirts. He had married a good plain Moslem woman who bore children and stamped her own chilies. He had a sudden vision of her at the duplicating machine, that night just before she was taken away, and he felt himself maddened, baffled, and hopeless. He had become the ghost of a victim, hanging about the scene of a crime whose motive he could not understand and had not had time to learn.

T he hunger strike at the prison went into the second week. Alone in the rattling cab of his lorry, he said things that he heard as if spoken by

260 someone else, and his heart burned in fierce agreement with them. "For a crowd of natives who'll smash our shops and kill us in our houses when their time comes." "She will starve herself to death there." "She will die there." "Devils who will burn and kill us." He fell into bed each night like a stone and dragged himself up in the mornings as a beast of burden is beaten to its feet.

---

12. **lorry:** truck.

⊕ **THEME AND PERSUASION**
How does Jimmy view his mother's political activity?

DIFFERENTIATED INSTRUCTION

FOR ENGLISH LANGUAGE LEARNERS

Vocabulary: Phrasal Verbs Discuss the meanings of these phrasal verbs: *run off* (line 26), *drifted off* (line 31), *gone over* (line 221), *putting aside* (line 235), *emptying out* (lines 235–236). Have students use the Think-Pair-Share activity and a dictionary to find other phrasal verbs associated with each main verb (underlined in the list) and then provide example sentences.

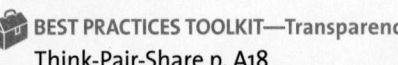 BEST PRACTICES TOOLKIT—Transparency
Think-Pair-Share p. A18

FOR STRUGGLING READERS

Develop Reading Fluency To help students understand the way the author constructs dialogue, read aloud lines 258–264 with expression. Then divide the class into two groups, and assign the role of Mr. Bamjee to one group and the narrator to the other. Have the groups read the lines aloud as you did. Distribute the copy masters and have students work in pairs to practice fluency.

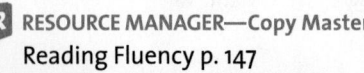 RESOURCE MANAGER—Copy Master
Reading Fluency p. 147

One of these mornings, Girlie appeared very early, while he was wolfing bread and strong tea—alternate sensations of dry solidity and stinging heat— at the kitchen table. Her real name was Fatima, of course, but she had adopted the silly modern name along with the clothes of the young factory girls among whom she worked. She was expecting her first baby in a week or two, and
270 her small face, her cut and curled hair, and the sooty arches drawn over her eyebrows did not seem to belong to her thrust-out body under a clean smock. She wore mauve lipstick and was smiling her cocky little white girl's smile, foolish and bold, not like an Indian girl's at all.

A Sketch of Two Figures at a Window, Nicholai Uvarov. 29.2 cm × 23.4 cm. Bonhams, London. Photo © Bridgeman Art Library.

A CHIP OF GLASS RUBY   **705**

Analyze Visuals

Activity Ask students to compare and contrast the woman in the painting with Girlie, as described in lines 265–273. *Possible answer: Like Girlie, the woman in the painting wears modern clothes (line 268), appears to have short hair (line 270), could be Indian, and is possibly pregnant. Her posture also suggests that, like Girlie, she might be "bold" (line 273).*

About the Art Russian artist Nicholai Uvarov (b. 1927) uses a quick, sketchy style to capture the dappled light of this domestic scene. By omitting details, such as the facial features of the two figures, he focuses instead on the interplay of colors and the relationship between the foreground and the background.

FOR ENGLISH LANGUAGE LEARNERS

Language: Modifiers Gordimer uses multiple adjectives to modify nouns and pronouns in descriptions such as these:

- "He pulled on . . . his dirty white hawker's coat" (line 175).
- "he felt himself maddened, baffled, and hopeless" (line 255).
- "She . . . was smiling her cocky little white girl's smile, foolish and bold" (lines 272–273).

Write these sentences on the board or on a transparency. Then ask students to provide similar sentences that relate to the story and that use multiple adjectives (for example, *Mrs. Bamjee was a strong, loving, and principled person*). To get students started, use these sentence starters:

- Mr. Bamjee was _____.
- The _____ children . . .
- Girlie acted as though _____.

"What's the matter?" he said.

She smiled again. "Don't you know? I told Bobby he must get me up in time this morning. I wanted to be sure I wouldn't miss you today."

"I don't know what you're talking about."

She came over and put her arm up around his unwilling neck and kissed the grey bristles at the side of his mouth. "Many happy returns! Don't you 280 know it's your birthday?"

"No," he said. "I didn't know, didn't think—" He broke the pause by swiftly picking up the bread and giving his attention desperately to eating and drinking. His mouth was busy, but his eyes looked at her, intensely black. She said nothing but stood there with him. She would not speak, and at last he said, swallowing a piece of bread that tore at his throat as it went down, "I don't remember these things."

The girl nodded, the Woolworth baubles in her ears swinging. "That's the first thing she told me when I saw her yesterday—don't forget it's Bajie's birthday tomorrow."

290 He shrugged over it. "It means a lot to children. But that's how she is. Whether it's one of the old cousins or the neighbor's grandmother, she always knows when the birthday is. What importance is my birthday, while she's sitting there in a prison? I don't understand how she can do the things she does when her mind is always full of woman's nonsense at the same time—that's what I don't understand with her." ⓘ

"Oh, but don't you see?" the girl said. "It's because she doesn't want anybody to be left out. It's because she always remembers; remembers everything— people without somewhere to live, hungry kids, boys who can't get educated— remembers all the time. That's how Ma is."

300 "Nobody else is like that." It was half a complaint.

"No, nobody else," said his stepdaughter.

She sat herself down at the table, resting her belly. He put his head in his hands. "I'm getting old"—but he was overcome by something much more curious, by an answer. He knew why he had desired her, the ugly widow with five children; he knew what way it was in which she was not like the others; it was there, like the fact of the belly that lay between him and her daughter. ❧

④ Targeted Passage

ⓘ **DRAW CONCLUSIONS**
How has Mrs. Bamjee been affected by her imprisonment?

READING SKILL

COMMON CORE
RL 1

ⓘ DRAW CONCLUSIONS

Possible answer: Imprisonment has not diminished Mrs. Bamjee's focus on other people, as implied by her reminder to Girlie about Bamjee's birthday (lines 287–289).

REVISIT THE BIG QUESTION

What would you
SACRIFICE for justice?

Discuss Based on lines 296–301, how does Mrs. Bamjee's sacrifice reflect her character? *Possible answer: Mrs. Bamjee has sacrificed her personal safety to stand up for the rights of people who are being excluded. As Girlie explains, Mrs. Bamjee "doesn't want anybody to be left out. . . . That's how Ma is."*

SELECTION WRAP–UP

READ WITH A PURPOSE Now that students have finished reading the selection, have them explain why Mrs. Bamjee was willing to sacrifice herself for a cause. *Possible answer: Mrs. Bamjee cares about people and doesn't want anyone to be left out.*

★ **CRITIQUE** Have students evaluate Gordimer's portrayal of Bamjee and Mrs. Bamjee. Ask students to evaluate the credibility of the two characters and to consider whether Gordimer's characterization of them is sufficiently developed.

INDEPENDENT READING

Students might enjoy reading *A Dry White Season* by Andre Brink, which tells the story of a white schoolteacher coming to terms with the reality of apartheid in South Africa.

DIFFERENTIATED INSTRUCTION

FOR STRUGGLING READERS

④ Targeted Passage [Lines 290–306]
This passage presents Bamjee's concluding realization about his wife.

- What does Bamjee tell Girlie that he doesn't understand about his wife? (lines 293–295)
- Both Bamjee and Girlie say that no one else is like Mrs. Bamjee. Do they mean the same thing? Explain. (lines 300–301)
- At the end, what does Bamjee realize about his reason for loving Mrs. Bamjee? (lines 304–306)

FOR ADVANCED LEARNERS/PRE–AP

Analyze and Evaluate Title Have students re-read lines 35–40. Then ask them to reflect on Gordimer's possible reasons for choosing "A Chip of Glass Ruby" as her title for this story. Have students write a brief essay analyzing the significance of the title. Students also should present their views about the effectiveness of the title, with supporting reasons. Invite students to exchange and compare essays.

Comprehension

1. **Recall** What political struggle is Mrs. Bamjee engaged in?

2. **Recall** How does Bamjee feel about his wife's political activities?

3. **Recall** What happens when the government finds out about Mrs. Bamjee's activities?

4. **Summarize** How do the members of Mrs. Bamjee's family react to what happens to her?

COMMON CORE

RL 1 Cite textual evidence to support analysis of what the text says explicitly as well as inferences drawn from the text. **RL 2** Determine a theme of a text and analyze in detail its development, including how it is refined by specific details. **RL 6** Analyze a particular point of view or cultural experience in a work of world literature.

Text Analysis

5. **Examine Character Traits** What traits does Gordimer give Mrs. Bamjee to make her a sympathetic character? Identify the traits in a graphic organizer like the one shown.

Mrs. Bamjee

6. **Analyze Theme** What main theme does Gordimer develop in the story to **persuade** readers? Is she successful? Support your responses.

7. **Interpret a Statement** Reread lines 296–299. What do you make of Girlie's explanation of Mrs. Bamjee's commitment to both her family and the anti-apartheid movement?

8. **Make Inferences** Reread lines 302–306. What does Bamjee come to realize about his feelings for his wife at the end of the story?

9. **Draw Conclusions** Review the chart you created as you read. What conclusion would you draw about the relationship between Bamjee and Mrs. Bamjee? Provide examples to support your conclusion.

10. **Make Judgments** Mrs. Bamjee's family makes sacrifices as a result of the government's actions against her. Should she have avoided political activity out of concern for their welfare? Give reasons for your opinion.

Text Criticism

11. **Critical Interpretations** The critic Brigitte Weeks once wrote that "Gordimer insists that her readers face South African life as she does: with affection and horror." How might this statement apply to "A Chip of Glass Ruby"?

What would you SACRIFICE for justice?
Would you be willing to fight for a cause that does not directly affect you?

---

10. *Some students may feel that Mrs. Bamjee's first responsibility is to her family. Others may argue that she is helping her family by being a role model and by fighting to make the world a better place for her children.*

Text Criticism
Possible answer:

11. *The statement applies because Gordimer shows courageous people like Mrs. Bamjee taking risks to help others (the "affection"), but she also shows racial injustice and the*

government taking the unsympathetic step of imprisoning the mother of nine children (the "horror").

What would you SACRIFICE
for justice? Students might consider causes that are current issues. Encourage students to think of possible benefits and difficulties that might result from their affiliation with such a cause.

Practice and Apply

For preliminary support of post-reading questions, use these copy masters:

R RESOURCE MANAGER—Copy Masters
Reading Check p. 144
Theme and Persuasion p. 137
Question Support p. 145

Additional selection questions are provided for teachers on page 131.

ANSWERS

Comprehension

1. *Mrs. Bamjee is engaged in the struggle against apartheid laws in South Africa.*

2. *Bamjee disapproves of her activism.*

3. *The government imprisons Mrs. Bamjee.*

4. *The children support Mrs. Bamjee, but Bamjee is angry and resentful.*

Text Analysis
COMMON CORE RL 1, RL 2, RL 6
Possible answers:

5. *Mrs. Bamjee is upbeat, compassionate, loving, considerate, unassuming, and selfless.*

6. ● **COMMON CORE FOCUS** *Theme and Persuasion The persuasive theme is that people have a responsibility to fight injustice, even if it doesn't directly affect them. Some students may feel that Gordimer is persuasive because Mrs. Bamjee is portrayed in such a positive light. Students who disagree may say that the story offers no evidence that Mrs. Bamjee's actions make a difference.*

7. *Girlie grasps her mother's essential character—that the same concern for others that leads Mrs. Bamjee to remember everyone's birthday also motivates her political activism. She doesn't want anyone to be left out, on any level.*

8. *Bamjee comes to realize that it is his wife's caring attitude toward others that made him fall in love with her in the first place.*

9. ■ **COMMON CORE FOCUS** *Draw Conclusions The Bamjees' relationship is strained because of differing attitudes, but Bamjee and Mrs. Bamjee make it work. Mrs. Bamjee pretends that her husband's indifference is "only a mannerism" (line 70), and he pretends that her activism is less risky than he knows it is.*

ANSWERS

Vocabulary in Context

▲ VOCABULARY PRACTICE

1. *presumption*   4. *disarm*
2. *repute*   5. *morose*
3. *patronize*

 **RESOURCE MANAGER**—Copy Master
Vocabulary Practice p. 142

ACADEMIC VOCABULARY IN WRITING

Sample response: Bamjee's main objective *is to preserve his family and live a traditional life. Mrs. Bamjee shares that* objective, *but she also hopes to help create a more just government in which all people have equal rights. They do not discuss their differing goals, so Mrs. Bamjee never* cites *specific reasons for her political work.*

VOCABULARY STRATEGY: USING A THESAURUS

COMMON CORE **L 4c**

- Explain that synonyms are not always interchangeable, because although they may have similar denotations (literal meanings), they may have different connotations (implied meanings). For example, *clever* generally has positive connotations, whereas *sly* generally has negative connotations.

- To extend the activity, challenge students to use a thesaurus to locate other pairs of synonyms with different connotations. Discuss several examples.

Possible answers:

1. *biased*   4. *engrossed*
2. *inheritance*   5. *prompted*
3. *solemnity*

 RESOURCE MANAGER—Copy Master
Vocabulary Strategy p. 143

Interactive Vocabulary   **THINK** central

Keywords direct students to a **WordSharp** tutorial on **thinkcentral.com** or to other types of vocabulary practice and review.

Vocabulary in Context

▲ VOCABULARY PRACTICE

WORD LIST
disarm
morose
patronize
presumption
repute

Choose the vocabulary word that is a **synonym,** or word that has a similar meaning, for each of the following words.

1. disrespect   4. soothe
2. fame   5. sullen
3. condescend

ACADEMIC VOCABULARY IN WRITING

- cite   - controversy   - convince   - objective   - statistic

How do Mrs. Bamjee's **objectives** lead to conflict and disagreement? Write a paragraph in which you analyze what Bamjee and Mrs. Bamjee want and the steps they take to achieve those goals. Use at least one Academic Vocabulary word in your response.

VOCABULARY STRATEGY: USING A THESAURUS

COMMON CORE

L 4c Consult specialized reference materials to determine or clarify a word's precise meaning or etymology.

A **thesaurus** is a book of synonyms and antonyms. You can use it to find a replacement for an overused word or to find a word with the precise shade of meaning that you need. The synonyms in a thesaurus entry are not always interchangeable. For example, *assumption* and *impudence* are both synonyms for the word *presumption,* but only *assumption* would be an appropriate replacement in the following sentence:

It is my presumption that the plane is late due to the bad weather.

PRACTICE Use a thesaurus to find appropriate synonyms for the boldfaced words.

1. The judge was **partial** to the defendant in the case.
2. We received a generous **legacy** from our benefactor.
3. She spoke with impressive **gravity** on the topic.
4. I was completely **immersed** in my studies.
5. His comment **provoked** laughter in the audience.

Interactive Vocabulary   **THINK** central
Go to **thinkcentral.com**.
KEYWORD: HML10-708

DIFFERENTIATED INSTRUCTION

FOR ENGLISH LANGUAGE LEARNERS

Vocabulary Strategy Practice To provide practice using a thesaurus, have pairs of students find synonyms and antonyms for these words from the selection: *endearing* (line 72), *bitterly* (line 103), *squat* (line 148), *shrill* (line 158), *keenly* (line 205), *animated* (line 217), *baffled* (line 255), *wolfing* (line 265). Have students complete a Three-Column Journal with these heads: *Word, Synonym, Antonym.*

 BEST PRACTICES TOOLKIT—Transparency
Three-Column Journal p. B10

FOR ADVANCED LEARNERS/PRE–AP

Vocabulary in Writing Challenge students to use as many vocabulary words as they can in a paragraph or two written from the imprisoned Mrs. Bamjee's point of view. Invite students to compare their responses in small groups to see the various ways in which they used the words and to discuss how their responses offer insights into Mrs. Bamjee's character.

Language

◆ GRAMMAR AND STYLE: Vary Sentence Structure

COMMON CORE

L 1b Use various types of clauses to convey specific meanings and add variety and interest to writing.

Review the **Grammar and Style** note on page 703. A **compound-complex sentence** consists of two or more independent clauses and at least one subordinate clause. By using this particular sentence structure, Gordimer, in just one sentence, connects ideas and answers such questions as *where, why, when, what kind,* and *which one.* In the following example, notice how Gordimer combines a subordinate clause (in green) with a series of independent clauses (in yellow) to form a compound-complex sentence:

> *When the Special Branch knocked steadily on the door in the small hours of Thursday morning, he did not wake up, for his return to consciousness was always set in his mind to half past four, and that was more than an hour away.* (lines 108–111)

In the following student model, the revisions in blue demonstrate how a series of simple sentences can be combined to form one compound-complex sentence. Note the use of independent and subordinate clauses, and make similar edits when you revise your own writing.

> **STUDENT MODEL**
>
> *Since*
> Mrs. Bamjee sacrifices for the good of others. She is always with those in
> *, and*
> need in spirit. This keeps her from being lonely.

READING-WRITING CONNECTION

 YOUR TURN Explore the themes of "A Chip of Glass Ruby" by responding to this prompt. Then use the **revising tip** to improve your writing.

WRITING PROMPT

Short Constructed Response: Analysis
A character in one of Gordimer's novels says, "The real definition of loneliness is to live without responsibility." Write **one or two paragraphs** in which you discuss how this quotation relates to the main theme of "A Chip of Glass Ruby."

REVISING TIP

Review your response. Have you used compound-complex sentences to vary sentence structure?

 **Interactive Revision** THINK central
Go to **thinkcentral.com**.
KEYWORD: HML10-709

A CHIP OF GLASS RUBY **709**

FOR STRUGGLING WRITERS

- Limit the length of the assignment to one well-developed paragraph.
- Help students analyze the meaning of the quotation. Discuss why a person with no sense of responsibility might feel lonely.
- Urge students to consider why Bamjee's apparent indifference toward black South Africans might make him feel isolated both during and at the end of the story.

Language

 COMMON CORE L 1b

◆ GRAMMAR AND STYLE

- Examine the student model, discussing how the revisions change the text.
- Write this passage on the board, and then ask students to combine the series of simple sentences into one compound-complex sentence.

Although Mrs. Bamjee may have violated the law., t~~T~~he law is unjust., and s~~S~~he should not be punished for her actions.

R RESOURCE MANAGER—Copy Master
Vary Sentence Structure p. 146

READING-WRITING CONNECTION

- Suggest that students first determine the theme of "A Chip of Glass Ruby" (for example: *People have a responsibility to oppose injustice*) and then reflect on the relationship of the quotation to that theme.

Writing Online  THINK central

The following tools are available online at **thinkcentral.com** and on **Write*Smart* CD-ROM**:
- **Interactive Graphic Organizers**
- **Interactive Student Models**
- **Interactive Revision Lessons**
For additional grammar instruction, see **GrammarNotes** on **thinkcentral.com**.

Assess and Reteach

Assess

DIAGNOSTIC AND SELECTION TESTS
Selection Test A pp. 203–204
Selection Test B/C pp. 205–206

Interactive Selection Test on **thinkcentral.com**

Reteach

Level Up Online Tutorials on **thinkcentral.com**

Reteaching Worksheets on **thinkcentral.com**
Literature Lesson 11: Theme, Motif, and Epiphany
Reading Lesson 9: Drawing Conclusions
Informational Text Lesson 15: Persuasive Techniques

Focus and Motivate

COMMON CORE FOCUS

RI 4 Determine the figurative and connotative meanings of words and phrases as they are used in a text. **RI 6** Determine an author's point of view or purpose in a text and analyze how an author uses rhetoric to advance that point of view or purpose. **W 2** Write explanatory texts to examine and convey complex ideas, concepts, and information clearly and accurately through the effective analysis of content. **W 9b (RI 6)** Draw evidence from informational texts to support analysis. **L 4b** Identify patterns of word changes that indicate different meanings or parts of speech.

SUMMARY

Excerpts from a speech by Desmond Tutu paint a vivid word picture of the division and alienation, the animosity, poverty, and suffering in South Africa that result from the practice of apartheid.

What's the Connection?

The story "A Chip of Glass Ruby" explores apartheid from the viewpoint of an outsider who desires to bring change to an unjust system, to help those who are left out. Desmond Tutu's speech describes the horror of apartheid from the perspective of an insider. As students read, have them keep a list of statements by Desmond Tutu that are illustrated by events in "A Chip of Glass Ruby."

Teach

Standards Focus: Analyze a Speech

Guide students through the elements of a persuasive speech discussed on this page. Point out that use of these elements make the difference between a speech heard and forgotten and words that resonate as deeply on the page as in the ear. Help students fill in their Skills Focus charts as they read.

The Question of South Africa

Speech by Desmond Tutu

COMMON CORE

RI 4 Determine the figurative and connotative meanings of words and phrases as they are used in a text; analyze the cumulative impact of specific word choices on meaning and tone. **RI 6** Determine an author's point of view or purpose in a text and analyze how an author uses rhetoric to advance that point of view or purpose. **L 4b** Identify patterns of word changes that indicate different meanings or parts of speech.

What's the Connection?

In "A Chip of Glass Ruby," Nadine Gordimer writes about the political activities of an Indian housewife in racially segregated South Africa. Now, in "The Question of South Africa," you will read an excerpt from a historical anti-apartheid speech by civil rights leader Desmond Tutu.

Standards Focus: Analyze a Speech

In a persuasive speech, the *way* a message is conveyed is often as important as the message itself. Good persuasive speakers use language to stir emotions. Here are some of the elements they use:

- **Syntax** is the arrangement of words in a sentence. A speaker may use **rhetorical devices** such as **repetition** of the same word, phrase, or sentence to emphasize his or her point. Another rhetorical device often found in speeches is **parallelism**±—the use of similar grammatical constructions to express related ideas. Repetition and parallelism can help advance a speaker's message.
- **Diction** is the choice of words. Often the words used will have strong **connotations**—positive or negative emotional associations.
- **Tone** is the speaker's attitude toward the subject, as expressed through choice of words and details.
- **Voice** is the way a speaker uses language to allow readers to "hear" a personality in a speech.
- **Imagery** includes words and phrases that re-create sensory experiences for readers. **Figurative language**—expressions that communicate meanings beyond their literal meanings—can give a concrete form to an abstract idea or unfamiliar situation.

Use a chart like the one shown below to identify the elements elements found in the following speech.

Element	Example
Syntax	
Diction	
Voice	
Tone	
Imagery	

Selection Resources

See resources on the **Teacher One Stop DVD-ROM** and on **thinkcentral.com**.

R RESOURCE MANAGER UNIT 6
Lesson Support, pp. 149–163

DIAGNOSTIC AND SELECTION TESTS
Selection Tests, pp. 207–210

BEST PRACTICES TOOLKIT
Two-Column Chart, p. A57

TECHNOLOGY

- Teacher One Stop DVD-ROM
- Student One Stop DVD-ROM
- Audio Anthology CD
- GrammarNotes DVD-ROM
- ExamView Generator on the Teacher One Stop

* Resources for Differentiation

The Question of South Africa

by Desmond Tutu

Desmond Tutu (1931–   ) was the first black archbishop (the head of the Anglican Church) in Capetown, a city in segregated South Africa. From this position of leadership, Tutu worked to end apartheid and create a just South African government. In 1984, Tutu was awarded the Nobel Peace Prize for his work. He gave the following speech to the United Nations Security Council shortly after receiving the prestigious award.

I speak out of a full heart, for I am about to speak about a land that I love deeply and passionately; a beautiful land of rolling hills and gurgling streams, of clear starlit skies, of singing birds, and gamboling[1] lambs; a land God has richly endowed with the good things of the earth, a land rich in mineral deposits of nearly every kind; a land of vast open 10 spaces, enough to accommodate all its inhabitants comfortably; a land capable of feeding itself and other lands on the beleaguered[2] continent of Africa, a veritable[3] breadbasket; a land that could contribute wonderfully to the material and spiritual development and prosperity of all Africa and indeed of the whole world. It is endowed with enough to satisfy the material and spiritual needs of 20 all its peoples. **A**

And so we would expect that such a land, veritably flowing with milk and honey, should be a land where peace and harmony and contentment reigned

supreme. Alas, the opposite is the case. For my beloved country is wracked by division, by alienation, by animosity, by separation, by injustice, by avoidable pain and suffering. It is a deeply fragmented 30 society, ridden by fear and anxiety, covered by a pall of despondency[4] and a sense of desperation, split up into hostile, warring factions.

It is a highly volatile[5] land, and its inhabitants sit on a powder keg with a very short fuse indeed, ready to blow us all up into kingdom come. There is endemic[6] unrest, like a festering sore that will not heal until not just the symptoms are treated 40 but the root causes are removed. **B**

South African society is deeply polarized. Nothing illustrates this more sharply than the events of the past week. While the black community was in the seventh heaven of delight because of the decision of that committee in Oslo, and while the world was congratulating the recipient of the Nobel Peace Prize,[7] the

---

1. **gamboling** *adj.*: playing, frolicking.
2. **beleaguered** *adj.*: stressed; threatened.
3. **veritable** *adj.*: genuine, real.
4. **pall of despondency** *n.*: a state of hopelessness.
5. **volatile** *adj.*: explosive.
6. **endemic** *adj.*: native.
7. **committee . . . Prize:** The committee is the Nobel Committee and the recipient is Tutu himself.

① Targeted Passage

A ANALYZE A SPEECH
What is unusual about the **syntax** of the first sentence of the speech? What effect does this have on the opening of this speech?

B ANALYZE A SPEECH
How does Tutu use **figurative language** to create vivid **imagery** in this paragraph?

COMMON CORE L 4b

Language Coach
Affixes By adding prefixes and suffixes to a base word, you create new words. For example, the word *alienation* (line 27) is a form of the word *alien*. Use a dictionary to define *alien* and to find other forms of the word.

Practice and Apply

READ WITH A PURPOSE
Help students set a purpose for reading. Ask them to identify three polarizations that result from apartheid.

INFORMATIONAL ANALYSIS   COMMON CORE   RI 4 RI 6

A ANALYZE A SPEECH
Possible answer: The first sentence is very long, with many long appositive phrases, separated by semicolons. The syntax creates a rhythmic flow that gives momentum to the introduction.

INFORMATIONAL ANALYSIS   COMMON CORE   RI 4 RI 6

B ANALYZE A SPEECH
Possible answer: He says the people "sit on a powder keg with a very short fuse," and compares the unrest to "a festering sore that will not heal" as long as the infection remains. The images suggest imminent danger and illness.

DIFFERENTIATED INSTRUCTION

FOR ENGLISH LANGUAGE LEARNERS

Language Coach   COMMON CORE L 4b
Derivations
Answer: Alien *means "foreign, strange." Derivations include* alienate, alienable, alienor, *and* alienee. Point out the words *injustice* and *avoidable* in line 28. Have students identify each word's prefix or suffix (*in-, -able*). Explain to students that the prefix *in-* means

"not," and adding it changes the meaning of *justice* from "fairness" to "not just" or "wrong." The suffix *-able* means "worthy of an action," and adding it changes the verb *avoid* to an adjective.

FOR STRUGGLING READERS

In combination with the *Audio Anthology CD*, use this Targeted Passage to ensure that students focus on key events, concepts, and skills. Targeted Passages are also good for English learners.

① Targeted Passage [Lines 21–33]
This passage sets up a contrast between what should be and what is.

- How does Tutu describe the richness of the land? (lines 21–23)
- With this richness, what should the land be like? (lines 23–25) What is the land like, in reality? (lines 26–33)
- What are words that contrast with peace, harmony, and contentment? (lines 27–33)

C Model the Skill: ANALYZE A SPEECH

To model how to evaluate diction, or word choice, in a speech, have a volunteer read aloud footnote 9. Then read lines 83–85 aloud, substituting "submissive followers" for *lackeys*. Point out that substituting this phrase for *lackeys* reduces the impact of the message. Discuss with students the connotations of *lackeys* and "submissive followers." Have students add this example to their Skills Focus charts.

Possible answer: *Lackeys* and stooges *are two words with very negative connotations that contrast with the more neutral official title "town councilors." The word choice explains the blacks' feelings.*

D ANALYZE A SPEECH

Possible answer: *The tone is indignation and anger. One detail that shows this tone is the accusation that not enough people have died at any one time to spur the international community to act. Words with negative connotations that Tutu uses to create his tone include* vicious, immoral, evil, *and* unchristian.

---

white government and most white South Africans, very sadly, were seeking to devalue that prize. An event that should have been the occasion of uninhibited joy and thanksgiving revealed a sadly divided society.

Before I came to this country in early September to go on sabbatical, I visited one of the trouble spots near Johannesburg. . . . In this black township, we met an old lady who told us that she was looking after her grandchildren and the children of neighbors while they were at work. On the day about which she was speaking, the police had been chasing black schoolchildren in that street, but the children had eluded the police, who then drove down the street past the old lady's house. Her wards[8] were playing in front of the house, in the yard. She was sitting in the kitchen at the back, when her daughter burst in, calling agitatedly for her. She rushed out into the living room. A grandson had fallen just inside the door, dead. The police had shot him in the back. He was six years old. Recently a baby, a few weeks old, became the first white casualty of the current uprisings. Every death is one too many. Those whom the black community has identified as collaborators with a system that oppresses them and denies them the most elementary human rights have met cruel death, which we deplore as much as any others. They have rejected these people operating within the system, whom they have seen as lackeys[9] and stooges, despite their titles of town councilors, and so on, under an apparently new dispensation[10] extending the right of local government to the blacks. **C**

Over 100,000 black students are out of school, boycotting—as they did in 1976—what they and the black community perceive as an inferior education designed deliberately for inferiority. An already highly volatile situation has been ignited several times and, as a result, over 80 persons have died. There has been industrial unrest, with the first official strike by black miners taking place, not without its toll of fatalities among the blacks.

Some may be inclined to ask: But why should all this unrest be taking place just when the South African government appears to have embarked on the road of reform? . . .

There is little freedom in this land of plenty. There is little freedom to disagree with the determinations of the authorities. There is large-scale unemployment because of the drought and the recession that has hit most of the world's economy. And it is at such a time that the authorities have increased the prices of various foodstuffs and also of rents in black townships—measures designed to hit hardest those least able to afford the additional costs. It is not surprising that all this has exacerbated[11] an already tense and volatile situation.

So the unrest is continuing, in a kind of war of attrition, with the casualties not being large enough at any one time to shock the world sufficiently for it to want to take action against the system that is the root cause of all this agony. We have warned consistently that unrest will be endemic in South Africa until its root cause is removed. And the root cause is apartheid—a vicious, immoral and totally evil, and unchristian system. . . . **D**

C ANALYZE A SPEECH
Reread lines 83–89. What is the effect of Tutu's choice of the words *lackeys* and *stooges*?

D ANALYZE A SPEECH
What is the **tone** of this paragraph? What words and details communicate this tone?

---

8. **wards** *n. pl.:* children who have been placed in the care of others because their parents are dead or incapable of caring for them.

9. **lackeys** *n. pl.:* submissive followers.

10. **dispensation** *n.:* a release from a rule or requirement.

11. **exacerbated** *v.:* made worse.

DIFFERENTIATED INSTRUCTION

FOR ADVANCED LEARNERS/PRE-AP

Compare and Contrast Have students build a two-column chart based on this selection. In the first column, have students list Tutu's descriptions of South Africa as it could be. In the second column, have them list how South Africa is. Then have students identify words and phrases that set the tone and voice of the speech. Discuss why particular words are more powerful than their synonyms.

BEST PRACTICES TOOLKIT—Transparency
Two-Column Chart p. A57

FOR STRUGGLING READERS

Develop Reading Fluency Read aloud lines 121–131 to model the cadence and flow of the syntax and diction. Ask students to identify powerful elements of persuasive speech in the lines. Then have them read the lines aloud as they believe Desmond Tutu would have. Read lines 121–131 aloud again, with students echoing your reading.

R RESOURCE MANAGER—Copy Master
Reading Fluency, p. 162

Comprehension

1. **Recall** Why has Desmond Tutu won the Nobel Prize?

2. **Recall** Why are black students boycotting school? What has happened because of the boycott?

3. **Clarify** How do reactions to the Nobel Prize Committee's award to Tutu illustrate the divisions in South African Society?

4. **Summarize** What examples does Tutu give to show that his nation is divided?

Text Analysis

1. **Analyze Speeches** Review the elements of a speech in the chart you created as you read. Choose an example of each element, and explain how it helps make the speech effective.

2. **Compare Texts** What similarities and differences do you see between South Africa as described by Desmond Tutu and the setting of "A Chip of Glass Ruby"? Explain your response using evidence from the texts.

Read for Information: Diction and Syntax

WRITING PROMPT

A writer's or speaker's effective use of language is essential to a work's success. How do diction and syntax contribute to Nadine Gordimer's "A Chip of Glass Ruby" and Desmond Tutu's "The Question of South Africa"? Cite evidence from both works in your response.

To answer this prompt, you will need to draw conclusions based on both texts. Use the following steps.

1. Reread "A Chip of Glass Ruby," looking for examples of diction and syntax that contribute to the story. Look especially for words with very strong connotations or sentences that slow down or speed up your rate of reading.

2. Review the chart you created as you read "The Question of South Africa." Find examples of diction and syntax you have noted.

3. Draw conclusions about the effect of diction and syntax on each text. Select 2–3 examples to use as evidence from each text.

4. Organize your response. Discuss one text first, then the other. Or you can discuss diction in both texts first, then syntax in both texts second.

5. As you compose your response, support your statements about the effects of diction and syntax with direct quotations from the texts. After presenting evidence, explain how it supports your statements.

COMMON CORE

RI 4 Determine the figurative and connotative meanings of words and phrases as they are used in a text; analyze the cumulative impact of specific word choices on meaning and tone. **RI 6** Determine an author's point of view or purpose in a text and analyze how an author uses rhetoric to advance that point of view or purpose. **W 2** Write explanatory texts to examine and convey complex ideas, concepts, and information clearly and accurately through the effective analysis of content. **W 9b (RI 6)** Draw evidence from informational texts to support analysis.

Read for Information

Suggest that students look particularly at the dialogue and vocalized thoughts of characters in "A Chip of Glass Ruby."

• Remind students to consider the reason the author of each selection chose particular words. Why is the word chosen more powerful than possible synonyms?

• Encourage students to read aloud phrases, particularly in the speech, to enable them to feel the flow that the author has built with the words.

• Remind students to think about the emotional impact created by particular words.

Practice and Apply

ANSWERS

Comprehension

1. *As head of the Anglican Church in segregated South Africa, Tutu worked for an end to apartheid and creation of a just government in his country.*

2. *The students want to point out to the world that blacks in South Africa receive an inferior education that is designed to keep them in inferior positions.*

3. *The black community celebrated while the white community belittled the accomplishment.*

4. *Examples Tutu gives to show his nation is divided include the divided reaction to his receipt of the Nobel Peace Prize, the police murder of a six-year-old child in his own yard, a white baby killed, perceived collaborators cruelly murdered, and student boycotts of their schools.*

Text Analysis
COMMON CORE RI 4, RI 6, W 2, W 9b

Possible answers:

1. *The final paragraph carries all the elements discussed. The syntax of the last phrase resonates in the head—"vicious, immoral and totally evil." Word choices such as* war *and* unrest *and* agony *bombard the hearer like bombs in battle. The tone of the author, in presenting the idea of war, is crying out for people to remember peace. The author's voice is a battle cry for freedom, and the imagery of war produces a vivid picture that contrasts with the world needing to be shocked enough to "take action."*

2. *Both readings provide a clear sense of the lack of freedom, the poverty, and the resentment against those who corroborate with an evil system. One example is the scene in "A Chip of Glass Ruby" when the police arrest Mrs. Bamjee. Part of Mr. Bamjee's anger was fueled by the realization that his wife was going to prison to help the very people who were arresting her (lines 129–131). Desmond Tutu points out the cruel murder of those "identified as collaborators with a system that oppresses them" (lines 78–80).*

Practice and Apply

COMMON CORE FOCUS

RI 7 Analyze various accounts of a subject told in different mediums, determining which details are emphasized in each account.

What's the Connection?

"A Chip of Glass Ruby" introduces the struggle for racial equality in South Africa. The action of the story never moves beyond Mrs. Bamjee's home, but the struggle outside invades even there. Excerpts from a speech by Desmond Tutu, "The Question of South Africa," skillfully picture a land torn apart by inequality and injustice. This poster, "Stop Apartheid Now" illustrates the deep divide described in the other two selections.

Poster

The poster below is from the apartheid era. It was created by Trócaire, an international relief and development agency of the Catholic Church in Ireland. Notice how the image and the words in this visual work together to convey meaning. Respond to the questions below, citing evidence from the visual to support your answers.

COMMON CORE

RI 7 Analyze various accounts of a subject told in different mediums.

STOP APARTHEID NOW!

 TRÓCAIRE The Catholic Agency for World Development 169 Booterstown Avenue, Co. Dublin. Phone: (01) 885385

1. INTERPRET
What is happening in this poster? What does the image represent? What purpose does it help the artist to achieve?

2. ANALYZE
What is the connection between the text in this poster and what the woman is doing?

ANALYZE VISUALS

COMMON CORE
RI 7

1. INTERPRET

Possible answer: The woman is standing up to oppression. She represents the anti-apartheid movement, and the tank represents apartheid. The purpose is to show that although apartheid may be bigger and stronger, people should still stand up to it.

ANALYZE VISUALS

COMMON CORE
RI 7

2. ANALYZE

Possible answer: The words say to "Stop Apartheid Now!" and the woman is stopping the tank.

Assessment Practice: Short Constructed Response

LITERARY TEXT: "A CHIP OF GLASS RUBY"

The title of a story is often a clue to its theme. When an assessment question asks about a story's title, it is often asking you to show the connection between a story's title and its theme. Use the **short constructed response question** below to practice this necessary skill.

> Why is "A Chip of Glass Ruby" a good title for the story? Support your answer with evidence from the story.

◀ **STRATEGIES IN ACTION**

1. Examine the title. Does it refer to a person, place, thing, event, or idea?
2. Reread the story, looking for **words** or **details** that relate to the **title**.
3. Consider the **themes** expressed in the story. Choose one that relates to the story's title.
4. Use **evidence** from the story in your response.

NONFICTION TEXT: "THE QUESTION OF SOUTH AFRICA"

The ability to make inferences based on the details of a text is a skill that all good readers possess. Practice this skill by answering the **short constructed response question** below.

> Why did the police shoot the six-year-old boy? Support your answer with evidence from the text.

◀ **STRATEGIES IN ACTION**

1. Reread the description of the event.
2. Consider the event's **context**—how this **anecdote** supports the ideas around it.
3. Draw on your own **experience and knowledge** to **infer** details that are not specifically given in the text.
4. Make sure your inferences are based on **evidence** from the text.

COMPARING LITERARY AND NONFICTION TEXTS

Assessment questions often ask you to compare literary and nonfiction texts. Practice this valuable skill by answering the following **short constructed response question** about "A Chip of Glass Ruby" and "The Question of South Africa."

> What is one characteristic shared by Mrs. Bamjee in "A Chip of Glass Ruby" and Desmond Tutu? Support your answer with evidence from the text.

◀ **STRATEGIES IN ACTION**

1. Skim both texts to refresh your memory about each person's **characteristics**.
2. Because the question asks only for **shared** characteristics, note only **similarities**.
3. Choose one characteristic that stands out for both people.
4. Use **evidence** from both texts to support your answer.

Assessment Practice: Short Constructed Response

LITERARY TEXT: "A CHIP OF GLASS RUBY"
Possible answer: *The chip of glass ruby refers to an outdated adornment from Mrs. Bamjee's childhood. Although she had abandoned this as too old-fashioned, she still considered herself a proper Muslim woman. Yet in spite of this, she was a mover and a shaker, housing a duplicating machine on her sideboard and turning out leaflets long after her husband had retired for the night.*

NONFICTION TEXT: "THE QUESTION OF SOUTH AFRICA" **Possible answer:** *The boy was shot and killed because the police were chasing black schoolchildren and the boy happened to be playing outside. The police probably explained that it was a case of mistaken identity. The boy was an innocent bystander in the wrong place at the wrong time.*

COMPARING LITERARY AND NONFICTION TEXTS **Possible answer:** *Both Mrs. Bamjee and Desmond Tutu believe in equality and both believe that it can become a reality. If Mrs. Bamjee did not believe this, she would not have been involved in the struggle for black equality, she would not have had a duplicating machine in her home, she would not have spent her time printing pamphlets. Desmond Tutu, in his speech, argues passionately for peace and justice. He wants the world to see what is happening so that the world will be shocked enough to take action and end apartheid.*

DIFFERENTIATED INSTRUCTION

FOR STRUGGLING WRITERS
Using the Elements of Writing Have students review **Standards Focus: Analyze a Speech** on page 710. Then remind students that the elements of syntax, diction, tone, voice, and imagery can become part of their own writing.

Have students develop a short descriptive paragraph based on a single statement, such as "The wind is blowing." Prompt students to think about the elements of language before they begin writing by asking: What kind of wind is blowing? Is it a gentle breeze, a strong wind, or a howling gale? What adjectives and sensory details best describe the wind? Why is one word better than another? What words express their feelings about the wind? Encourge students to include adjectives that appeal to the senses.

Focus and Motivate

⬡ COMMON CORE FOCUS

RL 1 Cite textual evidence to support analysis of what the text says explicitly as well as inferences drawn from the text. **RL 2** Determine a central idea of a text. **RL 4** Determine the meaning of words and phrases as they are used in a text. **RL 7** Analyze the representation of a subject in two different mediums, including what is emphasized or absent in each treatment. **W 9b (RI 7)** Draw evidence from literary or informational texts to support analysis; analyze various accounts of a subject told in different mediums. **L 5** Demonstrate an understanding of word relationships.

SUMMARIES

"How Much Land Does a Man Need?" Overhearing a peasant named Pakhom wish for "enough" land, the Devil decides to tempt him. After Pakhom aquires much land, the Bashkir people agree to sell all the land that he can mark off in a day. Pakhom dies trying to claim as much land as possible.

from **The New Testament** In this scriptural writing, Paul urges readers to be content and to avoid greed. He exhorts the rich to put God first and to use wealth to help others.

How important is WEALTH?

Pose the question, and then have students complete the *DISCUSS* activity.

Selection Resources

Comparing Across Genres

How Much Land Does a Man Need?
Allegory by Leo Tolstoy

HISTORY Video link at thinkcentral.com

from The New Testament
Scriptural Writing

How important is WEALTH?

⬡ **COMMON CORE**

RL 1 Cite textual evidence to support analysis of what the text says explicitly as well as inferences drawn from the text. **RL 4** Determine the meaning of words and phrases as they are used in a text. **RL 7** Analyze the representation of a subject in two different mediums, including what is emphasized or absent in each treatment.

We all need a certain amount of money just to survive. But many people strive to achieve more than a basic level of comfort, and some can't be satisfied unless they are rich. The two selections you will read address the dangers of pursuing wealth.

DISCUSS Think of three activities that make you happy. Then discuss with a partner what role money plays in these activities. Consider whether you would find it easier or harder to pursue the activities if you were wealthy.

716

See resources on the **Teacher One Stop DVD-ROM** *and on* **thinkcentral.com**.

HISTORY Video link at thinkcentral.com

R RESOURCE MANAGER UNIT 6
Plan and Teach, pp. 165–172
Summary, pp. 173–174†‡*
Text Analysis and Reading
  Skill, pp. 175–179†*
Vocabulary, pp. 180–182*

DIAGNOSTIC AND SELECTION TESTS
Selection Tests, pp. 211–214

📖 BEST PRACTICES TOOLKIT
Definition Mapping, p. E6
Analysis Frame: Theme, pp.
  D21, D32
Predicting, p. A10
Sequence Chain, p. B21

TECHNOLOGY
- Teacher One Stop DVD-ROM
- Student One Stop DVD-ROM
- Audio Anthology CD
- GrammarNotes DVD-ROM
- ExamView Test Generator
  on the **Teacher One Stop**

* Resources for Differentiation   **†** Also in Spanish   **‡** In Haitian Creole and Vietnamese

TEXT ANALYSIS: DIDACTIC LITERATURE

The selections you are about to read are examples of **didactic literature**—literature intended mainly to instruct or to convey a moral message. This message is sometimes conveyed through the characters' actions when faced with a **moral dilemma,** or choice between two difficult moral options. As you read, try to determine the moral message of each selection by paying attention to the following literary techniques:

In the Short Story	In the Bible Excerpt
plot and foreshadowing	direct statements
character traits and motivation	figurative language
irony	word choice and tone

"How Much Land Does A Man Need" is also an **allegory**—a story that operates on both literal and symbolic levels. Various elements of the story, including people, places, and events, have both a literal and symbolic meaning. As you read, consider what the various elements symbolize and how the allegory achieves its function of conveying a moral message.

Review: **Suspense**

◼ READING STRATEGY: SET A PURPOSE FOR READING

When you **set a purpose** for reading, you identify specific goals to accomplish as you read. In this case, you'll be asked, after reading these selections, to write an essay in which you compare each selection's message. As you read, think about:

- the moral message of each selection
- similarities and differences in the two messages

Review: **Predict**

▲ VOCABULARY IN CONTEXT

To see how many words you already know, substitute a different word or phrase for each boldfaced term.

1. You should not praise people and then **disparage** them behind their backs.
2. The club meeting was friendly and free of **discord.**
3. I was so hungry that I could not **forbear** eating my lunch early.
4. He lay **prostrate** on the table during the doctor's exam.

 Complete the activities in your **Reader/Writer Notebook.**

Meet the Author

Leo Tolstoy
1828–1910

Rise to Fame
Leo Tolstoy was born into an aristocratic Russian family. He became internationally famous for his novels *War and Peace* and *Anna Karenina,* which are among the finest ever written. However, shortly after *Anna Karenina* was published in 1877, Tolstoy suffered a profound spiritual crisis that led him to question whether his life and literary works had any meaning.

Tolstoy's New Faith
As a result of his crisis, Tolstoy began preaching a personal faith that emphasized love of humanity and rejection of traditional authority. Tolstoy worked among the poor and simplified his own life in the belief that material possessions—money or land—were not the answer to society's problems. He also became a pacifist and a vegetarian. Tolstoy's new outlook on life is reflected in his later fiction, including "How Much Land Does a Man Need?"

BACKGROUND TO THE SELECTION

The New Testament: Paul and His Letters
Paul the Apostle dedicated his life to promoting Christianity in parts of Asia and Europe during the first century A.D. His letters to followers, which make up a good portion of the New Testament, helped shape Christian beliefs. The passage you will read is from a letter traditionally thought to have been written by Paul to his disciple Timothy.

Author Online
THINK central
Go to **thinkcentral.com.**
KEYWORD: HML10-717

717

Teach

TEXT ANALYSIS — COMMON CORE RL 7

● Model the Skill: DIDACTIC LITERATURE

To model how to analyze didactic literature, mention a well-known and accessible allegory, such as one of Aesop's fables (for example, "The Ant and the Grasshopper" or "The Boy Who Cried Wolf"). Ask students to explain the function of the allegory. Recognizing the simple morals of such texts will help students understand the function of allegories in particular and of didactic literature in general.

GUIDED PRACTICE Ask students to give an example of didactic literature that they have read and to state the moral message it conveys.

R RESOURCE MANAGER—Copy Master
Didactic Literature p. 175 (for student use while reading the selection)

READING STRATEGY — COMMON CORE RL 1

◼ Model the Skill: SET A PURPOSE FOR READING

Discuss why people read movie reviews or newspaper editorials. Point out that people often read these articles to find out someone's opinion about something, such as a move or current events. That is their purpose for reading.

GUIDED PRACTICE Ask students to describe other things they have read and to share their reasons for reading that material.

COMMON CORE L 4

VOCABULARY SKILL

▲ VOCABULARY IN CONTEXT

DIAGNOSE WORD KNOWLEDGE Have all students complete Vocabulary in Context. Check their definitions against the following:

discord (dĭs'kôrd') *n.* disagreement; lack of harmony
disparage (dĭ-spăr'ĭj) *v.* to speak of in a negative or insulting way
forbear (fôr-bâr') *v.* to refrain from; resist
prostrate (prŏs'trāt') *adj.* lying in a flat, horizontal position

PRETEACH VOCABULARY Use the following copy master to help students predict the meaning of each boldfaced word.

R RESOURCE MANAGER—Copy Master
Vocabulary Study p. 180

1. Read the first sentence in Part A aloud, emphasizing *disparage.*
2. Point out the phrase "defended the peasant way of life." Elicit possible meanings for *disparage,* such as "to

criticize."

3. Repeat the procedure for items 2–4.

READ WITH A PURPOSE

Help students set a purpose for reading. Tell them to look for reasons why the Devil succeeded in getting Pakhom into his power.

Ⓐ DIDACTIC LITERATURE

Possible answer: *The younger sister knows that town life offers more wealth and luxury (lines 10–11), but she values a life that she describes as "free from anxiety" (line 10). She seems content in knowing that although she may never be rich, she will always have enough to eat (line 15).*

Extend the Discussion After listening to this speech, the older sister makes fun of the younger sister's values (lines 16–19). Why do you think that the older sister continues to press her point?

OWN THE WORD

disparage: Explain to students that Tolstoy uses *disparaged* in line 7 not only to be insulting but also to make light of the life of a tradesman. Have students compose sentences using *disparage*.

How Much Land Does a Man Need?

Leo Tolstoy

~ I ~

An elder sister came to visit her younger sister in the country. The elder was married to a tradesman in town, the younger to a peasant in the village. As the sisters sat over their tea talking, the elder began to boast of the advantages of town life: saying how comfortably they lived there, how well they dressed, what fine clothes her children wore, what good things they ate and drank, and how she went to the theater, promenades, and entertainments.

The younger sister was piqued, and in turn **disparaged** the life of a tradesman, and stood up for that of a peasant.

"I would not change my way of life for yours," said she. "We may live
10 roughly, but at least we are free from anxiety. You live in better style than we do, but though you often earn more than you need, you are very likely to lose all you have. You know the proverb, 'Loss and gain are brothers twain.'[1] It often happens that people who are wealthy one day are begging their bread the next. Our way is safer. Though a peasant's life is not a fat one, it is a long one. We shall never grow rich, but we shall always have enough to eat." Ⓐ

The elder sister said sneeringly:

"Enough? Yes, if you like to share with the pigs and the calves! What do you know of elegance or manners! However much your goodman may slave, you will die as you are living—on a dung heap—and your children the same."

---

1. **twain:** two.

Analyze Visuals ▶

Describe the **setting** and the way of life depicted in this image.

disparage (dĭ-spăr'ĭj) *v.* to speak of in a negative or insulting way

Ⓐ **DIDACTIC LITERATURE**
What values does the younger sister express in her speech? Cite specific words and phrases.

Late Night Guest (2002), A. Kurzov. Tradestone Gallery.

DIFFERENTIATED INSTRUCTION

FOR ENGLISH LANGUAGE LEARNERS

Vocabulary Support Use Definition Mapping to teach these words: *consented* (line 65), *obtained* (line 162), *documents* (line 162), *distributed* (line 245), *assemble* (line 313), *perceived* (line 407).

🧰 **BEST PRACTICES TOOLKIT—Transparency**
Definition Mapping p. E6

FOR ENGLISH LANGUAGE LEARNERS

Media and Language Have students work with proficient English speakers to record themselves as they read aloud the first paragraph of this story. Then, have them listen to their recordings and identify any words they do not know or that they found difficult to pronounce. By listening to their recordings and discussing unknown or difficult words, students will build and reinforce their understanding of difficult vocabulary.

BACKGROUND

Russian Peasants Until 1861, Russian peasants were serfs—tenant farmers who cultivated a plot of land that was owned by a lord. The Emancipation Manifesto of 1861 abolished serfdom, granting serfs personal freedoms and promising them land. However, freed serfs had to redeem their land through government loans and then make redemption payments for 49 years. Most peasants remained poor as they struggled to pay back their loans.

Land Ownership After emancipation, the land the peasants redeemed was jointly owned and controlled by a village commune, called a *mir*. The mir was responsible for allocating land to individual households and making communal redemption payments. Yet most villages did not receive enough land to support all their peasants, particularly as the Russian population grew dramatically in the late 19th century. While some peasants, like Pakhom, managed to achieve private land ownership, most did not.

Cultural Connection Attitudes toward land ownership have varied from culture to culture. For example, villages made a yearly allotment of land to individuals in early European society, even before feudalism. Pre-Columbian Native Americans would have found private ownership of land an alien concept: land was used by each group or nation for the benefit of all. Invite students to share their opinions about land ownership.

Analyze Visuals

Possible answer: The setting is rural, and the man and woman look like peasants who follow traditional roles and customs (seen in her offering food to him).

About the Art *Late Night Guest*, by contemporary Russian artist A. Kurzov, is painted on the lid of a lacquer box. Russian lacquer boxes are a unique form of miniature art. The painting style varies from region to region, but the overall technique is similar. It begins with painting a base coat on a papier-mâché box (which itself may take six to eight weeks to make). Then the artist applies a coat of lacquer, then layers of paint, then additional coats of lacquer. Lacquer-box paintings often depict fairy tales, poems, landscapes, battles, famous paintings, or scenes of country life, as in this example.

FOR ADVANCED LEARNERS/PRE–AP

Analyze Theme [small-group option] Point out to students that Tolstoy delivers several powerful messages about human beings in his story. Have students explore his messages by answering the questions in Analysis Frame: Theme.

BEST PRACTICES TOOLKIT—Transparency
Analysis Frame: Theme pp. D21, D32

Direct students to lines 20–38. Use these prompts to introduce students to Pakhom and his imminent struggle:

Connect Have you or someone you know wished for more than you had? Does that help you understand Pakhom's feelings? *Accept all reasonable responses.*

Analyze Why is the Devil happy about Pakhom's boast? *Possible answer: The Devil is happy about Pakhom's boast because it reveals both his pride and his weakness. Pakhom's pride is his belief that he is immune to the temptations that ensnare townspeople, and that he would not fear the Devil himself if only he had enough land (lines 29–30). Pakhom's weakness is his desire for land. The Devil now knows how to get Pakhom into his power because he knows exactly what temptation to use.*

Evaluate Do you think the Devil's plan will work? Why or why not? *Possible answer: Most likely the plan will work. Pakhom is poor and dissatisfied with what he has. If the Devil gives him land, Pakhom will probably want still more. The Devil knows human nature and is right to predict that Pakhom will respond to his temptation.*

---

20   "Well, what of that?" replied the younger. "Of course our work is rough and coarse. But, on the other hand, it is sure, and we need not bow to any one. But you, in your towns, are surrounded by temptations; today all may be right, but tomorrow the Evil One may tempt your husband with cards, wine, or women, and all will go to ruin. Don't such things happen often enough?"

  Pakhom, the master of the house, was lying on the top of the stove[2] and he listened to the women's chatter.

  "It is perfectly true," thought he. "Busy as we are from childhood tilling[3] mother earth, we peasants have no time to let any nonsense settle in our heads. Our only trouble is that we haven't land enough. If I had plenty of land, I 30 shouldn't fear the Devil himself!"

  The women finished their tea, chatted a while about dress, and then cleared away the tea-things and lay down to sleep.

  But the Devil had been sitting behind the stove, and had heard all that was said. He was pleased that the peasant's wife had led her husband into boasting, and that he had said that if he had plenty of land he would not fear the Devil himself.

  "All right," thought the Devil. "We will have a tussle. I'll give you land enough; and by means of that land I will get you into my power."

① Targeted Passage

∼ II ∼

C lose to the village there lived a lady, a small landowner who had an 40 estate of about three hundred acres. She had always lived on good terms with the peasants until she engaged as her steward[4] an old soldier, who took to burdening the people with fines. However careful Pakhom tried to be, it happened again and again that now a horse of his got among the lady's oats, now a cow strayed into her garden, now his calves found their way into her meadows—and he always had to pay a fine.

  Pakhom paid up, but grumbled, and going home in a temper, was rough with his family. All through that summer, Pakhom had much trouble because of this steward, and he was even glad when winter came and the cattle had to be stabled. Though he grudged the fodder[5] when they could no longer graze 50 on the pasture-land, at least he was free from anxiety about them.

  In the winter the news got about that the lady was going to sell her land and that the keeper of the inn on the high road was bargaining for it. When the peasants heard this they were very much alarmed.

---

2. **Pakhom** (på-kōm′) . . . **lying on the top of the stove:** The stoves and ovens in Russian peasant homes had large tops that were often used for sleeping because they provided extra warmth.

3. **tilling:** plowing land to prepare it for planting.

4. **steward:** a person in charge of the household affairs of a large estate.

5. **fodder:** food for livestock, such as hay or straw.

DIFFERENTIATED INSTRUCTION

FOR STRUGGLING READERS

In combination with the *Audio Anthology CD*, use one or more Targeted Passages (pp. 720, 725, 729, 732, 733) to ensure that students focus on key story events, concepts, and skills. Targeted Passages are also good for English learners.

① Targeted Passage [Lines 20–38]

In this passage, students learn that Pakhom is not satisfied with what he has, which the Devil takes as a dare to tempt Pakhom.

- Why does the younger sister think country life is better than life in town? (lines 21–24)
- What does Pakhom think is the trouble with their country life? (line 29)
- What does he think having plenty of land will protect him from? (lines 20–21, 27–30)
- How does the Devil feel when he overhears Pakhom's thoughts? What does he plan to do? (lines 34–38)

"Well," thought they, "if the innkeeper gets the land, he will worry us with fines worse than the lady's steward. We all depend on that estate."

So the peasants went on behalf of their commune,[6] and asked the lady not to sell the land to the innkeeper, offering her a better price for it themselves. The lady agreed to let them have it. Then the peasants tried to arrange for the commune to buy the whole estate, so that it might be held by them all in 60 common. They met twice to discuss it, but could not settle the matter; the Evil One sowed **discord** among them and they could not agree. So they decided to buy the land individually, each according to his means; and the lady agreed to this plan as she had to the other.

Presently Pakhom heard that a neighbor of his was buying fifty acres, and that the lady had consented to accept one half in cash and to wait a year for the other half. Pakhom felt envious.

"Look at that," thought he, "the land is all being sold, and I shall get none of it." So he spoke to his wife.

"Other people are buying," said he, "and we must also buy twenty acres 70 or so. Life is becoming impossible. That steward is simply crushing us with his fines."

So they put their heads together and considered how they could manage to buy it. They had one hundred rubles[7] laid by. They sold a colt and one half of their bees, hired out one of their sons as a laborer and took his wages in advance; borrowed the rest from a brother-in-law, and so scraped together half the purchase money.

Having done this, Pakhom chose out a farm of forty acres, some of it wooded, and went to the lady to bargain for it. They came to an agreement, and he shook hands with her upon it and paid her a deposit in advance. Then 80 they went to town and signed the deeds; he paying half the price down, and undertaking to pay the remainder within two years.

So now Pakhom had land of his own. He borrowed seed, and sowed it on the land he had bought. The harvest was a good one, and within a year he had managed to pay off his debts both to the lady and to his brother-in-law. So he became a landowner, plowing and sowing his own land, making hay on his own land, cutting his own trees, and feeding his cattle on his own pasture. When he went out to plow his fields, or to look at his growing corn, or at his grass-meadows, his heart would fill with joy. The grass that grew and the flowers that bloomed there seemed to him unlike any that grew elsewhere. 90 Formerly, when he had passed by that land, it had appeared the same as any other land, but now it seemed quite different. **B**

discord (dĭs'kôrd') *n.* disagreement; lack of harmony

B PREDICT
Will Pakhom remain content with the land that he has purchased? Why or why not?

---

6. **commune:** in late 19th-century Russia, a local organization of peasants that held land in common for its members. A peasant could also own land individually while still belonging to the commune.

7. **rubles** (rōō'bəlz): The ruble is the basic monetary unit of Russia.

REVISIT THE BIG QUESTION
How important is
WEALTH?

Discuss Based on lines 56–71, does jealousy lead to a desire for wealth, or does the desire for wealth lead to jealousy? Explain your interpretation. *Possible answer: The passage suggests that jealousy makes people want wealth (valuable possessions such as land) that they might not otherwise have wanted. Pakhom seems content to let the commune buy the lady's land until some villagers approach her on their own. Then he becomes jealous and wants to buy a farm for himself. However, the passage also suggests that Pakhom becomes envious of his neighbor precisely because the man is buying land (lines 64–66). So perhaps it is the desire for wealth that leads to Pakhom's jealousy rather than jealousy that leads to his desire for wealth.*

READING STRATEGY: *Review*  COMMON CORE RL 1

B PREDICT

Possible answer: Pakhom will most likely not remain content with the land. He has already shown signs of wanting what others have (lines 64–71). In addition, he enjoys being a landowner (lines 90–91). Furthermore, the Devil wants control over him (lines 37–38); for that to happen, the Devil will probably tempt Pakhom with more land.

IF STUDENTS NEED HELP . . . Direct their attention to lines 33–38 and 64–71. Use a Predicting chart to discuss clues that indicate Pakhom's lack of contentment with the land that he has.

 BEST PRACTICES TOOLKIT—Transparency Predicting p. A10

FOR ENGLISH LANGUAGE LEARNERS

Language Coach COMMON CORE RL 4

Homophones *Answer: Students should be able to use the context clue that Pakhom is sowing seed to figure out that* sowed *means "planted."* Brainstorm with students to identify other homophones, and have each student use a pair of homophones correctly in one or two sentences. Give students an example or two to get them started, such as heard/herd and buy/by.

FOR ADVANCED LEARNERS/PRE–AP

Research Communes [paired-activity option] Have students reread lines 56–63, footnote 6, and the Background on page 719. Then ask students to locate and share more information in answer to these questions:

• Historically, why have people formed communes?

• Where do communes exist today? Why were they formed?

• What appear to be the benefits and drawbacks to communes?

VOCABULARY COMMON CORE L 4

OWN THE WORD

discord: Have students complete the following sentence to demonstrate their understanding of *discord*. There was *discord* among the committee members because. . . .

So Pakhom was well-contented, and everything would have been right if the neighboring peasants would only not have trespassed on his corn-fields and meadows. He appealed to them most civilly, but they still went on: now the communal herdsmen would let the village cows stray into his meadows, then horses from the night pasture would get among his corn. Pakhom turned them out again and again, and forgave their owners, and for a long time he **forbore** to prosecute any one. But at last he lost patience and complained to the district court. He knew it was the peasants' want of land,
100 and no evil intent on their part, that caused the trouble, but he thought:
   "I cannot go on overlooking it or they will destroy all I have. They must be taught a lesson."
   So he had them up, gave them one lesson, and then another, and two or three of the peasants were fined. After a time Pakhom's neighbors began to bear him a grudge for this, and would now and then let their cattle on to his land on purpose. One peasant even got into Pakhom's wood at night and cut down five young lime trees for their bark. Pakhom passing through the wood one day noticed something white. He came nearer and saw the stripped trunks lying on the ground, and close by stood the stumps where the trees had been.
110 Pakhom was furious.

forbear (fôr-bâr') *v.* to refrain from; resist

Woodland Scenery with Cows, Ivanchuk. 15.5
x 6.5 x 3.5 cm. Vika's Russia Direct.

722   UNIT 6: ARGUMENT AND PERSUASION

TIERED DISCUSSION PROMPTS

Direct students to lines 92–110. Use these prompts to help students explore the new relationship between Pakhom and his peasant neighbors:

Connect Would you have treated Pakhom as his neighbors did? Why or why not? *Accept all reasonable responses.*

Analyze Why do you think the peasants acted as they did? *Possible answer: The peasants might have wanted more land, and therefore they may have been jealous of Pakhom's prosperity. Then, when Pakhom fines them for trespassing, they grow angry and want revenge.*

Evaluate Has Pakhom changed for the better or for the worse? How can you tell? *Possible answer: Pakhom has changed for the worse. He acts just as the landowner's despised steward once did toward Pakhom and the other peasants (lines 39–45).*

Analyze Visuals

Activity Ask students how this scene matches Tolstoy's description of Pakhom's land. *Possible answer: The scene shows a meadow with cows grazing (lines 95–96).*

About the Art *Woodland Scenery with Cows*, by Ivanchuk, is another example of a miniature painting on a Russian lacquer box. (See page 719.)

DIFFERENTIATED INSTRUCTION

FOR STRUGGLING READERS

Concept Support As students read lines 92–102, point out that Pakhom turns against his neighbors only after his efforts to deal with them amicably have failed. Explain that a gradual change suits this didactic tale well: Since the story is meant to show the corrupting power of greed, a sudden change from contentment to avarice would be less believable—and thus a weaker moral lesson for the reader.

FOR ADVANCED LEARNERS/PRE–AP

Evaluate a Character's Decision Have students debate whether it really is Pakhom's responsibility to teach his peasant neighbors a lesson (lines 101–102). Have one group of students defend Pakhom by saying what might have happened to his land if he had not responded to his neighbors the way he did. Have another group of students criticize Pakhom by suggesting how he might have handled his problem more effectively.

"If he had only cut one here and there it would have been bad enough," thought Pakhom, "but the rascal has actually cut down a whole clump. If I could only find out who did this, I would pay him out."[8]

He racked his brains as to who it could be. Finally he decided: "It must be Simon—no one else could have done it." So he went to Simon's homestead to have a look round, but he found nothing, and only had an angry scene. However, he now felt more certain than ever that Simon had done it, and he lodged a complaint. Simon was summoned. The case was tried, and retried, and at the end of it all Simon was acquitted, there being no evidence against
120 him. Pakhom felt still more aggrieved, and let his anger loose upon the elder and the judges.

"You let thieves grease your palms,"[9] said he. "If you were honest folk yourselves you would not let a thief go free."

So Pakhom quarreled with the judges and with his neighbors. Threats to burn his building began to be uttered. So though Pakhom had more land, his place in the commune was much worse than before. **C**

About this time a rumor got about that many people were moving to new parts.

"There's no need for me to leave my land," thought Pakhom. "But some of
130 the others might leave our village and then there would be more room for us. I would take over their land myself and make my estate a bit bigger. I could then live more at ease. As it is, I am still too cramped to be comfortable."

One day Pakhom was sitting at home when a peasant, passing through the village, happened to call in. He was allowed to stay the night, and supper was given him. Pakhom had a talk with this peasant and asked him where he came from. The stranger answered that he came from beyond the Volga[10] where he had been working. One word led to another, and the man went on to say that many people were settling in those parts. He told how some people from his village had settled there. They had joined the commune, and had had twenty-
140 five acres per man granted them. The land was so good, he said, that the rye sown on it grew as high as a horse, and so thick that five cuts of a sickle made a sheaf. One peasant, he said, had brought nothing with him but his bare hands, and now he had six horses and two cows of his own.

Pakhom's heart kindled with desire. He thought:

"Why should I suffer in this narrow hole, if one can live so well elsewhere? I will sell my land and my homestead here, and with the money I will start afresh over there and get everything new. In this crowded place one is always having trouble. But I must first go and find out all about it myself."

---

8. **pay him out:** get even with him.

9. **grease your palms:** bribe you.

10. **Volga** (vŏl′gə): the longest river in Russia, flowing from north of Moscow to the Caspian Sea.

G **DIDACTIC LITERATURE**
Reread lines 101–126. What **message** about private ownership does Tolstoy convey through this description of Pakhom's encounters with his neighbors?

C *Model the Skill:* **DIDACTIC LITERATURE**

Read lines 92–102. Point out that Pakhom understands the reason for the intrusion on his land, but he is also beginning to understand the trials of land ownership. Have students add information about Pakhom's character traits to their Text Analysis charts.

Possible answer: Tolstoy's message about private ownership is that it produces conflict among neighbors because it leads to envy and suspicion.

TEXT ANALYSIS   **COMMON CORE** RL 7

REVISIT THE BIG QUESTION
How important is
WEALTH?

Discuss Based on lines 127–148, ask students how they can tell that Pakhom's wealth will never be quite enough for him? *Possible answer: At first, when Pakhom learns that others are moving to new parts, he says that he has no need to leave, although he may expand his estate when others leave (lines 129–131). However, when the visiting peasant tells him of better land beyond the Volga, "Pakhom's heart kindled with desire" (line 144). Suddenly he refers to his estate as "this narrow hole" (line 145) and feels that he is suffering. Once again envious of what others possess, Pakhom decides to leave his home and acquire some of that better land for himself. It is clear that Pakhom will never be satisfied with what he has as long as someone else has—or appears to have—more.*

FOR STRUGGLING READERS

Comprehension Support As students read about Pakhom's worsening relationships with his neighbors and the arrival of a visitor, clarify these points:

- Early in the story (lines 37–38), the Devil predicts that he will get a victory over Pakhom by using land as a temptation. Pakhom begins quarreling with his neighbors, and though he has more land than he had ever had, he is not getting along well with his

community (lines 124–125). He is protective of his land, and he wants more.

- The visitor says little about himself. He mentions that there is very good, free land beyond the Volga (lines 140–143). Could he be the Devil in disguise, tempting Pakhom?

Storm Is Coming V. V. Sindyukov. 7.5 x 6 x 4 cm. Vika's Russia Direct.

Analyze Visuals

Possible answer: *The countryside is beautiful—just as Pakhom considered his farm—but the cloudy sky and the dark shading on the sides of the painting suggest a foreboding mood that hints at trouble to come. This mood matches Pakhom's experiences on his new farm: He loves his farm but cannot enjoy it. He begins to view it as a "narrow hole" (line 145) in which he is suffering—because of the behavior of his neighbors and his own desire for more land.*

About the Art *Storm Is Coming*, by contemporary Russian artist V. V. Sindyukov, is another example of a lacquer-box painting (see page 719). The date "1889" suggests that it may be a copy of a 19th-century painting.

Towards summer he got ready and started. He went down the Volga on a
150 steamer to Samara,[11] then walked another three hundred miles on foot, and at last reached the place. It was just as the stranger had said. The peasants had plenty of land: every man had twenty-five acres of communal land given him for his use and any one who had money could buy, besides, at two shillings an acre as much good freehold[12] land as he wanted.

Having found out all he wished to know, Pakhom returned home as autumn came on, and began selling off his belongings. He sold his land at a profit, sold his homestead and all his cattle, and withdrew from membership of the commune. He only waited till the spring, and then started with his family for the new settlement.

▲ **Analyze Visuals**

How does the **mood** of this image relate to Pakhom's experiences on his new farm?

---

11. **Samara** (sə-mâr′ə): a city in western Russia on the Volga River.
12. **freehold:** land held for life with the right to pass it along to one's heirs.

DIFFERENTIATED INSTRUCTION

FOR ENGLISH LANGUAGE LEARNERS

Comprehension: Transitions Help students identify words signaling a transition—"towards summer," "then," and "at last"—in the first paragraph on page 724. Explain that these transitions indicate when something happened or the sequence in which events took place. Then ask small groups of students to find two or more paragraphs that contain at least three sequence words. Have groups write short summaries about some aspect of Tolstoy's story using two or three sequence words.

FOR ADVANCED LEARNERS/PRE–AP

Evaluate Character After students finish this part of the story, pose this question: *Is Pakhom simply greedy, or is he showing good business sense?* Have students write a short persuasive essay or speech in which they define and defend their view. Encourage students to share their essays or speeches and compare their arguments.

∼ IV ∼

160 As soon as Pakhom and his family reached their new abode, he applied for admission into the commune of a large village. He stood treat[13] to the elders and obtained the necessary documents. Five shares of communal land were given him for his own and his sons' use: that is to say—125 acres (not all together, but in different fields) besides the use of the communal pasture. Pakhom put up the buildings he needed, and bought cattle. Of the communal land alone he had three times as much as at his former home, and the land was good corn-land. He was ten times better off than he had been. He had plenty of arable[14] land and pasturage, and could keep as many head of cattle as he liked.

170 At first, in the bustle of building and settling down, Pakhom was pleased with it all, but when he got used to it he began to think that even here he had not enough land. The first year, he sowed wheat on his share of the communal land and had a good crop. He wanted to go on sowing wheat, but had not enough communal land for the purpose, and what he had already used was not available; for in those parts wheat is only sown on virgin soil or on fallow[15] land. It is sown for one or two years, and then the land lies fallow till it is again overgrown with prairie grass. There were many who wanted such land and there was not enough for all; so that people quarreled about it. Those who were better off wanted it for growing wheat, and those who were poor wanted it to let to dealers, so that they might raise money to pay their taxes.

180 Pakhom wanted to sow more wheat, so he rented land from a dealer for a year. He sowed much wheat and had a fine crop, but the land was too far from the village—the wheat had to be carted more than ten miles. After a time Pakhom noticed that some peasant-dealers were living on separate farms and were growing wealthy; and he thought:

"If I were to buy some freehold land and have a homestead on it, it would be a different thing altogether. Then it would all be nice and compact."

The question of buying freehold land recurred to him again and again.

He went on in the same way for three years, renting land and sowing wheat. The seasons turned out well and the crops were good, so that he began to lay
190 money by. He might have gone on living contentedly, but he grew tired of having to rent other people's land every year, and having to scramble for it. Wherever there was good land to be had, the peasants would rush for it and it was taken up at once, so that unless you were sharp about it you got none. It happened in the third year that he and a dealer together rented a piece of pasture land from some peasants; and they had already plowed it up, when there was some dispute and the peasants went to law about it, and things fell out so that the labor was all lost.

② **Targeted Passage**

---

13. **stood treat:** paid for the cost of drinks or entertainment.

14. **arable:** land suitable for farming.

15. **fallow:** land left unplowed and unseeded during a growing season, usually to restore its fertility.

HOW MUCH LAND DOES A MAN NEED? **725**

REVISIT THE BIG QUESTION

How important is
WEALTH?

Discuss Based on lines 165–171, how much more wealth does Pakhom have now? Is it enough for him? ***Possible answer:*** *Having been given 125 acres, Pakhom now has three times as much communal land as he did previously. Overall, he is "ten times better off" (line 167). However, Pakhom decides that he still does not have enough land (lines 170–171).*

FOR STRUGGLING READERS

② **Targeted Passage** [Lines 165–187]

This passage helps students consider how greed is taking hold of Pakhom's life.

- Why is Pakhom at first content with his five shares of communal land? (lines 165–168)

- Why does he decide that he needs more land? How does he initially solve that problem? (lines 171–174)

- How does Pakhom's new land compare with his old land? In what ways is he better off?

- How do the rich and poor villagers differ in what they want to do with their land? With which group would you place Pakhom, and why? (lines 177–179; 180)

- Why does the idea of buying freehold land appeal to Pakhom? How much does he think about this idea? (lines 185–187)

- Suppose that Pakhom winds up buying freehold land. Will that be "land enough" for him? Why or why not? (lines 185–187)

Direct students to lines 200–221. Use these prompts to help students explore Pakhom's character:

Connect Does Pakhom's continuing search for more and better land disturb you? Why or why not? *Accept all reasonable responses.*

Analyze What does Pakhom's handling of the peasant (lines 200–205) tell you about Pakhom? *Possible answer: Pakhom haggles to get the lowest price he can for the land, even though he knows that the peasant is having financial problems. Pakhom now has more of the landowner mentality than the peasant mentality. He is not sympathetic toward people who are in the situation that he once was in himself.*

Evaluate Earlier in the story, Pakhom said that if he owned his own land, he would be independent and have a life without unpleasantness (lines 198–199). Considering what happens when the trader arrives (lines 204–221), do you think Pakhom has judged himself correctly? Explain. *Possible answer: Pakhom has not judged himself correctly. With the trader's news about the Bashkirs' land, Pakhom's greed takes over again. He appears to be becoming more and more enslaved by his need for acquiring possessions. Considering the unpleasantness that his greed has already caused him, it seems unlikely that following through on the trader's report will make Pakhom's life more pleasant.*

"If it were my own land," thought Pakhom, "I should be independent, and there would not be all this unpleasantness."

200   So Pakhom began looking out for land which he could buy; and he came across a peasant who had bought thirteen hundred acres, but having got into difficulties was willing to sell again cheap. Pakhom bargained and haggled with him, and at last they settled the price at 1,500 rubles, part in cash and part to be paid later. They had all but clinched the matter when a passing dealer happened to stop at Pakhom's one day to get a feed for his horses. He drank tea with Pakhom and they had a talk. The dealer said that he was just returning from the land of the Bashkirs,[16] far away, where he had bought thirteen thousand acres of land, all for 1,000 rubles. Pakhom questioned him further, and the tradesman said:

210   "All one need do is to make friends with the chiefs. I gave away about one hundred rubles worth of silk robes and carpets, besides a case of tea, and I gave wine to those who would drink it; and I got the land for less than a penny an acre." And he showed Pakhom the title-deeds, saying:

"The land lies near a river, and the whole prairie is virgin soil."

Pakhom plied him with questions, and the tradesman said:

"There is more land there than you could cover if you walked a year, and it all belongs to the Bashkirs. They are as simple as sheep, and land can be got almost for nothing."

"There now," thought Pakhom, "with my one thousand rubles, why should
220   I get only thirteen hundred acres, and saddle myself with a debt besides? If I take it out there, I can get more than ten times as much for the money."

∼ V ∼

P akhom inquired how to get to the place, and as soon as the tradesman had left him, he prepared to go there himself. He left his wife to look after the homestead, and started on his journey taking his man with him. They stopped at a town on their way and bought a case of tea, some wine, and other presents, as the tradesman had advised. On and on they went until they had gone more than three hundred miles, and on the seventh day they came to a place where the Bashkirs had pitched their tents. It was all just as the tradesman had said. The people lived on the steppes,[17] by a river, in felt-
230   covered tents. They neither tilled the ground, nor ate bread. Their cattle and horses grazed in herds on the steppe. The colts were tethered behind the tents, and the mares were driven to them twice a day. The mares were milked, and from the milk kumiss[18] was made. It was the women who prepared kumiss, and they also made cheese. As far as the men were concerned, drinking kumiss

---

16. **Bashkirs:** a group of people of Asiatic origin who lived in southwestern Russia.

17. **steppes:** vast semi-arid, grass-covered plains.

18. **kumiss:** a liquor made from fermented mare's or camel's milk.

Language Coach

Synonyms Words with the same or nearly the same meaning are **synonyms**. Reread lines 202–204. Which pair of words in this sentence are synonyms? What other words in the sentence help you understand the pair's meaning?

DIFFERENTIATED INSTRUCTION

FOR ENGLISH LANGUAGE LEARNERS

Language Coach   COMMON CORE RL 4

Synonyms *Answer:* Bargained *and* haggled *are synonyms. The phrase "at last they settled the price" shows the result of "bargained and haggled," suggesting that both words mean "discussed the details of a transaction in order to get the best deal."* Ask students to suggest synonyms for *clinched* in line 204 and *plied* in line 215. *Possible answers: settled, sealed, closed, finalized; badgered, hounded*

FOR ADVANCED LEARNERS/PRE–AP

Research the Bashkirs [paired-activity option] Ask students to find out more about the Bashkirs, whom Pakhom meets in this new section of the story. Have students research the Bashkirs' origins, their way of life in 19th-century Russia, and the way they live today. Invite students to share their findings in a format of their own choosing, with frequent references to Tolstoy's story.

and tea, eating mutton, and playing on their pipes, was all they cared about. They were all stout and merry, and all the summer long they never thought of doing any work. They were quite ignorant, and knew no Russian, but were good-natured enough. **D**

240 As soon as they saw Pakhom, they came out of their tents and gathered round their visitor. An interpreter was found, and Pakhom told them he had come about some land. The Bashkirs seemed very glad; they took Pakhom and led him into one of the best tents, where they made him sit on some down cushions placed on a carpet, while they sat round him. They gave him some tea and kumiss, and had a sheep killed, and gave him mutton to eat. Pakhom took presents out of his cart and distributed them among the Bashkirs, and divided the tea amongst them. The Bashkirs were delighted. They talked a great deal among themselves, and then told the interpreter to translate.

"They wish to tell you," said the interpreter, "that they like you, and that it is our custom to do all we can to please a guest and to repay him for his gifts.
250 You have given us presents, now tell us which of the things we possess please you best, that we may present them to you."

"What pleases me best here," answered Pakhom, "is your land. Our land is crowded and the soil is exhausted; but you have plenty of land and it is good land. I never saw the like of it."

The interpreter translated. The Bashkirs talked among themselves for a while. Pakhom could not understand what they were saying, but saw that they were much amused and that they shouted and laughed. Then they were silent and looked at Pakhom while the interpreter said:

"They wish me to tell you that in return for your presents they will gladly
260 give you as much land as you want. You have only to point it out with your hand and it is yours."

The Bashkirs talked again for a while and began to dispute. Pakhom asked what they were disputing about, and the interpreter told him that some of them thought they ought to ask their chief about the land and not act in his absence, while others thought there was no need to wait for his return.

∼ VI ∼

While the Bashkirs were disputing, a man in a large fox-fur cap appeared on the scene. They all became silent and rose to their feet. The interpreter said, "This is our chief himself."

Pakhom immediately fetched the best dressing-gown and five pounds of tea,
270 and offered these to the chief. The chief accepted them, and seated himself in the place of honor. The Bashkirs at once began telling him something. The chief listened for a while, then made a sign with his head for them to be silent, and addressing himself to Pakhom, said in Russian:

D DIDACTIC LITERATURE
Note how the Bashkirs' way of life compares with that of Pakhom and the other Russian peasants. What lesson does this comparison help teach?

HOW MUCH LAND DOES A MAN NEED? **727**

TEXT ANALYSIS

COMMON CORE

RL 7

D DIDACTIC LITERATURE

Possible answer: *The Bashkirs feel that they have all that they need, and they contentedly enjoy life. Unlike Pakhom and the other Russian peasants, they are not greedy for land or other possessions. The Bashkirs are generous with what they have, and they sell their land for almost nothing. Their example teaches that one can be happy without constantly trying to gain wealth.*

FOR ADVANCED LEARNERS/PRE–AP

Hypothesize Have students read the Bashkirs' response to Pakhom's request for their land (lines 255–258). Ask students why they think the Bashkirs are laughing and if it bodes well for Pakhom. Then have them collaborate in small groups to write the conversation that they imagine the Bashkirs have among themselves. Have students act out or read aloud their writings.

Activity Invite suggestions about ways in which this painting parallels Tolstoy's characterization of the Bashkirs. *Possible answer: The three figures in the painting seem to be conferring about something, just as the Bashkirs "talked among themselves" (line 255) about Pakhom's request for land.*

Tashkent Dervishes Wearing Their Festive Clothes (1870), Vasilij Vasil'evic Verescagin. Oil on canvas. © The State Tretyakov Gallery, Moscow. Photo © Anatoly Sapronenkov/Superstock.

"Well, let it be so. Choose whatever piece of land you like; we have plenty of it."

"How can I take as much as I like?" thought Pakhom. "I must get a deed to make it secure, or else they may say, 'It is yours,' and afterwards may take it away again."

"Thank you for your kind words," he said aloud. "You have much land, 280 and I only want a little. But I should like to be sure which bit is mine. Could it not be measured and made over to me? Life and death are in God's hands. You good people give it to me, but your children might wish to take it away again."

"You are quite right," said the chief. "We will make it over to you."

"I heard that a dealer had been here," continued Pakhom, "and that you gave him a little land, too, and signed title-deeds to that effect. I should like to have it done in the same way."

The chief understood.

"Yes," replied he, "that can be done quite easily. We have a scribe, and we will go to town with you and have the deed properly sealed."

DIFFERENTIATED INSTRUCTION

FOR STRUGGLING READERS

Compare Accounts Point out these comments from Pakhom to the Bashkir chief: "You have much land, and I only want a little.... I heard that a dealer had been here ... and that you gave him a little land, too" (lines 279–280 and 284–285). Have students compare this account to the account in lines 204–221. Discuss why Pakhom tells the chief that he only wants a little land when the dealer told him there was a great expanse of land available.

FOR ENGLISH LANGUAGE LEARNERS

Vocabulary: Idioms and Sayings Point out the saying "Life and death are in God's hands" (line 281). Explain that people sometimes say, "It's in God's hands" when they feel that there is nothing they can do to change a situation. Help students find and define the proverbial sayings in lines 12 and 423. Then, if possible, have them share similar sayings in their home languages.

TIERED DISCUSSION PROMPTS

Direct students to lines 323–340. Use these prompts to help students explore Pakhom's dream:

Summarize What happens in Pakhom's dream? *Possible answer: Pakhom dreams that he sees someone laughing. At first he thinks that it is the Bashkir chief—but then he sees that it is the dealer who told him about the Bashkirs, then the peasant who told him about the land beyond the Volga, and then the Devil—laughing over Pakhom's corpse.*

Analyze Why is the Devil laughing? How does his laughter foreshadow what may happen the next day? *Possible answer: The Devil is laughing because he has succeeded at getting Pakhom into his power (lines 37–38). So far, he has managed to manipulate Pakhom's greed by appearing in the guise of the peasant and the dealer to tempt Pakhom with more and better land. His laughter now may foreshadow Pakhom's death the next day during the attempt to cover as much land as possible before sunset.*

Evaluate Should Pakhom spend more time thinking about the dream? Why or why not? *Possible answer: Pakhom should think more about the dream. If he did, he might realize that it is a warning that the Devil is tempting him with the promise of land.*

VOCABULARY   COMMON CORE
                                       L 4

OWN THE WORD

prostrate: Tell students that *prostrate* comes from the Latin *prosternere* meaning "throw down." Explain that *prostrate* is used to indicate submission, adoration, or extreme weakness and incapacitation.

---

here long?" he saw that it was not the dealer, but the peasant who had come up from the Volga, long ago, to Pakhom's old home. Then he saw that it was not the peasant either, but the Devil himself with hoofs and horns, sitting there and chuckling, and before him lay a man barefoot, **prostrate** on the ground, with only trousers and a shirt on. And Pakhom dreamt that he looked more attentively to see what sort of man it was that was lying there, and he saw that the man was dead, and that it was himself! He awoke horror-struck.

"What things one does dream," thought he.

Looking round he saw through the open door that the dawn was breaking.

340   "It's time to wake them up," thought he. "We ought to be starting."

He got up, roused his man (who was sleeping in his cart), bade him harness; and went to call the Bashkirs.

"It's time to go to the steppe to measure the land," he said.

The Bashkirs rose and assembled, and the chief came too. Then they began drinking kumiss again, and offered Pakhom some tea, but he would not wait.

"If we are to go, let us go. It is high time," said he.

> *prostrate* (prŏs′trāt′) *adj.* lying in a flat, horizontal position

∼ VIII ∼

The Bashkirs got ready and they all started: some mounted on horses, and some in carts. Pakhom drove in his own small cart with his servant and took a spade with him. When they reached the steppe, the morning red was
350   beginning to kindle. They ascended a hillock (called by the Bashkirs a *shikhan*[19]) and dismounting from their carts and their horses, gathered in one spot. The chief came up to Pakhom and stretching out his arm toward the plain:

"See," said he, "all this, as far as your eye can reach, is ours. You may have any part of it you like."

Pakhom's eyes glistened: it was all virgin soil, as flat as the palm of your hand, as black as the seed of a poppy, and in the hollows different kinds of grasses grew breast high.

The chief took off his fox-fur cap, placed it on the ground and said:

"This will be the mark. Start from here, and return here again. All the
360   land you go round shall be yours."

Pakhom took out his money and put it on the cap. Then he took off his outer coat, remaining in his sleeveless under-coat. He unfastened his girdle[20] and tied it tight below his stomach, put a little bag of bread into the breast of his coat, and tying a flask of water to his girdle, he drew up the tops of his boots, took the spade from his man, and stood ready to start. He considered for some moments which way he had better go—it was tempting everywhere.

"No matter," he concluded, "I will go towards the rising sun."

He turned his face to the east, stretched himself, and waited for the sun to appear above the rim.

---

19. *shikhan* (shĭ-kän′).

20. **girdle:** a belt or sash that fastens around the waist.

DIFFERENTIATED INSTRUCTION

FOR ENGLISH LANGUAGE LEARNERS

Language: Verb Tenses Remind students of the differences in past-tense forms of regular and irregular verbs, using these examples:

Regular verbs: dreamt (line 335; another form of *dreamed*), looked (line 335), roused (line 341), assembled (line 344), offered (line 345)

Irregular verbs: saw (line 331), lay (line 334), was (line 337), thought (line 338), went (line 342), came (line 344), began (line 344)

Language: Pronouns Remind students that the pronoun *one* means "a person" or "you." Point out these examples: "What things one does dream" (line 338) and "The further one goes, the better the land seems" (lines 389–390). Reread the examples with either *you* or *a person* to aid understanding. Ask students if they have this impersonal usage in their home languages. (For example, Spanish uses *uno* or the passive *se*, and French uses *on*.)

370 "I must lose no time," he thought, "and it is easier walking while it is still cool."

The sun's rays had hardly flashed above the horizon, before Pakhom, carrying the spade over his shoulder, went down into the steppe.

Pakhom started walking neither slowly nor quickly. After having gone a thousand yards he stopped, dug a hole, and placed pieces of turf one on another to make it more visible. Then he went on; and now that he had walked off his stiffness he quickened his pace. After a while he dug another hole.

Pakhom looked back. The hillock could be distinctly seen in the sunlight, with the people on it, and the glittering tires of the cart-wheels. At a rough
380 guess Pakhom concluded that he had walked three miles. It was growing warmer; he took off his under-coat, flung it across his shoulder, and went on again. It had grown quite warm now; he looked at the sun, it was time to think of breakfast.

"The first shift is done, but there are four in a day, and it is too soon yet to turn. But I will just take off my boots," said he to himself.

He sat down, took off his boots, stuck them into his girdle, and went on. It was easy walking now.

"I will go on for another three miles," thought he, "and then turn to the left. This spot is so fine, that it would be a pity to lose it. The further one goes,
390 the better the land seems."

Forest Road. A. Karapaev. 18 x 13.5 x 6.5. Vika's Russia Direct.

Analyze Visuals

Activity Discuss whether this miniature landscape painting matches the description of the Bashkirs' land in the story. *Possible answer: The painting shows a flat, grassy, sunny landscape that matches the description of the Bashkirs' land as being "flat as the palm of your hand," with tall grasses (lines 355–357). The painting's glistening light captures the story's emphasis on sunlight (lines 372, 378, and 382). The land in the painting also appears to be uncultivated, like the "virgin soil" (line 355) in the story. However, there is no mention of trees in the story's description of the Bashkirs' land.*

About the Art *Forest Road* is a lacquer-box painting (see page 719) by Yuriy Vasiliyevich Karapaev (b. 1936), an honored Russian artist. Karapaev studied at the Fedoskino Art School, and his works have been exhibited in Russia and abroad.

FOR STRUGGLING READERS

Comprehension Support Help students locate these clues that may foreshadow the ending of the story:

- Pakhom knows that it is difficult to walk in the sun, and the day grows warmer (lines 380–382) as he walks farther away from his starting point.

- Pakhom finds it more comfortable to walk barefoot (lines 385–387), making him resemble the dreamlike image of himself (line 334).

- Pakhom ignores the heat because he wants more land (lines 388–390).

Develop Reading Fluency Point out to students that the final sections can be read in a manner that reflects Pakhom's initial excitement and his gradual exhaustion. Read lines 368–369 aloud, in an eager, confident voice. Then model how to read lines 435–439 with breathless exhaustion. Have student pairs practice reading both sets of lines until they are able to read them fluently and with expression.

Direct students to lines 394–405. Use these prompts to help students recognize the beginning of Pakhom's demise:

Connect If you were Pakhom, would you keep on claiming more land? Why or why not? *Accept all reasonable responses.*

Analyze What does the statement "An hour to suffer, a life-time to live" (lines 404–405) mean? Why does Pakhom make this statement? *Possible answer: The statement means that suffering for a short time is worthwhile if you can enjoy life for a long time afterward. Pakhom makes the statement as a way of encouraging himself to keep going.*

Evaluate Do you think that Pakhom's statement will prove to be true in the story? Explain your answer. *Possible answer: The statement probably will prove untrue. Pakhom is in a dangerous situation, and he could cause himself to suffer beyond his ability to recover. He will suffer and perhaps even die because of heat exhaustion; as a result, he will not have "a life-time to live" at the end of his suffering.*

VOCABULARY

COMMON CORE RL 4

⚠ AFFIXES

Tell students that another affix that means "not" is the Latin prefix *non-*. When *non-* is added to the beginning of a word, it negates its meaning, just as adding *un-* does. For example, *nonsense* means "no sense." *Possible answers: unhappy, unpleasant, uncover, unbreakable, unremarkable, undefeated, undependable*

He went straight on for a while, and when he looked round, the hillock was scarcely visible and the people on it looked like black ants, and he could just see something glistening there in the sun.

"Ah," thought Pakhom, "I have gone far enough in this direction, it is time to turn. Besides I am in a regular sweat, and very thirsty."

He stopped, dug a large hole, and heaped up pieces of turf. Next he untied his flask, had a drink, and then turned sharply to the left. He went on and on; the grass was high, and it was very hot. ⚠

Pakhom began to grow tired: he looked at the sun and saw that it was noon.

400   "Well," he thought, "I must have a rest."

He sat down, and ate some bread and drank some water; but he did not lie down, thinking that if he did he might fall asleep. After sitting a little while, he went on again. At first he walked easily: the food had strengthened him; but it had become terribly hot and he felt sleepy, still he went on, thinking: "An hour to suffer, a life-time to live."

He went a long way in this direction also, and was about to turn to the left again, when he perceived a damp hollow: "It would be a pity to leave that out," he thought. "Flax²¹ would do well there." So he went on past the hollow, and dug a hole on the other side of it before he turned the corner. Pakhom

410   looked towards the hillock. The heat made the air hazy: it seemed to be quivering, and through the haze the people on the hillock could scarcely be seen.

"Ah!" thought Pakhom, "I have made the sides too long; I must make this one shorter." And he went along the third side, stepping faster. He looked at the sun: it was nearly half-way to the horizon, and he had not yet done two miles of the third side of the square. He was still ten miles from the goal.

"No," he thought, "though it will make my land lop-sided, I must hurry back in a straight line now. I might go too far, and as it is I have a great deal of land."

So Pakhom hurriedly dug a hole, and turned straight towards the hillock.

～ IX ～

420   **P**akhom went straight towards the hillock, but he now walked with difficulty. He was done up with the heat, his bare feet were cut and bruised, and his legs began to fail. He longed to rest, but it was impossible if he meant to get back before sunset. The sun waits for no man, and it was sinking lower and lower.

"Oh dear," he thought, "if only I have not blundered trying for too much! What if I am too late?"

He looked towards the hillock and at the sun. He was still far from his goal, and the sun was already near the rim.

---

21. **flax:** a plant grown for its seed and for its fine fibers.

COMMON CORE RL 4

⚠ AFFIXES

Affixes are parts that can be added at the beginning or end of a word to change its meaning. The prefix *un-* means "not," and is added to the beginning of words to negate their meaning, or turn them into their opposite. For example, when *un-* is added to *tied*, as in *untied* in line 396, it forms a word that is the opposite of *tied*. Make a list of other words that begin with *un-* that negate the meaning of the root word.

COMMON CORE RL 4

Language Coach

Etymology The **etymology**, or history, of *blundered* is linked to that of *blind*. *Blunder* comes from on Old Norse word *blunda*, meaning "to shut the eyes." How is *blundered* more effective in line 425 than a similar expression, "made a mistake"?

④ **Targeted Passage**

DIFFERENTIATED INSTRUCTION

FOR STRUGGLING READERS

④ **Targeted Passage** [Lines 420–428]

This passage focuses on Pakhom's physical and mental condition as the story approaches its climax.

- Physically, how does Pakhom feel? What details lead you to that answer? (lines 421–423)

- What does Pakhom long to do? What will happen to him if he gives in? (lines 422–423)

FOR ENGLISH LANGUAGE LEARNERS

Language Coach

COMMON CORE RL 4

Etymology *Possible answer: In addition to being more concise than "made a mistake,"* blundered *suggests Pakhom's "blindness" to his greed.* Ask students to look at line 437 and the word *bellows.* Have a student read the footnote. Ask students why saying "he was gasping for breath" would be less effective.

Pakhom walked on and on; it was very hard walking but he went quicker
430 and quicker. He pressed on, but was still far from the place. He began running, threw away his coat, his boots, his flask, and his cap, and kept only the spade which he used as a support.

"What shall I do?" he thought again, "I have grasped too much and ruined the whole affair. I can't get there before the sun sets."

And this fear made him still more breathless. Pakhom went on running, his soaking shirt and trousers stuck to him and his mouth was parched. His breast was working like a blacksmith's bellows,[22] his heart was beating like a hammer, and his legs were giving way as if they did not belong to him. Pakhom was seized with terror lest he should die of the strain.

440 Though afraid of death, he could not stop. "After having run all that way they will call me a fool if I stop now," thought he. And he ran on and on, and drew near and heard the Bashkirs yelling and shouting to him, and their cries inflamed his heart still more. He gathered his last strength and ran on.

The sun was close to the rim, and cloaked in mist looked large, and red as blood. Now, yes now, it was about to set! The sun was quite low, but he was also quite near his aim. Pakhom could already see the people on the hillock waving their arms to hurry him up. He could see the fox-fur cap on the ground and the money on it, and the chief sitting on the ground holding his sides. And Pakhom remembered his dream.

450 "There is plenty of land," thought he, "but will God let me live on it? I have lost my life, I have lost my life! I shall never reach that spot!" **G**

Pakhom looked at the sun, which had reached the earth: one side of it had already disappeared. With all his remaining strength he rushed on, bending his body forward so that his legs could hardly follow fast enough to keep him from falling. Just as he reached the hillock it suddenly grew dark. He looked up—the sun had already set! He gave a cry: "All my labor has been in vain," thought he, and was about to stop, but he heard the Bashkirs still shouting, and remembered that though to him, from below, the sun seemed to have set, they on the hillock could still see it. He took a long breath and ran up the
460 hillock. It was still light there. He reached the top and saw the cap. Before it sat the chief laughing and holding his sides. Again Pakhom remembered his dream, and he uttered a cry: his legs gave way beneath him, he fell forward and reached the cap with his hands.

"Ah, that's a fine fellow!" exclaimed the chief. "He has gained much land!"

Pakhom's servant came running up and tried to raise him, but he saw that blood was flowing from his mouth. Pakhom was dead!

The Bashkirs clicked their tongues to show their pity.

His servant picked up the spade and dug a grave long enough for Pakhom to lie in, and buried him in it. Six feet from his head to his heels was all he
470 needed. 〰 **H**

G SUSPENSE
How does Tolstoy create suspense in lines 429–451?

5 Targeted Passage

H DIDACTIC LITERATURE
Land plays an important role in this allegory. What is its literal meaning? What do you think its symbolic meaning is?

22. **bellows:** a device with a flexible chamber that can be expanded to draw air in and contracted to force air out.

FOR STRUGGLING READERS

5 Targeted Passage [Lines 452–470]
This concluding passage resolves the story and answers the question posed in the title.

- Why does Pakhom cry, "All my labor has been in vain"? (line 456)
- Do you think that Pakhom should have stopped running? How might the outcome of the story have been different if he had? (lines 456–457)
- According to the narrator, how much land did Pakhom really need? What does he mean? (lines 469–470)

FOR ENGLISH LANGUAGE LEARNERS
Culture: Connect Ask students to think of a story or fable in their home culture with a lesson or moral that is similar to the one in this story, such as the story of the magic fish. Have them write a brief summary of the story and then share it with the class. In a follow-up discussion, have students compare and contrast their shared stories with one another and with "How Much Land Does a Man Need?"

TEXT ANALYSIS: *Review*

G SUSPENSE

Possible answer: *Tolstoy creates suspense by presenting Pakhom's internal dialogue, which expresses first self-doubt (lines 433–434) and then desperation (lines 450–451). Tolstoy also creates suspense through the physical details he presents about Pakhom, such as his breathlessness, perspiration, parched mouth, pounding heart, and unsteady legs (lines 435–438). The suggestion that Pakhom might die (line 439) also adds to the suspense.*

TEXT ANALYSIS COMMON CORE
RL 7

H DIDACTIC LITERATURE

Answer: *The literal meaning of land is a place for Pakhom to grow his crops and graze his animals. Symbolically, it represents wealth.*

REVISIT THE BIG QUESTION
How important is
WEALTH?

Discuss Based on lines 464–466, what is ironic about Pakhom's successful acquisition of wealth? *Possible answer: Pakhom has acquired more wealth than he probably could have imagined at the beginning of the story, but now he cannot enjoy it. His greed has overtaken him, and he never will be able to enjoy what he thought would make him the happiest.*

How important is
WEALTH?

Discuss Based on lines 3–7, what does Paul say about wealth? ***Possible answer:*** *Paul says that desiring wealth is dangerous. People who do so fall into temptation and may abandon their faith.*

Analyze Visuals

Possible answer: The people's wealth is seen in their fancy clothing and in the fact that they are counting money.

About the Art *The Money Lender and His Wife* shows the tendency of Flemish artist Quentin Metsys (c. 1466–1530) to focus on people and personal expression. Metsys is considered the first important painter of the Antwerp school.

TEXT ANALYSIS   COMMON CORE

❶ DIDACTIC LITERATURE   RL 7

Possible answer: *The phrase, linked to "the future" (line 11), refers to the afterlife. Paul says that if the rich are generous, they will be blessed in the afterlife.*

SELECTION WRAP–UP

READ WITH A PURPOSE Now that students have finished reading the selections, have them explain how the morals in "How Much Land Does a Man Need?" and the Bible excerpt are similar. ***Possible answer:*** *Accept all thoughtful answers.*

⭐ **CRITIQUE** Ask students what they consider the most memorable passage in each selection and to explain their choices.

INDEPENDENT READING

Students may also enjoy reading Leo Tolstoy's classic *War and Peace,* set during Napoleon's invasion of Russia in 1812.

The Money Lender and his Wife (1514), Quentin Metsys. Louvre, Paris. Photo © Erich Lessing/ Art Resource, New York.

◀ **Analyze Visuals**
What details indicate that the people depicted in the painting are wealthy?

The New Testament

There is great gain in godliness with contentment; for we brought nothing into the world, and we cannot take anything out of the world; but if we have food and clothing, with these we shall be content. But those who desire to be rich fall into temptation, into a snare, into many senseless and hurtful desires that plunge men into ruin and destruction. For the love of money is the root of all evils; it is through this craving that some have wandered away from the faith and pierced their hearts with many pangs. . . .

As for the rich of this world, charge them not to be haughty, nor to set their hopes on uncertain riches but on God who richly furnishes us with everything
10 to enjoy. They are to do good, to be rich in good deeds, liberal and generous, thus laying up for themselves a good foundation for the future, so that they may take hold of the life which is life indeed. ∾ ❶

❶ **DIDACTIC LITERATURE**
Reread lines 8–12. How do you interpret the phrase "the life which is life indeed"?

DIFFERENTIATED INSTRUCTION

FOR ENGLISH LANGUAGE LEARNERS
Culture: Clarify Some students may be unfamiliar with the New Testament. Explain that it is the second part of the Christian Bible— the writings that Christians consider sacred texts. The first part of the Christian Bible is the Old Testament, which is similar to the Hebrew Bible, the sacred text of Judaism, but with certain structural differences. According to tradition, the New Testament was written by Jesus' apostles, including Paul (see **Background**, p. 717).

FOR ADVANCED LEARNERS/PRE–AP
Compare and Contrast Didactic Literature
Ask students to use print or online reference sources (such as a concordance) to find other passages from the Bible or other spiritual texts that talk about wealth. Do the quotations seem to agree with Paul's and Tolstoy's views of wealth? How do these passages add to the messages in these selections? Invite students to meet in small groups to share, interpret, and discuss their findings.

Practice and Apply

Comprehension

1. **Recall** In "How Much Land Does a Man Need?" what conflicts does Pakhom have after buying his first farm?

2. **Recall** Why does Pakhom want to buy land from the Bashkirs?

3. **Summarize** What happens to Pakhom at the end of the story?

○ **COMMON CORE**

RL 1 Cite textual evidence to support analysis of what the text says explicitly as well as inferences drawn from the text. **RL 7** Analyze the representation of a subject in two different mediums, including what is emphasized or absent in each treatment.

Text Analysis

● 4. **Interpret Didactic Literature** Explain the meaning of the statement from the New Testament that "money is the root of all evils."

5. **Analyze Moral Dilemmas** Compare and contrast the moral dilemmas faced by Pakhom in "How Much Land Does a Man Need" and the wife in "The Blue Stones." How does each respond to the moral dilemma?

6. **Analyze Allegory** In a sentence or two, summarize what you think is the story's **allegorical meaning**—the symbolic meaning behind the surface narrative. What does that additional level of meaning add to your appreciation of the story?

Comparing Across Genres

Now that you have read both selections, you can identify their subjects. The questions in the **Points of Analysis** chart will help you get started. If a point of comparison is not included in a selection, leave the box blank.

Points of Analysis	In the Short Story	In the Bible Excerpt
What problem is identified with the desire for wealth?		
What idea, if any, does the title emphasize?		
What images strike you as important?		
Write a sentence stating the message as you interpret it.		
Which literary techniques are most important in conveying the message?		

> **How important is WEALTH?**
> How can seeking wealth lead to problems?

For preliminary support of post-reading questions, use these copy masters:

R RESOURCE MANAGER—Copy Masters
Comparing Across Genres p. 177
Reading Check p. 184
Question Support p. 185

Additional selection questions are provided for teachers on page 169.

ANSWERS

Comprehension

1. *Pakhom has conflicts with neighboring peasants and with local judges.*

2. *Pakhom wants to buy land from the Bashkirs because it is excellent land but especially because they are practically giving it away.*

3. *Pakhom returns just in time to claim his land, only to die from exhaustion.*

Text Analysis

○ COMMON CORE RL 1, RL 7

Possible answers:

4. ● **COMMON CORE FOCUS** *Didactic Literature* Paul means that a host of problems can result from loving money. He mentions wandering away from the faith (lines 6–7 and 9) and grieving in one's heart (line 7) as two of those problems. He also implies that a lack of charity can result (line 10).

5. *Both Pakhom and his wife let their jealousy and desire overwhelm their need for the people in their lives, and even for their own health. Answers will vary, but most students will conclude they did not make the right decisions.*

6. *Answers will vary. Students should express that this allegory illustrates the fact that greed and the search for wealth can destroy a person.*

Comparing Across Genres

Possible answers:
Row 1: Short Story inability to be content (lines 66, 132, 144–148, 198–199, and 317–322); *Bible* evil behavior and a loss of faith (lines 3–7)

Row 2: Short Story What material possessions do you really need in order to be content with life? *Bible* No answer needed.

Row 3: Short Story Pakhom running uphill (lines 459–463); servant digging Pakhom's grave

(lines 468–469); *Bible* the piercing of hearts (line 7); taking hold of life (lines 11–12)

Row 4: Short Story Do not covet wealth or possessions, or they will destroy you; *Bible* Do not love wealth, or you will do evil and perhaps abandon your faith.

Row 5: Short Story cause and effect, outcome of plot, allegory; *Bible* direct statements

> **How important is WEALTH?**
> Students should support their answers with specific examples based on their experiences or from their reading.

Vocabulary in Context

▲ VOCABULARY PRACTICE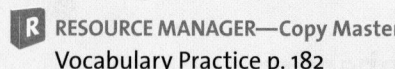

1. *compliment*
2. *discord*
3. *commence*
4. *vertical*

 **RESOURCE MANAGER—Copy Master**
Vocabulary Practice p. 182

ACADEMIC VOCABULARY IN WRITING

***Possible answer:** Pakhom is partly* convinced *by his wife's sister, who makes fun of the life of peasants. He also changes his* objectives *because he is influenced by the Devil.*

VOCABULARY STRATEGY: SIMILES AND METAPHORS

COMMON CORE L5

- Have students read each sentence and determine what two things are being compared.
- Ask students to look for the word *like* or *as* to see whether the sentence has a simile.

Possible answers:

1. *Metaphor; "discord" is compared to a "dark, ominous cloud."* Discord *means "discomfort" or "disagreement."*
2. *Simile; "I" is compared to a cranky alligator. When a person does not get sleep, that person could become very cranky.* Forbear *means "to abstain from."*
3. *Metaphor; "my heart" is compared to "shattered glass," which implies the person felt very bad or hurt.* Disparaged *means "spoke of in a negative way."*
4. *Simile; "the man" is being compared to "a rug on the floor," which usually lies flat.* Prostrate *means "down, in a flat position."*

 **RESOURCE MANAGER—Copy Master**
Vocabulary Strategy p. 182

Interactive Vocabulary **THINK central**

Keywords direct students to a **WordSharp** tutorial on **thinkcentral.com** or to other types of vocabulary practice and review.

Vocabulary in Context

▲ VOCABULARY PRACTICE

Identify the word that is not related in meaning to the other words in the set. If necessary, use a dictionary to look up the precise meanings of words you are unsure of.

1. disparage, compliment, belittle, insult
2. harmony, peace, discord, agreement
3. forbear, refrain, commence, withhold
4. vertical, prostrate, horizontal, flat

WORD LIST
discord
disparage
forbear
prostrate

ACADEMIC VOCABULARY IN WRITING

- cite - controversy - convince - objective - statistic

What **convinces** Pakhom to buy land? Write a paragraph in which you **cite** the reasons for his actions. Explain the results of his choices as well. Use at least one Academic Vocabulary word in your response.

VOCABULARY STRATEGY: SIMILES AND METAPHORS

A **simile** is a figure of speech that compares two things that are basically unlike each other but have something in common. In a simile, a word such as *like* or *as* signals the comparison. A **metaphor** is also a figure of speech that compares two things. However, unlike a simile, a metaphor does not use the words *like* or *as*. When an unfamiliar word appears in a sentence containing a simile or metaphor, you can often figure out its meaning by examining the comparison being made.

COMMON CORE

L5 Demonstrate an understanding of word relationships.

PRACTICE Explain what is being compared in each of the following sentences, and identify whether the figure of speech is a simile or a metaphor. Then decide what each comparison adds to your understanding of the boldfaced word.

1. The **discord** in the room was a dark, ominous cloud.
2. When I **forbear** sleeping, I'm as cranky as an alligator.
3. My heart was shattered glass after they **disparaged** me.
4. The man lay as **prostrate** as a rug on the floor.

Interactive Vocabulary THINK central
Go to **thinkcentral.com**.
KEYWORD: HML10-736

DIFFERENTIATED INSTRUCTION

FOR ENGLISH LANGUAGE LEARNERS

Vocabulary Strategy: Similes and Metaphors Ask small groups of students to find two similes and two metaphors in Tolstoy's story. Have groups write each simile and metaphor on an index card; then create a "class deck" with the cards. Have students take turns choosing a card, identifying whether the example is a simile or a metaphor, and explaining what is being compared.

FOR ADVANCED LEARNERS/PRE–AP

Vocabulary Strategy: Similes and Metaphors To extend the feature, have students create three similes and three metaphors that compare two things in Tolstoy's story. For example, students might compare the Devil to something, Pakhom's feelings or actions to something, features of the desired land to something, the Bashkirs to something, and so on. Call on volunteers to share their original figures of speech.

Writing for Assessment

COMMON CORE

RL 1, RL 2, W 9 (RI 7)

1. READ THE PROMPT

In writing assessments, you will often be asked to compare and contrast works that have a similar subject, such as the two selections you have just read. You are now going to practice writing an essay that involves this type of comparison.

The desire for wealth raises moral issues in many cultures. Consider how this subject is addressed in "How Much Land Does a Man Need?" and in the passage from the New Testament. In a well-developed essay, compare and contrast the selections, identifying the moral message in each selection and the techniques used to convey it. Note examples and details in the Tolstoy story that illustrate the points made in the Bible passage.

◀ **STRATEGIES IN ACTION**

1. *I need to write an essay that points out similarities and differences between the Bible passage and the Tolstoy story.*

2. *I need to discuss the techniques used to convey a* **moral message** *in each selection.*

3. *I need to identify* **examples** *of how the Tolstoy story supports ideas in the Bible passage.*

2. PLAN YOUR WRITING

- Review the **Points of Analysis** chart you created on page 735.
- Using your chart, find examples to use as evidence for the points you plan to develop in your essay. If necessary, review the selections again to identify more examples.
- Create an outline to organize your main points. You might want to base your outline on the **Points of Analysis** chart, as shown.

I. *Problems with wealth*
   A. Story
   B. Scripture
II. *Title*
   A. Story
   B. Scripture

3. DRAFT YOUR RESPONSE

Introduction Explain that you will be comparing a short story and scriptural writing that both deal with the desire for wealth. Be sure to identify the title of each work.

Body Cover each key point of comparison in its own paragraph. In one paragraph, for example, you might compare and contrast problems associated with the desire for wealth in each selection. Within each paragraph you write, give specific details to back up your points.

Conclusion Wrap up your essay by summarizing your main points.

Revision Be sure you have included details from both selections to support each key comparison. Also, check your use of transitional words and phrases to connect your ideas within and between paragraphs.

FOR STRUGGLING WRITERS

- Help students identify several cause-and-effect examples that provide clues to the moral message of Tolstoy's story.

- Review the last two questions in students' Points of Comparison charts on page 735 and discuss their chart entries.

- Limit the length of the assignment to no more than four paragraphs (introduction, two key points of comparison, conclusion).

Writing for Assessment

COMMON CORE RL 1 RL 2 W 9 (RI 7)

1. READ THE PROMPT

Review with students how the moral message of a story can be revealed through a character's actions and what happens to the character as a result of those actions. For example, in Tolstoy's story, Pakhom dies as a result of relentlessly chasing wealth.

2. PLAN YOUR WRITING

After students have reviewed the Points of Analysis chart on page 735, start an outline on the board. Have them suggest heads and subheads as well as details from each story, as in this example:

I. Moral Message in Selections

  A. Story—Pursuit of wealth leads to greed, envy, and ultimately death.

  B. New Testament—Pursuit of wealth leads to evil deeds and perhaps loss of faith.

II. Techniques Used to Convey Message

  A. Story—Cause and effect

  B. New Testament—Direct statement

3. DRAFT YOUR RESPONSE

Have students use their outline to draft the introduction, body, and conclusion of their essays. Urge students to use enough examples in the body of their essays to make their ideas clear. Remind students that they will have ample chance to revise their drafts.

Assess and Reteach

Assess

DIAGNOSTIC AND SELECTION TESTS
  Selection Test A pp. 211–212
  Selection Test B/C pp. 213–214

Interactive Selection Test on **thinkcentral.com**

Reteach

Level Up Online Tutorials on **thinkcentral.com**

Reteaching Worksheets on **thinkcentral.com**
  Reading Lesson 3: Determining Author's Purpose
  Vocabulary Lesson 12: Context Clues

Focus and Motivate

◌ COMMON CORE FOCUS

SL 2 Integrate multiple sources of information presented in diverse media or formats, evaluating the credibility and accuracy of each source. **SL 3** Evaluate a speaker's point of view, reasoning, and use of evidence and rhetoric, identifying any fallacious reasoning or exaggerated or distorted evidence. **SL 4** Present supporting evidence clearly such that listeners can follow the line of reasoning.

SUMMARY

The ad "Daisy" shows a black-and-white shot of a young girl in a field plucking and counting petals from a daisy. As she reaches ten, a voice-over counts down to a powerful nuclear blast. President Lyndon B. Johnson says ominously, "These are the stakes.... We must either love each other, or we must die."

The ad "America's Back" shows smiling Americans and evokes an optimistic view of life in small-town America. A girl rides a bicycle, a family moves into a new house, factory workers go to work, and an African-American man paints a picket fence.

How do candidates get your VOTE?

To help students explore the question, ask them to recall a recent political TV ad. Discuss the images or symbols that appear in the ad. Which persuasive techniques help "sell" the candidate? What music or voice-overs appeal to your emotions? Would you vote for this candidate, and why?

BACKGROUND

Senator William Benton from Connecticut may have been the first to use political ads on television. Benton, a former advertising executive, ran continuous campaign ads in his 1950 political campaign. In addition, Senator Benton had small kiosks with rear-projection screens set up in shopping centers and on street corners because at the time few Americans owned TV sets. Benton won a tight race against his opponent.

Media Study

Daisy
America's Back

Political Ads on Media ◆ Smart DVD-ROM

Essential Course of Study ECOS

How do candidates get your **VOTE?**

◌ COMMON CORE

SL 2 Integrate multiple sources of information presented in diverse media or formats. **SL 3** Evaluate a speaker's point of view, reasoning, and use of evidence and rhetoric, identifying any fallacious reasoning or exaggerated or distorted evidence.

Experience, leadership, honesty, compassion—in politics, a candidate's image is just as important as the issues he or she represents. In this lesson, you'll learn how political campaign advertisers use persuasive techniques to influence the way voters perceive candidates.

Background

Selling Candidates In a TV ad, most candidates have 30 seconds or less to "sell" their message and appeal to voters. Just how important is a 30-second commercial? In 1964, President Lyndon B. Johnson ran one of the most memorable ad campaigns in advertising and political history. The ad "Daisy" aired at a time when the threat of a nuclear war between the Soviet Union and the United States was a key issue for voters. It ran only one day, but it had a profound impact. Johnson's opponent, Barry Goldwater, lost the election.

While "Daisy" addressed viewers' deepest fears, President Ronald Reagan's 1984 ad "America's Back," captured the public's attention in a different way. The ad shows a series of images that set a positive tone, highlighting the theme of the campaign: America is "Prouder, Stronger, Better." By sending an optimistic message, the ad helped viewers associate positive feelings with the Reagan campaign.

Media Study Resources

See resources on the **Teacher One Stop DVD-ROM** *and on* **thinkcentral.com**.

R RESOURCE MANAGER UNIT 6
Plan and Teach pp. 186–188
Summary, pp. 189†*, 190‡*
Viewing Guide p. 191
Close Viewing p. 192
Produce Your Own Media p. 194

TECHNOLOGY
 Teacher One Stop DVD-ROM
● **Student One Stop DVD-ROM**
● **Media*Smart* DVD-ROM**
MediaScope on thinkcentral.com

* Resources for Differentiation   † Also in Spanish   ‡ In Haitian Creole and Vietnamese

Media Literacy: Persuasion in Political Ads

A well-designed ad can define a candidate's beliefs, values, and issues, but it can also present **rhetorical fallacies** (deliberately false or misleading statements) or **logical fallacies** (errors in reasoning). By using carefully chosen visuals, sounds, and persuasive techniques, political ads have the potential to sway voters' attitudes about candidates. The following types of political ads are commonly used by candidates, political organizations, and interest groups:

- **Biography ads** emphasize the candidate's personal and professional accomplishments.
- **Vision ads** provide a "vision" of the candidate's policies. These ads are intended to make viewers feel good about the country and the politician.
- **Negative ads** portray a candidate's opponent in an unfavorable light, often by distorting the facts or making personal attacks.
- **Scare ads** play on voters' fears and are usually combined with negative ads.

STRATEGIES FOR ANALYZING PERSUASION IN POLITICAL ADS

Visual Elements
- Notice a candidate's **physical appearance** and **body language.** A candidate's physical appearance and behavior are carefully planned to create an impression on a **target audience.** Members of a target audience often share such characteristics as age, gender, ethnicity, economic level, or values. For example, a target audience of voters who prefer a likable, approachable candidate will respond well to images of one who speaks informally, dresses casually, and shakes hands.
- **Symbols** are images that represent certain ideas or values. An image of the Statue of Liberty, for example, might be used to symbolize freedom.

Persuasive Techniques
- **Emotional appeals** create strong feelings such as fear, security, anger, patriotism, optimism, pity, distrust, and loyalty. Ask yourself: What emotions is the ad trying to create?
- **Glittering generalities** are general statements that sound important but are often vague or abstract. Their intended effect is to create a positive feeling about a candidate (for example, "A vote for Evan Smith is a vote for freedom and democracy").
- **"Plain folks" appeals** are attempts to persuade viewers that the candidate understands the average person, because he or she is one.

Sound Elements
- **Music** is used to trigger emotions such as optimism or nostalgia. Upbeat music inspires voters, while jarring or disturbing music gives a sense of mistrust.
- Some **voice-over** narrations can inspire trust or confidence. Other voice-overs can give a sense of unease or mistrust. Ask yourself: How is voice-over used to create a positive or negative image of a candidate?

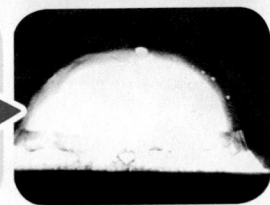

MEDIA STUDY   **739**

MEDIA STUDY: TEACHING OPTIONS

Teaching Option 1: The Basics (1–2 Days)
1. Begin the Media Study using the material provided on pages 738–739.
2. Show the Introduction on Media*Smart*. Then show the First Viewing. As they watch, have students use the Viewing Guide on page 740, along with the corresponding copy master on page 193 of the Resource Manager. Discuss their responses.
3. Return to the pupil book for the extension activities on page 741.

Teaching Option 2: In-Depth Study (2–3 Days)
1. Begin the Media Study using pages 738–739.
2. Show the Introduction and First Viewing from Media*Smart*. Then continue on Media*Smart* with the Media Lessons, using the teacher notes available in the Resources section.
3. Show the Guided Analysis presentation. Have students record their observations on the Student Viewing Guide available in the Resources section from Media*Smart*.
4. Return to the pupil book, page 741.

Media Literacy

COMMON CORE SL 2, SL 3

Review with students the definition of *persuasion*. Then ask them to recall political ads they have seen and to identify different elements these ads used to influence voters. On the board, list any responses that students may generate, such as *patriotic music, emotional appeals, slogans, vivid images, evocative symbols,* and so on. Make sure *persuasive techniques,* such as *emotional appeals* and *glittering generalities,* are included on the list. Then discuss the chart on page 739.

- **Visual Elements** To reinforce the importance of visual elements, have students name some powerful symbols they have seen in political ads, such as a soaring eagle, an American flag, or a dove. Ask them to tell how these symbols make them feel. Then help students understand the concept of target audience by helping them think about the kinds of product ads that might appear during children's cartoon programs, music video shows, and other programs.

- **Persuasive Techniques** Make sure students understand the persuasive techniques in the chart. Have them give examples of emotional appeals, glittering generalities, and "plain folks" appeals they have seen in either political ads or product ads. As students view the film clip, have them identify examples of these persuasive techniques.

- **Sound Elements** Have students compare and contrast different types of music or voice-over narrations in political ads. For example, eerie music might frighten voters, while a patriotic song like "America the Beautiful" might inspire them or make them feel proud. A soothing voice might gently encourage voters, while a deep, commanding voice might intimidate or compel them. Have students evaluate the clip with their eyes closed to emphasize the importance of sound elements.

Practice and Apply

1. Before students view the clip, tell them they will be asked to analyze persuasive techniques in the ads. Ask them to watch and listen for these elements:

   - **visual elements** that create an impression on the target audience, including how Ronald Reagan looks at the end of "America's Back" as well as images and symbols in each ad that reflect positive or negative ideas and values held by Presidents Reagan and Johnson or by their opponents

   - **persuasive techniques,** such as emotional appeals, glittering generalities, and "plain folks" appeals, that create strong positive or negative emotional responses in viewers about either President Reagan or President Johnson

   - **music, voice-over narration,** and sound effects in "America's Back" and "Daisy" that help stir viewers' emotions and keep their attention

2. To help students understand some of the historical context, explain that Reagan's 1984 ad focused on the effects of his economic policies, known as "Reaganomics." Reagan took office at a time when the nation's economy was struggling, and by the end of his first term, there had been some economic recovery.

R RESOURCE MANAGER—Copy Masters
Viewing Guide p. 193
Close Viewing p. 194
Viewing Activity p. 195

Use this resource with the Viewing Guide:

Media*Smart* DVD-ROM

Media*Scope* on **thinkcentral.com**

ANSWERS

FIRST VIEWING: Comprehension

1. *"America's Back":* All is well in America and there's no reason to change leadership now. *"Daisy":* If you don't vote for the peace-promoting Johnson, Goldwater might get us into a nuclear war.

2. *The American flag appears repeatedly.*

CLOSE VIEWING: Media Literacy

Possible answers:

3. *"America's Back":* This is a vision ad be-

Media Smart DVD-ROM
- Advertisement 1: "Daisy"
- Advertisement 2: "America's Back"
- Genre: Political Ads

Viewing Guide for
Political Ads

As you view the political ads, consider the times in which they were created. How had American society and culture changed in the twenty years between these ads? Both ads are regarded as classic by today's standards. Each serves a different purpose. "Daisy" capitalizes on voters' fears of a nuclear war with the Soviet Union. The ad was meant to scare viewers into voting for Johnson. "America's Back" uses images of peace and prosperity to persuade Americans to re-elect President Reagan.

Quickly review the persuasive techniques that appear on page 740 of this lesson as well as those listed on page 628. To analyze how persuasive techniques are used in political ads, view each ad more than once and answer the following questions.

NOW VIEW

FIRST VIEWING: Comprehension

1. **Summarize** Summarize the message in each ad.

2. **Recall** What symbol appears repeatedly in "America's Back"?

CLOSE VIEWING: Media Literacy

3. **Identify Type of Ad** How would you categorize each ad—biography ad, vision ad, negative ad, or scare ad? Give reasons.

4. **Identify Target Audience** Who do you think is the target audience of each ad—for example, new voters, retired voters, wealthy voters? Explain. How do the differences in target audience affect the formality and tone of the ads?

5. **Analyze Emotional Appeals** In "Daisy," what emotions do you think the visuals and voice-over are attempting to trigger?

6. **Analyze Persuasive Techniques** Identify the persuasive techniques used in "America's Back." How do these techniques help convey the ad's message?

7. **Compare Media** How different would these ads' messages and their impact have been in the more traditional media of print or radio? How might they be different today, delivered on the Internet?

740

---

cause it conveys Reagan's beliefs and ideas. *"Daisy":* This is both a negative ad and a scare ad. It implies that a vote for Johnson's opponent is dangerous, and it plays on voters' fears of nuclear war.

4. *"America's Back":* The target audience is adults with families, homes, and responsibilities. *"Daisy":* The target audience is any voter who is afraid of nuclear war.

5. *The image of a nuclear mushroom cloud is intended to scare people into thinking that the other candidate favors war. President Johnson's voice-over is intended to reassure viewers with the candidate's belief in peaceful solutions to problems.*

6. *"America's Back" uses emotional appeals to convey both patriotism (images of the flag) and optimism (sunny day; people smiling and looking upward). The images have a "plain folks" appeal (people buying homes or trucks; an elderly man relaxing and reading the newspaper). The calm voice-over reads glittering generalities ("Just about every place you look, things are looking up . . . ," "Life is better. America's back.")*

7. *The effectiveness of the ads requires both visual and sound elements and one or the other would be lost in print or radio. The impact would be the same or enhanced on the Internet.*

Write or Discuss

Evaluate the Message By contrasting the image of a little girl counting daisy petals with an image of a nuclear explosion, "Daisy" made a powerful and persuasive suggestion about Goldwater's position on war. Based on your viewing of "Daisy," do you think the ad's creators went too far to win votes for Johnson? Why or why not? Use evidence to support your opinion and also consider the following:

- persuasive techniques used in the ad to attract voters' attention and to influence their actions
- the use of visual and sound elements
- any information that you think is missing from the ad
- your reaction to the ad and how you think viewers responded

COMMON CORE

SL 2 Integrate multiple sources of information presented in diverse media or formats, evaluating the credibility and accuracy of each source. **SL 4** Present supporting evidence clearly such that listeners can follow the line of reasoning.

Produce Your Own Media

Design a Campaign Poster Imagine that you are a political consultant whose job it is to create a campaign poster for a candidate. Choose an existing candidate, a historical figure, or someone running for student government, and create a poster that projects a positive image of the candidate.

Media Tools **THINK** central
Go to thinkcentral.com.
KEYWORD: HML10-741

HERE'S HOW To help you create your poster, consider the following suggestions:

- Identify your target audience. What will they find persuasive?
- Determine whether you will focus on the candidate's image or the issues.
- Create a **slogan** that captures a major theme of a campaign or that highlights the candidate's personality and image. Remember that slogans are catchy phrases that voters remember and associate with a candidate.
- Plan the layout of the poster. What images, graphics, or words will stand out? What symbols or colors will get voters' attention?

Tech Tip

Use a software program to add design elements, such as color and special fonts, to your campaign poster.

MEDIA STUDY **741**

- **Sound Elements** Have students look back at the selections they have read in Unit 6 and suggest appropriate music and a voice-over summary to go with each.

Produce Your Own Media

Rubric An effective political campaign poster should

- center on a contemporary or historical candidate
- focus on the candidate's image or political issues

- emphasize the candidate's positive qualities
- include a catchy slogan
- incorporate strong visual elements, such as colors, fonts, symbols, and images, to grab voters' attention

R RESOURCE MANAGER—Copy Master
Produce Your Own Media p. 196

Write or Discuss

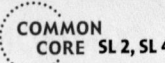
COMMON CORE SL 2, SL 4

Evaluate the Message In their written work or discussions, students should clearly state whether they felt "Daisy" was an appropriate ad. They should analyze the use of persuasion in the ad, referring to specific *symbols* (the innocence of the girl counting petals, the destruction of the nuclear blast); the *appeal to emotions* such as fear, anxiety, and distrust; and *glittering generalities* ("We must love each other, or we must die"). In their evaluations, students should mention any information that they think is missing from the ad. They should also share their personal reactions and speculate on how other viewers might have reacted.

MEDIA STUDY WRAP-UP

Have students summarize what they have learned about visual elements, persuasive techniques, and sound elements in political campaign ads. Encourage them to use terms such as *physical appearance, body language, symbols, emotional appeals, glittering generalities, "plain folks" appeals, music,* or *voice-overs* in their explanations.

RETEACH

For students who are unable to apply the Media Study skills, select from these reteaching options:

- **Visual Elements** Use pictures of several symbols, such as the school mascot or the Texas state flag, and ask students to explain the impression produced by each symbol. Then have the class suggest a target audience that would respond well to that symbol.
- **Persuasive Techniques** Divide the class into several small groups and assign each group one of the three persuasive techniques. Have each group draft a persuasive appeal for the importance of carrying an umbrella and present the appeal to the class. Have the class identify the technique the group is using.

Media Tools **THINK** central

Media study keywords point to **MediaScope,** a Web site that helps students strengthen media analysis and production skills.

Focus and Motivate

W 1a–e Write arguments to support claims in an analysis of substantive topics, using valid reasoning and relevant and sufficient evidence. **W 4** Produce clear and coherent writing appropriate to task, purpose, and audience. **W 5** Strengthen writing by planning, revising, editing, rewriting, or trying a new approach, addressing what is most significant for a specific purpose and audience. **W 10** Write routinely over shorter time frames for a range of tasks, purposes, and audiences. **L 1** Demonstrate command of the conventions of standard English grammar and usage. **L 2c** Spell correctly. **L 3** Apply knowledge of language to make effective choices for meaning or style.

WRITE WITH A PURPOSE

Tell students that the purpose of a persuasive essay is to convince an audience to agree with you and to take action. Emphasize that students should choose an issue about which they feel strongly.

COMMON CORE TRAITS

Review the *COMMON CORE TRAITS* with students, focusing primarily on the development of ideas. Compare the list of traits with the rubric on page 750.

ADDITIONAL TASK

Write About Fine Art Write a letter to the school board recommending that a specific piece of art be put on display at your school. **Possible subjects:** mural, painting, student art

Writing Online

The following tools are available online at **thinkcentral.com** and on Write*Smart* CD-ROM:
- **Interactive Graphic Organizers**
- **Interactive Student Models**
- **Interactive Revision Lessons**

Writing Workshop

ARGUMENT

Persuasive Essay

Essential Course of Study **ECOS**

Ideas and words can shape people's attitudes and influence their actions. Think of times you've tried to convince others to agree with you. How did you build your case? What words did you use to get others to take your side or take action? In this workshop, you will learn how to construct an argument and choose words that will have the greatest impact on others in a **persuasive essay**.

Complete the workshop activities in your **Reader/Writer Notebook**.

WRITE WITH A PURPOSE

WRITING TASK

Write a **persuasive essay** on an issue about which you have a strong opinion. In your essay, try to persuade a specific audience to agree with your position and take a stand or action on it.

Idea Starters
- an issue that affects your friends or family
- a current event discussed in a newspaper, on television, or on an online news site
- a possible action discussed by the student council, board of education, or your city council or town board

THE ESSENTIALS

Here are some common purposes, audiences, and formats for persuasive writing.

PURPOSES	AUDIENCES	FORMATS
• to sway others to adopt your position • to inspire others to take action	• classmates and teacher • parents • community members • school board • Web users	• essay for class • letter to editor • speech • blog • advertisement • message-board posting • podcast

COMMON CORE TRAITS

1. DEVELOPMENT OF IDEAS
- includes an **introduction** that identifies an issue and states a **precise claim**
- fairly develops the claim with **valid reasons** and **relevant evidence**
- anticipates **opposing claims** and counters them with well-supported **counterclaims**
- offers a **concluding section** that supports the claim

2. ORGANIZATION OF IDEAS
- establishes **clear, logical relationships** among claims, counterclaims, reasons, and evidence
- uses **transitions** to create cohesion and clarify relationships

3. LANGUAGE FACILITY AND CONVENTIONS
- maintains a **formal style** and **objective tone**
- uses the **subjunctive mood**
- employs correct **grammar, mechanics**, and **spelling**

Writing Online

Go to **thinkcentral.com**.
KEYWORD: HML10N-742

Writing Workshop Resources

R RESOURCE MANAGER UNIT 6

Plan and Teach, pp. 197–200
Prewriting–Editing, pp. 201–205
Writing Rubric, p. 206
Speaking and Listening, p. 207
Writing Support, p. 208*

BEST PRACTICES TOOLKIT

Writing Template: Persuasive Essay, pp. C16, C31
Analysis Frame: Persuasion, pp. D21, D44

TECHNOLOGY

- **Teacher One Stop DVD-ROM**
- **Student One Stop DVD-ROM**
- **Write*Smart* CD-ROM**
- **GrammarNotes DVD-ROM**

Writing Center on thinkcentral.com

See resources on the **Teacher One Stop DVD-ROM** *and on* **thinkcentral.com.**

* Resources for Differentiation

Planning/Prewriting

 COMMON CORE W 1a–e Write arguments to support claims in an analysis of substantive topics, using valid reasoning and relevant and sufficient evidence. **W 5** Develop and strengthen writing as needed by planning.

Getting Started

CHOOSE AN ISSUE

For your essay, you need to choose a **substantive issue** that matters to a great deal of people. Make a list of issues about which people have differing opinions. Then, select the issue that is most important to you.

▶ **ASK YOURSELF:**
- Which issue do I care about the most?
- What is my position on this issue?
- What reasons and evidence can I use to support my position?
- What opinions do other people have on this issue?

THINK ABOUT AUDIENCE AND PURPOSE

Your **purpose** is to convince others to share your opinion or to take your suggested course of action. Also, make sure you know your **audience**—people who either disagree with you or do not yet have an opinion on the issue. Understanding their views and concerns will help you build a more convincing argument.

▶ **ASK YOURSELF:**
- Who is my audience? What do I want my audience to believe or do?
- How can I make my audience care about this issue?
- What does my audience know about this issue? What background information might they need?
- What views might my audience have on this issue?
- What objections might my audience raise?

WRITE A CLAIM

To guide your writing, formulate a **precise claim**, a statement that makes your opinion clear. This statement should identify the issue and describe your position on it.

▶ **WHAT DOES IT LOOK LIKE?**

> Position   Issue
> **Claim:** Schools should allow fast food restaurants to offer menu items in the school cafeteria.

GATHER SUPPORT FOR YOUR CLAIM

To show why your opinion is correct, you'll need to provide **reasons** that explain your position. Make sure that each reason is **valid** (makes logical sense) and can be supported with evidence. Also, think ahead and brainstorm **opposing claims** that your audience might have. Prepare a **counterclaim** to refute each objection. An effective counterclaim can help you establish the strength of your claim over all other viewpoints.

▶ **WHAT DOES IT LOOK LIKE?**

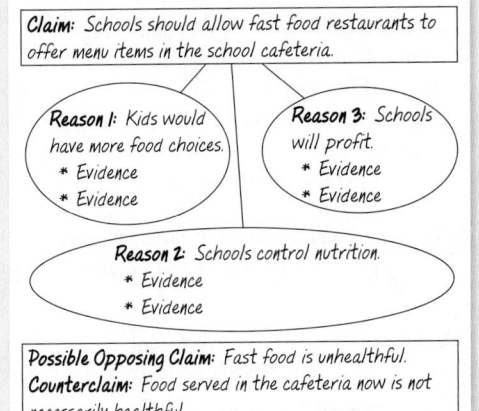

Teach

Planning/ Prewriting

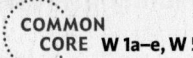 **COMMON CORE** W 1a–e, W 5

▶ **CHOOSE AN ISSUE** Stress that the issues students choose to address should be not only important but also debatable. Make sure students choose only issues that have opposing opinions. To make sure that the issues they list meet these criteria, have students make brief notes about the opposing views on each issue. If students are unable to identify at least two opinions on an issue, tell them to remove it from their list of possible essay topics.

▶ **THINK ABOUT AUDIENCE AND PURPOSE** Reiterate that the purpose for writing this essay is to persuade others to agree with a position and to take action. Point out that the audience will be individuals interested in the issue, whether they have an opinion on it yet or not.

▶ **WRITE A CLAIM** Tell students to begin by stating their claim, or position, simply, in one sentence. Explain that this sentence forms the controlling idea of their essays.

▶ **GATHER SUPPORT FOR YOUR CLAIM** Tell students to supply several reasons for their position on the issue. If students have difficulty identifying reasons, suggest that they read their claims aloud and then ask, "Why?" Direct students to list any ideas that come to mind and then select the reasons they can support with evidence.

🇷 **RESOURCE MANAGER—Copy Master**
Planning / Prewriting p. 201
Drafting p. 202
Revising pp. 203–204
Editing p. 205
Rubric p. 206
Writing Support p. 208

DIFFERENTIATED INSTRUCTION

FOR ENGLISH LANGUAGE LEARNERS

Language: Reinforce Persuasive Terms Write these terms on the board and review them with students:

position: an opinion on an issue

call to action: the writer's request to the reader to do, think, or say something

evidence: facts, expert opinions, explanations, examples, and other details used to support reasons in an argument

objection: an opposing claim

counterclaim: a claim made to respond to an objection

appeal: a request or call to somebody

Planning/Prewriting *continued*

▶ **COLLECT EVIDENCE** Review the different types of evidence and examples of each. Ask students to offer additional examples. Emphasize that an effective persuasive essay includes a wide range of evidence. Tell students to cite two or more pieces of evidence for each reason they have listed for their position.

▶ **USE APPROPRIATE APPEALS** Discuss the three forms of appeals, and note the types of evidence that are most effective with each form. Provide examples of each form of appeal, using the issue of fast food in school cafeterias. Urge students to include more than one form of appeal in their essays but to avoid too many emotional appeals.

YOUR TURN Give students time to choose an issue, form a controlling idea, and begin listing reasons and evidence in a graphic organizer. Have students present their issues, opinions, claims, and reasons to you. Direct students to research and locate evidence independently.

For interactive graphic organizers, see

💿 **Write*Smart* CD-ROM**

Writing Center on thinkcentral.com

Planning/Prewriting *continued*

Getting Started

COLLECT EVIDENCE

Support your claim with specific evidence that is relevant to your issue. Make sure your evidence is **sufficient**, or substantive enough to prove your point. Here are some types of evidence:

WHAT DOES IT LOOK LIKE?

Anecdotes: brief, personal stories that illustrate a point

▶ *My mother told me that when she was in school, students could leave school at lunchtime to go out to buy fast food.*

Examples: specific instances of an idea or situation

▶ *Now students have choices of fat-soaked meat and side orders lacking vitamins.*

Expert Opinions: quotations or paraphrases of statements made by people who are considered experts on your issue

▶ *"Kids get bored easily with the options we provide," noted cafeteria manager Ingrid Stone.*

Facts: statements that can be proven true

▶ *Many fast food companies are now preparing their food with zero trans fat.*

Statistics: information in numerical form

▶ *Each student spends about $2.00 a day in the cafeteria.*

USE APPROPRIATE APPEALS

Logical appeals rely on your audience's ability to use common sense; facts and expert opinions can help you make logical appeals.

Emotional appeals speak to your audience's emotions, such as fear and hope; anecdotes can create emotional appeal.

Ethical appeals speak to your audience's ethics and rely on commonly accepted beliefs or values; examples can be used to make ethical appeals.

▶ **TIP**

While emotional and ethical appeals can be powerful, they also can disguise flawed logic in weak arguments. For that reason, avoid relying too much on emotional and ethical appeals. Rather, start with sound logical appeals. Then, incorporate some of these other appeals to help you strengthen key points.

PEER REVIEW Read your claim aloud to a peer. Then, ask: What do you know about this issue? What would you like to know? What objections would you raise to my position?

YOUR TURN In your *Reader/Writer Notebook,* develop your writing plan. Draft a claim, and organize your reasons, evidence, and counterclaims. Consider these tips:

• Use reliable sources, such as books and trustworthy Web sites.
• Use at least two sources to find facts to back up your argument.

DIFFERENTIATED INSTRUCTION

FOR ENGLISH LANGUAGE LEARNERS

Writing: Persuasive Writing To reinforce the concept of persuasive writing, suggest that students locate editorial pieces in English language newspapers or newspapers in their native languages. Have students work individually or with partners to read and analyze the persuasive elements of the editorials: opinion, reasons, evidence, and forms of appeals.

FOR STRUGGLING WRITERS

Develop a Controlling Idea Have students use these sentence frames to start thinking about an issue, their position on it, and reasons for their position:

• I think more teenagers should _____ because _____.

• I think our school should _____ because _____.

• I think our community or neighborhood must _____ because _____.

• I think our government should _____ because _____.

Drafting

W 4 Produce clear and coherent writing appropriate to task, purpose, and audience.
L 1 Demonstrate command of the conventions of standard English grammar and usage when writing.

The following chart shows a structure for organizing your draft.

Organizing Your Persuasive Essay

INTRODUCTION
- Grab your audience's attention with a **question, anecdote,** or startling **statistic.**
- Provide **background information** to help your audience understand your issue.
- Include a **precise claim** that makes your position on the issue clear.

▼

BODY
- **Logically sequence ideas** to show how the claims, counterclaims, and evidence relate.
- Develop reasons with **relevant, sufficient,** and **varied evidence**.
- Fairly address opposing claims by acknowledging their strengths and limitations. Include a **well-supported counterclaim.**
- Use **transitions,** such as *one concern* and *another concern,* to create **cohesion,** or flow.
- Maintain a **formal style** by using a confident voice and avoiding slang. Use an **objective,** or controlled, **tone** that isn't defensive or overly emotional.

▼

CONCLUDING SECTION
- Restate, but do not repeat, your **opinion.** Summarize the reasons for it.
- End with a **call to action,** telling members of your audience what they can do.

GRAMMAR IN CONTEXT: SUBJUNCTIVE MOOD

Mood is the form a verb takes to indicate a certain attitude. The **indicative** mood expresses a fact, an opinion, or a question; the **imperative** mood expresses a direct command or a request; and the **subjunctive** mood expresses a suggestion, a requirement, a condition contrary to fact, or a wish. In persuasive writing, use the subjunctive mood to clarify that something is not currently the case but could be if your proposed course of action were taken. Read these paired sentences:

Indicative Mood	*Subjunctive Mood*
The school **tried** offering fast food. [fact]	I recommend that the school **try** offering fast food. [suggestion]
Because we **are** better fed, we can be more productive and positive. [fact]	It is essential that we **be** better fed, so that we can be more productive and positive. [requirement]
When students **are** offered a variety of choices, their morale **increases.** [fact]	If students **were** offered a variety of choices, their morale **would increase.** [wish]

YOUR TURN Develop a first draft following the structure outlined in the chart above. In your draft, use the subjunctive mood correctly to express a possibility.

FOR ENGLISH LANGUAGE LEARNERS

Subjunctive Mood For additional practice, write these sentences on the board, and have students identify the mood of the underlined verb as indicative or subjunctive.

- It is required that every student <u>eat</u> lunch at school. [*subjunctive*]
- I suggest that you <u>try</u> the soup. [*subjunctive*]
- The cooks <u>make</u> soup every day. [*indicative*]
- I <u>like</u> to bring my own lunch. [*indicative*]
- I wish the food at school <u>were</u> better. [*subjunctive*]

FOR STRUGGLING WRITERS

Organize an Argument Have students use an outline framework to organize the introduction and first paragraph of their essays:

  I. Introduction
    A. Attention-getting opening
    B. Claim
  II. Reason 1
    A. Evidence
    B. Evidence

Practice and Apply

Drafting

COMMON CORE **W 4, L 1**

▶ **INTRODUCTION** Explain that the opening sentences of a persuasive essay are critical to engaging readers' interest, holding their attention, and ultimately swaying their opinion. Have students identify the attention-grabbing opening in the Student Draft on page 747.

▶ **BODY** Point out that in each body paragraph in the Student Draft on pages 747–748, the writer discusses one reason for her claim and cites evidence to support it. Observe that the essay ends with the most important reason.

▶ **CONCLUDING SECTION** Remind students that the concluding section of a persuasive essay should offer readers a clear, specific action they can take or support. Have students locate the student writer's call to action on page 748.

GRAMMAR IN CONTEXT: SUBJUNCTIVE MOOD

For additional practice, have students identify the mood of the underlined verb in each of these sentences:

- If fast food <u>were</u> a choice, more students would eat lunch. [*subjunctive*]
- A menu that <u>caters</u> to students' food preferences is an excellent idea. [*indicative*]
- I propose that fast food <u>be</u> included on the cafeteria menu for three months. [*subjunctive*]

YOUR TURN Ask students to complete the **Your Turn** activity independently. Remind students to use the subjunctive mood where appropriate. Suggest that students double-space their drafts so that they can make revisions more easily later.

For a persuasive essay writing template, see

BEST PRACTICES TOOLKIT—Transparency
  Writing Template: Persuasive Essay, pp. C16, C31

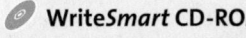 **Write*Smart* CD-ROM**

Writing Center on **thinkcentral.com**

Revising

COMMON CORE W 5, L 3

Model the Skill Using a draft essay on a transparency, model how to use the questions, tips, and strategies suggested in the chart to evaluate and revise. You might use a student's essay from a previous year, for example. Be sure to remove the student's name so that he or she remains anonymous.

 YOUR TURN Tell students to read their partner's essay with a critical eye, even if they agree with their partner's claim. After reading each other's drafts, partners should begin their feedback by identifying at least one positive quality of the draft. Explain that if they have not been persuaded by their partner's essay, they should tactfully identify places where the essay could be more persuasive.

For interactive revision tools, see

💿 **Write*Smart* CD-ROM**

Writing Center on thinkcentral.com

Revising

When you revise, you consider the development, organization, and style of your essay. The questions, tips, and strategies in the following chart can help you identify, revise, and rewrite the parts of your essay that need improvement.

PERSUASIVE ESSAY

Ask Yourself	Tips	Revision Strategies
1. Does the introduction grab the audience's attention and present a precise claim?	**Put a check mark** by sentences that get the audience interested. **Underline** the claim.	**Add** an interesting opening sentence. **Add** a claim that states your position on the issue. **Rework** the existing claim to make it more precise.
2. Does the introduction include background information on the issue?	**Put a star** by sentences that give background information on the issue.	**Add** background information to address any gaps in the audience's knowledge about the issue.
3. Do at least two valid reasons support the claim? Is each reason supported by relevant and sufficient evidence?	**Underline** each reason. **Circle** each piece of evidence, and **draw an arrow** to the reason it supports.	**Add** reasons or **rework** existing ones to make them more valid. **Add** relevant evidence to ensure that your support is sufficient.
4. Do I maintain an objective, or controlled, tone?	**Highlight** words or phrases that seem defensive, dismissive, or emotional.	**Reword** highlighted language to better express your command of the issue and confidence in your claim.
5. Are potential opposing claims anticipated and refuted with counterclaims?	**Draw a wavy line** under potential opposing claims. **Bracket** counterclaims that address those objections.	**Add** opposing claims and counterclaims to fairly address potential concerns the audience might have.
6. Does the concluding section restate the opinion? Does it include a call to action?	**Underline** the restatement of the position. **Put a check mark** next to the call to action.	**Add** a restatement of your position on the issue. **Add** a call to action.

 YOUR TURN **PEER REVIEW** Exchange your persuasive essay with a classmate, or read your essay aloud to your partner. Use the chart to make sure the claim, reasons, and evidence are communicated effectively. Help each other identify parts of the drafts that need strengthening or a new approach.

746 UNIT 6: ARGUMENT AND PERSUASION

DIFFERENTIATED INSTRUCTION

FOR ENGLISH LANGUAGE LEARNERS
Writing: Call to Action Provide students with sentence frames such as these to help them develop their call to action.

- I hope you will _____.
- I urge you to _____.
- Now is the time to _____.
- To help, you can _____.
- To learn more, you can _____.

FOR ADVANCED LEARNERS/PRE–AP
Ask a Peer Reader Have students use the questions in the Analysis Frame: Persuasion to analyze their own or a partner's draft.

 BEST PRACTICES TOOLKIT— Transparency Analysis Frame: Persuasion, pp. D21, D44

ANALYZE A STUDENT DRAFT

Read this draft; note the comments on its strengths as well the suggestions for improvement.

 COMMON CORE **W 5** Strengthen writing by revising, editing, rewriting, or trying a new approach, addressing what is most significant for a specific purpose and audience. **L 3** Apply knowledge of language to make effective choices for meaning or style.

Expand Our Food Choices

by Elizabeth Naglak, Searcy High School

1 How does the idea of eating real fast food at school sound? Recently some schools have been allowing fast food restaurants to serve lunch in their cafeterias. This is a brilliant idea because it gives students a variety of choices, a healthy and appealing menu, and an experience to enjoy. In doing so, the school would also acquire another way to earn money.

2 Ordinarily, students have the regular plate lunch or a salad every day. After a couple of months, these choices get old and unappetizing. "Kids get bored easily with the options we provide," noted cafeteria manager Ingrid Stone. I recommend that the school try offering fast food. Students would get more options for lunch. They would no longer have to eat the same foods on a daily basis. It is my hope that students be offered a variety of choices so that their morale might increase. The gourmet lunch options currently offered do nothing to get students excited about lunch. It is essential that we be better fed, so that we can be more productive and positive.

> Elizabeth grabs her audience's attention by asking a question. The question also sets up her **claim**.

> The **subjunctive mood** is used to express what would happen if Elizabeth's idea were approved.

> Elizabeth uses sarcasm in this paragraph. She should alert the reader to this use of sarcasm with quotation marks.

LEARN HOW Use Quotation Marks to Indicate Sarcasm or Irony In her second paragraph, Elizabeth uses sarcasm to emphasize that the current school lunch offerings are far from perfect. When used in writing, sarcasm and irony should be indicated by **quotation marks** to alert the reader. Elizabeth forgot to put quotation marks around the sarcastic phrase, however, to warn readers that she is not being completely serious. Therefore, her revision includes quotation marks around her use of irony.

> **ELIZABETH'S REVISION TO PARAGRAPH 2**
> The gourmet lunch options currently offered do nothing to get students excited about lunch.

FOR ENGLISH LANGUAGE LEARNERS

Writing: Use Transitions Explain that transitional words and phrases are used to link ideas in persuasive and other kinds of writing. Discuss these categories and examples:

- **addition:** *besides, moreover, in addition*
- **illustration:** *for example, including, such as, specifically*
- **comparison/contrast:** *likewise, similarly, however, nevertheless, in contrast, on the other hand*
- **time/sequence:** *in the past, before, later, meanwhile, eventually, first, to begin with, finally*
- **cause/effect:** *therefore, as a result, consequently*

Then give students sentence frames, and have them fill in the blank with an appropriate transition.

R RESOURCE MANAGER—Copy Master
Writing Support p. 208

ANALYZE A STUDENT DRAFT

Explain that the Student Draft on this page is the first half of a persuasive essay. Model reading the draft and the annotations in blue, and explain that the yellow highlighting illustrates the student's language choices. Explain that the following *Learn How* mini-lessons provide helpful information about ways to improve this student draft as well as their own.

LEARN HOW Use Quotation Marks to Indicate Sarcasm or Irony

- Define sarcasm as a remark or expression that makes fun of something, and define irony as the opposite of what is expected.
- Explain that writers often use quotation marks to indicate a word or phrase that is meant sarcastically or ironically, just as speakers sometimes use "air quotes" to indicate sarcasm or irony.
- Point out that the writer's description of lunch options as "gourmet" is sarcastic because the writer is obviously making fun of the lunch options.

Explain that the Student Draft is continued and completed on this page. Read the draft and annotations aloud, and discuss them. Ask students to comment on whether the writer followed the organizational plan for a persuasive essay outlined on page 745.

LEARN HOW Add Evidence to Strengthen an Argument

- Observe that the writer of the Student Draft includes clear factual evidence in her first draft of paragraph 4 to support her point about lunch as a source of revenue for schools. She includes the statistic that "on average, a student spends approximately $2.00 a day in the cafeteria."

- Remind students to pay attention to questions that come to mind as they revise their drafts. While revising her essay, the writer of the Student Draft notices, for example, that readers might wonder how much money schools would make if they added fast food to their menus. Point out that the writer strengthens support for her most important reason by adding evidence in paragraph 4 in response to this question.

- Challenge students to put a star next to two places in their drafts where they could add supporting evidence. Then have students research the factual support they need.

YOUR TURN Ask students to complete the **Your Turn** activity independently. Tell them to make sure they have used quotation marks to set off examples of sarcasm or irony in their drafts. Direct students to evaluate the effectiveness of their concluding section by asking these questions: Have I made the importance of the issue clear? Have I suggested a specific course of action to my audience?

For interactive revision tools, see

WriteSmart CD-ROM
Writing Center on thinkcentral.com

---

❸ One concern about offering fast food in schools is nutrition. While parents may be concerned with unhealthful fast food being offered in schools, there is nothing to fear. The school would have the power to allow into the lunchroom only those restaurants that offered healthy foods that met nutritional guidelines. The school and the restaurants would therefore be working jointly to create more varied and nutritious lunch options.

Elizabeth anticipates an opposing claim and then offers a counterclaim to refute the objection that fast food is not nutritious.

❹ Finally, lunch is an important source of revenue for a school. Students who buy their lunch from the cafeteria bring hundreds of dollars into the school each year. On average, a student spends approximately $2.00 a day in the cafeteria. When this is multiplied by one thousand students, the profit is astronomical.

Elizabeth gives her strongest reason in the final paragraph before the concluding section. Although she provides some support for this reason, more evidence is needed to strengthen her argument.

❺ Fast food restaurants in schools give students a plethora of choices without negatively effecting their health. If we were to allow fast food in our schools, everyone would benefit. Our school board should contact local fast food restaurants and ask them to provide school lunch options for our high school.

In the concluding section, Elizabeth summarizes the reasons for her position and includes a call to action.

LEARN HOW Add Evidence to Strengthen an Argument Elizabeth gives her most important reason last and supports it with facts and statistics. However, to make her argument as strong and effective as it can be, she needs to add more evidence to explain how fast food menu options would generate revenue for the school.

ELIZABETH'S REVISION TO PARAGRAPH ❹

When this is multiplied by one thousand students, the profit is astronomical. *Hungry students will buy more food, and the restaurants will pay a fee to operate in the school. In the Lakewood school district, the two high schools earned an extra #10,000 in the first year from fees paid by the restaurants, without diminishing the sales of regular cafeteria food. This demonstrates that our school is missing out on the money that students might spend on food if more choices were available.*

YOUR TURN Use the feedback from your peers and teacher as well as the two "Learn How" lessons to revise your essay. Evaluate how well you have clarified the importance of the issue, communicated the strength of your claim, and recommended a specific action for your audience to take.

DIFFERENTIATED INSTRUCTION

FOR STRUGGLING WRITERS
Identify Evidence Students may have difficulty identifying appropriate evidence to add to their essays. Have students choose partners and read aloud each other's drafts. After each paragraph, direct the reading partner to pause and ask, "What kind of evidence would help prove your point here?" and then discuss possible answers with the writer. After peer review, students should locate the evidence needed to support the reasons they have provided for their position.

FOR ADVANCED LEARNERS/PRE–AP
Reader Response Challenge students to write a paragraph in response to the argument in the Student Draft. Suggest that students research the nutritional value of popular fast food meals or the cost of offering organic, low-calorie, or locally grown food in school cafeterias. Remind students that their responses should either dispute or confirm the position taken in the Student Draft.

Editing and Publishing

In the editing stage, you proofread your essay to make sure that it is free of grammar, spelling, and punctuation errors. Mistakes will distract your audience from the issue and will likely cause them to question your authority.

COMMON CORE

W 5 Strengthen writing by revising, editing, rewriting, or trying a new approach. **L 1** Demonstrate command of the conventions of standard English grammar and usage. **L 2c** Spell correctly.

GRAMMAR IN CONTEXT: SPELLING

Always proofread what you have written so that you can eliminate careless spelling errors. Errors can suggest that you do not care enough about the issue to present your argument accurately. Incorrect spelling also undermines your argument by raising questions about your authority, giving your audience reason to mistrust your ideas.

Follow these general guidelines:

- Do not guess about correct spelling; use a dictionary.
- Do not rely solely on spell-checkers, which are not foolproof. They may overlook words that are spelled correctly but are used incorrectly.

EXAMPLE

The principle has assured us that she would be open to allowing fast food in the cafeteria.

[The word *principle* is spelled correctly but used incorrectly. A *principle* is a rule of conduct. The word *principal*, the head of a school, should be used.]

As Elizabeth edited her essay, she noticed that the word *effecting* in the sentence below is not correct. *Effect* refers to the result or consequence of an action, while *affect* refers to the action itself of having an impact on something.

> Fast food restaurants in schools give students a plethora of choices without negatively ~~effecting~~ their health.   *affecting*

PUBLISH YOUR WRITING

Finally, you can decide how best to make sure your intended audience considers your ideas. Here are some options:

- Condense your essay for publication in a local paper as a letter to the editor.
- Publish your essay on a school or community Web site.
- Adapt your essay into a persuasive speech; deliver it to an appropriate audience.

 YOUR TURN Proofread your essay for errors, including spelling errors. Correct any errors you find. Then, publish your final essay where it will reach its intended audience.

Editing and Publishing

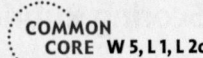 COMMON CORE W 5, L 1, L 2c

GRAMMAR IN CONTEXT: SPELLING

- Remind students that a dictionary is the most reliable source for the correct spelling of words.
- Emphasize that computer spell-checkers may accept spellings as correct that are not correct in the context of students' writing.
- Tell students to double-check their writing carefully for spelling errors even if a spell-checker has not found any.
- Urge students to prevent spelling errors by learning the difference between homonyms and other often-confused words.

PUBLISH YOUR WRITING

Brainstorm with students additional ways to publish their persuasive essays.

 YOUR TURN Allow students time to proofread their drafts. Remind them to use quotation marks to enclose sarcasm or irony. Also remind students to carefully check spelling in their essays.

FOR ENGLISH LANGUAGE LEARNERS

Spelling Have students work in pairs or small groups to create spelling notebooks of often-confused words. Have students include these and other words in their notebooks:

- *affect, effect*
- *complement, compliment*
- *coarse, course*
- *formally, formerly*
- *moral, morale*
- *principal, principle*
- *stationary, stationery*
- *than, then*
- *weather, whether*

Tell students to create an entry for each word that gives its part of speech, its definition, and a sample sentence using the word.

Scoring Rubric

Tell students that the best way to understand a scoring rubric is to use it to score actual writing. Have students use the rubric to evaluate student models of a persuasive essay found online at state assessment Web sites. Ask students to score the essays they read and then write a brief paragraph using the language of the rubric to explain the reasons for the score.

For Rubric Bank, see

 **Write*Smart* CD-ROM**

Writing Center on **thinkcentral.com**

Assess and Reteach

Assess

 RESOURCE MANAGER—Copy Master
Rubric for Evaluation p. 206

Online Essay Scoring on **thinkcentral.com**

Reteach

Level Up Online Tutorials on **thinkcentral.com**
Reteaching Worksheets on **thinkcentral.com**

Writing Lesson 15: Writing Introductions

Informational Texts Lesson 15: Persuasive Techniques

Scoring Rubric

Use the rubric below to evaluate your persuasive essay from the Writing Workshop or your response to the on-demand writing task on the next page.

PERSUASIVE ESSAY	
SCORE	**COMMON CORE TRAITS**
6	• **Development** Asserts a precise claim on a substantive topic; supports the claim with valid reasons and relevant, sufficient evidence; ably counters opposing claims with counterclaims; ends powerfully • **Organization** Is logically organized to persuasive effect; uses transitions to create cohesion and show the relationships among the claim, reasons, and evidence • **Language** Consistently maintains a formal style and objective tone; shows a strong command of conventions
5	• **Development** States a precise claim; offers valid reasons and evidence; counters opposing claims with counterclaims; ends with a strong concluding section • **Organization** Is logically organized; uses transitions to show the relationships among the claim, reasons, and evidence • **Language** Uses a formal style and objective tone; has a few errors in conventions
4	• **Development** States a clear claim; offers mostly valid support; needs to more fairly address opposing claims; has an adequate concluding section • **Organization** Reflects a logical organization, with one or two exceptions; could use a few more transitions • **Language** Mostly uses a formal style, but sounds defensive at times; includes a few distracting errors in conventions
3	• **Development** States a claim that could be more precise; provides some relevant support but not enough to be sufficient; unfairly dismisses other viewpoints; has a somewhat weak concluding section • **Organization** Has some flaws in organization; needs more transitions to show how ideas relate • **Language** Often lapses into an informal style or defensive tone; has several errors in conventions
2	• **Development** Has a vague claim; offers irrelevant reasons and insufficient evidence; fails to acknowledge other viewpoints; has a weak concluding section • **Organization** Has major organizational flaws; lacks transitions throughout • **Language** Uses an informal style and defensive tone; has many errors in conventions
1	• **Development** Lacks a claim; has no support; ignores opposing claims; ends abruptly • **Organization** Has no organization and transitions • **Language** Uses an inappropriate style and tone; has major problems with grammar, mechanics, and spelling

Preparing for Timed Writing

COMMON CORE

W 10 Write routinely over shorter time frames for a range of tasks, purposes, and audiences.

1. ANALYZE THE TASK 5 MIN

Read the task carefully. Then, read it again, noting the words that tell the topic, the purpose, the type of writing, and the audience.

> **WRITING TASK**
>
> Imagine that your school board is planning to no longer allow students to work [← Topic] during the school year. Write a persuasive essay convincing parents to agree with your position on this policy. [← Purpose] [Type of writing] [← Audience]

2. PLAN YOUR RESPONSE 10 MIN

Decide how you feel about the policy. Write a claim that states your viewpoint. Next, think of two to three reasons that support your position. Then, brainstorm evidence—anecdotes, examples, expert opinions, facts, and statistics—to support your reasons. Finally, consider opposing claims that your audience might raise. How could you counter those objections?

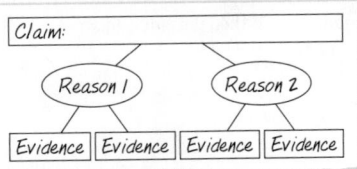

Claim:
Reason 1   Reason 2
Evidence Evidence Evidence Evidence

3. RESPOND TO THE TASK 20 MIN

Use your organizer to start drafting your essay. Begin with a question, anecdote, or statistic to grab your audience's attention. Consider these tips:

- In your introduction, provide background information on the issue and state your claim.
- In each body paragraph, explain one reason for your position and provide evidence to support it. Cite examples from your own or someone else's experience.
- Address at least one opposing claim and refute it with a counterclaim. Explain why your viewpoint is more valid.
- Conclude with a restatement of your position and a call to action.

4. IMPROVE YOUR RESPONSE 5–10 MIN

Revising Check your draft against the writing task. Does your draft clearly state your position? Will your reasons be convincing to your audience? Have you included enough supporting evidence? If not, add these elements or revise them to make them stronger.

Proofreading Find and correct errors in grammar, spelling, punctuation, and capitalization. Make sure your edits are neatly written and readable.

Checking Your Final Copy Before you turn in your response, read it one more time to make sure that you have not overlooked any errors. Does your final essay represent your best work?

DIFFERENTIATED INSTRUCTION

FOR ENGLISH LANGUAGE LEARNERS

Writing: Analyzing Tasks Make sure students understand the language used in the task (*school board, school year, policy*). Then have students meet in groups to read aloud and discuss possible responses to the task. After students write their drafts, have them meet with the same group to apply the guidelines outlined in the scoring rubric to their writing.

FOR STRUGGLING WRITERS

Brainstorm Ideas Suggest that students use a Cluster Diagram to brainstorm ideas for an opposing claim. Tell students to write the opposing claim in the center of the diagram and then add ways they would respond to it in a cluster around the opposing claim.

🧰 BEST PRACTICES TOOLKIT—Transparency
Cluster Diagram, pp. B18, B41

COMMON CORE FOCUS

W 10 Write routinely over shorter time frames for a range of tasks, purposes, and audiences.

Preparing for Timed Writing

1. **Analyze the Task** Before students begin writing, encourage them to answer the following questions:
   - What is my time limit?
   - What are the core traits assessed in the scoring rubric?
   - Who is my audience?
   - What is my purpose?

2. **Plan Your Response** Point out that the scoring rubric states specifically that the essay should support claims with valid reasons and relevant, sufficient evidence. Tell students to identify reasons for their position and to list at least two pieces of supporting evidence for each reason before they begin drafting.

3. **Respond to the Task** Remind students to address opposing claims in their essays. Students should provide convincing counterclaims that explain why their position is the right one.

4. **Improve Your Response** Note that the scoring rubric emphasizes the importance of thoroughly supporting one's position. Remind students to set aside time to review their essays to verify that they have successfully integrated varied and appropriate support where necessary.

Assess

Use the Scoring Rubric on page 750 to assess students' essays.

Focus and Motivate

COMMON CORE FOCUS

SL 3 Evaluate a speaker's point of view, reasoning, and use of evidence and rhetoric. **SL 4** Present information clearly, concisely, and logically. **SL 6** Adapt speech to a variety of contexts and tasks. **L 1a** Use parallel structure.

SPEAK WITH A PURPOSE

Tell students that the purpose, or goal, of their oral presentation is the same as that of their persuasive essay: to explain and support their position on an issue and to convince their audience to agree with it and to act. Tell students that the skills for effective speaking can be acquired through practice and hard work and that these skills will give them the confidence to share their opinions with audiences large and small.

COMMON CORE TRAITS

As students prepare to present their arguments, remind them to keep in mind the *COMMON CORE TRAITS* of a strong oral argument.

Practice and Apply

Adapting Your Essay

Model the Skill: ORGANIZATION

Draw a one-column, three-row chart on the board. Label the top row "Introduction." Label the middle row "Reasons," and leave space for three reasons. Label the bottom row "Concluding Section: Call to Action." Then, using the Student Draft on pages 747–748, demonstrate how you would make notes in each section of the organizer for an oral presentation.

GUIDED PRACTICE Have students fill in their own organizers with notes on the main parts of their presentations. Tell students that they can use the brief notes in their organizers to help them remember their key points, or they can transfer the notes to index cards and refer to the cards as they speak.

R RESOURCE MANAGER—Copy Master
Speaking and Listening p. 207

Speaking & Listening Workshop

Presenting an Argument

Essential Course of Study **ECOS**

When was the last time you presented an argument? Perhaps you tried to convince your parents or a teacher to see things your way. Maybe you attempted to persuade a group of friends to participate in an activity with you or to share your opinion. Good arguments can be made for or against almost any issue if the reasoning and evidence are logical, well organized, and delivered effectively.

Complete the workshop activities in your **Reader/Writer Notebook**.

SPEAK WITH A PURPOSE	COMMON CORE TRAITS
TASK Adapt your persuasive essay into an **oral presentation**. Practice your argument, and then present it to an appropriate audience.	**A STRONG ORAL ARGUMENT . . .** • focuses on a precise claim • presents information clearly, concisely, and logically • provides valid reasons and relevant evidence • fairly addresses potential opposing claims • employs **rhetoric**, or persuasive language • uses effective verbal and nonverbal speaking techniques

COMMON CORE

SL 3 Evaluate a speaker's point of view, reasoning, and use of evidence and rhetoric. **SL 4** Present information clearly, concisely, and logically. **SL 6** Adapt speech to a variety of contexts and tasks. **L 1a** Use parallel structure.

THINK central

Speaking & Listening Online

Go to **thinkcentral.com**.
KEYWORD: HML10-752

Adapting Your Essay

Follow these suggestions to turn your persuasive essay into an effective oral presentation.

- **Audience** As you plan your presentation, choose reasons and evidence that will resonate with your listeners. Acknowledge the concerns of audience members who might disagree with you. Be prepared with counterclaims.

- **Introduction** Grab your audience's interest from the start. Make your introduction dramatic by opening with a thought-provoking question, an illustrative anecdote, or a quotation from an expert on the subject.

- **Organization** Build interest and momentum by maintaining focus. Structure your ideas for maximum impact by presenting your reasons in order of importance, with the strongest reason last. Make brief notes to help you remember the key points you want to make. Make sure to state each point concisely, so that your audience doesn't lose interest in your ideas.

- **Effective Rhetoric** Experiment with language and sentence structures for persuasive effect. To make your ideas "stick," you might use **parallel structure**—the repeated use of words, phrases, and sentences with the same grammatical form.

- **Concluding Section** Sum up your argument. Then, end with a passionate call to action. Choose your last sentence carefully for the greatest impact.

DIFFERENTIATED INSTRUCTION

FOR ENGLISH LANGUAGE LEARNERS
Language: Reinforce Oral Argument Terms Reinforce key terms used in the Writing Workshop and this workshop:

- *position:* an opinion on an issue

- *anecdote:* a brief, personal story that illustrates a point

- *evidence:* facts and examples used to support key points

- *counterclaim:* reasons and evidence used to answer or disprove an opposing claim

- *call to action:* a request to the audience to do, think, or say something in response to the argument

Delivering Your Presentation

USE VERBAL TECHNIQUES

How you use your voice can be as persuasive as *what* you say. Practice these verbal techniques before giving your presentation.

- **Speak Loudly and Clearly** Project your voice so that everyone in your audience can hear you. Enunciate so that everyone can understand exactly what you say.
- **Adopt an Appropriate Tone** Choose a tone that is right for the audience you are addressing. In an informal group of classmates or friends, use a conversational tone. In a formal gathering, avoid slang, colloquialisms, and contractions.
- **Pace Your Presentation** To engage listeners and compel them to accept your claim, try speaking at a faster pace at the beginning of your presentation. Then speak more slowly to emphasize specific points in your argument. Pausing before and after key points is also effective.

USE NONVERBAL TECHNIQUES

Body language and graphic aids can also help make your presentation convincing.

- **Use Hand Gestures** Stress key points in your argument with gestures.
- **Vary Facial Expressions** Smile, frown, or raise your eyebrows to express agreement, disagreement, concern, worry, surprise, or shock.
- **Make Eye Contact** Connect with your audience by making frequent eye contact with individuals.
- **Change Your Pose** Approach the audience. Turn to face different parts of the audience.
- **Share Visuals** Use props such as charts, photos, and other visuals to keep your audience's interest and to support your argument.

YOUR TURN

As a Speaker Practice presenting your argument to a small group of friends. Try incorporating the verbal and nonverbal techniques described above for a speaking style that effectively conveys your message. After your presentation, ask for feedback on your delivery. Then, apply what you have learned from your friends' critique when you speak before a larger audience.

As a Listener Listen to a friend's presentation of an argument. Evaluate his or her claim, as well as the choice of reasons and evidence. Don't be swayed by **fallacious** (flawed) reasoning and distorted evidence that is inaccurate or taken out of context. In addition to the substance of the argument, evaluate the delivery of information. Share your ideas about how the presentation might be improved.

SPEAKING AND LISTENING WORKSHOP **753**

Delivering Your Presentation

Model the Skill: **USE VERBAL AND NONVERBAL TECHNIQUES**

Point out that a speaker's delivery affects the audience's response to an argument. Present the concluding section of the Student Draft on page 748 without using verbal and nonverbal techniques; then present it using the techniques. Discuss the difference in delivery, and ask students how it affected their response to the presentations.

GUIDED PRACTICE Have students practice delivering their presentations using verbal and nonverbal techniques.

YOUR TURN

Ask listeners to make notes about the speaker's use of verbal and nonverbal techniques and to offer specific feedback in the form of tips. Collect the feedback and compile a list of the most frequent and important tips that students offer. Post this list in the classroom for all students to review as they work to improve the delivery of their presentations.

Assess and Reteach

Assess

Use the *COMMON CORE TRAITS* to assess students' oral presentations.

A strong oral argument
- focuses on a precise claim, or position
- presents information clearly, concisely, and logically
- provides valid reasons and relevant evidence
- fairly addresses potential opposing claims
- employs persuasive rhetoric, or language
- uses effective verbal and nonverbal speaking techniques

Reteach

Have students meet in small groups to brainstorm ways they can build confidence for speaking in front of an audience. Ask each group to share its ideas, and urge students to apply the ideas in their oral presentations.

Speaking and Listening Online
- Public speaking tips
- Strategies for effective listening

Assessment Practice

RL 1 Cite textual evidence to support analysis of what the text says explicitly as well as inferences drawn from the text. **RL 2** Determine a theme or central idea of a text. **RI 1** Cite textual evidence to support analysis of what the text says explicitly as well as inferences drawn from the text. **RI 2** Determine a central idea of a text. **RI 5** Analyze how an author's ideas or claims are developed. **RI 6** Determine an author's point of view or purpose. **W 5** Strengthen writing by revising and editing.

CHECK READINESS

Read aloud the paragraph under **ASSESS** and stress to students that this is not the full Unit Test, but a way for them to check their readiness for it. Then have students examine the skills standards listed under **REVIEW** and look back in the unit or in the **Student Resource Bank** for any skills they need to review.

READ THE TEXTS

Remind students to keep unit goals in mind as they read each passage, paying particular attention to these literary and reading skills:

- theme
- draw conclusions
- analyze evidence

To help students focus on theme while reading, urge them to consider these questions:

- What message does each selection convey?
- How are the themes of the two selections similar? How do they differ?

ANSWER THE QUESTIONS

Direct students to pages R93–R101 of the **Handbook** to review test-taking strategies.

Remind students to read through all the choices, eliminate answers that are clearly wrong, and then choose the *best* answer.

Assessment Practice

ASSESS
Taking this practice test will help you assess your knowledge of these skills and determine your readiness for the Unit Test.

REVIEW
After you take the practice test, your teacher can help you identify any standards you need to review.

COMMON CORE

RL 1 Cite textual evidence to support analysis of what the text says explicitly as well as inferences drawn from the text. **RL 2** Determine a theme or central idea of a text. **RI 1** Cite textual evidence to support analysis of what the text says explicitly as well as inferences drawn from the text. **RI 2** Determine a central idea of a text. **RI 5** Analyze how an author's ideas or claims are developed. **RI 6** Determine an author's point of view or purpose. **W 5** Strengthen writing by revising and editing.

DIRECTIONS Read the two selections and the viewing and representing piece. Then, answer the questions that follow.

The Storyteller   *by Saki*

1   It was a hot afternoon, and the railway carriage was correspondingly sultry, and the next stop was at Templecombe, nearly an hour ahead. The occupants of the carriage were a small girl, and a smaller girl, and a small boy. An aunt belonging to the children occupied one corner seat, and the further corner seat on the opposite side was occupied by a bachelor who was a stranger to their party, but the small girls and the small boy emphatically occupied the compartment. Both the aunt and the children were conversational in a limited, persistent way, reminding one of the attentions of a housefly that refuses to be discouraged. Most of the aunt's remarks seemed to begin with "Don't," and nearly all of the children's remarks began with "Why?" The bachelor said nothing out loud.

2   "Don't, Cyril, don't," exclaimed the aunt, as the small boy began smacking the cushions of the seat, producing a cloud of dust at each blow.

3   "Come and look out of the window," she added.

4   The child moved reluctantly to the window. "Why are those sheep being driven out of that field?" he asked.

5   "I expect they are being driven to another field where there is more grass," said the aunt weakly.

6   "But there is lots of grass in that field," protested the boy; "there's nothing else but grass there. Aunt, there's lots of grass in that field."

7   "Perhaps the grass in the other field is better," suggested the aunt fatuously.[1]

8   "Why is it better?" came the swift, inevitable question.

9   "Oh, look at those cows!" exclaimed the aunt. Nearly every field along the line had contained cows or bullocks, but she spoke as though she were drawing attention to a rarity.

10 The frown on the bachelor's face was deepening to a scowl. He was a hard, unsympathetic man, the aunt decided in her mind. She was utterly unable to come to any satisfactory decision about the grass in the other field.

11 The smaller girl created a diversion by beginning to recite "On the Road to Mandalay."[2] She only knew the first line, but she put her limited knowledge to the fullest possible use. She repeated the line over and over again in a dreamy

---

1. **fatuously** (făch'ōō əs lē): foolishly

2. **"On the Road to Mandalay":** long poem by the English writer Rudyard Kipling (1865–1936). The first line is "By the old Moulmein pagoda, lookin' eastward to the sea."

Practice Test THINK central
Take it at **thinkcentral.com**.
KEYWORD: HML10-754

DIFFERENTIATED INSTRUCTION

FOR ENGLISH LANGUAGE LEARNERS
Assessment Practice: Work Backward Prepare students by having them read the questions *before* reading the passages. Have pairs find unfamiliar words in test directions and questions and follow these steps:

1. Write each word on an index card.

2. Look up the meaning in a dictionary and write it on the back of the card.

3. Use the cards to practice words with your partner and to teach them to others.

but resolute and very audible voice; it seemed to the bachelor as though someone had had a bet with her that she could not repeat the line aloud two thousand times without stopping. Whoever it was who had made the wager was likely to lose his bet.

12   "Come over here and listen to a story," said the aunt, when the bachelor had looked twice at her and once at the communication cord.[3]

13   The children moved listlessly towards the aunt's end of the carriage. Evidently her reputation as a storyteller did not rank high in their estimation.

14   In a low, confidential voice, interrupted at frequent intervals by loud, petulant questions from her listeners, she began an unenterprising and deplorably uninteresting story about a little girl who was good, and made friends with everyone on account of her goodness, and was finally saved from a mad bull by a number of rescuers who admired her moral character.

15   "Wouldn't they have saved her if she hadn't been good?" demanded the bigger of the small girls. It was exactly the question that the bachelor had wanted to ask.

16   "Well, yes," admitted the aunt lamely, "but I don't think they would have run quite so fast to her help if they had not liked her so much."

17   "It's the stupidest story I've ever heard," said the bigger of the small girls, with immense conviction.

18   "I didn't listen after the first bit, it was so stupid," said Cyril.

19   The smaller girl made no actual comment on the story, but she had long ago recommenced a murmured repetition of her favorite line.

20   "You don't seem to be a success as a storyteller," said the bachelor suddenly from his corner.

21   The aunt bristled in instant defense at this unexpected attack.

22   "It's a very difficult thing to tell stories that children can both understand and appreciate," she said stiffly.

23   "I don't agree with you," said the bachelor.

24   "Perhaps *you* would like to tell them a story," was the aunt's retort.

25   "Tell us a story," demanded the bigger of the small girls.

26   "Once upon a time," began the bachelor, "there was a little girl called Bertha, who was extraordinarily good."

27   The children's momentarily aroused interest began at once to flicker; all stories seemed dreadfully alike, no matter who told them.

GO ON ➡

---

3. **communication cord:** on a train, a cord that can be pulled to call the conductor.

ITEM ANALYSIS

COMPREHENSION AND WRITTEN RESPONSE	ITEMS	UNIT PAGES
Theme	2, 17, 18, 23	695
Tone	4	677
Draw Conclusions	1, 3, 4, 6, 8, 9, 10, 11, 12, 13, 15, 16, 19, 20	695
Analyze Evidence	14, 21, 22	647

VOCABULARY	ITEMS	UNIT PAGES
Synonyms	5	708
Word Roots	7	644

WRITING AND GRAMMAR	ITEMS	UNIT PAGES
Compound-Complex Sentences	2, 3	709
Organization	1, 4	745

Practice Test

On **thinkcentral.com** students can complete an interactive version of this practice test *and* receive remediation for the skills they have not yet mastered.

FOR STRUGGLING READERS

Assessment Support Consider these options for completing the Assessment Practice:

- Have students "work backward" to review the test questions before reading the passages.

- Select random questions in the Assessment and have students demonstrate *how* and *where* to look for answers.

- Ask students to locate unfamiliar vocabulary words in the Assessment. Elicit the words' meanings from the class.

- Have students record useful testing words and definitions in their journal for later reference.

- Read the selections or parts of them aloud to aid in student comprehension.

28   "She did all that she was told, she was always truthful, she kept her clothes clean, ate milk puddings as though they were jam tarts, learned her lessons perfectly, and was polite in her manners."

29   "Was she pretty?" asked the bigger of the small girls.

30   "Not as pretty as any of you," said the bachelor, "but she was horribly good."

31   There was a wave of reaction in favor of the story; the word horrible in connection with goodness was a novelty that commended itself. It seemed to introduce a ring of truth that was absent from the aunt's tales of infant life.

32   "She was so good," continued the bachelor, "that she won several medals for goodness, which she always wore, pinned onto her dress. There was a medal for obedience, another medal for punctuality, and a third for good behavior. They were large metal medals and they clicked against one another as she walked. No other child in the town where she lived had as many as three medals, so everybody knew that she must be an extra good child."

33   "Horribly good," quoted Cyril.

34   "Everybody talked about her goodness, and the Prince of the country got to hear about it, and he said that as she was so very good she might be allowed once a week to walk in his park, which was just outside the town. It was a beautiful park, and no children were ever allowed in it, so it was a great honor for Bertha to be allowed to go there."

35   "Were there any sheep in the park?" demanded Cyril.

36   "No," said the bachelor, "there were no sheep."

37   "Why weren't there any sheep?" came the inevitable question arising out of that answer.

38   The aunt permitted herself a smile, which might almost have been described as a grin.

39   "There were no sheep in the park," said the bachelor, "because the Prince's mother had once had a dream that her son would either be killed by a sheep or else by a clock falling on him. For that reason the Prince never kept a sheep in his park or a clock in his palace."

40   The aunt suppressed a gasp of admiration.

41   "Was the Prince killed by a sheep or by a clock?" asked Cyril.

42   "He is still alive, so we can't tell whether the dream will come true," said the bachelor unconcernedly; "anyway, there were no sheep in the park, but there were lots of little pigs running all over the place."

43   "What color were they?"

44   "Black with white faces, white with black spots, black all over, grey with white patches, and some were white all over."

45   The storyteller paused to let a full idea of the park's treasures sink into the children's imaginations; then he resumed:

756

DIFFERENTIATED INSTRUCTION

FOR ENGLISH LANGUAGE LEARNERS
Review Literary Terms On the board write the term *author's purpose*. Explain that an author usually writes for one or more of these purposes, and discuss each:

- to inform
- to persuade
- to entertain
- to describe or explain

Have students list these purposes in a two-column chart and work in pairs as they read to collect evidence in the story that supports each purpose. Tell them to record the evidence in their charts. After reading, have students use the evidence they have listed to determine the author's purpose in this selection. Point out that the row(s) in which they have recorded the most evidence should indicate the author's main purpose(s).

46   "Bertha was rather sorry to find that there were no flowers in the park. She
had promised her aunts, with tears in her eyes, that she would not pick any of
the kind Prince's flowers, and she had meant to keep her promise, so of course
it made her feel silly to find that there were no flowers to pick."

47   "Why weren't there any flowers?"

48   "Because the pigs had eaten them all," said the bachelor promptly. "The
gardeners had told the Prince that you couldn't have pigs and flowers, so he
decided to have pigs and no flowers."

49   There was a murmur of approval at the excellence of the Prince's decision; so
many people would have decided the other way.

50   "There were lots of other delightful things in the park. There were ponds
with gold and blue and green fish in them, and trees with beautiful parrots
that said clever things at a moment's notice, and hummingbirds that hummed
all the popular tunes of the day. Bertha walked up and down and enjoyed
herself immensely, and thought to herself: 'If I were not so extraordinarily
good I should not have been allowed to come into this beautiful park and
enjoy all that there is to be seen in it,' and her three medals clinked against
one another as she walked and helped to remind her how very good she really
was. Just then an enormous wolf came prowling into the park to see if it could
catch a fat little pig for its supper."

51   "What color was it?" asked the children, amid an immediate quickening of
interest.

52   "Mud-color all over, with a black tongue and pale grey eyes that gleamed
with unspeakable ferocity. The first thing that it saw in the park was Bertha;
her pinafore[4] was so spotlessly white and clean that it could be seen from a
great distance. Bertha saw the wolf and saw that it was stealing toward her,
and she began to wish that she had never been allowed to come into the park.
She ran as hard as she could, and the wolf came after her with huge leaps
and bounds. She managed to reach a shrubbery of myrtle bushes and she hid
herself in one of the thickest of the bushes. The wolf came sniffing among
the branches, its black tongue lolling out of its mouth and its pale grey eyes
glaring with rage. Bertha was terribly frightened, and thought to herself: 'If I
had not been so extraordinarily good I should have been safe in the town at
this moment.' However, the scent of the myrtle was so strong that the wolf
could not sniff out where Bertha was hiding, and the bushes were so thick that
he might have hunted about in them for a long time without catching sight of
her, so he thought he might as well go off and catch a little pig instead. Bertha
was trembling very much at having the wolf prowling and sniffing so near her,
and as she trembled the medal for obedience clinked against the medals for
good conduct and punctuality. The wolf was just moving away when he heard

GO ON ➡

---

4. **pinafore** (pĭn′ə fôr): apronlike garment that young girls used to wear over their dresses.

757

FOR STRUGGLING READERS

Assessment Support: Author's Purpose
Model how to determine the author's purpose. Tell students to pay attention to word choice and tone. Observe, for example, that Cyril is intelligent and inquisitive. He asks valid questions, but rather than encouraging these traits, the aunt wants Cyril to be quiet. She responds to his questions "weakly" and "fatuously." The bachelor, on the other hand, offers direct, interesting answers to each of Cyril's questions. Note that both the aunt's and the bachelor's choice of words and tone suggest that the writer's purpose is to describe relationships between adults and children.

the sound of the medals clinking and stopped to listen; they clinked again in a bush quite near him. He dashed into the bush, his pale grey eyes gleaming with ferocity and triumph, and dragged Bertha out and devoured her to the last morsel. All that was left of her were her shoes, bits of clothing, and the three medals for goodness."

53   "Were any of the little pigs killed?"

54   "No, they all escaped."

55   "The story began badly," said the smaller of the small girls, "but it had a beautiful ending."

56   "It is the most beautiful story that I ever heard," said the bigger of the small girls, with immense decision.

57   "It is the *only* beautiful story I have ever heard," said Cyril.

58   A dissentient[5] opinion came from the aunt.

59   "A most improper story to tell to young children! You have undermined the effect of years of careful teaching."

60   "At any rate," said the bachelor, collecting his belongings preparatory to leaving the carriage, "I kept them quiet for ten minutes, which was more than you were able to do."

61   "Unhappy woman!" he observed to himself as he walked down the platform of Templecombe station; "for the next six months or so those children will assail her in public with demands for an improper story!"

---

5. **dissentient** (dĭs sĕn′shənt): dissenting; disagreeing

DIFFERENTIATED INSTRUCTION

FOR STRUGGLING READERS
Assessment Support: Monitor Comprehension Guide students in answering these comprehension questions:

- What causes the wolf to find Bertha hiding in the myrtle bushes? [*The clanging of Bertha's medals (that is, her goodness) causes the wolf to find her.*]

- What is Bertha's fate? [*Bertha is devoured by the wolf.*]

- Which story—the aunt's or the bachelor's—do the children favor, and why? [*The children favor the bachelor's story because they find it "beautiful."*]

Harmless Fun? *from* World Almanac

1   Say what you want, but in Mortal Kombat: Armageddon, the latest version of the wildly popular Mortal Kombat video game, the character Taven's signature move is known as the "Ring of Hatred." That's when he pounds the ground with his fist, creating a shockwave of fire. If he executes it just right, he will obliterate his opponent, leaving small bits of flesh, blood and internal organs splattered across the screen.

2   And Taven is one of the good guys.

3   You can see from this example that in the world of violent video games, players can channel their aggressions and take on virtual foes, with instant and typically graphic results. Die-hard video game addicts will tell you it is all harmless fun—at worst, a way to let off steam. But don't be so sure.

4   In 1996, M. E. Ballard and J. R. Weist reported in the *Journal of Applied Social Psychology* that playing these kinds of games actually increased blood pressure in some players. Studies by P. J. Lynch in 1994 found that in aggressive children these games increased the flow of adrenaline. These two studies prove that video games cause aggression.

5   Can it be true, as profit-hungry game manufacturers claim, that virtual fights act as a substitute for actual fights? Are they a way to give a player his or her "adrenaline fix" harmlessly? Not necessarily. Researchers Craig A. Anderson, PhD, of Iowa State University, and Karen E. Dill, PhD, of Lenoir-Rhyne College, gathered 210 college students and had them play either a violent or a non-violent video game. Afterward, they had each student "punish" an opponent with loud blast of noise. The students who played the violent video game blasted the noise for a longer period of time than those who played the non-violent one. In addition, Anderson and Dill examined the video game habits of another 227 college students who had exhibited actual aggressiveness. Anderson and Dill concluded, in the American Psychological Association's *Journal of Personality and Social Psychology,* that violent video games prime the brain for aggressive thoughts. In the longer term, they found, violent video games get players used to using violent means to solve their problems.

6   "The player learns and practices new aggression-related scripts that can become more and more accessible for use when real-life conflict situations arise," said Anderson.

7   Who is most exposed to and damaged by these terrifying scripts? Children are. A study by the Kaiser Family Foundation found 83 percent of children between ages 8 and 18 have a video game console in their homes, and 40 percent had a console in their bedroom. And while the government began

GO ON

759

in 2000 to crack down on the marketing of violent video games to children, results are not so great. A 2007 investigation by the Federal Trade Commission found that out of 20 games with a rating of "M" (for Mature), 16 were advertised on Web sites popular among children. This must mean that young children are playing and learning from these hideous games without adult supervision.

8   Most grown-ups and young adults can distinguish between real violence and the virtual kind. They know where to draw the line. But what about those who don't? Children are still learning the boundaries of good behavior, and the do's and don'ts of problem solving. They are the real-life victims of video game manufacturers.

9   I'm not saying that violent video games are the root of all aggression in the world. But I don't see any evidence that the blood-soaked citizens of the screen world are doing anything to make the real world a better place.

760

DIFFERENTIATED INSTRUCTION

FOR STRUGGLING READERS

Assessment Support: Monitor Comprehension
Guide students in identifying these statements as true or false:

- Studies have shown that viewing violent video games increases aggression. *[T]*

- The author believes that children cannot tell the difference between real violence and violence in video games. *[T]*

- Scientists have proven conclusively that violent video games cause violent behavior. *[F]*

FOR ENGLISH LANGUAGE LEARNERS

Assessment Support: Describe and Interpret Visuals Tell students to describe what they see in the photograph on this page to a partner. Then, have students respond to questions their partner asks about the photograph, including this question: What is purpose of the photograph? Direct partners to switch roles and repeat the activity.

Reading Comprehension

Model a thinking process for answering multiple-choice questions.

1. **B is correct.** *The narrator is an all-knowing observer who sees into the minds of all the characters. A is incorrect because the narrator does not use first-person pronouns and is not one of the characters. C is incorrect because the narrator does not tell what only one character thinks, feels, or observes. D is incorrect because the story is not an account of something that happened before the story began.*

2. **D is correct.** *The children don't like the aunt's story because it teaches a lesson about goodness. A is incorrect because the bachelor's story shows that good behavior is sometimes punished. B is incorrect because in the aunt's story goodness does not cause problems. C is incorrect because the author's message has to do with people's behavior, not travel.*

3. **A is correct.** *The author characterizes the aunt as sanctimonious, and his portrayal of her supports the story's theme. B is incorrect because although the children are irritating, the author does not make fun of them. C is incorrect because bystanders do not figure in the story. D is incorrect because although the bachelor is annoyed by the aunt and children, rather than making fun of him, the author portrays him sympathetically as understanding children surprisingly well.*

4. **C is correct.** *The children like the bachelor's story better than the aunt's story. A is incorrect because the story offers no evidence that the bachelor is actually married. B is incorrect because traveling alone is not contrary to being a bachelor. D is incorrect because the story offers no evidence that the bachelor has children of his own.*

5. **D is correct.** *The narrator calls the conversation of the aunt and children "persistent" and compares it to a housefly "that refused to be discouraged." A and B are incorrect because one would not "discourage" something pleasant or polite. C is incorrect because one might not discourage a silly conversation.*

Reading Comprehension

> **Use "The Storyteller" (pp. 754–758) to answer questions 1–11.**

1. This story is told through —
   A. first-person point of view
   B. third-person omniscient point of view
   C. third-person limited point of view
   D. a flashback

2. The author's message is that —
   A. good behavior is always rewarded
   B. good behavior can cause problems
   C. travel is boring
   D. people do not like lectures on behavior

3. "The Storyteller" is a satire, or a story that makes fun of something to persuade people to change. The author is making fun of —
   A. self-righteous people, like the aunt
   B. irritating people, like the children
   C. bystanders, like the reader
   D. easily annoyed people, like the bachelor

4. In paragraph 1, the word *bachelor,* meaning an unmarried man without children, is ironic because —
   A. the character is actually married
   B. he is traveling by himself
   C. he understands the children better than the aunt
   D. he has children of his own

5. The word *persistent* in paragraph 1 means —
   A. pleasant
   B. polite
   C. silly
   D. stubborn

6. The aunt tells the children a story because she wants to —
   A. stop them from bothering the bachelor
   B. answer their questions
   C. show that she is a wonderful storyteller
   D. amuse herself

7. The word *deplorably* in paragraph 14 comes from the Latin root *deplorare,* meaning "to weep bitterly." *Deplorably* means —
   A. terribly
   B. praiseworthy
   C. excellent
   D. magnificent

8. The bachelor's purpose for telling the story about Bertha is to —
   A. keep the children occupied and annoy the aunt
   B. give the children more accurate answers to their questions
   C. point out the benefits of good behavior
   D. pass the time productively

9. The children become interested in the bachelor's story when —
   A. he introduces the wolf
   B. the pigs eat the flowers
   C. he says "horribly good"
   D. he talks about Bertha's medals

10. The aunt smiles during the bachelor's story because she —
    A. enjoys the bachelor's retelling of her story
    B. expects that the bachelor will have the same trouble she did
    C. thinks the boy's question is interesting
    D. is waiting for a question from one of the girls

---

6. **A is correct.** *The aunt begins telling a story after noticing that the bachelor is annoyed and may be about to call the conductor. B is incorrect because the aunt has already answered questions from the children and decides to tell them a story when she is unable to answer further questions. C is incorrect because the aunt is not confident as she begins to tell the children a story. D is incorrect because the aunt suggests that the children listen to a story only after tiring of answering the children's questions and noticing that the bachelor is annoyed.*

7. **A is correct.** *Terribly is an adverb and reflects the meaning of the root deplorare. B, C, and D are incorrect because all are adjectives, not adverbs like deplorably, and none reflect the meaning of the Latin root.*

8. **A is correct.** *The bachelor responds without hesitation to the children's request for a story and makes negative comments about the aunt's storytelling abilities. B is incorrect because the bachelor does not try to correct the aunt's answers to the children's questions. C is incorrect because in the*

11. The bachelor thinks that in the future the children will —
    A. make up new stories about Bertha to tell each other
    B. learn more about wolves
    C. take more train rides
    D. ask the aunt to tell improper stories

Use "Harmless Fun?" (pp. 759–760) to answer questions 12–16.

12. The author's purpose in writing this essay is to —
    A. convince readers that video games are harmless fun
    B. teach readers how to play video games
    C. show readers that video games are not harmless
    D. point out that video games teach important life skills

13. In paragraph 1, *obliterate* means —
    A. to wipe out
    B. to pay back
    C. to make someone owe
    D. to turn inside-out

14. To back up the article's main opinion, the author draws upon —
    A. personal experience playing video games
    B. studies of people playing video games
    C. studies of children at recess
    D. articles about crime from newspapers

15. Which word in paragraph 5 helps the reader understand the meaning of the words *adrenaline fix*?
    A. *actual*
    B. *fights*
    C. *play*
    D. *video*

16. The reader can conclude that —
    A. video games help children learn the boundaries of good behavior
    B. the author thinks video games have limited benefits for society
    C. fewer children are playing violent games without adult supervision
    D. the author has proven that video games cause an increase in blood pressure

Use "The Storyteller" and "Harmless Fun?" to answer questions 17–18.

17. "The Storyteller" and "Harmless Fun?" both address the topic of —
    A. entertaining children with whatever is available
    B. letting children behave inappropriately
    C. guiding children toward good behavior
    D. watching children carefully all the time

18. The authors of both selections —
    A. unintentionally encourage bad behavior among children
    B. understand that children are interested in topics that adults consider inappropriate
    C. use humor to communicate a message
    D. express strong feelings about how children pass their time

GO ON ➡

bachelor's story good behavior is punished. D is incorrect because the story is told to entertain, not to accomplish something.

9. **C is correct.** The children react favorably when they hear the word "horrible" used in connection with goodness. A and B are incorrect because the children show interest in the story long before the wolf is introduced or the pigs are mentioned. D is incorrect because there is no indication that the medals grab the children's interest.

10. **B is correct.** When the bachelor comments on the aunt's "success" as a storyteller before beginning his own story, her response suggests that he will not be any more successful than she. A is incorrect because her smile suggests self-satisfaction rather than enjoyment. C is incorrect because the aunt has never shown interest in the children's questions; she has viewed them as an annoyance. D is incorrect because one of the girls has already asked a question.

11. **D is correct.** The bachelor observes as much at the end of the selection. A is incorrect because at the end of the bachelor's story the wolf eats Bertha. B is incorrect because there is no indication that the children are interested in learning more about wolves. C is incorrect because the children found the train ride boring until the bachelor began telling a story.

12. **C is correct.** Evidence that proves that video games are not harmless is cited throughout the article. A is incorrect because the evidence cited in the article shows the opposite. B is incorrect because the article does not provide instructions for how to play video games. D is incorrect because the article does not discuss life skills that video games teach.

13. **A is correct.** The details about body parts being "splattered across the screen" support this meaning of obliterate. B is incorrect because there is no suggestion of payback as a goal of the video game; instead, the game's name suggests combat to the death. C is incorrect because it mistakes obliterate for obligate. D is a weaker answer because it does not convey the idea of total destruction.

14. **B is correct.** Throughout the article, the author cites studies and research about people playing video games. A is incorrect because the author makes no mention of

personal experience playing video games. C is incorrect because none of the studies discussed had to do with children at recess. D is incorrect because newspaper articles about crime are not cited in the article.

15. **B is correct.** This choice is supported by the connection between adrenaline and aggression established in paragraph 4. A and D are incorrect because they do not reflect how adrenaline increases energy. C is incorrect because play does not reflect the negative energy associated with adrenaline.

16. **B is correct.** The author proves that video games are not harmless. A is incorrect because the article focuses on violent behavior associated with video games. C is incorrect because the author does not provide such a statistic in the article but observes in general that young children play video games without adult supervision. D is incorrect because although the author cites a study that shows that playing video games increases blood pressure, the author's purpose in writing is not to prove that fact.

17. C is correct. *The aunt in "The Storyteller" tries to guide children toward good behavior, albeit unsuccessfully, and in paragraph 8 of "Harmless Fun?" the author suggests that children need guidance toward good behavior. A is a weaker answer because it is not a main topic of either selection. B is incorrect because although the inappropriate behavior of children is featured in both selections, in "The Storyteller" both adults take steps to correct children's inappropriate behavior. D is incorrect because "The Storyteller" does not suggest that children should be watched carefully all the time.*

18. B is correct. *The children in "The Storyteller" are fascinated by the story of a child whose goodness is punished, and studies cited in "Harmless Fun?" show that children are drawn to violence depicted in video games. A is incorrect because although the bachelor's story in the first selection might be seen to encourage bad behavior, the second selection does not promote violent behavior in any way. C is incorrect because although the satirical tone of the first selection involves some humor, the second selection is completely serious. D is incorrect because although the second selection does express such feelings, the first selection does not.*

19. A is correct. *The stance of the person in the photo shows discipline. B, C, and D are incorrect because the photo shows only one person and so does not suggest bullies, competition, or fighting.*

20. B is correct. *The karate student in the photo demonstrates balance and confidence. A is incorrect because the person in the photo is not engaged with an opponent. C is a weaker answer because although the person shown is a girl, nothing else in the photo promotes karate for girls specifically. D is incorrect because although the person in the photo is practicing karate outdoors, the photo suggests that karate is hard work more than fun.*

SHORT CONSTRUCTED RESPONSE

Possible responses:

21. *They thought the story was beautiful because after beginning "badly" with a girl who was recognized for her goodness, it*

Use the visual representation on page 761 to answer questions 19–20.

19. This Web page encourages people to try martial arts to —
    A. develop self-control
    B. end their fear of bullies
    C. win competitions
    D. become better fighters

20. The Web site designer probably choose this photo to show that —
    A. karate can be used to disarm opponents in a fight
    B. karate students develop discipline and self-control
    C. karate is a good activity for girls
    D. karate is a fun outdoor activity

764

SHORT CONSTRUCTED RESPONSE
Write a short constructed response to each question, using text evidence to support your response.

21. Why did the children think that the bachelor's story was "beautiful"? Use text evidence to support your response.

22. How does the author of "Harmless Fun?" prove the article's main point? Use text evidence to support your response.

Write a short constructed response to the following question, using text evidence from both selections to support your response.

23. How does the idea of adults' responsibility toward children apply to both selections? Support your response with text evidence from **both** selections.

---

ended beautifully with the good girl being devoured by a wolf (paragraphs 52, 55). It was beautiful because it had interesting details, such as flower-eating pigs (paragraphs 41, 43, 46) and a Prince who liked pigs more than flowers (paragraphs 46, 47). It also did not instruct the children to be good (the good girl in the story was punished instead of rewarded, paragraph 52).

22. *The author uses studies on the effect of violent video games on blood pressure and adrenaline (paragraph 4), research on the*

behavior of college students who played violent video games (paragraph 5), and statistics about children's exposure to violent video games (paragraph 7) to prove the article's main point.

23. *Both convey messages about behavior, but the message of the first selection is that people do not like to be lectured about behavior, and the second selection suggests that children need guidance about behavior.*

Revising and Editing

DIRECTIONS Read this passage, and answer the questions that follow.

(1) One company found two willing candidates. (2) The candidates wanted to fly to the International Space Station. (3) Each was ready to pay $20 million. (4) In the future, the company will offer more-affordable trips. (5) People will be able to take suborbital flights for just $100,000. (6) Civilian spaceships need to be built first. (7) Some people might want the experience without going there. (8) To meet this need, the company will offer a training-only session. (9) Others, might be interested in a short flight. (10) They'll have the option to fly just 15 miles high. (11) Space tourism is a lucrative business.

1. What is the most effective way to improve the organization of the paragraph?
   A. Move sentence 1 before sentence 6
   B. Move sentence 4 before sentence 8
   C. Move sentence 9 before sentence 3
   D. Move sentence 11 before sentence 1

2. What is the best way to rewrite sentences 1, 2, and 3 as one compound-complex sentence?
   A. One company found two willing candidates wanting to fly to the International Space Station, and each was ready to pay $20 million.
   B. One company found two willing candidates who wanted to fly to the International Space Station, and each was ready to pay $20 million.
   C. When one company found two willing candidates wanting to fly to the International Space Station, each being ready to pay $20 million.
   D. One company found two willing candidates wanting to fly to the International Space Station, with each ready to pay $20 million.

3. How could sentences 4, 5, and 6 be rewritten as one compound-complex sentence?
   A. In the future, the company will offer more affordable trips to people who will be able to take suborbital flights for just $100,000 when civilian spaceships are built.
   B. In the future, when civilian spaceships are built, the company will offer more affordable trips to people who will be able to take suborbital flights for just $100,000.
   C. In the future, when civilian spaceships are built, the company will offer more affordable trips; people will be able to take suborbital flights for just $100,000.
   D. In the future, civilian spaceships will be built, and the company will offer flights for just $100,000.

4. What transitional word or phrase should be used in sentence 7?
   A. However,   C. Then,
   B. If   D. Until then,

5. Which change, if any, should be made to sentence 9?
   A. Delete the comma
   B. Add **only** after *in*
   C. Change *flight* to **journey**
   D. Make no change

STOP

765

COMMON CORE FOCUS

RL 10 Read and comprehend literature, including dramas. **RI 10** Read and comprehend literary nonfiction.

INTRODUCE *GREAT READS*

In Unit 6, students have discussed a number of big questions. Invite students to tell which question they found most intriguing and why, and then focus attention on the three that appear on this page. Discuss the recommended books and their summaries, pointing out how each connects to the related question. Encourage students to choose one or more of these "great reads" to read independently.

Ideas for Independent Reading

What should people do to protect the rights of animals? to protect the rights of other people? The following books explore such questions.

COMMON CORE

RL 10 Read and comprehend literature. **RI 10** Read and comprehend literary nonfiction.

Do animals have rights?

The Pig Who Sang to the Moon
by Jeffrey Moussaieff Masson

Masson's observations of farm animals suggest that they, too, are capable of fear, happiness, and grief. Masson argues that if animals feel, their lives matter to them, and it is not right to confine and slaughter them for human food.

The Ten Trusts
by Jane Goodall and Marc Bekoff

The authors set out ways in which people can protect animals and the environment. True stories of animals are matched with the ten trusts, which include "Respect all life" and "Refrain from harming life in order to learn about it."

Speaking Out for Animals
edited by Kim W. Stallwood

A collection of interviews, this book sheds light on the reasons people have adopted the animal rights cause. Some names are well-known, such as that of the ex-Beatle Paul McCartney, but most of the subjects are ordinary people.

What would you sacrifice for justice?

To Kill a Mockingbird: The Screenplay
by Horton Foote

In the South before the civil rights era, the lawyer Atticus Finch courageously (and unpopularly) defends a black man against unjust charges. His story is told from the viewpoint of his young daughter, Scout.

Silver Rights
by Constance Curry

This book tells the true story of the Carters, a black Mississippi family who worked for justice by having 7 of their 13 children desegregate an all-white school system in 1965. There were threats and bullets in the middle of the night, but the family endured.

Eyewitness: A Filmmaker's Memoir of the Chicano Movement
by Jesús Salvador Treviño

Treviño's memoir reflects on the Mexican-American civil rights movement, which he helped document through his work as a filmmaker. This experience shaped the political principles that guide his work as a television producer and director.

How important is wealth?

A Christmas Carol
by Charles Dickens

This classic introduces readers to Ebenezer Scrooge, a wealthy and disagreeable 19th-century businessman. One Christmas Eve he receives a series of ghostly visits that change the way he lives his life.

The Pearl
by John Steinbeck

When Kino, a poor Mexican fisherman, finds a huge pearl, he thinks it will bring his family wealth and happiness. Instead, it places him in danger and causes him to lose what he values most.

Mean Spirit
by Linda Hogan

Based on historical events, this novel is set in 1920s Oklahoma, where oil was discovered on Osage Indian lands. The murder of Grace Blanket, the richest woman in the territory, is followed by other mysterious deaths. Who is responsible?

Get Novel Wise
THINK central

Go to **thinkcentral.com**.
KEYWORD: HML10-766

766

NovelWise
THINK central

The keyword on this page points to **NovelWise**, a Web site that helps students choose a novel or other book-length work to read. **NovelWise** also provides

- study guides
- reading strategies and literary elements instruction
- presentations to introduce classic novels
- project ideas

UNIT 7

Sound and Sense

THE LANGUAGE OF POETRY

767

About the Art Colorado artist Jen Thario (b. 1968) created *Graffiti Divas* in 2003. For more information, see page 822.

INTRODUCE THE UNIT

When you hear a ticking or tapping sound in your house, you usually can figure out what is making the noise. You may be hearing a wall clock in a quiet room, for example, or the dripping of a faucet. As children, we learn to make sense of the language we hear in everyday speech. However, special study is sometimes needed to make sense of and appreciate the unusual way words can be used in poetry.

Interpreting art often requires similar study. For example, this page makes a connection between a spotlight and the moon by setting two silhouetted figures side by side. Invite students to explore the meaning of these images by answering these questions:

- How are the painting and the photograph similar? How do they differ?
- What thoughts and feelings come to mind as you consider each image?
- What words would you choose to describe each image?
- What sounds might you associate with each image? Are the sounds similar or different?

Tell students that as they read the selections in this unit, they will learn techniques and strategies that will help them make sense of **the language of poetry.**

For help in planning this unit, see

R RESOURCE MANAGER UNIT 7
pp. 1–10

UNIT 7

COMMON CORE STRAND	Text Analysis Workshop: The Language of Poetry pp. 770–777	There Will Come Soft Rains/Meeting at Night/ The Sound of Night Poems pp. 778–785	I dwell in Possibility—/ Variation on a Theme by Rilke/blessing the boats Poems pp. 786–793	The Fish/Christmas Sparrow/The Sloth Poems pp. 794–801	Piano/Fifteen/Tonight I Can Write . . ./Puedo Escribir Los Versos . . . Poems pp. 802–809
Reading Literature	Form pp. 770–771 RL 5 Poetic Elements pp. 772–775 RL 4 Analyze the Text p. 776 RL 10	Sound Devices pp. 779–780, 783–784 RL 4 Reading Poetry pp. 779–780, 782, 784 RL 5, RL 10	Lyric Poetry pp. 787, 791–792 RL 2, RL 5 Figurative Language pp. 787–788, 790, 792 RL 4, RL 5 Compare and Contrast pp. 787, 790–792 RL 4, RL 10	Free Verse pp. 795–796, 801 RL 5, RL 10 Imagery pp. 795, 797–798, 800–801 RL 5, RL 10 Visualize pp. 795, 797, 799, 801 RL 4 Elements of Poetry p. 800 RL 10 Language Coach p. 796 RL 4	Sound Devices pp. 803–804, 806, 809 RL 4, RL 10 Understand Line Breaks pp. 803, 805, 809 RL 5 Line Length p. 806 RL 5 Make Inferences p. 806 RL 10
Reading Informational Text					Journal Article p. 808
Writing		Writing Prompt p. 785 W 9a (RL 2)	Quickwrite p. 786 Writing Prompt p. 793		Quickwrite p. 802 Writing Prompt p. 809 W 2b
Speaking and Listening		Discuss p. 778 SL 1		Discuss p. 794 SL 1	
Language		Use Precise Language p. 785 L 3 Language Coach p. 783 L 4b	Create Rhythm p. 793 L 1a	Language Coach p. 798 L 4b	

767A

Sonnet 18/Sonnet XXX of Fatal Interview Sonnets pp. 810–815	*Linked Selections*		**Writing Workshop: Analysis of a Poem** pp. 828–837 **Technology Workshop: Creating a Class Blog** pp. 838–839
	Lord Randall/Ballad/Balada/ Midwinter Blues Poems pp. 816–823	*from* **Blues Poems** Essay pp. 824–827	
		Lexile: 740 *Fry: 5* *Dale-Chall: 9.5*	
Sonnet pp. 811, 814, 815 RL 5, RL 10 Reading Sonnets pp. 811–812, 815 RL 2	Ballad pp. 817–818, 820, 822–823 RL 5, RL 10 Symbols p. 820 RL 4 Understand Dialect pp. 817–818, 822–823 RL 4		Analysis of a Poem pp. 828–837 RL 1
		Take Notes pp. 825–826 RI 2 Foreign Words in English p. 825 RI 4 Read for Information p. 827 RI 2, RI 4	
Writing Prompt p. 815 W 2b	Quickwrite p. 816 Writing Prompt p. 823 W 2f	Evaluate Poems p. 827 W 2	Writing an Analysis of a Poem pp. 828–837 W 2a–f, W 4, W 5, W 9a (RL 1), W 10 Creating a Class Blog pp. 838–839 W 2a, W 6
Brainstorm p. 810 SL 1			Creating a Class Blog pp. 838–839 SL 1c, SL 4, SL 5
			Drafting p. 831 L 2 Editing and Publishing p. 835 L 1

ECOS

To see the complete Essential Course of Study, see pp. T23–T28.

 For additional lesson planning help, see **Teacher One Stop DVD.**

Instructional Support

Resource Manager Unit 7

UNIT SUPPORT
Academic Vocabulary, p. 3

Additional Academic Vocabulary, p. 4

Grammar Focus p. 5

Text Analysis Workshop pp. 9–10

Writing Workshop: Analysis of a
   Poem p. 113

SELECTION SUPPORT*
Plan and Teach
   Lesson planning pages

   Additional leveled selection questions

   Extension activities

Student Copy Masters
   Selection summaries in four languages

   Skills copy masters in English and Spanish

   Vocabulary preteaching and support

   Reading Check and Question Support

   Reading Fluency

   * Available for all selections

   † Available on **thinkcentral.com**.

Language Handbook

Vocabulary Practice

Best Practices Toolkit†

PowerNotes DVD-ROM†

Connections: Nonfiction for
Common Core CD-ROM†

Teacher One Stop DVD-ROM

Student One Stop DVD-ROM

Media*Smart* DVD-ROM
Daisy / America's Back

Write*Smart* CD-ROM†

GrammarNotes DVD-ROM†

WordSharp CD-ROM†

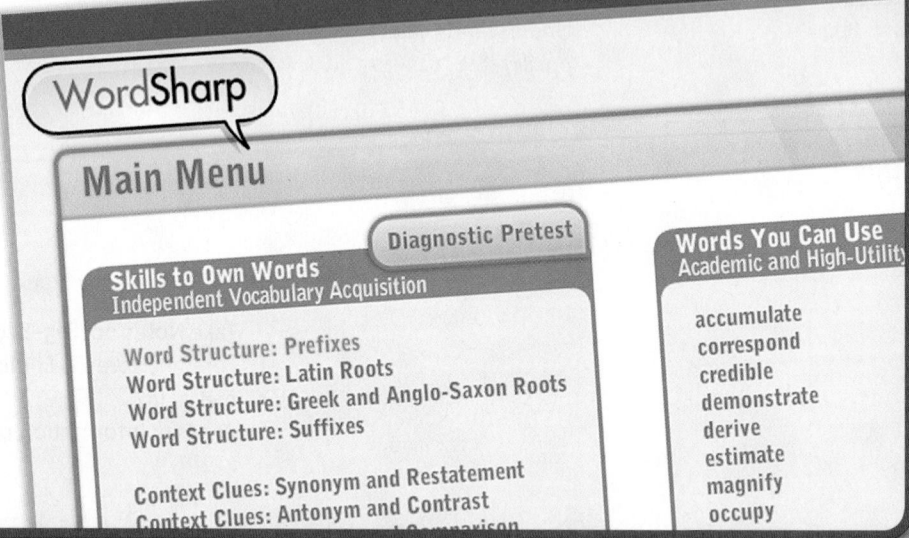

Differentiated Instruction

STRUGGLING READERS AND WRITERS

Resource Manager Unit 7
Additional Selection Questions

Question Support

Reading Fluency

Interactive Reader

Adapted Interactive Reader

Audio Tutor

Level Up Online Tutorials

Audio Anthology
(with Audio summaries)

Diagnostic and Selection Tests
Selection Tests A/B

ENGLISH LANGUAGE LEARNERS

Resource Manager Unit 7
Selection Summaries in English,
Spanish, Vietnamese and Haitian Creole

Skills Copymasters in Spanish

**English Language Learner Adapted
Interactive Reader Teacher's Guide**

ELL Adapted Interactive Reader

Audio Tutor

Guide to English for Newcomers

Audio Anthology

**Audio Summaries in Multiple
Languages** (on **thinkcentral.com**)

ADVANCED LEARNERS

Resource Manager Unit 7
Additional Selection Questions

Ideas for Extension

Diagnostic and Selection Tests
Selection Tests B/C

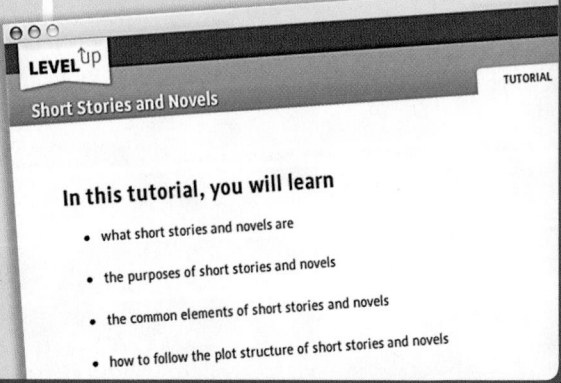

Assessment and Reteaching

Diagnostic and Selection Tests

Unit and Benchmark Tests

ThinkCentral Online Assessment:
- All program assessments
- Level Up Online Tutorials

ExamView Test Generator on the Teacher One Stop DVD-ROM

Online Essay Scoring on **thinkcentral.com**

ThinkCentral Online Reteaching:
- Level Up Online Tutorials
- Reteaching Worksheets

Holt McDougal **Online Essay Scoring**

Welcome to Holt McDougal Online Essay Scoring!

This site is designed to help you improve your writing skills and prepare for standardized writing tests. When you write and submit a response to one of the writing prompts on this site, the computerized scoring system will immediately score and deliver feedback on your essay. Other resources on this site will help you prepare, develop, and revise your essay.

STUDENTS

Get started by entering the **Writing Zone** →

Professional Development

Video Center Based on interviews with program consultants and other educational experts, these videos feature classroom-ready teaching strategies.

Teacher Toolkit Includes a Teacher Handbook as well as a range of articles and handouts by program consultants and other educators.

Janet Allen

Jim Burke

Kylene Beers

Carol Jago

 THINK central **at a Glance**

One Location, Endless Resources

Find Resources Browse all *Holt McDougal Literature* components for the ones that meet your students' needs and match your teaching style.

Assess Progress and Reteach Assign electronic versions of program assessments to measure your students' mastery of the Common Core State Standards. On thinkcentral.com, some tests deliver online remediation tutorials to students who have not mastered skills.

⚡ Interactive Whiteboard Lessons

Prepare your students for college and careers by teaching relevant, real-world skills through dynamic, interactive instruction. Go to **thinkcentral.com** to browse through all whiteboard lessons, including the following:

- Poetry: Language and Form
- Figurative Language and Imagery
- Comparing Texts
- Using Precise Language

 **HISTORY**

Together Holt McDougal and HISTORY® are revolutionizing the study of English/language arts with video that helps students relive and re-imagine the people, places, and events they are discovering through reading. Look for selections with the HISTORY® icon.

Where do you find
POETRY?

Read aloud the lines of "poetry" and call on volunteers to answer the questions that follow. Then read aloud the next paragraph. When the text reveals that the "poem" is actually advertising copy, invite comments. Ask students why the lines still seem like poetry. *Possible answers: The lines are short, and they break as poetic lines often do, instead of being written as a paragraph; the lines create images in the reader's mind; the lines explore someone's feelings at a personal moment.*

MAKE A LIST After students complete the activity, have them come together as a class to further discuss the definition of poetry. (For example, must poetry rhyme? Is it limited to certain subjects?) Then encourage students to think of other places—besides ads—in which it would be unusual to find poetry, but in which poetry might make a point effectively.

CHECK UNDERSTANDING Come to a class consensus about a working definition of poetry. Have students share what they learned from defining the term.

Where do you find
POETRY?

We drove to the cafe in silence.
When we arrived,
She whispered to the piano player,
Then took my hand. We danced.
And suddenly, something we had lost was back.

Where do you think these lines are from? Could they appear somewhere else in this anthology? in a volume of love poems? Perhaps they're from a song.

It might surprise you to learn that lines like these appeared in a magazine ad for a car. So are they poetry or not? Your answer probably depends on what you think poetry is and on the role it plays in your life.

MAKE A LIST On a sheet of paper, write your own definition of what poetry is. Then, on the basis of that definition, make a list of all the places you think poetry lives. When you're done, compare your definition and list with those of others in your class. Do any of the responses surprise you?

Find It Online! THINK central
Go to **thinkcentral.com** for the interactive version of this unit.

768

Unit Resources

See resources on the **Teacher One Stop DVD-ROM** *and on* **thinkcentral.com**.

R RESOURCE MANAGER UNIT 7

UNIT AND BENCHMARK TESTS

 **BEST PRACTICES TOOLKIT**

INTERACTIVE READER

ADAPTED INTERACTIVE READER

ELL ADAPTED INTERACTIVE READER

LANGUAGE HANDBOOK

VOCABULARY PRACTICE

TECHNOLOGY

- **Teacher One Stop DVD-ROM**
- **Student One Stop DVD-ROM**
- **PowerNotes DVD-ROM**
- **Write*Smart* CD-ROM**
- **Media*Smart* DVD-ROM**
- **GrammarNotes DVD-ROM**
- **Audio Anthology CD**
- **Audio Tutor CD**

THINK central

Find it Online!

The interactive version of this unit on **thinkcentral.com** includes
- video and **PowerNotes** introductions to key selections
- audio support—listen or download
- **ThinkAloud** models
- **WordSharp** vocabulary tutorials
- interactive review and remediation

Complete text of the Common Core Standards is found in the correlation on pp. T10–T22. Standards covered in this unit are found in the overview (pp. 767A–767B) and on the lesson pages where they are taught.

Preview Unit Goals

This page presents an overview of the skills and strategies covered in this unit. Explain to students that they can get more from their reading by previewing. Then ask them to skim the page to preview the skills that they will learn. Note that each strand or category of skill is color-coded on this page and throughout the unit.

COMMON
CORE

Preview Unit Goals

TEXT ANALYSIS	• Recognize characteristics of a variety of forms of poetry, including lyric poetry, ode, ballad, sonnet, and free verse • Analyze how an author chooses to structure poetry, including lines and stanzas • Analyze imagery, figurative language, including metaphor, simile, personification, and hyperbole • Analyze prosody and sound devices, including repetition, alliteration, assonance, consonance, onomatopoeia, rhythm, rhyme and rhyme scheme, and meter
READING	• Compare and contrast • Develop strategies for reading poetry • Understand and analyze dialect • Take notes and evaluate poems; cite evidence
WRITING AND LANGUAGE	• Write an analysis of a poem • Use precise language to express rhythm, sound, and imagery • Use parallelism to create rhythm
MEDIA AND VIEWING	• Create a class blog

KEY LARGO

769

Focus and Motivate

COMMON CORE FOCUS

RL 4 Determine the meaning of words and phrases as they are used in a text; analyze the cumulative impact of specific word choices on meaning.
RL 5 Analyze an author's choices concerning how to structure a text. **RL 10** Read and comprehend poems.

Teach

Part 1: Form

Have students read each poetry example silently as a volunteer reads aloud. Then help students analyze the examples.

Traditional Form

- Ask students how the rhyming pattern in Rossetti's poem is coordinated with the two different speakers. ***Possible answer:*** *The two questions rhyme, and the two answers rhyme.*

- Ask students how the length of lines 1 and 3 and their rising inflection as questions enhance the images described. ***Possible answer:*** *The length and rising inflection of these lines suggest a long, slow uphill journey.*

Organic Form

- Have a volunteer write the de Hoyos poem on the board as two prose sentences, using standard conventions, no ampersand, and no line breaks. Ask students to compare the two versions and explain how the poet's form reflects her message. ***Possible answer:*** *It doesn't waste precious time on inputting capitalization or punctuation, or even on spelling out the word* and.

- Discuss how the shortness of the last two lines adds to the poem's message. ***Possible answer:*** *It emphasizes the words and suggests that ideas are simple and easily stated, unlike the traditional, formal, time-consuming presentation of ideas.*

BEST PRACTICES TOOLKIT—Copy Master
Analysis Frame: Poetic Form and Structure
pp. D21, D40

Text Analysis Workshop

The Language of Poetry

Essential Course of Study ECOS

Emily Dickinson once wrote, "If I feel physically as if the top of my head were taken off, I know that is poetry." A good poem can make readers look at the world in a new way. A simple fork becomes the foot of a strange and unearthly bird; death itself appears as the driver of a carriage. After reading a poem, you might find yourself repeating lines in your mind or remembering images that "spoke" to you from the page. What gives poetry such power? Read a poem closely, and you'll see how it has been carefully crafted to affect you.

COMMON CORE

Included in this workshop:
RL 4 Determine the meaning of words and phrases as they are used in a text; analyze the cumulative impact of specific word choices on meaning.
RL 5 Analyze an author's choices concerning how to structure a text. **RL 10** Read and comprehend poems.

Part 1: Form

What you'll most likely notice first about a poem is its **form,** or the distinctive way the words are arranged on the page. Included in a poem's form are its **graphic elements,** such as the length and placement of **lines** and the way they are grouped into **stanzas.** Similar to a paragraph in narrative writing, each stanza conveys a unified idea and contributes to a poem's overall meaning.

Poems can be traditional or organic in form. Regardless of its **structure,** though, a poem's form is often deliberately chosen to echo its meaning.

TRADITIONAL

Characteristics
- follows fixed rules, such as a specified number of lines
- has a regular pattern of rhythm and rhyme
- includes the following forms: sonnet, ode, haiku, limerick, ballad, and epic

Example
Does the road wind up-hill all the way?
    Yes, to the very end.
Will the day's journey take the whole long day?
    From morn to night, my friend.

    —from "Up-hill" by Christina Rossetti

Analyze the Example
- Identify the rhyming words at the ends of the lines to see the rhyme pattern of the stanza.
- Read the lines aloud to hear their regular rhythm.
- Notice how the singsong musical quality emphasizes the comforting message.

ORGANIC

Characteristics
- does not have a regular pattern of rhythm and may not rhyme
- may use unconventional spelling, punctuation, and grammar
- includes the following forms: free verse and concrete poetry

Example
wear your colors
like a present person
        today is
        here & now

    —from "Look Not to Memories"
      by Angela de Hoyos

Analyze the Example
- Notice that this poem has no capitalization or end punctuation.
- Note the lack of rhyme and the use of an ampersand (&).
- Think about why this structure suits the "seize the day" message.

DIFFERENTIATED INSTRUCTION

FOR STRUGGLING READERS

Note Taking For students who need help with note taking, hand out the note-taking copy master before discussing this page. As volunteers read aloud each section, discuss the main points and have students record them on the copy master.

Define Organic Form Explain that the scientific term for a living thing is *organism,* so in its broadest sense *organic* refers to something living and natural. Point out that organic

poetry is informal and sounds the way real people speak or think.

 RESOURCE MANAGER—Copy Master
Note Taking p. 9

MODEL 1: TRADITIONAL FORM

The following two stanzas are from an **ode,** a complex lyric poem that addresses a serious theme, such as justice, truth, or the passage of time. While odes can follow just about any structure, "The Fire of Driftwood" is traditional in form because of its regular stanzas, rhythm, and rhyme. Here, the **speaker**—the voice that talks to the reader—sadly reflects on how he and his friends have grown apart.

---

from THE FIRE *of* DRIFTWOOD
Poem by **Henry Wadsworth Longfellow**

We spake of many a vanished scene,
    Of what we once had thought and said,
Of what had been, and might have been,
    And who was changed, and who was dead;

5 And all that fills the hearts of friends,
    When first they feel, with secret pain,
Their lives thenceforth have separate ends,
    And never can be one again.

Close Read

1. How is the form of the first stanza similar to that of the second? Consider the number and length of the lines, the pattern of the rhyme, and the rhythm.

2. Summarize the different ideas expressed in each stanza.

MODEL 2: ORGANIC FORM

This poem is written in **free verse,** with no regular pattern of rhythm and rhyme. Notice how its form differs from that of Longfellow's poem.

---

i am not done yet
Poem by **Lucille Clifton**

as possible as yeast
as imminent as bread
a collection of safe habits
a collection of cares
5 less certain than i seem
more certain than i was
a changed changer
i continue to continue
where i have been
10 most of my lives is
where i'm going

Close Read

1. Using the chart on the preceding page, identify two characteristics that make this poem organic in form.

2. Read the poem aloud. The short lines and the rhythm help to emphasize the ideas expressed in each line. Choose two lines and explain what the speaker is saying.

MODEL 1: TRADITIONAL FORM
Close Read

1. *Possible answer: Both stanzas have four lines of similar length, an* abab *rhyme scheme, and a weak-strong, weak-strong rhythm of beats.*

2. *Possible answer: First stanza: Two old friends share memories. Second stanza: Growing apart is painful.*

MODEL 2: ORGANIC FORM
Close Read

1. *Possible answer: The poem's organic characteristics include lack of capitalization, punctuation, rhyme, and a regular rhythm.*

2. *Possible answer: In the first two lines, the writer may be describing her sense of her own hidden potential. Yeast is not visible in bread dough, yet it makes the dough rise. Imminent means "about to happen."*

IF STUDENTS NEED HELP . . . Read the poem line by line with students, working together to paraphrase its meaning.

FOR STRUGGLING READERS
Analysis Support: Form Have students take turns reading the poems aloud to each other. Point out that the Longfellow excerpt is all one sentence. For the Clifton poem, ask students to notice the repeated words ("as," "collection," "continue," "certain," "where"), related ideas, and matching rhythms that connect pairs of lines. Point out that the last three lines form their own unit.

FOR ENGLISH LANGUAGE LEARNERS
Language: Punctuation and Print Cues Remind students that organic poems use unconventional spelling, punctuation, and grammar. Help students see this in the Clifton poem. For example, Clifton does not capitalize the first-person pronoun *I.* She also uses the plural noun *lives* where grammar rules would require the singular noun *life.*

Online Remediation

Are your students struggling with text analysis skills? Consider assigning them one or more **Level Up Online Tutorials** as remediation before beginning this unit. Log in to **thinkcentral.com** to view a list of the skills addressed by **Level Up.**

Teach

Part 2: Poetic Elements

After students read this page, direct them to the poem "Tell All the Truth But Tell It Slant" by Emily Dickinson (page 224). Ask a volunteer to read the poem aloud, and have the class chart the rhyme scheme *abcb*. Together, analyze the use of prosody and sound devices in the poem, and point out these examples:

- **alliteration:** "Tell ... Truth ... tell" (line 1); "Success ... Circuit" (line 2); "superb surprise" (line 4)

- **assonance:** the long *i* sound in "bright" and "delight" (line 3)

- **consonance:** the *l* sound in "Tell all.... tell ... slant" (line 1); the *k* sound in "Success ... Circuit" (line 2); the *r* and *p* sounds in "Truth's superb surprise" (line 4)

Describe the pattern of meter that repeats throughout the poem. *An unstressed syllable is followed by a stressed syllable.* Scan the poem for students, inviting their input.

Part 2: Poetic Elements

What gives one poem a brisk rhythm and another the sound of an everyday conversation? How can two poems on the same subject create dramatically different images in your mind? **Prosody,** the meter and rhyme of a poem, as well as other sound devices and imagery, give each poem its own character.

PROSODY AND SOUND DEVICES

Much of the power of poetry depends on **rhythm**—the pattern of stressed and unstressed syllables in each line. Poets use rhythm to emphasize ideas and to create a mood that suits their subject. Some poems have a regular pattern of rhythm, which is called **meter.** Analyzing the effects of a poem's rhythm begins with **scanning,** or marking, the meter. Unstressed syllables are marked with a (˘) and stressed syllables with a (´), as in these lines from "A Dirge" by Percy Bysshe Shelley:

Rŏugh wínd, / thăt móan / est lŏud	a
Gríef / tŏo sád / fŏr sóng;	b
Wíld wínd / whĕn súl / lĕn clóud	a
Knélls / all thĕ níght / lŏng.	b

A regular pattern of rhyme is called a **rhyme scheme.** Rhyme scheme is charted by assigning a letter of the alphabet to matching end rhymes, as shown in "A Dirge."

Poets also use many other sound devices to create specific effects. In each of the following examples, notice how the device helps to establish a mood, create a rhythm, and suggest different sounds and sights of the sea.

REPETITION
a sound, word, phrase, or line that is repeated for emphasis and unity

Break, break, break,
  On thy cold gray stones, O Sea!
  —from "Break, Break, Break" by Alfred, Lord Tennyson

ALLITERATION
the repetition of consonant sounds at the beginnings of words

The scraggy rock spit shielding the town's blue bay
  —from "Departure" by Sylvia Plath

ASSONANCE
the repetition of vowel sounds in words that do not end with the same consonant

The waves break fold on jewelled fold.
  —from "Moonlight" by Sara Teasdale

CONSONANCE
the repetition of consonant sounds within and at the ends of words

And black are the waters that sparkled so green.
  —from "Seal Lullaby" by Rudyard Kipling

DIFFERENTIATED INSTRUCTION

FOR STRUGGLING READERS

Note Taking For students who need help, hand out the note-taking copy master for this page. As they read and discuss the main points on pages 772–773, have students record them on the copy master.

R RESOURCE MANAGER—Copy Master
Note Taking p. 10

FOR ENGLISH LANGUAGE LEARNERS

Language: Skill Words Write these sentences on the board. Ask students to identify the underlined sound devices:

- Trees sh<u>i</u>vered in the b<u>i</u>tter w<u>i</u>nd. *assonance*

- <u>S</u>ing your <u>s</u>orrow, <u>s</u>ing your joy! *repetition*

- He tugge<u>d</u> an<u>d</u> dragge<u>d</u> the boat ashore. *consonance*

- The lion <u>r</u>ea<u>r</u>ed in <u>r</u>age and <u>r</u>oared. *alliteration*

MODEL 1: RHYTHM AND RHYME

The speakers in this next poem could be understood to be the collective voice of the pool players mentioned underneath the title. Read the poem aloud to hear its unique rhyme scheme and rhythm. In what ways do these elements reflect the fast-lane lifestyle that the speakers describe?

We Real Cool

The Pool Players.
Seven at The Golden Shovel.

Poem by **Gwendolyn Brooks**

We real cool. We
Left school. We

Lurk late. We
Strike straight. We

5   Sing sin. We
Thin gin. We

Jazz June. We
Die soon.

Close Read

1. Even though the rhyming words in this poem fall in the middle of the lines, they sound like end rhymes. If you treat these words as end rhymes, what is the rhyme scheme?

2. One way to read this poem is to stress every syllable. How would you describe the rhythm? Explain how it echoes the speakers' attitude toward life.

MODEL 2: OTHER SOUND DEVICES

This poem immerses you in the edge-of-your-seat excitement of a close baseball game. What sound devices has the poet used to create this effect?

THE BASE STEALER

Poem by **Robert Francis**

Poised between going on and back, pulled
Both ways taut like a tightrope-walker,
Fingertips pointing the opposites,
Now bouncing tiptoe like a dropped ball
5   Or a kid skipping rope, come on, come on,
Running a scattering of steps sidewise,
How he teeters, skitters, tingles, teases,
Taunts them, hovers like an ecstatic bird,
He's only flirting, crowd him, crowd him,
10   Delicate, delicate, delicate, delicate—now!

Close Read

1. Read the boxed text aloud. The use of alliteration emphasizes the tension that the base stealer feels. Find another example of alliteration and explain its effect.

2. Identify two other sound devices that the poet uses and describe their effects.

MODEL 1: RHYTHM AND RHYME

Close Read

1. *The rhyme scheme is* aa bb cc dd.

2. *Possible answer: The rhythm is very regular and monotonous, the lines short and abrupt. Readers can almost hear the bravado of the speakers as they brag about their fast-lane lifestyle and shrug their shoulders at the consequences.*

MODEL 2: OTHER SOUND DEVICES

Close Read

1. *Possible answer: In addition to the boxed text, examples of alliteration include "bouncing . . . ball" (line 4); "scattering . . . steps sidewise" (line 6); "teeters . . . tingles, teases, / Taunts" (lines 7–8).*

2. *Possible answers: Other sound devices in the poem: Repetition: "come on, come on" (line 5); "crowd him, crowd him" (line 9); "Delicate, delicate, delicate, delicate" (line 10); **Assonance:** the aw sound in "taut . . . walker" (line 2); the short i sound in "kid skipping" (line 5); the long e and short i sounds in "he teeters, skitters, tingles, teases" (line 7); **Consonance:** the t and p sounds within "tiptoe . . . dropped / . . . skipping rope . . . / teeters, skitters" (lines 4–7). Repetition helps to capture the suspense of the situation. Assonance and consonance help to create a sense of the base stealer's movements.*

FOR STRUGGLING READERS

Analysis Support: Sound Devices Have pairs of students read "We Real Cool" aloud to each other and find the sound devices. Provide these line numbers as clues:

- Repetition (throughout poem)
- Assonance (lines 1, 5)
- Alliteration (lines 3, 4, 5, 6–7)
- Consonance (lines 1–2, 3–4)

FOR ENGLISH LANGUAGE LEARNERS

Vocabulary: Idioms and Onomatopoeia For students who don't know what it means to steal a base, ask a volunteer to explain the term and demonstrate the movements of the base stealer in the poem. Then review the meaning of words such as *teeters, skeeters,* and *tingles.* Explain that the sound of these words helps the poet to convey meaning.

IMAGERY AND FIGURATIVE LANGUAGE

Draw on the board a large grid with four squares labeled *simile, metaphor, personification,* and *hyperbole.* Brainstorm with students for examples of everyday figurative language, and have them identify which category each example belongs in. Write the expression in the appropriate square.

simile:	metaphor:
sleep like a log	hard nut to crack
personification:	hyperbole:
eyes dancing with delight	died laughing

IMAGERY AND FIGURATIVE LANGUAGE

> *I can remember wind-swept streets of cities*
> *on cold and blustery nights, on rainy days;*
> *heads under shabby felts and parasols*
> *and shoulders hunched against a sharp concern.*
>
> —from "Memory" by Margaret Walker

Do these lines make you want to stay indoors, nestled under layers of blankets? If so, the reason is **imagery,** or words and phrases that re-create sensory experiences for readers. Through the highlighted images, the poet helps readers visualize the bleak scene—the way it looks, sounds, and even *feels*—in striking detail.

One way poets create strong imagery is through the use of **figurative language,** which conveys meanings beyond the literal meanings of words. Figurative language pops up all the time in everyday speech. For example, if you say "My heart sank when I heard the disappointing news," your friends will understand that your heart did not literally sink. Through this figurative expression, you are conveying the emotional depth of your disappointment.

In the following examples, notice what each technique helps to emphasize about the subject described.

FIGURATIVE LANGUAGE	EXAMPLE
SIMILE a comparison between two unlike things using the words *like, as,* or *as if*	I remember how you sang in your stone shoes light-voiced as dusk or feathers. —from "Elegy for My Father" by Robert Winner
METAPHOR a comparison between two unlike things but without the words *like* or *as*	The door of winter is frozen shut. —from "Wind Chill" by Linda Pastan
PERSONIFICATION a description of an object, an animal, a place, or an idea in human terms	Death, be not proud, though some have callèd thee Mighty and dreadful, for thou art not so. —from "Sonnet 10" by John Donne
HYPERBOLE an exaggeration for emphasis or humorous effect	Here once the embattled farmers stood And fired the shot heard round the world. —from "The Concord Hymn" by Ralph Waldo Emerson

---

DIFFERENTIATED INSTRUCTION

FOR STRUGGLING READERS

Note Taking As students read and discuss the main points on pages 774–775, have them record the main ideas on their note-taking copy masters.

 RESOURCE MANAGER—Copy Master
Note Taking p. 9–10

FOR ENGLISH LANGUAGE LEARNERS

Language: Skill Words Ask students to give examples of everyday figurative expressions in their home language. Have them give the literal and figurative translation of their examples and identify them as a simile, metaphor, personification, or hyperbole.

MODEL 3: IMAGERY

Notice the imagery this poet uses to transport you to the hot sands of an island in the West Indies.

Midsummer, Tobago

Poem by **Derek Walcott**

Broad sun-stoned beaches.

White heat.
A green river.

A bridge,
5 scorched yellow palms

from the summer-sleeping house
drowsing through August.

Days I have held,
days I have lost,

10 days that outgrow, like daughters,
my harbouring arms.

Close Read

1. The boxed image appeals to the senses of sight and touch. Identify three other images and describe the scene they conjure up in your mind.

2. How does the speaker feel about the summer days he or she describes? Explain how the image in lines 10–11 helps you to understand the speaker's emotions.

MODEL 4: FIGURATIVE LANGUAGE

The use of figurative language in this poem strengthens the contrast between a lifeless winter day and the vibrancy of the horses.

from Horses

Poem by **Pablo Neruda,** translated by Alastair Reid

I was in Berlin, in winter. The light
was without light, the sky skyless.

The air white like a moistened loaf.

From my window, I could see a deserted arena,
5 a circle bitten out by the teeth of winter.

All at once, led out by a man,
ten horses were stepping into the snow.

Emerging, they had scarcely rippled into existence
like flame, than they filled the whole world of my eyes,
10 empty till now. Faultless, flaming,
they stepped like ten gods on broad, clean hooves.

Close Read

1. One example of a simile is boxed. What does this comparison tell you about the air? Find another simile and explain the comparison.

2. In line 5, the poet uses personification to describe winter. What characteristics of winter does this comparison emphasize?

MODEL 3: IMAGERY
Close Read

1. ***Possible answers:*** *Three images and the scenes they conjure include "Broad sun-stoned beaches" (line 1), a wide beach covered with stones that radiate the sun's heat and brightness; "White heat" (line 2), intense heat, glaring light; "A green river" (line 3), cool, smooth water giving relief from the heat; "A bridge" (line 4), perhaps a wooden bridge over the river; "summer-sleeping house / drowsing" (lines 6–7), a house where there is little activity because of the heat; "Days I have held, / days I have lost" (lines 8–9), the speaker remembering the past with happiness and regret; "days that outgrow, like daughters, / my harbouring arms" (lines 10–11), the passing of happy times, like children who grow up and leave*

2. ***Possible answer:*** *The speaker feels nostalgic about the summer days. Lines 10–11 compare summer days to beloved daughters who outgrow the need for a parent's care and move on.*

MODEL 4: FIGURATIVE LANGUAGE
Close Read

1. ***Possible answers:*** *The boxed simile suggests that the air feels damp and heavy. Other similes and their meanings include: "rippled into existence / like flame" (lines 8–9): The horses appeared suddenly and with intense vividness; "Faultless, flaming, / they stepped like ten gods" (lines 10–11): The horses were perfect and majestic.*

2. ***Possible answer:*** *Line 5 uses personification to emphasize winter's biting cold and brutality.*

FOR STRUGGLING READERS

Comprehension Support: Figurative Language To help students connect the literal meanings and figurative uses of words, ask these questions and help students to answer them:

- Why does Walcott describe the heat as "white"? (line 2)
- What does *drowse* mean? In what way could a house seem to be "drowsing"? (lines 6–7)

- What characteristics do we associate with the sky? How could the sky in Neruda's poem seem "skyless"? (line 2)
- What characteristics do we associate with flame? Why might Neruda see the horses as "flaming"? (line 10)

Part 3: Analyze the Text

Close Read

1. **Possible answer:** Flick is taller than the gas pumps ("stands tall" among them—line 7). The pumps have a stupid look ("idiot pumps"—line 7), with round tops and dangling arms with "rubber elbows hanging loose and low" (line 9). The word ESSO (the oil company that subsequently became ExxonMobil) on one pump looks like a face (lines 10–11). One pump is short, wide, and headless, reminding the speaker of a "football type" (line 12).

2. **Possible answer:** The simile in the third stanza is "His hands were like wild birds" (line 18). It suggests that Flick was quick, had great natural instincts, and played with aggression, grace, and confidence.

3. **Possible answer:** The image of Pearl Avenue (lines 1–3) is like Flick in that the street ends abruptly after the high school, just as Flick's life went nowhere after high school.

4. **Possible answer:** In the last stanza, examples of alliteration include "kind of coiled" and "plays pinball" (line 26), "seldom says" (line 28), and "Necco . . . Nibs" (line 30).

Part 3: Analyze the Text

Apply what you have just learned about the forms, techniques, and effects of poetry by comparing the next two poems. The first describes the dead-end life of Flick Webb, a former high school basketball star. Read the poem a first time, looking for details that help you to understand the character of Flick. Then read the poem aloud to get the full impact.

EX-*Basketball Player*

Poem by **John Updike**

Pearl Avenue runs past the high-school lot,
Bends with the trolley tracks, and stops, cut off
Before it has a chance to go two blocks,
At Colonel McComsky Plaza. Berth's Garage
5 Is on the corner facing west, and there,
Most days, you'll find Flick Webb, who helps Berth out.

Flick stands tall among the idiot pumps—
Five on a side, the old bubble-head style,
Their rubber elbows hanging loose and low.
10 One's nostrils are two S's, and his eyes
An E and O. And one is squat, without
A head at all—more of a football type.

Once Flick played for the high-school team, the Wizards.
He was good: in fact, the best. In '46
15 He bucketed three hundred ninety points,
A county record still. The ball loved Flick.
I saw him rack up thirty-eight or forty
In one home game. His hands were like wild birds.

He never learned a trade, he just sells gas,
20 Checks oil, and changes flats. Once in a while,
As a gag, he dribbles an inner tube,
But most of us remember anyway.
His hands are fine and nervous on the lug wrench.
It makes no difference to the lug wrench, though.

25 Off work, he hangs around Mae's Luncheonette.
Grease-gray and kind of coiled, he plays pinball,
Smokes those thin cigars, nurses lemon phosphates.
Flick seldom says a word to Mae, just nods
Beyond her face toward bright applauding tiers
30 Of Necco Wafers, Nibs, and Juju Beads.

Close Read

1. In the second stanza, Flick stands next to gas pumps, which are personified as athletes. Citing details in the stanza, describe this image as you see it in your mind's eye.

2. Identify the simile in the third stanza. What does it tell you about Flick's athletic ability in high school?

3. Now that you know more about the character of Flick, reread lines 1–3. How does the image of Pearl Avenue remind you of him?

4. The poet uses alliteration in the last stanza. One example is boxed. Find two more examples.

DIFFERENTIATED INSTRUCTION

FOR STRUGGLING READERS
Analysis Support: Form

- **Stanza** Remind students that a stanza in poetry is like a paragraph in prose. Help them identify the main topic of each stanza in Updike's poem. *1, the setting; 2, the pumps; 3, Flick's talent; 4, his present work; 5, how he spends his leisure time*

- **Traditional vs. Organic** Review the characteristics of traditional and organic poetry on page 770. Using a Two-Column Chart on the board, help students distinguish the traditional and organic elements in Updike's poem. *Possible answers: Traditional: six-line stanzas; nearly all lines have five stressed syllables; conventional grammar and punctuation; Organic: meter varies somewhat; no rhyme*

    BEST PRACTICES TOOLKIT—Transparency
Two-Column Chart p. A25

The description of basketball players in this poem provides a sharp contrast to the sad portrait of Flick Webb in "Ex-Basketball Player."

Poem by **Yusef Komunyakaa**

Fast breaks. Lay ups. With Mercury's
Insignia on our sneakers,
We outmaneuvered to footwork
Of bad angels. Nothing but a hot
5   Swish of strings like silk
Ten feet out. In the roundhouse
Labyrinth our bodies
Created, we could almost
Last forever, poised in midair
10 Like storybook sea monsters.
A high note hung there
A long second. Off
The rim. We'd corkscrew
Up & dunk balls that exploded
15 The skullcap of hope & good
Intention. Lanky, all hands
& feet . . . sprung rhythm.
We were metaphysical when girls
Cheered on the sidelines.
20 Tangled up in a falling,
Muscles were a bright motor
Double-flashing to the metal hoop
Nailed to our oak.
When Sonny Boy's mama died
25 He played nonstop all day, so hard
Our backboard splintered.
Glistening with sweat,
We rolled the ball off
Our fingertips. Trouble
30 Was there slapping a blackjack
Against an open palm.
Dribble, drive to the inside,
& glide like a sparrow hawk.
Lay ups. Fast breaks.
35 We had moves we didn't know
We had. Our bodies spun
On swivels of bone & faith,
Through a lyric slipknot
Of joy, & we knew we were
40 Beautiful & dangerous.

Close Read

1. Is the form of this poem traditional or organic? Support your answer with specific examples.

2. Read the [boxed] lines aloud and identify two sound devices that are used. What does the rhythm in these lines remind you of?

3. The speaker describes the players as "Beautiful & dangerous" in line 40. Find two examples of figurative language that suggest either of these qualities. Explain your choices.

4. Contrast the two poems, citing three differences. Think about each poet's treatment of the subject, as well as his use of poetic techniques.

TEXT ANALYSIS WORKSHOP **777**

Close Read

1. *Possible answer: The poem is organic. It lacks a regular pattern of rhythm or rhyme or a traditional form in its lines. It breaks the rules of conventional grammar and punctuation with sentence fragments, such as "Fast breaks. Lay ups" (line 1), and ampersands as in line 14.*

2. *Possible answers: Two sound devices in the boxed text include alliteration, such as "Dribble, drive" (line 32), and assonance, as in "slapping . . . blackjack" (line 30). The rhythm may remind students of the fast pace of a basketball game.*

3. *Possible answers: Figurative language that suggests that the players are beautiful and dangerous includes "bad angels" (line 4), which combines the image of beautiful angels with the word "bad," and "Like storybook sea monsters" (line 10), which makes the players sound scary.*

4. *Possible answer: Differences between the two poems include: The Updike poem has more traditional elements: stanzas, a fairly regular meter, conventional grammar and punctuation. Updike's poem arouses pity rather than admiration, focusing on the emptiness of Flick's present life, while Komunyakaa focuses on the vitality and joy of the young players. Komunyakaa's poem has a fast pace that captures the energy and pace of the game. Updike's poem has a slower pace that reflects the sad routine of Flick's life.*

Assess and Reteach

Assess

Ask students to contrast traditional and organic poetry and to describe the poetic elements from the workshop, giving examples from any model on pages 773–775.

Reteach

For students who are unable to apply the workshop skills, use this reteaching activity:

Review the lesson note-taking copy masters.

1. Have pairs of students quiz each other on the meanings of the terms.

2. Have partners make a chart showing each term and an example from one of the models in the workshop.

FOR ENGLISH LANGUAGE LEARNERS
Vocabulary Support Explain these terms from "Slam, Dunk, & Hook":

- *fast break* (line 1), a rush to the basket
- *lay up* (line 1), a usually single-handed shot made close to the basket
- *Mercury's insignia* (lines 1–2), wings, which are the logo on the basketball shoes and also the symbol of the Roman messenger god Mercury
- *labyrinth* (line 7), a maze

- *blackjack* (line 30), a blunt stick with a short, flexible strap, used as a weapon

FOR ADVANCED LEARNERS/PRE–AP
Analysis Support Have students read the workshop independently for the purpose of noting the traditional and organic elements, sound devices, and figurative language the poets use.

Focus and Motivate

COMMON CORE FOCUS

RL 4 Analyze the cumulative impact of specific word choices on meaning. **RL 5** Analyze an author's choices concerning how to structure a text. **RL 10** Read and comprehend poems. **W 9a (RL 2)** Draw evidence from literary texts to support analysis; determine a theme and how it is refined by specific details. **L 3** Apply knowledge of language to make effective choices for meaning and style. **L 4b** Identify and correctly use patterns of word changes that indicate different meanings or parts of speech.

SUMMARIES

"There Will Come Soft Rains" The speaker contrasts nature's gentleness with humanity's warfare.

"Meeting at Night" The speaker journeys over sea and land to see his beloved.

"The Sound of Night" The speaker re-creates the symphony of animal and insect sounds that play on through the night while she is camping near a lake.

What is our place in NATURE?

Introduce the question. Then discuss how humans overpower nature and how nature overpowers humans. Have students complete the *DISCUSS* activity.

Selection Resources

There Will Come Soft Rains
Poem by Sara Teasdale

Meeting at Night
Poem by Robert Browning

The Sound of Night
Poem by Maxine Kumin

Essential Course of Study **ECOS**

What is our place in NATURE?

COMMON CORE

RL 4 Analyze the cumulative impact of specific word choices on meaning. **RL 5** Analyze an author's choices concerning how to structure a text. **RL 10** Read and comprehend poems. **L 4b** Identify and correctly use patterns of word changes that indicate different meanings or parts of speech.

Are humans more powerful than nature? Think of how we change landscapes, drive other species to extinction, and otherwise use nature for our own ends. Or are humans insignificant in the face of nature's power?

DISCUSS Think about a recent encounter you had with nature. What attitude did you express—admiration? indifference? In a small group, discuss your overall attitudes toward nature.

778

See resources on the **Teacher One Stop DVD-ROM** and on **thinkcentral.com**.

 RESOURCE MANAGER UNIT 7
Plan and Teach, pp. 11–18
Text Analysis and Reading
  Skill, pp. 19–22†*
Grammar and Style, p. 24

DIAGNOSTIC AND SELECTION TESTS
Selection Tests, pp. 215–218

INTERACTIVE READER

ADAPTED INTERACTIVE READER

ELL ADAPTED INTERACTIVE READER

TECHNOLOGY
- Teacher One Stop DVD-ROM
- Student One Stop DVD-ROM
- Audio Anthology CD
- GrammarNotes DVD-ROM
- Audio Tutor CD
- ExamView Test Generator
  on the **Teacher One Stop**

Find it Online!

Features on **thinkcentral.com** that support the selection include
- **PowerNotes** presentation
- **ThinkAloud** models to enhance comprehension
- **WordSharp** vocabulary tutorials
- interactive writing and grammar instruction

---

* Resources for Differentiation   † Also in Spanish   ‡ In Haitian Creole and Vietnamese

TEXT ANALYSIS: SOUND DEVICES

One common sound device used in poetry is **rhyme,** the repetition of sounds at the ends of words. **End rhyme** is rhyme at the ends of lines, as in this excerpt:

Whose woods these are I think I <u>know</u>.
His house is in the village <u>though</u>.

Another sound device is **alliteration,** the repetition of consonant sounds at the beginnings of words, as in *Droning a drowsy syncopated tune.*

Still another sound device is **onomatopoeia,** the use of words that imitate sounds, as in *The buzz saw snarled and rattled in the yard.* As you read the following poems about nature, notice their sound devices. Record examples on a chart.

Title	End Rhyme	Alliteration	Onomatopoeia
"There Will Come Soft Rains"	ground / sound (lines 1 and 2)		

READING STRATEGY: READING POETRY

Reading poetry requires paying attention not only to the meaning of the words but to the way they look and sound. The following strategies will help you.

- Notice how the lines are arranged on the page. Are they long lines, or short? Are they grouped into regular **stanzas** or irregular stanzas, or are they not divided into stanzas at all? Stanza breaks usually signal the start of a new idea.

- Pause in your reading where punctuation marks appear, just as you would when reading prose. Note that in poetry, punctuation does not always occur at the end of a line; a thought may continue for several lines.

- Read a poem aloud several times. As you read, notice whether the rhythm is regular or varied. Is there a **rhyme scheme,** or regular pattern of end rhyme? For example, you'll notice that "There Will Come Soft Rains" is written in **couplets,** two-line units with an *aa* rhyme scheme. Regular patterns of rhythm and rhyme give a musical quality to poems.

***Review:* Make Inferences**

 Complete the activities in your **Reader/Writer Notebook.**

Sara Teasdale
1884–1933

Love and War
Sara Teasdale explored the topic of love in all of its aspects. Drawing on her own experiences, she wrote about the beauty, pleasure, fragility, and heartache of love in exquisitely crafted lyric poems. In reaction to World War I, she also wrote antiwar poems, such as "There Will Come Soft Rains."

Robert Browning
1812–1889

Painter of Portraits
Robert Browning was a master at capturing psychological complexity. Using the **dramatic monologue,** a poem addressed to a silent listener, he conveyed the personalities of both fictional and historical figures. "Meeting at Night" is one of his shorter lyric poems.

Maxine Kumin
born 1925

Poet of Place
The poetry of Maxine Kumin is rooted in New England rural life. Using traditional verse forms, Kumin explores changes in nature, people's relationship to the land and its creatures, and human mortality, loss, and survival.

Authors Online
Go to **thinkcentral.com.** KEYWORD: HML10-779

THINK central

Teach

TEXT ANALYSIS — COMMON CORE — RL 4

● *Model the Skill:* SOUND DEVICES

To model how to identify sound devices, write these lines on the board and read them aloud:

> The wind whispered through the trees,
> Saying, "Winter left just yesterday."
> Now Spring basks in its bold display
> With hints of summer in the breeze.

Help students to identify the rhymes, alliteration, and onomatopoeia in these lines of poetry. Point out the following possibilities: **Rhymes:** trees/breeze, yesterday/display; **Alliteration:** <u>w</u>ind/<u>wh</u>ispered/<u>W</u>inter; <u>b</u>asks/<u>b</u>old/<u>b</u>reeze; **Onomatopoeia:** whispered.

GUIDED PRACTICE Have students create simple examples of each sound device.

R RESOURCE MANAGER—Copy Master
Sound Devices p. 19 (for student use while reading the selection)

READING STRATEGY — COMMON CORE — RL 5 RL 10

■ *Model the Skill:* READING POETRY

Use the example in Text Analysis to model the poetry reading strategies discussed on this page.

- Point out that the lines form a four-line stanza, and ask students to identify its rhyme scheme (*abba*).

- Help students identify the fairly regular rhythm of the stanza (*four strong beats and either three or four weak beats per line*).

- Elicit that lines 1, 2, and 4 have end punctuation, while line 3 does not. Model how to read these lines aloud to reflect their use of punctuation.

GUIDED PRACTICE Have students apply one or more of these reading strategies to a favorite poem or to the lyrics of a song.

DIFFERENTIATED INSTRUCTION

FOR STRUGGLING READERS
Concept Support Share these additional examples of alliteration and onomatopoeia, and have students identify the techniques used in each one:

- We could hear the clattering and clanging of Maxie washing dishes.
- Birds chirped and chattered in the trees.
- The wicked wind howled from the west.
- The startled snake hissed at the hikers.

FOR ENGLISH LANGUAGE LEARNERS
Language: Skill Words Explain to students that because some onomatopoeic words are invented especially to mimic sounds in certain situations, they may be unfamiliar and may not even be found in the dictionary. Explain to students that when they read such a word, they should say the word aloud to understand the sound it imitates. They should also carefully consider the words around it to help figure out its meaning.

READ WITH A PURPOSE

Help students set a purpose for reading. Tell students to look for similarities in the nature poems.

READING STRATEGY

COMMON CORE

A READING POETRY

RL 5
RL 10

Possible answer: The couplet sets up the expectation that the rest of the poem will also feature rhymed couplets.

TEXT ANALYSIS

COMMON CORE

RL 4

B Model the Skill: SOUND DEVICES

Read the first six lines of the poem aloud, emphasizing the repetition of consonant sounds at the beginnings of words. Point out that in line 1, *soft* and *smell* begin with consonants and are examples of alliteration. Have students use their Sound Devices charts to record other examples of alliteration in the poem.

Possible answer: Examples of alliteration include soft, smell, swallows, circling, sound (lines 1–2); wild, will, wear, wire (lines 4–6); white (line 4), whistling, whims (line 6); and feathery, fire, fence (lines 5–6).

REVISIT THE BIG QUESTION

What is our place in NATURE?

Discuss In lines 1–12, what differences can you identify between Teasdale's portrayal of nature and her portrayal of humankind?
Possible answer: *Nature: gentle and peaceful; Humans: combatant and destructive; Nature: self-sufficient, independent, enduring; Humans: self-destructive*

There Will Come
Soft Rains

Sara Teasdale

There will come soft rains and the smell of the ground,
And swallows circling with their shimmering sound;

And frogs in the pools singing at night,
And wild plum-trees in tremulous white;

5 Robins will wear their feathery fire
Whistling their whims on a low fence-wire; **B**

And not one will know of the war, not one
Will care at last when it is done.

Not one would mind, neither bird nor tree
10 If mankind perished utterly;

And Spring herself, when she woke at dawn,
Would scarcely know that we were gone.

A READING POETRY
Read the first stanza aloud. Notice that it is a rhymed **couplet.** What expectations are set up by this **end rhyme**?

B SOUND DEVICES
What examples of **alliteration** can you identify in lines 1–6?

Analyze Visuals ▶

What overall feeling do you get from this landscape?

Spring Landscape (1909), Constant Permeke. Constant Permeke Museum, Jabbeke, Belgium. © 2008 Artists Rights Society (ARS), New York/SABAM, Brussels.

DIFFERENTIATED INSTRUCTION

FOR ENGLISH LANGUAGE LEARNERS
Language Support Draw students' attention to the first line of "There Will Come Soft Rains." Point out that the poet has used inverted word order and that, in normal speech, the line would be read: "Soft rains and the smell of the ground will come." Explain to students that poets often use inverted word order so that they can maintain a rhyme scheme or regular rhythm (meter).

Vocabulary Support Verify that students understand the meanings of the following words in the contexts in which they are used in this poem:

• *tremulous* (line 4), "shaking or trembling"

• *whims* (line 6), "impulsive ideas"

• *utterly* (line 10), "absolutely; completely"

Reading Support

This selection on **thinkcentral.com** includes embedded **ThinkAloud** models–students "thinking aloud" about the story to model the kinds of questions a good reader would ask about a selection.

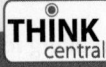

TIERED DISCUSSION PROMPTS

Direct students to lines 1–12. Use these prompts to help students connect their ideas about nature to those in the poem:

Connect Have you ever felt insignificant or small in the face of nature? Explain. *Accept all reasonable responses.*

Analyze At what point in the poem does the imagery change? How does this change affect the tone of the poem? ***Possible answer:*** *The poem's imagery changes in the fourth couplet (lines 7–8). In the first three couplets, the speaker presents vivid imagery and sensory details about nature: soft rains, the smell of the ground, swallows circling, shimmering sound (lines 1–2), frogs singing, wild plum-trees in blossom (lines 3–4), and robins in their "feathery fire / Whistling . . . on a low fence-wire" (lines 5–6). Starting in line 7, however, the tone of the poem becomes stark and desolate. Specific images of nature disappear, replaced by images of a post-war world that is empty of people who can witness nature.*

Analyze Visuals

Possible answer: *This landscape, with its shimmering light and glowing colors, evokes a feeling of serenity and delight in nature.*

About the Art The Flemish artist Constant Permeke (1886–1952) began his artistic career painting in the postimpressionist style, using luminous colors and small, textured brush-strokes, as in *Spring Landscape.* Later he became an expressionist, using flat areas of somber colors to depict massive, exaggerated figures that often blend into the landscape.

FOR STRUGGLING READERS

Develop Reading Fluency Have students read along in their texts as they listen to "There Will Come Soft Rains" on the *Audio Anthology CD* (also good for English language learners). Once students have listened to the audio recording, have them read the poem independently for comprehension. If students still have difficulty, encourage them to focus on one couplet at a time.

Distribute the copy masters and have students work in pairs or groups to practice fluency.

R RESOURCE MANAGER—Copy Master
Reading Fluency p. 25

FOR RELUCTANT READERS

Connect Have students work in pairs or small groups to brainstorm topics for nature poems. Tell students to consider subjects that appeal to them. Have each group pick one subject for a nature poem and write the first line for it. Have the group leaders explain to the class what subject they chose and present their first lines.

Prereading for this poem is found on page 778.

Analyze Visuals

Activity Ask students to identify words and phrases from the poem that match the painting. *Possible answer: Words and phrases include "gray sea" (line 1), "startled little waves that leap" (line 3), "the slushy sand" (line 6), and "warm sea-scented beach" (line 7). A "moon" (line 2) is also shown, except that in the picture the moon is a full moon, not a half moon as it is in the poem.*

READING STRATEGY

COMMON CORE RL 5 RL 10

C *Model the Skill:* **READING POETRY**

Model for students how to read poetry. Re-read lines 2 and 5 aloud. Explain that *low* and *prow* are called slant rhymes or near rhymes—partial or imperfect rhymes that often use assonance or consonance only. Then have students analyze the poem's end rhyme in a chart like this:

Line	End word	Rhyme
1	land	a
2	low	b
3	leap	c
4	sleep	c

Possible answer: *The poem's rhyme scheme is abccba deffed.*

READING STRATEGY: *Review*

COMMON CORE RL 10

D **MAKE INFERENCES**

Possible answer: The speaker arrives at a farm (line 8). Once there, the speaker taps at the window (line 9), and his beloved lights a lamp or candle, then greets and embraces the speaker (lines 10–12).

IF STUDENTS NEED HELP . . . Work with them to find the details in the poem that lead to these inferences. For example, "two hearts beating each to each!" (line 12) is the detail from which we infer that the speaker is embracing a loved one.

Moonrise (1906), Guillermo Gomez y Gil. Oil on canvas. Musée des Beaux-Arts, Pau, France. Photo © Giraudon/Bridgeman Art Library.

Meeting at Night
Robert Browning

1

The gray sea and the long black land;
And the yellow half-moon large and low;
And the startled little waves that leap
In fiery ringlets from their sleep,
5 As I gain the cove[1] with pushing prow,[2]
And quench its speed i' the slushy sand. **C**

2

Then a mile of warm sea-scented beach;
Three fields to cross till a farm appears;
A tap at the pane, the quick sharp scratch
10 And blue spurt of a lighted match,
And a voice less loud, through its joys and fears,
Than the two hearts beating each to each! **D**

C **READING POETRY**
Read the first stanza aloud. What **rhyme scheme** do you notice?

D **MAKE INFERENCES**
Where does the speaker arrive, and what happens once he is there?

---

1. **cove:** a small, partly enclosed body of water.
2. **prow** (prou): the front part of a boat.

DIFFERENTIATED INSTRUCTION

FOR STRUGGLING READERS

Options for Reading: Audio Recording Have students listen to "Meeting at Night" and "The Sound of Night" on the *Audio Anthology CD* (also recommended for English language learners). Then ask them to read through each poem a few times independently in order to understand the actions described.

Language Support To encourage deeper comprehension, have student pairs write a brief paraphrase of the action in "Meeting at Night." Urge them to use a dictionary to define unfamiliar words, such as *fiery* (line 4), *ringlets* (line 4), *quench* (line 6), and *slushy* (line 6). Finally, have pairs meet with one another to compare their paraphrased summaries.

The Sound of Night

Maxine Kumin

And now the dark comes on, all full of chitter noise.
Birds huggermugger[1] crowd the trees,
the air thick with their vesper[2] cries,
and bats, snub seven-pointed kites,
5 skitter across the lake, swing out,
squeak, chirp, dip, and skim on skates
of air, and the fat frogs wake and prink
wide-lipped, noisy as ducks, drunk
on the boozy black, gloating chink-chunk. **E**

10 And now on the narrow beach we defend ourselves from dark.
The cooking done, we build our firework
bright and hot and less for outlook
than for magic, and lie in our blankets
while night nickers around us. Crickets
15 chorus hallelujahs; paws, quiet
and quick as raindrops, play on the stones
expertly soft, run past and are gone;
fish pulse in the lake; the frogs hoarsen.

Now every voice of the hour—the known, the supposed, the strange,
20 the mindless, the witted, the never seen—
sing, thrum, impinge,[3] and rearrange
endlessly; and debarred[4] from sleep we wait
for the birds, importantly silent,
for the crease of first eye-licking light,
25 for the sun, lost long ago and sweet.
By the lake, locked black away and tight,
we lie, day creatures, overhearing night.

---

1. **huggermugger:** disorderly.
2. **vesper:** pertaining to the evening; a type of swallow that sings in the evening.
3. **impinge** (ĭm-pĭnj´): to strike or push upon.
4. **debarred:** prevented or hindered.

Trees at Night (c. 1900), Thomas Meteyard. Berry Hill Gallery, New York. Photo © Edward Owen/Art Resource, New York.

E SOUND DEVICES
What examples of **onomatopoeia** can you identify in the first stanza? What do they add to the poem?

COMMON CORE L 4b

Language Coach

Affixes An affix at the end of a word is a **suffix**. The suffix *-en*, meaning "to become," makes a verb when added to an adjective. In line 18, *hoarsen* is made from *-en* and what adjective? What does this new verb mean?

Prereading for this poem is found on page 778.

Analyze Visuals

Activity Ask students to compare and contrast the night scene in this painting with the night scene described in the poem. *Possible answer: The night scene in the painting appears peaceful and quiet. In contrast, the night scene in the poem is bustling with noisy animal and insect activity.*

About the Art Like many American artists of his period, Thomas Meteyard (1865–1928) lived as an expatriate in France, where he fell under the influence of the impressionists. His later work, like *Trees at Night*, reflects his involvement with the Nabis, a group of postimpressionists who used bold shapes and colors.

TEXT ANALYSIS COMMON CORE RL 4

E SOUND DEVICES

Possible answer: Examples of onomatopoeia include chitter *(line 1),* squeak, chirp *(line 6),* prink *(line 7), and* chink-chunk *(line 9). These words add to the rich sound imagery of the poem by re-creating the actual sounds that the animals and insects are making.*

SELECTION WRAP–UP

READ WITH A PURPOSE Ask students to identify the images in the poems they think are the most memorable and explain why. *Possible answer: Answers will vary. Students may be struck by images because they are pleasant or disturbing, or because of stylistic devices the poet used, such as alliteration.*

★ **CRITIQUE** Have students discuss what aspect of each poem they found most effective and why.

INDEPENDENT READING

If students are interested in reading more works about nature, suggest *In Deep Country Essays* by Maxine Kumin, a collection of essays and poems about life on her New Hampshire farm.

FOR ENGLISH LANGUAGE LEARNERS

Language Coach
COMMON CORE L 4b

Affixes *Answer:*
hoarse; "to make hoarse or rough sounding" Have students create other verbs by adding *-en* to the adjectives *thick* (line 3) and *fat* (line 7). Ask: What do these words mean? Have students use the verbs in sentences.

FOR ADVANCED LEARNERS/PRE–AP

Compare and Contrast: Mood Have students write two paragraphs comparing and contrasting the mood—the emotional feeling or atmosphere—in two of the three poems in this grouping. Urge students to use an adjective to name each poem's mood and to cite details from the poem to support their views. Invite volunteers to read their paragraphs aloud. If students disagree about a poem's mood, encourage them to discuss and defend their interpretations.

Practice and Apply

For preliminary support of post-reading questions, use these copy masters:

R RESOURCE MANAGER—Copy Masters
Reading Poetry p. 21
Question Support p. 23

Additional selection questions are provided for teachers on page 15.

ANSWERS

Comprehension

1. *The natural world would not notice or mind if "mankind perished utterly."*

2. *The speaker meets his beloved.*

3. *Kumin's poem describes a lake and the surrounding countryside at night.*

Text Analysis

COMMON CORE RL 4, RL 5, RL 10

Possible answers:

4. ■ **COMMON CORE FOCUS** *Reading Poetry
Answers should include a discussion of the poem's sound devices.*

5. *"There Will Come Soft Rains": regular rhyme scheme (aa bb cc dd ee ff); end rhyme (tree/utterly, dawn/gone) emphasizes the contrast between what remains in nature and what humans have lost. "Meeting at Night": regular rhyme scheme (abccba deffed); end rhyme (land/sand, beach/each) emphasizes the elements of the setting as the speaker's journey progresses. "The Sound of Night": no regular rhyme scheme; end rhyme (drunk/chunk, light/tight/night) emphasizes the idea that the sounds of the natural world are more noticeable to a listener who is wrapped in darkness.*

6. *Teasdale's poem makes the most obvious use of alliteration. The soft consonant sounds suggest the gentle coming of spring.*

7. ● **COMMON CORE FOCUS** *Sound Devices
"There Will Come Soft Rains" conveys the gentleness of nature through the use of alliteration. "Meeting at Night" conveys the sensual experience of a seascape and suggests the lulling motions of waves with its abccba rhyme scheme. "The Sound of Night" conveys the cacophony of nature sounds heard near a lake at night, partly through the use of onomatopoeia and alliteration.*

8. *"There Will Come Soft Rains" suggests that nature is indifferent, and perhaps even superior, to humans and will thus outlast them. "Meeting at Night" presents nature as a series of obstacles to be overcome before the speaker can be reunited with a loved one. "The Sound of Night" suggests that humans are mesmerized and distracted by nature at night, and find daylight more comfortable and familiar.*

Comprehension

1. **Clarify** According to the speaker in Teasdale's poem, how would the natural world react if "mankind perished utterly"?

2. **Clarify** Whom does the speaker in Browning's poem meet when he arrives at his destination?

3. **Clarify** What time and place are described in Kumin's poem?

⸬ COMMON CORE

RL 4 Analyze the cumulative impact of specific word choices on meaning. RL 5 Analyze an author's choices concerning how to structure a text. RL 10 Read and comprehend poems.

Text Analysis

4. ● **Reading Poetry** Which poem did you appreciate most when read aloud? Explain the qualities that were brought out in an oral reading.

5. **Analyze Rhyme** Describe how **end rhyme** is used in each poem. Which poems employ a regular **rhyme scheme**? What ideas are emphasized through end rhyme? Use a chart like the one shown to plan your answer.

	Rhyme Scheme	Important Rhyming Words
"There Will Come Soft Rains"		
"Meeting at Night"		
"The Sound of Night"		

6. **Recognize Alliteration** Which poem makes the most obvious use of alliteration? What feelings or ideas are suggested by these repeated consonant sounds?

7. **Relate Theme and Sound Devices** Describe the qualities of nature conveyed in each poem. How are sound devices used to suggest these qualities? Refer to your sound devices chart to plan your answer.

8. **Draw Conclusions** What does each poem suggest about humans and nature?

Text Criticism

9. **Critical Interpretations** According to one critic, Teasdale's poetry "expresses the fragility of human life where the only real certainty comes from nature." How does this comment apply to "There Will Come Soft Rains"?

What is our place in **NATURE**?

Do you think humans are part of nature? Why or why not?

Text Criticism

Possible answers:

9. *Teasdale's poem presents a world in which human lives are threatened by war (line 7), while the earth's creatures remain carefree and nature continues its cycle, unaffected.*

What is our place in **NATURE**?
Students might consider how humans interact with nature, even in a big city. They might also think about how their everyday actions make an impact on nature.

Language

◆ GRAMMAR AND STYLE: Use Precise Language

It is important for writers to choose words that effectively express the rhythm, sound, and imagery they wish to convey to their audience. Notice how Maxine Kumin's use of **precise verbs** in "The Sound of Night" makes the description livelier and more specific than if she had used verbs such as "fly" or "communicate."

> and bats, snub seven-pointed kites,
> skitter across the lake, swing out,
> squeak, chirp, dip, and skim on skates
> of air . . . (lines 4–7)

Careful consideration of word choice can be given to all types of writing, not just poetry. Notice that the revisions in blue are precise verbs that enhance the description in this first draft. Revise your response to the prompt by changing any dull, general verbs to more precise ones.

> **STUDENT MODEL**
>
> In "There Will Come Soft Rains," Sara Teasdale ~~asks~~ *urges* us to consider that nature will go on long after humans have ~~done away with~~ *annihilated* themselves.

READING-WRITING CONNECTION

YOUR TURN Broaden your understanding of the poems by responding to this prompt. Then use the **revising tip** to improve your writing.

WRITING PROMPT	REVISING TIP
Extended Constructed Response: Interpret Write **three-to-five paragraphs comparing** and contrasting the themes of each poem. In your response, consider the figurative language used in each poem. How does the figurative language reflect the time and place in which the poem was written and help illustrate its theme?	Review your response. Did you use precise language to enhance your comparisons? If not, revise your essay to include precise verbs.

Interactive Revision THINK central
Go to **thinkcentral.com**.
KEYWORD: HML10-785

DIFFERENTIATED INSTRUCTION

FOR STRUGGLING WRITERS

- Clarify that this prompt requires a discussion of all three poems, rather than just focusing on one.

- Remind students that a poem's subject and theme are not the same thing. A poem's subject may be nature, but its theme will share an insight about nature ("Humans and nature must maintain a delicate balance.")

Language

COMMON CORE W 9a (RL 2), L 3

◆ GRAMMAR AND STYLE

- After students examine the student model, discuss the different connotations suggested by the original and substitution verbs. (For more on using language effectively, see **Writing Handbook,** p. R29.)

- Write this sentence on the board. Have students suggest a more precise verb to replace each existing verb. (For more on using verbs, see **Grammar Handbook,** p. R55.)

> *Angrily, Peter* ~~walked~~ *stormed into the room,* ~~shut~~ *slammed the door, and* ~~sat~~ *flung himself in the chair.*

🅡 RESOURCE MANAGER—Copy Master
Use Precise Language p. 24

READING-WRITING CONNECTION

- Tell students to think about each poem's speaker, imagery, sound devices, and mood as they interpret its theme. Have them use a chart to organize textual evidence that supports their interpretations.

> **Writing Online**  THINK central
>
> The following tools are available online at **thinkcentral.com** and on Write*Smart* **CD-ROM:**
> - **Interactive Graphic Organizers**
> - **Interactive Student Models**
> - **Interactive Revision Lessons**
>
> For additional grammar instruction, see **GrammarNotes** on **thinkcentral.com**.

Assess and Reteach

Assess

DIAGNOSTIC AND SELECTION TESTS
Selection Test A pp. 215–216
Selection Test B/C pp. 217–218

Interactive Selection Test on **thinkcentral.com**

Reteach

Level Up Online Tutorials on **thinkcentral.com**

Reteaching Worksheets on **thinkcentral.com**
Literature Lesson 17: Structure of Poetry

Literature Lesson 21: Alliteration, Assonance, and Consonance

COMMON CORE

W 9a (RL 2) Draw evidence from literary texts to support analysis; determine a theme and how it is refined by specific details.
L 3 Apply knowledge of language to make effective choices for meaning or style.

Focus and Motivate

COMMON CORE FOCUS

RL 2 Determine a theme of a text. **RL 4** Determine the figurative meanings of words; analyze the cumulative impact of specific word choices on meaning. **RL 5** Analyze an author's choices concerning how to structure a text. **RL 10** Read and comprehend poems. **L 1a** Use parallel structure.

SUMMARIES

"I dwell in Possibility—" The speaker exalts the art form of poetry, comparing the writing of poetry to living in a limitless house that sets free the imagination.

"Variation on a Theme by Rilke" The speaker compares the idea of a special day's endless opportunity to the act of a king bestowing knighthood upon a subject.

"blessing the boats" The speaker shares her wishes for boats—and by extension, people—to have successful life journeys.

What if you couldn't FAIL?

Introduce the question. Ask students what the idea of endless possibility means to them. Then have students complete the *QUICKWRITE*.

Before Reading

I dwell in Possibility—
Poem by Emily Dickinson

Variation on a Theme by Rilke
Poem by Denise Levertov

blessing the boats
Poem by Lucille Clifton

What if you couldn't FAIL?

COMMON CORE

RL 2 Determine a theme of a text. **RL 4** Determine the figurative meanings of words; analyze the cumulative impact of specific word choices on meaning. **RL 5** Analyze an author's choices concerning how to structure a text. **RL 10** Read and comprehend poems.

Think about living in a world of endless possibility. You have no limitations, and you have every advantage available to you. If you want to sing, you have an extraordinary voice. If you want to feed the hungry, world leaders adopt your plans. What would you do in life if you knew that you could only succeed?

QUICKWRITE Make a short to-do list of things you'd like to accomplish if success were assured. Then, with a partner, discuss your list. What are some of the entries? How do you feel inside as you imagine completing these tasks?

786

Selection Resources

*See resources on the **Teacher One Stop DVD-ROM** and on **thinkcentral.com**.*

R RESOURCE MANAGER UNIT 7
Plan and Teach, pp. 27–34
Text Analysis and Reading
   Skill, pp. 35–38†*
Grammar and Style, p. 40

DIAGNOSTIC AND SELECTION TESTS
Selection Tests, pp. 219–222

BEST PRACTICES TOOLKIT
Two-Column Chart, p. A25
Cluster Diagram, p. B18

TECHNOLOGY
- **Teacher One Stop DVD-ROM**
- **Student One Stop DVD-ROM**
- **Audio Anthology CD**
- **GrammarNotes DVD-ROM**
- **ExamView Test Generator** on the **Teacher One Stop**

---

* Resources for Differentiation   † Also in Spanish   ‡ In Haitian Creole and Vietnamese

POETIC FORM: LYRIC POETRY

A **lyric poem** is a short poem in which a single speaker expresses personal thoughts and feelings on a subject. In ancient Greece, lyric poets expressed their feelings in song, accompanied by a lyre. While modern lyric poems are no longer sung, they still retain common characteristics such as:

- a sense of rhythm and melody
- imaginative language
- exploration of a single feeling or thought

Reading the lyric poems on the following pages aloud will help you appreciate these characteristics.

TEXT ANALYSIS: FIGURATIVE LANGUAGE

Figurative language is an expression of ideas beyond what the words literally mean. Three basic types of figurative language, or **figures of speech**, follow:

- A **simile** compares two unlike things that have something in common, using *like* or *as*. (*bats, sailing like kites*)
- A **metaphor** compares two unlike things by saying that one thing actually is the other. (*bats, snub seven-pointed kites*)
- **Personification** lends human qualities to an object, animal, or idea. (*bats, performing a graceful ballet*)

Poets use figurative language both to convey abstract thoughts and to offer a fresh outlook on everyday things. As you read the following poems, use a chart like this one to record and analyze examples of simile, metaphor, and personification.

Example	Type	Two Things Compared	Ideas Suggested
"I dwell in Possibility—/ A fairer House than Prose—"	metaphor	poetry/possibility and a house	

READING SKILL: COMPARE AND CONTRAST

Comparing and contrasting the poems—identifying the similarities and the differences between them—will help you understand each poem's central theme. As you read, compare the feelings expressed and the figurative language used. Also think about the time period in which each poem was written.

 Complete the activities in your **Reader/Writer Notebook.**

Meet the Authors

Emily Dickinson
1830–1886

Passionate Poet
As an adult, Emily Dickinson rarely left her father's home or welcomed visitors. Yet she managed to write poems that are remarkable for their originality and awareness of human passion. Using unusual imagery and syntax, she explored such powerful emotions as love, despair, and ecstasy.

Denise Levertov
1923–1997

A Poetic Vocation
Denise Levertov's view that writing poetry should be like a religious calling was influenced by the early 20th-century poet Rainer Maria Rilke, whom she claimed as a role model. Levertov often used her art in service of political ideals, tackling such issues as the Vietnam War and the nuclear arms race.

Lucille Clifton
born 1936

Honoring Heritage
Lucille Clifton's poetry honors African heritage and expresses optimism about life. Clifton is a professor of humanities at St. Mary's College, which boasts a premier varsity sailing program. Sailboat races there may have inspired "blessing the boats."

Authors Online
Go to **thinkcentral.com.** KEYWORD: HML10-787

THINK central

787

Teach

TEXT ANALYSIS COMMON CORE RL 4 RL 5

● Model the Skill: FIGURATIVE LANGUAGE

To model how to identify figurative language, write this sentence on the board:

> Opportunity is like a stranger who brushes past you on a crowded street.

Tell students that the word *like* in the first line indicates a simile. Tell students that this simile compares opportunity to a stranger. This comparison is also an example of personification, because opportunity, a nonhuman idea, is given human qualities. Then show students how to turn the simile into a metaphor. Write this metaphor on the board as one possible example:

> Opportunity is a stranger who brushes past you on a crowded street.

GUIDED PRACTICE Have students write original examples of the three types of figurative language discussed on this page.

R **RESOURCE MANAGER—Copy Master**
Figurative Language p. 35 (for student use while reading the selection)

READING SKILL COMMON CORE RL 4 RL 10

■ Model the Skill: COMPARE AND CONTRAST

To model how to compare and contrast, write this sentence on the board:

> Opportunity is an unexpected guest.

Compare and contrast this figure of speech with the one in the previous example. Explain that this figure of speech is a metaphor, while the previous example is a simile. Tell students that both comparisons are also examples of personification. Both give human qualities to the same idea—opportunity. However, the metaphor presents opportunity as a blessing that arrives unexpectedly, while the simile portrays it as a chance that slips away.

GUIDED PRACTICE Have students briefly compare and contrast two songs or movies about the same subject.

DIFFERENTIATED INSTRUCTION

FOR STRUGGLING READERS
Concept Support: Figurative Language Help students interpret the meaning of the examples on page 787. First ask students to identify the main subject of the comparisons (bats). Then model how to think beyond the literal meaning of the words. You might say: "Humans are the only real ballet dancers, but grace is a characteristic associated with them. I think the writer wants me to picture bats flying with a dancer's grace."

Concept Support: Lyric Poetry Point out to students that lyric poetry often has the rhythmic feel of a song. Review the features of lyric poetry and have students suggest and share other appropriate songs with lyric qualities.

787

Practice and Apply

READ WITH A PURPOSE

Help students set a purpose for reading. Have students look for the theme of each poem as they read.

REVISIT THE BIG QUESTION

What if you couldn't FAIL?

Discuss Direct students to lines 1–12. How would you feel about dwelling in a "house" of possibility? Do you think that limitless possibility is a good thing—or are limits and rules necessary? *Accept all thoughtful responses.*

I DWELL IN POSSIBILITY—

EMILY DICKINSON

I dwell in Possibility—
A fairer House than Prose—
More numerous of Windows—
Superior—for Doors— Ⓐ

5 Of Chambers as the Cedars—
Impregnable[1] of Eye—
And for an Everlasting Roof
The Gambrels[2] of the Sky— Ⓑ

Of Visitors—the fairest—
10 For Occupation—This—
The spreading wide my narrow Hands
To gather Paradise—

Ⓐ FIGURATIVE LANGUAGE
The speaker is not literally living in a House of Possibility. What idea is really being conveyed in this **metaphor**?

Ⓑ FIGURATIVE LANGUAGE
An **extended metaphor** compares two unlike things in more than one way. The house metaphor continues from the first stanza to the next. In lines 5–8, what is Dickinson saying about the size and scope of this house?

---

1. **Impregnable:** unconquerable.
2. **Gambrels:** a type of roof with two slopes on each side.

Detail of *Cape Cod Morning* (1950), Edward Hopper. Oil on canvas, 34¹/₈″ × 40¹/₄″. Smithsonian American Art Museum, Washington, D.C. © Heirs of Josephine N. Hopper, licensed by the Whitney Museum of American Art.

788 UNIT 7: THE LANGUAGE OF POETRY

DIFFERENTIATED INSTRUCTION

FOR ENGLISH LANGUAGE LEARNERS

Comprehension: Comparison Remind students that the purpose of a metaphor is to compare two unlike things by saying that one thing actually is the other. Have students reread lines 1 and 2. What is the poet comparing? Tell students that with the words *dwell* and *House*, Dickinson lets readers know that she will be using the image of a house as a metaphor for possibility or imagination. Have students identify other house-related words in the poem that extend the metaphor.

FOR STRUGGLING READERS

Develop Reading Fluency: Echo Reading Read "I dwell in Possibility—" aloud two lines at a time. Have students repeat each couplet, using the same intonation and rhythm that you modeled. Then explain that this is an example of a lyric poem. Have students identify characteristics of lyric poetry in "I dwell in Possibility—." Distribute the copy masters and have students work to practice fluency.

Ⓡ RESOURCE MANAGER—Copy Master
Reading Fluency p. 41

Analyze Visuals ▲

In what way does this image illustrate the feelings expressed in Dickinson's poem? Give specific **details**.

FOR STRUGGLING READERS

Language Support Have pairs of students paraphrase Dickinson's poem by "translating" her unusual diction (word choice) into simple, modern language and by revising her unconventional punctuation (frequent dashes) and capitalization to conform to standard usage. For example, suggest to students that they might paraphrase line 1 to read "I live in the world of possibilities" and line 10 to read "This is my job" or "This is the work I do."

Draw students' attention to the words "fairer" in line 2 and "fairest" in line 9. Explain that these words, as used in the context of the poem, might be translated as "finer" and "finest" or "more beautiful" and "most beautiful" in today's speech. Ask volunteers to share their paraphrases.

TIERED DISCUSSION PROMPTS

Direct students to lines 1–12. Use these prompts to help students understand the speaker's ideas about poetry and prose:

Connect Describe a time when you felt frustrated or confined by the limitations of a writing assignment. *Accept all reasonable responses.*

Analyze In the third stanza, what metaphor does the speaker use to describe her "Occupation"? How does this metaphor connect to the house metaphor? *Possible answer: The speaker describes her occupation— writing poetry—as gathering "Paradise" in her "narrow hands" (lines 11–12). The house metaphor presents poetry as an expansive dwelling, with numerous doors and windows, endless rooms, and the limitless sky itself for a roof. The Paradise metaphor presents the writing of poetry as an act of reaching out, perhaps through those windows and doors, to gather up something infinite and hold it in the confined space of one's hands.*

Evaluate Do you agree with the speaker's assertion that poetry is a more imaginative (limitless) form of writing than prose? Why or why not? *Students who disagree may argue that prose can be just as imaginative as poetry and also provides more styles and genres for different types of imaginative expression.*

Analyze Visuals

Possible answer: Both the painting and the poem express a feeling of anticipation and possibility. The woman in the painting gazes out the window as if surveying the possibilities of a new day, while the speaker in Dickinson's poem says that she dwells "in Possibility."

About the Art Edward Hopper (1882–1967) depicted ordinary American life in the first half of the 20th century—urban, small town, and country scenes that often suggest a sense of isolation and loneliness. Though the woman in Hopper's *Cape Cod Morning* projects a sense of anticipation as she gazes out the window, she also seems trapped within the house, as if separated from the object of her gaze.

Prereading for this poem is found on page 786.

TEXT ANALYSIS — COMMON CORE

C FIGURATIVE LANGUAGE RL 4 RL 5

Possible answer: Levertov uses personification to highlight the idea that the day gives the speaker the authority and strength to accomplish a great task, as a king would grant the privileges and opportunities of knighthood to a subject.

READING SKILL — COMMON CORE

D COMPARE AND CONTRAST RL 4 RL 10

To model for students how to compare and contrast poems, work with them to complete a Two-Column Chart like the one shown that gathers and compares thematic details from the two poems.

Levertov's Poem	Dickinson's Poem
"I can"	"Possibility"

 BEST PRACTICES TOOLKIT—Transparency
Two-Column Chart p. A25

Possible answer: Both poems express the idea that life is full of possibilities.

BACKGROUND

German poet Rainer Maria Rilke (1875–1926) experienced a self-described divine inspiration during a visit to a Russian monastery at the turn of the 20th century. The ritualistic prayers performed by the monks were based in part on a medieval religious text called the Book of Hours. The poems Rilke wrote as a product of that visit are contained in a collection of the same name.

Analyze Visuals

Activity Ask students whether they think this photograph works well as the image to accompany this poem. Why or why not? *Students who think the photograph works well with the poem will cite line 8, in which the speaker describes herself as "a bell awakened."*

Variation on a Theme by Rilke
(The Book of Hours, *Book I, Poem I, Stanza I*)

DENISE LEVERTOV

A certain day became a presence to me;
there it was, confronting me—a sky, air, light:
a being. And before it started to descend
from the height of noon, it leaned over
5 and struck my shoulder as if with
the flat of a sword, granting me
honor and a task. The day's blow **C**
rang out, metallic—or it was I, a bell awakened,
and what I heard was my whole self
10 saying and singing what it knew: *I can.* **D**

C FIGURATIVE LANGUAGE
In this poem, a day is given human qualities. What idea does Levertov highlight through this use of **personification**?

D COMPARE AND CONTRAST
How similar are the feelings expressed in this poem and Dickinson's poem?

790

DIFFERENTIATED INSTRUCTION

FOR STRUGGLING READERS

Options for Reading: Audio Recording Direct students to read along in their texts as they listen to this poem on the *Audio Anthology CD* (also recommended for English language learners). Then point out that this poem includes several different types of punctuation marks, and two lines include internal periods. Read the poem aloud, modeling how to read a poem in "sentences," stopping or pausing slightly when you reach a punctuation mark rather than at the ends of lines.

FOR ADVANCED LEARNERS/PRE–AP

Compare and Contrast Themes Invite students to read the poem that inspired "Variation on a Theme by Rilke" and compare the themes of the two poems. Ask students to focus their analyses on the stanza specified in Levertov's subtitle. Have students submit their ideas in a comparison-and-contrast essay. To extend the activity, have students discuss their ideas in a small group after they submit their essays.

blessing the boats
(at St. Mary's)

LUCILLE CLIFTON

may the tide
that is entering even now
the lip of our understanding
carry you out
5 beyond the face of fear
may you kiss
the wind then turn from it
certain that it will
love your back   may you
10 open your eyes to water
water waving forever
and may you in your innocence
sail through this to that

Ⓔ LYRIC POETRY
What feeling is the
speaker expressing?

Prereading for this poem is found on page 786.

REVISIT THE BIG QUESTION
What if you couldn't
FAIL?

Discuss In lines 1–13, how does the speaker's wish that the tide "carry you out / beyond the face of fear" (lines 4–5) connect to her wish that "you / open your eyes to water" (lines 9–10)? *Possible answer: The speaker is saying that overcoming fear is necessary if you are to open yourself to life's opportunities—everything that is **possible**.*

POETIC FORM   COMMON CORE

Ⓔ LYRIC POETRY   RL 2
                                      RL 5

Possible answer: The speaker is expressing the hope that people will have successful journeys that allow them to lose their fear and gain experience and confidence.

Analyze Visuals

Activity How does the photograph match the mood of Clifton's poem? *Possible answer: The calm waters and sunny sky match the speaker's gentle wishes and optimistic tone.*

SELECTION WRAP–UP

READ WITH A PURPOSE Now that students have finished reading the poems, ask: How have your ideas about possibility changed? Why? *Possible answer: Accept all reasonable and thoughtful answers.*

★ **CRITIQUE** Ask students which poem they found the most inspiring, and why.

INDEPENDENT READING

Students might enjoy reading selections from Lucille Clifton's poetic memoir *Generations*.

FOR STRUGGLING READERS

Options for Reading Read the poem aloud as students read along silently in their texts. Point out that the poem includes no punctuation, and ask them to think about where punctuation marks would normally go to create grammatically correct sentences (*at the end of line 5 and the middle of line 9*). Then have students read the poem aloud with you, pausing at the ends of sentences even though there are no punctuation marks.

Comprehension Support Have students break the poem into four parts, each part beginning with the words "may the" or "may you." Explain that these words often begin a statement that expresses a wish or a hope, as in "May all your dreams come true." Ask students to identify the four wishes made by the speaker in the poem. Also point out that "May you ..." is the traditional way to begin a blessing. Then have students work in small groups to discuss and interpret the figurative meaning of each wish.

Practice and Apply

For preliminary support of post-reading questions, use these copy masters:

R **RESOURCE MANAGER**—Copy Masters

Compare and Contrast p. 37

Question Support p. 39

Additional selection questions are provided for teachers on page 31.

ANSWERS

Comprehension

1. *The speaker's house is fairer than "Prose."*

2. *The speaker hears her whole self saying and singing "I can."*

3. *The speaker wishes the boats a successful journey in which passengers lose fear and gain experience.*

Text Analysis

COMMON CORE RL 2, RL 4, RL 5, RL 10

Possible answers:

4. ● **COMMON CORE FOCUS** *Metaphor The metaphor suggests that being a poet allows one to exist in a boundless realm of the imagination—a realm that is superior to the more confining realm of prose. Poetry provides limitless opportunities to imagine, to create, and to envision ideas—to gather "Paradise" in one's hands (lines 11–12).*

5. ● **COMMON CORE FOCUS** *Figurative Language Lines 4–7 personify the day as being a ruler who bends over and taps the speaker's shoulder. Lines 5–6 present a simile: "as if with the flat of a sword." The day is figuratively knighting the speaker, meaning that the speaker feels that she can accomplish great tasks on such a day. This figurative language shows that the day empowers the speaker.*

6. ● **COMMON CORE FOCUS** *Personification The boats are given human qualities: they kiss the wind, turn from it, open their eyes, and possess innocence. This personification suggests that people journey or sail through their lives as boats sail through the ocean.*

7. ■ **COMMON CORE FOCUS** *Compare and Contrast All three poems use figurative language to express the idea of limitless possibility. Dickinson suggests that it is specifically poets who enjoy limitless possibility, while Levertov and Clifton seem to apply the theme more broadly. Dickinson uses an extended metaphor, Levertov uses personification, and Clifton uses both*

Comprehension

1. **Recall** In Dickinson's poem, what is the speaker's house "fairer than"?

2. **Recall** What did the speaker of Levertov's poem hear when "the day's blow rang out"?

3. **Paraphrase** What does the speaker of Clifton's poem wish?

Text Analysis

● 4. Interpret Metaphor In Dickinson's poem, the house is the basis for a metaphor that is carried throughout the poem. What does this **extended metaphor** suggest about being a poet and living a life of the imagination?

● 5. Interpret Figurative Language Reread lines 4–7 in Levertov's poem and identify two examples of figurative language. What idea is conveyed? How does the figurative language illustrate the relationship between the speaker and the day?

● 6. Analyze Personification Find two or three examples of personification in Clifton's poem. What is given human qualities, and to what effect?

■ 7. Compare and Contrast Themes Complete a chart like the one shown. Then, use this information to compare and contrast the themes of the poems you've read. What does each poem say about possibility?

	Feelings Expressed	Figurative Language Used
"I dwell in Possibility"		
"Variation on a Theme by Rilke"		
"blessing the boats"		

● 8. Evaluate Lyric Poems Review the characteristics of lyric poetry listed on page 787. Which poem would work best as the lyrics of a song, and why?

Text Criticism

9. **Critical Interpretations** French poet Jean de La Fontaine said, "Man is so made that when anything fires his soul, impossibilities vanish." Evaluate the three poems against his statement. Do they support his claim? Why or why not?

What if you couldn't FAIL?

Does fear ever limit your possibilities? Explain.

COMMON CORE

RL 2 Determine a theme of a text. RL 4 Determine the figurative meanings of words and phrases; analyze the cumulative impact of specific word choices on meaning. RL 5 Analyze an author's choices concerning how to structure a text. RL 10 Read and comprehend poems.

---

personification and the metaphor of life as a journey.

8. ● **COMMON CORE FOCUS** *Lyric Poetry Many students may feel that Dickinson's poem would most readily lend itself to music because of its rhythm and rhyme.*

Text Criticism

Possible answers:

9. *All three poems support the claim that people can conquer seeming impossibilities. The speaker in Dickinson's poem can*

imagine any idea, the speaker in Levertov's poem can do anything, and the speaker in Clifton's poem imagines a journey past fear toward confidence and experience.

What if you couldn't FAIL?

Students might consider their goals and dreams and then ask themselves what factors, if any, cause them to hesitate or hold back from pursuing those goals.

Language

◆ **GRAMMAR AND STYLE: Create Rhythm**

Parallelism is the use of similar grammatical constructions to express ideas that are related or equal in importance. In the following excerpt from her poem "blessing the boats," Lucille Clifton uses parallelism to add rhythmic cadence to her writing. Notice how, in two different instances, she uses an inverted sentence structure that begins with the words "may you," followed by predicates.

may you kiss
the wind then turn from it
certain that it will
love your back   may you
open your eyes to water
water waving forever (lines 6–11)

Note how the revisions in blue use parallelism to improve this first draft. Revise your poem by making similar changes.

STUDENT MODEL

Through confusion, my mind becomes spaghetti.
Through   , my dreams become
Confusion ~~makes~~ meatballs ~~of my dreams~~.
∧   ∧

READING-WRITING CONNECTION

Broaden your understanding of lyrical poems by responding to this prompt. Then use the **revising tip** to improve your writing.

WRITING PROMPT	REVISING TIP
Short Constructed Response: Lyric Poem	Review your response.
In four or more lines, write a **poem** about a feeling you've had. Incorporate at least two examples of figurative language.	Have you used parallelism to add rhythm to your poem?

Interactive Revision

Go to **thinkcentral.com**.
KEYWORD: HML10-793

DIFFERENTIATED INSTRUCTION

FOR STRUGGLING WRITERS

- Help students identify a specific subject that is central to their chosen feeling.
- Tell students to use a Cluster Diagram to brainstorm ideas related to that subject.
- Suggest that students incorporate only one type of figurative language in their poems (simile is easiest).

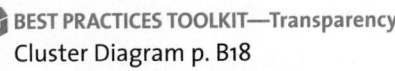 **BEST PRACTICES TOOLKIT—Transparency**
Cluster Diagram p. B18

Language

◆ **GRAMMAR AND STYLE**

- After students examine the student model, ask a volunteer to identify the two ideas that are balanced by the use of parallelism.

- Write these sentences on the board. Have students suggest revisions that incorporate parallelism.

  Don't worry about failing or to meet others' expectations.

  The poem suggests that people can overcome their fears, set new goals, and to move toward a hopeful future.

R **RESOURCE MANAGER—Copy Master**
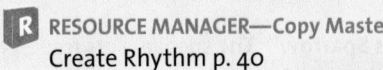
Create Rhythm p. 40

READING-WRITING CONNECTION

- Encourage students to review the explanation of lyric poetry on page 787. You might suggest that they use one of the three poems they just studied as a model for their own poems.

Writing Online

 **THINK** central

The following tools are available online at **thinkcentral.com** and on **WriteSmart CD-ROM**:
- **Interactive Graphic Organizers**
- **Interactive Student Models**
- **Interactive Revision Lessons**
For additional grammar instruction, see **GrammarNotes** on **thinkcentral.com**.

Assess and Reteach

Assess

DIAGNOSTIC AND SELECTION TESTS
Selection Test A pp. 219–220
Selection Test B/C pp. 221–222

Interactive Selection Test on **thinkcentral.com**

Reteach

Level Up Online Tutorials on **thinkcentral.com**

Reteaching Worksheets on **thinkcentral.com**
Literature Lesson 16: Narrative vs. Lyric Poetry

Literature Lesson 27: Simile and Metaphor

Reading Lesson 12: Comparing and Contrasting

Focus and Motivate

COMMON CORE FOCUS

RL 4 Determine the connotative meanings of words and phrases; analyze the cumulative impact of specific word choices on meaning. **RL 5** Analyze an author's choices concerning how to structure a text. **RL 10** Read and comprehend poems. **L 4b** Identify and correctly use patterns of word changes that indicate different meanings or parts of speech.

SUMMARIES

"The Fish" After studying a fish she caught, the speaker realizes that it has escaped many fishing lines in its long life. She decides to let the fish go.

"Christmas Sparrow" The speaker sets free a sparrow that was trapped in his home and ponders the frightful night it spent hiding in his Christmas tree.

"The Sloth" The speaker describes the laid-back manner of a sloth and suggests the attitudes that may be behind its inactivity.

What **ANIMAL** reminds you of yourself?

Introduce the question. Then invite volunteers to share stories about situations when animals such as their pets seemed "almost human." You might begin the discussion by sharing a personal anecdote. Then have students work in pairs to complete the *DISCUSS* activity.

Before Reading

The Fish
Poem by Elizabeth Bishop

Christmas Sparrow
Poem by Billy Collins

The Sloth
Poem by Theodore Roethke

What **ANIMAL** reminds you of yourself?

⦙ **COMMON CORE**

RL 4 Determine the connotative meanings of words and phrases; analyze the cumulative impact of specific word choices on meaning. **RL 5** Analyze an author's choices concerning how to structure a text. **L 4b** Identify and correctly use patterns of word changes that indicate different meanings or parts of speech.

Think about your pets or other animals you've seen at the zoo or on TV nature shows. Do animals ever behave in a way that seems almost human? Have you ever thought you knew what they were feeling? In the poems that follow, you will meet three animals with distinctive "human" qualities.

DISCUSS Choose one animal you identify with the most. Explain to a partner why you relate to it and what characteristics you share with it.

794

Selection Resources

See resources on the **Teacher One Stop DVD-ROM** *and on* <u>thinkcentral.com</u>.

R **RESOURCE MANAGER UNIT 7**
    Plan and Teach, pp. 43–50
    Text Analysis and Reading Skill,
      pp. 51–54†*

DIAGNOSTIC AND SELECTION TESTS
    Selection Tests, pp. 223–226

TECHNOLOGY

 **Teacher One Stop DVD-ROM**
⊘ **Student One Stop DVD-ROM**
⊘ **Audio Anthology CD**
⊘ **GrammarNotes DVD-ROM**
⊘ **ExamView Test Generator**
    on the **Teacher One Stop**

* **Resources for Differentiation**   † Also in Spanish   ‡ In Haitian Creole and Vietnamese

POETIC FORM: FREE VERSE

Most modern poems are written in **free verse,** a poetic form with no regular pattern of rhyme or rhythm. A free verse poem can be structured as one long, unbroken stanza, as in "The Fish," or with many stanzas of varying length, as in "Christmas Sparrow." The lines in free verse poems may also vary in length. Without a strict meter, the rhythm of free verse poetry often seems more like everyday speech. As you read, notice how the line length, sounds of words, and punctuation create a rhythm in each poem.

TEXT ANALYSIS: IMAGERY

Sometimes a poem can seem like a portrait. **Sensory language,** or words and phrases that appeal to the reader's senses, can help create **imagery**—visual portraits that reinforce ideas about the subject described. For example, in "The Fish," Bishop appeals to the senses of sight and touch when she describes the fish's skin. Lines like these help depict a fragile old fish.

hung in strips / like ancient wallpaper

shapes like full-blown roses / stained and lost through age

As you read the poems, record strong, evocative imagery on a chart like the one shown. Identify

- the sense the word or phrase appeals to
- the associations the imagery conjures up
- the idea that is being reinforced

Poem Title:			
Imagery	Sense(s)	Associations	Idea Reinforced

READING STRATEGY: VISUALIZE

Listen carefully as your teacher reads aloud the poems. **Visualize** the animals, settings, and events. Then read along with your teacher as he or she reads the poems a second time in a shared reading. Use your imagination and the word clues to "see" what the animals might look like. Then, read the poems again with a partner. Discuss how the shared and repeated readings helped you visualize the animals and understand the poems.

 Complete the activities in your **Reader/Writer Notebook.**

Meet the Authors

Elizabeth Bishop
1911–1979

Soulful Poet
The poetry of Elizabeth Bishop is marked by its exact and tranquil descriptions of the physical world. Hidden beneath her poems' air of serenity and simplicity, however, are underlying themes of great depth. When writing about loss and pain, the struggle to belong, and other themes, Bishop worked hard to ensure that "the spiritual [was] felt."

Billy Collins
born 1941

Poet for the People
Billy Collins remembers publishing a poem in his high school newspaper that was later confiscated. Rising to national and popular prominence years later, Collins became U.S. Poet Laureate (2001–2003) and launched the "Poetry 180" program, which aimed to get more high school students to read well-written, understandable poetry each day during the 180-day school year.

Theodore Roethke
1908–1963

Passion for Nature
"When I get alone under an open sky," wrote Theodore Roethke, "where man isn't too evident—then I'm tremendously exalted...." A passion for nature pervades Roethke's poetry. His poems also explore love, mortality, and the quest for spiritual wholeness.

 **THINK** central
Authors Online
Go to **thinkcentral.com.** KEYWORD: HML10-795

795

DIFFERENTIATED INSTRUCTION

FOR STRUGGLING READERS
Concept Support: Free Verse Explain to students that although free verse doesn't have a regular rhythm, it often includes rhythmic and sound effects—such as alliteration, repetition, and parallelism—and may even include some rhyme. Also point out that although the rhythm of free verse often sounds conversational, it is not random. The poet has carefully considered how the rhythm reinforces the meaning of the poem.

FOR ADVANCED LEARNERS/PRE–AP
Explore Imagery Enhance students' understanding and appreciation of imagery by challenging them to explore the technique from a different perspective. Ask students to choose one work of fine art in the pupil edition and write a brief poem re-creating the scene, using imagery that appeals to at least two senses. Encourage students to imagine sensations that the artwork suggests through its visual details.

Teach

TEXT ANALYSIS   COMMON CORE   RL 5   RL 10

● Model the Skill: IMAGERY

To model how to identify imagery, write these lines on the board and read them aloud:

> A jangling of tags and flapping of ears
> A soft, slurpy tongue
> Polishing my sleepy cheek
> Then a whisper of whimper
> Escalating to a whine:
> It's time to get up and walk the dog.

Help students identify the senses these lines appeal to and the specific words that appeal to each of those senses. Point out these examples: sound ("jangling," "flapping," "slurpy," "whisper," "whimper," "whine") and touch ("soft," "slurpy," "polishing").

GUIDED PRACTICE Have students write another line that appeals to the sense of sight or smell.

 RESOURCE MANAGER—Copy Master
   Imagery p. 51 (for student use while reading the selection)

READING STRATEGY   COMMON CORE   RL 4

■ Model the Skill: VISUALIZE

To model how to visualize, return to the lines written on the board. Help students visualize the experience the speaker is describing. Point out that the speaker is lying in bed, asleep. A dog wakes up the speaker by jangling its tags, flapping its ears, licking the speaker's face, and whimpering and whining to go out.

GUIDED PRACTICE Ask students to write another line that helps them visualize the dog, the speaker, or the setting.

795

READ WITH A PURPOSE

Help students set a purpose for reading. Tell students to find out what happens to the animal in each poem.

The Fish
Elizabeth Bishop

I caught a tremendous fish
and held him beside the boat
half out of water, with my hook
fast in a corner of his mouth.
5 He didn't fight.
He hadn't fought at all.
He hung a grunting weight,
battered and venerable
and homely. Here and there Ⓐ
10 his brown skin hung in strips
like ancient wallpaper,
and its pattern of darker brown
was like wallpaper:
shapes like full-blown roses
15 stained and lost through age.
He was speckled with barnacles,
fine rosettes of lime,
and infested
with tiny white sea-lice,
20 and underneath two or three
rags of green weed hung down.
While his gills were breathing in
the terrible oxygen
—the frightening gills,
25 fresh and crisp with blood,
that can cut so badly—
I thought of the coarse white flesh
packed in like feathers,
the big bones and the little bones,
30 the dramatic reds and blacks
of his shiny entrails,

POETIC FORM

COMMON CORE
RL 5
RL 10

Ⓐ *Model the Skill:* **FREE VERSE**

To model how to identify free verse, read the poem aloud for students, emphasizing its slow, unpatterned rhythm. Have students follow along in the textbook as you read, noting the line breaks and punctuation.

Possible answer: *The short lines affect the poem's rhythm by slowing it down, drawing the reader's attention to important words in those lines.*

Ⓐ **FREE VERSE**
Notice the different lengths of the lines in this poem. How do the short lines affect the poem's rhythm?

COMMON CORE RL 4

Language Coach

Connotations The images and feelings connected to a word are its **connotations**. In line 18, *infested* literally means *overrun* or *permeated*. What connotations do you associate with *infested*? Would you want to eat an infested fish?

DIFFERENTIATED INSTRUCTION

FOR ENGLISH LANGUAGE LEARNERS

Language Coach   **COMMON CORE RL 4**

Connotations *Answer:*
Infested *carries the imagery of parasites overrunning something. No, you would not want to eat an* infested *fish.* Have students point out other words describing the fish that have negative connotations. Ask students if the poem contains any adjectives for the fish that have positive connotations.

FOR STRUGGLING READERS

Develop Reading Fluency Read the poem aloud to students. Then guide them in reading the poem, pausing after each period for questions.

and the pink swim-bladder
like a big peony.
I looked into his eyes
35 which were far larger than mine
but shallower, and yellowed,
the irises backed and packed
with tarnished tinfoil
seen through the lenses
40 of old scratched isinglass.
They shifted a little, but not
to return my stare.
—It was more like the tipping
of an object toward the light. **B**
45 I admired his sullen face,
the mechanism of his jaw,
and then I saw
that from his lower lip
—if you could call it a lip—
50 grim, wet, and weaponlike,
hung five old pieces of fish-line,
or four and a wire leader
with the swivel still attached,
with all their five big hooks
55 grown firmly in his mouth.
A green line, frayed at the end
where he broke it, two heavier lines,
and a fine black thread
still crimped from the strain and snap
60 when it broke and he got away.
Like medals with their ribbons
frayed and wavering,
a five-haired beard of wisdom
trailing from his aching jaw. **C**
65 I stared and stared
and victory filled up
the little rented boat,
from the pool of bilge
where oil had spread a rainbow
70 around the rusted engine
to the bailer rusted orange,
the sun-cracked thwarts,
the oarlocks on their strings,
the gunnels—until everything
75 was rainbow, rainbow, rainbow!
And I let the fish go.

B VISUALIZE
Reread lines 34–44. What
aspects of the fish's
character can you "see" in
this description of its eyes?

C IMAGERY
What senses does this
description of the fish's
face appeal to? What
associations form in your
mind about the fish?

THE FISH **797**

FOR ADVANCED LEARNERS/PRE–AP

Analyze Symbolism Point out to students
that the rainbow has become a symbol of
hope over despair, of life over death. Have
students work in small groups to analyze the
rainbow's symbolic meaning in "The Fish."
Specifically, what does the speaker mean
toward the end of the poem when she says
that "everything / was rainbow, rainbow, rainbow!"? (lines 74–75) Ask students to consider
these questions:

- What, literally, has caused the rainbow?
- Why does this rainbow cause "victory" to
  fill up the boat? (lines 66–67)
- How do lines 74–75 relate to the speaker's
  decision to "let the fish go"? (line 76)

Analyze Visuals

Activity Ask students what details in the
photographs on pages 796 and 797 match the
description of the fish in the poem. *Possible
answer: Similar details include "brown skin"
(line 10); "pattern of darker brown . . . like wallpaper" (lines 12–13); "eyes . . . larger than mine /
but shallower, and yellowed" (lines 34–36); and
"sullen face" (line 45).*

READING STRATEGY   COMMON CORE
                                    RL 4

B *Model the Skill:* VISUALIZE

Point out the imagery and details in lines
34–44. Tell students that the adjectives
yellowed, tarnished, and *scratched* convey
overuse, neglect, and age.

Possible answer: *The description of the
fish's eyes characterizes the fish as old, tired,
and perhaps indifferent.*

Extend the Discussion Which details in
this description of the fish's eyes might
also apply to human eyes?

TEXT ANALYSIS   COMMON CORE
                              RL 5
                              RL 10

C IMAGERY

Possible answer: *This description appeals to the senses of sight and touch. The
description associates the fish with a wise
old soldier through the simile that associates fish hooks and lines with "medals with
their ribbons / frayed and wavering" (lines
61–62) and through the metaphor that calls
the hooks and lines "a five-haired beard of
wisdom" (line 63). These comparisons call
to mind age, strength, and resistance.*

IF STUDENTS NEED HELP . . . Encourage
them to use their Text Analysis charts to
classify the poem's imagery.

THE FISH   **797**

Prereading for this poem is found on page 794.

CHRISTMAS SPARROW

BILLY COLLINS

The first thing I heard this morning
was a rapid flapping sound, soft, insistent—

wings against glass as it turned out
downstairs when I saw the small bird
5 rioting in the frame of a high window,
trying to hurl itself through
the enigma of glass into the spacious light. **D**

Then a noise in the throat of the cat
who was hunkered on the rug
10 told me how the bird had gotten inside,
carried in the cold night
through the flap of a basement door,
and later released from the soft grip of teeth.

On a chair, I trapped its pulsations
15 in a shirt and got it to the door,
so weightless it seemed
to have vanished into the nest of cloth.

But outside, when I uncupped my hands,
it burst into its element,
20 dipping over the dormant garden
in a spasm of wingbeats
then disappeared over a row of tall hemlocks.

D IMAGERY
What images describe the bird in lines 1–7? What senses do these images appeal to?

COMMON CORE L 4b

Language Coach

Suffixes The word *pulsation* (line 14) is formed by adding the suffix *-ion*, meaning "the action of" to the base word *pulsate*, meaning "to throb or beat." Restate the definition of *pulsation* in your own words. Can you think of other words formed from a base word and the suffix *-ion*?

TEXT ANALYSIS

COMMON CORE

D IMAGERY

RL 5
RL 10

Possible answer: *Images describing the bird are "rapid flapping sound, soft, insistent"; "wings against glass"; "rioting in the frame of a high window"; and "trying to hurl itself through / the enigma of glass into the spacious light." These images appeal to the senses of hearing, sight, and touch.*

TIERED DISCUSSION PROMPTS

Direct students to lines 1–34. Use these prompts to help students understand the speaker's reaction to the bird:

Connect Have you or someone you know ever rescued a wild animal? How does that experience help you connect to the poem? *Accept all reasonable responses.*

Analyze How would you describe the speaker's tone? *Possible answer:* The *speaker's tone is tender and compassionate. He is alarmed by the bird's plight and feels a responsibility to help it escape. The speaker feels compassion and empathy for "the hours it must have spent" (line 26) trapped in the room.*

Evaluate In your opinion, should humans intervene to protect animals? Explain your opinion. *Accept all reasonable responses, but require support for students' views.*

DIFFERENTIATED INSTRUCTION

FOR STRUGGLING READERS

Options for Reading: Audio Recording Encourage students to read along in their texts as they listen to the *Audio Anthology CD* (also recommended for English language learners). Then have them listen again and answer these questions in order:

- How did the bird get in the house? (stanza 3)
- Was the speaker able to save the bird? (stanza 5)

FOR ENGLISH LANGUAGE LEARNERS

Language Coach   **COMMON CORE L 4b**

Suffixes *Possible answers:*
Pulsations *are rhythmic beats. Other words formed by adding* -ion *to a base word include* alteration, promotion, variation. Have students work in pairs to create original sentences using *pulsation* and at least one other word ending with the suffix *-ion.* Invite students to share their sentences with the class.

For the rest of the day,
I could feel its wild thrumming
25 against my palms as I wondered about
the hours it must have spent
pent in the shadows of that room,
hidden in the spiky branches
of our decorated tree, breathing there
30 among the metallic angels, ceramic apples, stars of yarn,
its eyes open, like mine as I lie in bed tonight **E**
picturing this rare, lucky sparrow
tucked into a holly bush now,
a light snow tumbling through the windless dark.

E VISUALIZE
What details help you imagine how the bird looks and feels as it hides in the Christmas tree?

E VISUALIZE

Possible answer: *Details such as "pent in the shadows"; "hidden in the spiky branches / of our decorated tree"; "breathing there"; "among the metallic angels, ceramic apples, stars of yarn"; and "its eyes open" help the reader visualize the bird as fearfully peeking out from the branches of a decorated tree.*

REVISIT THE BIG QUESTION

What ANIMAL reminds you of yourself?

Discuss Based on lines 23–24, why might the speaker feel a connection to this animal? ***Possible answer:*** *In line 31, the speaker compares his own eyes, open at night, to the bird's eyes, which he imagines were also open. The speaker might feel a strong connection to the animal because he saved it and because he spent the day imagining how the bird must have felt.*

Analyze Visuals

Activity Ask students how the photograph of the sparrow helps them to visualize the images in the poem. ***Possible answer:*** *The photograph emphasizes how small the sparrow is. Seeing the bird in its natural habitat helps us visualize the last two lines of the poem. It also helps us imagine how out of place the bird must have looked when it was trapped inside the house.*

FOR STRUGGLING READERS

Vocabulary Support Share with students definitions for these unfamiliar words:

- *insistent* (line 2), "demanding attention"
- *rioting* (line 5), "moving violently"
- *enigma* (line 7), "mystery; puzzle"
- *hunkered* (line 9), "crouched; squatted"
- *pulsations* (line 14), "rhythmic thumpings"
- *dormant* (line 20), "inactive; not growing"
- *spasm* (line 21), "sudden contraction"

- *hemlocks* (line 22), "a kind of pine tree"
- *thrumming* (line 24), "repetitive humming"
- *pent* (line 27), "confined"
- *spiky* (line 28), "with spikes or sharp points"
- *ceramic* (line 30), "made from heated and shaped clay"

Prereading for this poem is found on page 794.

Possible answer: This image suggests that the sloth is a gentle, peace-loving animal that has no interest in answering questions and no concern for anyone's opinion of him.

Read lines 6 and 7 aloud as students follow along. Then have students identify the punctuation mark at the end of each line. Point out that there is no punctuation at the end of line 4. Ask how students think that line should be read.

Possible answer: The dash gives a sense of the words trailing off, while the hyphens in the words slow the reader down. These forms of punctuation match the poem's subject, the sloth.

SELECTION WRAP-UP

READ WITH A PURPOSE Now that students have read the poems, have them compare and contrast how the speakers of the poems view these three animals. Ask students: Would you have treated the animals the same way? *Possible answers: The speaker in "The Fish" respects the grotesque animal and personally connects with it. In "Christmas Sparrow," the speaker feels compassion for the bird and finds joy in releasing it. The speaker in "The Sloth" views the animal with affectionate humor.*

⭐ **CRITIQUE** Have students discuss which of the poems' animals affected them most deeply and why.

INDEPENDENT READING

Students interested in other works by Billy Collins might enjoy reading *Sailing Alone Around the Room: New and Selected Poems.*

The Sloth

Theodore Roethke

In moving-slow he has no Peer.[1]
You ask him something in his Ear,
He thinks about it for a Year;

And, then, before he says a Word
5 There, upside down (unlike a Bird),
He will assume that you have Heard—

A most Ex-as-per-at-ing Lug.
But should you call his manner Smug,
He'll sigh and give his Branch a Hug; **G**

10 Then off again to Sleep he goes,
Still swaying gently by his Toes,
And you just *know* he knows he knows. **G**

---

1. **peer:** equal.

F IMAGERY
Reread line 9. What does this image suggest about the sloth?

G ELEMENTS OF POETRY
Poets often use punctuation to help illustrate their thoughts. In "The Sloth," Roethke uses a dash at the end of one line and hyphens in the middle of words to help bring to life the subject of his poem. Reread lines 6–7. What effect does this punctuation have on the way you read and interpret the poem?

DIFFERENTIATED INSTRUCTION

FOR STRUGGLING READERS

Vocabulary Support Share with students definitions of two unfamiliar words and one familiar word used in an unfamiliar way:

- *exasperating* (line 7), "irritating; annoying." Clarify that the hyphenation ("Ex-as-per-at-ing") is intended to mimic the speaker's sense of annoyance.

- *lug* (line 7), "clumsy fool." Point out that this slang word is somewhat old-fashioned.

- *should* (line 8), "if." Explain that the word should does not mean "must" in this context. Point out that this conditional usage for *should* is not common in American English.

Develop Reading Fluency To help students hear the rhythm of the poem, read the poem aloud one stanza at a time. Have students echo your reading, using the same intonation and rhythm.

Comprehension

1. **Recall** How does the fish in Bishop's poem react when it is caught?

2. **Recall** How did the bird in Collins's poem get trapped inside the house?

3. **Summarize** What is the sloth's response when asked a question?

Text Analysis

4. **Visualize** Describe in detail the mental picture you form of each animal in the poems.

5. **Analyze Imagery** Review the examples of imagery that you recorded in your chart. Identify some images that appeal to your sense of sight and others that appeal to your sense of touch. What is the most striking image in each poem? Why?

6. **Analyze Free Verse** How is the experience of reading Bishop's and Collins's free verse poems different from that of reading Roethke's more traditional poem?

7. **Interpret Themes** How are the three animals in these poems like people? What does each poem suggest about the relationship between human beings and animals?

8. **Compare and Contrast Texts** Compare and contrast "The Fish" and "Christmas Sparrow." In a chart like the one shown, consider the similarities and differences in subject, mood, and theme.

	"The Fish"	"Christmas Sparrow"	Similarities	Differences
Subject				
Mood				
Theme				

Text Criticism

9. **Critical Interpretations** According to Billy Collins, the best poems begin in clarity and end in mystery. Would you say that this is true for each of the three poems in this lesson? Why or why not?

> ### What **ANIMAL** reminds you of yourself?
> What can animals teach us about being human?

COMMON CORE

RL 4 Determine the figurative meanings of words and phrases; analyze the cumulative impact of specific word choices on meaning. **RL 5** Analyze an author's choices concerning how to structure a text.

Practice and Apply

For preliminary support of post-reading questions, use these copy masters:

R RESOURCE MANAGER—Copy Masters
 Visualize p. 53
 Question Support p. 55

 Additional selection questions are provided for teachers on page 47.

ANSWERS

Comprehension

1. *The fish doesn't fight but just hangs there.*

2. *The cat brought the bird indoors.*

3. *The sloth hugs his branch and goes to sleep.*

Text Analysis

COMMON CORE **RL 4, RL 5**

Possible answers:

4. ■ **COMMON CORE FOCUS** *Visualize*
fish: big, old, brown, mottled, yellowed eyes, hooks stuck in its mouth; sparrow: small, panicky, flapping its wings against the window, fluttering inside the speaker's shirt, hiding in the tree, then tucking itself into a holly bush; sloth: slow-moving, unsociable

5. ● **COMMON CORE FOCUS** *Imagery* *Accept any choice if it is well-supported with reasons.*

6. ● **COMMON CORE FOCUS** *Free Verse*
reading free verse poems was slower, required more attention; ideas in these poems more serious

Writing Online

The following tools are available online at **thinkcentral.com** and on **Write*Smart* CD-ROM**:
• Interactive Graphic Organizers
• Interactive Student Models
• Interactive Revision Lessons
For additional grammar instruction, see **GrammarNotes** on **thinkcentral.com**.

7. *The fish is an experienced survivor worthy of respect. The sparrow is caught up in a confusing, terrifying situation and wants its freedom. The sloth is exasperating and self-absorbed. Human beings often seem to see their own traits reflected in animals.*

8. *"The Fish"—Subject: A fish is caught by the speaker and then released; Mood: awe, triumph; Theme: Age and survival deserve respect. "Christmas Sparrow"—Subject: A sparrow is trapped and then released;*
Mood: compassion; Theme: Help those who cannot help themselves. Both speakers are ennobled by the act of freeing an animal.

Text Criticism

9. *Agree: Each poem begins by describing an animal but ends by exploring its mystery. Disagree: Other factors determine merit.*

> What **ANIMAL** reminds you of yourself? Students might consider why people feel attachment to pets.

Assess and Reteach

Assess

DIAGNOSTIC AND SELECTION TESTS
 Selection Tests A, B/C pp. 223–226

Interactive Selection Test on **thinkcentral.com**

Reteach

Level Up Online Tutorials on **thinkcentral.com**

Reteaching Worksheets on **thinkcentral.com**

Piano
Poem by D. H. Lawrence

Fifteen
Poem by William Stafford

Tonight I Can Write . . . /
Puedo Escribir Los Versos . . .
Poem by Pablo Neruda

COMMON CORE FOCUS

RL 4 Analyze the cumulative impact of specific word choices on meaning. **RL 5** Analyze an author's choices concerning how to structure a text. **RL 10** Read and comprehend poems. **W 2b** Develop the topic with quotations appropriate to the audience's knowledge of the topic.

SUMMARIES

"Piano" The sound of a woman singing and a piano being played evokes a deeply affecting memory of the speaker's childhood, his mother, and happier times.

"Fifteen" The speaker recalls the conflict he felt when he was 15 years old and came upon a wrecked motorcycle and its injured owner.

"Tonight I Can Write . . ." The speaker muses sadly over a lost love.

Which **MEMORIES** last?

Introduce the question. Suggest that some important life events often become lasting memories, such as the first day of school or the day you get your driver's license. Ask students to consider such memories as they complete the *QUICKWRITE*.

Which **MEMORIES** last?

COMMON CORE

RL 4 Analyze the cumulative impact of specific word choices on meaning. **RL 5** Analyze an author's choices concerning how to structure a text. **RL 10** Read and comprehend poems.

Think back to a moment from your past that evokes powerful feelings in you. Why has this memory made such a lasting impression? Was it the person you shared the experience with, or the activity itself? In the poems that follow, three speakers recall moments that have had a lasting impact.

QUICKWRITE In a short paragraph, describe a particular memory. Why is this recollection special? What feelings do you remember? Include sensory details that help present a clear picture.

802

See resources on the **Teacher One Stop DVD-ROM** *and on* **thinkcentral.com**.

 RESOURCE MANAGER UNIT 7
   Plan and Teach, pp. 57–64
   Text Analysis and Reading
      Skill, pp. 65–68†*

DIAGNOSTIC AND SELECTION
   TESTS
      Selection Tests, pp. 227–230

 BEST PRACTICES TOOLKIT
   Read Aloud, p. A34

TECHNOLOGY
   🔘 **Teacher One Stop DVD-ROM**
   🔘 **Student One Stop DVD-ROM**
   🔘 **Audio Anthology CD**
   🔘 **ExamView Test Generator**
      on the **Teacher One Stop**

* Resources for Differentiation   **† Also in Spanish**   **‡ In Haitian Creole and Vietnamese**

TEXT ANALYSIS: SOUND DEVICES

In the poems that follow, the poets use rhyme and other **sound devices** to convey rhythm and meaning:

- **Assonance**—the repetition of vowel sounds in words that don't rhyme

  We could find the end of a road, meet
  the sky on out Seventeenth. . . .

- **Consonance**—the repetition of consonant sounds within and at the ends of words

  Softly, in the dusk, a woman is singing to me;
  Taking me back down the vista of years, till I see

- **Repetition**—a sound, word, phrase, or line that is repeated

  I loved her, and sometimes she loved me too.
  She loved me, sometimes I loved her too.

Record examples of the various sound devices that establish in a chart like the one below.

	Assonance	Consonance	Repetition
"Piano"			
"Fifteen"			
"Tonight I Can Write…"			

READING SKILL: UNDERSTAND LINE BREAKS

End-stopped lines of poetry end at a normal speech pause, as in these lines from "Tonight I Can Write . . .":

The same night whitening the same trees.
We, of that time, are no longer the same.

This emphasizes the line endings and makes a reader view each line as a complete unit of meaning.

Enjambed lines run on without a natural pause, as in "Fifteen":

South of the bridge on Seventeenth
I found back of the willows one summer
day a motorcycle with engine running

Enjambment can create a tension and momentum until the thought is complete. As you read each poem, think about how line breaks affect rhythm and meaning.

***Review:* Make Inferences**

 Complete the activities in your **Reader/Writer Notebook.**

D. H. Lawrence
1885–1930

Writer of Experience
Although impoverished during his childhood, D. H. Lawrence found great pleasure in learning and culture, a love of which was instilled by his mother. Lawrence's confessional, earnest style is illustrated in the poem "Piano." He wrote it in memory of his mother.

William Stafford
1914–1993

Remembering the Past
William Stafford remembered, growing up in Kansas, being "surrounded by songs and stories and poems, and lyrical splurges of excited talk...." These memories eventually became the stuff of his poetry. "Fifteen" is part of a collection of poems that recall his past.

Pablo Neruda
1904–1973

Boy Wonder
Pablo Neruda was drawn to poetry at an early age, even though his working-class family scoffed at his literary ambitions. By age 20 he had achieved literary stardom with the publication of *Twenty Love Poems and a Song of Despair.* The book chronicles a passionate love story, from the couple's first meeting to eventual breakup. "Tonight I Can Write" is the 20th poem.

Authors Online
Go to thinkcentral.com. KEYWORD: HML10-803

THINKcentral

803

TEXT ANALYSIS

COMMON CORE
RL 4
RL 10

Model the Skill: SOUND DEVICES

To model how to identify sound devices, write these lines on the board and read them aloud:

> It's not enough to mourn
> Those blazing days of summer in
> The only home I ever knew.
> I can't go back, unlock the door
> Or click my heels. That place is gone.
> It's not enough to long for home.

Help students identify examples of assonance, consonance, and repetition in these lines. Point out these examples: **assonance:** "blazing / days," "only / home" "gone / long" "Oh / home"; **consonance:** "blazing / days," "back / unlock / click"; **repetition:** "not enough to" in lines 1 and 6.

GUIDED PRACTICE Have students write original examples of each of the sound devices discussed on this page.

R RESOURCE MANAGER—Copy Master
Sound Devices p. 65 (for student use while reading the selection)

READING SKILL

COMMON CORE
RL 5

Model the Skill: UNDERSTAND LINE BREAKS

Point out that end-stopped lines usually end with a period, semi-colon, comma, or other punctuation mark to show the natural pause in speech. Also explain that a line of poetry may include internal punctuation yet still be an enjambed line if the sentence continues onto the next line. Help students analyze the line breaks in the poetry example on the board, and then classify each line as either end-stopped or enjambed. Point out that lines 3, 5, and 6 are end-stopped lines, and lines 1, 2, and 4 are enjambed lines.

GUIDED PRACTICE Invite volunteers to read the examples of poetry in the pupil book and on the board. Make sure that they pause at the end of each end-stopped line and read on without pausing at the end of each enjambed line.

DIFFERENTIATED INSTRUCTION

FOR STRUGGLING READERS

Concept Support Point out that the best way to identify a poem's sound devices is to listen to it read aloud. Have students work with partners to read aloud the examples on the page. Tell students that they should read a poem several times with a different purpose for reading each time; for example, they might read once for comprehension and a second time to notice sound devices.

FOR ENGLISH LANGUAGE LEARNERS

Language: Skill Words Encourage students to use mnemonic devices to remember the names of the different sound devices. Remind them that *assonance* refers to the repetition of vowel sounds by pointing out that the word *assonance* begins with the vowel *a.* Similarly, consonance refers to the repetition of consonant sounds, and the word *consonance* begins with the consonant *c.* Also, tell students to think of end-stopped lines as those that stop at the end of the line.

READ WITH A PURPOSE

Help students set a purpose for reading. Tell students to identify the memories each poet writes about.

Analyze Visuals

Activity Ask students to compare the mood of the painting with the mood of Lawrence's poem. *Possible answer: The painting and the poem share an atmosphere of dreaminess and mystery. The painting's setting is dreamlike, the piano seems to grow out of a wall of leaves. In the poem, the speaker's memories suggest a dreamlike reverie.*

About the Art Thomas Wilmer Dewing (1851–1938) is best known for his elegant and mysterious paintings of idealized women, who are often depicted in dreamlike interiors. As in *The Spinet*, many of Dewing's works focus on a woman playing a musical instrument.

The Spinet (1902), Thomas Wilmer Dewing. Oil on wood, 15½" × 20". Smithsonian American Art Museum, Washington, D.C. Photo © Smithsonian American Art Museum, Washington, D.C./Art Resource, New York.

 **D. H. Lawrence**

TEXT ANALYSIS

COMMON CORE
RL 4
RL 10

A *Model the Skill:* **SOUND DEVICES**

Read lines 5–9 aloud twice. Before the first reading, direct students to focus on the vowel sounds as they listen. Emphasize assonance as you read. Before reading the lines a second time, emphasizing consonance, direct students to focus their attention on the internal consonant sounds. Have students record the sound devices in their Text Analysis charts.

Possible answer: *One can find assonance in the repetition of the short* i *vowel sound, in "insidious," "till," and "hymns"; the long* i *vowel sound in "spite" and "myself"; and the long* e *vowel sound in "me," "weeps," and "evenings." One can find consonance in the repetition of the* s *sound in "myself," "insidious," and "mastery."*

Softly, in the dusk, a woman is singing to me;
Taking me back down the vista of years, till I see
A child sitting under the piano, in the boom of the
    tingling strings
And pressing the small, poised feet of a mother who
    smiles as she sings.

5 In spite of myself, the insidious mastery of song
Betrays me back, till the heart of me weeps to belong
To the old Sunday evenings at home, with winter outside
And hymns in the cozy parlour, the tinkling piano
    our guide. **A**

So now it is vain for the singer to burst into clamour
10 With the great black piano appassionato. The glamour
Of childish days is upon me, my manhood is cast
Down in the flood of remembrance, I weep like a child
    for the past.

A **SOUND DEVICES**
Reread lines 5–9 aloud. Where can you find **assonance** and **consonance** in this stanza?

DIFFERENTIATED INSTRUCTION

FOR ENGLISH LANGUAGE LEARNERS

Comprehension: Definitions Tell students that some British English terms are spelled differently than the same American English terms. Write the words *parlour* (line 8) and *clamour* (line 9) on the board. Explain to students that that these words mean the same as *parlor* and *clamor*. Have students use context clues or a dictionary to determine the meanings of the two words.

FOR STRUGGLING READERS

Options for Reading Read the poem aloud stanza by stanza, pausing after each for questions, explanations, or discussion.

 BEST PRACTICES TOOLKIT—Transparency
Read Aloud p. A34

Fifteen

William Stafford

South of the bridge on Seventeenth
I found back of the willows one summer
day a motorcycle with engine running
as it lay on its side, ticking over
5 slowly in the high grass. I was fifteen.

I admired all that pulsing gleam, the
shiny flanks, the demure headlights
fringed where it lay; I led it gently
to the road and stood with that
10 companion, ready and friendly. I was fifteen. **B**

We could find the end of a road, meet
the sky on out Seventeenth. I thought about
hills, and patting the handle got back a
confident opinion. On the bridge we indulged
15 a forward feeling, a tremble. I was fifteen.

Thinking, back farther in the grass I found
the owner, just coming to, where he had flipped
over the rail. He had blood on his hand, was pale—
I helped him walk to his machine. He ran his hand
20 over it, called me good man, roared away.

I stood there, fifteen.

B LINE BREAKS
Notice how Stafford continues a thought or sentence from one line to the next. How does this **enjambment** affect the way you read the lines?

PIANO / FIFTEEN **805**

Prereading for this poem is found on page 802.

Analyze Visuals

Activity Ask students to connect lines of the poem to the photograph of the motorcycle and its rider. *Possible answer: Lines 11–12 connect to the photograph because the road seems to meet the sky, as in the poem.*

READING SKILL — COMMON CORE — RL 5

B *Model the Skill:* **LINE BREAKS**

Read the first stanza aloud, stopping at the end of every line. Then reread the stanza, pausing only at a punctuation mark or the completion of a thought. Point out that stopping at the end of each line breaks the rhythm of the poem.

Possible answer: This enjambment affects the speed at which one reads the lines. It slows the reader down and creates suspense that is resolved only at the end of the thought.

TIERED DISCUSSION PROMPTS

Direct students to lines 1–21. Use these prompts to help students understand the conflict the speaker feels over the motorcycle:

Connect Have you ever come upon something or someone that opened up new opportunities for you? Explain. *Students' answers will vary.*

Analyze Why do you think the speaker keeps repeating that he was fifteen? Does he mean the same thing every time he says his age? *Possible answer: In the first two stanzas, the speaker tells us that he was fifteen to explain how alluring the motorcycle was to him: he was at the age when it would have seemed like a ticket to freedom and adulthood. When he repeats his age at the end of the third stanza, it emphasizes the temptation he felt to hop on the motorcycle and ride off into the sunset. When the speaker repeats his age in the last line of the poem, the meaning has subtly changed again: he is now referring to how grown-up he felt after helping the injured rider and being called a "good man."*

FOR STRUGGLING READERS

Develop Reading Fluency Encourage students to listen to the selection on the *Audio Anthology CD* (also recommended for English language learners) as they read along. Then have student pairs practice reading the poem aloud to each other until they can read it fluently.

Distribute the copy masters and have students work in pairs or groups to practice fluency.

R RESOURCE MANAGER—Copy Master
Reading Fluency p. 70

FOR ADVANCED LEARNERS/PRE-AP

Analyze Symbolism Point out to students that elements of "Fifteen" could be interpreted as symbols for larger ideas. For example, the bridge might represent a limit or a border, as if on the edge of a town. Invite students to consider the symbolic meanings of the motorcycle, the road, and the owner. Have them discuss their interpretations—along with evidence from the poem—in small groups.

Tonight I Can Write . . .
Pablo Neruda

Prereading for this poem is found on page 802.

TEXT ANALYSIS

COMMON CORE
RL 4
RL 10

C SOUND DEVICES

Possible answer: *The repetition of the sentence (lines 1, 5, 11) emphasizes the overwhelming sadness that the speaker is feeling over a lost love.*

IF STUDENTS NEED HELP . . . Encourage them to record examples of repetition in their Sound Devices charts.

TEXT ANALYSIS

COMMON CORE
RL 5

D LINE LENGTH

Read line 1 aloud. Point out that the line is an example of an end-stopped line, because it ends at a normal speech pause and with a period. Read lines 17–18 aloud, and then have students echo the reading.

Possible answer: *Line 1 is one sentence and has a smooth rhythm. Line 17 has two sentences and a fragment, which slows the reader down, breaking the line's rhythm.*

READING SKILL: *Review*

COMMON CORE
RL 10

E MAKE INFERENCES

Possible answer: *Yes, the speaker still loves the woman because he is still thinking about her, missing her, and sad that he lost her. No, the speaker no longer loves the woman; he clearly states that as a fact in line 23. The speaker may not be certain how he feels about the woman.*

Extend the Discussion Identify the details that led you to your inference.

REVISIT THE BIG QUESTION
Which MEMORIES last?

Discuss What does the speaker suggest about memory with the words in line 28, "Love is so short, forgetting is so long"? *Possible answer: With these words the speaker suggests that certain memories will remain with us, even if we don't want them to; or that sometimes a memory of love can become bigger to us than the actual experience.*

Tonight I can write the saddest lines.

Write, for example, 'The night is shattered
and the blue stars shiver in the distance.'

The night wind revolves in the sky and sings.

5 Tonight I can write the saddest lines.
I loved her, and sometimes she loved me too.

Through nights like this one I held her in my arms.
I kissed her again and again under the endless sky.

She loved me, sometimes I loved her too.
10 How could one not have loved her great still eyes.

Tonight I can write the saddest lines. **C**
To think that I do not have her. To feel that I have lost her.

To hear the immense night, still more immense without her.
And the verse falls to the soul like dew to the pasture.

15 What does it matter that my love could not keep her.
The night is shattered and she is not with me.

This is all. In the distance someone is singing. In the distance. **D**
My soul is not satisfied that it has lost her.

My sight searches for her as though to go to her.
20 My heart looks for her, and she is not with me.

The same night whitening the same trees.
We, of that time, are no longer the same.

I no longer love her, that's certain, but how I loved her.
My voice tried to find the wind to touch her hearing.

25 Another's. She will be another's. Like my kisses before.
Her voice. Her bright body. Her infinite eyes.

I no longer love her, that's certain, but maybe I love her.
Love is so short, forgetting is so long.

Because through nights like this one I held her in my arms
30 my soul is not satisfied that it has lost her.

Though this be the last pain that she makes me suffer
and these the last verses that I write for her. **E**

Translated by W. S. Merwin

C SOUND DEVICES
What impact is created by the **repetition** of "Tonight I can write the saddest lines"?

COMMON CORE RL 5

D LINE LENGTH
The line is the core unit of a poem. **Line length** is an essential element of a poem's meaning and rhythm. Some **end-stopped** lines express complete thoughts, while other **enjambed lines** run on, their thoughts completed in one or more lines. Find examples of end-stopped and enjambed lines in the poem. What effects do these different line lengths create?

E MAKE INFERENCES
Reread lines 27–32. Do you think the speaker still loves the woman? Why or why not?

DIFFERENTIATED INSTRUCTION

FOR STRUGGLING READERS

Options for Reading: Choral Reading Read the first half of the poem aloud, through line 16, pausing if necessary for questions or discussion. Then alternate reading the rest of the poem in couplets, with either the whole class or individual volunteers reading every other couplet. As students read aloud, have them listen for rhythm and sound devices. Pause between students' readings to clarify concepts.

FOR ENGLISH LANGUAGE LEARNERS

Culture: Connect Invite a student whose native language is Spanish to read the original version of the poem on page 807. If you have more than one Spanish speaker in the class, invite each of them to share an oral reading of the poem by dividing the poem into sections. Encourage students to share any observations about the translation or the differences between the Spanish and English versions of the poem.

Puedo Escribir Los Versos . . .

Pablo Neruda

Puedo escribir los versos más tristes esta noche.

Escribir, por ejemplo: 'La noche está estrellada,
y tiritan, azules, los astros, a lo lejos.'

El viento de la noche gira en el cielo y canta.

5 Puedo escribir los versos más tristes esta noche.
Yo la quise, y a veces ella también me quiso.

En las noches como ésta la tuve entre mis brazos.
La besé tantas veces bajo el cielo infinito.

Ella me quiso, a veces yo también la quería.
10 Cómo no haber amado sus grandes ojos fijos.

Puedo escribir los versos más tristes esta noche.
Pensar que no la tengo. Sentir que la he perdido.

Oir la noche inmensa, más inmensa sin ella.
Y el verso cae al alma como al pasto el rocío.

15 Qué importa que mi amor no pudiera guardarla.
La noche está estrellada y ella no está conmigo.

Eso es todo. A lo lejos alguien canta. A lo lejos.
Mi alma no se contenta con haberla perdido.

Como para acercarla mi mirada la busca.
20 Mi corazón la busca, y ella no está conmigo.

La misma noche que hace blanquear los mismos árboles.
Nosotros, los de entonces, ya no somos los mismos.

Ya no la quiero, es cierto, pero cuánto la quise.
Mi voz buscaba el viento para tocar su oído.

25 De otro. Será de otro. Como antes de mis besos.
Su voz, su cuerpo claro. Sus ojos infinitos.

Ya no la quiero, es cierto, pero tal vez la quiero.
Es tan corto el amor, y es tan largo el olvido.

Porque en noches como ésta la tuve entre mis brazos,
30 mi alma no se contenta con haberla perdido.

Aunque éste sea el último dolor que ella me causa,
y éstos sean los últimos versos que yo le escribo.

Waiting (2001), Ben McLaughlin. Oil on board, 30.5 cm × 30.5 cm. Private collection. Photo © Bridgeman Art Library.

Analyze Visuals

Activity Ask students how the painting reflects the mood and subject of the poem. *Possible answer: Both the painting and the poem evoke a lonely, contemplative mood. The man in the painting is physically looking back, staring off into the distance. Similarly, the speaker in the poem is looking back at an episode in his past.*

About the Art Contemporary British painter Ben McLaughlin often paints solitary figures in familiar yet eerie settings that are starkly lit and viewed from unusual vantage points.

SELECTION WRAP–UP

READ WITH A PURPOSE Now that students have finished reading the selection, ask students which memory seems the most clear to them. Which one can they visualize best, and why? *Possible answer: Answers will vary. Students who are interested in music may find it easiest to relate to "Piano." "Fifteen" maybe appeal to students because of the age of the speaker." Tonight I Can Write . . ." has the universal theme of lost love.*

⭐ **CRITIQUE** Ask students what aspect of each poem they find most effective, and why.

INDEPENDENT READING

Students interested in more works by Pablo Neruda might enjoy *Neruda: Selected Poems*, a sampling of what some consider to be his best work.

FOR ENGLISH LANGUAGE LEARNERS

Connect Call on Spanish speakers to find examples of sound devices in the Spanish version of the poem. Students can point out instances of assonance, consonance, and repetition and read the lines aloud for non-English speakers to hear.

FOR ADVANCED LEARNERS/PRE–AP

Analyze Imagery Invite students to choose one image from the poem to examine more closely. Ask them to identify the sense or senses this image appeals to, as well as the mood or feeling it creates for the reader. Students should also interpret the role of the specific image in the larger picture painted by the poem. Have students discuss their ideas in small groups.

JOURNAL ARTICLE In 1971, nearly 50 years after writing "Tonight I Can Write ..." Pablo Neruda was awarded the Nobel Prize in Literature. For Neruda, this meant a prize of $450,000 and worldwide fame, although he was already quite famous in and around Chile, his native country. The following selection gives background on this prestigious award.

The Nobel Prize in Literature

In 1888, the well-known scientist and inventor Alfred Nobel experienced the shock of reading his own obituary. A French journalist had mistakenly reported his passing and described him as a "merchant of Death." The name was a reference to Nobel's most famous invention: dynamite.

This description troubled Nobel. He had often spoken out against violence and considered himself a pacifist. Many believe that he was moved to create a more positive legacy; for when he did die, his will specified that his fortune be used to honor people whose achievements enrich human life.

Since 1900, the Nobel Prize has rewarded some of the world's most dazzling achievements in the fields of physics, chemistry, medicine, economics, peace, and literature. Given out each year by the Swedish Academy, the prize consists of a gold medal, a diploma, and money (in 2000, it reached one million dollars), but its actual worth is much higher. Nobel winners, or laureates, are considered among the most important and influential people in the world. The Nobel Prize has both launched new careers and brought closure to long and successful ones.

Nobel's will required that a prize winner's work provide "the greatest benefit to mankind." For achievements in literature, however, Nobel had a second requirement: this work must

also be "in an ideal direction." Over the past century, there has been debate over what "ideal direction" means, and why any particular writer should be chosen. As a result, the prize has been used at different times to honor different things: talented but unknown writers, for example, or writers who pioneer new styles. Pablo Neruda falls into the "pioneers" category, while recent winning poets Seamus Heaney (1995) and Wislawa Szymborska (1996), were honored as "unknown masters."

When Neruda won his Nobel Prize in 1971, the Swedish Academy's presentation speech stated that "his work benefits mankind precisely because of its direction." Neruda's early poems describing "isolation and dissonance" gave way to later ones declaring "harmony with Man and the Earth." The academy saw this as an "ideal direction" for all of mankind to take. Neruda's work was also praised for its political content, particularly as it criticized the oppression of writers and artists.

In recent years, the Academy has moved away from determining "ideal direction" in favor of simply honoring writers for work which "furthers knowledge of man and his condition." This tendency might have pleased Neruda, who once stated, "The books that help you most are those which make you think the most . . . a great book that comes from a great thinker is a ship of thought, deep freighted with truth and beauty."

TIERED DISCUSSION PROMPTS

Use these prompts to help students understand Neruda's view of great literature and connect his view to his own work:

Connect Reread the quotation by Neruda that closes the article. What books have helped you the most or made you think the most? *Accept all reasonable responses.*

Analyze Explain Neruda's metaphor that is quoted at the end of the article. What two things is he comparing, and what point is he making? *Possible answer: Neruda uses a metaphor to compare a great book to a ship. The point of the comparison is that both a book and a ship transport something: a ship carries cargo and a book carries a message of "truth and beauty."*

Evaluate In your opinion, does "Tonight I Can Write . . ." fit Neruda's definition of a great piece of literature? Why or why not? *Possible answers: Yes, Neruda's poem does more than just sit on the page; it stays with you and makes you think about the nature of love and memory. No, Neruda's poem is too personal to inspire much thought about universal truths; it is only one man's experience of love and loss.*

Comprehension

1. **Recall** How does the speaker in Stafford's poem react to finding the motorcycle?

2. **Recall** What are some nature images in Neruda's poem?

3. **Summarize** In Lawrence's poem, what is the speaker remembering?

Text Analysis

4. **Visualize** Cite specific lines from both Lawrence's and Stafford's poems that helped you to visualize what the speakers remember. For example, what mental pictures did you form when reading lines 3 and 4 of Lawrence's poem?

5. **Analyze Sound Devices** What examples of sound devices did you list as you read? Explain what ideas are emphasized through **repetition** of words and phrases.

6. **Examine Line Breaks** Compare and contrast the poets' use of **end-stopped** and **enjambed** lines. How do their choices affect the rhythm of the poems?

7. **Compare and Contrast Themes** Compare and contrast the memories of the speakers in these poems. In your opinion, why have these memories endured?

8. **Evaluate** Read "The Nobel Prize in Literature" on page 808, and consider "Tonight I Can Write . . ." in light of the Swedish Academy's comments on Neruda's work. Does the poem have more to do with isolation and dissonance, or harmony?

READING-WRITING CONNECTION

YOUR TURN Explore the imagery in "Tonight I Can Write . . ." by responding to the prompt below. Then use the **revising tip** to improve your writing.

WRITING PROMPT	REVISING TIP
Extended Constructed Response: Analysis What do the images from nature in Neruda's poem reveal about the speaker's relationship with the woman? What do they tell the reader about the speaker's emotions? Use details from the poem to write a response in **three to five paragraphs**.	Review your response. Have you used quotation marks correctly when quoting text from the poem?

Which MEMORIES last?

What will you most remember about this period in your life?

COMMON CORE

RL 4 Analyze the cumulative impact of specific word choices on meaning. **RL 5** Analyze an author's choices concerning how to structure a text. **W 2b** Develop the topic with quotations appropriate to the audience's knowledge of the topic.

Practice and Apply

For preliminary support of post-reading questions, use these copy masters:

R RESOURCE MANAGER—Copy Masters
Understand Line Breaks p. 67
Question Support p. 69

Additional selection questions are provided for teachers on page 61.

ANSWERS

Comprehension

1. *He imagines riding away on it.*

2. *Neruda's nature images include "The night is shattered" (line 2), "blue stars shiver in the distance" (line 3), and "The same night whitening the same trees" (line 21).*

3. *The speaker remembers sitting under the piano in the parlor while his mother sang and played the piano on Sunday evenings.*

Text Analysis

COMMON CORE **RL 4, RL 5, W 2b**

Possible answers:

4. *Lawrence's poem: lines 3–4 and 7–10 Stafford's poem: lines 3–5, 7–9, 13–15, and 16–20*

5. ● **COMMON CORE FOCUS** *Sound Devices Accept all appropriate examples of assonance and consonance. Stafford's poem: repetition of "fifteen" emphasizes speaker's memories of youth Neruda's poem: repetition of title line emphasizes speaker's sadness*

6. ● **COMMON CORE FOCUS** *Line Breaks Only Neruda uses end-stopped lines, creating a slow, stately rhythm. The other poems sound more conversational.*

Assess and Reteach

7. *Accept all reasonable answers.*

8. *"Tonight I Can Write . . ." has more to do with isolation and dissonance, because the speaker is lonely and longing for something he has lost.*

Which MEMORIES last?

Students might think about big events and smaller, emotional moments in their lives.

READING-WRITING CONNECTION

Encourage students to use a three-column chart to record each image, what it reveals about the speaker's relationship, and what it reveals about his emotions.

Assess

DIAGNOSTIC AND SELECTION TESTS
Selection Test A pp. 227–228
Selection Test B/C pp. 229–230

Interactive Selection Test on **thinkcentral.com**

Reteach

Level Up Online Tutorials on **thinkcentral.com**

Reteaching Worksheets on **thinkcentral.com**
Literature Lesson 17: Structure of Poetry

Literature Lesson 21: Alliteration, Assonance, and Consonance

Focus and Motivate

COMMON CORE FOCUS

RL 2 Determine a central idea of a text . **RL 5** Analyze an author's choices concerning how to structure a text. **RL 10** Read and comprehend poems. **W 2b** Develop the topic with quotations appropriate to the audience's knowledge of the topic.

SUMMARIES

"Sonnet 18" The speaker assures his beloved that she is even more beautiful than a summer's day and declares that her beauty will be immortalized in this sonnet.

"Sonnet XXX" of *Fatal Interview* In this sonnet, the speaker observes that although love holds little practical value, she would not trade the love of her beloved, even for life's necessities.

What makes a good LOVE POEM?

Ask the question, and relate it to the comic strip. Ask students to share the titles of other poems or of songs they know that present ideas about love. Encourage students to keep these examples in mind as they complete the *BRAINSTORM* activity.

Essential Course of Study ECOS

Sonnet 18
Poem by William Shakespeare

Sonnet XXX of *Fatal Interview*
Poem by Edna St. Vincent Millay

VIDEO TRAILER THINK central KEYWORD: HML10-810

What makes a good LOVE POEM?

COMMON CORE

RL 2 Determine a central idea of a text. **RL 5** Analyze an author's choices concerning how to structure a text. **RL 10** Read and comprehend poems.

How do you describe something you cannot see or taste or touch? Like a love song, a love poem uses familiar objects and experiences to make sense of the mysterious feelings of love. As you'll see in "Sonnet 18" and "Sonnet XXX," the results can be as different as day and night.

BRAINSTORM In a group, brainstorm a list of comparisons you might use to describe how it feels to be in love. Think of song lyrics you know or poems you have read. As you create your list, discuss what aspect or quality of love each comparison communicates.

KAT! I DID IT! I WROTE A VALENTINE'S DAY POEM FOR HEART! TELL ME WHAT YOU THINK!

"I WANTED TO WRITE A POEM FOR HEART, BUT I DIDN'T KNOW JUST HOW I SHOULD START. AND SO I THINK I'LL SIMPLY SAY, 'BE MY VALENTINE TODAY!' NOW IT'S DONE AS YOU CAN SEE, SO I CAN GO AND WATCH TV."

MAYBE YOU SHOULD JUST GET HER PERFUME.

810

Selection Resources

R RESOURCE MANAGER UNIT 7
Plan and Teach, pp. 71–78
Text Analysis and Reading Skill, pp. 79–82†*

DIAGNOSTIC AND SELECTION TESTS
Selection Tests, pp. 231–234

BEST PRACTICES TOOLKIT
Read Aloud, p. A34
INTERACTIVE READER
ADAPTED INTERACTIVE READER
ELL ADAPTED INTERACTIVE READER

TECHNOLOGY
- Teacher One Stop DVD-ROM
- Student One Stop DVD-ROM
- PowerNotes DVD-ROM
- Audio Anthology CD
- Audio Tutor CD
- ExamView Test Generator on the Teacher One Stop

Video Trailer THINK central

Go to **thinkcentral.com** to preview the **Video Trailer** introducing this selection. Other features that support the selection include
- **PowerNotes** presentation
- **ThinkAloud** models to enhance comprehension
- **WordSharp** vocabulary tutorials
- interactive writing and grammar instruction

---

* Resources for Differentiation   † Also in Spanish   ‡ In Haitian Creole and Vietnamese

POETIC FORM: SONNET

The sonnet has been a popular poetic form for centuries, and, traditionally, love has been its subject. While different types of sonnets have been developed by various poets, there are some characteristics that are common to all sonnets.

- Typically, the **sonnet** is a 14-line lyric poem written with a strict pattern of rhyme and rhythm.
- The **English,** or **Shakespearean, sonnet** has a rhyme scheme of *abab cdcd efef gg.* Notice how this divides the poem into four distinct line groups: three **quatrains,** or four-line units, followed by a **couplet**—a pair of rhymed lines, or two-line unit.
- The **meter,** or the repeated pattern of rhythm, in each line of a sonnet is typically **iambic pentameter.** Each rhythmic unit of meter is known as a **foot.** The most commonly used metrical foot is an **iamb,** which is an unstressed syllable followed by a stressed syllable. Note the iambs in the following example from Shakespeare's "Sonnet 18":

> Sŏ lóng ăs mén căn bréathe, ŏr eýes căn sée,
>
> Sŏ lóng lĭves thís, ănd thĭs gĭves lĭfe tŏ thée.

In each line, notice that there are five units of iambs. When a line has five feet in it, it is referred to as **pentameter.** Therefore, this meter is called iambic pentameter.

As you read the poems in this lesson, compare their rhyme schemes and meter.

READING STRATEGY: READING SONNETS

Through their structure, sonnets often express complex ideas. These strategies will help you identify those ideas:

1. Identify the situation, problem, or question introduced at the beginning of the poem.
2. Identify the turning point, if there is one.
3. Determine how the situation is clarified, the problem resolved, or the question answered.

As you read, apply these strategies and record the results on a chart like the one shown.

Strategy	Sonnet 18	Sonnet XXX
Situation/Problem/Question		
Turning Point		
Solution/Resolution/Answer		

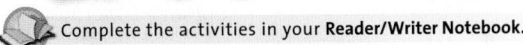 Complete the activities in your **Reader/Writer Notebook.**

Meet the Authors

William Shakespeare
1564–1616

Renaissance Man
Although Shakespeare is best known for his plays, he was also a brilliant poet. When Shakespeare began his career in the 1590s, the sonnet was a literary fashion in England, usually written as a longing tribute to a faraway beloved. In fact, many of Shakespeare's sonnets are addressed to a "dark lady" whose identity has never been discovered. First published in 1609, the complete series of 154 sonnets includes some of the finest love poems written in English. For more about Shakespeare, see the extended biography on page 1186.

Edna St. Vincent Millay
1892–1950

A True Original
Edna St. Vincent Millay was only 19 when her poem "Renascence" made her an instant celebrity. Although Millay's youth and free-spirited lifestyle fit the image of the rebellious artist, her highly crafted poems often took on traditional poetic forms, such as the sonnet. In 1923 she became the first woman to win the Pulitzer Prize in poetry, a tribute to her technical skill.

Authors Online
Go to **thinkcentral.com.** KEYWORD: HML10-811

Teach

POETIC FORM — COMMON CORE — RL 5 RL 10

● *Model the Skill:* **SONNET**

To help students understand characteristics of the sonnet, write these lines on the board and read them aloud:

> When men lament lost love, I think they lie:
>
> They sometimes fall apart, but rarely die.

Help students mark the stressed and unstressed syllables. Explain that these lines are written in iambic pentameter and that they form a couplet.

GUIDED PRACTICE Ask pairs of students to write and share an original couplet in iambic pentameter.

READING STRATEGY — COMMON CORE — RL 2

■ *Model the Skill:* **READING SONNETS**

Explain that in many Shakespearean sonnets, the first quatrain introduces the problem or question, the second quatrain expounds upon it, the third quatrain introduces a resolution, and the couplet provides a final commentary on the problem or sums up the proposed resolution.

GUIDED PRACTICE Ask students to imagine that the couplet written on the board is at the end of a sonnet. Have them suggest a situation or problem that the couplet could be commenting on or a solution that it could be summing up.

R RESOURCE MANAGER—Copy Master Reading Sonnets p. 81 (for student use while reading the selection)

DIFFERENTIATED INSTRUCTION

FOR STRUGGLING READERS

Concept Support Help students grasp the concept of meter by reading aloud the couplet from "Sonnet 18" or the one written on the board. Tap out the meter as you read, demonstrating that the lines are iambic pentameter, with five iambs per line. Then change one or two words so that the stresses are off—either the wrong number per line or the wrong pattern. Read the lines again while students tap out the meter with you.

FOR ADVANCED LEARNERS/PRE–AP

Compare and Contrast Meter Ask students to learn more about other types of poetic feet (such as the trochee, anapest, dactyl, and spondee). Also have them learn the names for the number of feet in a line of verse (such as dimeter, trimeter, and tetrameter). Ask each student to choose three classic poems, each of which illustrates a different type of regular meter (such as iambic tetrameter). Then have students share their examples in small groups.

READ WITH A PURPOSE

Help students set a purpose for reading. Tell them to look for the ways that the poets describe love.

READING STRATEGY COMMON CORE RL 2

A *Model the Skill:* **READING SONNETS**

Remind students that the second quatrain is elaborating on the question from the first quatrain. Direct students to line 1, and have them paraphrase the question. Tell them that this is the subject of the sonnet. Then move to the second quatrain. As students unravel the sonnet, have them record the details in their Reading Sonnets charts.

Possible answer: *The second quatrain describes the faults of summer days—too much heat (line 5) and frequent clouds (line 6)—and the fact that nothing stays beautiful forever (lines 7–8).*

Analyze Visuals ▶
Describe the relationship of the figures shown. What specific details support your **inferences**?

SONNET 18

WILLIAM SHAKESPEARE

Shall I compare thee to a summer's day?
Thou art more lovely and more temperate:[1]
Rough winds do shake the darling buds of May,
And summer's lease hath all too short a date:
5 Sometime too hot the eye of heaven shines,
And often is his gold complexion dimmed;
And every fair from fair sometime declines,
By chance or nature's changing course untrimmed;[2] **A**
But thy eternal summer shall not fade,
10 Nor lose possession of that fair thou owest;[3]
Nor shall Death brag thou wander'st in his shade,
When in eternal lines to time thou growest:
    So long as men can breathe, or eyes can see,
    So long lives this, and this gives life to thee.

A **READING SONNETS**
Reread the second **quatrain,** or grouping of four lines. What situation does it describe?

---

1. **temperate** (tĕm′pər-ĭt): moderate, mild.
2. **untrimmed:** stripped of beauty.
3. **thou owest** (*thou* ō′ĭst): you own; you possess.

Offering of the Heart (1400-1410). French tapestry from Arras. Wool and silk, 247 cm × 209 cm. Louvre, Paris. Photo © Réunion des Musées Nationaux/Art Resource, New York.

DIFFERENTIATED INSTRUCTION

FOR ENGLISH LANGUAGE LEARNERS

Language Work with students to untangle the sentence inversions throughout the sonnet. Write line 5 on the board and tell students that the word order is inverted. Write underneath it "Sometimes the eye of heaven shines too hot." Explain to students that this would be the normal word order for that sentence. Work through the remaining inverted lines, having students suggest normal word orders for the inversions.

FOR STRUGGLING READERS

Options for Reading Read "Sonnet 18" aloud, emphasizing the rhythm created by the rhyme scheme and iambic pentameter. Then ask students to listen to the poem on the *Audio Anthology CD* (also recommended for English language learners). Address students' questions and comments in a whole-group discussion.

 BEST PRACTICES TOOLKIT—Transparency
Read Aloud p. A34

Reading Support

This selection on **thinkcentral.com** includes embedded **ThinkAloud** models—students "thinking aloud" about the story to model the kinds of questions a good reader would ask about a selection.

BACKGROUND

Sonnet Forms The Petrarchan sonnet, named after the 14th-century Italian poet Petrarch, is divided into an octave (first 8 lines; *abbaabba*) and a sestet (last 6 lines; usually *cdecde*, or *cdccdc*). The Spenserian sonnet, named after 16th-century English poet Edmund Spenser, is a variation of the Shakespearean sonnet, with an interlocking rhyme scheme of *abab bcbc cdcd ee*.

Analyze Visuals

Possible answer: The people are in love. Details that support this inference include the lovely and secluded setting and the fact that the man is shown literally offering the woman a heart.

About the Art This tapestry comes from Arras, a town in northern France. Arras became so closely associated with the production of tapestries during the early Middle Ages that many people used the word *arras* as a synonym for *tapestry*. Shakespeare himself included an arras in a key scene in *Hamlet*, in which the character Polonius hides behind an arras and is killed.

REVISIT THE BIG QUESTION

What makes a good

LOVE POEM?

Discuss Based on lines 1–14, is "Sonnet 18" a love poem for today? Why or why not? *Possible answers: Yes; people today might use such ideas to express their feelings. No; although the ideas still make sense, the language and imagery are outdated.*

FOR STRUGGLING READERS

Language Support Pair students with proficient readers and ask them to work together to "translate" Shakespeare's sonnet into modern language. Encourage students to paraphrase one line at a time, keeping the main idea of each line but rewording it so that it is more accessible to a modern reader. Urge them to be sure that they are satisfied with each section of the sonnet before moving on to the next. Call on volunteers to share their translations with the class. After discussing the similarities and differences among the translations, work with students to create a final "translation" based on these versions. Discuss the class translation and ask students to comment on the timelessness of the ideas about love that the poem's speaker expresses.

Prereading for this poem is found on page 810.

BACKGROUND

Fatal Interview Millay published *Fatal Interview*, a collection of 52 sonnets, in 1931. "Sonnet XXX" also goes by the title "Love is not all."

Analyze Visuals

Activity Ask students to suggest one word that describes the aspect of love captured in the sculpture. *Possible answers: unity, togetherness, tenderness, commitment.* Be sure to point out the title, *The Cathedral,* and to ask students to consider its meaning.

About the Art French sculptor Auguste Rodin (1840–1917) achieved great acclaim during his lifetime and is today considered one of the greatest sculptors in the history of art. Perhaps his most famous work is *The Thinker* (1880).

POETIC FORM

COMMON CORE
RL 5
RL 10

B *Model the Skill:* **SONNET**

Model for students how to understand the sonnet. Read aloud lines 1–8 and ask students to point out which words rhyme. Tell students that *rain* and *again* count as rhyming words, even though they are near rhymes, not exact rhymes.

Possible answer: The rhyme scheme is the same as that of the first two quatrains of Shakespeare's sonnet: abab cdcd.

SELECTION WRAP–UP

READ WITH A PURPOSE Now that students have read the poems, ask: What topics do both speakers address in addition to love? *Possible answer: Both speakers discuss time, immortality, death, and change.*

⭐ **CRITIQUE** Ask students to cite their two favorite lines or images from each poem, and to explain their choices.

INDEPENDENT READING

Students might enjoy reading *The Collected Poetry of Edna St. Vincent Millay,* which contains some of her most popular poems.

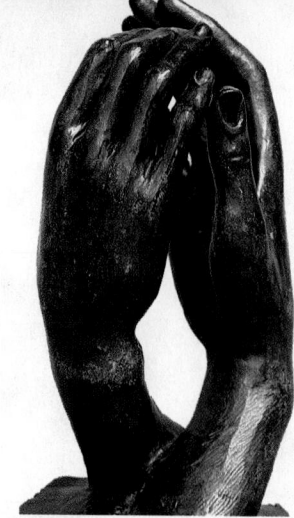

The Cathedral (1908), Auguste Rodin. Bronze, 24¹/₂″ × 10³/₄″ × 11³/₄″. Photo © Timothy McCarthy/Art Resource, New York.

Sonnet XXX
OF FATAL INTERVIEW

Edna St. Vincent Millay

Love is not all: it is not meat nor drink
Nor slumber nor a roof against the rain;
Nor yet a floating spar[1] to men that sink
And rise and sink and rise and sink again;
5 Love can not fill the thickened lung with breath,
Nor clean the blood, nor set the fractured bone;
Yet many a man is making friends with death
Even as I speak, for lack of love alone. **B**
It well may be that in a difficult hour,
10 Pinned down by pain and moaning for release,
Or nagged by want[2] past resolution's power,
I might be driven to sell your love for peace,
Or trade the memory of this night for food.
It well may be. I do not think I would.

B SONNET
How does the **rhyme scheme** of lines 1–8 compare with that of Shakespeare's sonnet?

---

1. **spar:** a pole used to support a ship's sails.
2. **want:** need.

DIFFERENTIATED INSTRUCTION

FOR STRUGGLING READERS

Develop Reading Fluency Guide students in performing an echo reading of "Sonnet XXX." Read the poem aloud, one phrase and one line at a time; have the class repeat after you, using the same speed and intonation. Then ask students to listen to the audio recording of the poem on the *Audio Anthology CD* (also recommended for English language learners).

R RESOURCE MANAGER—Copy Masters
Reading Fluency p. 84

FOR ADVANCED LEARNERS/PRE–AP

Analyze Sound Devices [paired-activity option] Assign students a specific sound device—alliteration, assonance, consonance, repetition, rhyme, or rhythm—and ask them to analyze its use in "Sonnet XXX." Instruct students to discuss the prevalence of the device and its effect on the poem's sound and meaning, providing examples to support their ideas. Have students summarize their findings in a paragraph or two and then meet with a few classmates to compare analyses.

After Reading

Comprehension

1. **Recall** What is the main comparison developed in "Sonnet 18"?

2. **Clarify** In "Sonnet 18," the speaker promises the subject of the poem that "thy eternal summer shall not fade." What is the basis for this promise?

3. **Recall** What contrast opens "Sonnet XXX"?

4. **Paraphrase** Reread the second quatrain of "Sonnet XXX." What is the speaker's claim about love in these lines?

COMMON CORE

RL 2 Determine a central idea of a text. **RL 5** Analyze an author's choices concerning how to structure a text. **W 2b** Develop the topic with quotations appropriate to the audience's knowledge of the topic.

Text Analysis

5. **Identify Metaphor** In poetry, an **extended metaphor** is a comparison between two things that is continued across a number of lines. What qualities does the extended metaphor in "Sonnet 18" help communicate?

6. **Interpret Imagery** Consider the images that Millay presents in describing what love is not, or what it cannot do. These images are examples of what kinds of human needs? What is the point of contrasting love with these needs? Use a chart like the one shown to record the images from the poem.

Love Is Not	Love Cannot
meat	fill the lung with breath

7. **Analyze Sonnet Structure** Review the chart you developed as you read. How do the ideas expressed in the sonnet relate to its quatrains and couplets? Cite evidence from the poems to explain your answer.

8. **Compare Form** Although they lived more than 300 years apart, Millay and Shakespeare both wrote poetry using the sonnet form. Determine the rhyme scheme and meter for both sonnets. Then reread the top of page 811. Is Millay's poem a Shakespearean sonnet? Explain your answer.

READING-WRITING CONNECTION

WRITING PROMPT

Extended Constructed Response: Interpret How would the speaker of each poem respond to the statement "Love lasts forever"? Use details from "Sonnet 18" and "Sonnet XXX" to **write a three- to five-paragraph response.**

REVISING TIP

Review your response. Have you correctly used quotation marks and commas to create embedded quotations when citing evidence?

What makes a good LOVE POEM?

Do the two sonnets agree with your own ideas about love?

(quatrains 1, 2): Love cannot give life, but people can die without it; **Turning Point** (quatrain 3): The speaker wonders if she would give her love away; **Solution** (couplet): She says that she would not give her love away.

8. ● **COMMON CORE FOCUS Sonnet Form** Yes, because it is written in iambic pentameter with the rhyme scheme abab cdcd efef gg.

What makes a good LOVE POEM? Accept all thoughtful and supported answers.

READING-WRITING CONNECTION

Have students summarize the main ideas in each poem. Then have them look for any statements the speakers make that relate to time, immortality, or change. Suggest that students use these details as they decide how each speaker would answer the question.

Practice and Apply

For preliminary support of post-reading questions, use these copy masters:

R RESOURCE MANAGER—Copy Masters
Sonnet p. 79
Question Support p. 83

Additional selection questions are provided for teachers on page 75.

ANSWERS

Comprehension

1. *The person addressed in the poem is compared to a summer day.*

2. *The basis for his promise is that he has captured his beloved's beauty in a poem that will last as long as there are people to read it.*

3. *Love is contrasted with food and drink.*

4. *Although love cannot cure physical ills, life may have little value without it.*

Text Analysis

COMMON CORE RL 2, RL 5, W 2b

Possible answers:

5. *The metaphor communicates the beauty and gentleness of the speaker's beloved.*

6. *Love Is Not: meat, drink, sleep, a roof, or a pole that saves one from drowning.* **Love Cannot:** *cure lung failure or blood diseases or mend broken bones. All the images are of physical needs. The contrast shows that love is an emotional need, not a physical need.*

7. ● **COMMON CORE FOCUS** *Sonnet Structure* **Sonnet 18: Situation** *(quatrains 1 and 2): The speaker's beloved is better than a summer day, and nature's beauty fades;* **Turning Point** *(quatrain 3): His beloved's beauty will be immortal;* **Solution** *(couplet): The poem grants immortality.* **Sonnet XXX: Situation**

Assess and Reteach

Assess

DIAGNOSTIC AND SELECTION TESTS
Selection Test A pp. 231–232
Selection Test B/C pp. 233–234

Interactive Selection Test on **thinkcentral.com**

Reteach

Level Up Online Tutorials on **thinkcentral.com**

Reteaching Worksheets on **thinkcentral.com**
Literature Lesson 13: Sonnet

Focus and Motivate

COMMON CORE FOCUS

RL 4 Analyze the cumulative impact of specific word choices on meaning. **RL 5** Analyze an author's choices concerning how to structure a text. **RL 10** Read and comprehend poems. **W 2f** Provide a concluding statement or section that follows from the information or explanation presented.

SUMMARIES

"Lord Randall" When Lord Randall returns home from hunting, his mother questions him and learns that her son has been poisoned by his true love.

"Ballad" The speaker describes the despair she feels after seeing her former love with a new love.

"Midwinter Blues" The speaker's man has left her and, although she loves him, she accepts his departure. She is saddened, however, that he left her without enough coal.

When does poetry SING?

Ask the question. Suggest to students that songs are like poems set to music, and that some poems are like song lyrics. Then have students complete the *QUICKWRITE*. Conclude the exploration with a class discussion in which groups share and compare the musical qualities they identified.

Selection Resources

Before Reading

Lord Randall
Anonymous Ballad

Essential Course of Study **ECOS**

Ballad / Balada
Poem by Gabriela Mistral

Midwinter Blues
Poem by Langston Hughes

 Video link at thinkcentral.com

VIDEO TRAILER THINK central KEYWORD: HML10-816

When does poetry SING?

COMMON CORE

RL 4 Analyze the cumulative impact of specific word choices on meaning. **RL 5** Analyze an author's choices concerning how to structure a text. **RL 10** Read and comprehend poems.

Have you ever found yourself singing lines from a song you'd forgotten you knew? As you'll see in this lesson, poems based on musical forms can be as catchy as song lyrics.

QUICKWRITE With a small group, write out the lyrics of a well-known song. Discuss the patterns you notice in the song, such as repetition and rhyme. Then, write a brief response to this question: What qualities make a poem "songlike"?

816

See resources on the **Teacher One Stop DVD-ROM** *and on* **thinkcentral.com**.

 RESOURCE MANAGER UNIT 7
Plan and Teach, pp. 85–92
Text Analysis and Reading
  Skill, pp. 93–96†*

DIAGNOSTIC AND SELECTION TESTS
Selection Tests, pp. 235–238

 BEST PRACTICES TOOLKIT
Read Aloud, p. A34

INTERACTIVE READER

ADAPTED INTERACTIVE READER

ELL ADAPTED INTERACTIVE READER

 Video link at thinkcentral.com

TECHNOLOGY

- 💿 **Teacher One Stop DVD-ROM**
- 💿 **Student One Stop DVD-ROM**
- 💿 **PowerNotes DVD-ROM**
- 💿 **Audio Anthology CD**
- 💿 **Audio Tutor CD**
- 💿 **ExamView Test Generator**
  on the **Teacher One Stop**

 **Video Trailer**

Go to **thinkcentral.com** to preview the **Video Trailer** introducing this selection. Other features that support the selection include

- **PowerNotes** presentation
- **ThinkAloud** models to enhance comprehension
- **WordSharp** vocabulary tutorials
- interactive writing and grammar instruction

● POETIC FORM: BALLAD

The earliest **ballads** were stories told in song, using the voice and language of everyday people. They were composed orally, and singers often added or changed details to make the songs meaningful for their audience. These early ballads, typical of the medieval period, are known as **folk ballads.**

Like a work of fiction, a ballad has characters, setting, and dialogue. Like a song, it uses repetition and has regular rhyme and meter. A **traditional ballad**—such as "Lord Randall," the written version of an older folk ballad—has these characteristics:

- consists of four-line stanzas with a simple rhyme scheme
- narrates a single tragic incident through dialogue

A ballad's rhyme scheme may be very loose or seem inconsistent. A loose rhyme scheme gave the singer more freedom to improvise lyrics. And, because pronunciations change over time, words that once rhymed may no longer sound alike.

As you read "Ballad" and "Midwinter Blues," consider how these poems expand the traditional ballad form.

● READING SKILL: UNDERSTAND DIALECT

People who inhabit a particular region or who belong to a particular social or ethnic group may speak in a **dialect,** a variation of a language. Their speech may differ in pronunciation, vocabulary, and grammar from the standard form of the language.

Dialect often provides clues about a poem's setting, as in "Lord Randall," which uses an 18th-century Scottish dialect. It can also reveal information about the speaker's identity, such as ethnicity and social class, as in "Midwinter Blues."

As you read "Lord Randall," record on a graphic organizer in your *Reader/Writer Notebook* all words and phrases written in dialect, and then rewrite them in standard English. Make a similar graphic organizer for "Midwinter Blues."

Title: "Lord Randall"	
Speaker's English	*Standard English*
What gat ye to your dinner?	*What did you eat?*

 Complete the activities in your **Reader/Writer Notebook.**

Gabriela Mistral
1899–1957

Voice of the Poor
Chilean poet Gabriela Mistral (mē-sträl') wrote about the lives of everyday people. She believed the poet had a duty to speak for his or her own people and age. "What the soul is to the body," she once remarked, "so is the artist to his people." Mistral's themes include love and loss, faith, childbearing, and motherhood. Many of her finest poems grappled with the suicide of her fiancé Romelio Ureta, who had left Mistral prior to his death. In 1945, Mistral became the first Latin American writer to receive the Nobel Prize for literature.

Langston Hughes
1902–1967

Man of the People
Langston Hughes was a central figure of the Harlem Renaissance, a cultural movement of the 1920s and 1930s celebrating African-American artistic expression. He was one of the first artists to champion the beauty of blues songs, which he called music from "black, beaten, but unbeatable throats." Blues songs, and the "low-down folks" who sang them, were a lifelong inspiration for Hughes, who drew on their rhythms, motifs, and themes in his poems, short stories, essays, and novels.

 **Authors Online**
Go to **thinkcentral.com.** KEYWORD: HML10-817

THINK central

817

POETIC FORM

COMMON CORE
RL 5
RL 10

● *Model the Skill:* **BALLAD**

To help students understand a ballad, write these lines on the board and read them aloud:

> "Oh, Mother, can you tell the tale
>   Of cousin Bobby Jean?"
> "Yes, my dear: she left her home
>   And never more was seen."

Identify the characteristics of the traditional ballad form in these lines. Point out that the lines form a four-line stanza, they have a simple rhyme scheme, and they use dialogue to narrate what seems to be a tragic story.

GUIDED PRACTICE Ask students to identify the rhyme scheme of the lines.

READING SKILL

COMMON CORE
RL 4

■ *Model the Skill:* **UNDERSTAND DIALECT**

To help students understand dialect, write these lines on the board, and then ask a volunteer to read them aloud:

> Mahty went down tuh Pawtland
> Tuh hahv a bowl a chowdah.
> Driving they-uh his cah broke down
> And he couldn't go any fahthah.

"Translate" these lines of Maine regional dialect into standard English, and then discuss how the "translation" is different from the original lines. Use this example: Marty went down to Portland / To have a bowl of chowder. / Driving there his car broke down / And he couldn't go any farther. Point out that this "translation" is easier to read, but without the dialect, the lines lose their distinctive regional flavor.

GUIDED PRACTICE Ask students to name movies or songs that include dialect.

 RESOURCE MANAGER—Copy Master Understand Dialect p. 95 (for student use while reading the selection)

DIFFERENTIATED INSTRUCTION

FOR STRUGGLING READERS

Concept Support Explain to students that a dialect consists of pronunciations, specific vocabulary, and distinctive grammatical constructions unique to a particular group or region. Ask pairs of students to examine their own dialects. Have them brainstorm pronunciations, words, and expressions that they and their friends use daily that are not found in other regions. Create a master list, and discuss with the class which items are and are not examples of dialect, and why.

FOR ADVANCED LEARNERS/PRE–AP

Analyze Dialect Ask students to find three other works of literature that include dialect. (They may use their pupil edition or other sources.) Have students consider why the authors of these works might have chosen to include dialect. Then have them discuss their findings in a group.

READ WITH A PURPOSE

Help students set a purpose for reading. Tell students to look for the way that each speaker was betrayed.

Ⓐ Model the Skill: DIALECT

Have students reread lines 1–4. Point out that the quotation marks indicate dialogue. Then have students note the words and phrases written in dialect in the stanza. Work with them to fill in the chart introduced on page 817.

Speaker's English	Standard English
ha'e ye	have you

Possible answer: The words "ha'e" (line 1), "wi'" (line 4), and "fain wald" (line 4) capture the way people spoke during the time in which "Lord Randall" was written.

Ⓑ BALLAD

Possible answer: The first four stanzas begin with the mother questioning her son, while the final stanza begins with her making an exclamation. The last line of the first four stanzas begins with Lord Randall saying he is "weary wi' hunting." The last line of the final stanza, however, begins with him saying, "I'm sick at the heart."

Analyze Visuals ▶

Which character in "Lord Randall" might this image represent? Cite **details** that support your answer.

Lord Randall
Anonymous

"Oh where ha'e ye[1] been, Lord Randall my son?
O where ha'e ye been, my handsome young man?"
"I ha'e been to the wild wood: mother, make my bed soon,
For I'm weary wi'[2] hunting, and fain[3] wald[4] lie down." Ⓐ

5 "Where gat ye[5] your dinner, Lord Randall my son?
Where gat ye your dinner, my handsome young man?"
"I dined wi' my true love: mother, make my bed soon,
For I'm weary wi' hunting, and fain wald lie down."

"What gat ye to your dinner, Lord Randall my son?
10 What gat ye to your dinner, my handsome young man?"
"I gat eels boiled in broo:[6] mother, make my bed soon,
For I'm weary wi' hunting and fain wald lie down."

"What became of your bloodhounds, Lord Randall my son?
What became of your bloodhounds, my handsome young man?"
15 "O they swelled and they died: mother, make my bed soon,
For I'm weary wi' hunting and fain wald lie down."

"O I fear ye are poisoned, Lord Randall my son!
O I fear ye are poisoned, my handsome young man!"
"Oh yes, I am poisoned: mother, make my bed soon,
20 For I'm sick at the heart, and I fain wald lie down." Ⓑ

---

1. **ha'e ye** (hā′ yē′): have you.
2. **wi'** (wĭ): with.
3. **fain** (fān): gladly, eagerly.
4. **wald** (wăld): would.
5. **gat ye** (găt yē): did you get.
6. **broo** (brōō): brew, broth.

Ⓐ **DIALECT**
Reread the first stanza. What words capture the qualities of spoken language?

Ⓑ **BALLAD**
How does the ballad's pattern of repetition change in this stanza?

The Vitriol Thrower (1894), Eugene Grasset. Color lithograph. Cecil Higgins Art Gallery, Bedford, Bedfordshire, United Kingdom. Photo © Bridgeman Art Library.

DIFFERENTIATED INSTRUCTION

FOR ENGLISH LANGUAGE LEARNERS

Conversational English Patterns Work with students to translate "Lord Randall" into modern, conversational English. Read aloud the first line, and then ask students how they would say the line. Continue working through the poem, having students rephrase the lines as you read each thought. Explain to students the importance of keeping the meaning of the lines unchanged.

FOR STRUGGLING READERS

Options for Reading: Audio Recording Have students listen to the selection on the *Audio Anthology CD* (also recommended for English language learners) as they read along in their texts. Then ask pairs of students to read the poem aloud, with one student reading Lord Randall's lines and the other student reading the mother's lines. Circulate through the room, and pause to reinforce pronunciation of dialect as necessary.

📖 BEST PRACTICES TOOLKIT—Transparency
Read Aloud p. A34

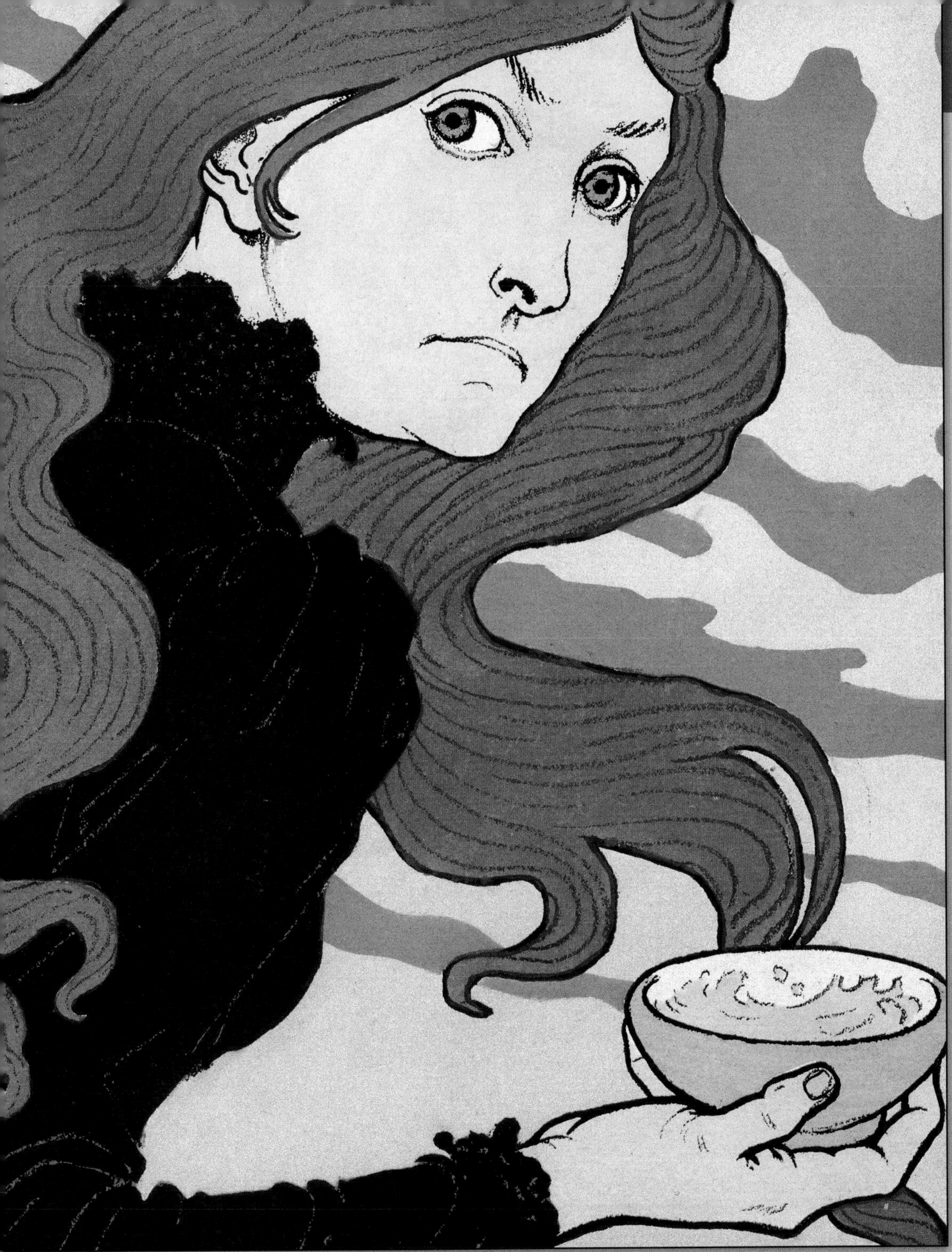

Reading Support

This selection on **thinkcentral.com** includes embedded **ThinkAloud** models—students "thinking aloud" about the story to model the kinds of questions a good reader would ask about a selection.

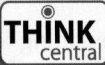

BACKGROUND

Ballad History "Lord Randall" is one of the oldest and best-known ballads in the English language. It is found in countless variations throughout the British Isles and North America, but the dialogue structure and basic story are always the same: a mother questions her son and discovers that he has been poisoned by his true love. Although most scholars believe that "Lord Randall" has its roots in an Italian ballad of the 1600s, one scholar has suggested that Lord Randall was Randolph, the sixth Earl of Chester, who was poisoned by his wife in 1232.

Analyze Visuals

Possible answer: *The character represented might be Lord Randall's "true love," the one who poisoned him. The woman is holding a bowl with liquid in it, and Lord Randall's true love fed him eels boiled in broth.*

About the Art Swiss-born artist Eugene Grasset (1845–1917) was a leader of the Art Nouveau movement, a style of art and architecture that flourished during the late 19th century. The curved lines and flowing patterns of *The Vitriol Thrower* are characteristic of the Art Nouveau style.

TIERED DISCUSSION PROMPTS

Direct students to lines 13–20. Then use these prompts to help students understand why the mother questions her son:

Recall When the mother asks Lord Randall what happened to his hunting dogs, what does he answer? ***Possible answer:*** *He says the dogs "swelled" and "died" (line 15).*

Interpret Why does Lord Randall's mother believe he has been poisoned? ***Possible answer:*** *She assumes that the dogs had eaten the eels and infers that that they were poisoned. As Lord Randall has also eaten the eels, he must be poisoned as well.*

FOR ADVANCED LEARNERS/PRE–AP

Analyze Character Ask students to look closely at Lord Randall's responses to his mother and use those responses to write an analysis of his character. Ask them to consider how Lord Randall feels about his mother, his true love, and his situation, citing details from the poem to support their interpretations. Have students share and discuss their work in small groups.

FOR RELUCTANT READERS

Connect Tell students that modern American folk-rock music has drawn inspiration from traditional ballads. For example, Bob Dylan's song "A Hard Rain's A-Gonna Fall" is loosely based on "Lord Randall." Have students work in groups to identify examples of other contemporary songs of any genre that feature the themes in "Lord Randall." Have groups share the titles and, if appropriate, the lyrics of the songs they have identified with the class.

Prereading for this poem is found on page 816.

REVIST THE BIG QUESTION

When does poetry SING?

Discuss In addition to repetition, what sound devices in lines 19–24 give them a musical quality? What mood do these sound devices create? *Possible answer: The sound devices that give these lines a musical quality are alliteration, assonance, and consonance. Repitition: "with another"; "He goes loving another/over the earth in bloom"; alliteration: "will/with" and "Sweet/skies/silent"; assonance: "skies/shine/silent"; consonance: "skies/wills." These sound devices create a melancholy mood that reflects the speaker's sadness because the man she loves is now in love with someone else.*

POETIC FORM   **COMMON CORE**

RL 5
RL 10

C *Model the Skill:* **BALLAD**

Model for students how to identify patterns of repetition in a ballad. Read aloud stanza 1, emphasizing the repeated words. Then have students read stanza 2 with emphasis on repetition.

Possible answer: In stanza 1, line 6 repeats part of line 2 ("saw him pass by"). In stanza 2, lines 11–12 repeat lines 7–8 ("He goes loving another/over the earth in bloom"). In lines 7 and 11, "another" is repeated from line 1.

TEXT ANALYSIS   **COMMON CORE**

RL 4

D **SYMBOLS**

Have students practice identifying symbols. Read aloud lines 7–12. Ask students to point out words in the stanza that give them clues to the meaning of the symbol "earth in bloom." Point out the words *hawthorn* and *flowering*, and ask students what those words bring to mind.

Possible answer: "My heart's blood" symbolizes the speaker's misery and heartache.

Ballad

Gabriela Mistral

He passed by with another;
I saw him pass by.
The wind ever sweet
and the path full of peace.
5 And these eyes of mine, wretched,
saw him pass by!

He goes loving another
over the earth in bloom.
The hawthorn[1] is flowering
10 and a song wafts by.
He goes loving another
over the earth in bloom! **C**

He kissed the other
by the shores of the sea.
15 The orange-blossom moon
skimmed over the waves.
And my heart's blood did not taint[2] **D**
the expanse of the sea!

He will go with another
20 through eternity.
Sweet skies will shine.
(God wills to keep silent.)
And he will go with another
through eternity!

Translated by Doris Dana

---

1. **hawthorn:** a spring-flowering shrub.
2. **taint** (tānt): contaminate.

C **BALLAD**
Reread stanzas 1 and 2. What examples of repetition can you identify?

COMMON CORE RL 4

D **SYMBOLS**
A **symbol** is a person, place, object, or activity that represents something beyond itself. Often that "something" is an abstract idea, such as hope. For example, chess pieces in a story may symbolize various characters, or a young person's car trip might represent the journey to adulthood. What do you think "my heart's blood" (line 17) symbolizes?

DIFFERENTIATED INSTRUCTION

FOR STRUGGLING READERS

Options for Reading: Echo Reading Read the poem aloud to students two lines at a time, and have students repeat the lines after you, using your intonation, pacing, and rhythm.

Comprehension Support Point out to students that most of the poem's ideas are contained in two-line units. Draw their attention to the punctuation to highlight

this point, emphasizing that periods and exclamation points represent the end of an idea, while commas and no punctuation indicate that an idea continues to the next line. Encourage students to study the poem two lines at a time and to provide a summary of each stanza. Finally, have pairs of students discuss their summaries and identify any parts of the poem that they still have difficulty understanding.

Balada

Gabriela Mistral

El pasó con otra;
yo le vi pasar.
Siempre dulce el viento
y el camino en paz.
5 ¡Y estos ojos míseros
le vieron pasar!

El va amando a otra
por la tierra en flor.
Ha abierto el espino;
10 pasa una canción.
¡Y él va amando a otra
por la tierra en flor!

El besó a la otra
a orillas del mar;
15 resbaló en las olas
la luna de azahar.
¡Y no untó mi sangre
la extensión del mar!

El irá con otra
20 por la eternidad
Habrá cielos dulces.
(Dios quiere callar.)
¡Y él irá con otra
por la eternidad!

Melancholy, Edvard Munch. National Gallery, Oslo, Norway. © 2008 The Munch Museum/The Munch-Ellingsen Group/ Artists Rights Society (ARS), New York. Photo © Scala/Art Resource, New York.

Analyze Visuals

Activity Ask students to describe how the painting reflects the details and emotions of the poem. *Possible answer: Both the painting and the poem evoke a lonely, melancholy mood. The woman in the painting is alone, holding her head in her hand in a pose that reflects the painting's title, Melancholy. Similarly, the speaker in the poem feels alone and melancholy because the man she loves is now in love with someone else. The bright red dress of the woman in the painting and the swirling brushstrokes that surround her match the passionate, turbulent emotions of the poem's speaker. The red dress in the painting also suggests the speaker's reference to her "heart's blood" (line 17), while the beach setting of the painting reflects the "shores of the sea," "waves," and "expanse of the sea" in the poem's third stanza.*

About the Art Norwegian painter and printmaker Edvard Munch (1863–1944) was no stranger to melancholy—his parents and a sister had died by the time he was in his mid-20s. Most famous for his painting *The Scream*, Munch was a major influence on the German Expressionists, a group of early 20th-century artists who used heightened color and distorted forms to express emotions. Like *Melancholy*, Munch's paintings are often symbolic depictions of intense psychological states, such as anguish, anxiety, and isolation.

FOR ADVANCED LEARNERS/PRE–AP

Analyze Imagery Have students use a three-column chart like the one shown to analyze the nature imagery in the poem by categorizing the central nature image in each stanza.

Stanza	Central Nature Image	Element of Nature
1	"The wind ever sweet"	wind
2	"the earth in bloom"	flowers

Have students discuss their charts in small groups and then continue to analyze the poem's nature imagery by answering these questions:

- How would you describe the pattern of nature imagery in the poem?

- How does each nature image connect to what the speaker is describing in that stanza about her former love?

- Taken as a whole, how do the nature images relate to the meaning of the poem?

Prereading for this poem is found on page 816.

Analyze Visuals

Activity Ask students to compare the emotional state of the woman in the painting with that of the speaker of the poem. *Possible answer: The woman looks forlorn and defeated, just as the poem's speaker sounds.*

About the Art Contemporary Denver artist Jen Thario (b. 1968) works in many styles and media. Like *Graffiti Divas*, her paintings frequently depict musicians.

POETIC FORM   COMMON CORE

E BALLAD   RL 5   RL 10

Possible answer: As in "Lord Randall," the poem's first statement is repeated. Both opening stanzas also end with the word "down."

READING SKILL   COMMON CORE

F DIALECT   RL 4

Possible answer: The speaker does not use standard English and may be poor and uneducated. The dialect spoken is similar to that used in blues songs with African-American roots.

SELECTION WRAP–UP

READ WITH A PURPOSE Ask students: Which speaker suffered the worst betrayal? Why? *Possible answer: Students may feel that Lord Randall suffered the worst betrayal because he died.*

⭐ **CRITIQUE** Ask students which of the three poems they can best imagine being set to music, and why.

INDEPENDENT READING

Students interested in lyrical poetry might enjoy *Lyrical Ballads and Other Poems* by William Wordsworth and Samuel T. Coleridge.

Midwinter Blues

Graffiti Divas (2003), Jen Thario. Spray paint on paper, 22″ × 22″. © Jen Thario.

Langston Hughes

In the middle of the winter,
Snow all over the ground.
In the middle of the winter,
Snow all over the ground—
5 'Twas the night befo' Christmas
My good man turned me down. **E**

Don't know's I'd mind his goin'
But he left me when the coal was low.
Don't know's I'd mind his goin'
10 But he left when the coal was low.
Now, if a man loves a woman
That ain't no time to go. **F**

He told me that he loved me
But he must a been tellin' a lie.
15 He told me that he loved me.
He must a been tellin' a lie.
But he's the only man I'll
Love till the day I die.

I'm gonna buy me a rose bud
20 An' plant it at my back door,
Buy me a rose bud,
Plant it at my back door,
So when I'm dead they won't need
No flowers from the store.

E BALLAD
Compare this opening stanza with that of "Lord Randall." What qualities do the poems share?

F DIALECT
Based on the dialect used in this poem, what do you learn about the speaker's identity?

DIFFERENTIATED INSTRUCTION

FOR STRUGGLING READERS

Develop Reading Fluency To focus students' attention on the musical quality of "Midwinter Blues," work with them to create a lively choral reading of the poem. Guide them in assigning lines and choosing proper pitch, pacing, and intonation. Allow the group ample time to practice reading, and invite them to perform their interpretations for the rest of the class.

R RESOURCE MANAGER—Copy Master
Reading Fluency p. 98

FOR ADVANCED LEARNERS/PRE–AP

Evaluate Speaker Ask students to work in small groups to discuss these questions about the speaker of "Midwinter Blues":

• Do any of the speaker's statements seem to contradict each other? Explain.

• How does the speaker feel about her man now? about life?

• Is Hughes, being a male poet, successful at portraying a female point of view through this speaker? Why or why not?

Comprehension

1. **Recall** Where has Lord Randall been, and what has happened to him?

2. **Clarify** Why is the speaker of "Ballad" so distressed?

3. **Summarize** In "Midwinter Blues," what is the speaker's situation?

COMMON CORE

RL 4 Analyze the cumulative impact of specific word choices on meaning. **RL 5** Analyze an author's choices concerning how to structure a text. **W 2f** Provide a concluding statement or section that follows from the information or explanation presented.

Text Analysis

4. **Identify Ballad** Reread "Lord Randall" and "Ballad." Using a chart like the one shown, compare how the elements of the traditional ballad are used in both poems. How does Mistral's poem depart from a traditional ballad?

Ballad Characteristics	Examples from "Lord Randall"	Examples from "Ballad"
Single tragic incident		
Repetition		
Dialogue		
Four-line stanzas		
Regular rhyme and meter		

5. **Analyze Dialect** Review your dialect chart. How does dialect help establish the voices of the speakers in "Lord Randall" and "Midwinter Blues"?

6. **Contrast Speakers** Contrast the attitudes of the speakers in "Ballad" and "Midwinter Blues." How does the language used in each poem communicate the speaker's emotional state?

READING-WRITING CONNECTION

WRITING PROMPT	REVISING TIP
Extended Constructed Response: Opinion Compare and contrast the experiences of each speaker. What do their experiences suggest about the nature of romantic love? Support your argument with details from the poems in a **three-to five-paragraph response.**	Review your response. Does it point out both similarities and differences ▶ between the speakers' experiences? Is the conclusion you formulated supported by details? If not, revise.

When does poetry SING?

Why are poems and songs so often about love and loss?

Practice and Apply

For preliminary support of post-reading questions, use these copy masters:

R RESOURCE MANAGER—Copy Masters
Ballad p. 93
Question Support p. 97

Additional selection questions are provided for teachers on page 89.

ANSWERS

Comprehension

1. *He has been hunting in the woods and has been poisoned by his true love.*

2. *The man she loves has a new love.*

3. *The speaker's man has left her without love or coal to heat her home for the winter.*

Text Analysis

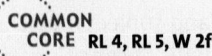
COMMON CORE RL 4, RL 5, W 2f

Possible answers:

4. ● **COMMON CORE FOCUS** *Ballad "Lord Randall":* Incident: Lord Randall's true love poisoned him; Repetition: question-and-answer format in each stanza and repeated phrases such as "my handsome young man" and "mother, make my bed soon"; Dialogue: yes; Four-line stanzas: yes; Rhyme and meter: loose rhyme, regular meter. "Ballad": Incident: speaker's love now loves another; Repetition: "another" and "other," lines 2/6, 7–8/11–12, and 20/24. Dialogue: no; Four-line stanzas: no; Rhyme and meter: not in English translation, loose in original. Mistral's ballad departs from a traditional ballad because it does not have four-line stanzas, does not use dialogue, and does not use regular meter and rhyme.*

Assess and Reteach

Assess

R DIAGNOSTIC AND SELECTION TESTS
Selection Test A pp. 235–236
Selection Test B/C pp. 237–238

Interactive Selection Test on **thinkcentral.com**

Reteach

Level Up Online Tutorials on **thinkcentral.com**

Reteaching Worksheets on **thinkcentral.com**
Literature Lesson 12: Ballad
Literature Lesson 41: Dialogue and Dialect

---

5. ● **COMMON CORE FOCUS** *Dialect* In "Lord Randall," dialect such as "ha'e ye" and "fain wald" show that the speakers are Scottish, from a previous era. In "Midwinter Blues," dialect such as "Don't know's I'd mind his goin'" show that the speaker might be uneducated or poor.

6. *"Ballad":* Emotionally charged language such as "wretched," "heart's blood," and "taint" reveal the speaker's despair. *"Midwinter Blues":* Emotionally understated language such as "Don't know's I'd mind his goin'" (line 7) suggest that the speaker is reconciled to her loss.

READING-WRITING CONNECTION

Suggest that students begin by listing each speaker's experiences. Then have them highlight related experiences in one color and unrelated experiences in another color.

When does poetry SING?

Students might consider how they express their feelings when they fall in love or lose someone they love.

Focus and Motivate

RI 2 Determine a central idea of a text, analyze its development over the course of a text, and how it is shaped by specific details. **RI 4** Determine the meaning of words and phrases as they are used in a text. **W 2** Write explanatory texts to examine and convey complex ideas, concepts, and information clearly and accurately through the effective analysis of content.

SUMMARY

In this essay, blues poet Kevin Young offers his description and interpretation of blues music and poetry. He begins by discussing the blues' roots in African-American culture; then offers some interpretations of the purpose, nature, and subject matter of the blues; and closes with observations about how the blues make us feel.

What's the Connection?

Encourage students to use the SQ3R strategy to study the selection. Guide students in surveying the essay, pointing out the margin notes, and discussing the focus of the Comprehension and Critical Analysis questions on page 827. Invite students to read the first and last paragraphs of the essay before they write their questions for consideration.

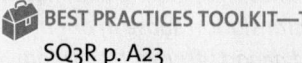 **BEST PRACTICES TOOLKIT—Transparency**
SQ3R p. A23

Teach

Standards Focus: Take Notes

Suggest that students pause after reading each paragraph and ask themselves: "What is this paragraph about?" The answer to that question is the main idea of each paragraph. Point out that the main idea of a paragraph is sometimes presented as a topic sentence, which is often the paragraph's first or last sentence. Once students know the main idea, they can review the paragraph to identify the details that support it. Have students continue this technique throughout the essay.

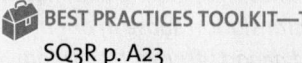 **RESOURCE MANAGER—Copy Master**
Take Notes p. 107

Reading for Information

from **Blues Poems**
Essay by Kevin Young

Use with "Lord Randall," "Ballad," and "Midwinter Blues," pages 818–822.

COMMON CORE

RI 2 Determine a central idea of a text, analyze its development over the course of a text, and how it is shaped by specific details. **RI 4** Determine the meaning of words and phrases as they are used in a text.

What's the Connection?

The speakers of the poems you just read all share the experience of lost love, a theme that runs through blues music. But sorrow isn't the only way to face hard times. In the following selection, you'll learn how people transform sorrow into solace by singing the blues.

Standards Focus: Take Notes

Note taking is a strategy for organizing information by showing how ideas relate to one another and support a passage's controlling idea and purpose. To take notes effectively, you need to identify which ideas are important (**main ideas**) and which facts or examples support those ideas (**supporting details**). Using a chart will help you see how main ideas connect with supporting details. To complete such a chart, follow these steps:

- Identify the topic of the selection—in this case, the blues. Write it at the top of the chart.
- On a first reading, examine the supporting details used to elaborate the topic, and organize them into categories. In this essay, you can organize the details the author provides into four main categories: the origin of the blues, the feeling of the blues, the form of blues music and poetry, and the subjects of the blues.

As you read the selection a second time, fill in the chart by relating the supporting details to the appropriate categories. Write down only the more important details, which most strongly support the selection's main ideas. This will prepare you to identify the main ideas the author presents about the blues.

The Blues	
Origin • Originated in African-American culture	Feeling
Form	Subjects

Selection Resources

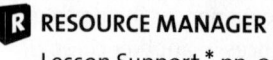

See resources on the **Teacher One Stop DVD-ROM** *and on* **thinkcentral.com**.

R RESOURCE MANAGER UNIT 7
Lesson Support,* pp. 99–112

DIAGNOSTIC AND SELECTION TESTS
Selection Tests, pp. 239–242

BEST PRACTICES TOOLKIT
Jigsaw Reading, p. A1
SQ3R, p. A23

TECHNOLOGY
- Teacher One Stop DVD-ROM
- Student One Stop DVD-ROM
- Audio Anthology CD
- ExamView Test Generator on the Teacher One Stop

* Resources for Differentiation

KEVIN YOUNG

There are feelings and states of mind that are hard to describe—some might say that don't properly exist—until we have a word for them. *Catharsis, angst, schadenfreude, duende, ennui:* all feelings we now know ▲ in English, but that still retain the tenor of their country and culture of origin. One could easily add *the blues* to this list. Indeed, you might say that the blues contain all these other words in one.

The blues, after all, describe a state of being, a feeling, a form and sound not yet named until their 12 bars and repeated refrains came into being—and now that black folks have invented and named the blues,

10 people all over the world speak them. Being part of our common language in no way denies the blues' origins in African American culture and mouths and hands. Too many people, however, mistake the feeling of the blues with the form of the blues themselves.

For in spite of navigating the depths of despair, the blues ultimately are about triumphing over that despair—or at least surviving it long enough to sing about it. With the blues, the form fights the feeling. Survival and loss, **B** sin and regret, boasts and heartbreak, leaving and loving, a pigfoot and a bottle of beer—the blues are a series of reversals, of finding love and losing it, of wanting to see yourself dead in the depths of despair, and then soon as

20 the train comes down the track, yanking your fool head back. . . . As one saying goes, the blues ain't nothin' but a good man (or woman) feelin' bad.

COMMON CORE RI 4

▲ FOREIGN WORDS IN ENGLISH
The word *schadenfreude* is a German word created from the words for "harm" and "joy" and meaning "pleasure taken from observing another person's misery." Although this word has been used in English for over a hundred years, it is still treated as a foreign word. Have you ever experienced *schadenfreude*? Why might a person feel pleasure at someone else's misfortune?

B TAKE NOTES
Paraphrase the first sentence of this paragraph. What point is the author making?

Practice and Apply

BACKGROUND

"Blues Poems" This essay appears as the foreword of an anthology titled *Blues Poems.* A "blues poet" himself, Kevin Young selected and edited this anthology, which includes lyrics by such famous blues legends as Robert Johnson, Bessie Smith, and Muddy Waters, as well as poems by such writers as Langston Hughes, Countee Cullen, and Gwendolyn Brooks. Young's selections reveal the far-reaching influence of the blues form through the inclusion of works by writers of various backgrounds and time periods, such as W. H. Auden, Allen Ginsberg, Joseph Brodsky, and Sherman Alexie.

VOCABULARY   COMMON CORE RI 4

▲ FOREIGN WORDS IN ENGLISH

Help students learn to pronounce *schaden-freude.* Guide students in looking up the pronunciation in a dictionary. Then say the word slowly, and have students repeat it until they can pronounce the word correctly.

Possible answer: Students should note times they felt pleasure at another's misfortune. Students may have benefited from another person's misfortune or disliked the other person.

INFORMATIONAL ANALYSIS   COMMON CORE RI 2

B TAKE NOTES

Possible answer: Although the blues describe pain, they are more about overcoming and surviving that pain. The author is making the point that singing or playing the blues helps a person get over sad feelings.

DIFFERENTIATED INSTRUCTION

FOR ENGLISH LANGUAGE LEARNERS
Options for Reading: Jigsaw Reading Divide students into pairs and distribute the essay's six paragraphs among them. Have each pair work together to identify the main idea and supporting details in each assigned paragraph. Then have all the pairs take turns reading their paragraphs aloud and sharing main ideas and details.

 **BEST PRACTICES TOOLKIT**
Jigsaw Reading p. A1

FOR STRUGGLING READERS
Vocabulary Support Share with students these definitions of unfamiliar words:

- *catharsis* (line 3), "emotional release or cleansing"
- *angst* (line 3), "anxiety; apprehension"
- *duende* (line 3), "charisma; charm"
- *ennui* (line 3), "boredom"
- *tenor* (line 4), "general sense or feeling"

COMMON CORE

RI 2

C *Model the Skill:* TAKE NOTES

Model for students how to take notes. Read lines 14–16 aloud. Ask students which contradiction the author talks about in these lines. Point out that *despair* and *triumph* are contradictory emotions indicated. Tell students to record details in their Take Notes charts.

Possible answer: *Contradictory emotions are important to the form of the blues because, as Young says, "the form fights the feeling" (line 16). To overcome the feeling of the blues, one must contradict it: sorrow is contradicted through the joyful expression of music. These contradictions, or "reversals" as Young calls them, reflect the basic function and power of the blues form.*

INFORMATIONAL ANALYSIS

COMMON CORE

RI 2

D TAKE NOTES

Possible answer: *The blues express an ironic or a comic attitude toward heartbreak and suffering. The blues singer never wholly gives in to pain or despair.*

C TAKE NOTES
How are contradictory emotions important to the form of the blues?

D TAKE NOTES
Review the author's list of blues subjects. What attitude do blues songs express about these subjects?

But another saying knows the opposite is true: the blues ain't nothin' but a bad woman (or man) feelin' good. **C**

. . . As Langston Hughes often said, the blues are "laughing to keep from crying"; the fact that this line also appears in the song "Trouble in Mind" tells us that even when there's trouble, we still can laugh about it. We must, the blues insist. Ralph Ellison puts it this way:

> The blues is an impulse to keep the painful details and episodes of a brutal experience alive in one's aching consciousness, to finger its
> 30 jagged grain, and then transcend it, not by the consolation of philosophy but by squeezing from it a near-tragic, near-comic lyricism. As a form, the blues is an autobiographical chronicle of personal catastrophe expressed lyrically.

Indeed, for me the blues provide a fresh way to express the lyric poem's mix of emotion and intensity, all the while evoking not so much strict autobiography as a personal metaphor for life's daily struggles. "You've been a good old wagon, but you done broke down."

The blues can be about work, or the lack of it; about losing hope or your home, your lover or your mind or your faith; or all of these at once! The
40 blues are unafraid of talking about violence, whether of the physical kind (as reflected in Hughes' "Beale Street Love" and Ma Rainey's "See See Rider Blues") or the often more troubling psychological sort. Still, the heartbreak the blues rails against and trains us to overcome is never far from ironic and even comic, and for every "Nobody Knows You When You're Down and Out," Bessie Smith declares "Tain't Nobody's Business if I Do." That Nobody sure is fickle. **D**

The blues ain't polite—they don't say please, though sometimes they say "Good Morning." They are, in the end, often more loyal than the sweet mistreater whom the singer loves but wants "to lay low". . . after feeling
50 low for days. Or nights—the blues after all, began as Saturday night entertainment, making us laugh and move and maybe even forget our troubles, not by pretending everything's all right, but by admitting it's a hard road full of forks and crossroad devils. By finding out that the powerful voice onstage, or on the jukebox, or coming from the radio, has been there too. The blues are loyal to a fault.

DIFFERENTIATED INSTRUCTION

FOR STRUGGLING READERS
Vocabulary Support Discuss with students these references and colloquial phrases:

- *pigfoot* (line 17), "pig's foot." It is used in recipes for soul food, the classic cuisine of African Americans in the South. Young is referring to a famous blues song, "Gimme a Pigfoot (And a Bottle of Beer)," by Bessie Smith.

- *fool head* (line 20), "foolish self"

- *done broke down* (line 37), "has broken, is no longer functioning"

- *Nobody* (line 46), Young is referring to the "nobody" described in the two titles of the songs that precede this reference.

- *lay low* (line 49), "hurt or kill"

Comprehension

1. **Recall** According to Young, what do the blues describe?

2. **Recall** What are some typical subjects found in blues music?

3. **Clarify** According to Ralph Ellison, how do the blues help us transcend personal tragedy?

Text Analysis

4. **Analyze Notes** Review the details you recorded in your chart. Based on these details, what are the main characteristics of blues music?

5. **Identify Tone** What tone, or attitude, toward blues music does Young convey in his essay? Cite specific words and phrases that help convey this tone.

Read for Information: Evaluate Poems

WRITING PROMPT

Of the three poems on pages 816–820, which best matches Young's description of the blues? Use excerpts from the poems and descriptive details from the essay to support your response.

To answer this prompt, follow these steps:

1. Review your chart to make sure you understand Young's main ideas about the blues. Restate his main ideas in your own words.

2. Analyze the poems to see how many characteristics of blues songs you can find in each. Decide which poem best matches Young's description of the blues.

3. State your conclusion(s) in a thesis. Then, support those conclusions with relevent evidence and well-chosen details from the poems.

Characteristics of the Blues	Characteristics of Poem 1	Characteristics of Poem 2	Characteristics of Poem 3
	✓		
		✓	✓
			✓

Conclusion:

COMMON CORE

RI 2 Determine a central idea of a text, analyze its development over the course of a text, and how it is shaped by specific details. **RI 4** Determine the meaning of words and phrases as they are used in a text. **W 2** Write explanatory texts to examine and convey complex ideas, concepts, and information clearly and accurately through the effective analysis of content.

Practice and Apply

For preliminary support of post-reading questions, use these copy masters:

R RESOURCE MANAGER—Copy Masters
Evaluate Poems p. 108
Reading Check p. 111
Question Support p. 112

Additional selection questions are provided for teachers on page 102.

ANSWERS

Comprehension

1. *The blues describe a state of being, a feeling, a form, and a sound.*

2. *Subjects found in the blues are contrasts: survival and loss, sin and regret, boasts and heartbreak, and loving and leaving.*

3. *According to Ellison, the blues help us transcend personal tragedy by allowing us to squeeze lyricism from painful experiences.*

Text Analysis COMMON CORE RI 2, RI 4

Possible answers:

4. *The blues originated in African-American culture; are about triumphing over despair; express emotion and intensity like a lyric poem; can be about many subjects, such as love, loss, work, hope, and violence; are ironic and comic; are not polite.*

5. *Words like "loyal" and "powerful" convey Young's admiring, appreciative tone.*

Read for Information: COMMON CORE W 2
Evaluate Poems

Writing Prompt Most students will choose Hughes's poem because its dialect places it in African-American culture. Encourage students to think beyond cultural associations.

Assess and Reteach

Assess

DIAGNOSTIC AND SELECTION TESTS
Selection Tests A, B/C pp. 239–242

Interactive Selection Test on **thinkcentral.com**

Reteach

Level Up Online Tutorials on **thinkcentral.com**

Reteaching Worksheets on **thinkcentral.com**
Reading Lesson 4: Recognizing Main Ideas and Details

FOR STRUGGLING WRITERS
Read for Information

- For the first step, suggest that students review their answers to question 4 under Critical Analysis.

- Invite students to work in pairs or small groups to discuss the characteristics of the blues that they find in the poems.

- Tell students to support their ideas by relating three quotations from the essay with three examples from the chosen poem.

FOR ADVANCED LEARNERS/PRE–AP

Read for Information Offer students this alternative writing prompt:

According to Young, people all over the world "speak" the blues (lines 9–10). Identify the characteristics of the blues, as defined by Young, in three other poems in your textbook. Include details from the poems and from Young's essay to support your ideas.

Focus and Motivate

COMMON CORE FOCUS

W 2a–f Write informative/explanatory texts to examine complex ideas clearly and accurately through the effective selection, organization, and analysis of content; use domain-specific vocabulary to manage the complexity of a topic. **W 4** Produce clear and coherent writing. **W 5** Develop and strengthen writing as needed by planning, revising, editing, rewriting, or trying a new approach. **W 9a (RL 1)** Draw evidence from literary texts to support analysis. **W 10** Write routinely over shorter time frames for a range of tasks, purposes, and audiences. **L 1** Demonstrate command of the conventions of standard English grammar and usage. **L 2** Demonstrate command of the conventions of standard English capitalization, punctuation, and spelling.

WRITE WITH A PURPOSE

Remind students that their audience is most likely to be their classmates and teacher. Read aloud the two purposes listed under "The Essentials." Point out that in a poem both meaning and language are important.

COMMON CORE TRAITS

Review the *COMMON CORE TRAITS* with students, concentrating on development of ideas and organization of ideas. Compare the list of traits with the rubric on page 836.

ADDITIONAL TASK

Blog About a Poem Choose a poem you enjoy from Unit 7. Write a blog entry explaining what makes the poet's message and use of stylistic elements effective.

Possible subjects: Sara Teasdale's "There Will Come Soft Rains," Lucille Clifton's "Blessing the Boats"

Writing Online   THINK central

The following tools are available online at **thinkcentral.com** and on **Write*Smart* CD-ROM**:
- Interactive Graphic Organizers
- Interactive Student Models
- Interactive Revision Lessons

Writing Workshop
INFORMATIVE TEXT

Analysis of a Poem

When you analyze a poem, you examine how its style reveals its deeper meaning. In this workshop, you will write an analysis of a poem in which you examine how a poet uses stylistic elements to create certain effects to convey meaning.

Essential Course of Study ECOS

Complete the workshop activities in your **Reader/Writer Notebook**.

WRITE WITH A PURPOSE

WRITING TASK

Choose a poem, and write an **analysis**. In your essay, analyze the poet's use of stylistic elements and their effects, using quotations and other evidence from the poem to support your ideas and help your audience gain a new understanding of the poem's meaning.

Idea Starters
- effects of imagery in Elizabeth Bishop's poem "The Fish"
- impact of sound effects in "Ex-Basketball Player" by John Updike
- effect of structure in William Shakespeare's "Sonnet 18"

THE ESSENTIALS

Here are some common purposes, audiences, and formats for a literary analysis.

PURPOSES	AUDIENCES	FORMATS
• to make sense of the meaning of a poem • to understand how a writer uses language to affect readers	• classmates and teacher • fans of a poet • readers of a literary magazine • Web users	• essay for class • journal • blog • oral presentation • podcast script • message-board posting

COMMON CORE TRAITS

1. DEVELOPMENT OF IDEAS
- presents an **engaging introduction**
- develops a **controlling idea** that offers an **analysis** of the poet's style
- supports key points of analysis with **relevant details** and **quotations from the poem**
- concludes with a **summary of key points** and **insights**

2. ORGANIZATION OF IDEAS
- **organizes** ideas in a logical way
- uses varied **transitions** to create **cohesion** and **connect ideas**

3. LANGUAGE FACILITY AND CONVENTIONS
- establishes and maintains a **formal style** and **objective tone**
- includes **precise language** and **domain-specific vocabulary**
- incorporates **complex sentences**
- employs correct **grammar**, **usage**, and **spelling**

Writing Online   THINK central

Go to **thinkcentral.com**.
KEYWORD: HML10N-828

Writing Workshop Resources

R **RESOURCE MANAGER UNIT 7**
Plan and Teach, pp. 113–116
Prewriting–Editing, pp. 117–121
Writing Rubric, p. 122
Technology, p. 123
Writing Support, p. 124*

BEST PRACTICES TOOLKIT
Evaluating a Poem, p. D62
Analysis Frame: Poetic Language/Style, pp. D38, D39

TECHNOLOGY
- **Teacher One Stop DVD-ROM**
- **Student One Stop DVD-ROM**
- **Write*Smart* CD-ROM**
- **GrammarNotes DVD-ROM**

Writing Center on thinkcentral.com

*See resources on the **Teacher One Stop DVD-ROM** and on **thinkcentral.com**.*

* Resources for Differentiation

Planning/Prewriting

 COMMON CORE **W 2a–f** Write informative/explanatory texts to examine complex ideas clearly and accurately through the effective selection, organization, and analysis of content. **W 5** Develop and strengthen writing by planning.

Getting Started

CHOOSE A POEM

For your essay, you need to choose a poem to analyze. Reread poems you have enjoyed. Consider what each means to you. Read each aloud to catch subtleties and deeper meanings through the sound of the language. Think about the **stylistic elements**—techniques such as word choice and imagery—that are used in each poem, and their **effects** on the reader.

▶ **ASK YOURSELF:**

- What does this poem mean to me?
- What stylistic elements does the poet use, and how do they affect my understanding of the poem's meaning?

THINK ABOUT AUDIENCE AND PURPOSE

As you begin to think about the poem you have selected, keep in mind that your **purpose** is to respond to stylistic elements that shape the poem's meaning and to share your insights with your **audience.** Your audience is likely to include people who have read the poem and have their own ideas about its meaning.

▶ **ASK YOURSELF:**

- Who is my audience? Why might they be interested in an analysis of this poem?
- What ideas might my audience already have about this poem?
- Will my audience be familiar with the necessary **background information** and **domain-specific vocabulary**? What might I need to provide?
- What insights can I share?

GATHER DETAILS

Read the poem a second or third time. Look for **stylistic elements** that the poet uses. List the elements you identify and record your ideas about their **effects** in a chart.

▶ **WHAT DOES IT LOOK LIKE?**

Stylistic Element	Ideas about Effect
repetition ("I was fifteen")	explains teen's thoughts and feelings; we understand and sympathize with him
personification (motorcycle)	conveys loneliness of being a teen; we identify with him
line breaks (run-on)	draws us into teen's world; we go with him and identify with him

WRITE A CONTROLLING IDEA

Review your chart and look for a **controlling idea** behind the stylistic elements you have listed. Then, draft a controlling idea that explains the overall effect of these stylistic elements.

▶ **WHAT DOES IT LOOK LIKE?**

In "Fifteen," William Stafford uses a variety of stylistic elements to draw readers into the confusing world of a teenager and help them experience the boy's feelings, dreams, and realities.

WRITING WORKSHOP **829**

DIFFERENTIATED INSTRUCTION

FOR ENGLISH LANGUAGE LEARNERS

Language: Reinforce Analysis Terms Write these terms on the board and review them with students:

- *transition:* word or phrase connecting one idea to the next, one sentence to the next, or one paragraph to the next

- *key point:* important idea, usually developed in at least one complete paragraph and stated in that paragraph's topic sentence

- *evidence:* support for key points, including quotations, summaries, and examples

Elicit from students the sorts of evidence they might use in an analysis of a poem.

Planning/ Prewriting

 **COMMON CORE W 2a–f, W 5**

▶ **CHOOSE A POEM** Tell students they may find it easier to write about a poem they like and connect to on a personal level. Suggest that students reread several of their favorite poems aloud to become more aware of stylistic elements and the effects of those elements on their understanding.

▶ **THINK ABOUT AUDIENCE AND PURPOSE** Explain to students that the audience is their classmates and teachers. Remind students that the audience's reaction to a poem may not be exactly like theirs. Have students focus on their audience and purpose by answering the Ask Yourself questions. Tell students that some poetry may contain unusual vocabulary that they will need to define for their audience.

▶ **GATHER DETAILS** Emphasize the point that poetry is about sound and imagery as well as meaning. Review with students the kinds of stylistic elements they should look for in their poems. Then, model how to fill out the chart by analyzing a poem that the class has read. Have students work with you to identify the poem's stylistic elements and their effects.

▶ **WRITE A CONTROLLING IDEA** Suggest that students focus on stylistic elements that draw attention to the controlling idea. They can then analyze how those elements promote the poem's controlling idea.

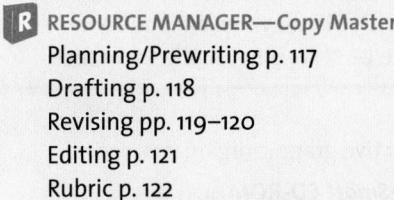 **RESOURCE MANAGER—Copy Masters**
Planning/Prewriting p. 117
Drafting p. 118
Revising pp. 119–120
Editing p. 121
Rubric p. 122
Writing Support p. 124

 BEST PRACTICES TOOLKIT—Transparencies
Evaluating a Poem p. D62
Analysis Frames: Poetic Language and Style pp. D38, D39; Poetic Form and Function pp. D40, D41

Planning/Prewriting *continued*

▶ **COLLECT EVIDENCE** Read aloud the examples of evidence listed in the chart. Point out that paraphrases and summaries allow students to incorporate their own ideas with the details from the poem.

▶ **ORGANIZE YOUR IDEAS** Remind students that organizing their ideas by order of importance means that they discuss the least important idea first and the most important one last—or the most important first and the least important last.

YOUR TURN Give students time to develop their writing plans, draft their controlling ideas, and fill in their charts. If students have trouble selecting a poem, ask them to think about which one they liked the most or remember the best. What did they like about it? Did they feel an emotional reaction to it? If so, what made them feel that way?

For interactive graphic organizers, see

WriteSmart CD-ROM

Writing Center on thinkcentral.com

Planning/Prewriting *continued*

Getting Started

COLLECT EVIDENCE

Gather relevant (related) **evidence** to support your controlling idea. Look for concrete details that support each of your key points about the effects of the stylistic elements. Cite the details in one of the following ways:

- **quotation:** quote exact words from the poem
- **paraphrase:** restate lines in your own words
- **summary:** sum up main ideas and important details

▶ **WHAT DOES IT LOOK LIKE?**

Key Point	Evidence
Use of personification helps you enter the world of the speaker and experience his loneliness as a teen	• **quotation**—"that / companion, ready and friendly" • **paraphrase**—When he touches the handle of the bike, it seems to respond. • **summary**—The description of parts of the motorcycle suggests it is a living being. Its engine sounds like a heartbeat. Its sides are called flanks. Its headlights look like shy eyes.

ORGANIZE YOUR IDEAS

Present your ideas in a **logical structure.** Think about how you can present your ideas to achieve your **purpose** and make your analysis clear to the **audience.** You can discuss each **stylistic element** separately by **order of importance.**

> Introduction and controlling idea
> A. Personification of motorcycle
>   1. Engine has heartbeat
>   2. Friendly, confident
>   3. Speaker's loneliness
> B. Run-on lines
>   1. Create a flow
>   2. Help you identify with speaker
> C. Repetition of "I was fifteen"
>   1. At end of first three stanzas
>   2. Explains teen's thoughts and feelings
>   3. Creates sympathy

PEER REVIEW Share your key points and supporting evidence with a classmate who is familiar with the poem. Ask him or her to identify which key points need more support in the form of quotations, paraphrases, or summaries. Use this feedback to collect additional supporting evidence.

YOUR TURN In your *Reader/Writer Notebook*, develop your writing plan. Record a working version of your controlling idea. Then, use a chart like the one above to organize your key points and evidence. Consider these tips as you gather evidence:

- Cite **evidence** to back up every statement you make. Explain exactly how each detail supports your ideas.
- Double-check any **quotations** you plan to use. Record the exact words from the poem and enclose them in quotation marks. Use ellipses (…) to indicate omitted words.
- In addition to quotations, use paraphrases and summaries as supporting **evidence.**

DIFFERENTIATED INSTRUCTION

FOR ENGLISH LANGUAGE LEARNERS

Writing: Respond to Poetry If students have difficulty articulating their reactions to poetry in words, suggest they draw a picture or make a collage based on imagery in the poems they select. Then have students describe the feelings shown in their pictures.

FOR ADVANCED LEARNERS/PRE-AP

Write a Poem Have advanced learners write poems of their own inspired by favorite poems in the unit. For example, after rereading Shakespeare's "Sonnet 18," a student might write a love poem comparing someone to a computer game or to landing on Mars. Hold a poetry reading, and have volunteers read their poems aloud to the class.

Drafting

The following chart shows how to organize your draft to create an effective analysis of a poem.

COMMON CORE

W 4 Produce clear and coherent writing. **W 9a (RL 1)** Draw evidence from literary texts to support analysis. **L 2** Demonstrate command of the conventions of standard English capitalization, punctuation, and spelling.

Organizing Your Analysis

INTRODUCTION
- Engage your **audience** by relating the **meaning** of the poem to experiences people share.
- Provide the **poet's name** and the **title** of the poem.
- Explain your analysis in a **controlling idea** that identifies the overall **effect** of **stylistic elements.**

▼

BODY
- Organize your key points by **order of importance** to help your audience follow your ideas.
- Cite **details**, **quotations**, and other **evidence** from the text to support each key point.
- Use appropriate and varied **transitions**—such as *also, by this point,* and *however*—to connect major sections and create cohesion.
- Establish and maintain a **formal style** and **objective tone.**
- Use **domain-specific vocabulary,** such as literary terms, to identify **stylistic elements.** (Consult the Handbook section.)

▼

CONCLUDING SECTION
- Summarize your **key points** and reflect on their overall **meaning.**
- End with a **question**, **statement**, or **insight** for your audience to consider.

GRAMMAR IN CONTEXT: USING QUOTATIONS CORRECTLY

When you include direct quotations from the poem as evidence, follow these rules:
- Use quotation marks at the beginning and end of material quoted directly from a poem.
- To indicate the end of a line in a poem, use a slash (/) and insert a space on either side of the slash.
- Follow the exact capitalization and punctuation of the poem in your quotation.
- Whenever possible, use the quotation in your own sentence to provide context.

Examples

The speaker is vague about where and when the action takes place, saying only that it was "back of the willows one summer / day."

There is nothing vague, however, about the motorcycle the boy finds: "it lay on its side, ticking over / slowly in the high grass."

YOUR TURN Develop a first draft of your essay, following the structure outlined in the chart above. As you write, use quotations correctly as supporting evidence for your key points.

FOR STRUGGLING WRITERS

Using Quotations Correctly Students may have difficulty punctuating sentences with quotations. Review the use of commas and colons before quotations: Colons are used after complete sentences. Commas follow phrases such as "he said" or "Millay writes." **After** *that,* there is no comma, as in "Many believe that . . . ."

Have students insert quotations from poems in Unit 7 in the following sentences:

- The poet provides a startling image when s/he says _____.
- There is evident humor in the poet's assertion that _____.
- Another example of the poet's use of alliteration is _____.

Have students work in pairs to make sure they have followed the rules for using quotations correctly.

Practice and Apply

Drafting
COMMON CORE W 4, W 9a (RL 1), L 2

▶ **INTRODUCTION** Offer students some examples of techniques they might use in their opening lines:

- Generalize about the human experience, such as "everybody falls in love."
- Ask a question addressing a generalization, such as "Have you ever been in love?"
- Quote a line from the poem that everyone knows, such as "Shall I compare thee to a summer's day?"

▶ **BODY** Remind students to use domain-specific language, such as literary terms, to help the reader to understand the meaning. Emphasize that students should check any unfamiliar terms in a dictionary, thesaurus, or glossary.

▶ **CONCLUDING SECTION** Tell students that their concluding sections should refer to the question or controlling idea posed in their introductions. Also, remind students that their concluding sections should offer audiences something to think about.

GRAMMAR IN CONTEXT: USING QUOTATIONS CORRECTLY

For additional practice, write these two quotations on the board:

- I saw the small bird
  rioting in the frame of a high window
- may you
  open your eyes to water
  water waving forever

Have students write sentences that incorporate all or part of one of the quotations. Remind students to use correct punctuation. For example: *Collins uses a surprising and effective image when he refers to the sparrow's frantic attempts to get out as "rioting" in these lines: "I saw the small bird / rioting in the frame of a high window."*

YOUR TURN Have students complete the **Your Turn** exercise on their own. When they are finished, have them exchange papers with another student and proofread each other's work. Remind students to include ample supporting evidence for key points and to correctly punctuate quotations.

 Write*Smart* CD-ROM

Writing Center on thinkcentral.com

Revising

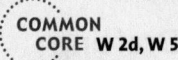

Model the Skill Using a draft poem analysis on a transparency, model how to use the questions, tips, and strategies suggested in the chart to evaluate and revise. You might use an essay by a student from another class or from last year. Be sure to remove the student's name from the essay so that he or she is anonymous.

YOUR TURN Suggest that, before exchanging papers with their partners, students make a list of questions they have about their own analyses. For example, students might want to know whether they have used a literary term correctly or provided enough support for a particular point. Allow students time to read their partner's draft and to make suggestions for improvement.

For interactive revision tools, see

💿 **Write*Smart* CD-ROM**

Writing Center on thinkcentral.com

Revising

When you revise, you consider the content, organization, and style of your essay. Your goal is to determine if you have achieved your purpose and effectively communicated your ideas to your intended audience. The questions, tips, and strategies in the following chart can help you revise and improve your draft.

LITERARY ANALYSIS

Ask Yourself	Tips	Revision Strategies
1. Does the introduction grab the audience's interest? Does it include the name of the poet and the title of the poem?	▶ **Put a star** by sentences that get the audience interested. **Put a check mark** by the name of the poet and the title of the poem.	▶ **Add** an interesting opening sentence. **Add** the name of the poet and the title of the poem.
2. Does the introduction identify the stylistic elements and state a controlling idea?	▶ **Circle** the stylistic elements and effects mentioned in the controlling idea.	▶ **Rewrite** your controlling idea to include an overarching idea about the effect of the author's stylistic elements.
3. Is each stylistic element illustrated with well-chosen and relevant textual evidence such as concrete details and quotations?	▶ **Underline** each piece of evidence. **Draw an arrow** from each item to the point it supports.	▶ **Add** evidence such as quotations, paraphrases, and summaries to support your key points. **Rearrange** evidence so that it is in the paragraph containing the point it supports.
4. Are appropriate and varied transitions used to link ideas?	▶ **Place a check mark** next to each transitional word or phrase.	▶ **Add** transitional words or phrases where needed to link ideas.
5. Does the writing establish and maintain a formal style and objective tone?	▶ **Bracket** contractions, casual slang, and informal or biased language.	▶ **Replace** informal or vague language with more formal, precise wording. **Revise** subjective wording to maintain a neutral tone.
6. Does the concluding section summarize key points and provide an insight into the effect of the author's style?	▶ **Place a check mark** above the restatement of the controlling idea and **circle** the concluding insight.	▶ **Add** a summary of key points or a statement regarding the connection between style and effect as necessary.

YOUR TURN **PEER REVIEW** Exchange your essay with a classmate, or read your analysis aloud to your partner. As you read and comment on your classmate's essay, focus on the controlling idea and supporting evidence. If necessary, provide concrete suggestions for improvement, using the revision strategies in the chart.

DIFFERENTIATED INSTRUCTION

FOR ENGLISH LANGUAGE LEARNERS

Writing: Paraphrasing Poetry Give students these tips for paraphrasing poetry to be used as evidence:

- Locate the main idea of the line or lines. Put that idea into your own words.

- List any supporting details in the same order they appear in the poem.

- Determine the tone of the poem—the attitude it expresses. Write the paraphrase so that it reflects the meaning and tone of the original.

FOR STRUGGLING WRITERS

Comprehension: Transitions Remind students that their ideas and key points should be logically organized by order of importance. Introduce transitions that are useful for this method: *for one thing, above all, equally important, furthermore, most important*. Have students suggest other appropriate signal words or phrases.

COMMON CORE

W 2d Use domain-specific vocabulary to manage the complexity of a topic.
W 5 Develop and strengthen writing as needed by revising, editing, rewriting, or trying a new approach.

ANALYZE A STUDENT DRAFT

Read this draft; note the comments on its strengths as well the suggestions for improvement.

Being Fifteen
by Allison Chen, Markham High School

① Have you ever wanted to escape into another world? In his poem "Fifteen," William Stafford creates a vivid snapshot of the dreams and realities of a teenager. Stafford's use of several stylistic elements helps readers enter the world of this fifteen-year-old and identify with his thoughts and feelings.

> The introduction presents Allison's **controlling idea,** or overarching analysis of the poem.

② Stafford draws readers into the teen's world immediately through the use of stylistic elements. The speaker is vague about where and when the action takes place, saying only that it was "back of the willows one summer / day." He does not reveal his name or describe himself except for the statement "I was fifteen." There is nothing vague, however, about the motorcycle the boy finds: "it lay on its side, ticking over / slowly in the high grass." The machine sounds almost like a living thing with a heartbeat.

> **Evidence** in the form of **quotations** from the poem supports Allison's **key points.**

③ Stafford also uses human qualities to describe the motorcycle to show us how the bike has captured the speaker's imagination. The speaker describes the motorcycle as a "companion, ready and friendly." He refers to its metal parts as flanks. Its headlights look shy to him. Through the figure of speech used to compare the bike to a person, we sense the teen's loneliness.

> Allison discusses the **effect** of the figure of speech here. She should, however, use the precise, domain-specific—or specialized—literary term for this **stylistic element.**

④ The speaker describes the adventures he is dreaming up for himself and his two-wheeled friend. The bike is ready to go, responding to a pat on its handle with "a confident opinion." By this point, we are ready to go, too. The line breaks in each stanza have helped transport us completely into the world of the speaker. Stafford does not end a sentence at the end of a line. He continues a sentence or thought from one line to the next. His use of run-on lines creates a flow that carries us along through the teen's fantasy.

> Allison explains the **effect** of the **stylistic element** used by the poet.

LEARN HOW Use Domain-Specific Vocabulary   In the third paragraph Allison discusses the figure of speech in which human qualities are given to an object, animal, or idea. She needs to refer to this device with the correct literary term, *personification.*

ALLISON'S REVISION TO PARAGRAPH ③

Stafford also uses ~~human qualities~~ *personification* to describe the motorcycle to show us how the bike has captured the speaker's imagination. . . . Through the ~~figure of speech used to compare~~ *personification of* the bike ~~to a person~~, we sense the teen's loneliness.

FOR ENGLISH LANGUAGE LEARNERS
Language: Literary Terms Explain that literary terms are words used to talk about literature. Then, write these terms on the board, and review them with students:

- *imagery:* descriptive words and phrases that recreate sensory experiences for the reader
- *repetition:* technique in which a sound, word, phrase, or line is repeated for emphasis or unity
- *personification:* giving human qualities to an object, animal, or idea

FOR STRUGGLING WRITERS
Recognize Stylistic Elements Write this list of stylistic elements on the board: *imagery, repetition, personification.* Have students review the poems in Unit 7 and identify an example of each element. Have volunteers share their examples with the class.

ANALYZE A STUDENT DRAFT
Explain that the Student Draft on this page is the first half of an analysis of a poem. Model reading the draft and the annotations in blue, and explain that the yellow highlighting illustrates the student's language choices. Explain that the following *Learn How* mini-lessons provide helpful information about ways to improve this student draft as well as their own.

LEARN HOW Use Domain-Specific Vocabulary

- Read aloud the sentences about personification from the draft. Then read aloud the suggested changes.
- Point out that the student writer uses the literary term *personification* to replace "human qualities" and "figure of speech used to compare" in her essay.
- Have students identify other literary terms in the draft on this and the next page. (*stylistic element, repetition, run-on lines*)

ANALYZE A STUDENT DRAFT *continued*

Explain that the Student Draft is continued and completed on this page. Read the draft and annotations aloud, and discuss them. Ask students to comment on the student writer's concluding section.

---

5   Another stylistic element used by the author is repetition, in this case, of the statement "I was fifteen." Why does the speaker repeat this? I think Stafford wants the statement to serve as an explanation of the thoughts, feelings, and dreams of the teen. Each time it appears, it tells us something else about the speaker. The repetition of "I was fifteen" helps us understand the speaker and sympathize with him.

> Allison states a key point of her analysis, but she needs to add evidence from the text to support her ideas.

6   The speaker starts thinking realistically about the situation. He goes looking for the owner of the motorcycle and finds him lying injured in the grass. When the motorcyclist thanks the speaker for his help, calling him "good man," we see the contrast between the two characters. The speaker dreams of being an adult. An adult can climb on a roaring machine and take off for exciting adventures. However, he is still just a boy. He is left behind as the motorcyclist speeds away. Stafford uses personification, run-on lines, and repetition to convey what it feels like to be a teenager, trapped between childhood and adulthood. "I stood there, fifteen," the boy says in the last line of the poem. Soon, but not yet, he will be old enough to "meet / the sky on out Seventeenth."

> The **structure** of Allison's discussion follows order of importance.

> In her **concluding section**, Allison summarizes her **key points** and ends with an insightful **statement**.

LEARN HOW   Add Evidence from the Text   As she reviewed her draft, Allison noticed that she had not included evidence from the text to support her key point about the use of repetition. She decided to add **paraphrases** as evidence.

ALLISON'S REVISION TO PARAGRAPH 5

At the end of the first stanza, the repetition of "I was fifteen" gives a reason for his excitement about finding the motorcycle. At the end of the second stanza, it helps explain why he imagines the bike as a companion. In the third stanza, the statement almost seems to be given as an excuse for his wild fantasies.

. . . Each time it appears, it tells us something else about the speaker. The repetition of "I was fifteen" helps us understand the speaker and sympathize with him.

YOUR TURN   Use the feedback from your peers and teacher as well as the two "Learn How" lessons to revise, rewrite, or try a new approach to your essay. Evaluate how well you conveyed your controlling idea and addressed what is most significant for your specific purpose and audience.

LEARN HOW   Add Evidence from the Text

- Have students explain how Allison's revision differs from her draft. *(The draft asserts, without evidence, that the repeated phrase "I was fifteen" says something different about the speaker each time it appears. The revision gives evidence to support that key point.)*

- Point out that the revision helps the reader understand Allison's idea.

YOUR TURN   Allow students to take time to revise their drafts. Tell them to include plenty of evidence from the text to support their key points. Remind them to use quotations, paraphrases, and summaries.

For interactive revision tools, see

🖱 **Write*Smart* CD-ROM**

Writing Center on <u>thinkcentral.com</u>

DIFFERENTIATED INSTRUCTION

FOR STRUGGLING WRITERS

Evidence   Since readers cannot ask writers questions, writers must provide sufficient evidence to support their ideas. Have students add one piece of evidence to support each of their key points—even if they think they have already provided enough evidence. Remind students that this evidence must be relevant to their ideas. Have students exchange papers and give one another constructive feedback about how well evidence supports key points.

FOR ENGLISH LANGUAGE LEARNERS

Complex Sentences   Remind students that when combining two sentences, they may need to add a comma between the clauses. Explain to students that a comma is needed when the subordinate clause defines the noun it modifies.

Write these sentence pairs on the board, and have students explain how adding commas changes the meaning:

- The movie-goers who were on time got in free. (*The ones who came late had to pay.*)

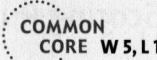

W 5 Develop and strengthen writing as needed. **L 1** Demonstrate command of the conventions of standard English grammar and usage.

Editing and Publishing

In the editing stage, you proofread your essay to make sure that it is free of grammar, spelling, usage, and punctuation errors. With this final step, you prepare your essay for public appearance.

GRAMMAR IN CONTEXT: COMPLEX SENTENCES

Using a variety of sentence structures is one way to keep your readers interested in your ideas. After drafting your essay, evaluate it for sentence variety. In addition to including simple and compound sentences, look for opportunities to create complex sentences.

A **complex sentence** contains one independent clause and at least one subordinate clause. If two sentences are unequal in importance, you can combine them into a complex sentence by turning the less important idea into a subordinate clause and attaching it to the other sentence (which then becomes an independent clause in the complex sentence).

While editing her essay, Allison sees an opportunity to combine two sentences that discuss the same idea into a single complex sentence.

> The speaker dreams of being an adult. ~~An adult~~ *who* can climb on a roaring machine and take off for exciting adventures. However, he is still just a boy. ~~He~~ *who* is left behind as the motorcyclist speeds away.

Allison then decides to expand this new sentence by turning it into a subordinate clause attached to another related sentence to create a new complex sentence.

> *Although*
> ~~The~~ speaker dreams of being an adult who can climb on a roaring machine and take off for exciting adventures. ~~However,~~ he is still just a boy who is left behind as the motorcyclist speeds away.

PUBLISH YOUR WRITING

Finally, you can decide how best to make sure your analysis reaches your intended audience. Here are some options:

- Submit your essay to a literary magazine.
- Share your essay in an online discussion group.
- Adapt your essay to deliver as an audio podcast.
- Include parts of your essay in an e-mail to a living poet.

YOUR TURN Proofread your essay for grammar, usage, and spelling errors. Revise to create sentence variety with complex sentences. Then, publish your final essay where your intended audience is likely to see it.

Editing and Publishing

COMMON CORE **W 5, L 1**

GRAMMAR IN CONTEXT: COMPLEX SENTENCES

Reread the definition of a complex sentence in the chart on this page. Identify the independent clause in the first sentence of the example: "The speaker dreams of being an adult." Then identify the dependent clause— "who can climb on a roaring machine and take off for exciting adventures."

Have volunteers identify the independent and dependent clauses in the second revised sentence. (*independent clause: "he is still just a boy"; dependent clause: "who is left behind"*)

PUBLISH YOUR WRITING

Brainstorm with students additional ways to publish their essays.

YOUR TURN Allow students time to revise their essays. Remind them to check for sentences that could be combined into complex sentences. Have students check to see whether they should add more evidence to support their key points.

- The movie-goers, who were on time, got in free. (*All the movie-goers got in free, and all of them were on time.*)

- My brother who lives in San Diego likes surfing. (*I have more than one brother, and the one in San Diego is the one who likes surfing.*)

- My brother, who lives in San Diego, likes surfing. (*I have one brother. He lives in San Diego and likes to surf.*)

Have students reread their essays to make sure they have used a variety of sentence structures, including complex sentences, in their essays.

Scoring Rubric

Tell students that the best way to understand a scoring rubric is to use it to score actual writing. Provide the class with copies of a student's essay with the student's name removed. Work as a class to evaluate the essay by using the scoring rubric. Have students score the essay and write a brief paragraph using the language of the scoring guide to explain the reasons for their score.

For Rubric Bank, see

 WriteSmart CD-ROM

Writing Center on **thinkcentral.com**

Assess and Reteach

Assess

R RESOURCE MANAGER—Copy Master
Rubric for Evaluation p. 122

Online Essay Scoring on **thinkcentral.com**

Reteach

Level Up Online Tutorials on **thinkcentral.com**

Reteaching Worksheets on **thinkcentral.com**

Writing Lesson 8: Creating Sentence Variety

Writing Lesson 20: Integrating Quotations

Literature Lesson 44: Style and Syntax

Scoring Rubric

Use the rubric below to evaluate your analysis from the Writing Workshop or your response to the on-demand task on the next page.

LITERARY ANALYSIS

SCORE	COMMON CORE TRAITS
6	• **Development** Has an engaging introduction; includes a controlling idea with an insightful analysis of the author's style; supports key points with relevant evidence; ends powerfully • **Organization** Arranges ideas in an effective, logical order; uses varied transitions to create cohesion and connect ideas • **Language** Consistently maintains a formal style and objective tone; uses precise language; shows a strong command of conventions
5	• **Development** Has an effective introduction; provides a controlling idea that offers an original analysis of the author's style; supports key points with evidence; has a strong concluding section • **Organization** Arranges ideas logically; uses transitions to connect ideas • **Language** Maintains a formal style and objective tone; uses precise language; has a few errors in conventions
4	• **Development** Has an introduction that could be more engaging; includes a controlling idea that states an analysis of the author's style; could use some more evidence; has an adequate concluding section • **Organization** Arranges ideas logically; could vary transitions more • **Language** Mostly maintains a formal style and objective tone; needs more precise language at times; has a few distracting errors in conventions
3	• **Development** Has an adequate, though not memorable, introduction; has a controlling idea that makes an obvious statement about the author's style; lacks sufficient support; has a routine concluding section • **Organization** Has some flaws in organization; needs transitions to connect ideas • **Language** Frequently lapses into an informal style or subjective tone; uses some vague word choices; has some significant errors in conventions
2	• **Development** Has a weak introduction and a controlling idea that does not relate to the writing task; lacks specific evidence; has a weak concluding section • **Organization** Has organizational flaws; lacks transitions throughout • **Language** Uses an informal style and vague or biased language; has many distracting errors in conventions
1	• **Development** Has no introduction or controlling idea; offers unrelated points as evidence; ends abruptly • **Organization** Includes a string of disconnected ideas with no overall organization • **Language** Uses an inappropriate style and vague, tired language; has major problems with grammar, mechanics, and spelling

Preparing for Timed Writing

COMMON CORE **W 10** Write routinely over shorter time frames for a range of tasks, purposes, and audiences.

1. ANALYZE THE TASK — 5 MIN

Read the task carefully. Then, read it again, noting the words in the task that tell the type of writing, the topic, the audience, and the purpose.

> **WRITING TASK**
>
> If I can stop one heart from breaking,
> I shall not live in vain;
> If I can ease one life the aching,
> Or cool one pain,
> Or help one fainting robin
> Unto his nest again,
> I shall not live in vain.
> —Emily Dickinson

Type of writing/Topic →
Write an <u>analysis of this poem</u> to post as a blog for <u>fans of the poet</u>. *← Audience*
In your essay, <u>explain the effects of stylistic elements,</u> using quotations and other
evidence from the poem to support your analysis. *→ Purpose*

2. PLAN YOUR RESPONSE — 10 MIN

First, identify stylistic elements in the poem, list examples of each, and record your ideas about their effects. Then, review your ideas and write a controlling idea that explains how the stylistic elements in the poem help shape its meaning as you understand it.

Stylistic Element	Examples	Effect
Controlling Idea:		

3. RESPOND TO THE TASK — 20 MIN

Begin drafting your analysis. Start with a question or comment about the subject of the poem. As you write, keep the following points in mind:
- In the introduction, include a controlling idea that explains your overarching analysis of the effect of stylistic elements in the poem.
- In the body, present evidence, such as quotations, paraphrases, and summaries that support your controlling idea.
- In the concluding section, include an insight based on your analysis.

4. IMPROVE YOUR RESPONSE — 5–10 MIN

Revising Compare your draft with the task. Does your draft analyze the effect of stylistic elements in the poem? Does your draft include evidence that supports your analysis? Do you conclude with an insightful comment?
Proofreading Find and correct any errors in grammar, punctuation, and spelling. Make sure that your analysis and any edits are neatly written and legible.
Checking Your Final Copy Make sure your final draft is your best work.

DIFFERENTIATED INSTRUCTION

FOR ENGLISH LANGUAGE LEARNERS

Writing: Proofreading Remind students that errors are almost inevitable when responding to a writing task in a timed situation. Suggest that students be aware of grammar, spelling, or usage errors that they frequently make and proofread for them carefully before turning in timed writings.

FOR STRUGGLING WRITERS

Understanding the Task Responding to a timed writing task can be challenging for students. Remind students to reread the task to be certain they understand it and then review the task again after they have finished writing to be sure they have followed the instructions.

COMMON CORE FOCUS

W 10 Write routinely over shorter time frames for a range of tasks, purposes, and audiences.

Preparing for Timed Writing

1. **Analyze the Task** Before students begin writing, encourage them to answer the following questions:
   - What is my time limit?
   - What are the core traits assessed in the scoring rubric?
   - Who is my audience?
   - What is my purpose?
2. **Plan Your Response** Remind students that all the key points should relate to the controlling idea and be supported by evidence.
3. **Respond to the Task** Remind students to use transitional words and phrases to connect ideas and convey their degrees of importance.
4. **Improve Your Response** Point out to students that the scoring rubric emphasizes the need for evidence. Remind them to use a variety of quotations, paraphrases, and summaries to support their key points. Also, remind students to make sure they are recording and punctuating quotations accurately.

Assess

Use the Scoring Rubric on page 836 to assess students' essays.

Focus and Motivate

W 2a Introduce a topic; include graphics and multimedia. **W 6** Use technology to produce writing products. **SL 1c** Incorporate others into discussions. **SL 4** Present information clearly. **SL 5** Make strategic use of digital media.

PRODUCE WITH A PURPOSE

Read aloud the elements of a strong class blog. Tell students that their posts should pose thought-provoking questions, comments, and opinions, with evidence to support each point.

COMMON CORE TRAITS

As students plan their blogs, remind them to keep in mind the *COMMON CORE TRAITS* of a strong class blog.

Practice and Apply

Planning and Producing the Blog

Have students work in groups based on their interest in a particular issue. Make sure to consult with each group, checking that their threads are manageable and will provide rich opportunities for discussion and analysis.

Enlist the help of your school technology coordinator when students are ready to create their blogs. He or she may have specific recommendations for safe blogging sites to use, as well as expertise in setting up the discussions.

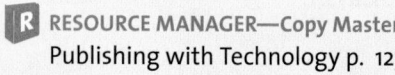
RESOURCE MANAGER—Copy Master
Publishing with Technology p. 123

Creating a Class Blog

Essential Course of Study **ECOS**

Whether you want to share your own review of a new blockbuster with moviegoers or a personal response to a favorite poem with other readers, creating a blog, or Web log, is an effective and direct way to exchange ideas.

Complete the workshop activities in your **Reader/Writer Notebook**.

PRODUCE WITH A PURPOSE	**COMMON CORE TRAITS**
TASK Create a **blog** in which you and your classmates can share ideas about topics of your choice. With a team of classmates, plan and build the blog. Then add posts, or messages, to spark discussion among your online community.	**A STRONG CLASS BLOG . . .** • focuses on topics that will prompt discussion • has a structure that allows for easy navigation • has a visually appealing home page • includes posts that have a respectful tone • is updated regularly

COMMON CORE

W 2a Introduce a topic; include graphics and multimedia. **W 6** Use technology to produce writing products. **SL 1c** Incorporate others into discussions. **SL 4** Present information clearly. **SL 5** Make strategic use of digital media.

Planning and Producing the Blog

Creating a class blog requires preparation. These tips can help you:

- **Decide on Your Topics** Which topics do you think would spark a lively discussion? Work with your classmates to set ground rules for choosing topics and develop a plan for settling potential disagreements. You might want to limit your categories to a few focused topics.

- **Determine Your Discussion Threads** Include a separate **discussion thread**—chain of related posts—for each topic you want users to discuss. Clearly label each thread. For example, "Top Ten Movies to See and Why" is a good label because it tells readers what to expect.

- **Map Out Your Home Page** Sketch the home page of your blog, visually representing how users will link to the different threads. Decide what other information and elements the page should feature. For instance, you might include interesting formats for headers, graphics such as figures or tables, or links to multimedia to make important connections and distinctions.

- **Assign Roles** As a class, decide how to divide the work equally. One person might research free Web sites that you can use to build your blog. Another might create a logo for the home page. In addition, each person should assume responsibility for writing the first post within one thread. Later, you can add posts that build on your classmates' ideas.

Media Tools
THINK central
Go to **thinkcentral.com**.
KEYWORD: HML10-838

- **Build a Blog** With the assistance of your teacher, the school technology coordinator, or another adult with technology expertise, assemble your blog using the Web site you chose.

DIFFERENTIATED INSTRUCTION

FOR ENGLISH LANGUAGE LEARNERS
Language: Reinforce Technology Terms
Review key technology terms used in this workshop:

- *blog:* contraction of "Web log"; a Web site where people provide regular commentary on current issues and events

- *blogger:* someone who posts entries on a blog site

- *posts:* entries in a blog

- *thread:* a group of posts on a single topic

- *home page:* the front or main page of a blog

Ask whether students are unfamiliar with any other terms, and help them learn the definitions.

Participating in an Online Discussion

Sharing your ideas in a blog is different from writing a review or a literary analysis or delivering it orally. Here are some tips for participating in a meaningful online discussion:

- **Clearly State and Support Your Ideas** Present your controlling idea, information, and supporting evidence clearly and logically so readers can follow your line of reasoning. Use a style and organization appropriate to your purpose and audience.

- **Make It Brief** Most bloggers don't want to scroll down indefinitely. Keep each post short and to the point. Formatting key ideas with bullet points can make them easier to read.

- **Use a Respectful Tone** In an online discussion, your audience can't see you face-to-face so it's important to maintain a polite tone. Though you don't have to agree with every idea proposed, you should welcome other perspectives and respond thoughtfully to them. Use these discussion starters in your conversation.

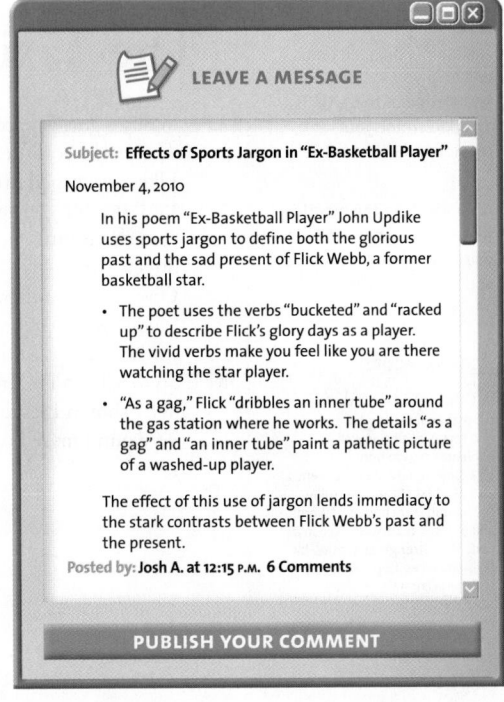

LEAVE A MESSAGE

Subject: Effects of Sports Jargon in "Ex-Basketball Player"

November 4, 2010

In his poem "Ex-Basketball Player" John Updike uses sports jargon to define both the glorious past and the sad present of Flick Webb, a former basketball star.

- The poet uses the verbs "bucketed" and "racked up" to describe Flick's glory days as a player. The vivid verbs make you feel like you are there watching the star player.

- "As a gag," Flick "dribbles an inner tube" around the gas station where he works. The details "as a gag" and "an inner tube" paint a pathetic picture of a washed-up player.

The effect of this use of jargon lends immediacy to the stark contrasts between Flick Webb's past and the present.

Posted by: **Josh A. at 12:15 P.M. 6 Comments**

PUBLISH YOUR COMMENT

> **Effective Discussion Starters**
>
> "I understand what you are saying, but I disagree because . . ."
>
> "That's a valid point, but . . ."
>
> "Have you thought about . . . ?"
>
> "Your evidence sounds reasonable, but I'm still not convinced that . . ."
>
> "Could you clarify your point about . . . ?"

- **Keep the Discussion Going** Participation is what makes a blog discussion successful. Incorporate others into the discussion by posing questions, and respond thoughtfully to the questions of others. Make connections between the discussion thread and larger ideas in order to broaden the perspective. Don't be afraid to challenge ideas or conclusions, but make sure you respect others' thoughts and opinions.

- **Invite Other Bloggers** Do you have friends, teachers, or family members who might be interested in the topics discussed in your blog? Motivate others to participate in the discussion by sending an e-mail with a link to your blog.

 YOUR TURN Plan and produce a blog using the guidelines on these pages. Once you've launched your blog, challenge yourself to post messages several times a week. As a team, plan to add a new discussion every couple of weeks.

TECHNOLOGY WORKSHOP **839**

FOR STRUGGLING STUDENTS

Evaluate Posts Show students several examples of successful blog posts. Then have students work with a partner to evaluate the posts using the core traits of a strong blog outlined on page 838. Finally, have students use their essays to practice writing their own posts.

Teach

Participating in an Online Discussion

Before students begin their blogs, review with them the guidelines for participating in a meaningful online discussion. Ask:

- How might an online discussion differ from a face-to-face conversation?

- What is an appropriate length for a post?

- How should users respond to posts they don't agree with?

- What are some effective strategies for starting a good discussion?

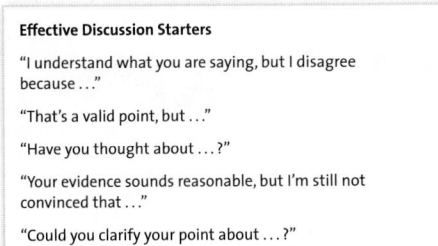 **YOUR TURN** Have students exchange drafts of their first posts with a partner. Tell students to check that the post includes a clear position supported by reasons and evidence.

Assess and Reteach

Assess

Use the ***COMMON CORE TRAITS*** to assess students' blogs.

A strong class blog
- focuses on topics that will prompt discussion
- has a structure that allows for easy navigation
- has a visually appealing home page
- includes posts that have a respectful tone
- is updated regularly

Reteach

Some students may have trouble mapping out a home page for their blogs. Make screenshots of several blogs from the Internet. Then work with students to evaluate the visual appeal and navigation of each home page.

 **THINK central**

> **Media Tools**
>
> Keywords for using technology direct students to **MediaScope,** a Web site that helps them strengthen media analysis and production skills.

TECHNOLOGY WORKSHOP **839**

Assessment Practice

COMMON CORE FOCUS

RL1 Cite textual evidence to support analysis of what the text says explicitly as well as inferences drawn from the text. **RL2** Determine a theme or central idea of a text. **RL4** Determine the figurative meanings of words and phrases as they are used in a text. **W5** Strengthen writing by revising and editing. **L6** Acquire and use accurately general academic and domain-specific words; demonstrate independence in gathering vocabulary knowledge.

CHECK READINESS

Read aloud the paragraph under **ASSESS** and stress to students that this is not the full Unit Test, but a way for them to check their readiness for it. Then have students examine the skills standards listed under **REVIEW** and look back in the unit or in the **Student Resource Bank** for any skills they need to review.

READ THE TEXTS

Remind students to keep unit goals in mind as they read the poems, paying particular attention to these literary and reading skills:

- poetic form
- imagery
- figurative language
- sound devices
- compare and contrast

To help students focus on imagery, encourage them to ask questions such as these as they read:

- What images describe the city in "The Taxi"?
- In "Reprise," what images help convey feelings of love?

ANSWER THE QUESTIONS

Direct students to pages R93–R101 of the **Handbook** to review test-taking strategies.

Urge students to use active reading strategies by asking questions as they read. Their questions can be in the form of notes on scrap paper. Such notes also might contain responses to passages and observations about literary elements.

COMMON CORE

ASSESS
Taking this practice test will help you assess your knowledge of these skills and determine your readiness for the Unit Test.

REVIEW
After you take the practice test, your teacher can help you identify any standards you need to review.

COMMON CORE

RL1 Cite textual evidence to support analysis of what the text says explicitly as well as inferences drawn from the text. **RL2** Determine a theme or central idea of a text. **RL4** Determine the figurative meanings of words and phrases as they are used in a text. **W5** Strengthen writing by revising and editing. **L6** Acquire and use accurately general academic and domain-specific words; demonstrate independence in gathering vocabulary knowledge.

Practice Test
THINK central
Take it at **thinkcentral.com**.
KEYWORD: HML10N-840

Assessment Practice

DIRECTIONS Read the following selections, and then answer the questions.

The Taxi *by Amy Lowell*

When I go away from you
The world beats dead
Like a slackened drum.
I call out for you against the jutted stars
5 And shout into the ridges of the wind.
Streets coming fast,
One after the other,
Wedge you away from me,
And the lamps of the city prick my eyes
10 So that I can no longer see your face.
Why should I leave you,
To wound myself upon the sharp edges of the night?

DIFFERENTIATED INSTRUCTION

FOR ENGLISH LANGUAGE LEARNERS
Assessment Practice: Work Backward
Prepare students by having them read the questions *before* reading the passage and supplementary selections. Have pairs find unfamiliar words in test directions and questions and follow these steps:

1. Write each word on an index card.
2. Look up the meaning in a dictionary and write it on the back of the card.

3. Use the cards to practice the words with your partner and to teach them to others.

Reprise   *by Ogden Nash*

Geniuses of countless nations
Have told their love for generations
Till all their memorable phrases
Are common as goldenrod or daisies.
5   Their girls have glimmered like the moon,
Or shimmered like a summer noon,
Stood like lily, fled like fawn,
Now the sunset, now the dawn,
Here the princess in the tower
10   There the sweet forbidden flower.
Darling, when I look at you
Every aged phrase is new,
And there are moments when it seems
I've married one of Shakespeare's dreams.

ITEM ANALYSIS

COMPREHENSION AND WRITTEN RESPONSE	ITEMS	UNIT PAGES
Poetic Form	1, 6	770–777, 795, 803, 811, 817
Imagery	3, 4, 5, 14	770–777, 795
Figurative Language	8, 9, 10, 13	770–777, 787
Sound Devices	2, 7	770–777, 779, 803
Compare and Contrast	11, 12, 14	787

WRITING AND GRAMMAR	ITEMS	UNIT PAGES
Precise Verbs	4, 6	785
Parallelism	2, 7	793

Practice Test

On **thinkcentral.com** students can complete an interactive version of this practice test *and* receive remediation for the skills they have not yet mastered.

FOR STRUGGLING READERS

Assessment Support Consider these options for completing the Assessment Practice:

- Have students "work backward" to review the test questions before reading the passage.

- Select random questions in the Assessment and have students demonstrate *how* and *where* to look for the answers.

- Ask students to locate unfamiliar vocabulary words in the Assessment. Elicit the words' meanings from the class.

- Have students record useful testing words and definitions in their journal for later reference.

- Read the selection or parts of it aloud to aid in student comprehension.

Reading Comprehension

Model a thinking process for answering multiple-choice questions.

1. **C is correct.** *"The Taxi" has neither rhyme nor meter, so B and D are incorrect. A is incorrect because in concrete poetry, the visual shape of the printed poem reflects the poem's topic.*

2. **A is correct.** *The drumlike sound is produced by d sounds, which alliterate in "dead" (line 2) and "drum" (line 3), and produce consonance in "world" (line 2) and "slackened" (line 3). B and C are incorrect because there is no rhyme in the lines. D is incorrect because there is no dialect in the lines.*

3. **B is correct.** *"Call" (line 4) and "shout" (line 5) create an image of distress; similarly, "the jutted stars" (line 4) and "the ridges of the wind" (line 5) suggest harshness and distress. A is incorrect because speed is not part of the imagery of these lines. C is incorrect because the setting is a city. D is incorrect because there is distress but no danger.*

4. **D is correct.** *D most vividly suggests that the speaker can be hurt. A, B, and C might convey emotional vulnerability but are weak in comparison with D.*

5. **B is correct.** *The succession of images creates a sense of movement. A is incorrect because the only details of the city are "streets" (line 6) and "lamps" (line 9). The poem's mood is sad, so C is incorrect. D is incorrect because the poem's nature images suggest pain.*

6. **A is correct.** *Each pair of lines in this poem rhymes. B is incorrect because the poem uses a four-foot line. C is incorrect because the poem is not divided into four-line units. D is wrong because the poem is not divided into separate groups of lines.*

7. **A is correct.** *Alliteration, the repetition of consonant sounds at the beginning of words, occurs only in the g sounds in "girls" and "glimmered." B and D illustrate rhyme; C illustrates assonance.*

Reading Comprehension

Use "The Taxi" (p. 840) to answer questions 1–5.	Use "Reprise" (p. 841) to answer questions 6–10.

1. "The Taxi" is an example of —
   - **A.** concrete poetry
   - **B.** a ballad
   - **C.** free verse
   - **D.** a sonnet

2. What sound devices used in lines 2–3 suggest the thump of a drum?
   - **A.** Alliteration and consonance
   - **B.** Rhyme and onomatopoeia
   - **C.** Assonance and end rhyme
   - **D.** Repetition and dialect

3. The images in lines 4–5 reinforce the idea that —
   - **A.** the taxi is traveling too fast
   - **B.** the speaker is distressed
   - **C.** nature is full of violence
   - **D.** the city is a dangerous place

4. Which image best conveys the speaker's feeling of vulnerability?
   - **A.** *Streets coming fast, / One after the other*
   - **B.** *And shout into the ridges of the wind*
   - **C.** *So that I can no longer see your face*
   - **D.** *To wound myself upon the sharp edges of the night*

5. The poet presents one image after another in rapid succession to —
   - **A.** paint a detailed picture of the city
   - **B.** create a sensation of movement
   - **C.** express the excitement of traveling
   - **D.** stress the transient beauty of nature

6. Which of the following terms best describes the rhymed lines of this poem?
   - **A.** Couplet
   - **B.** Iambic pentameter
   - **C.** Quatrain
   - **D.** Stanza

7. Which pair of words is an example of alliteration in the poem?
   - **A.** Girls, glimmered
   - **B.** Fawn, dawn
   - **C.** Every, aged
   - **D.** Seems, dreams

8. Which of the following lines contains a metaphor?
   - **A.** *Geniuses of countless nations*
   - **B.** *Are common as goldenrod or daisies*
   - **C.** *Or shimmered like a summer noon*
   - **D.** *There the sweet forbidden flower*

9. Line 7, "Stood like lily, fled like fawn," contains examples of —
   - **A.** metaphor
   - **B.** onomatopoeia
   - **C.** personification
   - **D.** simile

10. The speaker lists similes and metaphors used by other writers and calls them "memorable phrases" to emphasize that —
    - **A.** only geniuses can describe love
    - **B.** love is as common as goldenrod
    - **C.** love is hard to describe in new ways
    - **D.** every generation writes about love

842

DIFFERENTIATED INSTRUCTION

FOR ENGLISH LANGUAGE LEARNERS

Assessment Vocabulary To help students understand the Reading Comprehension questions, teach or review these key vocabulary words:

- Item 2: *suggest,* "remind you of"
- Item 3: *reinforce,* "support" or "make clear"
- Item 4: *conveys,* "shows"
- Items 8–9: *contains/contain,* "has"/"have"
- Item 10: *emphasize,* "show strongly"
- Item 12: *reflect on,* "explore personal thoughts about"

Use both selections to answer questions 11 and 12.

11. Which statement accurately compares the emotional state of the speakers in the two poems?

    A. Both speakers are lonely.

    B. Both speakers are angry.

    C. One speaker is content and one is unhappy.

    D. One speaker is frightened and one is optimistic.

12. In these poems, both poets reflect on —

    A. the sorrows that accompany being in love

    B. the strong feelings of someone in love

    C. the beauty and uniqueness of the loved one

    D. nature as a great comfort to those in love

SHORT CONSTRUCTED RESPONSE
Write three or four sentences to answer this question.

13. Why is the taxi a suitable metaphor for the emotions expressed in Lowell's poem? Support your answer with details from the poem.

Write two to three paragraphs to answer this question.

14. Compare and contrast the nature imagery in "The Taxi" and "Reprise." What do these images reveal about the two speakers' attitudes toward love?

GO ON

843

---

8. **D is correct.** The line compares girls to flowers without using *like* or *as*. A is incorrect because its language is literal. B and C are similes, not metaphors.

9. **D is correct.** The word *like* signals the use of simile. A is incorrect because a metaphor does not contain *like*. Onomatopoeia does not occur in line 7, so B is incorrect. C is incorrect because line 7 does not compare something nonhuman to something human.

10. **C is correct.** The list emphasizes how often previous poets have described love. The speaker never makes the claim noted in A. B names only one detail in the list. D is incorrect because the list refers to poetic descriptions of love, not to love itself.

11. **C is correct.** The speaker in "Reprise" is content (line 14); the speaker in "The Taxi" is unhappy, as evidenced in the poem's imagery. A and B are incorrect because only the speaker of "The Taxi" is lonely or angry. The speaker of "The Taxi" seems more unhappy than frightened, so D is incorrect.

12. **B is correct.** "The Taxi" stresses the intense loneliness and longing to be with the loved one, and "Reprise" focuses on the speaker's deep love for his wife. A is true only of "The Taxi." C is incorrect because "The Taxi" does not describe the loved one. D is incorrect because in "The Taxi" nature is not seen as comforting and because "Reprise" uses nature only for figurative comparisons.

SHORT CONSTRUCTED RESPONSE

Possible responses:

13. *Student responses should include evidence from the poem.*

14. *The nature images in "The Taxi" reflect the speaker's emotional pain: "jutted stars" (line 4); "ridges of the wind" (line 5); "sharp edges of the night" (line 12). These images grow more violent as the distance between the lovers grows.*

The nature images in "Reprise" are playfully romantic, comparing a loved one with beautiful objects in nature: "girls have glimmered like the moon" (line 5); "stood like lily, fled like fawn" (line 7); "sweet forbidden flower" (line 10). The positive imagery also makes a comparison to beautiful times of day: "noon" (line 6) and "dawn" (line 8).

FOR ENGLISH LANGUAGE LEARNERS
Review Literary Terms On the board, list the vocabulary terms shown in italics. Then give the examples in random order and have students classify them. Elicit additional examples from students.

- *imagery:* The sun-drenched beach curved along the edge of the glistening bay.

- *rhyme:* For that young pair, the heart's emotion/Soon became a true devotion.

- *alliteration:* "Darling," Dave declared, "I'm delighted that you decided to date me."

- *consonance:* With a meek wink, he took her hand, and they began to walk.

- *simile:* In the bright sunlight, the bay sparkled like diamonds. (This is also an example of *imagery*.)

- *metaphor:* The future was an unmapped road, but they would travel it together. (This is also an example of *imagery*.)

Revising and Editing

1. **B is correct.** *The verb must agree with the subject, which is plural. The comma is needed before "for example," so A is wrong. C is incorrect because "works" is a plural, not a possessive. Since a change is necessary, D is also incorrect.*

2. **C is correct.** *With this change, rhyme and rhythm are both nouns and objects of the preposition by. Neither A nor D addresses the lack of parallelism in the phrase "by rhyme and rhythmically," so they are both wrong. B changes the phrase but recreates the lack of parallelism, so it is also incorrect.*

3. **C is correct.** *In C, a participial phrase modifying poets combines the sentences. A is incorrect because there is no causal relationship between the two sentences. B is wrong because the poets did not travel only when they sang. Similarly, D is incorrect because they did not travel only while they were singing.*

4. **C is correct.** *Sparked is a metaphor relating to how a fire might start. For this reason, it conjures up the most precise image. A and D are incorrect because, while they share the concept of beginning something, they do not evoke such a clear image. B doesn't mean to begin something, but to help something that has already begun, so it is also incorrect.*

Revising and Editing

DIRECTIONS Read the passage, and answer the questions that follow.

(1) Although they are separated by nearly 3,000 years, Homer and hip-hop performers share certain traits. (2) Both has created works that use poetry and singing, for example. (3) In Homer's epics and in hip-hop, poetry is linked to song by rhyme and rhythmically. (4) Like hip-hop artists on tour, poets of the seventh-century B.C. were storytellers who went from town to town. (5) They sang epic works like Homer's *Odyssey* to educate and entertain the crowd. (6) With the advent of the printing press, poetry became more of a written art form. (7) Then, in the 1950s, poetry readings caused a strong resurgence in the oral tradition. (8) Further, energizing spoken poetry were poetry slams and hip-hop music in the 1980s and 1990s. (9) Today, hip-hop has worldwide attention. (10) The United States, France, and Japan are the three largest markets for hip-hop music, but countries in Africa and South America produce and appreciate it as well. (11) Hip-hop music and culture are even studied in universities. (12) Students and scholars are given grants to travel the world, visiting countries such as Senegal, Tanzania, Cuba, Mongolia, and Brazil to research this emerging musical form.

1. What change, if any, should be made in sentence 2?
   A. Delete the comma
   B. Change *has* to **have**
   C. Change *works* to **work's**
   D. Make no change

2. What is the most effective way to revise sentence 3 so that its elements are parallel?
   A. In Homer's epics and poetry and in hip-hop, there is a link to song by rhyme and rhythmically.
   B. In Homer's epics and in hip-hop, poetry is linked to song by rhyming and rhythm.
   C. In Homer's epics and in hip-hop, poetry is linked to song by rhyme and rhythm.
   D. Through rhyme and rhythmically, Homer's epics and hip-hop link poetry to song.

3. What is the most effective way to combine sentences 4 and 5?
   A. Like hip-hop artists on tour, poets of the seventh-century B.C. were storytellers who went from town to town; therefore, they sang epic works like Homer's *Odyssey* to educate and entertain the crowd.
   B. Like hip-hop artists on tour, poets of the seventh-century B.C. were storytellers who went from town to town when they sang epic works like Homer's *Odyssey* to educate and entertain the crowd.
   C. Like hip-hop artists on tour, poets of the seventh-century B.C. were storytellers who went from town to town, singing epic works like Homer's *Odyssey* to educate and entertain the crowd.
   D. Like hip-hop artists on tour, poets of the seventh-century B.C. were storytellers who went from town to town while they were singing epic works like Homer's *Odyssey* to educate and entertain the crowd.

844

DIFFERENTIATED INSTRUCTION

FOR ENGLISH LANGUAGE LEARNERS

Parallelism Remind students that parallelism refers to using the same word patterns in words, phrases, or clauses next to one another. Write these sentences on the board:

- Kara's favorite hobbies are riding horses, running marathons, and to sail boats. (*sailing boats*)

- Zack is getting a low grade because he has trouble paying attention in class, finishing his homework on time, and he never studies for tests. (*studying for tests*)

- Before the big game, the coach told the team to avoid eating too much and that they should get plenty of sleep. (either *to avoid eating too much and [to] get plenty of sleep*, or *that they should avoid eating too much and [that they should] get plenty of sleep*)

Have the students change the sentences to include parallel structures.

4. Which precise verb could replace *caused* in sentence 7?

   A. Began   **C.** Sparked

   B. Induced   **D.** Started

5. What change, if any, should be made in sentence 8?

   A. Delete comma after **Further**

   B. Change *energizing* to **energized**

   C. Change *1980s and 1990s* to **1980's and 1990's**

   D. Make no change

6. Which precise verb could replace *has* in sentence 9?

   A. Elicits   **C.** Makes

   B. Gets   **D.** Gathers

7. What is the most effective way to rewrite sentence 10 so that its elements are parallel?

   A. The three largest markets for hip-hop music are the United States, France, and Japan, but countries in Africa and South America are also producing and appreciating it.

   B. Becoming the three largest markets for hip-hop music are the United States, France, and Japan, but in countries in Africa and South America, hip-hop music is also produced and appreciated.

   C. The United States, France, and Japan are the three largest markets for hip-hop music, but countries in Africa and South America also produce and appreciate it.

   D. The United States, France, and Japan are the three largest markets for hip-hop music, but it is also produced and appreciated in countries in Africa and South America.

8. Which transitional word or phrase should be added to the beginning of sentence 11?

   A. As a result,

   B. Nevertheless,

   C. For example,

   D. In fact,

9. What change, if any, should be made to sentence 12?

   A. Insert a comma after **grants**

   B. Change *countries* to **country's**

   C. Change *such as* to **like**

   D. Make no change

5. A *is correct.* Further *does not link sentences 7 and 8, but modifies energizing.* B *would make the sentence ungrammatical, and* C *is not necessary, so they are both incorrect. Since a change is necessary,* D *is wrong.*

6. A *is correct.* Elicit *means "to draw out." Neither* B *nor* C *is precise.* D *is incorrect because to gather is to collect something that already exists.*

7. C *is correct.* *The subject of each clause tells where something happens, the object in each clause is the same, and the verb is in the simple present tense.* A *is incorrect because the verb in the second half is in progressive tense.* B *is poorly constructed, so it is wrong.* D *is incorrect because the object of the first clause is the subject of the second.*

8. D *is correct.* *The sentence elaborates on evidence supporting the topic sentence.* A *is incorrect because there is no causal relationship between sentences 10 and 11.* B *is incorrect because the sentence does not contradict the ideas that come before it but instead builds on them.* C *is incorrect because sentence 11 does not provide an example.*

9. D *is correct.* *No change is necessary.* A *and* B *would make the sentence ungrammatical.* C *is incorrect because* like *implies that the countries conducting research are not those listed but rather other countries that share similarities with the listed countries.*

FOR STRUGGLING READERS

Assessment Support: Precise Verbs Remind students that using precise verbs in writing helps to create more vivid images for readers. Tell students to keep this in mind when choosing their answers to the Revising and Editing questions.

COMMON CORE FOCUS

RL 10 Read and comprehend stories and poems.
RI 10 Read and comprehend literary nonfiction.

INTRODUCE *GREAT READS*

In Unit 7, students have discussed a number of big questions. Invite students to tell which question they found most intriguing and why, and then focus attention on the three that appear on this page. Discuss the recommended books and their summaries, pointing out how each connects to the related question. Encourage students to choose one or more of these "great reads" to read independently.

Ideas for Independent Reading

Which topics in Unit 7 inspired you most? Nature? Memories? Love? Explore them further with these additional works.

COMMON CORE

RL 10 Read and comprehend literature. **RI 10** Read and comprehend literary nonfiction.

What is our place in nature?

Any Small Thing Can Save You
by Christina Adam

A bestiary is a collection of writing about animals. This prose bestiary considers animals throughout the alphabet—from asp to goose, from porcupine to vulture—and the effect each has on humans.

Why I Wake Early
by Mary Oliver

Oliver is regarded as one of America's best nature poets. In this collection she describes elements of the natural world—toads, water, flowers—that cause her to wake early each morning, so as not to miss something extraordinary.

Danger on Peaks
by Gary Snyder

Several poems in this collection are about Washington State's Mount St. Helens, which Snyder first climbed in 1945. Pristine and quiet when he first scaled it, the mountain signaled its 1980 volcanic eruption with "growl stamp-dance, quiver swell, glow."

Which memories last?

An American Childhood
by Annie Dillard

In Dillard's memoir of her childhood years, she tells of diving into experiences fearlessly and without hesitation, whether pitching, throwing snowballs, or observing the natural world. Her full engagement in life provided many rich memories.

The Woman I Kept to Myself
by Julia Alvarez

Born in the Dominican Republic, Alvarez writes poems about her past and the forces and people that helped make her what she is today. Family, friends, animals, and jobs all formed her, and she looks to her past as a way of understanding who she is now.

I Can Hear the Cowbells Ring
by Lionel G. García

These hilarious autobiographical stories describe growing up in an extended Mexican-American family in south Texas after World War II. García creates indelible portraits of his stern grandmother and eccentric aunts and uncles.

What makes a good love poem?

Sonnets from the Portuguese
by Elizabeth Barrett Browning

These 44 sonnets that Browning wrote to her husband, Robert, are considered to be classics of love poetry. They celebrate the pair's marriage and the lasting nature of true love. Included is the famous "How do I love thee? . . ."

The Radiation Sonnets
by Jane Yolen

While her husband underwent 43 days of radiation and chemotherapy for an inoperable tumor, Jane Yolen wrote a sonnet a day to express her love and her fear, as well as her anger over the threat to his life. The sonnets have been inspirational to other cancer patients and their families.

Mother Love
by Rita Dove

Dove, the former poet laureate of the United States, examines the strong tie of love between mother and daughter in these sonnets. Several explore the classical myth of Demeter and Persephone, and one of Dove's major themes is a mother's obligation to let go.

Get Novel Wise

THINK central

Go to **thinkcentral.com.**
KEYWORD: HML10-846

846

NovelWise **THINK** central

The keyword on this page points to **NovelWise**, a Web site that helps students choose a novel or other book-length work to read. **NovelWise** also provides

- study guides
- reading strategies and literary elements instruction
- presentations to introduce classic novels
- project ideas

Signatures

AUTHOR'S STYLE AND VOICE

- In 19th-Century Writing
- In 20th-Century Writing

847

INTRODUCE THE UNIT

Most people think of *signature* as a synonym for *autograph*. *Signature* also can refer to a characteristic that distinguishes a creative effort. A poet's signature could include his or her habitual choice of poetic form, type of imagery, or tone. An artist's signature could include his or her habitual choice of subject matter, lighting, or color. For example, the painting on this page is by Vincent van Gogh. Its vivid colors and rough brushstrokes are two of van Gogh's signatures. These and other signatures work together to identify van Gogh's artistic style. The photograph shows how another artist interprets the same subject of sunflowers by using another medium, signature technique, composition, and style.

Have students consider their personal signatures. Ask:

- Think about your habitual way of dressing. Then identify or name your signature style of clothing or that of someone you admire.

- Is there a visual or musical artist whose signature or overall style you like? Explain.

- How would you describe your favorite style of writing? How would you describe your own writing style?

Tell students that throughout this unit they will explore the author's style in selections written in the 19th and 20th centuries.

For help in planning this unit, see

R RESOURCE MANAGER UNIT 8
   pp. 1–10

About the Art Vincent van Gogh (1853–1890) painted *Sunflowers* in 1889. The painting is one of a series of sunflower paintings that van Gogh made to prepare for a visit from fellow artist Paul Gauguin. Van Gogh had to paint the series quickly, for the flowers rapidly faded after they were picked.

COMMON CORE STRAND	ECOS **Text Analysis Workshop: Author's Style and Voice** pp. 850–855	ECOS **The Pit and the Pendulum/ The Lake** Short Story/Poem pp. 856–877 *Lexile: 1020/N/A Fry: 7.5/N/A Dale-Chall: 7.7/N/A*	**When I Heard the Learn'd Astronomer/ The Artilleryman's Vision** Poems pp. 878–885	ECOS **Birches/Mending Wall** Poems pp. 886–893
Reading Literature	Style in Literature pp. 850–851 RL 4 Style and Voice pp. 852–853 RL 4 Analyze the Text pp. 854–855 RL 4	Poe's Style pp. 857–858, 862–864, 867, 870, 873–875 RL 4 Paraphrase pp. 857, 860, 863–864, 866, 870, 874–875 RL 1 Language Coach pp. 861, 865 RL 4 Affixes p. 872 RL 4	Whitman's Style pp. 879, 883, 885 RL 5 Analyze Sensory Details pp. 879–880, 882, 885 RL 1, RL 4 Language Coach p. 882 RL 4	Frost's Style pp. 887–892 RL 4 Make Inferences pp. 887–889, 891–892 RL 1 Writing Prompt p. 893 RL 2
Reading Informational Text			Letter p. 884	
Writing		Writing Prompt p. 877 W 9a	Quickwrite p. 878	Quickwrite p. 886 Writing Prompt p. 893 W 9a
Speaking and Listening		Discuss p. 856 SL 1		
Language		Personification pp. 866, 877 L 3 Foreign Words Used in English p. 876 L 4b		Using Verbals Effectively p. 893 L 1b

The Pond/Fourth of July Night/The Red Wheelbarrow Poems pp. 894–899	Linked Selections		Writing Workshop: Online Feature Article pp. 914–921 Technology Workshop: Updating an Online Feature Article pp. 922–923
	Only Daughter/from Caramelo Personal Essay/Fiction pp. 900–909	Author Brings Back Memories of Not So Long Ago Newspaper Column pp. 910–913	
	Lexile: 800/N/A Fry: 10/N/A Dale-Chall: 6.9/N/A	Lexile: 1240 Fry: 5 Dale-Chall: 7.4	
Imagism pp. 895–896, 899 RL 4 Visualize pp. 895, 897–899 RL 1			
	Style and Voice pp. 901, 904, 906, 908 RI 4, RI 5, RI 6 Author's Purpose pp. 901, 902, 904, 906, 908 RI 6 Imagery in Nonfiction p. 905 RI 5 Language Coach p. 905 RI 4	Characteristics of a Critique pp. 911–913 RI 1, RI 8 Tone in Nonfiction p. 912 RI 4 Language Coach p. 911 RI 4	Online Feature Article pp. 914–921 RI 1
		Writing Prompt p. 913 W 9b	Writing an Online Feature Article pp. 914–921 W 2a–f, W 4, W 5, W 6, W 7, W 8, W 9b Updating an Online Feature Article pp. 922–923 W 6
Discuss p. 894 SL 1	Discuss p. 900 SL 1		Writing an Online Feature Article pp. 914–921 SL 5 Updating an Online Feature Article pp. 922–923 SL 1c, SL 5
	Etymology p. 909 L 4c		Drafting p. 917 L 3a Editing and Publishing p. 920 L 1b, L 2

To see the complete Essential Course of Study, see pp. T23–T28.

For additional lesson planning help, see **Teacher One Stop DVD.**

Instructional Support

Resource Manager Unit 8

UNIT SUPPORT
Academic Vocabulary p. 3
Additional Academic Vocabulary p. 4
Grammar Focus p. 5
Text Analysis Workshop pp. 9–10
Writing Workshop: Online Feature
  Article p. 109

SELECTION SUPPORT*

Plan and Teach
Lesson planning pages
Additional leveled selection questions
Extension activities

Student Copy Masters
Selection summaries in four languages
Skills copy masters in English and Spanish
Vocabulary preteaching and support
Reading Check and Question Support
Reading Fluency

*Available for all selections

† Available on **thinkcentral.com**.

Language Handbook
Vocabulary Practice
Best Practices Toolkit†
PowerNotes DVD-ROM†
Connections: Nonfiction for
Common Core CD-ROM†

Teacher One Stop DVD-ROM
Student One Stop DVD-ROM
Write*Smart* CD-ROM†
GrammarNotes DVD-ROM†
WordSharp CD-ROM†

Differentiated Instruction

STRUGGLING READERS AND WRITERS	ENGLISH LANGUAGE LEARNERS	ADVANCED LEARNERS
Resource Manager Unit 8 Additional Selection Questions Question Support Reading Fluency **Interactive Reader** **Adapted Interactive Reader** **Audio Tutor** **Level Up Online Tutorials** **Audio Anthology** (with Audio summaries) **Diagnostic and Selection Tests** Selection Tests A/B	**Resource Manager Unit 8** Selection Summaries in English, Spanish, Vietnamese and Haitian Creole Skills Copymasters in Spanish **English Language Learner Adapted** **Interactive Reader Teacher's Guide** **ELL Adapted Interactive Reader** **Audio Tutor** **Guide to English for Newcomers** **Audio Anthology** **Audio Summaries in Multiple** **Languages** (on **thinkcentral.com**)	**Resource Manager Unit 8** Additional Selection Questions Ideas for Extension **Diagnostic and Selection Tests** Selection Tests B/C 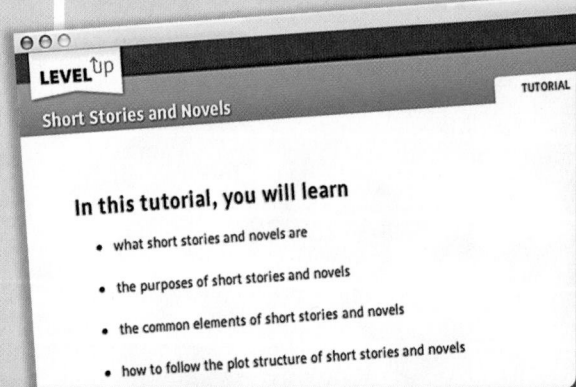

Assessment and Reteaching

Diagnostic and Selection Tests

Unit and Benchmark Tests

ThinkCentral Online Assessment:

- All program assessments
- Level Up Online Tutorials

ExamView Test Generator on the Teacher One Stop DVD-ROM

Online Essay Scoring on **thinkcentral.com**

ThinkCentral Online Reteaching:

- Level Up Online Tutorials
- Reteaching Worksheets

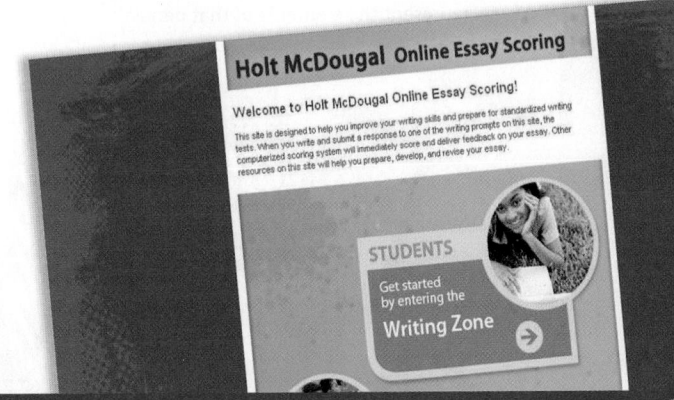

Holt McDougal Online Essay Scoring

Welcome to Holt McDougal Online Essay Scoring!

This site is designed to help you improve your writing skills and prepare for standardized writing tests. When you write and submit a response to one of the writing prompts on this site, the computerized scoring system will immediately score and deliver feedback on your essay. Other resources on this site will help you prepare, develop, and revise your essay.

STUDENTS

Get started by entering the

Writing Zone →

Professional Development

Video Center Based on interviews with program consultants and other educational experts, these videos feature classroom-ready teaching strategies.

Teacher Toolkit Includes a Teacher Handbook as well as a range of articles and handouts by program consultants and other educators.

Janet Allen

Kylene Beers

Jim Burke

Carol Jago

THINK central at a Glance

One Location, Endless Resources

Find Resources Browse all *Holt McDougal Literature* components for the ones that meet your students' needs and match your teaching style.

Assess Progress and Reteach Assign electronic versions of program assessments to measure your students' mastery of the Common Core State Standards. On thinkcentral.com, some tests deliver online remediation tutorials to students who have not mastered skills.

Interactive Whiteboard Lessons

Prepare your students for college and careers by teaching relevant, real-world skills through dynamic, interactive instruction. Go to **thinkcentral.com** to browse through all whiteboard lessons, including the following:

- Figurative Language and Imagery
- Word Choice and Tone
- Synthesizing Information

HISTORY

Together Holt McDougal and HISTORY® are revolutionizing the study of English/language arts with video that helps students relive and re-imagine the people, places, and events they are discovering through reading. Look for selections with the HISTORY® icon.

Who's got STYLE?

Introduce the question and opening paragraph. Encourage students to name figures in the media who convey a unique personal style. Start with these examples:

- the president of the United States
- a TV talk-show host
- a popular singer or rock star
- a star of action movies

Invite students to expand the list with names of celebrities with a memorable style. Have students describe the style of each celebrity they suggest. For example, the president of the United States might have a formal, official style. A rock star might have a unique or controversial style. An action-movie star might have a tough, no-nonsense style.

ACTIVITY Point out that an individual's personal style may be defined by clothing choices, speech mannerisms, writing style, or other signatures.

CHECK UNDERSTANDING Give as many students as possible the opportunity to share one element from their graphic and to explain how it is part of the person's style.

Who's got STYLE?

People in the public eye often cultivate an image that sets them apart from others. Some do it with the way they dress, others through the way they speak or act, and some with what they design or create. You recognize these people or their work by their style—that special blend of appearance, expression, and attitude that makes each person unique.

ACTIVITY Choose an individual whose personal or professional style you admire. This person could be someone you know, or a public figure such as a performer, a politician, or a businessperson. Draw a sketch or create a collage or illustration like the one shown to represent the elements of that person's style.

Find It Online! THINK central
Go to thinkcentral.com for the interactive version of this unit.

848

Unit Resources

See resources on the **Teacher One Stop DVD-ROM** *and on* thinkcentral.com.

R RESOURCE MANAGER UNIT 8

UNIT AND BENCHMARK TESTS

BEST PRACTICES TOOLKIT

INTERACTIVE READER

ADAPTED INTERACTIVE READER

ELL ADAPTED INTERACTIVE READER

LANGUAGE HANDBOOK

VOCABULARY PRACTICE

TECHNOLOGY

- Teacher One Stop DVD-ROM
- Student One Stop DVD-ROM
- PowerNotes DVD-ROM
- WriteSmart CD-ROM
- MediaSmart DVD-ROM
- GrammarNotes DVD-ROM
- Audio Anthology CD
- Audio Tutor CD

Find It Online! THINK central

The interactive version of this unit on thinkcentral.com includes

- video and **PowerNotes** introductions to key selections
- audio support—listen or download
- **ThinkAloud** models
- **WordSharp** vocabulary tutorials
- interactive review and remediation

Preview Unit Goals

TEXT ANALYSIS	• Identify elements of style, including diction, tone, and imagery • Recognize style of specific authors, including Poe, Whitman, Frost, and Cisneros
READING	• Make inferences about speaker • Identify author's purpose • Paraphrase; distinguish between a summary and a critique
WRITING AND LANGUAGE	• Write an online feature article • Incorporate quotations • Incorporate links to external sources • Use a variety of phrases
VOCABULARY	• Determine or clarify the precise meaning of foreign words used in English • Use a dictionary to determine or clarify a word's etymology
ACADEMIC VOCABULARY	• clarify • style • feature • transmit • precise
MEDIA AND VIEWING	• Update on online feature article

849

Complete text of the Common Core Standards is found in the correlation on pp. T10–T22. Standards covered in this unit are found in the overview (pp. 847A–847B) and on he lesson pages where they are taught.

Preview Unit Goals

The goals on this page present an overview of this unit's skills and strategies. Urge students to familiarize themselves with the goals as they prepare for the unit. Remind students that the colors for each skill strand create a code that students can track throughout the unit.

Draw students' attention to the Academic Vocabulary at the bottom of the page. Ask students to define familiar terms. Then have them record all the terms in their **Reader/ Writer Notebooks**, using a dictionary to help them define new terms. Encourage students to return to the definitions throughout Unit 8 as needed and to reinforce their understanding by using the terms as they discuss and write about the selections.

DIFFERENTIATED INSTRUCTION

FOR ENGLISH LANGUAGE LEARNERS

Academic Vocabulary Provide students with definitions of each Academic Vocabulary word.

clarify (klăr′ə fī′) *v.* to make clear or easier to understand

feature (fē′chər) *n.* a special quality or characteristic of something

precise (prē sīs′) *adj.* exact; accurately defined or stated

style (stīl) *n.* a distinctive or original manner of expression

transmit (trans mit′) *v.* to communicate; to send or hand off to others

Use the copy master to help students learn academic words they will use in this unit and on the Assessment Practice.

R RESOURCE MANAGER—Copy Masters
Academic Vocabulary p. 3
Additional Academic Vocabulary p. 4

849

RL 4 Determine the meaning of words and phrases as they are used in a text; analyze the cumulative impact of specific word choices on meaning and tone.

Teach

Part 1: Style in Literature

Style of an Individual Ask students to discuss how Ernest Hemingway's career as a reporter may have influenced his fiction writing. Students should be able to point out that his short, solid sentences reflect a journalistic quality. He also uses simple nouns and verbs to capture scenes or emotions directly.

Style of a Time Period Have students brainstorm a list of adjectives that can apply to style, such as *scientific, pompous, informal, grim, playful, ornate*. Give students a short passage from a newspaper, a fairy tale, or a selection from the previous unit. Have them "translate" the passage into another style such as the Hemingway journalistic style or the elaborate Victorian style shown here. Once students have shared their translations, discuss how audience and time period can influence the way writers convey information.

🧰 **BEST PRACTICES TOOLKIT—Transparency**
Analysis Frame: Author's Craft pp. D21, D24

Author's Style and Voice
Essential Course of Study **ECOS**

Jane Austen, Edgar Allan Poe, and Maya Angelou—why do works by authors such as these continue to captivate generations of readers? Not only have these authors crafted compelling stories, but they have expressed themselves in such individual, memorable ways. Austen's witty observations of society, Poe's dark tales of terror, and Angelou's deeply personal anecdotes all leave lasting impressions largely because of each author's distinctive style.

COMMON CORE

Included in this workshop:
RL 4 Determine the meaning of words and phrases as they are used in a text; analyze the cumulative impact of specific word choices on meaning and tone.

Part 1: Style in Literature

Style refers to the way a work of literature is written—not what is said, but *how* it is said. The "how" depends on many elements, including a writer's tone, sentence structures, and language. In the first example shown, notice how Ernest Hemingway's direct, journalistic style results from his use of simple words and sentences, among other elements.

Distinctive styles extend beyond individual writers, however. Sometimes writing produced during a particular time period, such as 19th-century England, has a recognizable style, as you'll notice in the second example.

STYLE OF AN INDIVIDUAL	STYLE OF A TIME PERIOD
Ernest Hemingway  Hemingway, who wrote during the 20th century, is known for his simple style. He avoided flowery language in favor of no-frills storytelling and short sentences.	**Victorian England**  Much of the writing produced in 19th-century England has an elaborate, formal style. Sentences are complex, and the vocabulary is sophisticated.
▼	▼
Example "Don't talk about the war," I said. The war was a long way away. Maybe there wasn't any war. There was no war here. Then I realized it was over for me. But I did not have the feeling that it was really over. —from *A Farewell to Arms*	**Example** Anyone who had looked at him as the red light shone upon his pale face, strange straining eyes, and meager form, would perhaps have understood the mixture of contemptuous pity, dread, and suspicion with which he was regarded by his neighbors. . . . —from *Silas Marner* by George Eliot
▼	▼
Characteristics of Hemingway's Style <ul><li>everyday words and sparse details</li><li>simple sentence structures</li><li>informal tone</li><li>matter-of-fact descriptions of characters' feelings</li></ul>	**Characteristics of Victorian Style** <ul><li>elevated language and vivid imagery</li><li>complex sentence structures</li><li>formal tone</li><li>involved focus on the narrator's and characters' observations and thoughts</li></ul>

DIFFERENTIATED INSTRUCTION

FOR STRUGGLING READERS

Note Taking For students who need help with note taking, hand out the note-taking copy master before discussing **Part 1: Style in Literature.** As you discuss the main points of the section, have students record them on the copy master.

🅡 **RESOURCE MANAGER—Copy Master**
Note Taking p. 9

MODEL 1: STYLE OF AN INDIVIDUAL

Now that you have learned the characteristics of Hemingway's style and have read a passage from *A Farewell to Arms*, examine this excerpt from one of his short stories.

from BIG TWO-HEARTED RIVER

Short story by **Ernest Hemingway**

Nick was hungry. He did not believe he had ever been hungrier. He opened and emptied a can of pork and beans and a can of spaghetti into the frying pan.

"I've got a right to eat this kind of stuff, if I'm willing to carry it," Nick said. His voice sounded strange in the darkening woods. He did not speak again.

5　He started a fire with some chunks of pine he got with the ax from a stump. Over the fire he stuck a wire grill, pushing the four legs down into the ground with his boot. Nick put the frying pan on the grill over the flames. He was hungrier. The beans and spaghetti warmed. Nick stirred them and mixed them together.

Close Read

1. Identify two characteristics of Hemingway's style that are evident in the boxed text.

2. Compare the excerpt from *A Farewell to Arms* with this one. What is the most striking stylistic similarity between them? Explain.

MODEL 2: STYLE OF A TIME PERIOD

Like George Eliot, Emily Brontë wrote in the sophisticated, ornate style that characterizes 19th-century English literature. In this excerpt from one of Brontë's novels, the narrator visits the estate of his landlord, Heathcliff.

from *Wuthering Heights*

Novel by **Emily Brontë**

Yesterday afternoon set in misty and cold. I had half a mind to spend it by my study fire, instead of wading through heath and mud to Wuthering Heights. On coming up from dinner, however, (N.B.[1]—I dine between twelve and one o'clock; the housekeeper, a matronly lady, taken as a fixture along with

5　the house, could not, or would not, comprehend my request that I might be served at five)—on mounting the stairs with this lazy intention, and stepping into the room, I saw a servant-girl on her knees surrounded by brushes and coal-scuttles, and raising an infernal dust as she extinguished the flames with heaps of cinders. This spectacle drove me back immediately; I took my hat,

10　and, after a four-miles' walk, arrived at Heathcliff's garden-gate just in time to escape the first feathery flakes of a snow-shower.

1. **N.B.:** an abbreviation of the Latin *nota bene*, "take notice."

Close Read

1. In what ways do Brontë's sentences—especially the one in the box—differ from Hemingway's?

2. Identify two stylistic similarities between Brontë's writing here and Eliot's writing in the excerpt from *Silas Marner* on the preceding page.

MODEL 1: STYLE OF AN INDIVIDUAL

Close Read

1. ***Possible answers:*** *Hemingway uses short and simple sentences. The vocabulary is plain and not overly descriptive, containing few adjectives and adverbs. These characteristics create a deceptively simple style.*

2. ***Possible answer:*** *The most striking similarity between the two Hemingway examples is the use of repetition. Both examples repeat words and phrases in short, simple sentences. This creates abrupt, matter-of-fact descriptions.*

MODEL 2: STYLE OF A TIME PERIOD

Close Read

1. ***Possible answer:*** *Brontë's sentences tend to be long and complex. The boxed text, for example, contains an aside separated with dashes, and several components separated by commas.*

2. ***Possible answers:*** *Both selections have sophisticated vocabulary ("contemptuous pity" in* Silas Marner *and "infernal dust" in* Wuthering Heights, *line 8). Both have long, complex sentence structures and vivid imagery ("his pale face, strange straining eyes, and meager form" in* Silas Marner *and "the first feathery flakes of a snow-shower" in* Wuthering Heights, *line 11). Both excerpts exhibit a formal, reserved style of writing ("with which he was regarded" in* Silas Marner *and "on mounting the stairs with this lazy intention" in* Wuthering Heights, *line 6).*

FOR STRUGGLING READERS

Explore Style To help students understand the concept of style, lead a class discussion about fashion or music styles. Have students brainstorm styles of clothing (such as formal, casual, preppy, athletic, hip-hop) or music (such as classical, country western, rock and roll, heavy metal, jazz, blues).

FOR ADVANCED LEARNERS/PRE–AP

Synthesize Style Give students a sentence from Model 1, such as "Nick was hungry," and have them brainstorm other ways of conveying the same information in words. Have students share their ideas. Point out that the styles they each selected—informal, simple, scientific—influence how an audience interprets the information.

THINK central

Online Remediation

Are your students struggling with text analysis skills? Consider assigning them one or more **Level Up Online Tutorials** as remediation before beginning this unit. Log in to **thinkcentral.com** to view a list of the skills addressed by **Level Up**.

Teach

Part 2: Style and Voice

Diction Tell students that there are many ways to evaluate a writer's word choice. One way to tell that diction is *appropriate* is if it is suited to the writer's topic and audience. For example, the diction in a magazine article aimed at teenagers will likely be informal. An explanation of tax codes designed for accountants is likely to use formal, mathematical language.

Voice and Tone Point out to students that it is the combination of voice and tone that gives a piece of writing its personality, distinction, and appeal. When the writer conveys strong feelings about the topic and audience, the reader feels an important connection with the writer and the writing. Ask students which of the two authors, Hawthorne or Naylor, appeals more to them. What are the reasons for the connections they feel?

CHECK UNDERSTANDING

Have students write their own definitions of diction, style, and voice.

Part 2: Style and Voice

You've started to consider how elements such as sentence structure and word choice help to create style. A closer look at the unique blend of three other key elements—**diction, tone,** and **imagery**—will help you to compare writing styles. You will also grasp how these elements contribute to a writer's or narrator's **voice**—the personality that comes across on the page.

Here, notice how diction, tone, and imagery help to distinguish Nathaniel Hawthorne's formal, ornate style from Gloria Naylor's playfully informal one.

COMPARING STYLES

She had dark and abundant hair, so glossy that it threw off the sunshine with a gleam, and a face which, besides being beautiful from regularity of feature and richness of complexion, had the impressiveness belonging to a marked brow and deep black eyes.

—from *The Scarlet Letter* by Nathaniel Hawthorne

She loaded that baby down with every name in the book: Charles Somebody Harrison Somebody-Else Duvall. We called him Chick. That's what he looked like, toddling around: little pecan head sitting on a scrawny neck, two bright buttons for eyes, and a feathery mess of hair she couldn't keep slicked down for nothing.

—from *Mama Day* by Gloria Naylor

DICTION

Diction includes both a writer's choice of words and his or her **syntax,** or arrangement of words into sentences. Hawthorne's formal style comes from his use of elevated vocabulary ("abundant hair"), complex phrases ("richness of complexion" rather than "great skin"), and long sentences. In contrast, Naylor's use of informal language, such as "slicked down for nothing," creates a conversational style.

TONE

Tone is a writer's attitude toward a subject, as expressed through choice of words and details. Naylor establishes a playful tone in her description of Chick's real name: "Charles Somebody Harrison Somebody-Else Duvall." Naylor's tone also helps readers to "hear" the no-nonsense voice of the narrator. Hawthorne's elegant diction, however, conveys a formal tone and style.

IMAGERY

You already know that **imagery** consists of words and phrases that re-create sensory experiences for readers. "Abundant hair, so glossy that it threw off the sunshine with a gleam" and "little pecan head"—image-laden descriptions like these are signatures of both Hawthorne's and Naylor's styles. The *kinds* of images the writers include, though, dramatically set their styles apart.

DIFFERENTIATED INSTRUCTION

FOR STRUGGLING READERS

Note Taking For students who need help, hand out the note-taking copy master before discussing **Part 2.** As you cover each element of style and voice, have students summarize main ideas. Later, have them list examples of each element.

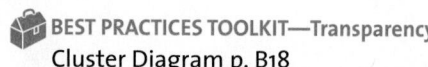 **RESOURCE MANAGER—Copy Master**
Note Taking p. 10

FOR ENGLISH LANGUAGE LEARNERS

Language: Skill Words To help students understand the impact of word choice, have them choose a noun, verb, or adjective from the Hawthorne or Naylor passage and write it in the center of a Cluster Diagram. In the surrounding circles, students should write how the word makes them feel, include similar words, and give a reason for why the author used the word.

BEST PRACTICES TOOLKIT—Transparency
Cluster Diagram p. B18

MODEL 1: ELEMENTS OF STYLE

Jamaica Kincaid's writing is rich with images that evoke the settings she describes. In this excerpt from one of Kincaid's novels, the narrator is leaving her home on the island of Antigua. As she rides a launch to her ship, she is overcome with emotion.

from
A WALK TO THE JETTY
from Annie John
Novel by **Jamaica Kincaid**

. . . My heart shriveled up and the words "I shall never see this again" stabbed at me. I don't know what stopped me from falling in a heap at my parents' feet.

When we were all on board, the launch headed out to sea. Away from the
5   jetty, the water became the customary blue, and the launch left a wide path in it that looked like a road. I passed by sounds and smells that were so familiar that I had long ago stopped paying any attention to them. But now here they were, and the ever-present "I shall never see this again" bobbed up and down inside me. There was the sound of the seagull diving down into the water and
10 coming up with something silverish in its mouth. There was the smell of the sea and the sight of small pieces of rubbish floating around in it.

Close Read

1. Identify two images that allow you to visualize the setting.

2. Reread the boxed details, noting such words as *stabbed* and *bobbed*. What does Kincaid's unique diction tell you about the narrator?

3. Would you describe Kincaid's tone as sympathetic or harsh? Explain your answer.

MODEL 2: ELEMENTS OF STYLE

Here, David Copperfield, the narrator of Charles Dickens's classic novel, reflects on an exciting time in his childhood—when he was preparing to leave *his* home. As you read, pay attention to the stylistic elements that help distinguish Dickens's writing from Kincaid's.

from
David Copperfield
Novel by **Charles Dickens**

The day soon came for our going. It was such an early day that it came soon, even to me, who was in a fever of expectation, and half afraid that an earthquake or a fiery mountain, or some other great convulsion of nature, might interpose to stop the expedition. We were to go in a carrier's cart, which
5   departed in the morning after breakfast. I would have given any money to have been allowed to wrap myself up overnight, and sleep in my hat and boots.

It touches me nearly now, although I tell it lightly, to recollect how eager I was to leave my happy home; to think how little I suspected what I did leave for ever.

Close Read

1. Consider Dickens's formal, dramatic diction, particularly evident in the boxed phrases. Through this stylistic element, what do you learn about young David?

2. What is the greatest difference between Kincaid's and Dickens's styles? Explain.

MODEL 1: ELEMENTS OF STYLE
Close Read

1. *Possible answer: Readers can visualize the setting with images such as "Away from the jetty, the water became the customary blue" (lines 4–5), "the sound of the seagull diving down . . . something silverish in its mouth" (lines 9–10), "the smell of the sea" (lines 10–11), and "the sight of small pieces of rubbish floating around in it" (line 11).*

2. *Possible answer: Kincaid's diction helps convey her narrator's emotional state. The diction emphasizes just how heartbroken the narrator is about leaving her home. Words like "stabbed," "bobbed," and "shriveled" give readers a physical sense of the narrator's emotional pain.*

3. *Possible answer: Kincaid's tone is sympathetic. Tenderness and understanding toward the narrator's feelings are shown in phrases such as "My heart shriveled up" and "'I shall never see this again.'" Kincaid's sympathy is also evident in her descriptions of the special things that the narrator will miss about her homeland.*

MODEL 2: ELEMENTS OF STYLE
Close Read

1. *Possible answer: Dickens's formal, dramatic diction emphasizes the emotional intensity that young David is feeling. The boxed phrases indicate David's dramatic tendency to experience each situation in an extreme way.*

2. *Possible answer: One major difference between Kincaid and Dickens is their diction. Kincaid chooses precise, colorful words such as "something silverish in its mouth" (line 10), while Dickens chooses more formal words and ornate sentence structures, such as "might interpose to stop the expedition" (line 4).*

DIFFERENTIATED INSTRUCTION

FOR STRUGGLING READERS

Analysis Support Give students a four-column chart and have them label each column with these heads: *Line/Page, Quotation, Element (tone, sentence structure, diction, or imagery),* and *Effect on Meaning.* Help students complete the first column using the example of *Wuthering Heights: line 1/"half a mind"/tone/informal.* Students can use the chart to analyze some or all of the models in the workshop.

FOR ENGLISH LANGUAGE LEARNERS

Vocabulary: Idioms Use New Word Analysis to teach these idioms from the Kincaid model: *My heart shriveled up* (line 1), "I felt sad"; *stabbed at me* (line 2), "hurt me"; *ever-present* (line 8), "familiar"; *bobbed up and down inside me* (lines 8–9), "kept coming into my mind."

Practice and Apply

Part 3: Analyze the Text

Close Read

1. **Possible answer:** *Austen's tone toward Emma's predicament seems gently mocking rather then completely serious. By including such details as "The hair was curled, and the maid sent away, and Emma sat down to think and be miserable" (lines 1–2), Austen seems to suggest that Emma's problem is not as serious as she thinks it is.*

2. **Possible answer:** *Austen's diction mixes complex vocabulary with informal sentences and even incomplete sentences. Repetition and parallel constructions such as "Such an overthrow" (line 2), "Such a development" (line 3), "Such a blow" (line 4), and "more mistaken—more in error—more disgraced" (line 7) emphasize how distraught Emma is. She replays the unfortunate incident in her mind, trying to find what went wrong.*

3. **Possible answer:** *Austen's use of dashes and exclamation points suggest that Emma is an emotional person who is caught up in a drama of the moment. Also, the dashes suggest a string of quick thoughts running through the character's head. This makes Emma seem like someone who has trouble focusing on a single thought.*

Part 3: Analyze the Text

Apply what you now know about style as you analyze these two excerpts. Each describes a connection between three people, one of whom will end up disappointed and unlucky in love.

This excerpt is taken from Jane Austen's novel *Emma*. Austen, who wrote during the early 19th century, is known for her ironic, amused observations of middle-class society in England. Here, Emma bemoans her foiled attempt to pair the sought-after Mr. Elton with her friend Harriet. Mr. Elton has fallen for Emma instead.

> *from*
> # Emma
> Novel by **Jane Austen**
>
> The hair was curled, and the maid sent away, and Emma sat down to think and be miserable.—It was a wretched business, indeed!—Such an overthrow of every thing she had been wishing for!—Such a development of every thing most unwelcome!—Such a blow for Harriet!—That was the worst of all. Every
> 5 part of it brought pain and humiliation, of some sort or other; but, compared with the evil to Harriet, all was light; and she would gladly have submitted to feel yet more mistaken—more in error—more disgraced by mis-judgment, than she actually was, could the effects of her blunders have been confined to herself.
> "If I had not persuaded Harriet into liking the man, I could have born any
> 10 thing. He might have doubled his presumption to me—But poor Harriet!"
> How she could have been so deceived!—He protested that he had never thought seriously of Harriet—never! She looked back as well as she could; but it was all confusion. She had taken up the idea, she supposed, and made every thing bend to it. His manners, however, must have been unmarked, wavering,
> 15 dubious, or she could not have been so misled.

Close Read

1. Consider the tone Austen uses to describe Emma's predicament. Is it mocking or serious? Support your answer.

2. Describe Austen's diction, citing details in the boxed text. What does her diction help to emphasize about Emma's current state of mind?

3. Austen's use of dashes and exclamation points helps to suggest Emma's personality and manner. What does this stylistic element tell you about the kind of person Emma is?

DIFFERENTIATED INSTRUCTION

FOR STRUGGLING READERS

Analysis Support: Sentence Structure and Tone To help students understand how punctuation such as Austen's dashes can affect style and tone, write this sentence on the board: *"The red jacket is mine," said Greg.* Then add a dash and an exclamation point: *"The red jacket is—mine!" said Greg.* Ask students to discuss how the additions change the tone of the sentence.

Possible answer: *The dash and exclamation indicate Greg's surprise in realizing the jacket is his. In the original statement, Greg is quietly or flatly identifying the jacket as his own.*

F. Scott Fitzgerald lived and wrote more than a century after Austen. Like Austen, he was a keen observer and recorder of society's manners and constraints. Though the authors explored similar subjects, their writing styles differed dramatically. As you read this excerpt from a short story by Fitzgerald, notice the stylistic elements that help to create this difference.

from

BERNICE BOBS HER HAIR

Short story by **F. Scott Fitzgerald**

Warren, who had grown up across the street from Marjorie, had long been "crazy about her." Sometimes she seemed to reciprocate his feeling with a faint gratitude, but she had tried him by her infallible test and informed him gravely that she did not love him. Her test was that when she was away from him she

5 forgot him and had affairs with other boys. Warren found this discouraging, especially as Marjorie had been making little trips all summer, and for the first two or three days after each arrival home he saw great heaps of mail on the Harveys' hall table addressed to her in various masculine handwritings. To make matters worse, all during the month of August she had been visited by her

10 cousin Bernice from Eau Claire, and it seemed impossible to see her alone. It was always necessary to hunt round and find some one to take care of Bernice. As August waned this was becoming more and more difficult.

Much as Warren worshiped Marjorie, he had to admit that Cousin Bernice was sorta dopeless. She was pretty, with dark hair and high color, but she was no

15 fun on a party. Every Saturday night he danced a long arduous duty dance with her to please Marjorie, but he had never been anything but bored in her company.

"Warren"—a soft voice at his elbow broke in upon his thoughts, and he turned to see Marjorie, flushed and radiant as usual. She laid a hand on his shoulder and a glow settled almost imperceptibly over him.

20 "Warren," she whispered, "do something for me—dance with Bernice. She's been stuck with little Otis Ormonde for almost an hour."

Warren's glow faded.

"Why—sure," he answered half-heartedly.

Close Read

1. Reread lines 1–8. In your opinion, is the writer's tone mocking or sympathetic toward the emotions and attitudes of young people in (and out of) love?

2. Through the boxed image, Fitzgerald helps readers to understand Warren's feeling of disappointment. Identify two more images.

3. Describe Fitzgerald's style, explaining whether you see any similarities between his writing and Austen's.

TEXT ANALYSIS WORKSHOP **855**

Close Read

1. *Possible answer: The writer's tone is both sympathetic and mocking toward the emotions and attitudes of young people in love. He indicates his understanding that Marjorie's unavailability during her cousin's long visit is hard for Warren. By using understatement in the phrase "Warren found this discouraging" (line 5), Fitzgerald pokes fun at Warren's slightly dense assessment of the situation.*

2. *Possible answer: Other images that show Warren's feelings are "long arduous duty dance" (line 15), "Warren's glow faded" (line 22), and "answered half-heartedly" (line 23).*

3. *Possible answer: Fitzgerald's style is generally looser and more informal than Austen's. Expressions such as "crazy about her" (line 2) and "sorta dopeless" (line 14) are slang and suggest diction typical of casual conversation. This is strikingly different from Austen's formal diction in "It was a wretched business, indeed!" (line 2). The only real similarity between the style of the two authors is the slightly mocking tone both use to describe the predicaments of their characters.*

Assess and Reteach

Assess

Have students describe the style in the excerpt from *Emma*, identifying the tone, diction, and imagery of the writing.

Reteach

For students who are unable to apply the workshop skills to the excerpt from *Emma*, select from these reteaching options:

1. Review with them the note-taking copy masters for this lesson. Confirm that students understand and can identify the terms *tone*, *diction*, and *imagery*.

2. Direct students back to the models on pages 851 and 853. Have them work in groups to describe the style of each, and to identify tone, diction, and imagery.

FOR STRUGGLING READERS

Vocabulary Support List context clues and help students use them to define these words from the Fitzgerald model:

- *reciprocate* (line 2), "feel in return"
- *infallible* (line 3), "certain not to fail"
- *waned* (line 12), "drew to an end"
- *arduous* (line 15), "requiring hard work"
- *imperceptibly* (line 19), "unnoticeably"

Next, construct accessible sentence starters ending in a semicolon and a write-on line for students' clarifying sentence:

Each year glaciers shrink imperceptibly;

_____.

Students can show that they know what *imperceptibly* means by completing the sentence with, for example, "only special measuring devices can tell how much glaciers shrink per year."

RL 1 Cite strong and thorough textual evidence to support inferences drawn from the text.
RL 4 Determine the meaning of words and phrases as they are used in a text; analyze the cumulative impact of specific word choices on meaning and tone. **W 9a** Draw evidence from literary texts to support analysis. **L 3** Apply knowledge of language to make effective choices for meaning or style. **L 4b** Consult reference materials to determine or clarify a word's meaning.

SUMMARIES

"The Pit and the Pendulum" A prisoner of the Spanish Inquisition is trapped in a dungeon. He escapes a pit and a pendulum to discover that his cell walls are closing in around him. At last, the French army saves him.

"The Lake" In this poem, the speaker describes a remote and frightening lake.

What breeds
TERROR?

Pose the question. After students complete the *DISCUSS* activity, ask a volunteer to summarize the results.

Before Reading

Essential Course of Study **ECOS**

The Pit and the Pendulum
Short Story by Edgar Allan Poe

Video link at
thinkcentral.com

The Lake
Poem by Edgar Allan Poe

VIDEO TRAILER THINK central KEYWORD: HML10-856

What breeds
TERROR?

COMMON CORE

RL 1 Cite strong and thorough textual evidence to support inferences drawn from the text.
RL 4 Determine the meaning of words and phrases as they are used in a text; analyze the cumulative impact of specific word choices on meaning and tone.

What causes your heart to race and your palms to sweat? Perhaps it's a deserted alley, a snarling dog, or a shadowy stranger. In the following selections by Edgar Allan Poe, you will read about both the physical and the psychological effects of fear.

DISCUSS With a large group, categorize the things that terrify people. What distinguishes the fear of snakes from the fear of being buried alive, for example? What categories do you come up with?

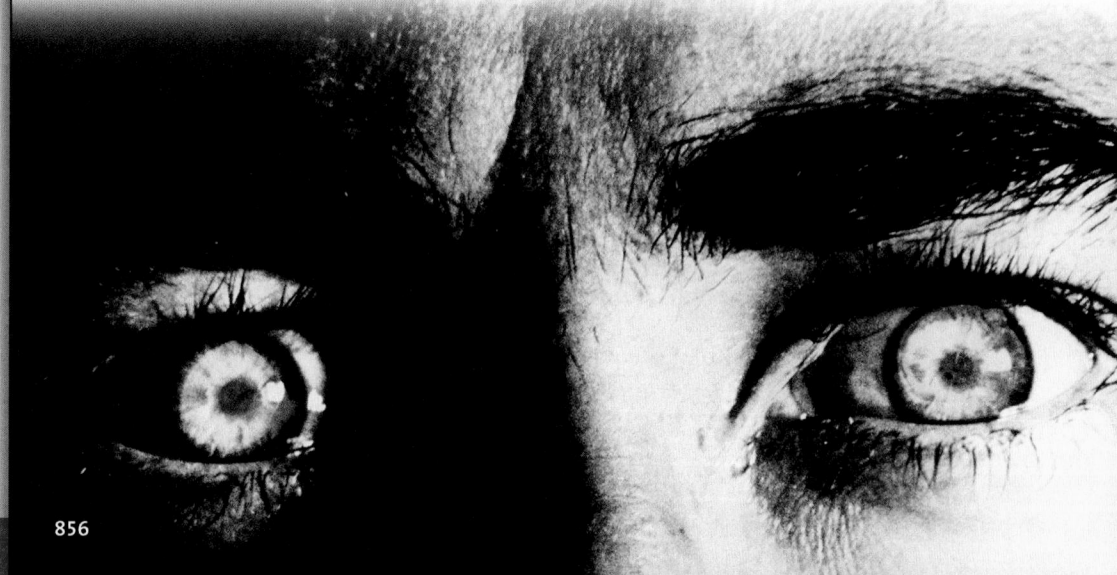

856

See resources on the **Teacher One Stop DVD-ROM** *and on* **thinkcentral.com**.

Video link at
HISTORY thinkcentral.com

 **RESOURCE MANAGER UNIT 8**
Plan and Teach, pp. 11–18
Summary, pp. 19–20†‡*
Text Analysis and Reading
  Skill, pp. 21–24†*
Vocabulary, pp. 25–27*
Grammar and Style, p. 30

**DIAGNOSTIC AND SELECTION
  TESTS**
Selection Tests, pp. 243–246

BEST PRACTICES TOOLKIT
Two-Column Chart, p. A25
Word Questioning, p. E9
Draw It, p. A2
Whip Around, p. B1

INTERACTIVE READER

ADAPTED INTERACTIVE READER

ELL ADAPTED INTERACTIVE READER

TECHNOLOGY
- **Teacher One Stop DVD-ROM**
- **Student One Stop DVD-ROM**
- **PowerNotes DVD-ROM**
- **Audio Anthology CD**
- **GrammarNotes DVD-ROM**
- **Audio Tutor CD**
- **ExamView Test Generator**
  on the **Teacher One Stop**

THINK central

Video Trailer

Go to **thinkcentral.com** to preview the **Video Trailer** introducing this selection. Other features that support the selection include
- **PowerNotes** presentation
- **ThinkAloud** models to enhance comprehension
- **WordSharp** vocabulary tutorials
- interactive writing and grammar instruction

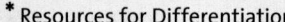 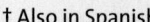

TEXT ANALYSIS: POE'S STYLE

A writer's **style** is the particular way he or she uses language to communicate ideas. Some writers are famous for their distinctive, innovative styles. This is true of Edgar Allan Poe, whose dark, suspenseful works helped create the genre of modern horror literature. The following characteristics frequently mark his style:

- a **first-person point of view** in which the narrator expresses emotional intensity, creating a **tone** of horror and terror
- repeated or italicized words
- unusual choice of words, phrases, and expressions
- long sentences or sentences with interruptions
- strange or grotesque **sensory images**

As you read, think about how Poe's choice of a narrator affects the tone of the work.

READING STRATEGY: PARAPHRASE

Poe's works can be challenging because they often feature unfamiliar words and complex sentences. One way that you can make sense of his writing as you read is to **paraphrase,** or restate information in your own words. A paraphrase is usually the same length as the original text but contains simpler language.

Poe's Words	Paraphrase
"Very suddenly there came back to my soul motion and sound...." (line 66)	I very quickly regained consciousness and was able to see and hear.

***Review:* Make Inferences**

▲ VOCABULARY IN CONTEXT

Many of Poe's words may seem unusual or old-fashioned. Review the list, noting any familiar roots, prefixes, or suffixes that might help you unlock the meanings of these words.

WORD LIST	confound	lethargy	pervade
	eloquent	lucid	supposition
	indeterminate	pertinacity	voracity
	insuperable		

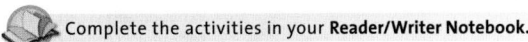

Complete the activities in your **Reader/Writer Notebook.**

Meet the Author

Edgar Allan Poe
1809–1849

Living a Nightmare
Edgar Allan Poe was born in Boston, the son of traveling actors. Following Poe's birth, his father deserted the family, and his mother moved to Virginia. She died in 1811, shortly after the move. An orphan, Poe was raised by his mother's friend Frances Allan and her husband, John, a merchant. In 1831, after brief studies at the University of Virginia and West Point, Poe, 21, sought work as a writer. Allan did not approve of Poe's literary ambitions and, in time, severed all ties with his foster son.

A Valuable Legacy
The 1845 publication of his eerie poem "The Raven" made Poe famous. His success, however, was soon marred by personal tragedy. In 1847, his wife, Virginia, fell victim to tuberculosis. Two years later, at, the age of 40, Poe himself grew ill and died. Although Poe's life was brief, his contribution to literature was great. He is widely credited with the invention of modern horror and detective literature.

BACKGROUND TO THE STORY

Tortured Times
"The Pit and the Pendulum" is set in the Spanish city of Toledo during the grim age of the Spanish Inquisition. Since the Middle Ages, the Roman Catholic Church had authorized priests to try heretics—people who opposed the teachings of the church. The priests, or inquisitors, frequently misused their power. Some suspects were tortured, and those found guilty were often executed at elaborate public ceremonies called *autos-da-fé.*

Author Online
THINK central
Go to **thinkcentral.com.**
KEYWORD: HML10-857

857

Teach

TEXT ANALYSIS   COMMON CORE
RL 4

● *Model the Skill:* POE'S STYLE

Share this sentence by Poe:

> After this I call to mind flatness and dampness; and all that is *madness*—the madness of a memory which busies itself among forbidden things.

Then identify elements in this passage that reflect Poe's writing style. Point out the first-person point of view, which contributes to tone; repetition ("madness"); italics; unusual phrase ("memory which busies itself"); a long, interrupted sentence; and a strange sensory image ("I call to mind flatness and dampness").

GUIDED PRACTICE Ask students to write a sentence or two that elicits terror, using a style like Poe's.

READING STRATEGY   COMMON CORE
RL 1

■ *Model the Skill:* PARAPHRASE

Write this sentence on the board:

> Despite his benevolent air, my interrogator proved to be, like the shearling wolf, a duplicitous fiend.

Then restate the sentence:

> Despite his kind manner, my questioner turned out to be a deceitful monster.

GUIDED PRACTICE Have students paraphrase an example of formal language.

R RESOURCE MANAGER—Copy Master
Paraphrase p. 23

VOCABULARY SKILL

▲ VOCABULARY IN CONTEXT

DIAGNOSE WORD KNOWLEDGE Have all students complete Vocabulary in Context. Check their definitions against the following:

confound (kən-found') *v.* to confuse or astonish
eloquent (ĕl'ə-kwənt) *adj.* vividly expressive
indeterminate (ĭn'dĭ-tûr'mə-nĭt) *adj.* not precisely known or determined
insuperable (ĭn-soo'pər-ə-bəl) *adj.* impossible to overcome
lethargy (lĕth'ər-jē) *n.* prolonged sluggishness;

unconsciousness
lucid (loo'sĭd) *adj.* clear; mentally sound
pertinacity (pûr'tn-ăs'ĭ-tē) *n.* unyielding persistence or adherence
pervade (pər-vād') *v.* to spread throughout
supposition (sŭp'ə-zĭsh'ən) *n.* something supposed; an assumption
voracity (vô-răs'ĭ-tē) *n.* greed for food

PRETEACH VOCABULARY Use the following copy master to help students predict meanings for each boldfaced word.

COMMON CORE
L 4

R RESOURCE MANAGER—Copy Master
Vocabulary Study p. 25

TEXT ANALYSIS	COMMON CORE RL 4

 Model the Skill: POE'S STYLE

To model how to determine characteristics of Poe's style, identify examples of repeated words and dashes. Record these examples in a Two-Column Chart drawn on the board.

Repeated Words	Dashes
sick (line 1)	line 1
sentence (line 3)	line 3
saw (line 8)	line 6

 BEST PRACTICES TOOLKIT—Transparency
Two-Column Chart p. A25

Possible answer: *Repeated words and dashes (lines 1, 3, 6, 9–11) reveal that the narrator is agitated and almost delirious.*

VOCABULARY	COMMON CORE L 4

OWN THE WORD

indeterminate: Have students explain or paraphrase the sentence in lines 4–5 to show they understand the use of *indeterminate* to describe the voices. **Possible answer:** *The voices merged together so that each individual voice could not be heard.*

The Pit and the Pendulum

Edgar Allan Poe

*Impia tortorum longos hic turba furores
Sanguinis innocui, non satiata, aluit.
Sospite nunc patriâ, fracto nunc funeris antro,
Mors ubi dira fuit vita salusque patent.*[1]

[Quatrain composed for the gates of a market to be erected upon the site of the Jacobin[2] Club House at Paris.]

I was sick—sick unto death with that long agony; and when they at length unbound me, and I was permitted to sit, I felt that my senses were leaving me. The sentence—the dread sentence of death—was the last of distinct accentuation which reached my ears. After that, the sound of the inquisitorial voices seemed merged in one dreamy **indeterminate** hum. It conveyed to my soul the idea of *revolution*—perhaps from its association in fancy with the burr of a millwheel. This only for a brief period; for presently I heard no more. Yet, for a while, I saw; but with how terrible an exaggeration! I saw the lips of the black-robed judges. They appeared to me white—whiter than the
10 sheet upon which I trace these words—and thin even to grotesqueness; thin with the intensity of their expression of firmness—of immoveable resolution—of stern contempt of human torture. I saw that the decrees of what to me was Fate, were still issuing from those lips. I saw them writhe with a deadly locution.[3]
I saw them fashion the syllables of my name; and I shuddered because no sound succeeded. I saw, too, for a few moments of delirious horror, the soft and nearly imperceptible waving of the sable draperies which enwrapped the walls of the apartment.[4] And then my vision fell upon the seven tall candles upon the table. At first they wore the aspect of charity, and seemed white

① Targeted Passage

indeterminate
(ĭn′dĭ-tûr′mə-nĭt) *adj.*
not precisely known or determined

Ⓐ POE'S STYLE
Reread lines 1–13, noting Poe's use of **repeated words** and **dashes**. What do these reveal about the narrator's state of mind?

---

1. **Impia . . . patent** *Latin:* Here the wicked crowd of tormentors, unsated, fed their long-time lusts for innocent blood. Now that our homeland is safe, now that the tomb is broken, life and health appear where once was dread death.
2. **Jacobin** (jăk′ə-bĭn): belonging to a radical French political group famous for its terrorist policies during the French Revolution.
3. **locution** (lō-kyōo′shən): speech.
4. **apartment:** room.

Analyze Visuals ▶

What details create the frightening **mood** of this illustration?

Illustrations © Cliff Nielson.

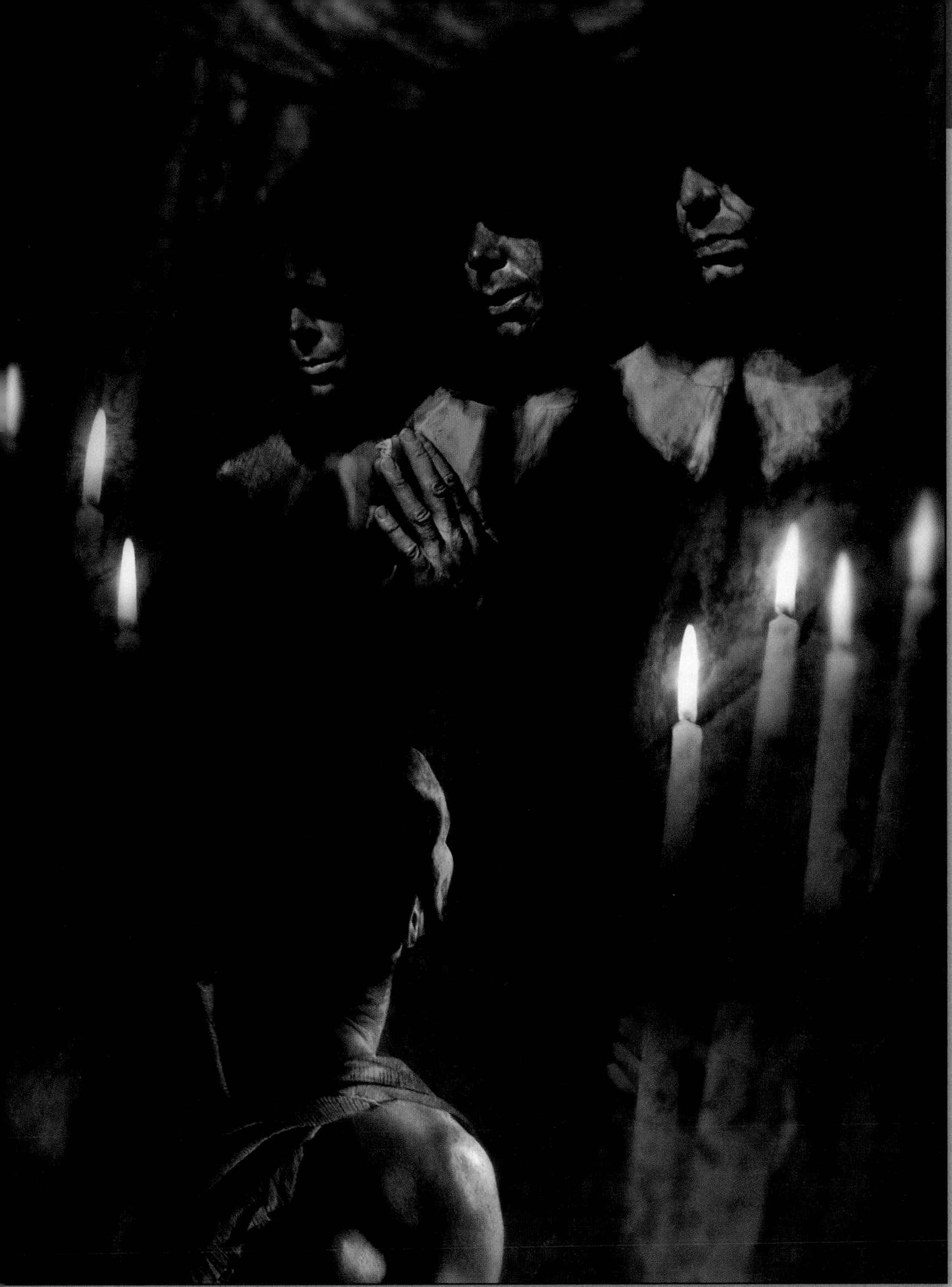

Reading Support

This selection on **thinkcentral.com** includes embedded **ThinkAloud** models–students "thinking aloud" about the story to model the kinds of questions a good reader would ask about a selection.

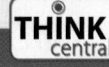

BACKGROUND

The Spanish Inquisition The Spanish Inquisition was an especially brutal outgrowth of the medieval Inquisition that the Catholic Church established in 1231 to uncover and punish heretics (see **Tortured Times** on p. 857). In 1478 King Ferdinand and Queen Isabella of Spain received the reluctant approval of the pope to establish a Spanish Inquisition that was controlled by the crown and not the Church. Its purpose was to prosecute Jews and Muslims who would not convert to Catholicism or whose forced conversion was considered insincere. The Spanish Inquisition later began to attack other so-called heretics such as Protestants.

The Grand Inquisitor The Spanish Inquisition's first grand inquisitor was Tomás de Torquemada (tôr' ke-mä' *thä*), a man famous for his use of torture, secret trials, and the notorious *auto-da-fé* ("act of faith"). This elaborate public religious ceremony culminated in the pronouncement of the victim's death sentence, and the condemned person was then turned over to civil authorities for execution, usually by being burned at the stake. Historians estimate that 2,000 people were executed this way during Torquemada's reign of terror.

The End of the Inquisition When Napoleon's army invaded Spain in 1808—the time period of the story—the Spanish Inquisition was temporarily stopped, but it was restored after Napoleon's defeat and not abolished until 1834.

Analyze Visuals

Possible answer: *Details that create the frightening mood of this illustration include dim light, shadows that obscure the people's eyes, the stern expression on each face, and placement of the foreground character below the others, as if he is under their power.*

- What does the narrator mean when he says that his "senses were leaving" him? (lines 2–3)
- What is the last thing that the narrator hears clearly? (lines 3–4)
- What is the judges' attitude toward torture? How do you know? (line 12; lines 9–11)
- When the judges appear to say the syllables of the narrator's name, why does "no sound" come out of their lips? (lines 14–15)

FOR STRUGGLING READERS

Journal Encourage students to keep a journal as they read, noting their questions, feelings, and responses to the character and events in the story. Students may also use their journals to paraphrase difficult passages. Tell students that they can refer to their journals as they work on other activities relating to this selection.

B PARAPHRASE

Possible answer: A possible paraphrase is "*I began to imagine that it would feel better to be dead, but then the judges vanished, the candles went out, and everything went black.*" His first thoughts are of death, and at first he is comforted by them.

TIERED DISCUSSION PROMPTS

Use these prompts to help students understand the narrator's thoughts about losing consciousness in lines 31–50:

Analyze The narrator compares fainting, dreaming, and death. What do these three experiences have in common? *Possible answer: Fainting, dreaming, and death are all states in which the mind and body are unaware of the outside world, and thoughts or perceptions are distorted.*

Evaluate In lines 45–50, the narrator suggests that he "who has never swooned" is somehow lacking in imagination or creativity—that fainting is a kind of window into the subconscious that only some people are able to experience. Do you agree with the narrator's interpretation? Why or why not? *Students who disagree with the narrator's view may argue that fainting is merely a physical reaction to illness or stress. Students who agree with the narrator may argue that the tendency to faint does suggest a heightened response to emotions, even if the response itself is physical.*

OWN THE WORD

- **eloquent:** Ask students if they have ever said something other people considered *eloquent*. What did students say? When did they say it?

- **lucid:** Have student pairs work together to create sentences using the word *lucid* correctly.

---

slender angels who would save me; but then, all at once, there came a most
20 deadly nausea over my spirit, and I felt every fiber in my frame thrill as if
I had touched the wire of a galvanic[5] battery, while the angel forms became
meaningless specters, with heads of flame, and I saw that from them there
would be no help. And then there stole into my fancy, like a rich musical note,
the thought of what sweet rest there must be in the grave. The thought came
gently and stealthily, and it seemed long before it attained full appreciation;[6]
but just as my spirit came at length properly to feel and entertain it, the figures
of the judges vanished, as if magically, from before me; the tall candles sank
into nothingness; their flames went out utterly; the blackness of darkness
supervened; all sensations appeared swallowed up in a mad rushing descent as of
30 the soul into Hades.[7] Then silence, and stillness, and night were the universe. **B**

    I had swooned;[8] but still will not say that all of consciousness was lost. What
of it there remained I will not attempt to define, or even to describe; yet all
was not lost. In the deepest slumber—no! In delirium—no! In a swoon—no!
In death—no! even in the grave all *is not* lost. Else there is no immortality for
man. Arousing from the most profound of slumbers, we break the gossamer
web of *some* dream. Yet in a second afterward, (so frail may that web have
been) we remember not that we have dreamed. In the return to life from
the swoon there are two stages; first, that of the sense of mental or spiritual;
secondly, that of the sense of physical, existence. It seems probable that if,
40 upon reaching the second stage, we could recall the impressions of the first, we
should find these impressions **eloquent** in memories of the gulf beyond. And
that gulf is—what? How at least shall we distinguish its shadows from those
of the tomb? But if the impressions of what I have termed the first stage, are
not, at will, recalled, yet, after long interval, do they not come unbidden, while
we marvel whence[9] they come? He who has never swooned, is not he who
finds strange palaces and wildly familiar faces in coals that glow; is not he who
beholds floating in midair the sad visions that the many may not view; is not
he who ponders over the perfume of some novel flower—is not he whose brain
grows bewildered with the meaning of some musical cadence which has never
50 before arrested his attention.

    Amid frequent and thoughtful endeavors to remember; amid earnest
struggles to regather some token of the state of seeming nothingness into
which my soul had lapsed, there have been moments when I have dreamed
of success; there have been brief, very brief periods when I have conjured
up remembrances which the **lucid** reason of a later epoch assures me could
have had reference only to that condition of seeming unconsciousness. These

---

B PARAPHRASE

Paraphrase lines 23–30. What are the narrator's thoughts immediately following his trial? How do these thoughts affect him?

eloquent (ĕl'ə-kwənt) *adj.* vividly expressive

lucid (lōō'sĭd) *adj.* clear; mentally sound

---

5. **galvanic** (găl-văn'ĭk): electric.
6. **attained full appreciation:** was fully understood.
7. **Hades** (hā'dēz): the underworld in Greek mythology.
8. **swooned:** passed out from weakness or distress.
9. **whence:** from where.

DIFFERENTIATED INSTRUCTION

FOR RELUCTANT READERS

Connect To help students connect with what the narrator is experiencing, ask them if they have ever felt faint, been delirious from a fever, or felt disoriented after waking from a deep, dream-filled sleep. Invite students to describe their experiences.

FOR ADVANCED LEARNERS/PRE-AP

Explore the Romantic Sensibility Have students work in small groups to continue to explore Poe's ideas about the relationship between the subconscious and artistic inspiration, as expressed by the narrator in lines 31–50. Explain that romanticism was an 18th- and 19th-century literary and artistic movement that valued strong emotion, the authority of imagination, and the importance of nature.

shadows of memory tell, indistinctly, of tall figures that lifted and bore me in silence down—down—still down—till a hideous dizziness oppressed me at the mere idea of the interminableness of the descent. They tell also of a vague
60 horror at my heart, on account of that heart's unnatural stillness. Then comes a sense of sudden motionlessness throughout all things; as if those who bore me (a ghastly train!) had outrun, in their descent, the limits of the limitless, and paused from the wearisomeness of their toil. After this I call to mind flatness and dampness; and that all is *madness*—the madness of a memory which busies itself among forbidden things.

VERY suddenly there came back to my soul motion and sound—the tumultuous motion of the heart, and, in my ears, the sound of its beating. Then a pause in which all is blank. Then again sound, and motion, and touch—a tingling sensation **pervading** my frame. Then the mere
70 consciousness of existence, without thought—a condition which lasted long. Then, very suddenly, *thought,* and shuddering terror, and earnest endeavor to comprehend my true state. Then a strong desire to lapse into insensibility. Then a rushing revival of soul and a successful effort to move. And now a full memory of the trial, of the judges, of the sable draperies, of the sentence, of the sickness, of the swoon. Then entire forgetfulness of all that followed; of all that a later day and much earnestness of endeavor have enabled me vaguely to recall. **C**

So far, I had not opened my eyes. I felt that I lay upon my back, unbound. I reached out my hand, and it fell heavily upon something damp and hard.
80 There I suffered[10] it to remain for many minutes, while I strove to imagine where and *what* I could be. I longed, yet dared not to employ my vision. I dreaded the first glance at objects around me. It was not that I feared to look upon things horrible, but that I grew aghast lest there should be *nothing* to see. At length, with a wild desperation at heart, I quickly unclosed my eyes. My worst thoughts, then, were confirmed. The blackness of eternal night encompassed me. I struggled for breath. The intensity of the darkness seemed to oppress and stifle me. The atmosphere was intolerably close. I still lay quietly, and made effort to exercise my reason. I brought to mind the inquisitorial proceedings, and attempted from that point to deduce my real
90 condition. The sentence had passed; and it appeared to me that a very long interval of time had since elapsed. Yet not for a moment did I suppose myself actually dead. Such a **supposition,** notwithstanding what we read in fiction, is altogether inconsistent with real existence;—but where and in what state was I? The condemned to death, I knew, perished usually at the *autos-da-fé,*[11] and

---

10. **suffered:** allowed.
11. ***autos-da-fé*** (ou'tōz-də-fā') *Portuguese:* acts of faith—public executions of people tried by the Inquisition, carried out by the civil authorities.

THE PIT AND THE PENDULUM   **861**

COMMON CORE RL 4

Language Coach

Etymology Reread the sentence in lines 56–59. The word *interminable* comes from the Latin root *terminus,* "a boundary or end." Using your knowledge of prefixes and suffixes, tell what *interminable* and then *interminableness* mean. Use a dictionary to check your answer.

pervade (pər-vād') *v.* to spread throughout

C MAKE INFERENCES
In lines 66–77, the narrator regains consciousness after having fainted. How does this account help create tension, or **suspense**?

2 Targeted Passage

supposition
(sŭp'ə-zĭsh'ən) *n.* something supposed; an assumption

READING STRATEGY: *Review*   **COMMON CORE RL 1**

C MAKE INFERENCES

Possible answer: *From the halting quality of the narrator's speech, the reader might infer that the narrator is delirious, and consequently we may question whether his perceptions are real. This sense of doubt creates suspense because we aren't sure what to believe.*

REVISIT THE BIG QUESTION

What breeds
TERROR?

Discuss In lines 80–92, what inspires the most fear in the narrator before he opens his eyes? How does he react when his fears are confirmed? ***Possible answer:*** *The narrator is not afraid of what he will see but of what he will not see. He is afraid there will be nothing but utter darkness. When he opens his eyes and is enveloped in the "blackness of eternal night," he has to struggle to breathe and to think clearly.*

FOR STRUGGLING READERS

2 Targeted Passage [Lines 78–94]

This passage describes the narrator's return to consciousness and attempt to determine where he is.

- Why is the narrator reluctant to open his eyes? (lines 82–84)
- After he opens his eyes, why does he find it hard to breathe? (lines 86–87)
- What does he think about? What does he realize? (lines 88–92)

FOR ENGLISH LANGUAGE LEARNERS

Language Coach   **COMMON CORE RL 4**

Etymology *Answer:*
Interminable *means "without end"; interminableness means "something that has an unending quality."* Identify other words that contain the Latin root *terminus* (*terminate, terminal*) and discuss their meanings. Then have students use *interminable* and other words with the root *terminus* in sentences related to the selection.

VOCABULARY   **COMMON CORE L 4**

OWN THE WORD

- **pervade:** Have students complete this sentence: *Pervading the narrator's body are. . . .*
- **supposition:** Tell students that the root of the noun *supposition* is the verb *suppose.* Have students use both words in sentences that show their understanding of both.

one of these had been held on the very night of the day of my trial. Had I been remanded to my dungeon, to await the next sacrifice, which would not take place for many months? This I at once saw could not be. Victims had been in immediate demand. Moreover, my dungeon, as well as all the condemned cells at Toledo, had stone floors, and light was not altogether excluded.

100   A fearful idea now suddenly drove the blood in torrents upon my heart, and for a brief period, I once more relapsed into insensibility. Upon recovering, I at once started to my feet, trembling convulsively in every fiber. I thrust my arms wildly above and around me in all directions. I felt nothing; yet dreaded to move a step, lest I should be impeded by the walls of the *tomb*. Perspiration burst from every pore and stood in cold big beads on my forehead. The agony of suspense grew at length intolerable, and I cautiously moved forward, with my arms extended, and my eyes straining from their sockets, in the hope of catching some faint ray of light. I proceeded for many paces; but still all was blackness and vacancy. I breathed more freely. It seemed evident that mine

110   was not, at least, the most hideous of fates. **D**

And now, as I still continued to step cautiously onward, there came thronging upon my recollection a thousand vague rumors of the horrors of Toledo. Of the dungeons there had been strange things narrated—fables I

D POE'S STYLE
Reread lines 100–110. What **unusual words and phrases** express the narrator's dread of the dungeon?

TEXT ANALYSIS

COMMON CORE   RL 4

D POE'S STYLE

Possible answer: *The narrator's dread of the dungeon is expressed in phrases such as "my eyes straining from their sockets, in the hope of catching some faint ray of light" (lines 107–108), "all was blackness and vacancy" (lines 108–109) and "I ... dreaded to move a step, lest I should be impeded by the walls of a tomb" (lines 103–104).*

Extend the Discussion What does the narrator consider "the most hideous of fates" (line 110)? Do you agree with him? Why or why not?

Analyze Visuals

Activity In what ways do the man and the dungeon in the illustration resemble the prisoner and the dungeon described in the story?
Possible answer: *The dungeon appears to have some small amount of light (line 99); both the man in the illustration and the man in the story are perspiring (lines 104–105); and the man in the illustration is reaching out, just as the prisoner in the story "cautiously moved forward, with [his] arms extended" (lines 106–107).*

DIFFERENTIATED INSTRUCTION

FOR STRUGGLING READERS

Vocabulary Support Work with students to understand the meanings of these unfamiliar words on this page:

- *remanded* (line 96), "sent back into custody or confinement, usually to await trial or further proceedings"
- *torrents* (line 100), "swift, violent streams"
- *relapsed* (line 101), "fell back into a former state"
- *convulsively* (line 102), "with spasms or violent shaking"
- *lest* (line 104), "for fear that"
- *impeded* (line 104), "blocked"
- *vacancy* (line 109), "empty space; blankness"
- *thronging upon* (line 112), "crowding into"

had always deemed them—but yet strange, and too ghastly to repeat, save in a whisper. Was I left to perish of starvation in the subterranean world of darkness; or what fate, perhaps even more fearful, awaited me? That the result would be death, and a death of more than customary bitterness, I knew too well the character of my judges to doubt. The mode and the hour were all that occupied or distracted me.

120 My outstretched hands at length encountered some solid obstruction. It was a wall, seemingly of stone masonry—very smooth, slimy, and cold. I followed it up! stepping with all the careful distrust with which certain antique narratives had inspired me. This process, however, afforded me no means of ascertaining the dimensions of my dungeon; as I might make its circuit, and return to the point whence I set out, without being aware of the fact; so perfectly uniform seemed the wall. I therefore sought the knife which had been in my pocket, when led into the inquisitorial chamber; but it was gone; my clothes had been exchanged for a wrapper of coarse serge.[12] I had thought of forcing the blade in some minute crevice of the masonry, so as to
130 identify my point of departure. The difficulty, nevertheless, was but trivial; although, in the disorder of my fancy, it seemed at first **insuperable.** I tore a part of the hem from the robe and placed the fragment at full length, and at right angles to the wall. In groping my way around the prison I could not fail to encounter this rag upon completing the circuit. So, at least I thought: but I had not counted upon the extent of the dungeon, or upon my own weakness. The ground was moist and slippery. I staggered onward for some time, when I stumbled and fell. My excessive fatigue induced me to remain prostrate; and sleep soon overtook me as I lay.

U PON awakening, and stretching forth an arm, I found beside me a loaf
140 and a pitcher with water. I was too much exhausted to reflect upon this circumstance, but ate and drank with avidity. Shortly afterward, I resumed my tour around the prison, and with much toil, came at last upon the fragment of the serge. Up to the period when I fell I had counted fifty-two paces, and upon resuming my walk, I counted forty-eight more;—when I arrived at the rag. There were in all, then, a hundred paces; and, admitting two paces to the yard, I presumed the dungeon to be fifty yards in circuit. I had met, however, with many angles in the wall, and thus I could form no guess at the shape of the vault; for vault I could not help supposing it to be.

I had little object—certainly no hope—in these researches; but a vague
150 curiosity prompted me to continue them. Quitting the wall, I resolved to cross the area of the enclosure. At first I proceeded with extreme caution, for the floor, although seemingly of solid material, was treacherous with slime. At length, however, I took courage, and did not hesitate to step firmly; endeavoring

---

12. **serge** (sûrj): a woolen cloth.

Side annotations

E PARAPHRASE
Paraphrase lines 111–119. What important realization about his situation does the narrator come to?

insuperable
(ĭn-sōō′pər-ə-bəl) *adj.* impossible to overcome

F POE'S STYLE
In lines 139–148, the narrator seems more clear minded than in earlier passages. What aspects of Poe's style help you understand this change in the narrator?

READING STRATEGY  COMMON CORE RL 1

E Model the Skill: PARAPHRASE

Model how to paraphrase by first reading lines 111–119 aloud and then restating the information in lines 111–116. Have students work in pairs to paraphrase lines 116–119 and record their paraphrases in their Reading Strategy charts.

Possible answer: *The lines can be paraphrased like this: "Now, as I stepped ahead cautiously, I remembered the terrible rumors I had heard about the Toledo dungeons. I had always considered them mere stories, too frightening to repeat except in a whisper. But now I wondered if I was left to starve to death in a dark, underground place, or if I would die in some even more terrible way. I knew I would die horribly— how and when I would die were all I could think about."* The narrator realizes that he is going to die a horrible death, but he doesn't know how or when.

TEXT ANALYSIS COMMON CORE RL 4

F POE'S STYLE

Possible answer: *The narrator's mind seems clearer because there are fewer dashes or repeated words. He uses many descriptive phrases to narrate what is happening, the sequence of events seems logical, and he makes mathematical calculations with relative ease.*

IF STUDENTS NEED HELP . . . Direct them to the last two sentences of the paragraph (lines 147–148) to help them focus on the narrator's realization.

VOCABULARY COMMON CORE L 4

OWN THE WORD

insuperable: The narrator at first thinks that marking the wall where he started was going to be *insuperable,* or impossible to overcome. Have students describe a task that might at first seem *insuperable.*

FOR STRUGGLING READERS

Comprehension Support Point out that the narrator describes his surroundings based not on what he sees but on what he feels. Ask students to find these descriptions. Then have them complete a Draw It activity to help them visualize the narrator's actions in the dungeon, such as his efforts to measure the chamber's size.

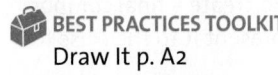 **BEST PRACTICES TOOLKIT**
Draw It p. A2

FOR ENGLISH LANGUAGE LEARNERS

Vocabulary: Prefixes Explain that in the word *insuperable* (line 131) the prefix *in-* means "not" and *superable* means "possible to overcome," so *insuperable* means "not possible to overcome." Then explain that *in-* can also mean "in, into, within, toward." Have students find words beginning with *in-*, such as *interminable.* Help students use a dictionary and context clues to determine the meaning of each word.

to cross in as direct a line as possible. I had advanced some ten or twelve paces in this manner, when the remnant of the torn hem of my robe became entangled between my legs. I stepped on it, and fell violently on my face.

In the confusion attending my fall, I did not immediately apprehend a somewhat startling circumstance, which yet, in a few seconds afterward, and while I still lay prostrate, arrested my attention. It was this—my chin rested
160 upon the floor of the prison, but my lips and the upper portion of my head, although seemingly at a less elevation than the chin, touched nothing. At the same time my forehead seemed bathed in a clammy vapor, and the peculiar smell of decayed fungus arose to my nostrils. I put forward my arm, and shuddered to find that I had fallen at the very brink of a circular pit, whose extent, of course, I had no means of ascertaining at the moment. Groping about the masonry just below the margin, I succeeded in dislodging a small fragment, and let it fall into the abyss. For many seconds I hearkened to its reverberations as it dashed against the sides of the chasm in its descent; at length there was a sullen plunge into water, succeeded by loud echoes. At
170 the same moment there came a sound resembling the quick opening, and as rapid closing of a door overhead, while a faint gleam of light flashed suddenly through the gloom, and as suddenly faded away.

I saw clearly the doom which had been prepared for me, and congratulated myself upon the timely accident by which I had escaped. Another step before my fall, and the world had seen me no more. And the death just avoided, was of that very character which I had regarded as fabulous and frivolous in the tales respecting the Inquisition. To the victims of its tyranny, there was the choice of death with its direst physical agonies, or death with its most hideous moral horrors. I had been reserved for the latter. By long suffering my nerves
180 had been unstrung, until I trembled at the sound of my own voice, and had become in every respect a fitting subject for the species of torture which awaited me.

Shaking in every limb, I groped my way back to the wall; resolving there to perish rather than risk the terrors of the wells, of which my imagination now pictured many in various positions about the dungeon. In other conditions of mind I might have had courage to end my misery at once by a plunge into one of these abysses; but now I was the veriest of cowards. Neither could I forget what I had read of these pits—that the *sudden* extinction of life formed no part of their most horrible plan. **H**
190 Agitation of spirit kept me awake for many long hours; but at length I again slumbered. Upon arousing, I found by my side as before, a loaf and a pitcher of water. A burning thirst consumed me, and I emptied the vessel at a draft. It must have been drugged; for scarcely had I drunk, before I became irresistibly drowsy. A deep sleep fell upon me—a sleep like that of death. How long it lasted of course, I know not; but when, once again, I unclosed my eyes, the

③ Targeted Passage

G POE'S STYLE
Reread lines 157–172, noting Poe's **sensory images**—words and phrases that appeal to the senses. Which details communicate the foulness of the pit?

H PARAPHRASE
Paraphrase this brief paragraph. Think about the narrator's opinion of himself. Do you agree or disagree with his view?

864 UNIT 8: AUTHOR'S STYLE AND VOICE

DIFFERENTIATED INSTRUCTION

FOR STRUGGLING READERS
③ Targeted Passage [Lines 157–182]
This passage provides the first link between the story's title and the narrator's fate.

• How does the narrator discover the "doom" (line 173) prepared for him? (lines 165–172)

• How does he escape this death? (lines 173–175)

• What are the two kinds of deaths imposed by the Inquisition? (lines 178–179)

• Why does the narrator think that he is a "fitting subject" for the second kind? (lines 179–182)

FOR ENGLISH LANGUAGE LEARNERS
Comprehension: Task Support Have students work independently to paraphrase lines 190–198. Then have them work in pairs to discuss the paraphrases and revise if necessary. Students should create a final composite paraphrase and present it to the class for discussion.

objects around me were visible. By a wild sulphurous luster,[13] the origin of which I could not at first determine, I was enabled to see the extent and aspect of the prison.

IN its size I had been greatly mistaken. The whole circuit of its walls did not
200 exceed twenty-five yards. For some minutes this fact occasioned me a world of vain trouble;[14] vain indeed! for what could be of less importance, under the terrible circumstances which environed me, than the mere dimensions of my dungeon? But my soul took a wild interest in trifles, and I busied myself in endeavors to account for the error I had committed in my measurement. The truth at length flashed upon me. In my first attempt at exploration I had counted fifty-two paces, up to the period when I fell; I must then have been within a pace or two of the fragments of serge; in fact, I had nearly performed the circuit of the vault. I then slept, and upon awaking, I must have returned upon my steps—thus supposing the circuit nearly double what it actually was.
210 My confusion of mind prevented me from observing that I began my tour with the wall to the left, and ended it with the wall to the right.

---

13. **sulphurous** (sŭl′fə-rəs) **luster:** fiery glow.
14. **occasioned . . . trouble:** caused me a great deal of useless worry.

I had been deceived, too, in respect to the shape of the enclosure. In feeling my way around I had found many angles, and thus deduced an idea of great irregularity; so potent is the effect of total darkness upon one arousing from **lethargy** or sleep! The angles were simply those of a few slight depressions, or niches, at odd intervals. The general shape of the prison was square. What I had taken for masonry seemed now to be iron, or some other metal, in huge plates, whose sutures or joints occasioned the depression. The entire surface of this metallic enclosure was rudely daubed in all the hideous and repulsive
220 devices to which the charnel superstitions[15] of the monks has given rise. The figures of fiends in aspects of menace, with skeleton forms, and other more really fearful images, overspread and disfigured the walls. I observed that the outlines of these monstrosities were sufficiently distinct, but that the colors seemed faded and blurred, as if from the effects of a damp atmosphere. I now noticed the floor, too, which was of stone. In the center yawned the circular pit from whose jaws I had escaped; but it was the only one in the dungeon. ✦

ALL this I saw distinctly and by much effort: for my personal condition had been greatly changed during slumber. I now lay upon my back, and at full length, on a species of low framework of wood. To this I was securely
230 bound by a long strap resembling a surcingle.[16] It passed in many convolutions about my limbs and body, leaving at liberty only my head, and my left arm to such extent that I could, by dint[17] of much exertion, supply myself with food from an earthen dish which lay by my side on the floor. I saw, to my horror, that the pitcher had been removed. I say to my horror; for I was consumed with intolerable thirst. This thirst it appeared to be the design of my persecutors to stimulate: for the food in the dish was meat pungently seasoned.

Looking upward I surveyed the ceiling of my prison. It was some thirty or forty feet overhead, and constructed much as the side walls. In one of its panels a very singular figure riveted my whole attention. It was the painted figure of
240 Time as he is commonly represented, save that, in lieu of a scythe, he held what, at a casual glance, I supposed to be the pictured image of a huge pendulum such as we see on antique clocks. There was something, however, in the appearance of this machine which caused me to regard it more attentively. While I gazed directly upward at it (for its position was immediately over my own) I fancied that I saw it in motion. In an instant afterward the fancy was confirmed. Its sweep was brief, and of course slow. I watched it for some minutes, somewhat in fear, but more in wonder. Wearied at length with observing its dull movement, I turned my eyes upon the other objects in the cell. ◗

lethargy (lĕth′ər-jē) *n.* prolonged sluggishness; unconsciousness

✦ **GRAMMAR AND STYLE**
In lines 225–226, Poe uses **personification**—describing the pit as an open mouth—to make the image seem particularly disturbing.

◗ **PARAPHRASE**
Paraphrase lines 227–248. What situation does the narrator find himself in?

---

15. **charnel** (chär′nəl) **superstitions:** ghastly irrational beliefs.
16. **surcingle** (sûr′sĭng′gəl): a band used to tie a pack or saddle to a horse.
17. **dint:** force.

A slight noise attracted my notice, and, looking to the floor, I saw several
250 enormous rats traversing it. They had issued from the well, which lay just
within view to my right. Even then, while I gazed, they came up in troops,
hurriedly, with ravenous eyes, allured by the scent of the meat. From this it
required much effort and attention to scare them away.

It might have been half an hour, perhaps even an hour, (for I could take but
imperfect note of time) before I again cast my eyes upward. What I then saw
confounded and amazed me. The sweep of the pendulum had increased in
extent by nearly a yard. As a natural consequence, its velocity was also much
greater. But what mainly disturbed me was the idea that it had perceptibly
descended. I now observed—with what horror it is needless to say—that its
260 nether extremity was formed of a crescent of glittering steel, about a foot in
length from horn to horn; the horns upward, and the under edge evidently as
keen as that of a razor. Like a razor also, it seemed massy and heavy, tapering
from the edge into a solid and broad structure above. It was appended to a
weighty rod of brass, and the whole *hissed* as it swung through the air.

I could no longer doubt the doom prepared for me by monkish ingenuity
in torture. My cognizance of the pit had become known to the inquisitorial
agents—*the pit* whose horrors had been destined for so bold a recusant[18] as
myself—*the pit*, typical of hell, and regarded by rumor as the Ultima Thule[19]
of all their punishments. The plunge into this pit I had avoided by the merest
270 of accidents, and I knew that surprise, or entrapment into torment, formed
an important portion of all the grotesquerie of these dungeon deaths. Having
failed to fall, it was no part of the demon plan to hurl me into the abyss; and
thus (there being no alternative) a different and a milder destruction awaited
me. Milder! I half smiled in my agony as I thought of such application of such
a term. **K**

What boots it[20] to tell of the long, long hours of horror more than mortal,
during which I counted the rushing vibrations of the steel! Inch by inch—
line by line—with a descent only appreciable at intervals that seemed ages—
down and still down it came! Days passed—it might have been that many
280 days passed—ere it swept so closely over me as to fan me with its acrid breath.
The odor of the sharp steel forced itself into my nostrils. I prayed—I wearied
heaven with my prayer for its more speedy descent. I grew frantically mad,
and struggled to force myself upward against the sweep of the fearful
scimitar.[21] And then I fell suddenly calm, and lay smiling at the glittering
death, as a child at some rare bauble.

confound (kən-found') *v.*
to confuse or astonish

4 **Targeted Passage**

K **POE'S STYLE**
In lines 254–275, Poe
includes various **italicized
words**. What effect do
they have on you as a
reader?

---

18. **recusant** (rĕk'yə-zənt): a religious dissenter; heretic.
19. **Ultima Thule** (ŭl'tə-mə thōō'lē): according to ancient geographers, the most remote region of the habitable world—here used figuratively to mean "most extreme achievement; summit."
20. **what boots it:** what good is it.
21. **scimitar** (sĭm'ĭ-tər): a curved, single-edged Asian sword.

THE PIT AND THE PENDULUM 867

REVISIT THE BIG QUESTION
What breeds
TERROR?

Discuss What else, other than the prospect of the actual pain of certain death, fills the narrator with fear and begins to drive him mad in lines 276–285? *Possible answer: The narrator fears the painful death that awaits him, but the long hours or, perhaps, days, of waiting are even more excruciating. Because the narrator cannot move, he is forced to watch the slow approach of the blade. His tormentors are torturing him by making him watch the slow approach of death.*

TEXT ANALYSIS   COMMON CORE
                                         RL 4
K **POE'S STYLE**

Possible answer: *The italicized words ("descended," "hissed," and "the pit") emphasize the dire situation of the narrator and allow the reader to share the narrator's terror as he describes his situation: The pendulum is descending toward his body, making a hissing noise as it lowers to slice him.*

VOCABULARY   COMMON CORE
                                          L 4
OWN THE WORD

confound: Ask students to think of a time when they were *confounded*. Ask them to explain when, how, and why they felt confused or astonished.

FOR STRUGGLING READERS

4 **Targeted Passage** [Lines 254–275]

This passage finally reveals the meaning of the story's title.

- What did the narrator see when he looked up? (lines 256–259)
- What new method of execution does the narrator now face? (lines 260–264)

- Why have the inquisitors developed a second plan for the narrator's death? (lines 269–270)
- Why would the torturers want their victims to be surprised or trapped by death? (lines 270–271)
- Does the narrator really find the term "milder" amusing? (lines 274–275)

Use these prompts to help students think about the idea the narrator begins to formulate in lines 294–316 as he watches the descent of the pendulum:

Connect How do you come up with your best ideas? Do they usually occur as the result of focused, analytical thought, or do they tend to pop into your head while you're doing something completely unrelated? *Accept all thoughtful answers.*

Analyze What exactly is the narrator doing when "a half formed thought of joy—of hope" (line 295) rushes into his mind, and what can we infer from his use of the words "joy" and "hope"? *Possible answer: The thought rushes into his head while the narrator is reaching for the small portion of the food that the rats haven't eaten. We can infer from his use of the words "joy" and "hope" that the thought has something to do with an escape plan.*

Evaluate Do you think the narrator has lost all his "ordinary powers of mind" (line 299), as he claims, or is he in fact thinking clearly? Defend your answer. *Students who think the narrator is losing his mind, or at least his "powers of mind," may cite his own assertion that he had become an "imbecile—an idiot" (line 300) and his statement that he "alternately laughed and howled" (line 316). Students who believe that the narrator is thinking clearly, despite his own assertions to the contrary and his obvious terror, may cite his "half formed thought," which is clearly the beginning of a plan, and his close observations of the pendulum.*

THERE was another interval of utter insensibility; it was brief; for, upon again lapsing into life there had been no perceptible descent in the pendulum. But it might have been long; for I knew there were demons who took note of my swoon, and who could have arrested the vibration at pleasure. 290 Upon my recovery, too, I felt very—oh, inexpressibly sick and weak, as if through long inanition.[22] Even amid the agonies of that period, the human nature craved food. With painful effort I outstretched my left arm as far as my bonds permitted, and took possession of the small remnant which had been spared me by the rats. As I put a portion of it within my lips, there rushed to my mind a half formed thought of joy—of hope. Yet what business had I with hope? It was, as I say, a half formed thought—man has many such which are never completed. I felt that it was of joy—of hope; but I felt also that it had perished in its formation. In vain I struggled to perfect—to regain it. Long suffering had nearly annihilated all my ordinary powers of mind. I was an 300 imbecile—an idiot.

The vibration of the pendulum was at right angles to my length. I saw that the crescent was designed to cross the region of the heart. It would fray the serge of my robe—it would return and repeat its operations—again—and again. Notwithstanding its terrifically wide sweep (some thirty feet or more) and the hissing vigor of its descent, sufficient to sunder these very walls of iron, still the fraying of my robe would be all that, for several minutes, it would accomplish. And at this thought I paused. I dared not go farther than this reflection. I dwelt upon it with a **pertinacity** of attention—as if, in so dwelling, I could arrest *here* the descent of the steel. I forced myself to ponder 310 upon the sound of the crescent as it should pass across the garment—upon the peculiar thrilling sensation which the friction of cloth produces on the nerves. I pondered upon all this frivolity until my teeth were on edge.

Down—steadily down it crept. I took a frenzied pleasure in contrasting its downward with its lateral velocity. To the right—to the left—far and wide— with the shriek of a . . . spirit; to my heart with the stealthy pace of the tiger! I alternately laughed and howled as the one or the other idea grew predominant.

Down—certainly, relentlessly down! It vibrated within three inches of my bosom! I struggled violently, furiously, to free my left arm. This was free only from the elbow to the hand. I could reach the latter, from the platter beside 320 me, to my mouth, with great effort, but no farther. Could I have broken the fastenings above the elbow, I would have seized and attempted to arrest the pendulum. I might as well have attempted to arrest an avalanche!

Down—still unceasingly—still inevitably down! I gasped and struggled at each vibration. I shrunk convulsively at its every sweep. My eyes followed its outward or upward whirls with the eagerness of the most unmeaning despair; they closed themselves spasmodically at the descent, although death would have been a relief, oh! how unspeakable! Still I quivered in every nerve to think how slight a sinking of the machinery would precipitate that keen, glistening

pertinacity
(pûr′tn-ăs′ĭ-tē) *n.*
unyielding persistence or adherence

Analyze Visuals

How effectively does this image convey the terror of the narrator's situation?

---

22. **inanition** (ĭn′ə-nĭsh′ən): wasting away from lack of food.

FOR STRUGGLING READERS

Vocabulary Support Work with students to understand the meanings of these unfamiliar words and phrases on this page:

• *arrested* (line 289), "stopped"

• *at pleasure* (line 289), "whenever it pleased them"

• *annihilated* (line 299), "destroyed; defeated"

• *serge* (line 303), "type of wool cloth"

• *notwithstanding* (line 304), "in spite of"

• *frivolity (line 312),* "unimportance; nonsense"

• *lateral* (line 314), "sideways"

• *predominant* (line 316), "more or most important"

• *precipitate* (line 328), "cause to happen"

Analyze Visuals

Possible answer: *The image is very effective. The reader can clearly see that the sharp blade is close to the narrator's chest and that he cannot escape. The narrator's partially opened mouth suggests a grimace or a scream, and the panic in his eyes reveals his terror at facing this gruesome death. The rats are shown in the corner of the illustration, which adds an extra element of horror to this grim scene.*

REVISIT THE BIG QUESTION

What breeds
TERROR?

Discuss What surprising physical and emotional responses does the narrator experience in lines 290–300, despite his fear? ***Possible answer:*** *The narrator experiences hunger and has brief flashes of joy and hope, as he begins to formulate a plan.*

FOR ENGLISH LANGUAGE LEARNERS
Vocabulary: Modifiers Poe uses adjectives and adverbs to convey terror powerfully. Remind students that the *-ly* ending signals adverbs, which modify verbs, adjectives, or other adverbs. Adjectives modify nouns. Write these examples on the board: **Adjectives:** *perceptible* (line 287), *hissing* (305), *frenzied* (313); **Adverbs:** *inexpressibly* (line 290), *terrifically* (304), *convulsively* (324).

Organize students into two teams, and provide each team with a Two-Column Chart labeled *Adjectives* and *Adverbs*. Team members should take turns adding an adjective and adverb from page 868 to their team's chart. The team with the most entries wins. Discuss the charts as a group.

BEST PRACTICES TOOLKIT—Transparency
Two-Column Chart p. A25

 POE'S STYLE

Possible answer: *First-person language takes readers inside the narrator's fear-stricken mind. Long sentences show how his mind is rambling. Repetition (particularly of "Down—" in lines 313, 317, and 323), dashes, exclamation points, and italicized words also help convey the narrator's agitation and growing fear.*

IF STUDENTS NEED HELP . . . Refer them back to the list of stylistic devices on page 857. Review the meaning of each device, and help students find examples of all the devices in this passage.

 PARAPHRASE

Possible answer: *A possible paraphrase is "The rats had eaten almost everything in the dish, despite my attempts to stop them. I regularly waved them away from the platter, but they got used to the movement and ignored it. In their greed, the rats often bit my fingers. I then rubbed the remaining bits of the greasy food on the straps that bound me. Then I raised my hand and lay motionless." The narrator wants the rats to chew through his bindings and free him.*

OWN THE WORD

voracity: Tell students that the adjective form of *voracity* is *voracious*. Explain that *voracious* connotes a person who is ravenous, gluttonous, or insatiable—much stronger words than *hungry*, for example. Explain that *voracious* can also be used to describe eager readers who "devour" books.

---

axe upon my bosom. It was *hope* that prompted the nerve to quiver—the frame
330 to shrink. It was *hope*—the hope that triumphs on the rack[23]—that whispers
to the death-condemned even in the dungeons of the Inquisition.

    I saw that some ten or twelve vibrations would bring the steel in actual contact with my robe, and with this observation there suddenly came over my spirit all the keen, collected calmness of despair. For the first time during many hours—or perhaps days—I *thought*. It now occurred to me that the bandage, or surcingle, which enveloped me, was *unique*. I was tied by no separate cord. The first stroke of the razor-like crescent athwart[24] any portion of the band, would so detach it that it might be unwound from my person by means of my left hand. But how fearful, in that case, the proximity of the
340 steel! The result of the slightest struggle how deadly! Was it likely, moreover, that the minions[25] of the torturer had not foreseen and provided for this possibility! Was it probable that the bandage crossed my bosom in the track of the pendulum? Dreading to find my faint, and, as it seemed, my last hope frustrated, I so far elevated my head as to obtain a distinct view of my breast. The surcingle enveloped my limbs and body close in all directions—*save in the path of the destroying crescent.*

    Scarcely had I dropped my head back into its original position, when there flashed upon my mind what I cannot better describe than as the unformed half of that idea of deliverance to which I have previously alluded, and of which a
350 moiety[26] only floated indeterminately through my brain when I raised food to my burning lips. The whole thought was now present—feeble, scarcely sane, scarcely definite,—but still entire. I proceeded at once, with the nervous energy of despair, to attempt its execution.

    For many hours the immediate vicinity of the low framework upon which I lay, had been literally swarming with rats. They were wild, bold, ravenous; their red eyes glaring upon me as if they waited but for motionlessness on my part to make me their prey. "To what food," I thought, "have they been accustomed in the well?"

    They had devoured, in spite of all my efforts to prevent them, all but a
360 small remnant of the contents of the dish. I had fallen into an habitual see-saw, or wave of the hand about the platter, and, at length, the unconscious uniformity of the movement deprived it of effect. In their **voracity** the vermin frequently fastened their sharp fangs into my fingers. With the particles of the oily and spicy viand[27] which now remained, I thoroughly rubbed the bandage wherever I could reach it; then, raising my hand from the floor, I lay breathlessly still. Ⓜ

    At first the ravenous animals were startled and terrified at the change—at the cessation of movement. They shrank alarmedly back; many sought the

---

Ⓛ **POE'S STYLE**
Reread lines 313–331. Which stylistic devices help convey the narrator's growing fear?

⑤ Targeted Passage

voracity (vô-răs′ĭ-tē) *n.* greed for food

Ⓜ **PARAPHRASE**
Paraphrase lines 359–366. What does the narrator hope to accomplish by wiping his greasy hands on his bindings?

---

23. **rack:** a device for torturing people by gradually stretching their bodies.
24. **athwart:** across.
25. **minions** (mĭn′yənz): followers; servants.
26. **moiety** (moi′ĭ-tē): half.
27. **viand** (vī′ənd): food.

DIFFERENTIATED INSTRUCTION

FOR STRUGGLING READERS

Vocabulary Support Have students reread lines 335–337. Make sure they understand that here, the word *unique* means "single." In other words, the narrator has just realized that he is tied by only a single bandage, or cord. Ask students why this realization is so important.

FOR ADVANCED LEARNERS/PRE-AP

Analyze a Paradox Point out the narrator's use of the word "despair" in lines 332–334 and lines 351–353. Have students discuss the apparent contradiction, or paradox, in these two statements about the "calmness of despair" and the "nervous energy of despair." Ask them if the narrator does, in fact, contradict himself, or if despair can produce both calmness and nervous energy. If so, how?

well. But this was only for a moment. I had not counted in vain upon their
370 voracity. Observing that I remained without motion, one or two of the boldest
leaped upon the framework, and smelt at the surcingle. This seemed the signal
for a general rush. Forth from the well they hurried in fresh troops. They clung
to the wood—they overran it, and leaped in hundreds upon my person. The
measured movement of the pendulum disturbed them not at all. Avoiding its
strokes they busied themselves with the anointed bandage. They pressed—they
swarmed upon me in ever accumulating heaps. They writhed upon my throat;
their cold lips sought my own; I was half stifled by their thronging pressure;
disgust, for which the world has no name, swelled my bosom, and chilled,
with a heavy clamminess, my heart. Yet one minute, and I felt that the struggle
380 would be over. Plainly I perceived the loosening of the bandage. I knew that
in more than one place it must be already severed. With a more than human
resolution I lay *still*.

Nor had I erred in my calculations—nor had I endured in vain. I at length
felt that I was *free*. The surcingle hung in ribands[28] from my body. But the
stroke of the pendulum already pressed upon my bosom. It had divided the
serge of the robe. It had cut through the linen beneath. Twice again it swung,
and a sharp sense of pain shot through every nerve. But the moment of escape

28. **ribands** (rĭbʹəndz): ribbons.

⑤ **Targeted Passage**
continued

 **MAKE INFERENCES**
Consider the narrator's thoughts and behavior up to this point in the story. Why might the church have considered him dangerous? What details help you make an inference?

N MAKE INFERENCES

Possible answer: *The church might have considered the narrator dangerous because he is unrepentant, intelligent, and able to withstand mental torture. He refers to "so bold a recusant as myself" (lines 267–268), he measures his cell, he thinks of a way to free himself from the table, and he endures extreme thirst and being overrun with rats.*

Analyze Visuals

Activity Ask students to discuss how this illustration reflects the atmosphere of the story. *Possible answer: The illustration reflects the story's atmosphere of horror and, specifically, the narrator's disgust at having the rats swarm all over him. The rats are portrayed as demonic with fiery red eyes, evoking the narrator's reference to his tormentors as "demons" (line 288).*

FOR STRUGGLING READERS

⑤ **Targeted Passage [Lines 354–384]**

This passage reveals the narrator's plan and suggests a possible resolution for the story.

- How does the narrator use the rats? (lines 374–375)
- Why does the narrator feel that he is free, and why does he then feel a sharp pain? (line 384)
- Do you think that he really is free? Explain.

FOR ADVANCED LEARNERS/PRE–AP

Imitating Poe's Style Ask students to write a paragraph describing a horrifying setting or scene, using Poe's description of the swarming rats (lines 370–382) as a model. Challenge students to imitate Poe's style, using complex sentences, repetition, italics, interruption, grotesque images, and so on. Tell students to avoid any references to violence, blood, or inappropriate subject matter. Invite volunteers to share their paragraphs with the class.

VOCABULARY

COMMON CORE

RL 4

△ AFFIXES

Have students look for other affixes in lines 392–429. Point out the word *distinctly* in line 400 as an example. Tell students the base word *distinct* is an adjective that means "clear." Adding the suffix *-ly* changes the word to an adverb.

Accept all reasonable answers.

ADDITIONAL TEACHING OPPORTUNITY

Narrator and Tone Explain to students that the point of view a writer uses greatly influences how a story is told—specifically, what readers learn about the characters and events. Remind students that Poe's story is told from the first-person point of view, with readers seeing everything that happens through the eyes of the unnamed narrator. Ask students to consider these questions:

- What is their impression of the narrator?
- How would they describe the story's tone— the writer's attitude toward the narrator?
- How would the story be different if it were told from the point of view of one of the torturers?

---

had arrived. At a wave of my hand my deliverers hurried tumultuously away. With a steady movement—cautious, sidelong, shrinking, and slow—I slid
390 from the embrace of the bandage and beyond the reach of the scimitar. For the moment, at least, *I was free.* △

Free!—and in the grasp of the Inquisition! I had scarcely stepped from my wooden bed of horror upon the stone floor of the prison, when the motion of the hellish machine ceased and I beheld it drawn up, by some invisible force, through the ceiling. This was a lesson which I took desperately to heart. My every motion was undoubtedly watched. Free!—I had but escaped death in one form of agony, to be delivered unto worse than death in some other. With that thought I rolled my eyes nervously around the barriers of iron that hemmed me in. Something unusual—some change which at first I could not
400 appreciate distinctly—it was obvious, had taken place in the apartment. For many minutes in a dreamy and trembling abstraction, I busied myself in vain, unconnected conjecture. During this period, I became aware, for the first time, of the origin of the sulphurous light which illuminated the cell. It proceeded from a fissure, about half an inch in width, extending entirely around the prison at the base of the walls, which thus appeared, and were, completely separated from the floor. I endeavored, but of course in vain, to look through the aperture.[29]

As I arose from the attempt, the mystery of the alteration in the chamber broke at once upon my understanding. I have observed that, although the
410 outlines of the figures upon the walls were sufficiently distinct, yet the colors seemed blurred and indefinite. These colors had now assumed, and were momentarily assuming, a startling and most intense brilliancy, that gave to the spectral and fiendish portraitures an aspect that might have thrilled even firmer nerves than my own. Demon eyes, of a wild and ghastly vivacity, glared upon me in a thousand directions, where none had been visible before, and gleamed with the lurid luster of a fire that I could not force my imagination to regard as unreal.

Unreal!—Even while I breathed there came to my nostrils the breath of the vapor of heated iron! A suffocating odor pervaded the prison! A deeper glow
420 settled each moment in the eyes that glared at my agonies! A richer tint of crimson diffused itself over the pictured horrors of blood. I panted! I gasped for breath! There could be no doubt of the design of my tormentors—oh! most unrelenting! oh! most demoniac of men! I shrank from the glowing metal to the center of the cell. Amid the thought of the fiery destruction that impended, the idea of the coolness of the well came over my soul like balm. I rushed to its deadly brink. I threw my straining vision below. The glare from the enkindled roof illumined its inmost recesses. Yet, for a wild moment, did my spirit refuse to comprehend the meaning of what I saw. At length it forced—it wrestled its way into my soul—it burned itself in upon

COMMON CORE RL 4

△ AFFIXES

Affixes are letters added to the beginning or end of a word to form a new word. An affix added to the beginning of a word is a prefix, while an affix added to the end of a word is a suffix. The word *tumultuously* in line 388 combines the base word *tumult* with two affixes, the Latin suffix *-ous* (meaning "full of") and the Old English suffix *-ly* (meaning "like"). Use *tumultuously* in a sentence of your own. Use a dictionary to help you if necessary.

---

29. **aperture** (ăp′ər-chər): opening.

DIFFERENTIATED INSTRUCTION

FOR STRUGGLING READERS

Develop Reading Fluency Have students read silently as you play the *Audio Anthology CD* recording of the last two paragraphs of the story. Instruct students to pay close attention to how the reader uses intonation and expression to convey punctuation and italics in the passage. Then have students work in pairs to practice reading the final paragraphs of the story aloud.

R RESOURCE MANAGER—Copy Masters
Reading Fluency p. 31

FOR ADVANCED LEARNERS/PRE–AP

Analyze Author's Purpose [small-group option] Read the **BACKGROUND** note in the side column of page 873 to students. Ask students to consider the ending of "The Pit and the Pendulum" and the timely arrival of General Lasalle within this literary context.

430 my shuddering reason.—Oh! for a voice to speak!—oh! horror!—oh! any horror but this! With a shriek, I rushed from the margin, and buried my face in my hands—weeping bitterly. ⓟ

The heat rapidly increased, and once again I looked up, shuddering as with a fit of the ague.[30] There had been a second change in the cell—and now the change was obviously in the form. As before, it was in vain that I, at first, endeavored to appreciate or understand what was taking place. But not long was I left in doubt. The Inquisitorial vengeance had been hurried by my two-fold escape, and there was to be no more dallying with the King of Terrors. The room had been square. I saw that two of its iron angles were now acute—
440 two, consequently, obtuse. The fearful difference quickly increased with a low rumbling or moaning sound. In an instant the apartment had shifted its form into that of a lozenge. But the alteration stopped not here—I neither hoped nor desired it to stop. I could have clasped the red walls to my bosom as a garment of eternal peace. "Death," I said, "any death but that of the pit!" Fool! might I have not known that *into the pit* it was the object of the burning iron to urge me? Could I resist its glow? or, if even that, could I withstand its pressure? And now, flatter and flatter grew the lozenge, with a rapidity that left me no time for contemplation. Its center, and of course, its greatest width, came just over the yawning gulf. I shrank back—but the closing walls pressed
450 me resistlessly onward. At length for my seared and writhing body there was no longer an inch of foothold on the firm floor of the prison. I struggled no more, but the agony of my soul found vent in one loud, long, and final scream of despair. I felt that I tottered upon the brink—I averted my eyes—

There was a discordant hum of human voices! There was a loud blast of many trumpets! There was a harsh grating as of a thousand thunders! The fiery walls rushed back! An outstretched arm caught my own as I fell, fainting, into the abyss. It was that of General Lasalle. The French army had entered Toledo. The Inquisition was in the hands of its enemies. ✑

ⓟ **POE'S STYLE**
Reread lines 418–432. What does the **punctuation** used by Poe suggest about the narrator's emotional state?

Ⓖ **Targeted Passage**

---

30. **the ague** (ā′gyōō): a feverish illness.

ⓟ **POE'S STYLE**

Possible answer: *The dashes and exclamation points suggest that the narrator is extremely frightened and is experiencing great mental anguish. These punctuation marks mirror the narrator's agitated, disjointed emotional state.*

REVISIT THE BIG QUESTION

What breeds
TERROR?

Discuss How do the inquisitors make use of the narrator's fear of the pit as they craft their plans for him in lines 433–453? ***Possible answer:*** *The inquisitors seem to know of the narrator's feelings to face "any death but that of the pit!" (line 444), so they present a horrible death for him to run to as a means of "escaping" the pit.*

BACKGROUND

The God in the Machine In ancient Greek and Roman drama, the plot was often resolved through a device called the *deus ex machina* (Latin for "god from a machine"). At the end of a play, a god would appear to solve the characters' problems. The god was literally lowered onto the stage by an overhead crane (the machine), as if appearing out of the sky. The term *deus ex machina* has come to refer to any unexpected and contrived "divine" intervention that a writer uses to resolve a plot—such as the last-minute appearance of the "queen's messenger" to announce the prisoner's pardon as he is about to be executed.

DIFFERENTIATED INSTRUCTION

FOR STRUGGLING READERS

Ⓖ **Targeted Passage** [Lines 433–453]

This passage presents the final phase of the torture endured by the narrator.

- What is the narrator's "two-fold escape"? (lines 437–438)

- Who is the "King of Terrors," and why is there to be no more "dallying" with him? (line 438)

- What is happening to the narrator's cell, and why? (lines 439–442)

- What does the narrator mean when he says, "I could have clasped the red walls to my bosom as a garment of eternal peace"? (lines 443–444)

- What is the "yawning gulf"? (line 449)

- Why did the walls move back? What saves the narrator? (lines 457–458)

Analyze Visuals

Activity Ask students how the painting conveys the mood and theme of the poem. *Possible answer: The painting's emphasis on light and shadow matches the poem's mood of "dark imagining" (line 20) and its theme that even within a beautiful setting, there is something shadowy and perhaps even terrifying.*

About the Art *Timeless*, by contemporary English painter Lee Campbell, reflects her interest in the play of light on surfaces.

TEXT ANALYSIS **COMMON CORE** **RL 4**

 POE'S STYLE

Possible answer: Words and phrases that convey the speaker's emotional intensity include "haunt" (line 2), "could not love the less" (line 3), "terror of that lone lake" (line 12), "tremulous delight" (line 14), and "darken'd mind" (line 16).

READING STRATEGY **COMMON CORE** **RL 1**

PARAPHRASE

Possible answer: "The lake could offer a comforting peace to someone suffering from dark thoughts."

SELECTION WRAP–UP

READ WITH A PURPOSE Ask students to compare and contrast the narrator in the story and speaker in the poem. How are the narrator in the story and the speaker in the poem alike? How do they differ? *Possible answer: Both display an emotional intensity and have a wild imagination, but the narrator's situation is truly terrifying, while the speaker finds comfort at the lake.*

★ **CRITIQUE** Ask students what they liked most and least about the story and the poem.

INDEPENDENT READING
Students may explore further works of Poe in *The Murders in the Rue Morgue*, a "locked room" mystery with a surprising ending.

Prereading for this poem is found on page 856.

Timeless, 2002, Lee Campbell. Private collection. Photo © The Bridgeman Art Library.

THE Lake
Edgar Allan Poe

In youth's spring, it was my lot
To haunt of the wide earth a spot
The which I could not love the less;
So lovely was the loneliness
5 Of a wild lake, with black rock bound,
And the tall pines that tower'd around.
But when the night had thrown her pall
Upon that spot—as upon all,
And the wind would pass me by
10 In its still melody,
My infant spirit would awake
To the terror of that lone lake.
Yet that terror was not fright—
But a tremulous delight,
15 And a feeling undefin'd,
Springing from a darken'd mind. **Q**
Death was in that poison'd wave
And in its gulf a fitting grave
For him who thence could solace bring
20 To his dark imagining;
Whose wild'ring thought could even make
An Eden of that dim lake. **R**

Q POE'S STYLE
Reread lines 1–16. Which words and phrases help communicate the emotional intensity of the speaker?

R PARAPHRASE
Paraphrase lines 17–22. What comfort does the speaker find in visiting the eerie lake?

874 UNIT 8: AUTHOR'S STYLE AND VOICE

DIFFERENTIATED INSTRUCTION

FOR STRUGGLING READERS
Options for Reading Have students listen as you read the entire poem aloud. Then organize students into small groups to read one of these sentences: lines 1–6, lines 7–12, lines 13–16, and lines 17–22. Tell groups to focus on the descriptive words in their sentences and to try to see, hear, or feel the sensations that these images suggest. Ask each group to paraphrase its sentence and share its content and images with the class.

FOR ENGLISH LANGUAGE LEARNERS
Language: Verb Tenses Point out the word *would* (lines 9, 11). Explain that here it reflects the habitual past tense, which describes an action done repeatedly in the past. In a Whip Around, have students name actions they did repeatedly in the past, using phrases such as "When I was ten _____" or "In eighth grade _____"

 **BEST PRACTICES TOOLKIT**
Whip Around p. B1

Comprehension

1. **Recall** What are the first two dangers the narrator faces in the story?

2. **Clarify** Who or what seems to save the narrator at the end?

3. **Summarize** In the poem, what effect does the lake have on the speaker?

Text Analysis

4. **Make Inferences About Character** Consider the narrator's words, thoughts, and actions in "The Pit and the Pendulum." What can you infer are his greatest strengths in his battle against the inquisitors? Support your answer with details from the story.

5. **Paraphrase the Ending** Paraphrase the story's conclusion, lines 454–458. Do you think the narrator is truly saved, or is he simply imagining a rescue as he falls? Cite evidence to support your opinion.

6. **Examine Sound Devices** Reread "The Lake," looking for examples of **alliteration** (repetition of consonant sounds at the beginnings of words) and **assonance** (repetition of vowel sounds). Which sound device does Poe use more extensively? What effect does this have on the reader?

7. **Analyze Imagery and Mood** Find several examples of sensory imagery—words and phrases that appeal to the senses—in the story and in the poem. In what way do these images help convey the **tone** of the story?

8. **Analyze Poe's Style** Poe has fascinated readers with his tales of horror and haunting poetry. Identify the stylistic characteristics that are common to both selections you have just read. Use the following list to help you:

   - a first-person point of view that expresses emotional intensity
   - repeated or italicized words
   - unusual choice of words, phrases, and expressions
   - long sentences or sentences with interruptions
   - strange or grotesque sensory images

Text Criticism

9. **Critical Interpretations** One literary critic has noted that Poe's "imagination is visual and three-dimensional. . . . If he had been alive today he probably would be a filmmaker." Do you think "The Pit and the Pendulum" would succeed as a movie? What would have to be changed in order to adapt the story for the screen? Explain.

> ## What breeds **TERROR?**
> What could a person do to overcome his or her fear?

COMMON CORE

RL 1 Cite strong and thorough textual evidence to support inferences drawn from the text. **RL 4** Determine the meaning of words and phrases as they are used in a text; analyze the cumulative impact of specific word choices on meaning and tone.

Practice and Apply

For preliminary support of post-reading questions, use these copy masters:

R RESOURCE MANAGER—Copy Masters
Reading Check p. 28
Poe's Style p. 21
Question Support p. 29

Additional selection questions are provided for teachers on page 15.

ANSWERS

Comprehension

1. *He almost falls into a pit, and then he is tied below a descending, razor-sharp pendulum.*

2. *General Lasalle, an officer of the conquering French army, seems to save the narrator.*

3. *The lake both terrifies and thrills the speaker.*

Text Analysis

COMMON CORE RL 1, RL 4

Possible answers:

4. *The narrator's greatest strengths are his observant, analytical mind, which comes up with the plan to use the rats, and his refusal to give up in the face of each new torture.*

5. ● **COMMON CORE FOCUS** *Paraphrase*
   The narrator hears voices, trumpets, and a loud grating sound. The walls push back and before he falls into the pit, he is caught by General Lasalle. Most students will believe that the narrator is really saved: The narrator speaks in the past tense and describes writing his story down (lines 9–10).

6. *Alliteration: "lot," "love," "less," "lovely," "loneliness," "lake" (lines 1–5); "tall," "tower'd," (line 6); "wind would" (line 9); "lone lake" (line 12); "fitting," "for" (lines 18–19). Assonance: "wild," "pines," "night" (lines 5–7); "in," "its," "still," "infant," "spirit" (lines 10–11). Poe uses alliteration more. Both sound devices create a musical effect.*

7. *Story: "They writhed upon my throat; their cold lips sought my own" (lines 376–377). Poem: "when the night had thrown her pall / Upon that spot" (lines 7–8). The images help convey a tone of fear and terror by making what the narrator fears very vivid and real to the reader.*

8. ● **COMMON CORE FOCUS** *Poe's Style*
   First-person: "I was sick—sick unto death with that long agony" (story, line 1), "My infant spirit would awake" (poem, line 11). *Repeated or italicized words:* "hope" (story, lines 329–330); "terror" (poem, lines 12, 13). *Word choice:* "Ultima Thule" (story, line 268), "wild'ring" (poem, line 21). *Long or interrupted sentences:* story, lines 9–12; poem, lines 7–12. *Strange images:* "Demon eyes, of a wild and ghastly vivacity" (story, line 414); "poison'd wave" (poem, line 17).

Text Criticism

Possible answer:

9. *The story would make an effective short film. The director might decide to use voice-over narration and to show the pit.*

> What breeds **TERROR?** *Possible answer:* Facing one's fear by actually experiencing what one is afraid of can be an effective method of overcoming fear.

ANSWERS

Vocabulary in Context

▲ **VOCABULARY PRACTICE**

1. *antonyms*	6. *synonyms*
2. *antonyms*	7. *antonyms*
3. *synonyms*	8. *synonyms*
4. *synonyms*	9. *antonyms*
5. *antonyms*	10. *synonyms*

 **RESOURCE MANAGER—Copy Master**
Vocabulary Practice p. 26

ACADEMIC VOCABULARY IN WRITING

Possible answer: *Poe's direct and vividly descriptive* style *and* precise *words bring the horror of the dungeon to vivid life. One powerful* feature *of the dungeon is its lighting. At first, the narrator is surrounded by "the blackness of eternal night." Later, the lighting changes to a "wild sulphurous luster," which* clarifies *the setting for the narrator. He sees the size of the room, as well as the pit and the pendulum that will terrify him.*

VOCABULARY STRATEGY: FOREIGN WORDS USED IN ENGLISH

COMMON CORE L 4b

1. *a Spanish fleet of ships sent against England in 1588*

2. *a Spanish ship of war*

3. *a Spanish-Portuguese irregular army member who fought against Napoleon*

 **RESOURCE MANAGER—Copy Master**
Vocabulary Strategy p. 27

Interactive Vocabulary THINK central

Keywords direct students to a **WordSharp** tutorial on **thinkcentral.com** or to other types of vocabulary practice and review.

Vocabulary in Context

▲ **VOCABULARY PRACTICE**

Indicate whether the words in each pair are synonyms or antonyms.

1. precise/indeterminate	6. insuperable/unconquerable
2. eloquent/inarticulate	7. lethargy/excitement
3. lucid/clear	8. bewilder/confound
4. spread/pervade	9. reluctance/pertinacity
5. supposition/evidence	10. hunger/voracity

ACADEMIC VOCABULARY IN WRITING

• clarify   • feature   • precise   • style   • transmit

Imagine that you are able to view the narrator in the dungeon. Write a paragraph to **transmit** your feelings about him and his circumstances. Highlight one **feature** that makes a strong impression on you, and choose **precise** words to describe it. Use at least one Academic Vocabulary word in your response.

VOCABULARY STRATEGY: FOREIGN WORDS USED IN ENGLISH

The English language changes all the time. Over its history, it has continually acquired new words from other languages and from historical events. For example, in line 94 of "The Pit and the Pendulum," Poe uses the term *autos-da-fé* (literally, "acts of faith"), which arose during the Spanish Inquisition to describe public executions, and then made its way into English usage. Other words that entered English from Spanish and Portuguese languages include *armada*, *galleon*, and *guerilla*.

PRACTICE Match each word below with its original meaning from Spanish. You can use a dictionary to help you.

1.	armada	a Spanish ship of war
2.	galleon	a Spanish-Portuguese irregular army member who fought against Napoleon
3.	guerilla	a Spanish fleet of ships sent against England in 1588

WORD LIST
confound
eloquent
indeterminate
insuperable
lethargy
lucid
pertinacity
pervade
supposition
voracity

COMMON CORE

L 4b Consult reference materials to determine or clarify a word's precise meaning.

Interactive Vocabulary THINK central
Go to **thinkcentral.com**.
KEYWORD: HML10-876

DIFFERENTIATED INSTRUCTION

FOR ENGLISH LANGUAGE LEARNERS

Vocabulary: Figurative Language To help students understand how to use language in abstract ways, have them first review the meanings of these vocabulary words: *confound, indeterminate, insuperable, lucid, pertinacity, supposition.* Then have students choose two words and work in groups to write a simile and metaphor using each word. Ask students to trade papers and discuss which examples work best.

FOR ADVANCED LEARNERS/PRE–AP

Vocabulary in Writing Ask students to use at least four vocabulary words and write either a scene from the perspective of the narrator in the story or a description of "The Lake" from the perspective of the speaker in the poem.

Language

◆ **GRAMMAR AND STYLE: Use Personification**

Review the **Grammar and Style** note on page 866. Poe uses a type of figurative language known as **personification**, in which a writer gives human characteristics to an animal, a thing, or an idea. To create personification, choose **nouns, verbs,** and **adjectives** that are usually used to refer to people. In the following example, Poe refers to the pendulum that moves to "fan" the narrator with its "breath":

> *Days passed—it might have been that many days passed—ere it swept so closely over me as to fan me with its acrid breath.* (lines 279–280)

Notice how the revisions in blue make the images in this first draft more memorable. Revise your response to the prompt by incorporating examples of personification.

> **STUDENT MODEL**
>
> In "The Pit and the Pendulum," the narrator is trapped between the pit ^hungry^
> and the ^menacing,^ enclosing walls, with the added danger of the sharp ^, sadistic^ pendulum
> above him.

COMMON CORE

W 9a Draw evidence from literary texts to support analysis.
L 3 Apply knowledge of language to make effective choices for meaning or style.

READING-WRITING CONNECTION

 YOUR TURN Broaden your understanding of Poe's works by responding to this prompt. Then use the **revising tip** to improve your writing.

WRITING PROMPT	**REVISING TIP**
Extended Constructed Response: Write Across Texts According to one critic, Poe's work is concerned with "death-in-life" and "life-in-death." How do "The Pit and the Pendulum" and "The Lake" deal with these themes? Using examples from the texts, write a **three- to five-paragraph response.**	Review your response. Have you used personification to make your descriptions memorable? If not, revise to give human characteristics to an animal, thing, or idea.

Interactive Revision THINK central

Go to **thinkcentral.com.**
KEYWORD: HML10-877

Language

COMMON CORE **W 9a, L 3**

◆ **GRAMMAR AND STYLE**

- After they review the note on page 866 and the student model, have students make up examples of personification.

- Write these sentences on the board. Have students suggest revisions that include personification.

> *The trees* ~~lifted~~ *stretched their* ~~branches~~ *bony arms toward the sky. Their leaves seemed to* ~~flutter toward~~ *claw at the clouds.*

R RESOURCE MANAGER—Copy Master
Use Personification p. 30

READING-WRITING CONNECTION

Have students decide which theme best fits the story and the poem. Then have them draft a thesis statement focusing on this one theme. Suggest that students discuss one example from the texts in each of their paragraphs.

 **Writing Online** THINK central

The following tools are available online at **thinkcentral.com** and on Write*Smart* **CD-ROM:**
- **Interactive Graphic Organizers**
- **Interactive Student Models**
- **Interactive Revision Lessons**
For additional grammar instruction, see **GrammarNotes** on **thinkcentral.com.**

Assess and Reteach

Assess

DIAGNOSTIC AND SELECTION TESTS
Selection Test A pp. 243–244
Selection Test B/C pp. 245–246

Interactive Selection Test on **thinkcentral.com**

Reteach

Level Up Online Tutorials on **thinkcentral.com**

Reteaching Worksheets on **thinkcentral.com**
Literature Lesson 27: Simile and Metaphor
Literature Lesson 44: Style and Syntax
Reading Lesson 8: Making Inferences

FOR STRUGGLING WRITERS

- Help students decide whether to write about "death-in-life" or "life-in-death."

- Have students present a statement of their thesis in the first paragraph.

- Have students work in small groups to identify and discuss supporting details.

Focus and Motivate

COMMON CORE FOCUS

RL 1 Cite evidence to support inferences drawn from the text. **RL 4** Analyze the cumulative impact of specific word choices on meaning and tone. **RL 5** Analyze an author's choices concerning how to structure a text and order the events within it.

SUMMARIES

"When I Heard the Learn'd Astronomer" In this poem, Whitman juxtaposes the speaker's boredom during an astronomy lecture with his enchantment with the night sky.

"The Artilleryman's Vision" A Civil War veteran relives the horror, trauma, and exhilaration of the battlefield in this poem.

What do we learn from EXPERIENCE?

Read the question. Ask students what they think happened to the driver in the photograph on this page. What possible lessons might someone learn from such an experience? Continue this exploration by having students complete the *QUICKWRITE*.

When I Heard the Learn'd Astronomer
Poem by Walt Whitman

The Artilleryman's Vision
Poem by Walt Whitman

 Video link at **thinkcentral.com**

What do we learn from EXPERIENCE?

COMMON CORE

RL 1 Cite evidence to support inferences drawn from the text. **RL 4** Analyze the cumulative impact of specific word choices on meaning and tone. **RL 5** Analyze an author's choices concerning how to structure a text and order the events within it.

We often gain valuable information through reading, watching television, and listening to people share their knowledge. But sometimes experience can be the most powerful teacher. In the following poems by Walt Whitman, you will meet two men who learn very different lessons through their life experiences.

QUICKWRITE Think about a time in which experiencing something firsthand helped you to learn about it. For example, maybe you gained appreciation for a distant city by actually visiting it. Or perhaps breaking a leg made you aware of some barriers to the disabled. Explain to a classmate how experience fostered your new understanding.

878

Selection Resources

See resources on the **Teacher One Stop DVD-ROM** and on **thinkcentral.com**.

 Video link at **thinkcentral.com**

 RESOURCE MANAGER UNIT 8
Plan and Teach, pp. 33–40
Text Analysis and Reading
Skill, pp. 41–44†*

DIAGNOSTIC AND SELECTION TESTS
Selection Tests, pp. 247–250

BEST PRACTICES TOOLKIT
Spider Map, p. B22

TECHNOLOGY
- Teacher One Stop DVD-ROM
- Student One Stop DVD-ROM
- Audio Anthology CD
- GrammarNotes DVD-ROM
- ExamView Test Generator on the Teacher One Stop

---

* Resources for Differentiation   **† Also in Spanish**   **‡ In Haitian Creole and Vietnamese**

TEXT ANALYSIS: WHITMAN'S STYLE

Like other poets of his day, Walt Whitman was deeply committed to celebrating the beauty and richness of America. Yet, while many of his contemporaries relied on conventional poetic forms such as sonnets and ballads, Whitman did not. Instead, he invented a new form to capture the spirit of the nation. Called **free verse,** this poetic form lacks traditional **prosody**—the regular patterns of rhyme and meter. As a result, the lines in free verse flow easily, resembling natural speech. Other aspects of style that distinguish Whitman's work are as follows:

- **repetition**—or repeated words and phrases
- **parallelism**—or ideas phrased in similar ways
- **onomatopoeia**—or words that imitate sounds
- **catalogs**—or lists of things, people, or attributes

As you read each poem, notice how Whitman's choice of form and stylistic devices help convey the speaker's experience.

READING SKILL: ANALYZE SENSORY DETAILS

In his poetry, Whitman praised life in all of its diversity. He often relied on sensory details to communicate a wealth of experiences to readers. You probably remember that **sensory details** are words and phrases that appeal to the five senses: sight, hearing, taste, smell, and touch. As you read Whitman's poetry, record various examples of sensory details and analyze their effectiveness. For each poem, use a chart like the one shown.

"When I Heard the Learn'd Astronomer"		
Details	Sense(s)	Why Effective
"When I heard ... When the proofs, the figures, were ranged in columns before me" (lines 1–2)	hearing and sight	They clearly place the speaker in a lecture hall.

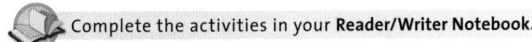 Complete the activities in your **Reader/Writer Notebook.**

Meet the Author

Walt Whitman
1819–1892

Jack-of-All-Trades
Born in 1819, Walt Whitman grew up in a hurry. He left school at age 11, and within a few years he was living on his own in New York City. He drifted from job to job, working as a printer, journalist, and carpenter. He loved to stroll around the city, taking in sights and sounds that he would later use in his poetry.

Pioneer of Poetry
In 1855, Whitman published *Leaves of Grass,* a volume of poems that captured the variety and tumult of 19th-century American life. Upon receiving a copy, the poet Ralph Waldo Emerson declared, "It is the most extraordinary piece of wit and wisdom that America has yet contributed." However, other writers denounced the book for its unorthodox form and content. Over the years, Whitman added to, revised, and rearranged the poems in *Leaves of Grass,* producing nine editions in total. Today, it is often regarded as the most influential collection of poetry in American literature.

Whitman and the Civil War
When Whitman learned that his younger brother had been wounded in Fredericksburg, Virginia, he immediately traveled to the front. There he saw the aftermath of one of the war's bloodiest battles. This experience convinced him to work in Washington, D.C., as a volunteer nurse. In caring for the wounded, Whitman witnessed the effects of war on men's bodies and minds. During this time, he wrote numerous poems, including the poignant "The Artilleryman's Vision." His years of nursing, he once wrote, were "the greatest privilege and satisfaction ... and, of course, the most profound lesson of my life."

Author Online
THINK central
Go to **thinkcentral.com.**
KEYWORD: HML10-879

879

Teach

879

Practice and Apply

READ WITH A PURPOSE

Help students set a purpose for reading. Tell them to read to compare and contrast the experiences of the speakers in the two poems.

A *Model the Skill:* **WHITMAN'S STYLE**

Use the Spider Map with students to model how to identify aspects of Whitman's style.

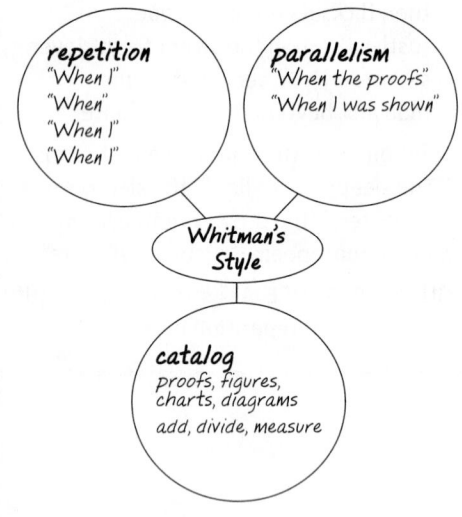

- **repetition** "When I" "When" "When I" "When I"
- **parallelism** "When the proofs" "When I was shown"
- **Whitman's Style**
- **catalog** proofs, figures, charts, diagrams add, divide, measure

🧰 BEST PRACTICES TOOLKIT—Transparency
Spider Map p. B22

Possible answer: *Whitman uses repetition of the words* When *and* When I; *he catalogs mathematical structures (proofs, figures, charts, and diagrams) and operations (add, divide, measure).*

B SENSORY DETAILS

Possible answer: *Students might say that "mystical moist night air" (line 7) or "Look'd up in perfect silence at the stars" (line 8) most effectively conveys his enjoyment of the night sky.*

When I Heard the Learn'd Astronomer

Walt Whitman

When I heard the learn'd astronomer,
When the proofs,[1] the figures, were ranged in columns before me,
When I was shown the charts and diagrams, to add, divide, and
    measure them,
When I sitting heard the astronomer where he lectured with much
    applause in the lecture-room, **A**
5 How soon unaccountable I became tired and sick,
Till rising and gliding out I wander'd off by myself,
In the mystical moist night air, and from time to time,
Look'd up in perfect silence at the stars. **B**

A WHITMAN'S STYLE
Notice Whitman's use of **parallelism** in lines 1–4. What other distinctive features of his style can you see in this poem?

B SENSORY DETAILS
Of the various sensory details, which most effectively conveys the speaker's enjoyment of the night sky?

---

1. **proofs:** formal scientific statements of evidence.

DIFFERENTIATED INSTRUCTION

FOR ENGLISH LANGUAGE LEARNERS

Language: Contractions Direct students' attention to the words *learn'd* (line 1), *wander'd* (line 6), and *Look'd* (line 8). Explain that elision, or striking out the final *e* in *ed* was commonly used by 19th-century poets. They dropped a syllable in order to enhance the flow and rhythm of lines. Have students find examples in "The Artilleryman's Vision": *brandish'd* (line 14), *fill'd* (line 15), and *color'd* (line 25).

FOR STRUGGLING READERS

Develop Reading Fluency Read aloud the poem. Point out the long clauses and hard sounds in the first four lines and the looser phrasing and softer sounds of the last four lines. Then read the poem aloud a second time, pausing at the ends of lines so that students can echo read. Emphasize the contrasting sound and structure of the first four lines and the last four lines.

R RESOURCE MANAGER—Copy Master
Reading Fluency p. 46

BACKGROUND

Popular Astronomy Astronomy sprang into the public consciousness in the 18th and 19th centuries. During that time major developments occurred, including the discovery of Neptune in 1846 and the moons of Mars in 1877. Observation of the Martian canals in 1877 and theories about vegetation on Mars caught the public imagination. The first photographs of the stars and planets brought the wonders of these sights to the public. And, possibly most importantly, astronomers such as Richard Anthony Proctor and Benjamin Martin began giving lectures and writing astronomy books for the public. Backyard stargazing became popular, and the first amateur astronomer associations formed.

Prereading for this poem is found on page 878.

Analyze Visuals

Activity Ask students to identify and explain details in the photograph that convey the idea of what cannon fire is like. *Possible answer: The fiery blast reflects the cannon's power and destructiveness. The soldiers are covering their ears, which suggests that cannon fire is painfully loud. The fact that five soldiers are involved with one cannon shows that it is a complicated and important operation.*

READING SKILL

COMMON CORE
RL 1
RL 4

C Model the Skill: SENSORY DETAILS

To model how to analyze sensory details, read the first three lines of the poem aloud. Then draw the Reading Skill chart from page 879 on the board. In the Details column, write the following: "I hear, just hear, the breath of my infant" (line 3). Ask students what sense the line appeals to, and record hearing in the second column. Explain to students that the detail is effective because it emphasizes the absolute stillness and quiet of the night, and record that in the third column. Have students continue to record details from lines 1–6 in their charts.

Possible answer: The details of the wife slumbering, the speaker's head resting on the pillow, and the sound of the baby breathing in the dark establish the peace and quiet of the night.

REVISIT THE BIG QUESTION

What do we learn from EXPERIENCE?

Discuss How does point of view help the audience share the speaker's experience of war in lines 1–10? What does the reader learn from this experience? *Possible answer: Whitman's use of the first-person point of view in an interior monologue helps the reader see the veteran's present situation and share his nightmarish memories of the battlefield.*

THE Artilleryman's VISION

Walt Whitman

While my wife at my side lies slumbering, and the wars are over long,
And my head on the pillow rests at home, and the vacant midnight passes,
And through the stillness, through the dark, I hear, just hear, the breath of my infant,
There in the room as I wake from sleep this vision presses upon me;
5　The engagement[1] opens there and then in fantasy unreal,
The skirmishers[2] begin, they crawl cautiously ahead, I hear the irregular snap! snap! **C**
I hear the sounds of the different missiles, the short *t-h-t! t-h-t!* of the rifle balls,
I see the shells exploding leaving small white clouds, I hear the great shells shrieking as they pass,
The grape[3] like the hum and whirr of wind through the trees, (tumultuous now the contest rages,)
10　All the scenes at the batteries[4] rise in detail before me again,
The crashing and smoking, the pride of the men in their pieces,
The chief-gunner ranges and sights his piece and selects a fuse of the right time,
After firing I see him lean aside and look eagerly off to note the effect;
Elsewhere I hear the cry of a regiment charging, (the young colonel leads himself this time with brandish'd[5] sword,)

---

1. **engagement:** battle.
2. **skirmishers:** soldiers sent out in advance of a main attack.
3. **grape:** grapeshot—small iron balls shot in a bunch from a cannon.
4. **batteries:** groups of cannons.
5. **brandish'd:** raised and waving.

882 UNIT 8: AUTHOR'S STYLE AND VOICE

C SENSORY DETAILS
Reread lines 1–6. Which sensory details help you to understand the situation described at the beginning of the poem?

COMMON CORE RL 4

Language Coach

Multiple Meanings In special contexts, some words that are usually nouns become verbs. What context gives you a clue to the meanings of *ranges* and *sights* in line 12? What do you think these words mean in this line?

DIFFERENTIATED INSTRUCTION

FOR ENGLISH LANGUAGE LEARNERS

Language Coach　COMMON CORE RL 4

Multiple Meanings *Answer: The context is firearms.* Ranges *and* sights *both seem to have to do with aiming a gun.* Ask students what context provides a clue to the meaning of *rages* in line 9. Then ask students what they think the verb means here. (*The context is battle;* rages *means "is violent."*)

FOR ADVANCED LEARNERS/PRE–AP

Analyze Repetition Point out that alliteration—the repetition of consonant sounds—is another of Whitman's stylistic devices. Ask students to identify which consonants he repeats and their frequency. Does he repeat different consonants at different places in the poem? What effect does this repetition have? How does it support the poem's themes and mood?

15 I see the gaps cut by the enemy's volleys,[6] (quickly fill'd up, no
    delay,)
I breathe the suffocating smoke, then the flat clouds hover low
    concealing all;
Now a strange lull for a few seconds, not a shot fired on either side, **D**
Then resumed the chaos louder than ever, with eager calls and
    orders of officers,
While from some distant part of the field the wind wafts to my ears
    a shout of applause, (some special success,)
20 And ever the sound of the cannon far or near, (rousing even in
    dreams a devilish exultation and all the old mad joy in the depths
    of my soul,)
And ever the hastening of infantry shifting positions, batteries,
    cavalry, moving hither and thither,
(The falling, dying, I heed not, the wounded dripping and red I heed
    not, some to the rear are hobbling,)
Grime, heat, rush, aide-de-camps[7] galloping by or on a full run,
With the patter of small arms, the warning *s-s-t* of the rifles, (these
    in my vision I hear or see,)
25 And bombs bursting in air, and at night the vari-color'd rockets. **E**

---

6. **volleys:** groups of cannonballs fired at the same time.
7. **aide-de-camps** (ād'dĭ-kămps'): assistants to military commanders.

THE ARTILLERYMAN'S VISION   **883**

D WHITMAN'S STYLE
Reread lines 7–17, noting the long **catalog** of combat activities. In what way is this stylistic element in keeping with the poem's speaker—a dreaming soldier?

E WHITMAN'S STYLE
What overall effect does Whitman create by using **free verse** in this poem?

THE ARTILLERYMAN'S VISION   **883**

TIERED DISCUSSION PROMPTS

Use these prompts to help students understand how Whitman's letter to his mother and his poem "The Artilleryman's Vision" present some similar reflections on war:

Connect Does an event on the news make more of an impression on you when it is narrated by an anchor or by a participant? Explain your answer. *Accept all reasonable answers.*

Analyze Why might Whitman have been interested in this particular Pennsylvania soldier? *Possible answer: While focusing on one infantryman, Whitman portrays the suffering and hardship experienced by tens of thousands of soldiers during the Civil War. The soldier's story of help from an enemy underscores the fact that although the soldiers fought each other in deadly combat, they were all Americans, and sometimes had grown up as friends, neighbors, or even brothers.*

Synthesize How did Whitman's wartime experience, as revealed in this letter, influence his poetry? *Possible answer: Though Whitman was not a soldier himself, his experiences as a battlefield nurse gave him a deep understanding of the hardships and suffering that soldiers endured and of the grim realities of the battlefield.*

Reading for Information

LETTER In this letter to his mother, Walt Whitman describes a meaningful encounter with a wounded Union soldier following the Battle of Fredericksburg.

January 29, 1865

Dear Mother—

Here is a case of a soldier I found among the crowded cots in the Patent hospital — (they have removed most of the men of late and broken up that hospital). He likes to have some one to talk to, and we will listen to him. He got badly wounded in the leg and side at Fredericksburg that eventful Saturday, 13th December. He lay the succeeding two days and nights helpless on the field, between the city and those grim batteries, for his company and his regiment had been compelled to leave him to his fate. To make matters worse, he lay with his head slightly down hill, and could not help himself. At the end of some fifty hours he was brought off, with other wounded, under a flag of truce.

We ask him how the Rebels treated him during those two days and nights within reach of them —whether they came to him —whether they abused him? He answers that several of the Rebels, soldiers and others, came to him, at one time and another. A couple of them, who were together, spoke roughly and sarcastically, but did no act. One middle-aged man, however, who seemed to be moving around the field among the dead and wounded for benevolent purposes, came to him in a way he will never forget. This man treated our soldier kindly, bound up his wounds, cheered him, gave him a couple of biscuits, gave him a drink and water, asked him if he could eat some beef. This good Secesh,[1] however, did not change our soldier's position, for it might have caused the blood to burst from the wounds where they were clotted and stagnated. Our soldier is from Pennsylvania; has had a pretty severe time; the wounds proved to be bad ones. But he retains a good heart, and is at present on the gain. . . .

Walt

---

1. **Secesh** (sĭ-sĕsh'): a secessionist from the Union; a Confederate.

Comprehension

1. **Recall** In "When I Heard the Learn'd Astronomer," what methods does the astronomer use to teach about the stars?

2. **Recall** In "The Artilleryman's Vision," where is the artilleryman when he experiences his vision?

3. **Summarize** Describe the sequence of events in "The Artilleryman's Vision."

Text Analysis

4. **Interpret Mood** Reread "When I Heard the Learn'd Astronomer." At what point does the mood, or atmosphere, of the poem change? Explain which words and phrases signal this shift.

5. **Understand Whitman's Style** In his poetry, Whitman often celebrates nature and its beauty. Which aspects of Whitman's style in "When I Heard the Learn'd Astronomer" help communicate the beauty of nature? If necessary, review the list of aspects of Whitman's style on page 879.

6. **Examine Diction and Tone** Reread lines 18–22 of "The Artilleryman's Vision," reviewing Whitman's diction, or choice of words. Considering phrases such as "devilish exultation" and "old mad joy," describe Whitman's tone, or attitude, toward war.

7. **Analyze Sensory Details** Review the charts that you created and your conclusions about Whitman's use of sensory details. Select one poem and explain how sensory details help make the speaker's firsthand experience vivid and engaging. Use examples from the poem to support your answer.

8. **Generalize About Poetic Form** Whitman uses **free verse** in both selections. How might your sense of the speakers and their experiences be different if the poems had been written in a form with a conventional metrical pattern and rhyme scheme?

9. **Compare Literary Works** Compare Whitman's depictions of Civil War soldiers in "The Artilleryman's Vision" and in his letter to his mother on page 884. Which offers a more disturbing view of the after-effects of war—the poem or the personal letter? Use information from both pieces to support your response.

Text Criticism

10. **Historical Context** When Whitman wrote "The Artilleryman's Vision" in the mid-1860s, psychology had yet to become a modern science. What does this fact reveal about Whitman and his handling of the poem's subject?

What do we learn from EXPERIENCE?
What could your life experiences teach someone else?

COMMON CORE

RL 1 Cite evidence to support inferences drawn from the text. **RL 4** Analyze the cumulative impact of specific word choices on meaning and tone. **RL 5** Analyze an author's choices concerning how to structure a text and order the events within it.

Practice and Apply

For preliminary support of post-reading questions, use these copy masters:

R RESOURCE MANAGER—Copy Masters
Whitman's Style p. 41
Question Support p. 45

Additional selection questions are provided for teachers on page 37.

ANSWERS

Comprehension

1. *The astronomer teaches by lecturing and displaying proofs, charts, and diagrams.*

2. *The artilleryman is in his bed at home.*

3. *The speaker is home in bed; he awakes and remembers a long-ago battle.*

Text Analysis
COMMON CORE RL 1, RL 4, RL 5

Possible answers:

4. *The mood changes in line 6, when the speaker escapes from the lecture. The words "rising," "gliding," "wander'd," "mystical," and "perfect silence" signal the shift in mood.*

5. ● **COMMON CORE FOCUS** *Whitman's Style Repetition in the first four lines makes the lecture seem monotonous. The freer feeling of the last four lines conveys the wonder of nature.*

6. *Through words like "eager" (line 18) and "applause" (line 19), Whitman implies that the excitement of war is attractive even though it is destructive.*

7. ■ **COMMON CORE FOCUS** *Analyze Sensory Details "The Artilleryman's Vision": Whitman re-creates the sights, sounds, and emotions of battle through images such as "suffocating smoke" (line 16)*

Assess and Reteach

Assess

DIAGNOSTIC AND SELECTION TESTS
Selection Test A pp. 247–248
Selection Test B/C pp. 249–250

Interactive Selection Test on **thinkcentral.com**

Reteach

Level Up Online Tutorials on **thinkcentral.com**

Reteaching Worksheets on **thinkcentral.com**
Literature Lesson 44: Style and Syntax

---

and "patter of small arms, the warning s-s-t of the rifles" (line 24). **"The Learn'd Astronomer":** Whitman re-creates the feeling of sitting in the lecture hall with "ranged in columns before me" (line 2), "was shown" (line 3), "with much applause" (line 4), "tired and sick" (line 5) and the stillness and peace of the night with "mystical moist night air" (line 7) and "perfect silence" (line 8).

8. *The speakers' experiences might not have seemed as authentic and immediate.*

9. *Some students may say the poem is more disturbing because the speaker cannot escape his memories. Other students may say*

that the letter is more disturbing because the soldier may not have survived.

Text Criticism
Possible answers:

10. *Whitman was observant, describing post-traumatic stress disorder before it was recognized or understood.*

What do we learn from EXPERIENCE?
Have students identify a particulary meaningful life experience and what they learned from it.

Focus and Motivate

SUMMARIES

"Birches" In this poem, the speaker describes a stand of ice-bent birch trees and reminisces about his youth, wistful for a respite from daily living.

"Mending Wall" In this poem, the speaker describes meeting his neighbor every spring to repair the stone walls that separate their properties. The speaker tries to understand the reason for the fences.

How can NATURE inspire you?

Introduce the question, and invite students to share their experiences with nature. Encourage students to try to visualize a place of natural beauty for their *QUICKWRITE*.

Selection Resources

Essential Course of Study **ECOS** ✓

Birches
Poem by Robert Frost

Mending Wall
Poem by Robert Frost

How can NATURE inspire you?

Spending time in nature often inspires us to think of things beyond our ordinary routines. Whether it's hiking through woods or canoeing down a river, for example, being in "the great outdoors" can help us appreciate our place in the world at large. In the following poems by Robert Frost, the speakers gain new insights into their own lives through their experiences with nature.

QUICKWRITE Think of an outdoor activity that says something about you and what you're like—such as birdwatching, fishing, climbing, or swimming. Write a paragraph describing the activity and what it has helped you realize about yourself.

886

See resources on the **Teacher One Stop DVD-ROM** and on **thinkcentral.com**.

R RESOURCE MANAGER UNIT 8
Plan and Teach, pp. 47–54
Text Analysis and Reading
Skill, pp. 55–58
Grammar and Writing, p. 60

DIAGNOSTIC AND SELECTION TESTS
Selection Tests, pp. 251–254

BEST PRACTICES TOOLKIT
Venn Diagram, p. A26
Draw It, p. A2

INTERACTIVE READER

ADAPTED INTERACTIVE READER

ELL ADAPTED INTERACTIVE READER

TECHNOLOGY
- Teacher One Stop DVD-ROM
- Student One Stop DVD-ROM
- PowerNotes DVD-ROM
- Audio Anthology CD
- GrammarNotes DVD-ROM
- Audio Tutor CD
- ExamView Test Generator on the Teacher One Stop

THINK central

Find it Online!
Features on **thinkcentral.com** that support the selection include
- **PowerNotes** presentation
- **ThinkAloud** models to enhance comprehension
- **WordSharp** vocabulary tutorials
- interactive writing and grammar instruction

TEXT ANALYSIS: FROST'S STYLE

In many ways, Robert Frost is a transitional figure between the 19th and 20th centuries. Like his predecessors, Frost loved and wrote about the natural world, particularly rural New England. His poems, however, contain more than his impressions of simple country life. In them, Frost often uses humor to point to more serious matters, such as themes of solitude and isolation. In this way, his writing anticipates later works of modern poetry and fiction. The following are key aspects of Frost's style:

- conversational or **colloquial language**
- rich sensory **imagery**
- imaginative **similes** and **metaphors**
- realistic **dialogue**
- a playful, mocking **tone**

As you read, notice how these stylistic techniques help make "Birches" and "Mending Wall" works of rare beauty and complexity.

READING SKILL: MAKE INFERENCES

In modern poetry, speakers do not often make direct statements about how they view the world. Instead, readers must use clues in the texts to **make inferences,** or logical guesses, about the speakers' ideas and feelings. For example, speculate about what the following lines from "Birches" reveal about the speaker's desires:

So was I once myself a swinger of birches.
And so I dream of going back to be.

As you read each poem, try to "read between the lines" and record your inferences in a chart like the one shown.

"Birches"		
Poem Details	My Associations	Inferences
"When I see birches bend to left and right/ Across the lines of straighter darker trees/ I like to think some boy's been swinging them."	Birches are white, flexible trees.	Seeing bent birches makes the speaker invent a playful explanation for them.

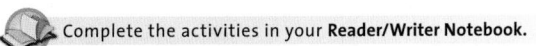 Complete the activities in your **Reader/Writer Notebook.**

Meet the Author

Robert Frost
1874–1963

Unruly Youth
Although Robert Frost is linked with rural New England in the public imagination, he spent his early years in cities. At age 11, Frost moved with his mother and sister from his birthplace, San Francisco, to the industrial city of Lawrence, Massachusetts. Undisciplined in grade school, Frost became co-valedictorian of his high school graduating class. However, he dropped out of the two universities he attended—Harvard and Dartmouth—because he disliked the discipline of academic life.

Farmer-Poet
In his 20s and 30s, Frost worked a 30-acre farm in Derry, New Hampshire. Captivated by Derry's inhabitants and rugged landscape, Frost wrote many of his most beloved poems while living there. He used traditional poetic devices—such as rhyme and meter—to capture the speech patterns of rural New Englanders. Frost's immense achievement was recognized with 4 Pulitzer Prizes in poetry and 44 honorary college degrees.

BACKGROUND TO THE POEMS
Nature's Splendor
In the selections, Frost captures the stark beauty of rural New England. In "Birches," he paints a vivid picture of the white-barked trees that adorn much of the countryside. The birch is a tall, delicate tree with a slender white trunk that can bend easily in a moderate wind. The title "Mending Wall" refers to the act of repairing the stone walls that divide farms and fields in New England. Farmers typically build these walls with stones removed from their own land.

Author Online
THINK central
Go to **thinkcentral.com.**
KEYWORD: HML10-887

887

Teach

TEXT ANALYSIS — COMMON CORE RL 4

● *Model the Skill:* **FROST'S STYLE**

To model how to identify aspects of Frost's style, write these lines on the board:

> When life was pure and summer days were long,
> We sisters stood under the apple tree
> To battle enemies beyond the fence.
> Our weapons were our long, slim willow sticks.
> Our ammunition, flying flinging apples.
> Oh, how we girls were feared by prairie weeds!

Point out how the style of these lines is similar to Frost's style. Explain that like passages from Frost, this passage uses imagery ("under the apple tree," "beyond the fence," long, slim willow sticks," "flying flinging apples," "prairie weeds"), metaphor ("Our weapons were . . . willow sticks," "Our ammunition, flying flinging apples"), and a playful tone ("Oh, how we girls were feared by prairie weeds!").

GUIDED PRACTICE Have students add realistic dialogue to the poem.

READING SKILL — COMMON CORE RL 1

■ *Model the Skill:* **MAKE INFERENCES**

To model how to make inferences, share these lines with students:

> I lay with grass tickling my neck,
> Imagining clowns in the clouds.

Explain to students that they can use clues in the lines to make inferences about the speaker. Point out that the speaker is relaxed, lying in a field or park, and daydreaming.

GUIDED PRACTICE Ask students what inferences they can make about the speaker in the lines on the board.

R RESOURCE MANAGER—Copy Master
Make Inferences p. 57 (for student use while reading the selection)

DIFFERENTIATED INSTRUCTION

FOR STRUGGLING READERS

Concept Support If students have difficulty making inferences, encourage them to ask questions about the passage they are having trouble with. To help clarify this point, refer students to this sentence in **Unruly Youth:**

"Undisciplined in grade school, Frost became co-valedictorian of his high school graduating class."

Pose these questions to students:

- How did Frost act in grade school?
- How might he have acted in high school?

Point out that the passage doesn't include much information about his behavior in high school; however, the reader can infer that his behavior was acceptable since he became co-valedictorian.

READ WITH A PURPOSE

Tell students to read to discover the views of the world and of life that the two poems convey.

TEXT ANALYSIS

COMMON CORE RL 4

Ⓐ FROST'S STYLE

Possible answer: Examples of colloquial language include "some boy's" (line 3), "heaps" (line 12), and "You'd" (line 13). The effect is that of a speaker talking informally.

TEXT ANALYSIS

COMMON CORE RL 4

Ⓑ *Model the Skill:* FROST'S STYLE

Review that sensory details appeal to the senses of hearing, seeing, touching, smelling, and tasting. Have students choose one sense, and create a concept web for it on the board. Ask students identify sensory details from the poem for you to record in the concept web.

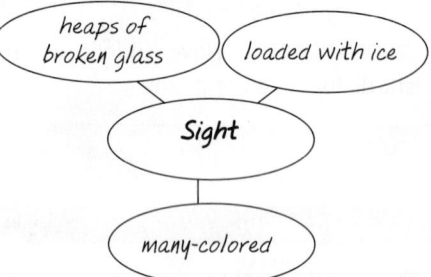

Possible answer: Sensory details that make the birches come alive include "Loaded with ice" (line 6), "click upon themselves . . . crazes their enamel" (lines 7–9), "crystal shells . . . on the snow-crust" (lines 10–11), "dragged to the withered bracken by the load" (line 14), and "trunks arching in the woods . . . to dry in the sun" (lines 17–20).

READING SKILL

COMMON CORE RL 1

Ⓒ MAKE INFERENCES

Possible answer: The speaker is imaginative ("Truth broke in / With all her matter-of-fact about the ice-storm," lines 21–22) and may have been a lonely child ("Some boy too far from town to learn baseball, / Whose only play was what he found himself," lines 25–27).

Birches

Robert Frost

When I see birches bend to left and right
Across the lines of straighter darker trees,
I like to think some boy's been swinging them.
But swinging doesn't bend them down to stay
5 As ice-storms do. Often you must have seen them
Loaded with ice a sunny winter morning
After a rain. They click upon themselves
As the breeze rises, and turn many-colored
As the stir cracks and crazes their enamel.
10 Soon the sun's warmth makes them shed crystal shells
Shattering and avalanching on the snow-crust—
Such heaps of broken glass to sweep away
You'd think the inner dome of heaven had fallen. Ⓐ
They are dragged to the withered bracken[1] by the load,
15 And they seem not to break; though once they are bowed
So low for long, they never right themselves:
You may see their trunks arching in the woods
Years afterwards, trailing their leaves on the ground
Like girls on hands and knees that throw their hair
20 Before them over their heads to dry in the sun. Ⓑ
But I was going to say when Truth broke in
With all her matter-of-fact about the ice-storm
I should prefer to have some boy bend them
As he went out and in to fetch the cows—
25 Some boy too far from town to learn baseball,
Whose only play was what he found himself,
Summer or winter, and could play alone. Ⓒ

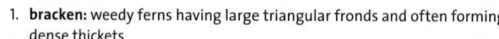

1. **bracken:** weedy ferns having large triangular fronds and often forming dense thickets.

Treetop Flier, Rod Frederick. Paper, 22⁵/₈″ × 4⁵/₈″. Courtesy of The Greenwich Workshop, Inc.

Ⓐ **FROST'S STYLE**
Frost uses plain and **colloquial words**— such as contractions— throughout this poem. Find one or two examples in lines 1–13. What effect do these everyday words create?

Ⓑ **FROST'S STYLE**
Which sensory details presented so far help the **image** of the birches come alive for you?

Ⓒ **MAKE INFERENCES**
Reread lines 21–27. What can you infer about the speaker?

DIFFERENTIATED INSTRUCTION

FOR ENGLISH LANGUAGE LEARNERS
Options for Reading Have students silently read along as they listen to the *Audio Anthology CD* recording of the selection. Play the recording a second time, stopping as needed for questions, discussion, or explanation. Then ask students to summarize the main ideas of the poem.

FOR STRUGGLING READERS
Develop Reading Fluency Read the complete poem aloud to students for enjoyment and to capture the mood of the lines. Then reread parts of the poem, and have students echo read, mimicking your intonation and pauses for punctuation. Invite students to participate in a final choral reading.

One by one he subdued[2] his father's trees
By riding them down over and over again
30 Until he took the stiffness out of them,
And not one but hung limp, not one was left
For him to conquer. He learned all there was
To learn about not launching out too soon
And so not carrying the tree away
35 Clear to the ground. He always kept his poise[3]
To the top branches, climbing carefully
With the same pains you use to fill a cup
Up to the brim, and even above the brim.
Then he flung outward, feet first, with a swish,
40 Kicking his way down through the air to the ground. **D**
So was I once myself a swinger of birches.
And so I dream of going back to be.
It's when I'm weary of considerations,
And life is too much like a pathless wood
45 Where your face burns and tickles with the cobwebs
Broken across it, and one eye is weeping
From a twig's having lashed across it open. **E**
I'd like to get away from earth awhile
And then come back to it and begin over.
50 May no fate willfully misunderstand me
And half grant what I wish and snatch me away
Not to return. Earth's the right place for love:
I don't know where it's likely to go better.
I'd like to go by climbing a birch tree,
55 And climb black branches up a snow-white trunk
Toward heaven, till the tree could bear no more,
But dipped its top and set me down again.
That would be good both going and coming back.
One could do worse than be a swinger of birches. **F**

---

2. **subdued:** brought under control.

3. **poise:** balance.

BIRCHES **889**

D FROST'S STYLE
In lines 28–40, Frost describes a boy swinging in the birches. Which words or phrases convey Frost's playful and energetic **tone?**

E FROST'S STYLE
Identify the **simile** used in lines 41–47. What ideas beyond the literal meaning of the words does this simile communicate?

F MAKE INFERENCES
Reread lines 48–59. Think of what this final passage suggests about the speaker. Does he accept or deny reality? Explain.

TEXT ANALYSIS — COMMON CORE RL 4

D FROST'S STYLE

Possible answer: A playful and energetic tone is conveyed through words and phrases such as "subdued his father's trees" (line 28), "conquer" (line 32), "not carrying the tree away / Clear to the ground" (lines 34–35), "flung outward" (line 39), and "swish" (line 39).

TEXT ANALYSIS — COMMON CORE RL 4

E FROST'S STYLE

Possible answer: The simile is "life is too much like a pathless wood" (line 44). It communicates the idea that going through life can be difficult and mysterious.

IF STUDENTS NEED HELP . . . Review that a simile is a comparison using the words *like* or *as.*

READING SKILL — COMMON CORE RL 1

F MAKE INFERENCES

Possible answer: The speaker accepts reality. He does not want to stop living or experiencing difficulties; he just wants to escape in order to play occasionally.

FOR STRUGGLING READERS

Comprehension Support Suggest that students use a Draw It strategy to make sense of the main image in lines 25–41. Have them work in pairs and draw a picture that illustrates the "swinger of birches." To provide additional practice, have students create several drawings that reflect different aspects of the image. Post the illustrations in the classroom.

BEST PRACTICES TOOLKIT
Draw It p. A2

FOR ADVANCED LEARNERS/PRE–AP

Analyze Imagery Distribute the following short excerpts among groups: lines 6–9, 37–38, 41–42, 45–47. Ask groups to discuss each passage, focusing on how imagery adds to the power of the poem. Have individual students then write a paragraph or short essay about the imagery and its power. Invite groups to share their writing.

Analyze Visuals

Activity In the painting on page 888, contemporary nature artist Rod Frederick captures the serene delicacy of birch trees. Ask students how the season portrayed in the painting differs from the seasons described or implied in the poem. *Possible answer: The birches in the poem are described in winter (lines 5–15) and summer (lines 25–35), whereas the leaves on the birches in the painting are changing color, as they would in autumn.*

Prereading for this poem is found on page 886.

Analyze Visuals

Possible answer: *The setting of the painting is like that of "Mending Wall" because it shows low stone walls. It is unlike that of "Mending Wall" because it does not show pine trees on one side of the wall and apple trees on the other.*

About the Art South African artist Derold Page (b. 1947) created *Cotswold Landscape* in 1981. Its peaceful, placid subject is typical of his work. It helps convey one of the most dominant themes in his work: that the natural world is precious and must be protected.

TEXT ANALYSIS	COMMON CORE
	RL 4

 FROST'S STYLE

Possible answer: *Some students may say that "Something" is the right word for the poem because it doesn't clearly define the force that opposes the walls. It gives the feeling of someone thinking out loud. Other students may prefer a more precise word, such as* Nature.

IF STUDENTS NEED HELP . . . Propose alternate words for students to accept or reject, such as *Nature, Winter,* or *A mystery.*

TIERED DISCUSSION PROMPTS

Use these prompts to discuss how the author explains the breaks in the wall in lines 1–11:

Analyze How does the speaker account for the broken walls in the poem? ***Possible answer:*** *The speaker says that "something" "sends the frozen-ground-swell under" the wall (lines 1–2), "creating gaps." In other words, the freezing winter weather causes the ground to swell, which, in turn, splits open the wall.*

Evaluate Why does the author give the gaps a mysterious quality in lines 10–11? Is this strategy effective? ***Possible answer:*** *The mystery of the gaps appearing in the spring makes the reader aware that a silent, unseen force of nature has been at work. The mystery engages the readers' interest.*

Mending Wall
Robert Frost

Cotswold Landscape (1981), Derold Page. Private collection. Photo © The Bridgeman Art Library.

◀ **Analyze Visuals**
In what ways might the **setting** shown in the painting represent that of "Mending Wall"? In what ways might it be different?

Something there is that doesn't love a wall,
That sends the frozen-ground-swell under it
And spills the upper boulders in the sun,
And makes gaps even two can pass abreast. **G**
5   The work of hunters is another thing:
I have come after them and made repair
Where they have left not one stone on a stone,
But they would have the rabbit out of hiding,
To please the yelping dogs.[1] The gaps I mean,
10 No one has seen them made or heard them made,
But at spring mending-time we find them there.

G FROST'S STYLE
Think about Frost's decision to use the informal, plain word *something* in line 1. In your opinion, would a more descriptive word have provided a better effect? Explain your opinion.

---

1. **The work . . . yelping dogs:** The speaker has replaced the stones hunters have removed from the wall when they have been pursuing rabbits.

DIFFERENTIATED INSTRUCTION

FOR STRUGGLING READERS

Comprehension Support Explain that one element of Frost's style is the way he concretely and simply refers to elements of daily existence in the country. Note that other poets, such as Poe, use unusual or exotic words to replace plain words, which creates a different style. Start a list of plain words from the poem: *wall* (line 1), *boulders* (line 3), *hunters* (line 5), *stone* (line 7), *rabbit* (line 8). Have students replace them with more exotic words and analyze the effect.

I let my neighbor know beyond the hill;
And on a day we meet to walk the line
And set the wall between us once again. **H**

15 We keep the wall between us as we go.
To each the boulders that have fallen to each.
And some are loaves and some so nearly balls
We have to use a spell to make them balance:
"Stay where you are until our backs are turned!"
20 We wear our fingers rough with handling them.
Oh, just another kind of outdoor game,
One on a side. It comes to little more:
There where it is we do not need the wall:
He is all pine and I am apple orchard.
25 My apple trees will never get across
And eat the cones under his pines, I tell him.
He only says, "Good fences make good neighbors."
Spring is the mischief in me, and I wonder
If I could put a notion in his head:
30 "*Why* do they make good neighbors? Isn't it
Where there are cows? But here there are no cows. **I**
Before I built a wall I'd ask to know
What I was walling in or walling out,
And to whom I was like to give offense.
35 Something there is that doesn't love a wall,
That wants it down." I could say "Elves" to him,
But it's not elves exactly, and I'd rather
He said it for himself. I see him there,
Bringing a stone grasped firmly by the top
40 In each hand, like an old-stone savage armed.
He moves in darkness as it seems to me,
Not of woods only and the shade of trees.
He will not go behind his father's saying,
And he likes having thought of it so well
45 He says again, "Good fences make good neighbors." **J**

H MAKE INFERENCES
Describe the speaker's feelings so far about mending the stone wall. Which words and phrases helped you make your inference?

I MAKE INFERENCES
Reread lines 23–31, looking for details that convey the speaker's opinion of his neighbor. Does the speaker admire him? Why or why not?

J FROST'S STYLE
Consider Frost's overall **tone,** or attitude, in this poem. Do you think the poet himself approves or disapproves of walls between neighbors? Explain.

MENDING WALL **891**

Practice and Apply

For preliminary support of post-reading questions, use these copy masters:

R RESOURCE MANAGER—Copy Masters
Frost's Style p. 55
Question Support p. 59

Additional selection questions are provided for teachers on page 51.

ANSWERS

Comprehension

1. *The speaker thinks that perhaps ice storms bent the trees or perhaps boys bent them by swinging on them.*

2. *The speaker says, "I should prefer to have some boy bend them" (line 23).*

3. *Careless hunters and an unknown "Something" cause the wall to fall apart.*

4. *There is no need for the wall because it separates fields of trees, not pastures with livestock that could stray.*

Text Analysis

COMMON CORE RL 1, RL 4

Possible answers:

5. ● **COMMON CORE FOCUS** *Make Inferences The speaker in "Birches" seems to be observant, playful, and a little weary of life. The speaker in "Mending Wall" seems to be playful also and critical of unquestioned ideas and unquestioning behavior.*

6. *"Good fences make good neighbors" suggests that setting clear boundaries helps people avoid disputes. Students may agree or may feel that walls bar close contact among good neighbors.*

7. *These sensory details convey Frost's playful tone:* **"Birches":** *boy riding the trees, taking the "stiffness" out of them, and kicking his feet on the way down (lines 28–40);* **"Mending Wall":** *apple trees leaping the wall to eat pine cones (lines 25–26).*

8. ● **COMMON CORE FOCUS** *Frost's Style* **Simile:** *"[L]ike a pathless wood" ("Birches," line 44) suggests that life is mysterious and full of obstacles. "[L]ike an old-stone savage armed" ("Mending Wall," line 40) suggests the neighbor is superstitious and ignorant.* **Metaphor:** *The words "enamel," "crystal shells," and "broken glass" ("Birches," lines 9, 10, 12) convey the ice's transparency and delicacy. In "Mending Wall," the words "some are loaves and some so nearly balls" (line 17) describe the shapes of the boulders.*

Comprehension

1. **Recall** In "Birches," what two explanations does the speaker give for the bent trees?

2. **Clarify** Which explanation does the speaker seem to prefer? Explain.

3. **Recall** According to the speaker of "Mending Wall," what two forces cause the stone wall to fall apart?

4. **Clarify** Why is there no practical need for the wall?

Text Analysis

5. **Make Inferences** Review the charts you made as you read. Think about the key inferences that helped you understand each speaker. What personality traits and values does each speaker appear to have?

6. **Interpret** In "Mending Wall," the neighbor reminds the speaker that "good fences make good neighbors." Paraphrase this statement. Do you agree or disagree? Explain your response.

7. **Analyze Tone Through Imagery** In his works, Frost often reveals a mischievous attitude toward his subjects through his choice of images. Review lines 23–42 in "Birches" and lines 15–26 in "Mending Wall." Which **sensory details** in each poem strongly convey Frost's playful tone?

8. **Analyze Frost's Style** One hallmark of Frost's style is his use of imaginative **similes** and **metaphors.** Identify two similes and two metaphors in the poems. Explain how they convey ideas beyond the literal meaning of the words.

9. **Generalize About Poetic Form** Frost often relied on conventional verse forms in his work. Both "Birches" and "Mending Wall" are written in **blank verse—** a form of unrhymed iambic pentameter favored by many English poets, including William Shakespeare. What does Frost's regular use of this poetic form suggest about him and his writing style?

Text Criticism

10. **Biographical Context** Sharing his understanding of good poetry, Frost once said: "A poem is never a put-up job, so to speak. It begins as a lump in the throat, a sense of wrong, a homesickness, a lovesickness.... It is at its best when it is a tantalizing vagueness." Select either poem and explain how it might fit Frost's standards. Use examples from the poem to support your response.

> **How can NATURE inspire you?**
> What can nature teach you about humanity?

COMMON CORE

RL 1 Cite strong and thorough textual evidence to support inferences drawn from the text. **RL 4** Analyze the cumulative impact of specific word choices on meaning and tone.

---

9. *Frost likes the freedom to write in an informal style, using unrhymed verse; yet he shows respect for traditional form by using a regular rhythm.*

Text Criticism

Possible answer:

10. *"Birches" explores an emotional weariness or pain; the speaker is weary of life but still sees the possibility of love and joy in it. The image of climbing trees toward heaven but then being set down is thrilling. "Mending Wall" suggests the speaker's sense that it is wrong for people to isolate themselves for no good reason. The force that mysteriously dismantles walls also has a "tantalizing vagueness."*

> How can **NATURE** inspire you?
> Encourage students to draw parallels between plants, animals, and natural phenomena and human behavior and relationships. Also have them consider ideas and issues that matter to people, and discuss insights nature has to offer.

Language

♦ **GRAMMAR AND STYLE: Use Verbals Effectively**

Poetry consists of words and phrases that are carefully chosen to create particular rhythms and effects. One kind of phrase that often appears in poetry is the **infinitive phrase,** which consists of an infinitive—a verb form that begins with *to*—plus its modifiers and complements. Infinitive phrases function as nouns, adjectives, or adverbs, but often they are able to provide more information than would one-word examples of these parts of speech. Here are some instances of Frost's use of infinitive phrases. Note how they function as a noun and adverbs in the poem.

> *I should prefer to have some boy bend them*
>
> *As he went out and in to fetch the cows—*
>
> *Some boy too far from town to learn baseball* ("Birches," lines 23–25)

In the following revision, notice how the writer uses an infinitive phrase to better describe the neighbor's wish. Use similar techniques to revise your responses to the prompt.

STUDENT MODEL

The speaker in "Mending Wall" doesn't understand his neighbor's wish. *to maintain the wall between their properties*

READING-WRITING CONNECTION

 YOUR TURN Broaden your understanding of Frost's poems by responding to this prompt. Then use the **revising tip** to improve your writing.

WRITING PROMPT	REVISING TIP
Extended Constructed Response: Analysis How does the dialogue and imagery in "Mending Wall" help illuminate the differences between the speaker and his neighbor? How do the differences between them help reveal the poem's theme? Using examples and direct quotations from the poem, write a **three- to five-paragraph response.**	Review your response. Did you use infinitive phrases to enhance your writing style? If not, revise your response.

Interactive Revision THINK central

Go to **thinkcentral.com.** KEYWORD: HML10-893

COMMON CORE

L 1b Use various types of phrases to convey specific meanings and add variety and interest to writing. **W 9a (RL 2)** Draw evidence from literary texts to support analysis; determine a theme and how it is refined by specific details.

DIFFERENTIATED INSTRUCTION

FOR STRUGGLING WRITERS

Distribute a Venn Diagram to help students contrast the speaker and his neighbor. Point out that since the essay focuses on contrast, the center part of the diagram may be empty. For each point of contrast, have students cite line numbers of dialogue that support the statement.

BEST PRACTICES TOOLKIT—Transparency Venn Diagram p. A26

Language

 COMMON CORE L 1b, W 9a (RL 2)

♦ **GRAMMAR AND STYLE**

- Explain that infinitive phrases should be used sparingly. Students should be careful to place infinitive phrases clearly in the sentence, so that the phrase does not muddy the meaning of the sentence. (For more on infinitives, see "Infinitives and Infinitive Phrases" on p. R61 in the **Grammar Handbook.**)

- After discussing the model, have students use infinitive phrases to revise sentences. Write these examples on the board. Discuss the effectiveness of the revisions.

  Hannah found herself wishing to see the loaves.

  Alexandra thought it would be fun to play out in the yard.

R RESOURCE MANAGER—Copy Master Grammar and Style p. 60

READING-WRITING CONNECTION

Have students begin by identifying and examining the few lines of dialogue in the poem. Point out that the dialogue in lines 24–26 is indirect and does not have quotation marks around it. Then, have students identify and analyze examples of imagery.

Writing Online THINK central

The following tools are available online at **thinkcentral.com** and on **Write*Smart* CD-ROM:**
- **Interactive Graphic Organizers**
- **Interactive Student Models**
- **Interactive Revision Lessons**

For additional grammar instruction, see **GrammarNotes** on **thinkcentral.com.**

Assess and Reteach

Assess

DIAGNOSTIC AND SELECTION TESTS Selection Test A, B/C pp. 251–254

Interactive Selection Test on **thinkcentral.com**

Reteach

Level Up Online Tutorials on **thinkcentral.com**

Reteaching Worksheets on **thinkcentral.com**

Focus and Motivate

COMMON CORE FOCUS

RL 1 Cite textual evidence to support analysis of what the text says explicitly as well as inferences drawn from the text. **RL 4** Analyze the cumulative impact of specific word choices on meaning and tone.

SUMMARIES

"The Pond" In this poem, the speaker re-creates the color, sounds, and feelings evoked by a pond at dusk.

"Fourth of July Night" In this poem, the speaker describes the appearance and beauty of the many fireworks that explode in the sky above a small boat.

"The Red Wheelbarrow" In this poem, the speaker describes a wheelbarrow and lets the reader wonder about its importance.

Can you paint a PICTURE with words?

Introduce the question. Point out that an image of a moment may appeal to the sensations of sight, sound, smell, taste, or touch. Then have students complete the *QUICKWRITE*.

Selection Resources

The Pond
Poem by Amy Lowell

Fourth of July Night Video link at **thinkcentral.com**
Poem by Carl Sandburg

The Red Wheelbarrow
Poem by William Carlos Williams

Can you paint a
PICTURE with words?

COMMON CORE

RL 1 Cite textual evidence to support analysis of what the text says explicitly as well as inferences drawn from the text. **RL 4** Analyze the cumulative impact of specific word choices on meaning and tone.

Think of a favorite photo and picture in your mind the scene it shows. What details help you visualize the scene? As you'll see, through carefully chosen details, a poem can capture the image of a moment in time.

QUICKWRITE William Carlos Williams famously remarked that a poem can be made out of anything. With a group, think of an animal or object that could be the subject of a poem. Without naming the animal or object, list details that illustrate its physical qualities and the feeling it creates in people who view it. Then, see if other groups can guess your subject from the details you chose.

894

See resources on the **Teacher One Stop DVD-ROM** *and on* **thinkcentral.com**.

 Video link at **thinkcentral.com**

 RESOURCE MANAGER UNIT 8
 Plan and Teach, pp. 61–68
 Text Analysis and Reading
  Skill, pp. 69–72†*

**DIAGNOSTIC AND SELECTION
 TESTS**
 Selection Tests, pp. 255–258

 BEST PRACTICES TOOLKIT
 Sensory Notes, p. B9
 Read Aloud/Think Aloud, p.
  A34

TECHNOLOGY
 ⦿ **Teacher One Stop DVD-ROM**
 ⦿ **Student One Stop DVD-ROM**
 ⦿ **Audio Anthology CD**
 ⦿ **GrammarNotes DVD-ROM**
 ⦿ **ExamView Test Generator**
  on the **Teacher One Stop**

* Resources for Differentiation   **†** Also in Spanish   **‡** In Haitian Creole and Vietnamese

TEXT ANALYSIS: IMAGISM

A style can be unique to an author, or it can reflect the shared artistic vision of a literary movement. **Imagism** was a style embraced by several influential English and American poets in the 1910s and 1920s. Rebelling against structured verse forms like the sonnet, imagists wanted poetry to be "swift, uncluttered, functional." Different poets interpreted the style in different ways, but most imagist poems include these characteristics:

- simple, unpretentious **language**
- flexible, natural **rhythms** instead of strict meter and rhyme
- concise, precise **descriptions**
- clear, vivid **images,** usually drawn from everyday life

While many poets use imagery, imagists wrote poems about single striking images or series of images. Every element of a poem—words, rhythm, structure—was carefully chosen to re-create the experience of seeing an image, whose meaning was never stated but only implied.

Imagism borrowed from several poetic traditions, including classical Greek lyric, Japanese haiku, and French symbolist poetry. **Free verse,** or unrhymed lines with irregular rhythms, was a hallmark of imagist style. As you read, note the elements of imagist style you find in each poem.

READING STRATEGY: VISUALIZE

When you **visualize,** you form mental pictures based on the details a writer supplies. Visualizing can help you understand the experience an imagist poem presents. Use the following strategies to visualize the scenes in these poems:

- Note **sensory details** in each poem, such as the "cold, wet leaves" in Amy Lowell's "The Pond."
- Think about the **mood** or idea each detail conveys.
- Sketch the mental images you "see" as you read each poem.

For each poem, use a chart to record descriptive phrases and words and the mental images that they evoke for you.

Title: "The Pond"	
Descriptive Words	Mental Pictures
"cold, wet leaves"	shivering; fallen leaves

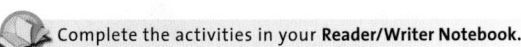 Complete the activities in your **Reader/Writer Notebook.**

Meet the Authors

Amy Lowell
1874–1925

Imagist Leader
Born into a well-known New England family, Amy Lowell was 28 when she decided to become a poet. She learned about imagism early in her career and became a tireless advocate for the new style. Her literary lectures and essays, as much as her creative work, helped transform American poetry.

Carl Sandburg
1878–1967

American Bard
A poet, reporter, folk musician, and traveler, Carl Sandburg chronicled the lives and landscapes of everyday America. His simple verse forms captured the bracing reality of a world he observed firsthand. Sandburg's colorful career and his best-selling biographies of Abraham Lincoln made him an American icon.

William Carlos Williams
1883–1963

Local Visionary
William Carlos Williams wrote nearly 50 books of fiction, drama, poetry, and essays while working full-time as a doctor in Rutherford, New Jersey. Using informal language and experimental forms, Williams wrote poems about objects, scenes, and people from his own life.

Authors Online
Go to **thinkcentral.com.** KEYWORD: HML10-895

Teach

● Model the Skill: IMAGISM

To model how to identify elements of imagist style, write these lines on the board:

> sticky shelf, puddle of milk
> last night's pasta
> crusty jar of mustard
> whiff of peeled onion
> close the fridge

Then, point out the simple language, natural rhythm, precise description, and vivid image of the refrigerator.

GUIDED PRACTICE Ask students to give the poem a title that suits the image it describes.

■ Model the Skill: VISUALIZE

To model how to visualize, read these descriptive phrases aloud. Then name the senses appealed to in each description that help readers to visualize each image.

- sweet fruit melting over pastry *(sight, taste, smell)*
- crash of drums *(sound)*
- explosion of colors across the sky *(sight)*

GUIDED PRACTICE Have students write an original description that creates a mental picture and then ask a partner to visualize it.

R RESOURCE MANAGER—Copy Master
   Visualize p. 71 (for student use while reading the selection)

DIFFERENTIATED INSTRUCTION

FOR STRUGGLING READERS

Concept Support To help students develop their skills at visualizing, distribute a Sensory Notes graphic organizer and encourage them to use it as they read the poetry in this group of selections. Using the organizer, students should note what they see, hear, feel, smell, taste, and think and then record the specific language that evokes that sensory response.

BEST PRACTICES TOOLKIT—Transparency
   Sensory Notes p. B9

FOR ADVANCED LEARNERS/PRE–AP

Research Imagist Poets Have students create a list of prominent imagist poets who are not showcased in this group of selections. Students should collect examples of several representative poems by each of these poets and then work in small groups to discuss how each poem demonstrates characteristics of the imagist movement. Invite volunteers to share their group's work with the class.

Practice and Apply

TEXT ANALYSIS

COMMON CORE
RL 4

Ⓐ Model the Skill: IMAGISM

To model how to identify elements of imagist style, use a graphic organizer to note words that appeal to the senses of sight, hearing, touch, smell, or taste.

sight	
hearing	
touch	
smell	
taste	

Possible answer: *The elements of imagist style in the poem are its simple language; its concise words and lack of rhyme; and its visual and auditory images that are clear, precise, and drawn from everyday life.*

Analyze Visuals

Possible answer: *The image on this page and the one on page 897 are both brightly colored. The image of the pond is made up of shades of blue and green, which combine to create a peaceful mood. The eye focuses on the single water lily, which suggests a mood of tranquillity. The image of the exploding fireworks conveys excitement and movement. The eye is first drawn to the bright patterns at the top and then moves downward to the dark sky, the illuminated trees, and the silhouettes of the crowd.*

REVISIT THE BIG QUESTION

Can you paint a
PICTURE with words?

Discuss How does the image in this poem capture a moment in time? *Possible answer: In the next moment, the leaves will move, the frogs will stop croaking, and the twilight will turn to night.*

The Pond
Amy Lowell

Cold, wet leaves
Floating on moss-coloured water,
And the croaking of frogs—
Cracked bell-notes in the twilight. Ⓐ

Ⓐ IMAGISM
What elements of imagist style can you identify in this poem?

◄ **Analyze Visuals**
Compare this image with the one on page 897. Which elements, such as color, subject, and composition, help establish the **mood** of each image?

DIFFERENTIATED INSTRUCTION

FOR ENGLISH LANGUAGE LEARNERS

Options for Reading Read the poem aloud. Then use the Read Aloud/Think Aloud strategy to help students understand how to go in depth with a very short poem. As you come to sensory words, point out how they help the reader visualize the poem. Then, stop after reading the first two lines to reflect out loud what students understand thus far.

 BEST PRACTICES TOOLKIT—Transparency
Read Aloud/Think Aloud p. A34

Fourth of July Night

Carl Sandburg

The little boat at anchor
in black water sat murmuring
to the tall black sky.

     A white sky bomb fizzed on a black line.
5   A rocket hissed its red signature into the west.
     Now a shower of Chinese fire alphabets,
     a cry of flower pots broken in flames,
     a long curve to a purple spray,
     three violet balloons—
10   Drips of seaweed tangled in gold,
          shimmering symbols of mixed numbers,
          tremulous arrangements of cream gold folds
          of a bride's wedding gown— **B**

A few sky bombs spoke their pieces,
15 then velvet dark.

The little boat at anchor
in black water sat murmuring
to the tall black sky.

B VISUALIZE
Reread the second stanza.
Which image is most
vivid, and why?

Prereading for this poem is found on page 894.

TIERED DISCUSSION PROMPTS

Use these prompts to help students appreciate
the intensity of Sandburg's description in lines
4–9:

Connect Look at the photograph or think
about fireworks displays you have seen.
Which lines from the poem best describe
your experience? *Answers should demonstrate an appreciation of the description in
the poem.*

Analyze What words does Sandburg use
instead of *fireworks*? How are they effective as descriptions? ***Possible answer:** "sky
bomb" (line 4), "rocket" (line 5), "fire alphabets" (line 6), "spray" (line 8), and "balloons"
(line 9). They appeal to the senses; they tell
how the fireworks look and sound.*

Evaluate Why does Sandburg not specifically name what he is describing? How
effective is this choice? ***Possible answer:** The
poet might not name the fireworks because
he wants the reader to really visualize what
he describes. His technique is very effective.
It is easy to visualize a fireworks display when
reading his description.*

READING STRATEGY   **COMMON CORE** RL 1

B VISUALIZE

*Students may feel that one of these images is
the most vivid: "Drips of seaweed tangled in
gold" (line 10), because it gives a sense of color,
movement, and texture, or "tremulous arrangements of cream gold folds / of a bride's
wedding gown" (lines 12–13), because it gives a
sense of bright and elaborate patterns.*

IF STUDENTS NEED HELP . . . Ask them to list
several images they feel are strong. Then
discuss as a class which one is strongest.

FOR STRUGGLING READERS

Concept Support Write several of the poem's
confusing images on the board, such as these:
"shower of Chinese fire alphabets" (line 6),
"a cry of flower pots broken in flames" (line
7), "Drips of seaweed" (line 10), "symbols of
mixed numbers" (line 11). Ask students to
identify what each image is referring to, using
the chart that they started on page 895 to
help them.

FOR ADVANCED LEARNERS/PRE–AP

Brainstorm [small-group option] Point out
that Sandburg uses many words to describe
the fireworks, but only one (*black*) to describe
the sky. Invite students to use a web to
brainstorm other descriptions for the sky that
might appear in the poem.

Prereading for this poem is found on page 894.

C *Model the Skill:* **VISUALIZE**

Read the poem aloud. Point out the descriptive words "red wheel barrow" in lines 3–4. Tell students you picture a shiny, bright red wheelbarrow. Have students record all the descriptive words and phrases they find in the poem in their Visualize charts. Then have them sketch the mental images they "see."

Possible answer: The visual contrast in the poem is the red wheelbarrow next to the white chickens.

REVISIT THE BIG QUESTION

Can you paint a
PICTURE with words?

Discuss Cover the picture on the page, and then read the poem. How does your mental image differ from the photograph? *Possible answer:* The mental image includes chickens, a glaze of rainwater, and no flowers.

SELECTION WRAP–UP

READ WITH A PURPOSE After students have finished reading the selections, ask them: How are the three poems in this group of selections similar? How are they different? *Possible answer:* All three poems focus on everyday images, feature natural rhythms, and use simple language and precise descriptions. "The Pond" and "The Red Wheelbarrow" offer a single striking image, while "Fourth of July Night" presents a series of images.

⭐ **CRITIQUE** Ask students to identify the element of each poem that they found most effective, and to explain why.

INDEPENDENT READING

Suggest that students read selected poems from Amy Lowell's Pulitzer Prize-winning collection, *What's O'clock.*

The Red Wheelbarrow

William Carlos Williams

so much depends
upon

a red wheel
barrow

5 glazed with rain
water

beside the white
chickens. **C**

C VISUALIZE
What visual contrast does this poem present?

DIFFERENTIATED INSTRUCTION

FOR STRUGGLING READERS

Concept Support Point out that the poem has no capitalization or punctuation, except for the period in the last line. Also point out that the poem is one sentence. Ask students to note where they would capitalize or add punctuation. (*Capitalize "so," and add a comma after "barrow" and "water."*)

Develop Reading Fluency Model reading the three poems aloud. Then have student pairs select one of the three poems to practice reading. Allow partners to decide whether to read the poem in unison or to read alternate lines or stanzas. Remind students to use punctuation as a guide while reading.

Comprehension

1. **Recall** What phrase does the speaker of "The Pond" use to describe the croaking of frogs?

2. **Clarify** What contrast does "Fourth of July Night" include?

3. **Recall** What sensory details does "The Red Wheelbarrow" provide?

Text Analysis

4. **Describe Mood** Amy Lowell's "The Pond" uses one simple image to communicate its message. Describe the mood of this poem. How does the image chosen help establish this mood?

5. **Interpret Form** In what way does the structure of "Fourth of July Night" mimic the action it describes?

6. **Make Inferences** Reread "The Red Wheelbarrow" without its opening stanza. How does the first stanza change your understanding of the poem?

7. **Visualize** Imagist poems present compact descriptions that leave many details implied or unstated. Choose an image from one of the charts you created earlier. Using the visualization strategy, write a more detailed description of the image.

8. **Evaluate Imagist Style** Use a chart to identify features of imagist style in each poem. Which of the poems is the best example of imagist style? Cite details to support your conclusion.

Title:	
Imagist Element	Example
Simple language	
Free verse	
Concise descriptions	
Striking images	

Text Criticism

9. **Historical Context** In the early decades of the 20th century, Europe and the United States experienced rapid technological and social change, as well as a devastating world war. How might these challenges to established traditions have fueled an experimental artistic movement like imagism?

Can you paint a PICTURE with words?

Would you prefer to use words or images to depict a scene? Why?

COMMON CORE

RL 1 Cite textual evidence to support analysis of what the text says explicitly as well as inferences drawn from the text. **RL 4** Analyze the cumulative impact of specific word choices on meaning and tone.

Practice and Apply

For preliminary support of post-reading questions, use these copy masters:

R RESOURCE MANAGER—Copy Masters
Imagism p. 69
Question Support p. 73

Additional selection questions are provided for teachers on page 65.

ANSWERS

Comprehension

1. *The phrase "Cracked bell-notes in the twilight" (line 4) describes the croaking.*

2. *The poem contrasts the image of a still boat in black water under a black sky with the riot of color, movement, and sound of the fireworks display.*

3. *The wheelbarrow is red, "glazed with rain water" (lines 5–6), and next to "white chickens" (lines 7–8).*

Text Analysis

COMMON CORE **RL 1, RL 4**

Possible answers:

4. *The image of cold, wet leaves floating on moss-colored water, as well as the lonely sound of the croaking frogs, creates a mood of isolation, chilliness, and decay. The image re-creates the sensation of being chilly and alone, looking at stagnant water.*

5. *The brief first and last stanzas of the poem contrast with the more elaborate burst of lines in the middle stanzas, as the dark night and still water contrast with the riot of fireworks.*

6. *The first stanza gives context to the wheelbarrow, as well as a sense of mystery and importance. Instead of simply presenting*

Assess and Reteach

Assess

DIAGNOSTIC AND SELECTION TESTS
Selection Test A, pp. 255–256
Selection Test B/C, pp. 257–258

Interactive Selection Test on **thinkcentral.com**

Reteach

Level Up Online Tutorials on **thinkcentral.com**

Reteaching Worksheets on **thinkcentral.com**
Literature Lesson 26: Imagery

---

the wheelbarrow, the poem suggests that readers must look beyond mere appearance to judge its value.

7. ■ **COMMON CORE FOCUS** *Visualize*
Students might describe the sounds of the firework, the color of leaves, or the shape of the wheelbarrow.

8. ● **COMMON CORE FOCUS** *Imagism* All of the poems show imagist style. "The Pond" demonstrates the purest image with simple language, concise description.*

Text Criticism

9. *Possible answer: Poets may have wanted to*

return to simple and basic means of expression, or they may have wanted to resist old, outdated forms of poetry. In a time of conflict, they may not have trusted words used for political ends.

Can you paint a PICTURE with words?
Students may prefer to use words, because words allow readers to create their own mental pictures. Other students might prefer to use images, because they provide the same pictures, perhaps not the same meaning.

Focus and Motivate

COMMON CORE FOCUS

RI 4 Determine the meaning of words and phrases as they are used in a text. **RI 5** Analyze in detail how an author's ideas are developed by portions of text. **RI 6** Determine an author's purpose in a text. **L 4c** Consult reference materials to determine or clarify the etymology of a word.

SUMMARIES

"Only Daughter" In this personal essay, Cisneros reflects on being the only daughter in a Mexican-American family of six sons. Her father treated her writing as a waste of time—until he read a story of hers that had been translated into Spanish.

From *Caramelo* In this novel excerpt, the narrator describes a family beach photograph in which she is missing. Nobody had noticed that she was off playing by herself.

What is your ROLE in your household?

Ask the question, then direct students' attention to the photographs. Encourage students to refer to the roles portrayed in these photos as they complete the *DISCUSS* activity.

Selection Resources

Before Reading

Only Daughter
Personal Essay by Sandra Cisneros

Essential Course of Study **ECOS**

from **Caramelo**
Fiction by Sandra Cisneros

What is your ROLE in your household?

COMMON CORE

RI 4 Determine the meaning of words and phrases as they are used in a text. **RI 5** Analyze in detail how an author's ideas are developed by portions of text. **RI 6** Determine an author's purpose in a text.

Think about the different roles that you play in your family and how you feel about them. Has your gender helped to determine these roles? In the following selections by Sandra Cisneros, you will learn what it means to be a daughter in a traditional Mexican-American family.

DISCUSS During the 1960s, many people began reexamining the role of women both at home and in society. Since then, ideas about the proper roles of males and females have changed dramatically. In a large group, share your thoughts about the roles of males and females today. Discuss gender roles at home, at school, in the workplace, and in the community.

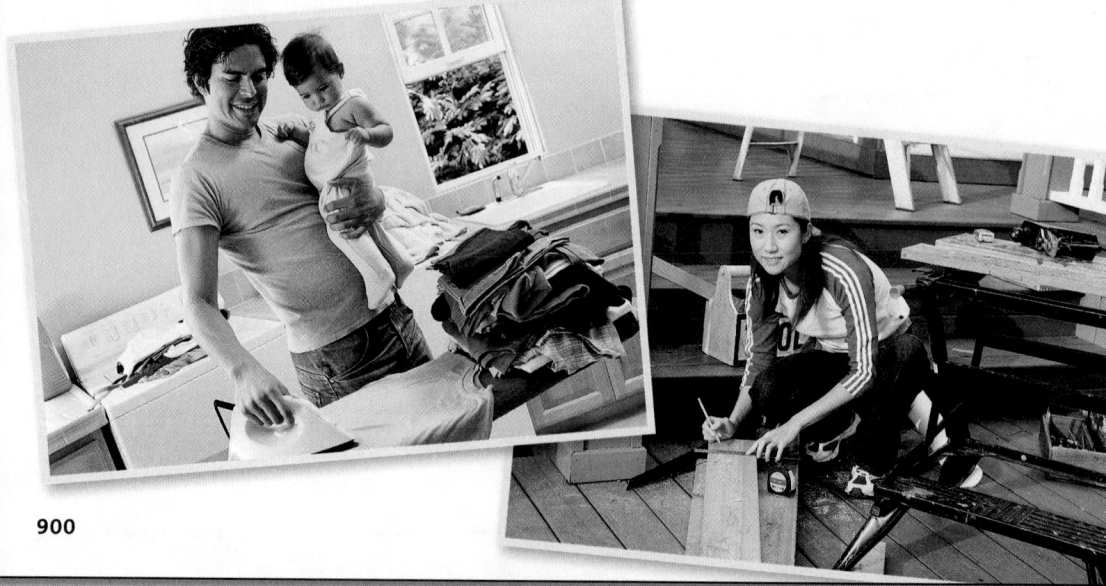

900

*See resources on the **Teacher One Stop DVD-ROM** and on **thinkcentral.com**.*

R RESOURCE MANAGER UNIT 8
Plan and Teach, pp. 75–82
Summary, pp. 83–84†‡*
Text Analysis and Reading Skill, pp. 85–88†*
Vocabulary, pp. 89–91*

DIAGNOSTIC AND SELECTION TESTS
Selection Tests, pp. 259–262

BEST PRACTICES TOOLKIT
Definition Mapping, p. E6
Two-Column Chart, p. A25

INTERACTIVE READER

ADAPTED INTERACTIVE READER

ELL ADAPTED INTERACTIVE READER

TECHNOLOGY
⊘ **Teacher One Stop DVD-ROM**
⊘ **Student One Stop DVD-ROM**
⊘ **PowerNotes DVD-ROM**
⊘ **Audio Anthology CD**
⊘ **GrammarNotes DVD-ROM**
⊘ **Audio Tutor CD**
⊘ **ExamView Test Generator** on the **Teacher One Stop**

Video Trailer **THINK central**

Go to **thinkcentral.com** to preview the **Video Trailer** introducing this selection. Other features that support the selection include
• **PowerNotes** presentation
• **ThinkAloud** models to enhance comprehension
• **WordSharp** vocabulary tutorials
• interactive writing and grammar instruction

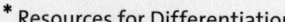
* Resources for Differentiation   † Also in Spanish   ‡ In Haitian Creole and Vietnamese

TEXT ANALYSIS: STYLE AND VOICE

Sandra Cisneros is a contemporary writer who is known for her vibrant writing style. Her work is easily recognizable because of her distinctive voice. In literature, a **voice** is a writer's use of language in a way that allows readers to "hear" a personality in his or her writing. In "Only Daughter," Cisneros states:

At Christmas, I flew home to Chicago. The house was throbbing, same as always; hot tamales and sweet tamales hissing in my mother's pressure cooker, and everybody—my mother, six brothers, wives, babies, aunts, cousins—talking too loud and at the same time....

Cisneros's use of conversational language, vivid images, and lyrical sentences gives readers a sense of her own lively spirit. As you read the two selections, think about the other stylistic elements that contribute to her voice.

READING SKILL: IDENTIFY AUTHOR'S PURPOSE

You may recall that an **author's purpose** is the reason why he or she creates a particular work. Often, an author's purpose directly relates to the form, or genre, of a text, as well as its structural pattern. Cisneros is a versatile writer whose body of work comprises different forms, including poetry, nonfiction, and fiction. As you read each selection, jot down answers to the following questions:

- What is the form, or genre, of this work?
- Why do writers usually write this type of work?
- Which words or phrases suggest a specific tone?
- Does the tone of the work suggest a specific purpose?

Later, you will use your answers to help you draw conclusions about Cisneros's purpose in each selection.

▲ VOCABULARY IN CONTEXT

The words in boldface help reveal what it's like to grow up in a traditional household. Restate each phrase, substituting a different word or words for each boldfaced word.

1. an **anthology** of short stories
2. fulfilling one's **destiny**
3. viewing events in **retrospect**
4. a **trauma** to the head
5. **nostalgia** for earlier days

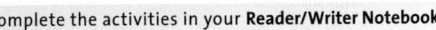 Complete the activities in your **Reader/Writer Notebook.**

Meet the Author

Sandra Cisneros
born 1954

A Writer Under Wraps
Born in Chicago in 1954, Sandra Cisneros (sĭs-nĕ'rôs) grew up with her Mexican father, Mexican-American mother, and six brothers. As a young girl, she had few friends because her family moved frequently between Chicago and Mexico City. To ward off loneliness, she often read stories and wrote poetry. As a teenager, she continued to write but was careful to keep her work away from family members, who disapproved of her writing.

A Proud Latina
While in graduate school, Cisneros began to embrace her own cultural heritage and experiences. She learned that the people and events that had shaped her life were different from those that had influenced the lives of her classmates. This discovery helped her find her own literary voice—one that reflected her unique Mexican-American background. In 1984, Cisneros published *The House on Mango Street*—a series of prose vignettes told by a girl living in a Chicago neighborhood. Since then, she has continued to tell stories drawn from her personal history.

BACKGROUND TO THE SELECTIONS
Traditional Roles
In "Only Daughter," Cisneros describes her father's ideas about the proper role of females. Coming from the culture of old Mexico, Cisneros's father held the patriarchal beliefs of many traditional cultures—that is, he considered men the heads of families and the leaders of society. According to his values, a woman needed only to "become someone's wife" and devote herself to her home and family.

Author Online **THINK** central
Go to **thinkcentral.com.**
KEYWORD: HML10-901

901

Teach

TEXT ANALYSIS COMMON CORE RI 4 RI 5 RI 6

● Model the Skill: STYLE AND VOICE

To model how to identify voice and its stylistic elements, share this example:

> To Mama, I was just the soon-to-be dutiful wife of someone's pampered son, so I had stopped telling her about my stories and my literary dreams, and I had stopped listening when she bubbled over about this one's fairy-tale wedding and that one's angelic baby.

Point out that the conversational language and sarcastic descriptions create a spirited, mocking voice.

GUIDED PRACTICE Have students write a brief passage with a different voice.

READING SKILL COMMON CORE RI 6

■ Model the Skill: IDENTIFY AUTHOR'S PURPOSE

Model how to identify author's purpose by explaining the purpose of **Meet the Author**.

Tell students that its purpose is to provide information about Cisneros that will enhance students' understanding.

GUIDED PRACTICE Ask students to predict Cisneros's purpose for writing "Only Daughter."

 RESOURCE MANAGER—Copy Master
Identify Author's Purpose p. 87

VOCABULARY SKILL COMMON CORE L 4

▲ VOCABULARY IN CONTEXT

DIAGNOSE WORD KNOWLEDGE Have all students complete Vocabulary in Context. Check their responses against the following:

anthology (ăn-thŏl'ə-jē) *n.* a collection of written works—such as poems, short stories, or plays— in a single book or set
destiny (dĕs'tə-nē) *n.* the determined fate of a particular person or thing; lot in life
nostalgia (nŏ-stăl'jə) *n.* a wistful longing for the past or the familiar

retrospect (rĕt'rə-spĕkt') *n.* a view or contemplation of something past
trauma (trô'mə) *n.* severe physical or emotional distress

PRETEACH VOCABULARY Use the following copy master to help students predict the meaning of each boldfaced word.

R RESOURCE MANAGER—Copy Master
Vocabulary Study p. 89
1. Read item 1 aloud, emphasizing *anthology*.

2. Point out the phrase "along with several others." Elicit possible meanings for *anthology*, such as "group of writings."
3. Have students record their predictions.
4. Repeat the procedure for items 2–5.

READ WITH A PURPOSE

Tell students to read to discover how Cisneros as portrayed in "Only Daughter" resembles the narrator in the second selection.

READING SKILL   COMMON CORE   RI 6

Ⓐ Model the Skill: AUTHOR'S PURPOSE

To model how to identify the author's purpose, read aloud the first three paragraphs of the essay. Point out the repetition of the phrase "only daughter." Explain that the author's purpose is to explain how being the only daughter in her family contributed to her career as a writer.

Possible answer: Cisneros's subject is how the experience of being the only daughter in her family has affected her, especially as a writer. Details include the repetition of "only daughter" (line 11) and the statement that being left out helped her prepare for becoming a writer (lines 13–15).

VOCABULARY   COMMON CORE   L 4

OWN THE WORD

- **anthology:** Tell students that *anthology* comes from the Greek word *anthologia*, meaning "gathering of flowers." Ask students how the Greek word's meaning relates to the way *anthology* is used in line 2.

- **destiny:** Have students complete the thought: The narrator says that her destiny is . . . .

- **retrospect:** Tell students that *retrospect* comes from the Latin prefix *retro-*, which means "backward" or "back," and *specere*, which means "look at."

ONLY DAUGHTER

Sandra Cisneros

Once, several years ago, when I was just starting out my writing career, I was asked to write my own contributor's note for an **anthology** I was part of. I wrote: "I am the only daughter in a family of six sons. *That* explains everything."

Well, I've thought about that ever since, and yes, it explains a lot to me, but for the reader's sake I should have written: "I am the only daughter in a *Mexican* family of six sons." Or even: "I am the only daughter of a Mexican father and a Mexican-American mother." Or: "I am the only daughter of a working-class family of nine." All of these had everything to do with who I
10   am today.

I was/am the only daughter and *only* a daughter. Being an only daughter in a family of six sons forced me by circumstance to spend a lot of time by myself because my brothers felt it beneath them to play with a *girl* in public. But that aloneness, that loneliness, was good for a would-be writer—it allowed me time to think and think, to imagine, to read and prepare myself. Ⓐ

Being only a daughter for my father meant my **destiny** would lead me to become someone's wife. That's what he believed. But when I was in the fifth grade and shared my plans for college with him, I was sure he understood. I remember my father saying, "*Que bueno, mi'ja,*[1] that's good." That meant a lot
20   to me, especially since my brothers thought the idea hilarious. What I didn't realize was that my father thought college was good for girls—good for finding a husband. After four years in college and two more in graduate school and still no husband, my father shakes his head even now and says I wasted all that education.

In **retrospect,** I'm lucky my father believed daughters were meant for husbands. It meant it didn't matter if I majored in something silly like English. After all, I'd find a nice professional eventually, right? This allowed me the liberty to putter about embroidering my little poems and stories without my father interrupting with so much as a "What's that you're writing?"

anthology (ăn-thŏl′ə-jē) *n.* a collection of written works—such as poems, short stories, or plays—in a single book or set

Ⓐ **AUTHOR'S PURPOSE** Reread lines 11–15. What specific experience is the **subject** of this personal essay? Identify the details that helped you draw your conclusion.

destiny (dĕs′tə-nē) *n.* the determined fate of a particular person or thing; lot in life

 **Targeted Passage**

retrospect (rĕt′rə-spĕkt′) *n.* a view or contemplation of something past

---

1. *Que bueno, mi'ja* (kĕ bwĕ′nô mē′hä) *Spanish:* That's good, my daughter. (*Mi'ja* is a shortened form of *mi hija.*)

Sandra Cisneros (2000), Raquel Valle Sentíes. Oil, 20″× 20″. www.soycomosoyyque.com

---

DIFFERENTIATED INSTRUCTION

FOR ENGLISH LANGUAGE LEARNERS

Vocabulary Support Use Definition Mapping to teach these words: *contributor* (line 2), *circumstance* (line 12), *majored* (line 26), *financial* (line 71).

 BEST PRACTICES TOOLKIT—Transparency Definition Mapping p. E6

FOR STRUGGLING READERS

In combination with the *Audio Anthology CD,* use one or more Targeted Passages (pp. 902, 905) to ensure that students focus on key story events, concepts, and skills. Targeted Passages are also good for English learners.

 **Targeted Passage** [Lines 16–29]

This passage introduces Cisneros's conflict with her very traditional father. It also explores how she adapted to her family circumstances.

BACKGROUND

An Era of Change Even as Cisneros's brothers laughed at her plans to go to college, new attitudes toward women's rights were opening the door to new opportunities. Title VII of the 1964 Civil Rights Act prohibited employment discrimination. In 1968, the Equal Employment Opportunity Commission ruled that it was illegal to specify help-wanted ads for "only men" or "only women." Title IX in the Education Amendment of 1972 gave women equal access to any educational program that receives federal funding.

Analyze Visuals

Activity Ask students what aspects of Cisneros's personality are suggested in Valle Sentíes's portrait of her. *Possible answer: The painting suggests Cisneros's introspective and contemplative qualities.*

About the Art Artist, poet, and playwright Raquel Valle Sentíes was born and raised in Laredo, Texas. She also lived in Veracrúz, Mexico, for many years. Like Cisneros, Valle Sentíes received little encouragement for her artistic interests as a child; she was left to explore them on her own, and she has done so to critical acclaim. This portrait of Cisneros is part of a series that Valle Sentíes painted in honor of Latina writers.

- What future did Cisneros's father want for his daughter? (lines 16–17)
- Why does he feel that she wasted her education? (lines 22–24)
- Why does Cisneros, looking back, feel "lucky" that he had this attitude? How did Cisneros use his attitude to her advantage? (lines 26–29)

FOR ADVANCED LEARNERS/PRE–AP

Analyze Characterization In this essay, Cisneros uses fictional techniques to present a vivid portrait of her father. Ask students to write a brief essay about the ways in which Cisneros develops the character of her father. How does she reveal his physical appearance, his manner of speaking, and his behavior? Is her father a static character, or does he change? Have students compare their ideas by sharing their essays in small groups.

TEXT ANALYSIS

COMMON CORE

RI 4
RI 5
RI 6

B Model the Skill:
STYLE AND VOICE

Have students identify what Cisneros's father was reading. Then have students tell which of these words they would use to describe his reading: *light, heavy, entertaining, serious.*

Possible answer: *Cisneros takes an affectionately mocking tone. Details such as "yet another sighting of La Virgen de* Guadalupe *on a tortilla" (lines 37–38), "bashing his skull in with a molcajete" (line 39), and "tragedy and trauma erupting from the characters' mouths in bubbles" (lines 41–42) convey her feelings.*

READING SKILL

COMMON CORE

RI 6

C AUTHOR'S PURPOSE

Possible answer: *These details suggest that Cisneros resented her father's pride in his sons at her expense: "As if he deserved a medal from the state" (lines 57–58); "I could feel myself being erased" (line 60); "Not seven sons. Six! and one daughter" (line 61).*

IF STUDENTS NEED HELP . . . Read lines 46–61 aloud with an expressive tone, urging students to listen for details and statements that sound like opinions.

VOCABULARY

COMMON CORE

L 4

OWN THE WORD

- **trauma:** Have students create a semantic map for the word *trauma.* On the board, write the word and its definition in the center circle. Draw spider legs from the center circle, and have students add synonyms to complete the map. *Possible answers: suffering, anguish, agony*

- **nostalgia:** Point out that *nostalgia* contains the Greek root *nostos*, which means "a return home." Explain that when one experiences *nostalgia*, one thinks of one's home or past.

---

30 But the truth is, I wanted him to interrupt. I wanted my father to understand what it was I was scribbling, to introduce me as "My only daughter, the writer." Not as "This is only my daughter. She teaches." *Es maestra*[2]—teacher. Not even *profesora*.[3]

In a sense, everything I have ever written has been for him, to win his approval even though I know my father can't read English words, even though my father's only reading includes the brown-ink *Esto* sports magazines from Mexico City and the bloody *¡Alarma!* magazines that feature yet another sighting of *La Virgen de Guadalupe*[4] on a tortilla or a wife's revenge on her philandering[5] husband by bashing his skull in with a *molcajete*[6] (a kitchen
40 mortar[7] made of volcanic rock). Or the *fotonovelas*,[8] the little picture paperbacks with tragedy and **trauma** erupting from the characters' mouths in bubbles. **B**

My father represents, then, the public majority. A public who is disinterested in reading, and yet one whom I am writing about and for and privately trying to woo.

When we were growing up in Chicago, we moved a lot because of my father. He suffered bouts of **nostalgia.** Then we'd have to let go our flat, store the furniture with mother's relatives, load the station wagon with baggage and bologna sandwiches, and head south. To Mexico City.
50 We came back, of course. To yet another Chicago flat, another Chicago neighborhood, another Catholic school. Each time, my father would seek out the parish priest in order to get a tuition break and complain or boast: "I have seven sons."

He meant *siete hijos*,[9] seven children, but he translated it as "sons." "I have seven sons." To anyone who would listen. The Sears Roebuck employee who sold us the washing machine. The short-order cook where my father ate his ham-and-eggs breakfasts. "I have seven sons." As if he deserved a medal from the state.

My papa. He didn't mean anything by that mistranslation, I'm sure. But
60 somehow I could feel myself being erased. I'd tug my father's sleeve and whisper: "Not seven sons. Six! and *one daughter*." **C**

When my oldest brother graduated from medical school, he fulfilled my father's dream that we study hard and use this—our heads, instead of this—our hands. Even now my father's hands are thick and yellow, stubbed by a history of hammer and nails and twine and coils and springs. "Use this,"

trauma (trô′mə) *n.* severe physical or emotional distress

B STYLE AND VOICE
Reread lines 34–42. Describe Cisneros's tone, or attitude, toward her father and his reading habits. Which details strongly convey her feelings?

nostalgia (nŏ-stăl′jə) *n.* a wistful longing for the past or the familiar

C AUTHOR'S PURPOSE
In personal essays, writers often express opinions on subjects. Which details in lines 46–61 suggest Cisneros's opinions?

---

2. **Es maestra** (ĕs mä-ĕs′trä) *Spanish:* She is a teacher.

3. **profesora** (prô-fĕ-sô′rä) *Spanish:* professor.

4. **La Virgen de Guadalupe** (lä vēr′hĕn dĕ gwä-dä-lōō′pĕ) *Spanish:* the Virgin of Guadalupe—a vision of Mary, the virgin mother of Jesus, said to have appeared on a hill outside Mexico City in 1531.

5. **philandering:** engaging in many casual love affairs.

6. **molcajete** (môl-kä-hĕ′tĕ) *Spanish.*

7. **mortar:** bowl for grinding grain.

8. **fotonovelas** (fô-tô-nô-vĕ′läs) *Spanish.*

9. **siete hijos** (syĕ′tĕ ē′hôs) *Spanish.* (*Hijos* can mean either "children" or "sons.")

904 UNIT 8: AUTHOR'S STYLE AND VOICE

DIFFERENTIATED INSTRUCTION

FOR STRUGGLING READERS

Develop Reading Fluency Explain that Cisneros uses sentence fragments to create a conversational tone, and identify lines 54–58 as an example. Note that the author's use of sentence fragments adds to her unique voice. Model how to read aloud lines 54–61, and then have students work in pairs to practice reading the same passage, with expression and at an appropriate pace.

FOR ENGLISH LANGUAGE LEARNERS

Culture: Connect In "Only Daughter," a language barrier contributes to the conflict between Cisneros and her father. It is not until one of Cisneros's stories has been translated into Spanish that her father is able to read and appreciate her writing for the first time. Invite students to share a time when a similar language barrier prevented understanding or appreciation of others' interests, dreams, or attitudes among family members.

my father said, tapping his head, "and not this," showing us those hands. He always looked tired when he said it.

Wasn't college an investment? And hadn't I spent all those years in college? And if I didn't marry, what was it all for? Why would anyone go to college
70 and then choose to be poor? Especially someone who had always been poor.

Last year, after ten years of writing professionally, the financial rewards started to trickle in. My second National Endowment for the Arts Fellowship.[10] A guest professorship at the University of California, Berkeley. My book, which sold to a major New York publishing house.

At Christmas, I flew home to Chicago. The house was throbbing, same as always; hot *tamales*[11] and sweet *tamales* hissing in my mother's pressure cooker, and everybody—my mother, six brothers, wives, babies, aunts, cousins— talking too loud and at the same time, like in a Fellini[12] film, because that's just how we are.

80 I went upstairs to my father's room. One of my stories had just been translated into Spanish and published in an anthology of Chicano[13] writing, and I wanted to show it to him. Ever since he recovered from a stroke two years ago, my father likes to spend his leisure hours horizontally. And that's how I found him, watching a Pedro Infante[14] movie on Galavisión[15] and eating rice pudding.

There was a glass filmed with milk on the bedside table. There were several vials of pills and balled Kleenex. And on the floor, one black sock and a plastic urinal that I didn't want to look at but looked at anyway. Pedro Infante was about to burst into song, and my father was laughing.

90 I'm not sure if it was because my story was translated into Spanish or because it was published in Mexico or perhaps because the story dealt with Tepeyac,[16] the *colonia* my father was raised in and the house he grew up in, but at any rate, my father punched the mute button on his remote control and read my story.

I sat on the bed next to my father and waited. He read it very slowly. As if he were reading each line over and over. He laughed at all the right places and read lines he liked out loud. He pointed and asked questions: "Is this So-and-so?"

"Yes," I said. He kept reading.

When he was finally finished, after what seemed like hours, my father
100 looked up and asked: "Where can we get more copies of this for the relatives?"

Of all the wonderful things that happened to me last year, that was the most wonderful. ∽

---

10. **National Endowment for the Arts Fellowship:** The National Endowment for the Arts (NEA)—a U.S. government agency—awards money in the form of fellowships to artists and writers.

11. *tamales* (tä-mä'lĕs) *Spanish:* rolls of cornmeal dough filled with meat and peppers and steamed in cornhusk wrappings.

12. **Fellini:** the Italian movie director Federico Fellini (1920–1993), famous for his noisy, energetic films.

13. **Chicano:** Mexican-American.

14. **Pedro Infante** (pā'drō ĭn-fän'tā): a popular Mexican film star.

15. **Galavisión:** cable TV network that features movies and programs in Spanish.

16. **Tepeyac** (tĕ-pĕ-yäk'): a district of Mexico City.

② **Targeted Passage**

Prereading for this fictional excerpt is found on page 900.

E AUTHOR'S PURPOSE

Possible answer: Such phrases suggest a purpose of entertaining readers through a vivid look at the narrator's family.

Extend the Discussion What do these phrases suggest about how well the various members of this family get along?

F STYLE AND VOICE

Possible answer: Cisneros's style suggests someone who has a zest for life and who cares about her family but who also has a sense of irony and is somewhat sarcastic.

Caramelo

Sandra Cisneros

Acuérdate de Acapulco,
de aquellas noches,
María bonita, María del alma;
acuérdate que en la playa,
con tus manitas las estrellitas
las enjuagabas.[1]
—*"María bonita," by Augustín Lara, version sung by the composer while playing the piano, accompanied by a sweet, but very, very sweet violin*

We're all little in the photograph above Father's bed. We were little in Acapulco. We will always be little. For him we are just as we were then.

Here are the Acapulco waters lapping just behind us, and here we are sitting on the lip of land and water. The little kids, Lolo and Memo, making devil horns behind each other's head; the Awful Grandmother holding them even though she never held them in real life. Mother seated as far from her as politely possible; Toto slouched beside her. The big boys, Rafa, Ito, and Tikis, stand under the roof of Father's skinny arms. Aunty Light-Skin hugging Antonieta Araceli to her belly. Aunty shutting her eyes when the shutter
10 clicks, as if she chooses not to remember the future, the house on Destiny Street sold, the move north to Monterrey. **E**

Here is Father squinting that same squint I always make when I'm photographed. He isn't *acabado*[2] yet. He isn't *finished*, worn from working, from worrying, from smoking too many packs of cigarettes. There isn't anything on his face but his face, and a tidy, thin mustache, like Pedro Infante, like Clark Gable.[3] Father's skin pulpy and soft, pale as the belly side of a shark.

The Awful Grandmother has the same light skin as Father, but in elephant folds, stuffed into a bathing suit the color of an old umbrella with an amber handle.

20 I'm not here. They've forgotten about me when the photographer walking along the beach proposes a portrait, *un recuerdo,* a remembrance literally. No one notices I'm off playing by myself building sand houses. They won't realize I'm missing until the photographer delivers the portrait to Catita's house, and I look at it for the first time and ask,—When was this taken? Where?

Then everyone realizes the portrait is incomplete. It's as if I didn't exist. It's as if I'm the photographer walking along the beach with the tripod camera on my shoulder asking.—¿*Un recuerdo?* A souvenir? A memory? **F**

E AUTHOR'S PURPOSE Reread lines 3–11. Consider your own reaction to phrases such as "making devil horns" and "the Awful Grandmother." What purpose do they suggest?

F STYLE AND VOICE Cisneros's style is often characterized by loosely structured sentences, such as those in lines 20–27. What aspect of Cisneros's **voice** comes through in this type of writing?

---

1. **Acuérdate de Acapulco . . . las enjuagabas** *Spanish:* Remember Acapulco, those nights, beautiful Maria, Maria of my soul; remember that in the sand, you washed the stars with your hands.
2. *acabado* (ä-kä-bä′dô) *Spanish:* finished.
3. **Clark Gable:** an American film star of the 1940s.

Black Jumper, Lucy Willis. British. Private collection. Photo © Curwen Gallery/The Bridgeman Art Library.

DIFFERENTIATED INSTRUCTION

FOR STRUGGLING READERS

Comprehension Support Help students understand these similes, metaphors, and unusual descriptions from the selection:

- *the lip of land and water* (line 4), "at the edge of the beach, where it meets the sea"
- *the roof of Father's skinny arms* (line 8), "Father's arms slope protectively down around the boys"
- *pale as the belly side of a shark* (line 16), "very light in color"

FOR ADVANCED LEARNERS/PRE–AP

Comparing Statements Have students write a paragraph comparing the narrator's statement "It's as if I didn't exist" (line 25) with Cisneros's statement "I could feel myself being erased" (line 60) in "Only Daughter." Ask students to share their comparisons in a small group and then choose a volunteer to present a summary of their ideas to the class.

Activity Ask students to compare and contrast the subject matter and mood of the painting with the excerpt. *Possible answer: Although the subject matter of the painting and the excerpt is similar—a day at the beach—it conveys different moods. The mood of the painting is cheerful and even serene, while the mood of the excerpt is darker, conveying the narrator's feelings of isolation and resentment.*

About the Art Prize-winning British artist Lucy Willis (b. 1954) has traveled, painted, and taught in Greece, India, and Africa and was an artist-in-residence at an English prison. A skilled watercolorist, Willis has had many solo exhibitions in London, and one of her paintings hangs in the National Portrait Gallery.

REVISIT THE BIG QUESTION
What is your ROLE
in your household?

Discuss In lines 20–24, what does the narrator's absence from the portrait suggest about her role in the family? In contrast, what do lines 25–27 suggest about her role? *Possible answer: Her absence from the portrait suggests that she plays an insignificant role in her family: no one even noticed that she was missing. However, lines 25–27 suggest that as a writer, her role is more important: to record her family's memories in words.*

SELECTION WRAP–UP

READ WITH A PURPOSE Ask students to explain how the narrator in this selection resembles Cisneros. What similarities are there between Cisneros in "Only Daughter" and the narrator in the excerpt from *Caramelo*? *Possible answers: Both are highly observant; both seem to appreciate the complexities of large, traditional families; both recall a childhood in which, to some extent, they felt left out and unimportant—"erased" and invisible.*

⭐ **CRITIQUE** Have students evaluate how effectively Cisneros portrays the two families in these selections.

FOR STRUGGLING READERS
Vocabulary Support Have partners work together to define these words, first using context and then a dictionary: *slouched* (line 7), "sit or stand in a drooped position"; *pulpy* (line 16), "soft and mushy"; *amber* (line 18), "brownish yellow"; *proposes* (line 21), "suggests; offers"; *tripod* (line 26), "three-legged stand for supporting a camera"

FOR ADVANCED LEARNERS/PRE–AP
Describe a Photograph Have students write a description of a family or other group photograph, modeled on the excerpt from *Caramelo*. Encourage them to use a distinctive voice in their descriptions and to focus on both the details of the image and its context—when, where, and why the photograph was taken. Invite volunteers to read their descriptions aloud and to share the photographs that inspired their writing.

Practice and Apply

For preliminary support of post-reading questions, use these copy masters:

R RESOURCE MANAGER—Copy Masters
Reading Check p. 92
Voice and Style p. 85
Question Support p. 93

Additional selection questions are provided for teachers on page 79.

ANSWERS

Comprehension

1. *Her father expected her to get married, preferably to a "nice professional" (line 27).*

2. *Cisneros went against her father's expectations by going to graduate school and becoming a writer instead of marrying and becoming a homemaker.*

3. *The photograph includes two little boys held by the grandmother, the mother sitting away from the grandmother with the middle boy beside her, the father with the three big boys under his arms, and the aunt holding a little girl. The narrator is missing from the photograph.*

4. *Neither is seen in the picture; both have created a remembrance of the narrator's family.*

Text Analysis

COMMON CORE RL 4, RI 4, RI 6

Possible answers:

5. *Cisneros communicates the theme that traditional female roles of daughter and wife can be stifling. Yet a motivated person can choose others roles and achieve her goals. She reveals this theme when she says that she felt "erased" (line 60) when her father forgot that he had a daughter; that not being taken seriously by him gave her the freedom to write (lines 25–29); and that everything she has written has been to win his approval (lines 34–35), which she eventually did.*

6. ● **COMMON CORE FOCUS** *Style and Voice* *With a more formal style, Cisneros would not come across as so lively or humorous. The reader might not find her as likeable or intriguing.*

7. *To the narrator, the photograph symbolizes her role in her family: an outsider who observes but does not participate, whose absence goes unnoticed but who is the keeper of family memories.*

8. *Her tone is honest and somewhat mocking. She projects loving sympathy for her overburdened father but is less tolerant of her "Awful Grandmother."*

9. ■ **COMMON CORE FOCUS** *Author's Purpose* *In both selections, Cisneros is writing to express how it feels to be overlooked in a family and to entertain readers with vivid descriptions of family life. In "Only Daughter" Cisneros's purpose is also to show the restrictive nature of gender roles.*

Text Criticism

Possible answer:

10. *Cisneros may have hoped to inspire young, single women to pursue their dreams, despite family expectations.*

> What is your **ROLE** in your household? Students may mention gender roles, traditions, personal preferences, and economic circumstances.

Comprehension

1. **Recall** According to "Only Daughter," what expectations did Cisneros's father have for her?

2. **Recall** In what way did Cisneros go against her father's expectations?

3. **Summarize** Describe the different family members included in the souvenir photograph in the excerpt from *Caramelo*. Who is missing from the picture?

4. **Clarify** Reread lines 25–27 of the excerpt. Why does the narrator compare herself to the photographer?

Text Analysis

5. **Identify Theme** In "Only Daughter," what theme about female roles does Cisneros communicate through her relationship with her father? Support your answer with evidence from the essay.

● 6. **Examine Style and Voice** Cisneros's writing style is often marked by a use of conversational language and fragmented sentences. How might your sense of Cisneros and her experiences be different if "Only Daughter" had been written with more formal words and sentence structures?

7. **Interpret Symbol** A person, a place, an activity, or an object that represents something beyond itself is called a symbol. In the excerpt from *Caramelo*, what does the souvenir photograph seem to symbolize to the narrator?

8. **Relate Imagery and Tone** Reread lines 12–19 of the excerpt, reviewing Cisneros's use of vivid sensory images. Considering words such as "squinting," "elephant folds," and "the color of an old umbrella," describe the narrator's tone, or attitude, toward her father and her grandmother.

■ 9. **Compare Author's Purposes** Review your answers to the questions on page 901. Identify Cisneros's purpose for writing each selection. What similarities or differences in purpose do you see between "Only Daughter" and the excerpt from *Caramelo*? Explain your response.

Text Criticism

10. **Social Context** "Only Daughter" was first published in *Glamour*, a monthly magazine that is read almost exclusively by women, many of whom are young and single. Does this information affect your understanding of Cisneros's purpose for writing the personal essay? Explain your response.

> **What is your ROLE in your household?**
> What has shaped the way your family members take on different roles?

Vocabulary in Context

▲ **VOCABULARY PRACTICE**

Select the vocabulary word that best completes each sentence.

1. Josh believed that his _____ would lead him to become a famous actor.
2. Someone with _____ often relives happy memories of earlier times.
3. Shirley is often seen carrying a(n) _____ of the works of Langston Hughes, her favorite author.
4. In _____, I wish I had done things differently.
5. The _____ of the accident would never completely leave Kyra.

WORD LIST
anthology
destiny
nostalgia
retrospect
trauma

ACADEMIC VOCABULARY IN WRITING

• clarify • feature • precise • style • transmit

Write a short narrative that shares a positive or negative experience from your childhood. Use your own personal **style** to help readers understand what happened. Specific details will help **clarify** the events for anyone who was not there. Use at least one Academic Vocabulary word in your response.

VOCABULARY STRATEGY: ETYMOLOGY

Etymology is the history of words, and knowing this history can often help you remember a word's meaning. For example, the word *nostalgia* derives from two Greek words: *nostos,* which means "homecoming," and *algos,* meaning "pain, grief, or distress." In modern English, this translates to "a sad or wistful yearning for the past."

> **nos•tal•gi•a** (nŏ-stăl′jə) *n.* **1.** a bittersweet longing. **2.** a sad or wistful yearning for the past. [Greek *nostos,* homecoming + Greek *algos,* pain, grief, or distress.]

PRACTICE Use the dictionary or an online reference to research the etymology of each word below. Study each word's derivation, meaning, and spelling.

1. anthology
2. retrospect
3. trauma

COMMON CORE

L 4c Consult reference materials to determine or clarify the etymology of a word.

Interactive Vocabulary
THINK central
Go to **thinkcentral.com**.
KEYWORD: HML10-909

DIFFERENTIATED INSTRUCTION

FOR STRUGGLING READERS

Comprehension: Vocabulary As students work through the Vocabulary Practice, help them find context clues. For example, in item 1, the phrase "would lead him to become" is a clue that the needed word (*destiny*) has something to do with fate. In item 2, the phrase "happy memories of earlier times" is a clue that the needed word has to do with a positive look at the past, a meaning that *nostalgia* fits better than does *retrospect.*

FOR ADVANCED LEARNERS/PRE–AP

Research Etymology Ask students to research the etymologies of five additional words from the Cisneros selections, using a print or online dictionary. Work with students to plan a format for sharing some of the most interesting results with the class.

ANSWERS

Vocabulary in Context

▲ **VOCABULARY PRACTICE**

1. *destiny*
2. *nostalgia*
3. *anthology*
4. *retrospect*
5. *trauma*

R RESOURCE MANAGER—Copy Master
Vocabulary Practice p. 90

ACADEMIC VOCABULARY IN WRITING

Possible answer: *When I saw the ocean for the first time, the features rushed at me all at once. The creeping tide! The endless beach! The smell of salt in the air! When I closed my eyes, the sounds transmitted a sense of peace and calm.*

VOCABULARY STRATEGY: ETYMOLOGY

COMMON CORE **L 4c**

Using *nostalgia* as an example, point out that the literal meaning derived from a word's etymology often is not an exact match for the modern meaning.

Possible answers:

1. *anthology:* Greek: *antho,* "flower," and *logos,* "gathering"
2. *retrospect:* Latin: *retro,* "backward," and *specere,* "to look at"
3. *trauma:* Greek: *trauma,* "wound," and Indo-European root *ter,* "to rub or turn"

R RESOURCE MANAGER—Copy Master
Vocabulary Strategy p. 91

Interactive Vocabulary
THINK central

Keywords direct students to a **WordSharp** tutorial on **thinkcentral.com** or to other types of vocabulary practice and review.

Assess and Reteach

Assess

DIAGNOSTIC AND SELECTION TESTS
Selection Test A, B/C pp. 259–262

Interactive Selection Test on **thinkcentral.com**

Reteach

Level Up Online Tutorials on **thinkcentral.com**

Reteaching Worksheets on **thinkcentral.com**

Focus and Motivate

RI 1 Cite textual evidence to support analysis of what the text says explicitly. **RI 4** Analyze the cumulative impact of specific word choices on meaning and tone. **RI 8** Delineate and evaluate the argument and specific claims in a text, assessing whether the reasoning is valid and the evidence is relevant and sufficient. **W 9b** Draw evidence from literary nonfiction to support analysis.

SUMMARY

In "Author Brings Back Memories of Not So Long Ago," Yvette Cabrera describes her anticipation about meeting Sandra Cisneros. She also explains how and why Cisneros's novel *The House on Mango Street* moved her profoundly years earlier.

What's the Connection?

Have students use a KWL chart to prepare for reading Cabrera's critique. In the first column of the chart, have students jot down what they already know about Cisneros, based on the two selections they have just read plus anything else they might have read by or about her. In the second column, have students write questions about what they would like to know about Cisneros or her work. After they have read Cabrera's critique, have students use the third column of the chart to record what they learned.

 BEST PRACTICES TOOLKIT—Transparency
KWL p. A21

Teach

Standards Focus: Identify the Characteristics of a Critique

Invite students to share what they know about critiques. Point out that a critique is more than a summary of the main points of a book or article. A critique also offers the writer's personal observations and opinions. As students read Cabrera's critique, urge them to consider her unique perspective on her subject.Standards Focus: Identify the Characteristics of a Critique

---

Author Brings Back Memories of Not So Long Ago
Critique

Use with "Only Daughter" and excerpt from *Caramelo*, pages 902–906.

RI 1 Cite textual evidence to support analysis of what the text says explicitly. **RI 4** Analyze the cumulative impact of specific word choices on meaning and tone. **RI 8** Delineate and evaluate the argument and specific claims in a text, assessing whether the reasoning is valid and the evidence is relevant and sufficient.

What's the Connection?

In the previous selections by Sandra Cisneros, you discovered how the author and one of her fictional characters feel about living in a Mexican-American family. In the newspaper column you are about to read, you will learn what one Latino writer thinks about Cisneros's 1984 novel *The House on Mango Street*.

Standards Focus: Identify the Characteristics of a Critique

A **critique** is a writer's response to another's work. While a **summary** simply states the main points of a book or article, a critique allows a writer to add personal observations, opinions, and perspective on the subject at hand. The essay you are about to read, "Author Brings Back Memories of Not So Long Ago," is a positive critique.

Most writers include a balance of negative and positive comments in their critiques. However, whether a writer's comments are positive or negative, he or she must offer support, or evidence, for the opinions offered. If a critique contains **unsubstantiated opinions,** or opinions without evidence, then that critique is not valid.

As you read Yvette Cabrera's critique, consider what descriptions of Cisneros's writing she provides, and what parts of the column are her own observations and opinions. Take notes in a chart like this one.

Descriptions of Cisneros's Writing	Cabrera's Observations and Opinions

---

Selection Resources

See resources on the **Teacher One Stop DVD-ROM** *and on* <u>thinkcentral.com</u>.

R RESOURCE MANAGER UNIT 8
Lesson Support,* pp. 95–108

DIAGNOSTIC AND SELECTION TESTS
Selection Tests, pp. 263–266

BEST PRACTICES TOOLKIT
KWL, p. A21

TECHNOLOGY
- Teacher One Stop DVD-ROM
- Student One Stop DVD-ROM
- ExamView Test Generator on the Teacher One Stop

* Resources for Differentiation

Author Brings Back Memories of Not So Long Ago

by Yvette Cabrera

Author Sandra Cisneros

Forget the boxes and the cobwebs; I was determined to find the book. I looked at my watch and out the window at the gray, misty morning outside my garage. It was already late.

I dived in frantically. It has to be here somewhere, but where in this mass of boxes and old furniture?

Five minutes later, still no luck. From
10 behind an old bookcase my boyfriend heard me half scream/half wail in frustration, as I pulled out box after box searching through my old college books.

Finally, the last box of books. My last hope. Please, I prayed, let this be my lucky day. In the last box, there it was: *The House on Mango Street* by Sandra Cisneros.

Slightly yellowed, with that com-
20 forting, worn appeal of your favorite pajamas, the book was just as I had left it.

A $9 soft-cover (the best a "working-three-jobs-a-week" college student could afford), its pages were dog-eared, my favorite paragraphs highlighted in fluorescent purples and pinks, and my notes scribbled on the borders.

With little time to spare, I sped off to work. Today, I was going to meet the
30 author of one of my favorite books.

Growing up, I studied books my high school English teachers said were written by the literary "greats"—must reads for a well-rounded education. Books like J.D. Salinger's *Catcher in the Rye*, Fyodor

Dostoyevsky's *Crime and Punishment* and Thomas Hardy's *Tess of the d'Urbervilles.*

It was literature with profound meaning that imparted important lessons. But
40 still, I felt a disconnection. *Beowulf* was an epic poem, but as my high school teacher went into great detail explaining what a mail[1] shirt was, I wondered what that had to do with my life.

It was that way all through high school, until the day in college when I was assigned to read *The House on Mango Street.* **A**

Mango. The word alone evoked
50 memories of my childhood—weekends when my family and I would pile into our sky-blue Chevrolet Malibu and head to Olvera Street's plaza in downtown Los Angeles.

At the time, the plaza was home to the Mexican consulate where my parents, Mexican immigrants, would deal with passport and residency paperwork.

The treat, for my sisters and I, for
60 behaving ourselves during the long

---

1. **mail:** flexible armor made of metal rings.

INFORMATIONAL ANALYSIS — COMMON CORE RI 1 RI 8

B CHARACTERISTICS OF A CRITIQUE

Possible answer: Cabrera uses lively verbs ("pile," "peeled," "impaled," "squeeze," "sprinkle") and evocative sensory details ("sky-blue Chevrolet Malibu," "juicy mango," "bright yellow slices") that bring the scene to life. Her words convey the voice of an observant, witty, and spirited personality with vivid childhood memories.

TEXT ANALYSIS — COMMON CORE RI 4

C TONE IN NONFICTION

Tell students that line 85, "I was hooked," is a clue to identifying the author's tone.

Possible answer: appreciative, admiring

INFORMATIONAL ANALYSIS — COMMON CORE RI 1 RI 8

D CHARACTERISTICS OF A CRITIQUE

Possible answer: Cabrera wants to reach young people like those who came to hear Cisneros speak: students who are a part of or who want to know more about the U.S. Latino experience (line 100).

INFORMATIONAL ANALYSIS — COMMON CORE RI 1 RI 8

E *Model the Skill:* CHARACTERISTICS OF A CRITIQUE

To model how to identify the characteristics of a critique, suggest this description of Cisneros's writing in lines 77–80: "A coming-of-age Chicana-feminist novel, the protagonist Esperanza, like Cisneros, grows up in a mainly Latino neighborhood in Chicago." Then point out Cabrera's personal observations in lines 135–138. Help students complete their Skill Focus charts.

Possible answer: Cabrera's excitement, her pleasure in reading Cisneros's autograph note, and her final comment that "Even her autographs are authentic!" convey an admiring, appreciative tone.

B CHARACTERISTICS OF A CRITIQUE
Describe the kinds of words Cabrera uses in lines 49–66. What do they reveal about her **voice**, or personality?

COMMON CORE RI 4

C TONE IN NONFICTION
Tone is the attitude or feelings that a writer has toward his or her subject. You can determine the tone of a nonfiction piece by noting the words and details the writer chooses. Reread lines 76–85. How would you define the tone of this critique? (Hint: Tone can usually be described in one or two words.)

D CHARACTERISTICS OF A CRITIQUE
Reread lines 86–100. What **audience** does Cabrera seem particularly interested in reaching?

E CHARACTERISTICS OF A CRITIQUE
Reread lines 135–145. Which details reveal Cabrera's **tone**, or attitude, toward Sandra Cisneros and her writing?

---

waits at the consulate, was a juicy mango on a stick sold at a fruit stand near the plaza's kiosk. Peeled and impaled on a stick for easy grip, we would squeeze lemon and sprinkle chile and salt over the bright yellow slices. **B**

Later, as an adult, whenever I had a reporting assignment near Olvera Street, I'd always take a minute to stop. 70 There, amid the smell of sizzling carne asada[2] in a nearby restaurant, the sounds of vendors negotiating prices in Spanish, and children licking a rainbow of raspados (shaved ice treats), I would bite into my mango and feel at home.

That's what *The House on Mango Street* did for me. A coming-of-age, Chicana-feminist novel, the protagonist Esperanza, like Cisneros, grows up in a 80 mainly Latino neighborhood in Chicago.

From the first page, when Esperanza explains how at school they say her name funny "as if the syllables were made out of tin and hurt the roof of your mouth," I was hooked. . . . **C**

That was a dozen years ago. Today, Latinos are the majority in cities like Santa Ana, California, where Cisneros spoke last week at Valley High School to 90 more than 1,000 students, as part of the Pathway Project, a collaborative effort among the University of California, Irvine, Santa Ana College and the city's school district.

Today, these students can pick from bookstore shelves filled with authors such as Julia Alvarez, Victor Villaseñor and Judith Ortiz Cofer—authors who go beyond census numbers to explain 100 what U.S. Latino life is about. **D**

It's about, as Cisneros explained to the students as she read from her novel *Caramelo*, a journey between two worlds.

It's about relishing truck-stop doughnut shops and bologna sandwiches on this side of the border, just as much as the strawberries in cream, the gelatins, and fruity *tejocote* bathed in caramel sauce on the other side of the border.

110 It was an hour of humorous storytelling that had the students busting with laughter and then crowding in line afterward, giddily waiting to get her autograph. . . .

Later, as I talk to Cisneros, she explains how much the literary world has changed since she finished writing *The House on Mango Street* 20 years ago. Back then, forget trying to get *The New* 120 *York Times* to review your book if you were Latino or getting a major bookseller to carry it, she says.

"I never questioned the Jim Crow[3] aspect of how our books were never reviewed—I was young," says Cisneros, 47, of San Antonio.

One thing has remained constant, something that Cisneros can see by the question that's most asked by students. 130 "They want to know, 'Is this real? Did this happen to you,'" Cisneros says. "They're so concerned and want to make sure this is my story, because it's their story, too."

As Cisneros autographed my book, I felt that same excitement I felt 12 years ago when I first discovered *The House on Mango Street.*

"Para la Yvette,[4] Sandra Cisneros," it 140 read. I chuckled. Mexicans just love to give nicknames, but sans[5] a nickname you attach a simple "la" in front of the name and suddenly you're extra special. Not just "Sandra," but "la Sandra" (that Sandra). Even her autographs are authentic! **E**

---

2. **carne asada** (kär'ně ä-sä'dä): grilled marinated steak.

3. **Jim Crow:** upholding or practicing discrimination against a minority population.

4. **para la Yvette** *Spanish:* for that Yvette.

5. **sans** (sănz): without.

DIFFERENTIATED INSTRUCTION

FOR STRUGGLING READERS

Vocabulary Support Help students understand the meaning of these words, as they are used in the column: *dog-eared* (line 24), "worn"; *imparted* (line 39), "revealed; conveyed"; *disconnection* (line 40), "lack of connection"; *kiosk* (line 63), "small, open structure"; *impaled* (line 63), "pierced through"; *collaborative* (line 91), "group"; *census* (line 99), "government population count"; *relishing* (line 104), "enjoying"; *giddily* (line 113), "excitedly."

FOR ADVANCED LEARNERS/PRE–AP

Analyze Flashback Have small groups of students discuss Cabrera's use of chronology. Encourage them to note how she moves back and forth between the present and the past and to consider the effect of this technique. Have students respond to these questions: What do the shifts in time reveal about Cabrera and the impact that *The House on Mango Street* has had on her? How does this technique prepare the reader for Cabrera's meeting with Cisneros?

Comprehension

1. **Recall** What childhood memory does the word *mango* evoke for Cabrera?

2. **Clarify** What question do students typically ask Cisneros, and why?

Text Analysis

3. **Identify Author's Purpose** Scan the first page of Cabrera's critique, including its title. What, in your opinion, is the main purpose of the critique? Explain your response.

4. **Analyze a Critique** Review the chart you developed as you read the article. What is Cabrera's perspective on Sandra Cisneros and her work? Why does she have this perspective?

5. **Compare Authors** What does Yvette Cabrera have in common with Sandra Cisneros? How were their childhoods different?

> **COMMON CORE**
>
> **RI 1** Cite textual evidence to support analysis of what the text says explicitly. **RI 8** Delineate and evaluate the argument and specific claims in a text, assessing whether the reasoning is valid and the evidence is relevant and sufficient. **W 9b** Draw evidence from literary nonfiction to support analysis.

Read for Information: Synthesizing Information from Multiple Sources

WRITING PROMPT

Many writing instructors believe that students should "write what they know." Find evidence in the nonfiction works of Sandra Cisneros and Yvette Cabrera that shows they have followed this advice.

The following steps will help you respond to the prompt:

1. Reread Cisneros's "Only Daughter" and Cabrera's critique, looking for direct statements, facts, and anecdotes about living as a Mexican American.

2. Record direct quotations and summarize longer passages that seem relevant to your response. For each, note the author, source, and page number.

3. **Synthesize** the information from both sources, and make connections between them.

4. As you compose your response, support your statements with direct quotations and citations of facts or anecdotes in the two sources. Make sure to use quotation marks around any direct quotations.

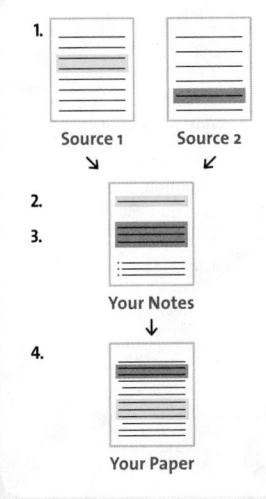

Source 1   Source 2

Your Notes

Your Paper

FOR STRUGGLING WRITERS

Read for Information

- Encourage students to start by writing a topic sentence that incorporates the language of the question.
- Remind students to support their topic sentence with various types of evidence about the two authors' subject matter and language. Also tell them to avoid irrelevant information.

FOR ADVANCED LEARNERS/PRE–AP

Read for Information Have students extend their essays to speculate on Cisneros's influence on Cabrera. In particular, ask them to discuss what literary lessons Cabrera may have learned from Cisneros. Encourage students to compare their responses.

Practice and Apply

For preliminary support of post-reading questions, use these copy masters:

R RESOURCE MANAGER—Copy Masters
  Reading Check p. 107
  Question Support p. 108
  Identify the Characteristics of a Critique p. 103

  Additional selection questions are provided for teachers on page 98.

ANSWERS

Comprehension

1. *eating juicy mangoes at a fruit stand*

2. *They ask if the things Cisneros writes about are "real," because her "story" validates their own experiences (lines 130–135).*

Text Analysis

COMMON CORE **RI 1, RI 8**

Possible answers:

3. *to convey Cabrera's strong feeling of connection to an author*

4. *Cabrera is deeply appreciative of Sandra Cisneros and her work for being a voice for the experiences of Latino people in the United States. Cabrera was unable to connect with literature that had little to do with her life, but she found a deep connection with Cisneros.*

5. *Both are Mexican-American writers. Cabrera has sisters, not brothers, and lived in Los Angeles.*

Read for Information: Synthesizing Information from Multiple Sources

COMMON CORE **W 9b**

Writing Prompt *Students should note that both authors draw upon childhood experiences and include Spanish words.*

Assess and Reteach

Assess

DIAGNOSTIC AND SELECTION TESTS
  Selection Test A, B/C pp. 263–266

Interactive Selection Test on **thinkcentral.com**

Reteach

Level Up Online Tutorials on **thinkcentral.com**

Focus and Motivate

COMMON CORE FOCUS

W 2a–f Write informative/explanatory texts to convey complex information; include formatting, graphics, and multimedia to aid comprehension. **W 4** Produce clear and coherent writing. **W 5** Develop and strengthen writing by revising, rewriting, editing, or trying a new approach. **W 6** Use technology to produce and publish individual writing products. **W 7** Conduct short research projects to answer a question. **W 8** Follow a standard format for citation. **W 9b (RI 1)** Draw evidence from informational texts to support research. **L 1b** Use absolute phrases to convey specific meanings and add interest. **L 2** Demonstrate command of the conventions of standard English capitalization, punctuation, and spelling. **L 3a** Conform to guidelines in a style manual. **SL 5** Make strategic use of digital media to enhance understanding and add interest.

WRITE WITH A PURPOSE

Tell students that their online article has a dual purpose—to inform and to entertain. An effective online article engages readers from start to finish. Students will best accomplish these purposes if they themselves are interested in learning about the topic they choose.

COMMON CORE TRAITS

Review the *COMMON CORE TRAITS* with students, focusing on the development of ideas. Clarify the structure and elements of online feature articles. Then compare the list of traits with the rubric on page 921.

ADDITIONAL TASKS

Write About a Social Issue Write an online feature article addressing what you see as a problem in today's society.
Possible topics: voter apathy, over-dependence on fossil fuels, violence

Write About Medicine Write an online feature article about a recent medical advance.
Possible topics: new cures or treatments for diseases or conditions, new vaccines

Writing Online   THINK central

The following tools are available online at **thinkcentral.com** and on Write*Smart* CD-ROM:
• Interactive Graphic Organizers
• Interactive Student Models
• Interactive Revision Lessons

Writing Workshop
INFORMATIVE TEXT

Online Feature Article

 **Essential Course of Study ECOS**

In this unit, you learned about the distinctive styles of Edgar Allan Poe, Walt Whitman, and Robert Frost. To learn more about these authors, you could turn to the vast network of information available on the World Wide Web. Now you will add your voice to this network by producing an **online feature article** on a topic that interests you.

 Complete the workshop activities in your **Reader/Writer Notebook**.

WRITE WITH A PURPOSE

WRITING TASK

Write an **online feature article** that informs your audience about a topic that interests you.

Idea Starters
• What are the physical and psychological effects of fear?
• What is imagist poetry?
• How has Edgar Allan Poe influenced pop culture?
• How can a beginning runner train for a 5K race?

THE ESSENTIALS

Here are some common purposes, audiences, and formats for informative/explanatory writing.

PURPOSES	AUDIENCES	FORMATS
• to increase your own understanding of a topic • to inform readers and provide them with new insights • to develop and maintain an online readership	• classmates and teacher • friends and family on a social networking site • members of online communities interested in the topic	• magazine article • news report • wiki article • encyclopedia entry

COMMON CORE TRAITS

1. DEVELOPMENT OF IDEAS
• begins with a compelling **introduction** and a **clear controlling idea**
• develops the topic with **evidence**, such as **relevant facts, definitions, quotations,** and **examples**
• provides a **concluding section** that supports the information

2. ORGANIZATION OF IDEAS
• logically **organizes** complex information
• includes **formatting, multimedia, links,** and **graphics**
• uses **varied transitions** to connect ideas
• **cites** and **links to sources**

3. LANGUAGE FACILITY AND CONVENTIONS
• uses **precise language** and **domain-specific vocabulary**
• maintains a **formal style** and **objective tone**
• uses **absolute phrases** to convey specific meanings and add detail
• employs correct **grammar, spelling,** and **punctuation**

Writing Online   THINK central
Go to **thinkcentral.com**.
KEYWORD: HML10N-914

Writing Workshop Resources

R RESOURCE MANAGER UNIT 8
Plan and Teach pp. 109–112
Prewriting–Editing pp. 113–117
Writing Support p. 119*

 BEST PRACTICES TOOLKIT
Writing Template: Informative Essay pp. C16, C29

TECHNOLOGY
⊘ **Teacher One Stop DVD-ROM**
⊘ **Student One Stop DVD-ROM**
⊘ **Write*Smart* CD-ROM**
⊘ **GrammarNotes DVD-ROM**

Writing Center on thinkcentral.com

See resources on the **Teacher One Stop DVD-ROM** *and on* **thinkcentral.com**.

* Resources for Differentiation

Planning/Prewriting

Getting Started

CHOOSE A TOPIC

Brainstorm ideas that interest you and are likely to appeal to others. Once you've selected a topic, do a quick online search to see how much information is available on it. Make sure your topic isn't too broad to cover well in a short article. Frame your topic with a focused **research question** to guide your planning and writing. (Consult the Idea Starters on the previous page for sample research questions.)

THINK ABOUT AUDIENCE AND PURPOSE

As you explore your topic, consider your **audience** and **purpose**. Understanding your audience will help you to determine what information to include or define, as well as where to post your final product. Consider online forums and community Web sites that are popular with your audience and that your teacher approves of.

FIND MULTIPLE SOURCES

Begin researching your topic by looking for sources in the library or on the Web. Determine the strengths and limitations of each source and consider whether it is appropriate for your audience and purpose.

Look for **credible** sources that have been written by experts in their fields or maintained by official government and educational institutions. Also, try to locate online sources that have graphics or multimedia that you could link to or obtain permission to include.

Record the title, author, and URL (Web address) or page number of each source. Take notes so that you know which information came from which source.

See pages 1323–1337 for more information on locating and evaluating potential sources.

▶ TIPS FOR GENERATING TOPIC IDEAS:

- Read popular news Web sites or RSS (really simple syndication) feeds.
- Visit blogs or wikis that your teachers or classmates recommend.
- Review school and community Web sites for interesting topics of conversation.
- Consider interests, sports, or hobbies that you pursue outside of school.

▶ ASK YOURSELF:

- Who will be interested in my topic?
- How knowledgeable is my audience about this topic? What background information should I include?
- What **domain-specific**, or specialized, terms will I need to define?
- Where will I publish, or post, my article?

▶ WHAT DOES IT LOOK LIKE?

Sources	Notes
Book: *Getting Unstuck: Breaking Through Your Barriers to Change* by Dr. Sidney B. Simon	Discusses ten effects of fear
Web site: *Fear and Phobia* http://kidshealth.org	Talks about how fear affects the brain

DIFFERENTIATED INSTRUCTION

FOR ENGLISH LANGUAGE LEARNERS

Language: Reinforce Terms Write these terms on the board and review them with students:

- *research:* careful study and investigation of a topic to find information
- *Web site:* collection of pages on the World Wide Web focusing on a specific topic
- *sources:* works that supply information, such as books and Web sites
- *link:* images or highlighted words or phrases on a Web page that connect to a new Web page or Web site

- *storyboard:* a drawing that shows how text features, words, and images will be organized in an online feature article
- *navigate:* to move from one section of a Web page to another
- *multimedia:* different forms of media, such as video, photographs, and music, used together to communicate information
- *formatting:* the way information is arranged on a page or screen

---

Planning/ Prewriting

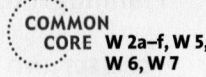

▶ **CHOOSE A TOPIC** Explain to students that if a topic is too broad, they will find it difficult to organize and present a coherent discussion. Searching general reference works and Web sites will help them understand the scope of their subject and identify a particular aspect of it that can be covered thoroughly in one article. Display a flowchart and model for students how to narrow their focus and phrase their research question, using one of their topics or an Idea Starter.

▶ **THINK ABOUT AUDIENCE AND PURPOSE** After students have chosen their topic, have them adapt the questions in the chart to interview one or more of their classmates. They should find out what their peers know about their topic, what interests them about it, and, if they have previously read online articles, what they found helpful or distracting. Have students keep this feedback in mind as they continue their research and begin their writing.

▶ **FIND MULTIPLE SOURCES** Tell students that they need to evaluate the credibility of their sources before they use them. Review these guidelines:

- Check that the publication date of print sources is recent. Make sure the books or articles have been published by well-respected publishers. Examine the credentials of the authors to see if they are qualified to write on the subject.

- Look for Web sites with addresses ending in *gov, org,* or *edu.* Check further to make sure that a respected institution is sponsoring the site and that the purpose is to share unbiased information. Avoid sites that have malfunctioning links, discrepancies in content, or any irregularities in their presentation of material.

R RESOURCE MANAGER—Copy Masters
Planning/Prewriting p. 113
Drafting p. 114
Revising and Editing pp. 115–116
Ask a Peer Reader p. 117
Writing Support p. 119

Planning/Prewriting *continued*

▶ **COLLECT AND SYNTHESIZE INFORMATION**
Review with students these guidelines for taking notes:

* Create a source card for each book, article, or Web site that looks promising. This card should include all essential bibliographical information, along with a card number. Place that number on every note taken from that source.

* Paraphrase (put details into your own words) or summarize (explain the main idea of a passage in your own words) the majority of your notes. Use direct quotations only when the original language is particularly powerful or unique.

▶ **DRAFT A CONTROLLING IDEA** Tell students that their controlling ideas should be the short answer to their research question. For example, the controlling idea "Fear can have a negative effect on both your mental and physical health" answers the research question "Can fear impair someone's health and well-being?" Encourage students to revisit and rework their controlling ideas as they organize and begin to draft their online articles.

▶ **GENERATE A STORYBOARD** As a class, visit several online feature articles. Have students identify elements that they like. Encourage them to apply some of these techniques in their own feature articles, noting them on their storyboards.

YOUR TURN Have students present their storyboards to small groups. As students view the storyboards, ask them to respond to these questions:

* Does the order of the main ideas seem logical?
* Does each storyboard have a balance of text and other elements?
* Would a reader be able to navigate easily?

Have students then rework their storyboards to reflect the comments they receive.

For interactive graphic organizers, see

WriteSmart CD-ROM

Writing Center on thinkcentral.com

Planning/Prewriting *continued*

Getting Started

COLLECT AND SYNTHESIZE INFORMATION

Use a graphic organizer to record **relevant quotations, facts, definitions,** and **examples.** Try to **synthesize** information—to draw conclusions using your prior knowledge and evidence from several sources. Keep your research question in mind as you review your notes.

▶ **WHAT DOES IT LOOK LIKE?**

When people are exposed to fear, they experience faster heart rates and breathing issues. —http://kidshealth.org	"Fear keeps you from asserting yourself and persuades you to settle..." Sidney B. Simon, Getting Unstuck
Fear affects our actions and reactions in many ways.	

DRAFT A CONTROLLING IDEA

Use your research question to write a **controlling idea** that states the main point you want to communicate. Modify your controlling idea as you develop your article.

▶ **WHAT DOES IT LOOK LIKE?**

Fear can have severe, negative effects on both mental and physical health.

GENERATE A STORYBOARD

Create a **storyboard** to map out the contents and layout of your article. Use **text features,** such as headings and links, to allow for easy reading and navigation. Decide what multimedia or graphics you will include. Keep in mind that Web users are more likely to notice elements along the top and left side of a screen.

▶ **WHAT DOES IT LOOK LIKE?**

The Debilitating Effects of Fear		
Sidebar	**Introduction**	
Contents	Introductory text	Photo
Links		
Discussion		Next

PEER REVIEW Exchange storyboards and ask: Does my article seem easy to navigate? Is the organization clear? Is my plan appropriate for my purpose and audience?

YOUR TURN List possible research questions in your *Reader/Writer Notebook.* Choose one that interests you, and locate a variety of reliable sources. Collect and synthesize evidence, and develop a controlling idea. Create a storyboard to plan your article.

DIFFERENTIATED INSTRUCTION

FOR ENGLISH LANGUAGE LEARNERS

Writing: Controlling Ideas Have students use these sentence starters to help them develop their controlling ideas and support:

* The topic of my article is _____.
* My article will explain _____, _____, and _____ about my topic.
* I want readers to understand _____ when they read my article.

FOR STRUGGLING WRITERS

Synthesizing Distribute copies of two brief informational passages on the same topic. Call on volunteers to read them aloud. Then note details from each on the board. Explaining each step that you follow, model how to use this strategy to develop an original insight about this information, for example, by making an inference. Group students and have them apply the same strategy to come up with their own insights. Call on groups to share their syntheses.

Drafting

W 4 Produce clear and coherent writing. **W 8** Follow a standard format for citation. **W 9b (RI 1)** Draw evidence from informational texts to support research. **L 3a** Conform to guidelines in a style manual.

The following chart shows a structure for outlining a clear and coherent online feature article.

Organizing Your Online Feature Article

INTRODUCTION

- Grab your audience's attention with a **compelling quotation, question, or anecdote**.
- Establish a **formal style** and an **objective tone** by using precise, unbiased language.
- Supply **background information** and **definitions** of domain-specific terms.
- Include a clear **controlling idea** that states the main point of your article.

▼

BODY

- Develop your ideas with **relevant facts, quotations, examples,** and **multimedia**. Organize your ideas and support in a logical way.
- Utilize **text features**, such as headings and links, to help readers navigate your article.
- Use **varied transitions**, such as *in addition* and *furthermore*, to link related ideas, sentences, and paragraphs.
- Document the **source** of each idea. See pages 1362–1363 for information on citations.

▼

CONCLUDING SECTION

- Restate your **controlling idea** and explain the significance of your topic.

GRAMMAR IN CONTEXT: INCORPORATING QUOTATIONS

Incorporating quotations into your article gives your writing more depth and authority. When using quotations, make sure to cite your sources both in the running text and in your Works Cited section. Use these guidelines to help you:

- Place quotation marks at the beginning and end of someone else's words.
- Integrate short quotations into your own sentences.
- Use ellipses to indicate that you've omitted words from the quotation.
- Enclose the author's last name and the page number of the quote in parentheses at the end of the sentence. If you mention the author, include only the page number, as shown below.
- Link your in-text citation to your Works Cited section.

> Dr. Sidney B. Simon said of the psychological effects of fear: "Fear is the great paralyzer" (212).

See pages 1362–1363 for Modern Language Association guidelines for creating a Works Cited list.

YOUR TURN

Draft your article in a word-processing document. Cite sources correctly. Follow your storyboard to input your draft into an online forum. Experiment with layout and navigation.

FOR ENGLISH LANGUAGE LEARNERS

Writing: Quotations Display these examples of quotations:

1. Coretta King called the rules of the Montgomery Bus Company "the most degrading" aspect of segregation.

2. Most people agreed with E. D. Nixon, who said, "We have taken this type of thing too long . . . we will not take this sort of thing any longer."

Discuss the internal punctuation of each quotation as well as the way it is framed in the sen-

tence. Then have students volunteer examples of direct quotations from their research. Work with the class to integrate them into sentences.

FOR STRUGGLING WRITERS

Integrate Quotations Display a paragraph from an informational text. Model how to take direct quotations from the original text and insert them into sentences. Then have students work in pairs to write their own sentences, integrating quotations from the paragraph. Have them write their sentences on the board or interactive whiteboard. As a class, review and revise them.

Practice and Apply

Drafting

COMMON CORE W 4, W 8, W 9b (RI 1), L 3a

▸ **INTRODUCTION** Review ways that students might choose to open their articles, making sure they understand that an anecdote is a brief but relevant story. Have pairs work together to draft possible openings for their articles. Remind students of the importance of establishing and maintaining a consistent style and tone.

▸ **BODY** Emphasize that students must develop their topic with relevant facts, extended definitions, and concrete details. They should write a draft for each of their storyboards. Explain also that although each screen presents material related to the main topic, the content should be self-sufficient. In other words, a reader should be able to navigate directly to that screen and understand the information that it contains.

▸ **CONCLUDING SECTION** Tell students that a major purpose of their concluding section is to show readers why they should care about the topic.

GRAMMAR IN CONTEXT: INCORPORATING QUOTATIONS

Give students these additional guidelines for incorporating quotations:

- Set quotations shorter than four lines within your paragraph, using quotation marks.

- Longer quotations should be introduced in your own words, followed by a colon. Set the quotation after the colon in block form: an indented paragraph without quotation marks.

YOUR TURN

Ask students to complete the **Your Turn** activity independently. Have them highlight quotations and parenthetical citations in their drafts and have a partner check them for accuracy. Suggest that students write their drafts double-spaced so that they can make revisions easily.

For an informative essay-writing template, see

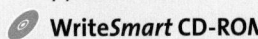

BEST PRACTICES TOOLKIT—Transparency
Writing Template: Informative Essay
pp. C16, C29

💿 **Write*Smart* CD-ROM**

Writing Center on thinkcentral.com

Revising

Model the Skill Using a draft feature article on a transparency or interactive whiteboard, model how to use the questions, tips, and strategies suggested in the chart to evaluate and revise. Consider using a feature article written by a student from a different class or from a previous year. Be sure to remove the writer's name from the article so that he or she remains anonymous.

YOUR TURN Before students work through the checklist, have them prepare their own list of questions for their peer reviewers. These questions should focus on parts of their article about which they have particular concerns. Have peer reviewers work through this list of questions before collaborating with their partners on the revision list.

For interactive revisions tools, see

WriteSmart CD-ROM

Writing Center on thinkcentral.com

Revising

The willingness to revise, rewrite, and try new approaches is an essential quality for effective writers. When you revise your online feature article, make sure your information is well organized and supports your controlling idea. The following chart can help you strengthen your draft.

ONLINE FEATURE ARTICLE

Ask Yourself	Tips	Revision Strategies
1. Does my introduction grab the audience's attention?	▶ **Highlight** attention-grabbing quotations, questions, anecdotes, or facts.	▶ **Add** a compelling question, quotation, or detail to engage your audience.
2. Is my controlling idea clear and appropriate for my task, purpose, and audience?	▶ **Underline** your controlling idea.	▶ **Add** a controlling idea if one is missing. **Rework** your existing controlling idea if it is unclear or doesn't fit your task, purpose, and audience.
3. Is my organization logical, effective, and easy to navigate?	▶ **Circle** headings, links, and menu options.	▶ **Group** related paragraphs under boldfaced headings. **Add** menu links to help users easily navigate your article.
4. Do I use relevant evidence and multimedia to support my controlling idea?	▶ **Underline** evidence or multimedia that doesn't support your controlling idea.	▶ **Delete** information that isn't relevant to your controlling idea. **Add** details and multimedia for unsupported ideas.
5. Does my concluding section restate my controlling idea and explain my topic's significance?	▶ **Highlight** your restated controlling idea. **Draw a star** next to your explanation of the topic's significance.	▶ **Add** a restatement of your controlling idea. **Insert** an explanation of your topic's significance.
6. Are all my sources correctly documented? See pages 1362–1363 for additional support.	▶ **Underline** each piece of evidence. **Circle** the corresponding citation and Works Cited entry.	▶ **Add** in-text citations and/or Works Cited entries for evidence that hasn't been properly cited.

YOUR TURN

PEER REVIEW Exchange drafts with another student. Answer each question in the chart to decide how your drafts can be improved. Ask: Is my controlling idea clear? Is my use of multimedia effective? Is my article easy to navigate?

DIFFERENTIATED INSTRUCTION

FOR ENGLISH LANGUAGE LEARNERS
Writing: Organizing Information Help students improve their organization by working through these sentence frames:

- My main idea is _____
- My first supporting fact, example, definition, or multimedia element is _____
- My second supporting detail is _____

Explain that students can use this organization for each paragraph in the body of their article.

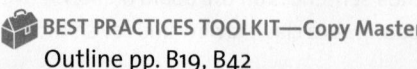 **BEST PRACTICES TOOLKIT—Copy Master**
Outline pp. B19, B42

FOR ADVANCED LEARNERS/PRE-AP
Develop Concluding Sections Remind students that the content of each screen must be complete in itself and yet connect to the preceding and succeeding parts as well. Challenge students to return to their article and develop short concluding sections for each of their screens. They should summarize the information on that page, show its relationship to the overall topic, and include a thought-provoking question or insight. Invite students to share their concluding sections in small groups.

ANALYZE A STUDENT DRAFT

Read this draft. Note the comments on its strengths and the suggestions for improvement.

⊙ **COMMON CORE**

W 2a Include formatting, graphics, and multimedia to aid comprehension. **W 5** Develop and strengthen writing by revising, rewriting, or trying a new approach. **SL 5** Make strategic use of digital media to enhance understanding and add interest.

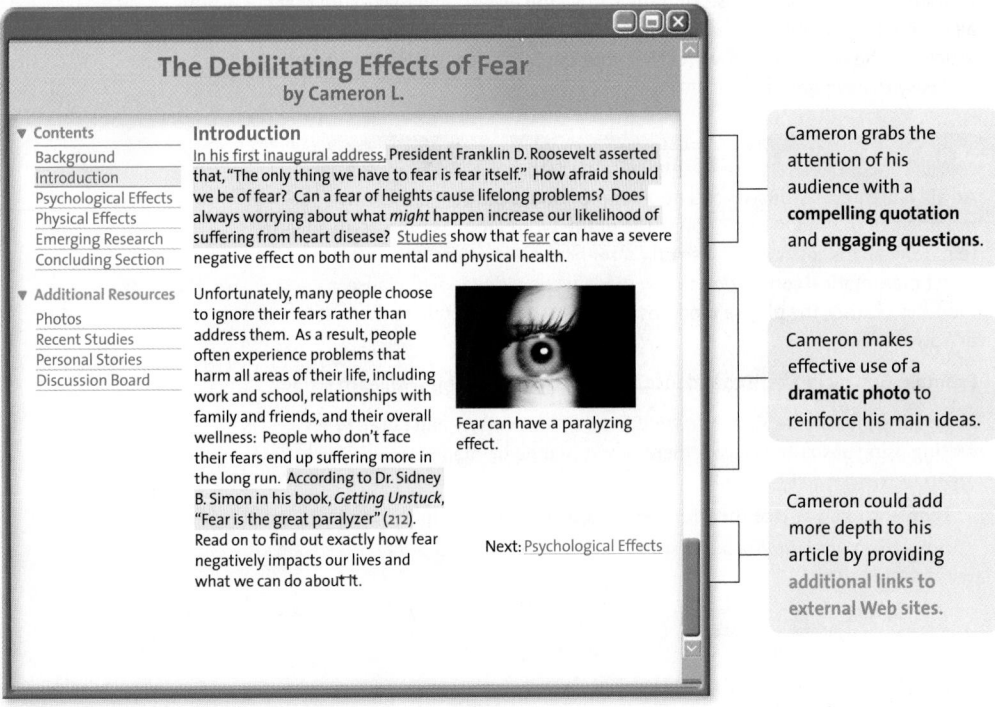

The Debilitating Effects of Fear
by Cameron L.

▾ Contents
Background
Introduction
Psychological Effects
Physical Effects
Emerging Research
Concluding Section

▾ Additional Resources
Photos
Recent Studies
Personal Stories
Discussion Board

Introduction

In his first inaugural address, President Franklin D. Roosevelt asserted that, "The only thing we have to fear is fear itself." How afraid should we be of fear? Can a fear of heights cause lifelong problems? Does always worrying about what *might* happen increase our likelihood of suffering from heart disease? Studies show that fear can have a severe negative effect on both our mental and physical health.

Unfortunately, many people choose to ignore their fears rather than address them. As a result, people often experience problems that harm all areas of their life, including work and school, relationships with family and friends, and their overall wellness: People who don't face their fears end up suffering more in the long run. According to Dr. Sidney B. Simon in his book, *Getting Unstuck,* "Fear is the great paralyzer" (212). Read on to find out exactly how fear negatively impacts our lives and what we can do about it.

Fear can have a paralyzing effect.

Next: Psychological Effects

Cameron grabs the attention of his audience with a **compelling quotation** and **engaging questions**.

Cameron makes effective use of a **dramatic photo** to reinforce his main ideas.

Cameron could add more depth to his article by providing additional links to external Web sites.

LEARN HOW Link to External Sites In his first paragraph, Cameron embeds links to other sites with more information or multimedia related to his topic. He could add more dimension to his article by following this approach in his second paragraph. Notice how he includes another link to a reliable source.

CAMERON'S REVISION TO *INTRODUCTION*

According to Dr. Sidney B. Simon in his book, *Getting Unstuck,* "Fear is the great paralyzer" (212).

Link to more information on this expert and his books

YOUR TURN Use the "Learn How" lesson and feedback from your teacher and peers to revise or rework your article.

FOR ENGLISH LANGUAGE LEARNERS

Links to Internal and External Web Sites As a class, view a live online feature article. Explain the difference between internal and external links, clicking on each to demonstrate. Then have pairs of students read a second online article. Using a two-column chart, have them list each link and what it leads to. Have pairs compare their charts in groups.

FOR STRUGGLING READERS

Develop Internal Links To help students insert internal links, have them work with a partner to locate and underline or highlight these elements in their article:

- words or terms explained more fully in another section of their article
- multimedia captions that relate to information in their article
- names of people, places, events, or concepts that are discussed in other parts of their article

---

ANALYZE A STUDENT DRAFT

Explain that the Student Draft on this page is the first screen of an online feature article. Model reading the draft and the annotations in blue that explain the student's language choices. Explain that the *Learn How* minilesson has helpful information about a way to improve the student draft as well as their own.

LEARN HOW Link to External Sites

- Tell students that links to external Web sites can add richness to their articles by providing additional information and by adding interactivity.
- Have students read through their drafts, looking for places that could benefit from links to external Web sites.

Remind students to link only to reliable and relevant, or related, Web sites. Suggest they look through their source material and *Works Cited* lists for possible links.

YOUR TURN Have students complete the **Your Turn** independently. Tell them to review their drafts to make sure they have provided enough background information and have incorporated quotations appropriately. Tell students to place asterisks in the margins next to places that could be improved by a link to an external Web site.

For interactive revisions tools, see

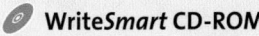 **WriteSmart CD-ROM**

Writing Center on thinkcentral.com

Editing and Publishing

GRAMMAR IN CONTEXT: ABSOLUTE PHRASES

Give students these additional examples:

- The decrepit truck rattled down the road, its fenders dragging on the ground and its door swinging loosely.
- The runner finished the marathon, sobbing breaths escaping from his chest.

Then have students return to their drafts and find one or two sentences to which they can add an absolute phrase. Ask volunteers to share an example of an absolute phrase they added with the class.

PUBLISH YOUR WRITING

Brainstorm with students about additional ways to publish their online feature articles.

 YOUR TURN Allow time for students to proofread their drafts. Then have them exchange articles and draw arrows to sentences that they think could be clarified by the addition of an absolute phrase.

Editing and Publishing

 COMMON CORE

W 5 Strengthen writing by editing. **L 1b** Use absolute phrases to convey specific meanings and add interest. **L 2** Demonstrate command of the conventions of standard English capitalization, punctuation, and spelling.

Errors in spelling, grammar, and punctuation can distract your audience from understanding and appreciating your ideas. In the editing stage, you proofread your article to eliminate these kinds of errors. You also should make sure that all your links and multimedia are functioning properly. Before you publish your article for the world to read, verify that your pages are formatted consistently and easy to navigate.

GRAMMAR IN CONTEXT: ABSOLUTE PHRASES

An **absolute phrase** consists of a noun or pronoun, a participle, and any modifiers of that noun or pronoun. The entire word group is used as an adverb to modify an independent clause of a sentence. An absolute phrase has no direct grammatical connection to any word in the independent clause it modifies. Rather, the phrase modifies the entire clause by telling *when, why,* or *how.*

Example: Sophia ran with confidence, **her fears disappearing with each stride.**

As he edited his article, Cameron tried to add more variety and detail to his writing using absolute phrases. Here is one change he made:

> People who don't face their fears end up suffering more in the long run, *their coping mechanism ultimately damaging their mental and physical health.*

PUBLISH YOUR WRITING

After you have finished proofreading your article, you are ready to post it online. Consider the following ideas:

- Send an e-mail or text message to friends and family notifying them that your article has been posted.
- Update your status on social media networks that you participate on to include a link to your article.
- Post a link to your article in forums or online communities that you frequently visit.

YOUR TURN Carefully proofread your article and correct any errors in conventions. Try to include at least one absolute phrase to add detail and variety to your writing. After you've completed these final touches, publish your online feature article for your audience to read.

DIFFERENTIATED INSTRUCTION

FOR ENGLISH LANGUAGE LEARNERS

Language: Phrases Display each sentence:

1. No doubts existing in her mind, she made her final decision.
2. He was not about to count on the win, his hopes having been dashed before.
3. The president toured the site, reporters following along behind him.
4. The small child—her face shining with happiness—accepted the gift.

Have students read each sentence aloud and identify the absolute phrase in each sentence.

FOR STRUGGLING WRITERS

Use Absolute Phrases Review with students the punctuation rules concerning absolute phrases: (1) An absolute phrase at the beginning of a sentence is followed by a comma. (2) An absolute phrase that interrupts the sentence is set off by parentheses, a pair of commas, or a pair of dashes. (3) An absolute phrase at the end of a sentence is preceded by a comma or a dash. Display sentences containing absolute phrases without the correct punctuation. Have students rewrite them correctly.

Scoring Rubric

Use the rubric below to evaluate your online feature article.

ONLINE FEATURE ARTICLE

SCORE	COMMON CORE TRAITS
6	• **Development** Effectively introduces a topic; states a well-researched controlling idea; develops the topic with relevant, varied evidence; ends powerfully • **Organization** Logically organizes information; uses varied transitions; includes formatting and multimedia that enhances the information; correctly cites sources • **Language** Ably uses precise language; maintains a formal style and objective tone; shows strong command of conventions
5	• **Development** Competently introduces a topic; states a clear controlling idea; offers relevant evidence; has a strong concluding section • **Organization** Logically organizes information; uses transitions; includes formatting and multimedia; correctly cites sources • **Language** Uses precise language; generally maintains a formal style and objective tone; has a few errors in conventions
4	• **Development** Sufficiently introduces a topic; states a controlling idea; offers mostly relevant evidence; has an adequate concluding section • **Organization** Is mostly logically organized; needs a few more transitions; could use more formatting and multimedia; cites most sources • **Language** Uses vague language in some places; mostly maintains a formal style and objective tone; includes a few distracting errors in conventions
3	• **Development** States a controlling idea, but the introduction could be more compelling; lacks enough evidence; has a somewhat weak concluding section • **Organization** Has some flaws in organization; lacks many transitions; has inconsistent formatting and distracting multimedia; does not cite all sources • **Language** Needs more precise words; has frequent lapses in style and tone; has some critical errors in conventions
2	• **Development** Has a weak controlling idea; does not support most ideas; ends abruptly • **Organization** Has serious flaws in organization; lacks transitions throughout; lacks formatting and multimedia; neglects to cite many sources • **Language** Lacks precise words or uses them incorrectly; uses an overly informal style and tone; has many errors in conventions
1	• **Development** Lacks a controlling idea, supporting evidence, and a concluding section • **Organization** Has no organization, formatting, or multimedia; plagiarizes or does not credit sources • **Language** Uses vague words; has an inappropriate style and tone; has major problems in conventions

Scoring Rubric

Tell students that the best way to understand a scoring rubric is to use it to evaluate an actual piece of writing. Provide students with a model online feature article. (To ensure anonymity, if the essay is from a different class or previous school year, remove the writer's name and any details that might reveal his or her identity.) Invite students to evaluate the article using the rubric. Then have them write a brief paragraph using the language of the rubric to explain the reasons for their score.

For Rubric Bank, see

 Write*Smart* **CD-ROM**

Writing Center on <u>thinkcentral.com</u>

Assess and Reteach

Assess

 RESOURCE MANAGER—Copy Master
Rubric for Evaluation p. 120

Online Essay Scoring at <u>thinkcentral.com</u>

Reteach

Level Up Online Tutorials at <u>thinkcentraol.com</u>

Focus and Motivate

:COMMON CORE FOCUS

W 6 Use technology to update individual writing products, link to other information, and display information flexibly and dynamically. **SL 1c** Pose and respond to questions. **SL 5** Make strategic use of digital media in presentations.

PRODUCE WITH A PURPOSE

Ask students to share positive experiences that they have had reading online articles. Have them discuss the common characteristics of these articles. For example, did they find the article easy to navigate? Did all of the links work as they should? Was the presentation of the content inviting? Was multimedia used effectively? Tell them that this workshop will help them provide a similar experience for their own readers.

COMMON CORE TRAITS

As students prepare to update their articles, remind them to keep in mind the *COMMON CORE TRAITS* of a successful update.

Practice and Apply

Maintaining Your Article

Model the Skill: **UPDATING LINKS AND RESPONDING TO FEEDBACK**

Model how to check for a dead or broken link. If any are found, show students how to search for a replacement link or how to delete the link.

- Tell students that replacing dead or broken links is an important part of their update.

- Explain that they may also want to replace links with others that offer more information or are more interesting.

Then model for students how to respond to reader feedback, using an example that you write on the board or interactive whiteboard.

GUIDED PRACTICE Help students to write a comment about a partner's article. Have partners draft a sample response. Call on volunteers to share them.

 BEST PRACTICES TOOLKIT—Copy Master
Peer Response Guide pp. C14, C54

Technology Workshop

Essential Course of Study **ECOS**

Updating an Online Feature Article

Because of the fluid nature of the World Wide Web, online content is continually being added, updated, reorganized, or deleted. As the author of an online feature article, you have a responsibility to maintain your published work and keep it current. In this workshop, you will learn how to effectively update, improve, and enhance your online feature article.

Complete the workshop activities in your **Reader/Writer Notebook.**

PRODUCE WITH PURPOSE	**COMMON CORE TRAITS**
TASK	**A SUCCESSFUL UPDATE . . .**
Update your online feature article to provide new information about your topic, replace dead (broken) links, and improve your site design and navigation.	• repairs dead links and removes outdated information • adds or revises content, using current and reliable sources • responds promptly and politely to readers' questions and feedback • modifies the site design to improve navigation • seeks new audiences and encourages return visitors

:COMMON CORE

W 6 Use technology to update individual writing products, link to other information, and display information flexibly and dynamically. **SL 1c** Pose and respond to questions. **SL 5** Make strategic use of digital media in presentations.

Maintaining Your Article

Revisit your online article so that you can respond to feedback or problems as they arise. Use these guidelines to help you:

- **Update Your Links** Because many Web sites undergo changes in content and organization, some of your links might break over time. Dead links make your article look unprofessional and outdated—and can frustrate your readers. For this reason, regularly verify that the Web addresses, or URLs, still function and connect to the correct information. Update each broken link to reflect the new URL, find a suitable replacement, or delete the link from your article.

- **Respond to Feedback** Promptly read and reply to all appropriate questions and comments posted on your article; delete inappropriate comments immediately. Thoughtful replies can stimulate discussion and promote reader participation, which in turn can attract new readers and encourage return visitors.

- **Include a** *Last Updated* **Date** Include a line of text at the beginning or end of your article that tells when your article was last updated. This note lets your readers know how current your information is.

Media Tools

THINK central

Go to **thinkcentral.com.**
KEYWORD: HML10N-922

DIFFERENTIATED INSTRUCTION

FOR ENGLISH LANGUAGE LEARNERS

Language: Reinforce Technology Terms
Write these terms on the board and review them with students:

- *link:* highlighted or underlined words or phrases on a Web page that connect to a new Web page or different Web site

- *dead link:* highlighted words or phrases or images on a Web page that do not connect to anything

- *forum:* discussion site on the World Wide Web

- *World Wide Web:* a system of linked documents that people access through the Internet

- *URL:* universal resource locator, or the address of a Web site

Modifying and Improving Your Article

Part of publishing online is the ability to modify and improve your article as you receive user feedback and as new information about your topic becomes available. Regular updates can encourage return visitors and attract new readers. You might modify your article for a variety of reasons, including:

- **To Improve Content** As you learn more about your topic, replace outdated information with new content, including links and multimedia. If you have chosen a topic about something that is likely to change frequently (such as a scientific phenomenon or a current event), you might add a Recent News or Updates section. Subscribing to a Web or RSS feed is a good way to stay current on your topic.

- **To Address User Feedback** Readers might question your facts or suggest improvements to your navigation and design. Be willing to revise your work or even try a new approach to address valid feedback.

- **To Redesign Your Article** You might apply a more contemporary design, try a new font, or reorganize your links and menu options for easier navigation. Make sure that any changes suit your overall purpose and don't distract from the content.

- **To Grow Your Readership** Whenever you make a change to your article, let readers know about it. To attract readers and to encourage them to return, try posting an update on social media networks, sending e-mail updates, or posting a link to your article on forums that your audience frequently visits.

> **Danielle** (reader) said...
>
> This is an interesting article, but do you know of any research on practical strategies for facing fears? Many people would find that useful!
>
> June 7, 3:59 p.m
>
> ---
>
> **Cameron** (Site Administrator) said...
>
> Thanks for your feedback, Danielle! I have read some articles that include the kind of strategies you're talking about. I'll add links to the articles that are online. Watch for updates!
>
> June 7, 8:37 p.m.

NEWS FEED

Cameron How much does fear affect *your* life? Check out my article on the debilitating effects of fear on our lives. I just added a new section with practical strategies for facing <u>fears</u>.

YOUR TURN Regularly review your online feature article. Verify that your links still function and then promptly update or delete dead links. Revise content to correct mistakes or add new content as more information on your topic becomes available. Politely respond to readers' comments, questions, and feedback.

TECHNOLOGY WORKSHOP **923**

Modifying and Improving Your Article

Model the Skill: UPDATING CONTENT

Have students consider the following points when they add or remove content from their articles:

- Prepare the new information that you want to include ahead of time, so that your article can be updated quickly. Readers who cannot access it a first time may not return again.
- If information is removed, make sure the coherence of the rest of the article is not affected.
- Post links instead of writing out information in an updates or news section.

GUIDED PRACTICE Have pairs of students work together to identify content in their articles that may need to be updated. Make a class list of these needed updates for future reference when students update or modify their articles.

YOUR TURN Have pairs of students access each other's online articles. Ask them to identify areas that need to be updated or could be improved by a modification, such as new headings.

Assess and Reteach

Assess

Use the *COMMON CORE TRAITS* to assess students' updates.

A strong update
- repairs dead (broken) links
- removes outdated information
- adds new content from current and reliable sources
- responds promptly and politely to reader questions, comments, and feedback
- improves viewing and navigation

Reteach

Organize students into pairs, making sure that one partner is tech savvy. Then have them perform one or two updating tasks on each of their articles as you circulate around the room, checking their progress.

Media Tools

Keywords for using technology direct students to **MediaScope,** a Web site that helps them strengthen media analysis and production skills.

Assessment Practice

RI 1 Cite textual evidence to support analysis of what the text says explicitly as well as inferences drawn from the text. **RL 4** Determine the meaning of words and phrases as they are used in a text; analyze the cumulative impact of specific word choices on meaning and tone. **W 5** Strengthen writing by revising and editing. **L 6** Acquire and use accurately general academic words and phrases; demonstrate independence in gathering vocabulary knowledge.

CHECK READINESS

Read aloud the paragraph under **ASSESS** and stress to students that this is not the full Unit Test, but a way for them to check their readiness for it. Then have students examine the skills standards listed under **REVIEW** and look back in the unit or in the **Student Resource Bank** for any skills they need to review.

READ THE TEXTS

Remind students to keep unit goals in mind as they read each passage, paying particular attention to these literary and reading skills:

- style
- make inferences
- author's purpose

To help students focus on style while reading, encourage them to ask questions such as

- Why does this selection hold my interest?
- How does Hawthorne's style compare to Hemingway's style?

ANSWER THE QUESTIONS

Direct students to pages R93–R101 of the **Handbook** to review test-taking strategies.

Urge students to use active reading strategies when they read test materials. For example, before they read a passage, suggest that they skim the questions that follow it.

COMMON CORE

ASSESS
Taking this practice test will help you assess your knowledge of these skills and determine your readiness for the Unit Test.

REVIEW
After you take the practice test, your teacher can help you identify any standards you need to review.

⋯ **COMMON CORE**

RL 1 Cite textual evidence to support analysis of what the text says explicitly as well as inferences drawn from the text. **RL 4** Determine the meaning of words and phrases as they are used in a text; analyze the cumulative impact of specific word choices on meaning and tone. **W 5** Strengthen writing by revising and editing. **L 6** Acquire and use accurately general academic words and phrases; demonstrate independence in gathering vocabulary knowledge.

Practice Test **THINK** central

Take it at **thinkcentral.com**. KEYWORD: HML10N-924

Assessment Practice

DIRECTIONS Read the following selections, and then answer the questions.

from The House of the Seven Gables
by Nathaniel Hawthorne

1   On entering the shop, she found an old man there, a humble resident of Pyncheon-street, and whom, for a great many years past, she had suffered to be a kind of familiar of the house. He was an immemorial personage, who seemed always to have had a white head and wrinkles, and never to have possessed but a single tooth, and that a half-decayed one, in the front of the upper jaw. Well advanced as Hepzibah was, she could not remember when Uncle Venner, as the neighborhood called him, had not gone up and down the street, stooping a little and drawing his feet heavily over the gravel or pavement. But still there was something tough and vigorous about him, that not only kept him in daily

10 breath, but enabled him to fill a place which would else have been vacant, in the apparently crowded world. To go of errands, with his slow and shuffling gait, which made you doubt how he ever was to arrive anywhere; to saw a small household's foot or two of firewood, or knock to pieces an old barrel, or split up a pine board, for kindling-stuff; in summer, to dig the few yards of garden-ground, appertaining to a low-rented tenement, and share the produce of his labor at the halves; in winter, to shovel away the snow from the sidewalk, or open paths to the wood-shed, or along the clothesline; —such were some of the essential offices which Uncle Venner performed among at least a score of families.

Old Man at the Bridge
by Ernest Hemingway

1   An old man with steel rimmed spectacles and very dusty clothes sat by the side of the road. There was a pontoon bridge across the river and carts, trucks, and men, women and children were crossing it. The mule-drawn carts staggered up the steep bank from the bridge with soldiers helping push against the spokes of the wheels. The trucks ground up and away heading out of it all and the peasants plodded along in the ankle deep dust. But the old man sat there without moving. He was too tired to go any farther.

2   It was my business to cross the bridge, explore the bridgehead beyond and find out to what point the enemy had advanced. I did this and returned over

---

DIFFERENTIATED INSTRUCTION

FOR ENGLISH LANGUAGE LEARNERS
Assessment Practice: Work Backward
Prepare students by having them read the questions *before* reading the passage and supplementary selections. Have pairs find unfamiliar words in test directions and questions and follow these steps:

1. Write each word on an index card.
2. Look up the meaning in a dictionary and write it on the back of the card.

3. Use the cards to practice the words with your partner and to teach them to others.

the bridge. There were not so many carts now and very few people on foot, but the old man was still there.

3   "Where do you come from?" I asked him.

4   "From San Carlos," he said, and smiled.

5   That was his native town and so it gave him pleasure to mention it and he smiled.

6   "I was taking care of animals," he explained.

7   "Oh," I said, not quite understanding.

8   "Yes," he said, "I stayed, you see, taking care of animals. I was the last one to leave the town of San Carlos."

9   He did not look like a shepherd nor a herdsman and I looked at his black dusty clothes and his gray dusty face and his steel rimmed spectacles and said, "What animals were they?"

10   "Various animals," he said, and shook his head. "I had to leave them."

11   I was watching the bridge and the African looking country of the Ebro Delta and wondering how long now it would be before we would see the enemy, and listening all the while for the first noises that would signal that ever mysterious event called contact, and the old man still sat there.

12   "What animals were they?" I asked.

13   "There were three animals altogether," he explained. "There were two goats and a cat and then there were four pairs of pigeons."

14   "And you had to leave them?" I asked.

15   "Yes. Because of the artillery. The captain told me to go because of the artillery."

16   "And you have no family?" I asked, watching the far end of the bridge where a few last carts were hurrying down the slope of the bank.

17   "No," he said, "only the animals I stated. The cat, of course, will be all right. A cat can look out for itself, but I cannot think what will become of the others."

18   "What politics have you?" I asked.

19   "I am without politics," he said. "I am seventy-six years old. I have come twelve kilometers now and I think now I can go no further."

20   "This is not a good place to stop," I said. "If you can make it, there are trucks up the road where it forks for Tortosa."

21   "I will wait a while," he said, "and then I will go. Where do the trucks go?"

22   "Towards Barcelona," I told him.

23   "I know no one in that direction," he said, "but thank you very much. Thank you again very much."

GO ON →

ITEM ANALYSIS

COMPREHENSION AND WRITTEN RESPONSE	ITEMS	UNIT PAGES
Style		850–855, 857, 879, 887, 901
Word Choice	3, 6, 12, 13	850–855
Sentence Structure	1, 5, 13	
Tone	3, 7, 13	850–855, 901
Imagery	2, 8, 12	850–855, 879, 895
Make Inferences	2, 10, 11, 12	887
Author's Purpose	4, 9, 11	901

VOCABULARY	ITEMS	UNIT PAGES
Etymology	1, 2, 3, 4, 5, 6, 7	909

WRITING AND GRAMMAR	ITEMS	UNIT PAGES
Personification	3	877

THINK central

Practice Test

On **thinkcentral.com** students can complete an interactive version of this practice test *and* receive remediation for the skills they have not yet mastered.

FOR STRUGGLING READERS

Assessment Support Consider these options for completing the Assessment Practice:

- Have students "work backward" to review the test questions before reading the passage.

- Select random questions in the Assessment and have students demonstrate *how* and *where* to look for the answers.

- Ask students to locate unfamiliar vocabulary words in the Assessment. Elicit the words' meanings from the class.

- Have students record useful testing words and definitions in their journal for later reference.

- Read the selection or parts of it aloud to aid in student comprehension.

Reading Comprehension

Model a thinking process for answering multiple-choice questions.

1. **B is correct.** *All five sentences in the paragraph are long. That fact alone eliminates A, C, and D.*

2. **B is correct.** *The statement effectively summarizes lines 9–11. A and C are not supported by any details in the passage. D is incorrect because "daily breath" (line 10) is figurative, not literal.*

3. **D is correct.** *The sentence describing Uncle Venner in lines 3–6 reflects the author's good-natured tone. A is incorrect because Hawthorne's tone is not harsh. B is incorrect because the tone is formal. C is incorrect because sentence variety and vivid details prevent monotony.*

4. **A is correct.** *Hawthorne packs the paragraph with vivid, positive description. B is incorrect because the description is gentle, not harsh. C is a weak choice because although Venner is poor, discussing poverty is secondary to characterization in the selection. D is incorrect because the community is kind, not indifferent, to Venner.*

5. **D is correct.** *Long sentences such as those in paragraph 11 alternate with the passage's mostly short sentences. A is untrue, and B is incorrect because close reading shows the presence of some long sentences. C is incorrect because most of the sentences are short but complete.*

6. **A is correct.** *Both in dialogue and in description, Hemingway uses everyday vocabulary. Therefore, C is incorrect. B can be eliminated because the overall purpose seems to describe the situation as it actually existed. D is incorrect because although terms such as* pontoon bridge *(paragraph 1) and* bridgehead *(paragraph 2) occur, they do not dominate the selection.*

7. **D is correct.** *The first paragraph is serious and straightforward. A is incorrect because although the narrator's feeling by the end of the selection might be described as bitter, it is not so at the beginning. B is incorrect because there is no sense of fun in the selection. C is incorrect because the narration is neither negative nor mocking.*

24 He looked at me very blankly and tiredly, then said, having to share his worry with some one, "The cat will be all right, I am sure. There is no need to be unquiet about the cat. But the others. Now what do you think about the others?"

25 "Why they'll probably come through it all right."

26 "You think so?"

27 "Why not," I said, watching the far bank where now there were no carts.

28 "But what will they do under the artillery when I was told to leave because of the artillery?"

29 "Did you leave the dove cage unlocked?" I asked.

30 "Yes."

31 "Then they'll fly."

32 "Yes, certainly they'll fly. But the others. It's better not to think about the others," he said.

33 "If you are rested I would go," I urged. "Get up and try to walk now."

34 "Thank you," he said and got to his feet, swayed from side to side and then sat down backwards in the dust.

35 "I was taking care of animals," he said dully, but no longer to me. "I was only taking care of animals."

36 There was nothing to do about him. It was Easter Sunday and the Fascists were advancing toward the Ebro. It was a gray overcast day with a low ceiling so their planes were not up. That and the fact that cats know how to look after themselves was all the good luck that old man would ever have.

Reading Comprehension

> **Use the excerpt from *The House of the Seven Gables* (p. 924) to answer questions 1–4.**

1. The author's style includes his use of sentences that are —
   A. all short sentences
   B. all long sentences
   C. mostly short sentences
   D. a mix of long and short sentences

2. From the imagery in lines 9–11, you can infer that Uncle Venner —
   A. succeeds through his charm
   B. survives by being useful
   C. is somewhat overweight
   D. has breathing problems

3. The author's style can best be characterized by his use of —
   A. long descriptions and a harsh tone
   B. lyrical language and an informal tone
   C. flowery language and a monotonous tone
   D. detailed descriptions and a good-natured tone

926

8. **D is correct.** *The repetition emphasizes that the old man sits for a long time; and paragraph 1 says, "He was too tired to go any farther." A is incorrect because although the man is in danger, he appears to know it. B is incorrect because the man sits patiently. C is incorrect because the man is friendly, not sad.*

9. **C is correct.** *The story describes the war's effects upon an elderly civilian. A has some relevance, but it ultimately is incorrect because the old man is the focus of the story. B can be eliminated because the old man's dismissal of politics is ironic in view of his plight. D is incorrect because although the soldier-narrator mentions his duties (paragraph 2), his chief focus is on the old man.*

10. **D is correct.** *Uncle Venner is serious about his errands; the old man is serious about his animals. A is incorrect because Venner is energetic. B is incorrect because neither character seems angry. C is incorrect because both characters are self-reliant.*

4. The author's purpose in this excerpt is most likely to —
   A. paint an affectionate portrait of a local character
   B. ridicule an eccentric old man
   C. illustrate the hardships of poverty
   D. highlight the indifference of the community

Use "Old Man at the Bridge" (pp. 924–926) to answer questions 5–9.

5. One element of the author's style is his use of —
   A. mostly long sentences
   B. all very short sentences
   C. long sentences and some incomplete sentences
   D. mostly short, simple sentences and some long sentences

6. The author's choice of words can best be characterized as —
   A. conversational   C. flowery
   B. exaggerated   D. technical

7. The tone in paragraph 1 is —
   A. bitter   C. sarcastic
   B. playful   D. somber

8. The author repeats variations of the phrase "the old man sat there" in paragraphs 1, 2, and 11 to create an impression of —
   A. foolishness   C. sorrow
   B. impatience   D. weariness

9. The author's primary purpose in writing this story is to —
   A. describe an elderly man's fondness for his animals
   B. persuade readers that politics is unimportant
   C. portray the effects of war on the citizens of a country
   D. evaluate the duties of a soldier in times of war

Use both selections to answer question 10.

10. What can you infer about the old men in the two selections?
    A. They are tired from all of the work that they do.
    B. One of them is sad and one is angry because they must work for other people.
    C. Because they are elderly, both must rely on others to care for them.
    D. Both take their work and responsibilities seriously.

SHORT CONSTRUCTED RESPONSE
Write three or four sentences to answer each question.

11. Why do you think the author has a soldier narrate "Old Man at the Bridge"? In what way does this choice help the author achieve his purpose?

12. List five words or images from the excerpt from *The House of the Seven Gables* that describe Uncle Venner. What can you infer about Venner from these words and images?

Write two to three paragraphs to answer this question.

13. Describe the differences in the two authors' writing styles. Give examples of word choice, sentence structure, and tone in your answer.

GO ON ➤

927

SHORT CONSTRUCTED RESPONSE
Possible responses:

11. *The soldier-narrator's view of the old man is both matter-of-fact and sympathetic. He communicates information to the reader that the old man could not: the nature of his mission and the imminent arrival of the enemy. The soldier's understanding of the old man's fate makes that fact seem more tragic. Through the soldier's eyes, the reader sees the point of the author's purpose (that is, showing the effects of war upon civilians)—namely, that those fighting a war feel helpless because they cannot protect the people for whom they are fighting.*

12. *Words and images include "old man"; "humble"; "a kind of familiar of the house"; "immemorial personage"; "seemed always to have had a white head and wrinkles"; "a single tooth"; "stooping"; "drawing his feet heavily"; "tough and vigorous"; and "slow and shuffling gait." The reader can infer that Venner is a poor, aged man, that he is well known locally, and that he is strong and energetic but slow-moving.*

13. *Hawthorne's style is formal, with elevated language and long descriptive sentences. Hemingway's style is informal and journalistic, using plain language and extensive dialogue. Most of Hawthorne's sentences are complex or compound-complex; most of Hemingway's are simple or compound. Hawthorne's tone is gently humorous; Hemingway's is somber. Student examples of word choice will vary.*

DIFFERENTIATED INSTRUCTION

FOR ENGLISH LANGUAGE LEARNERS
Assessment Vocabulary To help students understand the Reading Comprehension questions, teach or review these key vocabulary words:

- Items 3 and 6: *characterized*—"described"
- Item 4: *excerpt*—"part of a longer work"
- Item 5: *element*—"part"
- Item 8: *variations*—"different ways of saying the same thing"
- Item 9: *primary*—"main"

FOR ENGLISH LANGUAGE LEARNERS
Vocabulary Support On the board, list the terms shown in italics. Then give the examples in random order and have students classify them. Elicit additional examples from students.

- *tone:* Hawthorne's phrase "an immemorial personage" expresses affection for Uncle Venner.
- *diction:* In "Old Man at the Bridge," Hemingway uses military terms like *pontoon bridge* and *bridgehead.*

- *imagery:* Uncle Venner had "a single tooth, and that a half-decayed one, in the front of the upper jaw."
- *author's style:* Unlike Hawthorne, Hemingway writes mostly in short sentences.

Vocabulary

1. **A is correct.** The clue grave *clearly points to gravel.* B, C, *and* D *obviously have no etymological connection to* grave.

2. **A is correct.** *The somewhat obscure meaning of familiar—"domestic servant"—comes from* famulus. B *comes from a related Latin word, but the choice makes no sense in the context of the sentence.* C *and* D *are obviously unrelated to* famulus.

3. **B is correct.** *The connection between humilis and* humble *is evident.* A *is incorrect because although the word* low *appears in the definition of* humilis, garden-ground *does not derive from* humilis *and makes little sense in context.* C *and* D *are unrelated to* humilis.

4. **D is correct.** *In both sound and meaning,* stupian *is clearly close to* stooping. A *is untrue in both etymology and meaning.* B *is nonsensical, for it speaks of exiting by entering.* C *fits the meaning of the sentence but not the etymology.*

5. **C is correct.** Staggered *and* stakra *are similar in sound as well as meaning.* A, B, *and* D *have meanings that are conceivable in the sentence but are clearly not related to* stakra.

6. **C is correct.** *The prefix* con- *and the general sound of* tangere *are clues to the derivation of* contact. A, B, *and* D *lack any etymological resemblance to the clue words; and of the three choices, only* signal *would fit meaningfully into the sentence.*

7. **C is correct.** *The derivation of* politics *from* polis *is obvious in view of the meaning of* politics. A *and* D *can be eliminated because they show no resemblance to* polis. B *is incorrect because the presence of the letters* p *and* l *in* planes *is not enough to indicate a derivation from* polis.

Vocabulary

> Use the etymology clues to help you choose the correct modern English word from the reading selections.

1. Which of the following words from *The House of the Seven Gables* comes from the Old French word *grave*, meaning "pebbly shore"?
   A. Gravel
   B. Kindling-stuff
   C. Paths
   D. Pavement

2. The Latin word *famulus* means "servant." Which word in *The House of the Seven Gables* comes from the word *famulus*?
   A. Familiar
   B. Famous
   C. Personage
   D. Resident

3. Which of the following words from *The House of the Seven Gables* comes from the Latin word *humilis*, meaning "low"?
   A. Garden-Ground
   B. Humble
   C. Immemorial
   D. Vigorous

4. The Old English word *stupian* means "to bow or bend." Which word in *The House of the Seven Gables* comes from the word *stupian*?
   A. Appertaining
   B. Entering
   C. Shuffling
   D. Stooping

5. Which of the following words from "Old Man at the Bridge" is an alteration of the Old Norse word *stakra, staka*, meaning "to push"?
   A. Advanced
   B. Plodded
   C. Staggered
   D. Swayed

6. The Latin prefix *con-* means "together" and the past participle *tangere* means "to touch." Which of the following words from "Old Man at the Bridge" comes from *con-* + *tangere*?
   A. Bank
   B. Bridgehead
   C. Contact
   D. Signal

7. Which of the following words from "Old Man at the Bridge" comes from the Greek word *polis*, meaning "city"?
   A. Business
   B. Planes
   C. Politics
   D. Towns

Revising and Editing

DIRECTIONS Read this passage, and answer the questions that follow.

(1) Pablo Picasso's painting *Guernica* portrays the destruction of a town during the Spanish Civil War. (2) It is an abstract composition of colors and forms. (3) Tormented animals and tortured human image fill the canvas. (4) In the painting, a snorting bull and a writhing horse seem pained. (5) The painting also depicts human suffering. (6) Picasso painted a woman clutching her dead child. (7) His purpose was to expose the horrors of war.

1. What is the most effective way to combine sentences 1 and 2 into a complex sentence?
   A. Pablo Picasso's painting *Guernica* portrays the destruction of a town during the Spanish Civil War; however it is an abstract composition of colors and forms.
   B. Pablo Picasso's painting *Guernica* portrays the destruction of a town during the Spanish Civil War, it is an abstract composition of colors and forms.
   C. Pablo Picasso's painting *Guernica,* which is an abstract composition of colors and forms, portrays the destruction of a town during the Spanish Civil War.
   D. Pablo Picasso's painting *Guernica* portrays the destruction of a town during the Spanish Civil War in an abstract composition of colors and forms.

2. What change, if any, should be made in sentence 3?
   A. Change *tortured* to **torturing**
   B. Insert comma after *animals*
   C. Change *image* to **images**
   D. Make no change

3. What is the most effective way to revise sentence 5 to include personification?
   A. The painting also shows human suffering in great detail.
   B. The painting also cries out against human suffering.
   C. The painting also demonstrates examples of human suffering.
   D. The painting also displays images of human suffering.

4. Which transitional word or phrase should be added to the beginning of sentence 6?
   A. For instance,   C. Nevertheless,
   B. In conclusion,   D. On the other hand,

5. What change, if any, should be made to sentence 7?
   A. Change *horrors* to **horrors'**
   B. Change *expose* to **exposing**
   C. Change *war* to **wars**
   D. Make no change

STOP

929

Revising and Editing

1. **C *is correct.*** *Sentence 2 is included as a subordinate clause beginning with* which. *In A, there are two main clauses. B is wrong because it uses an ungrammatical comma splice between the two sentences. D combines the two sentences into one simple sentence in which the idea in sentence 2 has been reduced to a prepositional phrase.*

2. **C *is correct.*** *Two images fill the canvas—"tormented animals and tortured humans." A, B, and D do not correct the problem.*

3. **B *is correct.*** *The phrase "cries out" attributes a human emotional gesture to a painting. A, C, and D are incorrect because the verbs* shows, demonstrates, *and* displays *give literal rather than figurative descriptions and do not imply specifically human attributes.*

4. **A *is correct.*** *Sentence 6 provides an example of the suffering mentioned in sentence 5. B is incorrect because sentence 6 does not present a conclusion. C and D are incorrect because sentence 6 does not provide a contrast to the idea in sentence 5.*

5. **D *is correct.*** *The sentence is correct as written. The possessive form of* horrors *in A is wrong. B and C are also incorrect.*

DIFFERENTIATED INSTRUCTION

FOR STRUGGLING READERS

Assessment Support: Personification Remind students that personification is a figure of speech in which human qualities are given to an animal, object, or idea. Have students review the answer choices for item 3 to identify the sentence that gives human emotions to the painting.

COMMON CORE FOCUS

RL 10 Read and comprehend literature. **RI 10** Read and comprehend literary nonfiction.

INTRODUCE *GREAT READS*

In Unit 8, students have discussed a number of big questions. Invite students to tell which question they found most intriguing and why, and then focus attention on the three that appear on this page. Discuss the recommended books and their summaries, pointing out how each connects to the related question. Encourage students to choose one or more of these "great reads" to read independently.

UNIT 8 Great Reads

Ideas for Independent Reading

Extend your exploration of authors' styles and of provocative questions raised in this unit by reading the following works.

COMMON CORE

RL 10 Read and comprehend literature. **RI 10** Read and comprehend literary nonfiction.

What breeds terror?

Dracula
by Bram Stoker

Though books, films, and television series about vampires are now common, nothing terrifies readers like the original tale of Dracula, the undead count who hunts for young women he can turn into vampires.

It
by Stephen King

Readers could argue forever about which of King's horror novels is the most terrifying. This one pits seven teenagers against a clown-faced evil. They unite to banish it, only to see it reappear after they've grown to adulthood.

The Collector of Hearts: New Tales of the Grotesque
by Joyce Carol Oates

Oates, who claims Edgar Allan Poe as an influence, offers 27 macabre tales written in her own distinctive style. Several stories center on children, such as "Handpuppet," in which a ragged toy alters its young owner.

What do we learn from experience?

On the Blue Shores of Silence: Poems of the Sea
by Pablo Neruda

Chile's national poet, who admired Walt Whitman, loved to watch the sea outside his island home. In these poems Neruda captures the sea's continual movements—at times wild, at times calm—and its changes of color.

. . . And the Earth Did Not Devour Him
by Tomás Rivera

This kaleidoscopic collection of stories centers on a Mexican-American migrant community. The stories detail the people's hardships and hopes as they complete the yearly cycle of travel, labor, and return to Texas.

A Raisin in the Sun
by Lorraine Hansberry

In this famous play, an African-American family in Chicago dreams of what they will do with a $10,000 life insurance check. The son's rash decision teaches the family a painful yet ultimately ennobling lesson.

What is your role in your household?

The Joy Luck Club
by Amy Tan

This novel-in-stories explores the relationships of Chinese-immigrant mothers and their American-born daughters. The mothers struggle with painful memories as they adjust to a new culture. The daughters struggle with their mothers' high expectations of them.

Invent Radium, or I'll Pull Your Hair
by Doris Drucker

Doris Drucker grew up in an assimilated German-Jewish family who hoped they could outlast the Nazis. Her mother wanted her to be a scientist and forbade Doris to have opinions that differed from hers. This witty memoir gives insight into German culture under Hitler.

The Prize Winner of Defiance, Ohio
by Terry Ryan

Ryan's mother began entering contests as a young wife. She wrote jingles for products and earned enough to support ten children through years when her husband was unable to work. The family lived on her monetary winnings and the products that came with them.

Get Novel Wise **THINK central**

Go to **thinkcentral.com.**
KEYWORD: HML10-930

930

NovelWise **THINK central**

The keyword on this page points to **NovelWise,** a Web site that helps students choose a novel or other book-length work to read. **NovelWise** also provides

• study guides
• reading strategies and literary elements instruction
• presentations to introduce classic novels
• project ideas

UNIT 9

Product of the Times

HISTORY, CULTURE, AND THE AUTHOR

- In Nonfiction
- In Fiction
- In Poetry
- In Media

931

About the Art Malcah Zeldis created *Miss Liberty Celebration* to commemorate the 1986 centennial of the Statue of Liberty. The painting displays Zeldis's characteristic use of bright colors and a folk-art, storytelling style. It also is typical of her artistic themes, which include social awareness and celebrations.

INTRODUCE THE UNIT

A powdered wig, a piñata, a telephone with a rotary dial—each of these items reflects a historical era or culture. You could say that they are products of the times in which they were made and used. Similarly, every person is a product of his or her times. For example, if an elderly relative refuses to throw out any scrap of food, freezing it all to be used later, he or she might be a product of the Great Depression, an era when money was tight and food was too precious to throw out.

The images on this page can be described as products of the times, too. They express a similar theme, but each image depicts a specific culture and historical era. Use these questions to discuss the images:

- What elements in the images would you relate to mainstream American culture?
- How does the photograph evoke a historical era? What elements make it historically interesting?
- How would you describe "the times" that produced the painting?

Tell students that the selections in Unit 9 will show, in a particularly strong way, how **history, culture, and the author** can come together to produce meaningful works in nonfiction, fiction, poetry, and the media.

For help in planning this unit, see

R RESOURCE MANAGER UNIT 9
pp. 1–10

931

	COMMON CORE	ECOS Text Analysis Workshop: History, Culture, and the Author pp. 934–939	ECOS from Night Memoir pp. 940–951	ECOS from Farewell to Manzanar Memoir pp. 952–967	Linked Selections Montgomery Boycott Memoir pp. 968–979	A Eulogy for Dr. Martin Luther King Jr. Speech pp. 980–983
STRAND			Lexile: 440 Fry: 4 Dale-Chall: 5.2	Lexile: 1010 Fry: College Dale-Chall: 6.2	Lexile: 1020 Fry: 9 Dale-Chall: 6.8	Lexile: 1220 Fry: 9 Dale-Chall: 6.9
Reading Literature		Writer's Background pp. 934–935 RL 4, RL 6 Historical and Cultural Influences pp. 936–937 RL 4, RL 6 Analyze the Text pp. 938–939				
Reading Informational Text		Writer's Background pp. 934–935 RI 4, RI 6 Historical and Cultural Influences pp. 936–937 RI 4, RI 6 Analyze the Text pp. 938–939	Memoir pp. 941–942, 945, 949 RI 6 Connect pp. 941, 945, 947, 949 RI 1 Voice p. 947 RI 4 Language Coach p. 946 RI 4	Cultural Characteristics pp. 953–954, 958, 965 RI 6 Monitor pp. 953, 956, 959, 963, 965 RI 1 Foreign Words in English p. 960 RI 4 Language Coach pp. 960, 963 RI 4	Historical Events pp. 969–970, 973, 978 RI 6 Distinguish Fact from Opinion pp. 969, 972, 976, 978 RI 1, RI 4 Language Coach p. 975 RI 4	Rhetorical Devices pp. 980–983 RI 6, RI 9
Writing			Writing Prompt p. 951	Quickwrite p. 952 Writing Prompt p. 967 W 4	Cite Evidence p. 983 W 2	Writing Prompt p. 983 W 2
Speaking and Listening			Discuss p. 940 SL 1		Discuss p. 968 SL 1	
Language			Establish Tone pp. 944, 951 L 3 Connotation and Denotation p. 950 L 5b	Sentence Structure pp. 964, 967 L 1b Prefix in- p. 966 L 4c	Suffix -ion p. 979 L 4b	

Marriage is a Private Affair Short Story pp. 984–994	*Adam and Rosie/ Faces of Folklife* Transcript/Poster pp. 995–997	*On the Rainy River* Short Story pp. 998–1019	*The New Colossus/ Who Makes the Journey* Poems pp. 1020–1025	*Media Study: The Aftermath of September 11* Image Collection (Cartoon, Book Cover, Web Site) pp. 1026–1029	*Writing Workshop: Cause-and-Effect Essay* pp. 1030–1039 — *Speaking & Listening Workshop: Giving and Following Oral Instructions* pp. 1040–1041
Lexile: 830 Fry: 4 Dale-Chall: 6.0		Lexile: 940 Fry: 7 Dale-Chall: 6.2			
Moral Dilemma pp. 985–986, 988, 990, 992 RL 3, RL 6 Predict pp. 985, 989, 991–992 RL 1 Language Coach p. 988 RL 4		Historical Context pp. 999, 1002, 1004, 1009, 1016–1017 RL 2 Author's Perspective pp. 999, 1000, 1014, 1016–1017 RL 1 Language Coach pp. 1003, 1010 RL 4 Affixes p. 1005 RL 4	Literary Periods pp. 1021, 1023, 1025 RL 2 Sensory Details pp. 1021–1022, 1024–1025 RL 1 Allusion p. 1022 RL 2		
	Transcript p. 995 Poster p. 996 RI 7			History Through Media pp. 1027–1029 RI 7	
Writing Prompt p. 994 W 9b	Writing for Assessment p. 997	Writing Prompt p. 1019		Write or Discuss p. 1029 W 9b	Writing a Cause-and-Effect Essay pp. 1030–1039 W 2a–f, W 4, W 5, W 7, W 8, W 10
What's the Connection? p. 984 SL 1		Discuss p. 998 SL 1	Discuss p. 1020 SL 1	Write or Discuss p. 1029 SL 2	Giving and Following Oral Instructions pp. 1040–1041 SL 1, SL 4
Write Concisely pp. 988, 994 L 1b *kosmos* Word Family p. 993 L 4c		Establish Voice pp. 1005, 1019 L 5 Dictionary, Glossary, Thesaurus p. 1018 L 4c			Editing and Publishing p. 1037 L 1, L 2a

ECOS

To see the complete Essential Course of Study, see pp. T23–T28.

 For additional lesson planning help, see **Teacher One Stop DVD.**

Instructional Support

Resource Manager Unit 9

UNIT SUPPORT
Academic Vocabulary p. 3
Additional Academic Vocabulary p. 4
Grammar Focus p. 5
Text Analysis Workshop pp. 9–10
Writing Workshop: Analytical Essay:
   Cause and Effect p. 157

SELECTION SUPPORT*
Plan and Teach
   Lesson planning pages
   Additional leveled selection questions
   Extension activities

Student Copy Masters
   Selection summaries in four languages
   Skills copy masters in English and Spanish
   Vocabulary preteaching and support
   Reading Check and Question Support
   Reading Fluency

*Available for all selections

† Available on **thinkcentral.com**.

Language Handbook
Vocabulary Practice
Best Practices Toolkit†
PowerNotes DVD-ROM†
Connections: Nonfiction for
Common Core CD-ROM†

Teacher One Stop DVD-ROM
Student One Stop DVD-ROM
Media*Smart* DVD-ROM
The Aftermath of September 11
Write*Smart* CD-ROM†
GrammarNotes DVD-ROM†
WordSharp CD-ROM†

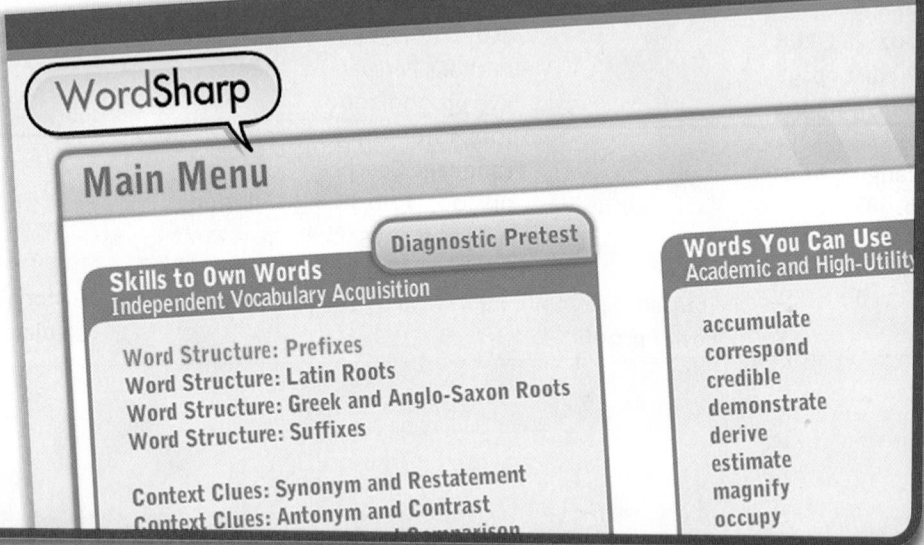

Differentiated Instruction

STRUGGLING READERS AND WRITERS	ENGLISH LANGUAGE LEARNERS	ADVANCED LEARNERS
Resource Manager Unit 9	**Resource Manager Unit 9**	**Resource Manager Unit 9**
Additional Selection Questions	Selection Summaries in English, Spanish, Vietnamese and Haitian Creole	Additional Selection Questions
Question Support	Skills Copymasters in Spanish	Ideas for Extension
Reading Fluency	**English Language Learner Adapted Interactive Reader Teacher's Guide**	**Diagnostic and Selection Tests**
Interactive Reader		Selection Tests B/C
Adapted Interactive Reader	**ELL Adapted Interactive Reader**	
Audio Tutor	**Audio Tutor**	
Level Up Online Tutorials	**Guide to English for Newcomers**	
Audio Anthology	**Audio Anthology**	
(with Audio summaries)	**Audio Summaries in Multiple Languages** (on **thinkcentral.com**)	
Diagnostic and Selection Tests		
Selection Tests A/B		

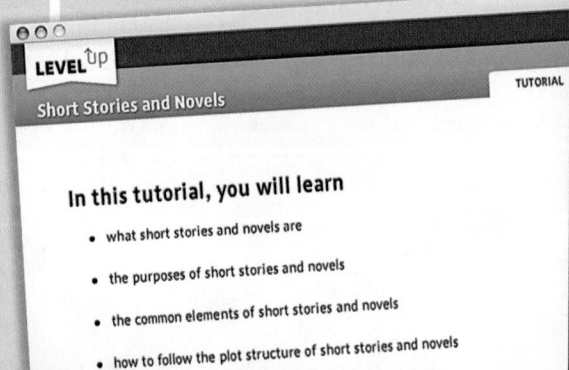

Assessment and Reteaching

Diagnostic and Selection Tests

Unit and Benchmark Tests

ThinkCentral Online Assessment:

- All program assessments
- Level Up Online Tutorials

ExamView Test Generator on the Teacher One Stop DVD-ROM

Online Essay Scoring on **thinkcentral.com**

ThinkCentral Online Reteaching:

- Level Up Online Tutorials
- Reteaching Worksheets

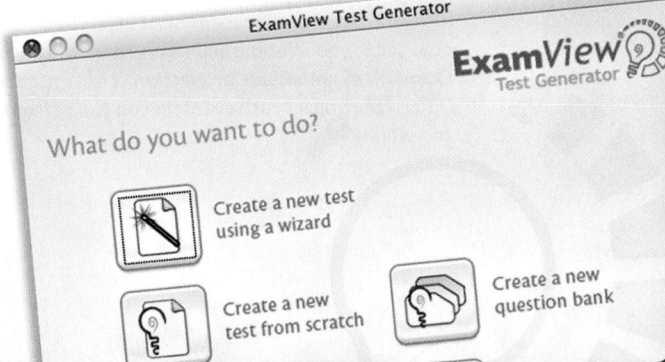

ExamView Test Generator

ExamView Test Generator

What do you want to do?

Create a new test using a wizard

Create a new test from scratch

Create a new question bank

Professional Development

Video Center Based on interviews with program consultants and other educational experts, these videos feature classroom-ready teaching strategies.

Teacher Toolkit Includes a Teacher Handbook as well as a range of articles and handouts by program consultants and other educators.

Janet Allen

Jim Burke

Kylene Beers

Carol Jago

THINK central at a Glance

One Location, Endless Resources

Find Resources Browse all *Holt McDougal Literature* components for the ones that meet your students' needs and match your teaching style.

Assess Progress and Reteach Assign electronic versions of program assessments to measure your students' mastery of the Common Core State Standards. On thinkcentral.com, some tests deliver online remediation tutorials to students who have not mastered skills.

 Interactive Whiteboard Lessons

Prepare your students for college and careers by teaching relevant, real-world skills through dynamic, interactive instruction. Go to **thinkcentral.com** to browse through all whiteboard lessons, including the following:

- Historical and Cultural Context
- Author's Purpose and Perspective
- Word Choice and Tone

HISTORY Together Holt McDougal and HISTORY® are revolutionizing the study of English/language arts with video that helps students relive and re-imagine the people, places, and events they are discovering through reading. Look for selections with the HISTORY® icon.

What **SHAPES**
your world?

Read and discuss the question and the open-ing paragraphs. Relate the discussion to the image and ask students to think about how the events of September 11, 2001, shaped their world. To spark students' thinking about the influence of daily realities, discuss how life might be different without these things that we take for granted:

- DVDs
- automobiles
- e-mail technology
- supermarkets

ACTIVITY As students meet in groups, urge them to consider events that have affected a large number of people. Once students have chosen the events, have them discuss personal and societal effects of each one. In a follow-up class discussion, invite group representatives to share one example and its effects.

CHECK UNDERSTANDING Ask students to define both concepts introduced in this unit opener: *a product of the times and something that shapes your world.* Correct any misunder-standings.

What **SHAPES**
your world?

Popular reality shows are fond of placing individuals in unfamiliar settings and situations. These shows can be fascinating because viewers see how a different environment, culture, or situation can transform the people involved.

Our own daily reality shapes each of us, usually without our even being aware of it. It affects how we live, how we behave, even how we think. It influences artists, musicians, and writers, as well; the times and places in which they work can affect their choice of subject matter, their perspective, and their popularity.

ACTIVITY In a small group, think of at least two events that have occurred in your lifetime and changed the way people think or act. Examples might include an election, a natural disaster, or a war. Discuss the impact each event had on you personally or on society as a whole.

Find It Online!  Go to thinkcentral.com for the interactive version of this unit.

932

Unit Resources

See resources on the **Teacher One Stop DVD-ROM** *and on* thinkcentral.com.

R RESOURCE MANAGER UNIT 9

UNIT AND BENCHMARK TESTS

BEST PRACTICES TOOLKIT

INTERACTIVE READER

ADAPTED INTERACTIVE READER

ELL ADAPTED INTERACTIVE READER

LANGUAGE HANDBOOK

VOCABULARY PRACTICE

TECHNOLOGY

- Teacher One Stop DVD-ROM
- Student One Stop DVD-ROM
- PowerNotes DVD-ROM
- Write*Smart* CD-ROM
- Media*Smart* DVD-ROM
- GrammarNotes DVD-ROM
- Audio Anthology CD
- Audio Tutor CD

Find It Online! THINK central

The interactive version of this unit on **thinkcentral.com** includes

- video and **PowerNotes** introductions to key selections
- audio support—listen or download
- **ThinkAloud** models
- **WordSharp** vocabulary tutorials
- interactive review and remediation

Preview Unit Goals

TEXT ANALYSIS
- Identify cultural characteristics in a work of world literature
- Analyze historical and cultural context
- Analyze influence of author's background
- Analyze influence of a literary period
- Analyze how complex characters interact and develop the theme

READING
- Use reading strategies, including connecting, monitoring, and predicting
- Determine an author's point of view or purpose
- Analyze rhetorical devices
- Identify and analyze sensory details

WRITING AND LANGUAGE
- Write an informative cause-and-effect essay
- Use simple, compound, complex, and compound-complex sentences; use gerund phrases

SPEAKING AND LISTENING
- Give and follow oral instructions

VOCABULARY
- Understand and use prefixes and suffixes to determine word meaning
- Use a dictionary to help determine a word's meaning and its etymology

ACADEMIC VOCABULARY
- acknowledge
- community
- contemporary
- culture
- role

MEDIA AND VIEWING
- Determine cultural influences in the creation of media messages

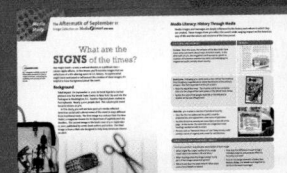

Media Smart DVD-ROM

Products of the Times

Find out how the events of September 11, 2001, influenced various creators of media.
Page 1026

933

Complete text of the Common Core State Standards is found in the correlation on p. T10. Standards covered in this unit are found in the standards overview (pp. 931A–931B) and on the lesson pages where they are taught.

Preview Unit Goals

Point out to students that these goals reflect the main skills and strategies taught in Unit 9. Have students read through the list and consider what they already know about each goal. Review the color-coding of the skill strands, reminding students that it will reappear throughout the unit.

Call on a volunteer to read aloud the Academic Vocabulary. Discuss the meaning of each term and especially the concept of *context*. Have students record each term and its definition in their **Reader/Writer Notebooks**. Encourage students to refer to the definitions as needed throughout the unit.

DIFFERENTIATED INSTRUCTION

FOR ENGLISH LANGUAGE LEARNERS

Academic Vocabulary Provide students with definitions of each Academic Vocabulary word.

acknowledge (ak näl'ij) *v.* to recognize and admit that something is true or accurate

community (kə myōō'nə tē) *n.* a group of individuals with a common interest or characteristic

contemporary (kən-tĕm'pə-rĕr´ē) *adj.* current; modern

culture (kŭl'chər) *n.* the attitudes, behavior, or customs that characterize a group; the particular group having such attitudes, behavior, or customs

role (rōl) *n.* a character played by an actor in a performance; a function or part assumed in a process

Use the copy master to help students learn academic words they will use in this unit and on the Assessment Practice.

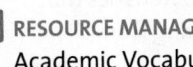 **RESOURCE MANAGER—Copy Masters**
Academic Vocabulary p. 3
Additional Academic Vocabulary p. 4

Focus and Motivate

COMMON CORE FOCUS

RL 4 Determine the figurative meaning of words as they are used in a text; analyze the cumulative impact of specific word choices on meaning and tone. **RL 6** Analyze a particular point of view or cultural experience reflected in a work of world literature. **RI 4** Analyze the cumulative impact of specific word choices on meaning and tone. **RI 6** Determine an author's point of view or purpose in a text.

Teach

Part 1: The Writer's Background

Using Background Point out to students that a literary work does not contain a fixed meaning. Instead, it is open to interpretation. Often, students can add information about an author and his or her cultural and historical period to their own personal experience and cultural context in order to create their own interpretation.

Background, Beliefs, and Values Caution students against making unwarranted connections between a writer's life and his or her work. The inferences and conclusions they draw should be supportable with examples from the text. For example, have students pick out details from "To Da-duh, in Memoriam" that support Marshall's description of the rivalrous relationship she had with her grandmother. ***Possible answer:*** *Marshall writes: "Da-duh watched me a long time before she spoke . . . , 'All right, now, tell me if you've got anything this tall in that place you're from.'"*

🗂 BEST PRACTICES TOOLKIT—Transparency
Analysis Frame: Literary Nonfiction
pp. D21, D48

Text Analysis Workshop

Essential Course of Study ECOS

COMMON CORE

Included in this workshop:
RL 4 Determine the figurative meaning of words as they are used in a text; analyze the cumulative impact of specific word choices on meaning and tone. **RL 6** Analyze a particular point of view or cultural experience reflected in a work of world literature. **RI 4** Analyze the cumulative impact of specific word choices on meaning and tone. **RI 6** Determine an author's point of view or purpose in a text.

History, Culture, and the Author

Behind every work of literature is a writer—the individual responsible for crafting the words on the page. A writer's words may entertain, inform, or inspire, but they may also reveal glimpses into his or her background, beliefs, or times. Perhaps the writer endured the horrors of a war you've only read about, or grew up in a family very different from your own. Learning more about writers and the forces that shaped their lives can help you discover unexpected layers of meaning in the literature you read.

Part 1: The Writer's Background

"Write what you know" is often the first piece of advice that writers receive. Whether they intentionally follow it or not, many writers produce works that are influenced by personal factors in their lives, such as heritage, national identity, customs, and values. For example, consider the following excerpt from Paule Marshall's short story "To Da-duh, in Memoriam." On one level, the work is a poignant story about family. But by reading the background and asking yourself a few questions, you can discover just how personal the story is.

from To Da-duh, in Memoriam

Short story by **Paule Marshall**

BACKGROUND Paule Marshall was born in Brooklyn, New York, but her family came from the island of Barbados. Her story draws on her memories of a childhood visit to her grandmother (nicknamed Da-duh). "Ours was a complex relationship," she has written, "close, affectionate yet rivalrous." Marshall has said that the rivalry between the grandmother and the granddaughter in the story is supposed to represent a struggle between cultures, old and new.

. . . She stopped before an incredibly tall royal palm which rose cleanly out of the ground, and drawing the eye up with it, soared high above the trees around it into the sky. It appeared to be touching the blue dome of sky, to be flaunting its dark crown of fronds right in the blinding white face of the late morning sun.

5   Da-duh watched me a long time before she spoke, and then she said, very quietly, "All right, now, tell me if you've got anything this tall in that place you're from."

I almost wished, seeing her face, that I could have said no. "Yes," I said. "We've got buildings hundreds of times this tall in New York."

QUESTIONS TO ASK

What beliefs and values are reflected in the writing?
Through the interaction between the characters, Marshall conveys a respect for the old (the palm tree) and an acknowledgment of the new (skyscrapers).

What aspects of the author's background are evident?
Though Marshall was born in New York, she too visited her grandmother in Barbados as a child.

What does the background reveal about the author's motivation for writing this story?
Marshall is communicating her understanding of cultural conflicts.

DIFFERENTIATED INSTRUCTION

FOR STRUGGLING READERS

Note Taking For students who need help with note taking, hand out the note-taking copy master. Review these definitions and have students record ideas:

- *heritage,* "ideas, traditions, and customs passed down by a previous generation"

- *national identity,* "characteristics that identify someone as being from a specific nation"

- *customs,* "accepted practices of people in a particular group or region"

- *values,* "standards or qualities viewed as worthwhile or desirable"

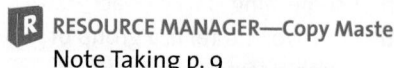 RESOURCE MANAGER—Copy Master
Note Taking p. 9

MODEL 1: ANALYZING A POEM

Read this poem "cold" first, noticing what images it calls to mind.

Women

Poem by **Alice Walker**

They were women then
My mama's generation
Husky of voice—Stout of
Step
5   With fists as well as
Hands
How they battered down
Doors
And ironed
10   Starched white
Shirts
How they led
Armies
Headragged Generals
15   Across mined
Fields
Booby-trapped
Kitchens
To discover books
20   Desks
A place for us
How they knew what we
Must know
Without knowing a page
25   Of it
Themselves.

Close Read

1. "Women" is full of images that suggest physical force. One is boxed. Find two more images.

2. What one word would you use to describe the women in the poem? Explain your choice.

3. Reread lines 19–26. What do you think the women did for their children?

MODEL 2: THE WRITER'S BACKGROUND

Now read this background information about Alice Walker. How does learning about the poet change or enhance your understanding of her poem?

BACKGROUND Alice Walker was born in Eatonton, Georgia, in 1944, a time of legal segregation and organized violence against African Americans. The eighth child in a family of sharecroppers, she grew up in a black community that nurtured and protected its children. Her mother and aunts were strong women
5   who maintained their independence despite racism and poverty and fought for a better future for the young. Inspired by these role models, Walker became a civil rights activist and writer.

Close Read

1. In line 14 of the poem, the speaker describes the women as generals. What might she see as the enemy they were fighting?

2. Using information from the background and the poem, explain why Walker may admire women of her mother's generation.

MODEL 1: ANALYZING A POEM

Close Read

1. *Possible answer: Other images that suggest physical force include "battered down doors" (lines 7–8), "led armies" (lines 12–13), "headragged generals across mined fields" (lines 14–16), and "booby-trapped kitchens" (lines 17–18).*

2. *Adjectives to describe the women in the poem may include* courageous, determined, powerful, tough, independent, *or* intimidating. *Students should give reasons for their choice.*

3. *Possible answer: The women fought to get an education for their children, something that they themselves never had.*

MODEL 2: THE WRITER'S BACKGROUND

Close Read

1. *Possible answer: Based on the background material, the women might have been fighting racism and poverty.*

2. *Possible answer: Walker seems to admire the almost intimidating strength and independence of the women of "my mama's generation" (line 2), whom the speaker describes as "husky of voice—stout of step" (lines 3–4). The background informs readers that Walker grew up in a community that "nurtured and protected its children" (line 4); it also says that Walker's mother and aunts "fought for a better future for the young" (line 6). In the poem, the women are described as doing all these things—from routine tasks like ironing to fighting for their children's future.*

FOR STRUGGLING READERS

Analysis Support: Interpreting the Poem
Have students discuss the poem without looking at Walker's background. Help them draw conclusions about the speaker and the speaker's voice, the subject of the poem and any key statements, the use of language and imagery, and the feelings evoked by reading the poem. Ask them what is important to Alice Walker, based on her poem.

FOR ADVANCED LEARNERS/PRE–AP

Analyze Themes A central theme in Walker's writing is her belief that not enough credit has been given to African-American women who have been repressed. Ask students to discuss where they see this theme revealed in the poem.

Online Remediation

THiNK central

Are your students struggling with text analysis skills? Consider assigning them one or more **Level Up Online Tutorials** as remediation before beginning this unit. Log in to **thinkcentral.com** to view a list of the skills addressed by **Level Up.**

Part 2: Historical and Cultural Influences

Context Have students imagine that they are writing a short story or a poem at this very moment in history. Have them brainstorm words and phrases that they would use to characterize their moment in order to capture it in a story or poem.

Analysis Questions Discuss how to determine the level of importance readers should give to historical and cultural connections when interpreting literature. Suggest asking questions such as these:

- What historical events does the work cover?
- In what ways did history affect the writer's outlook?
- In what ways did history affect the style, language, and content of the work?
- Did the writer change historical events? In what way and for what reasons?

CHECK UNDERSTANDING

Have students give examples of historical and cultural context.

Part 2: Historical and Cultural Influences

The historical and cultural setting of a work may also influence a writer's use of language, including **figurative language** and **diction**. To fully understand some works of literature, you need a sense of their **historical** and **cultural context**—the social and cultural conditions that influenced their creation. What was happening at the time a work was written, both in the writer's hometown and in the world at large? What issues or social problems were people grappling with? By uncovering answers to questions like these, you can often gain deeper insights into literature.

When John Steinbeck's novel *The Grapes of Wrath* was published in 1939, the Great Depression had been going on for ten long years. The novel presents a sympathetic portrayal of farmers who are forced to leave their land. Notice how reading the background and asking some questions can help you understand Steinbeck's work as social commentary on the harsh injustices of the time.

from *The Grapes of Wrath*

Novel by **John Steinbeck**

BACKGROUND During the Great Depression, life was especially difficult for farmers on the Great Plains, where a severe drought turned the land to desert. High winds brought terrible dust storms that killed crops and livestock and blotted out the sun for days. Some farmers gave up, abandoning their land. Others struggled to hold on, relying on government aid—"relief"—in the form of food, money, and jobs. Many were evicted when they couldn't pay their mortgages or when wealthy landowners replaced sharecroppers with mechanical tractors. Many farmers fled to California in search of promising jobs, only to find backbreaking, low-paying work.

This is an exchange between landowners and sharecroppers they are about to evict:

But if we go, where'll we go? How'll we go? We got no money.
We're sorry, said the owner men. The bank, the fifty-thousand-acre owner can't be responsible. You're on land that isn't yours. Once over the line maybe you can pick cotton in the fall. Maybe you can go on relief. Why don't you
5 go on west to California? There's work there, and it never gets cold. Why, you can reach out anywhere and pick an orange. Why, there's always some kind of crop to work in. Why don't you go there? And the owner men started their cars and rolled away.

QUESTIONS TO ASK

How does the conflict reflect the struggles of the times? The sharecroppers' conflict—being evicted from their land—was one that many poor farmers experienced during the Great Depression.

How are the characters portrayed? The pleas of the sharecroppers make them seem desperate. Expressions like "rolled away" make the landowners seem indifferent.

How does your knowledge of history help you understand what you are reading? Steinbeck knew that the reality of life in California did not measure up to the promise of "reach[ing] out anywhere and pick[ing] an orange." Therefore, the portrayal of California as a paradise becomes ironic.

936 UNIT 9: HISTORY, CULTURE, AND THE AUTHOR

DIFFERENTIATED INSTRUCTION

FOR STRUGGLING READERS

Note Taking For students who need help, hand out the note-taking copy master for page 936. As you discuss, have students jot down key ideas and questions that will help them apply historical and cultural influences to literary analysis. Assist them as needed.

R RESOURCE MANAGER—Copy Master
Note Taking p. 10

FOR ENGLISH LANGUAGE LEARNERS

Language: Skill Words List the literary terms shown in italics below. Have students provide examples of each from the Steinbeck model.

- *conflict*, "a struggle between opposing forces, such as between characters" (*The sharecroppers were in conflict with the wealthy landowners who were evicting them.*)
- *characters*, "individuals who play a part in a literary work" (*The sharecroppers are characters in the model.*)

MODEL 1: ANALYZING FICTION

This excerpt is from a short story that is set several years after the California gold rush of the mid-1800s. As you read it, consider what you already know about that time.

from *The Californian's Tale*

Short story by **Mark Twain**

Now and then, half an hour apart, one came across solitary log cabins of the earliest mining days, built by the first gold miners. . . . In some few cases these cabins were still occupied; and when this was so, you could depend upon it that the occupant was the very pioneer who had built the cabin; and . . .

5 that he was there because he had once had his opportunity to go home to the States rich, and had not done it; had rather lost his wealth, and had then in his humiliation resolved to sever all communication with his home relatives and friends, and be to them thenceforth as one dead. Round about California in that day were scattered a host of these living dead men— pride-smitten

10 poor fellows, grizzled and old at forty, whose secret thoughts were made all of regrets and longings —regrets for their wasted lives, and longings to be out of the struggle and done with it all.

It was a lonesome land! Not a sound in all those peaceful expanses of grass and woods but the drowsy hum of insects; no glimpse of man or beast;

15 nothing to keep up your spirits and make you glad to be alive.

Close Read

1. What do you learn about the men who live in the cabins? Cite details that help you understand their situation.

2. Identify four phrases or details that suggest a sense of desolation and hopelessness.

MODEL 2: HISTORICAL AND CULTURAL CONTEXT

The following background explains how the promise of gold lured thousands to California in 1848. As you read, consider how this information enhances your understanding of the "wasted lives" of the men in Twain's story.

BACKGROUND On a winter morning in 1848, workers discovered gold east of Sacramento, setting off an epidemic of "gold fever." Thousands of young men left their homes and traveled west in the hope that they would strike it rich. The first to arrive found that there was plenty of gold to go around—but

5 not much else. Prices for food and other supplies shot sky-high in the rough frontier towns. Newly rich miners let their fortunes slip away, confident they could get more. By mid-1849, however, gold became much harder to find. Soon, many gave up and left, turning the "boom" towns into ghost towns.

By the time Samuel Clemens went west in the early 1860s, the wild

10 hopes of the gold rush years had turned to bitter disillusionment. After a few unsuccessful months of working as a miner, Clemens gave up and began a new career as the writer Mark Twain."

Close Read

1. Reread the boxed details in Twain's story. What information in the background helps you understand the narrator's description of the land and its inhabitants?

2. In your opinion, is Twain's tone toward the miners sympathetic? Explain.

TEXT ANALYSIS WORKSHOP **937**

MODEL 1: ANALYZING FICTION

Close Read

1. *Possible answer: The men living in the cabins have been there since the earliest mining days. Many had the chance to go home rich but instead stayed and lost their wealth. Humiliated, they broke all ties with family members and stayed in California. Soon, these "pride-smitten poor fellows" (lines 9–10) became "living dead men" (line 9), who spent their days consumed with "regrets for their wasted lives" (line 11) and wishing they were done with the struggle of life.*

2. *Possible answers: Details that suggest **desolation:** "solitary log cabins" (line 1), "It was a lonesome land" (line 13), "Not a sound in all those peaceful expanses . . . of insects" (lines 13–14), and "no glimpse of man or beast" (line 14); **hopelessness:** "in his humiliation resolved . . . thenceforth as one dead" (lines 6–8), "living dead men" (line 9), "regrets for their wasted lives" (line 11), "longings to be out of the struggle and done with it all" (lines 11–12), and "nothing to . . . make you glad to be alive" (line 15).*

MODEL 2: HISTORICAL AND CULTURAL CONTEXT

Close Read

1. *Possible answer: "Let their fortunes slip away" (line 6) explains why those in the story have lost their wealth. The background says the gold supply dwindled (lines 7–8) helping readers understand why there were so many disillusioned miners left in the camps, but so few other people.*

2. *Possible answer: Twain's tone toward the miners is sympathetic. He describes them as "pride-smitten poor fellows" (lines 9–10), but he also acknowledges that the "lonesome land" (line 13) offers "nothing to keep up your spirits and make you glad to be alive" (line 15). Clemens himself had tried and failed at mining, which perhaps made him more understanding of the miners' situation.*

DIFFERENTIATED INSTRUCTION

FOR STRUGGLING READERS

Analysis Support: Personal Experience Ask students whether Model 2 is necessary to understand Model 1. Point out that Model 1 can stand alone; it is clear from its text that many people were not successful during the gold rush. However, the background information, with its suggestion of Twain's own gold rush experiences, helps readers understand the timing and scope of the mining situation and the author's sympathetic tone in the story.

FOR ENGLISH LANGUAGE LEARNERS

Vocabulary: Cognates List these words from "The Californian's Tale":

- *solitary* (line 1), "alone"
- *occupant* (line 4), "person living in it"
- *opportunity* (line 5), "chance"

Have students define the Spanish cognates, then use Word Questioning to understand the English words.

BEST PRACTICES TOOLKIT—Transparency
Word Questioning p. E9

TEXT ANALYSIS WORKSHOP **937**

Part 3: Analyze the Text

Approaching the Selections Organize the class into two groups. Have one group read the background information and the excerpt; have the second group read only the excerpt. After reviewing students' answers to the Close Read questions, discuss whether students who did not have the benefit of the background information had difficulty analyzing, interpreting, and connecting with the literature.

Communism and Chinese Literature Provide this additional background information and have students discuss it in relationship to the excerpt. How might these circumstances have influenced Zhang Jie?

- Communism has kept tight control over Chinese literature. Following the 1949 revolution, literature, like society in general, focused on great social transformations. Instead of developing believable conflicts and characters, writers were reduced to illustrating Communist Party doctrine.

- The Cultural Revolution (1966–1976), during which Zhang Jie was sent away to be re-educated, was the time to do away with the "four olds": ideas, culture, customs, and habits. It was more suppressive to writers than ever before. Every piece of literature that did not celebrate Mao Zedong's teachings was burned. In bookstores, the writings of Mao replaced classic works of prose and poetry.

Part 3: Analyze the Text

Zhang Jie is one of the most acclaimed writers from the People's Republic of China. Her story "Love Must Not Be Forgotten" takes place during the 1970s, when Communist ideals affected how people viewed the institution of marriage. Read this background about China during that time and about the life of Zhang Jie. Then use the information in the background to help you analyze an excerpt from her story.

BACKGROUND

A Writer in the People's Republic

For the Greater Good In 1949, Mao Zedong and his Communist forces took control of China. In 1966, Mao felt that new blood was needed to keep the ideals of
5 communism alive, so he implemented the Cultural Revolution. For the next several years, groups of young radicals removed and replaced older Communist Party leaders, who were executed or imprisoned.

Zhang Jie

10 Despite sweeping political changes, many Chinese customs were slow to change. For example, centuries-old traditions dictated that marriages be arranged by couples' families when the
15 couples were still young children. New laws enacted by the Communists allowed individuals to choose their own marriage partners. However, marrying for love was still frowned upon, because Communist
20 teachings encouraged individuals to suppress personal desires for the greater social good.

The Fight Against Injustice Both personal hardships and the harsh political
25 climate in Communist China helped shape the life of the writer Zhang Jie. She has written, "These circumstances made me sensitive to all injustice and inequality. . . . I determined to fight
30 injustice all my life." Born in 1937, Zhang Jie grew up in poverty during the war-torn years before communism. She dreamed of studying literature at the great university in Beijing and of
35 becoming a writer. Zhang Jie's dreams were put on hold when the government assigned her to a subject considered more useful to the nation: economics.

After graduation, Zhang Jie worked
40 as a statistician. She married a colleague and gave birth to their daughter in 1963. Then came the Cultural Revolution, when millions of educated white-collar workers were sent to harsh work camps to be "re-
45 educated" in Communist thought. Despite her loyalty to communism, Zhang Jie was sent thousands of miles away to a labor camp, where she spent four years tending pigs and slogging through rice paddies.

50 **A Writer at Last** Zhang Jie was 40 when she finally was able to publish her first story, which won a major award. Soon she was one of the most popular writers in China—and one of the most controversial.
55 "Love Must Not Be Forgotten" raised a storm of protest from party officials, who thought the story undermined traditional attitudes toward marriage.

DIFFERENTIATED INSTRUCTION

FOR STRUGGLING READERS

Analysis Support Have students organize the background information in a Main Idea and Details chart. Ask them to write a short paragraph summarizing what they learned.

Main Idea	Details
Cultural Revolution	1. help communism 2. customs slow to change

 BEST PRACTICES TOOLKIT—Transparency
Main Idea and Details p. B6

FOR ADVANCED LEARNERS/PRE–AP

Hypothesize Plot Based on the background information, ask students what they expect the story to be about. Why do they think the story was controversial? Have students share their thoughts with the class.

from

LOVE MUST NOT
BE FORGOTTEN

Short story by **Zhang Jie**

I am thirty, the same age as our People's Republic. For a republic thirty is still young. But a girl of thirty is virtually on the shelf.

Actually, I have a bona fide suitor. Have you seen the Greek sculptor Myron's *Discobolus*? Qiao Lin is the image of that discus thrower. Even the padded
5 clothes he wears in winter fail to hide his fine physique. Bronzed, with clear-cut features, a broad forehead and large eyes, his appearance alone attracts most girls to him.

But I can't make up my mind to marry him. I'm not clear what attracts me to him, or him to me.
10 I know people are gossiping behind my back, "Who does she think she is, to be so choosy?"

To them, I'm a nobody playing hard to get. They take offense at such preposterous behavior.

Of course, I shouldn't be captious.¹ In a society where commercial production
15 still exists, marriage like most other transactions is still a form of barter.

I have known Qiao Lin for nearly two years, yet still cannot fathom whether he keeps so quiet from aversion to talking or from having nothing to say. When, by way of a small intelligence test, I demand his opinion of this or that, he says "good" or "bad" like a child in kindergarten.
20 Once I asked, "Qiao Lin, why do you love me?" He thought the question over seriously for what seemed an age. I could see from his normally smooth but now wrinkled forehead that the little grey cells in his handsome head were hard at work cogitating. I felt ashamed to have put him on the spot.

Finally he raised his clear childlike eyes to tell me, "Because you're good!"
25 Loneliness flooded my heart. "Thank you, Qiao Lin!" I couldn't help wondering, if we were to marry, whether we could discharge our duties to each other as husband and wife. Maybe, because law and morality would have bound us together. But how tragic simply to comply with law and morality! Was there no stronger bond to link us?
30 When such thoughts cross my mind, I have the strange sensation that instead of being a girl contemplating marriage I am an elderly social scientist.

Perhaps I worry too much. We can live like most married couples, bringing up children together, strictly true to each other according to the law. . . . | Although living in the seventies of the twentieth century, people still consider marriage the
35 way they did millennia ago, as a means of continuing the race, a form of barter or a business transaction in which love and marriage can be separated.

---
1. **captious:** overly critical.

Close Read

1. Which details in the background help you understand why Zhang Jie chose to write about a woman who questions social values?

2. What values do you think Zhang Jie and her narrator share? Support your answer.

3. Reread the boxed text. How was marriage viewed in China during the 1970s? Does the narrator support this view? Explain.

4. What aspects of this story might Communist Party officials have considered controversial? Support your answer, using details from both texts.

Close Read

1. ***Possible answer:*** *Zhang Jie's words "These circumstances made me . . . determined to fight injustice all my life" (lines 27–30 in the background) help readers understand her motivation. The story narrator is not fighting any injustice but questions the institution of marriage as it is defined in China. Readers learn that the author and her narrator are women who won't simply accept laws without question.*

2. ***Possible answer:*** *Zhang Jie and her narrator share the value of making one's own decisions rather than simply following outside rules. Zhang Jie questioned traditional attitudes (lines 55–58 in the background), and her narrator questioned marrying just to "comply with law and morality" (line 28).*

3. ***Possible answer:*** *In China during the 1970s, marriage was a way of continuing the race, a "business transaction" in which emotions did not play a role. The narrator questions this belief in lines 28–29. Still, she admonishes herself for "worry[ing] too much" (line 32) and tries to talk herself into believing traditional views of marriage.*

4. ***Possible answer:*** *According to the background information, party officials viewed Zhang Jie's story as controversial because it "undermined traditional attitudes toward marriage" (lines 57–58 in the background). Perhaps the officials objected to the narrator questioning traditional views. Or they may have thought that the narrator valued her own personal desires over the greater social good, or that she shouldn't explore whether she loves her suitor.*

Assess and Reteach

Assess

Have students apply the Analysis Questions from pages 934 and 936 to "Love Must Not Be Forgotten." Then, invite students to tell how each background piece in the lesson helped their literary analysis.

Reteach

For students who cannot apply the workshop skills to Zhang Jie's story, review the note-taking copy masters for this lesson. Have volunteers define terms and concepts, then find examples in the Part 3 materials.

FOR STRUGGLING READERS

Vocabulary Support Preteach the vocabulary from the selection by listing the following words on the board:

- *republic* (line 1), "country"
- *bona fide* (line 3), "real, authentic"
- *physique* (line 5), "bodily shape"
- *preposterous* (line 13), "ridiculous"
- *fathom* (line 16), "understand"
- *aversion* (line 17), "discomfort with"
- *cogitating* (line 23), "thinking"
- *contemplating* (line 31), "considering"

Then have students read the context for each word and suggest a synonym to replace it.

Focus and Motivate

COMMON CORE FOCUS

RI 1 Cite strong and thorough textual evidence to support analysis of what the text says explicitly as well as inferences drawn from the text. **RI 4** Analyze the cumulative impact of specific word choices on meaning and tone. **RI 6** Determine an author's point of view in a text. **L 3** Apply knowledge of language to make effective choices for meaning or style. **L 5b** Analyze nuances in the meaning of words with similar denotations.

SUMMARY

In this excerpt from his memoir of survival in a Nazi death camp, Elie Wiesel recalls a day when Nazi doctors sent the weakest prisoners to the gas chamber. Wiesel spends anguished hours waiting to learn his father's fate.

Can HUMANITY
triumph over evil?

Read the question aloud. Ask students what the term *humanity* means to them. Encourage students to consider these definitions as they complete the *DISCUSS* activity.

Selection Resources

---

from **Night** Video link at **thinkcentral.com**

Memoir by Elie Wiesel

Can HUMANITY
triumph over evil?

COMMON CORE

RI 1 Cite textual evidence to support what the text says explicitly as well as inferences drawn from the text. **RI 4** Analyze the cumulative impact of specific word choices on meaning and tone. **RI 6** Determine an author's point of view in a text.

Elie Wiesel was imprisoned in a Nazi concentration camp when he was only 15. He later wrote his memoir *Night* so that the world would never forget the horrors he and his fellow prisoners experienced. Yet his book also shows how people in the most desperate circumstances can retain their humanity through acts of kindness and self-sacrifice.

DISCUSS As a class, recall two or three examples of world events in which cruelty was inflicted on groups of people. Discuss how individuals and governments responded to these events, and then list actions that should be taken to prevent similar tragedies from occurring.

> *Triumphing over Evil*
> 1. *Expose violations of human rights.*
> 2. *Prosecute leaders responsible for crimes.*
> 3.
> 4.

940

See resources on the **Teacher One Stop DVD-ROM** *and on* **thinkcentral.com**.

 Video link at **thinkcentral.com**

 RESOURCE MANAGER UNIT 9
Plan and Teach, pp. 11–18
Summary, pp. 19–20†‡*
Text Analysis and Reading
  Skill, pp. 21–24†*
Vocabulary, pp. 25–27*
Grammar and Style, p. 30

**DIAGNOSTIC AND SELECTION
  TESTS**
Selection Tests, pp. 267–270

 BEST PRACTICES TOOLKIT
New Word Analysis, p. E8
Observation Chart, p. C7

TECHNOLOGY
- **Teacher One Stop DVD-ROM**
- **Student One Stop DVD-ROM**
- **Audio Anthology CD**
- **GrammarNotes DVD-ROM**
- **ExamView Test Generator**
  on the **Teacher One Stop**

---

* Resources for Differentiation   † Also in Spanish   ‡ In Haitian Creole and Vietnamese

TEXT ANALYSIS: MEMOIR

A **memoir** is a personal account of the significant events and people in the author's life. In Elie Wiesel's memoir *Night*, for example, readers view through his eyes the terrifying experience of being imprisoned in a Nazi concentration camp. Unlike strictly historical accounts, most memoirs

- are first-person narratives in the writer's voice
- express the writer's feelings and opinions about events, giving insight into the impact of history on people's lives

As you read, record the insights you gain from Wiesel's personal history. Use a chart like the one shown.

Wiesel's Experience	Historical Insight
"I had been transferred to another unit ... where, twelve hours a day, I had to drag heavy blocks of stone about."	In the concentration camps, inmates were brutally overworked.

READING STRATEGY: CONNECT

Because a memoir offers a personal view of events, you will often have the opportunity to **connect** the content to your own experiences and knowledge. Although Wiesel describes cruel treatment that few readers will have experienced, at some point in your life you probably have felt emotions that he expresses, such as his sense of relief in this example:

"Well? So you passed?"
"Yes. And you?"
"Me too."
How we breathed again, now!

As you read, look for opportunities to connect with Wiesel's reactions to incidents in the concentration camp.

▲ VOCABULARY IN CONTEXT

The following words help to convey Wiesel's harrowing experience. To see how many words you know, substitute a different word or phrase for each boldfaced word in your *Reader/Writer Notebook*.

1. She heard the **din** of a dozen car horns.
2. I appeared **emaciated** after my long fast.
3. The basketball player had an imposing **stature**.
4. That long concert seemed **interminable**.

 Complete the activities in your **Reader/Writer Notebook**.

Meet the Author

Elie Wiesel
born 1928

Holocaust Survivor
Elie Wiesel was born in Transylvania, a region of Romania controlled by Hungary during World War II. In April 1944, the Nazis ordered the deportation of all Jews in the area. Wiesel and his family were forced to board a cattle train bound for the Auschwitz concentration camp in Poland, where his mother and one of his sisters were murdered. Wiesel and his father were later sent to another camp, Buchenwald, in Germany; his father died just three months before the camp was liberated. Wiesel's Holocaust experiences have led him to speak out against human rights violations in countries around the world. A U.S. citizen since 1963, Wiesel was awarded the Nobel Peace Prize in 1986.

BACKGROUND TO THE MEMOIR

The Holocaust
Soon after Adolf Hitler became chancellor of Germany in 1933, he began to persecute German Jews, gradually stripping them of their rights. Germany's invasion of Poland in 1939 marked the beginning of World War II. Two of Hitler's goals were to expand his empire across Europe and to eliminate the Jewish population. Jews from all areas under Nazi control were transported to concentration camps, along with gypsies, homosexuals, political opponents, and others. Prisoners at Auschwitz, the largest camp, had numbers tattooed on their arms for identification. Most of the 6 million Jews killed in the Holocaust died in concentration camps—in gas chambers, before firing squads, or from starvation, torture, or disease.

Author Online **THINK** central
Go to **thinkcentral.com**.
KEYWORD: HML10-941

941

Teach

● Model the Skill: MEMOIR

To model how to identify a memoir, read aloud this example:

> I was sick with worry every time I saw an SS man near my father. They preyed on the sickest, oldest prisoners.

Point out that this passage classifies as a memoir because it uses the first person point of view, expresses the writer's feelings, and comments on a historical issue.

GUIDED PRACTICE Ask students to name other memoirs written about significant historical events.

R RESOURCE MANAGER—Copy Master
Memoir p. 21 (for student use while reading the selection)

❏ Model the Skill: CONNECT

To model how to connect, share this example:

> I couldn't breathe. Would I have to clean our classroom's snake cages? No! I got to water the plants instead!

Point out that the writer expresses both the emotions of fear and relief in these lines. Ask students what emotions they connect to in this passage.

GUIDED PRACTICE Elicit examples of memoirs or personal essays that students have connected to their own experiences.

▲ VOCABULARY IN CONTEXT

DIAGNOSE WORD KNOWLEDGE Have all students complete Vocabulary in Context. Check their substitutions against the following:

din (dĭn) *n.* a deafening noise
emaciated (ĭ-mā′shē-ā′tĭd) *adj.* excessively thin as a result of starvation **emaciate** *v.*
interminable (ĭn-tûr′mə-nə-bəl) *adj.* having no limit or end
stature (stăch′ər) *n.* the height of a person, animal, or object in an upright position

PRETEACH VOCABULARY Use the following copy master to help students predict meanings for each boldfaced word.

R RESOURCE MANAGER—Copy Master
Vocabulary Study p. 25

1. Read item 1 aloud, emphasizing *din*.
2. Point out the phrase "loud, harsh roar." Elicit possible meanings for *din*, such as "noise."
3. Repeat the procedure for items 2–4.
4. Have students complete Part B.

Practice and Apply

READ WITH A PURPOSE

Help students set a purpose for reading. Tell students to look for historical references as they read.

REVISIT THE BIG QUESTION

Can **HUMANITY** triumph over evil?

Discuss Based on lines 12–22, what details suggest that the Nazis who work in the death camps may be losing their humanity? ***Possible answer:*** *They send weak prisoners to the gas chamber. They run camps in which many prisoners starve and freeze to death, and guards are ordered to kill prisoners daily.*

TEXT ANALYSIS · COMMON CORE · RI 6

Ⓐ Model the Skill: MEMOIR

Work with students to use the chart introduced on page 941 to record the insights they gained from this conversation.

Wiesel's Experience	Historical Insight
Veterans tell Wiesel, "This camp is paradise today, compared with what it was like two years ago."	Camp conditions were brutal but had been worse.

Possible answer: *Possible insights are that the camp conditions were brutal but had been worse (lines 16–22); that surviving in the camp for two years changed what the men could tolerate; and that newcomers like Wiesel were terribly frightened (lines 23–27).*

VOCABULARY · COMMON CORE · L 4

OWN THE WORD

stature: Have students describe their own *stature*. **Possible answers:** *tall, short, small, big*

Night

Elie Wiesel

> The SS[1] gave us a fine New Year's gift.
> We had just come back from work. As soon as we had passed through the door of the camp, we sensed something different in the air. Roll call did not take so long as usual. The evening soup was given out with great speed and swallowed down at once in anguish.
> I was no longer in the same block as my father. I had been transferred to another unit, the building one, where, twelve hours a day, I had to drag heavy blocks of stone about. The head of my new block was a German Jew, small of **stature,** with piercing eyes. He told us that evening that no one would
> 10 be allowed to go out after the evening soup. And soon a terrible word was circulating—selection.
> We knew what that meant. An SS man would examine us. Whenever he found a weak one, a *musulman* as we called them, he would write his number down: good for the crematory.
>
> After soup, we gathered together between the beds. The veterans said:
> "You're lucky to have been brought here so late. This camp is paradise today, compared with what it was like two years ago. Buna[2] was a real hell then. There was no water, no blankets, less soup and bread. At night we slept almost naked, and it was below thirty degrees. The corpses were collected in
> 20 hundreds every day. The work was hard. Today, this is a little paradise. The Kapos[3] had orders to kill a certain number of prisoners every day. And every week—selection. A merciless selection. . . . Yes, you're lucky."
> "Stop it! Be quiet!" I begged. "You can tell your stories tomorrow or on some other day."
> They burst out laughing. They were not veterans for nothing.
> "Are you scared? So were we scared. And there was plenty to be scared of in those days." Ⓐ

Analyze Visuals ▶

The painting shows a portion of a uniform worn by a concentration camp prisoner. What do the details on the uniform **symbolize**?

stature (stăch'ər) *n.* the height of a person, animal, or object in an upright position

① Targeted Passage

Ⓐ MEMOIR
Reread lines 15–27. What insights did you gain from this conversation between Wiesel and the camp veterans?

---

1. **SS:** an elite military unit of the Nazi party that served as Hitler's personal guard and as a special security force.
2. **Buna** (bōō'nə): a forced-labor camp in Poland, near the Auschwitz concentration camp.
3. **Kapos** (kä'pōz): the prisoners who served as foremen, or heads, of each building or cell block.

Auschwitz Prisoner's Uniform, from the series *Reclaiming My Family History* (1998), Lina Eve. Mixed media on canvas.

DIFFERENTIATED INSTRUCTION

FOR ENGLISH LANGUAGE LEARNERS

Vocabulary Support Use New Word Analysis to teach these words: *transferred* (line 6), *selection* (line 11), *sole* (line 105), *automatically* (line 107), *significance* (line 127).

 BEST PRACTICES TOOLKIT—Transparency New Word Analysis p. E8

FOR STRUGGLING READERS

In combination with the *Audio Anthology CD,* use one or more Targeted Passages (pp. 942, 944, 945, 947) to ensure that students focus on key story events, concepts, and skills. Targeted Passages are also good for English learners.

① Targeted Passage [Lines 1–14]

This passage introduces the memoir's setting and creates a bleak and suspenseful tone.

- Where is Wiesel, and what activities fill his days? (lines 2–8)
- What details does Wiesel use to create suspense? (lines 2–3, 9–11)
- What is a "selection"? (lines 12–14)
- Where is his father staying? (lines 6–7)

The old men stayed in their corner, dumb, motionless, haunted. Some were praying. **B**

B GRAMMAR AND STYLE
Reread lines 28–29. Notice how Wiesel's use of simple sentence structure and words such as *dumb*, *motionless*, and *haunted* helps to set a tone of sadness and despair.

30   An hour's delay. In an hour, we should know the verdict—death or a reprieve. And my father? Suddenly I remembered him. How would he pass the selection? He had aged so much. . . .

   The head of our block had never been outside concentration camps since 1933. He had already been through all the slaughterhouses, all the factories of death. At about nine o'clock, he took up his position in our midst:

   "Achtung!"[4]

   There was instant silence.

   "Listen carefully to what I am going to say." (For the first time, I heard his voice quiver.) "In a few moments the selection will begin. You must get

40   completely undressed. Then one by one you go before the SS doctors. I hope you will all succeed in getting through. But you must help your own chances. Before you go into the next room, move about in some way so that you give yourselves a little color. Don't walk slowly, run! Run as if the devil were after you! Don't look at the SS. Run, straight in front of you!"

   He broke off for a moment, then added:

   "And, the essential thing, don't be afraid!"

   Here was a piece of advice we should have liked very much to be able to follow.

   I got undressed, leaving my clothes on the bed. There was no danger of anyone stealing them this evening.

50   Tibi and Yossi, who had changed their unit at the same time as I had, came up to me and said:

   2 Targeted Passage

   "Let's keep together. We shall be stronger."

   Yossi was murmuring something between his teeth. He must have been praying. I had never realized that Yossi was a believer. I had even always thought the reverse. Tibi was silent, very pale. All the prisoners in the block stood naked between the beds. This must be how one stands at the last judgment.

   "They're coming!"

   There were three SS officers standing around the notorious Dr. Mengele,[5] who had received us at Birkenau.[6] The head of the block, with an attempt at a

60   smile, asked us:

   "Ready?"

   Yes, we were ready. So were the SS doctors. Dr. Mengele was holding a list in his hand: our numbers. He made a sign to the head of the block: "We can begin!" As if this were a game!

   The first to go by were the "officials" of the block: *Stubenaelteste*,[7] Kapos, foremen, all in perfect physical condition of course! Then came the ordinary

---

4. **Achtung!** (ŏk-tōōng′) *German:* Attention!

5. **Dr. Mengele** (mŭng′gĕ·lə): Josef Mengele, a German doctor who personally selected nearly half a million prisoners to die in gas chambers at Auschwitz. He also became infamous for his medical experiments on inmates.

6. **Birkenau** (bûr′kĭn-ou′): a large section of the Auschwitz concentration camp.

7. *Stubenaelteste* (shtyōō′bə-nĭl-tŭs′-tə): a rank of Kapos; literally "elders of the rooms."

TIERED DISCUSSION PROMPTS

Direct students to lines 38–47. Use these prompts to help students understand how the prisoners prepare for the terrifying selection:

Connect Have you ever been scared but needed to pretend that you were not? Explain. *Accept all reasonable responses.*

Analyze What does the brief speech by the head of the block reveal about his character? *Possible answer: His advice reveals his humanity and his wisdom in the face of crisis as he tries to help the prisoners survive. There was a "quiver" (line 39) in his voice, showing that he keenly felt the deep emotions of lives being at stake.*

Synthesize Based on what you know about the SS officers and the selection, why do you think it is essential that the prisoners hide their fear? *Possible answer: The SS men prey on the weakest people (lines 12–14), and showing fear may be taken as a sign of weakness. Fear might also cause a prisoner to look pale, rather than to have "a little color" (line 43).*

DIFFERENTIATED INSTRUCTION

FOR STRUGGLING READERS

Vocabulary Support Explain that the word *dumb* in line 28 means "temporarily unable to speak; silent." Have students discuss how this description of the men contributes to the mood of this scene.

2 Targeted Passage [Lines 36–64]

This passage creates tension when the head of the block gives instructions to the prisoners to prepare for the selection process.

- What does the head of the block say is about to begin? What will the prisoners have to do? (lines 38–41)

- How does he advise the prisoners to help their own chances? Why does he do this? (lines 41–46)

- Why do Tibi and Yossi want to stay together? (line 52)

- Why might the SS officers treat the selection as if it were a "game"? (line 64)

prisoners' turn. Dr. Mengele took stock of them from head to foot. Every now and then, he wrote a number down. One single thought filled my mind: not to let my number be taken; not to show my left arm.

70   There were only Tibi and Yossi in front of me. They passed. I had time to notice that Mengele had not written their numbers down. Someone pushed me. It was my turn. I ran without looking back. My head was spinning: you're too thin, you're too weak, you're too thin, you're good for the furnace. . . . The race seemed **interminable.** I thought I had been running for years. . . . You're too thin, you're too weak. . . . At last I had arrived exhausted. When I regained my breath, I questioned Yossi and Tibi:

"Was I written down?"

"No," said Yossi. He added, smiling: "In any case, he couldn't have written you down, you were running too fast. . . ."

80   I began to laugh. I was glad. I would have liked to kiss him. At that moment, what did the others matter! I hadn't been written down. **C**

Those whose numbers had been noted stood apart, abandoned by the whole world. Some were weeping in silence.

The SS officers went away. The head of the block appeared, his face reflecting the general weariness.

"Everything went off all right. Don't worry. Nothing is going to happen to anyone. To anyone."

Again he tried to smile. A poor, **emaciated,** dried-up Jew questioned him avidly in a trembling voice:

90   "But . . . but, *Blockaelteste,*[8] they did write me down!"

The head of the block let his anger break out. What! Did someone refuse to believe him!

"What's the matter now? Am I telling lies then? I tell you once and for all, nothing's going to happen to you! To anyone! You're wallowing in your own despair, you fool!"

The bell rang, a signal that the selection had been completed throughout the camp.

With all my might I began to run to Block 36. I met my father on the way. He came up to me:

100   "Well? So you passed?"

"Yes. And you?"

"Me too."

How we breathed again, now! My father had brought me a present—half a ration of bread obtained in exchange for a piece of rubber, found at the warehouse, which would do to sole a shoe. **D**

The bell. Already we must separate, go to bed. Everything was regulated by the bell. It gave me orders, and I automatically obeyed them. I hated it. Whenever I dreamed of a better world, I could only imagine a universe with no bells.

---

8. *Blockaelteste* (blä′kĭl-tüs′tə): a rank of Kapos; literally, "elders of the building."

---

interminable
(ĭn-tûr′mə-nə-bəl) *adj.* having no limit or end

3 Targeted Passage

C CONNECT
What experiences in your own life help you understand Wiesel's reaction after he gets through the selection process?

emaciated
(ĭ-mā′shē-ā′tĭd) *adj.* excessively thin as a result of starvation
emaciate *v.*

D MEMOIR
What do you learn in lines 103–105 about actions that prisoners could take to improve their situation?

C *Model the Skill:* CONNECT

Model for students how to connect. Point out Wiesel's reaction in line 80—he laughed! Ask students to think about why he laughed, why he was glad and wanted to kiss Yossi. Then tell students to recall times in their own lives when they felt similarly.

Possible answer: Students might recall passing a difficult exam, completing a public speech or performance, or making it through an athletic tryout, even though students' experiences are not life-threatening as Wiesel's ordeal was.

D MEMOIR

Possible answer: Prisoners could improve their situation by trading items they had found for food or other things they needed. They could also look out for one another.

REVISIT THE BIG QUESTION

Can **HUMANITY** triumph over evil?

Discuss The head of the block appears harsh, but what clues in lines 84–95 suggest that his behavior, even his anger, is rooted in his humanity and concern for the prisoners? *Possible answer: He tries to reassure the prisoners that they will be safe, even though he knows that some of them will be killed (lines 86–87). He tries to smile to lift their spirits (line 88). His anger is probably a release and cover for his despair.*

OWN THE WORD

- **interminable:** Ask students to list other things that seem *interminable*, or have no limit or end. *Possible answer: a boring lecture or concert*

- **emaciated:** Remind students that the connotation of *emaciated* is extremely low and unhealthy weight.

---

3 Targeted Passage [Lines 70–83]

This passage describes Wiesel's thoughts as he ran past Mengele and his reaction to learning that his number had not been written down.

- What was Wiesel thinking as he ran past the SS doctors? (lines 72–75)

- Does he notice anything beyond himself as he runs? Why not? (lines 72–79)

- What does he learn from Yossi and Tibi? (lines 77–78)

FOR ADVANCED LEARNERS/PRE–AP

Roundtable Discussion Have students hold a roundtable discussion about the statement the head of the block makes to the other prisoners: "Don't worry. Nothing is going to happen to anyone. To anyone" (lines 86–87). Ask students to consider these questions: Does this man have the right to mislead the other prisoners? Is he helping them by lessening their panic about a situation they can't control—or do the others have a right to know what is going to happen to them?

◀ **Analyze Visuals**
In what ways does this image reflect Wiesel's experiences in the camp?

Analyze Visuals

Possible answer: The people in the painting are wearing striped uniforms and are doing hard labor. The figures carry shovels, sledge hammers, and other tools.

About the Art The image is a close-up of a mural painted on a wall of the concentration camp at Birkenau, Poland.

TIERED DISCUSSION PROMPTS

Direct students to lines 116–130. Use these prompts to help students discuss the prisoners' responses to the selection:

Recall Why are the prisoners surprised that the head of the block has a list of numbers? *Possible answer: They thought—or convinced themselves—that the selection was over, and that all of them had passed.*

Analyze The condemned prisoners beg the head of the block to help them. Why do they think he has the power to help them? Does he? *Possible answer: They think he has power because he tried to help them before (lines 38–46), he works with the SS men, and he has his own room (line 121), which hints at status. However, he does not have much power.*

Synthesize On the basis of his actions so far, why does the head of the block leave the other prisoners without speaking and "shut himself up in his room" (line 130)? *Possible answer: He has tried to do what little he can to help the prisoners (lines 38–46, 86–87). When he realizes that he can do nothing, he shuts himself up in his room to avoid facing the prisoners.*

110   Several days had elapsed. We no longer thought about the selection. We went to work as usual, loading heavy stones into railway wagons. Rations had become more meager: this was the only change.

    We had risen before dawn, as on every day. We had received the black coffee, the ration of bread. We were about to set out for the yard as usual. The head of the block arrived, running.

    "Silence for a moment. I have a list of numbers here. I'm going to read them to you. Those whose numbers I call won't be going to work this morning; they'll stay behind in the camp."

    And, in a soft voice, he read out about ten numbers. We had understood.
120 These were numbers chosen at the selection. Dr. Mengele had not forgotten.

    The head of the block went toward his room. Ten prisoners surrounded him, hanging onto his clothes:

    "Save us! You promised . . . ! We want to go to the yard. We're strong enough to work. We're good workers. We can . . . we will . . . ."

    He tried to calm them to reassure them about their fate, to explain to them that the fact that they were staying behind in the camp did not mean much, had no tragic significance.

    "After all, I stay here myself every day," he added.

    It was a somewhat feeble argument. He realized it, and without another
130 word went and shut himself up in his room.

    The bell had just rung.

    "Form up!"

    It scarcely mattered now that the work was hard. The essential thing was to be as far away as possible from the block, from the crucible of death, from the center of hell.

    I saw my father running toward me. I became frightened all of a sudden.

    "What's the matter?"

COMMON CORE RI 4

Language Coach

Etymology The words *tragic* and *tragedy* come from a Greek word referring to serious plays about the problems of a central character. Over time, *tragedy* came to refer to sad events in real life as well as in drama. Reread lines 125–127. What does *tragic* mean?

DIFFERENTIATED INSTRUCTION

FOR STRUGGLING READERS

Develop Reading Fluency Read the dialogue on page 946 aloud, beginning with line 116. Then have students work in mixed-ability groups to practice reading the dialogue. Remind students that dialogue is indicated with quotation marks. Monitor the groups, and help students make adjustments to speed and pronunciation where needed.

Distribute the copy masters and have students work in pairs or groups to practice fluency.

R RESOURCE MANAGER—Copy Master
Reading Fluency p. 31

FOR ENGLISH LANGUAGE LEARNERS

Language Coach   **COMMON CORE RI 4**
Etymology *Answer: terrible, very sad*
Point out to students that *tragedy* is a noun. *Tragic* ends with the suffix *-ic*, which forms adjectives and means "having the character or form of." Have students write sentences with *tragedy* and *tragic*.

Out of breath, he could hardly open his mouth.

"Me, too . . . me, too . . . ! They told me to stay behind in the camp."

140 They had written down his number without his being aware of it.

"What will happen?" I asked in anguish.

But it was he who tried to reassure me.

"It isn't certain yet. There's still a chance of escape. They're going to do another selection today . . . a decisive selection."

I was silent.

He felt that his time was short. He spoke quickly. He would have liked to say so many things. His speech grew confused; his voice choked. He knew that I would have to go in a few moments. He would have to stay behind alone, so very alone.

150 "Look, take this knife," he said to me. "I don't need it any longer. It might be useful to you. And take this spoon as well. Don't sell them. Quickly! Go on. Take what I'm giving you!"

The inheritance. **E**

"Don't talk like that, Father." (I felt that I would break into sobs.) "I don't want you to say that. Keep the spoon and knife. You need them as much as I do. We shall see each other again this evening, after work." **F**

He looked at me with his tired eyes, veiled with despair. He went on:

"I'm asking this of you. . . . Take them. Do as I ask, my son. We have no time. . . . Do as your father asks."

160 Our Kapo yelled that we should start.

The unit set out toward the camp gate. Left, right! I bit my lips. My father had stayed by the block, leaning against the wall. Then he began to run, to catch up with us. Perhaps he had forgotten something he wanted to say to me. . . . But we were marching too quickly . . . Left, right!

We were already at the gate. They counted us, to the **din** of military music. We were outside.

> The whole day, I wandered about as if sleepwalking. Now and then Tibi and Yossi would throw me a brotherly word. The Kapo, too, tried to reassure me. He had given me easier work today. I felt sick at heart. How well they were
> 170 treating me! Like an orphan! I thought: even now, my father is still helping me.
>
> I did not know myself what I wanted—for the day to pass quickly or not. I was afraid of finding myself alone that night. How good it would be to die here!
>
> At last we began the return journey. How I longed for orders to run!
>
> The military march. The gate. The camp.
>
> I ran to Block 36.
>
> Were there still miracles on this earth? He was alive. He had escaped the second selection. He had been able to prove that he was still useful. . . . I gave him back his knife and spoon. 〰

④ Targeted Passage

COMMON CORE RI 4

E VOICE

Writers use language in unique ways, so much so that a reader can often "hear" personality in the words. This unique use of language is called **voice.** Sentence structure, diction, (specific word choices) and tone all contribute to the writer's voice. Reread lines 138–153. How does the voice in this passage affect you as a reader?

F CONNECT

Think about a time when you received some painful news. Why might Wiesel have been reluctant to accept the spoon and knife?

din (dĭn) *n.* a deafening noise

E VOICE

Tell students to glance over the lines before reading them. What do they notice about the sentence structure? (*short sentences, punctuation*) Then tell students to read the lines, paying attention to diction and to how the structure affects their reactions.

Possible answer: *The short sentences, exclamation points, ellipses, and desperate tone of the passage help the reader "hear" the horror and despair of the situation.*

READING STRATEGY   COMMON CORE   RI 1

F CONNECT

Possible answer: *doing so would be accepting the idea that his father is going to be killed*

REVISIT THE BIG QUESTION

Can HUMANITY
triumph over evil?

Discuss What details in lines 150–170 show that people can experience kindness, hope, and humanity even when they face unspeakable cruelty? ***Possible answer:*** *Wiesel's father tries to give his knife and spoon to his son, which shows he still tries to take care of him even in what he thinks are his last hours (lines 150–153). Wiesel's friends try to cheer him up (lines 167–168). The head of the block reveals some compassion by giving Wiesel a light work assignment (lines 168–170).*

SELECTION WRAP–UP

READ WITH A PURPOSE Ask students what historical references they noted. Then ask: How can a memoir serve as both a private and public record of events?

VOCABULARY   COMMON CORE   L 4

OWN THE WORD

din: The narrator says that they marched to the *din* of military music. Have students describe a circumstance in which they would experience *din*.

FOR STRUGGLING READERS

④ Targeted Passage [Lines 167–178]

This passage provides resolution about the fate of Wiesel's father.

- How does Wiesel feel his father is helping him? (lines 154, 169, 171)

- Why might Wiesel question the existence of "miracles on this earth"? What miracle does he experience? (lines 30; 176–178)

- Wiesel's father had been able to "prove that he was still useful." What does this state-

ment mean? (lines 23–24)

FOR ENGLISH LANGUAGE LEARNERS

Language: Pronoun Referents Read line 140 aloud, noting the second use of *his* in the sentence: "without *his* being aware of it." Explain that while many people use *him* in this situation, Wiesel is correct to use *his*. Explain that the possessive pronoun is correct because it precedes an *–ing* verb form that functions as a noun. Provide these models:

- I object to your talking during the movie.

- He left without our saying good-bye.

SPEECH The following is an excerpt from the speech that Elie Wiesel gave in 1986 at the ceremony in Oslo, Norway, where he was awarded the Nobel Peace Prize.

TIERED DISCUSSION PROMPTS

Use these prompts to help students understand the connection between the excerpt from *Night* and Elie Wiesel's remarks when he won the Nobel Peace Prize:

Connect When Wiesel won the Nobel Peace Prize, he said in his acceptance speech that he has "tried to keep memory alive." How has Wiesel's mission to keep the past alive affected you and your sense of history? *Accept all reasonable responses.*

Analyze What does Wiesel mean when he says that receiving the Nobel Prize "transcends him"? *Possible answer: He means that the award honors not only his own work, but also all the other people who were persecuted during World War II—the dead, the survivors, and the survivors' children.*

Evaluate In what ways does *Night* fulfill the goals Wiesel outlines in his acceptance speech? *Possible answer: Wiesel's goals are to keep the memory of the Holocaust alive, to fight "those who would forget," and to "never be silent whenever" there is suffering and humiliation. His memoir* Night *fulfills these goals by keeping his Holocaust experiences in the public memory and by not allowing people to forget the costs of oppression.*

Nobel Prize Acceptance Speech

ELIE WIESEL

It is with a profound sense of humility that I accept the honor you have chosen to bestow upon me. I know: your choice transcends me. This both frightens and pleases me.

It frightens me because I wonder: do I have the right to represent the multitudes who have perished? Do I have the right to accept this great honor on their behalf? I do not. That would be presumptuous. No one may speak for the dead, no one may interpret their mutilated dreams and visions.

It pleases me because I may say that this honor belongs to all the survivors and their children, and through us, to the Jewish people with whose destiny I have always identified.

I remember: it happened yesterday or eternities ago. A young Jewish boy discovered the kingdom of night. I remember his bewilderment, I remember his anguish. It all happened so fast. The ghetto. The deportation. The sealed cattle car. The fiery altar upon which the history of our people and the future of mankind were meant to be sacrificed.

I remember: he asked his father: "Can this be true? This is the 20th century, not the Middle Ages. Who would allow such crimes to be committed? How could the world remain silent?"

And now the boy is turning to me: "Tell me," he asks. "What have you done with my future? What have you done with your life?"

And I tell him that I have tried. That I have tried to keep memory alive, that I have tried to fight those who would forget. Because if we forget, we are guilty, we are accomplices.

And then I explained to him how naive we were, that the world did know and remained silent. And that is why I swore never to be silent whenever and wherever human beings endure suffering and humiliation. We must always take sides. Neutrality helps the oppressor, never the victim. Silence encourages the tormentor, never the tormented.

Comprehension

1. **Recall** What is the purpose of the camp's selection process?

2. **Recall** How do the prisoners try to avoid being chosen?

3. **Recall** Why does Wiesel's father give him his knife and spoon?

4. **Summarize** What happens after Wiesel's father stays behind at the camp?

Text Analysis

● 5. **Connect** How did the connections you made as you read deepen your understanding of Wiesel's experiences? Discuss specific examples in the selection.

● 6. **Analyze Memoir** Review the chart you created as you read. What insights did you gain about the hardships faced by the concentration camp prisoners? Support your response with examples from the text.

7. **Make Inferences** Reread lines 84–95. Why does the head of Wiesel's block insist so firmly that none of the prisoners is in danger? Cite evidence to support your answer.

8. **Draw Conclusions** Wiesel describes an encounter with veteran prisoners in lines 15–27. Based on this description, what would you conclude about the effects of living in a concentration camp over a long period of time?

9. **Interpret Title** Why do you think Wiesel chose to call his memoir *Night*?

10. **Examine Author's Purpose** What does the excerpt from Wiesel's Nobel Prize acceptance speech on page 948 suggest about his purpose for writing *Night*? Cite specific statements in your response.

Text Criticism

11. **Different Perspectives** Elie Wiesel once said, "Just as despair can come to one only from other human beings, hope, too, can be given to one only by other human beings." Which details or incidents in the selection from *Night* give you reason to be hopeful about humanity?

Can **HUMANITY** triumph over evil?

How do some people manage to keep their humanity in desperate circumstances?

COMMON CORE

RI 1 Cite textual evidence to support analysis of what the text says explicitly as well as inferences drawn from the text.
RI 6 Determine an author's point of view or purpose in a text.

NIGHT **949**

Practice and Apply

For preliminary support of post-reading questions, use these copy masters:

R RESOURCE MANAGER—Copy Masters
Reading Check p. 28
Connect p. 23
Question Support p. 29

Additional selection questions are provided for teachers on page 15.

ANSWERS

Comprehension

1. *The purpose is to choose the weakest prisoners to kill in the gas chamber.*

2. *They try to appear healthy, they run instead of walk past the SS men, they do not look at the SS men, and they try not to look afraid (lines 40–46).*

3. *His father thinks he is going to be killed, and he wants to give his son something of value and use (lines 150–152).*

4. *Wiesel worries about his father, but his father is not selected to be killed. Wiesel gives him back the knife and spoon (lines 167–178).*

Text Analysis

COMMON CORE RI 1, RI 6

Possible answers:

5. ■ COMMON CORE FOCUS *Connect Accept any connections students make to the experiences of being afraid or of relief when they or loved ones remain safe.*

6. ● COMMON CORE FOCUS *Memoir Students may say they learned that the prisoners got little to eat (lines 113–114), did heavy labor (lines 7–8), were in constant fear of death (lines 12–14), were occasionally cruel to one another, but also tried to help one another (lines 167–170).*

7. *He may want the prisoners to believe in his authority, he may want to spare them from feeling fear in the face of a situation that neither they nor he can control, or he may be unwilling to admit that he can't help them. His face probably reflects "weariness" (line 85) at his own sense of helplessness. His anger might reflect frustration over that helplessness or embarrassment because the old Jew knows he is lying (lines 88–92).*

8. *One might conclude that people become hardened to human emotions and think they are tougher than newcomers.*

---

9. *Wiesel may have chosen the title because he is in a place of metaphorical darkness, or unspeakable evil and constant fear.*

10. *Wiesel's purpose is "to keep memory [of the Holocaust] alive" and "to fight those who would forget."*

Text Criticism

Possible answers:

11. *The head of the block's advice for avoiding selection (lines 38–46), Wiesel's solidarity with Tibi and Yossi (lines 167–168), and the* love between Wiesel and his father (lines 150–159) give us reason to feel hopeful about humanity.

Can **HUMANITY** triumph over evil?
Answers will vary. People who at their core believe in the goodness of people and respect others as individuals keep their humanity no matter what the circumstances.

NIGHT **949**

ANSWERS

Vocabulary in Context

▲ VOCABULARY PRACTICE

1. *synonyms*	**3.** *antonyms*
2. *antonyms*	**4.** *synonyms*

 RESOURCE MANAGER—Copy Master
Vocabulary Practice p. 26

ACADEMIC VOCABULARY IN WRITING

Possible answer: *The prisoners create a* culture *in which people try to support one another and help one another survive. However, like any* community, *people take on different, sometimes opposing* roles. *For example, veterans boast of their experiences. Nazis destroy this* sense of community *by creating fear, which forces prisoners to think mainly of themselves and their own survival.*

VOCABULARY STRATEGY:
CONNOTATION AND
DENOTATION

 **COMMON CORE L 5b**

- Tell students to use context clues to figure out the best word. Have them consider the emotions each answer choice inspires and then which emotion best fits the sentence context.

- For instructional support, provide this example:

  > The puppy yapped (wildly/savagely) because she was so happy to see us.

  Explain that *wildly* is the better choice. If the puppy is happy, she will not react *savagely*.

Answers:

1. *anxious*	**4.** *lazy*
2. *confident*	**5.** *meticulous*
3. *naive*	

 RESOURCE MANAGER—Copy Master
Vocabulary Strategy p. 27

Interactive Vocabulary

Keywords direct students to a **WordSharp** tutorial on **thinkcentral.com** or to other types of vocabulary practice and review.

Vocabulary in Context

▲ VOCABULARY PRACTICE

Decide whether the words in each pair are synonyms (words with similar meanings) or antonyms (words with opposite meanings).

1. stature/height
2. interminable/finite
3. emaciated/portly
4. din/commotion

WORD LIST
din
emaciated
interminable
stature

ACADEMIC VOCABULARY IN WRITING

- acknowledge • community • contemporary • culture • role

How do the prisoners create their own society within the concentration camp? Write a paragraph in which you describe the **community** portrayed in Wiesel's memoir. Tell how the sense of community was threatened by the Nazis. Use at least one Academic Vocabulary word in your response.

VOCABULARY STRATEGY: CONNOTATION AND DENOTATION

A word's **denotation** is its basic dictionary meaning. Its **connotation** is the nuances of meaning that it may take on. Even if words are **synonyms**— have the same meaning—they can have different connotations. For example, *emaciated* and *skinny* both mean "very thin," but the connotation of *emaciated* makes it a better choice to describe someone who is suffering from starvation or illness. When you choose words in writing, be sure to consider whether their connotations fit the context.

PRACTICE From the choice of words supplied in each sentence, choose the one that fits best. You can use a dictionary or thesaurus to help you.

1. I feel (anxious/fearful) about my upcoming math quiz.
2. She admired his easy and (confident/presumptuous) attitude.
3. You are young and (naive/foolish), but you have a good head on your shoulders.
4. The new employee will not last long if he continues to be (lazy/leisurely).
5. I appreciate your (meticulous/picky) review of my term paper.

COMMON CORE

L 5b Analyze nuances in the meaning of words with similar denotations.

Interactive Vocabulary
Go to **thinkcentral.com**.
KEYWORD: HML10-950

DIFFERENTIATED INSTRUCTION

FOR STRUGGLING READERS

Vocabulary Support Have students work in pairs to provide each vocabulary word's denotation, or dictionary meaning. Then have students give an example that suggests each word's connotation. Work as a group to check the accuracy of definitions and connotative examples in a dictionary.

FOR ADVANCED LEARNERS/PRE-AP

Vocabulary in Writing Have students use the vocabulary words in a paragraph written from the point of view of the head of the block. Ask students to share these paragraphs with the class for discussion. Do students agree on the feelings and observations expressed in the paragraphs? Why or why not?

Language

◆ **GRAMMAR AND STYLE: Establish Tone**

Review the **Grammar and Style** note on page 944. Tone, or the writer's attitude toward a subject, is established through the use of **imagery, word choice,** and **formal** or **informal language.** Wiesel's short, simple sentences and stark imagery help to convey the serious tone of his piece, allowing the tragic events to speak for themselves. In your own writing, make sure the language you choose matches the tone you wish to convey to your reader. Here is another example from the text:

> *Those whose numbers had been noted stood apart, abandoned by the whole world. Some were weeping in silence.*
>
> *The SS officers went away. The head of the block appeared, his face reflecting the general weariness.* (lines 82–85)

Notice how the revisions in blue give this first draft a more serious tone. Revise your responses to the prompt by making sure your word choice, sentence structure, and use of imagery match the desired tone.

> **STUDENT MODEL**
>
> Although the Kapos ~~could push around~~ *had some authority over* other prisoners, they were completely under the control of Dr. Mengele. He had the power ~~to kill off~~ *of life and death*. ~~any guy.~~

READING-WRITING CONNECTION

 YOUR TURN Broaden your understanding of the selection from *Night* by responding to this prompt. Then use the **revising tip** to improve your writing.

WRITING PROMPT	REVISING TIP
Short Constructed Response: Journal Entry Suppose that you were one of the soldiers who liberated Auschwitz from the Nazis. In **three to five paragraphs,** write a journal entry describing what you found in the camp.	Review your response. Did you use language that matches the tone you want to convey to your reader? If not, revise to give your reponse the correct tone.

 **Interactive Revision** THINK central Go to **thinkcentral.com**. KEYWORD: HML10-951

FOR STRUGGLING WRITERS

- Have students explain their mission—to liberate the camp—in the first paragraph.
- Ask students to work in small groups to identify details that describe the camp.
- Suggest that students include at least one detail for each of the five senses.

COMMON CORE

L3 Apply knowledge of language to make effective choices for meaning or style.

Language

 COMMON CORE **L3**

◆ **GRAMMAR AND STYLE**

- After they review the note on page 944 and the student model, have students describe the tone of the lines in the student model and identify the language that conveys that tone.

- Write these sentences on the board. Have students suggest revisions that suggest a more emotional tone.

I was ~~happy~~ overjoyed to see my father. He had ~~made it through~~ survived the second selection. I ~~walked quickly~~ ran wildly toward him, blinded by tears ~~in my eyes~~.

 RESOURCE MANAGER—Copy Master Grammar and Style p. 30

READING-WRITING CONNECTION

Have students use an Observation Chart to describe conditions in the camp, based on details in the selection.

 BEST PRACTICES TOOLKIT—Transparency Observation Chart p. C7

>  THINK central
>
> **Writing Online**
>
> The following tools are available online at **thinkcentral.com** and on **Write*Smart* CD-ROM:**
> - **Interactive Graphic Organizers**
> - **Interactive Student Models**
> - **Interactive Revision Lessons**
>
> For additional grammar instruction, see **GrammarNotes** on **thinkcentral.com**.

Assess and Reteach

Assess

DIAGNOSTIC AND SELECTION TESTS
  Selection Test A pp. 267–268
  Selection Test B/C pp. 269–270

Interactive Selection Test on **thinkcentral.com**

Reteach

Level Up Online Tutorials on **thinkcentral.com**

Reteaching Worksheets on **thinkcentral.com**
  Literature Lesson 45: Author's Perspective
  Vocabulary Lesson 17: Denotation and Connotation

Focus and Motivate

SUMMARY

During World War II, the U.S. government forced Jeanne Wakatsuki and her family to move to an internment camp for Japanese Americans.

What if your government declared you the **ENEMY?**

Read the question aloud. As students begin the *QUICKWRITE*, point out that nearly two-thirds of the people affected by the order shown in the image were U.S. citizens, not "enemy aliens."

Before Reading

Essential Course of Study **ECOS**

from **Farewell to Manzanar**
Memoir by Jeanne Wakatsuki Houston and James D. Houston

VIDEO TRAILER THINK central KEYWORD: HML10-952

What if your government declared you the ENEMY?

What sort of government would harm innocent people just because of their ancestry? Unfortunately, such persecution has occurred in many nations, including our own. During World War II, the United States declared Japanese Americans to be enemy aliens and forced them into internment camps, a tragic event described in *Farewell to Manzanar.*

QUICKWRITE Governments often take unusual measures during times of crisis. Write one or two paragraphs discussing whether it is ever justifiable to limit the rights of citizens or legal residents who have committed no crimes.

UNITED STATES DEPARTMENT OF JUSTICE

NOTICE

ALIEN ENEMY
Prohibited Area
No. 33

The United States Government requires all aliens of German, Italian or Japanese Nationality to vacate this area by midnight, February 24, 1942. Go to your local Federal Social Security Board office for details.

952

Selection Resources

TEXT ANALYSIS: CULTURAL CHARACTERISTICS

In memoirs, writers often provide information about their culture or about a particular time period in which they lived. When reading such accounts, readers can learn about the beliefs, values, traditions, and customs that are characteristic of a culture. For example, in *Farewell to Manzanar*, Wakatsuki makes the following statement about the customs of the Japanese diet:

Among the Japanese . . . rice is never eaten with sweet foods, only with salty or savory foods.

As you read about the Wakatsuki family, identify cultural beliefs, customs, traditions, or values and how these influence the family's actions and perceptions of events.

READING STRATEGY: MONITOR

Memoirs often mix personal details with references to historical events. When you find it difficult to keep track of such information, you can use techniques such as the following to **monitor** your reading:

- Ask questions about events or ideas that are unclear, and then read to find the answers.
- Clarify your understanding by rereading passages, summarizing, or slowing down your reading pace.

As you read the excerpt from *Farewell to Manzanar*, use a chart to improve your comprehension of difficult passages.

Passage	Monitoring Technique
lines 1–13	I reread the paragraph to clear up my confusion about the different locations that are mentioned.

Review: Make Inferences

▲ VOCABULARY IN CONTEXT

The following words are used in *Farewell to Manzanar* to describe a family's ordeal. Which words do you already know? Use each of those words in a sentence. Write each sentence in your *Reader/Writer Notebook*. After you have read the selection, check your sentences to make sure you used the words correctly.

WORD LIST	inevitable	permeate	subordinate
	irrational	sinister	

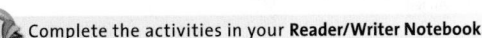 Complete the activities in your **Reader/Writer Notebook**.

Meet the Authors

Jeanne Wakatsuki Houston
(born 1934)

James D. Houston
(born 1933)

Coming to Terms
Jeanne Wakatsuki (wä-käts-ōō´kē) Houston was only seven when her family was forced to leave their home in California. The Wakatsukis were among the first Japanese Americans sent to the Manzanar internment camp and among the last to be released. Houston waited 25 years before describing her experience in *Farewell to Manzanar,* which she co-authored with her husband, James D. Houston. She says that writing was "a way of coming to terms with the impact these years have had on my entire life." The book won critical praise upon its publication in 1973 and helped publicize the unjust treatment of Japanese Americans during World War II.

BACKGROUND TO THE MEMOIR
Internment of Japanese Americans
After Japan attacked Pearl Harbor and drew the United States into World War II, some officials feared that Japanese Americans would secretly aid Japan's war effort, although there was no evidence of their disloyalty. In February 1942, President Franklin Roosevelt signed an order that led to the removal of almost 120,000 Japanese Americans from their homes on the West Coast. With little notice, they were bused to ten "relocation" centers in Western states and Arkansas, where they were confined for the duration of the war.

Author Online
THINK central
Go to **thinkcentral.com**.
KEYWORD: HML10-953

953

Teach

TEXT ANALYSIS · COMMON CORE · RI 6

● Model the Skill: CULTURAL CHARACTERISTICS

To model how to identify cultural characteristics, share this example:

> When facing something difficult, the older Japanese people would say, "It cannot be helped. It must be done."

Point out to students that this passage reveals that Japanese people try to accept what they are powerless to change.

GUIDED PRACTICE Ask volunteers to share a cultural characteristic that they know of.

READING STRATEGY · COMMON CORE · RI 1

■ Model the Skill: MONITOR

To model how to monitor reading, write this passage on the board:

> Block 16 was a cluster of 15 barracks, each of which was divided into 6 units the size of a living room—16 by 20 feet—and the 12 people in our family were assigned 2 of these small units.

Point out that by rereading, students have a better chance of keeping track of what they've read. Tell students that rereading is a monitoring strategy.

GUIDED PRACTICE Ask students when they would use this technique.

R RESOURCE MANAGER—Copy Master
Monitor p. 45 (for student use whilereading the selection)

VOCABULARY SKILL
COMMON CORE · L 4

▲ VOCABULARY IN CONTEXT

DIAGNOSE WORD KNOWLEDGE Have all students complete Vocabulary in Context. Check their sentences against the following:

inevitable (ĭn-ĕv´ĭ-tə-bəl) *adj.* unavoidable
irrational (ĭ-răsh´ə-nəl) *adj.* not possessed with reason or understanding
permeate (pûr´mē-āt´) *v.* to spread or flow throughout
sinister (sĭn´ĭ-stər) *adj.* threatening or foreshadowing evil

subordinate (sə-bôr´dn-āt´) *v.* to lower in rank or importance

PRETEACH VOCABULARY Use the following copy master to help students predict the meaning of each boldfaced word.

R RESOURCE MANAGER—Copy Master
Vocabulary Study p. 47

1. Read item 1 aloud, emphasizing *inevitable.*

2. Point out the phrase "with a score 20–1." Elicit possible meanings for *inevitable*, such as "certain."

3. Repeat the procedure for items 2–4, and then have students complete Part B.

READ WITH A PURPOSE

Help students set a purpose for reading. Tell students to note how the Wakatsuki family reacts to Manzanar.

Farewell *to* Manzanar

Jeanne Wakatsuki Houston and
James D. Houston

The American Friends Service[1] helped us find a small house in Boyle Heights, another minority ghetto, in downtown Los Angeles, now inhabited briefly by a few hundred Terminal Island refugees.[2] Executive Order 9066 had been signed by President Roosevelt, giving the War Department authority to define military areas in the western states and to exclude from them anyone who might threaten the war effort. There was a lot of talk about internment, or moving inland, or something like that in store for all Japanese Americans. I remember my brothers sitting around the table talking very intently about what we were going to do, how we would keep the family together. They had
10 seen how quickly Papa was removed, and they knew now that he would not be back for quite a while. Just before leaving Terminal Island, Mama had received her first letter, from Bismarck, North Dakota. He had been imprisoned at Fort Lincoln, in an all-male camp for enemy aliens.

Papa had been the patriarch. He had always decided everything in the family. With him gone, my brothers, like councilors in the absence of a chief, worried about what should be done. The ironic thing is, there wasn't much left to decide. These were mainly days of quiet, desperate waiting for what seemed at the time to be **inevitable.** There is a phrase the Japanese use in such situations, when something difficult must be endured.
20   You would hear the older heads, the Issei,[3] telling others very quietly, *"Shikata ga nai"* (It cannot be helped). *"Shikata ga nai"* (It must be done). **A**

---

1. **American Friends Service:** a Quaker charity that often aids political and religious refugees and other displaced persons.
2. **Terminal Island refugees:** Shortly after Pearl Harbor was attacked, Japanese fishermen and cannery workers were forced to leave Terminal Island, which is located near Los Angeles.
3. **Issei** (ē'sā): people born in Japan who immigrate to the United States.

954   UNIT 9: HISTORY, CULTURE, AND THE AUTHOR

Analyze Visuals ▶

Surrounded by her family's belongings, a young girl awaits transportation to an internment camp. Why might this photograph be used to support criticism of the internment policy?

① Targeted Passage

inevitable (ĭn-ĕv'ĭ-tə-bəl) *adj.* unavoidable

A CULTURAL CHARACTERISTICS
Reread lines 14–21. What does this passage reveal about traditional Japanese attitudes toward adversity?

A CULTURAL CHARACTERISTICS

Possible answer: *The passage reveals the traditional Japanese attitude that sometimes you cannot prevent something bad or difficult from happening and you must simply endure it.*

IF STUDENTS NEED HELP . . . Point out the English translations of the Issei's advice, and then have students restate that advice in their own words.

Extend the Discussion How might the family's reaction to the Executive Order have been different if they came from a culture that valued action above patience?

OWN THE WORD

inevitable: Ask students what the narrator thinks is *inevitable*. ***Possible answer:*** *The narrator thinks that the internment of her family is* inevitable.

DIFFERENTIATED INSTRUCTION

FOR ENGLISH LANGUAGE LEARNERS
Vocabulary Support Use Word Questioning to teach these words: *authority* (line 4), *exclude* (line 5), *issued* (line 90), *temporary* (line 223), *volunteers* (line 263).

 **BEST PRACTICES TOOLKIT—Transparency** Word Questioning p. E9

FOR STRUGGLING READERS
In combination with the *Audio Anthology CD*, use one or more Targeted Passages (pp. 954, 956, 960, 964) to ensure that students focus on key story events, concepts, and skills. Targeted Passages are also good for English learners.

 Targeted Passage [Lines 1–13]
This passage explains why the family was forced to evacuate their home.

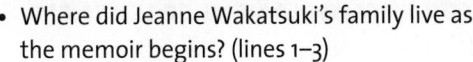

Reading Support

This selection on **thinkcentral.com** includes embedded **ThinkAloud** models—students "thinking aloud" about the story to model the kinds of questions a good reader would ask about a selection.

BACKGROUND

Government Reparations More than 20 years after Manzanar and the other Japanese-American internment camps closed and the internees were allowed to return home, public opinion about the internment began to change. The U.S. government started to consider how to compensate survivors for their loss of property and liberty. Not until 1988, however, did Congress pass legislation to grant each surviving internee $20,000 and officially denounce the internment as unjust. Eventually, reparation payments were made to more than 80,000 of the 120,000 Japanese Americans who had been interned during World War II, for a total of about $1.6 million. The Civil Liberties Act of 1988 also provided a formal presidential apology and created the Civil Liberties Public Education Fund to teach the public, particularly children, about the internment.

Analyze Visuals

Possible answer: This photograph could be used to support criticism of the internment policy because the girl does not look dangerous.

About the Art Photographer Ansel Adams documented the experience of the Japanese Americans at the Manzanar internment camp to show the injustice that they were enduring.

- Where did Jeanne Wakatsuki's family live as the memoir begins? (lines 1–3)
- Where had they been living before? Why had they been forced to leave? (lines 3–6)
- What did Executive Order 9066 authorize? Who had issued this order? (lines 3–6)
- Why had Papa been sent away? Where was he living? (lines 9–13)

FOR ADVANCED LEARNERS/PRE–AP

Research Critical Reviews Invite students to research the literary criticism written about *Farewell to Manzanar* in the library. In a brief report, have them share several positive or negative reviews of the book. Encourage students to use both the critics' words and their own words to summarize each literary review.

B MONITOR

Possible answer: *The teacher may have been unfriendly because many Americans had become suspicious and hostile toward Japanese Americans once the United States had gone to war with Japan.*

TIERED DISCUSSION PROMPTS

Direct students to lines 37–44. Use these prompts to help students appreciate the irony of the Wakatsukis' relief at their evacuation:

Connect Have you ever known someone who was misunderstood or treated badly because he or she was somehow different? Explain. *Accept all reasonable responses.*

Analyze Why is it ironic that Jeanne's older brothers and sisters felt relief when they were ordered to go to the internment camp? *Possible answer:* *It is ironic because things had gotten so bad that the Japanese Americans thought they might be better off leaving their homes and going to the internment camp. They had no idea what kind of living conditions awaited them.*

Evaluate Do you think the government ordered Japanese Americans into the camps to provide protection for them? *Possible answer:* *No, the government was reacting to racist fears. They intended to isolate people of Japanese descent not for their own protection but to "protect" other Americans.*

OWN THE WORD

irrational: Ask students why the American public's fear of Japanese people was *irrational.* *Possible answer:* *It was irrational because there was no basis for the fear. Japanese Americans were not the enemy.*

Mama and Woody went to work packing celery for a Japanese produce dealer. Kiyo and my sister May and I enrolled in the local school, and what sticks in my memory from those few weeks is the teacher—not her looks, her remoteness. In Ocean Park my teacher had been a kind, grandmotherly woman who used to sail with us in Papa's boat from time to time and who wept the day we had to leave. In Boyle Heights the teacher felt cold and distant. I was confused by all the moving and was having trouble with the classwork, but she would never help me out. She would have nothing to do with me. **B**

30   This was the first time I had felt outright hostility from a Caucasian. Looking back, it is easy enough to explain. Public attitudes toward the Japanese in California were shifting rapidly. In the first few months of the Pacific war, America was on the run. Tolerance had turned to distrust and **irrational** fear. The hundred-year-old tradition of anti-Orientalism on the west coast soon resurfaced, more vicious than ever. Its result became clear about a month later, when we were told to make our third and final move.

The name Manzanar meant nothing to us when we left Boyle Heights. We didn't know where it was or what it was. We went because the government ordered us to. And, in the case of my older brothers and sisters, we went with
40   a certain amount of relief. They had all heard stories of Japanese homes being attacked, of beatings in the streets of California towns. They were as frightened of the Caucasians as Caucasians were of us. Moving, under what appeared to be government protection, to an area less directly threatened by the war seemed not such a bad idea at all. For some it actually sounded like a fine adventure.

Our pickup point was a Buddhist church in Los Angeles. It was very early, and misty, when we got there with our luggage. Mama had bought heavy coats for all of us. She grew up in eastern Washington and knew that anywhere inland in early April would be cold. I was proud of my new coat, and I remember sitting on a duffel bag trying to be friendly with the Greyhound driver. I smiled at him.
50   He didn't smile back. He was befriending no one. Someone tied a numbered tag to my collar and to the duffel bag (each family was given a number, and that became our official designation until the camps were closed), someone else passed out box lunches for the trip, and we climbed aboard.

I had never been outside Los Angeles County, never traveled more than ten miles from the coast, had never even ridden on a bus. I was full of excitement, the way any kid would be, and wanted to look out the window. But for the first few hours the shades were drawn. Around me other people played cards, read magazines, dozed, waiting. I settled back, waiting too, and finally fell sleep. The bus felt very secure to me. Almost half its passengers were immediate relatives.
60   Mama and my older brothers had succeeded in keeping most of us together, on the same bus, headed for the same camp. I didn't realize until much later what a job that was. The strategy had been, first, to have everyone living in the same district when the evacuation began, and then to get all of us included under the same family number, even though names had been changed by marriage. Many families weren't as lucky as ours and suffered months of anguish while trying to arrange transfers from one camp to another.

B MONITOR
What might explain the unfriendly behavior of the teacher in Boyle Heights? To clarify, read on and check your answer.

irrational (ĭ-răsh'ə-nəl) *adj.* not possessed with reason or understanding

② Targeted Passage

DIFFERENTIATED INSTRUCTION

FOR STRUGGLING READERS

② **Targeted Passage** [Lines 37–66]

This passage explains why Jeanne was excited about going to the internment camp.

- Why are the Wakatsukis relieved to leave Boyle Heights? (lines 39–44)
- Where were they going? (line 37)
- How did their mother prepare for the trip? (lines 46–48)
- Why was the family lucky to have been kept together? (lines 64–66)

FOR ENGLISH LANGUAGE LEARNERS

Language: Verbs Write the verbs of being on the board: *be, become, feel, taste, seem, look, appear,* and *sound.* Explain that a verb of being has no object. Instead, it is often followed by an adjective that describes the subject. Help students identify the verb (*felt*) and the subject (*teacher*) that the adjectives (*cold, distant*) describe in this sentence: "In Boyle Heights the teacher felt cold and distant" (line 27). Repeat the procedure with sentences in lines 35 and 42–44.

These Japanese Americans are riding to an assembly center, where they will be held until their transfer to an internment camp.

We rode all day. By the time we reached our destination, the shades were up. It was late afternoon. The first thing I saw was a yellow swirl across a blurred, reddish setting sun. The bus was being pelted by what sounded like splattering
70 rain. It wasn't rain. This was my first look at something I would soon know very well, a billowing flurry of dust and sand churned up by the wind through Owens Valley.[4]

We drove past a barbed-wire fence, through a gate, and into an open space where trunks and sacks and packages had been dumped from the baggage trucks that drove out ahead of us. I could see a few tents set up, the first rows of black barracks, and beyond them, blurred by sand, rows of barracks that seemed to spread for miles across this plain. People were sitting on cartons or milling around, with their backs to the wind, waiting to see which friends or relatives might be on this bus. As we approached, they turned or stood up,
80 and some moved toward us expectantly. But inside the bus no one stirred. No one waved or spoke. They just stared out the windows, ominously silent. I didn't understand this. Hadn't we finally arrived, our whole family intact? I opened a window, leaned out, and yelled happily. "Hey! This whole bus is full of Wakatsukis!" **C**

Outside, the greeters smiled. Inside there was an explosion of laughter, hysterical, tension-breaking laughter that left my brothers choking and whacking each other across the shoulders.

C MAKE INFERENCES
Why were people in the bus "ominously silent" upon their arrival at the camp?

---

4. **Owens Valley:** the valley of the Owens River in south-central California west of Death Valley, where Manzanar was built. The once lush and green valley had become dry and deserted in the 1930s after water was diverted to an aqueduct supplying Los Angeles.

FAREWELL TO MANZANAR **957**

Activity What can you tell about the people riding on this train, based on their body language, clothing, and facial expressions? How do these details reflect the Wakatsukis' experience as described in this excerpt? What differences do you notice? *Possible answer: Some of the people on the train appear worried and uneasy. The man with his hand over his face appears ashamed or frightened. None of the people are smiling. They are all well dressed, suggesting that they have jobs, property, and homes, like Jeanne and her family. Also like the Wakatsukis, they are Japanese Americans on their way to an internment camp—but unlike Jeanne's family, they are traveling by train instead of bus and are first going to an assembly center. They do not seem to view their journey as an exciting adventure, the way Jeanne did.*

READING STRATEGY: *Review* COMMON CORE

C MAKE INFERENCES RI 1

Possible answer: The people on the bus were silent because they could see only sand and rows of barracks, and they did not want to believe they would be living in such a horrible place (lines 75–77).

IF STUDENTS NEED HELP... Encourage them to visualize the scene. Help them find details such as "rows of barracks that seemed to spread for miles across this plain" (lines 76–77).

FOR STRUGGLING READERS

Comprehension Support Have students reread lines 67–84, in which Jeanne describes her first view of Manzanar. Have students use a Setting Diagram to record setting features described in the passage. Encourage students to look for sensory details that give information about the setting.

BEST PRACTICES TOOLKIT—Transparency
Setting Diagram p. D12

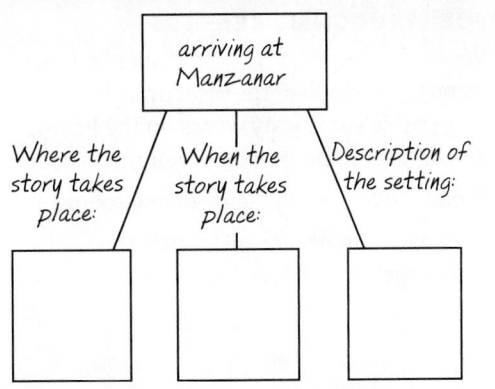

arriving at Manzanar

Where the story takes place:

When the story takes place:

Description of the setting:

We had pulled up just in time for dinner. The mess halls weren't completed yet. An outdoor chow line snaked around a half-finished building that broke
90 a good part of the wind. They issued us army mess kits, the round metal kind that fold over, and plopped in scoops of canned Vienna sausage, canned string beans, steamed rice that had been cooked too long, and on top of the rice a serving of canned apricots. The Caucasian servers were thinking that the fruit poured over rice would make a good dessert. Among the Japanese, of course, rice is never eaten with sweet foods, only with salty or savory foods. Few of us could eat such a mixture. But at this point no one dared protest. It would have been impolite. I was horrified when I saw the apricot syrup seeping through my little mound of rice. I opened my mouth to complain. My mother jabbed me in the back to keep quiet. We moved on through the line and joined the
100 others squatting in the lee[5] of half-raised walls, dabbing courteously at what was, for almost everyone there, an inedible concoction. **D**

After dinner we were taken to Block 16, a cluster of fifteen barracks that had just been finished a day or so earlier—although finished was hardly the word for it. The shacks were built of one thickness of pine planking covered with tarpaper. They sat on concrete footings, with about two feet of open space between the floorboards and the ground. Gaps showed between the planks,

---

5. **lee:** the side sheltered from the wind.

In the mess halls of internment camps, Japanese Americans were served unfamiliar foods such as sausages.

TEXT ANALYSIS

D *Model the Skill:* **CULTURAL CHARACTERISTICS**

To model how to identify cultural characteristics, read lines 90–101 aloud, and then ask students these questions:

- How did the Japanese Americans feel about the apricots and rice they were served?
- Why didn't they protest?
- What did they do with the food once it was on their plates?

Possible answer: *In lines 90–101, we learn about Japanese culinary customs and preferences—that they eat rice only with salty or savory foods, never with sweet foods. We also learn that they were too polite or scared to complain when the servers, ignorant of these customs, served them rice with canned apricots—food that the internees found "inedible." This cultural information lets readers understand how helpless, misunderstood, and disoriented the internees must have felt.*

Analyze Visuals

Activity How does the caption help you understand the details in the photograph?
Possible answer: *The caption indicates that the sausages were unfamiliar. That detail explains the uncertain expressions on the women's faces and the tentativeness with which they reach for the sausages.*

D CULTURAL CHARACTERISTICS How does the cultural information in lines 90–101 help you understand the experience of interned Japanese Americans?

DIFFERENTIATED INSTRUCTION

FOR STRUGGLING READERS

Vocabulary Support To help students understand the episode of the disastrous first meal, write these vocabulary words on the board, and be sure students know their meaning:

- *mess halls* (line 88), "large dining rooms"
- *Vienna sausage* (line 91), "small, spicy sausage"

- *Caucasian* (line 93), "people who are white or of European descent"
- *savory* (line 95), "salty or spicy"
- *inedible concoction* (line 101), "food that is too unappealing to eat"

and as the weeks passed and the green wood dried out, the gaps widened. Knotholes gaped in the uncovered floor.

Each barracks was divided into six units, sixteen by twenty feet, about 110 the size of a living room, with one bare bulb hanging from the ceiling and an oil stove for heat. We were assigned two of these for the twelve people in our family group; and our official family "number" was enlarged by three digits—16 plus the number of this barracks. We were issued steel army cots, two brown army blankets each, and some mattress covers, which my brothers stuffed with straw. **E**

The first task was to divide up what space we had for sleeping. Bill and Woody contributed a blanket each and partitioned off the first room: one side for Bill and Tomi, one side for Woody and Chizu and their baby girl. Woody also got the stove, for heating formulas.

120 The people who had it hardest during the first few months were young couples like these, many of whom had married just before the evacuation began, in order not to be separated and sent to different camps. Our two rooms were crowded, but at least it was all in the family. My oldest sister and her husband were shoved into one of those sixteen-by-twenty-foot compartments with six people they had never seen before—two other couples, one recently married like themselves, the other with two teenage boys. Partitioning off a room like that wasn't easy. It was bitter cold when we arrived, and the wind did not abate. All they had to use for room dividers were those army blankets, two of which were barely enough to keep one person warm. They argued over whose blanket should 130 be sacrificed and later argued about noise at night—the parents wanted their boys asleep by 9:00 P.M.—and they continued arguing over matters like that for six months, until my sister and her husband left to harvest sugar beets in Idaho. It was grueling work up there, and wages were pitiful, but when the call came through camp for workers to alleviate the wartime labor shortage, it sounded better than their life at Manzanar. They knew they'd have, if nothing else, a room, perhaps a cabin of their own.

That first night in Block 16, the rest of us squeezed into the second room— Granny; Lillian, age fourteen; Ray, thirteen; May, eleven; Kiyo, ten; Mama; and me. I didn't mind this at all at the time. Being youngest meant I got to 140 sleep with Mama. And before we went to bed I had a great time jumping up and down on the mattress. The boys had stuffed so much straw into hers, we had to flatten it some so we wouldn't slide off. I slept with her every night after that until Papa came back.

We woke early, shivering and coated with dust that had blown up through the knotholes and in through the slits around the doorway. During the night Mama had unpacked all our clothes and heaped them on our beds for warmth. Now our cubicle looked as if a great laundry bag had exploded and then been sprayed with fine dust. A skin of sand covered the floor. I looked over Mama's shoulder at Kiyo, on top of his fat mattress, buried under jeans and overcoats 150 and sweaters. His eyebrows were gray, and he was starting to giggle. He was looking at me, at my gray eyebrows and coated hair, and pretty soon we were

E MONITOR
What strategy would you use to clarify the information in lines 109–115?

RI 1

E *Model the Skill:* **MONITOR**

To model how to monitor reading, read lines 109–115 aloud. Then summarize the information about the barracks by drawing a diagram of them on the board. Remind students that to keep track of information, they can ask questions, and then read to find the answer. They can also reread passages and summarize to improve their comprehension. Have students fill in their Monitor charts to clarify their understanding of this passage.

Possible answer: *Students might use the strategies of rereading, visualizing, or drawing a diagram to clarify the information in the paragraph.*

REVISIT THE BIG QUESTION

What if your government declared you the **ENEMY?**

Discuss Direct students to lines 129–136. If the U.S. government considered Japanese Americans to be enemy aliens, why did it allow them to harvest sugar beets? *Some students may feel that the government's willingness to use Japanese Americans to alleviate wartime labor shortages proves that it did not really view them as a dangerous* **enemy.** *Other students may speculate that the government believed that Japanese Americans were not a threat if they were isolated in Idaho, away from the coast and their home communities.*

FOR ENGLISH LANGUAGE LEARNERS

Vocabulary: Idioms Have students record these idioms on their Personal Word Lists, along with a definition and sample sentence: *all in the family* (line 123), "only family members"; *tight as a barrel* (line 198), "without openings"; *making good* (line 221), "fulfilling"; *word would get around* (line 307), "everyone would find out"; *placed a high premium on* (line 316), "valued highly".

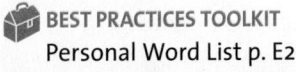 **BEST PRACTICES TOOLKIT**
Personal Word List p. E2

FOR STRUGGLING READERS

Develop Reading Fluency Point out Woody's conversational speaking style: for example, in "tell 'em" and "gonna" (lines 160–161). Explain that writers want characters to sound real, and that real people use shortened forms or leave out words when they talk. Model for students how to read the dialogue. Then have students echo the reading.

Distribute the copy masters.

R **RESOURCE MANAGER**—Copy Master
Reading Fluency p. 53

TIERED DISCUSSION PROMPTS

Direct students to lines 152–186. Use these prompts to discuss how the Wakatsuki family reacted to its situation:

Connect How do you feel about Woody at this point in the memoir? Why? *Accept all reasonable responses.*

Analyze What do Woody's words and actions reveal about his character?
Possible answer: Woody's friendly banter shows that he knows the power of having a positive outlook. His sack full of tin can lids shows that he is industrious and resourceful.

VOCABULARY  **COMMON CORE** RI 4

⚠ FOREIGN WORDS IN ENGLISH

Write the words *kimono* and *karate* on the board. Then, point out the words *shikata ga nai* (line 21), *arigato* (line 300), and *arigato gozaimas* (line 301). Ask students how these words are similar and how they are different. Point out that all these words are from the Japanese language. Although *kimono* and *karate* have become part of the English language, the other words have not. Thus, the authors provide translations for these terms and not for *karate* and *kimono*.

Answer: kimono

VOCABULARY **COMMON CORE** L 4

OWN THE WORD

sinister: Point out that the adjective *sinister* comes from the Latin word meaning "on the left, unlucky." Have students volunteer examples of nouns that could be described as *sinister*. **Possible answers:** *villains, traitors, tornadoes*

---

both giggling. I looked at Mama's face to see if she thought Kiyo was funny. She lay very still next to me on our mattress, her eyes scanning everything— bare rafters, walls, dusty kids—scanning slowly, and I think the mask of her face would have cracked had not Woody's voice just then come at us through the wall. He was rapping on the planks as if testing to see if they were hollow.

"Hey!" he yelled. "You guys fall into the same flour barrel as us?"

"No," Kiyo yelled back. "Ours is full of Japs."

All of us laughed at this.

160 "Well, tell 'em it's time to get up," Woody said. "If we're gonna live in this place, we better get to work."

He gave us ten minutes to dress, then he came in carrying a broom, a hammer, and a sack full of tin can lids he had scrounged somewhere. Woody would be our leader for a while now, short, stocky, grinning behind his mustache. He had just turned twenty-four. In later years he would tour the country with Mr. Moto, the Japanese tag-team wrestler, as his **sinister** assistant Suki— karate chops through the ropes from outside the ring, a chunky leg reaching from under his kimono to trip up Mr. Moto's foe. In the ring Woody's smile looked sly and crafty; he hammed it up. Offstage it was whimsical, as if

170 some joke were bursting to be told. ⚠ **Targeted Passage** ③

"Hey, brother Ray, Kiyo," he said. "You see these tin can lids?"

"Yeah, yeah," the boys said drowsily, as if going back to sleep. They were both young versions of Woody.

"You see all them knotholes in the floor and in the walls?"

They looked around. You could see about a dozen.

Woody said, "You get those covered up before breakfast time. Any more sand comes in here through one of them knotholes, you have to eat it off the floor with ketchup."

"What about sand that comes in through the cracks?" Kiyo said.

180 Woody stood up very straight, which in itself was funny, since he was only about five-foot-six.

"Don't worry about the cracks," he said. "Different kind of sand comes in through the cracks."

He put his hands on his hips and gave Kiyo a sternly comic look, squinting at him through one eye the way Papa would when he was asserting his authority. Woody mimicked Papa's voice: "And I can tell the difference. So be careful."

The boys laughed and went to work nailing down lids. May started sweeping out the sand. I was helping Mama fold the clothes we'd used for cover, when Woody came over and put his arms around her shoulder. He was

190 short; she was even shorter, under five feet.

He said softly, "You okay, Mama?"

She didn't look at him, she just kept folding clothes and said, "Can we get the cracks covered too, Woody?"

Outside the sky was clear, but icy gusts of wind were buffeting our barracks every few minutes, sending fresh dust puffs up through the floorboards. May's broom could barely keep up with it, and our oil heater could scarcely hold its own against the drafts.

---

sinister (sĭn′ĭ-stər) *adj.* threatening or foreshadowing evil

---

COMMON CORE RI 4

⚠ FOREIGN WORDS IN ENGLISH

Reread lines 165–168. The word *karate* first appeared in English in the 1950s. U.S. and British soldiers returning from World War II brought back karate techniques and the word *karate* from Japan. Which word in line 168 also comes from the Japanese language?

COMMON CORE RI 4

Language Coach

Roots and Affixes

Reread lines 184–186. Both *comic* and *mimic* originate in Greek theater. The root *kōmos* means "joyful activity," and *mimos* means "actor." Since the Greek affix *-ic* means "like, or akin to," what do you think the original meanings of *comic* and *mimic* are? What do these words mean in lines 184 and 186?

DIFFERENTIATED INSTRUCTION

FOR STRUGGLING READERS

③ **Targeted Passage** [Lines 171–186]

This passage shows that the family was able to share a positive spirit despite the difficult living conditions.

- What does Woody ask his brothers to do? (lines 171–178)

- What jokes does Woody make to amuse his family? (lines 180–186)

- Can Woody really tell if the sand comes in the cracks or the knotholes? Why does he insist that he can? (lines 184–187)

FOR ENGLISH LANGUAGE LEARNERS

Language Coach 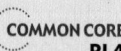 **COMMON CORE** RI 4

Roots and Affixes

Answer: *Etymologically,* comic *means "like joyful activity," and* mimic *means "akin to an actor." In line 184,* comic *means "funny," and in line 186* mimicked *means "imitated."* Point out that the noun form of *comic* is *comedy* and *mimic* is *mimicry*. Have students look up the noun forms and practice using them in original sentences.

Dust storms frequently blew through the 550-acre Manzanar internment camp, which was located 200 miles northeast of Los Angeles at the foot of the Sierra Nevada mountains.

"We'll get this whole place as tight as a barrel, Mama. I already met a guy who told me where they pile all the scrap lumber."

200   "Scrap?"

"That's all they got. I mean, they're still building the camp, you know. Sixteen blocks left to go. After that, they say maybe we'll get some stuff to fix the insides a little bit."

Her eyes blazed then, her voice quietly furious. "Woody, we can't live like this. Animals live like this."

It was hard to get Woody down. He'd keep smiling when everybody else was ready to explode. Grief flickered in his eyes. He blinked it away and hugged her tighter. "We'll make it better, Mama. You watch."

We could hear voices in other cubicles now. Beyond the wall Woody's baby
210 girl started to cry.

"I have to go over to the kitchen," he said, "see if those guys got a pot for heating bottles. That oil stove takes too long—something wrong with the fuel line. I'll find out what they're giving us for breakfast."

"Probably hotcakes with soy sauce," Kiyo said, on his hands and knees between the bunks.

"No." Woody grinned, heading out the door. "Rice. With Log Cabin syrup and melted butter."

I don't remember what we ate that first morning. I know we stood for half an hour in cutting wind waiting to get our food. Then we took it back to the

Analyze Visuals

Activity What details in the photograph help you understand what life was like in the internment camps? *Possible answer: The dust swirls around the ground, suggesting that the air and living quarters were dusty. The flag indicates that the camp is located in the United States. The long line of barracks shows that the camp housed many people in a bland and uniform setting. The mountains in the distance indicate that the location of the camp was remote. The lack of trees, shrubs, or grass shows the desolation of the location.*

REVISIT THE BIG QUESTION

What if your government declared you the ENEMY?

Discuss In lines 198–208, how do Woody and Mama respond to the living conditions? Do they view the U.S. government as the enemy? *Possible answer: Mama is deeply insulted that she is forced to live in primitive conditions; however, she does not directly condemn the government for the conditions (lines 204–205). Woody gives the government the benefit of the doubt, saying that life will improve once the camp is finished (lines 198–203).*

FOR ENGLISH LANGUAGE LEARNERS

Vocabulary: Multiple-Meaning Words List these words on the board:

- *passed out* (line 53)
- *mess* (lines 88, 90)
- *broke* (line 89)
- *mind* (line 139)
- *cutting* (line 219)
- *spoil* (line 261)

Point out that these words have multiple meanings. Invite students to determine the meaning of each word based on context clues. Then have them work in pairs to provide another definition and create sentences for both definitions. Encourage students to use a dictionary to check their definitions.

Analyze Visuals

Possible answer: *Two of the women are smiling, and the other two are working to keep
themselves and their room neat. Their attitude
seems to be positive and energetic. The people
depicted in the selection were also industrious,
working to improve their living quarters. They
tried to remain cheerful, especially Woody, and
like the people in the photograph, they made
the best of their situation by putting up privacy
barriers.*

Internees at Manzanar used boxes and scrap material to make their housing more comfortable.

◄ **Analyze
Visuals**
How does this
photograph reflect the
attitudes of people
depicted in the selection?

220 cubicle and ate huddled around the stove. Inside, it was warmer than when we
left, because Woody was already making good his promise to Mama, tacking
up some ends of lath[6] he'd found, stuffing rolled paper around the door frame.

Trouble was, he had almost nothing to work with. Beyond this temporary
weather stripping, there was little else he could do. Months went by, in fact,
before our "home" changed much at all from what it was the day we moved in—
bare floors, blanket partitions, one bulb in each compartment dangling from a
roof beam, and open ceilings overhead so that mischievous boys like Ray and
Kiyo could climb up into the rafters and peek into anyone's life.

The simple truth is the camp was no more ready for us when we got there
230 than we were ready for it. We had only the dimmest ideas of what to expect.
Most of the families, like us, had moved out from southern California with
as much luggage as each person could carry. Some old men left Los Angeles
wearing Hawaiian shirts and Panama hats and stepped off the bus at an altitude
of 4000 feet, with nothing available but sagebrush and tarpaper to stop the
April winds pouring down off the back side of the Sierras.[7]

The War Department was in charge of all the camps at this point. They
began to issue military surplus from the First World War—olive-drab knit caps,
earmuffs, peacoats, canvas leggings. Later on, sewing machines were shipped
in, and one barracks was turned into a clothing factory. An old seamstress
240 took a peacoat of mine, tore the lining out, opened and flattened the sleeves,
added a collar, put arm holes in and handed me back a beautiful cape. By fall,
dozens of seamstresses were working full-time transforming thousands of these

---

6. **lath** (lăth): a thin strip of wood.

7. **Sierras** (sē-ĕr'əz): the Sierra Nevada mountain range in eastern California.

DIFFERENTIATED INSTRUCTION

FOR ADVANCED LEARNERS/PRE–AP

Analyze Attitude Point out to students that
the conditions at the internment camp were
crowded and primitive, yet the members of
the author's family approached the problem
with industry and humor. Have students use
text examples to support this statement and
to analyze the attitude in its cultural context.
What does this attitude reveal about the
cultural values of the Japanese-American
internees? How might their reaction have

been different? Use students' completed
analyses to prompt a class-wide discussion
about the topic.

old army clothes into capes, slacks, and stylish coats. But until that factory got going and packages from friends outside began to fill out our wardrobes, warmth was more important than style. I couldn't help laughing at Mama walking around in army earmuffs and a pair of wide-cuffed, khaki-colored wool trousers several sizes too big for her. Japanese are generally smaller than Caucasians, and almost all these clothes were oversize. They flopped, they dangled, they hung.

250   It seems comical, looking back; we were a band of Charlie Chaplins[8] marooned in the California desert. But at the time, it was pure chaos. That's the only way to describe it. The evacuation had been so hurriedly planned, the camps so hastily thrown together, nothing was completed when we got there, and almost nothing worked.

    I was sick continually, with stomach cramps and diarrhea. At first it was from the shots they gave us for typhoid, in very heavy doses and in assembly-line fashion: swab, jab, swab, *Move along now,* swab, jab, swab, *Keep it moving.* That knocked all of us younger kids down at once, with fevers and vomiting. Later, it was the food that made us sick, young and old alike. The kitchens
260 were too small and badly ventilated. Food would spoil from being left out too long. That summer, when the heat got fierce, it would spoil faster. The refrigeration kept breaking down. The cooks, in many cases, had never cooked before. Each block had to provide its own volunteers. Some were lucky and had a professional or two in their midst. But the first chef in our block had been a gardener all his life and suddenly found himself preparing three meals a day for 250 people.

    "The Manzanar runs" became a condition of life, and you only hoped that when you rushed to the latrine,[9] one would be in working order.

    That first morning, on our way to the chow line, Mama and I tried to use the
270 women's latrine in our block. The smell of it spoiled what little appetite we had. Outside, men were working in an open trench, up to their knees in muck—a common sight in the months to come. Inside, the floor was covered with excrement, and all twelve bowls were erupting like a row of tiny volcanoes.

    Mama stopped a kimono-wrapped woman stepping past us with her sleeve pushed up against her nose and asked, "What do you do?"

    "Try Block Twelve," the woman said, grimacing. "They have just finished repairing the pipes."

    It was about two city blocks away. We followed her over there and found a line of women waiting in the wind outside the latrine. We had no choice but
280 to join the line and wait with them.

    Inside it was like all the other latrines. Each block was built to the same design just as each of the ten camps, from California to Arkansas, was built to a common master plan. It was an open room, over a concrete slab. The sink was a long metal trough against one wall, with a row of spigots for hot and cold

---

8. **Charlie Chaplins:** Charlie Chaplin, an actor and director, portrayed a tramp in baggy clothing in comedy films of the 1920s and 1930s.

9. **latrine:** a communal toilet in a camp or barracks.

COMMON CORE RI 4

Language Coach

Multiple-Meaning Words The word *maroon* has very different meanings as an adjective and as a verb. As an adjective, it means "purplish-red." As a verb, it means "stranded in an isolated place." Reread line 251. Which meaning of *maroon* is used? How do you know?

G MONITOR
How would you summarize the information in lines 255–266?

READING STRATEGY   COMMON CORE   RI 1

G MONITOR

Possible answer: *The people in camp got sick from typhoid shots and from spoiled food prepared by untrained cooks.*

IF STUDENTS NEED HELP . . . Distribute a Narrative summary frame, and help students adapt its questions to the brief narrative information in the passage.

BEST PRACTICES TOOLKIT—Transparency
Summary Frame: Narrative p. B13

TIERED DISCUSSION PROMPTS

Direct students to lines 225–273. Use these prompts to help students understand why the authors present such negative aspects of the camps in such detail:

Recall What conditions do the authors describe in the kitchens and the latrines? ***Possible answer:*** *The kitchens and latrines were unsanitary and insufficient.*

Analyze In your opinion, why did the authors describe the camp's unsanitary conditions in such detail? ***Possible answer:*** *The authors may believe that most readers will connect to the personal horror of unsanitary kitchen and bathroom facilities.*

Evaluate Do you think it is just or fair to require people to live in such conditions, particularly if they have not been convicted of any crime? *Most students will say that such conditions are unacceptable, even for those designated as "enemies" of a government.*

FOR STRUGGLING READERS

Comprehension Support As students read, have them use the Questioning the Author strategy to analyze the text. Focus on pages 963–964, and provide prompt questions such as these:

- What are the authors trying to say?
- What do the authors mean when they say that the experience was "a slap in the face you were powerless to challenge"? (line 323)

BEST PRACTICES TOOLKIT—Transparency
Questioning the Author p. D19

FOR ENGLISH LANGUAGE LEARNERS

Language Coach   COMMON CORE   RI 4

Multiple-Meaning Words *Answer: The verb meaning of* maroon *is used. The word uses a verb ending, -ed, and the context makes it clear that it means "stranded" or "isolated."* Point out "left" in line 260 as another multiple meaning word. *Left* can be an adjective related to direction or a side of the body, or it can be a verb, the past tense of *leave.* How is the word used in line 260?

water. Down the center of the room twelve toilet bowls were arranged in six pairs, back to back, with no partitions. My mother was a very modest person, and this was going to be agony for her, sitting down in public, among strangers.

One old woman had already solved the problem for herself by dragging in a large cardboard carton. She set it up around one of the bowls, like a three-sided screen. OXYDOL was printed in large black letters down the front. I remember this well, because that was the soap we were issued for laundry; later on, the smell of it would **permeate** these rooms. The upended carton was about four feet high. The old woman behind it wasn't much taller. When she stood, only her head showed over the top.

She was about Granny's age. With great effort she was trying to fold the sides of the screen together. Mama happened to be at the head of the line now. As she approached the vacant bowl, she and the old woman bowed to each other from the waist. Mama then moved to help her with the carton, and the old woman said very graciously, in Japanese, "Would you like to use it?"

Happily, gratefully, Mama bowed again and said, *"Arigato"* (Thank you). *"Arigato gozaimas"* (Thank you very much). "I will return it to your barracks."

"Oh, no. It is not necessary. I will be glad to wait."

The old woman unfolded one side of the cardboard, while Mama opened the other; then she bowed again and scurried out the door.

Those big cartons were a common sight in the spring of 1942. Eventually sturdier partitions appeared, one or two at a time. The first were built of scrap lumber. Word would get around that Block such and such had partitions now, and Mama and my older sisters would walk halfway across the camp to use them. Even after every latrine in camp was screened, this quest for privacy continued. Many would wait in line at night. Ironically, because of this, midnight was often the most crowded time of all. ◆

Like so many of the women there, Mama never did get used to the latrines. It was a humiliation she just learned to endure: *shikata ga nai*, this cannot be helped. She would quickly **subordinate** her own desires to those of the family or the community, because she knew cooperation was the only way to survive. At the same time, she placed a high premium on personal privacy, respected it in others and insisted upon it for herself. Almost everyone at Manzanar had inherited this pair of traits from the generations before them who had learned to live in a small, crowded country like Japan. Because of the first, they were able to take a desolate stretch of wasteland and gradually make it livable. But the entire situation there, especially in the beginning—the packed sleeping quarters, the communal mess halls, the open toilets—all this was an open insult to that other, private self, a slap in the face you were powerless to challenge. ∾

290

300

310

320

permeate (pûr'mē-āt')
v. to spread or flow throughout

◆ GRAMMAR AND STYLE
Reread lines 305–311. Notice how the authors use a variety of **simple**, **complex**, and **compound-complex sentences** to add rhythm and interest to their writing.

subordinate
(sə-bôr'dn-āt') *v.* to lower in rank or importance

④ Targeted Passage

GRAMMAR AND STYLE

COMMON CORE L 1b

Analyze Sentence Structure Point out to students that a series of simple sentences often creates a choppy style. Combining simple sentences makes writing sound smoother and more natural. To demonstrate, first review sentence structures, and then invite students to examine lines 22–29, 109–115, and 162–170, identifying the types of sentences used. Discuss how variety improves rhythm and interest.

VOCABULARY

COMMON CORE L 4

OWN THE WORD

- **permeate:** Have students use *permeate* in sentences to demonstrate their understanding of the word.

- **subordinate:** Have students complete this sentence: Mama would *subordinate* her own desires to those of family or community because. . . .

SELECTION WRAP–UP

READ WITH A PURPOSE Now that students have finished reading the selection, ask: What was the Wakatsuki family's overall attitude during their stay at Manzanar? *Possible answer: They mostly kept a positive attitude and made the best of the situation, enduring the humiliation and maintaining a sense of family and community.*

★ **CRITIQUE** Ask students to evaluate how effectively the authors conveyed the experience of living in an internment camp.

DIFFERENTIATED INSTRUCTION

FOR STRUGGLING READERS

④ **Targeted Passage** [Lines 312–323]

This passage summarizes how the internees coped with the difficulties of the camp.

- How did Mama feel about the latrines? (lines 312–314)

- Why do the authors use the phrase *shikata ga nai* to describe Mama's reaction to the humiliation she experienced at Manzanar? (lines 312–320)

- How did Japanese Americans learn to live in small, crowded conditions? (lines 317–320)

FOR RELUCTANT READERS

Connect Students may know of family members, friends, or others who were held in internment or concentration camps during World War II. Hold a class discussion about the impact this treatment had and may continue to have on individuals, families, communities, and societies.

Comprehension

1. **Recall** Why were the Wakatsukis sent to Manzanar?

2. **Recall** What kind of housing were they given?

3. **Recall** Why did Mama have to borrow the cardboard box?

4. **Summarize** How did the Wakatsukis and other Japanese Americans improve conditions at the camp?

Text Analysis

● 5. **Examine Monitoring Strategies** Review the chart you created as you read. Identify the strategy that you used most often to monitor your comprehension, and discuss why it was helpful.

● 6. **Identify Cultural Characteristics** What did you learn about Japanese beliefs, values, and customs as you read the memoir? Cite examples.

7. **Analyze Character Traits** What traits helped Jeanne and her siblings adjust to life at Manzanar? Cite evidence from the text to support your answer.

8. **Analyze Cause and Effect** The people in charge of Manzanar knew little about Japanese culture. How did their lack of knowledge affect conditions in the camp? Provide examples to support your answer.

9. **Compare Texts** Both Elie Wiesel and Jeanne Wakatsuki Houston were treated unjustly by their governments. Use a graphic organizer like the one shown to compare and contrast their experiences.

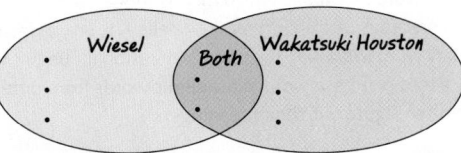

10. **Draw Conclusions** In the foreword to *Farewell to Manzanar*, Jeanne Wakatsuki Houston says, "It has taken me 25 years to reach the point where I could talk openly about Manzanar." Why might it have taken her so long to be able to discuss her experience?

Text Criticism

11. **Historical Context** In your opinion, could a forced internment, like the one experienced by the Wakatsuki family, happen in the United States today? Explain why or why not.

> **What if your government declared you the ENEMY?**
>
> Which rights would you be willing to give up during a time of national crisis?

COMMON CORE

RI 1 Cite textual evidence to support inferences drawn from the text. **RI 6** Determine an author's point of view or purpose in a text.

Practice and Apply

For preliminary support of post-reading questions, use these copy masters:

R RESOURCE MANAGER—Copy Masters
Reading Check p. 50
Cultural Characteristics p. 43
Question Support p. 51

Additional selection questions are provided for teachers on page 37.

ANSWERS

Comprehension

1. *The Wakatsukis were sent to Manzanar because the U.S. government isolated Japanese Americans in internment camps out of fear that they would threaten the war effort (lines 3–6).*

2. *They were housed in flimsy barracks of tarpaper-covered wood (lines 104–105).*

3. *Mama borrowed the box to gain privacy while using the latrine (lines 285–301).*

4. *They covered openings that let in wind and sand (lines 174–176), adapted army clothing (lines 239–243), and created partitions for privacy (lines 116–117, 288–290).*

Text Analysis

Possible answers:

COMMON CORE RI 1 RI 6

5. ● **COMMON CORE FOCUS** *Monitor It was most helpful to read slowly, to reread, or to visualize the reading material.*

6. ● **COMMON CORE FOCUS** *Cultural Characteristics The excerpt referenced: accepting difficulty without complaint (lines 20–21), courtesy despite one's true feelings, eating rice with savory foods (lines 94–97), valuing personal privacy (line 316).*

7. *They kept their senses of humor, helped one another, and worked to improve their surroundings (lines 150–190).*

8. *Administrators' ignorance of Japanese food preferences led to unappetizing meals (lines 88–101). Inattention to the Japanese value on personal privacy led to humiliating open latrines (lines 281–287).*

9. *Both Wiesel and Wakatsuki were held in camps because of their ethnicity. Both were assigned numbers and endured cold and lack of privacy, but Wiesel's conditions were much worse. He had to do heavy labor and, with his father, faced constant threat of death in the gas chamber. Wakatsuki was*

---

separated only from her father, and she and her family were not threatened with death.

10. *It might have taken Wakatsuki so long to discuss her experiences at Manzanar because the memories were humiliating or painful. She may also have thought that non–Japanese Americans did not want to hear her story or would not believe her account of what happened.*

Text Criticism

Possible answer:

11. *No, a forced internment could not happen because the country is now more sensitive to civil rights issues. Yes, a forced internment could happen in response to war or terrorism.*

> **What if your government declared you the ENEMY?** Students should consider the rights they enjoy as United States citizens, such as the right to free speech and the right to privacy. Rights are different than privileges, such as having a driver's license.

ANSWERS

Vocabulary in Context

▲ VOCABULARY PRACTICE

1. *false*
2. *false*
3. *true*
4. *true*
5. *false*

 **RESOURCE MANAGER—Copy Master**
Vocabulary Practice p. 48

ACADEMIC VOCABULARY IN WRITING

Possible answer: We must first of all acknowledge that the forced internment was unjust. By sending entire communities into relocation centers, the government took on the role of the oppressor. Although the policy may have seemed justified at the time, from a contemporary point of view such treatment seems immoral and undeserved.

VOCABULARY STRATEGY: THE PREFIX *in-*

COMMON CORE L 4c

- Clarify that the prefix *in-* and its spelling variants do not always mean "not." They can also mean "into, within, on, toward," as in *incline.*

- Suggest that students remove the prefix and then see if a complete word remains. If so, the prefix in that word probably means "not."

Possible answers:

1. *inconsiderate—not thoughtful; incompetent—not qualified or capable*

2. *insensitive—unfeeling; inattentive—not noticing*

3. *illiterate—unable to read or write; illogical—not reasonable*

4. *impartial—not biased; immortal—undying*

5. *irresponsible—not showing responsibility; irreversible—unable to be changed back*

 **RESOURCE MANAGER—Copy Master**
Vocabulary Strategy p. 49

Interactive Vocabulary

Keywords direct students to a **WordSharp** tutorial on **thinkcentral.com** or to other types of vocabulary practice and review.

Vocabulary in Context

▲ VOCABULARY PRACTICE

Decide whether each statement is true or false.

1. Something **inevitable** can be easily avoided.
2. A person who displays sound reasoning and judgment is **irrational.**
3. The stench of garbage can **permeate** the room.
4. A letter that talks of evil to come can be described as **sinister.**
5. To **subordinate** your feelings is to share them openly with others.

WORD LIST
inevitable
irrational
permeate
sinister
subordinate

ACADEMIC VOCABULARY IN WRITING

- acknowledge   - community   - contemporary   - culture   - role

What might a **contemporary** politician say if asked about the forced interment of Japanese Americans during World War II? Write a short statement from the politician's point of view in which you **acknowledge** and evaluate what happened. Use at least two Academic Vocabulary words in your response.

VOCABULARY STRATEGY: THE PREFIX *in-*

In- at the beginning of a word may be a Latin prefix meaning "not," as in the vocabulary word *inevitable*, which means "not evitable (avoidable)." When the prefix *in-* precedes certain letters, it is spelled *il-*, *im-*, or *ir-*. For example, the vocabulary word *irrational*, meaning "not rational," begins with *ir-*. If you can identify a root or a base word in academic words from different content areas, you can often figure out their meanings.

PRACTICE Use a dictionary or glossary to help you find two words in each academic vocabulary group that contain a prefix meaning "not." Then write a short definition of each word.

1. inconsiderate, incentive, incompetent
2. insensitive, inattentive, indulge
3. illiterate, illogical, illuminate
4. imaginary, impartial, immortal
5. irresponsible, irritable, irreversible

COMMON CORE

L 4c Consult reference materials to determine or clarify a word's precise meaning or its etymology.

Interactive Vocabulary
THINK central
Go to **thinkcentral.com.**
KEYWORD: HML10-966

DIFFERENTIATED INSTRUCTION

FOR ENGLISH LANGUAGE LEARNERS

Vocabulary: Multiple-Meaning Words Point out that the word *subordinate* can be used as a verb, an adjective, or a noun. Present these examples, and explain that the pronunciation changes depending on the part of speech:

- He is the director's subordinate.

- We subordinate our own personal wishes when we work in a group.

- The nurse's wishes were subordinate to the doctor's instructions.

FOR ADVANCED LEARNERS/PRE-AP

Connotations Note that most of the words in the vocabulary list have a negative connotation. Remind students, however, that the Wakatsuki family had a positive attitude. Challenge students to use each word in a positive, uplifting sentence that draws on content from the memoir. *Example: Using tin can lids, Ray and Kiyo made a game of stopping the dust that permeated the cabin.*

Language

◆ **GRAMMAR AND STYLE:** Vary Sentence Structure

Review the **Grammar and Style** note on page 964. To improve the cadence of your writing, be sure to employ a variety of sentence structures. A **simple** sentence consists of one independent clause and no subordinate clauses. A **compound** sentence consists of two or more independent clauses joined together. A **complex** sentence consists of one independent clause and one or more subordinate clauses. A **compound-complex** sentence consists of two or more independent clauses and one or more subordinate clauses. In the following example, notice how the writers use a variety of simple, complex, and compound-complex sentences to create an effective description.

> *I remember this well, because that was the soap we were issued for laundry; later on, the smell of it would permeate these rooms. The upended carton was about four feet high. The old woman behind it wasn't much taller. When she stood, only her head showed over the top.* (lines 290–294)

Notice how the revisions in blue relieve the monotony of this first draft by changing simple sentences to complex and compound-complex sentences.

> **STUDENT MODEL**
>
> *Although*
> ~~T~~he Japanese Americans in the camps have done nothing wrong, ~~Yet~~
>
> they receive worse treatment than most criminals. They live in drafty
> *, and*
> barracks. ~~T~~hey must use filthy latrines. *that* ~~O~~ften ~~the latrines~~ do not work.

READING-WRITING CONNECTION

YOUR TURN

Enhance your understanding of the selection from *Farewell to Manzanar* by responding to this prompt. Then use the **revising tip** to improve your writing.

WRITING PROMPT	REVISING TIP
Extended Constructed Response: Editorial Suppose that you worked for a newspaper during World War II. Write a **three-to-five-paragraph editorial** about the government's policy of interning "enemy" Japanese Americans. Be sure to consider your purpose, your 1940s audience, and the context of the war when organizing your argument.	Review your response. Have you used a variety of sentence structures? If not, revise to include ▶ subordinate clauses to create a mix of simple, complex, and compound-complex sentences.

Interactive Revision
THINK central
Go to **thinkcentral.com**.
KEYWORD: HML10-967

Language

COMMON CORE **L 1b, W 4**

◆ **GRAMMAR AND STYLE**

- After students examine the student model, review sentence structures. (For more on sentence structure, see **Grammar Handbook**, p. R63.)

- Write these simple sentences on the board. Have students combine sentences to make the ideas flow with a smoother rhythm.

> *Many of us at Manzanar had few clothes. Although ~~T~~the camp gave us army clothes~~.~~, ~~T~~they were too big~~.~~ ~~They~~ and did not fit us. Some of the women at the camp were seamstresses. They fixed the clothes~~.~~ by ~~They~~ cutting and seweding them ~~army clothes~~. ~~We got~~ into new clothes~~.~~ ~~The new clothes~~ that were fashionable~~.~~ ~~They~~ and fit us well.*

R RESOURCE MANAGER—Copy Master
Grammar and Style p. 30

READING-WRITING CONNECTION

- Explain that during World War II, many Americans supported the policy of interning Japanese Americans. Students should give thoughtful reasons for their position that might have persuaded people at the time.

>
> **Writing Online**
> THINK central
>
> The following tools are available online at **thinkcentral.com** and on *WriteSmart* CD-ROM:
> - **Interactive Graphic Organizers**
> - **Interactive Student Models**
> - **Interactive Revision Lessons**
> For additional grammar instruction, see **GrammarNotes** on **thinkcentral.com**.
>

FOR STRUGGLING WRITERS

- Limit essays to three paragraphs.

- Remind students that an editorial is persuasive writing. It requires a strong opinion statement and several persuasive facts and examples to support the opinion.

- Have students work in small groups to brainstorm supporting evidence for positions for or against the policy.

Assess and Reteach

Assess

DIAGNOSTIC AND SELECTION TESTS
Selection Test A pp. 271–272
Selection Test B/C pp. 273–274

Interactive Selection Test on **thinkcentral.com**

Reteach

Level Up Online Tutorials on **thinkcentral.com**

Reteaching Worksheets on **thinkcentral.com**
Reading Lesson 2: Monitoring

Focus and Motivate

SUMMARY

The widow of Dr. Martin Luther King, Jr. shares her memory of the beginning of the 1955 bus boycott in Montgomery, Alabama. She recalls the anxiety King felt as he took on the leadership of the boycott and the speech he gave that led that city's African Americans toward a peaceful protest.

How can we CHANGE society?

Read the question aloud. Then draw students' attention to the image of the war protester. Elicit suggestions about how the man pictured is attempting to change society. Use students' comments about the photograph to begin the *DISCUSS* activity.

Selection Resources

Montgomery Boycott

Memoir by Coretta Scott King

HISTORY. Video link at thinkcentral.com

How can we CHANGE society?

You don't have to be rich or powerful to change society. In "Montgomery Boycott," Coretta Scott King describes how a major triumph in the civil rights movement started when a seamstress refused to give up her seat on a bus.

DISCUSS Think of something you would like to change in your community. For example, you might see a need for more parks or afterschool programs. With a classmate, discuss specific actions you could take to help make this change.

968

See resources on the **Teacher One Stop DVD-ROM** *and on* **thinkcentral.com**.

HISTORY. Video link at thinkcentral.com

 RESOURCE MANAGER UNIT 9
Plan and Teach, pp. 55–62
Summary, pp. 63–64†‡*
Text Analysis and Reading
   Skill, pp. 65–68†*
Vocabulary, pp. 69–71*

DIAGNOSTIC AND SELECTION TESTS
Selection Tests, pp. 275–278

 BEST PRACTICES TOOLKIT
Word Squares, p. E10
Read Aloud/Think Aloud, p. A34
Character Traits and Textual Evidence, p. D6

TECHNOLOGY
 Teacher One Stop DVD-ROM
⦿ **Student One Stop DVD-ROM**
⦿ **GrammarNotes DVD-ROM**
⦿ **ExamView Test Generator** on the **Teacher One Stop**

---

* Resources for Differentiation   † Also in Spanish   ‡ In Haitian Creole and Vietnamese

TEXT ANALYSIS: HISTORICAL EVENTS IN MEMOIRS

Memoirs often contain information about historical events in which the writer was involved. For example, in "Montgomery Boycott," Coretta Scott King shares her memory of the events that sparked the 1955 bus boycott in Montgomery, Alabama. While reading a memoir such as King's, you can gain a new perspective on a historical event as well as learn in-depth information about it.

As you read, look for statements that convey information about the Montgomery bus boycott, the events leading up to it, and Dr. Martin Luther King, Jr.'s, involvement.

READING SKILL: DISTINGUISH FACT FROM OPINION

Memoirs can offer an intimate view of the past through a mixture of facts and opinions. A **fact** is a statement that can be verified using a reliable source, such as an encyclopedia. An **opinion** is a personal belief that cannot be proved. King often expresses opinions when she uses adjectives to describe people or historical circumstances.

As you read, use a chart like this one to identify important facts and the opinions of King or her husband. Underline parts of opinion statements that cannot be proved.

Facts	Opinions
"…in March 1955,… fifteen-year-old Claudette Colvin refused to give up her seat to a white passenger."	"Of all the facets of segregation in Montgomery, the most degrading were the rules of the Montgomery City Bus Lines."

▲ VOCABULARY IN CONTEXT

King uses the following boldfaced words to describe a crucial event in the civil rights movement. Figure out the meaning of each word from the context of the phrase. Record your answers in your *Reader/Writer Notebook*.

1. employees humiliated by **degrading** work conditions
2. a **boycott** of the company until our demands are met
3. a clever **tactic** to get what they want
4. angry members urging a more **militant** protest
5. ending the **perpetuation** of injustice
6. authorities using **coercion** to control people

 Complete the activities in your **Reader/Writer Notebook**.

Meet the Author

Coretta Scott King
1927–2006

Civil Rights Champion
As a child in Alabama, Coretta Scott had to walk five miles a day to a one-room schoolhouse while white children rode past her on a school bus. That experience and others made her determined to struggle for racial equality. She worked fearlessly with her husband, Dr. Martin Luther King, Jr., during his leadership of the civil rights movement, refusing to be intimidated after the 1956 bombing of their home. After her husband's assassination in 1968, she remained a tireless champion in the struggle for racial justice, most notably as founder of the Martin Luther King Jr. Center for Nonviolent Social Change in Atlanta, Georgia. "Montgomery Boycott" is taken from her book *My Life with Martin Luther King, Jr.*, which she wrote shortly after his death.

BACKGROUND TO THE MEMOIR

The Civil Rights Movement
Prior to 1954, many states, especially in the South, had laws to ensure segregation, the complete separation of the races in public places. After World War II, however, opponents of these laws began to challenge their legality. In 1954, the Supreme Court ruled that it was unconstitutional to force whites and blacks to attend separate schools. Soon afterward, African Americans in Montgomery, Alabama, began the bus boycott that is the subject of this selection. The Montgomery boycott, which lasted for 381 days, brought about an end to segregation on public buses.

Author Online THINK central
Go to **thinkcentral.com**.
KEYWORD: HML10-969

969

TEXT ANALYSIS
COMMON CORE
RI 6

● *Model the Skill:* HISTORICAL EVENTS IN MEMOIRS

To model how to understand historical events in memoirs, share this example:

> I joined the boycott, but it meant I had to leave home an hour earlier to get to work. I'd heard Reverend King preach about it, and I knew I had to take part.

Point out that the passage shows that the speaker participated in the Montgomery bus boycott.

GUIDED PRACTICE Ask students what kind of information this writer might be able to provide about the historical event.

READING SKILL
COMMON CORE
RI 1
RI 4

■ *Model the Skill:* DISTINGUISH FACT FROM OPINION

To model how to distinguish fact from opinion, read aloud these statements, and identify which statement is a fact and why:

1. The boycott lasted 381 days.
2. The boycott was the most exciting event in the civil rights movement.

Explain to students that statement 1 is a fact because it can be verified.

GUIDED PRACTICE Have students explain why statement 2 is an opinion be verified.

R RESOURCE MANAGER—Copy Master
Distinguish Fact from Opinion p. 67

VOCABULARY SKILL
COMMON CORE
L 4

▲ VOCABULARY IN CONTEXT

DIAGNOSE WORD KNOWLEDGE Have all students complete Vocabulary in Context. Compare their answers to the following definitions:

boycott (boi′kŏt′) *n.* a form of protest in which a group stops using a specific service or product in order to force a change
coercion (kō-ûr′zhən) *n.* the act of compelling by force or authority

degrading (dĭ-grā′dĭng) *adj.* tending or intended to cause dishonor or disgrace
militant (mĭl′ĭ-tənt) *adj.* aggressive or combative
perpetuation (pər-pĕch′oō-ā′shən) *n.* the act of continuing or prolonging something
tactic (tăk′tĭk) *n.* a planned action or maneuver to reach a certain goal

PRETEACH VOCABULARY Use the following copy master to help students predict the meaning of each boldfaced word.

R RESOURCE MANAGER—Copy Master
Vocabulary Study p. 69

1. Read item 1 aloud, emphasizing *boycott*.
2. Point out the phrase "choosing not to ride." Elicit possible meanings for *boycott*, such as "protest."
3. Have students record their predictions.
4. Repeat the procedure for items 2–6.

READ WITH A PURPOSE

Help students set a purpose for reading. Tell students to look for the ways that Dr. King affected the members of the Civil Rights movement.

TEXT ANALYSIS
COMMON CORE
RI 6

Ⓐ *Model the Skill:* HISTORICAL EVENTS

Model for students how to understand historical events. Point out that many reasons for the Montgomery boycott are included in lines 1–17. Two of the reasons are in lines 3–5: "it [the bus lines] treated them [blacks] like cattle" and "the first seats... were reserved for whites." Help students understand other information in lines 1–17 by asking them these questions:

• How would you expect African-American riders to feel in response to the way they were treated on buses?

• What options do you think African Americans would have had for fighting back?

Possible answer: This information helps readers understand the motivation for the boycott: African Americans were forced to give up their seats to white people (lines 7–9), buses sometimes drove off without blacks after they paid their fare (lines 10–12), and white bus drivers called them insulting names (lines 14–15). These details convey how abusive the bus system was and help readers understand why change was needed.

Montgomery
BOYCOTT

Coretta Scott King

Of all the facets of segregation in Montgomery, the most **degrading** were the rules of the Montgomery City Bus Lines. This northern-owned corporation outdid the South itself. Although seventy percent of its passengers were black, it treated them like cattle—worse than that, for nobody insults a cow. The first seats on all buses were reserved for whites. Even if they were unoccupied and the rear seats crowded, blacks would have to stand at the back in case some whites might get aboard; and if the front seats happened to be occupied and more white people boarded the bus, black people seated in the rear were forced to get up and give them their seats. Furthermore—and I don't think
10 northerners ever realized this—blacks had to pay their fares at the front of the bus, get off, and walk to the rear door to board again. Sometimes the bus would drive off without them after they had paid their fare. This would happen to elderly people or pregnant women, in bad weather or good, and was considered a joke by the drivers. Frequently the white bus drivers abused their passengers, calling them . . . black cows, or black apes. Imagine what it was like, for example, for a black man to get on a bus with his son and be subjected to such treatment. Ⓐ

There had been one incident in March 1955, when fifteen-year-old Claudette Colvin refused to give up her seat to a white passenger. The high
20 school girl was handcuffed and carted off to the police station. At that time Martin served on a committee to protest to the city and bus-company officials. The committee was received politely—and nothing was done.

The fuel that finally made that slow-burning fire blaze up was an almost routine incident. On December 1, 1955, Mrs. Rosa Parks, a forty-two-year-old seamstress whom my husband aptly described as "a charming person with a

degrading (dĭ-grā′dĭng) *adj.* tending or intended to cause dishonor or disgrace

① Targeted Passage

Ⓐ HISTORICAL EVENTS
What information in lines 1–17 helps you understand the motivation for the boycott?

Analyze Visuals ▶
What impression of Dr. Martin Luther King, Jr., do you get from this photograph?

VOCABULARY
COMMON CORE
L 4

OWN THE WORD

degrading: Ask students to explain what the most *degrading* facets of segregation were, according to the narrator. *Possible answer: The rules of the Montgomery City Bus Lines were the most* degrading *since they resulted in blacks being humiliated, insulted, and treated as inferior.*

DIFFERENTIATED INSTRUCTION

FOR ENGLISH LANGUAGE LEARNERS

Options for Reading Invite and answer any specific questions students have about the Background on page 969. Then have students read one section at a time and use follow-up questions to assess their comprehension.

FOR STRUGGLING READERS

Use one or more Targeted Passages (pp. 970, 972, 975, 977) to ensure that students focus on key ideas, concepts, and skills. Targeted Passages are also good for English learners.

① Targeted Passage [Lines 1–17]

This passage describes the segregation enforced by the bus company and implicitly approved of by the city of Montgomery.

BACKGROUND

Rosa Parks The woman who became the spark for the Montgomery bus boycott was not just a tired seamstress on her way home from work. Rosa Parks (1913–2005) was a community leader who held an important position with the Montgomery chapter of the NAACP (National Association for the Advancement of Colored People), a prominent civil rights group. By the time of her famous refusal to give up her seat on the bus, she had already had a few "incidents" with bus drivers, as had many other African-American bus riders in Montgomery. Parks was not the first person to be arrested for resisting orders to give up her seat to a white rider, but the civil rights movement had been waiting for someone like her, a community leader with a strong character, who would be able to withstand the pressure, scrutiny, and even death threats she would receive as the struggle against segregated busing progressed.

Analyze Visuals

Possible answer: *The photograph gives the impression that King is a thoughtful, serious man.*

- Who made up the majority of the bus passengers? (line 3)
- Where did the bus company make African Americans ride? (lines 4–9)
- How were white people treated? (lines 4–9)
- Where did African Americans board the bus? (lines 10–11)
- How were African Americans often treated by bus drivers? (lines 14–15)

FOR ADVANCED LEARNERS/PRE–AP

Research Rosa Parks Invite students to research the life of Rosa Parks. As a group, have students prepare a bulletin board display that shows a timeline of Parks's life, a summary of her civil rights activities, and any relevant visuals to illustrate her life.

Analyze Visuals

Activity From the photograph, what can you tell about Rosa Parks? How do these details reflect her actions as described in the memoir? *Possible answer: She is neat and respectful. She is not upset or frightened. She does not appear powerless or cowed by the white policeman. In the memoir Parks is described not as a revolutionary but as a calm person whose "cup had run over" (line 31), meaning that she was fed up with being treated badly.*

REVISIT THE BIG QUESTION

How can we
CHANGE society?

Discuss Based on lines 30–35, did Rosa Parks intend to change society when she refused to give up her seat? Why do you think she allowed herself to get arrested? *Possible answer: Parks would have known that refusing to give up her seat meant that she would be arrested, but she probably was not consciously planning the scope of change that she set in motion.*

READING SKILL   COMMON CORE   RI 1   RI 4

B DISTINGUISH FACT FROM OPINION

Possible answer: These details are facts: Nixon was from Alabama (line 36); he was a Pullman porter who had been active in the Brotherhood of Sleeping Car Porters and in civil rights activities (lines 36–38); phones began ringing all over the black section of the city (lines 40–41); the Women's Political Council suggested a one-day boycott of the buses (lines 41–42); Nixon agreed to organize it (line 42). These details are opinions: Nixon was fiery (line 36); he had had enough, and it seemed that every African American in Montgomery had had enough (lines 38–39); the response was "spontaneous combustion" (lines 39–40); Nixon was courageous (line 42).

VOCABULARY   COMMON CORE   L 4

OWN THE WORD

boycott: Ask students use *boycott* in sentences to show their understanding of the word.

Rosa Parks being fingerprinted by a Montgomery sheriff after she refused to give up her seat on a bus

radiant personality," boarded a bus to go home after a long day working and shopping. The bus was crowded, and Mrs. Parks found a seat at the beginning of the black section. At the next stop more whites got on. The driver ordered Mrs. Parks to give her seat to a white man who boarded; this meant that she
30 would have to stand all the way home. Rosa Parks was not in a revolutionary frame of mind. She had not planned to do what she did. Her cup had run over. As she said later, "I was just plain tired, and my feet hurt." So she sat there, refusing to get up. The driver called a policeman, who arrested her and took her to the courthouse. From there Mrs. Parks called E. D. Nixon, who came down and signed a bail bond for her.

    Mr. Nixon was a fiery Alabamian. He was a Pullman porter who had been active in A. Philip Randolph's Brotherhood of Sleeping Car Porters,[1] and in civil rights activities. Suddenly he also had had enough; suddenly, it seemed, almost every African American in Montgomery had had enough. It was
40 spontaneous combustion.[2] Phones began ringing all over the black section of the city. The Women's Political Council suggested a one-day **boycott** of the buses as a protest. E. D. Nixon courageously agreed to organize it.

 **Targeted Passage**

boycott (boi′kŏt′) *n.* a form of protest in which a group stops using a specific service or product in order to force a change

B DISTINGUISH FACT FROM OPINION

Which details in lines 36–42 are factual, and which ones are opinion?

---

1. **Pullman ... Sleeping Car Porters:** Pullman porters were railroad employees who served passengers on Pullman sleeping cars, which had seats that could be converted into beds. The Brotherhood of Sleeping Car Porters was the first successful black labor union.

2. **spontaneous combustion** (spŏn-tā′nē-əs kəm-bŭs′chən): literally, the situation that occurs when something bursts into flames on its own, without the addition of heat from an outside source.

972   UNIT 9: HISTORY, CULTURE, AND THE AUTHOR

DIFFERENTIATED INSTRUCTION

FOR STRUGGLING READERS

Targeted Passage [Lines 27–40]

This passage gives the details of Rosa Parks's arrest.

- Where was Parks sitting on the bus? (lines 27–28)

- Why did the bus driver tell her to get up? (lines 28–29)

- What happened as a result of her refusal? (lines 33–34)

- Who was E. D. Nixon? (lines 34–38)

- How did Nixon and the entire African-American community respond? (lines 38–42)

FOR ENGLISH LANGUAGE LEARNERS

Culture: Clarify Point out the words "bail bond" in line 35: "From there Mrs. Parks called E. D. Nixon, who came down and signed a bail bond for her." Clarify that a bail bond is a written promise that the arrested person will appear in court when summoned. Usually, money or some other form of security must be paid to guarantee the promise.

The first we knew about it was when Mr. Nixon called my husband early in the morning of Friday, December 2. He had already talked to Ralph Abernathy.[3] After describing the incident, Mr. Nixon said, "We have taken this type of thing too long. I feel the time has come to boycott the buses. It's the only way to make the white folks see that we will not take this sort of thing any longer."

Martin agreed with him and offered the Dexter Avenue Church as a meeting place. After much telephoning, a meeting of black ministers and civic leaders
50 was arranged for that evening. Martin said later that as he approached his church Friday evening, he was nervously wondering how many leaders would really turn up. To his delight, Martin found over forty people, representing every segment of African-American life, crowded into the large meeting room at Dexter. There were doctors, lawyers, businessmen, federal-government employees, union leaders, and a great many ministers. The latter were particularly welcome, not only because of their influence, but because it meant that they were beginning to accept Martin's view that "religion deals with both heaven and earth. . . . Any religion that professes to be concerned with the souls of men and is not concerned with the slums that doom them, the economic
60 conditions that strangle them, and the social conditions that cripple them, is dry-as-dust religion." From that very first step, the Christian ministry provided the leadership of our struggle, as Christian ideals were its source. **G**

Martin told me after he got home that the meeting was almost wrecked because questions or suggestions from the floor were cut off. However, after a stormy session, one thing was clear: however much they differed on details, everyone was unanimously for a boycott. It was set for Monday, December 5. Committees were organized; all the ministers present promised to urge their congregations to take part. Several thousand leaflets were printed on the church mimeograph machine, describing the reasons for the boycott and urging all
70 blacks not to ride buses "to work, to town, to school, or anyplace on Monday, December 5." Everyone was asked to come to a mass meeting at the Holt Street Baptist Church on Monday evening for further instructions. The Reverend A. W. Wilson had offered his church because it was larger than Dexter and more convenient, being in the center of the black district.

Saturday was a busy day for Martin and the other members of the committee. They hustled around town talking with other leaders, arranging with the black-owned taxi companies for special bulk fares and with the owners of private automobiles to get the people to and from work. I could do little to help because Yoki[4] was only two weeks old, and my physician, Dr. W.
80 D. Pettus, who was very careful, advised me to stay in for a month. However, I was kept busy answering the telephone, which rang continuously, and coordinating from that central point the many messages and arrangements.

Our greatest concern was how we were going to reach the fifty thousand black people of Montgomery, no matter how hard we worked. The white press,

G HISTORICAL EVENTS
What disagreement within the African-American community did King need to overcome in order to build an effective movement?

---

3. **Ralph Abernathy** (1926–1990): a minister who became a close colleague of Dr. Martin Luther King, Jr.'s, and an important civil rights leader.

4. **Yoki:** nickname of the Kings' daughter Yolanda.

TEXT ANALYSIS   COMMON CORE
                                                        RI 6

G HISTORICAL EVENTS

Possible answer: To build an effective movement, King needed to overcome the belief that churches should not be politically active (lines 55–61). By doing so, he was able to bring ministers into the movement.

IF STUDENTS NEED HELP . . . Have them complete a before/after chart with answers to these questions:
- How did ministers in Montgomery feel at first about getting involved in politics?
- How did ministers in Montgomery feel about getting involved in politics after hearing Martin Luther King Jr.'s views?

Before	After
They felt that they should not be involved in politics.	

FOR STRUGGLING READERS
Vocabulary Support Hyphenated Adjectives Point out these hyphenated adjectives on this page: *African-American* (line 53), *federal-government* (line 54), *dry-as-dust* (line 61), and *black-owned* (line 77). Explain that the hyphens are used only when the words act as adjectives and come before the noun. Ask students to think of other examples of hyphenated adjectives.

FOR ENGLISH LANGUAGE LEARNERS
Vocabulary Support Use Word Squares to teach these words: *federal* (line 54), *ministry* (line 61), *instructions* (line 72), *coordinating* (line 82), *resources* (line 86), *coherently* (line 125).

🧰 BEST PRACTICES TOOLKIT—Transparency
Word Squares p. E10

Direct students to lines 93–107. Use these
prompts to help students understand King's
interpretation of the morality of the boycott:

Connect Have you or anyone you know
ever participated in a protest or boycott?
If so, what was the reason for the action,
and what was the outcome?

Analyze How does King elaborate on Thoreau's statement "We can no longer lend
our cooperation to an evil system" (lines
103–104)? *Possible answer: King elaborates
on Thoreau's statement with his own statement: "He who accepts evil without protesting against it is really cooperating with it"
(lines 104–105). In other words, if you think
that something is evil, then you must protest
against it; otherwise, you are cooperating
with it.*

Evaluate Do you agree with King's statement? Why or why not? *Students who agree
may say that King's argument is similar to
the idea that if you are a bystander to an act
of racism or bullying and you don't speak up
on behalf of the victim, then your silence is
lending support to the racist or bully. Students
who disagree may argue that ordinary people
can't be expected to protest against every
wrongdoing in the world—and that as long
as they are not actively cooperating with the
"evil," then they are not condoning it.*

OWN THE WORD

tactic: Point out that the Greek word for
tactic is *taktika*, which means "matters
pertaining to arrangement." The *tactics* of an organization refers to how it
arranges the pieces of a plan of action.
Have students make a list of *tactics* that
might be used in a boycott of a company.
*Possible answers: avoiding using the
company's products or services, getting
information about the boycott out to the
general public*

---

in an outraged exposé, spread the word for us in a way that would have been
impossible with only our own resources.

As it happened, a white woman found one of our leaflets, which her black
maid had left in the kitchen. The irate woman immediately telephoned the
newspapers to let the white community know what the blacks were up to. We
90 laughed a lot about this, and Martin later said that we owed them a great debt.

On Sunday morning, from their pulpits, almost every African-American
minister in town urged people to honor the boycott.

Martin came home late Sunday night and began to read the morning paper.
The long articles about the proposed boycott accused the NAACP[5] of planting
Mrs. Parks on the bus—she had been a volunteer secretary for the Montgomery
chapter—and likened the boycott to the **tactics** of the White Citizens Councils.[6]
This upset Martin. That awesome conscience of his began to gnaw at him, and
he wondered if he was doing the right thing. Alone in his study, he struggled
with the question of whether the boycott method was basically unchristian.
100 Certainly it could be used for unethical ends. But, as he said, "We were using
it to give birth to freedom . . . and to urge men to comply with the law of
the land. Our concern was not to put the bus company out of business, but
to put justice in business." He recalled Thoreau's[7] words, "We can no longer
lend our cooperation to an evil system," and he thought, "He who accepts
evil without protesting against it is really cooperating with it." Later Martin
wrote, "From this moment on I conceived of our movement as an act of massive
noncooperation. From then on I rarely used the word 'boycott.'"

Serene after his inner struggle, Martin joined me in our sitting room. We
wanted to get to bed early, but Yoki began crying and the telephone kept
110 ringing. Between interruptions we sat together talking about the prospects for
the success of the protest. We were both filled with doubt. Attempted boycotts
had failed in Montgomery and other cities. Because of changing times and
tempers, this one seemed to have a better chance, but it was still a slender
hope. We finally decided that if the boycott was sixty percent effective we
would be doing all right, and we would be satisfied to have made a good start.

A little after midnight we finally went to bed, but at five-thirty the next
morning we were up and dressed again. The first bus was due at six o'clock at
the bus stop just outside our house. We had coffee and toast in the kitchen;
then I went into the living room to watch. Right on time, the bus came,
120 headlights blazing through the December darkness, all lit up inside. I shouted,
"Martin! Martin, come quickly!" He ran in and stood beside me, his face lit
with excitement. There was not one person on that usually crowded bus!

We stood together waiting for the next bus. It was empty too, and this was

tactic (tăk′tĭk) *n.* a
planned action or
maneuver to reach a
certain goal

---

5. **NAACP:** the National Association for the Advancement of Colored People, a prominent civil
   rights organization.

6. **White Citizens Councils:** groups that formed, first in Mississippi and then throughout the South,
   to resist the 1954 Supreme Court decision to desegregate the schools.

7. **Thoreau** (thə-rō′): Henry David Thoreau (1817–1862), American writer whose famous
   essay "Civil Disobedience" helped inspire the ideas of nonviolent resistance used in the civil
   rights movement.

DIFFERENTIATED INSTRUCTION

FOR STRUGGLING READERS

Concept Support Use the Read Aloud/Think
Aloud strategy to help students understand
King's debt in lines 87–90. Read the paragraph and then "think" aloud: *King said that
he owed the white newspapers a great debt.
I think his debt was that the papers helped his
boycott be successful by publicizing it in the
newspaper.*

 BEST PRACTICES TOOLKIT—Transparency
Read Aloud/Think Aloud p. A34

FOR RELUCTANT READERS

Connect Help students to connect to what
they just read by writing the following
questions on the board: Why did Dr. King
struggle with the idea of the boycott? How
was his struggle resolved? What happened
on the first day of the boycott? Then engage
students in a class discussion about what it
might have been like to have no transportation. Ask students what they would be willing to give up for something they believe in.

African Americans walking to work during the third month of the bus boycott

the most heavily traveled line in the whole city. Bus after empty bus paused at the stop and moved on. We were so excited we could hardly speak coherently. Finally Martin said, "I'm going to take the car and see what's happening other places in the city."

He picked up Ralph Abernathy and they cruised together around the city. Martin told me about it when he got home. Everywhere it was the same—a few
130 white people and maybe one or two blacks in otherwise empty buses. Martin and Ralph saw extraordinary sights—the sidewalks crowded with men and women trudging to work; the students of Alabama State College walking or thumbing rides; taxicabs with people clustered in them. Some of our people rode mules; others went in horse-drawn buggies. But most of them were walking, some making a round-trip of as much as twelve miles. Martin later wrote, "As I watched them I knew that there is nothing more majestic than the determined courage of individuals willing to suffer and sacrifice for their freedom and dignity."

Martin rushed off again at nine o'clock that morning to attend the trial of Mrs. Parks. She was convicted of disobeying the city's segregation ordinance
140 and fined ten dollars and costs. Her young attorney, Fred D. Gray, filed an appeal. It was one of the first clear-cut cases of an African American being convicted of disobeying the segregation laws—usually the charge was disorderly conduct or some such thing.

The leaders of the Movement called a meeting for three o'clock in the afternoon to organize the mass meeting to be held that night. Martin was a bit late, and as he entered the hall, people said to him, "Martin, we have elected you to be our president. Will you accept?"

Fear was an invisible presence at the meeting, along with courage and hope. Proposals were voiced to make the organization, which the leaders decided to
150 call the Montgomery Improvement Association, or MIA, a sort of secret society, because if no names were mentioned it would be safer for the leaders. E. D. Nixon opposed that idea. "We're acting like little boys," he said. "Somebody's name will be known, and if we're afraid, we might just as well fold up right now.

▲ **Analyze Visuals**

What do the facial expressions in the photograph suggest to you?

COMMON CORE RI 4

Language Coach

Informal Language In her memoir, King often uses informal language to narrate events. Reread lines 128–143 and note examples of King's informal language. How does King's choice of words affect the **tone** of the memoir?

③ **Targeted Passage**

Analyze Visuals

Possible answer: The facial expressions suggest that the people are serious and determined.

REVISIT THE BIG QUESTION

How can we
CHANGE society?

Discuss According to lines 128–137, what sacrifices did the African Americans who participated in the Montgomery bus boycott make in an attempt to change their society? ***Possible answer:*** *African Americans who participated in the bus boycott sacrificed time, convenience, and comfort by walking to work and school instead of taking the bus. Those who took cabs also sacrificed money. The boycotters were "willing to suffer and sacrifice" (line 137) to fight racist policies in their society—the city of Montgomery—that were undermining their "freedom and dignity" (line 137).*

FOR STRUGGLING READERS

③ **Targeted Passage** [Lines 128–143]

This passage describes King and Abernathy witnessing the first day of the boycott and also tells of Parks's unusual conviction for disobeying segregation laws.

- What did King and Abernathy see as they drove around the city? (lines 129–135)

- How were people getting where they needed to go without using buses? (lines 132–135)

- What was unusual about Parks's conviction? (lines 141–143)

FOR ENGLISH LANGUAGE LEARNERS

Language Coach   COMMON CORE RI 4

Informal Language *Possible answer:* Examples of informal language include "cruised together," "thumbing rides," "rushed off again," "or some such thing." The informal language makes the tone more conversational and friendly.

RI 1
RI 4

 Model the Skill: DISTINGUISH FACT FROM OPINION

Model for students how to distinguish fact from opinion. Read aloud the opinion statement in line 148, and then ask these questions:

- What were the MIA members afraid of?
- What was Nixon's argument against secrecy?
- What emotion did Nixon's comments probably inspire?

Tell students that the answers to these questions are the evidence to support the opinion statement. Have students add this information to their Reading Skill charts.

Possible answer: *The opinion in line 148—that fear was an invisible presence at the meeting—is supported by the fact that proposals were made to keep the MIA a secret society with no names mentioned (lines 149–151) and the fact that Nixon said they had to decide whether to be "fearless men or scared little boys" (lines 151–155).*

REVISIT THE BIG QUESTION
How can we CHANGE society?

Discuss On the basis of what you have read so far, why do you think King was able to inspire people to take action to change society? ***Possible answer:*** *King had thought about the ethical rationale for the boycott (lines 93–107), about his responsibility as the movement's leader (lines 159–160, 166–167), that he needed to "rouse people to action" (line 171) yet also prevent them from feeling "hate and resentment" (line 172).*

L 4

OWN THE WORD

militant: Tell students that the adjective *militant* and the noun *militia* both refer to soldiers or armies. Ask students to list the kinds of behavior or actions of someone who is *militant*. ***Possible answers:*** *dedicated support for a cause, belligerent, uncompromising*

The white folks are eventually going to find out anyway. We'd better decide now if we are going to be fearless men or scared little boys."

That settled that question. It was also decided that the protest would continue until certain demands were met. Ralph Abernathy was made chairman of the committee to draw up the demands.

Martin came home at six o'clock. He said later that he was nervous about
160 telling me he had accepted the presidency of the protest movement, but he need not have worried, because I sincerely meant what I said when I told him that night: "You know that whatever you do, you have my backing."

Reassured, Martin went to his study. He was to make the main speech at the mass meeting that night. It was now six-thirty and—this was the way it was usually to be—he had only twenty minutes to prepare what he thought might be the most decisive speech of his life. He said afterward that thinking about the responsibility and the reporters and television cameras, he almost panicked. Five minutes wasted and only fifteen minutes left. At that moment he turned to prayer. He asked God "to restore my balance and be with me in a time
170 when I need Your guidance more than ever."

How could he make his speech **militant** enough to rouse people to action and yet devoid of hate and resentment? He was determined to do both.

Martin and Ralph went together to the meeting. When they got within four blocks of the Holt Street Baptist Church, there was an enormous traffic jam. Five thousand people stood outside the church listening to loudspeakers and singing hymns. Inside it was so crowded, Martin told me, the people had to lift Ralph and him above the crowd and pass them from hand to hand over their heads to the platform. The crowd and the singing inspired Martin, and God answered his prayer. Later Martin said, "That night I understood what the older preachers
180 meant when they said, 'Open your mouth and God will speak for you.'"

First the people sang "Onward, Christian Soldiers" in a tremendous wave of five thousand voices. This was followed by a prayer and a reading of the Scriptures. Martin was introduced. People applauded; television lights beat upon him. Without any notes at all he began to speak. Once again he told the story of Mrs. Parks, and rehearsed some of the wrongs black people were suffering. Then he said,

> *But there comes a time when people get tired. We are here this evening to say to those who have mistreated us so long, that we are tired. Tired of being segregated and humiliated; tired of being kicked about by the brutal feet of oppression.*

The audience cheered wildly, and Martin said,

190 > *We have no alternative but to protest. We have been amazingly patient . . . but we come here tonight to be saved from that patience that makes us patient with anything less than freedom and justice.*

Taking up the challenging newspaper comparison with the White Citizens Councils and the Klan,[8] Martin said,

---

8. **Klan:** the Ku Klux Klan, a secret society trying to establish white power and authority by unlawful and violent methods directed against African Americans and other minority groups.

 **DISTINGUISH FACT FROM OPINION**
What factual evidence supports the statement of opinion in line 148?

militant (mĭl′ĭ-tənt) *adj.* aggressive or combative

DIFFERENTIATED INSTRUCTION

FOR STRUGGLING READERS

Comprehension Support: Character To help students understand Dr. Martin Luther King, Jr. more fully, have them complete a Character Traits and Textual Evidence graphic organizer about him. Remind students that a person's behavior can demonstrate beliefs and character traits. Ask volunteers to share details from their work.

 BEST PRACTICES TOOLKIT—Transparency
Character Traits and Textual Evidence p. D6

Character Trait: Contemplative

Quote (p. 975, lines 136–137): "I knew that there is nothing more majestic than the determined courage of individuals . . ."	Explanation: King feels inspired by his followers. He is interested in human nature.
Quote (p. 976, lines 159–160): "He said later that he was nervous about telling me he had accepted the presidency . . ."	Explanation: King knows the presidency will be a big job; he respects his wife's concerns.

Martin Luther King, Jr., speaking at a church in Montgomery

◀ **Analyze Visuals**

How does the photograph reflect the author's description of King's speaking ability?

They are protesting for the __perpetuation__ of injustice in the community; we're protesting for the birth of justice . . . their methods lead to violence and lawlessness. But in our protest there will be no cross-burnings, no white person will be taken from his home by a hooded Negro mob and brutally murdered . . . We will be guided by the highest principles of law and order.

perpetuation
(pər-pĕch′ōō-ā′shən) *n.*
the act of continuing or prolonging something

200 Having roused the audience for militant action, Martin now set limits upon it. His study of nonviolence and his love of Christ informed his words. He said,

No one must be intimidated to keep them from riding the buses. Our method must be persuasion, not __coercion.__ We will only say to the people, "Let your conscience be your guide." . . . Our actions must be guided by the deepest principles of the Christian faith. . . . Once again we must hear the words of Jesus, "Love your enemies. Bless them that curse you. Pray for them that despitefully use you." If we fail to do this, our protest will end up as a meaningless drama on the stage of history and its memory will be shrouded in the ugly garments of shame. . . . We must not become bitter and end up by
210 *hating our white brothers. As Booker T. Washington[9] said, "Let no man pull you so low as to make you hate him."*

coercion (kō-ûr′zhən) *n.*
the act of compelling by force or authority

Finally, Martin said,

If you will protest courageously, and yet with dignity and Christian love, future historians will say, "There lived a great people—a black people—who injected new meaning and dignity into the veins of civilization." This is our challenge and our overwhelming responsibility.

④ Targeted Passage

As Martin finished speaking, the audience rose cheering in exaltation. And in that speech my husband set the keynote and the tempo of the Movement he was to lead, from Montgomery onward. ◖◗

---

9. **Booker T. Washington** (1856–1915): an African-American educator and writer.

Analyze Visuals

Possible answer: The photograph reflects King's speaking ability because it shows a large and attentive audience, suggesting that he could rouse a crowd and energize a movement.

VOCABULARY · COMMON CORE · L 4

OWN THE WORD

- **perpetuation:** Have students complete this sentence: In his speech, King says that the newspaper argues for the *per-petuation* of. . . .
- **coercion:** Have students write sentences using *coercion* correctly.

SELECTION WRAP–UP

READ WITH A PURPOSE Now that students have read the selection, ask: What did Dr. King ask of the protesters? How did he wish them to act? ***Possible answer:*** *He encouraged protesters to act "with dignity and Christian love," "protest courageously," and use persuasion, not coercion.*

★ **CRITIQUE** Ask students what aspect of the memoir they found most effective and why.

INDEPENDENT READING
Recommend *Coretta: The Story of Coretta Scott King* by Octavia Vivian to students wanting to learn more about the author.

FOR STRUGGLING READERS
④ Targeted Passage [Lines 212–219]

This passage summarizes King's message to the protesters.

- In his speech, what qualities does King ask his followers to show in the protest? (line 213)
- How did the audience react to the speech? (line 217)
- Why was the speech important to King, to African Americans, and to the civil rights movement? (lines 217–219)

FOR STRUGGLING READERS
Develop Reading Fluency Model reading Dr. King's speech for students, starting with line 186. Tell students to note how intonation and pacing add impact to the words. Read each section aloud and then reread the passage with students in a choral reading.

Distribute the copy masters and have students work in pairs or groups to practice fluency.

R **RESOURCE MANAGER**—Copy Master
Reading Fluency p. 74

Practice and Apply

For preliminary support of post-reading questions, use these copy masters:

R RESOURCE MANAGER—Copy Masters
Reading Check p. 72
Historical Events in Memoirs p. 65
Question Support p. 73

Additional selection questions are provided for teachers on page 59.

ANSWERS

Comprehension

1. *African Americans had to sit in the back of the bus, give up their seats to whites, and board at the rear after paying in the front.*

2. *Rosa Parks was arrested for refusing to give up her seat to a white person.*

3. *The first day of the boycott was extremely successful. The buses were almost empty.*

4. *King urged them to avoid intimidating others into joining the boycott and to avoid feeling bitterness and hatred toward white people.*

Text Analysis

COMMON CORE RI 4, RI 6

Possible answers:

5. ● **COMMON CORE FOCUS** *Distinguish Fact from Opinion The protesters are presented as angry, courageous, and determined.*

6. ● **COMMON CORE FOCUS** *Historical Events in Memoirs Leadership: involvement of Christian ministers, other leaders from all segments of society (lines 52–62); Strategies: showed that nonviolent tactics guided by Christian ideals could be successful (lines 195–211).*

7. *In a standard historical account, the author would not have mentioned her own concerns, such as her new baby (line 79), or having coffee and toast in the kitchen (line 118). It might not have delved into Dr. King's personal feelings and fears (lines 97–107).*

8. *King was influenced by the values of freedom, justice, and Christian love. He stated that the boycott was to achieve freedom and justice (lines 100–103); he praised the boycotters who were "willing to suffer and sacrifice for their freedom and dignity" (line 137); he urged his supporters not to be coercive, violent, or full of hatred (lines 202–211).*

9. *Both groups were unfairly treated because of racism, but African Americans were not*

Comprehension

1. **Recall** What rules did African Americans have to follow on buses in Montgomery?

2. **Recall** What incident set off the bus boycott?

3. **Recall** How successful was the first day of the boycott?

4. **Summarize** What did Dr. Martin Luther King, Jr., urge his followers to avoid in his speech at the Holt Street Baptist Church?

Text Analysis

5. **Analyze Opinions** Review the chart you created as you read. Both the author and Dr. Martin Luther King, Jr., express opinions about the protesters who participated in the boycott. What character traits of the protesters are emphasized in these opinions?

6. **Examine Historical Events in Memoir** According to the author, how did the Montgomery boycott influence the civil rights movement? Use a chart like the one shown to record your answer.

Aspects of Civil Rights Movement	Influence of Boycott
Leadership	
Strategies	

7. **Analyze Memoir** In what ways might this selection have been different if the author had intended to write a standard historical account instead of a memoir? Be specific.

8. **Draw Conclusions About Leadership** What values influenced King's leadership during the boycott? Cite evidence from the text.

9. **Compare Texts** Compare and contrast the experiences of the African Americans in Montgomery with the experiences of Japanese Americans described in the excerpt from *Farewell to Manzanar*, which begins on page 954. What circumstances might explain the different ways in which these two groups responded to injustice?

Text Criticism

10. **Critical Interpretations** Some reviewers of Coretta Scott King's memoir *My Life with Martin Luther King, Jr.* complained that her portrayal of the civil rights leader is too idealized. Do you think that she should have shown more of her husband's flaws or weaknesses in "Montgomery Boycott"? Explain why or why not.

> **How can we CHANGE society?**
>
> What ordinary people do you know or know of who are working to change society?

COMMON CORE

RI 4 Cite textual evidence to support analysis of what the text says explicitly as well as inferences drawn from the text.
RI 6 Determine an author's point of view or purpose in a text.

---

interned, and anti-Japanese racism existed in the context of a war with Japan. While many Japanese Americans accepted mistreatment, African Americans protested. Japanese Americans may have been unwilling to protest because of cultural attitudes and because they were so outnumbered by whites.

Text Criticism

10. *Some students may say that including her husband's flaws would have given a more realistic picture of King; others may say that it would have diverted attention from his strengths and successes.*

> How can we **CHANGE** society?
> Students might think about causes such as civil rights that their friends and family members are involved in, as well as causes students think are important.

Vocabulary in Context

▲ VOCABULARY PRACTICE

Choose the word that is not related in meaning to the other words in the set.

1. boycott, cooperation, acceptance, participation
2. tactic, strategy, maneuver, hindrance
3. perpetuation, conclusion, cessation, interruption
4. compliant, militant, submissive, passive
5. coercion, compulsion, intimidation, influence
6. humiliating, demeaning, uplifting, degrading

WORD LIST

boycott

coercion

degrading

militant

perpetuation

tactic

ACADEMIC VOCABULARY IN SPEAKING

- acknowledge
- community
- contemporary
- culture
- role

Can an individual play a significant **role** in changing history? Share your response in a discussion, using details from Coretta Scott King's memoir to support your opinions. Use at least one Academic Vocabulary word in your response.

VOCABULARY STRATEGY: THE SUFFIX *-ion*

The suffix *-ion* means "the act, state, or result of." When this suffix is added to a verb, it changes the word to a noun. For example, in the vocabulary word *coercion,* the suffix *-ion* has changed the verb *coerce* into a noun meaning "the act of coercing." Notice that the final *e* in a word is dropped when a suffix that begins with a vowel is added. Sometimes a final consonant in a word is doubled or letters are changed when a suffix is added. If you can identify the root or the base word in a word with the suffix *-ion,* you can often figure out the word's meaning.

PRACTICE Add the suffix *-ion* to each word below, changing the last letter or letters of the base word if necessary. Then write a short definition of each word, referring to a dictionary if necessary.

1. perpetuate
2. conciliate
3. evacuate
4. imitate
5. expand
6. suspect

COMMON CORE

L 4b Identify and correctly use patterns of word changes that indicate different meanings or parts of speech.

Interactive Vocabulary

THINK central

Go to **thinkcentral.com**.
KEYWORD: HML10-979

DIFFERENTIATED INSTRUCTION

FOR ENGLISH LANGUAGE LEARNERS

Vocabulary Activity Point out to students that all the words in the Vocabulary Strategy practice end in *-tion, -sion,* or *-cion.* Ask students to list words from their home language that also have these endings. Do any of the words in the activity have counterparts in students' home language? If so, ask students to generalize to create a rule about these cognates.

FOR ADVANCED LEARNERS/PRE–AP

Vocabulary in Writing Have students write a newspaper article about the Montgomery bus boycott, using as many vocabulary words as possible.

ANSWERS

Vocabulary in Context

▲ VOCABULARY PRACTICE

1. *boycott*
2. *hindrance*
3. *perpetuation*
4. *militant*
5. *influence*
6. *uplifting*

R RESOURCE MANAGER—Copy Master
Vocabulary Practice p. 70

ACADEMIC VOCABULARY IN SPEAKING

Possible answer: *The* role *played by Dr. Martin Luther King, Jr., in* community *outreach helped to motivate people to fight for equal rights.*

VOCABULARY STRATEGY: THE SUFFIX *-ion*

COMMON CORE **L 4b**

- Model the strategy using these words: *frustrate–frustration,* "the result of an impediment to progress"; *segregate–segregation,* "the act of separating"

1. *perpetuation: the state of ongoing action*
2. *conciliation: the act of bringing together in harmony*
3. *evacuation: the act of removing or emptying*
4. *imitation: the act of copying*
5. *expansion: the act of enlarging*
6. *suspicion: doubt, or the act of distrusting*

R RESOURCE MANAGER—Copy Master
Vocabulary Strategy p. 71

THINK central

Interactive Vocabulary

Keywords direct students to a **WordSharp** tutorial on **thinkcentral.com** or to other types of vocabulary practice and review.

Assess and Reteach

Assess

DIAGNOSTIC AND SELECTION TESTS
Selection Test A, B/C pp. 275–278

Interactive Selection Test on **thinkcentral.com**

Reteach

Level Up Online Tutorials on **thinkcentral.com**

Reteacing Worksheets on **thinkcentral.com**

Focus and Motivate

COMMON CORE FOCUS

RI 6 Determine an author's point of view or purpose in a text and analyze how an author uses rhetoric to advance that point of view or purpose. **RI 9** Analyze seminal U.S. documents of historical and literary significance, including how they address related themes and concepts. **W 2** Write explanatory texts to examine and convey complex ideas, concepts, and information through the effective selection, organization, and analysis of content.

SUMMARY

Robert F. Kennedy pays tribute to the death of the great civil rights leader just hours after King's assassination. He shares his great sorrow with the audience of African Americans and implores all Americans to dedicate themselves anew to a peaceful solution to injustice.

What's the Connection?

Use a KWL chart to prepare students for the selection. For the first column, have students recall what they already know about Dr. Martin Luther King, Jr. In the second column, have them write questions about what they want to know. After reading, have students write what they have learned.

BEST PRACTICES TOOLKIT—Transparency
KWL p. A21

Teach

Standards Focus: Analyze Rhetorical Devices

Define the word *rhetoric* as "the art of using words effectively in speaking or writing." Have students consider the rhetorical devices that they feel make an effective speech. Ask:

- What speech have you heard that has been powerful or moving?
- What was it about the speech that made it powerful?

R RESOURCE MANAGER—Copy Master
Analyze Rhetorical Devices p. 83

Reading for Information

A Eulogy for Dr. Martin Luther King, Jr.
Speech

VIDEO TRAILER **THINK**central KEYWORD: HML10-980   *Essential Course of Study* **ECOS**

Use with "Montgomery Boycott," page 970.

COMMON CORE
RI 6 Determine an author's point of view or purpose in a text and analyze how an author uses rhetoric to advance that point of view or purpose. **RI 9** Analyze seminal U.S. documents of historical and literary significance, including how they address related themes and concepts.

What's the Connection?

In "Montgomery Boycott," Coretta Scott King recalls an important event in the civil rights movement that was also a turning point in Martin Luther King, Jr.'s career. Now, in "A Eulogy for Dr. Martin Luther King, Jr.," you will read a moving speech that Robert F. Kennedy delivered on the day of King's assassination.

Standards Focus: Analyze Rhetorical Devices

Rhetorical devices are techniques that allow writers to communicate ideas more effectively. Speeches often contain rhetorical devices, because they help keep an audience's attention. By analyzing rhetorical devices, you can gain insight into what makes a speech powerful or memorable.

Writers use **diction,** or word choice, as well as **syntax,** sentence structure, to help create rhetorical devices. One common rhetorical device is the **repetition** of the same word, phrase, or sentence for emphasis. Another device is **parallelism,** the use of similar grammatical constructions to express related ideas. The chart shows examples of these rhetorical devices from a speech delivered by Martin Luther King Jr. during the Montgomery bus boycott. Use a similar chart to identify examples of rhetorical devices in the following selection.

Device	Example
Repetition	"Tired of being segregated and humiliated; tired of being kicked about by the brutal feet of oppression."
Parallelism	"They are protesting for the perpetuation of injustice in the community; we're protesting for the birth of justice. . . ."

Selection Resources

See resources on the **Teacher One Stop DVD-ROM** *and on* **thinkcentral.com**.

R RESOURCE MANAGER UNIT 9
Lesson Support,* pp. 75–88

DIAGNOSTIC AND SELECTION TESTS
Selection Tests, pp. 279–282

BEST PRACTICES TOOLKIT
pp. A21, D21, D48

INTERACTIVE READER

ADAPTED INTERACTIVE READER

ELL ADAPTED INTERACTIVE READER

TECHNOLOGY
- Teacher One Stop DVD-ROM
- Student One Stop DVD-ROM
- PowerNotes DVD-ROM
- Audio Anthology CD
- Audio Tutor CD
- ExamView Test Generator on the Teacher One Stop

* Resources for Differentiation

A Eulogy for Dr. Martin Luther King, Jr.

by Robert F. Kennedy

On April 4, 1968, hundreds of African Americans gathered for what they thought would be an exciting political event. Presidential candidate Robert F. Kennedy was coming to speak to them. Before he was to deliver his speech, however, Kennedy was informed that Martin Luther King Jr. had been assassinated earlier that day. He nevertheless went to the rally, where he found the people upbeat in anticipation of his appearance. Realizing that they were unaware of the tragic event, he began his speech with the following words.

I have bad news for you, for all of our fellow citizens, and people who love peace all over the world, and that is that Martin Luther King was shot and killed tonight.

Martin Luther King dedicated his life to love and to justice for his fellow human beings, and he died because of that effort.

In this difficult day, in this difficult time for the United States, it is perhaps well to ask what kind of a nation we are and what direction we want to move in. For those of you who are black—considering the evidence there evidently is that there were white people who were
10 responsible—you can be filled with bitterness, with hatred, and a desire for revenge. We can move in that direction as a country, in great polarization—black people amongst black, white people amongst white, filled with hatred toward one another. **A**

Or we can make an effort, as Martin Luther King did, to understand and to comprehend, and to replace that violence, that stain of bloodshed that has spread across our land, with an effort to understand with compassion and love.

For those of you who are black and are tempted to be filled with hatred and distrust at the injustice of such an act, against all white people, I can
20 only say that I feel in my own heart the same kind of feeling. I had a member of my family killed, but he was killed by a white man. But we have to make an effort in the United States, we have to make an effort to understand, to go beyond these rather difficult times.

My favorite poet was Aeschylus. He wrote, "In our sleep, pain which cannot forget falls drop by drop upon the heart until, in our own despair, against our will, comes wisdom through the awful grace of God."

A RHETORICAL DEVICES
How does Kennedy use **parallelism** to emphasize the potential for American society to become more divided?

Practice and Apply

BACKGROUND

Robert F. Kennedy The speaker of this eulogy was the younger brother of John F. Kennedy, who had served as president from 1961 until his assassination in 1963. Robert, or "Bobby," began his political career in earnest after his brother's assassination, serving as a senator from New York. As Attorney General, Robert Kennedy was a tough supporter of the civil rights movement. In April 1968, he was running for president. Just two months after giving the eulogy of this selection, Robert Kennedy was also assassinated.

INFORMATIONAL ANALYSIS

COMMON CORE

RI 6
RI 9

A *Model the Skill:* RHETORICAL DEVICES

Model for students how to identify rhetorical devices. Direct students to follow along in the text as you read lines 1–13 aloud. Remind students that parallelism is the use of similar grammatical constructions to express related ideas. Point out an example of parallelism in lines 7–8. Ask students what other lines contain parallelism in this passage, and have them record these examples in their Skill Focus charts.

Possible answer: Kennedy uses parallelism in these examples: "what kind of nation we are and what direction we want to move in" (lines 7–8); "with bitterness, with hatred, and a desire for revenge" (lines 10–11); "black people amongst black, white people amongst white" (line 12).

Video Trailer

Go to **thinkcentral.com** to preview the **Video Trailer** introducing this selection. Other features that support the selection include
• **PowerNotes** presentation
• **ThinkAloud** models to enhance comprehension

DIFFERENTIATED INSTRUCTION

FOR ENGLISH LANGUAGE LEARNERS

Options for Reading To complete the chart on page 980, have students listen to the audio recording of the text on the *Audio Anthology CD* several times. After listening, have them read the eulogy silently, looking for the passages that contain repetition of words or parallel phrases.

Reading Online!

Features on **thinkcentral.com** that support the selection include
• **PowerNotes** presentation
• **ThinkAloud** models to enhance comprehension

Analyze Visuals

About the Art The photograph was taken at a special White House conference on civil rights in 1962. Pictured in the foreground, from left to right, are Dr. Martin Luther King, Jr., Attorney General Robert F. Kennedy, Roy Wilkins (Executive Director of the NAACP), and Vice President Lyndon B. Johnson. In the background are other civil rights leaders.

What we need in the United States is not division; what we need in the United States is not hatred; what we need in the United States is not violence or lawlessness but love and wisdom, and compassion toward one
30 another, and a feeling of justice towards those who still suffer within our country, whether they be white or they be black.

So I shall ask you tonight to return home, to say a prayer for the family of Martin Luther King, that's true, but more importantly to say a prayer for our own country, which all of us love—a prayer for understanding and that compassion of which I spoke.

We can do well in this country. We will have difficult times. We've had difficult times in the past. We will have difficult times in the future. It is not the end of violence; it is not the end of lawlessness; it is not the end of disorder. **B**

40 But the vast majority of white people and the vast majority of black people in this country want to live together, want to improve the quality of our life, and want justice for all human beings who abide in our land.

Let us dedicate ourselves to what the Greeks wrote so many years ago: to tame the savageness of man and to make gentle the life of this world.

Let us dedicate ourselves to that, and say a prayer for our country and for our people. **C**

B RHETORICAL DEVICES
What idea does Kennedy call attention to through **parallelism** in lines 36–39?

C RHETORICAL DEVICES
What does Kennedy suggest through the **repetition** of the phrase "let us dedicate ourselves" in lines 43–46?

Shown (left to right) are King, Kennedy, Roy Wilkins, and Lyndon Johnson.

DIFFERENTIATED INSTRUCTION

FOR STRUGGLING READERS
Comprehension Support: Nonfiction To help students analyze the writer's message, distribute the Analysis Frame: Literary Nonfiction. Use the Core Analysis questions to help students determine and evaluate the writer's purpose and effectiveness in the speech.

BEST PRACTICES TOOLKIT—Transparency
Analysis Frame: Literary Nonfiction
pp. D21, D48

FOR ENGLISH LANGUAGE LEARNERS
Concept Support Read aloud the Greek adage in line 44, and define any confusing words, such as *savageness*. Have students discuss the meaning of the quotation and discuss how this advice applies to the African Americans in the audience and to the white Americans who may hear or read the speech later.

Comprehension

1. **Recall** What personal experience has helped Kennedy understand the feelings of African Americans following King's assassination?

2. **Summarize** What kinds of reactions does Kennedy hope his speech will prevent?

Text Analysis

3. **Analyze Rhetorical Devices** Review the examples of rhetorical devices in the chart you created as you read. Choose an example of each device, and explain how it helps make the speech effective.

4. **Interpret Statement** What do you make of the statement by Aeschylus that Kennedy quotes in lines 24–26?

COMMON CORE

RI 6 Determine an author's point of view or purpose in a text and analyze how an author uses rhetoric to advance that point of view or purpose. **RI 9** Analyze seminal U.S. documents of historical and literary significance, including how they address related themes and concepts. **W 2** Write explanatory texts to examine and convey complex ideas, concepts, and information through the effective selection, organization, and analysis of content.

Read for Information: Cite Evidence

WRITING PROMPT

In "A Eulogy for Dr. Martin Luther King Jr.," Kennedy urges the audience to follow King's approach to fighting injustice. How do Martin Luther King Jr.'s words and actions in "Montgomery Boycott" support the message of Kennedy's speech?

To answer this prompt, you will need to identify Kennedy's message and cite evidence from "Montgomery Boycott" that supports this message. Use the following steps:

1. Reread Kennedy's speech, looking for statements about injustice to help you identify his message.

2. Reread "Montgomery Boycott" and keep track of statements, facts, and anecdotes that are relevant to Kennedy's message. Indicate line numbers for each item in your notes.

3. Review your notes and evaluate each item to see whether it supports Kennedy's message.

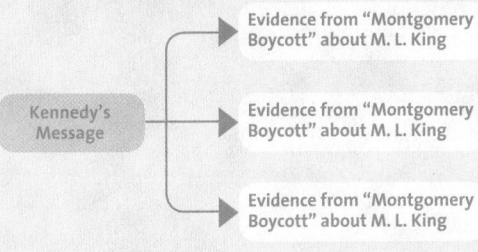

Kennedy's Message

Evidence from "Montgomery Boycott" about M. L. King

Evidence from "Montgomery Boycott" about M. L. King

Evidence from "Montgomery Boycott" about M. L. King

Practice and Apply

For preliminary support of post-reading questions, use these copy masters:

R RESOURCE MANAGER—Copy Masters
Reading Check p. 87
Question Support p. 88
Cite Evidence p. 84

Additional selection questions are provided for teachers on page 78.

ANSWERS

Comprehension

1. *His brother was assassinated.*

2. *racial hatred and violence*

Text Analysis

COMMON CORE **RI 6, RI 9, W 2**

Possible answers:

3. *Parallelism: "to understand and to comprehend, and to replace" (lines 14–15); lists alternatives to hate. **Repetition:** "What we need in the United States is not . . . " (lines 27–29); emphasizes what is not needed, reminds the listeners that they belong to one country, and makes them want to hear what actually is needed.*

4. *Students may interpret the Aeschylus passage as meaning that over time, deep pain softens people and makes them wiser even though they may resist it.*

Read for Information: Cite Evidence

Writing Prompt *Possible answer: Kennedy's message to use compassion, love, and understanding to gain justice (lines 14–17, 27–31) is supported by King's words ("Montgomery Boycott," lines 202–216) asking followers to use courage, dignity, and Christian love.*

Assess and Reteach

FOR STRUGGLING WRITERS
Read for Information

• Help students summarize Kennedy's message in a single statement, using line numbers to support their statement.

• As students read "Montgomery Boycott" for evidence, urge them to list details that support Kennedy's interpretation on index cards. Have them write a few words or a sentence telling why they think each detail is relevant to Kennedy's speech.

FOR ADVANCED LEARNERS/PRE–AP

Read for Information Have students read other famous speeches by Dr. Martin Luther King, Jr., to determine whether his overall message is in accordance with Kennedy's interpretation. Cite the details as evidence in the essay.

Assess

DIAGNOSTIC AND SELECTION TESTS
Selection Test A, B/C pp. 279–282

Interactive Selection Test on **thinkcentral.com**

Reteach

Level Up Online Tutorials on **thinkcentral.com**

Reteaching Worksheets on **thinkcentral.com**

Focus and Motivate

 COMMON CORE FOCUS

RL 1 Cite strong and thorough textual evidence to support inferences drawn from the text.
RL 3 Analyze how complex characters interact and develop the theme. **RL 6** Analyze a particular point of view or cultural experience reflected in a work of world literature. **W 9b** Draw evidence from literary text to support analysis and reflection.
L 1b Use various types of phrases to convey specific meanings and add variety and interest to writing.
L 4b Consult reference materials to determine or clarify a word's precise meaning and etymology.

SUMMARIES

"Marriage Is a Private Affair" When Nnaemeka chooses his own wife, his father renounces him. Years later, his wife sends Nnaemeka's father a letter concerning his grandsons, which sparks remorse and possible reconciliation.
"Adam and Rosie" Adam explains how he won the approval of Rosie's Korean parents.
"Festival of World Cultures" The poster shows nine people from different cultures.

Whose **LIFE** is it, anyway?

Read the question. Have students tell what parental approval means to them.

What's the Connection?

Lead students in a discussion about multicultural influences. How do influences from other cultures impact daily life? Ask students to consider the food they eat, the television programs they watch, and family and friends.

Selection Resources

Marriage Is a Private Affair
Short Story by Chinua Achebe

Adam and Rosie
Transcript

Festival of World Cultures
Poster

 **Essential Course of Study** ECOS

Whose **LIFE** is it, anyway?

 COMMON CORE

RL 1 Cite strong and thorough textual evidence to support inferences drawn from the text. **RL 3** Analyze how complex characters interact and develop the theme. **RL 6** Analyze a particular point of view or cultural experience reflected in a work of world literature.

Growing up means learning to make your own decisions. But parents are often reluctant to let go of their authority. In the traditional culture that Chinua Achebe portrays in the following selection, even adults are expected to get parental approval for some big decisions.

What's the Connection?

All cultures have expectations about parents' involvement in their children's lives. But when cultures come together, expectations may change—and even clash. You'll read about a moral dilemma arising from the clash of cultures in "Marriage Is a Private Affair." Then you'll read a transcript that explores the same topics and finally view a poster that provides another perspective.

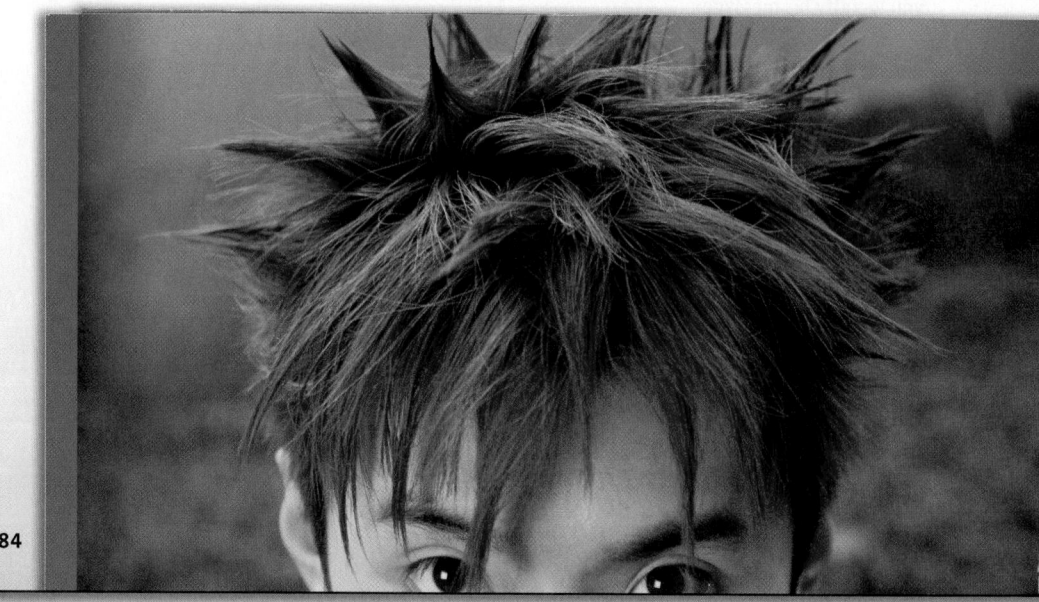

984

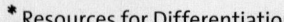

TEXT ANALYSIS: MORAL DILEMMA

A **moral dilemma** is a difficult decision in which either option results in violating one's moral principles. Moral dilemmas sometimes arise through cultural conflicts—a clash between the values and cultures of characters.

In "Marriage Is a Private Affair," a father and son face moral dilemmas as to how they should behave when the father's traditional values clash with his son's decisions. Achebe reveals this tension through a character's thoughts:

In the cosmopolitan atmosphere of the city it had always seemed to her something of a joke that a person's tribe could determine whom he married.

As you read, examine the forces that create the characters' moral dilemmas and how the characters respond to these dilemmas.

READING STRATEGY: PREDICT

You can use text clues in a story to make **predictions,** reasonable guesses about what will happen next. When making predictions,

- analyze characters' words, thoughts, and actions to gain a sense of how the characters might react in a situation
- tap into your own experiences and knowledge of human behavior

As you read, use a chart like this one to record your predictions and to see how they compare with actual outcomes.

Prediction	Reason for Prediction	Actual Outcome
Nnaemeka's father will be upset about the engagement.	Nnaemeka says villagers are unhappy when they do not get to arrange an engagement.	

▲ VOCABULARY IN CONTEXT

Achebe uses the following boldfaced words to portray family conflict. Determine the meaning of each word from the context. Record your answers in your *Reader/Writer Notebook*.

1. Her travels had given her a **cosmopolitan** attitude.
2. He **vehemently** denied any wrongdoing on his part.
3. She would not accept attempts at **dissuasion;** her mind was set.
4. It is important to show **deference** to your elders.
5. We can still **persevere,** despite all the obstacles ahead.

 Complete the activities in your **Reader/Writer Notebook.**

Meet the Author

Chinua Achebe
born 1930

Reclaiming Africa's Stories
Chinua Achebe (chē'nū-ä ä-chā'bä) is one of Africa's most famous contemporary authors. A member of the Ibo (ē'bō) people of eastern Nigeria, Achebe was born in the village of Ogidi (ô-gē-dē'), where his father taught at a Christian mission school. As a child, Achebe learned both Ibo and English, the language in which he usually writes. In addition to novels and short stories, Achebe has written children's books, essays, and poetry. Commenting on what made him consider becoming a writer, Achebe stated, "I read some appalling European novels about Africa . . . and realized that our story could not be told for us by anyone else."

BACKGROUND TO THE STORY

Nigerian Crossroads
This story takes place in the West African country of Nigeria. It focuses on a conflict between a father and son who belong to the Ibo, one of Nigeria's largest ethnic groups. The father lives in an Ibo village where people follow traditional practices, such as choosing spouses for their children. The son has moved to Lagos (lā'gŏs'), a large and ethnically diverse city. In Lagos and other urban areas, modern practices have displaced many of the village traditions. The tension between old and new ways of life sometimes creates conflict within families, especially between generations.

 **Author Online**
Go to **thinkcentral.com.** KEYWORD: HML10-985

Teach

TEXT ANALYSIS — COMMON CORE · RL 3 · RL 6

● *Model the Skill:* MORAL DILEMMA

To model how to analyze a moral dilemma, read aloud this example: "Unlike Leah's parents, her grandparents had two sets of dishes, one for meals with milk, another for meals with meat. They observed the laws of keeping kosher." Explain to students that a moral dilemma could arise for Leah's parents because the grandparents keep kosher, but the parents don't.

GUIDED PRACTICE Ask students to suggest what conflicts might arise from this cultural difference.

READING STRATEGY — COMMON CORE · RL 1

■ *Model the Skill:* PREDICT

To model how to make predictions, provide this scenario: "When Jake asked for money to pay for a new CD player, his mother said no. So Jake did some odd jobs and bought the player himself." By using knowledge of human behavior and the information, it is possible to predict that Jake's mother will be angry that he ignored her authority.

GUIDED PRACTICE Ask students to give reasons for this prediction.

R RESOURCE MANAGER—Copy Master
Predict p. 101

VOCABULARY SKILL — COMMON CORE · L 4

▲ VOCABULARY IN CONTEXT

DIAGNOSE WORD KNOWLEDGE Have all students complete Vocabulary in Context. Check their meanings against the following:

cosmopolitan (kŏz'mə-pŏl'ĭ-tn) *adj.* containing elements from all over the world; sophisticated
deference (dĕf'ər-əns) *n.* polite respect; submission to someone else's wishes
dissuasion (dĭ-swā'zhən) *n.* an attempt to deter a person from a course of action

persevere (pûr'sə-vîr') *v.* to persist in an action or belief despite difficulty
vehemently (vē'ə-mənt-lē) *adv.* in a fierce, intense manner

PRETEACH VOCABULARY Use the following copy master to help students predict meanings for each boldfaced word.

R RESOURCE MANAGER—Copy Master
Vocabulary Study p. 103

1. Read the first sentence and ask students to find clues to the meaning of *cosmopolitan.*
2. If necessary, point out the clue "much more sophisticated than the small village."
3. Have students record their ideas.
4. Repeat the procedure for items 2–5.

Marriage Is a PRIVATE Affair

Chinua Achebe

"Have you written to your dad yet?" asked Nene[1] one afternoon as she sat with Nnaemeka[2] in her room at 16 Kasanga Street, Lagos.

"No. I've been thinking about it. I think it's better to tell him when I get home on leave!"

"But why? Your leave is such a long way off yet—six whole weeks. He should be let into our happiness now."

Nnaemeka was silent for a while and then began very slowly as if he groped for his words: "I wish I were sure it would be happiness to him."

"Of course it must," replied Nene, a little surprised. "Why shouldn't it?"

10 "You have lived in Lagos all your life, and you know very little about people in remote parts of the country."

"That's what you always say. But I don't believe anybody will be so unlike other people that they will be unhappy when their sons are engaged to marry."

"Yes. They are most unhappy if the engagement is not arranged by them. In our case it's worse—you are not even an Ibo."

This was said so seriously and so bluntly that Nene could not find speech immediately. In the **cosmopolitan** atmosphere of the city it had always seemed to her something of a joke that a person's tribe could determine whom he married.

At last she said, "You don't really mean that he will object to your marrying 20 me simply on that account? I had always thought you Ibos were kindly disposed to other people."

"So we are. But when it comes to marriage, well, it's not quite so simple. And this," he added, "is not peculiar to the Ibos. If your father were alive and lived in the heart of Ibibio-land, he would be exactly like my father." **A**

"I don't know. But anyway, as your father is so fond of you, I'm sure he will forgive you soon enough. Come on then, be a good boy and send him a nice lovely letter . . ."

1. **Nene** (ně′-ně).
2. **Nnaemeka** (ĕn-nä′ĕ-mě′kä).

Analyze Visuals ▶

What does the painting suggest about the story's characters and setting?

① **Targeted Passage**

cosmopolitan
(kŏz′mə-pŏl′ĭ-tn) *adj.* containing elements from all over the world; sophisticated

A MORAL DILEMMA
Reread lines 1–24. What do you learn about the cultural backgrounds of Nene and Nnaemeka? How does Nnaemeka's background contribute to his moral dilemma?

Woman and Husband in Floating Agbada 1 (1997), D. Gbenga Orimoloye. Gouache, 25 cm × 20 cm. © www.Orimoloye.com.

G. ORIMOLOYE 1997

Reading Support

This selection on **thinkcentral.com** includes embedded **ThinkAloud** models–students "thinking aloud" about the story to model the kinds of questions a good reader would ask about a selection.

BACKGROUND

Lagos Nene and Nnaemeka's home is Nigeria's largest city and its economic center. Located on the Atlantic Ocean in the Gulf of Guinea, Lagos is also Nigeria's biggest port. The city served as the country's capital from 1960 to 1991, when Abuja became the capital.

Analyze Visuals

Possible answer: The painting suggests that the story takes place in Africa and that the characters are an African couple.

About the Art The "floating agbada," mentioned in the title of the painting (*Woman and Husband in Floating Agbada 1*), refers to the decorative robe the husband is wearing. That kind of robe was traditionally worn throughout Nigeria by men of power and wealth, and on important occasions.

- Where do Nene and Nnaemeka live? Where does Nnaemeka's father live? (line 2; line 10)
- Why does Nene want Nnaemeka to write to his father? (lines 5–6; 12–13)
- Why does Nnaemeka think that writing to his father might not be a good idea? (lines 8–15)

FOR ADVANCED LEARNERS/PRE–AP

Evaluate Realia As students read, have them pay attention to the three letter excerpts that appear in the story. After students have finished the story, have them compare the three letter excerpts and the effects of each one on their understanding of character. In a paragraph or two, have them evaluate whether the excerpts are as effective as dialogue might have been.

B GRAMMAR AND STYLE

COMMON CORE

L 1b

Evaluate Gerunds Ask students which sentence is more effective and why. *Possible answer: The sentence with the gerund is more effective, because it is less wordy; it avoids a third infinitive (to write) and repetition of the phrase to him.*

REVISIT THE BIG QUESTION

Whose LIFE is it, anyway?

Discuss Ask students what the letter in lines 38–44 shows about the attitude of Nnaemeka's father toward parental approval of a potential spouse. *Possible answer: The letter shows that Nnaemeka's father thinks it is very important to approve of—in fact, to choose—a son's potential wife. He believes that Nnaemeka wants parental approval of his future spouse.*

TEXT ANALYSIS

COMMON CORE

C MORAL DILEMMA

RL 3
RL 6

Possible answer: Nnaemeka's father will be angry that Nnaemeka is choosing his wife on his own, when he had expected to make that decision.

IF STUDENTS NEED HELP . . . Ask them what Nnaemeka answers when his father asks why it is impossible for him to marry Nweke (line 55). Then have them read his father's response (lines 59–60).

"It would not be wise to break the news to him by writing. A letter will bring it upon him with a shock. I'm quite sure about that."

30   "All right, honey, suit yourself. You know your father."

As Nnaemeka walked home that evening, he turned over in his mind different ways of overcoming his father's opposition, especially now that he had gone and found a girl for him. He had thought of showing his letter to Nene but decided on second thoughts not to, at least for the moment. He read it again when he got home and couldn't help smiling to himself. He remembered Ugoye[3] quite well, an Amazon[4] of a girl who used to beat up all the boys, himself included, on the way to the stream, a complete dunce at school.

I have found a girl who will suit you admirably—Ugoye Nweke, the eldest daughter of our neighbor, Jacob Nweke. She has a proper Christian
40   *upbringing. When she stopped schooling some years ago, her father (a man of sound judgment) sent her to live in the house of a pastor where she has received all the training a wife could need. Her Sunday school teacher has told me that she reads her Bible very fluently. I hope we shall begin negotiations when you come home in December.*

On the second evening of his return from Lagos Nnaemeka sat with his father under a cassia tree. This was the old man's retreat where he went to read his Bible when the parching December sun had set and a fresh, reviving wind blew on the leaves.

"Father," began Nnaemeka suddenly, "I have come to ask for forgiveness."
50   "Forgiveness? For what, my son?" he asked in amazement.

"It's about this marriage question."

"Which marriage question?"

"I can't—we must—I mean it is impossible for me to marry Nweke's daughter."

"Impossible? Why?" asked his father.

"I don't love her."

"Nobody said you did. Why should you?" he asked.

"Marriage today is different . . ."

"Look here, my son," interrupted his father, "nothing is different. What one
60   looks for in a wife are a good character and a Christian background." C

Nnaemeka saw there was no hope along the present line of argument.

"Moreover," he said, "I am engaged to marry another girl who has all of Ugoye's good qualities, and who . . ."

His father did not believe his ears. "What did you say?" he asked slowly and disconcertingly.

"She is a good Christian," his son went on, "and a teacher in a girls' school in Lagos."

"Teacher, did you say? If you consider that a qualification for a good wife,

---

3. **Ugoye** (ū-gō′yĕ).

4. **Amazon:** a woman who is tall, strong-willed, and aggressive.

988   UNIT 9: HISTORY, CULTURE, AND THE AUTHOR

B GRAMMAR AND STYLE

Reread line 28. Rather than writing, "It would not be wise to write to him to break the news to him," Achebe uses the **gerund** *writing*, a verb form that functions as a noun.

COMMON CORE RL 4

Language Coach

Etymology The Latin word *vivus*, "alive," is a root for many English words. Reread lines 46–48. What word contains *vivus* as its root? What do you think this word means? (Hint: *re-* means "again.")

C MORAL DILEMMA

What does the exchange of dialogue in lines 49–60 reveal about Nnaemeka's and his father's beliefs about marriage? What conflict is developing between the two sets of beliefs?

DIFFERENTIATED INSTRUCTION

FOR STRUGGLING READERS

Concept Support Have two fluent readers take the parts of Nnaemeka and his father and read lines 49–60. Then have them begin to fill in Character Analysis Charts for father and son.

 BEST PRACTICES TOOLKIT—Transparency
Character Analysis Chart p. D5

FOR ENGLISH LANGUAGE LEARNERS

Language Coach

COMMON CORE
RL 4

Etymology *Answer:*
Revive *contains the root* vivus. *It means "bring alive again."* Point out that related words with Latin roots that mean "live" include *vivacious* and *vivid.* Have students define these words, using a dictionary for reference if they need help.

I should like to point out to you, Emeka, that no Christian woman should
70 teach. St. Paul in his letter to the Corinthians says that women should keep
silence." He rose slowly from his seat and paced forwards and backwards. This
was his pet subject, and he condemned **vehemently** those church leaders who
encouraged women to teach in their schools. After he had spent his emotion
on a long homily, he at last came back to his son's engagement, in a seemingly
milder tone.

"Whose daughter is she, anyway?"

"She is Nene Atang."

"What!" All the mildness was gone again. "Did you say Neneataga; what
does that mean?"

80 "Nene Atang from Calabar.[5] She is the only girl I can marry." This was a
very rash reply, and Nnaemeka expected the storm to burst. But it did not.
His father merely walked away into his room. This was most unexpected and
perplexed Nnaemeka. His father's silence was infinitely more menacing than a
flood of threatening speech. That night the old man did not eat. **D**

When he sent for Nnaemeka a day later, he applied all possible ways of
dissuasion. But the young man's heart was hardened, and his father eventually
gave him up as lost.

"I owe it to you, my son, as a duty to show you what is right and what is
wrong. Whoever put this idea into your head might as well have cut your
90 throat. It is Satan's work." He waved his son away.

"You will change your mind, Father, when you know Nene."

"I shall never see her" was the reply. From that night the father scarcely
spoke to his son. He did not, however, cease hoping that he would realize
how serious was the danger he was heading for. Day and night he put him
in his prayers.

Nnaemeka, for his own part, was very deeply affected by his father's grief.
But he kept hoping that it would pass away. If it had occurred to him that
never in the history of his people had a man married a woman who spoke a
different tongue, he might have been less optimistic. "It has never been heard,"
100 was the verdict of an old man speaking a few weeks later. In that short sentence
he spoke for all of his people. This man had come with others to commiserate
with Okeke[6] when news went round about his son's behavior. By that time the
son had gone back to Lagos.

"It has never been heard," said the old man again with a sad shake of his head.

"What did Our Lord say?" asked another gentleman. "Sons shall rise against
their fathers; it is there in the Holy Book."

"It is the beginning of the end," said another.

The discussion thus tending to become theological, Madubogwu, a highly
practical man, brought it down once more to the ordinary level.

110 "Have you thought of consulting a native doctor about your son?" he asked
Nnaemeka's father.

---

5. **Calabar:** a seaport in southeastern Nigeria.

6. **Okeke** (ō-kě′-kě).

---

vehemently
(vē′ə-mənt-lē) *adv.* in a
fierce, intense manner

D PREDICT
Will Nnaemeka's father
change his mind after
thinking about his son's
marriage plans?

dissuasion (dĭ-swā′zhən)
n. an attempt to deter a
person from a course of
action

D *Model the Skill:* PREDICT

Model for students how to make predictions. Read lines 80–84 aloud. Point out
the details that give them information
about Nnaemeka's father, such as "His
father's silence" in line 83. Tell students
that their knowledge of human nature
and these details will help them make
their predictions. Have students record
their predictions, reasons, and the actual
outcome in their Predict charts.

*Possible answer: Most students may pre-
dict that Nnaemeka's father will not change
his mind, because his silence "was infinitely
more menacing than a flood of threatening
speech" (lines 83–84), and because he hasn't
shown any flexibility so far.*

TIERED DISCUSSION PROMPTS

Direct students to lines 82–95. Use these
prompts to help students understand that for
Nnaemeka and his father there is no ground
for compromise on the issue of Nnaemeka's
engagement to Nene:

Connect Ask students to suggest some
controversial subjects that divide people.
Why is it hard for people to compromise on
controversial issues? *Possible answer: People
find it hard to compromise when their beliefs
and feelings on a topic are extremely strong
and hardened.*

Analyze What does Nnaemeka's father say
that shows he is not at all willing to compromise? *Possible answer: He says that whoever
influenced Nnaemeka to choose his own
wife was evil and might as well have killed
Nnaemeka, and that he will never see Nene.*

OWN THE WORD

- **vehemently:** Have students create
  semantic maps for *vehemently*, inserting
  synonyms to complete the map.

- **dissuasion:** Ask students if they have
  ever used *dissuasion* to convince someone not to do something.

FOR ENGLISH LANGUAGE LEARNERS

Language: Phrasal Verbs Discuss the meaning of the following verbs in the context
of the story: *pass away* (line 97), "die down,
lessen"; *rise [up] against* (line 105), "throw
over the authority of"; *broke through* (line
149), "overcame, won over"; *give in* (line 167),
"relent, change one's mind"; *making it up to
(someone)* (line 181), "compensating for one's
past actions."

FOR STRUGGLING READERS

Develop Reading Fluency Direct students
to the conversation between Okeke and his
neighbors (lines 96–127). Write the following
proper nouns on the board: *Nnaemeka, Okeke,
Madubogwu, Lagos, Amalile,* and *Ochuba.*
Pronounce each name and have students
echo the pronunciations. Then lead students
in unison reading of the lines.

E *Model the Skill:* **MORAL DILEMMA**

Reread the short letter in lines 130–133 aloud. Then explain to students that these lines show the depth and complexity of the cultural conflict between father and son. The father values his views about marriage above almost anything else, including his relationship with his son and daughter-in-law.

Possible answer: Answers will vary. Some students will suggest that the issue may re-solve in time. Others may answer that the two cultures' expectations are so different that they cannot be resolved.

REVISIT THE BIG QUESTION

Whose **LIFE** is it, anyway?

Discuss Ask students, based on lines 130–143, what efforts Nnaemeka made to win parental approval for his marriage. *Possible answer: He sent his father a wedding picture and wrote him three times about coming home for a visit.*

OWN THE WORD

deference: Review the definition of *deference* with students. Then have students name people whom they would treat with *deference*.

"He isn't sick" was the reply.

"What is he then? The boy's mind is diseased, and only a good herbalist[7] can bring him back to his right senses. The medicine he requires is *Amalile,* the same that women apply with success to recapture their husbands' straying affection."

"Madubogwu is right," said another gentleman. "This thing calls for medicine."

"I shall not call in a native doctor." Nnaemeka's father was known to be obstinately ahead of his more superstitious neighbors in these matters. "I will not be another Mrs. Ochuba. If my son wants to kill himself, let him do it
120 with his own hands. It is not for me to help him."

"But it was her fault," said Madubogwu. "She ought to have gone to an honest herbalist. She was a clever woman, nevertheless."

"She was a wicked murderess," said Jonathan, who rarely argued with his neighbors because, he often said, they were incapable of reasoning. "The medicine was prepared for her husband, it was his name they called in its preparation, and I am sure it would have been perfectly beneficial to him. It was wicked to put it into the herbalist's food and say you were only trying it out."

Six months later, Nnaemeka was showing his young wife a short letter from his father:

130   *It amazes me that you could be so unfeeling as to send me your wedding*
         picture. I would have sent it back. But on further thought I decided just to
         cut off your wife and send it back to you because I have nothing to do with
         her. How I wish that I had nothing to do with you either.

When Nene read through this letter and looked at the mutilated picture, her eyes filled with tears, and she began to sob.

"Don't cry, my darling," said her husband. "He is essentially good-natured and will one day look more kindly on our marriage." But years passed, and that one day did not come. **E**

For eight years, Okeke would have nothing to do with his son, Nnaemeka.
140 Only three times (when Nnaemeka asked to come home and spend his leave) did he write to him.

"I can't have you in my house," he replied on one occasion. "It can be of no interest to me where or how you spend your leave—or your life, for that matter."

The prejudice against Nnaemeka's marriage was not confined to his little village. In Lagos, especially among his people who worked there, it showed itself in a different way. Their women, when they met at their village meeting, were not hostile to Nene. Rather, they paid her such excessive **deference** as to make her feel she was not one of them. But as time went on, Nene gradually broke through some of this prejudice and even began to make friends among
150 them. Slowly and grudgingly they began to admit that she kept her home much better than most of them.

The story eventually got to the little village in the heart of the Ibo country that Nnaemeka and his young wife were a most happy couple. But his father

E MORAL DILEMMA
Do you think there's a good way for Nnaemeka to resolve his moral dilemma? Why or why not?

deference (dĕf′ər-əns) *n.* polite respect; submission to someone else's wishes

---

7. **herbalist** (ûr′bə-lĭst): a person who is expert in the use of medicinal herbs.

990 UNIT 9: HISTORY, CULTURE, AND THE AUTHOR

DIFFERENTIATED INSTRUCTION

FOR STRUGGLING READERS

Comprehension Support Make sure students understand how each of the main characters is feeling six months after Nnaemeka's marriage to Nene.

• What does the letter show about how Nnaemeka's father is feeling?

• How did Nene feel after reading the letter?

• What does Nnaemeka say to make Nene feel better? What do his comments show?

FOR ADVANCED LEARNERS/PRE–AP

Compare and Contrast: Point of View Have students discuss Achebe's use of the om-niscient point of view in this story. Explain how it supports the story's theme: in time, love will overcome prejudice. How would the story have been different if written from the first- or third-person point of view?

Portrait 1 (1999), D. Gbenga Orimoloye. Watercolor, 30 cm × 20 cm. © www.Orimoloye.com.

was one of the few people in the village who knew nothing about this. He always displayed so much temper whenever his son's name was mentioned that everyone avoided it in his presence. By a tremendous effort of will he had succeeded in pushing his son to the back of his mind. The strain had nearly killed him, but he had **persevered** and won.

160 Then one day he received a letter from Nene, and in spite of himself he began to glance through it perfunctorily until all of a sudden the expression on his face changed and he began to read more carefully.

. . . Our two sons, from the day they learnt that they have a grandfather, have insisted on being taken to him. I find it impossible to tell them that you will not see them. I implore you to allow Nnaemeka to bring them home for a short time during his leave next month. I shall remain here in Lagos . . . **F**

The old man at once felt the resolution he had built up over so many years falling in. He was telling himself that he must not give in. He tried to steel his heart against all emotional appeals. It was a reenactment of that other struggle. He leaned against a window and looked out. The sky was overcast with heavy 170 black clouds, and a high wind began to blow, filling the air with dust and dry leaves. It was one of those rare occasions when even Nature takes a hand in a human fight. Very soon it began to rain, the first rain in the year. It came down in large sharp drops and was accompanied by the lightning and thunder which mark a change of season. Okeke was trying hard not to think of his two grandsons. But he knew he was now fighting a losing battle. He tried to hum a favorite hymn, but the pattering of large raindrops on the roof broke up the tune. His mind immediately returned to the children. How could he shut his door against them? By a curious mental process he imagined them standing, sad and forsaken, under the harsh angry weather—shut out from his house. 180 That night he hardly slept, from remorse—and a vague fear that he might die without making it up to them. ◊

persevere (pûr′sə-vîr′) *v.* to persist in an action or belief despite difficulty

F PREDICT
How will Nnaemeka's father react to this letter? Cite evidence.

② **Targeted Passage**

MARRIAGE IS A PRIVATE AFFAIR 991

Analyze Visuals

Ask students what qualities of Nene the painting illustrates. *Possible answer: Nene is thoughtful, intelligent, and determined. The painting reflects these qualities.*

About the Art Point out to students that the artist who painted *Portrait 1* also painted *Woman and Husband in Floating Agbada 1* on page 987.

SELECTION WRAP-UP

READ WITH A PURPOSE Now that students have finished reading the selection, ask students: Will Nnaemeka's childen change his relationship with his father? Why or why not? *Possible answer: Some students will say that Okeke will develop a relationship with his grandsons, but they do not think he will reunite with his son because Okeke is stubborn. Other students will say that beginning a relationship with the grandsons will lead to a relationship with the son. Accept all reasonable responses.*

★ **CRITIQUE** Have students evaluate whether Nnaemeka shares the blame with his father for the problems in their relationship.

INDEPENDENT READING
Students interested in reading another work by Chinua Achebe might enjoy reading his acclaimed novel *Things Fall Apart*.

FOR STRUGGLING READERS

② **Targeted Passage** [Lines 166–181]

This passage suggests how the conflict between Nnaemeka and his father will be resolved.

- What did Okeke do to try to keep his old resolve? (lines 167–168)
- What effect did the rain have on Okeke? (lines 174–179)
- Why did Okeke hardly sleep that night? (lines 180–181)

FOR ADVANCED LEARNERS/PRE-AP

Analyze Symbol and Theme Have students consider the rainstorm as a symbol. What does the narrator say about how Okeke was feeling before the rain started (lines 166–168)? What does the narrator say about the weather that night? How is this rainstorm different from other rainstorms? How does this rainstorm reflect Okeke's feelings? How does this symbol help to support the story's theme?

Practice and Apply

For preliminary support of post-reading questions, use these copy masters:

R RESOURCE MANAGER—Copy Masters
Reading Check p. 106
Moral Dilemma p. 99
Question Support p. 107

Additional selection questions are provided for teachers on page 93.

ANSWERS

Comprehension

1. *He opposes his son's choice because Nene is not from their Ibo ethnic group, and because he believes that it is the father's right to choose his son's spouse.*

2. *He cuts Nene out of the picture.*

3. *After Okeke receives Nene's letter revealing that his two grandsons want to meet him, he regrets his harsh attitude.*

Text Analysis

COMMON CORE RL 1, RL 3, RL 6

Possible answers:

4. ■ **COMMON CORE FOCUS** *Predict*
Many students probably predicted that Okeke would reject his daughter-in-law, but they may not have predicted that his stance would soften after learning about his grandsons.

5. ● **COMMON CORE FOCUS** *Moral Dilemma*
Nnaemeka believes that he should marry for love and select his own wife; Okeke believes that love is not important in marriage and that the father should choose; Nnaemeka does not think it necessary to marry within his ethnic group; Okeke opposes intermarriage; Nnaemeka values his wife's education and teaching job; Okeke believes a good Christian wife should not teach but should keep silent.

6. *In cities, people from different ethnic backgrounds interact; this interaction can break down prejudice and cause attitudes to change.*

7. *Family and bloodline are important to Okeke, and his grandsons are part of his lineage. As a grandfather, Okeke feels love for his grandchildren and wants to see them.*

8. *Though parental approval may not come quickly, it may come; Okeke feels remorse (line 180). Interactions with his grandsons may lead to reconciliation with his son and,*

Comprehension

1. **Recall** Why does Okeke oppose Nnaemeka's choice of a wife?

2. **Recall** What does Okeke do when his son sends him a wedding photo?

3. **Summarize** What happens at the end of the story?

Text Analysis

4. **Examine Predictions** Review the chart you created as you read. How accurate were your predictions about Okeke? Cite specific examples in your response.

5. **Analyze Moral Dilemmas** What beliefs cause moral dilemmas to develop for Nnaemeka and Okeke? Record your answer in a diagram like the one shown.

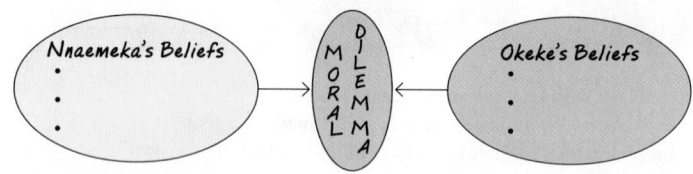

6. **Interpret Cultural Context** Why might living in a city influence Nnaemeka's attitude toward Ibo traditions?

7. **Make Inferences** Why does Nene's letter have such a powerful effect on Okeke?

8. **Draw Conclusions** Reread lines 166–181. Does the ending of the story suggest that Okeke will finally offer parental approval of Nnaemeka's marriage? Cite evidence for your conclusion.

9. **Make Judgments** How much sympathy do you have for Okeke as a character? Give reasons for your answer.

Text Criticism

10. **Critical Interpretations** The critic G. D. Killam has said about Achebe's work, "Through it all the spirit of man and the belief in the possibility of triumph endures." How might this comment apply to "Marriage Is a Private Affair"?

> ## Whose **LIFE** is it, anyway?
> How involved should parents be in their adult children's decisions?

COMMON CORE

RL 1 Cite textual evidence to support inferences drawn from the text. RL 3 Analyze how complex characters interact and develop the theme. RL 6 Analyze a particular point of view or cultural experience reflected in a work of world literature.

---

given time, possibly with Nene as well.

9. *Some students may not sympathize with Okeke because he is so intolerant and unyielding; others may sympathize with him because he is a villager with little outside experience and because he is obviously bewildered by his son's actions.*

Text Criticism

Possible answer:

10. *The ending of the story is triumphant because love and family ties finally overcome ignorance and prejudice.*

Whose **LIFE** is it, anyway?
Students might consider why parents need or want to be involved in some decisions. They might also consider the limitations on their own abilities and experience which could affect their decision-making skills.

Vocabulary in Context

▲ **VOCABULARY PRACTICE**

Decide whether the words in each pair are synonyms or antonyms.

1. cosmopolitan/provincial
2. vehemently/fiercely
3. persuasion/dissuasion
4. deference/respect
5. abandon/persevere

WORD LIST
cosmopolitan
deference
dissuasion
persevere
vehemently

ACADEMIC VOCABULARY IN WRITING

• acknowledge • community • contemporary • culture • role

In a paragraph, describe the moral dilemmas that Nnaemeka and Okeke face. How does the clash between **cultures** help create their dilemmas? How much does each **acknowledge** the other's point of view? Try to use at least two Academic Vocabulary words in your response.

VOCABULARY STRATEGY: THE *kosmos* WORD FAMILY

The root of the vocabulary word *cosmopolitan* can be traced to the Greek word *kosmos,* which means "world." This root has given rise to a family of words. If you are familiar with the other word parts in a word with the root *cosmo* or *cosm,* you can often figure out the word's meaning.

PRACTICE Using a dictionary or a glossary, find four words containing the root *cosmo* or *cosm.* Define each word.

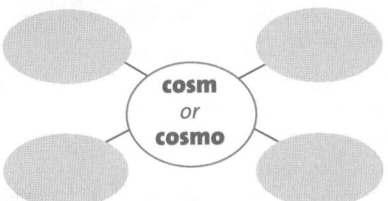

cosm
or
cosmo

COMMON CORE

L 4c Consult reference materials to determine or clarify a word's precise meaning or etymology.

Interactive Vocabulary
THINK central
Go to **thinkcentral.com**.
KEYWORD: HML10-993

DIFFERENTIATED INSTRUCTION

FOR ENGLISH LANGUAGE LEARNERS

Vocabulary: Word Families Have students who speak Latin languages list words in their home language that have the root *cosm* or *cosmo.* Ask them to write a definition for each word and to present their lists to their classmates.

FOR ADVANCED LEARNERS/PRE–AP

Vocabulary in Writing Have students write a paragraph about a conflict between cousins, one from the city and one from the country. Ask them to use as many of the vocabulary words as possible.

ANSWERS

Vocabulary in Context

▲ **VOCABULARY PRACTICE**

1. *antonyms*
2. *synonyms*
3. *antonyms*
4. *synonyms*
5. *antonyms*

R RESOURCE MANAGER—Copy Master
Vocabulary Practice p. 104

ACADEMIC VOCABULARY IN WRITING

***Possible answer:** Nnaemeka and Okeke both face a moral dilemma that stems from a clash between* cultures. *Okeke believes that it is his* role *to choose a wife for Nnaemeka; Nnaemeka wants to choose his own. Neither is able to reconcile his loyalty toward the other with his desire to make the decisions. Nnaemeka* acknowledges *his father's expectations, but his father refuses to see that the* contemporary *world is different from his way of life.*

VOCABULARY STRATEGY: THE *kosmos* WORD FAMILY

COMMON CORE L 4c

Invite students to tell how the root *kosmos* would help them figure out and remember the meaning of *cosmopolitan.* ***Possible answer:** Someone who is* cosmopolitan *is worldly or has experience with the larger world. The word has the expanded meaning of knowing the world or the universe as well.*

After students complete the Practice, ask them to tell how the root helps with figuring out the word.

***Possible answers: cosmic:** relating to the universe;* **cosmogony:** *study of the history and origins of the universe;* **cosmography:** *description of the universe;* **cosmology:** *study of the structure of the universe;* **cosmonaut:** *crew member on a spacecraft.*

R RESOURCE MANAGER—Copy Master
Vocabulary Strategy p. 105

Interactive Vocabulary
THINK central

Vocabulary keywords direct students to a **WordSharp** tutorial on **thinkcentral.com** or to other types of vocabulary practice and review.

Language

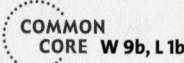

◆ **GRAMMAR AND STYLE**

To provide additional guided practice using gerunds or gerund phrases, write these sentences on the board. Have students suggest how to replace the words in parentheses with gerunds or gerund phrases.

- (To see) Seeing their children abandon traditions can be hard on parents.

- Her mistake was (that she failed) failing to understand Nnaemeka's point of view.

R **RESOURCE MANAGER**—Copy Master
  Grammar and Style p. 108

For more information on gerunds and gerund phrases, see p. R61 of the **Grammar Handbook**.

READING-WRITING CONNECTION

Suggest that students use a Two-Column Chart to list the moral dilemmas that arise from culture clashes in the two selections. Have them brainstorm ideas, including examples from the selections.

BEST PRACTICES TOOLKIT—Transparency
  Two-Column Chart p. A25

Writing Online

The following tools are available online at **thinkcentral.com** and on **Write*Smart* CD-ROM:**
- **Interactive Graphic Organizers**
- **Interactive Student Models**
- **Interactive Revision Lessons**
For additional grammar instruction, see **GrammarNotes** on **thinkcentral.com**.

Assess and Reteach

Assess

DIAGNOSTIC AND SELECTION TESTS
  Selection Test A pp. 283–284
  Selection Test B/C pp. 285–286

Interactive Selection Test on **thinkcentral.com**

Reteach

Level Up Online Tutorials on **thinkcentral.com**

Reteaching Worksheets on **thinkcentral.com**
  Literature Lesson 6: Conflict and Suspense
  Reading Lesson 1: Predicting

Language

◆ **GRAMMAR AND STYLE: Write Concisely**

Review the **Grammar and Style** note on page 988. Like Achebe, you can use **gerunds** and **gerund phrases** to make your writing more fluid and concise. A gerund is a verb form that ends in *–ing* and functions as a noun. A gerund phrase is a gerund plus its modifiers and complements. Here is an example of Achebe's use of a gerund phrase. Notice how "pattering of large raindrops on the roof" functions as a noun in the sentence.

> *He tried to hum a favorite hymn, but the pattering of large raindrops on the roof broke up the tune.* (lines 175–177)

The revisions in blue use a gerund phrase to make the following first draft more concise. Revise your response to the prompt by incorporating gerunds and gerund phrases into your writing.

STUDENT MODEL

When you choose a spouse, ~~you are making a decision that~~ is too personal

a decision to put in anyone else's hands.

READING-WRITING CONNECTION

 **YOUR TURN**   Enhance your understanding of "Marriage Is a Private Affair" by responding to this prompt. Then use the **revising tip** to improve your writing.

WRITING PROMPT	REVISING TIP
Extended Constructed Response: Analysis What kinds of moral dilemmas arise from a clash of cultures? How can these dilemmas be resolved? Write a three-to-five paragraph answer, using examples from "Marriage Is a Private Affair" and "Adam and Rosie" (page 995).	Review your response. Did you use gerunds and gerund phrases to make your writing more fluid and concise? If not, revise to incorporate more gerunds and gerund phrases.

COMMON CORE

L 1b Use various types of phrases to convey specific meanings and add variety and interest to writing. **W 9b** Draw evidence from literary text to support analysis and reflection.

Interactive Revision THINK central
Go to **thinkcentral.com**.
KEYWORD: HML10-994

DIFFERENTIATED INSTRUCTION

FOR STRUGGLING WRITERS

- Limit the length of the assignment to two paragraphs.

- Ask students to include in one paragraph their ideas about what the moral dilemmas are in the two selections, along with an example from each selection.

- Ask them to include in a second paragraph their ideas about how the dilemmas could be resolved, along with an example from each selection.

Transcript

In "Marriage Is a Private Affair," you read a fictional account of a moral dilemma created when cultures clash. Now you'll read a transcript of an actual, similar situation.

Case Study #51

Adam and Rosie

When we were first going out, Rosie's parents were extremely upset by her dating a non-Korean. They refused to meet me. One day Rosie decided to take me to visit her grandmother, who lived only a few blocks from Rosie's parents. It was hard to read her reaction. She didn't speak much English, and I didn't speak Korean. She offered us tea, and after a half hour we left. We started to visit her regularly, and even though Rosie's parents wouldn't accept our relationship, it was clear that her grandmother enjoyed our coming over. Finally she had a talk with Rosie's mother, and soon after that we received our first invitation to the house.

Now we have a child, and Rosie's parents have relaxed. I was really touched when her father said at the baby naming, "After a hundred generations our family tree has a different color branch grafted onto it. I was very worried about the colors harmonizing, but now that I can see the results, I am pleased."

I think if it wasn't for her grandmother, we would never have made it as a couple. When I visit my in-laws these days, I take my mother-in-law's hands and kiss them in front of her friends. She and her friends giggle like schoolgirls. In their culture they're not used to direct expressions of affection—especially between men and women. It wouldn't be considered proper nor would they tolerate that kind of behavior if Rosie had married another Korean. But my being white puts me in a different category. I think for them, as upset as they initially were by Rosie getting involved with me, they enjoy the novelty I have introduced into their lives.

ADAM AND ROSIE **995**

Transcript

Tell students that the transcript and the short story both illustrate the importance of finding common ground in cases of cultural conflict. As they read, ask students to consider whether this transcript or the short story more effectively show the power of love in overcoming cultural prejudice.

READING FOR INFORMATION

Point out that "Adam and Rosie" is a transcript. It is a taped interview with Adam about how he eventually won the approval of Rosie's Korean parents, even though he was non-Korean.

- Ask students how a transcript is similar to but different from a letter. ***Possible answer:*** *A transcript of an interview can contain a person's thoughts and words, just as a letter does. However, a transcript is based on an interview, and the person's words are usually in response to a question posed by the interviewer.*

- After students have read the transcript, ask them to suggest the question that the interviewer asked Adam to elicit this response. ***Possible answer:*** *The interviewer may have asked him how he and Rosie won parental approval of their relationship.*

TIERED DISCUSSION PROMPTS

Use these prompts to help students compare the transcript and the short story:

Connect Have you ever been in a situation in which someone refused to accept you? How did you respond? *Student responses will vary.*

Analyze How did Adam's relationship with Rosie's grandmother lead to her parents' acceptance of him into the family? ***Possible answer:*** *His efforts with the grandmother opened the door to the extended family. The grandmother's acceptance and support paved the way for Adam's winning parental approval.*

Practice and Apply

COMMON CORE FOCUS

RI 7 Analyze various accounts of a subject.

POSTER

Have students compare and contrast the ideas about culture that are represented in the short story, the transcript, and the poster. Ask students: What ideas, if any, do all three pieces have in common? Which ideas about culture do you share with the writers and the artist?

ANALYZE VISUALS | COMMON CORE RI 7

A. INTERPRET

Possible answer: Answers will vary. Students may suggest that the designer wanted to show the number of different ethnicities in Texas through the use of many small images.

ANALYZE VISUALS | COMMON CORE RI 7

B. ANALYZE

Answer: The poster is promoting a society in which everyone celebrates their own heritage, and respects other people's heritage, beliefs, and customs.

ANALYZE VISUALS | COMMON CORE RI 7

C. ANALYZE

Answer: Answers will vary. Students should support their answers with reasons, including reasons gathered from the short story and transcript they have just read.

Poster

Images can also help you consider what happens when different cultures interact. Think about the poster below in the context of the short story and transcript you have just read. The questions to the right will help you.

COMMON CORE

RI 7 Analyze various accounts of a subject told in different mediums, determining which details are emphasized in each account.

FESTIVAL OF WORLD CULTURES
2010
Brooklyn Arts League

A. INTERPRET
Why do you think the designer of the poster chose the format of nine small images?

B. ANALYZE
What view of society is the poster promoting?

C. ANALYZE
Do you think festivals like this can help prevent cultural clashes from occurring? Why or why not?

Assessment Practice: Short Constructed Response

LITERARY TEXT: "MARRIAGE IS A PRIVATE AFFAIR"

Assessments often expect you to analyze the relationship of literary elements featured in a literary text. Practice analyzing the relationship of setting and conflict by answering the **short constructed response question** below.

> At the end of "Marriage Is a Private Affair," a sentence reads "It was one of those rare occasions when even Nature takes a hand in a human fight." What effect does the thunderstorm have on Okeke's internal conflict? Support your answer with evidence from the story.

◄ **STRATEGIES IN ACTION**

1. Reread the section closely.
2. Identify what Okeke's internal conflict is. Then note what happens to this conflict as the storm builds.
3. Support your answer with evidence from the story.

NONFICTION TEXT: "ADAM AND ROSIE"

Assessments often expect you to identify and to analyze conflicts that are present in the texts you read. Practice these skills by answering the **short constructed response question** below.

> What is the cultural conflict in "Adam and Rosie," and how is it resolved? Support your answer with evidence from the selection.

◄ **STRATEGIES IN ACTION**

1. Notice that this question has two parts.
2. First, reread the transcript and note the conflict involved. Then read it a third time, looking for details that explain how the conflict ends.
3. Use evidence from the text in the form of a **direct quotation**, a **paraphrase**, or a **specific synopsis** to support your answers.

COMPARING LITERARY AND NONFICTION TEXTS

Tests often expect you to answer questions that ask you to make connections between literary and nonfiction texts and the everyday world. Practice this valuable skill by applying the following **short constructed response question** to "Marriage Is a Private Affair" and "Adam and Rosie."

> In "Marriage Is a Private Affair" and "Adam and Rosie," having grandchildren seems to help the parents accept their children's marriage to someone from a different culture. Why might grandchildren have this effect? Support your answer with evidence from both selections.

◄ **STRATEGIES IN ACTION**

1. This question is asking you to make an **inference**, an educated guess based on evidence in the texts and on your own knowledge or experiences.
2. Review the details in both texts, and connect that information with what you know about the grandparent and grandchild relationship. Use evidence from the texts and even your own life to support your answer.

Assessment Practice: Short Constructed Response

LITERARY TEXT: "MARRIAGE IS A PRIVATE AFFAIR" **Possible answer:** At the end of "Marriage Is a Private Affair" the storm reflects Okeke's internal struggle about whether or not to continue ignoring his son and his son's family. As the storm builds, the rain washes away Okeke's resistance. The storm leaves Okeke tormented by the image of his grandchildren standing outside in the storm, "sad and forsaken." For the first time, he feels remorse.

NONFICTION TEXT: "ADAM AND ROSIE" **Possible answer:** In "Adam and Rosie," the cultural conflict revolves around Adam, who is not Korean, marrying Rosie, who is. Rosie's parents are upset by the relationship. However, Rosie's grandmother plays a major role in resolving the cultural conflict when she intervenes on the couple's behalf. As a result, the parents begin allowing the couple to visit. The birth of a grandchild relaxes Rosie's parents even more.

COMPARING LITERARY AND NONFICTION TEXTS **Possible answer:** In "Marriage Is a Private Affair," Okeke will not consider accepting his son's marriage until he learns he has grandchildren. Similarly, in "Adam and Rosie," Rosie's parents become more relaxed about the marriage when their grandchild arrives. In both selections, the arrival of a new generation sparks emotional responses from the grandparents. As Okeke puts it, "How could he shut his door against them?"

DIFFERENTIATED INSTRUCTION

FOR STRUGGLING WRITERS

Create a Controlling Idea Write the short constructed response on the board. Have students work in pairs to paraphrase the question. Ask students to volunteer their paraphrases, and then record the paraphrases on the board. Help students change the question into a thesis statement. Suggest this prompt to get them started: Grandchildren help parents to accept their children's marriages because . . . . Write the students' suggestions on the board. Then have the pairs work on finishing their controlling idea and short answers to the short constructed response.

Focus and Motivate

COMMON CORE FOCUS

RL 1 Cite strong and thorough textual evidence to support analysis of what the text says explicitly as well as inferences drawn from the text. **RL 2** Determine a central theme or idea of a text and analyze its development over the course of the text, including how it emerges and is shaped and refined by specific details. **RL 4** Determine the meaning of words and phrases as they are used in a text. **L 4c** Consult general and specialized reference materials to find the pronunciation of a word or determine or clarify its precise meaning, its part of speech, or its etymology. **L 5** Demonstrate understanding of figurative language.

SUMMARY

The narrator recalls the summer of 1968, when he was drafted to fight in the Vietnam War. He faced a difficult choice: serve in a war he opposed or flee to Canada. Ultimately, he cannot bring himself to flee. He goes to Vietnam and fights, for which he considers himself a moral coward.

What is COWARDICE?

Have students read the question. Have students consider whether there are different kinds and degrees of cowardice. Extend the exploration by having groups complete the *DISCUSS* activity.

Selection Resources

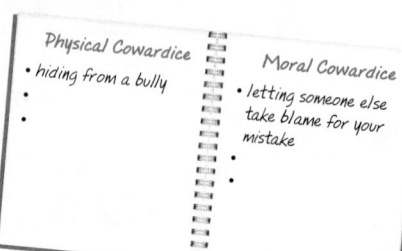
What is COWARDICE?

COMMON CORE

RL 1 Cite strong and thorough textual evidence to support inferences drawn from the text. **RL 2** Determine a central idea of a text and analyze its development over the course of the text, including how it emerges and is shaped and refined by specific details. **RL 4** Determine the meaning of words and phrases as they are used in a text.

Some people take great risks to avoid being accused of cowardice. Yet daring actions are not necessarily brave ones, especially if they are done for the wrong reasons. In "On the Rainy River," a young man must decide whether to risk his life fighting in a war he opposes.

DISCUSS With a small group of classmates, discuss the difference between physical cowardice and moral cowardice. Come up with several examples of each type of cowardice.

Physical Cowardice
• hiding from a bully
•
•

Moral Cowardice
• letting someone else take blame for your mistake
•

998

See resources on the **Teacher One Stop DVD-ROM** and on <u>thinkcentral.com</u>.

 RESOURCE MANAGER UNIT 9
Plan and Teach, pp. 111–118
Summary, pp. 119–120†‡*
Text Analysis and Reading
    Skill, pp. 121–124†*
Vocabulary, pp. 125–127*
Grammar and Style, p. 130

DIAGNOSTIC AND SELECTION TESTS
Selection Tests, pp. 287–290

 BEST PRACTICES TOOLKIT
Word Questioning, p. E9
T Charts, p. A25
Jigsaw Reading, p. A1
New Word Analysis, p. E8
Cluster Diagram, p. B18

 Video link at <u>thinkcentral.com</u>

TECHNOLOGY
⊘ **Teacher One Stop DVD-ROM**
⊘ **Student One Stop DVD-ROM**
⊘ **Audio Anthology CD**
⊘ **GrammarNotes DVD-ROM**
⊘ **ExamView Test Generator**
    on the **Teacher One Stop**

* Resources for Differentiation   † Also in Spanish   ‡ In Haitian Creole and Vietnamese

TEXT ANALYSIS: HISTORICAL CONTEXT

When you look at literature in its **historical context,** you examine the social conditions that inspired or influenced the creation of a literary work and that contribute to its **theme.** Sometimes you can obtain historical information from the work you are reading. For example, the narrator of Tim O'Brien's story often directly comments on the Vietnam War era:

America was divided on these and a thousand other issues. . . . The only certainty that summer was moral confusion.

You may also need to read background information to learn more about a work's historical context. Before you read "On the Rainy River," study the background information on this page. Then, as you read the story, use this information to gain insight into the narrator's actions and beliefs and into the story's theme.

READING SKILL: IDENTIFY AUTHOR'S PERSPECTIVE

An **author's perspective** is the combination of beliefs, values, and feelings through which a writer views a subject. Tim O'Brien's perspective was influenced by his rural upbringing, his education, and his experiences in Vietnam. These influences are reflected in statements by the narrator of "On the Rainy River," whose background and experiences are very similar to those of the author.

As you read, use a chart like the one shown to identify statements that reveal the author's perspective.

Statements	O'Brien's Perspective
"It was my view then, and still is, that you don't make war without knowing why."	The United States should not have entered the Vietnam War.

Review: Make Inferences, Predict

▲ VOCABULARY IN CONTEXT

O'Brien uses the following words to describe characters and attitudes. Put them into the categories "Words I Know Well," "Words I Think I Know," and "Words I Don't Know at All." Write brief definitions for words in the first two categories.

WORD LIST		
acquiescence	compassionate	preoccupied
censure	naive	reticence

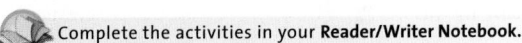 Complete the activities in your **Reader/Writer Notebook.**

Meet the Author

Tim O'Brien
born 1946

Fact and Fiction
"On the Rainy River" appears in *The Things They Carried* (1990), Tim O'Brien's collection of interrelated stories about the Vietnam War. Although the stories are fictional, they were inspired by O'Brien's wartime experiences. He even gave his own name to the narrator, who, like the real Tim O'Brien, grew up in Minnesota and was drafted into the U.S. Army after graduating from college. For O'Brien, the truths a story conveys are more important than whether the story is literally true: "I want you to feel what I felt. I want you to know why story truth is truer sometimes than happening truth."

BACKGROUND TO THE STORY

The Vietnam War
The Vietnam War (1954–1975) was one of the most controversial military conflicts in U.S. history. The United States entered the war in the 1960s to prevent the spread of Communism throughout Southeast Asia. During the course of the war, nearly 3 million Americans were sent overseas to defend the South Vietnamese government against a takeover by Communist North Vietnam and the Viet Cong, a South Vietnamese Communist rebel force. Although many volunteered for service, about two-thirds of American soldiers were drafted into the military. Draftees who opposed the war faced a difficult decision: whether to risk their lives in a foreign war they did not believe in or risk imprisonment at home by refusing to serve. Some chose to leave the country, most often by crossing the border into Canada.

Author Online **THINK** central
Go to **thinkcentral.com.**
KEYWORD: HML10-999

999

Teach

TEXT ANALYSIS — COMMON CORE — RL 2

● *Model the Skill:* HISTORICAL CONTEXT

To model how to understand historical context, read this example:

> Young men finishing school in 1968 had more to worry about than finding a job. They had to wonder if they would soon be dodging bullets in an Asian jungle.

Point out that the historical context described in the **Background** helps them understand the passage because it explains that Americans were being drafted to fight in Vietnam.

READING SKILL — COMMON CORE — RL 1

■ *Model the Skill:* IDENTIFY AUTHOR'S PERSPECTIVE

To model how to identify the author's perspective, read this example:

> I was eager to enlist. My dad and grandfather were army men. Fighting our nation's enemies was in my blood. There are no cowards in our family.

Point out that the passage reveals the author's perspective about the army: a strong belief in the use of military force.

GUIDED PRACTICE Ask for other possible insights to be gained.

 RESOURCE MANAGER—Copy Master
Identify Author's Perspective p. 123

VOCABULARY SKILL

COMMON CORE — L 4

▲ VOCABULARY IN CONTEXT

DIAGNOSE WORD KNOWLEDGE Have all students complete Vocabulary in Context. Check their definitions against the following:

acquiescence (ăk′wē-ĕs′əns) *n.* passive agreement; acceptance without protest
censure (sĕn′shər) *n.* harsh criticism or disapproval
compassionate (kəm-păsh′ə-nĭt) *adj.* feeling or sharing the suffering of others
naive (nī-ēv′) *adj.* unsophisticated, lacking worldly experience
preoccupied (prē-ŏk′yə-pīd′) *adj.* absorbed in one's thoughts; distracted
reticence (rĕt′ĭ-səns) *n.* the quality of keeping silent or reserved

PRETEACH VOCABULARY Use the following copy master to help students predict meanings for each boldfaced word.

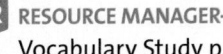 RESOURCE MANAGER—Copy Master
Vocabulary Study p. 125

1. Read item 1 aloud, emphasizing *acquiescence.*

2. Point out the phrase "allows it to continue." Elicit possible meanings for *acquiescence,* such as "acceptance."

3. Have students record their predictions.

4. Repeat the procedure for items 2–6.

READ WITH A PURPOSE

Help students set a purpose for reading. Tell students to look for the ways that Elroy influences O'Brien.

ON THE
Rainy River

Tim O'Brien

This is one story I've never told before. Not to anyone. Not to my parents, not to my brother or sister, not even to my wife. To go into it, I've always thought, would only cause embarrassment for all of us, a sudden need to be elsewhere, which is the natural response to a confession. Even now, I'll admit, the story makes me squirm. For more than twenty years I've had to live with it, feeling the shame, trying to push it away, and so by this act of remembrance, by putting the facts down on paper, I'm hoping to relieve at least some of the pressure on my dreams.

Still, it's a hard story to tell. All of us, I suppose, like to believe that in a
10 moral emergency we will behave like the heroes of our youth, bravely and forthrightly, without thought of personal loss or discredit. Certainly that was my conviction back in the summer of 1968. Tim O'Brien: a secret hero. The Lone Ranger. If the stakes ever became high enough—if the evil were evil enough, if the good were good enough—I would simply tap a secret reservoir of courage that had been accumulating inside me over the years. Courage, I seemed to think, comes to us in finite quantities, like an inheritance, and by being frugal and stashing it away, and letting it earn interest, we steadily increase our moral capital in preparation for that day when the account must be drawn down. It was a comforting theory. It dispensed with all those
20 bothersome little acts of daily courage; it offered hope and grace to the repetitive coward; it justified the past while amortizing the future. **Ⓐ**

Analyze Visuals ▸

Based on details in the collage, what do you **predict** the story will be about?

❶ Targeted Passage

Ⓐ AUTHOR'S PERSPECTIVE Reread lines 9–21. What does this passage suggest about the way the narrator's perspective has changed over time?

READING SKILL

COMMON CORE RL 1

Ⓐ *Model the Skill:* AUTHOR'S PERSPECTIVE

To model how to identify the author's perspective, point out that the narrator's use of past tense—"that was my conviction" (lines 11–12), "It was a comforting theory" (line 19)—suggests he now feels differently. Highlight other clues to the narrator's changed perspective, such as his statement that "it's a hard story to tell" (line 9) and his I'm-wiser-now tone: "Courage, I seemed to think . . ." (lines 15–16)

Have students record these statements in their Author's Perspective charts.

Possible answer: The passage suggests that the narrator once believed that he would act heroically "in a moral emergency" (lines 9–10), but is no longer convinced of this belief.

DIFFERENTIATED INSTRUCTION

FOR ENGLISH LANGUAGE LEARNERS

Vocabulary Support Use Word Questioning to teach these words: *justified* (line 21), *drafted* (line 23), *policy* (line 35), *radical* (line 42), *abstract* (line 46), *dimension* (line 363).

🧰 BEST PRACTICES TOOLKIT—Transparency
Word Questioning p. E9

FOR STRUGGLING READERS

In combination with the *Audio Anthology* CD, use one or more Targeted Passages (pp. 1000, 1003, 1005, 1014, 1016) to ensure that students focus on key story events, concepts, and skills. Targeted Passages are also good for English learners.

❶ Targeted Passage [Lines 1–15]

This passage establishes the story as a "confession" intended to make the narrator feel better. It also describes the narrator's perspective on courage.

U.S. Planes Attack North Vietnam Bases

Hanoi Charges U.S. Raid Far North of 20th Parallel

BACKGROUND

American Exiles in Canada Facing a draft notice calling him to the Vietnam War, the story's narrator considers fleeing to Canada. Beginning in 1965, many Americans fled to Canada to avoid military service in the Vietnam War. Estimates range anywhere from 20,000 to 90,000, including draft resisters ("draft dodgers") as well as military deserters. Some of these Americans returned to the United States after the war, but many did not. (In 1977, President Jimmy Carter granted amnesty to draft resisters, but not to deserters.)

Analyze Visuals

Possible answer: Details in the collage suggest that the story may be about growing U.S. involvement in the Vietnam War. Headlines about the war are superimposed on a partial map of the United States (Minnesota) and Canada. The rushing water shown in the picture may suggest that the United States is being swept into the conflict. It may also represent the Rainy River, which forms the border between Minnesota and Canada—a place to which many drafted men who opposed the war escaped.

REVISIT THE BIG QUESTION
What is
COWARDICE?

Discuss In lines 9–21, the narrator talks about what it means to behave like a hero "in a moral emergency" (lines 9–10). What kind of cowardice is the opposite of the kind of heroic behavior the narrator describes? *Possible answer:* The "heroes of our youth" that the narrator describes act "bravely and forthrightly, without thought of personal loss or discredit" (lines 10–11). By contrast, cowardice might involve being too concerned with personal loss.

Analyze Visuals

Activity After students read pages 1002–1003, ask them how the buttons displayed across these pages reflect the historical context of the story. *Possible answer: The buttons reflect antiwar sentiment during the Vietnam era.*

BACKGROUND

Students for a Democratic Society SDS was one of the groups pursuing what O'Brien describes as "radical . . . hothead stuff" (line 42). The group was founded in 1960 and became a central organizer of antiwar protests. In 1965, SDS organized protests against the Vietnam War that drew first 15,000 and then 30,000 people to Washington, D.C. In April 1968, just months before O'Brien's story takes place, members of SDS occupied a building at Columbia University to protest that institution's involvement in war research.

TEXT ANALYSIS   **COMMON CORE**   RL 2

ⓑ HISTORICAL CONTEXT

Possible answer: The narrator is opposed to the Vietnam War because there is no clarity or general agreement about the purpose or nature of the war or even about the facts that explain how it started. The narrator believes that "you don't make war without knowing why. . . . Once people are dead, you can't make them undead" (lines 37, 40).

VOCABULARY   **COMMON CORE**   L 4

OWN THE WORD

naive: Discuss the definition of *naive* with students. Then have students list possible synonyms for the word. *Possible answers: unaffected, ingenuous*

In June of 1968, a month after graduating from Macalester College, I was drafted to fight a war I hated. I was twenty-one years old. Young, yes, and politically **naive,** but even so the American war in Vietnam seemed to me wrong. Certain blood was being shed for uncertain reasons. I saw no unity of purpose, no consensus on matters of philosophy or history or law. The very facts were shrouded in uncertainty: Was it a civil war? A war of national liberation or simple aggression? Who started it, and when, and why? What really happened to the U.S.S. *Maddox* on that dark night in the Gulf of
30 Tonkin?[1] Was Ho Chi Minh[2] a Communist stooge, or a nationalist savior, or both, or neither? What about the Geneva Accords?[3] What about SEATO[4] and the Cold War?[5] What about dominoes?[6] America was divided on these and a thousand other issues, and the debate had spilled out across the floor of the United States Senate and into the streets, and smart men in pinstripes could not agree on even the most fundamental matters of public policy. The only certainty that summer was moral confusion. It was my view then, and still is, that you don't make war without knowing why. Knowledge, of course, is always imperfect, but it seemed to me that when a nation goes to war it must have reasonable confidence in the justice and imperative of its cause. You can't
40 fix your mistakes. Once people are dead, you can't make them undead. ⓑ

In any case those were my convictions, and back in college I had taken a modest stand against the war. Nothing radical, no hothead stuff, just ringing

naive (nī-ēv′) *adj.* unsophisticated, lacking worldly experience

ⓑ **HISTORICAL CONTEXT** Reread lines 22–40. Cite details that explain why the narrator is opposed to the Vietnam War.

---

1. **U.S.S. *Maddox* . . . Gulf of Tonkin** (tŏn′kĭn′): a reference to the alleged attack in 1964 on the U.S. destroyer *Maddox* in the Gulf of Tonkin, off the coast of North Vietnam, which provided a basis for expanding U.S. involvement in the Vietnam conflict.
2. **Ho Chi Minh** (hō′ chē′ mĭn′): a political leader who waged a successful fight against French colonial rule and established a Communist government in North Vietnam.
3. **Geneva Accords:** a 1954 peace agreement providing for the temporary division of Vietnam into North and South Vietnam and calling for national elections.
4. **SEATO:** the Southeast Asia Treaty Organization, an alliance of eight nations, including the United States, formed to halt Communist expansion in Southeast Asia after Communist forces defeated France in Indochina.
5. **Cold War:** the post–World War II struggle for influence between Communist and democratic nations.
6. **dominoes:** a reference to the domino theory, which holds that if a nation becomes a Communist state, it it will cause neighboring nations to also become Communist, as a falling domino will cause neighboring dominoes to fall too.

1002   UNIT 9: HISTORY, CULTURE, AND THE AUTHOR

DIFFERENTIATED INSTRUCTION

FOR ENGLISH LANGUAGE LEARNERS

Culture: Clarify To clarify the domino theory (line 32), display a map of Southeast Asia. Have students locate Vietnam and its neighboring nations, such as Cambodia, Laos, and Thailand. Explain that the domino theory was used to justify U.S. involvement in Vietnam. After U.S. troops left in 1973, Communists took over two nearby nations, Cambodia and Laos. Other countries in the region remained non-communist.

FOR ADVANCED LEARNERS/PRE–AP

Synthesize Perspectives In lines 27–32, the narrator poses questions to which there were no definite answers in 1968. Divide students into groups, and have each group research and attempt to answer one or more of these questions from a present-day perspective. Have groups share their conclusions with the class.

a few doorbells for Gene McCarthy,[7] composing a few tedious, uninspired editorials for the campus newspaper. Oddly, though, it was almost entirely an intellectual activity. I brought some energy to it, of course, but it was the energy that accompanies almost any abstract endeavor; I felt no personal danger; I felt no sense of an impending crisis in my life. Stupidly, with a kind of smug removal that I can't begin to fathom, I assumed that the problems of killing and dying did not fall within my special province.

50   The draft notice arrived on June 17, 1968. It was a humid afternoon, I remember, cloudy and very quiet, and I'd just come in from a round of golf. My mother and father were having lunch out in the kitchen. I remember opening up the letter, scanning the first few lines, feeling the blood go thick behind my eyes. I remember a sound in my head. It wasn't thinking, it was just a silent howl. A million things all at once—I was too *good* for this war. Too smart, too **compassionate,** too everything. It couldn't happen. I was above it. I had the world—Phi Beta Kappa and summa cum laude and president of the student body and a full-ride scholarship for grad studies at Harvard. A mistake, maybe—a foul-up in the paperwork. I was no soldier. I hated Boy Scouts. I
60   hated camping out. I hated dirt and tents and mosquitoes. The sight of blood made me queasy, and I couldn't tolerate authority, and I didn't know a rifle from a slingshot. I was a *liberal*: If they needed fresh bodies, why not draft some back-to-the-stone-age hawk? Or some dumb jingo[8] in his hardhat and Bomb Hanoi button? Or one of LBJ's[9] pretty daughters? Or Westmoreland's[10] whole family—nephews and nieces and baby grandson? There should be a law, I thought. If you support a war, if you think it's worth the price, that's fine, but you have to put your own life on the line. You have to head for the front and hook up with an infantry unit and help spill the blood. And you have to bring along your wife, or your kids, or your lover. A *law*, I thought.

70   I remember the rage in my stomach. Later it burned down to a smoldering self-pity, then to numbness. At dinner that night my father asked what my plans were.

---

7. **Gene McCarthy:** Eugene McCarthy, the U.S. senator from Minnesota and a critic of the Vietnam War, who unsuccessfully sought the 1968 Democratic presidential nomination.

8. **jingo** (jǐng'gō): one who aggressively supports his or her country and favors war as a means of settling political disputes.

9. **LBJ:** Lyndon B. Johnson, the U.S. president from 1963 to 1969.

10. **Westmoreland:** General William Westmoreland, the senior commander of U.S. forces in Vietnam from 1964 to 1968.

ON THE RAINY RIVER **1003**

COMMON CORE RL 4

Language Coach

Fixed Expressions In English, **fixed expressions** are words that are commonly used together to express a specific meaning. The expression *of course* (line 45) means "naturally" or "certainly." What does the fixed expression *above it* (line 56) mean? (Hint: check the context of the expression by reading the sentences around it.)

②

compassionate
(kəm-pǎsh'ə-nĭt) *adj.*
feeling or sharing the suffering of others

TIERED DISCUSSION PROMPTS
Direct students to lines 41–69. Use these prompts to help students understand the narrator's reaction to receiving a draft notice:

Connect The narrator is terribly upset by receiving a draft notice. Have you or someone you know ever received upsetting news? Explain the reactions. *Accept all reasonable responses.*

Analyze How does receiving the draft notice change the narrator's perspective? *Possible answer: Until he received the draft notice, thinking about the war "was almost entirely an intellectual activity" (lines 44–45) for the narrator. He felt far removed from the reality of war's killing and dying. Receiving the draft notice comes as both a shock and a wake-up call. All of a sudden, the narrator realizes that the war is now a personal reality for him.*

Synthesize As the narrator looks back on his state of mind before and after receiving the draft notice, what emotions do you think he is experiencing? Cite evidence to support your answer. *Possible answer: The narrator seems angry at his own naiveté, as evidenced by such statements as: "Stupidly, with a kind of smug removal that I can't begin to fathom, I assumed that the problems of killing and dying did not fall within my special province" (lines 47–49).*

VOCABULARY   COMMON CORE
                                          L 4
OWN THE WORD

compassionate: Have students list acts that could be considered *compassionate*.

FOR STRUGGLING READERS

② **Targeted Passage** [Lines 46–65]
This passage describes a pivotal event in the story—the arrival of the draft notice—and the narrator's reaction of shock and disbelief.

-   What key event in the narrator's life occurs on June 17, 1968? (line 50)

-   How did the narrator feel about the Vietnam War before this event? (lines 41–49)

-   Describe the narrator's reaction. (lines 52–71)

FOR ENGLISH LANGUAGE LEARNERS

Language Coach   COMMON CORE
                                          RL 4
Fixed Expressions *Answer:* Above it *means "better than."* Have students work in pairs to create two sentences of dialogue in which they use the expressions *of course* and *above it*. Invite student volunteers to read their sentences aloud to the class.

TIERED DISCUSSION PROMPTS

Direct students to lines 73–98. Use these prompts to help students understand the narrator's feelings about working at the meat-packing plant:

Connect Have you ever had an unpleasant job to do? Explain the job and your reaction. *Accept all reasonable responses.*

Analyze How does the author's use of sensory details help you understand the narrator's feelings about his job? Give examples. *Possible answer: The narrator finds his job very distasteful. The author conveys this feeling by comparing the job to "standing for eight hours a day under a lukewarm blood-shower" (lines 92–93) and describing the "dense greasy pig-stink that soaked deep into [his] skin and hair" (lines 95–96).*

Evaluate Considering the narrator's description of his job at the meat-packing plant, why do you think he continued to work there? *Possible answer: Perhaps it was the best or only job he could find as a 21-year-old home from college.*

TEXT ANALYSIS

COMMON CORE

RL 2

Ⓒ HISTORICAL CONTEXT

Possible answer: The narrator describes how young men had previously avoided being drafted to fight in Vietnam: they could get deferments by attending graduate school; they could join the National Guard or Army Reserves; they could try to be rejected for health reasons or exempted as conscientious objectors.

"Nothing," I said. "Wait."

I spent the summer of 1968 working in an Armour meat-packing plant in my hometown of Worthington, Minnesota. The plant specialized in pork products, and for eight hours a day I stood on a quarter-mile assembly line—more properly, a disassembly line—removing blood clots from the necks of dead pigs. My job title, I believe, was Declotter. After slaughter, the hogs were decapitated, split down the length of the belly, pried open, eviscerated,[11] and strung up by the hind hocks on a high conveyer belt. Then gravity took
80 over. By the time a carcass reached my spot on the line, the fluids had mostly drained out, everything except for thick clots of blood in the neck and upper chest cavity. To remove the stuff, I used a kind of water gun. The machine was heavy, maybe eighty pounds, and was suspended from the ceiling by a heavy rubber cord. There was some bounce to it, an elastic up-and-down give, and the trick was to maneuver the gun with your whole body, not lifting with the arms, just letting the rubber cord do the work for you. At one end was a trigger; at the muzzle end was a small nozzle and a steel roller brush. As a carcass passed by, you'd lean forward and swing the gun up against the clots and squeeze the trigger, all in one motion, and the brush would whirl and
90 water would come shooting out and you'd hear a quick splattering sound as the clots dissolved into a fine red mist. It was not pleasant work. Goggles were a necessity, and a rubber apron, but even so it was like standing for eight hours a day under a lukewarm blood-shower. At night I'd go home smelling of pig. I couldn't wash it out. Even after a hot bath, scrubbing hard, the stink was always there—like old bacon, or sausage, a dense greasy pig-stink that soaked deep into my skin and hair. Among other things, I remember, it was tough getting dates that summer. I felt isolated; I spent a lot of time alone. And there was also that draft notice tucked away in my wallet.

In the evenings I'd sometimes borrow my father's car and drive aimlessly
100 around town, feeling sorry for myself, thinking about the war and the pig factory and how my life seemed to be collapsing toward slaughter. I felt paralyzed. All around me the options seemed to be narrowing, as if I were hurtling down a huge black funnel, the whole world squeezing in tight. There was no happy way out. The government had ended most graduate school deferments; the waiting lists for the National Guard and Reserves[12] were impossibly long; my health was solid; I didn't qualify for CO status[13]—no religious grounds, no history as a pacifist. Moreover, I could not claim to be opposed to war as a matter of general principle. There were occasions, I believed, when a nation was justified in using military force to achieve its
110 ends, to stop a Hitler or some comparable evil, and I told myself that in such circumstances I would've willingly marched off to the battle. The problem, though, was that a draft board did not let you choose your war. Ⓒ

---

11. **eviscerated** (ĭ-vĭsʹə-rā′tĭd): having guts removed.

12. **National Guard and Reserves:** military reserve units run by each state in the United States. Some men joined these units to avoid service in Vietnam.

13. **CO status:** the status of a conscientious objector, a person exempted from military service because of strongly held moral or religious beliefs that do not permit participation in war.

1004 UNIT 9: HISTORY, CULTURE, AND THE AUTHOR

Ⓒ **HISTORICAL CONTEXT**
Reread lines 99–112, and then review the Background on page 999. What circumstances from that period are depicted here?

DIFFERENTIATED INSTRUCTION

FOR ENGLISH LANGUAGE LEARNERS

Language: Contractions Point out the contractions *would've* (line 111), *must've* (line 307), and *could've* (line 411), and help students determine their meaning from the context. List the contractions in a T Chart, along with *might've* and *should've*, and have students write out their long forms. Then ask students to write a short paragraph about how they might have felt about the Vietnam War if they had been draft-age young men in 1968.

Encourage students to use as many of the five contractions as they can in their paragraph.

Contraction	Long Form
would've	would have
must've	must have

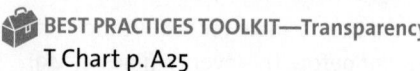 **BEST PRACTICES TOOLKIT—Transparency**
T Chart p. A25

Beyond all this, or at the very center, was the raw fact of terror. I did not want to die. Not ever. But certainly not then, not there, not in a wrong war. Driving up Main Street, past the courthouse and the Ben Franklin store, I sometimes felt the fear spreading inside me like weeds. I imagined myself dead. I imagined myself doing things I could not do—charging an enemy position, taking aim at another human being. **D**

At some point in mid-July I began thinking seriously about Canada. The border lay a few hundred miles north, an eight-hour drive. Both my conscience and my instincts were telling me to make a break for it, just take off and run like hell and never stop. In the beginning the idea seemed purely abstract, the word Canada printing itself out in my head; but after a time I could see particular shapes and images, the sorry details of my own future— a hotel room in Winnipeg, a battered old suitcase, my father's eyes as I tried to explain myself over the telephone. I could almost hear his voice, and my mother's. *Run*, I'd think. Then I'd think, *Impossible*. Then a second later I'd think, *Run.*

It was a kind of schizophrenia.[14] A moral split. I couldn't make up my mind. I feared the war, yes, but I also feared exile. I was afraid of walking away from my own life, my friends and my family, my whole history, everything that mattered to me. I feared losing the respect of my parents. I feared the law. I feared ridicule and **censure.** My hometown was a conservative little spot on the prairie, a place where tradition counted, and it was easy to imagine people sitting around a table at the old Gobbler Café on Main Street, coffee cups poised, the conversation slowly zeroing in on the young O'Brien kid, how the damned sissy had taken off for Canada. At night, when I couldn't sleep, I'd sometimes carry on fierce arguments with those people. I'd be screaming at them, telling them how much I detested their blind, thoughtless, automatic **acquiescence** to it all, their simple-minded patriotism, their prideful ignorance, their love-it-or-leave-it platitudes, how they were sending me off to fight a war they didn't understand and didn't want to understand. I held them responsible. By God, yes I *did*. All of them—I held them personally and individually responsible—the polyestered Kiwanis boys, the merchants and farmers, the pious churchgoers, the chatty housewives, the PTA and the Lions club and the Veterans of Foreign Wars and the fine upstanding gentry out at the country club. They didn't know Bao Dai[15] from the man in the moon. They didn't know history. They didn't know the first thing about Diem's[16] tyranny, or the nature of Vietnamese nationalism, or the long colonialism of the French—this was all too damned complicated, it required some reading— but no matter, it was a war to stop the Communists, plain and simple, which was how they liked things, and you were treasonous if you had second thoughts about killing or dying for plain and simple reasons. **A**

---

14. **schizophrenia** (skĭt′sə-frē′nē-ə): a mental disorder. Here, the narrator refers to a split personality.

15. **Bao Dai** (bä′ō dä′ē): the last emperor of Vietnam (1926–1945) and chief of state from 1949 to 1955.

16. **Diem:** Ngo Dinh Diem (nyō′ dĭn′ dē-ĕm′), the brutal and dictatorial first president of South Vietnam, who was murdered by his own generals in 1963.

ON THE RAINY RIVER **1005**

D GRAMMAR AND STYLE
Reread lines 113–118. Notice how O'Brien uses short sentences, sentence fragments, and figurative language to establish his **voice,** or the "sound" of his writing.

3 Targeted Passage

censure (sĕn′shər) *n.* harsh criticism or disapproval

acquiescence (ăk′wē-ĕs′əns) *n.* passive agreement; acceptance without protest

COMMON CORE RL 4

A AFFIXES
The affix *-ism* comes from the Greek *-ismos*, which was a suffix that turned verbs into nouns. In modern English, *-ism* forms nouns that mean "the condition of" or "characteristic of." Reread lines 140–149. What words contain the affix *-ism*? What do these words mean?

D GRAMMAR AND STYLE
COMMON CORE L 5

Establish Voice Point out that O'Brien's language ["the raw fact of terror" (line 113)], sentence structure, and figurative language ["fear spreading inside me like weeds" (line 116)] add drama to the narrative and help to convey the stress that the narrator is feeling. Ask students to find other passages in the text where O'Brien uses short sentences, fragments, or figurative language to create a similar effect. Read them aloud. *Possible answers: Lines 129–133, 175–182, 486–496*

VOCABULARY
COMMON CORE RL 4

A AFFIXES

Read lines 140–149 aloud as students follow along. Have students stop you when they hear a word ending with *-ism*. Write the words on the board as they are called out. Then ask students to brainstorm a list of other nouns that contain the affix *-ism*. *Answer: The words* patriotism, nationalism, *and* colonialism *contain the affix* -ism. Patriotism *means "love or devotion to country,"* nationalism *means "excessive devotion to country," and* colonialism *means "the taking of other countries as colonies, especially to exploit their resources."*

VOCABULARY
COMMON CORE L 4

OWN THE WORD

- **censure:** Review the definition of *censure* with students. A *censure* is an official reprimand. Ask students why someone might be *censured*.

- **acquiescence:** Ask students if they have ever *acquiesced* to something and if so, to explain the circumstances. Have students compare and contrast the connotations of *acquiescence* and agreement. *Possible answer: Both words convey agreement, but agreement is active, and acquiescence is passive, indicating giving in.*

FOR STRUGGLING READERS

3 Targeted Passage [Lines 119–142]

This passage highlights the narrator's conflict: his fear of the war versus his reluctance to exile himself to Canada.

- What conflict is the narrator experiencing? (lines 129–130)

- What would the narrator lose if he fled to Canada? (lines 130–133)

- How does the narrator anticipate his hometown will react if he goes to Canada? (lines 133–153)

FOR ENGLISH LANGUAGE LEARNERS

Culture: Connect Discuss the ideas presented in lines 133–153. Focus on why the hometown people would believe that "a war to stop the Communists" was worth fighting and dying for, "plain and simple" (line 151). Use a print or online encyclopedia to help students learn more about communism. Then, if possible, ask students to describe common views of communism in their home country.

ON THE RAINY RIVER **1005**

Direct students to lines 154–182. Use these prompts to help students understand the feelings that cause O'Brien to leave town:

Connect Have you ever felt so pressured that you took action without having a definite plan? Explain. *Accept all reasonable responses.*

Analyze What factors cause O'Brien to crack (line 158)? *Possible answer: O'Brien can't make up his mind whether to flee to Canada or to report for duty. This internal conflict, accompanied by a wide range of ever-changing emotions (lines 154–156), causes him so much stress that he finally gives way emotionally.*

Evaluate Would you describe O'Brien's drive north as a panic reaction? Why or why not? *Possible answer: "Panic" generally implies feelings of overwhelming fear or anxiety. In O'Brien's case, however, his actions seem to be dictated more by internal pressure from his inability to make a decision. While fear is certainly part of this pressure, it's not the only factor.*

I was bitter, sure. But it was so much more than that. The emotions went from outrage to terror to bewilderment to guilt to sorrow and then back again to outrage. I felt a sickness inside me. Real disease.

Most of this I've told before, or at least hinted at, but what I have never told is the full truth. How I cracked. How at work one morning, standing on the pig line, I felt something break open in my chest. I don't know what 160 it was. I'll never know. But it was real. I know that much, it was a physical rupture—a cracking-leaking-popping feeling. I remember dropping my water gun. Quickly, almost without thought, I took off my apron and walked out of the plant and drove home. It was midmorning, I remember, and the house was empty. Down in my chest there was still that leaking sensation, something very warm and precious spilling out, and I was covered with blood and hog-stink, and for a long while I just concentrated on holding myself together. I remember taking a hot shower. I remember packing a suitcase and carrying it out to the kitchen, standing very still for a few minutes, looking carefully at the familiar objects all around me. The old chrome toaster, the telephone, the 170 pink and white Formica on the kitchen counters. The room was full of bright sunshine. Everything sparkled. My house, I thought. My life. I'm not sure how long I stood there, but later I scribbled out a short note to my parents.

What it said exactly, I don't recall now. Something vague. Taking off, will call, love Tim.

I drove north.

It's a blur now, as it was then, and all I remember is a sense of high velocity and the feel of the steering wheel in my hands. I was riding on adrenaline.[17] A giddy feeling, in a way, except there was the dreamy edge of impossibility to it—like running a dead-end maze—no way out—it couldn't 180 come to a happy conclusion and yet I was doing it anyway because it was all I could think to do. It was pure flight, fast and mindless. I had no plan. Just hit the border at high speed and crash through and keep on running. Near dusk I passed through Bemidji, then turned northeast toward International Falls. I spent the night in the car behind a closed-down gas station a half mile from the border. In the morning, after gassing up, I headed straight west along the Rainy River, which separates Minnesota from Canada, and which for me separated one life from another. The land was mostly wilderness. Here and there I passed a motel or bait shop, but otherwise the country unfolded in great sweeps of pine and birch and sumac. Though it was still August, the air already 190 had the smell of October, football season, piles of yellow-red leaves, everything crisp and clean. I remember a huge blue sky. Off to my right was the Rainy River, wide as a lake in places, and beyond the Rainy River was Canada.

For a while I just drove, not aiming at anything, then in the late morning I began looking for a place to lie low for a day or two. I was exhausted, and

---

17. **adrenaline** (ə-drĕn′ə-lĭn): a hormone that is released into the bloodstream in response to physical or mental stress, such as fear, and that initiates or heightens several physical responses, including an increase in heart rate.

DIFFERENTIATED INSTRUCTION

FOR ENGLISH LANGUAGE LEARNERS
Vocabulary: Idioms Organize students into groups for a Jigsaw activity. Assign an idiom to a student in each group:

- *make a break for it* (line 121), "flee"
- *lie low* (line 194), "remain out of sight"
- *go off the* (psychic) *edge* (line 271), "go insane"

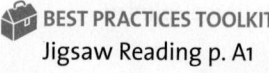 **BEST PRACTICES TOOLKIT**
Jigsaw Reading p. A1

FOR STRUGGLING READERS
Develop Reading Fluency Read lines 154–156 aloud to students. Point out that the emotions the narrator describes are reflected in the sentence structure and punctuation. Model reading lines 157–174 aloud and then engage the class in a choral reading of the same passage.

Distribute the copy masters and have students work in pairs or groups to practice fluency.

 RESOURCE MANAGER—Copy Master
Reading Fluency p. 131

Analyze Visuals

Activity Ask students to explain how the images in the collage are related to each other, using story events as a guide. *Possible answer: The collage shows someone behind the wheel of a car. Superimposed are headlines pertaining to the Vietnam War and a map of Minnesota. In the story, O'Brien is driving toward Canada, fleeing there to avoid military service in Vietnam.*

scared sick, and around noon I pulled into an old fishing resort called the Tip Top Lodge. Actually, it was not a lodge at all, just eight or nine tiny yellow cabins clustered on a peninsula that jutted northward into the Rainy River. The place was in sorry shape. There was a dangerous wooden dock, an old minnow tank, a flimsy tar paper boathouse along the shore. The main building,
200 which stood in a cluster of pines on high ground, seemed to lean heavily to one side, like a cripple, the roof sagging toward Canada. Briefly, I thought about turning around, just giving up, but then I got out of the car and walked up to the front porch.

The man who opened the door that day is the hero of my life. How do I say this without sounding sappy? Blurt it out—the man saved me. He offered exactly what I needed, without questions, without any words at all. He took me in. He was there at the critical time—a silent, watchful presence. Six days later, when it ended, I was unable to find a proper way to thank him, and I never have, and so, if nothing else, this story represents a small gesture of
210 gratitude twenty years overdue.

Even after two decades I can close my eyes and return to that porch at the Tip Top Lodge. I can see the old guy staring at me. Elroy Berdahl: eighty-one years old, skinny and shrunken and mostly bald. He wore a flannel shirt and brown work pants. In one hand, I remember, he carried a green apple, a small paring knife in the other. His eyes had the bluish gray color of a razor blade, the same polished shine, and as he peered up at me I felt a strange sharpness, almost painful, a cutting sensation, as if his gaze were somehow

ON THE RAINY RIVER **1007**

FOR ENGLISH LANGUAGE LEARNERS

Language: Modifiers Explain that lines 213–218 use noun-adjective combinations to create a detailed, vivid picture. Have students identify examples of these combinations. *Possible answers: flannel shirt; brown work pants; green apple; small paring knife; bluish gray eyes; polished shine; strange, painful sharpness; cutting sensation*

FOR ADVANCED LEARNERS/PRE–AP

Analyze Character's Emotions The narrator says that Elroy Berdahl "offered exactly what I needed, without questions, without any words at all" (lines 205–206). Have students reflect on this statement. What could Berdahl have offered the narrator? What was it the narrator needed? Have students write and share a brief essay analyzing the narrator's statement and, if possible, linking it to a personal experience they have had.

---

slicing me open. In part, no doubt, it was my own sense of guilt, but even so I'm absolutely certain that the old man took one look and went right to the heart of things—a kid in trouble. When I asked for a room, Elroy made a little clicking sound with his tongue. He nodded, led me out to one of the cabins, and dropped a key in my hand. I remember smiling at him. I also remember wishing I hadn't. The old man shook his head as if to tell me it wasn't worth the bother.

"Dinner at five-thirty," he said. "You eat fish?"

"Anything," I said.

Elroy grunted and said, "I'll bet."

We spent six days together at the Tip Top Lodge. Just the two of us. Tourist season was over, and there were no boats on the river, and the wilderness seemed to withdraw into a great permanent stillness. Over those six days Elroy Berdahl and I took most of our meals together. In the mornings we sometimes went out on long hikes into the woods, and at night we played Scrabble or listened to records or sat reading in front of his big stone fireplace. At times I felt the awkwardness of an intruder, but Elroy accepted me into his quiet routine without fuss or ceremony. He took my presence for granted, the same way he might've sheltered a stray cat—no wasted sighs or pity—and there was never any talk about it. Just the opposite. What I remember more than anything is the man's willful, almost ferocious silence. In all that time together, all those hours, he never asked the obvious questions: Why was I there? Why alone? Why so **preoccupied**? If Elroy was curious about any of this, he was careful never to put it into words.

My hunch, though, is that he already knew. At least the basics. After all, it was 1968, and guys were burning draft cards, and Canada was just a boat ride away. Elroy Berdahl was no hick. His bedroom, I remember, was cluttered with books and newspapers. He killed me at the Scrabble board, barely concentrating, and on those occasions when speech was necessary, he had a way of compressing large thoughts into small, cryptic packets of language. One evening, just at sunset, he pointed up at an owl circling over the violet-lighted forest to the west.

"Hey, O'Brien," he said. "There's Jesus."

The man was sharp—he didn't miss much. Those razor eyes. Now and then he'd catch me staring out at the river, at the far shore, and I could almost hear the tumblers clicking in his head. Maybe I'm wrong, but I doubt it.

preoccupied
(prē-ŏk′yə-pīd′) *adj.* absorbed in one's thoughts; distracted

---

One thing for certain, he knew I was in desperate trouble. And he knew
I couldn't talk about it. The wrong word—or even the right word—and I
would've disappeared. I was wired and jittery. My skin felt too tight. After
supper one evening I vomited and went back to my cabin and lay down for
a few moments and then vomited again; another time, in the middle of the
afternoon, I began sweating and couldn't shut it off. I went through whole
days feeling dizzy with sorrow. I couldn't sleep; I couldn't lie still. At night I'd
toss around in bed, half awake, half dreaming, imagining how I'd sneak down
to the beach and quietly push one of the old man's boats out into the river and
270 start paddling my way toward Canada. There were times when I thought I'd
gone off the psychic edge. I couldn't tell up from down, I was just falling, and
late in the night I'd lie there watching weird pictures spin through my head.
Getting chased by the Border Patrol—helicopters and searchlights and barking
dogs—I'd be crashing through the woods, I'd be down on my hands and
knees—people shouting out my name—the law closing in on all sides—my
hometown draft board and the FBI and the Royal Canadian Mounted Police.
It all seemed crazy and impossible. Twenty-one years old, an ordinary kid with
all the ordinary dreams and ambitions, and all I wanted was to live the life I
was born to—a mainstream life—I loved baseball and hamburgers and cherry
280 Cokes—and now I was off on the margins of exile, leaving my country forever,
and it seemed so impossible and terrible and sad. **F**

I'm not sure how I made it through those six days. Most of it I can't
remember. On two or three afternoons, to pass some time, I helped Elroy get
the place ready for winter, sweeping down the cabins and hauling in the boats,
little chores that kept my body moving. The days were cool and bright. The
nights were very dark. One morning the old man showed me how to split and
stack firewood, and for several hours we just worked in silence out behind his
house. At one point, I remember, Elroy put down his maul[18] and looked at me
for a long time, his lips drawn as if framing a difficult question, but then he
290 shook his head and went back to work. The man's self-control was amazing.
He never pried. He never put me in a position that required lies or denials.
To an extent, I supposed, his **reticence** was typical of that part of Minnesota,
where privacy still held value, and even if I'd been walking around with some
horrible deformity—four arms and three heads—I'm sure the old man would've
talked about everything except those extra arms and heads. Simple politeness
was part of it. But even more than that, I think, the man understood that words
were insufficient. The problem had gone beyond discussion. During that long
summer I'd been over and over the various arguments, all the pros and cons,
and it was no longer a question that could be decided by an act of pure reason.
300 Intellect had come up against emotion. My conscience told me to run, but
some irrational and powerful force was resisting, like a weight pushing me
toward the war. What it came down to, stupidly, was a sense of shame. Hot,
stupid shame. I did not want people to think badly of me. Not my parents,
not my brother and sister, not even the folks down at the Gobbler Café. I was

---

18. **maul** (môl): a heavy hammer with a wedge-shaped head.

F HISTORICAL CONTEXT
How does the historical
context of the work help
you understand the
narrator's feelings in lines
261–281?

reticence (rĕt′ĭ-səns) n.
the quality of keeping
silent or reserved

FOR STRUGGLING READERS
Comprehension Support In line 300, the
narrator says, "Intellect had come up against
emotion." To make sure students understand
this statement, help them use context clues
in the paragraph to reflect on its meaning.
(*My feelings were stronger than my rational
ideas.*) Help students compare what the narrator *thinks* he should do with what he *feels*
he should do.

FOR ADVANCED LEARNERS/PRE–AP
Synthesize Figurative Language In lines
300–302, the narrator uses a simile to help
convey the inner resistance he feels to the
idea of fleeing to Canada: "…like a weight
pushing me toward the war." Have students
mimic the author's style by writing two original similes or metaphors that would similarly
convey the inner conflict that the narrator
is experiencing.

F *Model the Skill:* **HISTORICAL CONTEXT**

To model how to understand historical
context, review the background information on page 999 with students, and then
reread lines 129–153 aloud. Explain that
the background information and the lines
you just read give context to, or help readers understand, the narrator's feelings in
the passage on this page. Ask students:

- What decision does O'Brien have to
make?

- What are the likely consequences if he
decides to go to Canada? What are the
likely consequences if he decides not to?

- How does facing an "impossible" decision make someone feel?

Possible answer: *The Vietnam War was
extremely controversial, and feelings ran
high among both war supporters and
protesters. Some young men facing the
draft found themselves with a difficult,
emotionally charged dilemma: kill and risk
being killed for a questionable cause or
flee the country and be viewed by some as
unpatriotic and cowardly. The pressure on
draftees was enormous, which helps readers
understand why the narrator is emotionally
distraught and filled with fear and sadness.*

Extend the Discussion What are the likely
long-term consequences of each decision?

OWN THE WORD

reticence: Have students complete this
sentence: Elroy's *reticence* was common
in his part of Minnesota and meant that
he never. . . .

What is
COWARDICE?

Discuss In lines 297–306, the narrator explains: "My conscience told me to run, but . . . I did not want people to think badly of me. . . . I was ashamed of my conscience. . . ." Is the conflict he is experiencing caused by cowardice? ***Possible answer:** To a large extent, the narrator's conflict is caused by cowardice—not physical, but moral. He is struggling to find the courage to act on his convictions.*

---

ashamed to be there at the Tip Top Lodge. I was ashamed of my conscience, ashamed to be doing the right thing.

Some of this Elroy must've understood. Not the details, of course, but the plain fact of crisis.

310 Although the old man never confronted me about it, there was one occasion when he came close to forcing the whole thing out into the open. It was early evening, and we'd just finished supper, and over coffee and dessert I asked him about my bill, how much I owed so far. For a long while the old man squinted down at the tablecloth.

"Well, the basic rate," he said, "is fifty bucks a night. Not counting meals. This makes four nights, right?"

I nodded. I had three hundred and twelve dollars in my wallet.

Elroy kept his eyes on the tablecloth. "Now that's an on-season price. To be fair, I suppose we should knock it down a peg or two." He leaned back in his chair. "What's a reasonable number, you figure?"

320 "I don't know," I said. "Forty?"

"Forty's good. Forty a night. Then we tack on food—say another hundred? Two hundred sixty total?"

"I guess."

He raised his eyebrows. "Too much?"

"No, that's fair. It's fine. Tomorrow, though . . . I think I'd better take off tomorrow."

Elroy shrugged and began clearing the table. For a time he fussed with the dishes, whistling to himself as if the subject had been settled. After a second he slapped his hands together.

330 "You know what we forgot?" he said. "We forgot wages. Those odd jobs you done. What we have to do, we have to figure out what your time's worth. Your last job—how much did you pull in an hour?"

"Not enough," I said.

"A bad one?"

"Yes. Pretty bad."

Slowly then, without intending any long sermon, I told him about my days at the pig plant. It began as a straight recitation of the facts, but before I could stop myself I was talking about the blood clots and the water gun and how the smell had soaked into my skin and how I couldn't wash it away. I went on for

340 a long time. I told him about wild hogs squealing in my dreams, the sounds of butchery, slaughterhouse sounds, and how I'd sometimes wake up with that greasy pig-stink in my throat.

When I was finished, Elroy nodded at me.

"Well, to be honest," he said, "when you first showed up here, I wondered about that. The aroma, I mean. Smelled like you was awful damned fond of pork chops." The old man almost smiled. He made a snuffling sound, then sat down with a pencil and a piece of paper. "So what'd this crud job pay? Ten bucks an hour? Fifteen?"

"Less."

> **COMMON CORE** RL 4
> **Language Coach**
> **Informal Language** O'Brien uses **informal language** in his characters' dialogue to replicate the natural rhythms of speech. Informal language has short, basic sentence structures and simple, ordinary word choices. Informal language can also include contractions, slang, and sentence fragments. Show that you understand lines 314–315 by rewriting them in formal language.

DIFFERENTIATED INSTRUCTION

FOR ENGLISH LANGUAGE LEARNERS

Language Coach COMMON CORE RL 4

Informal Language *Answer:*
"The basic rate," he said, "is fifty dollars a night, which does not include meals. Is four nights correct?" Have student pairs take turns reading the parts of Elroy and O'Brien in lines 319–335. Then have students rewrite the following lines in formal language: 321–322, 325–326, and 330–332. Have pairs share one of their rewritten passages with the class.

◄ **Analyze Visuals**

What details in the photograph help you form an impression of the Tip Top Lodge?

350 Elroy shook his head. "Let's make it fifteen. You put in twenty-five hours here, easy. That's three hundred seventy-five bucks total wages. We subtract the two hundred sixty for food and lodging. I still owe you a hundred and fifteen."

He took four fifties out of his shirt pocket and laid them on the table.

"Call it even," he said.

"No."

"Pick it up. Get yourself a haircut."

The money lay on the table for the rest of the evening. It was still there when I went back to my cabin. In the morning though, I found an envelope tacked to my door. Inside were the four fifties and a two-word note that said

360 EMERGENCY FUND.

The man knew.

Looking back after twenty years, I sometimes wonder if the events of that summer didn't happen in some other dimension, a place where your life exists before you've lived it, and where it goes afterward. None of it ever seemed real. During my time at the Tip Top Lodge I had the feeling that I'd slipped out of my own skin, hovering a few feet away while some poor yo-yo with my name and face tried to make his way toward a future he didn't

Analyze Visuals

Possible answer: *Details in the photograph that suggest an impression of the Tip Top Lodge include the stone hearth, the rustic furniture, the rag rug, and the oars and snowshoes above the fireplace. These details suggest a cozy, informal, secluded place.*

understand and didn't want. Even now I can see myself as I was then. It's like watching an old home movie: I'm young and tan and fit. I've got hair—lots of it. I don't smoke or drink. I'm wearing faded blue jeans and a white polo shirt. I can see myself sitting on Elroy Berdahl's dock near dusk one evening, the sky a bright shimmering pink, and I'm finishing up a letter to my parents that tells what I'm about to do and why I'm doing it and how sorry I am that I've never found the courage to talk to them about it. I ask them not to be angry. I try to explain some of my feelings, but there aren't enough words, and so I just say that it's a thing that has to be done. At the end of the letter I talk about the vacations we used to take up in this north country, at a place called Whitefish Lake, and how the scenery here reminds me of those good times. I tell them I'm fine. I tell them I'll write again from Winnipeg or Montreal or wherever I end up.

On my last full day, the sixth day, the old man took me out fishing on the Rainy River. The afternoon was sunny and cold. A stiff breeze came in from the north, and I remember how the little fourteen-foot boat made sharp rocking motions as we pushed off from the dock. The current was fast. All around us, I remember, there was a vastness to the world, an unpeopled rawness, just the trees and the sky and the water reaching out toward nowhere. The air had the brittle scent of October.

For ten or fifteen minutes Elroy held a course upstream, the river choppy and silver-gray, then he turned straight north and put the engine on full throttle. I felt the bow lift beneath me. I remember the wind in my ears, the sound of the old outboard Evinrude. For a time I didn't pay attention to anything, just feeling the cold spray against my face, but then it occurred to me that at some point we must've passed into Canadian waters, across that dotted line between two different worlds, and I remember a sudden tightness in my chest as I looked up and watched the far shore come at me. This wasn't a daydream. It was tangible and real. As we came in toward land, Elroy cut the engine, letting the boat fishtail lightly about twenty yards off shore. The old man didn't look at me or speak. Bending down, he opened up his tackle box and busied himself with a bobber and a piece of wire leader, humming to himself, his eyes down.

It struck me then that he must've planned it. I'll never be certain, of course, but I think he meant to bring me up against the realities, to guide me across the river and to take me to the edge and to stand a kind of vigil as I chose a life for myself. **G**

I remember staring at the old man, then at my hands, then at Canada. The shoreline was dense with brush and timber. I could see tiny red berries on the bushes. I could see a squirrel up in one of the birch trees, a big crow looking at me from a boulder along the river. That close—twenty yards—and I could see the delicate latticework of the leaves, the texture of the soil, the browned needles beneath the pines, the configurations of geology and human history.

G PREDICT
What choices will O'Brien make now that he can easily reach Canada? Cite evidence to support your prediction.

G PREDICT

Some students may predict that O'Brien will choose to swim to Canada, citing as evidence the letter he was writing to his parents telling them he will "write again from Winnipeg or Montreal" (line 379). Other students may predict that he will choose not to go to Canada, citing as evidence his fear and sadness at the thought of leaving his country forever or his reluctance to have people think badly of him for fleeing (lines 130–133).

IF STUDENTS NEED HELP... Review lines 130–133, 277–306 and 372–380. Help students speculate about O'Brien's likely choices.

DIFFERENTIATED INSTRUCTION

FOR STRUGGLING READERS
Vocabulary Support Explain these terms to students:

- *fishtail* (line 397), "have the back end slide from side to side while moving forward"
- *vigil* (line 403), "watch"
- *latticework* (line 409), "design consisting of crossed strips"
- *configurations* (line 410), "arrangements"

Vocabulary Support: Similes Elicit or explain that O'Brien often uses similes—comparisons using *like* or *as*—to bring his narrative to life. Help students identify what is being compared in this simile: "It's like watching an old home movie" (lines 368–369). Then examine the similes in lines 115–116 and 178–181. Challenge students to write similes of their own.

REVISIT THE BIG QUESTION
What is
COWARDICE?

Discuss Direct students to lines 371–376. In his letter to his parents, O'Brien apologizes because he "never found the courage" to discuss his dilemma with them. Do you think his failure to talk with them was a kind of cowardice? Why or why not? ***Possible answer: In a sense, it was a kind of cowardice because he was probably afraid that his parents would judge him negatively. By abruptly leaving, O'Brien avoided discussing the matter face to face with them.***

Analyze Visuals

Activity Ask students how the atmosphere of the picture reflects the story situation. ***Possible answer: In the story, O'Brien is facing a moment of truth as he contemplates fleeing to nearby Canada. Various picture elements blend together to capture this feeling: an expanse of still water, the boats' close proximity to land, and the superimposed headlines about the war.***

FOR ENGLISH LANGUAGE LEARNERS
Vocabulary: Compound Words Point out these compound words from the story:

- *hardhat* (line 63)
- *hometown* (line 74)
- *courthouse* (line 115)
- *churchgoers, housewives* (line 145)
- *boathouse* (line 199)
- *slaughterhouse* (line 341)
- *shoreline* (line 406)

Ask students to find others. Help students build meaning by identifying and defining the individual words within the compounds. Then have students in home-language groups list examples of similar words in their home language and share the meanings with the class.

 **AUTHOR'S PERSPECTIVE**

RL 1

Possible answer: *The passage suggests that the author believes in acting in accordance with one's convictions. He presents the narrator's "paralysis," his "moral freeze," as a source of embarrassment (lines 424–425).*

Extend the Discussion Do you think the narrator is judging himself too harshly?

REVISIT THE BIG QUESTION

What is
COWARDICE?

Discuss Direct students to lines 430–440. O'Brien says, "a great worldwide sadness came pressing down on me . . . sorrow like I had never known before" (lines 431–432). How is the sorrow that O'Brien describes linked to feelings of cowardice? **Possible answer:** *In reaching a decision, O'Brien realizes that "I would not do what I should do. . . . I would not be brave" (lines 435–438). In other words, he realizes that he does not have enough courage to do what he thinks is right.*

Analyze Visuals

Activity Ask students how the elements in the picture relate to the story and how they contrast with each other. *Possible answer: The picture shows hands holding a fishing rod, suggesting Berdahl calmly "humming a . . . little tune" (lines 429–430). This image contrasts with the superimposed headlines, which relate to the war and, by extension, to O'Brien's emotionally charged dilemma.*

Twenty yards. I could've done it. I could've jumped and started swimming for my life. Inside me, in my chest, I felt a terrible squeezing pressure. Even now, as I write this, I can still feel that tightness. And I want you to feel it—the wind coming off the river, the waves, the silence, the wooded frontier. You're at the bow of a boat on the Rainy River. You're twenty-one years old, you're scared, and there's a hard squeezing pressure in your chest.

What would you do?

Would you jump? Would you feel pity for yourself? Would you think about the family and your childhood and your dreams and all you're leaving behind?
420 Would it hurt? Would it feel like dying? Would you cry, as I did?

I tried to swallow it back. I tried to smile, except I was crying.

Now, perhaps, you can understand why I've never told this story before. It's not just the embarrassment of tears. That's part of it, no doubt, but what embarrasses me much more, and always will, is the paralysis that took my heart. A moral freeze: I couldn't decide, I couldn't act, I couldn't comport myself with even a pretense of modest human dignity.

All I could do was cry. Quietly, not bawling, just the chest-chokes.

At the rear of the boat Elroy Berdahl pretended not to notice. He held a fishing rod in his hands, his head bowed to hide his eyes. He kept humming a
430 soft, monotonous little tune. Everywhere, it seemed, in the trees and water and sky, a great worldwide sadness came pressing down on me, a crushing sorrow, sorrow like I had never known before. And what was so sad, I realized, was that Canada had become a pitiful fantasy. Silly and hopeless. It was no longer a possibility. Right then, with the shore so close, I understood that I would not do what I should do. I would not swim away from my hometown and my country and my life. I would not be brave. That old image of myself as a hero, as a man of conscience and courage, all that
440 was just a threadbare pipe dream.[19] Bobbing there on the Rainy River, looking back at the Minnesota shore, I felt a sudden swell of helplessness come over me, a drowning sensation, as if I had toppled overboard and was being swept away by the silver waves. Chunks of my own history flashed by. I saw a seven-year-old boy in a white cowboy hat and a Lone Ranger mask and a pair of holstered six-shooters; I saw a twelve-year-old Little League shortstop pivoting to turn a double play; I saw a
450 sixteen-year-old kid decked out for his first prom, looking spiffy in a white tux and a black bow tie, his hair cut short and flat, his shoes freshly polished. My whole life seemed to spill out into the river, swirling

④ **Targeted Passage**

 **AUTHOR'S PERSPECTIVE**
Reread lines 422–426. What insight into the author's values do you gain from this passage?

---

19. **pipe dream:** a daydream or fantasy that will never happen; vain hope.

DIFFERENTIATED INSTRUCTION

FOR STRUGGLING READERS

④ **Targeted Passage** [Lines 414–440]

In this passage, O'Brien faces the painful truth: he lacks the courage to go to Canada.

- Why does the narrator experience a "moral freeze"? (line 425)

- Why does the narrator conclude that "Canada had become a pitiful fantasy"? (line 433)

- What painful truth about himself does the narrator realize? (lines 435–440)

- Who is the narrator talking to in lines 414–420?

away from me, everything I had ever been or ever wanted to be. I couldn't get my breath; I couldn't stay afloat; I couldn't tell which way to swim. A hallucination, I suppose, but it was as real as anything I would ever feel. I saw my parents calling to me from the far shoreline. I saw my brother and sister, all the townsfolk, the mayor and the entire Chamber of Commerce and all my old teachers and girlfriends and high school buddies. Like some weird
460 sporting event: everybody screaming from the sidelines, rooting me on—a loud stadium roar. Hotdogs and popcorn—stadium smells, stadium heat. A squad of cheerleaders did cartwheels along the banks of the Rainy River; they had megaphones and pompoms and smooth brown thighs. The crowd swayed left and right. A marching band played fight songs. All my aunts and uncles were there, and Abraham Lincoln and Saint George,[20] and a nine-year-old girl named Linda who had died of a brain tumor back in fifth grade, and several members of the United States Senate, and a blind poet scribbling notes, and LBJ, and Huck Finn, and Abbie Hoffman,[21] and all the dead soldiers back from the grave, and the many thousands who were later to die—villagers
470 with terrible burns, little kids without arms or legs—yes, and the Joint Chiefs of Staff[22] were there, and a couple of popes, and a first lieutenant named Jimmy Cross, and the last surviving veteran of the American Civil War, and Jane Fonda dressed up as Barbarella,[23] and an old man sprawled beside a pigpen, and my grandfather, and Gary Cooper,[24] and a kind-faced woman carrying an umbrella and a copy of Plato's *Republic*,[25] and a million ferocious citizens waving flags of all shapes and colors—people in hardhats, people in headbands—they were all whooping and chanting and urging me toward one shore or the other. I saw faces from my distant past and distant future. My wife was there. My unborn daughter waved at me, and my two sons hopped
480 up and down, and a drill sergeant named Blyton sneered and shot up a finger and shook his head. There was a choir in bright purple robes. There was a cabbie from the Bronx. There was a slim young man I would one day kill with a hand grenade along a red clay trail outside the village of My Khe.[26] ▣

The little aluminum boat rocked softly beneath me. There was the wind and the sky.

I tried to will myself overboard.

I gripped the edge of the boat and leaned forward and thought, *Now.*

---

20. **Saint George:** a Christian martyr and the patron saint of England. According to legend, he slew a frightening dragon.

21. **Abbie Hoffman:** a social organizer and radical anti–Vietnam War activist known for his humor and politically inspired pranks.

22. **Joint Chiefs of Staff:** the principal military advisors of the U.S. president, including the chiefs of the army, navy, and air force and the commandant of the marines.

23. **Jane Fonda dressed up as Barbarella:** the actress and anti–Vietnam War activist Jane Fonda, who played the title character in the 1968 science fiction film *Barbarella*.

24. **Gary Cooper:** an American actor famous for playing strong, quiet heroes.

25. **Plato's *Republic*:** a famous work in which the ancient Greek philosopher Plato describes the ideal state or society.

26. **My Khe** (mē′ kā′).

▣ **MAKE INFERENCES**
In lines 457–483, notice the **extended simile** of a sporting event in which people are cheering for the narrator from both shores of the river. What can you infer about the narrator's state of mind from this simile?

What is
COWARDICE?

Discuss In lines 484–498, how is O'Brien's failure to jump overboard and swim to shore an act of cowardice? *Possible answer: O'Brien's behavior is caused by a kind of moral cowardice. For fear of "embarrassment," he "couldn't make [himself] be brave" (lines 494–495). Instead, he fails to act on his beliefs.*

READING SKILL
COMMON CORE · RL 1

J AUTHOR'S PERSPECTIVE

Possible answer: The author might view his character's decision as weak or cowardly. Or he might view it as sad, but understandable under the circumstances.

Extend the Discussion How might the author's perspective have changed over the years since he himself was 21?

TEXT ANALYSIS
COMMON CORE · RL 2

K HISTORICAL CONTEXT

Possible answer: If the setting were World War II, the protagonist might not have had the same moral dilemma about the justness of the war. If the setting were the Iraq War, he would not have been drafted into military service.

SELECTION WRAP–UP

READ WITH A PURPOSE Ask students how Elroy influenced O'Brien. Did he say or do something specific to help O'Brien make his decision? *Possible answer: Elroy influenced O'Brien indirectly by giving him the space and time he needed to make his decision. He brought O'Brien face to face with his decision by bringing him into Canadian waters.*

⭐ **CRITIQUE** Have students evaluate the story's ending. Ask whether it is effective, and discuss other ways that O'Brien might have concluded his story.

INDEPENDENT READING

Suggest that students read *For Whom the Bell Tolls* by Ernest Hemingway, which depicts the struggle between cowardice and bravery during war.

I did try. It just wasn't possible.

490 All those eyes on me—the town, the whole universe—and I couldn't risk the embarrassment. It was as if there were an audience to my life, that swirl of faces along the river, and in my head I could hear people screaming at me. Traitor! they yelled. Turncoat! I felt myself blush. I couldn't tolerate it. I couldn't endure the mockery, or the disgrace, or the patriotic ridicule. Even in my imagination, the shore just twenty yards away, I couldn't make myself be brave. It had nothing to do with morality. Embarrassment, that's all it was.

And right then I submitted.

I would go to the war—I would kill and maybe die—because I was embarrassed not to.

That was the sad thing. And so I sat in the bow of the boat and cried. It was
500 loud now. Loud, hard crying.

Elroy Berdahl remained quiet. He kept fishing. He worked his line with the tips of his fingers, patiently, squinting out at his red and white bobber on the Rainy River. His eyes were flat and impassive. He didn't speak. He was simply there, like the river and the late-summer sun. And yet by his presence, his mute watchfulness, he made it real. He was the true audience. He was a witness, like God, or like the gods, who look on in absolute silence as we live our lives, as we make our choices or fail to make them.

"Ain't biting," he said.

Then after a time the old man pulled in his line and turned the boat back
510 toward Minnesota.

I don't remember saying goodbye. That last night we had dinner together, and I went to bed early, and in the morning Elroy fixed breakfast for me. When I told him I'd be leaving, the old man nodded as if he already knew. He looked down at the table and smiled.

At some point later in the morning it's possible that we shook hands—I just don't remember—but I do know that by the time I'd finished packing the old man had disappeared. Around noon, when I took my suitcase out to the car, I noticed that his old black pickup truck was no longer parked in front of the house. I went inside and waited for a while, but I felt a bone certainty that
520 he wouldn't be back. In a way, I thought, it was appropriate. I washed up the breakfast dishes, left his two hundred dollars on the kitchen counter, got into the car, and drove south toward home.

The day was cloudy. I passed through towns with familiar names, through the pine forests and down to the prairie, and then to Vietnam, where I was a soldier, and then home again. I survived, but it's not a happy ending. I was a coward. I went to the war. ∽ K

J AUTHOR'S PERSPECTIVE
How might the author view his character's decision to go to war?

⑤ Targeted Passage

K HISTORICAL CONTEXT
How might the theme of this story have been different if it had been set during a different war, such as World War II or the Iraq War?

DIFFERENTIATED INSTRUCTION

FOR STRUGGLING READERS

⑤ Targeted Passage [Lines 493–526]

In this passage, the narrator regretfully decides that he will "go to the war ... because [he] was embarrassed not to."

- What decision does the narrator reach? (lines 493–498)

- Why does he come to this decision? (lines 497–498)

- Why does the narrator cry *after* he has made his decision? (lines 497–500)

- How does Elroy react to the narrator's sobs in the boat? (lines 501–504)

- What happens after they return to Minnesota? (lines 511–522)

- Why does the narrator feel that this story does not have a happy ending? (lines 525–526)

Comprehension

1. **Recall** What kind of notice does the narrator receive in the mail after graduating from college?

2. **Recall** Why does the narrator drive toward the Canadian border?

3. **Recall** How does the narrator meet Elroy Berdahl?

4. **Summarize** What happens when Elroy's boat brings the narrator within 20 yards of the Canadian shoreline?

Text Analysis

5. **Analyze Historical Context** The 1960s was a period in which many young people rebelled against the beliefs and traditions of older generations. How does "On the Rainy River" reflect this historical context?

6. **Identify Author's Perspective** Review the chart you created as you read. How might the author's upbringing in a small Minnesota town have influenced his view of events and people in the story? Cite evidence from the text.

7. **Analyze Symbol** A symbol is a person, a place, an object, or an activity that represents something beyond itself. What does the narrator's job at the meat-packing plant symbolize? Explain your answer.

8. **Draw Conclusions** The narrator describes Elroy as "the hero of my life." In a graphic organizer like the one shown, identify some of Elroy's admirable traits and actions. Then explain why he was so important to the narrator.

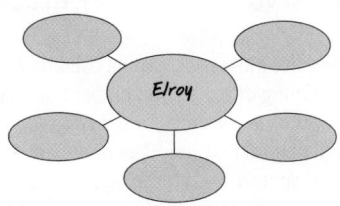

Elroy

9. **Make Judgments** Do you agree with the narrator that his decision to go to Vietnam was an act of cowardice? Give reasons for your answer.

10. **Evaluate** Would this story be as effective if Tim O'Brien had not served in Vietnam? Explain why or why not.

Text Criticism

11. **Social Context** How do the experiences of people entering the military today compare with the experiences of people in Tim O'Brien's generation? Cite examples from the text in your response.

> ### What is **COWARDICE?**
> When have you or has someone you know shown cowardice?

COMMON CORE

RL 1 Cite strong and thorough textual evidence to support analysis of what the text says explicitly as well as inferences drawn from the text.
RL 2 Determine a theme or central idea of a text and analyze its development over the course of the text, including how it emerges and is shaped and refined by specific details.

Practice and Apply

For preliminary support of post-reading questions, use these copy masters:

R RESOURCE MANAGER—Copy Masters
Reading Check p. 128
Historical Context p. 121
Question Support p. 129

Additional selection questions are provided for teachers on p. 115.

ANSWERS

Comprehension

1. *The narrator receives a draft notice.*

2. *The narrator plans to avoid the draft by fleeing to Canada.*

3. *Berdahl runs the Tip Top Lodge, where the narrator stops to consider his plans.*

4. *The narrator cannot summon the courage to swim to Canada. He just sits and cries.*

Text Analysis

COMMON CORE RL 1, RL 2

Possible answers:

5. ● **COMMON CORE FOCUS** *Historical Context Like many young men of the 1960s, the narrator resists being drafted and considers fleeing to Canada. Like millions of Americans of his time, he feels the war isn't justified and objects to the "simple-minded patriotism" (line 140) of war supporters.*

6. ■ **COMMON CORE FOCUS** *Identify Author's Perspective The author's upbringing in "a conservative . . . place where tradition counted" (lines 133–134) likely gave him a conservative outlook—at least until the rebellious '60s. Then he came to question the simplistic patriotism of his community. Still, a part of him wants its approval and fears its "patriotic ridicule" (line 493).*

7. *The narrator's job at the plant symbolizes the slaughter of Vietnam. Both are bloody places that the narrator wishes to avoid.*

8. *Elroy's admirable traits and actions: listening without pressure; offering work and money; taking the narrator close to Canada. Without judgment, Elroy lets O'Brien think things through. He is an understanding, supportive presence during O'Brien's intensely stressful time.*

9. *Some students may agree because the act was motivated by fear and went against the narrator's true beliefs. Others may disagree, stating that options such as fleeing one's country or going to jail were too negative to be seriously considered.*

10. *Accept all reasonable responses, but encourage students to support their answers with clear reasons.*

Text Criticism

Possible answer:

11. *Young men today don't face a draft, as they did in O'Brien's time. People support U.S. soldiers, but many have questioned U.S. involvement in Iraq and Afghanistan, much as they questioned Vietnam.*

> ### What is **COWARDICE?**
> Students might consider what the difference is between fear and cowardice.

ANSWERS

Vocabulary in Context

▲ **VOCABULARY PRACTICE**

1. *compassionate*   4. *naive*
2. *reticence*   5. *censure*
3. *preoccupied*   6. *acquiescence*

 RESOURCE MANAGER—Copy Master
Vocabulary Practice p. 126

ACADEMIC VOCABULARY IN SPEAKING

Possible answer: *American* culture *has changed since the 1960s. The end of the military draft took away the difficult moral choices young men like O'Brien's narrator had to make about military service and desertion. However, much of* contemporary *life is similar. Young people have similar roles, often taking difficult jobs for poor pay. Also, making a decision can often seem overwhelming, just as it did to the narrator.*

VOCABULARY STRATEGY: USING A DICTIONARY, GLOSSARY, OR THESAURUS

 **COMMON CORE L 4c**

- For practice, have students refer to the pronunciation guide on the selection pages to help them correctly pronounce each of the vocabulary words. Elicit or provide the sound of any phonetic symbols, such as the schwa (ə) in *censure*.

- Review with students that foreign words in etymologies appear in italic type and that dictionaries may use the symbol < to mean "derived from."

Answers:

1. *es*
2. *a verb or a noun*
3. *"to occupy the mind of"*
4. *humane*
5. *Latin*
6. *"showing a lack of sophistication and critical judgment"*

 RESOURCE MANAGER—Copy Master
Vocabulary Strategy p. 127

Interactive Vocabulary

Keywords direct students to a **WordSharp** tutorial on **thinkcentral.com** or to other types of vocabulary practice and review.

1018   UNIT 9

Vocabulary in Context

▲ **VOCABULARY PRACTICE**

Choose the vocabulary word that best completes each sentence.

1. We have to rely on _____ people to look out for the needy.
2. His _____ made him reluctant to take part in group discussions.
3. I am _____ with this issue; I can't think of anything else.
4. She was a _____ girl who knew nothing of the world outside her door.
5. The corrupt politician wanted to avoid public _____.
6. I have come to regret my _____ in this terrible decision.

WORD LIST
acquiescence
censure
compassionate
naive
preoccupied
reticence

ACADEMIC VOCABULARY IN SPEAKING

- acknowledge • community • contemporary • culture • role

How has American **culture** changed since the 1960s described in "On the Rainy River"? Share your opinions in a small group discussion. Give at least three specific examples that show how **contemporary** culture differs from or is similar to 1960s culture. Use at least two Academic Vocabulary words in your discussion.

VOCABULARY STRATEGY: USING A DICTIONARY, GLOSSARY, OR THESAURUS

Print and online **dictionaries,** like **glossaries,** can be used to determine or confirm the spelling and meaning of words and phrases. Also, you can use a dictionary or a **thesaurus** to look up a word's connotations and denotations. Dictionaries have additional helpful features. Dictionary entries may include a word's pronunciation, part of speech, and etymology, or origin and history. When a word has more than one meaning, the different definitions are numbered. Sometimes the most common meaning appears first. Other times, the entries are in historical order—that is, they are arranged with the oldest meaning of the word appearing first.

PRACTICE Use a dictionary to answer the following questions.

1. What syllable would you emphasize the most when pronouncing the word *acquiescence*?
2. What parts of speech can *censure* be?
3. What is the most common meaning of *preoccupy*?
4. What is a synonym for *compassionate*?
5. From which language did the word *reticent* originate?
6. Which meaning of *naive* is expressed in the following sentence? *Although the poem is full of clichés, the naive reader considered it a masterpiece.*

COMMON CORE

L 4c Consult general and specialized reference materials to find the pronunciation of a word or determine or clarify its precise meaning, its part of speech, or its etymology.

Interactive Vocabulary THINK central
Go to **thinkcentral.com**.
KEYWORD: HML10-1018

DIFFERENTIATED INSTRUCTION

FOR ENGLISH LANGUAGE LEARNERS

Vocabulary Activity For extra practice, have pairs of students check each other's practice answers as they use the dictionary's pronunciation guide to correctly pronounce these words: *reservoir* (line 14), *endeavor* (line 46), *vague* (line 173), *peninsula* (line 197), *ferocious* (line 239), *psychic* (line 271), *paralysis* (line 424), *impassive* (line 503). Then ask them to define the words and use them correctly in sentences. For *censure* and *naive*, have students find the etymology, or origin, for each word. From what language do these words originate?

FOR ADVANCED LEARNERS/PRE–AP

Vocabulary in Writing Ask students to use as many vocabulary words as they can in a brief essay expressing their opinions about the concept of a draft.

Language

◆ **GRAMMAR AND STYLE: Establish Voice**

Review the **Grammar and Style** note on page 1005. Voice is the unique way a writer uses vocabulary, sentence structure, and **figurative language** to express himself or herself. The particular characteristics of a writer's voice help to identify a piece as belonging to that writer. In "On the Rainy River," for example, O'Brien's use of short, simple sentences, sentence fragments, and similes distinguishes his writing from that of other writers. Here is an example:

> *His eyes were flat and impassive. He didn't speak. He was simply there, like the river and the late-summer sun. And yet by his presence, his mute watchfulness, he made it real. He was the true audience. He was a witness, like God, or like the gods, who look on in absolute silence as we live our lives. . . . (lines 503–507)*

In this first draft, notice how the revisions in blue better capture the writer's voice. Revise your own writing by tailoring your vocabulary sentence structures, and use of figurative language to make it sound more like you.

> **STUDENT MODEL**
>
> ~~If the narrator of~~ "On the Rainy River" ^would^ ~~had not presented an in-depth~~ *have had the same emotional*
> *impact if O'Brien had not included*
> ~~description of his reaction to the~~ ~~devastating~~ draft notice, ~~the literary work~~ *scene. By opening the narrator's*
> *heart and mind to the reader, O'Brien helps us think and feel as the narrator does.*
> ~~would not have contributed to the effectiveness of the story.~~

READING-WRITING CONNECTION

Broaden your understanding of "On the Rainy River" by responding to this prompt. Then use the **revising tip** to improve your writing.

WRITING PROMPT	REVISING TIP
Short Constructed Response: Analysis Reread the scene in which the narrator receives the draft notice (lines 50–72). How might the story have been different if the narrator hadn't presented an in-depth description of his reaction? Write **one or two paragraphs** in which you analyze how this scene contributes to the effectiveness of the story.	Review your response. Have you used vocabulary, sentence structure, and figurative language to establish your voice? If not, revise to make your writing sound more like you.

Interactive Revision
Go to **thinkcentral.com**.
KEYWORD: HML10-1019

ON THE RAINY RIVER **1019**

FOR STRUGGLING WRITERS

- Limit the length of the composition to a single well-developed paragraph.
- Help students review lines 50–72 and discuss the narrator's reaction to the draft notice.
- To help students understand the importance of the scene, discuss what the story would have been like without it.

COMMON CORE
L5 Demonstrate understanding of figurative language.

Language

COMMON CORE L5

◆ **GRAMMAR AND STYLE**

- As students examine the student model, analyze the specific changes made, and discuss their effect on sentence flow and overall feel.

- Write these sentences on the board. Have students suggest revisions to capture O'Brien's voice.

> *As I swam toward shore, I could see Elroy in the boat~~.~~, watching me like a sentry sta-tioned at a remote outpost. Even though the man hadn't spoken much, he had been many things to me. An advisor. A guide. A friend. ~~an advisor, a guide, and a friend to me.~~*

R RESOURCE MANAGER—Copy Master
Grammar and Style p. 130

READING-WRITING CONNECTION

- Stress that students are analyzing how the scene contributes to the effectiveness of the story, not narrator's reaction to the draft notice. Have students list what they learn about the narrator in lines 50–72 to gain an understanding of the importance of the de-tailed description of the narrator's reaction.

> **Writing Online**  THINK central
>
> The following tools are available online at **thinkcentral.com** and on **WriteSmart CD-ROM**:
> - **Interactive Graphic Organizers**
> - **Interactive Student Models**
> - **Interactive Revision Lessons**
> For additional grammar instruction, see **GrammarNotes** on **thinkcentral.com**.

Assess and Reteach

Assess

R DIAGNOSTIC AND SELECTION TESTS
Selection Test A, B/C pp. 287–290

Interactive Selection Test on **thinkcentral.com**

Reteach

Level Up Online Tutorials on **thinkcentral.com**

Reteaching Worksheets on **thinkcentral.com**
Literature Lessons 25, 45

ON THE RAINY RIVER **1019**

Focus and Motivate

COMMON CORE FOCUS

RL 1 Cite strong textual evidence to support analysis of what the text says explicitly as well as inferences drawn from the text. **RL 2** Determine a theme or central idea of a text and how it is shaped and refined by specific details.

SUMMARIES

"The New Colossus" The speaker contrasts the Statue of Liberty with a Greek statue representing the glories of the past. She presents Lady Liberty as a powerful symbol of welcome and acceptance to the lowly and needy who wish to enter the United States.

"Who Makes the Journey" The speaker describes an elderly woman, newly immigrated, who struggles to keep up with her family as they cross a busy street. The speaker likens the old woman's slow pace to the passage of history.

How does it feel to
START OVER?

Ask the question. Invite volunteers to share what they know about immigrants and immigration from their study of history or their present-day experiences. Urge students to use this prior knowledge of the subject to complete the *DISCUSS* activity. Have groups share and compare their lists.

Selection Resources

The New Colossus
 Video link at **thinkcentral.com**
Poem by Emma Lazarus

Who Makes the Journey
Poem by Cathy Song

How does it feel to
START OVER?

COMMON CORE

RL 1 Cite textual evidence to support analysis of what the text says explicitly as well as inferences drawn from the text. **RL 2** Determine a theme or central idea of a text and how it is shaped and refined by specific details.

The United States has welcomed millions of people fleeing religious and political persecution, as well as those who simply wanted to make a better life for themselves and their families. In the following poems, Emma Lazarus and Cathy Song reflect upon the ideals and the reality of the immigrant experience.

DISCUSS If your family moved away from the United States, what challenges would you face? With a group of classmates, make a list of challenges and discuss how hard they would be to overcome.

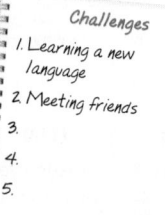

Challenges
1. Learning a new language
2. Meeting friends
3.
4.
5.

1020

See resources on the **Teacher One Stop DVD-ROM** and on **thinkcentral.com**.

R RESOURCE MANAGER UNIT 9
Plan and Teach, pp. 133–140
Text Analysis and Reading
    Skill, pp. 141–144†*
DIAGNOSTIC AND SELECTION TESTS
Selection Tests, pp. 291–294

BEST PRACTICES TOOLKIT
Question and Answer Note
    Taking, p. B7

TECHNOLOGY
- Teacher One Stop DVD-ROM
- Student One Stop DVD-ROM
- Audio Anthology CD
- GrammarNotes DVD-ROM
- ExamView Test Generator
  on the Teacher One Stop

* Resources for Differentiation   † Also in Spanish   ‡ In Haitian Creole and Vietnamese

TEXT ANALYSIS: LITERARY PERIODS

Just as there are trends in fashion and music, there are trends in literature. For example, poems from the same **literary period** often have similarities in style. The opening lines of "The New Colossus" exemplify the formal tone and diction common in 19th-century poetry.

Not like the brazen giant of Greek fame,
With conquering limbs astride from land to land;

In contrast, the opening of "Who Makes the Journey" has a relaxed, conversational tone that is more typical of contemporary poetry.

In most cases,
it is the old woman
who makes the journey;

Contemporary poets are also less likely than poets from earlier periods to follow regular patterns of rhyme and meter.

As you read, note how the two poems differ in style and form, and consider how the poets' attitudes toward their subjects may have been influenced by their literary periods.

READING SKILL: ANALYZE SENSORY DETAILS

Each of the poems you will read has a vivid central image—a towering statue or an old woman crossing the street. To create these images, Lazarus and Song use **sensory details,** appealing to the senses of sight, hearing, taste, smell, or touch.

As you read, use a chart like the one shown to analyze sensory details in each poem.

"Who Makes the Journey"		
Detail	Sense	What It Suggests
"the stooped gnome figure" (line 30)	sight	small and worn down

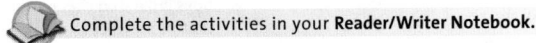 Complete the activities in your **Reader/Writer Notebook.**

Meet the Authors

Emma Lazarus
1849–1887

Voice of Liberty
In her brief lifetime, Emma Lazarus (lăz'ər-əs) saw the United States being transformed by a surge in immigration. Although her family had been in America since the 1600s, she strongly identified with immigrants, especially fellow Jews who had left eastern Europe to escape violence and oppression. She wrote her poem about the Statue of Liberty, "The New Colossus," in 1883 to raise funds to build a pedestal for the statue. The poem was later inscribed on the pedestal.

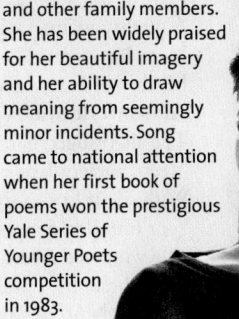

Cathy Song
born 1955

Family Ties
Born in Hawaii of Korean and Chinese ancestry, Cathy Song often writes about the experiences of her immigrant grandparents and other family members. She has been widely praised for her beautiful imagery and her ability to draw meaning from seemingly minor incidents. Song came to national attention when her first book of poems won the prestigious Yale Series of Younger Poets competition in 1983.

Authors Online
Go to **thinkcentral.com.** KEYWORD: HML10-1021

THINK central

1021

TEXT ANALYSIS

COMMON CORE
RL 2

● Model the Skill: LITERARY PERIODS

To model how to identify literary periods, write these lines on the board:

> Shall we venture whither the icy-breath'd wind blows?

> It doesn't matter to me where the letter came from.

Identify words that indicate each sentence's literary period. Point out that in the first sentence, *Shall, venture, whither,* and *icy-breath'd* reflect the formal language of an earlier time. In the second sentence, *doesn't matter to me* and *came from* suggest informal, modern speech.

GUIDED PRACTICE Ask students to list some characteristics that might distinguish a literary period.

READING SKILL

COMMON CORE
RL 1

■ Model the Skill: ANALYZE SENSORY DETAILS

To model how to analyze sensory details, review the first example in the **TEXT ANALYSIS** activity. Point out that the line "the icy-breath'd wind blows" strongly evokes the sense of touch and hearing.

GUIDED PRACTICE Ask students to write and share a sentence with sensory details that appeal primarily to the sense of sight or hearing.

R RESOURCE MANAGER—Copy Master
Analyze Sensory Details p. 143 (for student use while reading the selection)

DIFFERENTIATED INSTRUCTION

FOR STRUGGLING READERS

Concept Support Provide students with vivid examples of the contrast between the language of various literary periods. For example, you might contrast William Shakespeare's Elizabethan formality in such a title as "That Time of Year Thou May'st in Me Behold," the 19th-century informality of Walt Whitman's "When I Heard the Learn'd Astronomer," and the 20th-century slang of Langston Hughes's "Midwinter Blues."

FOR ADVANCED LEARNERS/PRE–AP

Analyze Literary Periods Ask students to locate in their textbook one or two other 19th-century poems and one or two other late 20th-century poems. After students have read the poems in this lesson, ask them to read the poems against the other poems that they found. Have them identify features that seem to be characteristic of each period, as well as features that may be unique to either Lazarus or Song. Have students share and compare their findings with partners or in small groups.

Practice and Apply

READ WITH A PURPOSE

Help students set a purpose for reading. Tell students to note a common theme in the two poems.

Analyze Visuals

Activity Ask students to identify details in the poem that reflect details in the photograph. **Possible answer:** *Details might include "sea-washed . . . gates" (line 3), "woman with a torch" (line 4), "her beacon-hand" (line 6), "The air-bridged harbor" (line 8), and possibly the description of the immigrants in lines 10–13.*

TEXT ANALYSIS · COMMON CORE · RL 2

Ⓐ ALLUSION

Tell students that the author alludes to, or references, the Greek statue in the phrase "the brazen giant of Greek fame." Point out to students that from this first line readers also know that the poet is contrasting the Statue of Liberty with the Greek statue, because she begins the line with "Not like." The Statue of Liberty, then, is not like the Greek statue.

Possible answer: *Students should note that Lazarus intends to contrast the Greek statue, which she portrays as standing for conquering other lands, with the Statue of Liberty, which welcomes people from other countries to the United States. The allusion helps portray the United States as a different sort of country that welcomes everyone.*

READING SKILL · COMMON CORE · RL 1

Ⓑ ANALYZE SENSORY DETAILS

Possible answer: *The sensory details suggest that the immigrants are weary, poor, and frightened and that they are oppressed and unwanted in their homelands.*

Extend the Discussion Review the words and phrases that describe the Statue of Liberty. How does that language reinforce the message that the statue expresses?

1022 UNIT 9

The New COLOSSUS
Emma Lazarus

Not like the brazen giant of Greek fame,[1] Ⓐ
With conquering limbs astride from land to land;
Here at our sea-washed, sunset gates shall stand
A mighty woman with a torch, whose flame
5 Is the imprisoned lightning, and her name
Mother of Exiles. From her beacon-hand
Glows world-wide welcome; her mild eyes command
The air-bridged harbor that twin cities[2] frame.
"Keep, ancient lands, your storied pomp!"[3] cries she
10 With silent lips. "Give me your tired, your poor,
Your huddled masses yearning to breathe free,
The wretched refuse of your teeming shore.
Send these, the homeless, tempest-tost[4] to me,
I lift my lamp beside the golden door!" Ⓑ

---

1. **giant of Greek fame:** the Colossus of Rhodes, a huge Greek statue of the sun god Helios.
2. **harbor . . . twin cities:** New York Harbor, where the Statue of Liberty is located. Brooklyn was a city separate from New York until 1898.
3. **storied pomp:** the splendor of your history.
4. **tempest-tost:** tossed by violent windstorms.

1022 UNIT 9: HISTORY, CULTURE, AND THE AUTHOR

COMMON CORE RL 2

Ⓐ ALLUSION

Allusions are references to a person, place, or event that is famous in literature or real life. In the first line of "The New Colossus," Lazarus makes an allusion to an ancient Greek statue. Reread lines 1–2. Why do you think she includes this allusion? What impact does it have on the central idea of the poem?

Ⓑ SENSORY DETAILS

What do the sensory details in lines 10–14 suggest about the experiences of some immigrants?

DIFFERENTIATED INSTRUCTION

FOR ENGLISH LANGUAGE LEARNERS

Language: Punctuation and Print Cues Write the words *world-wide* and *air-bridged* (lines 6–8) on the board. Explain to students that by hyphenating these words, the author has created adjectives describing a noun that follows. What nouns do these adjectives modify? (*World-wide modifies* welcome *and* air-bridged *modifies* harbor.)

FOR STRUGGLING READERS

Develop Reading Fluency Have students listen to "The New Colossus" on the *Audio Anthology CD* while they read along in their textbook. Then ask pairs of students to read the poem aloud, creating an informal choral reading. Circulate through the room to listen to students' readings and answer questions. Distribute the copy masters.

Ⓡ **RESOURCE MANAGER—Copy Master**
Reading Fluency p. 146

Who Makes the JOURNEY

Cathy Song

In most cases,
it is the old woman
who makes the journey;
the old man having had
5 the sense to stay
put and die at home.

You see her scurrying
behind her
newly arrived family.
10 She comes from the Azores[1]
and she comes from the Orient.
It makes no difference.
You have seen her before: **C**

C LITERARY PERIODS
What words and phrases in lines 7–13 help give the stanza a casual, contemporary tone?

the short substantial
15 legs buckle
under the weight
of the ghost child
she carried centuries

ago like a bundle of rags
20 who now turns in front
of your windshield,
transformed in Western clothes.

The grown woman stops
impatiently
25 and self-consciously
to motion *Hurry* to her mother.

---

1. **Azores:** a group of islands in the northern Atlantic Ocean.

Prereading for this poem is found on page 1020.

REVISIT THE BIG QUESTION

How does it feel to
START OVER?

Discuss In lines 1–6, what idea is the speaker trying to convey about the immigrant experience? *Possible answer: The speaker is conveying the idea that many immigrants share a similar experience when they first arrive in the United States. Many immigrants must adjust to a new culture.*

TEXT ANALYSIS

COMMON CORE
RL 2

C *Model the Skill:* LITERARY PERIODS

To model how to identify literary periods, reread a few lines from "The New Colossus" with students. Then read aloud a few lines from "Who Makes the Journey," and tell students to note how Lazarus's 19th-century language contrasts with Song's contemporary language. Then have students identify expressions in lines 7–13 that they think would be out of place in Lazarus's poem.

Possible answer: *"You see her scurrying," "She comes from . . . ," and "It makes no difference" help give the stanza a casual, contemporary tone.*

FOR STRUGGLING READERS

Comprehension Support Make sure students understand that the speaker is presenting this scene from a unique perspective—what the reader sees while sitting in a car stopped in traffic. Read the second stanza aloud while students close their eyes and visualize the scene. Draw students' attention to the word *you* in lines 7 and 13. Elicit that *you* refers to all readers of the poem.

FOR ADVANCED LEARNERS/PRE–AP

Analyze Speaker Ask students to discuss these questions in small groups:

- Who is the speaker in "Who Makes the Journey"? Describe him or her.

- Review the language of the poem. What impression do you have of the speaker?

- Why might the speaker present the old woman as if you, the reader, are observing her from inside a nearby car? What effect does this perspective create?

- Which of the details that the speaker presents would you be able to see for yourself if you were watching the scene from a car? Which details would you not be able to see? Why do you think the speaker shares both kinds of details?

- What is the speaker's opinion of the old woman? of the old woman's daughter? Which lines or details suggest that opinion?

- If the old woman were the poem's speaker, how would the poem be different?

D Model the Skill: ANALYZE SENSORY DETAILS

Model for students how to analyze sensory details. Point out that the details not only tell readers how the cabbage looks but also tell readers how the old woman will handle it. Have students record these details in their Analyze Sensory Details charts.

Possible answer: The details reveal that the old woman treasures the cabbages and that she may have at least some responsibility for cooking in her family.

Analyze Visuals

Possible answer: The photograph suggests a "stooped gnome figure" (line 30) who is "hauling her sack" (lines 32–33) and who may be wearing "a shapeless dress" (line 39). In addition, the cane suggests that the woman moves slowly, as does the old woman in the poem.

SELECTION WRAP–UP

READ WITH A PURPOSE Now that students have finished reading the two poems, ask them: In what ways are the two poems similar? *Possible answer: Both poems deal with the subject of immigrants and both deal with moving to the United States.*

★ **CRITIQUE** Ask students to explain the techniques that each poet uses to make the immigrant experience clear and memorable for the reader.

INDEPENDENT READING

Students might enjoy reading other works by Cathy Song. Suggest *Frameless Windows, Squares of Light: Poems.*

Seeping into your side view
mirror like a black mushroom
blooming in a bowl of water,
30 the stooped gnome figure
wades through the river
of cars hauling

her sack of cabbages,
the white and curved,
35 translucent leaves of which
she will wash individually
as if they were porcelain cups. D

Like black seed buttons
sewn onto a shapeless dress,
40 those cryptic eyes
rest on your small reflection

for an instant. Years pass.
History moves like an old woman
crossing the street.

D SENSORY DETAILS
What do the sensory details in lines 33–37 reveal about the old woman?

◄ **Analyze Visuals**
How does the photograph reflect Song's description of the old woman?

1024   UNIT 9: HISTORY, CULTURE, AND THE AUTHOR

DIFFERENTIATED INSTRUCTION

FOR STRUGGLING READERS

Review Key Details Use Question and Answer Note Taking to help students review this poem. Pose these questions: Where does this scene take place? What does the old woman look like? To what does the speaker compare her at the end of the poem? Have students pose and answer their own questions.

🧰 **BEST PRACTICES TOOLKIT—Transparency**
Question and Answer Note Taking p. B7

FOR ENGLISH LANGUAGE LEARNERS

Culture: Connect Students who are learning English may identify quickly with the subject of "Who Makes the Journey." If they are comfortable doing so, invite volunteers to compare their perspectives to those of the speaker.

After Reading

Comprehension

1. **Clarify** Who is being welcomed in "The New Colossus"?

2. **Recall** How does the old woman in "Who Makes the Journey" differ from her daughter?

3. **Clarify** What journey does the title of Cathy Song's poem refer to?

Text Analysis

4. **Compare and Contrast** In what ways is the Statue of Liberty unlike the ancient Greek colossus that Lazarus describes in lines 1–2 of "The New Colossus"? Cite evidence from the text.

5. **Analyze Literary Periods** How might Lazarus's poem be different if she had written it today? Be specific.

6. **Interpret Figurative Language** A **simile** is figurative language that makes a comparison using *like* or *as*. Reread lines 43–44 of "Who Makes the Journey." Explain the meaning of the simile at the end of Song's poem.

7. **Identify Sensory Details** Review the chart you created as you read "Who Makes the Journey." What details does Song include to help you visualize the old woman as if you were watching her from a car?

8. **Analyze Tone and Author's Purpose** How would you describe the tone and purpose of "Who Makes the Journey"? Cite passages as evidence.

9. **Synthesize** On the basis of these two poems, what conclusion can you draw about the immigrant experience? Use a graphic organizer like the one shown to record your answer.

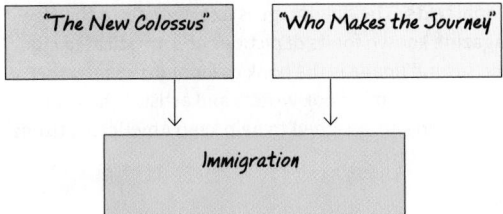

Text Criticism

10. **Biographical Context** During the early 1880s, Emma Lazarus met many Jewish refugees who had recently fled Russia to escape anti-Semitic massacres. What details in "The New Colossus" reflect this experience?

How does it feel to START OVER?
What challenges do immigrants face in the United States?

COMMON CORE
RL 1 Cite textual evidence to support analysis of what the text says explicitly as well as inferences drawn from the text.
RL 2 Determine a theme or central idea of a text and how is shaped and refined by specific details.

Practice and Apply

For preliminary support of post-reading questions, use these copy masters:

RESOURCE MANAGER—Copy Masters
Literary Periods p. 141
Question Support p. 145
Additional selection questions are provided for teachers on page 137.

ANSWERS
Comprehension
1. *Immigrants to the U.S. are welcomed.*
2. *The old woman moves slowly, unlike her daughter, and she may not be wearing Western clothes, as her daughter does.*
3. *The title refers to the journey to the United States from another country.*

Text Analysis
COMMON CORE RL 1, RL 2
Possible answers:
4. *The Statue of Liberty is female (line 4), motherly (line 6), welcoming (line 7), and mild of temperament (line 7), in contrast to the "brazen" male "giant" with its "conquering limbs" (lines 1–2).*
5. ● **COMMON CORE FOCUS** *Literary Periods* *If writing today, Lazarus might not allude to ancient Greece; she might not use regular meter and a rhyme scheme; she might use informal speech instead of such constructions as "storied pomp."*
6. *The simile suggests that history proceeds slowly during the busyness of everyday life.*
7. ● **COMMON CORE FOCUS** *Sensory Details* *Details that aid visualization include "your windshield" (line 21), "your side view mirror" (lines 27–28), "river of cars" (lines 31–32), and "your small reflection" (line 41).*

8. *The tone is admiring; the old woman is shown as substantial and strong. The purpose may be to have readers consider the history and importance of such women.*
9. *"The New Colossus": The immigrants are poor and weary but welcome. "Who Makes the Journey": The woman is overwhelmed but connected to her past. Immigration: Immigration is both challenging but positive.*

How does it feel to START OVER?
Immigrants must find new homes, jobs, and community connections, learn new laws and language.

Text Criticism
Possible answers:
10. *Such lines as "huddled masses yearning to breathe free" (line 11), "wretched refuse" (line 12), and "homeless, tempest-tost" (line 13) suggest the harsh experiences of Jewish refugees. The relief that they probably felt when reaching the United States is reflected in "Mother of Exiles" (line 6).*

Assess and Reteach

Assess
DIAGNOSTIC AND SELECTION TESTS
Selection Test A, B/C pp. 291–292, 293–294
Interactive Selection Test on **thinkcentral.com**

Reteach
Level Up Online Tutorials on **thinkcentral.com**
Reteaching Worksheets on **thinkcentral.com**
Literature Lessons 25, 26, 43, 44

Focus and Motivate

COMMON CORE FOCUS

RI 7 Analyze various accounts of a subject told in different mediums, determining which details are emphasized in each account. **W 9b** Draw evidence from informational texts to support analysis, reflection, and research. **SL 2** Integrate multiple sources of information presented in diverse media or formats, evaluating the credibility and accuracy of each source.

SUMMARY

Images in a *New Yorker* cartoon, book cover, and Web site refer to aspects or aftereffects of the 9/11 terrorist attacks. In the cartoon, a man in front of a restaurant focuses more on security than on the food quality. The book cover shows Superman admiring 9/11's heroes. The Web site shows an American flag and identifies locations and infrastructure elements in the United States that Homeland Security efforts intend to protect.

What are the SIGNS of the times?

Explore the question by asking what symbols students think reflect their time in U.S. history. iPods? e-mail? cell phones? Then ask them to think back to the events of 9/11. What images leap to mind? List images on the board. How do these images represent the event? What do they say about the event?

BACKGROUND

The World Trade Center was a group of seven buildings in lower Manhattan that included the famous twin towers, once the world's tallest buildings. By the end of September 11, 2001, all seven were either leveled or severely damaged. The Pentagon, the administrative center for the U.S. military, is the world's largest office building. The 9/11 attack damaged the western side. The Department of Homeland Security was authorized that November.

Media Study

The Aftermath of September 11
Image Collection on Media Smart DVD-ROM

What are the SIGNS of the times?

COMMON CORE

SL 2 Integrate multiple sources of information presented in diverse media or formats, evaluating the credibility and accuracy of each source.

Any major event—a war, a natural disaster, or a political crisis—causes ripple effects. In this lesson, you'll examine images that are reflections of a life-altering event in U.S. history. To explore what might have motivated or influenced the creation of these images, it's helpful to have background about the event.

Background

Total Impact On September 11, 2001, terrorist hijackers crashed jetliners into the World Trade Center in New York City and into the Pentagon in Washington, D.C. Another hijacked plane crashed in Pennsylvania. Nearly 3,000 people died. This catastrophic event became known as *9/11*.

In this study, you will see how post-9/11 media reflected American social and cultural views of the event in ways different from traditional texts. The first image is a cartoon from the *New Yorker,* a magazine known for its depictions of sophisticated city dwellers. The second image is the book cover of *9-11: September 11, 2001,* published by comic-book writers and artists. The third image is from a Web site designed to help keep American citizens on alert.

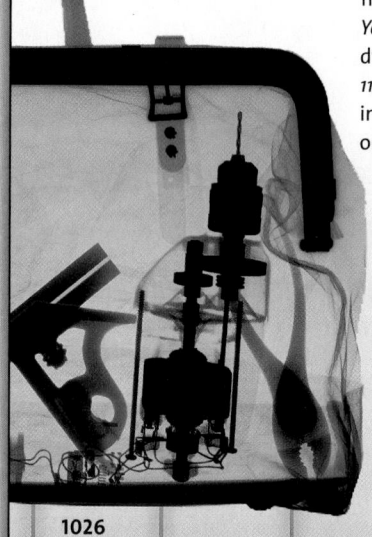

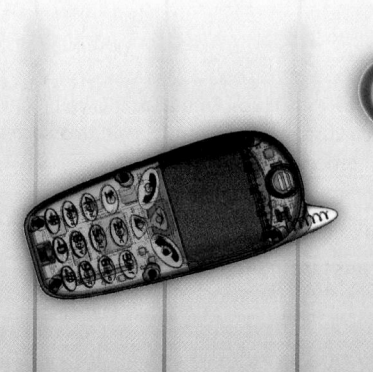

1026

Media Study Resources

See resources on the **Teacher One Stop DVD-ROM** and on **thinkcentral.com**.

R **RESOURCE MANAGER UNIT 9**
Plan and Teach, pp. 147–150
Summary, pp. 151†*, 152‡*
Viewing Guide, p. 153
Close Viewing, p. 154
Viewing Activity, p. 155
Produce Your Own Media, p. 156

TECHNOLOGY
- Teacher One Stop DVD-ROM
- Student One Stop DVD-ROM
- Media*Smart* DVD-ROM

MediaScope on **thinkcentral.com**

* Resources for Differentiation   † Also in Spanish   ‡ In Haitian Creole and Vietnamese

Media Literacy: History Through Media

Media images and messages are deeply influenced by the history and culture in which they are created. These images from 9/11 reflect the event's wide-ranging impact on the American way of life and the values and concerns of the time period.

CULTURAL INFLUENCES

IMAGES

Cartoon Since the 1920s, the cartoons of the *New Yorker* have made witty comments about major American events. In the aftermath of 9/11, the magazine's staff wanted to uphold its tradition of humorous commentary while acknowledging the heightened public anxiety about security.

Book Cover Following 9/11, comic book artists shifted the emphasis from imaginary superheroes to salute the heroism of the ordinary citizens—the first responders to the 9/11 attacks.

- Note the top of the cover. The shadow cast by the numbered title is in the shape of the twin towers of the World Trade Center.
- Notice the sizes of the people depicted on the billboard in relation to the size of Superman.

Web Site 9/11 marked a new era of homeland security.

- Sites like this one addressed the public's need for preparedness and tapped into a new sense of patriotism.
- Possible threats to security are menu items at the left of the page. At the center, the same links are categorized under headings worded as calls to action.
- Phrases such as "terrorism forces us" and "keep America safe" convey a sense of urgency and a need for watchfulness.

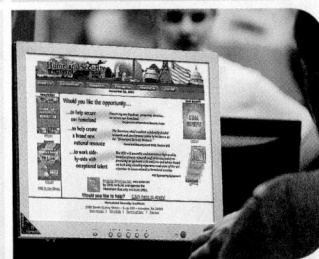

STRATEGIES FOR EXAMINING IMAGES

Use these questions to guide your examination of each image:

- What might the subject matter of the image reveal about the creator's life and times?
- What message does the image convey? Is any part of the image a potential symbol?
- What mood does the work reflect? What social and cultural beliefs or values?
- How does the difference in each image's intended audience and purpose affect its formality and tone?
- How do the design elements of **color, line, texture, shape,** and **words** work together to reinforce the work's message?

Media Literacy

COMMON CORE RI 7

Brainstorm with students to identify changes in people's values and concerns in the United States as a result of 9/11. List ideas on the board, such as *increased airport security, patriotism, and fear of terrorist attacks.*

- **Cartoon** Share additional *New Yorker* cartoons with students or bring in other political comic strips. For each example, have students identify the number of panels and the punchline. To help students recognize how cartoons can reflect the times, discuss the values and concerns the examples reflect.

- **Book Cover** Share with students book covers from recent nonfiction books or realistic works of fiction along with older book covers. Ask students to contrast the culture, values, and concerns reflected in the different covers.

- **Web Site** Have students explore how language can reflect societal values and concerns by searching Web sites related to a topic of interest. Ask them to list key words and phrases from each Web site that describe the topic. Is the language emotional or loaded? What cultural values does the language reflect? Have students share their reactions and ideas in small groups.

MEDIA STUDY: TEACHING OPTIONS

Teaching Option 1: The Basics (1–2 Days)

1. Begin the Media Study using the material provided on pages 1026–1027.
2. Show the Introduction on Media*Smart.* Have students use the Viewing Guide on page 1028, along with the corresponding copy master on page 153 of the Resource Manager. Discuss their responses.
3. Return to the pupil book for the extension activities on page 1029.

Teaching Option 2: In-Depth Study (2–3 Days)

1. Begin the Media Study using pages 1026–1027.
2. Show the Introduction from Media*Smart.* Then continue on Media*Smart* with the Media Lessons, using the teacher notes available in the Resources section.
3. Show the Guided Analysis presentation. Have students record their observations on the Student Viewing Guide available in the Resources section from Media*Smart.*
4. Return to the pupil book, page 1029.

Practice and Apply

VIEWING GUIDE

1. Before students look at the three images, inform them that they will be asked to analyze and draw conclusions about the messages in the images and the impressions the images seek to convey. Urge students to look for these elements:

   - how words and image work together in a **cartoon**

   - how a **book cover** can refer back to specific elements of an event through pictures as well as use of font

   - how a **Web site** can present a point of view with a group of images

   - how images use **color, line, texture,** and **shape** to create a message and convey an impression. For example, the use of color on the book cover conveys a sense of awe and glory by casting light on the faces of the workers.

2. Some students may not have clear memories of the events of 9/11 and therefore may not have a clear point of reference for the images. Remind these students of key elements of 9/11 and its aftermath, such as the bravery of firefighters and other people, the subsequent fear of terrorism and heightened security, and the formation of the Department of Homeland Security.

R RESOURCE MANAGER—Copy Masters

   Viewing Guide p. 153
   Close Viewing p. 154
   Viewing Activity p. 155

Use this resource with the Viewing Guide:

MediaSmart DVD-ROM

MediaScope on **thinkcentral.com**

ANSWERS

FIRST VIEWING: Comprehension

1. *Superman says "Wow."*

2. *The slogan encourages the public to react to terrorism with strength, not fear, by making preparations.*

CLOSE VIEWING: Media Literacy

Possible answers:

3. *The cartoonist extends the idea of heightened security concerns to public places such as restaurants. The cartoonist is also playing with the idea that the new focus on*

Media **Smart** DVD-ROM
- **Selection 1:** *New Yorker*
- **Type:** Cartoon
- **Selection 2:** *9-11*
- **Type:** Book cover
- **Selection 3:** U.S. Department of Homeland Security
- **Type:** Web site

Viewing Guide for

The Aftermath of September 11

Access the full-sized images of the cartoon, book cover, and Web site on the DVD. Begin by examining each image individually and carefully, jotting down your own initial impressions. To help you examine each in terms of color, line, texture, and shape, refer to the **Elements of Design** section of the **Media Handbook** (pages R91–R92). Then quickly review the purposes, additional details, and strategies on page 1027 and study the images again. Use questions like the following as well.

NOW VIEW

FIRST VIEWING: Comprehension

1. **Recall** What does Superman say as he looks at the billboard?

2. **Clarify** On the Web site of the U.S. Department of Homeland Security, what does the slogan encourage the public to do in response to terrorism?

CLOSE VIEWING: Media Literacy

3. **Analyze the Cartoon** In the aftermath of 9/11, airports, the White House, and other public buildings enforced stricter security measures. Nationwide, Americans had to adjust to the inconvenience of additional security checkpoints. In your own words, describe the message the cartoonist conveys in the *New Yorker* cartoon.

4. **Draw Conclusions** Look closely at the *9-11* book cover. What evidence can you find in the image that shows the artist is expressing America's strength and determination in the face of terrorism?

5. **Analyze the Web Site** Look at the images at the top of the homeland security Web site. The left-to-right presentation shows the official symbol of the U.S. Department of Homeland Security, the U.S. flag, and an ordinary citizen who appears calm, alert, and proud. What impressions do you think these images are intended to convey?

---

security is fashionable. The cartoon's overall message is that we have become afraid.

4. *The first responders—police officers, firefighters, healthcare workers—as well as average citizens shown in the image are all standing tall with expressions of defiance and strength. The figures' strong stance impresses Superman, a familiar superhero.*

5. *The images are intended to convey a sense of America's strength and steadfastness in the face of terrorist challenges. The symbol of the U.S. Department of Homeland Security reminds readers that the country has the*

power and resources to defend itself against terrorism. The U.S. flag conveys a sense of national pride and honor. The calm, proud citizen shows that people in the United States remain secure and strong.

Write or Discuss

Compare the Images You've focused on three images that in some way reflect the aftermath of September 11, 2001. In your opinion, which image communicates the mood of these times most effectively? Give specific reasons for your views. Think about

- the original purpose for each image and any message it conveys
- how clearly the message comes across years after the event
- the use of color, line, texture, shape, and words in the images

Produce Your Own Media

Create a Signs-of-the-Times Collage What are the signs of *your* times? In recent times, you've probably witnessed—directly and indirectly—a number of happenings on the American scene, involving social and cultural issues, technological advances, music, fashion, the environment, media, and so on. Depict the times in which you live in the form of a collage. Use the design template shown as a guide in selecting images or quotations.

HERE'S HOW Here are a few suggestions for making the collage:

- Individually or in small groups, brainstorm a list of current events and trends.
- Decide on a tone for the piece. It can be humorous, serious, or a combination—just be sure it's appropriate for your intended audience.
- Clip images and relevant headlines or quotations from a variety of old newspapers and magazines. Reflect your own distinct impression of the mood of the times.
- Think about how to incorporate such elements as color, line, texture, and shape into your collage. Which visual elements will appeal to your audience?

DESIGN TEMPLATE

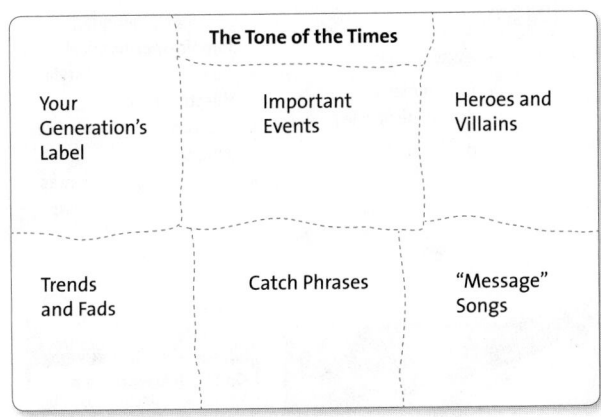

The Tone of the Times		
Your Generation's Label	Important Events	Heroes and Villains
Trends and Fads	Catch Phrases	"Message" Songs

COMMON CORE

RI 7 Analyze various accounts of a subject told in different mediums, determining which details are emphasized in each account
W 9b Draw evidence from informational texts to support analysis, reflection, and research.

Media Tools **THINK** central
Go to **thinkcentral.com**.
KEYWORD: HML10-1029

Tech Tip

You can use a word processing program to vary the typefaces of any headlines or quotes.

---

shop for books. Encourage them to think how a cover's color, images, and type face prompts them to pick up the book.

- **Web Site** Point out that the writing on Web sites may contain multi-colored text, short phrases instead of full sentences, bullet points, and graphics. Ask how Web writing reflects current ideas and values.

Produce Your Own Media

Rubric: Create a Signs-of-the-Times Collage
A strong signs-of-the-times collage should

- include a clear label for the generation
- include a variety of images and headlines or quotes from newspapers and magazines
- convey a recognizable mood of the times
- depict a variety of current events and trends
- use design elements effectively

R RESOURCE MANAGER—Copy Master
Produce Your Own Media p. 156

Assess and Reteach

Write or Discuss

COMMON CORE **RI 7**
W 9b
SL 2

Compare the Images In their opinion statements, students should make specific references to the purposes, messages, and design elements in the images. For example, if students choose the book cover, they might refer to the effective use of size, positioning, and color in juxtaposing Superman in his bright red cape with the more average-looking heroes of 9/11. The juxtaposition shows clearly the pride that the United States took in its heroes. Students might also point out the dignified and resilient way the heroes look, along with the clever use of the shadow of the twin towers as part of the "11" in the book title. Both point to the mood of defiance in the face of terrorist attacks.

MEDIA STUDY WRAP–UP

Have students summarize what they have learned about analyzing history through media. Encourage them to use terms such as *cartoon, book cover, Web site, color, line, texture, shape, words, panel, punchline,* and *frame* in their explanations.

RETEACH

For students who are unable to apply the Media Study Skills, select from these reteaching options:

- **Cartoon** Have students suggest subjects for political cartoons, and list their ideas on the board. Then have students work in groups to choose one of the topics for a cartoon they will create. Have the groups decide whether the cartoon should be one panel or several panels and brainstorm the images and captionss their cartoons should contain. Have students sketch their cartoons and present them to the class.
- **Book Cover** Point out that book covers are a form of marketing, and a strong visual can be a great way of conveying a message to viewers. Have students discuss the types of book covers that appeal to them when they

Media Tools **THINK** central

Media study keywords point to **MediaScope**, a Web site that helps students strengthen media analysis and production skills.

Focus and Motivate

COMMON CORE FOCUS

W 2a–f Write informative/explanatory texts to convey complex information; develop the topic with relevant, well-chosen, and sufficient evidence; use appropriate and varied transitions. **W 4** Produce clear and coherent writing appropriate to task, purpose, and audience. **W 5** Develop and strengthen writing by planning, revising, editing, rewriting, or trying a new approach, focusing on addressing what is most significant for a specific purpose and audience. **W 7** Conduct short research projects to answer a question. **W 8** Gather information from multiple authoritative sources. **W 10** Write routinely over shorter time frames for a range of tasks, purposes, and audiences. **L 1** Demonstrate command of the conventions of standard English grammar and usage. **L 2a** Use a semicolon.

WRITE WITH A PURPOSE

Tell students that their purpose in writing a cause-and-effect essay is to explain the *what* and *why* of an event or phenomenon. Have students consider what their audience wants to know.

COMMON CORE TRAITS

Review the *COMMON CORE TRAITS* with students, focusing on traits associated with the development and organization of ideas. Compare the list of traits with the rubric on page 1038.

ADDITIONAL TASKS

Write about Literature Write an essay that traces a cause-and-effect relationship in a work of fiction or nonfiction.
Possible subjects: a character's actions, a real-life tragedy

Write to Consumers Write an article that "sells" the effects that consumers can expect from a particular product.
Possible subjects: a car, a washing machine, athletic shoes

Writing Online  THINK central

The following tools are available online at **thinkcentral.com** and on **Write*Smart* CD-ROM**:
- **Interactive Graphic Organizers**
- **Interactive Student Models**
- **Interactive Revision Lessons**

Writing Workshop

INFORMATIVE TEXT

Essential Course of Study ECOS

Cause-and-Effect Essay

What happened and why? These are questions you ask every day about events in the news and situations closer to home and school. When you ask what happened and why, you want to know about the cause-and-effect relationships of events. In this workshop, you will write a cause-and-effect essay, which explores the connection between events.

 Complete the workshop activities in your **Reader/Writer Notebook**.

WRITE WITH A PURPOSE

WRITING TASK

Write a **cause-and-effect essay** in which you clearly and accurately explain a cause-and-effect relationship that you consider important or interesting. You can examine how multiple causes lead to a single effect or how a single cause leads to multiple effects. Develop the topic with sufficient evidence to support your controlling idea.

Idea Starters
- an event in your life, such as a personal experience or significant accomplishment
- a scientific phenomenon, such as an eclipse or the rise and fall of ocean tides
- a historical event, such as the French Revolution or the Great Depression

THE ESSENTIALS

Here are some common purposes, audiences, and formats for cause-and-effect writing.

PURPOSES	AUDIENCES	FORMATS
• to understand connections between events • to inform or entertain an audience	• classmates and teacher • newspaper or magazine readers • community members • Web users	• essay for class • newspaper or magazine article • documentary • blog • commercial/PSA • podcast

COMMON CORE TRAITS

1. DEVELOPMENT OF IDEAS
- introduces the topic and states a **controlling idea**
- includes **well-chosen, relevant,** and **sufficient evidence**
- makes clear **connections** and **distinctions** between causes and effects
- provides a **concluding section** that supports the information presented

2. ORGANIZATION OF IDEAS
- **organizes** complex ideas logically
- uses **appropriate transitions** to clarify cause-and-effect relationships

3. LANGUAGE FACILITY AND CONVENTIONS
- uses **precise language** and **domain-specific vocabulary**
- maintains a **formal style** and **objective tone**
- uses **compound sentence** structures
- reflects correct **grammar, mechanics,** and **spelling**

Writing Online **THINK** central
Go to **thinkcentral.com**.
KEYWORD: HML10N-1030

Writing Workshop Resources

** RESOURCE MANAGER UNIT 9**
Plan and Teach, pp. 157–160
Prewriting–Editing, pp. 161–165
Writing Rubric, p. 166
Speaking and Listening, p. 167
Writing Support, p. 168*

📖 BEST PRACTICES TOOLKIT
Cause-and-Effect Graphics, pp. B16, B37–B39

Writing Template: Cause and Effect, pp. C20, C21
TECHNOLOGY
💿 **Teacher One Stop DVD-ROM**
💿 **Student One Stop DVD-ROM**
💿 **Write*Smart* CD-ROM**
💿 **GrammarNotes DVD-ROM**

Writing Center on thinkcentral.com

*See resources on the **Teacher One Stop DVD-ROM** and on **thinkcentral.com**.*

* Resources for Differentiation

Planning/Prewriting

COMMON CORE W 2a–f Write informative/explanatory texts to convey complex information. W 5 Develop writing by planning. W 7 Conduct short research projects to answer a question. W 8 Gather information from multiple authoritative sources.

Getting Started

CHOOSE A TOPIC

Brainstorm **topics** for your essay, and list them in a cluster diagram. Think of topics that illustrate engaging cause-and-effect relationships. Include your own accomplishments, current events, natural phenomena, historical events, and any other ideas that come to mind. Then choose the topic that interests you most.

► WHAT DOES IT LOOK LIKE?

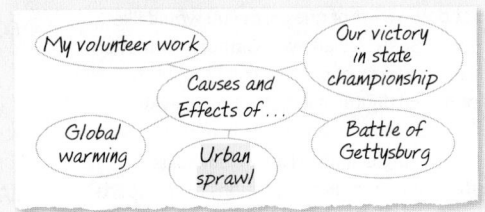

IDENTIFY CAUSES AND EFFECTS

Identify **causes** and **effects** related to your chosen topic. Remember that a cause can have several effects and that several causes can combine to produce one effect. Also, make sure that you select valid causes and effects. Just because one event follows another doesn't necessarily mean that the first event causes the second. List all the causes and effects you can. Then, review your list and select the most important causes and effects to discuss in your essay. Well-chosen examples should effectively support your topic. If you find you have too many related causes and effects, **narrow your topic** to focus on something more specific. If you can't generate a sufficient amount of relevant examples of causes and effects, then you need to **broaden your topic.**

► WHAT DOES IT LOOK LIKE?

Overall cause:	Overall effects:
urban sprawl	→ * damages city's economic and human resources * endangers farmland
Cause:	**Effects:**
suburbs grow	→ * population loss in city * loss of jobs in city * brain drain from city
Cause:	**Effect:**
brain drain from city	→ decline of school quality in city
Cause:	**Effect:**
redirection of resources to suburbs	→ decline of urban centers

THINK ABOUT AUDIENCE AND PURPOSE

Write sentences about your **purpose**—to explain causes and effects—and your **audience**. What **background information** might they need to understand the topic? What **domain-specific** (specialized) **vocabulary** might they not understand? How formal should your style should be?

► WHAT DOES IT LOOK LIKE?

Audience: This essay is for concerned citizens in my community.

Purpose: I want to inform community members about the effects of urban sprawl.

WRITE A CONTROLLING IDEA

Explain your **controlling idea,** or the overarching cause-and-effect relationship of your topic.

► WHAT DOES IT LOOK LIKE?

Controlling Idea: Urban sprawl affects the health of cities and rural areas.

WRITING WORKSHOP **1031**

DIFFERENTIATED INSTRUCTION

FOR ENGLISH LANGUAGE LEARNERS
Language: Reinforce Cause-and-Effect Terms
Write these terms on the board, and review them with students:

- *cause:* the reason an event happens
- *effect:* what happens as a result of an event
- *introduction:* the opening paragraph in an essay, which presents the topic and the controlling idea
- *controlling idea:* one or more sentences that state the overall cause-and-effect relationship

- *background information:* basic facts that an audience needs to know to understand a topic
- *organizational structure:* the way ideas are organized or presented
- *evidence:* facts, examples, quotations, observations, and other details that support a controlling idea
- *tone:* the writer's attitude toward the subject; the way in which a writer expresses his or her thoughts
- *transitions:* words and groups of words that link ideas

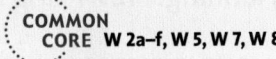
Teach

Planning/ Prewriting

COMMON CORE W 2a–f, W 5, W 7, W 8

▶ **CHOOSE A TOPIC** Have students work in pairs to free associate. Direct one partner to fill in the first circle of the cluster by writing a historical, news, scientific, or experiential topic. Then have the other partner add a related or new topic, connecting it to the first circle or starting a new branch. Tell students to continue the process until they have listed six or more topics. Have each partner then choose the topic that interests him or her most.

▶ **IDENTIFY CAUSES AND EFFECTS** Before students identify causes and effects related to their chosen topics, review the examples in the diagram on this page. Remind students that a cause can have several effects (see the "urban sprawl" entry, for example) and that several causes can combine to produce one effect.

▶ **THINK ABOUT AUDIENCE AND PURPOSE** Remind students that their primary purpose, or reason, for writing a cause-and-effect essay is to explain *why* something happened (state the effect, then explain the causes) or *what* happened (state the cause, then explain the effects).

▶ **WRITE A CONTROLLING IDEA** Emphasize that the controlling idea in a cause-and-effect essay states the overarching cause-and-effect relationship of the topic. Tell students to consider the causes and effects they have listed for their topic and then ask, "What is the idea that connects all of these causes and effects?"

R RESOURCE MANAGER—Copy Masters
Planning / Prewriting p. 161
Drafting p. 162
Revising pp. 163–164
Ask a Peer Reader p. 165
Rubric p. 166
Writing Support p. 168

BEST PRACTICES TOOLKIT—Transparency
Cause-and-Effect Graphics pp. B16, B37, B38, B39

WRITING WORKSHOP **1031**

Planning/Prewriting continued

▶ **COLLECT SUPPORTING EVIDENCE** Review the types of evidence students should look for when conducting their research.

- *fact*: information that can be proven
- *statistic*: a fact expressed with numerical information
- *example*: a specific instance of an idea or situation
- *expert opinion*: a statement by a person with special knowledge of a topic
- *quotation*: a person's exact words
- *anecdote*: a brief story that illustrates a point

▶ **CHOOSE AN ORGANIZATIONAL STRUCTURE** Point out that the writer of the Student Draft on pages 1035–1036 uses a cause-and-effect structure to discuss urban sprawl. Explain that time order and order of importance can also be used to organize ideas in a cause-and-effect essay. Structuring an essay according to time order is a good choice when discussing a series of causes and effects as they occurred. Order of importance highlights the relative importance of causes and effects to the central cause-and-effect relationship by presenting the most important cause or effect first or last.

YOUR TURN Give students time to choose a topic and research causes and effects. After students share their lists of causes and effects with each other, have them use their classmates' feedback to narrow their lists to the most important or interesting causes and effects. Direct students to collect supporting evidence for these causes and effects.

For interactive graphic organizers, see

💿 **WriteSmart CD-ROM**

Writing Center on thinkcentral.com

Planning/Prewriting continued

Getting Started

COLLECT SUPPORTING EVIDENCE

Jot down a list of questions you would like your research to answer. Gather information from a variety of sources, including both print and digital resources. Locate **evidence** for each cause or effect you plan to discuss. Supporting evidence can include facts, statistics, examples, quotations from experts and others, anecdotes, your own observations, and other carefully chosen details. Assess the usefulness of each source. If it doesn't include information that answers your questions, then it isn't likely to support your controlling idea.

▶ **WHAT DOES IT LOOK LIKE?**

Effect: Loss of farmland
* Bob Winfield of the U.S. Department of Agriculture: land used to develop housing and commercial areas in suburbs is best farmland, once used for crops of high value (fact, expert opinion)
* 332,800 acres of good farmland in Texas lost to developers between 1992 and 1997; more than any other state (statistic)

Effect: Smart growth
* laws to preserve farmland before developers can buy it (fact)
* improvement of public transportation (fact)
* more housing options in downtowns of cities (fact)
* Portland, Oregon (example)

CHOOSE AN ORGANIZATIONAL STRUCTURE

Use a **logical structure** to organize the causes and effects you have identified. You might describe an effect and then analyze its causes, or you might begin with a cause and trace its effect or effects. The writer of the student model names just one cause—urban sprawl—and discusses its effects.

▶ **WHAT DOES IT LOOK LIKE?**

Cause: Urban sprawl

Effect 1: Urban sprawl damages the economy and human resources of a city.
* evidence
* evidence

Effect 2: Urban sprawl endangers farmland.
* evidence
* evidence

Effect 3: Urban sprawl has led to smart growth.
* evidence
* evidence

PEER REVIEW Share your list of causes and effects with a classmate. Then, ask: Which causes and effects on my list do you think are most important? Why? Which cause-and-effect relationships interest you most? Why?

 YOUR TURN In your *Reader/Writer Notebook*, develop your writing plan. Use a diagram such as the one on page 1031 to list causes and effects. Then, draft a controlling idea. Consider the following tips as you research and gather evidence:

- Choose relevant facts and concrete details to clearly explain causes and effects.
- If you use quotations as supporting evidence, copy them word-for-word exactly as they appear in your source.
- If you can't find solid evidence to explain the causes and effects you have identified, consider choosing a new topic or trying a new approach.

1032 UNIT 9: HISTORY, CULTURE, AND THE AUTHOR

DIFFERENTIATED INSTRUCTION

FOR ENGLISH LANGUAGE LEARNERS

Writing: Developing Ideas As students prepare to draft their essays, suggest that they use these questions and sentence frames to help them focus:

- Who or what caused what to happen?
- Who or what was affected by what happened?
- _____ happens because of _____.
- _____ brings about _____.

FOR STRUGGLING WRITERS

Choose an Organizational Structure To help students organize their ideas, suggest that they write their main points on index cards and their supporting evidence on self-stick flags. Then have students manipulate cards and flags in several different ways until they find the best method of organization. Have students explain the structure they have chosen to a classmate to see if the cause-and-effect relationships are clear.

Drafting

W 2c Use appropriate and varied transitions.
W 4 Produce clear and coherent writing appropriate to task, purpose, and audience.

The following chart shows a structure for organizing your essay.

Organizing Your Cause-and-Effect Essay

INTRODUCTION

- Identify your **topic** and provide any **background information** your audience may need.
- Explain your **controlling idea**—the overarching cause-and-effect relationship of your topic.
- Establish a **formal style** and **objective tone** by avoiding contractions and slang, using precise language, and presenting information in a neutral, unbiased way.

▼

BODY

- Develop your topic by presenting causes and effects in a clear, **logical structure**. Depending on your topic, ideas may be presented in **sequence** or by **order of importance.**
- Cite **evidence** (facts, examples, quotations, anecdotes, observations) that supports your controlling idea, makes the nature of the cause-and-effect relationships clear, and is appropriate for your audience and purpose.
- Incorporate **transitional words and phrases** to connect ideas and to signal causes and effects.

▼

CONCLUDING SECTION

- Summarize the **key causes and effects** that support your controlling idea.
- Close with an **observation** about why the information is important.

GRAMMAR IN CONTEXT: TRANSITIONS THAT RELATE CAUSE AND EFFECT

You can use a variety of transitional words and phrases to link causes and effects. The following examples show how transitional words and phrases can appear in sentences at the beginning, middle, or end. Using transitions in a variety of locations will keep your sentences from sounding repetitive or formulaic.

Transitional Words and Phrases	Examples
Cause: *as, because, if, since, when*	**As** suburban areas explode in growth, urban areas lose population and jobs.
Effect: *as a result, consequently, for this reason, so, so that, then, therefore*	Cities also experience a "brain drain"; **consequently**, the quality of city schools declines. Urban centers suffer **as a result.**

 YOUR TURN
Develop a first draft of your cause-and-effect essay, using the evidence you have gathered, and following the structure outlined in the chart above. As you write, use a variety of transitional words and phrases in different sentence positions to clarify relationships between causes and effects.

FOR ENGLISH LANGUAGE LEARNERS

Transitions That Relate Cause and Effect Remind students that certain transitional words and phrases indicate that a writer is explaining the reason why something happened (cause) or the result of what happened (effect). Write these examples on the board:

- The weather gets too humid. Wooden doors swell and are difficult to open.
- If the weather gets too humid, then wooden doors swell and are difficult to open.

Ask students which example is easier to understand and why. *Possible answer: The second sentence is easier to understand, because the transition "if...then" makes the cause-and-effect relationship between the ideas clear.*

Have students suggest an appropriate transition for this sentence:

- _____ property taxes in the city are high, many businesses are moving to the suburbs. *Possible answer: Because*

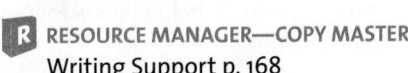 **RESOURCE MANAGER—COPY MASTER**
Writing Support p. 168

Practice and Apply

Drafting

 COMMON CORE W 2c, W 4

▶ **INTRODUCTION** Remind students that the introduction to an essay serves two purposes. It stimulates the audience's interest in the topic of the essay and establishes the essay's point. Point out that the writer of the Student Draft (see page 1035) adds a hook to her introduction to grab her readers' interest.

▶ **BODY** Emphasize the importance of including appropriate transitions in cause-and-effect essays. Have students locate examples of transitions that link ideas in the Student Draft on pages 1035–1036.

▶ **CONCLUDING SECTION** Explain that an effective concluding section not only summarizes but also leaves the reader with a new perspective on the topic or an interesting insight into it. Have students identify how the writer of the Student Draft makes her concluding section on page 1036 memorable for readers.

GRAMMAR IN CONTEXT: TRANSITIONS THAT RELATE CAUSE AND EFFECT

With students, review the transitional words and phrases that relate causes and effects. Point out that the examples of the transitions shown on this page are also highlighted on page 1035 in the Student Draft. Model how to use additional cause-and-effect transitions in these examples:

- Farmland has been lost *because* development has spread to rural areas.
- Many companies have moved to the suburbs; *therefore,* fewer jobs are available in the city.
- *When* companies leave a city, the downtown often declines.

 YOUR TURN
Ask students to complete the **Your Turn** activity independently. Remind students to use appropriate transitions to relate causes and effects. Suggest that students double-space their drafts so that they can make revisions more easily later.

For a cause-and-effect writing template, see

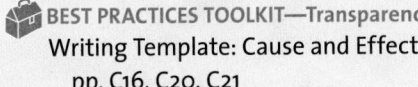 **BEST PRACTICES TOOLKIT—Transparency**
Writing Template: Cause and Effect, pp. C16, C20, C21

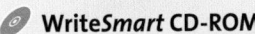 **WriteSmart CD-ROM**

Writing Center on thinkcentral.com

Revising

Model the Skill Using a draft essay on a transparency, model how to use the questions, tips, and strategies suggested in the chart to evaluate and revise. You might use the essay of a student from another class or from a previous year. Be sure to remove the student's name so that he or she remains anonymous.

Revising

As you revise, consider the controlling idea, evidence, and organization of your essay. The goal is to determine whether you've achieved your purpose and effectively communicated your ideas to your intended audience. The questions, tips, and strategies in the following chart will help you revise and improve your draft.

CAUSE-AND-EFFECT ESSAY

Ask Yourself	Tips	Revision Strategies
1. Does the introduction grab the audience's attention?	**Underline** sentences in the introduction that engage readers.	**Add** an interesting fact, example, or observation to get readers' attention.
2. Does the introduction identify the topic and state a controlling idea?	**Draw a star** next to the topic. **Bracket** the controlling idea.	**Add** an overarching statement that explains the controlling cause-and-effect relationship.
3. Are causes and effects clearly connected and organized in a logical way?	**Number** causes and effects in order of occurrence or importance. **Draw a line** from the first cause to its effect and so on.	**Rearrange** the order by putting the most important cause or effect first or last or by organizing causes and effects sequentially.
4. Is each cause or effect supported by accurate, concrete evidence?	**Circle** each piece of evidence. **Draw an arrow** to connect it to the cause or effect it supports.	**Add** evidence such as facts, examples, quotations, and observations for any cause or effect that does not have a corresponding circle.
5. Do transitional words and phrases clarify relationships among all parts of the essay?	**Place a check mark** next to each transitional word or phrase.	**Add** transitional words or phrases where needed to link parts of the text and relate causes and effects.
6. Does the concluding section summarize key causes and effects and explain why the information is important?	**Double underline** the summary. **Underline** the explanation of the information's importance.	**Add** a summary or a final observation about the importance of the information.

YOUR TURN

Remind students that a goal of their essays is to anticipate and answer readers' questions about what happened and why. Partners should feel free to point out where a student's essay does not adequately answer their questions about the reasons for an occurrence or its effects. Urge partners also to point out portions of the essay that address such questions clearly and completely. Tell students to consider seriously any comments their partners make about their drafts.

For interactive revision tools, see

WriteSmart CD-ROM

Writing Center on thinkcentral.com

YOUR TURN

PEER REVIEW Exchange your cause-and-effect essay with a classmate, or read it aloud to your partner. As you read and comment on your classmate's essay, focus on the controlling idea and supporting evidence. Discuss whether more evidence is needed for support and whether your tone is sufficiently objective. Provide suggestions for improvement, using the revision strategies in the chart.

1034 UNIT 9: HISTORY, CULTURE, AND THE AUTHOR

DIFFERENTIATED INSTRUCTION

FOR STRUGGLING WRITERS

Peer Review Have students work with a more proficient partner. These questions can help peer reviewers focus feedback and writers focus on specifics:

- What is the cause-and-effect relationship?
- Which paragraphs need more evidence to explain, develop, or support the cause-and-effect relationship?
- What transitions would help readers follow the writer's thinking?

FOR ADVANCED LEARNERS/PRE-AP

Analyze Tone Have students read the Student Draft to analyze its tone. Ask them to choose an adjective to describe the tone and to point out some of the ways the writer achieves it. Then have students read their own drafts aloud to confirm that the tone is appropriate for the topic, purpose, and audience and make adjustments in diction as needed.

ANALYZE A STUDENT DRAFT

Read this draft; notice the comments on its strengths as well as suggestions for improvement.

COMMON CORE

W 5 Strengthen writing as needed by revising, editing, rewriting, or trying a new approach, focusing on addressing what is most significant for a specific purpose and audience.

Urban Sprawl

by Rachel Langley, Lyndon Baines Johnson High School

❶   Urban sprawl is the unplanned, uncontrolled spread of urban development into areas adjoining the edge of a city. It occurs when a city's developers use spare land outside city limits to build new residential areas, which soon become supported by strip malls, businesses, grocery stores, and much more. Most people think of urban sprawl as a recent development, but the phenomenon can be traced as far back as colonial times. Puritans pushed west beyond Boston to settle Concord, settlers spread from New York to the Bronx and Staten Island, and the trend has continued. By 1950 seven million Americans occupied suburbs, or the areas surrounding cities. A problem now for more than 50 years, urban sprawl affects the health of both cities and rural areas.

❷   Although it is generally thought that urban sprawl contributes to economic growth, in the long run it actually causes major damage to a city's economy and human resources. As suburban areas explode in growth, urban areas lose population and jobs. Cities also experience a "brain drain"; consequently, the quality of city schools declines. Resources that could be used in the city are redirected to clearing land, building roads, and erecting new schools to accommodate new communities. Urban centers suffer as a result.

> Rachel identifies the **topic** of her essay in the first sentence of her **introduction,** but she needs to add a hook to grab readers' interest.

> A clear **controlling idea** explains the **cause-and-effect relationship** of the topic.

> Rachel uses various **transitional words and phrases** to clarify cause-and-effect relationships.

LEARN HOW   **Use a Hook to Grab Readers' Interest**   Rachel decides to open her essay with a startling statistic that will grab her audience's attention and interest them in her topic. She also adds a transition sentence to lead smoothly into her definition of urban sprawl.

RACHEL'S REVISION TO PARAGRAPH ❶

As of 2000, approximately 10.8 million people live in the suburbs of America's largest cities. This expansive growth has resulted in "urban sprawl."

Urban sprawl is the unplanned, uncontrolled spread of urban development into areas adjoining the edge of a city.

ANALYZE A STUDENT DRAFT

Explain that the Student Draft on this page is the first half of a cause-and-effect essay. Model reading the draft and the annotations in blue, and explain that the yellow highlighting illustrates the student's language choices. Explain that the following *Learn How* mini-lessons provide helpful information about ways to improve this draft as well as your students' drafts.

LEARN HOW   Use a Hook to Grab Readers' Interest

- Remind students that the opening sentences of their essays should grab readers' interest.
- Point out that the student writer realizes that opening her essay with a definition instead of an interesting fact might discourage her audience from reading further.
- Have students read the original and revised versions of the introduction of Rachel's essay. Then ask them how her addition of a statistic makes the introduction more interesting and helps hook her readers.

FOR STRUGGLING WRITERS

Connect Ideas Explain that an effective essay is more than a collection of individual sentences and paragraphs. An effective essay is made up of ideas that are related not only by the logic of what they say but also by the transitions between them. Review transitions that connect causes and effects, as identified on page 1033, and other common transitional words and phrases. Then have students use colored markers to highlight breaks between causes and effects and between sentences and paragraphs in their own essays. Tell students to add appropriate transitions as needed.

FOR ADVANCED LEARNERS/PRE-AP

Synthesize Have students discuss the practical advantages of analyzing causes and effects. Challenge them to identify and share real-world examples of these advantages, from their own experience or from current events. (*Students may mention that leaders may learn from past mistakes, scientists may learn about the causes or effects of diseases or other phenomena, and individuals may make wise decisions.*)

ANALYZE A STUDENT DRAFT *continued*

Explain that the Student Draft is continued and completed on this page. Read the draft and annotations aloud and discuss. Ask students to comment on whether the writer followed the organizational plan for a cause-and-effect essay outlined on pages 1032 and 1033.

❸   Urban sprawl also endangers America's farmland. As Bob Winfield of the U.S. Department of Agriculture notes, the land being used to develop suburban housing and commercial areas is the country's best farmland; it was previously used for crops of high value. Texas, for example, lost 332,800 acres of good farmland to developers between 1992 and 1997—more than any other state. With the country's population increasing, the loss of prime farmland to strip malls and apartment complexes is a serious problem that will affect our nation's economy for decades to come.

> As supporting **evidence** for her point about the loss of farmland, Rachel cites facts provided by an expert. She could strengthen her point by **incorporating** other **evidence** here.

❹   Has urban sprawl had a positive impact of any kind? The answer is yes. It has led to "smart growth." "Smart growth" involves passing laws to preserve farmland before developers can buy it, improving public transportation, and expanding housing options in downtown neighborhoods. One good example of an urban area that has applied the ideas of smart growth is Portland, Oregon, the city has curbed urban sprawl through legislation, community activism, and efficient city growth.

> Rachel restates her **controlling idea** and summarizes her key points about urban sprawl.

❺   Urban sprawl continues to threaten cities and rural areas, robbing urban communities of population and resources and gobbling up farmland for development. Not enough has been done to control it. Author Tom Clancy observes: "Terrorism is beyond our control, which is why it doesn't scare me. . . . We can control urban sprawl, but we choose not to; that is what is so frustrating." Will we rise to the challenge of preserving our farmland and honoring our cities by controlling urban sprawl?

> In her **concluding section** Rachel also offers an interesting quotation from a popular author and a question for her audience.

LEARN HOW Incorporating Evidence

- Tell students that personal testimony is another type of evidence that can be used to explain causes and effects. Point out that personal testimony is cited in the form of a quotation.

- Explain that adding quotations not only provides information from authoritative sources, it also adds a new voice to the writing. Note that Rachel's inclusion of a quotation shifts the text's point of view from objective to subjective, making the paragraph more interesting to read.

- Point out the transitional sentence Rachel inserts to prepare for the quotation from the Ohio farmer. Emphasize the importance of smoothly incorporating quotations and other kinds of evidence.

 YOUR TURN Ask students to complete the **Your Turn** activity independently. Tell them to make sure they hook their readers' interest in the opening sentences of their essays and seamlessly incorporate evidence in the essay's body to explain causes and effects.

For interactive revision tools, see

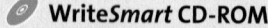 **Write*Smart* CD-ROM**

Writing Center on **thinkcentral.com**

LEARN HOW Incorporating Evidence Rachel decides to further support her point about urban sprawl's effect on farmland with a quotation, which she incorporates by adding a transitional sentence.

RACHEL'S REVISION TO PARAGRAPH ❸

. . . it was previously used for crops of high value. ⋏ *Owners of family farms feel pressure from both sides. Tom Spellmire, a farmer in Dayton, Ohio, explains: "When I'm out there on my tractor, the subdivision kids are hanging over the fence watching me. And you know what their parents say to me? 'You're not going to sell to developers, are you?'" Farmland is being replaced by development throughout the United States.*

 YOUR TURN Use the feedback from your peers and teacher as well as the two "Learn How" lessons to revise your essay. Evaluate how well you have explained significant causes and effects and addressed your audience.

1036 UNIT 9: HISTORY, CULTURE, AND THE AUTHOR

DIFFERENTIATED INSTRUCTION

FOR ENGLISH LANGUAGE LEARNERS

Writing: Adding Evidence Students who are not confident in their language skills may rely too heavily on direct quotations in their writing. Remind them to balance quoted and paraphrased or summarized material. Suggest that students work with more fluent partners to paraphrase or summarize some of the quotations in their drafts. Encourage students to use a dictionary or thesaurus to check the meanings and locate synonyms of difficult or unfamiliar words.

FOR STRUGGLING WRITERS

Check Accuracy Tell students to highlight quotations used in their drafts. Remind students that any quotation they incorporate in their essays should represent a person's exact words and be punctuated as it was in the source where students found it. Have students check quotations carefully against their sources to make sure that they are accurately recorded.

Editing and Publishing

In the editing stage, you proofread your essay to make sure that it is free of grammar, spelling, and punctuation errors, which can distract and confuse your audience.

COMMON CORE

W 2b Develop the topic with relevant, well-chosen, and sufficient evidence. **W 5** Strengthen writing by revising and editing. **L 1** Demonstrate command of the conventions of standard English grammar and usage. **L 2a** Use a semicolon.

GRAMMAR IN CONTEXT: PUNCTUATING COMPOUND AND COMPOUND-COMPLEX SENTENCES

Using a variety of sentence structures can make your writing more interesting to your readers. When using compound and compound-complex sentences, use correct punctuation to signal the relationships among your ideas clearly. Independent clauses can be joined with a comma and a coordinating conjunction, a semicolon, or a semicolon followed by a conjunctive adverb and a comma, as in these examples:

> *Most people think of urban sprawl as a recent development,* **but** *the phenomenon can be traced as far back as colonial times.*
>
> *Cities also experience a "brain drain"; consequently, the quality of city schools declines.*

The subordinate clause in a compound-complex sentence should be set off with commas from the independent clause to which it connects:

> *As Bob Winfield of the U.S. Department of Agriculture notes, the land being used to develop suburban housing and commercial areas is the country's best farmland; it was previously used for crops of high value.*
>
> [A comma sets off the subordinate clause "As Bob Winfield of the U.S. Department of Agriculture notes"; a semicolon joins the two independent clauses.]

As Rachel edits her essay, she discovers a compound sentence that is not correctly punctuated. She replaces the comma joining the independent clauses with a semicolon:

> *One good example of an urban area that has applied the ideas of smart growth is Portland, Oregon; the city has curbed urban sprawl through legislation, community activism, and efficient city growth.*

PUBLISH YOUR WRITING

Here are some options for sharing your essay with an audience:
- Present your essay as a speech for your classmates.
- Submit your essay to an online or print journal or magazine.
- Send your essay to a business concerned with your topic for its newsletter.

 YOUR TURN Correct any errors in your essay. Use correct punctuation in compound and compound-complex sentences. Make sure your style is consistent and appropriate for your audience. Then publish your essay in your intended format.

FOR ENGLISH LANGUAGE LEARNERS

Punctuating Compound and Compound-Complex Sentences Tell students that varying sentence structure adds rhythm and interest to writing and keeps an audience engaged. Have students combine simple sentences and subordinate ideas in their drafts to create compound and compound-complex sentences. Remind students to follow the punctuation rules. Then have volunteers read aloud examples of sentences from their essays—before and after editing—and have listeners comment on the differences.

Editing and Publishing

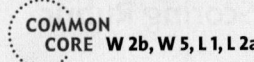
COMMON CORE W 2b, W 5, L 1, L 2a

GRAMMAR IN CONTEXT: PUNCTUATING COMPOUND AND COMPOUND-COMPLEX SENTENCES

- Review rules for punctuating compound and compound-complex sentences.
- Explain that in the first example from Rachel's draft, the independent clauses of the compound sentence are joined by a comma and the coordinating conjunction *but*.
- Observe that because a semicolon joins the independent clauses in the compound sentence in the second sentence, no coordinating conjunction is needed. Instead, the conjunctive adverb *consequently* followed by a comma introduces the second independent clause.
- Encourage students to vary sentence structure in their essays by including compound and compound-complex sentences and following the rules for punctuating these longer sentences correctly.

PUBLISH YOUR WRITING

Brainstorm with students additional ways to publish their cause-and-effect essays.

YOUR TURN Allow students time to proofread their drafts. Remind them to punctuate compound and compound-complex sentences correctly. Also remind students to include transitions that relate causes and effects where appropriate in their essays.

Scoring Rubric

Tell students that the best way to understand a scoring rubric is to use it to score actual writing. Have students use the rubric to evaluate a partner's cause-and-effect essay. Ask them to score the essays they read and then write a brief paragraph using the language of the rubric to explain the reasons for the score.

For Rubric Bank, see

 Write*Smart* CD-ROM

Writing Center on **thinkcentral.com**

Assess and Reteach

Assess

R RESOURCE MANAGER—Copy Master
Rubric for Evaluation p. 166

Online Essay Scoring on **thinkcentral.com**

Reteach

Level Up Online Tutorials on **thinkcentral.com**

Reteaching Worksheets on **thinkcentral.com**

Writing Lesson 5: Combining Sentences and Sentence Parts

Writing Lesson 13: Coherence in Paragraphs

Scoring Rubric

Use the rubric below to evaluate your cause-and-effect essay from the Writing Workshop or your response to the on-demand task on the next page.

CAUSE-AND-EFFECT ESSAY

SCORE	COMMON CORE TRAITS
	• **Development** Ably introduces a topic; states an insightful controlling idea; effectively relates causes and effects; supports ideas with sufficient, relevant evidence; ends powerfully • **Organization** Arranges ideas in an effective, logical order; uses varied transitions to link ideas • **Language** Consistently maintains a formal style and objective tone; uses precise language; shows a strong command of conventions
	• **Development** Has an effective introduction and controlling idea; relates causes and effects clearly; develops the topic with relevant evidence; has a strong concluding section • **Organization** Is logically organized; uses transitions to link ideas • **Language** Maintains a formal style and objective tone; has a few errors in conventions
	• **Development** Introduces the topic and controlling idea adequately; examines causes and effects, but could use more evidence; has an adequate concluding section • **Organization** Arranges ideas logically; needs more varied transitions • **Language** Mostly maintains an appropriate style and tone; needs more precise language; has a few distracting errors in conventions
	• **Development** Has a routine introduction; states a controlling idea but lacks sufficient support; has a routine concluding section • **Organization** Reflects some flaws in organization; needs more transitions • **Language** Frequently lapses into an informal style or subjective tone; has some significant errors in conventions
	• **Development** Has a weak controlling idea; lacks specific evidence; has an unrelated concluding section • **Organization** Has organizational flaws; lacks transitions throughout • **Language** Uses an informal style and vague language; has many distracting errors in conventions
	• **Development** Has no introduction or controlling idea; offers unrelated points as evidence; ends abruptly • **Organization** Includes a string of disconnected ideas with no overall organization • **Language** Uses an inappropriate style and language; has major problems with grammar, punctuation, and spelling

Preparing for Timed Writing

COMMON CORE — **W 10** Write routinely over shorter time frames for a range of tasks, purposes, and audiences.

1. ANALYZE THE TASK — 5 MIN

Read the task carefully. Then, read it again, noting the words that tell the type of writing, the topic, the audience, and the purpose.

> **WRITING TASK** *Type of writing* · *Audience* · *Purpose*
> Write a short essay to share with your classmates that explains the causes and effects of a personal accomplishment or an experience that changed your life in some way.
> *Possible topics*

2. PLAN YOUR RESPONSE — 10 MIN

Think about the cause-and-effect relationships of your topic. List them, beginning with the overall cause and effect, which will form your controlling idea. Review the other causes and effects you have listed, and circle the most significant ones to explain in your essay.

Overall Cause:	→	Overall Effect:
Cause:	→	Effect:
Cause:	→	Effect:
Cause:	→	Effect:

3. RESPOND TO THE TASK — 20 MIN

Begin drafting your essay. You might start with an observation or a brief scene related to your experience to grab your audience's attention. As you write, keep these tips in mind:
- In the introduction, present your topic, a controlling idea that explains the overall cause-and-effect relationship, and background information for your audience.
- In the body, use a logical structure to explain important causes or effects. Support each cause or effect with specific evidence.
- In the concluding section close with an observation about the importance of your experience and how it might affect you in the future.

4. IMPROVE YOUR RESPONSE — 5–10 MIN

Revising Compare your draft with the writing task. Does your draft explain the causes and effects of your topic? Do you support each cause or effect with relevant evidence? Do you use transitions to clarify relationships between ideas?
Proofreading Find and correct any errors in grammar, punctuation, or spelling. Make sure that your essay and any edits are neatly written and legible.
Checking Your Final Copy Before you submit your essay, examine it once more to make sure that you are presenting your best work.

COMMON CORE FOCUS

W 10 Write routinely over shorter time frames for a range of tasks, purposes, and audiences.

Preparing for Timed Writing

1. **Analyze the Task** Before students begin writing, encourage them to answer the following questions:
   - What is my time limit?
   - What are the core traits assessed in the scoring rubric?
   - Who is my audience?
   - What is my purpose?

2. **Plan Your Response** Point out that the scoring rubric emphasizes the importance of a logical structure and appropriate transitions. Suggest that students organize causes and effects from most important to least important. As they write, students should add transitional words that indicate the importance of each cause and effect.

3. **Respond to the Task** Remind students to consider their audience and purpose. Urge them to provide background information for their audience as needed. Also tell them to a formulate a controlling idea—a sentence that states the overall cause-and-effect relationship they will discuss in the essay.

4. **Improve Your Response** Note that the scoring rubric details the development of ideas and specifies that students include carefully selected supporting evidence. Tell students to elaborate on any key points that are insufficiently supported by adding facts, examples, and anecdotes.

Assess

Use the Scoring Rubric on page 1038 to assess students' essays.

DIFFERENTIATED INSTRUCTION

FOR ENGLISH LANGUAGE LEARNERS

Writing: Planning a Response As an alternative to the chart shown on page 1039, have students use small squares for causes and small circles for effects and connect them with arrows. By labeling the geometric shapes and then making physical connections, students may be better able to see relationships between causes and effects and the multiplicity of each.

FOR STRUGGLING WRITERS

Analyze the Task Point out that the task for this writing assignment specifies that students should focus on a personal accomplishment or experience rather than a current event or natural phenomenon about which facts and statistics might be available. Explain that in this case, students themselves are the experts, and their essays should feature personal observations and relevant examples and details to support the causes and effects they present.

Focus and Motivate

SL 1 Participate effectively in collaborative discussions. **SL 4** Present information clearly, concisely, and logically such that listeners can follow the line of reasoning.

SPEAK WITH A PURPOSE

Tell students that their purpose in giving oral instructions is to explain the steps in a process clearly to an audience and enable them to perform a task. Discuss with students how their approach to giving instructions, as well as the instructions themselves, might vary depending on their audience.

COMMON CORE TRAITS

As students prepare to give and follow instructions, remind them to keep in mind the *COMMON CORE TRAITS* of good oral instructions.

Practice and Apply

Planning Your Instructions

Model the Skill: IDENTIFY AND ORDER THE STEPS IN THE PROCESS

Draw a sequence chart on the board, and list the steps of a simple process, such as feeding a pet, in order in the chart. Keep your description of the steps brief so that they will fit in the boxes of the chart. Then list the numbers of the steps on the board and flesh out the instruction for each step. In the instructions include transitions that signal sequence.

GUIDED PRACTICE Have students fill in their own charts with brief notes on the steps in the process they have chosen to explain. When students have identified and ordered the steps, have them list the numbers for all the steps. Then, have them write fuller descriptions of each step incorporating appropriate transitions as needed.

R RESOURCE MANAGER—Copy Master
Speaking and Listening p. 167

Speaking & Listening Workshop

Essential Course of Study **ECOS**

Giving and Following Oral Instructions

Have you ever explained to a family member how to send pictures from a cell phone—or been taught to do that yourself by a friend? You might be surprised at how often you give and follow oral instructions. Like producing cause-and-effect writing, giving and following instructions orally involves making connections and clarifying relationships between a process and its end result. Direct a partner through a process using **oral instructions**—step-by-step verbal information that tells someone how to do something.

Complete the workshop activities in your **Reader/Writer Notebook**.

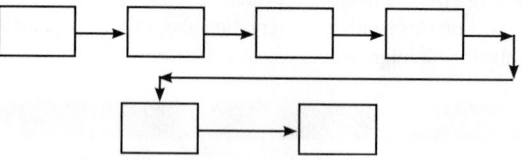

SPEAK WITH A PURPOSE	COMMON CORE TRAITS
TASK Give **oral instructions** to a partner regarding a process such as downloading a podcast or sending a text message. Have your partner follow your directions as you give them. Come prepared with the necessary equipment (for instance, a cell phone or a computer) to help your listener more easily follow your instructions.	**GOOD ORAL INSTRUCTIONS . . .** • present steps in a logical order • incorporate sequence words as transitions • contain clear and precise language • make domain-specific vocabulary understandable for listeners • meet the needs of the audience, purpose, and occasion

COMMON CORE

SL 1 Participate effectively in collaborative discussions.
SL 4 Present information clearly, concisely, and logically such that listeners can follow the line of reasoning.

Planning Your Instructions

Consider the sequence and language that you will use to present your instructions clearly and logically. Follow these suggestions to plan your instructions:

- **Identify and Order the Steps in the Process** Use a sequence chart like the one below to organize and develop the steps in the process. Number each step.

- **Write Step-by-Step Instructions** Write instructions for each of the steps in your sequence chart. Use concise sentences and precise language, and include sequence words such as *first, next, then,* and *finally*. Define any domain-specific, or specialized, terms that your audience may not know.

- **Revise for Audience and Purpose** Review your instructions to make sure you have included all the steps a listener needs to accomplish the task. Evaluate the substance and style of your text to ensure that it is appropriate for a peer. Make revisions as needed. As you give your instructions, you may revise further on the spot to help your partner follow your thinking, answer questions, or solve problems.

THINK central
Speaking & Listening Online
Go to **thinkcentral.com**.
KEYWORD: HML10-1040

DIFFERENTIATED INSTRUCTION

FOR ENGLISH LANGUAGE LEARNERS
Language: Reinforce Oral Instructions Terms
Reinforce key terms used in this workshop:

- *process:* a series of actions carried out to make or do something

- *instructions:* steps involved in making or doing something

- *sequence:* the order of steps in a process

- *steps:* individual actions to make or do something

Giving Instructions

As you lead your partner through the step-by-step process, use a variety of both verbal and nonverbal techniques to express yourself clearly.

Verbal	Nonverbal
• Speak slowly and pause frequently to allow your partner time to understand and perform each step. • Speak at a moderate volume and say each word clearly so that your partner can hear every word. • Emphasize important information by stressing certain words. • Respond to questions by clarifying important details as appropriate or necessary.	• Help listeners follow your oral directions by using gestures. For example, point to an area of a screen or to a key on a keyboard. • Emphasize the order of the steps and important details with gestures. • Use facial expressions to invite questions or encourage your partner as he or she performs the task.

Following Instructions

The goal of any set of instructions is to enable a listener to perform a task. However, it can be difficult to learn and master the steps in a complex task after a single instructional session. To perform the task correctly on subsequent occasions, you may need to take notes as you listen to oral instructions. Use these tips to take notes as your partner gives instructions:

• **Summarize** Use your own words to restate each step of the process.
• **Synthesize** Note how each step contributes to the whole process.
• **Highlight** Mark key words, phrases, or details.
• **Question** Ask questions about terms or steps that confuse you. Ask for clarification about how to perform particular steps.

YOUR TURN

As a Speaker Give oral instructions to your partner, using your voice effectively and incorporating gestures. Use your partner's questions to clarify or make adjustments to your instructions. Take part in this activity once as a speaker and once as a listener.

As a Listener Follow the oral instructions of your partner, taking notes and asking questions as needed to perform the task successfully. Ask your partner to clarify or elaborate on anything you do not understand, or that does not seem appropriate or necessary for completing the task. Pay attention to both the verbal and the nonverbal cues your partner provides to help you follow his or her instructions.

SPEAKING AND LISTENING WORKSHOP 1041

FOR STRUGGLING STUDENTS

Giving and Following Instructions Have students work in small groups. Tell the students in each group to draw a simple picture. Students should not show their pictures to anyone in the group. Next, have each student in turn describe his or her picture while the other members of the group listen and take notes. The listeners may also ask questions if necessary. Once the speaker has finished, the listeners should draw the picture described. Then have the speaker share his or her picture

and listeners compare and contrast their own renderings. Have students in each group conclude by discussing what they learned about giving and following instructions.

Giving Instructions

Model the Skill: VERBAL AND NONVERBAL TECHNIQUES

Demonstrate how to give instructions about how to feed a pet by speaking slowly, emphasizing important information, and using gestures. Then model how to summarize those instructions.

GUIDED PRACTICE Have students practice using verbal and nonverbal techniques to explain steps to a partner.

YOUR TURN

Ask listeners to make notes about the speaker's use of verbal and nonverbal techniques and offer specific feedback about which were most effective and which could be improved. Also encourage listeners to ask questions about steps that are confusing.

Assess and Reteach

Assess

Use the *COMMON CORE TRAITS* to assess students' oral instructions.

Good oral instructions

• include all steps sequentially
• incorporate sequence words as transitions
• contain clear and precise language
• make domain-specific, or specialized, terms understandable for listeners
• meet the needs of the audience, purpose, and occasion

Reteach

If students have difficulty listening and taking notes simultaneously, give them copies of written instructions. Read the instructions aloud, and have students highlight key words and phrases and put question marks next to terms or steps that are confusing. Then discuss items students highlighted and respond to questions about confusing terms or steps. Finally, have a volunteer describe how a step contributes to the whole process.

Speaking and Listening Online THINK central

• Public speaking tips
• Strategies for effective listening

Assessment Practice

RL1 Cite textual evidence to support analysis of what the text says explicitly as well as inferences drawn from the text. **RL2** Determine a theme or central idea of a text. **RL4** Determine the meaning of words and phrases as they are used in a text. **RI1** Cite textual evidence to support analysis of what the text says explicitly as well as inferences drawn from the text. **W5** Strengthen writing by revising and editing.

CHECK READINESS

Read aloud the paragraph under **ASSESS** and stress to students that this is not the full Unit Test, but a way for them to check their readiness for it. Then have students examine the skills standards listed under **REVIEW** and look back in the unit or in the **Student Resource Bank** for any skills they need to review.

READ THE TEXTS

Remind students to keep unit goals in mind as they read each passage, paying particular attention to these literary and reading skills:

- cultural context
- cultural influences on media
- monitor comprehension

To help students focus on cultural context, encourage them to ask questions such as

- How do cultural stereotypes influence people's views of one another?
- How do people overcome cultural stereotypes?

ANSWER THE QUESTIONS

Direct students to pages R93–R101 of the **Handbook** to review test-taking strategies.

ASSESS
Taking this practice test will help you assess your knowledge of these skills and determine your readiness for the Unit Test.

REVIEW
After you take the practice test, your teacher can help you identify any standards you need to review.

COMMON CORE
RL1 Cite textual evidence to support analysis of what the text says explicitly as well as inferences drawn from the text. **RL2** Determine a theme or central idea of a text. **RL4** Determine the meaning of words and phrases as they are used in a text. **RI1** Cite textual evidence to support analysis of what the text says explicitly as well as inferences drawn from the text. **W5** Strengthen writing by revising and editing.

Practice Test
Take it at thinkcentral.com.
KEYWORD: HML10N-1042

Assessment Practice

DIRECTIONS Read the two selections and the viewing and representing piece. Then, answer the questions that follow.

The Pale Mare *by Marian Flandrick Bray*

1   "But why?" I ask again, even though I know what he'll say.

2   "Because it's tradition."

3   He always says that. My papa. He's not a tall man, but he has much height in the soaring ways of our family and *la raza*, too.

4   Papa leans against the shiny side of our vendor truck with the black script that announces *Diaz Family Food*. The heavy smell of grease and corn hangs over us like a banner, an invisible proclamation: tradition.

5   Our family as always is at the *charreada*, the Mexican-style rodeo, to sell tamales, burritos, refried beans, and sweet bread. The real stuff. Not the Taco Bell version.

6   I try a different angle. After all, I'm good in geometry. "Papa, it's just this one, small weekend. Rafael can help."

7   My cousin. He helped last year when I had my appendix out. I wonder briefly if I have another body part to give out.

8   "Consuela," says Papa, then he bends over a sack of pinto beans. He lifts the fifty pounds as easy as my tiny baby sister and continues, "This is the final *charreada* and it is gonna be huge. I need your help. Not Rafael who goofs around."

9   I sigh. My expertise isn't what he needs. Any fool can take orders. It's not complicated to yell, "Four chicken burritos, one green sauce, three red, two large Cokes, two medium 7Ups." No, it's not my expertise in serving food that my precious parents want to preserve. It's that tradition again, our *familia* thing, the one that leads to *la raza*, the bigger picture of our people, who we are as Latin Americans. At least that's how Papa and Mama see it. But I don't see things just that way. Not anymore.

10   Papa goes into the house with the beans, for Mama to soak, then cook. I see my exit and in the dusk fling myself down the street, fast, furious, flying.

11   Kids play on the street, kicking soccer balls and riding bikes, rushing about like wasps from a knocked-down nest. As usual, it's the boys playing outside, with the rare girl running alongside until she can be gathered back into her house.

12   Papa is disgusted with my long walks. For once Mama tells him to let me be. She knows that I will explode like a star going nova if I am to stay home always.

DIFFERENTIATED INSTRUCTION

FOR ENGLISH LANGUAGE LEARNERS

Assessment Practice: Work Backward
Prepare students by having them read the questions *before* reading the passages. Have pairs find unfamiliar words in test directions and questions and follow these steps:

1. Write each word on an index card.

2. Look up the meaning in a dictionary and write it on the back of the card.

3. Use the cards to practice words with your partner and to teach them to others.

13   Each of my strides jars a different, recent memory. Earlier this week at school: my teacher exclaiming over my work in physics, "Excellent work, Consuela. I'll write a letter of recommendation for you. You should really apply to Cal Tech and MIT. You're coming to the weekend astronomy camp, right?" My heart sang. The stars. For the last two years, they are all I've wanted to do: Study them, chart their fierce light, listen to them, learn what they are saying. Stars do talk—really—with radio waves for words. But when I got home from school, an eclipse was on.

14   Parents, on the dark side: "You will not go to any camp. Isn't school during the week enough? You have to help us with the business."

15   Me, trying to remain calm in the light: "What about Manuel?" My brother, older by a year.

16   Parents, astonishment: "He has football practice."

17   "So what! I'm getting top honors in science! He's just playing junior varsity football!"

18   More genuine astonishment: "But he's the son." Meaning, of course, I'm only the daughter, only a girl. Maybe they don't mean to, but they're banishing me to the dark. I can't let that happen.

19   Later Mama tried to soothe me. "*M'ija*,[1] it's because we love you. We want you to be happy with a nice boy, to have a family."

20   "Are you saying being an astronomer and being happy with a nice boy are not compatible?"

21   She *was* saying that with her hands that touched my hair, with her liquid Spanish murmuring, with her eyes that lingered on my face, imploring me to stop struggling in this foolish manner.

22   I cross busy Lincoln Avenue and head up Rio Hondo Road, past the earth dam. The oil hills, scrubby with ugly bushes, prickled with derricks, bunch up on one side, then unfurl into the familiar, sandy, flattened flood plain.

23   The night is clear, rare in smoggy L.A. My science class is at this moment zooming away from L.A. for a weekend at Joshua Tree. They will observe the breathtaking stars from the desert floor.

24   A sob shakes my lungs. I didn't even know I was crying, but tears drip down my chin and onto my shirt collar. Why didn't I just go, like my friend Mia suggested? Because I have these stupid ideals, like honesty.

25   I find that, as suddenly as I started, I've stopped crying. The wind, fresh and sharp, brings the hot scent of livestock, dirt, and human sweat.

GO ON

---

1. **M'ija** (mē′ hă) *n.*: term of endearment, a contraction of *mi hija*, meaning "my daughter"

ITEM ANALYSIS

COMPREHENSION AND WRITTEN RESPONSE	ITEMS	UNIT PAGES
Cultural Context	1, 6, 11, 18, 19, 22, 23, 24	934–939, 953
Cultural Influences on Media	20, 21	1026–1029
Author's Perspective	2	934–939, 941, 999
Monitor Comprehension	3, 5, 7, 9, 10, 12, 13, 14, 15, 16, 17	953

VOCABULARY	ITEMS	UNIT PAGES
Word Meanings	4, 6, 8	1018

WRITING AND GRAMMAR	ITEMS	UNIT PAGES
Sentence Structure	1, 2, 3, 4, 6, 7	967, 1019
Gerund Phrases	5	994

Practice Test

On **thinkcentral.com** students can complete an interactive version of this practice test *and* receive remediation for the skills they have not yet mastered.

FOR STRUGGLING READERS

Assessment Support Consider these options for completing the Assessment Practice:

- Have students "work backward" to review the test questions before reading the passages.

- Select random questions in the Assessment and have students demonstrate *how* and *where* to look for answers.

- Ask students to locate unfamiliar vocabulary words in the Assessment. Elicit the words' meanings from the class.

- Have students record useful testing words and definitions in their journal for later reference.

- Read the selections or parts of them aloud to aid in student comprehension.

26   The *charreada*.

27   The grounds are quiet. The arena is smooth as flour tortilla. Many of the *charros'*[2] horses are stabled here in tidy, low barns, including the one belonging to *Tío* Jesús, Papa's brother. *Tío* Jesús' horse is an Andalusian, the color of very ripe plums.

28   The stock pens are on the far side, closest to the flood control, the citified riverbed that captures the water and hurries it to the sea, thirty miles away. Some of the water rushes from the San Gabriel Mountains, ten miles away, a dark stain in the north sky. The flood control is a hundred miles long, mountains to ocean. I've ridden this nearby stretch a million times, along its sandy path on my uncle's serious but kindly horse. Horses in the city— it sounds funny—the *charros*, they wouldn't have it any other way. Like my family. Life has to be a certain way. Their way.

29   Not for me though. Sorry, Papa, Mama. Your world isn't my world. It's not that I'm trying to pretend my Mexican blood doesn't course through my veins, it just means that my blood is calling to different things. That isn't wrong or bad.

30   Is it?

31   Mama, Papa, they just don't get it.

32   Or maybe they do. Perhaps that scares them.

33   I climb the sturdy metal pipe corral. I bypass the cattle, lumpy beasts dozing like logs in a stream, dull, empty life, cut off from their roots, and head out to the edge of the corrals.

34   I've been going to *charreadas* since I was a baby. The smell of dirt and animals was often overlaid by the stronger scent of greasy bean burritos, but I'd always sniff and sniff until the odor of hot horses and freshly shaken alfalfa flakes overtook me. When I was really little I'd clap my hands and crow, "*Char, char.*" I'd play I was a *charro* and swing astride the nearest fence, imagining I rode the finest horses—a Paso Fino, slate gray with white banners for a mane and tail, or a chestnut Andalusian, lifting his hooves high in the Spanish walk. The horse and I always moved as one—a seamless centaur.

35   What happened? Why did I change?

36   No moon tonight. My science class is observing stars tonight because a moonless night shows the stars the best. Starlight. I wish I could hold the light of those distant fires in my hands, bright and smooth as a sea stone, or maybe poured into a bowl and drunk.

37   The barns glow in the orange fog lights. Inside the stalls darkness swells, with an occasional flash of animal life. I hurry around them.

38   Farthest from the main arena is the mares' pen. I lean on the rails. The mares shy nervously, young wiry things, most of them rented for the weekend

---

2. **charros** (chä′ rrōs) *n.:* traditional horsemen or cowboys

FOR ENGLISH LANGUAGE LEARNERS
Review Literary Terms Write these literary terms on the board and review their meanings with students:

• *theme:* the message about life or human nature that a writer wants readers to understand

• *point of view:* the method of narration used in a story or work of nonfiction

• *symbol:* a person, a place, an object, or an activity that stands for something beyond itself

• *cultural context:* the traditions, beliefs, and customs that form the background of a story or influence a character's thoughts, feelings, and actions

from slaughterhouses. By Sunday night, they'll be off to the slaughterhouse stockyards. I never used to think about them. I mean, what was the point?

39   The last few months, though, I found I couldn't watch the horse-tripping. I'd busy myself in our truck, chopping chilis, slicing onions, refilling the Coke machine, anything. But even when I'd turn away from watching the *piales en el lienzo* and *mangana a caballo*,[3] *charros* performing their artistic ropework with the mares their targets, my stomach would still be tightened up because I knew how the mares would look when snared. If the *charro* does it right, the mare rolls on her shoulder, landing hard, but gets up, shaken, bruised, but walking. If he doesn't throw her correctly, she falls very hard and sometimes can't get up.

40   Don't get me wrong. Working the magic of the rope is hard, clever work. *Charros* are artists, as much as any writer, painter, singer, or astronomer. *Tío* Jesús trains and trains and he still screws up, snaring a mare wrong, crashing her spectacularly in a wild somersault, so she lands on her head. Sometimes the mares are so injured that the men who rented the mares started a "you broke 'em, you keep 'em" policy. If the horse is so damaged that she can't be loaded and trailered to the slaughterhouse, then they make you keep her.

41   I swing my leg over the top pipe and perch on the cold metal. One mare, pale as eggshells, whirls, ears up, like antennae, watching me. If she were a girl, she'd look like Fai, the Chinese girl in my class, also in the science club. Fai works long hours in her parents' Chinese takeout. Some nights, she's told me, she doesn't go to bed until two A.M. and then she has to get up at six to make it to school. Fai has deep smudges under her eyes and this little mare would, too, I bet, if horses got bags under their eyes.

42   I slip off the corral. Every head flings up, wild forelocks toss between pointed ears, and tension bolts up every leg. All senses lock on me, the intruder.

43   "Sorry," I whisper. Several mares whirl at my words and spin away across the pen to the far side. My little Chinese mare is brave. She continues to stare at me. She blinks her large, dark eyes. She shakes her neck and paws the ground with a dainty oval hoof, her gaze never shifting from my face.

44   Tomorrow will be different. She will burst, terrified, out of the chute. A *charro* will spur his pampered, well-groomed horse after his waif. He will snare her. He will throw her to the ground. Yes, artistically. But the ground is hard whether the rope is tossed prettily or not. In all fairness, I have to ask, is it any worse than roping calves, or goats? No. But it clutches at me with a tightness I can't ignore. I just know that I don't want to see her tomorrow frantically scrambling on her hind legs, trying to scale the arena's smooth walls, then spinning around the arena for any escape only to be slammed into the ground.

---

3. **piales en el lienzo** (pē ăl′ es en el lē en′ sō) *n.:* "roping of the feet"; and
mangana a caballo (măn gă′nă ă kă bī′ yō) *n.:* "forefooting on horseback"; two Mexican rodeo events

GO ON ➡

FOR STRUGGLING READERS

Assessment Support: Analyze Symbols To help students answer Reading Comprehension item 3, model how to analyze symbols in a literary text. Explain that a symbol is a person, a place, an object, or an activity that stands for something beyond itself. Observe that the pale mare might be a symbol in this story. Think aloud about what the mare might represent. List details from the story that support your interpretation in a chart like this:

Symbol	Story Details	Symbolic Meaning

45   I edge away along the fence line. The wind is cooler, tinged with sage and damp dirt. If I was at Joshua Tree I'd train my telescope near the Hercules constellation and study M-13, a cluster of stars so dense that if you lived on a planet nearby, night would never fall. There the sky would always be filled with brilliant starlight, clusters of stars like bunches of heavy grapes, plump, white, shining.

46   Never would there be night. How would that change a human's life? Change a mare's life?

47   I unlatch the gate. A packed dirt path leads one way to the arena. Another path, softer, less used, flickers up to the riverbed. I shove the gate wide.

48   I think the pale mare will realize she'll need to keep going north on the riverbed to the mountains beyond the city, to a place where there is no night for her.

49   The mares skitter from me like bugs over a pond as I walk toward them. The starlit mare is farthest away from me, but she locks onto my gaze, telescoping the distance between us, until we are closer than any binary star system. I close in. With a quiet dignity, she suddenly folds, turns, and walks calmly out of the open gate. The other mares see her outside and trot in circles, confused. Silly things. I raise my arms, shooing them out after the pale mare.

50   The remaining horses rush for the gate like the tail of a comet, fine, fiery. In the lead, the pale mare trots, her tail streaming ribbons. She passes under a fog light, an alien creature, then under another and another, until she is herself again, galloping away from the grounds, traveling light.

51   "That's right," I say admiringly. "Don't even look back." I turn and fade away into the night as shouts from security erupt from a nearby barn. The image of the starlit mare glows before me. Maybe I won't mind as much working tomorrow because in this darkness I'm beginning to see the path the stars have laid down for me. I hurry back home, my step lighter than it has been in a long time.

1046

Breaking Down Barriers

**A Vietnamese-American Football Star Brings
a Racially Divided Town Together**

by Adam Piore | *NEWSWEEK*

1   If any other group of kids had won the Rockport-Fulton youth soccer
championship in Texas, the parents of their opponents would surely have
applauded. But most of the members of Dat Nguyen's team were the children
of Vietnamese refugees. So when the proud victors rose to accept their trophies,
the crowd showered them with boos. It was the 1980s, and back then tensions
were so high in the small south Texas coastal community that white shrimpers
and their Vietnamese competitors sometimes carried rifles into the bay and took
potshots at one another from their boats. Dat Nguyen's domination on the soccer
field (he scored as many as 10 goals a game) didn't make his team any more
popular with the locals. "We weren't wanted in that community," Nguyen
recalled. "They wanted to kick us out. There was so much hatred between the
two cultures. My parents told me we couldn't trust anybody outside our family."

2   Nobody in Rockport would dare boo Dat Nguyen now. The hard-headed
kid who brawled on the field to defend himself against racist taunts grew up
to become the closest thing Texans have to royalty. Nguyen became a 5-foot,
11-inch, 231-pound football star. After leading Rockport-Fulton High School
to statewide renown, Nguyen went on to play at Texas A&M where he broke
the school record for tackles and in 1998 was named the best defensive player
in the country. Last week Nguyen, now 25, finished his second season as a
middle linebacker for "America's Team," the Dallas Cowboys. The easygoing,
quick-to-smile athlete has broken a lot of barriers. He is the first Vietnamese-
American ever to play pro football. He was the first Vietnamese-American to
start at linebacker for a major university in Texas.

3   But equally remarkable are the barriers Nguyen has broken down in this
tiny, racially divided corner of the United States. Thousands of Vietnamese
refugees moved to the gulf coast of Texas in the 1970s, many drawn by the
opportunity to make a living doing what they once did in Vietnam: shrimping.
According to the U.S. Census, 1,112 Asian-Americans, the vast majority
Vietnamese, live among a population of 23,129 in Nguyen's home county.
At last count well over 70,000 Vietnamese lived in Texas. Dat Nguyen is the
first to have a day named after him in his hometown, and the first to have his
picture plastered on a billboard displayed on the way into city limits. "That
boy never backed down for nobody," recalls Jimmy Hattenbach, Nguyen's
old soccer coach and mentor. "He has helped to mend this community—
everybody in this town believes that. When the football team started winning,
it really brought the town together. He became a role model."

GO ON ➡

FOR ENGLISH LANGUAGE LEARNERS

Assessment Support: Use Context Clues

Review how to use context clues to unlock the
meanings of unfamiliar words while reading.
Then have students work with partners to list
unfamiliar words in the selections and use
context clues to figure out their meanings.
Call on each pair to describe their process
and share the meanings they determined for
several words on their lists. Have students use
the new vocabulary in sample sentences.

4   Nobody would have believed that was possible just a few years ago. Dat Nguyen's family fled Ben Da, a fishing village on South Vietnam's Vung Tau Peninsula, in a fishing boat, the night shells began to rain down on their village in April, 1975. Ho Nguyen, Dat's brother, remembers soldiers firing artillery at their boat from the shore. After brief stops at an Arkansas refugee camp, where Nguyen was born, and in Michigan, the family landed in another war zone. Thousands of Vietnamese shrimpers had already begun new lives in the bays of south Texas. When they began pulling around-the-clock shifts, the locals felt their livelihoods were threatened. . . .

5   Nguyen broke down the barriers on the sports field. In eighth grade, he began to play football. Just as he had on the soccer field, he always seemed to know where the ball was. He was exceptionally quick, and soon learned to tackle hard. In an area where two thirds of the population have been known to caravan to championship high-school games, people took notice. Attitudes began to change. "He was a celebrity in high school," said Trish Wilson, who worked in the school district's central office for 18 years. "He was just one of those kids you don't see too often. If he was out there on the field, he was going to do something. He'd always get the extra yards, make the tackle, save the day." In college, he was one of the most popular Aggies ever. And when the Dallas Cowboys drafted him in 1999, he became a fan favorite. Critics who always said he was too small, and that an Asian would never make it (only four people of Asian ancestry had done so) had been proved wrong.

6   Now the town that once booed Dat Nguyen has claimed him as their own. Last year Rockport held a Dat Nguyen Day to honor him. Three hundred people showed up. (When a campaigning governor named George W. Bush came to town a few years earlier, only 200 people turned out.) At the local Wal-Mart, store managers have created a consumer shrine to the football star, with Dat Nguyen T shirts hanging off a rack and hats bearing his name. This year his neighbors chipped in $15,000 to erect the billboard on the road into town. . . .

7   Some residents actively opposed erecting the celebratory billboard. But they are in the minority. When Nguyen returns to his hometown he is mobbed for autographs. "There's always going to be people who are going to have some tension against us," Nguyen says. "But I think the tension died down. I opened a lot of doors for people to see that whatever background you come from, everybody can have an opportunity. I dreamed of being here all my life. And now I'm a Vietnamese boy living in America, playing the American sport, living the American dream, playing for America's Team. It doesn't get any better than that."

Editor's Note: In three of his five seasons with the Cowboys, Dat Nguyen led the team in tackles. In 2005, neck and knee injuries led him to retire. Then, less than two years later, the Cowboys hired him back as an assistant linebackers coach.

DIFFERENTIATED INSTRUCTION

FOR STRUGGLING READERS

Assessment Support: Monitor Comprehension
Guide students in identifying these statements
as true or false:

- Dat Nguyen became the first Vietnamese-American to play pro football. *(T)*

- Dat's performance on his high school football team helped change attitudes in his community toward the Vietnamese. *(T)*

- Racial tension in Dat's town disappeared. *(F)*

Diversity

"We become not a melting pot but a beautiful mosaic.
Different people, different beliefs, different yearnings,
different hopes, different dreams."

—Jimmy Carter

1049

Reading Comprehension

Model a thinking process for answering multiple-choice questions.

1. **C is correct.** *Consuela believes there is more for her than her culture's traditional role for women. A is incorrect because Consuela questions aspects of tradition. B is incorrect because Consuela's thoughts and actions suggest that the message of the story is broader than obedience to one's parents. D is incorrect because Consuela acknowledges the importance of her family's tradition.*

2. **B is correct.** *Consuela narrates and reveals her thoughts and feelings. A is incorrect because the story does not have a third-person omniscient narrator. C is incorrect because Mama is not the narrator. D is incorrect because Consuela can reveal only her perspective, not her entire family's.*

3. **D is correct.** *Consuela wants to break free of tradition and the boundaries it sets just as she helps the mare break out of the pen and the limits on its life. A is incorrect because the author is drawing a parallel between the horse and Consuela. B is incorrect because if she were a girl, the mare might look like Fai but does not represent her. C is incorrect because the pale mare ultimately breaks free from the pen, and tradition does not change.*

4. **D is correct.** *The context clue in paragraph 5, "Mexican-style rodeo," follows the first occurrence of the term in the story. A, B, and C are incorrect because neither the text nor footnotes support these definitions.*

5. **B is correct.** *Consuela plays on the multiple meanings of the word angle, which is a geometry term but also means "a special approach for accomplishing a goal." A is incorrect because there is no suggestion here that she is thinking of sneaking out. C is incorrect because her dream is not mentioned until later. D is incorrect because it is too literal.*

6. **C is correct.** *Consuela refers to* la raza *as "the bigger picture of our people." A is incorrect because* la raza *encompasses various family traditions of Latin Americans. B is incorrect because it is too specific. D is incorrect because its focus is on individual family members rather than the family group.*

Reading Comprehension

> Use "The Pale Mare" (pp. 1042–1046) to answer questions 1–10.

1. One theme of "The Pale Mare" is that —
   A. traditions should never be broken
   B. it is important to obey one's parents
   C. sometimes you have to break traditions to be true to yourself
   D. no tradition is good

2. The author writes the story in the first person so that readers —
   A. know what everyone is doing and thinking
   B. can understand how Consuela feels
   C. sympathize with Mama
   D. will trust the family's perspective

3. The pale mare that Consuela frees is a symbol for —
   A. nothing, it's just a horse
   B. her friend Fai
   C. tradition
   D. Consuela

4. The *charreada* is —
   A. the family's taco stand
   B. the family's hometown
   C. the local fairgrounds
   D. a rodeo

5. In paragraph 6, when Consuela jokes, "I try a different angle. After all, I'm good in geometry," she means that —
   A. she is going to sneak out
   B. she will try another way to convince her father
   C. she is giving up on her dream
   D. she enjoys math

6. In paragraph 9, Consuela explains that *la raza* is —
   A. tradition
   B. her grandfather
   C. the sense of who the family is as Latin Americans
   D. the sense of who each individual family member is

7. On this particular weekend, Consuela wants to —
   A. go to the mall with her friends
   B. learn more about her family's traditions
   C. go to astronomy camp
   D. work at the *charreada*

8. In paragraph 18, *banishing* means —
   A. allowing
   B. considering an idea
   C. rewarding
   D. sending away

9. In paragraphs 25–28 Consuela reaches the *charreada*, and the first thing she notices are the —
   A. horses
   B. people
   C. smells
   D. sounds

10. Consuela frees the mares —
    A. so that there will be no rodeo the next day
    B. because she is angry with her parents and her cultural traditions
    C. because she trips and opens the gate accidentally
    D. because she doesn't want to see the horses trapped the way she is

---

7. **C is correct.** *Consuela expresses her desire to go the weekend astronomy camp in paragraph 13. A is incorrect because Consuela does not mention wanting to go to the mall. B is incorrect because Consuela shows that she is disenchanted with her family's traditions. D is incorrect because Consuela does not like what happens to the horses at the charreada.*

8. **D is correct.** *The light side of the eclipse represents everything Consuela dreams of, while the dark side represents what her parents*

expect her to do; in her view, her parents are sending her away to the dark side. *A, B, and C are incorrect because they cannot be understood syntactically with the direct object "me" or the prepositional phrase "to the dark side."*

9. **C is correct.** *In paragraph 25 Consuela notes "the hot scent of livestock, dirt, and human sweat." A is incorrect because once she is at the grounds, it takes her time to make it to the pens. B is incorrect because the grounds are quiet, and no people are in sight. D is incorrect because Consuela does not*

Use "Breaking Down Barriers" (pp. 1047–1048) to answer questions 11–17.

11. One theme of "Breaking Down Barriers" is —
   A. there are no racial tensions in football
   B. many Vietnamese-Americans play professional football
   C. racial divides can sometimes be overcome
   D. the history of Vietnamese in the United States of America

12. Dat Nguyen's soccer team is booed mainly because —
   A. the other team thinks they cheated
   B. the players are children of Vietnamese refugees
   C. his team plays a poor game
   D. the other team wins the championship

13. According to the article, many Vietnamese settled in the Texas Gulf area because —
   A. they were shrimpers, like many of the people already living there
   B. they had family there
   C. they liked the weather because it reminded them of Vietnam
   D. there were good schools, and schooling was important to them

14. Dat's brother, Ho Nguyen, remembers —
   A. wishing he were more athletic himself
   B. working on the shrimp boats
   C. their parents pushing Dat to play football
   D. escaping as soldiers fired at the family's boat

15. According to the article, when the Vietnamese started shrimping in Texas, some of the local shrimpers —
   A. gave up shrimping
   B. felt threatened
   C. did nothing
   D. helped the Vietnamese

16. What happened when Dat was in eighth grade?
   A. He didn't back down, and people started to see him as an individual.
   B. His family went into politics, and people started to see him as an individual.
   C. He began playing football, and people started to see him as an individual.
   D. He faced the same problems as all the other students.

17. Critics thought that Dat could not play professional football because —
   A. he was a good soccer player and soccer players can't play football
   B. no good football players come from Texas
   C. he was not a good player in college
   D. he was small and of Asian descent

Use "The Pale Mare" and "Breaking Down Barriers" to answer questions 18–19.

18. The main barrier that Consuela and Dat must overcome is —
   A. problems associated with poverty
   B. difficulties with the English language
   C. strict rules from their parents
   D. stereotypes that might limit opportunities

GO ON ➡

1051

10. **D is correct.** Consuela frees the mares as a symbolic gesture of what she is going through. A is incorrect because Consuela understands people enjoy the artistry of the rodeo even though she doesn't like how the animals are treated. B is incorrect because freeing the mares will not change her parents or the traditions. C is incorrect because Consuela unlatches the gate on purpose.

11. **C is correct.** Dat Nguyen's story illustrates how a racial divide was overcome. A is incorrect because the article describes the racial tensions Dat experienced. B is incorrect because the article says that Dat was the first Vietnamese-American to play pro football. D is incorrect because it represents a topic rather than a theme.

12. **B is correct.** Paragraph 1 says the team was booed because most of the team members were children of Vietnamese refugees. A is incorrect because the article does indicate that the other team thinks Dat's team cheated. C and D are incorrect because the team played well enough to win the championship.

13. **A is correct.** According to paragraph 3, the immigrants could continue their work as shrimpers. B is incorrect because the Vietnamese were newcomers to Texas. C and D are incorrect because the article does not cite this information to explain Vietnamese settlement in the Texas Gulf area.

14. **D is correct.** In paragraph 4, Ho Nguyen remembers the family's escape from Vietnam in April 1975. A, B, and C are not included in the article.

15. **B is correct.** The Vietnamese shrimpers worked hard, which made the locals feel that their jobs were in jeopardy. A is incorrect because the local shrimpers continued to fish in competition with the Vietnamese. C is incorrect because local shrimpers fired shots from their boats at Vietnamese shrimpers. D is incorrect because the local shrimpers showed that they did not like the Vietnamese and did not want them in their community, and so would not have helped them.

16. **C is correct.** According to paragraph 5, when Dat started playing football in eighth grade, people's attitudes began to change. A is incorrect because it does not mention that Dat

started playing football in eighth grade. B is incorrect because there is nothing in the article about Dat's family going into politics. D is incorrect because although Dat may have experienced some of the same problems as other eighth graders, one can infer from information in the article that as a Vietnamese student he also faced different problems.

17. **D is correct.** Dat gave his full effort on the field, and he was quick which made up for his small size. A and B are incorrect because they are illogical generalizations. C is

incorrect because Dat broke a school record and was named best defensive player in the country while in college.

18. **D is correct.** Cultural stereotypes create a formidable barrier against which both Consuela and Dat struggle. A is incorrect because poverty is not mentioned as a barrier for Consuela or Dat. B is incorrect because although both Consuela and Dat may have had difficulties with the English language, such problems are not discussed in the selections. C is incorrect because strict parental rules are not a barrier for Dat.

19. B is correct. *Consuela's thoughts and Dat's experience illustrate that culture doesn't have to be a limitation. A is incorrect because Consuela's parents do not show signs of changing their ideas, and people's attitudes toward Dat and other Vietnamese in the Gulf area of Texas changed only after time. C is incorrect because it is a broad generalization that doesn't apply to Consuela's situation. D is incorrect because Consuela's success in school does not seem to be important to her parents, and there is no mention of Dat being academically successful.*

20. D is correct. *The repetition of* different *and the characterization* beautiful mosaic *suggest that diversity should be celebrated. A is incorrect because the quotation suggests that the differences that one sees are real, not deceptive. B and C are incorrect because the quotation does not refer to building bridges or bridging differences.*

21. D is correct. *The individuals in the photograph look different from each other and are clearly from different ethnic backgrounds. A is incorrect because the point of the poster is not physical beauty. B is incorrect because it is not clear that the students shown are artists. C is incorrect because students appear to be about the same age.*

SHORT CONSTRUCTED RESPONSE

Possible responses:

22. *Consuela's parents suggest that she should be content with their plans for her because they need her help with the business (paragraph 14), she is a girl (paragraphs 18 and 19), and they love her (paragraph 19).*

23. *Dat Nguyen helped break down barriers between the Vietnamese and others in his community in Texas (paragraphs 3, 5, 6). He also broke down barriers for Asians in football and other sports (paragraphs 1, 2, 5).*

24. *Cultural stereotypes about gender roles prevent Consuela's parents from supporting her dreams even though she shows ability (paragraphs 14–21). Cultural stereotypes create tensions between groups in Dat's community (paragraphs 1, 4) but are overcome to a certain extent when Dat becomes a local sports hero (paragraphs 2, 3, 5, 6, 7). Dat also overturns cultural stereo-*

types about Asians in professional football when he proves wrong the critics who said he was too small and would never make it (paragraphs 2, 5).

---

19. One message taught by "The Pale Mare" and "Breaking Down Barriers" is that —
  A. people change their ideas easily
  B. people do not have to accept cultural limitations
  C. hard work is always rewarded
  D. doing well in school is important to everyone

Use the visual representation on page 1049 to answer questions 20–21.

20. The quotation underscores the message of the poster that —
  A. appearances can be deceiving
  B. students should try and build bridges
  C. many differences are impossible to bridge
  D. diversity should be celebrated

21. The designer probably chose the photo to illustrate "not a melting pot but a beautiful mosaic" because the image is of —
  A. very attractive students
  B. artistic students
  C. students of a wide range of ages
  D. students from a variety of ethnic backgrounds

SHORT CONSTRUCTED RESPONSE
Write a short response to each question, using text evidence to support your response.

22. Why do Consuela's parents think that she should be content with their plans for her? Support your response with evidence from the selection.

23. Why is "Breaking Down Barriers" a good title for this selection? Support your response with evidence from the selection.

Write a short response to the following question, using text evidence from both selections to support your response.

24. How does the idea of cultural stereotypes apply to both selections? Support your response with evidence from **both** selections.

1052

Revising and Editing

DIRECTIONS Read this passage, and answer the questions that follow.

(1) In the 1950s, the United States investigated citizens. (2) They were considered Communist sympathizers. (3) U.S. senator Joseph McCarthy led the charge. (4) McCarthy who was known for his reckless accusations. (5) Under suspicion were even people who read foreign magazines. (6) As a result of these accusations, many people lost they're jobs. (7) Today, the term still describes the use of unfounded accusations. (8) This accusatory technique was known as McCarthyism.

1. What is the most effective way to improve the organization of the paragraph?
   A. Move sentence 3 to follow sentence 4.
   B. Move sentence 5 to follow sentence 7.
   C. Move sentence 6 to follow sentence 2.
   D. Move sentence 7 to follow sentence 8.

2. What is the most effective way to combine sentences 1 and 2?
   A. In the 1950s, the United States investigated citizens who were considered Communist sympathizers.
   B. In the 1950s, the United States investigated citizens, by thinking they were Communist sympathizers.
   C. In the 1950s, the United States investigated citizens; they were considered Communist sympathizers.
   D. In the 1950s, the United States investigated citizens and considered them Communist sympathizers.

3. What change, if any, should be made to sentence 3?
   A. Change *senator* to **Senator**
   B. Change *McCarthy* to **Mccarthy**
   C. Change *led* to **lead**
   D. Make no change

4. What change, if any, should be made in sentence 4?
   A. Insert a comma after *McCarthy*
   B. Delete *who*
   C. Change *was known* to **knew**
   D. Make no change

5. What would be the most effective way to rewrite sentence 5?
   A. Even reading foreign magazines was cause for suspicion.
   B. McCarthy was even suspicious of foreign magazine readers.
   C. To read a foreign magazine was enough cause for suspicion of people.
   D. To be considered suspicious, people read foreign magazines.

6. What change, if any, should be made to sentence 6?
   A. Change *lost* to **loosed**
   B. Insert a comma after *result*
   C. Change *they're* to **their**
   D. Make no change

7. What change, if any, should be made in sentence 8?
   A. Insert a comma after *technique*
   B. Change *technique* to **technical**
   C. Insert a colon after *as*
   D. Make no change

STOP

---

7. D is correct. The meaning of the sentence is clear, and punctuation, spelling, and mechanics in the sentence are correct. A is incorrect because a comma would separate the subject and predicate. B is incorrect because technical is an adjective and cannot function as the subject of the sentence. C is incorrect because a colon would separate the predicate noun McCarthyism from the rest of the sentence.

Revising and Editing

1. **D is correct.** Sentence 8 contains the term McCarthyism *to which sentence 7 refers, and so must precede sentence 7.* A *is incorrect because sentence 3 introduces McCarthy and must precede sentence 4.* B *is incorrect because if sentence 5 were moved,* foreign magazines *would seem to be the referent of* the term *in sentence 7.* C *is incorrect because if sentence 6 were moved to follow sentence 2, the referent and meaning of* these accusations *would not be clear.*

2. **A is correct.** A complex sentence contains at least one independent clause and one subordinate clause ("who were considered Communist sympathizers"). B is incorrect because it is a simple sentence with an independent clause and a participial phrase. C is a compound sentence. D is a simple sentence with a compound predicate.

3. **A is correct.** The title refers to a specific person and needs to be capitalized. B is incorrect because the spelling McCarthy is incorrect. C is incorrect because lead is the present tense, but the sentence is in past tense. D is incorrect because there is an error with capitalization.

4. **B is correct.** Deleting who makes this a sentence instead of a sentence fragment. A and C are incorrect because they do not form a complete sentence. D is incorrect because without deleting who it is still a sentence fragment.

5. **A is correct.** The gerund phrase "Even reading foreign magazines" balances the predicate noun cause following was. B is incorrect because it is important to vary the beginning of the sentences, and McCarthy is the subject of the previous two sentences. C is incorrect because of people is not necessary. D is incorrect because the main verb is not in the correct form.

6. **C is correct.** The possessive adjective their should be used instead of the contraction for "they are". A is incorrect because lost is the correct form of the verb and does not need to be changed. B is incorrect because a comma goes at the end of the clause, not in the middle. D is incorrect because of the incorrect word choice.

COMMON CORE FOCUS

RL 10 Read and comprehend literature. **RI 10** Read and comprehend literary nonfiction.

INTRODUCE *GREAT READS*

In Unit 9, students have discussed a number of big questions. Invite students to tell which question they found most intriguing and why, and then focus attention on the three that appear on this page. Discuss the recommended books and their summaries, pointing out how each connects to the related question. Encourage students to choose one or more of these "great reads" to read independently.

UNIT 9
Great Reads

Ideas for Independent Reading

Several profound questions were raised in Unit 9. Reading the following books may deepen your perspective on these questions.

COMMON CORE

RL 10 Read and comprehend literature. **RI 10** Read and comprehend literary nonfiction.

Can humanity triumph over evil?

Lord of the Flies
by William Golding

In this novel by a former schoolmaster, a group of English schoolboys is marooned with no adults on a Pacific island. They organize their own society, which soon disintegrates into savagely warring factions.

Jubilee
by Margaret Walker

The character Vyry, based on the novelist's great-grandmother, survives the brutality of slavery in the Old South only to have her family terrorized by the Ku Klux Klan after slavery's end. Through all her trials, she manages to keep a loving heart.

Schindler's List
by Thomas Keneally

Oskar Schindler was a German factory owner who managed to save 1,300 Polish Jews during the Holocaust by claiming that he needed their labor. Keneally's novel, based on true events, explores how a person can do good in the midst of the worst evil.

What if your government declared you the enemy?

Farewell to Manzanar
by Jeanne Wakatsuki Houston and James D. Houston

Read more about the Wakatsuki family's experiences in an internment camp. Learn how internees made the camp more homelike, planting gardens and setting up schools. Also discover how hard it was to adjust to life outside the camps once they were closed.

Resistance
by Barry Lopez

This collection of short fiction shows Americans abroad who are targeted by U.S. authorities for challenging government power. Each story is a farewell, explaining the events that are causing the narrator to flee and go underground.

Torn Between Two Cultures
by Maryam Qudrat Aseel

Aseel is a Muslim woman born in the United States to Afghan immigrant parents. She reflects on being considered an enemy in her own country after the terrorist attacks of September 11, 2001, and she attempts to correct misperceptions about Afghan culture and Islam.

What is cowardice?

Lord Jim
by Joseph Conrad

Jim, a ship's crew member, unthinkingly leaves the ship when it catches fire and sinks. Though the captain and other officials have also fled, Jim alone is tried for abandoning the passengers. For the rest of this novel, Jim tries to make up for this act of cowardice.

Confronting the War Machine
by Michael S. Foley

They were called cowards and worse. The men profiled in this book did not hide or seek draft deferments but refused to serve in Vietnam and were willing to take the consequences. Their resistance powered the U.S. antiwar movement.

Refusenik! Israel's Soldiers of Conscience
by Peretz Kidron

Refuseniks are Israeli soldiers who refuse orders on moral grounds. They believe in defending their country but oppose its occupation of territories outside its borders. Though praised by peace groups, refuseniks have not always had an easy time within Israeli society.

Get Novel Wise THINK central

Go to **thinkcentral.com**.
KEYWORD: HML10-1054

1054

Upholding Honor

UNIT 10

GREEK TRAGEDY AND MEDIEVAL ROMANCE

- In Drama
- In Fiction
- Across Genres

1055

About the Art British artist Edmund Blair Leighton (1853–1922) painted *The Accolade in* 1901. An *accolade* is a ceremony in which some-one is made a knight; in this scene, a queen bestows knighthood on a medieval warrior.

INTRODUCE THE UNIT

When someone is honored in a public cere-mony, he or she may become famous or may earn widespread respect. However, when someone upholds his or her personal honor, the private rewards may be far less obvious and may come at a cost. To illustrate, compare the public and private aspects of honor as suggested in the images on this page. When the queen bestows the honor of knighthood upon someone, she holds a public event. The knight takes a public oath to uphold the queen's honor, as well. In contrast, Don Quixote upholds honor, as he understands it, by envisioning himself as a knight. He then sets off on a personal journey to right the wrongs of the world—a journey that will bring him ridicule and little glory.

Ask students to define *honor* in their own words and to consider the challenges of up-holding honor in situations like these:

- a friend asks to copy your homework
- your coach asks if you know what went on at last weekend's party
- a classmate is the subject of an untrue ru-mor that is going around school

Tell students that as they read the selections in this unit, they will consider the various ways in which authors present and interpret the concept of honor in **drama,** in **fiction,** and **across genres.**

For help in planning this unit, see

R RESOURCE MANAGER UNIT 10
   pp. 1–9

UNIT 10

COMMON CORE

STRAND

	Text Analysis Workshop: Greek Tragedy and Medieval Romance pp. 1058–1063	*Classical Greek Drama* Informational Article pp. 1064–1065	*Antigone* Drama pp. 1066–1109	from *Le Morte d'Arthur: The Crowning of Arthur, Sir Launcelot du Lake* Romance pp. 1110–1129
				Lexile: 1130 Fry: 10 Dale-Chall: 7.2
Reading Literature	Greek Tragedy pp. 1058–1059 RL 2, RL 3, RL 6, RL 10 Medieval Romance pp. 1060–1061 RL 2, RL 3, RL 6, RL 10 Analyze the Text pp. 1062–1063 RL 2, RL 3, RL 6, RL 10	Greek Drama pp. 1064–1065 RL 6, RL 9	Classical Drama pp. 1067, 1077, 1080, 1082, 1084, 1091–1092, 1096, 1098, 1105–1106, 1107 RL 2, RL 3 Reading Classical Drama pp. 1067–1068, 1073, 1079, 1087, 1093, 1097, 1102 RL 1, RL 10 Motifs pp. 1074, 1083 RL 3 World Literature p. 1094 RL 6 Allegory p. 1106 RL 2 Language Coach pp. 1070, 1078, 1085, 1100, 1105 RL 4	Medieval Romance pp. 1111, 1114–1115, 1117–1118, 1120, 1122, 1126, 1128 RL 3, RL 5 Evaluate pp. 1111–1112, 1115, 1117, 1120–1121, 1125, 1128 RL 7 Archetype p. 1117 RL 5 Language Coach p. 1116 RL 4
Reading Informational Text				Historical Account p. 1127
Writing			Writing Prompt p. 1109 W 9b (RL 2)	
Speaking and Listening			Discuss p. 1066 SL 1	Discuss p. 1110 SL 1
Language			Vary Sentence Structure pp. 1079, 1109 L 3 Etymology p. 1108 L 4c Language Coach p. 1088	Analogies p. 1129 L 5 Foreign Words p. 1124 L 4c Language Coach p. 1124 L 4d

from _The Acts of King Arthur and His Noble Knights_
Romance
pp. 1130–1143

Lexile: 1130
Fry: 9
Dale-Chall: 6.4

from _Don Quixote/_
from _Man of La Mancha_
Novel/Musical Play
pp. 1144–1163

Lexile: 1130
Fry: 9
Dale-Chall: 7.6

Writing Workshop: Video Script
pp. 1164–1175

Technology Workshop: Producing a Drama
pp. 1174–1175

Style pp. 1131–1132, 1135, 1137, 1140–1141
RL 4
Make Inferences pp. 1131, 1134, 1135, 1137, 1138, 1140–1141 RL 1, RL 9
Analyze Character p. 1140 RL 9
Language Coach p. 1138 RL 4

Parody pp. 1145–1146, 1148, 1150–1151, 1153, 1155, 1157–1161 RL 5
Purpose p. 1145 RL 1, RL 7, RL 9
Archetypal Motifs p. 1158 RL 5
Language Coach pp. 1154, 1159 RL 4

Quickwrite p. 1130
Writing Prompt p. 1143 W 9a (RL 9)

Writing for Assessment p. 1163 W 2, W 5

Writing a Video Script pp. 1164–1173
W 2a, W 3a–e, W 4, W 5, W 6, W 10
Producing a Drama pp. 1174–1175 W 6

Discuss p. 1144 SL 1

Producing a Drama pp. 1174–1175 SL 2

Vary Sentence Beginnings pp. 1135, 1143 L 1b
Connotation p. 1142 L 5b

Similes and Metaphors p. 1162 L 5

ECOS

To see the complete Essential Course of Study, see pp. T23–T28.

For additional lesson planning help, see **Teacher One Stop DVD.**

Instructional Support

Resource Manager Unit 10

UNIT SUPPORT

Academic Vocabulary p. 5

Additional Academic Vocabulary p. 6

Grammar Focus p. 7

Text Analysis Workshop pp. 11–12

Writing Workshop: Video Script p. 96

SELECTION SUPPORT*

Plan and Teach

Lesson planning pages

Additional leveled selection questions

Extension activities

Student Copy Masters

Selection summaries in four languages

Skills copy masters in English and Spanish

Vocabulary preteaching and support

Reading Check and Question Support

Reading Fluency

* Available for all selections

† Available on **thinkcentral.com**.

Language Handbook

Vocabulary Practice

Best Practices Toolkit†

PowerNotes DVD-ROM†

Connections: Nonfiction for Common Core CD-ROM†

Teacher One Stop DVD-ROM

Student One Stop DVD-ROM

Write*Smart* CD-ROM†

GrammarNotes DVD-ROM†

WordSharp CD-ROM†

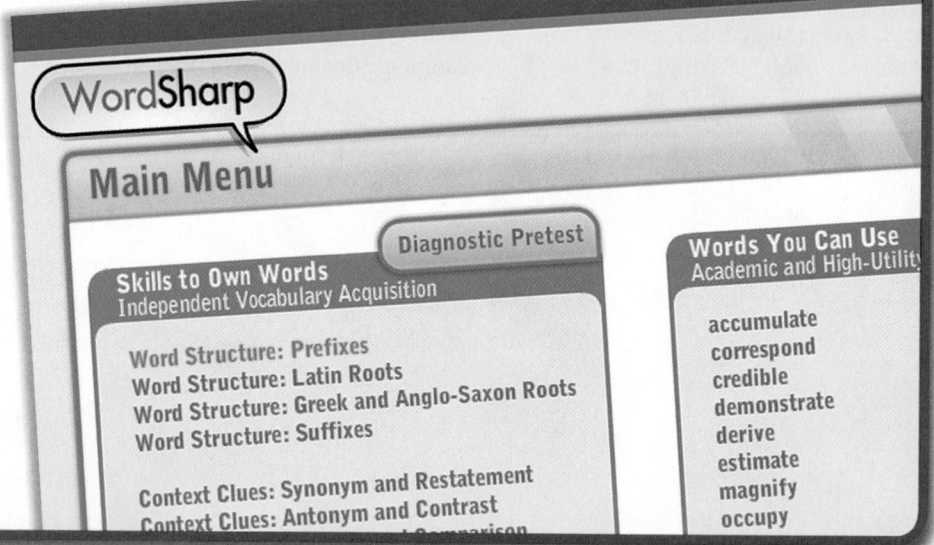

Differentiated Instruction

STRUGGLING READERS AND WRITERS

Resource Manager Unit 10

Additional Selection Questions

Question Support

Reading Fluency

Interactive Reader

Adapted Interactive Reader

Audio Tutor

Level Up Online Tutorials

Audio Anthology

(with Audio summaries)

Diagnostic and Selection Tests

Selection Tests A/B

ENGLISH LANGUAGE LEARNERS

Resource Manager Unit 10

Selection Summaries in English, Spanish, Vietnamese and Haitian Creole

Skills Copymasters in Spanish

English Language Learner Adapted Interactive Reader Teacher's Guide

ELL Adapted Interactive Reader

Audio Tutor

Guide to English for Newcomers

Audio Anthology

Audio Summaries in Multiple Languages (on **thinkcentral.com**)

ADVANCED LEARNERS

Resource Manager Unit 10

Additional Selection Questions

Ideas for Extension

Diagnostic and Selection Tests

Selection Tests B/C

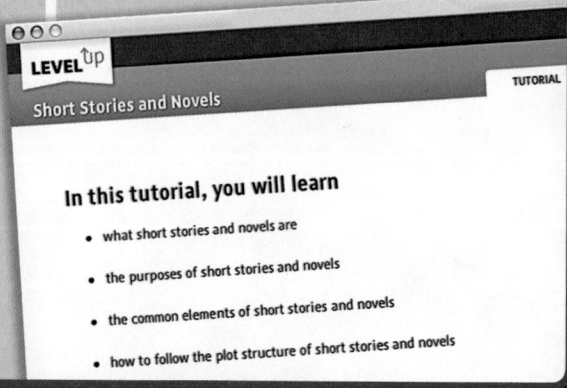

Assessment and Reteaching

Diagnostic and Selection Tests

Unit and Benchmark Tests

ThinkCentral Online Assessment:

- All program assessments
- Level Up Online Tutorials

ExamView Test Generator on the Teacher One Stop DVD-ROM

Online Essay Scoring on **thinkcentral.com**

ThinkCentral Online Reteaching:

- Level Up Online Tutorials
- Reteaching Worksheets

Holt McDougal Online Essay Scoring

Welcome to Holt McDougal Online Essay Scoring!

This site is designed to help you improve your writing skills and prepare for standardized writing tests. When you write and submit a response to one of the writing prompts on this site, the computerized scoring system will immediately score and deliver feedback on your essay. Other resources on this site will help you prepare, develop, and revise your essay.

STUDENTS

Get started by entering the

Writing Zone →

Professional Development

Video Center Based on interviews with program consultants and other educational experts, these videos feature classroom-ready teaching strategies.

Teacher Toolkit Includes a Teacher Handbook as well as a range of articles and handouts by program consultants and other educators.

Janet Allen

Jim Burke

Kylene Beers

Carol Jago

THINK central at a Glance

One Location, Endless Resources

Find Resources Browse all *Holt McDougal Literature* components for the ones that meet your students' needs and match your teaching style.

Assess Progress and Reteach Assign electronic versions of program assessments to measure your students' mastery of the Common Core State Standards. On thinkcentral.com, some tests deliver online remediation tutorials to students who have not mastered skills.

 Interactive Whiteboard Lessons

Prepare your students for college and careers by teaching relevant, real-world skills through dynamic, interactive instruction. Go to **thinkcentral.com** to browse through all whiteboard lessons, including the following:

- Character Development and Motivation
- Making Inferences
- Historical and Cultural Context

HISTORY

Together Holt McDougal and HISTORY® are revolutionizing the study of English/language arts with video that helps students relive and re-imagine the people, places, and events they are discovering through reading. Look for selections with the HISTORY® icon.

What **QUESTS** live on?

Call on a volunteer to read the introductory paragraph aloud. Supply background information about any of the historical figures that students find unfamiliar. Then offer these questions to prompt discussion:

- Why do you think that the people in these examples undertook a quest for the object named (the Golden Fleece, the Fountain of Youth, and so on)?

- What historical quests can you think of that had an idea rather than an object as their goal?

- What are the goals of some personal quests?

- How important is it for someone to have one or more personal quests in his or her lifetime?

Encourage students to offer examples as they continue to discuss the Big Question.

ACTIVITY To help students evaluate the quests, have them map out the details of each quest, including the number of people and the length of time that each quest is likely to take. Urge students to look for patterns to help them generalize about the factors that raise a quest to the status of a legend.

CHECK UNDERSTANDING Have students define *quest* in their own words. Invite examples of legendary quests and personal quests.

What **QUESTS** live on?

Jason and the Argonauts sailed from their homes to find the Golden Fleece. The knights of King Arthur spent years seeking the Holy Grail. Ponce de León explored unknown lands, hoping to discover the Fountain of Youth. All of these quests live on in history and legend. Why do they capture our imaginations so powerfully?

ACTIVITY On a chart, list each of the great quests mentioned above, and add to them any other historical or legendary quests that come to mind. Then think of modern quests that are equally captivating: the search for life on other planets, the plan to raise the *Titanic*. With a partner, try to identify the characteristics you think raise each quest to the level of legend. What do all of these quests have in common?

Find It Online!  **THINK** central

Go to **thinkcentral.com** for the interactive version of this unit.

See resources on the **Teacher One Stop DVD-ROM** *and on* **thinkcentral.com**.

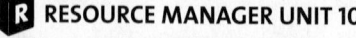 **RESOURCE MANAGER UNIT 10**

UNIT AND BENCHMARK TESTS

BEST PRACTICES TOOLKIT

INTERACTIVE READER

ADAPTED INTERACTIVE READER

ELL ADAPTED INTERACTIVE READER

LANGUAGE HANDBOOK

VOCABULARY PRACTICE

TECHNOLOGY

- Teacher One Stop DVD-ROM
- Student One Stop DVD-ROM
- PowerNotes DVD-ROM
- WriteSmart CD-ROM
- MediaSmart DVD-ROM
- GrammarNotes DVD-ROM
- Audio Anthology CD
- Audio Tutor CD

THINK central

Find It Online!

The interactive version of this unit on **thinkcentral.com** includes

- video and **PowerNotes** introductions to key selections
- audio support—listen or download
- **ThinkAloud** models
- **WordSharp** vocabulary tutorials
- interactive review and remediation

Preview Unit Goals

TEXT ANALYSIS	• Identify characteristics of classical world drama • Analyze characteristics of Greek tragedy, including tragic hero and tragic flaw • Analyze archetypes and motifs in drama • Analyze conventions of medieval romance, including romance hero • Identify characteristics of a parody • Analyze and evaluate style
READING	• Make inferences; cite evidence • Read and comprehend drama
WRITING AND LANGUAGE	• Write a narrative video script • Vary sentence structure by inverting sentences • Use a variety of phrases and clauses
VOCABULARY	• Use a dictionary to determine a word's etymology • Understand and use words with similar denotations
ACADEMIC VOCABULARY	• drama • encounter • underlie • emerge • globe
MEDIA AND VIEWING	• Produce a drama

UNIT GOALS

Included in this unit: RL 1, RL 2, RL 3, RL 4, RL 5, RL 6, RL 7, RL 9, RL 10, RI 10, W 2, W 2a, W 3a–e, W 4, W 5, W 6, W 9a, W 9b, W 10, SL 2, SL 5, L 1b, L 3, L 4a, L 4c, L 5, L 5b, L 6

Complete text of the Common Core State Standards is found in the correlation on p. T10. Standards covered in this unit are found in the standards overview (pp. 1055A–1055B) and on the lesson pages where they are taught.

Preview Unit Goals

Explain to students that these goals reflect the main skills and strategies presented in Unit 10. Encourage students to skim the list and to set some personal goals as they prepare for the unit. Note the color-coding, which distinguishes the skill strands.

Throughout the unit, model using the vocabulary. Encourage students to use the vocabulary in discussions and in writing, as well. By the end of Unit 10, students should have developed a clear, accurate, and useful definition of each term.

DIFFERENTIATED INSTRUCTION

FOR ENGLISH LANGUAGE LEARNERS

Academic Vocabulary Provide students with definitions of each Academic Vocabulary word.

drama (drä′ ma) literature in which plot and characters are developed through dialogue and action

emerge (ē mərj′) v. to become visible; to develop or become something new

encounter (ĕn-koun′tər) n. an unexpected meeting

globe (glōb) n. a round, ball-shaped model of the earth; the earth

underlie (un′dər lī′) v. to form the basis or foundation of

Use the copy master to help students learn academic words they will use in this unit and on the Assessment Practice.

R RESOURCE MANAGER—Copy Masters
Academic Vocabulary p. 3
Additional Academic Vocabulary p. 4

Focus and Motivate

COMMON CORE FOCUS

RL 2 Determine a theme or central idea of a text. **RL 3** Analyze how complex characters develop, interact with others, and advance the plot or develop the theme. **RL 6** Analyze a particular point of view or cultural experience reflected in a work of world literature. **RL 10** Read and comprehend stories and dramas.

Teach

Part 1: Greek Tragedy

Tragedy Point out to students that the tragic hero is neither completely good nor completely bad, but is a basically decent yet flawed person. Point out, too, that tragedy seeks to arouse pity and fear in viewers as they witness the hero's courage and dignity in the face of certain doom—what can happen to that hero can happen to anyone!

Catastrophe Tell students that to be properly tragic, a situation must have major implications beyond the tragic hero. The death of a grandparent, for example, would be sad, whereas the death of a general on the eve of a war's end is tragic and potentially catastrophic.

Fate Tell students that conflict in Greek tragedy revolves around a person who, attempting to escape fate, hurries directly toward it. As students read the excerpts from *Oedipus the King* and *Antigone,* have them consider these questions:

- What kind of person is each hero?
- To what extent are tragic heroes responsible for what happens to them?
- To what extent do tragic heroes try to avoid fate?
- What attitude toward the Greek gods does each play suggest?

🧰 **BEST PRACTICES TOOLKIT—Transparency**
   Core Analysis Frame: Drama pp. D21, D42

Greek Tragedy and Medieval Romance

In today's popular culture, heroes are celebrated in movies and TV shows. Centuries ago, other cultures immortalized their heroes in literature. Consider ancient Greek tragedy and medieval romance. One features ill-fated heroes who face defeat with dignity, and the other follows gallant, knightly heroes on perilous quests. Each type of hero reflects the values of its time and its society, but these values still appeal to us, many centuries later.

Essential Course of Study ✓ **ECOS**

○ **COMMON CORE**

Included in this workshop:
RL 2 Determine a theme or central idea of a text. **RL 3** Analyze how complex characters develop, interact with others, and advance the plot or develop the theme. **RL 6** Analyze a particular point of view or cultural experience reflected in a work of world literature. **RL 10** Read and comprehend stories and dramas.

Part 1: Greek Tragedy

In literature, a **tragedy** is a form of drama that shows the downfall of a dignified, superior character who participates in events of great significance. The ancient Greeks, who developed tragedy, used it to explore ideas about humans' relationship to the gods, often delving into such serious subjects as duty, suffering, and fate. These ideas were often developed through **motifs,** concepts or elements that recur throughout the play to help advance its plot and reveal its theme.

Familiarize yourself with the characteristics of Greek tragedy by examining this chart.

CHARACTERISTICS OF GREEK TRAGEDY	CENTRAL BELIEF
Tragic Hero The **tragic hero** at the center of a tragedy is a person of high rank who accepts his or her downfall with dignity. The tragic hero is one common **archetype**—a model from which similar heroes have been copied for centuries in mythic, traditional, and classical literature.	**Fate** The ancient Greeks believed in the idea of **fate,** or a destiny preordained by the gods no matter what action a person takes in the present. The Fates, or *Moirai,* were three goddesses who determined the length of a person's life and how much suffering it would contain. Greeks held that it was impossible to escape one's fate. This belief is reflected in such ancient tragedies as *Oedipus the King* and *Antigone.*
Tragic Flaw A **tragic flaw**—an error in judgment or a weakness in character, such as pride or arrogance—helps bring about the hero's downfall. The tragic hero recognizes this flaw and its consequences but only after it is too late to change the course of events.	
Catastrophe A tragedy ends with a **catastrophe**—a disastrous conclusion that usually involves multiple deaths. If the tragic hero does not die, then he or she suffers complete ruin.	
Chorus Throughout a tragedy, the **chorus**—a masked group of actors—observe and comment on the action through songs. Their responses and values were supposed to reflect those of the audience.	

DIFFERENTIATED INSTRUCTION

FOR STRUGGLING READERS

Note Taking For students who need help with note taking, hand out the note-taking copy master before discussing the characteristics of Greek tragedy. As you discuss the main points of the page, have students record them on the copy master.

R RESOURCE MANAGER—Copy Master
   Note Taking p. 9

FOR ADVANCED LEARNERS/PRE–AP

Examine Tragedy Before students read page 1058, have groups discuss tragedy by sharing examples from the literature or media. Challenge groups to develop a definition of tragedy based on their shared examples. Then have them compare this definition with the characteristics of Greek tragedy and tragic heroes.

Oedipus the King is one of the most famous Greek tragedies; the philosopher Aristotle based his definition of *tragedy* on this play. Which characteristics of Greek tragedy do you notice in this excerpt?

from OEDIPUS THE KING

Tragedy by **Sophocles,** translated by Robert Fagles

Oedipus. My father was Polybus, king of Corinth.
My mother, a Dorian, Merope. And I was held
the prince of the realm among the people there,
till something struck me out of nowhere,
5 something strange . . . worth remarking perhaps,
hardly worth the anxiety I gave it.
Some man at a banquet who had drunk too much
shouted out—he was far gone, mind you—
that I am not my father's son. Fighting words!
10 I barely restrained myself that day
but early the next I went to mother and father,
questioned them closely, and they were enraged
at the accusation and the fool who let it fly.
So as for my parents I was satisfied,
15 but still this thing kept gnawing at me,
the slander spread—I had to make my move.
                                   And so,
unknown to mother and father I set out for Delphi,
and the god Apollo spurned me, sent me away
denied the facts I came for,
20 but first he flashed before my eyes a future
great with pain, terror, disaster—I can hear him cry,
"You are fated to couple with your mother, you will bring
a breed of children into the light no man can bear to see—
you will kill your father, the one who gave you life!"
25 I heard all that and ran. I abandoned Corinth. . . .

At the end of the scene, the chorus sings.

Chorus. Destiny guide me always
Destiny find me filled with reverence
  pure in word and deed.
Great laws tower above us, reared on high
30 born for the brilliant vault of heaven—
  Olympian sky their only father,
nothing mortal, no man gave them birth. . . .

Close Read

1. What do you learn about the tragic hero Oedipus in lines 1–3? Consider his background and how others regard him.

2. What incident disturbs Oedipus' happy existence?

3. According to the god Apollo, what tragic fate awaits Oedipus?

4. Reread the boxed text. Consider Oedipus' response to the disturbing news at the banquet and the vision that Apollo flashes before his eyes. What possible tragic flaw does Oedipus display?

5. Summarize what the chorus says about destiny and the laws that rule human life.

MODEL: CHARACTERISTICS OF GREEK TRAGEDY

Close Read

1. *Possible answer: Oedipus is the son of a king. The people of Corinth regard him highly as "the prince of the realm" (line 3).*

2. *Possible answer: A drunken banquet guest makes an alarming revelation—that Oedipus is not really the son of Polybus, king of Corinth. Even though Oedipus' parents assure him it is not true, he continues to worry (lines 9–16).*

3. *Possible answer: The god Apollo prophesies that Oedipus will have children with his mother and kill his father (lines 22–24).*

4. *Possible answer: Oedipus makes the mistake of actively seeking answers and thinking he can change a preordained destiny instead of enduring his fate. He seems to think that his actions can help him escape his tragic fate, as when he says "I had to make my move" (line 16) and "I heard all that and ran" (line 25). Most ancient Greeks believed that it was impossible to escape one's fate.*

5. *Possible answer: The chorus chants words that reflect the Greek belief that destiny should be the guiding force in people's lives. The chorus says that "great laws" (line 29) are above them and that people should show their reverence for the power of destiny (lines 27–28).*

FOR STRUGGLING READERS

Build Background To help students access prior knowledge and discuss the selection, have them complete sentences like these:

- This reminds me of . . .
- I wonder why . . .
- What this means to me is . . .

Comprehension: Jigsaw Reading Organize students into five "home" groups and assign each student one Close Reading question. Have students regroup with other "expert" students who have the same question. Once groups have read the selection and answered their question, have students return to their "home" group and share discussion results.

BEST PRACTICES TOOLKIT
Jigsaw Reading p. A1

Online Remediation

Are your students struggling with text analysis skills? Consider assigning them one or more **Level Up Online Tutorials** as remediation before beginning this unit. Log in to **thinkcentral.com** to view a list of the skills addressed by **Level Up**.

Teach

Part 2: Medieval Romance

Romance Have students brainstorm connections to the word *romance*. Point out that although love plays a part in medieval romance, stories such as *Sir Gawain and the Green Knight* and *Le Morte D'Arthur* are not love stories. Instead, the hero is often inspired to undertake a journey or task to rescue or win the favor of an idealized woman. The emphasis is more on the virtues of the hero than it is on the relationship between the knight and his lady.

Heroic Virtues Have students brainstorm a list of virtues they associate with knights, such as courage, courtesy, honesty, faith, and others. Have them fill out a chart like this as they read the excerpt:

Virtue	Example
Courage	
Courtesy	
Honesty	
Faith	

The Supernatural Explain to students that many of the elements of the medieval romance come from the oral tradition. The more spectacular and magical the events, the better people would remember them and pass them along to their children and grandchildren.

CHECK UNDERSTANDING

Have students write a sentence using each of these terms:

- *tragic hero*
- *tragic flaw*
- *romance hero*
- *chivalry*

Part 2: Medieval Romance

The heroes who populate the pages of medieval romances are not suffering, flawed figures but knights in shining armor. A **romance** is an adventure tale that features extravagant characters, exotic places, heroic events, passionate love, and supernatural forces. Romances first appeared in Old French literature of the 12th century and quickly spread throughout Europe. The best-known English romances concern the legendary King Arthur and his Knights of the Round Table.

Romance literature expresses the ideals of chivalry, an elaborate code of honor that is described in the chart. As the stories entertain readers, they also convey medieval values of loyalty and Christian faith.

CONVENTIONS OF MEDIEVAL ROMANCE

Romance Hero
The **romance hero** is a knight of superhuman strength, intelligence, and virtue who follows the code of chivalry.

A Quest
The hero of a romance often proves his worth by undertaking a **quest**, a journey motivated by love, religious faith, or a desire for adventure. He must overcome many obstacles on this quest.

Exotic Setting
Romances are set in imaginary kingdoms with great castles, enchanted lakes, and forests populated with giants and monsters.

Supernatural Elements
Sorcerers and magic spells, giants and dragons, mysterious evil forces and foreknowledge of future events—such supernatural elements all play a part in romances.

Hidden Identities
In a romance, others are often unaware of a character's true identity. The truth is usually revealed at the climax of the tale.

Episodic Structure
Romances are not tightly structured; characters simply go from one adventure to the next.

CENTRAL BELIEF

Chivalry
The code of chivalry required that a knight
- swear allegiance to his lord
- fight to uphold Christianity
- seek to redress all wrongs
- honor truth by word and deed
- be faithful to one lady
- act with bravery, courtesy, and modesty

These ideals guide the behavior of the knights in the romance literature you will read.

DIFFERENTIATED INSTRUCTION

FOR STRUGGLING READERS

Note Taking For students who need help with note taking, hand out the note-taking copy master for this page. Have students record key words and phrases to clarify characteristics of medieval romance.

R RESOURCE MANAGER—Copy Master
Note Taking p. 10

Comprehension: Story Elements Write these story elements on the board and have students identify them as they read:

Main Characters: *Arthur, Sir Gawain, the Green Knight*

Main Plot Events: *Sir Gawain takes King Arthur's place in a contest with the Green Knight; Gawain cuts off the Green Knight's head, but the Green Knight doesn't die; the Green Knight reminds Gawain that he will return the blow in a year.*

MODEL: CONVENTIONS OF MEDIEVAL ROMANCE

Sir Gawain and the Green Knight is a famous romance originally composed in verse. Gawain is a knight of King Arthur's Round Table. On New Year's Day, when all are gathered at the court, a giant green knight issues an unusual challenge: any man may strike him with an axe, provided the Green Knight can return the blow a year later. Notice how Gawain responds to the challenge.

from *Sir Gawain and the* *Green Knight*

Romance retold by **Constance Hieatt**

The knight leaped down from his horse and handed the great axe to the king. While Arthur swung it to test its weight, the tall knight waited calmly. He tossed off his cloak, with no sign of fear.

But now Sir Gawain, who had remained quietly in his place at the table,
5 spoke courteously to Arthur: "I beg you, let this contest be mine, dear lord— allow me to take your place. It is not seemly that you, our king, should accept such a challenge when all around you sit the bravest knights in the world. I am the least of them, and my life is worth little. But I am the first to ask. Let me be the one to take this knight's dare."

After Gawain accepts the challenge, the Green Knight prepares for Gawain's blow.

10 The knight in green bent and pulled his long hair forward over his head, so that his neck was bare. Gawain gripped the weapon with both hands and raised it high over his head. He leaned forward on his left foot, and swung the axe down with such force that it went straight through the neck and bit into the floor. The Green Knight's head fell to the ground and tumbled toward the
15 high table, where knights and ladies drew back in horror as it rolled.

Yet the bleeding, headless body did not fall! The green man stood up, walked briskly over to his head, and picked it up by the long hair. Then he turned to his horse, caught hold of the bridle, and swung into the saddle, sitting there as easily as if nothing had happened. He held up the head,
20 turning it to face the high table. It opened its red eyes and spoke: "Gawain, Gawain, remember the promise you made before your king and this company. I am the knight of the Green Chapel. Next New Year's Day you will find me there. If you will look for me, you will find me. Therefore come, or be called coward by all men!"

Close Read

1. Reread Gawain's speech in the boxed text. In what ways does he show the traits of a romance hero?

2. What elements of the supernatural are evident in this tale? Cite specific details to support your answer.

3. If he does not meet the Green Knight next New Year's Day, how will Gawain violate the code of chivalry?

MODEL: CONVENTIONS OF MEDIEVAL ROMANCE

Close Read

1. **Possible answer:** *Gawain shows three traits of the romance hero: bravery by asking King Arthur to let him take the knight's dare; modesty by saying, "I am the least of them [brave knights], and my life is worth little" (lines 7–8); and steadfast allegiance when he "courteously" (line 5) asks to be allowed to take his king's place.*

IF STUDENTS NEED HELP . . . Have students create a character web with information about the typical romance hero, then add information about Gawain to each spoke:

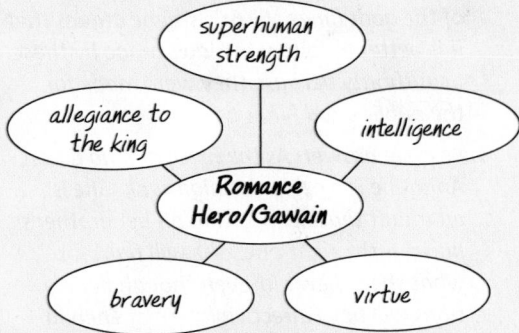

2. **Possible answer:** *What happens after Gawain strikes the Green Knight with an axe is supernatural. Although the head rolls off, the body does not fall. Then the body walks over to the head and picks it up. The head opens its eyes and reminds Gawain of his obligation (lines 16–24).*

3. **Possible answer:** *Gawain accepts both parts of the knight's challenge. The code of chivalry requires that knights honor truth by word and deed. Gawain would not honor his word if he failed to meet the Green Knight the next New Year's Day.*

DIFFERENTIATED INSTRUCTION

FOR ENGLISH LANGUAGE LEARNERS

Comprehension: Transitions Have students determine the organization method in the story and identify related transitions. ***Possible answer:*** *The organization method is chronological.* **Chronological transitions:** *"While" (line 2), "now" (line 4), "when" (line 7), "first" (line 8), "Then" (line 17), and "Next" (line 22).*

Vocabulary: Multiple Meanings Tell students that *before* usually means "earlier in time." In line 21, though, *before* means "in the presence of." Have students write sentences showing both meanings.

Practice and Apply

Part 3: Analyze the Text

Close Read

1. **Possible answer:** *Even though her brother has died fighting against Thebes, Antigone feels that he is entitled to a proper burial, considered by the gods to be a sacred and holy act. Even though Creon forbids her brother's burial, Antigone argues that the laws of the gods are more important to obey than the laws of the country (lines 58–61).*

2. **Possible answer:** *Antigone and Ismene's contrasting arguments represent the conflict between the dictates of conscience and the laws of the state. In contrast to Antigone, who makes a case for maintaining the laws of the gods (lines 56–61), Ismene argues that it is better to follow the laws made by those in authority because they were made for the public good (lines 62–63).*

3. **Possible answer:** *As the niece of King Creon, Antigone is a person of high rank. She is adamant that her position on her brother's burial is the right one. She will fight for what she believes in, even though her actions will be in direct violation of Theban law (lines 55–58). Her tragic flaw might be her unwavering nature. As Ismene says, Antigone is "fiery," rather than "cold with fear" (line 72). Antigone intends to do what she believes is right, regardless of the consequences.*

4. **Possible answer:** *Students may predict that Antigone will be caught in the act of burying her brother. Her conversation with Ismene foreshadows the tragic outcome. Antigone says, "and if I must die, I say that this crime is holy" (lines 55–56). Some may predict that Antigone will eventually be punished by death.*

Part 3: Analyze the Text

Now you will read two excerpts from works you will study in this unit. The first excerpt is from *Antigone* (ăn-tĭg'ə-nē), which tells the story of Oedipus' grown daughter and her conflict with Creon, her uncle and the king of Thebes. Here, Antigone tells her sister, Ismene, that she intends to bury their brother Polyneices, who died on the battlefield fighting against their country. Burying the dead is a sacred act, but Creon, by law, has forbidden this particular burial.

from ANTIGONE

Tragedy by **Sophocles,** translated by Dudley Fitts
and Robert Fitzgerald, Lines 47–72

Ismene. We cannot fight with men, Antigone!
The law is strong, we must give in to the law
In this thing, and in worse. I beg the dead
50 To forgive me, but I am helpless: I must yield
To those in authority. And I think it is dangerous business
To be always meddling.

Antigone.   If that is what you think,
I should not want you, even if you asked to come.
You have made your choice; you can be what you want to be.
55 But I will bury him [our brother]; and if I must die,
I say that this crime is holy: I shall lie down
With him in death, and I shall be as dear
To him as he to me.
         It is the dead,
Not the living, who make the longest demands:
60 We die forever. . . .
         You may do as you like,
Since apparently the laws of the gods mean nothing to you.

Ismene. They mean a great deal to me; but I have no strength
To break laws that were made for the public good.

Antigone. That must be your excuse, I suppose. But as for me,
65 I will bury the brother I love.

Ismene.   Antigone,
I am so afraid for you!

Antigone.   You need not be:
You have yourself to consider, after all.

Ismene. But no one must hear of this; you must tell no one!
I will keep it a secret, I promise!

Antigone.   Oh tell it! Tell everyone!
70 Think how they'll hate you when it all comes out
If they learn that you knew about it all the time!

Ismene. So fiery! You should be cold with fear.

Close Read

1. Reread the boxed text. What is Antigone's motivation for wanting to bury her brother?

2. What contrasting Greek social values are represented through the argument between Antigone and Ismene?

3. What traits of a tragic hero does Antigone exhibit? In your opinion, does she seem to have a tragic flaw? Explain.

4. A fearful Ismene hints that Antigone will have to face the terrible consequences of her future actions. What tragic outcome do you predict?

DIFFERENTIATED INSTRUCTION

FOR STRUGGLING READERS

Analysis Support: Tragedy Have students graphically portray the conflict Antigone faces on a Two-Column Chart, listing her positions and the obstacles in the two columns.

Antigone	Obstacles
Desire to obey the gods and display family loyalty by burying brother	Creon's pronouncements and laws against burying a traitor

Discuss how the contrast between the two sisters adds to the conflict by dividing Antigone's family loyalties. Then have students draw conclusions about how this scene represents characteristics of Greek tragedy. Help students recognize that because Antigone is willing to fight anyone who stands in her way, she is bound to face a downfall that affects more than just herself.

 BEST PRACTICES TOOLKIT—Transparency
Two-Column Chart p. A25

This excerpt is from *Le Morte d'Arthur,* a 15th-century English collection of Arthurian romances. Here, King Arthur discovers that King Pellinore has injured a young knight. Angered, Arthur challenges King Pellinore to a joust, a form of medieval combat in which two mounted knights armed with long spears try to unseat each other from their horses. Merlin, a prophet and magician, has accompanied Arthur to the challenge.

---

from Le Morte d'Arthur

Romance by **Sir Thomas Malory,** retold by Keith Baines

Merlin accompanied Arthur to the well, and when they arrived they found King Pellinore seated outside his pavilion. "Sir," said Arthur, "it would seem that no knight can pass this well without your challenging him."

"That is so," said King Pellinore.

5 "I have come to force you to change this custom of yours, so defend yourself!"

They jousted three times, each time breaking their spears, until the third time, when Arthur was flung from his horse. "Very well," said Arthur, "you have won the advantage jousting; now let us see what you can do on foot." King Pellinore was reluctant to dismount and lose the advantage he had

10 won; however, when Arthur rushed at him boldly with drawn sword, he grew ashamed and did dismount.

They fought until both collapsed from pain and exhaustion; their armor was splintered and the blood flowed from their wounds. They fought again, until Arthur's sword broke in his hand. "Now," said King Pellinore, "you shall

15 yield to me, or die."

"Not so!" Arthur shouted as he sprang at him, and grabbing him around the waist, threw him to the ground. Arthur was unlacing his helmet when, with a sudden fearful effort, King Pellinore overturned Arthur and clambered on top of him. King Pellinore had loosened Arthur's helmet and raised his

20 sword to strike off his head when Merlin spoke.

"Hold your hand!" he said; "you will endanger the whole realm. You do not realize who it is you are about to kill."

"Who is it, then?"

"King Arthur."

25 Hearing this, King Pellinore feared that he would receive little mercy from Arthur if he spared him—so he raised his sword once more. Merlin adroitly put him to sleep with a magic spell.

"You have killed him with your magic," said Arthur hotly. "I would rather that my whole realm were lost, and myself killed; he was a magnificent fighter."

30 "He is more whole than you are," Merlin replied. "He will not only live, but serve you excellently: It is to him that you will give your sister in marriage, and she will bear two sons—Sir Percivale and Sir Lamerok—who will be two of the most famous of the Knights of the Round Table."

Close Read

1. The code of chivalry required that knights act with bravery and courtesy. How are these qualities reflected in Arthur's and Pellinore's behavior and actions? Support your answer with specific details.

2. What common characteristic of medieval romance is revealed in the boxed lines?

3. How does the supernatural play a role in the story? Is it a force for good or evil?

4. Which knight—Pellinore or Arthur—displays more qualities of a romance hero? Cite details from the excerpt to support your opinion.

TEXT ANALYSIS WORKSHOP **1063**

Explain that this episode from *Le Morte D'Arthur* does not appear in the selection on pages 1110–1126. Instead, students will read other episodes from this medieval romance.

Close Read

1. ***Possible answer:*** *Arthur and Pellinore act bravely and courteously. Arthur addresses Pellinore as "Sir" (line 2), and after the two fight, he calls his opponent "a magnificent fighter" (line 29). Arthur tries to get Pellinore to change the challenge to a joust. Even after losing, Arthur tries at all costs to win succeeding conflicts (lines 14–16). Pellinore, too, is brave, overcoming fear to gain advantage (lines 9–11).*

2. ***Possible answer:*** *The boxed text reflects the **Hidden Identities** characteristic noted on page 1060. Pellinore does not realize the true identity of the knight he is about to kill until the climactic moment when he is about to strike Arthur (lines 21–24).*

3. ***Possible answer:*** *Merlin casts a spell on Pellinore to keep the knight from killing Arthur. Merlin's supernatural abilities are used here for a good purpose, to keep Pellinore from "endanger[ing] the whole realm" (line 21) of King Arthur.*

4. ***Possible answer:*** *Arthur displays more qualities of a romance hero than Pellinore as he acts bravely throughout the challenge, even while losing (lines 6–8, 16–17). Pellinore is also brave, though fear and reluctance seize him at critical moments (lines 9–11, 18). Also, the chivalric code requires knights to swear allegiance to the king. After discovering Arthur's identity, Pellinore prepares to kill Arthur for fear that the king will show him no mercy in the future (lines 25–26).*

Assess and Reteach

Assess

Have students identify characteristics of Greek tragedy and medieval romance in the excerpts from *Antigone* and *Le Morte d'Arthur.*

Reteach

For students who cannot apply the workshop skills to the two excerpts, review the note-taking copy masters and help students find examples for each noted definition.

FOR ENGLISH LANGUAGE LEARNERS

Vocabulary Support: Word Squares Give students Word Squares with these words:

- *pavilion* (line 2), "an ornate tent"
- *clambered* (line 18), "climbed with difficulty"
- *adroitly* (line 26), "skillfully or cleverly"

Have students list meanings, dictionary definitions, pictures, and sentences.

🧰 **BEST PRACTICES TOOLKIT—Transparency** Word Squares p. E10

FOR ADVANCED LEARNERS/PRE–AP

Compare and Contrast Have students fill in a Comparison Matrix to show similarities and differences between the two Greek heroes, the two romance heroes, or one from each category.

🧰 **BEST PRACTICES TOOLKIT—Transparency** Comparison Matrix p. A24

Classical Greek Drama

RL 6 Analyze a particular point of view or cultural experience reflected in a work of world literature. **RL 9** Analyze how an author draws on and transforms source material in a specific work.

BACKGROUND

Sophocles (496 B.C.?–406 B.C.) The author of *Antigone* is celebrated as one of the greatest Greek tragedians—along with Aeschylus (his senior) and Euripides (his younger contemporary). Sophocles won early fame. While still in his 20s, he placed first in a theatrical competition, defeating Aeschylus. During his long, productive career, he may have never placed lower than second, winning first place at least 20 times. Of Sophocles' 123 dramas, seven complete tragedies still exist, along with fragments of others. He was an innovator, the first known playwright to add a third actor and increase the size of the chorus. Sophocles also served Athens as a general and high official. After his death, he was honored as a hero.

READING SKILL

COMMON CORE
RL 6

DRAW CONCLUSIONS

After students read the first three sections of the article, ask them what conclusions they can draw about how classical Greek theater was different from today's theater. *Possible answer:* Unlike most modern theater, Greek theater was performed outdoors and depended on natural lighting. It was linked with religious celebrations, especially the festivals of Dionysus. Scenery was limited. The chorus played a central role.

CLASSICAL GREEK DRAMA

Masked chorus in a production of a classical Greek drama

COMMON CORE   **RL 6** Analyze a particular point of view or cultural experience reflected in a work of world literature. **RL 9** Analyze how an author draws on and transforms source material in a specific work.

Religious Origins The drama of ancient Greece and Rome is referred to as **classical drama.** It arose in Athens from religious celebrations in honor of the Greek god Dionysus (dī′ə-nī′səs). These celebrations included ritual chants and songs performed by a group called a chorus. Drama evolved from these celebrations during the sixth century B.C., when individual actors began entering into dialogue with the chorus to tell a story.

The Theater Greek drama was filled with the spectacle and pageantry of a religious festival. Attended by thousands, plays were performed during the day in an outdoor theater with seats built into a hillside. The action of each play was presented at the foot of the hill, often on a raised platform. A long building, called the **skene,** served as a backdrop for the action and as a dressing room. A spacious floor, the **orchestra,** was located between the skene and the audience, who sat in the **theatron.**

Actors and Chorus The actors—all men—wore elegant robes, huge masks, and often elevated shoes, all of which added to the grandeur of the spectacle. Sophocles (sŏf′ə-klēz′), an innovator in classical drama, used three actors in his plays;

between scenes, they changed costumes and masks when they needed to portray different characters. The **chorus**—a group of about 15—commented on the action, and the leader of the chorus, the **choragus** (kə-rā′gəs), participated in the dialogue. Between scenes, the chorus sang and danced to musical accompaniment in the orchestra, giving insights into the message of the play. The chorus has often been considered a kind of ideal spectator, representing the response of ordinary citizens to the events unfolding in the play. Typically, the chorus communicated the values, beliefs, and ideals that were central to Athenian society.

Tragedy and the Tragic Hero During Sophocles' lifetime, three playwrights were chosen each year to enter a theatrical competition in the festival of Dionysus. Each playwright would produce three tragedies, along with a satyr (sā′tər) play, a short comic interlude.

As you recall, a **tragedy** is a drama that recounts the downfall of a dignified, superior character—a **tragic hero**—who is involved in

Greek drama was first performed at festivals honoring Dionysus, depicted in this sculpture.

This illustration shows what scholars believe a Greek theater looked like.

1 skene
2 orchestra
3 theatron

historically or socially significant events. The philosopher Aristotle was the first to define tragedy, theorizing that the form evokes both pity and fear in audiences—pity because they feel sorry for the tragic hero, fear because they realize that the hero's struggles are perhaps a necessary part of human life. Tragedies often included **archetypes,** frequently used characters or events, and **motifs,** repeating elements that advanced the plot and illustrated the theme. At the end of a tragedy, an audience generally feels a sense of waste because a person who is in some way superior has been destroyed. Aristotle based his ideas about tragedy on Sophocles' *Oedipus the King,* which he considered the perfect tragedy. Other Greek tragedies, such as *Antigone,* may not fit his model so perfectly.

Mythological Sources The subjects of Greek tragedy are myths and legends that were very familiar to a Greek audience. **Myths,** as you may know, are traditional stories about gods and goddesses; **legends** are stories about people believed to have once lived. Gods and goddesses are often characters in tragedies, and even when they do not appear on stage, they influence the fates of human characters. Usually a tragic hero's downfall is the result of having offended the gods. The gods' wishes are frequently made known through specially gifted characters—such as the blind prophet Teiresias in *Antigone*—who communicate with the gods. Because the myths and legends were so familiar, often employing archetypal characters and events, the audience already knew the outcome of events and could realize the significance of words and actions the characters were blind to. When the audience knows more than the characters do, the result is **dramatic irony.**

Greek Deities Some knowledge of Greek deities is needed to understand classical drama, as the dialogue is filled with **allusions,** or references, to gods and rituals. The ancient Greeks believed that their gods ruled the world from the top of Mount Olympus, Greece's highest mountain. The gods' ruler was Zeus, whose weapons were thunderbolts. Other deities included Ares, the god of war; Aphrodite, the goddess of love and beauty; Athena, the goddess of wisdom, for whom Athens was named; and Dionysus, the god of wine and fertility in whose honor dramas were first performed. The characters in tragedies honor and fear their gods and struggle to live in proper relationship to them. These characters' struggles continue to fascinate audiences today.

CLASSICAL GREEK DRAMA **1065**

■ ANALYZE CAUSE AND EFFECT

After students read **Tragedy and the Tragic Hero,** ask them what, according to Aristotle, causes audiences at a tragedy to feel pity and fear. *Possible answer: They feel pity because they are sorry for the tragic hero and fear because they realize that the hero's struggles are a part of human life.* Point out to students that this cause-and-effect relationship is stated directly in the text. However, sometimes this kind of relationship is implied. When they read *Antigone,* they will need to look deeper to understand cause-and-effect relationships.

BACKGROUND

Great Dionysia Dionysus was the Greek god of wine and fertility—and patron of the performing arts. Two major Athenian festivals honored Dionysus. The most important was known as the City, or Great, Dionysia, held in late March. The Lenaea was a winter festival. After three tragedians were chosen to compete in the Great Dionysia, wealthy private citizens assumed the production costs.

Analyze Visuals

Activity Ask students what information the annotated illustration of the Greek theater shows that is not in the text. *Possible answer: The illustration shows statuary, stone columns, and the basic appearance of the theater. It also gives a clearer sense of the scale of the theater and the relationship between its main parts.*

Focus and Motivate

COMMON CORE FOCUS

RL 1 Cite strong textual evidence to support analysis of what the text says explicitly as well as inferences drawn from the text. **RL 2** Determine a theme or central idea of a text. **RL 3** Analyze how complex characters with conflicting motivations develop, interact with others, and advance the plot or develop the theme. **RL 4** Determine the meaning of words and phrases as they are used in a text, including connotative meaning. **RL 10** Read and comprehend dramas. **W 9a (RL 2)** Draw evidence from literary texts to support analysis and reflection; determine a theme of central idea of a text. **L 3** Make effective choices for meaning or style. **L 4c** Consult reference materials to clarify the etymology of a word.

SUMMARY

Antigone buries her slain brother, contravening the decree of her uncle, King Creon. When he learns of her action, his rage leads him to bury her alive, despite the pleas of his son, Antigone's fiancé. After a warning from the seer Teiresias, the king repents, but he's too late to prevent the suicides of Antigone, his son, and his wife.

What is your ultimate LOYALTY?

Ask students to define loyalty. Then read the question and discuss. Continue this exploration with the *DISCUSS* activity.

Antigone
Drama by Sophocles

What is your ultimate LOYALTY?

COMMON CORE

RL 1 Cite textual evidence to support analysis of what the text says explicitly as well as inferences drawn from the text. **RL 2** Determine a theme or central idea of a text. **RL 3** Analyze how complex characters with conflicting motivations develop, interact with others, and advance the plot or develop the theme. **RL 10** Read and comprehend dramas.

Do you feel more loyal to your family or your friends? to yourself or your country? Which of these gets your greatest loyalty?

DISCUSS Rank the principles shown on the list in order of their importance to you. Imagine situations that might bring these principles into conflict and think about which you would choose. With a small group, discuss your rankings and your reasoning.

> loyalty to family
> obedience to civil law
> protection of nation
> protection of personal dignity

1066

Selection Resources

See resources on the **Teacher One Stop DVD-ROM** *and on* **thinkcentral.com**.

R RESOURCE MANAGER UNIT 10
Plan and Teach, pp. 12–18
Summary, pp. 19–20†‡*
Text Analysis and Reading
  Skill, pp. 21–24†*
Vocabulary, pp. 25–27*
Grammar and Style, p. 30

DIAGNOSTIC AND SELECTION TESTS
Selection Tests, pp. 295–298

BEST PRACTICES TOOLKIT
Open Mind Diagram, p. D9
Three-Column Journal, p. B10
Definition Mapping, p. E6
Sequence Chain, p. B21
Two-Column Chart, p. A25
Story Map, p. D14

TECHNOLOGY
- Teacher One Stop DVD-ROM
- Student One Stop DVD-ROM
- Audio Anthology CD
- GrammarNotes DVD-ROM
- ExamView Test Generator on the **Teacher One Stop**

---

* Resources for Differentiation   † Also in Spanish   ‡ In Haitian Creole and Vietnamese

TEXT ANALYSIS: CLASSICAL DRAMA

Keep these characteristics of classical drama in mind as you read Sophocles' *Antigone*:

- A major form of classical drama is the **tragedy,** which recounts the downfall of a dignified, superior character—a **tragic hero.** The tragic hero may have **archetypal** elements, or elements that appear over and over again in literature. An error or weakness—the hero's **tragic flaw**—may contribute to his or her ruin.
- An important element of classical drama is the **chorus,** a group of actors who comment on the action in the play. Their leader is the **choragus.**
- **Dramatic irony**—the audience's awareness of things the characters do not know—is often present in classical drama.

Review: **Character, Conflict, Theme**

READING STRATEGY: READING CLASSICAL DRAMA

Use the following strategies to help you understand *Antigone*:

- **Visualize** the staging of the play, with its masked actors.
- **Clarify** unfamiliar references by using the marginal notes.
- **Infer** the traits, values, and motivations of the two main characters, Antigone and Creon. **Evaluate** these characters, who are in conflict.
- **Relate** the songs of the chorus to the action of the play. Use a chart to record notes about the song the chorus sings at the end of each scene.

	Summary of Song	Function of Song
Parodos	*Polyneices attacked Thebes but was defeated.*	*gives background for Creon's order not to bury Polyneices*
Ode 1		

▲ VOCABULARY IN CONTEXT

Define each vocabulary word you're familiar with. After reading the play, define the words that were unfamiliar.

WORD LIST		
anarchist	impassively	reverence
auspicious	insolence	sate
contempt	lamentation	sententiously
defile	perverse	transgress

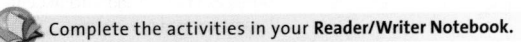 Complete the activities in your **Reader/Writer Notebook.**

Background

Sophocles

496?–406 B.C.

Doomed King
Sophocles was one of the great dramatists of ancient Greece, and his play *Antigone* is regarded as one of the finest examples of classical Greek tragedy. Along with *Oedipus the King* and *Oedipus at Colonus*, it is part of Sophocles' Theban trilogy. These three plays are based on the legend of Oedipus (ĕd'ə-pəs), the doomed Theban king who unknowingly killed his father and married his mother. Antigone (ăn-tĭg'ə-nē) is the daughter of Oedipus.

Family Feud
As the play begins, Antigone and her sister, Ismene (ĭs-mē'nē), recall their dead father. Upon discovering the truth about his marriage, Oedipus blinded himself and went into exile, where he was cared for by his two daughters until his death. His sons, Eteocles (ĭ-tē'ə-klēz') and Polyneices (pŏl'ə-nī'sēz), agreed to share the kingship of Thebes, ruling in alternate years. However, after Eteocles had served his first term as king, he refused to relinquish the throne to Polyneices, claiming that Polyneices was unfit to rule. Polyneices then enlisted an army from Argos, a long-standing enemy of Thebes, to fight his brother. In the course of battle, the brothers killed each other. Their uncle, Creon, who has become king, now faces the task of restoring order in Thebes. He plans to honor one corpse and dishonor the other.

Author Online
Go to **thinkcentral.com.** KEYWORD: HML10-1067

THiNK central

ANTIGONE **1067**

Teach

TEXT ANALYSIS
COMMON CORE
RL 2
RL 3
RL 4

● *Model the Skill:* **CLASSICAL DRAMA**

To model how to identify tragedy, a form of classical drama, read **Family Feud** aloud, and tell why the story of Oedipus is a tragedy. Point out that it is the story of the downfall of Oedipus, a tragic hero who was ruined.

GUIDED PRACTICE Have students identify facts about Oedipus in **Family Feud** that a Greek audience would know but not Oedipus (i.e., dramatic irony).

READING STRATEGY
COMMON CORE
RL 1
RL 10

■ *Model the Skill:* **READING CLASSICAL DRAMA**

Read aloud these lines.

> Blinded by his own hand, Oedipus stands among his advisors. He declares that he will wander in exile. His daughters come to him, weeping, and lead him away.

Tell students that as you read, you visualized that Oedipus is wounded and unseeing. He stands uncertainly. Each daughter takes one arm and they lead him slowly off.

GUIDED PRACTICE Have students infer traits of Antigone and Ismene from their description in **Family Feud.**

 RESOURCE MANAGER—Copy Master
Reading Classical Drama p. 24

VOCABULARY SKILL

COMMON CORE
L 4

▲ VOCABULARY IN CONTEXT

DIAGNOSE WORD KNOWLEDGE Have all students complete Vocabulary in Context. Check their definitions against the following:

anarchist (ăn'ər-kĭst) *n.* a person favoring the overthrow of government

auspicious (ô-spĭsh'əs) *adj.* promising success; favorable

contempt (kən-tĕmpt') *n.* an attitude of regarding someone or something as worthless or inferior

defile (dĭ-fīl') *v.* to make dirty, unclean, or impure

impassively (ĭm-păs'ĭv-lē) *adv.* in a way that shows no emotion or feeling

insolence (īn'sə-ləns) *n.* rudeness and disrespect

lamentation (lăm'ən-tā'shən) *n.* an expression of grief

perverse (pər-vûrs') *adj.* willfully determined to go against what is expected or desired

reverence (rĕv'ər-əns) *n.* awe and respect

sate (sāt) *v.* to satisfy fully

sententiously (sĕn-tĕn'shəs-lē) *adv.* in a pompous, moralizing manner

transgress (trăns-grĕs') *v.* to violate or break (a law, command, or moral code)

PRETEACH VOCABULARY Use the following copy master to help students predict meanings for each boldfaced word.

R RESOURCE MANAGER—Copy Master
Vocabulary Study p. 25

Practice and Apply

READ WITH A PURPOSE

Help students set a purpose for reading. Tell students to look for the hero's tragic flaw.

READING STRATEGY

COMMON CORE
RL 1
RL 10

■ READING CLASSICAL DRAMA

Remind students that *Antigone* is a story about a family torn by dissension. Have students preview the cast of characters. Ask them to identify those that are related and explain the relationship. ***Possible answers:*** *Antigone and Ismene are sisters; Creon is their uncle; Eurydice is Creon's wife and the aunt of Antigone and Ismene; Haemon is the son of Creon and Eurydice.*

ANTIGONE
Sophocles

CAST OF CHARACTERS

Antigone, daughter of Oedipus, former king of Thebes

Ismene, daughter of Oedipus

Creon (krē′ŏn′), king of Thebes, uncle of Antigone and Ismene

Haemon (hē′mŏn′), Creon's son, engaged to Antigone

Eurydice (yŏŏ-rĭd′ĭ-sē), wife of Creon

Teiresias (tī-rē′sē-əs), a blind prophet

Chorus, made up of about 15 elders of Thebes

Choragus, leader of the chorus

A Sentry

A Messenger

SCENE

Before the palace of Creon, king of Thebes. A central double door, and two doors at the side. A platform extends the length of the stage, and from this platform three steps lead down into the orchestra, or chorus ground.

TIME

Dawn of the day after the repulse of the Argive army from the assault on Thebes

PROLOGUE

(Antigone *and* Ismene *enter from the central door of the palace.*)

Antigone. Ismene, dear sister,
You would think that we had already suffered enough
For the curse on Oedipus:
I cannot imagine any grief
5 That you and I have not gone through. And now—
Have they told you the new decree of our king Creon?

Ismene. I have heard nothing: I know
That two sisters lost two brothers, a double death
In a single hour; and I know that the Argive army
10 Fled in the night; but beyond this, nothing.

9 Argive (är′jīv′): of Argos.

Martha Henry as Antigone and Philip Bosco as Creon in the Lincoln Center Repertory 1971 production

1068   UNIT 10: GREEK TRAGEDY AND MEDIEVAL ROMANCE

DIFFERENTIATED INSTRUCTION

FOR ENGLISH LANGUAGE LEARNERS

Concept Support Remind students of some terms used in the reading of dramatic works, including *cast, scene,* and *stage directions.* Help students to define each term. Point out that the stage directions appear in parentheses and italics (except for the names of characters). Note that, in addition to the Prologue, this play has five scenes, rather than five acts. Review the role of the chorus and choragus.

FOR ADVANCED LEARNERS/PRE–AP

Explore Oedipus Myth Ask students to research the tragedy of Oedipus. What role did prophecy play in the tragedy? How did the city of Thebes figure into the story? What part did Antigone and Ismene play? Discuss how this information helps them understand *Antigone.*

Get Into the Prologue
SUMMARY

Creon has decreed that only one of Antigone's two brothers will get a proper burial. Polyneices, he declared, was a traitor who attacked the city and shall remain unburied. Antigone believes it is her sacred duty to bury her brother and asks Ismene to help. Ismene refuses, fearing repercussions from disobeying the king's command.

Analyze Visuals

Activity Ask students what the photograph of the two actors suggests about the characters they play. *Possible answer: The photograph shows a confident, serious, determined Antigone; Creon appears confident to the point of arrogance, as his expression has a mocking quality.* Ask students why the photograph features Creon, who does not appear in the Prologue, rather than Ismene. *Possible answer: Creon will be one of the main characters in the play, whereas Ismene is a minor character. The major conflict occurs between Creon and Antigone.*

Creon decrees no one shall bury Polyneices.

↓

Antigone decides to bury her brother.

↓

Ismene refuses to help Antigone.

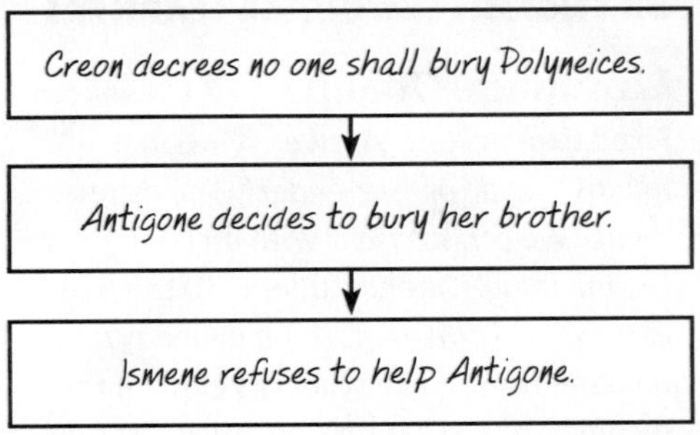

What is your ultimate
LOYALTY?

Discuss Based on lines 48–52, where does Ismene's greatest loyalty lie? *Possible answer: Ismene says that she is unwilling to disobey the decree, suggesting that her loyalty lies with the law of the land. She also admits to being guided by fear. Her first loyalty, it appears, is self-preservation.*

Antigone. I thought so. And that is why I wanted you
To come out here with me. There is something we must do.

Ismene. Why do you speak so strangely?

Antigone. Listen, Ismene:

15 Creon buried our brother Eteocles
With military honors, gave him a soldier's funeral,
And it was right that he should; but Polyneices,
Who fought as bravely and died as miserably—
They say that Creon has sworn

20 No one shall bury him, no one mourn for him,
But his body must lie in the fields, a sweet treasure
For carrion birds to find as they search for food.
That is what they say, and our good Creon is coming here
To announce it publicly; and the penalty—

25 Stoning to death in the public square!
                                         There it is,
And now you can prove what you are:
A true sister, or a traitor to your family.

Ismene. Antigone, you are mad! What could I possibly do?

Antigone. You must decide whether you will help me or not.

30 **Ismene.** I do not understand you. Help you in what?

Antigone. Ismene, I am going to bury him. Will you come?

Ismene. Bury him! You have just said the new law forbids it.

Antigone. He is my brother. And he is your brother, too.

Ismene. But think of the danger! Think what Creon will do!

35 **Antigone.** Creon is not strong enough to stand in my way.

Ismene. Ah sister!
Oedipus died, everyone hating him
For what his own search brought to light, his eyes
Ripped out by his own hand; and Jocasta died,

40 His mother and wife at once: she twisted the cords
That strangled her life; and our two brothers died,
Each killed by the other's sword. And we are left:
But oh, Antigone,
Think how much more terrible than these

45 Our own death would be if we should go against Creon
And do what he has forbidden! We are only women;
We cannot fight with men, Antigone!
The law is strong, we must give in to the law
In this thing, and in worse. I beg the dead

50 To forgive me, but I am helpless: I must yield
To those in authority. And I think it is dangerous business
To be always meddling.

---

① **Targeted Passage**

20–22 No one shall bury . . . search for food: The obligation to bury the dead with appropriate rites was considered sacred by the ancient Greeks. They believed that the soul of someone left unburied would never find peace.

39 Jocasta (jō-kăs'tə): the mother of Antigone and Ismene. Jocasta hanged herself when she realized the truth about her relationship with Oedipus.

COMMON CORE RL 4

Language Coach

Fixed Expressions Some verbs take on a special meaning when followed by a particular adverb. Reread lines 48–49. What does *give in* mean in these lines? What clue does line 47 provide?

DIFFERENTIATED INSTRUCTION

FOR ENGLISH LANGUAGE LEARNERS

Language Coach   **COMMON CORE RL 4**

Fixed Expressions *Answer:* Give in means "yield" or "surrender." The statement "We cannot fight with men" suggests the meaning. Direct students to the fixed expression *come to nothing* in line 137 on page 1106. Have students explain the meaning of the expression and point out the clues to understanding the phrase in lines 135–138.

FOR STRUGGLING READERS

In combination with the *Audio Anthology CD,* use one or more Targeted Passages (pp. 1070, 1074, 1077, 1080, 1085, 1088, 1090, 1093, 1097, 1098, 1103, 1106) to ensure that students focus on key events, concepts, and skills. Targeted Passages are also good for English learners.

Antigone.   If that is what you think,
I should not want you, even if you asked to come.
You have made your choice; you can be what you want to be.
55 But I will bury him; and if I must die,
I say that this crime is holy: I shall lie down
With him in death, and I shall be as dear
To him as he to me. **Ⓐ**
                    It is the dead,
Not the living, who make the longest demands:
60 We die forever. . . .
                    You may do as you like,
Since apparently the laws of the gods mean nothing to you.

Ismene. They mean a great deal to me; but I have no strength
To break laws that were made for the public good.

Antigone. That must be your excuse, I suppose. But as for me,
65 I will bury the brother I love.

Ⓐ CONFLICT
Note the seriousness of the conflict that is introduced. What is Antigone going to do, and what may happen to her as a result?

Tandy Cronyn as Ismene and Martha Henry as Antigone in the Lincoln Center Repertory 1971 production

ANTIGONE **1071**

TEXT ANALYSIS: *Review*   **COMMON CORE** RL 3

Ⓐ CONFLICT

Possible answer: *Antigone is going to bury her brother Polyneices, contravening the order of King Creon, and she may be killed for doing so.*

Analyze Visuals

Activity What does the photograph suggest about the relationship between Antigone and Ismene? ***Possible answer:*** *The photograph suggests that Antigone and Ismene share a close, loving, sisterly relationship, but that they have just realized that they have differing core values. Antigone looks stronger and more assertive than her sister, who kneels below her. Their expressions seem to show that they are deep in contemplation about how their loyalties will divide them.*

① Targeted Passage [Lines 15–31]

This passage establishes Antigone's motivation, her determination, and the penalty she will have to pay for her act of conscience.

- What does Antigone plan to do? (line 31)
- Why has she told Ismene about her plan? (lines 26–27)
- What will happen to the sisters if they bury Polyneices? (lines 24–25)

FOR ENGLISH LANGUAGE LEARNERS

Vocabulary Support Have students use context to determine the meaning of these common idioms and expressions:

- *do as you like* (line 60), "do whatever you want to do"
- *a great deal* (line 62), "very much"
- *break laws* (line 63), "go against the law"
- *for the public good* (line 63), "for the good of all the people"
- *as for me* (line 64), "myself"

ANTIGONE **1071**

Ismene.   Antigone,
I am so afraid for you!

Antigone.   You need not be:
You have yourself to consider, after all.

Ismene. But no one must hear of this; you must tell no one!
I will keep it a secret, I promise!

Antigone.   Oh tell it! Tell everyone!
70 Think how they'll hate you when it all comes out
If they learn that you knew about it all the time!

Ismene. So fiery! You should be cold with fear.

Antigone. Perhaps. But I am doing only what I must.

Ismene. But can you do it? I say that you cannot.

75 **Antigone.** Very well: when my strength gives out, I shall do no more.

Ismene. Impossible things should not be tried at all.

Antigone. Go away, Ismene:
I shall be hating you soon, and the dead will too,
For your words are hateful. Leave me my foolish plan:
80 I am not afraid of the danger; if it means death,
It will not be the worst of deaths—death without honor.

Ismene. Go then, if you feel that you must.
You are unwise,
But a loyal friend indeed to those who love you. **B**

(*Exit into the palace.* Antigone *goes off, left. Enters the* Chorus, *with* Choragus.)

PARODOS

Chorus. Now the long blade of the sun, lying
Level east to west, touches with glory
Thebes of the Seven Gates. Open, unlidded
Eye of golden day! O marching light
5 Across the eddy and rush of Dirce's stream,
Striking the white shields of the enemy
Thrown headlong backward from the blaze of morning!

Choragus. Polyneices their commander
Roused them with windy phrases,
10 He the wild eagle screaming
Insults above our land,

B CHARACTER
So far, what have you learned about Antigone, the **protagonist** of the play? How would you contrast her with her sister, Ismene?

Parodos (pär'ə-dŏs'): a song that marks the entry of the chorus, which represents the leading citizens of Thebes.

5 Dirce's (dûr'sēz) **stream:** a stream flowing past Thebes. The stream is named for a murdered queen who was thrown into it.

TEXT ANALYSIS: *Review*   COMMON CORE
RL 3

B CHARACTER

Possible answer: *Antigone is principled (line 31), fearless (lines 55–57, 80–81), and determined (lines 35, 73), unlike timid Ismene. Antigone places the laws of principle above the laws of the state, while Ismene supports authority, mostly out of fear (lines 32, 44–51, 62–63).*

IF STUDENTS NEED HELP . . . Use an Open Mind diagram to guide students in exploring what they know about Antigone and Ismene. Discuss how these characteristics reveal the characters' similarities and differences.

Her behavior: tries to persuade Ismene

Character: Antigone

Her thoughts: determined to bury brother, thinks Ismene is a coward

Her statements: "I'm going to bury him. I say that this crime is holy."

Her fears: none

Others' actions toward her: Ismene is afraid for her.

 BEST PRACTICES TOOLKIT—Transparency
Open Mind Diagram p. D9

DIFFERENTIATED INSTRUCTION

FOR STRUGGLING READERS

Background Point out that the words *chorus* and *ode* came from Greek words meaning "dance" and "song." Scholars believe that the Greek chorus, even in the time of Sophocles, likely danced and sang during the play. Encourage students to keep this in mind as they read the Parodos and the Odes at the end of each of the first four scenes.

FOR ENGLISH LANGUAGE LEARNERS

Vocabulary Support Define and discuss these phrases from the Parodos:

- *unlidded eye of golden day* (lines 3–4), "the sun"

- *windy phrases* (line 9), "empty words, speeches"

- *marshaled helms* (line 13), "helmets arranged (for battle)"

- *storming in fury* (line 30), "violently attacking"

- *matchless rage* (line 36), "greatest anger"

His wings their shields of snow,
His crest their marshaled helms.

Chorus. Against our seven gates in a yawning ring
15 The famished spears came onward in the night;
But before his jaws were **sated** with our blood,
Or pine fire took the garland of our towers,
He was thrown back; and as he turned, great Thebes—
No tender victim for his noisy power—
20 Rose like a dragon behind him, shouting war.

Choragus. For God hates utterly
The bray of bragging tongues;
And when he beheld their smiling,
Their swagger of golden helms,
25 The frown of his thunder blasted
Their first man from our walls.

Chorus. We heard his shout of triumph high in the air
Turn to a scream; far out in a flaming arc
He fell with his windy torch, and the earth struck him.
30 And others storming in fury no less than his
Found shock of death in the dusty joy of battle.

Choragus. Seven captains at seven gates
Yielded their clanging arms to the god
That bends the battle line and breaks it.
35 These two only, brothers in blood,
Face to face in matchless rage,
Mirroring each the other's death,
Clashed in long combat.

Chorus. But now in the beautiful morning of victory
40 Let Thebes of the many chariots sing for joy!
With hearts for dancing we'll take leave of war:
Our temples shall be sweet with hymns of praise,
And the long night shall echo with our chorus. **C**

14–15 seven gates: Thebes had seven gates, which the Argives attacked all at once.

sate (sāt) *v.* to satisfy fully

21–26 Zeus, the king of the gods, threw a thunderbolt, which killed the first Argive attacker.

32–34 When the seven captains were killed, their armor was offered as a sacrifice to Ares (âr'ēz), the god of war.

C READING CLASSICAL DRAMA
Summarize the background information that the **chorus** gives in its song. How does the chorus view Polyneices?

ANTIGONE **1073**

ANTIGONE **1073**

SCENE 1

Choragus. But now at last our new king is coming:
Creon of Thebes, Menoeceus' son.
In this **auspicious** dawn of his reign
What are the new complexities
5 That shifting Fate has woven for him?
What is his counsel? Why has he summoned
The old men to hear him?

(*Enter* Creon *from the palace. He addresses the* Chorus *from the top step.*)

Creon. Gentlemen: I have the honor to inform you that our ship of
state, which recent storms have threatened to destroy, has come
10 safely to harbor at last, guided by the merciful wisdom of heaven.
I have summoned you here this morning because I know that I
can depend upon you: your devotion to King Laius was absolute;
you never hesitated in your duty to our late ruler Oedipus; and
when Oedipus died, your loyalty was transferred to his children.
15 Unfortunately, as you know, his two sons, the princes Eteocles and
Polyneices, have killed each other in battle; and I, as the next in
blood, have succeeded to the full power of the throne.

I am aware, of course, that no ruler can expect complete loyalty
from his subjects until he has been tested in office. Nevertheless,
20 I say to you at the very outset that I have nothing but **contempt**
for the kind of governor who is afraid, for whatever reason, to
follow the course that he knows is best for the state; and as for
the man who sets private friendship above the public welfare—
I have no use for him, either. I call God to witness that if I
25 saw my country headed for ruin, I should not be afraid to
speak out plainly; and I need hardly remind you that I would
never have any dealings with an enemy of the people. No one **D**
values friendship more highly than I; but we must remember
that friends made at the risk of wrecking our ship are not real
30 friends at all. **E**

These are my principles, at any rate, and that is why I have
made the following decision concerning the sons of Oedipus:
Eteocles, who died as a man should die, fighting for his country,
is to be buried with full military honors, with all the ceremony
35 that is usual when the greatest heroes die; but his brother
Polyneices, who broke his exile to come back with fire and
sword against his native city and the shrines of his fathers'
gods, whose one idea was to spill the blood of his blood and
sell his own people into slavery—Polyneices, I say, is to have no
40 burial: no man is to touch him or say the least prayer for him;
he shall lie on the plain, unburied; and the birds and the
scavenging dogs can do with him whatever they like.

1074 UNIT 10: GREEK TRAGEDY AND MEDIEVAL ROMANCE

---

2 Menoeceus' (mə-nē'syōōs).

auspicious (ô-spĭsh'əs) *adj.*
promising success; favorable

 Targeted Passage

12 Laius (lā'əs): the father of Oedipus.

contempt (kən-tĕmpt') *n.* an attitude
of regarding someone or something
as worthless or inferior

COMMON CORE RL 3

D MOTIFS IN DRAMA
A **motif** is an element or concept
expressed by the characters
throughout a play that helps
develop the plot and theme.
Although this is only the first scene
of *Antigone*, the idea of treachery
versus loyalty has appeared several
times. How do you think this motif
might affect the plot?

E CHARACTER
This speech introduces Creon,
who acts as Antigone's **antagonist**.
According to him, what deserves
the highest loyalty? Read on to
learn his motives for forbidding
Polyneices' burial.

Philip Bosco as Creon in the Lincoln
Center Repertory 1971 production

Left column

TEXT ANALYSIS COMMON CORE RL 3

D MOTIFS IN DRAMA

Point out to students that Antigone introduces the treachery versus loyalty motif
with her speech starting in line 14. Discuss
with students that this motif has already
been introduced in lines 26–27 of the Prologue. Point out to students the repetition
of the motif reinforces its importance to
the audience. ***Possible answer:*** *Students
may predict that that a central conflict of
the play will revolve around issues of loyalty
and treachery and the fallout if Antigone
disobeys Creon's order and buries her
brother.*

TEXT ANALYSIS: *Review* COMMON CORE RL 3

E CHARACTER

Possible answer: *According to Creon, a ruler
who has been tested in office (and presumably performed well) deserves "complete
loyalty from his subjects" (lines 18–19). That
ruler should do what is "best for the state"
(line 22) and value "public welfare" above all
(line 23).*

VOCABULARY COMMON CORE L 4

OWN THE WORD

- **auspicious:** Tell students that *auspicious*
has the connotation of good luck. Have
students write sentences that demonstrate their understanding of *auspicious*.

- **contempt:** Have students list synonyms
for *contempt*. ***Possible answers:*** *disdain,
scorn, shame, dishonor, disgrace, dis-
repect, disobedience*

DIFFERENTIATED INSTRUCTION

FOR STRUGGLING READERS

 Targeted Passage [Lines 8–17]

This passage establishes Creon's credentials
and purpose for summoning the chorus.

- What "recent storm" does Creon refer to?
(line 9)

- Why has Creon called together the chorus?
(lines 11–12)

- How does he justify his succession to the
throne? (lines 15–17)

FOR ENGLISH LANGUAGE LEARNERS

Vocabulary Support Use Definition Mapping
to teach these words: *devotion* (scene 1, line
12), *enforce* (scene 1, line 49), *scheming* (scene
1, line 114), *analyze* (scene 1, line 133), *deny*
(scene 2, line 52), *licensed* (scene 2, line 102).

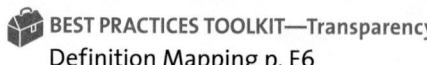 BEST PRACTICES TOOLKIT—Transparency
Definition Mapping p. E6

Get Into the Scene
SUMMARY

The chorus of Theban elders arrives, summoned by Creon. He justifies his decree, denying Polyneices a burial. After the chorus agrees to honor Creon's decree, a sentry enters with news that someone has thrown dust on Polyneices' corpse. Creon accuses the sentry of complicity and sends him to find the guilty man.

Analyze Visuals

Activity The actor in the photograph projects what qualities? Are these qualities consistent with Sophocles' Creon? ***Possible answer:*** *The actor projects self-assurance, nobility, firmness, pride, and gravity. These qualities are consistent with the character that Sophocles portrays.*

REVIST THE BIG QUESTION
What is your ultimate
LOYALTY?

Discuss Based on lines 18–30, why does a clash with Antigone appear to be inevitable, considering Creon's stated loyalty? ***Possible answer:*** *Creon's absolute loyalty to the state stands in stark contrast to Antigone's staunch loyalty to family and principle. Given these strong and competing loyalties—Creon's decree and Antigone's intention to defy it—a clash appears inevitable.*

FOR STRUGGLING READERS

Preview Ask students to listen carefully as you read the summary aloud. Encourage them to continue the Sequence Chain that they started at the beginning of the play.

🧰 **BEST PRACTICES TOOLKIT—Transparency** Sequence Chain p. B21 .

FOR ADVANCED LEARNERS/PRE–AP

Persuasive Argument Have students analyze Creon's speech as a persuasive argument. What is his position on the burial of Polyneices? What reasons does he use to support his claim? Is his argument logical? Does he deal with the "counterargument"? Have students write two or three paragraphs about their findings.

Use these prompts to help students understand the interaction between Creon and the sentry in lines 58–76:

Connect The sentry finds himself in the dangerous situation of telling the king bad news. How do you feel toward the sentry at this point. Why? *Students will be sympathetic toward the sentry. They may cite situations in which they have had to deliver bad news to a parent, teacher, or friend, and have had to suffer the consequences or anger directed at someone else.*

Analyze Why is the sentry afraid of telling Creon that somebody put dust on Polyneices' body? *Possible answer: The sentry is afraid that Creon will be angry at him for being the messenger of bad news or that the king will blame him and, perhaps, punish him.*

Synthesize What does the audience learn about Creon from this interaction with the sentry? *Possible answer: Creon has the power of life and death over his subjects and can mete out justice as he pleases, whether the subject is innocent or not. Also, he seems to be known as a demanding, temperamental leader who will not tolerate anyone going against his orders.*

VOCABULARY

COMMON CORE
L 4

OWN THE WORD

- **reverence:** Tell students that *reverence* is a noun that refers to feeling "awe and respect" for someone or something. *Revere* is the related verb that is the act of giving *reverence.* Have students list things that they *revere* or to which they would show *reverence.*

- **impassively:** Point out that the prefix *im-* and suffix *-ly* has been added to *passive* to create the adverb *impassively.* Have students use a dictionary to find other forms of the root *passive.*

This is my command, and you can see the wisdom behind it. As long as I am king, no traitor is going to be honored with the
45 loyal man. But whoever shows by word and deed that he is on the side of the state—he shall have my respect while he is living, and my **reverence** when he is dead.

Choragus. If that is your will, Creon son of Menoeceus, You have the right to enforce it: we are yours.

50 **Creon.** That is my will. Take care that you do your part.

Choragus. We are old men: let the younger ones carry it out.

Creon. I do not mean that: the sentries have been appointed.

Choragus. Then what is it that you would have us do?

Creon. You will give no support to whoever breaks this law.

55 **Choragus.** Only a crazy man is in love with death!

Creon. And death it is; yet money talks, and the wisest Have sometimes been known to count a few coins too many.

(*Enter* Sentry.)

Sentry. I'll not say that I'm out of breath from running, King, because every time I stopped to think about what I have to tell you, I felt like going back.
60 And all the time a voice kept saying, "You fool, don't you know you're walking straight into trouble?"; and then another voice: "Yes, but if you let somebody else get the news to Creon first, it will be even worse than that for you!" But good sense won out, at least I hope it was good sense, and here I am with a story that makes no sense at all; but I'll tell it anyhow, because, as they say,
65 what's going to happen's going to happen, and—

Creon. Come to the point. What have you to say?

Sentry. I did not do it. I did not see who did it. You must not punish me for what someone else has done.

Creon. A comprehensive defense! More effective, perhaps,
70 If I knew its purpose. Come: what is it?

Sentry. A dreadful thing . . . I don't know how to put it—

Creon. Out with it!

Sentry.   Well, then;
The dead man—
                    Polyneices—

(*Pause. The Sentry is overcome, fumbles for words. Creon waits **impassively**.*)

                    out there—
                              someone—
New dust on the slimy flesh!

reverence (rĕv'ər-əns) *n.* awe and respect

impassively (ĭm-păs'ĭv-lē) *adv.* in a way that shows no emotion or feeling

---

DIFFERENTIATED INSTRUCTION

FOR STRUGGLING READERS

Minor Characters Remind students that the choragus leads the chorus, which represents ordinary citizens. Ask them to describe the choragus' attitude toward Creon's decree.
Possible answer: The attitude of the choragus is that Creon has the right to make this decree and the power to enforce it (lines 48–49), yet the phrasing of the choragus' responses seems to question whether the decree is just (lines 48–49 and 102–103).

FOR ENGLISH LANGUAGE LEARNERS

Vocabulary Support Define and discuss these idioms, phrasal verbs, and expressions: *as long as I am* (line 44), "during the time when I am"; *do your part* (line 50), "fulfill your duty, job, or role"; *money talks* (line 56), "money influences people"; *won out* (line 63), "prevailed, succeeded"; *makes no sense* (line 64), "has no logic or explanation"; *Come to the point* (line 66), "Say your meaning or purpose."

(Pause. No sign from Creon.)

75 Someone has given it burial that way, and
Gone. . . .

(Long pause. Creon *finally speaks with deadly control.)*

Creon. And the man who dared do this? **F**

Sentry.   I swear I
Do not know! You must believe me!
                                        Listen:
The ground was dry, not a sign of digging, no,
80 Not a wheel track in the dust, no trace of anyone.
It was when they relieved us this morning: and one of them,
The corporal, pointed to it.
                                        There it was,
The strangest—
                        Look:
The body, just mounded over with light dust: you see?
85 Not buried really, but as if they'd covered it
Just enough for the ghost's peace. And no sign
Of dogs or any wild animal that had been there.

And then what a scene there was! Every man of us
Accusing the other: we all proved the other man did it;
90 We all had proof that we could not have done it.
We were ready to take hot iron in our hands,
Walk through fire, swear by all the gods,
It was not I!
I do not know who it was, but it was not I!

*(*Creon's *rage has been mounting steadily, but the* Sentry *is too
intent upon his story to notice it.)*

95 And then, when this came to nothing, someone said
A thing that silenced us and made us stare
Down at the ground: you had to be told the news,
And one of us had to do it! We threw the dice,
And the bad luck fell to me. So here I am,
100 No happier to be here than you are to have me:
Nobody likes the man who brings bad news. **G**

Choragus. I have been wondering, King: can it be that the gods
    have done this? **H**

Creon *(furiously).* Stop!
Must you doddering wrecks
105 Go out of your heads entirely? "The gods!"
Intolerable!
The gods favor this corpse? Why? How had he served them?

3 Targeted Passage

F CLASSICAL DRAMA
Who do you think buried the body?
Note the **dramatic irony** arising from
Creon's assumption that the person
who buried the body was a man.

G CHARACTER
Notice how the sentry, a **minor
character,** relates to Creon.
What does his attitude tell you
about Creon?

H CLASSICAL DRAMA
The **choragus** poses a reasonable
question. Judge Creon's response,
noting what attitude he shows
toward the gods.

ANTIGONE **1077**

What is your ultimate
LOYALTY?

Discuss At this point in the play, Creon doesn't know that Antigone has buried her brother out of loyalty to family and principle. In lines 111–120, what does he think is the reason for this refusal to obey his decree? *Possible answer: Creon believes that his enemies have bribed his guards to perform the burial; in his view, money and anarchy corrupt loyalty to the state.*

TEXT ANALYSIS: *Review*   COMMON CORE   RL 3

❶ CHARACTER

Possible answer: Students may have mixed feelings about Creon. They may admire him for wanting to do what is best for his city. However, they may criticize him for being judgmental, tyrannical, inflexible, and quick to anger.

VOCABULARY   COMMON CORE   L 4

OWN THE WORD

- **anarchist:** Tell students that an *anarchist* is a person who practices *anarchism*, the belief that all forms of government should be abolished. *Anarchy* is the state of political disorder where there is the absence of all political authority.

- **sententiously:** Remind students that the word *sententiously* refers to a person's "pompous, moralizing manner." Sophocles included this word in the script as a directive to help actors recite the lines with correct emotion. Read aloud the section of Creon's remarks beginning with line 110 through 120 using proper inflection to reflect a *sententious* delivery.

Tried to loot their temples, burn their images,
Yes, and the whole state, and its laws with it!
110 Is it your senile opinion that the gods love to honor bad men?
A pious thought!—
            No, from the very beginning
There have been those who have whispered together,
Stiff-necked **anarchists,** putting their heads together,
Scheming against me in alleys. These are the men,
115 And they have bribed my own guard to do this thing.
(*sententiously*) Money!
There's nothing in the world so demoralizing as money.
Down go your cities,
Homes gone, men gone, honest hearts corrupted,
120 Crookedness of all kinds, and all for money!
           (*to* Sentry)   But you—!
I swear by God and by the throne of God,
The man who has done this thing shall pay for it!
Find that man; bring him here to me, or your death
Will be the least of your problems: I'll string you up
125 Alive, and there will be certain ways to make you
Discover your employer before you die;
And the process may teach you a lesson you seem to have missed:
The dearest profit is sometimes all too dear.
That depends on the source. Do you understand me?
130 A fortune won is often misfortune.

Sentry. King, may I speak?

Creon.   Your very voice distresses me.

Sentry. Are you sure that it is my voice, and not your conscience?

Creon. By God, he wants to analyze me now!

Sentry. It is not what I say, but what has been done, that hurts you.

135 **Creon.** You talk too much.

Sentry.   Maybe; but I've done nothing.

Creon. Sold your soul for some silver: that's all you've done.

Sentry. How dreadful it is when the right judge judges wrong!

Creon. Your figures of speech
May entertain you now; but unless you bring me the man,
140 You will get little profit from them in the end. ❶

(*Exit* Creon *into the palace.*)

Sentry. "Bring me the man"—!
I'd like nothing better than bringing him the man!
But bring him or not, you have seen the last of me here.
At any rate, I am safe!

(*Exit* Sentry.)

anarchist (ăn′ər-kĭst) *n.* a person favoring the overthrow of government

sententiously (sĕn-tĕn′shəs-lē) *adv.* in a pompous, moralizing manner

---

COMMON CORE   RL 4

Language Coach

Denotations/Connotations The feelings associated with a word are its **connotations.** Some words can have either a positive or a negative connotation, depending on context. Sometimes writers use the same word in different ways for effect. In line 128, how are the connotations of *dearest* different from those of *dear?*

---

❶ CHARACTER
What do you think of Creon so far? What seem to be his virtues? his flaws?

DIFFERENTIATED INSTRUCTION

FOR STRUGGLING READERS
Comic Relief Point out to students that the sentry provides a bit of comic relief. He talks too much—so much so that Creon tells him to "come to the point" (line 66) and says the sentry's "very voice distresses me" (line 131). Finally, after his persuasive efforts fail, the sentry banters with Creon (lines 132–140). Call on two fluent readers to dramatize these lines, drawing out the irony and humor.

FOR ENGLISH LANGUAGE LEARNERS

Language Coach   COMMON CORE   RL 4
Denotations/Connotations
Answer: In both cases, dearest/dear have to do with value; "dearest profit" refers to something positive—a tidy sum. However, the cost of gaining that profit is "all too dear." In this case, dear connotes a price so high that it incurs damage. Point out the word loot in line 108. Have students use a dictionary to find one negative and one positive connotation of loot.

ODE 1

Chorus. Numberless are the world's wonders, but none
More wonderful than man; the storm-grey sea
Yields to his prows; the huge crests bear him high;
Earth, holy and inexhaustible, is graven
5 With shining furrows where his plows have gone
Year after year, the timeless labor of stallions.

The light-boned birds and beasts that cling to cover,
The lithe fish lighting their reaches of dim water,
All are taken, tamed in the net of his mind;
10 The lion on the hill, the wild horse windy-maned,
Resign to him; and his blunt yoke has broken
The sultry shoulders of the mountain bull.

Words also, and thought as rapid as air,
He fashions to his good use; statecraft is his,
15 And his the skill that deflects the arrows of snow,
The spears of winter rain: from every wind
He has made himself secure—from all but one:
In the late wind of death he cannot stand.

O clear intelligence, force beyond all measure!
20 O fate of man, working both good and evil!
When the laws are kept, how proudly his city stands!
When the laws are broken, what of his city then?
Never may the anarchic man find rest at my hearth,
Never be it said that my thoughts are his thoughts. 🄚

Ode: a song chanted by the chorus.

🄙 **GRAMMAR AND STYLE**
Reread line 1 of the ode. Notice how the subject *wonders* comes after, rather than before, the verb *are.* Writers sometimes use **inverted sentences** like this to add variety or emphasis to their writing.

🄚 **READING CLASSICAL DRAMA**
In your chart, summarize the message that this choral **ode** conveys about human beings. How would you relate the ode to the preceding scene?

🄙 **GRAMMAR AND STYLE**
COMMON CORE L 3

Inverted Sentences Ask students what word the inversion emphasizes in line 1.
Possible answer: It emphasizes the word "numberless" by placing it at the beginning of the sentence and making it the first word of the ode. What purpose does this serve?
Possible answer: It reinforces the idea that humans are truly wonderful, as they reign supreme in a world of many wonders.

READING STRATEGY
COMMON CORE
RL 1
RL 10

🄚 *Model the Skill:* **READING CLASSICAL DRAMA**

Model for students how to relate the songs of the chorus to the action of the play. Read Ode 1 aloud. Reread the final verse aloud. Point out line 22, "When the laws are broken, what of his city then?" Have students think about how this line in particular relates to the preceding scene. Then remind students to fill in the chart that they started on page 1067.
Possible answer: The ode conveys the message that human beings can subdue anything except death (lines 17–18). The final verse, in particular, relates to the preceding scene as it asks what happens to cities when laws are broken. The implied "lawbreaker" might refer either to the person who buried Polyneices or to Creon, who is breaking a higher law by leaving Polyneices unburied.

FOR ENGLISH LANGUAGE LEARNERS
Vocabulary Support Define and discuss these descriptive phrases from the first two verses of the ode:

- *Yields to his prows* (line 3), "gives way to (the forward part of) his ships"
- *huge crests bear him* (line 3), "giant waves carry him"
- *Earth . . . graven / With shining furrows where his plows have gone* (lines 4–5), "Earth is carved with bright plowed furrows"

FOR ADVANCED LEARNERS/PRE–AP
Metaphor Ask students to discuss Sophocles' use of metaphor and simile in the ode. Ask them to consider specific examples, such as *the net of his mind* (line 9), *thought as rapid as air* (line 13), *the arrows of snow* (line 15), *the spears of winter rain* (line 16), and *the late wind of death* (line 18). Then ask them to write a brief essay on how these examples of figurative language connect to the theme of the ode in particular and the play in general.

SCENE 2

(Reenter Sentry *leading* Antigone.)

Choragus. What does this mean? Surely this captive woman
Is the princess, Antigone. Why should she be taken?

Sentry. Here is the one who did it! We caught her
In the very act of burying him. Where is Creon?

5 **Choragus.** Just coming from the house.

(Enter Creon, *center.)*

Creon.   What has happened?
Why have you come back so soon?

Sentry (*expansively*).   O King,
A man should never be too sure of anything: **Ⓐ**
I would have sworn
That you'd not see me here again: your anger
10 Frightened me so, and the things you threatened me with;
But how could I tell then
That I'd be able to solve the case so soon?

No dice throwing this time: I was only too glad to come!

Here is this woman. She is the guilty one:
15 We found her trying to bury him.

Take her, then; question her; judge her as you will.
I am through with the whole thing now, and glad of it.

Creon. But this is Antigone! Why have you brought her here?

Sentry. She was burying him, I tell you!

Creon (*severely*).   Is this the truth?

20 **Sentry.** I saw her with my own eyes. Can I say more?

Creon. The details: come, tell me quickly!

Sentry.   It was like this:
After those terrible threats of yours, King,
We went back and brushed the dust away from the body.
The flesh was soft by now, and stinking,
25 So we sat on a hill to windward and kept guard.
No napping this time! We kept each other awake.
But nothing happened until the white round sun
Whirled in the center of the round sky over us:
Then, suddenly,
30 A storm of dust roared up from the earth, and the sky
Went out, the plain vanished with all its trees

Ⓐ **CLASSICAL DRAMA**
Reread line 7, and note the **dramatic irony.** How might the sentry's statement that "a man should never be too sure of anything" apply to Creon?

④ Targeted Passage

Martha Henry as Antigone and Philip Bosco as Creon in the Lincoln Center Repertory 1971 production

---

TEXT ANALYSIS

Ⓐ CLASSICAL DRAMA

Possible answer: *The statement could apply to Creon, who is all too sure that he knows what is best for the state, that he understands the will of the gods, and that his enemies are motivated by money. Also, Creon assumed that the lawbreaker was a man.*

IF STUDENTS NEED HELP . . . Reread Scene 1, lines 20–24, and ask students to describe Creon's attitude about following a course he believes is right. Then reread lines 55–57, and ask them to explain Creon's views on corruption. Finally, reread lines 102–110, and ask them to explain Creon's attitude toward the gods.

DIFFERENTIATED INSTRUCTION

FOR STRUGGLING READERS

④ Targeted Passage [Lines 17–31]

This passage describes the circumstances that preceded Antigone's capture.

- Why is Creon surprised to see Antigone? (lines 1–2)
- What did the sentry do when he returned to Polyneices' body? (lines 22–25)
- What strange things happened during the sentry's watch? (lines 27–34)

FOR RELUCTANT READERS

Connect Point out that Antigone is acting out against a law that she feels is unjust. Write the following discussion questions on the board: *Are there present-day rules or laws that you feel are unjust? What laws would you like to see changed, and why? What are some ways to protest an unjust law?* Have students work in small groups to develop answers to the questions. Then have a class discussion in which the groups share their answers and their reasons.

Get Into the Scene
SUMMARY

The sentry returns to Creon with Antigone. He explains how he caught her burying Polyneices a second time. Confronted, Antigone confesses, defending her actions by citing a higher law. Creon accuses Ismene of complicity, condemns both sisters to death, and has them taken away.

Analyze Visuals

Activity Ask students what emotions the actors in the photograph project. ***Possible answer:*** *Creon appears angry and overbearing, leaning toward Antigone, his fists clenched. Antigone stands her ground, defiant and self-possessed, looking her uncle straight in the eye.*

▪ DRAW CONCLUSIONS

Point out to students that the Greeks would have viewed unnatural events such as the sun whirling in the sky (lines 27–28) and a dust storm darkening everything (lines 30–31) as signs. Ask them what these events might signify. ***Possible answer:*** *They might signify the concern and, possibly, the displeasure of the gods.* What dramatic effects do these events serve? ***Possible answer:*** *They foreshadow the tragic events that lie ahead.*

FOR STRUGGLING READERS

Preview Ask students to listen carefully as you read the summary aloud. Then help them to continue the Sequence Chain that they started at the beginning of the play.

BEST PRACTICES TOOLKIT—Transparency
Sequence Chain p. B21

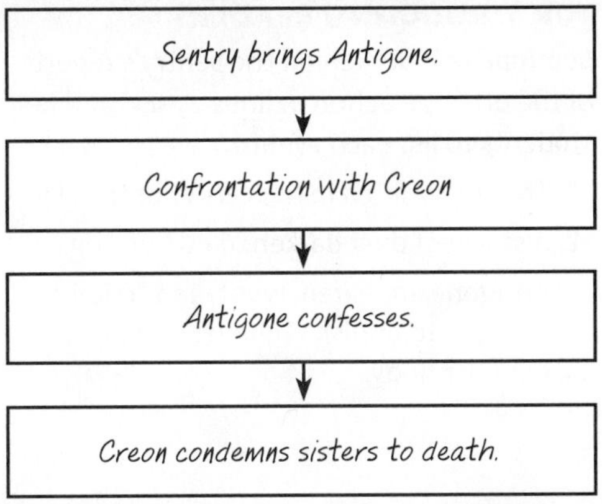

```
┌─────────────────────────────┐
│   Sentry brings Antigone.   │
└─────────────────────────────┘
              ↓
┌─────────────────────────────┐
│  Confrontation with Creon   │
└─────────────────────────────┘
              ↓
┌─────────────────────────────┐
│     Antigone confesses.     │
└─────────────────────────────┘
              ↓
┌─────────────────────────────┐
│ Creon condemns sisters to death. │
└─────────────────────────────┘
```

 Model the Skill: CLASSICAL DRAMA

Reread lines 35–42, and help students paraphrase the metaphor that compares Antigone to a mother bird whose chicks have been stolen. Ask them what emotion this comparison reveals in Antigone. Point out that this emotion creates sympathy for Antigone. Then have them find lines that show Antigone was not afraid (lines 43–44) and that the sentry felt some regret about turning her in (lines 47–48). Point out that the sentry's regret shows that he feels some sympathy for Antigone.

Possible answer: The sentry creates sympathy for Antigone by saying that she wept like a mother bird who has come back to an empty nest, by stating that she was unafraid and denied nothing, and by admitting that he regrets bringing death to "a friend."

TIERED DISCUSSION PROMPTS

Direct students to lines 14–49. Use these prompts to help students understand the sentry's mixed emotions:

Recall How does the sentry feel in Scene 1 when he leaves Creon to find out who had buried Polyneices? *Possible answer: He is terrified of being blamed and punished for the deed.*

Analyze How do the sentry's feelings change in Scene 2? *Possible answer: Having proved his own innocence, the sentry no longer fears punishment. Though he feels relief, he also feels regret about turning over Antigone.*

Evaluate Do you think that the sentry's strongest feelings are for himself or for Antigone? *Possible answer: The sentry's relief for his own safety is greater than his concern for Antigone; his final comment is: "There is nothing so comfortable as your own safe skin" (line 49).*

In the stinging dark. We closed our eyes and endured it.
The whirlwind lasted a long time, but it passed;
And then we looked, and there was Antigone!
35 I have seen
A mother bird come back to a stripped nest, heard
Her crying bitterly a broken note or two
For the young ones stolen. Just so, when this girl
Found the bare corpse, and all her love's work wasted,
40 She wept, and cried on heaven to damn the hands
That had done this thing.
                   And then she brought more dust
And sprinkled wine three times for her brother's ghost.
We ran and took her at once. She was not afraid,
Not even when we charged her with what she had done.
45 She denied nothing.
                 And this was a comfort to me,
And some uneasiness: for it is a good thing
To escape from death, but it is no great pleasure
To bring death to a friend. **B**
                 Yet I always say
There is nothing so comfortable as your own safe skin!
50 **Creon** (*slowly, dangerously*). And you, Antigone,
You with your head hanging—do you confess this thing?
Antigone. I do. I deny nothing.
Creon (*to* Sentry).   You may go.
(*Exit* Sentry.)
(*to* Antigone) Tell me, tell me briefly:
Had you heard my proclamation touching this matter?
55 **Antigone.** It was public. Could I help hearing it?
Creon. And yet you dared defy the law.
Antigone.   I dared.
It was not God's proclamation. That final Justice
That rules the world below makes no such laws.
Your edict, King, was strong,
60 But all your strength is weakness itself against
The immortal unrecorded laws of God.
They are not merely now: they were, and shall be,
Operative forever, beyond man utterly.
I knew I must die, even without your decree:
65 I am only mortal. And if I must die
Now, before it is my time to die,

B CLASSICAL DRAMA
In classical drama, much of the action takes place offstage and is reported by **minor characters**. How does the sentry's speech create sympathy for Antigone?

DIFFERENTIATED INSTRUCTION

FOR STRUGGLING READERS

Summarize Plot Reread the sentry's report of the offstage action in lines 25–45, and help students to list each event.

1. The sun whirled in the center of the sky.

2. A storm of dust darkened everything.

3. Antigone appeared, wept, and "cried on heaven" to punish whoever had uncovered the body.

4. She buried Polyneices again.

5. The sentries apprehended her and charged her.

Surely this is no hardship: can anyone
Living, as I live, with evil all about me,
Think Death less than a friend? This death of mine
70 Is of no importance; but if I had left my brother
Lying in death unburied, I should have suffered.
Now I do not. **C**

      You smile at me. Ah Creon,
Think me a fool, if you like; but it may well be
That a fool convicts me of folly.

75 **Choragus.** Like father, like daughter: both headstrong, deaf to reason!
She has never learned to yield.

Creon.   She has much to learn.
The inflexible heart breaks first, the toughest iron
Cracks first, and the wildest horses bend their necks
At the pull of the smallest curb.

          Pride? In a slave?
80 This girl is guilty of a double **insolence,**
Breaking the given laws and boasting of it.
Who is the man here,
She or I, if this crime goes unpunished? **D**
Sister's child, or more than sister's child,
85 Or closer yet in blood—she and her sister
Win bitter death for this!

      (*to servants*) Go, some of you,
Arrest Ismene. I accuse her equally.
Bring her: you will find her sniffling in the house there.

Her mind's a traitor: crimes kept in the dark
90 Cry for light, and the guardian brain shudders;
But how much worse than this
Is brazen boasting of barefaced anarchy! **E**

Antigone. Creon, what more do you want than my death?

Creon.   Nothing.
That gives me everything.

Antigone.   Then I beg you: kill me.
95 This talking is a great weariness: your words
Are distasteful to me, and I am sure that mine
Seem so to you. And yet they should not seem so:
I should have praise and honor for what I have done.
All these men here would praise me
100 Were their lips not frozen shut with fear of you.
(*bitterly*) Ah the good fortune of kings,
Licensed to say and do whatever they please! **F**

C CHARACTER
Reread lines 57–72. What does
Antigone believe is the supreme law?
What is her attitude toward death?

insolence (ĭn′sə-ləns) *n.* rudeness
and disrespect

D CONFLICT
How does Creon's perception of
Antigone as a threat to his manhood
heighten the **conflict** between them?

COMMON CORE RL 3

E MOTIFS IN DRAMA
A **motif** recurs throughout a play,
advancing the plot and illuminating
the theme. Look back over *Antigone*
so far. How has the **motif** of
treachery versus loyalty affected
the characters and events? Who is
motivated by loyalty and who by
treachery at this point in the play?

F THEME
Reread lines 99–102. What is
Antigone suggesting about the rule
of kings and its effect on citizens?

What is your ultimate
LOYALTY?

Discuss Direct students to lines 110–114. Which statement sums up Creon's outlook and loyalty? Which statement summarizes Antigone's position? *Possible answer: Creon sums up his viewpoint in line 112: "He made war on his country. Eteocles defended it." Antigone summarizes her viewpoint in line 113: "There are honors due all the dead."*

TEXT ANALYSIS

COMMON CORE

RL 2
RL 3

Ⓖ CLASSICAL DRAMA

Possible answer: Antigone asserts that the gods require her to honor the dead (line 113). Creon argues that the wicked do not deserve the same honors as others (line 114). Antigone says that people are not able to judge what the gods consider wicked (line 116). Creon thinks that "An enemy is an enemy, even dead" (line 117). In short, Creon claims the power to understand and interpret those "unrecorded laws of God" (line 61) that Antigone values so highly.

Creon. You are alone here in that opinion.

Antigone. No, they are with me. But they keep their tongues in leash.

105 **Creon.** Maybe. But you are guilty, and they are not.

Antigone. There is no guilt in reverence for the dead.

Creon. But Eteocles—was he not your brother too?

Antigone. My brother too.

Creon.   And you insult his memory?

Antigone (*softly*). The dead man would not say that I insult it.

110 **Creon.** He would: for you honor a traitor as much as him.

Antigone. His own brother, traitor or not, and equal in blood.

Creon. He made war on his country. Eteocles defended it.

Antigone. Nevertheless, there are honors due all the dead.

Creon. But not the same for the wicked as for the just.

115 **Antigone.** Ah Creon, Creon,
Which of us can say what the gods hold wicked? Ⓖ

Ⓖ **CLASSICAL DRAMA**
Greek **tragedy** explores humans' relationship to the gods. How does Antigone's thinking about the gods differ from Creon's thinking?

1084   UNIT 10: GREEK TRAGEDY AND MEDIEVAL ROMANCE

DIFFERENTIATED INSTRUCTION

FOR ADVANCED LEARNERS/PRE–AP

Analyze [small-group option] Have students discuss Antigone's statement "It is my nature to join in love, not hate" (line 118). In their discussion, have them consider the message about love that Sophocles is developing. Remind them also to keep in mind how Oedipus' illicit love flows beneath the surface of the play.

Creon. An enemy is an enemy, even dead.

Antigone. It is my nature to join in love, not hate.

Creon (*finally losing patience*). Go join them, then; if you must have your love,
120 Find it in hell!

Choragus. But see, Ismene comes:

(*Enter* Ismene, *guarded.*)

Those tears are sisterly; the cloud
That shadows her eyes rains down gentle sorrow.

Creon. You too, Ismene,
125 Snake in my ordered house, sucking my blood
Stealthily—and all the time I never knew
That these two sisters were aiming at my throne!

Ismene,
Do you confess your share in this crime or deny it?
Answer me.

130 **Ismene.** Yes, if she will let me say so. I am guilty.

COMMON CORE RL 4

Language Coach

Roots and Affixes An affix at the end of a word is a **suffix**. The suffix *-ly* can form either an adjective (modifying a noun) or an adverb (modifying a verb, adjective, or other adverb). Find both uses of *-ly* in lines 121–127.

⑤ **Targeted Passage**

Martha Henry as Antigone and Philip Bosco as Creon in the Lincoln Center Repertory 1971 production

FOR STRUGGLING READERS

⑤ **Targeted Passage** [Lines 117–130]

This passage illustrates the escalating conflict that is quickly moving events toward a tragic climax.

- What does Creon accuse the sisters of? (line 127)

- How does Ismene respond to his accusation? (line 130)

- How has Ismene changed since the beginning of the play? (lines 133–134)

FOR ENGLISH LANGUAGE LEARNERS

Language Coach   COMMON CORE
RL 4
Roots and Affixes
Answer: *In line 122, -ly makes an adjective from* sister. Context can help determine parts of speech. Read the following lines to students: Scene 1, lines 76–78; Scene 2, lines 124–127; Scene 3, lines 90–91; Scene 4, lines 29–30. Have students point out words with the affix *-ly*, and identify correct parts of speech for each word.

Antigone (*coldly*). No, Ismene. You have no right to say so.
You would not help me, and I will not have you help me.

Ismene. But now I know what you meant; and I am here
To join you, to take my share of punishment.

135 **Antigone.** The dead man and the gods who rule the dead
Know whose act this was. Words are not friends.

Ismene. Do you refuse me, Antigone? I want to die with you:
I too have a duty that I must discharge to the dead.

Antigone. You shall not lessen my death by sharing it.

140 **Ismene.** What do I care for life when you are dead?

Antigone. Ask Creon. You're always hanging on his opinions.

Ismene. You are laughing at me. Why, Antigone?

Antigone. It's a joyless laughter, Ismene.

Ismene.   But can I do nothing?

Antigone. Yes. Save yourself. I shall not envy you.

145 There are those who will praise you; I shall have honor, too.

Ismene. But we are equally guilty!

Antigone.   No, more, Ismene.
You are alive, but I belong to Death.

Creon (*to the* Chorus). Gentlemen, I beg you to observe these girls:
One has just now lost her mind; the other,

150 It seems, has never had a mind at all.

Ismene. Grief teaches the steadiest minds to waver, King.

Creon. Yours certainly did, when you assumed guilt with the guilty!

Ismene. But how could I go on living without her?

Creon.   You are.
She is already dead.

Ismene.   But your own son's bride!

155 **Creon.** There are places enough for him to push his plow.
I want no wicked women for my sons!

Ismene. O dearest Haemon, how your father wrongs you! ❶

Creon. I've had enough of your childish talk of marriage!

Choragus. Do you really intend to steal this girl from your son?

160 **Creon.** No; Death will do that for me.

Choragus.   Then she must die?

Creon. You dazzle me.

                        —But enough of this talk!

1086   UNIT 10: GREEK TRAGEDY AND MEDIEVAL ROMANCE

Ⓗ CHARACTER
What does Antigone's treatment of her sister reveal about her character?

❶ CONFLICT
Ismene reveals that Antigone is engaged to Creon's son Haemon. What new issues could arise from the conflict between Antigone and Creon?

TEXT ANALYSIS: *Review*   COMMON CORE   RL 3

Ⓗ CHARACTER

Possible answer: *Antigone refuses to let Ismene share her guilt, because Ismene did not join her from the start. She reveals herself to be, like Creon, unbending, stubborn, and self-righteous.*

TEXT ANALYSIS: *Review*   COMMON CORE   RL 3

❶ CONFLICT

Possible answer: *Haemon could side with his father, provoking Antigone by his disloyalty; he could try to stop Creon; or he could resent Creon for hurting the woman he loves.*

Extend the Discussion Encourage students to predict which scenario is most likely. Ask them to support their opinions with evidence.

DIFFERENTIATED INSTRUCTION

FOR STRUGGLING READERS

Personification Remind students that, in personification, human qualities are given to objects, animals, or ideas. Point out that Antigone and Creon both personify death during their exchange (Antigone: line 147; Creon: lines 160, 164). Explain that these personifications reinforce the idea that tragedy and death are near.

Ask students what traits each character attributes to death. ***Possible answer:*** *Antigone says that she belongs to death, suggesting that death is like a spouse, a friend, or a kind master. By contrast, Creon says that death is a thief who will "steal" Antigone from his son (line 160), as well as a frightening antagonist (lines 163–164).*

(*to guards*) You, there, take them away and guard them well:
For they are but women, and even brave men run
When they see Death coming.

(*Exeunt* Ismene, Antigone, *and guards.*)

ODE 2

Chorus. Fortunate is the man who has never tasted God's vengeance!
Where once the anger of heaven has struck, that house is shaken
Forever: damnation rises behind each child
Like a wave cresting out of the black northeast,
5 When the long darkness under sea roars up
And bursts drumming death upon the wind-whipped sand.

I have seen this gathering sorrow from time long past
Loom upon Oedipus' children: generation from generation
Takes the compulsive rage of the enemy god.
10 So lately this last flower of Oedipus' line
Drank the sunlight! but now a passionate word
And a handful of dust have closed up all its beauty. **J**

What mortal arrogance
Transcends the wrath of Zeus?
15 Sleep cannot lull him, nor the effortless long months
Of the timeless gods: but he is young forever,
And his house is the shining day of high Olympus.
  All that is and shall be,
  And all the past, is his.
20 No pride on earth is free of the curse of heaven.

The straying dreams of men
May bring them ghosts of joy:
But as they drowse, the waking embers burn them;
Or they walk with fixed eyes, as blind men walk.
25 But the ancient wisdom speaks for our own time:
  Fate works most for woe
  With Folly's fairest show.
Man's little pleasure is the spring of sorrow. **K**

J READING CLASSICAL DRAMA
Judging from this choral **ode,** how do the gods feel toward the family of Oedipus? Make notes in your chart.

K READING CLASSICAL DRAMA
Explain the last three lines of the **ode.** Whom do you think these lines apply to?

FOR ENGLISH LANGUAGE LEARNERS
Vocabulary Support Define and discuss these similes and metaphors from the ode:

- *damnation rises behind each child like a wave* (lines 3–4), "tragedy follows the children of Oedipus"

- *So lately this last flower of Oedipus' line / Drank the sunlight!* (lines 10–11), "Oedipus' daughters were alive and beautiful"

- *Or they walk with fixed eyes, as blind men walk* (line 24), "they are not aware of the truth"

Possible answer: *The gods are angry with the house of Oedipus and have punished each generation with the "compulsive rage of the enemy god" (line 9). Antigone and Ismene are the last of the doomed line.*

READING STRATEGY COMMON CORE

RL 1
RL 10

K **READING CLASSICAL DRAMA**

Possible answer: *The last three lines of the ode suggest that just when things appear to be going well for someone, circumstances may suddenly change and bring sorrow. Students might apply this perception to King Creon: although he appears the victor in his conflict with Antigone, it may yet lead to grief.*

IF STUDENTS NEED HELP . . . Make sure that they understand these words: *fate,* "destiny or fortune"; *woe,* "misery"; *folly,* "foolishness"; *spring,* "source."

TIERED DISCUSSION PROMPTS

Direct students to lines 1–28. Use these prompts to help students understand how the ode expands on the subject of death:

Recall What punishment has Creon just ordered for Antigone and Ismene? ***Possible answer:*** *He has promised to have them killed.*

Analyze How does the sea imagery in the first verse of the ode underscore the idea that Antigone and Ismene are doomed? ***Possible answer:*** *The image of an enormous, unstoppable wave "cresting out of the black northeast" (line 4) reinforces the feeling that the sisters cannot escape death, which is closely following them.*

Synthesize The first half of the poem refers to the house of Oedipus, the second half to the house of Creon. What does the poem suggest about how the two houses are linked? ***Possible answer:*** *The ode suggests that the two houses have both drawn the vengeance and rage of the gods upon them through pride and arrogance.*

SCENE 3

Choragus. But here is Haemon, King, the last of all your sons.
Is it grief for Antigone that brings him here,
And bitterness at being robbed of his bride?

(*Enter* Haemon.)

Creon. We shall soon see, and no need of diviners.

                                                 —Son,

5 You have heard my final judgment on that girl:
Have you come here hating me, or have you come
With deference and with love, whatever I do?

Haemon. I am your son, Father. You are my guide.
You make things clear for me, and I obey you.
10 No marriage means more to me than your continuing wisdom.

Creon. Good. That is the way to behave: subordinate
Everything else, my son, to your father's will.
This is what a man prays for, that he may get
Sons attentive and dutiful in his house,
15 Each one hating his father's enemies,
Honoring his father's friends. But if his sons
Fail him, if they turn out unprofitably,
What has he fathered but trouble for himself
And amusement for the malicious? **A**

                                  So you are right

20 Not to lose your head over this woman.
Your pleasure with her would soon grow cold, Haemon,
And then you'd have a hellcat in bed and elsewhere.
Let her find her husband in hell!
Of all the people in this city, only she
25 Has had contempt for my law and broken it.

Do you want me to show myself weak before the people?
Or to break my sworn word? No, and I will not.
The woman dies.

I suppose she'll plead "family ties." Well, let her.
30 If I permit my own family to rebel,
How shall I earn the world's obedience?
Show me the man who keeps his house in hand,
He's fit for public authority.

                             I'll have no dealings
With lawbreakers, critics of the government:
35 Whoever is chosen to govern should be obeyed—
Must be obeyed, in all things, great and small,

4 diviners (dĭ-vī′nərz): those who predict the future.

A THEME
Reread lines 11–19. What is Creon's view of family relationships?

Language Coach

Oral Fluency Many words can be either nouns or verbs. In some cases, as in *permit*, the noun's stress is on the first syllable, while the verb's stress is on the second. Reread line 30. Choose the correct pronunciation for the two verbs in the line.

G Targeted Passage

Philip Bosco as Creon in the Lincoln Center Repertory 1971 production

---

TEXT ANALYSIS: *Review*

COMMON CORE
RL 2

A THEME

Possible answer: Creon voices strong patriarchal views of family: sons should obey their fathers absolutely (lines 11–12), hate their fathers' enemies (line 15), and honor their fathers' friends (line 16).

DIFFERENTIATED INSTRUCTION

FOR STRUGGLING READERS

G **Targeted Passage [Lines 20–36]**

This passage illustrates Creon's determination to stick by his decree.

- What reassurance does Creon offer Haemon for the loss of Antigone? (lines 19–22)

- Why does Creon fear breaking his word? (line 27)

- Why does Creon decide to ignore family ties? (lines 30–33)

FOR ENGLISH LANGUAGE LEARNERS

Vocabulary Support Creon's belief that a son must subordinate himself to his father (lines 11–19) is linked with his authoritarian view of kingship (lines 20–44). Make sure students understand that *subordinate* means "to be submissive or obedient." Then teach these interrelated words from Creon's monologue.

- *attentive* (line 14), "considerate, thoughtful"

- *dutiful* (line 14), "obedient"

- *authority* (line 33), "power"

Language Coach

Oral Fluency *Answer:* /per mit′/; /re bel′/ Have students work in pairs to practice using the two forms of the words. Then have students write sentences of dialogue in which they use each form of *permit* and *rebel* once. Have students practice saying their sentences aloud. Monitor students for correct pronunciations. Invite student volunteers to share the examples with the class.

Get Into the Scene
SUMMARY

Haemon, who is engaged to Antigone, first flatters his father. Then he supports Antigone's position and suggests she has widespread sympathy. Finally, he threatens that Antigone's death will lead to others (Haemon's). Yet Creon remains unmoved.

Analyze Visuals

Activity Ask students what they learn about the relationship between Creon and Haemon from the actors' expressions, gestures, posture, and positions in the photograph. *Possible answer: Creon has his back to Haemon, his hands on his hips, and a disdainful, haughty expression; Haemon approaches his father like a supplicant, his eyes downcast, his hands stretched out in a gesture of appeal. The staging suggests that Creon is as domineering and unyielding with his son as he has been with his subjects and nieces.*

REVISIT THE BIG QUESTION

What is your ultimate
LOYALTY?

Discuss Based on lines 11–36, to whom, according to Creon, does Haemon owe his loyalty? Is this view in keeping with Creon's view of the public's duty? Explain. *Possible answer: According to Creon, Haemon owes his loyalty to his father, Creon, the head of the household, just as the public owes its duty to the king, the head of government.*

READING SKILL: *Review*

☐ DRAW CONCLUSIONS

How does Creon's perception of his position in his family and in the government heighten his conflict with Antigone? *Possible answer: Creon believes in his supreme authority as head of his household and government. Thus, Antigone's actions, in his view, represent a rebellion against him in both capacities. This viewpoint heightens the conflict, putting Creon into a double bind: he must punish Antigone for disobeying him as head of household and as head of government.*

FOR STRUGGLING READERS

Preview Ask students to listen carefully as you read the summary aloud. Then help them to continue the Sequence Chain that they started at the beginning of the play.

🧰 BEST PRACTICES TOOLKIT—Transparency
Sequence Chain p. B21

Haemon tries to flatter his father.
↓
Haemon argues with Creon.
↓
Haemon threatens to kill himself.

B THEME

Possible answer: *Creon believes that "who-ever is chosen to govern should be obeyed" completely (line 35), and those who know how to obey will be steadfast in the face of trouble (lines 40–41). He also believes that anarchy is the greatest evil, destroying governments and cities.*

C CONFLICT

Possible answer: *Creon believes that men should be stronger than women and that it would be shameful to allow Antigone to influence him and Haemon. This opinion heightens the conflict by linking his need to "be the man" with his unwillingness to be influenced by Antigone's argument.*

D THEME

Possible answer: *Haemon believes that leaders should be open to the opinions of others. A king cannot know everything the people think and should be wary of being told only what he wants to hear.*

Just and unjust! O Haemon,
The man who knows how to obey, and that man only,
Knows how to give commands when the time comes.
40 You can depend on him, no matter how fast
The spears come: he's a good soldier; he'll stick it out.

Anarchy, anarchy! Show me a greater evil!
This is why cities tumble and the great houses rain down;
This is what scatters armies! **B**
45 No, no: good lives are made so by discipline.
We keep the laws then, and the lawmakers,
And no woman shall seduce us. If we must lose,
Let's lose to a man, at least! Is a woman stronger than we? **C**

Choragus. Unless time has rusted my wits,
50 What you say, King, is said with point and dignity.

Haemon (*boyishly earnest*). Father:
Reason is God's crowning gift to man, and you are right
To warn me against losing mine. I cannot say—
I hope that I shall never want to say!—that you
55 Have reasoned badly. Yet there are other men
Who can reason, too; and their opinions might be helpful.
You are not in a position to know everything
That people say or do, or what they feel:
Your temper terrifies them—everyone
60 Will tell you only what you like to hear. **D**
But I, at any rate, can listen; and I have heard them
Muttering and whispering in the dark about this girl.
They say no woman has ever, so unreasonably,
Died so shameful a death for a generous act:
65 "She covered her brother's body. Is this indecent?
She kept him from dogs and vultures. Is this a crime?
Death? She should have all the honor that we can give her!"

This is the way they talk out there in the city.

You must believe me:
70 Nothing is closer to me than your happiness.
What could be closer? Must not any son
Value his father's fortune as his father does his?
I beg you, do not be unchangeable:
Do not believe that you alone can be right.
75 The man who thinks that,

B THEME
Reread lines 35–44. What are Creon's views about government and his role as king?

C CONFLICT
How does Creon's perception of women contribute to his conflict with Antigone?

7 Targeted Passage

D THEME
Reread lines 55–60. How do Haemon's views of government differ from Creon's?

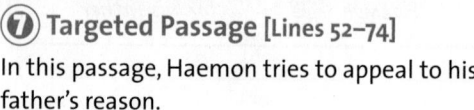

DIFFERENTIATED INSTRUCTION

FOR STRUGGLING READERS

7 Targeted Passage [Lines 52–74]

In this passage, Haemon tries to appeal to his father's reason.

- Which words show that Haemon is trying to coax his father gently? (lines 51–56)

- What does Haemon tell Creon people are saying about Antigone's actions and his punishment? (lines 61–68)

- What does Haemon say about his feelings for Creon? (lines 70–72)

FOR ENGLISH LANGUAGE LEARNERS

Vocabulary Support Point out these expressions and idioms: *stick it out* (line 41), "persevere, manage"; *in a position* (line 57), "in circumstances, in a situation"; *at any rate* (line 61), "at least"; *to go astray* (line 90), "to do something wrong, make mistakes"; *What does my age matter?* (line 98), "What difference does my age make?"; *Not at all* (line 100), "No!"; *to a man* (line 102), "all the people"; *sold out to* (line 108), "been corrupted by."

The man who maintains that only he has the power
To reason correctly, the gift to speak, the soul—
A man like that, when you know him, turns out empty.

It is not reason never to yield to reason!

80 In flood time you can see how some trees bend,
And because they bend, even their twigs are safe,
While stubborn trees are torn up, roots and all.
And the same thing happens in sailing:
Make your sheet fast, never slacken—and over you go,

85 Head over heels and under: and there's your voyage. **E**
Forget you are angry! Let yourself be moved!
I know I am young; but please let me say this:
The ideal condition
Would be, I admit, that men should be right by instinct;

90 But since we are all too likely to go astray,
The reasonable thing is to learn from those who can teach.

Choragus. You will do well to listen to him, King,
If what he says is sensible. And you, Haemon,
Must listen to your father. Both speak well. **F**

95 **Creon.** You consider it right for a man of my years and experience
To go to school to a boy?

Haemon. It is not right
If I am wrong. But if I am young, and right,
What does my age matter?

Creon. You think it right to stand up for an anarchist?

100 **Haemon.** Not at all. I pay no respect to criminals.

Creon. Then she is not a criminal?

Haemon. The city would deny it, to a man.

Creon. And the city proposes to teach me how to rule?

Haemon. Ah. Who is it that's talking like a boy now?

105 **Creon.** My voice is the one voice giving orders in this city!

Haemon. It is no city if it takes orders from one voice.

Creon. The state is the king!

Haemon. Yes, if the state is a desert. **G**

(*pause*)

Creon. This boy, it seems, has sold out to a woman.

Haemon. If you are a woman: my concern is only for you.

110 **Creon.** So? Your "concern"! In a public brawl with your father!

E THEME
Compare Haemon's words to Creon with Creon's words in Scene 2, beginning "The inflexible heart breaks first . . ." (line 77, page 1083). What do both speeches suggest about inflexibility?

F CLASSICAL DRAMA
How does the **choragus** respond to Creon's and Haemon's arguments? How similar is your response?

G THEME
Interpret Haemon's reply.

ANTIGONE **1091**

ANTIGONE **1091**

H CLASSICAL DRAMA

Possible answer: Haemon may be suggesting that he will kill himself. Creon, however, thinks that Haemon is threatening him.

TIERED DISCUSSION PROMPTS

Direct students to lines 111–134. Use these prompts to help students understand how Haemon's confrontation only exacerbates Creon's outrage and accelerates the tragic momentum:

Connect Think of a situation in which somebody intercedes on behalf of a friend who is being punished unfairly. Why might this intervention make things worse? *Possible answer: The person who is confronted might feel as though the interceding person is being intrusive, or might realize the unfairness of his or her actions but be too embarrassed to back down.*

Analyze How does the tone of the dialogue between Creon and Haemon change from the beginning to the end of the scene? *Possible answer: The tone becomes increasingly angry and more threatening. Creon becomes condescending, calling his son an "adolescent fool" (line 114). Haemon gets quietly angry, trying to speak respectfully but making it clear that his father has lost his respect.*

Evaluate Do you think that there is anything that Haemon could say or do to change Creon's mind about Antigone? Why or why not? *Possible answer: No, Creon is inflexible, certain that he is right, and determined to punish Antigone.*

Haemon. How about you, in a public brawl with justice?

Creon. With justice, when all that I do is within my rights?

Haemon. You have no right to trample on God's right.

Creon (*completely out of control*). Fool, adolescent fool! Taken in by a woman!

115 **Haemon.** You'll never see me taken in by anything vile.

Creon. Every word you say is for her!

Haemon (*quietly, darkly*).   And for you.
And for me. And for the gods under the earth.

Creon. You'll never marry her while she lives.

Haemon. Then she must die. But her death will cause another.

120 **Creon.** Another?
Have you lost your senses? Is this an open threat? H

Haemon. There is no threat in speaking to emptiness.

Creon. I swear you'll regret this superior tone of yours!
You are the empty one!

Haemon.   If you were not my father,

125 I'd say you were **perverse.**

Creon. You girl-struck fool, don't play at words with me!

Haemon. I am sorry. You prefer silence.

Creon.   Now, by God—!
I swear, by all the gods in heaven above us,
You'll watch it; I swear you shall!
       (*to the servants*) Bring her out!

130 Bring the woman out! Let her die before his eyes,
Here, this instant, with her bridegroom beside her!

Haemon. Not here, no; she will not die here, King.
And you will never see my face again.
Go on raving as long as you've a friend to endure you.

(*Exit* Haemon.)

135 **Choragus.** Gone, gone.
Creon, a young man in a rage is dangerous!

Creon. Let him do, or dream to do, more than a man can.
He shall not save these girls from death.

Choragus.   These girls?
You have sentenced them both?

Creon.   No, you are right.

140 I will not kill the one whose hands are clean.

H CLASSICAL DRAMA

Note the **dramatic irony.** What might Haemon mean? What does Creon think he means?

perverse (pər-vûrs') *adj.* willfully determined to go against what is expected or desired

---

OWN THE WORD

perverse: Have students create a semantic map for the word *perverse*. Write the word and its definition in a center circle. Draw spider legs out from the center circle, and have students add synonyms for this definition to complete the map. *Possible answers: contrary, difficult, ornery, bullheaded, headstrong, obstinate*

DIFFERENTIATED INSTRUCTION

FOR STRUGGLING READERS

Summarize Plot Help students use a Two-Column Chart to summarize the strategies and arguments that Haemon uses to try to change Creon's mind, as well as Creon's responses.

 BEST PRACTICES TOOLKIT—Transparency
Two-Column Chart p. A25

Haemon's Strategies	Creon's Responses
flatters Creon (lines 8–9)	lectures Haemon (lines 11–48)
begs Creon to be flexible (lines 73–92)	gets angry (lines 95–96)
gets angry; says people do not agree with Creon (line 102)	gets angrier; says he is the state (line 107)
restates Antigone's argument (line 113)	resorts to insults (line 114)
threatens Creon (line 119)	bullies Haemon (lines 121, 123–124)

Choragus. But Antigone?

Creon (*somberly*).   I will carry her far away,
Out there in the wilderness, and lock her
Living in a vault of stone. She shall have food,
As the custom is, to absolve the state of her death.
145 And there let her pray to the gods of hell:
They are her only gods:
Perhaps they will show her an escape from death,
Or she may learn,
                though late,
That piety shown the dead is pity in vain.

(*Exit* Creon.)

ODE 3

> **Chorus.** Love, unconquerable 🄹
> Waster of rich men, keeper
> Of warm lights and all-night vigil
> In the soft face of a girl:
> 5 Sea wanderer, forest visitor!
> Even the pure immortals cannot escape you,
> And mortal man, in his one day's dusk,
> Trembles before your glory.
>
> Surely you swerve upon ruin
> 10 The just man's consenting heart,
> As here you have made bright anger
> Strike between father and son—
> And none has conquered but Love!
> A girl's glance working the will of heaven:
> 15 Pleasure to her alone who mocks us,
> Merciless Aphrodite.

🄸 **CHARACTER**
What do you make of Creon's decision to bury a person alive when he has refused to bury a person who is dead?

🄹 **READING CLASSICAL DRAMA**
In your chart, summarize the message about love expressed in this **ode.** How does the ode relate to the exchange between Creon and Haemon?

⑧ **Targeted Passage**

16 Aphrodite (ăf'rə-dī'tē): the goddess of love and beauty.

TEXT ANALYSIS: *Review*   COMMON CORE   RL 3

🄸 **CHARACTER**

Possible answer: *Students may say that Creon is being unnecessarily cruel and assigning himself the power of the gods; his decision shows the depth of his anger and self-righteousness.*

READING STRATEGY   COMMON CORE   RL 1   RL 10

🄹 **READING CLASSICAL DRAMA**

Possible answer: *The ode expresses the message that love is more powerful than human beings and can ruin them. The ode mentions the anger between Haemon and Creon, attributing it to Haemon's love for Antigone (lines 9–13). Neither Haemon nor Creon wins this battle; instead, Love conquers them both and works the will of the gods.*

FOR STRUGGLING READERS

⑧ **Targeted Passage** [Lines 1–16]

Remind students that personification is a type of figurative language in which human qualities are assigned to an object, an animal, or an idea. In the ode, love is personified as a conqueror and destroyer.

- According to the first verse, whom does Love conquer and destroy? (lines 6–8)

- According to the second verse, what does Love do to a just man? (lines 9–13)

- According to the second verse, who gets pleasure from the work of Love? (line 16)

What is your ultimate
LOYALTY?

Discuss In lines 11–14 and 33–36, how does the chorus view Antigone's punishment for her act of conscience and loyalty? *Possible answer: The chorus says that her punishment comes with praise and honor (lines 11–12), though they suggest fate may have played a part (lines 35–36).*

TEXT ANALYSIS

COMMON CORE
RL 6

Ⓐ **WORLD LITERATURE**

Read lines 28–30 aloud. Point out to students that this is an example of personification because Antigone gives human qualities to the sacred places. She talks to them as if they can hear her and as though they can see her and think about her.

Possible answer: Antigone's call to the sacred places shows the importance of these natural places to the Greeks, as she calls upon them when she is about to be executed to bear witness to her unjust execution.

🌸 SCENE 4

Choragus (*as Antigone enters, guarded*). But I can no longer stand
in awe of this,
Nor, seeing what I see, keep back my tears.
Here is Antigone, passing to that chamber
Where all find sleep at last.

5 **Antigone.** Look upon me, friends, and pity me
Turning back at the night's edge to say
Good-bye to the sun that shines for me no longer;
Now sleepy Death
Summons me down to Acheron, that cold shore:
10 There is no bride song there, nor any music.

Chorus. Yet not unpraised, not without a kind of honor,
You walk at last into the underworld;
Untouched by sickness, broken by no sword.
What woman has ever found your way to death?

15 **Antigone.** How often I have heard the story of Niobe,
Tantalus' wretched daughter, how the stone
Clung fast about her, ivy-close: and they say
The rain falls endlessly
And sifting soft snow; her tears are never done.
20 I feel the loneliness of her death in mine.

Chorus. But she was born of heaven, and you
Are woman, woman-born. If her death is yours,
A mortal woman's, is this not for you
Glory in our world and in the world beyond?

25 **Antigone.** You laugh at me. Ah, friends, friends,
Can you not wait until I am dead? O Thebes,
O men many-charioted, in love with Fortune,
Dear springs of Dirce, sacred Theban grove,
Be witnesses for me, denied all pity,
30 Unjustly judged! and think a word of love
For her whose path turns
Under dark earth, where there are no more tears. Ⓐ

Chorus. You have passed beyond human daring and come at last
Into a place of stone where Justice sits.
35 I cannot tell
What shape of your father's guilt appears in this.

Antigone. You have touched it at last: that bridal bed
Unspeakable, horror of son and mother mingling:
Their crime, infection of all our family!
40 O Oedipus, father and brother!
Your marriage strikes from the grave to murder mine.

9 Acheron (ăk'ə-rŏn'): in Greek mythology, one of the rivers bordering the underworld, the place inhabited by the souls of the dead.

15–20 Niobe (nī'ə-bē) was a queen of Thebes whose children were killed by the gods because she had boasted that she was greater than a goddess. After their deaths, she was turned to stone but continued to shed tears.

COMMON CORE RL 6

Ⓐ **WORLD LITERATURE**
Antigone's **figurative language**, or language that conveys more than its literal meaning, in this passage reflects the historical and cultural setting of the play. The ancient Greeks had a deep reverence for sacred places, which were sometimes groves of trees or springs. Reread lines 25–32. Why does Antigone call upon these sacred places? What do her words tell you about ancient Greek culture?

Martha Henry as Antigone in the Lincoln Center Repertory 1971 production

1094 UNIT 10: GREEK TRAGEDY AND MEDIEVAL ROMANCE

DIFFERENTIATED INSTRUCTION

FOR STRUGGLING READERS
Allusion and Personification Make sure students understand the allusions to Greek mythology in the opening lines of Scene 4: Acheron (line 9), Niobe (lines 15–20), Dirce (line 28), and Oedipus (line 40). Point out that these references all link Antigone to doomed figures. The personification of Death (line 8), Fortune (line 27), and Justice (line 34) reinforces this sense of doom.

Develop Reading Fluency Help students to understand the effect of the Chorus. Read Ode 3 aloud to students. Then reread the Ode with the class as a choral reading. Ask students what they notice about how the two readings differ.

Distribute the copy masters and have students work in pairs or groups to practice fluency.

 RESOURCE MANAGER—Copy Master Reading Fluency p. 31

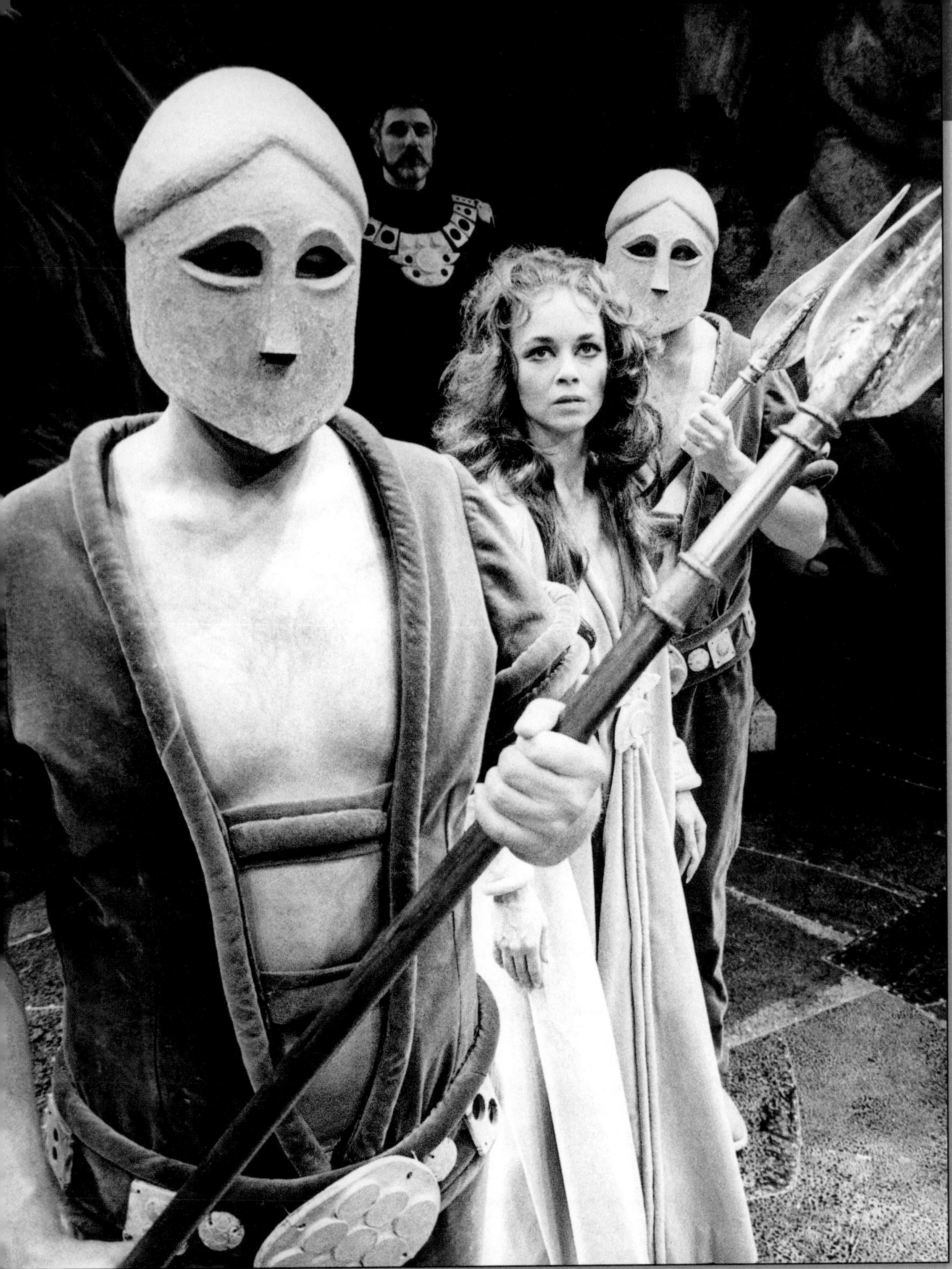

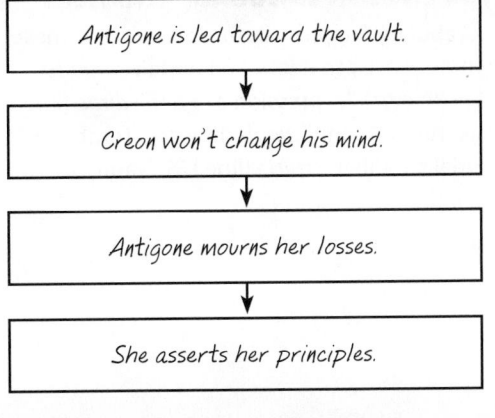

Get Into the Scene

SUMMARY

As Antigone is led toward the vault, she bemoans the absence of pity and justice and mourns the life she is losing. When Creon remains impassive and unyielding, Antigone again asserts the correctness of her principles.

Analyze Visuals

Activity Ask students to evaluate how well this photograph conveys Antigone's predicament. ***Possible answer:*** *Standing between the two nameless, faceless guards who lead her to her doom, Antigone looks small and vulnerable. Creon, meanwhile, stands behind them, aloof, arrogant, and unyielding as his niece is led away.*

READING STRATEGY: ***Review***

PREDICT

Ask students to predict how the rest of the play will unfold. ***Possible answer:*** *Antigone will die, Haemon will kill himself or his father, and Ismene will die from grief.*

FOR STRUGGLING READERS

Preview Ask students to listen carefully as you read the summary aloud. Then help them to continue the Sequence Chain that they started at the beginning of the play.

BEST PRACTICES TOOLKIT—Transparency Sequence Chain p. B21

Antigone is led toward the vault.
↓
Creon won't change his mind.
↓
Antigone mourns her losses.
↓
She asserts her principles.

B CLASSICAL DRAMA

Possible answer: *The chorus says that Antigone has brought on her own death through her conscious choice to break the law.*

C CLASSICAL DRAMA

Some students may feel that Antigone faces death with courage, still insisting on the justness of her actions. Like a tragic hero, she is dignified, with a tragic flaw— "the blasphemy of [her] birth" (line 44).

TIERED DISCUSSION PROMPTS

Direct students to lines 53–74. Use these prompts to help students understand that Creon's rage has dulled his reason and compassion:

Connect Have you or anyone you know ever gotten so angry that you had a hard time thinking clearly? What was it like? *Students may recall various incidents.*

Analyze How would you describe Creon's rage? *Possible answer: He is so angry that he has no pity for Antigone, no sympathy for his son, and no comprehension of what he himself stands to lose.*

Evaluate Antigone says that Creon's voice is "like the voice of death" (line 73). Do you think her description is a good characterization of Creon's words and actions? *Possible answer: Creon, like death, is unyielding, unforgiving, and without compassion.*

OWN THE WORD

lamentation: Remind students that *lamentation* means "an expression of grief." The verb form is *lament.* Have students give examples of situations in which they might *lament.* *Possible answer: death of loved one; loss of a significant opportunity*

I have been a stranger here in my own land:
All my life
The blasphemy of my birth has followed me.

45 **Chorus.** Reverence is a virtue, but strength
Lives in established law: that must prevail.
You have made your choice;
Your death is the doing of your conscious hand. **B**

Antigone. Then let me go, since all your words are bitter,
50 And the very light of the sun is cold to me.
Lead me to my vigil, where I must have
Neither love nor **lamentation**; no song, but silence.

(Creon *interrupts impatiently.*)

Creon. If dirges and planned lamentations could put off death,
Men would be singing forever.

(*to the servants*) Take her, go!
55 You know your orders: take her to the vault
And leave her alone there. And if she lives or dies,
That's her affair, not ours: our hands are clean.

Antigone. O tomb, vaulted bride-bed in eternal rock,
Soon I shall be with my own again
60 Where Persephone welcomes the thin ghosts underground:
And I shall see my father again, and you, Mother,
And dearest Polyneices—

dearest indeed
To me, since it was my hand
That washed him clean and poured the ritual wine:
65 And my reward is death before my time!

And yet, as men's hearts know, I have done no wrong;
I have not sinned before God. Or if I have,
I shall know the truth in death. But if the guilt
Lies upon Creon who judged me, then, I pray,
70 May his punishment equal my own. **C**

Choragus. O passionate heart,
Unyielding, tormented still by the same winds!

Creon. Her guards shall have good cause to regret their delaying.

Antigone. Ah! That voice is like the voice of death!

Creon. I can give you no reason to think you are mistaken.

75 **Antigone.** Thebes, and you my fathers' gods,
And rulers of Thebes, you see me now, the last
Unhappy daughter of a line of kings,
Your kings, led away to death. You will remember
What things I suffer, and at what men's hands,

44 blasphemy of my birth: Antigone is referring to her father's marriage to his own mother, an incestuous relationship that resulted in her birth. This type of relationship was considered a sin against the gods.

B CLASSICAL DRAMA
Reread lines 45–48. To what does the **chorus** attribute Antigone's **tragic** downfall?

lamentation (lăm'ən-tā'shən) *n.* an expression of grief

60 Persephone (pər-sĕf'ə-nē): wife of Hades (hā'dēz) and queen of the underworld.

C CLASSICAL DRAMA
How do you judge the way Antigone accepts her death? Consider whether she shows qualities of a **tragic hero.**

DIFFERENTIATED INSTRUCTION

FOR ENGLISH LANGUAGE LEARNERS

Vocabulary Support Define and discuss these words related to death and burial: *lamentation* (line 52), "expression of grief"; *dirge* (line 53), "funeral song"; *vault* (line 55), "tomb; burial chamber"; *tomb* (line 58), "vault, burial chamber."

80 Because I would not **transgress** the laws of heaven.
(*to the guards, simply*) Come: let us wait no longer. **D**
(*Exit* Antigone, *left, guarded.*)

ODE 4

Chorus. All Danae's beauty was locked away
In a brazen cell where the sunlight could not come:
A small room, still as any grave, enclosed her.
Yet she was a princess too,
5 And Zeus in a rain of gold poured love upon her.
O child, child,
No power in wealth or war
Or tough sea-blackened ships
Can prevail against untiring Destiny!

10 And Dryas' son also, that furious king,
Bore the god's prisoning anger for his pride:
Sealed up by Dionysus in deaf stone,
His madness died among echoes.
So at the last he learned what dreadful power
15 His tongue had mocked:
For he had profaned the revels
And fired the wrath of the nine
Implacable sisters that love the sound of the flute.

And old men tell a half-remembered tale
20 Of horror done where a dark ledge splits the sea
And a double surf beats on the grey shores:
How a king's new woman, sick
With hatred for the queen he had imprisoned,
Ripped out his two sons' eyes with her bloody hands
25 While grinning Ares watched the shuttle plunge
Four times: four blind wounds crying for revenge,

Crying, tears and blood mingled. Piteously born,
Those sons whose mother was of heavenly birth!
Her father was the god of the north wind,
30 And she was cradled by gales;
She raced with young colts on the glittering hills
And walked untrammeled in the open light:
But in her marriage deathless Fate found means
To build a tomb like yours for all her joy. **E**

transgress (trăns-grĕs′) *v.* to violate or break (a law, command, or moral code)

D THEME
What is Antigone's highest **loyalty**?

1–5 The princess Danae (dăn′ə-ē′) was imprisoned by her father because it had been predicted that her son would one day kill him. After Zeus visited Danae in the form of a shower of gold, she gave birth to his son Perseus, who did eventually kill his grandfather.

10–18 King Lycurgus (lī-kûr′gəs), son of **Dryas** (drī′əs), was driven mad and eaten by horses for objecting to the worship of Dionysus. The **nine implacable sisters** are the Muses, the goddesses who presided over literature, the arts, and the sciences. Once offended, they were impossible to appease.

9 Targeted Passage

19–34 These lines refer to the myth of King Phineus (fĭn′yŏŏs), who imprisoned his first wife, the daughter of the north wind, and allowed his new wife to blind his sons from his first marriage.

E READING CLASSICAL DRAMA
What insights into Antigone's situation do you get from the **myths** that this **ode** alludes to? Summarize your thoughts in your chart.

ANTIGONE **1097**

✿ SCENE 5

(Enter blind Teiresias, *led by a boy. The opening speeches of* Teiresias *should be in singsong contrast to the realistic lines of* Creon.)

Teiresias. This is the way the blind man comes, princes, princes,
Lock step, two heads lit by the eyes of one.

Creon. What new thing have you to tell us, old Teiresias?

Teiresias. I have much to tell you: listen to the prophet, Creon.

5 **Creon.** I am not aware that I have ever failed to listen.

Teiresias. Then you have done wisely, King, and ruled well.

Creon. I admit my debt to you. But what have you to say?

Teiresias. This, Creon: you stand once more on the edge of fate.

Creon. What do you mean? Your words are a kind of dread.

10 **Teiresias.** Listen, Creon:
I was sitting in my chair of augury, at the place
Where the birds gather about me. They were all a-chatter,
As is their habit, when suddenly I heard
A strange note in their jangling, a scream, a
15 Whirring fury; I knew that they were fighting,
Tearing each other, dying
In a whirlwind of wings clashing. And I was afraid.
I began the rites of burnt offering at the altar,
But Hephaestus failed me: instead of bright flame,
20 There was only the sputtering slime of the fat thigh-flesh
Melting: the entrails dissolved in grey smoke;
The bare bone burst from the welter. And no blaze!

This was a sign from heaven. My boy described it,
Seeing for me as I see for others.

25 I tell you, Creon, you yourself have brought
This new calamity upon us. Our hearths and altars
Are stained with the corruption of dogs and carrion birds
That glut themselves on the corpse of Oedipus' son.
The gods are deaf when we pray to them; their fire
30 Recoils from our offering; their birds of omen
Have no cry of comfort, for they are gorged
With the thick blood of the dead. **Ⓐ**
⠀⠀⠀⠀⠀⠀⠀⠀⠀⠀⠀⠀O my son,
These are no trifles! Think: all men make mistakes,
But a good man yields when he knows his course is wrong,
35 And repairs the evil. The only crime is pride.

Give in to the dead man, then: do not fight with a corpse—
What glory is it to kill a man who is dead?

1098 UNIT 10: GREEK TRAGEDY AND MEDIEVAL ROMANCE

Side notes (right column)

1–7 Teiresias is physically blind but spiritually sighted. As a prophet, he is an agent of the gods in their dealings with humans. His revelation of the truth to Oedipus had led Oedipus to leave Thebes, thus indirectly helping Creon to become king.

⑩ Targeted Passage

11–17 chair of augury: the place where Teiresias sits to hear the birds, whose sounds reveal the future to him. The fighting among the birds suggests that the anarchy infecting Thebes has spread even to the world of nature.

19 Hephaestus (hĭ-fĕs′təs): the god of fire.

26–32 According to Teiresias, the birds and dogs that have eaten the corpse of Polyneices have become corrupt, causing the gods to reject the Thebans' offerings and prayers.

Ⓐ CLASSICAL DRAMA
Reread lines 18–32. What do they suggest about how the gods view Creon's refusal to allow Polyneices to be buried?

Sydney Walker as Teiresias in the Lincoln Center Repertory 1971 production

---

Left column box

TEXT ANALYSIS   COMMON CORE

Ⓐ CLASSICAL DRAMA   RL 2 RL 3

Possible answer: *The failure of the animal sacrifices to burn properly (lines 18–22), the gods' rejection of the offerings (lines 29–30), and the strange behavior of the birds of omen (lines 30–32) suggest that the gods are angered by Creon's refusal to bury Polyneices.*

IF STUDENTS NEED HELP . . . Reread lines 18–22, and ask students to summarize what happened when Teiresias tried to offer a sacrifice. Then reread lines 30–32 and ask them why the birds can't cry.

DIFFERENTIATED INSTRUCTION

FOR STRUGGLING READERS

⑩ Targeted Passage [Lines 1–17]
This passage establishes Teiresias' credentials as a prophet and his prior relationship with Creon.

• What is Creon's initial attitude toward Teiresias? (lines 3–7)

• Why is he indebted to Teiresias? (lines 7, 64)

• Why has Teiresias come to Creon now? (lines 8–40)

FOR ENGLISH LANGUAGE LEARNERS
Vocabulary Support Define and discuss these words related to prophecy: *augury* (line 11), "foretelling"; *rites* (line 18), "ceremonial acts"; *burnt offering* (line 18), "animal sacrifice"; *altar* (lines 18, 26), "elevated structure for sacrifices"; *omen* (line 30), "prophecy."

Get Into the Scene
SUMMARY

The blind prophet Teiresias warns Creon about the dire danger of leaving Polyneices unburied. Creon refuses to recant his decree and accuses the seer of corruption. After Teiresias leaves, Creon relents, fearing the seer's prophecy. He buries Polyneices and then goes to free Antigone. Creon's change of heart comes too late: Antigone and Haemon have killed themselves, and the suicide of Eurydice soon follows.

Analyze Visuals

Activity Ask students what qualities the actor playing Teiresias projects in the photograph. *Possible answer: He appears to be serene and self-possessed. His expression suggests inner strength. Is this a character whom the audience would take seriously? Why or why not? Possible answer: Yes, the audience would take Teiresias' self-assurance and calm demeanor as a sign that he should be treated with seriousness and consideration.*

READING STRATEGY: *Review*

■ MONITOR

Ask students to summarize the status of the characters at the start of Scene 5. *Possible answer: Antigone has been buried alive in a vault for contravening Creon's order. Haemon has threatened to kill himself if Antigone is punished. Ismene has been reprieved. Have students predict what will happen to the characters after Creon receives yet another warning. Possible answer: Creon will remain unbending; Antigone and Haemon will die along with Ismene.*

FOR STRUGGLING READERS

Preview Ask students to listen carefully as you read the summary aloud. Then help them to continue the Sequence Chain that they started at the beginning of the play.

BEST PRACTICES TOOLKIT—Transparency Sequence Chain p. B21

| Teiresias warns Creon. |
↓

| Creon won't recant his decree. |
↓
| Creon changes his mind. |
↓
| Creon buries Polyneices. |
↓
| Antigone and Haemon kill themselves. |
↓
| Eurydice kills herself. |

BACKGROUND

The Prophet Teiresias The blind prophet was a recurrent figure in Greek mythology. Teiresias understood far more than most mortals, and he always spoke the truth. The seer explained to Hercules that Zeus was his real father. Odysseus dared to travel to the underworld so that he might consult with Teiresias. It was Teiresias who finally revealed to Oedipus the dreadful facts of his birth. Considering this, Creon should understand the wisdom of treating Teiresias with respect, and should fear the consequences of turning a deaf ear to his warnings.

TIERED DISCUSSION PROMPTS

Direct students to lines 48–69. Use these prompts to help students understand how Creon's rage leads him to level unfounded charges:

Recall At what other point in the play has Creon leveled charges of corruption? ***Possible answer:*** *Creon accused the sentry of taking money to allow Polyneices' burial (Scene 1, lines 115–130).*

Analyze How and why does Creon's attitude toward Teiresias change during the scene? ***Possible answer:*** *Creon becomes hostile and angry, leveling charges of corruption against the prophet (lines 49–53) because Teiresias has told Creon what he does not want to hear: that he should bury Polyneices.*

Evaluate Why do you think Creon levels charges of corruption against an acknowledged wise man? ***Possible answer:*** *This is Creon's normal response when he hears unwelcome news or information. He seems to be paranoid and impulsive.*

Think, I beg you:
It is for your own good that I speak as I do.
40 You should be able to yield for your own good.
Creon. It seems that prophets have made me their especial province.
All my life long
I have been a kind of butt for the dull arrows
Of doddering fortunetellers!
　　　　　No, Teiresias:
45 If your birds—if the great eagles of God himself—
Should carry him stinking bit by bit to heaven,
I would not yield. I am not afraid of pollution:
No man can **defile** the gods.
　　　　　　　　Do what you will;
Go into business, make money, speculate
50 In India gold or that synthetic gold from Sardis,
Get rich otherwise than by my consent to bury him.
Teiresias, it is a sorry thing when a wise man
Sells his wisdom, lets out his words for hire!
Teiresias. Ah Creon! Is there no man left in the world—
55 **Creon.** To do what? Come, let's have the aphorism!
Teiresias. No man who knows that wisdom outweighs any wealth?
Creon. As surely as bribes are baser than any baseness.
Teiresias. You are sick, Creon! You are deathly sick!
Creon. As you say: it is not my place to challenge a prophet.
60 **Teiresias.** Yet you have said my prophecy is for sale.
Creon. The generation of prophets has always loved gold.
Teiresias. The generation of kings has always loved brass.
Creon. You forget yourself! You are speaking to your king.
Teiresias. I know it. You are a king because of me.
65 **Creon.** You have a certain skill; but you have sold out.
Teiresias. King, you will drive me to words that—
Creon. 　　　　　　　　　　　　Say them, say them!
Only remember: I will not pay you for them.
Teiresias. No, you will find them too costly.
Creon. 　　　　　　　　　No doubt. Speak:
Whatever you say, you will not change my will.
70 **Teiresias.** Then take this, and take it to heart!
The time is not far off when you shall pay back
Corpse for corpse, flesh of your own flesh.
You have thrust the child of this world into living night;
You have kept from the gods below the child that is theirs:

defile (dĭ-fīl´) *v.* to make dirty, unclean, or impure

50 Sardis (sär´dĭs): the capital of ancient Lydia, where metal coins were first produced.

COMMON CORE RL 4

Language Coach

Word Definitions Sometimes the definition of an unknown word can be discovered from **context**—the surrounding text. One type of context clue is an example that illustrates a word's meaning. Reread lines 54–56. How do Teiresias's words help you figure out the meaning of *aphorism*?

VOCABULARY
　　　　　　　　　　　COMMON CORE
　　　　　　　　　　　　　　L 4

OWN THE WORD

defile: To help students better understand the word *defile*, have them use a thesaurus or dictionary to create a list of synonyms and antonyms for this word. ***Possible answers:*** *synonyms: contaminate, pollute, besmirch, dirty, sully, corrupt, violate; antonyms: honor, hallow, consecrate, sanctify*

DIFFERENTIATED INSTRUCTION

FOR ENGLISH LANGUAGE LEARNERS

Vocabulary: Outdated Forms Point out that some words and expressions in this translation are not used in modern English. Provide the following terms and their definitions. Then have students reread the lines, substituting the definitions for the words or phrases: *especial province* (line 41), "special target"; *a sorry thing* (line 52), "a terrible or unfortunate thing"; *lets out his words for hire* (line 53), "sells himself or his work"; *my mind misgives* (line 106), "I am not thinking clearly."

FOR ENGLISH LANGUAGE LEARNERS

Language Coach　　　**COMMON CORE**
　　　　　　　　　　　　　　RL 4
Word Definitions
Answer: *Teiresias says "Is there no man left in the world . . . who knows that wisdom outweighs any wealth?"* This rhetorical question expresses the principle that wisdom is more valuable than wealth—an example of an *aphorism, a wise saying or statement of principle.* Have students use context clues and dictionaries to define other unfamiliar words in the play.

75 The one in a grave before her death, the other,
  Dead, denied the grave. This is your crime:
  And the Furies and the dark gods of hell
  Are swift with terrible punishment for you.

  Do you want to buy me now, Creon?
                              Not many days,
80 And your house will be full of men and women weeping,
  And curses will be hurled at you from far
  Cities grieving for sons unburied, left to rot before the walls of Thebes.

  These are my arrows, Creon: they are all for you.

  (to boy) But come, child: lead me home.
85 Let him waste his fine anger upon younger men.
  Maybe he will learn at last
  To control a wiser tongue in a better head.  B

  (Exit Teiresias.)

  Choragus. The old man has gone, King, but his words
  Remain to plague us. I am old, too,
90 But I cannot remember that he was ever false.

  Creon. That is true. . . . It troubles me.
  Oh it is hard to give in! but it is worse
  To risk everything for stubborn pride.

  Choragus. Creon: take my advice.

  Creon.   What shall I do?

95 Choragus. Go quickly: free Antigone from her vault
  And build a tomb for the body of Polyneices.

  Creon. You would have me do this?

  Choragus.   Creon, yes!
  And it must be done at once: God moves
  Swiftly to cancel the folly of stubborn men.

100 Creon. It is hard to deny the heart! But I
  Will do it: I will not fight with destiny. C

  Choragus. You must go yourself; you cannot leave it to others.

  Creon. I will go.
                  —Bring axes, servants:
  Come with me to the tomb. I buried her; I
105 Will set her free.
                    Oh quickly!
  My mind misgives—
  The laws of the gods are mighty, and a man must serve them
  To the last day of his life!

  (Exit Creon.)

---

77 Furies: three goddesses who avenge crimes, especially those that violate family ties.

B CHARACTER
What does Creon's exchange with the **minor character** Teiresias reveal about Creon's view of himself and others? Predict how Teiresias's prophecy might be fulfilled.

C CHARACTER
Why does Creon change his mind?

REVISIT THE BIG QUESTION
What is your ultimate
LOYALTY?

Discuss In lines 70–83, Creon has accused Teiresias of selling out. To what does Teiresias say one should pay his loyalty? *Possible answer: Teiresias suggests that people must pay their loyalty to the gods who demand burial for all the dead.*

TEXT ANALYSIS: *Review*    COMMON CORE
                                              RL 3

B CHARACTER
Possible answer: *Creon insults and threatens Teiresias and finally says, "you will not change my will" (line 69), revealing once again his belief that he is right and that he knows the will of the gods. Students may predict that Teiresias' prophecy will be fulfilled through Creon's death, Haemon's death, or worse.*

TEXT ANALYSIS: *Review*   COMMON CORE
                                              RL 3

C CHARACTER
Possible answer: *Creon changes his mind because he knows that Teiresias' prophecies have always proved true, because the choragus advises him to undo what he has done, and because he fears the gods' punishment.*

IF STUDENTS NEED HELP . . . Reread Teiresias' final warning to Creon (lines 70–83) and the choragus' advice to the king (lines 88–90 and 95–96).

FOR ADVANCED LEARNERS/PRE-AP
Analyze Irony Have students discuss the significance of the confrontation between a blind prophet who sees the truth and the "seeing" king who is deaf to reason and blind to the truth. How does this confrontation support the play's themes, irony, and images of light and dark? What message is Sophocles suggesting about the nature of Truth? Have students write one or two paragraphs about their conclusions.

BACKGROUND

Cadmus, Dionysus, and the House of Thebes

In this paean, Sophocles alludes to the relationship between Dionysus—in whose honor the play was written and performed—and the house of Thebes. Dionysus was the son of Semele and Zeus; and Semele was a daughter of Cadmus, who founded Thebes. (According to tradition, Cadmus civilized Greece and introduced the alphabet to Greece.) Creon and Oedipus were also descendents of Cadmus—great-great grandsons. Thus, both tragic kings were distantly related to Dionysus and the gods: Cadmus was Dionysus' grandfather. Sophocles' allusions add dramatic texture and reinforce the irony of the play, written about doomed members of Dionysus' own family.

READING STRATEGY

COMMON CORE

D **READING CLASSICAL DRAMA**

RL 1
RL 10

Possible answer: *The paean creates an ominous mood. The chorus, begging Dionysus for his help, recognizes the danger that Creon is bringing upon himself and his land: "The shadow of plague is upon us," they sing (line 13).*

PAEAN

Choragus. God of many names

Chorus.   O Iacchus
                                                    son
of Cadmean Semele
                            O born of the thunder!
guardian of the West
                              regent
of Eleusis' plain
                    O prince of maenad Thebes
5   and the Dragon Field by rippling Ismenus:

Choragus. God of many names

Chorus.   the flame of torches
flares on our hills
                    the nymphs of Iacchus
dance at the spring of Castalia:
from the vine-close mountain
                                        come ah come in ivy:
10 *Evohé evohé!* sings through the streets of Thebes

Choragus. God of many names

Chorus.   Iacchus of Thebes
heavenly child
                    of Semele bride of the Thunderer!
The shadow of plague is upon us:
                                    come
with clement feet
                    oh come from Parnassus
15 down the long slopes
                            across the lamenting water

Choragus. Io Fire! Chorister of the throbbing stars!
O purest among the voices of the night!
Thou son of God, blaze for us!

Chorus. Come with choric rapture of circling Maenads
20 Who cry *Io Iacche!*
                    God of many names! **D**

Paean (pē'ən): a hymn that is an appeal to the gods for assistance. In this paean, the chorus praises Dionysus, or Iacchus (yā'kəs), and calls on him to come to Thebes to show mercy and drive out evil.

2 Cadmus was the legendary founder of Thebes. Dionysus was the son of Cadmus' daughter **Semele** (sə-mē'lē) and Zeus, who is referred to here as thunder.

4–5 These lines name locations near Athens and Thebes. A **maenad** (mē'năd') was a priestess of Dionysus.

8–9 **Castalia:** a spring on the sacred mountain Parnassus. Grapevines and ivy were symbols of Dionysus.

10 **evohé** (ĕ-woi'): hallelujah.

D **READING CLASSICAL DRAMA**
What **mood** is created by this **paean** to the god Dionysus?

DIFFERENTIATED INSTRUCTION

FOR STRUGGLING READERS

Mythology Point out to students the significance of a paean to Dionysus immediately following the climactic scene between Creon and Teiresias: after advising Creon to bury Polyneices and save Antigone, the chorus asks Dionysus to help, before it is too late. Remind them that Sophocles wrote this play for the Great Dionysia, an Athenian festival honoring Dionysus.

EXODOS

(*Enter* Messenger.)

Messenger. Men of the line of Cadmus, you who live
Near Amphion's citadel:
                 I cannot say
Of any condition of human life, "This is fixed,
This is clearly good, or bad." Fate raises up,
5 And Fate casts down the happy and unhappy alike:
No man can foretell his fate.
                   Take the case of Creon:
Creon was happy once, as I count happiness:
Victorious in battle, sole governor of the land,
Fortunate father of children nobly born.
10 And now it has all gone from him! Who can say
That a man is still alive when his life's joy fails?
He is a walking dead man. Grant him rich;
Let him live like a king in his great house:
If his pleasure is gone, I would not give
15 So much as the shadow of smoke for all he owns.

Choragus. Your words hint at sorrow: what is your news for us?

Messenger. They are dead. The living are guilty of their death.

Choragus. Who is guilty? Who is dead? Speak!

Messenger.   Haemon.
Haemon is dead; and the hand that killed him
20 Is his own hand.

Choragus.   His father's? or his own?

Messenger. His own, driven mad by the murder his father had done.

Choragus. Teiresias, Teiresias, how clearly you saw it all!

Messenger. This is my news: you must draw what conclusions you can from it.

> **Choragus.** But look: Eurydice, our queen:
> 25 Has she overheard us?
>
> (*Enter* Eurydice *from the palace, center.*)
>
> **Eurydice.** I have heard something, friends:
> As I was unlocking the gate of Pallas' shrine,
> For I needed her help today, I heard a voice
> Telling of some new sorrow. And I fainted
> 30 There at the temple with all my maidens about me.
> But speak again: whatever it is, I can bear it:
> Grief and I are no strangers.

 Targeted Passage

Exodos: the last episode in the play. It is followed by a final speech made by the choragus and addressed directly to the audience.

2 Amphion (ăm-fī'ən), Niobe's husband, built a wall around Thebes by charming the stones into place with music.

27 Pallas (păl'əs): Athena, the goddess of wisdom.

32 Megareus (mə-găr'yōōs), the older son of Eurydice and Creon, had died in the battle for Thebes.

TIERED DISCUSSION PROMPTS

Direct students to lines 44–72. Use these prompts to help students understand the parallels between the house of Oedipus and the house of Creon:

Recall What has happened to Antigone's family—the house of Oedipus? *Possible answer: Queen Jocasta killed herself; Polyneices and Eteocles killed each other; Oedipus died; and now Antigone has also died by her own hand. Only Ismene survives.*

Analyze What similarities can you identify so far between the fate of the house of Oedipus and the house of Creon? *Possible answer: The sons of both Creon and Oedipus have died, leaving none to rule Thebes or continue the line. Within the two houses, family members have been responsible for the death of other family members.*

Evaluate What effect do these parallels have on the mood of the scene? *Possible answer: They increase the ominous mood, the tension, and the sense of tragedy unfolding. They also underscore the powerlessness of humans against the gods and the inevitability of fate.*

Messenger. Dearest lady,
I will tell you plainly all that I have seen.
I shall not try to comfort you: what is the use,
35 Since comfort could lie only in what is not true?
The truth is always best.
                    I went with Creon
To the outer plain where Polyneices was lying,
No friend to pity him, his body shredded by dogs.
We made our prayers in that place to Hecate
40 And Pluto, that they would be merciful. And we bathed
The corpse with holy water, and we brought
Fresh-broken branches to burn what was left of it,
And upon the urn we heaped up a towering barrow
Of the earth of his own land.
                    When we were done, we ran
45 To the vault where Antigone lay on her couch of stone.
One of the servants had gone ahead,
And while he was yet far off he heard a voice
Grieving within the chamber, and he came back
And told Creon. And as the king went closer,
50 The air was full of wailing, the words lost,
And he begged us to make all haste. "Am I a prophet?"
He said, weeping. "And must I walk this road,
The saddest of all that I have gone before?
My son's voice calls me on. Oh quickly, quickly!
55 Look through the crevice there, and tell me
If it is Haemon, or some deception of the gods!"

We obeyed; and in the cavern's farthest corner
We saw her lying:
She had made a noose of her fine linen veil
60 And hanged herself. Haemon lay beside her,
His arms about her waist, lamenting her,
His love lost underground, crying out
That his father had stolen her away from him.
When Creon saw him, the tears rushed to his eyes,
65 And he called to him: "What have you done, child? Speak to me.
What are you thinking that makes your eyes so strange?
O my son, my son, I come to you on my knees!"
But Haemon spat in his face. He said not a word,
Staring—
                    and suddenly drew his sword
70 And lunged. Creon shrank back; the blade missed, and the boy,
Desperate against himself, drove it half its length
Into his own side and fell. And as he died,
He gathered Antigone close in his arms again,

39–40 Hecate (hĕk′ə-tē) **and Pluto:** other names for Persephone and Hades, the queen and king of the underworld.

43–44 Note the contrast between the barrow, or burial mound, erected by Creon and the handful of dirt used by Antigone to cover her brother.

60 Note that this is the same way in which Jocasta, Antigone's mother, killed herself.

DIFFERENTIATED INSTRUCTION

FOR ADVANCED LEARNERS/PRE–AP

Synthesize The messenger reports that Creon had asked this question: "Am I a prophet?" (line 51) Ironically, when Creon appears in person, he takes on a truth-teller role. Encourage students to find specific lines spoken by Creon that echo those spoken by Teiresias. What truths does Creon tell? Have students discuss the meaning of Creon's transformation and then present their findings to the class.

Choking, his blood bright red on her white cheek.
75 And now he lies dead with the dead, and she is his
At last, his bride in the houses of the dead. **E**

(*Exit* Eurydice *into the palace.*)

Choragus. She has left us without a word. What can this mean?

Messenger. It troubles me, too; yet she knows what is best;
Her grief is too great for public lamentation,
80 And doubtless she has gone to her chamber to weep
For her dead son, leading her maidens in his dirge.

Choragus. It may be so: but I fear this deep silence.

(*pause*)

Messenger. I will see what she is doing. I will go in.

(*Exit* Messenger *into the palace. Enter* Creon *with attendants, bearing* Haemon's *body.*)

Choragus. But here is the king himself: oh look at him,
85 Bearing his own damnation in his arms.

Creon. Nothing you say can touch me any more.
My own blind heart has brought me
From darkness to final darkness. Here you see
The father murdering, the murdered son—
90 And all my civic wisdom!
Haemon my son, so young, so young to die,
I was the fool, not you; and you died for me.

Choragus. That is the truth; but you were late in learning it.

Creon. This truth is hard to bear. Surely a god
95 Has crushed me beneath the hugest weight of heaven,
And driven me headlong a barbaric way
To trample out the thing I held most dear.
The pains that men will take to come to pain! **F**

(*Enter* Messenger *from the palace.*)

Messenger. The burden you carry in your hands is heavy,
100 But it is not all: you will find more in your house.

Creon. What burden worse than this shall I find there?

Messenger. The queen is dead.

Creon. O port of death, deaf world,
Is there no pity for me? And you, angel of evil,
105 I was dead, and your words are death again.
Is it true, boy? Can it be true?
Is my wife dead? Has death bred death?

Messenger. You can see for yourself.

E CLASSICAL DRAMA
Summarize the **tragic** catastrophe that events have led to.

COMMON CORE RL 4

Language Coach

Synonyms Words with the same or similar meanings are **synonyms**. The word *lamentation*, meaning "an expression of grief," is related to the noun *lament*, which can be a musical expression of grief. What word in line 81 is a possible synonym for *lament*?

F CLASSICAL DRAMA
Reread lines 86–98. How does Creon view his actions?

ANTIGONE **1105**

TEXT ANALYSIS — COMMON CORE — RL 2 / RL 3

E CLASSICAL DRAMA

Possible answer: *Before Creon could free Antigone, she hung herself. Grieving, Haemon tried to kill Creon but ended up killing himself.*

REVISIT THE BIG QUESTION

What is your ultimate LOYALTY?

Discuss In lines 86–92, what does Creon suggest was the effect of his unbending loyalty to the laws of the state? ***Possible answer:*** *He suggests that his unbending loyalty caused his son's death, making him, in effect, a murderer.*

TEXT ANALYSIS — COMMON CORE — RL 2 / RL 3

F CLASSICAL DRAMA

Possible answer: *Creon understands that he has been blind and foolish (lines 86–88). He wonders whether a god has cruelly driven him to act in a way that could only lead to grief (lines 94–97).*

FOR STRUGGLING READERS

Plot Explain that the messenger's speech represents the play's resolution by tying up loose ends. Ask students to identify the climax. ***Possible answer:*** *The climax occurs when Creon rejects Teiresias, who has just given a final and compelling warning.*

Help students complete a Story Map to fit together the pieces of the plot.

📦 **BEST PRACTICES TOOLKIT—Transparency**
Story Map p. D14

FOR ENGLISH LANGUAGE LEARNERS

Language Coach — COMMON CORE RL 4

Synonyms *Answer: dirge* Have students work in pairs and use a dictionary or thesaurus to find synonyms for the following words: *doubtless* (line 80), *trample* (line 97), *briefest* (line 126), and *rash* (line 134).

G CLASSICAL DRAMA

Possible answer: Some students may say that Creon's realization of his guilt makes him a tragic hero. Others may suggest that he has not displayed enough greatness and nobility to be considered heroic.

H ALLEGORY

Tell students that to understand the lesson the allegory is trying to teach, they should look for lessons learned by the characters in the allegory. Ask: In *Antigone*, who learned a hard lesson? *(Creon)*

Possible answer: Antigone is sentenced to death, but she is joined in death by her fiancé, and dies in the knowledge that she has done what she knows is right. Creon, however, has his entire family die around him, and hopes for death. Although both characters have unpleasant fates, the play can still be read as an allegory for submission to the gods since Antigone's death is more positive than Creon's life will be after the close of the play.

SELECTION WRAP–UP

READ WITH A PURPOSE Now that students have finished reading the selection, ask: What is Creon's tragic flaw? Which character in the drama do they sympathize with the most? Why? *Possible answer: Creon's tragic flaw is pride, but students may not think he is the hero of the story. Students may sympathize most with Antigone because of her love for her family and her willingness to stand up for what she feels is right.*

⭐ **CRITIQUE** Have students consider why *Antigone* still holds interest for modern audiences.

INDEPENDENT READING

Students may also enjoy reading the other Oedipus plays of Sophocles: *Oedipus the King* and *Oedipus at Colonus*.

(*The doors are opened, and the body of* Eurydice *is disclosed within.*)

Creon. Oh pity!
110 All true, all true, and more than I can bear!
O my wife, my son!

Messenger. She stood before the altar, and her heart
Welcomed the knife her own hand guided,
And a great cry burst from her lips for Megareus dead,
115 And for Haemon dead, her sons; and her last breath
Was a curse for their father, the murderer of her sons.
And she fell, and the dark flowed in through her closing eyes.

Creon. O God, I am sick with fear.
Are there no swords here? Has no one a blow for me?

120 **Messenger.** Her curse is upon you for the deaths of both.

Creon. It is right that it should be. I alone am guilty.
I know it, and I say it. Lead me in,
Quickly, friends.
I have neither life nor substance. Lead me in. **G**

125 **Choragus.** You are right, if there can be right in so much wrong.
The briefest way is best in a world of sorrow.

Creon. Let it come;
Let death come quickly and be kind to me.
I would not ever see the sun again.

130 **Choragus.** All that will come when it will; but we, meanwhile,
Have much to do. Leave the future to itself.

Creon. All my heart was in that prayer!

Choragus. Then do not pray any more: the sky is deaf.

Creon. Lead me away. I have been rash and foolish.
135 I have killed my son and my wife.
I look for comfort; my comfort lies here dead.
Whatever my hands have touched has come to nothing.
Fate has brought all my pride to a thought of dust.

(*As Creon is being led into the house, the* Choragus *advances and speaks directly to the audience.*)

Choragus. There is no happiness where there is no wisdom;
140 No wisdom but in submission to the gods.
Big words are always punished,
And proud men in old age learn to be wise. **H**

Translated by Dudley Fitts and Robert Fitzgerald

G CLASSICAL DRAMA
Creon assumes responsibility for the terrible events that have occurred. To what extent is he a **tragic hero**?

⑫ **Targeted Passage**

COMMON CORE RL 2

H ALLEGORY
An **allegory** is a story that functions on two levels: a literal and a symbolic level. Allegories often teach a moral lesson through their symbolic meaning. *Antigone* can be read as an allegory about obedience, or as the choragus says, "submission to the gods." How does the ultimate fate of each character support this reading of *Antigone*? Give specific examples from the text in your answer.

DIFFERENTIATED INSTRUCTION

FOR STRUGGLING READERS

⑫ **Targeted Passage [Lines 121–138]**

In this passage, Creon fully acknowledges his guilt.

- Creon says that Eurydice was right to curse him. Why? (lines 121–122)

- What words does Creon use to describe himself and his actions? (lines 121, 124, 134, 137, 138)

- What tragic flaw does he blame for his downfall? (lines 134–138)

Comprehension

1. **Recall** Why is Antigone determined to bury her brother?

2. **Recall** What punishment does Antigone receive for disobeying Creon?

3. **Clarify** How does Antigone die?

Text Analysis

4. **Identify Conflict** Describe the conflict between Antigone and Creon. What arguments support each one's position? You may want to reread Scene 2, lines 105–118 (pages 1084–1085).

● 5. **Understand Classical Drama** In what way do the comments and songs of the **chorus** influence your understanding of characters and events? Refer to the chart you filled out as you read.

6. **Make Judgments** How responsible is Creon for the deaths of Antigone, Haemon, and Eurydice?

7. **Analyze Minor Characters** How do the minor characters—such as Ismene, Teiresias, Haemon, Eurydice, the sentry, and the messenger—help you judge Antigone and Creon?

8. **Analyze Tragedy** Who better fits the definition of an archetypal **tragic hero**, Antigone or Creon? Use a chart like the one shown to help you plan your answer.

	Antigone	Creon
Dignified, Superior Character		
Meets Tragic End		
Possesses Tragic Flaw		
Recognizes Flaw and Consequences		

9. **Analyze Dramatic Irony** Discuss the dramatic irony in the play. At what points do you know more than the characters know?

10. **Interpret Themes** What does the play suggest about where a person's highest loyalty should lie? What other themes are revealed in the play? Give evidence to support your interpretations.

11. **Apply Themes** What relevance do the themes of *Antigone* have in modern times? Explain your opinion, offering examples.

Text Criticism

12. **Biographical Context** Sophocles was not only a playwright; he also served in the Athenian government. What messages does *Antigone* contain about democracy and the government of states?

> **What is your ultimate LOYALTY?**
> Is it more important to do what you think is right or to follow the rules? Why?

COMMON CORE

RL 1 Cite textual evidence to support analysis of what the text says explicitly as well as inferences drawn from the text. **RL 2** Determine a theme or central idea of a text. **RL 3** Analyze how complex characters with conflicting motivations develop, interact with others, and advance the plot or develop the theme. **RL 10** Read and comprehend dramas.

10. *It suggests a person's highest loyalty should be to the laws of conscience. Other themes: pride will be punished; the ways of gods are mysterious; humans suffer.*

11. *The themes have relevance today when people have conflicting duties to conscience and state; when they consider breaking laws they perceive as unjust; and when they wonder how much people can know.*

Text Criticism
Possible answer:
12. *Democracy is preferable to tyranny; leaders should listen to the people; universal laws supersede human laws; there is greatness in defying a corrupt government.*

> **What is your ultimate LOYALTY?** Student answers should acknowledge the difficulties in choosing between rules and conscience and might also explore the idea of compromise.

Practice and Apply

For preliminary support of post-reading questions, use these copy masters:

R RESOURCE MANAGER—Copy Masters
Reading Check p. 28
Classical Drama p. 23
Question Support p. 29

Additional selection questions are provided for teachers on page 15.

ANSWERS
Comprehension

1. *She buries him out of duty to higher laws.*

2. *She is sealed alive in a vault.*

3. *She hangs herself with a veil in the vault.*

Text Analysis
COMMON CORE RL 1, RL 2, RL 3, RL 10
Possible answers:
4. *Creon denies burial to Polyneices as punishment for being a traitor. Antigone buries Polyneices out of duty to higher laws, believing that no king can ignore those laws.*

5. ● **COMMON CORE FOCUS** *Classical Drama* *The chorus provides background, foreshadows the future, and hints at larger meanings.*

6. *Some students may blame Creon for the suicides that resulted from his punishment of Antigone; others may say that each person chose suicide over other choices.*

7. *They help you see Creon's stubbornness, suspicion, pride, rage, and insolence. The messenger arouses sympathy for Creon. Ismene calls attention to Antigone's principles and her coldness. The sentry shows Antigone as a loving sister.*

8. *Antigone: for her moral principles, death, and her flaws of inflexibility and caring too little for life. Creon: for his desire to protect Thebes, his acceptance of blame, and his flaws of stubbornness and pride.*

9. *The reader learns before Creon does that Antigone has buried the body, yet Creon assumes a man has done it (Scene 1, line 77); also, when Haemon threatens that Antigone's death "will cause another" (Scene 3, line 119), Creon mistakenly thinks his son threatens him. Such incidents heighten the suspense and the tragedy.*

ANSWERS

Vocabulary in Context

▲ **VOCABULARY PRACTICE**

1. *false*	7. *false*
2. *true*	8. *false*
3. *true*	9. *false*
4. *true*	10. *true*
5. *false*	11. *false*
6. *true*	12. *false*

R RESOURCE MANAGER—Copy Master
   Vocabulary Practice p. 26

ACADEMIC VOCABULARY IN SPEAKING

Suggest that individual students brainstorm advice for Antigone and record their ideas in a Two-Column Chart. In the first column, have them list Creon's questions about her actions. In the second column, have students list ways Antigone could answer Creon. Students should then share this information with their partner.

 BEST PRACTICES TOOLKIT—Transparency
   Two-Column Chart p. A57

VOCABULARY STRATEGY: ETYMOLOGY

COMMON CORE L 4c

Remind students that word histories are good mnemonic devices, but often etymologies do not provide an exact meaning or definition.

1. *contempt:* from the Latin *contemptus,* meaning "despise"

2. *transgress:* from the Latin *transgred,* meaning "to step across"

3. *insolence:* from the Latin *insolens,* meaning "arrogant"

4. *perverse:* from the Latin *pervertere,* meaning "to pervert"

R RESOURCE MANAGER—Copy Master
   Vocabulary Strategy p. 27

Interactive Vocabulary

Keywords direct students to a **WordSharp** tutorial on **thinkcentral.com** or to other types of vocabulary practice and review.

Vocabulary in Context

▲ **VOCABULARY PRACTICE**

Decide if each statement is true or false.

1. To **sate** a desire is to make it stronger.
2. An **auspicious** event is promising and hopeful.
3. To have **contempt** for someone is to show scorn and disdain.
4. To have **reverence** for others is to love and respect them.
5. To do something **impassively** is to do it with energy and enthusiasm.
6. An **anarchist** wants to overthrow a country's government.
7. To speak **sententiously** is to do so in a respectful, humble manner.
8. Teachers appreciate **insolence** in their students.
9. A **perverse** child is one who is obedient.
10. A **lamentation** might occur at a funeral or burial site.
11. People who **transgress** the law are those who enforce it.
12. To **defile** something is to make it more beautiful in appearance.

WORD LIST

anarchist
auspicious
contempt
defile
impassively
insolence
lamentation
perverse
reverence
sate
sententiously
transgress

ACADEMIC VOCABULARY IN SPEAKING

• drama • emerge • encounter • globe • underlie

Imagine that Antigone **emerged** from this **drama** and wants to ask your advice on how she should answer Creon's questions about her actions. Prepare for a cooperative learning interaction by first taking notes on helpful advice you would offer Antigone in this situation. Share your ideas and information with a partner. Then, practice giving and following oral instructions, with one of you taking on the role of Antigone and the other of a modern advisor. Then switch roles. As the advisor, give Antigone specific suggestions, speaking slowly and repeating yourself if necessary. As Antigone, listen carefully to your partner's suggestions and demonstrate what you have learned by rephrasing his or her ideas in your own words in your sample answers to Creon's questions. Use at least two Academic Vocabulary words in your discussion.

COMMON CORE

L 4c Consult reference materials to clarify the etymology of a word.

VOCABULARY STRATEGY: ETYMOLOGY

An **etymology** is the history of a word. Knowing a word's history can often help you remember the word's meaning. For example, the word *anarchy* comes from the Greek prefix *an-,* "without," plus the Greek root *archos,* "leader." Use a dictionary, thesaurus, or glossary to research the etymology of each word below. Study each word's origin, meaning, and spelling.

1. contempt: _____
2. trangress: _____
3. insolence: _____
4. perverse: _____

Interactive Vocabulary
THINK central
Go to **thinkcentral.com**.
KEYWORD: HML10-1108

DIFFERENTIATED INSTRUCTION

FOR ENGLISH LANGUAGE LEARNERS

Vocabulary Activity After students complete the vocabulary practice, ask them to list words that are cognates, or words related in origin, in their home languages. Challenge them to write a short paragraph in English, using as many of the vocabulary words as possible. Then have them write the same paragraph in their home language.

Language

◆ **GRAMMAR AND STYLE:** Vary Sentence Structure

Review the **Grammar and Style** note on page 1079. Most sentences you write will have subjects preceding verbs; however, you may occasionally use inverted sentences when you want to add variety or emphasis. In an inverted sentence, the subject comes after the verb or part of the verb phrase. Here is an example from *Antigone*:

> **Chorus.** *Fortunate is the man who has never tasted God's vengeance!*
> (Ode 2, line 1)

Notice how the revisions in blue in this response to the prompt make the writing more interesting and effective.

STUDENT MODEL

Creon even suspects Teiresias of disloyalty at the end of the play. ~~The old seer~~

~~the old seer~~
had ~~never~~ been driven to such anger.

READING-WRITING CONNECTION

YOUR TURN Broaden your understanding of the play by responding to the prompt. Then use the **revising tip** to improve your writing.

WRITING PROMPT	REVISING TIP
Extended Constructed Response: Analysis How does the motif of blindness in *Antigone* affect the plot and theme of the play? In your answer, examine the archetype of the blind prophet as portrayed by Teiresias. How does the prophet's appearance advance the plot of the play? Who else is "blind" in the play? Write a three-to-five-paragraph response.	Review your response. Have you used inverted sentences to add variety or emphasis? If not, revise to make your writing more interesting and effective.

Interactive Revision THINK central
Go to **thinkcentral.com**.
KEYWORD: HML10-1109

FOR STRUGGLING WRITERS

- Limit the length of the assignment to two paragraphs.
- Ask students to include two examples of how the prophet advances the plot in the first paragraph.
- Ask them to include two examples of other characters who are "blind" in the second paragraph.

Language

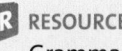
COMMON CORE L 3, W 9b (RL 2)

COMMON CORE
L 3 Make effective choices for meaning or style. W 9b (RL 2) Draw evidence from literary texts to support analysis and reflection; determine a theme of central idea of a text.

◆ **GRAMMAR AND STYLE**

- After students read **Vary Sentence Structure,** ask them to change the word order in this sentence:

  The ruler is wise who listens to the will of his people. ***Possible answer:*** *Wise is the ruler who listens to the will of his people.*

- Write this model on the board. Have students suggest one or more changes in sentence order for variety.

  The new-to-town, inexperienced candidate had won the election by a landslide. ~~The people of the town had not foreseen such an outcome. They wondered who could have expected the newcomer to win.~~ *Such an outcome had not been foreseen by the people of the town. Who, they wondered, expected the newcomer to win?*

R RESOURCE MANAGER—Copy Master
Grammar and Style p. 30

READING-WRITING CONNECTION

Suggest that students begin their analyses of the play by listing lines where references to blindness, eyes, or sight appear.

Writing Online THINK central

The following tools are available online at **thinkcentral.com** and on **Write*Smart* CD-ROM:**
- **Interactive Graphic Organizers**
- **Interactive Student Models**
- **Interactive Revision Lessons**
For additional grammar instruction, see **GrammarNotes** on **thinkcentral.com**.

Assess and Reteach

Assess

DIAGNOSTIC AND SELECTION TESTS
  Selection Test A pp. 295–296
  Selection Test B/C pp. 297–298

Interactive Selection Test on **thinkcentral.com**

Reteach

Level Up Online Tutorials on **thinkcentral.com**

Reteaching Worksheets on **thinkcentral.com**

Focus and Motivate

COMMON CORE FOCUS

RL 3 Analyze how complex characters develop, interact with others, and advance the plot or develop the theme. **RL 4** Determine the meaning of words and phrases as they are used in a text. **RL 5** Analyze how an author's choices concerning how to structure a text and order events within it to create such effects as mystery, tension, or surprise. **RL 7** Analyze the representation of a subject in two different mediums. **L 4c** Consult reference materials to determine a word's meaning or clarify etymology. **L 4d** Verify the preliminary determination of the meaning of a word. **L 5** Demonstrate understanding of figurative language, word relationships, and nuances in words.

SUMMARIES

from *Le Morte d'Arthur*: The Crowning of Arthur This Arthurian legend explains Arthur's parentage and describes how Arthur becomes king after freeing a sword from a stone.

from *Le Morte d'Arthur*: Sir Launcelot du Lake In this tale, Launcelot and his nephew, Sir Lyonel, are captured—Lyonel by Sir Tarquine, Launcelot by Morgan le Fay. When a woman aids his escape, Launcelot jousts for her father. He then kills Tarquine and frees Lyonel.

Could you be a KNIGHT?

Introduce the question, and link it to the photograph. Have students share their thoughts about the term *chivalry*. Help students begin the *DISCUSS* activity by reminding them that even simple acts can demonstrate chivalric traits.

Selection Resources

from Le Morte d'Arthur

 Video link at **thinkcentral.com**

The Crowning of Arthur
Sir Launcelot du Lake
Romance by Sir Thomas Malory
Retold by Keith Baines

Could you be a KNIGHT?

COMMON CORE

RL 3 Analyze how complex characters develop, interact with others, and advance the plot or develop the theme.
RL 4 Determine the meaning of words and phrases as they are used in a text. **RL 5** Analyze how an author's choices concerning how to structure a text and order events within it create such effects as mystery, tension, or surprise.

The time of knights—roughly 1100 to 1400—is often called the age of chivalry. The term *chivalry* refers to the code of conduct that medieval knights were expected to follow. Chivalry promoted the idea of the knight as both a warrior and a gentleman. He was to be courageous, honest, loyal, generous to enemies, and protective of women and the weak. In the following selections, you will read about the legendary King Arthur and his Knights of the Round Table and see how they lived up to the standards of medieval knighthood.

DISCUSS Could you be a knight? With a partner, discuss the traits associated with knights. Then try to provide examples from your own life that demonstrate each trait. Afterward, review your partner's responses. Four or five examples mean that he or she is worthy to join the company of the Round Table.

Chivalric Traits	My Examples
1. Courage	
2. Honesty	
3. Loyalty	
4. Generosity	
5. Kindness	

1110

See resources on the **Teacher One Stop DVD-ROM** and on **thinkcentral.com**.

 Video link at **thinkcentral.com**

 RESOURCE MANAGER UNIT 10
Plan and Teach, pp. 34–40
Summary, pp. 41–42†‡*
Text Analysis and Reading
   Skill, pp. 43–46†*
Vocabulary, pp. 47–49*

DIAGNOSTIC AND SELECTION
   TESTS
Selection Tests, pp. 299–302

BEST PRACTICES TOOLKIT
Word Squares, p. E10
Definition Mapping, p. E6
Sequence Chain, p. B21
New Word Analysis, p. E8
Venn Diagram, p. A26

TECHNOLOGY
- Teacher One Stop DVD-ROM
- Student One Stop DVD-ROM
- Audio Anthology CD
- ExamView Test Generator
   on the Teacher One Stop

*Resources for Differentiation   † Also in Spanish   ‡ In Haitian Creole and Vietnamese

TEXT ANALYSIS: MEDIEVAL ROMANCE

In the 12th century, a new literary form—the **romance**—developed in France and spread throughout Europe. The main purpose of a romance was to recount the heroic deeds of knights and to celebrate their chivalric way of life. Romances typically involved **archetypes,** or familiar elements of traditional literature, such as a hero and his quest. As you read the selections, notice these other elements of medieval romance:

- idealized noble characters
- exaggerated or larger-than-life behavior
- a hero's journey or quest, which is motivated by love, religious faith, or a desire for adventure
- supernatural or magical elements
- unusual or exotic settings
- incidents involving hidden or mistaken identity

READING SKILL: EVALUATE

The chivalric code is of great importance in the world Malory describes. As you read, **evaluate,** or make judgments about, how well the main characters follow the code. Complete a chart like the one shown. For each character listed, place a check mark by the chivalric traits he demonstrates.

	Uther	Arthur	Launcelot	Tarquine
Courage				
Honesty				
Loyalty				
Generosity				
Kindness				

◢ VOCABULARY IN CONTEXT

The following words are used in the selections. Some of these words may seem unusual or antiquated. Review the list, noting any familiar roots, prefixes, and suffixes that might help you unlock the meanings of the words.

WORD LIST	abash	ignominiously	succession
	adversary	prowess	vindicate
	fidelity	recompense	

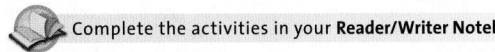 Complete the activities in your **Reader/Writer Notebook.**

Meet the Author

A Knight Himself
The man who wrote *Le Morte d'Arthur* called himself "Syr Thomas Maleore, knight." He also indicated that he completed this work in the ninth year of Edward IV's reign (1469 or 1470), and he added a prayer that he be delivered from prison. Although his precise identity remains uncertain, most historians believe him to be Sir Thomas Malory (1405?–1471), an English knight who lived at the end of the Middle Ages.

Behind Bars
As a youth, Malory fought bravely for England during the Hundred Years' War with France. In the 1440s, however, he embarked on a life of crime. From 1451 on, Malory was imprisoned several times, accused of such crimes as highway robbery and attempted murder. In 1462, he joined rebel forces opposing Edward IV in the Wars of the Roses. Accused of treason, he spent the remainder of his life in London's Newgate Prison, where historians believe he wrote *Le Morte d'Arthur.*

BACKGROUND TO THE ROMANCE
Legendary King
The legend of King Arthur is one of the most popular and enduring legends in Western culture. Some scholars believe the tales of King Arthur were inspired by the heroic deeds of an actual Celtic chieftain or warlord who defended Britain against Anglo-Saxon (Germanic) invaders during the 5th or 6th century. However, the historical Arthur was undoubtedly very different from the king of legend, who ruled an idealized world of knights, damsels, and dragons.

The earliest tales of Arthur come from Welsh literature. Malory drew upon these ancient tales and several 13th-century French romances in writing *Le Morte d'Arthur.* Most English-speaking readers know of the Arthurian legend through this work or one of its modern retellings.

Author Online

 Go to **thinkcentral.com**. KEYWORD: HML10-1111

1111

Teach

● *Model the Skill:* MEDIEVAL ROMANCE

To model how to analyze medieval romance, read aloud this example:

> "For Giliana, please spare my life, Sir," moaned Sir Crispus.
>
> "As you speak of the fairest of ladies," replied Sir Finley, "I beg your forgiveness for having wounded you."

Point out that the example includes conventions of medieval romance, such as noble characters and a reference to love as a motivating force.

GUIDED PRACTICE Discuss how students might add other conventions of medieval romance to the example.

■ *Model the Skill:* EVALUATE

To model how to evaluate the chivalric traits listed on the Evaluate chart, urge students to consider these types of evidence:

- what the character says or does
- what the narrator or other characters say about the character

GUIDED PRACTICE Ask students to name specific "knightly" words or actions that might help them evaluate the characters about whom Malory writes.

R RESOURCE MANAGER—Copy Master
Evaluate p. 45

◢ VOCABULARY IN CONTEXT

DIAGNOSE WORD KNOWLEDGE Have all students complete Vocabulary in Context. Check their responses against the following:

abash (ə-băsh′) *v.* to make ashamed or embarrass
adversary (ăd′vər-sĕr′ē) *n.* an opponent; enemy
fidelity (fĭ-dĕl′ĭ-tē) *n.* faithfulness to duties; loyalty and devotion
ignominiously (ĭg′nə-mĭn′ē-əs-lē) *adv.* shamefully
prowess (prou′ĭs) *n.* superior skill, strength, or

courage, especially in battle
recompense (rĕk′əm-pĕns′) *n.* amends for damage or payment for service
succession (sək-sĕsh′ən) *n.* the sequence in which one person after another acquires a title, dignity, or estate
vindicate (vĭn′dĭ-kāt′) *v.* to clear of suspicion, doubt, or blame

PRETEACH VOCABULARY Use the following copy master to help students self-assess their knowledge of each boldfaced word.

R RESOURCE MANAGER—Copy Master
Vocabulary Study p. 47

1. Read item 1 aloud, emphasizing *abashed.*
2. Point out the clue "an embarrassing defeat." Elicit possible meanings for *abashed,* such as "ashamed" or "humiliated."
3. Repeat the procedure for items 2–8.

READ WITH A PURPOSE

Help students set a purpose for reading. Tell students to look for characters behaving chivalrously.

READING SKILL

COMMON CORE

RL 7

A EVALUATE

Possible answer: King Uther hears that Igraine, the wife of his enemy, the Duke of Tintagil, is beautiful, so he declares a truce and invites them to dinner. He asks Igraine to be his mistress; she refuses, and she and the duke sneak away. Enraged, King Uther wages war on the duke but cannot defeat him. Most students will say that Uther behaves dishonorably because he tries to seduce another man's wife and then starts a bloody war when she rejects him.

IF STUDENTS NEED HELP . . . point out lines 7–8 and line 14. Ask students what the king's actions have in common. *Possible answer:* The actions are motivated by emotion, not logic, and they do harm rather than good.

from LE MORTE D'ARTHUR

The CROWNING of ARTHUR

Sir Thomas Malory

King Uther Pendragon,[1] ruler of all Britain, had been at war for many years with the Duke of Tintagil in Cornwall when he was told of the beauty of Lady Igraine,[2] the duke's wife. Thereupon he called a truce and invited the duke and Igraine to his court, where he prepared a feast for them, and where, as soon as they arrived, he was formally reconciled to the duke through the good offices of his courtiers.[3]

In the course of the feast, King Uther grew passionately desirous of Igraine and, when it was over, begged her to become his paramour.[4] Igraine, however, being as naturally loyal as she was beautiful, refused him.

10 "I suppose," said Igraine to her husband, the duke, when this had happened, "that the king arranged this truce only because he wanted to make me his mistress. I suggest that we leave at once, without warning, and ride overnight to our castle." The duke agreed with her, and they left the court secretly.

The king was enraged by Igraine's flight and summoned his privy council.[5] They advised him to command the fugitives' return under threat of renewing the war; but when this was done, the duke and Igraine defied his summons. He then warned them that they could expect to be dragged from their castle within six weeks.

The duke manned and provisioned[6] his two strongest castles: Tintagil for 20 Igraine, and Terrabyl, which was useful for its many sally ports,[7] for himself. Soon King Uther arrived with a huge army and laid siege to Terrabyl; but despite the ferocity of the fighting, and the numerous casualties suffered by both sides, neither was able to gain a decisive victory. **A**

Still enraged, and now despairing, King Uther fell sick. His friend Sir Ulfius came to him and asked what the trouble was. "Igraine has broken my heart," the king replied, "and unless I can win her, I shall never recover."

Analyze Visuals ▶

The two scenes shown are from a medieval manuscript about King Arthur. What event does each scene seem to depict?

① Targeted Passage

A EVALUATE
Summarize the events that lead King Uther to renew his battle with the duke of Tintagil. Do you think King Uther behaves honorably? Why or why not?

1. **Uther Pendragon** (ōō'thər pĕn-drăg'ən): Uther took the name *Pendragon* after seeing a dragon-shaped comet, which foretold his ascension to power. *Pendragon* refers to a supreme chief or leader.
2. **Igraine** (ē-grān').
3. **offices of his courtiers** (kôrt'tē-ərz): services of his court attendants.
4. **paramour** (păr'ə-mŏŏr'): sweetheart or lover.
5. **privy** (prĭv'ē) **council:** a group of advisers who serve a ruler.
6. **provisioned:** supplied.
7. **sally ports:** gates or doors in the walls of fortifications, from which troops can make sudden attacks.

Arthur Extracting the Sword (1280) from *Histoire de Merlin.* MS Fr.95, f.159v 14tr. Bibliothèque Nationale de France, Paris. Photo © Bibliotheque Nationale de France, Paris.

1112 UNIT 10: GREEK TRAGEDY AND MEDIEVAL ROMANCE

DIFFERENTIATED INSTRUCTION

FOR ENGLISH LANGUAGE LEARNERS

Vocabulary Support Use Word Squares to teach these words: *despite* (line 22), *conceived* (line 50), *task* (line 58), *identity* (line 88), *estates* (line 89), *projected* (line 130).

BEST PRACTICES TOOLKIT—Transparency Word Squares p. E10

FOR STRUGGLING READERS

In combination with the *Audio Anthology CD,* use one or more Targeted Passages (pp. 1112, 1116, 1117, 1118, 1121, 1124, 1126) to ensure that students focus on key ideas, concepts, and skills. Targeted Passages are also good for English learners.

① Targeted Passage [Lines 7–26]

This passage reveals a key plot event and insights into the characters of Uther and Igraine.

Direct students to lines 31–48. Use these prompts to help students understand Merlin and Uther's alliance:

Summarize What agreement do Merlin and Uther reach? *Merlin will arrange for Uther to be with Igraine; Uther will let Merlin rear the child that will be born from that union.*

Analyze How do the motives of Uther and Merlin differ in the plot to deceive Igraine? *Possible answer: Uther is motivated only by his desire for Igraine, but Merlin seems to have an ulterior motive, as he confides to Sir Ulfius that the plan will be to Uther's benefit more than his own (lines 33–34).*

Evaluate How might a present-day audience react to Merlin's plan? *Possible answer: An audience today might take a negative view of the plan because it sanctions adultery and treats a baby (and its mother) as a prize.*

TEXT ANALYSIS

COMMON CORE

Ⓑ MEDIEVAL ROMANCE

RL 3
RL 5

Possible answer: Merlin demonstrates his magical powers by appearing as a beggar, by knowing that Ulfius is seeking him, and by making Uther appear to be the duke and Ulfius and himself appear to be the duke's knights.

"Sire," said Sir Ulfius, "surely Merlin the Prophet[8] could find some means to help you? I will go in search of him."

Sir Ulfius had not ridden far when he was accosted by a hideous beggar. 30 "For whom are you searching?" asked the beggar; but Sir Ulfius ignored him.

"Very well," said the beggar, "I will tell you: you are searching for Merlin, and you need look no further, for I am he. Now go to King Uther and tell him that I will make Igraine his if he will reward me as I ask; and even that will be more to his benefit than to mine."

"I am sure," said Sir Ulfius, "that the king will refuse you nothing reasonable."

"Then go, and I shall follow you," said Merlin.

Well pleased, Sir Ulfius galloped back to the king and delivered Merlin's message, which he had hardly completed when Merlin himself appeared at the entrance to the pavilion.[9] The king bade him welcome.

40 "Sire," said Merlin, "I know that you are in love with Igraine; will you swear, as an anointed[10] king, to give into my care the child that she bears you, if I make her yours?"

The king swore on the gospel that he would do so, and Merlin continued: "Tonight you shall appear before Igraine at Tintagil in the likeness of her husband, the duke. Sir Ulfius and I will appear as two of the duke's knights: Sir Brastius and Sir Jordanus. Do not question either Igraine or her men, but say that you are sick and retire to bed. I will fetch you early in the morning, and do not rise until I come; fortunately Tintagil is only ten miles from here."

The plan succeeded: Igraine was completely deceived by the king's 50 impersonation of the duke, and gave herself to him, and conceived Arthur. The king left her at dawn as soon as Merlin appeared, after giving her a farewell kiss. But the duke had seen King Uther ride out from the siege on the previous night and, in the course of making a surprise attack on the king's army, had been killed. When Igraine realized that the duke had died three hours before he had appeared to her, she was greatly disturbed in mind; however, she confided in no one. Ⓑ

 nce it was known that the duke was dead, the king's nobles urged him to be reconciled to Igraine, and this task the king gladly entrusted to Sir Ulfius, by whose eloquence it was soon accomplished. "And 60 now," said Sir Ulfius to his fellow nobles, "why should not the king marry the beautiful Igraine? Surely it would be as well for us all."

The marriage of King Uther and Igraine was celebrated joyously thirteen days later; and then, at the king's request, Igraine's sisters were also married: Margawse, who later bore Sir Gawain, to King Lot of Lowthean and Orkney; Elayne, to King Nentres of Garlot. Igraine's daughter, Morgan le Fay, was put to school in a nunnery; in after years she was to become a witch, and to be married to King Uryens of Gore, and give birth to Sir Uwayne of the Fair Hands.

---

8. **Merlin the Prophet:** Merlin possesses the ability to prophesy, or predict future events.

9. **pavilion:** a large tent, often with a peaked top.

10. **anointed:** installed in office with a religious ceremony.

Ⓑ MEDIEVAL ROMANCE
Reread lines 29–56. Describe the ways in which Merlin demonstrates his **magical powers** to Sir Ulfius and King Uther.

DIFFERENTIATED INSTRUCTION

FOR STRUGGLING READERS

Comprehension Support As students begin this next section of the story, make sure they understand that the wedding of Uther and Igraine serves several purposes:

- It fulfills and legitimizes Uther's desire to be with Igraine.

- It merges their realms (Britain and Cornwall).

- It ensures that Arthur will not be born out of wedlock.

- It forges alliances with the realms ruled by the new husbands of Igraine's sisters.

FOR ENGLISH LANGUAGE LEARNERS

Vocabulary: Multiple-Meaning Words Have students use Definition Mapping to master varying definitions of each of these multiple-meaning words: *swear* (line 40), *retire* (line 47), *course* (line 53), *celebrated* (line 62), *bore* (line 64), *checked* (line 100), *plain* (line 102).

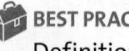 **BEST PRACTICES TOOLKIT—Transparency**
Definition Mapping p. E6

A few months later it was seen that Igraine was with child, and one night, as she lay in bed with King Uther, he asked her who the father might be. Igraine was greatly **abashed.**

"Do not look so dismayed," said the king, "but tell me the truth, and I swear I shall love you the better for it."

"The truth is," said Igraine, "that the night the duke died, about three hours after his death, a man appeared in my castle—the exact image of the duke. With him came two others who appeared to be Sir Brastius and Sir Jordanus. Naturally I gave myself to this man as I would have to the duke, and that night, I swear, this child was conceived."

"Well spoken," said the king; "it was I who impersonated the duke, so the child is mine." He then told Igraine the story of how Merlin had arranged it, and Igraine was overjoyed to discover that the father of her child was now her husband. **C**

Sometime later, Merlin appeared before the king. "Sire," he said, "you know that you must provide for the upbringing of your child?"

"I will do as you advise," the king replied.

"That is good," said Merlin, "because it is my reward for having arranged your impersonation of the duke. Your child is destined for glory, and I want him brought to me for his baptism.[11] I shall then give him into the care of foster parents who can be trusted not to reveal his identity before the proper time. Sir Ector would be suitable: he is extremely loyal, owns good estates, and his wife has just borne him a child. She could give her child into the care of another woman, and herself look after yours."

Sir Ector was summoned and gladly agreed to the king's request, who then rewarded him handsomely. When the child was born, he was at once wrapped in a gold cloth and taken by two knights and two ladies to Merlin, who stood waiting at the rear entrance to the castle in his beggar's disguise. Merlin took the child to a priest, who baptized him with the name of Arthur, and thence to Sir Ector, whose wife fed him at her breast. **D**

Two years later King Uther fell sick, and his enemies once more overran his kingdom, inflicting heavy losses on him as they advanced. Merlin prophesied that they could be checked only by the presence of the king himself on the battlefield, and suggested that he should be conveyed there on a horse litter.[12] King Uther's army met the invader on the plain at St. Albans, and the king duly appeared on the horse litter. Inspired by his presence, and by the lively leadership of Sir Brastius and Sir Jordanus, his army quickly defeated the enemy, and the battle finished in a rout. The king returned to London to celebrate the victory.

But his sickness grew worse, and after he had lain speechless for three days and three nights, Merlin summoned the nobles to attend the king in his chamber on the following morning. "By the grace of God," he said, "I hope to make him speak."

---

11. **baptism:** a religious sacrament that marks the admission of a person into the Christian faith. In Arthurian legend, Arthur represents the ideal Christian knight and monarch.

12. **horse litter:** a stretcher pulled by a horse.

LE MORTE D'ARTHUR   **1115**

abash (ə-băsh') v. to make ashamed or embarrass

C MEDIEVAL ROMANCE
Think about Malory's depiction of Igraine up to this point. What details suggest that she is an **idealized character?**

D EVALUATE
Reread lines 82–97. In what way does Merlin show his loyalty to King Uther and the Britons?

C Model the Skill: MEDIEVAL ROMANCE

Remind students that idealized characters are one of the conventions of medieval romance. Point out lines 70–73 in which Igraine tells the truth despite being embarrassed to do so. Explain that she is an idealized character in part because she is truthful.

Possible answer: *Details suggesting that Igraine is an idealized character are her beauty and loyalty. She also lacks anger for Uther for deceiving and taking advantage of her and for being the indirect cause of the duke's death. In fact, she is said to be "overjoyed" at learning that Uther is the father of her mysteriously conceived child (lines 80–81).*

Extend the Discussion If you added Igraine to the evaluation chart on page 1111, how would she rate, compared to Uther?

D EVALUATE

Possible answer: *Merlin shows his loyalty by protecting Uther's child: having Arthur baptized, arranging for his rearing outside the court, and concealing his identity until the proper time.*

IF STUDENTS NEED HELP . . . Ask these questions about Merlin's description of his plan (lines 85–91):

• What future does Merlin predict for Arthur?

• What does Merlin's plan suggest about his motivation?

OWN THE WORD

abash: Remind students that the definition for *abash* is "to make ashamed or embarrassed." Have students write sentences using the word correctly.

FOR STRUGGLING READERS

Comprehension Support Have students create a Sequence Chain to review the events between the death of the Duke of Tintagil and the death of King Uther.

Uther marries the widowed Igraine and finds husbands for her sisters.

↓

Igraine describes her mysterious pregnancy and is happy to learn that Uther is the father.

↓

Merlin asks to rear Arthur; Uther agrees.

↓

The baby is given to the household of Sir Ector.

↓

Uther falls gravely ill and names Arthur as his successor before he dies.

🛠 **BEST PRACTICES TOOLKIT—Transparency**
Sequence Chain p. B21

Direct students to lines 110–133. Use these prompts to help students grasp the difficulty of Arthur's succession:

Summarize What wish does King Uther make from his deathbed concerning his successor? *Possible answer: King Uther declares his wish that Arthur should succeed him as king.*

Analyze What do lines 118–120 indicate about the state of affairs in Britain following King Uther's death? *Possible answer: Ambitious barons were fighting each other for the throne, unaware that King Uther had already named an heir.*

Evaluate Is this plan for succession a wise one? Why or why not? *Possible answer: The plan is wise if Arthur is the only person who can free the sword from the stone.*

VOCABULARY

COMMON CORE L 4

OWN THE WORD

succession: *Succession* refers to a sequence or order of how things are arranged. In line 123, *succession* refers to which person was next in line to become the British king. Have students offer examples of other things that follow in *succession*.

---

110   In the morning, when all the nobles were assembled, Merlin addressed the king: "Sire, is it your will that Arthur shall succeed to the throne, together with all its prerogatives?"[13]

The king stirred in his bed and then spoke so that all could hear: "I bestow on Arthur God's blessing and my own, and Arthur shall succeed to the throne on pain of forfeiting my blessing." Then King Uther gave up the ghost.[14] He was buried and mourned the next day, as befitted his rank, by Igraine and the nobility of Britain.

D   uring the years that followed the death of King Uther, while Arthur was still a child, the ambitious barons fought one another for the
120   throne, and the whole of Britain stood in jeopardy. Finally the day came when the Archbishop of Canterbury,[15] on the advice of Merlin, summoned the nobility to London for Christmas morning. In his message the archbishop promised that the true **succession** to the British throne would be miraculously revealed. Many of the nobles purified themselves during their journey, in the hope that it would be to them that the succession would fall.

The archbishop held his service in the city's greatest church (St. Paul's), and when matins[16] were done, the congregation filed out to the yard. They were confronted by a marble block into which had been thrust a beautiful sword. The block was four feet square, and the sword passed through a steel
130   anvil which had been struck in the stone, and which projected a foot from it. The anvil had been inscribed with letters of gold:

WHOSO PULLETH OUTE THIS SWERD OF THIS STONE AND ANVYLD
IS RIGHTWYS KYNGE BORNE OF ALL BRYTAYGNE[17]

The congregation was awed by this miraculous sight, but the archbishop forbade anyone to touch the sword before mass had been heard. After mass, many of the nobles tried to pull the sword out of the stone, but none was able to, so a watch of ten knights was set over the sword, and a tournament proclaimed for New Year's Day, to provide men of noble blood with the opportunity of proving their right to the succession.
140   Sir Ector, who had been living on an estate near London, rode to the tournament with Arthur and his own son Sir Kay, who had been recently knighted. When they arrived at the tournament, Sir Kay found to his annoyance that his sword was missing from its sheath, so he begged Arthur to ride back and fetch it from their lodging.

Arthur found the door of the lodging locked and bolted, the landlord and his wife having left for the tournament. In order not to disappoint his brother, he rode on to St. Paul's, determined to get for him the sword which was lodged

---

13. **prerogatives:** rights and privileges.
14. **gave up the ghost:** died.
15. **Archbishop of Canterbury:** the leader of the Christian community in England.
16. **matins** (măt'nz): morning prayers.
17. **Whoso pulleth . . . all Brytaygne:** Whoever pulls this sword from this stone and anvil is rightfully king of all Britain.

1116   UNIT 10: GREEK TRAGEDY AND MEDIEVAL ROMANCE

---

② **Targeted Passage**

succession (sək-sĕsh'ən) *n.* the sequence in which one person after another acquires a title, dignity, or estate

---

COMMON CORE RL 4

Language Coach

Roots and Affixes A word's **root** may contain its core meaning. The word *proclaimed* (line 138) comes from the Latin root *clamare*, "to cry out." *Proclaimed* means "announced officially." What other words with this root do you know, and what do those words mean?

DIFFERENTIATED INSTRUCTION

FOR STRUGGLING READERS

② **Targeted Passage** [Lines 110–124]

This passage focuses on Merlin's power in steering the fate of Britain.

- What important step does Merlin take at King Uther's deathbed? (lines 110–115)
- How would you describe Merlin's role in the succession of power? (lines 106–115)
- How important is magic in Merlin's role? (lines 106–115)

FOR ENGLISH LANGUAGE LEARNERS

Language Coach   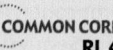 COMMON CORE RL 4

Roots and Affixes

Possible answer: claim, *"to assert"*; exclaim, *"to say in surprise"*; acclaim, *"to praise loudly"*; reclaim, *"to demand the return of"*. Have students work in pairs and use each of the words in original sentences. Then have student volunteers share their sentences with the class.

in the stone. The yard was empty, the guard also having slipped off to see the tournament, so Arthur strode up to the sword, and, without troubling
150 to read the inscription, tugged it free. He then rode straight back to Sir Kay and presented him with it.

Sir Kay recognized the sword and, taking it to Sir Ector, said, "Father, the succession falls to me, for I have here the sword that was lodged in the stone." But Sir Ector insisted that they should all ride to the churchyard, and once there bound Sir Kay by oath to tell how he had come by the sword. Sir Kay then admitted that Arthur had given it to him. Sir Ector turned to Arthur and said, "Was the sword not guarded?"

"It was not," Arthur replied.

"Would you please thrust it into the stone again?" said Sir Ector. Arthur
160 did so, and first Sir Ector and then Sir Kay tried to remove it, but both were unable to. Then Arthur, for the second time, pulled it out. Sir Ector and Sir Kay both knelt before him.

"Why," said Arthur, "do you both kneel before me?" **E**

"My lord," Sir Ector replied, "there is only one man living who can draw the sword from the stone, and he is the true-born King of Britain." Sir Ector then told Arthur the story of his birth and upbringing.

"My dear father," said Arthur, "for so I shall always think of you—if, as you say, I am to be king, please know that any request you have to make is already granted."

170 Sir Ector asked that Sir Kay should be made Royal Seneschal,[18] and Arthur declared that while they both lived it should be so. Then the three of them visited the archbishop and told him what had taken place. **F**

All those dukes and barons with ambitions to rule were present at the tournament on New Year's Day. But when all of them had failed, and Arthur alone had succeeded in drawing the sword from the stone, they protested against one so young, and of ignoble[19] blood, succeeding to the throne.

The secret of Arthur's birth was known only to a few of the nobles surviving from the days of King Uther. The archbishop urged them to make Arthur's cause their own; but their support proved ineffective. The tournament was
180 repeated at Candlemas and at Easter, and with the same outcome as before.

Finally at Pentecost,[20] when once more Arthur alone had been able to remove the sword, the commoners arose with a tumultuous cry and demanded that Arthur should at once be made king. The nobles, knowing in their hearts that the commoners were right, all knelt before Arthur and begged forgiveness for having delayed his succession for so long. Arthur forgave them and then, offering his sword at the high altar, was dubbed[21] first knight of the realm. The coronation took place a few days later, when Arthur swore to rule justly, and the nobles swore him their allegiance. ❧ **G**

③ Targeted Passage

---

18. **Royal Seneschal** (sĕn′ə-shəl): the representative of a king in judicial and domestic matters.
19. **ignoble**: not noble; common.
20. **Candlemas . . . Easter . . . Pentecost** (pĕn′tĭ-kôst′): Christian holidays.
21. **dubbed**: granted knighthood by being tapped on the shoulder.

COMMON CORE RL 5

E ARCHETYPE
An **archetype** is a pattern that reappears in literature throughout history and in different cultures. One archetype that appears in this romance is hidden identity—a noble or ruler whose true parentage is hidden. What other stories have you encountered that contain this archetype? Why do you think this idea appeals to readers?

F EVALUATE
Compare the behavior of Sir Kay with that of Arthur. Which character better illustrates the chivalric traits of a knight? Explain.

G MEDIEVAL ROMANCE
Reread lines 173–188. How do Arthur's actions fit the conventions of medieval romance?

TEXT ANALYSIS

COMMON CORE RL 5

E ARCHETYPE

Read lines 152–166 aloud. Point out that Arthur fits the archetype of hidden identity. Elicit explanations from students about why Arthur fits this archetype.

Possible answer: *Students may mention characters such as Harry Potter, Oedipus, or Oliver Twist. They may suggest that this idea appeals to readers as a way for people to find a wonderful destiny in store for them, despite their original circumstances.*

READING SKILL

COMMON CORE RL 7

F Model the Skill: EVALUATE

Remind students that chivalric traits include courage, honesty, loyalty, generosity, and kindness. Have students use their Evaluate charts to determine and record which of the traits apply to Sir Kay and which apply to Arthur. Ask: How do the two men compare?

	Uther	Arthur
Courage	✓	✓
Honesty		✓
Loyalty		✓
Generosity		✓
Kindness		✓

Possible answer: *Arthur better illustrates the chivalric traits of a knight. Sir Kay, who lies about how he got the sword (lines 152–153), wants to claim the throne for himself. Arthur, on the other hand, is truthful and humbly acts in service of others. When he learns that he may be king, he thinks not about himself but about how he can help his family (lines 167–169).*

TEXT ANALYSIS

COMMON CORE RL 3 RL 5

G MEDIEVAL ROMANCE

Possible answer: *Arthur's actions fit the conventions of medieval romance through magical elements, when he pulls the sword from the stone; generosity, when he gives the sword to Kay; loyalty, when he affirms Ector's fatherhood and bestows a rank upon Kay; and kindness, when he offers to grant any request from Ector.*

FOR STRUGGLING READERS

③ Targeted Passage [Lines 173–188]

This passage shows how Arthur finally becomes king of Britain.

- What action does Arthur perform in the tournament on New Year's Day? Why is it significant? (lines 140–151)
- How do the nobles react to Arthur's success in the tournament on New Year's Day? (lines 173–176)

Develop Reading Fluency Read lines 148–169 aloud. Then have students practice reading the parts of Sir Ector, Sir Kay, Arthur, and the narrator in groups of four. After students can read the passage fluently, invite volunteers to read the exchange in front of the class.

Distribute the copy masters and have students work in pairs or groups to practice fluency.

R RESOURCE MANAGER—Copy Master
Reading Fluency p. 52

Prereading for this selection is found on page 1110.

from LE MORTE D'ARTHUR

Sir Launcelot du Lake

Sir Thomas Malory

When King Arthur returned from Rome, he settled his court at Camelot, and there gathered about him his knights of the Round Table, who diverted themselves with jousting[22] and tournaments. Of all his knights one was supreme, both in **prowess** at arms and in nobility of bearing, and this was Sir Launcelot, who was also the favorite of Queen Gwynevere, to whom he had sworn oaths of **fidelity**.

One day Sir Launcelot, feeling weary of his life at the court, and of only playing at arms,[23] decided to set forth in search of adventure. He asked his nephew Sir Lyonel to accompany him, and when both were suitably armed
10 and mounted, they rode off together through the forest. ⊕

At noon they started across a plain, but the intensity of the sun made Sir Launcelot feel sleepy, so Sir Lyonel suggested that they should rest beneath the shade of an apple tree that grew by a hedge not far from the road. They dismounted, tethered their horses, and settled down.

"Not for seven years have I felt so sleepy," said Sir Launcelot, and with that fell fast asleep, while Sir Lyonel watched over him.

Soon three knights came galloping past, and Sir Lyonel noticed that they were being pursued by a fourth knight, who was one of the most powerful he had yet seen. The pursuing knight overtook each of the others in turn and,
20 as he did so, knocked each off his horse with a thrust of his spear. When all three lay stunned, he dismounted, bound them securely to their horses with the reins, and led them away.

Without waking Sir Launcelot, Sir Lyonel mounted his horse and rode after the knight and, as soon as he had drawn close enough, shouted his challenge. The knight turned about, and they charged at each other, with the result that Sir Lyonel was likewise flung from his horse, bound, and led away a prisoner.

prowess (prou'ĭs) *n.* superior skill, strength, or courage, especially in battle

fidelity (fĭ-dĕl'ĭ-tē) *n.* faithfulness to duties; loyalty and devotion

⊕ **MEDIEVAL ROMANCE**
Reread lines 7–10. What motivates Sir Launcelot to begin his **quest**?

① **Targeted Passage**

Analyze Visuals ▶

How does the use of color and active figures affect the **mood** of this illustration? Contrast the mood with that of the illustration on page 1113.

---

22. **jousting:** combat between two knights who charge each other with lances while riding horses.
23. **playing at arms:** fighting with weapons as sport.

Tournament jousting at the court of Caerleon (1468). *Les Chroniques de Hainaut.* MS. 9243, fol. 45. Bibliotheque Royale Albert I, Brussels, Belgium. Photo © Art Resource, New York.

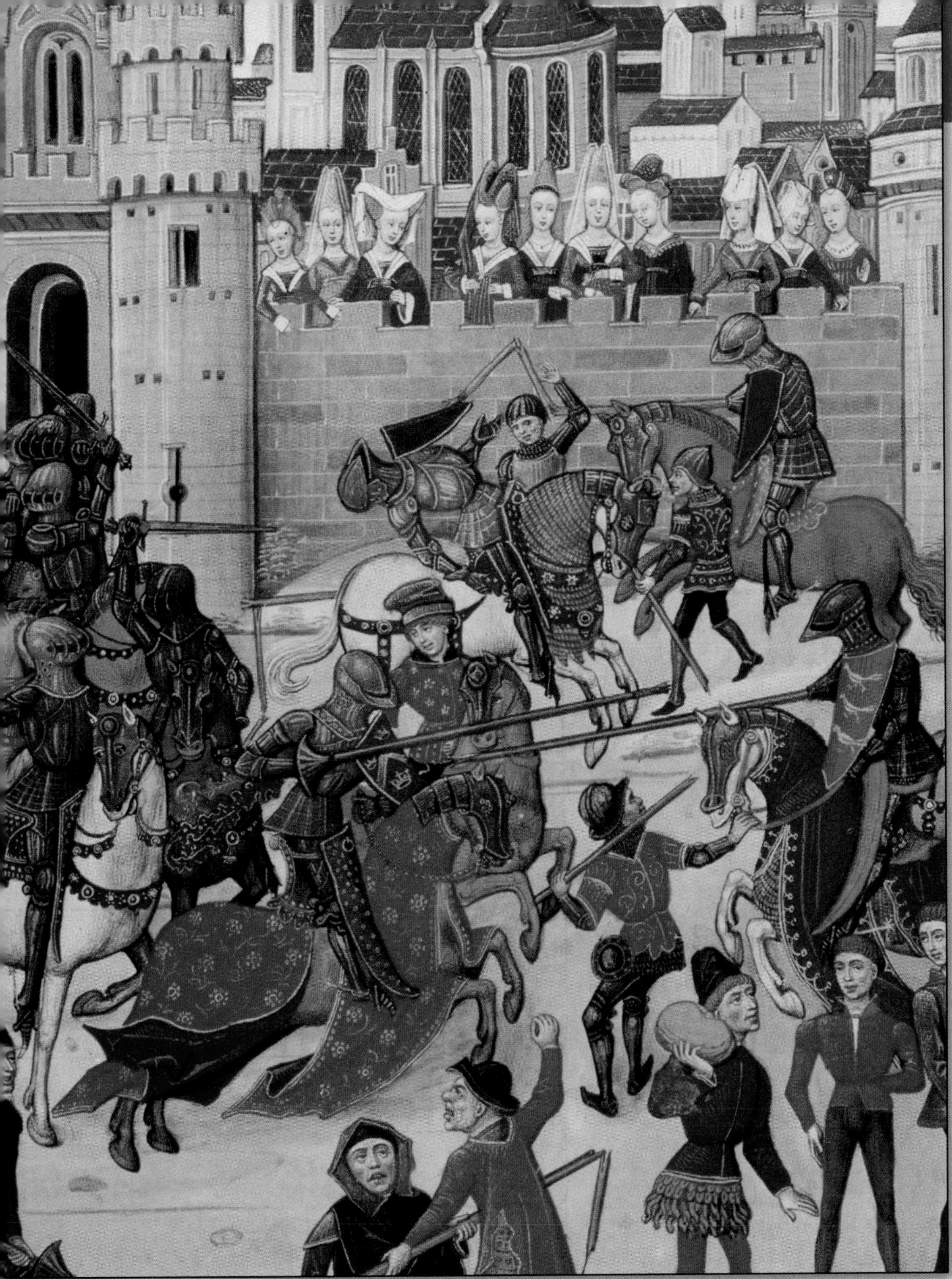

BACKGROUND

Jousting and Tournaments The words *joust* and *tournament* are often used interchangeably. In strict terms, however, jousting featured combat between only two horsemen armed with lances, whereas a tournament (as the illustration on this page shows) was a bloody brawl between groups of armored knights. The tournament arose in France in the mid-11th century and spread to the West by the mid-12th century. In the 13th century, officials developed the "joust of peace," which used no metal weapons. Still, participants in tournaments often were gravely injured or even killed. Such gatherings were banned by the Church, only to resurface later.

Analyze Visuals

Possible answer: *The colors and active figures help create a mood of excitement, intensity, and festivity. It is in contrast with the quieter, more stately mood of the illustration on page 1113.*

About the Art *Tournament jousting at the court of Caerleon* is characteristic of Burgundian Golden Age. This scene— which depicts an element of court life with which Sir Launcelot has grown dissatisfied (lines 7–8)—comes from the illuminated manuscript *Les chroniques de Hainaut*. The chronicles recount the tales of King Arthur. Caerleon, a town in Britain's South Wales, is thought by many to be the basis for Camelot, where Arthur settled his court (lines 1–3).

FOR ENGLISH LANGUAGE LEARNERS

Vocabulary Support Use New Word Analysis to teach these words: *pursued* (line 18), *challenge* (line 24), *encounter* (line 48), *assure* (line 154), *liberally* (line 249).

BEST PRACTICES TOOLKIT—Transparency
New Word Analysis p. E8

FOR ADVANCED LEARNERS/PRE–AP

Compare and Contrast Motifs [paired-activity option] Explain that "the quest" is a literary **motif**—a theme or concept that appears in literature across cultures and time periods. Then ask students to compare and contrast Launcelot's quest with other quests that they have read about or seen in movies. Invite students to prepare a graphic organizer to record their comments about the quests. Then have them share their comments with the class.

Could you be a KNIGHT?

Discuss In lines 31–35, what do Sir Ector's actions and words suggest about his sense of chivalry? Explain. **Possible answer:** *Sir Ector's willingness to follow Sir Launcelot shows bravery and loyalty. His polite words to the forester suggest that he is a gentleman. These are all traits of a chivalrous knight.*

---

❶ MEDIEVAL ROMANCE   RL 3   RL 5

Possible answer: *Unusual or exotic details of setting include a moated castle (lines 36 and 44); a tree from which knights' shields dangle ominously (lines 38–39 and 44–45); and a caldron (cauldron) that, when struck, brings on an adventure (lines 39–42 and 46–47).*

---

❷ EVALUATE   RL 7

Possible answer: *Sir Tarquine appreciates a skilled opponent and fights fairly. After defeating Sir Ector, he asks only Ector's parole as his prisoner (lines 54–56), so he seems to treat Ector fairly. However, when Ector refuses, Tarquine unfairly strips him, beats him, and locks him up, as he has done to others (lines 57–60).*

IF STUDENTS NEED HELP . . . Guide them to form opinions by considering these points:

- Chivalry stemmed, in part, from physical prowess.
- Punishing captives of rival kingdoms was not considered cruel in medieval times.

The victorious knight, whose name was Sir Tarquine,[24] led his prisoners to his castle and there threw them on the ground, stripped them naked, and beat them with thorn twigs. After that he locked them in a dungeon where many
30 other prisoners, who had received like treatment, were complaining dismally.

Meanwhile, Sir Ector de Marys,[25] who liked to accompany Sir Launcelot on his adventures, and finding him gone, decided to ride after him. Before long he came upon a forester.

"My good fellow, if you know the forest hereabouts, could you tell me in which direction I am most likely to meet with adventure?"

"Sir, I can tell you: less than a mile from here stands a well-moated castle. On the left of the entrance you will find a ford where you can water your horse, and across from the ford a large tree from which hang the shields of many famous knights. Below the shields hangs a caldron, of copper and
40 brass: strike it three times with your spear, and then surely you will meet with adventure—such, indeed, that if you survive it, you will prove yourself the foremost knight in these parts for many years."

"May God reward you!" Sir Ector replied.

The castle was exactly as the forester had described it, and among the shields Sir Ector recognized several as belonging to knights of the Round Table. After watering his horse, he knocked on the caldron, and Sir Tarquine, whose castle it was, appeared.

They jousted, and at the first encounter Sir Ector sent his opponent's horse spinning twice about before he could recover.

50 "That was a fine stroke; now let us try again," said Sir Tarquine.

This time Sir Tarquine caught Sir Ector just below the right arm and, having impaled him on his spear, lifted him clean out of the saddle and rode with him into the castle, where he threw him on the ground.

"Sir," said Sir Tarquine, "you have fought better than any knight I have encountered in the last twelve years; therefore, if you wish, I will demand no more of you than your parole[26] as my prisoner."

"Sir, that I will never give."

"Then I am sorry for you," said Sir Tarquine, and with that he stripped and beat him and locked him in the dungeon with the other prisoners. There Sir
60 Ector saw Sir Lyonel. ❷

"Alas, Sir Lyonel, we are in a sorry plight. But tell me, what has happened to Sir Launcelot? for he surely is the one knight who could save us."

"I left him sleeping beneath an apple tree, and what has befallen him since I do not know," Sir Lyonel replied; and then all the unhappy prisoners once more bewailed their lot.

---

❶ MEDIEVAL ROMANCE
Reread lines 31–47, and think about the **setting** in which Sir Ector de Marys finds himself. What details suggest that this is an unusual or exotic place?

❷ EVALUATE
Consider Sir Tarquine's behavior up to this point. Does he treat his opponents fairly both on and off the battlefield? Explain.

---

24. **Tarquine** (tär'kwĭn).
25. **Sir Ector de Marys** (măr'əs): the brother of Launcelot.
26. **parole:** the promise of a prisoner to abide by certain conditions in exchange for full or partial freedom.

DIFFERENTIATED INSTRUCTION

FOR STRUGGLING READERS

Concept Support As you discuss lines 36–47, help students grasp that the shields and caldron (cauldron) represent Sir Tarquine's open challenge to any passing knight who might want to engage him in a fight. The shields indicate the knights that he already has defeated and serve as an intimidating symbol to other knights or potential rescuers. Challengers who refuse to be intimidated can use the caldron, like a gong, to summon Sir Tarquine to battle.

FOR ENGLISH LANGUAGE LEARNERS

Vocabulary Support Help students use context clues to grasp words and phrases related to the setting and to the diction of the genre:

- *well-moated* (line 36), "with a good moat, or protective band of water, around it"
- *caldron* (line 39), "large metal pot"
- *dungeon* (line 59), "castle prison, often below ground"
- *bewailed their lot* (line 65), "complained about their situation"

W hile Sir Launcelot still slept beneath the apple tree, four queens started across the plain. They were riding white mules and accompanied by four knights who held above them, at the tips of their spears, a green silk canopy, to protect them from the sun. The party
70 was startled by the neighing of Sir Launcelot's horse and, changing direction, rode up to the apple tree, where they discovered the sleeping knight. And as each of the queens gazed at the handsome Sir Launcelot, so each wanted him for her own.

"Let us not quarrel," said Morgan le Fay. "Instead, I will cast a spell over him so that he remains asleep while we take him to my castle and make him our prisoner. We can then oblige him to choose one of us for his paramour."

Sir Launcelot was laid on his shield and borne by two of the knights to the Castle Charyot, which was Morgan le Fay's stronghold. He awoke to find himself in a cold cell, where a young noblewoman was serving him supper.
80 "What cheer?"[27] she asked.

"My lady, I hardly know, except that I must have been brought here by means of an enchantment."

② Targeted Passage

"Sir, if you are the knight you appear to be, you will learn your fate at dawn tomorrow." And with that the young noblewoman left him. Sir Launcelot spent an uncomfortable night, but at dawn the four queens presented themselves and Morgan le Fay spoke to him:

"Sir Launcelot, I know that Queen Gwynevere loves you, and you her. But now you are my prisoner, and you will have to choose: either to take one of us for your paramour, or to die miserably in this cell—just as you please. Now I
90 will tell you who we are: I am Morgan le Fay, Queen of Gore; my companions are the queens of North Galys, of Estelonde, and of the Outer Isles. So make your choice."

"A hard choice! Understand that I choose none of you, lewd sorceresses that you are; rather will I die in this cell. But were I free, I would take pleasure in proving it against any who would champion you that Queen Gwynevere is the finest lady of this land."

"So, you refuse us?" asked Morgan le Fay.

"On my life, I do," Sir Launcelot said finally, and so the queens departed. **K**
Sometime later, the young noblewoman who had served Sir Launcelot's
100 supper reappeared.

"What news?" she asked.

"It is the end," Sir Launcelot replied.

"Sir Launcelot, I know that you have refused the four queens, and that they wish to kill you out of spite. But if you will be ruled by me, I can save you. I ask that you will champion my father at a tournament next Tuesday, when he has to combat the King of North Galys, and three knights of the Round Table, who last Tuesday defeated him **ignominiously**."

"My lady, pray tell me, what is your father's name?"

K EVALUATE
Reread lines 87–98. What does Launcelot's response to the ultimatum of the four queens reveal about his character?

ignominiously
(ĭg′nə-mĭn′ē-əs-lē) *adv.* shamefully

---

27. **What cheer?:** How are you?

LE MORTE D'ARTHUR 1121

FOR STRUGGLING READERS

② Targeted Passage [Lines 66–82]

This passage focuses on the supernatural element found in many medieval romances.

- What effect does the sleeping Launcelot have upon the four queens? (lines 71–73)

- What is Morgan le Fay's plan? How does magic figure into her plan? (lines 74–76)

- What does Sir Launcelot understand about how he was taken captive? (lines 81–82)

FOR ADVANCED LEARNERS/PRE–AP

Analyze Conflict Ask students to analyze the nature of the conflicts that Sir Lyonel and Sir Launcelot have undergone since embarking upon their adventure. Have them write a brief analysis of these conflicts, taking into account each character's antagonist, means of defeat, and manner in which the conflict is resolved. As students share their analyses, discuss how Malory uses conflict to portray character.

TIERED DISCUSSION PROMPTS

Direct students to lines 58–79. Use these prompts to help students consider how details about imprisonment heighten conflict and suspense in this tale:

Connect Imagine being imprisoned without a trial. How would you feel about your captor? About other prisoners? *Accept all reasonable responses.*

Analyze How do the imprisonments of Ector and Launcelot enhance the plot? *Possible answer: Ector's imprisonment heightens the conflict between Sir Tarquine and the knights of the Round Table; Launcelot's imprisonment adds suspense.*

Synthesize Compare these imprisonments to the earlier imprisonment of Lyonel. What do you think must happen to resolve the story's conflict? *Possible answer: The imprisonment of Lyonel, then Ector, and then Launcelot suggests that a resolution will show the freeing of these captives and perhaps the punishment of the captors (Sir Tarquine and Morgan le Fay).*

READING SKILL   COMMON CORE   RL 7

K EVALUATE

Possible answer: Launcelot's response reveals that he is brave, pure, and loyal to Gwynevere.

IF STUDENTS NEED HELP . . . Have them re-read Morgan le Fay's words in lines 87–89 and Lancelot's response in lines 93–96. Next, have students record Launcelot's chivalric traits in their Evaluate charts. Then assist students in using what they know about the chivalric code to infer the character traits that Launcelot exhibits.

VOCABULARY   COMMON CORE   L 4

OWN THE WORD

ignominiously: Tell students that *ignominious* is the adjective form of the noun *ignominy*, and *ignominiously* is the adverb. Have students give examples of *ignominious* behavior.

Ⓛ MEDIEVAL ROMANCE
RL 3
RL 5

Possible answer: The noblewoman is idealized in that she is virtuous and polite, even as she takes risks in helping Launcelot escape. Launcelot is idealized because although he is in prison, he is courteous and waits to know that her father is honorable before he commits to helping him.

Ⓜ MEDIEVAL ROMANCE
RL 3
RL 5

Possible answer: This scene of hidden identity, involving an amorous knight, is a misunderstanding that creates humor. The earlier scene, in which King Uther is disguised as the duke, involves an intentional deception, and it creates a mysterious and tense mood.

IF STUDENTS NEED HELP . . . Guide them in creating a Venn Diagram that compares and contrasts the two scenes.

Mistaken Identity Scenes

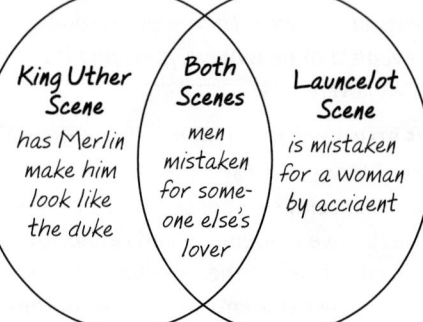

King Uther Scene — has Merlin make him look like the duke

Both Scenes — men mistaken for someone else's lover

Launcelot Scene — is mistaken for a woman by accident

 BEST PRACTICES TOOLKIT—Transparency Venn Diagram p. A26

OWN THE WORD
L 4

adversary: Have students use *adversary* in sentences to show their understanding of the word.

"King Bagdemagus."[28]

110   "Excellent, my lady; I know him for a good king and a true knight, so I shall be happy to serve him."

"May God reward you! And tomorrow at dawn I will release you and direct you to an abbey[29] which is ten miles from here, and where the good monks will care for you while I fetch my father."

"I am at your service, my lady."

As promised, the young noblewoman released Sir Launcelot at dawn. When she had led him through the twelve doors to the castle entrance, she gave him his horse and armor, and directions for finding the abbey.

"God bless you, my lady; and when the time comes, I promise I shall not
120 fail you." Ⓛ

Sir Launcelot rode through the forest in search of the abbey but at dusk had still failed to find it and, coming upon a red silk pavilion, apparently unoccupied, decided to rest there overnight and continue his search in the morning.

He had not been asleep for more than an hour, however, when the knight who owned the pavilion returned and got straight into bed with him. Having made an assignation[30] with his paramour, the knight supposed at first that Sir Launcelot was she and, taking him into his arms, started kissing him. Sir Launcelot awoke with a start and, seizing his sword, leaped out of bed and out
130 of the pavilion, pursued closely by the other knight. Once in the open they set to with their swords, and before long Sir Launcelot had wounded his unknown **adversary** so seriously that he was obliged to yield.

The knight, whose name was Sir Belleus, now asked Sir Launcelot how he came to be sleeping in his bed and then explained how he had an assignation with his lover, adding:

"But now I am so sorely wounded that I shall consider myself fortunate to escape with my life."

"Sir, please forgive me for wounding you; but lately I escaped from an enchantment, and I was afraid that once more I had been betrayed. Let us go
140 into the pavilion, and I will staunch your wound." Ⓜ

Sir Launcelot had just finished binding the wound when the young noblewoman who was Sir Belleus's paramour arrived and, seeing the wound, at once rounded in fury on Sir Launcelot.

"Peace, my love," said Sir Belleus. "This is a noble knight, and as soon as I yielded to him, he treated my wound with the greatest care." Sir Belleus then described the events which had led up to the duel.

"Sir, pray tell me your name, and whose knight you are," the young noblewoman asked Sir Launcelot.

"My lady, I am called Sir Launcelot du Lake."

---

28. **Bagdemagus** (băg'də-măg'əs).

29. **abbey:** a place where monks or nuns live.

30. **assignation** (ăs'ĭg-nā'shən): an appointment for a meeting between lovers.

Ⓛ **MEDIEVAL ROMANCE**
Review the exchange between Sir Launcelot and the noblewoman in lines 99–120. Why might they be considered **idealized characters**?

adversary (ăd'vər-sĕr'ē) *n.* an opponent; enemy

Ⓜ **MEDIEVAL ROMANCE**
Hidden identity is a common element in romances. Compare the scene in lines 121–140 with the scene in lines 40–56 on page 1114. What different effects do these scenes create?

DIFFERENTIATED INSTRUCTION

FOR STRUGGLING READERS

Concept Support Help students see that although the mistaken-identity scene in lines 121–140 is a convention of medieval romance, it is meant as broad comedy. Use these questions to reinforce the scene's purpose and meaning:

- Is this scene meant to be realistic?
- If you were watching this scene performed, when would you start laughing? Why?
- Why might Malory have written this scene?

FOR ENGLISH LANGUAGE LEARNERS

Vocabulary Support Help students use context clues to find the meaning of this scene's genre-related words and phrases:

- *pavilion* (line 122), "large tent with a peaked top"
- *set to* (lines 130–131), "began to fight"
- *staunch* (line 140), "stop the bleeding of"
- *rounded in fury on* (line 143), "turned and angrily faced"
- *sovereign* (line 155), "king or ruler"

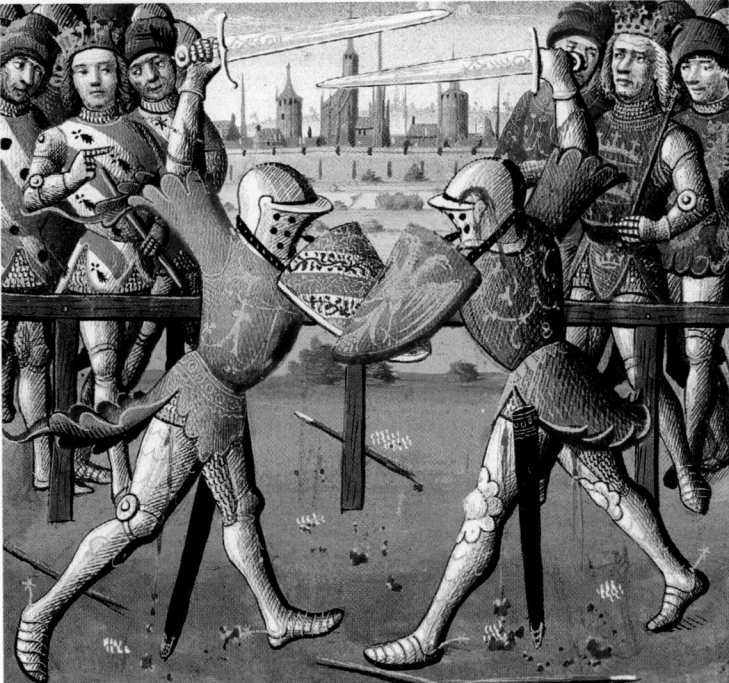

Combat between Lancelot and Gawain (1400s) from the *Cycle de Lancelot*. MS Fr. 120, f. 590v.107a. Bibliothèque Nationale de France, Paris. Photo © Bibliothèque Nationale de France, Paris.

150   "As I guessed, both from your appearance and from your speech; and indeed I know you better than you realize. But I ask you, in **recompense** for the injury you have done my lord, and out of the courtesy for which you are famous, to recommend Sir Belleus to King Arthur, and suggest that he be made one of the knights of the Round Table. I can assure you that my lord deserves it, being only less than yourself as a man-at-arms, and sovereign of many of the Outer Isles."

    "My lady, let Sir Belleus come to Arthur's court at the next Pentecost.[31] Make sure that you come with him, and I promise I will do what I can for him; and if he is as good a man-at-arms as you say he is, I am sure Arthur will accept him."

160   As soon as it was daylight, Sir Launcelot armed, mounted, and rode away in search of the abbey, which he found in less than two hours. King Bagdemagus's daughter was waiting for him and, as soon as she heard his horse's footsteps in the yard, ran to the window and, seeing that it was Sir Launcelot, herself ordered the servants to stable his horse. She then led him to her chamber, disarmed him, and gave him a long gown to wear, welcoming him warmly as she did so.

---

31. **Pentecost:** In Arthurian legend, Pentecost is one of the times at which the knights meet at Camelot to renew their oaths and receive new missions.

recompense
(rĕk′əm-pĕns′) *n.* amends for damage or payment for service

Analyze Visuals

Activity This is a fight between Launcelot and Sir Gawain, who is representing King Arthur against Launcelot and his army. Which knight seems more likely to win this fight? Why do you think so? *Possible answer: The knight on the left seems more likely to win. He is the less severely wounded of the combatants; in addition, the group watching him (and wearing the same colors) seems more confident than the other group of onlookers.*

About the Art This illustration from a French manuscript of the *Cycle of Lancelot* depicts what may be the most dramatic clash in Arthurian legend. It began over Launcelot's affair with Arthur's wife, Queen Gwynevere. The knights Mordred and Agraviane plot to expose and destroy the pair. Though Gawain is loyal to Arthur, he wants no part of this scheme. With Gwynevere set to burn at the stake, Launcelot attacks the execution guard, killing Agraviane and wounding Mordred in the process. Gawain's desire for revenge plays a key role in the downfall of the Round Table.

VOCABULARY   COMMON CORE   L 4

OWN THE WORD

recompense: Tell students that *recompense* comes from Latin for "to compensate." What is another English phrase for "to compensate"? What did the noblewoman request as *recompense* for Sir Belleus? *Possible answers: make up for, pay back, reimburse; The noblewoman requested that Sir Belleus be made one of King Arthur's knights of the Round Table.*

FOR STRUGGLING READERS

Comprehension Support Lines 160–165 open the scene in which Launcelot honors his pledge to the woman who helped him escape from Morgan le Fay. Explain that the phrase "a long gown to wear" (line 165) is a reference to a type of old-fashioned pajamas or nightclothes, pulled over the head and worn by men as well as women. The woman has "disarmed" Launcelot and has replaced his armor and riding clothes with soft, lightweight clothes for relaxing.

FOR ADVANCED LEARNERS/PRE–AP

Evaluate Character Have students write and share one-paragraph evaluations of the two women who interact with Launcelot on pages 1121–1123. Suggest that students evaluate the women's motivations in dealing with Launcelot, using questions such as these:

- Are the women motivated by idealism?
- How do they gain a position of control?
- Do they get what they want?

TIERED DISCUSSION PROMPTS

Direct students to lines 171–191. Use these prompts to help students explore the unstated internal conflict and looming external conflict that Launcelot faces by keeping his promise to the noblewoman:

Connect How would you feel if you had to fight three friends to keep a promise? *Accept all reasonable responses.*

Analyze Why does Launcelot ask King Bagdemagus for "plain armor" (lines 177–179)? *Possible answer: Launcelot wants to hide his identity from the three Round Table knights whom he will have to face when he fights for King Bagdemagus.*

Evaluate Consider Launcelot's moral dilemma. Is he making the right decision to fight against his Round Table friends? Use what you know about chivalry to defend your opinion. *Possible answers: Launcelot is making the right decision: His promise to the noblewoman, who may have saved his life, must take priority over his friendship with his fellow knights. Launcelot is making the wrong decision: Loyalty is part of the chivalric code, and Launcelot committed his loyalty to the Round Table long before he became involved in this situation.*

Ⓝ FOREIGN WORDS

Point out to students that the word *galloped* in line 192 is from the Old French word *galoper*. Tell students that the English language adds words constantly to adapt to changing times, many of them foreign words. Brainstorm with students to identify present-day examples of foreign words or phrases that have been added to the English language.

Answer: Retinue *comes from the Old French word for "retain," and was used in the sense of "hired as a servant." Tournament comes from the Medieval French sport in which armored knights fought for prizes. Armor comes via Old French from the Latin "armature" and was used in the middle ages to describe a defensive suit of metal.*

King Bagdemagus's castle was twelve miles away, and his daughter sent for him as soon as she had settled Sir Launcelot. The king arrived with his retinue[32] and embraced Sir Launcelot, who then described his recent enchantment, and the great obligation he was under to his daughter for 170 releasing him.

"Sir, you will fight for me on Tuesday next?"

"Sire, I shall not fail you; but please tell me the names of the three Round Table knights whom I shall be fighting."

"Sir Modred, Sir Madore de la Porte, and Sir Gahalantyne. I must admit that last Tuesday they defeated me and my knights completely."

"Sire, I hear that the tournament is to be fought within three miles of the abbey. Could you send me three of your most trustworthy knights, clad in plain armor, and with no device,[33] and a fourth suit of armor which I myself shall wear? We will take up our position just outside the tournament field and 180 watch while you and the King of North Galys enter into combat with your followers; and then, as soon as you are in difficulties, we will come to your rescue and show your opponents what kind of knights you command." Ⓝ

This was arranged on Sunday, and on the following Tuesday Sir Launcelot and the three knights of King Bagdemagus waited in a copse,[34] not far from the pavilion which had been erected for the lords and ladies who were to judge the tournament and award the prizes.

The King of North Galys was the first on the field, with a company of ninescore knights; he was followed by King Bagdemagus with fourscore[35] knights, and then by the three knights of the Round Table, who remained 190 apart from both companies. At the first encounter King Bagdemagus lost twelve knights, all killed, and the King of North Galys six.

With that, Sir Launcelot galloped on to the field, and with his first spear unhorsed five of the King of North Galys's knights, breaking the backs of four of them. With his next spear he charged the king and wounded him deeply in the thigh.

"That was a shrewd blow," commented Sir Madore and galloped onto the field to challenge Sir Launcelot. But he too was tumbled from his horse, and with such violence that his shoulder was broken.

Sir Modred was the next to challenge Sir Launcelot, and he was sent 200 spinning over his horse's tail. He landed headfirst, his helmet became buried in the soil, and he nearly broke his neck, and for a long time lay stunned.

Finally Sir Gahalantyne tried; at the first encounter both he and Sir Launcelot broke their spears, so both drew their swords and hacked vehemently at each other. But Sir Launcelot, with mounting wrath, soon struck his opponent a blow on the helmet which brought the blood streaming from eyes, ears, and

---

32. **retinue** (rĕt′n-ōō′): attendants.

33. **device:** an emblem or design used as an identifying mark.

34. **copse** (kŏps): a thicket of small trees.

35. **ninescore . . . fourscore:** A score is a set of 20; thus, ninescore is 180 and fourscore is 80.

Ⓝ FOREIGN WORDS

The English language often takes words from other languages. Many words specific to the plots of medieval romances come from Old French. These words entered English after 1066, when the French-speaking Normans invaded England. The words *retinue* (line 168), *tournament* (line 176), and *armor* (line 178), all come from Old French words. Use a dictionary or encyclopedia to discover the meaning and origin of each of these words.

③ Targeted Passage

Language Coach

Multiple Meaning Words Some words have more than one meaning, depending on how they are used in a sentence. When the knights "drew" their swords (line 203), they pulled them out. What other meanings does the word *drew* have? Use a dictionary for help.

DIFFERENTIATED INSTRUCTION

FOR STRUGGLING READERS

③ Targeted Passage [Lines 187–204]

This passage spotlights the warrior side rather than the gentlemanly side of medieval knights.

- Who are the opponents in this tournament? (lines 187–190)

- What happens when Launcelot joins the fight? (lines 192–195)

- How does Launcelot deal with his fellow Round Table knights? (lines 196–207)

FOR ENGLISH LANGUAGE LEARNERS

Multiple Meaning Words *Possible answers: pulled, dragged; inhaled; extracted, elicited; earned, received; depicted with lines; formulated; composed* Have students use a dictionary or thesaurus to help them understand other multiple meaning words in the selection, such as *judge* in line 185 and *spear* in line 192.

mouth. Sir Gahalantyne slumped forward in the saddle, his horse panicked, and he was thrown to the ground, useless for further combat.

Sir Launcelot took another spear and unhorsed sixteen more of the King of North Galys's knights and, with his next, unhorsed another twelve; and in each
210 case with such violence that none of the knights ever fully recovered. The King of North Galys was forced to admit defeat, and the prize was awarded to King Bagdemagus.

That night Sir Launcelot was entertained as the guest of honor by King Bagdemagus and his daughter at their castle and before leaving was loaded with gifts.

"My lady, please, if ever again you should need my services, remember that I shall not fail you."

The next day Sir Launcelot rode once more through the forest and by chance came to the apple tree where he had previously slept. This time he met
220 a young noblewoman riding a white palfrey.[36]

"My lady, I am riding in search of adventure; pray tell me if you know of any I might find hereabouts."

"Sir, there are adventures hereabouts if you believe that you are equal to them; but please tell me, what is your name?"

"Sir Launcelot du Lake."

"Very well, Sir Launcelot, you appear to be a sturdy enough knight, so I will tell you. Not far away stands the castle of Sir Tarquine, a knight who in fair combat has overcome more than sixty opponents whom he now holds prisoner. Many are from the court of King Arthur, and if you can rescue them,
230 I will then ask you to deliver me and my companions from a knight who distresses us daily, either by robbery or by other kinds of outrage."

"My lady, please first lead me to Sir Tarquine; then I will most happily challenge this miscreant knight of yours."

When they arrived at the castle, Sir Launcelot watered his horse at the ford and then beat the caldron until the bottom fell out. However, none came to answer the challenge, so they waited by the castle gate for half an hour or so. Then Sir Tarquine appeared, riding toward the castle with a wounded prisoner slung over his horse, whom Sir Launcelot recognized as Sir Gaheris, Sir Gawain's brother and a knight of the Round Table.
240 "Good knight," said Sir Launcelot, "it is known to me that you have put to shame many of the knights of the Round Table. Pray allow your prisoner, who I see is wounded, to recover, while I **vindicate** the honor of the knights whom you have defeated."

"I defy you, and all your fellowship of the Round Table," Sir Tarquine replied.

"You boast!" said Sir Launcelot.

At the first charge the backs of the horses were broken and both knights stunned. But they soon recovered and set to with their swords, and both struck so lustily that neither shield nor armor could resist, and within two hours they

---

36. **palfrey:** a gentle riding-horse.

○ EVALUATE
Reread lines 192–212. Which aspects of the chivalric code does Sir Launcelot uphold in his performance at the jousting tournament?

vindicate (vĭn′dĭ-kāt′)
v. to clear of suspicion, doubt, or blame

READING SKILL COMMON CORE RL 7

○ EVALUATE

Possible answer: Launcelot upholds loyalty by supporting King Bagdemagus as promised; he upholds courage by taking on dozens of knights in battle; he upholds prowess by defeating his opponents.

IF STUDENTS NEED HELP . . . Guide them in using their Evaluate charts to record Launcelot's chivalric traits.

VOCABULARY COMMON CORE L 4

OWN THE WORD

vindicate: Tell students that *vindicate* is from the Latin word *vindex* meaning "avenger." Have students write sentences demonstrating their understanding of *vindicate.*

FOR ENGLISH LANGUAGE LEARNERS
Vocabulary: Outdated Forms Help students use context clues to determine the meaning of these out-of-use terms in the dialogue between Launcelot and the young noblewoman:

- *pray tell me* (line 221), "please tell me"
- *hereabouts* (line 222), "around here"
- *deliver me and my companions* (line 230), "save me and my friends"
- *miscreant* (line 233), "rogue, criminal"

FOR ADVANCED LEARNERS/PRE–AP
Evaluate Plot [small-group activity] Have students evaluate the plot of "Sir Launcelot du Lake" by considering the nature of the characters and events that Launcelot encounters in this adventure. They should consider the conditions under which he meets various people, the battles that he fights, and the degree of difficulty in resolving his conflicts (both external and internal). Students can then present a written or oral evaluation, rating the quality of the story.

Could you be a KNIGHT?

Discuss What traits of chivalry does Launcelot exemplify in lines 263–276? *Possible answer: Launcelot exemplifies the chivalric traits of grace and politeness in his words; honor and courage in not trying to hide who he is to avoid danger; prowess in his fight with Tarquine; and honor and humility in proclaiming his service to the noblewoman after beheading Tarquine.*

TEXT ANALYSIS

COMMON CORE

Ⓟ MEDIEVAL ROMANCE

RL 3
RL 5

Possible answer: Details suggesting exaggeration include the fact that Launcelot and Tarquine fight for two hours without pause (lines 247–249); that Tarquine uses hyperbole when he speaks with Launcelot (lines 254–256); that the opponents must fight to the death (lines 261–262); and that Launcelot beheads Tarquine with one blow (lines 272–274).

SELECTION WRAP-UP

READ WITH A PURPOSE Now that students have finished reading the selections, ask students whether they think the chivalric traits are important in today's world. Which ones are the most important, and why? *Possible answer: Accept all thoughtful answers.*

⭐ **CRITIQUE** Ask students to evaluate Malory's characterizations, as interpreted by modern readers.

INDEPENDENT READING

Recommend Jane Yolen's *Sword of the Rightful King* to students interested in an imaginative variation of the Arthurian legend.

---

were cutting each other's flesh, from which the blood flowed liberally. Finally
250 they paused for a moment, resting on their shields.

"Worthy knight," said Sir Tarquine, "pray hold your hand for a while and, if you will, answer my question."

"Sir, speak on."

"You are the most powerful knight I have fought yet, but I fear you may be the one whom in the whole world I most hate. If you are not, for the love of you I will release all my prisoners and swear eternal friendship."

"What is the name of the knight you hate above all others?"

"Sir Launcelot du Lake; for it was he who slew my brother, Sir Carados of the Dolorous Tower, and it is because of him that I have killed a hundred
260 knights and maimed as many more, apart from the sixty-four I still hold prisoner. And so, if you are Sir Launcelot, speak up, for we must then fight to the death."

"Sir, I see now that I might go in peace and good fellowship or otherwise fight to the death; but being the knight I am, I must tell you: I am Sir Launcelot du Lake, son of King Ban of Benwick, of Arthur's court, and a knight of the Round Table. So defend yourself!"

"Ah! this is most welcome."

Now the two knights hurled themselves at each other like two wild bulls; swords and shields clashed together, and often their swords drove into the
270 flesh. Then sometimes one, sometimes the other, would stagger and fall, only to recover immediately and resume the contest. At last, however, Sir Tarquine grew faint and unwittingly lowered his shield. Sir Launcelot was swift to follow up his advantage and, dragging the other down to his knees, unlaced his helmet and beheaded him. Ⓟ

Sir Launcelot then strode over to the young noblewoman: "My lady, now I am at your service, but first I must find a horse."

Then the wounded Sir Gaheris spoke up: "Sir, please take my horse. Today you have overcome the most formidable knight, excepting only yourself, and by so doing have saved us all. But before leaving, please tell me your name."

280 "Sir Launcelot du Lake. Today I have fought to vindicate the honor of the knights of the Round Table, and I know that among Sir Tarquine's prisoners are two of my brethren, Sir Lyonel and Sir Ector, also your own brother, Sir Gawain. According to the shields there are also Sir Brandiles, Sir Galyhuddis,[37] Sir Kay, Sir Alydukis,[38] Sir Marhaus, and many others. Please release the prisoners and ask them to help themselves to the castle treasure. Give them all my greetings and say I will see them at the next Pentecost. And please request Sir Ector and Sir Lyonel to go straight to the court and await me there." ∽

④ **Targeted Passage**

Ⓟ MEDIEVAL ROMANCE
Reread lines 246–274. Which details suggest that the clash between Sir Tarquine and Sir Launcelot is **exaggerated** or larger than life?

---

37. **Galyhuddis** (găl′ĭ-hōͦd′əs).
38. **Alydukis** (ăl′ĭ-dōͦ′kəs).

DIFFERENTIATED INSTRUCTION

FOR STRUGGLING READERS

④ **Targeted Passage** [Lines 254–274]
In this passage Malory brings details together to create the tale's climax.

- What backstory, or events that took place before the tale, does Tarquine reveal? How does the information add to the importance of the fight? (lines 254–262)

- How does the ending of this fight differ from the other battles in this tale? (lines 271–274)

FOR ENGLISH LANGUAGE LEARNERS

Vocabulary Support Help students paraphrase these stilted phrases from this climactic scene:

- *pray hold your hand* (line 251), "please stop"

- *the one whom in the whole world I most hate* (line 255), "the person whom I hate the most in the world"

- *it was he who slew my brother* (line 258), "he is the one who killed my brother"

- *most welcome* (line 267), "good news"

HISTORICAL ACCOUNT In *A Distant Mirror*, the historian Barbara Tuchman offers a glimpse of the actual conditions medieval knights faced in battle.

from A Distant Mirror:
The Calamitous 14th Century

Barbara Tuchman

To fight on horseback or foot wearing 55 pounds of plate armor, to crash in collision with an opponent at full gallop while holding horizontal an eighteen-foot lance half the length of an average telephone pole, to give and receive blows with sword or battle-ax that could cleave a skull or slice off a limb at a stroke, to spend half of life in the saddle through all weathers and for days at a time, was not a weakling's work. Hardship and fear were part of it. "Knights who are at the wars . . . are forever swallowing their fear," wrote the companion and biographer of Don Pero Niño, the "Unconquered Knight" of the late 14th century. "They expose themselves to every peril; they give up their bodies to the adventure of life in death. Moldy bread or biscuit, meat cooked or uncooked; today enough to eat

The Knight (1400s), Jacques de Cessoles. From *Livre des eschecs moralises,* translated by Jean Ferron. MS. 3066, fol. 21. Bibliotheque Municipale, Rouen, France. Photo © Giraudon/Art Resource, New York.

and tomorrow nothing, little or no wine, water from a pond or a butt,[1] bad quarters, the shelter of a tent or branches, a bad bed, poor sleep with their armor still on their backs, burdened with iron, the enemy an arrow-shot off. 'Ware! Who goes there? To arms! To arms!' With the first drowsiness, an alarm; at dawn, the trumpet. 'To horse! To horse! Muster! Muster!' As lookouts, as sentinels, keeping watch by day and by night, fighting without cover, as foragers, as scouts, guard after guard, duty after duty. 'Here they come! Here! They are so many—No, not as many as that—This way—that—Come this side—Press them there—News! News! They come back hurt, they have prisoners—no, they bring none back. Let us go! Let us go! Give no ground! On!' Such is their calling."

---

1. **butt:** water cask.

TIERED DISCUSSION PROMPTS

Use these prompts to help students appreciate the connection between the legends in *Le Morte d'Arthur* and the real-life challenges of medieval knights:

Recall What was the life of a knight really like? *Possible answer: The life of a knight was difficult and unglamorous. At times, there was little to eat, little shelter, and little glory.*

Analyze How does Barbara Tuchman use source material to enhance her account? *Possible answer: Tuchman quotes the biographer of Don Pero Niño, a real-life knight, to make her account more immediate and believable.*

Evaluate In your opinion, does Tuchman's account capture the excitement of being a knight as well as Malory's tales do? Defend your opinion. *Possible answer: Although Tuchman's account is more grim and realistic, the quotation of breathless orders recounted by the knight's biographer briefly captures the excitement of being a knight as well as Malory's tales do.*

Practice and Apply

For preliminary support of post-reading questions, use these copy masters:

R RESOURCE MANAGER—Copy Masters
Reading Check p. 50
Medieval Romance p. 43
Question Support p. 51

Additional selection questions are provided for teachers on page 37.

ANSWERS

Comprehension

1. *King Uther is motivated by the desire to have Igraine, the duke's wife, as his own.*

2. *Uther dies of an illness about two years after Arthur's birth, following a defeat of invading enemies.*

3. *Launcelot repays the noblewoman by championing her father in a tournament.*

4. *Tarquine wants to kill Launcelot because Launcelot killed Tarquine's brother.*

Text Analysis

COMMON CORE **RL 3, RL 5, RL 7**

Possible answers:

5. *Secrecy will protect Arthur from enemies and will keep his identity from being revealed until the moment is right.*

6. *Arthur may forgive because he is of noble character and because he knows that peace and reconciliation are better for the kingdom than revenge.*

7. *Launcelot's chivalrous actions include refusing to choose one of the four queens as his lover (lines 93–94), keeping a pledge to champion the king (lines 167–173), and facing Sir Tarquine (lines 237–245). Unworthy actions include being too quick to fight the knight who mistook him for a lover (lines 128–132) and harming fellow Round Table knights (lines 196–207).*

8. *Morgan le Fay poses the bigger threat, for she uses magic to tempt Launcelot. Tarquine merely wants to fight, and Launcelot can comply without losing honor.*

9. ● **COMMON CORE FOCUS** *Examine Medieval Romance Students should back up the examples with textual evidence.*

10. ■ **COMMON CORE FOCUS** *Evaluate Sir Launcelot most closely follows the code of chivalry: He is courageous, fighting dozens of knights; honest, in keeping his promise to Bagdemagus; loyal to Gwynevere;*

generous, in offering the knights Tarquine's treasures; and kind to women.

11. *Malory glamorizes knighthood, as when "Launcelot galloped on to the field, and ... unhorsed five ... knights" (lines 192–193). Tuchman is more realistic, listing hardship and danger; for example, she notes that knights wore "55 pounds of plate armor" and that a battle-ax "could cleave a skull."*

Text Criticism

12. *During a period of recovery from war,*

After Reading

Comprehension

1. **Recall** What motivates King Uther to resume war against the duke of Tintagil?

2. **Summarize** Describe the reign of King Uther following Arthur's birth.

3. **Recall** How does Sir Launcelot repay the noblewoman who releases him from the four queens?

4. **Clarify** Why does Sir Tarquine wish to kill Sir Launcelot?

Text Analysis

5. **Make Inferences** Reread lines 82–97 of "The Crowning of Arthur" (page 1115). Why does Merlin want Arthur to be raised in secrecy and away from the royal court?

6. **Draw Conclusions** In "The Crowning of Arthur," the nobles repeatedly reject Arthur as their true-born ruler. Why do you think Arthur chooses to forgive them rather than punish them once he is crowned king?

7. **Analyze Character** In "Sir Launcelot du Lake," identify at least three of Sir Launcelot's actions that are worthy of a chivalric knight. What, if anything, does he do that seems unworthy of his position?

8. **Compare Characters** Who seems to pose a greater threat to Launcelot's honor—Morgan le Fay or Sir Tarquine? Cite evidence to support your answer.

9. Examine Medieval Romance Review the elements of medieval romance on page 1111. Choose one selection and try to find examples of each element. To what extent does the selection reflect all of these elements? Explain.

10. **Evaluate** Review the chart you created as you read. In your opinion, which of the four characters most closely follows the code of chivalry? Support your answer with details from your chart.

11. **Compare Literary Texts** Compare "Sir Launcelot du Lake" with the excerpt from *A Distant Mirror* on page 1127. How do these two pieces—a medieval romance and a historical account—differ in their depictions of knighthood? Use information from both texts to support your response.

Text Criticism

12. **Historical Context** At the end of the 15th century, England was recovering from both the Hundred Years' War with France and its own civil conflicts—the Wars of the Roses. Why do you think Malory wrote *Le Morte d'Arthur* during this turbulent period?

> ### Could you be a KNIGHT?
>
> Would you want to live by the code of chivalry? Why or why not?

COMMON CORE

RL 3 Analyze how complex characters develop, interact with others, and advance the plot or develop the theme. **RL 5** Analyze how an author's choices concerning how to structure a text and order events within it to create such effects as mystery, tension, or surprise. **RL 7** Analyze the representation of a subject in two different mediums.

Malory and his readers may have been attracted to a vision of England as a great and unified land, in which honor reigned and evil was punished.

> ### Could you be a KNIGHT?
> Students might compare and contrast the code of honor or ethics they follow now with chivalry. Students might also think about the physical and mental demands of the code of chivalry.

Vocabulary in Context

▲ VOCABULARY PRACTICE

Decide whether each pair of words are synonyms, words with the same meaning, or antonyms, words with opposite meanings.

1. abash/encourage
2. sequence/succession
3. prowess/skill
4. disloyalty/fidelity
5. ignominiously/disgracefully
6. supporter/adversary
7. recompense/payment
8. accuse/vindicate

WORD LIST
abash
adversary
fidelity
ignominiously
prowess
recompense
succession
vindicate

ACADEMIC VOCABULARY IN WRITING

• drama • emerge • encounter • globe • underlie

What thoughts about medieval culture and value **emerge** as you read the legends of King Arthur? Write a paragraph identifying at least three core beliefs that **underlie** these tales. Use at least one Academic Vocabulary word in your response.

VOCABULARY STRATEGY: ANALOGIES

Analogies express relationships between pairs of words. Some common relationships are described in the chart that follows.

COMMON CORE

L 5 Demonstrate understanding of word relationships.

Type	Relationship
synonym	means the same as
antonym	means the opposite of
characteristic	distinguishes or describes

Write the letter of the word pair that expresses a relationship similar to that of the first pair. Indicate what kind of relationship is being expressed.

1. dog : fidelity :: (a) chicken : egg, (b) fox : cleverness, (c) wolf : timidity, (d) whale : mammal
2. prowess : gladiator :: (a) tact : diplomat, (b) honesty : thief, (c) wisdom : fool, (d) shyness : actor
3. adversary : friend :: (a) cat : pet, (b) hunter : trapper, (c) servant : ruler, (d) member : club

Interactive Vocabulary
THINK central
Go to **thinkcentral.com**.
KEYWORD: HML10-1129

DIFFERENTIATED INSTRUCTION

FOR ENGLISH LANGUAGE LEARNERS

Vocabulary: Cognates Point out that the Spanish words *fidelidad* and *sucesión* are similar in form and meaning to the English words *fidelity* and *succession*. Encourage students who speak Latin-based languages to search for and explain five words in the story that are similar to those in their home language.

FOR ADVANCED LEARNERS/PRE–AP

Vocabulary: Analogies Have students create and share analogies using words from the selections. As a class, work through the process for the word *defied* ("The Crowning of King Arthur," line 16). Then have groups work on their own analogies.

ANSWERS

Vocabulary in Context

▲ VOCABULARY PRACTICE

1. *antonyms*
2. *synonyms*
3. *synonyms*
4. *antonyms*
5. *synonyms*
6. *antonyms*
7. *synonyms*
8. *antonyms*

 **RESOURCE MANAGER—Copy Master**
Vocabulary Practice p. 48

ACADEMIC VOCABULARY IN WRITING

Possible answer: *A clear impression of the medieval world and values begins to* emerge *in these tales. Underlying all of the Arthurian tales is a belief in the powers of good and evil. Characters strive to behave morally and ethically. Those who misuse violence are revealed as villains.*

VOCABULARY STRATEGY: ANALOGIES

COMMON CORE L 5

Urge students to follow these steps: (1) Determine the relationship between the given pair of words. (2) Identify the relationship in each word pair. (3) Choose the word pair that correctly expresses the same relationship as that in the given pair of words.

1. *b; characteristic*
2. *a; characteristic*
3. *c; antonym*

 **RESOURCE MANAGER—Copy Master**
Vocabulary Strategy p. 49

Interactive Vocabulary **THINK** central

Keywords direct students to a **WordSharp** tutorial on **thinkcentral.com** or to other types of vocabulary practice and review.

Assess and Reteach

Assess

DIAGNOSTIC AND SELECTION TESTS
Selection Tests A, B/C pp. 299–302

Interactive Selection Test on **thinkcentral.com**

Reteach

Level Up Online Tutorials on **thinkcentral.com**

Reteaching Worksheets on **thinkcentral.com**

Focus and Motivate

COMMON CORE FOCUS

RL 1 Cite strong textual evidence to support inferences drawn from the text. **RL 4** Analyze the cumulative impact of specific word choices on meaning. **RL 9** Analyze how an author draws on and transforms source material in a specific work. **W 9a (RL 9)** Draw evidence from literary texts to support analysis; analyze how an author draws on and transforms source material in a specific work. **L 1b** Use various types of phrases and clauses to convey specific meanings and add variety and interest to writing. **L 5b** Analyze nuances in the meaning of words with similar denotations.

SUMMARY

In this excerpt from John Steinbeck's telling of the Arthurian legend, King Arthur asks Lancelot to join him and Queen Guinevere in his chamber. There, Lancelot and the queen hide their love during a tense chat. Later, they steal a passionate kiss; then Lancelot leaves, weeping with guilt.

Do heroes get to be HUMAN?

Introduce the question. Have students name some "heroes" who have—or have not—lived up to an image of perfection. Then help students with the *QUICKWRITE*.

---

from The Acts of King Arthur and His Noble Knights

Romance by John Steinbeck

Do heroes get to be HUMAN?

COMMON CORE

RL 1 Cite textual evidence to support inferences drawn from the text. **RL 4** Analyze the cumulative impact of specific word choices on meaning. **RL 9** Analyze how an author draws on and transforms source material in a specific work.

Think about people whom you regard as heroes. How do you expect them to behave? What kinds of virtues should they possess? In this modern retelling of Arthurian legend, John Steinbeck depicts Sir Lancelot as a knight whose private ambitions clash with his public image of perfection.

QUICKWRITE Write a paragraph or two about what it might be like to live in the public eye and be held to a high standard of behavior. Then discuss when, if ever, we allow our heroes to show human weaknesses.

1130

Selection Resources

See resources on the **Teacher One Stop DVD-ROM** *and on* **thinkcentral.com**.

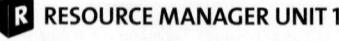 **RESOURCE MANAGER UNIT 10**
  Plan and Teach, pp. 53–60
  Summary, pp. 61–62†‡*
  Text Analysis and Reading
    Skill, pp. 63–66†*
  Vocabulary, pp. 67–69*
  Grammar and Style, p. 72

**DIAGNOSTIC AND SELECTION
  TESTS**
  Selection Tests, pp. 303–306

BEST PRACTICES TOOLKIT
  New Word Analysis, p. E8
  Writing Template: Compare-
    Contrast (by Points),
    pp. C16, C23

TECHNOLOGY
  ⊘ **Teacher One Stop DVD-ROM**
  ⊘ **Student One Stop DVD-ROM**
  ⊘ **Audio Anthology CD**
  ⊘ **GrammarNotes DVD-ROM**
  ⊘ **ExamView Test Generator**
    on the **Teacher One Stop**

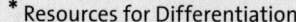

TEXT ANALYSIS: STYLE

In his introduction to *The Acts of King Arthur and His Noble Knights,* John Steinbeck states his aim: to set down the story of King Arthur in "present-day speech," avoiding the archaic language of Malory's version. As you read the selection, notice how the following stylistic techniques transform his source material into a retelling that appeals to modern readers:

- plain, contemporary language
- detailed characterizations
- vivid sensory images
- rich figurative language, including similes and metaphors
- long, flowing sentences
- realistic dialogue
- a sympathetic tone

READING SKILL: MAKE INFERENCES

In his work, Steinbeck presents Lancelot (spelled *Launcelot* by Malory) as a complex character—one who struggles to maintain integrity in both his public and his private life. To fully appreciate Lancelot, you will need to use details in the text and your own knowledge to **make inferences,** or logical guesses, about his feelings and behavior. As you read, keep track of your inferences in a chart like the one shown.

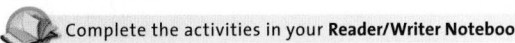

Details About Lancelot	My Experiences	My Inferences
"Some said he nodded and perhaps dozed...." (line 26)	Traveling can be tiring. Award ceremonies can be tedious.	Lancelot is weary from his journey and bored by the speeches.

▲ VOCABULARY IN CONTEXT

To see how many vocabulary words you already know, match each boldfaced vocabulary word in the first column with a word that has a similar meaning in the second column.

1. **disparagement**	a. revenge
2. **exalt**	b. exhausted
3. **haggard**	c. wandering
4. **intemperate**	d. praise
5. **reprisal**	e. denigration
6. **vagrant**	f. excessive

Complete the activities in your **Reader/Writer Notebook.**

Meet the Author

John Steinbeck
1902–1968

Voice of the Common People
John Steinbeck, who believed that a writer's first duty is to "set down his time as nearly as he can understand it," managed perhaps better than anyone else to tell the stories of ordinary people caught up in the Great Depression of the 1930s. His masterpiece, *The Grapes of Wrath*, depicts the hardships of an Oklahoma farm family forced to migrate west for work. Like his other novels, it shows deep sympathy for working people and outrage over social injustice.

"Dazzled and Swept Up"
Steinbeck was born in Salinas, California, in one of the nation's most productive farming regions. A shy young man, he enjoyed spending time alone by the seashore in Monterey, where he basked in the raw, untamed power of nature. For adventure, he turned to literature. In particular, he felt "dazzled and swept up" by the legends of King Arthur.

Steinbeck and Arthur
As an adult, Steinbeck attempted to set down a retelling of Arthurian legend that his two sons could enjoy. He researched the legend in England and Italy, studying rare manuscripts, and wrote in a room he named Joyous Garde, after Lancelot's castle. Unfortunately, Steinbeck died before he completed his version of the legend. In 1976, his unfinished work was published as *The Acts of King Arthur and His Noble Knights*. The excerpt you are about to read offers a fresh perspective on some of the events in Malory's tale of Sir Launcelot.

1131

Teach

TEXT ANALYSIS — COMMON CORE — RL 4

● Model the Skill: STYLE

To model how to analyze style, write this example on the board:

> Feeling the weight of the public's expectations like an oxen's yoke, Lancelot recalled a day when he had wished for fame.

Describe the style by noting word choice and language. Point out that the example has a plainspoken style, a vivid simile, and a sympathetic tone.

GUIDED PRACTICE Have students create sentences with different styles—for example, an angry tone with no figurative language.

READING SKILL — COMMON CORE — RL 1 / RL 9

■ Model the Skill: MAKE INFERENCES

Explain to students how personal experience can help them understand complex characters. For example, students' personal experiences could help them make an inference about a talkative boy who blushes and falls silent when a certain girl joins his group. Ask students if they would agree that the boy has a crush on the girl.

GUIDED PRACTICE Discuss how students connected the blush to the crush, eliciting the concept of personal knowledge.

R RESOURCE MANAGER—Copy Master
Make Inferences p. 65 (for student use while reading the selection)

VOCABULARY SKILL

COMMON CORE — L 4

▲ VOCABULARY IN CONTEXT

DIAGNOSE WORD KNOWLEDGE Have all students complete Vocabulary in Context. Check their answers against the following:

disparagement (dǐ-spăr′ǐj-mənt) *n.* belittlement
exalt (ǐg-zôlt′) *v.* to glorify, praise, or honor
haggard (hăg′ərd) *adj.* appearing worn and exhausted
intemperate (ǐn-tĕm′pər-ǐt) *adj.* extreme
reprisal (rǐ-prī′zəl) *n.* retaliation in the form of harm or injury similar to that received

vagrant (vā′grənt) *adj.* wandering

PRETEACH VOCABULARY Use the following copy master to help students predict the meaning of each boldfaced word.

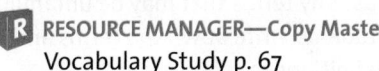

R RESOURCE MANAGER—Copy Master
Vocabulary Study p. 67

1. Read item 1 aloud, emphasizing *disparagement*.

2. Point out the phrase "contemptuous words." Elicit possible meanings for *disparagement*, such as "ridicule."

3. Repeat the procedure for items 2–6.

READ WITH A PURPOSE

Help students set a purpose for reading. Tell students to look for what Arthur, Lancelot, and Guinevere lose in the story.

Ⓐ *Model the Skill:* **STYLE**

To model how to understand style, read the lines aloud, twice. The first time, have students listen for enjoyment. The second time, ask students to think about the images that come to mind as they listen. Relate the unfolding of images to the flow of the sentences. Explain to students that this is part of Steinbeck's style.

Possible answer: *Steinbeck begins with long, flowing sentences to draw readers into the story and to set the scene in such a way that readers can envision a wide range of details—as if they were witnessing all of bustling Winchester at once and in person.*

Extend the Discussion Rewrite the first two sentences of the paragraph, breaking them up into shorter sentences. When you compare the results with Steinbeck's original, what insights do you get about the crafting that a writer does?

OWN THE WORD

disparagement: Tell students that *disparagement* is a noun for the verb *disparage*, which means "to speak of in a disrespectful way; belittle." Have students use *disparagement* and *disparage* in sentences.

The Acts of King Arthur
and His Noble Knights

John Steinbeck

King Arthur held Whitsun[1] court at Winchester, that ancient royal town favored by God and His clergy as well as the seat and tomb of many kings. The roads were clogged with eager people, knights returning to stamp in court the record of their deeds, of bishops, clergy, monks, of the defeated fettered to their paroles,[2] the prisoners of honor. And on Itchen water, pathway from Solent[3] and the sea, the little ships brought succulents, lampreys, eels and oysters, plaice and sea trout, while barges loaded with casks of whale oil and casks of wine came tide borne. Bellowing oxen walked to the spits on their own four hooves, while geese and swans, sheep and swine, waited their turn
10 in hurdle pens. Every householder with a strip of colored cloth, a ribbon, any textile gaiety, hung it from a window to flap its small festival, and those in lack tied boughs of pine and laurel over their doors. **Ⓐ**

In the great hall of the castle on the hill the king sat high, and next below the fair elite company of the Round Table, noble and decorous as kings themselves, while at the long trestle boards the people were as fitted as toes in a tight shoe.

Then while the glistening meat dripped down the tables, it was the custom for the defeated to celebrate the deeds of those who had overcome them, while the victor dipped his head in **disparagement** of his greatness and fended off
20 the compliments with small defensive gestures of his hands. And as at public penitence sins are given stature they do not deserve, little sins grow up and baby sins are born, so those knights who lately claimed mercy perchance might raise the exploits of the brave and merciful beyond reasonable gratitude for their lives and in anticipation of some small notice of value.

This no one said of Lancelot, sitting with bowed head in his golden-lettered seat at the Round Table. Some said he nodded and perhaps dozed, for the testimony to his greatness was long and the monotony of his victories

---

1. **Whitsun:** another name for Pentecost. In Arthurian legend, Pentecost is one of the times at which the knights meet at Camelot to renew their oaths and receive new missions.
2. **fettered to their paroles:** bound by their word of honor to lay down arms.
3. **Itchen . . . Solent:** waterways in southern England.

Ⓐ STYLE
Reread lines 1–12, noting Steinbeck's **long, flowing sentences.** Why do you think Steinbeck begins this part of his retelling of Arthurian legend in this way?

disparagement
(dĭ-spărʹĭj-mənt) *n.* belittlement

① **Targeted Passage**

Analyze Visuals ▶

What **character traits** are suggested in this portrait of King Arthur?

Detail of *King Arthur* (1903), Charles Ernest Butler. Oil on canvas, 123.2 cm × 73.7 cm. Private collection. Christopher Wood Gallery, London. © Bridgeman Art Library.

DIFFERENTIATED INSTRUCTION

FOR ENGLISH LANGUAGE LEARNERS
Develop Reading Fluency Have students listen to *The Acts of King Arthur and His Noble Knights* on the *Audio Anthology CD*, pausing to discuss any terms that may be unfamiliar. Have students write down the terms and their definitions to refer to later.

FOR STRUGGLING READERS
In combination with the *Audio Anthology CD*, use one or more Targeted Passages (pp. 1132, 1137, 1140) to ensure that students focus on key story ideas, concepts, and skills. Targeted Passages are also good for English learners.

① **Targeted Passage [Lines 13–24]**

This passage provides a transition from the overview of Winchester to the royal court. It sets the scene for the public exaltation of Lancelot, a key element in this story.

REVISIT THE BIG QUESTION

Do heroes get to be
HUMAN?

Discuss In lines 20–24, what details in Stein-beck's description suggest that the legendary Arthurian court is not a place of total perfec-tion? *Possible answer: The court falls short of perfection because lying, cowardice, and greed have a place there. An important court activity is the retelling of knightly deeds, and Steinbeck notes that some who tell those tales elaborate upon them in hopes of saving their lives or advancing their fortunes.*

Analyze Visuals

Possible answer: Suggested traits include nobility, purity, and a sense of mission.

About the Art Charles Ernest Butler (1864–1918) was known for his Victorian depictions of Arthurian legend. This painting captures the youthfulness and integrity of Arthur. Further-more, the light on Arthur's face and the tilt of his head suggest that his coronation is an act of divine will. Like other painters of the time, Butler brought to his work a loftiness of spirit—something more idealized or spiritual than what is seen in Steinbeck's introductory word pictures.

- Where in Winchester does this scene occur? (line 13)

- How can you tell which participants are more important than others? (lines 13–16)

- What details show the popularity and the bounty of the feast? (lines 3–12, 15–17)

- What are conquered knights supposed to do at the feast? How are victorious knights supposed to react? (lines 17–20)

FOR ADVANCED LEARNERS/PRE–AP

Compare and Contrast Point out that the Arthurian legend has been retold by many writers over the centuries. Challenge students to create their own retellings of the story with present-day characters and settings. Have students work in small groups to outline their versions of the Arthurian tale for contempo-rary audiences. Then have the groups share their ideas with the class and compare and contrast their updated versions with the two selections in this unit.

continued for many hours. Lancelot's immaculate fame had grown so great that men took pride in being unhorsed by him—even this notice was an
30 honor. And since he had won many victories, it is possible that knights he had never seen claimed to have been overthrown by him. It was a way to claim attention for a moment. And as he dozed and wished to be otherwise, he heard his deeds **exalted** beyond his recognition, and some mighty exploits once attributed to other men were brought bright-painted out and laid on the shining pile of his achievements. There is a seat of worth beyond the reach of envy whose occupant ceases to be a man and becomes the receptacle of the wishful longings of the world, a seat most often reserved for the dead, from whom neither **reprisal** nor reward may be expected, but at this time Sir Lancelot was its unchallenged tenant. And he vaguely heard his strength
40 favorably compared with elephants, his ferocity with lions, his agility with deer, his cleverness with foxes, his beauty with the stars, his justice with Solon,[4] his stern probity with St. Michael, his humility with newborn lambs; his military niche would have caused the Archangel Gabriel[5] to raise his head. Sometimes the guests paused in their chewing the better to hear, and a man who slopped his metheglin[6] drew frowns. **B**

Arthur on his dais[7] sat very still and did not fiddle with his bread, and beside him sat lovely Guinevere, still as a painted statue of herself. Only her inward eyes confessed her **vagrant** thoughts. And Lancelot studied the open pages of his hands—not large hands, but delicate where they were not knobby
50 and scarred with old wounds. His hands were fine-textured—soft of skin and very white, protected by the pliant leather lining of his gauntlets. **C**

The great hall was not still, not all upturned listening. Everywhere was movement as people came and went, some serving huge planks of meat and baskets of bread, round and flat like a plate. And there were restless ones who could not sit still, while everyone under burden of half-chewed meat and the floods and freshets of mead and beer found necessity for repeated departures and returns.

Lancelot exhausted the theme of his hands and squinted down the long hall and watched the movement with eyes so nearly closed that he could not see
60 faces. And he thought how he knew everyone by carriage. The knights in long full floor-brushing robes walked lightly or thought their feet barely touched the ground because their bodies were released from their crushing boxes of iron. Their feet were long and slender because, being horsemen, they had never widened and flattened their feet with walking. The ladies, full-skirted, moved like water, but this was schooled and designed, taught to little girls with the help of whips on raw ankles, while their shoulders were bound back with nail-studded harnesses and their heads held high and rigid by painful collars

---

4. **Solon:** an Athenian statesman and lawgiver who lived in the sixth century B.C.

5. **St. Michael . . . Archangel Gabriel:** In several religious traditions, Michael and Gabriel are archangels, the chief messengers of God. Both are celebrated as warriors against evil.

6. **metheglin** (mə-thĕg′lĭn): a liquor made from honey.

7. **dais** (dā′ĭs): a raised platform used for a seat of honor.

1134 UNIT 10: GREEK TRAGEDY AND MEDIEVAL ROMANCE

DIFFERENTIATED INSTRUCTION

FOR STRUGGLING READERS

Paraphrase Theme Steinbeck uses challenging word choice and sentence structure to state a thematic point in lines 35–39. Help students paraphrase the point so that it reads something like this: *There is a very special seat that envy cannot reach. The person who sits in that seat is no longer a man; he is the symbol of what everyone else wants to be. This seat usually is meant for dead people. But now it was Lancelot's, and no one challenged him for it.*

FOR ENGLISH LANGUAGE LEARNERS

Vocabulary Support Use New Word Analysis to teach these words: *exploits* (line 33), *attributed* (line 34), *theme* (line 58), *rigid* (line 67), *aspect* (line 91), *device* (line 199).

 BEST PRACTICES TOOLKIT—Transparency
New Word Analysis p. E8

of woven willow or, for the forgetful, by supports of painted wire, for to learn the high proud head on a swan's neck, to learn to flow like water, is not easy
70 for a little girl as she becomes a gentlewoman. But knights and ladies both matched their movements to their garments; the sweep and rhythm of a long gown informs the manner of its moving. It is not necessary to inspect a serf or a slave, his shoulder wide and sloping from burdens, legs short and thick and crooked, feet splayed and widespread, the whole frame slowly crushed by weights. In the great hall the serving people walked under burdens with the slow weight of oxen and scuttled like crabs, crooked and nervous when the weight was gone. **D**

A pause in the recital of his virtues drew Lancelot's attention. The knight who had tried to kill him in a tree had finished, and among the benches Sir
80 Kay was rising to his feet. Lancelot could hear his voice before he spoke, reciting deeds like leaves and bags and barrels. Before his friend could reach the center of the hall, Sir Lancelot wriggled to his feet and approached the dais. "My lord king," he said, "forgive me if I ask leave to go. An old wound has broken open."

Arthur smiled down on him. "I have the same old wound," he said. "We'll go together. Perhaps you will come to the tower room when we have attended to our wounds." And he signed the trumpets to end the gathering, and the bodyguards to clear the hall. **E**

The stone stairway to the king's room was in the thickness of the wall of
90 the round tower of the keep. At short intervals a deep embrasure[8] and a long, beveled arrow slit commanded some aspect of the town below.

No armed men guarded this stairway. They were below and had passed Sir Lancelot in. The king's room was round, a horizontal slice of the tower, windowless save for the arrow slits, entered by a narrow arched door. It was a sparsely furnished room, carpeted with rushes. A wide bed, and at its foot a carved oaken chest, a bench before the fireplace, and several stools completed the furnishing. But the raw stone of the tower was plastered over and painted with solemn figures of men and angels walking hand in hand. Two candles and the reeky fire gave the only light. **F**

100 When Lancelot entered, the queen stood up from the bench before the fire, saying, "I will retire, my lords."

"No, stay," said Arthur.

"Stay," said Lancelot.

The king was stretched comfortably in the bed. His bare feet projecting from his long saffron[9] robe caressed each other, the toes curled downward.

The queen was lovely in the firelight, all lean, down-flowing lines of green samite.[10] She wore her little mouth-corner smile of concealed amusement, and

---

8. **embrasure** (ĕm-brā′zhər): an opening in a wall, narrowing toward the outside.
9. **saffron**: golden yellow, like the spice of that name.
10. **samite**: a heavy silk fabric.

D STYLE
In lines 60–77, Steinbeck describes various members of medieval society. What **similes** and **metaphors** help you understand these people and their differences?

E MAKE INFERENCES
Reread lines 78–88. What can you infer about Lancelot and Arthur on the basis of their sudden departure from the banquet hall?

F GRAMMAR AND STYLE
Reread lines 92–99. Notice how Steinbeck varies the beginnings of his sentences, here through the use of adjectives, conjunctions, pronouns, and articles.

TEXT ANALYSIS   COMMON CORE   RL 4

D STYLE

Possible answer: *The metaphor "crushing boxes of iron" (lines 62–63) conveys the weight of a knight's armor. The metaphor "on a swan's neck" and the simile "flow like water" (line 69) convey the grace of the ladies. The simile "scuttled like crabs" (line 76) conveys the servants' nervous busyness.*

READING SKILL   COMMON CORE   RL 1 RL 9

E Model the Skill: MAKE INFERENCES

Model for students how to make inferences. Point out that Lancelot has been inattentive during the recitation of his deeds (line 78). Tell students to note the details about how Arthur reacts to Lancelot's leaving (lines 83–85). Point out that Arthur not only joins Lancelot, he smiles at him. Remind students that these details and their personal knowledge will enable them to make an inference about Lancelot and Arthur. Have students use the chart that they started on page 1131 to make an inference about Lancelot—and, by extension, about Arthur.

Details About Lancelot	My Experiences	My Inferences
"Lancelot could hear his voice before he spoke..." (line 80)	Hearing the same stories repeated gets boring.	Lancelot is bored—tired of hearing his praises repeated.

Possible answer: *It can be inferred that these characters are bored and tired and that they understand each other well.*

F GRAMMAR AND STYLE   COMMON CORE   L 1b

Vary Sentence Beginnings Explain that varied sentence beginnings add interest to writing. Invite students to comment on this stylistic element as they continue reading.

FOR ENGLISH LANGUAGE LEARNERS
Vocabulary: Outdated Forms Explain that Steinbeck uses some outdated language to evoke a long-ago, legendary setting. Provide these terms and definitions; then have students reread the lines, substituting the definitions.

- *otherwhere* (line 32), "somewhere else"
- *gentlewoman* (line 70), "upper-class woman"
- *ask leave to go* (line 83), "request permission to leave"
- *reeky* (line 99), "smoky"

FOR ADVANCED LEARNERS/PRE–AP
Analyze Grammar and Style Have students analyze the sentence beginnings in lines 92–99. Lead students to these findings:

- Four sentences (those that begin in lines 92, 93, 95, and 98) begin with noun phrases, one of which is a compound subject.
- The remaining sentences begin with single words—twice with a pronoun (lines 92 and 94) and once with a conjunction (line 97).

Analyze Visuals

Activity How does the artist suggest the virtue of Queen Guinevere? *Possible answer: Collier suggests the queen's virtue by using the color white—dressing her in a white gown, seating her on a white horse, and surrounding her with branches of white blossoms.*

About the Art British artist John Collier (1850–1934) is best known for his portraits, including one of Charles Darwin that is displayed in Britain's National Portrait Gallery. This detail from *Queen Guinevere's Maying* offers an idealized view of the queen: Collier places Guinevere at the center of the Mayday celebration, where she embodies the youth, freshness, and sensuousness associated with springtime. The distant look on her face echoes Steinbeck's description that "her inward eyes confessed her vagrant thoughts" (lines 47–48).

REVISIT THE BIG QUESTION

Do heroes get to be
HUMAN?

Discuss In lines 120–141, what happens to indicate that the private life of the king and queen does not match their public image of perfection? *Possible answer: Guinevere's flirtatious talk and the touch that thrills Lancelot indicate that her marriage to Arthur is not entirely happy and that she is looking for love elsewhere. Arthur's seeming obliviousness to his wife's behavior also suggests a marriage that is less than ideal.*

Queen Guinevere's Maying, John Collier. Bradford Art Galleries and Museums, West Yorkshire, UK. Photo © Bridgeman Art Library.

1136   UNIT 10: GREEK TRAGEDY AND MEDIEVAL ROMANCE

DIFFERENTIATED INSTRUCTION

FOR STRUGGLING READERS

Explore Cause and Effect Have students reread page 1137, focusing on Lancelot's comments about the heroism that others see in him. Then invite them to discuss the effect that people's views of Lancelot may have had upon the knight, especially with regard to his feelings for Guinevere. Have students suggest reasons for Lancelot's feelings for the queen and the possible effect of giving in to those feelings.

FOR ENGLISH LANGUAGE LEARNERS

Culture: Clarify On page 1137, Steinbeck refers to the roles of church and state in medieval times. Clarify these terms:

- *secular* (line 134), "related to worldly rather than spiritual things"
- *The Church* (line 134), "the institution of the Christian church"
- *nunneries* (line 136), "residences for nuns"
- *archbishop* (line 137), "chief bishop, high church official"

her bold golden eyes were the same color as her hair, and odd it was that her
lashes and slender brows were dark, an oddity contrived with kohl[11] brought
110 in a small enameled pot from an outland by a far-wandering knight.

"How are you holding up?" Arthur asked.

"Not well, my lord. It's harder than the quest."

"Did you really do all the things they said you did?"

Lancelot chuckled. "Truthfully, I don't know. It sounds different when
they tell about it. And most of them feel it necessary to add a little. When
I remember leaping eight feet, they tell it at fifty, and frankly I don't recall
several of those giants at all." **G**

The queen made room for him on the fire bench, and he took his seat, back
to the fire.

120   Guinevere said, "The damsel—what's her name—talked about fair queen
enchantresses,[12] but she was so excited that her words tumbled over each other.
I couldn't make out what happened."

Lancelot looked nervously away. "You know how excitable young girls are,"
he said. "A little back-country necromancy[13] in a pasture."

"But she spoke particularly of queens."

"My lady, I think everyone is a queen to her. It's like the giants—makes the
story richer."

"Then they were not queens?"

"Well, for that matter, when you get into the field of enchantment, everyone
130 is a queen, or thinks she is. Next time she tells it, the little damsel will be a
queen. I do think, my lord, there's too much of that kind of thing going on.
It's a bad sign, a kind of restlessness, when people go in for fortunetelling and
all such things. Maybe there should be a law about it."

"There is," said Arthur. "But it's not in secular hands. The Church is
supposed to take care of that."

"Yes, but some of the nunneries are going in for it."

"Well, I'll put a bug in the archbishop's ear."[14]

The queen observed, "I gather you rescued damsels by the dozen." She
put her fingers on his arm and a searing shock ran through his body, and his
140 mouth opened in amazement at a hollow ache that pressed upward against his
ribs and shortened his breath. **H**

After a moment she said, "How many damsels did you rescue?"

His mouth was dry. "Of course there were a few, madame. There always are."

"And all of them made love to you?"

"That they did not, madame. There you protect me."

"I?"

"Yes. Since with my lord's permission I swore to serve you all my life

---

11. **kohl:** a cosmetic preparation used as eye makeup.
12. **fair queen enchantresses:** Morgan le Fay and three other queens, the four of whom, as related in
"Sir Launcelot du Lake," imprisoned Launcelot, demanding that he take one of them as his lover.
13. **necromancy:** magic.
14. **put a bug in the archbishop's ear:** alert the archbishop in a quiet way.

THE ACTS OF KING ARTHUR AND HIS NOBLE KNIGHTS   **1137**

G MAKE INFERENCES
How are Lancelot's
remarks in lines 114–117
consistent with his earlier
behavior at the banquet?
Explain.

2 Targeted Passage

H STYLE
Review the **dialogue** in
lines 120–138. Which
words and phrases in
this exchange sound
particularly realistic?
Explain.

READING SKILL   COMMON CORE
                      RL 1
                      RL 9

G MAKE INFERENCES

*Possible answer: Lancelot's remarks are
self-effacing, or meant to play down his
achievements. He did not enjoy hearing his
feats exaggerated at the feast, either.*

TEXT ANALYSIS   COMMON CORE
                      RL 4

H STYLE

*Possible answer: Phrases such as "what's
her name," "going in for it," and "put a bug
in the archbishop's ear" sound very realistic
because they are so much a part of modern
conversational style.*

TIERED DISCUSSION PROMPTS

Direct students to lines 120–144. Use these
prompts to help students consider Steinbeck's
skill at characterization:

Summarize What happens in this passage?
*Possible answer: During a conversation, Gui-
nevere touches Lancelot's arm.*

Analyze Based on their behavior, how
would you describe Guinevere and Arthur?
*Possible answer: Guinevere seems quick-
witted, playful, and aware of her effect on
Lancelot; Arthur seems decent, content, and
unaware of his wife's behavior.*

Evaluate How well does Steinbeck balance the characters' nobility and humanity? Explain. *Possible answer: Steinbeck
balances nobility and humanity well in the
men, as when Lancelot tries to rise above his
feelings throughout the scene. In Guinevere,
Steinbeck shows humanity over nobility by
portraying her more as a flirtatious woman
than a royal wife.*

FOR STRUGGLING READERS

2 Targeted Passage [Lines 120–145]

In this passage, Lancelot plays down what
people say about his deeds and tries to evade
Guinevere's suggestive questions.

• Who brings up the subject of royal
enchantresses? (lines 120–121)

• How does Lancelot feel about such talk?
What does he seem to think about magic?
(lines 123–133)

FOR ADVANCED LEARNERS/PRE–AP

Research Marriage Law Ask students to
consider the attraction between Lancelot and
Guinevere. Have them use print or electronic
resources to research and report on answers to
these questions about medieval marriage law:

• How was marriage viewed at the time?

• What role did the church play in the creation and enforcement of marriage laws?

• Were marriage laws enforced across social
classes? If not, why not?

and gave my knightly courtly love[15] to you, I am sheltered from damsels by your name."

150   "And do you want to be sheltered?"

"Yes, my lady. I am a fighting man. I have neither time nor inclination for any other kind of love. I hope this pleases you, my lady. I sent many prisoners to ask your mercy."

"I never saw such a crop of them," Arthur said. "You must have swept some counties clean."

Guinevere touched him on the arm again and with side-glancing golden eyes saw the spasm that shook him. "While we are on this subject, I want to mention one lady you did not save. When I saw her, she was a headless corpse and not in good condition, and the man who brought her in was

160 half crazed."[16]

"I am ashamed of that," said Lancelot. "She was under my protection, and I failed her. I suppose it was my shame that made me force the man to do it. I'm sorry. I hope you released him from the burden."

"Not at all," she said. "I wanted him away before the feast reeked up the heavens. I sent him with his burden to the Pope. His friend will not improve on the way. And if his loss of interest in ladies continues, he may turn out to be a very holy man, a hermit or something of that nature, if he isn't a maniac first."

The king rose on his elbow. "We will have to work out some system," he said. "The rules of errantry[17] are too loose, and the quests overlap. Besides, I

170 wonder how long we can leave justice in the hands of men who are themselves unstable. I don't mean you, my friend. But there may come a time when order and organization from the crown will be necessary."

The queen stood up. "My lords, will you grant me permission to leave you now? I know you will wish to speak of great things foreign and perhaps tiresome to a lady's ears."

The king said, "Surely, my lady. Go to your rest."

"No, sire—not rest. If I do not lay out the designs for the needlepoint, my ladies will have no work tomorrow."

"But these are feast days, my dear."

180   "I like to give them something every day, my lord. They're lazy things and some of them so woolly in the mind that they forget how to thread a needle from day to day. Forgive me, my lords."

She swept from the room with proud and powerful steps, and the little breeze she made in the still air carried a strange scent to Lancelot, a perfume which sent a shivering excitement coursing through his body. It was an odor he did not, could not, know, for it was the smell of Guinevere distilled by her

---

15. **courtly love:** a sentimental reflection of the feudal relationship between a knight and his lord. The knight serves his chosen lady with the same obedience and loyalty he owes his lord. The knight's love for the lady inspires him to seek adventure and achieve great deeds.

16. **When I saw her . . . half crazed:** Guinevere is referring to a woman Lancelot was unable to save—a woman who was beheaded by her jealous husband. As punishment, Lancelot commanded the husband to take the woman's body to Guinevere and to throw himself on her mercy.

17. **errantry** (ĕr′ən-trē): the knightly pursuit of adventure.

READING SKILL

COMMON CORE
RL 1
RL 9

MAKE INFERENCES

Possible answer: *Lancelot feels chivalric loyalty to Guinevere, but he is personally attracted to her, as well. Lancelot speaks of his "knightly courtly love" (line 148), but he is thrilled when she touches him (lines 138–141, 156–157).*

MAKE INFERENCES
Reread lines 138–157. Describe Lancelot's feelings for Guinevere. Which details helped you make your inference?

COMMON CORE RL 4

Language Coach

Commonly Confused Words The words *tiresome* (line 175) and *tiring* are easy to confuse. Although both can mean "causing fatigue," one has the connotation, or associated meaning, of "causing annoyance." Which word has this negative connotation?

Analyze Visuals ▶

How does this painting depict Lancelot as an ideal knight?

DIFFERENTIATED INSTRUCTION

FOR STRUGGLING READERS

Comprehension Support As students reread lines 157–172, make these points to show the foreshadowing purpose of this dialogue:

- The case that Arthur and Lancelot discuss involves a jealous husband and at least the suspicion of adultery. According to legend, Arthur later will be cast in the role of a jealous husband.

- Lancelot is ashamed that he failed to protect the jealous husband's wife. According to legend, Lancelot later stands up to protect Guinevere in a similar situation.

- Arthur worries that his knights are getting out of control, but he does not so accuse Lancelot. According to legend, Arthur later loses his control over Lancelot.

FOR ENGLISH LANGUAGE LEARNERS

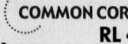

Language Coach   **COMMON CORE** RL 4

Commonly Confused Words *Answer:* Tiresome *has negative connotations.* Give students practice differentiating between *tiring* and *tiresome.* Write the words *tiring* and *tiresome* on the board. Have students suggest a list of things that are *tiring* and a list of things that are *tiresome.* Write their suggestions on the board. Monitor the suggestions for accuracy, and make adjustments and clarifications as necessary.

Detail of *Lancelot and Guinevere*, Herbert James Draper. Private collection. Bohams, London. Photo © Bridgeman Art Library.

Do heroes get to be
HUMAN?

Discuss What does the exchange in lines 147–163 show about the different views of perfection held by Lancelot and Guinevere?
Possible answer: *Lancelot seems to view perfection as a superhuman ideal that he constantly must uphold. Guinevere seems to relish the fact that she doesn't need to be perfect—and that Lancelot is really just a man, not some perfect being.*

Analyze Visuals

Possible answer: *The painting idealizes Lancelot by portraying him as handsome, straight of posture, and noble and sensitive in expression. He holds a laurel-wreathed lance, wears fine armor, and bears a shield decorated with a lion in its coat of arms.*

About the Art Like the Collier painting on page 1136, Herbert James Draper's *Lancelot and Guinevere* suggests an innate grandness in British nobility. Also like Collier, Draper (1864–1920) was favored as a painter of society portraits and peaked in appeal near the end of Victoria's reign. This work, also known as *Queen of the Tournament*, shows Lancelot after winning a joust. His face bears scratches from the battle. In the full scene, Guinevere, flanked by fair maidens on the royal dais, looks down gracefully upon her champion.

FOR ADVANCED LEARNERS/PRE–AP
Analyze Tone [small-group activity] Have students analyze Steinbeck's tone from Guinevere's exit to the end of the story. Suggest that they consider the connotation of key descriptive words and phrases in the text (such as *bleak, cold,* and *bitterly*). Extend the analysis by having students contrast the tone of Steinbeck's description with the tone of the dialogue, especially the words of King Arthur.

FOR RELUCTANT READERS
Connect Write the following critical thinking questions on the board: Do you think humans can achieve perfection? Is the pursuit of perfection a worthy goal? Have students support their opinions with examples from their own experiences or from things they've read or seen in TV and film. Ask students what modern endeavors, if any, seek perfection as a goal.

TEXT ANALYSIS

J STYLE

Possible answer: *The image of Guinevere as she "swept from the room," leaving the "perfume" of her scent, excites Lancelot. The fact that the room goes "bleak" and Lancelot feels "dog-weary" upon her exit shows her effect upon him.*

TEXT ANALYSIS
COMMON CORE
RL 9

K ANALYZE CHARACTER

Steinbeck's Lancelot is brave and gallant but his greatness isolates him; he is often lonely. He is not always comfortable being "the greatest knight in Christendom." Steinbeck draws a portrait of a strong but humble Lancelot. "When I remember leaping eight feet, they tell it at fifty, and frankly I don't recall several of those giants at all."

READING SKILL
COMMON CORE
RL 1
RL 9

L MAKE INFERENCES

Possible answer: *He is attracted to the wife of his friend and king.*

VOCABULARY
COMMON CORE
L 4

OWN THE WORD

• **intemperate:** Tell students that *intemperate* is formed by adding the prefix *in-*, meaning "not," to the word *temperate*, which means "exercising moderation and self-restraint."

• **haggard:** Have students suggest reasons that a person might look *haggard*.

SELECTION WRAP–UP

READ WITH A PURPOSE Ask students which character suffered the greatest loss. *Possible answer: Students may think Lancelot lost the most, because he lost his honor.*

⭐ **CRITIQUE** Have students evaluate the realism in Steinbeck's tale.

---

own skin. And as she passed through the door and descended the steps, he saw himself leap up and follow her, although he did not move. And when she was gone, the room was bleak, and the glory was gone from it, and Sir Lancelot
190 was dog-weary, tired almost to weeping. **J**

"What a queen she is," said King Arthur softly. "And what a woman equally. Merlin was with me when I chose her. He tried to dissuade me with his usual doomful prophecies. That was one of the few times I differed with him. Well, my choice has proved him fallible. She has shown the world what a queen should be. All other women lose their sheen when she is present."

Lancelot said, "Yes, my lord," and for no reason he knew, except perhaps the **intemperate** dullness of the feast, he felt lost, and a cold knife of loneliness pressed against his heart.

The king was chuckling. "It is the device of ladies that their lords have great
200 matters to discuss, when if the truth were told, we bore them. And I hope the truth is never told. Why, you look **haggard,** my friend. Are you feverish? Did you mean that about an old wound opening?"

"No. The wound was what you thought it was, my lord. But it is true that I can fight, travel, live on berries, fight again, go without sleeping, and come out fresh and fierce, but sitting still at Whitsun feast has wearied me to death."

Arthur said, "I can see it. We'll discuss the realm's health another time. Go to your bed now. Have you your old quarters?"

"No—better ones. Sir Kay has cleared five knights from the lovely lordly rooms over the north gate. He did it in memory of an adventure which we,
210 God help us, will have to listen to tomorrow. I accept your dismissal, my lord."

And Lancelot knelt down and took the king's beloved hand in both of his and kissed it. "Good night, my liege lord, my liege friend," he said and then stumbled blindly from the room and felt his way down the curving stone steps past the arrow slits.

As he came to the level of the next landing, Guinevere issued silently from a darkened entrance. He could see her in the thin light from the arrow slit. She took his arm and led him to her dark chamber and closed the oaken door.

"A strange thing happened," she said softly. "When I left you, I thought you followed me. I was so sure of it I did not even look around to verify it. You
220 were there behind me. And when I came to my own door, I said good night to you, so certain I was that you were there."

He could see her outline in the dark and smell the scent which was herself. "My lady," he said, "when you left the room, I saw myself follow you as though I were another person looking on."

Their bodies locked together as though a trap had sprung. Their mouths met, and each devoured the other. Each frantic heartbeat at the walls of ribs trying to get to the other until their held breaths burst out and Lancelot, dizzied, found the door and blundered down the stairs. And he was weeping bitterly. ✎ **K** **L**

③ Targeted Passage

Reread lines 183–190, noting Steinbeck's **imagery**—words that appeal to the senses. Which images help you understand Guinevere and her effect on Lancelot?

intemperate
(ĭn-tĕm′pər-ĭt) *adj.* extreme

haggard (hăg′ərd) *adj.* appearing worn and exhausted

COMMON CORE RL 9

K ANALYZE CHARACTER
Now that you've read Steinbeck's modern retelling of Le Morte d'Arthur, think about how Steinbeck transforms the character of Sir Lancelot. What qualities does Steinbeck emphasize? What details does he leave out? Cite evidence from the texts in your answer.

L MAKE INFERENCES
Reread the final paragraph of the selection. Why does Lancelot weep?

DIFFERENTIATED INSTRUCTION

FOR STRUGGLING READERS

③ Targeted Passage [Lines 211–229]

In this conclusion, Lancelot leaves the king, only to succumb to Guinevere's passionate kiss.

• How do Lancelot's farewell words to the king indicate his allegiance to Arthur? (line 212)

• What action does Guinevere take? What does that action show about her? (lines 215–226)

• What do Guinevere's words to Lancelot indicate about her view of their relationship? (lines 218–221)

• Why is Lancelot's reply significant? (lines 222–224)

FOR ENGLISH LANGUAGE LEARNERS

Vocabulary: Idioms Remind students that Steinbeck occasionally uses idioms to infuse the dialogue of this centuries-old story with a contemporary realism. Discuss these idioms:

• *dog-weary* (line 190), "extremely tired"

• *to death* (line 205), "extremely"

To check understanding, have students use these idioms in sentences.

After Reading

Comprehension

1. **Recall** Why is Lancelot praised at the feast?

2. **Clarify** Why does Lancelot leave the feast?

3. **Summarize** Describe what happens after Lancelot leaves the king's room.

Text Analysis

4. **Make Inferences** Review the chart you created as you read. Do you think Lancelot sees himself as others do—as a model of perfection? Cite evidence.

5. **Draw Conclusions** Reread lines 183–198. What conclusions can you draw about the **internal conflict** Lancelot experiences? Support your answer.

6. **Interpret Theme** What theme about knighthood does Steinbeck communicate in the selection? Cite evidence to support your answer.

7. **Understand Style** Steinbeck's style features many tightly constructed **characterizations.** Choose a passage of at least five lines that illustrates the author's ability to create a brief, effective portrait. Explain your choice.

8. **Examine Figurative Language** Identify three examples of figurative language—similes and metaphors—in the selection. Explain how each helps to clarify an idea or enliven a scene.

9. **Compare Literary Texts** Review Keith Baines's retelling of Malory's *Le Morte d'Arthur* on pages 1112–1126. Then compare Baines's writing style with Steinbeck's. Complete a chart like the one shown. In your opinion, did Steinbeck do a good job of transforming his source material? Why or why not?

	Baines	Steinbeck
Characterization		
Sensory Details		
Dialogue		
Word Choice		
Tone		

Text Criticism

10. **Social Context** In *King Arthur and His Noble Knights,* what does Steinbeck suggest were the roles and responsibilities of noblewomen in medieval society? Cite evidence to support your response.

> **Do heroes get to be HUMAN?**
>
> Do you want to know about your heroes' human weaknesses? Why or why not?

THE ACTS OF KING ARTHUR AND HIS NOBLE KNIGHTS **1141**

COMMON CORE

RL 1 Cite textual evidence to support inferences drawn from the text. **RL 4** Analyze the cumulative impact of specific word choices on meaning. **RL 9** Analyze how an author draws on and transforms source material in a specific work.

Practice and Apply

For preliminary support of post-reading questions, use these copy masters:

R RESOURCE MANAGER—Copy Masters
Reading Check p. 70
Grammar and Style p. 72
Question Support p. 71

Additional selection questions are provided for teachers on page 57.

ANSWERS

Comprehension

1. *Lancelot is praised because he has defeated so many opponents.*

2. *Lancelot leaves because he is bored by all the praise and exaggeration of his deeds.*

3. *As Lancelot descends the stairs, Guinevere appears and leads him to her chamber. They kiss; then Lancelot leaves in tears.*

Text Analysis

 COMMON CORE RL 1, RL 4, RL 9

Possible answers:

4. ■ **COMMON CORE FOCUS** *Make Inferences Lancelot does not see himself as perfect. For example, he admits that people exaggerate his deeds (lines 113–117).*

5. *Lancelot's internal conflict is his allegiance to Arthur versus his feelings for Guinevere (seen in the way that she moves him and in his lonely feeling when Arthur praises her).*

6. *Steinbeck communicates the theme that people glorify knights to quell their own longings. He shows how Lancelot's inner feelings are at odds with his public image. He also says, specifically, "There is a seat of worth beyond the reach of envy whose occupant ceases to be a man. . . ." (lines 35–39).*

7. ● **COMMON CORE FOCUS** *Style The description of Lancelot in lines 25–35 shows that he is uncomfortable about having been turned into a near-god against his will.*

8. *People "as fitted as toes in a tight shoe" (lines 15–16) shows how crowded the feast room was; "a cold knife of loneliness pressed against his heart" (lines 197–198) makes the reader feel the pain of Lancelot's hidden love; "Their bodies locked together as though a trap had sprung" (line 225) indicates the force of the characters' love.*

---

9. **Characterization:** *Baines—flat; Steinbeck—complex and realistic*
Sensory details: *Baines—few; Steinbeck—many*
Dialogue: *Baines—stiff and archaic; Steinbeck—informal and modern*
Word choice: *Baines—elevated; Steinbeck—concrete*
Tone: *Baines—distant; Steinbeck—sympathetic*
Although Baines's version is more exciting, Steinbeck's has more detail and inner drama.

Text Criticism

Possible answer:

10. *Steinbeck suggests that the role of noblewomen was to be beautiful and graceful, to inspire the knights, and to supervise the work of lower-ranking women.*

> **Do heroes get to be HUMAN?**
> *Knowing heroes' human weaknesses helps readers connect with them. Although perfection might be admired, it can never attained by mortals. Characters who are perfect are cold and off-putting.*

THE ACTS OF KING ARTHUR AND HIS NOBLE KNIGHTS **1141**

ANSWERS

Vocabulary in Context

▲ VOCABULARY PRACTICE

1. *a*   **3.** *a*   **5.** *c*

2. *a*   **4.** *b*   **6.** *a*

 RESOURCE MANAGER—Copy Master
Vocabulary Practice p. 68

ACADEMIC VOCABULARY IN WRITING

Sample response: Lancelot's body language and physical responses often reflect feelings that he does not want others to witness. At the banquet, he is bored by the elegies to his heroism, and even dozes. Later, when Guinevere touches his arm, he feels "a searing shock" that reveals the intensity that underlies his feelings for her.

VOCABULARY STRATEGY: CONNOTATION

COMMON CORE L 5b

• To give students a sense of connotation, urge them to imagine the words applied in some way to themselves.

• Have students explain their placement of the words on each continuum.

Possible answers:

1. *intemperate (negative), bold (positive), extreme (positive or negative)*

2. *worn (negative), haggard (negative), tired (neutral)*

3. *exalt (positive), boast (negative), praise (positive)*

4. *retaliation (negative), reprisal (neutral), revenge (negative)*

 RESOURCE MANAGER—Copy Master
Vocabulary Strategy p. 69

Interactive Vocabulary   THINK central

Keywords direct students to a **WordSharp** tutorial on **thinkcentral.com** or to other types of vocabulary practice and review.

Vocabulary in Context

▲ **VOCABULARY PRACTICE**

Choose the letter of the word that differs most in meaning from the others in the set. If necessary, use a dictionary to check the precise meanings of words you are unsure of.

1. (a) encouragement, (b) belittlement, (c) disparagement, (d) ridicule
2. (a) motionless, (b) vagrant, (c) drifting, (d) wandering
3. (a) mercy, (b) reprisal, (c) punishment, (d) revenge
4. (a) glorify, (b) condemn, (c) exalt, (d) acclaim
5. (a) intemperate, (b) excessive, (c) mild, (d) extreme
6. (a) refreshed, (b) rundown, (c) worn, (d) haggard

WORD LIST
disparagement
exalt
haggard
intemperate
reprisal
vagrant

ACADEMIC VOCABULARY IN WRITING

• drama   • emerge   • encounter   • globe   • underlie

How does body language reflect **underlying** feelings? A clear portrait of a character often **emerges** when you consider the character's words and actions. Write a paragraph about how Lancelot's responses and physical actions reveal his feelings for both Arthur and Guinevere. Use at least one Academic Vocabulary word in your response.

VOCABULARY STRATEGY: CONNOTATION

A **connotation** is an attitude or a feeling associated with a word. For example, *vagrant* and *rambling* could both be defined as "moving in a random fashion," but Steinbeck's use of *vagrant* to describe Guinevere's thoughts does not convey the negativity associated with *rambling*. Writers are aware of the connotations of words and often use them to evoke particular moods.

COMMON CORE

L 5b Analyze nuances in the meaning of words with similar denotations.

PRACTICE Place the words in each group on a continuum to show the positive, neutral, or negative connotation of each word. Use a dictionary, glossary, or thesaurus to help you. Then compare your answers with those of a classmate.

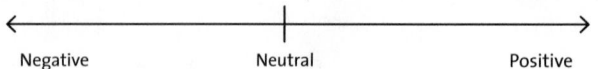

Negative   Neutral   Positive

1. intemperate, bold, extreme
2. worn, haggard, tired
3. exalt, boast, praise
4. retaliation, reprisal, revenge

Interactive Vocabulary THINK central
Go to **thinkcentral.com**.
KEYWORD: HML10-1142

DIFFERENTIATED INSTRUCTION

FOR ENGLISH LANGUAGE LEARNERS

Vocabulary Strategy Have students work in small groups, using a thesaurus for help, to create connotation triads like those in the Vocabulary Strategy. Students might begin with these words from the story: *decorous* (line 14), *ferocity* (line 40), *rigid* (line 67), *excitable* (line 123), *tiresome* (line 175), and *scent* (line 222). Then have group representatives read out triads to other groups, who will respond by suggesting an appropriate order for the words.

FOR ADVANCED LEARNERS/PRE–AP

Vocabulary Strategy: Apply Connotations Challenge students to form new triads using these words from the story: *decorous* (line 14), *ferocity* (line 40), *rigid* (line 67), *excitable* (line 123), *tiresome* (line 175), and *scent* (line 222). Then have them write and share a brief essay evaluating Lancelot and Guinevere in terms of their passionate kiss and thus disloyalty to King Arthur. Have students use in their essays one synonym from each of the six triads.

Language

◆ **GRAMMAR AND STYLE: Vary Sentence Beginnings**

Review the **Grammar and Style** note on page 1135. In the selection, Steinbeck uses a variety of sentence beginnings that help to enliven his work. Your writing, too, will be more interesting if you use an assortment of **phrases, clauses,** and **words** to begin sentences. In the following examples, notice how Steinbeck starts one sentence with a series of prepositional phrases and another sentence with an adverbial clause:

> *In the great hall of the castle on the hill the king sat high . . . while at the long trestle boards the people were as fitted as toes in a tight shoe.* (lines 13–16)
> *Then while the glistening meat dripped down the tables, it was the custom for the defeated to celebrate the deeds of those who had overcome them. . . .* (lines 17–18)

Note how the revisions in blue make the following draft less repetitive. Revise your responses to the prompt by varying your sentence beginnings.

> **STUDENT MODEL**
> *In* <u>Le Morte d'Arthur,</u>   *His*
> Malory portrays Launcelot as the true gallant knight. ~~Malory's~~ Launcelot
>
> clanks swords with sworn enemies before dramatically riding off across
>   *While*
> the countryside. Steinbeck's knight is just as brave as Malory's, ~~Steinbeck's~~
>
> ~~Lancelot~~ is much more distracted by thoughts of Guinevere, ~~though.~~

READING-WRITING CONNECTION

Broaden your understanding of the selections by responding to this prompt. Then use the **revising tip** to improve your writing.

WRITING PROMPT	REVISING TIP
Extended Constructed Response: Comparison Launcelot, or Lancelot, is an archetypal hero. How does Malory's portrayal of the knight differ from Steinbeck's? What aspects of the archetypal hero do Launcelot and Lancelot have in common? Compare and contrast the way the two authors depict this famous knight in a **three-to-five-paragraph response.** What about him is not heroic?	Review your response. Have you varied your sentence beginnings to make your writing interesting? If not, revise to begin your sentences with different phrases, clauses, and words.

Interactive Revision THINK central
Go to **thinkcentral.com**.
KEYWORD: HML10-1143

THE ACTS OF KING ARTHUR AND HIS NOBLE KNIGHTS **1143**

COMMON CORE

L 1b Use various types of phrases and clauses to convey specific meanings and add variety and interest to writing. **W 9a (RL 9)** Draw evidence from literary texts to support analysis; analyze how an author draws on and transforms source material in a specific work.

FOR STRUGGLING WRITERS

- Find and contrast one example from each story—for instance, how Lancelot does or does not reflect the chivalric code when at (in Steinbeck's account) or away from (in Malory's account) the Round Table.

- Have students generalize the differences between the two versions of Lancelot.

- Remind students that their contrasts need to make an overall point. Help students express their opinion in a thesis statement in the opening paragraph.

Language

◆ **GRAMMAR AND STYLE**

COMMON CORE **L 1b**
W 9a (RL 9)

- Write this passage on the board. Have students suggest alternative sentence beginnings to enliven the style:

> ~~The~~ In Malory's Le Morte d'Arthur, *Launcelot* ~~in Malory's Le Morte d'Arthur~~ is every bit the brave and honorable knight, battling evil and protecting women but never quite seeming human. Although the ~~The~~ Lancelot in Steinbeck's updating of the legend receives praise for his bravery, ~~but~~ he also seems like a real person.

- Remind students to use a thesaurus when they write for an audience that responds best to formal language.

R RESOURCE MANAGER—Copy Master
Grammar and Style p. 72

READING-WRITING CONNECTION

Suggest that students use a Compare-Contrast template to record their ideas.

🧰 BEST PRACTICES TOOLKIT—Transparency
Writing Template: Compare-Contrast
(by Points) pp. C16, C23

Writing Online  THINK central

The following tools are available online at **thinkcentral.com** and on **WriteSmart** CD-ROM:
- **Interactive Graphic Organizers**
- **Interactive Student Models**
- **Interactive Revision Lessons**
For additional grammar instruction, see **GrammarNotes** on **thinkcentral.com**.

Assess and Reteach

Assess

DIAGNOSTIC AND SELECTION TESTS
     Selection Test A pp. 303–304
     Selection Test B/C pp. 305–306

Interactive Selection Test on **thinkcentral.com**

Reteach

Level Up Online Tutorials on **thinkcentral.com**

Reteaching Worksheets on **thinkcentral.com**
     Literature Lesson 44, Writing Lessons 8, 28

Focus and Motivate

RL 1 Cite evidence to support analysis of what the text says explicitly as well as inferences drawn from the text. **RL 4** Determine the meaning of words and phrases as they are used in a text. **RL 5** Analyze how an author's choices concerning how to structure a text and order events within it to create such effects as mystery, tension, or surprise. **RL 7** Analyze the representation of a subject in two different artistic mediums, including what is emphasized or absent in each treatment. **RL 9** Analyze how an author draws on and transforms source material in a specific work. **W 2** Write informative/explanatory texts to examine and convey complex ideas, concepts, and information clearly and accurately through the effective selection, organization, and analysis of content. **W 5** Develop and strengthen writing by planning and revising, focusing on addressing what is most significant for a specific purpose and audience. **L 5** Demonstrate understanding of figurative language, word relationships, and nuances in words.

SUMMARIES

from *Don Quixote* A man imagines himself to be Don Quixote, a knight-errant and sets out on a heroic quest with Sancho Panza.

from *Man of La Mancha* Cervantes play-acts the role of Don Quixote.

Why do we admire DREAMERS?

Have students read the question and suggest definitions of the word *dream*. Then have students complete the *DISCUSS* activity.

Selection Resources

Comparing Across Genres

from **Don Quixote**
Novel by Miguel de Cervantes

from **Man of La Mancha**
Musical Play by Dale Wasserman

Essential Course of Study **ECOS**

Why do we admire DREAMERS?

COMMON CORE

RL 5 Analyze how an author's choices concerning how to structure a text and order events within it create such effects as mystery, tension, or surprise.
RL 7 Analyze the representation of a subject in two different artistic mediums, including what is emphasized or absent in each treatment. **RL 9** Analyze how an author draws on and transforms source material in a specific work.

Think of people you know or have heard of who have pursued their dreams even when the dreams seemed foolish or impossible to achieve. Which of their qualities do you admire the most? In these two selections, you will meet a character whose devotion to an impossible dream has inspired countless readers.

DISCUSS With a small group, generate a list of people who have been considered dreamers—Mahatma Gandhi, for example. Then discuss these questions: What traits do these individuals share? How have their actions affected the way you look at the world?

1144

See resources on the **Teacher One Stop DVD-ROM** *and on* **thinkcentral.com**.

R RESOURCE MANAGER UNIT 10
Plan and Teach, pp. 73–80
Summary, pp. 81–82†‡*
Text Analysis, pp. 83–87†*
Vocabulary, pp. 88–90*

DIAGNOSTIC AND SELECTION TESTS
Selection Tests, pp. 307–310

BEST PRACTICES TOOLKIT
Venn Diagram, p. A26
Definition Mapping, p. E6
Character Traits and Textual Evidence, p. D6
Core Analysis Frame: Fiction, pp. D21, D22

INTERACTIVE READER

ADAPTED INTERACTIVE READER

ELL ADAPTED INTERACTIVE READER

TECHNOLOGY
- **Teacher One Stop DVD-ROM**
- **Student One Stop DVD-ROM**
- **PowerNotes DVD-ROM**
- **Audio Anthology CD**
- **Audio Tutor CD**
- **ExamView Test Generator** on the Teacher One Stop

THINK central

Video Trailer
Go to **thinkcentral.com** to preview the **Video Trailer** introducing this selection. Other features that support the selection include
- **PowerNotes** presentation
- **ThinkAloud** models to enhance comprehension
- **WordSharp** vocabulary tutorials
- interactive writing and grammar instruction

---

* Resources for Differentiation   † Also in Spanish   ‡ In Haitian Creole and Vietnamese

TEXT ANALYSIS: PARODY ACROSS GENRES

A **parody** is a comic imitation of another work or of a type of literature. The following two selections are parodies of medieval romances, rambling tales of heroic knights and their fearless search for adventure. These parodies may include the same archetypes, or common features, of traditional romances, but they turn the reader's understanding of the archetypes inside out. Use the descriptions on pages 1110 and 1111 to review characteristics of the chivalric code and of medieval romance.

The novel and play excerpts you will read both portray the same ridiculous hero on his hopeless quest, but they use different techniques to get the joke across. The following chart shows how genre influences the comic strategies each writer uses.

In the Novel	In the Play
• character traits and motivations conveyed through description	• character traits and motivations conveyed through dialogue, song, and action
• verbal humor, such as exaggerated descriptions, puns, and irony	• visual humor, such as non-realistic staging, sight gags, and pratfalls
• language that imitates the style of a chivalric romance	• comic misunderstandings that highlight the unrealistic ideals of the chivalric code
• absurd situations that parallel the actions of a chivalric hero	

READING STRATEGY: SET A PURPOSE FOR READING

When you **set a purpose for reading,** you decide what to look for as you read. In this lesson, you are reading to compare and contrast two selections that parody the medieval romance. As you read, note the specific ideas each writer is mocking and the techniques he uses to achieve his comic effects. After you read, you will use the Points of Comparison chart on page 1161 to analyze the two selections.

▲ VOCABULARY IN CONTEXT

Test your knowledge by substituting a different word or phrase for each boldfaced term.

1. **resurrect** the dead
2. expose the **fictitious** alibi
3. a smiling and **affable** host
4. **burnish** the silver
5. his **incongruous** garb
6. swore undying **enmity**
7. split up the **hapless** couple
8. a mile-long **cavalcade**

Complete the activities in your **Reader/Writer Notebook.**

Miguel de Cervantes
1547–1616

Disenchanted Hero
Miguel de Cervantes led a life of adventure. As a young soldier fighting for Spain, he was wounded in battle, nearly losing his left hand. On his journey home, he was captured by pirates and was enslaved for five years. In 1580, when his family raised the money to pay his ransom, he returned to Spain, hoping to be honored for his sacrifices. Instead, he struggled to make a living from odd jobs and landed in debtor's prison.

A Lasting Influence
In 1605, after 25 years of failures, Cervantes found fame with *Don Quixote.* Written to parody both romances and romantic ideals, the book's inspired use of irony and realistic details changed the way novels were written. Today, Cervantes's work is one of the most widely published books in the world.

Dale Wasserman
born 1917

Man of the Theater
Dale Wasserman was inspired to write *Man of La Mancha* by his admiration for Cervantes and his groundbreaking novel. Wasserman's reinvention of Don Quixote for the stage became one of the longest-running musicals of the 1960s. His long career includes more than 70 works for television, 17 feature films, and approximately 24 plays and musicals.

Authors Online
Go to **thinkcentral.com.** KEYWORD: HML10-1145

THINK central

● Model the Skill: PARODY ACROSS GENRES

To model how to analyze parody, read aloud this example:

> The knight boldly announced that he would joust with anyone who spoke against his lady's honor. Alas, his challenge went unanswered, as he had neglected to mention his lady's name.

Explain the element of parody in these sentences. Point out that the sentences imitate a knightly tale but present a forgetful, foolish knight.

GUIDED PRACTICE Ask students to name and describe books, movies, or songs that are parodies.

R RESOURCE MANAGER—Copy Master
Parody Across Genres p. 84

■ Model the Skill: SET A PURPOSE FOR READING

Point out that students are reading to consider parody of ideas and parody of techniques. Have students review the characteristics of medieval romance.

GUIDED PRACTICE Ask students to name the kinds of details that they will want to watch for as they read these two selections.

▲ VOCABULARY IN CONTEXT

DIAGNOSE WORD KNOWLEDGE Have all students complete Vocabulary in Context. Check their words or phrases against the following:

affable (ăf'ə-bəl) *adj.* warm and friendly
burnish (bûr'nĭsh) *v.* to polish
cavalcade (kăv'əl-kād') *n.* a procession of people on horseback
enmity (ĕn'mĭ-tē) *n.* hostility and ill will
fictitious (fĭk-tĭsh'əs) *adj.* fabricated; created by the imagination

hapless (hăp'lĭs) *adj.* pitiful; unfortunate
incongruous (ĭn-kŏng'grōō-əs) *adj.* unsuitable; incompatible
resurrect (rĕz'ə-rĕkt') *v.* to bring back to life

PRETEACH VOCABULARY Use the following copy master to help students predict meanings for each boldfaced word.

R RESOURCE MANAGER—Copy Master
Vocabulary Study p. 88

1. Read the first two sentences in the passage aloud, emphasizing *cavalcade.*

2. Point to the details about the riders and their mounts. Elicit meanings for *cavalcade,* such as "a group of riders."

3. Help students find a similar definition in Part B (item 8). Repeat the procedure.

READ WITH A PURPOSE

Help students set a purpose for reading. Tell students to look in both the novel and the play for qualities they admire in Don Quixote.

TEXT ANALYSIS　　　COMMON CORE

Ⓐ PARODY　　　RL 5

Possible answer: *Unlike Malory's heroes, this person has an unimpressive horse and armor. He is middle-aged rather than young, and he seems to prefer life at home to adventurous quests.*

IF STUDENTS NEED HELP . . . Have them use a Venn Diagram to contrast Malory's type of knight with Quejana.

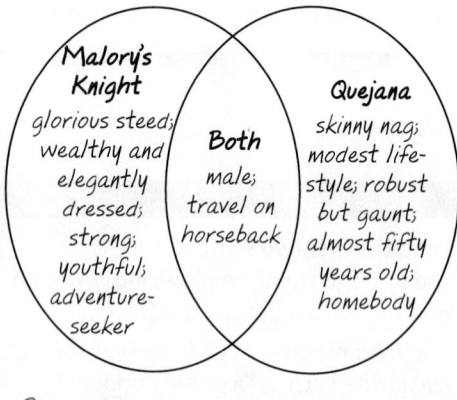

Malory's Knight: glorious steed; wealthy and elegantly dressed; strong; youthful; adventure-seeker

Both: male; travel on horseback

Quejana: skinny nag; modest life-style; robust but gaunt; almost fifty years old; homebody

🧰 **BEST PRACTICES TOOLKIT—Transparency**
Venn Diagram p. A26

Don Quixote

Miguel de Cervantes

❦ Part 1, Chapter 1 ❦

In a village of La Mancha[1] the name of which I have no desire to recall, there lived not so long ago one of those gentlemen who always have a lance in the rack, an ancient buckler,[2] a skinny nag, and a greyhound for the chase. A stew with more beef than mutton in it, chopped meat for his evening meal, scraps for a Saturday, lentils on Friday, and a young pigeon as a special delicacy for Sunday, went to account for three-quarters of his income.

The rest of it he laid out on a broadcloth greatcoat[3] and velvet stockings for feast days, with slippers to match, while the other days of the week he cut a figure in a suit of the finest homespun. Living with him were a housekeeper in
10 her forties, a niece who was not yet twenty, and a lad of the field and market place who saddled his horse for him and wielded the pruning knife.

This gentleman of ours was close on to fifty, of a robust constitution but with little flesh on his bones and a face that was lean and gaunt. He was noted for his early rising, being very fond of the hunt. They will try to tell you that his surname was Quijada or Quesada—there is some difference of opinion among those who have written on the subject—but according to the most likely conjectures we are to understand that it was really Quejana.[4] But all this means very little so far as our story is concerned, providing that in the telling of it we do not depart one iota from the truth. **Ⓐ**

20 You may know, then, that the aforesaid gentleman, on those occasions when he was at leisure, which was most of the year around, was in the habit of reading books of chivalry with such pleasure and devotion as to lead him almost wholly to forget the life of a hunter and even the administration of his estate. So great was his curiosity and infatuation in this regard that he even sold many acres of tillable land in order to be able to buy and read the books that he loved, and he would carry home with him as many of them as he could obtain.

---

1. **La Mancha:** a high, flat, barren region in central Spain.
2. **buckler:** a small, round shield carried or worn on the arm.
3. **broadcloth greatcoat:** a heavy wool overcoat.
4. **Quijada** (kē-hä′dä) . . . **Quesada** (kē-sä′dä) . . . **Quejana** (kē-hä′nä).

Analyze Visuals ▶

What details in this photograph evoke the heroic image of the ideal knight?

Ⓐ PARODY

Reread the opening paragraphs. Compare this passage with the idealized descriptions of Malory's heroes. What details establish a pointed contrast with the romance hero?

❶ **Targeted Passage**

John Lithgow in the TNT production of *Don Quixote*

DIFFERENTIATED INSTRUCTION

FOR ENGLISH LANGUAGE LEARNERS

Vocabulary Support Use Definition Mapping to teach these words: *administration* (line 23), *author* (line 44), *constantly* (line 48), *indicate* (line 116), *appropriate* (line 236).

🧰 **BEST PRACTICES TOOLKIT—Transparency**
Definition Mapping p. E6

FOR STRUGGLING READERS

In combination with the *Audio Anthology CD*, use one or more Targeted Passages (pp. 1146, 1149, 1154, 1155, 1159, 1160) to ensure that students focus on key story ideas, concepts, and skills. Targeted Passages are also good for English learners.

❶ **Targeted Passage** [Lines 20–26]

This passage establishes the hero's passion for reading books of chivalry.

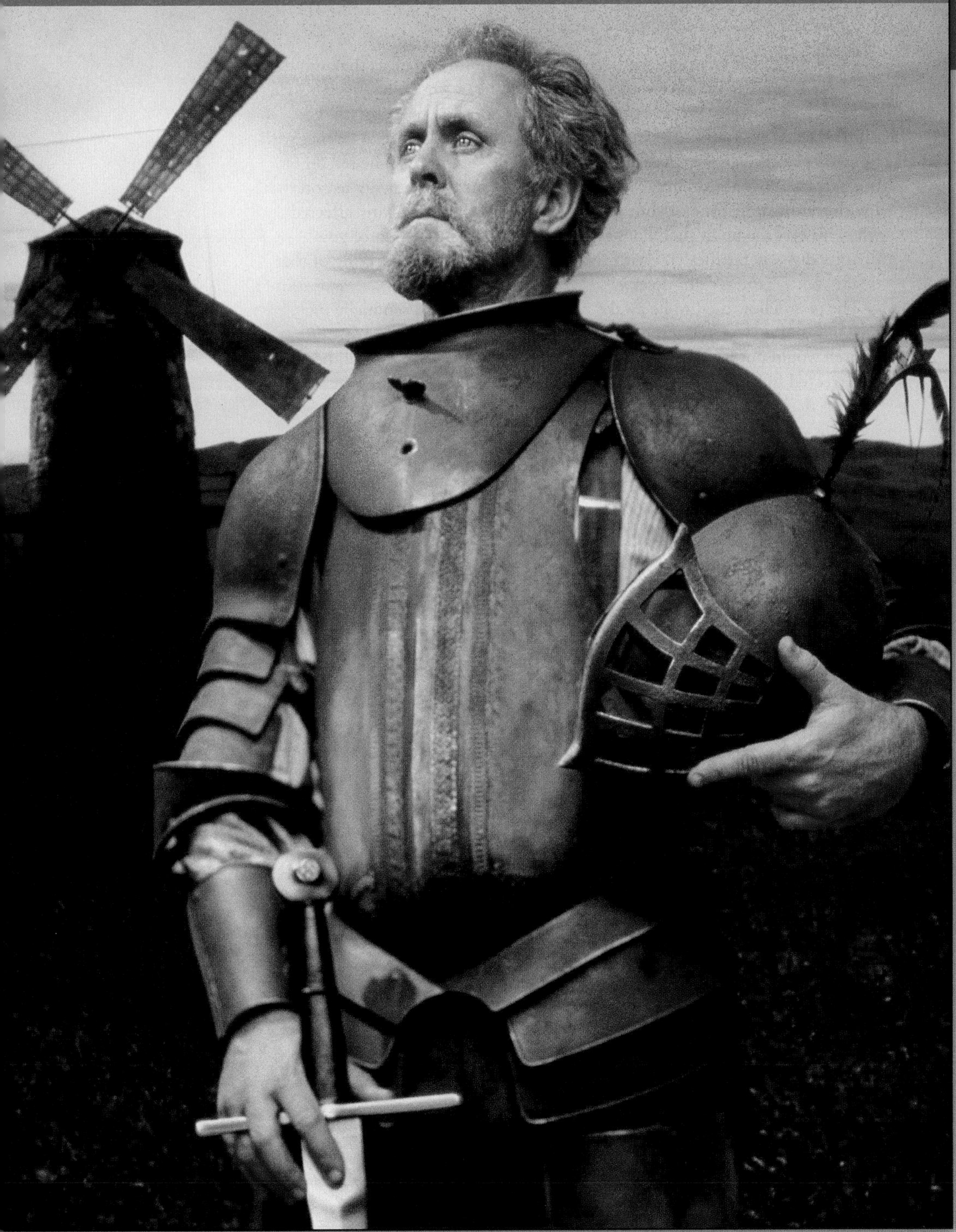

Reading Support

THINK central

This selection on **thinkcentral.com** includes embedded **ThinkAloud** models–students "thinking aloud" about the story to model the kinds of questions a good reader would ask about a selection.

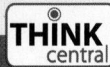

BACKGROUND

An Unconventional Hero *Don Quixote* was published in two parts, the first in 1605, and the second in 1615, a year before Cervantes's death. Early readers focused on the novel's comedic elements (the novel's parody of chivalric material was itself parodied, when a fake "sequel" was published in 1614). Contemporary readers have noted that, with its examination of the psychological development of its characters, *Don Quixote* is one of the first examples of a modern novel.

Cultural Connection The 400th anniversary of the publication of *Don Quixote* was celebrated around the world in 2005. One million free copies of the novel were distributed in Venezuela, BBC Radio produced a 10-part adaptation, and Peru published a translation in Quechua, an indigenous language spoken in the Andean region of South America.

Analyze Visuals

Possible answer: *To evoke the heroic image of the ideal knight, the photograph shows Don Quixote (Quejana) staring resolutely into the distance, as if looking ahead to his destiny. Although his armor and sword are rusty, he bears them with dignity.*

- How much reading time does Quejana have? (lines 20–24)
- How does he feel about books on chivalry? (lines 21–26)
- What activities does he ignore so that he can spend more time reading? (lines 23–24)
- What does he sell so that he can buy more books? (lines 24–25)
- Given these details, what words would describe Quejana's interest in chivalry? (lines 20–26)

FOR ADVANCED LEARNERS/PRE-AP

Analyze Engage students in a discussion about parody. Point out that parody can be used to bring attention to issues or subjects that might otherwise be too difficult, or taboo, to approach. Ask students to give examples of parodies they have seen or read. Then have them discuss how effective the paradoy was in presenting its subject or portraying a character. Have students offer support for their opinions.

B PARODY

Possible answer: The tone of the passage is one of amusement. The narrator seems to view the books of chivalry and Quejana's passion for them as ridiculous.

IF STUDENTS NEED HELP . . . Direct them to specific lines in the passage and ask:

- Why do the quotations from the stories of Feliciano de Silva (lines 31–36) sound humorous? *Possible answer: The quotations are marked by overly repeated words, and they are so formal and complex that they are almost incomprehensible.* How does knowing that Quejana loves this writer's work help you understand the narrator's point? *Possible answer: Knowing that Quejana delights in reading this incomprehensible writer's books helps the reader understand that the narrator doesn't take Quejana too seriously.*

- What humorous exaggerations does Cervantes use in lines 28–29 and 37–40? *Possible answer: Cervantes compares de Silva's words to pearls but also says that even Aristotle, if resurrected, could not understand de Silva's writing.*

- In lines 43–48, what final action helps portray Quejana as ridiculous? *Possible answer: The final ridiculous action is that Quejana loves de Silva's stories so much he wanted to write a sequel to one of them but always got distracted.*

OWN THE WORD

resurrect: Have students complete this sentence: The narrator says that even if Aristotle had been *resurrected* for one purpose, he would not....

Of all those that he thus devoured none pleased him so well as the ones that had been composed by the famous Feliciano de Silva,[5] whose lucid prose style and involved conceits[6] were as precious to him as pearls; especially when he 30 came to read those tales of love and amorous challenges that are to be met with in many places, such a passage as the following, for example: "The reason of the unreason that afflicts my reason, in such a manner weakens my reason that I with reason lament me of your comeliness." And he was similarly affected when his eyes fell upon such lines as these: ". . . the high Heaven of your divinity divinely fortifies you with the stars and renders you deserving of that desert your greatness doth deserve."

The poor fellow used to lie awake nights in an effort to disentangle the meaning and make sense out of passages such as these, although Aristotle[7] himself would not have been able to understand them, even if he had been 40 **resurrected** for that sole purpose. He was not at ease in his mind over those wounds that Don Belianís[8] gave and received; for no matter how great the surgeons who treated him, the poor fellow must have been left with his face and his entire body covered with marks and scars. Nevertheless, he was grateful to the author for closing the book with the promise of an interminable adventure to come; many a time he was tempted to take up his pen and literally finish the tale as had been promised, and he undoubtedly would have done so, and would have succeeded at it very well, if his thoughts had not been constantly occupied with other things of greater moment. **B**

He often talked it over with the village curate,[9] who was a learned man, a 50 graduate of Sigüenza,[10] and they would hold long discussions as to who had been the better knight, Palmerin of England or Amadis of Gaul; but Master Nicholas, the barber of the same village, was in the habit of saying that no one could come up to the Knight of Phoebus,[11] and that if anyone could compare with him it was Don Galaor, brother of Amadis of Gaul, for Galaor was ready for anything—he was none of your finical[12] knights, who went around whimpering as his brother did, and in point of valor he did not lag behind him.

In short, our gentleman became so immersed in his reading that he spent whole nights from sundown to sunup and his days from dawn to dusk in poring over his books, until, finally, from so little sleeping and so much 60 reading, his brain dried up and he went completely out of his mind. He had

resurrect (rĕz′ə-rĕkt′) *v.* to bring back to life

B PARODY
Describe the **tone** of lines 27–48. How does the narrator seem to view books of chivalry and Quejana's passion for them?

---

5. **Feliciano de Silva:** a Spanish author of fictional books about knights.

6. **conceits:** lengthy, exaggerated comparisons.

7. **Aristotle:** a Greek philosopher (384–322 B.C.) widely known for his wisdom.

8. **Don Belianís** (dôn bĕ-lyä-nēs′): the hero of a chivalric romance.

9. **curate** (kyŏŏr′ĭt): a religious official in charge of a parish.

10. **Sigüenza** (sē-gwĕn′sä): a "minor" university of Spain, whose graduates were often mocked.

11. **Palmerin of England . . . Amadis** (ä′mə-dĭs) **of Gaul . . . Knight of Phoebus** (fē′bəs): romance heroes who exemplified knightly perfection.

12. **finical** (fĭn′ĭ-kəl): finicky; picky.

1148 UNIT 10: GREEK TRAGEDY AND MEDIEVAL ROMANCE

DIFFERENTIATED INSTRUCTION

FOR STRUGGLING READERS

Paraphrase a Passage Point out to students that the quotations in lines 31–36 are not from a real book. Read the quotations aloud, and then help students to paraphrase them to read something like "I am confused by your beauty" and "You will be rewarded for your greatness." Make sure students understand that the reason for the extra words and unnecessary repetition is to create humor—specifically, to show what the narrator sees as the ridiculousness of chivalric literature.

FOR ADVANCED LEARNERS/PRE–AP

Write a Dialogue [small-group option] In lines 49–56, Cervantes notes that the curate, the barber, and Quejana share an interest in the chivalric heroes of literature. Challenge students to write a dialogue in which the three characters debate the merits of the literary heroes mentioned on pages 1148–1149. Invite students to perform their dialogue for the class and to share insights they gained during the activity.

filled his imagination with everything that he had read, with enchantments, knightly encounters, battles, challenges, wounds, with tales of love and its torments, and all sorts of impossible things, and as a result had come to believe that all these **fictitious** happenings were true; they were more real to him than anything else in the world. He would remark that the Cid Ruy Díaz[13] had been a very good knight, but there was no comparison between him and the Knight of the Flaming Sword,[14] who with a single backward stroke had cut in half two fierce and monstrous giants. He preferred Bernardo del Carpio,[15] who at Roncesvalles had slain Roland despite the charm the latter bore, availing 70 himself of the stratagem which Hercules employed when he strangled Antaeus, the son of Earth, in his arms.

fictitious (fĭk-tĭsh′əs) *adj.* fabricated; created by the imagination

He had much good to say for Morgante[16] who, though he belonged to the haughty, overbearing race of giants, was of an **affable** disposition and well brought up. But, above all, he cherished an admiration for Rinaldo of Montalbán,[17] especially as he beheld him sallying forth from his castle to rob all those that crossed his path, or when he thought of him overseas stealing the image of Mohammed which, so the story has it, was all of gold. And he would have liked very well to have had his fill of kicking that traitor Galalón,[18] a privilege for which he would have given his housekeeper with his niece 80 thrown into the bargain.

affable (ăf′ə-bəl) *adj.* warm and friendly

At last, when his wits were gone beyond repair, he came to conceive the strangest idea that ever occurred to any madman in this world. It now appeared to him fitting and necessary, in order to win a greater amount of honor for himself and serve his country at the same time, to become a knight-errant[19] and roam the world on horseback, in a suit of armor; he would go in quest of adventures, by way of putting into practice all that he had read in his books; he would right every manner of wrong, placing himself in situations of the greatest peril such as would redound[20] to the eternal glory of his name. As a reward for his valor and the might of his arm, the poor fellow could already 90 see himself crowned Emperor of Trebizond[21] at the very least; and so, carried away by the strange pleasure that he found in such thoughts as these, he at once set about putting his plan into effect.

② Targeted Passage

---

13. **Cid Ruy Díaz** (sēd′ rwē′ dē′äs): Rodrigo (or Ruy) Díaz de Vivar, known as the Cid, was an actual Spanish military leader and national hero about whom an epic poem was written.

14. **Knight of the Flaming Sword:** Amadis of Greece, a romance hero whose symbol was a red sword.

15. **Bernardo del Carpio** (kär′pyô): a legendary Spanish hero who, in some tales, killed the hero of *The Song of Roland* by strangling him in midair, as Hercules had done to the giant Antaeus.

16. **Morgante** (môr-gän′tĕ): a ferocious giant, in an Italian romantic poem, who later became sweet and loving.

17. **Rinaldo of Montalbán** (môn-täl-bän′): the hero in a series of French epic poems.

18. **Galalón** (gä-lä-lôn′): Ganelon, the stepfather and betrayer of Roland, the French epic hero.

19. **knight-errant:** a knight who wanders the countryside in search of adventure to prove his chivalry.

20. **redound:** contribute.

21. **Trebizond:** a former Greek empire, often mentioned in stories of knighthood.

TIERED DISCUSSION PROMPTS

Direct students to lines 81–92. Use these prompts to help students explore Quejana's decision to become a knight-errant:

Connect Think of a time when something that you read made you decide to take action. What do your and Quejana's decisions suggest about the power of writing? *Possible answer: Such decisions suggest that writing has the power to effect change, including changing the direction of one's life.*

Analyze To what emotions is Quejana responding when he decides to become a knight-errant? *Possible answer: Quejana is showing admiration for his fictional heroes and a desire to be like them. In what sense could Quejana's goals be seen as prideful? Possible answer: Quejana wants to right wrongs, but he also wants to earn eternal glory and to be crowned Emperor of Trebizond. Since some of his goals are self-glorifying, Quejana's idealism seems to be tainted by pride.*

Evaluate Do you think that Quejana's decision to become a knight-errant is reasonable, or is he a madman, as the narrator suggests? Explain. *Possible answer: Quejana's decision is not reasonable, for he is relatively old and poor. His quest to "right every manner of wrong" (line 87) is too lofty to achieve, as well. However, his decision is probably motivated by idealism rather than by madness.*

VOCABULARY

COMMON CORE
L 4

OWN THE WORD

- **fictitious:** Point out that *fictitious* is an adjective. In line 64, it modifies the noun *happenings*. Have students give examples of other nouns that could be described as *fictitious*. *Possible answers: name, person, character, story*

- **affable:** Review the definition of *affable* with students. Then have students describe character traits of someone who is *affable*. *Possible answers: friendly, easy to talk with, inviting*

FOR STRUGGLING READERS

② Targeted Passage [Lines 81–92]

This passage reveals Quejana's decision to become a knight-errant and his goals for his journey.

- What inspires Quejana to make his decision to become a knight-errant? (lines 74–84)

- What kind of life can Quejana expect as a knight-errant? (lines 85–90)

- What rewards does Quejana hope to achieve as a knight-errant? (lines 88–90)

Concept Support As students read about Quejana's decision, point out that the goals identified in lines 82–88 are exactly the kinds of goals that one might find in a chivalric romance. Explain that the parody lies in the fact that, according to the narrator, Quejana becomes a knight-errant because he has been inspired by literature of questionable quality and because he has gone insane.

Why do we admire
DREAMERS?

Discuss In lines 93–107, as Quejana begins to prepare for the life of a knight-errant, what qualities in him reflect the nobility of his dream? Explain. *Possible answer: In his first steps of polishing some old family armor and remodeling a helmet, Quejana shows himself to be careful and deliberate. He is thoughtful about the image that he wants to create as a knight-errant and righter of wrongs, so he spends time on small details that will help make his noble dream a reality.*

The first thing he did was to **burnish** up some old pieces of armor, left him by his great-grandfather, which for ages had lain in a corner, moldering and forgotten. He polished and adjusted them as best he could, and then he noticed that one very important thing was lacking: there was no closed helmet, but only a morion, or visorless headpiece, with turned up brim of the kind foot soldiers wore. His ingenuity, however, enabled him to remedy this, and he proceeded to fashion out of cardboard a kind of half-helmet, which, when
100 attached to the morion, gave the appearance of a whole one. True, when he went to see if it was strong enough to withstand a good slashing blow, he was somewhat disappointed; for when he drew his sword and gave it a couple of thrusts, he succeeded only in undoing a whole week's labor. The ease with which he had hewed it to bits disturbed him no little, and he decided to make it over. This time he placed a few strips of iron on the inside, and then, convinced that it was strong enough, refrained from putting it to any further test; instead, he adopted it then and there as the finest helmet ever made.

After this, he went out to have a look at his nag; and although the animal had more *cuartos,* or cracks, in its hoof than there are quarters in a real,[22]
110 and more blemishes than Gonela's steed[23] which *tantum pellis et ossa fuit,*[24] it nonetheless looked to its master like a far better horse than Alexander's Bucephalus or the Babieca of the Cid.[25] He spent all of four days in trying to think up a name for his mount; for—so he told himself—seeing that it belonged to so famous and worthy a knight, there was no reason why it should not have a name of equal renown. The kind of name he wanted was one that would at once indicate what the nag had been before it came to belong to a knight-errant and what its present status was; for it stood to reason that, when the master's worldly condition changed, his horse also ought to have a famous, high-sounding appellation, one suited to the new order of things and the new
120 profession that it was to follow.

After he in his memory and imagination had made up, struck out, and discarded many names, now adding to and now subtracting from the list, he finally hit upon "Rocinante," a name that impressed him as being sonorous and at the same time indicative of what the steed had been when it was but a hack, whereas now it was nothing other than the first and foremost of all the hacks[26] in the world. **⊙**

Having found a name for his horse that pleased his fancy, he then desired to do as much for himself, and this required another week, and by the end of that period he had made up his mind that he was henceforth to be known as

burnish (bûr′nĭsh) *v.* to polish

PARODY
What does the horse's name imply about the hero's lofty goals?

---

22. **quarters in a real** (rā-äl′): A real was a coin worth about five cents.
23. **Gonela's steed:** the horse of the Italian court comedian Pietro Gonela, which was famous for having gas.
24. *tantum pellis et ossa fuit Latin:* was only skin and bones.
25. **Alexander's Bucephalus** (byōō-sĕf′ə-ləs) **or the Babieca** (bä-byĕ′kä) **of the Cid:** famous horses. Alexander is Alexander the Great, the early conqueror of Asia.
26. **Rocinante** (rô-sĕ-nän′tĕ) **. . . foremost of all the hacks:** *Rocin* means "nag" or "hack" in Spanish; *ante* means "before" or "first." So the name Rocinante indicates that the horse is the first, or chief, nag.

1150 UNIT 10: GREEK TRAGEDY AND MEDIEVAL ROMANCE

---

130 Don Quixote,[27] which, as has been stated, has led the authors of this veracious history to assume that his real name must undoubtedly have been Quijada, and not Quesada as others would have it. But remembering that the valiant Amadis was not content to call himself that and nothing more, but added the name of his kingdom and fatherland that he might make it famous also, and thus came to take the name Amadis of Gaul, so our good knight chose to add his place of origin

140 and become "Don Quixote de la Mancha"; for by this means, as he saw it, he was making very plain his lineage and was conferring honor upon his country by taking its name as his own.

And so, having polished up his armor and made the morion over into a closed helmet, and having given himself and his horse a name, he naturally found but one thing lacking still: he must seek out a lady of whom he could become enamored; for a knight-errant without a ladylove was like a tree

150 without leaves or fruit, a body without a soul.

"If," he said to himself, "as a punishment for my sins or by a stroke of fortune I should come upon some giant hereabouts, a thing that very commonly happens to knights-errant, and if I should slay him in a hand-to-hand encounter or perhaps cut him in two, or, finally, if I should vanquish and subdue him, would it not be well to have someone to whom I may send him as a present, in order that he, if he is living, may come in, fall upon his knees in front of my sweet lady, and say in a humble and submissive tone of voice, 'I, lady, am the giant Caraculiambro,[28] lord of the island Malindrania, who has been overcome in

160 single combat by that knight who never can be praised enough, Don Quixote de la Mancha, the same who sent me to present myself before your Grace that your Highness may dispose of me as you see fit'?" **D**

Oh, how our good knight reveled in this speech, and more than ever when he came to think of the name that he should give his lady! As the story goes, there was a very good-looking farm girl who lived near by, with whom he had once been smitten, although it is generally believed that she never knew or suspected it. Her name was Aldonza Lorenzo, and it seemed to him that she was the one upon whom he should bestow the title of mistress of his thoughts. For her he wished a name that should not be **incongruous** with his

170 own and that would convey the suggestion of a princess or a great lady; and,

John Lithgow and Vanessa Williams in the TNT production of *Don Quixote*

D PARODY
Reread lines 127–162, and note Cervantes's imitation of the style of medieval romance. What romance conventions does Cervantes mock here?

incongruous
(ĭn-kŏng'grōō-əs) *adj.* unsuitable; incompatible

27. **Quixote** (kē-hō'tĕ): The word literally denotes a piece of armor that protects the thigh.
28. **Caraculiambro** (kä-rä-kōō-lyäm'brô).

Analyze Visuals

Activity Ask students to locate story details on this page that explain the photograph. *Possible answer: The photograph shows Don Quixote and his "ladylove" (lines 147–150)—his idealization of the farm girl Aldonza Lorenzo, whom he envisions as "a princess or a great lady" (line 170).*

TEXT ANALYSIS COMMON CORE RL 5

D PARODY

Possible answer: *Cervantes mocks the romance conventions of grand names for knights, their devotion to a "ladylove," their battles with larger-than-life opponents, and the practice of sending defeated opponents as a gift to a ladylove. Using the elevated language style of romances to describe these elements adds to the mocking tone.*

IF STUDENTS NEED HELP . . . Ask them to reread the lines, making note of details in the thoughts and plans of Quejana/Don Quixote that remind them of other heroic stories that they know.

VOCABULARY COMMON CORE L 4

OWN THE WORD

incongruous: Review the definition of *incongruous* with students, and remind them that the prefix *in-* means "not."

FOR STRUGGLING READERS

Explore Character Have pairs or small groups of students use a Character Traits and Textual Evidence chart to note Don Quixote's character traits. At the end of the selection, discuss the character traits and invite opinions about why such an unlikely hero as Don Quixote continues to be cherished by readers today.

BEST PRACTICES TOOLKIT—Transparency
Character Traits and Textual Evidence p. D6

FOR ADVANCED LEARNERS/PRE–AP

Analyze Names Have students write and share a brief essay that considers these questions about the importance of names:

- In what ways might a person's name influence his or her personality?
- Why do you think that Quejana took such care in choosing names for himself, his horse, and his "ladylove"?

TIERED DISCUSSION PROMPTS

Direct students to lines 174–192. Use these prompts to help students consider the wisdom of destroying Don Quixote's books:

Recall Why do Don Quixote's family and friends burn his books? *Possible answer: His family and friends act because they believe that the books have inspired Don Quixote to perform harmful actions and because they want to spare him from further folly.*

Analyze What does Cervantes mean by saying that "the innocent must sometimes pay for the sins of the guilty" (line 178)? *Possible answer: Cervantes uses "the innocent" to refer to the people who would like to read the burned books and "the guilty" to refer to Don Quixote. He means that readers are punished by not having the chance to read the books that had to be burned to save Don Quixote.*

Synthesize Reread lines 24–26. How would destroying the books probably affect the value of Don Quixote's estate? Explain. *Possible answer: Since the books were extremely valuable and were purchased after selling parcels of land, destroying them probably would mean a significant loss of value to Don Quixote's estate.*

accordingly, he resolved to call her "Dulcinea del Toboso,"[29] she being a native of that place. A musical name to his ears, out of the ordinary and significant, like the others he had chosen for himself and his appurtenances.[30]

After completing his preparations, Don Quixote sets off on his first adventure, which lasts three days. He persuades an innkeeper to dub him a knight. Then he "rescues" a servant boy from his master's beating, but as soon as "our knight" leaves, the master beats the boy even harder. Next, Don Quixote mistakes a traveling group of merchants for hostile knights. After insulting the merchants for failing to swear to the beauty of Dulcinea del Toboso, he is badly beaten. A neighbor finds him on the road and carries him home, to the great relief of his family and friends. They blame Don Quixote's mad behavior on his reading habits, so for his own good they decide to burn his books.

⟡ from Part 1, Chapter 7 ⟡

. . . That night the housekeeper burned all the books there were in the stable yard and in all the house; and there must have been some that went up in smoke which should have been preserved in everlasting archives, if the one who did the scrutinizing had not been so indolent. Thus we see the truth of the old saying, to the effect that the innocent must sometimes pay for the sins of the guilty.

One of the things that the curate and the barber advised as a remedy for 180 their friend's sickness was to wall up the room where the books had been, so that, when he arose, he would not find them missing—it might be that the cause being removed, the effect would cease—and they could tell him that a magician had made away with them, room and all. This they proceeded to do as quickly as possible. Two days later, when Don Quixote rose from his bed, the first thing he did was to go have a look at his library, and, not finding it where he had left it, he went from one part of the house to another searching for it. Going up to where the door had been, he ran his hands over the wall and rolled his eyes in every direction without saying a word; but after some little while he asked the housekeeper where his study was with all his books.

190 She had been well instructed in what to answer him. "Whatever study is your Grace talking about?" she said. "There is no study, and no books, in this house; the devil took them all away."

"No," said the niece, "it was not the devil but an enchanter who came upon a cloud one night, the day after your Grace left here; dismounting from a serpent that he rode, he entered your study, and I don't know what all he did there, but after a bit he went flying off through the roof, leaving the house full of smoke;

---

29. **Dulcinea del Toboso** (dōōl-sē-nĕ'ä dĕl tô-bô'sô): The name comes from *dulce*, the Spanish word for sweet.

30. **appurtenances:** appendages; accessories.

1152 UNIT 10: GREEK TRAGEDY AND MEDIEVAL ROMANCE

DIFFERENTIATED INSTRUCTION

FOR ENGLISH LANGUAGE LEARNERS

Vocabulary: Idioms Have pairs of students determine meaning from context and/or from a dictionary for these idioms:

- *went up in smoke* (line 175), "were destroyed by fire"
- *wall up the room* (line 180), "seal the entrance with a wall"
- *made away with* (line 183), "stolen"
- *have a look at* (line 185), "inspect"

- *ran his hands over* (line 187), "explored by touching"
- *rolled his eyes* (line 188), "looked"
- *I can't say as to that* (line 204), "I don't have an answer for that"
- *in the course of time* (line 208), "eventually"

and when we went to see what he had done, there was no study and not a book in sight. There is one thing, though, that the housekeeper and I remember very well: at the time that wicked old fellow left, he cried out in a loud voice that it
200 was all on account of a secret **enmity** that he bore the owner of those books and that study, and that was why he had done the mischief in this house which we would discover. He also said that he was called Muñatón the Magician."

"Frestón, he should have said," remarked Don Quixote.

"I can't say as to that," replied the housekeeper, "whether he was called Frestón or Fritón;[31] all I know is that his name ended in a *tón*."

"So it does," said Don Quixote. "He is a wise enchanter, a great enemy of mine, who has a grudge against me because he knows by his arts and learning that in the course of time I am to fight in single combat with a knight whom he favors, and that I am to be the victor and he can do nothing to prevent
210 it. For this reason he seeks to cause me all the trouble that he can, but I am warning him that it will be hard to gainsay or shun that which Heaven has ordained." . . . **E**

In the meanwhile Don Quixote was bringing his powers of persuasion to bear upon a farmer who lived near by, a good man—if this title may be applied to one who is poor—but with very few wits in his head. The short of it is, by pleas and promises, he got the **hapless** rustic to agree to ride forth with him and serve him as his squire. Among other things, Don Quixote told him that

---

31. **Frestón** (frĕs-tôn′) **or Fritón** (frē-tôn′): Frestón, a magician, was thought to be the author of *History of Belianis of Greece.*

enmity (ĕn′mĭ-tē) *n.* hostility and ill will

E PARODY
Would Don Quixote's response in lines 206–212 make sense in the context of a traditional romance? Explain.

hapless (hăp′lĭs) *adj.* pitiful; unfortunate

Bob Hoskins and John Lithgow in the TNT production of *Don Quixote*

DON QUIXOTE **1153**

Use these prompts to help students examine the relationship between Don Quixote and Sancho Panza in lines 213–222:

Restate What argument persuades Sancho Panza to serve as Don Quixote's squire?
Possible answer: Sancho Panza is persuaded by the argument that their adventures might win them an island, of which he would become the governor.

Analyze What advantages does this relationship offer to Sancho Panza? To Don Quixote? *Possible answer: The relationship offers Sancho Panza the adventure of riding with a knight and the possibility of power and wealth. It offers Don Quixote the comfort of a companion and a partner to help him recover when he gets into trouble.*

Synthesize What themes can Cervantes explore by establishing this relationship?
Possible answer: Cervantes can explore themes relating to the responsibility of caring for others, the value of friendship, and the lure of possible adventure.

he ought to be more than willing to go, because no telling what adventure might occur which would win them an island, and then he (the farmer) would
220 be left to be the governor of it. As a result of these and other similar assurances, Sancho Panza forsook his wife and children and consented to take upon himself the duties of squire to his neighbor.

Next, Don Quixote set out to raise some money, and by selling this thing and pawning that and getting the worst of the bargain always, he finally scraped together a reasonable amount. He also asked a friend of his for the loan of a buckler and patched up his broken helmet as well as he could. He advised his squire, Sancho, of the day and hour when they were to take the road and told him to see to laying in a supply of those things that were most necessary, and, above all, not to forget the saddlebags. Sancho replied that he
230 would see to all this and added that he was also thinking of taking along with him a very good ass that he had, as he was not much used to going on foot.

With regard to the ass, Don Quixote had to do a little thinking, trying to recall if any knight-errant had ever had a squire thus asininely[32] mounted. He could not think of any, but nevertheless he decided to take Sancho with the intention of providing him with a nobler steed as soon as occasion offered; he had but to appropriate the horse of the first discourteous knight he met. Having furnished himself with shirts and all the other things that the innkeeper had recommended, he and Panza rode forth one night unseen by anyone and without taking leave of wife and children, housekeeper or niece.
240 They went so far that by the time morning came they were safe from discovery had a hunt been started for them. . . .

~ from Part 1, Chapter 8 ~

At this point they caught sight of thirty or forty windmills which were standing on the plain there, and no sooner had Don Quixote laid eyes upon them than he turned to his squire and said, "Fortune is guiding our affairs better than we could have wished; for you see there before you, friend Sancho Panza, some thirty or more lawless giants with whom I mean to do battle. I shall deprive them of their lives, and with the spoils from this encounter we shall begin to enrich ourselves; for this is righteous warfare, and it is a great service to God to remove so accursed a breed from the face of the earth."
250 "What giants?" said Sancho Panza.

"Those that you see there," replied his master, "those with the long arms some of which are as much as two leagues in length."

"But look, your Grace, those are not giants but windmills, and what appear to be arms are their wings which, when whirled in the breeze, cause the millstone to go."

③ Targeted Passage

---

32. **asininely:** foolishly; ridiculously (derived from Latin *asinus*, "ass"). The statement is both a literal description and a sly joke about Sancho's unheroic appearance.

COMMON CORE RL 4

Language Coach

Multiple Meanings The word *appropriate* can be either an adjective meaning "fitting" or a verb meaning "to take for one's own." As an adjective, it is pronounced /ə-prō′ prē-ĭt′/, as a verb, /ə-prō′prē-āt′/. Which version is used in line 236?

DIFFERENTIATED INSTRUCTION

FOR STRUGGLING READERS

③ Targeted Passage [Lines 242–255]

This passage introduces the famous scene in which Don Quixote does battle with a windmill.

- How does Don Quixote misidentify the windmills? (lines 244–246)

- What does Sancho Panza say to correct him? Does Don Quixote listen to him? (lines 250, 253–255)

- Why does Don Quixote want to attack the windmills? (lines 246–249)

FOR ENGLISH LANGUAGE LEARNERS

Language Coach COMMON CORE RL 4

Multiple Meanings *Answer: the verb, meaning "to take for one's own, pronounced* /ə-prō′prē-āt′/. Have students work in pairs to write brief dialogues using both forms of *appropriate*. Then have students practice reading their dialogues aloud to each other. Monitor students for correct pronunciations.

"It is plain to be seen," said Don Quixote, "that you have had little experience in this matter of adventures. If you are afraid, go off to one side and say your prayers while I am engaging them in fierce, unequal combat."

260 Saying this, he gave spurs to his steed Rocinante, without paying any heed to Sancho's warning that these were truly windmills and not giants that he was riding forth to attack. Nor even when he was close upon them did he perceive what they really were, but shouted at the top of his lungs, "Do not seek to flee, cowards and vile creatures that you are, for it is but a single knight with whom you have to deal!"

At that moment a little wind came up and the big wings began turning.

"Though you flourish as many arms as did the giant Briareus,"[33] said Don Quixote when he perceived this, "you still shall have to answer to me."

He thereupon commended himself with all his heart to his lady Dulcinea, beseeching her to succor him in this peril; and, being well covered with his 270 shield and with his lance at rest, he bore down upon them at a full gallop and fell upon the first mill that stood in his way, giving a thrust at the wing, which was whirling at such a speed that his lance was broken into bits and both horse and horseman went rolling over the plain, very much battered indeed. Sancho upon his donkey came hurrying to his master's assistance as fast as he could, but when he reached the spot, the knight was unable to move, so great was the shock with which he and Rocinante had hit the ground.

④ Targeted Passage

"God help us!" exclaimed Sancho, "did I not tell your Grace to look well, that those were nothing but windmills, a fact which no one could fail to see unless he had other mills of the same sort in his head?"

280 "Be quiet, friend Sancho," said Don Quixote. "Such are the fortunes of war, which more than any other are subject to constant change. What is more, when I come to think of it, I am sure that this must be the work of that magician Frestón, the one who robbed me of my study and my books, and who has thus changed the giants into windmills in order to deprive me of the glory of overcoming them, so great is the enmity that he bears me; but in the end his evil arts shall not prevail against this trusty sword of mine." **F**

"May God's will be done," was Sancho Panza's response. And with the aid of his squire the knight was once more mounted on Rocinante, who stood there with one shoulder half out of joint. And so, speaking of the adventure 290 that had just befallen them, they continued along the Puerto Lápice[34] highway; for there, Don Quixote said, they could not fail to find many and varied adventures, this being a much traveled thoroughfare. . . .

Translated by Samuel Putnam

F PARODY
Compare Don Quixote's quest with the heroic journeys of the knights-errant of romance. What point is Cervantes making about using chivalry as a practical guide to life?

33. **Briareus** (brē-ăr′yŏŏs): a mythological giant with 100 arms.
34. **Puerto Lápice** (pwĕr′tô lä′pē-sĕ).

REVISIT THE BIG QUESTION
Why do we admire
DREAMERS?

Discuss In lines 287–292, how does Don Quixote's response to his defeat show that his dream is still alive? *Possible answer: Don Quixote's failure to be discouraged by this setback, his determination to continue, and his overall optimism show that he still intends to fulfill his dream of fighting for justice and personal glory.*

TEXT ANALYSIS   COMMON CORE
                                        RL 5

F PARODY

Possible answer: Unlike the heroic journeys of the knights-errant in fictional romance, Don Quixote's quest ends in defeat. His opponents are not even real; they are mere windmills. Don Quixote makes the proper knightly challenges, but they are of no use in the real world, and they only get him hurt. Cervantes's point seems to be that chivalry is useless—in fact, it even may be harmful—as a guide to life.

FOR STRUGGLING READERS

④ Targeted Passage [Lines 265–276]

This passage presents the battle between Don Quixote and the windmills.

- What does Don Quixote think is happening when the windmill starts turning? (lines 266–267)

- Why does he think of Dulcinea? (lines 268–269)

- Step by step, what happens in the battle between Don Quixote and the windmill? (lines 269–273)

- What does Sancho Panza do when the battle is over? (lines 273–276)

FOR ADVANCED LEARNERS/PRE–AP

Evaluate Literary Importance As students read this excerpt from *Don Quixote*, have them fill out the Core Analysis Frame: Fiction. When they have finished, have them review and reflect upon their notes. Then ask them to meet in small groups to discuss these questions:

- Based on this excerpt, why do you think that Cervantes's novel is called a literary classic?

- What elements in the story or in Cervantes's storytelling style remind you of modern stories that you have read? Give examples.

Invite group representatives to share insights with the class.

BEST PRACTICES TOOLKIT—Transparency
Core Analysis Frame: Fiction pp. D21, D22

Prereading for this play is found on page 1144.

Analyze Visuals

Possible answer: The details that establish the subject as a comic character are his old rusty armor; his wooden horse; and his look of otherworldly intensity, which stands in marked contrast to his armor and horse.

BACKGROUND

Wasserman's Interpretation When *Man of La Mancha* opened in 1965, ticket sales were slow, but the show received rave reviews from critics. As the musical continued, word of its power spread. Ultimately, the play grew into a Broadway success story, with "The Impossible Dream," the highlight of its score, becoming a hit on popular radio. Wasserman interprets the character of Don Quixote not as a doddering fool, but as a great idealist and devoted dreamer.

Man of La Mancha

A Musical Play by Dale Wasserman
Lyrics by Joe Darion, Music by Mitch Leigh

Brian Stokes Mitchell as Don Quixote in a 2002 Broadway production of *Man of La Mancha*

▲ **Analyze Visuals**
What details establish the subject of the photo as a comic character?

DIFFERENTIATED INSTRUCTION

FOR STRUGGLING READERS
Develop Reading Fluency Students may gain a better understanding of this script if they see it performed or listen to part of its score. Find a copy of the 1972 film version of the musical and play this scene for the class. Alternately, find a cast recording of *Man of La Mancha* and play several famous songs from it for the class. To develop reading fluency, have students follow along or read along with the text as they listen.

FOR ADVANCED LEARNERS/PRE–AP
Analyze Drama [paired-activity option] Challenge students to think critically about this selection by asking them to complete the Core Analysis Frame: Drama as they read. Urge students to refer to their notes as they participate in class discussions or write about the play.

 BEST PRACTICES TOOLKIT—Transparency Core Analysis Frame: Drama pp. D21, D42

Basing his work partly on Cervantes's life experiences, Wasserman set his play in a Spanish prison, where Cervantes and his fellow prisoners act out scenes from Don Quixote.

Cervantes. I shall impersonate a man . . . enter into my imagination and see him! His name is Alonso Quijana . . . a country squire, no longer young. Bony and hollow-faced . . . eyes that burn with the fire of inner vision. Being retired, he has much time for books. He studies them from morn to night, and often through the night as well. And all he reads oppresses him . . . fills him with indignation at man's murderous ways toward man. He broods . . . and broods . . . and broods—and finally from so much brooding his brains dry up! He lays down the melancholy burden of sanity and conceives the
10 strangest project ever imagined . . . to become a knight-errant and sally forth into the world to right all wrongs. No longer shall he be plain Alonso Quijana . . . but a dauntless knight known as—Don Quixote de La Mancha!!!

(*The* Prisoners *giggle appreciatively as the transformation of* Cervantes *into* Don Quixote *takes place before their eyes. The* Manservant, *who will become* Sancho Panza, *assists with costume elements, props, and so forth.*)

Don Quixote (*singing, a little tongue-in-cheek; an actor aware that he's performing*).
20 Hear me now, oh thou bleak and unbearable world!
Thou art base and debauched as can be;
And a knight with his banners all bravely unfurled
Now hurls down his gauntlet to thee!

I am I, Don Quixote,
The Lord of La Mancha,
My destiny calls and I go;
And the wild winds of fortune will carry me onward,
Oh whithersoever they blow.

Whithersoever they blow,
30 Onward to glory I go! **G**

Sancho.
I'm Sancho! Yes, I'm Sancho!
I'll follow my master till the end.
I'll tell all the world proudly
I'm his squire! I'm his friend!

G PARODY
Reread lines 1–30. What dramatic techniques does the playwright use to introduce Don Quixote and explain his transformation?

TIERED DISCUSSION PROMPTS
Use these prompts to help students consider the opening monologue in lines 1–13:

Connect How do you feel about Cervantes when he finishes this monologue? *Accept all reasonable responses.*

Analyze How does Cervantes's explanation help you understand what the story is about? *Possible answer: Cervantes's explanation gives the audience an immediate grasp of Don Quixote's origin and motivation.*

Evaluate Do you think that it was a wise idea for the playwright to tell the story through the persona of Cervantes? Why or why not? *Possible answer: Using the persona of Cervantes was a wise idea. Doing so adds a level of interest for audience members who are familiar with Don Quixote's story. In addition, knowing that Don Quixote is only imagined makes it easier for the audience to accept his improbable adventures.*

TEXT ANALYSIS   COMMON CORE
                                      RL 5
G PARODY

Possible answer: The playwright uses the dramatic technique of a story within a story when he has Cervantes describe Don Quixote in a monologue (another dramatic technique) and then transform himself to play the role. The stage directions explain how the transformation occurs. The song that Cervantes sings reveals Don Quixote's self-perception and goals.

FOR ENGLISH LANGUAGE LEARNERS
Vocabulary Support Write these challenging terms on the board and have students find definitions. Urge students to substitute the definition for the term as they read the excerpt from the play.

- *melancholy* (line 9), "gloomy"
- *sally forth* (line 11), "to begin a journey"
- *tongue-in-cheek* (line 18), "jokingly"
- *debauched* (line 21), "morally corrupt"
- *gauntlet* (line 23), "a knight's glove"

("hurls down a gauntlet" means "issues a challenge")

- *whithersoever* (line 28), "wherever"
- *squire* (line 34), "a knight's attendant"
- *dastardly* (line 36), "evil but cowardly"
- *ogre* (line 87), "monster"
- *dubbed* (line 111), "given a title"
- *drubbing* (line 113), "beating; defeat"
- *amidst the crags* (line 128), "set within a steep mass of rock"

 ARCHETYPAL MOTIFS

Remind students that this is a parody. Explain that although the archetypes are familiar, they are subject to the same comic treatment as everything else. In a parody, everything is fair game for a joke.

Possible answer: The mentions of "destiny" and "wild winds of fortune" in these lines make the ideas look foolish and silly as they come out of the mouth of Don Quixote in song form.

TEXT ANALYSIS

COMMON CORE
RL 5

① PARODY

Possible answer: The dialogue establishes a contrast between Don Quixote, who is lofty and imaginative, and Sancho Panza, who is a practical, down-to-earth person.

IF STUDENTS NEED HELP . . . Ask:

• How does Don Quixote describe what he and Sancho Panza are doing? *Possible answer: Don Quixote describes it as "adventuring"—an activity that will lead them to "amazing sights." How does Sancho Panza describe it? Possible answer: Sancho Panza describes it as traveling on a familiar road to "buy chickens cheap."*

• What do the differing interpretations tell you about the characters? *Possible answer: The difference suggests that Sancho Panza is a realist and that Don Quixote sees only what he wants to see.*

Extend the Discussion How would you describe the language that each character uses? How do the language differences increase the contrast between the characters?

VOCABULARY

COMMON CORE
L 4

OWN THE WORD

cavalcade: Point out that the Latin root for *cavalcade* is *caballicare*, which means "ride on horseback." A *cavalcade* is a procession of people riding on horses. Have students use *cavalcade* in sentences.

Don Quixote.
Hear me, heathens and wizards and serpents of sin!
All your dastardly doings are past;
For a holy endeavor is now to begin,
And virtue shall triumph at last!

40 (*They mount the "horses"—two dancers with wooden frames attached— and ride away. As they ride, the horses dance a spirited flamenco and* Don Quixote *points out to* Sancho *the sights along the way. They sing together.*)

Don Quixote.
I am I, Don Quixote,
The Lord of La Mancha,
My destiny calls and I go;
And the wild winds of
    fortune will carry
    me onward,
Oh whithersoever they
    blow!

Sancho.
I'm Sancho! Yes, I'm
    Sancho!
I'll follow my master till
    the end.
I'll tell all the world
    proudly
I'm his squire!
I'm his friend!

Don Quixote and Sancho.
50   Whithersoever they blow,
    Onward to glory we go! ⓗ

(*At the conclusion of the song, they dismount and* Sancho *leads the "horses" to the well to drink.*)

Don Quixote. Well, Sancho—how dost thou like adventuring?

Sancho. Oh, marvelous, Your Grace. But it's peculiar—to me this great highway to glory looks exactly like the road to El Toboso where you can buy chickens cheap.

Don Quixote. Like beauty, my friend, 'tis all in the eyes of the beholder. Only wait and thou shalt see amazing sights. ①

60 **Sancho.** What kind?

Don Quixote. There will be knights and nations, warlocks, wizards . . . a **cavalcade** of vast, unending armies!

Sancho. They sound dangerous!

Don Quixote. They *are* dangerous. But one there'll be who leads them . . . and he will be most dangerous of all!

Sancho. Well, who is he? Who?

Don Quixote. The Great Enchanter. Beware him, Sancho . . . for his thoughts are cold and his spirit shriveled. He has eyes like little machines, and where he walks the earth is blighted. But one day I
70 shall meet him face to face . . . and on that day—!

(*He shakes his lance ferociously.*)

COMMON CORE RL 5

ⓗ ARCHETYPAL MOTIFS

Many romances include **archetypal motifs**—familiar patterns or themes such as destiny, fate, and fortune, that help move the plot forward. The tale of Don Quixote, though it includes these same concepts, often turns them inside out. Reread lines 42–51. What function do the mentions of "destiny" and "wild winds of fortune" play in these lines?

① PARODY

What contrast between Don Quixote and Sancho does the **dialogue** in lines 54–59 establish?

cavalcade (kăv′əl-kād′) *n.* a procession of people on horseback

---

DIFFERENTIATED INSTRUCTION

FOR ENGLISH LANGUAGE LEARNERS

Vocabulary: Outdated Forms Explain that as he portrays Don Quixote, Cervantes purposely uses outdated language to create a sense of high breeding and formality. Provide these terms and definitions; then have students reread the lines, substituting the definitions.

• *Thou art* (line 21), "You are"

• *thee* (line 23), "you"

• *dost* (line 54), "do"

• *'tis* (line 58), "it is"

• *thou shalt* (line 59), "you will"

• *blighted* (line 69), "made unable to support plant life"

• *Can'st not see* (line 84), "Can't you see"

• *Avast* (line 93), "Stop, halt"

• *Avaunt* (line 93), "Go away"

Sancho (*sensibly*). Well, I wouldn't get upset, Your Grace. As I always say, have patience and shuffle the cards.

Don Quixote. Do you never run out of proverbs?

Sancho. No, Your Grace. I was born with a bellyful of them. I always say—

Don Quixote (*looking off as the projected shadows of a great windmill's sails cross the stage*). Aah-hah!

Sancho. What is it?

80 **Don Quixote.** How long since we sallied forth?

Sancho. About two minutes?

Don Quixote. So soon shall I engage in brave, unequal combat!

Sancho. Combat? Where?

Don Quixote. Can'st not see? (*pointing*) A monstrous giant of infamous repute!

Sancho (*looking vainly; the "horses" are interested, too*). *What* giant?

Don Quixote.
It is that dark and dreaded ogre
By the name of Matagoger!
You can tell him by the four great arms awhirling on his back!

90 **Sancho.** It's a windmill.

Don Quixote (*shouting*).
Ho! Feckless giant standing there!
Avast! Avaunt! On guard! Beware!
(*He charges off.*)

Sancho. No, no, Your Grace, I swear by my wife's little black mustache, that's not a giant, it's only a— (*Offstage a crash; the horses run for cover. To musical accompaniment the combat continues as* Sancho *dances about, dodging first* Quixote's *helmet which comes flying back onstage, then the butt of his lance, splayed and splintered. The final crash;* 100 *and* Quixote *crawls back into view, his sword a corkscrew. A doleful picture, he comes rolling downstage as* Sancho *hurries to plump himself down and stop him.*) Didn't I tell you? Didn't I say, "Your Grace, that's a windmill"? **J**

Don Quixote (*hollowly*). The work of my enemy.

Sancho. The Enchanter?

Don Quixote. He changed that giant into a windmill at the last moment. He will take any advantage in order to— (*a pause; an illumination*) Sancho, it comes to me!

Sancho. What, Your Grace?

COMMON CORE RL 4

Language Coach

Fixed Expressions The verb *sally* is seldom seen without the word *forth*. It is **cognate** with, or similar to, the Spanish *salir*, "to go out." In English, it has the **connotation**, or association, of troops going on the attack. How would you paraphrase line 80?

---

1 **Targeted Passage**

J **PARODY**
Identify three examples of **visual humor** in lines 96–102.

TIERED DISCUSSION PROMPTS

Direct students to lines 80–93. Use these prompts to help students explore the humor of the windmill scene:

Connect How is this scene like other comic movies or performances that you have seen? *Students should identify familiar qualities of slapstick comedy, such as the misguided hero, the clear-seeing servant, the flying equipment, and the physical tumbling.*

Analyze How do Don Quixote and Sancho Panza work together to create the humor in this scene? *Possible answer: Don Quixote takes everything seriously, leaving Sancho Panza to make wry comments and attend to him when he is defeated.*

Synthesize Why do you think that Wasserman chose to depict Don Quixote as such a fool in this scene? *Possible answer: Wasserman may have chosen this depiction to increase the entertainment value of the scene and to endear Don Quixote to the audience.*

TEXT ANALYSIS

COMMON CORE RL 5

J **PARODY**

Possible answer: Examples of visual humor are the horses running for cover (lines 96–97), Sancho Panza's dodge of Quixote's helmet and lance (lines 97–99), the transformation of the sword into a corkscrew (line 100), and Sancho Panza's attempt to stop Don Quixote from rolling (lines 101–102).

FOR STRUGGLING READERS

1 **Targeted Passage** [Lines 95–103]

In this passage, the audience sees the result of the battle with the windmill.

- What does Sancho try to tell Don Quixote about the giant? Why doesn't Don Quixote listen to him? (lines 95–107)

- What happens to Don Quixote in the battle? (lines 96–102)

- How can you tell that Don Quixote has not won the battle against the giant? (lines 96–102)

FOR ENGLISH LANGUAGE LEARNERS

Language Coach

COMMON CORE RL 4

Fixed Expressions *Possible answer: How long since we went out on an attack?* Have students work in pairs to paraphrase the following lines containing the verb *sally*: "He lays down the melancholy burden of sanity and conceives the strangest project ever imagined . . . to become a knight-errant and sally forth into the world to right all wrongs" (lines 9–11 on page 1157). Invite volunteers to share their paraphrases with the class.

Why do we admire
DREAMERS?

Discuss In lines 110–122, how does Don Quixote's desire to be properly knighted relate to his overall dream? *Possible answer: Don Quixote believes that he will not have the power to defeat some of his enemies if he has not been properly knighted (lines 110–111). Since his dream is "to right all wrongs" (line 11), it is understandable that he would want to be properly knighted so that he could gain as much power as possible.*

TEXT ANALYSIS

COMMON CORE

RL 5

Ⓚ PARODY

Possible answer: The cause of the misunderstanding is that Don Quixote does not see things as they really are; his mind transforms everything into an element of a chivalric romance. Sancho Panza does not share Don Quixote's fantasies; he sees an inn where Don Quixote imagines a castle.

SELECTION WRAP–UP

READ WITH A PURPOSE Ask students which portrayal of Don Quixote they found funnier. Why? Have students cite passages that support their opinions. *Possible answer: Answers will vary. Some students may prefer the wit in Cervantes' writing style while others may prefer the silliness expressed by the characters in the musical.*

★ **CRITIQUE** Ask students to tell what element in both the novel and the play they liked the most and to explain why.

INDEPENDENT READING

For students who would like to read another parody, suggest "The Secret Life of Walter Mitty" by James Thurber. The humor in the short story centers on the chaos of contemporary American life.

---

110 **Don Quixote.** How he was able to upset me. It is because I have never properly been dubbed a knight.

Sancho. That's no problem. Just tell me how it's done and I'll be glad to take care of this drubbing.

Don Quixote. Dubbing. Thank you, my friend, but it may only be done by another knight.

Sancho (*dismayed*). *That's* a problem. I've never *seen* another knight.

Don Quixote. The lord of some castle would do. Or a king or a duke.

Sancho (*helping* Quixote *to his feet*). Very well. I'll keep an eye out for any kings or dukes as we go.

120 **Don Quixote** (*looking off*). Ahaaa!

Sancho (*apprehensively*). Now what?

Don Quixote. The very place!

Sancho. Where?

Don Quixote. There!

Sancho. If Your Grace would just give me a hint . . . ?

Don Quixote. There in the distance. A castle!

Sancho (*peering vainly*). Castle.

Don Quixote. Rockbound amidst the crags!

Sancho. Crags.

130 **Don Quixote.** And the banners—ah, the brave banners flaunting in the wind!

Sancho. Anything on 'em?

Don Quixote (*shielding his eyes*). I see a cat crouching on a field tawny . . . and beneath it the inscription "Miau"!

Sancho. Oh, that's fine, Your Grace. Maybe this is where you can get yourself drubbed.

Don Quixote. Dubbed. (*excitedly*) Blow thy bugle that a dwarf may mount the battlements and announce our coming!

Sancho (*under the spell, lifts his bugle then hesitates*). But I don't *see*
140 a castle. I do see something . . . maybe it's an inn. Ⓚ

Don Quixote (*sadly*). An inn.

Sancho. We'd better pass it by, Your Grace. Those roadside places are full of rough men and women.

Don Quixote. Come. We shall ride straight to the drawbridge of yon castle, and there thy vision may improve!

(*The lights fade to transition lighting as* Quixote *and* Sancho *drop out of character.*)

Ⓚ PARODY
Reread lines 120–140. What causes the misunderstanding between Sancho Panza and Don Quixote?

❷ Targeted Passage

DIFFERENTIATED INSTRUCTION

FOR STRUGGLING READERS

❷ Targeted Passage [Lines 139–147]

This concluding passage reveals that Don Quixote has not learned his lesson after the fight with the windmill.

- When Don Quixote thinks that he sees a castle, what is he really seeing? (line 141)

- How does Sancho Panza try to talk him out of stopping there? (lines 142–143)

- At the end of this scene, what does Don Quixote intend to do? Why? (lines 144–145)

FOR ADVANCED LEARNERS/PRE–AP

Research Knighthood [paired-activity option] Challenge students to research the process whereby a medieval courtly warrior was dubbed a knight. Have them collect details of the process, including the oath of loyalty that a knight would make to his lord and the duties that such an oath would entail. As students share their findings, discuss how the duties of a "properly dubbed" knight compare with Don Quixote's goals.

Comprehension

1. **Recall** What causes Don Quixote to lose his mind?

2. **Clarify** Why does Don Quixote decide to become a knight-errant?

3. **Clarify** Why does Sancho Panza agree to become Don Quixote's squire?

Text Analysis

4. **Identify Hyperbole** The romances Cervantes parodied often used **hyperbole,** or exaggerated descriptions, to emphasize the perfection of their heroes. Reread the description of Don Quixote's horse in lines 108–126 (page 1150), and give two examples of exaggerated details in this description. What kinds of details does Cervantes choose to exaggerate?

5. **Analyze Character Traits** A **foil** is a character whose traits contrast sharply with those of a main character. List three traits that make Sancho Panza a foil for Don Quixote. How does the contrast between these characters bring out the humor of Don Quixote's behavior?

● 6. **Analyze Parodies** Both Cervantes and Wasserman use **diction,** or unique word choices and speech patterns, to make Don Quixote a vivid character. What is distinctive about Don Quixote's manner of speaking? How does the hero's diction help the authors communicate the point of their **parodies?**

Comparing Across Genres

Now you are ready to compare the ways in which both authors parody chivalric romances. To get started, complete the following Points of Comparison chart. If a point of comparison is not covered in one of the selections, leave the box blank.

Points of Comparison	In the Novel	In the Play
What motivates the main character?		
How do the main character's traits compare with those of a romance hero?		
What absurd events occur in the story?		
What romance conventions are being mocked?		
Which descriptions, dialogue, or visual images were particularly funny?		

Why do we admire DREAMERS?

Is it foolish or inspiring to dream about what seems impossible?

COMMON CORE

RL 1 Cite evidence to support analysis of what the text says explicitly as well as inferences drawn from the text. **RL 7** Analyze the representation of a subject or a key scene in two different artistic mediums, including what is emphasized or absent in each treatment. **RL 9** Analyze how an author draws on and transforms source material in a specific work.

Practice and Apply

For preliminary support of post-reading questions, use these copy masters:

R **RESOURCE MANAGER**—Copy Masters

Reading Check p. 91

Comparing Across Genres p. 84

Question Support p. 92

Additional selection questions are provided for teachers on page 77.

ANSWERS

Comprehension

1. *Don Quixote loses his mind by sleeping too little and reading too much.*

2. *Don Quixote becomes a knight-errant to right wrongs and to win honor for himself and his country.*

3. *Sancho Panza agrees to become a squire because Don Quixote offers him the possibility of governing an island.*

Text Analysis

COMMON CORE RL 1, RL 7, RL 9

Possible answers:

4. *Exaggerated details include the number of cracks in the horse's hoof (line 109) and its number of blemishes (line 110). Cervantes exaggerates the horse's physical defects.*

5. *Sancho Panza is a farmer, but Don Quixote is a gentleman; Sancho Panza does not read and does not know literary romance, but Don Quixote makes his life into a romance; Sancho Panza speaks plainly, in contrast to Don Quixote's formality. The contrast between these characters creates humor by showing the difference between what a realist (Sancho Panza) sees and what a dreamer (Don Quixote) imagines.*

6. ● **COMMON CORE FOCUS** *Analyze Parodies Don Quixote uses elevated, archaic, and dramatic diction that sounds like the language of literary romance. His diction shows how much he has been influenced by romances; it adds to the parody by suggesting that literature can cause someone to become disconnected from the real world.*

Comparing Across Genres

Possible answers:

Motivation: Novel desire for glory; Play desire to right wrongs

Character traits: Novel and play Don Quixote resembles a romance hero in his desire for glory,

---

his flowery speech, and his chivalric ideals. He is unlike a romance hero because he is aging, relatively poor, and deluded.

Absurd events: Novel and play a fight against windmills; Play seeing an inn as a castle

Mocked conventions: Novel elevated style, battles, grand names, glorious armor, and devotion to a ladylove; Play stock characters such as enchanters, giants, ogres, and dwarves

Funny elements: Novel the opening description of the hero (lines 1–19), the quotations from romances (lines 31–36), Don Quixote's helmet

(lines 93–107), his imagined presentation of the giant to his ladylove (lines 151–162); Play Don Quixote's song (lines 20–30), his dialogue with Sancho Panza (lines 54–70), and his fight with the windmill (lines 95–103).

Why do we admire DREAMERS? *Possible answer:*

Dreaming impossible dreams inspires people to accomplish great things.

ANSWERS

Vocabulary in Context

▲ VOCABULARY PRACTICE

1. *incongruous*
2. *hapless*
3. *resurrect*
4. *enmity*

5. *fictitious*
6. *cavalcade*
7. *burnish*
8. *affable*

 RESOURCE MANAGER—Copy Master
Vocabulary Practice p. 89

ACADEMIC VOCABULARY IN SPEAKING

Sample response: Don Quixote and Sancho travel to the frozen tundra of northern Russia. Along the coast they encounter *an iceberg that Don Quixote mistakes for a terrible giant. He attacks the iceberg, even though Sancho assures him it is not dangerous. The theme of Don Quixote's illusions and misinterpretations* emerges *and the* underlying *relationships remain the same.*

VOCABULARY STRATEGY: SIMILES AND METAPHORS

 COMMON CORE L5

- Illustrate the instruction with these examples:
  Similes: hair like silk; as strong as Hercules; runs as if being chased by a bear
  Metaphors: the cold was a slap in the face; a rainbow of possibilities

- Stress the importance of *like, as,* and *as if* in distinguishing a simile from a metaphor.

- Explain that parts of a comparison may be separated by other words (as in items 2 and 5).

Possible answers:

1. simile
2. metaphor
3. simile

4. metaphor
5. simile

 RESOURCE MANAGER—Copy Master
Vocabulary Strategy p. 90

Interactive Vocabulary

Keywords direct students to a **WordSharp** tutorial on **thinkcentral.com** or to other types of vocabulary practice and review.

Vocabulary in Context

▲ VOCABULARY PRACTICE

Choose the word that best completes the sentence.

1. Her quirky courtroom outfit looked _____ next to the conservative suits of those around her.
2. This _____ child seems always to have bad luck.
3. That noise was loud enough to _____ the dead!
4. He was distressed and puzzled by the _____ of his rival.
5. Although they seem real, the characters in her story are _____.
6. The _____ of mounted police led the parade.
7. She left orders to _____ the trophies until they gleamed.
8. People easily warm up to your _____ personality.

WORD LIST
affable
burnish
cavalcade
enmity
fictitious
hapless
incongruous
resurrect

ACADEMIC VOCABULARY IN SPEAKING

- drama • emerge • encounter • globe • underlie

How might Don Quixote's adventures have been different on another part of the **globe?** Briefly retell one of his adventures, setting the scene in a very different location. Consider how the central themes will **emerge** in your alternate version. Use at least one Academic Vocabulary word in your response.

VOCABULARY STRATEGY: SIMILES AND METAPHORS

A **simile** is a figure of speech in which *like, as,* or *as if* signals that a comparison is being made. A **metaphor** is a comparison in which one thing is talked about as if it were another. The comparison is implied; there are no signal words to show that it is not literal. Similes and metaphors can provide clues to the meanings of unfamiliar words.

COMMON CORE

L5 Demonstrate understanding of figurative language, word relationships, and nuances in words.

PRACTICE Indicate whether each sentence contains a simile or a metaphor. Ask yourself what two things are being compared. Then ask what the comparison suggests about the meaning of the boldfaced word.

1. He was **hapless** and confused, like a boy who had lost his mother in a store.
2. The **enmity** of his former friend was a dark cloud over his happiness.
3. The comment was as **incongruous** as a pink tutu on a hippo.
4. The story was **fictitious,** a richly embroidered veil for the truth.
5. The **cavalcade** of invaders stretched to the horizon like a deadly carpet.

Interactive Vocabulary

THINK central

Go to **thinkcentral.com.**
KEYWORD: HML10-1162

DIFFERENTIATED INSTRUCTION

FOR ENGLISH LANGUAGE LEARNERS

Vocabulary Support Point out to students that learning one word often will help them learn other words in the same word family. Demonstrate using vocabulary words such as *resurrect (resurrection), affable (affably), fictitious (fiction, fictional), incongruous (incongruity, incongruent),* and *enmity (enemy).* Have students predict the meaning of the words in the word family and look up any words that they do not know.

FOR ADVANCED LEARNERS/PRE–AP

Vocabulary in Writing Have students use at least three vocabulary words as they write a poem about the character of Don Quixote. (For an additional challenge, instruct them to include at least one simile and one metaphor, as well.) Work with students to create a format for sharing their poems.

Writing for Assessment

1. READ THE PROMPT

In writing-assessment tests, you will often be asked to **compare and contrast** two works of literature that treat a similar subject. You are now going to practice writing an essay that requires this type of focus.

> Both Cervantes and Wasserman poke fun at the form of medieval romances and at the chivalric code of behavior. Compare and contrast the writers' parodies of romances. Do they mock the same ideas, customs, and behaviors? In what ways do their parodies differ? Support your points with evidence from the texts.

◀ **STRATEGIES IN ACTION**

1. I need to consider how each writer ridicules the style and content of **chivalric romances**.

2. I need to write an essay that **compares and contrasts** two parodies.

3. I need to support my ideas with **details and quotations** from each work.

2. PLAN YOUR WRITING

- Review the **Points of Comparison** chart you created on page 1161.
- Using your chart, find examples to use as evidence for the points you will develop in your essay. If necessary, review the selections to identify more examples.
- Create an outline to organize your main points.

3. DRAFT YOUR RESPONSE

Introduction Introduce the topic—making fun of chivalric romances—and then explain that you will discuss how the two works accomplish this goal.

Organization Use the topics in your **Points of Comparison** chart as a guide to the key points of your comparison. In one paragraph, for example, you might point out how the authors choose similar targets for their humor. In another, you might focus on the different comic techniques the authors use.

Conclusion Wrap up your essay with a restatement of your main idea and a brief summary of your main points.

Revision Check to make sure that your essay is not repetitive or bland. Add interest to your writing by replacing dull language with vivid and fresh nouns, adjectives, and verbs.

FOR STRUGGLING WRITERS

- Limit the length of the essay to three paragraphs (introduction, one well-developed point of comparison, conclusion).
- Discuss the **Points of Comparison** chart, as necessary, to make sure that students have a grasp of most or all of the points.
- Suggest that students base their essays on two contrasting quotations, one from the play and one from the novel.

- Brainstorm with students for a list of appropriate transitions for comparisons and contrasts, such as *likewise, similarly, on the other hand, unlike,* and *however.*
- As students revise, urge them to review their introduction and conclusion to be sure that they state and restate the premise of the essay accurately and vividly.

Writing for Assessment

1. *READ THE PROMPT*

Review that a compare-and-contrast essay must address both similarities and differences. Point out that the prompt asks students to compare and contrast only the works' treatment of chivalric romances, not other elements of the stories. Suggest that students review the characteristics of medieval romances in the Text Analysis Workshop (pages 1058–1063) before they begin writing.

2. *PLAN YOUR WRITING*

After students have reviewed the Points of Comparison chart on page 1161, start an outline on the board. Encourage students to suggest points, as in this example:

I. Cervantes, *Don Quixote*

   A. Elevated language

   B. Grand names

   C.

II. Wasserman, *Man of La Mancha*

   A. Elevated language

   B. Stock characters

   C.

3. *DRAFT YOUR RESPONSE*

Have students use their outline to organize their essay and to plan the placement of supporting material. Students can recast their outline with complete sentences and appropriate transitions.

Assess and Reteach

Assess

DIAGNOSTIC AND SELECTION TESTS

   Selection Test A pp. 307–308

   Selection Test B/C pp. 309–310

Interactive Selection Test on **thinkcentral.com**

Reteach

Level Up Online Tutorials on **thinkcentral.com**

Reteaching Worksheets on **thinkcentral.com**

   Literature Lesson 37

   Writing Lessons 23, 28

   Vocabulary Lesson 12

Focus and Motivate

COMMON CORE FOCUS

W 2a Introduce a topic; organize complex ideas, concepts, and information to make important connections and distinctions. **W 3a–e** Write narratives to develop real or imagined experiences or events using effective technique, well-chosen details, and well-structured event sequences. **W 4** Produce clear and coherent writing in which the development, organization, and style are appropriate to a task, purpose, and audience. **W 5** Develop and strengthen writing as needed by planning, revising, editing, rewriting, or trying a new approach, focusing on addressing what is most significant for a specific purpose and audience. **W 6** Use technology to produce and publish individual writing products. **W 10** Write routinely over shorter time frames for a range of tasks, purposes, and audiences.

WRITE WITH A PURPOSE

Have students think of difficult choices they have made in their lives, the conflicts they faced, and the consequences of their choices. Remind students that their purpose in writing a video script is not only to entertain but also to express an observation about life.

COMMON CORE TRAITS

Review the *COMMON CORE TRAITS* with students, focusing primarily on development and organization of ideas. Compare the list of traits with the rubric on page 1172.

ADDITIONAL TASKS

Write About a Movie Character Write a reinterpretation of one dramatic scene from a favorite movie in which a character struggles with the consequences of a choice.
Possible subjects: choosing between two loves, revealing a lie

Write From Fine Art Use a work of art to help you craft a story for a video script. Look for ideas in art books or on museum Web sites.
Possible subjects: solitary figures, people standing out from a crowd

---

Writing Online

The following tools are available online at **think*central*.com** and on **Write*Smart* CD-ROM**:
• Interactive Graphic Organizers
• Interactive Student Models
• Interactive Revision Lessons

Writing Workshop
NARRATIVE

Video Script

Essential Course of Study **ECOS**

Although visual images and special effects grab the attention of a TV or movie audience, viewers connect to characters because of what they say and do. The words and actions of actors originate in the written word in the form of a script. In this workshop, you will learn to write a **video script** that tells a story and develops the characters, mood, and theme through dialogue and action.

Complete the workshop activities in your **Reader/Writer Notebook.**

WRITE WITH A PURPOSE

WRITING TASK

Write a **video script** about a character who is struggling with the consequences of a choice. In your script, develop and resolve the conflict the character faces. Make sure your script uses dialogue and well-chosen details that create a vivid picture of the events you want to present in your video.

Idea Starters
• a choice that hurts others, such as joining a clique that excludes certain friends
• a choice that jeopardizes popularity, such as resisting peer pressure
• a choice that affects academic performance, such as participating in a sport or extracurricular activity

THE ESSENTIALS

Here are some common purposes, audiences, and formats for script writing.

PURPOSES	AUDIENCES	FORMATS
• to entertain	• classmates and teacher	• video
• to express a theme or observation about life	• family and community	• performance for classmates
	• drama club members	• Readers' Theater
	• Internet video viewers	

COMMON CORE TRAITS

1. DEVELOPMENT OF IDEAS
• introduces, develops, and resolves a **central conflict**
• introduces and develops distinctive **characters**
• uses techniques such as **dialogue** and **description** to develop the plot and the characters
• provides a **resolution** that follows from and reflects on the events in the story

2. ORGANIZATION OF IDEAS
• presents a smooth **sequence of events** that build on one another to create a coherent story
• uses effective **pacing** to advance the plot
• uses appropriate **formatting** to aid comprehension

3. LANGUAGE FACILITY AND CONVENTIONS
• includes **precise words and phrases, telling details,** and **sensory language** to convey a vivid picture of the events, setting, and characters
• employs correct **grammar, usage,** and **spelling**

 Writing Online  **THINK** central

Go to **think*central*.com**.
KEYWORD: HML10N-1164

Writing Workshop Resources

 RESOURCE MANAGER UNIT 10
Plan and Teach, pp. 93–96
Prewriting–Editing, pp. 97–100
Technology p. 103
Writing Support p. 104*

 BEST PRACTICES TOOLKIT
Writing Template: Dramatic Scene, p. C26

TECHNOLOGY
🔘 **Teacher One Stop DVD-ROM**
🔘 **Student One Stop DVD-ROM**
🔘 **Write*Smart* CD-ROM**
🔘 **GrammarNotes DVD-ROM**

Writing Center on think*central*.com

See resources on the **Teacher One Stop DVD-ROM** *and on* **think*central*.com**.

* Resources for Differentiation

Planning/Prewriting

 COMMON CORE **W 3a–e** Write narratives to develop real or imagined experiences or events using effective technique, well-chosen details, and well-structured event sequences. **W 5** Develop and strengthen writing as needed by planning.

Getting Started

CONSIDER NARRATIVE STRUCTURE

Movies and videos need screenplays for their stories. A screenplay is literature in script form. Like other forms of fiction, a script uses a well-structured sequence of events to tell its story. It engages and orients the audience in the **exposition**, where the **characters, setting,** and **conflict**—or problem—are introduced. In the **rising action**, events build smoothly on one another until they reach a **climax**, the most exciting or important part in the plot. The **falling action** then leads to the **resolution**, where the conflict is solved.

THINK ABOUT AUDIENCE AND PURPOSE

As you begin to think about the story your video script will tell, keep in mind your **purpose**—to convey to your **audience** how an individual deals with the consequences of a choice.

IDENTIFY DRAMATIC ELEMENTS

Now define the **setting, characters, conflict,** and **theme** for your video script. The **theme** is the message about life or human nature that you want to communicate to your **audience.** The theme may be explicit (stated directly by a character) or implicit (suggested by the **resolution** of the conflict).

▶ **WHAT DOES IT LOOK LIKE?**

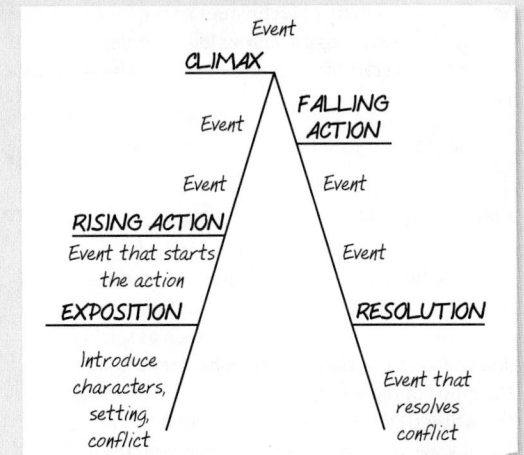

▶ **ASK YOURSELF:**

- Who is my target audience?
- What message do I want to communicate to my audience?
- To what characters and situations might my chosen audience relate?

▶ **WHAT DOES IT LOOK LIKE?**

Dramatic Elements
Setting: Central High School
Characters: Rosa (main character, student), Maddie and Dante (other students), Ms. Eaton (teacher, yearbook adviser)
Conflict: Rosa's grades are suffering because of her work on the yearbook staff.
Resolution: Rosa accepts help from other staff.
Theme: No one can do everything.

WRITING WORKSHOP **1165**

Teach

Planning/ Prewriting

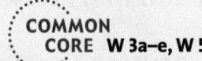 **COMMON CORE** **W 3a–e, W 5**

▶ **CONSIDER NARRATIVE STRUCTURE** Remind students that good stories or dramas have a problem that is solved in the end. Suggest that students use the Narrative Structure diagram on page 1165 to help them plan their video scripts. Have students jot down the ideas for characters, the setting and conflict, events that lead to the climax, and how they would like the conflict to resolve along the points of the diagram.

▶ **THINK ABOUT AUDIENCE AND PURPOSE** Remind students to keep the needs of their audience in mind as they craft their scripts. Suggest that students include characters and situations that audience members will understand or want to learn about.

▶ **IDENTIFY DRAMATIC ELEMENTS** Model for students how to define the dramatic elements in a script. Give students a sample story for a video script (example: cheating in school); then work as a class to define the dramatic elements that will be included in the script. Project the Dramatic Elements chart on the board, and work with students to fill in each element.

R RESOURCE MANAGER—Copy Masters
Planning / Prewriting p. 97
Drafting p. 98
Revising pp. 99–100
Ask a Peer Reader p. 101
Rubric p. 102
Writing Support p. 104

DIFFERENTIATED INSTRUCTION

FOR ENGLISH LANGUAGE LEARNERS
Language: Reinforce Video Script Terms
Write these terms on the board and review them with students:

- *script:* the text of a play, film, or video
- *characters:* the people in a story
- *conflict:* a struggle between opposing forces. An external conflict is a struggle between a character and an outside force. An internal conflict is a struggle between opposing desires or emotions within a person.

- *dialogue:* written conversation between two or more characters
- *stage directions:* instructions that describe the setting and actions for the actors, director, set and lighting designers, and readers

Planning/Prewriting *continued*

▶ **DEVELOP A SEQUENCE OF EVENTS** Remind students that chronological order is time order, or the order in which events occur. Explain that to help an audience follow the sequence of the plot, students need to write clear transitions from one scene or event to the next.

▶ **EMPLOY NARRATIVE TECHNIQUES** Ask students to look at the chart on page 1166. From the details about the setting and character, how would they describe the mood of the narrative? They might suggest that it's stressful, worried, or rushed. Have students use the chart to help them plan and organize details in their own scripts that will convey the mood that best fits their purpose, audience, and theme.

 YOUR TURN Give students time to identify their characters, conflict, and theme. Remind students that as they begin to develop their scripts, they might need to reword or revise elements of their writing plan to make their scripts more effective.

For interactive graphic organizers, see

WriteSmart CD-ROM

Writing Center on thinkcentral.com

Planning/Prewriting *continued*

Getting Started

DEVELOP A SEQUENCE OF EVENTS

You can use a variety of techniques to sequence events. One way is to use **chronological order**. Another is to start in the present and **flash back** to past events.

▶ **ASK YOURSELF:**
- What happens first?
- How will I sequence the events?
- How does each event relate to the conflict?
- Which event marks the climax, or point of greatest suspense?
- How is the conflict resolved?

EMPLOY NARRATIVE TECHNIQUES

Writers of scripts use their own specialized narrative techniques, such as **dialogue** and **stage directions**. Stage directions are **descriptions** of important visual or sensory details such as **settings** and **characters' actions** or emotions. They often set the mood of the script, which is the overall feeling the writer creates for the audience. Jot down notes about ways you can use settings, dialogue, and actions to tell your story.

▶ **WHAT DOES IT LOOK LIKE?**

Subject: Teen dealing with consequences of a choice

Setting: Opening scene busy, crowded school hallway; students hurrying by; Rosa is standing in front of her locker, frantically shuffling through her papers

Dialogue: Rosa talks to herself; Rosa talks to other students in short, quick sentences

Actions: At first Rosa seems rushed and preoccupied; acts panicked and overwhelmed; at end she acts relieved and confident

 **PEER REVIEW** Describe to a peer the purpose and audience of your script and its theme. Then, ask: How do I tell my story using dialogue, descriptions, and characters? Does the sequence of events develop the story effectively? Do I need to try a new approach?

 YOUR TURN In your *Reader/Writer Notebook*, develop your writing plan. Use a chart such as the one at the bottom of page 1165 to identify your characters, conflict, and theme. Consider these tips as you plan your script:

- Use **dialogue** to reveal character traits and to move the plot forward.
- Insert **stage directions** to provide details about visual elements, such as the setting, a character's behavior, or the entrance or exit of characters.
- Consider whether to have a character state the **theme** directly or to suggest it through one or more characters' words and actions.

DIFFERENTIATED INSTRUCTION

FOR ENGLISH LANGUAGE LEARNERS
Vocabulary Support Review these terms:

- *plot:* the sequence of events in a story. A plot focuses on a central conflict or problem faced by the main character.
- *resolution:* how the conflict is worked out. Resolution comes after the climax and falling action of the plot.
- *setting:* the time and place of the action of a drama. Setting is one of the main elements in fiction and often plays an important role in what happens and why.

FOR STRUGGLING WRITERS
Determining Mood Students may have difficulty understanding what mood is. Explain to students that mood is the feeling or atmosphere that a writer creates, and it is intended to shape the audience's emotional response. Mood may be described by a single word, such as *serious, humorous, formal, informal, somber, sarcastic, playful, scary, romantic,* or *thrilling.*

Drafting

COMMON CORE

W 4 Produce clear and coherent writing in which the development, organization, and style are appropriate to a task, purpose, and audience.

The following chart shows a structure for organizing an effective video script.

Organizing Your Video Script

EXPOSITION

- Provide background information about **characters** and **setting** and begin to set the **mood** through **stage directions** (see below).
- Introduce **characters** and **setting** through opening lines of **dialogue** and **stage directions**.
- Explain the **conflict** through **dialogue** and **action**.

▼

RISING ACTION AND CLIMAX

- Continue to develop **characters** and **plot** through **dialogue** and **action**.
- Sequence events so they build on one another, creating a well-paced and smooth progression toward the **climax.**
- Convey the **mood** through **dialogue** and **stage directions.**

▼

FALLING ACTION AND RESOLUTION

- Explain through **dialogue** or **actions** how the **conflict** is resolved.
- Make the **theme** clear, either by having a character directly state the theme or by implying the theme through the **resolution** of the conflict.

GRAMMAR IN CONTEXT: STAGE DIRECTIONS

Writers usually include stage directions at the beginning of a video script to set the scene. **Stage directions** describe the time and place of the scene, as well as characters' actions. Sensory language in the stage directions also often help set the mood. Do you want the story to be serious, funny, scary, romantic?

> *Students hurry down a hall at Central High School to their afternoon classes. Some stop at lockers, others pause in pairs or groups to talk. Rosa is standing at her locker, frantically shuffling through a pile of papers. Rosa looks worried.*

These stage directions tell the director or reader that the time is afternoon, and the place is Central High School. The setting is a school hallway filled with students engaged in various activities, including the main character, Rosa. The details in the stage directions suggest that the mood is bustling.

 YOUR TURN Develop a first draft of your video script following the structure outlined in the *Organizing Your Video Script* chart. Include stage directions at the beginning of your script to set the scene. Provide details that tell time and place and use sensory language to describe characters' actions and suggest the mood.

FOR ENGLISH LANGUAGE LEARNERS

Stage Directions Have students reread the stage directions in the example on page 1167. Ask students: What parts of the stage directions refer to the setting? *("hall at Central High School," "afternoon")* Which stage directions refer to how the set should look *("hall," "lockers")* What stage directions set the mood? (*"Students hurry," "frantically shuffling," "Rosa looks worried.")*

FOR STRUGGLING WRITERS

Organize a Draft Have students use these sentence starters to help them plan their scripts:

- The theme of my script is _____.
- The setting is _____.
- The characters are _____ and _____.
- The main conflict is _____.
- The mood I want to convey is _____.

Practice and Apply

Drafting

COMMON CORE W 4

▶ *EXPOSITION* Tell students to look at the Student Draft on page 1169 for an example of how to effectively set the scene through the exposition. Remind students that their expositions should engage readers' interest and provide information about characters and setting.

▶ *RISING ACTION AND CLIMAX* Remind students to remain true to the development of their characters. Have students think about what each character would do, say, or feel. Have students create dialogue that is realistic, well-paced, reveals who the characters are, and advances the plot to a convincing climax.

▶ *FALLING ACTION AND RESOLUTION* Stress that after reading a video script, the audience should be able to understand what happened in the plot and how the conflict was resolved.

GRAMMAR IN CONTEXT: STAGE DIRECTIONS

For additional practice, have students write brief stage directions for one of the following scenes. Tell students to include the setting (time and place), a description of the setting, and the actions of one or more characters:

- a football game
- the school cafeteria at lunch time
- a classroom before a test

 YOUR TURN Ask students to complete the **Your Turn** activity independently. Remind students to include stage directions in the exposition of their video scripts. Suggest that students write their drafts double-spaced so that they can make revisions more easily later.

For a dramatic scene writing template, see

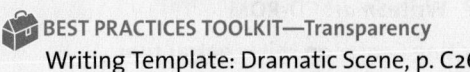 BEST PRACTICES TOOLKIT—Transparency
    Writing Template: Dramatic Scene, p. C26

 **Write*Smart* CD-ROM**

Writing Center on thinkcentral.com

Revising

Model the Skill Using a draft video script on a transparency, model how to use the questions, tips, and strategies suggested in the chart to evaluate and revise. You might use the script of a student from another class or from last year. Be sure to remove the student's name from the script so that he or she is anonymous.

YOUR TURN Suggest that students, after reading their partners' draft scripts, take one minute to freewrite a response that explains why the mood and theme were or were not addressed through dialogue and action. Then allow students a few minutes to share their responses with one another. Students should begin by making positive comments, followed by clear suggestions on how their partners can address the tone, mood, and theme more clearly.

For interactive revision tools, see

WriteSmart CD-ROM

Writing Center on thinkcentral.com

Revising

As you revise, consider the characters, sequence of events, dialogue, and pacing of your video script. The goal is to determine whether you've achieved your purpose and effectively communicated your ideas to your intended audience. The questions, tips, and strategies in the following chart will help you revise and improve your draft.

VIDEO SCRIPT

Ask Yourself	Tips	Revision Strategies
1. Do the initial stage directions and opening dialogue introduce the characters and the setting?	**Circle** details about the characters. **Underline** information about the setting.	**Add** details to develop the characters and setting for the audience.
2. Is the conflict introduced early in the script?	**Place a star** next to actions or dialogue that describe the conflict.	**Revise** actions or dialogue as necessary to introduce conflict early in the script.
3. Do dialogue and action convincingly develop characters and advance the plot?	**Double underline** dialogue and actions that reveal character traits. **Highlight** lines that advance the plot.	**Delete** or **revise** dialogue or actions that do not develop characters or advance the plot. **Add** new dialogue or actions, if necessary.
4. Are plot events sequenced so they build on one another and keep the pace of the story moving?	**Number** events in chronological order in the margin and **note** how each event relates to the plot and helps build to the climax.	**Delete** or **revise** events that do not relate to or add anything to the conflict and slow the pace. **Reorder** events to build on one another.
5. Does the script convey vivid pictures of the settings, events, and characters?	**Draw a wiggly line** under words or phrases that help the audience picture the characters, actions, and settings through dialogue, stage directions, and descriptions.	**Add** descriptive details and sensory language to the stage directions and dialogue to allow the audience to picture the events and characters in the script.
6. Does the resolution of the conflict follow from the events of the narrative?	**Put brackets** around dialogue and actions that reveal the resolution.	**Add** dialogue or actions to reveal or elaborate on the resolution.

YOUR TURN

PEER REVIEW Exchange your video script with a classmate, or read your script aloud to a partner. As you read and discuss your classmate's script, focus on plot, characters, and pacing and how well they are addressed through dialogue and action. If necessary, provide concrete suggestions for improvement, using the revision strategies in the chart.

1168 UNIT 10: GREEK TRAGEDY AND MEDIEVAL ROMANCE

DIFFERENTIATED INSTRUCTION

FOR STRUGGLING WRITERS

Bring, or have student volunteers bring, printed copies of video scripts for students to study. Movie, television, and other scripts may be available at libraries, bookstores, or on the Internet. Have students study the structure and organization of the scripts to identify stage directions and how dialogue is written.

FOR ADVANCED LEARNERS/PRE–AP

Suggest that students conduct a table reading of their scripts as a way to hear and revise dialogue. Have student writers assign roles to student volunteers and lead the cast in a reading of a scene or two. After the reading, have student writers ask for feedback: Does the dialogue develop characters and advance the plot? Does the dialogue convey the proper mood? Does the dialogue suggest the theme? Then, have writers revise the dialogue as needed.

ANALYZE A STUDENT DRAFT

Read this draft; notice the comments on its strengths as well as suggestions for improvement.

COMMON CORE

W 5 Develop and strengthen writing as needed by revising, editing, rewriting, or trying a new approach, focusing on addressing what is most significant for a specific purpose and audience.

Who Can Do It All?
by Anita Jindal, East High School

Students hurry down a hall at Central High School to their afternoon classes. Some stop at lockers, others pause in pairs or groups to talk. Rosa is standing at her locker frantically, shuffling through a pile of papers. Rosa looks worried.

Rosa. *[With growing panic.]* Now, where's that civics assignment? Is this it? No, that's my short story draft. It's due today and still needs work. I'm going to miss the deadline. But where's the civics project? If I don't start the research on it today, I'll never get it in by Friday. Ah, here it is!

[Rosa *closes her locker and hurries toward the yearbook office.* Maddie *joins her.*]

Maddie. Hey Rosa! Wanna go to the basketball game after school?

Rosa. Sorry, Maddie, I'd like to, but I have to line up some more ads for the yearbook. Then I've got to do research for civics.

Maddie. *[In awe.]* I don't know how you juggle everything.

Rosa. I don't either. Being advertising editor for the yearbook is a lot more work than I thought. I'm barely keeping up with my classes. I don't know what I'm going to do.

Maddie. But you always have everything under control.

Rosa. Not this year.

Maddie. If there's anything I can do to help, just let me know. I've got to get to math class. Later!

Rosa. Bye!

[*Exit* Maddie. Rosa *enters the yearbook office.*]

Rosa. *[Sitting at a computer.]* OK, I've got an hour. Now what can I get done?

> The stage directions and opening lines of **dialogue** introduce the main character, Rosa.

> These lines of **dialogue** between Rosa and Maddie introduce the **conflict** to the **audience.** However, the audience does not have enough information to understand it. Anita needs to add details to explain the conflict.

> Stage directions describe **characters' actions.**

LEARN HOW Add Details to Explain the Conflict To clarify the conflict, Anita adds details to Rosa's dialogue with Maddie. The additional details also help contribute to the mood of panic.

ANITA'S REVISION TO DIALOGUE

I've got C's in almost every class and I'm running out of time to make up work or do extra credit. All the yearbook ad copy is due next week, too.

Rosa. . . . I'm barely keeping up with my classes. I don't know what I'm going to do.

Maddie. But you always have everything under control.

Rosa. Not this year. *I need a B average to stay on the yearbook staff.*

WRITING WORKSHOP **1169**

ANALYZE A STUDENT DRAFT

Explain that the Student Draft on this page is the first half of a video script. Model reading the draft and the annotations in blue, and explain that the yellow highlighting illustrates the student's language choices. Explain that the following *Learn How* mini-lessons hold helpful information about ways to improve this student draft as well as your students' own drafts.

LEARN HOW Add Details to Explain the Conflict

- Explain that dialogue between characters should reveal the internal and external struggles a character or characters face.

- Point out that dialogue leads the audience through the scene and offers clues to a character's feelings and thoughts.

- Ask students to think about whether the writer includes enough details to explain the conflict. Then ask them to think of other details that the writer could add.

- Have students identify at least two places in their drafts where they can add details that help explain the conflict in more depth.

ANALYZE A STUDENT DRAFT *continued*

[*Enter* Dante.]

Dante. Rosa, do you need help recording or filing anything?

Rosa. [*Confidently.*] Thanks, Dante, but I've got my own system. I can do it myself.

Dante. Sure thing, just asking.

[*Exit* Dante *into next room.*]

Rosa. [*Looking at her computer; to herself.*] Whoa, It's going to take at least an hour to answer all these e-mails. [*Noticing a new folder on the computer desktop.*] Hmm, what's in this new folder? A file for the Daisy Mini-Mart ad and here's one for Butterworth Bakery. I wonder who filed these?

[*Enter* Ms. Eaton, *yearbook adviser. She pauses to look over* Rosa's *shoulder at what's on the computer.*]

Ms. Eaton. Well, Rosa, I see you've got everything organized, as usual.

[Ms. Eaton *goes into her office.*]

Rosa. [*To herself.*] Actually, someone else must have done this when the ads came in. It's not how I would have done it, but their system seems to work. Maybe I really <u>could</u> use some help. That would sure make this job a lot less stressful. I'd have more time for classwork, and I could get my grades back up. [*Calling into the next room.*] Dante, are you still there?

Both the **stage directions** and **dialogue** help develop the character of Rosa. They reveal that she can be confident and organized.

The **plot** reaches its **climax,** or point of greatest suspense, as Rosa finds a mountain of e-mails that need to be answered, and then discovers some work has been done for her.

These lines of dialogue contain the **resolution** of the **conflict** and the implied **theme.** Additional stage directions are needed to convey Rosa's feelings.

LEARN HOW Use Stage Directions to Show Point of View When stage directions describe what a character is thinking or feeling, they allow the actor and reader to understand an event from that character's point of view. Anita adds stage directions to indicate Rosa's shift in mood from panic to relief.

ANITA'S REVISION TO DIALOGUE

, annoyed at first, then almost grateful

Rosa. [*To herself.*] Actually, someone else must have done this when the ads

came in. . . . Maybe I really <u>could</u> use some help. That would sure make this

[*Sounding relieved*]

job a lot less stressful. I'd have more time for classwork. . . .

YOUR TURN Use the feedback from your peers and teacher as well as the two "Learn How" lessons to revise your video script. Evaluate how well you have used dialogue, action, and stage directions to convey mood and theme. If any of these elements do not work well, consider trying a new approach.

ANALYZE A STUDENT DRAFT *continued*

Explain that the Student Draft is continued and completed on this page. Read the draft and annotations aloud and discuss. Ask students to comment on the student writer's use of narrative structure.

LEARN HOW Use Stage Directions to Show Point of View

- Explain that a common mistake students make when creating video scripts is not writing clear stage directions.

- Point out how Anita's additional stage directions clarify the transition from panic to relief.

- Have students place asterisks next to places in their drafts that might be strengthened by adding more detailed stage directions.

YOUR TURN Ask students to complete the **Your Turn** activity independently. Remind students to find places in their scripts where they can effectively add stage directions to help convey mood and theme.

For interactive revision tools, see

🔘 **Write*Smart* CD-ROM**

Writing Center on thinkcentral.com

DIFFERENTIATED INSTRUCTION

FOR STRUGGLING WRITERS

Stage Directions Have students review the original and revised stage directions in the Student Model on page 1170. Point out that the words *confidently, annoyed, grateful,* and *relieved* describe how Rosa is feeling and tell the actor how to deliver the lines in order to convey those feelings to the audience. Have students go back over their own scripts to add details to their stage directions.

Editing and Publishing

COMMON CORE

W 5 Strengthen writing by revising, editing, rewriting, or trying a new approach. **W 6** Use technology to produce and publish individual writing products.

During the editing process, read your video script to make sure that it is free of grammar, spelling, and punctuation errors. Mechanical mistakes will make it difficult for actors to read and understand your script.

GRAMMAR IN CONTEXT: FORMATTING A SCRIPT

Scripts for video, movies, or stage productions follow a variety of formatting styles. The constant is that a script's formatting must be consistent and easy to follow. This helps producers, directors, and actors easily understand and visualize all the elements used to tell the story. Use these guidelines to apply formatting to your script:

Font/Type Size Choose an easy-to-read font and type size.
Spacing Align character names, dialogue, and stage directions that are not part of the dialogue with the left margin.
Capital Letters or Boldfacing Use all capitals or boldface type for names of characters and for headings.
Italics Use italics for stage directions.
Brackets Use brackets and italics for stage directions within dialogue, such as details about the entrance or exit of characters. Within brackets, do not italicize character names.
Underscore Underline words or phrases that should be emphasized in dialogue.

PUBLISH YOUR WRITING

Finally, think about ways to share your script with your intended audience. Here are some possibilities:
- Create a short video using your script and host a viewing or post it on the Internet.
- Cast your script with friends or members of a drama club, and perform it.
- Submit your script to a screenplay contest.

YOUR TURN Correct any spelling, punctuation, or grammar errors in your script. Format it correctly. Then, publish it for your audience.

FOR STRUGGLING WRITERS

Formatting a Script Have students work in pairs to check their scripts for consistency in formatting. Suggest that students review their partners' scripts and ask

- Is the font/type easy to read?
- Are the characters' names, dialogue, and stage directions that are not part of the dialogue aligned at the left margin?
- Are names of characters capitalized or boldfaced?
- Are the stage directions bracketed and set in italics?

Then have student pairs check for and correct errors in grammar, spelling, and punctuation.

FOR ENGLISH LANGUAGE LEARNERS

Culture: Connect Students may have incorporated words and phrases from their native language into the dialogue to reflect how their characters talk and think. Remind students to build clues into the dialogue that will help the audience understand what the words and phrases mean.

Editing and Publishing

COMMON CORE **W 5, W 6**

GRAMMAR IN CONTEXT: FORMATTING A SCRIPT

Remind students that proper formatting is essential in creating a good video script. The differences in stage directions, characters, and dialogue should be apparent in the choice of font size, spacing, and word treatment. For practice, have students format the stage directions in the following lines from *Man of La Mancha* in the student edition, page 1159.

1. Sancho. [looking vainly; the "horses" are interested, too] *What **giant?*** *(Align left and boldface "Sancho"; italicize stage directions.)*

2. Don Quixote. It is that dark and dreaded ogre / By the name of Matagoger! *(Align left and boldface "Don Quixote.")*

3. Don Quixote [shouting]. Ho! Feckless giant standing there! / Avast! Avaunt! On guard! Beware! [He charges off.] *(Align left and boldface "Don Quixote"; italicize "shouting"; italicize "He charges off," and align at left margin, as the stage direction is not part of the dialogue.)*

PUBLISH YOUR WRITING

Brainstorm with students about additional ways to publish their video scripts.

YOUR TURN Allow students time to proofread their drafts. Remind them to pay close attention to where stage directions and additional points of dialogue might need to be added. Also remind students to use consistent formatting as they publish their scripts.

Scoring Rubric

Tell students that the best way to understand a scoring rubric is to use it to score actual writing. Provide the class with copies of a student's video script with the student's name removed. Work as a class to evaluate the script by using the scoring rubric. Have students score the script and write a brief paragraph using the language of the scoring guide to explain the reasons for their score.

For Rubric Bank, see

WriteSmart CD-ROM

Writing Center on thinkcentral.com

Assess and Reteach

Assess

Online Essay Scoring on thinkcentral.com

Reteach

Level Up Online Tutorials on thinkcentral.com
Reteaching Worksheets on thinkcentral.com
Writing Lesson 32: Writing Dialogue

Scoring Rubric

Use the rubric below to evaluate and revise your video script.

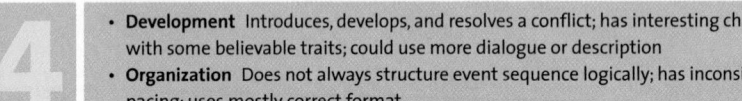

SCORE	COMMON CORE TRAITS
6	• **Development** Skillfully introduces, develops, and resolves a conflict; develops compelling, believable characters; effectively uses dialogue and description • **Organization** Has a smooth, coherent event sequence that builds to a strong resolution; uses effective pacing; uses correct formatting • **Language** Conveys vivid pictures by using well-chosen details and sensory language; shows a strong command of conventions
5	• **Development** Effectively introduces, develops, and resolves a conflict; develops interesting, believable characters; ably uses dialogue and description • **Organization** Has a coherent event sequence that builds to a resolution; uses mostly effective pacing; uses correct format • **Language** Includes sensory language and details to convey images; has a few errors in conventions
4	• **Development** Introduces, develops, and resolves a conflict; has interesting characters with some believable traits; could use more dialogue or description • **Organization** Does not always structure event sequence logically; has inconsistent pacing; uses mostly correct format • **Language** Needs more sensory language; has a few distracting errors in conventions
3	• **Development** Introduces and resolves a conflict, but needs more development; has some underdeveloped characters; needs better dialogue or description • **Organization** Has a confusing sequence; has sluggish pacing; formatting is inconsistent • **Language** Lacks details and sensory language; has some significant errors in conventions
2	• **Development** Introduces a conflict but does not develop or resolve it; inadequately develops characters; lacks descriptions and convincing dialogue • **Organization** Uses events unrelated to the conflict and a confusing sequence; has choppy pacing; formatting is very erratic • **Language** Does not present actions, characters, or imagery clearly; has many distracting errors in conventions
1	• **Development** Has no identifiable conflict; includes underdeveloped characters; lacks dialogue or description that develop the plot • **Organization** Has no apparent organization and little formatting • **Language** Does not use language effectively; has major problems with conventions

Preparing for Timed Writing

COMMON CORE

W 2a Introduce a topic; organize complex ideas, concepts, and information to make important connections and distinctions. **W 10** Write routinely over shorter time frames for a range of tasks, purposes, and audiences.

1. ANALYZE THE TASK — 5 MIN

Read the task carefully. Then, read it again, noting the words that tell the type of writing, the topic, the audience, and the purpose.

WRITING TASK

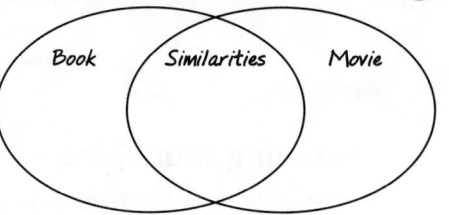

Identify a book you have read and enjoyed and a film version of it with which you are familiar. In a short article for an online site devoted to film, compare and contrast the book with the film it inspired.

Topic ↘
↖ *Audience*   ↖ *Purpose*
Type of Writing

2. PLAN YOUR RESPONSE — 10 MIN

Use a Venn diagram to list similarities and differences between the book and its film version. Consider aspects of each, such as plot, setting, mood, theme, characters, and dialogue.

Book   Similarities   Movie

3. RESPOND TO THE TASK — 20 MIN

Begin drafting your essay. Remember to use a point-by-point or block organizational structure. As you write, keep the following tips in mind:
- In the introduction, identify the subjects and include a controlling idea.
- In the body, state several points of comparison and contrast. Develop each point through examples, explanation, and evidence.
- Conclude by summarizing the key ideas and providing a final, insightful thought.

4. IMPROVE YOUR RESPONSE — 5–10 MIN

Revising Compare your draft with the task. Does your draft compare and contrast a book with a film version? Will the information help readers understand key similarities and differences between the subjects?

Proofreading Find and correct any errors in grammar, usage, or mechanics. Make sure that your article and any edits are neatly written and legible.

Checking Your Final Copy Before you submit your article, examine it once more to make sure that you are presenting your best work.

DIFFERENTIATED INSTRUCTION

FOR ENGLISH LANGUAGE LEARNERS

Vocabulary Support Review these terms in the timed writing task with students:

- *article:* an essay appearing in a publication such as a journal or Web site
- *compare:* identify similarities in two or more subjects
- *contrast:* identify differences in two or more subjects
- *point-by-point organization:* compares and contrasts two works one element at a time
- *block organization:* also called subject-by-subject; discusses all the elements of one work first, then all the elements of the other

FOR STRUGGLING WRITERS

Organize the Essay Suggest to students an alternative method of planning their responses: organizing ideas on index cards. Tell students to write each of their "similar" points on white index cards and each of their "different" points on colored index cards.

COMMON CORE FOCUS

W 2a Introduce a topic; organize complex ideas, concepts, and information to make important connections and distinctions. **W 10** Write routinely over shorter time frames for a range of tasks, purposes, and audiences.

Preparing for Timed Writing

1. **Analyze the Task** Before students begin writing, encourage them to answer the following questions:
   - What is my time limit?
   - What are the core traits assessed in the scoring rubric?
   - Who is my audience?
   - What is my purpose?

2. **Plan Your Response** Point out to students that the scoring rubric emphasizes the importance of clearly stating the similarities and differences between subjects. Remind students to consider different aspects of the two subjects as they plan their responses.

3. **Respond to the Task** Remind students to use a clear organizational structure in the opening paragraphs of their responses. They should include examples that support their controlling ideas and an observation in their concluding sections.

4. **Improve Your Response** Point out that the scoring rubric emphasizes using an effective organizational strategy—either block or point-by-point. Remind students to use transitions to ensure a smooth and clear writing style.

Assess

Use the Scoring Rubric on page 1172 to assess student's responses.

Focus and Motivate

W 6 Use technology to produce individual or shared writing products. **SL 2** Integrate multiple sources of information in diverse media. **SL 5** Make strategic use of digital media.

PRODUCE WITH A PURPOSE

Ask volunteers to compare live plays or concerts that they have seen with recorded productions on television or on the Web. Have students brainstorm to identify the strengths and weakness of a recorded performance and list the results on the board. Encourage them to take advantage of these strengths as they produce their own dramas.

COMMON CORE TRAITS

As students plan their productions, remind them to keep in mind the *COMMON CORE TRAITS* of a successful video.

Practice and Apply

Planning Your Video

WALK THROUGH EACH SCENE

As students walk through their scenes, remind them to follow their storyboards when they position cameras and actors. If they decide to change a shot, make sure that they revise the storyboard and consider the change's effect on adjacent scenes. Also, point out one advantage of recording a drama: the performers can act much more subtly because they don't have to convey their emotions to a relatively distant audience.

Technology Workshop

Producing a Drama

Essential Course of Study ECOS

Creating a video of your drama can help you reach a larger audience and present a more polished final product. You can control what the audience sees by experimenting with different camera shots, adding special effects and music, and editing any mistakes.

Complete the workshop activities in your **Reader/Writer Notebook**.

PRODUCE WITH A PURPOSE	COMMON CORE TRAITS
TASK **Produce a video** of your dramatic script, using visuals and sounds to develop plot, character, and mood.	**A SUCCESSFUL VIDEO . . .** • shows evidence of planning and rehearsal • effectively uses camera shots, music, and sound effects to convey mood, develop characters, and advance the plot • achieves coherence and an appropriate pace through strategic editing

COMMON CORE

W 6 Use technology to produce individual or shared writing products. **SL 2** Integrate multiple sources of information in diverse media. **SL 5** Make strategic use of digital media.

Media Tools

THINK central

Go to thinkcentral.com.
KEYWORD: HML10N-1174

Planning Your Video

Before the camera starts rolling, prepare for production using these guidelines:

• **Create a Storyboard** Referring to your script, identify each shot that will appear in your drama. Draw simple sketches of these shots in a series of frames, like a comic strip. Label each frame with its number in the sequence and a description of the action and the actors involved.

• **Choose Dramatic Elements** Decide on your set design and obtain your props and costumes. Keeping them simple will allow your audience to focus on the actors' words, gestures, and expressions.

• **Walk Through Each Scene** Have the actors read through their lines and practice their gestures and movements for each shot. As they rehearse, decide where each actor should stand. Then work with the technical crew to check the lighting and to prepare the camera shots and movement, keeping in mind the purpose of each shot.

DIFFERENTIATED INSTRUCTION

FOR ENGLISH LANGUAGE LEARNERS

Language: Reinforce Media Terms Write the following media terms on the board and review them with students:

• *camera angle:* the specific place where the camera is positioned to record a shot

• *props:* short for theatrical properties, the objects that actors touch or use during their performance

• *rough cut:* an early sequence of scenes assembled after all footage has been imported into the editing program.

• *scenery:* everything used to make up the setting for a production

• *sound effects:* audio elements other than speech or music inserted into a presentation

• *special effects:* artificial images created by technological means.

• *transitional devices:* the many methods used to connect one shot to another, such as cuts, dissolves, fades, and wipes

• *walk-through:* a brief rehearsal on the set

Producing Your Video

The camera shots, angles, and movements that you choose can convey important ideas about character, mood, setting, and plot. Use this chart to help you decide which camera techniques can help you achieve the effect you want.

Camera Technique	Effect
Close-up shot: detailed view of a subject	*Develops the character; creates emotion; shows a reaction*
Medium shot: view of one or more people from the waist up	*Reveals character interactions and relationships*
Long shot: wide view of characters or a setting shot from a distance	*Shows relationships among members of a group; establishes setting*
High-angle shot: shot of a subject or scene from above	*Can be used deliberately to make the character seem powerless and insignificant*
Low-angle shot: shot of a subject or scene from below	*Can be used deliberately to make the subject look imposing or threatening*
Pan: movement of the camera from side to side	*Shows the sweeping expanse of a setting; emphasizes a transition*
Zoom: movement of the camera toward or away from a subject	*Captures and focuses audience's attention on a specific detail or on a character's face*

When you edit your video, integrate a variety of media elements to add impact. Make sure that you acquire permission to use any copyrighted components.

- **Music** Add background music to the video, or use music strategically to reflect a character's emotions, echo the action, or heighten a mood, such as suspense.
- **Sound Effects** Sound effects, such as doors slamming, glasses breaking, or screams, can indicate action taking place off screen, clarify what the audience is seeing, contribute to the mood, or emphasize a point.
- **Special Effects** Slow down or speed up some sequences in your film, intersperse photographs or animations, or include clips from other videos to give an added dimension.

Assemble the scenes of your video in a way that creates coherence and maintains momentum. Use transitional devices, such as **dissolves**, a transition in which one shot fades into another, to move smoothly from one scene to the next.

 YOUR TURN Plan camera techniques, actors' positions, and lighting before you shoot the scene. When you edit, insert at least one media element, such as sound effects. Show an early "rough cut" of your video to a small audience, and make changes based on feedback.

TECHNOLOGY WORKSHOP **1175**

Assessment Practice

COMMON CORE FOCUS

RL 1 Cite textual evidence to support analysis of what the text says explicitly as well as inferences drawn from the text. **RL 3** Analyze how complex characters develop over the course of a text, interact with other characters, and advance the plot or develop the theme. **W 5** Strengthen writing by revising or editing. **L 4a** Use context as a clue to the meaning of a word or phrase. **L 6** Acquire and use accurately general academic words and phrases; demonstrate independence in gathering vocabulary knowledge.

CHECK READINESS

Read aloud the paragraph under **ASSESS** and stress to students that this is not the full Unit Test, but a way for them to check their readiness for it. Then have students examine the skills standards listed under **REVIEW** and look back in the unit or in the **Student Resource Bank** for any skills they need to review.

READ THE TEXTS

Remind students to keep unit goals in mind as they read the passage, paying particular attention to these literary and reading skills:

- characteristics of classical drama
  - tragic hero
  - tragic flaw
- conventions of medieval romance
  - romance hero
  - code of chivalry

To help students focus on the tragic hero while reading, encourage them to ask questions such as

- What is Antigone's reason for refusing to obey Creon?
- Is Antigone admirable? Why or why not?

ANSWER THE QUESTIONS

Direct students to pages R93–R101 of the **Handbook** to review test-taking strategies.

Remind students to check their answers if they have time. This is something they should do on all tests, including standardized tests.

COMMON CORE

ASSESS
Taking this practice test will help you assess your knowledge of these skills and determine your readiness for the Unit Test.

REVIEW
After you take the practice test, your teacher can help you identify any standards you need to review.

COMMON CORE

RL 1 Cite textual evidence to support analysis of what the text says explicitly as well as inferences drawn from the text. **RL 3** Analyze how complex characters develop over the course of a text, interact with other characters, and advance the plot or develop the theme. **W 5** Strengthen writing by revising or editing. **L 4a** Use context as a clue to the meaning of a word or phrase. **L 6** Acquire and use accurately general academic words and phrases; demonstrate independence in gathering vocabulary knowledge.

Practice Test
THINK central
Take it at **thinkcentral.com**.
KEYWORD: HML10N-1176

Assessment Practice

DIRECTIONS Read the following selections, and then answer the questions.

In this excerpt from Scene 2, Creon confronts Antigone for disobeying his proclamation.

from Antigone   *by Sophocles*

Creon (*slowly, dangerously*). And you, Antigone,
You with your head hanging—do you confess this thing?

Antigone. I do. I deny nothing.

Creon (*to* Sentry).   You may go.

(*Exit* Sentry.)

(*to* Antigone) Tell me, tell me briefly:
Had you heard my proclamation touching this matter?

55 **Antigone.** It was public. Could I help hearing it?

Creon. And yet you dared defy the law.

Antigone.   I dared.
It was not God's proclamation. That final Justice
That rules the world below makes no such laws.

Your edict, King, was strong,
60 But all your strength is weakness itself against
The immortal unrecorded laws of God.
They are not merely now: they were, and shall be,
Operative forever, beyond man utterly.

I knew I must die, even without your decree:
65 I am only mortal. And if I must die
Now, before it is my time to die,
Surely this is no hardship: can anyone
Living, as I live, with evil all about me,
Think Death less than a friend? This death of mine
70 Is of no importance; but if I had left my brother
Lying in death unburied, I should have suffered.
Now I do not.
              You smile at me. Ah Creon,
Think me a fool, if you like; but it may well be
That a fool convicts me of folly.

75 **Choragus.** Like father, like daughter: both headstrong, deaf to reason!
She has never learned to yield.

1176   UNIT 10: GREEK TRAGEDY AND MEDIEVAL ROMANCE

DIFFERENTIATED INSTRUCTION

FOR ENGLISH LANGUAGE LEARNERS
Assessment Practice: Work Backward
Prepare students by having them read the questions *before* reading the passages. Have pairs find unfamiliar words in test directions and questions and follow these steps:

1. Write each word on an index card.

2. Look up the meaning in a dictionary and write it on the back of the card.

3. Use the cards to practice the words with your partner and to teach them to others.

1176   UNIT 10

Creon.   She has much to learn.
The inflexible heart breaks first, the toughest iron
Cracks first, and the wildest horses bend their necks
At the pull of the smallest curb.
                        Pride? In a slave?
80 This girl is guilty of a double insolence,
Breaking the given laws and boasting of it.
Who is the man here,
She or I, if this crime goes unpunished?
Sister's child, or more than sister's child,
85 Or closer yet in blood—she and her sister
Win bitter death for this!
                    (*to servants*) Go, some of you,
Arrest Ismene. I accuse her equally.
Bring her: you will find her sniffling in the house there.
Her mind's a traitor: crimes kept in the dark
90 Cry for light, and the guardian brain shudders;
But how much worse than this
Is brazen boasting of barefaced anarchy!

Antigone. Creon, what more do you want than my death?

Creon.   Nothing.
That gives me everything.

Antigone.   Then I beg you: kill me.
95 This talking is a great weariness: your words
Are distasteful to me, and I am sure that mine
Seem so to you. And yet they should not seem so:
I should have praise and honor for what I have done.
All these men here would praise me
100 Were their lips not frozen shut with fear of you.
(*bitterly*) Ah the good fortune of kings,
Licensed to say and do whatever they please!

Creon. You are alone here in that opinion.

Antigone. No, they are with me. But they keep their tongues in leash.

105 **Creon.** Maybe. But you are guilty, and they are not.

Antigone. There is no guilt in reverence for the dead.

GO ON ➡

ITEM ANALYSIS

COMPREHENSION AND WRITTEN RESPONSE	ITEMS	UNIT PAGES
Characteristics of Classical Drama		
Tragic Hero	4, 8, 10	1058–1063
Tragic Flaw	1, 2, 5	1058–1063
Chorus	3	1058–1063
Conventions of		
Medieval Romance	6	1111
Romance Hero	7, 8	1111
Chivalry	8, 9	1111

VOCABULARY	ITEMS	UNIT PAGES
Etymology	1, 2, 3	1108
Connotation	4, 5, 6	1142

WRITING AND GRAMMAR	ITEMS	UNIT PAGES
Vary Sentence Beginnings	2, 4, 6	1143
Inverted Sentences	5	1109
Sentence Structure	1, 3	

Practice Test

On **thinkcentral.com** students can complete an interactive version of this practice test *and* receive remediation for the skills they have not yet mastered.

FOR STRUGGLING READERS

Assessment Support Consider these options for completing the Assessment Practice:

- Have students "work backward" to review the test questions before reading the passages.

- Select random questions in the Assessment, and have students demonstrate *how* and *where* to look for the answers.

- Ask students to locate unfamiliar vocabulary words in the Assessment. Elicit the words' meanings from the class.

- Have students record useful testing words and definitions in their *Reader/Writer Notebooks* for later reference.

- Read the selections or parts of it aloud to aid in student comprehension.

Reading Comprehension

Model a thinking process for answering multiple-choice questions.

1. **B is correct.** Antigone's crime was to disobey Creon's order to leave her brother unburied (lines 70–71). A is incorrect because Antigone's rudeness was not as serious as that crime. There is no evidence for C or D.

2. **D is correct.** All of the answer choices suggest pride, but D is the only statement that contradicts Creon. A is incorrect because it emphasizes honesty. B is incorrect because it emphasizes disrespect. C is incorrect because it emphasizes Antigone's willingness to die.

3. **B is correct.** The function of the choragus is to comment, and lines 75–76 illustrate that function. A can be eliminated because the lines do not allude to the future. C is incorrect because although Greek tragedy was originally chanted to music, the words provide the main function. D is incorrect because the choragus supports Creon.

4. **D is correct.** Antigone accepts the fate of an untimely death (lines 65–67). A is incorrect because the passage does not mention Antigone's descent. B is incorrect because Antigone shows disrespect for Creon. C is incorrect because Antigone shows strong emotion.

5. **B is correct.** In lines 69–71, Antigone says, "...This death of mine/Is of no importance; but if I had left my brother/Lying in death unburied, I should have suffered." A and C are contradicted by those lines. D is incorrect because saving her sister would bring Antigone joy.

6. **B is correct.** Initially, Launcelot hides his identity from Sir Tarquine. There is no evidence for A or D. C is incorrect because the setting is not identified.

7. **A is correct.** Launcelot responds to a challenge to "you, and all your fellowship of the Round Table" (paragraph 2). B is incorrect because his reputation is already established. C is incorrect because he has no magical powers. D can be eliminated because he treats Tarquine courteously.

8. **A is correct.** Antigone is loyal to her brother; Launcelot is loyal to King Arthur and the Round Table. B is incorrect because Antigone's actions do not lead to adventure. C is incorrect because Launcelot makes no reference to God. D is incorrect because Antigone is motivated by a desire to honor her brother.

from Le Morte d' Arthur

by Sir Thomas Malory

1   "Good knight," said Sir Launcelot, "it is known to me that you have put to shame many of the knights of the Round Table. Pray allow your prisoner, who I see is wounded, to recover, while I vindicate the honor of the knights whom you have defeated."

2   "I defy you, and all your fellowship of the Round Table," Sir Tarquine replied.

3   "You boast!" said Sir Launcelot.

4   At the first charge the backs of the horses were broken and both knights stunned. But they soon recovered and set to with their swords, and both struck so lustily that neither shield nor armor could resist, and within two hours they were cutting each other's flesh, from which the blood flowed liberally. Finally they paused for a moment, resting on their shields.

5   "Worthy knight," said Sir Tarquine, "pray hold your hand for a while and, if you will, answer my question."

6   "Sir, speak on."

7   "You are the most powerful knight I have fought yet, but I fear you may be the one whom in the whole world I most hate. If you are not, for the love of you I will release all my prisoners and swear eternal friendship."

8   "What is the name of the knight you hate above all others?"

9   "Sir Launcelot du Lake; for it was he who slew my brother, Sir Carados of the Dolorous Tower, and it is because of him that I have killed a hundred knights and maimed as many more, apart from the sixty-four I still hold prisoner. And so, if you are Sir Launcelot, speak up, for we must then fight to the death."

10   "Sir, I see now that I might go in peace and good fellowship or otherwise fight to the death; but being the knight I am, I must tell you: I am Sir Launcelot du Lake, son of King Ban of Benwick, of Arthur's court, and a knight of the Round Table. So defend yourself!"

11   "Ah! this is most welcome."

12   Now the two knights hurled themselves at each other like two wild bulls; swords and shields clashed together, and often their swords drove into the flesh. Then sometimes one, sometimes the other, would stagger and fall, only to recover immediately and resume the contest. At last, however, Sir Tarquine grew faint and unwittingly lowered his shield. Sir Launcelot was swift to follow up his advantage and, dragging the other down to his knees, unlaced his helmet and beheaded him.

1178

Reading Comprehension

1. Creon is angry with Antigone because she —

  A. spoke rudely to him in public

  B. buried her brother in defiance of his order

  C. tried to seize his throne and kill him

  D. lied to protect herself and her sister

2. In which of the following statements does Antigone most clearly express her attitude?

  A. *I do. I deny nothing.*

  B. *Could I help hearing it?*

  C. *Creon, what more do you want than my death?*

  D. *I should have praise and honor for what I have done.*

3. The function of the choragus in lines 75–76 is to —

  A. foreshadow the action

  B. comment on the characters

  C. provide a musical backdrop

  D. influence Creon

4. Which quality of a tragic hero does Antigone exhibit in the face of Creon's anger?

  A. Descent from royal lineage

  B. Respect for political authority

  C. Ability to control emotions

  D. Willingness to accept fate

5. According to Antigone in lines 65–72, the experience which would cause her the most suffering would be —

  A. being condemned to death by Creon

  B. leaving her brother unburied

  C. dying while she is still young

  D. not saving her sister's life

6. Which element of medieval romance is reflected in this battle scene?

  A. A supernatural occurrence

  B. A hidden identity

  C. An exotic setting

  D. A romantic quest

7. Launcelot is a hero in a medieval romance because he fights to —

  A. defend the honor of his fellow knights

  B. establish his reputation as a warrior

  C. exhibit his magical powers in battle

  D. bring public shame upon Tarquine

8. Antigone and Launcelot are motivated by —

  A. personal loyalty

  B. desire for adventure

  C. reverence for God

  D. excessive ambition

SHORT CONSTRUCTED RESPONSE
Write three or four sentences to answer this question.

9. What are two ways Tarquine and Launcelot practice the code of chivalry? Provide evidence from the text.

Write two to three paragraphs to answer this question.

10. What do the actions of Antigone and Creon reveal about their individual views of loyalty? Support your answer with details from the excerpt.

GO ON

SHORT CONSTRUCTED RESPONSE

Possible responses:

9. *Launcelot and Tarquine treat each other with respect (paragraphs 5–7, for example); both fight bravely in a battle motivated by loyalty (paragraphs 8–11); both are honest.*

10. *Antigone's actions reveal that she values family loyalty over political allegiance and that her ultimate loyalty is to the gods, who have ordained the laws of burial (lines 59–61 and 69–72). Creon's actions reveal that he is loyal to the law of the land and to his own political authority (lines 53–56).*

Vocabulary

1. **B is correct.** *Bræsen sounds like* brazen, *and* brassy *can be substituted for* brazen. *A has no connection to* bræsen. *C and D begin with the same letter as* bræsen, *but the resemblance is no closer than that.*

2. **D is correct.** *With the* s *dropped,* disfidare *sounds like* defy. *A is incorrect despite some similarity in sound, because it means "to reject." B and C are not related to* disfidare.

3. **D is correct.** *If the vowel* o *is changed to* u, stunned *and* stonen *are clearly related. A shows no relation to* stonen. *B and C begin similarly to* stonen *but are less similar than* stunned.

4. **D is correct.** *Sniffling implies crying, and the context implies that Ismene is hiding out of fear. Both A and B have negative connotations but not the same connotation of whimpering fear that* sniffling *has. C is incorrect because secretive people would be silent rather than sniffling audibly.*

5. **D is correct.** *A barefaced person is unashamed to show a dishonorable aspect. A can be eliminated because Creon sees the opposite of courtesy in* Antigone. *B is incorrect because the context refers to Antigone's boldness, not to her honesty. C can be eliminated because rareness is unimportant to the context.*

6. **B is correct.** *The phrase "like two wild bulls" is a context clue. This same clue contradicts choices A and C. D is incorrect because the passage emphasizes the knights' power, not their speed.*

Vocabulary

> Use the etymological clues provided to answer the following questions.

1. The Old English word *bræsen* means "made of brass." Which of the following words from *Antigone* comes from *bræsen*?
   A. Bitter
   B. Brazen
   C. Briefly
   D. Brother

2. The Latin prefix *dis-* means "without" and the infinitive *fidare* means "to trust." Which of the following words from the selections comes from *dis-* + *fidare*?
   A. Deny
   B. Defeat
   C. Defend
   D. Defy

3. The Middle English word *stonen* comes from the Latin *tonare*, meaning "to thunder." Which of the following words from *Le Morte d'Arthur* comes from *stonen*?
   A. Shields
   B. Stagger
   C. Struck
   D. Stunned

> Use context clues and your knowledge of connotation to answer the following questions.

4. The word *sniffling* in line 88 of *Antigone* has a connotation of —
   A. desperation
   B. meanness
   C. secretiveness
   D. weakness

5. In line 92 of *Antigone*, the word *barefaced* has a connotation of —
   A. courtesy
   B. honesty
   C. rareness
   D. shamelessness

6. The word *hurled* in paragraph 12 of *Le Morte d'Arthur* has a connotation of —
   A. clumsiness
   B. forcefulness
   C. hesitation
   D. speed

DIFFERENTIATED INSTRUCTION

FOR ENGLISH LANGUAGE LEARNERS

Vocabulary Support On the board, list the vocabulary terms shown in italics. Then give the examples in random order and have students classify them. Elicit additional examples from students.

- *classical drama:* Antigone is an ancient Greek play about the downfall of a brave and virtuous woman.

- *tragic hero:* Antigone stands by her principles even though doing so will result in her death.

- *medieval romance:* The tales of the Round Table include knights who set out on quests of adventure.

- *romance hero:* Launcelot was the greatest knight of the Round Table.

Revising and Editing

DIRECTIONS Read this passage, and answer the questions that follow.

> (1) Medieval nobles were much more powerful then peasants under the feudal system. (2) Medieval nobles and peasants endured similarly harsh living conditions. (3) Medieval castles were built for defense, nor comfort. (4) So, though a lord's castle might be large, it was rarely inviting. (5) It was built of thick stone and had few windows. (6) It had damp, dark, and cold rooms. (7) It had bedrooms with lice-infested mattresses.

1. What change, if any, should be made in sentence 1?
   A. Insert a comma after **peasants**
   B. Change **then** to **than**
   C. Change **much more powerful** to **most powerful**
   D. Make no change

2. Which transitional word or phrase should be added to the beginning of sentence 2?
   A. After all,
   B. Likewise,
   C. Nevertheless,
   D. Thus,

3. What change, if any, should be made in sentence 3?
   A. Change **built** to **build**
   B. Change **nor** to **not**
   C. Change **comfort** to **comfortable**
   D. Make no change

4. What is the most effective sentence to add after sentence 4?
   A. Certainly it was nothing like a fairy-tale castle.
   B. In other words, castles were unbelievably luxurious.
   C. The era of castle building ended with the advent of the cannon.
   D. Who would have wanted to visit?

5. What is the most effective way to revise sentence 5 for variety?
   A. The castle, built of thick stone and having few windows.
   B. The castle was built of thick stone, and the castle had few windows.
   C. Built of thick stone was the castle, and with few windows.
   D. Built of thick stone, it had few windows.

6. What change, if any, should be made to vary sentences 6 and 7?
   A. Damp, dark, cold rooms it had. In the bedrooms, mattresses were lice infested.
   B. Rooms were damp, dark, and cold. Lice infested the mattresses in the bedrooms.
   C. It had damp, dark, and cold rooms, yet it had bedrooms with lice-infested mattresses.
   D. Make no change

STOP

1181

Revising and Editing

1. **B is correct.** The word then is incorrectly used as an adverb in the sentence. Than is a conjunction that means "in comparison with." A is incorrect because a comma is not needed in this sentence. C is incorrect because a comparative adjective is needed, not a superlative adjective. D is incorrect because a change is needed.

2. **C is correct.** Nevertheless means "yet" or "in spite of," which supports the idea in sentence 1. A is incorrect because after all is a transitional phrase that is used to summarize information. B is incorrect because likewise means "in addition to." D is incorrect because thus, meaning "consequently," does not show an accurate relationship between the ideas in sentences 1 and 2.

3. **B is correct.** The word nor would make sense if paired with neither— "castles were built neither for defense nor for comfort," but the meaning of the resulting sentence would be false. A is incorrect because changing "built" to "build" would make the verb present tense instead of past tense. C is incorrect because "comfort" is used correctly as a noun. D is incorrect because a change is needed to the sentence.

4. **A is correct.** The phrase "nothing like a fairy-tale castle" supports the phrase "rarely inviting" in sentence 4. B is incorrect because "unbelievably luxurious" is the opposite of "rarely inviting." C and D are incorrect because they do not make sense in this paragraph.

5. **D is correct.** The sentence correctly inverts, or changes the word order, of the sentence and maintains the meaning of the sentence. A is incorrect because it is a fragment. B is incorrect because the dependent clauses are repetitive. Punctuation and grammar are wrong in C.

6. **B is correct.** The sentences are both varied and grammatically correct. Word order in A is awkward. C is incorrect because the transition word "yet" would indicate a contrast between the two clauses. D is incorrect because the existing sentences are repetitive and lack variety.

FOR STRUGGLING READERS

Assessment Support: Inverted Word Order
Remind students that poets throughout history have used inverted word order to make their lines fit a rhyme scheme or rhythm. Have students create their own short poem with inverted word order in one line.

COMMON CORE FOCUS

RL 10 Read and comprehend literature. **RI 10** Read and comprehend literary nonfiction.

INTRODUCE *GREAT READS*

In Unit 10, students have discussed a number of big questions. Invite students to tell which question they found most intriguing and why, and then focus attention on the three that appear on this page. Discuss the recommended books and their summaries, pointing out how each connects to the related question. Encourage students to choose one or more of these "great reads" to read independently.

NovelWise

The keyword on this page points to **NovelWise**, a Web site that helps students choose a novel or other book-length work to read. **NovelWise** also provides

- study guides
- reading strategies and literary elements instruction
- presentations to introduce classic novels
- project ideas

UNIT 10 Great Reads

Ideas for Independent Reading

What ideas about honor did you gain from reading Greek drama and medieval romances? Expand on your thoughts with these related readings.

COMMON CORE

RL 10 Read and comprehend literature. **RI 10** Read and comprehend literary nonfiction.

What is your ultimate loyalty?

Antigone
by Jean Anouilh

French playwright Anouilh wrote his version of *Antigone* when the Nazis occupied France during World War II. The play is often interpreted as an allegory of the French Resistance. Read to see how it differs from the original.

Jane Eyre
by Charlotte Bronte

Poor, plain, and honest Jane Eyre is a governess. Her employer, Mr. Rochester, is attracted by her directness, and the two fall in love. On the day of their wedding, Jane learns a secret that forces her to make a hard choice.

Grey Is the Color of Hope
by Irina Ratushinskaya

This memoir is by a deeply religious Russian poet who spent four years as a political prisoner in a Soviet labor camp. She and other female prisoners refused to submit to rules that would strip them of their humanity.

Could you be a knight?

The Once and Future King
by T. H. White

White's retelling of Malory's *Le Morte d'Arthur* is a classic of English literature. Written at the outbreak of World War II, it entertains while commenting on political ideas of the time. King Arthur rejects the philosophy that "might makes right" and conceives the Round Table to use might *for* right.

Perceval: The Story of the Grail
by Chrétien de Troyes

This 12th-century French romance in verse introduced the legend of the Holy Grail. Perceval is a naïve boy who lives in the forest with his mother. Awestruck after seeing a knight for the first time, he vows to become one. Eventually he joins the Round Table.

Ramón Lull's Book of Knighthood and Chivalry
by Ramón Lull

This "training manual for squires" was written by a 13th-century Spanish knight who later became a theologian. Among the advice it offers: "The knight must possess such riches as to support his office, lest he be forced to robbery."

Why do we admire dreamers?

Encounters with the Archdruid
by John McPhee

The author describes conversations between David Brower, one of America's most uncompromising conservationists, and three of his opponents—a developer, a mining engineer, and a dam builder.

Mountains Beyond Mountains
by Tracy Kidder

Kidder profiles Dr. Paul Farmer, a Harvard-trained physician and anthropologist whose mission is to fight disease among the world's poor. Much of Farmer's work was done in rural Haiti, battling drug-resistant tuberculosis.

They All Laughed . . .
by Ira Flatow

This book is subtitled "From Light Bulbs to Lasers: The Fascinating Stories Behind the Great Inventions That Have Changed Our Lives." Many of these discoveries were ridiculed when first publicized.

Get Novel Wise THINK central

Go to **thinkcentral.com**.
KEYWORD: HML10-1182

1182

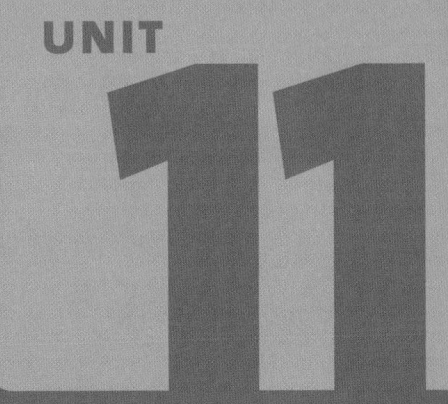

Shakespearean Drama

THE TRAGEDY OF JULIUS CAESAR

- In Drama
- In Media

1183

About the Art *Emperor Julius Caesar* was painted by Flemish painter Peter Paul Rubens (1577–1640).

INTRODUCE THE UNIT

Shakespeare was a great poet, but he may be best known for his plays—plays that were written hundreds of years ago but that remain relevant because of their universal themes and the excellence of their execution. Invite students to name some of Shakespeare's plays; as they do, point out that these plays continue to be performed (in both traditional and current interpretations) around the world today.

Explain that the painting and the photograph both reference *The Tragedy of Julius Caesar* and suggest the timelessness of the play. Both images also focus on Mark Antony, an important character in the play. Use these questions to get students thinking about the drama that the images suggest:

- How would you describe each image? Why?
- What emotion or emotions does Mark Antony seem to express?
- If you look at both images, what story do you think they tell?

Tell students that in this unit they will read the **Shakespearean drama** of *The Tragedy of Julius Caesar*. They also will consider how the play has been interpreted in modern media— and the responses with which some of the interpretations have been met.

For help in planning this unit, see

 RESOURCE MANAGER UNIT 11
pp. 1–7

UNIT 11

ECOS ECOS ECOS ECOS

	COMMON CORE STRAND	*Shakespeare's World* Informational Article pp. 1186–1189	*Text Analysis Workshop: Shakespearean Drama* pp. 1190–1197	*The Tragedy of Julius Caesar, Act One* Drama pp. 1198–1219	*The Tragedy of Julius Caesar, Act Two* Drama pp. 1220–1237	*The Tragedy of Julius Caesar, Act Three* Drama pp. 1238–1257
Reading Literature			Characteristics of Shakespearean Tragedy pp. 1190–1191 The Language of Shakespeare pp. 1192–1193 Reading Shakespearean Drama pp. 1194–1195 Analyze the Text pp. 1196–1197 RL 3, RL 5, RL 9, RL 10	Shakespearean Tragedy pp. 1199, 1215, 1219 RL 3, RL 4, RL 5, RL 9 Reading Shakespearean Drama pp. 1199, 1219 RL 1, RL 10 Motifs in Drama p. 1206 RL 2 Blank Verse pp. 1210, 1212 RL 4 Soliloquy p. 1214 RL 3, RL 5 English Roots p. 1202 RL 4 Language Coach p. 1209 RL 4	Tragedy pp. 1225, 1236, 1237 RL 3, RL 4, RL 5, RL 9 Soliloquy p. 1223 RL 3, RL 5 Tragic Hero p. 1232 RL 3 Dramatic Irony p. 1234 RL 3 Reading Shakespearean Drama p. 1237 RL 1, RL 10 Language Coach, pp. 1223, 1227, 1232 RL 4 Word Origins p. 1220 RL 4	Tragedy pp. 1243, 1247 RL 3, RL 4, RL 5, RL 9 Tragic Hero p. 1240 RL 3 Analyze Motivations p. 1248 RL 3 Rhetorical Devices pp. 1251, 1252, 1254, 1257 RL 3 Reading Shakespearean Drama p. 1239, 1257 RL 1, RL 10 Language Coach pp. 1245, 1253 RL 4
Reading Informational Text	Read Nonfiction Text pp. 1186-1189		Set Design, p. 1213 RI 7	Casting p. 1229 RI 7	Blocking, p. 1242 RI 7
Writing			Quickwrite p. 1198		
Speaking and Listening					Rhetorical Devices pp. 1251, 1252, 1254, 1257 SL 3
Language			Shakespearean Language pp. 1190–1197 L 6		Adjective Clauses p. 1249 L 1b

The Tragedy of Julius Caesar, Act Four Drama pp. 1258–1273	Linked Selections		Media Study: from Julius Caesar Film Clip pp. 1294–1297	Writing Workshop: Critical Review pp. 1298–1307 Speaking & Listening Workshop: Participating in a Critics' Debate pp. 1308–1309
	The Tragedy of Julius Caesar, Act Five Drama pp. 1274–1289	Julius Caesar at the Public Theater Theater Reviews pp. 1290–1293		
Tragic Hero pp. 1261, 1264, 1265, 1270, 1271, 1273 RL 3 Allusion p. 1266 RL 2 Reading Shakespearean Drama p. 1273 RL 1, RL 10 Language Coach p. 1271 RL 4	Tragedy pp. 1281, 1282, 1288 RL 3, RL 4, RL 5, RL 9 Tragic Hero pp. 1279, 1285 RL 3 Reading Shakespearean Drama p. 1288 RL 1, RL 10 Language Coach p. 1284 RL 4		Shakespearean Drama on Film pp. 1294–1297 RL 7	
Costume Design p. 1263 RI 7	Promotion p. 1287 RI 7	Theater Review pp. 1290–1293 RI 1, RI 8 Language Coach p. 1292 RI 4		
	Writing Prompt p. 1289	Writing Prompt p. 1293 W 2	Write a Shooting Script p. 1297 W 2	Writing a Critical Review pp. 1298–1307 W 1a–e, W 4, W 5, W 9a (RL 7, 9), W 10
			Discuss p. 1297 SL 1	Participating in a Critics' Debate pp. 1308–1309 SL 1a–d, SL 3, SL 4
	Descriptive Details p. 1289 L 1b			Editing and Publishing p. 1305 L 2a

ECOS

To see the complete Essential Course of Study, see pp. T23–T28.

For additional lesson planning help, see **Teacher One Stop DVD.**

Instructional Support

Resource Manager Unit 11

UNIT SUPPORT
Academic Vocabulary, p. 3
Additional Academic Vocabulary, p. 4
Grammar Focus p. 5
Text Analysis Workshop pp. 9–10
Writing Workshop: Critical Review p. 115

SELECTION SUPPORT*
Plan and Teach
Lesson planning pages
Additional leveled selection questions
Extension activities

Student Copy Masters
Selection summaries in four languages
Skills copy masters in English and Spanish
Vocabulary preteaching and support
Reading Check and Question Support
Reading Fluency

* Available for all selections

† Available on **thinkcentral.com**.

Language Handbook
Vocabulary Practice
Best Practices Toolkit†
PowerNotes DVD-ROM†
Connections: Nonfiction for Common Core CD-ROM†

Teacher One Stop DVD-ROM
Student One Stop DVD-ROM
Media*Smart* DVD-ROM
from Julius Caesar
Write*Smart* CD-ROM†
GrammarNotes DVD-ROM†
WordSharp CD-ROM†

Differentiated Instruction

STRUGGLING READERS AND WRITERS	ENGLISH LANGUAGE LEARNERS	ADVANCED LEARNERS
Resource Manager Unit 11	**Resource Manager Unit 11**	**Resource Manager Unit 11**
Additional Selection Questions	Selection Summaries in English, Spanish, Vietnamese and Haitian Creole	Additional Selection Questions
Question Support		Ideas for Extension
Reading Fluency	Skills Copymasters in Spanish	**Diagnostic and Selection Tests**
Interactive Reader	**English Language Learner Adapted Interactive Reader Teacher's Guide**	Selection Tests B/C
Adapted Interactive Reader		
Audio Tutor	**ELL Adapted Interactive Reader**	
Level Up Online Tutorials	**Audio Tutor**	
Audio Anthology (with Audio summaries)	**Guide to English for Newcomers**	
Diagnostic and Selection Tests	**Audio Anthology**	
Selection Tests A/B	**Audio Summaries in Multiple Languages** (on **thinkcentral.com**)	

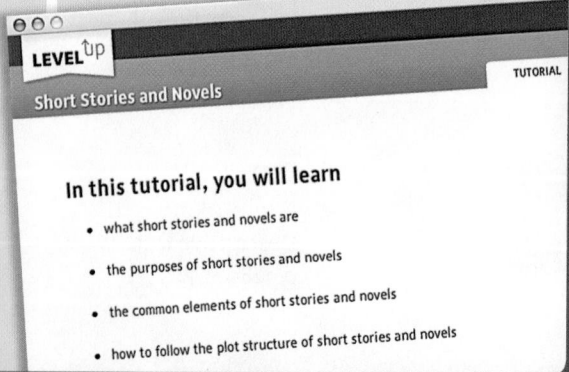

Assessment and Reteaching

Diagnostic and Selection Tests

Unit and Benchmark Tests

ThinkCentral Online Assessment:
- All program assessments
- Level Up Online Tutorials

ExamView Test Generator on the Teacher One Stop DVD-ROM

Online Essay Scoring on thinkcentral.com

ThinkCentral Online Reteaching:
- Level Up Online Tutorials
- Reteaching Worksheets

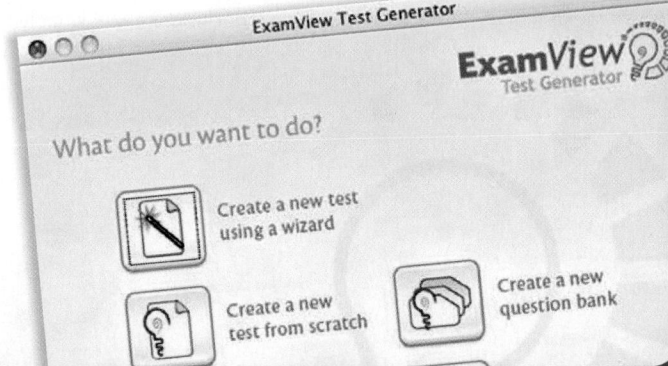

Professional Development

Video Center Based on interviews with program consultants and other educational experts, these videos feature classroom-ready teaching strategies.

Teacher Toolkit Includes a Teacher Handbook as well as a range of articles and handouts by program consultants and other educators.

Janet Allen

Jim Burke

Kylene Beers

Carol Jago

 **at a Glance**

One Location, Endless Resources

Find Resources Browse all *Holt McDougal Literature* components for the ones that meet your students' needs and match your teaching style.

Assess Progress and Reteach Assign electronic versions of program assessments to measure your students' mastery of the Common Core Standards. On thinkcentral.com, some tests deliver online remediation tutorials automatically to students who have not mastered skills.

 Interactive Whiteboard Lessons

Prepare your students for college and careers by teaching relevant, real-world skills through dynamic, interactive instruction. Go to **thinkcentral.com** to browse through all whiteboard lessons, including the following:

- Irony and Satire
- Comparing Texts
- Writing Effective Arguments

 Together Holt McDougal and HISTORY® are revolutionizing the study of English/language arts with video that helps students relive and re-imagine the people, places, and events they are discovering through reading. Look for selections with the HISTORY® icon.

When does ambition
lead to **TRAGEDY?**

Introduce the page by reading aloud the question and the opening paragraph. Call on volunteers to define *ambition* (linking it to "power or fame at any cost") and *tragedy* (linking it to "unexpected cost"). Then ask students to comment and expand upon this list of potentially tragic events:

- academic failure
- romantic rejection
- financial ruin
- military defeat
- death (of self or of a loved one)

Ask students what role ambition might play in each tragic event discussed. Point out that tragedy can be a largely personal matter; that is, a certain situation might destroy one person, while someone else may weather the same events with courage and grace.

ACTIVITY To begin the brainstorming session, suggest that students consider people who have been in the news lately due to difficult circumstances or scandal. As students share their thoughts, guide them to conclude that tragedy often is the result of greedy, selfish ambition.

CHECK UNDERSTANDING Review the question at the top of the page. Elicit that ambition can lead to tragedy because an obsessive desire can blind a person to reality.

Unit Resources

When does ambition
lead to **TRAGEDY?**

History, politics, and literature are filled with stories of people who sought power or fame at any cost. But success can ultimately have a dark side, as many of those individuals learned. Some were stripped of the power they found, and others found that their success came at an unexpected cost. Why do you think so many of these stories end in tragedy?

ACTIVITY As a class, brainstorm examples of individuals whose ambition led to tragedy. These can be characters from literature or real people from business, politics, or history. Analyze what happened in each case, and draw conclusions about what led to each person's downfall.

Find It Online! THINK central

Go to **thinkcentral.com** for the interactive version of this unit.

1184

See resources on the **Teacher One Stop DVD-ROM** *and on* **thinkcentral.com**.

R **RESOURCE MANAGER UNIT 11**

UNIT AND BENCHMARK TESTS

BEST PRACTICES TOOLKIT

INTERACTIVE READER

ADAPTED INTERACTIVE READER

ELL ADAPTED INTERACTIVE READER

LANGUAGE HANDBOOK

VOCABULARY PRACTICE

TECHNOLOGY

- **Teacher One Stop DVD-ROM**
- **Student One Stop DVD-ROM**
- **PowerNotes DVD-ROM**
- **Write*Smart* CD-ROM**
- **Media*Smart* DVD-ROM**
- **GrammarNotes DVD-ROM**
- **Audio Anthology CD**
- **Audio Tutor CD**

THINK central

Find It Online!

The interactive version of this unit on **thinkcentral.com** includes

- video and **PowerNotes** introductions to key selections
- audio support—listen or download
- **ThinkAloud** models
- **WordSharp** vocabulary tutorials
- interactive review and remediation

Preview Unit Goals

TEXT ANALYSIS	• Identify characteristics of Shakespearean tragedy, including tragic hero and tragic flaw • Analyze complex characters and how they interact with others and advance the plot or develop the theme • Identify and analyze dramatic irony and rhetorical devices • Determine a theme and analyze its development
READING	• Read and comprehend Shakespearean drama • Draw conclusions; cite textual evidence • Analyze a theater review
WRITING AND LANGUAGE	• Write an argument (critical review) • Develop and strengthen counterclaims • Use phrases and clauses to link major sections of text
SPEAKING AND LISTENING	• Participate in a critics' debate
MEDIA AND VIEWING	• Identify, analyze, and evaluate mise en scène • Compare your response to a critical review • Create a shooting script

Media Smart DVD-ROM

Shakespearean Tragedy on Film

Analyze how film and performance techniques add intrigue to a pivotal scene in *Julius Caesar*. Page 1294

1185

COMMON CORE **UNIT GOALS**

Included in this unit: **RL 1, RL 2, RL 3, RL 4, RL 5, RL 7, RL 9, RL 10, RI 1, RI 4, RI 7, RI 8, RI 10, W 1a–e, W 2, W 4, W 5, W 9a, W 10, SL 1, SL 3, SL 4, L 1b, L 6**

Complete text of the Common Core is found in the correlation on p. T10. Standards covered in this unit are found in the standards overview (pp. 1183A–1183B) and on the lesson pages where they are taught.

Preview Unit Goals

Point out to students that these goals are the main skill focus of Unit 11. Have students familiarize themselves with the list and set some personal goals as they prepare to read. Remind students that each skill is color-coded, both here and throughout the unit.

Shakespeare's World

Shakespeare's England

Cultural Blossoming
William Shakespeare is considered by many to be the world's greatest playwright. Shakespeare lived in England during the Renaissance, the blossoming of European learning that followed the Middle Ages. During the Middle Ages, the European world view had focused on God and the afterlife, but with the Renaissance came a renewal of interest in individual human achievement. This new emphasis spurred human beings to expand their horizons in all sorts of ways—scientifically, geographically, commercially, philosophically, artistically. In 1564, when Shakespeare was born, England had already embraced the spirit of Renaissance creativity. In the decades that followed, Shakespeare himself would help carry the Renaissance to even greater heights.

**William Shakespeare
1564–1616**

Queen of the Arts Six years before Shakespeare was born, Elizabeth I became queen of England, and the period of her reign, from 1558 to 1603, is known as the Elizabethan Age. Elizabeth I supported all the arts—literature, painting, sculpture, music, and theater. She was also a frugal and clever leader who, despite frequent political in-fighting and religious turmoil, managed to steer England down a middle road to stability and prosperity.

During Elizabeth's reign, London, the capital of the nation, flourished as a great commercial center, the hub of England's growing overseas empire. London was also the hub of the artistic efforts that Elizabeth championed, and it attracted talented and ambitious individuals from all over the land.

**Queen Elizabeth I
1533–1603**

Because a true Renaissance figure was supposed to excel in many fields, Elizabeth's courtiers often dabbled in writing. In fact, some of them, like Sir Walter Raleigh, produced memorable poetry that is still being read today. Topping the list of the era's fine literature, however, was its verse drama, plays in which the dialogue consists mostly or entirely of poetry. Several outstanding dramatists appeared, none more notable than William Shakespeare; and by the end of the 16th century, London had more theaters than any other city in Europe.

Shakespeare's Theater

The World's a Stage From the early 1590s, Shakespeare was affiliated with a theater company known as the Lord Chamberlain's Men. Its chief sponsors were a father and son who served consecutively as England's Lord Chamberlain, an influential member of Elizabeth's court. Shakespeare not only wrote the company's plays but also was a company shareholder, or part owner, and even performed occasionally as an actor. In 1599, with the other company shareholders, he became part owner of the Globe Theatre, the new London home of the Lord Chamberlain's Men. Four years later, when Queen Elizabeth died, the company at the Globe acquired a new sponsor, King James I, and became known as the King's Men.

Located on the south bank of the Thames (tĕmz) River, just outside of central London, the Globe Theatre was a three-story wooden building that held up to 3,000 theatergoers. In the center was an open-air courtyard with a platform stage on which the plays were performed. Those paying the lowest admission charges, known as groundlings, stood in the pit, the part of the courtyard right near the stage. Wealthier theatergoers sat in the building's interior galleries, which surrounded all sides of the courtyard except for the part of the building directly behind the stage.

Insight and Excitement Judging from the success of Shakespeare's company, all classes of theatergoers seem to have enjoyed his plays. That's probably because they included something for everyone—powerful speeches, fancy sword fights, humor, eerie supernatural events, and insightful observations about human nature. Such a mixture was important to Shakespeare. As a playwright, he wanted to explore human behavior, to understand how different people deal with universal problems. Yet he was also part of a commercial venture, writing for an audience that wanted, first and foremost, to be entertained. He made sure that his plays included enough action and excitement to keep just about anyone interested. The groundlings were particularly loud in their appreciation, cheering the heroes, yelling insults at the villains, and laughing loudly at humorous characters and jokes. In fact, by the standards of today's theater, Elizabethan performances were rather rowdy events.

Since the Globe had no artificial lighting or heat, performances were given in daylight in warmer weather. The stage also had no scenery; usually, lines of dialogue told the audience where a scene was taking place.

Despite the lack of scenery, productions were by no means drab. Costumes could be quite ornate, and props such as swords, shields, and swirling banners added to the colorful display. From behind the stage came sound effects—the chiming of a clock, for instance, or the sound of a cannon. The stage had no curtain. Instead, performers usually walked on and off in full view of the audience.

THE GLOBE THEATRE

The Globe was rebuilt in 1996.

1. raised platform stage
2. the pit
3. inner balconies
4. doors for actors' entrances

Analyze Visuals

Activity Read **The World's a Stage** and look at the picture of the reconstructed Globe Theatre. How does the picture help you visualize what is described in the text? From where did the groundlings and the wealthier people watch the stage? According to the picture, which part of the building do you think offered the best view? *Possible answer: The picture helps the reader understand where the different types of theatergoers gathered and what the building and its stage looked like. The groundlings watched from the pit (#2); wealthier people watched from inner balconies (#3). The inner balconies would probably offer the best view because their height would allow viewers to see everything happening on the stage. The pit, however, offered only an eye-level view.*

READING SKILL

■ MAKE INFERENCES

Discuss whether theatergoers would have appreciated Shakespeare's plays as much if he had explored human behavior simply through dialogue and omitted dramatic action. *Possible answer: Theatergoers—from the wealthy to the groundlings—probably would not have enjoyed the plays as much, nor would they have grasped Shakespeare's exploration of human behavior as readily. Their chief wish was to be entertained. Shakespeare understood that wish, so he made sure that there was excitement and action in his plays, as well as meaningful dialogue.*

Analyze Visuals

Shakespeare's Life

Mystery Man Though the works of William Shakespeare have probably been seen or read by more people worldwide than those of any other author, the man himself remains something of a mystery. This is particularly true of his early life, before he became a famous playwright. Literary biographies were uncommon in the Elizabethan period, and Shakespeare did not belong to a prominent family. What we know of his early life and family background comes from scanty documentary evidence—church records and property deeds, for example.

A Small-Town Boy According to those records, an infant named William Shakespeare was baptized in April 1564 in the local church in Stratford-upon-Avon, a bustling town on the River Avon, northwest of London. His father was a tanner and glove-maker and also served as a local politician. It is likely that Shakespeare attended Stratford's grammar school, where he would have studied Latin, the language of ancient Rome; classical literature written in Latin; and translations from ancient Greek. It is here that he would have been introduced to the writings of the ancient Greek biographer Plutarch, whose *Parallel Lives* provides the historical basis for the events in *Julius Caesar.*

Shakespeare's birthplace at Stratford-upon-Avon

Off to London Records further tell us that in 1582 William Shakespeare married one Anne Hathaway, probably the daughter of a well-to-do Stratford farm family, and that over the next three years the couple had three children, an older daughter named Susanna and twins named Hamnet (a male) and Judith. After the birth of the twins in 1585, nothing is known about Shakespeare for the next several years, after which he turns up again, living in London and working as an actor and a playwright. Clearly he was recognized as a promising talent, for he became a shareholder in the prestigious acting company the Lord Chamberlain's Men, which had strong ties to Elizabeth's court. Shakespeare's plays helped make the company even more successful, and he was soon allowed—probably even encouraged—to give up acting in order to focus on his writing.

The Years of Fame By 1599, the year in which *Julius Caesar* was first produced, Shakespeare is known to have written 18 of his 38 plays, including early pieces such as his history *Richard III,* his comedy *The Taming of the Shrew,* and his tragedy *Romeo and Juliet.* He was also a rich man. As a shareholder in the Lord Chamberlain's Men, he was now one of the owners of the company's new home, the Globe Theatre. He also made money by having his plays produced and by publishing some of his nondramatic poetry, although his sonnets did not appear in print until 1609.

The Final Years About a year before the sonnets appeared, Shakespeare began curtailing his theater activities. He seems to have spent less time in London and more back in Stratford. He wrote no plays after 1613, when he probably moved back to Stratford permanently. No one knows for sure just when, where, or how he died, but his gravestone in Stratford's Holy Trinity Church lists the date of his death as April 23, 1616.

A scene from Franco Zeffirelli's 1990 film *Hamlet*

A scene from the film *O*, Tim Blake Nelson's 2001 update of *Othello*

Shakespeare's Legacy

The Test of Time Some of the most familiar lines in the English language come from the plays of Shakespeare: "Friends, Romans, countrymen, lend me your ears" *(Julius Caesar),* "O Romeo, Romeo! wherefore art thou Romeo?" *(Romeo and Juliet),* "To be or not to be" *(Hamlet).* Why do readers and theatergoers continue to enjoy Shakespeare's plays four centuries after they were written? One answer is that Shakespeare thoroughly understood the theater and knew all the tricks of stagecraft—how to move an audience, create an exciting scene, and sketch out a setting using only the spoken word. Another answer lies in Shakespeare's language— the beautiful lines and phrases that resound in the minds of all who experience his plays. No other writer, before or since, has developed the potential of the English language to such heights. Still another answer lies in Shakespeare's profound understanding of human psychology, revealed in the unforgettable characters he created. Today, as much as ever, to understand Shakespeare's plays is to understand what is most important about being human and about life.

OTHER PLAYS BY WILLIAM SHAKESPEARE

As You Like It (1599)
King Lear (1605)
Macbeth (1606)
The Merchant of Venice (1596–1597)
A Midsummer Night's Dream (1595–1596)
Richard II (1595)
The Tempest (1611)
Twelfth Night (1601–1602)

Author Online
Go to **thinkcentral.com.** KEYWORD: HML10-1189

THINK central

Analyze Visuals

Activity What do the photographs show? What do they and their captions indicate about the legacy of Shakespeare? *Possible answer: The photographs are stills from film productions of two of Shakespeare's plays:* Hamlet *and* Othello. *Both photographs show two characters speaking closely together, suggesting that character and dialogue remain central to modern versions of Shakespeare's plays. The photographs and captions relate to Shakespeare's legacy because they indicate that his plays are still relevant and able to be adapted and interpreted in many formats. Indeed, these plays reach more people today than they did in Shakespeare's lifetime.*

READING SKILL

■ IDENTIFY MAIN IDEAS

Ask students to identify the main idea of **The Test of Time.** *Possible answer: Shakespeare's plays remain popular because Shakespeare understood theater and knew how to hold an audience, because he wrote lines and phrases that still resonate with people, and because he understood timeless aspects of human psychology and of life itself.*

Focus and Motivate

COMMON CORE FOCUS

RL 3 Analyze how complex characters develop over the course of a text, interact with other characters, and advance the plot or develop the theme. **RL 5** Analyze how an author's choices concerning how to structure a text, order events within it, and manipulate time create effects such as mystery, tension, or surprise. **RL 9** Analyze how an author draws on and transforms source material in a specific work. **RL 10** Read and comprehend dramas. **L 6** Acquire domain-specific words.

Teach

Part 1: Characteristics of Shakespearean Tragedy

Main Character (Tragic Hero) Emphasize that the Shakespearean tragic hero is a powerful person who goes off course due to a weakness (such as ambition or jealousy) and who realizes his mistake too late. Encourage students to use a Three-Column Journal to explore the qualities of a tragic hero (in this case, Brutus), following these directions:

- In the first column, note key details about the tragic hero.
- In the second column, list the character's positive traits.
- In the third column, list the character's negative traits.
- Look for connections between the details and the traits that they suggest.

Tragic Hero: Brutus	Positive Traits	Negative Traits
leader in Republican Rome	patriotic	too trusting

 **BEST PRACTICES TOOLKIT—Transparency**
Three-Column Journal p. B10

Dramatic Conventions Point out that dramatic irony is largely a matter of plot and that soliloquy and aside are largely matters of language. Using the dramatic irony discussed in the text—Caesar's ignorance of the plot against him—discuss what might be said in a soliloquy by Caesar and in asides by the people who are plotting against him.

 **BEST PRACTICES TOOLKIT—Transparency**
Core Analysis Frame: Drama pp. D21, D42

Shakespearean Drama
Essential Course of Study **ECOS**

In Elizabethan times, Shakespeare's plays captivated diverse crowds of theatergoers, ranging from wealthy nobility to common groundlings. But even Shakespeare may have been surprised that his works have so resonated with contemporary audiences, centuries after the plays were first performed. One reason Shakespeare has endured may be that his characters—figures from history and his imagination—transcend any particular time or place. Many of these characters are **archetypes**—familiar character types that appear over and over again in literature. The scheming characters and conspiracies at the heart of *The Tragedy of Julius Caesar* are as relevant today as they were in Shakespeare's time.

COMMON CORE

Included in this workshop:
RL 3 Analyze how complex characters develop over the course of a text, interact with other characters, and advance the plot or develop the theme.
RL 5 Analyze how an author's choices concerning how to structure a text, order events within it, and manipulate time create effects such as mystery, tension, or surprise. **RL 9** Analyze how an author draws on and transforms source material in a specific work. **RL 10** Read and comprehend dramas. **L 6** Acquire domain-specific words.

Part 1: Characteristics of Shakespearean Tragedy

Perhaps the most powerful of Shakespeare's plays are his tragedies. A **tragedy** is a drama in which a series of actions leads to the downfall of the main character, called the **tragic hero.** The plot builds to a **catastrophe,** or a disastrous final outcome, that usually involves the death of the hero and many others.

To create suspense before this inevitable outcome and to help the audience understand the characters, Shakespeare used certain dramatic conventions—the **soliloquy,** the **aside,** and **dramatic irony**—which are described in the chart.

MAIN CHARACTER	DRAMATIC CONVENTIONS
Tragic Hero • is of high social rank—a king, a prince, or a general • has a **tragic flaw**—an error in judgment or a character defect—that ultimately leads to his or her downfall • suffers complete ruin or death • faces his or her downfall with courage and dignity 	*Dramatic Irony* • results when the audience knows more than one or more of the characters—for example, Caesar does not know that people are plotting against him, but the audience does • helps build suspense *Soliloquy* • is a speech given by a character alone on stage, used to reveal his or her private thoughts and feelings • may help the audience understand a character's motivation *Aside* • is a character's remark, either to the audience or to another character, that no one else on stage is supposed to hear • lets the audience in on a character's thoughts or secrets

---

DIFFERENTIATED INSTRUCTION

FOR STRUGGLING READERS

Note Taking For students who need help with note taking, hand out the note-taking copy master before discussing Part 1. Explain that some literary terms are key to understanding Shakespearean drama but that they apply to the reading of modern plays, as well. Have students record notes on the copy master as you discuss the definition of each boldfaced term in Part 1.

archetypes
tragedy
tragic hero
catastrophe

tragic flaw
dramatic irony
soliloquy
aside

When you teach Part 2, have students record notes about the remaining terms.

 **RESOURCE MANAGER—Copy Master**
Note Taking p. 9

MODEL 1: TRAGIC HERO

Many critics believe that the tragic hero in *Julius Caesar* is not Caesar himself but Brutus, a respected Roman. As you read this excerpt, consider what Brutus' words reveal about his character.

---

from  Act One

Scene 2   Lines 79–89

Brutus. What means this shouting? I do fear the people
80 Choose Caesar for their king.
    Cassius.   Ay, do you fear it?
    Then must I think you would not have it so.
    Brutus. I would not, Cassius, yet I love him well.
    But wherefore do you hold me here so long?
    What is it that you would impart to me?
85 If it be aught toward the general good,
    Set honor in one eye and death i' the other,
    And I will look on both indifferently;
    For let the gods so speed me as I love
    The name of honor more than I fear death.

85–87 Brutus declares that he would not care whether he faced death if the matter Cassius has in mind concerns the public welfare (**general good**).

Close Read

1. Reread the boxed lines. What noble qualities does Brutus display? Cite specific details to support your answer.

2. What possible flaw might Brutus' mindset suggest?

MODEL 2: SOLILOQUY

Early in the play, Brutus must make a critical choice. Should he continue to live under Caesar's rule, or should he assassinate Caesar before the dictator becomes too power-hungry? Notice what you learn about Brutus from this soliloquy.

---

from  Act Two

Scene 1   Lines 10–17

10 **Brutus.** It must be by his death; and for my part,
    I know no personal cause to spurn at him,
    But for the general. He would be crowned.
    How that might change his nature, there's the question.
    It is the bright day that brings forth the adder,
15 And that craves wary walking. Crown him that,
    And then I grant we put a sting in him
    That at his will he may do danger with.

10–12 It must... general: Caesar would need to be killed, and I have no personal reason to attack him, only concern for the general welfare.

15 craves: demands.

Close Read

1. In the boxed text, Brutus compares Caesar to a poisonous snake (adder). Explain how this analogy helps you understand Brutus' concern about Caesar.

2. What is Brutus' motive for opposing Caesar? Given what you've just learned about Brutus, does his motive surprise you? Explain.

MODEL 1: TRAGIC HERO
Close Read

1. ***Possible answer:*** *Brutus displays selflessness and courage. He indicates that he would be willing to die to aid "the general good" (lines 85–87), and he emphasizes his feeling by taking an oath to the gods (line 88).*

   IF STUDENTS NEED HELP... Problems with comprehension may lie in a lack of familiarity with Shakespearean language. Show students how the side note provides a paraphrase and how the paraphrase signals the qualities of courage and selflessness.

2. ***Possible answer:*** *Brutus' flaw may be that he is too idealistic and perhaps unable to see himself realistically. He thus may be duped into joining a noble-sounding but destructive cause.*

MODEL 2: SOLILOQUY
Close Read

1. ***Possible answer:*** *Most people would be fearful of a poisonous snake. Saying that crowning Caesar would be like making a snake poisonous ("put[ting] a sting" into it, line 16) indicates Brutus' fear of how gaining kingly power might turn Caesar into a harmful person.*

2. ***Possible answer:*** *Brutus' motive is not personal; rather, he is motivated by concern for the Roman Republic and its people, both of which he fears may suffer if Caesar becomes king. This motive is consistent with Brutus' statement in Model 1 that he values the public good above his own welfare.*

FOR ENGLISH LANGUAGE LEARNERS

Language: Skill Words Point out that some literary terms in this workshop have everyday meanings related to, but not exactly the same as, their literary meanings. Write the words *tragedy, hero, catastrophe,* and *aside* on the board. To the left of each word, write the meaning as provided by students, based on this workshop. Then have students (using a dictionary, if needed) supply an everyday meaning for each word. As you note their responses to the right of each word, compare and contrast the meanings.

FOR ADVANCED LEARNERS/PRE–AP

Analyze Character Ask students to describe Brutus, based on what they have read in the two models. Have students list and share some questions about what more they would want to learn about Brutus as they read the play.

Online Remediation

Are your students struggling with text analysis skills? Consider assigning them one or more **Level Up Online Tutorials** as remediation before beginning this unit. Log in to **thinkcentral.com** to view a list of the skills addressed by **Level Up**.

Part 2: The Language of Shakespeare

Blank Verse To help students sense the rhythm of blank verse, have them read the two italicized lines aloud at least twice. The first time, have students tap their desks or clap their hands at each stressed syllable. The second time, have them read the lines as if speaking them naturally. Invite comments about the differences in the rhythms of the two readings. Explain that although actors speak the lines with a natural, conversational rhythm, the iambic meter can be sensed, just the same.

Rhetorical Devices As students read the chart, note the following:

- Repetition and parallelism can occur over several lines, not just in the concentrated examples in the chart.

- Rhetorical questions are asked without the expectation of an answer; rather, they are meant chiefly to make a point and to get the audience to think.

Then challenge students to develop original examples of each type of rhetorical device, such as these:

- *Repetition:* "I come before you to discuss a problem. I come before you to suggest a solution."

- *Parallelism:* "I ask you to listen, to think, and to join me in taking action."

- *Rhetorical Questions:* "How much longer must we wait for reform?"

CHECK UNDERSTANDING

Have students write the main idea they learned about Shakespearean drama and the main idea they learned about Shakespearean language.

Part 2: The Language of Shakespeare

Shakespearean language is more grand, more rhythmic, and, admittedly, less comprehensible than everyday modern speech. If you familiarize yourself with Shakespeare's language, though, you will find yourself getting caught up in the intriguing plot that drives *Julius Caesar*.

BLANK VERSE

Shakespeare's plays are **verse dramas,** in which most of the dialogue is written in the metrical patterns of poetry. Shakespeare wrote primarily in **blank verse,** or unrhymed lines of iambic pentameter. **Iambic pentameter** is a pattern of rhythm that has five unstressed syllables (˘), each followed by a stressed syllable (´). Read these lines aloud, noticing how the rhythm mimics that of everyday speech:

> *Such men as he be never at heart's ease*
> *Whiles they behold a greater than themselves,*

Most of *Julius Caesar* is written in blank verse. In some places, however, Shakespeare broke the pattern to vary the rhythm, create dramatic tension, or distinguish certain characters from others.

RHETORICAL DEVICES

Julius Caesar is about power, ambition, and betrayal. The characters are constantly trying to persuade themselves, each other, and the audience of the rightness of their cause. As a result, the play is full of speeches that make masterful use of rhetorical devices, such as those shown in the chart.

RHETORICAL DEVICE	EXAMPLE
REPETITION the use of words and phrases more than once to emphasize ideas	Therein, ye gods, you make the weak most strong; Therein, ye gods, you tyrants do defeat. —Act One, Scene 3, Lines 91–92
PARALLELISM the repetition of grammatical structures to express ideas that are related or of equal importance	Not that I loved Caesar less, but that I loved Rome more. —Act Three, Scene 2, Line 20
RHETORICAL QUESTIONS the use of questions that require no answer to make the speaker's rightness seem self-evident	Wherein hath Caesar thus deserved your loves? Alas, you know not! —Act Three, Scene 2, Lines 232–233

ELIZABETHAN WORDS TO KNOW

Here are words that you will encounter often while reading *Julius Caesar*:

an: if

aught: anything

beseech: beg

but: only

durst: dared

ere: before

hie: hurry

hither: here

mark: notice

marry: a short form of "by the Virgin Mary" and so a mild exclamation

prithee: pray thee, or please

save: except

soft: wait a minute

thither: there

wherefore: why

whither: when

withal: also

DIFFERENTIATED INSTRUCTION

FOR STRUGGLING READERS

Comprehension: Elizabethan Words After students have read the list of *ELIZABETHAN WORDS TO KNOW* at least twice, have them work in pairs to create everyday statements and questions and to rephrase them using the Elizabethan words. Provide these examples:

"Please wait a minute!" → "Prithee, soft!"

"If they want anything, they need only ask." → "An they want aught, they need but ask."

FOR ENGLISH LANGUAGE LEARNERS

Vocabulary: Multiple-Meaning Words Call students' attention to the fact that some words listed in *ELIZABETHAN WORDS TO KNOW* exist in modern English but with different meanings. These words are *an, but, mark, marry, save,* and *soft.* Write these words on the board, then call on volunteers to explain each word as it is used today. Write the modern definition next to each word.

MODEL 1: BLANK VERSE

In the following excerpt, Casca, one conspirator plotting against Caesar, speaks excitedly to the senator Cicero about a violent thunderstorm that is occurring. As you read, notice the rhythmic variation in the lines.

from

Scene 3

Lines 3–13

Casca. Are you not moved when all the sway of earth
Shakes like a thing unfirm? O Cicero,
5 I have seen tempests when the scolding winds
Have rived the knotty oaks, and I have seen
The ambitious ocean swell and rage and foam
To be exalted with the threat'ning clouds;
But never till tonight, never till now,
10 Did I go through a tempest dropping fire.
Either there is a civil strife in heaven,
Or else the world, too saucy with the gods,
Incenses them to send destruction.

3 sway of earth: the natural order of things.

5 tempests: storms.

6 rived: torn.

8 To be exalted with: to raise themselves to the level of.

11–13 Either . . . destruction: Either there is a civil war in heaven or the world has so insulted the gods that they want to destroy us.

Close Read

1. Read the boxed lines aloud and scan the stressed and unstressed syllables. Where are the breaks in the pattern?

2. Point out the key words that are emphasized by the rhythm in lines 3–7. Why might Shakespeare have chosen to stress them?

MODEL 2: RHETORICAL DEVICES

This speech is given by Marullus, a Roman official loyal to Caesar's rival, Pompey. As the play opens, Romans take to the streets to celebrate Caesar's victory over Pompey, an occasion that spurs the official's anger. What rhetorical devices does Marullus use in his address to the crowd?

from

Act One

Scene 1

Lines 36–42 and 48–51

Marullus. . . . O you hard hearts, you cruel men of Rome!
Knew you not Pompey? Many a time and oft
Have you climbed up to walls and battlements,
To tow'rs and windows, yea, to chimney tops,
40 Your infants in your arms, and there have sat
The livelong day, with patient expectation,
To see great Pompey pass the streets of Rome. . . .

And do you now put on your best attire?
And do you now cull out a holiday?
50 And do you now strew flowers in his way
That comes in triumph over Pompey's blood?

37 Pompey: a former Roman ruler defeated by Caesar in 48 B.C. Pompey was murdered a year after his defeat.

49 cull out: select.

Close Read

1. Consider the use of parallelism in the boxed lines. What words or phrases are parallel?

2. Notice the rhetorical questions that Marullus asks in line 37 and in lines 48–51. Through this rhetorical device, what is he trying to emphasize?

MODEL 1: BLANK VERSE
Close Read

1. **Possible answer:** *Slight variations are possible; but in this scansion, the breaks occur in lines 4, 5, and 7:*

˘ / ˘ / ˘ / ˘ / ˘ /
Are you not moved when all the sway of earth

/ ˘ ˘ / ˘ / ˘ / /˘˘
Shakes like a thing unfirm? O Cicero,

/ ˘ / ˘ / ˘ / ˘ /
I have seen tempests when the scolding winds

˘ / ˘ / ˘ / ˘ / ˘ /
Have rived the knotty oaks, and I have seen

˘ ˘ / ˘ / ˘ / ˘ / ˘ /
The ambitious ocean swell and rage and foam

2. **Possible answer:** *Emphasized words include "moved," "sway," "earth," "Shakes," "unfirm," "tempests," "scolding winds," "rived," "knotty oaks," "ambitious ocean," "swell," "rage," and "foam." Shakespeare might have emphasized these words to convey both Casca's excitement and the severity of the storm that Casca describes.*

MODEL 2: RHETORICAL DEVICES
Close Read

1. **Possible answer:** *The parallel phrases are "to walls and battlements," "To tow'rs and windows," and "to chimney tops."*

2. **Possible answer:** *Marullus' question in line 37 emphasizes the people's prior support of Pompey. His questions in lines 48–51 emphasize what he sees as the hypocrisy of the people in so quickly switching their loyalty to Caesar, the general who defeated Pompey.*

FOR STRUGGLING READERS

Analysis Support: Inverted Word Order
Point out that in lines of poetry, word order may be inverted, usually to preserve rhythm. If the reader mentally switches the order to reflect modern English, a difficult line can become clear. For example, "Knew you not Pompey?" (line 37) can be updated to "Didn't you know Pompey?" Elicit that the beginning of line 38, "Have you climbed," becomes "You have climbed" in modern English.

FOR ADVANCED LEARNERS/PRE–AP

Research Rhetorical Devices Explain that the techniques discussed in Part 2 are only three of the dozens of rhetorical devices that writers and speakers use to make their ideas more powerful or memorable. Invite small groups of students to research these additional rhetorical devices:

allusion	hyperbole
antithesis	litotes
enumeratio	metonymy
exemplum	sententia

Part 3: Reading Shakespearean Drama

Reading Tragedy Point out that the strategies listed can be used in reading a wide range of plays, including modern ones. Shakespeare, however, uses fewer stage directions than most modern playwrights do. To illustrate, direct students to line 24. Explain that a modern playwright might have included a stage direction indicating Caesar's tone (such as "arrogantly") but that Shakespeare leaves the interpretation of the line up to the actor or reader. Suggest that students ask themselves as they read, "How would I say this if I were the actor?"

Reading Shakespeare's Language Emphasize the importance of rereading, explaining that the more familiar students become with Shakespeare's language, the more natural the language will sound. Encourage students to consider these rereading options when approaching a passage from *Julius Caesar*:

- First read the passage without referring to the side notes, just to get a feel for the language; then reread it, using the side notes.

- First read the passage, using the side-notes to aid understanding; then reread the passage by itself to get a feel for the language.

To illustrate the concept of paraphrasing, have students turn back to page 1191 and reread Scene 2, lines 85–89. Model paraphrasing the passage so that it reads something like this: "If you want to tell me anything that will be good for Rome, then—whether it is a matter of honor or a matter of death—I will listen. May the gods help me as long as I love honor more than I fear death."

Part 3: Reading Shakespearean Drama

Understanding Shakespearean drama can be challenging for modern readers. Unusual vocabulary and grammatical structures can be difficult to decipher, and certain dramatic conventions can be tricky to track. Use these strategies to help you appreciate and analyze *Julius Caesar*.

READING TRAGEDY

- Study the opening **cast of characters,** which in *Julius Caesar* will tell you who is conspiring against the title character and who is supporting him.

- Try to visualize the setting and the action by using information in the **stage directions,** the **dialogue,** and the **synopsis** at the beginning of each scene.

- Keep track of the characters, and think about what their speech and actions reveal about their traits. Caesar, Cassius, Brutus, and Mark Antony are the ones to watch in *Julius Caesar*. At the end, consider how closely each fits the model of a **tragic hero.**

- Note examples of **foreshadowing,** using a chart like the one shown. Think about how each example can help you both **predict** events and better understand the characters' personalities.

- As you read each **scene,** consider it both in isolation and in how it contributes to the plot as a whole.

- Keep in mind the **historical background** on page 1199 as you read the play. *Julius Caesar* is based on ancient Roman figures and events that Shakespeare views from an Elizabethan perspective. Shakespeare knew his audience had divided opinions about Caesar, and he exploits that tension throughout the play.

READING SHAKESPEARE'S LANGUAGE

- Use the **side notes,** context clues, and the word list on page 1192 to help you understand unfamiliar words and expressions.

- Be aware that the English spoken in Shakespeare's time contains grammatical forms and structures that are no longer used today. Using a chart like the one shown, jot down difficult lines and then reword them to read like modern speech.

- Remember that the end of a line does not necessarily mean the end of a thought. Look closely at each line's punctuation, and try to figure out the meaning of the complete sentence or phrase.

- Paraphrase passages to help you understand characters' public personas as well as their private schemes. When you **paraphrase** a passage, you restate its key points in your own words.

STRATEGIES IN ACTION

Act One

Scene 2   Lines 22–24

Caesar. What say'st thou to me now? Speak once again.

Soothsayer. Beware the ides of March.

Caesar. He is a dreamer; let us leave him. Pass.

Example of Foreshadowing	My Impressions
Soothsayer (fortune-teller) gives Caesar a mysterious warning about March 15 (ides)	• shows that Caesar is not superstitious or easily rattled • suggests that something terrible may happen to Caesar on that day

Lines from Play	Modern Rewording
"…you and I will yet ere day See Brutus at his house. Three parts of him Is ours already, and the man entire Upon the next encounter yields him ours." (Act One, Scene 3, Lines 153–156)	Before the end of the day, you and I will see Brutus at his house. We've already won over three parts of him. The next time we see him, we'll win him over entirely.

DIFFERENTIATED INSTRUCTION

FOR STRUGGLING READERS

Note Taking For students who need help with note taking, hand out the second note-taking copy master before discussing Part 3. Explain that this copy master is about reading tools and strategies for understanding Shakespearean tragedy and Shakespearean language and that students can use the tools and strategies throughout the whole play.

 RESOURCE MANAGER—Copy Master
Note Taking p. 10

FOR ENGLISH LANGUAGE LEARNERS

Language: Skill Words The **READING TRAGEDY** section includes terms that students have seen in previous units but that are not redefined here. If students need a refresher, have them use resources in this text or a dictionary to define these terms:

cast of characters	foreshadowing
stage directions	predict
dialogue	scene
synopsis	historical background
tragic hero	

MODEL: READING SHAKESPEAREAN DRAMA

This scene takes place on the streets as Caesar returns from a public festival. Many characters are on stage at the same time, but Brutus and Cassius speak privately in asides, as do Caesar and Antony. Use the stage directions and sidenotes to help you understand the scene.

from
Act One

Scene 2   Lines 178–201

[*Voices and music are heard approaching.*]

Brutus. The games are done, and Caesar is returning.

Cassius. As they pass by, pluck Casca by the sleeve,
180 And he will (after his sour fashion) tell you
What hath proceeded worthy note today.

[*Reenter* Caesar *and his train of followers.*]

Brutus. I will do so. But look you, Cassius!
The angry spot doth glow on Caesar's brow,
And all the rest look like a chidden train.
185 Calpurnia's cheek is pale, and Cicero
Looks with such ferret and such fiery eyes
As we have seen him in the Capitol,
Being crossed in conference by some senators.

Cassius. Casca will tell us what the matter is.

[Caesar *looks at* Cassius *and turns to* Antony.]

190 **Caesar.** Antonius.

Antony. Caesar?

Caesar. Let me have men about me that are fat,
Sleek-headed men, and such as sleep o' nights.
Yond Cassius has a lean and hungry look;
195 He thinks too much, such men are dangerous.

Antony. Fear him not, Caesar, he's not dangerous.
He is a noble Roman, and well given.

Caesar. Would he were fatter! But I fear him not.
Yet if my name were liable to fear,
200 I do not know the man I should avoid
So soon as that spare Cassius. . . .

181 worthy note: worthy of notice.

184 chidden train: a group of followers who have been scolded.

185–188 Cicero was a highly respected senator. Brutus says he has the angry look of a **ferret** (a fierce little animal), the look he gets when other senators disagree with him.

190–214 Brutus and Cassius take Casca aside. The conversation Caesar has with Antony is not heard by any of the other characters around them.

197 Antony says that Cassius, despite his appearance, is a supporter of Caesar.

Close Read

1. Paraphrase what Cassius is saying to Brutus in lines 179–181.

2. Reread the boxed lines and visualize the action unfolding in your mind. Cite details from the stage directions and Brutus' dialogue that helped you form a mental image of the characters' movements.

3. Consider what Caesar says about Cassius in lines 192–195. What do his words reveal about the character traits of Cassius and of Caesar himself?

4. How do you think Caesar will act toward Cassius in the future? Give reasons to support your prediction.

DIFFERENTIATED INSTRUCTION

FOR STRUGGLING READERS

Comprehension: Summary Ask pairs of students to collaborate on a two- or three-sentence summary of the passage on this page. *Possible answer: Caesar and his followers are returning from a public festival. Cassius and Brutus remark upon the mood of Caesar's group. Caesar notices them; he comments that Cassius is dangerous but claims that he does not fear Cassius.* Invite students to comment upon the reading strategies that helped them create the summaries.

FOR ENGLISH LANGUAGE LEARNERS

Language: Conjunctions Discuss with students the use of coordinating conjunctions in this passage's dialogue.

- *and*: introduces additional facts and details (lines 178, 184, 185, 186, 193, 194, and 197); expresses a result (line 180)

- *but*: expresses a contrast (lines 182 and 198)

- *yet*: expresses a contrast (line 199)

MODEL 1: READING SHAKESPEAREAN DRAMA

Close Read

1. *Possible answer: As Caesar and his crew pass by, stop Casca. He'll tell us (in his usual grumpy way) what important things happened today.*

2. *Possible answer: The stage directions help the reader visualize a powerful leader followed by an adoring throng. Brutus' dialogue helps the reader visualize an angry Caesar (line 183), a pale Calpurnia (line 185), and a fierce Cicero (lines 185–186).*

    IF STUDENTS NEED HELP . . . On the board, draw this simple diagram: Brutus and Cassius, side by side, are to one side of the front of the stage; Caesar, with Antony alongside him, enters and proceeds toward the front and center of the stage; followers trail after them, unidentified except for Casca. Urge students to keep this setup in mind as they read and to relate the image to the dialogue in these lines.

    ```
                              /////////
                               //////
                                ////
                                 ///
    Brutus  Cassius         Casca / /

                            Caesar  Anthony
    ```

3. *Possible answer: Caesar's words suggest that the "lean and hungry" Cassius has a keen, thoughtful mind but also that he seeks some kind of satisfaction. The words imply that Caesar feels insecure and threatened by powerful personalities such as Cassius and that he prefers meek followers.*

4. *Possible answer: Although he claims not to be afraid (line 198), Caesar sounds quite nervous about Cassius. The reference to avoiding Cassius (lines 199–201) suggests that Caesar plans to be wary of Cassius in the future.*

Practice and Apply

Part 4: Analyze the Text

Close Read

1. **Possible answer:** *Examples of rhetorical questions: "And why should Caesar be a tyrant then?" (line 103); "But, O grief, / Where hast thou led me?" (lines 111–112).* **Examples of parallelism:** *"I know he would not be a wolf / But that he sees the Romans are but sheep; / He were no lion, were not Romans hinds" (lines 104–106); "What trash is Rome, / What rubbish and what offal" (lines 108–109). Cassius wants Casca to accept the ideas that a weak-minded Roman public has made Caesar's rise possible and that Caesar deserves contempt for taking advantage of the people.*

2. **Possible answer:** *Cassius: "What am I saying? You might be a loyal supporter of Caesar and report my words to him. I'll pay the price then—but I don't really care because I'm armed and I'm indifferent to danger." Casca: "You're talking to me, and I'm not a tattletale. If you form a group to correct the wrongs you've just described, count me in. I will do as much for this cause as anyone."*

3. **Possible answer:** *The emphasized words are "honorable," "dangerous," and (to a slightly lesser extent) "consequence."*

Part 4: Analyze the Text

Use what you've learned about Shakespearean drama to analyze this scene from *Julius Caesar*. In the scene, Cassius finally persuades Casca to join the conspiracy against Caesar. When Cinna, another conspirator, enters, they discuss winning over Brutus. Notice how Cassius manipulates the others, and consider what effect the events in this scene will have on the play's plot.

from 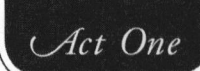 **Act One**

Scene 3   Lines 103–164

Cassius. And why should Caesar be a tyrant then?
Poor man! I know he would not be a wolf
105 But that he sees the Romans are but sheep;
He were no lion, were not Romans hinds.
Those that with haste will make a mighty fire
Begin it with weak straws. What trash is Rome,
What rubbish and what offal, when it serves
110 For the base matter to illuminate
So vile a thing as Caesar! But, O grief,
Where hast thou led me? I, perhaps, speak this
Before a willing bondman. Then I know
My answer must be made. But I am armed,
115 And dangers are to me indifferent.

Casca. You speak to Casca, and to such a man
That is no fleering telltale. Hold, my hand.
Be factious for redress of all these griefs,
And I will set this foot of mine as far
120 As who goes farthest.

Cassius.   There's a bargain made.
Now know you, Casca, I have moved already
Some certain of the noblest-minded Romans
To undergo with me an enterprise
Of honorable-dangerous consequence;
125 And I do know, by this they stay for me
In Pompey's Porch; for now, this fearful night,
There is no stir or walking in the streets,
And the complexion of the element
In favor's like the work we have in hand,
130 Most bloody, fiery, and most terrible.

[*Enter* Cinna.]

Casca. Stand close awhile, for here come one in haste.

Cassius. 'Tis Cinna. I do know him by his gait.
He is a friend. Cinna, where haste you so?

Side notes

103–111 Cassius says the only reason for Caesar's strength is the weakness of the Romans, who are female deer (**hinds**) and trash (**offal**) for allowing such a person as Caesar to come to power.

111–114 Cassius says that he will have to pay the penalty for his words if Casca is a submissive slave (**willing bondsman**).

117 fleering telltale: sneering tattletale.

118–120 Be factious . . . farthest: Form a group, or faction, to correct (**redress**) these wrongs, and I will go as far as any other man.

125–126 by this . . . Porch: Right now, they wait (**stay**) for me at the entrance to the theater Pompey built.

128–130 the complexion . . . terrible: The sky (**element**) looks like the work we have ahead of us—bloody, full of fire, and terrible.

132 gait: manner of walking.

Close Read

1. Find examples of rhetorical questions and parallelism that Cassius uses in lines 103–115. What ideas does he want Casca to accept?

2. Reword the exchange between Cassius and Casca in lines 111–120 to sound like modern speech. Use the sidenotes to help you.

3. Read lines 121–124 aloud as you think Cassius would say them. What words are emphasized by the variation in the rhythm of line 124?

DIFFERENTIATED INSTRUCTION

FOR STRUGGLING READERS

Analysis Support: Reading Tragedy Point out ways in which the reading strategies on page 1194 can aid understanding of this page (lines 103–134):

- Based on the dialogue, you can assume that Cassius, Casca, and Cinna all would be listed among the conspirators in the play's **cast of characters.**

- The fact that there is only one **stage direction** emphasizes the importance of **dialogue.**

- The reference to bad weather (lines 128–130) is a **foreshadowing** of the turmoil that these characters may cause if Cassius' enterprise (lines 121–124) is carried out.

Explore Metaphor Discuss these metaphors in the dialogue on this page:

- a comparison of Caesar and his followers to animals (lines 104–106)

- a comparison of Caesar's ambition to a fire and his followers to straw (lines 107–108)

- a comparison of people to garbage (lines 108–110)

Elicit that Cassius uses these metaphors to express a negative view not only of Caesar but also of the Roman people.

FOR STRUGGLING READERS

Comprehension: Update the Scene After students have read and discussed the side notes and the scene on these two pages, call on three volunteers to play the parts of

Cinna. To find out you. Who's that? Metellus Cimber?

135 **Cassius.** No, it is Casca, one incorporate
To our attempts. Am I not stayed for, Cinna?

Cinna. I am glad on't. What a fearful night is this!
There's two or three of us have seen strange sights.

Cassius. Am I not stayed for? Tell me.

Cinna.   Yes, you are.

140 O Cassius, if you could
But win the noble Brutus to our party—

Cassius. Be you content. Good Cinna, take this paper
And look you lay it in the praetor's chair,
Where Brutus may but find it, and throw this

145 In at his window. Set this up with wax
Upon old Brutus' statue. All this done,
Repair to Pompey's Porch, where you shall find us.
Is Decius Brutus and Trebonius there?

Cinna. All but Metellus Cimber, and he's gone

150 To seek you at your house. Well, I will hie
And so bestow these papers as you bade me.

Cassius. That done, repair to Pompey's Theater.

[*Exit* Cinna.]

Come, Casca, you and I will yet ere day
See Brutus at his house. Three parts of him

155 Is ours already, and the man entire
Upon the next encounter yields him ours.

Casca. O, he sits high in all the people's hearts,
And that which would appear offense in us,
His countenance, like richest alchemy,

160 Will change to virtue and to worthiness.

Cassius. Him and his worth and our great need of him
You have right well conceited. Let us go,
For it is after midnight, and ere day
We will awake him and be sure of him.

[*Exeunt.*]

135–136 it is . . . stayed for: This is Casca, who is now part of our plan (**incorporate / To our attempts**). Are they waiting for me?

142–146 Cassius tells Cinna to place letters for Brutus at several locations, including the seat of the praetor, a position held by Brutus.

150–151 I will . . . bade me: I'll hurry (**hie**) to place (**bestow**) these papers as you instructed me.

154–156 Three parts . . . yields him ours: We've already won over three parts of Brutus. The next time we meet him, he will be ours completely.

157–160 he sits . . . worthiness: The people love Brutus. What would seem offensive if we did it will, like magic (**alchemy**), become good and worthy because of his involvement.

162 conceited: judged.

Close Read

4. Review the boxed details. What might the thunderstorm foreshadow about the conspirators' plans?

5. What qualities of Brutus make him so valued by the conspirators?

6. How would you describe the character of Cassius, judging by his words and actions in this scene? Support your answer.

Close Read

4. *Possible answer: The thunderstorm might foreshadow that something will go awry with the conspirators' plans or that the plans will result in an upset of society.*

5. *Possible answer: Brutus' nobility (line 141) and popularity (lines 157–160) make him valued by the conspirators.*

6. *Possible answer: Cassius' winning-over of Casca (lines 103–115) shows Cassius' intelligence and ability to manipulate. He is a calculating planner: In lines 142–148 he knows exactly what he wants Cinna to do in recruiting Brutus. He is also a master of "spin"; for example, in lines 128–130 he equates the storm with the work of the conspiracy, justifying the violent plan by equating it with a violent act of nature.*

IF STUDENTS NEED HELP . . . Work with them to complete a Character Traits and Textual Evidence transparency for this scene.

 BEST PRACTICES TOOLKIT—Transparency
Character Traits and Textual Evidence p. D6

Assess and Reteach

Assess

Have students summarize what they have learned from this workshop about reading Shakespearean drama. Discuss how the information helped them understand the excerpt from *Julius Caesar*, Act One, Scene 3, on these two pages.

Reteach

For students who are unable to apply the workshop skills to the excerpts from *Julius Caesar*, select from these reteaching options:

1. Review with them the note-taking copy masters for this workshop. Have students
   - take turns reading aloud the terms
   - take turns reading aloud their responses, having peers identify the applicable terms

2. Return to the excerpt from Act One, Scene 2 (Model 1). Guide students to use the skills and terms learned later in the workshop to help them understand that brief excerpt.

Cassius, Casca, and Cinna. Given a few minutes to prepare, the actors should improvise a dialogue in which they state the same basic ideas and feelings as Shakespeare's characters, but in modern language. Afterward, invite constructive comments from both the actors and the class.

FOR ENGLISH LANGUAGE LEARNERS

Culture: Connect Explain that the events of *Julius Caesar* had happened more than 1,600 years before Shakespeare wrote about them,

yet his audience found the play interesting because they could connect it to the politics of their own time and place. Ask students if they know of examples from history of leaders who quickly rose to power and faced plots against them. Invite volunteers to share information about any of them.

Focus and Motivate

COMMON CORE FOCUS

RL 1 Cite strong and thorough textual evidence to support analysis of what the text says explicitly as well as inferences drawn from the text. **RL 2** Determine the theme or central idea of a text. **RL 3** Analyze how complex characters with conflicting motivations develop, interact with others, and advance the plot or develop the theme. **RL 4** Determine the figurative and connotative meanings of words and phrases as they are used in a text. **RL 5** Analyze how an author's choices concerning how to structure a text and order events within it create such effects as mystery, tension, or surprise. **RL 9** Analyze how an author draws on and transforms source material in a specific work. **RL 10** Read and comprehend dramas. **RI 7** Analyze various accounts of a subject told in different mediums. **SL 3** Evaluate a speaker's point of view, reasoning, and use of evidence and rhetoric. **L 1b** Use various types of clauses to convey specific meanings and add variety and interest to writing.

SUMMARY

Julius Caesar begins in 44 B.C., as Caesar celebrates his victory in Rome's civil war. Commoners favor him and support his rule, but many Roman leaders find him too ambitious. While pretending loyalty, they plot his murder. Brutus, Cassius, and other conspirators murder Caesar. Mark Antony, devoted to Caesar, seeks revenge. He defeats the conspirators' armies and prompts Brutus and Cassius to kill themselves.

Can your CONSCIENCE mislead you?

Ask the question, and discuss the role of conscience in decision-making. Then have students complete the *QUICKWRITE* activity.

Selection Resources

Essential Course of Study ✓ **ECOS**

The Tragedy of Julius Caesar
Drama by William Shakespeare

Video link at **thinkcentral.com**

Can your CONSCIENCE mislead you?

COMMON CORE

RL 3 Analyze how complex characters with conflicting motivations develop, interact with others, and advance the plot or develop the theme. **RL 4** Determine the figurative and connotative meanings of words and phrases as they are used in a text. **RL 9** Analyze how an author draws on and transforms source material in a specific work. **RL 10** Read and comprehend dramas.

When making a difficult decision, you may be urged to let your conscience be your guide—in other words, to rely on an internal sense of what is right and wrong. But how foolproof is your conscience? In *The Tragedy of Julius Caesar*, a man guided by the highest ideals fails to foresee the consequences of his actions.

QUICKWRITE Think of a time when you made a wrong decision, even though your intention was good. Write a paragraph explaining why you had this unexpected outcome.

See resources on the **Teacher One Stop DVD-ROM** and on **thinkcentral.com**.

 Video link at **thinkcentral.com**

R **RESOURCE MANAGER UNIT 11**
Plan and Teach, pp. 11–17, 31–36, 45–50, 59–64, 73–80
Summary, pp. 19–22, 37–40, 51–54, 65–68, 81–84†‡*
Text Analysis and Reading Skill, pp. 23–26, 41–42, 55–56, 69–70, 85–86†*
Grammar and Style, p. 89

DIAGNOSTIC AND SELECTION TESTS
Selection Tests, pp. 311–330

BEST PRACTICES TOOLKIT
pp. C9, D9, B21, B20, B10, B39, A2, A57

INTERACTIVE READER

ADAPTED INTERACTIVE READER

ELL ADAPTED INTERACTIVE READER

TECHNOLOGY
- **Teacher One Stop DVD-ROM**
- **Student One Stop DVD-ROM**
- **PowerNotes DVD-ROM**
- **Audio Anthology CD**
- **GrammarNotes DVD-ROM**
- **Audio Tutor CD**
- **ExamView Test Generator** on the **Teacher One Stop**

THINK central

Video Trailer

Go to **thinkcentral.com** to preview the **Video Trailer** introducing this selection. Other features that support the selection include
- **PowerNotes** presentation
- **ThinkAloud** models to enhance comprehension
- **WordSharp** vocabulary tutorials
- interactive writing and grammar instruction

---

* Resources for Differentiation   † Also in Spanish   ‡ In Haitian Creole and Vietnamese

TEXT ANALYSIS: SHAKESPEAREAN TRAGEDY

A **tragedy** is a drama in which a series of actions leads to the downfall of the main character, or **tragic hero.** In Shakespeare's tragedies, the hero is usually the title character. However, many critics believe that the tragic hero of *Julius Caesar* is not Caesar but another character, a prominent Roman named Brutus.

As you read, pay attention to these characteristics of Shakespearean tragedy:

- Because the tragic hero is a person of high rank, his or her fate has an impact on all of society.

- The hero has a **tragic flaw**—a fatal error in judgment or a weakness in character—that contributes to his or her downfall.

- Characters sometimes reveal their motives in **soliloquies** or **asides,** speeches that express thoughts that are hidden from other characters.

READING STRATEGY: READING SHAKESPEAREAN DRAMA

Shakespeare's plays, with their unusual vocabulary, grammar, and word order, can be challenging for modern readers. The following reading strategies can help:

- Read the synopsis, or summary, at the beginning of each scene to get an idea of what will happen in the scene.

- If you have trouble understanding a passage, use the sidenotes to figure out the meaning of unfamiliar words and gain helpful information. However, you do not necessarily need to understand every word to understand and enjoy the play.

- Rearrange sentences that have unusual word order to create a familiar sentence structure.

- Use the stage directions and details in dialogue to help you visualize the play's settings and action.

- As you read, use a chart like the one shown to help you identify and analyze important characters in the play. Revise the chart as you learn more about the characters.

Important Characters	Who Are They?	Personality
Julius Caesar	dictator of Rome	

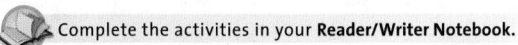

Complete the activities in your **Reader/Writer Notebook.**

Past and Present

Julius Caesar is a history play as well as a tragedy. For the Elizabethans, the ancient past offered important lessons about their own political problems. Like Rome under Caesar, England was governed by a strong ruler, Elizabeth I. The queen had survived several plots against her life, and by 1599, when Shakespeare wrote his play, she was an elderly woman. Many English people feared that her death would lead to civil unrest.

Caesar's Rise to Power

The story of Julius Caesar, a Roman general, politician, and orator who lived from 100 to 44 B.C., was well- known in Shakespeare's time. One of the greatest military leaders in Roman history, Caesar is famous for conquering Gaul, a land that corresponds roughly to modern-day France and Belgium. Caesar's growing power alarmed Rome's senators, who feared that he would seize control of the government. In 49 B.C., the Senate ordered him to give up his command in one of Rome's provinces. Caesar refused the order and crossed with his troops into Italy, starting a civil war. Caesar was opposed by Pompey, a former friend and ally. By 45 B.C., Caesar had defeated his opponents and was governing as an absolute ruler. Generous in victory, Caesar gave important positions to men who had recently been his enemies. However, many members of the nobility resented his disregard for their traditional authority, and some began to plot against him.

Bust of Julius Caesar

Author Online

Go to thinkcentral.com. KEYWORD: HML10-1199

THINK
central

1199

TEXT ANALYSIS

COMMON CORE
RL 3
RL 4
RL 5
RL 9

● *Model the Skill:*
SHAKESPEAREAN TRAGEDY

To model the skill of analyzing Shakespearean tragedy, have students read **Caesar's Rise to Power** and discuss possible tragic flaws of Caesar. Point out that he liked power too much and trusted people he should not have trusted.

GUIDED PRACTICE Ask students to name other tragic heroes they know of from literature or movies, along with these heroes' tragic flaws.

READING STRATEGY

COMMON CORE
RL 1
RL 10

■ *Model the Skill:* **READING SHAKESPEAREAN DRAMA**

Emphasize the importance of the scene summaries and the side notes. Direct students to page 1202, and point out the summary for Act One, Scene 1. Then have students skim through the side notes on the page. Read aloud lines 2–5, and model how to use the side notes—matching the side note to the correct lines of text and taking note of the boldfacing. Elicit that the side notes make the dialogue clearer to the modern reader.

GUIDED PRACTICE Ask students to read the rest of the side notes on page 1202. Have them summarize what is happening on the page.

R RESOURCE MANAGER—Copy Master
Reading Shakespearean Drama p. 25 (for student use while reading the selection)

DIFFERENTIATED INSTRUCTION

FOR ENGLISH LANGUAGE LEARNERS

Concept Support Point out to students that this play has five *acts* and that each act comprises *scenes*. Remind students of other terms used in the reading of dramatic works, including *cast, characters, stage, stage directions,* and *curtain*. Help students define each term. Point out that stage directions for this play are italicized (except for the names of characters) and that they appear within brackets.

FOR ADVANCED LEARNERS/PRE–AP

Compare and Contrast Rulers Note that *Julius Caesar* is both a historical play and a tragedy. Also tell students that they will learn only limited factual information about Caesar in this play. Have them research his life and write a brief biographical summary.

READ WITH A PURPOSE

Help students set a purpose for reading. Tell them to look for the steps taken by Brutus on his path from honored friend of Caesar at the beginning of Act One to his death on the battlefield at the end of Act Five.

GO BEHIND THE CURTAIN

COMMON CORE RI 7

As students read and discuss **Go Behind the Curtain,** explain that *stagecraft* refers to theatrical devices and techniques. Then have students turn to page 1213, the first appearance of the **Behind the Curtain** feature, and tell what the photographs show. *Possible answer: The photographs show set designs from various productions of* Julius Caesar. Point out that set design is one of the many elements of stagecraft.

READING STRATEGY

■ *Model the Skill:* MONITOR

Suggest that students place a bookmark at page 1201, which lists the play's cast of characters. Doing so will help them find the list if they need a quick refresher on the identity of a character, including the conspirators and the rulers after Caesar's death. Remind students to use their Reading Strategy charts to record information about the characters as they read.

1200

COMMON CORE RI 7

Go Behind the Curtain

This photograph shows the interior of London's Globe Theatre, a reconstruction of Shakespeare's original theater. As you read the play, you will see photographs from the Globe Theatre Company's 1999 production of *Julius Caesar*. Photographs from other productions appear in the **Behind the Curtain** feature pages, which explore the stagecraft used to create exciting theatrical productions of this famous play.

DIFFERENTIATED INSTRUCTION

FOR STRUGGLING READERS

Develop Reading Fluency To help students become comfortable with the names of the characters in the play, read the cast list aloud. Then have students practice reading the list aloud to gain an oral familiarity with the names. Point out that there are two characters named Cinna: one listed as a conspirator, the other identified as a poet. Also explain that *Caesar* is a title and that Octavius Caesar had that title because (in history as well as in the play) Julius Caesar had named him as his heir.

Distribute the copy masters and have students work in pairs or groups to practice fluency.

R RESOURCE MANAGER—Copy Master
Reading Fluency p. 29

The Tragedy of
JULIUS CÆSAR
William Shakespeare

CAST OF CHARACTERS

Julius Caesar

TRIUMVIRS AFTER THE DEATH OF JULIUS CAESAR

Octavius Caesar
Marcus Antonius
M. Aemilius Lepidus

SENATORS

Cicero
Publius
Popilius Lena

CONSPIRATORS AGAINST JULIUS CAESAR

Marcus Brutus
Cassius
Casca
Trebonius
Ligarius
Decius Brutus
Metellus Cimber
Cinna

Flavius and Marullus, *tribunes of the people*
Artemidorus of Cnidos, *a teacher of Rhetoric*

A Soothsayer
Cinna, *a poet*
Another Poet

FRIENDS TO BRUTUS AND CASSIUS

Lucilius
Titinius
Messala
Young Cato
Volumnius

SERVANTS TO BRUTUS

Varro
Clitus
Claudius
Strato
Lucius
Dardanius

Pindarus, *servant to Cassius*
Calpurnia, *wife to Caesar*
Portia, *wife to Brutus*
The Ghost of Caesar
Senators, Citizens, Guards, Attendants, Servants, etc.

TIME	PLACE
44 B.C.	Rome; the camp near Sardis; the plains of Philippi

1201

Practice and Apply

Get Into the Act
SUMMARY
As Act One opens, tribunes Marullus and Flavius criticize commoners who celebrate Julius Caesar's return. Caesar himself is met with a soothsayer's warning: "Beware the ides of March." Cassius and Brutus privately voice distrust of Caesar, even when they hear that he has refused the crown that Mark Antony has offered him. One month later, on a night filled with omens, Cassius meets other conspirators to plan Caesar's murder.

Analyze Visuals

Activity What part of the Globe Theatre does this photograph show? *Possible answer: the inner balconies as they would appear from the stage—that is, from the actors' perspective*

READING STRATEGY

■ PREDICT
Have students read through the cast list, noting the heading under which each character appears and any notes beside the names. Ask students what they can predict will happen in the play, based on this information. ***Possible answer:*** *Several people will conspire against Caesar. Brutus, who has many friends and servants, will be a key figure. Three people will rule after Caesar dies. Caesar's ghost will appear, perhaps to haunt those who had conspired against him.*

Resources for Act One

See resources on the **Teacher One Stop DVD-ROM** *and on* **thinkcentral.com**.

R RESOURCE MANAGER UNIT 11
Plan and Teach, pp. 11–17
Summary, pp. 19–22†‡*
Text Analysis and Reading Skill, pp. 23–26†*

DIAGNOSTIC AND SELECTION TESTS
Selection Tests, pp. 311–314

BEST PRACTICES TOOLKIT
Reporter's Questions, p. C9
Open Mind, p. D9
Sequence Chain, p. B21

INTERACTIVE READER

ADAPTED INTERACTIVE READER

ELL ADAPTED INTERACTIVE READER

TECHNOLOGY
- Teacher One Stop DVD-ROM
- Student One Stop DVD-ROM
- PowerNotes DVD-ROM
- Audio Anthology CD
- GrammarNotes DVD-ROM
- Audio Tutor CD
- ExamView Test Generator on the **Teacher One Stop**

Video Trailer
Go to **thinkcentral.com** to preview the **Video Trailer** introducing this selection. Other features that support the selection include
- **PowerNotes** presentation
- **ThinkAloud** models to enhance comprehension
- **WordSharp** vocabulary tutorials
- interactive writing and grammar instruction

---
* Resources for Differentiation   † Also in Spanish   ‡ In Haitian Creole and Vietnamese

JULIUS CAESAR **1201**

Practice and Apply

⚠ ENGLISH ROOTS

Point out that the word *war* (in the first paragraph of the introduction to the scene) is another English word from a Germanic root. *War* comes from the Middle English *werre*, which is related to the Germanic *werra*, meaning "strife."

Possible answer: *Answers will vary. The word* start *has an Indo-European base,* commence *is from a Latin root and affix, and* initiate *is from Latin.*

Scene 1 *A street in Rome.*

The play begins on February 15, the religious feast of Lupercal. Today the people have a particular reason for celebrating. Julius Caesar has just returned to Rome after a long civil war in which he defeated the forces of Pompey, his rival for power. Caesar now has the opportunity to take full control of Rome. ⚠

In this opening scene, a group of workmen, in their best clothes, celebrate in the streets. They are joyful over Caesar's victory. The workers meet Flavius and Marullus, two tribunes—government officials—who supported Pompey. The tribunes express their anger at the celebration, and one worker responds with puns. Finally, the two tribunes scatter the crowd.

Flavius. Hence! home, you idle creatures, get you home!
Is this a holiday? What, know you not,
Being mechanical, you ought not walk
Upon a laboring day without the sign
5 Of your profession? Speak, what trade art thou?

First Commoner. Why, sir, a carpenter.

Marullus. Where is thy leather apron and thy rule?
What dost thou with thy best apparel on?
You, sir, what trade are you?

10 **Second Commoner.** Truly sir, in respect of a fine workman I am
but, as you would say, a cobbler.

Marullus. But what trade art thou? Answer me directly.

Second Commoner. A trade, sir, that I hope I may use with a safe
conscience, which is indeed, sir, a mender of bad soles.

15 **Flavius.** What trade, thou knave? Thou naughty knave, what trade?

Second Commoner. Nay, I beseech you, sir, be not out with me.
Yet if you be out, sir, I can mend you.

Marullus. What mean'st thou by that? Mend me, thou saucy fellow?

Second Commoner. Why, sir, cobble you.

20 **Flavius.** Thou art a cobbler, art thou?

Second Commoner. Truly, sir, all that I live by is with
the awl. I meddle with no tradesman's matters nor
women's matters, but with all. I am indeed, sir, a
surgeon to old shoes. When they are in great
25 danger, I recover them. As proper men as ever trod
upon neat's leather have gone upon my handiwork.

⚠ ENGLISH ROOTS

English words stem from a variety of root languages. Many words come from Latin and Greek, but some, such as *begin*, come from Germanic origins. In Old English, *begin* was formed *beginnan*, from the German *beginnen*. Use a thesaurus to investigate synonyms of *begin*, then use a dictionary to determine the etymology of these words.

2–5 What, know . . . profession: Since you are craftsmen (**mechanical**), you should not walk around on a workday without your work clothes and tools (**sign / Of your profession**). *What is Flavius's attitude toward these workers?*

10–26 In this conversation, a shoemaker (**cobbler**) makes a series of puns about his trade, which Marullus and Flavius fail to understand. Imagine the workmen laughing as Marullus and Flavius grow increasingly angry, wondering what is so funny.

15–16 Flavius accuses the commoner of being a wicked, sly person (**naughty knave**), but the commoner begs Flavius not to be angry with him (**be not out with me**).

18 Marullus thinks the cobbler means "I can mend your behavior." He accuses the cobbler of being disrespectful (**saucy**).

21–23 The cobbler jokes about the similarity of **awl** (a shoemaker's tool) to the word *all*.

26 neat's leather: calfskin, used to make expensive shoes. The cobbler means that even rich people come to him for shoes.

Julius Caesar in the Globe Theatre's 1999 production

DIFFERENTIATED INSTRUCTION

FOR ENGLISH LANGUAGE LEARNERS

Task Support Have students read the question in the side note for lines 2–5. Remind students that Flavius is a tribune, not a craftsperson or common laborer. ***Possible answer:*** *Flavius has an attitude of superiority toward these workers, shown in his calling them "idle creatures." He seems offended that they are not doing their jobs (and, as the scene synopsis implies, he is also unhappy with them because they support Julius Caesar).*

FOR STRUGGLING READERS

Preview Have students read the italicized scene synopsis to give them an overview of Scene 1. Help them fill in a Reporter's Questions chart to record the key events.

Who is in this scene?	Marullus, Flavius, commoners
What are they doing?	reacting to Caesar's return

Where does the scene take place?	a street in Rome
When does the scene take place?	February 15 (the feast of Lupercal)
Why are the people joyful?	they are glad for Caesar's triumph
How do Marullus and Flavius feel?	they are angry about the defeat of Pompey

 BEST PRACTICES TOOLKIT—Transparency
Reporter's Questions p. C9

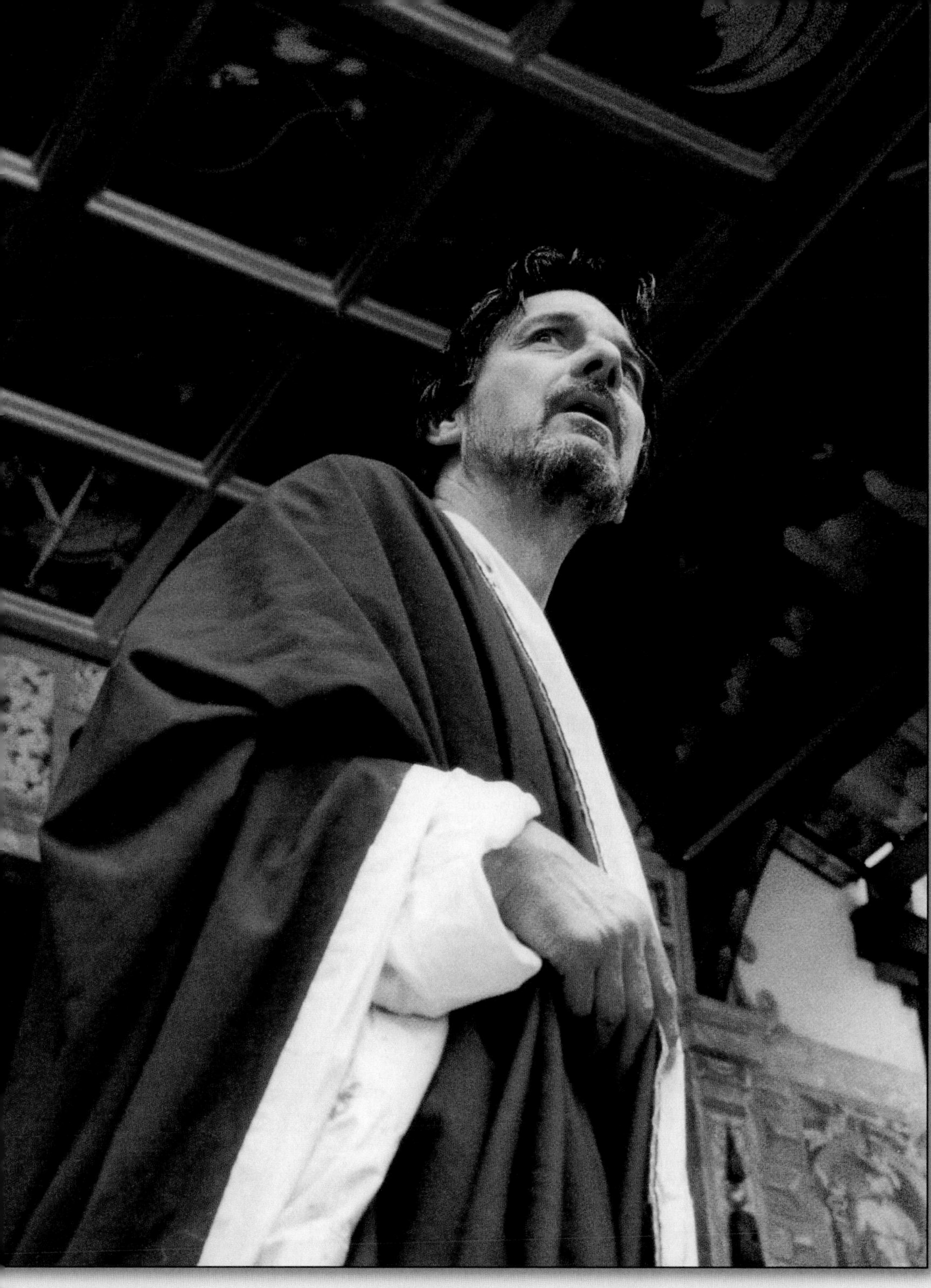

Reading Support

THINK central

This selection on **thinkcentral.com** includes embedded **ThinkAloud** models–students "thinking aloud" about the story to model the kinds of questions a good reader would ask about a selection.

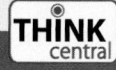

BACKGROUND

The Feast of Lupercal The celebration of Lupercal (or Lupercalia) honored the gods Lupercus and Faunus and the twin brothers Romulus and Remus, the legendary founders of Rome. Julius Caesar actually returned from Spain in October of 45 B.C.; but Shakespeare uses dramatic license to make a connection between the founders of Rome (Romulus and Remus) and Caesar, founder of the new Rome. Furthermore, since the Romans worshiped many gods, linking Caesar's return with a religious holiday makes Caesar seem godlike.

Republican Rome Although Caesar was a military dictator, Rome was officially considered a republic. Its chief officials were the triumvirs, the rulers who shared powers as a threesome; the senators, who represented nobility and landowners; and the tribunes, who represented the common people.

Analyze Visuals

Activity After you have read the scene synopsis, look at this photograph of an actor portraying Julius Caesar. How might the angle suggest his position in Rome? ***Possible answer:*** *The photograph shows Caesar in an elevated position, as if the viewer were beneath him and looking up at him. As the play opens, Caesar is in a position of power, and the commoners "look up to," or admire, him.*

FOR STRUGGLING READERS

In combination with the *Audio Anthology CD,* use one or more Targeted Passages (pp. 1204, 1211, 1218) to ensure that students focus on key story events, concepts, and skills. Targeted Passages are also good for English learners.

FOR ENGLISH LANGUAGE LEARNERS

Vocabulary Support Explain that Shakespeare often included puns, or humorous uses of words that suggest two or more meanings, in dialogue. For example, in Shakespeare's time, the word *cobbler* (line 11) meant both "a person who repairs shoes" and "a clumsy worker." Discuss these other puns on page 1202: "mender of bad soles" (lines 14–18), "awl" (lines 21–23), and "recover" (line 25).

Can your
CONSCIENCE
mislead you?

Discuss Given the conversation in lines 53–62, why do Marullus and Flavius think that the commoners should have a guilty conscience and show remorse for their behavior? *Possible answer: Flavius thinks that the commoners should have a guilty conscience about having abandoned their jobs (lines 1–5 and 27–28). More important, as Marullus points out, the commoners should feel guilty about cheering for Caesar when once they had been strong supporters of Pompey. Marullus and Flavius agree that the commoners should have such a guilty conscience that they should weep and beg for mercy from the gods.*

Flavius. But wherefore art not in thy shop today?
Why dost thou lead these men about the streets?

Second Commoner. Truly, sir, to wear out their shoes, to get
30 myself into more work. But indeed, sir, we make holiday to see
Caesar and to rejoice in his triumph.

Marullus. Wherefore rejoice? What conquest brings he home?
What tributaries follow him to Rome
To grace in captive bonds his chariot wheels?
35 You blocks, you stones, you worse than senseless things!
O you hard hearts, you cruel men of Rome!
Knew you not Pompey? Many a time and oft
Have you climbed up to walls and battlements,
To tow'rs and windows, yea, to chimney tops,
40 Your infants in your arms, and there have sat
The livelong day, with patient expectation,
To see great Pompey pass the streets of Rome.
And when you saw his chariot but appear,
Have you not made an universal shout,
45 That Tiber trembled underneath her banks
To hear the replication of your sounds
Made in her concave shores?
And do you now put on your best attire?
And do you now cull out a holiday?
50 And do you now strew flowers in his way
That comes in triumph over Pompey's blood?
Be gone!
Run to your houses, fall upon your knees,
Pray to the gods to intermit the plague
55 That needs must light on this ingratitude.

Flavius. Go, go, good countrymen, and for this fault
Assemble all the poor men of your sort;
Draw them to Tiber banks, and weep your tears
Into the channel, till the lowest stream
60 Do kiss the most exalted shores of all.

[*Exeunt all the* Commoners.]

See, whe'r their basest metal be not moved.
They vanish tongue-tied in their guiltiness.
Go you down that way towards the Capitol;
This way will I. Disrobe the images
65 If you do find them decked with ceremonies.

Marullus. May we do so?
You know it is the feast of Lupercal.

Flavius. It is no matter. Let no images
Be hung with Caesar's trophies. I'll about

---

27 wherefore: why.

33–34 What . . . wheels: What captured prisoners march chained to the wheels of his chariot?

37 Pompey: a former Roman ruler, defeated by Caesar in 48 B.C. Pompey was murdered a year after his defeat.

① **Targeted Passage**

45 Tiber: a river that runs through Rome.

46 replication: echo.

49 cull out: select.

51 Pompey's blood: Caesar is returning to Rome in triumph after defeating Pompey's sons in Spain.

54–55 intermit . . . ingratitude: hold back the deadly illness that might be just punishment for your behavior.

58–60 weep . . . of all: weep into the Tiber River until it overflows.

Exeunt (Latin): They leave.

61 Flavius and Marullus are now alone, having shamed the workers into leaving the street. Flavius says that they will now see if they have touched (**moved**) the workers' poor characters (**basest metal**).

64–65 Disrobe . . . ceremonies: Strip the statues of any decorations you find on them.

DIFFERENTIATED INSTRUCTION

FOR STRUGGLING READERS

① **Targeted Passage** [Lines 32–52]

This passage uses the words of one character to define the play's main conflict.

- How does Marullus insult the commoners? (lines 35–36)

- According to Marullus, what did the commoners once think about Pompey? (lines 37–47)

- How do the commoners now treat Caesar? What does Marullus think that they should do instead? Why? (lines 48–51, 52)

FOR ENGLISH LANGUAGE LEARNERS

Vocabulary: Outdated Forms Have students begin a language journal. Explain that some words and expressions in the play are outdated. Provide these terms and definitions; then have students reread the lines, substituting the definitions.

- *wherefore art not* (line 27), "why aren't you"

- *dost thou* (line 28), "do you"

- *Many a time and oft* (line 37), "Often"

- *whe'r* (line 61), "whether"

70 And drive away the vulgar from the streets.
   So do you too, where you perceive them thick.
   These growing feathers plucked from Caesar's wing
   Will make him fly an ordinary pitch,
   Who else would soar above the view of men
75 And keep us all in servile fearfulness.

   [*Exeunt.*]

Scene 2   *A public place in Rome.*

As Caesar attends the traditional race at the festival of Lupercal, a soothsayer warns him to beware the ides of March, or March 15. (The middle day of each month was called the ides.) When Caesar leaves, Cassius and Brutus speak. Cassius tries to turn Brutus against Caesar by using flattery, examples of Caesar's weaknesses, and sarcasm about Caesar's power. Caesar passes by again, expressing his distrust of Cassius. Cassius and Brutus learn of Caesar's reluctant rejection of a crown that his friend Antony has offered him. They agree to meet again to discuss what must be done about Caesar.

[*A flourish of trumpets announces the approach of Caesar. A large crowd of Commoners has assembled; a* Soothsayer *is among them. Enter* Caesar, *his wife* Calpurnia, Portia, Decius, Cicero, Brutus, Cassius, Casca, *and* Antony, *who is stripped for running in the games.*]

Caesar. Calpurnia.

Casca.   Peace, ho! Caesar speaks.

Caesar.   Calpurnia.

Calpurnia. Here, my lord.

Caesar. Stand you directly in Antonius' way
   When he doth run his course. Antonius.

5 **Antony.** Caesar, my lord?

Caesar. Forget not in your speed, Antonius,
   To touch Calpurnia; for our elders say
   The barren, touched in this holy chase,
   Shake off their sterile curse.

Antony.   I shall remember.
10 When Caesar says "Do this," it is performed.

Caesar. Set on, and leave no ceremony out.

[*Flourish of trumpets. Caesar starts to leave.*]

Soothsayer. Caesar!

Caesar. Ha! Who calls?

Casca. Bid every noise be still. Peace yet again!

15 **Caesar.** Who is it in the press that calls on me?
   I hear a tongue shriller than all the music

69–71 I'll about...thick: I'll go around and scatter the rest of the commoners. Do the same yourself wherever they are forming a crowd.

72–75 These...fearfulness: Flavius compares Caesar to a bird. He hopes that turning away some of Caesar's supporters (**growing feathers**) will prevent him from becoming too powerful.

3–9 Stand...curse: Antony (Antonius) is about to run in a race that is part of the Lupercal celebration. Caesar refers to the superstition that a **sterile** woman (one unable to bear children) can become fertile if touched by one of the racers.

9–10 I shall...performed: *What do these lines tell you about Antony's attitude toward Caesar?*

12–15 The fortuneteller (**soothsayer**) who calls out Caesar's name can hardly be heard above the noise of the crowd (**press**). Casca tells the crowd to quiet down.

JULIUS CAESAR: ACT ONE, SCENE 2   **1205**

B MOTIFS IN DRAMA

Explain to students that an omen is something believed to be a sign of future good or evil. Elicit from students that this omen is a sign of evil. Have students watch for other omens as they read the play.

Possible answer: A soothsayer warns Caesar to beware the ides of March. This omen adds tension to the play at this point, for both Caesar and the audience.

TIERED DISCUSSION PROMPTS

Direct students to lines 32–47. Use these prompts to help students begin to understand the character of Brutus, a key figure in *Julius Caesar*:

Connect Have you or someone you know ever given someone a look that was misinterpreted? How does that experience help you understand Cassius' comment? *Students should note Cassius' concern that Brutus may no longer be his friend.*

Analyze Is Brutus angry with Cassius? What has caused the change in his behavior? *Possible answer: Brutus is not angry with Cassius. He tells Cassius that conflicting emotions have affected his behavior (lines 37–42) and that Cassius should not take it personally (lines 43–47).*

Evaluate Does Brutus seem to be a positive character? Explain your answer. *Possible answer: Although Brutus is troubled at this moment, he seems to be a positive character in many ways. He has a conscience and thinks seriously about things. He admits that he is troubled, suggesting that he is not deceitful. He is thoughtful and compassionate toward Cassius, showing that he respects his friends.*

Cry "Caesar!" Speak. Caesar is turned to hear.

Soothsayer. Beware the ides of March. B

Caesar.   What man is that?

Brutus. A soothsayer bids you beware the ides of March.

20 **Caesar.** Set him before me; let me see his face.

Cassius. Fellow, come from the throng; look upon Caesar.

Caesar. What say'st thou to me now? Speak once again.

Soothsayer. Beware the ides of March.

Caesar. He is a dreamer; let us leave him. Pass.

[*Trumpets sound. Exeunt all but* Brutus *and* Cassius.]

25 **Cassius.** Will you go see the order of the course?

Brutus. Not I.

Cassius. I pray you do.

Brutus. I am not gamesome. I do lack some part
Of that quick spirit that is in Antony.

30 Let me not hinder, Cassius, your desires.
I'll leave you.

Cassius. Brutus, I do observe you now of late;
I have not from your eyes that gentleness
And show of love as I was wont to have.

35 You bear too stubborn and too strange a hand
Over your friend that loves you.

Brutus.   Cassius,
Be not deceived. If I have veiled my look,
I turn the trouble of my countenance
Merely upon myself. Vexed I am

40 Of late with passions of some difference,
Conceptions only proper to myself,
Which give some soil, perhaps, to my behaviors;
But let not therefore my good friends be grieved
(Among which number, Cassius, be you one)

45 Nor construe any further my neglect
Than that poor Brutus, with himself at war,
forgets the shows of love to other men.

Cassius. Then, Brutus, I have much mistook your passion,
By means whereof this breast of mine hath buried

50 Thoughts of great value, worthy cogitations.
Tell me, good Brutus, can you see your face?

Brutus. No, Cassius, for the eye sees not itself
But by reflection, by some other things.

18 **ides of March:** March 15.

COMMON CORE RL 2

B MOTIFS IN DRAMA

A **motif** is an element or concept that appears throughout a play and helps develop the plot and theme. In *The Tragedy of Julius Caesar,* one motif is the appearance of omens foreshadowing doom for Caesar and turmoil for Rome. What omen appears in lines 17–19? How do you think this omen might affect the plot of the play?

25–28 Cassius asks if Brutus is going to watch the race (**the order of the course**), but Brutus says he is not fond of sports (**gamesome**).

32–34 I do observe . . . to have: Lately I haven't seen the friendliness in your face that I used to see (**was wont to have**).

37–42 Brutus explains that if he has seemed distant, it is only because he has been preoccupied with conflicting emotions (**passions of some difference**), and that these private thoughts may have stained his conduct.

48–50 I have . . . cogitations: I have misunderstood your feelings. As a result, I have kept certain thoughts to myself.

DIFFERENTIATED INSTRUCTION

FOR STRUGGLING READERS

Inverted Word Order Explain that Shakespeare often inverted the word order of sentences, stating the verb before the subject. Model these examples:

- *Vexed I am* (line 39), "I am vexed (bothered)"

- *be you one* (line 44), "you are one"

- *What means this shouting?* (line 79), "What does this shouting mean?"

FOR ENGLISH LANGUAGE LEARNERS

Concept Support Explain that a soothsayer is someone who claims to predict the future. (*Sooth* is an archaic word meaning "truth.") Have students reread the passage that contains the soothsayer's warning to Caesar (lines 18–24); elicit that Caesar disregards the soothsayer's warning. Briefly discuss foreshadowing and then invite students to predict what might happen on the ides of March.

Cassius. 'Tis just.

55 And it is very much lamented, Brutus,
That you have no such mirrors as will turn
Your hidden worthiness into your eye,
That you might see your shadow. I have heard
Where many of the best respect in Rome

60 (Except immortal Caesar), speaking of Brutus
And groaning underneath this age's yoke,
Have wished that noble Brutus had his eyes.

Brutus. Into what dangers would you lead me, Cassius,
That you would have me seek into myself

65 For that which is not in me?

Cassius. Therefore, good Brutus, be prepared to hear;
And since you know you cannot see yourself
So well as by reflection, I, your glass,
Will modestly discover to yourself

70 That of yourself which you yet know not of.
And be not jealous on me, gentle Brutus.
Were I a common laugher, or did use
To stale with ordinary oaths my love
To every new protester; if you know

75 That I do fawn on men and hug them hard,
And after scandal them; or if you know
That I profess myself in banqueting
To all the rout, then hold me dangerous.

[*Flourish and shout.*]

Brutus. What means this shouting? I do fear the people

80 Choose Caesar for their king.

Cassius.   Ay, do you fear it?
Then must I think you would not have it so.

Brutus. I would not, Cassius, yet I love him well.
But wherefore do you hold me here so long?
What is it that you would impart to me?

85 If it be aught toward the general good,
Set honor in one eye and death i' the other,
And I will look on both indifferently;
For let the gods so speed me as I love
The name of honor more than I fear death.

90 **Cassius.** I know that virtue to be in you, Brutus,
As well as I do know your outward favor.
Well, honor is the subject of my story.
I cannot tell what you and other men
Think of this life, but for my single self,

95 I had as lief not be as live to be

55–62 it is . . . eyes: It is too bad you don't have a mirror that would show you your inner qualities (**hidden worthiness**). In fact, many respected citizens suffering under Caesar's rule (**this age's yoke**) have wished that Brutus could see how things stand. *What is Cassius suggesting to Brutus?*

66–70 Therefore . . . not of: Listen, Brutus, since you cannot see yourself, I will be your mirror (**glass**) and show you what you truly are.

71 jealous on me: suspicious of me.

72–78 Were I . . . dangerous: If you think I am a fool (**common laugher**) or someone who pretends to be the friend of everyone I meet, or if you believe that I show friendship and then talk evil about my friends (**scandal them**) behind their backs, or that I try to win the affections of the common people (**all the rout**), then consider me dangerous.

85–87 Brutus declares that he would not care whether he faced death if the matter Cassius has in mind concerns the public welfare (**general good**).

91 outward favor: physical appearance.

REVISIT THE BIG QUESTION

Can your
CONSCIENCE
mislead you?

Discuss Based on lines 79–89, what evidence in these lines suggests that Brutus has a "good" conscience? *Possible answer: When Brutus is trying to ascertain what Cassius is trying to tell him, he tells Cassius that if it will further the general good, then he will listen. He also declares that he loves honor more than he fears death (lines 84–89).*

FOR ENGLISH LANGUAGE LEARNERS

Task Support Have students read the side note and question about lines 55–62. Ask students to look for the compliment that Cassius pays Brutus and the criticism that he makes of Caesar. In addition, explain that "had his eyes" (line 62) means "saw the situation the way that others [namely, "many of the best respect in Rome" (line 59)] see it." *Possible answer: Cassius is suggesting that Brutus, not Caesar, should be the leader of Rome.*

FOR ADVANCED LEARNERS/PRE–AP

Evaluate Character Have students meet in small groups to discuss how and why Cassius uses flattery in speaking with Brutus in Scene 2. Ask them to discuss whether Brutus seems to be the type of person who would be swayed by flattery. Urge them to find textual support for their views. When discussion has concluded, invite group representatives to share their evaluations with the class.

Direct students to lines 97–131. Use these prompts to help students better understand Cassius' views and plans with regard to Caesar:

Recall What does Cassius say about Caesar's strength compared to other mortals? *Cassius does not see Caesar as any stronger than the rest of them. He witnessed Caesar's weakness when swimming the Tiber (lines 105–115) and during a fever (lines 120–128).*

Analyze Why does Cassius says these things about Caesar to Brutus? *Possible answer: Cassius says these things because he is frustrated over Caesar's ascendancy. More important, he wants Brutus to think less of Caesar and to consider opposing him.*

Synthesize Does Cassius' depiction of Caesar coincide with the way that the commoners see Caesar and the way that Caesar has portrayed himself? Explain. *Possible answer: Cassius' depiction does not coincide with the view that others have. Since the commoners treat Caesar as a hero, they must think of Caesar as better than they are. Caesar's acceptance of their praise suggests that he agrees with their vision.*

In awe of such a thing as I myself.
I was born free as Caesar, so were you;
We both have fed as well, and we can both
Endure the winter's cold as well as he.
100 For once, upon a raw and gusty day,
The troubled Tiber chafing with her shores,
Caesar said to me, "Dar'st thou, Cassius, now
Leap in with me into this angry flood
And swim to yonder point?" Upon the word,
105 Accoutered as I was, I plunged in
And bade him follow. So indeed he did.
The torrent roared, and we did buffet it
With lusty sinews, throwing it aside
And stemming it with hearts of controversy.
110 But ere we could arrive the point proposed,
Caesar cried, "Help me, Cassius, or I sink!"
I, as Aeneas, our great ancestor,
Did from the flames of Troy upon his shoulder
The old Anchises bear, so from the waves of Tiber
115 Did I the tired Caesar. And this man
Is now become a god, and Cassius is
A wretched creature and must bend his body
If Caesar carelessly but nod on him.
He had a fever when he was in Spain,
120 And when the fit was on him, I did mark
How he did shake. 'Tis true, this god did shake.
His coward lips did from their color fly
And that same eye whose bend doth awe the world
Did lose his luster. I did hear him groan.
125 Ay, and that tongue of his that bade the Romans
Mark him and write his speeches in their books,
Alas, it cried, "Give me some drink, Titinius,"
As a sick girl! Ye gods! it doth amaze me
A man of such a feeble temper should
130 So get the start of the majestic world
And bear the palm alone.

[*Shout. Flourish.*]

Brutus. Another general shout?
I do believe that these applauses are
For some new honors that are heaped on Caesar.

135 **Cassius.** Why, man, he doth bestride the narrow world
Like a Colossus, and we petty men
Walk under his huge legs and peep about
To find ourselves dishonorable graves.

95–96 I had ... I myself: I would rather not live, than to live in awe of someone no better than I am.

101 troubled ... shores: The Tiber River was rising in the middle of a storm.

105 Accoutered: dressed.

107–109 we did ... controversy: We fought the raging river with strong muscles (**lusty sinews**), conquering it with our spirit of competition (**hearts of controversy**).

110 ere: before.

112–115 I, as Aeneas ... Caesar: Aeneas (ĭ-nē′əs), the mythological founder of Rome, carried his father, Anchises (ăn-kī′sēz′), out of the burning city of Troy. Cassius says he did the same for Caesar when he became exhausted.

117 bend his body: bow.

122 His coward ... fly: His lips turned pale.

123 bend: glance.

125–131 that tongue ... alone: The same tongue that has led Romans to memorize his speeches cried out in the tone of a sick girl. I'm amazed that such a weak man should get ahead of the rest of the world and appear as the victor (**bear the palm**) all by himself. (A palm leaf was a symbol of victory in war.)

135–136 he doth ... Colossus: Cassius compares Caesar to Colossus, the huge statue of the Greek god Apollo at Rhodes. The statue supposedly spanned the entrance to the harbor and was so high that ships could sail through the space between its legs. *What is Cassius's tone in these lines?*

DIFFERENTIATED INSTRUCTION

FOR ENGLISH LANGUAGE LEARNERS

Task Support Call attention to the question in the side note for lines 135–136. As students consider their answer, point to *narrow world, Colossus,* and *petty men* to help them identify Cassius' tone. Also remind students that Cassius has just spoken very critically about Caesar to Brutus (lines 93–131). *Possible answer: Cassius' tone is sarcastic, bitter, and resentful. He refers to Caesar as "Colossus" and to everyone else as "petty," but he does not believe that those descriptions are deserved.*

FOR ADVANCED LEARNERS/PRE–AP

Rewrite the Play Have pairs or small groups of students rewrite the conversation between Brutus and Cassius (lines 51–178) as contemporary prose. They should focus on Cassius' attempt to persuade Brutus to see Caesar from the conspirators' point of view and on Brutus' measured responses. Remind students that tone of voice, facial expressions, and body language also convey meaning. Invite students to present their dialogues for the class to discuss and enjoy.

Men at some time are masters of their fates.

140 The fault, dear Brutus, is not in our stars,
But in ourselves, that we are underlings.
"Brutus," and "Caesar." What should be in that "Caesar"?
Why should that name be sounded more than yours?
Write them together: yours is as fair a name.

145 Sound them, it doth become the mouth as well.
Weigh them, it is as heavy. Conjure with 'em:
"Brutus" will start a spirit as soon as "Caesar."
Now in the names of all the gods at once,
Upon what meat doth this our Caesar feed

150 That he is grown so great? Age, thou are shamed!
Rome, thou hast lost the breed of noble bloods!
When went there by an age since the great Flood
But it was famed with more than with one man?
When could they say (till now) that talked of Rome

155 That her wide walls encompassed but one man?
Now is it Rome indeed, and room enough,
When there is in it but one only man!
O, you and I have heard our fathers say
There was a Brutus once that would have brooked

160 The eternal devil to keep his state in Rome
As easily as a king.

Brutus. That you do love me I am nothing jealous.
What you would work me to, I have some aim.
How I have thought of this, and of these times,

165 I shall recount hereafter. For this present,
I would not (so with love I might entreat you)
Be any further moved. What you have said
I will consider; what you have to say
I will with patience hear, and find a time

170 Both meet to hear and answer such high things.
Till then, my noble friend, chew upon this:
Brutus had rather be a villager
Than to repute himself a son of Rome
Under these hard conditions as this time

175 Is like to lay upon us.

Cassius.   I am glad
That my weak words have struck but thus much show
Of fire from Brutus.

[*Voices and music are heard approaching.*]

Brutus. The games are done, and Caesar is returning.

Cassius. As they pass by, pluck Casca by the sleeve,
180 And he will (after his sour fashion) tell you

140–141 The fault ... underlings: It is not the stars that have determined our fate; we are inferiors through our own fault.

146 Conjure: call up spirits.

150 Age ... shamed: It is a shameful time (**Age**) in which to be living.

159–161 There was ... a king: Cassius is referring to an ancestor of Brutus who drove the last of the ancient kings from Rome.

162 am nothing jealous: am sure.

163 have some aim: can guess.

164–167 How I have ... moved: I will tell you later (**recount hereafter**) my thoughts about this topic. For now, I ask you as a friend not to try to convince me further. *What does this request suggest about Brutus's character?*

170 meet: appropriate.

COMMON CORE RL 4

Language Coach

Roots and Affixes A word's **root** may contain the word's core meaning. The Latin root *put*, as in *reputation* and *computer*, means "think over." What do you think to *repute himself* means in line 173?

BACKGROUND

Brutus in History and in Shakespeare When the Roman civil war began in 49 B.C., Marcus Junius Brutus joined Pompey's army to fight against Caesar. Brutus was taken prisoner in Greece the next year, when Pompey was defeated. Caesar, however, not only pardoned Brutus but later made him a regional governor and a praetor. Brutus had reason to be loyal to Caesar, but history records that he loved the republican form of government, which Caesar threatened to end. In *Julius Caesar*, Cassius knows Brutus' history and realizes that he must gain Brutus' favor to mount a conspiracy against Caesar. Thus, Cassius' argument in Scene 2 focuses on Caesar's self-importance and on Brutus' allegiance to Rome rather than to Caesar.

FOR ENGLISH LANGUAGE LEARNERS

Concept Support Reread and discuss lines 151–161, guiding students to grasp these points:

- Cassius wonders whether there ever has been a time in which one man has had Caesar's influence. He feels that under Caesar, Rome has room for only one man.

- Cassius depicts Caesar as a dictator, and he knows that Brutus—like his famous ancestor— loves Rome too much to let a dictator rule.

Task Support Point students to the question in the side note for lines 164–167 and reread the lines with them. Elicit that Brutus asks Cassius to stop talking to him about the subject for now. *Possible answer: His request suggests that Brutus is thoughtful, deliberate, and cautious; he will not make major decisions on the spur of the moment. He values Cassius' friendship, however, and he promises to share his thoughts with Cassius in a later discussion.*

Language Coach   COMMON CORE
                            RL 4
Roots and Affixes *Answer: It must mean "to think of himself as."* Ask students to find another example on this page of a word in which the root contains its core meaning. Have them identify the root word and think of another word with the same root. *Possible answers: encompassed, compass, compassed (line 155); recount, count, account (line 165); entreat, treat, treaty (line 166)*

JULIUS CAESAR: ACT ONE, SCENE 2   **1209**

What hath proceeded worthy note today.

[Reenter Caesar *and his train of followers.]*

Brutus. I will do so. But look you, Cassius!
The angry spot doth glow on Caesar's brow,
And all the rest look like a chidden train.
185 Calpurnia's cheek is pale, and Cicero
Looks with such ferret and such fiery eyes
As we have seen him in the Capitol,
Being crossed in conference by some senators.

Cassius. Casca will tell us what the matter is.

*[Caesar *looks at* Cassius *and turns to* Antony.]*

190 **Caesar.** Antonius.

Antony. Caesar?

Caesar. Let me have men about me that are fat,
Sleek-headed men, and such as sleep o' nights.
Yond Cassius has a lean and hungry look;
195 He thinks too much, such men are dangerous.

Antony. Fear him not, Caesar, he's not dangerous.
He is a noble Roman, and well given.

Caesar. Would he were fatter! But I fear him not.
Yet if my name were liable to fear,
200 I do not know the man I should avoid
So soon as that spare Cassius. He reads much,
He is a great observer, and he looks
Quite through the deeds of men. He loves no plays
As thou dost, Antony; he hears no music.
205 Seldom he smiles, and smiles in such a sort
As if he mocked himself and scorned his spirit
That could be moved to smile at anything.
Such men as he be never at heart's ease
Whiles they behold a greater than themselves,
210 And therefore are they very dangerous.
I rather tell thee what is to be feared
Than what I fear, for always I am Caesar.
Come on my right hand, for this ear is deaf,
And tell me truly what thou think'st of him. **C**

[Trumpets sound. Exeunt Caesar *and all his train except* Casca, *who stays behind.]*

215 **Casca.** You pulled me by the cloak. Would you speak with me?

Brutus. Ay, Casca. Tell us what hath chanced today
That Caesar looks so sad.

Casca. Why, you were with him, were you not?

---

181 worthy note: worthy of notice.

184 chidden train: a group of followers who have been scolded.

185–188 Cicero was a highly respected senator. Brutus says he has the angry look of a **ferret** (a fierce little animal), the look he gets when other senators disagree with him.

190–214 Brutus and Cassius take Casca aside. The conversation Caesar has with Antony is not heard by any of the other characters around them.

197 Antony says that Cassius, despite his appearance, is a supporter of Caesar.

202–203 he looks . . . deeds of men: He sees hidden motives in men's actions.

C BLANK VERSE
Reread lines 208–214 aloud, tapping out the stressed syllables with your finger. Which line in this passage varies from strict iambic pentameter?

216 hath chanced: has happened.

1210 UNIT 11: SHAKESPEAREAN DRAMA

C *Model the Skill:* **BLANK VERSE**

Remind students that iambic pentameter consists of five metrical feet, each one consisting of one unstressed syllable followed by one stressed syllable. Begin a scansion of these lines by tapping out line 208 while a volunteer reads the line aloud. Help students recognize the pattern by saying *da-DUM* (weak-strong) as you read the line again. Continue with the other lines in question, but as you tap out line 212, elicit that you ended on an extra, unstressed syllable. Point out that although iambic pentameter sounds rather stylized (or "sing-songy") when read in this fashion, it is closer to spoken English than are other metrical patterns. Illustrate by rereading these lines more naturally.

Possible answer: *Line 212 varies slightly because it ends with an extra unstressed syllable.*

DIFFERENTIATED INSTRUCTION

FOR STRUGGLING READERS

Paraphrasing Shakespeare After students reread the summary of lines 190–214 in the side note, model this paraphrase of lines 205–207: *He [Cassius] does not smile often, but when he does, he smiles in a way that makes it seem as if he is making fun of himself for smiling.* Then call on volunteers to paraphrase lines 208–209. ***Possible answer:*** *People like him [Cassius] will never be comfortable as long as they see a superior in power.*

Discuss why Caesar would call such people "dangerous" (line 210).

FOR ENGLISH LANGUAGE LEARNERS

Vocabulary: Outdated Forms Discuss these examples of Shakespearean terms that have passed from use: *hath* (line 181), "has"; *doth* (line 183), "does"; *Yond* (line 194), "Yonder," "Over there"; *Whiles* (line 209), "While," "As long as"; *thee* (line 211), "you"; *think'st* (line 214), "think."

Brutus. I should not then ask Casca what had chanced.

220 **Casca.** Why, there was a crown offered him; and being offered him, he put it by with the back of his hand, thus. And then the people fell a-shouting.

Brutus. What was the second noise for?

Casca. Why, for that too.

225 **Cassius.** They shouted thrice. What was the last cry for?

Casca. Why, for that too.

Brutus. Was the crown offered him thrice?

Casca. Ay, marry, was't! and he put it by thrice, every time gentler than other; and at every putting-by mine honest
230 neighbors shouted.

Cassius. Who offered him the crown?

Casca. Why, Antony.

Brutus. Tell us the manner of it, gentle Casca.

Casca. I can as well be hanged as tell the manner of it. It was
235 mere foolery; I did not mark it. I saw Mark Antony offer him a crown—yet 'twas not a crown neither, 'twas one of these coronets—and, as I told you, he put it by once. But for all that, to my thinking, he would fain have had it. Then he offered it to him again; then he put it by again; but to my thinking, he was
240 very loath to lay his fingers off it. And then he offered it the third time. He put it the third time by; and still as he refused it, the rabblement hooted, and clapped their chapped hands, and threw up their sweaty nightcaps, and uttered such a deal of stinking breath because Caesar refused the crown that it had,
245 almost, choked Caesar; for he swounded and fell down at it. And for mine own part, I durst not laugh, for fear of opening my lips and receiving the bad air.

Cassius. But soft, I pray you. What, did Caesar swound?

Casca. He fell down in the market place and foamed at mouth
250 and was speechless.

Brutus. 'Tis very like. He hath the falling sickness.

Cassius. No, Caesar hath not it; but you, and I, And honest Casca, we have the falling sickness.

Casca. I know not what you mean by that, but I am sure Caesar
255 fell down. If the tag-rag people did not clap him and hiss him, according as he pleased and displeased them, as they use to do the players in the theater, I am no true man.

Brutus. What said he when he came unto himself?

221 **put it by:** pushed it aside.

228 **Ay, marry, was't:** Yes, indeed, it was. *Marry* was a mild oath used in Shakespeare's time (but not in ancient Rome). The word means "by the Virgin Mary."

237 **coronets:** small crowns.

238 **fain:** gladly.

240 **loath:** reluctant.

242 **rabblement:** unruly crowd.

245 **swounded:** fainted.

② **Targeted Passage**

248 **soft:** Wait a moment.

251 **falling sickness:** epilepsy.

252–253 Cassius's pun on the term **falling sickness** suggests that they have fallen low under Caesar's rule.

D BLANK VERSE

Possible answer: Casca has two character traits that inspire prose dialogue: He is both blunt and cynical. These traits come across clearly in his prose comments. For example, Casca speaks bluntly when he tells Brutus and Cassius that Caesar "offered ... his throat to cut" (line 261) and when he says, "I would I might go to hell among the rogues" (line 263). He also is quite cynical when he gives this opinion about the women who forgave Caesar: "If Caesar had stabbed their mothers, they would have done no less" (lines 268–269).

Casca. Marry, before he fell down, when he perceived the
260 common herd was glad he refused the crown, he plucked me ope
his doublet and offered them his throat to cut. An I had been a
man of any occupation, if I would not have taken him at a word
I would I might go to hell among the rogues. And so he fell.
When he came to himself again, he said, if he had done or said
265 anything amiss, he desired their worships to think it was his
infirmity. Three or four wenches where I stood cried, "Alas,
good soul!" and forgave him with all their hearts. But there's no
heed to be taken of them. If Caesar had stabbed their mothers,
they would have done no less. **D**

270 **Brutus.** And after that, he came thus sad away?

Casca. Ay.

Cassius. Did Cicero say anything?

Casca. Ay, he spoke Greek.

Cassius. To what effect?

275 **Casca.** Nay, an I tell you that, I'll ne'er look you i' the face again.
But those that understood him smiled at one another and shook
their heads; but for mine own part, it was Greek to me. I could
tell you more news, too. Marullus and Flavius, for pulling scarfs
off Caesar's images, are put to silence. Fare you well. There was
280 more foolery yet, if I could remember it.

Cassius. Will you sup with me tonight, Casca?

Casca. No, I am promised forth.

Cassius. Will you dine with me tomorrow?

Casca. Ay, if I be alive, and your mind hold, and your
285 dinner worth eating.

Cassius. Good. I will expect you.

Casca. Do so. Farewell both.

[*Exit.*]

Brutus. What a blunt fellow is this grown to be!
He was quick mettle when he went to school.

290 **Cassius.** So is he now in execution
Of any bold or noble enterprise,
However he puts on this tardy form.
This rudeness is a sauce to his good wit,
Which gives men stomach to digest his words
295 With better appetite.

Brutus. And so it is. For this time I will leave you.
Tomorrow, if you please to speak with me,
I will come home to you; or if you will,
Come home to me, and I will wait for you.

260–261 plucked me ... doublet: tore open his jacket.

261–263 An ... rogues: If (**An**) I had been a worker with a proper tool, may I go to hell with the sinners (**rogues**) if I would not have done as he asked (**taken him at a word**).

265 amiss: wrong.

265–266 his infirmity: due to his sickness.

266 wenches: common women.

D BLANK VERSE
Notice that Shakespeare chose prose instead of blank verse for Casca's speeches. Which of Casca's **character traits** may have inspired this choice?

279 put to silence: silenced by removal from office, exile, or death. *What does this detail suggest about Caesar's rule?*

282 I am promised forth: I have another appointment.

289 quick mettle: clever, intelligent.

290–295 So is ... appetite: Casca can still be intelligent in carrying out an important project. He only pretends to be slow (**tardy**). His rude manner makes people more willing to accept (**digest**) the things he says.

DIFFERENTIATED INSTRUCTION

FOR ENGLISH LANGUAGE LEARNERS

Language Support Point out Casca's statement "it was Greek to me" (line 277) and ask students if they have heard or read this expression before. Explain that the expression *it's Greek to me* has become part of modern English and today means "I do not understand (the words or their meanings) at all." Explain that this comment supports the characterization of Casca as blunt and unsophisticated, as already seen in lines 259–269.

Task Support Refer students to the side note for line 279 and read the question aloud. Remind them that Marullus and Flavius are the two characters from Scene 1 who first spoke against Caesar. *Possible answer: This detail— swift punishment for critics—suggests that Caesar's rule is absolute and that he will not tolerate anyone who opposes him.*

Behind the Curtain

Set Design

In a theatrical production, the **set design** helps audiences imagine the time and place in which the action occurs. Some designers use scenery and props to create the illusion of specific rooms or outdoor locations. Others try to suggest the essence of a play's setting through elements such as platforms, stairs, and columns. How do the features of these sets for *Julius Caesar* differ?

Set for the Shakespeare Theatre's 1993–1994 production

Set for a 2005 production at the Warf1 Theatre

Set for a 2005 production at the Belasco Theatre

BEHIND THE CURTAIN    COMMON CORE RI 7

Set Design Explain to students that a set includes all of the furnishings and backdrops that create the play's environment. For example, the background scenery, the furniture and props, and the steps and platforms are all part of a set's design. Note, too, that a set can change as the play's action moves from scene to scene but that the set designer's overall intent is usually apparent throughout. *Possible answer: The Shakespeare Theatre set is dark. Its scattered platforms, which look like ruins, suggest that the action is taking place outdoors and perhaps in the future. The Wharf Theatre (Sydney, Australia) set is also dark, and even more bare and grim. The sand on the floor of the stage suggests that the scene occurs outside. Both modern and ancient costumes are used in this production. Similarly, the set design for the Belasco Theatre mixes elements of both the ancient and the modern world. This production shows a long table and overturned chairs, indicating that the action most likely is occurring inside a building.*

FOR ADVANCED LEARNERS/PRE–AP

Create a Set Design Divide students into three groups and have each group create a set design for one of the three scenes in Act One. As students consider various designs, remind them that a set can express an overall mood as well as depict specific, concrete details. Instruct groups to work together to sketch their designs and write a paragraph or two to explain the elements. Display the finished set designs. Invite comments about the designs and compare designs created for the same scene.

E SOLILOQUY

Possible answer: *Cassius explains that he is going to leave forged letters at Brutus' house—letters that compliment Brutus and subtly critique Caesar's ambition (lines 308–314). If Brutus knew that Cassius was trying to manipulate him, Brutus would be much more cautious about listening to him.*

IF STUDENTS NEED HELP . . . Use an Open Mind diagram to help students clarify Cassius' secret thoughts.

> Caesar dislikes me but loves Brutus.
>
> I can manipulate Brutus even though he doesn't want to listen to me.
>
> I will leave phony letters at his house.
>
> All of the letters will praise Brutus but hint at distrust of Caesar.

 BEST PRACTICES TOOLKIT—Transparency
Open Mind p. D9

---

300 **Cassius.** I will do so. Till then, think of the world.

[*Exit* Brutus.]

Well, Brutus, thou art noble; yet I see
Thy honorable mettle may be wrought
From that it is disposed. Therefore it is meet
That noble minds keep ever with their likes;
305 For who so firm that cannot be seduced?
Caesar doth bear me hard, but he loves Brutus.
If I were Brutus now and he were Cassius,
He should not humor me. I will this night,
In several hands, in at his windows throw,
310 As if they came from several citizens,
Writings, all tending to the great opinion
That Rome holds of his name; wherein obscurely
Caesar's ambition shall be glanced at.
And after this let Caesar seat him sure,
315 For we will shake him, or worse days endure. **E**

[*Exit.*]

Scene 3 *A street in Rome.*

It is the night of March 14. Amid violent thunder and lightning, a terrified Casca fears that the storm and other omens predict terrible events to come. Cassius interprets the storm as a sign that Caesar must be overthrown. Cassius and Casca agree that Caesar's rise to power must be stopped by any means. Cinna, another plotter, enters, and they discuss how to persuade Brutus to follow their plan.

[*Thunder and lightning. Enter, from opposite sides,* Casca, *with his sword drawn, and* Cicero.]

Cicero. Good even, Casca. Brought you Caesar home?
Why are you breathless? and why stare you so?

Casca. Are not you moved when all the sway of earth
Shakes like a thing unfirm? O Cicero,
5 I have seen tempests when the scolding winds
Have rived the knotty oaks, and I have seen
The ambitious ocean swell and rage and foam
To be exalted with the threat'ning clouds;
But never till tonight, never till now,
10 Did I go through a tempest dropping fire.
Either there is a civil strife in heaven,
Or else the world, too saucy with the gods,
Incenses them to send destruction.

Cicero. Why, saw you anything more wonderful?

15 **Casca.** A common slave—you know him well by sight—
Held up his left hand, which did flame and burn

302 Thy . . . wrought: Your honorable nature can be manipulated.

306 bear me hard: hold a grudge against me.

308 He should . . . me: I wouldn't let him influence me.

308–312 I will . . . his name: Cassius plans to leave messages at Brutus's home that appear to be from several people.

E SOLILOQUY

Why would Cassius not want Brutus to hear the thoughts he expresses in lines 301–315?

3 sway of earth: the natural order of things.

5 tempests: storms.

6 rived: torn.

8 To be exalted with: to raise themselves to the level of.

11–13 Either . . . destruction: Either there is a civil war in heaven, or the world has so insulted the gods that they want to destroy us.

14 saw . . . wonderful: Did you see anything else that was strange?

DIFFERENTIATED INSTRUCTION

FOR STRUGGLING READERS

Preview Read through the italicized scene synopsis with students to give them an overview of Scene 3. Help them create a Sequence Chain to organize the plot events.

 BEST PRACTICES TOOLKIT—Transparency
Sequence Chain p. B21

> Casca declares that the storm warns of terrible future events.
>
> ↓
>
> Cassius says that the storm proves the need to overthrow Caesar.
>
> ↓
>
> Cassius and Casca agree that Caesar must be stopped.
>
> ↓
>
> Cinna, Cassius, and Casca discuss how to get Brutus to join the conspiracy.

Concept Support Elicit that a storm is raging as Scene 3 opens. Point out that it creates a mysterious, ominous mood. Note that characters can interpret the storm's meaning to meet their own needs (as Cicero points out in lines 33–34). Ask students how Casca interprets the storm in lines 11–13 and how Cassius does so later. Discuss whether the two interpretations are similar or different—or whether both interpretations could be true.

Like twenty torches joined; and yet his hand,
Not sensible of fire, remained unscorched.
Besides—I ha' not since put up my sword—
20 Against the Capitol I met a lion,
Who glared upon me, and went surly by
Without annoying me. And there were drawn
Upon a heap a hundred ghastly women,
Transformed with their fear, who swore they saw
25 Men, all in fire, walk up and down the streets.
And yesterday the bird of night did sit
Even at noonday upon the market place,
Hooting and shrieking. When these prodigies
Do so conjointly meet, let not men say,
30 "These are their reasons, they are natural,"
For I believe they are portentous things
Unto the climate that they point upon. **F**

Cicero. Indeed it is a strange-disposed time.
But men may construe things after their fashion,
35 Clean from the purpose of the things themselves.
Comes Caesar to the Capitol tomorrow?

Casca. He doth, for he did bid Antonius
Send word to you he would be there tomorrow.

Cicero. Good night then, Casca. This disturbed sky
40 Is not to walk in.

Casca.   Farewell, Cicero.

[*Exit* Cicero.]

[*Enter* Cassius.]

Cassius. Who's there?

Casca.   A Roman.

Cassius.   Casca, by your voice.

Casca. Your ear is good. Cassius, what night is this!

Cassius. A very pleasing night to honest men.

Casca. Who ever knew the heavens menace so?

45 **Cassius.** Those that have known the earth so full of faults.
For my part, I have walked about the streets,
Submitting me unto the perilous night,
And, thus unbraced, Casca, as you see,
Have bared my bosom to the thunder-stone;
50 And when the cross blue lightning seemed to open
The breast of heaven, I did present myself
Even in the aim and very flash of it.

18 **Not sensible of fire:** not feeling the fire.

19–20 **I ha' not . . . lion:** I haven't put my sword back into its scabbard since I saw a lion at the Capitol building.

22–23 **drawn . . . heap:** huddled together.

23 **ghastly:** ghostly white.

26 **bird of night:** the owl, usually seen only at night.

28–32 **When these . . . upon:** When strange events (**prodigies**) like these happen at the same time (**conjointly meet**), no one should say there are natural explanations for them. I believe they are bad omens (**portentous things**) for the place where they happen.

33–35 Cicero agrees that the times are strange, but he says that people can misinterpret events.

F TRAGEDY
How does Casca's speech in lines 15–32 help build **suspense?**

41 **Who's there?:** Cassius probably has his sword out; with no light other than moonlight, it could be dangerous to come upon a stranger in the street.

46–52 Cassius brags that he offered himself to the dangerous night, with his coat open (**unbraced**), exposing his chest to the lightning. *Why might he do this?*

JULIUS CAESAR: ACT ONE, SCENE 3 **1215**

Can your
CONSCIENCE
mislead you?

Discuss Based on lines 62–80, does Cassius have a guilty conscience for thinking and speaking as he does about Caesar? Explain your answer. *Possible answer: Cassius does not have a guilty conscience. He is emphatic in telling Casca that the reason heaven has brought about such foreboding happenings is to warn the people about the "man / Most like this dreadful night" (lines 72–73): Caesar. Cassius is angry that Caesar, who has not proven himself to be any more courageous than Cassius or Casca, is "prodigious grown" (lines 76–77), and he wants Caesar to be removed. He seems to feel no guilt at all for these accusatory, defiant thoughts.*

Casca. But wherefore did you so much tempt the heavens?
It is the part of men to fear and tremble
55 When the most mighty gods by tokens send
Such dreadful heralds to astonish us.

Cassius. You are dull, Casca, and those sparks of life
That should be in a Roman you do want,
Or else you use not. You look pale, and gaze,
60 And put on fear, and cast yourself in wonder,
To see the strange impatience of the heavens.
But if you would consider the true cause
Why all these fires, why all these gliding ghosts,
Why birds and beasts, from quality and kind;
65 Why old men fool and children calculate;
Why all these things change from their ordinance,
Their natures, and preformed faculties,
To monstrous quality, why, you shall find
That heaven hath infused them with these spirits
70 To make them instruments of fear and warning
Unto some monstrous state.
Now could I, Casca, name to thee a man
Most like this dreadful night
That thunders, lightens, opens graves, and roars
75 As doth the lion in the Capitol;
A man no mightier than thyself or me
In personal action, yet prodigious grown
And fearful, as these strange eruptions are.

Casca. 'Tis Caesar that you mean. Is it not, Cassius?

80 **Cassius.** Let it be who it is. For Romans now
Have thews and limbs like to their ancestors.
But woe the while! our fathers' minds are dead,
And we are governed with our mothers' spirits,
Our yoke and sufferance show us womanish.

85 **Casca.** Indeed, they say the senators tomorrow
Mean to establish Caesar as king,
And he shall wear his crown by sea and land
In every place save here in Italy.

Cassius. I know where I will wear this dagger then;
90 Cassius from bondage will deliver Cassius.
Therein, ye gods, you make the weak most strong;
Therein, ye gods, you tyrants do defeat.
Nor stony tower, nor walls of beaten brass,
Nor airless dungeon, nor strong links of iron,
95 Can be retentive to the strength of spirit;
But life, being weary of these worldly bars,

54–56 It is ... astonish us: Men are supposed to be frightened when the gods send dreadful signs (**tokens**) of what is to come.

58 want: lack.

62–71 Cassius insists that heaven has brought about such things as birds and animals that change their natures (**from quality and kind**) and children who predict the future (**calculate**)—all these beings that act unnaturally (**change from their ordinance / Their natures, and preformed faculties**). Heaven has done all this, he says, to warn the Romans of an evil condition that they should correct.

77 prodigious grown: become enormous and threatening.

80–84 Romans ... womanish: Modern Romans have muscles (**thews**) and limbs like our ancestors, but we have the minds of our mothers, not our fathers. Our acceptance of servitude (**yoke and sufferance**) shows us to be like women, not like men. (In Shakespeare's time—and in ancient Rome—women were considered weak creatures.)

88 save: except.

89–90 I know ... deliver Cassius: I will free myself from slavery (**bondage**) by killing myself (**wear this dagger**).

91 Therein: through suicide.

95 be retentive to: hold in.

DIFFERENTIATED INSTRUCTION

FOR ENGLISH LANGUAGE LEARNERS

Concept Support Explain that some of Cassius' statements on these pages are not literally true; rather, Shakespeare has him make comparisons by using figurative language. In lines 80–84, Cassius compares citizens of Rome to women. The analogy is supposed to illustrate their weakness to Caesar's power. Today, it would not be appropriate to make this kind of analogy.

Never lacks power to dismiss itself.
If I know this, know all the world besides,
That part of tyranny that I do bear
100 I can shake off at pleasure.

[*Thunder still.*]

Casca.   So can I.
So every bondman in his own hand bears
The power to cancel his captivity.

Cassius. And why should Caesar be a tyrant then?
Poor man! I know he would not be a wolf
105 But that he sees the Romans are but sheep;
He were no lion, were not Romans hinds.
Those that with haste will make a mighty fire
Begin it with weak straws. What trash is Rome,
What rubbish and what offal, when it serves
110 For the base matter to illuminate
So vile a thing as Caesar! But, O grief,
Where hast thou led me? I, perhaps, speak this
Before a willing bondman. Then I know
My answer must be made. But I am armed,
115 And dangers are to me indifferent.

Casca. You speak to Casca, and to such a man
That is no fleering telltale. Hold, my hand.
Be factious for redress of all these griefs,
And I will set this foot of mine as far
120 As who goes farthest.

Cassius.   There's a bargain made.
Now know you, Casca, I have moved already
Some certain of the noblest-minded Romans
To undergo with me an enterprise
Of honorable-dangerous consequence;
125 And I do know, by this they stay for me
In Pompey's Porch; for now, this fearful night,
There is no stir or walking in the streets,
And the complexion of the element
In favor's like the work we have in hand,
130 Most bloody, fiery, and most terrible.

[*Enter* Cinna.]

Casca. Stand close awhile, for here comes one in haste.

Cassius. 'Tis Cinna. I do know him by his gait.
He is a friend. Cinna, where haste you so?

Cinna. To find out you. Who's that? Metellus Cimber?

89–100 *What impression does Cassius convey of himself in this speech?*

103–111 Cassius says the only reason for Caesar's strength is the weakness of the Romans, who are female deer (**hinds**) and trash (**offal**) for allowing such a person as Caesar to come to power.

111–114 Cassius says that he will have to pay the penalty for his words if Casca is a submissive slave (**willing bondsman**). *Why does Cassius suggest that he may have spoken too freely to Casca?*

117 fleering telltale: sneering tattletale.

118–120 Be factious . . . farthest: Form a group, or faction, to correct (**redress**) these wrongs, and I will go as far as any other man.

125–126 by this . . . Porch: Right now, they wait (**stay**) for me at the entrance to the theater Pompey built.

128–130 the complexion . . . terrible: The sky (**element**) looks like the work we have ahead of us—bloody, full of fire, and terrible.

132 gait: manner of walking.

TIERED DISCUSSION PROMPTS

Direct students to lines 103–120. Use these prompts to help students grasp Cassius' persuasive abilities:

Connect Have you ever had to defend your opinion? How did you go about doing it? *Accept all reasonable responses.*

Analyze What kind of support does Cassius use to defend his opinion of Caesar? How effective is his argument? *Possible answer: Cassius appears to support his views with emotions, not facts. He uses dramatic and exaggerated language to insult both the Romans and Caesar (lines 103–111). His argument seems quite effective, however: Casca immediately promises to keep quiet about what Cassius has said and to help Cassius form a group to deal with these wrongs (lines 116–120).*

Evaluate Is Cassius an honest person? Defend your response. *Possible answer: Cassius is not an honest person. Although he may have valid concerns about Caesar's ascendancy and fitness to rule, he is very manipulative and therefore dishonest in the way that he recruits Casca to join the conspiracy.*

FOR ENGLISH LANGUAGE LEARNERS

Task Support Draw students' attention to the question in the side note for lines 89–100. Point out that Cassius makes this speech immediately after Casca tells him that Caesar will be made king the next day (lines 85–88). Also have students summarize Cassius' previously expressed opinion of Caesar. *Possible answer: Cassius conveys the impression that he would rather commit suicide than live under Caesar's rule (lines 89–90 and 96–100).*

Task Support Point out the side note and question for lines 111–114. Have students consider Cassius' manipulative character as they answer the question. *Possible answer: Cassius makes this suggestion because he needs to know where Casca's loyalty lies. However, he does it in a way that flatters Casca, so that Casca will think of himself as defiant and brave if he allies himself with Cassius.*

FOR ADVANCED LEARNERS/PRE–AP

Hypothesize In lines 116–120, Casca proves that he is no "willing bondman" of Caesar's (line 113) by pledging his support to Cassius. Suppose, however, that Casca had been noncommittal—or, worse yet, that he had affirmed his loyalty to Caesar. Have students write and share a paragraph in which they discuss what Cassius might say or do, and whether his words and actions would make a major difference in Cassius' plans for Caesar.

Can your CONSCIENCE mislead you?

Discuss Based on lines 157–160, how would the support of Brutus ease the conscience of conspirators, like Casca, who recognize the offensiveness of the action they are planning? *Possible answer: Brutus is considered a worthy, virtuous man. His support would ease the conspirators' conscience by making the overthrow of Caesar seem to be a worthy, virtuous action.*

ACT ONE WRAP-UP

READ WITH A PURPOSE Now that students have finished reading Act One, have them list the steps Brutus has taken away from friendship with Caesar. Has he yet made any irrevocable decisions? *Possible answer: Brutus has listened to the words of Cassius and has agreed to speak further to him. Brutus has begun to see Caesar as dangerous, but he has not yet acted in any way that sets him against Caesar.*

★ **CRITIQUE** Ask students whether they think that Caesar is as bad a character as he is depicted by others (especially Cassius) in Act One. Have students cite evidence to support their opinions.

---

135 **Cassius.** No, it is Casca, one incorporate
To our attempts. Am I not stayed for, Cinna?

Cinna. I am glad on't. What a fearful night is this!
There's two or three of us have seen strange sights.

Cassius. Am I not stayed for? Tell me.

Cinna. Yes, you are.
140 O Cassius, if you could
But win the noble Brutus to our party—

Cassius. Be you content. Good Cinna, take this paper
And look you lay it in the praetor's chair,
Where Brutus may but find it, and throw this
145 In at his window. Set this up with wax
Upon old Brutus' statue. All this done,
Repair to Pompey's Porch, where you shall find us.
Is Decius Brutus and Trebonius there?

Cinna. All but Metellus Cimber, and he's gone
150 To seek you at your house. Well, I will hie
And so bestow these papers as you bade me.

Cassius. That done, repair to Pompey's Theater.
[*Exit* Cinna.]

Come, Casca, you and I will yet ere day
See Brutus at his house. Three parts of him
155 Is ours already, and the man entire
Upon the next encounter yields him ours.

Casca. O, he sits high in all the people's hearts,
And that which would appear offense in us,
His countenance, like richest alchemy,
160 Will change to virtue and to worthiness.

Cassius. Him and his worth and our great need of him
You have right well conceited. Let us go,
For it is after midnight, and ere day
We will awake him and be sure of him.

[*Exeunt.*]

135–136 it is...stayed for: This is Casca, who is now part of our plan (**incorporate / To our attempts**). Are they waiting for me?

142–146 Cassius tells Cinna to place letters for Brutus at several locations, including the seat of the praetor, a position held by Brutus.

150–151 I will...bade me: I'll hurry (**hie**) to place (**bestow**) these papers as you instructed me.

154–156 Three parts...yields him ours: We've already won over three parts of Brutus. The next time we meet him, he will be ours completely.

157–160 he sits...worthiness: The people love Brutus. What would seem offensive if we did it will, like magic (**alchemy**), become good and worthy because of his involvement.

162 conceited: judged.

③ **Targeted Passage**

DIFFERENTIATED INSTRUCTION

FOR STRUGGLING READERS

③ **Targeted Passage** [Lines 153–164]

This passage concludes Act One but also lets the reader know that an important meeting is likely to take place in Act Two.

- How soon does Cassius plan to meet with Brutus? Why is he in such a hurry? (lines 153–154, lines 154–156)

- What does Cassius expect to be the result of this meeting? Why is he so optimistic? (lines 154–156)

- Why do the conspirators have "great need" of Brutus? (lines 157–160)

Concept Support Remind students that the letters to which Cassius refers in lines 142–146 are the letters that he spoke of forging in Scene 2 (lines 308–313). Elicit that the varied placement of the letters is one more way of fooling Brutus into thinking that the letters were written by several citizens of Rome.

Comprehension

1. **Recall** Why do the tribunes Flavius and Marullus become angry with the commoners at the beginning of the play?

2. **Recall** How does Caesar respond to the Soothsayer's warning?

3. **Recall** According to Casca, what happened at the games when Mark Antony offered Caesar a crown?

4. **Clarify** Why does Cassius send letters to Brutus that appear to have been written by other people?

Text Analysis

5. **Examine Blank Verse** Identify which characters speak in blank verse and which ones speak in prose in Act One, Scene 1. What can you tell about the characters in this scene based on whether their dialogue is in verse or prose?

6. **Analyze Suspense** In Scene 3, Shakespeare creates excitement about what will happen next in the play. Use a graphic organizer like the one shown to identify details in the scene that help build suspense.

7. **Reading Shakespearean Drama** Review the chart you created as you read, and compare the personalities of Brutus and Cassius. In your opinion, which character would make a better leader? Give reasons for your answer.

8. **Draw Conclusions About Motivation** In Scenes 2 and 3, Cassius explains why he is opposed to Caesar. Does Cassius seem motivated more by personal rivalry or by concern for the future of Rome? Cite details to support your conclusion.

9. **Make Judgments** Reread Casca's description of Caesar's behavior at the games in lines 215–287 of Scene 2. Do Caesar's words and actions suggest that he is becoming a tyrant? Support your answer with evidence from the play.

Text Criticism

10. **Historical Context** When Shakespeare wrote *Julius Caesar*, Europe did not have any democratically elected leaders; most nations were governed by powerful monarchs such as England's Queen Elizabeth I. How might a modern audience's reaction to the events in Act One differ from the reaction of an Elizabethan audience? Discuss specific examples in your response.

COMMON CORE

RL 3 Analyze how complex characters with conflicting motivations develop, interact with others, and advance the plot or develop the theme. **RL 5** Analyze how an author's choices concerning how to structure a text and order events within it create such effects as mystery, tension, or surprise.

Practice and Apply

For preliminary support of post-reading questions, use these copy masters:

R RESOURCE MANAGER—Copy Masters
Reading Check p. 27
Shakespearean Tragedy p. 23
Question Support p. 28

Additional selection questions are provided for teachers on page 15.

ANSWERS

Comprehension

1. *The tribunes are opposed to Caesar, but the commoners are celebrating him.*

2. *Caesar does not take it seriously.*

3. *Caesar refused the crown three times, but reluctantly so.*

4. *Cassius wants Brutus to think that many people oppose Caesar; he wants Brutus to lead the opposition.*

Text Analysis

COMMON CORE RL 3, RL 5

Possible answers:

5. *The reader can tell the status of the characters by the way they speak. The tribunes, members of the upper class, speak in blank verse; the commoners, in prose.*

6. *Details that build suspense: the storm, supernatural omens, Cassius' attempt to learn Casca's loyalty, the placement of the*

Assess and Reteach

Assess

DIAGNOSTIC AND SELECTION TESTS
Selection Test A pp. 311–312
Selection Test B/C pp. 313–314

Interactive Selection Test on **thinkcentral.com**

Reteach

Level Up Online Tutorials on **thinkcentral.com**

Reteaching Worksheets on **thinkcentral.com**
Literature Lesson 20: Rhythm and Meter
Literature Lesson 35: Rhetorical Devices
Literature Lesson 36: Irony
Literature Lessons 23, 24: Elements of Drama

---

forged letters as Cassius prepares to win Brutus to his side

7. **■ COMMON CORE FOCUS** *Reading Shakespearean Drama Brutus would be a better ruler because he considers his actions carefully and is noble. Cassius would be a better leader because he is shrewd and forceful.*

8. *Cassius is motivated by personal rivalry. He describes Caesar's physical frailties and frequently mentions his equal stature to Caesar (Scene 2, lines 97–131 and 135–150; Scene 3, lines 76–78 and 103–111).*

9. *If Casca is correct in saying that Caesar would have liked to wear the crown that he refused, then Caesar may be becoming a tyrant.*

Text Criticism

Possible answer:

10. *A modern audience might be more sympathetic toward the conspirators, believing that a dictator (which is how Caesar is depicted) has no right to rule.*

Practice and Apply

Get Into the Act
SUMMARY

Act Two begins with Brutus considering why Caesar may need to be killed. He reads one of Cassius' false letters, meets with the conspirators, and agrees that Caesar must die. Brutus tries to ease the worries of Portia, his wife. Caesar decides to go to the Capitol. Artemidorus and a soothsayer plan to warn Caesar; Portia awaits news of Brutus and Caesar.

VOCABULARY

COMMON CORE RL 4

⚠ WORD ORIGINS

Point out that *assassinate* is a verb, and *assassin* is the noun form that means "a murderer, especially of a prominent person."

Possible answer: *The Roman conspirators are, like the original assassins, plotting to kill a military leader.*

READING STRATEGY

◼ *Model the Skill:* SUMMARIZE

Read the synopsis aloud. Point out the date, and call to mind the soothsayer from Act One, Scene 2. Ask students what Brutus will do and what his reason will be.

Possible answer: *Brutus has decided that Caesar must die for the good of Rome.*

Resources for Act Two

Act Two

Scene 1   *Brutus' orchard in Rome.*

It is a few hours before dawn on March 15—the ides of March. Brutus, unable to sleep, walks in his garden. He faces a crucial decision: accept Caesar's growing power or kill Caesar and thus end his rule. While considering the problem, Brutus receives an anonymous letter (from Cassius) suggesting that Brutus take action against Caesar. Shortly after, Cassius and the conspirators visit Brutus, and they all agree to assassinate Caesar that day. After the conspirators leave, Brutus' wife, Portia, asks him to confide what has been troubling him. ⚠

Brutus. What, Lucius, ho!
I cannot by the progress of the stars
Give guess how near to day. Lucius, I say!
I would it were my fault to sleep so soundly.
5   When, Lucius, when? Awake, I say! What, Lucius!

[*Enter* Lucius *from the house.*]

Lucius. Called you, my lord?

Brutus. Get me a taper in my study, Lucius.
When it is lighted, come and call me here.

Lucius. I will, my lord.

[*Exit.*]

[Brutus *returns to his brooding.*]

10   **Brutus.** It must be by his death; and for my part,
I know no personal cause to spurn at him,
But for the general. He would be crowned.
How that might change his nature, there's the question.
It is the bright day that brings forth the adder,
15   And that craves wary walking. Crown him that,
And then I grant we put a sting in him
That at his will he may do danger with.
The abuse of greatness is when it disjoins
Remorse from power. And to speak truth of Caesar,
20   I have not known when his affections swayed
More than his reason. But 'tis a common proof
That lowliness is young ambition's ladder,
Whereto the climber-upward turns his face;
But when he once attains the upmost round,
25   He then unto the ladder turns his back,
Looks in the clouds, scorning the base degrees
By which he did ascend. So Caesar may.

1220   UNIT 11: SHAKESPEAREAN DRAMA

COMMON CORE RL 4

⚠ WORD ORIGINS

The word *assassin* is derived from an Arabic word for fighters during the Crusades who tried to kill leaders of the European armies. Reread the introduction to this scene. Given what you know of the etymology of *assassin*, why does it apply to this situation?

4 **I would . . . soundly:** I wish I could sleep so soundly.

7 **taper:** candle.

10–12 **It must . . . general:** Caesar would need to be killed; and I have no personal reason to attack him, only concern for the general welfare.

15 **craves:** demands.

19 **Remorse:** compassion.

20 **affections swayed:** passions ruled.

21–27 Brutus says that for an ambitious person, humility (**lowliness**) is like a ladder that only remains useful until the climber reaches the top rung (**round**). *How does this metaphor relate to the argument for overthrowing Caesar?*

Brutus and Portia in the Globe Theatre's 1999 production

---

*See resources on the **Teacher One Stop DVD-ROM** and on **thinkcentral.com**.*

R **RESOURCE MANAGER UNIT 11**

Plan and Teach, pp. 45–50
Summary, pp. 51–54†‡*
Text Analysis, pp. 55–56†*

DIAGNOSTIC AND SELECTION TESTS

Selection Tests, pp. 315–318

🧰 BEST PRACTICES TOOLKIT

Problem-and-Solution Charts, p. B20
Three-Column Journal, p. B10
Cause-and-Effect Chain, p. B39
Draw It, p. A2
Sequence Chain, p. B21

INTERACTIVE READER

ADAPTED INTERACTIVE READER

ELL ADAPTED INTERACTIVE READER

TECHNOLOGY

💿 **Teacher One Stop DVD-ROM**
💿 **Student One Stop DVD-ROM**
💿 **PowerNotes DVD-ROM**
💿 **Audio Anthology CD**
💿 **GrammarNotes DVD-ROM**
💿 **Audio Tutor CD**
💿 **ExamView Test Generator** on the **Teacher One Stop**

Video Trailer  THINK central

Go to **thinkcentral.com** to preview the **Video Trailer** introducing this selection. Other features that support the selection include

• **PowerNotes** presentation
• **ThinkAloud** models to enhance comprehension
• **WordSharp** vocabulary tutorials
• interactive writing and grammar instruction

---

* **Resources for Differentiation**   † Also in Spanish   ‡ In Haitian Creole and Vietnamese

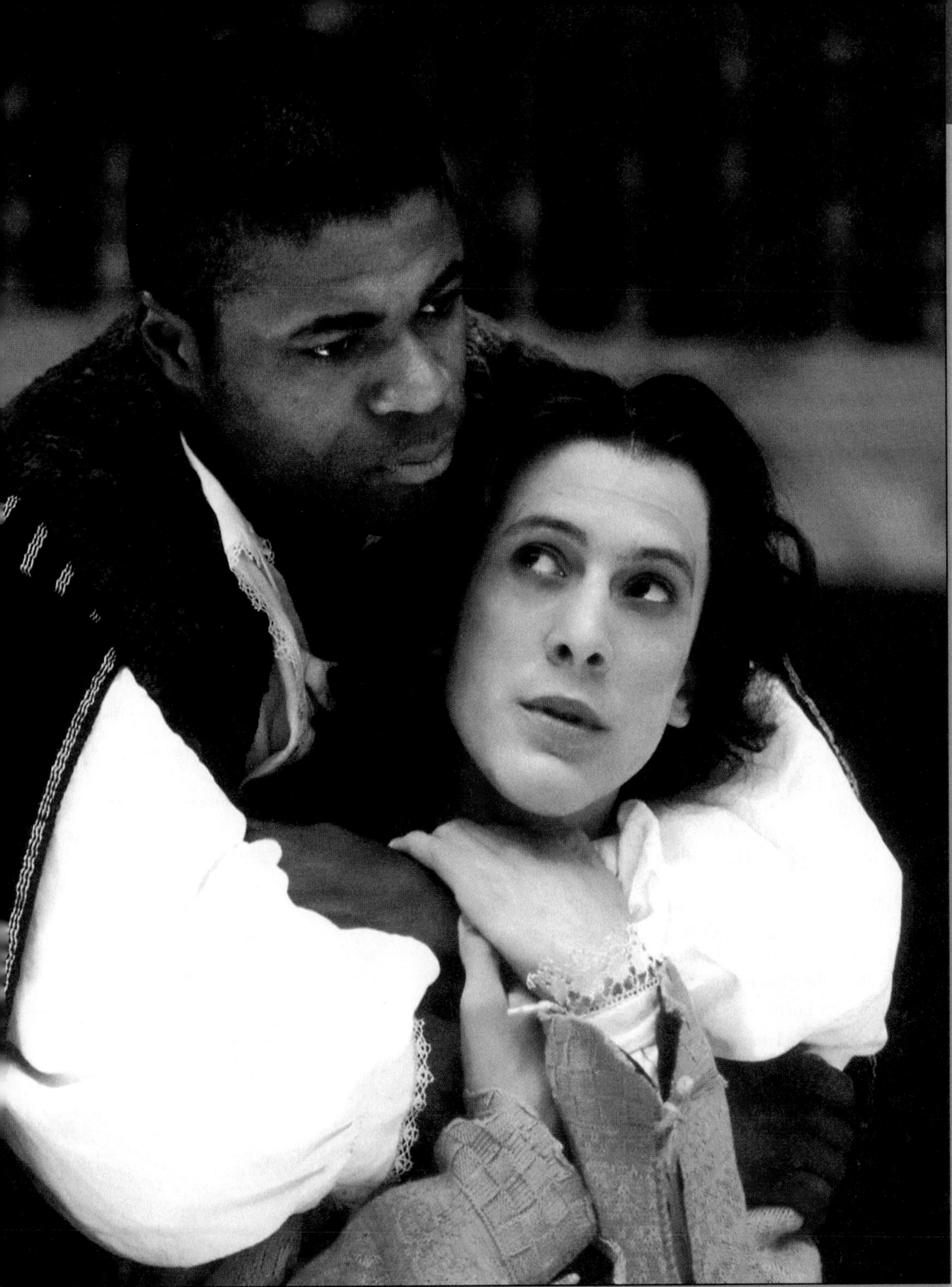

Reading Support

THINK central

This selection on **thinkcentral.com** includes embedded **ThinkAloud** models–students "thinking aloud" about the story to model the kinds of questions a good reader would ask about a selection.

Analyze Visuals

Activity What does this photograph suggest about Brutus' and Portia's emotions? Explain. ***Possible answer:*** *The photograph suggests that Brutus is troubled, for he is staring into the distance in a thoughtful way and seems to be embracing Portia for support. Portia seems concerned, as well, for she clasps his arm and looks toward his face, as if trying to figure out what is bothering him.*

TIERED DISCUSSION PROMPTS

Direct students to lines 10–27. Use these prompts to help students explore Brutus' brooding thoughts:

Connect Have you ever struggled with a difficult decision? How does that experience help you understand Brutus' soliloquy? *Accept all reasonable responses.*

Analyze What does Brutus fear will happen if Caesar is crowned? Why? ***Possible answer:*** *Brutus fears that after being crowned, Caesar will discard his appearance of humility, turn his back on his past, and abuse his power (lines 12–19 and 21–27). Popular wisdom says that people who are granted power often use it to harm those who granted them that power (lines 14–19 and 21–27).*

Evaluate Brutus says that he has no hard evidence that Caesar is becoming the kind of person who would harm Rome (lines 11 and 19–21). Given that, do you think that Brutus is being fair? Why or why not? ***Possible answers:*** *Brutus is not fair; he is thinking only of what might happen, and Caesar has not had the chance to prove himself. Brutus is fair; he is thinking of what has happened to others in Caesar's position and what he himself believes is best for Rome.*

DIFFERENTIATED INSTRUCTION

FOR ENGLISH LANGUAGE LEARNERS

Task Support Point out the question in the side note for lines 21–27. Explain that "the climber-upward" in line 23 is a reference to Caesar. ***Possible answer:*** *Brutus uses a ladder metaphor to suggest that when Caesar rises in power (climbs to the top), he will no longer feel the need to be humble. He then may look down on people (those on lower rungs) and abuse his power (lines 25–26). Someone like that, Brutus reasons, should be overthrown.*

FOR STRUGGLING READERS

In combination with the *Audio Anthology CD*, use one or more Targeted Passages (pp. 1222, 1228, 1235) to ensure that students focus on key story events, concepts, and skills. Targeted Passages are also good for English learners.

Preview After students have read the Scene 1 synopsis, have them use Problem-and-Solution Charts to record its key events.

BEST PRACTICES TOOLKIT—Transparency
Problem-and-Solution Charts p. B20

Can your
CONSCIENCE
mislead you?

Discuss Based on lines 10–34, what factors seem to be shaping Brutus' conscience when he decides that Caesar must die? Explain.

Possible answer: Brutus' conscience is shaped by two main factors. One factor is his fear of the unknown. Although he does not know for sure how Caesar will act when he becomes king (lines 11–13 and 19–21), Brutus is aware of the popular wisdom that says that someone in Caesar's position will change for the worse. The other factor is Brutus' patriotism. He loves Rome as a republic, and he does not want to see it change (lines 10–12). Because of these factors, Brutus decides that it would be right to kill Caesar before he begins to abuse his power and harm Rome (lines 28–34).

Then lest he may, prevent. And since the quarrel
Will bear no color for the thing he is,
30 Fashion it thus: that what he is, augmented,
Would run to these and these extremities;
And therefore think him as a serpent's egg,
Which, hatched, would as his kind grow mischievous,
And kill him in the shell.

[*Reenter* Lucius *with a letter.*]

35 **Lucius.** The taper burneth in your closet, sir.
Searching the window for a flint, I found
This paper, thus sealed up, and I am sure
It did not lie there when I went to bed.

[*Gives him the letter.*]

Brutus. Get you to bed again; it is not day.
40 Is not tomorrow, boy, the ides of March?

Lucius. I know not, sir.

Brutus. Look in the calendar and bring me word.

Lucius. I will, sir.

[*Exit.*]

Brutus. The exhalations, whizzing in the air,
45 Give so much light that I may read by them.

[*Opens the letter and reads.*]

"Brutus, thou sleep'st. Awake, and see thyself!
Shall Rome, etc. Speak, strike, redress!"
"Brutus, thou sleep'st. Awake!"
Such instigations have been often dropped
50 Where I have took them up.
"Shall Rome, etc." Thus must I piece it out:
Shall Rome stand under one man's awe? What, Rome?
My ancestors did from the streets of Rome
The Tarquin drive when he was called a king.
55 "Speak, strike, redress!" Am I entreated
To speak and strike? O Rome, I make thee promise,
If the redress will follow, thou receivest
Thy full petition at the hand of Brutus!

[*Reenter* Lucius.]

Lucius. Sir, March is wasted fifteen days.

[*Knocking within.*]

60 **Brutus.** 'Tis good. Go to the gate, somebody knocks.

[*Exit* Lucius.]

Since Cassius first did whet me against Caesar,
I have not slept.

28–34 lest … shell: Rather than let Caesar do that, I should take steps to prevent it. Since our case against Caesar is weak (**Will bear no color**) at present, we must shape (**Fashion**) our argument against him in the following way: We know what kind of person Caesar is now. If his true nature were allowed to develop (**augmented**), it would reach terrible extremes. So we must treat him as a serpent's egg and kill him before he hatches.

35 closet: private room.

44 exhalations: meteors.

① Targeted Passage

47 redress: right a wrong. The letter is meant to suggest certain things to Brutus, without actually spelling them out.

49 instigations: suggestions.

51 Thus … out: I must guess the rest of the sentence.

52 Shall … awe: Should Rome have such fear and respect for just one man?

53–54 My ancestors … king: Brutus refers to an ancestor who drove out Rome's last king. After that, rule by the Senate was established.

56–58 I make … Brutus: I promise you, Rome, if a remedy for our troubles can follow from my action, you will get what you need from Brutus.

61 whet me: sharpen my appetite.

DIFFERENTIATED INSTRUCTION

FOR STRUGGLING READERS

① Targeted Passage [Lines 44–58]

In this passage, Brutus reads the forged letter and declares himself loyal to Rome, not to Caesar.

- What does the letter urge Brutus to do? (lines 46–47)

- What must Brutus figure out about the parts where the letter is vague? (line 51)

- What fact about his ancestors does Brutus recall? Why is that fact important to him? (lines 53–54)

- What does Brutus promise to Rome? (lines 57–58)

FOR ENGLISH LANGUAGE LEARNERS

Vocabulary Support Work with students to clarify the meanings of these words:

- *flint* (line 36), "a kind of stone used to create a spark"

- *strike* (line 47), "to attack"

- *petition* (line 58), "a request"

Between the acting of a dreadful thing
And the first motion, all the interim is
65 Like a phantasma or a hideous dream.
The genius and the mortal instruments
Are then in council, and the state of man,
Like to a little kingdom, suffers then
The nature of an insurrection.

[*Reenter* Lucius.]

70 **Lucius.** Sir, 'tis your brother Cassius at the door,
Who doth desire to see you.

Brutus.   Is he alone?

Lucius. No, sir, there are more with him.

Brutus.   Do you know them?

Lucius. No, sir. Their hats are plucked about their ears
And half their faces buried in their cloaks,
75 That by no means I may discover them
By any mark of favor.

Brutus.   Let 'em enter.

[*Exit* Lucius.]

They are the faction. O conspiracy,
Sham'st thou to show thy dang'rous brow by night,
When evils are most free? O, then by day
80 Where wilt thou find a cavern dark enough
To mask thy monstrous visage? Seek none,
conspiracy, hide it in smiles and affability!
For if thou path, thy native semblance on,
No Erebus itself were dim enough
85 To hide thee from prevention. **B**

[*Enter the conspirators,* Cassius, Casca, Decius, Cinna, Metellus
Cimber, *and* Trebonius.]

Cassius. I think we are too bold upon your rest.
Good morrow, Brutus. Do we trouble you?

Brutus. I have been up this hour, awake all night.
Know I these men that come along with you?

90 **Cassius.** Yes, every man of them; and no man here
But honors you; and every one doth wish
You had but that opinion of yourself
Which every noble Roman bears of you.
This is Trebonius.

Brutus.   He is welcome hither.

95 **Cassius.** This, Decius Brutus.

Brutus.   He is welcome too.

63–69 Between...insurrection: The time between the earliest thought of a terrible act and the actual performance of it is a nightmare. The soul (**genius**) and body (**mortal instruments**) debate the subject, while the man himself feels like a kingdom undergoing a civil war.

70 brother: Cassius, the husband of Brutus' sister, is his brother-in-law.

75–76 by no...favor: There is no way I can tell who they are.

77–85 O conspiracy...prevention: If these plotters are afraid to be seen at night, how will they keep these terrible plans from showing on their faces during the day? They must smile and show friendliness (**affability**). If they go out showing their true natures (**native semblance**), even the dark gateway to hell (**Erebus** ĕr′ə-bəs) could not hide them.

B SOLILOQUY
Reread lines 61–69 and 77–85. What feelings does Brutus reveal in these two soliloquies?

86 I think...rest: I think we may have come too early.

COMMON CORE RL 4

Language Coach

Multiple Meanings *But,* which usually means *except,* has other meanings, especially in older writings. In lines 90–91, *but* creates a double negative (with "no man"), which, according to the laws of mathematics and English grammar, results in a positive. Rephrase these lines in positive terms.

TEXT ANALYSIS  COMMON CORE

B *Model the Skill:* SOLILOQUY   RL 3 RL 5

To model how to analyze Shakespearean tragedy, read aloud lines 61–69 and 77–85. Then read the side note on lines 63–69. Elicit from students why Brutus is at war within himself. Have a student read the side note for lines 77–85, and then ask the class what concerns Brutus has about the conspirators.

Possible answer: *In the first soliloquy, Brutus reveals that he has not slept (line 62) and that he feels uneasy (lines 63–69) while waiting for events to play out. In the second soliloquy, Brutus reveals that he feels rather doubtful about his fellow conspirators' ability to keep the plot a secret (lines 77–85).*

FOR ENGLISH LANGUAGE LEARNERS

Vocabulary Support Brutus now joins the conspiracy. Discuss these words and phrases that relate to the hidden nature of a conspiracy:

- *discover* (line 75), "identify"
- *faction* (line 77), "minority group"
- *dang'rous brow by night* (line 78), "dangerous face at night"
- *a cavern dark enough* (line 80), "a dark enough cave"
- *mask* (line 81), "hide"

Language Coach   COMMON CORE RL 4

Multiple Meanings *Answer:*
Every man here honors you . . . Ask students to identify the meaning of *but* in line 92.
(only or merely)

FOR ADVANCED LEARNERS/PRE-AP

Analyze Allusions [paired-activity option]
Point out that Shakespeare, like many Renaissance writers, frequently alludes to Greek mythology. Ask students to research Brutus' reference to Erebus in line 84. Have students prepare to share information about (1) who Erebus is, (2) why Brutus would have referenced him in this soliloquy, and (3) how the allusion adds to the overall mood of the scene.

TIERED DISCUSSION PROMPTS

Direct students to lines 114–140. Use these prompts to help students consider this argument that Brutus makes to his fellow conspirators:

Summarize What is the main point of Brutus' argument in this passage? *Possible answer: The main point is that there are many reasons for the conspirators to refrain from taking an oath to assassinate Caesar.*

Analyze How does Brutus appeal to the conspirators' pride? *Possible answer: Brutus appeals to their pride by saying that their cause is noble and that Romans are honorable and honest enough to need no oath (lines 119–128). He points out that only lesser people need oaths (lines 129–132) and says again that Romans are known for being faithful (lines 132–140).*

Evaluate Do you think that Brutus is being completely honest? Why else might he not want to swear an oath? *Possible answer: Brutus is not being completely honest. He does not want to swear an oath because he does not want the murder to look dishonorable and secretive. Brutus already knows that he must cast their actions in a positive light, and here he tries to do that by saying that their act is honorable and noble and that it thus does not require an oath.*

Cassius. This, Casca; this, Cinna; and this, Metellus Cimber.

Brutus. They are all welcome.
What watchful cares do interpose themselves
Betwixt your eyes and night?

100 **Cassius.** Shall I entreat a word?

[*They whisper.*]

Decius. Here lies the east. Doth not the day break here?

Casca. No.

Cinna. O, pardon, sir, it doth; and yon grey lines
That fret the clouds are messengers of day.

105 **Casca.** You shall confess that you are both deceived.
Here, as I point my sword, the sun arises,
Which is a great way growing on the south,
Weighing the youthful season of the year.
Some two months hence, up higher toward the north
110 He first presents his fire; and the high east
Stands as the Capitol, directly here.

[Brutus *and* Cassius *rejoin the others.*]

Brutus. Give me your hands all over, one by one.

Cassius. And let us swear our resolution.

Brutus. No, not on oath. If not the face of men,
115 The sufferance of our souls, the time's abuse—
If these be motives weak, break off betimes,
And every man hence to his idle bed.
So let high-sighted tyranny range on
Till each man drop by lottery. But if these
120 (As I am sure they do) bear fire enough
To kindle cowards and to steel with valor
The melting spirits of women, then, countrymen,
What need we any spur but our own cause
To prick us to redress? what other bond
125 Than secret Romans that have spoke the word
And will not palter? and what other oath
Than honesty to honesty engaged
That this shall be, or we will fall for it?
Swear priests and cowards and men cautelous,
130 Old feeble carrions and such suffering souls
That welcome wrongs; unto bad causes swear
Such creatures as men doubt; but do not stain
The even virtue of our enterprise,
Nor the insuppressive mettle of our spirits,
135 To think that or our cause or our performance
Did need an oath when every drop of blood

98–99 What watchful...night: What troubles keep you awake at night?

100 Shall I entreat a word?: Cassius asks Brutus to step aside and talk privately with him. While they talk, the others chatter about the sky (lines 101–111), pretending to be not at all interested in what Cassius and Brutus are discussing.

104 fret: stripe.

107–108 Which is...year: from a southerly direction, since it is still early in the year.

114–119 If not...lottery: We do not need to swear our loyalty to one another. The sadness of people's faces, our own suffering, and the awful time we live in—if these aren't strong enough to hold us together, then let us all go back to bed. In that case, let tyranny live, while we die off, one at a time, by chance (**by lottery**).

126 palter: go back on our word.

129–131 Swear priests...wrongs: Swearing oaths is for priests, crafty men, old men on the verge of death, and wretches who welcome injustice.

134 insuppressive mettle: unconquerable courage.

135 or our cause...performance: either our cause or our actions.

DIFFERENTIATED INSTRUCTION

FOR STRUGGLING READERS

Inverted Word Order Have students reread lines 129–131. Explain that *cautelous* means "crafty" and that *carrion* means "dead and putrefying flesh." (Shakespeare uses *carrions* to mean "people who are about to die and decay.") Point out that Shakespeare inverts the word order by placing the adjective after the noun that it modifies and placing the verb at the beginning of the sentence. Elicit this rephrasing: "Priests, cowards, crafty men, men who are near death, and men who welcome injustice swear oaths."

FOR ENGLISH LANGUAGE LEARNERS

Vocabulary: Outdated Forms Urge students to continue adding outdated terms to their language journal. (See the For English Language Learners note on page 1204.) Provide these terms and their definitions. Then have students reread the lines noted and substitute the definitions for the words.

- *Betwixt* (line 99), "Between"
- *prick us to redress* (line 124), "make us do what is right"
- *no whit* (line 148), "not at all"
- *it is not meet* (line 155), "it is not right"

That every Roman bears, and nobly bears,
Is guilty of a several bastardy
If he do break the smallest particle
140 Of any promise that hath passed from him.

Cassius. But what of Cicero? Shall we sound him?
I think he will stand very strong with us.

Casca. Let us not leave him out.

Cinna.   No, by no means.

Metellus. O, let us have him! for his silver hairs
145 Will purchase us a good opinion
And buy men's voices to commend our deeds.
It shall be said his judgment ruled our hands;
Our youths and wildness shall no whit appear,
But all be buried in his gravity.

150 **Brutus.** O, name him not! Let us not break with him,
For he will never follow anything
That other men begin.

Cassius.   Then leave him out.

Casca. Indeed he is not fit. **C**

Decius. Shall no man else be touched but only Caesar?

155 **Cassius.** Decius, well urged. I think it is not meet
Mark Antony, so well beloved of Caesar,
Should outlive Caesar. We shall find of him
A shrewd contriver; and you know, his means,
If he improve them, may well stretch so far
160 As to annoy us all; which to prevent,
Let Antony and Caesar fall together.

Brutus. Our course will seem too bloody, Caius Cassius,
To cut the head off and then hack the limbs,
Like wrath in death and envy afterwards;
165 For Antony is but a limb of Caesar.
Let us be sacrificers, but not butchers, Caius.
We all stand up against the spirit of Caesar,
And in the spirit of men there is no blood.
O that we then could come by Caesar's spirit
170 And not dismember Caesar! But, alas,
Caesar must bleed for it! And, gentle friends,
Let's kill him boldly, but not wrathfully;
Let's carve him as a dish fit for the gods,
Not hew him as a carcass fit for hounds.
175 And let our hearts, as subtle masters do,
Stir up their servants to an act of rage
And after seem to chide 'em. This shall make

---

138 **guilty ... bastardy:** not truly Roman.

141 **sound him:** see what he thinks of the matter.

144–146 **his silver ... deeds:** his old age will win us popular support.

C TRAGEDY
The development of the conspiracy is an important part of the **plot** of *Julius Caesar.* Who seems to be in charge in lines 112–153, Brutus or Cassius? Cite details to support your answer.

169–170 Brutus wishes they could remove Caesar's soul without having to destroy his body.

174 **Not ... hounds:** Let's not chop him up like the body of an animal to be fed to dogs.

TEXT ANALYSIS	COMMON CORE
	RL 3 RL 5

C TRAGEDY

Possible answer: *Brutus seems to be in charge. Brutus is the one who decides that they will not swear an oath, thus overruling Cassius (lines 112–114). When Cassius asks whether they should include Cicero in the conspiracy, and several conspirators think that they should, Brutus says no, and the conspirators immediately reverse their opinion so that they can show themselves to be in agreement with him (lines 141–153).*

FOR STRUGGLING READERS

Summarize Explain that Mark Antony will become a more important character as the play progresses. Ask students to reread and then summarize Brutus' argument against killing Antony (lines 162–183). Elicit that Brutus wants to spare Antony so that the conspirators will look like sacrificers rather than butchers, which is how they would be viewed if they killed Antony as well as Caesar. Also elicit that Brutus thinks that Antony can do nothing if Caesar is gone.

FOR ADVANCED LEARNERS/PRE–AP

Analyze Character Motivation Remind students that Brutus makes three important decisions on pages 1224–1225. Have students use a Three-Column Journal to explain what each decision is, why they think that Brutus has made the decision, and whether or not they think that the decision will prove to be a good one.

🧰 BEST PRACTICES TOOLKIT—Transparency
Three-Column Journal p. B10

Decision	Reason for Decision	Good/Bad Decision
Brutus decides against an oath.	He wants the murder to look better than it is.	
Brutus decides against including Cicero.		
Brutus decides against killing Antony.		

BACKGROUND

The Conspirators: Decius Brutus and Trebonius Caesar would have been quite surprised to learn that Decius Brutus (Decius) and Trebonius were plotting against him, because he considered both of them good friends. Caesar had appointed Trebonius chief magistrate of Rome, which was both an honorable and an influential position. Caesar was so close to Decius Brutus that he had named him as an heir in the event of the death of Octavius, Caesar's primary heir.

Our purpose necessary, and not envious;
Which so appearing to the common eyes,
180 We shall be called purgers, not murderers.
And for Mark Antony, think not of him;
For he can do no more than Caesar's arm
When Caesar's head is off.

Cassius.   Yet I fear him,
For in the ingrafted love he bears to Caesar—

185 **Brutus.** Alas, good Cassius, do not think of him!
If he love Caesar, all that he can do
Is to himself—take thought, and die for Caesar.
And that were much he should; for he is given
To sports, to wildness, and much company.

190 **Trebonius.** There is no fear in him. Let him not die,
For he will live and laugh at this hereafter.

[*Clock strikes.*]

Brutus. Peace! Count the clock.

Cassius.   The clock hath stricken three.

Trebonius. 'Tis time to part.

Cassius.   But it is doubtful yet
Whether Caesar will come forth today or no;
195 For he is superstitious grown of late,
Quite from the main opinion he held once
Of fantasy, of dreams, and ceremonies.
It may be these apparent prodigies,
The unaccustomed terror of this night,
200 And the persuasion of his augurers
May hold him from the Capitol today.

Decius. Never fear that. If he be so resolved,
I can o'ersway him; for he loves to hear
That unicorns may be betrayed with trees
205 And bears with glasses, elephants with holes,
Lions with toils, and men with flatterers;
But when I tell him he hates flatterers,
He says he does, being then most flattered.
Let me work,
210 For I can give his humor the true bent,
And I will bring him to the Capitol.

Cassius. Nay, we will all of us be there to fetch him.

Brutus. By the eighth hour. Is that the uttermost?

Cinna. Be that the uttermost, and fail not then.

175–180 let our hearts ... murderers: Let our hearts treat our hands (**servants**) the way sly masters do; we will let our hands do our dirty work, then later scold (**chide**) them for what they have done. This attitude will make us seem to the public (**common eyes**) to be healers (**purgers**) instead of murderers.

184 ingrafted: deep-rooted.

188–189 And that ... company: And that is unlikely, for he loves sports, wild times, and socializing.

190 There is no fear in him: We have nothing to fear from Antony.

193–201 But it is ... Capitol today: We don't know if Caesar will leave his house (**come forth**) today. Lately he has become superstitious, in contrast to the strong views (**main opinion**) he once had of such beliefs. The cause may be these strange events and the arguments of his fortunetellers (**augurers**). These things may keep him from coming to the Capitol today.

203 o'ersway him: change his mind.

204–208 Decius tells of ways to trap shrewd animals. He says that Caesar, who loves to hear such stories, can also be trapped—by flattery.

210 I can give ... true bent: I can get him into the right mood.

213 By the ... uttermost: By eight o'clock. Do we all agree that eight is the latest we will be there?

DIFFERENTIATED INSTRUCTION

FOR ENGLISH LANGUAGE LEARNERS

Vocabulary: Outdated Forms Have pairs of students work together to figure out the meanings of these outdated words and phrases:

- *Count the clock* (line 192), "Tell the time"
- *hath stricken* (line 192), "has struck"
- *or no* (line 194), "or not"
- *Nay* (line 212), "No"

- *He loves me well* (line 219), "He likes/respects me very much"
- *The morning comes upon's* (line 221), "It is almost morning"
- *Wherefore rise you now?* (line 234), "Why are you getting up now [so early]?"
- *yesternight* (line 238), "last night"
- *Gave sign* (line 247), "Signaled"

FOR STRUGGLING READERS

Recognize Irony Have students reread lines 202–211, in which Decius says that Caesar loves to hear stories of shrewd animals that can be trapped. Point out the irony: Caesar himself is about to become the "shrewd animal" that Decius will help the conspirators trap.

Metellus. Caius Ligarius doth bear Caesar hard,
215 Who rated him for speaking well of Pompey.
I wonder none of you have thought of him.

Brutus. Now, good Metellus, go along by him.
He loves me well, and I have given him reasons.
220 Send him but hither, and I'll fashion him.

Cassius. The morning comes upon's. We'll leave you, Brutus.
And, friends, disperse yourselves; but all remember
What you have said and show yourselves true Romans.

Brutus. Good gentlemen, look fresh and merrily.
225 Let not our looks put on our purposes,
But bear it as our Roman actors do,
With untired spirits and formal constancy.
And so good morrow to you every one.

[*Exeunt all but* Brutus.]

Boy! Lucius! Fast asleep? It is no matter.
230 Enjoy the honey-heavy dew of slumber.
Thou hast no figures nor no fantasies
Which busy care draws in the brains of men;
Therefore thou sleep'st so sound.

[*Enter* Portia, *Brutus' wife.*]

Portia.   Brutus, my lord!

Brutus. Portia! What mean you? Wherefore rise you now?
235 It is not for your health thus to commit
Your weak condition to the raw cold morning.

Portia. Nor for yours neither. Y'have ungently, Brutus,
Stole from my bed. And yesternight at supper
You suddenly arose and walked about,
240 Musing and sighing with your arms across;
And when I asked you what the matter was,
You stared upon me with ungentle looks.
I urged you further, then you scratched your head
And too impatiently stamped with your foot.
245 Yet I insisted, yet you answered not,
But with an angry wafture of your hand
Gave sign for me to leave you. So I did,
Fearing to strengthen that impatience
Which seemed too much enkindled, and withal
250 Hoping it was but an effect of humor,
Which sometime hath his hour with every man.
It will not let you eat nor talk nor sleep,
And could it work so much upon your shape
As it hath much prevailed on your condition,

215–217 Caius . . . of him: Caius Ligarius has a grudge against Caesar, who criticized him for supporting Pompey. I don't know why you haven't asked him to join our plot.

220 fashion: persuade.

225 Let not . . . purposes: Let's not let our appearances give away (**put on**) what we are planning to do.

233 *As you read the conversation between Brutus and his wife, think about the kind of relationship they have.*

245 Yet: still.

246 wafture: waving.

249 withal: also.

250 humor: mood.

REVISIT THE BIG QUESTION

Can your CONSCIENCE mislead you?

Discuss Based on lines 229–233, how is Lucius able to sleep but Brutus is not? What might Lucius' ability to sleep suggest about his conscience? *Possible answer: Lucius is able to sleep because he is not a conspirator. As such, he has a clean conscience. He is not about to be guilty of an assassination, nor is he tortured by the soul-searching, plotting, and manipulation of others that Brutus has experienced.*

FOR ENGLISH LANGUAGE LEARNERS

Concept Support Explain to students that in lines 224–228, Brutus is comparing the conspirators to Roman actors who hide their personal feelings and play their assigned parts. Brutus makes this comparison as a way of urging his fellow conspirators to put on a fearless, united front and to keep hidden any indication that they know of or are involved in a plot against Caesar.

Task Support Have students read the side note for line 233. Help students analyze the couple's relationship by pointing out the words with which Portia greets Brutus (line 233) and the fact that Brutus seems concerned about his wife's health (line 235–236). *Possible answer: Brutus and Portia have a good relationship in that each respects and cares about the other. Their relationship is also somewhat typical of the time in that Portia refers to him as "my lord" and that Brutus accepts this authoritative role.*

Language Coach   (COMMON CORE RL 4)

Multiple Meanings *Answer: It means "to move secretly." Today, we would say* stolen, *to form the present perfect correctly.* Point out "rise" in line 234 as another example of a multiple meaning word. Tell students that the word can mean "to stand up after lying, sitting, or kneeling," and it can also mean "to increase in number." Ask students which meaning is intended in line 234.

BACKGROUND

Portia in History and in Shakespeare Portia was Brutus' first cousin and his second wife. She reminds Brutus (line 295) that she is the daughter of Marcus Porcius Cato, a statesman who was remembered for his conservative views but also for his honesty. In Rome's civil war, Cato was a leader in Pompey's army and fought against Julius Caesar in Africa; at the end of a key battle, he killed himself rather than surrender to Caesar. Shakespeare presents Portia, Cato's daughter, as a strong woman who is unafraid of confronting Brutus and who is frustrated at Brutus' unwillingness to share his thoughts with her. She reminds him of her heritage to persuade him that she is stronger than typical wives are.

---

255 I should not know you Brutus. Dear my lord,
Make me acquainted with your cause of grief.

Brutus. I am not well in health, and that is all.

Portia. Brutus is wise and, were he not in health,
He would embrace the means to come by it.

260 **Brutus.** Why, so I do. Good Portia, go to bed.

Portia. Is Brutus sick, and is it physical
To walk unbraced and suck up the humors
Of the dank morning? What, is Brutus sick,
And will he steal out of his wholesome bed
265 To dare the vile contagion of the night,
And tempt the rheumy and unpurgéd air,
To add unto his sickness? No, my Brutus.
You have some sick offense within your mind,
Which by the right and virtue of my place
270 I ought to know of; and upon my knees
I charm you, by my once commended beauty,
By all your vows of love, and that great vow
Which did incorporate and make us one,
That you unfold to me, yourself, your half,
275 Why you are heavy, and what men tonight
Have had resort to you; for here have been
Some six or seven, who did hide their faces
Even from darkness.

Brutus.   Kneel not, gentle Portia.

Portia. I should not need if you were gentle Brutus.
280 Within the bond of marriage, tell me, Brutus,
Is it excepted I should know no secrets
That appertain to you? Am I yourself
But, as it were, in sort or limitation?
To keep with you at meals, comfort your bed,
285 And talk to you sometimes? Dwell I but in the suburbs
Of your good pleasure? If it be no more,
Portia is Brutus' harlot, not his wife.

Brutus. You are my true and honorable wife,
As dear to me as are the ruddy drops
290 That visit my sad heart.

Portia. If this were true, then should I know this secret.
I grant I am a woman, but withal
A woman that Lord Brutus took to wife.
I grant that I am a woman, but withal
295 A woman well reputed, Cato's daughter.
Think you I am no stronger than my sex,
Being so fathered and so husbanded?

253–255 And could ... you Brutus: If a mood like that could change your appearance (**shape**) the way it has changed your personality (**condition**), I would not recognize you.

257 *Why do you think Brutus lies to Portia?*

261–267 Is Brutus ... sickness: Do you expect me to believe that you're sick? Is it healthy to walk without a coat (**unbraced**) and breathe the air of a damp morning or the unhealthy night air that is not yet cleansed (**unpurged**) by the sun?

268–270 You have ... know of: You have a sickness of the mind; as your wife, I have a right to know what it is.

275 heavy: sad.

② **Targeted Passage**

281 excepted: made an exception that.

283 in sort or limitation: only in part.

289–290 the ruddy ... heart: my blood.

DIFFERENTIATED INSTRUCTION

FOR STRUGGLING READERS

② **Targeted Passage** [Lines 263–287]

This passage offers insights into Portia's character, including her intelligence and strength.

- How does Portia know that Brutus is not physically ill? (lines 264–267)

- What does Portia say is wrong with Brutus? (line 268)

- What questions does Portia ask toward the end of this passage? Why? (lines 281–286)

FOR ENGLISH LANGUAGE LEARNERS

Task Support Direct students' attention to the side note question for line 257. Urge students to read the entire page before they answer.
Possible response: Brutus lies to Portia because he does not want her to know about the plot to kill Caesar. He loves and honors her (lines 288–290). He most likely wants to protect her from worry or from being implicated in the murder—or he is concerned that if she knows the truth, she might try to change his mind.

Concept Support Have pairs of students reread Portia's words in lines 268–278. Explain that Portia says that she is using her beauty, which captivated Brutus when they were younger, to charm him into answering her now. Elicit that she also uses the fact that she is his wife ("that great vow / Which did incorporate and make us one" [lines 272–273]) to persuade Brutus to tell her what is bothering him.

COMMON CORE RI 7

Casting

When **casting** roles for a Shakespearean play, directors don't necessarily try to match the race or even the gender of a character. (Originally, all of the roles were played by males.) However, physical traits are still important; a plump actor would generally not be chosen to play the "lean and hungry" Cassius. These photographs show three pairs of actors who have played Brutus and Portia. What traits set them apart? Which actors would you have chosen for the roles? Explain your response.

Brutus and Portia in the Shakespeare Theatre's 1993–1994 production

Brutus and Portia in the New York Shakespeare Festival's 1988 production

Brutus and Portia in the Globe Theatre's 1999 production

BEHIND THE CURTAIN

COMMON CORE RI 7

Casting Explain to students that casting the actors for a play is important because the choice affects the way in which the audience responds to the characters and to the play as a whole. Both the physical traits and the stage presence of the actors are important to consider when casting roles. *Possible answer: The three pairs of actors are distinct in several ways. First, the actors playing Brutus in the Shakespeare Theatre and the New York Shakespeare Festival productions are Caucasian and appear older than the African-American man playing Brutus in the Globe Theatre production. The actor playing Portia in the Shakespeare Theatre production looks to be pleading with Brutus. The actor playing Portia in the New York Shakespeare Festival production is embracing Brutus; she looks as if she is concerned but trying to be comforting. The actress playing Portia in the Globe Theatre production is turned away from Brutus and does not appear as loving. Readers may choose the pair of actors from the Shakespeare Theatre production because Portia seems to be kneeling (line 278) as she pleads with Brutus.*

FOR ADVANCED LEARNERS/PRE–AP

Analyze Casting Have small groups of students prepare a list of all of the characters they have met so far in *Julius Caesar*. Then ask them to cast those roles with present-day actors and to explain their choices. Encourage groups to compare their lists to see if they have any actors in common.

REVIST THE BIG QUESTION

Can your CONSCIENCE mislead you?

Discuss Based on lines 298–309, how do you think that keeping the plot to kill Caesar from Portia affects Brutus' guilty conscience? Explain your answer. *Possible answer: Not telling Portia probably makes Brutus' guilty conscience worse. Brutus prays that he would be "worthy of this noble wife" (line 303). He also promises Portia that he will tell her later what is bothering him (lines 305–308).*

Tell me your counsels; I will not disclose 'em.
I have made strong proof of my constancy,
300 Giving myself a voluntary wound
Here, in the thigh. Can I bear that with patience,
And not my husband's secrets?

Brutus. O ye gods,
Render me worthy of this noble wife!

[*Knocking within.*]

Hark, hark! one knocks. Portia, go in awhile,
305 And by-and-by thy bosom shall partake
The secrets of my heart.
All my engagements I will construe to thee,
All the charactery of my sad brows.
Leave me with haste.

[*Exit* Portia.]

Lucius, who's that knocks?

[*Reenter* Lucius *with* Caius Ligarius.]

310 **Lucius.** Here is a sick man that would speak with you.

Brutus. Caius Ligarius, that Metellus spake of.
Boy, stand aside. Caius Ligarius, how?

Caius. Vouchsafe good morrow from a feeble tongue.

Brutus. O, what a time have you chose out, brave Caius,
315 To wear a kerchief! Would you were not sick!

Caius. I am not sick if Brutus have in hand
Any exploit worthy the name of honor.

Brutus. Such an exploit have I in hand, Ligarius,
Had you a healthful ear to hear of it.

320 **Caius.** By all the gods that Romans bow before,
I here discard my sickness! Soul of Rome!
Brave son, derived from honorable loins!
Thou like an exorcist has conjured up
My mortified spirit. Now bid me run,
325 And I will strive with things impossible;
Yea, get the better of them. What's to do?

Brutus. A piece of work that will make sick men whole.

Caius. But are not some whole that we must make sick?

Brutus. That must we also. What it is, my Caius,
330 I shall unfold to thee as we are going
To whom it must be done.

Caius. Set on your foot,
And with a heart new-fired I follow you,
To do I know not what; but it sufficeth

296–302 Think you ... secrets: How can you consider me merely a typical woman when I am the daughter of Cato (**a highly respected Roman**) and the wife of Brutus? So tell me your secret. I have proven my strength by wounding myself here in the thigh. If I can put up with that pain, I can certainly deal with my husband's secrets.

307–308 All may ... brows: I will explain all my dealings and the reason for my sad looks.

313 Vouchsafe ... tongue: Accept a good morning from a sick man.

315 kerchief: a covering to protect the head during sickness.

317 exploit: deed.

322 derived ... loins: descended from noble Romans.

323 exorcist: someone who can call up spirits.

328 *What is Caius hinting at?*

331 Set on your foot: Lead the way.

333 it sufficeth: It is enough.

DIFFERENTIATED INSTRUCTION

FOR ENGLISH LANGUAGE LEARNERS

Task Support Have students read the side note question for line 328 and then reread lines 316–328. Explain that Brutus and Caius are not using the literal definition of *sick* and that Caius commits to Brutus even before he knows what Brutus is planning. Elicit that earlier in this scene, Brutus joined the conspiracy. *Possible answer: Caius is hinting at the plot to overthrow Caesar. In other words, he is asking, "Isn't there a healthy man whom we need to harm?"*

Vocabulary: Outdated Forms Ask students to add these words to their language journals (see the For English Learners note on page 1204).

- *Render* (line 303), "Make"
- *by-and-by thy bosom shall partake* (line 305), "soon your heart will share"
- *spake of* (line 311), "talked about"
- *bid me run* (line 324), "ask me to run"
- *What's to do?* (line 326), "What needs to be done?"

FOR ADVANCED LEARNERS/PRE–AP

Analyze Motif [paired-activity option] Have students consider how Shakespeare has used the motif of illness so far (Caesar's deafness and epilepsy; Caius' sickness). Ask students to make and share some notes about how (1) the motif affects the mood of the play, and (2) Shakespeare might be using the motif to comment about humankind in general. Urge students to note other references to illness as they continue to read.

That Brutus leads me on.

[*Thunder.*]

Brutus.   Follow me then.

[*Exeunt.*]

Scene 2   *Caesar's house in Rome.*

It is now past dawn on March 15. Like everyone else in Rome, Caesar and his wife have slept badly because of the storm. There is still some lightning and thunder. Caesar prepares to go to the Capitol; but because of the many threatening omens, his wife, Calpurnia, insists that he stay home. Caesar agrees, for Calpurnia's sake. He changes his mind, however, when Decius, one of the conspirators, persuades him that he must not seem swayed by his wife's superstitions. Although Caesar doesn't know it, the other conspirators are on their way to his house to make sure he does not decide to stay at home.

[*Enter Caesar in his nightgown.*]

Caesar. Nor heaven nor earth have been at peace tonight.
Thrice hath Calpurnia in her sleep cried out
"Help, ho! They murder Caesar!" Who's within?

[*Enter a Servant.*]

Servant. My lord?

5 **Caesar.** Go bid the priests do present sacrifice,
And bring me their opinions of success.

Servant. I will, my lord.

[*Exit.*]

[*Enter Caesar's wife, Calpurnia, alarmed.*]

Calpurnia. What mean you, Caesar? Think you to walk forth?
You shall not stir out of your house today.

10 **Caesar.** Caesar shall forth. The things that threatened me
Ne'er looked but on my back. When they shall see
The face of Caesar, they are vanished.

Calpurnia. Caesar, I never stood on ceremonies,
Yet now they fright me. There is one within,
15 Besides the things that we have heard and seen,
Recounts most horrid sights seen by the watch.
A lioness hath whelped in the streets,
And graves have yawned and yielded up their dead.
Fierce fiery warriors fought upon the clouds
20 In ranks and squadrons and right form of war,
Which drizzled blood upon the Capitol.
The noise of battle hurtled in the air,
Horses did neigh, and dying men did groan,
And ghosts did shriek and squeal about the streets.

5–6 Go bid … success: Roman priests would kill an animal as a sacrifice to the gods. Then they would cut the animal open and examine its internal organs for signs of future events.

10–12 The things … vanished: When I turn to face the things that threaten me, they disappear.

13–26 Caesar, I never … fear them: Calpurnia tells Caesar that she has never before believed in omens (**stood on ceremonies**), but now she is frightened. She describes the terrible things she has heard of from the men who were on guard during the night.

Direct students to lines 1–24. Use these prompts to help students explore Caesar's relationship with Calpurnia:

Connect Have you or someone you know ever had an uneasy feeling that resulted in a change of plans? How does that experience help you understand the beginning of this scene? *Accept all reasonable responses.*

Analyze As the scene opens, how does Caesar show that he gives some consideration to Calpurnia's warning? *Possible answer: He shows his hesitation by asking for a sacrifice that may confirm or contradict the warning that Calpurnia cried out in her sleep (lines 1–6).*

Synthesize If Caesar's relationship with Calpurnia were more like Brutus' relationship with Portia, how might the dialogue be different? *Possible answer: Caesar might show a more personal side; he might treat Calpurnia with more respect and be more understanding of her concerns.*

FOR STRUGGLING READERS

Preview Read through the italicized scene synopsis to give students an overview of Scene 2. Help them create a Cause-and-Effect Chain to record Caesar's actions.

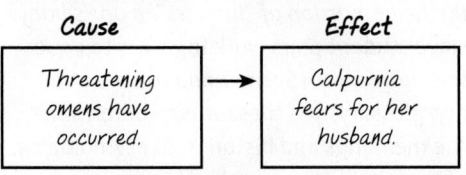

Cause → Effect

Cause	Effect
Threatening omens have occurred.	Calpurnia fears for her husband.

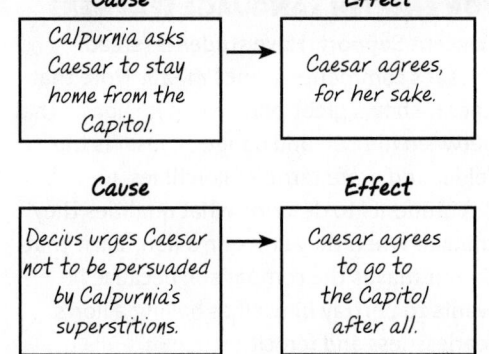

Cause	Effect
Calpurnia asks Caesar to stay home from the Capitol.	Caesar agrees, for her sake.
Decius urges Caesar not to be persuaded by Calpurnia's superstitions.	Caesar agrees to go to the Capitol after all.

 **BEST PRACTICES TOOLKIT—Transparency**
Cause-and-Effect Chain p. B39

Paraphrasing Shakespeare Point students to the side note for lines 13–26 and then model this paraphrase of lines 13–14: *Caesar, I never have considered omens of any kind, but now they frighten me.* Ask students to paraphrase lines 17–18. *Possible answer: A lioness has given birth in the streets; graves have opened, releasing the dead people within them.*

D TRAGIC HERO

Possible answer: Caesar's attitude seems to be a mix of courage and resignation. He does not fear death, because he knows that death is inevitable (lines 35–37). He does not think he can avoid fate, and he appears to consider himself one of the "valiant" who "never taste of death but once" (line 33).

25 O Caesar, these things are beyond all use,
And I do fear them!

Caesar.   What can be avoided
Whose end is purposed by the mighty gods?
Yet Caesar shall go forth, for these predictions
Are to the world in general as to Caesar.

30 **Calpurnia.** When beggars die there are no comets seen;
The heavens themselves blaze forth the death of princes.

Caesar. Cowards die many times before their deaths;
The valiant never taste of death but once.
Of all the wonders that I yet have heard,
35 It seems to me most strange that men should fear,
Seeing that death, a necessary end,
Will come when it will come. **D**

[*Reenter* Servant.]

                    What say the augurers?

Servant. They would not have you to stir forth today.
Plucking the entrails of an offering forth,
40 They could not find a heart within the beast.

Caesar. The gods do this in shame of cowardice.
Caesar should be a beast without a heart
If he should stay at home today for fear.
No, Caesar shall not. Danger knows full well
45 That Caesar is more dangerous than he.
We are two lions littered in one day,
And I the elder and more terrible,
And Caesar shall go forth.

Calpurnia.   Alas, my lord!
Your wisdom is consumed in confidence.
50 Do not go forth today. Call it my fear
That keeps you in the house and not your own.
We'll send Mark Antony to the Senate House,
And he shall say you are not well today.
Let me upon my knee prevail in this.

55 **Caesar.** Mark Antony shall say I am not well,
And for thy humor I will stay at home.

[*Enter* Decius.]

Here's Decius Brutus, he shall tell them so.

Decius. Caesar, all hail! Good morrow, worthy Caesar!
I come to fetch you to the Senate House.

60 **Caesar.** And you are come in very happy time
To bear my greetings to the senators

25 beyond all use: unlike anything we are accustomed to.

26–29 Caesar insists that if these are omens and if the gods have destined that certain things will happen, no one can avoid them. He will go out, since the predictions, he believes, apply to the whole world, not only to himself.

D TRAGIC HERO
Reread lines 32–37. What is Caesar's attitude toward his fate?

46 littered in one day: born at the same time.

COMMON CORE RL 4

Language Coach

Etymology A word's **etymology** is its history. The word *humor* was originally a Latin word meaning "fluid." The ancients believed the human body contained four "humors" whose relative proportions determined an individual's personality. How is this etymology related to *humor's* meaning in line 56?

DIFFERENTIATED INSTRUCTION

FOR STRUGGLING READERS

Paraphrasing Shakespeare Direct students to the side note for lines 26–29. Model this paraphrase of Caesar's question in lines 26–27: *If the mighty gods have decided that something will happen, who can avoid their plan?* Ask students to paraphrase lines 28–29. **Possible answer:** *I [Caesar] will go out anyway, for these omens of evil are directed to everyone, not just to me [Caesar].*

FOR ENGLISH LANGUAGE LEARNERS

Concept Support Have students reread Caesar's comments in lines 41–48. Note that Caesar shows great pride when he boasts that between himself and danger, Caesar is the "elder and more terrible" lion (lines 46–47). Ask students to describe what qualities they think of when they envision a lion. Elicit that Caesar makes the comparison because he wants to portray himself as having a lion's fearlessness and ferocity.

Language Coach   COMMON CORE RL 4

Etymology *Answer: In line 56 it seems to mean "mood," which would, according to the ancient theory, be affected by the proportion of "humors" in one's body.* Have student pairs work together to choose five words from Scene 2 and use a dictionary, glossary, or a thesaurus to determine the meanings and histories, or etymologies, of the words. Have each pair choose one word history to share with the class.

And tell them that I will not come today.
Cannot, is false; and that I dare not, falser.
I will not come today. Tell them so, Decius.

65 **Calpurnia.** Say he is sick.

Caesar.   Shall Caesar send a lie?
Have I in conquest stretched mine arm so far
To be afeard to tell greybeards the truth?
Decius, go tell them Caesar will not come.

Decius. Most mighty Caesar, let me know some cause,
70 Lest I be laughed at when I tell them so.

Caesar. The cause is in my will: I will not come.
That is enough to satisfy the Senate;
But for your private satisfaction,
Because I love you, I will let you know.
75 Calpurnia here, my wife, stays me at home.
She dreamt tonight she saw my statue,
Which, like a fountain with an hundred spouts,
Did run pure blood, and many lusty Romans
Came smiling and did bathe their hands in it.
80 And these does she apply for warnings and portents
And evils imminent, and on her knee
Hath begged that I will stay at home today.

Decius. This dream is all amiss interpreted;
It was a vision fair and fortunate.
85 Your statue spouting blood in many pipes,
In which so many smiling Romans bathed,
Signifies that from you great Rome shall suck
Reviving blood, and that great men shall press
For tinctures, stains, relics, and cognizance.
90 This by Calpurnia's dream is signified.

Caesar. And this way have you well expounded it.

Decius. I have, when you have heard what I can say:
And know it now, the Senate have concluded
To give this day a crown to mighty Caesar.
95 If you shall send them word you will not come,
Their minds may change. Besides, it were a mock
Apt to be rendered, for some one to say
"Break up the Senate till another time,
When Caesar's wife shall meet with better dreams."
100 If Caesar hide himself, shall they not whisper
"Lo, Caesar is afraid"?
Pardon me, Caesar, for my dear dear love
To your proceeding bids me tell you this,
And reason to my love is liable.

65–68 Shall ... not come: Caesar is appalled by his wife's suggestion that he lie to a bunch of old men (**greybeards**) about his reason for not going to the Senate.

80 portents: signs of evil to come.

83 amiss: wrongly.

83–90 Decius has to think fast. He promised the others that he could flatter Caesar into believing anything. Now he must give Caesar a new interpretation of Calpurnia's dream, one that will get him out of the house.

88–89 great men ... cognizance: Great men will come to you for honors and souvenirs to remember you by.

96–97 it were ... rendered: It's likely that someone will make a sarcastic comment.

102–104 my dear ... liable: My sincere interest in your career (**proceeding**) makes me tell you this. My feeling for you overtakes my intelligence (**reason**).
What arguments does Decius use to change Caesar's mind?

Can your
CONSCIENCE
mislead you?

Discuss Based on lines 60–70, is Caesar's insistence on a truthful message to the Senate driven purely by his conscience? Might he have another motive? *Possible answer: Caesar's carefulness in telling the truth—that is, that he will not go to the Senate House because he chooses not to go, not because he is afraid to go—seems to be driven by his pride, not his conscience. Decius has seen that Calpurnia wants Caesar to offer an excuse of illness, and Caesar does not want Decius or the Senate to think that Calpurnia makes his decisions for him. Caesar acts as if he is too moral to tell a lie, but the truth is that he does not want to appear vulnerable, fearful, or weak.*

FOR STRUGGLING READERS

Explore Theme Discuss how Decius persuades Caesar to go to the Capitol: flattery [reinterpreting Calpurnia's dream (lines 83–90)] and manipulation [saying that Caesar might not become king and he will be laughed at for listening to Calpurnia (lines 92–104)]. Elicit that Decius exemplifies a theme of *Julius Caesar*: People manipulate others to achieve their own ends. Also elicit that Cassius has done the same with Brutus and that Caesar has done so with the people of Rome.

FOR ENGLISH LANGUAGE LEARNERS

Task Support As students read the side note and question for lines 102–104, remind them that Decius met with Brutus and the other conspirators in Scene 1. Elicit that Decius is not being truthful with Caesar. *Possible answer: Decius' argument is that if Caesar does not come, members of the Senate may change their minds and not give Caesar the crown, after all. Decius also says that they will joke that Caesar is ruled by his wife's dreams.*

FOR ADVANCED LEARNERS/PRE–AP

Evaluate a Statement In line 32, Caesar comments, "Cowards die many times before their deaths." Challenge students to write a brief opinion essay that explains whether they agree or disagree with this statement and that gives examples that either support or contradict the statement. Urge students to use examples from movies, literature, or current events, rather than from their own lives. Invite students to choose an example or two to share in small groups or with the entire class.

105 **Caesar.** How foolish do your fears seem now, Calpurnia!
I am ashamed I did yield to them.
Give me my robe, for I will go.

[*Enter* Brutus, Ligarius, Metellus, Casca, Trebonius, Cinna, *and* Publius.]

And look where Publius is come to fetch me.

Publius. Good morrow, Caesar.

Caesar.   Welcome Publius.
110 What Brutus, are you stirred so early too?
Good morrow, Casca. Caius Ligarius,
Caesar was ne'er so much your enemy
As that same ague which hath made you lean.
What is't o'clock?

Brutus.   Caesar, 'tis strucken eight.

113 ague: sickness.

115 **Caesar.** I thank you for your pains and courtesy.

[*Enter* Antony.]

See! Antony, that revels long o'nights,
Is notwithstanding up. Good morrow, Antony.

116–117 Antony . . . up: Even Antony, who parties (**revels**) late into the night, is up early today.

Antony. So to most noble Caesar.

Caesar.   Bid them prepare within.
I am to blame to be thus waited for.
120 Now, Cinna, now, Metellus. What, Trebonius!
I have an hour's talk in store for you;
Remember that you call on me today;
Be near me, that I may remember you.

Trebonius. Caesar, I will. [*Aside.*] And so near will I be
125 That your best friends shall wish I had been further.

124 Aside: privately, in a way that keeps the other characters from hearing what is said. Think of it as a whisper that the audience happens to overhear.

Caesar. Good friends, go in and taste some wine with me,
And we (like friends) will straightway go together. ⓔ

Brutus. [*Aside.*] That every like is not the same, O Caesar,
The heart of Brutus yearns to think upon.

[*Exeunt.*]

ⓔ **DRAMATIC IRONY**
Why are Caesar's remarks in lines 126–127 an example of dramatic irony?

Scene 3 *A street in Rome near the Capitol.*

In this brief scene, Caesar has still another chance to avoid the path that leads to his death. Artemidorus, a supporter of Caesar, has learned about the plot. He reads a letter he has written to warn Caesar, and then waits in the street for Caesar to pass by on his way to the Capitol.

[*Enter* Artemidorus, *reading a paper.*]

Artemidorus. "Caesar, beware of Brutus; take heed of Cassius; come not near Casca; have an eye to Cinna;

TEXT ANALYSIS

COMMON CORE

RL 3

ⓔ **DRAMATIC IRONY**

Possible answer: *Caesar's remarks are an example of dramatic irony because the audience knows that the people whom Caesar invites to drink wine with him are not really his friends. The audience also knows that when Caesar trusts these people and goes with them, he is walking toward his own death.*

FOR STRUGGLING READERS

Preview Read through the italicized scene synopsis with students. Then have students use the Draw It activity to represent what happens in this scene. Students should represent the fact that Artemidorus writes a letter in hopes of saving Caesar's life. They can convey this action in cartoon strip form, in character and thought bubble form, and so on.

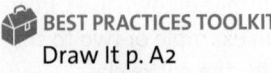 **BEST PRACTICES TOOLKIT**
Draw It p. A2

FOR ENGLISH LANGUAGE LEARNERS

Vocabulary: Outdated Forms Suggest that students add these outdated terms to their language journals. (See the For English Language Learners note on page 1204.)

From Scene 2

• *Good morrow* (line 109), "Good morning"

• *ne'er* (line 112), "never"

• *Bid them* (line 118), "Ask them to"

From Scene 3

• *have an eye to* (line 2), "watch"

• *beest* (line 6), "be"

• *mayst* (line 15), "may"

From Scene 4

• *prithee* (line 1), "pray thee" (used to make a request)

• *get thee gone* (line 2), "leave"

• *'tween* (line 7), "between"

trust not Trebonius; mark well Metellus Cimber;
Decius Brutus loves thee not; thou hast wronged Caius
5 Ligarius. There is but one mind in all these men,
and it is bent against Caesar. If thou beest not
immortal, look about you. Security gives way to
conspiracy. The mighty gods defend thee!

                                    "Thy Lover,   9 **Lover:** devoted friend.
                              "ARTEMIDORUS."

10

> Here will I stand till Caesar pass along
> And as a suitor will I give him this.
> My heart laments that virtue cannot live
> Out of the teeth of emulation.
> 15 If thou read this, O Caesar, thou mayst live;
> If not, the Fates with traitors do contrive.

③ **Targeted Passage**

12 **suitor:** a person making a petition or request.

13–14 **My heart ... emulation:** My heart is sad that Caesar's greatness cannot escape jealousy (**the teeth of emulation**).

16 **contrive:** plot.

[*Exit.*]

Scene 4 *In front of Brutus' house.*

Brutus' wife, Portia, feels anxious about the conspiracy. She nervously orders the servant Lucius to go and see what is happening at the Capitol. She next meets the Soothsayer, who makes her even more anxious as he continues to predict danger for Caesar.

[*Enter* Portia *and* Lucius.]

Portia. I prithee, boy, run to the Senate House.
Stay not to answer me, but get thee gone!
Why dost thou stay?

Lucius.   To know my errand, madam.

Portia. I would have had thee there and here again
5 Ere I can tell thee what thou shouldst do there.
O constancy, be strong upon my side,
Set a huge mountain 'tween my heart and tongue!
I have a man's mind, but a woman's might.
How hard it is for women to keep counsel!
10 Art thou here yet?

Lucius.   Madam, what should I do?
Run to the Capitol and nothing else?
And so return to you and nothing else?

Portia. Yes, bring me word, boy, if thy lord look well,
For he went sickly forth; and take good note
15 What Caesar doth, what suitors press to him.
Hark, boy! What noise is that?

Lucius. I hear none, madam.

5 **Ere:** before.

6 **constancy:** determination

9 **keep counsel:** keep a secret. *What does Portia seem to have learned from Brutus since their last scene together?*

15 **what suitors press to him:** what petitioners stand near him.

JULIUS CAESAR: ACT TWO, SCENE 4   **1235**

REVISIT THE BIG QUESTION

Can your
CONSCIENCE
mislead you?

Discuss Based on lines 1–10, how does Artemidorus follow his conscience in this scene? *Possible answer: Artemidorus follows his conscience by writing a letter to warn Caesar about the conspirators.* How does his comment in lines 13–14 reflect his conscience? *Possible answer: In these lines, Artemidorus grieves to think that some people are jealous of virtuous Caesar. The comment shows that he is thinking seriously about matters of right and wrong.*

FOR STRUGGLING READERS

Preview Have students read through the italicized scene synopsis for Scene 4. Help them create a Sequence Chain to organize plot events.

> Nervous about the conspiracy, Portia orders Lucius to go to the Capitol.

> Portia meets the Soothsayer.

> The Soothsayer's predictions make Portia even more nervous.

BEST PRACTICES TOOLKIT—Transparency
Sequence Chain p. B21

③ **Targeted Passage** [Scene 3, Lines 11–16]
This passage offers a different perspective on the conspiracy.

- Why does Artemidorus think that the conspirators want to kill Caesar? (line 14)
- How does Artemidorus portray the conspirators? What does he call them? (line 16)
- Do you think that Caesar will read this letter? Explain your answer.

FOR ENGLISH LANGUAGE LEARNERS

Task Support Have students read the side note and question about Scene 4, line 9. Note Portia's nervousness as the scene opens. Also remind students that in Scene 2, Caesar decided to go to the Capitol. *Possible answer: Portia seems to have learned about the plot to kill Caesar. She is insistent that Lucius go to the Capitol (where Caesar is most likely to appear).*

JULIUS CAESAR: ACT TWO, SCENE 4   **1235**

Portia.   Prithee, listen well.
I heard a bustling rumor like a fray,
And the wind brings it from the Capitol.

20 **Lucius.** Sooth, madam, I hear nothing.

[*Enter the* Soothsayer.]

Portia. Come hither, fellow. Which way hast thou been?

Soothsayer. At mine own house, good lady.

Portia. What is't o'clock?

Soothsayer   About the ninth hour, lady.

Portia. Is Caesar yet gone to the Capitol?

25 **Soothsayer.** Madam, not yet. I go to take my stand,
To see him pass on to the Capitol.

Portia. Thou hast some suit to Caesar, hast thou not?

Soothsayer. That I have, lady. If it will please Caesar
To be so good to Caesar as to hear me,
30 I shall beseech him to befriend himself.

Portia. Why, know'st thou any harm's intended towards him?

Soothsayer. None that I know will be, much that I fear may chance.
Good morrow to you. Here the street is narrow.
The throng that follows Caesar at the heels,
35 Of senators, of praetors, common suitors,
Will crowd a feeble man almost to death.
I'll get me to a place more void and there
Speak to great Caesar as he comes along.

[*Exit.*]

Portia. I must go in. Ay me, how weak a thing
40 The heart of woman is! O Brutus,
The heavens speed thee in thine enterprise—
Sure the boy heard me.—Brutus hath a suit
That Caesar will not grant.—O, I grow faint.—
Run, Lucius, and commend me to my Lord;
45 Say I am merry. Come to me again
And bring me word what he doth say to thee. **ⓕ**

[*Exeunt severally.*]

---

18 a bustling . . . fray: a noise like a fight.

20 Sooth: truly.

21 The Soothsayer is the same fortune-teller who warned Caesar to beware the ides of March. He is now on his way to the street near the Capitol building where he usually sits.

27 suit: petition.

32 None . . . chance: I'm not sure of any danger, but I fear that some may occur.

37 void: empty.

42–43 Fearing that Lucius has overheard her mention of the plot against Caesar, Portia pretends to worry about a petition that Brutus is going to present today.

ⓕ **TRAGEDY**
Which details in this scene help build **suspense**?

severally: separately.

1236   UNIT 11: SHAKESPEAREAN DRAMA

TEXT ANALYSIS

COMMON CORE
RL 3
RL 4
RL 5

ⓕ TRAGEDY

Possible answer: Suspense-building details include Portia's nervousness, Portia's hearing "a bustling rumor like a fray" (line 18), and the Soothsayer's plan to warn Caesar before he arrives at the Capitol (lines 28–38).

ACT TWO WRAP-UP

READ WITH A PURPOSE Now that students have finished reading Act Two, ask them what factors they believe have moved Brutus from friend of Caesar to co-conspirator. *Possible answer: Brutus has been manipulated by the flattery and stratagems of Cassius to believe that killing Caesar is a noble act.*

★ CRITIQUE Ask students whether they think that Brutus remains as honorable as he appeared in Act One. Encourage students to cite textual evidence from Act One and Act Two to support their views.

DIFFERENTIATED INSTRUCTION

FOR ENGLISH LANGUAGE LEARNERS
Concept Support Remind students that in Scene 1, lines 291–297, Portia said that she was stronger than typical women. In Scene 4, lines 8–9, she says that she has "a man's mind, but a woman's might." In lines 39–40, she says that her woman's heart is weak. Discuss with students how Portia's behavior in Scene 4 differs from what it was in Scene 1 and what might have caused it to change.

FOR ADVANCED LEARNERS/PRE-AP
Research and Analyze Women's Roles [small-group option] Have students research the role of married women in ancient Rome. For example, did a married woman have many rights? Could she speak against her husband? Ask students to present their findings, including an analysis of the relationship between Portia and Brutus and between Caesar and Calpurnia. Is either woman presented as a traditional wife?

After Reading

Comprehension

1. **Recall** Why is Portia upset with Brutus?

2. **Recall** What has made Calpurnia concerned about Caesar's safety?

3. **Recall** Why are Artemidorus and the Soothsayer trying to reach Caesar as he makes his way to the Capitol?

4. **Summarize** How does Decius convince Caesar to change his mind about staying home?

Text Analysis

● 5. **Reading Shakespearean Drama** Review the chart you created as you read. What have you learned about Caesar in Act Two?

● 6. **Analyze Shakespearean Tragedy** Using a chart like the one shown, identify soliloquies and asides in Act Two, and explain what each one reveals about the speaker. Which technique gives you more insight into a character's way of thinking? Explain your response.

Scene and Line Nos.	Speaker	Soliloquy or Aside?	What It Reveals

7. **Identify Mood** What mood do the two brief scenes at the end of Act Two help create? Cite details in your response.

8. **Make Inferences About Characters** Contrast the relationship between Caesar and Calpurnia with the relationship between Brutus and Portia. What do the differences suggest about the character of each man?

9. **Draw Conclusions** Is Brutus's decision to join the conspiracy driven more by his **conscience** or by Cassius's manipulation? Support your conclusion with evidence from the text.

10. **Evaluate Argument** Reread Brutus's soliloquy in lines 10–34 of Scene 1. Are you persuaded by his argument on the need to kill Caesar? Why or why not?

Text Criticism

11. **Critical Interpretations** According to some critics, one reason *Julius Caesar* is so complex is that it offers widely differing views of the title character. Do you agree that the play allows you to form different impressions of Caesar as you read, or is his character portrayed consistently? Cite evidence to support your opinion.

COMMON CORE

RL 3 Analyze how complex characters with conflicting motivations develop, interact with others, and advance the plot or develop the theme. **RL 10** Read and understand dramas.

JULIUS CAESAR: ACT TWO **1237**

Practice and Apply

For preliminary support of post-reading questions, use these copy masters:

R **RESOURCE MANAGER—Copy Masters**
Reading Check p. 43
Soliloquy / Aside p. 41
Question Support p. 44

Additional selection questions are provided for teachers on page 35.

ANSWERS

Comprehension

1. *Brutus has been keeping a secret.*

2. *Calpurnia has had a nightmare about Caesar's murder and is aware of several frightening omens that night.*

3. *They want to warn Caesar of the plot.*

4. *He reinterprets Calpurnia's dream.*

Text Analysis

COMMON CORE **RL 3, RL 10**

Possible answers:

5. ● **COMMON CORE FOCUS** *Reading Shakespearean Drama Caesar is superstitious (Scene 2, lines 5–6), is proud (Scene 2, lines 10–12), believes in fate (Scene 2, lines 35–37), and is easily flattered (Scene 2, lines 83–107).*

6. ● **COMMON CORE FOCUS** *Shakespearean Tragedy Scene 1, lines 77–85; Brutus; soliloquy; Brutus knows murder is not defendable. Scene 2, lines 124–125; Trebonius; aside; Trebonius is a conspirator and deceitful. Scene 2, lines 128–129; Brutus; aside; Brutus knows he's not a friend to Caesar. Soliloquies give more insight into a character's thoughts because they explore a character's mind more than asides do.*

---

7. *Portia's anxiousness and the Soothsayer's warnings create a suspenseful mood.*

8. *Brutus respects and loves Portia (Scene 1, lines 288–290 and 303–309). Caesar disregards and is impersonal with Calpurnia (Scene 2, lines 10–12 and 105–107).*

9. *Brutus joins the conspiracy because his conscience tells him that Caesar may become a tyrant (Scene 1, lines 10–34). Brutus is also manipulated by Cassius' forged letters (Scene 1, lines 44–58).*

10. *Most students may suggest that it is wrong to kill someone for an action that he or she may take in the future.*

Text Criticism

Possible answer:

11. *Different impressions are possible. Caesar is portrayed as a friend, as aging and fragile, as indecisive and prideful.*

Assess and Reteach

Assess

DIAGNOSTIC AND SELECTION TESTS
Selection Tests A, B/C pp. 315–316, 317–318

Interactive Selection Test on **thinkcentral.com**

Reteach

Level Up Online Tutorials on **thinkcentral.com**

Reteaching Worksheets on **thinkcentral.com**
Literature Lesson 5: Elements of Plot

Literature Lesson 36: Irony

JULIUS CAESAR: ACT TWO **1237**

Practice and Apply

Get Into the Act
SUMMARY

As Act Three opens, Caesar arrives at the Capitol, where he rejects Artemidorus and the Soothsayer's warnings. The conspirators approach, pretending to petition Caesar; they then attack and stab Caesar to death. Antony appears to make peace with the murderers but privately vows revenge. At the funeral, Brutus convinces the crowd that Caesar would have been a tyrant, but Antony's powerful eulogy changes the people's minds. The crowd revolts against the conspirators, and Brutus and Cassius flee.

Act Three

Scene 1   *The Capitol in Rome.*

Outside the Capitol, Caesar refuses to look at Artemidorus' letter of warning. Caesar next moves into the Capitol. There, the conspirators surround him, pretending to plead a case. Suddenly, they stab him to death. Mark Antony flees, but Brutus persuades the conspirators to let him live. Brutus himself promises to explain the killing and its reasons to the Roman people. Antony returns and pretends to be an ally of the conspirators. Secretly, however, he plans to strike back with help from Octavius Caesar, who is now on his way to Rome.

[*The Senate sits on a higher level, waiting for* Caesar *to appear.* Artemidorus *and the* Soothsayer *are among the crowd. A flourish of trumpets. Enter* Caesar, Brutus, Cassius, Casca, Decius, Metellus, Trebonius, Cinna, Antony, Lepidus, Popilius, *and others.* Caesar *stops in front of the* Soothsayer.]

Caesar. The ides of March are come.

Soothsayer. Ay, Caesar, but not gone.

[Artemidorus *steps up to* Caesar *with his warning.*]

Artemidorus. Hail, Caesar! Read this schedule.

[Decius *steps up quickly with another paper.*]

    Decius. Trebonius doth desire you to o'erread
5 (At your best leisure) this his humble suit.

Artemidorus. O Caesar, read mine first, for mine's a suit
That touches Caesar nearer. Read it, great Caesar!

Caesar. What touches us ourself shall be last served.

[Caesar *pushes the paper aside and turns away.*]

Artemidorus. Delay not, Caesar! Read it instantly!

10 **Caesar.** What, is the fellow mad?

    Publius.   Sirrah, give place.

[Publius *and the conspirators force* Artemidorus *away from* Caesar.]

Cassius. What, urge you your petitions in the street?
Come to the Capitol.

[Caesar *goes into the Senate House, the rest following.* Popilius *speaks to* Cassius *in a low voice.*]

Popilius. I wish your enterprise today may thrive.

Cassius. What enterprise, Popilius?

Popilius.   Fare you well.

[*Advances to* Caesar.]

3 schedule: document.

4–5 o'erread: read over. *Why does Decius interrupt Artemidorus's request by presenting Caesar with a petition from someone else?*

7 touches Caesar nearer: more closely concerns Caesar.

10 Sirrah: a form of address used toward a servant or inferior, often to express anger or disrespect; **give place:** get out of the way.

13 I wish . . . thrive: I hope your venture is successful.

Antony mourns Julius Caesar in the Globe Theatre's 1999 production

Resources for Act Three

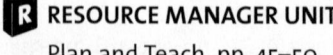

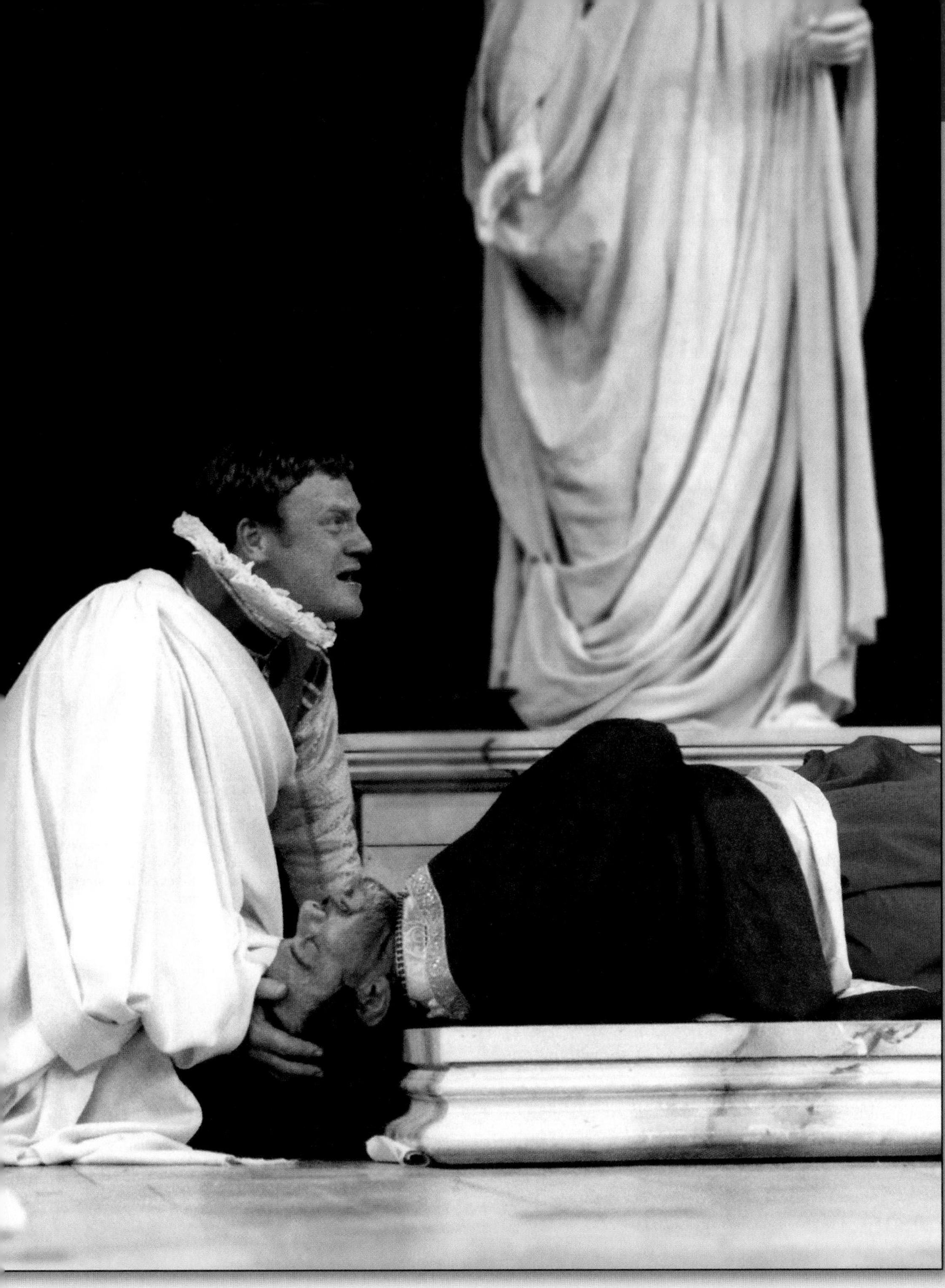

Reading Support

THINK central

This selection on **thinkcentral.com** includes embedded **ThinkAloud** models–students "thinking aloud" about the story to model the kinds of questions a good reader would ask about a selection.

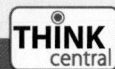

Analyze Visuals

Activity Based on this photograph, how does Antony probably feel about Caesar and his murder? ***Possible answer:*** *Since Antony is protectively cradling Caesar's head and has a look of agony on his face, he probably cares deeply for Caesar and is outraged at his murder.*

TIERED DISCUSSION PROMPTS

Direct students to lines 1–12. Use these prompts to help students set the scene for Caesar's assassination:

Recall How was Caesar already warned about this moment? ***Possible answer:*** *Caesar was warned already by the Soothsayer, by Calpurnia's dream, and by the omens that were witnessed during the night.*

Analyze How do the conspirators influence Caesar to disregard Artemidorus? ***Possible answer:*** *Decius puts a second document into Caesar's hands, making Artemidorus insistent and seemingly troublesome. Cassius steps in with a reminder that petitions should be dealt with at the Capitol, not in the street.*

DIFFERENTIATED INSTRUCTION

FOR ENGLISH LANGUAGE LEARNERS

Task Support As students read the question in the side note for lines 4–5, point out that according to the stage directions, Decius moves in quickly. ***Possible answer:*** *Decius does not want Caesar to read of any possible warning of the murder plot. His petition (probably prepared ahead of time, for just such a circumstance) is meant to distract Caesar or to annoy him so much that he refuses to read either one.*

FOR STRUGGLING READERS

In combination with the *Audio Anthology CD*, use one or more Targeted Passages (pp. 1241, 1247, 1249, 1256) to ensure that students focus on key story events, concepts, and skills. Targeted Passages are also good for English learners.

Preview Have students organize key events from the Scene 1 synopsis into a Sequence Chain.

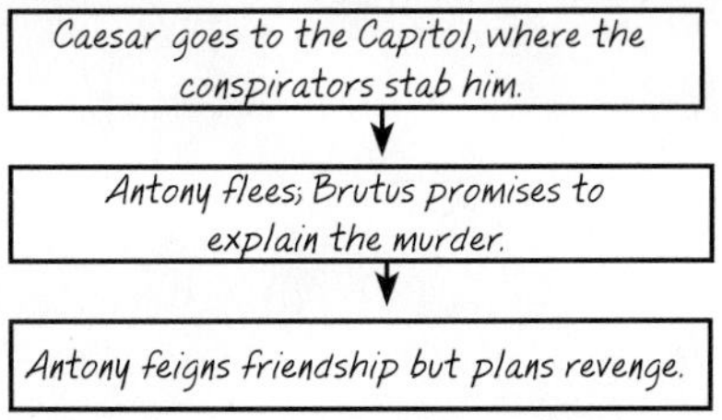

Caesar goes to the Capitol, where the conspirators stab him.
Antony flees; Brutus promises to explain the murder.
Antony feigns friendship but plans revenge.

BEST PRACTICES TOOLKIT—Transparency
Sequence Chain p. B21

A TRAGIC HERO

Possible answer: The characters' behavior is quite different. When it seems that the plot may have been detected, Cassius panics and acts fearful, threatening suicide if they are discovered (lines 17 and 19–22). Brutus, on the other hand, does not panic. He urges Cassius to be calm, and he rationally points out that Popilius is smiling and that Caesar's demeanor has not changed (lines 22–24).

BACKGROUND

The Roman View of Suicide To the Elizabethan—mostly Christian—audience, suicide was viewed as a sin. The Romans, however, considered suicide an act of heroism if the person committing suicide did so to avoid living a life that was contradictory to his or her morals. Cassius could not imagine living under Caesar's rule; for him, therefore, suicide would be an honorable escape (lines 20–22).

---

15 **Brutus.** What said Popilius Lena?

Cassius. He wished today our enterprise might thrive.
I fear our purpose is discovered.

Brutus. Look how he makes to Caesar. Mark him.

Cassius. Casca, be sudden, for we fear prevention.
20 Brutus, what shall be done? If this be known,
Cassius or Caesar never shall turn back,
For I will slay myself.

Brutus.   Cassius, be constant.
Popilius Lena speaks not of our purposes,
For look, he smiles, and Caesar doth not change. **A**

25 **Cassius.** Trebonius knows his time, for look you, Brutus,
He draws Mark Antony out of the way.

[*Exeunt* Antony *and* Trebonius.]

Decius. Where is Metellus Cimber? Let him go
And presently prefer his suit to Caesar.

Brutus. He is addressed. Press near and second him.

30 **Cinna.** Casca, you are the first that rears your hand.

[Caesar *seats himself in his high Senate chair.*]

Caesar. Are we all ready? What is now amiss
That Caesar and his Senate must redress?

Metellus. Most high, most mighty, and most puissant Caesar,
Metellus Cimber throws before thy seat
35 An humble heart.

[*Kneeling.*]

Caesar.   I must prevent thee, Cimber.
These couchings and these lowly courtesies
Might fire the blood of ordinary men
And turn preordinance and first decree
Into the law of children. Be not fond
40 To think that Caesar bears such rebel blood
That will be thawed from the true quality
With that which melteth fools—I mean, sweet words,
Low-crookèd curtsies, and base spaniel fawning.
Thy brother by decree is banished.
45 If thou dost bend and pray and fawn for him,
I spurn thee like a cur out of my way.
Know, Caesar doth not wrong, nor without cause
Will he be satisfied.

Metellus. Is there no voice more worthy than my own,
50 To sound more sweetly in great Caesar's ear
For the repealing of my banished brother?

19 prevention: being prevented from carrying out our task.

22 constant: calm.

A TRAGIC HERO
How does Brutus's behavior in this dangerous moment compare with that of Cassius?

28 presently prefer: immediately present.

29 addressed: ready.

33 puissant: powerful.

36–46 Caesar declares that he will not be influenced by low bows and humble appeals, which might cause ordinary men to overlook established laws (**preordinance and first decree**). No amount of pleading will cause him to end the banishment of Metellus's brother.

DIFFERENTIATED INSTRUCTION

FOR STRUGGLING READERS

Paraphrasing Shakespeare Have students reread the summary in the side note for lines 36–46. Then model this paraphrase of lines 39–43: *Do not think that Caesar is like a fool, whose mind can be changed by pleasing words, bowing, and flattery.* Ask students to paraphrase lines 44–46. **Possible answer:** *Your brother has been banished by law. If you beg for him, I will kick you out of my way like a dog.*

Concept Support Point out to students that Metellus' petition is simply part of the conspirators' plan. Metellus does not think that Caesar will release his brother, and whatever decision Caesar makes, he still will be killed. Offering the petition, however, gives the conspirators the chance they need to move in close to Caesar and then stab him.

Brutus. I kiss thy hand, but not in flattery, Caesar,
Desiring thee that Publius Cimber may
Have an immediate freedom of repeal.

55 **Caesar.** What, Brutus?

Cassius.   Pardon, Caesar! Caesar, pardon!
As low as to thy foot doth Cassius fall
To beg enfranchisement for Publius Cimber.

Caesar. I could be well moved, if I were as you;
If I could pray to move, prayers would move me;
60 But I am constant as the Northern Star,
Of whose true-fixed and resting quality
There is no fellow in the firmament.
The skies are painted with unnumbered sparks,
They are all fire, and every one doth shine;
65 But there's but one in all doth hold his place.
So in the world: 'tis furnished well with men.
And men are flesh and blood, and apprehensive,
Yet in the number I do not know but one
That unassailable holds on his rank,
70 Unshaked of motion; and that I am he,
Let me a little show it, even in this,
That I was constant Cimber should be banished
And constant do remain to keep him so.

Cinna. O Caesar!

Caesar.   Hence! Wilt thou lift up Olympus?

75 **Decius.** Great Caesar!

Caesar.   Doth not Brutus bootless kneel?

Casca. Speak hands for me!

[*They stab* Caesar. Casca, *the others in turn, then* Brutus.]

Caesar. *Et tu, Brute?*—Then fall Caesar!

[*Dies.*]

Cinna. Liberty! Freedom! Tyranny is dead!
Run hence, proclaim, cry it about the streets!

80 **Cassius.** Some to the common pulpits and cry out
"Liberty, freedom, and enfranchisement!"

Brutus. People and Senators, be not affrighted.
Fly not; stand still. Ambition's debt is paid.

Casca. Go to the pulpit, Brutus.

Decius   And Cassius, too.

85 **Brutus.** Where's Publius?

Cinna. Here, quite confounded with this mutiny.

---

54 freedom of repeal: the right to return to Rome from exile.

57 enfranchisement: restoration of citizenship.

59 If I . . . move: if, like you, I could plead with others to change their minds.

60–70 Caesar compares himself to the North Star, which always appears at the same place in the sky. Like that star, which has no equal in the sky (**fellow in the firmament**), Caesar cannot be moved from his decisions. *Has Caesar been as firm in his decisions as he claims to be?*

74 Olympus: the mountain where the Greek gods were believed to live.

75 Doth not . . . kneel: Can't you see that even Brutus's kneeling is useless?

① **Targeted Passage**

77 Et tu, Brute? (ĕt tōō brōō-tā) *Latin:* Even you, Brutus?

80–83 Some . . . pulpits: Some of you go to the speakers' platforms. *What do Cassius and Brutus fear might occur following the assassination?*

86 confounded with this mutiny: stunned by this turmoil.

Can your CONSCIENCE mislead you?

Discuss Based on lines 60–73, what factor or factors have shaped Caesar's conscience so that he finds it wrong to consider forgiving Publius Cimber? *Possible answer: A high regard for Roman law seems to be a factor. Caesar's response to Cassius suggests an even more powerful factor: his pride, which assures him that he is above others and must stay constant to appear strong.*

BACKGROUND

The Conspirators' Pact Each member of the conspiracy agreed to stab Caesar at least once so that they would be equally involved in the murder. Therefore, Caesar was stabbed 23 times, with Brutus inflicting the final wound. Caesar's murder certainly must have appeared bloody and barbaric, rather than as a sacrificial "dish fit for the gods," as Brutus described it to the other conspirators in Act Two (Scene 1, lines 162–174).

FOR STRUGGLING READERS

① **Targeted Passage [Lines 74–83]**

This passage focuses on the moment of Caesar's assassination and its immediate aftermath.

- Does Caesar seem aware that he is in great danger? How can you tell? (lines 74, 75)
- Who stabs Caesar first? last? (between lines 76 and 77)
- What are Caesar's final words to Brutus? (line 77)

FOR ENGLISH LANGUAGE LEARNERS

Task Support Direct students to the side note for lines 60–70 and have them read the question. Ask students to recall what caused Caesar to come to the Capitol. *Possible answer: Caesar has not always been firm in his decisions. Shortly before this scene, he listened to Calpurnia and decided not to come to the Capitol that day, but then he changed his mind (largely due to Decius' persuasive words).*

Task Support Have students read the side note question for lines 80–83. Elicit that Cinna shouts that liberty and freedom have come because tyranny is dead. Elicit that Cassius asks others to say similar things from the pulpit and that both they and Brutus act quickly. *Possible answer: Cassius and Brutus fear that if the people do not understand the reason for the assassination, they will attack the conspirators.*

BEHIND THE CURTAIN

Blocking Explain to students that directors generally follow stage directions to help them set up the blocking for a play, but that *Julius Caesar* offers few stage directions related to Caesar's assassination. The blocking illustrated in these photographs reflects different directors' interpretations of that moment in the play. ***Possible answer:*** *In the 2004 production, the conspirators are not as close to Caesar and are not facing him. In the 1993 production, the conspirator is looking at and holding Caesar as he stabs him. In the 2001 production, one conspirator stabs Caesar while another holds him. The two photographs from the Royal Shakespeare Company productions give the strongest impressions of violence. In the 2001 production, the blocking helps show Caesar's shock; in the 2004 production, the blocking helps show Caesar's outrage at his betrayal.*

Behind the Curtain

Blocking

During theater rehearsals, the director works out the positions and movements of actors on stage in a process called **blocking.** Some of these decisions are simple ones, such as figuring out how an actor will enter and exit. But blocking can have an important influence on the impact of a scene. How does the blocking of Caesar's assassination differ in these photographs? Which photograph gives the greatest impression of violence, and why?

Caesar's assassination in the Royal Shakespeare Company's 2004 production

Caesar's assassination in the Stratford 1993 production

Caesar's assassination in the Royal Shakespeare Company's 2001 production

DIFFERENTIATED INSTRUCTION

FOR ADVANCED LEARNERS/PRE–AP

Hypothesize and Evaluate Have small groups of students select a scene that they have read thus far. Ask them to diagram the scene, with written blocking directions for the actors. Volunteer actors within each group should follow those directions as they enact the scene; then the group should discuss how the blocking affected their interpretation of the scene. Invite representatives to share each group's insights with the class.

FOR RELUCTANT READERS

Connect Read and discuss the information about blocking with the class. Then divide the class into two groups. Assign one group Scene 1, lines 30–120, and the other group Scene 2, lines 160–257. Have each group practice reading its scene, determine what to accomplish visually in the scene, and then work together to block the scene. When blocking is completed, have each group present the sequence to the class and allow the other group to evaluate the impact of the blocking.

Metellus. Stand fast together, lest some friend of Caesar's
Should chance—

Brutus. Talk not of standing! Publius, good cheer.
90 There is no harm intended to your person
Nor to no Roman else. So tell them, Publius.

Cassius. And leave us, Publius, lest that the people,
Rushing on us, should do your age some mischief.

Brutus. Do so, and let no man abide this deed
95 But we the doers.

[*Reenter* Trebonius.]

Cassius.   Where is Antony?

Trebonius. Fled to his house amazed.
Men, wives, and children stare, cry out, and run,
As it were doomsday.

Brutus.   Fates, we will know your pleasures.
That we shall die, we know; 'tis but the time,
100 And drawing days out, that men stand upon.

Cassius. Why, he that cuts off twenty years of life
Cuts off so many years of fearing death.

Brutus. Grant that, and then is death a benefit.
So are we Caesar's friends, that have abridged
105 His time of fearing death. Stoop, Romans, stoop,
And let us bathe our hands in Caesar's blood
Up to the elbows and besmear our swords.
Then walk we forth, even to the market place,
And waving our red weapons o'er our heads,
110 Let's all cry, "Peace, freedom, and liberty!" **B**

Cassius. Stoop then and wash. How many ages hence
Shall this our lofty scene be acted over
In states unborn and accents yet unknown!

Brutus. How many times shall Caesar bleed in sport,
115 That now on Pompey's basis lies along
No worthier than the dust!

Cassius.   So oft as that shall be.
So often shall the knot of us be called
The men that gave their country liberty.

Decius. What, shall we forth?

Cassius.   Ay, every man away.
120 Brutus shall lead, and we will grace his heels
With the most boldest and best hearts of Rome.

[*Enter a* Servant.]

Brutus. Soft! who comes here? A friend of Antony's.

92–93 Cassius wants Publius, an old man, to leave before he gets hurt by the crowd.

94 **abide:** suffer for.

B TRAGEDY
What message is Brutus trying to convey by having the conspirators go out in public smeared with Caesar's blood?

111–113 Cassius predicts that far into the future, the assassination will be reenacted in plays performed around the world. *Why might Shakespeare have added this speech?*

115 **Pompey's basis:** the base of Pompey's statue.

REVISIT THE BIG QUESTION

Can your
CONSCIENCE
mislead you?

Discuss Based on lines 98–105, how do both Brutus and Cassius show that their consciences have been corrupted—that is, that their standards of right and wrong are now far from normal? *Possible answer: Both murderers state that they have done Caesar a favor by relieving him of years of fearing death. Such rationalization suggests that their standards are corrupt; such an unrealistic reason for killing someone would be almost universally condemned.*

TEXT ANALYSIS   COMMON CORE
                                              RL 3
B TRAGEDY   RL 5

Possible answer: Brutus' main message is that the conspirators are unashamed of and feel justified in their actions: They have removed Caesar for the public good, so that the Roman people could have "[P]eace, freedom, and liberty" (line 110). The image of bloody hands also recalls the idea from Act Two that the conspirators should be sacrificers rather than butchers (Scene 1, line 166).

FOR STRUGGLING READERS

Understand Irony Point out to students that according to lines 114–116, Caesar's body is lying at the base of Pompey's statue. Explain that it is ironic that Caesar lies dead at the base of the statue of the enemy whom he defeated in Rome's civil war. Note that even Brutus seems to recognize the irony in this moment.

FOR ENGLISH LANGUAGE LEARNERS

Task Support Have students read the side note for lines 111–113 and the question that it asks. *Possible answer: Shakespeare might have added this speech because it underscores the historic importance of the events portrayed in the play. It also is an ironic acknowledgment that this, in fact, is a play (seen especially in the term "this our lofty scene" in line 112).*

FOR ADVANCED LEARNERS/PRE-AP

Analyze Imagery [paired-activity option] Have students complete a concept web that details the images associated with blood in this scene and the symbolic meanings of those images. Challenge students to consider what the blood might symbolize specifically related to Caesar's death—to the conspirators, to Antony, to the people of Rome, and to themselves as readers. Invite students to compare their responses.

Direct students to lines 123–137. Use these prompts to help students explore the message that Antony sends Brutus:

Connect How do you think most people would feel if something terrible happened to a good friend? How does that response help you understand Antony's request? *Accept all reasonable responses.*

Analyze What does Antony's message indicate about the cause for his absence? *Possible answer: Antony asks for a promise of safe passage (lines 130–131), so he probably is in hiding out of fear that he, as a vocal supporter of Caesar, is also marked for death.*

Evaluate In what sense might Antony's argument and language be a warning to Brutus about Antony's role in future events? *Possible answer: Antony's argument is logical, and the language is flattering. The message also tells Brutus what he probably most wants to hear. In short, Antony shows that he, too, can manipulate and flatter people; that ability may later enable him to turn Rome against the conspirators.*

Servant. Thus, Brutus, did my master bid me kneel;
    Thus did Mark Antony bid me fall down;
125 And being prostrate, thus he bade me say:
    Brutus is noble, wise, valiant, and honest;
    Caesar was mighty, bold, royal, and loving.
    Say I love Brutus and I honor him;
    Say I feared Caesar, honored him, and loved him.
130 If Brutus will vouchsafe that Antony
    May safely come to him and be resolved
    How Caesar hath deserved to lie in death,
    Mark Antony shall not love Caesar dead
    So well as Brutus living, but will follow
135 The fortunes and affairs of noble Brutus
    Through the hazards of this untrod state
    With all true faith. So says my master Antony.
Brutus. Thy master is a wise and valiant Roman.
    I never thought him worse.
140 Tell him, so please him come unto this place,
    He shall be satisfied and, by my honor,
    Depart untouched.
Servant.   I'll fetch him presently.
    [*Exit.*]
Brutus. I know that we shall have him well to friend.
Cassius. I wish we may. But yet have I a mind
145 That fears him much; and my misgiving still
    Falls shrewdly to the purpose.
    [*Reenter* Antony.]
Brutus. But here comes Antony. Welcome, Mark Antony.
Antony. O mighty Caesar! Dost thou lie so low?
    Are all thy conquests, glories, triumphs, spoils,
150 Shrunk to this little measure? Fare thee well.
    I know not, gentlemen, what you intend,
    Who else must be let blood, who else is rank.
    If I myself, there is no hour so fit
    As Caesar's death's hour; nor no instrument
155 Of half that worth as those your swords, made rich
    With the most noble blood of all this world.
    I do beseech ye, if you bear me hard,
    Now, whilst your purpled hands do reek and smoke,
    Fulfill your pleasure. Live a thousand years,
160 I shall not find myself so apt to die;
    No place will please me so, no mean of death,
    As here by Caesar, and by you cut off,
    The choice and master spirits of this age.

130–137 If Brutus...faith: If Brutus will guarantee Antony's safety so that he may come and receive a satisfactory explanation for Caesar's death, then Antony will faithfully support Brutus through the dangers of this crisis.

142 presently: immediately.

144–146 Unlike Brutus, Cassius doesn't trust Antony. He adds that his doubts (**misgiving**) in matters like this are usually accurate.

152 Who else...rank: who else is so diseased (**rank**) that they must be "cured" by bloodshed.

153–163 Antony says that if they have hard feelings toward him, he would be honored to be killed at this time and place by the same great men who killed Caesar. *Does Antony seem sincere? Why or why not?*

DIFFERENTIATED INSTRUCTION

FOR STRUGGLING READERS

Paraphrasing Shakespeare Direct students to the summary in the side note for lines 153–163. Model this paraphrase of lines 153–159: *If you intend to kill me, then kill me now, in the same way that you killed noble Caesar.* Ask students to paraphrase lines 159–163. **Possible answer:** *If I lived for 1,000 years, no place would be better for me to die than by Caesar's side and at the hands of such noble people as yourselves.*

FOR ENGLISH LANGUAGE LEARNERS

Task Support Have students read the side note for lines 153–163 and the question that it contains. Elicit that Antony's tone in these lines is flattering rather than angry. **Possible answer:** Antony may give the appearance of sincerity; however, he is too flattering, and he gives the conspirators permission to kill him if they do not accept him (lines 157–163). Readers would expect him to be angry with the murderers and fearful that they may kill him.

Brutus. O Antony, beg not your death of us!
165 Though now we must appear bloody and cruel,
As by our hands and this our present act
You see we do, yet see you but our hands
And this the bleeding business they have done.
Our hearts you see not. They are pitiful;
170 And pity to the general wrong of Rome
(As fire drives out fire, so pity pity)
Hath done this deed on Caesar. For your part,
To you our swords have leaden points, Mark Antony.
Our arms in strength of malice, and our hearts
175 Of brothers' temper, do receive you in
With all kind of love, good thoughts, and reverence.

Cassius. Your voice shall be as strong as any man's
In the disposing of new dignities.

Brutus. Only be patient till we have appeased
180 The multitude, beside themselves with fear,
And then we will deliver you the cause
Why I, that did love Caesar when I struck him,
Have thus proceeded.

Antony.   I doubt not of your wisdom.
Let each man render me his bloody hand.
185 First, Marcus Brutus, will I shake with you;
Next, Caius Cassius, do I take your hand;
Now, Decius Brutus, yours; now yours, Metellus;
Yours, Cinna; and, my valiant Casca, yours.
Though last, not least in love, yours, good Trebonius.
190 Gentlemen all—Alas, what shall I say?
My credit now stands on such slippery ground
That one of two bad ways you must conceit me,
Either a coward or a flatterer.
That I did love thee, Caesar, O, 'tis true!
195 If then thy spirit look upon us now,
Shall it not grieve thee dearer than thy death
To see thy Antony making his peace,
Shaking the bloody fingers of thy foes,
Most noble! in the presence of thy corse?
200 Had I as many eyes as thou hast wounds,
Weeping as fast as they stream forth thy blood,
It would become me better than to close
In terms of friendship with thine enemies.
Pardon me, Julius! Here wast thou bayed, brave hart;
205 Here didst thou fall; and here thy hunters stand,
Signed in thy spoil, and crimsoned in thy lethe.
O world, thou wast the forest to his hart;

---

169 pitiful: full of pity.

171 As fire . . . pity: Just as one fire may extinguish another, our pity for Rome overcame our pity for Caesar.

172–176 Brutus assures Antony that as far as he is concerned, their swords are harmless, and their arms as well as their hearts are friendly toward him.

Language Coach

Fixed Expressions Many verbs followed by a particular preposition have a special meaning. The term *disposing of* can mean "attending to" or "getting rid of." Which meaning fits best in line 178? What does it mean here? *The scout troop set about disposing of the trash.*

191 credit: reputation.

192 conceit: think of.

194–210 These lines are addressed to the corpse (**corse**) of Caesar.

204 Here . . . hart: This is the place where you were trapped (**bayed**) like a hunted deer (**hart**).

206 Signed . . . lethe: marked with the signs of your slaughter and reddened by your bloodshed.

JULIUS CAESAR: ACT THREE, SCENE 1   **1245**

REVISIT THE BIG QUESTION

Can your
CONSCIENCE
mislead you?

Discuss Based on lines 164–176, how is Brutus still able to present himself as having a clear conscience when to others, like Antony, it would seem that he should have a guilty conscience? *Possible answer: Brutus is able to present himself as having a clear conscience because he believes in the assurances that he gives to Antony—namely, that (1) they killed Caesar because of their greater love for Rome (lines 170–172) and (2) they mean to welcome Antony as a friend, not to harm him because of his previous support of Caesar (lines 172–176).*

FOR STRUGGLING READERS

Inverted Word Order Have students reword these inversions to achieve a more natural word order:

- *beg not your death* (line 164), "do not beg your death"
- *yet see you* (line 167), "yet [but] you see"
- *That I did love thee, Caesar, O, 'tis true* (line 194), "O, 'tis [it is] true that I did love thee, Caesar"

Explore Character Motivation Have students reread lines 183–193, then discuss why Antony is shaking hands with the conspirators. Be sure students understand that Antony is taking this action so that the conspirators will trust him (because in their eyes, he is identifying himself with them) and not suspect that he has plans for revenge (which, as students will see in lines 254–275, he definitely has).

FOR ENGLISH LANGUAGE LEARNERS

Language Coach

Fixed Expressions *Answer: In line 178, disposing of means "attending to." In the new sentence, it means "getting rid of."* Ask students to rephrase Cassius' words in lines 177–178 in modern speech. *(Your opinion will be equal with ours in attending to privileges in the new government.)*

TIERED DISCUSSION PROMPTS

Direct students to lines 226–242. Use these prompts to help students grasp Antony's cunning, Brutus' naiveté, and the beginning of the plot complication:

Restate What does Antony want to do? *Possible answer: Antony wants to present Caesar's body to the public and to be allowed to speak at Caesar's funeral.*

Analyze Why does Cassius not want Antony to speak at the funeral? *Possible answer: Cassius does not trust Antony and is unsure of what Antony will say. He is concerned that the people will be affected (against the conspirators) by Antony's words.*

Synthesize What does Brutus' response reveal about his character? *Possible answer: Brutus' response—that he will speak to the people first and allow Antony to speak only by permission—shows his naiveté (in his quickness to believe Antony) and an overestimation of his own influence over the Roman people.*

And this indeed, O world, the heart of thee!
How like a deer, strucken by many princes,
210 Dost thou here lie!

Cassius. Mark Antony—

Antony.   Pardon me, Caius Cassius.
The enemies of Caesar shall say this;
Then, in a friend, it is cold modesty.

Cassius. I blame you not for praising Caesar so;
215 But what compact mean you have with us?
Will you be pricked in number of our friends,
Or shall we on, and not depend on you?

Antony. Therefore I took your hands; but was indeed
Swayed from the point by looking down on Caesar.
220 Friends am I with you all, and love you all,
Upon this hope, that you shall give me reasons
Why and wherein Caesar was dangerous.

Brutus. Or else were this a savage spectacle.
Our reasons are so full of good regard
225 That were you, Antony, the son of Caesar,
You should be satisfied.

Antony.   That's all I seek;
And am moreover suitor that I may
Produce his body to the market place
And in the pulpit, as becomes a friend,
230 Speak in the order of his funeral.

Brutus. You shall, Mark Antony.

Cassius.   Brutus, a word with you.

[*Aside to* Brutus.]

You know not what you do. Do not consent
That Antony speak in his funeral.
Know you how much the people may be moved
235 By that which he will utter?

Brutus.   By your pardon,

[*Aside to* Cassius.]

I will myself into the pulpit first
And show the reason of our Caesar's death.
What Antony shall speak, I will protest
He speaks by leave and by permission,
240 And that we are contented Caesar shall
Have all true rites and lawful ceremonies.
It shall advantage more than do us wrong.

215 compact: agreement.

216 pricked: listed; marked down.

218 Therefore . . . hands: That is why I shook hands with all of you (because I intend to be counted as an ally of yours).

223 Or else . . . spectacle: If we could not give you reasons for what we have done, it would be nothing but a display of savagery.

226–230 Antony asks permission to present Caesar's body in public and make a funeral speech.

238 protest: explain.

242 It shall . . . wrong: His speech will do us more good (**advantage more**) than harm.

DIFFERENTIATED INSTRUCTION

FOR ENGLISH LANGUAGE LEARNERS

Vocabulary Support: Elliptical Language
Explain that to fit the meter of blank verse, Shakespeare sometimes leaves out words that normally would be included. Have students reread lines 214–217 and then rephrase them, adding words when necessary. *Possible answer: I do not blame you for praising Caesar so; / But what agreement <u>do you mean to have</u> with us? / Will you be counted <u>in the number</u> of our friends, / Or shall we <u>go on</u>, and not depend on you?*

Cassius.

[*Aside to* Brutus.]

I know not what may fall. I like it not. **C**

Brutus. Mark Antony, here, take you Caesar's body.
245 You shall not in your funeral speech blame us,
But speak all good you can devise of Caesar,
And say you do't by our permission.
Else shall you not have any hand at all
About his funeral. And you shall speak
250 In the same pulpit whereto I am going,
After my speech is ended.

Antony.   Be it so.
I do desire no more.

Brutus. Prepare the body then, and follow us.

[*Exeunt all but* Antony, *who looks down at* Caesar *body.*]

Antony. O, pardon me, thou bleeding piece of earth,
255 That I am meek and gentle with these butchers!
Thou art the ruins of the noblest man
That ever lived in the tide of times.
Woe to the hand that shed this costly blood!
Over thy wounds now do I prophesy
260 (Which, like dumb mouths, do ope their ruby lips
To beg the voice and utterance of my tongue),
A curse shall light upon the limbs of men;
Domestic fury and fierce civil strife
Shall cumber all the parts of Italy;
265 Blood and destruction shall be so in use
And dreadful objects so familiar
That mothers shall but smile when they behold
Their infants quartered with the hands of war,
All pity choked with custom of fell deeds;
270 And Caesar's spirit, ranging for revenge,
With Até by his side come hot from hell,
Shall in these confines with a monarch's voice
Cry "Havoc!" and let slip the dogs of war,
That this foul deed shall smell above the earth
275 With carrion men, groaning for burial.

[*Enter* Octavius' Servant.]

You serve Octavius Caesar, do you not?

Servant. I do, Mark Antony.

Antony. Caesar did write for him to come to Rome.

C TRAGEDY
Cassius remains concerned about Brutus's decision to let Antony give a funeral speech. How might this decision lead to complications in the play's **plot**?

254–275 Now that Antony is alone with Caesar's corpse, he speaks truthfully. His speech shows what he really thinks of the men who have just left and what he intends to do about the murder.

257 **in the tide of times:** in all of history.

② Targeted Passage

263–269 **Domestic fury . . . deeds:** Rome (Italy) will be torn by civil war. People will become so accustomed to horrible sights that mothers will simply smile when they see their children cut into pieces (**quartered**). Pity will disappear among so much cruelty.

271 **Até** (ā'tē): the Greek goddess of revenge.

273 **"Havoc!":** Kill without mercy.

275 **With carrion . . . burial:** like rotting corpses begging to be buried.

276 Antony is interrupted by a servant of Octavius, Caesar's grandnephew and adopted son.

TEXT ANALYSIS   COMMON CORE

C *Model the Skill:* **TRAGEDY**   RL 3 RL 5

Point out that Cassius remains skeptical of Antony and is afraid of what he might say. Ask students to predict what might happen if Antony should decide to betray the conspirators.

Possible answer: Brutus is hoping to justify Caesar's murder to the people so that they will support the conspirators rather than seek revenge against them. If Brutus allows Caesar's close friend Antony to speak, he may undermine Brutus' explanation and move the people to support an avenging Antony. If that were to happen, then instead of a quiet outcome after Caesar's murder, the plot may be complicated by violence.

IF STUDENTS NEED HELP . . . Ask them to put themselves in Antony's place. Have them explain why they would want to speak at Caesar's funeral—and how their reasons might differ from those of Brutus.

FOR STRUGGLING READERS

② Targeted Passage [Lines 254–275]

In this passage, Antony reveals his true feelings and intentions regarding Caesar's assassination.

- What does Antony call the conspirators? (line 255)
- What does Antony say about Caesar? How does he feel about Caesar? (lines 256–258)
- Will Antony support the conspirators? How can you tell? (lines 255–258, 270–275)

- What future does Antony predict for Rome? (lines 263–269)

FOR ENGLISH LANGUAGE LEARNERS

Vocabulary Support Discuss and explain these references to murder, revenge, and civil disorder in Antony's soliloquy:

- *bleeding piece of earth* (line 254), "Caesar's bloody body"
- *butchers* (line 255), "murderers of Caesar"
- *the ruins* (line 256), "Caesar's corpse"

- *the tide of times* (line 257), "the coming and going of the years"
- *ruby lips* (line 260), "Caesar's wounds"
- *ranging* (line 270), "hunting"
- *hot from hell* (line 271), "directly [and eagerly] from hell"
- *let slip the dogs of war* (line 273), "release the circumstances that will create war"

Can your CONSCIENCE mislead you?

Discuss A body of people or a culture is sometimes said to have a collective, or group, conscience. In lines 288–289, how does Antony describe Rome's conscience? According to him, what are the people of Rome thinking at this point? *Possible answer: Antony says that the people of Rome are in mourning and that the mood in Rome is dangerous. The people are unsettled because their leader has just been killed. Rome's conscience is unsettled, as well—unsure of the right and wrong of the situation and not knowing what to think or believe.*

TEXT ANALYSIS

COMMON CORE RL 3

D ANALYZE MOTIVATIONS

Read the synopsis aloud to students. To help students contrast the views of Brutus and Mark Antony, draw a Two-Column Chart on the board. With help from students, fill the first column with what Brutus says about Caesar and the other with what Mark Antony says about Caesar.

BEST PRACTICES TOOLKIT
Two-Column Chart p. A25

Possible answer: Students may predict that the scene will result in increased tensions between the two Roman factions.

Servant. He did receive his letters and is coming,
280 And bid me say to you by word of mouth—
O Caesar!

Antony. Thy heart is big. Get thee apart and weep.
Passion, I see, is catching, for mine eyes,
Seeing those beads of sorrow stand in thine,
285 Began to water. Is thy master coming?

Servant. He lies tonight within seven leagues of Rome.

Antony. Post back with speed and tell him what hath chanced.
Here is a mourning Rome, a dangerous Rome,
No Rome of safety for Octavius yet.
290 Hie hence and tell him so. Yet stay awhile.
Thou shalt not back till I have borne this corse
Into the market place. There shall I try
In my oration how the people take
The cruel issue of these bloody men,
295 According to the which thou shall discourse
To young Octavius of the state of things.
Lend me your hand.

[*Exeunt with* Caesar's *body.*]

286 He lies . . . Rome: Octavius will set up camp tonight about 21 miles (**seven leagues**) outside Rome.

287–297 Antony tells the servant to hurry back and tell Octavius what has happened. Then he tells the servant to wait. He wants the servant to listen to his funeral speech and report to Octavius how the crowd responds to it.

Scene 2 *The forum in Rome.* D

Brutus speaks before a group of "citizens," or common people of Rome. He explains why Caesar had to be slain for the good of Rome. Then Brutus leaves and Antony speaks to the citizens. A far better judge of human nature than Brutus, Antony cleverly manages to turn the crowd against the conspirators by telling them of Caesar's good works and his concern for the people, as proven by the slain ruler's will. He has left all his wealth to the people. As Antony stirs the citizens to pursue the assassins and kill them, he learns that Octavius has arrived in Rome and that Brutus and Cassius have fled.

[*Enter* Brutus *and* Cassius *and a throng of* Citizens, *disturbed by the death of* Caesar.]

Citizens. We will be satisfied! Let us be satisfied!

Brutus. Then follow me and give me audience, friends.
Cassius, go you into the other street
And part the numbers.
5 Those that will hear me speak, let 'em stay here;
Those that will follow Cassius, go with him;
And public reasons shall be rendered
Of Caesar's death.

First Citizen. I will hear Brutus speak.

Second Citizen. I will hear Cassius, and compare their reasons
10 when severally we hear them rendered.

COMMON CORE RL 3

D **ANALYZE MOTIVATIONS**
This famous scene in *The Tragedy of Julius Caesar* marks a turning point in the play, and illustrates the conflicting motivations of Brutus and Mark Antony. As you read this scene, think about what motivates each character and predict how the scene will contribute to the plot as a whole.

3–8 Brutus tells Cassius to divide the crowd (**part the numbers**) so they can explain their reasons for killing Caesar to separate groups.

DIFFERENTIATED INSTRUCTION

FOR STRUGGLING READERS

Preview Have students create a cartoon, like this one, that records key details in the synopsis for Scene 2:

Caesar had to die for the good of Rome!

Caesar was a good leader. He loved you and left you all something in his will!

Brutus

Antony

[*Exit* Cassius, *with some of the* Citizens. Brutus *goes into the pulpit.*]

Third Citizen. The noble Brutus is ascended. Silence!

Brutus. Be patient till the last.

Romans, countrymen, and lovers, hear me for my cause, and be silent, that you may hear. Believe me for mine honor, and have
15 respect to mine honor, that you may believe. Censure me in your wisdom, and awake your senses, that you may the better judge. If there be any in this assembly, any dear friend of Caesar's, to him I say that Brutus' love to Caesar was no less than his. If then that friend demand why Brutus rose against Caesar, this is my answer:
20 Not that I loved Caesar less, but that I loved Rome more. Had you rather Caesar were living, and die all slaves, than that Caesar were dead, to live all freemen? As Caesar loved me, I weep for him; as he was fortunate, I rejoice at it; as he was valiant, I honor him; but—as he was ambitious, I slew him. There is tears for his love; joy for his
25 fortune; honor for his valor; and death for his ambition. Who is here so base that would be a bondman? If any, speak, for him have I offended. Who is here so rude that would not be a Roman? If any, speak, for him have I offended. Who is here so vile that will not love his country? If any, speak, for him have I offended. I pause
30 for a reply.

All. None, Brutus, none!

Brutus. Then none have I offended. I have done no more to Caesar than you shall do to Brutus. The question of his death is enrolled in the Capitol; his glory not extenuated, wherein he was
35 worthy, nor his offenses enforced, for which he suffered death.

[*Enter* Antony *and others, with* Caesar's *body.*]

Here comes his body, mourned by Mark Antony, who though he had no hand in his death, shall receive the benefit of his dying, a place in the commonwealth, as which of you shall not? With this  I depart, that, as I slew my best lover for the good of Rome, I
40 have the same dagger for myself when it shall please my country to need my death.

All. Live, Brutus! live, live!

First Citizen. Bring him with triumph home unto his house.

Second Citizen. Give him a statue with his ancestors.

45 **Third Citizen.** Let him be Caesar.

Fourth Citizen.   Caesar's better parts
Shall be crowned in Brutus.

First Citizen. We'll bring him to his house with shouts and clamors.

Brutus. My countrymen—

Second Citizen.   Peace! silence! Brutus speaks.

---

13 lovers: friends.

15 Censure me: Judge me.

16 senses: reason.

③ Targeted Passage

25–26 Who is . . . bondman: Which of you is so low that you would prefer to be a slave?

27 rude: uncivilized.

33–35 The question . . . death: The reasons for his death are on record in the Capitol. We have not belittled (**extenuated**) his accomplishments or overemphasized (**enforced**) the failings for which he was killed.

ⓔ GRAMMAR AND STYLE
Reread lines 36–38. Here, Shakespeare uses the **adjective clause** "who . . . shall receive the benefit of his dying" to convey Brutus's implication that Antony will gain from Caesar's death.

42–48 *What is the mood of the crowd as Brutus finishes his speech?*

45 parts: qualities.

JULIUS CAESAR: ACT THREE, SCENE 2   **1249**

ⓔ GRAMMAR AND STYLE  COMMON CORE L 1b

Explain that writers often use adjective clauses to convey ideas that are difficult or impossible to express with one word. Like one-word adjectives, however, adjective clauses answer questions such as "What kind of?" and "Which one?" As you discuss the example in lines 36–38 and these additional examples from the early part of Scene 2 (in which the adjective clauses are underlined), point out that adjective clauses often begin with *which, that,* or *who.*

• "Those that will hear me speak, let 'em stay here; / Those that will follow Cassius, go with him" (lines 5–6)

• "Tending to Caesar's glories which Mark Antony, / By our permission, is allowed to make." (lines 53–54)

FOR STRUGGLING READERS

③ Targeted Passage [Lines 13–30]
This passage reveals more about Brutus' character and shows how he argued for the necessity of Caesar's death.

• Why does Brutus say that the people should listen to and believe him? (lines 14–15)

• What does Brutus say would have happened to the Roman people if Caesar had lived? (lines 20–22)

• Which of Caesar's qualities does Brutus applaud? According to Brutus, which quality required that Caesar die? (lines 22–24)

Understand Irony Point out that the people are so moved by Brutus' speech that they want to crown Brutus as their ruler (lines 45–46). Ironically, they want to replace Caesar with his killer; even more ironically, they want to create a dictator out of the man who helped to eliminate the dictator Caesar.

FOR ENGLISH LANGUAGE LEARNERS

Task Support Refer students to the side note question for lines 42–48. After students reread those lines, discuss what honors the crowd wants to pay Brutus and what feelings might motivate such a desire. *Possible answer: The crowd's mood is positive and satisfied. The people believe that Brutus' arguments are valid, and they think that he not only should be honored but that he should be their new ruler.*

Can your
CONSCIENCE
mislead you?

Discuss Based on lines 61–68, what does the Roman people's conscience tell them about Caesar and about Brutus? Explain. ***Possible answer:*** *The Roman people believe that Caesar was a tyrant—that is, they now see him as evil—and that they are fortunate to have him gone (both ideas are stated directly in lines 65–67). They also think that Brutus is honorable—that is, they now see him as good—for they become offended at even the possibility that Antony might speak against him (line 64).*

First Citizen. Peace ho!

50 **Brutus.** Good countrymen, let me depart alone,
And, for my sake, stay here with Antony.
Do grace to Caesar's corpse, and grace his speech
Tending to Caesar's glories which Mark Antony,
By our permission, is allowed to make.
55 I do entreat you, not a man depart,
Save I alone, till Antony have spoke.

[*Exit.*]

First Citizen. Stay, ho! and let us hear Mark Antony.

Third Citizen. Let him go up into the public chair.
We'll hear him. Noble Antony, go up.

60 **Antony.** For Brutus' sake I am beholding to you.

[*Goes into the pulpit.*]

Fourth Citizen. What does he say of Brutus?

Third Citizen.   He says for Brutus'
Sake he finds himself beholding to us all.

Fourth Citizen. 'Twere best he speak no harm of Brutus here!

65 **First Citizen.** This Caesar was a tyrant.

Third Citizen.   Nay, that's certain.
We are blest that Rome is rid of him.

Second Citizen. Peace! Let us hear what Antony can say.

Antony. You gentle Romans—

All.   Peace, ho! Let us hear him.

70 **Antony.** Friends, Romans, countrymen, lend me your ears;
I come to bury Caesar, not to praise him.
The evil that men do lives after them;
The good is oft interred with their bones.
So let it be with Caesar. The noble Brutus
75 Hath told you Caesar was ambitious.
If it were so, it was a grievous fault,
And grievously hath Caesar answered it.
Here, under leave of Brutus and the rest
(For Brutus is an honorable man;
80 So are they all, all honorable men),
Come I to speak in Caesar's funeral.
He was my friend, faithful and just to me;
But Brutus says he was ambitious,
And Brutus is an honorable man.
85 He hath brought many captives home to Rome,
Whose ransoms did the general coffers fill.
Did this in Caesar seem ambitious?

52 grace his speech: Listen to him respectfully.

56 Save: except.

58 public chair: speaker's platform.

60 beholding: indebted.

70–134 In this famous speech, notice how Antony gradually turns the citizens away from their support of the conspirators.

72–74 Antony says that Caesar's good deeds should be buried (**interred**) with him; let him be remembered by his faults.

76 grievous: serious.

78 under leave of: with the permission of.

86 general coffers: the Roman government's treasury.

DIFFERENTIATED INSTRUCTION

FOR ENGLISH LANGUAGE LEARNERS

Vocabulary: Outdated Forms Encourage students to add these words to their language journals. (See "For English Language Learners" page 1204.)

- *'Twere* (line 64), "It would be"
- *blest* (line 67), "blessed," "fortunate"
- *oft* (line 73), "often"
- *Methinks* (line 105), "I think," "It seems to me"

FOR ADVANCED LEARNERS/PRE–AP

Analyze and Evaluate a Speech [small-group option] Have students prepare a list of effective public-speaking skills and persuasive techniques. Then have them analyze and evaluate Antony's speech as they answer these questions:

- Does the text of the speech suggest good public-speaking skills? Cite examples.
- Does the speech include some nontraditional techniques? Explain.

- What is Antony's most effective technique? Why do you think so?
- If you had been in the crowd, would you have been persuaded by Antony's words? Why or why not?
- Would you give Antony's speech a good grade? Why or why not?

When that the poor have cried, Caesar hath wept;
Ambition should be made of sterner stuff.
90 Yet Brutus says he was ambitious;
And Brutus is an honorable man.
You all did see that on the Lupercal
I thrice presented him a kingly crown,
Which he did thrice refuse. Was this ambition?
95 Yet Brutus says he was ambitious;
And sure he is an honorable man. **Ⓕ**
I speak not to disprove what Brutus spoke,
But here I am to speak what I do know.
You all did love him once, not without cause.
100 What cause withholds you then to mourn for him?
O judgment, thou art fled to brutish beasts,
And men have lost their reason! Bear with me,
My heart is in the coffin there with Caesar,
And I must pause till it come back to me.

105 **First Citizen.** Methinks there is much reason in his sayings.

Second Citizen. If thou consider rightly of the matter,
Caesar has had great wrong.

Third Citizen.   Has he, masters?
I fear there will a worse come in his place.

Fourth Citizen. Marked ye his words? He would not take the crown;
110 Therefore 'tis certain he was not ambitious.

First Citizen. If it be found so, some will dear abide it.

Second Citizen. Poor soul! his eyes are red as fire with weeping.

Third Citizen. There's not a nobler man in Rome than Antony.

Fourth Citizen. Now mark him. He begins again to speak.

115 **Antony.** But yesterday the word of Caesar might
Have stood against the world. Now lies he there,
And none so poor to do him reverence.
O masters! If I were disposed to stir
Your hearts and minds to mutiny and rage,
120 I should do Brutus wrong, and Cassius wrong,
Who, you all know, are honorable men.
I will not do them wrong. I rather choose
To wrong the dead, to wrong myself and you,
Than I will wrong such honorable men.
125 But here's a parchment with the seal of Caesar.
I found it in his closet; 'tis his will.
Let but the commons hear this testament,
Which (pardon me) I do not mean to read,
And they would go and kiss dead Caesar's wounds
130 And dip their napkins in his sacred blood;

93 thrice: three times.

Ⓕ RHETORICAL DEVICES
Reread lines 74–96 and pay attention to Antony's **repetition** of the words *ambitious* and *honorable*. What does he emphasize through the repetition of these words?

111 some will dear abide it: Some will pay dearly for it.

115 But: only.

117 And none ... reverence: And no one is low enough to show respect for him.

127–134 Antony says that if the people heard Caesar's will, they would dip their handkerchiefs (**napkins**) in his blood or beg for one of his hairs, and then upon their own deaths their children (**issue**) would inherit these valuable mementos. *Why does Antony tell the crowd that he does not plan to read the will?*

JULIUS CAESAR: ACT THREE, SCENE 2   **1251**

Yea, beg a hair of him for memory,
And dying, mention it within their wills,
Bequeathing it as a rich legacy
Unto their issue.

135 **Fourth Citizen.** We'll hear the will! Read it, Mark Antony.

All. The will, the will! We will hear Caesar's will!

Antony. Have patience, gentle friends, I must not read it.
It is not meet you know how Caesar loved you.
You are not wood, you are not stones, but men;
140 And being men, hearing the will of Caesar,
It will inflame you, it will make you mad.
'Tis good you know not that you are his heirs,
For if you should, O, what would come of it?

Fourth Citizen. Read the will! We'll hear it, Antony!
145 You shall read us the will, Caesar's will!

Antony. Will you be patient? Will you stay awhile?
I have o'ershot myself to tell you of it.
I fear I wrong the honorable men
Whose daggers have stabbed Caesar; I do fear it.

150 **Fourth Citizen.** They were traitors. Honorable men!

All. The will! the testament!

Second Citizen. They were villains, murderers! The will!
Read the will!

Antony. You will compel me then to read the will?
155 Then make a ring about the corpse of Caesar
And let me show you him that made the will.
Shall I descend? and will you give me leave?

All. Come down.

Second Citizen. Descend.

160 **Third Citizen.** You shall have leave.

[Antony *comes down.*]

Fourth Citizen. A ring! Stand round.

First Citizen. Stand from the hearse! Stand from the body!

Second Citizen. Room for Antony, most noble Antony!

Antony. Nay, press not so upon me. Stand far off.

165 **All.** Stand back! Room! Bear back!

Antony. If you have tears, prepare to shed them now.
You all do know this mantle. I remember
The first time ever Caesar put it on.
'Twas on a summer's evening in his tent,
170 That day he overcame the Nervii.

138 meet: proper.

147 I have . . . of it: I have gone too far in even mentioning it to you.

G RHETORICAL DEVICES
Reread lines 146–157. What does Antony's use of **rhetorical questions** suggest about his relationship with the crowd?

167 mantle: Caesar's toga.

170 the Nervii: a Belgian tribe that Caesar defeated 13 years earlier.

1252 UNIT 11: SHAKESPEAREAN DRAMA

TEXT ANALYSIS

COMMON CORE
RL 3
SL 3

G RHETORICAL DEVICES

Possible answer: Antony asks the crowd rhetorical questions (lines 146, 154, and 157) to make his listeners think that they have a say in what he is doing or even that they are controlling him. The crowd's response to these questions (lines 150–153 and 158–160) shows that the people are reacting just as Antony wants them to react. Antony, in fact, is manipulating them, yet his questioning keeps them from realizing it.

BACKGROUND

Mantle Misstatement In lines 166–170, Antony shows the people Caesar's bloody mantle. He tells them that he remembers that Caesar first put on the mantle during the conquest of the Nervii, a tribe living in Gaul. History notes that Antony did not join Caesar in Gaul until three years after the defeat of the Nervii; thus, it is unlikely that Antony remembered the battle or knew about the specific robe that Caesar wore.

DIFFERENTIATED INSTRUCTION

FOR ENGLISH LANGUAGE LEARNERS

Concept Support Reread Antony's words in lines 127–143 with students. Point out that Antony is telling his listeners exactly how he wants them to react when he reads the will to them. He also leaks the news that they are Caesar's heirs (line 142) before he reads the will. Antony manipulates them so that their reaction will begin to fulfill Antony's earlier prophecy: "Cry 'Havoc!' and let slip the dogs of war" (Scene 1, line 273).

1252 UNIT 11: SHAKESPEAREAN DRAMA

Look, in this place ran Cassius' dagger through.
See what a rent the envious Casca made.
Through this the well-beloved Brutus stabbed;
And as he plucked his cursed steel away,
175 Mark how the blood of Caesar followed it,
As rushing out of doors to be resolved
If Brutus so unkindly knocked or no;
For Brutus, as you know, was Caesar's angel.
Judge, O you gods, how dearly Caesar loved him!
180 This was the most unkindest cut of all;
For when the noble Caesar saw him stab,
Ingratitude, more strong than traitors' arms,
Quite vanquished him. Then burst his mighty heart;
And in his mantle muffling up his face,
185 Even at the base of Pompey's statue
(Which all the while ran blood) great Caesar fell.
O, what a fall was there, my countrymen!
Then I, and you, and all of us fell down,
Whilst bloody treason flourished over us.
190 O, now you weep, and I perceive you feel
The dint of pity. These are gracious drops.
Kind souls, what, weep you when you but behold
Our Caesar's vesture wounded? Look you here!
Here is himself, marred, as you see, with traitors.
[*Pulls the cloak off* Caesar's *body*.]

195 **First Citizen.** O piteous spectacle!

Second Citizen. O noble Caesar!

Third Citizen. O woeful day!

Fourth Citizen. O traitors, villains!

First Citizen. O most bloody sight!

200 **Second Citizen.** We will be revenged.

All. Revenge! About! Seek! Burn! Fire! Kill! Slay!
Let not a traitor live!

Antony. Stay, countrymen.

First Citizen. Peace there! Hear the noble Antony.

205 **Second Citizen.** We'll hear him, we'll follow him, we'll die with him!

Antony. Good friends, sweet friends, let me not stir you up
To such a sudden flood of mutiny.
They that have done this deed are honorable.
What private griefs they have, alas, I know not,
210 That made them do it. They are wise and honorable,
And will no doubt with reasons answer you.
I come not, friends, to steal away your hearts.

172 rent: tear, hole.

175 Mark: notice.

176–177 As rushing . . . or no: as if it rushed out of that opening to find out if it really was Brutus who had made the wound.

183 vanquished: defeated.

191 dint: force.

192–194 weep you . . . traitors: Do you cry when you look only at his wounded clothing (**vesture**)? Here, look at his body!

COMMON CORE RL 4
Language Coach
Denotations/Connotations The words *mutiny* and *treason* mean "opposition to authority," though each has different **connotations** (associated images and feelings). *Mutiny* connotes an uprising of soldiers or sailors against authority. *Treason* connotes disloyalty. Why does Antony use *treason* in line 189 but *mutiny* in line 207?

TIERED DISCUSSION PROMPTS
Direct students to lines 171–194. Use these prompts to help students see how Antony craftily continues to get the crowd to react in the way that he wishes:

Connect Can you think of examples of people who have been untruthful to get other people to do things their way? *Accept all reasonable responses.*

Analyze How and why does Antony focus on Brutus? How does he want the people to feel? *Possible answer: Since Caesar considered Brutus a great friend (line 178), Antony focuses on Brutus' stabbing of Caesar to highlight the traitorous, devastating nature of the murder. He makes Caesar appear to be the innocent, undeserving victim because he wants the people to feel pity and anger (lines 190–194).*

Evaluate Do Antony's ends justify his means? In other words, is it acceptable for Antony to be untruthful so that the crowd will become enraged? *Possible answers: Yes, because the people should avenge Caesar's unjustified murder. No, it is never appropriate to be untruthful, even if you are trying to right a wrong.*

FOR ENGLISH LANGUAGE LEARNERS
Concept Support As students read lines 171–174, remind them that Trebonius took Antony away from the Capitol before the assassination (Scene 1, lines 25–26); thus, Antony would not have known who made each rent (tear) in Caesar's robe. Antony continues to be untruthful to support his argument.

Language Coach   COMMON CORE RL 4
Denotations/Connotations
Possible answer: Antony uses treason *to describe Brutus' acts because he wants the crowd to see Brutus as a criminal; Antony uses* mutiny *to describe the feeling of the crowd he is trying, subtly, to incite.* Point out that treason is committed by a traitor—"one who betrays one's country." Have students determine whether *treason, traitor,* and *mutiny* have positive, neutral, or negative connotations and explain their reasoning.

I am no orator, as Brutus is,
But (as you know me all) a plain blunt man
215 That love my friend; and that they know full well
That gave me public leave to speak of him.
For I have neither wit, nor words, nor worth,
Action, nor utterance, nor the power of speech
To stir men's blood. I only speak right on.
220 I tell you that which you yourselves do know,
Show you sweet Caesar's wounds, poor poor dumb mouths,
And bid them speak for me. But were I Brutus,
And Brutus Antony, there were an Antony
Would ruffle up your spirits, and put a tongue
225 In every wound of Caesar that should move
The stones of Rome to rise and mutiny. ⒣

All. We'll mutiny.

First Citizen. We'll burn the house of Brutus.

Third Citizen. Away then! Come, seek the conspirators.

Antony. Yet hear me, countrymen. Yet hear me speak.

230 **All.** Peace, ho! Hear Antony, most noble Antony!

Antony. Why, friends, you go to do you know not what.
Wherein hath Caesar thus deserved your loves?
Alas, you know not! I must tell you then.
You have forgot the will I told you of.

235 **All.** Most true! The will! Let's stay and hear the will.

Antony. Here is the will, under Caesar's seal.
To every Roman citizen he gives,
To every several man, seventy-five drachmas.

Second Citizen. Most noble Caesar! We'll revenge his death!

240 **Third Citizen.** O royal Caesar!

Antony. Hear me with patience.

All. Peace, ho!

Antony. Moreover, he hath left you all his walks,
His private arbors, and new-planted orchards,
245 On this side Tiber; he hath left them you,
And to your heirs for ever—common pleasures,
To walk abroad and recreate yourselves.
Here was a Caesar! When comes such another?

First Citizen. Never, never! Come, away, away!
250 We'll burn his body in the holy place
And with the brands the traitors' houses.
Take up the body.

Second Citizen. Go fetch fire!

TEXT ANALYSIS

COMMON CORE
RL 3
SL 3

⒣ RHETORICAL DEVICES

Possible answer: *Antony uses the rhetorical devices of repetition (pages 1250–1251) and rhetorical questions (page 1252). Antony also uses parallelism in lines 139 and 141. Antony's words in lines 213–219 are ironic because he is, in fact, a better public speaker than Brutus. He does not love the conspirators, and although they gave him permission to speak, they did not want him to say what he has just said. Antony is perfectly capable of stirring men's blood (line 219), and that is exactly what he has done.*

⒣ **RHETORICAL DEVICES**
Identify examples of rhetorical devices in Antony's funeral speech, lines 70–226. What is **ironic** about his claim in lines 213–219?

238 several: individual; **drachmas:** silver coins, worth quite a bit to poor people such as those in the crowd.

243–247 Antony tells the crowd that Caesar has left all his private parks and gardens on this side of the Tiber River to be used by the public.

251 brands: pieces of burning wood.

DIFFERENTIATED INSTRUCTION

FOR ENGLISH LANGUAGE LEARNERS

Vocabulary: Outdated Forms Suggest that students add these outdated terms and phrases to their language journal. (See the For English Language Learners note on page 1204.) Then have students go back and reread the lines, inserting the new definitions.

- *'dumb* (line 221), "speechless"
- *bid them speak* (line 222), "let them speak"
- *Away then!* (line 228), "Let's go!"

- *windows* (line 255), "shutters"
- *How now?* (line 257), "What is going on?"
- *I have no will to wander forth of doors* (Scene 3, line 3), "I have no desire to go outside"

FOR ADVANCED LEARNERS/PRE–AP

Analyze Imagery [paired-activity option]
Have students reflect on the fire imagery on this page through the end of Act Three. Ask them to explain how Shakespeare uses fire to create both positive and negative images. (For example, how is the people's talk of burning Caesar's body different from their talk of burning the conspirators' houses?)

Third Citizen. Pluck down benches!

255 **Fourth Citizen.** Pluck down forms, windows, anything!

[*Exeunt* Citizens *with the body.*]

Antony. Now let it work. Mischief, thou art afoot,
Take thou what course thou wilt.

[*Enter a* Servant.]

How now, fellow?

Servant. Sir, Octavius is already come to Rome.

Antony. Where is he?

260 **Servant.** He and Lepidus are at Caesar's house.

Antony. And thither will I straight to visit him.
He comes upon a wish. Fortune is merry,
And in this mood will give us anything.

Servant. I heard him say Brutus and Cassius

265 Are rid like madmen through the gates of Rome.

Antony. Belike they had some notice of the people,
How I had moved them. Bring me to Octavius.

[*Exeunt.*]

Scene 3   *A street in Rome.*

This scene involves a famous Roman poet named Cinna. (He is not the same Cinna who took part in the assassination.) The angry Roman citizens come upon the poet and believe he is Cinna the conspirator. Soon they realize he is the wrong man, yet they are so enraged that they slay him anyway. Then they rush through the city after the true killers of Caesar.

[*Enter* Cinna, *the poet, and after him the* Citizens, *armed with sticks, spears, and swords.*]

Cinna. I dreamt tonight that I did feast with Caesar,
And things unluckily charge my fantasy.
I have no will to wander forth of doors,
Yet something leads me forth.

5 **First Citizen.** What is your name?

Second Citizen. Whither are you going?

Third Citizen. Where do you dwell?

Fourth Citizen. Are you a married man or a bachelor?

Second Citizen. Answer every man directly.

10 **First Citizen.** Ay, and briefly.

Fourth Citizen. Ay, and wisely.

Third Citizen. Ay, and truly, you were best.

256–257 Now let . . . wilt: Alone, Antony gloats over what he has just accomplished. Let things take their course, he says. Whatever happens, happens.

261 thither . . . him: I will go right there to see him.

262–263 Antony says that Octavius has arrived just as he hoped. Antony believes that Fortune, the goddess of fate, is on his side.

265 Are rid: have ridden.

266 Belike: probably.

2 things . . . fantasy: Recent events have caused me to imagine awful things.

6 Whither: where.

REVISIT THE BIG QUESTION

Can your CONSCIENCE mislead you?

Discuss Based on lines 256–257 and 266–267, does Antony seem to have a guilty conscience for enraging the crowd to imminent violence? Cite evidence. ***Possible answer:*** *Antony does not have a guilty conscience. He has intentionally incensed the people (line 267). He knows that they are up to mischief (line 256), and he is willing to let mischief happen (line 257) rather than attempt to stop it.*

FOR STRUGGLING READERS

Preview Have students read through the italicized scene synopsis for Scene 3. Help them create a Sequence Circle to organize plot events.

 BEST PRACTICES TOOLKIT—Transparency
Sequence Circle p. B21

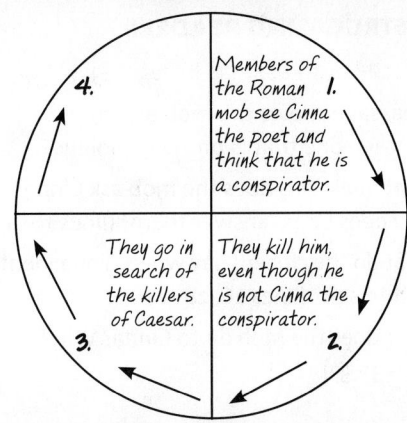

4.

1. Members of the Roman mob see Cinna the poet and think that he is a conspirator.

2. They kill him, even though he is not Cinna the conspirator.

3. They go in search of the killers of Caesar.

READ WITH A PURPOSE Now that students have finished reading Act Three, ask them to think about the step Brutus took in preserving Antony's life. Was Brutus the weak link in the conspiracy or the only person of honor involved? *Possible answer: Brutus was a weak link because he spared Antony in order to make himself look good and honorable.*

⭐ **CRITIQUE** Ask students whether they feel that the mob is justified in its actions. Was it right for these people to kill Cinna? Should they go after the conspirators and kill them? What alternatives do they have?

Cinna. What is my name? Whither am I going? Where do I dwell? Am I a married man or a bachelor? Then, to answer every man
15 directly and briefly, wisely and truly: wisely I say, I am a bachelor.

Second Citizen. That's as much to say they are fools that marry. You'll bear me a bang for that, I fear. Proceed—directly.

Cinna. Directly I am going to Caesar's funeral.

First Citizen. As a friend or an enemy?

20 **Cinna.** As a friend.

Second Citizen. That matter is answered directly.

Fourth Citizen. For your dwelling—briefly.

Cinna. Briefly, I dwell by the Capitol.

Third Citizen. Your name, sir, truly.

25 **Cinna.** Truly, my name is Cinna.

First Citizen. Tear him to pieces! He's a conspirator.

Cinna. I am Cinna the poet! I am Cinna the poet!

Fourth Citizen. Tear him for his bad verses! Tear him for his bad verses!

30 **Cinna.** I am not Cinna the conspirator.

Fourth Citizen. It is no matter; his name's Cinna! Pluck but his name out of his heart, and turn him going.

Third Citizen. Tear him, tear him!

[*They attack* Cinna.]

Come, brands, ho! To Brutus', to Cassius'! Burn all!
35 Some to Decius' house and some to Casca's; some to Ligarius'! Away, go!

[*Exeunt all the* Citizens.]

16–17 That's ... fear: This response shows that Cinna is in danger. The citizen threatens to beat him (**You'll bear me a bang**), even though Cinna's comment was not meant to be insulting.

④ **Targeted Passage**

31–32 Pluck ... going: Let's just tear the name out of his heart and send him away.

DIFFERENTIATED INSTRUCTION

FOR STRUGGLING READERS

④ **Targeted Passage** [Lines 13–33]

This passage shows the mob as a minor character—one that is prone to violence.

- What questions does the mob ask Cinna? How does Cinna answer them? (lines 13–14)
- What do the citizens say when Cinna identifies himself? (lines 26, 28–29)
- What does the mob do to Cinna? Why? (lines 31–33)

FOR ENGLISH LANGUAGE LEARNERS

Concept Support Explain that as Act Three concludes, the mob sets torches ablaze and goes off to burn down the houses of Brutus, Cassius, Decius, Casca, and Ligarius. The people who have listened to Antony's speech, now enraged beyond rational thought, intend to kill the conspirators—or, at least, to destroy their property.

Comprehension

1. **Recall** What request do the conspirators make just before killing Caesar?

2. **Recall** What disagreement do Brutus and Cassius have about the plans for Caesar's funeral?

3. **Recall** What information does Antony reveal to the crowd during his funeral speech?

4. **Clarify** Why does the crowd attack Cinna the poet?

Text Analysis

● 5. **Reading Shakespearean Drama** Review the chart you created. How do the events in Act Three affect your impression of Brutus?

6. **Examine Dramatic Irony** What dramatic irony does Shakespeare create in lines 1–2 of Act Three, Scene 1?

7. **Identify Motivation** Reread Mark Antony's soliloquy in lines 254–275 of Scene 1. What does this speech reveal about the motivation for Antony's actions in the rest of Act Three?

8. **Analyze Rhetorical Devices** In a chart like the one shown, analyze examples of rhetorical devices in the funeral speeches delivered by Brutus and Antony in Act Three, Scene 2, lines 13–42 and 70–248. How does Antony use **repetition** to contradict assertions in Brutus' speech?

Example	Speaker	Type of Rhetorical Device	What It Suggests or Emphasizes

9. **Compare and Contrast** Why does Antony's funeral speech have a much more powerful effect on the crowd than Brutus' speech? Cite details in your response.

10. **Draw Conclusions About Plot** Act Three begins and ends with violent events. What does the murder of Cinna the poet in Scene 3 suggest about the use of violence to achieve political goals? Cite evidence to support your conclusion.

Text Criticism

11. **Critical Interpretations** The novelist and critic E. M. Forster wrote that Brutus "cannot realize that men seek their own interests, for he has never sought his own, he has lived nobly among noble thoughts, wedded to a noble wife." How is this limitation reflected in Brutus's words and actions in Act Three? Cite examples from the text.

COMMON CORE

RL 3 Analyze how complex characters with conflicting motivations develop, interact with others, and advance the plot or develop the theme. **SL 3** Evaluate a speaker's point of view, reasoning, and use of evidence and rhetoric.

Practice and Apply

For preliminary support of post-reading questions, use these copy masters:

R **RESOURCE MANAGER**—Copy Masters
Reading Check p. 57
Rhetorical Devices p. 55
Question Support p. 58

Additional selection questions are provided for teachers on page 49.

ANSWERS

Comprehension

1. *that Caesar pardon Metellus' brother*

2. *Cassius doesn't want Antony to speak at Caesar's funeral, but Brutus allows it.*

3. *what Caesar left the people in his will*

4. *The crowd mistakes Cinna for a conspirator with the same name and kills him even when the truth is known.*

Text Analysis

COMMON CORE RL 3, SL 3

Possible answers:

5. ● **COMMON CORE FOCUS** *Reading Shakespearean Drama* *Brutus no longer seems as honorable. He excuses murder (Scene 1, lines 103–105), allows Antony to speak at Caesar's funeral (Scene 1, lines 236–251), and assumes that the mob will find the murder honorable (Scene 2, lines 13–15).*

6. *Ironically, Caesar believes that he is safe because it is already the ides of March; readers, however, know that the conspirators will kill him shortly.*

7. *The speech reveals that Antony is motivated by revenge (lines 259–275).*

8. *Lines 13–15, 20, and 22–25; Brutus; parallelism and repetition; reinforces his ideas, makes speech more memorable. Lines 20–22, 25–26, and 28–29; Brutus; rhetorical questions; encourages listeners to see themselves on his side.*

9. *Antony contradicts Brutus' characterization of Caesar (Scene 2, lines 82–96). He dramatically shows Caesar's corpse (lines 166–194), and reveals that the people are in Caesar's will (lines 125–130).*

10. *The murder suggests that violence leads only to more violence and social disorder (Scene 3, lines 13–36).*

Text Criticism

Possible answers:

11. *Brutus fails to understand Antony's motives (Scene 1, lines 231–242). He thinks that he can win the people's support (Scene 2, lines 13–30).*

Assess and Reteach

Assess

DIAGNOSTIC AND SELECTION TESTS
Selection Test A pp. 319–320
Selection Test B/C pp. 321–322

Interactive Selection Test on **thinkcentral.com**

Reteach

Level Up Online Tutorials on **thinkcentral.com**

Reteaching Worksheets on **thinkcentral.com**
Literature Lessons 23, 24: Elements of Drama
Literature Lesson 35: Rhetorical Devices

Practice and Apply

Get Into the Act

SUMMARY

Act Four presents the power struggle that follows Caesar's death. In Rome, Antony, Octavius, and Lepidus discuss their enemies. They consider who must die and how they will defeat the forces that Brutus and Cassius have gathered. In Sardis, Brutus and Cassius argue over Cassius' acceptance of bribes. They later reconcile, and Brutus tells Cassius of Portia's suicide. Cassius reluctantly consents to Brutus' decision to fight the forces of Rome at Philippi.

READING STRATEGY

 **Model the Skill: REVIEW**

To model how to review information, re-read Act Three, Scene 2, lines 236–238 and 243–247 aloud as students follow along. Elicit from students the specific items Antony says Caesar left the people of Rome in his will, and write this information on the board. Ask students whether they think the people will actually receive this bounty.

Possible answer: *Antony told the people that Caesar had left each of them 75 drachmas, as well as his arbors and orchards for public use (lines 236–247).*

Resources for Act Four

Act Four

Scene 1 *At a table in Antony's house in Rome.*

Antony, Octavius, and Lepidus now rule Rome as a triumvirate—a committee of three. The scene opens on the triumvirate, meeting to draw up a list of their enemies who must be killed. They also discuss changing Caesar's will. As Lepidus goes to fetch the will, Antony expresses his low opinion of Lepidus as a leader. Then, Antony and Octavius begin to discuss how to defeat the armies of Brutus and Cassius.

[*Enter* Antony, Octavius, *and* Lepidus.]

Antony. These many, then, shall die; their names are pricked.

Octavius. Your brother too must die. Consent you, Lepidus?

Lepidus. I do consent.

Octavius.   Prick him down, Antony.

Lepidus. Upon condition Publius shall not live,
5 Who is your sister's son, Mark Antony.

Antony. He shall not live. Look, with a spot I damn him.
But Lepidus, go you to Caesar's house.
Fetch the will hither, and we shall determine
How to cut off some charge in legacies.

10 **Lepidus.** What? shall I find you here?

Octavius. Or here or at the Capitol.

[*Exit* Lepidus.]

Antony. This is a slight unmeritable man,
Meet to be sent on errands. Is it fit,
The threefold world divided, he should stand
15 One of the three to share it?

Octavius.   So you thought him,
And took his voice who should be pricked to die
In our black sentence and proscription.

Antony. Octavius, I have seen more days than you;
And though we lay these honors on this man
20 To ease ourselves of divers sland'rous loads,
He shall but bear them as the ass bears gold,
To groan and sweat under the business,
Either led or driven as we point the way;
And having brought our treasure where we will,
25 Then take we down his load, and turn him off
(Like to the empty ass) to shake his ears
And graze in commons.

1 pricked: marked down.

6 with a spot ... him: I condemn him by marking him on this list.

8–9 Fetch ... legacies: Bring Caesar's will here, so we can figure out how to lower the amounts left to the people. *What impression of Antony do you get from this remark?*

13 meet: fit.

13–15 Antony questions whether it is fitting for Lepidus to share control of Rome's lands in Europe, Asia, and Africa (**the threefold world**).

17 black sentence and proscription: death sentences.

19–27 Antony says that they are giving Lepidus temporary power only so that he will bear the burden of public criticism of their actions.

27 commons: public land for grazing.

Cassius and Brutus in the Globe Theatre's 1999 production

1258 UNIT 11: SHAKESPEAREAN DRAMA

See resources on the **Teacher One Stop DVD-ROM** and on **thinkcentral.com**.

R **RESOURCE MANAGER UNIT 11**
Plan and Teach, pp. 59–64
Summary, pp. 65–68†‡*
Text Analysis, pp. 69–70†*

DIAGNOSTIC AND SELECTION TESTS
Selection Tests, pp. 323–326

 BEST PRACTICES TOOLKIT
Cluster Diagram, p. B18
Open Mind, p. D9
Sequence Chain, p. B21

INTERACTIVE READER

ADAPTED INTERACTIVE READER

ELL ADAPTED INTERACTIVE READER

TECHNOLOGY
- Teacher One Stop DVD-ROM
- Student One Stop DVD-ROM
- PowerNotes DVD-ROM
- Audio Anthology CD
- GrammarNotes DVD-ROM
- Audio Tutor CD
- ExamView Test Generator on the Teacher One Stop

 **Video Trailer**

Go to **thinkcentral.com** to preview the **Video Trailer** introducing this selection. Other features that support the selection include
- **PowerNotes** presentation
- **ThinkAloud** models to enhance comprehension
- **WordSharp** vocabulary tutorials
- interactive writing and grammar instruction

---

* Resources for Differentiation   † Also in Spanish   ‡ In Haitian Creole and Vietnamese

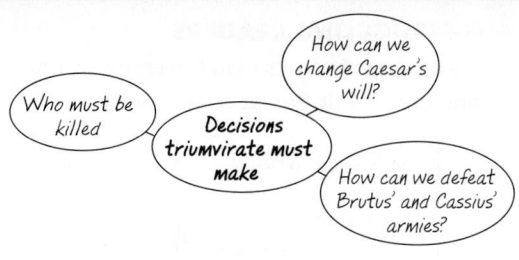 (photograph spanning the left portion of the page)

Reading Support

This selection on **thinkcentral.com** includes embedded **ThinkAloud** models—students "thinking aloud" about the story to model the kinds of questions a good reader would ask about a selection.

BACKGROUND

The Second Triumvirate in History and in Shakespeare Shakespeare's text gives the impression that Caesar's funeral was followed almost immediately by the forming of the Second Triumvirate. In fact, more than a year and a half passed between the events. During that time, Octavius had the Senate recognize him as Caesar's rightful heir and declare Antony an enemy. However, Antony remained a powerful figure. In 43 B.C., Antony, Octavius, and Lepidus, a member of a distinguished Roman family and an ally of Antony, agreed to form the Second Triumvirate—a trio of rulers. (The First Triumvirate had consisted of Caesar, Pompey, and Crassus.)

Analyze Visuals

Activity How does this photograph reflect the way in which Brutus and Cassius seem to relate to each other? *Possible answer: The photograph shows Brutus speaking to Cassius and pointing with his index finger, as if he is instructing Cassius. Cassius is looking at and listening to Brutus. In much of the play, Brutus tells Cassius what to do, and Cassius obeys, even if he disagrees.*

TIERED DISCUSSION PROMPTS

Direct students to lines 18–40. Use these prompts to help students explore Antony's revealing description of Lepidus:

Connect Have you ever seen or read about someone who used people as a means to an end instead of treating them as individuals with feelings? *Accept all reasonable responses.*

Analyze To what nonhuman things does Antony compare Lepidus? *Possible answer: Antony compares Lepidus to an ass who does not understand the value of the burden that others have him carry (lines 18–27), to a horse who has to be trained and told what to do (lines 34–35), and to property (line 40).* What does that kind of language suggest about what Antony is really like (or what he has become)? *Possible answer: The language suggests that Antony is (or has become) cruel and that he disregards the value of an individual. He seems to care only about using people to achieve his own purposes.*

Synthesize How does Antony's description of Lepidus add to what he has already revealed about himself in Scene 1? *Possible answer: Antony has already spoken of reducing the people's inheritance from Caesar (lines 8–9), the very people whom he once claimed that he cared for and wanted to help. The description of Lepidus reinforces the idea that Antony now cares only for himself.*

Octavius.   You may do your will;
But he's a tried and valiant soldier.

   Antony. So is my horse, Octavius, and for that
30 I do appoint him store of provender.
It is a creature that I teach to fight,
To wind, to stop, to run directly on,
His corporal motion governed by my spirit.
And, in some taste is Lepidus but so.
35 He must be taught, and trained, and bid go forth:
A barren-spirited fellow; one that feeds
On objects, arts and imitations
Which, out of use and staled by other men,
Begin his fashion. Do not talk of him,
40 But as a property. And now, Octavius,
Listen great things. Brutus and Cassius
Are levying powers. We must straight make head.
Therefore let our alliance be combined,
Our best friends made, and our best means stretched out;
45 And let us presently go sit in council
How covert matters may be best disclosed
And open perils surest answered.

   Octavius. Let us do so; for we are at the stake
And bayed about with many enemies;
50 And some that smile have in their hearts, I fear,
Millions of mischiefs.

   [*Exeunt.*]

30 appoint … provender: give him a supply of hay.

31–40 Antony says that like a horse, Lepidus must be taught to turn (**wind**), stop, and run straight. Lepidus is merely a tool (**property**) who fills his head with borrowed ideas that have gone out of fashion.

41–42 Listen … head: Listen to important (**great**) matters. Brutus and Cassius are raising an army (**levying powers**). We must move fast (**straight make head**) to build up our own army.

45–47 let us … answered: Let us decide the best way to uncover hidden (**covert**) dangers and to deal with the threats we know about.

48–51 we are … mischiefs: We are like a bear tied to a stake and taunted by barking dogs. Some of the people who smile at us may have evil intentions (**mischiefs**) in mind for us.

Scene 2   *A military camp near Sardis. In front of Brutus' tent.*

Displeased at the way events are developing, Brutus tells his servant about Cassius' new cold and distant attitude. Cassius arrives, and he and Brutus go into the tent to talk about their disagreements.

[*Sound of drums. Enter* Brutus, Lucilius, Lucius, *and* Soldiers. Titinius *and* Pindarus, *from Cassius' army, meet them.*]

Brutus. Stand ho!

Lucilius. Give the word, ho! and stand!

Brutus. What now, Lucilius? Is Cassius near?

Lucilius. He is at hand, and Pindarus is come
5 To do you salutation from his master.

   Brutus. He greets me well. Your master, Pindarus,
In his own change, or by ill officers,
Hath given me some worthy cause to wish
Things done undone; but if he be at hand,
10 I shall be satisfied.

5 do you salutation: bring you greetings.

6–9 He greets … undone: Cassius sends a good man to greet me, but he has given me reason to be regretful, either because he has changed or because he is poorly served by subordinates. *What might Brutus wish to have "undone"?*

1260   UNIT 11: SHAKESPEAREAN DRAMA

DIFFERENTIATED INSTRUCTION

FOR STRUGGLING READERS

Preview Have students read the scene synopsis and then list Brutus' actions in Scene 2.

> In Scene 2, Brutus . . .
> ○ • is unhappy about his situation.
>   • complains to his servant about Cassius.
>   • meets with Cassius to
> ○ discuss the problem.

FOR ENGLISH LANGUAGE LEARNERS

Task Support Have students read the marginal note and question about lines 6–9 in Scene 2. Briefly discuss what actions Brutus has participated in since the play began. *Possible answer: Brutus might wish that he could undo Caesar's murder or his military alliance with Cassius.*

Vocabulary: Outdated Forms Encourage students to add these terms and definitions from Scene 2 to their language journal. (See the For English Language Learners note on page 1204.)

- *word* (line 2), "command"
- *if he be at hand* (line 9), "if he is nearby"
- *regard* (line 12), "respect"
- *of old* (line 18), "in the past"
- *gently* (line 31), "slowly"
- *wrangle* (line 45), "argue"

Pindarus.   I do not doubt
But that my noble master will appear
Such as he is, full of regard and honor.

Brutus. He is not doubted. A word, Lucilius,
How he received you. Let me be resolved.

15 **Lucilius.** With courtesy and with respect enough,
But not with such familiar instances
Nor with such free and friendly conference
As he hath used of old.

Brutus.   Thou has described
A hot friend cooling. Ever note, Lucilius,
20 When love begins to sicken and decay
It useth an enforced ceremony.
There are no tricks in plain and simple faith;
But hollow men, like horses hot at hand,
Make gallant show and promise of their mettle;

[*Low march within.*]

25 But when they should endure the bloody spur,
They fall their crests, and like deceitful jades
Sink in the trial. Comes his army on?

Lucilius. They mean this night in Sardis to be quartered.
The greater part, the horse in general,
30 Are come with Cassius.

Brutus.   Hark! He is arrived.
March gently on to meet him.

[*Enter* Cassius *and his army.*]

Cassius. Stand, ho!

Brutus. Stand, ho! Speak the word along.

First Soldier. Stand!

35 **Second Soldier.** Stand!

Third Soldier. Stand!

Cassius. Most noble brother, you have done me wrong.

Brutus. Judge me, you gods! wrong I mine enemies?
And if not so, how should I wrong a brother? Ⓐ

40 **Cassius.** Brutus, this sober form of yours hides wrongs,
And when you do them—

Brutus.   Cassius, be content.
Speak your griefs softly. I do know you well.
Before the eyes of both our armies here
(Which should perceive nothing but love from us)
45 Let us not wrangle. Bid them move away.

13–14 A word . . . resolved: Brutus takes his officer aside and asks him privately how he was treated when he met Cassius. *Why does Brutus want to know this?*

17 conference: conversation.

⓵ **Targeted Passage**

20–27 Brutus says that when affection begins to cool, it turns into awkward politeness. He compares insincere (**hollow**) men to horses who show spirit and courage (**mettle**) at first but fail like worn-out nags when put to the test.

28 They . . . quartered: Cassius and his army intend to stay here (**in Sardis**) tonight.

29 horse in general: entire cavalry.

34–36 The soldiers are passing the order to stop marching (**Stand**) along the lengthy column that has followed Cassius into camp.

Ⓐ **TRAGIC HERO**
What **tragic flaw** is revealed in Brutus's suggestion that he has never even wronged his enemies?

41 content: calm.

Ⓐ *Model the Skill:*
TRAGIC HERO

To model how to analyze Shakespearean tragedy, read lines 38–39 aloud. Point out that Brutus believes he killed Caesar for noble purposes (line 38). Remind students that Brutus' tragic flaw—an error in judgment or a weakness in character—will cause his downfall.

Possible answer: *Brutus' tragic flaw is his belief in his own nobility, regardless of the facts. He does not consider that he has wronged his enemies (line 38) because he believes that he participated in Caesar's murder for noble reasons, not out of envy or a desire for gain.*

IF STUDENTS NEED HELP . . . Use an Open Mind diagram to help students explore Brutus' attitude.

I loved Rome as a republic.

I feared that Caesar would tyrannize Rome.

I admired Caesar, but I had greater love for Rome.

Cassius talked me into joining the conspiracy.

💼 **BEST PRACTICES TOOLKIT—Transparency**
Open Mind p. D9

FOR STRUGGLING READERS

⓵ **Targeted Passage** [Lines 13–30]

This passage reveals that the friendship between Brutus and Cassius is disintegrating.

• What kind of change did Lucilius sense in Cassius? (lines 15–18)

• What does Brutus think of his relationship with Cassius now? How can you tell? (lines 18–24)

• To what does Brutus compare "hollow men"? What is his point? (lines 23–27)

FOR ENGLISH LANGUAGE LEARNERS

Task Support As you direct students to the side note and question about lines 13–14, remind them that the relationship between Cassius and Brutus is not as ideal as it once was (lines 8–10). ***Possible answer:*** *Brutus wants to know how Cassius acted toward Lucilius, Brutus' representative, so that he can get a clearer idea about how Cassius might feel or act toward Brutus himself.*

Can your CONSCIENCE mislead you?

Discuss Based on Scene 3, lines 9–28, how does Brutus think that the condition of his conscience compares to that of Cassius? How can you tell? *Possible answer: Brutus feels that his conscience is superior to that of Cassius. He speaks condemningly to Cassius about accepting bribes (lines 9–10). He also asserts that they killed Caesar for the sake of justice (line 19) and that he would rather be a dog than contaminate his fingers with bribes (lines 23–28). What is ironic about Brutus' view? Possible answer: Ironically, Brutus' conscience is not nearly as superior as he claims it to be. He participated in a political assassination that some would call unjustified.*

Then in my tent, Cassius, enlarge your griefs,
And I will give you audience.

    Cassius.   Pindarus,
Bid our commanders lead their charges off
A little from this ground.

50 **Brutus.** Lucilius, do you the like, and let no man
Come to our tent till we have done our conference.
Let Lucius and Titinius guard our door.

[Exeunt.]

46 **enlarge your griefs:** freely express your grievances.

Scene 3   *Inside Brutus' tent at Sardis.*

Brutus and Cassius argue angrily, as Brutus accuses Cassius of corruption and greed. After a while, though, they calm down and become friendly once again. Brutus informs Cassius of Portia's death. Soon after, Massala enters. He tells of all the killings in Rome and of Antony and Octavius approaching with their armies. Brutus persuades Cassius that their forces must meet the enemy at Philippi, in Greece. Later, as Brutus reads, the ghost of Caesar appears and promises to see Brutus at Philippi.

[Enter Brutus and Cassius.]

Cassius. That you have wronged me doth appear in this:
You have condemned and noted Lucius Pella
For taking bribes here of the Sardians;
Wherein my letters, praying on his side,
5 Because I knew the man, were slighted off.

2 **noted:** publicly disgraced.

5 **slighted off:** ignored.

  Brutus. You wronged yourself to write in such a case.

  Cassius. In such a time as this it is not meet
That every nice offense should bear his comment.

7–8 **it is not ... comment:** It is not appropriate for every tiny (**nice**) offense to be criticized.

  Brutus. Let me tell you, Cassius, you yourself
10 Are much condemned to have an itching palm,
To sell and mart your offices for gold
To undeservers.

10 **to have an itching palm:** to be always looking for bribes.

11 **mart:** market.

    Cassius.   I an itching palm?
You know that you are Brutus that speaks this,
Or, by the gods, this speech were else your last!

15 **Brutus.** The name of Cassius honors this corruption,
And chastisement doth therefore hide his head.

15–16 **The name ... head:** Because Cassius's name is linked to the bribery (**corruption**), no one dares talk about punishment (**chastisement**) for those who accept the bribes.

  Cassius. Chastisement?

  Brutus. Remember March; the ides of March remember.
Did not great Julius bleed for justice' sake?
20 What villain touched his body that did stab
And not for justice? What, shall one of us,
That struck the foremost man of all this world

DIFFERENTIATED INSTRUCTION

FOR STRUGGLING READERS

Preview Have students read the Scene 3 synopsis and use a Sequence Chain to organize the plot events mentioned.

> Brutus and Cassius argue but then reestablish their friendship.

↓

> Brutus tells Cassius that Portia is dead.

↓

> Massala announces that Antony and Octavius' armies are approaching.

↓

> Brutus persuades Cassius to have their forces meet the enemy at Philippi.

↓

> The ghost of Caesar appears and tells Brutus that he will see him at Philippi.

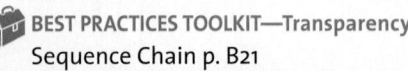
BEST PRACTICES TOOLKIT—Transparency
Sequence Chain p. B21

FOR ENGLISH LANGUAGE LEARNERS

Concept Support As students read lines 9–16, explain that Cassius is so upset by Brutus' accusations that he declares that he would kill anyone other than Brutus who said such a thing to him (lines 13–14). Discuss whether Cassius says this because of their past friendship, their role as co-conspirators in Caesar's murder, or some other reason.

Behind the Curtain

Brutus and Cassius in the Royal Shakespeare Company's 2001 production

Brutus and Cassius in the New York Shakespeare Festival's 1988 production

Brutus and Cassius in the Shakespeare Theatre's 1993–1994 production

Costume Design

In addition to providing information about a character's occupation and social class, a **stage costume** may offer clues to the character's personality. Costume designers often have to do careful research to create historically accurate styles of clothing. For a production that is not realistic, the designer may mix fashions from different periods. How do the costumes of Brutus and Cassius differ in these photographs? What do they suggest about the characters?

JULIUS CAESAR: ACT FOUR, SCENE 3 **1263**

BEHIND THE CURTAIN COMMON CORE RI 7

Costume Design Explain to students that because *The Tragedy of Julius Caesar* concerns real people who lived during a specific historical period, costume designers often try to re-create realistic costumes for the actors in this play. Still, costumes may reflect the attitudes of the characters or a director's unique interpretation of a play, as well— and sometimes that means wholly original costume designs. *Possible answer: The 1988 production seems historically accurate, but the 2001 and 1993–1994 productions mix fashions from different periods. In the 2001 production, Brutus and Cassius wear a mix of togas and more modern military uniforms, but Brutus is wearing a red and possibly more royal outfit than Cassius' green one. In the 1988 production, Brutus is dressed as a nobleman and Cassius is outfitted as a soldier, suggesting that Brutus is the rational "thinker" whereas Cassius is the impulsive "doer." In the 1993–1994 production, both men are dressed the same (suits or vests beneath their Roman robes), as noblemen and thinkers. This picture suggests that they are the most equal in stature.*

FOR ENGLISH LANGUAGE LEARNERS

Vocabulary Support Discuss these expressions with students:

From Scene 2

• *do you the like* (line 50), "you do the same"

From Scene 3

• *That you have wronged me doth appear in this* (line 1)—"Here is the proof that you have treated me unfairly"

• *Wherein my letters, praying on his side* (line 4), "In which my letters, supporting him"

FOR ADVANCED LEARNERS/PRE–AP

Research and Create Costumes [small-group option] Have students research the Rome of Caesar's time to find out what soldiers, nobles, senators, and common people wore. Then have students select three characters from the play (at least two of which must be of different classes) and design costumes for them. Students may either physically create the costumes or illustrate them. Have students share their costume designs with the class and explain their choices.

Elizabethans and Their Humors In lines 39 and 43, Brutus accuses Cassius of being "choleric." The Elizabethans believed that a person's physical and emotional health depended upon the mixture of four fluids, called "humors"—blood, phlegm, choler (yellow bile), and melancholy (black bile)—in his or her body. If these fluids were properly proportioned, the person would be generally healthy and would have a stable personality. If the mixture was off, the person would become ill or would think and act erratically. When Brutus says that Cassius is choleric, he implies that Cassius has too much choler in his system, making him hot-tempered and impulsive.

TEXT ANALYSIS

COMMON CORE

RL 3

B TRAGIC HERO

Possible answer: The character trait that Brutus implies is necessary for a good leader is control over one's emotions. He criticizes Cassius for fretting (line 42) and goes so far as to call Cassius "testy" (line 46), "waspish" (line 50), and "a madman" (line 40).

But for supporting robbers—shall we now
Contaminate our fingers with base bribes,
25 And sell the mighty space of our large honors
For so much trash as may be grasped thus?
I had rather be a dog and bay the moon
Than such a Roman.

Cassius.   Brutus, bait not me!
I'll not endure it. You forget yourself
30 To hedge me in. I am a soldier, I,
Older in practice, abler than yourself
To make conditions.

Brutus.   Go to! You are not, Cassius.

Cassius. I am.

Brutus. I say you are not.

35 **Cassius.** Urge me no more! I shall forget myself.
Have mind upon your health, tempt me no farther.

Brutus. Away, slight man!

Cassius. Is't possible?

Brutus.   Hear me, for I will speak.
Must I give way and room to your rash choler?
40 Shall I be frighted when a madman stares?

Cassius. O ye gods, ye gods! Must I endure all this?

Brutus. All this? Ay, more! Fret till your proud heart break.
Go show your slaves how choleric you are
And make your bondmen tremble. Must I budge?
45 Must I observe you? Must I stand and crouch
Under your testy humor? By the gods,
You shall digest the venom of your spleen,
Though it do split you; for from this day forth
I'll use you for my mirth, yea, for my laughter,
50 When you are waspish. **B**

Cassius.   Is it come to this?

Brutus. You say you are a better soldier;
Let it appear so. Make your vaunting true,
And it shall please me well. For mine own part,
I shall be glad to learn of noble men.

55 **Cassius.** You wrong me every way! You wrong me, Brutus!
I said an elder soldier, not a better.
Did I say "better"?

Brutus.   If you did, I care not.

Cassius. When Caesar lived he durst not thus have moved me.

Brutus. Peace, peace! You durst not so have tempted him.

---

23 But for supporting robbers: because he supported corrupt officials. (This is not one of the charges the conspirators originally made against Caesar.)

27 bay: howl at.

28 bait: provoke.

32 make conditions: arrange matters.

B TRAGIC HERO
In lines 39–50, Brutus refers to Cassius's quick temper (**rash choler**), irritable mood (**testy humor**), and his spleen, which was once believed to be the source of emotions such as anger and spite. What **character trait** does Brutus imply is necessary in a good leader?

52 vaunting: bragging. *What challenge does Brutus make?*

58 he durst . . . me: Even Caesar would not have dared to provoke me this way.

DIFFERENTIATED INSTRUCTION

FOR ENGLISH LANGUAGE LEARNERS

Vocabulary Support Discuss the meanings of these expressions to help students better grasp the argument between Brutus and Cassius:

- *Contaminate our fingers with base bribes (line 24)*, "Dirty our hands with dishonest money paid to influence our behavior"

- *sell . . . For so much trash (lines 25–26)*, "trade our honor for dishonest gain"

- *digest the venom of your spleen (line 47)*, "swallow the poison of your anger"

- *use you for my mirth (line 49)*, "laugh at you"

- *waspish (line 50)*, "annoyed"

- *terror . . . in your threats (line 66)*, "fear in your intimidations"

- *faults (lines 89 and 90)*, "weaknesses"

Task Support Ask students to read the question in the side note for line 52. Have them review lines 30–32, where Cassius says that he is a soldier and that he has more experience than Brutus. *Possible answer: Brutus challenges Cassius to act like the better soldier that Cassius claims to be. He implies that he would then respect Cassius as a "noble" man (line 54).*

60   **Cassius.** I durst not?

    Brutus. No.

    Cassius. What, durst not tempt him?

    Brutus.   For your life you durst not.

    Cassius. Do not presume too much upon my love.
    I may do that I shall be sorry for.

65   **Brutus.** You have done that you should be sorry for.
    There is no terror, Cassius, in your threats;
    For I am armed so strong in honesty
    That they pass by me as the idle wind,
    Which I respect not. I did send to you

70   For certain sums of gold, which you denied me,
    For I can raise no money by vile means—
    By heaven, I had rather coin my heart
    And drop my blood for drachmas than to wring
    From the hard hands of peasants their vile trash

75   By any indirection. I did send
    To you for gold to pay my legions,
    Which you denied me. Was that done like Cassius?
    Should I have answered Caius Cassius so?
    When Marcus Brutus grows so covetous

80   To lock such rascal counters from his friends,
    Be ready, gods, with all your thunderbolts,
    Dash him to pieces! **C**

    Cassius.   I denied you not.

    Brutus. You did.

    Cassius. I did not. He was but a fool that brought

85   My answer back. Brutus hath rived my heart.
    A friend should bear his friend's infirmities,
    But Brutus makes mine greater than they are.

    Brutus. I do not, till you practice them on me.

    Cassius. You love me not.

    Brutus.   I do not like your faults.

90   **Cassius.** A friendly eye could never see such faults.

    Brutus. A flatterer's would not, though they do appear
    As huge as high Olympus.

    Cassius. Come, Antony, and young Octavius, come!
    Revenge yourselves alone on Cassius.

95   For Cassius is aweary of the world:
    Hated by one he loves; braved by his brother;
    Checked like a bondman, all his faults observed,
    Set in a notebook, learned and conned by rote
    To cast into my teeth. O, I could weep

71–75 For I can . . . indirection: I cannot raise money by dishonest (**vile**) methods. I would rather make coins out of my heart and blood than steal money from peasants by lying (**indirection**).

76 legions: armies.

79–82 When . . . pieces: When I become such a miser as to deny cheap coins (**rascal counters**) to my friends, may the gods destroy me.

C TRAGIC HERO
What conclusion would you draw about Brutus's honesty in light of his request for money from Cassius? Explain your answer.

85 rived: torn apart.

86 infirmities: shortcomings.

96 braved: defied.

97 Checked like a bondman: scolded like a slave.

98 conned by rote: memorized by repetition.

TEXT ANALYSIS   COMMON CORE

C TRAGIC HERO   RL 3

Possible answer: *The reader can conclude that Brutus is not as honest as he says he is. It is hypocritical for Brutus to blame Cassius for taking bribes and then to ask him for money. He is being dishonest either with himself or with Cassius.*

IF STUDENTS NEED HELP . . . Focus on Brutus' hypocrisy by having them reread lines 9–12 and 18–28 and note Brutus' declaration of his high moral standards. Then have students reread lines 71–77. Point out that Brutus there says that he cannot use dishonest means to raise money to pay his troops, yet he has no qualms about asking Cassius to give him money, which Brutus knows was raised by dishonest means (bribery).

FOR ADVANCED LEARNERS/PRE–AP

Analyze Character [paired-activity option]
In this scene, Cassius—seen earlier in the play as a cunning manipulator and the first proponent of Caesar's assassination—is almost comical as he becomes more and more emotional and overdramatic in Brutus' presence. Ask students to reflect upon his argument with Brutus in this scene. Then have them write a character analysis that acknowledges Cassius' earlier strengths and explains the internal conflicts that may be driving him to be so melodramatic in this scene. (As part of the latter point, students might speculate about why Brutus' friendship seems so important to Cassius.) As volunteers share their analyses with the class, discuss the insights that are presented most often.

TEXT ANALYSIS

ⓓ ALLUSION

Point out that Romans living in the time period of the play would have quickly understood a reference to Pluto, or other mythological characters, in conversation, and that these allusions could serve multiple functions.

Possible answer: *Students may say that these allusions serve to make Shakespeare's characters believable people of their time and place, and to create the atmosphere of ancient Rome.*

TIERED DISCUSSION PROMPTS

Direct students to lines 93–123. Use these prompts to help students grasp the reconciliation of Brutus and Cassius:

Summarize What does Cassius say and do in lines 93–107? *Cassius says that Brutus has turned against him and is accusing him unfairly. He is so unhappy over this situation that he offers Brutus his dagger and urges Brutus to kill him.*

Analyze How does Brutus' response make reconciliation possible? *Possible answer: Seeing Cassius' extreme behavior, Brutus backs down and describes himself as a lamb that cannot stay angry (lines 110–113). His backing down makes it possible for Cassius to do so, as well. How does Cassius then take the next step toward reconciliation? Possible answer: Cassius then admits that he acted out of ill temper, prompting Brutus to make the same admission (lines 113–116). Once they both have confessed that they were wrong, they can be friends again (lines 117–118).*

Evaluate Think about the exchange that ends this passage (lines 119–123). In your opinion, have Brutus and Cassius just made a permanent reconciliation? Defend your view. *Possible answer: The reconciliation probably is not permanent. Cassius predicts that he will have angry outbursts in the future; when he does, it remains to be seen if Brutus will be able to overlook them, as he says that he will. In addition, the accusations that both men have made during this argument remain unresolved.*

---

100 My spirit from mine eyes! There is my dagger,
 And here my naked breast; within, a heart
 Dearer than Pluto's mine, richer than gold:
 If that thou be'st a Roman, take it forth.
 I, that denied thee gold, will give my heart.
105 Strike as thou didst at Caesar; for I know,
 When thou didst hate him worst, thou lov'dst him better
 Than ever thou lov'dst Cassius. ⓓ

   Brutus.   Sheathe your dagger.
 Be angry when you will; it shall have scope.
 Do what you will; dishonor shall be humor.
110 O Cassius, you are yoked with a lamb
 That carries anger as the flint bears fire;
 Who, much enforced, shows a hasty spark,
 And straight is cold again.

   Cassius.   Hath Cassius lived
 To be but mirth and laughter to his Brutus
115 When grief and blood ill-tempered vexeth him?

   Brutus. When I spoke that, I was ill-tempered too.

   Cassius. Do you confess so much? Give me your hand.

   Brutus. And my heart too.

   Cassius.   O Brutus!

   Brutus.   What's the matter?

   Cassius. Have you not love enough to bear with me
120 When that rash humor which my mother gave me
 Makes me forgetful?

   Brutus.   Yes, Cassius, and from henceforth,
 When you are over-earnest with your Brutus,
 He'll think your mother chides, and leave you so.

   [*Enter a* Poet *followed by* Lucilius, Titinius, *and* Lucius.]

   Poet. Let me go in to see the generals!
125 There is some grudge between 'em. 'Tis not meet
 They be alone.

   Lucilius. You shall not come to them.

   Poet. Nothing but death shall stay me.

   Cassius. How now? What's the matter?

130 **Poet.** For shame, you generals! What do you mean?
 Love and be friends, as two such men should be,
 For I have seen more years, I'm sure, than ye.

   Cassius. Ha, ha! How vilely doth this cynic rhyme!

   Brutus. Get you hence, sirrah! Saucy fellow, hence!
135 **Cassius.** Bear with him, Brutus. 'Tis his fashion.

ⓓ ALLUSION

An **allusion** is a reference in a work of literature to a famous person, event, or idea in literature, history, or mythology. Allusions can help define the setting, add depth to characters, and even hint at themes. In this passage, Cassius makes an allusion to the Roman god Pluto, god of the underworld and of mines. Reread the allusion in line 102. What function does this allusion and Shakespeare's other references to Roman mythology serve?

108–113 Brutus tells Cassius not to restrain his anger; he will no longer take offense at Cassius's insults. He describes himself as a mild man (**lamb**) who may flare up when provoked but whose anger immediately cools.

113–115 Recalling Brutus's remark in lines 49–50, Cassius asks whether his moodiness has made him a joke to Brutus.

120 rash humor: quick temper.

124–138 The poet who interrupts Brutus and Cassius is called a rude fellow (**cynic**) and other insulting terms. *Why might Shakespeare have included this brief scene with the poet?*

DIFFERENTIATED INSTRUCTION

FOR STRUGGLING READERS

Paraphrasing Shakespeare Have students reread lines 124–138. Model this paraphrase of lines 125–126: *There are bad feelings between the two generals. It is not good to leave them alone with each other.* Then ask students to paraphrase lines 128–129. **Possible answer: Poet.** *You will have to kill me to keep me away.* / **Cassius.** *What is going on now? What is wrong?*

FOR ENGLISH LANGUAGE LEARNERS

Task Support After students read the question in the side note for lines 124–138, have them reread lines 130–132 and consider the advice that the Poet gives to the two generals. **Possible answer:** *Shakespeare might have included this brief scene both to make the audience laugh (that is, for comic relief) and to emphasize what Brutus and Cassius should keep in mind if they truly want to succeed.*

Cassius and Poet in the Globe Theatre's 1999 production

Brutus. I'll know his humor when he knows his time.
What should the wars do with these jigging fools?
Companion, hence!

Cassius.   Away, away, be gone!

[*Exit* Poet.]

Brutus. Lucilius and Titinius, bid the commanders
140 Prepare to lodge their companies tonight.

Cassius. And come yourselves, and bring Messala with you
Immediately to us.

[*Exeunt* Lucilius *and* Titinius.]

Brutus.   Lucius, a bowl of wine.

[*Exit* Lucius.]

Cassius. I did not think you could have been so angry.

Brutus. O Cassius, I am sick of many griefs.

145 **Cassius.** Of your philosophy you make no use
If you give place to accidental evils.

Brutus. No man bears sorrow better. Portia is dead.

Cassius. Ha! Portia?

Brutus. She is dead.

150 **Cassius.** How scaped I killing when I crossed you so?

145–146 Of your . . . evils: You aren't making use of your philosophy if you let chance happenings get you down. (Brutus was a Stoic, one who believed that pain and suffering should be endured calmly.)

148 Ha: Cassius is not laughing but is so shocked by the news of Portia's death that he gasps.

150 How . . . so: How did I escape being killed when I angered you, with such a terrible thing on your mind?

Analyze Visuals

Activity What does this photograph suggest about the way in which Cassius and Brutus view the Poet? *Possible answer: The photograph suggests a reason that Cassius and Brutus do not take the Poet seriously. The Poet is standing on a table; he looks more like a jester than a poet. Cassius' hands are on his hips, as if he is an adult who is scolding an irresponsible, bothersome child.*

FOR ENGLISH LANGUAGE LEARNERS

Vocabulary: Outdated Forms Encourage students to add these terms to their language journals. (See the For English Language Learners note on page 1204.)

- *didst* (line 106), "did"
- *lov'dst* (line 106), "loved"
- *vexeth* (line 115), "bother"
- *'Tis not meet* (line 125), "It is not proper"
- *stay* (line 128), "stop"
- *Saucy* (line 134), "Disrespectful"
- *Bear* (line 135), "Be patient"
- *jigging* (line 137), "joking"
- *give place* (line 146), "allow [yourself] to think about"
- *accidental* (line 146), "unexpected"

Can your
CONSCIENCE
mislead you?

Discuss Based on lines 152–159, does Brutus seem to have a guilty conscience about Portia's death? Should he? Explain. *Possible answer: No, Brutus does not seem to feel guilty about Portia's death, but perhaps he should. He mentions Portia's death in a calm manner (line 147), then placidly explains to Cassius that Portia killed herself because she was worried about his absence and the power of Octavius and Antony (lines 152–156). Cassius seems to be more upset about Portia's death than Brutus is, for he cries out when he hears the news— only to have Brutus tell him to be quiet (lines 157–158, 166).*

BACKGROUND

Marcus Tullius Cicero (106 B.C.–43 B.C.) Considered by many to be the greatest orator and prose stylist of ancient Rome, Cicero was an ardent believer in the ideals of the Roman Republic. Following the death of Julius Caesar, Cicero supported the conspirators and opposed Mark Antony, a political rival. He urged the Senate to name Brutus governor of Cisalpine Gaul (modern-day northern Italy) and declare Antony an enemy of the state. After the formation of the Second Triumverate, Cicero was among those condemned for his opposition to their authority. He was apprehended at his villa and decapitated on December 7, 43 B.C.

O insupportable and touching loss!
Upon what sickness?

Brutus.   Impatient of my absence,
And grief that young Octavius with Mark Antony
Have made themselves so strong—for with her death

155 That tidings came—with this she fell distract,
And (her attendants absent) swallowed fire.

Cassius. And died so?

Brutus.   Even so.

Cassius.   O ye immortal gods!

[*Reenter* Lucius, *with wine and tapers.*]

Brutus. Speak no more of her. Give me a bowl of wine.
In this I bury all unkindness, Cassius.

[*Drinks.*]

160 **Cassius.** My heart is thirsty for that noble pledge.
Fill, Lucius, till the wine o'erswell the cup.
I cannot drink too much of Brutus' love.

[*Drinks. Exit* Lucius.]

[*Reenter* Titinius, *with* Messala.]

Brutus. Come in, Titinius! Welcome, good Messala.
Now sit we close about this taper here

165 And call in question our necessities.

Cassius. Portia, art thou gone?

Brutus.   No more, I pray you.
Messala, I have here received letters
That young Octavius and Mark Antony
Come down upon us with a mighty power,

170 Bending their expedition toward Philippi.

Messala. Myself have letters of the selfsame tenure.

Brutus. With what addition?

Messala. That by proscription and bills of outlawry
Octavius, Antony, and Lepidus

175 Have put to death an hundred senators.

Brutus. Therein our letters do not well agree.
Mine speak of seventy senators that died
By their proscriptions, Cicero being one.

Cassius. Cicero one?

Messala.   Cicero is dead,
180 And by that order of proscription.
Had you your letters from your wife, my lord?

152–156 Impatient . . . fire: She was worried about my absence and about the armies of Antony and Octavius. These things made her insane (**she fell distract**). When her servants were not around, she swallowed burning coals.

161 o'erswell: overflow.

164–165 Now sit . . . necessities: Let's sit around this candle and talk about what we must do.

170 Bending . . . Philippi: leading their armies to Philippi (**a city in northern Greece**).

171 Myself . . . tenure: I have received letters that say the same thing.

173 proscription . . . outlawry: death sentences and lists of condemned people.

DIFFERENTIATED INSTRUCTION

FOR STRUGGLING READERS

Summarize Remind students that although this scene has focused on the conflict between two characters, it takes place in the context of a much larger conflict. Ask students to summarize lines 167–175 in terms of that conflict. Elicit that Octavius and Mark Antony have a powerful army that is headed toward Philippi to put down the assassins' opposition, as they put down opposition within Rome's government by executing many senators.

Brutus. No, Messala.

Messala. Nor nothing in your letters writ of her?

Brutus. Nothing, Messala.

Messala. That methinks is strange.

185 **Brutus.** Why ask you? Hear you aught of her in yours?

Messala. No, my lord.

Brutus. Now as you are a Roman, tell me true.

Messala. Then like a Roman bear the truth I tell,
For certain she is dead, and by strange manner.

190 **Brutus.** Why, farewell, Portia. We must die, Messala.
With meditating that she must die once,
I have the patience to endure it now.

Messala. Even so great men great losses should endure.

Cassius. I have as much of this in art as you,

195 But yet my nature could not bear it so.

Brutus. Well, to our work alive. What do you think
Of marching to Philippi presently?

Cassius. I do not think it good.

Brutus. Your reason?

Cassius. This it is:
'Tis better that the enemy seek us.

200 So shall he waste his means, weary his soldiers,
Doing himself offense, whilst we, lying still,
Are full of rest, defense, and nimbleness.

Brutus. Good reasons must of force give place to better.
The people 'twixt Philippi and this ground

205 Do stand but in a forced affection,
For they have grudged us contribution.
The enemy, marching along by them,
By them shall make a fuller number up,
Come on refreshed, new-added, and encouraged;

210 From which advantage we cut him off
If at Philippi we do face him there,
These people at our back.

Cassius. Hear me, good brother.

Brutus. Under your pardon. You must note beside
That we have tried the utmost of our friends,

215 Our legions are brimful, our cause is ripe.
The enemy increaseth every day;
We, at the height, are ready to decline.

There is a tide in the affairs of men
Which, taken at the flood, leads on to fortune;

181–195 Brutus seems to know nothing about Portia's death in this passage, although earlier he describes her fate to Cassius in lines 149–158. Many scholars believe that the first account of Portia's death was a revision and that Shakespeare intended to delete this second account. *How does Brutus's reaction to Portia's death differ in the two accounts?*

194 in art: in theory, in my beliefs.

② **Targeted Passage**

203–212 Good ... our back: Good reasons have to give way to better ones. The people between (**'twixt**) here and Philippi are friendly only because they have to be (**stand but in a forced affection**). They have given us aid grudgingly. If the enemy marches through, they will find recruits. If we face them at Philippi, we'll eliminate this advantage and keep these unfriendly people behind us.

213–217 Brutus interrupts with another reason for his plan: Their army is now at peak strength, while the enemy is growing stronger.

218–221 Comparing life to a sea voyage, Brutus says that if you miss the high tide when it comes, you can be stuck at shore forever.

TIERED DISCUSSION PROMPTS
Direct students to lines 187–193. Use these prompts to help students draw a parallel between Brutus and Caesar:

Restate What news does Messala bring to Brutus? *Messala tells Brutus that Portia is dead.*

Analyze How is Brutus' response to the news similar to what Caesar says about death in Act Two, Scene 2? *Possible answer: Brutus dispassionately says that everyone must die. His comment is similar to Caesar's statement "Seeing that death, a necessary end, / Will come when it will come" (Act Two, Scene 2, lines 36–37).*

Synthesize Why might Brutus be responding to Messala in a Caesar-like fashion? *Possible answer: Brutus is concerned with his public image and might be acting this way so that Messala will be impressed (which he is, line 193). Brutus cares about what people think of him and wants to project a certain public image, as Caesar did. He wants people to consider him worthy of honor and respect, as Caesar did. Brutus also has a high opinion of himself, as Caesar did.*

FOR STRUGGLING READERS

② **Targeted Passage** [Lines 196–217]

This passage reveals Cassius' and Brutus' differing opinions about traveling to Philippi.

• Why does Cassius want to wait for the enemy's arrival at Sardis? (lines 199–202)

• What reasons does Brutus give for having their armies march to Philippi right away? (lines 204–210)

• How can you tell that Brutus believes that his ideas are superior to those of Cassius,

the more experienced soldier? (lines 203, 213–217)

Task Support Direct students to the side note for lines 181–195 and ask them to read the question. Then have them reread lines 149–162 and compare Brutus' first reaction to his second one. *Possible answer: At first, Brutus is sorrowful (line 147) and will not speak of it (line 158), but later he seems to accept her death calmly and almost without emotion (lines 190–192).*

Ⓔ TRAGIC HERO

Possible answer: *The tragic flaw that Brutus reveals is his inability—or his refusal—to consider the ideas of other people. He assumes that his plan for doing battle with the enemy is superior to Cassius' plan (line 203). Even when Cassius, an experienced soldier, asks Brutus to listen, Brutus interrupts with another reason (lines 213–215) and then waxes philosophical about the importance of seizing moments of destiny (lines 218–224).*

220 Omitted, all the voyage of their life
Is bound in shallows and in miseries.
On such a full sea are we now afloat,
And we must take the current when it serves
Or lose our ventures. Ⓔ

Cassius. Then, with your will, go on.
225 We'll along ourselves and meet them at Philippi.

Brutus. The deep of night is crept upon our talk
And nature must obey necessity,
Which we will niggard with a little rest.
There is no more to say?

Cassius. No more. Good night.
230 Early tomorrow will we rise and hence.

Brutus. Lucius!

[*Reenter* Lucius.]

My gown.

[*Exit* Lucius.]

Farewell, good Messala.
Good night, Titinius. Noble, noble Cassius,
235 Good night and good repose!

Cassius. O my dear brother,
This was an ill beginning of the night!
Never come such division 'tween our souls!
Let it not, Brutus.

[*Reenter* Lucius, *with the gown.*]

Brutus. Everything is well.

Cassius. Good night, my lord.

Brutus. Good night, good brother.

240 **Titinius and Messala.** Good night, Lord Brutus.

Brutus. Farewell every one.

[*Exeunt all but* Brutus *and* Lucius.]

Give me the gown. Where is thy instrument?

Lucius. Here in the tent.

Brutus. What, thou speak'st drowsily?
Poor knave, I blame thee not, thou art o'erwatched.
Call Claudius and some other of my men;
245 I'll have them sleep on cushions in my tent.

Lucius. Varro and Claudius!

[*Enter* Varro *and* Claudius.]

Varro. Calls my lord?

Brutus. I pray you, sirs, lie in my tent and sleep.

Ⓔ **TRAGIC HERO**
Reread lines 196–224. What **tragic flaw** does Brutus reveal in his response to Cassius' concerns about marching their armies to Philippi? Cite details to support your answer.

228 Which . . . rest: We will reluctantly satisfy nature by getting a little rest.

232 gown: nightgown.

242–243 What . . . o'erwatched: I see you're sleepy. It's no wonder, since you've been watching and waiting for so long.

DIFFERENTIATED INSTRUCTION

FOR ENGLISH LANGUAGE LEARNERS

Concept Support As students reread Brutus' words in lines 218–224, explain that this is an extended metaphor. Brutus is comparing life to a voyage on a ship. On such voyages, following the high tide can lead to good fortune (lines 218–219). People who do not follow the tide, however, may spend the rest of their lives in shallow water and misery (lines 220–221). Our tide comes now, Brutus insists to Cassius, and we must act now (lines 222–224).

Vocabulary Support Explain to students that Shakespeare's use of elliptical sentences—the omission of words that are assumed to be understood—can make reading the dialogue difficult. Point out these elliptical sentences and their "translations":

• *We'll along ourselves and meet them at Philippi* (line 225), "We'll move along ourselves and meet them at Philippi"

• *Never come such division 'tween our souls* (line 237), "May such division between our souls never come again"

• *I was sure your lordship did not give it me* (line 256), "I was sure that your lordship did not give it to me"

• *Where I left reading* (line 276), "Where I left off reading"

It may be I shall raise you by-and-by
250 On business to my brother Cassius.

Varro. So please you, we will stand and watch your pleasure.

Brutus. I will not have it so. Lie down, good sirs.
It may be I shall otherwise bethink me.

[*Varro* and Claudius *lie down.*]

Look, Lucius, here's the book I sought for so;
255 I put it in the pocket of my gown.

Lucius. I was sure your lordship did not give it me.

Brutus. Bear with me, good boy, I am much forgetful.
Canst thou hold up by thy heavy eyes awhile,
And touch thy instrument a strain or two?

260 **Lucius.** Ay, my lord, an't please you.

Brutus.   It does, my boy.
I trouble thee too much, but thou art willing.

Lucius. It is my duty, sir.

Brutus. I should not urge thy duty past thy might.
I know young bloods look for a time of rest.

265 **Lucius.** I have slept, my lord, already.

Brutus. It was well done; and thou shalt sleep again;
I will not hold thee long. If I do live,
I will be good to thee. **ⓕ**

[*Music, and a song. Lucius* falls asleep as he sings.]

This is a sleepy tune. O murd'rous slumber!
270 Layest thou thy leaden mace upon my boy,
That plays thee music? Gentle knave, good night.
I will not do thee so much wrong to wake thee.
If thou dost nod, thou break'st thy instrument;
I'll take it from thee; and, good boy, good night.
275 Let me see, let me see. Is not the leaf turned down
Where I left reading? Here it is, I think.

[*Sits.*]

[*Enter the* Ghost of Caesar.]

How ill this taper burns! Ha! Who comes here?
I think it is the weakness of mine eyes
That shapes this monstrous apparition.
280 It comes upon me. Art thou anything?
Art thou some god, some angel, or some devil,
That mak'st my blood cold and my hair to stare?
Speak to me what thou art.

Ghost. Thy evil spirit, Brutus.

249–253 **It may ... bethink me:** Brutus wants them to be handy in case he needs to send a message to Cassius. Varro offers to stand guard all night. Brutus insists the men sleep, not stand guard. He says he may change his mind (**otherwise bethink me**) about sending messages to Cassius.

COMMON CORE RL 4

Language Coach

Slang Slang words are informal, sometimes made-up words that substitute for formal words. You can often figure out the meaning of slang by its context. To what does *bloods* refer in line 264? How can you tell?

ⓕ TRAGIC HERO
What **character traits** are revealed in Brutus's dialogue with Lucius?

270 **mace:** a rod used as a symbol of authority. Brutus is addressing slumber as though it were an officer of the law who has arrested Lucius.

❸ Targeted Passage

277 **How ... burns:** How poorly this candle burns. Everyone in the tent is asleep except Brutus. At first he thinks the thing he sees is only the result of poor eyesight. Then he realizes that something is really there.

282 **stare:** stand on end.

TEXT ANALYSIS   COMMON CORE RL 3

ⓕ TRAGIC HERO

Possible answer: *Brutus' dialogue reveals his concern and caring for others. He seems to show this side of himself only in private.*

IF STUDENTS NEED HELP ... Work with them to identify and record statements that Brutus makes to Lucius and note what each statement reveals about Brutus.

FOR STRUGGLING READERS

❸ Targeted Passage [Lines 275–284]

This passage presents the arrival of what may be Caesar's ghost—and Brutus' confused reaction.

• What is Brutus doing when the Ghost of Caesar arrives? (line 276)

• At first, how does Brutus explain the vision? (lines 278–279)

• How does he admit to feeling as he continues to look at it? (line 282)

• What does Brutus ask the Ghost? Does the Ghost respond clearly? Explain. (lines 283, 284)

FOR ENGLISH LANGUAGE LEARNERS

Language Coach   COMMON CORE RL 4

Slang *Answer: young men; Earlier, Brutus repeatedly refers to Lucius as "my boy." Substituting* boys *for* bloods *makes sense.* Remind students that slang words are informal and substitute for formal words. Ask students to suggest current slang terms that could be substituted in place of *bloods.* (dudes, guys)

Can your CONSCIENCE mislead you?

Discuss Based on lines 289–300 and 308–310, does Brutus' conscience seem to have been bothered by the appearance of the Ghost of Caesar? Cite evidence. *Possible answer: Brutus' conscience has been bothered—temporarily. He does say that he wanted to talk more with the Ghost (line 290), and he asks whether Lucius saw anything (line 299). However, Brutus then orders the men to tell Cassius to get his armies moving (lines 308–309). In short, seeing the Ghost of Caesar does not make Brutus rethink his actions enough to repent and take a course of action other than war.*

ACT FOUR WRAP–UP

READ WITH A PURPOSE Now that students have finished reading Act Four, ask them to decide whether Brutus was a victim of circumstances and explain their answers. *Possible answer: Brutus was not a victim of circumstances, but he was a victim of his pride. He made conscious decisions, such as listening to arguments for the death of Caesar, deciding to spare Antony's life, and determining where to fight the final battle. These decisions were all made with a proud certainty of his own nobility.*

★ **CRITIQUE** Ask students to comment on whether they think that Cassius and Brutus have a right to fight Antony and Octavius. Ask students to speculate about other options that Cassius and Brutus might have.

Brutus.   Why com'st thou?

285 **Ghost.** To tell thee thou shalt see me at Philippi.

Brutus. Well; then I shall see thee again?

Ghost. Ay, at Philippi.

Brutus. Why, I will see thee at Philippi then.

[*Exit* Ghost.]

Now I have taken heart thou vanishest.

290 Ill spirit, I would hold more talk with thee.
Boy! Lucius! Varro! Claudius! Sirs! Awake!
Claudius!

Lucius. The strings, my lord, are false.

Brutus. He thinks he still is at his instrument.

295 Lucius, awake!

Lucius. My lord?

Brutus. Didst thou dream, Lucius, that thou so criedst out?

Lucius. My lord, I do not know that I did cry.

Brutus. Yes, that thou didst. Didst thou see anything?

300 **Lucius.** Nothing, my lord.

Brutus. Sleep again, Lucius. Sirrah Claudius!

[*To* Varro.]

Fellow thou, awake!

Varro. My lord?

Claudius. My lord?

305 **Brutus.** Why did you so cry out, sirs, in your sleep?

Both. Did we, my lord?

Brutus.   Ay. Saw you anything?

Varro. No, my lord, I saw nothing.

Claudius.   Nor I, my lord.

Brutus. Go and commend me to my brother Cassius.
Bid him set on his pow'rs betimes before,
310 And we will follow.

Both.   It shall be done, my lord.

[*Exeunt.*]

289 Now…vanishest: Now that I have my courage back, you disappear.

293 false: out of tune. Lucius, only half awake, thinks he is playing the instrument that Brutus took from him earlier.

308 commend me: give my respects to.

309 Bid…before: Tell him to get his army (**pow'rs**) moving early in the morning.

DIFFERENTIATED INSTRUCTION

FOR ADVANCED LEARNERS/PRE–AP

Analyze an Interpretation Point out that in the play, the Ghost of Caesar really appears and that both the Elizabethans and the Romans generally believed in ghosts. Then ask students to consider and find evidence to support another interpretation—that the Ghost is a figment of Brutus' imagination. Students might consider these possibilities:

• Brutus has been so anxious about his argument with Cassius, Portia's death, the senators' killings, and the impending battle that he imagined the Ghost.

• The Ghost identifies itself as "Thy evil spirit" (line 284). It actually is Brutus' conscience, telling him that the murder of Caesar and the armed opposition are wrong.

Then have students discuss these questions:

• Which interpretation do you like better? Why?

• How do the different interpretations affect your view of Brutus?

Comprehension

1. **Recall** Which three characters have taken control of Rome after Caesar's assassination?

2. **Recall** What has strained the relationship between Brutus and Cassius?

3. **Recall** What happened to Portia after Brutus fled from Rome?

4. **Paraphrase** What arguments do Brutus and Cassius make regarding whether they should march to Philippi to fight their enemies?

Text Analysis

● 5. **Analyze Shakespearean Drama** What flaw or flaws does Brutus show in Act Four, Scene 3? How do these flaws make him a tragic hero? Cite details to support your answer.

● 6. **Reading Shakespearean Drama** Review your notes on Antony's personality in the chart you created as you read. Are Antony's words and actions in Act Four, Scene 1, consistent with your impression of him earlier in the play? Support your answer with evidence from the text.

7. **Make Inferences** Why might Brutus choose to tell Cassius the news about Portia after they have resolved their quarrel?

8. **Predict Outcome** What do you predict will be the outcome of Brutus's decision to meet his enemies at Philippi? Give reasons for your prediction.

9. **Draw Conclusions** Do the Romans seem better off or worse off under their new rulers than they were under Julius Caesar? Cite evidence to support your answer.

10. **Make Judgments** Reread lines 1–123 of Scene 3. Is Brutus justified in his complaints about Cassius? Explain why or why not.

Text Criticism

11. **Critical Interpretations** Some critics have argued that *Julius Caesar* dramatizes the difficulty of balancing private values and public leadership. Do you agree that this conflict between values and effective leadership is an important **theme** in the play? Provide specific examples in your response.

COMMON CORE

RL 1 Cite textual evidence to support analysis of what the text says explicitly as well as inferences drawn from the text. **RL 3** Analyze how complex characters develop over the course of a text, interact with others, and advance the plot or develop the theme. **RL 10** Read and comprehend drama.

Practice and Apply

For preliminary support of post-reading questions, use these copy masters:

R RESOURCE MANAGER—Copy Masters
Reading Check p. 71
Tragic Hero p. 69
Question Support p. 72

Additional selection questions are provided for teachers on page 63.

ANSWERS

Comprehension

1. *Antony, Octavius, and Lepidus*

2. *Brutus has accused Cassius of corruption.*

3. *Portia killed herself.*

4. *Cassius wants to wait so that the enemy will waste provisions and tire themselves out by marching toward them. Brutus thinks that it is better to march toward the enemy because his army is stronger now and he fears that the enemy will be able to gain new recruits.*

Text Analysis
Possible answers:

COMMON CORE RL 1, RL 3, RL 10

5. ● **COMMON CORE FOCUS** *Analyze Shakespearean Tragedy Brutus is intolerant of other people's flaws and blind to contradictions in his own behavior. These flaws are weaknesses in his character and will lead to his downfall. He chastises Cassius for being corrupt, yet he becomes angry with Cassius for not sharing the bribes (Scene 3, lines 69–75).*

6. ● **COMMON CORE FOCUS** *Reading Shakespearean Drama In Scene 1, Antony seems*

more power-hungry and cynical. He shows little of his earlier concern for the people of Rome, and he uses people to get what he wants (lines 8–9 and 19–27).

7. *Brutus wants to explain why he lost his temper with Cassius.*

8. *The warning from the Ghost of Caesar foreshadows a bad outcome for Brutus.*

9. *The Romans seem worse off because there is civil strife again (including the execution of many government officials, Scene 3, lines 175, 177).*

10. *Brutus is justified because corruption will cause the people to turn against the conspirators; Brutus is not justified because he also asks Cassius to give him some of the bribe money to pay his troops.*

Text Criticism
Possible answer:

11. *This conflict is an important theme. Brutus wants to act nobly at all times, yet he must make compromises to support his army and to avoid offending his allies.*

Assess and Reteach

Assess

DIAGNOSTIC AND SELECTION TESTS
Selection Test A pp. 323–324
Selection Test B/C pp. 325–326

Interactive Selection Test on **thinkcentral.com**

Reteach

Level Up Online Tutorials on **thinkcentral.com**

Reteaching Worksheets on **thinkcentral.com**
Literature Lesson 1: Characters
Literature Lessons 23, 24: Elements of Drama

Practice and Apply

Get Into the Act
SUMMARY

Act Five begins on the battlefield, with Antony and Octavius (whom Antony now addresses as "Caesar") exchanging insults with Brutus and Cassius. In battle, Brutus bests Octavius, but Cassius loses to Antony. When Pindarus mistakenly reports Titinius' capture, Cassius despairs and has Pindarus stab him. Facing defeat in the next battle, Brutus kills himself. Arriving on the scene, Antony calls Brutus "the noblest Roman of them all," and Octavius declares a peace.

READING SKILL

■ *Model the Skill:* **CLARIFY**

Read lines 1–6 aloud. Discuss each line to help clarify the actions of the conspirators. Point out that Octavius is pleased with the enemy's behavior (line 1). ***Possible answer:*** *Instead of staying in the hills, the conspirators are going to meet the enemy (Octavius and Antony and their armies) at Philippi.*

Resources for Act Five

Act Five

Scene 1   *The plains of Philippi in Greece.*

Antony and Octavius enter the battlefield with their army. Brutus and Cassius enter with their forces. The four leaders meet, but they only exchange insults and taunts. Antony and Octavius leave to prepare for battle. Cassius expresses his fears to Messala. Finally, Brutus and Cassius say their final farewells, in case they should die in battle.

[*Enter* Octavius, Antony, *and their Army.*]

Octavius. Now Antony, our hopes are answered.
You said the enemy would not come down
But keep the hills and upper regions.
It proves not so, their battles are at hand.
5 They mean to warn us at Philippi here,
Answering before we do demand of them.

> **Antony.** Tut! I am in their bosoms and I know
> Wherefore they do it. They could be content
> To visit other places, and come down
> 10 With fearful bravery, thinking by this face
> To fasten in our thoughts that they have courage.
> But 'tis not so.
>
> [*Enter a* Messenger.]
>
> **Messenger.**   Prepare you, generals,
> The enemy comes on in gallant show;
> Their bloody sign of battle is hung out,
> 15 And something to be done immediately.
>
> **Antony.** Octavius, lead your battle softly on
> Upon the left hand of the even field.
>
> **Octavius.** Upon the right hand I. Keep thou the left.
>
> **Antony.** Why do you cross me in this exigent?
>
> 20 **Octavius.** I do not cross you; but I will do so.

[*March.*]

[*Drum. Enter* Brutus, Cassius, *and their Army;* Lucilius, Titinius, Messala, *and others.*]

Brutus. They stand and would have parley.

Cassius. Stand fast, Titinius. We must out and talk.

Octavius. Mark Antony, shall we give sign of battle?

Antony. No, Caesar, we will answer on their charge.
25 Make forth. The generals would have some words.

3 keep . . . regions: stay in the higher areas (where they could defend themselves more easily).

5 warn: challenge.

7–11 I am . . . courage: I know their secrets (**am in their bosoms**) and why they have done this. They would rather be in other places, but they come down with a show of bravery, thinking they will convince us they have courage.

① Targeted Passage

14 sign of battle: a red flag symbolizing readiness for battle.

19 exigent: moment of crisis.

21 They . . . parley: They are standing and waiting for a conference.

24 answer on their charge: respond to their attack.

Antony speaks over the body of Brutus in the Globe Theatre's 1999 production.

1274   UNIT 11: SHAKESPEAREAN DRAMA

See resources on the **Teacher One Stop** DVD-ROM *and on* **thinkcentral.com**.

 RESOURCE MANAGER UNIT 11
Plan and Teach, pp. 73–80
Summary, pp. 81–84†‡*
Text Analysis and Reading
   Skill, pp. 85–86†*
Grammar and Style, p. 89

DIAGNOSTIC AND SELECTION
   TESTS
Selection Tests, pp. 327–330

 BEST PRACTICES TOOLKIT
Sequence Chain, p. B21

INTERACTIVE READER

ADAPTED INTERACTIVE READER

ELL ADAPTED INTERACTIVE
   READER

TECHNOLOGY
🅰 **Teacher One Stop DVD-ROM**
🅰 **Student One Stop DVD-ROM**
🅰 **PowerNotes DVD-ROM**
🅰 **Audio Anthology CD**
🅰 **GrammarNotes DVD-ROM**
🅰 **Audio Tutor CD**
🅰 **ExamView Test Generator**
   on the **Teacher One Stop**

 **Video Trailer**

Go to **thinkcentral.com** to preview the **Video Trailer** introducing this selection. Other features that support the selection include
• **PowerNotes** presentation
• **ThinkAloud** models to enhance comprehension
• **WordSharp** vocabulary tutorials
• interactive writing and grammar instruction

---

* Resources for Differentiation   † Also in Spanish   ‡ In Haitian Creole and Vietnamese

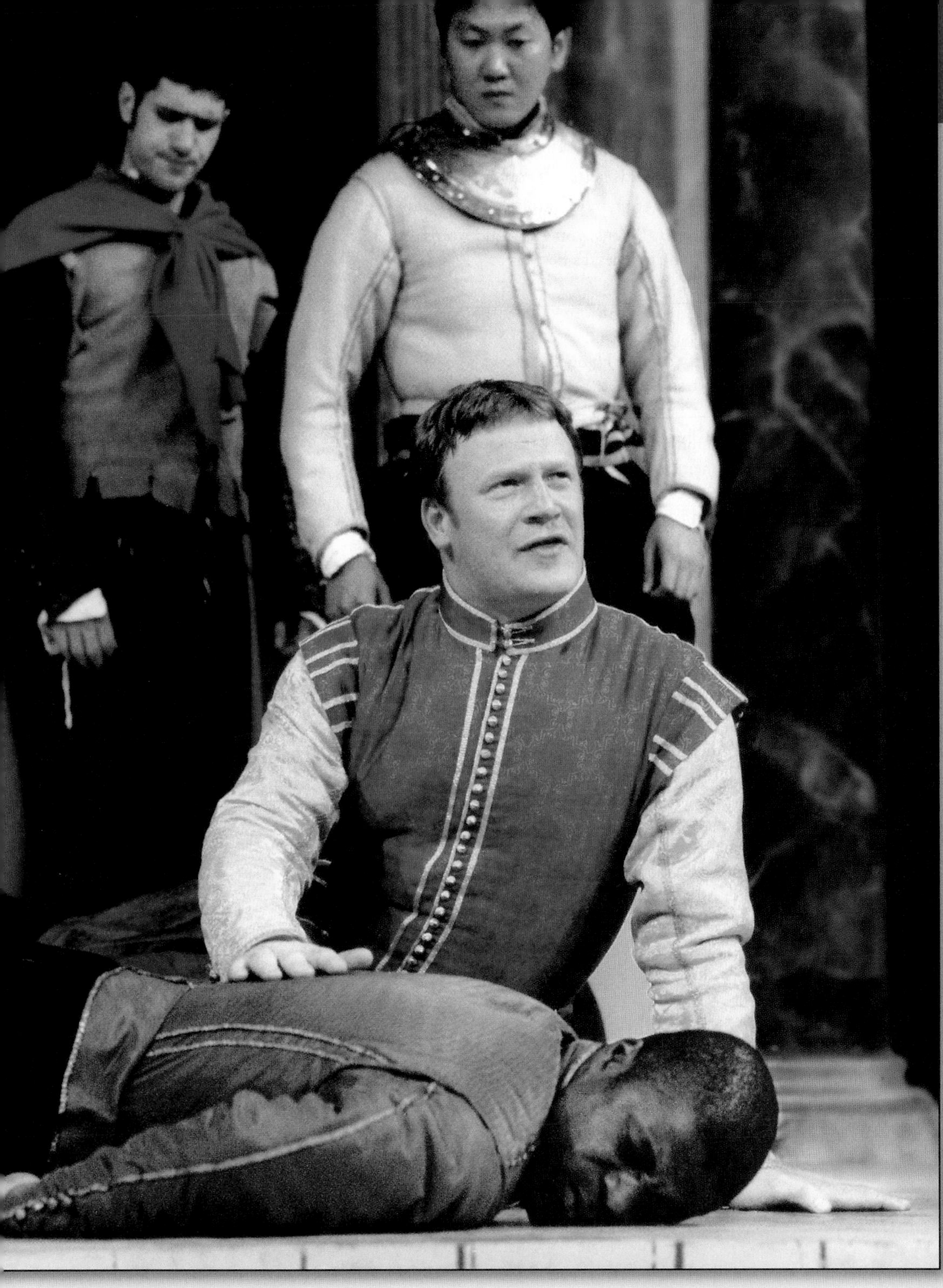

Reading Support

THINK central

This selection on **thinkcentral.com** includes embedded **ThinkAloud** models—students "thinking aloud" about the story to model the kinds of questions a good reader would ask about a selection.

BACKGROUND

The First Battle After the Ghost of Caesar appeared to Brutus (Act Four, Scene 3), Brutus demanded that the conspirators' armies march toward Philippi, a city in the province of Macedonia, several hundred miles to the east of Rome. A skirmish between the armies of Brutus and Cassius and the armies of Antony and Octavius occurred before Act Five, Scene 1 opened. During that fight, the outnumbered armies of Brutus and Cassius seized the hills, the better strategic position. Brutus and Cassius may well have triumphed if they had just waited in the hills and left the armies of Antony and Octavius to try to survive on the unprotected, swampy plains beneath them. Instead, Brutus and Cassius marched to face the enemy head-on.

Analyze Visuals

Activity What seems strange about what Antony is doing in this photograph? What does this image suggest about Antony's attitude toward Brutus? *Possible answer: It seems strange that Antony, who has been Brutus' enemy since Caesar's murder, is gently touching Brutus' corpse. The image suggests that Antony has some respect for Brutus.*

BACKGROUND

Words Before Blows The "words before blows" tradition (line 27) is more medieval than Roman, for it was traditional during the Middle Ages for men to insult each other before doing battle. By invoking this tradition, Shakespeare can use verbal combat instead of physical combat to show how much each side despises the other. It is difficult to show a large battle on a small stage; therefore, Shakespeare uses verbal slights, quick action and scene changes, and one-to-one combat to make the battle seem bigger to the audience.

REVISIT THE BIG QUESTION

Can your
CONSCIENCE
mislead you?

Discuss Direct students to lines 50–60. As Brutus speaks with Octavius, does he seem to be regretful or to have a guilty conscience about his actions? Cite evidence. *Possible answer: Brutus shows no regret or guilt. He does not see himself as a traitor (lines 56–57), despite his role in the murder of Caesar. He also thinks that he is still so noble that it would be an honor for Octavius to die by his sword (lines 59–60). These are comments that someone with a guilty conscience probably would not make.*

Octavius. Stir not until the signal.

[Brutus, Cassius, Octavius, *and* Antony *meet in the center of the stage.*]

Brutus. Words before blows. Is it so, countrymen?

Octavius. Not that we love words better, as you do.

Brutus. Good words are better than bad strokes, Octavius.

30 **Antony.** In your bad strokes, Brutus, you give good words;
Witness the hole you made in Caesar's heart,
Crying "Long live! Hail, Caesar!"

Cassius.   Antony,
The posture of your blows are yet unknown;
But for your words, they rob the Hybla bees,
35 And leave them honeyless.

Antony.   Not stingless too.

Brutus. O yes, and soundless too!
For you have stol'n their buzzing, Antony,
And very wisely threat before you sting.

Antony. Villains! you did not so when your vile daggers
40 Hacked one another in the sides of Caesar.
You showed your teeth like apes, and fawned like hounds,
And bowed like bondmen, kissing Caesar's feet;
Whilst damned Casca, like a cur, behind
Struck Caesar on the neck. O you flatterers!

45 **Cassius.** Flatterers? Now, Brutus, thank yourself!
This tongue had not offended so today
If Cassius might have ruled.

Octavius. Come, come, the cause! If arguing make us sweat,
The proof of it will turn to redder drops.
50 Look,
I draw a sword against conspirators.
When think you that the sword goes up again?
Never, till Caesar's three-and-thirty wounds
Be well avenged, or till another Caesar
55 Have added slaughter to the sword of traitors.

Brutus. Caesar, thou canst not die by traitors' hands
Unless thou bring'st them with thee.

Octavius.   So I hope.
I was not born to die on Brutus' sword.

Brutus. Oh, if thou wert the noblest of thy strain,
60 Young man, thou couldst not die more honorable.

Cassius. A peevish schoolboy, worthless of such honor,
Joined with a masker and a reveller!

Antony. Old Cassius still.

33–35 The posture . . . honeyless: We don't know yet how effective you'll be as a soldier, but your words are sweeter than honey. (Hybla is a mountain in Sicily known for its sweet honey.)

39–44 you did not so . . . neck: You didn't give warning before you killed Caesar. Instead, you acted like loving pets and slaves while Casca, like a dog (**cur**), stabbed Caesar in the neck.

45–47 Cassius angrily tells Brutus that they wouldn't be listening to these insults if he had gotten his way (**ruled**) when arguing that Antony should be killed.

48 cause: business at hand.

49 proof of it: testing of the argument in battle.

54–55 or till . . . traitors: or until a second Caesar (that is, Octavius himself—Caesar's grandnephew and adopted son) has been killed by the traitors.

59 strain: family line.

62–63 Cassius insults Antony by calling him a partygoer and a playboy. Same old Cassius (**Old Cassius still**), Antony replies.

DIFFERENTIATED INSTRUCTION

FOR ENGLISH LANGUAGE LEARNERS

Concept Support As students reread lines 28–32, help them interpret this exchange. Explain that Octavius says that Brutus loves to talk, and Brutus responds by saying that good words are better than bad actions. Antony turns Brutus' statement back on him by reminding Brutus that he said kind words about Caesar before killing him.

FOR STRUGGLING READERS

Understand Character Remind students of the times since Caesar's murder that Cassius has clashed with Brutus. Elicit that Cassius is a person who is ruled by his emotions. Help students see that in this meeting with Antony and Octavius, he cannot control his anger at not having gotten his way when he and Brutus discussed killing Antony (Act Three, Scene 1), and his whining "I told you so" rant (lines 45–47) reveals a weakness that the opposition may be able to exploit.

Octavius.   Come, Antony. Away!
Defiance, traitor, hurl we in your teeth.
65 If you dare fight today, come to the field;
If not, when you have stomachs.

[*Exeunt* Octavius, Antony, *and their Army.*]

Cassius. Why, now blow wind, swell billow, and swim bark!
The storm is up, and all is on the hazard.

Brutus. Ho, Lucilius! Hark, a word with you.

[Lucilius *and* Messala *stand forth.*]

Lucilius.   My lord?

[Brutus *and* Lucilius *converse apart.*]

70 **Cassius.** Messala.

Messala   What says my general?

Cassius.   Messala,
This is my birthday; as this very day
Was Cassius born. Give me thy hand, Messala.
Be thou my witness that against my will
(As Pompey was) am I compelled to set
75 Upon one battle all our liberties.
You know that I held Epicurus strong
And his opinion. Now I change my mind
And partly credit things that do presage.
Coming from Sardis, on our former ensign
80 Two mighty eagles fell, and there they perched,
Gorging and feeding from our soldiers' hands,
Who to Philippi here consorted us.
This morning are they fled away and gone,
And in their steads do ravens, crows, and kites
85 Fly o'er our heads and downward look on us
As we were sickly prey. Their shadows seem
A canopy most fatal, under which
Our army lies, ready to give up the ghost.

Messala. Believe not so.

Cassius.   I but believe it partly,
90 For I am fresh of spirit and resolved
To meet all perils very constantly.

Brutus. Even so, Lucilius.

Cassius.   Now, most noble Brutus,
The gods today stand friendly, that we may,
Lovers in peace, lead on our days to age!
95 But since the affairs of men rest still incertain,
Let's reason with the worst that may befall.

66 stomachs: enough nerve.

68 all . . . hazard: Everything is at stake.

74–75 to set . . . liberties: to gamble our freedom in one battle.

76–88 Epicurus was a philosopher who did not believe omens. Cassius says that he once was a follower of this philosophy, but now he sometimes believes in things that predict the future (**credit things that do presage**). Cassius then tells Messala of two eagles that accompanied the army from Sardis to Philippi. The eagles have been replaced by ravens, crows, and hawks (**kites**)—birds that symbolize death.

79 former ensign: the flag that was carried at the head of the army's march.

91 constantly: with determination.

96 Let's . . . befall: Let's think about the worst that might happen to us.

Analyze Visuals

Activity Based on this photograph, how do you think Cassius feels about his situation? Explain. **Possible answer:** *Cassius feels a mix of determination and fear. He grips the banner firmly and seems to be glaring (perhaps at the oncoming army), but there is also a trace of fear in his look. He may feel determined to fight but also resigned to be defeated, captured, or killed.*

Cassius carrying laurel wreath and banner in the Globe Theatre's 1999 production

If we do lose this battle, then is this
The very last time we shall speak together.
What are you then determined to do?

100 **Brutus.** Even by the rule of that philosophy
By which I did blame Cato for the death
Which he did give himself—I know not how,
But I do find it cowardly and vile,
For fear of what might fall, so to prevent
105 The time of life—arming myself with patience
To stay the providence of some high powers
That govern us below.

    Cassius.   Then, if we lose this battle,
You are contented to be led in triumph
Through the streets of Rome.

110 **Brutus.** No, Cassius, no. Think not, thou noble Roman,
That ever Brutus will go bound to Rome.
He bears too great a mind. But this same day
Must end that work the ides of March begun,
And whether we shall meet again I know not.
115 Therefore our everlasting farewell take.

100–107 Even . . . govern us below: According to the Stoic philosophy that Brutus follows, people should endure their troubles. Brutus therefore finds suicide to be dishonorable (**cowardly and vile**). He mentions Cato, a famous Roman who killed himself after Pompey lost to Caesar.

108 in triumph: as a captive in a victory parade.

115 our . . . take: Let's make a final farewell to each other.

DIFFERENTIATED INSTRUCTION

FOR ENGLISH LANGUAGE LEARNERS

Vocabulary Support Review these comments with students to emphasize that Brutus and Cassius are unsure about the outcome of their impending battle and think that they may never see each other again. Be sure to clarify the word inversions in the second and third comments.

• *fear of what might fall* (line 104), "fear of the future"

• *whether we shall meet again I know not* (line 114), "I do not know whether we shall see one another again"

• *our everlasting farewell take* (lines 115), "say a final good-bye"

• *For ever and for ever farewell* (line 116), "Good-bye forever"

• *parting* (line 118), "separation; departure"

FOR ADVANCED LEARNERS/PRE–AP

Research and Analyze [paired-activity option] Remind students that Cassius is an Epicurean (line 76) and that Brutus is a Stoic (side note for lines 100–107). Explain that now that Brutus and Cassius are facing possible death, they question their beliefs. Have students do some research into each philosophy. Then have them write and share a paragraph or two about how these two characters' actions in the play thus far demonstrate their beliefs.

For ever and for ever farewell, Cassius!
If we do meet again, why, we shall smile;
If not, why then this parting was well made. **Ⓐ**

Cassius. For ever and for ever farewell, Brutus!
120 If we do meet again, we'll smile indeed;
If not, 'tis true this parting was well made.

Brutus. Why then, lead on. O that a man might know
The end of this day's business ere it come!
But it sufficeth that the day will end,
125 And then the end is known. Come, ho! Away!

[*Exeunt.*]

Scene 2   *The battlefield.*

Brutus sends Messala with orders for the forces across the field.

[*Alarum. Enter* Brutus *and* Messala.]

Brutus. Ride, ride, Messala, ride, and give these bills
Unto the legions on the other side.

[*Loud alarum.*]

Let them set on at once; for I perceive
But cold demeanor in Octavius' wing,
5 And sudden push gives them the overthrow.
Ride, ride, Messala! Let them all come down.

[*Exeunt.*]

Scene 3   *Another part of the battlefield.*

Cassius retreats, losing the battle to Antony's forces. He sends Titinius to see if nearby forces are friend or enemy. From a hill, Pindarus believes he sees Titinius killed. Completely discouraged, Cassius asks Pindarus to kill him. Titinius returns to find Cassius' body and kills himself. Brutus and others arrive, having defeated Octavius army. Messala has brought them to see the body of Cassius. Now they see that Titinius is also dead. Brutus mourns the two, but also looks to a second battle with his enemies.

[*Enter* Cassius *and* Titinius.]

Cassius. O, look, Titinius, look! The villains fly!
Myself have to mine own turned enemy.
This ensign here of mine was turning back;
I slew the coward and did take it from him.

5 **Titinius.** O Cassius, Brutus gave the word too early,
Who, having some advantage on Octavius,
Took it too eagerly. His soldiers fell to spoil,
Whilst we by Antony are all enclosed.

[*Enter* Pindarus.]

Ⓐ TRAGIC HERO
Reread lines 110–112. What **character trait** would lead Brutus to overlook his philosophical objection to suicide if he were captured?

4 cold demeanor: lack of courage.
How does Brutus feel about the battle at this point?

1–4 Dismayed that his troops are fleeing from the battle, Cassius says that when he saw his flag-bearer (**ensign**) start to retreat, he killed him and took his flag.

7 His … spoil: Brutus's soldiers began looting (instead of fighting the enemy).

JULIUS CAESAR: ACT FIVE, SCENE 3   **1279**

FOR STRUGGLING READERS
Preview Have students use a graphic like this one to organize the Scene 2 synopsis:

B R U T U S	Wants…	Thinks…
	Messala to give orders to his army on the other side	that Octavius' army lacks courage and can be defeated

FOR ENGLISH LANGUAGE LEARNERS
Task Support Have students reread lines 3–6; then elicit that Brutus believes that Octavius' army lacks courage. Ask them to read the question in the side note for Scene 2, line 4.
Possible answer: *Brutus believes that he can win the battle if he acts quickly, because he thinks that Octavius' army has been weakened by a lack of courage.*

FOR STRUGGLING READERS
Preview Help students create a cause-and-effect diagram to record the events in the Scene 3 synopsis.

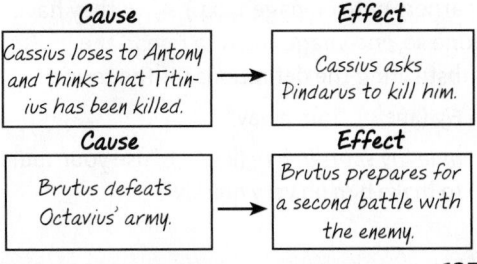

Cause		Effect
Cassius loses to Antony and thinks that Titinius has been killed.	→	Cassius asks Pindarus to kill him.

Cause		Effect
Brutus defeats Octavius' army.	→	Brutus prepares for a second battle with the enemy.

Direct students to lines 14–36. Use these prompts to help students gain insight into Cassius' character right before his death:

Connect Have you or someone you know ever asked someone to do something important for you in the name of friendship? How does that experience help you to understand why Cassius might make the request that he does of Titinius? *Accept all reasonable responses.*

Analyze How does Cassius feel at this point? Cite evidence. *Possible answer: He thinks that he might die. He believes that his life is coming full circle now (lines 23–25).*

Synthesize Why does Titinius' supposed capture bother Cassius so much? What might he think is the honorable thing to do next? *Possible answer: Cassius has shown himself to value friendship, even to his own detriment. He now feels that he has failed his friend Titinius by sending him into a dangerous situation. A rescue attempt might be honorable; however, Cassius might think that the honorable thing to do would be to kill himself.*

Pindarus. Fly further off, my lord! fly further off!
10 Mark Antony is in your tents, my lord.
Fly, therefore, noble Cassius, fly far off!

Cassius. This hill is far enough. Look, look, Titinius!
Are those my tents where I perceive the fire?

Titinius. They are, my lord.

Cassius.   Titinius, if thou lovest me,
15 Mount thou my horse and hide thy spurs in him
Till he have brought thee up to yonder troops
And here again, that I may rest assured
Whether yond troops are friend or enemy.

Titinius. I will be here again even with a thought.

[*Exit.*]

20 **Cassius.** Go, Pindarus, get higher on that hill.
My sight was ever thick. Regard Titinius,
And tell me what thou not'st about the field.

[*Pindarus ascends the hill.*]

This day I breathed first. Time is come round,
And where I did begin, there shall I end.
25 My life is run his compass. Sirrah, what news?

Pindarus.

[*Above.*]

O my lord!

Cassius. What news?

Pindarus.

[*Above.*]

Titinius is enclosed round about
With horsemen that make to him on the spur.
30 Yet he spurs on. Now they are almost on him.
Now, Titinius!
Now some light. O, he lights too! He's ta'en.

[*Shout.*]

And hark!
They shout for joy.

Cassius.   Come down; behold no more.
35 O coward that I am to live so long
To see my best friend ta'en before my face!

[*Enter* Pindarus *from above.*]

Come hither, sirrah.
In Parthia did I take thee prisoner,
And then I swore thee, saving of thy life,

Marginal notes:

15–18 Mount . . . enemy: Ride my horse to those troops over there, and come back to tell me if they are friend or enemy.

19 even with a thought: as fast as you can think of it.

25 is run his compass: has come full circle.

29 make to . . . spur: ride to him at top speed.

32 light: dismount; **ta'en:** taken prisoner.

38–46 In Parthia . . . the sword: When I saved your life in Parthia (an ancient Asian land), you swore to do whatever I asked. Now keep your oath and become a free man. I'll cover my face as you stab me (**search this bosom**) with the same sword that killed Caesar. Don't argue (**Stand not to answer**). *Why does Cassius finally decide to kill himself?*

FOR ENGLISH LANGUAGE LEARNERS
Vocabulary: Outdated Forms Have students add these terms and definitions to their language journals. (See the For English Language Learners note on page 1204.) After they have done so, encourage them to reread the lines, substituting the definitions for the terms:

• *Fly* (line 9), "Run away"

• *hide thy spurs in him* (line 15), "use your spurs to make him go very quickly"

• *My sight was ever thick* (line 21), "My sight has never been clear; I cannot see well"

• *not'st* (line 22), "notice; observe"

• *ta'en* (line 36), "taken"

• *hither* (line 37), "here"

• *whatsoever I did bid thee do, / Thou shouldst attempt it* (lines 40–41), "whatever I asked you to do, you should try to do"

Task Support Direct students to the question in the marginal note for lines 38–46. Ask them to reread lines 34–36 before answering the question. *Possible answer: Cassius believes that the battle is lost, and he thinks that it was cowardly of him to let his best friend be captured.*

40 That whatsoever I did bid thee do,
   Thou shouldst attempt it. Come now, keep thine oath.
   Now be a freeman, and with this good sword,
   That ran through Caesar's bowels, search this bosom.
   Stand not to answer. Here, take thou the hilts,
45 And when my face is covered, as 'tis now,
   Guide thou the sword.

   [*Pindarus stabs him.*]

                        —Caesar, thou are revenged
   Even with the sword that killed thee.

   [*Dies.*]

   Pindarus. So, I am free, yet would not so have been,
   Durst I have done my will. O Cassius!
50 Far from this country Pindarus shall run,
   Where never Roman shall take note of him.

   [*Exit.*]

   [*Reenter* Titinius *with* Messala.]

   Messala. It is but change, Titinius; for Octavius
   Is overthrown by noble Brutus' power,
   As Cassius' legions are by Antony.

55 **Titinius.** These tidings will well comfort Cassius.

   Messala. Where did you leave him?

   Titinius.   All disconsolate,
   With Pindarus his bondman, on this hill.

   Messala. Is not that he that lies upon the ground?

   Titinius. He lies not like the living. O my heart!

60 **Messala.** Is not that he?

   Titinius.   No, this was he, Messala,
   But Cassius is no more. O setting sun,
   As in thy red rays thou does sink to night
   So in his red blood Cassius' day is set!
   The sun of Rome is set. Our day is gone;
65 Clouds, dews, and dangers come; our deeds are done!
   Mistrust of my success hath done this deed. **B**

   Messala. Mistrust of good success hath done this deed.
   O hateful Error, Melancholy's child,
   Why dost thou show to the apt thoughts of men
70 The things that are not? O Error, soon conceived,
   Thou never com'st unto a happy birth,
   But kill'st the mother that engend'red thee!

   Titinius. What, Pindarus! Where art thou, Pindarus?

   Messala. Seek him, Titinius, whilst I go to meet

JULIUS CAESAR: ACT FIVE, SCENE 3   **1281**

---

② **Targeted Passage**

48–49 So...will: I am free, but I wouldn't have been if I had done what I wanted (that is, refused to kill Cassius).

52–54 It is...Antony: It's an even exchange. Just as Antony has defeated Cassius, Brutus has defeated Octavius.

56 disconsolate: extremely sad.

B TRAGEDY
Titinius says that Cassius killed himself because he believed that Titinius had failed in his mission. How might Cassius's decision to commit suicide affect the final outcome of the **plot**?

68–72 Messala says that depression can lead people to misperceive events; such errors end up killing the minds that gave birth to them.

TEXT ANALYSIS   COMMON CORE

B TRAGEDY   RL 3
                                       RL 5

Possible answer: Cassius' suicide probably will cause his troops to become discouraged; Titinius and Messala show their discouragement right away (lines 60–72). Their forces have lost an important, experienced military leader, and now their chances of prevailing in battle are much slimmer.

IF STUDENTS NEED HELP... Discuss these points:

- Of the conspirators, only Brutus and Cassius have high positions of leadership. They are the ones who control the rebel army.

- Cassius has more military knowledge and experience than Brutus; in theory, Cassius has a better chance of securing a final victory than Brutus does.

- The conspirators have been fighting on two fronts (one front battling Antony, the other battling Octavius). With Cassius gone, the reader wonders who will take his place or whether Brutus can command a combined force effectively.

FOR STRUGGLING READERS

② **Targeted Passage [Lines 40–51]**

This passage shows what happened to Cassius and suggests that, in a sense, Caesar's spirit may have haunted Cassius, too.

- What does Cassius tell Pindarus to do? Does Pindarus protest? Does he obey? (lines 45–46)

- What is ironic about the weapon that Pindarus uses? (lines 42–43, 47)

- How does Pindarus feel about what has just happened? How can you tell? (lines 48–49)

FOR ADVANCED LEARNERS/PRE–AP

Analyze Figurative Language Have students analyze Titinius' last words about Cassius (lines 61–66). Elicit these points about the figurative comparisons that Titinius makes:

- Titinius compares Cassius' life to the course of the sun in a day.

- The sunset represents Cassius' death.

- The sun's red rays represent Cassius' red blood.

- The dampness that follows the sunset represents Rome's bleak future.

Can your CONSCIENCE mislead you?

Discuss Based on lines 81–91, how would you characterize Titinius' conscience at this point? Cite evidence. *Possible answer: Titinius seems to have a slightly guilty conscience. He is upset about Cassius' death and feels responsible for it. Titinius chooses to honor his friend Cassius and relieve his own conscience by killing himself with Cassius' sword (lines 87–91).*

ⓒ TRAGEDY

Possible answer: The theme is that the murderous act will not go unpunished. Whether Caesar's spirit is considered to be real or whether it is a metaphor for his influence, the fact remains that the people who murdered Caesar are "haunted" by him and will meet a sad end.

---

75 The noble Brutus, thrusting this report
Into his ears. I may say "thrusting" it;
For piercing steel and darts envenomed
Shall be as welcome to the ears of Brutus
As tidings of this sight.

Titinius.   Hie you, Messala,
80 And I will seek for Pindarus the while.

[*Exit* Messala.]

[Titinius *looks at* Cassius.]

Why didst thou send me forth, brave Cassius?
Did I not meet thy friends, and did not they
Put on my brows this wreath of victory
And bid me give it thee? Didst thou not hear their shouts?
85 Alas, thou hast misconstrued everything!
But hold thee, take this garland on thy brow.
Thy Brutus bid me give it thee, and I
Will do his bidding. Brutus, come apace
And see how I regarded Caius Cassius.
90 By your leave, gods. This is a Roman's part.
Come, Cassius' sword, and find Titinius' heart.

[*Dies.*]

[*Alarum. Enter* Brutus, Messala, Young Cato, Strato, Volumnius, *and* Lucilius.]

Brutus. Where, where, Messala, doth his body lie?

Messala. Lo, yonder, and Titinius mourning it.

Brutus. Titinius' face is upward.

Cato.   He is slain.

95 **Brutus.** O Julius Caesar, thou art mighty yet!
Thy spirit walks abroad and turns our swords
In our own proper entrails. ⓒ

[*Low alarums.*]

Cato.   Brave Titinius!
Look whe'r he have not crowned dead Cassius.

Brutus. Are yet two Romans living such as these?
100 The last of all the Romans, fare thee well!
It is impossible that ever Rome
Should breed thy fellow. Friends, I owe more tears
To this dead man than you shall see me pay.
I shall find time, Cassius; I shall find time.
105 Come therefore, and to Thasos send his body.
His funerals shall not be in our camp,
Lest it discomfort us. Lucilius, come;
And come, young Cato. Let us to the field.

77 **darts envenomed:** poisoned darts.

79 **Hie you:** Hurry.

88 **apace:** quickly.

90 **This ... part:** This (killing myself) is the proper thing for a brave Roman to do.

ⓒ TRAGEDY

What **theme** is expressed in Brutus's remark about Caesar's spirit?

98 **whe'r:** whether.

❸ Targeted Passage

105 **Thasos** (thā'sŏs'): an island near Philippi.

107 **discomfort us:** discourage our troops.

102 **fellow:** equal.

DIFFERENTIATED INSTRUCTION

FOR STRUGGLING READERS

❸ **Targeted Passage** [Lines 99–108]

In this passage, Brutus responds to the death of Cassius.

• How does Brutus refer to Cassius now? Does he think that Cassius is honorable? Cite evidence. (lines 99–100)

• Does Brutus become upset when learning about Cassius' death? (lines 102–104)

• Why does Brutus want Cassius' body to be sent to Thasos? (lines 106–107)

FOR ENGLISH LANGUAGE LEARNERS

Vocabulary: Outdated Forms Have students add these words to their language journals:

From Scene 3

• *the while* (line 80), "in the meantime"

• *regarded* (line 89), "honored"

• *part* (line 90), "task; role"

• *our own proper* (line 97), "our very own"

• *battles* (line 109), "troops"

From Scene 4

• *diest* (line 10), "die"

Labeo and Flavius set our battles on.
110 'Tis three o'clock; and, Romans, yet ere night
We shall try fortune in a second fight.

[*Exeunt.*]

Scene 4   *Another part of the battlefield.*

During the battle, Young Cato is killed, and Lucilius is taken prisoner. Brought to Antony, Lucilius insists that Brutus will never be taken alive.

[*Alarum. Enter* Brutus, Messala, Young Cato, Lucilius, *and* Flavius.]

Brutus. Yet, countrymen, O, yet hold up your heads!

Cato. What fellow doth not? Who will go with me?
I will proclaim my name about the field.
I am the son of Marcus Cato, ho!
5 A foe to tyrants, and my country's friend.
I am the son of Marcus Cato, ho!

[*Enter Soldiers and fight.*]

Brutus. And I am Brutus, Marcus Brutus I!
Brutus, my country's friend! Know me for Brutus!

[*Exit.*]

[*Young Cato falls.*]

Lucilius. O young and noble Cato, art thou down?
10 Why, now thou diest as bravely as Titinius,
And mayst be honored, being Cato's son.

First Soldier. Yield, or thou diest.

Lucilius.   Only I yield to die.

[*Offering money.*]

There is so much that thou wilt kill me straight.
Kill Brutus, and be honored in his death.

15 **First Soldier.** We must not. A noble prisoner!

[*Enter* Antony.]

Second Soldier. Room ho! Tell Antony Brutus is ta'en.

First Soldier. I'll tell the news. Here comes the general.
Brutus is ta'en! Brutus is ta'en, my lord!

Antony. Where is he?

20 **Lucilius.** Safe, Antony; Brutus is safe enough.
I dare assure thee that no enemy
Shall ever take alive the noble Brutus.
The gods defend him from so great a shame!
When you do find him, or alive or dead,
25 He will be found like Brutus, like himself.

Antony. This is not Brutus, friend; but, I assure you,

4 Marcus Cato: Portia's father, a greatly respected Roman.

12 Yield: surrender.

13–14 Pretending to be Brutus, Lucilius offers the soldier money to kill him immediately. *Why would Lucilius want the enemy to think he is Brutus?*

24 or alive or dead: either alive or dead. *How do you interpret Lucilius's remark that Brutus will be found "like Brutus, like himself"?*

FOR STRUGGLING READERS

Preview As you read through Scene 4, use a web to help students identify what happens to Lucilius.

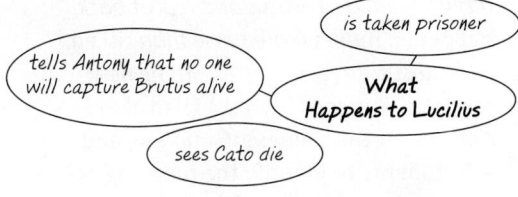

- tells Antony that no one will capture Brutus alive
- is taken prisoner
- **What Happens to Lucilius**
- sees Cato die

FOR ENGLISH LANGUAGE LEARNERS

Task Support After students read the question in the side note for lines 13–14, remind them that Lucilius is Brutus' loyal servant. Have them imagine what they would do in Lucilius' place. ***Possible answer:*** *Lucilius would want the enemy to think that he is Brutus because doing so would make the enemy spend time and energy upon him (Lucilius). In the meantime, Brutus might have an opportunity to overcome the enemy in battle or might have time to escape.*

Task Support Have students read the side note and question about line 24. Refer students to Scene 1, lines 110–113, and elicit that Brutus generally thinks himself quite honorable and noble. ***Possible answer:*** *Lucilius means that Brutus will not be found in a position to be captured or humiliated. He will be found in a way that does not tarnish his honor.*

Can your
CONSCIENCE
mislead you?

Discuss Based on Scene 4, lines 27–32, what evidence of change do you see in Antony? How is his conscience guiding him differently now? *Possible answer: Antony was very angry and bitter toward the conspirators and did not intend to show them any mercy. Here, however, he shows kindness to Lucilius, ordering that Lucilius be kept safe and suggesting that he would like Lucilius to be his friend. Antony's conscience is guiding him to extend compassion rather than hatred to his enemies.*

A prize no less in worth. Keep this man safe;
Give him all kindness. I had rather have
Such men my friends than enemies. Go on,
30 And see whe'r Brutus be alive or dead;
And bring us word unto Octavius' tent
How everything is chanced.

[*Exeunt.*]

Scene 5   *Another part of the battlefield.*

Facing defeat, Brutus' forces rest. Brutus feels that all is lost. He asks three men to kill him, but each refuses. Finally, Strato agrees to hold the sword as Brutus kills himself on it. Antony, Octavius, and others arrive. Antony mourns Brutus, calling him the "noblest Roman." Octavius promises him a noble funeral as the play ends.

[*Enter* Brutus, Dardanius, Clitus, Strato, *and* Volumnius.]

Brutus. Come, poor remains of friends, rest on this rock.

Clitus. Statilius showed the torchlight but, my lord,
He came not back. He is or ta'en or slain.

Brutus. Sit thee down, Clitus. Slaying is the word.
5 It is a deed in fashion. Hark thee, Clitus.

[*Whispers.*]

Clitus. What, I, my lord? No, not for all the world!

Brutus. Peace then. No words.

Clitus.   I'll rather kill myself.

Brutus. Hark thee, Dardanius.

[*Whispers.*]

Dardanius.   Shall I do such a deed?

Clitus. O Dardanius!

10 **Dardanius.** O Clitus!

Clitus. What ill request did Brutus make to thee?

Dardanius. To kill him, Clitus. Look he meditates.

Clitus. Now is that noble vessel full of grief,
That it runs over even at his eyes.

15 **Brutus.** Come hither, good Volumnius. List a word.

Volumnius. What says my lord?

Brutus.   Why this, Volumnius.
The ghost of Caesar hath appeared to me
Two several times by night—at Sardis once,
And this last night here in Philippi fields.
20 I know my hour is come.

Volumnius.   Not so, my lord.

COMMON CORE RL 4

Language Coach

Multiple Meanings The word *chanced* has more than one meaning. It can mean "risked" or "happened." Which meaning makes more sense in line 32? How can you tell? What does it mean in this sentence: *Frank chanced his last dollar on the raffle ticket.*

2–3 Statilius . . . slain: Statilius (**our scout**) signaled with his torch that all was well at our camp. But since he hasn't come back, he has been either captured or killed.

4–5 Brutus says that it has become fashionable to kill, not to capture.

15 List: listen to.

18 Two several times: twice.

DIFFERENTIATED INSTRUCTION

FOR ENGLISH LANGUAGE LEARNERS

Concept Support Reread lines 5–12 with students. Explain that Brutus' "Hark thee, Clitus" means that he wants Clitus to listen to him. Next, point out the stage direction in brackets (*Whispers.*) and read Clitus' response. Help students infer that Brutus has asked Clitus to kill him. Point out that once Clitus refuses, Brutus whispers the same question to Dardanius. It is only when Clitus and Dardanius compare notes that the audience knows for sure what Brutus has whispered.

Language Coach   COMMON CORE RL 4

Multiple Meanings *Answer: Since Antony is asking his men to find out what has happened to Brutus and report back,* happened *makes more sense than* risked *as a substitute for* chanced. *In the new sentence, it means "risked." Read aloud Act One, Scene 2, lines 216 and 219, and ask students to identify the meaning of* chanced *in these lines. (happened)*

Brutus. Nay, I am sure it is, Volumnius.
Thou seest the world, Volumnius, how it goes.
Our enemies have beat us to the pit.

[*Low alarums.*]

It is more worthy to leap in ourselves
25 Than tarry till they push us. Good Volumnius,
Thou know'st that we two went to school together.
Even for that our love of old, I prithee
Hold thou my sword-hilts whilst I run on it.

Volumnius. That's not an office for a friend, my lord.

[*Alarum still.*]

30 **Clitus.** Fly, fly, my lord! There is no tarrying here.

Brutus. Farewell to you; and you; and you, Volumnius.
Strato, thou hast been all this while asleep.
Farewell to thee too, Strato. Countrymen,
My heart doth joy that yet in all my life
35 I found no man but he was true to me.
I shall have glory by this losing day
More than Octavius and Mark Antony
By this vile conquest shall attain unto.
So fare you well at once, for Brutus' tongue
40 Hath almost ended his life's history.
Night hangs upon mine eyes; my bones would rest,
That have but labored to attain this hour. **D**

[*Alarum. Cry within:* Fly, fly, fly!]

Clitus. Fly, my lord, fly!

Brutus.   Hence! I will follow.

[*Exeunt* Clitus, Dardanius, *and* Volumnius.]

I prithee, Strato, stay thou by thy lord.
45 Thou art a fellow of a good respect;
Thy life hath had some smatch of honor in it.
Hold then my sword, and turn away thy face
While I do run upon it. Wilt thou, Strato?

Strato. Give me your hand first. Fare you well, my lord.

50 **Brutus.** Farewell, good Strato. Caesar, now be still.
I killed not thee with half so good a will.

[*Dies.*]

[*Alarum. Retreat. Enter* Octavius, Antony, Messala, Lucilius,
and the Army.]

Octavius. What man is that?

Messala. My master's man. Strato, where is thy master?

Strato. Free from the bondage you are in, Messala.

---

23 pit: a hole into which hunted animals are forced.

25 tarry: wait.

27–28 I prithee . . . on it: I beg you to hold my sword while I run into it.

29 That's . . . friend: That's no duty for a friend to perform.

41–42 my bones . . . hour: My tired bones have worked to reach this final hour.

D TRAGIC HERO
Reread lines 31–42. Which details in Brutus's farewell speech show his courage and dignity in defeat?

46 smatch: little bit.

51 I killed . . . will: I didn't kill you (Caesar) half as willingly as I kill myself.

52 man: servant.

REVISIT THE BIG QUESTION

Can your
CONSCIENCE
mislead you?

Discuss Based on lines 31–48, does Brutus express sorrow for any of his actions as he prepares to die? Is his conscience driving him to kill himself? Explain. ***Possible answer:*** *Brutus does not appear to show any remorse for his actions, including his role in Caesar's assassination. He says that all men have been loyal to him (lines 34–35). He does not mention feeling shame or regret about what he has done; indeed, his only regret seems to be that he has lost to Octavius and Antony (lines 36–38). Brutus' conscience does not drive him to kill himself out of guilt; rather, Brutus wants to kill himself with the help of a man who is somewhat honorable (lines 45–46) to preserve his own honor.*

TEXT ANALYSIS   COMMON CORE
                                           RL 3

D TRAGIC HERO

Possible answer: *Brutus' praise of his followers' loyalty (lines 35–38) shows dignity in that he does not blame others for his defeat. His claim of glory (lines 41–42) shows his courage and nobility in that he does not regret any of his decisions.*

FOR ADVANCED LEARNERS/PRE–AP

Analyze Character Ask students to reread lines 31–42, considering what Brutus' statements suggest about his character and his examination of his life. Have small groups discuss these questions to analyze Brutus' character; then have groups compare answers:

• Have all of the men really been true to Brutus (line 35)? Which man in the play do you think has been the most true to Brutus? Explain.

• What is ironic in Brutus' statement about the "vile conquest" that Octavius and Antony have achieved? (line 38)

• Do you think that Brutus paints a realistic picture of his "life's history"? (line 40) Explain and cite evidence.

READ WITH A PURPOSE Now that students have finished reading the entire play, ask them to decide whether they believe Antony was correct in his assessment of the character of Brutus (lines 68–72). Why or why not? *Possible answer: Antony says Brutus was noble and honest, yet many of Brutus' actions, such as having Antony speak to the people and deciding where to fight, sprang from pride rather than honor.*

⭐ **CRITIQUE** Have students recall the main characters in the play, the principles that they espouse, and the character qualities that they possess. Then ask students what they found most memorable about the characters.

INDEPENDENT READING

Students might enjoy reading another of Shakespeare's tragedies, such as *King Lear* or *Romeo and Juliet*.

---

55 The conquerors can but make a fire of him;
For Brutus only overcame himself,
And no man else hath honor by his death.

Lucilius. So Brutus should be found. I thank thee, Brutus,
That thou hast proved Lucilius' saying true.

60 **Octavius.** All that served Brutus, I will entertain them.
Fellow, wilt thou bestow thy time with me?

Strato. Ay, if Messala will prefer me to you.

Octavius. Do so, good Messala.

Messala. How died my master, Strato?

65 **Strato.** I held the sword, and he did run on it.

Messala. Octavius, then take him to follow thee,
That did the latest service to my master.

Antony. This was the noblest Roman of them all.
All the conspirators save only he
70 Did that they did in envy of great Caesar;
He, only in a general honest thought
And common good to all, made one of them.
His life was gentle, and the elements
So mixed in him that Nature might stand up
75 And say to all the world, "This was a man!"

Octavius. According to his virtue let us use him,
With all respect and rites of burial.
Within my tent his bones tonight shall lie,
Most like a soldier, ordered honorably.
80 So call the field to rest, and let's away
To part the glories of this happy day.

[*Exeunt.*]

58–59 So Brutus . . . true: That is just how Brutus should be found. Thank you, Brutus, for proving me correct (in saying you would never be taken alive).

60 All . . . them: All those who served Brutus will now be welcome in my army.

62 prefer: recommend.

66–67 Octavius . . . master: Octavius, I recommend him for your army; he performed the last favor for Brutus (**my master**).

69 save: except.

72 made one of them: joined the conspirators.

④ **Targeted Passage**

76 According . . . him: Let us treat him as he deserves.

81 part: divide up.

DIFFERENTIATED INSTRUCTION

FOR STRUGGLING READERS

④ **Targeted Passage** [Lines 68–81]

This concluding passage focuses on the honors paid to Brutus in his death.

- How does Antony characterize Brutus? (line 68)
- According to Antony, how did Brutus' reason for killing Caesar differ from the other conspirators' reasons? (lines 69–72)

- How does Octavius plan to treat Brutus' corpse? (lines 76–79)
- Why does Octavius call the day a "happy" one? (line 81)

FOR ENGLISH LANGUAGE LEARNERS

Concept Support Point out to students that Octavius is the final character to speak in this play. Discuss how the fact that he presents the final words may foreshadow Octavius' future leadership role. Tell students that historically Octavius eventually deposed Lepidus and then Antony, the other two members of the Second Triumvirate, and ruled Rome as emperor.

Behind the Curtain

COMMON CORE RI 7

Promotion

How do producers get people to see a new Shakespeare production? They mainly rely on good reviews and **promotional** items, such as posters. What do the images in these posters suggest about how the producers have chosen to "sell" the play? Which poster do you find most interesting? Explain your responses.

BEHIND THE CURTAIN

COMMON CORE RI 7

Promotion Explain to students that the design and use of promotional items, such as posters, for a theatrical production may vary widely, depending upon what the promoters think would most entice their target audience. Their goal is to attract the greatest number of ticket-buyers possible. ***Possible answer:*** *All three posters suggest that* Julius Caesar *contains death and most likely murder, as signified by the bloody letters of "Caesar" in the purple poster, by the red robe that Antony wears in the poster for the production at St. James's Theatre, and by the red background of the Denzel Washington poster. The purple poster is the most interesting one because it contains the mysterious warning "Beware the Ides of March." The viewer also wonders whose face is shown and what terrible thing will happen to Caesar.*

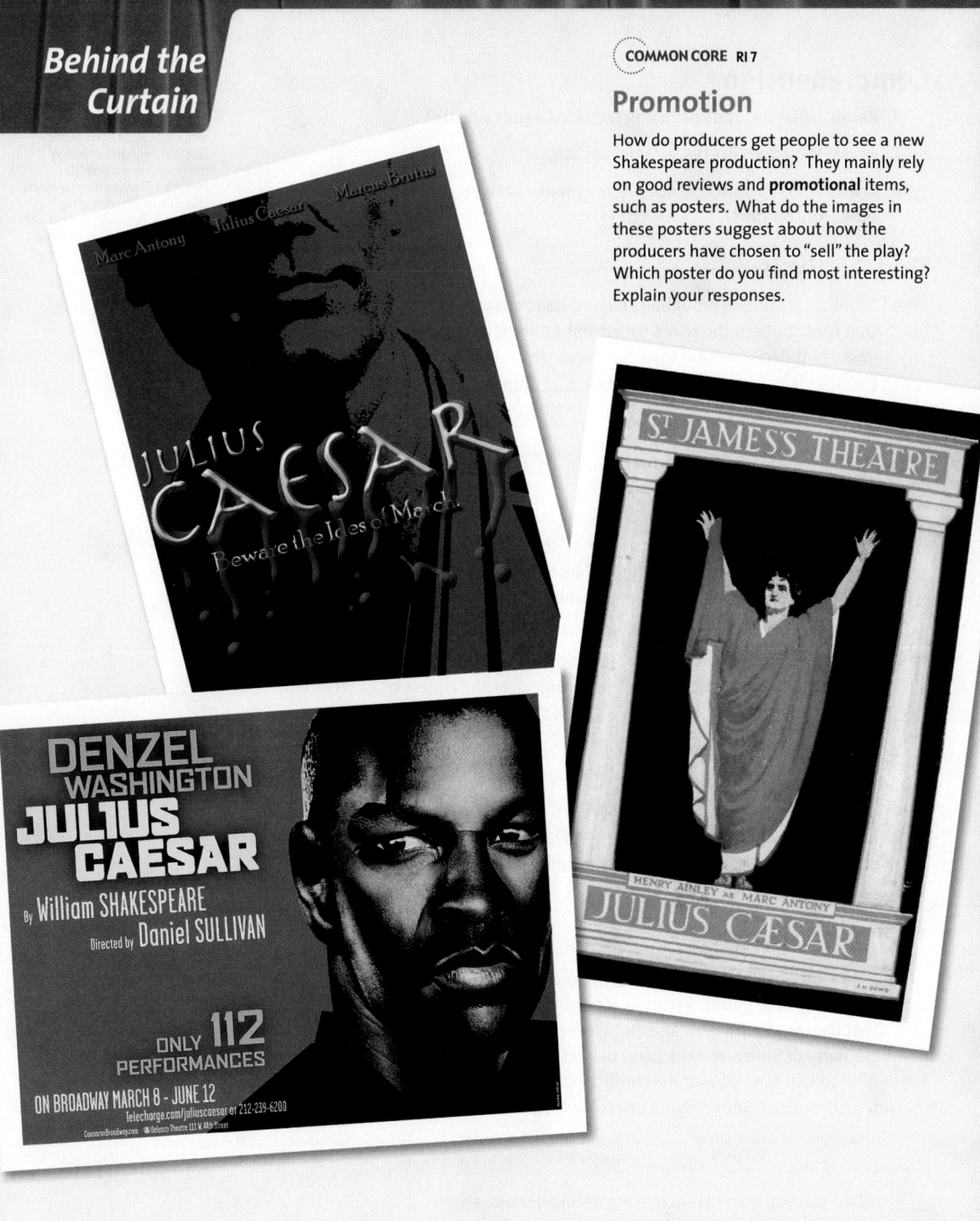

FOR RELUCTANT READERS

Create a Poster Have small groups take the role of the promotional team for an upcoming public performance of *Julius Caesar*. Instruct each group to create a poster that its members feel would persuade people to buy tickets. Urge students to consider the characters and themes of the play as they plan and to experiment with a few design ideas before they develop one in full. Invite group representatives to share the finished posters and explain the various designs.

Practice and Apply

For preliminary support of post-reading questions, use these copy masters:

R RESOURCE MANAGER—Copy Masters

Reading Check p. 87
Shakespearean Tragedy p. 85
Question Support p. 88

Additional selection questions are provided for teachers on page 77.

ANSWERS

Comprehension

1. *Cassius mistakenly thinks that Titinius has been captured by enemy troops.*

2. *Brutus knows that the battle is lost, and he does not want to be captured and humiliated.*

3. *Antony says that Brutus acted from noble motives but that the others acted from envy of Caesar.*

Text Analysis

COMMON CORE **RL 1, RL 3, RL 10**

Possible answers:

4. ● **COMMON CORE FOCUS**
   ***Shakespearean Tragedy Decision:** Brutus attacks too early. **Consequence:** leaves Cassius exposed to attack **Decision:** Cassius kills himself. **Consquence:** deprives Brutus of most important ally*

5. *Brutus is the tragic hero because he could have prevented his own death by making better decisions and by not believing so much in his own nobility; Caesar is the tragic hero because he thought himself too great and because he failed to think that "friends" would oppose him so strongly that they would assassinate him.*

6. ■ **COMMON CORE FOCUS** *Reading Shakespearean Drama In Acts One and Two, Cassius appeared forceful and manipulative with Brutus. However, after Brutus joined the conspiracy in Act Two, Cassius deferred to Brutus' authority and became obsessive about having Brutus as his friend.*

7. *The reappearance of Caesar's ghost to Brutus (Scene 5, lines 17–20) may have influenced Brutus' suicide. Cassius' mistaken assumption that Titinius was captured may have been influenced by the omen that he describes to Messala (Scene 1, lines 79–88).*

8. *Brutus will gain more glory, but not because he killed himself. Brutus will gain more*

1288 UNIT 11: SHAKESPEAREAN DRAMA

Comprehension

1. **Recall** What misunderstanding leads to Cassius's death?

2. **Recall** Why does Brutus commit suicide?

3. **Clarify** What distinction does Antony make between Brutus and the other conspirators?

Text Analysis

● 4. **Examine Tragedy** Throughout *Julius Caesar*, characters make flawed decisions that contribute to the play's catastrophe. In a chart like the one shown, list important decisions and their consequences. Then identify decisions in Act Five that lead to the death of Brutus. Cite details from the chart in your answer.

Decisions	Consequences

5. **Analyze Tragedy** Brutus and Julius Caesar both have traits that are associated with tragic heroes. In your opinion, which character is really the **tragic hero** of the play? Explain your response.

● 6. **Reading Shakespearean Drama** Review the chart you created as you read. How did your impression of Cassius change over the course of *Julius Caesar*? Support your response with details from the play.

7. **Identify Cause and Effect** Which of Brutus's and Cassius's actions in Act Five may have been influenced by an omen or a supernatural occurrence? Cite evidence.

8. **Make Judgments** Reread lines 33–38 of Scene 5. Do you agree with Brutus's statement that despite his defeat, he will gain more glory from the Battle of Philippi than Octavius and Antony will? Explain why or why not.

Text Criticism

9. **Critical Interpretations** According to the critic Maurice Charney, *Julius Caesar* is "… deeply ambiguous. We grow increasingly certain after the middle of the play that the conspirators will lose, but we feel a strange balancing of values between the party of Brutus and the party of Caesar." Do you agree that Shakespeare offers a balanced view of the conflict, or does he portray one side more favorably than the other? Support your opinion with evidence from the play.

> ### Can your CONSCIENCE mislead you?
> What can you do to avoid making wrong decisions?

COMMON CORE

RL 1 Cite textual evidence to support analysis of what the text says explicitly as well as inferences drawn from the text. **RL 3** Analyze how complex characters with conflicting motivations develop, interact with others, and advance the plot or develop the theme. **RL 10** Read and comprehend dramas.

---

glory because, as Antony and Octavius agree, he died because he put Rome before his personal interests.

Text Criticism

Possible answer:

9. *Shakespeare's view is balanced: He shows not only the strengths but also the weaknesses of Cassius (manipulative), Brutus (impressed by his own nobility and blind to his flaws), Antony (angry and greedy), and Octavius (desirous of power). He portrays*

his characters as human beings with flaws, therefore showing the negative aspects of their ambitions or desires. As a result, readers are left wondering if either side was right.

> Can your **CONSCIENCE** mislead you? *Possible answer:* Students should cite logical reasons and ideas that could help them avoid making poor decisions.

Language

◆ **GRAMMAR AND STYLE:** Add Descriptive Details

Review the **Grammar and Style** note on page 1249. **Adjective clauses** are subordinate clauses that modify nouns and pronouns in the same way adjectives do. They are useful for adding details that help to explain, support, and connect ideas. Adjective clauses are introduced by the **relative pronouns** *that, which, who, whom,* and *whose,* and the **relative adverbs** *where, when,* and *why.* Note Shakespeare's use of adjective clauses in the following excerpts.

> *Against the Capitol I met a lion,/Who glared upon me....* (Act One, Scene 3, lines 20–21)

> *All this done,/Repair to Pompey's Porch, where you shall find us.* (Act One, Scene 3, lines 146–147)

You can also use the **reciprocal pronouns**—*each other, one another*—to add interest to your writing. Notice how the revisions in blue add more descriptive details to the following first draft. Revise your response to the prompt by using adjective clauses to help support your ideas.

STUDENT MODEL

who remains loyal to Caesar even after his death.

Mark Antony proves himself to be a good friend ~~to Caesar.~~ Through a

that he delivers at Caesar's funeral,

powerful speech ∧ he turns Rome's citizens against the conspirators and even

each other

the conspirators against ∧ ~~themselves.~~

READING-WRITING CONNECTION

Broaden your understanding of *Julius Caesar* by responding to the prompt. Then use the **revising tip** to improve your writing.

WRITING PROMPT	REVISING TIP
Short Constructed Response: Analysis To what extent do you consider Mark Antony to be motivated by **conscience?** Using examples from the text, write a **one- or two-paragraph response** that explains how Antony's decisions reflect his internal sense of what is right and wrong.	▶ Review your response. Have you used adjective clauses and reciprocal pronouns to add descriptive details? If not, revise your response.

Interactive Revision

THINKcentral

Go to **thinkcentral.com.** KEYWORD: HML10-1289

JULIUS CAESAR: ACT FIVE **1289**

DIFFERENTIATED INSTRUCTION

FOR STRUGGLING WRITERS

- Help students write a statement that reflects what they believe Antony's conscience told him to do.

- Have students look together for examples that support the idea that Antony followed that statement.

- Remind students that Antony's internal sense of right and wrong may not have been the same as that for other characters.

Language

COMMON CORE L 1b

◆ **GRAMMAR AND STYLE**

1. Elicit from students that in the excerpts, the first adjective clause modifies *lion* and is introduced by the relative pronoun *Who.* The second adjective clause modifies *Pompey's Porch* and is introduced by the relative adverb *where.*

2. In the student model, have students identify each relative pronoun or adverb and what each modifies. ***Possible answer:*** *The relative pronoun* who *modifies* Antony; *the relative pronoun* that *modifies* speech.

3. For practice, have students add an adjective clause to this statement: *Cassius, who despaired at Titinius' supposed capture, asked Pindarus to kill him.*

R RESOURCE MANAGER—Copy Master Grammar and Style p. 89

READING-WRITING CONNECTION

Suggest that students focus on Antony's soliloquy in Act Three, Scene 1, lines 254–275, and his funeral oration in Act Three, Scene 2. Have students consider and compare those thoughts to what they find in Act Four, Scene 1, lines 6–9 and 29–47, and then Act Five, Scene 5, lines 68–75.

THINKcentral

Writing Online

The following tools are available online at **thinkcentral.com** and on **Write*Smart* CD-ROM:**
- **Interactive Graphic Organizers**
- **Interactive Student Models**
- **Interactive Revision Lessons**

For additional grammar instruction, see **GrammarNotes** on **thinkcentral.com.**

Assess and Reteach

Assess

DIAGNOSTIC AND SELECTION TESTS
Selection Test A pp. 327–328
Selection Test B/C pp. 329–330

Interactive Selection Test on **thinkcentral.com**

Reteach

Level Up Online Tutorials on **thinkcentral.com**

JULIUS CAESAR: ACT FIVE **1289**

COMMON CORE

L 1b Use various types of clauses to convey specific meanings and add variety and interest to writing.

Focus and Motivate

COMMON CORE FOCUS

RI 1 Cite textual evidence to support analysis of what the text says explicitly. **RI 4** Determine the meaning of words and phrases as they are used in a text, including connotative meanings. **RI 7** Analyze various accounts of a subject told in different mediums, determining which details are emphasized in each account. **RI 8** Delineate and evaluate the argument and specific claims in a text, assessing whether the reasoning is valid and the evidence is relevant and sufficient. **W2** Write explanatory texts to examine and convey complex ideas.

SUMMARIES

"Review of *Julius Caesar*" In his review of a performance of *Julius Caesar,* Thomas M. Disch decries the dullness of the play itself and of the actors' interpretation of it.

"Hail, Caesar!" In her positive review of the same production, Edith Oliver focuses on the cast's apt, thoughtful acting.

What's the Connection?

Use the Read Aloud/Think Aloud activity to help students identify and contrast the initial tone of each reviewer.

- Read aloud the first paragraph of "Review of *Julius Caesar,*" emphasizing words like *dullest* and phrases like *so flensed* and *without danger of awakening their interest.*

- Read aloud lines 4–13 of "Hail, Caesar," emphasizing phrases like *towering performance* and *the rest of the casting . . . is mostly very good.*

- Elicit that the initial tone of the first review is negative and that the initial tone of the second review is positive. Invite students to predict the general opinion of both reviewers.

 **BEST PRACTICES TOOLKIT—Transparency**
Read Aloud/Think Aloud p. A34

Teach

Standards Focus: Analyze a Theater Review

Explain that since a theater review is subjective, students should look for opinions and personal statements. Even so, for a reviewer to be taken seriously, he or she must support opinions with details from the performance. Urge students to look for such details in each review and to record them in the chart.

R **RESOURCE MANAGER—Copy Master**
Analyze a Theater Review p. 99

1290 UNIT 11: SHAKESPEAREAN DRAMA

Reading for Information

Julius Caesar at the Public Theater

Theater Reviews

Use with *Julius Caesar,*
page 1200.

COMMON CORE

RI 1 Cite textual evidence to support analysis of what the text says explicitly. **RI 7** Analyze various accounts of a subject told in different mediums, determining which details are emphasized in each account. **RI 8** Delineate and evaluate the argument and specific claims in a text, assessing whether the reasoning is valid and the evidence is relevant and sufficient.

What's the Connection?

Now that you have read *Julius Caesar,* you are familiar with the characters and plot of William Shakespeare's tragedy. But the text is just the starting point for a play, which comes to life through the artistic choices of directors, actors, set designers, and other theater professionals. In the following selections, two critics respond very differently to the same production at the Public Theater in New York City.

Standards Focus: Analyze a Theater Review

A **theater review** is an essay in which the writer presents opinions about a theatrical production. Use the following steps to analyze a theater review:

- Identify the reviewer's **criteria,** the standards on which his or her opinions are based. For example, a reviewer might evaluate an actor's performance on how clearly the actor delivers lines of dialogue and on his or her ability to suggest a character's emotions. Sometimes a reviewer states criteria, but often you must infer the criteria from the reviewer's opinions.

- Note **details** about the production that the reviewer uses to support opinions. These details might include descriptions of the stage set and costumes or particular movements and gestures that actors make in their performances.

- Identify the **tone,** the writer's attitude toward the production. For example, does the writer seem enthusiastic, even-handed, or sarcastic? Consider what the tone suggests about the reviewer's general opinion of the production.

As you read, use a chart like the one shown to help you analyze each review.

Review by Thomas Disch	
Criteria	A production of Julius Caesar should be judged by its stateliness, pageantry, and music.
Details of the Performance	
Tone	
General Opinion	

1290 UNIT 11: SHAKESPEAREAN DRAMA

Selection Resources

See resources on the **Teacher One Stop DVD-ROM** *and on* **thinkcentral.com***.*

R **RESOURCE MANAGER UNIT 11**
Lesson Support,* pp. 91–104

DIAGNOSTIC AND SELECTION TESTS
Selection Tests, pp. 331–334

BEST PRACTICES TOOLKIT
pp. A34

TECHNOLOGY

- Teacher One Stop DVD-ROM
- Student One Stop DVD-ROM
- Audio Anthology CD
- ExamView Test Generator on the Teacher One Stop

* Resources for Differentiation

Review of

Julius Caesar

by Thomas M. Disch

Julius Caesar is at once the dullest and the most familiar of Shakespeare's tragedies. It has become the most familiar precisely because it is the dullest, a tale so flensed[1] of dramatic meat that it can be presented to any group of teenagers, however rowdy, without danger of awakening their interest.

Given all these liabilities, the best one
10 can hope for from any production of *Julius Caesar* is stateliness, pageantry and music, . . . and these aren't qualities likely to be in large supply at the Public Theater, which undertook *Julius Caesar* as the second production of its six-year assault on the whole oeuvre.[2] It was stoically[3] done. Without the ghost of an idea for making it new, director Stuart Vaughan had his cast trot through their
20 lines as best they could and the devil take the hindmost.[4] The hindmost was indisputably Martin Sheen as Brutus. He declaimed every line in the same hoarse timbre[5] and indicated every statement with alphabet-block simplicity: a thump of his hand to his heart when that organ was mentioned, or a finger pointing to his head, when "thoughts" had to be glossed. He was not left to die
30 entirely by himself, however, but fell upon his sword with careful choreography, and nothing in his role became him like the leaving of it. **A**

Al Pacino as Mark Antony seemed ill. This was an Antony whose protestations of a lack of eloquence can be taken at face value. Had he had to contend against any Brutus but Sheen's, the Romans' preference for him would have
40 been unaccountable. But he did remember all the lines of that long oration, which, you'll recall, is very long indeed. Bravo, Al. Now, my advice to you is get some rest, eat sensibly, exercise, and take Geritol every day. **B**

---

1. **flensed** (flĕnsd): stripped of the fat or skin; said of an animal.
2. **oeuvre** (œ′vrə): the sum of the lifework of an artist, a writer, or a composer.
3. **stoically** (stō′ĭk-ə-lē): in a manner unaffected by pain or pleasure.
4. **devil take the hindmost**: let others manage as best they can.
5. **timbre** (tăm′bər): the distinctive tone of an instrument or a voice.

A THEATER REVIEW
Reread lines 17–29. What **details** does the reviewer include to support his opinion of Martin Sheen's performance as Brutus?

B THEATER REVIEW
Describe the reviewer's **tone** in lines 34–45.

INFORMATIONAL ANALYSIS — COMMON CORE

A *Model the Skill:* **THEATER REVIEW**

RI 1
RI 7
RI 8

To teach how to interpret a review, read aloud lines 21–33. Help students expand the graphic organizer from page 1290 to include details Disch provides about Martin Sheen.

Possible answer: The reviewer says that the director had no idea how to make the performance fresh, so he had the actors recite their lines "as best they could" (lines 17–20). Details that the reviewer includes about Sheen's performance are "declaimed every line in the same hoarse timbre" (lines 23–24) and the gestures that "indicated every statement with alphabet-block simplicity" (lines 24–25).

INFORMATIONAL ANALYSIS — COMMON CORE

B THEATER REVIEW

RI 1
RI 7
RI 8

Possible answer: The reviewer's tone is sarcastic. He says that "Al Pacino . . . seemed ill" (line 34) and that the Romans might have preferred him only because Sheen's performance was worse (lines 37–40). He also criticizes Pacino's physical appearance and mockingly prescribes Geritol (a vitamin supplement) for him (lines 43–45).

DIFFERENTIATED INSTRUCTION

FOR STRUGGLING READERS

Build Comprehension To help students complete the analytical chart on page 1290, have them read the reviews as a group, listing (with line references) details of each performance and words that indicate each reviewer's tone. Have the group review the lists; then offer assistance as group members work together to write a general opinion of each reviewer.

FOR ADVANCED LEARNERS/PRE–AP

Evaluate Tone Disch's review is very bitter— and very personal. Why does he make such a point of belittling director Stuart Vaughan and actors Martin Sheen and Al Pacino? Is it fair for him to do so? Ask students to write one or two paragraphs in which they discuss the purpose and effectiveness of writing a review using such a bitter, personal tone. Have students exchange and compare their responses.

INFORMATIONAL ANALYSIS

COMMON CORE
RI 1
RI 7
RI 8

C THEATER REVIEW

Possible answer: *Students may note the opinion that "the casting is mostly very good." Oliver follows up this assertion by describing several strong actors' performance in the lead roles.*

INFORMATIONAL ANALYSIS

COMMON CORE
RI 1
RI 7
RI 8

D THEATER REVIEW

Possible answer: *Oliver's criteria seem to be based on how well an actor suggests his or her character's emotions and his or her effect upon other characters. For example, Oliver says that Sheen plays a self-questioning, melancholy, virtuous, and brave Brutus, "a man whose honesty, even innocence, makes him an easy mark for more devious types" (lines 20–22). Oliver also admires Herrmann's forcefulness and clarity (lines 8–12) and Pacino's skill at portraying Antony's sinister sullenness (lines 23–32).*

TIERED DISCUSSION PROMPTS

Direct students to lines 43–60. Use these prompts to help students explore Oliver's other criticisms of the production:

Connect When you see a play or movie, what do you notice besides the actors? *Accept all reasonable responses.*

Analyze How does Oliver's opinion of the director differ from Disch's opinion? *Possible answer: Oliver calls him "sensible"; Disch feels that he was inept.* How would you describe Oliver's opinion of the set, lighting, and costumes? *Possible answer: She approves of all of them but is not excessively enthusiastic.*

Synthesize How might Oliver have reviewed this production if she had seen it several years earlier? Explain. *Possible answer: Oliver might have appreciated the actors but not the staging and presentation. She explains that it took her a long time to appreciate the kind of production that has been staged at the Public Theater (lines 48–49).*

C THEATER REVIEW
A **critique** is a writer's comments on another work. Theater reviews provide a critique of a performance of a play. Throughout a critique, writers offer their own opinions—but these opinions must be substantiated, or backed up by examples and evidence. Identify an opinion that this writer states. What evidence or examples does she offer to support it?

D THEATER REVIEW
Reread lines 4–42, and note the qualities that the reviewer admires in the performances of Edward Herrmann, Martin Sheen, and Al Pacino. What can you infer about her **criteria** for evaluating the casting of a play?

COMMON CORE RI 4

Language Coach

Connotations A word's **connotations** are the feelings and images connected to it. Read lines 43–60. How do words like *sensible*, *effective*, and *appropriate* rate on a scale of passion, with 1 being least passionate? What do these words tell you about the reviewer's attitude toward the performance?

Hail, Caesar!
by Edith Oliver

Herewith some impressions of "Julius Caesar," the second entry in the Shakespeare Marathon, at the Public: **C**

This is the first "Caesar" I've ever seen that is dominated by Cassius, in Edward Herrmann's towering performance— towering physically, too, with a lean, but hardly hungry, look. Mr. Herrmann brings an intellectual clarity and force to
10 the character which make him seem the focus of the play, the instigator of the action. And the rest of the casting, as is usual at the Public, is mostly very good. Martin Sheen, a memorable Hamlet there twenty years ago (he recited the "To be, or not to be" soliloquy in a Hispanic accent), now makes the step to Brutus seem inevitable. His Brutus is self-questioning, often melancholy,
20 and virtuous and brave—a man whose honesty, even innocence, makes him an easy mark for more devious types. Which, of course, brings us to Al Pacino's Mark Antony, a devious type if ever there was one, so obviously scheming and sinister right from the start that I doubt he could fool even this Brutus into allowing him to deliver Caesar's funeral oration. (He doesn't fool
30 Cassius.) A sullen, sharp-witted Antony,

Mr. Pacino takes the curse of "set piece" off that oration. John McMartin is a surprising but, as it turns out, excellent choice for a Caesar who is aristocratic, cheerful, and friendly—just the sort of ruler to inspire the devotion of Brutus, among others, and perhaps the distrust of Cassius. His very soft "Et tu, Brute!" at the stabbing is indelible. I also admired
40 Joan MacIntosh, in her one passionate, loving scene with Brutus, and, come to think of it, almost everyone else. **D**

Under the sensible direction of Stuart Vaughan, the performance as a whole is always absorbing and always clear. If you sense some extra enthusiasm in my praise, you're probably right. It is the fervor of the convert;[1] it took me a long time to enjoy and appreciate the kind
50 of American Shakespeare presented by Joseph Papp at the Public or in the Park. (There have been some lemons, too.) The handsome setting for "Julius Caesar"—a bare stage with a flight of steps at center leading to a platform and surrounded by square, sky-high columns of brick—was designed by Bob Shaw and effectively lighted by Arden Fingerhut; the appropriate costumes
60 were designed by Lindsay W. Davis.

---

1. **fervor of the convert:** the intensity of emotion experienced by one who has changed one set of beliefs for another.

DIFFERENTIATED INSTRUCTION

FOR STRUGGLING READERS

Comprehension Support As you discuss Oliver's words about Al Pacino's performance (lines 23–32), make sure students understand that in Oliver's view, Pacino presents Antony as such an obvious schemer that she is surprised that Brutus (even this "innocent" Brutus, as played by Sheen) allows Antony to speak at Caesar's funeral. Remind students that Shakespeare did not intend for Brutus to suspect that Antony would use the funeral oration (Act Three, Scene 2) to turn the people against Brutus.

FOR ENGLISH LANGUAGE LEARNERS

Language Coach

COMMON CORE RI 4

Connotations *Answer:*
All of the words suggest a rather muted response to the performance. Although the review is positive, it is not what you would call a "rave review." Ask students to think of more passionate words, with positive connotations, to replace *sensible, effective,* and *appropriate* in lines 43–60. Explain to students that words such as *stunning* would be part of a rave review.

Comprehension

1. **Recall** According to Thomas Disch, which actor gave the worst performance in *Julius Caesar*?

2. **Recall** Why did Edward Herrmann's performance as Cassius surprise Edith Oliver?

3. **Summarize** What general opinion does each reviewer express about the production?

Text Analysis

4. **Analyze a Theater Review** Look over the charts you created as you read. Which reviewer offers better support for the opinions expressed in his or her review? Cite evidence to support your response.

5. **Make Inferences** A theater review may be influenced by factors outside of the production, such as the reviewer's opinion of the play itself and past experiences with the theater company. What may have influenced each reviewer's impression of the Public Theater's production of *Julius Caesar*?

COMMON CORE

RI 1 Cite textual evidence to support analysis of what the text says explicitly as well as inferences drawn from the text. RI 7 Analyze various accounts of a subject told in different mediums. RI 8 Delineate and evaluate the argument and specific claims in a text. W 2 Write explanatory texts to examine and convey complex ideas.

Read for Information: Draw Conclusions

WRITING PROMPT
What choices in casting, set design, and costumes would you make if you were in charge of a production of *Julius Caesar*? How do you suppose Thomas Disch or Edith Oliver would respond to your production?

To answer this prompt, you will need to **draw conclusions,** making judgments based on information from the two reviews and your own knowledge of the play. Use the following steps:

1. Reread both reviews to remind yourself of the reviewers' opinions about casting, set design, and costumes. Use these opinions as the starting point for your planning.

2. Describe the choices you would make about the casting, the set design, and the costumes in a production of the play.

3. Draw conclusions about how Disch and Oliver would likely respond to your production. Cite evidence from the reviews to support your prediction.

Information from Reviews		My Knowledge of the Play
Casting:	Set Design:	Costumes:

FOR STRUGGLING WRITERS
Read for Information

- Have students use a three-column chart to record their decisions for casting, set design, and costumes.

- Have students use their answers to the chart on page 1290 to help determine how Disch and Oliver would respond to their choices.

- Help students draft two summary statements that tell how Disch and Oliver would like their production.

FOR ADVANCED LEARNERS/PRE–AP
Read for Information Adopting the persona of either Disch or Oliver, have students write a short theater review of the production described in the prompt. Remind students to think about the criteria that each reviewer used to review the Public Theater production play as well as the tone that each reviewer took.

Practice and Apply

For preliminary support of post-reading questions, use these copy masters:

R RESOURCE MANAGER—Copy Masters
   Reading Check p. 103
   Question Support p. 104
   Draw Conclusions p. 100

Additional selection questions are provided for teachers on page 95.

ANSWERS

Comprehension

1. *Martin Sheen as Brutus*

2. *Herrmann was the only Cassius that she had seen dominate* Julius Caesar.

3. *Disch strongly disliked the production, but Oliver liked it very much.*

Text Analysis
COMMON CORE RI 1, RI 7, RI 8

Possible answers:

4. *Oliver describes more performances in detail, but her details are often vague. Disch focuses on fewer characters and frequently resorts to insults, but he gives very specific details about actors' performances.*

5. *Disch was influenced by his inherent bias against Shakespeare's play (lines 1–8); he also does not like the Public Theater's work in general (lines 12–14). Oliver was influenced by her recent "conversion" to the Public Theater's style of presentation (lines 45–51).*

Read for Information: Draw Conclusions
COMMON CORE W 2

Writing Prompt *Responses will vary, but students should support their choices with specific details.*

Assess and Reteach

Assess

DIAGNOSTIC AND SELECTION TESTS
   Selection Test A pp. 331–332
   Selection Test B pp. 333–334

Interactive Selection Test on **thinkcentral.com**

Reteach

Level Up Online Tutorials on **thinkcentral.com**

Reteaching Worksheets on **thinkcentral.com**
   Informational Text Lesson 16

Focus and Motivate

⋯ **COMMON CORE FOCUS**

RL 7 Analyze the representation of a key scene in two different artistic mediums, including what is emphasized or absent in each treatment.
W 2 Write explanatory texts to convey complex ideas, concepts and information clearly through the effective selection, organization, and analysis of content. **SL 1** Come to discussions prepared, having read and researched material under study; explicitly draw on that preparation by referring to evidence from texts and other research.

SUMMARY

In this film clip from *The Tragedy of Julius Caesar*, Brutus follows his murder of Caesar with a speech at Caesar's funeral, arguing to the crowd that Caesar deserved death. After Brutus leaves, Mark Antony enters with Caesar's body. He skillfully paints Caesar's killers as traitors and Caesar as a good leader unfairly murdered. Mark Antony then reads Caesar's will, which promises money and land to all. The furious crowd disperses, ready to kill Caesar's murderers.

What gives a
SCENE its power?

Ask students to name forceful, influential, or moving speeches they know, such as Martin Luther King, Jr.'s, "I Have a Dream" speech, or Abraham Lincoln's "Gettysburg Address." Ask students what makes these speeches memorable.

BACKGROUND

Based on what Greek historian Appian of Alexandria (c. 95–165), wrote about Caesar's funeral, Shakespeare's version was accurate. The funeral crowd seemed willing to grant amnesty to Caesar's killers until Mark Antony spoke. At first Antony calmed the crowd, urging them not to do anything that would return Rome to civil war. However, as he went on, he worked himself and the crowd into a frenzy. Then someone raised an effigy of Caesar's body, which clearly displayed 23 wounds savagely inflicted on his body and face. This led the crowd to rebellion. Citizens burned the Senate where Caesar had been killed and began the hunt for his murderers.

Media Study

from Julius Caesar **Essential Course of Study** **ECOS**
Film Clip on **Media ◯ Smart** DVD-ROM

What gives a
SCENE its power?

⋯ **COMMON CORE**

RL 7 Analyze the representation of a key scene in two different artistic mediums, including what is emphasized or absent in each treatment.

Some of the world's greatest **speeches** have inspired and moved audiences. Others have initiated change by creating cultural and political awareness. A few, like Shakespeare's version of Mark Antony's funeral oration, have stirred a crowd to mob action. In this lesson, you'll see how certain filmmaking techniques enhance the performance of Mark Antony's famous speech.

Background

"Friends, Romans, Countrymen . . ." If you've ever seen a live performance of a Shakespearean play, then you understand why film directors have long been interested in bringing Shakespearean drama to film. Shakespeare's understanding of human nature—the flaws, strengths, and ambitions of his characters—remains universal and timeless.

One of the most memorable speeches in literary history. Mark Antony's funeral oration is brief. However, its ability to stir an audience from sadness and compassion to anger and rage shows the emotional range of Shakespearean drama.

Media Study Resources

*See resources on the **Teacher One Stop DVD-ROM** and on **thinkcentral.com**.*

R RESOURCE MANAGER UNIT 11
Plan and Teach pp. 105–108
Summary, pp. 109†*, 110‡*
Viewing Guide p. 111
Close Viewing p. 112
Viewing Activity p. 113
Produce Your Own Media p. 114

TECHNOLOGY
⊘ **Teacher One Stop DVD-ROM**
⊘ **Student One Stop DVD-ROM**
⊘ **Media*Smart* DVD-ROM**
MediaScope on **thinkcentral.com**

---

* Resources for Differentiation   † Also in Spanish   ‡ In Haitian Creole and Vietnamese

Media Literacy: Shakespearean Drama on Film

One key ingredient directors use to bring Shakespearean drama to the big screen is **mise en scène** (mēz′ än sĕn′). This French term refers to the arrangement and the use of setting, props, costumes, lighting, and acting in a scene. Once the visual elements come together, directors use a careful selection of **camera shots.** Here are some of the ways directors use these techniques.

FILMMAKING TECHNIQUES	STRATEGIES FOR VIEWING	
Mise en Scène Directors use elements of mise en scène to provide clues about the setting, to create relationships between characters, and to show the behavior and motivation of characters.	• Pay close attention to the **setting,** the **props,** and the **costumes.** They not only establish the time and place in which a story is set but may also be essential to the plot in other ways. For example, a director may use a prop as a symbol. Keep track of when and how a prop is used. • Study the **performances.** An actor's performance consists of his or her appearance, body movements, facial expressions, gestures, and voice. • Notice how characters are positioned within a frame. For example, a main character may be placed in the center of the frame to emphasize his or her importance in a scene.	
Camera Shots In the realm of theater, directors achieve effective onstage performances through precise positioning of the actors. Film directors do this as well, but they also use camera shots to draw viewers' attention to something important, and to create an impression or feeling in the audience.	• Study the types of shots a director uses to convey the action in a scene. An **extreme long shot,** or **establishing shot,** is used to provide a view of a large area or to establish the scene. To show how characters interact within their surroundings, a director may use a **long shot.** • Notice how **close-up shots** can suggest a character's inner thoughts and feelings. Likewise, a **reaction shot** may be used to show how a character reacts to something in a previous shot.	

MEDIA STUDY **1295**

Media Literacy

Discuss Shakespearean plays with which students are familiar. Ask them what staged or film versions of these plays look like or might look like. What do actors wear? What is the scenery? What kinds of props might be used? On the board, list answers that note the use of period costumes, props, and setting. Then discuss the chart on this page.

• **Mise en Scène** To help students recognize the impact of mise en scène in film, ask them to compare a film set in the Old West and one set in modern times. How are the **settings** different? What kinds of **props** are used? What **costumes** do actors wear? How do **performances** help viewers recognize the film's time period?

• **Camera Shots** To help students understand different camera shots, have volunteers play the role of cameraperson. Ask volunteers to pantomime framing an **extreme long shot** of the room and then describe what he or she sees. Repeat the procedure with a **long shot** and a **close-up shot**. To help students visualize a **reaction shot**, have a pair pantomime a scene in which one student tells the other a dark secret. Have the cameraperson frame and describe a reaction shot of the person who hears the secret.

MEDIA STUDY: TEACHING OPTIONS

Teaching Option 1: The Basics (1–2 Days)
1. Begin the Media Study using the material provided on pages 1294–1295.
2. Show the Introduction on Media*Smart.* Then show the First Viewing. As they watch, have students use the Viewing Guide on page 1296, along with the corresponding copy master on page 111 of the Resource Manager. Discuss their responses.
3. Return to the pupil book for the extension activities on page 1297.

Teaching Option 2: In-Depth Study (2–3 Days)
1. Begin the Media Study using pages 1294–1295.
2. Show the Introduction and First Viewing from Media*Smart.* Then continue on Media*Smart* with the Media Lessons, using the teacher notes available in the Resources section.
3. Show the Guided Analysis presentation. Have students record their observations on the Student Viewing Guide available in the Resources section from Media*Smart.* Return to the pupil book, page 1297.

MEDIA STUDY **1295**

Practice and Apply

VIEWING GUIDE

1. Before students view the film clip, explain that they will be asked to identify and analyze elements of mise en scène and camera shots used to re-create a famous speech on film. Urge students to look for these elements in the film clip:

   - how the director uses different kinds of **camera shots** to reveal the intentions of Brutus and Mark Antony and the crowd's reactions

   - how **setting, props,** and **costumes** establish the time and place of events in ancient Rome

   - how the actors' **performances**, including their appearance, movements, expressions, gestures, and voice, convey information, attitude, and emotion

2. Some students may find it useful to follow along with a printed version of the play while viewing. Encourage students to mark comments on the printed version as they watch.

R RESOURCE MANAGER—Copy Masters
   Viewing Guide p. 111
   Close Viewing p. 112
   Viewing Activity p. 113

Use this resource with the Viewing Guide:

💿 **Media*Smart* DVD-ROM**

Media*Scope* on **thinkcentral.com**

ANSWERS

FIRST VIEWING: Comprehension

1. *An extreme long shot, or establishing shot, is used to open the scene and show where the scene takes place.*

2. *Props include the parchment containing Caesar's will, the bloody cloth covering Caesar, and the corpse of Caesar.*

CLOSE VIEWING: Media Literacy

Possible answers:

3. *The reaction shots isolate the three men from the crowd and put them in physical opposition to Mark Antony.*

4. *Mise en scène elements that show the film's historical setting include:* **Setting:** *The building appears to be a classical, ancient style.* **Props:** *Caesar's will is on a rolled-up parchment, his body is on a pallet under a bloody*

Media🎞Smart DVD-ROM
- **Film Clip:** *Julius Caesar,* 1970
- **Director:** Stuart Burge
- **Genre:** Drama
- **Running Time:** 10 minutes

1296

Viewing Guide for
Julius Caesar

Prepare to view an interpretation of one of the most famous speeches in Shakespearean drama. How might the experience of watching this scene performed on screen differ from the experience of reading or watching the stage performance? As you view, think about these questions.

NOW VIEW

FIRST VIEWING: Comprehension

1. **Recall** What type of **camera shot** is used to open the scene?

2. **Recall** Name one prop that is used in this scene.

CLOSE VIEWING: Media Literacy

3. **Make Inferences** Throughout the scene, the director cuts to the reactions of three men. What do the **reaction shots** convey about these men?

4. **Analyze Mise en Scène** What elements of mise en scène indicate that the film takes place in the past?

5. **Analyze Camera Shots** Which camera shot is used the most? Why do you think this shot is important to the scene?

6. **Evaluate the Performance** The actor's performance is an important element of **mise en scène.** How would you rate the performance of the actor who plays Mark Antony? Think about

   - how the actor uses facial expressions and gestures to convey the character's emotions

   - the actor's tone of voice and delivery of the lines

   - your own expectations of the character of Mark Antony and how the actor would portray any traits you associate with him

---

mantle. **Costumes:** *The flowing tunics suggest ancient Roman times.* **Dialogue:** *The dialogue is formal, spoken in iambic pentameter.*

5. *Long shots are used most often. They convey the event's public nature, Caesar's importance to his subjects, and the crowd's changing reactions to Mark Antony's appeals and incitements.*

6. *The actor playing Mark Antony, Charlton Heston, gives a strong performance. His facial expressions reflect Antony's sadness and anger and convey Antony's hidden agenda.*

The actor commands attention with his deep voice, impassioned delivery of the lines, strong gestures, movements up and down the stairs and into the crowd, and gestures with the bloody mantle. Students may say that they expected Mark Antony to be clever and manipulative and that the actor successfully conveyed these attributes.

Write or Discuss

Evaluate the Film Clip The 1970 adaptation of *Julius Caesar* received mixed reviews. Read an excerpt from a review by critic Roger Ebert. Explain whether you agree or disagree with his statements. Remember that, in a critique (a review of another's work), opinions should be substantiated, or backed up by evidence.

> When the crowds gather for Mark Antony's funeral oration, they group themselves like refugees from a particularly orderly Renaissance painting. When we get close-ups of the conspirators, they're arranged like mannequins in a department-store window. . . . And then Charlton Heston leaps in with his Mark Antony speech. Heston does a fine job. . . . But just when Heston gets into high gear, we cut away to a long shot of the crowd and lose all the personal emotion in Heston's face.
>
> Roger Ebert, *Chicago Sun-Times,* March 17, 1971

COMMON CORE

RL 7 Analyze the representation of a key scene in two different artistic mediums, including what is emphasized or absent in each treatment. **W 2** Write explanatory texts to examine and convey complex ideas, concepts, and information clearly and accurately through the effective selection, organization, and analysis of content. **SL 1** Come to discussions prepared, having read material under study; draw on that preparation by referring to evidence from texts.

Produce Your Own Media

Write a Shooting Script Before filming, directors often create a **shooting script.** A shooting script is a split-page document that describes camera shots on the left, and sound (dialogue, voice-over narration, music, and sound effects) on the right. Choose a scene (or part of a scene) from *Julius Caesar* and create a shooting script that describes how the scene is shot.

HERE'S HOW Use the model and the tip to help you create a shooting script.

- Determine the setting, the place and time in which the scene takes place.
- Vary the **camera placement** to show characters' actions and emotions.
- Consider how **sound** contributes to the scene.

Media Tools **THINK** central

Go to **thinkcentral.com**.
KEYWORD: HML10-1297

STUDENT MODEL

SHOT DESCRIPTIONS	SOUND	
FADE IN EXT—DAY		
1. MS, CASCA AND BRUTUS. Begin slow zoom out to reveal Brutus pulling Casca's cloak. Casca has turned to face Brutus.	CASCA:	You pulled me by the cloak. Would you speak with me?
	BRUTUS:	Ay, Casca. Tell us what hath chanced today that Caesar looks so sad.
2. CU—CASCA LOOKS CONFUSED.	CASCA:	Why you were with him, were you not?

PRODUCTION TIP

Use the following abbreviations to indicate camera placement:

ELS = extreme long shot

LS = long shot

CU = close-up shot

MS = medium shot

POV = point-of-view shot

MEDIA STUDY **1297**

Produce Your Own Media

Rubric: Write a Shooting Script A strong shooting script should

- show character names and accurately tell what the characters in the scene say
- establish the place and time of the scene
- use variations in camera placement, including extreme long shots, long shots, close-up shots, medium shots, and point-of-view shots, to give variety and drama to the scene
- use sound effects when appropriate

- follow the shooting script model in the placement of and terminology for shot descriptions and sound

R RESOURCE MANAGER—Copy Master
Produce Your Own Media p. 114

Assess and Reteach

Write or Discuss
COMMON CORE RL 7, W 2, SL 1

Evaluate the Film Clip In their evaluations, students should cite specific comments in Ebert's review and elements from the clip. For example, students might disagree with Ebert's comment that "just when Heston gets into high gear," the cutaway to the crowd loses the emotion building in Heston's face. They might assert that the crowd's reactions are mirrors of Antony's emotional fervor and that it is not necessary to show Antony's face to know how he is looking and behaving.

MEDIA STUDY WRAP–UP

Have students summarize what they have learned about mise en scène as used to film Shakespearean drama. Encourage them to use terms such as *mise en scène, setting, props, costumes, performances, camera shots, extreme long shot, establishing shot, long shot, close-up shot,* and *reaction shot* in their explanations.

RETEACH

For students who are unable to apply the Media Study skills, select from these reteaching options:

- **Mise en Scène** Ask students to look back at **Behind the Curtain** on pages 1213, 1229, 1242, and 1263. Ask them to identify the elements of mise en scène in the photographs. Discuss how differences in set design, props, and costumes impact the look and feel of the play. Ask students how these elements are different in film than in theater. Remind students that movies are often filmed on location. What are other ways in which films can be more elaborate?

- **Camera Shots** Assign students to work in groups as directors of Act One, Scene 1 in *The Tragedy of Julius Caesar*. Have each group decide where to use extreme long shots, long shots, close-up shots, and reaction shots. Ask each group to explain why a particular shot was selected and what they wished to accomplish by using that shot.

Media Tools **THINK** central

Media study keywords point to **MediaScope**, a Web site that helps students strengthen media analysis and production skills.

Focus and Motivate

COMMON CORE FOCUS

W 1a–e Write arguments to support claims using valid reasoning and relevant evidence; develop claims and counterclaims fairly, supplying evidence for each; use words, phrases, and clauses to create cohesion; maintain a formal style; provide a concluding statement that supports the argument. **W 4** Produce coherent writing appropriate to task, purpose, and audience. **W 5** Develop and strengthen writing by planning, revising, editing, rewriting, or trying a new approach. **W 9a (RL 7, 9)** Draw evidence from literary texts; analyze a scene in two mediums; analyze how an author transforms source material. **W 10** Write routinely over shorter time frames for a range of tasks, purposes, and audiences. **L 2a** Use semicolons to link independent clauses.

WRITE WITH A PURPOSE

Tell students that they should choose a scene in which they can locate several examples from both the text and film adaptation to support their claim. Encourage them to also consider their audience when choosing a scene.

COMMON CORE TRAITS

Review the *COMMON CORE TRAITS* with students, focusing on the use of valid reasons and relevant evidence. Compare the list of traits with the rubric on page 1306.

ADDITIONAL TASKS

Write About Geography Evaluate a travel article or brochure about an exotic place. Determine whether the writing and layout are convincing you to travel to the destination.

Possible topics: Florida, Greece, Brazil, Egypt

Write About School Attend a high school musical or theater production. Write a critical review in which you evaluate how well the actors and set pieces captured the mood or another aspect of the play.

Possible topics: theater production or set design, orchestra performance, show choir performance

---

Writing Workshop
ARGUMENT

Critical Review

Essential Course of Study **ECOS**

Shakespeare's plays have inspired writers, artists, and directors to adapt them for new audiences. Although these adaptations are all based on Shakespeare's timeless texts, they can differ widely in their approach and execution. In this workshop, you will write a critical review of an adaptation of a specific scene from the play *The Tragedy of Julius Caesar.*

 Complete the workshop activities in your **Reader/Writer Notebook.**

WRITE WITH A PURPOSE

WRITING TASK

Write a **critical review** of a key scene in a movie or theater adaptation of Shakespeare's *The Tragedy of Julius Caesar.* Assert and support a claim that states whether the adaptation does justice to the text of Shakespeare's play.

Idea Starters
- Act Two, Scene 1 (the murder of Caesar)
- Act Three, Scene 2 (Mark Antony's funeral oration)
- Act Five, Scene 5 (Cassius' suicide and Antony's speech over Brutus)

THE ESSENTIALS

Here are some common purposes, audiences, and formats for writing a critical review.

PURPOSES	AUDIENCES	FORMATS
• to convince others to agree with your claim • to evaluate the success of the adaptation	• classmates and teacher • fans of movies, theater, and Shakespeare • newspaper and magazine readers • Web users	• essay for class • film or theater review in a school or local newspaper • speech • podcast • blog

COMMON CORE TRAITS

1. DEVELOPMENT OF IDEAS
- includes an **engaging introduction** that states a **precise claim**
- provides **valid reasons** and **relevant evidence** to support the claim
- acknowledges **opposing claims** and effectively refutes them with **counterclaims**
- offers a **concluding section** that supports the argument presented

2. ORGANIZATION OF IDEAS
- **organizes** reasons and evidence in a **logical** way
- uses **transitions** to create cohesion and clarify the relationships among ideas

3. LANGUAGE FACILITY AND CONVENTIONS
- maintains a **formal style** and **objective tone**
- uses **semicolons** correctly and effectively
- employs correct **grammar, mechanics,** and **spelling**

Writing Online
Go to **thinkcentral.com**.
KEYWORD: HML10N-1298

Writing Workshop Resources

* Resources for Differentiation

Planning/Prewriting

 COMMON CORE

W 1a–e Write arguments to support claims using valid reasoning and relevant evidence. **W 5** Develop writing by planning. **W 9a (RL 7, 9)** Draw evidence from literary texts; analyze a scene in two mediums; analyze how an author transforms source material.

Getting Started

CHOOSE A SCENE

Decide which film or theatrical adaptation of *Julius Caesar* you will use as the basis for your critical review. Then list scenes from the play that have made an impression on you. (Consult the Idea Starters on page 1298 for some sample scenes.) Review your list, and then choose a scene that is critical to the play. Jot down notes about how the scene is the same as or different from the original. Include your ideas about the adaptation's set design, casting, pacing, and other elements that reveal the influence of its director.

▶ **WHAT DOES IT LOOK LIKE?**

the funeral oration scene in *Julius Caesar*

Similarities/Differences
- Setting is a central public square just outside a classic Roman building. (same)
- Some minor dialogue is cut. (difference)

Film Techniques
- Long shots reveal the setting; close-ups capture the characters' grief
- The absence of music enhances the intensity of the scene

THINK ABOUT AUDIENCE AND PURPOSE

To write an effective critical review, you must first identify your **purpose**—to persuade your **audience** to accept your **claim**, or position, on the adaptation. Be sure to consider what your audience likely knows—and may not know—about the original play and the adaptation. You also need to anticipate opinions that they may already have.

▶ **ASK YOURSELF:**
- Who is my audience?
- What background information do I need to include for my audience to follow my argument?
- What opinions might my audience already have on the adaptation? How will they affect my choice of reasons and evidence?

STATE YOUR CLAIM AND REASONS

The foundation of your argument is a precise **claim**. Make sure you can support your claim with at least two or three valid **reasons**—ones that are logical and make sense. If you realize that your claim can't be sufficiently supported, you should rework it or try a new approach. For example, consider whether the reasons you've thought about support a different claim.

▶ **WHAT DOES IT LOOK LIKE?**

Claim: The funeral oration scene in the 1970 version of Shakespeare's *Julius Caesar* is as powerful as Shakespeare's original text.

Reason 1	Reason 2
The set's classical Roman architecture captures the time and place of Shakespeare's setting.	Charlton Heston as Mark Antony gives the scene a believable tragic hero.

Teach

Planning/ Prewriting

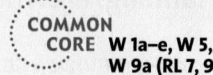 COMMON CORE W 1a–e, W 5, W 9a (RL 7, 9)

▶ **CHOOSE A SCENE** To help students determine which scene to evaluate, ask the following questions:

- Do you feel strongly enough about this scene to make a claim?
- Is there enough evidence in this scene to support your claim?

If students are unable to make or support a claim, encourage them to consider another scene.

▶ **THINK ABOUT AUDIENCE AND PURPOSE** Explain to students that their audience may not agree with their claim. As they acknowledge any opposing claims in their critical review, they should be prepared to offer effective counterclaims.

▶ **STATE YOUR CLAIM AND REASONS** Encourage students to evaluate the validity of each of their reasons. Have them ask themselves: Is this reason logical? Does it make sense? If they answer *no* to any of these questions, have them replace the reason with a valid one. If too many of their reasons seem weak, remind students to revise or rework their claim.

R **RESOURCE MANAGER**—Copy Masters
Planning/Prewriting p. 119
Drafting p. 120
Revising and Editing pp. 121–123
Writing Support p. 126

DIFFERENTIATED INSTRUCTION

FOR ENGLISH LANGUAGE LEARNERS

Language: Reinforce Critical Terms Write these terms on the board and review them with students:

- *claim:* a sentence that states the writer's position on an issue
- *reasons:* explanation of why the writer believes a claim

- *evidence:* valid and relevant information that supports a reason
- *opposing claim:* a viewpoint on the issue that is different from the writer's
- *counterclaim:* the writer's response to an opposing claim

Planning/Prewriting *continued*

- ▶ **GATHER EVIDENCE** Remind students to gather evidence about the scene in both the play and the film adaptation. Explain that exploring the similarities and differences between the two versions may help strengthen their argument.

- ▶ **ANTICIPATE OPPOSING CLAIMS** Have students state their claim and explain their reasons to a partner. Their partner should then express an opposing claim. If students are unable to offer a convincing counterclaim, encourage them to rethink their stance on the scene.

- ▶ **PLAN YOUR CONCLUDING SECTION** Have students brainstorm and list several possible thought-provoking insights or quotations to include in their concluding section. Have them work with a partner to determine which option works best in their critical review.

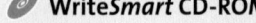 Have students complete the **Your Turn** activity independently. Then ask them to discuss their ideas with a partner. Have partners brainstorm ways their comparisons could be used as relevant evidence to support a claim or reason in a critical review.

For interactive graphic organizers, see

💿 **Write*Smart* CD-ROM**

Writing Center on <u>thinkcentral.com</u>

Planning/Prewriting *continued*

Getting Started

GATHER EVIDENCE

Each of your reasons should be supported by **relevant**, or related, **evidence**. This evidence should include direct quotations, description, examples, and other details from both works.

- **direct quotation:** "Friends, Romans, countrymen, lend me your ears."
- **description:** outside a classical Roman building in a public square
- **example:** there is no music, enhancing the realism and intensity of the scene

▶ **TIPS**

- Create a graphic organizer to track the evidence that you collect in support of each reason. Then, choose the reasons for which you have the most convincing evidence.
- If you find that the evidence you gathered suggests an alternative view of the scene, reconsider your claim and try a new approach.

ANTICIPATE OPPOSING CLAIMS

For your critical review to be persuasive, you need to address any **alternative** or **opposing claims** and point out their weaknesses. Brainstorm a list of possible opposing claims that viewers might have. For each opposing claim, list a **counterclaim** that refutes the opposition and explains why your viewpoint is more valid.

▶ **WHAT DOES IT LOOK LIKE?**

Opposing Claim: The omission of some dialogue from the film version of this scene detracts from the effectiveness of the adaptation.

Counterclaim: The cuts, which are done sparingly, are mostly of repetitive asides from the crowd and take nothing away from the tension of the scene.

PLAN YOUR CONCLUDING SECTION

To complete your argument, end with a compelling concluding section. Remember to restate your claim and summarize your reasons. Consider presenting a thought-provoking quotation, question, or insight to keep your audience thinking about the ideas you have presented. Jot down a brief outline of the details you want to include.

▶ **WHAT DOES IT LOOK LIKE?**

restatement: The 1970 film Julius Caesar is as compelling as Shakespeare's original text.

summary of reasons: The set design, camera techniques, and other filmmaking decisions support the strong casting and are faithful to Shakespeare's text.

insight: This scene—set in ancient Rome, written in Elizabethan England, and adapted for the screen in the 20th century—shows the timeless power of rhetoric.

PEER REVIEW Share with a peer your claim, reasons, and evidence. Then ask: What can I rework or add to strengthen my argument?

 In your *Reader/Writer Notebook*, list key scenes from an adaptation of *Julius Caesar*. Then choose a scene, and write a precise claim. Use a graphic organizer to list reasons, evidence, and opposing claims.

DIFFERENTIATED INSTRUCTION

FOR ENGLISH LANGUAGE LEARNERS

Writing: Gather Support Have students use these sentence starters to help them develop their claims and relevant evidence:

- My claim is _____.
- One reason for my claim is _____.
- This reason is supported by the following (quotation, description, technique, detail): _____.

FOR STRUGGLING WRITERS

Providing Counterclaims Explain that counterclaims address an opposing claim and give examples of why the original claim is still valid. Have students write a list of possible opposing claims. Then ask: How would you convince someone that this opposing claim is inaccurate or irrelevant? Students should use evidence in the form of quotations, descriptions, techniques, or details to refute the counterclaim.

Drafting

COMMON
CORE

W 1c Use words, phrases, and clauses to create cohesion.
W 4 Produce coherent writing appropriate to task, purpose, and audience.

The following chart shows how to organize your draft to create a coherent critical review.

Organizing Your Critical Review

INTRODUCTION
- Grab the audience's attention with a **provocative question** or **insightful quotation**.
- Introduce the **play**, the **author**, and the **adaptation**. Provide any **background** about your chosen scene that the audience may need to understand your review.
- State your opinion in a **precise claim**.

▼

BODY
- Present your reasons in a **logical order**, such as by order of importance.
- Support each reason with **direct quotations**, **examples**, **descriptive details**, and other types of **evidence** from the text and adaptation.
- Acknowledge **opposing claims** fairly. Provide **counterclaims** to strengthen your claim and emphasize the limitations of other viewpoints.
- Use **transitions**—such as *additionally, although,* or *so that*—to create **cohesion**.
- Maintain a **formal style** by avoiding casual, conversational language, and use an **objective tone** that shows respect for opposing views.

▼

CONCLUDING SECTION
- Restate your **claim**. Conclude with a **thought-provoking question** or **insight**.

GRAMMAR IN CONTEXT: USING TRANSITIONS

Transitions are words, phrases, and clauses that show relationships among ideas in a text. Using appropriate transitions will lend clarity and cohesion to your writing. Examples of transitions include those that introduce new ideas or examples—such as *one reason, for example,* and *most important*—and those that signal contrast, such as *however, yet,* and *although*.

Examples

__Although__ I enjoyed reading Shakespeare's play, I preferred watching the 1970 film adaptation.

__One reason__ the scene works is Heston's intensity as he delivers the speech.

__Much as__ Antony turns the crowd in his favor without ever actually condemning Brutus, filmmaking techniques in the adaptation are also subtle but effective.

YOUR TURN Develop a draft of your critical review by following the plan outlined in the chart. Include words, phrases, and clauses to connect your ideas and create a cohesive argument.

FOR ENGLISH LANGUAGE LEARNERS

Language: Transitions Write the following sentences on the board:

_____ I would like to see the film adaptation, I have decided to read the original play first. _____ I have decided to do this is because I want to understand what the playwright had originally intended. _____ when I see the film, I would like to recognize how the director changed the material.

Help students use transitions to fill in the blanks and connect the sentences.

Possible answer: *Although I would like to see the film adaptation, I have decided to read the original play first. One reason I have decided to do this is because I want to understand what the playwright had originally intended. Furthermore, when I see the film I would like to recognize how the director changed the material.*

Practice and Apply

Drafting

COMMON CORE W 1c, W 4

▶ **INTRODUCTION** Have students think about why they chose the scene in the first place. What about it made a strong impression on them? Encourage students to use their own motivations as a starting point for their introductions.

▶ **BODY** Remind students that the details in the body of their critical review should all be working together to support their claim. Students will be listing reasons, including relevant evidence, acknowledging opposing claims, and providing counterclaims. Have students review their draft and eliminate any extraneous details that do not support their claims.

▶ **CONCLUDING SECTION** Remind students that their concluding sections should not only restate their claims, but also leave readers with some powerful insight based on the adaptation and the significance of both works. Have students work with a partner to brainstorm ways to strengthen their concluding sections.

GRAMMAR IN CONTEXT: USING TRANSITIONS

For practice, have students write a short paragraph that states their claim and gives three reasons that support it. Encourage them to use transitions to create cohesion among the reasons. Have volunteers share their paragraphs with the class. To extend this activity, display a paragraph that lacks effective transitions on the board or interactive whiteboard. Then ask volunteers to revise or rework the paragraph, using transitions effectively.

YOUR TURN Ask students to complete the **Your Turn** activity independently. Have them circle transitional words and phrases and insert more if there are not enough. Suggest that students write their drafts double-spaced so that they can make revisions easily later.

For a critical review writing template, see

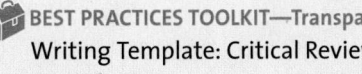
BEST PRACTICES TOOLKIT—Transparency
Writing Template: Critical Review
pp. C16, C25

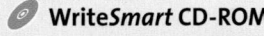
WriteSmart CD-ROM

Writing Center on thinkcentral.com

Revising

Model the Skill Using a draft of a critical review on a transparency or interactive whiteboard, model how to use the questions, tips, and strategies suggested in the chart to evaluate and revise. Consider using a critical review written by a student from a different class or from a previous year. Be sure to remove the writer's name and any other identifying information from the critical review so that the student is anonymous.

YOUR TURN As students review each other's drafts, remind them to think of all possible opposing claims. Have them identify any argument or evidence that needs strengthening by asking themselves: Does this convince me that this claim is correct?

For interactive revision tools, see

⊘ **Write*Smart* CD-ROM**

Writing Center on thinkcentral.com

Revising

When you revise, check that you have met the writing task, achieved your purpose, and provided enough evidence to convince your audience of the soundness of your argument. Use the chart shown to help you revise, rewrite, and rework to improve your critical review.

CRITICAL REVIEW

Ask Yourself	Tips	Revision Strategies
1. Do I capture the audience's attention with a compelling introduction?	**Bracket** interesting statements or thought-provoking questions.	**Add** an attention-getting question, statement, or quotation.
2. Does my introduction identify the play, author, and adaptation? Do I state a precise claim about one scene?	**Draw boxes** around the name of the play, the author, and the information that identifies the adaptation. **Underline** your claim.	**Add** information that identifies the play, author, and adaptation. **Revise** the claim to more precisely describe your opinion of a key scene.
3. Are there at least two valid reasons that support my claim? Does relevant evidence support each reason?	**Highlight** the reasons that support your claim. **Circle** the evidence that supports each reason. **Draw an arrow** from the evidence to the reason.	**Add** valid examples, anecdotes, or quotations to bolster unsupported reasons. **Elaborate** on evidence by adding more details or explanation.
4. Do I use transitions to clarify the relationships among my claim, counterclaim, reasons, and evidence?	Draw a **star** next to each transition.	**Check** your starred transitions and **add** variety if necessary. **Reread** the parts that lack stars. **Add** appropriate transitions to link related ideas.
5. Do I acknowledge and address opposing claims fairly?	**Draw a wavy line** under the opposing claims and your responses to them.	**Add** a counterclaim that points out the limitations of the opposing claims and the merits of your opinion.
6. Does my concluding section restate my claim and give the audience something important to consider?	**Put a check mark** next to the restatement. **Underline** the sentence that leaves the reader with an important insight or observation.	**Add** a restatement of the claim if it is missing. **Add** a thought-provoking question or insightful statement about the adaptation of the play.

YOUR TURN **PEER REVIEW** Working with a peer, review your drafts together. Answer each question in the chart to decide which parts of your drafts need improvement.

DIFFERENTIATED INSTRUCTION

FOR ENGLISH LANGUAGE LEARNERS

Writing: Introduction Provide students with sentence frames such as these to help them develop insights they can share in their introduction:

- In my claim, I have determined that _____.
- I strongly believe this because _____.
- A quotation, description, technique, or detail that supports this is _____.

Work with students to reorder the information in these sentences to make for a compelling and attention-grabbing introduction.

FOR ADVANCED LEARNERS/PRE–AP

Analyze Concluding Sections Work with students to create a self-evaluation form and have them complete it individually, jotting down their responses. Then have them exchange essays and carry out the same analysis of their partner's work, using a new form. Students should compare evaluations to help them determine what to focus on when revising their critical reviews.

ANALYZE A STUDENT DRAFT

Use this student's draft and the comments as a model for your review.

COMMON CORE

W 5 Strengthen writing by revising, editing, rewriting, or trying a new approach.

Mark Antony Works the Crowd
by Rupert Alterio, Springfield Regional High School

❶ Do you think graphic violence on film and TV is a modern phenomenon in entertainment? In fact, ancient Greek playwrights drew huge audiences with their tales of blood and gore. Centuries later, Shakespeare's violent tragedies were very popular with Elizabethan audiences. Today, many of Shakespeare's plays have found new fans through film adaptations. Take, for example, the 1970 film version of Shakespeare's *The Tragedy of Julius Caesar,* which succeeds as an interpretation that is true to the original work. One of the chief reasons for the film's success is its depiction of a key scene, the funeral oration of Mark Antony, which is brilliantly performed by Charlton Heston within a realistic ancient Roman setting.

❷ One technique that contributes to the power of the funeral oration scene in this adaptation is mise-en-scène, or the arrangement and use of sets, props, costumes, and performers. The scene takes place in the ancient Roman Forum, where the mutilated body of Caesar is placed before the crowd, establishing the time and place in line with the play. Look for this splendid feature of the set design: eye-catching friezes on the ancient building, portraying Romans on parade. These friezes form a striking backdrop to Antony as he addresses the crowd.

> In his introduction, Rupert grabs his audience's attention with a **provocative question**.

> Rupert clearly states a **precise claim**.

> To convince his audience that his reason is valid, Rupert needs to add more details about the set design and costumes.

LEARN HOW Use Valid Reasoning In his second paragraph, Rupert states his first reason—that the adaptation is successful because the film set, props, and costumes are true to the text. However, he does not provide enough evidence to show that this reason is valid. He made the following revisions, adding more detailed evidence, to support and strengthen his argument.

The setting is characteristically Roman—a classical, architecturally impressive structure, with columns and wide arches.

Some of the figures carry weapons, and they wear similar clothing to the Romans assembled before Antony.

RUPERT'S REVISION TO PARAGRAPH ❷

The ~~scene~~ *action* takes place in the ancient Roman Forum, where the mutilated body of Caesar is placed before the crowd, *thus* establishing the time and place in line with the play. Look for this splendid feature of the set design: eye-catching friezes on the ancient building, portraying Romans on parade. ~~These friezes~~ *are prominent on both sides of the center steps and* form a striking backdrop to Antony as he addresses the crowd.

ANALYZE A STUDENT DRAFT

Explain that the Student Draft on this page is the first half of a critical review. Model reading the draft and the annotations in blue that explain the student's language choices. Explain that the *Learn How* mini-lesson has helpful information about ways to improve the student draft as well as their own.

LEARN HOW Use Valid Reasoning

- Remind students that the use of valid reasoning will strengthen and make their claims more credible.

- Read Rupert's revision to Paragraph 2 and ask: Why is Rupert's reasoning now valid? *(because it relates to the evidence and directly supports the claim)*

- Have students read through their drafts, looking for places where they can replace faulty or weak reasons with valid or stronger ones.

FOR ENGLISH LANGUAGE LEARNERS

Writing: Valid Reasoning Guide students in completing sentence frames that support a claim with valid reasons. For example:

Claim: A movie adaptation of a Shakespeare play helps modern audiences better appreciate it.

Reason: Seeing actors on the screen helps _____. *(bring the characters to life)*

Focus students on one aspect of adaptations to help them understand how to develop valid reasons, such as characters.

FOR STRUGGLING WRITERS

Use Valid Reasoning Explain to students that valid reasons make sense because they relate to the topic and support the claim. Give students the following scenario: The principal is proposing to start school an hour later. Have students list two reasons that support or argue against this proposal. Then have them work with a partner to determine whether their reasons are valid.

📦 BEST PRACTICES TOOLKIT—Transparency
Character Analysis Chart pp. D5, D50

ANALYZE A STUDENT DRAFT *continued*

❸   Charlton Heston's performance as Antony also contributes to the effectiveness of the scene. With passion and conviction, he delivers the famous opening lines: "Friends, Romans, countrymen, lend me your ears; / I come to bury Caesar, not to praise him." As the scene progresses, Antony makes contradictory statements that hold his motives in question. The scene requires skillful acting, and Heston brings just that to the role. The close-up shots of Heston's anguished face and the statement "My heart is in the coffin there with Caesar" make it seem as if Heston, as Antony, is speaking in genuine grief.

Rupert includes **quotations** from the text to support his **reason** that Heston delivers a powerful performance.

❹   Then, when Antony walks down into the crowd after asking "Shall I descend?" he becomes one of them. An effective close-up shot shows him standing over Caesar's corpse. Finally, Antony plays his trump card: "But here's a parchment with the seal of Caesar. / I found it in his closet; 'tis his will." Brilliantly, he has swayed the crowd to his camp. In addition, because very little dialogue has been cut from the play, we get nearly the full force of Shakespeare's words.

Rupert uses **effective transitions** to clarify the relationships among his ideas.

❺   Some viewers might contest that this scene is ineffective because the supporting cast is not realistic. Perhaps it would be more effective if they talked back or shook their fists in defiance? Also, the crowd, in spite of many long shots, seems too sparse to represent the Roman populous. Those criticisms aside, the adaptation boasts a realistic set design, compelling camera shots, and a powerful performance. Most viewers will be riveted by the film. The 1970 film adaptation of *Julius Caesar* has all the ingredients of a good Shakespearean tragedy—murder, revenge, and betrayal.

Rupert acknowledges an **opposing claim**. However, he needs to develop a counterclaim in response.

LEARN HOW Develop Your Counterclaim In his concluding section, Rupert neglects to offer **counterclaims** that state why his stance is more valid. Notice how Rupert improved his argument with this revision:

RUPERT'S REVISION TO PARAGRAPH ❺

No, I think their blood-stained hands are enough to convey their murderous deed.

Some viewers might contest that this scene is ineffective because the supporting cast is not realistic. Perhaps it would be more effective if they talked back or shook their fists in defiance? Also, the crowd, in spite of many long shots, seems too sparse to represent the Roman populous.

Does this not suggest only that the film was made on a tight budget? Besides, viewers should judge the strength of this scene on the effectiveness of its star performer—Heston—not on inconsequential background actors.

YOUR TURN Use feedback from your peers and teacher as well as the two "Learn How" lessons to revise your critical review. Evaluate how well you persuade your audience to adopt your claim.

ANALYZE A STUDENT DRAFT *continued*

Explain that the Student Draft is continued and completed on this page. Read the draft and annotations aloud and discuss. Ask students how well the writer's response to an opposing claim addresses possible reader concerns.

LEARN HOW Develop Your Counterclaim
- Read aloud the original draft of Rupert's paragraph. Then read the revised version. Ask students how adding a question and example strengthened the effectiveness of his counterclaim.
- Have volunteers suggest other questions or examples Rupert could have added to his counterclaim to make it more convincing.
- Suggest students return to their own critical reviews to see how they might strengthen their counterclaims.

YOUR TURN Before students complete the **Your Turn** activity, have them pair up and discuss each other's counterclaims. Ask partners to evaluate whether the counterclaim adequately addresses the opposing claim. Have them offer suggestions for strengthening the counterclaim.

For interactive revision tools, see

🔘 **Write*Smart* CD-ROM**

Writing Center on thinkcentral.com

DIFFERENTIATED INSTRUCTION

FOR ENGLISH LANGUAGE LEARNERS
Writing: Strengthen Your Counterclaim
Students may need help strengthening their counterclaims. Suggest that students list each of their opposing claims and debate them with a partner. Then have students record any counterclaims that were strong enough to withstand the debate. Work with students to include these in their critical reviews.

FOR STRUGGLING WRITERS
Strengthen Your Counterclaim For practice, display the following claim and counterclaim. Invite students to cite reasons and evidence (such as anecdotes, examples, and facts) that would strengthen the counterclaim:

Opposing claim: Having school on Saturday morning would improve test scores.
Counterclaim: No student wants to go to school on Saturdays.

Editing and Publishing

COMMON CORE

W 1b Develop claims and counterclaims fairly, supplying evidence for each. **W 5** Strengthen writing by editing. **L 2a** Use semicolons to link independent clauses.

In the editing stage, you proofread your essay to make sure it is free of grammar, spelling, and punctuation errors. You don't want mistakes to distract your readers while they read your critical review or to prevent them from accepting the validity of your argument.

> **GRAMMAR IN CONTEXT: SEMICOLONS AND CONJUNCTIVE ADVERBS**
>
> **Conjunctive adverbs** act as transitions between complete ideas, indicating the logical connections between them. Common conjunctive adverbs include *consequently, however, nevertheless,* and *furthermore.* A **semicolon** shows the close relationship between two independent clauses. In general, place a semicolon before the conjunctive adverb and then a comma after the conjunctive adverb.
>
> When Rupert proofread his critical review, he noticed he could make it more coherent by using semicolons and conjunctive adverbs. For example:
>
> Those criticisms aside, the adaptation boasts a realistic set design, compelling camera shots, and a powerful performance. ~~Most~~ viewers will be riveted by the film.
> ; consequently, most

PUBLISH YOUR WRITING

Share your critical review with an audience.

- Make copies of your writing and distribute them to your classmates.
- Participate in an informal discussion in which you and a small group debate how effectively the scene in the adaptation does justice to Shakespeare's play.
- Post your review on a blog and invite other classmates to post their viewpoints. Elicit others' opinions on the adaptation and your claim.

 YOUR TURN Correct any errors in your review by carefully proofreading it. Also look for places where you might strengthen the connections among your ideas by inserting semicolons and conjunctive adverbs. Then publish your final product where it is likely to reach your intended audience.

FOR STRUGGLING WRITERS

Semicolons and Conjunctive Adverbs Review with students that semicolons and conjunctive adverbs help to connect two independent clauses. Have students practice linking together the following sentences:

1. I arrived at school early. I had time to set up the auditorium. *(I arrived at school early; therefore, I had time to set up the auditorium.)*

2. Last night, the play started later than usual. The stagehands had to stay later to break down the set. *(Last night, the play started later than usual; consequently, the stagehands had to stay later to break down the set.)*

Editing and Publishing

COMMON CORE **W 1b, W 5, L 2a**

GRAMMAR IN CONTEXT: SEMICOLONS AND CONJUNCTIVE ADVERBS

- Provide practice by displaying the following example on the board or interactive whiteboard and then have students improve it by using semicolons and conjunctive adverbs, as well as by making other changes:

  Julius Caesar was one of the great leaders of the ancient world and someone we should study today. *(**Possible answer:** Julius Caesar was one of the great leaders of the ancient world; therefore, we should study his life today.)*

- Next, have students read their final drafts and identify areas where they need to connect ideas better.

- Encourage them to work with a partner to link these ideas by adding semicolons and conjunctive adverbs.

PUBLISH YOUR WRITING

Brainstorm with students about additional ways to publish their critical reviews.

 YOUR TURN Allow time for students to proofread their drafts for any grammar, punctuation, or spelling errors. Remind them to use semicolons and conjunctive adverbs correctly.

Scoring Rubric

Explain to students that the best way to understand a scoring rubric is to use it to evaluate an actual piece of writing. Provide students with copies of a sample critical review from the state assessment Web site. Ask students to score the critical review, then write a brief paragraph using the language of the rubric to explain the reasons for their score.

For Rubric Bank, see

WriteSmart CD-ROM

Writing Center on thinkcentral.com

Assess and Reteach

Assess

R RESOURCE MANAGER—Copy Master
Rubric for Evaluation, p. 124

Online Essay Scoring at thinkcentral.com

Reteach

Level Up Online Tutorials at thinkcentral.com

Scoring Rubric

Use the rubric below to evaluate your critical review from the Writing Workshop or your response to the on-demand writing task on the next page.

CRITICAL REVIEW

SCORE	COMMON CORE TRAITS
 **6**	• **Development** Effectively presents a precise claim; supports the claim with valid reasons and relevant, sufficient evidence; ably counters opposing claims with counterclaims; has a powerful concluding section • **Organization** Arranges reasons and evidence persuasively; effectively uses transitions to create cohesion and show relationships among the claim, reasons, and evidence • **Language** Consistently maintains a formal style and objective tone; shows a strong command of conventions
 **5**	• **Development** Presents a precise claim; supports the claim with clear reasons and relevant evidence; counters opposing claims with counterclaims; has a strong concluding section • **Organization** Logically organizes reasons and evidence; uses transitions to show the relationships among the claim, reasons, and evidence • **Language** Maintains a formal style and objective tone; has a few errors in conventions
 **4**	• **Development** States a claim; offers mostly valid reasons and evidence; needs to more thoroughly address opposing claims; has an adequate concluding section • **Organization** Arranges the reason and evidence logically with some exceptions; needs more transitions • **Language** Mostly maintains a formal style and tone; includes a few distracting errors in conventions
 **3**	• **Development** States a claim that could be more precise; provides some relevant support but not enough to be sufficient; unfairly dismisses other viewpoints; has a concluding section that repeats ideas • **Organization** Arranges reasons and evidence in a somewhat confusing way; needs more transitions to show how ideas are linked • **Language** Often lapses into an informal style or inappropriate tone; has several errors in conventions
 **2**	• **Development** Has a weak claim; offers some unclear reasons and needs more evidence; fails to acknowledge other viewpoints; has a weak concluding section • **Organization** Arranges reasons and evidence in a confusing way; uses few transitions • **Language** Uses an informal style and inappropriate tone; has many errors in conventions
1	• **Development** Lacks a claim; has no support; ignores opposing claims; ends abruptly • **Organization** Has no organization and transitions • **Language** Uses an inappropriate style and tone; has major problems with grammar, mechanics, and spelling

Preparing for Timed Writing

COMMON CORE

W 10 Write routinely over shorter time frames for a range of tasks, purposes, and audiences.

1. ANALYZE THE TASK 5 MIN

Read the task carefully. Then read it again, underlining words that tell the topic, the audience, and the purpose. Circle the type of writing you are being asked to do.

> **WRITING TASK**
>
> *Audience* ⟶
> Your school drama club newsletter wants you to write about a movie you've seen recently *Topic* ⟶
> that has been adapted from a play. Write a ⟨critical review⟩ in which you evaluate whether
> the movie adaptation does justice to the original play. ⟶ *Type of Writing*
> ↳ *Purpose*

2. PLAN YOUR RESPONSE 10 MIN

First, jot down titles of movies you have seen recently that are based on a play. After choosing one, identify the ways in which the movie is similar to or different from the original work. Consider how the director presents the characters and key scenes. Note other aspects of the film that you do or do not like. Then use what you have listed to assert your claim and major reasons. Support each reason with evidence. Also identify an opposing claim and plan a response to it.

Claim:	
Reason 1:	Evidence:
Reason 2:	Evidence:
Possible Opposing Claim: My Counterclaim:	

3. RESPOND TO THE TASK 20 MIN

As you write your review, keep these guidelines in mind:
- In the introduction, capture your audience's interest, provide sufficient background information about the film, and precisely state your claim.
- In each body paragraph, provide a reason and the evidence that clearly supports it.
- Acknowledge an opposing claim and present an effective counterclaim in response.
- Conclude by restating your claim and sharing an insightful observation.

4. IMPROVE YOUR RESPONSE 5–10 MIN

Revising Review your draft, checking it against the writing task. Do you state a precise claim? Do you include enough convincing support? Do you acknowledge and respond to at least one opposing claim?

Proofreading Neatly correct any errors in grammar, spelling, and mechanics.

Checking Your Final Copy Before you turn in your critical review, read it once more to catch any errors you may have missed and to apply any finishing touches.

COMMON CORE FOCUS

W 10 Write routinely over shorter time frames for a range of tasks, purposes, and audiences.

Preparing for Timed Writing

1. **Analyze the Task** Before students begin writing, encourage them to answer the following questions:
   - What is my time limit?
   - What are the key skills assessed in the scoring rubric?
   - Who is my audience?
   - What is my purpose?

2. **Plan Your Response** Remind students that the critical review rubric emphasizes supporting a claim with reasons and evidence. Tell students that they should state their claim in their introduction and that every detail in their critical review should support their claim.

3. **Respond to the Task** Tell students that the rubric stresses the importance of addressing counterclaims. Tell them that within the body of their critical review, they should include a possible opposing claim and a claim addressing that concern.

4. **Improve Your Response** Point out that the scoring rubric emphasizes the use of transitions to create cohesion and show relationships among the claim, reasons, and evidence. Encourage students to check that they have included transitional words and phrases that show the organization of their critical review and link their ideas logically.

Assess

Use the scoring rubric on p. 1306 to assess students' critical reviews.

DIFFERENTIATED INSTRUCTION

FOR ENGLISH LANGUAGE LEARNERS

Writing: Plan a Response Have students write their claims in the center of a word web. Help them identify three reasons that support their claims and record them in the web. Remind students that each reason needs to be supported with evidence, such as a quotation, description, technique, or detail. Have students identify evidence for each of their reasons before writing their critical reviews.

FOR STRUGGLING WRITERS

Organize Ideas Have students use the following outline to record details they will include in the body of their critical reviews.

Body
- Reason 1: _____
- Evidence: _____
- Reason 2: _____
- Evidence: _____
- Opposing Claim: _____
- Counterclaim: _____

Focus and Motivate

COMMON CORE FOCUS

SL 1a–d Participate in discussions; come prepared; work with peers to set rules; respond to questions; respond to diverse perspectives. **SL 3** Evaluate a speaker's point of view, reasoning, and use of evidence and rhetoric. **SL 4** Present information clearly.

SPEAK WITH A PURPOSE

Tell students that they will be using the scene they evaluated in the critical review to participate in a debate. Students should be prepared to defend their claims to their peers and offer counterclaims.

COMMON CORE TRAITS

As students plan their debates, remind them to keep in mind the *COMMON CORE TRAITS* of a strong debate.

Practice and Apply

Planning the Debate

Model the Skill: PREPARE DEBATE NOTES

Students may struggle to determine how to adapt their critical reviews for the debate. If students are asked to support a position that is similar to what they wrote in their critical review, show them how to expand on the arguments and evidence listed in their essay. If they are on the opposite side of the issue from their critical review, help them brainstorm new reasons and gather evidence to support their claim.

GUIDED PRACTICE Have small groups of students discuss helpful ways to prepare notes for their debate. Ask students to share their ideas and make a class list.

R RESOURCE MANAGER—Copy Master
Speaking and Listening p. 125

Speaking & Listening Workshop

Participating in a Critics' Debate

Have you ever disagreed with your friends about the merits of a popular form of entertainment? If so, you have probably engaged in an informal debate—in which two or more people evaluate other speakers' evidence and the validity of their claims.

Essential Course of Study ECOS

📖 Complete the workshop activities in your **Reader/Writer Notebook**.

SPEAK WITH A PURPOSE	COMMON CORE TRAITS
TASK Actively **participate in a critics' debate**. Evaluate and respond to other speakers' reviews of a scene from an adaptation of a Shakespearean play.	**PARTICIPANTS IN AN EFFECTIVE DEBATE . . .** • present precise claims, supported by reasons and evidence • respond thoughtfully to diverse perspectives and justify their own views • analyze each speaker's reasoning, evidence, and **rhetoric**, or persuasive language

COMMON CORE

SL 1a–d Participate in discussions; come prepared; work with peers to set rules; respond to questions; respond to diverse perspectives.
SL 3 Evaluate a speaker's point of view, reasoning, and use of evidence and rhetoric.
SL 4 Present information clearly.

Planning the Debate

Follow these suggestions for planning your debate:

- **Identify Debate Teams** Form groups of six members based on the issue you want to debate. Consider using topics from students' critical reviews of an adaptation of *Julius Caesar*. Three members will form one team and argue for the affirmative side of the issue. The other three members will argue for the negative side of the issue. For example:

  Affirmative: *Yes, the funeral oration scene in the 1970 film* Julius Caesar *is a successful adaptation of Shakespeare's original text.*

  Negative: *No, the funeral oration scene in the 1970 film version of* Julius Caesar *does not measure up to Shakespeare's original text.*

- **Prepare Debate Notes** Outline your claim, reasons, and supporting evidence. Refer to these notes during your debate. Be sure to anticipate possible opposing claims and compile evidence to counter those claims.

- **Appoint a Moderator** The moderator will present the topic and goals of the debate, keep track of the time, and begin and end the debate.

- **Assign Debate Roles** One member will introduce the first team's claim and support. The other team members will respond to questions and opposing claims in an exchange with members of the opposing team. Determine what your group hopes to accomplish as a result of this debate. For example, will you reach a consensus on whether or not the scene is effective?

Speaking & Listening Online

Go to **thinkcentral.com**.
KEYWORD: HML10N-1308

DIFFERENTIATED INSTRUCTION

FOR ENGLISH LANGUAGE LEARNERS

Language: Reinforce Debate Terms Review with students the following terms used in the Workshop:

- *formal:* following standard rules; not casual or sloppy

- *team:* in a debate, a group of people who support the same claim; an *opposing team* argues against the claim

- *affirmative:* in favor of; describes the team that says "yes" to a claim

- *negative:* against; describes the team that says "no" to a claim

- *moderator:* in a debate, a person who does not belong to a team but who tells team members when they can speak and when they are out of time

- *closing argument:* a concluding statement that summarizes a team's claim

Holding the Debate

When you debate literary topics, you have the opportunity to share your insights, as well as hear others' interpretations. Use the tips on this page to present your viewpoints effectively and to evaluate other speakers' claims.

PRESENTING AND EVALUATING CLAIMS

Whether you are presenting information or evaluating what you hear, keep the following in mind:

Speaker	Role	Time
Affirmative Speaker 1	Use direct language to present the claim and supporting evidence for the "pro" side of the argument. Avoid words such as *possibly* or *maybe*, which make a speaker appear less confident.	5 minutes
Negative Speaker 1	Ask probing questions that will prompt the other team to address flaws in their argument.	3 minutes
Affirmative Speaker 2	Listen closely while the other team responds. Answer the questions posed by the opposing team and counter opposing views, but also ask yourself: In what way, if any, do other perspectives change or modify my viewpoint?	3 minutes
Negative Speaker 2	Present the claim and evidence for the "con" side of the argument. Think about whether the other team's reasons lack validity.	5 minutes
Affirmative Speaker 3	Summarize the claim and evidence for the affirmative side, and explain why your reasoning is more valid. Make sure that listeners can follow your line of reasoning.	3 minutes
Negative Speaker 3	Summarize the claim and evidence for the negative side of the argument and explain why your reasoning is more valid.	3 minutes

As a Speaker Do a self-evaluation of your planned opening speech before delivering it, referring to the ideas on these pages. Make sure to use formal English appropriate for a structured debate.

As a Listener Evaluate each speaker's, claim, reasons, and evidence. Jot down notes, identifying points of disagreement. Also note any **fallacious**, or flawed, reasoning, and any exaggerated evidence.

1309

Holding the Debate

Model the Skill: **PRESENTING AND EVALUATING CLAIMS**

Students may struggle with presenting their claims and reasons in an organized and logical manner. Remind students to use their debate notes. If additional ideas and questions occur to them during the debate, students should jot them down.

GUIDED PRACTICE Work with students before the debate to organize their notes.

After the debate, have students evaluate their roles as speakers and listeners. Students should ask themselves: As a speaker, how well did I answer questions and address comments? As a listener, how well did I offer opposing claims? Have students suggest ways they can improve their performance in future debates.

Assess and Reteach

Assess

Use the *COMMON CORE TRAITS* to assess students' debates.

A strong debate
- demonstrates productive teamwork
- presents claims, reasons, and evidence
- responds to diverse perspectives
- is delivered in clear, persuasive speech using standard formal English
- includes an evaluation of other speakers' arguments

Reteach

Explain that during a debate, two sides argue opposing views on an issue. For a debate to be lively and informative, each team needs to supply valid reasons and evidence in support of their claim.

FOR ENGLISH LANGUAGE LEARNERS
Language: Prepare Notes To help students prepare for the debate, emphasize the importance of having good notes. Have them use index cards to write several prepared statements they can use when it is their turn to speak. Warn them that they may also need to improvise, or "think on their feet" during the debate.

FOR STRUGGLING STUDENTS
Politely Challenge Others Explain that when a listener challenges a speaker's reasons, it keeps a debate lively and thought provoking. Both the speaker and listener may learn something new from this exchange. Have pairs work together to challenge each other's claims and reasons politely and with respect. Suggest that they use the following format: *While I agree that _____, I think _____.*

Speaking and Listening Online THINK central
- Public speaking tips
- Strategies for effective listening

Assessment Practice

○ COMMON CORE FOCUS

RL1 Cite textual evidence to support analysis of what the text says explicitly as well as inferences drawn from the text. **RL3** Analyze how complex characters interact with others and advance the plot or develop the theme. **RL4** Determine the meanings of words and phrases as they are used in a text. **W5** Strengthen writing by revising and editing.

CHECK READINESS

Read aloud the paragraph under **ASSESS** and stress to students that this is not the full Unit Test, but a way for them to check their readiness for it. Then have students examine the skills standards listed under **REVIEW** and look back in the unit or in the **Student Resource Bank** for any skills they need to review.

READ THE TEXT

Remind students to keep unit goals in mind as they read the passage, paying particular attention to these literary and reading skills:

- characteristics of tragedy
- soliloquy
- blank verse

To help students focus on soliloquy, encourage them to ask questions such as

- How can I tell that this passage is a soliloquy, not a dialogue?
- Who is the speaker? What is the main idea of his or her words?

ANSWER THE QUESTIONS

Direct students to page R93–R101 of the **Handbook** to review test-taking strategies.

- Remind students to read through all the answer choices, eliminate any that are clearly wrong, and then choose the *best* answer—the one that is the most accurate.

- Remind students to take a little time to plan their written responses before writing them. Students can use simple prewriting strategies such as making a concept web.

COMMON CORE

Assessment Practice

ASSESS
Taking this practice test will help you assess your knowledge of these skills and determine your readiness for the Unit Test.

REVIEW
After you take the practice test, your teacher can help you identify any standards you need to review.

○ **COMMON CORE**

RL1 Cite textual evidence to support analysis of what the text says explicitly as well as inferences drawn from the text. **RL3** Analyze how complex characters interact with others and advance the plot or develop the theme. **RL4** Determine the meanings of words and phrases as they are used in a text. **W5** Strengthen writing by revising and editing.

DIRECTIONS Read the following selection, and then answer the questions.

from The Tragedy of Julius Caesar
by William Shakespeare

Lucius. Sir, March is wasted fifteen days.

[*Knocking within.*]

60 **Brutus.** 'Tis good. Go to the gate, somebody knocks.

[*Exit* Lucius.]

Since Cassius first did whet me against Caesar,
I have not slept.
Between the acting of a dreadful thing
And the first motion, all the interim is
65 Like a phantasma or a hideous dream.
The genius and the mortal instruments
Are then in council, and the state of man,
Like to a little kingdom, suffers then
The nature of an insurrection.

[*Reenter* Lucius.]

70 **Lucius.** Sir, 'tis your brother Cassius at the door,
Who doth desire to see you.

Brutus.   Is he alone?

Lucius. No, sir, there are more with him.

Brutus.   Do you know them?

Lucius. No, sir. Their hats are plucked about their ears
And half their faces buried in their cloaks,
75 That by no means I may discover them
By any mark of favor.

Brutus.   Let 'em enter.

[*Exit* Lucius.]

They are the faction. O conspiracy,
Sham'st thou to show thy dang'rous brow by night,
When evils are most free? O, then by day

Practice Test — THINK central
Take it at **thinkcentral.com**.
KEYWORD: HML10-1310

DIFFERENTIATED INSTRUCTION

FOR ENGLISH LANGUAGE LEARNERS
Assessment Practice: Work Backward
Prepare students by having them read the questions *before* reading the passage. Have pairs find unfamiliar words in test directions and questions and follow these steps:

1. Write each word on an index card.
2. Look up the meaning in a dictionary and write it on the back of the card.

3. Use the cards to practice the words with your partner and to teach them to others.

80 Where wilt thou find a cavern dark enough
To mask thy monstrous visage? Seek none,
conspiracy, hide it in smiles and affability!
For if thou path, thy native semblance on,
No Erebus itself were dim enough
85 To hide thee from prevention.

[*Enter the conspirators,* Cassius, Casca, Decius, Cinna, Metellus
Cimber, *and* Trebonius.]

Cassius. I think we are too bold upon your rest.
Good morrow, Brutus. Do we trouble you?

Brutus. I have been up this hour, awake all night.
Know I these men that come along with you?

90 **Cassius.** Yes, every man of them; and no man here
But honors you; and every one doth wish
You had but that opinion of yourself
Which every noble Roman bears of you.
This is Trebonius.

Brutus.   He is welcome hither.

95 **Cassius.** This, Decius Brutus.

Brutus.   He is welcome too.

Cassius. This, Casca; this, Cinna; and this, Metellus Cimber.

Brutus. They are all welcome.
What watchful cares do interpose themselves
Betwixt your eyes and night?

100 **Cassius.** Shall I entreat a word?

[*They whisper.*]

Decius. Here lies the east. Doth not the day break here?

Casca. No.

Cinna. O, pardon, sir, it doth; and yon grey lines
That fret the clouds are messengers of day.

105 **Casca.** You shall confess that you are both deceived.
Here, as I point my sword, the sun arises,
Which is a great way growing on the south,
Weighing the youthful season of the year.

GO ON →

ITEM ANALYSIS

COMPREHENSION AND WRITTEN RESPONSE	ITEMS	UNIT PAGES
Characteristics of Tragedy		
Conflict	2, 11, 15	1190–1197
Character	1, 3, 6, 8, 12, 13	1190–1197
Plot	7, 9, 14, 16	1190–1197
Soliloquy	1, 2, 5	1190–1197
Blank Verse	4, 10	1190–1197

WRITING AND GRAMMAR	ITEMS	UNIT PAGES
Adjective Clauses	1	1289
Sentence Structure	2, 3, 4, 5	

Practice Test

On **thinkcentral.com** students can complete
an interactive version of this practice test
and receive remediation for the skills they
have not yet mastered.

FOR STRUGGLING READERS

Assessment Support Consider these options
for completing the Assessment Practice:

- Have students "work backward" to review the
test questions before reading the passage.

- Select random questions in the Assessment
and have students demonstrate *how* and
where to look for the answers.

- Ask students to locate unfamiliar vocabulary words in the Assessment. Elicit the
words' meanings from the class.

- Have students record useful testing words
and definitions in their journal for later
reference.

- Read the selection or parts of it aloud to aid
in student comprehension.

Reading Comprehension

Model a thinking process for answering multiple-choice questions.

1. **B is correct.** *Brutus gives the cause when he says, "Since Cassius first did whet me against Caesar,/I have not slept" (lines 61–62). A is incorrect because Brutus does not say that phantoms appear in his dreams. C is incorrect because the reference to a battle (line 69) is implied and is not literal. D is incorrect because the soliloquy refers to thoughts before a dreadful action.*

2. **A is correct.** *This thought is expressed in "...the state of man,/...suffers then/The nature of an insurrection" (lines 67–69). B, C, and D are incorrect because Brutus compares an uprising in a kingdom only to his internal conflict.*

3. **C is correct.** *Brutus calls the planned assassination "a dreadful thing" (line 63) and speaks of the conspiracy's "monstrous visage" (line 81). A is incorrect because Brutus is not looking forward to what is to come. B is incorrect because Brutus' character wavers during the scene. D is incorrect because although Brutus is troubled, he does seem mentally sound.*

4. **A is correct.** *Blank verse is unrhymed iambic pentameter. B, C, and D can be eliminated because they are not required to have iambic pentameter; if they sometimes are written in iambic pentameter, it is purely by the writer's choice.*

5. **D is correct.** *Brutus voices that opinion when he says, "Hide it in smiles and affability!" (line 82). A is incorrect because Brutus does not say that the conspirators lack courage. B states the opposite of D and therefore is incorrect. C may seem reasonable because Brutus implies that the conspirators have evil thoughts, but it is incorrect because he does not say that such thoughts consume them.*

Some two months hence, up higher toward the north
110 He first presents his fire; and the high east
Stands as the Capitol, directly here.

[Brutus *and* Cassius *rejoin the others.*]

Brutus. Give me your hands all over, one by one.

Cassius. And let us swear our resolution.

Brutus. No, not on oath. If not the face of men,
115 The sufferance of our souls, the time's abuse—
If these be motives weak, break off betimes,
And every man hence to his idle bed.
So let high-sighted tyranny range on
Till each man drop by lottery. But if these
120 (As I am sure they do) bear fire enough
To kindle cowards and to steel with valor
The melting spirits of women, then, countrymen,
What need we any spur but our own cause
To prick us to redress? what other bond
125 Than secret Romans that have spoke the word
And will not palter? and what other oath
Than honesty to honesty engaged
That this shall be, or we will fall for it?
Swear priests and cowards and men cautelous,
130 Old feeble carrions and such suffering souls
That welcome wrongs; unto bad causes swear
Such creatures as men doubt; but do not stain
The even virtue of our enterprise,
Nor the insuppressive mettle of our spirits,
135 To think that or our cause or our performance
Did need an oath when every drop of blood
That every Roman bears, and nobly bears,
Is guilty of a several bastardy
If he do break the smallest particle
140 Of any promise that hath passed from him.

1312

Reading Comprehension

Use the excerpt from *The Tragedy of Julius Caesar* (pp. 1310–1312) to answer questions 1–16.

1. In the soliloquy in lines 61–69, Brutus reflects on his sleeplessness and tells the audience that it is caused by —
   A. bad dreams of phantoms
   B. thoughts of going against Caesar
   C. pains suffered in battle
   D. dreadful acts he has witnessed

2. In lines 66–69 of his soliloquy, Brutus compares an uprising in a kingdom to —
   A. his internal conflict
   B. a conflict between rulers
   C. Caesar's internal conflict
   D. battlefield conflicts

3. Brutus's sleeplessness is a sign of —
   A. enthusiasm for what is to come
   B. strength of character
   C. feelings of guilt
   D. mental instability

4. This excerpt is written mostly in iambic pentameter, a meter that is used primarily in —
   A. blank verse
   B. dialogue
   C. prose
   D. regular speech

5. In his soliloquy in lines 77–85, Brutus reveals his opinion that the conspirators —
   A. lack the courage to murder Caesar
   B. should reveal their true feelings about the conspiracy
   C. are consumed with evil thoughts
   D. must disguise their plot

6. In which statement does Brutus reveal his willingness to engage in trickery?
   A. *Hide it in smiles and affability!*
   B. *Give me your hands all over, one by one.*
   C. *So let high-sighted tyranny range on / Till each man drop by lottery.*
   D. *What other bond / Than secret Romans that have spoke the word*

7. Cassius and the conspirators visit Brutus before the sun has risen because —
   A. it is the only time of day they can all agree to meet
   B. they are afraid of being detected as they conspire
   C. they are kept awake by their concern for Rome's citizens
   D. they must set off early so that they can return by nightfall

8. Which motive is most likely behind Cassius's comment to Brutus in lines 91–93 that
   "*. . . every one doth wish / You had but that opinion of yourself / Which every noble Roman bears of you*"?
   A. He wants to encourage Brutus to be more confident in his leadership abilities.
   B. He knows that Caesar respects Brutus more than any other Roman citizen.
   C. He hopes to flatter Brutus so that he will join the conspiracy.
   D. He thinks Brutus does not know that most Romans admire him.

GO ON

1313

6. **A is correct.** The quoted line welcomes trickery. B and C can be eliminated because they imply honorable unity. D can be eliminated because although the comment mentions secrecy, secrecy does not necessarily mean trickery.

7. **B is correct.** Lines 73–81 speak of the conspirators' fear of being discovered. There is no evidence for A or C, and D is incorrect because night already has fallen.

8. **C is correct.** Brutus has just told Cassius, "I have been . . . awake all night" (line 88), implying his uncertainty about the cause, so the canny Cassius responds with compliments. A is incorrect because Cassius does not address this idea and because at this point, Cassius is leading the conspiracy. There is no evidence for B. D may seem possible, but Cassius does not address this idea.

9. **D is correct.** The three characters speak of the direction of sunrise, a trivial concern. A and B are incorrect because their conversation has nothing to do with the conspiracy or their oath. C is incorrect because the characters are not speaking about Cassius or Brutus.

10. **B is correct.** An iambic foot has no other definition. A and C are untrue (and C describes trochaic meter). D is incorrect because rhyme is irrelevant to a definition of meter.

DIFFERENTIATED INSTRUCTION

FOR ENGLISH LANGUAGE LEARNERS
Assessment Vocabulary To help students understand the Reading Comprehension questions, teach or review these key vocabulary words:

- Item 1: *reflects*—"thinks seriously about"
- Item 5: *reveals*—"shows"
- Item 6: *engage*—"to participate"
- Item 8: *motive*—"reason for doing something"
- Item 13: *oath*—"promise," "vow"
- Item 13: *allegiance*—"loyalty"
- Item 16: *further*—"to help make something happen"
- Item 16: *Support*—"to give evidence for"

11. A *is correct.* *In line 113, Cassius says, "And let us swear our resolution," and in line 114, Brutus replies, "No, not on oath." B is wrog because there is no disagreement about proceeding with the plan. C is incorrect because there is no discussion of dying for the cause. D is wrong because the mention of women (line 122) does not imply involving them in the conspiracy.*

12. B *is correct.* *The statement "[D]o not stain/ The even virtue of our enterprise,/Nor the insuppressive mettle of our spirits" (lines 132–134) reveals Brutus' nobility. A is incorrect because cowardice is the opposite of the tone of the speech. C is incorrect because Brutus does not exhibit rashness in this speech. D is incorrect because Brutus wants to depose a tyrant, not to become one.*

13. B *is correct.* *In lines 132–140, Brutus claims that a noble Roman's promise is so trustworthy that it does not require an oath. A is incorrect because Brutus has been portrayed as honorable. Brutus says nothing that would apply C or D to himself.*

SHORT CONSTRUCTED RESPONSE

Possible responses:

14. *He is a man of great personal integrity and moral conscience.*

15. *Internal conflict: Brutus struggles with his conscience about his right to murder Caesar (lines 61–69). External conflict: Brutus clashes with Cassius over whether to swear an oath of allegiance (lines 112–117).*

16. *1. Cassius brings the conspirators to Brutus' house in the early morning. 2. Brutus joins the conspirators. 3. Cassius asks them all to swear an oath of allegiance. 4. Brutus refuses to swear an oath.*

This series of actions furthers the plot by setting the stage for Caesar's assassination. Brutus' joining of the group strengthens the conspirators' resolve, and his refusal to swear an oath reaffirms their integrity. The conspirators can move forward with their plans because they see themselves as men of honor, acting for the good of Rome.

---

9. Decius, Casca, and Cinna argue in lines 101–111 —
   A. to define their roles in the conspiracy
   B. because they want to justify swearing an oath
   C. because they do not trust Cassius or Brutus
   D. to pass the time while Cassius and Brutus speak privately

10. The rhythm of iambic pentameter in line 116 comes from a pattern of —
    A. two stressed syllables followed by an unstressed syllable
    B. an unstressed syllable followed by a stressed syllable
    C. a stressed syllable followed by an unstressed syllable
    D. two rhyming words within the line

11. In lines 112–128, Brutus and Cassius disagree about whether they should —
    A. swear allegiance to one another
    B. proceed with their plans for assassination
    C. be willing to die for their cause
    D. involve women in the conspiracy

12. Which character trait does Brutus reveal in his speech in lines 114–140?
    A. Cowardice
    B. Nobility
    C. Rashness
    D. Tyranny

13. Brutus believes that swearing an oath of allegiance is unnecessary because he has —
    A. ulterior motives
    B. personal integrity
    C. powerful friends
    D. Roman ancestors

SHORT CONSTRUCTED RESPONSE
Write three or four sentences to answer each question.

14. What is ironic about someone of Brutus's character taking part in a conspiracy?

15. Identify one internal and one external conflict faced by Brutus in this excerpt. Provide a short quotation from the excerpt that illustrates each conflict.

Write two to three paragraphs to answer this question.

16. List the main actions of Cassius and Brutus in this excerpt. Explain how their actions further the plot. Support your explanation with details from the excerpt.

DIFFERENTIATED INSTRUCTION

FOR ENGLISH LANGUAGE LEARNERS
Review Literary Terms On the board, list the Literary terms shown in italics. Then give the examples in random order and have students classify them. Elicit additional examples or elaboration from students.

- *Shakespearean tragedy:* In *The Tragedy of Julius Caesar,* Shakespeare tells the story of honorable people who bring destruction upon themselves.

- *tragic hero:* Brutus' pride in his sense of public duty gets him entangled in violence.

- *soliloquy:* In lines 61–69 of this excerpt, Brutus muses aloud to himself about his troubled thoughts.

- *blank verse:* "No, not on oath. If not the face of men,/The sufferance of our souls, the time's abuse—/If these be motives weak, break off betimes,/And every man hence to his idle bed" (lines 114–117).

Revising and Editing

DIRECTIONS Read this passage, and answer the questions that follow.

(1) The word *ides* was a calendar term used during the time of Caesar. (2) The term which dates back to the earliest Roman calendar. (3) The ides fell on the fifteenth day in March, May, July, and October and on the thirteenth day in the other months. (4) The ides' significance grown following the death of Caesar. (5) The ides of March was viewed as a day of foreboding and gloom.

1. What is the most effective way to add descriptive details to sentence 1 using an adjective clause?

A. In ancient Rome, people used the word *ides* as a calendar term.

B. The word *ides* was a calendar term used during the time of Caesar, a Roman general and politician.

C. The word *ides* was a calendar term used in ancient Rome; it means "to divide."

D. The word *ides*, which means "to divide," was a calendar term used during the time of Caesar.

2. What change, if any, should be made in sentence 2?

A. Change *dates* to **date**

B. Insert a comma after *term*

C. Delete *which*

D. Make no change

3. What change, if any, should be made in sentence 4?

A. Change *grown* to **grew**

B. Delete the apostrophe

C. Change *significance* to **significant**

D. Make no change

4. Which transitional word or phrase should be added to the beginning of sentence 5?

A. After all,

B. From then on,

C. Otherwise,

D. Similarly,

5. Where is the best place for the writer to add the following sentence?

The Romans once celebrated the ides of March with a military parade to honor Mars, the god of war.

A. At the beginning of the paragraph

B. After sentence 1

C. After sentence 2

D. After sentence 3

STOP

1315

RL 10 Read and comprehend literature. **RI 10** Read and comprehend literary nonfiction.

INTRODUCE *GREAT READS*

In Unit 11, students read *The Tragedy of Julius Caesar,* an important work by William Shakespeare. Discuss the recommended books and their summaries. Point out to students that some selections will introduce them to additional examples of Shakespeare's work, while other selections can help them learn more about Julius Caesar. Encourage students to choose one or more of these "great reads" to read independently.

UNIT 11
Great Reads

Ideas for Independent Reading

Satisfy your curiosity about the real Julius Caesar and other topics related to Shakespeare's play by reading the following works.

COMMON CORE

RL 10 Read and comprehend literature. **RI 10** Read and comprehend literary nonfiction.

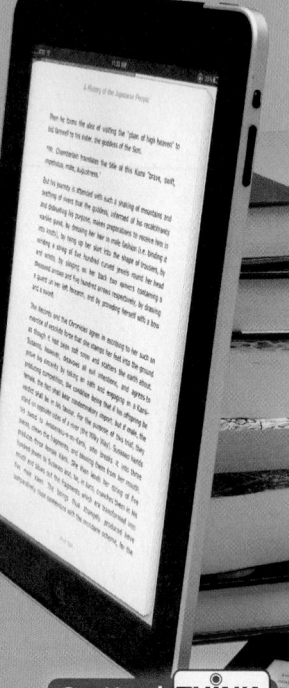

Antony and Cleopatra
by William Shakespeare

This is another tragedy based on historical events in ancient Rome. After Julius Caesar's assassination, Mark Antony, Octavius Caesar, and Lepidus jointly rule the Roman Empire. Antony has fallen in love with Julius Caesar's former mistress, Cleopatra, the queen of Egypt. He lives with her in Alexandria, neglecting his duties in Rome. Gradually, the ruling alliance falls apart, and Antony finds himself at war with Octavius Caesar. Has Antony's love for Cleopatra ruined him as a military leader?

Hamlet
by William Shakespeare

Like Brutus in Julius Caesar, the main character in this play also considers murdering his country's ruler. One night Hamlet, the prince of Denmark, is visited by the ghost of his father. The ghost claims that he has been murdered by Hamlet's uncle Claudius, who now is king and is married to Hamlet's mother. Should Hamlet trust the vision he has seen and kill the king in revenge? The decision undoes him, until he thinks of a clever plan to test his uncle's guilt. Hamlet finds out what he wants to know, but it is not the end of his troubles.

Plutarch's Lives, Vol. II
by Plutarch

The ancient Roman historian Plutarch wrote many biographies of famous Greeks and Romans, including Julius Caesar, Brutus, and Mark Antony. Shakespeare used an English translation of *Plutarch's Lives* as his source for the historical events in *Julius Caesar* and *Antony and Cleopatra.* Read the life stories of Caesar and Brutus in this volume to see how faithful Shakespeare was to his source.

The Ides of March
by Thornton Wilder

Author Thornton Wilder, who also wrote the play *Our Town,* describes this work as "a fantasia on certain events and persons in the last days of the Roman Republic." It is an epistolary novel, composed entirely of fictional letters, journal entries, and other documents relating to the reign and assassination of Julius Caesar. Wilder imagines an idealistic Caesar who knew of the plot against him and hoped he would be killed by someone interested only in the welfare of Rome.

The October Horse
by Colleen McCullough

This is the sixth and final volume in McCullough's acclaimed Masters of Rome series. As it opens, Julius Caesar is the busy ruler of Rome, wondering how he can ever get anything done if all his actions must be favorably foretold. The novel goes on to describe his romance with the Egyptian queen Cleopatra and the plots against him by his enemies, who, surprisingly, include Mark Antony. The story builds to Caesar's assassination and its aftermath.

Assassinations: History's Most Shocking Moments of Murder, Betrayal, and Madness
by R. G. Grant

This oversize book contains more than 100 accounts of notorious assassinations and is illustrated with paintings, photographs, diagrams, maps, and timelines. It covers the assassinations of Julius Caesar, Abraham Lincoln, Mahatma Gandhi, and John F. Kennedy. The backgrounds and motives of the assassins are described, and so are the repercussions of the acts.

Get Novel Wise

THINK central

Go to **thinkcentral.com.**
KEYWORD: HML10-1316

NovelWise

THINK central

The keyword on this page points to **NovelWise,** a Web site that helps students choose a novel or other book-length work to read. **NovelWise** also provides
- study guides
- reading strategies and literary elements instruction
- presentations to introduce classic novels
- project ideas

The Power of Research

12

RESEARCH WORKSHOPS

- Research Strategies
- Writing Research Papers

1317

INTRODUCE THE UNIT

This research unit consists of two interactive workshops that guide students through the search for information and the writing process.

The **Research Strategies Workshop,** starting on page 1320, offers strategies for organizing, selecting, and evaluating information to answer academic as well as practical questions. Students learn how to access and navigate Web-based, electronic, audio-visual, and print resources. A wide range of activities gives them opportunities to apply their learning in concrete situations.

The **Writing Workshop,** beginning on page 1342, provides a systematic approach for students to use in writing a research report and helps them apply the strategies they have learned. As students adapt the procedures to their own projects, they master each step through reflection and practice.

For help in planning this unit, see

R RESOURCE MANAGER UNIT 12
pp. 1–10

UNIT 12

COMMON CORE

STRAND

ECOS

Research Strategies Workshop
pp. 1320–1341

Reading Literature	
Reading Informational Text	
Writing	Plan and Focus Research pp. 1321–1322, 1340 W 7, W 8, W 9
	Narrow or Broaden Your Research Inquiry p. 1322 W 7
	Take Notes p. 1322
	Use the Internet to Select and Assess Relevant Sites pp. 1323–1325 W 7, W 8, W 9
	Navigate Relevant Internet Sites pp. 1324, 1325 W 8
	Use Library or Media Center Resources, Including Databases and Online Catalogs pp. 1326–1327, 1330 W 8
	Distinguish Between Primary and Secondary Sources pp. 1328–1329, 1332
	Use Parts of a Book to Locate Information p. 1331
	Choose and Evaluate Information and Sources by Applying Evaluation Criteria pp. 1333– 1337 W 8
	Use Evaluation Criteria to Evaluate a Web Site pp. 1334–1335 W 8
	Use Evaluation Criteria to Evaluate Nonfiction Books, Periodicals, and Newspapers pp. 1336–1337 W 8, W 9
	Collect Original Data for a Report pp. 1338–1339
Speaking and Listening	
Language	

Writing Workshop: Research Paper
pp. 1342–1365

Technology Workshop: Creating a Web Site
pp. 1364–1365

Writing a Research Paper pp. 1342–1365   W 2a-f, W 4, W 5, W 7, W 8, W 9b (RI 1), W 10
Creating a Web Site pp. 1364–1365   W 6

Creating a Web Site pp. 1364–1365   SL 2, SL 4, SL 5

Drafting pp. 1350–1351   L 1, L 3a
Editing and Publishing p. 1360   L 2, L 2b
MLA Citation Guidelines pp. 1362–1363   L 3a

To see the complete
Essential Course
of Study, see
pp. T23–T28.

For additional
lesson planning
help, see **Teacher
One Stop DVD.**

Instructional Support

Resource Manager Unit 12

UNIT SUPPORT
Academic Vocabulary, p. 2
Additional Academic Vocabulary, p. 3
Writing Workshop: Research Paper
   pp. 5–33

SELECTION SUPPORT*
Plan and Teach
Student Copy Masters

   *Available for all selections

   † Available on **thinkcentral.com**.

Language Handbook
Best Practices Toolkit†
PowerNotes DVD-ROM†
Connections: Nonfiction for Common Core CD-ROM†

Teacher One Stop DVD-ROM
Student One Stop DVD-ROM
Write*Smart* CD-ROM†
GrammarNotes DVD-ROM†

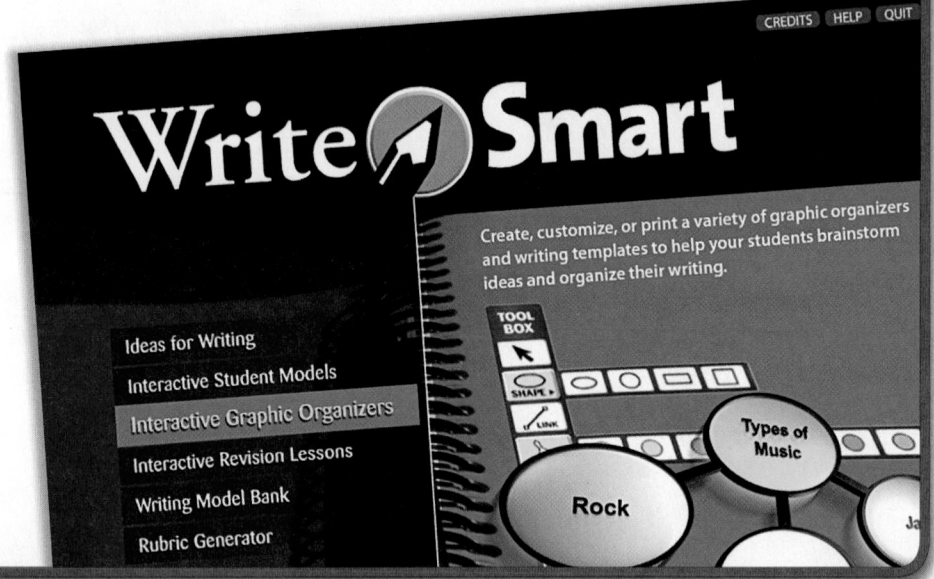

Differentiated Instruction

STRUGGLING READERS AND WRITERS

Level Up Online Tutorials

ENGLISH LANGUAGE LEARNERS

English Language Learner Adapted Interactive Reader Teacher's Guide

Guide to English for Newcomers

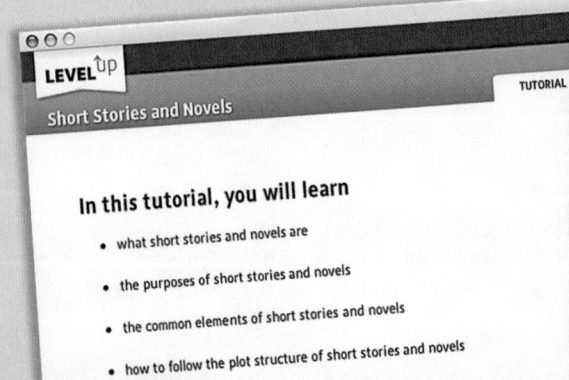

Assessment and Reteaching

Diagnostic and Selection Tests

Unit and Benchmark Tests

ThinkCentral Online Assessment:
- All program assessments
- Level Up Online Tutorials

ExamView Test Generator on the Teacher One Stop DVD-ROM

Online Essay Scoring on thinkcentral.com

ThinkCentral Online Reteaching:
- Level Up Online Tutorials
- Reteaching Worksheets

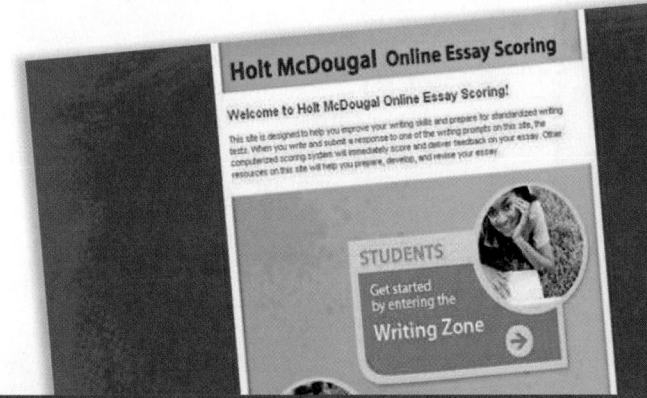

Professional Development

Video Center Based on interviews with program consultants and other educational experts, these videos feature classroom-ready teaching strategies.

Teacher Toolkit Includes a Teacher Handbook as well as a range of articles and handouts by program consultants and other educators.

Janet Allen

Jim Burke

Kylene Beers

Carol Jago

THINK central at a Glance

One Location, Endless Resources

Find Resources Browse all *Holt McDougal Literature* components for the ones that meet your students' needs and match your teaching style.

Assess Progress and Reteach Assign electronic versions of program assessments to measure your students' mastery of the Common Core State Standards. On thinkcentral.com, some tests deliver online remediation tutorials to students who have not mastered skills.

 Interactive Whiteboard Lessons

Prepare your students for college and careers by teaching relevant, real-world skills through dynamic, interactive instruction. Go to **thinkcentral.com** to browse through all whiteboard lessons, including the following:

- Conducting Research on the Web
- Evaluating Sources
- Synthesizing Information
- Writing Informative Texts

 Together Holt McDougal and HISTORY® are revolutionizing the study of English/language arts with video that helps students relive and re-imagine the people, places, and events they are discovering through reading. Look for selections with the HISTORY® icon.

Why do **RESEARCH?**

Read the introductory paragraph, and help students develop a working definition of *research,* such as "a search for information." Stress that finding information is a crucial skill in school and in everyday life.

Conduct a quick survey to determine how many days each week students answer questions or get information from these sources:

- the Internet
- newspapers or magazines
- a library
- television

Create a bar graph reflecting the data, and discuss results with students. Urge students to identify other sources of information that they use regularly.

ACTIVITY To help students formulate additional questions, suggest topics such as public transportation, the environment, family history, and health.

CHECK UNDERSTANDING Have students identify a place they would like to visit, define a question about it, and suggest a source that might help them answer the question.

Why do **RESEARCH?**

When you read the classified ads to find a summer job, gather information to write a research paper, or call the local multiplex to find out what time a certain movie is playing, you are doing research. Answers to your questions are out there. You just need to know how to find them. This unit will point you in the right direction.

ACTIVITY Make a list of questions concerning topics that you have always wanted to know more about. Next to each question, write two or three possible sources of information on the topic. Here are some questions to get you started:

- How can I find out which jobs and careers best match my skills and interests?
- What was my city, town, or neighborhood like a hundred years ago?
- What kind of diet will help a person live to be 100?
- I "freeze up" whenever I take a test. How can I stay relaxed and improve my memory?

Find It Online! **THINK** central

Go to **thinkcentral.com** for the interactive version of this unit.

Unit Resources

See resources on the **Teacher One Stop DVD-ROM** *and on* **thinkcentral.com**.

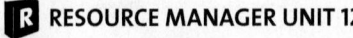 **RESOURCE MANAGER UNIT 12**

BEST PRACTICES TOOLKIT

LANGUAGE HANDBOOK

VOCABULARY WORKSHOP

READER/WRITER NOTEBOOK

TECHNOLOGY

- **Teacher One Stop DVD-ROM**
- **Student One Stop DVD-ROM**
- **Write***Smart* **CD-ROM**
- **GrammarNotes DVD-ROM**

Writing and Research in a Digital Age on **thinkcentral.com**

Find It Online!

The interactive version of this unit on **thinkcentral.com** includes

- **Writing and Research in a Digital Age**
- **Citation Guide**

Preview Unit Goals

DEVELOPING RESEARCH SKILLS
- Plan research
- Use library and media center resources
- Distinguish between primary and secondary sources
- Evaluate information and sources, including nonfiction books, periodicals, and Web sites
- Collect your own data

WRITING
- Write a research paper
- Formulate a major research question
- Develop a plan for conducting research
- Locate sources and assess their usefulness
- Take notes
- Prepare a source list
- Summarize, paraphrase, and quote directly
- Integrate information selectively, avoiding plagiarism
- Document sources correctly, using a standard format for citations
- Format your paper

ACADEMIC VOCABULARY
- authoritative
- compile
- debates
- inquiry
- relevance

MEDIA AND VIEWING
- Create a Web site

Writing and Research in a Digital Age

THINK central
KEYWORD: HML10-1319

When it comes to doing research, you can find a range of technology to help you, from online databases to podcasts and more. Find out how to find the best information the best way.

1319

UNIT GOALS

Included in this unit: **W 2a-f, W 4, W 5, W 6, W 7, W 8, W 9b (RI 1), W 10, L 1, L 2, L 2a, SL 2, SL 4, SL 5, L 2b, L 3a**

Complete text of the Common Core State Standards is found in the correlation on p. T10. Standards covered in this unit are found in the standards overview (pp. 1317A–1317B) and on the lesson pages where they are taught.

Preview Unit Goals

This page provides an overview of the unit research skills and strategies, which differ from those presented in previous units. Remind students that previewing prepares them for understanding and remembering what they read. Have them preview the page by skimming over the list of unit skills. Point out that the skills are grouped according to four color-coded categories that appear throughout the unit: Developing Research Skills; Writing; Listening and Speaking; and Academic Vocabulary.

Model how to generate preliminary definitions for Academic Vocabulary. Suggest that students copy and write in their journals definitions based on their current knowledge. Encourage students to practice using these terms in discussion and writing. Ask them to refine their initial definitions as they work through the unit.

DIFFERENTIATED INSTRUCTION

FOR ENGLISH LANGUAGE LEARNERS

Academic Vocabulary Provide students with definitions of each Academic Vocabulary word.

authoritative (ə-thôr′ĭ-tā′tĭv) *adj.* backed by evidence and showing deep knowledge

compile (kəm-pīl′) *v.* to gather things together to form a whole

debates (dĭ-bātz′) *n.* public discussions involving opposing points

inquiry (ĭn-kwīr′ē) *n.* a close examination in search for information

relevance (rĕl′ə-vənse) *n.* pertaining to a matter at hand; significance

Use the copy master to help students learn academic words they will use in this unit and on the Assessment Practice.

R RESOURCE MANAGER—Copy Masters
Academic Vocabulary p. 2
Additional Academic Vocabulary p. 3

Focus and Motivate

COMMON CORE FOCUS

W 7 Conduct sustained research projects to answer a question or solve a problem; narrow or broaden a research inquiry; synthesize multiple sources on a research subject. **W 8** Gather relevant information from multiple authoritative print and digital sources; use advanced searches effectively; assess the usefulness of each source. **W 9** Draw evidence from informational texts to support research.

Tell students that this unit presents strategies that will help them with all kinds of research, not just research for school assignments. Explain that the unit is divided into two parts:

- the **Research Strategies Workshop,** which includes instruction on selecting and using print and electronic sources as well as activities that will strengthen students' ability to use reference sources and tools.

- the **Writing Workshop,** in which students will apply the strategies to write a research paper.

Where is the
INFORMATION
I need?

Have students read the question. Ask them to identify a product they would like to purchase and to brainstorm ways to find information about quality and prices. For example, they might search the Internet or look in a consumer magazine. Then have students complete the *QUICKWRITE.* After they finish, ask them how career research might be similar to research for a product.

Research Workshop Resources

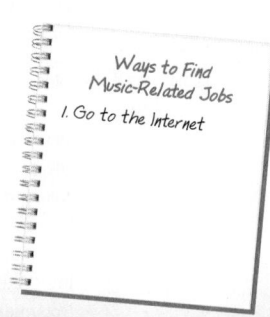

Essential Course of Study ECOS

Where is the
INFORMATION
I need?

COMMON CORE

Included in this workshop:
W 7 Conduct sustained research projects to answer a question or solve a problem; narrow or broaden a research inquiry; synthesize multiple sources on a research subject. **W 8** Gather relevant information from multiple authoritative print and digital sources; use advanced searches effectively; assess the usefulness of each source. **W 9** Draw evidence from informational texts to support research.

Knowing how to find accurate information quickly can help you, whether you are choosing elective classes, researching a purchase, or making plans for your future.

QUICKWRITE Imagine that you have enjoyed playing music by yourself and with friends since you were a child and have started wondering whether a career in music might be right for you. What are some ways to find out what kinds of jobs are available and what qualifications are required? With a group, brainstorm possible answers. Then list places where more information might be available.

Ways to Find Music-Related Jobs
1. Go to the Internet

1320

See resources on the **Teacher One Stop DVD-ROM** and on **thinkcentral.com**.

R RESOURCE MANAGER UNIT 12
Plan and Teach, pp. 6–10

BEST PRACTICES TOOLKIT
Classification Chart, p. B17
Outline, p. B19
Question and Answer Note Taking, p. B7
Three-Column Journal, p. B10
Comparison Matrix, p. A24

T Chart, p. A25
Y Chart, p. A27
Sequence Chain, p. B21
Venn Diagram, p. A26
KWL, p. A21

INTERACTIVE READER

ADAPTED INTERACTIVE READER

ELL ADAPTED INTERACTIVE READER

TECHNOLOGY
- **Teacher One Stop DVD-ROM**
- **Student One Stop DVD-ROM**
- **GrammarNotes DVD-ROM**
- **ExamView Test Generator** on the **Teacher One Stop**

Planning Your Research

It's easy to be overwhelmed by all the information sources out there. How can you refine and focus your search?

Getting Started

To avoid wasting time and getting frustrated, take a few minutes to think about what you want to accomplish.

CLARIFY YOUR GOAL

Putting your ideas on paper can help you clarify your thoughts.

> **GENERAL GOAL:** Find out about jobs that have to do with music.
>
> **WAYS TO ACCOMPLISH IT:**
> - Talk to performers and to people who work behind the scenes. How did they get started? What is a typical day on the job like?
> - Look in the careers section at the library.
> - See what I can find on the Internet.
>
> **SPECIFIC GOAL:** I want to do research and conduct interviews to find out about entry-level jobs and careers in the music industry.

GET AN OVERVIEW

Now that you have a goal, your next step is to get a broad overview of your subject. Use one or all of the following techniques:

- **Talk to people.** Friends and relatives might be able to provide answers themselves or might guide you to someone who can.
- **Use Internet search engines.** Think of words and phrases that are related to your subject. For instance, you might use the phrase *recording studio* and the name of your city or town. Plug the words into search engines and look at relevant Web sites.
- **Head for your school's media center or the local public library.** A research librarian might suggest reference works, books, magazines, or online sources.
- **Be creative.** Flip through the telephone book to see if there are local businesses or organizations that you might call for information. If you know someone who has a job that interests you, consider asking permission to "shadow" him or her—in other words, to spend a few hours or an entire day on the job with that person.

As you find out more about your subject, you might change the focus of your research. For example, spending a day with a local musician may make you want to investigate schools and colleges that offer degree programs in music.

Research Tools THINK central

Go to **thinkcentral.com**.
KEYWORD: HML10-1321

DIFFERENTIATED INSTRUCTION

FOR ENGLISH LANGUAGE LEARNERS

Concept Support Assess students' understanding of the concepts on this page by asking them to paraphrase the information here. Elicit answers to the following questions: What is the difference between a broad overview and a specific focus? What does it mean to "clarify your goal"? Work with students to clarify these concepts.

FOR STRUGGLING READERS

Concept Support For practice in narrowing a topic, have partners read a brief encyclopedia article about a general type of music: jazz, blues, classical, or rock. Ask them to identify two specific topics related to this music, such as a composer, performer, or time period. They should record their findings in a Classification Chart or concept web.

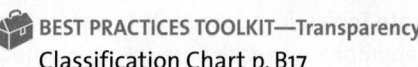

BEST PRACTICES TOOLKIT—Transparency
Classification Chart p. B17

Planning Your Research

COMMON CORE **W 7 W 8 W 9**

Getting Started

CLARIFY YOUR GOAL

- Explain that examples in this unit, beginning with the *QUICKWRITE* on page 1320, refer to careers in music.

- Point out the informal outline on this page, and explore how to develop a specific goal from a general one. List some general goals such as *learn about radio DJ careers* or *learn about composing careers*. Have groups work to refine them into specific goals, such as *identify training needed for radio DJ career* or *identify education needed for composing career.*

- Have small groups use a two-step chart to develop a specific goal related to another career area, such as music therapist.

GET AN OVERVIEW

- As students review each research method, they should think about it in relation to their favorite ways of learning. For example, if they learn well by listening, they may want to include interviewing as part of their research. Recognizing their personal learning style will help them conduct effective and productive research.

- Point out to students that the bulleted subheads correspond to information that is examined in depth in other parts of the unit. Have students preview the unit to locate the additional information. *Bullets 1 and 4 are covered on pages 1338–1339. Bullets 2–4 are covered on pages 1323–1332.*

Research Tools THINK central

Research keywords for **thinkcentral.com** connect students to the web site, **Writing and Research in a Digital Age**. This resource contains PowerPoint presentations covering all aspects of the research process, including research planning and selecting sources.

Focusing Your Research

NARROW OR BROADEN YOUR RESEARCH INQUIRY

- Have students read the sample questions and identify key terms. Note that key terms make questions more specific and offer search terms for research.

- Invite students to consider questions that combine music and another field. Offer examples and highlight key terms:

  Could a job selling <u>musical equipment</u> lead to other careers in the music industry?

  Should I go to a <u>teaching college</u> or <u>music school</u> if I want to teach music?

- Have small groups generate two questions about another career path and identify key terms. Urge students to share ideas.

CHOOSE A NOTE-TAKING METHOD

- Discuss the uses and benefits of each note-taking method, and urge students to describe their experiences with each.

- **Note cards** help organize information from texts, reference materials, magazines, newspapers, and other materials. Researchers often quote, summarize, or paraphrase on note cards.

- **Category charts** help list related information, such as music schools with entrance qualifications, number of students, location, and so on.

- **A pro/con chart** can help students weigh two sides of an issue or option such as teaching college versus music school as training for a career in teaching music.

- Additional note-taking methods include outlining and Question and Answer Note Taking.

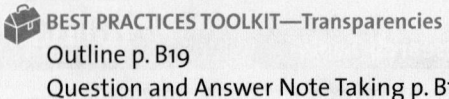 BEST PRACTICES TOOLKIT—Transparencies
Outline p. B19
Question and Answer Note Taking p. B7

Reteaching Worksheets on **thinkcentral.com**
Research and Study Skills Lesson 1:
Research Questions and Topic
Research and Study Skills Lesson 8: Source
Cards and Notecards

 RESOURCE MANAGER—Copy Master
Develop Research Questions p.11

Focusing Your Research

Once you have specific goals, you can narrow the focus of your research to help you find the most relevant information.

NARROW OR BROADEN YOUR RESEARCH INQUIRY

To narrow or broaden your inquiry, develop a set of specific questions that you would like answered, and use those questions to guide your research.

> - What careers are there in the music industry?
> - Could I make a living as a professional songwriter or musician? Would having a college degree from a music school help?
> - What entry-level jobs related to music are available, and what qualifications do I need to get one?

CHOOSE A NOTE-TAKING METHOD

To avoid being overwhelmed by facts, figures, and details, record the information you find in a way that matches your purpose. Here are some examples:

- If you are doing research for a formal report, you should probably use **electronic** or **written note cards**. See page 1347 to learn more.
- A **category chart** is another useful way to organize information.

Music-Related Jobs and Internships

Name and Location	Job Description	Pay
McNulty Audio Recording, 1622 Davis	production assistant (duplicating CDs, data entry)	minimum wage
WLCT Radio, 780 Skyline Dr.	intern (data entry, filing, phone calls)	none
Fort Square Church, 155 Lakeside Ave.	guitarist at Sunday evening worship services	$15 per service

- If you are trying to choose between two options, consider a **pro-con chart**.

Interning at WLCT

Advantages	Disadvantages
• can learn about careers in radio • can get there in about 20 minutes	• no pay • minimum 10 hrs/week

Working at McNulty Audio Recording

Advantages	Disadvantages
• a paying job • can learn about audio recording	• takes almost an hour to get there • have to work every Saturday

---

DIFFERENTIATED INSTRUCTION

FOR ENGLISH LANGUAGE LEARNERS

Vocabulary Support Make sure that students understand the vocabulary related to the category and pro/con charts:

- *category,* "grouping, types, kinds"
- *pro,* "in favor of, for"
- *con,* "against, anti, opposed to"

FOR ADVANCED LEARNERS/PRE–AP

Generate Topics Invite students to generate a topic appropriate to each note-taking method.

Have partners work together to discuss the topics and methods. Ask them to answer these questions in their discussion:

- Why did you match this method and topic?
- What are the advantages of this method?
- What are the disadvantages?

Invite groups to share results with the class.

Using the Internet

How can you find accurate, up-to-date information quickly from all the information available on the Internet?

Understanding the Web

The World Wide Web is accessible through the Internet, a vast system of linked computers. The Web includes hundreds of millions of Web sites and literally billions of Web pages.

Each Web address, or URL, ends with an abbreviation. Knowing what these abbreviations mean can help you understand the purpose of each Web site you visit.

WEB ABBREVIATIONS AND MEANINGS

.COM commercial—product information and sales; personal sites; some combinations of products and information, such as World Book Online

.EDU education—information about schools, courses, campus life, and research projects; students' and teachers' personal sites

.GOV United States government—official sites of the White House, NASA, the FBI, and other government agencies

.MIL United States military—official sites of the Army, Navy, Air Force, and Marines, as well as the Department of Defense and related agencies

.NET network—product information and sales

.ORG organization—charities, libraries, and other nonprofits; political parties

SEARCH THE WEB

Keyword Search Begin with a **search engine,** a Web site that lets you look for information using a phrase or term related to your subject. This is called a **keyword search.** Keep these tips in mind while searching:

- Be specific. Instead of *music,* try *music careers.* Look at your research questions for ideas.
- Try putting exact phrases in quotation marks. For instance, *"recording studio"* will give you sites that include those words in that order.
- Some search engines let you replace the end of a word with an asterisk. For example, the keyword *music** leads to sites that contain *music, musician,* and *musicianship.*

TIP The most common search engines used today are Google and Yahoo!

Using the Internet

COMMON
CORE W 7
        W 8
        W 9

Understanding the Web

TERMS FOR THE INTERNET

Write the terms on the board. Elicit or provide preliminary definitions, but urge students to refine those definitions as they read the terms on pages 1323–1324.

WEB ABBREVIATIONS AND MEANINGS

After students read the Web abbreviations and meanings, have them predict possible purposes of each of these Web sites:

- www.movies.go.com
- www.uscg.mil
- www.irish-music.net
- www.nws.noaa.gov
- www.kidshealth.org

Explain that many search engines allow researchers to limit the search results to Web sites that end with certain abbreviations. For example, for academic research, Google's advanced search feature can be set to return results only from sites that end with *.org, .gov,* or *.edu,* thus avoiding commercial sites that end with *.com.*

SEARCH THE WEB

Keyword Search

- Ask volunteers to identify useful search engines, such as Google and Yahoo! Then have groups use different search engines to carry out, report, and compare searches using keywords like "music careers" or "recording studio."

- After students read the **TIP**, have them repeat the searches on a metasearch engine such as Mamma.com and share the differences they noticed.

Reteaching Worksheets on thinkcentral.com
   Research and Study Skills Lesson 4:
      Using a Web Site for Research

FOR STRUGGLING READERS

Task Support Have knowledgeable students demonstrate how to find the search engines Google and Yahoo! Urge students to learn how to bookmark these on the classroom computer or to list them on a paper reference.

FOR ADVANCED LEARNERS/PRE–AP

Explain Terms for the Internet Challenge students to create a study card defining one of the terms for other students. Tell them that their study cards should explain the term in a way that would be helpful for someone who did not understand it. Allow time for students to share their cards and teach each term.

ADDITIONAL TEACHING OPPORTUNITY

Boolean Searches

- Make sure students understand that using AND and NOT will narrow and focus their keyword search, while using OR will broaden that search. Stress that the most effective searches are focused and narrow but that broad searches may be necessary as starting points.

- Have students read the **TIP** and locate the "Advanced Search" link on the picture of the Google Web page. Explain that using this feature often means that the searcher does not have to do a Boolean search because Advanced Search is preset for such a task. Researchers must enter keywords but need not enter AND, NOT, or OR (or the equivalent symbols). Advanced Search can also search for an entire phrase without the need for quotation marks.

ASSESS AND SELECT RELEVANT SITES

- Remind students that URLs, or Web addresses, are given with each Web site listed in a search. Refer them to page 1323 for information about the abbreviations that come at the end of URLs. Students should also skim through the text in black print that describes each site.

YOUR TURN   **Close Read**

Possible answers:

1. *The keywords are "music industry jobs." They are effective because of their specificity.*

2. *There are about 4,690 sites. The search could be made more specific by adding a city, state, or region name, or by using a specific type of job, such as "songwriting job."*

IF STUDENTS NEED HELP . . . Have them complete the original search, then add a specific job to the keyword.

3. *Students may say that they would be less likely to click on a sponsored link included for profit, not relevance.*

R RESOURCE MANAGER—Copy Master
Select Relevant Web Sites p. 12

Boolean Searches A Boolean search lets you specify how the keywords in your search are related.

- Using the word AND tells the search engine to find all documents that contain both words (*internship* AND *radio*). Some search engines use a plus sign in front of the words instead (*+internship +radio*).

- The word OR broadens the search to include all documents that contain either word (*job* OR *career*).

- The word NOT—or, for some search engines, a minus sign—excludes unwanted terms from the search (*songwriting* NOT *commercials*).

TIP Look for a "Search Tips" or "Advanced Search" hyperlink on each search engine you use. Click on it to find out whether that search engine allows Boolean searches.

ASSESS AND SELECT RELEVANT SITES

Your search will result in a list of sites sorted either by date or by relevance. Most search engines base relevance on how often your search terms appear on a particular page and on whether any or all of your search terms appear in the page's URL. However, just because a site is at the top of the list doesn't mean that it is the best or most relevant for you. Read the descriptions of listed items, looking for words that are related to your goals and needs.

YOUR TURN   **Look at Search Engine Results**

A search for music-industry jobs resulted in a number of possibilities. Which sites would you choose to explore?

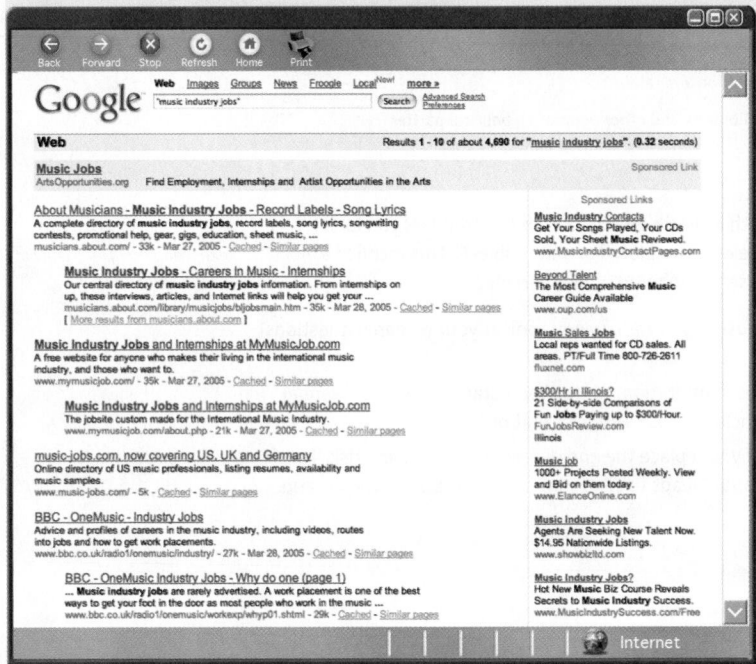

Close Read

1. What keywords did this student use? What makes them an effective combination?

2. What was the total number of sites found? How could this search be made more specific?

3. The results labeled "Sponsored Links" are paid advertisements. Would you be more or less likely to click on a sponsored link? Why?

DIFFERENTIATED INSTRUCTION

FOR STRUGGLING READERS

Concept Support Have partners experiment with keyword and Boolean searches for the topic "how to prepare for a job as a recording engineer." Suggest that they use a Three-Column Journal to list keyword sets, number of results, and most helpful sites. Ask students to share what they learned.

 **BEST PRACTICES TOOLKIT—Transparency**
Three-Column Journal p. B10

FOR ENGLISH LANGUAGE LEARNERS

Vocabulary: Jargon Review meaning, usage, or pronunciation of these terms:

- *.com*, pronounced "dot com"

- *URL*, pronounced as letters "U" "R" "L"

- *hits*, the number of times a Web site is visited

- *window*, "boxed frame around a Web site image or other document on a computer"

EXPLORE WEB SITES

After selecting a few sites, you will need to know how to read them and use the special features they contain. Most Web pages include features that aren't used in books.

TIP To evaluate the usefulness and accuracy of the information on a Web site, use the evaluation guidelines on page 1226.

- Underlined or highlighted words are called **hyperlinks** or links. Clicking on these words leads you to related information on another page on the site or to a different site.
- **Icons** are small pictures or symbols that work the same way as hyperlinks.
- Most Web pages include at least one **menu,** or list of choices. These are often on one side of the page, at the top, or at the bottom.
- Look for a "last updated" reference (often at the bottom of the page) to determine if the Web page you are reading is up-to-date.

Read a Web Site

YOUR TURN

Take a close look at this Web site. What information does this site provide?

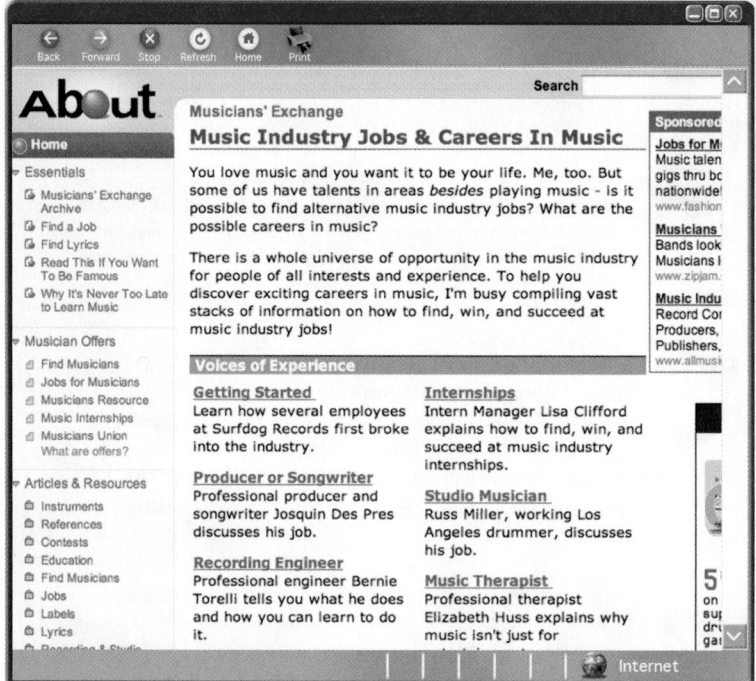

Close Read

1. Is this site appropriate for someone looking for information about entry-level jobs in the music industry? Give reasons for your answer.
2. Which three menu items would you click on to learn more about paid positions in the music industry?
3. Who is Lisa Clifford? Which hyperlink would you click on to learn more about her opinions?

FOR STRUGGLING READERS

Task Support Have small groups explore Web sites, such as those cited on page 1323. Ask groups to record specific *hyperlinks, icons, menus,* and *other features* on spokes of a concept web, with the Web site address in the center.

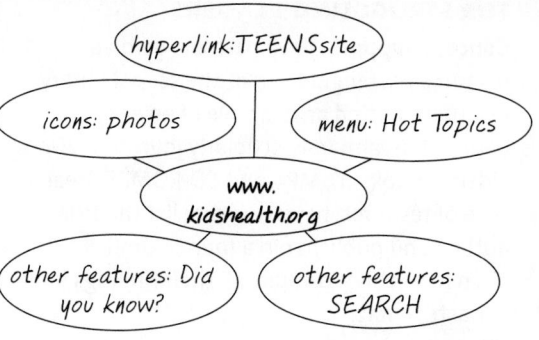

EXPLORE WEB SITES

Use the Google results and the About site on pages 1324–1325 to help explain these features of Web sites:

- **Hyperlinks** Point out that these electronic links often appear in a color, which identifies and highlights them. For example, the hyperlinks on the About Web site are red and blue. Encourage students to identify the color of the Google links. (*blue and green*) Clarify that text is a link if moving the cursor over it changes the cursor into a "hand" icon.
- **Icons** Note that the icons at the top of both Web pages offer operations such as printing. Clicking on the icon starts the operation.
- **Menus** Direct students to the sets of menus on the About page: "Voices of Experience" in the middle of the page and "Essentials," "Musician Offers," and "Articles & Resources" on the left side.
- Direct students to the **TIP**, and review the evaluation guidelines. Note that hyperlinks and icons connect to pages such as "Contact Us" that help users evaluate a site's usefulness and accuracy.

YOUR TURN

Close Read

Possible answers:

1. *The site is appropriate because it includes information about entry-level jobs in the music industry.*
2. *Three items with information about paid positions in the music industry include: "Find a Job," "Jobs for Musicians," and "Getting Started."*
3. *Lisa Clifford is an intern manager. The "Internships" hyperlink under "Voices of Experience" gives her opinions.*

Reteaching Worksheets on **thinkcentral.com**
Research and Study Skills Lesson 4: Using a Web Site for Research

R RESOURCE MANAGER—Copy Master
Navigate Relevant Web Sites p. 13

Using the Library or Media Center

COMMON CORE W7 W8 W9

TERMS FOR THE LIBRARY

Read the terms aloud; then invite volunteers to share situations in which they have found some of these resources helpful, using either school or community libraries. Again, elicit preliminary definitions, which students can refine as they read and discuss the page.

Understanding Today's Library

LIBRARY AND MEDIA CENTER RESOURCES

- Survey students about their library habits. Point out the importance of not relying exclusively on the Internet for research.

- Display examples of the listed library and media-center resources. As you review each type, ask students to find samples.

  Books Invite students to name their favorite fiction titles. What nonfiction books have they read in the last year? Where are fiction and nonfiction books housed in the school or local library?

  Newspapers and Periodicals Stress that these materials offer information and opinions on current ideas, trends, scientific and medical advances, and the arts. Invite students to give examples.

  Reference Have students explain the kinds of information they would find in an encyclopedia, almanac, and atlas. Then ask which would be most helpful in finding the six fastest animals in the world. (*almanac or encyclopedia*)

  Electronic Resources Tell students that many materials, such as novels, plays, encyclopedias, and magazines, come in nontraditional formats. For example, students can listen to books on audiotape, CD, or MP3; read them on a computer; or watch them on a DVD.

R RESOURCE MANAGER—Copy Master
Use Library and Media Center Sources p. 14

TERMS FOR THE LIBRARY

You will use these terms when doing research in the library or media center:
- catalog
- microfilm
- microfiche
- abstract
- primary source
- secondary source
- database
- bibliography
- index
- glossary

Using the Library or Media Center

How can the people, materials, and technologies at your local library or media center help you find information?

Understanding Today's Library

Libraries and media centers are treasure troves of information. Your school's media center or your local public library will probably have most or all of these departments.

LIBRARY AND MEDIA CENTER RESOURCES

BOOKS
Nonfiction books are arranged by subject. See "Library Detective" on page 1340 to learn about the two systems for classifying nonfiction books.
Fiction books are shelved alphabetically by the author's last name.

NEWSPAPERS AND PERIODICALS
Periodicals include magazines, newsletters, and scholarly journals.
Microforms are newspapers, periodicals, and reports stored on film (microfilm) or cards (microfiche) and viewable on special machines.

REFERENCE WORKS
Reference books include encyclopedias, atlases, almanacs, and dictionaries. These usually cannot be checked out of the library.
Search tools include databases, directories, indexes, and the library's catalog. One search tool that can save you time is an index of abstracts. An **abstract** is a short summary of a journal article. By looking at abstracts, you can determine which articles are most closely related to your topic.

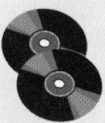

ELECTRONIC RESOURCES
DVDs and videos of documentaries and other films and television programs are available at most libraries for free or for a small fee.
E-books are books available in electronic form. They are readable on a personal computer or on various hand-held electronic devices.
Audio resources include books, music, and speeches on CD or MP3.
CD-ROMs of encyclopedias, maps, and other resources are available at many libraries.

OTHER RESOURCES
Your library may have a careers section, a college-search section, maps, music scores, genealogy resources to help you trace your family tree, or one-of-a-kind resources to help you learn about local history.

DIFFERENTIATED INSTRUCTION

FOR STRUGGLING READERS

Concept Support Have partners go on a resource scavenger hunt at the school library. Ask them to find an example of an encyclopedia, atlas, almanac, scholarly journal, DVD, video, e-book, CD, MP3, and CD-ROM. For each type of resource, have students list the title, author, and publisher in a four-column chart. Then have them compile all their findings into a master chart.

FOR ADVANCED LEARNERS/PRE–AP

Compare Have students use a Comparison Matrix to compare library and media-center resources within categories; for example, magazines, newsletters, and scholarly journals; encyclopedias, atlases, and almanacs; databases, directories, and online catalogs; DVDs, e-books, and CD-ROMs; or e-books, CDs, and MP3s.

 BEST PRACTICES TOOLKIT—Transparency
Comparison Matrix p. A24

Finding What You Need

Where should you start your library search? Ask a librarian, or consult the library's online resources.

THE RESEARCH LIBRARIAN

Librarians are information detectives. These experts can help you

- determine what you need to know
- choose the most useful print, electronic, and audiovisual sources
- operate equipment, such as microfilm readers
- use interlibrary catalogs to expand your research to other libraries

THE LIBRARY'S CATALOG

The catalog is your road map through the library's resources. Here are four ways to search for a source:

- author   • title   • subject   • keyword

In addition to the item's author, title, and publication date, the catalog entry will include a brief summary of its content, the subject categories it addresses, where it is shelved, and whether it is available.

YOUR TURN

Search a Library Catalog

The following example of a catalog entry shows information about a specific book.

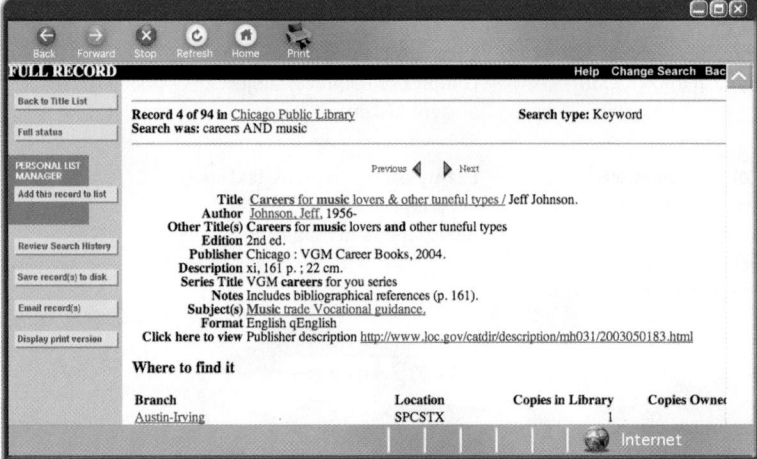

Close Read

1. What two search terms did this student use? Why is it important to include both terms instead of just one?

2. When was this book published? Why is a recent copyright date important when searching for information on careers?

FOR STRUGGLING READERS

Comprehension Support Have small groups answer questions about the book catalog entry pictured on page 1327.

- Who are the author and publisher of the book? (*Jeff Johnson; VGM Career Books*)
- How long is the book? (*161 pages*)
- What link takes readers to a description of the book? (*publisher description*)
- In which library branch is the book available? (*Austin-Irving*)

FOR ADVANCED LEARNERS/PRE–AP

Predict and Compare Have students predict the better search option—keyword or subject—for a search on "musical instrument design." Ask them to conduct both searches and record their results in a T Chart and then review their predictions. What were the pros and cons of each kind of search?

 BEST PRACTICES TOOLKIT—Transparency
T Chart p. A25

Finding What You Need

THE RESEARCH LIBRARIAN

Point out that research librarians often have a specific area of expertise, such as history or art. Help students identify questions to begin a search for information on "musical instrument design," such as: Where can I find books on the history of violin design?

THE LIBRARY'S CATALOG

Direct students to the label "Search type" in the catalog entry shown on page 1327. Ask them what kind of search was used to find the entry. (*a keyword search*) Then review each search type and its best uses.

- **Author** This type of search requires the exact spelling of an author's name. Entering this name pulls up book titles by that author and data about each book.

- **Title** This is the narrowest type of search, useful only when locating a specific book for which the exact title is known.

- **Subject** Clarify that library catalog systems use specific subject headings. Urge students to ask librarians for phrasing their system will recognize.

- **Keyword** A keyword related to a particular topic leads to books that contain that keyword in its catalog entry. Point out the keywords used for the search *careers AND music.* Then guide students to see that the word *career* appears three times in the catalog entry shown on page 1327.

YOUR TURN

Close Read

Possible answers:

1. *The search terms were "careers" and "music." Using only one term would have made the search too broad to be useful.*

2. *The book was published in 2004. A recent copyright is important because new technologies often change job requirements and career options. Contact information needed for a job search may also become outdated quickly.*

Reteaching Worksheets on thinkcentral.com
Research and Study Skills Lesson 2: Using Library Catalogs

Choosing Sources

PRIMARY AND SECONDARY SOURCES

As students read the chart, have them compare the two kinds of sources. Review how each difference might affect the quality, reliability, and usefulness of information.

- **Primary Sources** Explain that primary sources are sources that bear direct witness on something. Primary sources can be written in first person, second person, or third person. Personal writing can describe feelings, experiences, and events, as do letters, diaries, and autobiographies. Informational documents, on the other hand, contain raw data: public documents, interviews, graphs, or surveys. Other examples of primary sources include photographs, maps, or musical recordings.

- **Secondary Sources** Secondary sources must rely on primary sources for their information. Their main purpose is to convey analysis or information about a topic.

Have students use a Y Chart to compare a diary written by a participant in a weekend music festival with a magazine article about the festival. Discuss how information in the diary and article might differ.

 BEST PRACTICES TOOLKIT—Transparency
Y Chart p. A27

Reteaching Worksheets on thinkcentral.com
Research and Study Skills Lesson 5:
Using Primary and Secondary Sources

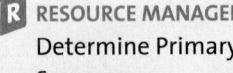 **RESOURCE MANAGER—Copy Master**
Determine Primary and Secondary Sources p. 15

Choosing Sources

You have looked at the library's online catalog, and you're overwhelmed by the amount of information available on your subject. How can you choose the right sources for your needs?

PRIMARY AND SECONDARY SOURCES

One of the first steps in choosing a source is to determine whether it is a primary or a secondary source. This chart explains the differences.

PRIMARY SOURCES	SECONDARY SOURCES
Definition: materials written or created by people who were present at events, either as participants or observers	**Definition:** records of events; created after the events occurred; created by people who were not directly involved in those events
▼	▼
Advantages: firsthand information; can help the researcher understand the attitudes and beliefs of a particular time and place; may contain very specific details	**Advantages:** sometimes include excerpts from many primary sources; often have a broad perspective and many viewpoints; good for getting an overview of a topic
▼	▼
Disadvantages: limited perspective; may need interpretation; may be biased	**Disadvantages:** only as reliable as the sources used; may be biased
▼	▼
Often used when researching: current events, biographical information	**Often used when researching:** complex or technical subjects, ancient history
▼	▼
Examples: autobiographies, letters, interviews, e-mails, diaries, speeches, travelogues, photographs, public documents such as census reports, first-person newspaper and magazine articles	**Examples:** biographies, textbooks, encyclopedias, third-person newspaper and magazine articles

DIFFERENTIATED INSTRUCTION

FOR STRUGGLING READERS

Comprehension Support Have small groups create original primary sources about a school event, such as a variety show, a band competition, or a musical. Each group should produce three different primary sources about the event—for example, an interview, a photograph, and a first-person account.

FOR ENGLISH LANGUAGE LEARNERS

Vocabulary Support Make sure that students understand these terms:

- *autobiography,* "the story of a person's life written by that person"

- *interview,* "a conversation in which one person asks questions of another person"

- *travelogue,* "writing that describes a travel experience"

- *census report,* "a survey of information about the nation's population and economy"

- *first-person newspaper article,* "an article written from the point of view of the writer, using the pronoun *I*"

- *third-person newspaper article,* "an article written from a third-person point of view"

- *biography,* "the story of a person's life written by another person"

REFERENCE SOURCES

A good way to find primary and secondary sources is to examine the library's reference collection. Use reference works to narrow your topic and create research questions. Many reference materials are available on CD-ROMs and online.

REFERENCE SOURCES	EXAMPLES
ENCYCLOPEDIAS **General:** Detailed articles on many subjects **Specialized:** Articles on a specific field, such as music, science, or history	*Encyclopedia.com, Encyclopaedia Britannica* *The Billboard Illustrated Encyclopedia of Music*
DICTIONARIES **General:** Word meanings, origins, spellings, pronunciations, and usage **Specialized:** Words and terms used in a specific field, such as medicine or music	*The American Heritage Dictionary* *The Harvard Dictionary of Music*
ALMANACS AND YEARBOOKS Statistics and other facts	*The World Almanac and Book of Facts*
THESAURI Synonyms and antonyms	*The American Heritage Thesaurus for Learners of English*
BIOGRAPHICAL REFERENCES Information on the lives of noteworthy people	*The Riverside Dictionary of Biography*
ATLASES Maps and other geographic information	*National Geographic Atlas of the World*
DIRECTORIES Names, addresses, and phone numbers of people and organizations	Telephone books; lists of business organizations, agencies, and publications
INDEXES Alphabetical lists of information	*The Readers' Guide to Periodical Literature*

REFERENCE SOURCES

- After students read through the text, invite them to name other specific reference sources they have used and to share advice they would offer to someone else using the resource.
- Have students identify projects and activities that lend themselves to each type of resource. Offer these examples, and ask students to name a resource they would use and explain why they would use it:

  Find synonyms for *rhythm, beat,* and *harmony* for a paper on the blues. ***Possible answer:*** *a thesaurus, because it contains synonyms for words*
  Identify countries that share a border with India. ***Possible answer:*** *an atlas, because it is a quick way to find geographical information*
  Find the top 100 songs of the century. ***Possible answer:*** *an almanac, because it contains many offbeat facts, including lists of entertainment trivia*
  Write a report on singer Billie Holiday. ***Possible answers:*** *an encyclopedia, because it contains articles on many subjects; a biographical reference, because it contains information on lives of famous people; a music encyclopedia, because it contains information about people in music*

Reteaching Worksheets on **thinkcentral.com**
  Research and Study Skills Lesson 3: Using Reference and Search Tools

  Vocabulary Lesson 24: Using Vocabulary Reference Sources

FOR STRUGGLING READERS

Concept Support Distribute various reference books among small groups of students. Ask each group to work together to study a reference source and to create an illustrated chart showing basic information about that source. The chart should explain how to use the reference book; its purpose; examples of information it contains, including illustrations, graphics, and maps; and types of questions it answers.

FOR ENGLISH LANGUAGE LEARNERS

Vocabulary Support Make sure that students understand the terms used to describe the different reference sources:

- *origins,* "word histories; etymologies"
- *noteworthy,* "well known"
- *geographic,* "relating to the earth and its features"
- *periodical literature,* "magazines and scholarly journals"

DATABASES

- Preview the three questions that the text answers about databases. Have a volunteer reread each question and the text that follows it. Then have students test their understanding by writing the question on the front of a note card and summarizing the answer on the back.

- Point out that many databases, such as the *Books In Print* page shown, are electronic bibliographies of books or periodicals. Explain that other databases contain links to full-text articles or e-books, government documents, photographs, music recordings, maps, health resources, reference sources, and newspaper articles.

- Make sure students understand that databases are useful for a variety of research projects in and outside of school. Britannica Online is a good place to start for an overview of many topics. Students might then use InfoTrac, a database of full-text articles from magazines, newspapers, and reference books. InfoTrac is available to members of many school and local libraries.

YOUR TURN

Close Read

Possible answers:

1. *Answers will vary based on students' choices of topics but should be thoughtful and precise.*

2. *Entries 1, 3, and 4 all appear to be useful sources of information about music industry jobs, especially entry 4, as it includes the terms "career opportunities" and "music business" in its title. Entry 2 is a history of a particular television program, so it is unlikely to have information on current jobs and careers.*

DATABASES

What Are Databases? A database is a collection of information that has been arranged so that it is easy to search. Some online databases, such as the Internet Movie Database and the Web Music Database, are free. Others charge a fee, but your local library may have access to them. For instance, ancestry.com is a database of census records, immigration records, and other resources to help people learn more about their family history. Noticias is a database of Spanish-language articles.

What Makes Them Useful? Database searches are more targeted than Web searches because most databases filter out advertisements. Also, most databases are collections of only one type of material—only newspaper articles, only scientific papers, and so on.

When Should I Use Them? Databases are especially helpful when you have narrowed your topic and have a good idea of what information you are seeking. To find out which databases would be most useful for you, ask a librarian.

YOUR TURN

Examine a Database

Books in Print, a database of book titles and descriptions, gives this information about careers in music.

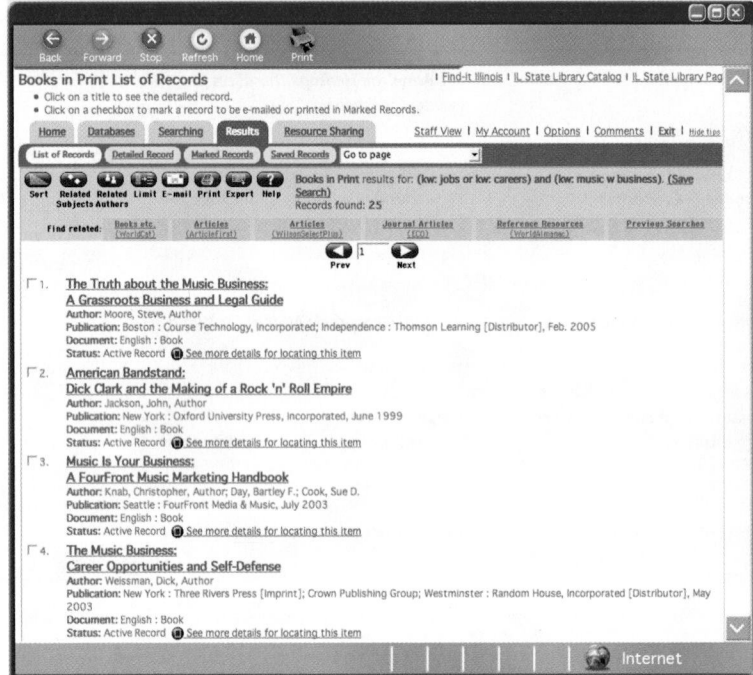

Close Read

1. This student did a Boolean search for "jobs OR careers AND 'music business.'" What keywords might you use to search for your topic on a database like this one?

2. Of the four entries shown, which would be good sources for someone looking for information on jobs that are available in the music industry? Give reasons for your answers.

DIFFERENTIATED INSTRUCTION

FOR STRUGGLING READERS

Task Support Review these databases that might help with research on music topics:

- The Encyclopedia Smithsonian: Musical History (http://www.si.edu/resources/faq/nmah/music.htm)

- American Memory at the Library of Congress (http://rs6.loc.gov)

- LookSmart Find Articles (www.findarticles.com)

FOR ADVANCED LEARNERS/PRE-AP

Mapping a Search Have students map a database search on a Sequence Chain. Ask them to record keywords and Web addresses, starting with the database, and then to list links that they used to find a useful primary or secondary source. Invite volunteers to describe their searches.

 BEST PRACTICES TOOLKIT—Transparency
Sequence Chain p. B21

NONFICTION BOOKS

As you search databases and library shelves, you may find many books that address your topic. How can you quickly determine which ones are right for you?

- Read the book's **title** (and the **subtitle,** if there is one) to get an idea of the general subject matter. Also skim **chapter titles** and **headings.**
- Look for the date of publication on the **copyright page,** which is usually located right after the title page. If you need up-to-the-minute information, don't depend on a book that is several years old.
- Read the **table of contents** at the front of the book, and skim the **index** at the back for terms related to your subject.
- Some books have a **bibliography** or a **recommended readings** section. Either of these can give you ideas for other sources to consult.
- If the book contains difficult technical terms, look for a **glossary** at the back. A glossary lists specialized terms along with their definitions.

YOUR TURN

Examine the Parts of a Book
Use what you have learned about the parts of a book as you look at the examples below.

BREAKING INTO THE MUSIC INDUSTRY

Your Guide to Jobs and Careers

Raquel Seldera, Ed.D.

SCHNARR PUBLISHING
Danbury, Connecticut

© 2008 by Raquel L. Seldera

All rights reserved. This book may not be duplicated in any form without the written permission of the publisher, except in the form of brief excerpts or quotations for the purpose of review.

First Edition
Printed in the United States

Contents

INTRODUCTION: The Pros and Cons of Working in the Music Business   **3**

CHAPTER 1: Touring Musicians   **7**

CHAPTER 2: Session Musicians   **13**

CHAPTER 3: Composers, Songwriters, and Jingle Writers   **21**

CHAPTER 4: Recording Engineers and Remixers   **29**

Bibliography

Crouch, Tanja L. *100 Careers in the Music Business.* New York: Barron's, 2001.

Field, Shelly. *Career Opportunities in the Music Industry.* 4th ed. New York: Facts on File, 2000.

Goldberg, Jan. *Great Jobs for Music Majors.* Chicago: NTC/Contemporary, 2001.

Hatschek, Keith. *How to Get a Job in the Music and Recording Industry.* Boston: Berklee, 2001.

Tieger, Paul D., and Barbara Barron-Tieger. *Do What You Are: Discover the Perfect Career for You Through the Secrets of Personality Type.* 3rd ed. New York: Little, Brown, 2001.

Index

A
A & R (Artists and Repertoire), 37–44
Academic assessment, 138
Advanced degree programs. *See* Graduate schools
Agents, 53–58
American Association for Music Therapy, 80
American Choral Directors Association, 205
American Federation of Musicians, 9, 15, 180

American Symphony Orchestra League, 10
Aptitude tests, 201–206
Assistant engineer, 30–32

B
Booking agencies, 167
Brass and woodwind instrument repairers, 101
Broadcasting, 96–99
Budgets, 5
Business of music. *See* Music business

Close Read

1. In your own words, what is the subject of this book?

2. When was this book published? Is it recent enough to be useful?

3. What are some of the careers this book discusses? Where did you find this information?

4. Which page would you consult to find more resources on this topic?

FOR STRUGGLING READERS

Concept Support Have partners use the Index and Contents pages shown here to compare these two book parts. Then ask them to answer these questions:

- What function does the Contents page serve? *It identifies chapter topics and pages.*

- What is the function of the Index page? *The index helps readers find topics by subject.*

- When would they use each page? *Contents: to learn general topics of the book; Index: to locate specific information*

Have students present their information in a Venn Diagram.

 BEST PRACTICES TOOLKIT—Transparency
Venn Diagram p. A26

NONFICTION BOOKS

As students read about nonfiction books, check their understanding by asking about the book parts shown or described on this page.

- **Title Page** Ask students to identify the information found on a title page (title and subtitle, if there is one; author, publisher, and publisher's location). Have them name the book's title, subtitle, and author. (Breaking into the Music Industry: Your Guide to Jobs and Careers; *Raquel Seldera, Ed.D.*)

- **Copyright Page** Point out that the copyright page reminds readers of the ownership of the book and the need to credit information taken from it. Ask students to read the copyright date. (*2008*)

- **Table of Contents** Point out that only part of the Table of Contents is shown here. Ask students what information Chapter 1 covers. (*musicians who go on tour*) What chapter covers different kinds of music writers? (*Chapter 3*) On what page does Chapter 4 begin? (*page 29*)

- **Index** Remind students that an index lists topics alphabetically, then gives the page numbers on which the topics appear. If a scan of a book's index shows a researcher's topic listed on many pages, that book is likely to be a useful source.

- **Bibliography** Suggest that students use authors, titles, or subjects from bibliography entries as keywords in their own searches.

- **Glossary** Ask students which terms in the Table of Contents might also be included in the glossary, and why. *Possible answers: jingle, remixers; they are technical terms.*

YOUR TURN

Close Read
Possible answers:

1. *The book's subject is getting started in a music-related career.*

2. *The book was published in 2008, recently enough to be useful.*

3. *Students may cite examples of careers from the Contents page or from the Index.*

4. *The Bibliography contains additional books on the topic.*

R RESOURCE MANAGER—Copy Master
Use Parts of a Book to Locate Information p. 17

NEWSPAPERS AND PERIODICALS

Provide a variety of magazines, newspapers, and journals for students to examine. Point out important features of each type.

- **Magazine features:** long and short articles, special sections and features, weekly to semi-annual issues, ads, specialized or general readership

- **Newspaper features:** headlines; daily issues; current news; editorials; special sections and features, classified ads in back section; general readership by location

- **Journal features:** specialized topics, serious content, infrequent issues, paid subscriptions, limited and specialty ads

Distribute periodicals to small groups. Have groups study the periodicals, answer questions, and exchange findings.

- What information is in the Table of Contents?
- Who is the audience?
- What kinds of articles are included?
- What special features are included?
- Are there ads? If so, what kind?
- How much does it cost?

DOCUMENTARIES AND OTHER FILMS

- Although facts may be adjusted for dramatic purposes, fictional films can be helpful in creating context for a topic. For example, the film *Gone with the Wind,* set during the American Civil War, can give viewers some idea of what clothing and buildings in that time were like. In contrast, documentaries are intended to inform the audience, although they may also reflect the filmmaker's point of view. They often use historical footage or archival materials.

- Provide examples of documentaries and films on similar topics, such as Ken Burns's documentary *The Civil War* and the movie *Gone with the Wind;* the documentary *Biography—Mahatma Gandhi: Pilgrim of Peace* and the movie *Gandhi.* Discuss differences.

NEWSPAPERS AND PERIODICALS

Newspapers, magazines, and academic journals provide concise information on specific topics.

TYPES OF PUBLICATIONS	EXAMPLES
MAGAZINES General: For most readers Specialized: Articles on specific topics	*Newsweek, Time, Life Musician, Rolling Stone* 
NEWSPAPERS General: For most readers in a specific geographic area Specialized: For readers interested in a certain subject, such as investing	*The Austin American-Statesman, The Miami Herald Investor's Business Daily* 
JOURNALS Journals provide highly specialized information. They are designed for experts. Journals have fewer advertisements than magazines and usually have a more formal writing style.	*Journal of Music Theory International Journal of Music Education* 

Use these tips to help you find an article on your topic:

- Ask a research librarian. He or she may know of specialized magazines or journals on your topic.
- Use databases of articles, such as InfoTrac or America's Newspapers, to help you find information on your subject in many sources.

DOCUMENTARIES AND OTHER FILMS

Some of the sources you find may be on DVD or videocassette. To quickly assess whether these sources are worth watching, ask yourself these questions:

- Is this a **fiction** or **nonfiction** source? To identify a nonfiction film, read the library's online catalog description. Look for the words *documentary* or *interview.* A fictional film probably does not have enough factual information to serve as a reliable source.
- How recent is the **copyright date**? The online description or the back cover should tell you. Recent documentaries are usually based on updated research.
- What kind of **information** does the film contain? Read the online catalog description and the front and back covers of the DVD or videocassette case. Does the film include **primary sources,** such as speeches or interviews? Did the filmmakers shoot their own footage, or are they using archived materials?

DIFFERENTIATED INSTRUCTION

FOR ENGLISH LANGUAGE LEARNERS
Vocabulary Support Work with students to understand the meanings of these unfamiliar words related to films:

- *documentary,* "a film that presents factual events, often with oral narration"
- *footage,* "film; news film"
- *archival materials,* "historical footage or documents"

FOR ADVANCED LEARNERS/PRE–AP
Compare Historical Films Ask students to select a documentary and a movie on the same topic, such as *Biography—Mahatma Gandhi: Pilgrim of Peace* and *Gandhi.* Have students review both films in an oral presentation, comparing and contrasting reliability and coverage as well as point of view and entertainment value. Which film did they prefer? Which film contains more material suitable for research? Would they recommend both? Ask them to give reasons.

Evaluating Information

Once you have found several sources, you need to figure out which ones are **authoritative** and reliable.

Applying General Evaluation Guidelines

Use the questions in this chart to help you look critically at each source—in print or online—and decide whether you can trust the information in it.

Evaluating Sources — **THINK** central
Go to **thinkcentral.com**.
KEYWORD: HML10-1333

EVALUATING SOURCES

Is the information up-to-date?	Check the copyright page or look for a "last updated" reference. Topics in science, medicine, or sports often require recently updated information. Older publications can be helpful for historical topics.
Is the information accurate?	Can the facts be verified by more than one source? Most print and online encyclopedias, dictionaries, directories, and almanacs are considered reliable because they are updated regularly and go through a rigorous review process.
What is the author's background?	Does the author have a job that qualifies him or her as an expert on the topic? Has he or she written other materials on this topic?
What kinds of materials does the publisher produce?	Magazines that publish trendy articles and gossip are not as reliable as university presses, newsmagazines, or science magazines.
Is there evidence of bias in the source?	Why does the source exist? Does the author list goals in the foreword, preface, or introduction? Is the source designed to inform, persuade, entertain, or some combination of these? Does the author use loaded language, such as "It should be clear to every intelligent person that this plan will be a disaster"?
How much information does the source cover?	Does the source give general or specific information? Does it support other information you have read, or does it add new information? Start by looking at the table of contents, the index, or the menu.
Is the source relevant and appropriate?	Does the source cover aspects of the topic that interest you? Is it written at a level that you can understand?

FOR ENGLISH LANGUAGE LEARNERS
Vocabulary Support Point out and define these informal terms and examples of jargon:
- *up-to-date*, "current"
- *updated*, "made current"
- *bias*, "unfair preference or dislike"
- *trendy*, "relating to current fashions"
- *loaded language*, "words with strong emotional impact"

FOR ADVANCED LEARNERS/PRE–AP
Investigate and Evaluate Challenge students to investigate recent instances when reporters used unreliable or inaccurate sources in high-profile media, such as Dan Rather's 2004 reporting on *60 Minutes* about President George W. Bush's Air National Guard service. Have them review articles, profiles, and footage about the cases and then create a bulletin board of their findings.

Evaluating Information

COMMON CORE W 7 / W 8 / W 9

Applying General Evaluation Guidelines

Discuss the information in the **Evaluating Sources** chart with students, providing clarification and additional instruction as needed. You may also wish to incorporate these activities:

- **Accuracy/Bias** Clarify that bias can be more subtle than a writer's stated opinion, appearing, for example, in the writer's choice of information presented or in the use of words with negative or positive connotations.

- **Credentials** Stress that an author's credentials can support his or her reliability. Students might also perform a search on the author to identify other published works and educational background.

- **Coverage** Display a wide range of newspapers, from reliable sources such as the *New York Times* to sensationalist tabloids. Have small groups review each sample to report on its coverage. Ask groups to determine what percentage of the stories cover a particular topic—for example, national or international news. Students can then decide if a source is appropriate as a general or specific source.

- **Usefulness/Relevance** Have partners create criteria for determining a source's usefulness or relevance. Invite volunteers to share and compare their criteria.

Reteaching Worksheets on **thinkcentral.com**
    Reading Lesson 5: Distinguishing Fact from Opinion
    Informational Text Lesson 16: Evaluating Evidence

R RESOURCE MANAGER—Copy Master
Identify Bias p. 16

Evaluating Sources — **THINK** central

Go to **thinkcentral.com** to preview instructional presentations on evaluating sources—part of the **Writing and Research in a Digital Age** Web site.

Evaluating Specific Sources

EVALUATE WEB SITES

Before students read this page, write the words *Author* and *Purpose* on the board, and have students read the first **TIP**. Remind students to use what they know about authors' purposes (entertain, express, persuade, inform) to help them evaluate a source. Stress also that if students have questions about the accuracy or reliability of a Web site's sources or author, they should check the information against other sources or ask their teacher for advice.

Commercial Web Sites Point out that many *.com* or *.net* sites are not primarily for profit but may still have commercial interests, such as promoting an organization (for example, Rock and Roll Hall of Fame, www.rockhall.com). Also call students' attention to helpful .com sites such as www.britannica.com (*Encyclopedia Britannica*) and www.nytimes.com (*New York Times*).

Organization Web Sites Tell students to consider carefully how a .org site gets its information. For example, anyone can add or edit the entries at www.wikipedia.org. As a result, this source is not considered reliable. Share the World Bank Web site (www.worldbank.org), which is useful for many high school research projects.

Personal Web Sites Have students read the second **TIP**. Review that one way to verify a Web site's information is to read information on the home page or at "About This Site," "Mission Statement," or "Contact Us" links. If there are no links to connect to this information, students can shorten the URL to include only information up to and including the first .org or equivalent ending.

Reteaching Worksheets on thinkcentral.com
Research and Study Skills Lesson 7:
Evaluating Electronic Sources

R RESOURCE MANAGER—Copy Master
Evaluate Web Sites Using Criteria p. 18

Evaluating Specific Sources

These tips, questions, and exercises will give you practice in evaluating specific types of sources.

EVALUATE WEB SITES

Web sites are easy to access but difficult to evaluate. They are often a mix of helpful information and attempts to promote a point of view or to sell something.

Commercial Web sites As you learned on page 1323, URLs ending in *.com* or *.net* are sometimes for-profit sites. When you look at a commercial site, ask yourself these questions:

- **Who created the site?** Look for a link called "About This Site" or "Contact Us."
- **Why was it created?** If the site is designed to sell you something, the site's creators may leave out negative information.

Organization (.org) Web sites Many *.org* sites are nonprofit organizations, such as the United Way. Political parties also have URLs with *.org* in them. Think about whether the site you are evaluating is promoting a particular point of view.

- **When was it last updated?** Look for a link titled "About Us" or "Mission Statement." If there is no way to find the creator of the site, then you should be cautious about the content.
- **What supporting evidence does the site offer?** Look for supporting evidence in links to respected institutions or publications.

Personal Web sites Anyone can post anything on the World Wide Web, so millions of personal Web sites exist. Some have misleading URLs. For example, students and faculty can post personal Web sites on their university's server, and their Web addresses will contain a university URL. However, these sites might not be reviewed, evaluated, or in any way sanctioned by the institution.

- **How can I tell if a site is personal even though the address includes the name of an institution?** Look for a forward slash and tilde (/~) and a name or initials following *.edu* in the URL.
- **What does the lack of an official institution logo tell me?** Don't expect the information to be reviewed or approved by the institution.
- **What if most of the links on the site don't work or connect to other items by the same author?** The author may be careless, or he or she may lack outside support.

TIP Knowing who created a site can help you figure out why the site exists and whether it will help you in your research.

TIP Not all personal Web sites are unreliable, but be cautious.

DIFFERENTIATED INSTRUCTION

FOR STRUGGLING READERS

Concept Support Discuss how an organization's profit or nonprofit status affects the information on its Web site. Point out that nonprofit organizations are often raising money for a cause or point of view, just as commercial organizations are selling something. Both may have a bias linked to their goal. Students must identify and consider bias to evaluate the site's information. Other questions to ask include:

- What is the site's goal, mission, or purpose? Is it charitable (www.redcross.org), political (www.dnc.org), or educational (www.sierraclub.org)?
- What aspects of the topic does the site stress?
- What, if anything, does the site ask readers to do, to buy, or to think?

YOUR TURN

Examine Web Sites

Examine these Web sites. What information do they offer?

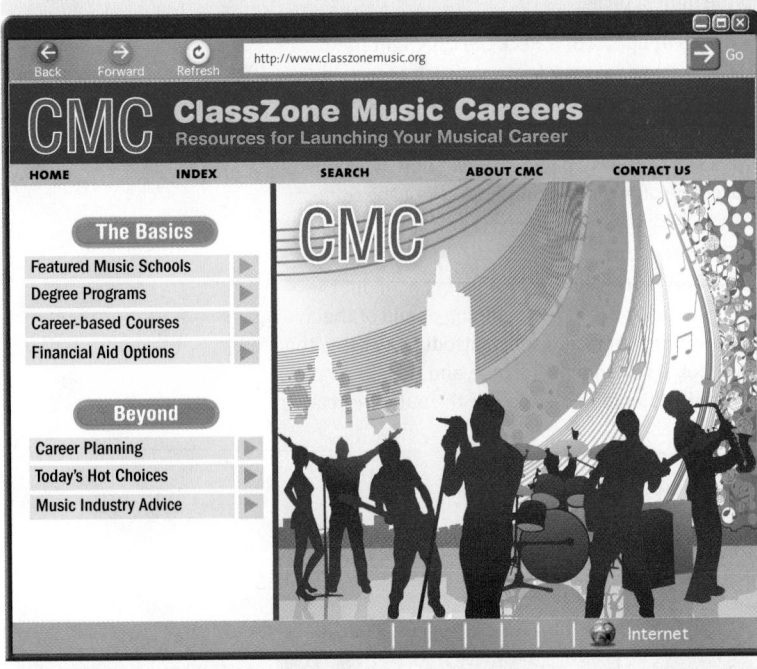

Close Read

1. Which link would you click on to find out more about the sponsoring organization?

2. Why was this site created?

3. Who is the intended audience?

4. Is this is a nonprofit site? How do you know?

5. Each of the questions in the thought bubbles is a link to further information. Which question would you click on to find out more about scholarships to music schools?

TIP To figure out how a particular Web site is organized, look for a link titled "Site Map" or "Home."

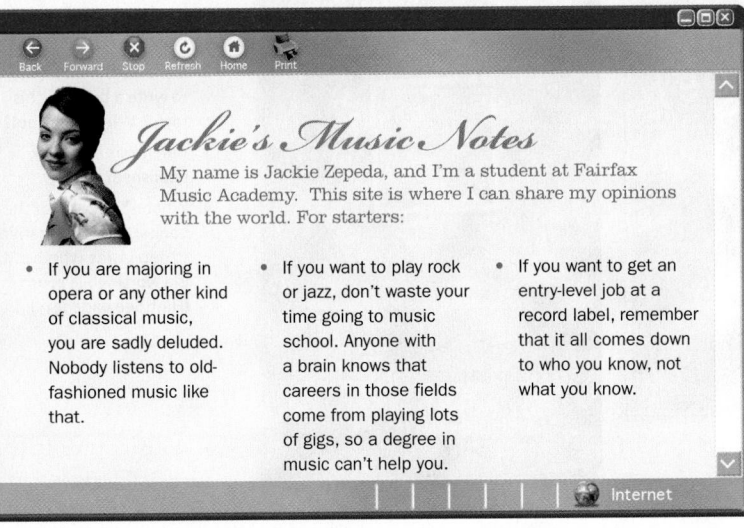

Close Read

1. Who created this site?

2. Why was this site created?

3. Is this an educational site or a personal site? How do you know?

4. What supporting evidence is included?

Before students complete the Close Read questions, refer them to the **TIP**. Ask them what link they would use on the CMC site to determine the site's organization. *Possible answer:* Home

YOUR TURN

Close Read

Possible answers:

1. *"About CMC"*

2. *This site was created to distribute information about the ClassZone Music Careers organization and the education and career resources it provides for people who want to pursue careers in music.*

3. *The intended audience is people interested in music careers or music education.*

4. *The .org in the Web address suggests that it is a nonprofit organization.*

5. *The "Financial Aid Options" link probably leads to information about scholarships to music schools.*

Close Read

Possible answers:

1. *Jackie Zepeda, a student at Fairfax Music Academy, created the site.*

2. *Zepeda created the site to share her opinions about music.*

3. *It is a personal site. The type of material presented is clearly opinion. The informal tone and sarcastic comments also suggest the site is not reliable.*

4. *The author does not provide any supporting evidence—facts, statistics, or examples—to back up her opinions.*

FOR STRUGGLING READERS

Comprehension Support Have small groups work together to answer additional questions about the information in the Web sites shown on this page.

- Which link would you click on to find out how to get in touch with the National Association for Music Education? (*"Contact Us"*)

- Where would you click to learn about performance programs? (*Degree Programs or Career-based Courses*)

- What organization made Jackie Zepeda's Web site possible? (*Fairfax Music Academy*) What question does this raise? (*Is Jackie's site reliable and unbiased?*)

EVALUATE NONFICTION BOOKS

Explain that an evaluation is a way to preview reading. The purpose of evaluation is to determine whether to use a source.

Bibliography Point out that a bibliography reveals the depth and breadth of an author's research, which suggests whether sources are reliable, current, and unbiased.

Appendix Explain that an appendix is a supplement with materials that enhance a reader's understanding. Appendices often include graphs, tables, polls, maps, and other raw data that amplifies text information.

Preface Tell students that this feature is often part mission statement, part biography. A preface may reveal information about the author's research or writing process, or suggest the author's reliability or bias. Give each student a nonfiction book from the school library. Does the book contain a preface? If so, what kind of information is in the preface?

Close Read

Possible answers:

1. *The subject is how to have a performance career with or without a college education; this information is contained in the subtitle.*

2. *As a former singer and professional career counselor with many years of singing experience, the author is probably qualified to write this book. Research into the National Career Development Association could confirm the author's qualifications.*

3. *The "Updated for 2008" notice on the back cover implies that the book was published in 2008. The book may have been published earlier and been revised and reprinted in 2008.*

4. *To determine usefulness, examine the book's chapter titles, headings, copyright page, table of contents, index, bibliography or "recommended readings" section, and glossary.*

R RESOURCE MANAGER—Copy Master
Evaluate Nonfiction Books p. 19

EVALUATE NONFICTION BOOKS

Nonfiction books can give you detailed information on your topic. Asking these questions will help you find the right sources:

- **When was the book copyrighted or updated?** Check the **copyright notice**, which is usually right after the title page. Look for terms such as *revised edition* and *updated edition* on the copyright page or the cover. If a book has gone through many updates and printings, it is likely to be reliable.

- **What sources did the writer use?** Look for a **bibliography**. Some books also include an **appendix**—a collection of additional material about the subject. Notes within the book, such as footnotes, endnotes, or cross-references, can also give you clues about sources.

- **What makes the author an expert on this subject?** Look for an "About the Author" description on the book jacket or at the beginning or end of the book. The author may have written a **preface**, a short introductory essay that explains the purpose of the book, its intended audience, and the research on which it is based. If the source is a biography, find out if the author is related to the person he or she is writing about.

Examine a Nonfiction Book

Using what you have learned about nonfiction books and about the parts of a book (page 1331),decide whether this book is a relevant source for someone interested in a music career.

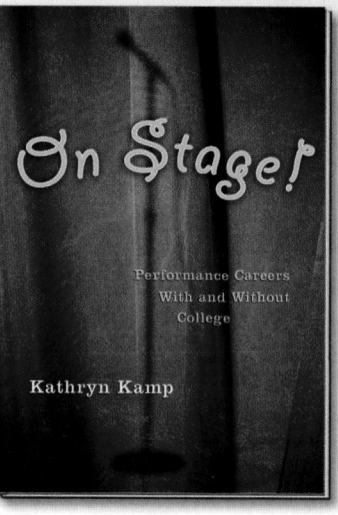

Close Read

1. What is the subject of this book? How do you know?

2. Is the author qualified to write a book on this topic? Why or why not?

3. When was this book published?

4. What other parts of the book should you examine to determine whether it is a worthwhile source? (Hint: See page 1331.)

1336 UNIT 12: THE POWER OF RESEARCH

DIFFERENTIATED INSTRUCTION

FOR STRUGGLING READERS

Comprehension Support Give pairs of students a nonfiction book from the school library. Have them create an "information sheet" about the book. The sheet should identify the title and subtitle, the number of chapters, the number of pages, the copyright date, and any special features, such as preface, index, appendix, bibliography or "recommended readings" section, and glossary.

FOR ADVANCED LEARNERS/PRE–AP

Nonfiction Checklist Ask students to create evaluation checklists for nonfiction based on information from the text and class discussions. Then have small groups compare their individual checklists and develop a master evaluation checklist. Have each group evaluate a book using this checklist and report on what they learned.

1336 UNIT 12: THE POWER OF RESEARCH

EVALUATE NEWSPAPERS AND PERIODICALS

Newspapers, magazines, and journals are available in the form of printed paper copies, online, or on microfilm or microfiche. Evaluating articles can be challenging because you need to assess the publication itself, the author of the specific article, and the content. Here are some basic questions to ask:

- **Is the publication well known and respected?** Most large-circulation newspapers and national magazines are reliable sources. Beware of sensationalist publications, such as the *National Enquirer,* however.

- **When was the article published?** Old is not always bad. Out-of-date newspaper and magazine articles can be excellent sources about historical events.

- **Who wrote the article?** You can usually assume that articles by the staff writers or contributing editors are as reliable as the periodical they're published in.

- **Was the article originally published in another source?** If so, make sure the original source is reliable, such as *Scientific American* or a news service such as AP (Associated Press).

- **Can the facts in the article be verified?** Consult other sources, either on paper, online, or in person.

TIP Whenever possible, check facts in more than one source. Even the most reliable sources may contain errors.

YOUR TURN

Examine a Newspaper Article
Use what you have learned about evaluating sources as you examine this article.

---

from **The Charlotte Observer**

Girlfriend Led Him to Music—Tuba Kept Him There

BY STEVEN BROWN, STAFF WRITER

When Neptune takes flight across the waters in Ottorino Respighi's "The Fountains of Rome," the orchestra's tuba helps pour out the big tune that escorts him on his way. In the Charlotte Symphony's concerts Friday and Saturday, David Mills will be Neptune's bass-clef companion. Mills has been in the orchestra since 1976.
Hometown: Albemarle.
In the beginning was the ulterior motive: "I joined the band," Mills recalled, "so I could sit next to my then-girlfriend. About two weeks later, she quit." That was in the fifth grade. Obviously, Mills—who played the trumpet at the time—stuck with music.

"Once I got started doing it," Mills said, "I loved it. It was the one activity in middle school and high school that I really was crazy about."
Working his way down: To get himself into the marching band, Mills

See TUBA, *page* A17

Close Read

1. In your own words, what is this article about?

2. Knowing that Charlotte is a large city in North Carolina and that the *Observer* is its major newspaper, would you expect this article to be a reliable information source?

3. At the end of the article, there is an e-mail address that allows readers to contact the reporter who wrote the article. Why is this important?

FOR ADVANCED LEARNERS/PRE-AP

Compare and Contrast Have students find two articles describing the same event, one from a highly reliable newspaper, the other from a sensationalist tabloid. Have them evaluate both articles, using the tools described in this lesson and the Comparison Matrix activity. Have them also indicate if they believe any additional tools might be useful for evaluating these publications.

BEST PRACTICES TOOLKIT—Transparency
Comparison Matrix p. A24

EVALUATE NEWSPAPERS AND PERIODICALS

Call on volunteers to read each question and response. Provide clarification and additional instruction as needed. You might also want to distribute copies of newspapers and magazines to pairs of students and incorporate these activities:

- Ask students whether the newspaper or magazine they received is reliable. How can they tell? Then have students read the *TIP*. Point out that small or local newspapers often pick up press releases or wire stories about world or national events from other sources. Discuss where else students could check facts in their sources.

- Direct students to the masthead of a periodical and discuss the information provided. Have partners check the publication date of the newspaper or periodical. Is the information up to date? Are the contributors reliable?

- Have partners skim through the top story or cover story in their publication. Ask students to identify the writer and his or her sources if possible.

YOUR TURN

Close Read
Possible answers:

1. *The article describes how David Mills became a professional tuba player.*

2. *Given that it is a major city newspaper, the information is likely to be reliable.*

3. *Readers could e-mail the reporter to ask a question, verify a fact, or find out more about the subject and related information.*

Reteaching Worksheets on **thinkcentral.com**
Research and Study Skills Lesson 6: Evaluating Print Sources

R RESOURCE MANAGER—Copy Master
Evaluate Periodicals p. 20

Collecting Your Own Data

Using People as Primary Sources

INDEPENDENT OBSERVATION AND FIELD RESEARCH

Field Research Explain that students who like hands-on learning experiences will probably enjoy field research. Have small groups brain-storm places to do field research to learn about music-related careers, such as music business attorney, music critic, film music editor, vocal-ist, elementary music teacher, and retail music salesperson. Invite groups to share their ideas.

Planning Being prepared will help students to make the most of their field research. Before conducting an interview or a visit, students might consider these options:

- Start a KWL chart, focusing on topics that they know about and those they hope to cover. Help students use the chart to devel-op a list of questions to ask or find answers to during their visit.

- Make a checklist of things they need to do to get ready: make an appointment, get permis-sion to record or photograph, call to confirm, collect note cards and pencils, get a tape recorder, dress appropriately.

- Do preliminary research to learn how to find their destinations and obtain the names of the people they plan or hope to meet.

 BEST PRACTICES TOOLKIT—Transparency
KWL p. A21

INTERVIEWS WITH EXPERTS

After reading the text, have volunteers list the steps in the interview process. (*identify people to interview, set up an interview, prepare ques-tions, take notes*) Point out that a tape record-er is a useful tool for interviewing—especially when used with note taking—but remind stu-dents that they must first get permission from the person being interviewed. Then ask small groups to use their field-research discussion to generate categories of people they might interview to find out more about each career.

Collecting Your Own Data

Sometimes it isn't possible to find the answers to your questions in a library or on a Web site. How can you collect your own data?

Using People as Primary Sources

For some topics, your own observations and data are your best source of information. Use these techniques to become your own search engine.

INDEPENDENT OBSERVATION AND FIELD RESEARCH

Doing **field research** means going somewhere and making focused, purposeful observations. For instance, you might visit a recording studio to learn more about a career as a recording engineer. Be sure to call ahead, ask permission, and make an appointment. Take notes while you are visiting.

> *Notes on Visit to McNulty Audio Recording, 5/2/2009*
>
> - *4 full-time employees plus 5 to 6 part-time production assistants*
> - *some analog equipment, but the studio is mostly digital*
> - *studio records some singers and bands but mostly does commercial audio (radio, TV, Internet)*
> - *2 to 3 part-time interns; Jenna Tinucci trains interns, coordinates scheduling*
> - *Ms. Tinucci says that Dave Zinn, a recording engineer at McNulty, might agree to an interview.*

For some topics, you may want to set up a **field study** in which you do multiple observations and collect specific types of data. For other topics, you might be able to attend a **lecture** at your school, at a public library, or at a nearby community center.

INTERVIEWS WITH EXPERTS

Try tapping the knowledge of people who have experience with your topic. For example, to research careers in music, you might interview musicians, music teachers, or students who have completed music-related internships. You might interview someone in person, over the telephone, or by e-mail. Ask if the person is willing to talk with you, and set a date and time for the interview. Prepare a list of clear, open-ended questions that must be answered with specific information, not just yes or no. Also, take thorough notes. Take a look at these sample interview questions.

DIFFERENTIATED INSTRUCTION

FOR STRUGGLING READERS

Comprehension Support Give students these suggestions for interview methods:

- Write each question on a separate index card with space to record the response.

- If anything is confusing, clarify it immedi-ately with the person being interviewed.

- Put questions in order, but be flexible about following new lines of thought.

Then have students work in pairs to generate and organize interview questions on topics of interest to each student.

> **Questions for Dave Zinn**
> 1. What is a typical day like at your job?
> 2. To get a job like yours, does it make more sense to have a college degree or on-the-job experience?
> 3. How much of your job is technical and how much is creative?
> 4. What are the best and worst parts of your job?

See pages R81–R82: Interview

If you are able to identify an expert, you may wish to send a polite and specific question by e-mail or letter. You can gain an inside track to a group of experts by joining a relevant Internet discussion group called a list server. For instance, ProAudio is a discussion group for professionals in the recording industry.

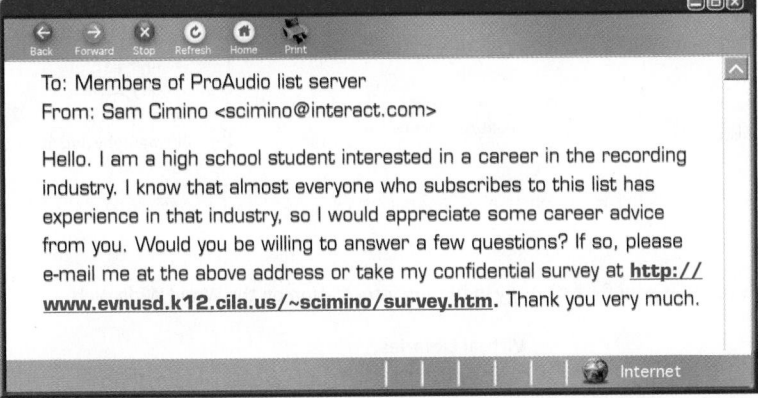

To: Members of ProAudio list server
From: Sam Cimino <scimino@interact.com>

Hello. I am a high school student interested in a career in the recording industry. I know that almost everyone who subscribes to this list has experience in that industry, so I would appreciate some career advice from you. Would you be willing to answer a few questions? If so, please e-mail me at the above address or take my confidential survey at **http://www.evnusd.k12.cila.us/~scimino/survey.htm**. Thank you very much.

QUESTIONNAIRES AND SURVEYS

You can collect questionnaire and survey information by e-mail, by mail, by telephone, through a Web site, or in person. Keep the names of participants confidential to protect their privacy.

TIP For safety reasons, give only an e-mail address to survey participants. Don't post or give out your home address or your telephone number.

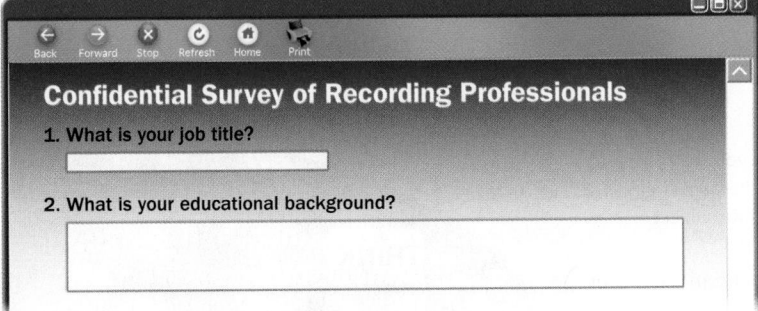

Confidential Survey of Recording Professionals

1. What is your job title?

2. What is your educational background?

Share these interviewing tips with students:

- Tell students that the way they prepare and plan for an interview will determine its usefulness. Have small groups review the information about interviewing and create a "to do" checklist to prepare for the content of an interview.

- Have groups select one interviewee and write five interview questions that they might ask to learn more about that career.

- Stress the importance of taking very careful notes. Interviewers should ask interviewees to repeat information, confirm quotations, and clarify statements as needed. Students should then check facts and spellings of people, businesses, or organizations. Tell students that most interviewees will gladly take a follow-up call to verify facts or information.

- Encourage students to end an interview by asking for suggestions of additional information sources. They should then quickly summarize important information in their notes while it is fresh, in particular filling in any holes in their notes, fleshing out details, and clarifying abbreviations.

- For e-mail interviews, remind students to use formal language and letter format, and to check grammar, punctuation, and spelling.

- Always remember to write a note thanking the interviewee for his or her time.

QUESTIONNAIRES AND SURVEYS

After students read through the text, point out the *TIP*. Stress that students should give out their e-mail addresses to individuals, not organizations, and then only to people associated with reliable groups. Brainstorm reasons why confidentiality is important.

FOR STRUGGLING READERS

Concept Support Have small groups work together to develop an e-mail message requesting an interview about careers in music education. Suggest that they use the e-mail message on page 1339 as a model.

FOR ADVANCED LEARNERS/PRE–AP

Questionnaire Invite partners to develop a questionnaire that they might send to people in music-related careers—music business attorney, music critic, film music editor, vocalist, elementary music teacher, or retail music salesperson. Discuss the similarities and differences between a questionnaire and an interview. Have students share their questionnaires with the class.

Research Tips and Strategies

COMMON CORE W 7 W 8 W 9

Library Detective

- Before students read through the information on the library classification systems, ask them to share their experiences looking for books in the school or local library. What problems did they face? Did they find the catalog system difficult or easy to use? Why?

- Have students identify the section of the school library where they would find books with these identification numbers. Then have them tell what topics books in this section cover, and what Library of Congress letter would apply to this topic.

  614 (Technology; T)

  225 (Religion; B)

  77 (General works; A)

  189 (Philosophy/psychology; B)

- Ask students which classification system your school and town library use. If students have used both systems, ask which they prefer and why. Have students visit the library and answer questions: Which numbers and letters have the most books? Which have they used most often?

Web Tools

- Point out to students that some search engines, such as Google, allow users to search specifically for images or to conduct a more scholarly search (scholar.google.com).

- Share another Web resource, http:// newslink.org. This Web site provides links to most newspapers in the country, organized by type. Invite students to name resources they have found useful.

- Assign small groups a section of the chart to review—search engines, metasearch engines, directories, virtual libraries, and other Web resources. Have groups report to the class on which search tool of that type they recommend most highly and why.

Reteaching Worksheets on thinkcentral.com
Research and Study Skills Lesson 3: Using Reference and Search Tools

---

Research Tips and Strategies

Library Detective

Two basic systems are used to classify nonfiction books. Most high school and public libraries use the Dewey decimal system. University and research libraries generally use the Library of Congress system.

DEWEY DECIMAL SYSTEM

000–099	General works
100–199	Philosophy and psychology
200–299	Religion
300–399	Social science
400–499	Language
500–599	Natural sciences and mathematics
600–699	Technology (applied sciences)
700–799	Arts and recreation
800–899	Literature and rhetoric
900–999	Geography and history

LIBRARY OF CONGRESS SYSTEM

A	General works		L	Education
B	Philosophy, psychology, religion		M	Music
C	History		N	Fine arts
D	General history and history of Europe		P	Language and literature
E–F	American history		Q	Science
G	Geography, anthropology, recreation		R	Medicine
H	Social sciences		S	Agriculture
J	Political science		T	Technology
K	Law		U	Military science
			V	Naval science
			Z	Bibliography and library science

Web Tools

Knowing what search tools to use is your first strategy in finding information on the World Wide Web.

Search Engines

Each search engine has its own method of searching and differs in speed, size of database, and other variables.

- Google   • Yahoo!   • MSN   • Ask.com

Metasearch Engines

A metasearch engine can save you time by searching multiple search engines simultaneously.

- Dogpile   • SurfWax   • Fazzle

Directories

Directories are useful when you are researching a general topic because they arrange Internet resources into subject categories.

- Lycos   • Galaxy   • About.com   • Yahoo!

Virtual Libraries

At a virtual library, you can look up information in encyclopedias, directories, and indexes. You can even e-mail a question to a librarian.

- Internet Public Library
- Librarians' Index to the Internet

Other Web Resources

Library catalogs: Library of Congress
Encyclopedias: Grolier Online
Newspaper archives: America's Newspapers
News associations: Associated Press, AFP
Specialized databases: Medline

Writing and Research in a Digital Age

THINK central   Discover a wealth of Web search tools and resources.

KEYWORD: HML10-1340

DIFFERENTIATED INSTRUCTION

FOR STRUGGLING READERS

Comprehension Support Explain that the Dewey decimal system incorporates many categories from the Library of Congress system. For example, a Library of Congress "R" book would fit in the Dewey decimal's 500s category: natural sciences and mathematics. Give students a selection of nonfiction books or book titles. Point out the Dewey decimal call number on the book and discuss why it fits in that particular category.

FOR ADVANCED LEARNERS/PRE-AP

Consumer Report Challenge individuals or partners to create a rating chart of one section of Web Tools presented on this page. Explain that other students should be able to use the chart to determine which of the tools is most effective. Refer students to *Consumer Reports* magazine for ideas and for examples of similar charts.

Checklist for Evaluating Sources

The information . . .

☑ is relevant to the topic you are researching

☑ is up to date (This point is especially important when researching time-sensitive topics in areas such as science, medicine, and sports.)

☑ is from an author who is qualified to write about the topic

☑ is from a trusted source that is updated or reviewed regularly

☑ makes the author's or institution's purpose for writing clear

☑ is written at the right level for your needs (For example, a children's book is probably too simplistic, while a scientific paper may be too complex.)

☑ has the level of detail you need—neither too general nor too specific

☑ can be verified in more than one source

Sharing Your Research

At last you have established your research goals, located sources of information, evaluated the materials, and taken notes on what you learned. Now you have a chance to share the results with people in your world—and even beyond. Here are some options:

- Give a speech to your classmates or to people in your community.
- Create a power presentation using presentation software and share it with classmates, friends, or family members.
- Describe your research findings on your own Web site.
- Summarize the information in a newsletter or brochure.
- Share the results of your research in a formal research paper. **See the following pages. ▶**

See pages 1364–1365 for more information about publishing with technology.

Checklist for Evaluating Sources

After students review the checklist, remind them that this information is covered in detail on pages 1333–1337. Ask them to study the list and answer these questions:

- Which criteria are most important for evaluating sources?
- What criteria, if any, would you add to the list?

Sharing Your Research

Options Call on a volunteer to read the workshop summary and options for sharing. List some additional suggestions:

- Create a graphic novel or comic book about your topic.
- Develop a workshop to teach your topic to middle-school students.
- Make a documentary video or DVD about your findings.

Ask students which options they would choose and why.

Summary Invite students to tell what information from this part of the unit was new to them, and what information was review. You might want to hold a roundtable discussion of related questions:

- How can strong research strategies help me make better decisions as a consumer?
- How can strong research strategies help me use my time more efficiently?
- How can strong research strategies help me in work and in life?

Reteaching Worksheets on thinkcentral.com
   Research and Study Skills Lesson 6: Evaluating Print Sources
   Research and Study Skills Lesson 7: Evaluating Electronic Sources

FOR STRUGGLING READERS

Comprehension Support To evaluate and review students' understanding of the Research Strategies Workshop, organize small groups to create a graphic/visual summary of the workshop concepts and methods. Have groups share their graphic displays with the class.

FOR ADVANCED LEARNERS/PRE–AP

Presentation Options Challenge small groups to brainstorm additional presentation options, based on topics discussed in this workshop. Urge students to suggest possible visual or sound aids, or interactive or other multimedia elements for a presentation. Invite groups to present their ideas to the class, with examples where possible.

Focus and Motivate

COMMON CORE FOCUS

W 2a–f Write informative/explanatory texts to examine complex ideas clearly and accurately.
W 4 Produce clear and coherent writing.
W 5 Develop and strengthen writing as needed by planning, revising, editing, rewriting, or trying a new approach. **W 7** Conduct research projects to answer a question or solve a problem. **W 8** Gather relevant information from multiple sources; assess the usefulness of each source. **W 9b (RI 1)** Draw and cite evidence from informational texts to support research. **L 1** Demonstrate command of the conventions of standard English grammar and usage. **L 2** Demonstrate command of standard English capitalization, punctuation, and spelling. **L 2b** Use a colon to introduce a quotation. **L 3a** Write and edit work so it conforms to guidelines in a style manual.

WRITE WITH A PURPOSE

Tell students that their purpose in writing a research paper is not only to inform readers about a topic but also to keep them engaged. Challenge students to choose a topic that they and their target audience will find interesting.

COMMON CORE TRAITS

Review the *COMMON CORE TRAITS* with students, focusing mainly on development and organization of ideas. Compare the list of traits with the rubric on page 1361.

ADDITIONAL TASKS

Write About a Career Write a research paper that explores training in a field of interest to you or other young people.

Possible topics: music, communications, health care

Write About History Write a research paper about people enduring a national crisis.

Possible topics: Great Depression, World War II

Writing Online

The following tools are available online at **thinkcentral.com** and on **WriteSmart CD-ROM**:
- **Interactive Graphic Organizers**
- **Interactive Student Models**
- **Interactive Revision Lessons**

Writing Workshop
INFORMATIVE TEXT

Research Paper
Essential Course of Study 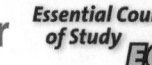 **ECOS**

Now that you have thoroughly explored a variety of research strategies, it's time to put what you have learned to work by conducting a research project to answer a question of your choosing. To start your investigation, refer to the information below.

 Complete the workshop activities in your **Reader/Writer Notebook**.

WRITE WITH A PURPOSE

WRITING TASK

Write a **research paper** to answer a question that interests you.

Idea Starters
- How have recent space expeditions expanded our knowledge of the universe?
- How do historians' depictions of Julius Caesar compare with Shakespeare's depiction?
- How do car manufacturers plan to help reduce carbon emissions and slow global warming?

THE ESSENTIALS

Here are some common purposes, audiences, and formats for research-based writing.

PURPOSES	AUDIENCES	FORMATS
• to inform or enlighten others with an interest in your subject	• classmates and teacher	• essay for class
	• community members	• encyclopedia article
• to offer a unique perspective on a subject	• readers of journals in special fields	• oral report
		• multimedia presentation
• to learn more about a subject	• Web users	• Web site publication

COMMON CORE TRAITS

1. DEVELOPMENT OF IDEAS
- introduces a clearly defined **topic**
- states a **controlling idea** that answers a research question
- supports the **main points** of the topic with **evidence** from multiple authoritative sources
- ends with a **concluding section** that follows from and supports the information presented

2. ORGANIZATION OF IDEAS
- **organizes** ideas, information, and evidence in a logical way
- uses varied **transitions** to create **cohesion** and **connect ideas**

3. LANGUAGE FACILITY AND CONVENTIONS
- maintains a **formal style** and **objective tone**
- uses **precise language** and **domain-specific vocabulary**
- correctly integrates **quotations**
- employs correct **grammar**, **usage**, and **spelling**

Writing Online THINK central

Go to **thinkcentral.com**.
KEYWORD: HML10N-1342

Writing Workshop Resources

 RESOURCE MANAGER UNIT 12
Plan and Teach, pp. 5–10
Prewriting–Editing, pp. 11–31
Scoring Rubric, p. 32
Technology, p. 33
Writing Support, p. 34*

BEST PRACTICES TOOLKIT
Writing Template: Informative Essay, pp. C16, C19

TECHNOLOGY
- **Teacher One Stop DVD-ROM**
- **Student One Stop DVD-ROM**
- **WriteSmart CD-ROM**
- **GrammarNotes DVD-ROM**

Writing Center on thinkcentral.com

See resources on the **Teacher One Stop DVD-ROM** *and on* **thinkcentral.com**.

* Resources for Differentiation

Planning/Prewriting

COMMON CORE

W 2a–f Write informative/explanatory texts to examine complex ideas clearly and accurately.
W 5 Develop and strengthen writing by planning.
W 7 Conduct research projects to answer a question or solve a problem.

Teach

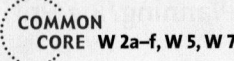

Getting Started

SELECT A TOPIC

Because possible research topics are limitless, it can be difficult to know where to start. Start with topics that fascinate you and might interest potential readers as well. Then, brainstorm a list of possible topics.

NARROW YOUR FOCUS

Your topic should be broad enough to support a full-length paper but not so broad that it could fill a book. Use a graphic organizer to investigate different aspects of your topic. Then, **narrow** your topic to one aspect to research. Consult with your teacher, a librarian, or an expert on your topic to make sure that your focus is compelling and complex enough for a detailed paper.

TIP To find out how much information is available on your topic, check the following resources at your school or local library or online:

- Card or online book catalog
- *Readers' Guide to Periodical Literature*
- Online databases, such as InfoTrac
- General or specialized reference books or CD-ROMs
- World Wide Web and online services

If there's too little available information, **broaden** your focus; if there's too much, consider narrowing your focus.

THINK ABOUT AUDIENCE AND PURPOSE

Focus on what is most significant for your specific **purpose** and **audience**. Write clearly and coherently in a style appropriate to your purpose and audience. Consider your audience's knowledge of the topic and what information will hold their interest.

▶ TIPS

- Skim your textbooks and the nonfiction section of the library for topics.
- Look for topics in the news, such as new laws, world events, or scientific breakthroughs.
- Watch documentaries on interesting topics.
- Browse the Internet, using a search engine to explore topics.
- Think about interesting historical or literary figures you have studied.

▶ WHAT DOES IT LOOK LIKE?

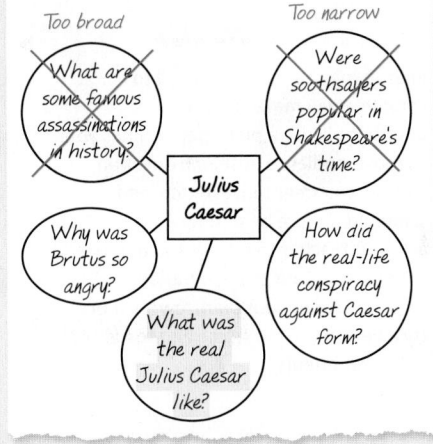

Too broad — What are some famous assassinations in history?
Too narrow — Were soothsayers popular in Shakespeare's time?
Julius Caesar
Why was Brutus so angry?
How did the real-life conspiracy against Caesar form?
What was the real Julius Caesar like?

▶ ASK YOURSELF:

- Who would be most interested in my topic?
- What does this audience already know (or think they know) about my topic?
- What background information and explanations of **domain-specific** (specialized) **vocabulary** might they need?

DIFFERENTIATED INSTRUCTION

FOR ENGLISH LANGUAGE LEARNERS

Language: Reinforce Research Terms Write these terms on the board and review them with students:

- *introduction:* the opening paragraphs, which present the topic and the focus
- *transition:* a word or phrase that links ideas
- *evidence:* facts, examples, quotations, observations, and other supporting details

- *summary:* a brief retelling of the main ideas of a source in one's own words
- *paraphrase:* a restatement of information
- *source:* anything that supplies information
- *tone:* the writer's attitude toward the topic, conveyed through word choice
- *format:* a way of arranging information

Planning/ Prewriting

COMMON CORE W 2a–f, W 5, W 7

▶ **SELECT A TOPIC** Remind students to look at the Idea Starters on page 1342 if they need help identifying possible topics. Students may also wish to freewrite for several minutes, recording their own ideas and questions. Encourage students to think of works of literature and other topics that interest them but are also somewhat new or unfamiliar to them.

▶ **NARROW YOUR FOCUS** Explain to students that narrowing their focus will make researching, developing a controlling idea, and organizing ideas easier to manage. Suggest that students use these questions to help narrow their focus to a more specific and manageable research topic:

- Is there enough information known about this topic to find research materials?
- Are there enough different resources available on the topic?
- Does my controlling idea offer an interesting or new angle on the topic?

▶ **THINK ABOUT AUDIENCE AND PURPOSE** Remind students that a primary purpose of a research paper is to provide information on a topic for an audience. As they plan, research, and write their papers, students should consider what their audience needs or wants to know about the topic. Point out that their audience's needs or interests may require students to cover certain additional aspects of their topic before discussing others. For example, if students write about a historical event, their readers may need to know about events leading up to the event to understand it. If there is domain-specific vocabulary for the topic, students may need to include definitions or explanations of these terms.

R **RESOURCE MANAGER—Copy Masters**

Planning / Prewriting pp. 11–22
Researching pp. 23–27
Drafting pp. 28–29
Ask a Peer Reader p. 30
Proofreading / Editing p. 31
Scoring Rubric p. 32
Writing Support p. 34

Planning/Prewriting *continued*

▶ **WRITE A RESEARCH QUESTION** Tell students that initially they will have many questions about their topics, but their papers should ultimately answer one main research question.

- Point out that as students read and take notes, related questions will evolve naturally from their main question. Note how each of the student model questions helps answer the main question "What was the real Julius Caesar like?"

- After students write their own research questions, have them evaluate each one by asking: "Does this question help to answer my main question?"

- Remind students that their questions should begin with one of the following words: *who, where, what, why, when,* or *how.* Questions that begin with why or how are likely to be more complicated and more interesting to research than questions that begin with *where, who,* or *when.*

▶ **DEVELOP A RESEARCH PLAN** Have students copy the template provided and use it to develop a research plan. Tell them to customize the template by adding other headings as they feel necessary.

YOUR TURN Give students time to select and focus a topic, write a research question and identify related questions, and sketch out a research plan. After students share their research questions and plan with a partner, have them make changes or additions based on their partner's feedback.

For interactive graphic organizers, see

WriteSmart CD-ROM

Writing Center on <u>thinkcentral.com</u>

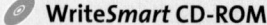 **RESOURCE MANAGER—Copy Masters**
Develop Research Questions p. 11
Narrowing a Research Topic p. 21
Planning / Prewriting p. 22

Planning/Prewriting *continued*

Getting Started

WRITE A RESEARCH QUESTION

Next, convert your focused topic into a research question to answer in your paper. This question will keep you on track as you identify sources and gather information. Make sure your research question cannot be answered in a single word; it should require investigation.

Also, develop more detailed questions related to your main question. These questions will guide your search for sources you can **synthesize**, or combine, to develop and demonstrate an understanding of the topic.

▶ WHAT DOES IT LOOK LIKE?

Topic: Julius Caesar

Research Question: What was the real Julius Caesar like?

Related Questions:

- How much of Julius Caesar is based on historical fact?
- How does Shakespeare portray Caesar?
- How did historians of Caesar's time describe him?
- How does Shakespeare's Caesar compare with the actual historical figure?

DEVELOP A RESEARCH PLAN

Identifying the tasks you need to complete will make research less daunting. Write a plan that outlines your purpose, audience, research question, sources you might investigate, and schedule. Before beginning your research, ask your teacher to review and approve your plan. If your teacher has any concerns about your plan, rework it or try a new approach, according to his or her comments.

▶ TEMPLATE FOR A RESEARCH PLAN

Student Name: _____
Purpose: _____
Audience: _____
Research Question: _____

Potential Sources: _____
_____

SCHEDULE
Research Completed: _____
First Draft Due: _____
Final Draft Due: _____

Teacher Approval: _____

PEER REVIEW Exchange research plans with a classmate. Review each other's research question, and ask: What related questions would you expect to be answered in my paper? What sources do you think I should investigate?

 YOUR TURN List four or five topic ideas in your *Reader/Writer Notebook,* and determine which one would be best for your paper. Then, narrow your topic and develop a controlling idea to guide your research. With your purpose and audience in mind, formulate a research plan using a template like the one above.

DIFFERENTIATED INSTRUCTION

FOR STRUGGLING WRITERS

Develop Research Questions Provide this form to help students generate research questions:

My main topic is _____
_____
_____.

To develop this topic, I need to know:
1. _____
_____
_____

2. _____
_____
_____
_____

3. _____
_____
_____

Researching

COMMON CORE

W 8 Gather relevant information from multiple sources; assess the usefulness of each source. **W 9b (RI 1)** Draw and cite evidence from informational texts to support research.

Following Your Research Plan

LOCATE SOURCES

Gather information from reliable, verifiable print and digital sources. When conducting research using digital sources or the Internet, make effective use of advanced searches by filling in as many of the search parameters as you can. This will help filter out any unwanted sources or Web sites, narrowing down the number of sources you need to review. Remember that **primary sources** contain original, firsthand information that is usually unfiltered and unedited. They include letters, diaries, autobiographies, speeches, historical documents, and eyewitness accounts. **Secondary sources** provide other people's interpretations of primary materials, in the form of encyclopedia articles, newspaper and journal articles, biographies, and textbooks.

Compile a list of useful sources, including the title of each potential source and where you found it. Also, include comments to remind you why the source might be useful.

See pages 1326–1332 of this unit for more information about the references and research tools available to you.

▶ WHAT DOES IT LOOK LIKE?

Sources	Comments
World Wide Web (bookmarked)	
"Julius Caesar." *Encyclopedia Britannica Online*	solid biography
"Bestriding the World." *Julius Caesar: The Last Dictator*	quotations from many primary sources
"Gaius Julius Caesar." Found through Search.com	lots of info
"Julius Caesar." *Columbia Encyclopedia*	useful biography
School Library	
Julius Caesar by Rupert Matthews (xBiog CaesJ MatthR)	fun to read
Cleopatra by Dorothy Hoobler (xBiog Cleopat HooblD)	interesting info
Public Library	
Materialist Shakespeare: A History by Ivo Kamps (822331)	very complicated
"Power Play: 'Friends, Generals and Captains of Industry, Lend Me Your Ears'" by Bruce Weber. *New York Times*	more about business than Shakespeare

ASSESS EACH SOURCE

Assessing your sources is an important step in the research process. A source is useful in answering the research question if it is

- **relevant**—contains information directly related to your research question
- **authoritative**—contains information by an expert on the topic
- **objective**—offers multiple viewpoints on the topic and is not biased, or showing favor to one view of the topic

▶ ASK YOURSELF:

- Is this a primary or secondary source? In what ways will it be useful to me?
- Is the information up-to-date, especially if my topic is timely?
- Are the facts accurate? How can I go about verifying them?
- What qualifies the author to write about this topic? Is he or she an **authority,** or expert, in this field of study?
- What, if any, biases does the source have?

Practice and Apply

Researching

COMMON CORE **W 8, W 9b (RI 1)**

▶ **LOCATE SOURCES** Tell students that they will probably read many more secondary sources than primary sources in the course of their research. Challenge students to locate and consult at least one primary source for every two secondary sources. Explain that one way to identify relevant primary sources is to read the footnotes and bibliographies of secondary sources. Many secondary sources will draw information from the same primary sources. Also point out that a primary source may be included in another primary or secondary source. For example, a primary source may quote from a contemporary speech or letter. A secondary source may quote from a primary source. In such cases, students should look at the footnotes or Works Cited page for the original source.

▶ **ASSESS EACH SOURCE** Tell students that to assess a source on their list, they must examine it thoroughly. If possible, using a source from the list on this page, such as one of the encyclopedia articles on Julius Caesar, model how to assess a source by examining the work and asking the questions provided.

FOR STRUGGLING WRITERS

Create an Evaluation Checklist Have students create and fill in this checklist as they find and assess sources:

Author:

_____

Title:

_____

Publication Date:

_____

❏ Primary source ❏ Secondary source

How I know

_____

This source is ❏ relevant ❏ accurate ❏ objective

How I know

_____

❏ I will use this source for my research because

_____

❏ I will not use this source for my research because

_____

 RESOURCE MANAGER—Copy Masters

Evaluate Web Sites Using Criteria p. 18
Evaluate Nonfiction Books p. 19
Evaluate Periodicals p. 20

Researching *continued*

▶ **PREPARE A SOURCE LIST** Tell students to use an electronic file or index cards to list all the sources they have identified as reliable.

- Explain that the information students list for each source will help them later to prepare a Works Cited page. As you review the information that students should include for each kind of source, point out the correct punctuation, capitalization, and other formatting. For practice, give students several books, periodicals, and articles from the Web and have them record the necessary information about each source.

- Tell students that it is important to number each source and later to use the corresponding number to identify any notes they take on information in that source. If students take a large number of notes on one source, tell them also to alphabetize their notes, using both the source number and a letter, to keep them in order. Explain that such a system is helpful for a longer paper, when notes may be mixed together during writing.

R RESOURCE MANAGER—Copy Master
Sources p. 23

Researching *continued*

Following Your Research Plan

PREPARE A SOURCE LIST

Once you have sorted through your initial list of sources, create an electronic file or use index cards to record information about the sources you plan to use. Special note-taking software is another option. Check with your school librarian or media specialist to see whether this option is available to you.

Include the following details in your list of sources, making sure to number each source. You can use this list later to build your Works Cited list.

World Wide Web source
- author's name (if given)
- title of article and Web page
- name of sponsoring organization or institution
- date created or posted
- medium of publication (Web)
- date of access

Book
- author or editor
- title
- location and publisher
- year of publication
- medium of publication (Print)

Encyclopedia article
- author (if given)
- title of article
- name and year of encyclopedia
- location and publisher
- year and medium of publication (CD-ROM)

Newspaper or magazine article
- author
- title of article
- name of periodical
- day, month, and year of publication
- beginning page number of article
- medium of publication (Print)

▶ **WHAT DOES IT LOOK LIKE?**

World Wide Web source

> **Source #:** 3
> **Type:** Article on Web site
>
> Cross, Suzanne. "Bestriding the World." *Julius Caesar: The Last Dictator.* 2004. Web. 30 Apr. 2010.

Book

> **Source #:** 6
> **Type:** Book
>
> Schanzer, Ernest. *The Problem Plays of Shakespeare.* New York: Schocken, 1965. Print.

Encyclopedia article

> **Source #:** 1
> **Type:** CD-ROM encyclopedia
>
> "Caesar, Julius." *Britannica Student Encyclopedia.* 2004 ed. Chicago: Encyclopaedia Britannica, 2004. CD-ROM.

Newspaper or magazine article

> **Source #:** 4
> **Type:** Newspaper article
>
> Weber, Bruce. "Power Play: 'Friends, Generals and Captains of Industry, Lend Me Your Ears.'" *New York Times* 31 Jan. 2005: B1+. Print.

DIFFERENTIATED INSTRUCTION

FOR STRUGGLING WRITERS

Identify Source Data To make sure that students understand the standard bibliographic formats used to record sources, ask these questions about the sample sources on this page:

- What type of source is Suzanne Cross's article "Bestriding the World" in *Julius Caesar: The Last Dictator?* *(Web)*

- Who is the publisher of Ernest Schanzer's The Problem Plays of Shakespeare? *(Schocken)*

- In which encyclopedia did the article on Mark Antony appear? *(Britannica Student Encyclopedia)* Was it found in print or on a CD-ROM? *(CD-ROM)*

- Where did Bruce Weber's article "Power Play" appear? *(New York Times)*

Researching *continued*

Following Your Research Plan

TAKE NOTES

When taking notes from sources, record only the information you think you will use. Skim each source and look for information that answers your research question. Also, look for new facts and expert opinions relevant to your topic. Record each piece of useful information in an electronic file (one for each source), on a separate index card, or using special note-taking software. Consult with your teacher to determine the option you should use.

For each entry, include
- a heading that tells the main idea
- the number of the source (from your source list)
- a page number, section name, or other way of locating the information in the source

If you are not quoting directly from a source, restate the information in your own words. You can either paraphrase the information or summarize it.

When you **paraphrase,** you restate all the ideas of the original.

When you **summarize,** you restate only the most important ideas from your source.

TIP Consider adding comments or questions. For example, note whether the information is puzzling or whether it supports or contradicts what you already know.

▶ WHAT DOES IT LOOK LIKE?
Original Source

> By the time of Caesar, Rome had a long-established republican government headed by two consuls with joint powers. Praetors were one step below consuls in the power chain and handled judicial matters. A body of citizens forming the Senate proposed legislation, which general people's assemblies then approved by vote. A special temporary office, that of dictator, was established for use only during times of extreme civil unrest.
>
> Vernon, Jennifer. "Ides of March Marked Murder of Julius Caesar." *National Geographic News*

Paraphrase

Source #: 1
Roman government
During Caesar's time, Rome was a republic. Two consuls who had equal authority were the leaders. Just below them, praetors dealt with legal issues. Senators suggested laws, and general assemblies voted on whether to approve the suggestions. The position of dictator was used only when there were serious outbreaks of lawlessness.
Comments/Questions: Find out who else besides Caesar was named dictator.

Summary

Source #: 1
Roman government
Rome's republican government was made up of consuls, praetors, a senate, and people's assemblies. The position of dictator was temporary and used only during emergencies.
Comments/Questions: Why was Caesar named dictator?

Researching *continued*

▶ **TAKE NOTES** Discuss how to take and organize notes.

- Emphasize that unless students are using note-taking software, they should use a separate electronic file or index card for each item of information they record. Explain that if students include too many pieces of information in the same file or on the same card, they may have difficulty locating and organizing the information later.

- Make sure that students understand how to quote, paraphrase, and summarize the information they gather. To help students decide which note-taking technique to use, have them follow these tips:

  If the source succinctly states the information better than you can state it, quote it.

  If the source provides information you want to restate in your own words, paraphrase it.

  If the source provides a substantial amount of information you want to distill into a main idea, summarize it.

- Refer students to the *TIP*. Suggest that they highlight their annotations about inconsistencies so that they will not forget these observations at a later date.

R RESOURCE MANAGER—Copy Masters
Summarize and Paraphrase 1 p. 24
Summarize and Paraphrase 2 p. 25

FOR STRUGGLING WRITERS

Use Summary Criteria Have students use these criteria as guidelines when writing a summary:

- A good summary runs one-quarter to one-third the length of the original.

- It contains the main points of the original.

- It includes important details only.

- It is accurate.

Point out the difference in length between the model summary and paraphrase. Explain that a paraphrase is useful when presenting background information and that it is roughly as long as the original. A summary is often useful when referring to a story or encapsulating key events.

Researching continued

▶ **QUOTE WELL-STATED IDEAS DIRECTLY**
Review procedures for quoting from sources, including using ellipses and brackets.

- Discuss steps students should take to make sure, when quoting, that they copy original sources exactly: copy only a few words at a time; check each section copied against the original; when finished, compare the quotation to the original source.

- After students read the information and the **TIP**, ask them how many ellipses are included in the quotation shown *(two)*, what word has been added by the student writer *(He)*, and to whom the pronoun in brackets refers *(Julius Caesar)*.

- For practice have students copy a quotation from the original source on page 1347. Then, ask them to include one ellipsis and to insert a word or phrase in brackets. Have partners exchange and check each other's quotations for accuracy.

▶ **AVOID PLAGIARISM** To emphasize the seriousness of plagiarism, write the words NEVER PLAGIARIZE on the board. Then have a student read aloud the text under "Avoid Plagiarism" and summarize it. *Possible answer: Any text that directly uses another writer's ideas must be credited, even if it is not quoted directly.*

- Point out that while the unauthorized use of others' words or ideas is sometimes deliberate, carelessness with source files or cards can also lead to plagiarism.

- Explain that the plagiarized example on this page should have had the same documentation as the correctly documented example.

- To underscore the importance of correct documentation, hold a discussion of plagiarism. Ask students what punishment plagiarism should bring about.

R RESOURCE MANAGER—Copy Masters
  Avoid Plagiarism 1 p. 26
  Avoid Plagiarism 2 p. 27

Researching continued

Following Your Research Plan

QUOTE WELL-STATED IDEAS DIRECTLY

Sometimes an idea is expressed so well in a source that you want to use the author's own words. In recording **direct quotations,** copy the material exactly as it appears in the original, word for word, and put quotation marks around it.

TIP When you cite a source, consider not only what the text says explicitly, or directly, but what it infers, or implies.

AVOID PLAGIARISM

Plagiarism—the unauthorized use of others' words or ideas—is not honest. Avoid plagiarism by carefully documenting the sources of any ideas that aren't common knowledge. Do this whether you are paraphrasing, summarizing, or directly quoting the material.

TIP Remember that quoting word-for-word several sentences or more without documenting the source is not the only type of plagiarism. When you include others' phrases within your paraphrase or summary and do not use quotation marks, you are plagiarizing.

▶ **GUIDELINES FOR RECORDING QUOTATIONS:**

- Enclose all original material in quotation marks.
- If you want to leave out unneeded words, use ellipses (. . .).
- If you add a clarifying word or phrase, enclose it in brackets [].

> **Source #:** 3
> **The problems with Shakespeare's Caesar**
>
> "There is no hint of the personal charm for which he was famous, the wit and magnetism. . . . [He] was infinitely more complex . . . than Shakespeare's version" (online, no page number).

▶ **WHAT DOES IT LOOK LIKE?**
Original Source

> His friends he treated with invariable kindness and consideration. . . . He advanced some of his friends to the highest positions, even though they were of the humblest origin, and when taken to task for it, flatly declared that if he had been helped in defending his honor by brigands and cut-throats, he would have requited even such men in the same way.
>
> Suetonius. *The Lives of the Caesars.* Trans. J. C. Rolfe

Plagiarized

> Caesar treated his friends with invariable kindness and consideration. When he was criticized for appointing his friends to high position, he flatly declared that if pirates and cut-throats had helped him, he would have rewarded them in the same way.

Correctly Documented

> Caesar often appointed friends, even those of low birth, to high positions. When he was criticized for this practice, Caesar "flatly declared that if he had been helped in defending his honor by brigands [thieves] and cut-throats, he would have requited [rewarded] even such men in the same way" (Suetonius 93).

DIFFERENTIATED INSTRUCTION

FOR ENGLISH LANGUAGE LEARNERS
Language: Skill Words Write these terms on the board and review them with students:

plagiarize: to use other people's words or ideas without giving them credit

uncredited: not given recognition, not identified

documented: has the source identified

original source: where information used in an essay first appears in print, CD-ROM, audio-visual, or online. Original sources should be credited, or cited.

Researching *continued*

Following Your Research Plan

DRAFT A CONTROLLING IDEA

Review the material you've gathered from your sources. What answer does it suggest to your original research question? Write a statement that describes the controlling idea of your paper. You may also want to hint in your controlling idea at the answers you've found.

TIP You may discover that the information you've gathered answers a different question than the one you initially asked. Revise your question and then draft a new controlling idea that accurately conveys the information you plan to present.

CREATE AN OUTLINE

Create an outline of your ideas before writing. Read through your files or cards and group them by similar headings or main ideas. Organize the main ideas in the order in which you will present the information in your paper. Your arrangement should show the relationship between complex ideas and reflect their logical development. Choose the method or methods that best fit your topic:

Chronological order presents events in the order in which they happened.

Logical order groups related ideas together—explaining the parts of a whole or comparing two subjects, for instance.

Order of importance places the least important ideas first and moves to the most important (or vice versa).

Then, develop an outline in which each main idea is listed as a Roman numeral. Supporting details, facts, and examples should be identified as sublevels of your outline. As you draft your paper, you will use this outline to guide your writing.

▶ **A STRONG CONTROLLING IDEA SHOULD . . .**

- introduce the topic of your paper
- state your research question
- be a statement that can be supported with evidence
- reveal your point of view on the topic, rather than simply state a fact

▶ **WHAT DOES IT LOOK LIKE?**

> **Capturing Julius Caesar**
> I. Introduction
>   A. Shakespeare
>   B. Historians and scholars
> II. Shakespeare's portrayal
>   A. Vain, arrogant, lacks humor
>   B. Some scholars disagree (Cross)
>   1. Charm, wit, magnetism
>   2. Intellectual and complex man
> III. The historical record
>   A. Proud, ruthless, driven, but also kind, loyal (Suetonius)
>   B. An intellectual (Cicero)
>   C. Driven by pride, ambition (Plutarch)
> IV. Concluding section
>   A. Complex man
>   B. Shakespeare plus historical record provides balanced view

YOUR TURN Locate and assess sources, jotting notes about their relevance and reliability in your *Reader/Writer Notebook*. Gather various quotations, paraphrases, and summaries that help answer your question. Use this information to write a controlling idea and develop an outline. Periodically review your research process, and make adjustments as needed.

Researching *continued*

▶ **DRAFT A CONTROLLING IDEA** Emphasize that a draft of a controlling idea is a "work in progress." Encourage students to revisit their controlling idea often as they organize and begin drafting their papers. Tell them they may want to reword or revise their controlling ideas if they seem too broad or too narrow. Remind students that all the information in their papers should be related to their controlling ideas. If they find an interesting new angle to their topics as they do research, they should revise their controlling ideas to include it.

▶ **CREATE AN OUTLINE** Tell students to prepare to create an outline by following these steps to organize their research:

- Read through your files or note cards.
- Group files or cards that address the same major ideas.
- Arrange the major ideas in the order in which you want to present them.

Explain that the arrangement students settle on should show the relationships between ideas and reflect their logical development.

YOUR TURN Direct students to pause periodically to review their research process and revise their plans. Tell them that they may discover that they need additional sources or evidence for a particular point, and if so, they should pursue additional research.

R RESOURCE MANAGER—Copy Masters
Write a Controlling Idea p. 28

FOR ENGLISH LANGUAGE LEARNERS

Writing: Main Ideas and Supporting Details
Students may need extra guidance to organize their main points and supporting evidence. They may want to use a modified Microtheme frame to help them get started. Ask students guiding questions to help them complete the form.

- What is one main point you want to make?
- What information do you have to support this point?

> Introduction: _____
> Body:
> Main point: Supporting evidence:
> • _____
>   • _____
>   • _____
> Concluding section: _____
> _____

BEST PRACTICES TOOLKIT
Microtheme pp. C13, C53

Drafting 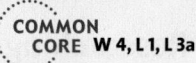 COMMON CORE W 4, L 1, L 3a

▶ **INTRODUCTION** Remind students that the purpose of an introduction is to identify the topic, and to give readers a brief overview of what the paper will cover, including any background information they may need. Point out that the controlling idea is often stated in either the first or last sentence of the introduction. Ask students where the writer of the Student Draft on page 1353 places his controlling idea.

▶ **BODY** Tell students that although much of their papers will focus on presenting information they located during research, their own ideas are important, too, and can also be supported by facts, examples, and other evidence they have found. Discuss these methods of generating original ideas and interpretations:

• React to a traditional or accepted view of a topic.

• Offer an alternative interpretation of a traditional or accepted view of a topic.

• Provide a new angle or a new approach by connecting a topic to new topics.

• Give an interesting, offbeat, or unexpected explanation.

Note that the writer of the Student Draft offers his own interpretation in the second paragraph on page 1355.

▶ **CONCLUDING SECTION** Discuss the various meanings of *concluding*: coming to an end, summarizing, deducing, or inferring. Point out that a concluding section often serves multiple purposes in a research paper. It is an opportunity for the writer to summarize, elaborate, and offer a final original insight. Refer students to the concluding section on page 1358 of the Student Draft and observe that it not only summarizes the content of the paper but leaves readers with something to think about.

▶ **WORKS CITED LIST** Point out that a Works Cited list differs from a bibliography. A bibliography is a list of all of the sources a writer has consulted during research for a paper, including sources used just to verify facts or gather background information. A Works Cited list includes only those sources the writer has actually quoted or paraphrased in the paper, and thus documented in parenthetical citations.

Drafting

The following chart offers a framework for drafting a research paper.

Organizing Your Research Paper

INTRODUCTION

• Grab your audience's attention with a **quotation,** an **anecdote,** or a **question.**
• Supply enough **background information** for readers to understand the topic.
• Include a clear **controlling idea** that introduces the research question your paper will answer.

▼

BODY

• Incorporate the **main ideas** from your outline into the body of your paper. Make sure each idea directly relates to your controlling idea.
• Support your ideas with **relevant facts, concrete details, extended definitions,** and **quotations.** Integrate information into the text selectively, and not randomly, to maintain the flow.
• Document the **source** of each idea in parentheses at the end of each sentence. Consult the "Learn How" lesson on the next page for help.
• Arrange main ideas and evidence in a **logical order.** Use **transitions** to create cohesion and to clarify relationships among ideas.
• **Synthesize** ideas from **multiple sources.**
• Use clear, specific, and **precise language** to convey your ideas.
• Maintain a **formal style** and **objective tone** appropriate to a research paper.
• Look for opportunities to include **formatting** and **graphics**—subheadings, maps, time lines, and charts—to aid understanding.

▼

CONCLUDING SECTION

• Sum up the **answer** you have found to your research question.
• Leave your audience with something interesting to think about, such as the overall **importance** of your topic, **questions** that remain unanswered, or **suggestions** for additional research.

▼

WORKS CITED LIST

• Include a **Works Cited list** as a separate page at the end of your draft.
• Use a **style manual,** such as the *MLA Handbook for Writers of Research Papers* or the *Chicago Manual of Style,* to ensure that you are correctly documenting your sources according to your teacher's preference. Refer to the MLA Citation Guidelines on pages 1362–1363.
• List sources in **alphabetical order** by the authors' last names (or by title for works with no author listed).
• Begin each entry on a **separate line,** aligned with the left margin; additional lines in an entry should be indented one-half inch.

DIFFERENTIATED INSTRUCTION

FOR STRUGGLING WRITERS

Write a Concluding Section Tell students that one way to draft a concluding section is to write a sentence restating each major idea in their paper. Explain that the sentences should refer to the major subtopics or sections of the paper but state the ideas using different words. Students can then link these sentences with transitions that show how the ideas are related and write a concluding statement that shares a final reflection or insight.

FOR ADVANCED LEARNERS/PRE–AP

Explore Openings Emphasize that an engaging opening is as important in a research paper as in an analytical essay. Have students brainstorm ways, in addition to those listed, to open a research paper. Then, ask them to share their ideas and provide an example of each that relates to their research topic and could function as an engaging opening sentence.

LEARN HOW Document Your Sources To avoid the serious academic offense of plagiarism, credit the source of each paraphrase, summary, or quotation as a parenthetical citation at the end of the sentence. If the same information can be found in most sources on your topic, it is considered common knowledge and does not require documentation. Use these guidelines to format parenthetical citations. When you finish your draft, highlight each citation. Then, use this information to help you assemble your Works Cited list.

COMMON CORE

W 4 Produce clear and coherent writing.
L 1 Demonstrate command of the conventions of standard English grammar and usage.
L 3a Write and edit work so it conforms to guidelines in a style manual.

Guidelines for Citing Sources Within a Paper

Source with one author	▶ Author's last name, page number (if any) of the work cited: (Garber 45)
Author unknown	▶ Shortened title of the work, page number (if any): ("Julius Caesar")
Multiple authors	▶ Last names of all authors, page number (if any): (McIver and Stevenson 52). For more than three authors, use the first author's last name and *et al.*: (Bennett et al. 45).
More than one work by an author	▶ Author's last name, title of work, page number (if any): (Hartman, *Selections* 39).
More than one source supporting an idea	▶ First author's last name, page number (if any); second author's last name, page number; and so on: (Garber 49; Vernon)
Author already mentioned in the sentence	▶ Page number only: (22)
Quotation from another source	▶ (qtd. in Schanzer 12)

GRAMMAR IN CONTEXT: CAPITALIZING TITLES

Use the rules below to correctly capitalize titles.

Capitalize first and last words and principal words, including those that follow hyphens in compound words. Capitalize the first word of a subtitle after a colon.	▶	"Shakespeare's Best-Known Tragedy" Julius Caesar: The Last Dictator
Do not capitalize these parts of speech when they are in the middle of a title: articles, prepositions, coordinating conjunctions, the word *to* in infinitives.	▶	Lives of the Caesars "Caesar and Antony" "The Conspiracy to Assassinate Caesar"

 YOUR TURN Using your outline and the chart on the preceding page, develop a first draft of your research paper. Remember to credit all sources in parenthetical citations. Use correct capitalization for any titles.

FOR ENGLISH LANGUAGE LEARNERS
Capitalizing Titles To help students capitalize titles of works correctly, review these grammatical terms:

- *hyphen:* a punctuation mark (-) used to join two words
- *compound word:* a word made up of more than one word
- *colon:* a punctuation mark (:) used to introduce a subtitle
- *article:* a special type of adjective used to refer to one of a general group of people, places, things, or ideas (*a, an*) or to a specific person, place, thing, or idea (*the*)
- *preposition:* a word that relates a noun or pronoun to another word
- *coordinating conjunction:* a word used to join words or groups of words (*and, but, or, nor, for*)
- *infinitive:* a verb form that combines the word *to* and the base form of a verb

Drafting *continued*

LEARN HOW Document Your Sources
Provide students with the following examples of parenthetical citations from the Student Draft. Have students explain the format of each based on the guidelines for documenting sources within a paper.

- Shakespeare's Caesar is a proud and arrogant man, superstitious and lacking humor (Cross, "Bestriding"; Garber). *(more than one source supporting an idea; more than one work by an author)*

- According to Suetonius, he was "tall of stature, with a fair complexion, shapely limbs, a somewhat full face, and keen black eyes" (45). *(author already mentioned in sentence)*

- Cicero supposedly wrote, "Do you know any man who . . . can speak better than Caesar? Or anyone who makes so many witty remarks? Or whose vocabulary is so varied and yet so exact?" (qtd. in Cross, "Private"). *(quoted from another source)*

GRAMMAR IN CONTEXT: CAPITALIZING TITLES

Have students correctly capitalize these titles:
- the problem plays of Shakespeare (*The Problem Plays of Shakespeare*)

- "bestriding the world." Julius Caesar: the last dictator ("Bestriding the World." *Julius Caesar: The Last Dictator*)

- Dream in Shakespeare: from metaphor to metamorphosis (*Dream in Shakespeare: From Metaphor to Metamorphosis*)

Note that underscored titles would be italicized on a computer.

 YOUR TURN Allow class time for students work independently to begin their drafts as suggested in the **Your Turn** activity. Have students exchange papers with a classmate, and have partners check to see if the beginning of the draft matches the outline. Remind students that as they continue working on their drafts, they should follow the guidelines for crediting their sources and correctly capitalize titles.

 Write*Smart* CD-ROM

Writing Center on thinkcentral.com

Revising

Model the Skill Using a draft research paper on a transparency, model how to use the questions, tips, and strategies suggested in the chart to evaluate and revise. You might use the research paper of a student from another class or from a previous year. Make sure to remove the student's name from the research paper so that the writer remains anonymous.

YOUR TURN Remind peer reviewers to offer constructive comments to their partners. Suggest that as students read each other's drafts, they jot down several "What if . . . ?" questions. For example, students might ask, "What if you opened your paper with an interesting anecdote or statistic?" "What if you added a quotation from this source to support your point?" or "What if you moved this idea from the end of the paragraph to the beginning?"

For interactive revision tools, see

Write*Smart* CD-ROM

Writing Center on thinkcentral.com

Revising

Once you have developed a draft of your ideas, evaluate its content, structure, and style with your purpose and audience in mind. Use this chart to help you revise.

RESEARCH PAPER

Ask Yourself	Tips	Revision Strategies
1. Does the controlling idea clearly state the research question?	▶ **Underline** the controlling idea. **Draw a box** around the part that states the research question.	▶ **Add** a controlling idea or **revise** the existing one to more clearly state the research question.
2. Is evidence given to support each main idea?	▶ **Label** each main idea in the margin. Then, **label** evidence.	▶ **Add** evidence for any main ideas that have too little support.
3. Is the organization clear and logical? Do subheadings and transitions help guide readers?	▶ **Circle** subheadings and transitions.	▶ **Rearrange** supporting evidence so it appears in the same paragraph as its main idea. **Add** a subheading and/or transition at the beginning of each main idea.
4. Are direct quotations smoothly integrated? Are all sources given proper credit within the paper?	▶ **Draw an arrow** from each direct quotation to the words that introduce the quotation. **Place check marks** by parenthetical citations.	▶ **Reword** the text around quotations so that the flow of ideas is not disrupted. **Add** parenthetical citations for direct quotations, paraphrases, or summaries that lack check marks.
5. Does the concluding section sum up the answer to the research question and leave readers with something more to think about?	▶ **Circle** the part of the concluding section that answers the research question. **Draw a wavy line** under the sentences that present an insightful idea or question.	▶ **Add** an answer to the research question. **Insert** sentences that describe the importance of the topic, raise unanswered questions, or recommend additional research.
6. Does a Works Cited list correctly document all sources?	▶ **Number** each source used in your paper, and repeat that number in your Works Cited list.	▶ **Add** entries to the Works Cited list as needed for sources used in your paper. **Delete** unused entries.

YOUR TURN **PEER REVIEW** Have a peer evaluate and suggest improvements to your paper using the chart on this page. Ask him or her the following: Do I answer the research question? If not, what additional evidence do I need to include? Where should I use more formal words or phrases? How can I improve my introduction or concluding section?

DIFFERENTIATED INSTRUCTION

FOR ADVANCED LEARNERS/PRE-AP

Apply Guidelines Students may wish to apply the questions, tips, and strategies on this page and the framework on page 1350 to a research paper they wrote in a different content area, such as science, civics, or history. Suggest that students work in small groups to revise and improve their papers and provide peer review.

ANALYZE A STUDENT DRAFT

Read this draft; notice the comments on its strengths and weaknesses as well as the suggestions for improvement.

COMMON CORE

W 5 Develop and strengthen writing as needed by revising, editing, rewriting, or trying a new approach.

Ferguson 1

Kevin Ferguson
Ms. Lin
English 10
20 May 2011

Capturing Julius Caesar

❶   Julius Caesar was a very important person in his own time. Declared a god by the Senate after his death, Caesar was further immortalized in William Shakespeare's drama *The Tragedy of Julius Caesar.* In fact, much of what most people know about Caesar the man comes from Shakespeare's play. As the Caesar scholar Suzanne Cross points out, "It is difficult, now, to separate the most famous Roman of them all from the most famous author of them all" ("Bestriding"). Still, modern readers wonder if Shakespeare's interpretation of Caesar is accurate. A close look at the writings of Caesar's era suggests that Julius Caesar was a much more complex man than the arrogant, aloof, and superstitious tyrant who appears so briefly in Shakespeare's play.

> The opening sentence of the paper is weak. Kevin needs to craft an **introduction** that will grab his readers' attention.

> Kevin provides **background information** to refresh his audience's memory about Caesar's accomplishments.

> A clear **controlling idea** presents the paper's research question.

LEARN HOW Craft an Attention-Getting Introduction To engage his readers, Kevin needs to begin his paper with a thought-provoking question, a powerful quotation, or a vivid description. Notice how the revision in blue improves Kevin's introduction.

KEVIN'S REVISION TO PARAGRAPH ❶

Julius Caesar is one of the most recognized figures of any historical era. His exploits in war, his rise to become dictator of the Roman Empire, and his brutal assassination in the Senate at the hands of conspirators—including his great friend Brutus—are legendary.

~~Julius Caesar was a very important person in his own time.~~ Declared a god by the Senate after his death, Caesar was further immortalized in William Shakespeare's drama *The Tragedy of Julius Caesar.*

FOR STRUGGLING WRITERS

Craft an Attention-Getting Introduction

Have students use these questions to review their own introductions:

- Does the opening of my introduction grab readers' attention?
- Is the topic of my paper clear?
- Do I include background information my readers might need to understand my topic?
- Does my controlling idea reflect my main research question about my topic?

FOR ADVANCED LEARNERS/PRE-AP

Use Lively Language Have students work individually or in small groups to develop a list of ten clichés and ten overused words or phrases to avoid in writing. Ask them to identify alternatives that are more specific, lively, and energetic. Post students' findings on a bulletin board for all to reference.

ANALYZE A STUDENT DRAFT

Explain that the Student Draft on this page is the beginning of a research paper. Model reading the draft and the annotations in blue, and explain that the yellow highlighting illustrates the student's language choices. Explain that the following *Learn How* mini-lessons provide helpful information about ways to improve this draft as well as their own.

LEARN HOW Craft an Attention-Getting Introduction

- Point out that the original opening sentence of the Student Draft is weak because it is vague. Tell students to avoid clichés and overused words and phrases such as "very important."

- Emphasize the importance of using specific information and details not only in the introduction to a paper but throughout one's writing to grab readers' attention and hold their interest.

- Have students read the revised version of the introduction and compare the specific information about Julius Caesar that the writer has included to his original, general statement about Caesar's importance.

- **Controlling Idea** Remind students that the controlling idea in a research paper springs from a research question that interests the writer. Ask students what question might have generated the controlling idea in the Student Draft. ***Possible answer:*** *How is Shakespeare's Julius Caesar like the real historical figure?*

Explain that the Student Draft is continued on this page. Read the draft and annotations aloud and discuss. Ask students to comment on how the student writer presents quotations from Shakespeare's play.

Ferguson 2

Shakespeare's Portrait of Caesar

❷ Shakespeare based his play on the writings of the Greek author Plutarch, who was born just two years after Caesar's assassination. Plutarch profiled Caesar, Brutus, and Mark Antony in his collection of biographies, *Parallel Lives*. These biographies contributed to both the plot of Shakespeare's play and the personalities of its principal characters (Schanzer 46; Vernon).

❸ Shakespeare's Caesar is a proud and arrogant man, superstitious and lacking humor (Cross, "Bestriding"; Garber). On the day of Caesar's assassination, Cassius warns his co-conspirators about Caesar's growing superstitious nature:

> But it is doubtful yet
> Whether Caesar will come forth today or no;
> For he is superstitious grown of late,
> Quite from the main opinion he held once …
>   (2.1.193–196)

❹ Caesar's arrogance is apparent in his vain boasting about his own invincibility. Before he leaves for the Senate on the day of his death, Caesar tells his fearful wife Calpurnia: "Danger knows full well / That Caesar is more dangerous than he" (2.2.44–45).

Subheadings organize the paper into sections to make important connections and distinctions.

Kevin **summarizes** research in two sources.

The correct **format** is used for a long quotation, introducing the quotation with a **colon**, indenting, and citing the source in **parentheses**.

An example from the play is offered as **evidence,** but a source quotation would provide stronger support and add interest.

LEARN HOW Support Ideas with Quotations Don't expect readers to accept the conclusions you draw. Support your ideas with quotations from your sources.

KEVIN'S REVISION TO PARAGRAPH ❹

Cross notes that "power vindicated, but did not create, his self-confidence" ("Private").
. . . more dangerous than he" (2.2.44–45).

LEARN HOW Support Ideas with Quotations

- Point out that to support his idea about Caesar's arrogance in paragraph 4 the student writer has cited an example from Shakespeare's *Tragedy of Julius Caesar,* quoting Caesar's words to Calpurnia on the day of this death.

- Note that in his revision of the paragraph the writer strengthens support for his idea by adding a quotation from a secondary source, Suzanne Cross's online article "The Private Man."

- Remind students that quotations can serve several purposes in a research paper: they can support a point, provide an example, and add interest and variety.

R RESOURCE MANAGER—Copy Master
Use Quotations Effectively p. 29

DIFFERENTIATED INSTRUCTION

FOR ENGLISH LANGUAGE LEARNERS
Writing: Source Citations Point out the parenthetical citation provided for the quotation from Shakespeare's play *The Tragedy of Julius Caesar.* Note that quotations from Shakespeare's plays are cited as follows: title of play, act, scene, line numbers. Since the play has already been identified in the text, the title is omitted in the citation. Have students read the citation aloud: "act 2, scene 1, lines 193–196."

FOR STRUGGLING WRITERS
Use Correct Format Have students compare and contrast the formats for long and short quotations. Point out that while the short quotation in paragraph 4 is run into the text, the long quotation in paragraph 3 is set off and indented. The format of the long quotation preserves the appearance of the lines in the play. Students should note that the citation format is the same for both types of quotation.

Ferguson 3

❺   On the other hand, some scholars fault Shakespeare for his narrow characterization of the Roman dictator. Suzanne Cross maintains that Shakespeare failed to offer a full picture of the man: "There is no hint of the personal charm for which he was famous, the wit and magnetism . . . the teenage rebel refusing to do the bidding of the killer-dictator, Sulla; the intellectual second only to Cicero as a speaker [and] writer. The man himself was infinitely more complex and interesting than Shakespeare's version" ("Bestriding").

❻   You have to remember that Caesar shows up in just three scenes. He isn't on stage often enough or long enough for anyone to figure him out. Historians of Caesar's era, however, offer many fascinating glimpses into his character.

A Look at the Historical Record

❼ In his biographical text *The Lives of the Caesars,* the Roman historian Suetonius describes Caesar's appearance. According to Suetonius, he was "tall of stature, with a fair complexion, shapely limbs, a somewhat full face,

> **Appropriate and varied transitions** connect sections of the text and create cohesion.

> Kevin includes his own **interpretation** of an aspect of his topic but in doing so does not maintain the formal style and objective tone appropriate for a research paper.

LEARN HOW Maintain a Formal Style and Objective Tone It is important to share original interpretations, observations, and conclusions, but a casual tone and slang are not appropriate. Kevin substitutes words and phrases that are objective and serious, though he is careful not to sound stuffy or overly formal.

KEVIN'S REVISION TO PARAGRAPH ❻

In Shakespeare's defense, it is important   *appears only*   *during the play. Caesar*
~~You have~~ to remember that Caesar ~~shows up in just~~ three scenes. ~~He~~ isn't on
                  a well-rounded portrait to emerge
stage often enough or long enough for ~~anyone to figure him out.~~

ANALYZE A STUDENT DRAFT *continued*

Explain that the Student Draft is continued on this page. Read the draft and annotations aloud and discuss. Ask students to comment on the writer's use of transitions.

- **Transitions** Tell students that a transitional word or phrase often appears in the first sentence of a new paragraph and acts as a bridge between paragraphs and ideas. Read aloud paragraphs 4 and 5. Explain that the transition "On the other hand" indicates that the ideas in paragraph 5 stand in contrast to Shakespeare's Caesar as described in paragraph 4.

LEARN HOW Maintain a Formal Style and Objective Tone

- Tell students that it is important to maintain a formal style and objective tone in a research paper. A formal style and objective tone, combined with the presentation of facts and sources, helps students' ideas gain credibility.

- Review the changes the student writer makes to correct the tone in paragraph 6.

- Suggest that students read the first draft of their paper aloud to identify where the style and tone may be too conversational, or informal. Have students use these questions to evaluate the style and tone of their paper: Have I avoided first-person pronouns, contractions, and slang? Is my language formal enough to earn my audience's confidence? Are my style and tone consistent throughout the paper?

FOR ENGLISH LANGUAGE LEARNERS

Writing: Transitions Help students generate a list of useful transitional phrases for a research paper.

1. Work together to group these transitions according to function:

- *on the other hand, however, in contrast, nevertheless:* contrast

- *similarly, likewise, in the same way:* comparison

- *furthermore, in addition:* addition

- *as a result, consequently, therefore:* cause-effect

- *for example, for instance, one reason, another reason:* illustration

2. Give students a list of related sentences, such as these:

   The best day of the week is Friday.

   The whole weekend is ahead of you.

   You can unwind from a hard week.

   You can plan for some fun events.

   Saturday is a contender for "best day."

3. Ask groups of students to add transitions from the list to connect the sentences.

R RESOURCE MANAGER—Copy Master
   Writing Support p. 34

Explain that the Student Draft is continued on this page. Read the draft and annotations aloud and discuss. Ask students to comment on the writer's use of ellipses.

LEARN HOW Use Ellipses Correctly

Explain that ellipses are used to tighten up quotations so that they present only the information that is relevant to a writer's discussion.

- Point out that in the long quotation from Suetonius the details about Caesar's superfluous hair and baldness and the steps he took to deal with both are not really needed to make the point that he cared about his appearance.

- Discuss the use of ellipsis points to mark the omission of text in the quotation. Note that four points are used only when one or more sentences are omitted.

- Ask a student to read the passage aloud without ellipses and then with ellipses.

Ferguson 4

and keen black eyes" (45). Suetonius's description also hints at Caesar's pride:

> He was somewhat overnice in the care of his person, being not only carefully trimmed and shaved, but even having superfluous hair plucked out, as some have charged; while his baldness was a disfigurement which troubled him greatly, since he found that it was often the subject of the gibes of his detractors. Because of it he used to comb forward his scanty locks from the crown of his head, and of all the honours voted him by the senate and people there was none he received or made use of more gladly than the privilege of wearing a laurel wreath at all times. They say, too, that he was remarkable in his dress (45).

A **quotation** is provided as **evidence,** but it is too long and rambling. Kevin should use *ellipses* to tighten it up.

LEARN HOW Use Ellipses Correctly When only parts of a quotation are relevant, they can be omitted and replaced with ellipses (. . .). Three ellipsis points are used in place of omitted words in the middle of a sentence. Four ellipsis points show that one or more sentences have been omitted. Kevin uses ellipses to shorten the quotation from Suetonius so that it contains only those details that are directly related to the point he is making.

KEVIN'S REVISION TO PARAGRAPH 7

> He was somewhat overnice in the care of his person, being ~~not only~~ carefully trimmed and shaved, ~~but even having superfluous hair plucked out, as some have charged; while his baldness was a disfigurement which troubled him greatly, since he found that it was often the subject of the gibes of his detractors. Because of it he used to comb forward his scanty locks from the crown of his head, and~~ of all the honours voted him by the senate and people there was none he received or made use of more gladly than the privilege of wearing a laurel wreath at all times. They say, too, that he was remarkable in his dress (45).

DIFFERENTIATED INSTRUCTION

FOR ENGLISH LANGUAGE LEARNERS

Writing: Paraphrasing Remind students that paraphrasing is restating a text in their own words. Explain that paraphrasing is one alternative to quoting directly from a source. To practice paraphrasing, have students restate and properly credit Suetonius's description of Caesar. *Possible answer: Julius Caesar was tall, well-built, and handsome. He paid careful attention to his appearance. He kept his hair cut and was clean-shaven. He thought being able to wear a laurel wreath was the greatest honor the senate and people had given him. He also dressed well (Suetonius 45).*

FOR STRUGGLING WRITERS

Insert Ellipses For practice using ellipses to tighten quotations, give students one or two long quotations. Ask students to insert at least one set of three ellipsis points and one set of four ellipsis points in each quotation. Tell students to be careful to preserve the overall meaning of each quotation as they insert ellipses. Have students read aloud the before- and after-versions of the quotations.

Ferguson 5

⑧   Suetonius goes on to describe a man who was ruthless, cunning, and driven to succeed at all costs. At the same time, Suetonius notes, Caesar could be kind, forgiving, and witty (Cross, "Private").

⑨   Caesar exhibited a ruthless streak at an early age. In 74 B.C., he was traveling to Rhodes to study with Apollonius Molo, a famous orator. Pirates captured Caesar and held him for 38 days, until ransom was paid. As soon as he was set free, Caesar raised a fleet, caught the fleeing pirates, and, fulfilling a promise he had made to his captors while he was their prisoner, had them all crucified (Cross, "Private"; Suetonius 7).

> Kevin **synthesizes** information from **multiple sources,** demonstrating an understanding of the subject under investigation.

⑩   Yet even while putting his captors to death, Caesar demonstrated a strange kind of mercy. Not wanting the pirates to endure the slow, agonizing death that was crucifixion, Caesar ordered that their throats be slit before they were hoisted onto their crosses (Suetonius 95).

> Kevin supports his research by citing relevant textual **evidence** and analyzing what the text says and infers.

⑪   Caesar was also known for his kindness and loyalty. He often appointed friends, even those of low birth, to high positions. When he was criticized for this practice, Caesar "flatly declared that if he had been helped in defending his honor by brigands [thieves] and cut-throats, he would have requited [rewarded] even such men in the same way" (Suetonius 93).

> Brackets are the correct **format** for Kevin's clarification of words in the quotation.

⑫   The ancient historians who chronicled Caesar's life did so with a mixture of admiration and disapproval. The Roman statesman and scholar Marcus Tullius Cicero disapproved strongly of Caesar's dictatorship. Yet he praised Caesar's intellectual abilities. Cicero supposedly wrote, "Do you know any man who . . . can speak better than Caesar? Or anyone who makes so many witty remarks? Or whose vocabulary is so varied and yet so exact?" (qtd. in Cross, "Private").

> An interesting **quotation** from a **primary source** is provided to support a main idea. Kevin uses correct **format** and **style** to show that he found the quotation in a **secondary source.**

ANALYZE A STUDENT DRAFT *continued*

Explain that the Student Draft is continued on this page. Read the draft and annotations aloud and discuss. Ask students to comment on the writer's presentation of evidence.

- **Evidence** Discuss the different methods the student writer uses to present evidence and support his main points: quoting a primary or secondary source, quoting from a literary source, paraphrasing a primary or secondary source. Ask students why it is important to use a variety of sources in a research paper. *Possible answer: Using a variety of sources helps to confirm that a source is trustworthy, supports personal interpretations, and adds color and variety to text.*

- **Brackets** Point out that the student writer uses brackets to enclose an explanation of words in the quotation from Suetonius in paragraph 11. Note that the words in brackets are synonyms for the words they follow in the text. Tell students to review quotations in their paper to determine whether words or ideas need to be clarified for readers. If so, encourage students to use brackets to enclose a brief explanation.

FOR STRUGGLING WRITERS

Use Correct Format Point out that the author's last name is included in the source citation unless it has been mentioned in the text or a preceding citation. In that case, simply using a page number is sufficient. Online sources may also be cited with the title of the article or Web page. Ask students to identify the two authors cited on pages 1356–1357 *(Suetonius* and *Cross)* Refer students to page 1351 for complete guidelines on parenthetical documentation of sources.

ADVANCED LEARNERS/PRE-AP

Document Sources Have students identify examples of books, periodicals, and online sources in their own research papers that fit the citation guidelines on page 1351. Tell them to use these examples to created annotated guidelines that illustrate how to document each kind of source.

Explain that the Student Draft is continued on this page. Read the draft and annotations aloud and discuss. Ask students to comment on the writer's concluding section.

- **Concluding Section** Explain that a concluding section revisits the important points of a paper. Ideally, it brings these ideas together in a meaningful way that sheds further light on the topic and leaves readers thinking. Stress that the concluding section leaves a "final impression" and should offer a way to take the paper's main ideas a step further.

Ask students what main points the student writer summarizes in his concluding section. **Possible answer:** *(1) Shakespeare could not convey the depth of Julius Caesar's complex character; (2) He did, however, communicate Caesar's charismatic personality; (3) Shakespeare's portrayal of Caesar alongside contemporary portraits gives us a more complete picture of Caesar.*

Ferguson 6

⑬   As with most tragic figures, Caesar's undoing was his pride, which blinded him to everything but his own ambition. Plutarch maintains that Caesar had "an insatiable desire to reign" and says in his biography of Caesar that "the chiefest cause that made him mortally hated was the covetous desire he had to be called king" (qtd. in Schanzer 12). As further evidence of Caesar's pride and ambition, consider this: Caesar's image appeared on Roman coins during his own lifetime. Until Caesar, only the dead had been so honored (Vernon).

Direct quotations are seamlessly integrated into the paper to maintain the flow.

⑭   Julius Caesar was so complex a character that William Shakespeare was able to just scratch the surface of his personality. Still, the Elizabethan playwright managed to portray the characteristics of one who truly did "bestride the narrow world / Like a Colossus" (1.2.135–136). When Shakespeare's portrait is combined with biographical anecdotes from Caesar's contemporaries, the picture comes into sharper focus, providing a more complete measure of the man who ruled Rome and changed the history of the Western world.

The **concluding section** follows from and supports the information presented and reflects on the paper's significance.

DIFFERENTIATED INSTRUCTION

FOR ADVANCED LEARNERS/PRE-AP

Analyze Development Ask students to examine "A Look at the Historical Record" on pages 1355–1358. Challenge them to analyze how the writer developed the ideas in this section. Students should focus on the writer's organization, transitions, and evidence and consider the effectiveness of each. Invite students to share their analyses in an essay or an oral presentation.

Ferguson 7

Works Cited

"Caesar, Julius." *Encyclopaedia Britannica Online.* Encyclopaedia
 Britannica. 2009. Web. *15 May 2010.*

Cross, Suzanne. "Bestriding the World." *Julius Caesar: The Last
 Dictator.* 2004. Web. *30 Apr. 2010.*

---. "The Private Man." *Julius Caesar: The Last Dictator.* 2004.
 Web. *30 Apr. 2010.*

Garber, Marjorie B. "Dream and Interpretation: *Julius Caesar.*" *Dream
 in Shakespeare: From Metaphor to Metamorphosis.* New Haven:
 Yale UP, 1974. Rpt. In *William Shakespeare's Julius Caesar.* Ed.
 Harold Bloom. Modern Critical Interpretations. New York:
 Chelsea, 1988. 43–52. Print.

Schanzer, Ernest. *The Problem Plays of Shakespeare.* New York:
 Schocken, 1965. *Print.*

Shakespeare, William. *The Tragedy of Julius Caesar. McDougal Littell
 Literature.* Evanston, IL: McDougal, 2008. 1097–1182. Print.

Suetonius. *The Lives of the Caesars.* Trans. J. C. Rolfe. Suetonius. Vol. 1.
 Loeb Classical Library. Cambridge: Harvard UP, 1997. Print.

Vernon, Jennifer. "Ides of March Marked Murder of Julius Caesar."
 National Geographic News. Natl. Geographic Soc. 12 Mar.
 2004. *Web. 18 May 2010.*

 YOUR TURN Use the feedback from your peers and teacher as well as the four "Learn How" lessons to revise, rewrite, or try a new approach to your essay as needed. Evaluate how well you conveyed your controlling idea and addressed what is most significant for your specific purpose and audience.

LEARN HOW Format a Works Cited List Correctly

When writing a research paper, it's critical that you not only give credit where credit is due but also cite *all* your sources according to the guidelines your teacher gives you. In developing his Works Cited list using MLA guidelines, Kevin did not adhere to the following guidelines:

- End each entry with a period.

- Indent the second and subsequent lines of entries one-half inch (or five spaces).

- Include the date of access for online sources.

- Include the medium of publication for all sources.

Kevin revised his Works Cited list, making the corrections in blue.

ANALYZE A STUDENT DRAFT *continued*

Explain that the Student Draft is continued and completed on this page. Read the draft and annotations aloud and discuss. Ask students to comment on the writer's Works Cited list.

LEARN HOW Format a Works Cited List Correctly

Explain that a Works Cited list is an alphabetical listing of all the works a writer quotes from or directly refers to in a research paper. Point out that the list includes both print and nonprint sources.

- Review the different kinds of sources cited in the Student Draft: online sources, essay, play, book, primary-source book. Have students identify these sources in the Works Cited list on this page.

- Have students used the Works Cited list to answer these questions:

 What are some different kinds of online sources? ***Possible answer:*** *Online sources include articles, books, and periodicals.*

 How do the entries for online sources differ from those for print sources? ***Possible answer:*** *Online source entries include the date of the Internet site and the date of access.*

 What does a dash at the beginning of an entry indicate? ***Possible answer:*** *The work cited has the same author as the preceding work.*

 How do entries for online periodical articles differ from those for encyclopedia articles? ***Possible answer:*** *The author's name is included in the entries for online periodical articles.*

 YOUR TURN Ask students to complete the **Your Turn** activity independently. Remind students to craft an effective introduction, support ideas with quotations, maintain a formal style and objective tone, use ellipses, and format their Works Cited list correctly.

FOR ENGLISH LANGUAGE LEARNERS

Language: Skill Words Write these terms on the board and review them with students:

- *online source:* an informational resource published on the Internet—for example, the Web site of a company or organization or the online edition of an encyclopedia

- *periodical:* a publication that is issued on a regular basis (such as daily or monthly)—for example, a magazine or newspaper

FOR STRUGGLING WRITERS

Order Works Ask students to tell where these sources would fit in the Works Cited list above: Plutarch's *Life of Caesar*; George Bernard Shaw's *Caesar and Cleopatra*; Julius Caesar's *Civil War*; Christian Meier's *Caesar.*
Possible answers: *Plutarch, after Garber; Shaw, after Shakespeare; Julius Caesar's* Civil War *before "Caesar, Julius"; Meier, after Garber and before Plutarch.*

Editing and Publishing

COMMON
CORE W 5, L 2, L 2b

GRAMMAR IN CONTEXT: INTEGRATING QUOTATIONS

- Discuss the treatment of quotations shorter than four lines and those longer than four lines. Point out that in addition to being set off from the text and indented, quotations longer than four lines are not enclosed in quotation marks.

- Locate examples of shorter and longer quotations included in the Student Draft, and have students examine how they are introduced and punctuated.

PUBLISH YOUR WRITING

Brainstorm with students additional ways to publish their research papers.

YOUR TURN Allow students time to proofread their drafts. Tell them to check that they have integrated quotations correctly. Also remind students to capitalize titles of works correctly.

Editing and Publishing

To accurately communicate what you have learned, edit carefully for errors in grammar, usage, punctuation, and spelling. You should also format your paper according to the following guidelines:
- Leave one-inch margins at the top, bottom, and sides of each page.
- On separate lines at the top left of the first page, type your name, your teacher's name, the class, and the date.
- On the rest of the pages, type your last name and the page number one-half inch from the top, in the upper right corner.
- Double-space all text, including quotations and the Works Cited list.
- Indent the first line of each paragraph one-half inch from the left margin. Indent set-off quotations one inch from the left margin.

GRAMMAR IN CONTEXT: INTEGRATING QUOTATIONS

Place quotations shorter than four lines within your own sentences, and use quotation marks. For quotations longer than four lines, describe the quotation in your own words. Then, use a colon to introduce the quotation. Indent the entire quotation, and do not use quotation marks.

Kevin revised his draft to fix an incorrectly formatted a long quotation:

> On the other hand, some scholars fault Shakespeare for his narrow characterization of the Roman dictator. Suzanne Cross maintains that Shakespeare failed to offer a full picture of the man: "There is no hint of the personal charm for which he was famous, the wit and magnetism . . . the teenage rebel refusing to do the bidding of the killer-dictator, Sulla; the intellectual second only to Cicero as a speaker [and] writer. The man himself was infinitely more complex and interesting than Shakespeare's version ("Bestriding").

PUBLISH YOUR WRITING

Here are some suggestions for sharing your research with an audience:
- See whether a group in your field of research will publish your paper in its newsletter or journal or on its Web site.
- Create your own Web site to publish your findings, adding appropriate graphics, formatting, and sound for a multimedia presentation of your topic.
- Deliver an oral report to classmates or interested community members.

YOUR TURN Proofread your draft for punctuation and spelling errors. Be sure you have correctly integrated quotations. Then, publish your research using one of the options on this page.

1360 UNIT 12: THE POWER OF RESEARCH

DIFFERENTIATED INSTRUCTION

FOR STRUGGLING WRITERS
Integrating Quotations Work with students to generate a list of transitional words and phrases for introducing quotations, such as *for instance, for example, as _____ points out, according to, _____ suggests that, as _____ suggests,* and so on.

COMMON CORE

W 5 Develop and strengthen writing by editing. **L 2** Demonstrate command of English conventions. **L 2b** Use a colon to introduce a quotation.

Scoring Rubric

Use the following rubric to evaluate and revise your research paper.

RESEARCH PAPER

SCORE	COMMON CORE TRAITS
6	• **Development** Effectively introduces the topic; states an insightful, well-researched controlling idea; supports main points with the most significant and relevant evidence; ends powerfully • **Organization** Arranges ideas in an effective, logical order; uses appropriate and varied transitions effectively to connect ideas • **Language** Maintains a formal style and objective tone; uses precise language and domain-specific vocabulary; shows a strong command of conventions; cites all sources correctly
5	• **Development** Has an effective introduction; states a well-researched controlling idea; supports main points with relevant evidence; has a strong concluding section • **Organization** Arranges ideas logically; uses transitions effectively to connect ideas • **Language** Maintains a formal style and objective tone; uses precise language; has a few errors in conventions; cites most sources correctly
4	• **Development** Has an introduction that could be more effective; states a clear controlling idea; could use more evidence; has an adequate concluding section • **Organization** Arranges ideas logically; could vary transitions more • **Language** Mostly maintains a formal style; needs more precise language at times; has a few distracting errors in conventions; incorrectly cites some sources
3	• **Development** Has an introduction that could be more effective; controlling idea is unclear; lacks sufficient evidence; has a routine concluding section • **Organization** Reflects some flaws in organization; needs more transitions to link related ideas • **Language** Frequently lapses into an informal style; has some significant errors in conventions; incorrectly cites some sources
2	• **Development** Has a weak controlling idea that does not relate to the writing task; lacks specific evidence; has a weak concluding section • **Organization** Has organizational flaws; lacks transitions throughout • **Language** Uses an informal style and subjective tone; has many distracting errors in conventions; does not cite all sources and cites many incorrectly
1	• **Development** Has no introduction or controlling idea; offers unrelated points as evidence; ends abruptly • **Organization** Includes a string of disconnected ideas with no overall organization • **Language** Uses an inappropriate style and subjective tone; has major problems with grammar, usage, and spelling; plagiarizes or does not credit sources

WRITING WORKSHOP **1361**

Scoring Rubric

Tell students that the best way to understand a scoring rubric is to use it to score actual writing. Provide the class with copies of a student's essay with the student's name removed. Work as a class to evaluate the essay by using the scoring rubric. Have students score the essay and write a brief paragraph using the language of the scoring guide to explain reasons for their score.

For Rubric Bank, see

 **Write*Smart* CD-ROM**

Writing Center on <u>thinkcentral.com</u>

Assess and Reteach

Assess

R RESOURCE MANAGER—Copy Master
Rubric for Evaluation p. 32

Online Essay Scoring on <u>thinkcentral.com</u>

Reteach

Level Up Online Tutorials on <u>thinkcentral.com</u>

Reteaching Worksheets on <u>thinkcentral.com</u>

Research and Study Skills Lesson 1: Research Questions and Topic

Research and Study Skills Lesson 3: Using Reference and Search Tools

Research and Study Skills Lesson 9: Avoiding Plagiarism

Review MLA Guidelines

Before discussing MLA citation guidelines, point out that there are other style manuals besides MLA. Clarify your requirements for style reference.

- Name each type of source and ask students to describe the correct format. For example,

BOOKS

One author: author's last name (comma); author's first name (period); book title (*italicized, or underlined if handwritten*, period); location of publisher (colon); publisher's name (comma); copyright date (period).

- Point out that only titles of complete works are italicized or underlined. Titles of articles, poems, short stories, and chapters should be enclosed in quotation marks.

- Direct students' attention to the second citation on the page. Point out the abbreviation *eds.*, and explain that it is an abbreviation for *editors*. Note that when only one editor is listed, the abbreviation should be *ed*. Remind students that an editor is listed when a book is an anthology or collection of articles or essays.

MLA Citation Guidelines

Today, you can find free Web sites that generate ready-made citations for research papers, using the information you provide. Although using such sites can save you some time, always check your citations carefully before you turn in your final paper. If you are following MLA style, use these guidelines to evaluate and finalize your work.

BOOKS

One author
Schanzer, Ernest. *The Problem Plays of Shakespeare.* New York: Schocken, 1965. Print.

Two authors or editors
McIver, Bruce, and Ruth Stevenson, eds. *Teaching Shakespeare: Critics in the Classroom.* Newark: U of Delaware Press, 1994. Print.

Three authors
Bennett, Josephine W., Oscar Cargill, and Vernon Hall, Jr., eds. *Studies in the English Renaissance Drama.* New York: New York UP, 1959. Print.

Four or more authors
The abbreviation et al. *means "and others." Use* et al. *instead of listing all the authors.*
Wells, Stanley, et al. *The Complete Works of William Shakespeare.* New York: Oxford UP, 1986. Print.

No author given
Elizabethan Literature. New York: Capital, 1957. Print.

An author and a translator
Suetonius. *Lives of the Caesars.* Trans. Catherine Edwards. New York: Oxford UP, 2000. Print.

An author, a translator, and an editor
Moretti, Salvatore. *Essays on Julius Caesar.* Trans. Jonathan Walsh. Ed. Louis Kind. New York: Devonshire, 1962. Print.

PARTS OF BOOKS

An introduction, a preface, a foreword, or an afterword written by someone other than the author(s) of a work
Heminge, John, and Henry Condell. Preface. *Dramatic Works of Shakespeare.* Edinburgh: William Peterson, 1883. Print.

A poem, a short story, an essay, or a chapter in a collection of works by one author
Roe, John. "'Character' in Plutarch and Shakespeare: Brutus, Julius Caesar, and Mark Antony." *Shakespeare and the Classics.* Ed. Charles Martindale and A. B. Taylor. New York: Cambridge, 2004. Print.

DIFFERENTIATED INSTRUCTION

FOR ENGLISH LANGUAGE LEARNERS
Language: Vocabulary Support Write these terms on the board, and review the meaning of each:

- *preface:* the introduction to a work, usually written by the author to explain his or her purpose for writing

- *foreword:* the introduction to a work, often written by someone other than the author

- *afterword:* a section that sometimes follows the main body of a work, often written by someone other than the author

- *anthology:* a collection of literary pieces or passages within a single book

FOR STRUGGLING WRITERS
Practice MLA Guidelines Give books as well as print and online articles to small groups of students. First, have them identify which format they would use to cite each work as a source. Then, have them use the MLA Citation Guidelines to write a source card for each.

COMMON CORE L3a Write and edit work so it conforms to guidelines in a style manual.

A novel or a play in an anthology

Shakespeare, William. *The Tragedy of Julius Caesar*. Ed. John Jowett. *William Shakespeare: The Complete Works*. Ed. Stanley Wells and Gary Taylor. Compact ed. Oxford: Clarendon, 1988. 599–626. Print.

MAGAZINES, NEWSPAPERS, AND ENCYCLOPEDIAS

An article in a newspaper

Weber, Bruce. "Power Play: "Friends, Generals and Captains of Industry, Lend Me Your Ears.'" *New York Times* 31 Jan. 2005: B1+. Print.

An article in a magazine

Tynan, William. "Cleopatra." *Time* 24 May 1999: 37–38. Print.

An article in an encyclopedia

"Julius Caesar." *Encyclopaedia Britannica*. 2004 ed. Print.

MISCELLANEOUS PRINT AND NONPRINT SOURCES

An interview

Covington, Nigel. Personal Interview. 1 Feb. 2011.

A video recording

Julius Caesar. Lions Gate, 2000. DVD.

ELECTRONIC PUBLICATIONS

A CD-ROM

"Antony, Mark." *Britannica Student Encyclopedia*. 2004 ed. Chicago: Encyclopaedia Britannica, 2004. CD-ROM.

A document from an Internet site

Entries for online sources should contain as much of the information shown as available.

Author or compiler | Title or description of document
Vernon, Jennifer. | "Ides of March Marked Murder of Julius Caesar."

Title of Internet site | Site sponsor | Date of Internet site
National Geographic News. | Natl. Geographic Soc. | 12 Mar. 2004.

Medium of publication | Date of access
Web. | 18 May 2011.

Review MLA Guidelines *continued*

- Continue the procedure from page 1362:

Identify each source type, and ask students to describe the correct format for citing it. For example,

ELECTRONIC PUBLICATIONS

A CD-ROM: name of article (period); title of publication (*italicized, or underlined if hand-written,* period); date edited (ed.) (period); CD-ROM (period); location of publisher (colon); publisher's name (comma); copyright date (period).

- Point out the page numbers listed for most of the citations. Clarify that these are all print sources. Nonprint sources such as interviews, films, or online articles do not need page numbers.

- Note to students that the MLA recommends not citing URLs, or Web addresses, given their frequent instability and length. There are two exceptions to this recommendation, however. Students should cite URLs when source information cannot be located without them, or when you specifically require your students to include URLs. If included in Works Cited, a URL is always set within angled brackets, whether it refers to an article from a database, to an e-book, or to a page from a Web site.

FOR ENGLISH LANGUAGE LEARNERS

Language: Vocabulary Support Write these terms on the board, and review the meaning of each:

- *compiler:* a person who gathers materials, such as documents or statistics, from one or more sources

- *site sponsor:* the person or organization responsible for a Web site

- *angled brackets:* marks (< >) that enclose words or characters in certain situations—such as a URL, when citing a Web site

FOR STRUGGLING WRITERS

Sequence Your Works Cited List Clarify with students that the MLA guidelines discuss sources in different categories to help students understand citation rules. When students create a Works Cited list, however, they should alphabetize entries from all categories into one list. Students should alphabetize according to the first item in the entry, such as author's last name or title. Have students check the alphabetization of their Works Cited list.

Focus and Motivate

COMMON CORE FOCUS

W 6 Use technology to produce writing products.
SL 2 Integrate multiple sources of information.
SL 4 Present information clearly. **SL 5** Make strategic use of digital media.

PRODUCE WITH A PURPOSE

Tell students that an effective Web site uses a variety of media to present information and engage its audience. Point out that although a Web site may serve more than one purpose, students' sites should have one main purpose.

COMMON CORE TRAITS

As students plan their Web sites, remind them to keep in mind the *COMMON CORE TRAITS* of an effective Web site.

Practice and Apply

Planning the Web Site

Urge students to select topics with a variety of visual possibilities. Help students locate print and online resources for appropriate photographs, images, clip art, and video clips that are free when used for educational purposes.

Organizing the Web Site

Point out that like storyboards for a comic strip, Web site storyboards tell a story—the story of how the information flows on the site. Suggest that students use the Storyboard organizer to plot the pages of their Web sites.

As students identify different media to include, remind them that the visual and audio elements of the Web site should work together and not overload or confuse the viewer.

BEST PRACTICES TOOLKIT—Transparency
Storyboard pp. C11, C51

Technology Workshop

Creating a Web Site  *Essential Course of Study* **ECOS**

You visit Web sites to gather information and learn about others' ideas on an array of subjects. Now that you have learned a great deal about your topic, you can share your expertise with others by creating a Web site of your own.

Complete the workshop activities in your **Reader/Writer Notebook.**

PRODUCE WITH A PURPOSE	COMMON CORE TRAITS
TASK	**AN EFFECTIVE WEB SITE . . .**
Create a **Web site** that uses text, graphics, images, sound, and links to present information and evidence clearly, concisely, and logically.	• focuses on a compelling controlling idea • has an inviting organization and style that suits the task, purpose, and audience • presents information and evidence clearly, concisely, and logically

COMMON CORE

W 6 Use technology to produce writing products. **SL 2** Integrate multiple sources of information. **SL 4** Present information clearly. **SL 5** Make strategic use of digital media.

Planning the Web Site

Creating a Web site requires careful planning. Follow these steps:

- **Choose a Topic** Adapt your research paper or select another topic that you will enjoy researching. Narrow or broaden your topic as needed.

- **Consider Your Audience and Purpose** Who will likely be drawn to your site—students, teachers, people unfamiliar with your subject? Make sure the organization, substance, and style you use to present your information is appropriate to your purpose and audience.

- **Research Your Topic** Gather relevant information from multiple sources. Use search engines and advanced searches (see pages 1323–1325) as well as library resources. Evaluate the usefulness, credibility, and accuracy of each source. Be aware that sites created by individuals rather than institutions may be biased. Select information that you can combine to maintain a smooth flow. Add links to other sites that might be useful. Look for relevant maps, illustrations, photos, videos, and other resources that will make your site stand out.

Organizing the Web Site

Next, think about the design of your Web site. Here are some tips:

- **Map the Site** Create a flow chart to help you determine how many pages you will need and where to create links to other parts of your site or to other sites. Organize the information clearly and logically, making sure your audience will be able to follow your line of reasoning.

- **Create a Storyboard for Each Page** Make sketches showing how you want the pages to look, including the placement of text, images, buttons, and links.

Media Tools — **THINK central**

Go to **thinkcentral.com**.
KEYWORD: HML10-1364

DIFFERENTIATED INSTRUCTION

FOR ENGLISH LANGUAGE LEARNERS
Language: Reinforce Technology Terms
Reinforce key terms used in this workshop:

- *Web site:* a location on the World Wide Web

- *audio:* sound

- *video:* moving images

- *search engine:* a tool used to find specific information in a database about sites on the World Wide Web

- *animation:* the rapid display of images to give the feeling of movement

- *storyboard:* a plan for each page of a Web site, showing the elements that will be included

- *link:* a connection in a Web document that redirects the user to another Web document

- **Write the Text** Using your site map and storyboard, include clear, concise text instead of long descriptions. Incorporate boldface subheadings to make the text easy for your readers to navigate.
- **Make It Multimedia** Use digital media—such as graphics, audio and/or video clips, and hyperlinks to other sites—to make your Web site dynamic and engaging. Write captions for photographs, illustrations, or clips. Make sure there is a clear purpose for any element you add and that each supports your controlling idea.

Caesar's Personality: Shakespeare's View

Picture of Caesar goes here

* **Physically weak:** Brutus and Casca say that Caesar has "the falling sickness"-probably epilepsy (Act One, Scene 2).
* **Easily flattered:** Decius says about Caesar: "...when I tell him he hates flatterers, / He says he does, being then most flattered" (Act Two, Scene 1).
* **Arrogant:** Caesar tell his wife, "Danger knows full well / That Caesar is more dangerous than he" (Act Two, Scene 2).
* **Obstinate:** Caesar tells someone who asks him for mercy, "I could be well moved, if I were as you....But I am constant as the Northern Star" (Act Three, Scene 1).

Read about historians' opinions of Caesar
See a video clip from Act Two, Scene 2
Hear an audio version of the entire play

(Home) (Politics) (Personality) (Legacy)

Producing the Web Site

Now you are ready to get your Web site up and running. Follow these steps:

- **Prepare the Features of Your Site** Follow the instructions of your school media specialist to scan graphics or save electronic elements to your project file. Be careful when using elements that may be protected by copyright. Some Web sites have "terms and conditions" statements for media elements. These statements may specify that students can use media elements in school projects.
- **Select an Authoring Program** Your school may have an authoring program. If not, ask the technology administrator for permission to download one from the Internet. Follow the program's instructions for importing media elements. Choose colors, fonts, buttons, and a layout based on the storyboards you prepared earlier. As you build your site, keep these guidelines in mind: Text must be large and clear enough to be read easily, and choose contrasting colors for the text and background. Buttons with the same function should have the same design. Brief titles for each page of your site will help visitors understand what information they will find there.
- **Review and Revise the Site** Proofread each page of your site for errors. Make sure all links are working properly. Which parts of the site grab your attention? Which visual or audio elements add value to the site, and which are distracting? Use the feedback to edit, revise, or reformat your site.
- **Upload Your Site** Launch your site on your school's internal server or on the Web. Ask your school's technology administrator for permission first.

YOUR TURN Plan and produce a Web site using the guidelines on these pages. Visit your Web site often, and keep the content fresh by updating information and images.

TECHNOLOGY WORKSHOP **1365**

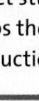

Student Resource Bank

COMMON CORE FOCUS

RL 2 Determine a theme or central idea of a text and analyze in detail its development over the course of the text, including how it emerges and is shaped and refined by specific details; provide an objective summary of the text. **RL 3** Analyze how complex characters develop over the course of a text, interact with other characters, and advance the plot or develop the theme. **RL 4** Determine the meaning of words and phrases as they are used in the text, including figurative and connotative meanings; analyze the cumulative impact of specific word choices on meaning and tone. **RI 2** Determine a central idea of a text and analyze its development over the course of the text, including how it emerges and is shaped and refined by specific details; provide an objective summary of the text. **RI 3** Analyze how the author unfolds an analysis or series of ideas or events, including the order in which the points are made, how they are introduced and developed, and the connections that are drawn between them. **RI 4** Determine the meaning of words and phrases as they are used in a text, including figurative, connotative, and technical meanings; analyze the cumulative impact of specific word choices on meaning and tone. **RI 8** Delineate and evaluate the argument and specific claims in a text, assessing whether the reasoning is valid and the evidence is relevant and sufficient; identify false statements and fallacious reasoning.

Reading any text—short story, poem, magazine article, newspaper, Web page—requires the use of special strategies. For example, you might plot events in a short story on a diagram, while you may use text features to spot main ideas in a magazine article. You also need to identify patterns of organization in the text. Using such strategies can help you read different texts with ease and also help you understand what you're reading.

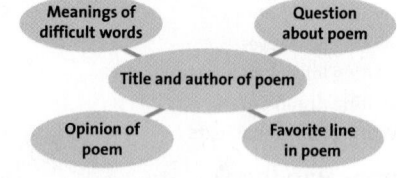

COMMON CORE
Included in this handbook:
RL 2–4, RI 2–4, RI 8

1 Reading Literary and Nonfiction Texts

Literary texts include short stories, novels, poems, and dramas. **Nonfiction** includes biographies, autobiographies, and essays. To appreciate and analyze literary and nonfiction texts, you will need to understand the characteristics of each type of text.

1.1 READING A SHORT STORY
Strategies for Reading

- Read the title. As you read the story, you may notice that the title has a special meaning.
- Keep track of events as they happen. Plot the events on a diagram like this one.

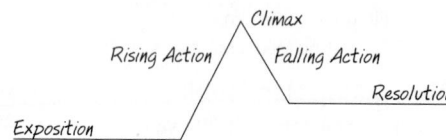

- From the details the writer provides, **visualize** the characters. **Predict** what they might do next.
- Look for specific adjectives that help you visualize the **setting**—the time and place in which events occur.

1.2 READING A POEM
Strategies for Reading

- Notice the **form** of the poem, or the number of its lines and their arrangement on the page.
- Read the poem aloud a few times. Listen for **rhymes** and **rhythms.**
- **Visualize** the images and comparisons.
- Determine the meaning of the poem's figurative language.
- Create a word web or another **graphic organizer** to record your reactions and questions.

1.3 READING A PLAY
Strategies for Reading

- Read the stage directions to help you **visualize** the setting and characters.
- **Question** what the title means and why the playwright chose it.
- Identify the main conflict (struggle or problem) in the play. To **clarify** the conflict, make a chart that shows what the conflict is and how it is resolved.
- **Evaluate** the characters. What do they want? How do they change during the play? Make a chart that lists each complex character's name, appearance, and traits.

1.4 READING NONFICTION TEXTS
Strategies for Reading

- If you are reading a diary or memoir, pay attention to the author's voice, tone, and use of imagery.
- When reading an essay or speech, **evaluate** the writer's ideas and reasoning. Does the writer present a central idea? How does the author's syntax and diction affect the text?

2 Reading Informational Texts: Text Features

An **informational text** is writing that provides factual or procedural information. Informational materials, such as chapters in textbooks and articles in magazines, encyclopedias, and newspapers, usually contain elements that help the reader recognize their purposes, organizations, and key ideas. These elements are known as **text features.**

2.1 UNDERSTANDING TEXT FEATURES

Text features are design elements of a text that indicate its organizational structure or otherwise make its controlling idea and details understandable. Text features include titles, headings, subheadings, boldface type, bulleted and numbered lists, and graphics, such as charts, graphs, illustrations, and photographs. Notice how the text features help you find key information on the textbook page shown.

A The **title** identifies the topic.

B A **subheading** indicates the start of a new topic or section and identifies the focus of that section.

C **Boldface type** is used to make key terms obvious.

D A **bulleted list** shows items of equal importance.

E **Graphics,** such as illustrations, photographs, charts, graphs, diagrams, maps, and timelines, often clarify ideas in the text.

PRACTICE AND APPLY

1. What are the subheadings on the textbook page shown?

2. What are the key terms on the page? How do you know?

3. What does the graph tell you about a snow line? Can you find this information elsewhere on the page?

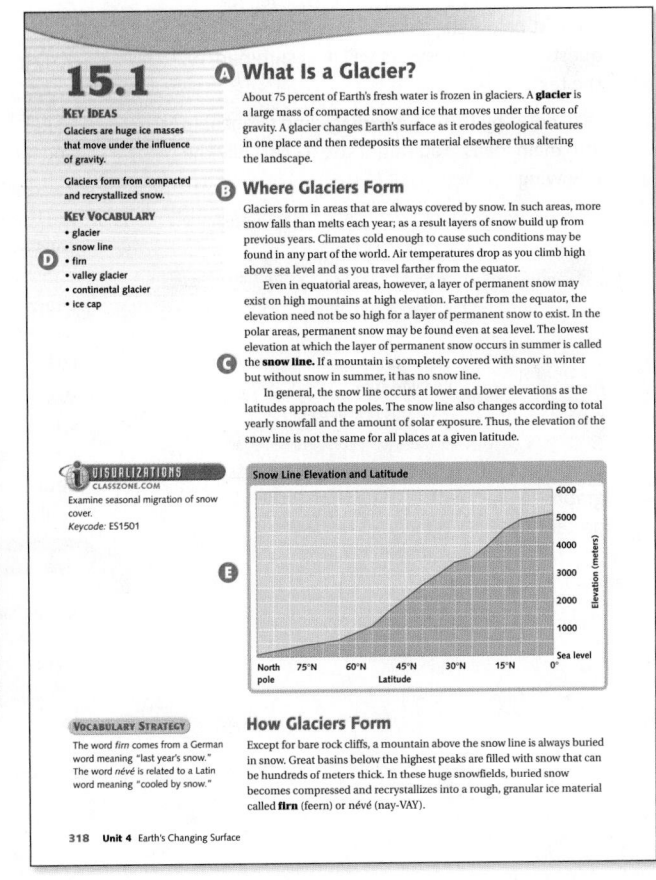

PRACTICE AND APPLY

ANSWERS

1. *Where Glaciers Form; How Glaciers Form*

2. *The key terms include* glacier, snow line, *and* firn. *They are listed in boldface type. Also, these terms are listed under **Key Vocabulary:*** *glacier, snowline, firn, valley glacier, continental glacier, ice cap.*

3. ***Possible answer:*** *The graph explains that the snow line occurs at lower and lower elevation as the latitude approaches the poles. The information can also be found in the second paragraph under the subheading "Where Glaciers Form."*

PRACTICE AND APPLY

ANSWERS

Students' outlines will vary. They should follow the format on page R4, including a main idea for each Roman-numeral entry, a subheading for each capital-letter entry, and a detail(s) for each numbered entry. The following is an example of a partial outline:

I. *Generational ties*

   A. *Adults as grandparents*

      1. *New names*

      2. *New roles*

   B. *Changes in grandparenthood*

      1. *Impediments*

         a. *high divorce and remarriage rates*

         b. *job stresses*

         c. *global economy*

         d. *bias against age*

      2. *Innovations*

         a. *increased travel*

         b. *technological advances*

         c. *improved social understanding*

         d. *advancements in health and life expectancy*

   C. *Grandparent and grandchild relationship*

      1. *Children learn values*

      2. *Grandparents feel vindicated*

II. *Technological aids*

   A. *Grandparents and technology*

      1. *Computer users*

      2. *Electronic communication*

         a. *e-mail*

         b. *digital cameras*

         c. *family sites*

   B. *Advantages of e-communication*

      1. *Accessibility*

      2. *Frequency of communication*

      3. *Open communication*

2.2 USING TEXT FEATURES

You can use text features to locate information, to help you understand it, and to categorize it. Just use the following strategies when you encounter informational text.

Strategies for Reading

- Scan the title, headings, and subheadings to get an idea of the main concepts and the way the text is organized.

- Before you begin reading the text more thoroughly, read any questions that appear at the end of a lesson or chapter. Doing this will help you set a purpose for your reading.

- Turn subheadings into questions. Then use the text below the subheadings to answer the questions. Your answers will be a summary of the text.

- Take notes by turning headings and subheadings into main ideas. You might use a chart like the following.

What Is a Glacier?		Main Heading
Where glaciers form	Notes: 1. in areas that are always covered by snow 2. elevation of snow line varies at different latitudes	Subheading

- Synthesize information from maps, charts, and graphs to draw conclusions about tthe ideas presented.

2.3 TURNING TEXT HEADINGS INTO OUTLINE ENTRIES

You can also use text features to take notes in outline form. The following outline shows how one student used text headings from the sample page on page R3. Study the outline and use the strategies that follow to create an outline based on text features.

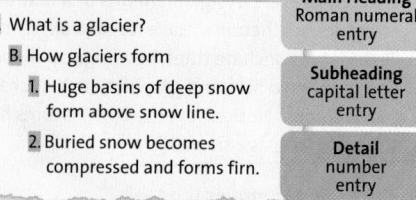

I. What is a glacier? — **Main Heading** Roman numeral entry

  B. How glaciers form — **Subheading** capital letter entry

    1. Huge basins of deep snow form above snow line. — **Detail** number entry

    2. Buried snow becomes compressed and forms firn.

Strategies for Using Text Headings

- Preview the headings and subheadings in the text to get an idea of what different kinds there are and what their positions might be in an outline.

- Be consistent. Note that subheadings that are the same size and color should be used consistently in Roman-numeral or capital-letter entries in the outline. If you decide that a chapter heading should appear with a Roman numeral, then that's the level at which all other chapter headings should appear.

- Write the headings and subheadings that you will use as your Roman-numeral and capital-letter entries first. As you read, fill in numbered details from the text under the headings and subheadings in your outline.

PRACTICE AND APPLY

Reread "Simply Grand: Generational Ties Matter," pages 247–250. Use text features in the selection to take notes in outline form.

Preview the subheadings in the text to get an idea of the different kinds. Write the headings and subheadings you are using as your Roman-numeral and capital-letter entries first. Then fill in the details.

2.4 GRAPHICS

Information is communicated not only with words but also with graphics. **Graphics** are visual representations of verbal statements. They can be charts, webs, diagrams, graphs, photographs, or other visual representations of information. Graphics usually make complex information easier to understand. For that reason, graphics are often used to organize, simplify, and summarize information for easy reference.

Graphs

Graphs are used to illustrate statistical information. A **graph** is a drawing that shows the relative values of numerical quantities. Different kinds of graphs are used to show different numerical relationships.

Strategies for Reading

Ⓐ Read the title.

Ⓑ Find out what is being represented or measured.

Ⓒ In a circle graph, compare the sizes of the parts.

Ⓓ In a line graph, study the slant of the line. The steeper the line, the faster the rate of change.

Ⓔ In a bar graph, compare the lengths of the bars.

A **circle graph,** or **pie graph,** shows the relationships of parts to a whole. The entire circle equals 100 percent. The parts of the circle represent percentages of the whole.

MODEL: CIRCLE GRAPH

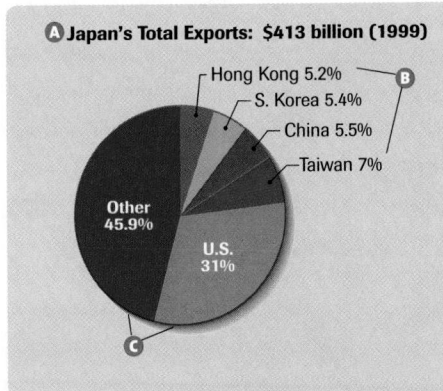

Ⓐ Japan's Total Exports: $413 billion (1999)
Ⓑ Hong Kong 5.2%
S. Korea 5.4%
China 5.5%
Taiwan 7%
Other 45.9%
U.S. 31%
Ⓒ

Line graphs show changes in numerical quantities over time and are effective in presenting trends such as global average temperatures over 120 years. A line graph is made on a grid. Here, the vertical axis indicates degrees of temperature, and the horizontal axis shows years. Points on the graph indicate data. The line that connects the points highlights a trend or pattern.

MODEL: LINE GRAPH

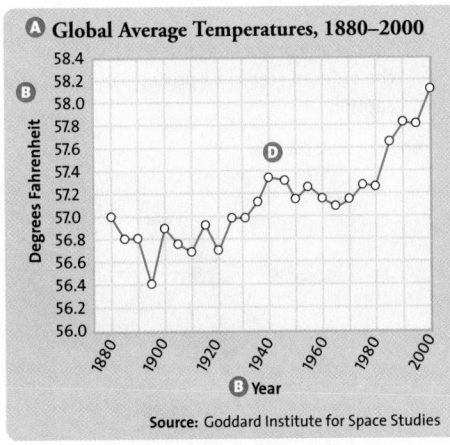

Ⓐ Global Average Temperatures, 1880–2000
Ⓑ Degrees Fahrenheit
Ⓓ
Ⓑ Year

Source: Goddard Institute for Space Studies

In a **bar graph,** vertical or horizontal bars are used to show or compare categories of information, such as the length of major world rivers. The lengths of the bars indicate the quantities.

MODEL: BAR GRAPH

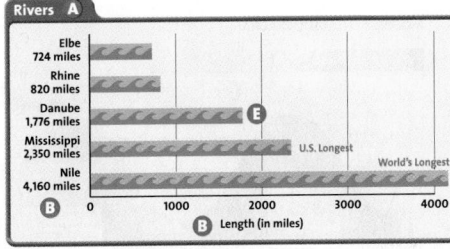

Rivers Ⓐ
Elbe 724 miles
Rhine 820 miles
Danube 1,776 miles Ⓔ
Mississippi 2,350 miles — U.S. Longest
Nile 4,160 miles — World's Longest
Ⓑ 0   1000   2000   3000   4000
Ⓑ Length (in miles)

WATCH OUT! Carefully evaluate the information presented in graphs. For example, circle graphs show major factors and differences well but tend to minimize smaller factors and differences.

Diagrams

A **diagram** is a drawing that shows how something works or how its parts relate to one another.

A **picture diagram** is a picture or drawing of the subject being discussed.

Strategies for Reading

Ⓐ Read the title.

Ⓑ Read each label and look at the part it identifies.

Ⓒ Follow any arrows or numbers that show the order of steps in a process, and read any captions.

MODEL: PICTURE DIAGRAM

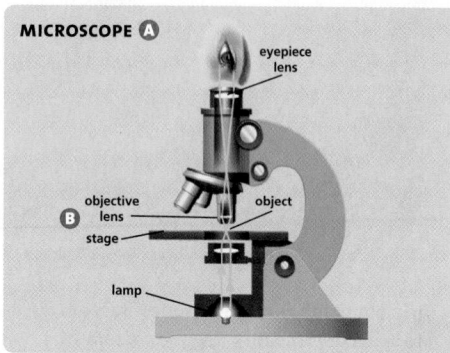

In a **schematic diagram,** lines, symbols, and words are used to help readers visualize processes or objects they wouldn't normally be able to see.

MODEL: SCHEMATIC DIAGRAM

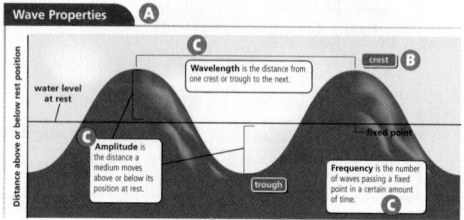

Charts and Tables

A **chart** presents information, shows a process, or makes comparisons, usually in rows or columns. A **table** is a specific type of chart that presents a collection of facts in rows and columns and shows how the facts relate to one another.

Strategies for Reading

Ⓐ Read the title to learn what information the chart or table covers.

Ⓑ Study column headings and row labels to determine the categories of information presented.

Ⓒ Look down columns and across rows to find specific information.

MODEL: CHART

Adult Literacy Rates in South Asia by Gender, 2003 estimates Ⓐ

Country	Male	Female	Total
Bangladesh	53.9%	31%	43%
Bhutan	56%	28%	42% Ⓒ
India	70%	48%	59%
Maldives	97%	97%	97%
Nepal	62%	27%	45%
Sri Lanka	94%	90%	92%
Pakistan	61%	35%	48%

Source: CIA, *The World Fact Book*

MODEL: TABLE

Amendments to the U. S. Constitution After the Bill of Rights Ⓐ

Amendment	Year Proposed by Congress	Year Adopted	What It Does Ⓑ
11	1794	1798	Gives states immunity from certain legal actions Ⓒ
12	1803	1804	Changes the selection of president and vice-president through the electoral college
13	1865	1865	Abolishes slavery
14	1866	1868	Defines citizenship and citizen rights; provides due process and equal protection of the laws
15	1869	1870	Extends the right to vote to all African Americans, including former slaves
16	1909	1913	Gives power to impose income tax

Maps

A **map** visually represents a geographic region, such as a state or country. It provides information about areas through lines, colors, shapes, and symbols. There are different kinds of maps.

- **Political maps** show political features, such as national borders.
- **Physical maps** show the landforms in areas.
- **Road or travel maps** show roads and highways.
- **Thematic maps** show information on a specific topic, such as climate, weather, or natural resources.

Strategies for Reading

Ⓐ Read the title to find out what kind of map it is.

Ⓑ Read the labels to get an overall sense of what the map shows.

Ⓒ Look at the **key** or **legend** to find out what the symbols and colors on the map stand for.

MODEL: THEMATIC MAP

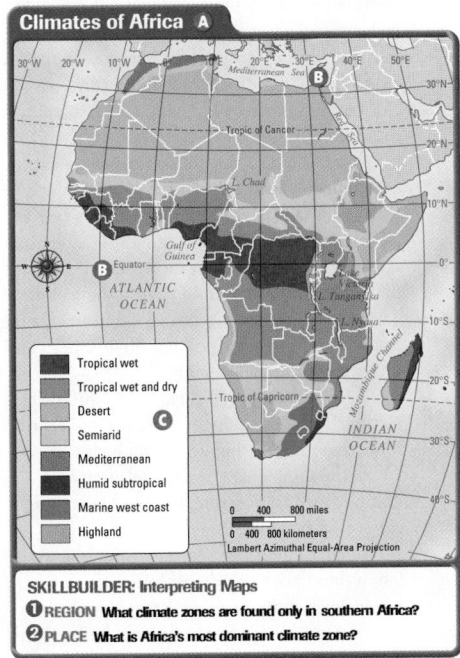

Climates of Africa Ⓐ

SKILLBUILDER: Interpreting Maps
❶ REGION What climate zones are found only in southern Africa?
❷ PLACE What is Africa's most dominant climate zone?

MODEL: PHYSICAL MAP

Map of Egypt Ⓐ

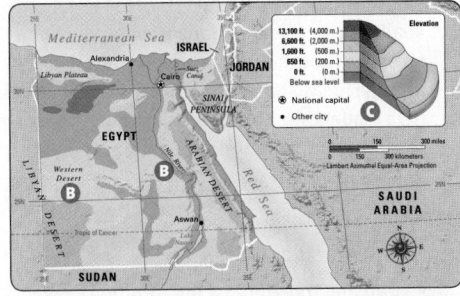

PRACTICE AND APPLY

Use the graphics shown on pages R5–R7 to answer the following questions:

1. According to the circle graph, did Japan export more to South Korea or to Taiwan in 1999?

2. According to the line graph, in what year were global average temperatures at their lowest?

3. Is the Nile River approximately four or five times longer than the Rhine River, according to the bar graph?

4. How many lenses does a microscope have?

5. Use the information in the schematic diagram to write a definition of a wavelength.

6. In general, according to the chart, were literacy rates in 2003 in South Asia higher for males or for females?

7. In what year was the right to vote guaranteed to African Americans, according to the table?

8. What is one major feature of the natural landscape shown on the physical map of Egypt?

9. Using the key on the climate map of Africa, identify the general area of Africa that is the wettest.

PRACTICE AND APPLY

ANSWERS

1. *Taiwan*

2. *1895*

3. *approximately five times longer*

4. *two lenses (eyepiece and objective)*

5. *Wavelength is the distance from one crest or trough of a wave to the next.*

6. *Literacy rates were higher for males.*

7. *1870*

8. ***Possible answers:*** *Nile River, Red Sea, Mediterranean Sea, Arabian Desert, Western Desert, Libyan Plateau, Libyan Desert*

9. *Central Africa*

3 Reading Informational Texts: Patterns of Organization

Reading any type of writing is easier once you recognize how it is organized. Writers usually arrange ideas and information in ways that best help readers see how they are related. There are several common patterns of organization:

- order of importance
- chronological order
- cause-effect organization
- compare-and-contrast organization

3.1 ORDER OF IMPORTANCE

Order of importance is a pattern of organization in which information is arranged by its degree of importance. The information is often arranged in one of two ways: from **most important to least important** or from **least important to most important.** In the first way, the most important quality, characteristic, or fact is presented at the beginning of the text, and the remaining details are presented in an order ending with the least significant. The second pattern is the reverse: the text builds from the less important elements to the most important one at the conclusion. Order of importance is frequently used in persuasive writing.

Strategies for Reading

- To identify order of importance in a piece of writing, skim the text to see if it moves from items of greater importance to items of lesser importance, or the reverse.

- Next, read the text carefully. Look for words and phrases such as *first, second, mainly, more important, less important, least important* and *most important* to indicate the relative importance of the ideas and information.

- Identify the topic of the text and what aspect of it is being discussed—its complexity, size, effectiveness, varieties, and so on. Note what the most important fact or idea seems to be.

- If you are having difficulty understanding the topic, try asking *who, what, when, where, why,* and *how* about the ideas or events.

Notice how the ideas move from the most important to the least in the following model.

Subject	Words showing order of importance

MODEL

If you spend any time outdoors in the summer, at some point you probably will find yourself covered with mosquito bites. The word *mosquito* means "little fly" in Spanish, but the impact these pesky insects have on people is anything but small.

The most important thing to know about mosquitoes is that they can transmit serious diseases such as yellow fever, malaria, and encephalitis. These diseases are not limited to developing countries, either. Outbreaks of West Nile virus, which is related to viruses that can cause encephalitis, have occurred recently in the United States. The symptoms of all these mosquito-borne illnesses include high fever and headaches.

Luckily, not all mosquitoes carry serious diseases. While the bites of these "safe" mosquitoes may not seem as important because they're less life-threatening, they can be extremely annoying. Just thinking about those raised red bumps that itch like crazy is enough to make anyone start scratching frantically.

Although exactly what happens when you get bitten by a mosquito is less important than the bite itself, the mechanism is surprising. First, only female mosquitoes "bite." Second, since the insects lack jaws, they don't actually bite at all. Instead, the mosquito punctures the victim's skin with sharp stylets on the proboscis used for piercing and injects her saliva into the wound. The saliva keeps the victim's blood from clotting, so the mosquito can drink her fill—sometimes up to 150 times her weight.

The saliva sets off an allergic reaction in the victim. Ironically, though, if the person lets the mosquito finish eating, there will be less saliva left in the skin. Therefore, the swelling and itching won't be as severe. Nice to know, but easier said than done.

The best ways to prevent mosquito bites or to lessen the effect if you do get bitten are to stay inside when mosquitoes are out—from dusk to dawn; to use mosquito repellant at all times; and, if you do get bitten, to refrain from scratching!

PRACTICE AND APPLY

Read the following passage, and then do the following:

1. Identify whether the order is from most important to least important or from least important to most important.

2. Identify one phrase that helped you figure out the order.

Of the four acknowledged heroes of the event, three are able to account for their behavior. Donald Usher and Eugene Windsor, a park police helicopter team, risked their lives every time they dipped the skids into the water to pick up survivors. On television, side by side in bright blue jumpsuits, they described their courage as all in the line of duty. Lenny Skutnik, a twenty-eight-year-old employee of the Congressional Budget Office, said: "It's something I never thought I would do"—referring to his jumping into the water to drag an injured woman to shore. Skutnik added that "somebody had to go in the water," delivering every hero's line that is no less admirable for its repetitions. In fact, nobody had to go into the water. That somebody actually did so is part of the reason this particular tragedy sticks in the mind.

But the person most responsible for the emotional impact of the disaster is the one known at first simply as "the man in the water." (Balding, probably in his fifties, an extravagant mustache.) He was seen clinging with five other survivors to the tail section of the airplane. This man was described by Usher and Windsor as appearing alert and in control. Every time they lowered a lifeline and flotation ring to him, he passed it on to another of the passengers.

—Roger Rosenblatt, "The Man in the Water"

3.2 CHRONOLOGICAL ORDER

Chronological order is the arrangement of events in their order of occurrence. This type of organization is used in fictional narratives, historical writing, biographies, and autobiographies. To indicate the order of events, writers use words such as *before, after, next,* and *later* and words and phrases that identify specific times of day, days of the week, and dates, such as *the next morning, Tuesday,* and *on July 4, 1776.*

Strategies for Reading

- Look in the text for headings and subheadings that may indicate a chronological pattern of organization.
- Look for words and phrases that identify times, such as *in a year, three hours earlier, in 1871,* and *the next day.*
- Look for words that signal order, such as *first, afterward, then, during,* and *finally,* to see how events or steps are related.
- Note that a paragraph or passage in which ideas and information are arranged chronologically will have several words or phrases that indicate time order, not just one.
- Ask yourself: Are the events in the paragraph or passage presented in time order?

Notice the words and phrases that signal time order in the first three paragraphs of the following model.

MODEL
The Career of Alexander Graham Bell

In 1871, Alexander Graham Bell came to Boston for a few weeks to lecture on his father's system for teaching speech to the deaf. What he didn't know was that this brief trip would have a dramatic impact on his life. Bell's lectures amazed audiences, prompting other Bostonians to extend similar invitations to him. Within the year, the Scottish-born teacher and scientist found himself living in Boston—although he had moved with his parents from London, England, to Ontario, Canada, just a year before.

Time words and phrases

Events

Order words and phrases

PRACTICE AND APPLY
ANSWERS

1. *Paragraph one: least important to most important; Paragraph two: most important to least important*

2. *Possible answers: Paragraph one:* Of the four; *Paragraph two:* But the person most responsible

By 1872, Bell had opened a school in Boston for training teachers of the deaf. In 1873, he accepted a teaching position at Boston University as professor of vocal physiology.

During this period, Bell also met Thomas Watson, a young repair mechanic and model maker. Watson teamed up with Bell in early 1875. For over two years the men worked together to create an apparatus for transmitting sound by electricity. Then, on April 6, 1875, Bell acquired a patent for a multiple telegraph. A little less than a year later, on the heels of their first success, the two created the first telephone.

The first transmission of human speech took place on March 10, 1876. On that day, Bell called to his assistant over a new transmitter he was trying out, "Mr. Watson! Come here! I want you!" and Mr. Watson heard him.

There was more work to do before others would have actual telephone service, of course. By 1915, however, coast-to-coast telephone communication was a reality.

By then, the two had also succeeded in inventing many other useful devices. In fact, although Bell is best known for inventing the telephone, he was also the father of many other equally amazing devices and scientific advancements.

PRACTICE AND APPLY

Refer to the preceding model to do the following:

1. List at least five words in the last three paragraphs that indicate time or order.

2. Draw a timeline beginning with Bell's arrival in Ontario, Canada, in 1870 and ending with the availability of coast-to-coast phone service in 1915. Chart on the timeline each major event described in the model.

3. A writer may use more than one pattern of organization in a text. In the last paragraph of the model, what pattern of organization does the writer use? How does this pattern contribute to your understanding of the passage?

3.3 CAUSE-EFFECT ORGANIZATION

Cause-effect organization is a pattern of organization that expresses causal relationships between events, ideas, and trends. Cause-effect relationships may be directly stated or merely implied by the order in which the information is presented. Writers often use the cause-effect pattern in historical and scientific writing. Cause-effect relationships may take several forms.

One cause with one effect

One cause with multiple effects

Multiple causes with a single effect

A chain of causes and effects

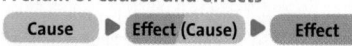

Strategies for Reading

- Look for headings and subheadings that indicate a cause-effect pattern of organization, such as "Effects of Population Density."
- To find the effect or effects, read to answer the question, What happened?
- To find the cause or causes, read to answer the question, Why did it happen?
- Look for words and phrases that help you identify specific relationships between events, such as *because, since, so, had the effect of, led to, as a result, resulted in, for that reason, due to, therefore, if . . . then,* and *consequently.*
- Evaluate each cause-effect relationship. Do not assume that because one event happened before another, the first event caused the second event.
- Use graphic organizers like the diagrams shown to record cause-effect relationships as you read.

PRACTICE AND APPLY

ANSWERS

1. first; March 10, 1876; On that day; By 1915; By then

2. *Possible answers (as timeline): 1870: Alexander Graham Bell moves from London, England, to Ontario, Canada. 1871: Bell visits Boston to lecture on his father's system for teaching speech to the deaf. 1872: Bell opens a school in Boston for training teachers of the deaf. 1873: Bell accepts a teaching position at Boston University. 1873: Bell meets Thomas Watson. 1873–75: Bell and Watson work together to create an apparatus for transmitting sound by electricity. 1875: Bell acquires a patent for a multiple telegraph. 1876: Bell and Watson create the first "telephonic communication." 1915: Coast-to-coast telephone service becomes available.*

3. *Possible answers: The writer uses order of importance (least important to most important) in the last paragraph. The pattern emphasizes the point that although Bell is known for inventing the telephone, he was also responsible for many other technological and scientific advancements.*

Notice the words that signal causes and effects in the following model.

MODEL

The Creation of National Parks

In 1870 and 1871, two expeditions were led through Montana. These men were awestruck by the deep canyons, dense pine forests, and refreshing rivers and waterfalls of Yellowstone, Montana. They were so moved by the area's natural wonders, in fact, that they immediately wanted to protect them. So they trooped off to Washington, D.C., to demand that Yellowstone lands be set aside for public use. There, before Congress, with the help of breathtaking paintings and photographs by artists who had ventured to Yellowstone with government land surveyors, these passionate preservationists presented their case. Dazzled, Congress responded to their pleas by creating the first national park, Yellowstone National Park.

> **Causes**

> **Effect that in turn becomes a cause**

> **Signal words and phrases**

The next several national parks owe their establishment primarily to the enthusiasm and persuasive abilities of one nature lover, John Muir. Muir took influential friends such as Ralph Waldo Emerson and Theodore Roosevelt on spectacular hikes through the Sierras. While on these hikes, he expressed his love of nature in passionate arguments for its preservation. In 1890, largely as a result of Muir's efforts, Yosemite, Sequoia, and General Grant national parks were established.

Interestingly, however, some of today's national parks owe their preservation to looters—or rather, to a Congress roused into action by looters. In 1906, because Congress was concerned that widespread plundering of precious Southwestern archaeological sites was destroying important artifacts, it enacted a law to prevent such plundering. This law, called the Antiquities Act, authorized the president to set aside as national monuments extremely precious or threatened lands. Consequently, by calling on the powers granted to him under this law, President Theodore Roosevelt was able to put under government protection many sites that might otherwise have been destroyed. These sites would eventually earn national-park status.

PRACTICE AND APPLY

Refer to the preceding model to do the following:

1. Use the pattern of multiple causes with a single effect illustrated on page R10 to make a graphic organizer showing the causes described in the text and the effect of those causes.

2. List two words that the writer uses to signal cause and effect in the last paragraph.

3.4 COMPARE-AND-CONTRAST ORGANIZATION

Compare-and-contrast organization is a pattern of organization that serves as a framework for examining similarities and differences in two or more subjects. A writer may use this pattern of organization to analyze two or more subjects, such as characters or movies, in terms of their important points or characteristics. These points or characteristics are called points of comparison. The compare-and-contrast pattern of organization may be developed in either of two ways:

Point-by-point organization—The writer discusses one point of comparison for both subjects, then goes on to the next point.

Subject-by-subject organization—The writer covers all points of comparison for one subject and then all points of comparison for the next subject.

Strategies for Reading

• Look in the text for headings, subheadings, and sentences that may suggest a compare-and-contrast pattern of organization, such as "Plants Share Many Characteristics." These will help you identify where similarities and differences are addressed.

PRACTICE AND APPLY

ANSWERS

1. *Possible answers (as graphic organizer): Causes: Tourists petitioned Congress to set aside Yellowstone lands for public use. John Muir, a nature lover, took influential friends on spectacular hikes through the Sierras and argued for the preservation of nature. Congress passed the Antiquities Act, authorizing the president to set aside precious or threatened lands as national monuments. Effect: The national park system was established, ensuring the preservation and protection of lands that might have been otherwise destroyed.*

2. because *and* consequently

- To find similarities, look for words and phrases such as *like, similarly, both, also,* and *in the same way.*

- To find differences, look for words and phrases such as *unlike, but, on the other hand, in contrast,* and *however.*

- Use a graphic organizer, such as a Venn diagram or a compare-and-contrast chart, to record points of comparison and similarities and differences.

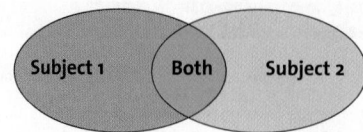

	Subject 1	Subject 2
Point 1		
Point 2		
Point 3		

Read the following models. As you read, use the signal words and phrases to identify the similarities and differences between the subjects and how the details are organized in each text.

MODEL 1

Two Favorite Chips

Tortilla and potato chips are top snack choices among Americans of all ages. Some snackers are happy munching on anything salty that crunches. Others are devoted fans of one chip or the other. Here's a look at some facts about these popular snacks.

While tortilla chips are made from corn, potato chips are made from—you guessed it, potatoes. Both chips are traditionally prepared by frying in vegetable oil with lots of salt, although baked versions are also available. Surprisingly, tortilla chips are lighter than potato chips. A one-ounce serving includes about 24 tortilla chips as opposed to 20 potato chips—about 17 percent more.

> **Subjects**

> **Contrast words and phrases**

> **Comparison words**

Neither snack is featured in weight-loss diets, though, and for good reason. Each is loaded with calories and fat—between 140 and 150 calories per serving, 70–90 of which come from fat. Although both chips are salty, tortilla chips are relatively less so.

As for nutrition, a serving of either tortilla or potato chips contains 2 grams of protein. That's not much, considering that the same amount of dry cereal offers about 300 percent more. It's probably a good thing, in that case, that people choose chips for their taste and texture, not for their food value.

Both chips come in numerous flavors. Tortilla-chip lovers can choose chips made from yellow or blue corn seasoned with salsa, nacho spices, ranch dressing, or guacamole. Similarly, potato chips are made from white or sweet potatoes and are available with barbecue, cheese, sour-cream-and-onion, dill pickle, and salt-and-vinegar flavors, to name just some options.

So choose your chip—just make sure that your snack is only part of a nutritious, well-balanced diet.

MODEL 2

Two Traditions

Almost every culture has a ceremony to mark the passage of young people from childhood to adulthood. In the Latin culture, this rite of passage for girls is *la quinceañera*. For American girls, it is the sweet 16 birthday party.

[Subjects]

Quinceañera means "15th birthday," and the occasion is celebrated when a girl reaches that age. The origin of *la quinceañera* is uncertain, although it may have roots in the Aztec, Maya, or Toltec culture. It generally involves celebration of a thanksgiving mass followed by a lavish party for the extended family and friends.

The *quinceañera* arrays herself to look as adult as possible, usually in a long, frilly dress in white or pastel colors. Her ensemble is topped by a hat or headdress. A highlight of the celebration is a waltz that she dances with her father and other male relatives. In Mexico, the celebrant may give her guests a memento taken from a handmade *quinceañera* doll.

The sweet 16 party, in contrast, takes place when a girl is a year older than the *quinceañera*. Unlike the Latin occasion, the sweet 16 celebration does not include a religious component and is designed more for the girl's friends than for the family. Like *la quinceañera*, the sweet 16 party often takes place in a hotel or reception hall. The guests at both celebrations are often treated to a live band, plentiful food, and a many-tiered birthday cake.

[Contrast words and phrases]

[Comparison words]

Similar to their Latin counterparts, sweet 16s dress to reflect their new adult status, many also choosing white or pastel gowns. On the other hand, sweet 16 attire can run the gamut from frothy and frilly to sleek and sophisticated, depending on the girl's personality.

Whether a girl celebrates *la quinceañera* or her sweet 16, however, the message from the world is the same—"Welcome to adulthood!"

PRACTICE AND APPLY

Refer to the preceding models to answer the following questions:

1. Which model is organized by subject? Which model is organized by points of comparison?

2. Identify two words or phrases in each model that signal a compare-and-contrast pattern of organization. Do not choose words or phrases that have already been highlighted.

3. List at least three points that the writer of each model compares and contrasts.

4. Use a Venn diagram or a compare-and-contrast chart to identify at least two points of comparison and the similarities and differences in model 2.

PRACTICE AND APPLY

ANSWERS

1. *Model 1 is organized by points of comparison. Model 2 is organized by subject.*

2. *Possible answers: Model 1: some; others; than; relatively less; either; same; similarly. Model 2: more; than; like; also; on the other hand; same*

3. *Possible answers: Model 1: ingredients, or what the chips are made from; how the chips are prepared; weight; calories and fat; nutritional value; availability of different flavors. Model 2: age; type of celebration; where the celebration takes place; who celebrates with the girls; girl's attire or dress*

4. *Students should create a Venn diagram or a compare-contrast chart like the one on page R12. Possible points of comparison include dress, type of celebration, location, and age.*

   *Possible answers: **Dress:** La Quinceañera—long, frilly gown accompanied by a hat or headdress; Sweet Sixteen—the dress's style reflects the taste of the teen; Similarities—both dresses reflect the adult status of the teen, both dresses are pastel or white. **Kind of Celebration:** La Quinceañera— follows a traditional religious ceremony, designed for friends and family; Sweet Sixteen—no religious component, designed for friends only; Similarities—both are lavish parties.*

4 Reading Informational Texts: Forms

Magazines, newspapers, Web pages, and consumer, public, and workplace documents are all examples of informational materials. To understand and analyze informational texts, pay attention to text features and patterns of organization.

4.1 READING A MAGAZINE ARTICLE

Because people often skim magazines, magazine publishers use devices to attract attention to articles.

Strategies for Reading

A Notice whether **graphics** or **quotations** attract your attention. Sometimes a publisher pulls a quotation out of the text and displays it to get your attention. Such quotations are called **pull quotes.**

B Once you decide that you're interested in the article, read the title and other headings to find out more about its topic and organization.

C Notice whether the article has a **byline,** a line naming the author.

D Sometimes an article will be accompanied by a **sidebar,** a short article that presents additional information. This sidebar also has a **title.** Is your understanding of the main article enhanced by the information in the sidebar?

PRACTICE AND APPLY

ANSWERS

1. *Possible answer:* The title grabs readers' interest and entices them to read further.

2. *The pull quote is taken from the last sentence in the second paragraph.*

3. *Possible answer: Like the article, the sidebar provides names of other inventions and inventors who are not as well known or as popular as Thomas Edison and Alexander Graham Bell.*

B Shouldn't We Know Who Invented the Windshield Wiper?

C by James T. Terry

We know the famous ones—the Thomas Edisons and the Alexander Graham Bells—but what about the less famous inventors? What about the people who invented the traffic light and the windshield wiper? Shouldn't we know who they are?

Joan McLean thinks so. In fact, McLean, a professor of physics at Mountain University in Range, Colorado, feels so strongly about this matter that she's developed a course on the topic. In addition to learning "who" invented "what," however, McLean also likes her students to learn the answers to the "why" and "how" questions. According to McLean, "When students learn the answers to these questions, they are better prepared to recognize opportunities for inventing and more motivated to give inventing a try."

Her students agree. One young man with a patent pending for an unbreakable umbrella is walking proof of McLean's statement. "If I had not heard the story of the windshield wiper's invention," said Tommy Lee, a senior physics major, "I never would have dreamed of turning my frustration during a rainstorm into something so constructive." Lee is currently negotiating to sell his patent to an umbrella manufacturer once it is approved.

So, just what is the story behind the windshield wiper? Well, Mary Anderson came up with the idea in 1902 after a visit to New York City. The day was cold and blus-

"When students learn the answers to these questions, they are better prepared to recognize opportunities for **A** *inventing...."*

tery, but Anderson still wanted to see the sights, so she hopped aboard a streetcar. Noticing that the driver was struggling to see through the sleet and snow covering the windshield, she found herself wondering why there couldn't be a built-in device for cleaning the window. Still wondering about this when she returned home to Birmingham, Alabama, Anderson started sketching out solutions. One of her ideas, a lever on the inside of a vehicle that would control an arm on the outside, became the first windshield wiper.

Today we benefit from countless inventions and innovations. It's hard to imagine getting by without Garrett A. Morgan's traffic light. It's equally impossible to picture a world without Katherine J. Blodgett's innovation that makes glass invisible. Can you picture life without transparent windows and eyeglasses?

As I think about stories like these, I am convinced that they will help untold numbers of inventors. So, only one question nags: how did we ever manage to give rise to so many inventors before McLean invented this class?

D

Someone Also Invented . . .

Dishwashers	Josephine Cochran
Disposable Diapers	Marion Donovan
Fire Escapes	Anna Connelly
Peanut Butter	George Washington Carver

PRACTICE AND APPLY

1. What is the effect of using a question for the title?

2. From what part of the article is the pull quote taken?

3. What is the relationship of the information in the sidebar to the article?

4.2 READING A TEXTBOOK

Each textbook that you use has its own system of organization based on the content in the book. Often an introductory unit will explain the book's organization and special features. If your textbook has such a unit, read it first.

Strategies for Reading

Ⓐ Before you begin reading the lesson or chapter, read any **questions** that appear at the end of it. Then use the questions to set your purpose for reading.

Ⓑ **Read slowly and carefully** to better understand and remember the ideas presented in the text. When you come to an unfamiliar word, first try to figure out its meaning from **context clues.** If necessary, find the meaning of the word in a **glossary** in the textbook or in a dictionary. Avoid interrupting your reading by constantly looking up words in a dictionary.

Ⓒ Use the book's graphics, such as illustrations, diagrams, and captions, to clarify your understanding of the text.

Ⓓ Take notes as you read. Use text features such as **subheadings** and boldfaced terms to help you organize your notes. Use graphic organizers, such as cause-effect charts, to help you clarify relationships among ideas.

PRACTICE AND APPLY

1. How would you find the definition of *equatorial*?

2. Where on the page can you find out the names of different types of glaciers?

3. Use the text on this page and on page R3 to answer the second question in the Section Review.

Firn resembles the ice of a packed snowball. It is not fluffy, such as new-fallen snow, nor is it as hard as solid ice. The granules of firn start out no larger than grains of sand. As the layer of firn thickens, the firn's crystals may grow as large as kernels of corn. Within a layer of firn, the weight of the material at the top compresses the firn below, turning that firn into solid ice. Under the weight of the overlying snow and firn, the ice begins to flow downward or outward. This moving mass of snow and ice is a glacier.

Types of Glaciers Ⓓ

There are two main types of glaciers, valley glaciers and continental glaciers. A **valley glacier** is a glacier that moves within valley walls. A **continental glacier** is a glacier that covers a large part of a continent.

Valley Glaciers Ⓓ

Many mountain ranges in the world have peaks and valleys high enough so that snowfall there exceeds snowmelt. The snow builds up and changes to ice as it accumulates in the valleys of such mountain ranges. The ice stays within valley walls, forming a large river of ice and snow, which moves slowly downhill under the influence of gravity. This long, slow-moving, wedge-shaped stream of ice is a valley glacier. Valley glaciers are also known as alpine glaciers, after the Alps in south-central Europe.

Ⓑ Valley glaciers form in regions where mountains are high enough to be in the colder part of Earth's atmosphere. Valley glaciers even form in equatorial regions where mountains are located at high elevations. Valley glaciers exist on all continents except Australia.

Valley glaciers vary in size. Small valley glaciers may be less than 2-kilometers long. Large valley glaciers may be over 100 kilometers long and hundreds of meters thick. Some of the world's largest valley glaciers are in southern Alaska. The world's tallest mountains, the Himalayas, also have very large valley glaciers.

DENALI NATIONAL PARK Muldrow Glacier, a valley glacier in Alaska, is about 56 kilometers long.

Ⓒ

Section Review Ⓐ

- What is the snow line?
- Describe how a glacier forms.
- **Critical Thinking** The graph on page 318 shows how snow-line elevations change north of the equator. Predict how snow-line elevations change as latitude increases south of the equator.

PRACTICE AND APPLY

ANSWERS

1. *Possible answers: using context clues; looking up the word in a glossary of the textbook; looking for the word in a dictionary*

2. *The names of the different composite glaciers can be found under the subheading "Types of Glaciers."*

3. *Possible answer: Glaciers form when layers of thick snow build up in the great basins below the highest mountain peaks. The buried snow becomes compressed and re-crystallizes into firn. The weight of the material at the top compresses the firn below, turning the firn into solid ice. Under the weight of the overlying snow and firn, the ice begins to flow downward or outward.*

4.3 READING A CONSUMER DOCUMENT

Consumer documents are materials that accompany products and services. They usually provide information about the use, care, operation, or assembly of the products they accompany. Some common consumer documents are contracts, warranties, manuals, instructions, schedules, and Web pages. Two examples of consumer documents follow.

Strategies for Reading

Ⓐ Read the **title** to identify the purpose of the document.

Ⓑ Read the general directions to get started.

Ⓒ Look for **numbers** or **letters** that indicate the order in which the steps should be followed. If you do not find letters or numbers, look for signal words such as *first, next, then,* and *finally* to see the order in which the steps should be followed.

Ⓓ Look at the **visuals** that accompany the numbered instructions. Follow the steps in order.

Ⓔ Look for **verbs that describe actions** you should take, such as *press, select,* and *click.*

INSTRUCTIONS FOR CREATING A HOME PAGE

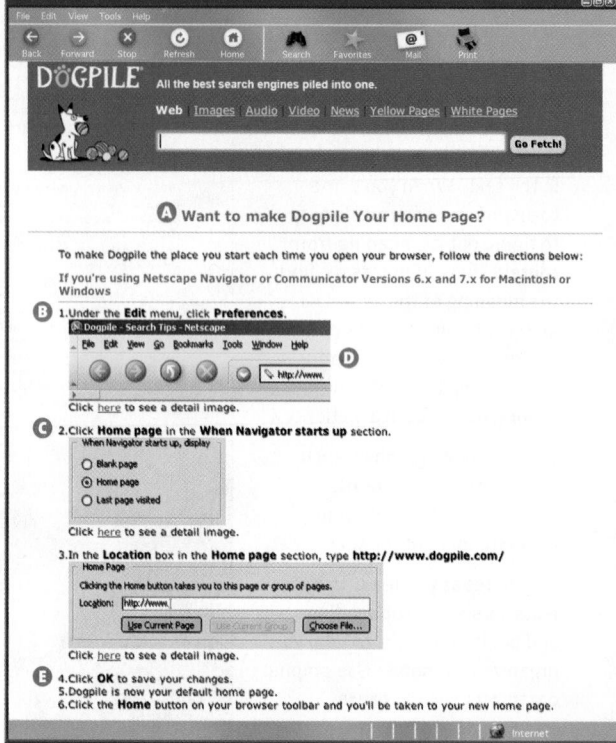

PRACTICE AND APPLY

ANSWERS

1. *Click OK.*

2. *Click the Home button on the browser toolbar.*

PRACTICE AND APPLY

Reread the Web page telling how to create a home page, and then answer the following questions:

1. Once you have input your preferences for your home page, what must you do to save your changes?

2. After you have saved your changes, how do you get taken straight to your new home page?

The instructions on this page are from a manual for operating a graphing calculator.

Strategies for Reading

A Read the **heading** to learn the kind of operation this section of the manual explains.

B Look for **numbers** that indicate the order in which the steps should be followed.

C Look for **verbs that describe actions** you should take, such as *open, move, press, position,* and *select.*

D Examine **graphics** that illustrate steps. If you have trouble completing the process, the graphics can help you pinpoint what you are doing wrong.

INSTRUCTIONS FOR OPERATING A GRAPHING CALCULATOR

A **Drawing a Triangle**

B 1. Open the F2 menu, move the pointer to **Triangle**, and press ENTER. The tool icon at the top left of the screen indicates that the Triangle tool is active. The pointer shape changes to a pen to indicate that you can draw a new point by pressing ENTER at that position.

C

2. Move the pointer to a convenient location for the first vertex of the triangle, and then press ENTER.

3. Move the pointer and then press ENTER to fix the second vertex and continue the same way for the last vertex.

D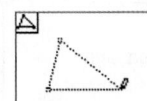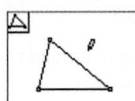

Changing the Shape of the Triangle

1. Press CLEAR to quit the Triangle tool.

2. Move the pointer close to one of the vertices that you drew. The pointer changes to a hollow arrow and the object that can be selected (the vertex) blinks.

PRACTICE AND APPLY

Reread the page from the manual and then answer the following questions:

1. What does this page explain how to do?

2. What key do you press to begin?

3. What tells you that you can begin drawing a new point?

4. How do you quit the Triangle tool?

Refer to the documents on pages R16–R17 to answer the following question:

5. Compare the document on page R16 with the document on this page. In terms of text features and organization, are they more alike or more different? Support your answer.

PRACTICE AND APPLY

ANSWERS

1. *The page explains how to draw a triangle using a graphing calculator.*

2. *F2*

3. *The pointer shape changes into a pen to indicate that you can draw a new point by pressing ENTER.*

4. *Press CLEAR.*

5. *Possible answer: The documents are similar in that they each use a title or heading to identify the purpose of the document. Both documents use numbers and visuals to demonstrate a step or procedure. The organization in the two documents is easy to follow.*

Public documents are documents that are written for the public to provide information that is of public interest or concern. These documents are often free. They can be federal, state, or local government documents. They can be speeches or historical documents. They may even be laws, posted warnings, signs, or rules and regulations. The following is one type of public document.

Strategies for Reading

Ⓐ Look at the **title** on the page to discover what the text is about.

Ⓑ Read any lists of **bulleted items** carefully. The bulleted points are usually the essential pieces of information.

Ⓒ Be sure to read the text that immediately precedes a visual. This **lead-in text** can help you understand what the visual is intended to show.

Ⓓ Pay attention to **captions** with pictures or drawings. These will help you interpret what you are seeing.

Ⓔ Study **graphics** and **illustrations** closely. These will help you interpret what you are reading and may even provide information not covered in the text.

PAGE FROM A DRIVER EDUCATION MANUAL

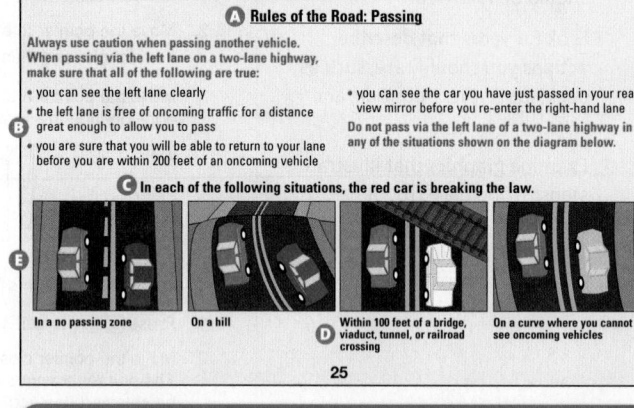

Ⓐ **Rules of the Road: Passing**

Always use caution when passing another vehicle. When passing via the left lane on a two-lane highway, make sure that all of the following are true:

Ⓑ
- you can see the left lane clearly
- the left lane is free of oncoming traffic for a distance great enough to allow you to pass
- you are sure that you will be able to return to your lane before you are within 200 feet of an oncoming vehicle
- you can see the car you have just passed in your rear-view mirror before you re-enter the right-hand lane

Do not pass via the left lane of a two-lane highway in any of the situations shown on the diagram below.

Ⓒ In each of the following situations, the red car is breaking the law.

In a no passing zone | On a hill | Ⓓ Within 100 feet of a bridge, viaduct, tunnel, or railroad crossing | On a curve where you cannot see oncoming vehicles

25

PRACTICE AND APPLY

Reread the page from the driving-instruction manual and then answer the following questions:

1. What essential piece of information does the lead-in text provide about the illustrations on this page?

2. What are the four driving situations described in which a driver should not pass another vehicle?

3. What do all of the bulleted items concern?

4. What information about lane markings can you gain from the visual that you do not learn from the text on this page?

For more information, see Reading Informational Texts: Text Features, pages R3–R7.

PRACTICE AND APPLY

ANSWERS

1. *In each illustration, the red car is breaking the law.*

2. *in a no passing zone; on a hill; within 100 feet of a bridge, viaduct, tunnel, or railroad crossing; on a curve where you cannot see oncoming vehicles*

3. *The bulleted items highlight precautions that should be taken when passing another vehicle in the left lane on a two-lane highway.*

4. *Lane markings are used to signal when a driver is allowed to pass another car. The visuals show examples of illegal passing that you can't learn from the text. A solid line means a no-passing zone.*

4.5 READING A WORKPLACE DOCUMENT

Workplace documents are materials that are produced or used within a workplace, usually to aid in the functioning of a business. These may be documents generated by a business to monitor itself, such as minutes of a meeting or a sales report. These documents may also explain company policies, organizational structures, and operating procedures. Workplace documents include memos, business letters, job applications, and résumés.

Strategies for Reading

A Read a workplace document slowly and carefully, as it may contain **details** that should not be overlooked.

B Notice how to contact the creator of the document. You will need this information to clear up anything that you don't understand.

C **Take notes** to help you remember times, dates, deadlines, and actions required. In particular, note whether you are expected to respond to the document, whether there is a deadline for your response, and to whom you should address your reply.

PRACTICE AND APPLY

Refer to both workplace documents to answer the following questions:

1. Why might the letter from Benjamin Blake be classified as a workplace document?

2. According to the details in Blake's letter, what actions should Ms. Ramirez take?

3. How does Ms. Ramirez use text features, such as graphics and headings, to get her message across clearly and quickly?

4. What actions is Ms. Keene expected to take?

LETTER

B **Benjamin Blake,**
Guidance Counselor
West High School
100 Oak Lane
Timber Creek, NJ 00000
(000) 000-0000
benj80@blake.com

August 8, 2010 **A**

Ramona Ramirez, Vice-President
Packer Press
200 Maple Lane
Timber Creek, NJ 00000

Dear Ms. Ramirez:

C In a recent conversation with your assistant, Kathy Keene, I learned of the list of workplace skills that you give to your employees. Would it **A** be possible for me to have a copy of this document to use with my students this fall? I would, of course, give full credit to your company. **C** Thank you for your consideration of my request.

Sincerely,
Benjamin Blake

MEMO

To: Kathy Keene
B **From:** Ramona Ramirez
Re: Teacher Request
Date: August 9, 2010

C Kathy, we can give permission to Mr. Blake to use our skills document. Please send him a copy of the following list to see if these categories will fit his needs:

- Resources
- Interpersonal skills
- Systems
- Technology

A Also, please tell him that we will need a signed agreement from him when we make the arrangements. Thanks.

READING HANDBOOK **R19**

PRACTICE AND APPLY

ANSWERS

1. *Possible answer: The letter can be classified as a workplace document because it is written in the form of a business letter, including a business address, date, greeting, body, and closing.*

2. *Possible answer: Ms. Ramirez should provide Mr. Blake with a response that either approves or denies his use of the workplace skills document. If she approves his request, she should also enclose a copy of the document.*

3. *Possible answer: The heading provides the necessary contact information, along with the purpose of the memo. Bulleted points draw attention to the categories of skills documents that are available. The bulleted list also allows the recipient to scan the memo for important information.*

4. *Possible answer: Ms. Keene is expected to contact Mr. Blake, approving his request for the workplace documents. In addition, she should send him a list of skills categories that are available, and she should request a signed agreement from Mr. Blake.*

PRACTICE AND APPLY

ANSWERS

1. *http://brookfieldzoo.org/*

2. *The* What's New *link gives updated information about the site.*

3. *Click on the* En Español *link that is located at the bottom of the Information category.*

4.6 READING ELECTRONIC TEXT

Electronic text is any text that is in a form that a computer can store and display on a screen. Electronic text can be part of Web pages, CD-ROMs, search engines, and documents that you create with your computer software. Like books, Web pages often provide aids for finding information. However, each Web page is designed differently, and information is not in the same location on each page. It is important to know the functions of different parts of a Web page so that you can easily find the information you want.

Strategies for Reading

Ⓐ Look at the **title** of a page to determine what topics it covers.

Ⓑ For an online source, such as a Web page or search engine, note the **Web address,** known as a **URL** (Universal Resource Locator). You may want to make a note of it if you need to return to that page.

Ⓒ Look for a **menu bar** along the top, bottom, or side of a Web page. Clicking on an item in a menu bar will take you to another part of the Web site.

Ⓓ Notice any hyperlinks to related pages. **Hyperlinks** are often underlined or highlighted in a contrasting color. You can click on a hyperlink to get to another page—one that may or may not have been created by the same person or organization.

Ⓔ For information that you want to keep for future reference, save documents on your computer or print them. For online sources, you can pull down the **Favorites** or **Bookmarks** menu and bookmark pages so that you can easily return to them or print the information you need. Printing the pages will allow you to highlight key ideas on a hard copy.

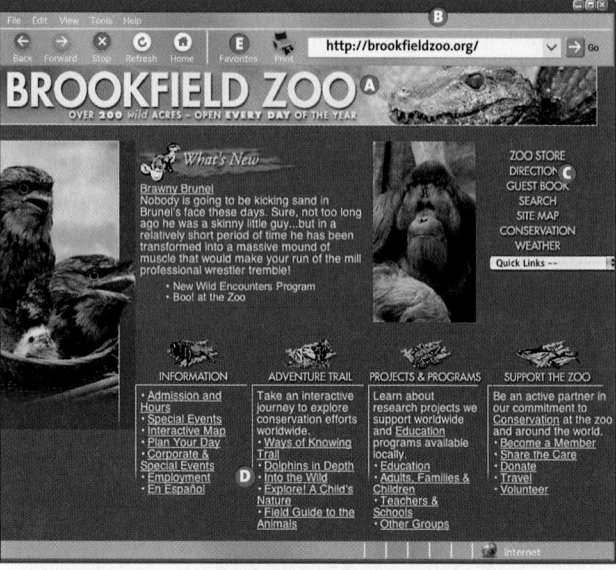

PRACTICE AND APPLY

1. What is the URL of the Web page shown?

2. How do you know that this Web site is regularly updated?

3. What would you do to get the text in Spanish?

5 Reading Persuasive Texts

5.1 ANALYZING AN ARGUMENT

An **argument** expresses a position on an issue or problem and supports it with reasons and evidence. Being able to analyze and evaluate arguments will help you distinguish between claims you should accept and those you should not. A sound argument should appeal strictly to reason. However, arguments are often used in texts that also contain other types of persuasive devices. An argument includes the following elements:

- A **claim** is the writer's position on an issue or central idea.

- **Support** is any material that serves to prove a claim. In an argument, support usually consists of reasons and evidence.

- **Reasons** are declarations made to justify an action, a decision, or a belief—for example, "My reason for thinking we will be late is that we can't make it to the appointment in five minutes."

- **Evidence** is the specific references, quotations, facts, examples, and opinions that support a claim. Evidence may also consist of statistics, reports of personal experience, or the views of experts.

- A **counterargument** or counterclaim is an argument made to oppose another argument. A good argument anticipates the opposition's objections and provides counterarguments to disprove or answer them.

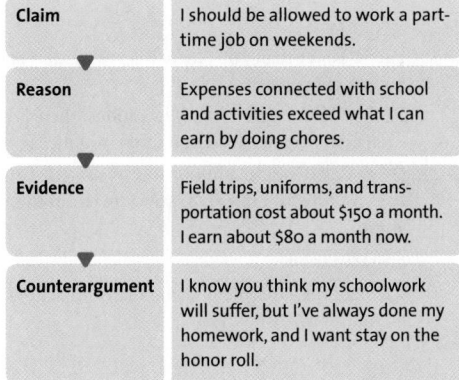

Claim	I should be allowed to work a part-time job on weekends.
Reason	Expenses connected with school and activities exceed what I can earn by doing chores.
Evidence	Field trips, uniforms, and transportation cost about $150 a month. I earn about $80 a month now.
Counterargument	I know you think my schoolwork will suffer, but I've always done my homework, and I want stay on the honor roll.

PRACTICE AND APPLY

Read the following editorial and use a chart like the one shown to identify the claim, reason, evidence, and counterargument.

Extracurricular Sports Should Satisfy State Physical Education Requirement

Track, football, soccer, baseball, basketball, and other sports attract dedicated student athletes who often practice every day after school and then participate in weekend games. Should these students be forced to give up an elective class period to take a required physical education class? In order to meet the state's physical education (P.E.) course requirements, that is exactly what Whitman High School asks them to do. I believe that this policy doesn't make any sense. Instead, the [Montgomery County public schools] should exempt student athletes from taking P.E. classes.

First of all, participating in an extracurricular sport meets the objectives of the state's course requirements. Those objectives are to promote fitness and improve athletic skill, according to the Whitman course catalog. Involvement in either a varsity or a club sport for one season already makes a student fit and athletically skilled.

A second reason to change the policy is that the physical education requirement forces students to give up an elective class period. High school students can generally choose only eight elective courses from dozens of class offerings. By eliminating the P.E. requirement for student athletes, the county would give students more freedom in selecting their courses.

Finally, exposing students to different sports is one goal of the P.E. requirement, but this objective alone is not important enough to require students to take P.E. class. Students seldom take P.E. class as seriously as they would an extracurricular sport, so students do not always appreciate sports they sample in P.E. class.

Varsity and club sports require a great deal of time and effort from athletes. The county should recognize that team sports encourage physical activity more effectively than P.E. class. It is more important for student athletes to become well-rounded academically by taking electives than to take P.E. class.

PRACTICE AND APPLY

ANSWERS

Students should create a chart like the one on page R21. The chart should include details similar to the ones below.

Claim *Montgomery County public schools should exempt student athletes from taking P.E. classes.*

Reason *Students involved in sports are forced to give up an elective course in order to meet the state's physical education course requirements.*

Evidence *Participating in extracurricular sports meets the objectives of the state's course requirements.*

Evidence *According to the Whitman High School course catalog, the objective of P.E. class is to promote fitness and improve athletic skill. Involvement in a varsity or club sport for one season already makes a student fit and athletically skilled.*

Counterargument *Exposing students to different sports is also one goal of the P.E. requirement, but this objective alone is not important enough to require students to take P.E. class. Students seldom take P.E. as seriously as they would an extracurricular sport and don't appreciate the different sports they sample in class.*

PRACTICE AND APPLY

ANSWERS

Possible answers:

Appeals by Association bandwagon appeal: "Join your friends and neighbors in serving others today."

Emotional Appeals appeals to pity, fear, vanity: "caring people everywhere are opening their hearts and wallets to those who are less fortunate"; "how important it is to share that good fortune"; "Make this holiday—and all the days that follow—a time of true giving."

Word Choice glittering generality: "Charity and community service show democracy in action, and Mayor Adam Miner's actions are setting a good example for village residents."

5.2 RECOGNIZING PERSUASIVE TECHNIQUES

Arguments typically rely on more than just the logical appeal of an argument to be convincing. They also depend on **persuasive techniques**—devices that can sway you to adopt a position or take an action.

The chart shown here explains several ways a writer may attempt to sway you to adopt his or her position. Learn to recognize these techniques, and you are less likely to be influenced by them.

Persuasive Technique	Example
Appeals by Association	
Bandwagon appeal Suggests that a person should believe or do something because "everyone else" does	Be where it's at—shop the Magnificent Mall.
Testimonial Relies on endorsements from well-known people or satisfied customers	Links Lorimer, winner of the Wide World Open, uses Gofar golf balls. Shouldn't you?
Snob appeal Taps into people's desire to be special or part of an elite group	Dine at the elite Plaza Inn, where you will be treated like royalty.
Transfer Connnects a product, candidate, or cause with a positive emotion or idea	One spray of Northwoods air freshener and you'll find inner peace.
Appeal to loyalty Relies on people's affiliation with a particular group	Show your support for the Tidewater Tigers by wearing the new Win-Team windbreaker.
Emotional Appeals	
Appeals to pity, fear, or vanity Use strong feelings, rather than facts, to persuade	Don't these abandoned animals deserve a chance? Adopt a pet today.
Word Choice	
Glittering generality Makes a generalization that includes a word or phrase with positive connotations, such as *freedom* and *honor*, to promote a product or idea.	Hop on a Swiftee moped and experience pure freedom.

Identify the persuasive techniques used in this model.

The True Holiday Spirit

The holiday season is almost upon us, and caring people everywhere are opening their hearts and wallets to those who are less fortunate. Charity and community service show democracy in action, and Mayor Adam Miner's actions are setting a good example for village residents. For the last three years, he has volunteered once a week at the local Meals for the Many program. Busing tables, serving soup, and helping wash dishes has made him aware of how fortunate he is and how important it is to share that good fortune. In his Thanksgiving address last week, he urged citizens, "Make this holiday—and all the days that follow—a time of true giving. Join your friends and neighbors in serving others today."

5.3 ANALYZING LOGIC AND REASONING

When you evaluate an argument, you need to look closely at the writer's logic and reasoning. To do this, it is helpful to identify the type of reasoning the writer is using.

The Inductive Mode of Reasoning

When a writer leads from specific evidence to a general principle or generalization, that writer is using **inductive reasoning.** Here is an example of inductive reasoning.

SPECIFIC FACTS

Fact 1 Fewer than 100 Arizona agave century plants remain in existence.

Fact 2 Over the last three generations, there has been a 50 percent reduction in the number of African elephants.

Fact 3 Only 50 Hawaiian crows are left in the world.

GENERALIZATION

Extinction is a problem facing many classes of living things.

Strategies for Determining the Soundness of Inductive Arguments

Ask yourself the following questions to evaluate an inductive argument:

- **Is the evidence valid and sufficient support for the conclusion?** Inaccurate facts lead to inaccurate conclusions.

- **Does the conclusion follow logically from the evidence?** From the facts listed in the previous example, the conclusion that extinction is a problem facing *all* living things would be too broad a generalization.

- **Is the evidence drawn from a large enough sample?** Even though there are only three facts listed above, the sample is large enough to support the claim. If you wanted to support the conclusion that extinction is a problem facing all classes of living things, the sample would not be large enough.

The Deductive Mode of Reasoning

When a writer arrives at a conclusion by applying a general principle to a specific situation, the writer is using **deductive reasoning.** Here's an example.

Green is a good color for redheads to wear.	General principle or premise
Iris has red hair.	Specific situation
Iris will look good in green.	Specific conclusion

Strategies for Determining the Soundness of Deductive Arguments

Ask yourself the following questions to evaluate a deductive argument:

- **Is the general principle stated, or is it implied?** Note that writers often use deductive reasoning in an argument without stating the general principle. They just assume that readers will recognize and agree with the principle. You may want to identify the general principle for yourself.

- **Is the general principle sound?** Don't just assume the general principle is sound. Ask yourself whether it is really true.

- **Is the conclusion valid?** To be valid, a conclusion in a deductive argument must follow logically from the general principle and the specific situation.

The following chart shows two conclusions drawn from the same general principle.

All government offices were closed last Monday.	
Accurate Deduction	**Inaccurate Deduction**
West Post Office is a government office; therefore, West Post Office was closed last Monday.	Soon-Lin's Spa was closed last Monday; therefore, Soon-Lin's Spa is a government office.

Soon-Lin might have closed her spa because there would be fewer customers in town when government offices were closed—or for another reason entirely.

PRACTICE AND APPLY

Identify the mode of reasoning used in the following paragraph.

> About a year ago, Dave Champlin and his two roommates lived in what their friends at the University of Missouri called the House of Fat. . . . By sticking to the low-carb, high-protein diet, Champlin lost about 45 pounds, and his roommates each lost about 50 to 60 pounds. Despite being pleased with the results, all three were off the diet by this past summer and have gained back some of the weight.
>
> A study by NPD Group, an independent marketing information company, found that the percentage of American adults on any low-carb diet in 2004 peaked at 9.1 percent in February and dropped to 4.9 percent by early November. Further, it said only one of four people surveyed was significantly cutting carbs and "virtually none" were reducing carbs as much as the diets recommended.
>
> That means many companies that rode the low-carb wave are either out of business or refocusing their strategies.
>
> —Margaret Stafford, *Associated Press*

PRACTICE AND APPLY

ANSWER

Inductive mode of reasoning. The writer comes to her conclusion (companies who made low-carb products are either out of business or re-focusing their strategies) through details about Americans' eating habits.

Identifying Faulty Reasoning

Sometimes an argument at first appears to make sense but isn't valid because it is based on a fallacy. A **fallacy** is an error in logic. Learn to recognize these common rhetorical and logical fallacies.

TYPE OF FALLACY	DEFINITION	EXAMPLE
Circular reasoning	Supporting a statement by simply repeating it in different words	Wearing a bicycle helmet should be required because **cyclists should use protective headgear.**
Either/or fallacy	A statement that suggests that there are only two choices available in a situation that really offers more than two options	**Either** you eat a balanced diet, **or** you'll die before you're 50.
Oversimplification	An explanation of a complex situation or problem as if it were much simpler than it is	Shared interests lead to a **successful relationship.**
Overgeneralization	A generalization that is too broad. You can often recognize overgeneralizations by the use of words such as *all, everyone, every time, anything, no one,* and *none.*	**Everyone** wants to go to college.
Stereotyping	A dangerous type of overgeneralization. Stereotypes are broad statements about people on the basis of their gender, ethnicity, race, or political, social, professional, or religious group.	**Men** just don't know how to express their emotions.
Personal attack or name-calling	An attempt to discredit an idea by attacking the person or group associated with it. Candidates often engage in name-calling during political campaigns.	**Mr. Edmonds drives a beat-up car and never mows his lawn,** so you shouldn't take music lessons from him.
Evading the issue	Refuting an objection with arguments and evidence that do not address its central point	I know I didn't clean up my room, **but that gave me more time to study and improve my grades.**
Non sequitur	A statement that uses irrelevant "proof" to support a claim. A non sequitur is sometimes used to win an argument by diverting the reader's attention to proof that can't be challenged.	I'll probably flunk the driving test. **I was late for school today.**
False dilemma	The mistake of assuming that because one event occurred after another event in time, the first event caused the second one to occur	Marc wore his new goggles in the swim meet and **as a result won with his best time ever.**
False analogy	A comparison that doesn't hold up because of a critical difference between the two subjects	I bet my little brother will be a great skier when he grows up **because he loves playing on the slide.**
Hasty generalization	A conclusion drawn from too little evidence or from evidence that is biased	**I got sick after eating at the pizzeria,** so Italian food must be bad for me.
Commonly held opinions	An argument that is deemed correct just because everyone else supposedly thinks it is correct.	**Everyone knows** that cats make better pets than dogs.
Appeal to pity	An argument that uses pity to make you feel sorry for someone.	I couldn't finish my homework **because my dog was sick.**

Look for examples of logical fallacies in the following argument. Identify each one and explain why you identified it as such.

> Everyone agrees that running is the best form of exercise. All you need is a good pair of shoes and you're ready to hit the road. I've run a mile twice this week, so I should know. As a result, I've slept better and my tone on the clarinet has improved. When you run, your heart beats faster because your pulse rate increases. That means that your cells get more oxygen, which is the second most common gas in the earth's atmosphere. You also get to enjoy the beauty of the world around you as you build up your stamina. So if you don't want to be a hopeless couch potato, get going and run for your life!

5.4 EVALUATING ARGUMENTS

Learning how to evaluate arguments and identify bias will help you become more selective when doing research and also help you improve your own reasoning and arguing skills. **Bias** is an inclination for or against a particular opinion or viewpoint. A writer may reveal a strongly positive or negative opinion on an issue by presenting only one way of looking at it or by heavily weighting the evidence on one side of the argument. Additionally, the presence of either of the following is often a sign of bias:

Loaded language consists of words with strongly positive or negative connotations that are intended to influence a reader's attitude.

EXAMPLE: *People who mistreat animals are subhuman and deserve to be locked up for life.* (*Subhuman* and *locked up* have very negative connotations.)

Propaganda is any form of communication that is so distorted that it conveys false or misleading information. Some politicians create and distribute propaganda. Many logical fallacies, such as name-calling, the either/or fallacy, and

false causes, are often used in propaganda. The following example shows an oversimplification. The writer uses one fact to support a particular point of view but does not reveal another fact that does not support that viewpoint.

EXAMPLE: *Since we moved to the city, our gas and electric bills have gone down.* (The writer does not include the fact that the move occurred in the spring, when the demand for heat or air conditioning is low anyway.)

For more information, see **Identifying Faulty Reasoning,** page R24.

Strategies for Evaluating Evidence

It is important to have a set of standards by which you can evaluate persuasive texts. Use the questions below to help you critically assess facts and opinions that are presented as evidence.

- **Are the facts presented verifiable?** Facts can be proved by eyewitness accounts, authoritative sources such as encyclopedias and almanacs, experts, or research.

- **Are the opinions presented well informed?** Any opinions offered should be supported by facts, be based on research or eyewitness accounts, or be the opinions of experts on the topic.

- **Is the evidence thorough?** Thorough evidence leaves no reasonable questions unanswered. If a choice is offered, background for making the choice should be provided. Any shifts in perspective in arguments should be explained and supported.

- **Is the evidence biased?** Be alert to evidence that contains loaded language and other signs of bias.

- **Is the evidence authoritative?** The people, groups, or organizations that provided the evidence should have credentials that verify their credibility.

- **Is it important that the evidence be current?** Where timeliness is crucial, as in the areas of medicine and technology, the evidence should reflect the latest developments in the areas.

ANSWERS

Possible answer:

Overgeneralizations: "Everyone agrees that running is the best form of exercise." Explanation: The writer uses words such as everyone and best to make a broad generalization about how people feel about running.

Oversimplification: "All you need is a good pair of shoes and you're ready to hit the road." Explanation: The writer makes the point of running a simple issue that does not take into account other factors.

Non sequitur: "I've run a mile twice this week, so I should know." Explanation: The statement does not provide sufficient evidence or proof to support the claim.

False cause: "As a result, I've slept better and my tone on the clarinet has improved." Explanation: The writer makes the assumption that one event has caused the other but does not take into account other causes.

Circular reasoning: "When you run, your heart beats faster because your pulse rate increases." Explanation: The writer simply restates the statement using different words.

Evading the issue: "which is the second most common gas in the earth's atmosphere. You also get to enjoy the beauty of the world around you." Explanation: The statements do not address the real issue.

Hasty generalization: "if you don't want to be a hopeless couch potato." Explanation: The statement draws the conclusion that people who do not run will become couch potatoes, but it is not based on adequate or appropriate evidence.

PRACTICE AND APPLY

ANSWERS

Possible answers:

Facts: "Cell phone users in a German study, for example, were three times more likely to develop eye cancer than controls"; "Another study done in Sweden showed that people who used cell phones for ten years or more increased their risk of brain cancer by 77 percent."

Opinions: "I think those disgusting machines should be banned. Using the dumb things while driving or riding a bicycle distracts the user and creates a serious hazard"; "People should wise up and stop harming themselves and bothering everybody else."

Elements of Bias: "I think those disgusting machines should be banned."; "Although other researchers found no connection between cell phones and cancer, those studies stink"; choosing to quote only studies that claim cell phones cause cancer.

PRACTICE AND APPLY

ANSWERS

Students' responses will vary, but they should evaluate the strength of the claim, the evidence supporting the claim, and the counterarguments.

Possible answer: Overall, the editorial is a poor example of an argument. The claim—that swimming is the most important skill and is the school's responsibility—is based on faulty reasoning and overgeneralization. The evidence is also based on faulty reasoning and does not adequately support the claim. A statement such as "it not only isn't preparing us for life, but it could actually be responsible for our deaths someday" is not sound. Moreover, the writer resorts to name-calling and attacks throughout the editorial and does not adequately refute the counterarguments. Ultimately, the writer's biased tone, faulty reasoning, inadequate evidence, and accusatory language discredit his or her argument.

Read the argument below. Identify the facts, opinion, and elements of bias.

> Are you tired of listening to people talking on their cell phones? I think those disgusting machines should be banned. Using the dumb things while driving or riding a bicycle distracts the user and creates a serious hazard. The phones also give off energy frequencies that can cause cancer. Cell phone users in a German study, for example, were three times more likely to develop eye cancer than controls. Another study done in Sweden showed that people who used cell phones for ten years or more increased their risk of brain cancer by 77 percent. Although other researchers found no connection between cell phones and cancer, those studies stink. People should wise up and stop harming themselves and bothering everybody else.

Strategies for Determining a Strong Argument

Make sure that all or most of the following statements are true:

- The argument presents a claim or thesis.
- The claim is connected to its support by a general principle that most readers would readily agree with. Valid general principle: *It is the job of a school to provide a well-rounded physical education program.* Invalid general principle: *It is the job of a school to produce healthy, physically fit people.*
- The reasons make sense.
- The reasons are presented in a logical and effective order.
- The claim and all reasons are adequately supported by sound evidence.
- The evidence is adequate, accurate, and appropriate.
- The logic is sound. There are no instances of faulty reasoning.

- The argument adequately anticipates and addresses reader concerns and counterclaims with counterarguments.

Use the preceding criteria to evaluate the strength of the following editorial.

> This school needs a swimming pool. Swimming is the most important skill there is, and I believe it is the responsibility of the school to provide this essential part of students' education.
>
> Everybody knows that the school's mission is to educate the whole person—mind and body—and to prepare students to be productive citizens. In addition to our academic subjects, we are taught how to eat right, budget our money, and drive a car. But since the school doesn't teach us water safety skills, it not only isn't preparing us for life, but it could actually be responsible for our deaths someday.
>
> The community and school board are irresponsible idiots, because they repeatedly have refused to fund the building of a pool. They think that the school has more important needs. As one board member put it, "Students can take swimming lessons at the local health club. A high school isn't a recreation center."
>
> That reason is crazy because it just doesn't make sense. Most students can't afford lessons at the health club; and those who have the money don't have the time. After completing homework, taking part in school activities, and working at weekend jobs, we're lucky to get enough sleep to just keep going.
>
> Students' fitness will improve if we have a pool because swimming keeps you in shape. Even if knowing how to swim never saves your life, it can improve its quality. So either this school gets a pool or the education it offers us will be worthless.

6 Adjusting Reading Rate to Purpose

You may need to change the way you read certain texts in order to understand what you read. To properly adjust the way you read, you need to be aware of what you want to get out of what you are reading. Once you know your purpose for reading, you can adjust the speed at which you read in response to your purpose and the difficulty of the material.

Determine Your Purpose for Reading

You read different types of materials for different purposes. You may read a novel for enjoyment. You may read a textbook unit to learn a new concept or to master the content for a test. When you read for enjoyment, you naturally read at a pace that is comfortable for you. When you read for information, you need to read material more slowly and thoroughly. When you are being tested on material, you may think you have to read fast, especially if the test is being timed. However, you can actually increase your understanding of the material if you slow down.

Determine Your Reading Rate

The rate at which you read most comfortably is called your **independent reading level.** It is the rate that you use to read materials that you enjoy. To learn to adjust your reading rate to read materials for other purposes, you need to be aware of your independent reading level. You can figure out your reading level by following these steps:

1. Select a passage from a book or story you enjoy.
2. Have a friend or classmate time you as you begin reading the passage silently.
3. Read at the rate that is most comfortable for you.
4. Stop when your friend or classmate tells you one minute has passed.
5. Determine the number of words you read in that minute and write down the number.
6. Repeat the process at least two more times, using different passages.
7. Add the numbers and divide the sum by the number of times your friend timed you.

Reading Techniques for Informational Texts

Use the following techniques to adapt your reading for informational texts, to prepare for tests, and to better understand what you read:

- **Skimming** is reading quickly to get the general idea of a text. To skim, read only the title, headings, graphic aids, highlighted words, and first sentence of each paragraph. In addition, read any introduction, conclusion, or summary. Skimming can be especially useful when taking a test. Before reading a passage, you can skim questions that follow it in order to find out what is expected and better focus on the important ideas in the text.

  When researching a topic, skimming can help you determine whether a source has information that is pertinent to your topic.

- **Scanning** is reading quickly to find a specific piece of information, such as a fact or a definition. When you scan, your eyes sweep across a page, looking for key words that may lead you to the information you want. Use scanning to review for tests and to find answers to questions.

- **Changing pace** is speeding up or slowing down the rate at which you read parts of a particular text. When you come across familiar concepts, you might be able to speed up without misunderstanding them. When you encounter unfamiliar concepts or material presented in an unpredictable way, however, you may need to slow down to process and absorb the information better.

WATCH OUT! Reading too slowly can affect your ability to comprehend what you read. Make sure you aren't just reading one word at a time.

PRACTICE AND APPLY

Find an article in a magazine or textbook. Skim the article. Then answer the following questions:

1. What did you notice about the organization of the article from skimming it?
2. What is the central idea of the article?

PRACTICE AND APPLY

ANSWERS

Accept answers that provide an accurate description of the organization of the article and its main ideas.

COMMON CORE FOCUS

W 1a–e Write arguments to support claims in an analysis of substantive topics or texts, using valid reasoning and relevant and sufficient evidence. **W 2a–f** Write informative/explanatory texts to examine and convey complex ideas, concepts, and information clearly and accurately through the effective selection, organization, and analysis of content. **W 3a–e** Write narratives to develop real or imagined experiences or events using effective technique, well-chosen details, and well-structured event sequences. **W 4** Produce clear and coherent writing in which the development, organization, and style are appropriate to task, purpose, and audience. **W 5** Develop and strengthen writing as needed by planning, revising, editing, rewriting, or trying a new approach, focusing on addressing what is most significant for a specific purpose and audience. **W 6** Use technology, including the Internet, to produce, publish, and update individual or shared writing products, taking advantage of technology's capacity to link to other information and to display information flexibly and dynamically.

Writing is a process, a journey of discovery in which you can explore your thoughts, experiment with ideas, and search for connections. Through writing, you can explore and record your thoughts, feelings, and ideas for yourself alone or you can communicate them to an audience.

> **COMMON CORE**
> Included in this handbook:
> W 1a–e, W 2a–f, W 3a–e, W 4, W 5, W 6

1 The Writing Process

The writing process consists of the following stages: prewriting, drafting, revising and editing, proofreading, and publishing. These are not stages that you must complete in a set order. Rather, you may return to an earlier stage at any time to improve your writing.

1.1 PREWRITING

In the prewriting stage, you explore what you want to write about, what your purpose for writing is, whom you are writing for, and what form you will use to express your ideas. Ask yourself the following questions to get started.

Topic	• Is my topic assigned, or can I choose it? • What am I interested in writing about?
Purpose	• Am I writing to entertain, to inform, or to persuade—or for some combination of these purposes? • What effect do I want to have on my readers?
Audience	• Who is the audience? • What might the audience members already know about my topic? • What about the topic might interest them?
Genre	• Which genre will work best? Essay? Poem? Speech? Short story? Article? Research paper?

Find Ideas for Writing

- Browse through magazines, newspapers, and Web sites.

- Start a file of articles you want to save for future reference.

- With a group, brainstorm as many ideas as you can. Compile your ideas into a list.

- Interview someone who is an expert on a particular topic.

- Write down anything that comes into your head.

- Use a cluster map to explore subordinate ideas that relate to a general topic.

Organize Ideas

Once you've chosen a topic, you will need to compile and organize your ideas. If you are writing a description, you may need to gather sensory details. For an essay or a research paper, you may need to record information from different sources. To record notes from sources you read or view, use any or all of these methods:

- **Summarize:** Briefly retell the main ideas of a piece of writing in your own words.

- **Paraphrase:** Restate all or almost all of the information in your own words.

- **Quote:** Record the author's exact words.

Depending on what form your writing takes, you may also need to arrange your ideas in a certain pattern.

*For more information, see the **Writing Handbook**, pages R34–R41.*

1.2 DRAFTING

In the drafting stage, you put your ideas on paper and allow them to develop and change as you write. You don't need to worry about correct grammar and spelling at this stage. There are two ways that you can draft:

Discovery drafting is a good approach when you are not quite sure what you think about your subject. You just start writing and let your feelings and ideas lead you in developing the topic.

Planned drafting may work better if you know that your ideas have to be arranged in a certain way, as in a research paper. Try making a writing plan or an informal outline before you begin drafting.

1.3 REVISING AND EDITING

The revising and editing stage allows you to polish your draft and make changes in its content, organization, and style. Use the questions that follow to assess problems and determine what changes would improve your work.

- Does my writing have a **controlling idea?** Is my main idea clear?

- Have I used **precise** nouns, verbs, and modifiers?

- Have I incorporated **adequate detail** and **evidence?** Where might I include a telling detail, a revealing statistic, or a vivid example?

- Is my writing **unified?** Do all ideas and supporting details pertain to my controlling idea or advance my thesis?

- Is my writing clear and **coherent?** Is the flow of sentences and paragraphs smooth and logical?

- Have I used a consistent **point of view?**

- Do I need to add **transitional words, phrases,** or **sentences** to create cohesion and clarify and connect relationships among ideas?

- Have I used a **variety of sentence types?** Are the sentences well constructed? Which ones might I combine to improve the rhythm of my writing?

- Have I used a **tone** appropriate for my audience, purpose, and genre?

1.4 PROOFREADING

When you are satisfied with your revision, proofread your paper for mistakes in grammar, usage, and mechanics. You may want to do this several times, looking for a different type of mistake each time. Use the following questions to help you correct errors:

- Have I corrected any errors in **subject-verb agreement** and **pronoun-antecedent agreement?**

- Have I double-checked for errors in **confusing word pairs,** such as *it's/its, than/then,* and *too/to?*

- Have I corrected any **run-on sentences** and **sentence fragments?**

- Have I followed rules for **correct capitalization?**

- Have I used **punctuation marks** correctly?

- Have I checked the **spellings of all unfamiliar words** in the dictionary?

> **TIP** If possible, don't begin proofreading just after you've finished writing. Put your work away for at least a few hours. When you return to it, identifying and correcting mistakes will seem easier.

For more information, see the Grammar Handbook and the Vocabulary and Spelling Handbook, pages R46–R75.

Use the proofreading symbols in the chart to mark changes on your draft.

1.5

Proofreading Symbols	
∧ Add letters or words.	/ Make a capital letter lowercase.
⊙ Add a period.	¶ Begin a new paragraph.
≡ Capitalize a letter.	✗ Delete letters or words.
⊃ Close up space.	∿ Switch the positions of letters or words.
∧ Add a comma.	

PUBLISHING AND REFLECTING

Always consider sharing your finished writing with a wider audience. Reflecting on your writing is another good way to finish a project.

Publishing Ideas
- Post your writing on a Weblog.

- Create a multimedia presentation and share it with classmates.

- Publish your writing in a school newspaper, local newspaper, or literary magazine.

- Present your work orally in a report, speech, reading, or dramatic performance.

Reflecting on Your Writing
Think about your writing process and whether you would like to add what you have written to your writing portfolio. You might attach a note in which you answer questions like these:

- Which parts of the process did I find easiest? Which parts were more difficult?

- What was the biggest problem I faced during the writing process? How did I solve the problem?

- What changes have occurred in my writing style?

- Have I noticed any features in the writing of

published authors or my peers that I can apply to my own work?

1.6 PEER RESPONSE

Peer response consists of the suggestions and comments you make about the writing of your peers and also the comments and suggestions they make about your writing. You can ask a peer reader for help at any time in the writing process.

Using Peer Response as a Writer

- Indicate whether you are more interested in feedback about your ideas or about your presentation of them.

- Ask questions that will help you get specific information about your writing. Open-ended questions that require more than yes-or-no answers are more likely to give you information you can use as you revise.

- Encourage your readers to be honest.

Being a Peer Reader

- Respect the writer's feelings.

- Offer positive reactions first.

- Make sure you understand what kind of feedback the writer is looking for, and then respond accordingly.

For more information on the writing process, see the Introductory Unit, pages 18–21.

2 Building Blocks of Good Writing

Whatever your purpose in writing, you need to capture your reader's interest and organize your thoughts clearly.

2.1 INTRODUCTIONS

An introduction should present a controlling idea and capture your reader's attention.

Kinds of Introductions

There are a number of ways to write an introduction. The one you choose depends on who the audience is and on your purpose for writing.

Make a Surprising Statement Beginning with a startling statement or an interesting fact can arouse your reader's curiosity about a subject, as in the following model.

> **MODEL**
>
> September should be the seventh month, and October should be the eighth. Any Latin student knows that the root *septem* is "seven" and *octo* is "eight." Where did the calendar makers go wrong? The truth is that when the months acquired their names, during Roman times, the year started in March.

Provide a Description A vivid description sets a mood and brings a scene to life for your reader.

Here, details about a lion observing possible prey set the tone for an essay on survival in the wild.

> **MODEL**
>
> Cool and cunning eyes followed the impala herd from a sturdy low-slung tree branch. The young female lion watched hungrily to see whether any of the impalas might be sickly or slower than the others. She kept every muscle quiet, though tense and ready to spring if an opportunity arose.

Pose a Question Beginning with a question can make your reader want to read on to find out the answer. The following introduction asks questions about the incredible persistence of racial segregation.

> **MODEL**
>
> How is it possible that as late as the mid-20th century in the United States of America, "the land of the free," riders on public buses were segregated by race? How is it possible that even today there are segregated social events, schools, and towns, no longer segregated by law but with effects just as real and damaging?

Relate an Anecdote Beginning with an anecdote, or brief story, can hook your reader and help you make a point in a dramatic way. The following anecdote introduces an essay about the downside of self-closing shoe straps.

MODEL

My five-year-old nephew, Ali, has never tied a shoelace. All of his shoes have self-closing straps. He is developing his large muscles by throwing and climbing, but I wonder if he will ever have the dexterity to handle bows on packages or ties that he wears with his suits.

Address the Reader Speaking directly to your reader establishes a friendly, informal tone and involves the reader in your topic.

MODEL

If you've ever wondered how to avoid using pesticides in your garden, you can find answers from Natural Gardens, Inc. It's easy to protect the environment and have pest-free plants.

Begin with a Controlling Idea A statement expressing a controlling idea may be woven into both the beginning and the end of a piece of writing. The following is a statement that introduces an essay on the relationship between caring for pets and caring for children.

MODEL

Pet owners who are casual about their pet's health and safety are likely to be the same ones who are casual about the health and safety of their children.

TIP To write the best introduction for your paper, you may want to try more than one of the methods and then decide which is the most effective for your purpose and audience.

2.2 PARAGRAPHS

A paragraph is made up of sentences that work together to develop an idea or accomplish a purpose. Whether or not it contains a topic sentence stating the main idea, a good paragraph must have unity and coherence.

Unity

A paragraph has unity when all the sentences support and develop one stated or implied idea. Use the following techniques to create unity in your paragraphs:

Write a Topic Sentence A topic sentence states the main idea of the paragraph; all other sentences in the paragraph provide supporting details. A topic sentence is often the first sentence in a paragraph. However, it may also appear later in a paragraph or at the end, to summarize or reinforce the main idea, as shown in the model that follows.

MODEL

Plastic that does not rust, rot, or shatter is useful, of course, but does add to the ever-increasing problems of waste disposal. It is possible to add chemicals to plastic that make it dissolvable by other chemicals. There are plastics that slowly disintegrate in sunlight. Biodegradable plastic is available and should be preferred over non-biodegradable plastic.

Relate All Sentences to an Implied Main Idea A paragraph can be unified without a topic sentence as long as every sentence supports an implied, or unstated, main idea. In the example, all the sentences work together to create a unified impression of a swim meet.

MODEL

The swimmers lined up along the edge of the pool. Toes curled over the edge, arms swung back in the ready position, and bodies leaned forward. The swimmers' eyes looked straight ahead. Their ears were alert for the starting signal.

Coherence

A paragraph is coherent when all its sentences are related to one another and each flows logically to the next. The following techniques will help you achieve coherence in paragraphs:

- Present your ideas in the most logical order.
- Use pronouns, synonyms, and repeated words to connect ideas.
- Use transitional devices to show relationships among ideas.

In the model shown here, the writer used some of these techniques to create a unified paragraph.

> **MODEL**
>
> As we experience day and night repeatedly, it is hard to imagine the enormous significance of that change. We have day and night because our planet rotates on its axis. We have seasons because Earth revolves around our solar system's star, the sun. Our solar system, along with many others, rotates with the Milky Way Galaxy. The universe is a gigantic structure of which our daily experiences of day and night, summer and winter are tiny parts.

2.3 TRANSITIONS

Transitions are words and phrases that show connections between details. Clear transitions help show how your ideas relate to one another.

Kinds of Transitions

The types of transitions you choose depend on the ideas you want to convey.

Time or Sequence Some transitions help to clarify the sequence of events over time. When you are telling a story or describing a process, you can connect ideas with such transitional words as *first, second, always, then, next, later, soon, before, finally, after, earlier, afterward,* and *tomorrow.*

> **MODEL**
>
> Teaching a puppy to come when called takes patience from the owner and the puppy. First, tie a lightweight rope to the dog's collar and go to a large play area. Play with the pup a while and then call to it. At the same time, pull gently on the rope. Always praise the puppy for coming when called. Next, allow the puppy to play again. Carry out this exercise several times a day.

Spatial Relationships Transitional words and phrases such as *in front, behind, next to, along, nearest, lowest, above, below, underneath, on the left,* and *in the middle* can help your reader visualize a scene.

> **MODEL**
>
> On the porch, wicker chairs stand in casual disorder along the red wall of the house. Next to the red-and-white porch railing, orange day lilies nod in the breeze. Overhead, a flycatcher perches on a bare branch, alert for her next meal. Beyond the lawn, a small stream flows from beneath an arched stone bridge.

Degree of Importance Transitional words such as *mainly, strongest, weakest, first, second, most important, least important, worst,* and *best* may be used to rank ideas or to show degrees of importance.

> **MODEL**
>
> The Repertory Theater performed six plays last year. All the plays were exciting, but the most outstanding one was *Master Class.*

Compare and Contrast Words and phrases such as *similarly, likewise, also, like, as, neither . . . nor,* and *either . . . or* show similarity between details. *However, by contrast, yet, but, unlike, instead, whereas,* and *while* show difference. Note the use of both types of transitions in the model.

> **MODEL**
>
> Dr. Herriot was a successful veterinarian. Mrs. Donovan also took care of sick animals. He cured his patients with medical treatments and laboratory medications. Mrs. Donovan, by contrast, used home remedies and constant affection.

TIP Both *but* and *however* can be used to join two independent clauses. When *but* is used as a coordinating conjunction, it is preceded by a comma. When *however* is used as a conjunctive adverb, it is preceded by a semicolon and followed by a comma.

Cause and Effect When you are writing about a cause-effect relationship, use transitional words and phrases such as *since, because, thus, therefore, so, due to, for this reason,* and *as a result* to help clarify that relationship and make your writing coherent.

> **MODEL**
>
> Because we never feed our dog from the table, she doesn't beg for food while we are eating. We are happy to take credit for her one good habit.

2.4 CONCLUSIONS

A conclusion should leave readers with a strong final impression.

Kinds of Conclusions

Good conclusions sum up ideas in a variety of ways. Here are some techniques you might try:

Restate Your Controlling Idea A good way to conclude an essay is by restating your controlling idea in different words. The following conclusion restates the controlling idea introduced on page R31.

> **MODEL**
>
> Although each pet has a personality of its own just as each child does, there are many ways of encouraging the best behavior in each. Love, persistence, patience, and consistency make all the difference in training pets as well as in raising children.

Ask a Question Try asking a question that sums up what you have said and gives your reader something new to think about. The following question concludes an appeal to support a local politician.

> **MODEL**
>
> Have you noticed that the roads are in better repair and that there are more safe playgrounds and parks since Mayor Ballwin has been in office?

Make a Recommendation When you are persuading your audience to take a position on an issue, you can conclude by recommending a specific course of action.

> **MODEL**
>
> You can make your research work much easier by taking advantage of the Internet. Develop a list of key words that will help you narrow your search of the Internet.

Make a Prediction Readers are concerned about matters that may affect them and therefore are moved by a conclusion that predicts the future.

> **MODEL**
>
> If the government continues to spend money from Social Security taxes for current operations, we will create a disastrous burden of debt for future generations.

Summarize Your Information Summarizing reinforces your main idea, leaving a strong, lasting impression. The model concludes with a statement that summarizes a film review.

> **MODEL**
>
> The movie *The Postman* shows the tremendous influence of the Chilean poet Pablo Neruda on a young Italian man—not only in his love life but also in his acquired self-confidence and his dedication to a cause.

2.5 ELABORATION

Elaboration is the process of developing an idea by providing specific supporting details that are relevant and appropriate to the purpose and form of your writing.

Facts and Statistics A fact is a statement that can be verified, and a statistic is a fact expressed as a number. Make sure the facts and statistics you supply are from reliable, up-to-date sources.

MODEL

Our entire solar system speeds through the Milky Way Galaxy at a speed of 180 miles a second. One could worry about the ability of any of us to stay in place with our feet on the ground. Or one could marvel at the magnificence of a universe that keeps everything whirling with such constancy.

Sensory Details Details that show how something looks, sounds, tastes, smells, or feels can enliven a description, making readers feel they are actually experiencing what you are describing.

MODEL

The campers hardly dared to breathe inside their tent as they considered the power of the massive beast they'd glimpsed through the tent flap. Snuffling and crackling brought news that the black bear had found something delectable inside the garbage can.

Incidents From our earliest years, we are interested in hearing stories. One way to illustrate a point powerfully is to relate an incident or tell a story, as shown in the example.

MODEL

January 24, 1848, began one of the most colorful periods of United States history. On that day James Marshall found gold at Sutter's Mill in California. That discovery brought on massive immigration from around the world. It also brought many new images and words—*gold rush, gold miners,* and *forty-niners,* to name a few.

Examples An example can help make an abstract idea concrete or can serve to clarify a complex point for your reader.

MODEL

The mere mention of the names of some writers causes distinct reactions, even from those who have not read the writers' works. For example, the mention of William Shakespeare causes many people to take in a sharp breath of admiration and others to think of something long and tedious.

Quotations Choose quotations that clearly support your points, and be sure that you copy each quotation word for word. Remember always to credit the source.

MODEL

In her book *How to Talk to Your Cat,* Patricia Moyes replies to certain authorities who claim that cats cannot smile: "I can only presume that these people have never owned a cat in the true sense of the word." She describes the cat's smile as a "relaxed upward tilting of the corners of the mouth."

3 Writing Descriptions

Descriptive writing allows you to paint word pictures about anything, from events of global importance to the most personal feelings. It is an essential part of almost every piece of writing.

> **RUBRIC: Standards for Writing**
>
> **Successful descriptive writing should**
> - have a clear focus and sense of purpose
> - use sensory details and precise words to create a vivid image, establish a mood, or express emotion
> - present details in a logical order

3.1 KEY TECHNIQUES

Consider Your Goals What do you want to accomplish with your description? Do you want to show why something is important to you? Do you want to make a person or scene more memorable? Do you want to explain an event?

Identify Your Audience Who will read your description? How familiar are they with your subject? What background information will they need? Which details will they find most interesting?

Think Figuratively What figures of speech might help make your description vivid and interesting? What simile or metaphor comes to mind? What imaginative comparisons can you make? What living thing does an inanimate object remind you of?

Gather Sensory Details Which sights, smells, tastes, sounds, and textures make your subject come alive? Which details stick in your mind when you observe or recall your subject? Which senses does it most strongly affect?

You might want to use a chart like the one shown here to collect sensory details about your subject.

Sights	Sounds	Textures	Smells	Tastes

Create a Mood What feelings do you want to evoke in your readers? Do you want to soothe them with comforting images? Do you want to build tension with ominous details? Do you want to evoke sadness or joy?

3.2 OPTIONS FOR ORGANIZATION

Option 1: Spatial Order Choose one of these options to show the spatial order of elements in a scene you are describing.

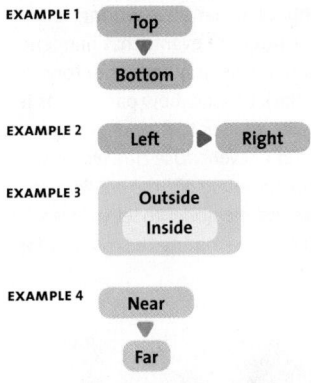

MODEL

Thunder's nostrils quivered as he was led into the barn. How would this be as a place to spend nights from now on? In the stall to the left, the straw smelled fresh. Beyond that stall, a saddle hung from rough boards. To the right of his stall was another, from which a mare looked at him curiously.

Option 2: Order of Impression Order of impression is the order in which you notice details.

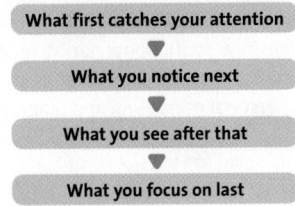

MODEL

As her foot slipped on the pebbles, her first thought was of whether she would sprain an ankle sliding into the surf. Her heart began a dangerous thumping, but soon the soft sand provided a comfortable seat so that her body responded by calming down. She realized that the water was shallow and warm. Her hat would shade her eyes and prevent sunburn.

TIP Use transitions that help readers understand the order of the impressions you are describing. Some useful transitions are *after, next, during, first, before, finally,* and *then.*

Option 3: Order of Importance You can use order of importance as the organizing structure for a description.

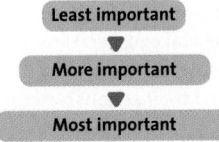

MODEL

I checked my backpack for the comforting essentials. Book? Yes. Journal and pencil? Yes. Water bottle? Yes. Tissues? Yes. Then I checked for the required essentials. Passport? Yes. Airline ticket? Yes. Map? Yes. Last of all, I checked the most important possessions for this trip—a light heart and a sense of adventure. I was beginning my first real vacation.

For more information, see **Transitions,** *page R32.*

4 Writing Narratives

Narrative writing tells a story. If you write a story from your imagination, it is a fictional narrative. A true story is a nonfictional narrative. Narrative writing can be found in short stories, novels, news articles, personal narratives, and biographies.

> **RUBRIC: Standards for Writing**
>
> **A successful narrative should**
>
> - hook the reader's attention with a strong introduction
> - include descriptive details and dialogue to develop the characters, setting, and plot
> - have a clear beginning, middle, and end
> - have a logical organization, with clues and transitions that help the reader understand the order of events
> - maintain a consistent tone and point of view
> - use language that is appropriate to the audience
> - demonstrate the significance of events or ideas

*For more information, see **Writing Workshop: Short Story,** pages 280–289.*

4.1 KEY TECHNIQUES

Identify the Main Events What are the most important events in your narrative? Is each event needed to tell the story?

Describe the Setting When do the events occur? Where do they take place? How can you use setting to create mood and to set the stage for the characters and their actions?

Depict Characters Vividly What do your characters look like? What do they think and say? How do they act? What details can show what they are like?

TIP Dialogue is an effective means of developing characters in a narrative. As you write dialogue, choose words that express your characters' personalities and that show how the characters feel about one another and about the events in the plot.

4.2 OPTIONS FOR ORGANIZATION

Option 1: Chronological Order One way to organize a piece of narrative writing is to arrange the events in chronological order, as shown in the following example.

EXAMPLE

It is the middle of March in Rome. It is also the first time that young Marius has been able to go into the city.	**Introduction** *Characters and setting*
A crowd gathers to watch the senators arrive. Marius hurries toward the front of the crowd.	**Event 1**
Marius sees that the emperor has arrived. There is great commotion, with shouts and screams.	**Event 2**
Marius witnesses the assassination of Julius Caesar. He then goes home with a premonition that there are bad times ahead for Rome.	**End** *Perhaps showing the significance of the events*

Option 2: Flashback In narrative writing, it is also possible to introduce events that happened sometime before the beginning of the story. You can use a flashback to show how past events led up to the present situation or to provide background about a character or event. Use clue words such as *last summer, as a young girl, the previous school year,* and *his earliest memories* to let your reader know that you are interrupting the main action to describe earlier events.

Notice how the flashback interrupts the action in the model.

MODEL

Greg and his friends rejoiced at being the first in line to buy the coveted concert tickets. Greg remembered when his favorite band came to town two years ago. Then, when he and his friends approached the ticket office, the line was five blocks long.

Option 3: Focus on Conflict When a fictional narrative focuses on a central conflict, the story's plot may be organized as shown in the following example.

EXAMPLE

A railroad porter notices a woman boarding the train and pulling along a young child.

> **Describe main characters and setting.**

The porter senses that the child is frightened, so he finds several excuses to appear at their compartment door. When he hears the child crying, he goes to the compartment and sees the glint of gunmetal inside a partially open market basket.

> **Present conflict.**

The porter begins to plan how to identify the woman and child and to separate the child from the woman.

- The porter finds out from a radio news report that a child has been kidnapped.
- He befriends the pair and offers to play with the child while the woman visits the dining car.
- He alerts the police, who then wait at an unscheduled stop.

> **Relate events that make conflict complex and cause characters to change.**

When the train stops, the woman becomes suspicious and begins to search the train for the child. She spots the porter with the child and fires her gun in his direction. Though wounded, the porter manages to throw the child from the train into the arms of a federal agent.

> **Present resolution or outcome of conflict.**

5 Writing Informative Texts

Expository writing informs and explains. You can use it to evaluate the effects of a new law, to compare two movies, to analyze a piece of literature, or to examine the problem of greenhouse gases in the atmosphere. There are many types of expository writing. Think about your topic and select the type that presents the information most clearly.

5.1 COMPARISON AND CONTRAST

Compare-and-contrast writing examines the similarities and differences between two or more subjects. You might, for example, compare and contrast two short stories, the main characters in a novel, or two movies.

> **RUBRIC: Standards for Writing**
>
> **Successful compare-and-contrast writing should**
>
> - hook the reader's attention with a strong introduction
> - clearly identify the subjects that are being compared and contrasted
> - include specific, relevant details
> - follow a clear plan of organization
> - use language and details appropriate to the audience
> - use transitional words and phrases to clarify similarities and differences

Options for Organization

Compare-and-contrast writing can be organized in different ways. The examples that follow demonstrate point-by-point organization and subject-by-subject organization.

Option 1: Point-by-Point Organization

EXAMPLE

I. How true smiles and false smiles are alike   **Point 1**

    Subject A. True smiles; show pleasure; corners of mouth curve up

    Subject B. False smiles; show pleasure; corners of mouth curve up

II. How true smiles and false smiles are different   **Point 2**

    Subject A. True smiles; cheeks move up; no furrow between eyebrows; crow's-feet form

    Subject B. False smiles; cheeks may move up; furrow between eyebrows; no crow's-feet

Option 2: Subject-by-Subject Organization

> **EXAMPLE**
>
> I. True smiles   **Subject A**
>   - Point 1. Show pleasure, corners of mouth curve up
>   - Point 2. Cheeks move up
>   - Point 3. No furrow between eyebrows
>   - Point 4. Crow's-feet form
>
> II. False smiles   **Subject B**
>   - Point 1. Show pleasure, corners of mouth curve up
>   - Point 2. Cheeks may move up
>   - Point 3. Furrow between eyebrows
>   - Point 4. No crow's-feet

*For more information, see **Writing Workshop: Informative Text: Literary Analysis**, pages 148–157, **Informative Text: Analysis of Literary Nonfiction**, pages 390–399, **Informative Text: Comparison-Contrast Essay**, pages 498–507, **Informative Text: Cause-and-Effect Essay**, pp. 1030–1039.*

5.2 CAUSE AND EFFECT

Cause-effect writing explains why something happened, why certain conditions exist, or what resulted from an action or a condition. You might use cause-effect writing to explain a character's actions, the progress of a disease, or the outcome of a war.

RUBRIC: Standards for Writing

Successful cause-effect writing should

- hook the reader's attention with a strong introduction
- clearly state the cause-and-effect relationship
- show clear connections between causes and effects
- present causes and effects in a logical order and use transitions effectively
- use facts, examples, and other details to illustrate each cause and effect
- use language and details appropriate to the audience

Options for Organization

Your organization will depend on your topic and your purpose for writing.

Option 1: Effect-to-Cause Organization If you want to explain the causes of an event, such as the closing of a factory, you might first state the effect and then examine its causes.

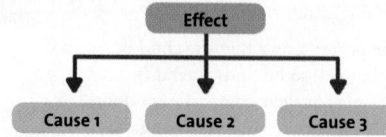

Option 2: Cause-to-Effect Organization If your focus is on explaining the effects of an event, such as the passage of a law, you might first state the cause and then explain the effects.

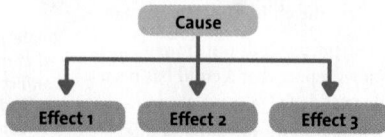

Option 3: Cause-Effect Chain Organization Sometimes you'll want to describe a chain of cause-effect relationships to explore a topic, such as the disappearance of tropical rain forests or the development of home computers.

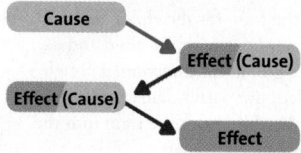

For an example of cause-effect writing, see page R11.

TIP Don't assume that a cause-effect relationship exists just because one event follows another. Look for evidence that the later event could not have happened if the first event had not caused it.

5.3 PROBLEM-SOLUTION

Problem-solution writing clearly states a problem, analyzes the problem, and proposes a solution to the problem. It can be used to identify and solve a conflict between characters, investigate global warming, or tell why the home team keeps losing.

RUBRIC: Standards for Writing

Successful problem-solution writing should

- hook the reader's attention with a strong introduction
- identify the problem and help the reader understand the issues involved
- analyze the causes and effects of the problem
- include quotations, facts, and statistics
- explore possible solutions to the problem and recommend the best one(s)
- use language, details, and a tone appropriate to the audience

Options for Organization

Your organization will depend on the goal of your problem-solution piece, your intended audience, and the specific problem you have chosen to address. The organizational methods that follow are effective for different kinds of problem-solution writing.

Option 1: Simple Problem-Solution

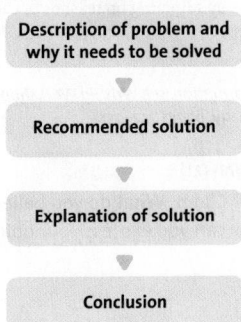

Option 2: Deciding Between Solutions

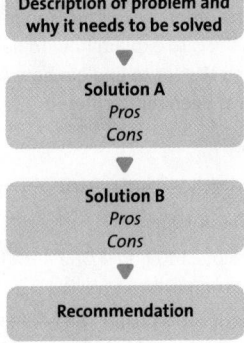

5.4 ANALYSIS

In writing an analysis, you explain how something works, how it is defined, or what its parts are.

RUBRIC: Standards for Writing

A successful analysis should

- hook the reader's attention with a strong introduction
- clearly define the subject and its parts
- use a specific organizing structure to provide a logical flow of information
- show connections among facts and ideas through transitional words and phrases
- use language and details appropriate for the audience

Options for Organization

Organize your details in a logical order appropriate to the kind of analysis you're writing. Use one of the following options:

Option 1: Process Analysis A process analysis is usually organized chronologically, with steps or stages in the order they occur. You might use a process analysis to explain how to bake a pie or prepare for a test, or to explain how Arthurian legends have been reinterpreted.

EXAMPLE

Arthurian legends reinterpreted

British ruler in 500s

Step 1: Around 1469, *Le Morte d'Arthur* is compiled.

Step 2: Between 1842 and 1885, *Idylls of the King* is published.

Step 3: In 1960, the musical *Camelot* opens.

> Introduce process.

> Give background.

> Explain steps.

Option 2: Definition Analysis You can organize the details of a definition analysis in order of importance or impression. Use a definition analysis to explain a quality (such as honor or loyalty), the distinguishing features of a sonnet, or the parts of the brain.

EXAMPLE

Honor

Honor defined as integrity, dignity, and pride.

Quality 1: Integrity

Quality 2: Dignity

Quality 3: Pride

> Introduce term and definition.

> Explain features.

Option 3: Parts Analysis The following parts analysis explores three elements of a medieval knight's code of chivalry.

EXAMPLE

Code of chivalry

Part 1: Uphold to Christianity

Part 2: Protect the defenseless

Part 3: Fight injustices, never surrender

> Introduce subject.

> Explain parts.

6 Writing Arguments

Persuasive writing allows you to use the power of language to inform and influence others. It includes speeches, persuasive essays, newspaper editorials, advertisements, and critical reviews.

RUBRIC: Standards for Writing

Successful persuasive writing should

- hook the reader's attention with a strong introduction
- state the issue and the writer's position
- give opinions and support them with facts or reasons
- have a reasonable and respectful tone
- answer opposing views
- use sound logic and effective language
- conclude by summing up reasons or calling for action

*For more information, see **Writing Workshop: Argument: Persuasive Essay**, pages 742–751.*

6.1 KEY TECHNIQUES

Clarify Your Claim What do you believe about the issue? How can you express your opinion most clearly?

Know Your Audience Who will read your writing? What do they already know and believe about the issue? What objections to your position might they have? What additional information might they need? What tone and approach would be most effective?

Support Your Opinion Why do you feel the way you do about the issue? What facts, statistics, examples, quotations, anecdotes, or expert opinions support your view? What reasons will convince your readers? What evidence can answer their objections?

Support for Your Argument	
Statistics	facts that are stated in numbers
Examples	specific instances that explain points
Observations	events or situations you yourself have seen
Anecdotes	brief stories that illustrate points
Quotations	direct statements from authorities

For more information, see **Identifying Faulty Reasoning,** *page R24.*

Begin and End with a Bang How can you hook your readers and make a lasting impression? What memorable quotation, anecdote, or statistic will catch their attention at the beginning or stick in their minds at the end? What strong summary or call to action can you conclude with?

MODEL

Beginning

A recent research report finds there is more rain on weekends than during the week. Scientists attribute this to the extra work week pollution that builds throughout the week.

End

We need to plan for more carpooling, efficient heating and cooling, and consolidation of some bus schedules to improve our air quality—and provide better weekend weather.

6.2 OPTIONS FOR ORGANIZATION

In a two-sided persuasive essay, you want to show the weaknesses of the other opinion as you explain the strengths of your own.

Option 1: Reasons for Your Opinion

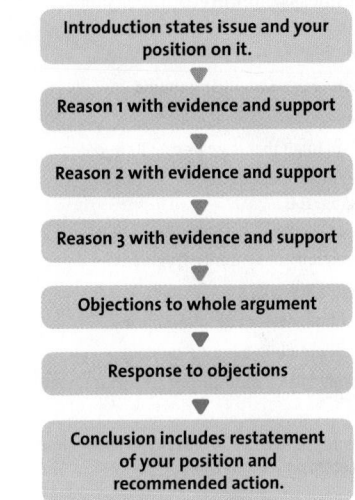

Option 2: Point-by-Point Basis

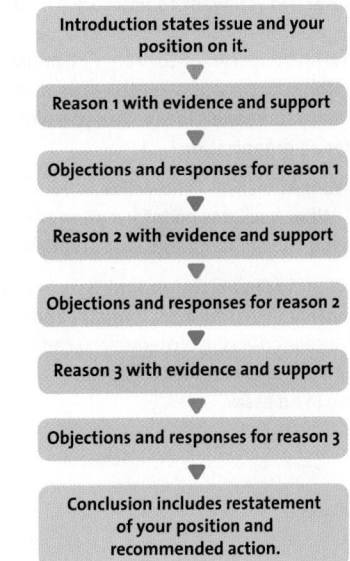

7 Writing Functional Texts

Business writing is writing done in a workplace to support the work of a company or business. Several types of formats, such as memos, letters, e-mails, applications, and bylaws, have been developed to make business communication easier.

> **RUBRIC: Standards for Writing**
>
> **Successful business writing should**
>
> - be courteous
> - use language that is geared to its audience
> - state the purpose clearly in the opening sentences or paragraph
> - have a formal tone and not contain slang, contractions, or sentence fragments
> - use precise words
> - present only essential information
> - present details in a logical order
> - conclude with a summary of important points

*For more information, see **Writing Workshop: Argument: Business Letter,** pages 610–619.*

7.1 KEY TECHNIQUES

Think About Your Purpose Why are you doing this writing? Do you want to promote yourself to a college admissions committee or a job interviewer? Do you want to order or complain about a product? Do you want to set up a meeting or respond to someone's ideas? Are you writing bylaws for an organization?

Identify Your Audience Who will read your writing? What background information will they need? What tone or language is appropriate?

Use a Pattern of Organization That Is Appropriate to the Content If you have to compare and contrast two products in a memo, you can use the same compare-and-contrast organization that you would use in an essay.

Support Your Points What specific details might clarify your ideas? What reasons do you have for your statements?

Finish Strongly How can you best sum up your statements? What is your main point? What action do you want the recipients to take?

Revise and Proofread Your Writing Just as you are graded on the quality of an essay you write for a class, you will be judged on the quality of your writing in the workplace.

7.2 MATCHING THE FORMAT TO THE OCCASION

E-mail messages, memos, and letters have similar purposes but are used in different situations. The chart shows how each format can be used.

Format	Occasion
Memo	Use to send correspondence **inside** the workplace only.
E-mail message	Use to send correspondence **inside or outside** the company.
Letter	Use to send correspondence **outside** the company.

TIP Memos are often sent as e-mail messages in the workplace. Remember that both require formal language and standard spelling, capitalization, and punctuation.

PRACTICE AND APPLY

Refer to the documents on page R43 to complete the following:

1. Draft a response to the letter. Then revise your letter as necessary according to the rubric at the beginning of this section. Make sure you have included the necessary information and have written in an appropriate tone. Proofread your letter for grammatical errors and spelling mistakes. Follow the format of the model and use appropriate spacing between elements.

2. Write a memo in response to the memo. Tell the recipient what actions you have taken. Follow the format of the model.

PRACTICE AND APPLY

ANSWERS

1. *Students' responses will vary. The letter should include a heading, inside address, salutation, body, and closing. Students should acknowledge that they have read Ms. LaPorta's letter and explain that they will pass along the information to the company engineers and designers. They should also thank her and let her know that they appreciate their customer's input and suggestions. They should also let her know that a brochure explaining the reasons for the current design is enclosed.*

2. *Students' responses will vary. The memo should include a heading and body. In their reply, students should indicate that they have sent out a letter and brochure to Ms. LaPorta. They should also explain that they have forwarded the suggestions to the engineers.*

7.3 FORMATS

Business letters usually have a formal tone and a specific format as shown below. The key to writing a business letter is to get to the point as quickly as possible and to present your information clearly.

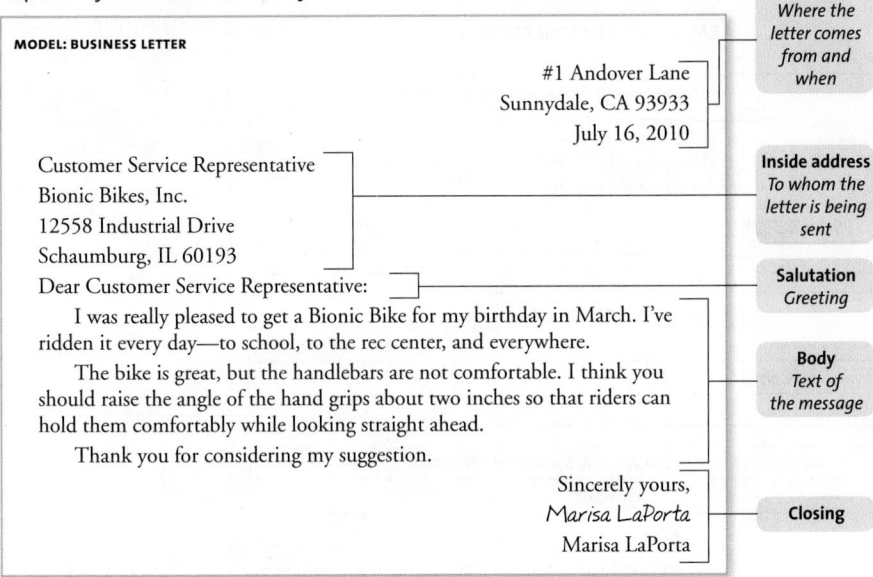

MODEL: BUSINESS LETTER

#1 Andover Lane
Sunnydale, CA 93933
July 16, 2010

Customer Service Representative
Bionic Bikes, Inc.
12558 Industrial Drive
Schaumburg, IL 60193
Dear Customer Service Representative:

    I was really pleased to get a Bionic Bike for my birthday in March. I've ridden it every day—to school, to the rec center, and everywhere.

    The bike is great, but the handlebars are not comfortable. I think you should raise the angle of the hand grips about two inches so that riders can hold them comfortably while looking straight ahead.

    Thank you for considering my suggestion.

Sincerely yours,
Marisa LaPorta
Marisa LaPorta

Heading
Where the letter comes from and when

Inside address
To whom the letter is being sent

Salutation
Greeting

Body
Text of the message

Closing

Memos are often used in workplaces as a way of conveying information in a direct and concise manner. They can be used to announce or summarize meetings and to request actions or specific information.

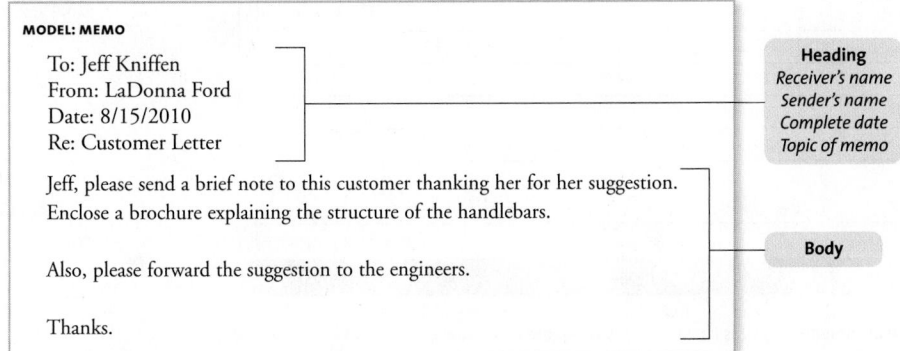

MODEL: MEMO

To: Jeff Kniffen
From: LaDonna Ford
Date: 8/15/2010
Re: Customer Letter

Jeff, please send a brief note to this customer thanking her for her suggestion. Enclose a brochure explaining the structure of the handlebars.

Also, please forward the suggestion to the engineers.

Thanks.

Heading
Receiver's name
Sender's name
Complete date
Topic of memo

Body

TIP Don't forget to write the topic of your memo in the subject line. This will help the receiver determine the importance of your memo.

When you apply for a job, you may be asked to fill out an application form. Application forms vary, but most of them ask for similar kinds of information. If you are mailing your application, you may want to include a brief letter.

EMPLOYMENT APPLICATION

PERSONAL INFORMATION

LAST NAME	FIRST NAME	MIDDLE NAME	IF UNDER 18, AGE
Kohl	Rachel	Elaine	16

STREET ADDRESS	CITY	STATE	ZIP
3240 Maple Dr.	St. Augustine	FL	32080

IF EMPLOYED, AND YOU ARE UNDER 16, CAN YOU FURNISH A WORK PERMIT? YES / NO   YES

TELEPHONE NUMBER	SOCIAL SECURITY NUMBER
904/555-1234	525-88-0723

POSITIONS APPLIED FOR: FULL TIME _____   PART TIME X   TEMPORARY _____

EDUCATION

	NAME OF SCHOOL AND ADDRESS	GRADUATED? YES / NO	NUMBER OF YEARS COMPLETED
HIGH SCHOOL	Riverside High School	No	2
COLLEGE			

AVAILIBILITY: PLEASE LIST ALL TIMES AVAILABLE TO WORK

SUN	MON	TUES	WED	THURS	FRI	SAT
9am–5pm					5pm–9pm	9am–5pm

REFERENCES

NAME	OCCUPATION	COMPANY	TELEPHONE NUMBER
Monica Lewis	Teacher	Riverside High	904/555-6789

PRACTICE AND APPLY

ANSWERS

1. *If possible, ask students to visit a local business to obtain a job application. Have students fill out the application. Encourage them to verify that the information is correct before turning in their applications.*

2. *Students' bylaws should include a purpose, membership requirements, meetings and rules of order, officers and their duties, and other pertinent information.*

PRACTICE AND APPLY

Refer to the documents on pages R44 and R45 to complete the following:

1. Visit a business and request an employment application for a job you would like to have. Make sure you understand what each question is asking before you begin to write. Fill out the application as neatly and completely as possible.

2. Write a set of bylaws for an organization that you already belong to or one that you would like to form. Follow the format of the document on page R45.

Sometimes you may have to write technical documents, such as a list of procedures for conducting a meeting, a manual on rules of behavior, or the minutes of a meeting. These documents contain written descriptions of rules, regulations, and meetings and enable organizations and businesses to run smoothly.

These bylaws for an astronomy club include a description of the organization and detailed information about how the club operates. The writer began each section with a heading so that readers could easily find information. The writer was also very specific so that readers would not misunderstand the rules.

MODEL: BYLAWS DOCUMENT

North High School Astronomy Club Bylaws

PURPOSE

1. To understand astronomy
2. To make science enjoyable
3. To inform the school and the community about astronomy

MEMBERSHIP REQUIREMENTS

To qualify for membership, a candidate must

1. be a student at North High School
2. participate in all club fundraisers
3. assist in the production of the newsletter

MEETINGS AND RULES OF ORDER

1. Meetings will be held once a month on a day designated by the vote of the regular membership.
2. Meetings will be held in the Science Lab.
3. All meetings will be conducted according to Robert's Rules of Order.
4. A quorum of seven members must be present for discussion of business items and voting.
5. All officers are voting members of the astronomy club; however, the President votes only when there is a tie.

OFFICERS AND THEIR DUTIES

1. The astronomy club will be governed by a panel of officers elected at the start of each school year.
2. Elected officers will consist of President, Vice-President, Secretary, and Treasurer.
3. Officers will meet twice a month.
4. An officers' meeting requires the attendance of either the President or the Vice-President and the Secretary and Treasurer.
5. Officers may appoint heads to any committee.
6. The President will preside over regular and special meetings.
7. The Vice-President will guide activities of appointed committees.
8. The Secretary will record and distribute meeting minutes.
9. The Treasurer will be responsible for all money collected by the club.

Writing Online

THINK central

Go to **thinkcentral.com**.
KEYWORD: HML10N-R28

Writing Online   **THINK** central

The keyword on this page directs students to interactive models, revision lessons, and other resources designed to support the writing process.

COMMON CORE FOCUS

L 1a–b Use parallel structure; use various types of phrases (noun, verb, adjectival, adverbial, participial, prepositional, absolute) and clauses (independent, dependent; noun, relative, adverbial) to convey specific meanings and add variety and interest to writing or presentations. **L 2a–b** Use a semicolon (and perhaps a conjunctive adverb) to link two or more closely related independent clauses; use a colon to introduce a list or quotation.

Writing that has many mistakes can confuse or even annoy a reader. For example, a business letter with a punctuation error might lead to miscommunication and delay a reply, or an essay that includes a sentence fragment might earn its writer a lower grade. Paying attention to grammar, punctuation, and capitalization rules can make your writing clearer and easier to read.

COMMON CORE

Included in this handbook:
L 1a–b, L 2a–b

Quick Reference: Parts of Speech

PART OF SPEECH	FUNCTION	EXAMPLES
Noun	names a person, a place, a thing, an idea, a quality, or an action	
Common	serves as a general name, or a name common to an entire group	boat, anchor, water, sky
Proper	names a specific person, place, or thing	Nile River, Acapulco, Swahili
Singular	refers to a single person, place, thing, or idea	map, berry, deer, mouse
Plural	refers to more than one person, place, thing, or idea	maps, berries, deer, mice
Concrete	names something that can be perceived by the senses	stone, crate, wall, knife
Abstract	names something that cannot be perceived by the senses	courage, caution, tyranny, importance
Compound	expresses a single idea through a combination of two or more words	toothbrush, sister-in-law, South Carolina
Collective	refers to a group of people or things	herd, family, team, staff
Possessive	shows who or what owns something	Kenya's, Les's, women's, waitresses'
Pronoun	takes the place of a noun or another pronoun	
Personal	refers to the person making a statement, the person(s) being addressed, or the person(s) or thing(s) the statement is about	I, me, my, mine, we, us, our, ours, you, your, yours, she, he, it, her, him, hers, his, its, they, them, their, theirs
Reflexive	follows a verb or preposition and refers to a preceding noun or pronoun	myself, yourself, herself, himself, itself, ourselves, yourselves, themselves
Intensive	emphasizes a noun or another pronoun	(same as reflexives)
Demonstrative	points to one or more specific persons or things	this, that, these, those
Interrogative	signals a question	who, whom, whose, which, what
Indefinite	refers to one or more persons or things not specifically mentioned	both, all, most, many, anyone, everybody, several, none, some
Relative	introduces an adjective clause by relating it to a word in the clause	who, whom, whose, which, that
Reciprocal	expresses a mutual action or relationship	each other, one another

PART OF SPEECH	FUNCTION	EXAMPLES
Verb	expresses an action, a condition, or a state of being	
Action	tells what the subject does or did, physically or mentally	run, reaches, listened, consider, decides, dreamed
Linking	connects the subject to something that identifies or describes it	am, is, are, was, were, sound, taste, appear, feel, become, remain, seem
Auxiliary	precedes the main verb in a verb phrase	be, have, do, can, could, will, would, may, might
Transitive	directs the action toward someone or something; always has an object	Mom **broke** the plate.
Intransitive	does not direct the action toward someone or something; does not have an object	The plate **broke.**
Adjective	modifies a noun or pronoun	**frightened** man, **two** epics, **enough** time
Adverb	modifies a verb, an adjective, or another adverb	walked **out, really** funny, **far** away
Preposition	relates one word to another word	at, by, for, from, in, of, on, to, with
Conjunction	joins words or word groups	
Coordinating	joins words or word groups used the same way	and, but, or, for, so, yet, nor
Correlative	used as a pair to join words or word groups used the same way	both . . . and, either . . . or, neither . . . nor
Subordinating	introduces a clause that cannot stand by itself as a complete sentence	although, after, as, before, because, when, if, unless
Interjection	expresses emotion	whew, yikes, uh-oh

Quick Reference: The Sentence and Its Parts

The diagrams that follow will give you a brief review of the essentials of a sentence and some of its parts.

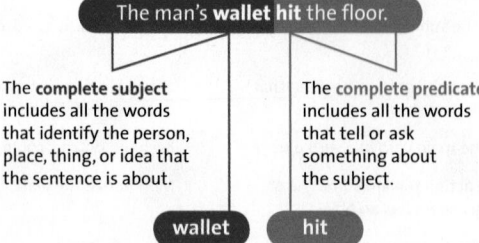

The man's **wallet hit** the floor.

The **complete subject** includes all the words that identify the person, place, thing, or idea that the sentence is about.

The complete predicate includes all the words that tell or ask something about the subject.

wallet

hit

The **simple subject** tells exactly whom or what the sentence is about. It may be one word or a group of words, but it does not include modifiers.

The simple predicate, or verb, tells what the subject does or is. It may be one word or several, but it does not include modifiers.

Every word in a sentence is part of a complete subject or a complete predicate.

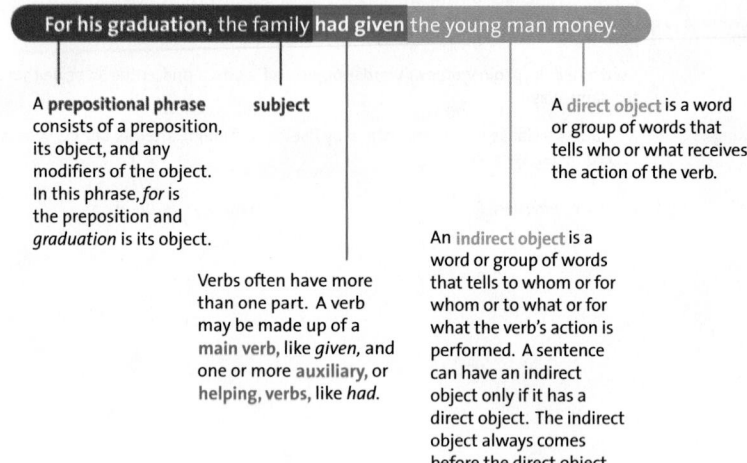

For his graduation, the family **had given** the young man money.

A **prepositional phrase** consists of a preposition, its object, and any modifiers of the object. In this phrase, *for* is the preposition and *graduation* is its object.

subject

A direct object is a word or group of words that tells who or what receives the action of the verb.

Verbs often have more than one part. A verb may be made up of a main verb, like *given,* and one or more auxiliary, or helping, verbs, like *had.*

An indirect object is a word or group of words that tells to whom or for whom or to what or for what the verb's action is performed. A sentence can have an indirect object only if it has a direct object. The indirect object always comes before the direct object.

Quick Reference: Punctuation

MARK	FUNCTION	EXAMPLES
End Marks period, question mark, exclamation point	ends a sentence	The games begin today. Who is your favorite contestant? What a play Jamie made!
period	follows an initial or abbreviation **Exception:** postal abbreviations of states	Prof. Ted Bakerman, D. H. Lawrence, Houghton Mifflin Co., P.M., A.D., oz., ft., Blvd., St. NE (Nebraska), NV (Nevada)

period	follows a number or letter in an outline	I. Volcanoes
		  A. Central-vent
		    1. Shield

Comma	separates parts of a compound sentence	I have never disliked poetry, but now I really love it.
	separates items in a series	She is brave, loyal, and kind.
	separates adjectives of equal rank that modify the same noun	The slow, easy route is best.
	sets off a term of address	O Wind, if winter comes … Come to the front, children.
	sets off a parenthetical expression	Hard workers, as you know, don't quit. I'm not a quitter, believe me.
	sets off an introductory word, phrase, or dependent clause	Yes, I forgot my key. At the beginning of the day, I feel fresh. While she was out, I was here. Having finished my chores, I went out.
	sets off a nonrestrctive phrase or clause and contrasting expressions	Ed Pawn, the captain of the chess team, won. Ed Pawn, who is the captain, won. The two leading runners, sprinting toward the finish line, finished in a tie.
	sets off parts of dates and addresses	Send it by August 18, 2010, to Cherry Jubilee, Inc., 21 Vernona St., Oakland, Minnesota.
	follows the salutation and closing of a letter	Dear Jim, Sincerely yours,
	separates words to avoid confusion	By noon, time had run out. What the minister does, does matter. While cooking, Jim burned his hand.
Semicolon	separates items that contain commas in a series	We invited my sister, Jan; her boyfriend, Don; my uncle Jack; and Mary Dodd.
	separates parts of a compound sentence that are not joined by a coordinating conjunction	The last shall be first; the first shall be last. I read the Bible; however, I have not memorized it.
	separates parts of a compound sentence when the parts contain commas	After I ran out of money, I called my parents; but only my sister was home, unfortunately.

MARK	FUNCTION	EXAMPLES
Colon	introduces a list	Those we wrote were the following: Dana, John, and Will.
	introduces a long quotation	Susan B. Anthony said: "Woman must not depend upon the protection of man. . . ."
	follows the salutation of a business letter	To Whom It May Concern: Dear Ms. Costa:
	separates certain numbers	1:28 P.M., Genesis 2:5
Dash	indicates an abrupt break in thought and adds emphasis to parenthetical information	I was thinking of my mother—who is arriving tomorrow—just as you walked in.
Parentheses	enclose less important material	Throughout her life (though some might think otherwise), she worked hard. The temperature on this July day (would you believe it?) is 65 degrees!
Hyphen	joins parts of a compound adjective before a noun	She lives in a first-floor apartment.
	joins part of a compound with *all-*, *ex-*, *self-*, or *-elect*	The president-elect is a well respected.
	joins part of a compound number (to ninety-nine)	Today I turn twenty-one.
	joins part of a fraction	My cup is one-third full.
	joins a prefix to a word beginning with a capital letter	Is this a pre-Bronze Age artifact? Caesar had a bad day in mid-March.
	indicates that a word is divided at the end of a line	Finding the right title has been a challenge for the committee.
Apostrophe	used with *s* to form the possessive of a noun or an indefinite pronoun	my friend's book, my friends' books, anyone's guess, somebody else's problem
	replaces one or more omitted letters in a contraction or numbers in a date	don't (omitted *o*), he'd (omitted *woul*), the class of '99 (omitted *19*)
	used with *s* to form the plural of a letter	I had two A's on my report card.
Quotation Marks	set off a speaker's exact words	Sara said, "I'm finally ready." "I'm ready," Sara said, "finally." Did Sara say, "I'm ready"? Sara said, "I'm ready!"
	set off the title of a story, an article, a short poem, an essay, a song, or a chapter	We read Hansberry's "On Summer" and Alvarez's "Exile."
	indicate sarcasm or irony	Oh she's an "expert" all right.
Ellipses	replace material omitted from a quotation	"Neither slavery nor involuntary servitude . . . shall exist within the United States. . . ."
Italics	indicate the title of a book, a play, a magazine, a long poem, an opera, a film, or a TV series, or the name of a ship	*The Mists of Avalon, Julius Caesar, Newsweek, Paradise Lost, La Bohème, ET, The West Wing,* USS *John F. Kennedy*

Quick Reference: Capitalization

CATEGORY	EXAMPLES
People and Titles	
Names and initials of people	Alice Walker, E. B. White
Titles used before or in place of names	Professor Holmes, Senator Long
Deities and members of religious groups	Jesus, Allah, Buddha, Zeus, Baptists, Roman Catholics
Names of ethnic and national groups	Hispanics, Jews, African Americans
Geographical Names	
Cities, states, countries, continents	Charleston, Nevada, France, Asia
Regions, bodies of water, mountains	the Midwest, Lake Michigan, Mount Everest
Geographic features, parks	Continental Divide, Everglades, Yellowstone
Streets and roads, planets	361 South Twenty-third Street, Miller Avenue, Jupiter, Saturn
Organizations, Events, Etc.	
Companies, organizations, teams	Monsanto, the Elks, Chicago Bulls
Buildings, bridges, monuments	the Alamo, Golden Gate Bridge, Lincoln Memorial
Documents, awards	the Constitution, World Cup
Special named events	Super Bowl, World Series
Government bodies, historical periods and events	the Supreme Court, Congress, the Middle Ages, Boston Tea Party
Days and months, holidays	Tuesday, October, Thanksgiving, Valentine's Day
Specific cars, boats, trains, planes	Cadillac, Titanic, Orient Express
Proper Adjectives	
Adjectives formed from proper nouns	Doppler effect, Mexican music, Elizabethan age, Midwestern town
First Words and the Pronoun I	
First word in a sentence or quotation	This is it. He said, "Let's go."
First word of sentence in parentheses that is not within another sentence	The spelling rules are covered in another section. (Consult that section for more information.)
First words in the salutation and closing of a letter	Dear Madam, Very truly yours,
First word in each line of most poetry Personal pronoun *I*	Then am I A happy fly If I live Or if I die.
First word, last word, and all important words in a title	*A Tale of Two Cities*, "The World Is Too Much with Us"

1 Nouns

A **noun** is a word used to name a person, a place, a thing, an idea, a quality, or an action. Nouns can be classified in several ways.

*For more information on different types of nouns, see **Quick Reference: Parts of Speech**, page R46.*

1.1 COMMON NOUNS

Common nouns are general names, common to entire groups.

1.2 PROPER NOUNS

Proper nouns name specific, one-of-a-kind things.

Common	Proper
motor, tree, time, children	Bradbury, Eastern Standard Time, Maine

*For more information, see **Quick Reference: Capitalization**, page R51.*

1.3 SINGULAR AND PLURAL NOUNS

A noun may take a singular or a plural form, depending on whether it names a single person, place, thing, or idea or more than one. Make sure you use appropriate spellings when forming plurals.

Singular	Plural
rocket, sky, life	rockets, skies, lives

*For more information, see **Forming Plural Nouns**, page R74.*

1.4 POSSESSIVE NOUNS

A **possessive noun** shows who or what owns something.

*For more information, see **Forming Possessives**, page R74.*

2 Pronouns

A **pronoun** is a word that is used in place of a noun or another pronoun. The word or word group to which the pronoun refers is called its **antecedent.**

2.1 PERSONAL PRONOUNS

Personal pronouns change their form to express person, number, gender, and case. The forms of these pronouns are shown in the following chart.

	Nominative	Objective	Possessive
Singular			
First person	I	me	my, mine
Second person	you	you	your, yours
Third person	she, he, it	her, him, it	her, hers, his, its
Plural			
First person	we	us	our, ours
Second person	you	you	your, yours
Third person	they	them	their, theirs

2.2 AGREEMENT WITH ANTECEDENT

Pronouns should agree with their antecedents in number, gender, and person.

If an antecedent is singular, use a singular pronoun.

> EXAMPLE: ***Malcolm** waved as he boarded the bus to the airport.*

If an antecedent is plural, use a plural pronoun.

> EXAMPLES:
>
> ***Malcolm** and **Hal** shared a sandwich as they waited to board the plane.*
>
> ***Delores** and **Arnetta** rode their bikes to the park.*

The gender of a pronoun must be the same as the gender of its antecedent.

> EXAMPLES:
>
> ***William** will give his final performance tonight.*
>
> ***Marla** played her trumpet.*

The person of the pronoun must be the same as the person of its antecedent. As the chart in Section 2.1 shows, a pronoun can be in first-, second-, or third-person form.

> EXAMPLE: *You classical music fans still have time to buy your tickets.*

Rewrite each sentence so that the underlined pronoun agrees with its antecedent.

1. "The Possibility of Evil" tells about a woman in a small town and <u>its</u> strange ideas.
2. Adela thinks the town is hers because her grandfather built <u>them</u>.
3. Adela writes anonymous letters to people in the town and hurts <u>its</u> feelings.
4. Helena Crane worried about her baby; she thought <u>it</u> might be slow.
5. A boy delivers the letter to Don Crane and <u>they</u> take revenge by destroying her roses.

2.3 PRONOUN CASE

Personal pronouns change form to show how they function in sentences. Different functions are shown by different **cases.** The three cases are **nominative, objective,** and **possessive.** For examples of these pronouns, see the chart in Section 2.1.

A **nominative pronoun** is used as a subject or a predicate nominative in a sentence.

An **objective pronoun** is used as a direct object, an indirect object, or the object of a preposition.

SUBJECT	OBJECT	OBJECT OF PREPOSITION
↓	↓	↓

She brought him to us.

A **possessive pronoun** shows ownership. The pronouns *mine, yours, hers, his, its, ours,* and *theirs* can be used in place of nouns.

EXAMPLE: *This book is mine.*

The pronouns *my, your, her, his, its, our,* and *their* are used before nouns.

EXAMPLE: *This is my book.*

WATCH OUT! Don't confuse the possessive pronouns *its* and *their* with the contractions *it's* and *they're.*

TIP To decide which pronoun to use in a comparison, such as "He runs faster than (I *or* me)," fill in the missing word(s): *He runs faster than I do.*

Replace the underlined words in each sentence with an appropriate pronoun and identify the pronoun as a nominative, an objective, or a possessive pronoun.

1. <u>Sophocles</u> was a famous playwright in ancient Greece.
2. *Antigone* is one of <u>Sophocles'</u> most important dramas.
3. <u>Antigone and Ismene</u> are two of the main characters.
4. Creon condemns <u>Antigone and Ismene</u>.
5. <u>The Greek chorus</u> represents the ordinary citizens.

2.4 REFLEXIVE AND INTENSIVE PRONOUNS

These pronouns are formed by adding *-self* or *-selves* to certain personal pronouns. Their forms are the same, and they differ only in how they are used.

A **reflexive pronoun** follows a verb or preposition and reflects back on an earlier noun or pronoun.

EXAMPLES:
He likes himself too much.
Kiyoko treated herself to dessert.

Intensive pronouns intensify or emphasize the nouns or pronouns to which they refer.

EXAMPLES:
The merchants themselves enjoyed sampling the foods.
You did it yourself.

WATCH OUT! Avoid using *hisself* or *theirselves.* Standard English does not include these forms.

NONSTANDARD: *The children sang theirselves to sleep.*

STANDARD: *The children sang themselves to sleep.*

2.5 RECIPROCAL PRONOUNS

Reciprocal pronouns express mutual actions or relationships between the members they represent. Reciprocal pronouns also take the possessive forms *each other's* and *one another's.*

EXAMPLES:
The children exchanged gifts with one another.
Sean and Julie laughed at each other's jokes.

GRAMMAR PRACTICE
ANSWERS

1. *"The Possibility of Evil" tells about a woman in a small town and <u>her</u> strange ideas.*
2. *Adela thinks the town is hers because her grandfather built <u>it</u>.*
3. *Adela writes anonymous letters to people in the town and hurts <u>their</u> feelings.*
4. *Helena Crane worried about her baby; she thought <u>she</u> (or he) might be slow.*
5. *A boy delivers the letter to Don Crane, and <u>he</u> takes revenge by destroying her roses.*

GRAMMAR PRACTICE
ANSWERS

1. *He; nominative*
2. *his; possessive*
3. *They; nominative*
4. *them; objective*
5. *It; nominative*

2.6 DEMONSTRATIVE PRONOUNS

Demonstrative pronouns point out things and persons near and far.

	Singular	Plural
Near	this	these
Far	that	those

2.7 INDEFINITE PRONOUNS

Indefinite pronouns do not refer to specific persons or things and usually have no antecedents. The chart shows some commonly used indefinite pronouns.

Singular	Plural	Singular or Plural	
another	both	all	none
anybody	few	any	some
no one	many	more	most
neither	several		

TIP Indefinite pronouns that end in *one*, *body*, or *thing* are always singular.

INCORRECT: *Everyone brought their clarinet.*
CORRECT: *Everyone brought his or her clarinet.*

If the indefinite pronoun might refer to either a male or a female, *his* or *her* may be used to refer to it, or the sentence may be rewritten.

EXAMPLES: *Did everybody play his or her part well?*
Did all the students play their parts well?

2.8 INTERROGATIVE PRONOUNS

An **interrogative pronoun** tells a reader or listener that a question is coming. The interrogative pronouns are *who, whom, whose, which,* and *what.*

EXAMPLES: *Who wrote that song?*
From whom did you get the answer?

TIP *Who* is used as a subject, *whom* as an object. To find out which pronoun you need to use in a question, change the question to a statement.

QUESTION: *(Who/Whom) are you speaking to?*
STATEMENT: *You are speaking to (?).*

Since the verb has a subject (*you*), the needed word must be the object form, *whom.*

EXAMPLE: *Whom are you speaking to?*

WATCH OUT! A special problem arises when you use an interrupter, such as *do you think,* within a question.

EXAMPLE: *(Who/Whom) do you think is the better singer?*

If you eliminate the interrupter, it is clear that the word you need is *who.*

2.9 RELATIVE PRONOUNS

Relative pronouns relate, or connect, adjective clauses to the words they modify in sentences. The noun or pronoun that a relative clause modifies is the antecedent of the relative pronoun. Here are the relative pronouns and their uses.

Replaces	Subject	Object	Possessive
Person	who	whom	whose
Thing	which	which	whose
Thing/Person	that	that	whose

Often short sentences with related ideas can be combined by using a relative pronoun to create a more effective sentence.

SHORT SENTENCE: *Joan Aiken decided to become a writer at an early age.*
RELATED SENTENCE: *Joan Aiken's father was a poet.*
COMBINED SENTENCE: *Joan Aiken, whose father was a poet, decided to become a writer at an early age.*

GRAMMAR PRACTICE

Write the correct form of each incorrect pronoun.

1. Whom has read "By the Waters of Babylon"?
2. Stephen Vincent Benét, which is a famous American author, wrote the story.
3. In "By the Waters of Babylon," him who touches the metal in the Dead Places must be a priest or son of a priest.
4. The narrator's father hisself questioned him.
5. When John saw a heap of broken stones, he cautiously approached them stones.

R54 GRAMMAR HANDBOOK

GRAMMAR PRACTICE

ANSWERS

1. *Who has read "By the Waters of Babylon"?*
2. *Stephen Vincent Benét, who is a famous American author, wrote the story.*
3. *In "By the Waters of Babylon," he who touches the metal in the Dead Places must be a priest or son of a priest.*
4. *The narrator's father himself questioned him.*
5. *When John saw a heap of broken stones, he cautiously approached them.*

2.10 PRONOUN REFERENCE PROBLEMS

The referent of a pronoun should always be clear. Avoid problems by rewriting sentences.

An **indefinite reference** occurs when the pronoun *it, you,* or *they* does not clearly refer to a specific antecedent.

> UNCLEAR: *In the article, it claims that the new Pink Blur CD is terrific.*
>
> CLEAR: *The article claims that the new Pink Blur CD is terrific.*

A **general reference** occurs when the pronoun *it, this, that, which,* or *such* is used to refer to a general idea rather than a specific antecedent.

> UNCLEAR: *Trudy practices the guitar every day. This has improved her playing.*
>
> CLEAR: *Trudy practices the guitar every day. Practicing has improved her playing.*

Ambiguous means "having more than one possible meaning." An **ambiguous reference** occurs when a pronoun could refer to two or more antecedents.

> UNCLEAR: *Jeb talked to Max while he listened to music.*
>
> CLEAR: *While Jeb listened to music, he talked to Max.*

GRAMMAR PRACTICE

Rewrite the following sentences to correct indefinite, ambiguous, and general pronoun references.

1. In the story "To Build A Fire," it tells about a man trying to survive in extremely cold conditions.

2. The man almost stepped in a trap. This made him use the dog to test the trail.

3. An old-timer told the miner that running would make his feet freeze faster.

4. Snow from a tree fell and put out the man's fire. This made him panic.

3 Verbs

A **verb** is a word that expresses an action, a condition, or a state of being.

For more information, see Quick Reference: Parts of Speech, page R47.

3.1 ACTION VERBS

Action verbs express mental or physical activity.

> EXAMPLE: *You hit the target.*

3.2 LINKING VERBS

Linking verbs join subjects with words or phrases that rename or describe them.

> EXAMPLE: *She is our queen.*

3.3 PRINCIPAL PARTS

Action and linking verbs typically have four principal parts, which are used to form verb tenses. The principal parts are the **present,** the **present participle,** the **past,** and the **past participle.**

Action verbs and some linking verbs also fall into two categories: regular and irregular. A **regular verb** is a verb that forms its past and past participle by adding *-ed* or *-d* to the present form.

Present	Present Participle	Past	Past Participle
perform	(is) performing	performed	(has) performed
hope	(is) hoping	hoped	(has) hoped
stop	(is) stopping	stopped	(has) stopped
marry	(is) marrying	married	(has) married

An **irregular verb** is a verb that forms its past and past participle in some other way than by adding *-ed* or *-d* to the present form.

Present	Present Participle	Past	Past Participle
bring	(is) bringing	brought	(has) brought
swim	(is) swimming	swam	(has) swum
steal	(is) stealing	stole	(has) stolen
grow	(is) growing	grew	(has) grown

3.4 VERB TENSE

The **tense** of a verb indicates the time of the action or state of being. An action or a state of being can occur in the present, the past, or the future. There are six tenses, each expressing a different range of time.

GRAMMAR PRACTICE

ANSWERS

1. *The story "To Build A Fire" tells about a man trying to survive in extremely cold conditions.*

2. *The man almost stepped in a trap. After this close call, he decided to use the dog to test the trail.*

3. *An old-timer told the miner that running would make the miner's feet freeze faster.*

4. *Snow from a tree fell and put out the man's fire. The incident made him panic.*

GRAMMAR PRACTICE

ANSWERS

1. *In her stories, Alice Walker <u>shows</u> the dignity of people who are her subjects. (present tense)*

2. *Alice Walker <u>wrote</u> "Everyday Use." (past tense)*

3. *The mother in the story <u>knows</u> both her daughters well. (present tense)*

4. *The mother <u>sweeps</u> the yard. (present tense)*

5. *Their other house <u>burned</u> down. (past tense)*

6. *The story <u>shows</u> how the mother respects the everyday use of the quilts. (present tense)*

7. *Maggie wants the quilts and <u>appreciates</u> their value. (present tense)*

8. *Dee wants the <u>quilts</u> and she <u>wants</u> to display them. (present tense)*

9. *Maggie and her mother <u>had known</u> the quilts could be used as bedcovers. (past perfect tense)*

10. *Dee <u>had argued</u> with her family. (past perfect tense)*

The **present tense** expresses an action or a state that is happening at the present time, occurs regularly, or is constant or generally true. Use the present part.

> **NOW:** *This soup tastes delicious.*
>
> **REGULAR:** *I make vegetable soup often.*
>
> **GENERAL:** *Crops require sun, rain, and rich soil.*

The **past tense** expresses an action that began and ended in the past. Use the past part.

> **EXAMPLE:** *The diver bought a shark cage.*

The **future tense** expresses an action or a state that will occur. Use *shall* or *will* with the present part.

> **EXAMPLE:** *The shark will destroy this cage.*

The **present perfect tense** expresses an action or a state that (1) was completed at an indefinite time in the past or (2) began in the past and continues into the present. Use *have* or *has* with the past participle.

> **EXAMPLE:** *The diver has used shark cages before.*

The **past perfect tense** expresses an action in the past that came before another action in the past. Use *had* with the past participle.

> **EXAMPLE:** *He had looked everywhere for a cage.*

The **future perfect tense** expresses an action in the future that will be completed before another action in the future. Use *shall have* or *will have* with the past participle.

> **EXAMPLE:** *Before the day ends, the shark will have destroyed three cages.*

TIP A past-tense form of an irregular verb is not used with an auxiliary verb, but a past-participle main irregular verb is always used with an auxiliary verb.

> **INCORRECT:** *I have saw her somewhere before.*
>
> **CORRECT:** *I have seen her somewhere before.*
>
> **INCORRECT:** *I seen her somewhere before.*

3.5 PROGRESSIVE FORMS

The progressive forms of the six tenses show ongoing actions. Use forms of *be* with the present participles of verbs.

PRESENT PROGRESSIVE: *We are dancing.*

PAST PROGRESSIVE: *We were dancing.*

FUTURE PROGRESSIVE: *We will be dancing.*

PRESENT PERFECT PROGRESSIVE: *We have been dancing.*

PAST PERFECT PROGRESSIVE: *We had been dancing.*

FUTURE PERFECT PROGRESSIVE: *We will have been dancing.*

WATCH OUT! Do not shift from tense to tense needlessly. Watch out for these special cases:

- In most compound sentences and in sentences with compound predicates, keep the tenses the same.

  > **INCORRECT:** *I keyed in the password, but I get an error message.*
  >
  > **CORRECT:** *I keyed in the password, but I got an error message.*

- If one past action happened before another, do shift tenses.

  > **INCORRECT:** *They wished they started earlier.*
  >
  > **CORRECT:** *They wished they had started earlier.*

GRAMMAR PRACTICE

Rewrite each sentence, using a form of the verb in parentheses. Identify each form that you use.

1. In her stories, Alice Walker (show) the dignity of people who are her subjects.

2. Alice Walker (write) "Everyday Use."

3. The mother in the story (know) both her daughters well.

4. The mother (sweep) the yard.

5. Their other house (burn) down.

6. The story (show) how the mother respects the everyday use of the quilts.

Rewrite each sentence to correct an error in tense.

7. Maggie wants the quilts and appreciated their value.

8. Dee wants the quilt and she wanted to display them.

9. Maggie and her mother had knew the quilts could be used as bedcovers.

10. Dee have argued with her family.

3.6 ACTIVE AND PASSIVE VOICE

The voice of a verb tells whether its subject performs or receives the action expressed by the verb. When the subject performs the action, the verb is in the **active voice.** When the subject is the receiver of the action, the verb is in the **passive voice.**

Compare these two sentences:

ACTIVE: *Her sunglasses hid her face.*

PASSIVE: *Her face was hidden by her sunglasses.*

To form the passive voice, use a form of *be* with the past participle of the verb.

WATCH OUT! Use the passive voice sparingly. It can make writing awkward and less direct.

AWKWARD: *She was given the handmade quilts by her mother.*

BETTER: *Her mother gave her the handmade quilts.*

There are occasions when you will choose to use the passive voice because

- you want to emphasize the receiver: *The king was shot.*
- the doer is unknown: *My books were stolen.*
- the doer is unimportant: *French is spoken here.*

4️⃣ Modifiers

Modifiers are words or groups of words that change or limit the meanings of other words. Adjectives and adverbs are common modifiers.

4.1 ADJECTIVES

Adjectives modify nouns and pronouns by telling which one, what kind, how many, or how much.

WHICH ONE: *this, that, these, those*
EXAMPLE: *These tomatoes have grown quickly.*

WHAT KIND: *tiny, impressive, bold, rotten*
EXAMPLE: *The bold officer stood in front of the crowd.*

HOW MANY: *some, few, ten, none, both, each*
EXAMPLE: *Some diners had sweet potatoes.*

HOW MUCH: *more, less, enough, fast*
EXAMPLE: *There was enough chicken to serve everyone.*

4.2 PREDICATE ADJECTIVES

Most adjectives come before the nouns they modify, as in the preceding examples. A **predicate adjective,** however, follows a linking verb and describes the subject.

EXAMPLE: *My friends are very intelligent.*

Be especially careful to use adjectives (not adverbs) after such linking verbs as *look, feel, grow, taste,* and *smell.*

EXAMPLE: *The weather grows cold.*

4.3 ADVERBS

Adverbs modify verbs, adjectives, and other adverbs by telling where, when, how, or to what extent.

WHERE: *The children played outside.*
WHEN: *The author spoke yesterday.*
HOW: *We walked slowly behind the leader.*
TO WHAT EXTENT: *He worked very hard.*

Adverbs may occur in many places in sentences, both before and after the words they modify.

EXAMPLES: *Suddenly the wind shifted.*

The wind suddenly shifted.

The wind shifted suddenly.

4.4 ADJECTIVE OR ADVERB?

Many adverbs are formed by adding *-ly* to adjectives.

EXAMPLES: *sweet, sweetly; gentle, gently*

However, *-ly* added to a noun will usually yield an adjective.

EXAMPLES: *friend, friendly; woman, womanly*

4.5 COMPARISON OF MODIFIERS

Modifiers can be used to compare two or more things. The form of a modifier shows the degree of comparison. Both adjectives and adverbs have **comparative** and **superlative** forms.

The **comparative form** is used to compare two things, groups, or actions.

EXAMPLES:

His emperor's chariots are faster than mine.
Brutus' speech was more effective than Cassius' speech.

The **superlative form** is used to compare more than two things, groups, or actions.

EXAMPLES:

The emperor's chariots are the fastest.

Antony's speech was the most effective of all.

4.6 REGULAR COMPARISONS

Most one-syllable and some two-syllable adjectives and adverbs have comparatives and superlatives formed by adding -er and -est. All three-syllable and most two-syllable modifiers have comparatives and superlatives formed with *more* or *most*.

Modifier	Comparative	Superlative
tall	taller	tallest
kind	kinder	kindest
droopy	droopier	droopiest
expensive	more expensive	most expensive
wasteful	more wasteful	most wasteful

WATCH OUT! Note that spelling changes must sometimes be made to form the comparatives and superlatives of modifiers.

EXAMPLES:

friendly, friendlier (Change *y* to *i* and add the ending.)

sad, sadder (Double the final consonant and add the ending.)

4.7 IRREGULAR COMPARISONS

Some commonly used modifiers have irregular comparative and superlative forms. They are listed in the following chart.

Modifier	Comparative	Superlative
good	better	best
bad	worse	worst
far	farther *or* further	farthest *or* furthest
little	less *or* lesser	least
many	more	most
well	better	best
much	more	most

4.8 PROBLEMS WITH MODIFIERS

Study the tips that follow to avoid common mistakes:

Farther and Further Use *farther* for distances; use *further* for everything else.

Double Comparisons Make a comparison by using -er/-est or by using *more/most.* Using -er with *more* or using -est with *most* is incorrect.

INCORRECT: *I like her more better than she likes me.*

CORRECT: *I like her better than she likes me.*

Illogical Comparisons An illogical or confusing comparison results when two unrelated things are compared or when something is compared with itself. The word *other* or the word *else* should be used in a comparison of an individual member to the rest of a group.

ILLOGICAL: *The narrator was more curious about the war than any student in his class.* (implies that the narrator isn't a student in the class)

LOGICAL: *The narrator was more curious about the war than any other student in his class.* (identifies that the narrator is a student)

Bad vs. Badly *Bad,* always an adjective, is used before a noun or after a linking verb. *Badly,* always an adverb, never modifies a noun. Be sure to use the right form after a linking verb.

INCORRECT: *Ed felt badly after his team lost.*

CORRECT: *Ed felt bad after his team lost.*

Good vs. Well *Good* is always an adjective. It is used before a noun or after a linking verb. *Well* is often an adverb meaning "expertly" or "properly." *Well* can also be used as an adjective after a linking verb when it means "in good health."

INCORRECT: *Helen writes very good.*

CORRECT: *Helen writes very well.*

CORRECT: *Yesterday I felt bad; today I feel well.*

Double Negatives If you add a negative word to a sentence that is already negative, the result will be an error known as a double negative. When using *not* or -n't with a verb, use *any-* words, such as

anybody or *anything*, rather than *no-* words, such as *nobody* or *nothing*, later in the sentence.

INCORRECT: *I don't have no money.*

CORRECT: *I don't have any money.*

Using *hardly, barely,* or *scarcely* after a negative word is also incorrect.

INCORRECT: *They couldn't barely see two feet ahead.*

CORRECT: *They could barely see two feet ahead.*

Misplaced Modifiers Sometimes a modifier is placed so far away from the word it modifies that the intended meaning of the sentence is unclear. Prepositional phrases and participial phrases are often misplaced. Place modifiers as close as possible to the words they modify.

MISPLACED: *The ranger explained how to find ducks in her office.* (The ducks were not in the ranger's office.)

CLEARER: *In her office, the ranger explained how to find ducks.*

Dangling Modifiers Sometimes a modifier doesn't appear to modify any word in a sentence. Most dangling modifiers are participial phrases or infinitive phrases.

DANGLING: *Coming home with groceries, our parrot said, "Hello!"*

CLEARER: *Coming home with groceries, we heard our parrot say, "Hello!"*

GRAMMAR PRACTICE

Choose the correct word or words from each pair in parentheses.

1. The play *Julius Caesar* is about the death of the (powerfulest, most powerful) emperor of Roman times.

2. The emperor didn't pay (no, any) attention to the soothsayer who warned him about the ides of March.

3. Caesar (could, couldn't) hardly know what lay in store for him.

4. He thought Brutus loved him (well, good).

GRAMMAR PRACTICE

Rewrite each sentence that contains a misplaced or dangling modifier. Write "correct" if the sentence is written correctly.

1. Ballerinas were on the television screen with weights.

2. Looking at the television, a buzzer sounded in George's head.

3. White and trembling, tears were in his eyes.

4. Being above average was not allowed in the story "Harrison Bergeron," making people like everyone else.

5 The Sentence and Its Parts

A **sentence** is a group of words used to express a complete thought. A complete sentence has a subject and a predicate.

*For more information, see **Quick Reference: The Sentence and Its Parts**, page R48.*

5.1 KINDS OF SENTENCES

There are four basic types of sentences.

Type	Definition	Example
Declarative	states a fact, a wish, an intent, or a feeling	I read White's essay last night.
Interrogative	asks a question	Did you like the essay?
Imperative	gives a command or direction	Read this paragraph aloud.
Exclamatory	expresses strong feeling or excitement	I wish I had thought of that!

5.2 COMPOUND SUBJECTS AND PREDICATES

A compound subject consists of two or more subjects that share the same verb. They are typically joined by the coordinating conjunction *and* or *or.*

EXAMPLE: *Ray and Joe write about families.*

A compound predicate consists of two or more predicates that share the same subject. They too are typically joined by a coordinating conjunction, usually *and, but,* or *or.*

GRAMMAR PRACTICE

ANSWERS

1. *most powerful*

2. *any*

3. *could*

4. *well*

GRAMMAR PRACTICE

ANSWERS

1. *Ballerinas with weights were on the television screen.*

2. *Looking at the television, George heard a buzzer in his head.*

3. *White and trembling, his eyes were full of tears.*

4. *In the story "Harrison Bergeron," people were made to be like everyone else; no one was allowed to be above average.*

EXAMPLE: *The father in "Those Winter Sundays" got up early and dressed in the dark.*

5.3 COMPLEMENTS

A **complement** is a word or group of words that completes the meaning of the sentence. Some sentences contain only a subject and a verb. Most sentences, however, require additional words placed after the verb to complete the meaning of the sentence. There are three kinds of complements: direct objects, indirect objects, and subject complements.

Direct objects are words or word groups that receive the action of action verbs. A direct object answers the question *what* or *whom*.

> **EXAMPLES:**
>
> *The students asked many questions.* (Asked what?)
>
> *The teacher quickly answered the students.* (Answered whom?)

Indirect objects tell to whom or what or for whom or what the actions of verbs are performed. Indirect objects come before direct objects. In the examples that follow, the indirect objects are highlighted.

> **EXAMPLES:**
>
> *My sister usually gave her friends good advice.* (Gave to whom?)
>
> *Her brother sent the store a heavy package.* (Sent to what?)

Subject complements come after linking verbs and identify or describe the subjects. A subject complement that names or identifies a subject is called a **predicate nominative.** Predicate nominatives include **predicate nouns** and **predicate pronouns.**

> **EXAMPLES:**
>
> *My friends are very hard workers.*
>
> *The best writer in the class is she.*

A subject complement that describes a subject is called a **predicate adjective.**

> **EXAMPLE:** *The pianist appeared very energetic.*

6 Phrases

A **phrase** is a group of related words that does not contain a subject and a predicate but functions in a sentence as a single part of speech.

6.1 PREPOSITIONAL PHRASES

A **prepositional phrase** is a phrase that consists of a preposition, its object, and any modifiers of the object. Prepositional phrases that modify nouns or pronouns are called **adjective phrases.** Prepositional phrases that modify verbs, adjectives, or adverbs are **adverb phrases.**

> **ADJECTIVE PHRASE:** *The central character of the story is a villain.*
>
> **ADVERB PHRASE:** *He reveals his nature in the first scene.*

6.2 APPOSITIVES AND APPOSITIVE PHRASES

An **appositive** is a noun or pronoun that identifies or renames another noun or pronoun. An **appositive phrase** includes an appositive and modifiers of it.

An appositive can be either **essential** or **nonessential.** An **essential appositive** provides information that is needed to identify what is referred to by the preceding noun or pronoun.

> **EXAMPLE:** *This poem was written by author Walt Whitman.*

A **nonessential appositive** adds extra information about a noun or pronoun whose meaning is already clear. Nonessential appositives and appositive phrases are set off with commas.

> **EXAMPLE:** *He wrote this poem, a sad remembrance of war, about an artilleryman.*

7 Verbals and Verbal Phrases

A **verbal** is a verb form that is used as a noun, an adjective, or an adverb. A **verbal phrase** consists of a verbal along with its modifiers and complements. There are three kinds of verbals: **infinitives, participles,** and **gerunds.**

7.1 INFINITIVES AND INFINITIVE PHRASES

An **infinitive** is a verb form that usually begins with *to* and functions as a noun, an adjective, or an adverb. An **infinitive phrase** consists of an infinitive plus its modifiers and complements. The examples that follow show several uses of infinitive phrases.

NOUN: *To know her is my only desire.* (subject)
I'm planning to walk with you. (direct object)
Her goal was to promote women's rights. (predicate nominative)
ADJECTIVE: *We saw his need to be loved.* (adjective modifying *need*)
ADVERB: *She wrote to voice her opinions.* (adverb modifying *wrote*)

Because *to,* the sign of the infinitive, precedes infinitives, it is usually easy to recognize them. However, sometimes *to* may be omitted.

EXAMPLE: *Let no one dare [to] enter this shrine.*

7.2 PARTICIPLES AND PARTICIPIAL PHRASES

A **participle** is a verb form that functions as an adjective. Like adjectives, participles modify nouns and pronouns. Most participles are present-participle forms, ending in *-ing,* or past-participle forms ending in *-ed* or *-en.* In the examples that follow, the participles are highlighted.

MODIFYING A NOUN: *The smiling man ate another fried chicken wing.*
MODIFYING A PRONOUN: *Ignored, she slipped out of the room unnoticed.*

Participial phrases are participles with all their modifiers and complements.

MODIFYING A NOUN: *Visiting gardens, butterflies flit among the flowers.*
MODIFYING A PRONOUN: *Driven by instinct, they use the flowers as meal stops.*

7.3 DANGLING AND MISPLACED PARTICIPLES

A participle or participial phrase should be placed as close as possible to the word that it modifies. Otherwise the meaning of the sentence may not be clear.

MISPLACED: *The boys were looking for squirrels searching the trees.*
CLEARER: *The boys searching the trees were looking for squirrels.*

A participle or participial phrase that does not clearly modify anything in a sentence is called a **dangling participle.** A dangling participle causes confusion because it appears to modify a word that it cannot sensibly modify. Correct a dangling participle by providing a word for the participle to modify.

DANGLING: *Running like the wind, my hat fell off.* (The hat wasn't running.)
CLEARER: *Running like the wind, I lost my hat.*

7.4 GERUNDS AND GERUND PHRASES

A **gerund** is a verb form ending in *-ing* that functions as a noun. Gerunds may perform any function nouns perform.

SUBJECT: *Running is my favorite pastime.*
DIRECT OBJECT: *I truly love running.*
INDIRECT OBJECT: *You should give running a try.*
SUBJECT COMPLEMENT: *My deepest passion is running.*
OBJECT OF PREPOSITION: *Her love of running keeps her strong.*

Gerund phrases are gerunds with all their modifiers and complements.

SUBJECT: *Wishing on a star never got me far.*
OBJECT OF PREPOSITION: *I will finish before leaving the office.*
APPOSITIVE: *Her avocation, flying airplanes, finally led to full-time employment.*

GRAMMAR PRACTICE

ANSWERS

1. **Possible answer:** *Living in Moscow, Tolstoy was orphaned by age nine.*

2. **Possible answer:** *The novel* War and Peace *was published in 1869.*

3. **Possible answer:** *Ivan tried to convince his wife to dance.*

4. **Possible answer:** *Ivan was happy dancing at the ball.*

5. **Possible answer:** *Ivan gradually lost interest in the colonel's daughter, Varenka.*

Rewrite each sentence, adding the type of phrase shown in parentheses.

1. Tolstoy was orphaned by age nine. (participial phrase)

2. *War and Peace* was published in 1869. (appositive phrase)

3. Ivan tried to convince his wife. (infinitive phrase)

4. Ivan was happy. (gerund phrase)

5. Ivan gradually lost interest in Varenka. (appositive phrase)

8 Clauses

A **clause** is a group of words that contains a subject and a verb. There are two kinds of clauses: independent clauses and subordinate clauses.

8.1 INDEPENDENT AND SUBORDINATE CLAUSES

An **independent clause** can stand alone as a sentence, as the word *independent* suggests.

> INDEPENDENT CLAUSE: *Emily Dickinson did not wish her poems to be published.*

A sentence may contain more than one independent clause.

> EXAMPLE: *Emily Dickinson did not wish her poems to be published, but seven were published during her lifetime.*

In the preceding example, the coordinating conjunction *but* joins two independent clauses.

For more information, see **Coordinating Conjunction,** *page R47.*

A **subordinate clause** cannot stand alone as a sentence. It is subordinate to, or dependent on, an independent clause.

> EXAMPLE: *Emily Dickinson did not wish her poems to be published, although she shared them with friends.*

The highlighted clause cannot stand by itself.

8.2 ADJECTIVE CLAUSES

An **adjective clause** is a subordinate clause used as an adjective. It usually follows the noun or pronoun it modifies.

> EXAMPLE: *Robert Frost wrote about birch tree branches that boys swing on.*

Adjective clauses are typically introduced by the relative pronoun *who, whom, whose, which,* or *that.*

For more information, see **Relative Pronouns,** *page R54.*

> EXAMPLES:
>
> *One song that we like became our theme song.*
>
> *Emily Dickinson, whose poems have touched many, lived a very quiet life.*

An adjective clause can be either restrictive or nonrestrictive. A **restrictive adjective clause** provides information that is necessary to identify the preceding noun or pronoun.

> EXAMPLE: *The candidate whom we selected promised to serve us well.*

A **nonrestrictive adjective clause** adds additional information about a noun or pronoun whose meaning is already clear. Nonrestrictive clauses are set off with commas.

> EXAMPLE: *Brookhaven National Laboratory, which employs Mr. Davis, is in Upton, New York.*

> **TIP** The relative pronouns *whom, which,* and *that* may sometimes be omitted when they are objects in adjective clauses.
>
> EXAMPLE: *Frost is a writer [whom] millions enjoy.*

8.3 ADVERB CLAUSES

An **adverb clause** is a subordinate clause that is used to modify a verb, an adjective, or an adverb. It is introduced by a subordinating conjunction.

For examples of subordinating conjunctions, see **Noun Clauses,** *page R63.*

Adverb clauses typically occur at the beginning or end of sentences.

> MODIFYING A VERB: *When we need you, we will call.*
>
> MODIFYING AN ADVERB: *I'll stay here where there is shelter from the rain.*
>
> MODIFYING AN ADJECTIVE: *Roman felt as good as he had ever felt.*

8.4 NOUN CLAUSES

A **noun clause** is a subordinate clause that is used as a noun. A noun clause may be used as a subject, a direct object, an indirect object, a predicate nominative, or an object of a preposition. Noun clauses are introduced either by pronouns, such as *that, what, who, whoever, which,* and *whose,* or by subordinating conjunctions, such as *how, when, where, why,* and *whether.*

For more subordinating conjunctions, see **Quick Reference: Parts of Speech,** *page R47.*

TIP Because the same words may introduce adjective and noun clauses, you need to consider how a clause functions within its sentence. To determine if a clause is a noun clause, try substituting *something* or *someone* for the clause. If you can do it, it is probably a noun clause.

> **EXAMPLES:** *I know whose woods these are.*
> ("I know *something.*" The clause is a noun clause, direct object of the verb *know.*)
> *Give a copy to whoever wants one.* ("Give a copy to *someone.*" The clause is a noun clause, object of the preposition *to.*)

GRAMMAR PRACTICE

Add descriptive details to each sentence by writing the type of clause indicated in parentheses.

1. Mr. Davis is a scientist. (adjective clause)
2. He has invented many things. (adjective clause)
3. He works. (adverb clause)
4. He does his best thinking at night. (adverb clause)
5. He should invent a better backpack. (adjective clause)

9 The Structure of Sentences

When classified by their structure, there are four kinds of sentences: simple, compound, complex, and compound-complex.

9.1 SIMPLE SENTENCES

A **simple sentence** is a sentence that has one independent clause and no subordinate clauses.

The fact that such a sentence is called simple does not mean that it is uncomplicated. Various parts of simple sentences may be compound, and simple sentences may contain grammatical structures such as appositive and verbal phrases.

> **EXAMPLES:**
> *Mark Twain, an unsuccessful gold miner, wrote many successful satires and tall tales.* (appositive and compound direct object)
> *Pablo Neruda, drawn to writing poetry at an early age, won celebrity at age 20.* (participial and gerund phrases)

9.2 COMPOUND SENTENCES

A **compound sentence** consists of two or more independent clauses. The clauses in compound sentences are joined with commas and coordinating conjunctions (*and, but, or, nor, yet, for, so*) or with semicolons. Like simple sentences, compound sentences do not contain any subordinate clauses.

> **EXAMPLES:**
> *I enjoyed Bradbury's story "The Utterly Perfect Murder," and I want to read more of his stories.*
> *Amy Lowell's poem "The Taxi" has powerful images; however, it does not use the word* taxi *anywhere in it.*

WATCH OUT! Do not confuse compound sentences with simple sentences that have compound parts.

> **EXAMPLE:** *A subcommittee drafted a document and immediately presented it to the entire group.* (Here *and* joins parts of a compound predicate, not a compound sentence.)

9.3 COMPLEX SENTENCES

A **complex sentence** consists of one independent clause and one or more subordinate clauses. Each subordinate clause can be used as a noun or as a modifier. If it is used as a modifier, a subordinate clause usually modifies a word in the independent clause, and the independent clause can stand alone. However, when a subordinate clause is a noun clause, it is a part of the independent clause; the two cannot be separated.

GRAMMAR PRACTICE

ANSWERS

1. *Possible answer: Mr. Davis is a scientist who works at the local university.*
2. *Possible answer: He has invented many things that are useful to everyone.*
3. *Possible answer: He works wherever his company sends him.*
4. *Possible answer: He does his best thinking at night when it is quiet.*
5. *Possible answer: He should invent a better backpack that will benefit all students.*

MODIFIER: *One should not complain unless one has a better solution.*

NOUN CLAUSE: *We sketched pictures of whomever we wished.* (The noun clause is the object of the preposition *of* and cannot be separated from the rest of the sentence.)

9.4 COMPOUND-COMPLEX SENTENCES

A **compound-complex sentence** contains two or more independent clauses and one or more subordinate clauses. Compound-complex sentences are, simply, both compound and complex. If you start with a compound sentence, all you need to do to form a compound-complex sentence is add a subordinate clause.

COMPOUND: *All the students knew the answer, yet they were too shy to volunteer.*

COMPOUND-COMPLEX: *All the students knew the answer that their teacher expected, yet they were too shy to volunteer.*

9.5 PARALLEL STRUCTURE

When you write sentences, make sure that coordinate parts are equivalent, or **parallel,** in structure.

NOT PARALLEL: *Erin loved basketball and to play hockey.* (*Basketball* is a noun; *to play hockey* is a phrase.)

PARALLEL: *Erin loved basketball and hockey.* (*Basketball* and *hockey* are both nouns.)

NOT PARALLEL: *He wanted to rent an apartment, a new car, and traveling around the country.* (*To rent* is an infinitive, *car* is a noun, and *traveling* is a gerund.)

PARALLEL: *He wanted to rent an apartment, to drive a new car, and to travel around the country.* (*To rent, to drive,* and *to travel* are all infinitives.)

🔟 Writing Complete Sentences

Remember, a sentence is a group of words that expresses a complete thought. In formal writing, try to avoid both sentence fragments and run-on sentences.

10.1 CORRECTING FRAGMENTS

A **sentence fragment** is a group of words that is only part of a sentence. It does not express a complete thought and may be confusing to a reader or listener. A sentence fragment may be lacking a subject, a predicate, or both.

FRAGMENT: *Waited for the boat to arrive.* (no subject)

CORRECTED: *We waited for the boat to arrive.*

FRAGMENT: *People of various races, ages, and creeds.* (no predicate)

CORRECTED: *People of various races, ages, and creeds gathered together.*

FRAGMENT: *Near the old cottage.* (neither subject nor predicate)

CORRECTED: *The burial ground is near the old cottage.*

In your writing, fragments may be a result of haste or incorrect punctuation. Sometimes fixing a fragment will be a matter of attaching it to a preceding or following sentence.

FRAGMENT: *We saw the two girls. Waiting for the bus to arrive.*

CORRECTED: *We saw the two girls waiting for the bus to arrive.*

10.2 CORRECTING RUN-ON SENTENCES

A **run-on sentence** is made up of two or more sentences written as though they were one. Some run-ons have no punctuation within them. Others may have only commas where conjunctions or stronger punctuation marks are necessary. Use your judgment in correcting run-on sentences, as you have choices. You can make a run-on two sentences if the thoughts are not closely connected. If the thoughts are closely related, you can keep the run-on as one sentence by adding a semicolon or a conjunction.

RUN-ON: *We found a place for the picnic by a small pond it was three miles from the village.*

MAKE TWO SENTENCES: *We found a place for the picnic by a small pond. It was three miles from the village.*

RUN-ON: *We found a place for the picnic by a small pond it was perfect.*

USE A SEMICOLON: *We found a place for the picnic by a small pond; it was perfect.*

ADD A CONJUNCTION: *We found a place for the picnic by a small pond, and it was perfect.*

WATCH OUT! When you form compound sentences, make sure you use appropriate punctuation: a comma before a coordinating conjunction, a semicolon when there is no coordinating conjunction. A very common mistake is to use a comma alone instead of a comma and a conjunction. This error is called a **comma splice.**

INCORRECT: *He finished the apprenticeship, he left the village.*

CORRECT: *He finished the apprenticeship, and he left the village.*

11 Subject-Verb Agreement

The subject and verb in a clause must agree in number. Agreement means that if the subject is singular, the verb is also singular, and if the subject is plural, the verb is also plural.

11.1 BASIC AGREEMENT

Fortunately, agreement between subjects and verbs in English is simple. Most verbs show the difference between singular and plural only in the third person of the present tense. In the present tense, the third-person singular form ends in -s.

Present-Tense Verb Forms	
Singular	**Plural**
I jog	we jog
you jog	you jog
she, he, it jogs	they jog

11.2 AGREEMENT WITH *BE*

The verb *be* presents special problems in agreement, because this verb does not follow the usual verb patterns.

Forms of *Be*			
Present Tense		**Past Tense**	
Singular	**Plural**	**Singular**	**Plural**
I am	we are	I was	we were
you are	you are	you were	you were
she, he, it is	they are	she, he, it was	they were

11.3 WORDS BETWEEN SUBJECT AND VERB

A verb agrees only with its subject. When words come between a subject and a verb, ignore them when considering proper agreement. Identify the subject, and make sure the verb agrees with it.

EXAMPLES:

A story in the newspapers tells about the 1890s.

Dad as well as Mom reads the paper daily.

11.4 AGREEMENT WITH COMPOUND SUBJECTS

Use plural verbs with most compound subjects joined by the word *and*.

EXAMPLE: *My father and his friends play chess every day.*

To confirm that you need a plural verb, you could substitute the plural pronoun *they* for *my father and his friends.*

If a compound subject is thought of as a unit, use a singular verb. Test this by substituting the singular pronoun *it*.

EXAMPLE: *Peanut butter and jelly [it] is my brother's favorite sandwich.*

Use a singular verb with a compound subject that is preceded by *each, every,* or *many a*.

EXAMPLE: *Each novel and short story seems grounded in personal experience.*

When the parts of a compound subject are joined by *or, nor,* or the correlative conjunctions *either . . . or* or *neither . . . nor,* make the verb agree with the noun or pronoun nearest the verb.

EXAMPLES:

Cookies or ice cream is my favorite dessert.

Either Cheryl or her friends are being invited.

Neither ice storms nor snow is predicted today.

11.5 PERSONAL PRONOUNS AS SUBJECTS

When using a personal pronoun as a subject, make sure to match it with the correct form of the verb *be*. (See the chart in Section 11.2.) Note especially that the pronoun *you* takes the forms *are* and *were*, regardless of whether it is singular or plural.

WATCH OUT! *You is* and *you was* are nonstandard forms and should be avoided in writing and speaking. *We was* and *they was* are also forms to be avoided.

> INCORRECT: *You was helping me.*
> CORRECT: *You were helping me.*
> INCORRECT: *They was hoping for this.*
> CORRECT: *They were hoping for this.*

11.6 INDEFINITE PRONOUNS AS SUBJECTS

Some indefinite pronouns are always singular; some are always plural.

Singular Indefinite Pronouns			
another	either	neither	one
anybody	everybody	nobody	somebody
anyone	everyone	no one	someone
anything	everything	nothing	something
each	much		

EXAMPLES:

Each of the writers was given an award.

Somebody in the room upstairs is sleeping.

Plural Indefinite Pronouns			
both	few	many	several

EXAMPLES:

Many of the books in our library are not in circulation.

Few have been returned recently.

Still other indefinite pronouns may be either singular or plural.

Singular or Plural Indefinite Pronouns		
all	more	none
any	most	some

The number of the indefinite pronoun *any* or *none* often depends on the intended meaning.

EXAMPLES:

Any of these topics has potential for a good article. (any one topic)

Any of these topics have potential for good articles. (all of the many topics)

The indefinite pronouns *all, some, more, most,* and *none* are singular when they refer to quantities or parts of things. They are plural when they refer to numbers of individual things. Context will usually give a clue.

EXAMPLES:

All of the flour is gone. (referring to a quantity)

All of the flowers are gone. (referring to individual items)

11.7 INVERTED SENTENCES

Problems in agreement often occur in inverted sentences beginning with *here* or *there*; in questions beginning with *how, when, why, where,* or *what*; and in inverted sentences beginning with phrases. Identify the subject—wherever it is—before deciding on the verb.

EXAMPLES:

There clearly are far too many cooks in this kitchen.

What is the correct ingredient for this stew?

Far from the embroiled cooks stands the master chef.

1. Most scholars (think, thinks) the author of *Le Morte d'Arthur* is Sir Thomas Malory.

2. (Is, Are) the author Syr Thomas Maleore, knight, the same as Sir Thomas Malory?

3. Sir Thomas himself, who lived during the Middle Ages, (was, were) a knight.

4. There (is, are) many knights and ladies in the tales of King Arthur.

5. One of the greatest prose works in the English language, *Le Morte d'Arthur* (was, were) based on French versions that were told earlier.

6. Many legends of King Arthur (was, were) also preserved in Wales.

7. Nearly everyone reading these tales (enjoy, enjoys) the adventures of the knights and ladies.

8. Several times Malory (was, were) put in prison.

9. He spent the last three years of his life in prison; he wrote *Le Morte d'Arthur* while he (was, were) there.

10. These tales featuring King Arthur (was, were) published after Malory's death.

11.8 SENTENCES WITH PREDICATE NOMINATIVES

When a predicate nominative serves as a complement in a sentence, use a verb that agrees with the subject, not the complement.

EXAMPLES:

The tales of King Arthur are a great work of literature. (*Tales* is the subject and it takes the plural verb *are*.)

A great work of literature is the tales of King Arthur. (The subject is the singular noun *work*.)

11.9 *DON'T* AND *DOESN'T* AS AUXILIARY VERBS

The auxiliary verb *doesn't* is used with singular subjects and with the personal pronouns *she, he,* and *it*. The auxiliary verb *don't* is used with plural subjects and with the personal pronouns *I, we, you,* and *they*.

SINGULAR: *She doesn't want to be without her cane. Doesn't the school provide help?*

PLURAL: *They don't know what it's like to be hungry. Bees don't like these flowers by the door.*

11.10 COLLECTIVE NOUNS AS SUBJECTS

Collective nouns are singular nouns that name groups of persons or things. *Team,* for example, is the collective name of a group of individuals. A collective noun takes a singular verb when the group acts as a single unit. It takes a plural verb when the members of the group act separately.

EXAMPLES:

Our team usually wins. (The team as a whole wins.)

Our team vote differently on most issues. (The individual members vote.)

11.11 RELATIVE PRONOUNS AS SUBJECTS

When the relative pronoun *who, which,* or *that* is used as a subject in an adjective clause, the verb in the clause must agree in number with the antecedent of the pronoun.

SINGULAR: *Have you selected **one** of the poems that **is** meaningful to you?*

The antecedent of the relative pronoun *that* is the singular *one;* therefore, *that* is singular and must take the singular verb *is.*

PLURAL: *The younger **redwoods,** which grow in a circle around an older tree, **are** also very tall.*

The antecedent of the relative pronoun *which* is the plural *redwoods.* Therefore, *which* is plural, and it takes the plural verb *grow.*

GRAMMAR PRACTICE

ANSWERS

1. *think*
2. *Is*
3. *was*
4. *are*
5. *was*
6. *were*
7. *enjoys*
8. *was*
9. *was*
10. *were*

COMMON CORE FOCUS

RL 4 Determine the meaning of words and phrases as they are used in the text, including figurative and connotative meanings; analyze the cumulative impact of specific word choices on meaning and tone (e.g., how the language evokes a sense of time and place; how it sets a formal or informal tone). **RI 4** Determine the meaning of words and phrases as they are used in a text, including figurative, connotative, and technical meanings; analyze the cumulative impact of specific word choices on meaning and tone (e.g., how the language of a court opinion differs from that of a newspaper). **L 2c** Spell correctly. **L 3** Apply knowledge of language to understand how language functions in different contexts, to make effective choices for meaning or style, and to comprehend more fully when reading or listening. **L 4a–d** Determine or clarify the meaning of unknown and multiple-meaning words and phrases, choosing flexibly from a range of strategies. **L 6** Acquire and use accurately general academic and domain-specific words and phrases, sufficient for reading, writing, speaking, and listening at the college and career readiness level; demonstrate independence in gathering vocabulary knowledge when considering a word or phrase important to comprehension or expression.

The key to becoming an independent reader is to develop a toolkit of vocabulary strategies. By learning and practicing the strategies, you'll know what to do when you encounter unfamiliar words while reading. You'll also know how to refine the words you use for different situations—personal, school, and work.

Being a good speller is important when communicating your ideas in writing. Learning basic spelling rules and checking your spelling in a dictionary will help you spell words that you may not use frequently.

COMMON CORE

Included in this handbook:
RL 4, RI 4, L 2c, L 3, L 4a–d, L 6

1 Using Context Clues

A word's context includes the words, sentences, and paragraphs surrounding it. A word's context can give you important clues about its meaning and help you distinguish between its denotative and connotative meanings.

1.1 GENERAL CONTEXT

Sometimes you need to infer the meaning of an unfamiliar word by reading all the information in a passage.

> On extremely hot days, Mariah *languidly* tends her garden. First she moseys to the yard to water her plants. Then she sits under a shady tree.

You can figure out from the context that *languidly* means "very slowly."

1.2 SPECIFIC CONTEXT CLUES

Sometimes writers help you understand the meanings of words by providing specific clues of the kinds shown in the chart.

1.3 IDIOMS, SLANG, AND FIGURATIVE LANGUAGE

An **idiom** is an expression whose overall meaning is different from the meaning of the individual words. **Slang** is informal language in which made-up words and ordinary words are used to mean something different from their meanings in formal English. **Figurative language** is language that communicates meaning beyond the literal meaning of words. Use context clues to figure out the meanings of idioms, slang, and figurative language.

> Trying to find the ring was like *looking for a needle in a haystack*. (idiom; conveys idea of "difficulty")

> When Brenda couldn't find her ring right away, she *went ballistic*. (slang; means "became angry")

> Mr. Gray has had the same car for over 20 years. Now it is just a *rusty tin can*. (figurative language; rusty tin can symbolizes the age and condition of the car)

Specific Context Clues		
Type of Clue	**Key Words/ Phrases**	**Example**
Definition or restatement of the meaning of the word	or, which is, that is, in other words, also known as, also called	A lichen is an example of *symbiosis,* **a relationship in which two living things live closely together and at least one benefits.**
Example following an unfamiliar word	such as, like, as if, for example, especially, including	*Prokaryotes,* which **include bacteria and blue-green algae,** are among the oldest forms of animal life.
Comparison with a more familiar word or concept	as, like, also, similar to, in the same way, likewise	He was as much a *prankster* **as** his brother was a **practical joker.**
Contrast with a familiar word or experience	unlike, but, however, although, on the other hand, on the contrary	Most organisms **need oxygen to survive, but** many types of bacteria are *anaerobic*.
Cause-and-effect relationship in which one term is familiar	because, since, when, consequently, as a result, therefore	**Because** they have a system of *membranes,* fish can use their **skin and gill tissue** to adjust to different salt levels in the water.

For more information, see **Vocabulary Strategy: Connotation,** *pages 436, 686, 1142.*

2 Analyzing Word Structure

Many words can be broken into smaller parts. These word parts include base words, roots, prefixes, and suffixes.

2.1 BASE WORDS

A **base word** is a word part that by itself is also a word. Other words or word parts can be added to base words to form new words.

2.2 ROOTS

A **root** is a word part that contains the core meaning of the word. Many English words contain roots that come from older languages such as Greek, Latin, Old English (Anglo-Saxon), and Norse. Knowing the meaning of the word's root can help you determine the word's meaning.

Root	Meaning	Example
anthrop (Greek)	human being	anthropology
hydr (Greek)	water	dehydrate
quer, quest (Latin)	ask, seek	question
pend, pens (Latin)	hang	pendulum
hēadfod (Old English)	head, top	headfirst

*For more information, see **Vocabulary Strategy: Word Roots**, pages 46, 236, 274, 335, 372, 380, and 597.*

2.3 PREFIXES

A **prefix** is a word part attached to the beginning of a word. Most prefixes come from Greek, Latin, or Old English.

Prefix	Meaning	Example
anti-	opposed to	**anti**social
de-	down, away from	**de**grade
sub-	under	**sub**marine

*For more information, see **Vocabulary Strategy: Prefixes**, pages 62, 76, 472, and 993.*

2.4 SUFFIXES

A **suffix** is a word part that appears at the end of a root or base word to form a new word. Some suffixes do not change word meaning. These suffixes are

- added to nouns to change the number of persons or objects
- added to verbs to change the tense
- added to modifiers to change the degree of comparison

Suffixes	Meaning	Examples
-s, -es	to change the number of a noun	trunk + s = trunks
-d, -ed, -ing	to change verb tense	sprinkle + d = sprinkled
-er, -est	to change the degree of comparison in modifiers	cold + er = colder icy + est = iciest

Other suffixes can be added to a root or base to change the word's meaning. These suffixes can also determine a word's part of speech.

Suffix	Meaning	Example
-ic	characterized by	sarcastic
-ion	process of	capitalization
-ness	condition of	uneasiness

*For more information, see **Vocabulary Strategy: Suffix -ion**, page 979.*

Strategies for Understanding Unfamiliar Words

- Look for any prefixes or suffixes. Remove them to isolate the base word or the root.
- See if you recognize any elements—prefix, suffix, root, or base—of the word. You may be able to guess its meaning by analyzing one or two elements.
- Consider the way the word is used in the sentence. Use the context and the word parts to make a logical guess about the word's meaning.
- Consult a dictionary to see whether you are correct.

3 Understanding Word Origins

3.1 ETYMOLOGIES

Etymologies show the origin and historical development of a word. When you study a word's history and origin, you can find out when, where, and how the word came to be.

> **co•ma¹** (kō′mə) *n., pl.* **–mas** A state of deep, often prolonged unconsciousness, usually the result of injury, disease, or poison, in which an individual is incapable of sensing or responding to external stimuli and internal needs. [Greek *kōma,* deep sleep.]
>
> **gar•lic** (gär′lĭk) *n.* **1.** An onionlike plant of southern Europe having a bulb that breaks into separate cloves with a strong distinctive odor and flavor. **2.**The bulb of this plant. [Middle English, from Old English *gārlēac : gār,* spear + *lēac,* leek.]
>
> **vin•dic•tive** (vĭn-dĭk′tĭv) *adj.* **1.** Disposed to seek revenge; revengeful. **2.** Marked by or resulting from a desire to hurt; spiteful. (From Latin *vindicta,* vengeance, from *vindex, vindic-,* surety, avenger.]

*For more information, see **Vocabulary Strategy: Etymology,** pages 644, 909, and 1108.*

3.2 WORD FAMILIES

Words that have the same root make up a word family and have related meanings. The chart shows a common Greek and a common Latin root. Notice how the meanings of the example words are related to the meanings of their roots.

Latin Root	*spect:* "see"
English	**inspect** look at carefully
	respect look at with esteem
	spectator someone who watches an event

Greek Root	*phil:* "love"
English	**philharmonic** devoted to music
	philosophy love and pursuit of wisdom
	philanthropy love of humankind

*For more information, see **Vocabulary Strategy: The Kosmos Word Family,** page 993.*

3.3 WORDS FROM CLASSICAL MYTHOLOGY

The English language includes many words from classical mythology. You can use your knowledge of Greek, Roman, and Norse myths to understand the origins and meanings of these words. For example, *herculean task* refers to the strongman Hercules. Thus *herculean task* probably means "a job that is large or difficult." The chart shows a few common words from mythology.

Greek	Roman	Norse
nemesis	insomnia	Thursday
atlas	fury	berserk
adonis	Saturday	rune
mentor	January	valkyrie

PRACTICE AND APPLY

Look up the etymology of each word in the chart and locate the myth associated with it. Use the information from the myth to explain the origin and meaning of each word.

3.4 FOREIGN WORDS

The English language includes words from diverse languages such as French, Dutch, Spanish, Italian, and Chinese. Many words stayed the way they were in their original language.

French	Dutch	Spanish	Italian
mirage	cookie	tornado	studio
vague	snoop	bronco	ravioli
beau	hook	salsa	opera

4 Synonyms and Antonyms

4.1 SYNONYMS

A **synonym** is a word with a meaning similar to that of another word. You can find synonyms in a thesaurus or a dictionary. In a dictionary, synonyms are often given as part of the definition of a word. The following word pairs are synonyms:

dry/arid   enthralled/fascinated   gaunt/thin

4.2 ANTONYMS

An **antonym** is a word with a meaning opposite that of another word. The following word pairs are antonyms:

friend/enemy   absurd/logical

courteous/rude   languid/energetic

5 Denotation and Connotation

5.1 DENOTATION

A word's dictionary meaning is called its **denotation.** For example, the denotation of the word *rascal* is "an unethical, dishonest person."

5.2 CONNOTATION

The images or feelings you connect to a word add a finer shade of meaning, called **connotation.** The connation of a word goes beyond its basic dictionary definition. Writers use connotations of words to communicate positive or negative feelings.

Positive	Neutral	Negative
save	store	hoard
fragrance	smell	stench
display	show	flaunt

Make sure you understand the denotation and connotation of a word when you read it or use it in your writing.

For more information, see **Vocabulary Strategy: Connotation and Denotation,** *pages 97, 216, 686, and 1142.*

6 Analogies

An **analogy** is a comparison between two things that are similar in some way but are otherwise dissimilar. Analogies are sometimes used in writing when unfamiliar subjects or ideas are explained in terms of familiar ones. Analogies often appear on tests as well, usually in a format like this:

TERRIER : DOG :: A) rat : fish
                      B) kitten : cat
                      C) trout : fish
                      D) fish : trout
                      E) poodle : collie

Follow these steps to determine the correct answer:

- Read the part in capital letters as "terrier is to dog as. . . ."
- Read the answer choices as "rat is to fish," "kitten is to cat," and so on.
- Ask yourself how the words *terrier* and *dog* are related. (A terrier is a type of dog.)
- Ask yourself which of the choices shows the same relationship. (A kitten is a kind of cat, but not in the same way that a terrier is a kind of dog. Therefore, the answer is C.)

For more information, see **Vocabulary Strategy: Analogies** *pages 450, 570, 676, and 1129.*

7 Homonyms and Homophones

7.1 HOMONYMS

Homonyms are words that have the same spelling and sound but have different origins and meanings.

> *I don't want to bore you with a story about how I had to bore through the living room wall.*

Bore can mean "cause a person to lose interest," but an identically spelled word means "to drill a hole."

> *My dog likes to bark while it scratches the bark on the tree in the backyard.*

Bark can mean "the sound made by a dog." However, another identically spelled word means "the outer covering of a tree." Each word has a different meaning and its own dictionary entry.

Sometimes only one of the meanings of a homonym may be familiar to you. Use context clues to help you figure out the meaning of an unfamiliar word.

7.2 HOMOPHONES

Homophones are words that sound alike but have different meanings and spellings. The following homophones are frequently misused:

it's/its   they're/their/there

to/too/two   stationary/stationery

Many misused homophones are pronouns and contractions. Whenever you are unsure whether to write *your* or *you're* and *who's* or *whose*, ask yourself if you mean *you are* and *who is/has*. If you do, write the contraction. For other homophones, such as *scent* and *sent*, use the meaning of the word to help you decide which one to use.

8 Words with Multiple Meanings

Over time, some words have acquired additional meanings that are based on the original meaning.

EXAMPLES: *I was in a hurry, so I jammed my clothes into the suitcase. Unfortunately, I jammed my finger in the process.*

These two uses of *jam* have different meanings, but both of them have the same origin. You will find all the meanings of this word listed in one entry in the dictionary.

9 Specialized Vocabulary

Specialized vocabulary is special terms suited to a particular domain, field of study or work. For example, science, mathematics, and history all have their own domain-specific, technical or specialized vocabularies. To figure out specialized terms, you can use context clues and reference sources, such as dictionaries on specific subjects, atlases, or manuals.

*For more information, see **Vocabulary Strategy: Specialized Vocabulary**, pages 134, 546, and 661.*

10 Using Reference Sources

10.1 DICTIONARIES

A **general dictionary** will tell you not only a word's definitions but also its pronunciation, parts of speech, and history and origin. A **specialized dictionary** focuses on terms related to a particular field of study or work. Use a dictionary to check the spelling of any word you are unsure of in your English class and other classes as well.

*For more information, see **Vocabulary Strategy: Using a Dictionary**, page 909.*

10.2 THESAURI

A **thesaurus** (plural, *thesauri*) is a dictionary of synonyms. A thesaurus can be especially helpful when you find yourself using the same modifiers over and over again.

*For more information, see **Vocabulary Strategy: Using a Thesaurus**, page 708.*

10.3 SYNONYM FINDERS

A **synonym finder** is often included in word-processing software. It enables you to highlight a word and be shown a display of its synonyms.

10.4 GLOSSARIES

A **glossary** is a list of specialized terms and their definitions. It is often found in the back of a book and sometimes includes pronunciations. Many textbooks contain glossaries. In fact, this textbook has four glossaries: the **Glossary of Literary and Nonfiction Terms**, the **Glossary of Reading & Informational Terms**, the **Glossary of Academic Vocabulary in English & Spanish**, and the **Glossary of Vocabulary in English & Spanish**. Use these glossaries to help you understand how terms are used in this textbook.

11 Spelling Rules

11.1 WORDS ENDING IN A SILENT *E*

Before adding a suffix beginning with a vowel or *y* to a word ending in a silent *e*, drop the *e* (with some exceptions).

> amaze + -ing = amazing
> love + -able = lovable
> create + -ed = created
> nerve + -ous = nervous

Exceptions: *change + -able = changeable; courage + -ous = courageous*

When adding a suffix beginning with a consonant to a word ending in a silent *e*, keep the *e* (with some exceptions).

> late + -ly = lately
> spite + -ful = spiteful
> noise + -less = noiseless
> state + -ment = statement

Exceptions: *truly, ninth, wholly, awful,* and others.

When a suffix beginning with *a* or *o* is added to a word with a final silent *e,* the final *e* is usually retained if it is preceded by a soft *c* or a soft *g.*

> bridge + -able = bridgeable
> peace + -able = peaceable
> outrage + -ous = outrageous
> advantage + -ous = advantageous

When a suffix beginning with a vowel is added to words ending in *ee* or *oe,* the final, silent *e* is retained.

> agree + -ing = agreeing   free + -ing = freeing
> hoe + -ing = hoeing   see + -ing = seeing

11.2 WORDS ENDING IN Y

Before adding most suffixes to a word that ends in *y* preceded by a consonant, change the *y* to *i.*

> easy + -est = easiest
> crazy + -est = craziest
> silly + -ness = silliness
> marry + -age = marriage

Exceptions: *dryness, shyness,* and *slyness.*

However, when you add *-ing,* the *y* does not change.

> empty + -ed = emptied   but
> empty + -ing = emptying

When you add a suffix to a word that ends in *y* preceded by a vowel, the *y* usually does not change.

> play + -er = player
> employ + -ed = employed
> coy + -ness = coyness
> pay + -able = payable

11.3 WORDS ENDING IN A CONSONANT

In one-syllable words that end in one consonant preceded by one short vowel, double the final consonant before adding a suffix beginning with a vowel, such as *-ed* or *-ing.* These are sometimes called 1+1+1 words.

> dip + -ed = dipped   set + -ing = setting
> slim + -est = slimmest   fit + -er = fitter

The rule does not apply to words of one syllable that end in a consonant preceded by two vowels.

> feel + -ing = feeling   peel + -ed = peeled
> reap + -ed = reaped   loot + -ed = looted

In words of more than one syllable, double the final consonant when accent is on the last syllable and remains there once the suffix is added, as in the following examples:

> be•gin´ + -ing = be•gin´ ning = beginning
> per•mit´ + -ed = per•mit´ ted = permitted

However, do not double the final consonant when the accent is on the final consonant but does not remain there when the suffix is added.

> tra´vel + er = tra´vel•er = traveler
> mar´ket + er = mar´ket•er = marketer

Do not double the final consonant when the accent is on the first syllable, as in the following examples:

> re•fer´ + -ence = ref´er•ence = reference
> con•fer´ + -ence = con´fer•ence = conference

11.4 PREFIXES AND SUFFIXES

When adding a prefix to a word, do not change the spelling of the base word. When a prefix creates a double letter, keep both letters.

> dis- + approve = disapprove
> re- + build = rebuild
> ir- + regular = irregular
> mis- + spell = misspell
> anti- + trust = antitrust
> il- + logical = illogical

When adding *-ly* to a word ending in *l,* keep both *l*'s. When adding *-ness* to a word ending in *n,* keep both *n*'s.

> careful + -ly = carefully
> sudden + -ness = suddenness
> final + -ly = finally
> thin + -ness = thinness

11.5 FORMING PLURAL NOUNS

To form the plural of most nouns, just add **-s**.

prizes   dreams   circles   stations

For most singular nouns ending in **o**, add **-s**.

solos   halos   studios   photos   pianos

For a few nouns ending in **o**, add **-es**.

heroes   tomatoes   potatoes   echoes

When the singular noun ends in **s, sh, ch, x**, or **z**, add **-es**.

waitresses   brushes   ditches
axes   buzzes

When a singular noun ends in **y** with a consonant before it, change the **y** to **i** and add **-es**.

army—armies   candy—candies
baby—babies   diary—diaries
ferry—ferries   conspiracy—conspiracies

When a vowel (**a, e, i, o, u**) comes before the **y**, just add **-s**.

boy—boys   way—ways
array—arrays   alloy—alloys
weekday—weekdays   jockey—jockeys

For most nouns ending in **f** or **fe**, change the **f** to **v** and add **-es** or **-s**.

life—lives   calf—calves   knife—knives
thief—thieves   shelf—shelves loaf—loaves

For some nouns ending in **f**, add **-s** to make the plural.

roofs   chiefs   reefs   beliefs

Some nouns have the same form for both singular and plural.

deer   sheep   moose   salmon   trout

For some nouns, the plural is formed in a special way.

man—men   goose—geese
ox—oxen   woman—women
mouse—mice   child—children

For a compound noun written as one word, form the plural by changing the last word in the compound to its plural form.

stepchild—stepchildren   firefly—fireflies

If a compound noun is written as a hyphenated word or as two separate words, change the most important word to the plural form.

brother-in-law—brothers-in-law
life jacket—life jackets

11.6 FORMING POSSESSIVES

If a noun is singular, add **'s**.

mother—my mother's car   Ross—Ross's desk

Exception: The **s** after the apostrophe is dropped after *Jesus', Moses',* and certain names in classical mythology (*Zeus'*). These possessive forms can thus be pronounced easily.

If a noun is plural and ends with **s**, just add an apostrophe.

parents—my parents' car
the Santinis—the Santinis' house

If a noun is plural but does not end in **s**, add **'s**.

people—the people's choice
women—the women's coats

11.7 SPECIAL SPELLING PROBLEMS

Only one English word ends in **-sede**: *supersede.* Three words end in **-ceed**: *exceed, proceed,* and *succeed.* All other verbs ending in the sound "seed" are spelled with **-cede.**

concede   precede   recede   secede

In words with **ie** or **ei**, when the sound is long **e** (as in *she*), the word is spelled **ie** except after **c** (with some exceptions).

i before *e*	thief	relieve	field
	piece	grieve	pier
except after *c*	conceit	perceive	ceiling
	receive	receipt	
Exceptions:	either	neither	weird
	leisure	seize	

12 Commonly Confused Words

WORDS	DEFINITIONS	EXAMPLES
accept/except	The verb *accept* means "to receive or believe"; *except* is usually a preposition meaning "excluding."	**Except** for some of the more extraordinary events, I can **accept** that the *Odyssey* recounts a real journey.
advice/advise	*Advise* is a verb; *advice* is a noun naming that which an *adviser* gives.	I **advise** you to take that job. Whom should I ask for **advice?**
affect/effect	As a verb, *affect* means "to influence." *Effect* as a verb means "to cause." If you want a noun, you will almost always want *effect*.	Did Circe's wine **affect** Odysseus' mind? It did **effect** a change in Odysseus' men. In fact, it had an **effect** on everyone else who drank it.
all ready/already	*All ready* is an adjective meaning "fully ready." *Already* is an adverb meaning "before or by this time."	He was **all ready** to go at noon. I have **already** seen that movie.
allusion/illusion	An *allusion* is an indirect reference to something. An *illusion* is a false picture or idea.	There are many **allusions** to the works of Homer in English literature. The world's apparent flatness is an **illusion.**
among/between	*Between* is used when you are speaking of only two things. *Among* is used for three or more.	**Between** *Hamlet* and *King Lear,* I prefer the latter. Emily Dickinson is **among** my favorite poets.
bring/take	*Bring* is used to denote motion toward a speaker or place. *Take* is used to denote motion away from a person or place.	**Bring** the books over here, and I will **take** them to the library.
fewer/less	*Fewer* refers to the number of separate, countable units. *Less* refers to bulk quantity.	We have **less** literature and **fewer** selections in this year's curriculum.
leave/let	*Leave* means "to allow something to remain behind." *Let* means "to permit."	The librarian will **leave** some books on display but will not **let** us borrow any.
lie/lay	*Lie* means "to rest or recline." It does not take an object. *Lay* always takes an object.	Rover loves to **lie** in the sun. We always **lay** some bones next to him.
loose/lose	*Loose* (lo͞os) means "free, not restrained"; *lose* (lo͞oz) means "to misplace or fail to find."	Who turned the horses **loose?** I hope we won't **lose** any of them.
precede/proceed	*Precede* means "to go or come before." Use *proceed* for other meanings.	Emily Dickinson's poetry **precedes** that of Alice Walker. You may **proceed** to the next section of the test.
than/then	Use *than* in making comparisons; use *then* on all other occasions.	Who can say whether Amy Lowell is a better poet **than** Denise Levertov? I will read Lowell first, and **then** I will read Levertov.
two/too/to	*Two* is the number. *Too* is an adverb meaning "also" or "very." Use *to* before a verb or as a preposition.	Meg had **to** go **to** town, **too.** We had **too** much reading **to** do. **Two** chapters is **too** many.
their/there/they're	*Their* means "belonging to them." *There* means "in that place." *They're* is the contraction for "they are."	**There** is a movie playing at 9 P.M. **They're** going to see it with me. Sakara and Jessica drove away in **their** car after the movie.

Interactive Vocabulary

Go to **thinkcentral.com**. KEYWORD: HML10-R68

Interactive Vocabulary

The keyword on this page directs students to **WordSharp** tutorials on key vocabulary strategies.

COMMON CORE FOCUS

SL 1a–d Initiate and participate effectively in a range of collaborative discussions with diverse partners, building on others' ideas and expressing their own clearly and persuasively. **SL 3** Evaluate a speaker's point of view, reasoning, and use of evidence and rhetoric, identifying any fallacious reasoning or exaggerated or distorted evidence. **SL 4** Present information, findings, and supporting evidence clearly, concisely, and logically such that listeners can follow the line of reasoning and the organization, development, substance, and style are appropriate to purpose, audience, and task.

Effective oral communication occurs when the audience understands a message the way the speaker intends it. Good speakers and listeners do more than just talk and hear. They use specific techniques to present their ideas effectively, and they are attentive and critical listeners.

COMMON CORE
Included in this handbook:
SL 1a–d, SL 3, SL 4

1 Speech

In school, in business, and in community life, a speech is one of the most effective means of communicating.

1.1 AUDIENCE, PURPOSE, AND OCCASION

When developing and delivering a speech, your goal is to deliver a focused, coherent presentation that conveys your ideas clearly and relates to the background of your audience. By understanding your audience, you can tailor your speech to them appropriately and effectively.

- **Know Your Audience** What kind of group are you presenting to? Fellow classmates? A group of teachers? What are their interests and backgrounds? Understanding their different points of view can help you organize the information so that they understand and are interested in it.

- **Understand Your Purpose** Keep in mind your purpose for speaking. Are you trying to convince the audience to do something? Perhaps you simply want to entertain them by sharing a story or experience. Your reason for giving the speech will guide you in organizing your thoughts and deciding on how to deliver it.

- **Know the Occasion** Are you speaking at a special event? Is it formal? Will others be giving speeches besides you? Knowing what the occasion is will help you tailor the language and the length for the event.

1.2 PREPARING YOUR SPEECH

There are several approaches to preparing a speech. Your teacher may tell you which one to use.

Manuscript	Prepare a complete script of the speech in advance and use it to deliver the speech. Use for formal occasions, such as graduation speeches and political addresses, and to present technical or complicated information.
Memory	Prepare a written text in advance and then memorize it in order to deliver the speech word for word. Use for short speeches, as when introducing another speaker or accepting an award.
Extemporaneous	Prepare the speech and deliver it using an outline or notes. Use for informal situations, for persuasive messages, and to make a more personal connection with the audience.

1.3 DRAFTING YOUR SPEECH

If you are writing your speech beforehand, rather than working from notes, use the following guidelines to help you:

- **Create a Unified Speech** Do this first by organizing your speech into paragraphs, each of which develops a single central idea. Then make sure that just as all the sentences in a paragraph support the central idea of the paragraph, all the paragraphs in your speech support the controlling idea of the speech.

- **Use Appropriate Language** The subject of your speech—and the way you choose to present it—should match your audience, your purpose, and the occasion. You can use informal language, such as slang, to share a story with your classmates. For a persuasive or argumentative speech in front of a school assembly, use formal, standard American English. If you are giving an informative or explanatory presentation, be sure to explain any terms that the audience may not be familiar with.

- **Provide Evidence** Include relevant facts, statistics, and incidents; quote experts to support your ideas and opinions. Elaborate—provide specific details, perhaps with visual or media displays—to clarify what you are saying.

- **Emphasize Important Points** To help your audience follow the main ideas and concepts of your speech, be sure to draw attention to important points. You can use rhyme, repetition, and other rhetorical devices.

- **Use Precise Language** Use precise language to convey your ideas, and vary the structure and length of your sentences. You can keep the audience's attention with a word that elicits strong emotion. You can use a question or interjection to make a personal connection with the audience.

- **Start Strong, Finish Strong** As you begin your speech, consider using a "hook"—an interesting question or statement meant to capture your audience's attention. At the end of the speech, restate your central ideas simply and clearly. Perhaps conclude with a powerful example or anecdote to reinforce your message.

- **Revise Your Speech** After you write your speech, revise, edit, and proofread it as you would a written report. Use a variety of sentence structures to achieve a natural rhythm. Check for correct subject-verb agreement and consistent verb tense. Correct run-on sentences and sentence fragments. Use parallel structure to emphasize ideas. Make sure you use complete sentences and correct punctuation and capitalization, even if no one else will see it. Your written speech should be clear and error-free. If you notice an error in your notes during the speech, you may not remember what you actually wanted to say.

1.4 DELIVERING YOUR SPEECH

Confidence is the key to a successful presentation. Use these techniques to help you prepare and present your speech:

Prepare

- **Review Your Information** Reread your notes and review any background research. You'll feel more confident during your speech.

- **Organize Your Notes** Some people prefer to include only key points. Others prefer the entire script. Write each main point, or each paragraph, of your speech on a separate numbered index card. Be sure to include your most important evidence and examples.

- **Plan Your Visual Aids** If you are planning on using visual aids, such as slides, posters, charts, graphs, video clips, overhead transparencies, or computer projections, now is the time to design them and decide how to work them into your speech.

Practice

- **Rehearse** Rehearse your speech several times, possibly in front of a practice audience. Maintain good posture by standing with your shoulders back and your head up. If you are using visual aids, practice handling them. Adapt your rate of speaking, pitch, and tone of voice to your audience and setting. Glance at your notes to refresh your memory, but avoid reading them word for word. Your style of performance should express the purpose of your speech. Use the following chart to help you.

Purpose	Pace	Pitch	Tone
To convince or present a claim	fast but clear	even	urgent
To inform	using plenty of pauses	even	authoritative
To entertain	usually building to a "punch"	varied to create characters or drama	funny or dramatic

- **Use Audience Feedback** If you had a practice audience, ask them specific questions about your delivery: Did I use enough eye contact? Was my voice at the right volume? Did I stand straight, or did I slouch? Use the audience's comments to evaluate the effectiveness of your delivery and to set goals for future rehearsals.

- **Evaluate Your Performance** When you have finished each rehearsal, evaluate your performance. Did you pause to let an important point sink in or use gestures for emphasis? Make a list of the aspects of your presentation that you will try to improve for your next rehearsal.

Present

- **Begin Your Speech** Try to look relaxed and smile.

- **Make Eye Contact** Try to make eye contact with as many audience members as possible. This will establish personal contact and help you determine if the audience understands your speech.

- **Remember to Pause** A slight pause after important points will provide emphasis and give your audience time to think about what you're saying.

- **Speak Clearly** Speak loud enough to be heard clearly, but not so loud that your voice is overwhelming. Use a conversational tone.

- **Maintain Good Posture** Stand up straight and avoid nervous movements that may distract the audience's attention from what you are saying.

- **Use Expressive Body Language** Use facial expressions to show your feelings toward your topic. Lean forward when you make an important point; move your hands and arms for emphasis. Use your body language to show your own style and reflect your personality.

- **Watch the Audience for Responses** If they start fidgeting or yawning, speak a little louder or get to your conclusion a little sooner. Use what you learn to evaluate the effectiveness of your speech and to decide what areas need improvement for future presentations.

- **Close your speech by thanking your audience.**

Respond to Questions

Depending on the content of your speech, your audience may have questions. Follow these steps to make sure that you answer questions in an appropriate manner:

- Think about what your audience may ask and prepare answers before your speech.

- Tell your audience at the beginning of your speech that you will take questions at the end. This helps prevent audience interruptions, which could make your speech hard to follow.

- Call on audience members in the order in which they raise their hands.

- Repeat each question before you answer it to ensure that everyone has heard it. This step also gives you time to prepare your answer.

2 Different Types of Oral Presentations

2.1 INFORMATIVE SPEECH

When you deliver an informative or explanatory speech, you give the audience new information, provide a better understanding of information, or enable the audience to use the information in a new way. An informative speech is presented in an objective way.

Use the following questions to evaluate the presentation of a peer or a public figure, or your own presentation.

Evaluate an Informative Speech

- Did the speaker have a specific, clearly focused topic?
- Did the speaker take the audience's previous knowledge into consideration?
- Did the speaker cite sources for the information?
- Did the speaker communicate the information logically and objectively?
- Did the speaker explain technical terms?
- Did the speaker use visual aids effectively?
- Did the speaker anticipate and address any audience concerns or misunderstandings?

2.2 PERSUASIVE SPEECH

When you deliver a persuasive or argumentative speech, you offer a thesis or clear statement on a subject, you provide relevant evidence to support your position, and you attempt to convince the audience to accept your point of view.

Use the following questions to evaluate the presentation of a peer or a public figure, or your own presentation.

Evaluate a Persuasive Speech

- Did the speaker present a clear thesis or argumentative claim?
- Did the speaker anticipate and address audience concerns, biases, and counterarguments?
- Did the speaker use sound logic and reasoning in developing the argument, avoiding the use of fallacious reasoning?
- Did the speaker support the argument with valid evidence, examples, facts, expert opinions, and quotations, avoiding the use of exaggerated or distorted evidence?
- Did the speaker use rhetorical devices, such as emotional appeals, to support assertions?
- Did the speaker hold the audience's interest with an effective voice, facial expressions, and gestures?
- Is your reaction to the speech similar to other audience members'?

2.3 DEBATE AN ISSUE

A debate is a balanced argument covering both sides of an issue. In a debate, two teams compete to win the support of the audience. In a formal debate, two teams, each with two members, present their arguments on a given proposition or policy statement. One team argues for the proposition or statement and the other argues against it. Each debater must consider the proposition closely and must research both sides of it. To argue convincingly either for or against a proposition, a debater must be familiar with both sides of the issue.

Use the following guidelines to evaluate a debate.

Evaluate a Team in a Debate

- Did the team prove that a significant problem does or does not exist? How thorough was the team's analysis of the problem?
- How did the team convince you that the proposition is or is not the best solution to the problem?
- How effectively did the team present reasons and evidence supporting the case?
- How effectively did the team refute and rebut arguments made by the opposing team?
- Did the speakers maintain eye contact and speak at an appropriate rate and volume?
- Did the speakers observe proper debate etiquette?

PRACTICE AND APPLY

View a political debate for a local, state, or national election. Use the preceding criteria to evaluate it.

2.4 NARRATIVE SPEECH

When you deliver a narrative speech, you tell a story or present a subject using a story-type format. A good narrative keeps an audience informed and entertained. It also allows you to deliver a message in a creative way.

Use the following questions to evaluate a speaker or your own presentation.

Evaluate a Narrative Speech

- Did the speaker choose a context that makes sense and contributes to a believable narrative?
- Did the speaker locate scenes and incidents in specific places?
- Does the plot flow well?
- Did the speaker use words that convey the appropriate mood and tone?
- Did the speaker use sensory details that allow the audience to experience the sights, sounds, and smells of a scene and the specific actions, gestures, and thoughts of the characters?
- Did the speaker use a range of narrative devices to keep the audience interested?
- Is your reaction to the presentation similar to other audience members'?

2.5 DESCRIPTIVE SPEECH

Description is part of most presentations. In a descriptive speech, you describe a subject that you are personally involved with. A good description will enable your listeners to tell how you feel toward your subject through the images you provide.

Use the following questions to evaluate a speaker or your own presentation.

Evaluate a Descriptive Speech

- Did the speaker make clear his or her point of view toward the subject being described?
- Did the speaker use sensory details, figurative language, and factual details?
- Did the speaker use tone and pitch to emphasize important details?
- Did the speaker use facial expressions to emphasize his or her feelings toward the subject?
- Did the speaker change vantage points to help the audience see the subject from another position?
- Did the speaker change perspectives to show how someone else might feel toward the subject or place?

2.6 ORAL INTERPRETATION

When you perform an oral reading, you use appropriate vocal intonations, facial expressions, and gestures to bring a literature selection to life.

Use the following questions to evaluate an artistic performance by a peer or a public presenter, a media presentation, or your own performance.

Evaluate an Oral Interpretation

- Did the speaker speak clearly, enunciating each word carefully?
- Did the speaker maintain eye contact with the audience?
- Did the speaker control his or her volume, projecting without shouting?
- Did the speaker vary the rate of speech appropriately to express emotion, mood, and action?
- Did the speaker use a different voice for the character(s)?
- Did the speaker stress important words or phrases?

- Did the speaker use voice, tone, and gestures to enhance meaning?
- Did the speaker's presentation allow you to identify and appreciate elements of the text such as character development, rhyme, imagery, and language?

PRACTICE AND APPLY

Listen to an oral reading by a classmate or view a dramatic performance in a theater or on television. Use the preceding criteria to evaluate it.

2.7 ORAL RESPONSE TO LITERATURE

An oral response to literature is a personal analytic interpretation of a writer's story, novel, poem, or drama. It demonstrates to an audience a solid and comprehensive understanding of what that piece means to you.

For more information, see Speaking and Listening: Presenting a Response to a Short Story, page 158.

Use the following questions to evaluate a speaker or your own presentation.

Evaluate an Oral Response to Literature

- Did the speaker choose an interesting piece that he or she understands and feels strongly about?
- Did the speaker make a judgment that shows an understanding of significant ideas from the text?
- Did the speaker direct the audience to specific parts of the piece that support his or her idea?
- Did the speaker identify and analyze the use of artistic elements such as imagery, figurative language, and character development?
- Did the speaker demonstrate an appreciation of the author's style?
- Did the speaker discuss any ambiguous or difficult passages and the impact of those passages on the audience?

PRACTICE AND APPLY

Listen as a classmate delivers an oral response to a selection you have read. Use the preceding criteria to evaluate the presentation.

3 Other Types of Communication

3.1 CONVERSATION

Conversations are informal, but they are important means of communicating. When two or more people exchange messages, it is equally important that each person contribute and actively listen.

3.2 GROUP DISCUSSION

Successful groups assign a role to each member. These roles distribute responsibility among the members and help keep discussions focused.

Leader or Chairperson

- Introduces topic
- Explains goal or purpose
- Participates in discussion and keeps it on track
- Helps resolve conflicts
- Helps group reach goal

Recorder

- Takes notes on discussion
- Reports on suggestions and decisions
- Organizes and writes up notes
- Participates in discussion

Participants

- Contribute relevant facts or ideas to discussion
- Respond constructively to one another's ideas
- Reach agreement or vote on final decision

Guidelines for Discussion

- Come to discussions prepared.
- Participate in the discussion.
- Don't talk while someone else is talking.
- Support statements and opinions with facts and examples.
- Listen attentively; be courteous and respectful of others' viewpoints.
- Work toward the goal; avoid getting sidetracked.

*For more information, see **Speaking and Listening: Participating in a Group Discussion**, page 508.*

3.3 INTERVIEW

An **interview** is a formal type of conversation with a definite purpose and goal. To conduct a successful interview, use the following guidelines:

Prepare for the Interview

- Select your interviewee carefully. Identify who has the kind of knowledge and experience you are looking for.
- Set a time, a date, and a place. Ask permission to tape-record the interview.
- Learn all you can about the person you will interview or the topic you want information on.
- Prepare a list of questions. Create questions that encourage detailed responses instead of yes-or-no answers.
- Arrive on time with everything you need.

Conduct the Interview

- Ask your questions clearly and listen to the responses carefully. Give the person whom you are interviewing plenty of time to answer.
- Be flexible; follow up on responses.
- Avoid arguments; be tactful and polite.
- Even if you record an interview, take notes.
- Thank the person for the interview, and ask if you can call with any follow-up questions.

Follow Up on the Interview

- Summarize your notes or make a written copy of the recording as soon as possible.
- If any points are unclear or if information is missing, call and ask more questions.
- Select the most appropriate quotations to support your ideas.
- If possible, have the person you interviewed review your work to make sure you haven't misrepresented what he or she said.
- Send a thank-you note to the person in appreciation of his or her time and effort.

3.4 ORAL INSTRUCTIONS

You may be called upon to follow or give oral instructions to perform specific tasks, answer questions, solve problems, and complete processes.

Evaluate your ability to follow oral instructions by asking yourself these questions:

- Did I **restate** each step in my own words?
- Did I **consider** how each step fits into the process or problem as a whole?
- Did I **ask** for clarification if necessary?

Evaluate your ability to give oral instructions by asking yourself these questions:

- Did I **plan** my instructions carefully?
- Did I **speak slowly** so my audience could follow each step?
- Did I **repeat** important details as necessary?
- Did I provide **diagrams or visual aids** to illustrate my instructions?

4 Active Listening

Active listening is the process of receiving, interpreting, evaluating, and responding to a message. Whether you listen to a class discussion or a formal speech, use the following strategies to get as much as you can from the message.

Listening with a Purpose		
Situation	**Reason for Listening**	**How to Listen**
A friend tells a story.	enjoyment	Maintain eye contact; visualize images and events.
A friend tells you a problem.	concern for your friend's well-being	Imagine the person's feelings; don't feel that you have to solve the problem.

Before Listening

- Learn what the topic is beforehand. You may need to read background information about the topic or learn technical terms in order to interpret the speaker's message.
- Think about what you know or want to know.
- Be prepared to take notes.
- Establish a purpose for listening.

While Listening

- Focus your attention on the speaker. Your facial expressions and body language should demonstrate your interest in hearing the topic.
- Listen for the speaker's purpose (usually stated at the beginning), which alerts you to main ideas.
- To help you interpret the speaker's message, listen for words or phrases that signal important points, such as *to begin with, in addition, most important, finally,* and *in conclusion.*
- Listen carefully for explanations of technical terms. Use these terms to help you understand.
- Listen for ideas that are repeated for emphasis.
- Take notes. Write down only the most important points.
- If possible, use an outline or list format to organize main ideas and supporting points.
- Note comparisons and contrasts, causes and effects, or problems and solutions.
- As you take notes, use phrases, abbreviations, and symbols to keep up with the speaker.
- To aid your comprehension, note how the speaker uses word choice, voice pitch, posture, and gestures to convey meaning.

After Listening

- Ask relevant questions to clarify anything that was unclear or confusing.
- Review your notes right away to make sure you understand what was said.
- Summarize and paraphrase the speaker's ideas.

- If you like, compare your interpretation of the speech with the interpretations of others who listened to it.

4.1 CRITICAL LISTENING

Critical listening involves interpreting and analyzing a spoken message to judge its accuracy and reliability. You can use the following strategies as you listen to messages from advertisers, politicians, lecturers, and others:

- **Determine the Speaker's Purpose** Think about the background, viewpoint, and possible motives of the speaker. Separate facts from opinions. Listen carefully to details and evidence that a speaker uses to support the message.

- **Listen for the Central Idea** Figure out the speaker's main message before allowing yourself to be distracted by seemingly convincing facts and details.

- **Recognize the Use of Persuasive Techniques** Pay attention to a speaker's choice of words. Speakers may slant information to persuade you to buy a product or accept an idea. Persuasive devices such as inaccurate generalizations, either/ or reasoning, and bandwagon or snob appeal may represent faulty reasoning and provide misleading information.

  *For more information, see **Persuasive Techniques**, pages 634 and R22.*

- **Observe Nonverbal Messages** A speaker's gestures, facial expressions, and tone of voice should reinforce the message. If they don't, you should doubt the speaker's sincerity and his or her message's reliability.

- **Give Appropriate Feedback** An effective speaker looks for verbal and nonverbal cues from you, the listener, to gauge how the message is being received. If you understand or agree with the message, you might nod your head. If possible, during or after a presentation, ask questions to clarify understanding.

4.2 VERBAL FEEDBACK

At times you will be asked to give direct feedback to a speaker. You may be asked to evaluate the way the speaker delivered the presentation as well as the content of the presentation.

Evaluate Delivery

- Did the speaker articulate words clearly and distinctly?
- Did the speaker pronounce words correctly?
- Did the speaker vary his or her rate?
- Did the speaker's voice sound natural and not strained?
- Was the speaker's voice loud enough?

Evaluate Content

Here's how to give constructive suggestions for improvement:

Be Specific Don't make statements like "Your charts need work." Offer concrete suggestions, such as "Please make the type bigger so we can read the poster from the back of the room."

Discuss Only the Most Important Points Don't overload the speaker with too much feedback about too many details. Focus on important points, such as:

- Is the topic too advanced for the audience?
- Are the supporting details well organized?
- Is the conclusion weak?

Give Balanced Feedback Tell the speaker not only what didn't work but also what did work: "Consider dropping the last two slides, since you covered those points earlier. The first two slides got my attention."

Every day you are exposed to hundreds of images and messages from television, radio, movies, newspapers, and the Internet. What is the effect of all this media? What do you need to know to be a smart media consumer? Being **media literate** *means that you have the ability to think critically about media messages. It means that you are able to analyze and evaluate media messages and how they influence you and your world. To become media literate, you'll need the tools to study media messages.*

.·.
:   :
 COMMON CORE
·.   .·
 ·. .·

Included in this handbook:
SL 3

1 Five Core Concepts in Media Literacy

from The Center for Media Literacy

The five core concepts of media literacy provide you with the basic ideas you can consider when examining media messages.

All media messages are "constructed." All media messages are made by someone. In fact, they are carefully thought out and researched and have attitudes and values built into them. Much of the information that you use to make sense of the world comes from the media. Therefore, it is important to know how media are put together so you can better understand the messages they convey.

Media messages are constructed using a creative language with its own rules. Each means of communication—whether it be film, television, newspapers, magazines, radio, or the Internet—has its own language and design. Therefore, a message must use the language and design of the medium that conveys the message. Thus, the medium actually shapes the message. For example, a horror film may use music to heighten suspense, or a newspaper may use a big headline to signal the significance of a story. Understanding the language of each medium can increase your enjoyment of it as well as alert you to obvious and subtle influences.

Different people experience the same media messages differently. Personal factors such as age, education, and experience will affect the way a person responds to a media message. How many times has your interpretation of a film or book differed from that of a friend? Everyone interprets media messages through his or her own personal lens.

Media have embedded values and points of view. Media messages carry underlying values, which are purposely built into them by the creators of the message. For example, a commercial's main purpose may be to persuade you to buy something, but it also conveys the value of a particular lifestyle. Understanding not only the core message but also the embedded points of view will help you decide whether to accept or reject the message.

Most media messages are constructed to gain profit and/or power. The creators of media messages often provide a commodity, such as information or entertainment, in order to make money. The bigger the audience, the more the media outlet can charge for advertising. Consequently, media outlets want to build large audiences in order to bring in more revenue from advertising. For example, a television network creates programming that appeals to the largest audience possible, and then uses the viewer ratings to attract more advertising dollars.

2 Media Basics

2.1 MESSAGE

When a film or TV show is created, it becomes a media product. Each media product is created to send a **message,** or an expression of belief or opinion, that serves a specific purpose. In order to understand the message, you will need to deconstruct it.

Deconstruction of a media presentation is the process of analyzing it. To analyze a media presentation you will need to look at its content, its purpose, the audience it's aimed at, and the techniques and elements that are used to create certain effects.

2.2 AUDIENCE

A **target audience** is a specific group of people that a product or presentation is aimed at. The members of a target audience usually share certain characteristics, such as age, gender, ethnic background, values, or lifestyle. For example, a target audience may be adults ages 40 to 60 who want to exercise and eat healthful foods.

Demographics are the characteristics of populations, including age, gender, profession, income, education, ethnicity, and geographical location. Media decision makers use demographics to shape their content to suit the needs and tastes of a target audience.

Nielsen ratings are the system used to track TV audiences and their viewing preferences. Nielsen Media Research, the company that provides this system, monitors TV viewing in a random sample of 5,000 U.S. households.

2.3 PURPOSE

The **purpose,** or intent, of a media presentation is the reason it was made. Most media offerings have more than one purpose. However, every media message has a **core purpose.** To discover that purpose, think about why its creator paid for and produced the message. For example, an ad might entertain you with humor, but its core purpose is to persuade you to buy something.

2.4 TYPES AND GENRES OF MEDIA

The term *media* refers to television, newspapers, magazines, radio, movies, and the Internet. Each is a **medium,** or means for carrying information, entertainment, and advertisements to a large audience. Each type of medium has different characteristics, strengths, and weaknesses. Understanding how different types of media work and the role they play will help you become more informed about the choices you make in response to the media.

*For more information, see **Types of Media**, page 10.*

2.5 PRODUCERS AND CREATORS

People who control the media are known as **gatekeepers.** Gatekeepers decide what information to share with the public and the ways it will be presented. The following diagram gives some examples.

Who Controls the Media?

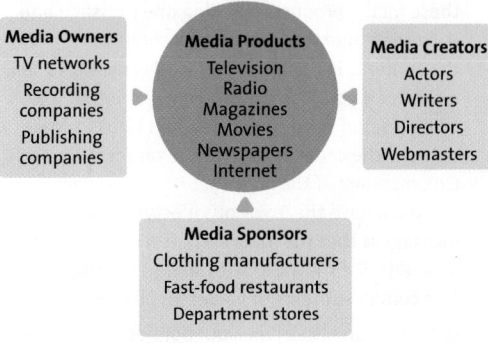

Media Owners	Media Products	Media Creators
TV networks	Television	Actors
Recording companies	Radio	Writers
Publishing companies	Magazines	Directors
	Movies	Webmasters
	Newspapers	
	Internet	

Media Sponsors
Clothing manufacturers
Fast-food restaurants
Department stores

Some forms of media are independently owned, while others are part of a corporate family. Some corporate families might own several different kinds of media. For example, a company may own three radio stations, five newspapers, a publishing company, and a small television station. Often a corporate "parent" decides the content for all of its holdings.

Media Tools THINK central
Go to **thinkcentral.com**.
KEYWORD: HML10-R84

Media Tools THINK central
The keyword on this page points to **MediaScope,** a Web site that helps students strengthen media analysis and production skills.

2.6 LAWS GOVERNING MEDIA

Four main laws and policies affect the content, delivery, and use of mass media.

The First Amendment to the Constitution forbids Congress to limit speech or the press.

Copyright law protects the rights of authors and other media creators against the unauthorized publishing, reproduction, and selling of their works.

Laws prohibit **censorship,** any attempt to suppress or control people's access to media messages.

Laws prohibit **libel,** the publication of false statements that damage a person's reputation.

2.7 INFLUENCE OF MEDIA

By sheer volume alone, media influences our very existence, values, opinions, and beliefs. Our environment is saturated with media messages from television, billboards, radio, newspapers, magazines, video games, and so on. Each of these media products is selling one message and conveying another—a message about values—in the subtext. For example, a car ad is meant to sell a car, but if you look closer, you will see that it is using a set of values, such as a luxurious lifestyle, to make the car attractive to the target audience. One message of the ad is that if you buy the car, you'll have the luxurious lifestyle. The other message is that the luxurious lifestyle is good and desirable. TV shows, movies, and news programs also convey subtexts of values and beliefs.

Media can also shape your opinions about the world. For example, news about crime shapes our understanding about how much and what type of crime is prevalent in the world around us. TV news items, talk show interviews, and commercials may shape our perception of a political candidate, a celebrity, an ethnic group, a country, or a regional area. As a consequence, our knowledge of someone or someplace may be completely based on the information we receive from the television.

3 Film and TV

Films and television programs come in a variety of types. Films include comedies, dramas, documentaries, and animated features. Televison programs cover an even wider array, including dramas, sitcoms, talk shows, reality shows, newscasts, and so on. Producers of films and producers of television programs rely on many of the same elements to convey their messages. Among these elements are scripts, visual and sound elements, special effects, and editing.

3.1 SCRIPT AND WRITTEN ELEMENTS

The writer and editor craft a story for television or film using a script and storyboard. A **script** is the text or words of a film or television show. A **storyboard** is a device often used to plan the shooting of a film and to help the director envision and convey what the finished product will look like. It consists of a sequence of sketches showing what will appear in the film's shots, often with explanatory notes and dialogue written beside or underneath them, as shown in the example.

*For more information, see **Media Study: Produce Your Own Media,** page 139.*

3.2 VISUAL ELEMENTS

Visual elements in film and television include camera shots, angles, and movements, as well as film components such as mise en scène, set design, props, and visual special effects.

A **camera shot** is a single, continuous view taken by a camera. **Camera angle** is the angle at which the camera is positioned during the recording of a shot or image. Each angle is carefully planned to create an effect. The chart shows what different shots are used for.

Camera Shot/Angle	Effect
Establishing shot introduces viewers to the location of a scene, usually by presenting a wide view of an area	establishes the setting of a film
Close-up shot shows a detailed view of a person or an object	helps to create emotion and make viewers feel as if they know the character
Medium shot shows a view wider than a close-up but narrower than an establishing or a long shot	shows part of an object or a character from the knees or waist up
Long shot is a wide view of a scene, showing the full figure(s) of a person or group and the surroundings	allows the viewer to see the "big picture" and shows the relationship between characters and the environment
Reaction shot shows someone reacting to something that occurred in a previous shot	allows the viewer to see how the subject feels in order to create empathy in the viewer
Low-angle shot looks up at an object or a person	makes a character, an object, or a scene appear more important or threatening
High-angle shot looks down on an object or a person	makes a character, an object, or a scene seem vulnerable or insignificant
Point-of-view (POV) shot shows a part of the story through a character's eyes	helps viewers identify with that character

Camera movement can create energy, reveal information, or establish a mood. The following chart shows some of the ways filmmakers move the camera to create an effect.

Camera Movement	Effect
Pan is a shot in which the camera scans a location from right to left or left to right	reveals information by showing a sweeping view of an area
Tracking shot is a shot in which the camera moves with the subject	establishes tension or creates a sense of drama
Zoom is the movement of the camera as it closes in on or moves farther away from the subject	captures action or draws the viewer's attention to detail

Mise en scène is a French term that refers to the arrangement of actors, props, and action on a film set. It is used to describe everything that can be seen in a frame, including the setting, lighting, visual composition, costumes, and action.

Framing is capturing people and objects within the "frame" of a screen or image. Framing is what the camera sees.

Composition is the arrangement of objects, characters, shapes, and colors within a frame and the relationship of the objects to one another.

3.3 SOUND ELEMENTS

Sound elements in film and television include music, voice-over, and sound effects.

Music may be used to set the mood and atmosphere in a scene. Music can have a powerful effect on the way viewers feel about a story. For example, fast-paced music helps viewers feel excited during an action scene.

Voice-over is the voice of the unseen commentator or narrator of a film, TV program, or commercial.

Sound effects are the sounds added to films, TV programs, and commercials during the editing process. Sound effects, such as laugh tracks or the sounds of punches in a fight scene, can create humor, emphasize a point, or contribute to the mood.

3.4 SPECIAL EFFECTS

Special effects include computer-generated animation, manipulated video images, and fast- or slow-motion sequences in films, TV programs, and commercials.

Animation on film involves the frame-by-frame photography of a series of drawings or objects. When these frames are projected—at a rate of 24 per second—the illusion of movement is achieved.

A **split screen** is a special-effects shot in which two or more separate images are shown in the same frame. One example is when two people, actually a distance apart, are shown talking to each other.

3.5 EDITING

Editing is the process of selecting and arranging shots in a sequence. The editor decides which scenes or shots to use, as well as the length of each shot, the number of shots, and their sequence. Editing establishes pace, mood, and a coherent story.

Cut is the transition from one shot to another. To create excitement, editors often use quick cuts, which are a series of short shots strung together.

Dissolve is a transitional device in which one scene fades into another.

Fade-in is a transitional device in which a white or black shot fades in to reveal the beginning of a new scene.

Fade-out is a transitional device in which a shot fades to darkness to end a scene.

Jump cut is an abrupt and jarring change from one shot to another. A jump cut shows a break in time or continuity.

Pace is the length of time each shot stays on the screen and the rhythm that is created by the transitions between shots. Short, quick cuts create a fast pace in a story. Long cuts slow down a story.

Parallel editing is a technique that cuts from one shot to another so as to suggest simultaneous action—often in different locations.

4 News

The **news** is information on events, people, and places in your community, your region, the nation, and the world. The news can be categorized by type, as shown in the chart.

Type	Description	Examples
Hard news	fact-based accounts of current events	local newspapers, newscasts, online wire services
Soft news	human-interest stories and other accounts that are less current or urgent than hard news	magazines and tabloid TV shows such as *Sports Illustrated, Access Hollywood*
News features	stories that elaborate on news reports	documentaries such as history reports on PBS
Commentary and opinion	essays and perspectives by experts, professionals, and media personalities	editorial pages, personal Web pages

4.1 CHOOSING THE NEWS

Newsworthiness is the significance of an event or action that makes it worthy of media reporting. Journalists and their editors usually weigh the following criteria in determining which stories should make the news:

Timeliness is the quality of being very current. Timely events usually take priority over previously reported events. For example, a car accident with fatalities will be timely on the day it occurs. Because of its timeliness it may be on the front page of a newspaper or may be the lead story on a newscast.

Impact measures the importance of an event and the number of people it could affect. The more widespread the impact of an event, the more likely it is to be newsworthy.

Proximity gauges the nearness of an event to a particular city, region, or country. People tend to be more interested in stories that take place locally and affect them directly.

Human interest is a quality of stories that cause readers or listeners to feel emotions such as happiness, anger, or sadness. People are interested in reading stories about other people.

Uniqueness belongs to uncommon events or circumstances that are likely to be interesting to an audience.

Compelling video and **photographs** grab people's attention and stay in their minds.

4.2 REPORTING THE NEWS

While developing a news story, a journalist makes a variety of decisions about how to construct the story, such as what information to include and how to organize it. The following elements are commonly used in news stories:

5 *W*'s and *H* are the six questions reporters answer when writing news stories—*who, what, when, where, why,* and *how*. It is a journalist's job to answer these questions in any type of news report. These questions also serve as a structure for writing and editing a story.

Inverted pyramid is the means of organizing information according to importance. In the inverted pyramid diagram below, the most important information (the answers to the 5 *W*'s and *H*) appears at the top of the pyramid. The less important details appear at the bottom. Not all stories are reported using the inverted pyramid form. The style remains popular, however, because it enables a reader to get the essential information without reading the entire story. Notice the following example.

> Men known as swan uppers have protected swans on the River Thames in London for more than eight centuries.
>
> Every July, the men, dressed in dark red or blue jackets, row three or more boats up the middle of the river to up, or check on the condition of, the swans.
>
> The term *upping* is believed to mean simply "going up the river."

Angle or slant is the point of view from which a story is written. Even an objective report must have an angle.

Consider these two headlines that describe a library program.

Patrons Should Return Books to Help Dwindling Collection

Library Offers Amnesty for Overdue Books

PHOENIX, March 17 —

The first headline focuses on an opinion and has a negative slant. The second headline focuses on facts about the program.

These two headlines reveal their writers' differing perceptions of the same event. A reporter's biases or perceptions about a subject can influence how he or she covers it—which can also influence how readers understand and react to the issue.

Standards for News Reporting

The ideal of journalism is to present news in a way that is objective, accurate, and thorough. The best news stories thus contain the following elements:

- **Objectivity** The story takes a balanced point of view on the issues; it is not biased, nor does it reflect a specific attitude or opinion.
- **Accuracy** The story presents factual information that can be verified.
- **Thoroughness** The story presents all sides of an issue; it includes background information, telling *who, what, when, where, why,* and *how*.

Balanced Versus Biased Reporting

Objectivity in news reporting can be measured by how balanced or biased the story is.

Balanced reporting represents all sides of an issue equally and fairly.

A balanced news story

- represents people and subjects in a neutral light
- treats all sides of an issue equally
- does not include inappropriate questions

- does not show stereotypes or prejudice toward people of a particular race, gender, age, religion, or other group
- does not leave out important background information that is needed to establish a context

Biased reporting is reporting in which one side is favored over another or in which the subject is unfairly represented. Biased reporting may show an overly negative view of a subject, or it may encourage racial, gender, or other stereotypes and prejudices. A viewer who receives news from a biased media source without evaluating the source and understanding the bias may end up misunderstanding events—which can lead to a skewed view of the world. It is important to evaluate reporting for bias and to search out objective media in order to receive an accurate view of events.

Sources are the people interviewed for the news report and also any written materials and documents the journalist used for background information. From each source, the journalist gets a different point of view. To decide whether news reporting is balanced or biased, you will need to pay attention to the sources. It is important to evaluate the **credibility,** or the believability and trustworthiness, of both a source and the report itself. The following chart shows which sources are credible.

Sources for News Stories	
Credible Sources	**Weak Sources**
• experts in a field • people directly affected by the reported event (eyewitnesses) • published reports that are specifically mentioned or shown	• unnamed or anonymous sources • people who are not involved in the reported event (for example, people who heard about a story from a friend) • research, data, or reports that are not specifically named or are referred to only in vague terms (for example, "Research shows that …")

5 Advertising

Advertising is a sponsor's paid use of various media to promote products, services, or ideas. Some common forms of advertising are shown in the chart.

Type of Ad	Characteristic
Billboard	a large outdoor advertising sign
Print ad	typically appears in magazines and newspapers; uses eye-catching graphics and persuasive copy
Flyer	a print ad that is circulated by hand or mail
Infomercial	an extended ad on TV that usually includes detailed product information, demonstrations, and testimonials
Public service announcement	a message aired on radio or TV to promote ideas that are considered to be in the public interest
Political ad	broadcast on radio or TV to promote political candidates
Trailer	a short film promoting an upcoming movie, TV show, or video game

Marketing is the process of transferring products and services from producer to consumer. It involves determining the packaging and pricing of a product, how it will be promoted and advertised, and where it will be sold. One way companies market their product is by becoming media sponsors.

Sponsors pay for their products to be advertised. These companies hire advertising agencies to create and produce specific campaigns for their products. They then buy television or radio airtime or magazine, newspaper, or billboard space to feature ads where the target audience is sure to see them. Because selling time and space to advertisers generates much of the income the media need to function, the media need advertisers just as much as advertisers need the media.

Product placement is the intentional and identifiable featuring of brand-name products in movies, television shows, video games, and other media. The intention is to have viewers feel positive about a product because they see a favorite character using it. Another purpose may be to promote product recognition.

5.1 PERSUASIVE TECHNIQUES

Persuasive techniques are the methods used to convince an audience to buy a product or adopt an idea. Advertisers use a combination of visuals, sound, special effects, and words to persuade their target audience. Recognizing the following techniques can help you evaluate persuasive media messages and identify misleading information:

Emotional appeals use strong feelings rather than factual evidence to persuade consumers. An example of an emotional appeal is "Is your home safe? ProAlarm Systems will make sure it is."

Bandwagon appeals use the argument that a person should believe or do something because "everyone else" does. These appeals take advantage of people's desire to be socially accepted by other people. Purchasing a popular product seems less risky to those concerned about making a mistake. An example of a bandwagon appeal is "More and more people are making the switch to Discountline long-distance service."

Slogans are memorable phrases used in advertising campaigns. Slogans substitute catchy phrases for factual information.

Logical appeals rely on logic and facts, appealing to a consumer's reason and his or her respect for authority. Two examples of logical appeals are expert opinions and product comparison.

Celebrity ads use one of the following two categories of spokesperson:

- **Celebrity authorities** are experts in a particular field. Advertisers hope that audiences will transfer the respect or admiration they have for the person to the product. For example, a famous chef may endorse a particular brand of cookware. The manufacturers of the cookware want you to think that it is a good product because a cooking expert wouldn't endorse pots and pans that didn't perform well.
- **Celebrity spokespeople** are famous people who endorse a product. Advertisers hope that audiences will associate the product with the celebrity.

Product comparison is comparing between a product and its competition. Often mentioned by name, the competing product is portrayed as inferior. The intended effect is for people to question the quality of the competing product and to believe the featured product is superior.

6 Elements of Design

The design of a media message is just as important as the words are in conveying the message. Like words, visuals are used to persuade, inform, and entertain. Graphics and images, such as charts, diagrams, maps, timelines, photographs, illustrations, cartoons, and symbols, present information that can be quickly and easily understood. The following basic elements are used to give meaning to visuals:

Color can be used to highlight important elements such as headlines and subheads. It can also create mood, because many colors have strong emotional or psychological impacts on the reader or viewer. For example, warm colors more readily draw the eye and are often associated with happiness and comfort. Cool colors are often associated with feelings of peace and contentment or sometimes sadness.

Lines—strokes or marks—can be thick or thin, long or short, and smooth or jagged. They can focus attention and create a feeling of depth. They can frame an object. They can also direct a viewer's eye or create a sense of motion.

Texture is the surface quality or appearance of an object. For example, an object's texture can be glossy, rough, wet, or shiny. Texture can be used to create contrast. It can also be used to make an object look "real." For example, a pattern on wrapping paper can create a feeling of depth even though the texture is only visual and cannot be felt.

Shape is the external outline of an object. Shapes can be used to symbolize living things or geometric objects. They can emphasize visual elements and add interest. Shapes can symbolize ideas.

Notice how this movie poster uses design elements.

- **Texture** Texture is used to show the contrast of the baby penguin's downy feathers to the adult penguin's smoother feathers.
- **Shape** The shape of the adult penguin's body and the downward slope of its head emphasize the bird's parental nature.
- **Color** Grayish blues and whites suggest the arctic environment that the penguins live in.

7 Evaluating Media Messages

Being able to respond critically to media images and messages will help you evaluate the reliability of the content and make informed decisions. Here are six questions to ask about any media message:

Who made—and who sponsored—this message, and for what purpose? The source of the message is a clue to its purpose. If the source of the message is a private company, that company may be trying to sell you a product. If the source is a government agency, that agency may be trying to promote a program or philosophy. To discover the purpose, think about why its creator paid for and produced the message.

Who is the target audience and how is the message specifically tailored to it? Think about the age group, ethnic group, gender, and/or profession the message is targeting. Decide how it relates to you.

What are the different techniques used to inform, persuade, entertain, and attract attention? Analyze the elements, such as humor, music, special effects, and graphics, that have been used to create the message. Think about how visual and sound effects, such as symbols, color, photographs, words, and music, support the purpose behind the message.

What messages are communicated (and/or implied) about certain people, places, events, behaviors, lifestyles, and so forth? The media try to influence who we are, what we believe, how we view things, and what values we hold. Look or listen closely to determine whether certain types of behavior are being depicted and if judgments or values are communicated through those behaviors. What are the biases in the message?

How current, accurate, and credible is the information in this message? Think about the reputation of the source. Note the broadcast or publication date of the message and whether the message might change quickly. If a report or account is not supported by facts, authoritative sources, or eyewitness accounts, you should question the credibility of the message.

What is left out of this message that might be important to know? Think about what the message is asking you to believe. Also think about what questions come to mind as you watch, read, or listen to the message.

Strategies and Practice for the SAT, ACT, and Other Standardized Tests

The test items in this section are modeled after test formats that are used on the SAT. The strategies presented here will help you prepare for that test and others. This section offers general test-taking strategies and tips for answering multiple-choice items, as well as short constructed response and extended constructed response questions in critical reading and writing. It also includes guidelines and samples for impromptu writing and essay writing. For each test, read the tips in the margin. Then apply the tips to the practice items. You can also apply the tips to Assessment Practice Tests in this book.

1 General Test-Taking Strategies

- Arrive on time and be prepared. Be sure to bring either sharpened pencils with erasers or pens—whichever you are told to bring.

- If you have any questions, ask them before the test begins. Make sure you understand the test procedures, the timing, and the rules.

- Read the test directions carefully. Look at the passages and questions to get an overview of what is expected.

- Tackle the questions one at a time rather than thinking about the whole test.

- Refer back to the reading passages as needed. For example, if a question asks about an author's attitude, you might have to reread a passage for clues.

- If you are not sure of your answer, make a logical guess. You can often arrive at the correct answer by reasoning and eliminating wrong answers.

- As you fill in answers on your answer sheet, make sure you match the number of each test item to the numbered space on the answer sheet.

- Don't look for patterns in the positions of correct choices.

- Only change an answer if you are sure your original choice is incorrect. If you do change an answer, erase your original choice neatly and thoroughly.

- Look for central or main ideas as you read passages. They are often stated at the beginning or the end of a paragraph. Sometimes the central idea is implied.

- Check your answers and reread your essay.

2 Critical Reading

Most tests contain a critical reading section that measures your ability to read, understand, and interpret passages. The passages may be either fiction or nonfiction, and they can be 100 words or 500 to 800 words. They are drawn from literature, the humanities, social studies, and the natural sciences.

Directions: Read the following passage. Base your answers to questions 1 and 2 on what is stated or implied in the passage.

PASSAGE

Every four years, Greek statesmen and peasants, merchants and philosophers traveled the roads and waterways leading to Olympia. . . . A festival atmosphere prevailed as hawkers peddled their wares, old friends reunited, orators expounded their ideas, and men consumed vast quantities of food and drink. It was noisy, hot, and crowded. Nevertheless, thousands returned time and time again because Olympia offered something unique: the best athletes in the Greek world fighting for supremacy in its most prestigious contest—the Olympic Games. . . .

. . . The competitions celebrated the godlike qualities inherent in man. Victory brought great fame and glory both to the athletes and to their families and hometown. A fifth century B.C. Olympic winner named Diagoras fathered two sons who in turn won Olympic crowns at the 448 B.C. games. The devoted sons placed their wreaths on Diagoras's head and carried him about the stadium on their shoulders. A friend called out as they passed, saying in essence: "Die now, Diagoras, for you have nothing but the heights of Olympus left to scale."

—What Life Was Like at the Dawn of Democracy, *Time-Life Books*

---

① [stem]

1. The (outcome) of the Olympic Games brought ②
   (A) shame to the hometowns of the losers

③ [choices]
   (B) fame and glory to the hometowns of the victors
   (C) fame and fortune to the merchants of Olympia
   (D) war to the towns of the competing athletes ④
   (E) money to the parents of victorious athletes

2. Which statement most likely explains the remark "Die now, Diagoras"? ⑤
   (A) Diagoras's sons shamed him by losing.
   (B) The friend was challenging Diagoras to a duel.
   (C) Diagoras already had achieved great honors.
   (D) Diagoras would die climbing Mount Olympus.
   (E) The friend was from a different city-state.

Tips: Multiple Choice

A multiple-choice question consists of a stem and a set of choices. The stem is usually in the form of a question or an incomplete sentence. One of the choices correctly answers the question or completes the sentence.

① Read the stem carefully and try to answer the question without looking at the choices.

② Pay attention to key words in the stem. They may direct you to the correct answer.

③ Read all of the choices before determining the correct answer.

④ After reading all of the choices, eliminate any that you know are incorrect. In question 1, you can immediately eliminate choice (D), because the passage does not mention this idea.

⑤ Some questions ask you to interpret a statement or figure of speech. In question 2, Diagoras's friend is not ordering him to die. The friend means that no matter how long Diagoras lives, he will never surpass the honors he and his sons earned at the Olympic Games.

Answers: 1 (B), 2 (C)

Directions: Following are two passages from a true story of a black youth's life under South Africa's policy of racial discrimination during the 1970s. Base your answers to questions 1 and 2 on these passages.

PASSAGE 1

❸

I don't believe in schools, woman," my father said emphatically. "Just look at all those so-called educated people. What has education done for them? ❹ They pick garbage, wash cars, work as garden boys and delivery boys." . . .

One of his strong points whenever he argued with my mother about the pros and cons of schooling was that blacks, before the coming of the white man to Africa, had always taught their offspring ways of being useful and productive in the villages while they were still in the cradle, and that by the time boys and girls were five, six, seven, and eight years old they were already making meaningful contributions to tribal society.

—Mark Mathabane, *Kaffir Boy*

PASSAGE 2

"I want you to go to school because I believe that an education is the key you need to open up a new world and a new life for yourself, a world and life different from that of either your father's or mine. It is the only key that can do that, and only those who seek it earnestly and perseveringly will get anywhere in the white man's world. Education will open doors where none ❺ seem to exist."

—Mark Mathabane, *Kaffir Boy*

1. Which statement best describes the two speakers' attitudes toward education? ❶

(A) The speaker in passage 1 thinks that a white person's education is a waste of time for black people. The speaker in passage 2 thinks that education is the key to success in life.

(B) The speaker in passage 1 thinks that education should be free. The speaker in passage 2 thinks that education is worth any price.

(C) The speaker in passage 1 thinks that people should not be overeducated. The speaker in passage 2 thinks that education is only for those who want it.

(D) The speaker in passage 1 thinks that blacks and whites should be educated differently. The speaker in passage 2 thinks that both races should receive an equal education.

(E) The speaker in passage 1 thinks that there are no jobs for black South Africans. The speaker in passage 2 thinks that you can't get ahead in the black world without an education.

2. What does the speaker in passage 2 mean by "Education will open doors where ❶ none seem to exist"?

(A) Education is a one-time opportunity.

(B) Education presents its own obstacles.

(C) Education will open imaginary doors.

(D) People will open the door for educated people.

(E) Education will provide new opportunities.

Tips: Two Passages

❷ Questions are sometimes based on a pair of related passages. The passages might express completely different points of view, or they might explore different aspects of the same subject.

❶ Before reading the passages, skim the questions to see what information you will need. The questions here ask about attitudes toward education. Knowing this, you can focus on the key parts of the passages.

❷ Sometimes, it helps to know the historical context of a passage. The directions may provide that information.

❸ Look for a topic sentence in each passage and ask yourself whether the body of the passage supports or refutes that statement.

❹ Analyze the attitudes that are expressed in the readings. When the speaker in passage 1 calls black people who have gone to school "so-called educated people," he conveys his contempt for the white educational system.

❺ Analyze any figures of speech in the readings. How do the images advance the point of view? The speaker in passage 2 compares education to a key that will open doors.

Answers: 1 (A), 2 (E)

Directions: Read the following passage. Base your answers to questions 1 through 4 on what is stated or implied in the passage.

Now the winter was come upon them. In the forests all summer long, the branches of the trees do battle for light, and some of them lose and die; and then come the raging blasts, and the storms of snow and hail, and strew the ground with these weaker branches. Just so it was in Packingtown; the
5 whole district braced itself for the struggle that was an agony, and those whose time was come died off in hordes. All the year round they had been serving as cogs in the great packing machine; and now was the time for the renovating of it, and the replacing of damaged parts. There came pneumonia and grippe, stalking among them, seeking for weakened constitutions; there
10 was the annual harvest of those whom tuberculosis had been dragging down. There came cruel, cold, and biting winds, and blizzards of snow, all testing relentlessly for failing muscles and impoverished blood. Sooner or later came the day when the unfit one did not report for work; and then, with no time lost in waiting, and no inquiries or regrets, there was a chance for a new
15 hand.

The new hands were here by the thousands. All day long the gates of the packing houses were besieged by starving and penniless men; they came, literally, by the thousands every single morning, fighting with each other for a chance for life. Blizzards and cold made no difference to them, they
20 were always on hand; they were on hand two hours before the sun rose, an hour before the work began. Sometimes their faces froze, sometimes their feet and their hands; sometimes they froze all together—but still they came, for they had no other place to go. One day Durham advertised in the paper for two hundred men to cut ice; and all that day the homeless and starving
25 of the city came trudging through the snow from all over its two hundred square miles. That night forty score of them crowded into the station house of the stockyards district—they filled the rooms, sleeping in each other's laps, toboggan fashion, and they piled on top of each other in the corridors, till the police shut the doors and left some to freeze outside. On the morrow, before
30 daybreak, there were three thousand at Durham's and the police reserves had to be sent for to quell the riot. Then Durham's bosses picked out twenty of the biggest; the "two hundred" proved to have been a printer's error.

—Upton Sinclair, *The Jungle*

Tips: Reading Text

❶ Sometimes, test questions will ask you to interpret an image or comparison. Note how the author uses the first three sentences in the opening paragraph to set up the comparison of trees in the forest to the work situation in Packingtown.

❷ Use words in the passage to help you visualize the people, places, and events as you read. The "cruel wind," "blizzards of snow," and "impoverished blood" depict the harshness of the packinghouse workers' lives.

❸ Analyze the tone of a piece. The author notes that when an unfit worker did not report to work, "there was a chance for a new hand." The stark language conveys the cold reality of survival of the fittest.

❹ Look beyond a literal interpretation. The author writes that the number 200 was a printer's error, but you might consider the possibility that the company had asked for 200 men so that it would have a large pool of applicants from which to pick its 20 men.

Answers: 1 (D), 2 (C), 3 (C), 4 (E)

1. In lines 1–4, the author compares the fallen branches of trees to
   (A) damaged machine parts
   (B) failing muscles
   (C) weak blood
   (D) dying packinghouse workers
   (E) biting winds

2. In line 19, the phrase "a chance for life" refers to
   (A) the decision in a boxing match
   (B) a place out of the cold
   (C) a job in the stockyard district
   (D) recovery from a disease such as tuberculosis
   (E) a life sentence for rioting

3. In line 7, comparing the workers to "cogs in the great packing machine" suggests that they are
   (A) lazy
   (B) well-trained
   (C) replaceable
   (D) unskilled
   (E) mechanized

4. The main idea of this passage is that
   (A) packinghouse workers got sick because they didn't take care of themselves
   (B) unemployed workers were ungrateful for an opportunity to work
   (C) winter was especially cold that year, so many workers were fired
   (D) the great packinghouse machine had many broken parts
   (E) packinghouse owners took advantage of the surplus supply of workers

The critical reading section may feature sentence completion questions that test your knowledge of vocabulary. They may also measure your ability to figure out how different parts of a sentence logically fit together.

Directions: Choose the word or set of words that, when inserted, best fits the meaning of each of the following sentences.

1. *A Christmas Carol* by Charles Dickens illustrates the literary _____ of a man who is driven by _____ greed. ❶
   (A) conflicts . . illicit
   (B) motif . . voracious
   (C) metaphor . . intermittent
   (D) stratagem . . abject
   (E) sophistry . . overweening ❷

2. The Beatles' _____ style of music reflects sounds as _____ as the American blues guitar and the Indian sitar. ❸
   (A) esoteric . . innate
   (B) ephemeral . . ebullient
   (C) incendiary . . potent
   (D) obscure . . ubiquitous
   (E) eclectic . . disparate ❸

3. (Because) they need to be kept _____ , golf courses in arid regions like the American Southwest can _____ water shortages. ❹
   (A) verdant . . exacerbate
   (B) utopian . . presage
   (C) torrid . . ameliorate
   (D) brackish . . effect
   (E) fallow . . instigate

4. Nelson Mandela _____ the movement against apartheid in South Africa.
   (A) gleaned
   (B) permeated
   (C) proscribed
   (D) galvanized ❺
   (E) pillaged

Tips: Sentence Completion

❶ When you are completing sentences with two words missing, look at both blanks and think about what kinds of words will fill them.

❷ If one of the words in an answer choice is wrong, you can eliminate that set of words. In sentence 1, the word *overweening* is an appropriate description of Scrooge's greed, but *sophistry*, a philosophical term, doesn't fit here.

❸ If you don't know the exact meaning of a word, look for clues in the sentence. In sentence 2, the instruments from different cultures are a clue. The prefix *dis-* in the word *disparate* means "apart."

❹ Look for words or phrases that link the ideas in a sentence. The word *because* in sentence 3 indicates a cause-and-effect relationship between golf courses and water shortages.

❺ You might recognize some words from a completely different context. *Galvanize* means "to subject to the action of applying an electric current." Nelson Mandela energized the anti-apartheid movement.

Answers: 1(B), 2 (E), 3 (A), 4 (D)

3 Writing

To measure your ability to express ideas clearly and correctly, tests ask you to identify errors in grammar and usage and to improve sentences and paragraphs.

> **Directions:** Select the one underlined part that must be changed to make the following sentence correct. There is no more than one error in the sentence. If the sentence is correct as written, select answer choice E.

1. When we look at the seven continents today, <u>it's</u> difficult <u>for you</u> to imagine
                 (A) ❷   (B) ❸

 that at one point in the earth's geologic history, they were a <u>contiguous</u> land mass
                                                  (C) ❹

 <u>that</u> was connected by an area called Pangaea. <u>No error</u> ❶
 (D)   (E)

> **Directions:** Determine if the underlined part of the following sentence needs improvement and select the best change presented in the five choices.

2. The national forest system in the United States stretches over 191 million acres, <u>which is including</u> temperate rainforests of the Northwest, the hardwood forests of the Southeast, and high-desert pines of the Great Basin.

 (A) which is including ❺
 (B) which include
 (C) that includes
 (D) including both
 (E) and including

> **Directions:** Read the following passage and answer the question.

> (1) One of New Hampshire's most recognizable residents was the Old Man of the Mountain, a natural rock formation. (2) The profile of the craggy-faced man appears on the reverse of the New Hampshire state quarter, making it America's first two-headed coin. (3) It's a good piece to use in a coin toss. (4) If you call heads, you're sure to win!

3. What is the *best* way to combine sentences 3 and 4? ❻

 (A) It's a good piece to use in a coin toss, because if you call heads you're sure to win.
 (B) It's a good piece to use in a coin toss, if you call heads you're sure to win.
 (C) It's a good piece to use in a coin toss if you call heads; you're sure to win.
 (D) If you call heads you're sure to win because this is a good piece to use in a coin toss.
 (E) Knowing that if you call heads you're sure to win makes it a good piece to use in a coin toss.

Tips: Grammar and Style

❶ Read the entire sentence or passage to grasp its overall meaning. Pay particular attention to any underlined portions.

❷ Misuse of the apostrophe in *its* and *it's* is a common grammatical error. The usage is correct in sentence 1.

❸ A good sentence maintains a consistent point of view. If the subject of one clause is *we*, it should be carried through in the next clause.

❹ Use prefixes to aid your reading comprehension. You may not know what *contiguous* means in sentence 1, but if you know that the prefix *con-* means "together," you can figure out that the land masses were joined in some way.

❺ In choosing a revision, read through all of the choices before you decide which one is best. Choose answer (A) only if the sentence is correct as it appears originally.

❻ To combine sentences, determine how ideas are related. Are they contrasting ideas? Do they express a cause-and-effect relationship? Are they chronological?

Answers: 1 (B), 2 (B), 3 (A)

Some tests may measure your understanding of a passage by asking you to write a response.

> **Directions:** Read the passage. Then follow the directions.

> Back then, boys could learn by working on their cars without expensive tools, computers, and complex training, and any who discovered their mechanical talents followed their fathers happily into the factories, where they found financial security, a sense of professionalism, and a pathway up. Michael Summers was young, but he had a sense of that history, and he missed it. "Kids today do not have the ability to work on mechanical things," he said. "We're in a throwaway society where the lawn mower breaks, you don't tear apart this little two-cycle engine. You throw it out and you get another one. . . . [We have a] shortage of tool and dye makers and fluid power mechanics, the guys who are basically screwing things together and building systems. People who are good at that are good because they like it, they have an aptitude for it, and they've had exposure to it. There are a lot of kids who would be good at it, but they have no clue that they have mechanical interest."
>
> —David Shipler, *The Working Poor*

SHORT CONSTRUCTED RESPONSE

Give a short definition of a throwaway society.

> **SAMPLE SHORT CONSTRUCTED RESPONSE**
>
> A throwaway society is one in which things are used just a few times and then thrown away. A good example is the disposable DVD, which automatically erases so that you can't view it again. **❶**

EXTENDED CONSTRUCTED RESPONSE

In the passage, Michael Summers argues that kids today never get the chance to discover whether they have an aptitude for fixing things. Explain in one or two paragraphs why you agree or disagree with him. **❷**

> **SAMPLE EXTENDED CONSTRUCTED RESPONSE**
>
> I agree that young people today are not learning traditional manual skills, but we do have opportunities to figure out how things work. Today we use different tools. **❸**
>
> With computers, we can learn about anything we are interested in and even get hands-on experience. Last year I searched the Internet to find out how windmills produce electricity. With that information I designed a model windmill that I entered into a science fair. A friend of mine in the school orchestra downloaded an inexpensive computer program for composing music. He was able to compose a sonata for violin. **❸ ❹**
>
> Computers can give you experience in figuring things out. With experience comes confidence in your own abilities.

Tips: Responding to Writing Prompts

❶ Short-constructed-response prompts are often fact based rather than interpretive. Get to the point in your answer, and stick to the facts.

❷ Make sure you write about the assigned topic. If you are asked to agree or disagree with a passage, don't just restate the author's arguments. Develop your own point of view and support it with examples.

❸ When you are writing an extended constructed response, build your paragraphs around clear topic sentences that will pull your ideas together.

❹ Don't try to cover the entire subject in your response. Focus on one or two main points.

❺ Proofread your response for errors in capitalization, punctuation, spelling, and grammar.

4 Essay

To determine how well you can develop and support your thoughts, many tests ask you to write an essay in response to an assignment, or prompt. The essay will represent a first draft and will be scored based on the following:

- **Focus** Establish a point of view in the opening paragraph.
- **Organization** Maintain a logical progression of ideas.
- **Support for Ideas** Use details and examples to develop an argument.
- **Style/Word Choice** Use words accurately and vary sentences.
- **Grammar** Use standard English and proofread for errors.

Think carefully about the issue presented in these quotations and the assignment that follows.

> The fact is there is a responsible case to be made for driving SUVs. It can be summed up in three words: "This is America."
>
> —Reg Henry, *Pittsburgh Post-Gazette*
>
> If you buy an SUV, you're buying your safety at the expense of another's. Hit someone and you'll kill them.
>
> —Randy Cohen, *New York Times*

Assignment: What is your view on the idea that sport utility vehicles (SUVs) are being driven on city streets and highways?

SAMPLE ESSAY

Today, light trucks and sport utility vehicles (SUVs) account for nearly half of all new vehicle sales. Although there are some legitimate uses for these oversized vehicles, they are generally unnecessary for today's city and suburban lifestyle. ①

Sport utility vehicles are designed for off-road travel. That means dirt roads and other rugged terrain. The elevated chassis, four-wheel drive, and heavier body are wasted on the paved streets and highways that we use to get to work or to the shopping malls. Even when we travel across the country, we ride on a system of well-maintained highways. ②

Some people say SUVs are safer because of their size and weight. That's true only if you are in the SUV. In fact, the bigger vehicles pose a serious risk to the dwindling number of people who still drive compact cars. In a side impact crash, the driver of an SUV might not even be scratched, but the people in the sedan will be severely injured or killed. ③

The strongest argument against SUVs is environmental. The law allows SUVs to have far worse fuel economy than regular-size cars, and they do. Many popular SUVs get only 12 to 15 miles per gallon of gas. The law also allows SUVs to emit higher levels of toxic pollution.

SUVs have their place, but many of them are not being used appropriately. If we can't convince people not to buy big vehicles they don't need, we can certainly improve the SUVs' fuel economy and emissions. ④

Tips: Writing an Essay

The SAT allows only 25 minutes for you to write an essay. So before you begin writing, take a few minutes to gather your thoughts. Write down the main points you want to make. Allow time to reread your essay before you hand it in. Make sure your handwriting is legible.

① When you're writing a persuasive essay, state your point of view in the introduction.

② Concrete examples make your writing come to life, no matter what the topic is. Use examples in the body of your essay to clarify your points and strengthen your arguments. The writer of this essay uses facts and personal observations to bolster the arguments.

③ Take the opposing point of view into consideration and respond to it.

④ Make sure your essay has a conclusion, even if it's just a single sentence. A conclusion pulls your ideas together and lets the reader know you have finished.

⑤ Allow enough time to reread what you have written. If you have to make a correction, do so neatly and legibly.

Glossary of Literary & Nonfiction Terms

Act An act is a major division within a play, similar to a chapter in a book. Each act may be further divided into smaller sections, called scenes. Plays can have as many as five acts, as in Shakespeare's *Julius Caesar*. Anton Chekhov's *A Marriage Proposal* is a one-act play.

Allegory An allegory is a work with two levels of meaning—a literal one and a symbolic one. In such a work, most of the characters, objects, settings, and events represent abstract qualities. Personification is often used in traditional allegories. As in a fable or a parable, the purpose of an allegory may be to convey truths about life, to teach religious or moral lessons, or to criticize social institutions.

Alliteration Alliteration is the repetition of consonant sounds at the beginning of words. Note the repetition of the *h* and *s* sounds in these lines.

> Mother whose heart hung humble as a button
> On the bright splendid shroud of your son,
> —Stephen Crane,
> "Do not weep, maiden, for war is kind"

See pages 478, 772.
See also **Consonance.**

Allusion An allusion is an indirect reference to a famous person, place, event, or literary work. The title of Stephen Vincent Benét's "By the Waters of Babylon" is an allusion to the beginning of Psalm 137 in the Bible: "By the rivers of Babylon, there we sat down, yea, we wept, when we remembered Zion."
See page 310.

Analogy An analogy is a point-by-point comparison between two things that are alike in some respect. Often, writers use analogies in nonfiction to explain unfamiliar subjects or ideas in terms of familiar ones.
See also **Extended Metaphor; Metaphor; Simile.**

Antagonist An antagonist is a principal character or force in opposition to a **protagonist,** or main character. The antagonist is usually another character but sometimes can be a force of nature, a set of circumstances, some aspect of society, or a force within the protagonist. In Guy de Maupassant's "Two Friends," the German officer who encounters the fishermen is the main antagonist. In Isabel Allende's "And of Clay Are We Created," the destructive force unleashed by the volcano may be considered an antagonist.
See pages 79, 438, 584.

Archetype An archetype is a pattern in literature that is found in a variety of works from different cultures throughout the ages. An archetype can be a plot, a character, an image, or a setting. For example, the association of death and rebirth with winter and spring is an archetype common to many cultures.

Argumentative Essay *See* **Essay.**

Aside In drama, an aside is a short speech directed to the audience, or another character, that is not heard by the other characters on stage. In the following example from *Julius Caesar,* the aside reveals Trebonius' murderous intentions after Caesar has asked him to stand near him in the Forum:

> Trebonius. Caesar, I will. [*aside*] And so near will I be
> That your best friends shall wish I had been further.
> —William Shakespeare, *Julius Caesar*

See pages 259, 1198.
See also **Soliloquy.**

Assonance Assonance is the repetition of vowel sounds within nonrhyming words. An example of assonance is the repetition of the short *u* sound in the following line.

> He hung a grunting weight,
> —Elizabeth Bishop, "The Fish"

Author's Perspective An author's perspective or point of view is a unique combination of ideas, values, feelings, and beliefs that influences the way the writer looks at a topic. **Tone,** or attitude, often reveals an author's perspective. In "A Chip of Glass Ruby," Nadine Gordimer writes from a perspective that reflects her experiences as a South African.
See pages 239, 526, 585, 696.
See also **Author's Purpose; Tone.**

Author's Purpose A writer usually writes for one or more of these purposes: to express thoughts or feelings, to inform or explain, to persuade, or to entertain. For example, David McCullough's purpose for writing *The Johnstown Flood* is to inform readers of a natural phenomenon that made history.
See also **Author's Perspective.**

Autobiography An autobiography is a writer's account of his or her own life. In almost every case, it is told from the first-person point of view. Generally, an autobiography focuses on the most significant events and people in the writer's life over a period of time. Shorter

autobiographical narratives include **journals, diaries,** and **letters.** An **autobiographical essay,** another type of short autobiographical work, focuses on a single person or event in the writer's life. Examples of autobiographical writing include Jeanne Wakatsuki Houston's *Farewell to Manzanar* and Coretta Scott King's *Montgomery Boycott.*

See pages 952, 968.

See also **Memoir.**

Ballad A ballad is a type of narrative poem that tells a story and was originally meant to be sung or recited. Because it tells a story, a ballad has a setting, a plot, and characters. **Traditional ballads** are written in four-line stanzas with regular rhythm and rhyme. **Folk ballads** were composed orally and handed down by word of mouth. These ballads usually tell about ordinary people who have unusual adventures or perform daring deeds. A **literary ballad** is a poem written by a poet in imitation of the form and content of a folk ballad. "Lord Randall" is an example of a traditional ballad.

Biography A biography is the true account of a person's life, written by another person. As such, a biography is usually told from a third-person point of view. The writer of a biography usually researches his or her subject in order to present accurate information. The best biographers strive for honesty and balance in their accounts of their subjects' lives.

Blank Verse Blank verse is unrhymed poetry written in **iambic pentameter.** That is, each line of blank verse has five pairs of syllables. In most pairs, an unstressed syllable is followed by a stressed syllable. The most versatile of poetic forms, blank verse imitates the natural rhythms of English speech.

Much of Shakespeare's drama is in blank verse. The following lines, spoken by the conspirator Casca, describe one of the wonders Casca observed during the storm on the night before Caesar's assassination. Note the iambic pentameter and the lack of end rhyme.

> Ă commŏn slăve—yŏu knŏw hĭm wĕll bў sĩght—
> Hĕld ŭp hĭs lĕft hănd, whĭch dĭd flăme ănd bŭrn
> —William Shakespeare, *Julius Caesar*

See also **Iambic Pentameter.**

Cast of Characters In the script of a play, a cast of characters is a list of all the characters in the play, usually in order of appearance. It may include a brief description of each character.

Central Idea *See* **Theme.**

Character Characters are the individuals who participate in the action of a literary work. Like real people, characters display certain qualities, or **character traits;** they develop and change over time; and they usually have **motivations,** or reasons, for their behaviors. Complex characters can have multiple or conflicting motivations.

Main characters: Main characters are the most important characters in literary works. Generally, the plot of a short story focuses on one main character, but a novel may have several main characters.

Minor characters: The less prominent characters in a literary work are known as minor characters. Minor characters support the plot. The story is not centered on them, but they help carry out the action of the story and help the reader learn more about the main character.

Dynamic character: A dynamic character is one who undergoes important changes as a plot unfolds. The changes occur because of his or her actions and experiences in the story. The change is usually internal and may be good or bad. Main characters are usually, though not always, dynamic.

Static character: A static character is one who remains the same throughout a story. The character may experience events and have interactions with other characters, but he or she is not changed because of them.

Round character: A round character is one who is complex and highly developed and has a variety of traits and different sides to his or her personality. Some of the traits may create conflict in the character. Round characters tend to display strengths, weaknesses, and a full range of emotions. The writer provides enough detail for the reader to understand their feelings and emotions.

Flat character: A flat character is one who is not highly developed. A flat character is a one-sided character: he or she usually has one outstanding trait, characteristic, or role. Flat characters exist mainly to advance the plot, and they display only the traits needed for their limited roles. Minor characters are usually flat characters.

See page 174.

See also **Characterization.**

Characterization The way a writer creates and develops characters' personalities is known as characterization. There are four basic methods of characterization:

- The writer may make direct comments about a character's personality or nature through the voice of the narrator.
- The writer may describe the character's physical appearance.

- The writer may present the character's own thoughts, speech, and actions.
- The writer may present pertinent thoughts, speech, and actions of other characters.

See pages 176, 227.

See also **Character.**

Chorus In the theater of ancient Greece, the chorus was a group of actors who commented on the action of the play. Between scenes the chorus sang and danced to musical accompaniment in the orchestra—the circular floor between the stage and the audience—giving insights into the message of the play. The chorus is often considered a kind of ideal spectator, representing the response of ordinary citizens to the tragic events that unfold. In Sophocles' *Antigone,* the chorus represents the leading citizens of Thebes.

See pages 1058, 1059, 1064, 1066.

See also **Drama.**

Climax In a plot, the climax is the point of maximum interest or tension. Usually the climax is a turning point in the story, after the reader has understood the **conflict** and become emotionally involved with the characters. The climax sometimes, but not always, points to the **resolution** of the conflict.

Example: In Stephen Vincent Benét's "By the Waters of Babylon," John's discovery of the dead "god" can be considered the climax of the story. As a result of his discovery, John realizes the truth about the past.

See pages 30, 308.

See also **Plot.**

Comedy A comedy is a dramatic work that is light and often humorous in tone, usually ending happily with a peaceful resolution of the main conflict. A comedy differs from a farce by having a more believable plot, more realistic characters, and less boisterous behavior.

Comic Relief Comic relief consists of humorous scenes, incidents, or speeches that are included in a serious drama to provide a reduction in emotional intensity. Because it breaks the tension, comic relief allows an audience to prepare emotionally for events to come. In many of Shakespeare's plays, comic relief is provided by a fool or through scenes with servants or common folk.

Complex Character *See* **Character.**

Complication A complication is an additional factor or problem introduced into the rising action of a story to make the conflict more difficult. Often, a plot complication makes it seem as though the main character is getting farther away from the thing he or she wants.

Conflict A conflict is a struggle between opposing forces. Almost every story has a main conflict—a conflict that is the story's focus. An **external conflict** involves a character pitted against an outside force, such as nature, a physical obstacle, or another character. An **internal conflict** is one that occurs within a character.

Examples: In "To Build a Fire," the man and the dog are in conflict with the external environment. At the same time, the man experiences internal conflict as he tries to think of ways he might be able to survive this extreme setting. In some stories, such as Chinua Achebe's "Marriage Is a Private Affair," the source of the conflict is cultural; that is, it arises from differences in beliefs and values.

See pages 30, 37, 78, 984.

See also **Plot.**

Connotation A connotation is an attitude or a feeling associated with a word, in contrast to the word's **denotation,** which is its literal, or dictionary, meaning. The connotations of a word may be positive or negative. For example, *enthusiastic* has positive associations, while *rowdy* has negative ones. Connotations of words can have an important influence on style and meaning and are particularly important in poetry.

Consonance Consonance is the repetition of consonant sounds within and at the end of words, as in "lonely afternoon." Consonance is unlike rhyme in that the vowel sounds preceding or following the repeated consonant sounds differ. Consonance is often used together with **alliteration, assonance,** and **rhyme** to create a musical quality, to emphasize certain words, or to unify a poem.

See also **Alliteration.**

Couplet A couplet is a rhymed pair of lines. A couplet may be written in any rhythmic pattern.

> So long as men can breathe, or eyes can see,
> So long lives this, and this gives life to thee.
> —William Shakespeare, "Sonnet 18"

See also **Stanza.**

Critical Essay *See* **Essay.**

Denotation *See* **Connotation.**

Dénouement *See* **Falling Action.**

Dialect A dialect is a form of language that is spoken in a particular geographic area or by a particular social or ethnic group. A group's dialect is reflected in its pronunciations,

vocabulary, expressions, and grammatical structures. Writers use dialects to capture the flavors of locales and to bring characters to life, re-creating the way they actually speak.

Dialogue Dialogue is written conversation between two or more characters. Writers use dialogue to bring characters to life and to give readers insights into the characters' qualities, traits, and reactions to other characters. Realistic, well-paced dialogue also advances the plot of a narrative. In fiction, dialogue is usually set off with quotation marks. In drama, stories are told primarily through dialogue. Playwrights use stage directions to indicate how they intend the dialogue to be interpreted by actors.

Diary A diary is a daily record of a writer's thoughts, experiences, and feelings. As such, it is a type of autobiographical writing. The terms *diary* and *journal* are often used synonymously.

Diction A writer's or speaker's choice of words and way of arranging the words in sentences is called diction. Diction can be broadly characterized as formal or informal. It can also be described as technical or common, abstract or concrete, and literal or figurative. A writer for *Scientific American* would use a more formal, technical, and possibly abstract diction than would a writer for the science section of a local newspaper.
See pages 533, 852.
See also **Style.**

Drama Drama is literature in which plots and characters are developed through dialogue and action; in other words, it is literature in play form. Drama is meant to be performed. Stage plays, radio plays, movies, and television programs are types of drama. Most plays are divided into acts, with each act having an emotional peak, or climax. Certain modern plays, such as *A Marriage Proposal*, have only one act. Most plays contain stage directions, which describe settings, lighting, sound effects, the movements and emotions of actors, and the ways in which dialogue should be spoken.

Dramatic Irony *See* **Irony.**

Dramatic Monologue A dramatic monologue is a lyric poem in which a speaker addresses a silent or absent listener in a moment of high intensity or deep emotion, as if engaged in private conversation. The speaker proceeds without interruption or argument, and the effect on the reader is that of hearing just one side of a conversation. This technique allows the poet to focus on the feelings, personality, and motivations of the speaker. "Exile" by Julia Alvarez is a dramatic monologue.
See page 140.
See also **Lyric Poetry; Soliloquy.**

Dynamic Character *See* **Character.**

Elegy An elegy is an extended meditative poem in which the speaker reflects on death—often in tribute to a person who has died recently—or on an equally serious subject. Most elegies are written in formal, dignified language and are serious in tone.

Epic An epic is a long narrative poem on a serious subject, presented in an elevated or formal style. It traces the adventures of a great hero whose actions reflect the ideals and values of a nation or race. Epics address universal concerns, such as good and evil, life and death, and sin and redemption. Homer's *Iliad* and *Odyssey* are famous epics in the Western tradition. The *Ramayana* is a great epic of India.

Epic Hero An epic hero is a larger-than-life figure who embodies the ideals of a nation or race. Epic heroes take part in dangerous adventures and accomplish great deeds. Many undertake long, difficult journeys and display great courage and superhuman strength.

Essay An essay is a short work of nonfiction that deals with a single subject. Some essays are **formal**—that is, tightly structured and written in an impersonal style. Others are **informal,** with a looser structure and a more personal style. Generally, an **informative** or **expository essay** presents or explains information and ideas. A **personal essay** is typically an informal essay in which the writer expresses his or her thoughts and feelings about a subject, focusing on the meaning of events and issues in his or her own life. In a **reflective essay,** the author makes a connection between a personal observation or experience and a universal idea, such as love, courage, or freedom. A **critical essay** evaluates a situation, a course of action, or a work of art. In an **argumentative** or **persuasive essay,** the author attempts to convince readers to adopt a certain viewpoint or to take a particular stand.
Examples: E. M. Forster's essay "Tolerance" seeks to persuade its audience to adopt a different attitude toward people around the world. In "The Man in the Water," Roger Rosenblatt reflects on current events and therefore combines qualities of both the reflective and expository essays.
See pages 374, 482.

Exposition Exposition is the first stage of a typical story plot. The exposition provides important background information and introduces the setting and the important characters. The conflict the characters face may also be introduced in the exposition, or it may be introduced later, in the rising action.
See page 30.
See also **Plot.**

Expository Essay *See* **Essay.**

Extended Metaphor An extended metaphor is a figure of speech that compares two essentially unlike things at some length and in several ways. It does not contain the word *like* or *as*. For example, Shakespeare makes a comparison between ambition and a ladder in this extended metaphor:

> That lowliness is young ambition's ladder,
> Whereto the climber-upward turns his face;
> But when he once attains the upmost round,
> He then unto the ladder turns his back,
> Looks in the clouds, scorning the base degrees
> By which he did ascend.
> —William Shakespeare, *Julius Caesar*

See also **Metaphor.**

External Conflict *See* **Conflict.**

Fable A fable is a brief tale told to illustrate a moral or teach a lesson. Often the moral of a fable appears in a distinct and memorable statement near the tale's beginning or end.

Falling Action In a plot, the falling action follows the climax and shows the results of the important decision or action that happened at the climax. Tension eases as the falling action begins; however, the final outcome of the story is not yet fully worked out at this stage. Events in the falling action lead to the **resolution,** or **dénouement,** of the plot.
Example: In Stephen Vincent Benét's "By the Waters of Babylon," the falling action occurs after the main character has discovered the dead "god." During the falling action, John realizes the truth about the past and the destruction of a way of life.
See pages 30, 308.
See also **Climax; Plot.**

Fantasy Fantasy is a type of fiction that is highly imaginative and portrays events, settings, or characters that are unrealistic. The setting might be a nonexistent world, the plot might involve magic or the supernatural, and the characters might employ superhuman powers.

Farce Farce is a type of exaggerated comedy that features an absurd plot, ridiculous situations, and humorous dialogue. The main purpose of a farce is to keep an audience laughing. The characters are usually stereotypes, or simplified examples of individual traits or qualities. Comic devices typically used in farces include mistaken identity, deception, physical comedy, wordplay—such as puns and double meanings—and exaggeration. Anton Chekhov's *A Marriage Proposal* is an example of a farce.

Fiction Fiction is prose writing that consists of imaginary elements. Although fiction can be inspired by actual events and real people, it usually springs from writers' imaginations. The basic elements of fiction are plot, character, setting, and theme. The novel and the short story are forms of fiction.
See also **Character; Novel; Plot; Setting; Short Story; Theme.**

Figurative Language Figurative language is language that communicates meanings beyond the literal meanings of the words. In figurative language, words are often used to symbolize ideas and concepts they would not otherwise be associated with. Writers use figurative language to create effects, to emphasize ideas, and to evoke emotions. Simile, metaphor, extended metaphor, hyperbole, and personification are examples of figurative language.
Example: The narrator in Alice Walker's "Everyday Use" says of Dee's hair, "It stands straight up like the wool on a sheep. It is black as night and around the edges are two long pigtails that rope around like small lizards disappearing behind her ears." Obviously, Dee's pigtails do not literally move like lizards, but the passage vividly suggests the look of Dee's hair.
See pages 48, 140, 774, 786, 877.
See also **Hyperbole; Metaphor; Onomatopoeia; Personification; Simile.**

Figure of Speech *See* **Figurative Language; Hyperbole; Metaphor; Personification; Simile; Understatement.**

First-Person Point of View *See* **Point of View.**

Flashback A flashback is an account of a conversation, an episode, or an event that happened before the beginning of a story. Often a flashback interrupts the chronological flow of a story to give the reader information needed for the understanding of a character's present situation. Haruki Marakami's "The Seventh Man" is told almost exclusively through flashback. Flashbacks can help create such effects as mystery, tension, or surprise.

Foil A foil is a character who provides a striking contrast to another character. By using a foil, a writer can call attention to certain traits possessed by a main character or simply enhance a character by contrast.

Foreshadowing Foreshadowing is a writer's use of hints or clues to suggest events that will occur later in a story. The hints and clues might be included in a character's dialogue or behavior, or they might be included in details of description. Foreshadowing can create mystery, suspense, or surprise, and make readers eager to find out what will happen.

Form *Form* refers to the principles of arrangement in a poem—the ways in which lines are organized. Form in poetry includes the following elements: the length of lines, the placement of lines, and the grouping of lines into stanzas.
See also **Stanza.**

Frame Story A frame story exists when a story is told within a narrative setting, or "frame"; it creates a story within a story. This storytelling technique has been used for over one thousand years and was employed in famous works such as *One Thousand and One Arabian Nights* and Geoffrey Chaucer's *The Canterbury Tales.*

Free Verse Free verse is poetry that does not contain regular patterns of rhythm or rhyme. The lines in free verse often flow more naturally than do rhymed, metrical lines and thus achieve a rhythm more like that of everyday speech. Although free verse lacks conventional meter, it may contain various rhythmic and sound effects, such as repetitions of syllables or words. Free verse can be used for a variety of subjects. Elizabeth Bishop's poem "The Fish" is one of several examples of free verse included in this book.
See pages 770, 794, 878.
See also **Meter; Rhyme.**

Genre The term *genre* refers to a category in which a work of literature is classified. The major genres in literature are fiction, nonfiction, poetry, and drama.

Haiku Haiku is a form of Japanese poetry in which 17 syllables are arranged in three lines of 5, 7, and 5 syllables. The rules of haiku are strict. In addition to the syllabic count, the poet must create a clear picture that will evoke a strong emotional response in the reader. Nature is a particularly important source of inspiration for Japanese haiku poets, and details from nature are often the subjects of their poems.

Hero A hero is a main character or protagonist in a story. In older literary works, heroes tend to be better than ordinary humans. They are typically courageous, strong, honorable, and intelligent. They are protectors of society who hold back the forces of evil and fight to make the world a better place.

The term **tragic hero,** first used by the Greek philosopher Aristotle, refers to a central character in a drama who is dignified or noble. According to Aristotle, a tragic hero possesses a defect, or **tragic flaw,** that brings about or contributes to his or her downfall. This flaw may be poor judgment, pride, weakness, or an excess of an admirable quality. The tragic hero, noted Aristotle, recognizes his or her own flaw and its consequences, but only after it is too late to change the course of events. Brutus is often considered the tragic hero of Julius Caesar.

The term **cultural hero** refers to a hero who represents the values of his or her culture. King Arthur, for example, represents the physical courage, moral leadership, and loyalty that were valued in Anglo-Saxon society. Antigone can also be considered a cultural hero because her sense of duty to family and the gods, as well as her courage, reflects the values of ancient Greece.
See pages 1058, 1064.
See also **Tragedy.**

Historical Fiction A short story or novel can be classified as historical fiction when the settings and details of the plot include real places and real events of historical importance. Historical figures may appear as major or minor characters, as Napoleon does in Leo Tolstoy's classic novel *War and Peace.* In historical fiction, the setting generally influences the plot in important ways.

Horror Fiction Horror fiction contains strange, mysterious, violent, and often supernatural events that create suspense and terror in the reader. Edgar Allan Poe is an author famous for his horror fiction.

Humor In literature, there are three basic types of humor, all of which may involve exaggeration or irony. **Humor of situation** arises out of the plot of a work. It usually involves exaggerated events or situational irony, which arises when something happens that is different from what was expected. **Humor of character** is often based on exaggerated personalities or on characters' failure to recognize their own flaws, a form of dramatic irony. **Humor of language** may include sarcasm, exaggeration, puns, or verbal irony, in which what is said is not what is meant.
See also **Irony.**

Hyperbole Hyperbole is a figure of speech in which the truth is exaggerated for emphasis or humorous effect. The expression "I'm so hungry I could eat a horse" is an example of hyperbole.

Iambic Pentameter Iambic pentameter is a metrical pattern of five feet, or units, each of which is made up of two syllables, the first unstressed and the second stressed. Iambic

pentameter is the most common meter used in English poetry; it is the meter used in blank verse and in the sonnet. The following lines are examples of iambic pentameter.

> Thĭs wăs ăn ĭll bĕgīnnĭng ŏf thĕ nīght!
> —William Shakespeare, *Julius Caesar*

See pages 810, 1192.
See also **Blank Verse; Sonnet.**

Idiom An idiom is a common figure of speech whose meaning is different from the literal meaning of its words. For example, the phrase "raining cats and dogs" does not literally mean that cats and dogs are falling from the sky; the expression means "raining heavily."

Imagery Imagery consists of descriptive words and phrases that re-create sensory experiences for the reader. Imagery usually appeals to one or more of the five senses—sight, hearing, smell, taste, and touch—to help the reader imagine exactly what is being described. In D. H. Lawrence's "Piano," the phrase "the boom of the tingling strings" appeals to the sense of hearing and touch.

See pages 253, 539, 772, 852.

Informative Essay *See* **Essay.**

Internal Conflict *See* **Conflict.**

Interview An interview is a conversation conducted by a writer or a reporter, in which facts or statements are elicited from another person, recorded, and then broadcast or published. "Jhumpa Lahiri: Pulitzer Prize Winner" is an example of an interview.
See page 470.

Irony Irony **is a special kind of contrast between appearance and reality—usually one in which reality is the opposite of what it seems.** One type of irony is **situational irony,** a contrast between what a reader or character expects and what actually exists or happens. Another type of irony is **dramatic irony,** where the reader or viewer knows something that a character does not know. **Verbal irony** exists when someone knowingly exaggerates or says one thing and means another.
Examples: In Guy de Maupassant's "Two Friends," the reader expects the Frenchmen to eat the fish they have caught. However, it is the German officer who eats the fish, after he executes the men (**situational irony**). Julius Caesar goes to the Senate on the Ides of March in the belief that he may receive the crown. The audience knows, however, that the conspirators are planning his assassination (**dramatic irony**).

The speaker in Stephen Crane's famous war poem "Do not weep, maiden . . ." continually repeats that "war is kind" while presenting images that suggest quite the opposite (**verbal irony**).
See pages 438, 476, 1198.

Journal *See* **Diary.**

Legend A legend is a story handed down from the past, especially one that is popularly believed to be based on historical events. Though legends often incorporate supernatural or magical elements, they claim to be the story of a real human being and are often set in a particular time and place. These characteristics separate a legend from a myth. The story of the rise and fall of King Arthur is a famous example of a legend.
See pages 1111, 1130.
See also **Myth.**

Limited Point of View *See* **Point of View.**

Line The line is the core unit of a poem. In poetry, line length is an essential element of the poem's meaning and rhythm. **Line breaks,** where a line of poetry ends, may coincide with grammatical units. However, a line break may also occur in the middle of a grammatical or syntactical unit, creating a meaningful pause or emphasis. Poets use a variety of line breaks to play with sense, grammar, and syntax and thereby create a wide range of effects.

Literary Criticism Literary criticism is a form of writing in which works of literature are compared, analyzed, interpreted, or evaluated. Two common forms of literary criticism are book reviews and critical essays.

Literary Nonfiction Literary nonfiction is nonfiction that is recognized as being of artistic value or that is about literature. Autobiographies, biographies, essays, and eloquent speeches typically fall into this category.

Lyric Poetry A lyric poem is a short poem in which a single speaker expresses personal thoughts and feelings. Most poems other than dramatic and narrative poems are lyric poems. In ancient Greece, lyric poetry was meant to be sung. Modern lyrics are usually not intended for singing, but they are characterized by strong melodic rhythms. Lyric poetry has a variety of forms and covers many subjects, from love and death to everyday experiences.

Magical Realism Magical realism is a literary genre that combines fantastic or magical events with realistic occurrences in a matter-of-fact way to delight or surprise the reader. A famous example of magical realism is Gabriel García Márquez's novel *One Hundred Years of Solitude.*

Memoir A memoir is a form of autobiographical writing in which a writer shares his or her personal experiences and observations of significant events or people. Often informal or even intimate in tone, memoirs usually give readers insight into the impact of historical events on people's lives. Coretta Scott King's "Montgomery Boycott" is an example of a memoir.

See pages 940, 952, 968.

See also **Autobiography.**

Metaphor A metaphor is a figure of speech that makes a comparison between two things that are basically unlike but have something in common. Unlike similes, metaphors do not contain the word *like* or *as*. In "By the Waters of Babylon" by Stephen Vincent Benét, the narrator uses the metaphor "Truth is a hard deer to hunt" to convey his difficulty in finding out what really happened in the Place of the Gods.

See also **Extended Metaphor; Figurative Language; Simile.**

Meter Meter is a regular pattern of stressed and unstressed syllables in a poem. The meter of a poem emphasizes the musical quality of the language. Each unit of meter, known as a **foot,** consists of one stressed syllable and one or two unstressed syllables. In representations of meter, a stressed syllable is indicated by the symbol ´; an unstressed syllable, by the symbol ˘. The four basic types of metrical feet are the **iamb,** an unstressed syllable followed by a stressed syllable (˘´); the **trochee,** a stressed syllable followed by an unstressed syllable (´˘); the **anapest,** two unstressed syllables followed by a stressed syllable (˘˘´); and the **dactyl,** a stressed syllable followed by two unstressed syllables (´˘˘).

See pages 772, 810, 1192.

See also **Rhythm.**

Mise en Scène *Mise en scène* is a term from the French that refers to the various physical aspects of a dramatic presentation, such as lighting, costumes, scenery, makeup, and props.

Mood In a literary work, mood is the feeling or atmosphere that a writer creates for the reader. Descriptive words, imagery, and figurative language contribute to the mood of a work, as do the sound and rhythm of the language used. In "The Pit and the Pendulum," Edgar Allan Poe creates a mood of dread and horror.

See pages 28, 65, 107.

See also **Tone.**

Motivation *See* **Character.**

Myth A myth is a traditional story, usually concerning some superhuman being or unlikely event, that was once widely believed to be true. Frequently, myths were attempts to explain natural phenomena, such as solar and lunar eclipses or the cycle of the seasons. For some peoples, myths were both a kind of science and a religion. In addition, myths served as literature and entertainment, just as they do for modern-day audiences.

Many classical Greek dramas were based on myths that would have been familiar to audiences in ancient Greece. The origins of *Antigone,* for example, can be traced to myths about the family of King Oedipus.

Narrative Nonfiction Narrative nonfiction is writing that reads much like fiction, except that the characters, setting, and plot are real rather than imaginary. Its purpose is usually to entertain or to express opinions or feelings. Narrative nonfiction includes, but is not limited to, autobiographies, biographies, memoirs, diaries, and journals.

Narrative Poetry Narrative poetry tells a story or recounts events. Like a short story or a novel, a narrative poem has the following elements: plot, characters, setting, and theme. Joy Harjo's poem "Crossing the Border" is a narrative poem.

Narrator The narrator of a story is the character or voice that relates the story's events to the reader.

See also **Persona; Point of View.**

Nonfiction Nonfiction is writing that tells about real people, places, and events. Unlike fiction, nonfiction is mainly written to convey factual information, although writers of nonfiction shape information in accordance with their own purposes and attitudes. Nonfiction can be a good source of information, but readers frequently have to examine it carefully in order to detect biases, notice gaps in the information provided, and identify errors in logic. Nonfiction includes a diverse range of writing—newspaper articles, letters, essays, biographies, movie reviews, speeches, true-life adventure stories, advertising, and more.

Novel A novel is an extended work of fiction. Like a short story, a novel is essentially the product of a writer's imagination. Because a novel is considerably longer than a short story, a novelist can develop a wider range of characters and a more complex plot. George Orwell's *Animal Farm* is an example of a novel.

GLOSSARY OF LITERARY & NONFICTION TERMS R109

Novella A novella is a work of fiction that is longer than a short story but shorter than a novel. A novella differs from a novel in that it concentrates on a limited cast of characters, a relatively short time span, and a single chain of events. The novella is an attempt to combine the compression of the short story with the development of the novel.

Ode An ode is a complex lyric poem that develops a serious and dignified theme. Odes appeal to both the imagination and the intellect, and many commemorate events or praise people or elements of nature.

Omniscient Point of View *See* **Point of View.**

Onomatopoeia Onomatopoeia is the use of words whose sounds echo their meanings, such as *buzz, whisper, gargle,* and *murmur*. Onomatopoeia as a literary technique goes beyond the use of simple echoic words, however. Skilled writers, especially poets, choose words whose sounds intensify images and suggest meanings. In "The Sound of Night," for example, Maxine Kumin makes use of words such as *skitter* and *prink* to add sensory richness to the natural scene she describes.

Oxymoron An oxymoron is a special kind of concise paradox that brings together two contradictory terms, such as "venomous love" or "sweet bitterness."

Paradox A paradox is a seemingly contradictory or absurd statement that may nonetheless suggest an important truth.

Parallelism Parallelism is the use of similar grammatical constructions to express ideas that are related or equal in importance.

> Love is not all: it is not meat nor drink
> Nor slumber nor a roof against the rain;
> Nor yet a floating spare to men that sink
> —Edna St. Vincent Millay, "Sonnet XXX"

Parallel Plot A parallel plot is a particular type of plot in which two stories of equal importance are told simultaneously. The story moves back and forth between the two plots.

Parody A parody is an imitation of another work, a type of literature, or a writer's style, usually for the purpose of poking fun. It may serve as an element of a larger work or be a complete work in itself. The purpose of parody may be to ridicule through broad humor, deploying such techniques as exaggeration or the use of inappropriate subject matter. Such techniques may even provide insights into the original work.

Pastoral A pastoral is a poem presenting shepherds in rural settings, usually in an idealized manner. The language and form of a pastoral tends to be formal. English Renaissance poets were drawn to the pastoral as a means of conveying their own emotions and ideas, particularly about love.

Persona A persona is a voice that a writer assumes in a particular work. A persona is like a mask worn by the writer, separating his or her identity from that of the speaker or the narrator. It is the persona's voice—not the writer's voice—that narrates a story or speaks in a poem.
See also **Narrator; Speaker.**

Personal Essay *See* **Essay.**

Personification Personification is a figure of speech in which human qualities are given to an object, animal, or idea. Notice the use of personification in this excerpt of poetry:

> In moving-slow he has no Peer.
> You ask him something in his Ear,
> He thinks about it for a Year;
> —Theodore Roethke, "The Sloth"

See pages 772, 794, 876.
See also **Figurative Language.**

Persuasive Essay *See* **Essay.**

Play *See* **Drama.**

Plot The sequence of events in a story is called the plot. A plot focuses on a central **conflict** or problem faced by the main character. The actions that the characters take to resolve the conflict build toward a climax. In general, it is not long after this point that the conflict is resolved and the story ends. A plot typically develops in five stages: exposition, rising action, climax, falling action, and resolution.
See pages 30, 36, 48.
See also **Climax; Exposition; Falling Action; Rising Action.**

Poetry Poetry is a type of literature in which words are carefully chosen and arranged to create certain effects. Poets use a variety of sound devices, imagery, and figurative language to express emotions and ideas.
See also **Alliteration; Assonance; Ballad; Free Verse; Imagery; Meter; Rhyme; Rhythm; Stanza.**

Point of View *Point of view* refers to the method of narration used in a short story, novel, narrative poem, or work of nonfiction. In a work told from a **first-person** point

of view, the narrator is a character in the story, as in "The Pit and the Pendulum" by Edgar Allan Poe. In a work told from a **third-person** point of view, the narrative voice is outside the action, not one of the characters. If a story is told from a **third-person omniscient,** or all-knowing, point of view, as in "The Doll's House" by Katherine Mansfield, the narrator sees into the minds of all the characters. If events are related from a **third-person limited** point of view, as in Hwang Sunwŏn's "Cranes," the narrator tells what only one character thinks, feels, and observes.

See pages 302, 308, 342, 856.
See also **Narrator.**

Prologue A prologue is an introductory scene in a drama. Some Elizabethan plays include prologues that comment on the theme or moral point that will be revealed in the play. The prologue is a feature of all Greek drama.

Prop The word *prop,* originally an abbreviation of the word *property,* refers to any physical object that is used in a drama.

Prose Generally, *prose* refers to all forms of written or spoken expression that are not in verse. The term, therefore, may be used to describe very different forms of writing—short stories as well as essays, for example.

Protagonist A protagonist is the main character in a work of literature, who is involved in the central conflict of the story. Usually, the protagonist changes after the central conflict reaches a climax. He or she may be a hero and is usually the one with whom the audience tends to identify. In R. K. Narayan's "Like the Sun," the protagonist is Sekhar, a man who encounters problems while seeking to tell the truth.

Quatrain A quatrain is a four-line stanza, or group of lines, in poetry. The most common stanza in English poetry, the quatrain can have a variety of meters and rhyme schemes.

Realistic Fiction Realistic fiction is fiction that is a truthful imitation of ordinary life. "On the Rainy River" by Tim O'Brien and "Shoofly Pie" by Naomi Shihab Nye are examples of realistic fiction.

Recurring Theme *See* **Theme.**

Reflective Essay *See* **Essay.**

Refrain A refrain is one or more lines repeated in each stanza of a poem.
See also **Stanza.**

Repetition Repetition is a technique in which a sound, word, phrase, or line is repeated for emphasis or unity. Repetition often helps to reinforce meaning and create

an appealing rhythm. The term includes specific devices associated with both prose and poetry, such as alliteration and parallelism.
See pages 772, 794.
See also **Alliteration; Parallelism; Sound Devices.**

Resolution *See* **Falling Action.**

Rhetorical Devices Rhetorical devices are techniques writers use to enhance their arguments and communicate more effectively. Rhetorical devices include **analogy, parallelism, rhetorical questions,** and **repetition.**
See also **Analogy; Repetition.**

Rhyme Rhyme is the occurrence of similar or identical sounds at the end of two or more words, such as *suite, heat,* and *complete.* Rhyme that occurs within a single line of poetry is **internal rhyme.** Rhyme that occurs at the ends of lines of poetry is called **end rhyme.** End rhyme that is not exact but approximate is called **slant rhyme,** or **off rhyme.** Notice the following example of slant rhyme involving the words *low* and *prow.*

> The gray sea and the long black land;
> And the yellow half-moon large and <u>low</u>;
> And the startled little waves that leap
> In the fiery ringlets from their sleep,
> As I gain the cove with the pushing <u>prow</u>,
> And quench its speed i' the slushy sand.
> —Robert Browning, "Meeting at Night"

See pages 772, 778, 810, 816.

Rhyme Scheme A rhyme scheme is a pattern of end rhymes in a poem. A rhyme scheme is noted by assigning a letter of the alphabet, beginning with *a,* to each line. Lines that rhyme are given the same letter. Notice the rhyme scheme of the first four lines of this poem.

> There will come soft rains and the smell of the ground, *a*
> And swallows circling with their shimmering sound; *a*
> And frogs in the pools singing at night, *b*
> And wild plum-trees in tremulous white; *b*
> —Sara Teasdale, "There Will Come Soft Rains"

See pages 772, 778.

Rhythm Rhythm is a pattern of stressed and unstressed syllables in a line of poetry. Poets use rhythm to bring out the musical quality of language, to emphasize ideas, to create moods, to unify works, and to heighten emotional

responses. Devices such as alliteration, rhyme, assonance, consonance, and parallelism often contribute to creating rhythm.

See pages 772, 778.

See also **Meter.**

Rising Action Rising action is the stage of a plot in which the conflict develops and story events build toward a climax. During this stage, complications arise that make the conflict more intense. Tension grows as the characters struggle to resolve the conflict.

See page 30.

See also **Plot.**

Romance A romance refers to any imaginative story concerned with noble heroes, chivalric codes of honor, passionate love, daring deeds, and supernatural events. Writers of romances tend to idealize their heroes as well as the eras in which the heroes live. Medieval romances, such as Malory's *Le Morte d'Arthur,* include stories of kings, knights, and ladies who are motivated by love, religious faith, or simply a desire for adventure.

See pages 1060, 1111.

Satire Satire is a literary technique in which ideas, customs, behaviors, or institutions are ridiculed for the purpose of improving society. Satire may be gently witty, mildly abrasive, or bitterly critical, and it often involves the use of irony and exaggeration to force readers to see something in a critical light.

Scansion Scansion is the notation of stressed and unstressed syllables in poetry. A stressed syllable is often indicated by the symbol ´; an unstressed syllable, by the symbol ˘. Using scansion can help you determine the rhythm and meter of a poem.

See page 772.

See also **Meter.**

Scene In drama, the action is often divided into acts and scenes. Each scene presents an episode of the play's plot and typically occurs at a single place and time.

See also **Act.**

Scenery Scenery is a painted backdrop or other structures used to create the setting for a play.

Science Fiction Science fiction is fiction in which a writer explores unexpected possibilities of the past or the future, using known scientific data and theories as well as his or her creative imagination. Most science fiction writers create believable worlds, although some create fantasy worlds that have familiar elements. Ray Bradbury, the author of the story "There Will Come Soft Rains," is famous for his science fiction.

See also **Fantasy.**

Screenplay A screenplay is a play written for film.

Script The text of a play, film, or broadcast is called a script.

Sensory Details Sensory details are words and phrases that appeal to the reader's senses of sight, hearing, touch, smell, and taste. For example, the sensory detail "a fine film of rain" appeals to the senses of sight and touch. Sensory details stimulate the reader to create images in his or her mind.

See also **Imagery.**

Setting Setting is the time and place of the action of a short story, drama, novel, narrative poem, or narrative nonfiction work. In addition to time and place, setting sometimes includes the larger historical and cultural contexts that form the background for a narrative. Setting is one of the main elements in fiction and often plays an important role in what happens and why.

See pages 28, 64, 78, 420, 427.

See also **Fiction.**

Short Story A short story is a work of fiction that centers on a single idea and can be read in one sitting. Generally, a short story has one main conflict that involves the characters, keeps the story moving, and stimulates readers' interest.

See also **Fiction.**

Simile A simile is a figure of speech that makes a comparison between two unlike things using the word *like* or *as.*

His brown skin hung in strips
like ancient wallpaper,
—Elizabeth Bishop, "The Fish"

See page 794.

See also **Epic Simile; Figurative Language; Metaphor.**

Situational Irony See **Irony.**

Soliloquy In drama, a soliloquy is a speech in which a character speaks his or her thoughts aloud. Generally, the character is on the stage alone, not speaking to other characters and perhaps not even consciously addressing an audience. *Julius Caesar* has several soliloquies. For example,

Casca begins plotting how to win over Brutus in a soliloquy that begins with these lines.

> Well, Brutus, thou art noble; yet I see
> Thy honorable mettle may be wrought
> From that it is disposed.
> —William Shakespeare, *Julius Caesar*

See also **Aside; Dramatic Monologue.**

Sonnet A sonnet is a lyric poem of 14 lines, commonly written in **iambic pentameter.** Sonnets are often classified as Petrarchan or Shakespearean. The Shakespearean, or Elizabethan, sonnet consists of three quatrains, or four-line units, and a final couplet. The typical rhyme scheme is *abab cdcd efef gg.*
See also **Iambic Pentameter; Rhyme Scheme.**

Sound Devices Sound devices, or uses of words for their auditory effect, can convey meaning and mood or unify a work. Some common sound devices are **alliteration, assonance, consonance, meter, onomatopoeia, repetition, rhyme,** and **rhythm.** The following lines contain alliteration, repetition, assonance, consonance, rhyme, and rhythm, all of which combine to help convey both meaning and mood.
See page 772.
See also **Alliteration; Assonance; Consonance; Meter; Onomatopoeia; Repetition; Rhyme; Rhythm.**

Speaker In poetry the speaker is the voice that "talks" to the reader, similar to the narrator in fiction. The speaker is not necessarily the poet. For example, in Rita Dove's "Lady Freedom Among Us," the experiences related may or may not have happened to the poet.
See page 841.
See also **Persona.**

Speech A speech is a talk or public address. The purpose of a speech may be to entertain, to explain, to present a claim, to inspire, or any combination of these aims. "On Nuclear Disarmament" by Carl Sagan was written and delivered in order to persuade an audience.
See page 652.

Stage Directions A play typically includes instructions called stage directions, which are usually printed in italic type. They serve as a guide to directors, set and lighting designers, performers, and readers. When stage directions appear within passages of dialogue, parentheses are usually used to set them off from the words spoken by characters.
See pages 7, 259, 1066, 1144, 1198.

Stanza A stanza is a group of two or more lines that form a unit in a poem. A stanza is comparable to a paragraph in prose. Each stanza may have the same number of lines, or the number of lines may vary.
See also **Couplet; Form; Poetry; Quatrain.**

Static Character *See* **Character.**

Stereotype In literature, a simplified or stock character who conforms to a fixed pattern or is defined by a single trait is known as a stereotype. Such a character does not usually demonstrate the complexities of a real person. Familiar stereotypes in popular literature include the absent-minded professor and the busybody.

Stream of Consciousness Stream of consciousness is a literary technique developed by modern writers, in which thoughts, feelings, moods, perceptions, and memories are presented as they randomly flow through a character's mind.

Structure Structure is the way in which the parts of a work of literature are put together. In poetry, structure involves the arrangement of words and lines to produce a desired effect. A common structural unit in poetry is the stanza, of which there are numerous types. In prose, structure is the arrangement of larger units or parts of a work. Paragraphs, for example, are basic units in prose, as are chapters in novels and acts in plays. The structure of a poem, short story, novel, play, or nonfictional work usually emphasizes certain important aspects of content.
See also **Act; Stanza.**

Style *Style* refers to the particular way in which a work of literature is written—not *what* is said but *how* it is said. It is the writer's unique way of communicating ideas. Many elements contribute to style, including word choice, sentence structure and length, tone, figurative language, and point of view. A literary style may be described in a variety of ways, such as formal, informal, journalistic, conversational, wordy, ornate, poetic, or dynamic.

Surprise Ending A surprise ending is an unexpected plot twist at the end of a story. The surprise may be a sudden turn in the action or a piece of information that gives a different perspective to the entire story. Saki is famous for using this device, as exemplified in his story "The Interlopers."
See page 426.

Suspense Suspense is the excitement or tension that readers feel as they wait to find out how a story ends or a conflict is resolved. Writers create suspense by raising questions in readers' minds about what might happen next.

The use of **foreshadowing** and **flashback** are two ways in which writers create suspense.

See also **Foreshadowing; Flashback.**

Symbol A symbol is a person, a place, an object, or an activity that stands for something beyond itself. For example, a flag is a colored piece of cloth that stands for a country. A white dove is a bird that represents peace.

Example: In "Cranes" by Hwang Sunwon, the birds represent the childhood friendship of the two main characters, as well as peace and tranquility.

See pages 418, 439.

Tall Tale A tall tale is a humorously exaggerated story about impossible events, often involving the supernatural abilities of the main character. Stories about folk heroes such as Pecos Bill and Paul Bunyan are typical tall tales.

Theme A theme or central idea, is an underlying message about life or human nature that a writer wants the reader to understand. It is a perception about life or human nature that the writer shares with the reader. In most cases, themes are not stated directly but must be inferred. A theme may imply how a person should live but should not be confused with a **moral.**

Example: Kurt Vonnegut Jr., in "Harrison Bergeron," never directly states his criticism of society and government. The reader must put details and events together in order to identify Vonnegut's theme about the damage that can be done when people go to extremes in the service of equality.

Recurring themes are themes found in a variety of works. For example, authors from varying backgrounds might convey similar themes having to do with the importance of family values. **Universal themes** are themes that are found throughout the literature of all time periods.

See pages 418, 426, 453, 477.

See also **Moral.**

Third-Person Point of View *See* **Point of View.**

Tone Tone is the attitude a writer takes takes toward a subject. Unlike mood, which is intended to shape the reader's emotional response, tone reflects the feelings of the writer. A writer communicates tone through choice of words and details. Tone may often be described by a single word, such as *serious, humorous, formal, informal, somber,*

sarcastic, playful, ironic, bitter, or *objective.* For example, the tone of the essay "The Man in the Water" by Roger Rosenblatt might be described as somber and reflective, whereas John Updike's poem "Ex-Basketball Player" has an ironic, somewhat humorous tone.

See pages 532, 852.

See also **Author's Perspective; Mood.**

Tragedy A tragedy is a dramatic work that presents the downfall of a dignified character (**tragic hero**) or characters who are involved in historically or socially significant events. The events in a tragic plot are set in motion by a decision that is often an error in judgment (**tragic flaw**) on the part of the hero. Succeeding events are linked in a cause-and-effect relationship and lead inevitably to a disastrous conclusion, usually death. Shakespeare's *Julius Caesar* is a tragedy.

Tragic Flaw *See* **Hero; Tragedy.**

Tragic Hero *See* **Hero; Tragedy.**

Traits *See* **Character.**

Turning Point *See* **Climax.**

Understatement Understatement is a technique of creating emphasis by saying less than is actually or literally true. It is the opposite of **hyperbole,** or exaggeration. One of the primary devices of irony, understatement can be used to develop a humorous effect, to create satire, or to achieve a restrained tone.

See also **Hyperbole; Irony.**

Universal Theme *See* **Theme.**

Verbal Irony *See* **Irony.**

Voice Voice is a writer's unique use of language that allows a reader to "hear" a human personality in the writer's work. Elements of style that contribute to a writer's voice include sentence structure, **diction,** and **tone.** Voice can reveal much about the author's personality, beliefs, and attitudes.

Word Choice *See* **Diction.**

Glossary of Reading & Informational Terms

Almanac *See* **Reference Works.**

Analogy *See Glossary of Literary and Nonfiction Terms, page R102.*

Argument An argument is speech or writing that presents a claim about an issue or problem and supports it with reasons and evidence. An argument often takes into account other points of view, anticipating and answering objections that opponents of the position might raise.
See also **Claim; Counterargument; Evidence.**

Assumption An assumption is an opinion or belief that is taken for granted. It can be about a specific situation, a person, or the world in general. Assumptions are often unstated.

Author's Message An author's message is the main idea or theme of a particular work.
See also **Main Idea; Theme,** *Glossary of Literary and Nonfiction Terms, page R114.*

Author's Perspective *See Glossary of Literary and Nonfiction Terms, page R102.*

Author's Position An author's position is his or her opinion on an issue or topic.
See also **Claim.**

Author's Purpose *See Glossary of Literary and Nonfiction Terms, page R102.*

Autobiography *See Glossary of Literary and Nonfiction Terms, page R102.*

Bias Bias is an inclination toward a particular judgment on a topic or issue. A writer often reveals a strongly positive or strongly negative opinion by presenting only one way of looking at an issue or by heavily weighting the evidence. Words with intensely positive or negative connotations are often a signal of a writer's bias.

Bibliography A bibliography is a list of books and other materials related to the topic of a text. Bibliographies can be good sources of works for further study on a subject.
See also **Works Consulted.**

Biography *See Glossary of Literary and Nonfiction Terms, page R103.*

Business Correspondence Business correspondence includes all written business communications, such as business letters, e-mails, and memos. In general, business correspondence is brief, to the point, clear, courteous, and professional.

Cause and Effect A **cause** is an event or action that directly results in another event or action. An **effect** is the direct or logical outcome of an event or action. Basic **cause-and-effect relationships** include a single cause with a single effect, one cause with multiple effects, multiple causes with a single effect, and a chain of causes and effects. The concept of cause and effect also provides a way of organizing a piece of writing. It helps a writer show the relationships between events or ideas.
See also **False Cause,** *Reading Handbook, page R24.*

Central Idea *See* **Main Idea.**

Chronological Order Chronological order is the arrangement of events in their order of occurrence. This type of organization is used in both fictional narratives and in historical writing, biography, and autobiography.

Claim In an argument, a claim is the writer's position on an issue or problem. Although an argument focuses on supporting one claim, a writer may make more than one claim in a work.
See also **Argument; Thesis Statement.**

Clarify Clarifying is a reading strategy that helps a reader to understand or make clear what he or she is reading. Readers usually clarify by rereading, reading aloud, or discussing.

Classification Classification is a pattern of organization in which objects, ideas, or information is presented in groups, or classes, based on common characteristics.

Cliché A cliché is an overused expression. "Better late than never" and "hard as nails" are common examples. Good writers generally avoid clichés unless they are using them in dialogue to indicate something about characters' personalities.

Compare and Contrast To compare and contrast is to identify similarities and differences in two or more subjects. Compare-and-contrast organization can be used to structure a piece of writing, serving as a framework for examining the similarities and differences in two or more subjects.

Conclusion A conclusion is a statement of belief based on evidence, experience, and reasoning. A **valid conclusion** is a conclusion that logically follows from the facts or statements upon which it is based. A **deductive conclusion** is one that follows from a particular generalization or premise. An **inductive conclusion** is a broad conclusion or generalization that is reached by arguing from specific facts and examples.

Connect Connecting is a reader's process of relating the content of a text to his or her own knowledge and experience.

Consumer Documents Consumer documents are printed materials that accompany products and services. They are intended for the buyers or users of the products or services and usually provide information about use, care, operation, or assembly. Some common consumer documents are applications, contracts, warranties, manuals, and schedules.

Context Clues When you encounter an unfamiliar word, you can often use context clues as aids for understanding. Context clues are the words and phrases surrounding the word that provide hints about the word's meaning.

Controlling Idea A controlling idea, or main idea, is the central or most important idea about a topic that a writer or speaker conveys. It can be the main idea of an entire work or of just a paragraph. The controlling idea of a paragraph is often expressed in a topic sentence, but it may also be implied, or suggested by details.

Counterargument A counterargument is an argument made to answer an opposing argument, or counterclaim. A good argument anticipates opposing viewpoints and provides counterarguments to refute (disprove) or answer them.

Counterclaim *See* **Counterargument**.

Credibility *Credibility* refers to the believability or trustworthiness of a source and the information it contains.

Critique A critique is an evaluation by a reviewer or critic. Different types of reviews include film reviews, book reviews, music reviews, and art-show reviews.

Database A database is a collection of information that can be quickly and easily accessed and searched and from which information can be easily retrieved.

Debate A debate is a structured argument. In academic settings, *debate* usually refers to a formal contest in which two opposing teams defend and attack a proposition.
See also **Argument.**

Deductive Reasoning Deductive reasoning is a way of thinking that begins with a generalization, presents a specific situation, and then advances with facts and evidence to a logical conclusion. The following passage has a deductive argument imbedded in it: "All students in the drama class must attend the play on Thursday. Since Ava is in the class, she had better show up." This deductive argument can be broken down as follows: generalization—all students in the drama class must attend the play on Thursday; specific situation—Ava is a student in the drama class; conclusion—Ava must attend the play.
See also **Analyzing Logic and Reasoning,** *Reading Handbook, pages R22–R23.*

Dictionary *See* **Reference Works.**

Draw Conclusions To draw a conclusion is to make a judgment or arrive at a belief based on evidence, experience, and reasoning.

Editorial An editorial is an opinion piece that usually appears on the editorial page of a newspaper or as part of a news broadcast. The editorial section of a newspaper presents opinions rather than objective news reports.
See also **Op-Ed Piece.**

Either/Or Fallacy An either/or fallacy is a statement that suggests that there are only two possible ways to view a situation or only two options to choose from. In other words, it is a statement that falsely frames a dilemma, giving the impression that no options exist but the two presented—for example, "Either we stop the construction of a new airport, or the surrounding suburbs will become ghost towns."
See also **Identifying Faulty Reasoning,** *Reading Handbook, page R24.*

Emotional Appeals Emotional appeals are messages that evoke strong feelings—such as fear, pity, or vanity—in order to persuade instead of using facts and evidence to make a point. An **appeal to fear** is a message that taps into people's fear of losing their safety or security. An **appeal to pity** taps into people's sympathy and compassion for others to build support for an idea, a cause, or a proposed action. An **appeal to vanity** attempts to persuade by tapping into people's desire to feel good about themselves.
See also **Recognizing Persuasive Techniques,** *Reading Handbook, pages R21–R22.*

Encyclopedia *See* **Reference Works.**

Essay *See Glossary of Literary and Nonfiction Terms, page R105.*

Evaluate To evaluate is to examine something carefully and judge its value or worth. Evaluating is an important skill for gaining insight into what you read. A reader can evaluate the actions of a particular character, for example, or can form an opinion about the value of an entire work.

Evidence Evidence is the specific pieces of information that support a claim. Evidence can take the form of facts, quotations, examples, statistics, or personal experiences, among others.

Expository Essay *See* **Essay,** *Glossary of Literary and Nonfiction Terms, page R105.*

Fact versus Opinion A **fact** is a statement that can be proved or verified. An **opinion,** on the other hand, is a statement that cannot be proved because it expresses a person's beliefs, feelings, or thoughts.
See also **Inference; Generalization.**

Fallacy A fallacy is an error in reasoning. Typically, a fallacy is based on an incorrect inference or a misuse of evidence. Some common logical fallacies are **circular reasoning, either/or fallacy, oversimplification, overgeneralization,** and **stereotyping.**
See also **Either/Or Fallacy, Logical Appeal, Overgeneralization; Identifying Faulty Reasoning,** *Reading Handbook, page R24.*

Faulty Reasoning *See* **Fallacy.**

Feature Article A feature article is a main article in a newspaper or a cover story in a magazine. A feature article is focused more on entertaining than informing. Features are lighter or more general than hard news and tend to be about human interest or lifestyles.

Functional Documents *See* **Consumer Documents; Workplace Documents.**

Generalization A generalization is a broad statement about a class or category of people, ideas, or things, based on a study of only some of its members.
See also **Overgeneralization.**

Government Publications Government publications are documents produced by government organizations. Pamphlets, brochures, and reports are just some of the many forms these publications may take. Government publications can be good resources for a wide variety of topics.

Graphic Aid A graphic aid is a visual tool that is printed, handwritten, or drawn. Charts, diagrams, graphs, photographs, and maps can all be graphic aids.
See also **Graphic Aids,** *Reading Handbook, pages R5–R7.*

Graphic Organizer A graphic organizer is a "word picture"—that is, a visual illustration of a verbal statement—that helps a reader understand a text. Charts, tables, webs, and diagrams can all be graphic organizers. Graphic organizers and graphic aids can look the same. For example, a table in a science article will not be constructed differently from a table that is a graphic organizer. However, graphic organizers and graphic aids do differ in how they are used. Graphic aids are the visual representations that people encounter when they read informational texts. Graphic organizers are visuals that people construct to help them understand texts or organize information.

Historical Documents Historical documents are writings that have played a significant role in human events or are themselves records of such events. The Declaration of Independence, for example, is a historical document.

How-To Book A how-to book is a book that is written to explain how to do something—usually an activity, a sport, or a household project.

Implied Controlling Idea An implied controlling idea is one that is suggested by details rather than stated explicitly.
See also **Controlling Idea.**

Index The index of a book is an alphabetized list of important topics and details covered in the book and the page numbers on which they can be found. An index can be used to quickly find specific information about a topic.

Inductive Reasoning Inductive reasoning is the process of logical reasoning from observations, examples, and facts to a general conclusion or principle.
See also **Analyzing Logic and Reasoning,** *Reading Handbook, pages R22–R23.*

Inference An inference is a logical assumption that is based on observed facts and one's own knowledge and experience.

Informational Nonfiction Informational nonfiction is writing that provides factual information. It often explains ideas or teaches processes. Examples include news reports, science textbooks, software instructions, and lab reports.

Internet The Internet is a global, interconnected system of computer networks that allows for communication through e-mail, listservers, and the World Wide Web. The Internet connects computers and computer users throughout the world.

Journal A journal is a periodical publication issued by a legal, medical, or other professional organization. Alternatively, the term may be used to refer to a diary or daily record.

Loaded Language Loaded language consists of words with strongly positive or negative connotations intended to influence a reader's or listener's attitude.

Logical Appeal A logical appeal relies on logic and facts, appealing to people's reasoning or intellect rather than to their values or emotions. Flawed logical appeals—that is, errors in reasoning—are considered logical fallacies.
See also **Fallacy.**

Logical Argument A logical argument is an argument in which the logical relationship between the support and the claim is sound.

Main Idea *See* **Controlling Idea.**

Make Inferences *See* **Inference.**

Monitor Monitoring is the strategy of checking your comprehension as you are reading and modifying the strategies you are using to suit your needs. Monitoring may include some or all of the following strategies: **questioning, clarifying, visualizing, predicting, connecting,** and **rereading.**

Narrative Nonfiction *See Glossary of Literary and Nonfiction Terms, page R109.*

News Article A news article is a piece of writing that reports on a recent event. In newspapers, news articles are usually written in a concise manner to report the latest news, presenting the most important facts first and then more detailed information. In magazines, news articles are usually more elaborate than those in newspapers because they are written to provide both information and analysis. Also, news articles in magazines do not necessarily present the most important facts first.

Nonfiction *See Glossary of Literary and Nonfiction Terms, page R109.*

Op-Ed Piece An op-ed piece is an opinion piece that usually appears opposite ("op") the editorial page of a newspaper. Unlike editorials, op-ed pieces are written and submitted by named writers.

Organization *See* **Pattern of Organization.**

Overgeneralization An overgeneralization is a generalization that is too broad. You can often recognize overgeneralizations by the appearance of words and phrases such as *all, everyone, every time, any, anything, no one,* and *none.* Consider, for example, this statement: "None of the sanitation workers in our city really care about keeping

the environment clean." In all probability, there are many exceptions. The writer can't possibly know the feelings of every sanitation worker in the city.
See also **Identifying Faulty Reasoning,** *Reading Handbook, page R24.*

Overview An overview is a short summary of a story, a speech, or an essay. It orients the reader by providing a preview of the text to come.

Paraphrase Paraphrasing is the restating of information in one's own words.
See also **Summarize.**

Pattern of Organization A pattern of organization is a particular arrangement of ideas and information. Such a pattern may be used to organize an entire composition or a single paragraph within a longer work. The following are the most common patterns of organization: **cause-and-effect, chronological order, compare-and-contrast, classification, deductive, inductive, order of importance, problem-solution, sequential,** and **spatial.**
See also **Cause and Effect; Chronological Order; Classification; Compare and Contrast; Problem-Solution Order; Sequential Order; Analyzing Patterns of Organization,** *Reading Handbook, pages R14–R20.*

Periodical A periodical is a publication that is issued at regular intervals of more than one day. For example, a periodical may be a weekly, monthly, or quarterly journal or magazine. Newspapers and other daily publications generally are not classified as periodicals.

Personal Essay *See* **Essay,** *Glossary of Literary and Nonfiction Terms, page R105.*

Persuasion Persuasion is the art of swaying others' feelings, beliefs, or actions. Persuasion normally appeals to both the intellect and the emotions of readers. **Persuasive techniques** are the methods used to influence others to adopt certain opinions or beliefs or to act in certain ways. Types of persuasive techniques include emotional appeals, logical appeals, and loaded language. When used properly, persuasive techniques can add depth to writing that's meant to persuade. Persuasive techniques can, however, be misused to cloud factual information, disguise poor reasoning, or unfairly exploit people's emotions in order to shape their opinions.
See also **Emotional Appeals; Loaded Language; Logical Appeal; Recognizing Persuasive Techniques,** *Reading Handbook, pages R21–R22.*

Predict Predicting is a reading strategy that involves using text clues to make a reasonable guess about what will happen next in a story.

Primary Source Primary source refers to materials created by people who participated in or observed an event directly. For example, an e-mail message describing the experience of being caught in an avalanche or a blog posting relating the writer's reactions to hearing a famous politician speak are primary sources. Other types of primary sources include letters, journals, and autobiographies.
See also **Sources.**

Prior Knowledge Prior knowledge is the knowledge a reader already possesses about a topic. This information might come from personal experiences, expert accounts, books, films, or other sources.

Problem-Solution Order Problem-solution order is a pattern of organization in which a problem is stated and analyzed and then one or more solutions are proposed and examined. Writers use words and phrases such as *propose, conclude, reason for, problem, answer,* and *solution* to connect ideas when writing about problems and solutions.

Procedural Texts *See* **Consumer Documents; Workplace Documents.**

Propaganda Propaganda is a form of communication that may use distorted, false, or misleading information. It usually refers to manipulative political discourse.

Public Documents Public documents are documents that were written for the public to provide information that is of public interest or concern. They include government documents, speeches, signs, and rules and regulations.
See also **Government Publications.**

Reference Works General reference works are sources that contain facts and background information on a wide range of subjects. More specific reference works contain in-depth information on a single subject. Most reference works are good sources of reliable information because they have been reviewed by experts. The following are some common reference works: **encyclopedias, dictionaries, thesauri, almanacs, atlases, biographical dictionaries,** and **directories.**

Review *See* **Critical Review.**

Rhetorical Devices *See Glossary of Literary and Nonfiction Terms, page R111.*

Rhetorical Questions Rhetorical questions are those that do not require a reply. Writers use them to suggest that their arguments make the answer obvious or self-evident.

Scanning Scanning is the process of searching through writing for a particular fact or piece of information. When you scan, your eyes sweep across a page, looking for key words that may lead you to the information you want.

Secondary Source *See* **Sources.**

Sequential Order A pattern of organization that shows the order in which events or actions occur is called sequential order. Writers typically use this pattern of organization to explain steps or stages in a process.

Setting a Purpose The process of establishing specific reasons for reading a text is called setting a purpose.

Sidebar A sidebar is additional information set in a box alongside or within a news or feature article. Popular magazines often make use of sidebar information.

Signal Words Signal words are words and phrases that indicate what is to come in a text. Readers can use signal words to discover a text's pattern of organization and to analyze the relationships among the ideas in the text.

Sources A source is anything that supplies information. **Primary sources** are materials written by people who were present at events, either as participants or as observers. Letters, diaries, autobiographies, speeches, and photographs are primary sources. **Secondary sources** are records of events that were created sometime after the events occurred; the writers were not directly involved or were not present when the events took place. Encyclopedias, textbooks, biographies, most newspaper and magazine articles, and books and articles that interpret or review research are secondary sources.

Spatial Order Spatial order is a pattern of organization that highlights the physical positions or relationships of details or objects. This pattern of organization is typically found in descriptive writing. Writers use words and phrases such as *on the left, to the right, here, over there, above, below, beyond, nearby,* and *in the distance* to indicate the arrangement of details.

Speech *See Glossary of Literary and Nonfiction Terms, page R113.*

Stereotyping Stereotyping is a dangerous type of overgeneralization. Stereotypes are broad statements made about people on the basis of their gender, ethnicity, race, or political, social, professional, or religious group.

Summarize To summarize is to briefly retell, or encapsulate, the main ideas of a piece of writing in one's own words.
See also **Paraphrase.**

Support Support is any material that serves to prove a claim. In an argument, support typically consists of reasons and evidence. In persuasive texts and speeches, however, support may include appeals to the needs and values of the audience.

Supporting Detail *See* **Controlling Idea.**

Synthesize To synthesize information is to take individual pieces of information and combine them with other pieces of information and with prior knowledge or experience to gain a better understanding of a subject or to create a new product or idea.

Text Features Text features are design elements that indicate the organizational structure of a text and help make the key ideas and the supporting information understandable. Text features include headings, boldface type, italic type, bulleted or numbered lists, sidebars, and graphic aids such as charts, tables, timelines, illustrations, and photographs.

Thesaurus *See* **Reference Works.**

Thesis Statement In an argument, a thesis statement is an expression of the claim that the writer or speaker is trying to support. In an essay, a thesis statement is an expression, in one or two sentences, of the main idea or purpose of the piece of writing.
See also **Claim.**

Topic Sentence The topic sentence of a paragraph states the paragraph's controlling idea. All other sentences in the paragraph provide supporting details.

Visualize Visualizing is the process of forming a mental picture based on written or spoken information.

Web Site A Web site is a collection of "pages" on the World Wide Web that is usually devoted to one specific subject. Pages are linked together and are accessed by clicking hyperlinks or menus, which send the user from page to page within the site. Web sites are created by companies, organizations, educational institutions, branches of the government, the military, and individuals.

Workplace Documents Workplace documents are materials that are produced or used within a work setting, usually to aid in the functioning of the workplace. They include job applications, office memos, training manuals, job descriptions, procedural documents, and sales reports.

Works Cited A list of works cited lists names of all the works a writer has referred to in his or her text. This list often includes not only books and articles but also nonprint sources.

Works Consulted A list of works consulted names all the works a writer consulted in order to create his or her text. It is not limited just to those works cited in the text.
See also **Bibliography.**

acknowledge (ăk-nŏl′ ĭj) *v.* to recognize and admit that something is true or accurate
  reconocer *v.* admitir y aceptar que algo es verdadero o exacto

affect (ə-fĕkt′) *v.* to influence; to create an effect upon
  afectar *v.* influir; crear un efecto

alter (ôl′tər) *v.* to change or modify some details
  alterar *v.* cambiar o modificar algunos detalles

author (ô′thər) *n.* a writer; a creator of something
  autor *sust.* escritor; creador de algo

authoritative (ə-thôr′ĭ-tā′tĭv) *adj.* backed by evidence and showing deep knowledge
  fidedigno *adj.* que se sostiene con pruebas y que demuestra un conocimiento profundo

cite (sīt) *v.* to quote from some source such as a book, internet article, or speech
  citar *v.* mencionar parte de una fuente, como un libro, un artículo de Internet o un discurso

clarify (klăr′ə fī′) *v.* to make clear or easier to understand
  aclarar *v.* hacer que algo sea más claro o fácil de comprender

communicate (kə myōō′nĭ kāt′) *v.* to share or exchange information or ideas
  comunicar *v.* compartir o intercambiar información o ideas

community (kə myōō′nĭ tē) *n.* a group of individuals with a common interest or characteristic
  comunidad *sust.* grupo de personas con intereses o características en común

compile (kəm-pīl′) *v.* to gather things together to form a whole
  compilar *v.* reunir cosas para formar un todo

consequent (kŏn′sĭ kwĕnt′) *adj.* following as an effect or result
  consiguiente *adj.* que sigue como efecto o resultado

contemporary (kən-tĕm′pə-rĕr′ē) *adj.* current; modern
  contemporáneo *adj.* actual; moderno

controversy (kŏn′trə vûr′sē) *n.* a debate or quarrel over opposing opinions
  controversia *sust.* debate o discusión con respecto a opiniones opuestas

convince (kən vĭns′) *v.* to overcome any doubts with argument or persuasion
  convencer *v.* superar las dudas por medio de argumentos o persuasiones

crucial (krōō′shəl) *adj.* extremely important; critical
  crucial *adj.* sumamente importante; crítico

culture (kŭl′chər) *n.* the attitudes, behavior, or customs that characterize a group; the particular group having such attitudes, behavior, or customs
  cultura *sust.* actitudes, conductas o costumbres que caracterizan a un grupo; grupo particular que tiene esas actitudes, conductas o costumbres

debates (dĭ-bātz′) *n.* public discussions involving opposing points
  debates *sust.* discusiones públicas sobre puntos opuestos

definite (dĕf′ə nĭt) *adj.* certain; unquestionable
  definitivo *adj.* seguro; incuestionable

document (dŏk′yə mənt) *n.* something printed or written that provides a record; something that provides evidence
  documento *sust.* algo impreso o escrito que sirve como registro; algo que proporciona pruebas

drama (drä′mə) *n.* literature in which plot and characters are developed through dialogue and action
  drama *sust.* literatura en la que la trama y los personajes se desarrollan mediante el diálogo y la acción

dynamic (dī năm′ik) *adj.* energetic; changing; in motion
  dinámico *adj.* enérgico; cambiante; en movimiento

emerge (ĭ mûrj′) *v.* to develop; to become something new
  surgir *v.* desarrollarse; convertirse en algo nuevo

encounter (ĕn-koun′tər) *n.* an unexpected meeting
  encuentro *sust.* reunión inesperada

establish (ĭ stăb′ lĭsh) *v.* to make stable or firm
  establecer *v.* hacer que algo esté estable o firme

feature (fē′chər) *n.* a special quality or characteristic of something
  rasgo *sust.* cualidad o característica especial de algo

globe (glōb) *n.* a round, ball-shaped model of the earth; the earth
  globo *sust.* modelo redondo y con forma de pelota de la Tierra; la Tierra

goal (gōl) *n.* an aim, purpose, or specific result one tries to achieve
　meta *sust.* fin, propósito o resultado específico que se busca alcanzar

identify (ī-děn'tə-fī') *v.* to find or name the characteristics, nature, or qualities of someone or something
　identificar *v.* hallar o nombrar las características, la naturaleza o las cualidades de alguien o algo

individual (ĭn'də-vĭj'ōō-əl) *adj.* existing as a single, separate thing or being
　individual *adj.* que existe como cosa o ser único o singular

initial (ĭ-nĭsh'əl) *adj.* occurring at the beginning
　inicial *adj.* que ocurre al principio

inquiry (ĭn-kwĭr'ē) *n.* a close examination in search for information
　averiguación *sust.* evaluación exhaustiva para buscar información

issue (ĭsh'ōō) *n.* a concern or problem
　cuestión *sust.* asunto o problema

layer (lā'ər) *n.* a single thickness, fold, or level
　capa *sust.* veta, pliegue o nivel individual

motive (mō'tĭv) *n.* incentive; inner drive or desire that causes someone to act
　motivo *sust.* incentivo; impulso o deseo interno que hace que una persona actúe

objective (əb-jĕk'tĭv) *n.* something worked toward or striven for
　objetivo *sust.* finalidad del trabajo o el esfuerzo

precise (prĭ-sīs') *adj.* exact; accurately defined or stated
　preciso *adj.* exacto; definido o expuesto con precisión

relevant (rĕl'ə-vənt) *adj.* pertaining to a matter at hand; significance
　relevante *adj.* relacionado con un tema; importante

role (rōl) *n.* a character played by an actor in a performance; a function or part assumed in a process
　papel *sust.* personaje que representa un actor en una obra; función o posición que se asume en un proceso

seek (sēk) *v.* to look for or try to find
　buscar *v.* rastrear o intentar hallar

shift (shĭft) *v.* to change course; to move or transfer
　correr *v.* cambiar el curso; mover o transferir

statistic (stə-tĭs'tĭk) *n.* numerical fact or quantity
　estadística *sust.* dato numérico o cantidad

style (stīl) *n.* a distinctive or original manner of expression
　estilo *sust.* forma de expresión distintiva u original

survive (sər-vīv') *v.* to live longer than expected; to remain in existence
　sobrevivir *v.* vivir más de lo esperado; conservar la existencia

symbol (sĭm'bəl) *n.* something that represents or suggests another thing
　símbolo *sust.* algo que representa o sugiere otra cosa

theme (thēm) *n.* a topic or subject of a discussion or piece of writing
　tema *sust.* materia o asunto de un debate o un escrito

transmit (trăns-mĭt') *v.* to communicate; to send or hand off to others
　transmitir *v.* comunicar; enviar o entregar a otros

undergo (ŭn'dər-gō') *v.* to endure, go through, or experience
　soportar *v.* sobrellevar, vivir o experimentar

underlie (ŭn'dər-lī') *v.* to form the basis or foundation of
　subyacer *v.* formar la base o los cimientos de algo

unify (yōō' nə-fī') *v.* to make into one; to bring together into a unit
　unificar *v.* unir en uno solo; juntar para formar una unidad

vision (vĭzh'ən) *n.* a mental or imaginative image; something seen in a dream or trance
　visión *sust.* imagen mental o intelectual; algo que se ve en un sueño o un trance

Glossary of Vocabulary in English & Spanish

abash (ə-băsh′) *v.* to make ashamed or embarrass
  avergonzar *v.* mortificar o humillar

acquiesce (ăk′wē-ĕs′) *v.* to agree or give in to
  consentir *v.* aceptar o ceder

acquiescence (ăk′wē-ĕs′əns) *n.* passive agreement; acceptance without protest
  conformidad *s.* aceptación pasiva; consentimiento

adaptation (ăd′ăp-tā′shən) *n.* the process of adjusting to suit one's surroundings
  adaptación *s.* proceso de acostumbrarse a lo que nos rodea

adversary (ăd′vər-sĕr′ē) *n.* an opponent; enemy
  adversario *s.* opositor; enemigo

affable (ăf′ə-bəl) *adj.* warm and friendly
  afable *adj.* cálido y amistoso

afford (ə-fôrd′) *v.* to provide or offer
  proveer *v.* dar u ofrecer

alleviate (ə-lē′vē-āt′) *v.* to make easier or provide relief
  aliviar *v.* facilitar o calmar

anarchist (ăn′ər-kĭst) *n.* a person favoring the overthrow of government
  anarquista *s.* persona a favor del derrocamiento del gobierno

annihilate (ə-nī′ə-lāt′) *v.* to destroy completely
  aniquilar *v.* destruir por completo

anthology (ăn-thŏl′ə-jē) *n.* a collection of written works—such as poems, short stories, or plays—in a single book or set
  antología *s.* colección de obras escritas —poemas, cuentos u obras de teatro— encuadernadas en un libro o una colección

apprehension (ăp′rĭ-hĕn′shən) *n.* fear and worry for the future
  aprensión *s.* temor y preocupación por el futuro

ascertain (ăs′ər-tān′) *v.* to discover with certainty
  determinar *v.* establecer con certeza

assail (ə-sāl′) *v.* to attack or deliver a blow
  atacar *v.* asaltar o agredir

atrocity (ə-trŏs′ĭ-tē) *n.* a very cruel or brutal act
  atrocidad *s.* acto muy cruel o brutal

auspicious (ô-spĭsh′əs) *adj.* promising success; favorable
  propicio *adj.* que promete éxito; favorable

autonomy (ô-tŏn′ə-mē) *n.* freedom; independence
  autonomía *s.* libertad; independencia

avidly (ăv′ĭd-lē) *adv.* with great eagerness and enthusiasm
  ávidamente *adv.* con mucho entusiasmo

boisterous (boi′stər-əs) *adj.* noisy and lacking in restraint or discipline
  escandaloso *adj.* alborotado y sin control o disciplina

boycott (boi′kŏt′) *n.* a form of protest in which a group stops using a specific service or product in order to force a change
  boicot *s.* forma de protesta en que un grupo deja de usar un servicio o un producto a fin de buscar un cambio

burnish (bûr′nĭsh) *v.* to polish
  bruñir *v.* sacar brillo

capricious (kə-prĭsh′əs) *adj.* impulsive, unpredictable
  caprichoso *adj.* impulsivo, inestable

carnage (kär′nĭj) *n.* massive slaughter
  matanza *s.* gran mortandad

catalyst (kăt′l-ĭst) *n.* something or someone that brings about change
  catalizador *s.* algo o alguien que causa un cambio o acción

cavalcade (kăv′əl-kād′) *n.* a procession of people on horseback
  cabalgata *s.* procesión de gente a caballo

censure (sĕn′shər) *n.* harsh criticism or disapproval
  censura *s.* crítica o desaprobación fuerte

chaotic (kā-ŏt′ĭk) *adj.* extremely confused or disordered
  caótico *adj.* extremadamente confuso o desordenado

coercion (kō-ûr′zhən) *n.* the act of compelling by force or authority
  coerción *s.* uso de poder o amenazas para obligar a actuar

collaborative (kə-lăb′ə-rə′tĭv) *adj.* done in cooperation with others
  en colaboración *adj.* hecho en cooperación

commiserate (kə-mĭz′ə-rāt′) *v.* to express sorrow or pity for another's troubles
  conmiserarse *v.* expresar dolor o piedad por los problemas de otro

compassionate (kəm-păsh'ə-nĭt) *adj.* feeling or sharing the suffering of others
    compasivo *adj.* que comparte el sufrimiento ajeno

compatriot (kəm-pā'trē-ət) *n.* a person from one's own country
    compatriota *s.* persona del mismo país que uno

complicity (kəm-plĭs'ĭ-tē) *n.* association or partnership in a crime or offense
    complicidad *adj.* participación en un delito u ofensa

concede (kən-sēd') *v.* to admit or acknowledge, often reluctantly
    reconocer *v.* admitir o aceptar

conceivably (kən-sēv'ə-blē) *adv.* possibly
    concebible *adj.* posible

condolence (kən-dō'ləns) *n.* an expression of sympathy
    condolencia *s.* pésame

conflagration (kŏn'flə-grā'shən) *n.* a large, destructive fire
    conflagración *s.* incendio destructivo

confound (kən-found') *v.* to confuse or astonish
    confundir *v.* desconcertar o sorprender

conjectural (kən-jĕk'chər-əl) *adj.* involving guesswork
    conjetural *adj.* basado en suposiciones

conspire (kən-spīr') *v.* to plan or plot secretly
    conspirar *v.* complotar en secreto

consternation (kŏn'stər-nā'shən) *n.* confused amazement or fear
    consternación *s.* abatimiento o disgusto

contempt (kən-tĕmpt') *n.* an attitude of regarding someone or something as worthless or inferior
    desdén *s.* actitud de desprecio

contemptuous (kən-tĕmp'chōō-əs) *adj.* scornful or disrespectful
    desdeñoso *adj.* despectivo o irrespetuoso

contending (kən-tĕn'dĭng) *adj.* struggling in rivalry **contend** *v.*
    contendiente *adj.* rival, contrario **contender** *v.*

contingent (kən-tĭn'jənt) *n.* a gathering of people representative of a larger group
    contingente *s.* reunión de representantes de un grupo mayor

contrary (kŏn'trĕr'ē) *adj.* stubbornly uncooperative or contradictory
    contrario *adj.* opuesto o adverso

cosmopolitan (kŏz'mə-pŏl'ĭ-tn) *adj.* containing elements from all over the world; sophisticated
    cosmopolita *adj.* que tiene elementos de muchos países; sofisticado

cower (kou'ər) *v.* to crouch down in fear
    encogerse *v.* doblarse con miedo

deference (dĕf'ər-əns) *n.* polite respect; submission to someone else's wishes
    deferencia *s.* respeto cortés; sumisión a los deseos ajenos

deficit (dĕf'ĭ-sĭt) *n.* a shortfall or deficiency
    déficit *s.* cantidad que falta para llegar al nivel necesario

defile (dĭ-fīl') *v.* to make dirty, unclean, or impure
    profanar *v.* ensuciar o deshonrar; quitarle la pureza

deflect (dĭ-flĕkt') *v.* to fend off or avert the direction of something
    desviar *v.* evitar o cambiar la dirección

degraded (dĭ-grā'dĭd) *adj.* corrupted, depraved
    degradado *adj.* corrupto, depravado

degrading (dĭ-grā'dĭng) *adj.* tending or intended to cause dishonor or disgrace
    degradante *adj.* que busca quitar dignidad u honor

dejectedly (dĭ-jĕk'tĭd-lē) *adv.* in a disheartened, depressed way
    abatido *adj.* desalentado, con el ánimo por los suelos

delirium (dĭ-lîr'ē-əm) *n.* a temporary state of mental confusion usually resulting from high fever or shock
    delirio *s.* estado pasajero de confusión mental por fiebre o shock

destiny (dĕs'tə-nē) *n.* the determinded fate of a particular person or thing; lot in life
    destino *s.* suerte o función de determinada persona o cosa; sino

din (dĭn) *n.* a deafening noise
    estruendo *s.* mezcla de ruidos fuertes

disarm (dĭs-ärm') *v.* to win over; to make less hostile
    desarmar *v.* reducir sospecha u hostilidad

discord (dĭs′kôrd′) *n.* disagreement; lack of harmony
   discordia *s.* desacuerdo; falta de armonía

disengage (dĭs′ĕn-gāj′) *v.* to detach or remove oneself
   desconectarse *v.* soltarse o retirarse

disparage (dĭ-spăr′ĭj) *v.* to speak of in a negative or insulting way
   menospreciar *v.* tratar de modo negativo o insultante

disparagement (dĭ-spăr′ĭj-mənt) *n.* belittlement
   menosprecio *s.* desprecio

dissuasion (dĭ-swā′zhən) *n.* an attempt to deter a person from a course of action
   disuasión *s.* utilización de razones para cambiar la opinión o el propósito de alguien

doctrine (dŏk′trĭn) *n.* a set of rules, beliefs, or values held by a group
   doctrina *s.* conjunto de principios o reglas de un grupo

draft (drăft) *n.* a gulp or swallow
   sorbo *s.* trago

eccentric (ĭk-sĕn′trĭk) *adj.* strange; peculiar
   excéntrico *adj.* extraño; peculiar

edict (ē′dĭkt′) *n.* a command issued by an authority
   edicto *s.* orden de una persona de autoridad

eloquent (ĕl′ə-kwənt) *adj.* vividly expressive
   elocuente *adj.* que se expresa con emoción

emaciated (ĭ-mā′shē-ā′tĭd) *adj.* excessively thin as a result of starvation **emaciate** *v.*
   emaciado *adj.* en los huesos; muy delgado por pasar hambre **emaciarse** *v.*

emblemized (ĕm′blə-mīzd′) *adj.* represented; symbolized **emblemize** *v.*
   emblemático *adj.* simbolizado **emblematizar** *v.*

embody (ĕm-bŏd′ē) *v.* to give shape to or visibly represent
   encarnar *v.* dar forma concreta o representar

emphatically (ĕm-făt′ĭk-lē) *adv.* with strong emphasis
   enfáticamente *adv.* con énfasis; con fuerza

enmity (ĕn′mĭ-tē) *n.* hostility and ill will
   enemistad *s.* hostilidad y odio

exalt (ĭg-zôlt′) *v.* to glorify, praise, or honor
   exaltar *v.* glorificar, alabar u honrar

fanatical (fə-năt′ĭ-kəl) *adj.* extremely enthusiastic
   fanático *adj.* extremadamente entusiasta

fictitious (fĭk-tĭsh′əs) *adj.* fabricated; created by the imagination
   ficticio *adj.* inventado; creado por la imaginación

fidelity (fĭ-dĕl′ĭ-tē) *n.* faithfulness to duties; loyalty and devotion
   fidelidad *s.* responsabilidad hacia obligaciones; dedicación y lealtad

flailing (flā′lĭng) *adj.* waving vigorously **flail** *v.*
   agitar *v.* sacudir, ondear

forbear (fôr-bâr′) *v.* to refrain from; resist
   abstenerse *v.* restringirse

fortitude (fôr′tĭ-tōōd′) *n.* strength of mind; courage
   fortaleza *s.* fuerza emocional; valor

furtive (fûr′tĭv) *adj.* sneaky, secretive
   furtivo *adj.* solapado; que tiene un motivo o propósito oculto

glutton (glŭt′n) *n.* a person who eats too much
   glotón *s.* persona que come mucho

haggard (hăg′ərd) *adj.* appearing worn and exhausted
   ojeroso *adj.* de aspecto cansado y exhausto

hapless (hăp′lĭs) *adj.* pitiful; unfortunate
   desafortunado *adj.* desventurado; lastimoso

heritage (hĕr′ĭ-tĭj) *n.* something passed down through generations, such as tradition, values, property
   herencia *s.* tradiciones, valores o propiedades transmitidas de generación en generación

hiatus (hī-ā′təs) *n.* a gap or break in continuity
   pausa *s.* interrupción momentánea

ignominiously (ĭg′nə-mĭn′ē-əs-lē) *adv.* shamefully
   ignominiosamente *adv.* vergonzosamente

impassively (ĭm-păs′ĭv-lē) *adv.* in a way that shows no emotion or feeling
   impasivamente *adv.* sin emoción

impeccably (ĭm-pĕk′ə-blē) *adv.* perfectly; flawlessly
   impecablemente *adv.* sin falla; perfectamente

impede (ĭm-pēd′) *v.* to obstruct or hinder
   impedir *v.* obstruir o dificultar

imperative (ĭm-pĕr′ə-tĭv) *adj.* urgently necessary
  imperativo *adj.* urgentemente necesario

imperceptible (ĭm′pər-sĕp′tə-bəl) *adj.* impossible or difficult to notice
  imperceptible *adj.* imposible o difícil de captar

implacable (ĭm-plăk′ə-bəl) *adj.* impossible to calm or satisfy; relentless
  implacable *adj.* imposible de apaciguar o satisfacer; despiadado

incongruous (ĭn-kŏng′grōō-əs) *adj.* unsuitable; incompatible
  inapropiado *adj.* fuera de lugar; incompatible

indeterminate (ĭn′dĭ-tûr′mə-nĭt) *adj.* not precisely known or determined
  indeterminado *adj.* que no se conoce con precisión

indomitable (ĭn-dŏm′ĭ-tə-bəl) *adj.* not easily discouraged or defeated
  indomable *adj.* que no se deja desalentar, derrotar o someter

inevitable (ĭn-ĕv′ĭ-tə-bəl) *adj.* unavoidable
  inevitable *adj.* que no se puede evitar

infatuated (ĭn-făch′ōō-ā′tĭd) *adj.* intensely fond
  encaprichado *adj.* enamorado

innovative (ĭn′ə-vā′tĭv) *adj.* able to create new, original ideas
  innovador *adj.* que tiene ideas nuevas y originales

insolence (ĭn′sə-ləns) *n.* rudeness and disrespect
  insolencia *s.* grosería y falta de respeto

insuperable (ĭn-sōō′pər-ə-bəl) *adj.* impossible to overcome
  insuperable *adj.* imposible de vencer

intangible (ĭn-tăn′jə-bəl) *adj.* unable to be perceived with the senses
  intangible *adj.* que no se puede percibir con los sentidos

intemperate (ĭn-tĕm′pər-ĭt) *adj.* extreme
  inmoderado *adj.* extremado; desmedido

interloper (ĭn′tər-lō′pər) *n.* one that intrudes in a place, a situation, or an activity
  intruso *s.* el que se mete en un lugar, situación o actividad

interminable (ĭn-tûr′mə-nə-bəl) *adj.* having no limit or end
  interminable *adj.* que no tiene final

irrational (ĭ-răsh′ə-nəl) *adj.* not possessed with reason or understanding
  irracional *adj.* que no se guía por la razón

isolated (ī′sə-lā′tĭd) *adj.* separated from others
  aislado *adj.* separado

lamentation (lăm′ən-tā′shən) *n.* an expression of grief
  lamentación *s.* expresión de dolor

languor (lăng′gər) *n.* a lack of feeling or energy
  languidez *s.* abatimiento físico o emocional

laudable (lô′də-bəl) *adj.* worthy of high praise
  loable *adj.* digno de alabanza

lethargy (lĕth′ər-jē) *n.* prolonged sluggishness; unconsciousness
  letargo *s.* sopor; inconsciencia

lucid (lōō′sĭd) *adj.* clear; mentally sound
  lúcido *adj.* que comprende claramente

malice (măl′ĭs) *n.* a desire to harm others
  malicia *s.* deseo de hacer daño

mandate (măn′dāt′) *n.* a command or instruction
  mandato *s.* orden u instrucción

manipulate (mə-nĭp′yə-lāt′) *v.* to move, operate, or handle
  manipular *v.* mover, manejar

marauder (mə-rôd′ər) *n.* one who raids and loots
  maleante *s.* persona que roba y saquea

meditate (mĕd′ĭ-tāt′) *v.* to consider for a long time
  meditar *s.* considerar por largo tiempo

mentor (mĕn′tôr′) *n.* a wise and trusted counselor or teacher
  mentor *s.* maestro sabio y de confianza

militant (mĭl′ĭ-tənt) *adj.* aggressive or combative
  militante *adj.* de espíritu de lucha o combativo

morose (mə-rōs′) *adj.* gloomy; sullen
  moroso *adj.* lento; triste

naive (nī-ēv′) *adj.* unsophisticated, lacking worldly experience
  ingenuo *adj.* sin malicia ni experiencia

negotiable (nĭ-gō′shə-bəl) *adj.* able to be bargained with
  negociable *adj.* que se puede cambiar o rebajar

neutralize (nōō'trə-līz') *v.* to counteract or cancel out the effect of
neutralizar *v.* contrarrestar o cancelar un efecto

nostalgia (nŏ-stăl'jə) *n.* a wistful longing for the past or the familiar
nostalgia *s.* recuerdo triste del pasado o de lo conocido

oblivious (ə-blĭv'ē-əs) *adj.* paying no attention, completely unaware
distraído *adj.* que no pone atención, ajeno a lo que sucede

ominous (ŏm'ə-nəs) *adj.* menacing; threatening
ominoso *adj.* amenazante

pandemonium (păn'də-mō'nē-əm) *n.* a wild uproar or noise
pandemonio *s.* alboroto o escándalo incontrolable

paranoia (păr'ə-noi'ə) *n.* an irrational fear of danger or misfortune
paranoia *s.* temor irracional

patronize (pā'trə-nīz') *v.* to behave in a manner that shows feelings of superiority
condescender *v.* actuar con superioridad

pensive (pĕn'sĭv) *adj.* thoughtful in a wistful, sad way
pensativo *adj.* meditabundo; triste o preocupado

peremptorily (pə-rĕmp'tə-rə-lē) *adv.* in a commanding way that does not allow for refusal or contradiction
perentorio *adj.* autoritario; que no permite contradicción

permeate (pûr'mē-āt') *v.* to spread or flow throughout
impregnar *v.* calar, penetrar

perpetuation (pər-pĕch'ōō-ā'shən) *n.* the act of continuing or prolonging something
perpetuación *s.* continuación a largo plazo

persevere (pûr'sə-vîr') *v.* to persist in an action or belief despite difficulty
perseverar *v.* persistir; seguir adelante a pesar de dificultades

pertinacity (pûr'tn-ăs'ĭ-tē) *n.* unyielding persistence or adherence
pertinacia *s.* terquedad; persistencia

pervade (pər-vād') *v.* to spread throughout
dominar *v.* invadir; impregnar

perverse (pər-vûrs') *adj.* willfully determined to go against what is expected or desired
perverso *adj.* que contraría con intención

pestilential (pĕs'tə-lĕn'shəl) *adj.* likely to spread and cause disease
pestilente *adj.* que contagia; de mal olor

pinioned (pĭn'yənd) *adj.* restrained or immobilized **pinion** *v.*
inmovilizado *adj.* restringido **inmovilizar** *v.*

precipitous (prĭ-sĭp'ĭ-təs) *adj.* extremely steep
escarpado *adj.* muy inclinado

precursor (prĭ-kûr'sər) *n.* something that comes before and signals or prepares the way for what will follow
precursor *s.* algo que precede o prepara el camino para lo que sigue

predisposed (prē'dĭ-spōzd') *v.* inclined to something in advance
predispuesto *v.* inclinado de antemano a hacer algo

premonition (prē'mə-nĭsh'ən) *n.* a hunch or feeling about the future; a foreboding
premonición *s.* corazonada o presentimiento del futuro

preoccupied (prē-ŏk'yə-pīd') *adj.* absorbed in one's thoughts; distracted
preocupado *adj.* absorto en sus pensamientos; distraído

prestigious (prĕ-stē'jəs) *adj.* having a great reputation; highly respected
prestigioso *adj.* de muy buena reputación; altamente respetado

presumption (prĭ-zŭmp'shən) *n.* behavior or language that is boldly arrogant or offensive
presunción *s.* conducta o lenguaje arrogante u ofensivo

proponent (prə-pō'nənt) *n.* a person who pleads for or supports a cause
defensor *s.* persona que apoya una causa

prostrate (prŏs'trāt') *adj.* lying in a flat, horizontal position
postrado *adj.* en posición horizontal

prowess (prou'ĭs) *n.* superior skill, strength, or courage, especially in battle
valor *s.* gran fuerza, valentía y arrojo, especialmente en la batalla

rapt (răpt) *adj.* fully absorbed; entranced
    embelesado *adj.* totalmente absorto

recompense (rĕk′əm-pĕns′) *n.* amends for damage or payment for service
    recompensa *s.* pago como premio o a cambio de un servicio

recompose (rē′kəm-pōz′) *v.* to restore to calm, to settle again
    serenar *v.* recobrar la calma, poner en orden

reconcile (rĕk′ən-sīl′) *v.* to restore friendly relations
    reconciliarse *v.* volver a las amistades

reconciliation (rĕk′ən-sĭl′ē-ā′shən) *n.* the act of settling or resolving
    reconciliación *s.* acto de arreglar o resolver

reiterate (rē-ĭt′ə-rāt′) *v.* to repeat
    reiterar *v.* repetir

rejuvenated (rĭ-jōō′və-nā′tĭd) *adj.* made new or young again **rejuvenate** *v.*
    rejuvenecido *adj.* que ha recuperado la juventud
    rejuvenecer *v.*

replenish (rĭ-plĕn′ĭsh) *v.* to fill again
    reponer *v.* volver a llenar

reprehensible (rĕp′rĭ-hĕn′sə-bəl) *adj.* deserving blame and criticism
    reprensible *adj.* que merece culpa y crítica

reprisal (rĭ-prī′zəl) *n.* retaliation in the form of harm or injury similar to that received
    represalia *s.* venganza con daños o heridas similares a los recibidos

repute (rĭ-pyōōt′) *n.* reputation; fame
    renombre *s.* reputación; fama

resignation (rĕz′ĭg-nā′shən) *n.* passive acceptance of something; submission
    resignación *s.* aceptación pasiva; sumisión

respite (rĕs′pĭt) *n.* a period of rest or relief
    respiro *s.* período breve de descanso o alivio

resurrect (rĕz′ə-rĕkt′) *v.* to bring back to life
    resucitar *v.* traer de vuelta a la vida

reticence (rĕt′ĭ-səns) *n.* the quality of keeping silent or reserved
    reticencia *s.* reserva; prudencia y discreción

retrospect (rĕt′rə-spĕkt′) *n.* a view or contemplation of something past
    retrospectiva *s.* contemplación del pasado

reverence (rĕv′ər-əns) *n.* awe and respect
    reverencia *s.* admiración y respeto

rhetoric (rĕt′ər-ĭk) *n.* grand but empty talk
    retórica *s.* discurso grandilocuente y vacío

rigorous (rĭg′ər-əs) *adj.* strict, uncompromising
    riguroso *adj.* estricto, intransigente

robustly (rō-bŭst′lē) *adv.* in a strong, powerful way
    enérgicamente *adv.* con fuerza y vigor

rudimentary (rōō′də-mĕn′tə-rē) *adj.* very basic, in the beginning stages
    rudimentario *adj.* básico, en las etapas iniciales

sate (sāt) *v.* to satisfy fully
    saciar *v.* satisfacer por completo

savagery (săv′ĭj-rē) *n.* extreme violence or cruelty
    salvajismo *s.* violencia o crueldad extremas

savoring (sā′vər-ĭng) *n.* a full appreciation and enjoyment **savor** *v.*
    sabor *s.* aprecio y gusto **saborear** *v.*

sententiously (sĕn-tĕn′shəs-lē) *adv.* in a pompous, moralizing manner
    sentenciosamente *adv.* en tono pomposo y regañón

sentiment (sĕn′tə-mənt) *n.* feeling or emotion
    sentimiento *s.* emoción

silhouette (sĭl′ōō-ĕt′) *n.* an outline that appears dark against a light background
    silueta *s.* perfil que se destaca sobre un fondo claro

sinister (sĭn′ĭ-stər) *adj.* threatening or foreshadowing evil
    siniestro *adj.* que amenaza un mal

smite (smīt) *v.* to inflict a heavy blow on; *past tense*—smote (smōt)
    golpear *v.* dar un fuerte golpe

sovereignty (sŏv′ər-ĭn-tē) *n.* complete independence and self-governance
   soberanía *s.* independencia completa y autogobierno

speculative (spĕk′yə-lə-tĭv) *adj.* based on guesses and theories rather than fact
   especulativo *adj.* basado en suposiciones y no en hechos

stark (stärk) *adj.* harsh or grim
   crudo *adj.* duro o agreste

stature (stăch′ər) *n.* the height of a person, animal, or object in an upright position
   estatura *s.* altura de una persona, animal u objeto en posición vertical

stealth (stĕlth) *n.* a concealed manner of acting
   secreto *s.* conducta callada u oculta

stratagem (străt′ə-jəm) *n.* a clever trick or device for obtaining an advantage
   estratagema *s.* truco o maquinación para conseguir ventaja

stridently (strīd′nt-lē) *adv.* harshly; conspicuously
   estridentemente *adj.* con dureza y escándalo

stupor (stōō′pər) *n.* a state of mental numbness, as from shock
   estupor *s.* pasmo; profundo asombro

sublime (sə-blīm′) *adj.* supreme, splendid
   sublime *adj.* supremo, espléndido

subordinate (sə-bôr′dn-āt′) *v.* to lower in rank or importance
   subordinar *v.* bajar de rango o importancia

succession (sək-sĕsh′ən) *n.* the sequence in which one person after another acquires a title, dignity, or estate
   sucesión *s.* secuencia en que se transmiten títulos, rango o propiedades de una persona a otra

succor (sŭk′ər) *n.* help in a difficult situation
   socorro *s.* ayuda en una situación difícil

supposition (sŭp′ə-zĭsh′ən) *n.* something supposed; an assumption
   suposición *s.* conjetura; creencia

synchronize (sĭng′krə-nīz′) *v.* to match the timing of
   sincronizar *v.* hacer que dos cosas ocurran al mismo tiempo

tact (tăkt) *n.* an understanding of the proper thing to do or say around others
   tacto *s.* sensibilidad para tratar a otras personas con delicadeza

tactic (tăk′tĭk) *n.* a planned action or maneuver to reach a certain goal
   táctica *s.* acción o maniobra planeada para alcanzar una meta

tenacity (tə-năs′ĭ-tē) *n.* the quality of holding persistently to something; firm determination
   tenacidad *s.* tesón y constancia; obstinación

trajectory (trə-jĕk′tə-rē) *n.* the path of a moving body through space
   trayectoria *s.* camino que sigue un objeto en movimiento en el espacio

transgress (trăns-grĕs′) *v.* to violate or break (a law, command, or moral code)
   transgredir *v.* violar una ley, una orden o un código moral

translucent (trăns-lōō′sənt) *adj.* allowing light to shine through
   translúcido *adj.* que deja pasar la luz

trauma (trô′mə) *n.* severe physical or emotional distress
   trauma *s.* daño físico o emocional fuerte

tremulous (trĕm′yə-ləs) *adj.* trembling, unsteady
   trémulo *adj.* tembloroso

tribulation (trĭb′yə-lā′shən) *n.* great distress or suffering
   tribulación *s.* gran sufrimiento o preocupación

unavailing (ŭn′ə-vā′lĭng) *adj.* useless, ineffective
   inservible *adj.* inútil, ineficaz

unperturbed (ŭn′pər-tûrbd′) *adj.* calm and serene; untroubled
   impasible *adj.* calmo y sereno; impertérrito

usurper (yōō-sûrp′ər) *n.* someone who wrongfully takes possession of something
   usurpador *s.* el que toma posesión de algo que no le corresponde

vagrant (vā′grənt) *adj.* wandering
   vagabundo *adj.* que va de un lado al otro sin rumbo fijo

vehemently (vē′ə-mənt-lē) *adv.* in a fierce, intense manner
   vehementemente *adv.* con intensidad

vigilance (vĭj′ə-ləns) *n.* alert attention, watchfulness
   vigilancia *s.* atención alerta, cuidado

vindicate (vĭn′dĭ-kāt′) *v.* to clear of suspicion, doubt, or blame
   vindicar *v.* exculpar de sospecha o duda

voluble (vŏl′yə-bəl) *adj.* especially talkative, fluent with words
   locuaz *adj.* hablador, charlatán

voracity (vô-răs′ĭ-tē) *n.* greed for food
   voracidad *s.* apetito ansioso

wince (wĭns) *v.* to shrink or flinch involuntarily, especially in pain
   estremecerse *v.* encogerse o contraerse involuntariamente por dolor

wizened (wĭz′ənd) *adj.* withered and dry
   arrugado *adj.* seco y marchito

Pronunciation Key

Symbol	Examples	Symbol	Examples	Symbol	Examples
ă	**a**t, g**a**s	m	**m**an, see**m**	v	**v**an, sa**ve**
ā	**a**pe, d**ay**	n	**n**ight, mitt**en**	w	**w**eb, t**w**ice
ä	f**a**ther, b**a**rn	ng	si**ng**, ha**ng**er	y	**y**ard, law**y**er
âr	f**air**, d**are**	ŏ	**o**dd, n**o**t	z	**z**oo, rea**s**on
b	**b**ell, ta**b**le	ō	**o**pen, r**oa**d, gr**ow**	zh	trea**s**ure, gara**ge**
ch	**ch**in, lun**ch**	ô	**aw**ful, b**ough**t, h**o**rse	ə	**a**wake, ev**e**n, penc**i**l,
d	**d**ig, bore**d**	oi	c**oi**n, b**oy**		pil**o**t, foc**u**s
ĕ	**e**gg, t**e**n	ŏŏ	l**oo**k, f**u**ll	ər	p**er**form, lett**er**
ē	**e**vil, s**ee**, m**ea**l	ōō	r**oo**t, gl**ue**, thr**ough**		
f	**f**all, lau**gh**, **ph**rase	ou	**ou**t, c**ow**	**Sounds in Foreign Words**	
g	**g**old, bi**g**	p	**p**ig, ca**p**	KH	*German* i**ch**, au**ch**;
h	**h**it, in**h**ale	r	**r**ose, sta**r**		*Scottish* lo**ch**
hw	**wh**ite, every**wh**ere	s	**s**it, fa**ce**	N	*French* e**n**tre, bo**n**, fi**n**
ĭ	**i**nch, f**i**t	sh	**sh**e, ma**sh**	œ	*French* f**eu**, c**œu**r;
ī	**i**dle, m**y**, tr**ie**d	t	**t**ap, hop**ped**		*German* sch**ö**n
îr	d**ear**, **h**ere	th	**th**ing, wi**th**	ü	*French* **u**tile, r**ue**;
j	**j**ar, **g**em, ba**dge**	*th*	**th**en, o**th**er		*German* gr**ü**n
k	**k**eep, **c**at, lu**ck**	ŭ	**u**p, n**u**t		
l	**l**oad, ratt**le**	ûr	f**ur**, **ear**n, b**ir**d, w**or**m		

Stress Marks

′ This mark indicates that the preceding syllable receives the primary stress. For example, in the word *language*, the first syllable is stressed: lăng′gwĭj.

′ This mark is used only in words in which more than one syllable is stressed. It indicates that the preceding syllable is stressed, but somewhat more weakly than the syllable receiving the primary stress. In the word *literature*, for example, the first syllable receives the primary stress, and the last syllable receives a weaker stress: lĭt′ər-ə-chŏŏr′.

Adapted from *The American Heritage Dictionary of the English Language,* fourth edition. Copyright © 2006 by Houghton Mifflin Harcourt Publishing Company. Used with the permission of Houghton Mifflin Harcourt Publishing Company.

Index of Skills

Compound predicates, R59
Compound sentences, 967, 1037, R49, R63
Comprehension. *See* Assessment; Reading skills and strategies.
Computer software. *See* Software.
Conciseness in writing, 381, 451, 994
Conclusions
    deductive, 647–651, R115
    drawing, 11, 37–45, 75, 79, 133, 199, 215, 235, 322, 325–334, 353, 379, 449, 453–471, 487, 675, 685, 695–707, 784, 949, 965, 978, 992, 1017, 1128, 1141, 1219, 1237, 1257, 1273, 1293, R33, R116
    graphic organizer for, 11, 37, 325
    inaccurate, R23
    inductive, 653, 660, R115, R117
    kinds of, R33
    in own writing, 616, 827, 1033, 1036, 1300, 1350, 1358, R33
    in speeches, R77
    strengthening, 154, 616, 1302
    valid, R115
Conflict, 30–35, R104
    analyzing, 37–45, 49–61, 79–96
    central, R37
    character and, 49–61, 79–96, 141, 219, 453, 985
    cultural, 985
    in drama, 1071, 1083, 1107, *also* 1169, R2
    external, R104
    identifying, 435, 1107
    internal, R104
    in narrative poetry, 141
    in narrative writing, 280, 284, 302, 336, R37
    plot and, 30–35, 37–45, 420, R104
    resolution of, 49
    setting and, 28, 79–96, 427
    suspense and, 30, 113
    theme and, 420, 427, 453
Conjunctions
    coordinating, 130, 135, R47
    correlative, R47, R65
    run-on sentences and, R64
    subordinating, R47
Conjunctive adverbs, 1305
Connecting, 98–103, 183–199, 246–251, 336–339, 343–353, 537, 548–551, 552–555, 572–575, 598–601, 824–827, 910–913, 941–949, 980–983, 1290–1293
Connections, making, 11, 78, 98, 104, 324, 336, 340, 452, 470, 474, 694, 710, 714, 984, 995, 996
Connotation, 74, 97, 216, 223, 264, 350, 386, 436, 540, 634, 668, 686, 796, 905, 950, 1078, 1138, 1142, 1159, 1253, 1292, R71, R104. *See also* Denotation.

Consonance, 772, 803, R104
Consumer documents, R17, R116. *See also* Business writing; Workplace and technical writing; Workplace documents.
Content-area vocabulary. *See* Academic vocabulary; Domain-specific vocabulary; Specialized vocabulary.
Context clues, 865, 882, 1100, 1271, R15, R68, R71, R116. *See also* Vocabulary, in context.
    biographical, 245, 449
    cause-and-effect, R68
    comparison, R68
    contrast, R68
    cultural, 936–937, R112
    definition or restatement, R68
    examples of, R68
    general, R68
    historical, 999
    Shakespearean language, 1194
    social, 215, 908
    specific, R68
    word roots and, R68
Contractions
    avoiding, in formal language, 317, 323
    in dialogue, 70, 77
Contracts, R116
Contrasts, recognizing, 545
Contrasting expressions, 501
Controlling idea. *See also* Main idea. 148, 149, 150, 151, 152, 390, 395, 498, 499, 829, 833, 916, 1030, 1031, 1035, 1342, 1349, 1353, R31, R120
Conversation, R81
Copyright page, 1331, 1336
Correspondence, business, R115
Costumes
    design of, 1263, 1290
    as mise en scène, 1295, R87, R109
Counterclaims, 632–633, 651, 679–685, 742, 748, 1300, 1304, R21, R116
Couplet, 779, 811, R104
Credibility, 577, R90, R92, R116. *See also* Sources.
Crisis. *See* Climax.
Critical essays, R105
Critical interpretation, 45, 115, 225, 257, 273, 353, 371, 379, 435, 707, 784, 792, 801, 875, 978, 992, 1237, 1257, 1273, 1288
Critical listening, R83
Critical reading. *See* Reading skills and strategies; Test-taking strategies.
Critical reviews, writing, R116
Critical thinking. *See* Text analysis; Reading skills and strategies.
Criticism. *See* Text criticism.

Critique, 679–685, 910–913, R116
Cultural characteristics, analysis of, 953–965
Cultural conflict, analysis of, 985–992
Cultural influences, 934–939, 1027
Currency of sources. *See* Sources.

D

Dactyl, R109
Dashes, 317, 617, R50
Databases, 1330, R116. *See also* References.
Debates, 238, R79, R116
    evaluating, R79
    holding, 1309
    planning, 1308
Deductive reasoning, 647–651, R23, R115, R116
Definition analysis, R40
Degree of importance, R32, R35
Delivery. *See* Speaking strategies.
Demographics, R85
Denotation, 97, 216, 223, 264, 350, 386, 540, 950, 1078, R71, R104. *See also* Connotation.
Denouement. *See* Resolution.
Derivations of words, 332, 595, 1140, R69. *See also* Word parts, analyzing.
Descriptive language. *See* Details.
Descriptive speech, R80
Descriptive writing, 473, R34–R35. *See also* Writing skills and strategies.
    key techniques in, R34–R35
    options for organization, R35
    rubric for, R34
Design, elements of, R91–R92
Design, visual. *See* Visual elements.
Details, 129
    concrete, 392
    descriptive, 12, 55, 63, 107, 286, 361, 373, 458, 473, 544, 565, 571, 1249, 1289
    sensory, 383–389, 879–885, 895, 1021–1025, R34, R35, R79, R80, R112
    supporting, 246–251, 375, 539, 824
Dewey decimal system, 1340
Diagrams, 119, 557, 1031, R6. *See also* Graphic aids; Graphic organizers.
    elements of design, R91
    picture diagrams, R6
    as reading strategy, 119, 557, R6, R15
    schematic diagrams, 549, R6
    sentence, R48
    of story events, R2
    Venn, 115, 353, 499, 601, 609, R12
Dialect, 817–823, R104. *See also* Standard English.
Dialogue, 259, R105. *See also* Monologue.
    in drama, 7, 1064, 1166, 1169, 1186–1187, 1194, 1199, 1290

persuasive, 742–751

text analysis, R39–R40

Ethical appeal, 634

Etymologies, 93, 120, 146, 558, 600, 607, 644, 732, 861, 909, 946, 988, 1108, 1232, R70. *See also* Word origins.

Evaluation

  of arguments, 487, 634, 637, 643, 685, R23, R25–R26

  of information, 339, 371, 651, 660, 913, 983, R14–R20

  of interpretations, 545

  of literature, 45, 75, 96, 103, 133, 147, 215, 225, 322, 389, 471, 481, 487, 537, 545, 569, 792, 809, 827, 899, 1017

  of media messages, 10, R84, R92

  of oral presentations, R78–R81

  of sources, 1333–1338, 1341, 1345

  of writing, 1361

Everyday texts. *See* Consumer documents; Job applications; Public documents; Workplace documents.

Evidence, 12, 148, 251, 325, 339, 375, 390, 393, 395, 498, 500, 632, 639–643, 647, 653, 748, 834, 913, 983, 1032, 1034, 1036, 1300, 1333, 1342, R21–R26, R38, R41, R79, R83, R115, R116

  analysis of, 483–487, 647–651

  bias in, R25, R115

  citing, FM46, 913, 983, 1354

  collecting, 744, 1032

  deductive reasoning and, R116

  versus emotional appeals, 634, R116

  generalizations, 251

  inductive reasoning and, 653–660, R22–R23

  inferences based on, 12

  from multiple sources, 915, 1354

  and organization, R41

  in speeches, R77–R78

  types of, 1326, 1333–1341, R24

  variety of, 395,

Exaggeration. *See* Hyperbole; Irony, verbal.

Exclamation points, 854, R49

Expert opinion, 639, 647, 744, R25, R41, R79, R91

Explanatory writing. *See* Informative writing.

Exposition, of plot, 30, R2, R105. *See also* Plot.

Expressive writing. *See* Narrative writing.

Extemporaneous speeches, R76. *See also* Oral presentations.

Extended metaphors, 788, 792, R106

External conflict, 30, 453, R104

Eye contact, while speaking, 159, 401, 753, R78–R80

F

Fable, R106

Facial expression in speeches, R78–R80, R82–R83

Facts, 744, R116–R117. *See also* Evidence; Supporting statements.

  in elaboration, R33

  media credibility and, 577, 739

  versus opinion, 639–643, 969–978, R24, R83, R116–R117

  synthesizing, 336–339, 913

  verifying, R25

Fallacy, R24, R116, R117

Falling action, 30, R2, R106. *See also* Plot.

False analogy, R24

False cause, R25

False dilemma, R24

Fantasy, R106

Farce, 4, 258, R106

  characters in, 259–273

Faulty reasoning, R24

Fear, appeals to, 634, R22, R116

Feature articles, 4, 8, 336, 526–531, 633, R117

Feedback. *See* Peer response.

Fiction, strategies for reading, 5, 11–15, R2. *See also* Reading skills and strategies.

Fiction, types of, 4, 5

  fantasy, R106

  historical, 5, R107

  horror, R107

  novellas, 4, 5, R110

  novels, 4, 5, R109

  realistic, R111

  science fiction, 5, 324, R112

  short stories, 4, 5, R112

Field research, 1338

Figurative language, 6, 54, 141, 489, 774, 775, 787–792, 1094, 1131, R68, R106

  extended metaphors, 788, 792, R106

  hyperbole, 774, 1161, R106, R107, R114

  metaphors, 736, 774, 787, 788, 792, 815, 1162, R106, R109

  onomatopoeia, 779, 783, 879–885, R110

  paradox, R110

  personification, 331, 774–775, 787, 790, 792, 866, 877, R110

  similes, 373, 736, 774–775, 787, 887, 1131, 1162, R112

Figures of speech. *See* Figurative language.

Film reviews, R33, R116

Films, 136, 276, 1294–1297, R86–R88. *See also* Camera shots in film and video; Editing, of films and video; Media elements and techniques.

  characterization in, 276–279, 1295

  documentaries, 1326, 1332

  editing of, 291, R88

feature, 10, 136, 276, 1294

  and product placement, 10, R91

  as research source, 1326, 1332

  script and written elements, 290, R86

  setting in, 136–139, 1295

  sound in, 137, R87

  special effects in, R88

  storyboards, 139, 290, R86

  visual elements in, 137–139, 277, 1027–1029, R87–R88

Firsthand and expressive writing. *See* Narrative writing.

First-person narrators. *See* Narrators.

First-person point of view. *See* Point of view.

Fixed expressions, 446, 1003, 1070, 1245

Flashbacks, 304–305, 307, 334, 355–371, 594, R36, R106

Flat characters, 176–177, R103

Flow chart, 417, 1365

Foils (character), 199, 1161, R106

Folk ballads, 817, R103

Folk tales. *See* Oral tradition.

Foreign words in English, 825, 876, 960, 1124, R70, R129

Foreshadowing, 79, 304, 355–371, 1194

  to create suspense, R107, R113

Formal language, 312, 317, 323, 615, 677, 684, 687, 911, 951, 1131, R42, R76

Formatting

  persuasive letter, 610, 615, 616

  quotations, 1359, 1354, R50

  research paper, 1360

  script, 1171

  workplace documents, R42–R44

  works cited, 1359, 1362–1363

Form in poetry, 770–771, 787, 795–801, 811, 815, 817, 879, R107

Forms of writing. *See* Writing skills and strategies.

Fragments. *See* Sentence fragments.

Frame (on screen), 277, 1295, R87, R88

Frame story, R107

Free verse, 770–771, 795–801, 895–899, R107

Freewriting, 23, 149. *See also* Quickwriting.

Functional reading, R3–R20

Functional texts, 8, 552–555. *See also* Consumer documents; Workplace documents.

G

Generalizations, R117

  in deductive reasoning, 647–651, R23, R115, R116

  hasty, 632, R24

  in inductive reasoning, 653–660, R22–R23, R115, R117

  making, 251, 379

overgeneralization, 653, R24, R118. *See also* Stereotyping.

General pronoun reference, R55

Genre, 4, 901, 1145, R107. *See also* Drama; Fiction; Informational texts; Literary nonfiction; Poetic forms.
  argument across, 629, 717–735, 1298–1307
  author's message across, 489–496
  comparing across, 415, 489–496, 717–735, 1145–1161
  parody across, 1145–1161
  Gerunds and gerund phrases, 566, 988, 994, R60, R61

Gestures, while speaking, R78

Glittering generality, 739, R22

Glossary, 134, 546, 1018, R72, R102, R115, R121

Government publications, R117

Grammar, R46–R65. *See also specific grammar concepts*.
  and style, 43, 47, 55, 63, 70, 77, 111, 116, 130, 135, 195, 200, 209, 217, 232, 237, 263, 275, 317, 323, 361, 373, 377, 381, 432, 437, 451, 458, 473, 544, 547, 565, 571, 642, 645, 657, 662, 668, 677, 684, 687, 703, 709, 785, 793, 866, 877, 893, 944, 951, 964, 967, 988, 994, 1005, 1019, 1079, 1109, 1135, 1143, 1249, 1289, R99

Grammar in Context, 151, 155, 283, 287, 393, 397, 501, 505, 613, 617, 745, 749, 831, 835, 917, 1033, 1037, 1167, 1171, 1305

Graphic aids, 548–551, 552–555, R5–R7, R14
  captions, 548, 598, 599, R3, R6, R15, R18
  charts, R6
  in consumer documents, R17
  cutaway diagrams, 550
  diagrams, 549, 550, 552, R6
  graphs, R5
  interpreting, 548–551, 572–575, 580–583
  maps, 580–583, R7
  photographs, 549, 599
  pie graphs, R5
  in public documents, R6
  schematic diagrams, 549
  strategies for reading, 552–555, R15, R17, R18, R27
  synthesizing information from, 572–575
  tables, R6

Graphic organizers, 557, R117
  balance scales, 678
  category chart, 1322
  for cause-and-effect, 11, 539, 557, 1031, R10, R38

charts, 45, 580, 1111, 1161, 1257
  for chronological order, 557
  cluster diagrams, 1031
  diagrams, 557, 1031
  pro/con chart, 1322
  points of comparison chart, 496
  for spatial order, 557
  story maps or story graphs, 281, 1165, R21
  timelines, 557
  Venn diagrams, 115, 353, 499, 601, 609
  webs, R2

Graphing calculator, R17

Greek drama, 1064–1065. *See also* Greek tragedy.

Greek tragedy, 1058–1059, 1067–1107
  analysis of, 1062, 1067–1107

Greek word parts, 46, 93, 120, 549, 648, 649, 909, 960, 963, 993, 1005, 1108, R69–R70. *See also* Word roots.

Group discussion, FM46, 291, 508–509, R81

H

Haiku, 6, 770, 895, R107

Harlem Renaissance literature, 817

Hasty generalizations, 632, R24

Hero, 1060–1061, R105, R107. *See also* Protagonist; Tragic hero.

Hierarchical organization. *See* Order of importance.

Historical context of literature, 49, 65, 107, 119, 239, 259, 309, 325, 343, 375, 383, 439, 453, 483, 557, 585, 647, 653, 695, 717, 857, 941, 953, 969, 985, 999, 1111, 1186–1189, 1194
  analyzing, 322, 481, 885, 899, 936–937, 965, 969–978, 999–1017, 1128, 1219

Historical documents, 734, 980, R18, R117

Historical fiction, 5, R107

Historical narratives, 106
  mood in, 107–115

Homonyms, R71

Homophones, 84, 430, 464, 721, R71

Horror fiction, R107

Humor, 259, 532, 1027, 1145, R107. *See also* Comedy; Farce; Parody; Understatement.

Hyperbole, 774, 1161, R106, R107, R114

Hyperlinks, 10, 919, 1325, R20

Hyphens, R50, R74

I

Iamb, 811, R109. *See also* Blank verse; Iambic pentameter; Sonnet.

Iambic pentameter, 811, 892, 1192, 1210, R103, R107, R113. *See also* Blank verse; Sonnet.

Ideas, 4, 11, 20, 533, R29. *See also* Main ideas.
  finding, for writing, 281, 610, 742, R28
  identifying main, 246–251
  organizing. *See* Patterns of organization.
  supporting, with details, 246–251, R101
  synthesizing, 336–339
  using transitions to connect, R32

Idioms, 196, 231, 268, 314, R68, R108

Illogical comparisons, R58

Imagery, 253, 774–775, 802, R108
  analysis of, 496, 539, 795–801
  and author's purpose, 539, 603–609
  creating, xxx
  in nonfiction, 668
  in poetry, 6, 253, 772, 774–775, 795–801, 895
  sensory, 545, 887
  in speech, 710–713
  tone and, 668, 677, 951

Imagism, 895–899

Implied main idea, R31

Indefinite pronouns, R55

Independent (main) clauses, R32, R62

Independent observation, 1338

Independent reading level, 15, R27

Indexes, R117. *See also* References.
  as part of a book, 1331
  in virtual libraries, 1340

Indirect objects, R48, R53, R60

Inductive reasoning, 653–660, R22–R23, R115, R117

Inferences, making, 49–61, 133, 141, 147, 225, 235, 245, 253–257, 309–322, 481, 603, 609, 675, 806, 992, 1128, 1273
  about authors, 887–892
  about characters, 49, 203–215, 245, 277, 379, 389, 439–449, 707, 875, 1131–1141, 1237
  about memoirs, 949
  about poetry, 603–609, 887, 899
  about setting, 309, 322
  about speakers, 141, 253–257

Infinitives and infinitive phrases, 893, R59, R61

Inflection. *See* Speaking strategies.

Informal language, 53, 69, 323, 677, 852, 911, 951, 1010, R68, R76. *See also* Slang.

Information. *See also* Electronic media; Informational texts; References; Sources.
  evaluating, 1333–1337, 1345
  from multiple sources, 551, 915, 1350
  reading for, 60, 117, 201, 246–251, 370, 470, 548, 598, 608, 663, 808, 824, 884, 910–913, 948, 980, 995, 1127, 1290

oral interpretations, R80
oral response to literature, 159, R80–R81
persuasive speech, 710–713, R79, R83
presenting a literary analysis, 158–159, 400–401
props, R87, R111
Oral tradition
fables, R106
folk ballad, 817, R103
legends, R108
myths, 1065, 1097, R108, R109
tall tales, R114
Order of importance, 98, 830, 834, R8, R35
Order of impression, R35
Order words and phrases, R9
Organizational patterns. *See* Patterns of organization.
Organizing. *See* Graphic organizers; Patterns of organization.
Origin of words, 644, R70. *See also* Word roots.
Outlines, 737, 1031, 1349
drafting from, 21
for taking notes, R4
Overgeneralization, 653, R24, R118
Oversimplification, R24, R117
Overview, 1321, 1328, R118, R93
Oxymoron, R110

P

Pace, 280, 289, 753, 953, R27, R77, R88
Pacing. *See* Speaking strategies.
Paradox, R110
Paragraphs
coherence of, R31–R32
organizing, R31
topic sentence in, R31, R120
transitions in, R32–R33
unity of, R31
Parallelism, 505, 636, 637, 653–660, 793, 879–885, 983, 1192–1193, 1196, R110
Parallel structure, 498, 505, R64
Paraphrasing, 103, 551, 689–693, 830, 857–875, 1194, 1347, R28, R118
Parentheses, 98, 101, R50
Parenthetical documentation, 1351, 1354. *See also* Works cited.
Parodies, 1156, R110
analysis of, 1145–1161
Participles and participial phrases, 287, 547, R61
to add details, 544, 547
dangling, R61
misplaced, R61
past, R55
present, R55
Parts analysis, R40

Parts of a book, 1331
Parts of speech. *See also specific parts of speech.*
reference chart, R46–R47
Passive voice. *See* Voice.
Past participle verb forms, R55
Pastoral, R110
Patterns of organization, 528–529, 539–545, R8–R13, R41, R118
cause-effect, 528–529, 1030–1039, R10–R11, R38, R115
chronological order, 107–115, 304, 325–334, 533, 1166, R8, R36, R115
classification, 528, R115
comparison-contrast, 498–507, 528–529, 737, R11–R13, R37–R38, R113
deductive, 647–651, R23, R116
effect-to-cause, R38
hierarchical, R35
inductive, 653–660, R22–R23, R117
logical, 647–651, R22–R23, R38, R117, R118
main idea and supporting details, R8–R9
order of importance, R8, R38
order of impression, R35
point-by-point, 503, R11, R37, R41
problem-solution, R39, R119
sequential, R119
signal words for, 528
spatial order, R35, R119
subject-by-subject, R11, R38
Peer review, 21, 23, 152, 284, 394, 502, 614, 746, 832, 918, 1032, 1034, 1168, 1302, 1352, R30
Performing arts. *See* Drama.
Periodicals, 1326, 1329, 1332, 1337, R118
Periods (punctuation), R49
Persona, R110. *See also* Speakers.
Personal essay, 900–908, R105
Personal narrative, 21, R36
Personification, 331, 774–775, 787, 790, 792, 866, 877, R110
Perspective. *See also* Point of view.
author's, 239–245, 343, 375, 526–527, 585, 910, 999–1017, R102
shifts in, 674, 682
Persuasion, 634–637, R118. *See also* Argumentative techniques.
in fiction, 695–707
in the media, 635
in political advertising, 738–741
in speeches, 635, 710–713
techniques for. *See* Argumentative techniques.
text analysis of, 695–707
theme and, 695–707, 699
Persuasive letter, writing, 610–619
Philosophical assumptions. *See* Assumptions.
Philosophical context, 96

Photographs, 8, 23, 548, 598, 1328, 1365, R3, R5, R89, R91, R117, R119, R120
Phrases
absolute, 920
adjective, R60
adverb, R60
appositive, 381, R60
gerund, R60, R61
infinitive, R61
introductory, 503
participial, R61
prepositional, 55, 63, 1143, R47, R48, R53, R59, R60
transitional, 504
verbal, 547, R60–R61
Pie graph, R5
Plagiarism, 1348. *See also* Parenthetical documentation; Works cited.
Planned drafting, R28
Planning/prewriting, 21, 23, 149–150, 281–282, 391–392, 499–500, 611–612, 743–744, 829–830, 915–916, 1031–1032, 1165–1166, 1299–1300, 1343–1344, R28
Plays. *See* Drama.
Plot, 30–35, R110
analysis of, 30–35, 37–45
characters and, 176, 178
climax, 30, 35, 45, 59, 61, 435, R2, R104, R105, R106
complications in, 30, 137, 1247, R104, R112
conflict and, 30–35, 37–45, 75, 420, R104
development of, 30, 1164
diagram of, 30
in drama, 1168, 1190
exposition, 30, R2, R105
falling action, 30, R2, R106
flashback and, 304–305
foreshadowing and, 79, 304, 355
in narrative writing, 141, R109
organization of, R37
parallel, R110
point of view and, 141
reading strategies for, 12, 15, 30
resolution, 30, 49, R2
rising action, 30, 41, R2, R104, R105, R112
stages of, 30–35. *See also* climax; exposition; falling action; resolution; rising action, *above*.
surprise ending, 427, R113
suspense and, 30, 133, 569, R113
Plot lines, multiple, 281
Poetic devices and elements, R110. *See also* Poetic forms.

INDEX OF TITLES & AUTHORS

Page numbers that appear in italics refer to biographical information.

ACKNOWLEDGMENTS

INTRODUCTORY UNIT

Naomi Shihab Nye: "Making a Fist," from *Hugging the Jukebox* by Naomi Shihab Nye. Copyright © 1982 by Naomi Shihab Nye. By permission of the author, Naomi Shihab Nye.

International Creative Management: Excerpt from "Twelve Angry Men," from *Six Television Plays* by Reginald Rose. Published by Simon & Schuster, Inc. Copyright © 1956 by Reginald Rose. Reprinted by permission of International Creative Management, Inc.

Scribner: Excerpt from *Kaffir Boy: The True Story of a Black Youth's Coming of Age in Apartheid South Africa* by Mark Mathabane. Copyright © 1986 by Mark Mathabane. All rights reserved. Reprinted with the permission of Scribner, a Division of Simon & Schuster, Inc.

Scholastic: From "South Africa's Decade of Freedom" by Michael Wines. Published in *The New York Times Upfront*, September 6, 2004. Copyright © 2004 by Scholastic Inc. Reprinted by permission of Scholastic Inc.

HarperCollins Publishers and John Hawkins & Associates: Excerpt from "Where Is Here?," from *Where Is Here?: Stories* by Joyce Carol Oates. Copyright © 1992 by The Ontario Review, Inc. All rights reserved. Reprinted by permission of HarperCollins Publishers and John Hawkins & Associates, Inc.

UNIT 1

University of Pittsburgh Press: "The Bass, the River, and Sheila Mant," from *The Man Who Loved Levittown* by W. D. Wetherell, © 1985. Reprinted by permission of the University of Pittsburgh Press.

Dell Publishing: "Harrison Bergeron," from *Welcome to the Monkey House* by Kurt Vonnegut, Jr. Copyright © 1961 by Kurt Vonnegut, Jr. Used by permission of Dell Publishing, a division of Random House, Inc.

Houghton Mifflin Harcourt: "Everyday Use," from *In Love & Trouble: Stories of Black Women* by Alice Walker. Copyright © 1973 by Alice Walker. Reprinted by permission of Houghton Mifflin Harcourt Publishing Company.

Roland L. Freeman: "Alice Walker on Quilting" by Alice Walker, from *A Communion of the Spirits* by Roland L. Freeman. Copyright © 2008 Roland L. Freeman. Published by Rutledge Hill Press. Reprinted by permission of Roland L. Freeman.

Brandt & Hochman Literary Agents: "Searching for Summer," from *The Green Flash and Other Tales of Horror, Suspense, and Fantasy* by Joan Aiken. Copyright © 1957, 1958, 1959, 1960, 1965, 1968, 1969, 1971 by Joan Aiken. Used by permission of Brandt & Hochman Literary Agents, Inc. All rights reserved.

W. W. Norton & Company: From *Deep Survival: Who Lives, Who Dies, and Why* by Laurence Gonzales. Copyright © 2003 by Laurence Gonzales. Used by permission of W. W. Norton & Company, Inc.

Simon & Schuster Adult Publishing Group: Excerpt from *The Johnstown Flood* by David G. McCullough. Copyright © 1968 by David G. McCullough, and renewed © 1996, by David G. McCullough. Reprinted with the permission of Simon & Schuster, Inc.

People Weekly: Excerpt from "Nine-Year-Old Amber Colvin Rides Out a Killer Flood in Ohio" by Michael Neill and Ken Myers, *People Weekly*, 2 July 1990. Copyright © 1990 Time Inc. All rights reserved. Reprinted from People Magazine with permission.

Crown Business: From *The Leadership Moment: Nine True Stories of Triumph and Disaster and Their Lessons for Us All* by Michael Useem. Copyright © 1998 by Michael Useem. Used by permission of Crown Business, a division of Random House, Inc.

Susan Bergholz Literary Services: "Exile," from *The Other Side/ El Otro Lado* by Julia Alvarez. Copyright © 1995 by Julia Alvarez. Published by Plume/Penguin, a division of Penguin Group (USA). Reprinted by permission of Susan Bergholz Literary Services, New York, NY and Lamy, NM. All rights reserved.

Joy Harjo: "Crossing the Border," from *How We Became Human: New and Selected Poems* by Joy Harjo. W. W. Norton, New York, NY, 2002. Copyright © 2002 by Joy Harjo. Reprinted by permission of the author.

Don Congdon Associates: "Embroidery" by Ray Bradbury. Published in *Marvel Science Fiction*, November 1951. Copyright © 1951 by Stadium Publishing, renewed 1979 by Ray Bradbury. Reprinted by permission of Don Congdon Associates, Inc.

New York Times: Excerpt from "Staying in Galveston, a Park Bench for Shelter" by Ian Urbina and John Schwartz, *The New York Times*, September 14, 2008. Copyright © 2008 by the New York Times Co. All rights reserved. Used by permission and protected by the Copyright Laws of the United States. The printing, copying, redistribution, or retransmission of the Material without express written permission is prohibited.

UNIT 2

Academy Chicago Publishers: Excerpt from "The Opportunity," from *Thirteen Uncollected Stories* by John Cheever. Copyright © 1994 Academy Chicago Publishers. Used by permission of Academy Chicago Publishers.

Coffee House Press: Excerpts from *A Place Where the Sea Remembers*, pp. 87–88 by Sandra Benítez. Copyright © 1993 by Sandra Benítez. Reprinted with the permission of Coffee House Press, Minneapolis, Minnesota, www.coffeehousepress.org.

HarperCollins Publishers and Faber & Faber: Two brief excerpts from pp. 286 & 293 "Initiation," used as a literary model, from *Johnny Panic and the Bible of Dreams* by Sylvia Plath. Copyright 1952, 1953, 1954, 1955, 1956, 1957, 1960, 1961, 1962, 1963 by Sylvia Plath. Copyright © 1977, 1979 by Ted Hughes. Used by permission of HarperCollins Publishers.

Elizabeth Walsh Peavoy: Excerpt from "Brigid," from *Collected Stories of Mary Lavin* by Mary Lavin, published by Houghton Mifflin Company, 1971. Originally published in *Long Ago and Other Stories*, Little, Brown and Company. Copyright © 1971 by Mary Lavin. Reprinted by permission of Elizabeth Walsh Peavoy.

Naomi Shihab Nye: "Shoofly Pie" by Naomi Shihab Nye. Copyright © 2001 by Naomi Shihab Nye. First published in *The*

UNIT 4

Peter H. Lee: "Cranes" by Hwang Sunwon, translated by Peter H. Lee, from *Flowers of Fire: Twentieth-Century Korean Stories,* edited by Peter H. Lee. Translation copyright © 1997 Peter H. Lee. Used with the permission of the translator.

Arnold Kellett: "Two Friends" by Guy de Maupassant, from *The Dark Side of Guy de Maupassant,* translated by Arnold Kellett. Copyright © 1972, 1976, 1989 by Arnold Kellett. Reprinted by permission of Arnold Kellett.

Houghton Mifflin Harcourt: "When Mr. Pirzada Came to Dine," from *Interpreter of Maladies* by Jhumpa Lahiri. Copyright © 1999 by Jhumpa Lahiri. Reprinted by permission of Houghton Mifflin Harcourt Publishing Company. All rights reserved.

MacNeil-Lehrer Productions: Excerpt from "Interview with Jhumpa Lahiri," from *The NewsHour with Jim Lehrer,* 12 April 2000. Copyright © 2000 MacNeil-Lehrer Productions. Reprinted by permission.

Brooks Permissions: "the sonnet-ballad," from *Blacks* by Gwendolyn Brooks (Chicago: Third World Press, 1991). Copyright © 1991 by Gwendolyn Brooks. Reprinted by consent of Brooks Permissions.

Houghton Mifflin Harcourt, the Provost and Scholars of King's College, Cambridge, and the Society of Authors: Excerpt from "Tolerance," from *Two Cheers for Democracy* by E. M. Forster. Copyright © 1951 by E. M. Forster and renewed 1979 by Donald Parry. Reprinted by permission of Houghton Mifflin Harcourt Publishing Company, the Provost and Scholars of King's College, Cambridge, and the Society of Authors as the Literary Representatives of the E. M. Forster Estate.

Andrew Lam: "Letter to a Young Refugee from Another" by Andrew Lam. Copyright © 1999 by Andrew Lam. Reprinted by permission of the author.

Columbia University Press: "Song of P'eng-ya" by Tu Fu, from *The Columbia Book of Chinese Poetry,* translated and edited by Burton Watson. Copyright © 1984 Columbia University Press. Reprinted with permission of the publisher.

René Saldaña Jr.: "The Heartbeat of the Soul of the World" by René Saldaña Jr. Copyright © 2004 by René Saldaña Jr. Reprinted by permission of the author.

Mary Lou Falcone, Publicist: "Overture," from *Nadja on My Way* by Nadja Salerno-Sonnenberg. Copyright © 1989 by Nadja Salerno-Sonnenberg. Reprinted by permission of Mary Lou Falcone, Publicist, on behalf of the author.

UNIT 5

Skiing: Excerpt from "Go Faster, Turn Easier" by Chris Anthony, *Skiing,* January 2004. Copyright © 2004 Time4 Media, Inc. All rights reserved. Used with permission.

Dave Barry: Excerpt from "Something in the Air" by Dave Barry, *The Miami Herald,* February 12, 1995. Copyright © 1995 by Dave Barry. Used by permission of the author.

Outside: Excerpt from "At Home in the Discomfort Zone" by Kevin Foley, *Outside,* April 2002. Copyright © 2002 Mariah Media, Inc. All rights reserved. Used by permission of Outside Magazine.

New York Times: "Observer: The Plot Against People" by Russell Baker, *The New York Times,* June 18, 1968. Copyright © 1968 by The New York Times. All rights reserved. Used by permission and protected by the Copyright Laws of the United States. The printing, copying, redistribution, or retransmission of the Material without express written permission is prohibited.

Random House: "Why the Leaves Turn Color in the Fall," from *A Natural History of the Senses* by Diane Ackerman. Copyright © 1990 by Diane Ackerman. Used by permission of Random House, Inc.

W. W. Norton & Company and Stuart Krichevsky Literary Agency: Excerpts from "Blowup: What Went Wrong at Storm King Mountain," from *Fire* by Sebastian Junger. Copyright © 2001 by Sebastian Junger. Used by permission of W. W. Norton & Company, Inc. and the Stuart Krichevsky Literary Agency, Inc.

Scribner: "And of Clay Are We Created," from *The Stories of Eva Luna* by Isabel Allende. Copyright © 1989 by Isabel Allende. English translation copyright © 1991 by Macmillan Publishing Company. All rights reserved. Reprinted with the permission of Scribner, a Division of Simon & Schuster, Inc.

Boston Globe: "Girl, Trapped in Water for 55 Hours, Dies Despite Rescue Efforts" by Julia Preston, *The Boston Globe,* November 17, 1985. Copyright © 1985 The Boston Globe. All rights reserved. Used by permission and protected by the Copyright Laws of the United States. The printing, copying, redistribution, or retransmission of the Material without express written permission is prohibited.

Arte Público Press: "Peruvian Child," from *My Own True Name: New and Selected Poems for Young Adults* by Pat Mora (Houston: Arte Público Press–University of Houston, 2000). Text copyright © 2000 by Pat Mora. Reprinted with permission from the publisher.

Rita Dove: "Lady Freedom Among Us," from *On the Bus with Rosa Parks* by Rita Dove, W. W. Norton & Company. Copyright © 1999 by Rita Dove. Reprinted by permission of the author.

Doubleday: Excerpts from "Interview with Rita Dove" by Bill Moyers, from *The Language of Life: A Festival of Poets* by Bill Moyers. Copyright © 1995 by Public Affairs Television, Inc., and David Grubin Productions, Inc. Used by permission of Doubleday, a division of Random House, Inc.

Discovery Books: Excerpt from *Discovery Channel: Insects & Spiders.* Copyright © Discovery Communications, Inc. Reprinted by permission of Discovery Books, a division of Random House, Inc.

Viking Penguin: Excerpt from "How to Write a Letter," from *We Are Still Married: Stories & Letters* by Garrison Keillor. Copyright © 1989 by Garrison Keillor. Used by permission of Viking Penguin, a division of Penguin Group (USA) Inc.

UNIT 6

The Advertising Council: Excerpts from "Youth Civic Engagement/Voter Participation," from the Advertising Council Website (http://www.adcouncil.org/issues/voting). Copyright © 2005 the Advertising Council. All rights reserved. Reprinted by permission of the Advertising Council.

International Creative Management: Excerpt from "Mount Holyoke Commencement Speech" by Anna Quindlen. Copyright © 1999 by Anna Quindlen. Reprinted by permission of International Creative Management, Inc. "Doing Nothing Is Something" by Anna Quindlen. Copyright © 2002 by Anna Quindlen. Reprinted by permission of International Creative Management, Inc.

Pinto & F. W. Roberts. Copyright © 1964, 1971 by Angelo Ravagli and C. M. Weekley, Executors of the Estate of Frieda Lawrence Ravagli. Used by permission of Viking Penguin, a division of Penguin Group (USA) Inc and Pollinger Limited.

Graywolf Press: "Fifteen," from *The Way It Is: New & Selected Poems* by William Stafford. Copyright © 1966, 1998 by the Estate of William Stafford. Reprinted with the permission of Graywolf Press, Saint Paul, Minnesota.

Agencia Literaria Carmen Balcells and Random House UK: Original "Poema 20" from the work *Veinte Poemas de Amor y Una Canción Desesperada* by Pablo Neruda. © Fundación Pablo Neruda, 1924. Used by permission of Agencia Literaria Carmen Balcells, S. A. "Puedo Escribir Los Versos . . ."/"Tonight I Can Write. . . ," from *Selected Poems* by Pablo Neruda, translated by W. S. Merwin, edited by Nathaniel Tarn and published by Jonathan Cape. Used by permission of the Random House Group Limited.

Elizabeth Barnett, Literary Executor: Sonnet XXX of *Fatal Interview* by Edna St. Vincent Millay. From **Collected Poems,** HarperCollins. Copyright 1931, 1958 by Edna St. Vincent Millay and Norma Millay Ellis. All rights reserved. Reprinted by permission of Elizabeth Barnett, literary executor.

Writers House: "Ballad"/"Balada," from *Selected Poems: A Bilingual Edition* by Gabriela Mistral, translated by Doris Dana (Baltimore: the Johns Hopkins University Press, 1971). Copyright © 1961, 1964, 1970, 1971 by Doris Dana. Reprinted with the permission of Writers House, LLC, New York, on behalf of the proprietors.

Alfred A. Knopf: "Midwinter Blues," from *The Collected Poems of Langston Hughes* by Langston Hughes, edited by Arnold Rampersad and David Roessel, Associate Editor. Copyright © 1994 by the Estate of Langston Hughes. Used by permission of Alfred A. Knopf, a division of Random House, Inc.

Everyman's Library: From *Blues Poems,* edited by Kevin Young. Copyright © 2003 by Everyman's Library. Used by permission of Everyman's Library, a division of Random House, Inc.

Harvard University Press: "If I can stop one Heart from breaking" by Emily Dickinson. Reprinted by permission of the publishers and the Trustees of Amherst College, from *The Complete Poems of Emily Dickinson,* Thomas H. Johnson, ed., Cambridge, Mass.: The Belknap Press of Harvard University Press. Copyright © 1951, 1955, 1979, 1983 by the President and Fellows of Harvard College.

Little, Brown and Company: "Reprise," from *Versus* by Ogden Nash. Copyright © 1950 by Odgen Nash. By permission of Little, Brown and Company.

UNIT 8

Scribner: Excerpt from "Big Two-Hearted River," from *The Nick Adams Stories* by Ernest Hemingway. Copyright © 1972 The Ernest Hemingway Foundation. Reprinted with the permission of Scribner, a Division of Simon & Schuster, Inc.

Farrar, Straus & Giroux: Excerpt from "A Walk to the Jetty," from *Annie John* by Jamaica Kincaid. Copyright © 1985 by Jamaica Kincaid. Reprinted by permission of Farrar, Straus & Giroux, LLC.

Henry Holt and Company: "Birches" and "Mending Wall" by Robert Frost, from *The Poetry of Robert Frost,* edited by Edward

Connery Lathem. Copyright © 1967 by Lesley Ballantine Frost. Copyright © 1944, 1958 by Robert Frost. Copyright 1916, 1930, © 1969 by Henry Holt and Company, copyright 1944, 1958 by Robert Frost, copyright © 1967 by Lesley Frost Ballentine. Reprinted by permission of Henry Holt and Company, LLC.

Houghton Mifflin Harcourt: "Fourth of July Night," from *Wind Song* by Carl Sandburg. Copyright © 1960 by Carl Sandburg, and renewed 1988 by Margaret Sandburg, Janet Sandburg, and Helga Sandburg Crile. Reprinted by permission of Houghton Mifflin Harcourt Publishing Company. All rights reserved.

New Directions: "The Red Wheelbarrow," from *Collected Poems: 1909–1930, Volume I* by William Carlos Williams. Copyright © 1938 by New Directions Publishing Corp. Reprinted by permission of New Directions Publishing Corp.

Susan Bergholz Literary Services: "Only Daughter" by Sandra Cisneros. Copyright © 1990 by Sandra Cisneros. First published in *Glamour,* November 1990. Reprinted by permission of Susan Bergholz Literary Services, New York, NY and Lamy, NM. All rights reserved. From *Caramelo* by Sandra Cisneros. Copyright © 2002 by Sandra Cisneros. Published by Vintage Books in paperback in 2003 and originally in hardcover by Alfred A. Knopf, Inc. Reprinted by permission of Susan Bergholz Literary Services, New York, NY and Lamy, NM. All rights reserved.

Fairyland Music: Excerpt from the song lyric "Moon Men Mambo," words and music by Paul Parnes. Copyright © by Fairyland Music (ASCAP). All rights reserved. Reprinted by permission of Fairyland Music.

The Orange County Register: "Author brings back memories of not so long ago" by Yvette Cabrera, *The Orange County Register,* 15 April 2002. Copyright © 2002 by The Orange County Register. Reprinted by permission.

Scribner: "Old Man at the Bridge," from *The Short Stories of Ernest Hemingway* by Ernest Hemingway. Copyright 1938 by Ernest Hemingway, renewal copyright © 1966 by Mary Hemingway. Reprinted with the permission of Scribner, a Division of Simon & Schuster, Inc.

UNIT 9

The Feminist Press: Excerpt from "To Da-duh, in Memoriam," from *Reena and Other Stories* by Paule Marshall. Copyright © 1983 by The Feminist Press. All rights reserved. Reprinted by permission of The Feminist Press.

Houghton Mifflin Harcourt and the Wendy Weil Agency: "Women," from *Revolutionary Petunias & Other Poems* by Alice Walker. Copyright © 1970 and renewed 1998 by Alice Walker. Reprinted by permission of Houghton Mifflin Harcourt Publishing Company and the Wendy Weil Agency.

Viking Penguin: Excerpt from *The Grapes of Wrath* by John Steinbeck. Copyright 1939 by John Steinbeck. Copyright renewed 1967 by John Steinbeck. Used by permission of Viking Penguin, a division of Penguin Group (USA) Inc.

Zhang Jie: Excerpt from "Love Must Not Be Forgotten" by Zhang Jie. Copyright © Zhang Jie. Reprinted by permission of the author.

Hill and Wang: Excerpt from *Night* by Elie Wiesel, translated by Stella Rodway. Copyright © 1960 by MacGibbon & Kee. Copyright renewed 1988 by the Collins Publishing Group. Reprinted by permission of Hill and Wang, a division of Farrar, Straus and Giroux, LLC.

Nobel Foundation: Excerpt from Nobel Prize acceptance speech by Elie Wiesel. Copyright © 1986 the Nobel Foundation. Reprinted by permission of the Nobel Foundation.

Houghton Mifflin Harcourt: Excerpt from *Farewell to Manzanar* by James D. Houston and Jeanne Wakatsuki Houston. Copyright © 1973 by James D. Houston. Reprinted by permission of Houghton Mifflin Harcourt Publishing Company. All rights reserved.

Writers House: Excerpt from *My Life with Martin Luther King, Jr.* by Coretta Scott King. Copyright © 1969 Coretta Scott King. Reprinted by arrangement with The Heirs to the Estate of Martin Luther King Jr., c/o of Writers House as agent for the proprietor New York, NY.

Doubleday and The Wylie Agency: "Marriage Is a Private Affair," from *Girls At War and Other Stories* by Chinua Achebe. Copyright © 1972, 1973 by Chinua Achebe. Used by permission of Doubleday, a division of Random House, Inc., and The Wylie Agency LLC.

Fawcett Books: Excerpt from *Mixed Matches: How to Create Successful Interracial, Interethnic, and Interfaith Relationships* by Joel Crohn, Ph.D. Copyright © 1995 by Joel Crohn, Ph.D. Used by permission of Fawcett Books, a division of Random House, Inc.

Houghton Mifflin Harcourt: "On the Rainy River," from *The Things They Carried* by Tim O'Brien. Copyright © 1990 by Tim O'Brien. Reprinted by permission of Houghton Mifflin Harcourt Publishing Company. All rights reserved.

Cathy Song: "Who Makes the Journey" by Cathy Song, from *Breaking Silence: An Anthology of Contemporary Asian American Poets,* edited by Joseph Bruchac. Reprinted by permission of the author.

Scholastic: "The Pale Mare" by Marian Flandrick Bray, from *Stay True: Short Stories for Strong Girls* compiled by Marilyn Singer. Scholastic Inc./Scholastic Press. Copyright © 1998 by Marian Flandrick Bray. Used by permission of Scholastic Inc.

Adam Piore: Excerpt from "Breaking Down Barriers: A Vietnamese-American Football Star Brings a Racially Divided Town Together" by Adam Piore, *Newseek,* January 8, 2001. Copyright © 2001 by Adam Piore. Reprinted by permission of the author.

UNIT 10

Viking Penguin: Excerpt from "Oedipus the King," by Sophocles, from *Three Theban Plays* by Sophocles, translated by Robert Fagles. Copyright © 1982 by Robert Fagles. Used by permission of Viking Penguin, a division of Penguin Group (USA) Inc.

Constance Hieatt: Excerpt from *Sir Gawain and the Green Knight,* retold by Constance Hieatt. Copyright © 1967 by Constance Hieatt. Reprinted by permission of the author.

Houghton Mifflin Harcourt: Excerpts from *The Antigone of Sophocles, An English Version* by Dudley Fitts and Robert Fitzgerald. Copyright 1939 by Houghton Mifflin Harcourt Publishing Company, and renewed 1967 by Dudley Fitts and Robert Fitzgerald. Reprinted by permission of the publisher. CAUTION: All rights, including professional, amateur, motion picture, recitation, lecturing, performance, public reading, radio broadcasting, and television, are strictly reserved. Inquiries on all rights should be addressed to Houghton Mifflin Harcourt Publishing Company, Permissions Department, Orlando, FL 32887-6777.

Dutton Signet: Excerpts from "The Tale of King Arthur," from *Le Morte d'Arthur* by Sir Thomas Malory, translated by Keith Baines. Copyright © 1962 by Keith Baines, renewed © 1990 by Francesca Evans. Used by permission of Dutton Signet, a division of Penguin Group (USA) Inc.

Houghton Mifflin Harcourt: *The Antigone of Sophocles, An English Version* by Dudley Fitts and Robert Fitzgerald. Copyright 1939 by Houghton Mifflin Harcourt Publishing Company, and renewed 1967 by Dudley Fitts and Robert Fitzgerald. Reprinted by permission of the publisher. CAUTION: All rights, including professional, amateur, motion picture, recitation, lecturing, performance, public reading, radio broadcasting, and television, are strictly reserved. Inquiries on all rights should be addressed to Houghton Mifflin Harcourt Publishing Company, Permissions Department, Orlando, FL 32887-6777.

Dutton Signet: Excerpt from "The Tale of King Arthur," and "The Tale of Sir Launcelot du Lake," from *Le Morte d'Arthur* by Sir Thomas Malory, translated by Keith Baines. Copyright © 1962 by Keith Baines, renewed © 1990 by Francesca Evans. Used by permission of Dutton Signet, a division of Penguin Group (USA) Inc.

Alfred A. Knopf: Excerpt from *A Distant Mirror: The Calamitous 14th Century* by Barbara W. Tuchman. Copyright © 1978 by Barbara W. Tuchman. Used by permission of Alfred A. Knopf, a division of Random House, Inc.

Viking Penguin and McIntosh and Otis: Excerpt from "The Noble Tale of Sir Lancelot of the Lake," from *The Acts of King Arthur and His Noble Knights* by John Steinbeck. Copyright © 1976 by Elaine Steinbeck. Used by permission of Viking Penguin, a division of Penguin Group (USA) Inc. and McIntosh and Otis, Inc.

Viking Penguin: Excerpt from *Don Quixote* by Miguel de Cervantes Saavedra, translated by Samuel Putnam. Copyright 1949 by The Viking Press, Inc. Used by permission of Viking Penguin, a division of Penguin Group (USA) Inc.

Random House, Alan S. Honig, and Dale Wasserman: Excerpt from *Man of La Mancha* by Dale Wasserman, lyrics by Joe Darion, and music by Mitch Leigh. Copyright © 1966 by Dale Wasserman. Copyright © 1965 by Helena Music Corp. and Andrew Scott, Inc. Used by permission of Random House, Inc., Alan S. Honig, administrator for the Estate of Joe Darion, and Dale Wasserman.

Houghton Mifflin Harcourt: Excerpt from *The Antigone of Sophocles, An English Version* by Dudley Fitts and Robert Fitzgerald. Copyright 1939 by Houghton Mifflin Harcourt Publishing Company, and renewed 1967 by Dudley Fitts and Robert Fitzgerald. Reprinted by permission of the publisher. CAUTION: All rights, including professional, amateur, motion picture, recitation, lecturing, performance, public reading, radio broadcasting, and television, are strictly reserved. Inquiries on all rights should be addressed to Houghton Mifflin Harcourt Publishing Company, Permissions Department, Orlando, FL 32887-6777.

Dutton Signet: Excerpt from *Le Morte d'Arthur* by Sir Thomas Malory, translated by Keith Baines. Copyright © 1962 by Keith Baines, renewed © 1990 by Francesca Evans. Used by permission of Dutton Signet, a division of Penguin Group (USA) Inc.

UNIT 11

The Nation: Excerpt from "Review of Julius Caesar" by Thomas M. Disch. Reprinted with permission from the April 23, 1998, issue of the *Nation.* For subscription information, call 1-800-333-8536. Portions of each week's *Nation* magazine can be accessed at http://www.thenation.com.

Diane Goldsmith: "Hail, Caesar!" by Edith Oliver. Originally published in the *New Yorker,* 28 March 1988. Copyright © 1988 Edith Oliver. Reprinted by permission of Diane Goldsmith on behalf of the Estate of Edith Oliver.

UNIT 12

The Charlotte Observer: Excerpt from "Girlfriend Led Him to Music—Tuba Kept Him There" by Steven Brown, the *Charlotte Observer,* 8 May 2005. Copyright © 2005 the Charlotte Observer. Reprinted by permission of the Charlotte Observer.

STUDENT RESOURCE BANK

Time: Excerpt from "The Man in the Water" by Roger Rosenblatt, *Time,* 25 January 1982. Copyright © 1982 Time Inc. Reprinted by permission.

Texas Instruments: "How to Draw a Triangle," from TI-84 Plus Cabri® Jr. Application Web page (http://education.ti.com/US/products/apps/cabrijr.html). Copyright © 1995–2005 Texas Instruments Incorporated. Used with permission of copyright owner, Texas Instruments.

Alfred A. Knopf: Excerpt from "The Daunting Workplace," from *The Working Poor* by David Shipler. Copyright © 2004 by David K Shipler. Reprinted by permission of Alfred A. Knopf, a division of Random House, Inc.

Associated Press: Excerpt from "Low-carb dieters losing interest," by Margaret Stafford, *Associated Press,* 20 December 2004. Copyright © 2004 Associated Press. Reprinted by permission of the Associated Press.

Elizabeth Barnett, Literary Executor: From Sonnet XXX of *Fatal Interview* by Edna St. Vincent Millay. From **Collected Poems,** HarperCollins. Copyright 1931, 1958 by Edna St. Vincent Millay and Norma Millay Ellis. All rights reserved. Reprinted by permission of Elizabeth Barnett, literary executor.

Doubleday: From "The Sloth," from *The Collected Poems of Theodore Roethke* by Theodore Roethke. Copyright 1950 by Theodore Roethke. Used by permission of Doubleday, a division of Random House, Inc.

Farrar, Straus & Giroux: From "The Fish," from *The Complete Poems 1927–1979* by Elizabeth Bishop. Copyright © 1979, 1983 by Alice Helen Methfessel. Reprinted by permission of Farrar, Straus & Giroux, LLC.

ART CREDITS

CONSULTANTS

Janet Allen © Duane McCubrey; *Arthur Applebee* © Mark Schmidt; *Kylene Beers* © Sam Dudgeon/Houghton Mifflin Harcourt; *Jim Burke* © Bruce Forrester; *Douglas Carnine* © Houghton Mifflin Harcourt; *Carol Jago* © Maggie's Photography, Pacific Palisades, CA; *Yvette Jackson* © Howard Gollub; *Robert Jimenez* © Tamra Stallings; *Judith Langer* © Mark Schmidt; *Robert Marzano* © Robert J. Marzano; *Donna Ogle* © Houghton Mifflin Harcourt; *Carol Booth Olson* © Dawson & Associates Photography; *Carol Tomlinson* © Gitchell's Studio; *May Lou McClosky* © Michael Romeo; *Lydia Stack* © Monica Ani; *William McBride* © William McBride; *David Considine* © Bill Caldwell; *Larkin Pauluzzi* © Gabriel Pauluzzi; *Lisa Scheffler* © Steven Scheffler.

TABLE OF CONTENTS

STUDENT GUIDE TO ACADEMIC SUCCESS

THE POWER OF IDEAS

UNIT 1

© Mary Iverson/Corbis; **70** *Entrance to Erchless* (1900s), Victoria Crowe. Oil on canvas, 96.5 cm x 111.7 cm. The Fleming-Wyfold Art Foundation. Photo © Bridgeman Art Library; **73** *Yellow Dress* (2003), Jeffrey T. Larson. Oil on linen, 12" x 16". © Daylight Fine Art; **78** © Chase Swift/Corbis; **79** © Underwood & Underwood/Corbis; **81** © Jeff Vanuga/Corbis; **83** © Gordon Wiltsie/Getty Images; *inset* © Ted Wood/Getty Images; **86** © Tim Thompson/Corbis; *inset* © Don Farrall/Getty Images; **91** © Ragnar Sigurdsson/Getty Images; *inset* © Herman Agopian/Getty Images; **95** © Anthony Nagelmann/Getty Images; *inset* © James Martin/Getty Images; **99** © Ted Streshinsky/Corbis; **100** © Photo by Ric Potter; **104** Illustration by Rolin Graphics; **106** © David W. Hamilton/Getty Images; **107** AP/Wide World Photos; **109** © Corbis; **112** © Bettmann/Corbis; **114** © Corbis; **117** ©1990 Michael A. Smith/Time Life Pictures/Getty Images; **118** © Bettmann/Corbis; **119** Wharton Communication, University of Pennsylvania; **121** NASA; **123** © Bettmann/Corbis; **124, 129, 131** NASA; **132** © Bettmann/Corbis; **136** NASA; **137** *top, center, bottom* © 1995 Universal City Studios, Inc./Courtesy of Universal Studios Licensing LLLP; **138** *top, center* © 1995 Universal City Studios, Inc./Courtesy of Universal Studios Licensing LLLP; *bottom* © Richard Wahlstrom/Getty Images; **140** © Erin Patrice O'Brien/Getty Images; **141** *top* AP/Wide World Photos; *bottom* Christopher Felver/Corbis; **143** *Utopie* (1999), Bob Lescaux. Oil on canvas, 81 cm x 65 cm. Private collection. Photo © Bridgeman Art Library; **146** © Todd Davidson/Getty Images; **148** © Craig Aurness/Corbis; **159** © Charles Gupton/Corbis; **167** Department of Homeland Security; **172** © Siede Preis/Getty Images.

UNIT 2

173 *left* © Illustration Works/Getty Images; *right* © Benno de Wilde/Imageshop-Zefa Visual Media, UK, Ltd./Alamy Images; **174–175** © Phil Schermeister/Corbis; **174** *left* Public Domain; *right* © Bettmann/Corbis; **178** *top left* © Volker Möhrke/Corbis; *top right* © Don Johnston/Stone/Getty Images; *bottom* © Alberto Incrocci/The Image Bank/Getty Images; **180** © Getty Images; **182** © Steve Taylor/Getty Images; **183** Photo by Madison Nye; **185** © Ray Laskowitz/Lonely Planet Images; **188** © Getty Images; **192** © Helen King/Corbis; **194** © Steve Lovegrove/Picture Tasmania Photo Library; **198** © Gary Conner/Index Stock/PictureQuest/Jupiterimages Corporation; **201** © Foodpix/Jupiterimages Corporation; **202** © The Image Bank/Getty Images; **203** AP/Wide World Photos; **205** Art by Michelle Warner. © Illustration Works/Getty Images; **207** © Images.com/Corbis; **209** *The House With Roses* (1936), Henri Le Sidaner. Oil on canvas. Private Collection. Photo © Visual Arts Library/Art Resource, New York; **211** *Mailboxes & Cosmos,* Carl Schmalz, W.H.S. Watercolor. Courtesy Pamela Dykstra; **212** © Images.com/Corbis; **214** © Getty Images; **218** © Vaide Seskauskiene/Shutterstock; **219** © Marilyn Silverstone/Magnum Photos; **221** Detail of *The Dance of Krishna* (about 1650). Mewar, Rajasthan, India. From a manuscript of the Sur-Sagar. Opaque watercolor on paper, 11" x 8 1/8". Collection Gopi Krishna, Patna, India; **224** © Delphoto/PictureQuest/Jupiterimages Corporation; **226** © Duomo/Corbis; **227** AP/Wide World Photos; **229** © Eddie Adams; **230, 231, 233** © Courtesy Nicholas Gage; **238** © Buzz Bailey/Getty Images; **239** Courtesy of Mimi; **241** © Adalberto Rios Szalay/age fotostock america, inc.; **242** © Peter Horee/Alamy Ltd.; **247** © Leland Bobbé/Corbis; **252** © Tom Stewart/Corbis; **253** *top* © 2002 Margaretta K. Mitchell; *bottom* © Pach Brothers/Corbis; **255** *Interwoven Hands,* Todd Davidson. © Images.com/Corbis; **256** *Vigour,* Martine Levy. Musée d'Art Moderne, Troyes, France. Photo © Gerard Blot/Réunion

des Musées Nationaux/Art Resource, New York; **258** © Chris Collins/Corbis; **259** © Hulton Archive/Getty Images; **261** *The Promenade* (1917), Marc Chagall. Oil on canvas. Russian State Museum, St. Petersburg, Russia. Photo © Scala/Art Resource, New York. © 2008 Artists Rights Society (ARS), New York/ADAGP, Paris; **262** *The Window at the Country House* (1915), Marc Chagall. Tretyakov Gallery, Moscow, Russia. Photo © Scala/Art Resource, New York. © 2008 Artists Rights Society (ARS), New York/ADAGP, Paris; **265** *Woman Reaping* (before 1930), Marc Chagall. National Gallery, Prague, Czech Republic. Photo © Nimatallah/Art Resource, New York. © 2008 Artists Rights Society (ARS), New York/ADAGP, Paris; **266** *The Harvest,* Natalia Goncharova. Russian State Museum, St. Petersburg, Russia. Photo © Scala/Art Resource, New York. © 2008 Artists Rights Society (ARS), New York/ADAGP, Paris; **270** *Dog Lying in the Snow* (1910–1911), Franz Marc. Oil on canvas. 62.5 cm x 105 cm. Stadelsches Kunstinstitut und Stadtische Galerie, Frankfurt am Main, Germany. Photo © Artothek; **277** *right, left, Finding Forrester.* Courtesy of Columbia Pictures; **278** *top, center, Finding Forrester.* Courtesy of Columbia Pictures; *background* Photo by Sharon Hoogstraten; **279** *left* © Andersen Ross/Getty Images; *right* © David Young-Wolff/Getty Images; **280** © Joseph Sohm/ChromoSohm Inc./Corbis; **291** © Rachel Epstein/PhotoEdit; **298** © Siede Preis/Getty Images.

UNIT 3

299 *left* Detail of *Sudden Shower over Shin-Ohashi Bridge and Atake* (1800s), Ando Hiroshige or Utagawa. Plate 58 from *One Hundred Famous Views of Edo.* Woodblock color print. © Brooklyn Museum of Art, Brooklyn, New York/Bridgeman Art Library; *right* © Michael S. Yamashita/Corbis; **300–301** Photo by Gordon Lewis; **304** *top left* © Erik Simonsen/Getty Images; *top center left* © Corbis; *top center right* © Firefly Productions/Corbis; *top right* © Photofest; *bottom left* © Photofest; *bottom center left* © Jon Deshler/Corbis; *bottom right center* © Michael Keller/Corbis; *bottom right* © Jon Deshler/Corbis; **308** © Kathleen Finlay/Masterfile; **309** National Archives; **311** *Birsay Ceremony* (1996), Gloria Wallington. Monotype. Private Collection. Photo © Bridgeman Art Library; **314** *Midsummer Night, 1994* (1994), Gloria Wallington. Monotype, 24 cm x 31 cm. Private Collection. Photo © The Bridgeman Art Library; **319** *Selassie Monoliths, 1998* (1998), Charlie Millar. Oil on canvas, 111.7 cm x 96.5 cm. Private Collection. Photo © Bridgeman Art Library; **324** © www.CartoonStock.com; **325** © Bassouls Sophie/Corbis Sygma; **327, 329, 331, 332, 337** © Getty Images; **340** *foreground* © Bettmann/Corbis; *background* © Getty Images; **342** © Philip Gould/Corbis; **343** The Granger Collection, New York; **345** Illustration by Dave Henderson/Mendola Ltd.; **347** *The Daughters of Edward Darley Boit* (1882), John Singer Sargent. Oil on canvas, 221.93 cm x 222.57 cm. Gift of Mary Louisa Boit, Julia Overing Boit, Jane Hubbard Boit and Florence D. Boit in memory of Edward Darley Boit. Museum of Fine Arts, Boston. Photo © Museum of Fine Arts, Boston; **350** *Apple Picking* (1878), Winslow Homer. Watercolor and gouache on paper laid down on board, 7" x 8 3/8". Daniel J. Terra Collection 1992.7. Photo © Terra Foundation for American Art, Chicago, Illinois/Art Resource, New York; **352** Illustration by Dave Henderson/Mendola Ltd.; **354** © Paul Conklin/PhotoEdit; **355** © Rune Hellestad/Corbis; **357** *Katsura Moonlight* (1982), Clifton Karhu. 30/100. Woodblock, 40 cm x 30 cm. The Tolman Collection, Tokyo; **359** *Sudden Shower over Shin-Ohashi Bridge and Atake* (1800s), Ando Hiroshige or Utagawa. Plate 58 from *One Hundred Famous Views of Edo.* Woodblock color print. © Brooklyn

Museum of Art, Brooklyn, New York/Bridgeman Art Library; **363** Detail of *Under the Wave off Kanagawa*, Hokusai. © Historical Picture Archive/Corbis; **368** *The Wave* (1800s), Ando Hiroshige or Utagawa. From the series *One Hundred Views of the Provinces.* Woodblock print, 37.3 cm x 25.5 cm. Galerie Janette Oster, Paris. Photo © Bridgeman Art Library; **370** © Getty Images; **374** AP/Wide World Photos; **375** © Mario Ruiz/Time Life Pictures/Getty Images; **377** AP/Wide World Photos; **382** © A. Ramey/PhotoEdit; **383** © Patrick Sylvain; **385** Detail of *Dance* (1996), Francks Deceus. Mixed media on canvas, 76.2 cm x 101.6 cm. © Francks Deceus/Bridgeman Art Library; **390** © Daryl Benson/Masterfile; **401** © Michael Newman/PhotoEdit; **410** *left* © 2009 Jupiterimages Corporation; *top right* © JGI/Getty Images; *bottom right* © 2009 Jupiterimages Corporation; **414** © Siede Preis/Getty Images.

UNIT 4

415 *left*, "Civilization is a method of living, an attitude of equal respect for all men." From the series, *Great Ideas of Western Men* (1955), George Giusti. India ink and goache on paper, 24 7/8" x 18 5/16". Gift of the Container Corporation of America. Smithsonian American Art Museum, Washington, D.C. Photo © Smithsonian American Art Museum, Washington, D.C./Art Resource, New York; *right* AP/Wide World Photos; **416–417** AP/Wide World Photos; **418** *left* © British Library, London/akg-images, London; *center, Venus, hunting, appears to Aeneas,* Pietro da Cortona. Louvre, Paris. © Erich Lessing/Art Resource, New York; *right* TM and © 2005 Marvel Characters, Inc. Used with permission; **426** © Matthew Antrobus/Getty Images; **427** The Granger Collection, New York; **429** © Johner/Getty Images; **431** © Brad Wilson/Getty Images; **434** © Chase Swift/Corbis; **438** © Digital Vision/Getty Images; **439** © Chris Hellier/Corbis; **441** *At the Inn of Mother Anthony* (1866), Pierre Auguste Renoir. Oil on canvas. National Museum, Stockholm, Sweden. Photo © Bridgeman Art Library; **444** *Line Fishermen,* study for *La Grande Jatte* (1883), Georges Seurat. Oil on canvas, 16 cm x 25 cm. Musée d'Art Moderne, Troyes, France. Photo © Réunion des Musées Nationaux/Art Resource, New York; **447** Detail of *Execution of the Emperor Maximilian* (1867), Edouard Manet. Oil on canvas, 77 1/8" x 102 1/4". Museum of Fine Arts, Boston. Gift of Mr. and Mrs. Frank Gair Macomber. 30.444; **452** *foreground* © Olson Scott/Corbis Sygma; *background* © Artbeats; **453** © Mark Mainz/Getty Images; **455** © David Papazian Photography, Inc./Getty Images; **459** Photo by Sharon Hoogstraten; **460** Photo by Sharon Hoogstraten; *TV picture* AP/Wide World Photos; *TV, curtain* © Getty Images; **462, 465** Photo by Sharon Hoogstraten; **468** Photo by Sharon Hoogstraten; *TV picture* AP/Wide World Photos; *TV* © Getty Images; **470** © Getty Images; **474** *top left* © Michael D. Brown/ShutterStock; *top right* AP/Wide World Photos; *bottom left* © Neil Lang/ShutterStock; *bottom center* © Bianda Ahmad Hisham/ShutterStock; *bottom right* © Michael D. Brown/ShutterStock; **476** © Philip James Corwin/Corbis; **477** *top* The Granger Collection, New York; *bottom* Photo © Nancy Crampton; **479** *Gloria Triptych,* right panel detail of despairing woman, Giuseppe Mentessi. Galleria d'Arte Moderna, Rome. Photo © Dagli Orti/The Art Archive; **480** *Lamentation: Memorial for Ernst Barlach* (1940), Käthe Kollwitz. Bronze. Photo © SuperStock, Inc. © 2008 Artists Rights Society (ARS), New York/VG Bild-Kunst, Bonn; **482** © Jeff Greenberg/PhotoEdit; **483** The Granger Collection, New York; **485** "Civilization is a method of living, an attitude of equal respect for all men." From the series, *Great Ideas of Western Men* (1955), George Giusti. India ink and goache on paper, 24 7/8" x 18 5/16".

Gift of the Container Corporation of America. Smithsonian American Art Museum, Washington, D.C. Photo © Smithsonian American Art Museum, Washington, D.C./Art Resource, New York; **488** © Peter Turnley/Corbis; **489** *top* Courtesy of the author; *bottom* China Stock Photography; **491** © Reuters/Corbis; **495** © Corbis; **498** © Richard Sisk/Jupiter Images; **509** © Spencer Grant/PhotoEdit; **517** © Juan Manuel Ordoñez/ShutterStock; **522** © Siede Preis/Getty Images.

UNIT 5

523 *left* © Bob Rowan; Progressive Image/Corbis; *right* Detail of *Path Through the Forest* (1914), Suzanne Valadon. Oil on canvas. Musée Fabre, Montpelier, France. Photo © Superstock, Inc./SuperStock © 2007 Artists Rights Society (ARS), New York/ADAGP, Paris; **524–525** © David McLain/Getty Images; **526** © Ross Anania/Getty Images; **532** © Rob Casey/Getty Images; **533** AP/Wide World Photos; **535** *Toasters on Hills* (1998), Charles Kaufman. Acrylic on canvas, 60 cm x 80 cm. © 2002 Charles Kaufman; **538** © Wayne Bennett/Corbis; **539** © Nancy Crampton; **541** © Charles Krebs/Corbis; **542** © Kennan Ward/Corbis; **544** © Getty Images; **549** *top center* © Biophoto Associates/Photo Researchers, Inc.; *bottom* Illustration by Keith Kasnot; **550** *top left* © Getty Images; *center left* Illustration by Debbie Maizels; *right* © Donna Disario/Corbis; **553** © GeoNova LLC; **554** Illustration by Precision Graphics; **556** AP/Wide World Photos; **557** © David Katzenstein/Corbis; **559** © Sarah Doehring; **564** © Sarah Doehring; **567** © Wayne Williams/Smokejumper Center/USDA Forest Service; **568** AP/Wide World Photos; **573, 574** Illustrations by Mick Posen/The Art Agency; **576** © W. Perry Conway/Corbis; **577** *top* © Getty Images; *center left* © NBC News Archives; *center right* © NBC News Archives; *bottom left* © Comstock Images/Punchstock; *bottom right* © Getty Images; **578** *top left* © NBC News Archives; *center left* © Comstock Images/Punchstock; *background* © Sam Barricklow/Workbookstock.com/Jupiterimages Corporation; **581, 582** Metropolitan Transit Authority of Harris County, Houston, Texas; **584** © Phil Hunt/Getty Images; **585** AP/Wide World Photos; **587** *Niña* (1943), Julia Diaz. Oil on canvas. 30 cm x 35 cm. Courtesy of the Julia Diaz Foundation; **590** *Sosteniendo el Tiempo* (1998), Satenik Tekyan. Mixed media, 95 cm x 80 cm. www.artesur.com/satenik; **593** *Resurrection* (2000), Stevie Taylor. Pastel on paper. Private Collection. Photo © Bridgeman Art Library; **599** Rex USA; **600** *top* Rex USA; *bottom* © GeoNova LLC; **602** AP/Wide World Photos; **603** *top* Courtesy Pat Mora/Photo by Cheron Bayna; *bottom* © Photograph of Rita Dove by Fred Viebahn; **605** © Galen Rowell/Corbis; **607** *left, right* The Architect of the Capitol, Office of the Curator, March 2001; **608** PBS ® and the PBS logo are registered trademarks of the Public Broadcasting Service and are used with permission. All rights reserved; **610** © Daryl Benson/Masterfile; **621** © Mark Richards/PhotoEdit; **628** © Siede Preis/Getty Images.

UNIT 6

629 *left, The Merry Jesters* (1906), Henri Rousseau. © Philadelphia Museum of Art/Corbis; *right* © Michael Nichols/Getty Images; **630** © Getty Images; **635** *left* © Jon Riley/Stone/Getty Images; *right* © Robin Nelson/PhotoEdit; **637** © ThinkStock/SuperStock; **638** © Ron Fehling/Masterfile; **639** © Bernard Gotfryd/Hulton Archive/Getty Images; **640** © Tom Stewart/Corbis; **646** © Francisco Cruz/Superstock; **647** © Time Life Pictures/Getty Images; **648** © Corbis; **650** © Charles O'Rear/Corbis; **652** © Craig Aurness/Corbis; **653** AP/Wide World Photos; **655** © Corbis; **656** © Lester Lefkowitz/Corbis;

659 © Kevin Fleming/Corbis; **664** © Alan Schein Photography/ Corbis; **665** AP/Wide World Photos; **667** © Michael Nichols/Getty Images; **669** © Tom Brakefield/Corbis; **670** Photo © Susan Farley; **673** © Martin Harvey; Gallo Images/Corbis; **678** © Charles E. Rotkin/ Corbis; **680** © LWA-Paul Chmielowiec/Corbis; **683** © Bettmann/ Corbis; **688** © Jupiterimages Corporation; **689** © Bettmann/Corbis; **691** Photo © Alfredo Dagli Orti/Naval Museum of Milan, Italy/The Art Archive; **692** © Jupiterimages Corporation; *inset* © Henry Chaplin/ istockphoto.com; **694, 695** AP/Wide World Photos; **697** © Arun K. Mishra/Dinodia Photo Library; **701** © Dinodia Photo Library; **705** *A Sketch of Two Figures at a Window,* Nicholai Uvarov. 29.2 cm x 23.4 cm. Bonhams, London. Photo © Bridgeman Art Library; **714** © Radu Sigheti/Reuters News Picture Archive; **716** © Michael Keller/Corbis; **717** © Michael Nicholson/Corbis; **719** *Late Night Guest* (2002). A. Kurzov. 3.4" x 1.75". Tradestone Gallery; **722** *Woodland Scenery with Cows,* Ivanchuk. 15.5 cm x 6.5 cm x 3.5 cm. Vika's Russia Direct; **724** *Storm is Coming,* V. V. Sindyukov. 7.5 cm x 6 cm x 4 cm. Vika's Russia Direct; **728** *Tashkent Dervishes Dressed in Festive Costume* (1870), Vasilij Vasil'evic Verescagin. Oil on canvas. © The State Tretyakov Gallery, Moscow. Photo © Anatoly Sapronenkov/Superstock; *frame* © Getty Images; **731** *Forest Road,* A. Karapaev. 18 cm x 13.5 cm x 6.5 cm. Vika's Russia Direct; **734** *The Money Lender and His Wife* (1514), Quentin Metsys. Louvre, Paris. Photo © Erich Lessing/Art Resource, New York; **738** © Richard Levine/Alamy Images; **739** *top right, center right* Courtesy of Ronald Reagan Presidential Library; *bottom right* Courtesy Democratic National Committee; **740** *top left, background* Courtesy Democratic National Committee; *bottom left* Courtesy of Ronald Reagan Presidential Library; **741** © Paul Barton/Corbis; **742** © J. David Andrews/Masterfile; **753** © Michelle D. Bridwell/PhotoEdit; **761** © Liane Cary/photolibrary; **764** © Siede Preis/Getty Images.

UNIT 7

767 *left, Graffiti Divas* (2003), Jen Thario. Spray paint on paper, 22" x 22". © Jen Thario; *right* © Galen Rowell/Corbis; **768–769** © Massimo Mastrorillo/Corbis; **772** © Paul Edmondson/Botanica/ Jupiterimages Corporation; **778** © David W. Hamilton/Getty Images; **779** *top* © Getty Images; *center* The Granger Collection, New York; *bottom* © Nancy E. Crampton; **781** *Spring Landscape* (1909), Constant Permeke. Constant Permeke Museum, Jabbeke, Belgium. © 2008 Artists Rights Society (ARS), New York/SABAM, Brussels. Photo © Dagli Orti/The Art Archive; **782** *Moonrise* (1906), Guillermo Gomez y Gil. Oil on canvas. Musee des Beaux-Arts, Pau, France. Photo © Giraudon/Bridgeman Art Library; **783** *Trees at Night* (about 1900), Thomas Meteyard. Berry Hill Gallery, New York. Photo © Edward Owen/Art Resource, New York; **786** © oote boe/Alamy Images; **787** *top* The Granger Collection. New York; *center* © Christopher Felver/ Corbis; *bottom* © Michael S. Glaser/St. Mary's College of Maryland; **789** Detail of *Cape Cod Morning* (1950), Edward Hopper. Oil on canvas, 34 1/8" x 40 ¼". Smithsonian American Art Museum, Washington, D.C. © Heirs of Josephine N. Hopper, licensed by the Whitney Museum of American Art. Photo © Smithsonian American Art Museum, Washington, D.C./Art Resource, New York; **790** © Brooks Walker/Getty Images; **791** © James Marshall/Corbis; **794** © Corbis; **795** *top* © Bettmann/Corbis; *center* © Christopher Felver/ Corbis; *bottom* © Bettmann/Corbis; **796, 797** © Davies & Starr/Getty Images; **799** © Getty Images; **800** © Tom Brakefield/Corbis; **802** © Brooklyn Productions/Getty Images; **803** *top* The Granger Collection, New York; *center* AP/Wide World Photos; *bottom* © Getty Images;

804 *The Spinet* (1902), Thomas Wilmer Dewing. Oil on wood, 15 1/2" x 20". Smithsonian American Art Museum, Washington, D.C. Photo © Smithsonian American Art Museum, Washington, D.C./ Art Resource, New York; **805** © Robert Houser/Index Stock Imagery; **807** *Waiting* (2001), Ben McLaughlin. Oil on board, 30.5 cm x 30.5 cm. Private collection. Photo © Bridgeman Art Library; **808** © The Nobel Foundation; **810** HEART OF THE CITY © 2000 Mark Tatulli. Distributed by UNIVERSAL PRESS SYNDICATE. Reprinted with permission. All rights reserved; **811** *top* © Pixtal/Age Fotostock America, Inc.; *bottom* © Bettmann/Corbis; **813** *Offering of the Heart* (1400–1410). French tapestry from Arras. Wool and silk, 247 cm x 209 cm. Louvre, Paris. Photo © Réunion des Musées Nationaux/ Art Resource, New York; **814** *The Cathedral* (1908), Auguste Rodin. Bronze, 24 1/2" x 10 3/4" x 11 3/4". Photo © Timothy McCarthy/ Art Resource, New York; **816** © Peter Mason/Getty Images; **817** *top* © Bettmann/Corbis; *bottom* © Corbis; **819** *The Vitriol Thrower* (1894), Eugene Grasset. Lithograph. Cecil Higgins Art Gallery, Bedford, Bedfordshire, United Kingdom. Photo © Bridgeman Art Library; **821** *Melancholy,* Edvard Munch. National Gallery, Oslo, Norway. © 2008 The Munch Museum/The Munch-Ellingsen Group/Artists Rights Society (ARS), New York. Photo © Scala/Art Resource, New York; **822** *Graffiti Divas* (2003), Jen Thario. Spray paint on paper, 22" x 22". © Jen Thario; **825** © Manuela Hoefer/Getty Images; **828** © Jason Ernst/ Age Fotostock America, Inc.; **846** © Siede Preis/Getty Images.

UNIT 8

847 *left* Detail of *Sunflowers,* Vincent van Gogh. © Philadelphia Museum of Art/Corbis; *right* © Evan Sklar/Botanica/Jupiterimages Corporation; **848–849** © Thomas Hoepker/Magnum Photos; **850** *left* © Hulton-Deutsch Collection/Corbis; *right* © Getty Images; **852** *left* Detail of *Nathaniel Hawthorne* (1840), Charles Osgood. Oil on canvas. © Peabody Essex Museum, Salem, Massachusetts/Bridgeman Art Library; *right* © Getty Images; **856** © Tomek Sikora/Getty Images; **857** © Bettmann/Corbis; **859, 862, 865, 869, 871** Illustration © Cliff Nielson; **874** *Timeless, 2002,* Lee Campbell. Private Collection. Photo © The Bridgeman Art Library; **878** © Albert Normandin/ Masterfile; **879** National Archives; **881** © Peter Casolino/Corbis; **882–883** © Kevin Fleming/Corbis; **884** © Time Life Pictures/Getty Images; **886** © Michael DeYoung/Corbis; **887** National Archives; **888** *Treetop Flier,* Rod Frederick. Paper. 22 5/8" x 4 5/8". Courtesy of The Greenwich Workshop, Inc.; **890** *Cotswold Landscape* (1981), Derold Page. Private collection. Photo © The Bridgeman Art Library; **894** © Getty Images; **895** *top, center* © Bettmann/Corbis; *bottom* National Archives; **896** © Farrell Grehan/Corbis; **897** © Firefly Productions/ Corbis; **898** © Evan Sklar/Botanica/Jupiterimages Corporation; **900** *left* © Banana Stock/Age Fotostock America, Inc.; *right* © Scott Tysick/ Masterfile; **901** © Gene Blevins/Corbis; **903** *Sandra Cisneros* (2000), Raquel Valle Senties. Oil, 20" x 20". www.soycomosoyyque.com; **907** *Black Jumper,* Lucy Willis. British. Private collection. Photo © Curwen Gallery/The Bridgeman Art Library; **911** © Gene Blevins/Corbis; **914** © Alain Choisnet/Getty Images; **919** © Getty Images; **923** © Michael Newman/PhotoEdit; **930** © Siede Preis/Getty Images.

UNIT 9

931 *left, Miss Liberty* (1987), Malcah Zeldis. Oil on corrugated cardboard. Smithsonian American Art Museum, Washington, D.C. Photo © Smithsonian American Art Museum, Washington, D.C./

ArenaPal/Topham/The Image Works, Inc.; **1229** *top* Helen Carey as Portia and Robert Stattel as Marcus Brutus in The Shakespeare Theatre's 1993–1994 production of *Julius Caesar.* Directed by Joe Dowling. Photo by Richard Anderson; *center* ©1988 Martha Swope/Time Inc.; *bottom* Photo © Pete Jones/ArenaPal/Topham/The Image Works; **1239** © International Shakespeare Globe Centre, Ltd.; **1242** *top* Photo by Manuel Harlan. © Royal Shakespeare Company; *center* Photo © Clive Barda/ArenaPal/Topham/The ImageWorks; *bottom* Photo by Manuel Harlan. © Royal Shakespeare Company; **1259** © Colin Willoughby/ArenaPal/Topham/The Image Works; **1263** *top* Photo by Manuel Harlan. © Royal Shakespeare Company; *center* Photo by Martha Swope © Time Inc.; *bottom* Robert Stattel as Marcus Brutus and Philip Goodwin as Caius Cassius in The Shakespeare Theatre's 1993–1994 production of William Shakespeare's *Julius Caesar.* Directed by Joe Dowling. Photo by Richard Anderson; **1267, 1275, 1278** © International Shakespeare Globe Centre, Ltd.; **1287** *left* © 2005 Eddie Guy; *center* © Teacher's Discovery, Auburn Hills, Michigan; *right* © Michael Diamond/ArenaPal/Topham/The Image Works, Inc.; **1294** *Mark Antony's Oration,* George Edward Robertson. Oil on canvas. © Hartlepool Museum Service, Cleveland, United Kingdom. Photo © Bridgeman Art Library; **1295** *top, center, bottom* Clip from *Julius Caesar.* Courtesy of Paramount Pictures; **1296** *top, center* Clip from *Julius Caesar.* Courtesy of Paramount Pictures; *background* © M. Angelo/Corbis; **1298** © Neil Emmerson/Getty Images; **1309** © Houghton Mifflin Harcourt; **1316** © Siede Preis/Getty Images.

UNIT 12

1317 *left* © Michael Newman/PhotoEdit; **1318–1319** © William Whitehurst/Corbis; **1320** © Michael Newman/PhotoEdit; **1324** © Google; **1325** © 2008 by Heather McDonald (http://musicians.about.com). Used with permission of About, Inc. which can be found online at www.about.com. All rights reserved; **1327** © Chicago Public Library, Chicago, Illinois; **1328** *left* © CMCD, Inc.; *background-left* © 1994 Artbeats; *right* © Bryan Mullennix/Getty Images; *background-right* © 1994 Artbeats; **1329** *top* Cover from *The Concise Animal Encyclopedia.* © Kingfisher Publications Plc 2003. Reprinted by permission of Kingfisher Publications Plc., an imprint of Houghton Mifflin

Company. All rights reserved; *bottom* Cover of *National Geographic Atlas of the World, Eighth Edition*© 2004. Published by permission of the National Geographic Society, Washington, D.C.; **1330** The WorldCat screen shot is used with OCLC's permission. FirstSearch™ and WorldCat™ are registered trademarks of OCLC Online Computer Library Center, Inc./The (WorldCat/First Search) screen shot contains bibliographic records from Books In Print ® .Books In Print ® is a registered trademark of R.R. Bowker LLC. Used with permission; **1332** *top* © Time Life Pictures/Getty Images; *center* © Crain's Chicago Business; *bottom* Cover of *The Instrumentalist Magazine.* Photo © University of Illinois, Champaign, Illinois; **1335** *Careers in Music Website* © istockphoto.com; © Nicholas Monu/istockphoto.com; © Paola Condreas/istockphoto.com; *bottom* © Getty Images; **1336** © Getty Images; **1337** *top* © The Charlotte Observer. Reprinted by permission of The Charlotte Observer; *bottom* © Digital Vision/Getty Images ; **1341** © Antonello Turchetti/Getty Images; **1342** © Claver Carroll/Jupiter Images; **1365** © Sonny T. Senser/Age Fotostock America, Inc.

STUDENT RESOURCE BANK

R6 Illustration by Dan Stuckenschneider; **R7** *top, bottom* © GeoNova LLC; **R14** © Corbis; **R15** © E. R. Degginger/Color-Pic, Inc.; **R16** © 2007 Infospace, Inc. All rights reserved. Reprinted with permission of Infospace, Inc.; **R20** © Brookfield Zoo, Brookfield, Illinois; **R84** © Digital Vision/Getty Images; **R92** © Photofest.

BACK COVER

(tl) Marko Shark/Corbis; (c) Offering of the Heart (1400–1410). French tapestry from Arras. Wool and silk, 247 cm × 209 cm. Louvre, Paris. Photo © Réunion des Musées Nationaux/Art Resource, New York; (bl) McDougal Littell; (br) Bettmann/Corbis.